O MAP PAGES

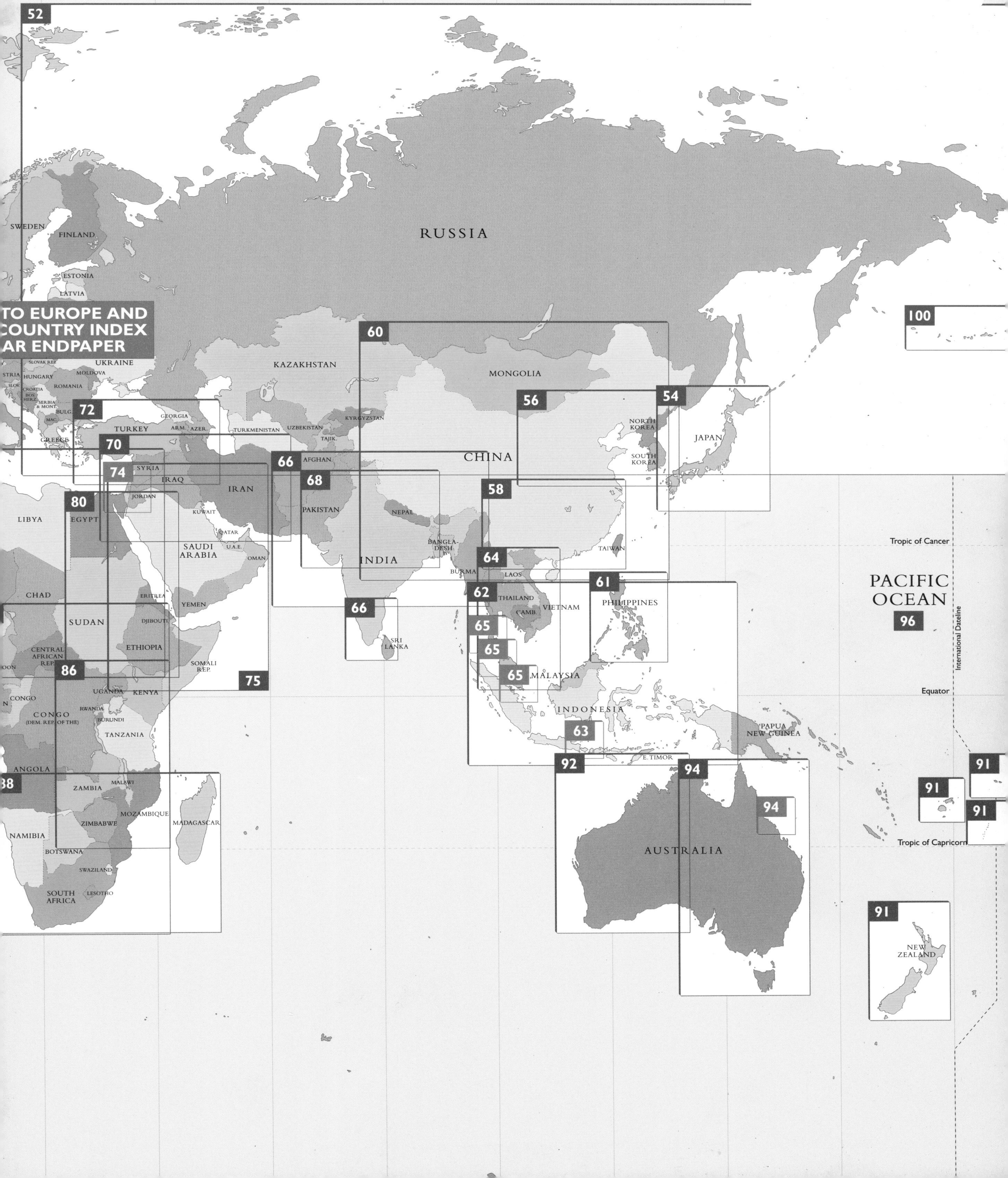

52

TO EUROPE AND
COUNTRY INDEX
AR ENDPAPER

RUSSIA

SWEDEN
FINLAND
ESTONIA
LATVIA
UKRAINE
SLOVAK REP.
MOLDOVA
HUNGARY
ROMANIA
CROATIA
BOS. HERZ.
SERBIA & MONT.
BULG.
MAC.
GREECE
KAZAKHSTAN
MONGOLIA
GEORGIA
ARM.
AZER.
TURKEY
TURKMENISTAN
UZBEKISTAN
KYRGYZSTAN
TAJIK.
SYRIA
IRAQ
IRAN
AFGHAN.
CHINA
NORTH KOREA
SOUTH KOREA
JAPAN
JORDAN
LIBYA
EGYPT
KUWAIT
PAKISTAN
NEPAL
QATAR
U.A.E.
SAUDI ARABIA
OMAN
BANGLA-DESH
INDIA
TAIWAN
BURMA
LAOS
CHAD
ERITREA
YEMEN
THAILAND
VIETNAM
CAMB.
PHILIPPINES
SUDAN
DJIBOUTI
ETHIOPIA
SRI LANKA
CENTRAL AFRICAN REP.
SOMALI REP.
MALAYSIA
UGANDA
KENYA
CONGO
RWANDA
BURUNDI
CONGO (DEM. REP. OF THE)
TANZANIA
INDONESIA
PAPUA NEW GUINEA
E. TIMOR
ANGOLA
MALAWI
ZAMBIA
MOZAMBIQUE
ZIMBABWE
MADAGASCAR
NAMIBIA
BOTSWANA
SWAZILAND
SOUTH AFRICA
LESOTHO
AUSTRALIA
NEW ZEALAND
PACIFIC OCEAN
Tropic of Cancer
Equator
Tropic of Capricorn
International Dateline

60 54 56 72 70 66 68 74 58 80 64 61 62 66 65 65 65 86 75 63 92 94 94 91 91 91 91 96 100 88

PHILIP'S

WORLD REFERENCE ATLAS

PHILIP'S

WORLD REFERENCE ATLAS

IN ASSOCIATION WITH

THE ROYAL GEOGRAPHICAL SOCIETY

WITH THE INSTITUTE OF BRITISH GEOGRAPHERS

NATIONS OF THE WORLD
Text
Keith Lye

IMAGES OF EARTH
All satellite images in this section supplied by NPA Ltd, Edenbridge, Kent, UK (www.satmaps.com)

© **NPA Remote Sensing Department: Processing by Richard Chiles and Paul Karwinski:** pages 65, 66 (bottom left), 67 (top), 67 (bottom), 68 (left), 68 (top right), 68 (bottom right), 69 (top left), 69 (bottom), 70 (top), 70 (bottom), 70–71, 72 (top), 72 (bottom left), 72 (bottom right), 73 (top left), 73 (bottom), 74 (top), 75 (bottom right), 76 (top), 76 (bottom), 76–77, 77 (top left), 77 (bottom right), 78 (bottom left), 78–79, 79 (top), 79 (bottom right)

Image courtesy Jacques Descloitres, MODIS Land Rapid Response Team at NASA GSFC: pages 66 (bottom right), 75 (bottom left)

Image courtesy Jeff Schmaltz, MODIS Land Rapid Response Team at NASA GSFC: page 66 (top)

Courtesy of the NOAA Coastal Services Center Hawai'i Land Cover Analysis project: page 77 (top right)

Satellite image courtesy of Space Imaging: pages 73 (top right), 74 (bottom), 75 (top)

Image provided by the USGS EROS Data Center Satellite Systems Branch: pages 69 (top right), 71 (top left), 78 (top)

Image by Jesse Allen, NASA Earth Observatory, based on expedited ASTER data provided by the NASA/GSFC/MITI/ERSDAC/JAROS, and US/Japan ASTER Science Team: page 71 (top right)

Image courtesy NASA/GSFC/MITI/ERSDAC/JAROS, and US/Japan ASTER Science Team: page 80

Published in Great Britain in 2005
by Philip's,
a division of Octopus Publishing Group Limited,
2–4 Heron Quays, London E14 4JP

Cartography by Philip's

ISBN-13 978-0-540-08825-6
ISBN-10 0-540-08825-0

A CIP catalogue record for this book is available from the British Library.

Printed in Hong Kong

Details of other Philip's titles and services can be found on our website at: www.philips-maps.co.uk

Philip's World Atlases are published in association with The Royal Geographical Society (with The Institute of British Geographers).

The Society was founded in 1830 and given a Royal Charter in 1859 for 'the advancement of geographical science'. It holds historical collections of national and international importance, many of which relate to the Society's association with and support for scientific exploration and research from the 19th century onwards. It was pivotal in establishing geography as a teaching and research discipline in British universities close to the turn of the century, and has played a key role in geographical and environmental education ever since.

Today the Society is a leading world centre for geographical learning – supporting education, teaching, research and expeditions, and promoting public understanding of the subject.

The Society welcomes those interested in geography as members. For further information, please visit the website at: www.rgs.org

Philip's World Maps

The reference maps which form the main body of this atlas have been prepared in accordance with the highest standards of international cartography to provide an accurate and detailed representation of the Earth. The scales and projections used have been carefully chosen to give balanced coverage of the world, while emphasizing the most densely populated and economically significant regions. A hallmark of Philip's mapping is the use of hill shading and relief colouring to create a graphic impression of landforms: this makes the maps exceptionally easy to read. However, knowledge of the key features employed in the construction and presentation of the maps will enable the reader to derive the fullest benefit from the atlas.

MAP SEQUENCE

The atlas covers the Earth continent by continent: first Europe, then its land neighbour Asia (mapped north before south, in a clockwise sequence), followed by Africa, Australia and Oceania, North America and South America. This is the classic arrangement adopted by most cartographers since the 16th century. For each continent, there are maps at a variety of scales. First, physical relief

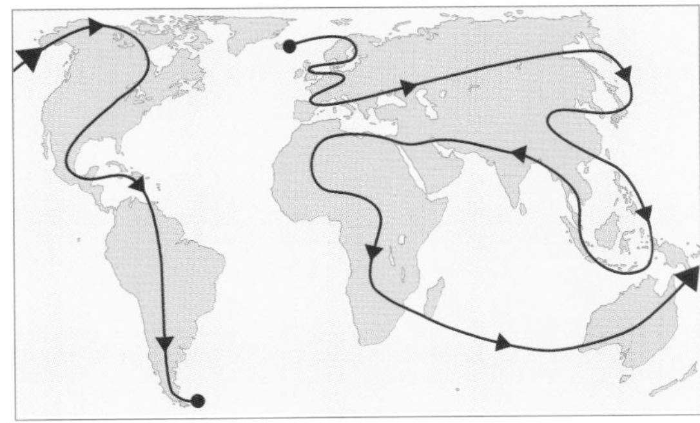

and political maps of the whole continent; then a series of larger-scale maps of the regions within the continent, each followed, where required, by still larger-scale maps of the most important or densely populated areas. The governing principle is that by turning the pages of the atlas, the reader moves steadily from north to south through each continent, with each map overlapping its neighbours.

MAP PRESENTATION

With very few exceptions (for example, for the Arctic and Antarctica), the maps are drawn with north at the top, regardless of whether they are presented upright or sideways on the page. In the borders will be found the map title; a locator diagram showing the area covered; continuation arrows showing the page numbers for maps of adjacent areas; the scale; the projection used; the degrees of latitude and longitude; and the letters and figures used in the index for locating place names and geographical features. Physical relief maps also have a height reference panel identifying the colours used for each layer of contouring.

MAP SYMBOLS

Each map contains a vast amount of detail which can only be conveyed clearly and accurately by the use of symbols. Points and circles of varying sizes locate and identify the relative importance of towns and cities; different styles of type are employed for administrative, geographical and regional place names to aid identification. A variety of pictorial symbols denote landscape features such as glaciers, marshes and coral reefs, and man-made structures including roads, railways, airports, canals and dams. International borders are shown by red lines. Where neighbouring countries are in dispute, for example in parts of the Middle East, the maps show the *de facto* boundary between nations, regardless of the legal or historical situation. The symbols are explained on the first page of the *World Maps* section of the atlas.

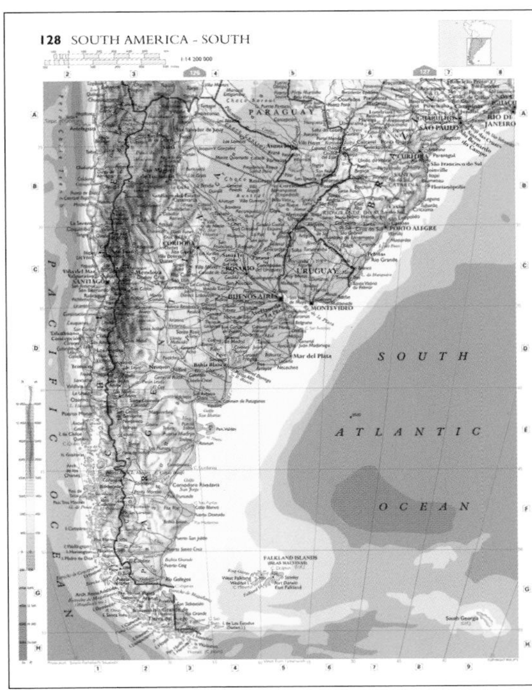

MAP SCALES

1:16 000 000
1 inch = 252 statute miles

The scale of each map is given in the numerical form known as the 'representative fraction'. The first figure is always one, signifying one unit of distance on the map; the second figure, usually in millions, is the number by which the map unit must be multiplied to give the equivalent distance on the Earth's surface. Calculations can easily be made in centimetres and kilometres, by dividing the Earth units figure by 100 000 (i.e. deleting the last five 0s). Thus 1:1 000 000 means 1 cm = 10 km. The calculation for inches and miles is more laborious, but 1 000 000 divided by 63 360 (the number of inches in a mile) shows that 1:1 000 000 means approximately 1 inch = 16 miles. The table below provides distance equivalents for scales down to 1:50 000 000.

LARGE SCALE		
1:1 000 000	1 cm = 10 km	1 inch = 16 miles
1:2 500 000	1 cm = 25 km	1 inch = 39.5 miles
1:5 000 000	1 cm = 50 km	1 inch = 79 miles
1:6 000 000	1 cm = 60 km	1 inch = 95 miles
1:8 000 000	1 cm = 80 km	1 inch = 126 miles
1:10 000 000	1 cm = 100 km	1 inch = 158 miles
1:15 000 000	1 cm = 150 km	1 inch = 237 miles
1:20 000 000	1 cm = 200 km	1 inch = 316 miles
1:50 000 000	1 cm = 500 km	1 inch = 790 miles
SMALL SCALE		

MEASURING DISTANCES

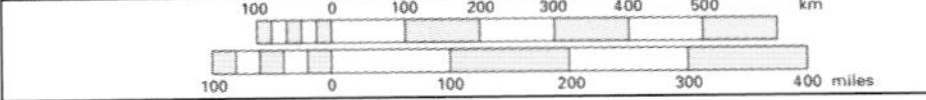

Although each map is accompanied by a scale bar, distances cannot always be measured with confidence because of the distortions involved in portraying the curved surface of the Earth on a flat page. As a general rule, the larger the map scale (that is, the lower the number of Earth units in the representative fraction), the more accurate and reliable will be the distance measured. On small-scale maps such as those of the world and of entire continents, measurement may only be accurate along the 'standard parallels', or central axes, and should not be attempted without considering the map projection.

MAP PROJECTIONS

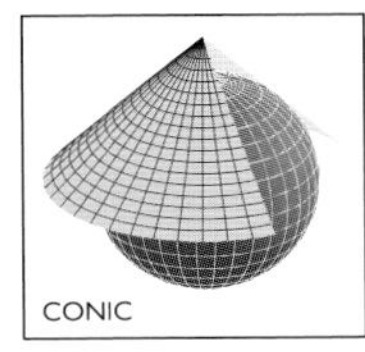

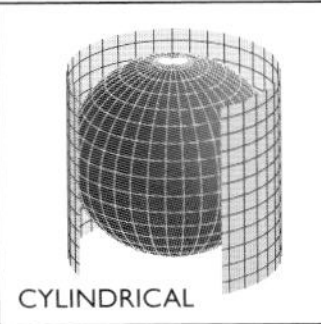

Unlike a globe, no flat map can give a true scale representation of the world in terms of area, shape and position of every region. Each of the numerous systems that have been devised for projecting the curved surface of the Earth on to a flat page involves the sacrifice of accuracy in one or more of these elements. The variations in shape and position of landmasses such as Alaska, Greenland and Australia, for example, can be quite dramatic when different projections are compared. For this atlas, the guiding principle has been to select projections that involve the least distortion of size and distance. The projection used for each map is noted in the border. Most fall into one of three categories – conic, azimuthal or cylindrical – whose basic concepts are shown above. Each involves plotting the forms of the Earth's surface on a grid of latitude and longitude lines, which may be shown as parallels, curves or radiating spokes.

LATITUDE AND LONGITUDE

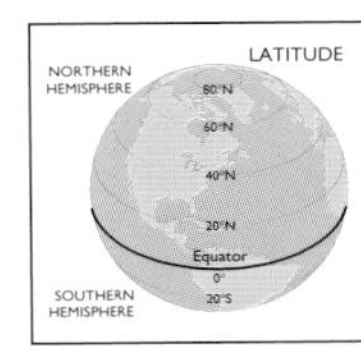

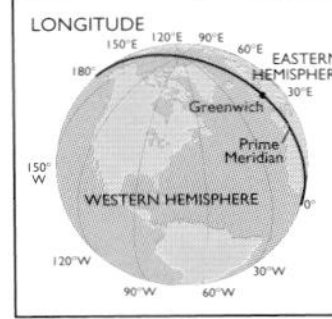

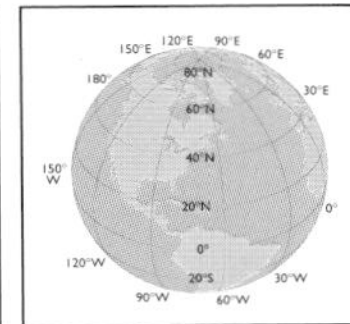

Accurate positioning of individual points on the Earth's surface is made possible by reference to the geometrical system of latitude and longitude. Latitude *parallels* are drawn west–east around the Earth and numbered by degrees north and south of the Equator, which is designated 0° of latitude. Longitude *meridians* are drawn north–south and numbered by degrees east and west of the *prime meridian*, 0° of longitude, which passes through Greenwich in England. By referring to these co-ordinates and their subdivisions of minutes (1/60th of a degree) and seconds (1/60th of a minute), any place on Earth can be located to within a few hundred metres. Latitude and longitude are indicated by blue lines on the maps; they are straight or curved according to the projection employed. Reference to these lines is the easiest way of determining the relative positions of places on different maps, and for plotting compass directions.

NAME FORMS

For ease of reference, both English and local name forms appear in the atlas. Oceans, seas and countries are shown in English throughout the atlas; country names may be abbreviated to their commonly accepted form (for example, Germany, not The Federal Republic of Germany). Conventional English forms are also used for place names on the smaller-scale maps of the continents. However, local name forms are used on all large-scale and regional maps, with the English form given in brackets only for important cities – the large-scale map of Russia and Central Asia thus shows Moskva (Moscow). For countries that do not use a Roman script, place names have been transcribed according to the systems adopted by the British and US Geographic Names Authorities. For China, the Pin Yin system has been used, with some more widely known forms appearing in brackets, as with Beijing (Peking). Both English and local names appear in the index, the English form being cross-referenced to the local form.

Contents

WORLD STATISTICS

The World 8–9

Europe and Russia 10

Asia 11

Africa 12

Oceania and Antarctica 13

North America 14

South America 15

World: Regions in the News 16

NATIONS OF THE WORLD

An A–Z Gazetteer of Countries 17–64

IMAGES OF EARTH

Europe 65–67

Middle East and Asia 68–69

Asia 70–71

Africa 72–73

Australia and Oceania 74–75

North America 76–77

South America 78–80

WORLD MAPS

Map Symbols 1

The World: Political 2–3
1:71 100 000

Arctic Ocean 4
1:31 100 000

Antarctica 5
1:31 100 000

EUROPE

Europe: Physical 6
1:17 800 000

Europe: Political 7
1:17 800 000

Scandinavia 8–9
1:4 400 000
Iceland 1:4 400 000

Denmark and Southern Sweden 10–11
1:2 200 000

Ireland 12
1:1 800 000

Scotland 13
1:1 800 000

England and Wales 14–15
1:1 800 000

British Isles 16
1:4 400 000

Netherlands, Belgium and Luxembourg 17
1:2 200 000

Northern France 18–19
1:2 200 000

Southern France 20–21
1:2 200 000

Central Europe 22–23
1:4 400 000

Germany and Switzerland 24–25
1:2 200 000

Austria, Czech Republic and Slovak Republic 26–27
1:2 200 000

Hungary, Romania and the Lower Danube 28–29
1:2 200 000

Poland and the Southern Baltic 30–31
1:2 200 000

Baltic States, Belarus and Ukraine 32–33
1:4 400 000

The Volga Basin and the Caucasus 34–35
1:4 400 000

Western Spain and Portugal 36–37
1:2 200 000

Eastern Spain 38–39
1:2 200 000

Northern Italy, Slovenia and Croatia 40–41
1:2 200 000

Southern Italy 42–43
1:2 200 000

Serbia and Montenegro, Bulgaria and Northern Greece 44–45
1:2 200 000

Southern Greece and Western Turkey 46–47
1:2 200 000

The Balearics, the Canaries and Madeira 48
1:900 000 / 1:1 800 000

Malta, Crete, Corfu, Rhodes and Cyprus 49
1:900 000 / 1:1 200 000

ASIA

Asia: Physical 50
1:44 400 000

Asia: Political 51
1:44 400 000

Russia and Central Asia 52–53
1:17 800 000

Japan 54–55
1:4 400 000

Northern China and Korea 56–57
1:5 300 000

Southern China 58–59
1:5 300 000

China 60
1:17 800 000

The Philippines 61
1:6 700 000

Indonesia and the Philippines 62–63
1:11 100 000
Java and Madura 1:6 700 000
Bali 1:1 800 000

Mainland South-east Asia 64–65
1:5 300 000
Ko Phuket 1:900 000
Ko Samui 1:900 000
Pinang 1:900 000
Singapore 1:900 000

South Asia 66–67
1:8 900 000

Northern India and Nepal 68–69
1:5 300 000
Jammu and Kashmir 1:5 300 000

The Middle East 70–71
1:6 200 000

Turkey and Transcaucasia 72–73
1:4 400 000

The Near East 74
1:2 200 000

Arabia and the Horn of Africa 75
1:13 300 000

AFRICA

Africa: Physical 76
1:37 300 000

Africa: Political 77
1:37 300 000

Northern Africa 78–79
1:13 300 000

The Nile Valley 80–81
1:7 100 000
The Nile Delta 1:3 600 000

West Africa 82–83
1:7 100 000

Central and Southern Africa 84–85
1:13 300 000

East Africa 86–87
1:7 100 000

Southern Africa 88–89
1:7 100 000
Madagascar 1:7 100 000

AUSTRALIA AND OCEANIA

Australia and Oceania: Physical and Political 90
1:44 400 000

New Zealand 91
1:5 300 000
Samoan Islands 1:10 700 000
Fiji and Tonga 1:10 700 000

Western Australia 92–93
1:7 100 000

Eastern Australia 94–95
1:7 100 000
Whitsunday Islands 1:2 200 000
Tasmania 1:7 100 000

Pacific Ocean 96–97
1:48 000 000

NORTH AMERICA

North America: Physical 98
1:31 100 000

North America: Political 99
1:31 100 000

Canada 100–101
1:13 300 000
Alaska 1:26 700 000

Western Canada 102–103
1:6 200 000

Eastern Canada 104–105
1:6 200 000

United States 106–107
1:10 700 000
Hawai'i 1:8 900 000

Western United States 108–109
1:5 300 000

Central and Southern California and Western Washington 110–111
1:2 200 000

Middle United States 112–113
1:5 300 000

Eastern United States 114–115
1:5 300 000

North-eastern United States 116–117
1:2 200 000

Mexico 118–119
1:7 100 000

Central America and the West Indies 120–121
1:7 100 000
Jamaica 1:2 700 000
Guadeloupe 1:1 800 000
Martinique 1:1 800 000
Puerto Rico 1:2 700 000
Virgin Islands 1:1 800 000
St Lucia 1:890 000
Barbados 1:890 000

SOUTH AMERICA

South America: Physical 122
1:31 100 000

South America: Political 123
1:31 100 000

South America – North 124–125
1:14 200 000
Trinidad and Tobago 1:2 200 000

Central South America 126–127
1:7 100 000

South America – South 128
1:14 200 000

INDEX TO WORLD MAPS

129–224

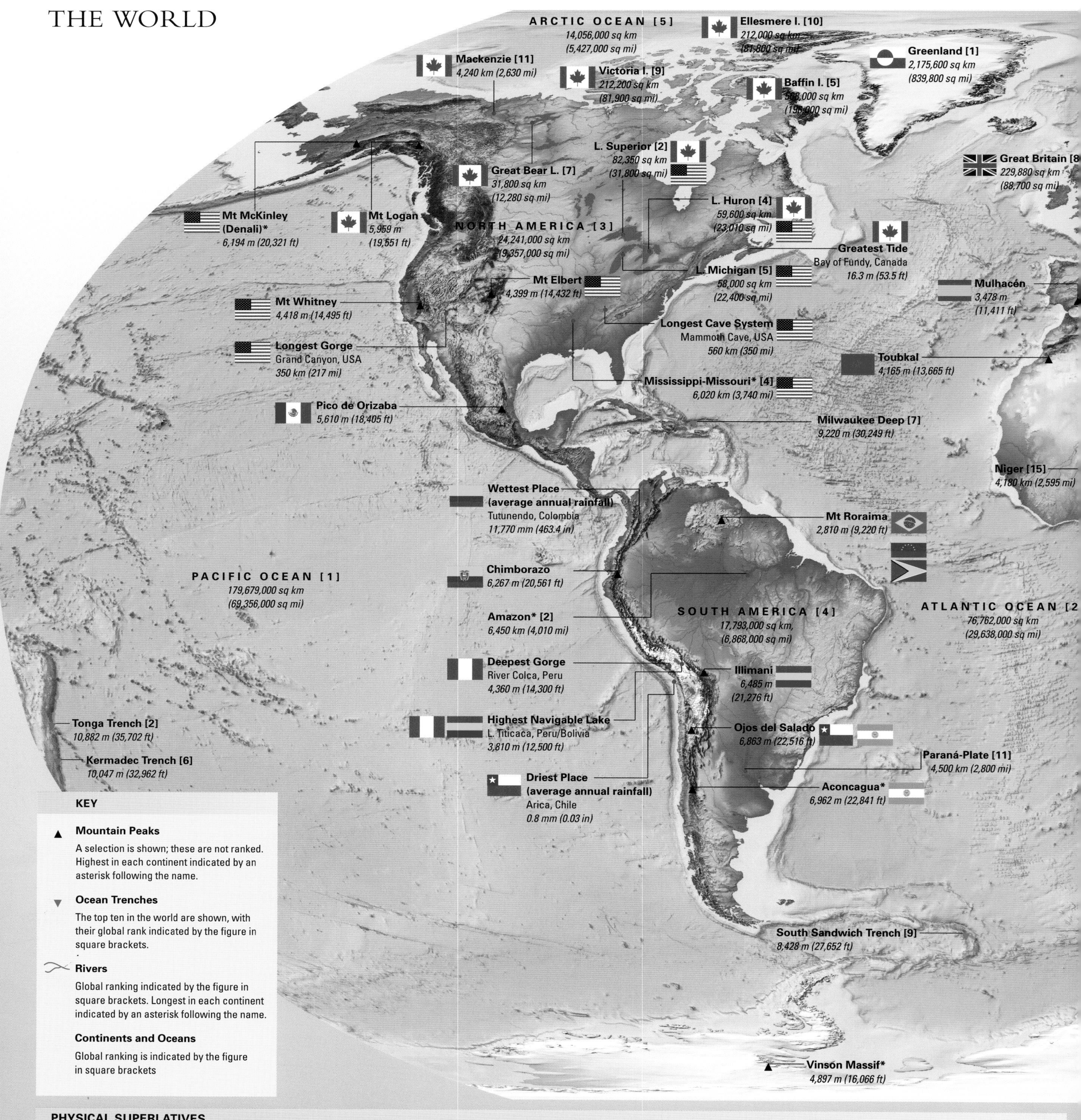

KEY

▲ **Mountain Peaks**
A selection is shown; these are not ranked. Highest in each continent indicated by an asterisk following the name.

▼ **Ocean Trenches**
The top ten in the world are shown, with their global rank indicated by the figure in square brackets.

Rivers
Global ranking indicated by the figure in square brackets. Longest in each continent indicated by an asterisk following the name.

Continents and Oceans
Global ranking is indicated by the figure in square brackets

PHYSICAL SUPERLATIVES

Highest Mountains

1	Everest, Asia *8,850 m (29,035 ft)*
2	K2 (Godwin Austen), Asia *8,611 m (28,251 ft)*
3	Kanchenjunga, Asia *8,598 m (28,208 ft)*
4	Lhotse, Asia *8,516 m (27,939 ft)*
5	Makalu, Asia *8,481 m (27,824 ft)*
6	Cho Oyu, Asia *8,201 m (26,906 ft)*
7	Dhaulagiri, Asia *8,172 m (26,811 ft)*
8	Manaslu, Asia *8,156 m (26,758 ft)*
9	Nanga Parbat, Asia *8,126 m (26,660 ft)*
10	Annapurna, Asia *8,078 m (26,502 ft)*

Longest Rivers

1	Nile, Africa *6,670 km (4,140 mi)*
2	Amazon, S. America *6,450 km (4,010 mi)*
3	Yangtze, Asia *6,380 km (3,960 mi)*
4	Mississippi-Missouri, N. America *6,020 km (3,740 mi)*
5	Yenisey-Angara, Asia *5,550 km (3,445 mi)*
6	Huang He, Asia *5,464 km (3,395 mi)*
7	Ob-Irtysh, Asia *5,410 km (3,360 mi)*
8	Congo, Africa *4,670 km (2,900 mi)*
9	Mekong, Asia *4,500 km (2,795 mi)*
10	Amur, Asia *4,440 km (2,760 mi)*

Largest Lakes and Inland Seas

1	Caspian Sea, Asia *371,000 sq km (143,000 sq mi)*
2	Lake Superior, N. America *82,350 sq km (31,800 sq mi)*
3	Lake Victoria, Africa *68,000 sq km (26,000 sq mi)*
4	Lake Huron, N. America *59,600 sq km (23,010 sq mi)*
5	Lake Michigan, N. America *58,000 sq km (22,400 sq mi)*
6	Lake Tanganyika, Africa *33,000 sq km (13,000 sq mi)*
7	Great Bear Lake, N. America *31,800 sq km (12,280 sq mi)*
8	Lake Baikal, Asia *30,500 sq km (11,780 sq mi)*
9	Lake Malawi/Nyasa, Africa *29,600 sq km (11,430 sq mi)*
10	Aral Sea, Asia *28,687 sq km (11,086 sq mi)*

Largest Islands

1	Greenland, N. America *2,175,600 sq km (839,800 sq mi)*
2	New Guinea, Oceania *821,030 sq km (317,000 sq mi)*
3	Borneo, Asia *744,360 sq km (287,400 sq mi)*
4	Madagascar, Africa *587,040 sq km (226,660 sq mi)*
5	Baffin Island, N. America *508,000 sq km (196,100 sq mi)*
6	Sumatra, Asia *473,600 sq km (182,860 sq mi)*
7	Honshu, Asia *230,500 sq km (88,980 sq mi)*
8	Great Britain, Europe *229,880 sq km (88,700 sq mi)*
9	Victoria Island, N. America *212,200 sq km (81,900 sq mi)*
10	Ellesmere Island, N. America *212,000 sq km (81,800 sq mi)*

INSIDE THE EARTH

Layer	Density (water = 1)	Temperature		State	Thickness	
Crust (continental)	2.8	<500°C	(930°F)	Solid	*c.* 40 km	(*c.* 25 mi)
Crust (oceanic)	2.9	<1,100°C	(2,010°F)	Solid	*c.* 7 km	(*c.* 4 mi)
Upper mantle	4.3	<1,400°C	(2,550°F)	Molten	*c.* 900 km	(*c.* 560 mi)
Lower mantle	5.5	<1,700°C	(3,090°F)	Solid	*c.* 1,900 km	(*c.* 1,180 mi)
Outer core	10.0	<2,300°C	(7,170°F)	Molten	*c.* 2,200 km	(*c.* 1,370 mi)
Inner core	13.5	<5,500°C	(9,930°F)	Solid	*c.* 1,300 km	(*c.* 810 mi)

EARTH'S DIMENSIONS

Mean distance from the Sun	149.6 million km (93 million mi)
Average speed around the Sun	108,000 km/h (66,600 mph)
Age	4,600 million years
Mass	5.9×10^{21} tonnes
Density (water = 1)	5.52
Volume	$1{,}083{,}230 \times 10^6$ cu km ($260{,}000 \times 10^6$ cu mi)
Area	510 million sq km (197 million sq mi)
Land surface	149 million sq km (58 million sq mi) = 29.3% of total area
Water surface	361 million sq km (139 million sq mi) = 70.7% of total area
Equatorial circumference	40,074 km (24,901 mi)
Polar circumference	40,008 km (24,860 mi)
Equatorial diameter	12,756 km (7,926 mi)
Polar diameter	12,714 km (7,900 mi)

EUROPE AND RUSSIA

COUNTRIES: AREA

	Country/Territory	Area sq km (thousands)	Area sq mi (thousands)
Largest			
1	Russia	17,075	6,593
2	Ukraine	604	233
3	France	552	213
4	Spain	498	192
5	Sweden	450	174
6	Germany	357	138
7	Finland	338	131
8	Norway	324	125
9	Poland	323	125
10	Italy	301	116
11	United Kingdom	242	93.4
12	Romania	238	92.0
13	Belarus	208	80.2
14	Greece	132	50.9
15	Bulgaria	111	42.8
16	Iceland	103	39.8
17	Serbia & Montenegro	102	39.4
18	Hungary	93.0	35.9
19	Portugal	88.8	34.3
20	Austria	83.9	32.4
Smallest			
1	Vatican City	0.0004	0.0002
2	Monaco	0.001	0.0004
3	Gibraltar (UK)	0.006	0.002
4	San Marino	0.06	0.02
5	Liechtenstein	0.16	0.06
6	Malta	0.32	0.12
7	Andorra	0.47	0.18
8	Færoe Is. (Denmark)	1.4	0.54
9	Luxembourg	2.6	1.0
10	Slovenia	20.3	7.8

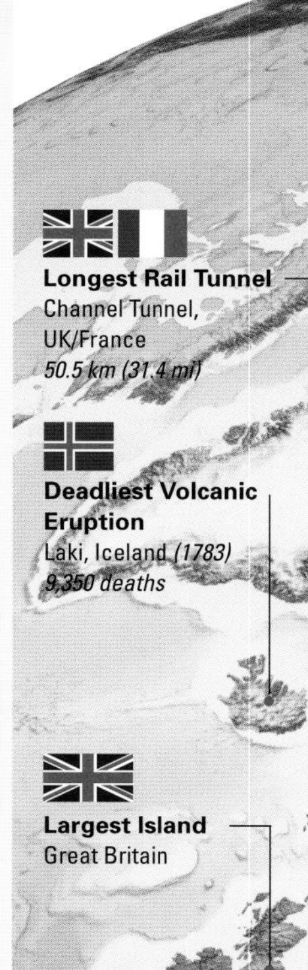

Longest Rail Tunnel
Channel Tunnel, UK/France
50.5 km (31.4 mi)

Deadliest Volcanic Eruption
Laki, Iceland *(1783)*
9,350 deaths

Largest Island
Great Britain

Richest Country
Luxembourg

Highest Dam
Grande Dixence, Switzerland
285 m (935 ft)

Tallest Building
Commerzbank Tower, Frankfurt
259 m (850 ft)

Highest Waterfall
Utigård, Jostedal Glacier, Norway
800 m (2,625 ft)

Longest Road Tunnel
Lærdal, Norway
24.5 km (15.8 mi)

Largest Lake
Lake Ladoga

Longest Suspension Bridge
Store Bælt, Denmark
1,624 m (5,328 ft)

Largest Country
Russia

Most Populous Country

Country with Longest Land Border
19,990 km (12,414 mi)

Largest Hydroelectric Plant
Sayano-Shushensk, Russia
6,400 MW

Longest River
Volga

Lowest Point
Caspian Sea
–28 m (–92 ft)

Highest Mountain
Elbrus

Largest Subway System
London
415 km (258 mi)

Busiest Airport
London (Heathrow)
63.5 million passengers per year

Largest City
Paris

Oldest Country
San Marino *(301)*

Deadliest Earthquake
Messina, Italy *(1908)*
70,000–100,000 deaths

Poorest Country
Bosnia-Herzegovina

Newest Countries
Czech Republic & Slovak Republic
(January 1993)

COUNTRIES: POPULATION

	Country/Territory	Population (thousands)
Most Populous		
1	Russia	143,782
2	Germany	82,425
3	France	60,424
4	United Kingdom	60,271
5	Italy	58,057
6	Ukraine	47,732
7	Spain	40,281
8	Poland	38,626
9	Romania	22,356
10	Netherlands	16,318
11	Serbia & Montenegro	10,826
12	Greece	10,648
13	Portugal	10,524
14	Belgium	10,348
15	Belarus	10,311
16	Czech Republic	10,246
17	Hungary	10,032
18	Sweden	8,986
19	Austria	8,175
20	Bulgaria	7,518
Least Populous		
1	Vatican City	1
2	Gibraltar (UK)	28
3	San Marino	29
4	Monaco	32
5	Liechtenstein	33
6	Færoe Islands (Denmark)	47
7	Andorra	70
8	Iceland	294
9	Malta	397
10	Luxembourg	463

LARGEST CITIES

	City	Population (thousands)
1	Paris, France	9,630
2	Moscow, Russia	8,367
3	London, UK	8,089
4	St Petersburg, Russia	4,635
5	Lisbon, Portugal	3,861
6	Berlin, Germany	3,387
7	Athens, Greece	3,116
8	Madrid, Spain	3,017
9	Rome, Italy	2,649
10	Kiev, Ukraine	2,621
11	Birmingham, UK	2,373
12	Manchester, UK	2,353
13	Bucharest, Romania	2,001
14	Porto, Portugal	1,940
15	Budapest, Hungary	1,819
16	Vienna, Austria	1,807
17	Minsk, Belarus	1,717
18	Hamburg, Germany	1,705
19	Belgrade, Serbia & Mont.	1,673
20	Warsaw, Poland	1,626
21	Stockholm, Sweden	1,612
22	Barcelona, Spain	1,527
23	Kharkov, Ukraine	1,521
24	Tbilisi, Georgia	1,406
25	Lyons, France	1,353
26	Nizhniy Novgorod, Russia	1,332
27	Copenhagen, Denmark	1,332
28	Novosibirsk, Russia	1,321
29	Marseilles, France	1,290
30	Yekaterinburg, Russia	1,218

COUNTRIES: WEALTH

	Country/Territory	Annual Income (US$ per capita)
Richest		
1	Luxembourg	48,900
2	San Marino	34,600
3	Norway	33,000
4	Switzerland	32,000
5	Iceland	30,200
6	Ireland	29,300
7	Belgium	29,200
8	Denmark	28,900
9	Austria	27,900
10	Netherlands	27,200
Poorest		
1	Bosnia-Herzegovina	1,900
2	Serbia & Montenegro	2,200
3	Moldova	2,600
4	Albania	4,400
5	Ukraine	4,500
6	Macedonia (FYROM)	5,100
7	Bulgaria	6,500
8	Romania	7,600
9	Lithuania	8,400
10	Belarus	8,700

PHYSICAL SUPERLATIVES

Land Area
9,957,000 sq km (3,843,000 sq mi)

Highest Mountains
1. Elbrus, Russia *5,642 m (18,510 ft)*
2. Mont Blanc, France/Italy *4,807 m (15,771 ft)*
3. Monte Rosa, Italy/Switzerland *4,634 m (15,203 ft)*
4. Dom, Switzerland *4,545 m (14,911 ft)*
5. Liskamm, Switzerland *4,527 m (14,852 ft)*

Longest Rivers
1. Volga *3,700 km (2,300 mi)*
2. Danube *2,850 km (1,770 mi)*
3. Ural *2,535 km (1,575 mi)*
4. Dnepr *2,285 km (1,420 mi)*
5. Kama *2,030 km (1,260 mi)*

Largest Lakes and Inland Seas
1. Lake Ladoga, Russia *17,700 sq km (6,800 sq mi)*
2. Lake Onega, Russia *9,700 sq km (3,700 sq mi)*
3. Saimaa system, Finland *8,000 sq km (3,100 sq mi)*
4. Vänern, Sweden *5,500 sq km (2,100 sq mi)*
5. Rybinsk Reservoir, Russia *4,700 sq km (1,800 sq mi)*

Largest Islands
1. Great Britain, UK *229,880 sq km (88,700 sq mi)*
2. Iceland, Atlantic Ocean *103,000 sq km (39,800 sq mi)*
3. Ireland, Ireland/UK *84,400 sq km (32,600 sq mi)*
4. Novaya Zemlya (N.), Russia *48,200 sq km (18,600 sq mi)*
5. W. Spitzbergen, Norway *39,000 sq km (15,100 sq mi)*

Note: If a territory is not completely independent, the country it is associated with is also named (in brackets). The area figures give the total area of land, inland water and ice. The population figures are 2004 estimates where available. The annual income is the Gross Domestic Product per capita (measured using the purchasing-power parity method, enabling comparisons to be made between countries through their purchasing power) in US dollars; the figures are the latest available, usually 2002 estimates. The city population figures are taken from the most recent census or estimate available, and as far as possible are the population of the metropolitan area or urban agglomeration (for example, greater New York or Paris).

COUNTRIES: AREA

	Country/Territory	Area sq km (thousands)	Area sq mi (thousands)
Largest			
1	China	9,597	3,705
2	India	3,287	1,269
3	Kazakhstan	2,725	1,052
4	Saudi Arabia	2,150	830
5	Indonesia	1,905	735
6	Iran	1,648	636
7	Mongolia	1,567	605
8	Pakistan	796	307
9	Turkey	775	299
10	Burma (= Myanmar)	677	261
11	Afghanistan	652	252
12	Yemen	528	204
13	Thailand	513	198
14	Turkmenistan	488	188
15	Uzbekistan	447	173
16	Iraq	438	169
17	Japan	378	146
18	Vietnam	332	128
19	Malaysia	330	127
20	Oman	310	119
Smallest			
1	Macau (China)	0.02	0.007
2	Maldives	0.30	0.12
3	Gaza Strip (OPT)	0.36	0.14
4	Singapore	0.68	0.26
5	Bahrain	0.69	0.27
6	Hong Kong (China)	1.1	0.42
7	Brunei	5.8	2.2
8	West Bank (OPT)	5.9	2.3
9	Cyprus	9.3	3.6
10	Lebanon	10.4	4.0

COUNTRIES: POPULATION

	Country/Territory	Population (thousands)
Most Populous		
1	China	1,298,848
2	India	1,065,071
3	Indonesia	238,453
4	Pakistan	159,196
5	Bangladesh	141,340
6	Japan	127,333
7	Philippines	86,242
8	Vietnam	82,690
9	Iran	69,019
10	Turkey	68,894
11	Thailand	64,866
12	South Korea	48,598
13	Burma (= Myanmar)	42,720
14	Afghanistan	28,514
15	Nepal	27,071
16	Uzbekistan	26,410
17	Saudi Arabia	25,796
18	Iraq	25,375
19	Malaysia	23,522
20	Taiwan	22,750
Least Populous		
1	Maldives	339
2	Brunei	365
3	Macau (China)	445
4	Bahrain	678
5	Cyprus	776
6	Qatar	840
7	East Timor	1,019
8	Gaza Strip (OPT)	1,325
9	Bhutan	2,186
10	Kuwait	2,258

LARGEST CITIES

	City	Population (thousands)
1	Mumbai (Bombay), India	16,086
2	Kolkata (Calcutta), India	13,058
3	Shanghai, China	12,887
4	Dhaka, Bangladesh	12,519
5	Delhi, India	12,441
6	Tokyo, Japan	12,064
7	Jakarta, Indonesia	11,018
8	Beijing, China	10,839
9	Karachi, Pakistan	10,032
10	Manila, Philippines	9,950
11	Seoul, South Korea	9,888
12	Tianjin, China	9,156
13	Istanbul, Turkey	8,953
14	Bangkok, Thailand	7,372
15	Tehran, Iran	6,979
16	Hong Kong, China	6,860
17	Yokohama, Japan	6,427
18	Chennai (Madras), India	6,353
19	Bangalore, India	5,567
20	Lahore, Pakistan	5,452
21	Hyderabad, India	5,445
22	Wuhan, China	5,169
23	Chongqing, China	4,900
24	Baghdad, Iraq	4,865
25	Shenyang, China	4,828
26	Ho Chi Minh City, Vietnam	4,619
27	Ahmadabad, India	4,427
28	Rangoon, Burma (Myanmar)	4,393
29	Singapore City, Singapore	4,131
30	Guangzhou, China	3,893

COUNTRIES: WEALTH

	Country/Territory	Annual Income (US$ per capita)
Richest		
1	Japan	28,700
2	Hong Kong (China)	27,200
3	Singapore	25,200
4	United Arab Emirates	22,100
5	Qatar	20,100
6	South Korea	19,600
7	Israel	19,500
8	Brunei	18,600
9	Macau (China)	18,500
10	Kuwait	17,500
Poorest		
1	East Timor	500
2	Gaza Strip (OPT)	600
3	Afghanistan	700
4	Syria	700
5	West Bank (OPT)	800
6	Yemen	800
7	North Korea	1,000
8	Bhutan	1,300
9	Tajikistan	1,300
10	Nepal	1,400

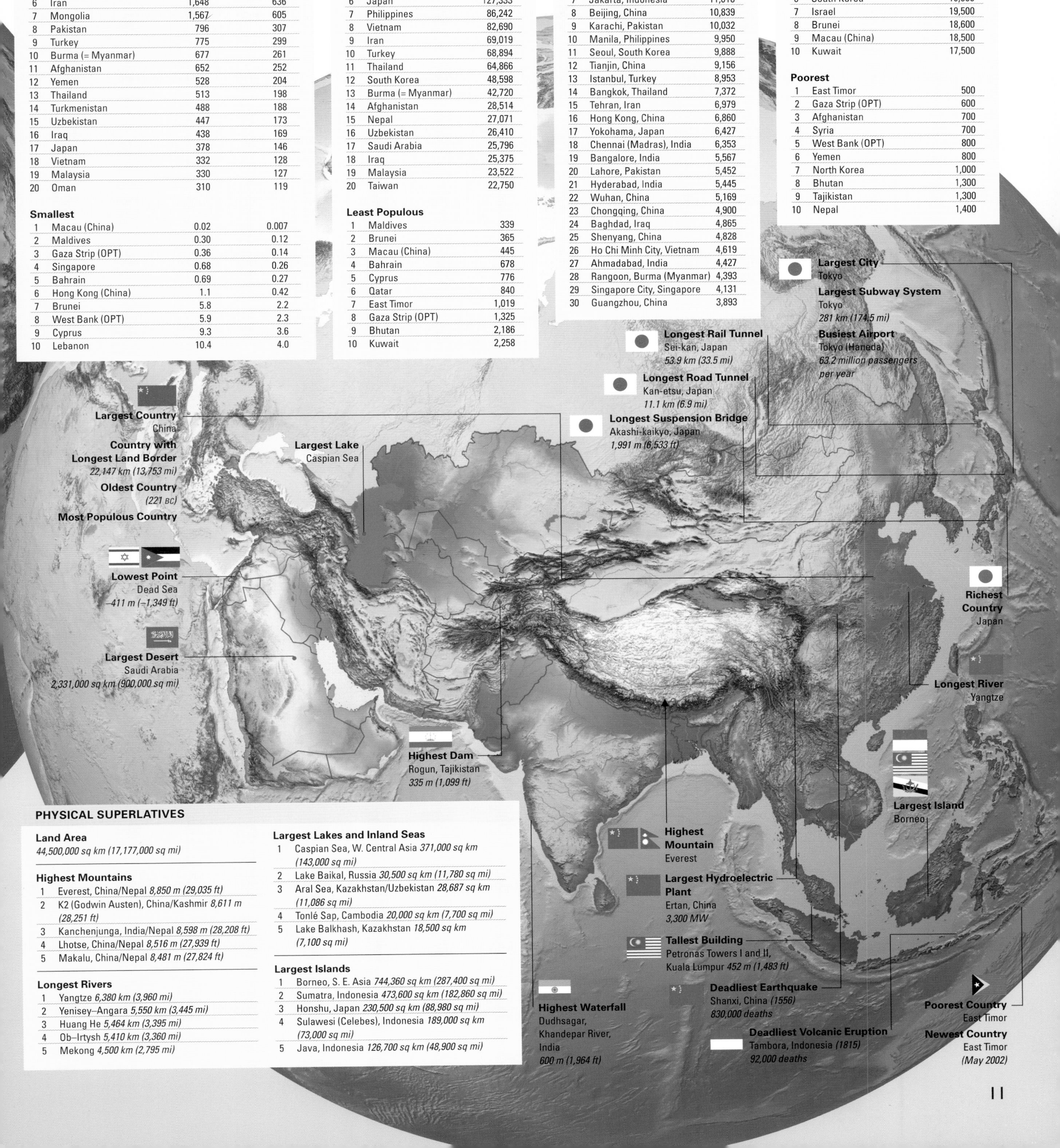

Largest City
Tokyo

Largest Subway System
Tokyo
281 km (174.5 mi)

Busiest Airport
Tokyo (Haneda)
63.2 million passengers per year

Longest Rail Tunnel
Sei-kan, Japan
53.9 km (33.5 mi)

Longest Road Tunnel
Kan-etsu, Japan
11.1 km (6.9 mi)

Longest Suspension Bridge
Akashi-kaikyo, Japan
1,991 m (6,533 ft)

Largest Country
China

Country with Longest Land Border
22,147 km (13,753 mi)

Oldest Country
(221 BC)

Most Populous Country

Largest Lake
Caspian Sea

Lowest Point
Dead Sea
–411 m (–1,349 ft)

Largest Desert
Saudi Arabia
2,331,000 sq km (900,000 sq mi)

Highest Dam
Rogun, Tajikistan
335 m (1,099 ft)

Richest Country
Japan

Longest River
Yangtze

Largest Island
Borneo

Highest Mountain
Everest

Largest Hydroelectric Plant
Ertan, China
3,300 MW

Tallest Building
Petronas Towers I and II, Kuala Lumpur *452 m (1,483 ft)*

Deadliest Earthquake
Shanxi, China *(1556)*
830,000 deaths

Deadliest Volcanic Eruption
Tambora, Indonesia *(1815)*
92,000 deaths

Highest Waterfall
Dudhsagar, Khandepar River, India
600 m (1,964 ft)

Poorest Country
East Timor

Newest Country
East Timor
(May 2002)

PHYSICAL SUPERLATIVES

Land Area
44,500,000 sq km (17,177,000 sq mi)

Highest Mountains
1. Everest, China/Nepal *8,850 m (29,035 ft)*
2. K2 (Godwin Austen), China/Kashmir *8,611 m (28,251 ft)*
3. Kanchenjunga, India/Nepal *8,598 m (28,208 ft)*
4. Lhotse, China/Nepal *8,516 m (27,939 ft)*
5. Makalu, China/Nepal *8,481 m (27,824 ft)*

Longest Rivers
1. Yangtze *6,380 km (3,960 mi)*
2. Yenisey–Angara *5,550 km (3,445 mi)*
3. Huang He *5,464 km (3,395 mi)*
4. Ob–Irtysh *5,410 km (3,360 mi)*
5. Mekong *4,500 km (2,795 mi)*

Largest Lakes and Inland Seas
1. Caspian Sea, W. Central Asia *371,000 sq km (143,000 sq mi)*
2. Lake Baikal, Russia *30,500 sq km (11,780 sq mi)*
3. Aral Sea, Kazakhstan/Uzbekistan *28,687 sq km (11,086 sq mi)*
4. Tonlé Sap, Cambodia *20,000 sq km (7,700 sq mi)*
5. Lake Balkhash, Kazakhstan *18,500 sq km (7,100 sq mi)*

Largest Islands
1. Borneo, S. E. Asia *744,360 sq km (287,400 sq mi)*
2. Sumatra, Indonesia *473,600 sq km (182,860 sq mi)*
3. Honshu, Japan *230,500 sq km (88,980 sq mi)*
4. Sulawesi (Celebes), Indonesia *189,000 sq km (73,000 sq mi)*
5. Java, Indonesia *126,700 sq km (48,900 sq mi)*

AFRICA

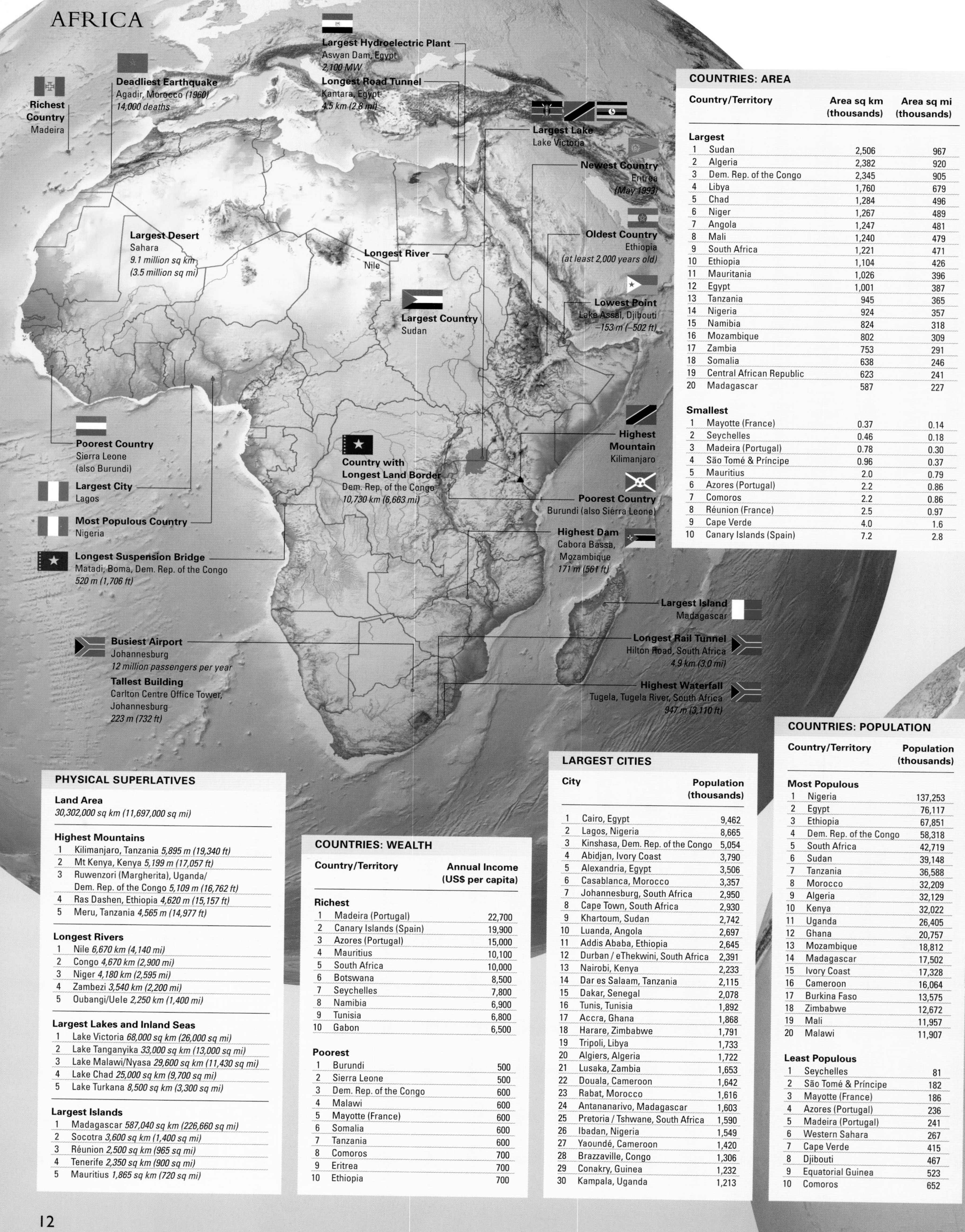

COUNTRIES: AREA

	Country/Territory	Area sq km (thousands)	Area sq mi (thousands)
Largest			
1	Sudan	2,506	967
2	Algeria	2,382	920
3	Dem. Rep. of the Congo	2,345	905
4	Libya	1,760	679
5	Chad	1,284	496
6	Niger	1,267	489
7	Angola	1,247	481
8	Mali	1,240	479
9	South Africa	1,221	471
10	Ethiopia	1,104	426
11	Mauritania	1,026	396
12	Egypt	1,001	387
13	Tanzania	945	365
14	Nigeria	924	357
15	Namibia	824	318
16	Mozambique	802	309
17	Zambia	753	291
18	Somalia	638	246
19	Central African Republic	623	241
20	Madagascar	587	227
Smallest			
1	Mayotte (France)	0.37	0.14
2	Seychelles	0.46	0.18
3	Madeira (Portugal)	0.78	0.30
4	São Tomé & Príncipe	0.96	0.37
5	Mauritius	2.0	0.79
6	Azores (Portugal)	2.2	0.86
7	Comoros	2.2	0.86
8	Réunion (France)	2.5	0.97
9	Cape Verde	4.0	1.6
10	Canary Islands (Spain)	7.2	2.8

PHYSICAL SUPERLATIVES

Land Area
30,302,000 sq km (11,697,000 sq mi)

Highest Mountains
1. Kilimanjaro, Tanzania *5,895 m (19,340 ft)*
2. Mt Kenya, Kenya *5,199 m (17,057 ft)*
3. Ruwenzori (Margherita), Uganda/Dem. Rep. of the Congo *5,109 m (16,762 ft)*
4. Ras Dashen, Ethiopia *4,620 m (15,157 ft)*
5. Meru, Tanzania *4,565 m (14,977 ft)*

Longest Rivers
1. Nile *6,670 km (4,140 mi)*
2. Congo *4,670 km (2,900 mi)*
3. Niger *4,180 km (2,595 mi)*
4. Zambezi *3,540 km (2,200 mi)*
5. Oubangi/Uele *2,250 km (1,400 mi)*

Largest Lakes and Inland Seas
1. Lake Victoria *68,000 sq km (26,000 sq mi)*
2. Lake Tanganyika *33,000 sq km (13,000 sq mi)*
3. Lake Malawi/Nyasa *29,600 sq km (11,430 sq mi)*
4. Lake Chad *25,000 sq km (9,700 sq mi)*
5. Lake Turkana *8,500 sq km (3,300 sq mi)*

Largest Islands
1. Madagascar *587,040 sq km (226,660 sq mi)*
2. Socotra *3,600 sq km (1,400 sq mi)*
3. Réunion *2,500 sq km (965 sq mi)*
4. Tenerife *2,350 sq km (900 sq mi)*
5. Mauritius *1,865 sq km (720 sq mi)*

COUNTRIES: WEALTH

	Country/Territory	Annual Income (US$ per capita)
Richest		
1	Madeira (Portugal)	22,700
2	Canary Islands (Spain)	19,900
3	Azores (Portugal)	15,000
4	Mauritius	10,100
5	South Africa	10,000
6	Botswana	8,500
7	Seychelles	7,800
8	Namibia	6,900
9	Tunisia	6,800
10	Gabon	6,500
Poorest		
1	Burundi	500
2	Sierra Leone	500
3	Dem. Rep. of the Congo	600
4	Malawi	600
5	Mayotte (France)	600
6	Somalia	600
7	Tanzania	600
8	Comoros	700
9	Eritrea	700
10	Ethiopia	700

LARGEST CITIES

	City	Population (thousands)
1	Cairo, Egypt	9,462
2	Lagos, Nigeria	8,665
3	Kinshasa, Dem. Rep. of the Congo	5,054
4	Abidjan, Ivory Coast	3,790
5	Alexandria, Egypt	3,506
6	Casablanca, Morocco	3,357
7	Johannesburg, South Africa	2,950
8	Cape Town, South Africa	2,930
9	Khartoum, Sudan	2,742
10	Luanda, Angola	2,697
11	Addis Ababa, Ethiopia	2,645
12	Durban / eThekwini, South Africa	2,391
13	Nairobi, Kenya	2,233
14	Dar es Salaam, Tanzania	2,115
15	Dakar, Senegal	2,078
16	Tunis, Tunisia	1,892
17	Accra, Ghana	1,868
18	Harare, Zimbabwe	1,791
19	Tripoli, Libya	1,733
20	Algiers, Algeria	1,722
21	Lusaka, Zambia	1,653
22	Douala, Cameroon	1,642
23	Rabat, Morocco	1,616
24	Antananarivo, Madagascar	1,603
25	Pretoria / Tshwane, South Africa	1,590
26	Ibadan, Nigeria	1,549
27	Yaoundé, Cameroon	1,420
28	Brazzaville, Congo	1,306
29	Conakry, Guinea	1,232
30	Kampala, Uganda	1,213

COUNTRIES: POPULATION

	Country/Territory	Population (thousands)
Most Populous		
1	Nigeria	137,253
2	Egypt	76,117
3	Ethiopia	67,851
4	Dem. Rep. of the Congo	58,318
5	South Africa	42,719
6	Sudan	39,148
7	Tanzania	36,588
8	Morocco	32,209
9	Algeria	32,129
10	Kenya	32,022
11	Uganda	26,405
12	Ghana	20,757
13	Mozambique	18,812
14	Madagascar	17,502
15	Ivory Coast	17,328
16	Cameroon	16,064
17	Burkina Faso	13,575
18	Zimbabwe	12,672
19	Mali	11,957
20	Malawi	11,907
Least Populous		
1	Seychelles	81
2	São Tomé & Príncipe	182
3	Mayotte (France)	186
4	Azores (Portugal)	236
5	Madeira (Portugal)	241
6	Western Sahara	267
7	Cape Verde	415
8	Djibouti	467
9	Equatorial Guinea	523
10	Comoros	652

OCEANIA

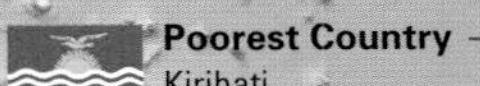
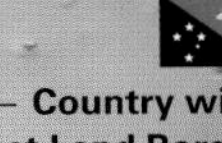

PHYSICAL SUPERLATIVES

Land Area
8,557,000 sq km (3,303,000 sq mi)

Highest Mountains

1. Puncak Jaya, Indonesia *5,029 m (16,499 ft)*
2. Puncak Trikora, Indonesia *4,730 m (15,518 ft)*
3. Puncak Mandala, Indonesia *4,702 m (15,427 ft)*
4. Mt Wilhelm, Papua New Guinea *4,508 m (14,790 ft)*
5. Mauna Kea, USA (Hawai'i) *4,205 m (13,796 ft)*

Longest Rivers

1. Murray–Darling *3,750 km (2,330 mi)*
2. Darling *3,070 km (1,905 mi)*
3. Murray *2,575 km (1,600 mi)*
4. Murrumbidgee *1,690 km (1,050 mi)*
5. Lachlan *1,370 km (850 mi)*

Largest Lakes and Inland Seas

1. Lake Eyre, Australia *8,900 sq km (3,400 sq mi)*
2. Lake Torrens, Australia *5,800 sq km (2,200 sq mi)*
3. Lake Gairdner, Australia *4,800 sq km (1,900 sq mi)*
4. Lake Mackay, Australia *3,490 sq km (1,380 sq mi)*
5. Lake Amadeus, Australia *1,032 sq km (400 sq mi)*

Largest Islands

1. New Guinea, Indon./Papua NG *821,030 sq km (317,000 sq mi)*
2. New Zealand (S.), Pacific Ocean *150,500 sq km (58,100 sq mi)*
3. New Zealand (N.), Pacific Ocean *114,700 sq km (44,300 sq mi)*
4. Tasmania, Australia *67,800 sq km (26,200 sq mi)*
5. New Britain, Papua NG *37,800 sq km (14,600 sq mi)*

COUNTRIES: AREA

	Country/Territory	Area sq km (thousands)	Area sq mi (thousands)
1	Australia	7,741	2,989
2	Papua New Guinea	463	179
3	New Zealand	271	104
4	Solomon Islands	28.9	11.2
5	New Caledonia (France)	18.6	7.2
6	Fiji Islands	18.3	7.1
7	Vanuatu	12.2	4.7
8	French Polynesia (France)	4.0	1.5
9	Samoa	2.8	1.1
10	Kiribati	0.73	0.28
11	Fed. States of Micronesia	0.70	0.27
12	Tonga	0.65	0.25
13	Guam (US)	0.55	0.21
14	Northern Mariana Islands (US)	0.46	0.18
15	Palau	0.46	0.18
16	Cook Is. (NZ)	0.24	0.09
17	American Samoa (US)	0.20	0.08
18	Wallis & Futuna Islands (France)	0.20	0.08
19	Marshall Islands	0.18	0.07
20	Tuvalu	0.03	0.01
21	Nauru	0.02	0.008

COUNTRIES: POPULATION

	Country/Territory	Population (thousands)
1	Australia	19,913
2	Papua New Guinea	5,420
3	New Zealand	3,994
4	Fiji Islands	881
5	Solomon Islands	524
6	French Polynesia (France)	266
7	New Caledonia (France)	214
8	Vanuatu	203
9	Samoa	178
10	Guam (US)	166
11	Tonga	110
12	Fed. States of Micronesia	108
13	Kiribati	101
14	Northern Mariana Is. (US)	78
15	American Samoa (US)	58
16	Marshall Islands	58
17	Cook Islands (NZ)	21
18	Palau	20
19	Wallis & Futuna Is. (France)	16
20	Nauru	13
21	Tuvalu	11

COUNTRIES: WEALTH

	Country/Territory	Annual Income (US$ per capita)
1	Australia	26,900
2	Guam (US)	21,000
3	New Zealand	20,100
4	New Caledonia (France)	14,000
5	Northern Mariana Is. (US)	12,500
6	Palau	9,000
7	American Samoa (US)	8,000
8	Fiji Islands	5,600
9	Samoa	5,600
10	Cook Islands (NZ)	5,000
11	French Polynesia (France)	5,000
12	Nauru	5,000
13	Vanuatu	2,900
14	Samoa	2,200
15	Papua New Guinea	2,100
16	Fed. States of Micronesia	2,000
17	Wallis & Futuna Is. (France)	2,000
18	Solomon Islands	1,700
19	Marshall Islands	1,600
20	Tuvalu	1,100
21	Kiribati	800

LARGEST CITIES

	City	Population (thousands)
1	Sydney, Australia	4,086
2	Melbourne, Australia	3,466
3	Brisbane, Australia	1,627
4	Perth, Australia	1,381
5	Auckland, New Zealand	1,102
6	Adelaide, Australia	1,096

ANTARCTICA

PHYSICAL SUPERLATIVES

Land Area
14,100,000 sq km (5,443,000 sq mi)

Highest Mountains

1. Vinson Massif, W. Antarctica *4,897 m (16,066 ft)*
2. Mt Tyree, W. Antarctica *4,852 m (15,920 ft)*
3. Mt Kirkpatrick, Transantarctic Mountains *4,528 m (14,855 ft)*
4. Mt Markham, Transantarctic Mountains *4,349 m (14,268 ft)*
5. Mt Jackson, Antarctic Peninsula *4,191 m (13,751 ft)*

Largest Islands

1. Berkner, Ronne Ice Shelf *47,920 sq km (18,500 sq mi)*
2. Alexander, Bellingshausen Sea *43,200 sq km (16,630 sq mi)*
3. Thurston, Amundsen Sea *15,700 sq km (6,045 sq mi)*
4. Carney, Amundsen Sea *8,500 sq km (3,275 sq mi)*
5. Roosevelt, Ross Ice Shelf *7,500 sq km (2,890 sq mi)*

NORTH AMERICA

COUNTRIES: AREA

	Country/Territory	Area sq km (thousands)	Area sq mi (thousands)
Largest			
1	Canada	9,971	3,850
2	United States of America	9,629	3,718
3	Greenland (Denmark)	2,176	840
4	Mexico	1,958	756
5	Nicaragua	130	50.2
6	Honduras	112	43.3
7	Cuba	111	42.8
8	Guatemala	109	42.0
9	Panama	75.5	29.2
10	Costa Rica	51.1	19.7
11	Dominican Republic	48.5	18.7
12	Haiti	27.8	10.7
13	Belize	23.0	8.9
14	El Salvador	21.0	8.1
15	Bahamas	13.9	5.4
16	Jamaica	11.0	4.2
17	Puerto Rico (US)	8.9	3.4
18	Trinidad & Tobago	5.1	2.0
19	Guadeloupe (France)	1.7	0.66
20	Martinique (France)	1.1	0.43
Smallest			
1	Bermuda (UK)	0.05	0.02
2	Anguilla (UK)	0.10	0.04
3	Montserrat (UK)	0.10	0.04
4	Virgin Islands (UK)	0.15	0.06
5	Aruba (Netherlands)	0.19	0.07
6	Cayman Islands (UK)	0.26	0.10
7	St Kitts & Nevis	0.26	0.10
8	Grenada	0.34	0.13
9	Virgin Islands (US)	0.35	0.13
10	St Vincent & the Grenadines	0.39	0.15

COUNTRIES: POPULATION

	Country/Territory	Population (thousands)
Most Populous		
1	United States of America	293,028
2	Mexico	104,960
3	Canada	32,508
4	Guatemala	14,281
5	Cuba	11,309
6	Dominican Republic	8,834
7	Haiti	7,656
8	Honduras	6,824
9	El Salvador	6,588
10	Nicaragua	5,360
11	Costa Rica	3,957
12	Puerto Rico (US)	3,898
13	Panama	3,000
14	Jamaica	2,713
15	Trinidad & Tobago	1,097
16	Guadeloupe (France)	445
17	Martinique (France)	430
18	Bahamas	300
19	Barbados	278
20	Belize	273
Least Populous		
1	Montserrat (UK)	9
2	Anguilla (UK)	13
3	Turks & Caicos Is. (UK)	20
4	Virgin Islands (UK)	22
5	St Kitts & Nevis	39
6	Cayman Islands (UK)	43
7	Greenland (Denmark)	56
8	Bermuda (UK)	65
9	Antigua & Barbuda	68
10	Dominica	69

LARGEST CITIES

	City	Population (thousands)
1	Mexico City, Mexico	18,066
2	New York, USA	17,800
3	Los Angeles, USA	11,789
4	Chicago, USA	8,308
5	Philadelphia, USA	5,149
6	Miami, USA	4,919
7	Toronto, Canada	4,881
8	Dallas-Fort Worth, USA	4,146
9	Boston, USA	4,032
10	Washington, USA	3,934
11	Detroit, USA	3,903
12	Houston, USA	3,823
13	Guadalajara, Mexico	3,697
14	Montréal, Canada	3,511
15	Atlanta, USA	3,500
16	Monterrey, Mexico	3,267
17	Guatemala City, Guatemala	3,242
18	San Francisco, USA	3,229
19	Phoenix, USA	2,907
20	Seattle, USA	2,712
21	San Diego, USA	2,674
22	Santo Domingo, Dom. Rep.	2,563
23	Minneapolis–St Paul, USA	2,389
24	Havana, Cuba	2,256
25	San Juan, Puerto Rico	2,217
26	Vancouver, Canada	2,079
27	St Louis, USA	2,078
28	Baltimore, USA	2,076
29	Tampa–St Petersburg, USA	2,062
30	Denver, USA	1,985

PHYSICAL SUPERLATIVES

Land Area
24,241,000 sq km (9,357,000 sq mi)

Highest Mountains

1. Mt McKinley (Denali), USA (Alaska) *6,194 m (20,321 ft)*
2. Mt Logan, Canada *5,959 m (19,551 ft)*
3. Pico de Orizaba, Mexico *5,610 m (18,405 ft)*
4. Mt St Elias, Canada/USA *5,489 m (18,008 ft)*
5. Popocatépetl, Mexico *5,452 m (17,887 ft)*

Longest Rivers

1. Mississippi–Missouri *6,020 km (3,740 mi)*
2. Mackenzie *4,240 km (2,630 mi)*
3. Mississippi *4,120 km (2,560 mi)*
4. Missouri *3,780 km (2,350 mi)*
5. Yukon *3,185 km (1,980 mi)*

Largest Lakes and Inland Seas

1. Lake Superior, Canada/USA *82,350 sq km (31,800 sq mi)*
2. Lake Huron, Canada/USA *59,600 sq km (23,010 sq mi)*
3. Lake Michigan, USA *58,000 sq km (22,400 sq mi)*
4. Great Bear Lake, Canada *31,800 sq km (12,280 sq mi)*
5. Great Slave Lake, Canada *28,500 sq km (11,000 sq mi)*

Largest Islands

1. Greenland, Atlantic Ocean *2,175,600 sq km (839,800 sq mi)*
2. Baffin Island, Canada *508,000 sq km (196,100 sq mi)*
3. Victoria Island, Canada *212,200 sq km (81,900 sq mi)*
4. Ellesmere Island, Canada *212,000 sq km (81,800 sq mi)*
5. Cuba, Caribbean Sea *110,860 sq km (42,800 sq mi)*

COUNTRIES: WEALTH

	Country/Territory	Annual Income (US$ per capita)
Richest		
1	United States of America	36,300
2	Bermuda (UK)	35,200
3	Cayman Islands (UK)	35,000
4	Canada	29,300
5	Aruba (Netherlands)	28,000
6	Greenland (Denmark)	20,000
7	Virgin Islands (US)	19,000
8	Virgin Islands (UK)	16,000
9	Bahamas	15,300
10	Barbados	15,000
Poorest		
1	Haiti	1,400
2	Nicaragua	2,200
3	Honduras	2,500
4	Cuba	2,700
5	St Vincent & the Grenadines	2,900
6	Montserrat (UK)	3,400
7	Jamaica	3,800
8	Guatemala	3,900
9	El Salvador	4,600
10	Belize	4,900

COUNTRIES: AREA

	Country/Territory	Area sq km (thousands)	Area sq mi (thousands)
1	Brazil	8,514	3,287
2	Argentina	2,780	1,074
3	Peru	1,285	496
4	Colombia	1,139	440
5	Bolivia	1,099	424
6	Venezuela	912	352
7	Chile	757	292
8	Paraguay	407	157
9	Ecuador	284	109
10	Guyana	215	83

COUNTRIES: POPULATION

	Country/Territory	Population (thousands)
1	Brazil	184,101
2	Colombia	42,311
3	Argentina	39,145
4	Peru	27,544
5	Venezuela	25,017
6	Chile	15,824
7	Ecuador	13,213
8	Bolivia	8,724
9	Paraguay	6,191
10	Uruguay	3,399

LARGEST CITIES

	City	Population (thousands)
1	São Paulo, Brazil	17,962
2	Buenos Aires, Argentina	12,024
3	Rio de Janeiro, Brazil	10,652
4	Lima, Peru	7,443
5	Bogotá, Colombia	6,771
6	Santiago, Chile	5,467
7	Belo Horizonte, Brazil	4,224
8	Pôrto Alegre, Brazil	3,757
9	Recife, Brazil	3,346
10	Salvador, Brazil	3,238
11	Caracas, Venezuela	3,153
12	Fortaleza, Brazil	3,066
13	Medellín, Colombia	2,866
14	Curitiba, Brazil	2,562
15	Cali, Colombia	2,233
16	Guayaquil, Ecuador	2,118
17	Brasília, Brazil	2,051
18	Maracaibo, Venezuela	1,901
19	Valencia, Venezuela	1,893
20	Barranquilla, Colombia	1,683
21	Belém, Brazil	1,658
22	Quito, Ecuador	1,616
23	La Paz, Bolivia	1,487
24	Manaus, Brazil	1,467
25	Campinas, Brazil	1,434
26	Córdoba, Argentina	1,368
27	Montevideo, Uruguay	1,324
28	Rosario, Argentina	1,279
29	Santos, Brazil	1,270
30	Asunción, Paraguay	1,262

PHYSICAL SUPERLATIVES

Land Area
17,793,000 sq km (6,868,000 sq mi)

Highest Mountains

1. Aconcagua, Argentina *6,962 m (22,841 ft)*
2. Bonete, Argentina *6,872 m (22,546 ft)*
3. Ojos del Salado, Argentina/Chile *6,863 m (22,516 ft)*
4. Pissis, Argentina *6,779 m (22,241 ft)*
5. Mercedario, Argentina/Chile *6,770 m (22,211 ft)*

Longest Rivers

1. Amazon *6,450 km (4,010 mi)*
2. Paraná–Plate *4,500 km (2,800 mi)*
3. Purus *3,350 km (2,080 mi)*
4. Madeira *3,200 km (1,990 mi)*
5. São Francisco *2,900 km (1,800 mi)*

Largest Lakes and Inland Seas

1. Lake Titicaca, Bolivia/Peru *8,300 sq km (3,200 sq mi)*
2. Lake Poopo, Bolivia *2,800 sq km (1,100 sq mi)*
3. Lake Mar Chiquita, Argentina *2,000 sq km (780 sq mi)*
4. Lake General Carrera (Buenos Aires), Argentina/Chile *1,850 sq km (720 sq mi)*
5. Lake Argentino, Argentina *1,470 sq km (575 sq mi)*

Largest Islands

1. Tierra del Fuego, Argentine/Chile *47,000 sq km (18,100 sq mi)*
2. Chiloe, Chile *8,400 sq km (3,235 sq mi)*
3. Falkland Is. (East), Atlantic Ocean *6,800 sq km (2,600 sq mi)*
4. Wellington, Chile *5,560 sq km (2,140 sq mi)*
5. Riesco, Chile *5,110 sq km (1,970 sq mi)*

COUNTRIES: WEALTH

	Country/Territory	Annual Income (US$ per capita)
1	French Guiana (France)	14,400
2	Argentina	10,500
3	Chile	10,100
4	Uruguay	7,900
5	Brazil	7,600
6	Colombia	6,100
7	Venezuela	5,400
8	Peru	5,000
9	Paraguay	4,300
10	Guyana	3,800

World: Regions in the News

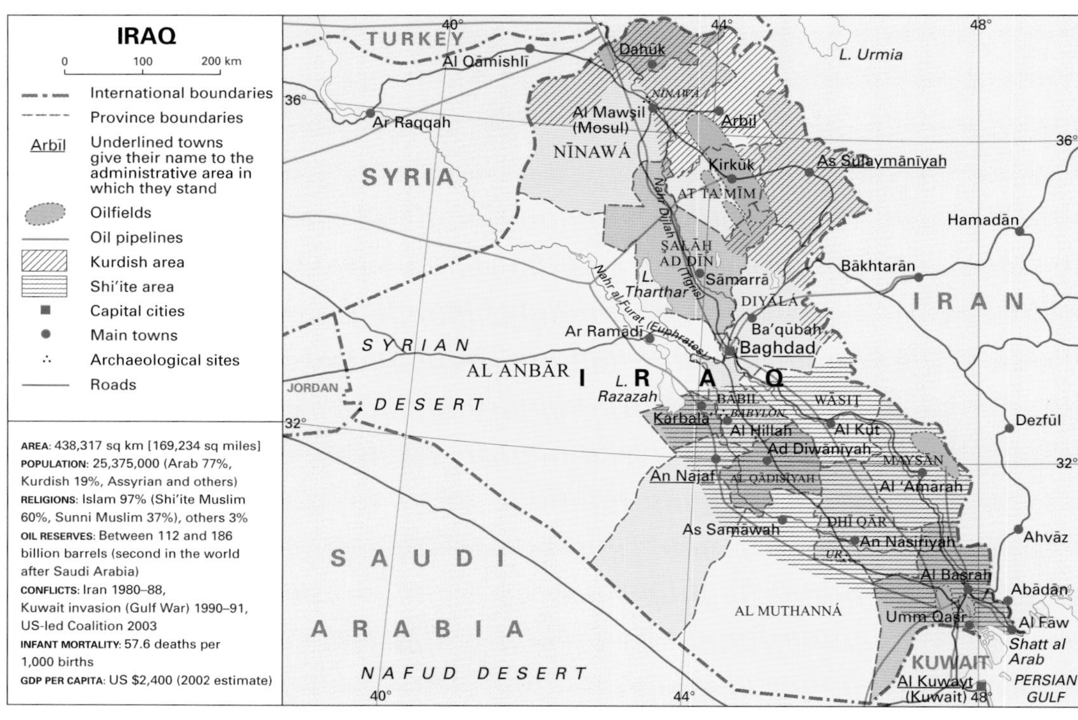

AREA: 438,317 sq km [169,234 sq miles]
POPULATION: 25,375,000 (Arab 77%, Kurdish 19%, Assyrian and others)
RELIGIONS: Islam 97% (Shi'ite Muslim 60%, Sunni Muslim 37%), others 3%
OIL RESERVES: Between 112 and 186 billion barrels (second in the world after Saudi Arabia)
CONFLICTS: Iran 1980–88, Kuwait invasion (Gulf War) 1990–91, US-led Coalition 2003
INFANT MORTALITY: 57.6 deaths per 1,000 births
GDP PER CAPITA: US $2,400 (2002 estimate)

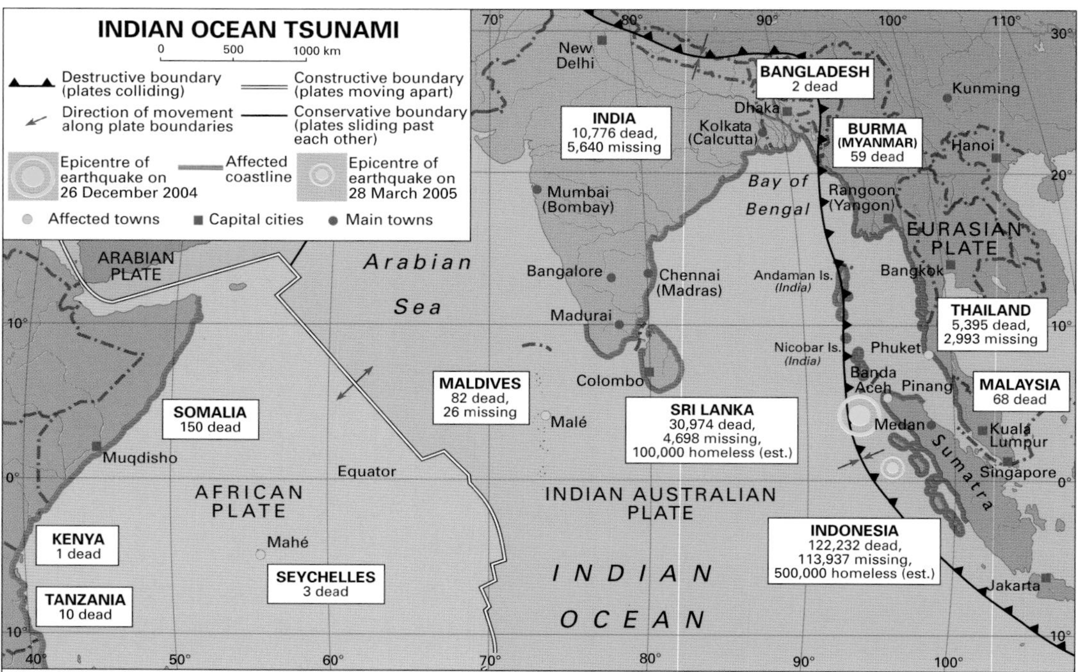

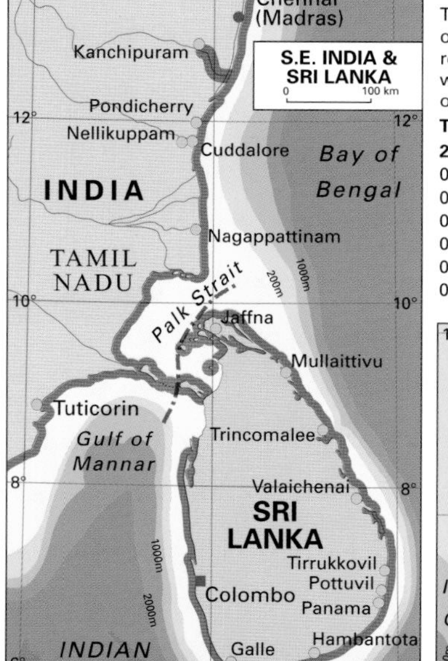

Total death toll: 169,752 dead, 127,294 missing

The 26 December 2004 earthquake measured 9.3 on the Richter Scale, whereas the earthquake on 28 March 2005 measured 8.7. The Richter Scale is a logarithmic scale, so in terms of energy released, the earthquake on 26 December was five times larger than the one on 28 March and was the second largest in recorded history. The December earthquake generated waves that, once they reached the land, were up to 20 m [65 ft] in height.

Timeline:

26 December 2004

0100 GMT	Earthquake occurs
0130 GMT	Tsunami hits Sumatra
0230 GMT	Thailand hit
0300 GMT	Sri Lanka and India hit
0430 GMT	Maldives hit
0700 GMT	East Africa hit

Aid Recipients:

Recipient	Pledges	Donations received (at 22 March 2005)
Indonesia	US $929 million	US $220.8 million
Sri Lanka	US $413.5 million	US $249 million
India	US $57.9 million	US $56.7 million
Thailand	US $13.3 million	US $7.5 million
Somalia	US $9.4 million	US $3 million

S. THAILAND

W. INDONESIA

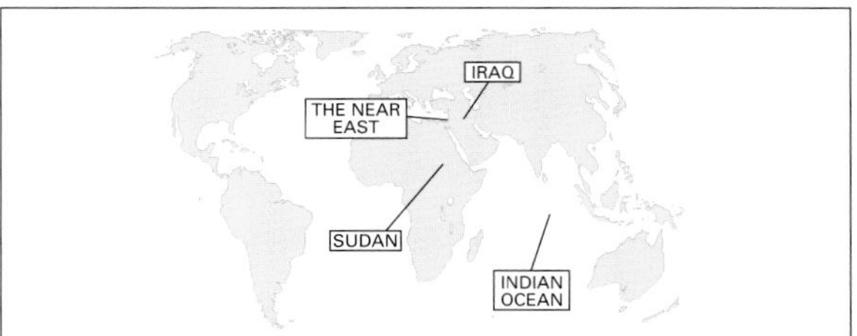

ISRAEL
POPULATION: 6,199,000 (inc. Israeli settlers in West Bank, Gaza Strip and Golan Heights)
INFANT MORTALITY: 6.2 deaths per 1,000 births
GDP PER CAPITA: US $19,500 (2002 estimate)

West Bank
POPULATION: 2,311,000 (Muslim 75%, Jewish 17%)
INFANT MORTALITY: 21.2 deaths per 1,000 births
GDP PER CAPITA: US $800 (2002 estimate)

Gaza Strip
POPULATION: 1,325,000 (Muslim 98.7%, Christian 0.7%, Jewish 0.6%)
INFANT MORTALITY: 24.8 deaths per 1,000 births
GDP PER CAPITA: US $600 (2002 estimate)

JORDAN
POPULATION: 5,611,000 (Palestinian Arab 50%)

LEBANON
POPULATION: 3,777,000 (Palestinian Arab 11%)

AREA: 2,505,813 sq km [967,494 sq miles]
POPULATION: 39,148,000 (Black 52%, Arab 39%, Beja 6%, others)
RELIGIONS: Islam 70% (mainly Sunni Muslim), traditional beliefs 25%, Christianity 5%
BIRTH RATE: 35.79 births per 1,000 population
DEATH RATE: 9.37 deaths per 1,000 population
INFANT MORTALITY: 64.05 deaths per 1,000 births
GDP PER CAPITA: US $1,400 (2002 estimate)

Sudan has more internally displaced people than any other country (4.4 million in 2004). Up to 1.6 million people have left their homes and 70,000 are estimated to have been killed since conflict began in the Darfur region in early 2003.

The largest country in Africa, Sudan is one quarter the size of the USA, or 10 times the size of the UK. The country's inhabitants are divided into three main groups: those in the north, consisting of Muslim Arab and Nubian peoples; those in the south, consisting of traditional Nilotic and Bantu peoples; and those in the west, most of whom immigrated from western Africa in the 20th century.

NATIONS OF THE WORLD

Afghanistan 18
Albania 18
Algeria 18
American Samoa 18
Andorra 18
Angola 18
Anguilla 19
Antigua and Barbuda 19
Argentina 19
Armenia 19
Aruba 19
Australia 19
Austria 20
Azerbaijan 20

Bahamas 20
Bahrain 20
Bangladesh 20
Barbados 20
Belarus 20
Belgium 21
Belize 21
Benin 21
Bermuda 21
Bhutan 21
Bolivia 21
Bosnia-Herzegovina 22
Botswana 22
Brazil 22
Brunei 23
Bulgaria 23
Burkina Faso 23
Burma (Myanmar) 23
Burundi 23

Cambodia 24
Cameroon 24
Canada 24
Cape Verde 25
Cayman Islands 25
Central African Republic 25
Chad 25
Chile 25
China 26
Colombia 26
Comoros 26
Congo 26
Congo (Dem. Rep. of the) 27
Costa Rica 27
Croatia 27
Cuba 27
Cyprus 28
Czech Republic 28

Denmark 28
Djibouti 29
Dominica 29
Dominican Republic 29

East Timor 29
Ecuador 29
Egypt 29
El Salvador 30
Equatorial Guinea 30
Eritrea 30
Estonia 30
Ethiopia 31

Falkland Islands 31
Færoe Islands 31
Fiji Islands 31
Finland 31
France 31
French Guiana 32
French Polynesia 32

Gabon 32
Gambia, The 32
Georgia 33
Germany 33
Ghana 33
Gibraltar 34
Greece 34
Greenland 34
Grenada 34
Guadeloupe 34
Guam 34
Guatemala 34
Guinea 34
Guinea-Bissau 35
Guyana 35

Haiti 35
Honduras 35
Hungary 36

Iceland 36
India 36
Indonesia 36
Iran 37
Iraq 37
Ireland 37
Israel 38
Italy 38
Ivory Coast 38

Jamaica 39
Japan 39
Jordan 39

Kazakhstan 39
Kenya 40
Kiribati 40
Korea, North 40
Korea, South 41
Kuwait 41
Kyrgyzstan 41

Laos 41
Latvia 41
Lebanon 42
Lesotho 42
Liberia 42
Libya 43
Liechtenstein 43
Lithuania 43
Luxembourg 43

Macedonia (FYROM) 43
Madagascar 44
Malawi 44
Malaysia 44
Maldives 45
Mali 45
Malta 45
Marshall Islands 45
Martinique 45
Mauritania 45
Mauritius 46
Mexico 46
Micronesia 46
Moldova 46
Monaco 46
Mongolia 46
Montserrat 47
Morocco 47
Mozambique 47

Namibia 47
Nauru 47
Nepal 47
Netherlands 48
Netherlands Antilles 48
New Caledonia 48
New Zealand 48
Nicaragua 48
Niger 49
Nigeria 49
Northern Mariana Islands 49
Norway 49

Oman 49

Pakistan 50
Palau 50
Panama 50
Papua New Guinea 50
Paraguay 50
Peru 51
Philippines 51
Pitcairn 51
Poland 51
Portugal 52
Puerto Rico 52

Qatar 52

Réunion 52
Romania 52
Russia 52
Rwanda 53

St Helena 53
St Kitts and Nevis 53
St Lucia 53
St Vincent and the Grenadines 53
Samoa 53
San Marino 53
São Tomé and Príncipe 53
Saudi Arabia 54
Senegal 54
Serbia and Montenegro 54
Seychelles 54
Sierra Leone 54
Singapore 55
Slovak Republic 55
Slovenia 55
Solomon Islands 56
Somalia 56
South Africa 56
Spain 56
Sri Lanka 57
Sudan 57
Suriname 57
Swaziland 57
Sweden 58
Switzerland 58
Syria 58

Taiwan 58
Tajikistan 59
Tanzania 59
Thailand 59
Togo 59
Tonga 60
Trinidad and Tobago 60
Tunisia 60
Turkey 60
Turkmenistan 60
Turks and Caicos Islands 61
Tuvalu 61

Uganda 61
Ukraine 61
United Arab Emirates 61
United Kingdom 61
United States of America 62
Uruguay 62
Uzbekistan 63

Vanuatu 63
Vatican City 63
Venezuela 63
Vietnam 63
Virgin Islands, British 64
Virgin Islands, US 64

Wallis and Futuna Islands 64

Yemen 64

Zambia 64
Zimbabwe 64

NOTE: This alphabetical list includes the principal countries and territories of the world. The area figures give the total area of land, inland water and ice. The population figures are 2004 estimates where available. The capital city population is for the 'city proper' (rather than its urban agglomeration) where available, using the latest census or estimate.

AFGHANISTAN

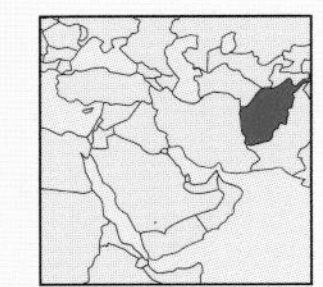

AREA 652,090 sq km [251,772 sq mi]
POPULATION 28,514,000
CAPITAL (POPULATION) Kabul (1,565,000)
GOVERNMENT Transitional
ETHNIC GROUPS Pashtun (Pathan) 44%, Tajik 25%, Hazara 10%, Uzbek 8%, others 13%
LANGUAGES Pashtu, Dari/Persian (both official), Uzbek
RELIGIONS Islam (Sunni Muslim 84%, Shi'ite Muslim 15%), others 1%
CURRENCY Afghani = 100 puls

GEOGRAPHY The Republic of Afghanistan is a landlocked, mountainous country in southern Asia. The central highlands reach a height of more than 7,000 m [22,966 ft] in the east and make up nearly three-quarters of Afghanistan. The main range is the Hindu Kush, which is cut by deep, fertile valleys.

In winter, northerly winds bring cold, snowy weather to the mountains, but summers are hot and dry.

POLITICS & ECONOMY The modern history of Afghanistan began in 1747, when the various tribes in the area united for the first time. In the 19th century, Russia and Britain struggled for control of the country. Following Britain's withdrawal in 1919, Afghanistan became fully independent. Soviet troops invaded Afghanistan in 1979 to support a socialist regime in Kabul, but they withdrew in 1989. By the early 21st century, a group called the Taliban ('Islamic students') controlled 90% of the country. In 2001, following the refusal of the Taliban government to hand over the terrorist leader Osama bin Laden, an international force overthrew the Taliban regime and a coalition government was set up, led by Hamid Karzai, who was sworn into office in 2002. Despite ongoing conflict, a draft constitution was approved in January 2004. Presidential elections, which were won by Karzai, followed in October.

Afghanistan is one of the world's poorest countries. About 60% of the people live by farming. Many people are semi-nomadic herders. Natural gas is produced, together with some coal, copper, gold, precious stones and salt.

ALBANIA

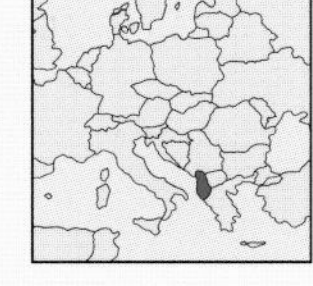

AREA 28,748 sq km [11,100 sq mi]
POPULATION 3,545,000
CAPITAL (POPULATION) Tirana (300,000)
GOVERNMENT Multiparty republic
ETHNIC GROUPS Albanian 95%, Greek 3%, Macedonian, Vlachs, Gypsy
LANGUAGES Albanian (official)
RELIGIONS Many people say they are non-believers; of the believers, 70% follow Islam and 30% follow Christianity (Orthodox 20%, Roman Catholic 10%)
CURRENCY Lek = 100 qindars

GEOGRAPHY The Republic of Albania lies in the Balkan peninsula, facing the Adriatic Sea. About 70% of the land is mountainous, but most Albanians live on the coastal lowlands. Albania's coastal areas have a typical Mediterranean climate, with fairly dry, sunny summers and cool, moist winters. The mountains have a severe climate, with heavy snowfalls in winter.

POLITICS & ECONOMY Albania is one of Europe's poorest nations. A former Communist country, Albania adopted a multiparty system in the early 1990s. The change proved difficult. But after elections in 1997, a socialist government committed to a market system took office. In 2001, the stability of the region was threatened when Albanian-speaking Kosovars and Macedonians, many of whom favoured the creation of a Greater Albania, fought with government forces in north-western Macedonia.

In the early 21st century, agriculture employed nearly 62% of the people. Private ownership has been encouraged since 1991 but change has been slow. Albania has some minerals, and chromite, copper and nickel are exported.

ALGERIA

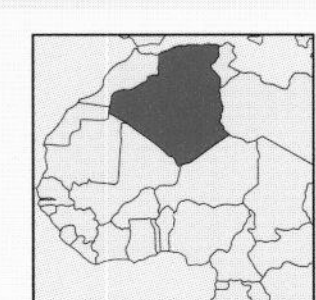

AREA 2,381,741 sq km [919,590 sq mi]
POPULATION 32,129,000
CAPITAL (POPULATION) Algiers (1,722,000)
GOVERNMENT Socialist republic
ETHNIC GROUPS Arab-Berber 99%
LANGUAGES Arabic and Berber (official), French
RELIGIONS Sunni Muslim 99%
CURRENCY Algerian dinar = 100 centimes

GEOGRAPHY The People's Democratic Republic of Algeria is Africa's second largest country after Sudan. Most Algerians live in the north, on the fertile coastal plains and hill country bordering the Mediterranean Sea. Four-fifths of Algeria is in the Sahara. The coast has a Mediterranean climate, but the arid Sahara is hot by day and cool at night.

POLITICS & ECONOMY France ruled Algeria from 1830 until 1962, when the socialist FLN (National Liberation Front) formed a one-party government. Following the recognition of opposition parties in 1989, a Muslim group, the FIS (Islamic Salvation Front), won an election in 1991. The FLN cancelled the elections and civil conflict broke out. About 100,000 people were killed in the 1990s. In 1999, following the withdrawal of the other candidates who alleged fraud, Abdelaziz Bouteflika, who was assumed to be favoured by the army, was elected president. Violence was reduced. In 2005, the government agreed to accept long-standing demands by the Berber minority.

Algeria is a developing country, whose chief resources are oil and natural gas. The natural gas reserves are among the world's largest, and gas and oil account for 90% of Algeria's exports. Cement, iron and steel, textiles and vehicles are manufactured.

AMERICAN SAMOA

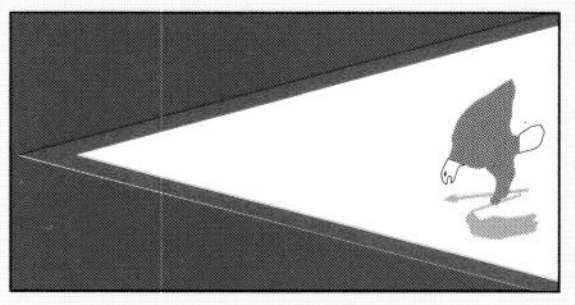
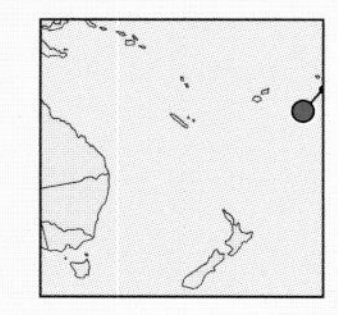

AREA 199 sq km [77 sq mi]
POPULATION 58,000
CAPITAL (POPULATION) Pago Pago (4,000)

An 'unincorporated territory' of the United States, American Samoa lies in the south-central Pacific Ocean. Two islands are coral islands. The other five are extinct volcanoes. The US took control of the islands between 1900 and 1904. The main industry is tuna canning and fish products dominate the economy.

ANDORRA

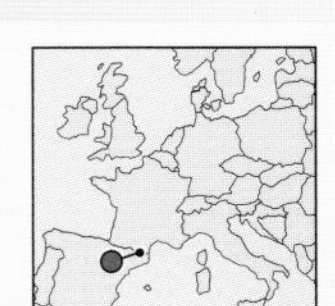

AREA 468 sq km [181 sq mi]
POPULATION 70,000
CAPITAL (POPULATION) Andorra La Vella (22,000)

A mini-state situated in the Pyrenees Mountains, Andorra is a co-principality ruled by the 'princes' of Andorra – namely the Bishop of Urgel, Spain, and the government of France. However, Catalan is the official language. The first known ruler of Andorra was the Spanish Count of Urgel in the 9th century. Today, most Andorrans live in the six valleys (the Valls) that drain the River Valira. The chief activity is tourism, including skiing in winter.

ANGOLA

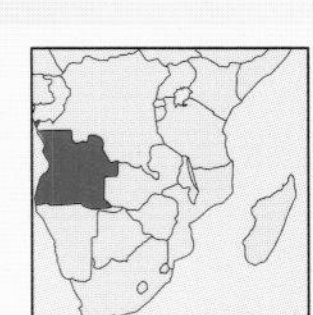

AREA 1,246,700 sq km [481,351 sq mi]
POPULATION 10,979,000
CAPITAL (POPULATION) Luanda (2,500,000)
GOVERNMENT Multiparty republic
ETHNIC GROUPS Ovimbundu 37%, Kimbundu 25%, Bakongo 13%, others 25%
LANGUAGES Portuguese (official), many others
RELIGIONS Traditional beliefs 47%, Roman Catholic 38%, Protestant 15%
CURRENCY Kwanza = 100 lwei

GEOGRAPHY The Republic of Angola is a large country in south-western Africa. Much of the country is part of the plateau that forms most of southern Africa, with a narrow coastal plain in the west.

Angola has a tropical climate, with temperatures of over 20°C [68°F] throughout the year, though the highest areas are cooler. The coastal regions are dry, but the rainfall increases to the east and north. Tropical savanna covers much of the country, with forests in the south and north-east.

POLITICS & ECONOMY The earliest inhabitants of Angola were probably hunter-gatherers, but Bantu-speaking peoples from the north displaced them in the 13th century. Later, several major kingdoms developed, including the Kong in the north and the Mbundu in the south. From the mid-17th century, the Portuguese controlled the coast from which they exported slaves to the Portuguese territory of Brazil. The Portuguese extended their control inland in the late 19th century and ruled the territory until independence was achieved in 1975, following a guerrilla war that began in the 1960s.

From 1975, rival nationalist groups fought for power. A long-running civil war ensued, which, despite a cease-fire in the mid-1990s, continued until 2002, when Jonas Savimbi, leader of the chief rebel group UNITA, was killed in action and his successors negotiated peace. However, the disruption caused by the war led to widespread famine.

Angola is a developing country, where 70% of the people are poor farmers. The main food crops are cassava and maize. Coffee is exported. Angola has much economic potential. It has oil reserves near Luanda and in the Cabinda enclave, which is separated from Angola by a strip of land belonging to Congo (Dem. Rep.). Oil is the leading export. Angola also produces diamonds and has reserves of copper, manganese and phosphates.

ANGUILLA

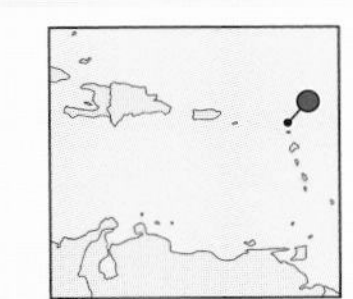

AREA 96 sq km [37 sq mi]
POPULATION 13,000
CAPITAL The Valley

A British colony in 1650, Anguilla was linked with St Kitts (then St Christopher) and Nevis in 1883. St Kitts and Nevis became a British associated state in 1967, but the people of Anguilla voted to become a British dependency (now a British overseas territory) in 1980. The main activity is tourism, although lobster still accounts for half of the island's exports.

ANTIGUA AND BARBUDA

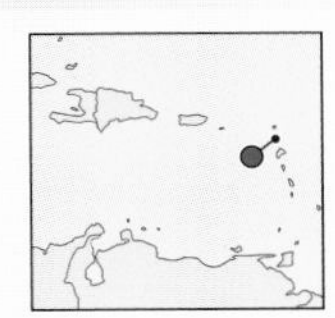

AREA 442 sq km [171 sq mi]
POPULATION 68,000
CAPITAL (POPULATION) St John's (22,000)

Britain made Antigua a colony in 1632. The islands of Barbuda and Redonda were later added to the colony, which was known as Antigua. Britain brought African slaves to the colony and most of the population today is of African descent. Antigua and Barbuda became independent in 1981. Tourism is the main industry.

ARGENTINA

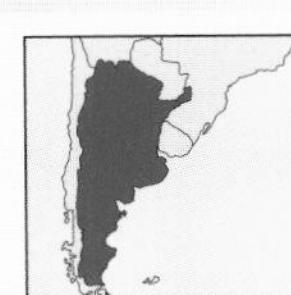

AREA 2,780,400 sq km [1,073,512 sq mi]
POPULATION 39,145,000
CAPITAL (POPULATION) Buenos Aires (2,965,000)
GOVERNMENT Federal republic
ETHNIC GROUPS European 97%, Mestizo, Amerindian
LANGUAGES Spanish (official)
RELIGIONS Roman Catholic 92%, Protestant 2%, Jewish 2%, others
CURRENCY Argentine peso = 10,000 australs

GEOGRAPHY The Argentine Republic is South America's second largest and the world's eighth largest country. The Andes range in the west contains Mount Aconcagua, the highest peak in the Americas. In the south, the Andes overlook Patagonia, an arid plateau region. In east-central Argentina lies a fertile, well-watered plain called the *pampas*. Temperatures vary from subtropical to temperate.

POLITICS & ECONOMY The earliest people of Argentina were American Indians, but they were relatively few in number. Today, about 86% of the population is of European ancestry. Spain took control of the country in the 16th century and ruled until independence was achieved in 1816. Argentina later suffered from instability and periods of military rule. In 1982, the government, led by the army chief General Leopoldo Galtieri, invaded the Falkland (Malvinas) Islands. But Britain regained the islands later that year and civilian rule was restored in 1983. In 1994, Argentina adopted a new constitution.

According to the World Bank, Argentina is an 'upper-middle-income' developing country. Large areas are fertile and the main agricultural products are beef, maize and wheat. But about 90% of the people live in cities and towns. Industries include food processing and the manufacture of cars, electrical equipment and textiles. Oil is the chief natural resource. Major exports include meat, wheat, maize, vegetable oils, hides and skins, and wool. In 1991, Argentina, Brazil, Paraguay and Uruguay set up Mercosur, an alliance aimed to create a common market. In 2001, a severe economic crisis threatened anarchy. The government worked to restore confidence and the economy began to grow again in 2003 and 2004.

ARMENIA

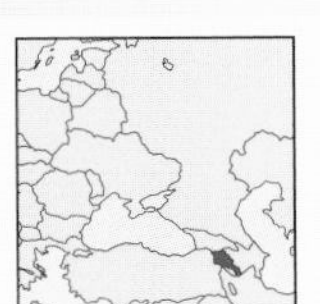

AREA 29,800 sq km [11,506 sq mi]
POPULATION 2,991,000
CAPITAL (POPULATION) Yerevan (1,249,000)
GOVERNMENT Multiparty republic
ETHNIC GROUPS Armenian 93%, Russian 2%, Azeri 1%, others (mostly Kurds) 4%
LANGUAGES Armenian (official)
RELIGIONS Armenian Apostolic 94%
CURRENCY Dram = 100 couma

GEOGRAPHY The Republic of Armenia is a landlocked country in south-western Asia. Most of Armenia consists of a rugged plateau, criss-crossed by long faults (cracks). Movements along the faults cause earthquakes. The highest point is Mount Aragats, at 4,090 m [13,419 ft] above sea level. Because of the high altitude, winters are severe and summers cool. The rainfall is generally low.

POLITICS & ECONOMY In 1920, Armenia became a Communist republic and, in 1922, it became, with Azerbaijan and Georgia, part of the Transcaucasian Republic within the Soviet Union. But the three territories became separate Soviet Socialist Republics in 1936. After the break-up of the Soviet Union in 1991, Armenia became an independent republic. Fighting broke out over Nagorno-Karabakh, an area enclosed by Azerbaijan where the majority of the people are Armenians. In 1992, Armenia occupied the territory between it and Nagorno-Karabakh. A cease-fire in 1994 left Armenia in control of about 20% of Azerbaijan's land area. With Azerbaijan and its ally Turkey blockading its borders, Armenia became increasingly dependent on Iran and Georgia for access to the outside world.

The World Bank classifies Armenia as a 'lower-middle-income' economy. After 1992, the government encouraged free enterprise, but the conflict with Azerbaijan damaged the economy.

ARUBA

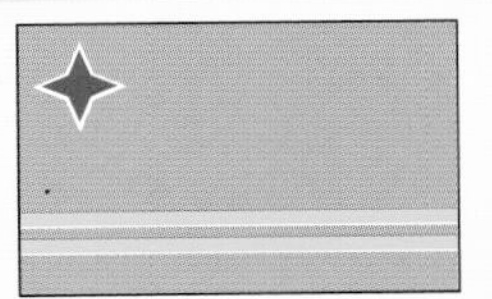
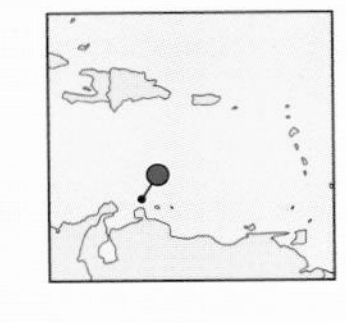

AREA 193 sq km [75 sq mi]
POPULATION 71,000
CAPITAL (POPULATION) Oranjestad (20,000)

Formerly part of the Netherlands Antilles, Aruba became a separate self-governing Dutch territory in 1986. The Netherlands is responsible for Aruba's defence and foreign affairs. Aruba is a hilly island with little agriculture. However, its warm, dry climate and fine beaches make tourism a major activity.

AUSTRALIA

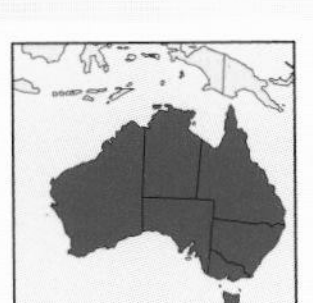

AREA 7,741,220 sq km [2,988,885 sq mi]
POPULATION 19,913,000
CAPITAL (POPULATION) Canberra (309,000)
GOVERNMENT Federal constitutional monarchy
ETHNIC GROUPS Caucasian 92%, Asian 7%, Aboriginal 1%
LANGUAGES English (official)
RELIGIONS Roman Catholic 26%, Anglican 26%, other Christian 24%, non-Christian 24%
CURRENCY Australian dollar = 100 cents

GEOGRAPHY The Commonwealth of Australia, the world's sixth largest country, is also a continent. Australia is the flattest of the continents and the main highland area is in the east. Here the Great Dividing Range separates the eastern coastal plains from the Central Plains. This range extends from the Cape York Peninsula to Victoria in the far south. The longest rivers, the Murray and Darling, drain the south-eastern part of the Central Plains. The Western Plateau makes up two-thirds of Australia. A few mountain ranges break the monotony of the generally flat landscape.

Only 10% of Australia has an average yearly rainfall of more than 1,000 mm [39 in]. These areas include the tropical north, where Darwin is situated, the north-east coast, and the south-east, where Sydney is located. The interior is dry, and water is quickly evaporated in the heat. Deserts cover about a third of Australia. They include the Gibson, Great Sandy, Great Victoria and Simpson deserts.

POLITICS & ECONOMY The Aboriginal people of Australia entered the continent from South-east Asia more than 50,000 years ago. The first European explorers were Dutch in the 17th century, but they did not settle. In 1770, the British Captain Cook explored the east coast and, in 1788, the first British settlement was established for convicts on the site of what is now Sydney. Australia has strong ties with the British Isles. But in the last 50 years, people from other parts of Europe and, most recently, from Asia have settled in Australia. Ties with Britain were also weakened by Britain's membership of the European Union. Many Australians believe that they should become more involved with the nations of eastern Asia and the Americas rather than with Europe. In 1999, Australia held a referendum on whether the country should become a republic or remain a constitutional monarchy. By a majority of about 55 to 45, the country retained its status as a monarchy, with Queen Elizabeth II remaining its titular head of state. In 2003, Australian troops joined the coalition forces in the invasion of Iraq. In 2004, the conservative prime minister John Howard won a fourth successive general election victory.

Australia is a prosperous country. Crops can be grown on only 6% of the land, but dry pasture covers another 58%. Yet the country remains a major producer and exporter of farm products, particularly cattle, wheat and wool. Grapes grown for wine-making are also important. The country is a major producer of minerals, including bauxite, coal, copper, diamonds, gold, iron ore, manganese, nickel, silver, tin, tungsten and zinc. Australia also produces oil and natural gas. Metals, minerals and farm products account for the bulk of exports. Australia's imports are mostly manufactured products, although the country makes many factory products, especially consumer goods. Imports include machinery.

AUSTRIA

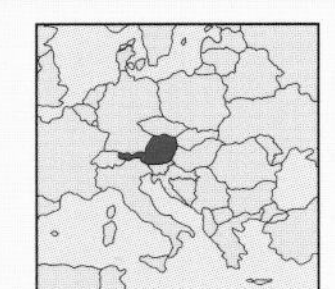

AREA 83,859 sq km [32,378 sq mi]
POPULATION 8,175,000
CAPITAL (POPULATION) Vienna (1,560,000)
GOVERNMENT Federal republic
ETHNIC GROUPS Austrian 90%, Croatian, Slovene, others
LANGUAGES German (official)
RELIGIONS Roman Catholic 78%, Protestant 5%, Islam and others 17%
CURRENCY Euro = 100 cents

GEOGRAPHY Austria is a landlocked country in Europe. Northern Austria contains the valley of the River Danube, which flows from Germany to the Black Sea, and the Vienna basin. Southern Austria contains ranges of the Alps, their highest point at Grossglockner, 3,797 m [12,457 ft] above sea level.

The climate is influenced by westerly and easterly winds. Moist westerly winds bring rain and snow, and moderate temperatures. Dry easterly winds bring cold weather in winter and hot weather in summer.

POLITICS & ECONOMY Formerly part of the monarchy of Austria-Hungary, which collapsed in 1918, Austria was annexed by Germany in 1938. After World War II, the Allies partitioned and occupied the country. In 1955, Austria became a neutral federal republic. It joined the European Union on 1 January 1995, but was a focus of controversy when, in 2000, a coalition government was formed by the right-wing People's Party and the extreme right-wing Freedom Party. The Freedom Party lost much of its support in 2002, but it remained part of the ruling coalition.

Austria has a highly developed economy, with plenty of hydroelectric power and some oil, gas and coal reserves. The chief activity is manufacturing metals or metal products. Crops are grown on 18% of the land, and another 24% is pasture. Farming products include dairy and livestock products, barley, potatoes, rye, sugar beet and wheat. Tourism is a major activity.

AZERBAIJAN

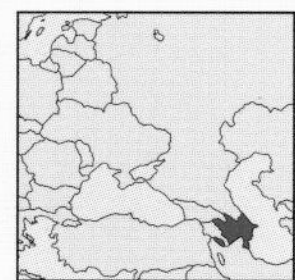

AREA 86,600 sq km [33,436 sq mi]
POPULATION 7,868,000
CAPITAL (POPULATION) Baku (1,792,000)
GOVERNMENT Federal multiparty republic
ETHNIC GROUPS Azeri 90%, Dagestani 3%, Russian, Armenian, others
LANGUAGES Azerbaijani (official), Russian, Armenian
RELIGIONS Islam 93%, Russian Orthodox 2%, Armenian Orthodox 2%
CURRENCY Azerbaijani manat = 100 gopik

GEOGRAPHY The Azerbaijani Republic is a country in the south-west of Asia, facing the Caspian Sea to the east. It includes an area called the Naxçivan Autonomous Republic, which is completely cut off from the rest of Azerbaijan by Armenian territory. The Caucasus Mountains border Russia in the north.

Azerbaijan has hot summers and cool winters. The plains are fairly dry, but the mountains are rainy.

POLITICS & ECONOMY After the Russian Revolution of 1917, attempts were made to form a Transcaucasian Federation made up of Armenia, Azerbaijan and Georgia. When this failed, Azerbaijanis set up an independent state. But Russian forces occupied the area in 1920. In 1922, the Communists set up a Transcaucasian Republic consisting of Armenia, Azerbaijan and Georgia under Russian control. In 1936, the three areas became separate Soviet Socialist Republics within the Soviet Union. In 1991, following the break-up of the Soviet Union, Azerbaijan became an independent nation. After independence, the country's economic progress was slow, partly because of the conflict with Armenia over the enclave of Nagorno-Karabakh, a region in Azerbaijan where the majority of people are Armenians. A cease-fire in 1994 left Armenia in control of about 20% of Azerbaijan's area, including Nagorno-Karabakh. Subsequent attempts to resolve the problem have failed.

In the mid-1990s, the World Bank classified Azerbaijan as a 'lower-middle-income' economy. Yet by the late 1990s, the enormous oil reserves in the Baku area on the Caspian Sea, and in the sea itself, held out great promise for the future. Oil extraction and manufacturing, including oil refining and the production of chemicals, machinery and textiles, are now the most valuable activities.

BAHAMAS

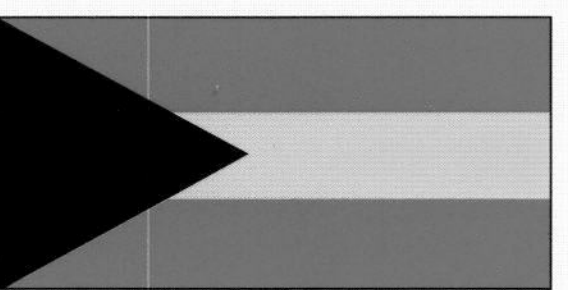

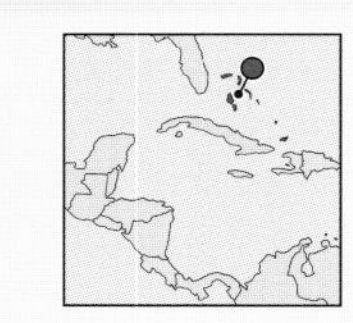

AREA 13,878 sq km [5,358 sq mi]
POPULATION 300,000
CAPITAL (POPULATION) Nassau (172,000)

A coral-limestone archipelago off the coast of Florida, the Bahamas became independent from Britain in 1973, and has since developed strong ties with the United States. Tourism and banking are major activities.

BAHRAIN

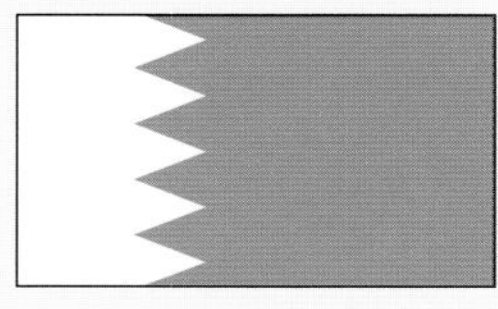

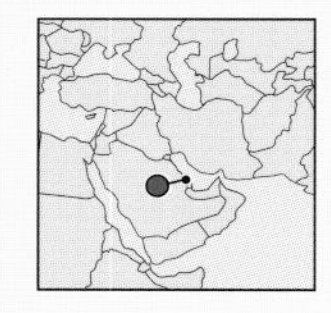

AREA 694 sq km [268 sq mi]
POPULATION 678,000
CAPITAL (POPULATION) Manama (140,000)

The Kingdom of Bahrain, an island nation in the Gulf, became independent from the UK in 1971. Oil accounts for about 70% of Bahrain's exports.

BANGLADESH

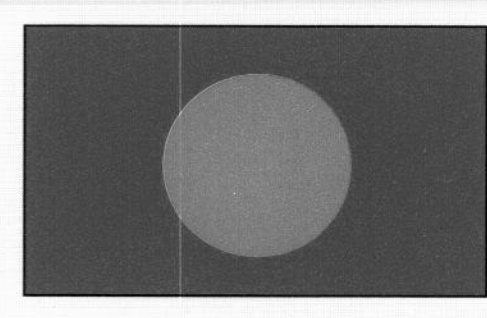

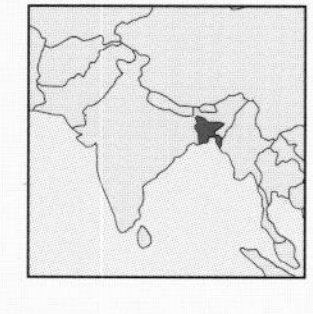

AREA 143,998 sq km [55,598 sq mi]
POPULATION 141,340,000
CAPITAL (POPULATION) Dhaka (3,839,000)
GOVERNMENT Multiparty republic
ETHNIC GROUPS Bengali 98%, tribal groups
LANGUAGES Bengali (official), English
RELIGIONS Islam 83%, Hinduism 16%
CURRENCY Taka = 100 paisas

GEOGRAPHY The People's Republic of Bangladesh is one of the world's most densely populated countries. Apart from hilly regions in the far north-east and south-east, most of the land is flat and covered by fertile alluvium spread over the land by the Ganges, Brahmaputra and Meghna rivers. Bangladesh has a tropical monsoon climate. Dry northerly winds blow in winter, but, in summer, moist winds from the south bring monsoon rains. Floods occur when rivers overflow or cyclones (hurricanes) batter the coast, though Bangladesh emerged relatively unscathed by the tsunami in the Indian Ocean in December 2004.

Contaminated water has long been a health hazard. In the early 2000s, the government disclosed that the water from wells sunk in the 1970s and 1980s to obtain safe water contains arsenic and large numbers of people were suffering from arsenic poisoning.

POLITICS & ECONOMY In 1947, British India was partitioned between the mainly Hindu India and the Muslim Pakistan. Pakistan consisted of two parts, West and East Pakistan, which were separated by about 1,600 km [1,000 mi] of Indian territory. Differences developed between West and East Pakistan. In 1971, the East Pakistanis rebelled. After a nine-month civil war, they declared East Pakistan to be a separate nation named Bangladesh.

Bangladesh is one of the world's poorest countries. Its economy depends mainly on agriculture, which employs over half the population.

BARBADOS

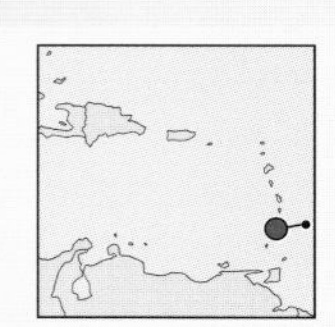

AREA 430 sq km [166 sq mi]
POPULATION 278,000
CAPITAL (POPULATION) Bridgetown (7,000)

Britons settled on Barbados in 1615 and the island became a British colony in 1652. The island became independent as a constitutional monarchy in 1966. However, in 2000, moves began to make the country a republic. The most easterly of the Caribbean islands, Barbados is also one of the region's most prosperous, with agriculture, manufacturing and tourism all making contributions to the economy.

BELARUS

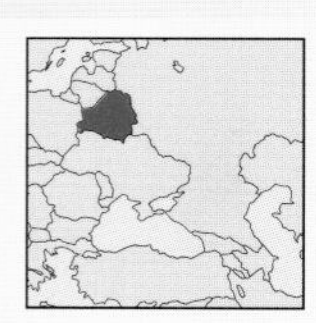

AREA 207,600 sq km [80,154 sq mi]
POPULATION 10,311,000
CAPITAL (POPULATION) Minsk (1,677,000)
GOVERNMENT Multiparty republic
ETHNIC GROUPS Belarusian 81%, Russian 11%, Polish, Ukrainian, others
LANGUAGES Belarusian, Russian (both official)
RELIGIONS Eastern Orthodox 80%, others 20%
CURRENCY Belarusian rouble = 100 kopecks

GEOGRAPHY The Republic of Belarus is a landlocked country in Eastern Europe. The land is low-lying and mostly flat. In the south, much of the land is marshy and this area contains Europe's largest marsh and peat bog, the Pripet Marshes. The climate is affected by both the moderating influence of the Baltic Sea and continental conditions to the east. The winters are cold and the summers warm.

POLITICS & ECONOMY In 1918, Belarus (White Russia) became an independent republic, but Russia invaded the country and, in 1919, a Communist state was set up. In 1922, Belarus became a founder republic of the Soviet Union. In 1991, Belarus again became an independent republic, though Belarus continued to support reunification with Russia. In 1998, Belarus and Russia set up a 'union state', with plans to have a common currency, a customs union, and common foreign and defence policies. But any surrender of sovereignty was not expected. In 2003, the Russian President Vladimir Putin agreed to deepen ties with Belarus, but also stated that he did not wish to create anything like the Soviet Union.

The World Bank classifies Belarus as an 'upper-middle-income' economy. Like other former republics of the Soviet Union, it faces many problems in turning from Communism to a free-market economy.

BELGIUM

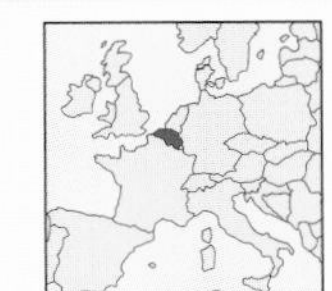

AREA 30,528 sq km [11,787 sq mi]
POPULATION 10,348,000
CAPITAL (POPULATION) Brussels (136,000)
GOVERNMENT Federal constitutional monarchy
ETHNIC GROUPS Belgian 89% (Fleming 58%, Walloon 31%), others 11%
LANGUAGES Dutch, French, German (all official)
RELIGIONS Roman Catholic 75%, others 25%
CURRENCY Euro = 100 cents

GEOGRAPHY The Kingdom of Belgium is a densely populated country in western Europe. Behind the coastline on the North Sea, which is 63 km [39 mi] long, lie its coastal plains. Central Belgium consists of low plateaux and the only highland region is the Ardennes in the south-east.

Belgium has a cool, temperate climate. Moist winds from the Atlantic Ocean bring fairly heavy rain, especially in the Ardennes. In January and February much snow falls on the Ardennes.

POLITICS & ECONOMY In 1815, Belgium and the Netherlands united as the 'low countries', but Belgium became independent in 1830. Belgium's economy was weakened by the two World Wars, but, from 1945, the country recovered quickly, first through collaboration with the Netherlands and Luxembourg, which formed a customs union called Benelux, and later through its membership of the European Union.

A central political problem in Belgium has been the tension between the Dutch-speaking Flemings and the French-speaking Walloons. In the 1970s, the government divided the country into three economic regions: Dutch-speaking Flanders, French-speaking Wallonia and bilingual Brussels. In 1993, Belgium adopted a federal constitution, with each region having its own parliament. Elections under this system were held in 1995, 1999 and 2003. The 2003 elections were won comfortably by the ruling centre-left coalition, which was headed by Prime Minister Guy Verhofstadt.

Belgium is a major trading nation, with a highly developed economy. Its main products include chemicals, processed food and steel. The textile industry is important. It has existed since medieval times in the Belgian province of Flanders. The steel industry was once based on Belgium's coalfields, but today the steelworks lie near to ports because they are powered by petroleum. In 2002, the parliament voted to phase out the use of nuclear energy by 2025.

Agriculture employs less than 2% of the people, but Belgian farmers produce most of the food needed by the people. The chief crops are barley and wheat, but the most valuable activities are dairy farming and livestock rearing.

BELIZE

AREA 22,966 sq km [8,867 sq mi]
POPULATION 273,000
CAPITAL (POPULATION) Belmopan (8,000)
GOVERNMENT Constitutional monarchy
ETHNIC GROUPS Mestizo 49%, Creole 25%, Mayan Indian 11%, Garifuna 6%, others 9%
LANGUAGES English (official), Spanish, Creole
RELIGIONS Roman Catholic 50%, Protestant 27%, others
CURRENCY Belizean dollar = 100 cents

GEOGRAPHY Behind the southern coastal plain, the land rises to the Maya Mountains, which reach 1,120 m [3,674 ft] at Victoria Peak. The north is mostly low-lying and swampy. Temperatures are high all year round, while the average annual rainfall ranges from 1,300 mm [51 in] in the north to over 3,800 mm [150 in] in the south. Hurricanes sometimes occur. One in 2001 killed 22 people and left 12,000 homeless.

POLITICS & ECONOMY From 1862, Belize (then called British Honduras) was a British colony. Full independence was achieved in 1981, but Guatemala, which had claimed the area since the early 19th century, opposed Belize's independence and British troops remained to prevent a possible invasion. In 1983, Guatemala reduced its claim to the southern fifth of Belize. Improved relations in the early 1990s led Guatemala to recognize Belize's independence and, in 1992, Britain agreed to withdraw its troops from the country.

The World Bank classifies Belize as a 'lower-middle-income' developing country. Its economy is based on agriculture, and sugar cane is the chief commercial crop and export. Other crops include bananas, beans, citrus fruits, maize and rice. Forestry, fishing and tourism are other important activities.

BENIN

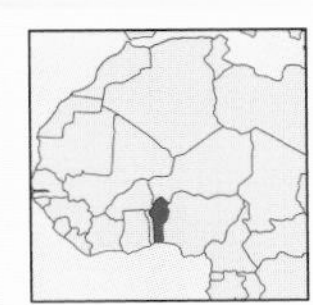

AREA 112,622 sq km [43,483 sq mi]
POPULATION 7,250,000
CAPITAL (POPULATION) Porto-Novo (233,000)
GOVERNMENT Multiparty republic
ETHNIC GROUPS Fon, Adja, Bariba, Yoruba, Fulani
LANGUAGES French (official), Fon, Adja, Yoruba
RELIGIONS Traditional beliefs 50%, Christianity 30%, Islam 20%
CURRENCY CFA franc = 100 centimes

GEOGRAPHY The Republic of Benin is one of Africa's smallest countries. It extends north–south for about 620 km [390 mi]. Lagoons line the short coastline, and the country has no natural harbours.

Benin has a hot, wet climate. The average annual temperature on the coast is about 25°C [77°F], and the average rainfall is about 1,330 mm [52 in]. The inland plains are wetter than the coast.

POLITICS & ECONOMY After slavery was ended in the 19th century, the French began to gain influence in the area. Benin became self-governing in 1958 and fully independent in 1960. After much instability and many changes of government, a military group took over in 1972. The country, renamed Benin in 1975, became a one-party socialist state. Socialism was abandoned in 1989. Multiparty elections were held throughout the 1990s and the early 2000s.

Benin is a developing country. About 55% of the people earn their living by farming, though many remain at subsistence level. The chief exports include cotton, petroleum and palm products.

BERMUDA

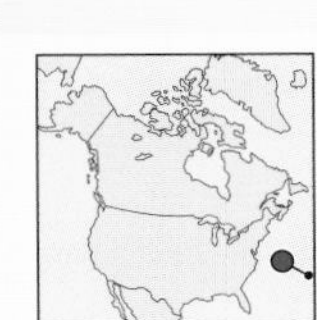

AREA 53 sq km [21 sq mi]
POPULATION 65,000
CAPITAL (POPULATION) Hamilton (1,000)

A group of about 150 small islands situated 920 km [570 miles] east of the United States. British settlers first arrived in 1610 and the islands became a British colony in 1684. Bermuda has a long tradition of self-rule. Tourism is the leading industry.

BHUTAN

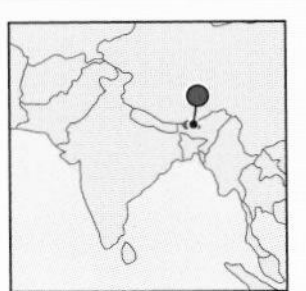

AREA 47,000 sq km [18,147 sq mi]
POPULATION 2,186,000
CAPITAL (POPULATION) Thimphu (35,000)
GOVERNMENT Constitutional monarchy
ETHNIC GROUPS Bhutanese 50%, Nepalese 35%
LANGUAGES Dzongkha (official)
RELIGIONS Buddhism 75%, Hinduism 25%
CURRENCY Ngultrum = 100 chetrum

GEOGRAPHY A mountainous, isolated Himalayan country located between India and Tibet. The climate is similar to that of Nepal, being dependent on altitude and affected by monsoonal winds.

POLITICS & ECONOMY The monarch of Bhutan is head of both state and government and this predominantly Buddhist country remains, even in the Asian context, both conservative and poor. Bhutan is the world's most 'rural' country, with about 87% of the population dependent on agriculture. In 2004, Bhutan imposed a ban on all tobacco products. The ban did not apply to foreigners.

BOLIVIA

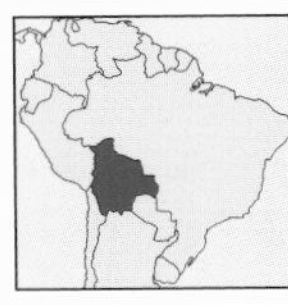

AREA 1,098,581 sq km [424,162 sq mi]
POPULATION 8,724,000
CAPITAL (POPULATION) La Paz (seat of government, 940,000); Sucre (legal capital/seat of judiciary, 177,000)
GOVERNMENT Multiparty republic
ETHNIC GROUPS Mestizo 30%, Quechua 30%, Aymara 25%, White 15%
LANGUAGES Spanish, Aymara, Quechua (all official)
RELIGIONS Roman Catholic 95%
CURRENCY Boliviano = 100 centavos

GEOGRAPHY The Republic of Bolivia is a landlocked country which straddles the Andes Mountains in central South America. The Andes rise to a height of 6,520 m [21,399 ft] at Nevado Sajama in the west.

About 40% of Bolivians live on a high plateau called

the Altiplano in the Andean region, while the sparsely populated east is essentially a vast lowland plain. The Andean peaks are permanently snow-covered, while the eastern plains are hot and humid.

POLITICS & ECONOMY American Indians have lived in Bolivia for at least 10,000 years. The main groups today are the Aymara and Quechua people.

In the last 50 years, Bolivia, an independent country since 1825, has been ruled by a succession of civilian and military governments, which violated human rights. Constitutional government was restored in 1982. From the 1980s, Bolivia has pursued economic reforms and free-market policies.

Bolivia is one of the poorest countries in South America. It has several natural resources, including tin, silver and natural gas, but the chief activity is agriculture. Coca, which is used to make cocaine, is exported illegally. In 2002–3, the production of coca plummeted, causing social unrest. In 2004, the people voted in favour of a government plan to export natural gas via a port in Peru.

BOSNIA-HERZEGOVINA

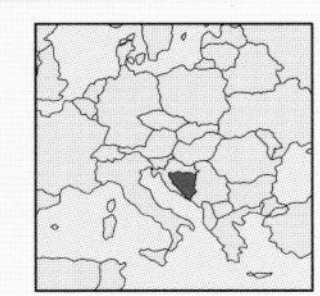

AREA 51,197 sq km [19,767 sq mi]
POPULATION 4,008,000
CAPITAL (POPULATION) Sarajevo (529,000)
GOVERNMENT Federal republic
ETHNIC GROUPS Bosnian 48%, Serb 37%, Croat 14%
LANGUAGES Bosnian, Serbian, Croatian
RELIGIONS Islam 40%, Serbian Orthodox 31%, Roman Catholic 15%, others 14%
CURRENCY Convertible marka = 100 convertible pfenniga

GEOGRAPHY The Republic of Bosnia-Herzegovina is one of the five republics to emerge from the former Federal People's Republic of Yugoslavia. Much of the country is mountainous or hilly, with an arid limestone plateau in the south-west. The River Sava, which forms most of the northern border with Croatia, is a tributary of the River Danube. Because of the country's odd shape, the coastline is limited to a stretch of 20 km [13 mi] on the Adriatic coast.

A Mediterranean climate, with dry, sunny summers and moist, mild winters, prevails only near the coast. Inland, the weather becomes more severe, with hot, dry summers and bitterly cold, snowy winters.

POLITICS & ECONOMY In 1918, Bosnia-Herzegovina became part of the Kingdom of the Serbs, Croats and Slovenes, which was renamed Yugoslavia in 1929. Germany occupied the area during World War II (1939–45). From 1945, Communist governments ruled Yugoslavia as a federation containing six republics, one of which was Bosnia-Herzegovina. In the 1980s, Communist policies proved unsuccessful and differences arose between ethnic groups.

Free elections were held in Bosnia-Herzegovina in 1990 and the non-Communists won a majority. A Muslim, Alija Izetbegovic, was elected president. In 1991, Croatia and Slovenia, other parts of the former Yugoslavia, declared themselves independent. In 1992, Bosnia-Herzegovina held a vote on independence. Most Bosnian Serbs boycotted the vote, while the Muslims and Bosnian Croats voted in favour. Many Bosnian Serbs, opposed to independence, started a war against the non-Serbs. They soon occupied more than two-thirds of the land. The Bosnian Serbs were accused of 'ethnic cleansing' – that is, the killing or expulsion of other ethnic groups from Serb-occupied areas. The war was later extended when Croat forces seized other parts of the country.

In 1995, the warring parties agreed to a solution to the conflict. This involved keeping the present boundaries of Bosnia-Herzegovina, but dividing it into two self-governing provinces, one Bosnian Serb and the other Muslim-Croat, under a central unified government. The country faced many problems, but, with the help of a NATO-led force, it soon became stable. In December 2004, when its problems were economic rather than political, a European Union force took over from NATO.

The economy of Bosnia-Herzegovina, the least developed of the six republics of the former Yugoslavia apart from Macedonia, was shattered by the war in the early 1990s. Before the war, manufactures were the main exports, including electrical equipment, machinery and transport equipment, and textiles. Farm products include fruits, maize, tobacco, vegetables and wheat, but the country has to import food.

BOTSWANA

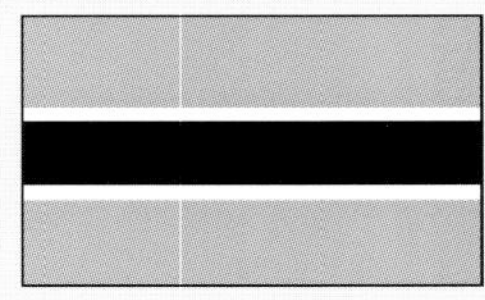

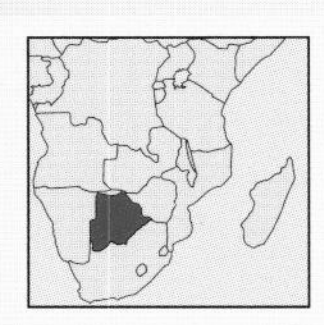

AREA 581,730 sq km [224,606 sq mi]
POPULATION 1,562,000
CAPITAL (POPULATION) Gaborone (186,000)
GOVERNMENT Multiparty republic
ETHNIC GROUPS Tswana (or Setswana) 79%, Kalanga 11%, Basarwa 3%, others
LANGUAGES English (official), Setswana
RELIGIONS Traditional beliefs 85%, Christianity 15%
CURRENCY Pula = 100 thebe

GEOGRAPHY The Republic of Botswana is a landlocked country in southern Africa. The Kalahari, a semi-desert area covered mostly by grasses and thorn scrub, covers much of the country. Most of the south has no permanent streams. But large depressions in the north are inland drainage basins. In one of them, the Okavango River, which rises in Angola, forms a large, swampy delta.

Temperatures are high in the summer months (October to April), but the winter months are much cooler. In winter, night-time temperatures sometimes drop below freezing point. The average annual rainfall ranges from over 400 mm [16 in] in the east to less than 200 mm [8 in] in the south-west.

POLITICS & ECONOMY Around 20,000 years ago, the area that is now Botswana was occupied by nomadic Khoisan people. Some of them, the Khoikhoi, developed a cattle-rearing culture, while others, the San (also called Bushmen) were nomadic hunters and gatherers. During the first millennium AD, Bantu-speaking peoples moved into the area, displacing the Khoisan and introducing a farming culture. Today, the main group of people in Botswana are Bantu-speaking Tswana, though there is a small San minority. The Khoikhoi are now extinct as a separate ethnic group.

Britain ruled the area as the Bechuanaland Protectorate between 1885 and 1966. When the country became independent, it was renamed Botswana. Since then, the country has been a stable, multiparty democracy. However, a major setback occurred in the early 21st century, when health officials announced that around 25% of the people were infected with HIV/AIDS.

In 1966, Botswana was extremely poor, depending on meat and live cattle for its exports. But the discovery of minerals, including coal, cobalt, copper, diamonds and nickel, has boosted the economy. About 16% of the people now depend on agriculture, raising cattle and growing crops. Industries include the processing of farm products.

BRAZIL

AREA 8,514,215 sq km [3,287,338 sq mi]
POPULATION 184,101,000
CAPITAL (POPULATION) Brasília (2,016,000)
GOVERNMENT Federal republic
ETHNIC GROUPS White 55%, Mulatto 38%, Black 6%, others 1%
LANGUAGES Portuguese (official)
RELIGIONS Roman Catholic 80%
CURRENCY Real = 100 centavos

GEOGRAPHY The Federative Republic of Brazil is the world's fifth largest country. It contains three main regions. The Amazon basin in the north covers more than half of Brazil. The Amazon, the world's second longest river, has a far greater volume than any other river. The second region, the north-east, consists of a coastal plain and the *sertão*, which is the name for the inland plateaux and hill country. The main river in this region is the São Francisco. The third region is made up of the plateaux in the south-east. This region, which covers about a quarter of the country, is the most developed and densely populated part of Brazil. Its main river is the Paraná, which flows south through Argentina.

Manaus has high temperatures all through the year. The rainfall is heavy, though the period from June to September is drier than the rest of the year. The capital, Brasília, and the city Rio de Janeiro also have tropical climates, with much more marked dry seasons than Manaus. The far south has a temperate climate. The north-eastern interior is the driest region, with an average annual rainfall of only 250 mm [10 in] in places. The rainfall is also unreliable and severe droughts are common in this region.

POLITICS & ECONOMY The Portuguese explorer Pedro Alvarez Cabral claimed Brazil for Portugal in 1500. With Spain occupied in western South America, the Portuguese began to develop their colony, which was more than 90 times as big as Portugal. To do this, they enslaved many local Amerindian people and introduced about 4 million African slaves. Brazil declared itself an independent empire in 1822 and a republic in 1889. From the 1930s, Brazil faced periods of military rule and widespread corruption. Civilian rule was restored in 1985, and a new constitution was adopted in 1988.

The United Nations has described Brazil as a 'Rapidly Industrializing Country', or RIC. Its total volume of production is one of the largest in the world. But many people, including poor farmers and residents of the *favelas* (city slums), do not share in the country's fast economic growth. Widespread poverty, together with high inflation and unemployment, led to the election as president of left-winger Luiz Inácio Lula da Silva (popularly known as 'Lula') in 2002.

By the early 1990s, industry was the most valuable activity, employing 25% of the people. Brazil is among the world's top producers of bauxite, chrome, diamonds, gold, iron ore, manganese and tin. It is also a major manufacturing country. Its products include aircraft, cars, chemicals, processed food, including raw sugar, iron and steel, paper and textiles.

Brazil is one of the world's leading farming countries and agriculture employs 22% of the people. Coffee is a major export. Other leading products include bananas, citrus fruits, cocoa, maize, rice, soybeans and sugar cane. Brazil is also the top producer of eggs, meat and milk in South America. Forestry is a major industry, though many people fear that the exploitation of the rainforests, with 1.5% to 4% of Brazil's forest being destroyed every year, is a disaster for the entire world.

BRUNEI

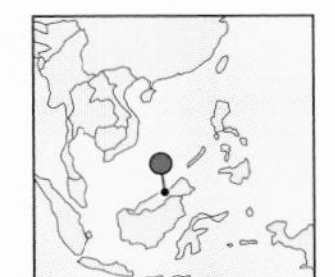

AREA 5,765 sq km [2,226 sq mi]
POPULATION 365,000
CAPITAL (POPULATION) Bandar Seri Begawan (50,000)

Brunei was a major trading centre on the north coast of Borneo around 1,400 years ago. The first sultan took power in the 13th century, but Britain took over the area in the 19th century. Brunei became a British protectorate in 1888 and it declined in importance. But the discovery of oil in 1929 revived the economy and Brunei became independent on 1 January 1984. The modern Islamic Republic of Brunei is prosperous, the result of its abundant oil and natural gas, and the Sultan is said to be one of the world's richest men. The climate is tropical and rainforests cover large areas.

BULGARIA

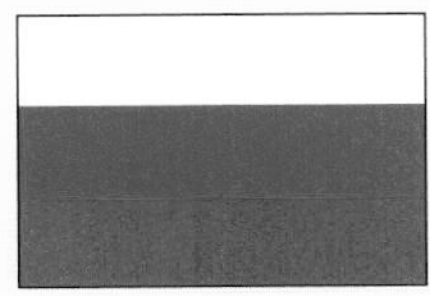
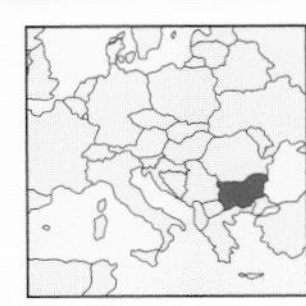

AREA 110,912 sq km [42,823 sq mi]
POPULATION 7,518,000
CAPITAL (POPULATION) Sofia (1,139,000)
GOVERNMENT Multiparty republic
ETHNIC GROUPS Bulgarian 84%, Turkish 9%, Gypsy 5%, Macedonian, Armenian, others
LANGUAGES Bulgarian (official), Turkish
RELIGIONS Bulgarian Orthodox 83%, Islam 12%, Roman Catholic 2%, others
CURRENCY Lev = 100 stotinki

GEOGRAPHY The Republic of Bulgaria is a country in the Balkan peninsula, facing the Black Sea in the east. The heart of Bulgaria is mountainous. The main ranges are the Balkan Mountains in the centre and the Rhodope (or Rhodopi) Mountains in the south.

Summers are hot and winters are cold, though seldom severe. The rainfall is moderate.

POLITICS & ECONOMY Ottoman Turks ruled Bulgaria from 1396 and ethnic Turks still form a sizeable minority in the country. In 1879, Bulgaria became a monarchy, and in 1908 it became fully independent. Bulgaria was an ally of Germany in World War I (1914–18) and again in World War II (1939–45). In 1944, Soviet troops invaded Bulgaria and, after the war, the monarchy was abolished and the country became a Communist ally of the Soviet Union. In the late 1980s, reforms in the Soviet Union led Bulgaria's government to introduce a multiparty system in 1990. A non-Communist government was elected in 1991, the first free elections in 44 years. In 2001, a coalition led by the former King Siméon, who had left Bulgaria in 1948, won the elections. Siméon became prime minister. Bulgaria's efforts to improve relations with the West were rewarded in 2004, when the country became a member of NATO.

According to the World Bank, Bulgaria in the 1990s was a 'lower-middle-income' developing country. Bulgaria has some deposits of minerals, including brown coal, manganese and iron ore. But manufacturing is the leading economic activity, though problems arose in the early 1990s because much of the industrial technology was outdated. The main products are chemicals, processed foods, metal products, machinery and textiles. Manufactures are Bulgaria's leading exports.

BURKINA FASO

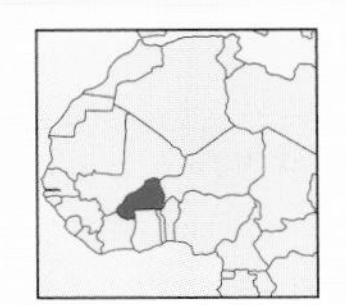

AREA 274,000 sq km [105,791 sq mi]
POPULATION 13,575,000
CAPITAL (POPULATION) Ouagadougou (637,000)
GOVERNMENT Multiparty republic
ETHNIC GROUPS Mossi 40%, Gurunsi, Senufo, Lobi, Bobo, Mande, Fulani
LANGUAGES French (official), Mossi, Fulani
RELIGIONS Islam 50%, traditional beliefs 40%, Christianity 10%
CURRENCY CFA franc = 100 centimes

GEOGRAPHY The Democratic People's Republic of Burkina Faso is a landlocked country in West Africa. It consists of a plateau, between about 300 m and 700 m [650 ft to 2,300 ft] above sea level.

The capital city, Ouagadougou, in central Burkina Faso, has high temperatures throughout the year. Most of the rain falls between May and September, but the rainfall is erratic and droughts are common.

POLITICS & ECONOMY The people of Burkina Faso are divided into two main groups. The Voltaic group includes the Mossi, who form the largest single group, and the Bobo. The French conquered the Mossi capital of Ouagadougou in 1897 and they made the area a protectorate. In 1919, the area became a French colony called Upper Volta. After independence in 1960, Upper Volta became a one-party state. But it was unstable – military groups seized power several times and political killings took place. In 1984, the country's name was changed to Burkina Faso. In 1991 and 1998, the former military leader, Captain Blaise Compaoré, was elected president, but the military continued to play an important part in the government.

Burkina Faso is one of the world's 20 poorest countries and is highly dependent on foreign aid. The main food crops are beans, maize, millet, rice and sorghum. Cotton, groundnuts and shea nuts are grown for export. Cattle are also exported.

The country has few resources and manufacturing is on a small scale. There are some deposits of manganese, zinc, lead and nickel in the north of the country, but exploitation awaits improvements to the transport system there. Many young men seek jobs abroad in Ghana and Ivory Coast. The money they send home is important to the country's economy.

BURMA (MYANMAR)

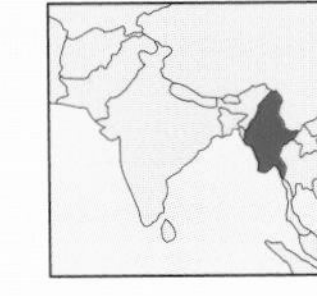

AREA 676,578 sq km [261,227 sq mi]
POPULATION 42,720,000
CAPITAL (POPULATION) Rangoon (2,513,000)
GOVERNMENT Military regime
ETHNIC GROUPS Burman 68%, Shan 9%, Karen 7%, Rakhine 4%, Chinese, Indian, Mon
LANGUAGES Burmese (official); minority ethnic groups have their own languages
RELIGIONS Buddhism 89%, Christianity, Islam
CURRENCY Kyat = 100 pyas

GEOGRAPHY The Union of Burma is now officially known as the Union of Myanmar; its name was changed in 1989. Mountains border the country in the east and west, with the highest mountains in the north. Burma's highest mountain is Hkakabo Razi, which is 5,881 m [19,294 ft] high. Between these ranges is central Burma, which contains the fertile valleys of the Irrawaddy and Sittang rivers. The Irrawaddy delta on the Bay of Bengal is one of the world's leading rice-growing areas. Burma also includes the long Tenasserim coast in the south-east.

Burma has a tropical monsoon climate. There are three seasons. The rainy season runs from late May to mid-October. A cool, dry season follows, between late October and the middle part of February. The hot season lasts from late February to mid-May, though temperatures remain high during the humid rainy season.

POLITICS & ECONOMY Many groups settled in Burma in ancient times. Some, called the hill peoples, live in remote mountain areas where they have retained their own cultures. The ancestors of the country's main ethnic group today, the Burmese, arrived in the 9th century AD.

Britain conquered Burma in the 19th century and made it a province of British India. But, in 1937, the British granted Burma limited self-government. Japan conquered Burma in 1942, but the Japanese were driven out in 1945. Burma became a fully independent country in 1948.

Revolts by Communists and various hill people led to instability in the 1950s. In 1962, Burma became a military dictatorship and, in 1974, a one-party state. Attempts to control minority liberation movements and the opium trade led to repressive rule. The National League for Democracy led by Aung San Suu Kyi won the elections in 1990, but the military continued their repressive rule, earning Burma the reputation for having one of the world's worst human rights records. Its admission to ASEAN (Association of South-east Asian Nations) may have implied recognition of the regime. However, in 2004, a United Nations report criticized the regime for holding more than 1,800 political detainees and for its failure to release opposition leader Aung San Suu Kyi from house arrest.

Agriculture is the main activity, employing 66% of the people. The chief crop is rice. Maize, pulses, oilseeds and sugar cane are other major products. Forestry is important. Teak and rice together make up about two-thirds of the total value of the exports. Burma has many mineral resources, though they are mostly undeveloped, but the country is famous for its precious stones, especially rubies. Manufacturing is mostly on a small scale.

BURUNDI

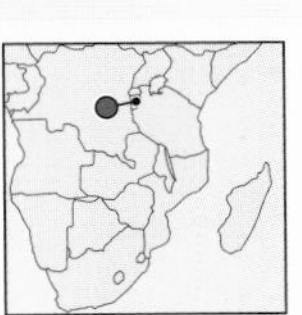

AREA 27,834 sq km [10,747 sq mi]
POPULATION 6,231,000
CAPITAL (POPULATION) Bujumbura (235,000)
GOVERNMENT Republic
ETHNIC GROUPS Hutu 85%, Tutsi 14%, Twa (Pygmy) 1%
LANGUAGES French and Kirundi (both official)
RELIGIONS Roman Catholic 62%, traditional beliefs 23%, Islam 10%, Protestant 5%
CURRENCY Burundi franc = 100 centimes

GEOGRAPHY The Republic of Burundi is the fifth smallest country in mainland Africa. It is also the second most densely populated after its northern neighbour, Rwanda. Part of the Great African Rift Valley, which runs throughout eastern Africa into south-western Asia, lies in western Burundi. It includes part of Lake Tanganyika.

The capital city, Bujumbura, on the shores of Lake Tanganyika, has a warm climate. A dry season runs from June to September, but the rest of the year is rainy. The highlands are cooler and wetter, though the rainfall decreases to the east.

POLITICS & ECONOMY The Twa, a pygmy people, were the first known inhabitants of Burundi. About 1,000 years ago, the Hutu, a people who speak a Bantu language, gradually began to settle the area, pushing the Twa into remote areas.

From the 15th century, the Tutsi, a cattle-owning people from the north-east, gradually took over the country. The Hutu, although greatly outnumbering the Tutsi, were forced to serve the Tutsi overlords.

Germany conquered the area that is now Burundi and Rwanda in the late 1890s. The area, called Ruanda-Urundi, was taken by Belgium during World War I (1914–18). In 1961, the people of Urundi voted to become a monarchy, while the people of Ruanda voted to become a republic. The two territories became fully independent as Burundi and Rwanda in 1962. After 1962, the rivalries between the Hutu and Tutsi led to periodic outbreaks of fighting. The Tutsi monarchy was ended in 1966 and Burundi became a republic. Instability continued, with massacres of thousands of people in ethnic violence. In 2001, a power-sharing agreement was reached, but conflict continued. Progress towards democracy was slow but a new constitution was approved in a referendum held in February 2005.

Burundi is one of the world's ten poorest countries. About 93% of the people are farmers who live mostly at subsistence level. The main food crops are beans, cassava, maize and sweet potatoes. Cattle, goats and sheep are raised and fishing is also important. However, Burundi has to import food.

CAMBODIA

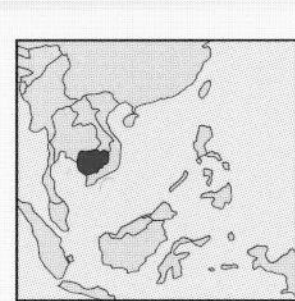

AREA 181,035 sq km [69,898 sq mi]
POPULATION 13,363,000
CAPITAL (POPULATION) Phnom Penh (1,000,000)
GOVERNMENT Constitutional monarchy
ETHNIC GROUPS Khmer 90%, Vietnamese 5%, Chinese 1%, others
LANGUAGES Khmer (official), French, English
RELIGIONS Buddhism 95%, others 5%
CURRENCY Riel = 100 sen

GEOGRAPHY The Kingdom of Cambodia is a country in South-east Asia. Low mountains border the country except in the south-east. But most of Cambodia consists of plains drained by the River Mekong, which enters Cambodia from Laos in the north and exits through Vietnam in the south-east. The north-west contains Tonlé Sap (or Great Lake). In the dry season, this lake drains into the River Mekong. But in the wet season, the level of the Mekong rises and water flows in the opposite direction from the river into Tonlé Sap – the lake then becomes the largest freshwater lake in Asia.

Cambodia has a tropical monsoon climate, with high temperatures all through the year. The dry season, when winds blow from the north or north-east, runs from November to April. During the rainy season, from May to October, moist winds blow from the south or south-east. The high humidity and heat often make conditions unpleasant. The rainfall is heaviest near the coast, and rather lower inland.

POLITICS & ECONOMY From 802 to 1432, the Khmer people ruled a great empire, which reached its peak in the 12th century. The Khmer capital was at Angkor. The Hindu stone temples built there and at nearby Angkor Wat form the world's largest group of religious buildings. France ruled the country between 1863 and 1954, when the country became an independent monarchy. But the monarchy was abolished in 1970 and Cambodia became a republic.

In 1970, US and South Vietnamese troops entered Cambodia but left after destroying North Vietnamese Communist camps in the east. The country became involved in the Vietnamese War, and then in a civil war as Cambodian Communists of the Khmer Rouge organization fought for power. The Khmer Rouge took over Cambodia in 1975 and launched a reign of terror in which between 1 million and 2.5 million people were killed. In 1979, Vietnamese and Cambodian troops overthrew the Khmer Rouge government. But fighting continued between several factions. Vietnam withdrew in 1989, and in 1991 Prince Sihanouk was recognized as head of state. Elections were held in May 1993, and in September 1993 the monarchy was restored, with Sihanouk as king. Elections were held in 1998 and 2003. In 2001, the government set up courts to try leaders of the Khmer Rouge. In 2004, Sihanouk abdicated because of ill health and his son, Prince Norodom Sihamoni, succeeded him.

Cambodia is a poor country whose economy has been wrecked by war. Until the 1970s, the country's farmers produced most of the food needed by the people. But by 1986, it was only able to supply 80% of its needs. Recovery was slow. Farming is still the main activity. Rice, rubber and maize are important. Manufacturing is on a small scale. Tourism is increasing – the impressive Angkor temples are a major attraction.

CAMEROON

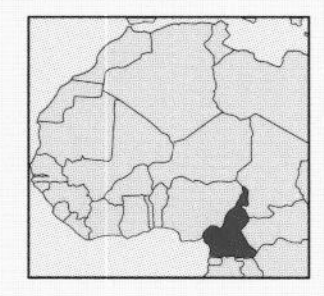

AREA 475,442 sq km [183,568 sq mi]
POPULATION 16,064,000
CAPITAL (POPULATION) Yaoundé (649,000)
GOVERNMENT Multiparty republic
ETHNIC GROUPS Cameroon Highlanders 31%, Bantu 27%, Kirdi 11%, Fulani 10%, others
LANGUAGES French and English (both official), many others
RELIGIONS Christianity 40%, traditional beliefs 40%, Islam 20%
CURRENCY CFA franc = 100 centimes

GEOGRAPHY The Republic of Cameroon in West Africa derived its name from the Portuguese word *camarões*, or prawns. This name was used by Portuguese explorers who fished for prawns along the coast. Behind the narrow coastal plains on the Gulf of Guinea, the land rises to a series of plateaux, with a mountainous region in the south-west where the volcano Mount Cameroon is situated. In the north, the land slopes down towards the Lake Chad basin.

The rainfall is heavy, especially in the highlands. The rainiest months near the coast are June to September. The rainfall decreases to the north and the far north has a hot, dry climate. Temperatures are high on the coast, whereas the inland plateaux are cooler.

POLITICS & ECONOMY Germany lost Cameroon during World War I (1914–18). The country was then divided into two parts, one ruled by Britain and the other by France. In 1960, French Cameroon became the independent Cameroon Republic. In 1961, after a vote in British Cameroon, part of the territory joined the Cameroon Republic to become the Federal Republic of Cameroon – the other part joined Nigeria. In 1972, Cameroon became a unitary state called the United Republic of Cameroon. It adopted the name Republic of Cameroon in 1984, but the country had two official languages. In 2002, the International Court of Justice gave Cameroon sovereignty over the disputed oil-rich Bakassi peninsula. But Nigeria failed to reach the deadline for the hand-over of the area in 2004.

Like most countries in tropical Africa, Cameroon's economy is based on agriculture, which employs 73% of the people. Food crops include maize, millet, sweet potatoes and yams, and coffee and cocoa are exported. Cameroon has some oil, which has become the chief export, and bauxite. There are few manufactures, but the mineral exports and self-sufficiency in food production make it one of tropical Africa's better-off countries.

CANADA

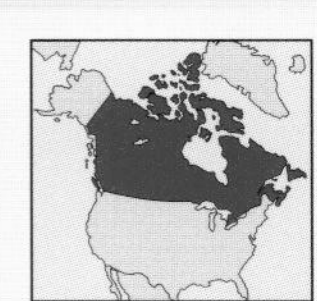

AREA 9,970,610 sq km [3,849,653 sq mi]
POPULATION 32,508,000
CAPITAL (POPULATION) Ottawa (774,000)
GOVERNMENT Federal multiparty constitutional monarchy
ETHNIC GROUPS British origin 28%, French origin 23%, other European 15%, Amerindian/Inuit 2%, others
LANGUAGES English and French (both official)
RELIGIONS Roman Catholic 46%, Protestant 36%, Judaism, Islam, Hinduism
CURRENCY Canadian dollar = 100 cents

GEOGRAPHY Canada is the world's second largest country after Russia. It is thinly populated, however, with much of the land too cold or too mountainous for human settlement. Most Canadians live within 300 km [186 mi] of the southern border.

Western Canada is rugged. It includes the Pacific ranges and the mighty Rocky Mountains. East of the Rockies are the interior plains. In the north lie the bleak Arctic islands, while to the south lie the densely populated lowlands around lakes Erie and Ontario and in the St Lawrence River valley.

Canada has a cold climate. In winter, temperatures fall below freezing point throughout most of Canada. But the south-western coast has a relatively mild climate. Along the Arctic Circle, mean temperatures are below freezing for seven months a year.

Western and south-eastern Canada experience high rainfall, but the prairies are dry with 250 mm to 500 mm [10 in to 20 in] of rain every year.

POLITICS & ECONOMY Canada's first people, the ancestors of the Native Americans, or Indians, arrived in North America from Asia around 40,000 years ago. Later arrivals were the Inuit (Eskimos), who also came from Asia. Europeans reached the Canadian coast in 1497 and a race began between Britain and France for control of the territory.

France gained an initial advantage, and the French founded Québec in 1608. But the British later occupied eastern Canada. In 1867, Britain passed the British North America Act, which set up the Dominion of Canada, which was made up of Québec, Ontario, Nova Scotia and New Brunswick. Other areas were added, the last being Newfoundland in 1949. Canada fought alongside Britain in both World Wars and many Canadians feel close ties with Britain. Canada is a constitutional monarchy, and the British monarch is Canada's head of state.

Rivalries between French- and English-speaking Canadians continue. In 1995, Québeckers voted against a move to make Québec a sovereign state. The majority was less than 1%. Opinion polls then suggested that support for independence had begun to fall. In 2003, the separatist Parti Québecois was defeated in provincial elections, ending nine years of rule by the pro-independence party. Another problem concerns the rights of Aboriginal minorities. To this end, in 1999, Canada created the territory of Nunavut for the Inuit population in the north. Nunavut covers about 64% of what was formerly the eastern part of the Northwest Territories.

Canada is a highly developed and prosperous country. Although farmland covers only 8% of the country, Canadian farms are highly productive. Canada is one of the world's leading producers of barley, wheat, meat and milk. Forestry and fishing are other important industries. It is rich in natural resources, especially oil and natural gas. Canada exports minerals, including copper, gold, iron ore, uranium and zinc. Manufacturing is important, mainly in the cities where 79% of the people live. Canada processes farm and mineral products. It also produces cars, chemicals, electronic goods, machinery, paper and timber products.

CAPE VERDE

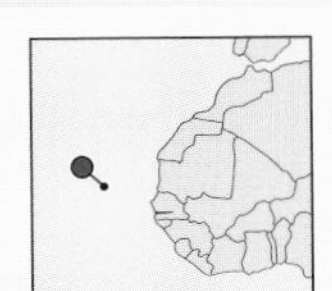

AREA 4,033 sq km [1,557 sq mi]
POPULATION 415,000
CAPITAL (POPULATION) Praia (95,000)

Cape Verde consists of ten large and five small islands, and is situated 560 km [350 mi] west of Dakar in Senegal. The islands have a tropical climate, with high temperatures throughout the year.

Portuguese explorers discovered the islands in the 15th century. They became an assembly point for African slaves, but the abolition of slavery in the 19th century, combined with severe droughts, ended the islands' prosperity. In 1951, Cape Verde became an overseas province of Portugal, but it became a fully independent republic in 1975. The World Bank rates Cape Verde as a 'low-income' developing country. Only 10% to 15% of the land is suitable for farming.

CAYMAN ISLANDS

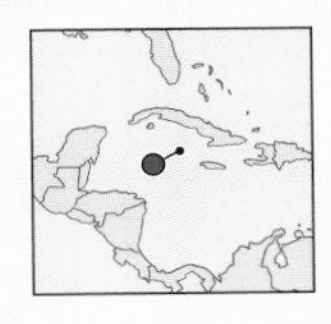

AREA 264 sq km [102 sq mi]
POPULATION 43,000
CAPITAL (POPULATION) George Town (14,000)

The Cayman Islands are an overseas territory of the UK. There are three low-lying islands: Grand Cayman, Little Cayman and Cayman Brac. Discovered by Christopher Columbus in 1503, they were recognized as British possessions in 1670. The islands were governed as part of Jamaica from 1863, but they became a separate dependency when Jamaica became independent in 1962. Financial services are the main economic activity and the islands offer a tax haven to many companies and banks. Farm production is limited and food is imported.

CENTRAL AFRICAN REPUBLIC

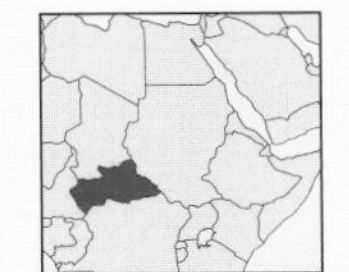

AREA 622,984 sq km [240,534 sq mi]
POPULATION 3,742,000
CAPITAL (POPULATION) Bangui (553,000)
GOVERNMENT Multiparty republic
ETHNIC GROUPS Baya 33%, Banda 27%, Mandjia 13%, Sara 10%, Mboum 7%, Mbaka 4%, others
LANGUAGES French (official), Sangho
RELIGIONS Traditional beliefs 35%, Protestant 25%, Roman Catholic 25%, Islam 15%
CURRENCY CFA franc = 100 centimes

GEOGRAPHY The Central African Republic is a remote, landlocked country in the heart of Africa. It consists mostly of a plateau lying between 600 m and 800 m [1,970 ft to 2,620 ft] above sea level. The Ubangi drains the south, while the Chari (or Shari) River flows from the north to the Lake Chad basin.

The climate is warm throughout the year, while the annual average rainfall in the capital Bangui totals 1,574 mm [62 in]. The north is drier, with an average annual rainfall of about 800 mm [31 in].

POLITICS & ECONOMY France set up an outpost at Bangui in 1899 and ruled the country as a colony from 1894. Known as Ubangi-Shari, the country was ruled by France as part of French Equatorial Africa until it gained independence in 1960.

Central African Republic became a one-party state in 1962, but army officers seized power in 1966. The head of the army, Jean-Bedel Bokassa, made himself emperor in 1976. The country was renamed the Central African Empire, but after a brutal reign, the tyrannical Bokassa was overthrown in a military coup in 1979. The country again became a republic.

The country adopted a new constitution in 1991, but a coup in 2003 brought General François Bozize to power. A new constitution was introduced in 2004, followed by elections in 2005.

The World Bank classifies Central African Republic as a 'low-income' developing country. Over 80% of the people are farmers, mostly at subsistence level. Bananas, maize, manioc, millet and yams are food crops, while cotton, timber and tobacco are exported. The country depends on aid, especially from France.

CHAD

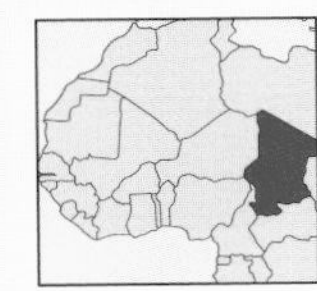

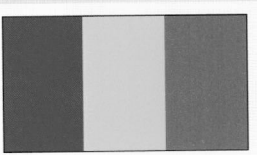

AREA 1,284,000 sq km [495,752 sq mi]
POPULATION 9,539,000
CAPITAL (POPULATION) Ndjamena (530,000)
GOVERNMENT Multiparty republic
ETHNIC GROUPS 200 distinct groups: mostly Muslim in the north and centre; mostly Christian or animist in the south
LANGUAGES French and Arabic (both official), many others
RELIGIONS Islam 51%, Christianity 35%, animist 7%
CURRENCY CFA franc = 100 centimes

GEOGRAPHY The Republic of Chad is a landlocked country in north-central Africa. It is Africa's fifth largest country. Ndjamena in central Chad has a hot, tropical climate, with a dry season from November to April. The south of the country is wetter, with an average yearly rainfall of around 1,000 mm [39 in]. The hot desert in the north has an average yearly rainfall of less than 130 mm [5 in].

POLITICS & ECONOMY Chad straddles two worlds. Muslim Arabs and Berbers live in the north, while black Africans, followers of traditional beliefs or Christianity, live in the south.

French explorers were active in the area in the late 19th century. France finally made Chad a colony in 1902. Since becoming independent in 1960, Chad has been hit by ethnic conflict. The 1970s were marked by civil war and coups. Chad and Libya agreed a truce in 1987 and, in 1994, the International Court of Justice ruled against Libya's claim on the Aozou Strip. Chad enjoyed more stability in the 1990s, but, in 2004, Chad forces clashed with pro-Sudanese militias as the conflict in Sudan's Darfur province spilled over the border.

Hit by drought and civil war, Chad is one of the world's poorest countries. Farming, fishing and livestock raising employ 83% of the people. Groundnuts, millet, rice and sorghum are major food crops in the south, but the chief export crop is cotton. Chad has few manufacturing industries, but its oil reserves hold out hope for development in the 21st century.

CHILE

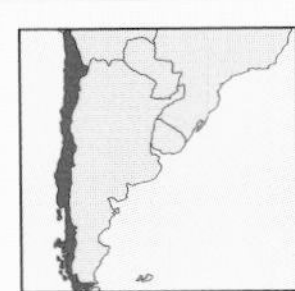

AREA 756,626 sq km [292,133 sq mi]
POPULATION 15,824,000
CAPITAL (POPULATION) Santiago (4,789,000)
GOVERNMENT Multiparty republic
ETHNIC GROUPS Mestizo 95%, Amerindian 3%
LANGUAGES Spanish (official)
RELIGIONS Roman Catholic 89%, Protestant 11%
CURRENCY Chilean peso = 100 centavos

GEOGRAPHY The Republic of Chile stretches about 4,260 km [2,650 mi] from north to south, although the maximum east–west distance is only about 430 km [267 mi]. The high Andes Mountains form Chile's eastern borders with Argentina and Bolivia. To the west are basins and valleys, with coastal uplands overlooking the shore. Most people live in the central valley, where Santiago is situated.

Santiago has a Mediterranean climate, with hot, dry summers and mild, moist winters. The Atacama Desert in the north is one of the world's driest places, while southern Chile is cold and stormy.

POLITICS & ECONOMY Amerindian people reached the southern tip of South America 8,000 years ago. In 1520, Portuguese navigator Ferdinand Magellan was the first European to sight Chile. The country became a Spanish colony in the 1540s. Chile became independent in 1818. During a war (1879–83), it gained mineral-rich areas from Peru and Bolivia.

In 1970, Salvador Allende became the first Communist leader to be elected democratically. He was overthrown in 1973 by army officers, who were supported by the CIA. General Augusto Pinochet then ruled as a dictator. A new constitution was introduced in 1981 and elections were held in 1989. Pinochet, who had been charged with presiding over acts of torture, was found to be too ill to stand trial in 2001. But new charges were brought against him in 2004 and, in 2005, he was placed under house arrest.

The World Bank classifies Chile as a 'lower-middle-income' developing country. Copper is mined and minerals are exported. The main activity is manufacturing, including processed foods, metals, iron and steel, transport equipment and textiles.

CHINA

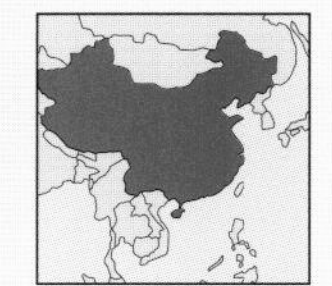

AREA 9,596,961 sq km [3,705,387 sq mi]
POPULATION 1,298,848,000
CAPITAL (POPULATION) Beijing (7,362,000)
GOVERNMENT Single-party Communist republic
ETHNIC GROUPS Han Chinese 92%, many others
LANGUAGES Mandarin Chinese (official)
RELIGIONS Atheist (official)
CURRENCY Renminbi yuan = 10 jiao = 100 fen

GEOGRAPHY The People's Republic of China is the world's third largest country. Most people live in the east – on the coastal plains or in the fertile valleys of the Huang He (Hwang Ho or Yellow River), the Chang Jiang (Yangtze Kiang), which is Asia's longest river at 6,380 km [3,960 mi], and the Xi Jiang (Si Kiang).

Western China is thinly populated. It includes the bleak Tibetan plateau which is bounded by the Himalaya, the world's highest mountain range. Other ranges include the Kunlun Shan, the Altun Shan and the Tian Shan. Deserts include the Gobi Desert along the Mongolian border and the Taklimakan Desert in the far west.

Beijing in north-eastern China has cold winters and warm summers, with a moderate rainfall. Shanghai, in the east-central region of China, has milder winters and more rain. The south-east has a wet, subtropical climate. In the west, the climate is severe. Lhasa has very cold winters and a low rainfall.

POLITICS & ECONOMY China is one of the world's oldest civilizations, going back 3,500 years. Under the Han dynasty (202 BC to AD 220), the Chinese empire was as large as the Roman empire. Mongols conquered China in the 13th century, but Chinese rule was restored in 1368. The Manchu people of Mongolia ruled the country from 1644 to 1912, when the country became a republic.

War with Japan (1937–45) was followed by civil war between the nationalists and the Communists. The Communists triumphed in 1949, setting up the People's Republic of China. In the 1980s, following the death of the revolutionary leader Mao Zedong (Mao Tse-tung) in 1976, China encouraged formerly forbidden policies, namely private enterprise and foreign investment. But the Communist leaders have not permitted political freedom. Opponents are still harshly treated, while attempts to negotiate some degree of autonomy for Tibet have been rejected.

China's economy has expanded greatly since the 1970s, with many Communist policies being abandoned. Foreign investors have helped to set up many new industries in the east. Between 1989 and 2004, the economy grew by an average of more than 9% per year. By 2005, China had the world's sixth largest economy and it had overtaken Japan to become the fourth largest exporter to the United States.

China has benefited from the return of Hong Kong in 1997 and its admission to the World Trade Organization in 2001. China would also like to regain the island of Taiwan, which it regards as a renegade province. This seems unlikely in the near future, although Taiwan's economy is closely tied to that of the mainland. In 2005, the 56-year ban on direct passenger flights from Taiwan to mainland China was lifted.

Despite its recent success, China remains a poor country. In the late 1990s, agriculture still employed nearly half of the people, although only 10% of the land is farmed. In 2004, the government announced that it planned to slow down the country's rapid economic growth in order to help the rural poor, who had become relatively worse off as China's industries expanded. Farm products include rice, sweet potatoes, tea and wheat, and many fruits and vegetables. Livestock farming is also important. Pork is popular. China has more than a third of the world's pigs.

Resources include coal, iron ore and other metals. Leading manufactures include cement, chemicals, fertilizers, machinery, telecommunications and recording equipment, and textiles. In recent years, China has also become one of the world's leading producers of consumer goods.

COLOMBIA

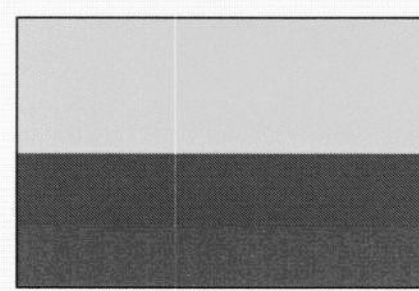
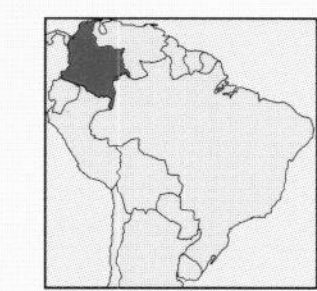

AREA 1,138,914 sq km [439,735 sq mi]
POPULATION 42,311,000
CAPITAL (POPULATION) Bogotá (6,545,000)
GOVERNMENT Multiparty republic
ETHNIC GROUPS Mestizo 58%, White 20%, Mulatto 14%, Black 4%
LANGUAGES Spanish (official)
RELIGIONS Roman Catholic 90%
CURRENCY Colombian peso = 100 centavos

GEOGRAPHY The Republic of Colombia, in north-eastern South America, is the only country in the continent to have coastlines on both the Pacific and the Caribbean Sea. Colombia also contains the northernmost ranges of the Andes Mountains.

There is a tropical climate in the lowlands. But the altitude greatly affects the climate of the Andes. The capital, Bogotá, which stands on a plateau in the eastern Andes at about 2,800 m [9,200 ft] above sea level, has mild temperatures throughout the year. The rainfall is heavy, especially on the Pacific coast.

POLITICS & ECONOMY Amerindian people have lived in Colombia for thousands of years. But today, only a small proportion of the people are of unmixed Amerindian ancestry. Mestizos (people of mixed white and Amerindian ancestry) form the largest group, followed by whites and mulattos (people of mixed European and African ancestry).

Spaniards opened up the area in the early 16th century. They set up a territory known as the Viceroyalty of the New Kingdom of Granada, including Colombia, Ecuador, Panama and Venezuela. In 1819, the area became independent, but Ecuador and Venezuela soon split away, followed by Panama in 1903. Instability has marked its recent history. Political rivalries led to civil wars in 1899–1902 and 1949–57, when a coalition government was formed. The coalition ended in 1986 when the Liberal Party was elected. Colombia faces economic and security problems, notably combating left-wing guerrillas and right-wing paramilitaries, while controlling a large illicit drug industry. In the early 2000s, the US provided aid to help Colombia fight drug-trafficking. Andrés Pastrana, who had been elected president in 1998, tried hard to end the guerrilla war, but peace talks collapsed in 2002 and full-scale fighting was resumed. His successor, President Uribe, elected in 2002, declared a tough line against the rebels.

The World Bank classifies Colombia as a 'lower-middle-income' developing country. Agriculture is important and coffee is the leading export crop. Other crops include bananas, cocoa, maize and tobacco. Colombia exports coal and oil, and it also produces emeralds and gold. The main manufacturing centre is the capital, Bogotá, together with Cali and Medellín.

COMOROS

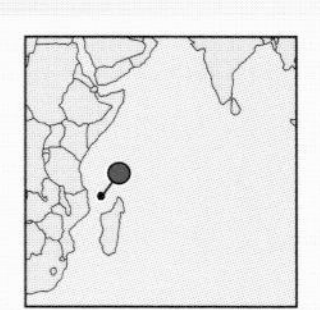

AREA 2,235 sq km [863 sq mi]
POPULATION 652,000
CAPITAL (POPULATION) Moroni (30,000)

The Union des Isles Comores, as the Comoros is officially called, consists of three large volcanic islands and some smaller ones, lying at the northern end of the Mozambique Channel in the Indian Ocean. France took over one of the islands, Mayotte, in 1843, and, in 1886, the other islands came under French protection.

The Comoros became independent in 1974, but the people of Mayotte opted to remain French. In the late 1990s, separatists on the islands of Anjouan and Mohéli sought to secede, but, in 2004, each of the large islands was granted autonomy, with its own president and legislature.

The Comoros is a poor country. Most people are subsistence farmers. The main exports are cloves, perfume oils and vanilla.

CONGO

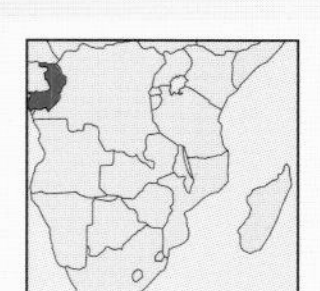

AREA 342,000 sq km [132,046 sq mi]
POPULATION 2,998,000
CAPITAL (POPULATION) Brazzaville (938,000)
GOVERNMENT Military regime
ETHNIC GROUPS Kongo 48%, Sangha 20%, Teke 17%, M'bochi 12%
LANGUAGES French (official), many others
RELIGIONS Christianity 50%, animist 48%, Islam 2%
CURRENCY CFA franc = 100 centimes

GEOGRAPHY The Republic of Congo is a country on the River Congo in west-central Africa. The Equator runs through the centre of the country. Congo has a narrow coastal plain on which its main port, Pointe Noire, stands. Behind the plain are uplands through which the River Niari has carved a fertile valley. Central Congo consists of high plains. The north contains large swampy areas in the valleys of the tributaries of the River Congo.

Congo has a hot, wet equatorial climate. Brazzaville has a dry season between June and September. The coast is drier and cooler than the rest of Congo, because of the cold offshore Benguela ocean current.

POLITICS & ECONOMY Part of the huge Kongo kingdom between the 15th and 18th centuries, the coast of the Congo later became a centre of the European slave trade. The area came under French protection in 1880. It was later governed as part of a larger region called French Equatorial Africa. The country remained under French control until 1960.

Congo became a one-party state in 1964 and a military group took over the government in 1968. In 1970, Congo declared itself a Communist country, though it continued to seek aid from Western countries. The government officially abandoned its Communist policies in 1990. Multiparty elections were held in 1992, but the elected president, Pascal Lissouba, was overthrown in 1997 by former president Denis Sassou-Nguesso. Civil war again occurred in January 1999, but peace was restored and a peace accord was signed in 2003.

The World Bank classifies Congo as a 'lower-middle-income' developing country. Agriculture is the most important activity, employing about 60% of the people. But many farmers produce little more than they need to feed their families. Major food crops include bananas, cassava, maize and rice, while the leading cash crops are coffee and cocoa. Congo's main exports are oil (which makes up 90% of the total) and timber. Manufacturing is relatively unimportant at the moment, still hampered by poor transport links. Inland, rivers form the main lines of communication, and Brazzaville is linked to the port of Pointe-Noire by the Congo-Ocean Railway.

CONGO (DEM. REP. OF THE)

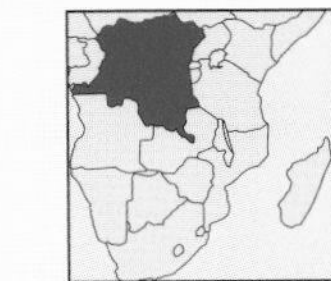

AREA 2,344,858 sq km [905,350 sq mi]
POPULATION 58,318,000
CAPITAL (POPULATION) Kinshasa (4,665,000)
GOVERNMENT Single-party republic
ETHNIC GROUPS Over 200; the largest are Mongo, Luba, Kongo, Mangbetu-Azande
LANGUAGES French (official), tribal languages
RELIGIONS Roman Catholic 50%, Protestant 20%, Islam 10%, others
CURRENCY Congolese franc = 100 centimes

GEOGRAPHY The Democratic Republic of the Congo, formerly known as Zaïre, is the world's 12th largest country. Much of the country lies within the drainage basin of the huge River Congo. The river reaches the sea along the country's coastline, which is 40 km [25 mi] long. Mountains rise in the east, where the country's borders run through lakes Tanganyika, Kivu, Edward and Albert.

The equatorial region has high temperatures and heavy rainfall throughout the year.

POLITICS & ECONOMY Pygmies were the first inhabitants of the region, with Portuguese navigators not reaching the coast until 1482, but the interior was not explored until the late 19th century. In 1885, the country, called Congo Free State, became the personal property of King Léopold II of Belgium. In 1908, the country became a Belgian colony.

The Belgian Congo became independent in 1960 and was renamed Zaïre in 1971. Ethnic rivalries caused instability until 1965, when the country became a one-party state, ruled by President Mobutu. The government allowed the formation of political parties in 1990, but elections were repeatedly postponed. In 1996, fighting broke out in eastern Zaïre, as the Tutsi–Hutu conflict in Burundi and Rwanda spilled over. The rebel leader Laurent Kabila took power in 1997, ousting Mobutu and renaming the country. A rebellion against Kabila broke out in 1998. Rwanda and Uganda supported the rebels, while Angola, Chad, Namibia and Zimbabwe assisted Kabila. A peace treaty was signed in 1999, but fighting continued. Kabila was assassinated in 2001. His son, Major-General Joseph Kabila, who became president, worked to end a war which, by early 2003, had claimed over 2 million lives. In 2003, under a peace agreement, Kabila was installed as interim president of a transitional government. But unrest continued into 2005.

The World Bank classifies the Democratic Republic of the Congo as a 'low-income' developing country, despite its reserves of copper, the main export, and other minerals. Agriculture, mainly at subsistence level, employs 63% of the people.

COSTA RICA

AREA 51,100 sq km [19,730 sq mi]
POPULATION 3,957,000
CAPITAL (POPULATION) San José (337,000)
GOVERNMENT Multiparty republic
ETHNIC GROUPS White (including Mestizo) 94%, Black 3%, Amerindian 1%, Chinese 1%, others
LANGUAGES Spanish (official), English
RELIGIONS Roman Catholic 76%, Evangelical 14%
CURRENCY Costa Rican colón = 100 céntimos

GEOGRAPHY The Republic of Costa Rica in Central America has coastlines on the Pacific Ocean and the Caribbean Sea. Mountain ranges, plateaux and volcanoes lie inland where the tropical climate is tempered by the altitude. Heavy rain occurs on the Caribbean coast, but the highlands and the Pacific coast are less rainy.

POLITICS & ECONOMY Christopher Columbus reached the Caribbean coast in 1502 and rumours of treasure soon attracted many Spaniards to settle in the country. Spain ruled the country until 1821, when Spain's Central American colonies broke away to join Mexico in 1822. In 1823, the Central American states broke with Mexico and set up the Central American Federation. Later, this large union broke up and Costa Rica became fully independent in 1838. From the late 19th century, Costa Rica experienced a number of revolutions, dictatorships and periods of democracy. In 1948 the army was abolished. Since then, Costa Rica has been a stable democracy, much admired in Latin America. However, in 2004, its image was tarnished when two former presidents were imprisoned on charges of graft.

The World Bank rates Costa Rica as a 'lower-middle-income' developing country. It is one of Central America's most prosperous nations with high educational standards and an average life expectancy of 78 years. Agriculture employs 19% of the people. Costa Rica's resources include its forests, but it lacks minerals apart from some bauxite and manganese. Manufacturing and tourism are increasing. The United States is Costa Rica's chief trading partner.

CROATIA

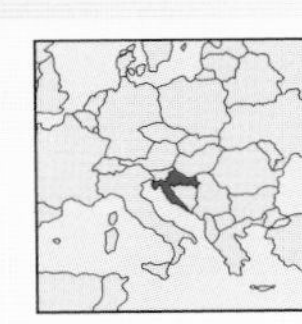

AREA 56,538 sq km [21,829 sq mi]
POPULATION 4,497,000
CAPITAL (POPULATION) Zagreb (779,000)
GOVERNMENT Multiparty republic
ETHNIC GROUPS Croat 90%, Serb 5%, others
LANGUAGES Croatian 96%
RELIGIONS Roman Catholic 88%, Orthodox 4%, Islam 1%, others
CURRENCY Kuna = 100 lipas

GEOGRAPHY The Republic of Croatia was one of the six republics that made up the former Communist country of Yugoslavia until it became independent in 1991. The region bordering the Adriatic Sea is called Dalmatia. It includes the coastal ranges, which contain large areas of bare limestone. Most of the rest of the country consists of the fertile Pannonian plains.

The coastal area has a typical Mediterranean climate, with hot, dry summers and mild, moist winters. Inland, the climate becomes more continental. Winters are cold, while temperatures often soar to 38°C [100°F] in the summer months.

POLITICS & ECONOMY Slav people settled in the area around 1,400 years ago. In 803, Croatia became part of the Holy Roman empire and the Croats soon adopted Christianity. Croatia was an independent kingdom in the 10th and 11th centuries. In 1102, the king of Hungary also became king of Croatia, creating a union that lasted 800 years. In 1526, part of Croatia came under the Turkish Ottoman empire, while the rest came under the Austrian Habsburgs.

After Austria–Hungary was defeated in World War I (1914–18), Croatia became part of the new Kingdom of the Serbs, Croats and Slovenes. This kingdom was renamed Yugoslavia in 1929. Germany occupied Yugoslavia during World War II (1939–45). Croatia was proclaimed independent, but it was really ruled by the invaders.

After the war, Communists took power with Josip Broz Tito as the country's leader. Despite ethnic differences between the people, Tito held Yugoslavia together until his death in 1980. In the 1980s, economic and ethnic problems, including a deterioration in relations with Serbia, threatened stability. In the 1990s, Yugoslavia split into five nations, one of which was Croatia, which declared itself independent in 1991.

After Serbia supplied arms to Serbs living in Croatia, war broke out between the two republics, causing great damage. Croatia lost more than 30% of its territory. But in 1992, the United Nations sent a peacekeeping force to Croatia, which effectively ended the war with Serbia. In 1992, when war broke out in Bosnia-Herzegovina, Bosnian Croats occupied parts of the country. But, in 1994, Croatia helped to end Croat–Muslim conflict, and, in 1995, it helped to draw up the Dayton Peace Accord which ended the civil war there.

The wars of the early 1990s disrupted Croatia's economy, but following the election of a pro-democratic coalition government in 2000, stability, which is so vital for the valuable tourist industry, appeared to be increasing. Manufacturing is the main activity. In 2004, the European Union agreed that accession talks with Croatia would begin in 2005, but many problems stood in the way.

CUBA

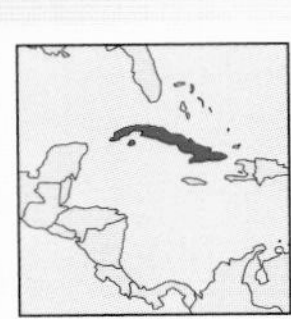

AREA 110,861 sq km [42,803 sq mi]
POPULATION 11,309,000
CAPITAL (POPULATION) Havana (2,192,000)
GOVERNMENT Socialist republic
ETHNIC GROUPS Mulatto 51%, White 37%, Black 11%
LANGUAGES Spanish (official)
RELIGIONS Christianity
CURRENCY Cuban peso = 100 centavos

GEOGRAPHY The Republic of Cuba is the largest island country in the Caribbean Sea. It consists of one large island, Cuba, the Isle of Youth (Isla de la Juventud) and about 1,600 small islets. Mountains and hills cover about a quarter of Cuba. The highest mountain range, the Sierra Maestra in the south-east, reaches 2,000 m [6,562 ft] above sea level. The rest of the land consists of gently rolling country or coastal plains, crossed by fertile valleys carved by the short, mostly shallow and narrow rivers.

Cuba lies in the tropics. But sea breezes moderate the temperature, warming the land in winter and cooling it in summer.

POLITICS & ECONOMY Christopher Columbus discovered the island in 1492 and Spaniards began to settle there from 1511. Spanish rule ended in 1898, when the United States defeated Spain in the Spanish–American War. American influence in Cuba remained strong until 1959, when revolutionary forces under Fidel Castro overthrew the dictatorial government of Fulgencio Batista.

The United States opposed Castro's policies, when he turned to the Soviet Union for assistance. In 1961, Cuban exiles attempting an invasion were defeated. In 1962, the US learned that nuclear missile bases armed by the Soviet Union had been established in Cuba. The US ordered the Soviet Union to remove the missiles and bases and, after a few days, when many people feared that a world war might break out, the Soviet Union agreed to the American demands.

Cuba's relations with the Soviet Union remained strong until 1991, when the Soviet Union was broken up. The loss of Soviet aid greatly damaged Cuba's economy, but Castro maintained his left-wing policies. In 2000, the United States lifted its food embargo on Cuba, but, in 2004, following a United States crackdown on currency and travel, Cuba declared that US dollars would no longer be accepted as payments for goods and services.

The government runs Cuba's economy and owns 70% of the farmland. Agriculture is important and sugar is the chief export, followed by refined nickel ore. Other exports include cigars, citrus fruits, fish, medical products and rum. Before 1959, US companies owned most businesses. Under Castro, the government took them over. After the collapse of the Soviet Union in 1991, Cuba worked to increase its trade with Latin America and China.

CYPRUS

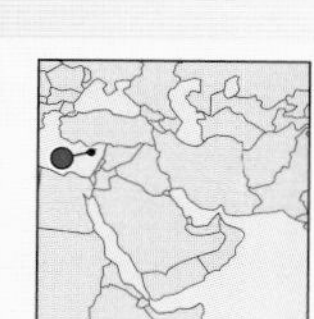

AREA 9,251 sq km [3,572 sq mi]
POPULATION 776,000
CAPITAL (POPULATION) Nicosia (198,000)
GOVERNMENT Multiparty republic
ETHNIC GROUPS Greek Cypriot 77%, Turkish Cypriot 18%, others
LANGUAGES Greek and Turkish (both official), English
RELIGIONS Greek Orthodox 78%, Islam 18%
CURRENCY Cypriot pound = 100 cents

GEOGRAPHY The Republic of Cyprus is an island nation in the north-eastern Mediterranean Sea. Geographers regard it as part of Asia, but it resembles southern Europe in many ways. Its scenic mountain ranges include the southern Troodos Mountains, which reach 1,951 m [6,401 ft] at Mount Olympus, and the Kyrenia range in the north. Between them lies the broad Mesaoria plain.

The climate is Mediterranean, with hot dry summers and mild, moist winters. But the island's proximity to south-western Asia makes it hotter than places in the western Mediterranean.

POLITICS & ECONOMY Greeks settled on Cyprus around 3,200 years ago. From AD 330, the island was part of the Byzantine empire. In the 1570s, Cyprus became part of the Turkish Ottoman empire. Turkish rule continued until 1878 when Cyprus was leased to Britain. Britain annexed the island in 1914 and proclaimed it a colony in 1925.

In the 1950s, Greek Cypriots, who made up four-fifths of the population, began a campaign for *enosis* (union) with Greece. Their leader was the Greek Orthodox Archbishop Makarios. A secret guerrilla force called EOKA attacked the British, who exiled Makarios. Cyprus became an independent country in 1960, although Britain retained two military bases. Independent Cyprus had a constitution which provided for power-sharing between the Greek and Turkish Cypriots. But the constitution proved unworkable and fighting broke out. In 1964, the United Nations sent in a peacekeeping force, but communal clashes recurred in 1967.

In 1974, Cypriot forces led by Greek officers overthrew Makarios. This led Turkey to invade northern Cyprus, a territory occupying about 40% of the island. Many Greek Cypriots fled from the north which, in 1979, was proclaimed an independent state called the Turkish Republic of Northern Cyprus, but the only country to recognize it was Turkey.

In 2002, the European Union invited Cyprus to become a member in 2004. In April 2004, the people voted on a UN plan to reunify the island. The Turkish-Cypriots voted in favour of the plan, but the Greek-Cypriots in the south voted against. Hence, only the south was admitted to membership of the EU on 1 May 2004.

Cyprus got its name from the Greek word *kypros*, meaning copper. But little copper remains and the chief minerals today are asbestos and chromium. However, the most valuable activity in Cyprus is tourism. In the early 1990s, the United Nations reclassified Cyprus as a developed rather than a developing country. But the economy of the Turkish-Cypriot north lags behind that of the more prosperous Greek-Cypriot south.

CZECH REPUBLIC

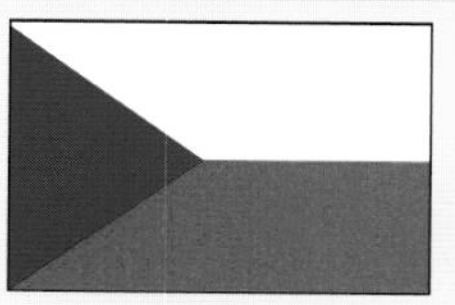

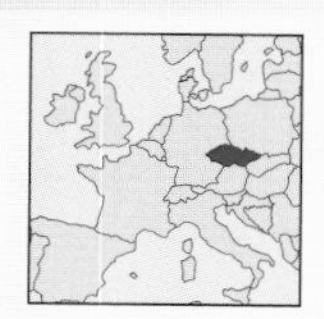

AREA 78,866 sq km [30,450 sq mi]
POPULATION 10,246,000
CAPITAL (POPULATION) Prague (1,193,000)
GOVERNMENT Multiparty republic
ETHNIC GROUPS Czech 81%, Moravian 13%, Slovak 3%, Polish, German, Silesian, Gypsy, Hungarian, Ukrainian
LANGUAGES Czech (official)
RELIGIONS Atheist 40%, Roman Catholic 39%, Protestant 4%, Orthodox 3%, others
CURRENCY Czech koruna = 100 haler

GEOGRAPHY The Czech Republic is the western three-fifths of the former country of Czechoslovakia. It contains two regions: Bohemia in the west and Moravia in the east. Mountains border much of the country in the west. The Bohemian basin in the north-centre is a fertile lowland region, with Prague, the capital city, as its main centre. Highlands cover much of the centre of the country, with lowlands in the south-east.

The climate is influenced by its landlocked position in east-central Europe. Prague has warm, sunny summers and cold winters. The average rainfall is moderate, with 500 mm to 750 mm [20 in to 30 in] every year in lowland areas.

POLITICS & ECONOMY After World War I (1914–18), Czechoslovakia was created. Germany seized the country in World War II (1939–45). In 1948, Communist leaders took power and Czechoslovakia was allied to the Soviet Union. When democratic reforms were introduced in the Soviet Union in the late 1980s, the Czechs also demanded reforms. Free elections were held in 1990, but differences between the Czechs and the Slovaks led to the partitioning of the country on 1 January 1993. The government continued to develop ties with Western Europe when it became a member of NATO in 1992. On 1 May 2004, the Czech Republic became a member of the European Union. This followed a referendum in 2003 in which 77% of Czechs voted in favour of their country joining the EU.

Under Communist rule the Czech Republic became one of the most industrialized parts of Eastern Europe. The country has deposits of coal, uranium, iron ore, magnesite, tin and zinc. Manufacturing employs about 30% of the Czech Republic's entire workforce. Farming is also important. Under Communism, the government owned the land, but private ownership is now being restored. The country was admitted into the OECD in 1995.

DENMARK

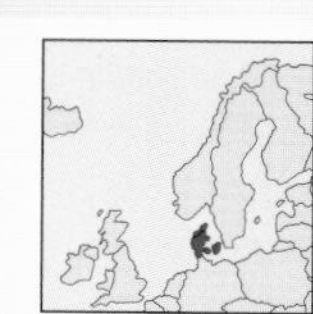

AREA 43,094 sq km [16,639 sq mi]
POPULATION 5,413,000
CAPITAL (POPULATION) Copenhagen (499,000)
GOVERNMENT Parliamentary monarchy
ETHNIC GROUPS Scandinavian, Inuit, Færoese, German
LANGUAGES Danish (official), English, Færoese
RELIGIONS Evangelical Lutheran 95%
CURRENCY Danish krone = 100 øre

GEOGRAPHY The Kingdom of Denmark is the smallest country in Scandinavia. It consists of a peninsula, called Jutland (or Jylland), which is joined to Germany, and more than 400 islands, 89 of which are inhabited.

The land is flat and mostly covered by rocks dropped there by huge ice-sheets during the last Ice Age. The highest point in Denmark is on Jutland. It is only 173 m [568 ft] above sea level.

Denmark has a cool but pleasant climate, except during cold spells in the winter when The Sound between Sjælland and Sweden may freeze over. Summers are warm. Rainfall occurs all through the year.

POLITICS & ECONOMY Danish Vikings terrorized much of Western Europe for about 300 years after AD 800. Danish kings ruled England in the 11th century. In the late 14th century, Denmark formed a union with Norway and Sweden (which included Finland). Sweden broke away in 1523, while Denmark lost Norway to Sweden in 1814.

After 1945, Denmark played an important part in European affairs, becoming a member of the North Atlantic Treaty Organization (NATO). In 1973, Denmark joined the European Union, although it rejected the adoption of the euro in 2000. The Danes now enjoy some of the world's highest living standards, although the cost of welfare provisions was high. The election of a Liberal-Conservative coalition in 2001 led to cutbacks. Under Prime Minister Anders Fogh Rasmussen, who won a second term in 2005, the government also tightened immigration controls, causing criticism by the UN High Commissioner for Refugees.

Denmark has few natural resources apart from some oil and gas from wells deep under the North Sea. But the economy is highly developed. Manufacturing industries, which employ about 16% of all workers, produce a wide variety of products, including furniture, processed food, machinery, television sets and textiles. Farms cover about three-quarters of the land. Farming employs only 4% of the workers, but it is highly scientific and productive. Meat and dairy farming are the chief activities.

DJIBOUTI

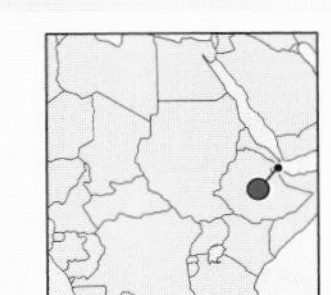

AREA 23,200 sq km [8,958 sq mi]
POPULATION 467,000
CAPITAL (POPULATION) Djibouti (317,000)
GOVERNMENT Multiparty republic
ETHNIC GROUPS Somali 60%, Afar 35%
LANGUAGES Arabic and French (both official)
RELIGIONS Islam 94%, Christianity 6%
CURRENCY Djiboutian franc = 100 centimes

GEOGRAPHY The Republic of Djibouti in eastern Africa occupies a strategic position where the Red Sea meets the Gulf of Aden. Djibouti has one of the world's hottest and driest climates.

POLITICS & ECONOMY France set up a territory called French Somaliland in 1888. Its capital, Djibouti, became important when a railway was built to Addis Ababa and Djibouti became the main outlet for Ethiopian trade. In 1967, France renamed the dependency the French Territory of the Afars and Issas, but it became Djibouti on independence in 1977.

Djibouti became a one-party state in 1981, but a new constitution (1992) permitted four parties which had to maintain a balance between the country's ethnic groups. Conflict flared up between the Afars and the Issas in 1992, but a peace agreement was signed in 1994. The economy is based largely on the revenue it gets from its port and railway.

DOMINICA

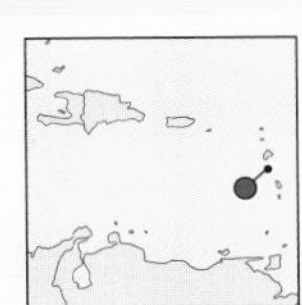

AREA 751 sq km [290 sq mi]
POPULATION 69,000
CAPITAL (POPULATION) Roseau (16,000)

The Commonwealth of Dominica, a former British colony, became independent in 1978. The island has a mountainous spine and less than 10% of the land is cultivated. Yet agriculture employs a substantial proportion of the people. Manufacturing, mining and tourism are other minor activities.

DOMINICAN REPUBLIC

AREA 48,511 sq km [18,730 sq mi]
POPULATION 8,834,000
CAPITAL (POPULATION) Santo Domingo (2,061,000)
GOVERNMENT Multiparty republic
ETHNIC GROUPS Mulatto 73%, White 16%, Black 11%
LANGUAGES Spanish (official)
RELIGIONS Roman Catholic 95%
CURRENCY Dominican peso = 100 centavos

GEOGRAPHY Second largest of the Caribbean nations in both area and population, the Dominican Republic shares the island of Hispaniola with Haiti. The country is mountainous, and the generally hot and humid climate eases with altitude.

POLITICS & ECONOMY The Dominican Republic has chaotic origins, having been held by Spain, France, Haiti and the United States at various times. Civil war broke out in 1966 but the conflict soon ended after US intervention. Since 1966, a young democracy has survived violent elections under the watchful eye of the USA.

EAST TIMOR

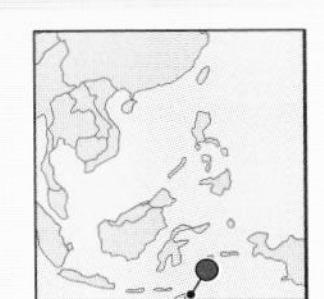

AREA 14,874 sq km [5,743 sq mi]
POPULATION 1,019,000
CAPITAL (POPULATION) Dili (52,000)

The Republic of East Timor became fully independent and the world's newest country on 20 May 2002. The land is mainly rugged. Temperatures are generally high and the rainfall is moderate. Portugal ruled the area from the late 19th century, when it was called Portuguese Timor. Portugal withdrew in 1975 and Indonesia seized the area. Guerrilla activity mounted under Indonesian rule and, in 1999, the people voted for independence. Agriculture is the main activity. East Timor is dependent on foreign aid. Offshore oil and natural gas deposits hold out hope for the future, though some oilfields are disputed with Australia.

ECUADOR

AREA 283,561 sq km [109,483 sq mi]
POPULATION 13,213,000
CAPITAL (POPULATION) Quito (1,616,000)
GOVERNMENT Multiparty republic
ETHNIC GROUPS Mestizo (mixed White/Amerindian) 65%, Amerindian 25%, White 7%, Black 3%
LANGUAGES Spanish (official), Quechua
RELIGIONS Roman Catholic 95%
CURRENCY US dollar = 100 cents

GEOGRAPHY The Republic of Ecuador straddles the Equator on the west coast of South America. Three ranges of the high Andes Mountains form the backbone of the country. Between the towering, snow-capped peaks of the mountains, some of which are volcanoes, lie a series of high plateaux, or basins. Nearly half of Ecuador's population lives on these plateaux.

The climate in Ecuador depends on the height above sea level. Though the coastline is cooled by the cold Peruvian Current, temperatures are between 23°C and 25°C [73°F to 77°F] all through the year. In Quito, at 2,500 m [8,200 ft] above sea level, temperatures are 14°C to 15°C [57°F to 59°F], though the city is just south of the Equator.

POLITICS & ECONOMY The Inca people of Peru conquered much of what is now Ecuador in the late 15th century. They introduced their language, Quechua, which is widely spoken today. Spanish forces defeated the Incas in 1533 and took control of Ecuador. The country became independent in 1822, following the defeat of a Spanish force in a battle near Quito. In the 19th and 20th centuries, Ecuador suffered from political instability, while successive governments failed to tackle the country's social and economic problems. A war with Peru in 1941 led to a loss of territory. Disputes continued until 1995, but a border agreement was signed in January 1998. Economic crises in the early 21st century led the government to abolish the sucre, its official currency, and replace it with the US dollar.

The World Bank classifies Ecuador as a 'lower-middle-income' developing country. Agriculture employs 10% of the people and bananas, cocoa and coffee are all important crops. Fishing, forestry, mining and manufacturing are other activities.

EGYPT

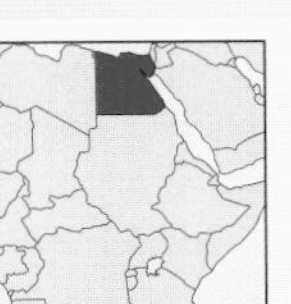

AREA 1,001,449 sq km [386,659 sq mi]
POPULATION 76,117,000
CAPITAL (POPULATION) Cairo (6,801,000)
GOVERNMENT Republic
ETHNIC GROUPS Egyptians/Bedouins/Berbers 99%
LANGUAGES Arabic (official), French, English
RELIGIONS Islam (mainly Sunni Muslim) 94%, Christianity (mainly Coptic Christian) and others 6%
CURRENCY Egyptian pound = 100 piastres

GEOGRAPHY The Arab Republic of Egypt is Africa's second largest country by population after Nigeria, though it ranks 13th in area. Most of Egypt is desert. Almost all the people live either in the Nile Valley and its fertile delta or along the Suez Canal, the artificial waterway between the Mediterranean and Red seas. This canal shortens the sea journey between the United Kingdom and India by 9,700 km [6,027 mi]. Recent attempts have been made to irrigate parts of the western desert.

Apart from the Nile Valley, Egypt has three other main regions. The Western and Eastern deserts are parts of the Sahara. The Sinai peninsula (Es Sina), to the east of the Suez Canal, is a mountainous desert region, geographically within Asia. It contains Egypt's highest peak, Gebel Katherina (2,637 m [8,650 ft]); few people live in this area.

Egypt is a dry country. The low rainfall occurs, if at all, in winter and the country is one of the sunniest places on Earth.

POLITICS & ECONOMY Ancient Egypt, which was founded about 5,000 years ago, was one of the great early civilizations. Throughout the country, pyramids, temples and richly decorated tombs are memorials to its great achievements. After Ancient Egypt declined, the country came under successive foreign rulers. Arabs occupied Egypt in AD 639–42. They introduced the Arabic language and Islam. Their influence was so great that most Egyptians now regard themselves as Arabs.

Egypt came under British rule in 1882, but it gained partial independence in 1922, becoming a monarchy. The monarchy was abolished in 1952, when Egypt became a republic. The creation of Israel in 1948 led Egypt into a series of wars in 1948–9, 1956, 1967 and 1973. Since the late 1970s, Egypt has sought for peace. In 1979, Egypt signed a peace treaty with Israel and regained the Sinai region which it had lost in a war in 1967. Extremists opposed contacts with Israel and, in 1981, President Sadat, who had signed the treaty, was assassinated.

While Egypt plays a major part in Arab affairs, most of its people are poor. Some Islamic fundamentalists, who dislike Western influences on their way of life, have resorted to violence. In the 1990s, attacks on foreign visitors caused a decline in the valuable tourist industry. In 1999, Hosni Mubarak, president since 1981, was himself attacked by extremists, but he was re-elected to a fourth term in office. But, in 2005, he announced that a vote on democratic reform would be held.

Most people are poor, although Egypt is Africa's second most industrialized country. Oil and textiles are exported.

EL SALVADOR

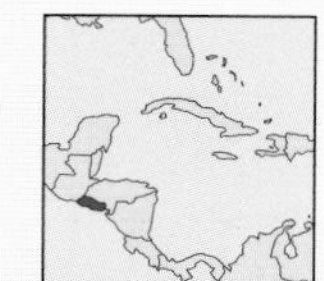

AREA 21,041 sq km [8,124 sq mi]
POPULATION 6,588,000
CAPITAL (POPULATION) San Salvador (473,000)
GOVERNMENT Republic
ETHNIC GROUPS Mestizo (mixed White and Amerindian) 90%, White 9%, Amerindian 1%
LANGUAGES Spanish (official)
RELIGIONS Roman Catholic 83%
CURRENCY US dollar = 100 cents

GEOGRAPHY The Republic of El Salvador is the only country in Central America which does not have a coast on the Caribbean Sea. El Salvador has a narrow coastal plain along the Pacific Ocean. Behind the coastal plain, the coastal range is a zone of rugged mountains, including volcanoes, which overlooks a densely populated inland plateau. Beyond the plateau, the land rises to the sparsely populated interior highlands.

The coast has a hot, tropical climate. Inland, the climate is moderated by the altitude. Rain falls on practically every afternoon between May and October.

POLITICS & ECONOMY Amerindians have lived in El Salvador for thousands of years. The ruins of Mayan pyramids built between AD 100 and 1000 are found in the west. Spanish soldiers conquered the area in 1524–5 and Spain ruled until 1821.

In 1823, all the Central American countries, apart from Panama, set up a Central American Federation. El Salvador withdrew in 1840 and declared its independence in 1841. Instability plagued El Salvador in the 19th century. The 20th century saw some improvements, but, from 1931, military dictatorships alternated with elected governments.

In the 1970s, El Salvador was plagued by conflict as protesters demanded that the government introduce reforms to help the poor. Kidnappings and murders committed by left- and right-wing groups caused instability. A civil war broke out in 1979 between the US-backed, right-wing government forces and left-wing guerrillas. In 12 years, 750,000 people died. A cease-fire was agreed in 1992 and, by 2003, the economy had shown signs of recovery.

The World Bank classifies El Salvador as a 'lower-middle-income' economy. About 70% of the land is farmed. Coffee is the main export, followed by sugar and cotton. Fishing for lobsters and shrimps is important, but manufacturing is on a small scale.

EQUATORIAL GUINEA

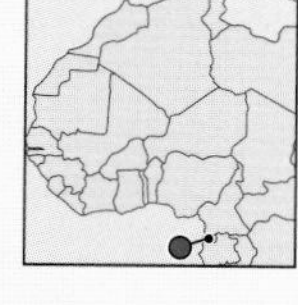

AREA 28,051 sq km [10,830 sq mi]
POPULATION 523,000
CAPITAL (POPULATION) Malabo (30,000)
GOVERNMENT Multiparty republic (transitional)
ETHNIC GROUPS Bubi (on Bioko), Fang (in Rio Muni)
LANGUAGES Spanish and French (both official)
RELIGIONS Christianity
CURRENCY CFA franc = 100 centimes

GEOGRAPHY The Republic of Equatorial Guinea is a small republic in west-central Africa. It consists of a mainland territory which makes up 90% of the land area, called Rio Muni, between Cameroon and Gabon, and five offshore islands in the Bight of Bonny, the largest of which is Bioko. The island of Annobon lies 560 km [350 mi] south-west of Rio Muni. Rio Muni consists mainly of hills and plateaux behind the coastal plains.

The climate is hot and humid. Bioko is mountainous, with the land rising to 3,008 m [9,869 ft], and hence it is particularly rainy. However, there is a marked dry season between the months of December and February. Mainland Rio Muni has a similar climate, though the rainfall diminishes inland.

POLITICS & ECONOMY Portuguese navigators reached the area in 1471. In 1778, Portugal granted Bioko, together with rights over Rio Muni, to Spain.

In 1959, Spain made Bioko and Rio Muni provinces of overseas Spain and, in 1963, it gave the provinces a degree of self-government. Equatorial Guinea became independent in 1968.

The first president of Equatorial Guinea, Francisco Macias Nguema, proved to be a tyrant. He was overthrown in 1979 and a group of officers, led by Lt.-Col. Teodoro Obiang Nguema Mbasogo, set up a Supreme Military Council to rule the country. In 1991, the people voted to set up a multiparty democracy. Elections were held in the 1990s, but accusations of human rights abuses continued. In 2004, a coup attempt by mercenaries was foiled and its leaders were arrested.

Agriculture employs over half of the people and the most valuable crop is coffee. However, oil has been produced since 1966 and, by 2002, it accounted for more than 80% of the country's exports. Yet despite the rapid expansion of the economy, a UN human rights report stated that 65% of the people were still living in 'extreme poverty'.

ERITREA

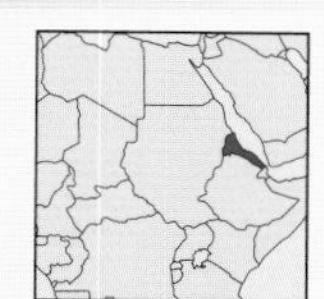

AREA 117,600 sq km [45,405 sq mi]
POPULATION 4,447,000
CAPITAL (POPULATION) Asmara (358,000)
GOVERNMENT Transitional government
ETHNIC GROUPS Tigrinya 50%, Tigre and Kunama 40%, Afar 4%, Saho 3%, others
LANGUAGES Afar, Arabic, Tigre and Kunama, Tigrinya
RELIGIONS Islam, Coptic Christian, Roman Catholic
CURRENCY Nakfa = 100 cents

GEOGRAPHY The State of Eritrea consists of a hot, dry coastal plain facing the Red Sea, with a fairly mountainous area in the centre. Most people live in the cooler highland area.

POLITICS & ECONOMY From the 1st century AD, Eritrea formed part of the ancient Kingdom of Axum, which adopted Christianity in the 4th century. Axum reached its greatest period of prosperity in the 4th century, but it began to decline in the 7th century. The Ottoman Turks took over the area in the 16th century and, in the 1880s, it became an Italian colony. The Italians were driven out in 1941 and, in 1952, it became part of Ethiopia.

A guerrilla struggle launched in 1961 ended in 1993, when Eritrea became independent. But economic recovery was hampered by conflict with Yemen over three islands in the Red Sea. Then, in 1998–9, clashes with Ethiopia flared up along the frontier. A peace agreement was signed in 2000, but arguments again broke out in 2003 over the proposed redrawing of the boundaries proposed by the Boundary Commission in The Hague. Farming and livestock rearing are the main activities in Eritrea. The country has a few manufacturing industries, based mainly in Asmara.

ESTONIA

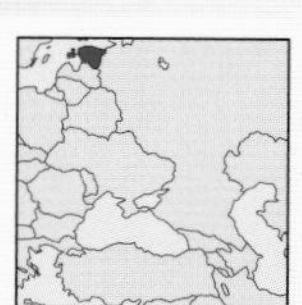

AREA 45,100 sq km [17,413 sq mi]
POPULATION 1,342,000
CAPITAL (POPULATION) Tallinn (418,000)
GOVERNMENT Multiparty republic
ETHNIC GROUPS Estonian 65%, Russian 28%, Ukrainian 3%, Belarusian 2%, Finnish 1%
LANGUAGES Estonian (official), Russian
RELIGIONS Lutheran, Russian and Estonian Orthodox, Methodist, Baptist, Roman Catholic
CURRENCY Estonian kroon = 100 senti

GEOGRAPHY The Republic of Estonia is the smallest of the three states on the Baltic Sea, which were formerly part of the Soviet Union, but which became independent in the early 1990s. Estonia consists of a generally flat plain which was covered by ice-sheets during the Ice Age. The land is strewn with moraine (rocks deposited by the ice).

The country is dotted with more than 1,500 small lakes, and water, including the large Lake Peipus (Chudskoye Ozero) and the River Narva makes up much of Estonia's eastern border with Russia. Estonia has more than 800 islands, which together make up about a tenth of the country. The largest island is Saaremaa (Sarema).

Despite its northerly position, Estonia has a fairly mild climate because of its nearness to the sea. This is because sea winds tend to warm the land in winter and cool it in summer.

POLITICS & ECONOMY The ancestors of the Estonians, who are related to the Finns, settled in the area several thousand years ago. German crusaders, known as the Teutonic Knights, introduced Christianity in the early 13th century. By the 16th century, German noblemen owned much of the land in Estonia. In 1561, Sweden took the northern part of the country and Poland the south. From 1625, Sweden controlled the entire country until Sweden handed it over to Russia in 1721.

Estonian nationalists campaigned for their independence from around the mid-19th century. Finally, Estonia was proclaimed independent in 1918. In 1919, the government began to break up the large estates and distribute land among the peasants.

In 1939, Germany and the Soviet Union agreed to take over parts of Eastern Europe. In 1940, Soviet forces occupied Estonia, but they were driven out by the Germans in 1941. Soviet troops returned in 1944 and Estonia became one of the 15 Soviet Socialist Republics of the Soviet Union. The Estonians strongly opposed Soviet rule. Many of them were deported to Siberia.

Political changes in the Soviet Union in the late 1980s led to renewed demands for freedom. In 1990, the Estonian government declared the country independent and, finally, the Soviet Union recognized this act in September 1991, shortly before the Soviet Union was dissolved. Estonia adopted a new constitution in 1992, when multiparty elections were held for a new national assembly. In 1993, Estonia negotiated an agreement with Russia to withdraw its troops.

Under Soviet rule, Estonia was the most prosperous of the three Baltic states. Since 1988, Estonia has restructured its economy. Turning increasingly to the West, it became a member of NATO and the European Union in 2004. Its industries produce fertilizers, processed food, machinery, petrochemical products, wood products and textiles. Agriculture and fishing are also important.

ETHIOPIA

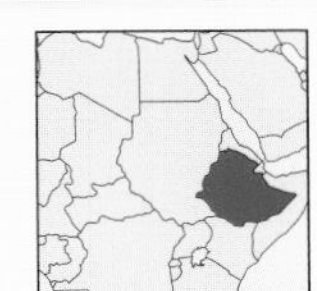

AREA 1,104,300 sq km [426,370 sq mi]
POPULATION 67,851,000
CAPITAL (POPULATION) Addis Ababa (2,424,000)
GOVERNMENT Federation of nine provinces
ETHNIC GROUPS Oromo 40%, Amhara and Tigre 32%, Sidamo 9%, Shankella 6%, Somali 6%, others
LANGUAGES Amharic (official), many others
RELIGIONS Islam 47%, Ethiopian Orthodox 40%, traditional beliefs 12%
CURRENCY Birr = 100 cents

GEOGRAPHY Ethiopia is a landlocked country in north-eastern Africa. The land is mainly mountainous, though there are extensive plains in the east, bordering southern Eritrea, and in the south, bordering Somalia. The highlands are divided into two blocks by the Great Rift Valley. To the north, the land is rugged, rising to 4,620 m [15,157 ft] at Ras Dashen. South-east of Ras Dashen is Lake Tana, source of the River Abay (Blue Nile).

The climate in Ethiopia is greatly affected by the altitude. Addis Ababa, at 2,450 m [8,000 ft], has an average yearly temperature of 20°C [68°F]. The rainfall is generally more than 1,000 mm [39 in]. But the lowlands are hot and arid.

POLITICS & ECONOMY Ethiopia was the home of an ancient monarchy, which became Christian in the 4th century. In the 7th century, Muslims gained control of the lowlands, but Christianity survived in the highlands. Ethiopia resisted attempts to colonize it, but Italy invaded the country in 1935. The Italians were driven out in 1941 during World War II.

In 1952, Eritrea, on the Red Sea coast, was federated with Ethiopia. But in 1961, Eritrean nationalists demanded their freedom and began a struggle that ended in their independence in 1993. Clashes along the border with Eritrea occurred in 1998 and 1999, but a peace agreement was signed in 2000, though a disagreement arose in 2003 about the status of Badme, the village where the conflict began. In 1995, to appease minorities, the country was divided into nine provinces, each with its own assembly.

Ethiopia is one of the world's poorest countries, particularly in the 1970s and 1980s when it was plagued by civil war and famine caused partly by droughts. Agriculture remains the main activity. In 2004, a UN report stated that Ethiopia remained on the brink of disaster, with spiralling population growth, slow economic growth and environmental degradation.

FALKLAND ISLANDS

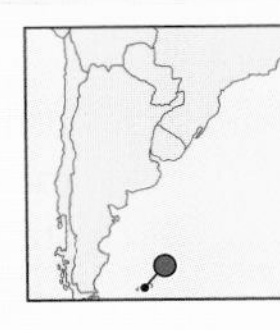

AREA 12,173 sq km [4,700 sq mi]
POPULATION 3,000
CAPITAL (POPULATION) Stanley (1,600)

Comprising two main islands and over 200 small islands, the Falkland Islands lie 480 km [300 mi] from South America. Sheep farming is the main activity, though the search for oil and diamonds holds out hope for the future of this treeless environment. Argentina claims the islands, which it calls Las Malvinas, and occupied them briefly in 1982.

FÆROE ISLANDS

AREA 1,399 sq km [540 sq mi]
POPULATION 47,000
CAPITAL (POPULATION) Tórshavn (15,000)

The Færoe Islands are a group of 18 volcanic islands and some reefs in the North Atlantic Ocean. The islands have been Danish since 1380 when they, and Norway, passed to Danish control. They were administratively separated from Norway in 1709. Since 1948, the Færoe Islands have been largely self-governing and, in 1998, the government of the Faeroes announced its intention of becoming independent.

FIJI ISLANDS

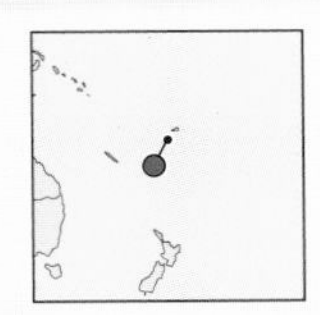

AREA 18,274 sq km [7,056 sq mi]
POPULATION 881,000
CAPITAL (POPULATION) Suva (70,000)

The Fiji Islands is a republic, comprising more than 800 Melanesian islands. The two largest islands are Viti Levu and Vanua Levu. Together they make up 87% of the land area. The climate is tropical, with south-east trade winds blowing throughout the year.

A former British colony, Fiji became independent in 1970 and a republic in 1987. Its recent history has been marred by violent coups as the ethnic Fijians have sought to impose their rule, stopping members of the ethnic Indian community from holding senior cabinet posts. Their actions have provoked international criticism. The country's name was changed from Fiji to Fiji Islands in 1998.

FINLAND

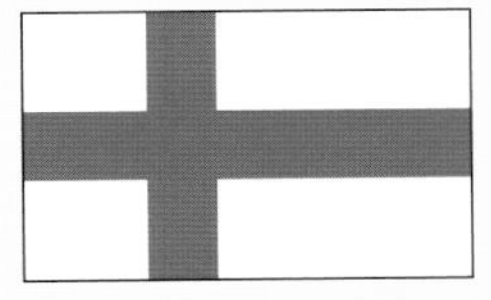
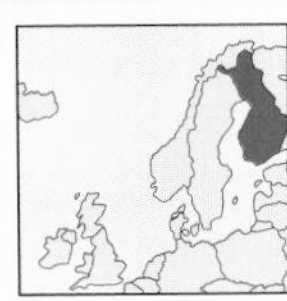

AREA 338,145 sq km [130,558 sq mi]
POPULATION 5,215,000
CAPITAL (POPULATION) Helsinki (549,000)
GOVERNMENT Multiparty republic
ETHNIC GROUPS Finnish 93%, Swedish 6%
LANGUAGES Finnish and Swedish (both official)
RELIGIONS Evangelical Lutheran 89%
CURRENCY Euro = 100 cents

GEOGRAPHY The Republic of Finland is a beautiful country in northern Europe. In the south, behind the coastal lowlands where most Finns live, lies a region of sparkling lakes worn out by ice-sheets in the Ice Age. The thinly populated northern uplands cover about two-fifths of the country.

Helsinki, the capital city, has warm summers, but the average temperatures between the months of December and March are below freezing point. Snow covers the land in winter. The north has less precipitation than the south, but it is much colder.

POLITICS & ECONOMY Between 1150 and 1809, Finland was under Swedish rule. The close links between the countries continue today. Swedish remains an official language in Finland and many towns have Swedish as well as Finnish names.

In 1809, Finland became a grand duchy of the Russian empire. It finally declared itself independent in 1917, after the Russian Revolution and the collapse of the Russian empire. But during World War II (1939–45), the Soviet Union declared war on Finland and took part of Finland's territory. Finland allied itself with Germany, but it lost more land to the Soviet Union at the end of the war.

After World War II, Finland became a neutral country and negotiated peace treaties with the Soviet Union. Finland also strengthened its relations with other northern European countries and became an associate member of the European Free Trade Association (EFTA) in 1961. Finland became a full member of EFTA in 1986, but in 1992, along with most of its fellow EFTA members, it applied for membership of the European Union, which it finally achieved on 1 January 1995. On 1 January 2002, the euro became Finland's sole official unit of currency. Finland has also discussed the possibility of joining NATO. However, polls since the events of 11 September 2001 in the United States suggest that a majority of Finns favour non-alliance.

Forests are Finland's most valuable resource, and forestry accounts for about 35% of the country's exports. The chief manufactures are wood products, pulp and paper. Since World War II, Finland has set up many other industries, producing such things as machinery and transport equipment. Its economy has expanded rapidly, but there has been a large increase in the number of unemployed people.

FRANCE

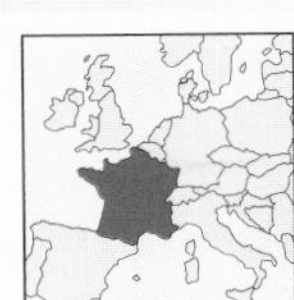

AREA 551,500 sq km [212,934 sq mi]
POPULATION 60,424,000
CAPITAL (POPULATION) Paris (2,152,000)
GOVERNMENT Multiparty republic
ETHNIC GROUPS Celtic, Latin, Arab, Teutonic, Slavic
LANGUAGES French (official)
RELIGIONS Roman Catholic 85%, Islam 8%, others
CURRENCY Euro = 100 cents

GEOGRAPHY The Republic of France is the largest country in Western Europe. The scenery is extremely varied. The Vosges Mountains overlook the Rhine valley in the north-east, the Jura Mountains and the Alps form the borders with Switzerland and Italy in the south-east, while the Pyrenees straddle France's border with Spain. The only large highland area entirely within France is the Massif Central in southern France.

Brittany (Bretagne) and Normandy (Normande) form a scenic hill region. Fertile lowlands cover most of northern France, including the densely populated Paris basin. Another major lowland area, the Aquitanian basin, is in the south-west, while the Rhône-Saône valley and the Mediterranean lowlands are in the south-east.

The climate of France varies from west to east and from north to south. The west comes under the moderating influence of the Atlantic Ocean, giving generally mild weather. To the east, summers are warmer and winters colder. The climate also becomes warmer as one travels from north to south. The Mediterranean Sea coast has hot, dry summers and mild, moist winters. The Alps, Jura and Pyrenees mountains have snowy winters. Winter sports centres are found in all three areas. Large glaciers occupy high valleys in the Alps.

POLITICS & ECONOMY The Romans conquered France (then called Gaul) in the 50s BC. Roman rule began to decline in the 5th century AD and, in 486, the Frankish realm (as France was called) became independent under a Christian king, Clovis. In 800, Charlemagne, who had been king since 768, became emperor of the Romans. He extended France's boundaries, but, in 843, his empire was divided into three parts and the area of France contracted. After the Norman invasion of England in 1066, large areas of France came under English rule, but this was finally ended in 1453.

France later became a powerful monarchy. But the French Revolution (1789–99) ended absolute rule by French kings. In 1799, Napoleon Bonaparte took power and fought a series of brilliant military campaigns before his final defeat in 1815. The monarchy was restored until 1848, when the Second Republic was founded. In 1852, Napoleon's nephew became Napoleon III, but the Third Republic was established in 1875. France was the scene of much fighting during World War I (1914–18) and World War II (1939–45), causing great loss of life and much damage to the economy.

In 1946, France adopted a new constitution, establishing the Fourth Republic. But political instability and costly colonial wars slowed France's post-war recovery. In 1958, Charles de Gaulle was elected president and he introduced a new constitution, giving the president extra powers and inaugurating the Fifth Republic.

Since the 1960s, France has made rapid economic progress, becoming one of the most prosperous nations in the European Union. But France's government faced a number of problems, including unemployment, pollution and the growing number of elderly people, who find it difficult to live when inflation rates are high. One social problem concerns the presence in France of large numbers of immigrants from Africa and southern Europe, many of whom live in poor areas.

A socialist government under Lionel Jospin was elected in June 1997. Under Jospin, France adopted the euro, the single European currency, and shortened the working week. The French system of high social security seemed likely to continue. However, in 2002, centre-right parties won a resounding victory and Jean-Pierre Raffarin replaced Jospin as prime minister. France has a long record of independence in foreign affairs and, in 2003, it angered the US and some of its allies in the European Union by opposing the invasion of Iraq, arguing that the UN inspectors should be given more time to search for weapons of mass destruction or nuclear weapons in Iraq. France's stance angered some US congressmen who called for a boycott of French goods. The number of US tourists to France also fell.

France is one of the world's most developed countries. Its natural resources include its fertile soil, together with deposits of bauxite, coal, iron ore, oil and natural gas, and potash. France is also one of the world's top manufacturing nations, and it has often innovated in bold and imaginative ways. The TGV, Concorde and hypermarkets are all typical examples. Paris is a world centre of fashion industries, but France has many other industrial towns and cities. Major manufactures include aircraft, cars, chemicals, electronic products, machinery, metal products, processed food, steel and textiles.

Agriculture employs about 2% of the people, but France is the largest producer of farm products in Western Europe, producing most of the food it needs. Wheat is the leading crop and livestock farming is of major importance. Fishing and forestry are leading industries. Tourism is also important. Paris is one of the world's great cities and major cultural centres, with many magnificent public buildings.

FRENCH GUIANA

AREA 90,000 sq km [34,749 sq mi]
POPULATION 191,000
CAPITAL (POPULATION) Cayenne (51,000)
GOVERNMENT Overseas department of France
ETHNIC GROUPS Black or Mulatto 66%, East Indian/Chinese and Amerindian 12%, White 12%, others 10%
LANGUAGES French (official)
RELIGIONS Roman Catholic
CURRENCY Euro = 100 cents

GEOGRAPHY French Guiana is the smallest country in mainland South America. The coastal plain is swampy in places, but some dry areas are cultivated. Inland lies a plateau, with the low Tumachumac Mountains in the south. Most of the rivers run north towards the Atlantic Ocean.

French Guiana has a hot, equatorial climate, with high temperatures throughout the year. The rainfall is heavy, especially between December and June, but it is dry between August and October. The north-east trade winds blow constantly across the country.

POLITICS & ECONOMY The first people to live in what is now French Guiana were Amerindians. Today, only a few of them survive in the interior. The first Europeans to explore the coast arrived in 1500 and French merchants founded Cayenne in 1637. The area became a French colony in the late 17th century. France used the colony as a penal settlement for political prisoners from the times of the French Revolution in the 1790s. From the 1850s to 1945, the country became notorious for the harsh treatment of prisoners.

In 1946, French Guiana became an overseas department of France, and in 1974 it also became an administrative region. An independence movement developed in the 1980s, but most people want to retain their links with France and continue to obtain financial aid to develop their territory.

Although it has rich forest and mineral resources, such as bauxite (aluminium ore), French Guiana is a developing country. It depends greatly on France for money to run its services and the government is the country's biggest employer. Since 1968, Kourou in French Guiana, the European Space Agency's rocket-launching site, has earned money for France by sending communications satellites into space.

FRENCH POLYNESIA

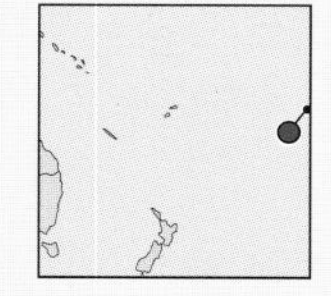

AREA 4,000 sq km [1,544 sq mi]
POPULATION 266,000
CAPITAL (POPULATION) Papeete (24,000)

French Polynesia consists of 130 islands, scattered over 4 million sq km [1.5 million sq mi] of the Pacific Ocean. Tribal chiefs in the area agreed to a French protectorate in 1843. They gained increased autonomy in 1984, but the links with France ensure a high standard of living. However, some people favour independence. Following a struggle for power in 2004, the pro-independence Union for Democracy party, led by Oscar Timaru, ousted the pro-French ruling party led by Gaston Flosse.

GABON

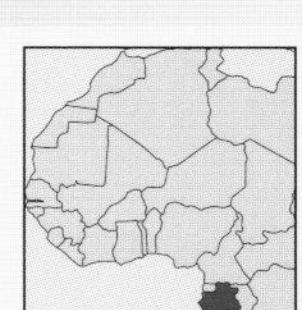

AREA 267,668 sq km [103,347 sq mi]
POPULATION 1,355,000
CAPITAL (POPULATION) Libreville (362,000)
GOVERNMENT Multiparty republic
ETHNIC GROUPS Four major Bantu tribes: Fang, Bapounou, Nzebi and Obamba
LANGUAGES French (official), Fang, Myene, Nzebi, Bapounou/Eschira, Bandjabi
RELIGIONS Christianity 75%, animist, Islam
CURRENCY CFA franc = 100 centimes

GEOGRAPHY The Gabonese Republic lies on the Equator in west-central Africa. Behind the narrow, partly lagooned 800 km [500 mi] long coastline, the land rises to hills, plateaux and mountains divided by deep valleys carved by the River Ogooué.

Most of Gabon has an equatorial climate, with high temperatures and humidity throughout the year. The rainfall is heavy and the skies are often cloudy.

POLITICS & ECONOMY Gabon became a French colony in the 1880s, but it achieved full independence in 1960. In 1964, an attempted coup was put down when French troops intervened and crushed the revolt. In 1967, Bernard-Albert Bongo, who later renamed himself El Hadj Omar Bongo, became president. He declared Gabon a one-party state in 1968. Opposition parties were legalized in 1991 and Bongo won successive victories in presidential elections. In 2003, constitutional changes enabled Bongo to stand as president as many times as he wished.

Gabon's abundant natural resources include its forests, oil and gas deposits near Port Gentil, together with manganese and uranium. These mineral deposits make Gabon one of Africa's better-off countries. But agriculture still employs about 41% of the population and many farmers produce little more than they need to support their families.

GAMBIA, THE

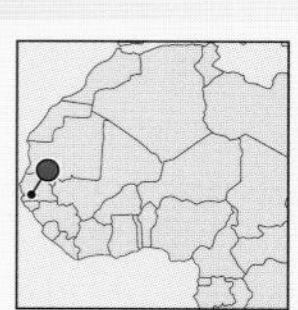

AREA 11,295 sq km [4,361 sq mi]
POPULATION 1,547,000
CAPITAL (POPULATION) Banjul (42,000)
GOVERNMENT Military regime
ETHNIC GROUPS Mandinka 42%, Fula 18%, Wolof 16%, Jola 10%, Serahuli 9%, others
LANGUAGES English (official), Mandinka, Wolof, Fula
RELIGIONS Islam 90%, Christianity 9%, traditional beliefs 1%
CURRENCY Dalasi = 100 butut

GEOGRAPHY The Republic of The Gambia is the smallest country in mainland Africa. It consists of a narrow strip of land bordering the River Gambia. The Gambia is almost entirely enclosed by Senegal, except along the short Atlantic coastline.

The Gambia has hot and humid summers, but the winter temperatures (November to May) drop to around 16°C [61°F]. In the summer, moist south-westerlies bring rain, which is heaviest on the coast.

POLITICS & ECONOMY English traders bought rights to trade on the River Gambia in 1588, and in 1664 the English established a settlement on an island in the river estuary. In 1765, the British founded a colony called Senegambia, which included parts of The Gambia and Senegal. In 1783, Britain handed this colony over to France.

In the 1860s and 1870s, Britain and France discussed the exchange of The Gambia for some other French territory. But no agreement was reached and Britain made The Gambia a British colony in 1888. It remained under British rule until it achieved full independence in 1965. In 1970, The Gambia became a republic. In 1981, a coup in The Gambia was put down with the help of Senegalese troops. In 1982, The Gambia and Senegal set up a defence alliance, called the Confederation of Senegambia. But this alliance was dissolved in 1989. In July 1994, a military group overthrew the president, Sir Dawda Jawara, who fled into exile. Captain Yahya Jammeh, who took power, was elected president in 1996 and re-elected in 2001.

Agriculture is the main activity, though the government announced in 2004 that large oil reserves had been discovered. Food crops include cassava, millet and sorghum. Groundnuts and groundnut products are the chief exports. Tourism is a growing industry.

GEORGIA

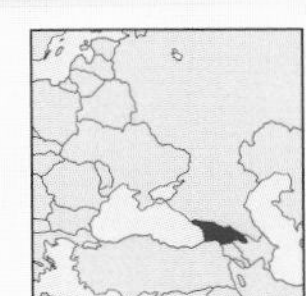

AREA 69,700 sq km [26,911 sq mi]
POPULATION 4,694,000
CAPITAL (POPULATION) Tbilisi (1,268,000)
GOVERNMENT Multiparty republic
ETHNIC GROUPS Georgian 70%, Armenian 8%, Russian 6%, Azeri 6%, Ossetian 3%, Greek 2%, Abkhaz 2%, others 3%
LANGUAGES Georgian (official), Russian
RELIGIONS Georgian Orthodox 65%, Islam 11%, Russian Orthodox 10%, Armenian Apostolic 8%
CURRENCY Lari = 100 tetri

GEOGRAPHY Georgia is a country on the borders of Europe and Asia, facing the Black Sea. The land is rugged with the Caucasus Mountains forming its northern border. The highest mountain in this range, Mount Elbrus (5,642 m [18,510 ft]), lies over the border in Russia. The Black Sea plains have hot summers and mild winters. The rainfall is heavy, though inland areas are drier.

POLITICS & ECONOMY The first Georgian state was set up nearly 2,500 years ago. But for much of its history, the area was ruled by various conquerors. Christianity was introduced in AD 330. Georgia freed itself of foreign rule in the 11th and 12th centuries, but Mongol armies attacked in the 13th century. From the 16th to the 18th centuries, Iran and the Turkish Ottoman empire struggled for control of the area, and in the late 18th century Georgia sought the protection of Russia and, by the early 19th century, Georgia was part of the Russian empire. After the Russian Revolution of 1917, Georgia declared its independence, but Russia invaded, making the country part of the Soviet regime. Georgia declared itself independent in 1991. It became a separate country when the Soviet Union was dissolved in December 1991.

Georgia contains three regions containing minority peoples: Abkhazia in the north-west, South Ossetia in north-central Georgia, and Adjaria (also spelled Adzharia) in the south-west. Civil war broke out in South Ossetia in the early 1990s, while fierce fighting continued in Abkhazia until the late 1990s. In 2000, Georgia agreed to recognize Adjaria's autonomy in the country's constitution. In 2002, Russian and Georgian troops attacked Chechen rebels in Pankisi Gorge in north-eastern Georgia. The USA also alleged that other Islamic terrorists were hiding in the area. In 2004, Mikhail Saakashvili was elected president, but his authority was challenged by separatists in the three minority regions.

Georgia is a developing country. Agriculture is important. Major products include barley, citrus fruits, grapes for wine-making, vegetables, maize, tobacco and tea. Food processing and silk and perfume-making are other important activities. Sheep and cattle are reared.

GERMANY

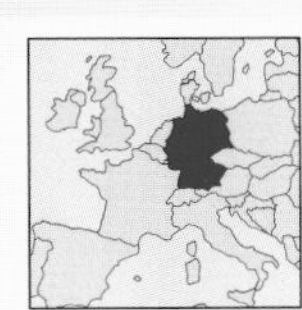

AREA 357,022 sq km [137,846 sq mi]
POPULATION 82,425,000
CAPITAL (POPULATION) Berlin (3,387,000)
GOVERNMENT Federal multiparty republic
ETHNIC GROUPS German 92%, Turkish 3%, Serbo-Croatian, Italian, Greek, Polish, Spanish
LANGUAGES German (official)
RELIGIONS Protestant (mainly Lutheran) 34%, Roman Catholic 34%, Islam 4%, others
CURRENCY Euro = 100 cents

GEOGRAPHY The Federal Republic of Germany is the fourth largest country in Western Europe, after France, Spain and Sweden. The North German plain borders the North Sea in the north-west and the Baltic Sea in the north-east. Major rivers draining the plain include the Weser, Elbe and Oder.

The central highlands contain plateaux and highlands, including the Harz Mountains, the Thuringian Forest (Thüringer Wald), the Ore Mountains (Erzgebirge), and the Bohemian Forest (Böhmerwald) on the Czech border. South Germany is largely hilly, but the land rises in the south to the Bavarian Alps, which contain Germany's highest peak, Zugspitze, at 2,962 m [9,718 ft] above sea level. The scenic Black Forest (Scharzwald) overlooks the River Rhine, which flows through a rift valley in the south-west. The Black Forest contains the source of the River Danube.

North-western Germany has a mild climate, but the Baltic coastlands are cooler. To the south, the climate becomes more continental, especially in the highlands. The precipitation is greatest on the uplands, many of which are snow-capped in winter.

POLITICS & ECONOMY Germany and its allies were defeated in World War I (1914–18) and the country became a republic. Adolf Hitler came to power in 1933 and ruled as a dictator. His order to invade Poland led to the start of World War II (1939–45), which ended with Germany in ruins.

In 1945, Germany was divided into four military zones. In 1949, the American, British and French zones were amalgamated to form the Federal Republic of Germany (West Germany), while the Soviet zone became the German Democratic Republic (East Germany), a Communist state. Berlin, which had also been partitioned, became a divided city. West Berlin was part of West Germany, while East Berlin became the capital of East Germany. Bonn was the capital of West Germany.

Tension between East and West mounted during the Cold War, but West Germany rebuilt its economy quickly. In East Germany, the recovery was less rapid. In the late 1980s, reforms in the Soviet Union led to unrest in East Germany. Free elections were held in East Germany in 1990 and, on 3 October 1990, Germany was reunited.

The united Germany adopted West Germany's official name, the Federal Republic of Germany. Elections in December 1990 returned Helmut Kohl, West Germany's Chancellor (head of government) since 1982, to power. In 1998, Kohl was succeeded by Social Democrat Gerhard Schröder. In 1999, Germany's parliament moved from Bonn to the rebuilt Reichstag building in Berlin.

Since reunification, Germany has faced many problems, some arising from the weak economy of eastern Germany and others involving racist violence and the resurgence of far-right groups. In 2003, Germany opposed the US-led invasion of Iraq, but it offered help in Iraq's reconstruction.

Germany is one of the world's leading economic powers. However, in the early 2000s, the economy became sluggish and Schröder introduced unpopular cuts in the welfare system. Manufacturing is the main economic sector and manufactures make up the bulk of Germany's exports. Leading manufactures include cars and other vehicles, cement, chemicals, computers, electrical equipment, processed food, machinery, scientific instruments, ships, steel, textiles and tools. Germany has some coal, potash and rock salt deposits, but it imports many raw materials.

Germany also imports food. Major agricultural products include fruits, grapes for wine-making, potatoes, sugar beet and vegetables. Beef and dairy cattle are raised, together with many other livestock.

GHANA

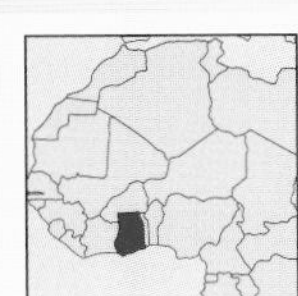

AREA 238,533 sq km [92,098 sq mi]
POPULATION 20,757,000
CAPITAL (POPULATION) Accra (949,000)
GOVERNMENT Republic
ETHNIC GROUPS Akan 44%, Moshi-Dagomba 16%, Ewe 13%, Ga 8%, Gurma 3%, Yoruba 1%
LANGUAGES English (official), Akan, Moshi-Dagomba, Ewe, Ga
RELIGIONS Christianity 63%, traditional beliefs 21%, Islam 16%
CURRENCY Cedi = 100 pesewas

GEOGRAPHY The Republic of Ghana faces the Gulf of Guinea in West Africa. It was formerly called the Gold Coast. Behind the thickly populated southern plains lies a plateau in the south-west. Lying just north of the Equator, it has a hot tropical climate. The south is rainy, but the north is drier.

POLITICS & ECONOMY Portuguese explorers reached the area in 1471 and named it the Gold Coast. The area became a centre of the slave trade in the 17th century. The slave trade was ended in the 1860s and, gradually, the British took control of the area. After independence in 1957, attempts were made to develop the economy by creating large state-owned manufacturing industries. But debt and corruption, together with falls in the price of cocoa, the chief export, caused economic problems. This led to instability and frequent coups. In 1981, power was invested in a Provisional National Defence Council, led by Flight-Lieutenant Jerry Rawlings.

The government steadied the economy and, in 1992, it reintroduced multiparty elections. Rawlings was elected president in 1992 and served until his retirement in 2000. He was succeeded by John Kufuor, who was re-elected in 2004.

The World Bank classifies Ghana as a 'low-income' developing country. Most people are poor and farming employs 55% of the population.

GIBRALTAR

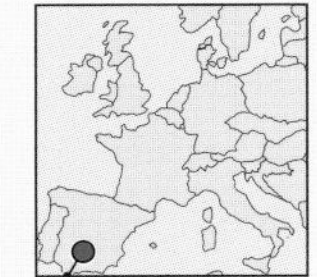

AREA 6 sq km [2.3 sq mi]
POPULATION 28,000
CAPITAL (POPULATION) Gibraltar Town (28,000)

Gibraltar occupies a strategic position on the south coast of Spain where the Mediterranean meets the Atlantic. Formerly held by Moors from North Africa and later by Spain, it was recognized as a British possession in 1713. Despite Spanish claims, its population has consistently voted to retain its contacts with Britain.

GREECE

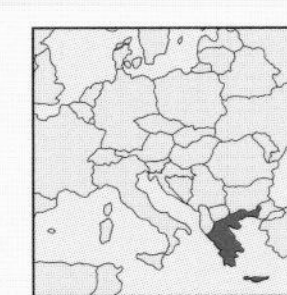

AREA 131,957 sq km [50,949 sq mi]
POPULATION 10,648,000
CAPITAL (POPULATION) Athens (772,000)
GOVERNMENT Multiparty republic
ETHNIC GROUPS Greek 98%
LANGUAGES Greek (official)
RELIGIONS Greek Orthodox 98%
CURRENCY Euro = 100 cents

GEOGRAPHY The Hellenic Republic, as Greece is officially called, is a rugged country situated at the southern end of the Balkan peninsula. Olympus, at 2,917 m [9,570 ft], is the highest peak. Islands make up about a fifth of the land.

Low-lying areas in Greece have mild, moist winters and hot, dry summers. The east coast has more than 2,700 hours of sunshine a year and only about half of the rainfall of the west. The mountains have a more severe climate, with snow on the higher slopes in winter.

POLITICS & ECONOMY Around 2,500 years ago, Greece became the birthplace of Western civilization. Ancient Greek ruins and art still attract millions of tourists to the country. The first civilization – the Minoan, centred on Crete – flourished between about 3000 and 1400 BC. Following the end of the related Mycaenean period on the mainland(1580–1100 BC), a 'dark age' lasted until about 800 BC. But from 750 BC, Greeks became rich traders and the city-state of Athens reached its peak in 461–431 BC. Greece became a Roman province in 146 BC and, in AD 365, it became part of the Byzantine Empire.

The Byzantine Empire fell to the Turks in 1453. But Greece became an independent monarchy in 1830. After World War II (1939–45), when Germany ruled Greece, a civil war broke out between Communists and nationalists. It ended in 1949 and a military dictatorship took power in 1967. The monarchy was abolished in 1973 and democracy was resumed in 1974. Greece joined the European Community (now the EU) in 1981. On 1 January 2002, the euro became the sole unit of currency.

Greece is one of the EU's poorer nations. Manufactured products include processed food, cement, chemicals, metal products, textiles and tobacco. Greece also mines lignite (brown coal), bauxite and chromite. Farmland covers about a third of the country and grazing land another 40%. Crops include barley, grapes for wine-making, dried fruits, olives, potatoes, sugar beet and wheat. Livestock farming is also important, as is tourism.

GREENLAND

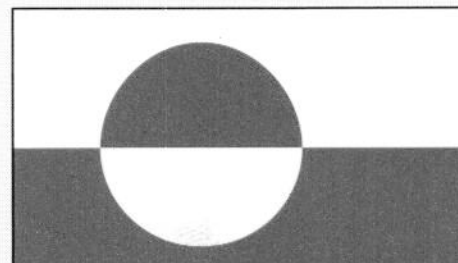
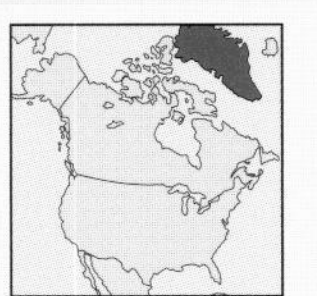

AREA 2,175,600 sq km [838,999 sq mi]
POPULATION 56,000
CAPITAL (POPULATION) Nuuk (Godthåb) (14,000)

Greenland is the world's largest island. Settlements are confined to the coast, because an ice-sheet covers four-fifths of the land. Greenland became a Danish possession in 1380. Full internal self-government was granted in 1981 and, in 1997, Danish place names were superseded by Inuit name forms. Its official name in the local language is Kalaallit Nunaat. However, Greenland remains heavily dependent on Danish subsidies.

GRENADA

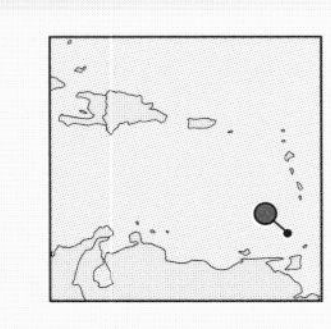

AREA 344 sq km [133 sq mi]
POPULATION 89,000
CAPITAL (POPULATION) St George's (4,000)

The most southerly of the Windward Islands in the Caribbean Sea, Grenada became independent from the UK in 1974. A military group seized power in 1983, when the prime minister was killed. US troops intervened and restored order. Agriculture and tourism are the chief activities. Exports include bananas, cocoa, mace, nutmeg and textiles. In 2004, a hurricane destroyed 90% of the island's buildings.

GUADELOUPE

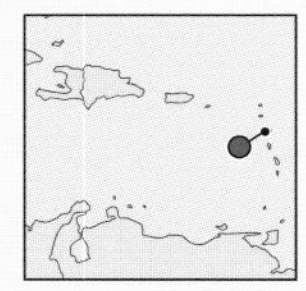

AREA 1,705 sq km [658 sq mi]
POPULATION 445,000
CAPITAL (POPULATION) Basse-Terre (12,000)

Guadeloupe is a French overseas department which includes seven Caribbean islands, the largest of which is Basse-Terre. French settlers arrived in 1635 and Guadeloupe has remained French except for a period of British rule in 1759–1813. French aid has helped to maintain reasonable living standards for the people.

GUAM

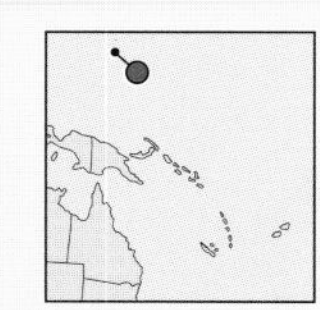

AREA 549 sq km [212 sq mi]
POPULATION 166,000
CAPITAL (POPULATION) Agana (1,000)

Guam, a strategically important 'unincorporated territory' of the USA, is the largest of the Mariana Islands in the Pacific Ocean. It is composed of a coralline limestone plateau. Guam was ruled by Spain from 1668 until it was ceded to the United States in 1898 after the Spanish–American War.

GUATEMALA

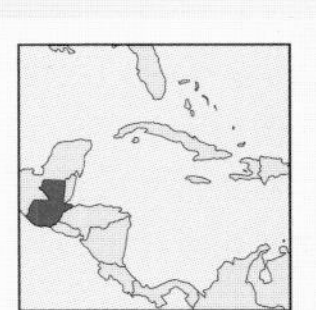

AREA 108,889 sq km [42,042 sq mi]
POPULATION 14,281,000
CAPITAL (POPULATION) Guatemala City (1,007,000)
GOVERNMENT Republic
ETHNIC GROUPS Ladino (mixed Hispanic and Amerindian) 55%, Amerindian 43%, others 2%
LANGUAGES Spanish (official), Amerindian languages
RELIGIONS Christianity, indigenous Mayan beliefs
CURRENCY US dollar; Quetzal = 100 centavos

GEOGRAPHY The Republic of Guatemala in Central America contains a thickly populated mountain region, with fertile soils. The mountains, which run in an east–west direction, contain many volcanoes, some of which are active. Volcanic eruptions and earthquakes are common in the highlands. South of the mountains lie the thinly populated Pacific coastlands, while a large inland plain occupies the north.

Guatemala lies in the tropics. The lowlands are hot and rainy. But the central mountain region is cooler and drier. Guatemala City, at about 1,500 m [5,000 ft] above sea level, has a pleasant, warm climate, with a marked dry season between November and April.

POLITICS & ECONOMY In 1823, Guatemala joined the Central American Federation. But it became fully independent in 1839. Since independence, Guatemala has been plagued by instability and violence.

Guatemala has a long-standing claim over Belize, but this was reduced in 1983 to the southern fifth of the country. Violence became widespread in Guatemala from the early 1960s, because of conflict between left-wing groups and government forces. A peace accord was signed in 1996, ending a 36-year war that had claimed perhaps 200,000 lives. In 2004, US$35 million was paid in damages to victims of the civil war.

The World Bank classifies Guatemala as a 'lower-middle-income' developing country. Agriculture employs nearly half of the population and coffee, sugar, bananas and beef are the leading exports. Other important crops include the spice cardamom and cotton, while maize is the chief food crop. But Guatemala still has to import food to feed the people.

GUINEA

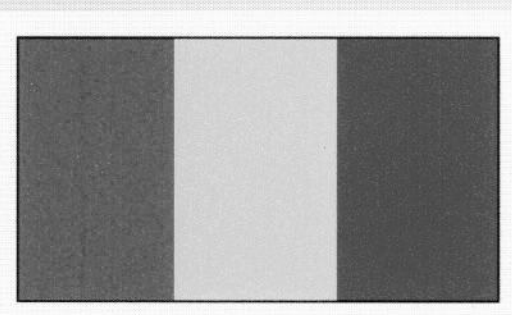
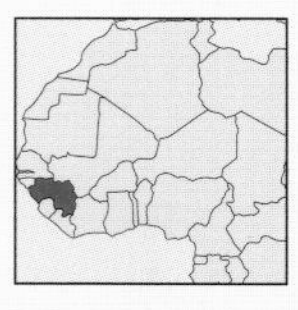

AREA 245,857 sq km [94,925 sq mi]
POPULATION 9,246,000
CAPITAL (POPULATION) Conakry (1,232,000)
GOVERNMENT Multiparty republic
ETHNIC GROUPS Peuhl 40%, Malinke 30%, Soussou 20%, others 10%
LANGUAGES French (official)
RELIGIONS Islam 85%, Christianity 8%, traditional beliefs 7%
CURRENCY Guinean franc = 100 cauris

GEOGRAPHY The Republic of Guinea faces the Atlantic Ocean in West Africa. A flat, swampy plain borders the coast. Behind this plain, the land rises to a plateau region called Fouta Djalon. The Upper Niger plains are in the north-east.

Guinea has a tropical climate and Conakry, on the coast, has heavy rains between May and November.

This is also the coolest period in the year. During the dry season, hot, dry harmattan winds blow south-westwards from the Sahara Desert.

POLITICS & ECONOMY Guinea became independent in 1958. Its president, Sékou Touré, pursued socialist policies, though he had to resort to repressive policies to hold on to power. After his death in 1984, a military government, under President Lansana Conté, introduced free-enterprise policies. A multiparty system was restored in 1992 and Conté was elected president in 1993. He was re-elected in 1998 and 2002. From the late 1990s, Guinea was drawn into the civil conflicts that were taking place in neighbouring Liberia and Sierra Leone.

The World Bank classifies Guinea as a 'low-income' developing country. It has several natural resources, including bauxite (aluminium ore), diamonds, gold, iron ore and uranium. Bauxite and alumina (processed bauxite) account for 60% of the value of the exports. Agriculture, however, employs 78% of the people, many of whom produce little more than they need for their own families. Guinea has some manufacturing industries. Products include alumina, processed food and textiles.

GUINEA-BISSAU

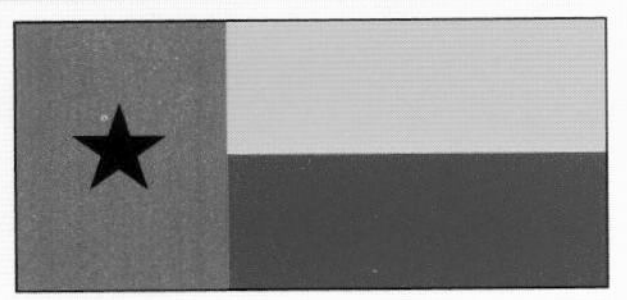

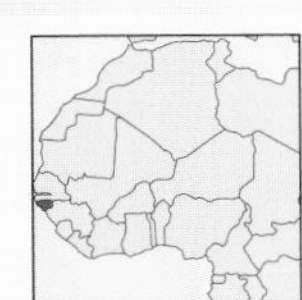

AREA 36,125 sq km [13,948 sq mi]
POPULATION 1,388,000
CAPITAL (POPULATION) Bissau (200,000)
GOVERNMENT 'Interim' government
ETHNIC GROUPS Balanta 30%, Fula 20%, Manjaca 14%, Mandinga 13%, Papel 7%
LANGUAGES Portuguese (official), Crioulo
RELIGIONS Traditional beliefs 50%, Islam 45%, Christianity 5%
CURRENCY CFA franc = 100 centimes

GEOGRAPHY The Republic of Guinea-Bissau, formerly known as Portuguese Guinea, is a small country in West Africa. The land is mostly low-lying, with a broad, swampy coastal plain and many flat offshore islands, including the Bijagós Archipelago.

The country has a tropical climate, with one dry season (December to May) and a rainy season from June to November.

POLITICS & ECONOMY Portugal appointed a governor to administer Guinea-Bissau and the Cape Verde Islands in 1836, but in 1879 the two territories were separated and Guinea-Bissau became a colony, then called Portuguese Guinea. But development was slow, partly because the territory did not attract settlers on the same scale as Portugal's much healthier African colonies of Angola and Mozambique.

In 1956, African nationalists in Portuguese Guinea and Cape Verde founded the African Party for the Independence of Guinea and Cape Verde (PAIGC). Because Portugal seemed determined to hang on to its overseas territories, the PAIGC began a guerrilla war in 1963. By 1968, it held two-thirds of the country. In 1972, a rebel National Assembly, elected by the people in the PAIGC-controlled area, voted to make the country independent as Guinea-Bissau.

The independent nation faced many problems arising from its under-developed economy and its lack of trained personnel. Its leaders wanted to unite their country with Cape Verde, but, in 1980, military leaders seized power. The Revolutionary Council, which took over, opposed unification with Cape Verde. Guinea-Bissau ceased to be a one-party state in 1991 and elections were held in 1994. Civil war broke out in 1998 and a military coup occurred in 1999. Kumba Ialá was elected president in 2000, but he was overthrown in a coup in 2003. Civilian government was restored in 2004, when parliamentary elections were held.

Guinea-Bissau is a poor country. Agriculture employs more than 70% of the people, but most farming is at subsistence level. Major crops include beans, coconuts, groundnuts, maize and rice.

GUYANA

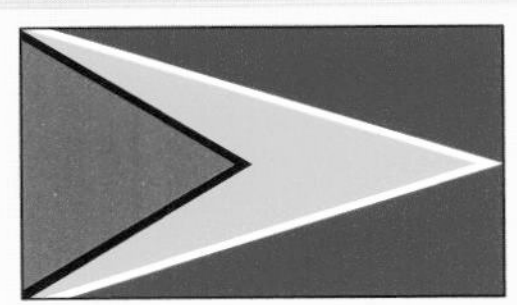

AREA 214,969 sq km [83,000 sq mi]
POPULATION 706,000
CAPITAL (POPULATION) Georgetown (150,000)
GOVERNMENT Multiparty republic
ETHNIC GROUPS East Indian 50%, Black 36%, Amerindian 7%, others
LANGUAGES English (official), Creole, Hindi, Urdu
RELIGIONS Christianity 50%, Hinduism 35%, Islam 10%, others
CURRENCY Guyanese dollar = 100 cents

GEOGRAPHY The Co-operative Republic of Guyana is a country facing the Atlantic Ocean in north-eastern South America. The coastal plain is flat and much of it is below sea level.

The climate is hot and humid, though the interior highlands are cooler than the coast. The rainfall is heavy, occurring on more than 200 days a year.

POLITICS & ECONOMY Britain gained control of the area in 1814 and set up the colony of British Guiana in 1831. British Guiana became independent as Guyana in 1966. A black lawyer, Forbes Burnham, became the first prime minister. Under a new constitution adopted in 1980, the president's powers were increased. Burnham became president until he died in 1985. He was succeeded by Hugh Desmond Hoyte, who was defeated in 1993 by an ethnic Indian, Cheddi Jagan. Jagan died in 1997 and was succeeded by his wife, Janet. In 1999, Bharrat Jagdeo was elected president. He was re-elected in 2001.

Guyana is a poor country. Its resources include gold, bauxite (aluminium ore) and other minerals, forests and fertile soils. Sugar cane and rice are leading crops. Electric power is in short supply, although the country has great potential for producing hydroelectricity from its many rivers.

HAITI

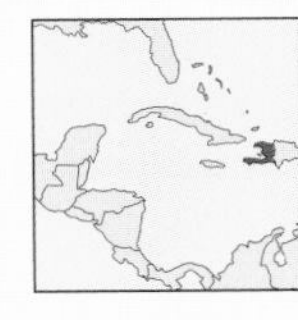

AREA 27,750 sq km [10,714 sq mi]
POPULATION 7,656,000
CAPITAL (POPULATION) Port-au-Prince (917,000)
GOVERNMENT Multiparty republic
ETHNIC GROUPS Black 95%, Mulatto/White 5%
LANGUAGES French and Creole (both official)
RELIGIONS Roman Catholic 80%, Voodoo
CURRENCY Gourde = 100 centimes

GEOGRAPHY The Republic of Haiti occupies the western third of Hispaniola in the Caribbean. The land is mainly mountainous. The climate is hot and humid, though the northern highlands, with about 200 mm [79 in], have more than twice as much rainfall as the southern coast.

POLITICS & ECONOMY Visited by Christopher Columbus in 1492, Haiti was later developed by the French. The African slaves revolted in 1791 and the country became independent in 1804. Since independence, Haiti has suffered from instability, violence and dictatorial rule. Elections in 1990 returned Jean-Bertrand Aristide as president, but he was overthrown in 1991. Following US intervention, he returned in 1994. In 1995, René Préval was elected president, but Aristide was again elected president in 2000 amid accusations of vote-rigging. In 2004, rebel activity forced Aristide to flee the country. A US-backed government was set up to restore order, but rising levels of violence in the capital and hurricane damage caused unrest in late 2004.

Haiti is the poorest country in the Americas. More than half of the people work on farms, producing barely enough to feed their families. Haiti has few industries.

HONDURAS

AREA 112,088 sq km [43,277 sq mi]
POPULATION 6,824,000
CAPITAL (POPULATION) Tegucigalpa (850,000)
GOVERNMENT Republic
ETHNIC GROUPS Mestizo 90%, Amerindian 7%, Black (including Black Carib) 2%, White 1%
LANGUAGES Spanish (official), Amerindian dialects
RELIGIONS Roman Catholic 97%
CURRENCY Honduran lempira = 100 centavos

GEOGRAPHY The Republic of Honduras is the second largest country in Central America. The northern coast on the Caribbean Sea extends more than 600 km [373 mi], but the Pacific coast in the south-east is only about 80 km [50 mi] long.

Honduras has a tropical climate, but the highlands, where the capital Tegucigalpa is situated, have a cooler climate than the hot coastal plains. The months between May and November are the rainiest. Hurricanes often strike the coast. In 1998, Hurricane Mitch caused great destruction.

POLITICS & ECONOMY Western Honduras was part of the Maya civilization and the ancient ruins of Copán in Honduras are testimony to the greatness of the Mayas. In 1502, Christopher Columbus claimed the land for Spain and Spain ruled the country from 1625 until 1821. It became part of the Central American Federation but it withdrew in 1838.

In the 1890s, American companies developed plantations in Honduras to grow bananas, which soon became the country's chief source of income. The companies exerted great political influence in Honduras and the country became known as a 'banana republic', a name that was later applied to several other Latin American nations.

Instability has continued to mar the country's progress. In 1969, Honduras fought the short 'Soccer War' with El Salvador. The war was sparked off by the treatment of fans during a World Cup soccer series. However, the real reason was that Honduras had forced Salvadoreans in Honduras to give up land. Since 1980, civilian governments have ruled Honduras, though the military remain influential.

Honduras is a developing country – one of the poorest in the Americas and the least industrialized in Central America. It has few resources besides some silver, lead and zinc, and agriculture dominates the economy. Bananas and coffee are the leading exports, and maize is the main food crop. Manufactures include processed food, textiles, and a variety of wood products.

HUNGARY

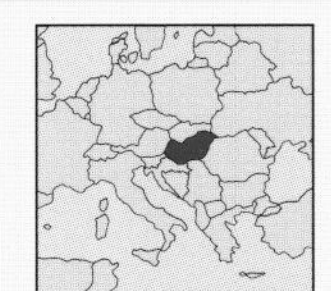

AREA 93,032 sq km [35,920 sq mi]
POPULATION 10,032,000
CAPITAL (POPULATION) Budapest (1,819,000)
GOVERNMENT Multiparty republic
ETHNIC GROUPS Magyar 90%, Gypsy, German, Serb, Romanian, Slovak
LANGUAGES Hungarian (official)
RELIGIONS Roman Catholic 68%, Calvinist 20%, Lutheran 5%, others
CURRENCY Forint = 100 fillér

GEOGRAPHY The Hungarian Republic is a landlocked country in central Europe. The land is mostly low-lying and drained by the Danube (Duna) and its tributary, the Tisza. Most of the land east of the Danube belongs to a region called the Great Plain (Nagyalföld), which covers about half of Hungary.

Hungary lies far from the moderating influence of the sea. As a result, summers are warmer and sunnier, and the winters colder than in Western Europe.

POLITICS & ECONOMY Hungary entered World War II (1939–45) in 1941, as an ally of Germany, but the Germans occupied the country in 1944. The Soviet Union invaded Hungary in 1944 and, in 1946, the country became a republic. The Communists gradually took over the government, taking complete control in 1949. From 1949, Hungary was an ally of the Soviet Union. In 1956, Soviet troops crushed an anti-Communist revolt. But in the 1980s, reforms in the Soviet Union led to the growth of anti-Communist groups in Hungary. In 1989, Hungary adopted a new constitution making it a multiparty state. Elections held in 1990 led to a victory for the non-Communist Democratic Forum. In 2002, the Hungarian Socialist Party, in alliance with the liberal Free Democrats, won a majority in parliament. In 2004, Hungary became a member of NATO and the EU.

Before World War II, Hungary's economy was based mainly on agriculture. But the Communists set up many manufacturing industries. The new factories were owned by the government, as also was most of the land. From the late 1980s, the government worked to increase private ownership. This created many problems. Manufacturing is the chief economic activity. Products include aluminium, chemicals, and electrical and electronic goods.

ICELAND

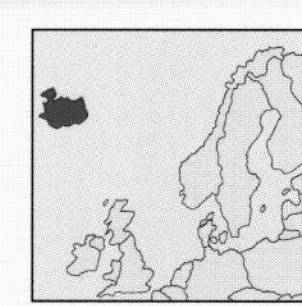

AREA 103,000 sq km [39,768 sq mi]
POPULATION 294,000
CAPITAL (POPULATION) Reykjavik (108,000)
GOVERNMENT Multiparty republic
ETHNIC GROUPS Icelandic 97%, Danish 1%
LANGUAGES Icelandic (official)
RELIGIONS Evangelical Lutheran 87%, other Protestant 4%, Roman Catholic 2%, others
CURRENCY Icelandic króna = 100 aurar

GEOGRAPHY The Republic of Iceland, in the North Atlantic Ocean, is closer to Greenland than Scotland. Iceland sits astride the Mid-Atlantic Ridge. It is slowly getting wider as the ocean is being stretched apart by continental drift.

Iceland has around 200 volcanoes, and eruptions are frequent. An eruption under the Vatnajökull ice-cap in 1996 created a subglacial lake which subsequently burst, causing severe flooding. Geysers and hot springs are other features. Ice-caps and glaciers cover about an eighth of the land. The only habitable areas are the coastal lowlands.

Although it lies far to the north, Iceland's climate is moderated by the warm waters of the Gulf Stream. The port of Reykjavik is ice-free all the year round.

POLITICS & ECONOMY Norwegian Vikings colonized Iceland in AD 874, and in 930 the settlers founded the world's oldest parliament, the Althing.

Iceland united with Norway in 1262. But when Norway united with Denmark in 1380, Iceland came under Danish rule. Iceland became a self-governing kingdom, united with Denmark, in 1918. It became a fully independent republic in 1944, following a referendum in which 97% of the people voted to break their country's ties with Denmark.

Iceland has played an important part in European affairs and is a member of the North Atlantic Treaty Organization. But Iceland has been involved in fishing disputes. In 1992, it left the International Whaling Commission because of its alleged anti-whaling policy. It rejoined in 2002, but, in 2003, it undertook its first whale hunt for 15 years, stating that it was a 'scientific catch' to study the impact of whales on fish stocks.

Iceland has few resources besides the fishing grounds which surround it. Fishing and fish processing are major industries which dominate Iceland's overseas trade. Barely 1% of the land is used to grow crops, but 23% of the country can be used for grazing sheep and cattle.

INDIA

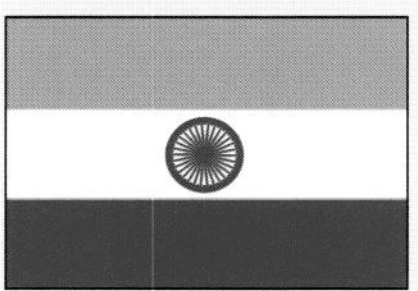
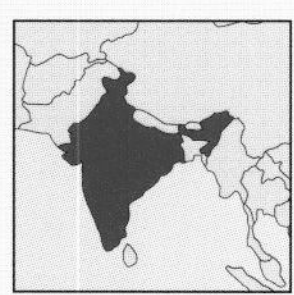

AREA 3,287,263 sq km [1,269,212 sq mi]
POPULATION 1,065,071,000
CAPITAL (POPULATION) New Delhi (295,000)
GOVERNMENT Multiparty federal republic
ETHNIC GROUPS Indo-Aryan (Caucasoid) 72%, Dravidian (Aboriginal) 25%, others (mainly Mongoloid) 3%
LANGUAGES Hindi, English, Telugu, Bengali, Marathi, Tamil, Urdu, Gujarati, Malayalam, Kannada, Oriya, Punjabi, Assamese, Kashmiri, Sindhi and Sanskrit are all official languages
RELIGIONS Hinduism 82%, Islam 12%, Christianity 2%, Sikhism 2%, Buddhism and others
CURRENCY Indian rupee = 100 paisa

GEOGRAPHY The Republic of India is the world's seventh largest country. In population, it ranks second only to China. The north is mountainous, with mountains and foothills of the Himalayan range. Rivers, such as the Brahmaputra and Ganges (Ganga), rise in the Himalaya and flow across the fertile northern plains. Southern India consists of a large plateau, called the Deccan. The Deccan is bordered by two mountain ranges, the Western Ghats and the Eastern Ghats.

India has three main seasons. The cool season runs from October to February. The hot season runs from March to June. The rainy monsoon season starts in the middle of June and continues into September. Delhi has a moderate rainfall, with about 640 mm [25 in] a year. The south-western coast and the north-east have far more rain. Darjeeling in the north-east has an average annual rainfall of 3,040 mm [120 in]. But parts of the Thar Desert in the north-west have only 50 mm [2 in] of rain per year.

POLITICS & ECONOMY In southern India, most of the people are descendants of the dark-skinned Dravidians, who were among India's earliest people. Most northerners are descendants of lighter-skinned Aryans who arrived around 3,500 years ago.

India was the birthplace of several major religions, including Hinduism, Buddhism and Sikhism. Islam was introduced from about AD 1000. The Muslim Mughal empire was founded in 1526. From the 17th century, Britain began to gain influence. From 1858 to 1947, India was ruled as part of the British empire. An independence movement began after the Sepoy Rebellion (1857–9) and, in 1885, the Indian National Congress was formed. In 1920, Mohandas K. Gandhi became its leader and it soon became a mass movement. When independence was finally achieved in 1947, British India was divided into modern India and Muslim Pakistan. Partition was marred by mass slaughter as Hindus and Sikhs fled from Pakistan, and Indian Muslims poured into Pakistan. In the ensuing disputes, some 1 million people were killed.

Although India has 15 major languages and hundreds of minor ones, together with many religions, the country remains the world's largest democracy. It has faced many problems, especially with Pakistan, over the disputed territory of Jammu and Kashmir. Two wars in 1965 and 1972 failed to alter greatly the 1948 cease-fire lines. In the late 1980s, Kashmiri nationalists in the Indian-controlled area waged a campaign, demanding either integration into Pakistan or independence. India sent in troops and accused Pakistan of intervention. In the 1990s, Pakistani-backed guerrillas fought to break India's hold on the Srinigar valley, Kashmir's most populous region. The situation was aggravated when both India and Pakistan tested nuclear devices in 1998. Between 2003 and 2005, the countries launched a series of peace moves, but conflict continued on the ground.

Economic development has been a major problem and, according to the World Bank, India is a 'low-income' developing country. After socialist policies failed to raise the living standards of the poor, the government introduced private enterprise. Farming employs 64% of the people. The main crops are rice, wheat, millet, sorghum, peas and beans. India has more cattle than any other country. Milk is produced but Hindus do not eat beef. India has reserves of coal, iron ore and oil, and manufacturing has expanded greatly since 1947. By 2004, India had the world's 11th largest economy, producing high-tech goods, iron and steel, machinery, refined petroleum, textiles, jewellery and transport equipment.

INDONESIA

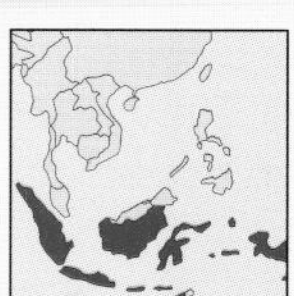

AREA 1,904,569 sq km [735,354 sq mi]
POPULATION 238,453,000
CAPITAL (POPULATION) Jakarta (9,374,000)
GOVERNMENT Multiparty republic
ETHNIC GROUPS Javanese 45%, Sundanese 14%, Madurese 7%, coastal Malays 7%, approximately 300 others
LANGUAGES Bahasa Indonesian (official), many others
RELIGIONS Islam 88%, Roman Catholic 3%, Hinduism 2%, Buddhism 1%
CURRENCY Indonesian rupiah = 100 sen

GEOGRAPHY The Republic of Indonesia is an island nation in South-east Asia. In all, Indonesia contains about 13,600 islands, less than 6,000 of which are inhabited. Three-quarters of the country is made up of five main areas: the islands of Sumatra, Java and Sulawesi (Celebes), together with Kalimantan (southern Borneo) and Irian Jaya (western New Guinea). The islands are generally mountainous and volcanic. The larger islands have extensive coastal lowlands. The climate is hot and humid, with a high rainfall. Only Java and the Sunda Islands have relatively dry seasons.

POLITICS & ECONOMY Indonesia is the world's most populous Muslim nation, though Islam was introduced as recently as the 15th century. The Dutch became active in the area in the early 17th century and Indonesia became a Dutch colony in 1799. After a long struggle, the Netherlands recognized Indonesia's independence in 1949. The economy has expanded, but ethnic and religious conflict have slowed down economic progress.

In the early 21st century, Indonesia faced considerable internal disorder. Separatists were operating in Aceh province in northern Sumatra and in West Papua (formerly Irian Jaya), Christian–Muslim clashes led to loss of life in the Moluccas, while East (formerly Portuguese) Timor became independent in 2002.

In December 2004, more than 120,000 people were killed in Indonesia by a tsunami. Worst hit was Aceh, where the tragedy provoked government negotiations with the separatists in 2005.

Indonesia is a developing country. Its resources include oil, natural gas, tin and other minerals, its fertile volcanic soils and its forests. Oil and gas are major exports. Timber, textiles, rubber, coffee and tea are also exported. The principal food crop is rice. Manufacturing is increasing, particularly on Java.

IRAN

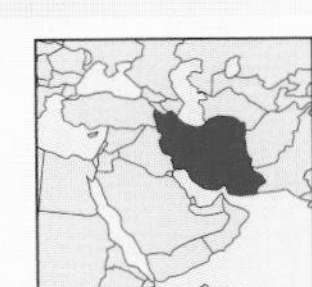

AREA 1,648,195 sq km [636,368 sq mi]
POPULATION 69,019,000
CAPITAL (POPULATION) Tehran (7,723,000)
GOVERNMENT Islamic republic
ETHNIC GROUPS Persian 51%, Azeri 24%, Gilaki and Mazandarani 8%, Kurd 7%, Arab 3%, Lur 2%, Baluchi 2%, Turkmen 2%
LANGUAGES Persian 58%, Turkic 26%, Kurdish
RELIGIONS Islam (Shi'ite Muslim 89%)
CURRENCY Iranian rial = 100 dinars

GEOGRAPHY The Republic of Iran contains a barren central plateau which covers about half of the country. It includes the Dasht-e-Kavir (Great Salt Desert) and the Dasht-e-Lut (Great Sand Desert). The Elburz Mountains north of the plateau contain Iran's highest peak, Damavand, while narrow lowlands lie between the mountains and the Caspian Sea. West of the plateau are the Zagros Mountains, beyond which the land descends to the Persian Gulf.

Much of Iran has a severe, dry climate, with hot summers and cold winters. In Tehran, rain falls on only about 30 days in the year and the annual temperature range is more than 25°C [45°F]. The climate in the lowlands, however, is generally milder.

POLITICS & ECONOMY Iran was called Persia until 1935. The empire of Ancient Persia flourished between 550 and 350 BC, when it fell to Alexander the Great. Islam was introduced in AD 641.

Britain and Russia competed for influence in the area in the 19th century, and in the early 20th century the British began to develop the country's oil resources. In 1925, the Pahlavi family took power. Reza Khan became shah (king) and worked to modernize the country. The Pahlavi dynasty was ended in 1979 when a religious leader, Ayatollah Ruhollah Khomeini, made Iran an Islamic republic. In 1980–8, Iran and Iraq fought a war over disputed borders. Khomeini died in 1989, but his fundamentalist views and anti-Western attitudes continued to dominate politics. In 1997, Mohammad Khatami, a liberal, was elected president, but conservative clerics made actual reform difficult. Between 2003 and 2005, the United States accused Iran of developing nuclear weapons, a charge Iran denied.

Iran's prosperity is based on its oil production and oil accounts for 95% of the country's exports. However, the economy was severely damaged by the Iran–Iraq war in the 1980s. Oil revenues have been used to develop a growing manufacturing sector. Agriculture is important even though farms cover only a tenth of the land. The main crops are wheat and barley. Livestock farming and fishing are other important activities, although Iran has to import much of the food it needs.

IRAQ

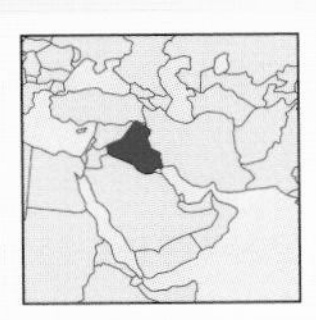

AREA 438,317 sq km [169,234 sq mi]
POPULATION 25,375,000
CAPITAL (POPULATION) Baghdad (4,865,000)
GOVERNMENT Republic
ETHNIC GROUPS Arab 77%, Kurdish 19%, Assyrian and others
LANGUAGES Arabic (official), Kurdish (official in Kurdish areas), Assyrian, Armenian
RELIGIONS Islam 97%, Christianity and others
CURRENCY New Iraqi dinar

GEOGRAPHY The Republic of Iraq is a south-west Asian country at the head of the Gulf. Rolling deserts cover western and south-western Iraq, with mountains in the north-east. The northern plains, across which flow the rivers Euphrates (Nahr al Furat) and Tigris (Nahr Dijlah), are dry. But the southern plains, including Mesopotamia, and the delta of the Shatt al Arab, the river formed south of Al Qurnah by the combined Euphrates and Tigris, contain irrigated farmland, together with marshes. The climate of Iraq ranges from temperate in the north to subtropical in the south.

POLITICS & ECONOMY Mesopotamia was the home of several great civilizations, including Sumer, Babylon and Assyria. It later became part of the Persian empire. Islam was introduced in AD 637 and Baghdad became the brilliant capital of the powerful Arab empire. But Mesopotamia declined after the Mongols invaded it in 1258. From 1534, Mesopotamia became part of the Turkish Ottoman empire. Britain invaded the area in 1916. In 1921, Britain renamed the country Iraq and set up an Arab monarchy. Iraq finally became independent in 1932.

By the 1950s, oil dominated Iraq's economy. In 1952, Iraq agreed to take 50% of the profits of the foreign oil companies. This revenue enabled the government to pay for welfare services and development projects. But many Iraqis felt that they should benefit more from their oil.

Since 1958, when army officers killed the king and made Iraq a republic, the country has undergone turbulent times. In the 1960s, the Kurds, who live in northern Iraq and also in Iran, Turkey, Syria and Armenia, asked for self-rule. The government rejected their demands and war broke out. A peace treaty was signed in 1975, but conflict has continued.

In 1979, Saddam Hussein became Iraq's president. Under his leadership, Iraq invaded Iran in 1980, starting an eight-year war. Iraqi Kurds supported Iran and the Iraqi government attacked Kurdish villages with poison gas. In 1990, Iraqi troops occupied Kuwait, but an international force drove them out in 1991. Since 1991, Iraqi troops have attacked Shi'ite Marsh Arabs and Kurds. In 1998, Iraq's failure to permit UN inspectors, charged with disposing of Iraq's deadliest weapons, access to suspect sites led to the Western bombardment of Iraqi military sites. Another major offensive occurred in February 2001.

In 2002 and 2003, pressure mounted on Iraq to dispose of its alleged weapons of mass destruction. Its failure to do so led to a coalition force, headed by the United States and the UK, to invade Iraq and overthrow the Saddam regime in March–April 2003. The coalition forces rapidly achieved their main objectives, but sporadic violence continued even after the capture of Saddam Hussein in December 2003. Although largely boycotted by the Sunni Arabs, who make up about a fifth of the population, elections took place in Iraq in 2005.

Civil war, war damage in 1991 and 2003, UN sanctions, and mismanagement have all contributed to economic chaos. Oil remains Iraq's main resource, but a UN trade embargo in 1990 halted oil exports. Farmland, including pasture, covers about a fifth of the land. Products include barley, cotton, dates, fruit, livestock, wheat and wool, but Iraq still has to import food. Industries include oil refining and the manufacture of petrochemicals and consumer goods.

IRELAND

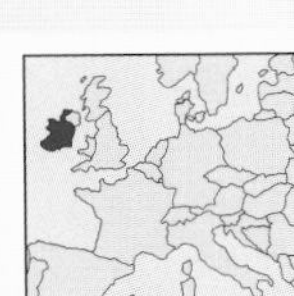

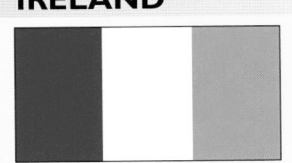

AREA 70,273 sq km [27,132 sq mi]
POPULATION 3,970,000
CAPITAL (POPULATION) Dublin (482,000)
GOVERNMENT Multiparty republic
ETHNIC GROUPS Irish 94%
LANGUAGES Irish (Gaelic) and English (both official)
RELIGIONS Roman Catholic 92%, Protestant 3%
CURRENCY Euro = 100 cents

GEOGRAPHY The Republic of Ireland occupies five-sixths of the island of Ireland. The country consists of a large lowland region surrounded by a broken rim of low mountains. The uplands include the Mountains of Kerry where Carrauntoohill, Ireland's highest peak at 1,041 m [3,415 ft], is situated. The River Shannon is the longest in the British Isles. It flows through three large lakes, loughs Allen, Ree and Derg.

Ireland has a mild, damp climate greatly influenced by the warm Gulf Stream current that washes its shores. The effects of the Gulf Stream are greatest in the west. Dublin in the east is cooler than places on the west coast. Rain occurs throughout the year.

POLITICS & ECONOMY In 1801, the Act of Union created the United Kingdom of Great Britain and Ireland. But Irish discontent intensified in the 1840s when a potato blight caused a famine in which a million people died and nearly a million emigrated. Britain was blamed for not having done enough to help. In 1916, an uprising in Dublin was crushed, but between 1919 and 1922 civil war occurred. In 1922, the Irish Free State was created as a Dominion in the British Commonwealth. But Northern Ireland remained part of the UK.

Ireland became a republic in 1949. Since then, Irish governments have sought to develop the economy, and it was for this reason that Ireland joined the

European Community in 1973. In 1998, Ireland took part in the negotiations to produce a constitutional settlement in Northern Ireland. As part of this 'Good Friday Agreement', Ireland agreed to give up its constitutional claim on Northern Ireland. But despite the efforts of the Irish and British governments, the agreement proved difficult to implement.

Major farm products in Ireland include barley, cattle and dairy products, pigs, potatoes, poultry, sheep, sugar beet and wheat, while fishing provides another valuable source of food. Farming is now profitable, aided by European Union grants, but manufacturing is the leading economic sector. Many factories produce food and beverages. Chemicals and pharmaceuticals, electronic equipment, machinery, paper and textiles are also important.

ISRAEL

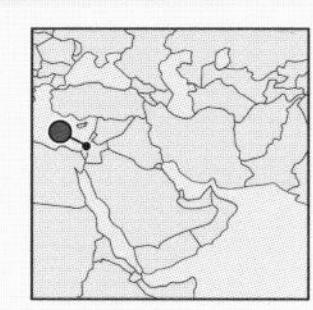

AREA 20,600 sq km [7,954 sq mi]
POPULATION 6,199,000
CAPITAL (POPULATION) Jerusalem (685,000)
GOVERNMENT Multiparty republic
ETHNIC GROUPS Jewish 80%, Arab and others 20%
LANGUAGES Hebrew and Arabic (both official)
RELIGIONS Judaism 80%, Islam (mostly Sunni) 14%, Christianity 2%, Druze and others 2%
CURRENCY New Israeli shekel = 100 agorat

GEOGRAPHY The State of Israel is a small country in the eastern Mediterranean. It includes a fertile coastal plain, where Israel's main industrial cities, Haifa (Hefa) and Tel Aviv-Jaffa are situated. Inland lie the Judaeo-Galilean highlands, which run from northern Israel to the northern tip of the Negev Desert. To the east lies part of the Great Rift Valley which contains the River Jordan, the Sea of Galilee and the Dead Sea.

Summers are hot and dry. Winters on the coast are mild and moist, but the rainfall decreases from west to east and from north to south.

POLITICS & ECONOMY Israel is part of a region called Palestine. Some Jews have always lived in the area, though most modern Israelis are descendants of immigrants who began to settle there from the 1880s. Britain ruled Palestine from 1917. Large numbers of Jews escaping Nazi persecution arrived in the 1930s, provoking an Arab uprising against British rule. In 1947, the UN agreed to partition Palestine into an Arab and a Jewish state. Fighting broke out after Arabs rejected the plan. The State of Israel came into being in May 1948, but fighting continued into 1949. Other Arab–Israeli wars in 1956, 1967 and 1973 led to land gains for Israel.

In 1978, Israel signed a treaty with Egypt which led to the return of the occupied Sinai peninsula to Egypt in 1979. But conflict continued between Israel and the PLO (Palestine Liberation Organization). In 1993, the PLO and Israel agreed to establish Palestinian self-rule in two areas: the occupied Gaza Strip, and in the town of Jericho in the occupied West Bank. The agreement was extended in 1995 to include more than 30% of the West Bank. Israel's prime minister, Yitzhak Rabin, was assassinated in 1995. In 1996, his successor, Simon Peres, was defeated by the right-wing Benjamin Netanyahu, under whom the peace process stalled. In 1999, the left-wing Ehud Barak defeated Netanyahu and revived the peace process. But, following violence between the Palestinians and Israeli forces, Barak resigned. In 2001, Barak was defeated by the right-wing Ariel Sharon, who adopted a hardline policy against the Palestinians. In late 2004, the death of hardline Palestinian leader Yasser Arafat held out hope for the creation of a Palestinian state.

Israel's most valuable activity is manufacturing and the country's products include chemicals, electronic equipment, fertilizers, military equipment, plastics, processed food, scientific instruments and textiles. Fruits and vegetables are leading exports.

ITALY

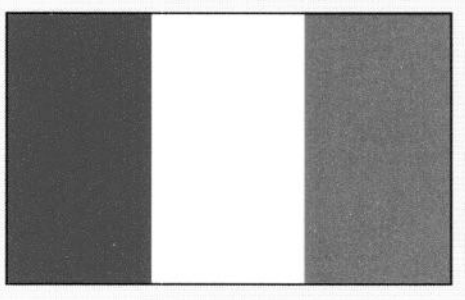

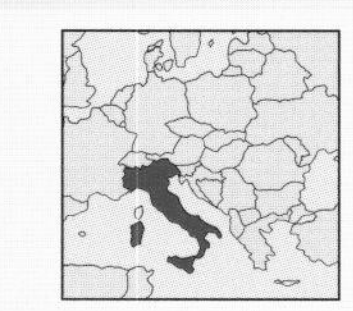

AREA 301,318 sq km [116,339 sq mi]
POPULATION 58,057,000
CAPITAL (POPULATION) Rome (2,460,000)
GOVERNMENT Multiparty republic
ETHNIC GROUPS Italian 94%, German, French, Albanian, Slovene, Greek
LANGUAGES Italian (official), German, French, Slovene
RELIGIONS Predominantly Roman Catholic
CURRENCY Euro = 100 cents

GEOGRAPHY The Republic of Italy is famous for its history and traditions, its art and culture, and its beautiful scenery. Northern Italy is bordered in the north by the high Alps, with their many climbing and skiing resorts. The Alps overlook the northern plains – Italy's most fertile and densely populated region – drained by the River Po. The rugged Apennines form the backbone of southern Italy. Bordering the range are scenic hilly areas and coastal plains. Southern Italy contains a string of volcanoes, stretching from Vesuvius, through the Lipari Islands, to Etna on Sicily, the largest Mediterranean island.

Northern Italy has cold, often snowy, winters, but the summer months are warm and sunny, with brief summer thunderstorms. Rainfall is abundant. The south has mild, moist winters and warm, dry summers.

POLITICS & ECONOMY Magnificent ruins throughout Italy testify to the glories of the ancient Roman Empire, which was founded, according to legend, in 753 BC. It reached its peak in the AD 100s. It finally collapsed in the 400s, although the Eastern Roman empire, also called the Byzantine empire, survived for another 1,000 years.

In the Middle Ages, Italy was split into many tiny states. These states made a great contribution to the revival of art and learning, called the Renaissance, in the 14th to 16th centuries. Beautiful cities, such as Florence (Firenze) and Venice (Venézia), testify to the artistic achievements of this period.

Italy finally became a united kingdom in 1861, although the Papal Territories (a large area ruled by the Roman Catholic Church) was not added until 1870. The Pope and his successors disputed the takeover of the Papal Territories. The dispute was finally resolved in 1929, when the Vatican City was set up in Rome as a fully independent state.

Italy fought in World War I (1914–18) alongside the Allies – Britain, France and Russia. In 1922, the dictator Benito Mussolini, leader of the Fascist party, took power. Under Mussolini, Italy conquered Ethiopia. During World War II (1939–45), Italy at first fought on Germany's side against the Allies. But in late 1943, Italy declared war on Germany. Italy became a republic in 1946. It has played an important part in European affairs. It was a founder member of the North Atlantic Treaty Organization (NATO) in 1949 and also of what has now become the European Union in 1958.

After the setting up of the European Union, Italy's economy developed quickly. But the country faced many problems. For example, much of the economic development was in the north. This forced many people to leave the poor south to find jobs in the north or abroad. Social problems, corruption at high levels of society, and a succession of weak coalition governments all contributed to instability. Elections in 1996 were won by the left-wing Olive Tree alliance led by Romano Prodi, who was replaced in 1998 by an ex-Communist, Massimo d'Alema, who tried but failed to introduce a two-party system. In 2001, a centre-right coalition won a substantial majority in parliament and its leader, media tycoon Silvio Berlusconi, became prime minister.

Only 50 years ago, Italy was a mainly agricultural society – today it is a leading industrial power. It lacks mineral resources, and imports most of the raw materials used in industry. Manufactures include textiles, processed food, machinery, cars and chemicals. The chief industrial region is in the north-west.

Farmland covers around 42% of the land, pasture 17%, and forest and woodland 22%. Major crops include citrus fruits, grapes which are used to make wine, olive oil, sugar beet and vegetables. Livestock farming is important, though meat is imported.

IVORY COAST

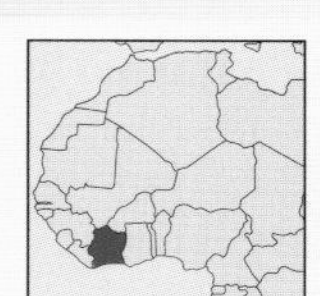

AREA 322,463 sq km [124,503 sq mi]
POPULATION 17,328,000
CAPITAL (POPULATION) Yamoussoukro (107,000)
GOVERNMENT Multiparty republic
ETHNIC GROUPS Akan 42%, Voltaiques 18%, Northern Mandes 16%, Krous 11%, Southern Mandes 10%
LANGUAGES French (official), many native dialects
RELIGIONS Islam 40%, Christianity 30%, traditional beliefs 30%
CURRENCY CFA franc = 100 centimes

GEOGRAPHY The Republic of the Ivory Coast, in West Africa, is officially known as Côte d'Ivoire. The south-east coast is bordered by sand bars that enclose lagoons. The south-west coast is lined by rocky cliffs.

Ivory Coast has a hot and humid tropical climate, with high temperatures all year. The south has two rainy seasons: between May and July, and from October to November. Inland, the rainfall decreases and the north has one dry and one rainy season.

POLITICS & ECONOMY From 1895, Ivory Coast was governed as part of French West Africa, a massive union which also included what are now Benin, Burkina Faso, Guinea, Mali, Mauritania, Niger and Senegal. In 1946, Ivory Coast became a territory in the French Union.

Ivory Coast became fully independent in 1960. Its first president, Félix Houphouët-Boigny, became the longest serving head of state in Africa with an uninterrupted period in office which ended with his death in 1993. Houphouët-Boigny, a pro-Western leader, made Ivory Coast a one-party state. In 1983, the National Assembly voted to make Yamoussoukro, the president's birthplace, the new capital. In 1999, a military coup occurred, but civilian rule was restored in 2000, when Laurent Gbagbo was elected president. However, conflict began in 2002. By 2004, the country was divided into the government-held south and the rebel-held, mainly Muslim, north.

Agriculture employs about two-thirds of the people, and farm products make up nearly half the value of the exports. Manufacturing has grown in importance since 1960; products include fertilizers, processed food, refined oil, textiles and timber.

JAMAICA

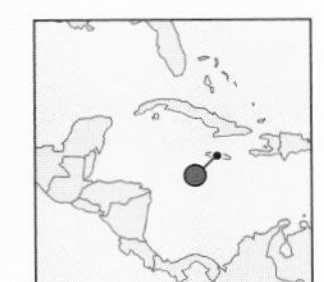

AREA 10,991 sq km [4,244 sq mi]
POPULATION 2,713,000
CAPITAL (POPULATION) Kingston (104,000)
GOVERNMENT Constitutional monarchy
ETHNIC GROUPS Black 91%, Mixed 7%, East Indian 1%
LANGUAGES English (official), patois English
RELIGIONS Protestant 61%, Roman Catholic 4%
CURRENCY Jamaican dollar = 100 cents

GEOGRAPHY Third largest of the Caribbean islands, half of Jamaica lies above 300 m [1,000 ft] and moist south-east trade winds bring rain to the central mountain range. The 'cockpit country' in the north-west of the island is an inaccessible limestone area of steep broken ridges and isolated basins.

POLITICS & ECONOMY Christopher Columbus reached the island in 1494 and claimed it for Spain. Britain took Jamaica from Spain in the 17th century and, despite slave and peasant revolts, the island did not achieve independence until 1962.

Some economic progress was made by the socialist government in the 1980s, but migration and unemployment remain high. Farming is important and sugar cane is the chief crop, but bauxite and alumina production dominate the exports and provide much of the country's income. Jamaica has some industries and tourism is a major industry.

JAPAN

AREA 377,829 sq km [145,880 sq mi]
POPULATION 127,333,000
CAPITAL (POPULATION) Tokyo (8,130,000)
GOVERNMENT Constitutional monarchy
ETHNIC GROUPS Japanese 99%, Chinese, Korean, Brazilian and others
LANGUAGES Japanese (official)
RELIGIONS Shintoism and Buddhism 84% (most Japanese consider themselves to be both Shinto and Buddhist), others
CURRENCY Yen = 100 sen

GEOGRAPHY Japan's four largest islands – Honshu, Hokkaido, Kyushu and Shikoku – make up 98% of the country. But Japan contains thousands of small islands. The four largest islands are mainly mountainous, while many of the small islands are the tips of volcanoes. Japan has more than 150 volcanoes, about 60 of which are active. Volcanic eruptions, earthquakes and tsunamis (destructive sea waves triggered by underwater earthquakes and eruptions) are common because the islands lie in an unstable part of our planet, where continental plates are always on the move. One powerful recent earthquake killed more than 5,000 people in Kobe in 1995.

The climate of Japan varies greatly from north to south. Hokkaido in the north has cold, snowy winters. At Sapporo, temperatures below –20°C [4°F] have been recorded between December and March. But summers are warm, with temperatures sometimes exceeding 30°C [86°F]. Rain falls throughout the year, though Hokkaido is one of the driest parts of Japan. Tokyo has higher rainfall and temperatures, while the southern islands of Shikoku and Kyushu have warm temperate climates. Summers are long and hot. Winters are cold.

POLITICS & ECONOMY In the late 19th century, Japan began a programme of modernization. Under its new imperial leaders, it began to look for lands to conquer. In 1894–5, it fought a war with China and, in 1904–5, it defeated Russia. Soon its overseas empire included Korea and Taiwan. In 1930, Japan invaded Manchuria (north-east China) and, in 1937, it began a war against China. In 1941, Japan launched an attack on the US base at Pearl Harbor in Hawaii. This drew both Japan and the United States into World War II.

Japan surrendered in 1945 when the Americans dropped atomic bombs on two cities, Hiroshima and Nagasaki. The United States occupied Japan until 1952. During this period, Japan adopted a democratic constitution. The emperor, who had previously been regarded as a god, became a constitutional monarch. Power was vested in the prime minister and cabinet, who are chosen from the Diet (elected parliament).

From the 1960s, Japan experienced many changes as the country rapidly built up new industries. By the early 1990s, Japan had become the world's second richest economic power after the US. But economic success has brought problems. For example, the rapid growth of cities has led to housing shortages and pollution. Another problem is that the proportion of people over 65 years of age is steadily increasing.

Japan has the world's second highest gross domestic product (GDP) after the United States. [The GDP is the total value of all goods and services produced in a country in one year.] The most important sector of the economy is industry. Yet Japan has to import most of the raw materials and fuels it needs for its industries. Its success is based on its use of the latest technology, its skilled and hard-working labour force, its vigorous export policies and its comparatively small government spending on defence. Manufactures dominate its exports, which include machinery, electrical and electronic equipment, vehicles and transport equipment, iron and steel, chemicals, textiles and ships. However, from the late 1990s, Japan experienced an economic slowdown, which merged in a recession in the early 21st century.

Japan is one of the world's top fishing nations and fish is an important source of protein. Because the land is so rugged, only 15% of the country can be farmed. Yet Japan produces about 70% of the food it needs. Rice is the chief crop, taking up about half of the total farmland. Other major products include fruits, sugar beet, tea and vegetables. Livestock farming has increased since the 1950s.

JORDAN

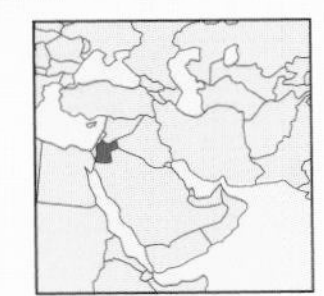

AREA 89,342 sq km [34,495 sq mi]
POPULATION 5,611,000
CAPITAL (POPULATION) Amman (1,148,000)
GOVERNMENT Constitutional monarchy
ETHNIC GROUPS Arab 98%, of which Palestinians make up roughly half
LANGUAGES Arabic (official)
RELIGIONS Islam (mostly Sunni) 94%, Christianity (mostly Greek Orthodox) 6%
CURRENCY Jordanian dinar = 1,000 fils

GEOGRAPHY The Hashemite Kingdom of Jordan is an Arab country in south-western Asia. The Great Rift Valley in the west contains the River Jordan and the Dead Sea, which Jordan shares with Israel. East of the Rift Valley is the Transjordan plateau, where most Jordanians live. To the east and south lie vast areas of desert.

Amman has a much lower rainfall and longer dry season than the Mediterranean lands to the west. The Transjordan plateau, on which Amman stands, is a transition zone between the Mediterranean climate zone to the west and the desert climate to the east.

POLITICS & ECONOMY In 1921, Britain created a territory called Transjordan east of the River Jordan. In 1923, Transjordan became self-governing, but Britain retained control of its defences, finances and foreign affairs. This territory became fully independent as Jordan in 1946.

Jordan has suffered from instability arising from the Arab–Israeli conflict since the creation of the State of Israel in 1948. After the first Arab–Israeli War in 1948–9, Jordan acquired East Jerusalem and a fertile area called the West Bank. In 1967, Israel occupied this area. In Jordan, the presence of Palestinian refugees led to civil war in 1970–1.

In 1974, Arab leaders declared that the PLO (Palestine Liberation Organization) was the sole representative of the Palestinian people. In 1988, King Hussein of Jordan renounced Jordan's claims to the West Bank and passed responsibility for it to the PLO. Opposition parties were legalized in 1991 and elections were held in 1993. In October 1994, Jordan and Israel signed a peace treaty, ending a state of war that had lasted more than 40 years. Jordan's King Hussein commanded respect for his role in Middle Eastern affairs until his death in 1999. He was succeeded by his eldest son who became Abdullah II.

Following the path of his father, Abdullah has sought to further the Israeli–Palestinian peace process, hosting a summit attended by the Israeli prime minister, Ariel Sharon, and President George W. Bush in 2003. At the same time, he has worked to consolidate his country's relations with other nations in the region. Despite local opposition to the invasion of Iraq in 2003, he supported the US-led war on terrorism and worked to improve relations with Israel.

Jordan lacks natural resources, apart from phosphates and potash, and the economy depends substantially on aid. The World Bank classifies Jordan as a 'lower-middle-income' developing country. Less than 6% of the land is farmed or used as pasture. Jordan has an oil refinery and manufactures include cement, ceramics, pharmaceuticals, processed food, fertilizers, shoes and textiles. Jordan depends on foreign aid and remittances sent home by Jordanians who have taken jobs abroad. Service industries, including tourism, employ more than 70% of the people.

KAZAKHSTAN

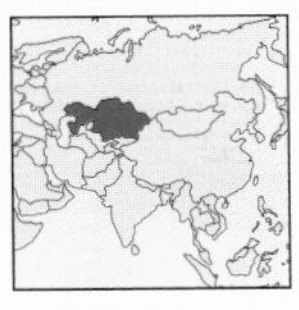

AREA 2,724,900 sq km [1,052,084 sq mi]
POPULATION 15,144,000
CAPITAL (POPULATION) Astana (322,000)
GOVERNMENT Multiparty republic
ETHNIC GROUPS Kazakh 53%, Russian 30%, Ukrainian 4%, German 2%, Uzbek 2%
LANGUAGES Kazakh (official); Russian, the former official language, is widely spoken
RELIGIONS Islam 47%, Russian Orthodox 44%
CURRENCY Tenge = 100 tiyn

GEOGRAPHY Kazakhstan is a large country in west-central Asia. In the west, the Caspian Sea lowlands include the Karagiye depression, which reaches 132 m [433 ft] below sea level. The lowlands extend eastwards through the Aral Sea area. The north contains high plains, but the highest land is along the eastern and southern borders. These areas include parts of the Altai and Tian Shan mountain ranges.

Eastern Kazakhstan contains several freshwater lakes, the largest of which is Lake Balkhash. The water in the rivers has been used for irrigation, causing ecological problems. For example, the Aral Sea, deprived of water, shrank from 66,900 sq km [25,830 sq mi] in 1960 to 33,642 sq km [12,989 sq mi] in 1993. Large areas are now barren desert.

Kazakhstan has an extreme climate. Winters are cold and snow covers the land for about 100 days at Almaty. The rainfall is generally low.

POLITICS & ECONOMY After the Russian Revolution of 1917, many Kazakhs wanted to make their country independent. But the Communists prevailed and in 1936 Kazakhstan became a republic of the Soviet Union, called the Kazakh Soviet Socialist Republic. During World War II and also after the war, the Soviet government moved many people from the west into Kazakhstan. From the 1950s, people were encouraged to work on a 'Virgin Lands' project, which involved bringing large areas of grassland under cultivation.

Reforms in the Soviet Union in the 1980s led to the break-up of the country in December 1991. Kazakhstan maintained contacts with Russia through the Commonwealth of Independent States (CIS). In 1997, the government moved its capital from Almaty to Aqmola (later renamed Astana), a town in the Russian-dominated north. It hoped that this would bring some Kazakh identity to the area. In the early 21st century, Kazakhstan's economy was in better shape than any other of the Central Asian ex-Soviet republics. However, its President Nursultan Nazarbaev was criticized for his authoritarian rule and the elections in 2004, won by his Otan party, were widely considered to be flawed.

The World Bank classifies Kazakhstan as a 'lower-middle-income' developing country. Livestock farming, especially sheep and cattle, is an important activity, and major crops include barley, cotton, rice and wheat. The country is rich in mineral resources, including coal and oil reserves, together with bauxite, copper, lead, tungsten and zinc. Manufactures include chemicals, food products, machinery and textiles. Oil is exported via a pipeline through Russia, though, to reduce dependence on Russia, Kazakhstan signed an agreement in 1997 to build a new pipeline to China. Other exports include metals, chemicals, grain, wool and meat.

KENYA

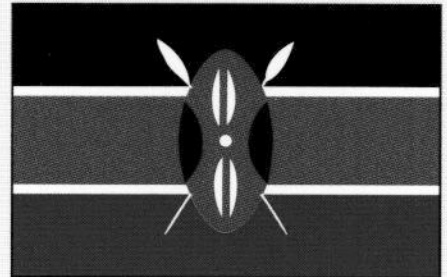

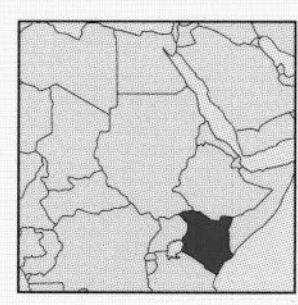

AREA 580,367 sq km [224,080 sq mi]
POPULATION 32,022,000
CAPITAL (POPULATION) Nairobi (2,143,000)
GOVERNMENT Multiparty republic
ETHNIC GROUPS Kikuyu 22%, Luhya 14%, Luo 13%, Kalenjin 12%, Kamba 11%, others
LANGUAGES Kiswahili and English (both official)
RELIGIONS Protestant 45%, Roman Catholic 33%, traditional beliefs 10%, Islam 10%
CURRENCY Kenyan shilling = 100 cents

GEOGRAPHY The Republic of Kenya is a country in East Africa which straddles the Equator. It is slightly larger in area than France. Behind the narrow coastal plain on the Indian Ocean, the land rises to high plains and highlands, broken by volcanic mountains, including Mount Kenya, the country's highest peak at 5,199 m [17,057 ft]. Crossing the country is an arm of the Great Rift Valley, on the floor of which are several lakes, including Baringo, Magadi, Naivasha, Nakuru and, on the northern frontier, Lake Turkana (formerly Lake Rudolf).

Mombasa on the coast is hot and humid. But inland, the climate is moderated by the height of the land. As a result, Nairobi, in the thickly populated south-western highlands, has summer temperatures which are 10°C [18°F] lower than Mombasa. Nights can be cool, but temperatures do not fall below freezing. Nairobi's main rainy season is from April to May, with 'little rains' in November and December. However, only about 15% of the country has a reliable rainfall of 800 mm [31 in].

POLITICS & ECONOMY The Kenyan coast has been a trading centre for more than 2,000 years. Britain took over the coast in 1895 and soon extended its influence inland. In the 1950s, a secret movement, called Mau Mau, launched an armed struggle against British rule. Although Mau Mau was eventually defeated, Kenya became independent in 1963.

Many Kenyans felt that Kenya should have a strong central government, and Kenya was a one-party state for much of the time since 1963. But democracy was restored in the early 1990s and elections were held in 1992, 1997 and 2002. In 1999, Kenya, with Tanzania and Uganda, set up an East African Community, which aimed to create a customs union, a common market, a monetary union, and, ultimately, a political union.

When it became a republic in 1964, Kenya's first president was the nationalist veteran Jomo Kenyatta, who died in 1978. He was succeeded by the vice-president, Daniel arap Moi, who stood down in 2002 after having been criticized for his autocratic rule, as well as corruption. The veteran Mwai Kibaki was elected president in 2002, promising to stamp out corruption. But, by 2005, he was widely criticized for failing to fulfil his election pledge.

According to the United Nations, Kenya is a 'low-income' developing country. Agriculture employs about 80% of the people, but many Kenyans are subsistence farmers, growing little more than they need to support their families. The chief food crop is maize. The main cash crops and leading exports are coffee and tea. Manufactures include chemicals, leather and footwear, processed food, petroleum products and textiles.

KIRIBATI

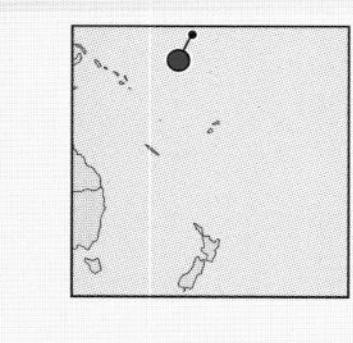

AREA 726 sq km [280 sq mi]
POPULATION 101,000
CAPITAL (POPULATION) Tarawa (32,000)

The Republic of Kiribati comprises three groups of low-lying coral atolls scattered over 5 million sq km [2 million sq mi], which are threatened by global warming and consequent rising sea levels. Kiribati straddles the Equator and temperatures are high throughout the year. The rainfall is abundant.

The Gilbert and Ellice Islands became a British protectorate in 1892 and a colony in 1915. In 1975, the Ellice Islands, following a referendum, officially severed its links with the Gilbert Islands and became a separate territory called Tuvalu in 1978. In 1979, the Gilbert Islands became fully independent as the Republic of Kiribati. The main export is copra and the country depends heavily on foreign aid.

KOREA, NORTH

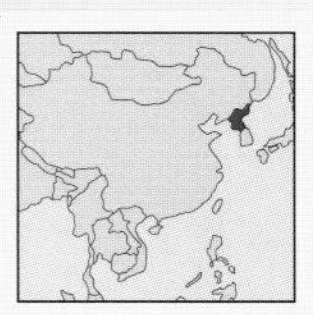

AREA 120,538 sq km [46,540 sq mi]
POPULATION 22,698,000
CAPITAL (POPULATION) Pyŏngyang (2,725,000)
GOVERNMENT Single-party people's republic
ETHNIC GROUPS Korean 99%
LANGUAGES Korean (official)
RELIGIONS Buddhism and Confucianism
CURRENCY North Korean won = 100 chon

GEOGRAPHY The Democratic People's Republic of Korea occupies the northern part of the Korean peninsula which extends south from north-eastern China. Mountains form the heart of the country, with the highest peak, Paektu-san, reaching 2,744 m [9,003 ft] on the northern border. In winter, winds blow from across central Asia, bringing snow and freezing conditions. In summer, moist oceanic winds bring rain.

POLITICS & ECONOMY North Korea was created in 1945, when the peninsula, a Japanese colony since 1910, was divided into two parts. Soviet forces occupied the north, with US forces in the south. Soviet occupation led to a Communist government being established in 1948 under the leadership of Kim Il Sung. He created a Stalinist regime and ruled as a dictator. He also became the world's most durable Communist leader.

The Korean War began in June 1950 when North Korean troops invaded the south. North Korea, aided by China and the Soviet Union, fought with South Korea, which was supported by troops from the United States and other UN members. The war ended in July 1953. An armistice was signed but no permanent peace treaty was agreed. After the war, North Korea adopted a hostile policy towards South Korea in pursuit of its policy of reunification.

The ending of the Cold War in the late 1980s eased the situation and both North and South Korea joined the United Nations in 1991. The two countries made several agreements, including one in which they agreed not to use force against each other. However, North Korea remained as isolated as ever.

In 1993, North Korea began a new international crisis by announcing that it was withdrawing from the Nuclear Non-Proliferation Treaty. This led to suspicions that North Korea, which had signed the Treaty in 1985, was developing its own nuclear weapons. Kim Il Sung, who had ruled as a virtual dictator from 1948 until his death in 1994, was succeeded by his son, Kim Jong Il.

In the early 2000s, attempts were made to reconcile the two Koreas, though the prospect of reunification seemed remote. In 2003, North Korea's relations with the United States deteriorated when the US accused the country of having a secret nuclear weapons programme. In 2005, North Korea withdrew from international talks, stating that it had already produced nuclear weapons.

North Korea has considerable resources, including coal, copper, iron ore, lead, tin, tungsten and zinc. Under Communism, North Korea has concentrated on developing heavy, state-owned industries. Manufactures include chemicals, iron and steel, machinery, processed food and textiles. Agriculture employs about a third of the people of North Korea and rice is the leading crop. Economic decline and mismanagement, aggravated by three successive crop failures caused by floods in 1995 and 1996 and a drought in 1997, led to famine on a large scale.

KOREA, SOUTH

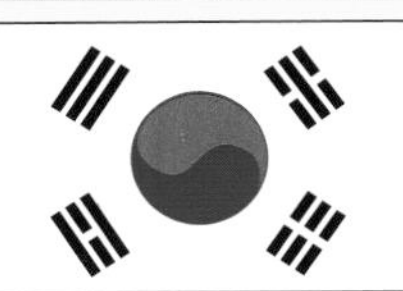

AREA 99,268 sq km [38,327 sq mi]
POPULATION 48,598,000
CAPITAL (POPULATION) Seoul (9,888,000)
GOVERNMENT Multiparty republic
ETHNIC GROUPS Korean 99%
LANGUAGES Korean (official)
RELIGIONS No affiliation 46%, Christianity 26%, Buddhism 26%, Confucianism 1%
CURRENCY South Korean won = 100 chon

GEOGRAPHY The Republic of Korea, as South Korea is officially known, occupies the southern part of the Korean peninsula. Mountains cover much of the country. The southern and western coasts are major farming regions. Many islands are found along the west and south coasts. The largest is Cheju-do, which contains South Korea's highest peak, which rises to 1,950 m [6,398 ft].

Like North Korea, South Korea is chilled in winter by cold, dry winds blowing from central Asia. Snow often covers the mountains in the east. The summers are hot and wet, especially in July and August.

POLITICS & ECONOMY After Japan's defeat in World War II (1939–45), North Korea was occupied by troops from the Soviet Union, while South Korea was occupied by United States forces. Attempts to reunify Korea failed and, in 1948, a National Assembly was elected in South Korea. This Assembly created the Republic of Korea, while North Korea became a Communist state. North Korean troops invaded the South in June 1950, sparking off the Korean War (1950–3).

In the 1950s, South Korea had a weak economy, which had been further damaged by the destruction caused by the Korean War. From the 1960s to the 1980s, South Korean governments worked to industrialize the economy. The governments were dominated by military leaders, who often used authoritarian methods and flouted human rights. In 1987, a new constitution was approved, enabling presidential elections to be held every five years. In 1991, South and North Korea became members of the United Nations and they signed agreements, including one in which they agreed not to use force against each other. Tensions continued, though hopes were raised by South Korea's 'sunshine policy', which involved negotiations between the two countries which took place in the early 21st century.

The World Bank classifies South Korea as an 'upper-middle-income' developing country. It is also one of the world's fastest growing industrial economies. The country's resources include coal and tungsten, and its main manufactures are processed food and textiles. Since partition, heavy industries have been built up, making chemicals, fertilizers, iron and steel, and ships. South Korea has also developed the production of such things as computers, cars and television sets. In late 1997, however, the dramatic expansion of the economy was halted by a market crash which affected many of the booming economies of Asia. However, South Korea recovered faster than any other country in the region, and huge inflows of foreign investment and strict financial measures, including the restructuring of its short-term debt, led to the restoration of confidence and economic growth.

Farming remains important in South Korea. Rice is the chief crop, together with fruit, grains and vegetables, while fishing provides a major source of protein.

KUWAIT

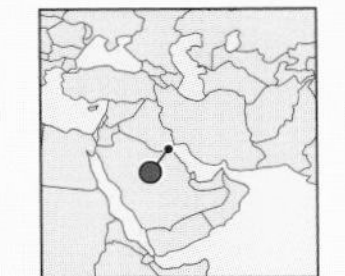

AREA 17,818 sq km [6,880 sq mi]
POPULATION 2,258,000
CAPITAL (POPULATION) Kuwait City (29,000)

The State of Kuwait at the north end of the Persian Gulf is largely made up of desert. Temperatures are high and the rainfall low. Kuwait became independent from Britain in 1961 and revenues from its oil wells have made it prosperous. Iraq invaded Kuwait in 1990 and much damage was inflicted in the conflict in 1991 when Kuwait was liberated. In 2004, the government announced draft legislation for women to vote and stand for parliament.

KYRGYZSTAN

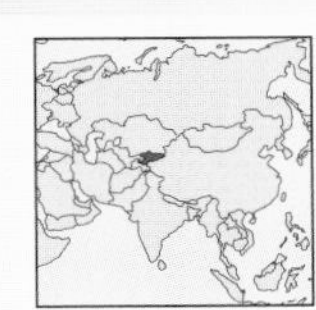

AREA 199,900 sq km [77,181 sq mi]
POPULATION 5,081,000
CAPITAL (POPULATION) Bishkek (753,000)
GOVERNMENT Multiparty republic
ETHNIC GROUPS Kyrgyz 65%, Russian 13%, Uzbek 13%, Ukrainian 1%, others
LANGUAGES Kyrgyz and Russian (both official)
RELIGIONS Islam 75%, Russian Orthodox 20%
CURRENCY Kyrgyzstani som = 100 tyiyn

GEOGRAPHY The Republic of Kyrgyzstan is a landlocked country between China, Tajikistan, Uzbekistan and Kazakhstan. The country is mountainous, with spectacular scenery. The highest mountain, Pik Pobedy in the Tian Shan range, reaches 7,439 m [24,406 ft] in the east. The lowlands have warm summers and cold winters. But January temperatures in the mountains plummet to –28°C [–18°F]. Kyrgyzstan has a low annual rainfall.

POLITICS & ECONOMY In 1876, Kyrgyzstan became a province of Russia and Russian settlement in the area began. In 1916, Russia crushed a rebellion among the Kyrgyz, and many subsequently fled to China. In 1922, the area became an autonomous *oblast* (self-governing region) of the newly formed Soviet Union but, in 1936, it became one of the Soviet Socialist Republics. Under Communist rule, local customs and religious worship were suppressed, but education and health services were greatly improved.

In 1991, Kyrgyzstan became an independent country following the break-up of the Soviet Union. The Communist party was dissolved, but the country maintained ties with Russia through an organization called the Commonwealth of Independent States. Elections were held under a new constitution adopted in 1994. However, massive protests followed flawed parliamentary elections in 2005. Askar Akaev, who had served as president since 1990 but who had monopolized power and his country's limited resources, fled into exile.

In the early 1990s, when Kyrgyzstan was working to reform its economy, the World Bank classified it as a 'lower-middle-income' developing country. Agriculture, especially livestock rearing, is the chief activity. The chief products include cotton, eggs, fruits, grain, tobacco, vegetables and wool. But food must be imported. Industries are mainly concentrated around the capital Bishkek.

LAOS

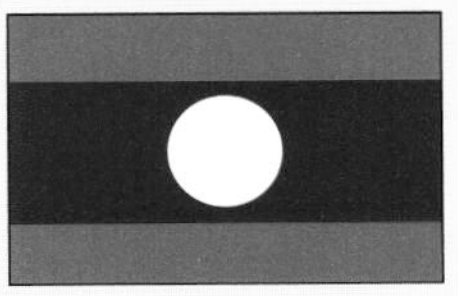

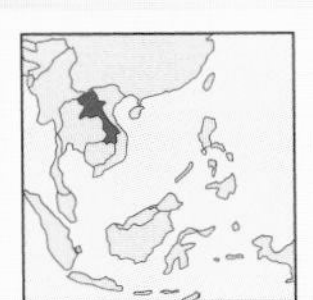

AREA 236,800 sq km [91,428 sq mi]
POPULATION 6,068,000
CAPITAL (POPULATION) Vientiane (528,000)
GOVERNMENT Single-party republic
ETHNIC GROUPS Lao Loum 68%, Lao Theung 22%, Lao Soung 9%
LANGUAGES Lao (official), French, English
RELIGIONS Buddhism 60%, traditional beliefs and others 40%
CURRENCY Kip = 100 at

GEOGRAPHY The Lao People's Democratic Republic is a landlocked country in South-east Asia. Mountains and plateaux cover much of Laos. Most people live on the plains bordering the River Mekong and its tributaries. The Mekong, one of Asia's longest rivers, forms much of the country's western borders.

Laos has a tropical monsoon climate. Winters are dry and sunny, with winds blowing from the north-east. The temperatures rise until April, when the wind directions are reversed. Moist south-westerly winds then arrive, heralding the start of the wet monsoon season.

POLITICS & ECONOMY France made Laos a protectorate in the late 19th century and ruled it as part of French Indo-China, a region which also included Cambodia and Vietnam. Laos became a member of the French Union in 1948 and an independent kingdom in 1954.

After independence, Laos suffered from instability caused by a long power struggle between royalist government forces and a pro-Communist group called the Pathet Lao. A civil war broke out in 1960 and continued into the 1970s. The Pathet Lao took control in 1975 and the king abdicated. Laos then came under the influence of Communist Vietnam, which had used Laos as a supply base during the Vietnam War (1957–75). From the early 1980s, the economy deteriorated and opposition appeared when bombings occurred in Vientiane in 2000. They were attributed to rebels in the minority Hmong tribe or to politicians who wanted faster economic reforms.

Laos is one of the world's poorest countries. Agriculture employs 76% of the people. Rice is the main crop, and timber and coffee are exported. But the most valuable export is electricity, which is produced at hydroelectric power stations on the River Mekong and is exported to Thailand. Laos also produces opium.

LATVIA

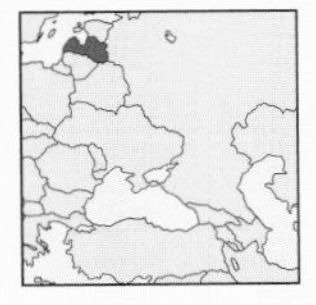

AREA 64,600 sq km [24,942 sq mi]
POPULATION 2,306,000
CAPITAL (POPULATION) Riga (793,000)
GOVERNMENT Multiparty republic
ETHNIC GROUPS Latvian 58%, Russian 30%, Belarusian, Ukrainian, Polish, Lithuanian
LANGUAGES Latvian (official), Lithuanian, Russian
RELIGIONS Lutheran, Roman Catholic, Russian Orthodox
CURRENCY Latvian lat = 10 santimi

GEOGRAPHY The Republic of Latvia is one of three states on the south-eastern corner of the Baltic Sea which were ruled as parts of the Soviet Union between 1940 and 1991. Latvia consists mainly of flat plains separated by low hills.

Riga has warm summers, but temperatures between December and March are subzero. Moderate rainfall occurs throughout the year, with light snow in winter.

POLITICS & ECONOMY In 1800, Russia was in control of Latvia, but Latvians declared their independence after World War I. In 1940, under a German-Soviet pact, Soviet troops occupied Latvia, but they were driven out by the Germans in 1941. Soviet troops returned in 1944 and Latvia became part of the Soviet Union. Under Soviet rule, many Russian immigrants settled in Latvia and many Latvians feared that the Russians would become the dominant ethnic group.

In the late 1980s, when reforms were being introduced in the Soviet Union, Latvia's government ended absolute Communist rule and made Latvian the official language. In 1990, it declared the country to be independent, an act which was finally recognized by the Soviet Union in September 1991.

Latvia held its first free elections to its parliament (the Saeima) in 1993. Voting was limited only to citizens of Latvia on 17 June 1940 and their descendants. This meant that about 34% of Latvian residents were unable to vote. In 1994, Latvia restricted the naturalization of non-Latvians, including many Russian settlers, who were not allowed to vote or own land. However, in 1998, the government agreed that all children born since independence should have automatic citizenship. Its cultivation of closer ties to the West proved successful in 2004, when Latvia was admitted to membership of both the North Atlantic Treaty Organization (NATO) and the European Union (EU).

The World Bank classifies Latvia as a 'lower-middle-income' country and, in the 1990s, it faced many problems in turning its economy into a free-market system. Products include electronic goods, farm machinery, fertilizers, processed food, plastics, radios and vehicles. Latvia produces only about a tenth of the electricity it needs. It imports the rest from Belarus, Russia and Ukraine.

LEBANON

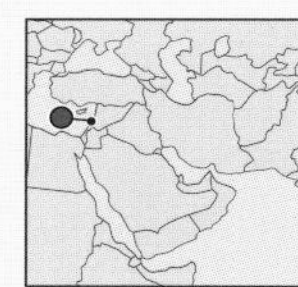

AREA 10,400 sq km [4,015 sq mi]
POPULATION 3,777,000
CAPITAL (POPULATION) Beirut (1,148,000)
GOVERNMENT Multiparty republic
ETHNIC GROUPS Arab 95%, Armenian 4%, others
LANGUAGES Arabic (official), French, English, Armenian
RELIGIONS Islam 70%, Christianity 30%
CURRENCY Lebanese pound = 100 piastres

GEOGRAPHY The Republic of Lebanon is a country on the eastern shores of the Mediterranean Sea. Behind the coastal plain are the rugged Lebanon Mountains (Jabal Lubnan). Between this range and the Anti-Lebanon Mountains (Al Jabal ash Sharqi) lies the fertile Bekaa (Beqaa) Valley. The coast has hot dry summers and mild wet winters. Inland, in winter, onshore winds bring heavy rain and snow to the western slopes of the mountains.

POLITICS & ECONOMY Lebanon was ruled by Turkey from 1516 until World War I. France ruled the country from 1923, but Lebanon became independent in 1946. After independence, the Muslims and Christians agreed to share power, and Lebanon made rapid economic progress. But from the late 1950s, development was slowed by periodic conflict between Sunni and Shia Muslims, Druze and Christians. The situation was further complicated by the presence of Palestinian refugees who used bases in Lebanon to attack Israel.

In 1975, civil war broke out as private armies representing the many factions struggled for power. This led to intervention by Israel in the south and Syria in the north. UN peacekeeping forces arrived in 1978, but bombings, assassinations and kidnappings became almost everyday events in the 1980s. From 1991, Lebanon enjoyed an uneasy peace. But, Israel continued to occupy an area in the south. In the 1990s, Israel launched several attacks on pro-Iranian Hezbollah guerrillas in Lebanon, but all Israeli troops were withdrawn in 2000. The assassination in 2005 of Rafik Hariri, former prime minister, who had helped to rebuild his shattered country, was blamed by many on Syria, which maintained a military force in Lebanon. Syria promised to withdraw its forces.

Lebanon's civil war almost destroyed valuable trade and financial services that had been Lebanon's chief source of income, together with tourism. Manufacturing, which had formerly been a major activity, was badly hit.

LESOTHO

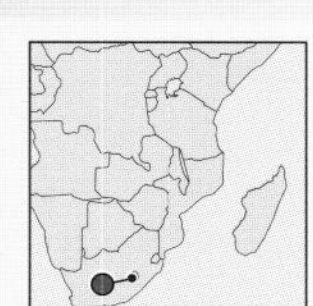

AREA 30,355 sq km [11,720 sq mi]
POPULATION 1,865,000
CAPITAL (POPULATION) Maseru (109,000)
GOVERNMENT Constitutional monarchy
ETHNIC GROUPS Sotho 99%
LANGUAGES Sesotho and English (both official)
RELIGIONS Christianity 80%, traditional beliefs 20%
CURRENCY Loti = 100 lisente

GEOGRAPHY The Kingdom of Lesotho is a landlocked country, completely enclosed by South Africa. The land is mountainous, rising to 3,482 m [11,424 ft] on the north-eastern border. The Drakensberg range covers most of the country.

The climate of Lesotho is greatly affected by the altitude, because most of the country lies above 1,500 m [4,921 ft]. Maseru has warm summers, but the temperatures fall below freezing in the winter. The mountains are colder. The rainfall varies, averaging around 700 mm [28 in].

POLITICS & ECONOMY The Basotho nation was founded in the 1820s by King Moshoeshoe I, who united various groups fleeing from tribal wars in southern Africa. Britain made the area a protectorate in 1868 and, in 1871, placed it under the British Cape Colony in South Africa. But in 1884, Basutoland, as the area was called, was reconstituted as a British protectorate, where whites were not allowed to own land.

The country finally became independent in 1966 as the Kingdom of Lesotho, with Moshoeshoe II, great-grandson of Moshoeshoe I, as its king. Since independence, Lesotho has suffered instability. The military seized power in 1986 and stripped Moshoeshoe II of his powers in 1990, installing his son, Letsie III, as monarch. After elections in 1993, Moshoeshoe II was restored to office in 1995. But after his death in a car crash in 1996, Letsie III again became king. In 1998, an army revolt, following an election in which the ruling party won 79 out of the 80 seats, caused much damage to the economy. In 2004, the government declared a state of emergency following three years of drought.

Lesotho is a 'low-income' developing country. It lacks natural resources. Agriculture employs two-thirds of the people, but most farmers live at subsistence level. Livestock farming is important. Other sources of incomes include the products of light manufacturing and remittances sent home by Basotho working abroad.

LIBERIA

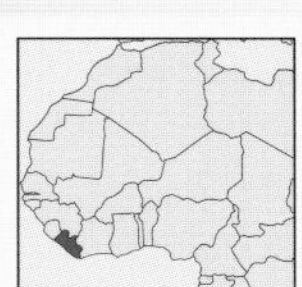

AREA 111,369 sq km [43,000 sq mi]
POPULATION 3,391,000
CAPITAL (POPULATION) Monrovia (421,000)
GOVERNMENT Multiparty republic
ETHNIC GROUPS Indigenous African tribes 95% (including Kpelle, Bassa, Grebo, Gio, Kru, Mano)
LANGUAGES English (official), ethnic languages
RELIGIONS Christianity 40%, Islam 20%, traditional beliefs and others 40%
CURRENCY Liberian dollar = 100 cents

GEOGRAPHY The Republic of Liberia is a country in West Africa. Behind the coastline, 500 km [311 mi] long, lies a narrow coastal plain. Beyond, the land rises to a plateau region, with the highest land along the border with Guinea.

Liberia has a tropical climate with high temperatures and high humidity all through the year. The rainfall is abundant all year round, but there is a particularly wet period from June to November. The rainfall generally increases from east to west.

POLITICS & ECONOMY In the late 18th century, some white Americans in the United States wanted to help freed black slaves to return to Africa. In 1816, they set up the American Colonization Society, which bought land in what is now Liberia.

In 1822, the Society landed former slaves at a settlement on the coast which they named Monrovia. In 1847, Liberia became a fully independent republic with a constitution much like that of the United States. For many years, the Americo-Liberians controlled the country's government. US influence remained strong and the American Firestone Company, which ran Liberia's rubber plantations, was especially influential. Foreign companies were also involved in exploiting Liberia's mineral resources, including its huge iron-ore deposits.

In 1980, a military group composed of people from the local population killed the Americo-Liberian president, William R. Tolbert. An army sergeant, Samuel K. Doe, was made president of Liberia. Elections held in 1985 resulted in victory for Doe.

From 1989, the country was plunged into civil war between various ethnic groups. Doe was assassinated in 1990 and the struggle with rebel groups continued. West African peacekeeping forces arrived in Liberia and, in 1995, a cease-fire was agreed. A council of state, composed of former warlords, was set up and, in 1997, one of the warlords, Charles Taylor, was elected president. Conflict continued and Taylor finally left the country in 2003. Since then, the United Nations has worked to restore order.

Liberia's civil war devastated its economy. Three out of every four people depend on agriculture, though many of them grow little more than they need to feed their families. Major food crops include cassava, rice and sugar cane, while rubber, cocoa and coffee are exported. But the most valuable export is iron ore.

Liberia also obtains revenue from its 'flag of convenience', which is used by about one-sixth of the world's commercial shipping, exploiting low taxes.

LIBYA

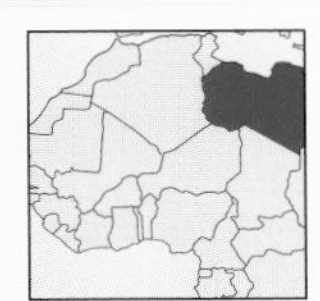

AREA 1,759,540 sq km [679,358 sq mi]
POPULATION 5,632,000
CAPITAL (POPULATION) Tripoli (1,500,000)
GOVERNMENT Single-party socialist state
ETHNIC GROUPS Libyan Arab and Berber 97%
LANGUAGES Arabic (official), Berber
RELIGIONS Islam (Sunni Muslim) 97%
CURRENCY Libyan dinar = 1,000 dirhams

GEOGRAPHY The Socialist People's Libyan Arab Jamahiriya, as Libya is officially called, is a large country in North Africa. Most people live on the coastal plains in the north-east and north-west. The Sahara, which occupies 95% of Libya, reaches the Mediterranean coast along the Gulf of Sidra (Khalij Surt). The north-eastern and north-western coastal plains have Mediterranean climates, with hot, dry summers and mild, moist winters. Inland, the average annual rainfall drops to 100 mm [4 in] or less.

POLITICS & ECONOMY Italy took over Libya in 1911, but lost it during World War II. Britain and France then jointly ruled Libya until 1951, when the country became an independent kingdom.

In 1969, a military group headed by Colonel Muammar Gaddafi deposed the king and set up a military government. Under Gaddafi, the government took control of the economy and used money from oil exports to finance welfare services and development projects. Gaddafi was criticized for supporting terrorist groups around the world, and Libya became isolated from the mid-1980s. In 1998, he tried to restore Libya's reputation by surrendering for trial two Libyans suspected of planting a bomb on a PanAm plane which exploded over the Scottish town of Lockerbie in 1988. In 2003, Libya announced an agreement to pay compensation to victims of the bombing. In 2004, Libya announced that it was abandoning programmes to produce weapons of mass destruction. Libya's initiatives were rewarded by visits to Libya by several Western leaders.

The discovery of oil and natural gas in 1959 led to the transformation of Libya's economy. Once one of the world's poorest countries, it has become Africa's richest in terms of its per capita income. It remains a developing country because of its dependence on oil, which accounts for nearly all of its export revenues.

Agriculture is important, although Libya has to import food. Crops include barley, citrus fruits, dates, olives, potatoes and wheat. Cattle, sheep and poultry are raised. Libya has oil refineries and petrochemical plants. Other manufactures include cement and steel.

LIECHTENSTEIN

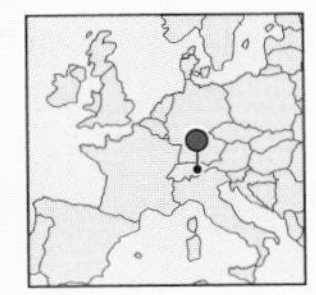

AREA 160 sq km [62 sq mi]
POPULATION 33,000
CAPITAL (POPULATION) Vaduz (5,000)

The tiny Principality of Liechtenstein is sandwiched between Switzerland and Austria. The River Rhine flows along its western border, while Alpine peaks rise in the east and south. The climate is relatively mild, with the annual precipitation averaging about 890 mm [35 in].

Liechtenstein has been an independent principality since 1719, except for a brief period in the early 19th century when it was controlled by Napoleon I of France. After World War I (1914–18), Switzerland represented Liechtenstein abroad and Swiss currency was adopted in 1921. Since 1924, Liechtenstein has been in a customs union with Switzerland. Taxation is low and the country is a haven for foreign companies. In 2003, the people voted to give their head of state, Prince Hans Adam III, sovereign powers. In 2004, he handed over the running of the country to his son, Prince Alois, while remaining the titular head of state.

LITHUANIA

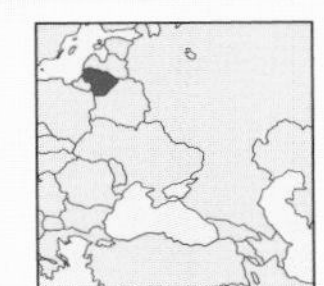

AREA 65,200 sq km [25,174 sq mi]
POPULATION 3,608,000
CAPITAL (POPULATION) Vilnius (578,000)
GOVERNMENT Multiparty republic
ETHNIC GROUPS Lithuanian 80%, Russian 9%, Polish 7%, Belarusian 2%
LANGUAGES Lithuanian (official), Russian, Polish
RELIGIONS Mainly Roman Catholic
CURRENCY Litas = 100 centai

GEOGRAPHY The Republic of Lithuania is the southernmost of the three Baltic states which were ruled as part of the Soviet Union between 1940 and 1991. Much of the land is flat or gently rolling, with the highest land in the south-east.

Winters are cold. January's temperatures average –3°C [27°F] in the west and –6°C [21°F] in the east. Summers are warm, with average temperatures in July of 17°C [63°F]. The average rainfall in the west is about 630 mm [25 in]. Inland areas are drier.

POLITICS & ECONOMY The Lithuanian people were united into a single nation in the 12th century, and later joined a union with Poland. In 1795, Lithuania came under Russian rule. After World War I (1914–18), Lithuania declared itself independent, and in 1920 it signed a peace treaty with the Russians, though Poland held Vilnius until 1939. In 1940, the Soviet Union occupied Lithuania, but the Germans invaded in 1941. Soviet forces returned in 1944, and Lithuania was integrated into the Soviet Union. In 1988, when the Soviet Union was introducing reforms, the Lithuanians demanded independence. Their language is one of the oldest in the world, and the country was always the most homogenous of the Baltic states, staunchly Catholic and resistant of attempts to suppress their culture. Pro-independence groups won the national elections in 1990 and, in 1991, the Soviet Union recognized Lithuania's independence.

Since 1991, Lithuania has sought to reform its economy and introduce a private enterprise system, which was close to completion a decade later. Lithuania has also drawn closer to the West and, in 2004, Lithuania became a member of the North Atlantic Treaty Organization (NATO) and, on 1 May, a member of the European Union.

The World Bank classifies Lithuania as a 'middle-income' country. In 2001, agriculture accounted for 7% of the gross domestic product, industry 24% and services 60%. Lithuania's main exports include mineral fuels, textiles and clothing, machinery, food products and chemical products. By 2001, the leading buyers of Lithuania's exports were the United Kingdom, Latvia and Germany, but Russia still supplied about 25% of the country's imports.

LUXEMBOURG

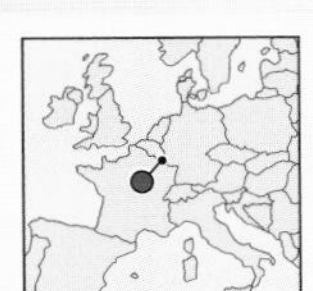

AREA 2,586 sq km [998 sq mi]
POPULATION 463,000
CAPITAL (POPULATION) Luxembourg (77,000)
GOVERNMENT Constitutional monarchy (Grand Duchy)
ETHNIC GROUPS Luxembourger 71%, Portuguese, Italian, French, Belgian, Slavs
LANGUAGES Luxembourgish (official), French, German
RELIGIONS Roman Catholic 87%, others 13%
CURRENCY Euro = 100 cents

GEOGRAPHY The Grand Duchy of Luxembourg is one of the smallest and oldest countries in Europe. The north belongs to an upland region which includes the Ardenne in Belgium and Luxembourg, and the Eifel highlands in Germany.

Luxembourg has a temperate climate. The south has warm summers and autumns, when grapes ripen in sheltered south-eastern valleys. Winters are sometimes severe, especially in upland areas.

POLITICS & ECONOMY Germany occupied Luxembourg in World Wars I and II. In 1944–5, northern Luxembourg was the scene of the famous Battle of the Bulge. In 1948, Luxembourg joined Belgium and the Netherlands in a union called Benelux and, in the 1950s, it was one of the six founders of what is now the European Union. Luxembourg has played a major role in Europe. Its capital contains the headquarters of several international agencies, including the European Coal and Steel Community and the European Court of Justice. The city is also a major financial centre.

Luxembourg has iron-ore reserves and is a major steel producer. It also has many high-technology industries, producing electronic goods and computers. Steel and other manufactures, including chemicals, rubber products, glass and aluminium, dominate the country's exports. Other major activities include tourism and financial services.

MACEDONIA (FYROM)

AREA 25,713 sq km [9,928 sq mi]
POPULATION 2,071,000
CAPITAL (POPULATION) Skopje (430,000)
GOVERNMENT Multiparty republic
ETHNIC GROUPS Macedonian 64%, Albanian 25%, Turkish 4%, Romanian 3%, Serb 2%
LANGUAGES Macedonian and Albanian (official)
RELIGIONS Macedonian Orthodox 70%, Islam 29%
CURRENCY Macedonian denar = 100 paras

GEOGRAPHY The Republic of Macedonia is a country in south-eastern Europe, which was once one of the six republics that made up the former Federal People's Republic of Yugoslavia. This landlocked country is largely mountainous or hilly.

Macedonia has hot summers, though highland areas are cooler. Winters are cold and snowfalls are often heavy. The climate is fairly continental in character and rain occurs throughout the year.

POLITICS & ECONOMY Until the 20th century, Macedonia's history was closely tied to a larger area, also called Macedonia, which included parts of northern Greece and south-western Bulgaria. This region reached its peak in power at the time of Philip II (382–336 BC) and his son Alexander the Great (336–323 BC). After Alexander's death, his empire was split up and it gradually declined. The area became a Roman province in the 140s BC and part of the Byzantine Empire from AD 395.

In the 6th century, Slavs from eastern Europe settled in the area, followed by the Bulgars from central Asia in the 9th century. The Byzantine Empire regained control in 1018, but Serbia took Macedonia in the early 14th century. In 1371, the Ottoman Turks conquered the area and ruled it for more than 500 years. The Ottoman Empire began to collapse in the late 19th century. In 1913, at the end of the Balkan Wars, the area was divided between Serbia, Bulgaria and Greece. At the end of World War I, Serbian Macedonia became part of the Kingdom of the Serbs. Croats and Slovenes, which was renamed Yugoslavia in 1929. After World War II, Yugoslavia became a Communist country under ex-partisan leader Josip Broz Tito.

Tito died in 1980 and, in the early 1990s, the country broke up into five separate republics. Macedonia declared its independence in September 1991. Greece objected to this territory using the name Macedonia, which it considered to be a Greek name. It also objected to a symbol on Macedonia's flag and a reference in the constitution to the desire to reunite the three parts of the old Macedonia. In 1993, the United Nations accepted the new republic as a member under the name of The Former Yugoslav Republic of Macedonia (FYROM).

By the end of 1993, all the countries of the EU, except Greece, were establishing diplomatic relations with the FYROM. In 1995, Greece lifted its trade ban, when Macedonia agreed to redesign its flag and remove territorial claims from its constitution. In 2001, fighting along the Kosovo border spilled over into Macedonia. It was attributed to nationalists who wanted to create a Greater Albania. The uprising ended when Macedonian Albanian-speakers were given increased rights. In 2004, the USA recognized the name Republic of Macedonia instead of FYROM. Other nations were expected to follow this lead, despite Greek objections.

The World Bank describes Macedonia as a 'lower-middle-income' developing country. Manufactures dominate the country's exports. Macedonia mines coal, but imports all its oil and natural gas. The country is self-sufficient in its basic food needs.

MADAGASCAR

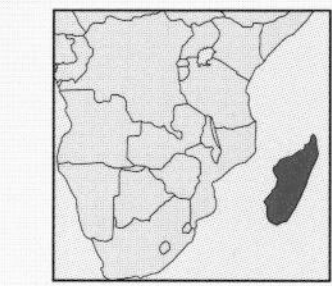

AREA 587,041 sq km [226,657 sq mi]
POPULATION 17,502,000
CAPITAL (POPULATION) Antananarivo (1,250,000)
GOVERNMENT Republic
ETHNIC GROUPS Merina, Betsimisaraka, Betsileo, Tsimihety, Sakalava and others
LANGUAGES Malagasy and French (both official)
RELIGIONS Traditional beliefs 52%, Christianity 41%, Islam 7%
CURRENCY Malagasy franc = 100 centimes

GEOGRAPHY The Democratic Republic of Madagascar, in south-eastern Africa, is an island nation, which has a larger area than France. Behind the narrow coastal plains in the east lies a highland zone, mostly between 610 m and 1,220 m [2,000 ft to 4,000 ft] above sea level. Broad plains border the Mozambique Channel in the west.

Temperatures in the highlands are moderated by the altitude. The winters (from April to September) are dry, but heavy rains occur in summer. The eastern coastlands are warm and humid. The west is drier and the south and south-west are hot and dry.

POLITICS & ECONOMY People from South-east Asia began to settle on Madagascar around 2,000 years ago. Subsequent influxes from Africa and Arabia added to the island's diverse heritage, culture and language.

French troops defeated a Malagasy army in 1895 and Madagascar became a French colony. In 1960, it achieved full independence as the Malagasy Republic. In 1972, army officers seized control and, in 1975, under the leadership of Lt-Commander Didier Ratsiraka, the country was renamed Madagascar. Parliamentary elections were held in 1977, but Ratsiraka remained president of a one-party socialist state. In 2002, the country came close to civil war when Ratsiraka and his opponent, Marc Ravalomanana, both claimed victory in presidential elections. Ravalomanana was eventually recognized as president and Ratsiraka went into exile.

Madagascar is one of the world's poorest countries. The land has been badly eroded because of the cutting down of the forests and overgrazing of the grasslands. Farming, fishing and forestry employ about 80% of the people. The country's food crops include bananas, cassava, rice and sweet potatoes. Coffee is the leading export.

MALAWI

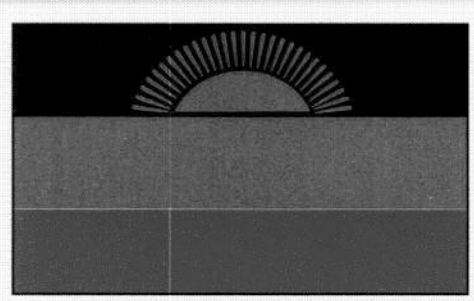

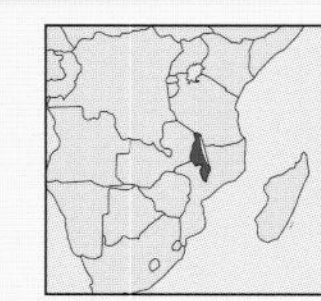

AREA 118,484 sq km [45,747 sq mi]
POPULATION 11,907,000
CAPITAL (POPULATION) Lilongwe (440,000)
GOVERNMENT Multiparty republic
ETHNIC GROUPS Chewa, Nyanja, Tonga, Tumbuka, Lomwe, Yao, Ngoni and others
LANGUAGES Chichewa and English (both official)
RELIGIONS Protestant 55%, Roman Catholic 20%, Islam 20%
CURRENCY Malawian kwacha = 100 tambala

GEOGRAPHY The Republic of Malawi includes part of Lake Malawi, which is drained by the River Shire, a tributary of the River Zambezi. The land is mostly mountainous. The highest peak, Mulanje, reaches 3,000 m [9,843 ft] in the south-east.

While the low-lying areas of Malawi are hot and humid all year round, the uplands have a pleasant climate. Lilongwe, at about 1,100 m [3,609 ft] above sea level, has a warm and sunny climate. Frosts sometimes occur in July and August, in the middle of the long dry season.

POLITICS & ECONOMY Malawi, then called Nyasaland, became a British protectorate in 1891. In 1953, Britain established the Federation of Rhodesia and Nyasaland, which also included what are now Zambia and Zimbabwe. Black African opposition, led in Nyasaland by Dr Hastings Kamuzu Banda, led to the dissolution of the federation in 1963.

In 1964, Nyasaland became independent as Malawi, with Banda as prime minister. Banda became president when the country became a republic in 1966 and, in 1971, he was made president for life. Banda ruled autocratically through the only party, the Malawi Congress Party. A multiparty system was restored in 1993 and Bakili Muluzi became president. He was succeeded in 2004 by Bingu wa Mutharika.

Malawi is one of the world's poorest countries. More than 80% of the people are farmers, but many grow little more than they need to feed their families. Crops include cotton, groundnuts, maize, sorghum and sugar cane. The leading exports are tobacco, sugar and tea. Malawi has few manufacturing industries.

MALAYSIA

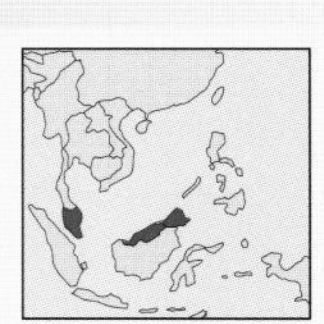

AREA 329,758 sq km [127,320 sq mi]
POPULATION 23,522,000
CAPITAL (POPULATION) Kuala Lumpur (1,145,000); Putrajaya (administrative capital awaiting completion)
GOVERNMENT Federal constitutional monarchy
ETHNIC GROUPS Malay and other indigenous groups 58%, Chinese 24%, Indian 8%, others
LANGUAGES Malay (official), Chinese, English
RELIGIONS Islam, Buddhism, Daoism, Hinduism, Christianity, Sikhism
CURRENCY Ringgit = 100 cents

GEOGRAPHY The Federation of Malaysia consists of two main parts. Peninsular Malaysia, which is joined to mainland Asia, contains about 80% of the population. The other main regions, Sabah and Sarawak, are in northern Borneo, an island which Malaysia shares with Indonesia. Much of the land is mountainous, with coastal lowlands bordering the rugged interior. The highest peak, Kinabalu, reaches 4,101 m [13,455 ft] in Sabah.

Malaysia has a hot equatorial climate. The temperatures are high all through the year, though the mountains are much cooler than the lowland areas. The rainfall is heavy throughout the year.

POLITICS & ECONOMY The Malay peninsula has long been a crossroads for trade. Around 1,200 years ago, Indian traders introduced Hinduism and Buddhism to the area, while Arab traders introduced Islam in the 15th century. Portuguese traders reached Melaka in 1509 and the Dutch took over in 1641. The British East India Company became established in the area in 1786. Britain gradually extended its control in the 19th century.

Japan occupied the area during World War II (1939–45), but British rule was re-established in 1945. In the 1940s and 1950s, British troops fought against Communist guerrillas, but Peninsular Malaysia (then called Malaya) became independent in 1957. Malaysia was created in 1963, when Malaya, Singapore, Sabah and Sarawak agreed to unite, but Singapore withdrew in 1965.

From the 1970s, Malaysia achieved rapid economic progress and, by the mid-1990s, it was playing a major part in regional affairs, especially through its membership of ASEAN (Association of South-east Asian Nations). However, together with several other countries in eastern Asia, Malaysia was hit by economic recession in 1997, including a major fall in stock market values. In response to the crisis, the government ordered the repatriation of many temporary foreign workers and initiated a series of austerity measures. In 2003, Mahathir bin Mohamad, who had served as prime minister since 1981, handed over power to Abdullah Ahmad Bud.

The World Bank classifies Malaysia as an 'upper-middle-income' developing country. Malaysia is a leading producer of palm oil, rubber and tin. Manufacturing now plays a major part in the economy. Manufactures are diverse, including cars, chemicals, a wide range of electronic goods, plastics, textiles, rubber and wood products.

MALDIVES

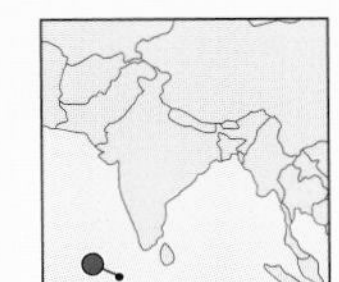

AREA 298 sq km [115 sq mi]
POPULATION 339,000
CAPITAL (POPULATION) Malé (74,000)

The Republic of the Maldives, Asia's smallest independent country, consists of about 1,200 low-lying coral islands, south of India. The highest point is 24 m [79 ft] above sea level. From the 16th century, the islands came under Portuguese and, later, Dutch rule, before the islands officially became a British territory until independence in 1965. Various crops are grown, but tourism and fishing are the main industries and fish are the main export. A tsunami struck the islands in December 2004, killing 82 people. In 2005, President Maumoon Abdul Gayoom, who had been in office since 1978, announced plans to introduce a multiparty democracy.

MALI

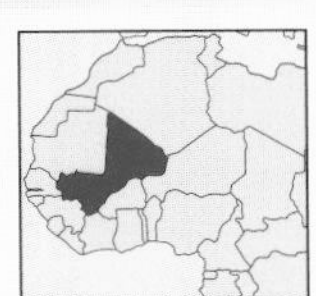

AREA 1,240,192 sq km [478,838 sq mi]
POPULATION 11,957,000
CAPITAL (POPULATION) Bamako (1,016,000)
GOVERNMENT Multiparty republic
ETHNIC GROUPS Mande 50% (Bambara, Malinke, Soninke), Peul 17%, Voltaic 12%, Songhai 6%, Tuareg and Moor 10%, others
LANGUAGES French (official), many African languages
RELIGIONS Islam 90%, traditional beliefs 9%, Christianity 1%
CURRENCY CFA franc = 100 centimes

GEOGRAPHY The Republic of Mali is a landlocked country in northern Africa. The land is generally flat, with the highest land in the Adrar des Iforhas on the border with Algeria.

Northern Mali is part of the Sahara, with a hot, practically rainless climate. But the south has enough rain for farming.

POLITICS & ECONOMY Between the 4th and 16th centuries, present-day Mali formed part of three major African empires which grew rich because of trans-Saharan trade. They were ancient Ghana, ancient Mali and Songhay. Islam was introduced from North Africa around 1,000 years ago and Tombouctou (Timbuktu) became a great centre of Muslim learning. However, following the defeat of the Songhay empire by Morocco in 1591, the area was divided into small kingdoms. France ruled the area, then known as French Sudan, from 1893 until the country achieved independence as Mali in 1960.

The first socialist government was overthrown in 1968 by an army group led by Moussa Traoré, but he was ousted in 1991. Multiparty democracy was restored in 1992 and Alpha Oumar Konaré was elected president. Konaré stood down in 2002 and Ahmadou Toure, who had restored democracy in 1992, was elected president.

Mali is one of the world's poorest countries and 70% of the land is desert or semi-desert. Only about 2% of the land is used for growing crops, while 25% is used for grazing animals. Despite this, agriculture employs nearly 80% of the people, many of whom still subsist by nomadic livestock rearing.

MALTA

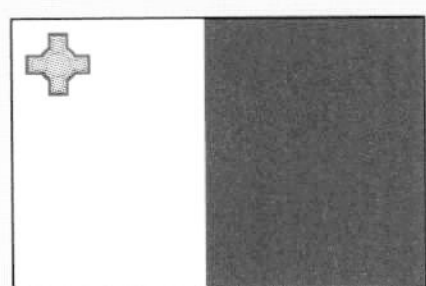

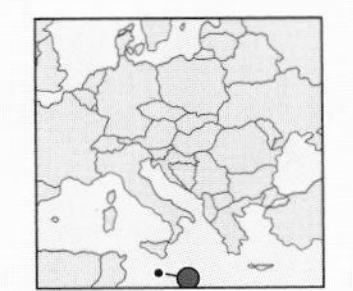

AREA 316 sq km [122 sq mi]
POPULATION 397,000
CAPITAL (POPULATION) Valletta (9,000)
GOVERNMENT Multiparty republic
ETHNIC GROUPS Maltese 96%, British 2%
LANGUAGES Maltese and English (both official)
RELIGIONS Roman Catholic 98%
CURRENCY Maltese lira = 100 cents

GEOGRAPHY The Republic of Malta consists of two main islands, Malta and Gozo, a third, much smaller island called Comino lying between the two large islands, and two tiny islets. Malta's climate is typically Mediterranean, with hot, dry summers and mild, wet winters. The sirocco, a hot wind from North Africa, may raise temperatures considerably during spring.

POLITICS & ECONOMY Malta's colourful history dates back to the Stone and Bronze Age remains that have been found there. The islands later came under Phoenician, Greek, Carthaginian, Roman and Arab rule. In about 1090, Malta came under the Norman kings of Sicily and, from 1530, the Knights Hospitallers. France took the islands in 1798, but the British drove them out in 1800. British rule was officially recognized in 1815.

During World War I (1914–18), Malta was an important British naval base. In World War II (1939–45), Italian and German aircraft bombed the islands. In recognition of the bravery of the Maltese, the British King George VI awarded the George Cross to Malta in 1942. In 1953, Malta became a base for NATO (North Atlantic Treaty Organization). Malta became independent in 1964 and it became a republic in 1974. In 1979, Britain's military agreement with Malta expired and Malta ceased to be a British military base. In the 1980s, Malta was declared a neutral country. On 1 May 2004, it became a member of the European Union.

The World Bank classifies Malta as an 'upper-middle-income' developing country. It lacks natural resources, and most people work in the former naval dockyards, which are now used for commercial shipbuilding and repairs, in manufacturing, and in tourism. Manufactures include chemicals, processed food and chemicals. Farming is difficult, because of the rocky soils. Crops include barley, fruits, potatoes and wheat. Fishing is also important.

MARSHALL ISLANDS

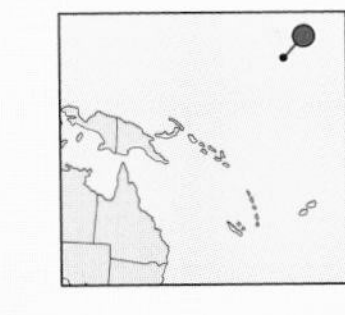

AREA 181 sq km [70 sq mi]
POPULATION 58,000
CAPITAL (POPULATION) Majuro (20,000)

The Republic of the Marshall Islands consists of 31 coral atolls, five single islands and more than 1,000 islets. It lies north of Kiribati in a region called Micronesia. The islands came under German rule in 1885 and became a Japanese mandate after World War I (1914–18). US forces took the main islands in 1944 and the territory became a US Trust Territory in 1947. Independence was achieved in 1991, but the islands remain heavily dependent on US aid. The main activities are agriculture and tourism.

MARTINIQUE

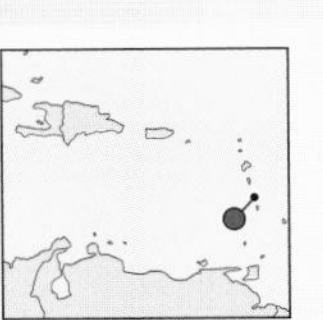

AREA 1,102 sq km [425 sq mi]
POPULATION 430,000
CAPITAL (POPULATION) Fort-de-France (100,000)

Martinique, a volcanic island nation in the Caribbean, was visited by Christopher Columbus in 1502 and colonized by France in 1635. It became a French department in 1946. Tourism and agriculture are major activities. French government aid makes up a substantial part of the gross domestic product, allowing for a good standard of living.

MAURITANIA

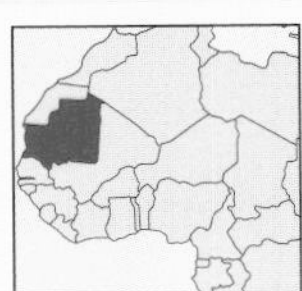

AREA 1,025,520 sq km [395,953 sq mi]
POPULATION 2,999,000
CAPITAL (POPULATION) Nouakchott (735,000)
GOVERNMENT Multiparty Islamic republic
ETHNIC GROUPS Mixed Moor/Black 40%, Moor 30%, Black 30%
LANGUAGES Arabic and Wolof (both official), French
RELIGIONS Islam
CURRENCY Ouguiya = 5 khoums

GEOGRAPHY The Islamic Republic of Mauritania in north-western Africa is nearly twice the size of France. But France has more than 28 times as many people. Part of the world's largest desert, the Sahara, covers northern Mauritania and most Mauritanians live in the south-west.

The amount of rainfall and the length of the rainy season increase from north to south. Much of the land is desert, with dry north-east and easterly winds throughout the year. But south-westerly winds bring summer rain to the south.

POLITICS & ECONOMY Originally part of the great African empires of Ghana and Mali, France set up a protectorate in Mauritania in 1903, attempting to exploit the trade in gum arabic. The country became a territory of French West Africa and a French colony in 1920. French West Africa was a huge territory, which included present-day Benin, Burkina Faso, Guinea, Ivory Coast, Mali, Niger and Senegal, as well as Mauritania. In 1958, Mauritania became a self-governing territory in the French Union and it became fully independent in 1960.

In 1976, Spain withdrew from Spanish (now Western) Sahara, a territory bordering Mauritania to the north. Morocco occupied the northern two-thirds of this territory, while Mauritania took the rest. But Saharan guerrillas belonging to POLISARIO (the Popular Front for the Liberation of Saharan Territories) began an armed struggle for independence. In 1979, Mauritania withdrew from the southern part of Western Sahara, which was then occupied by Morocco. In 1991, the country adopted a new constitution when the people voted to create a multiparty government. Multiparty elections were held in 1992, 1997 and 2001.

The World Bank classifies Mauritania as a 'low-income' developing country. Agriculture employs 38% of the people. Some are nomads with herds of cattle and sheep, though droughts and plagues of locusts, as in 2004, cause severe damage.

MAURITIUS

AREA 2,040 sq km [788 sq mi]
POPULATION 1,220,000
CAPITAL (POPULATION) Port Louis (148,000)

The Republic of Mauritius, an Indian Ocean nation lying to the east of Madagascar, was previously ruled by France and Britain until it achieved independence in 1968. It became a republic in 1992. Sugar production is in decline but tourism is vital to the economy.

MEXICO

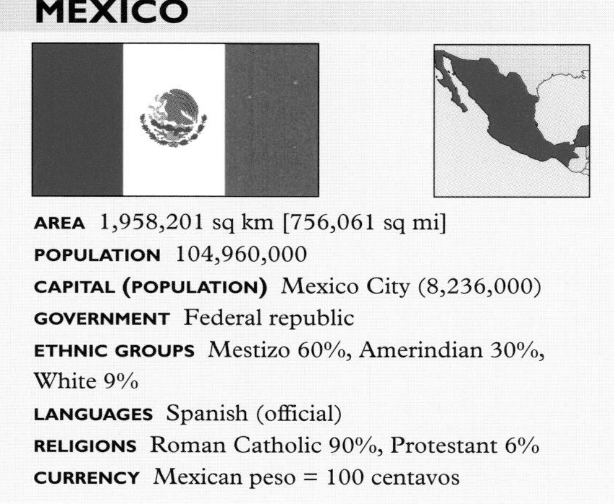

AREA 1,958,201 sq km [756,061 sq mi]
POPULATION 104,960,000
CAPITAL (POPULATION) Mexico City (8,236,000)
GOVERNMENT Federal republic
ETHNIC GROUPS Mestizo 60%, Amerindian 30%, White 9%
LANGUAGES Spanish (official)
RELIGIONS Roman Catholic 90%, Protestant 6%
CURRENCY Mexican peso = 100 centavos

GEOGRAPHY The United Mexican States, as Mexico is officially named, is the world's most populous Spanish-speaking country. Much of the land is mountainous, although most people live on the central plateau. Mexico contains two large peninsulas, Lower (or Baja) California in the north-west and the flat Yucatán peninsula in the south-east.

The climate varies according to the altitude. The resort of Acapulco on the south-west coast has a dry and sunny climate. Mexico City, at about 2,300 m [7,546 ft] above sea level, is much cooler. Most rain occurs between June and September. The rainfall decreases north of Mexico City and northern Mexico is mainly arid.

POLITICS & ECONOMY In the mid-19th century, Mexico lost land to the United States, and between 1910 and 1921 violent revolutions created chaos.

Reforms were introduced in the 1920s and, in 1929, the Institutional Revolutionary Party (PRI) was formed. The PRI ruled Mexico effectively as a one-party state until it was finally defeated in 2001. The new president, Vicente Fox, faced many problems, including unemployment and rapid urbanization especially around Mexico City, demands for indigenous rights by Amerindian groups, and illegal emigration to the United States.

The World Bank classifies Mexico as an 'upper-middle-income' developing country. Agriculture is important. Food crops include beans, maize, rice and wheat, while cash crops include coffee, cotton, fruits and vegetables. Beef cattle, dairy cattle and other livestock are raised and fishing is also important.

But oil and oil products are the chief exports, while manufacturing is the most valuable activity. Many factories near the northern border assemble goods, such as car parts and electrical products, for US companies. These factories are called *maquiladoras*. Hope for the future lies in increasing economic co-operation with the USA and Canada through NAFTA (North American Free Trade Agreement), which came into being on 1 January 1994.

MICRONESIA

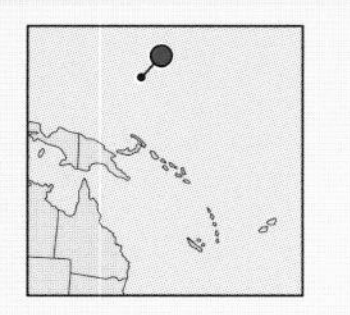

AREA 702 sq km [271 sq mi]
POPULATION 108,000
CAPITAL (POPULATION) Palikir (5,000)

The Federated States of Micronesia consist of about 600 islands spread across a vast area in the western Pacific. US forces took the islands in World War II (1939–45). From 1947, they were ruled by the United States, becoming fully independent in 1991. Copra is exported. Fishing and tourism are also important.

MOLDOVA

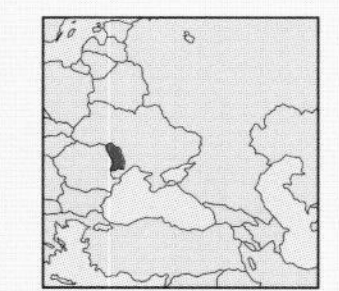

AREA 33,851 sq km [13,070 sq mi]
POPULATION 4,446,000
CAPITAL (POPULATION) Chişinău (658,000)
GOVERNMENT Multiparty republic
ETHNIC GROUPS Moldovan/Romanian 65%, Ukrainian 14%, Russian 13%, others
LANGUAGES Moldovan/Romanian and Russian (official)
RELIGIONS Eastern Orthodox 98%
CURRENCY Moldovan leu = 100 bani

GEOGRAPHY The Republic of Moldova is a small country sandwiched between Ukraine and Romania. It was formerly one of the 15 republics that made up the Soviet Union. Much of the land is hilly and the highest areas are near the centre of the country.

Moldova has a moderately continental climate, with warm summers and fairly cold winters. Most of the rain comes in the warmer months.

POLITICS & ECONOMY In the 14th century, the Moldavians formed a state called Moldavia. It included part of Romania and Bessarabia (now the modern country of Moldova). The Ottoman Turks took the area in the 16th century, but in 1812 Russia took over Bessarabia. In 1861, Moldavia and Walachia united to form Romania. Russia retook southern Bessarabia in 1878.

After World War I (1914–18), all of Bessarabia was returned to Romania, but the Soviet Union did not recognize this act. From 1944, the Moldovan Soviet Socialist Republic was part of the Soviet Union.

In 1989, the Moldovans asserted their independence and ethnicity by making Romanian the official language and, at the end of 1991, Moldova became an independent country. In 1992, fighting occurred between Moldovans and Russians in Trans-Dniester, a mainly Russian-speaking area east of the River Dniester which had declared its autonomy.

Multiparty elections were held in 1994, but economic problems made the government unpopular. In 2001, Moldova became the first former Soviet republic to return the Communist party to power in a general election. The Communist party was re-elected in 2005, though it now advocates close ties with the West, a matter of some concern to Russia.

In terms of its GNP per capita, Moldova is Europe's poorest country. Agriculture is the leading activity and products include fruits, maize, tobacco and wine. Moldova has few natural resources and it imports materials and fuels for its industries. Light industries, such as food processing and factories making household appliances, are increasing.

MONACO

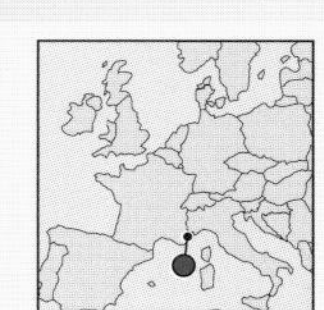

AREA 1 sq km [0.4 sq mi]
POPULATION 32,000
CAPITAL (POPULATION) Monaco (30,000)

The tiny Principality of Monaco consists of a narrow strip of coastline and a rocky peninsula on the French Riviera. Its considerable wealth is derived largely from banking, finance, gambling and tourism. Monaco's citizens do not pay any state tax. Its attractions include the Monte Carlo casino and such sporting events as the Monte Carlo Rally and the Monaco Grand Prix.

MONGOLIA

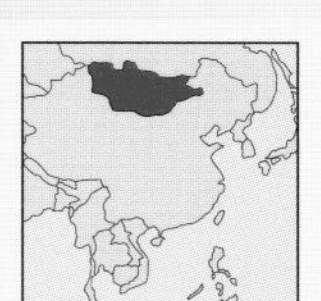

AREA 1,566,500 sq km [604,826 sq mi]
POPULATION 2,751,000
CAPITAL (POPULATION) Ulan Bator (760,000)
GOVERNMENT Multiparty republic
ETHNIC GROUPS Khalkha Mongol 85%, Kazakh 6%
LANGUAGES Khalkha Mongolian (official), Turkic, Russian
RELIGIONS Tibetan Buddhist Lamaism 96%
CURRENCY Tugrik = 100 möngös

GEOGRAPHY The State of Mongolia is the world's largest landlocked country. It consists mainly of high plateaux, with the Gobi Desert in the south-east. Ulan Bator has bitterly cold winters. Summer temperatures are moderated by the altitude.

POLITICS & ECONOMY In the 13th century, Genghis Khan united the Mongolian peoples and built up a great empire. Under his grandson, Kublai Khan, the Mongol empire extended from Korea and China to eastern Europe and present-day Iraq.

The Mongol empire broke up in the late 14th century. In the early 17th century, Inner Mongolia came under Chinese control, and by the late 17th century Outer Mongolia had become a Chinese province. In 1911, the Mongolians drove the Chinese out of Outer Mongolia and made the area a Buddhist kingdom. But in 1924, under Russian influence, the Communist Mongolian People's Republic was set up. From the 1950s, Mongolia supported the Soviet Union in its disputes with China. In 1990, the people demonstrated for more freedom, and free elections in June 1990 resulted in victory for the Mongolian People's Revolutionary Party, which was composed of Communists. Communist rule ended in 1996, when the Democratic Union coalition won power. But the Communists regained power in 2000. However, a coalition government was set up in 2004 following disputed elections.

The World Bank classifies Mongolia as a 'lower-middle-income' developing country. Most people were once nomads, who moved around with their herds of sheep, cattle, goats and horses. Under Communist rule, most people were moved into permanent homes on government-owned farms. But livestock and animal products remain leading exports. The Communists also developed industry, especially the mining of coal, copper, gold, molybdenum, tin and tungsten, and manufacturing. Minerals and fuels now account for around half of Mongolia's exports.

MONTSERRAT

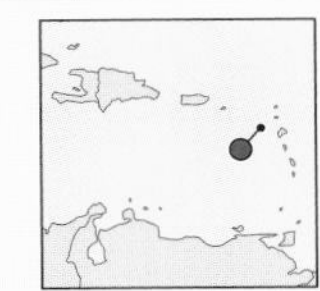

AREA 102 sq km [39 sq mi]
POPULATION 9,000 (prior to the volcanic activity)
CAPITAL Plymouth

Monserrat is a British overseas territory in the Caribbean Sea. It was colonized by Britain in 1632 and settled initially by Irish people. The climate is tropical and hurricanes cause much damage. Periodic eruptions of the Soufrière Hills volcano between 1995 and 1998, and again in 2003, led to the emigration of many inhabitants and the virtual destruction of Plymouth, the capital, in the south.

MOROCCO

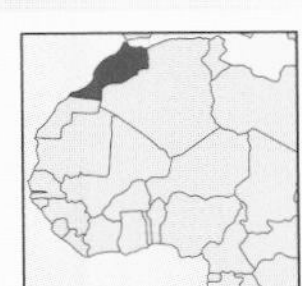

AREA 446,550 sq km [172,413 sq mi]
POPULATION 32,209,000
CAPITAL (POPULATION) Rabat (1,220,000)
GOVERNMENT Constitutional monarchy
ETHNIC GROUPS Arab-Berber 99%
LANGUAGES Arabic (official), Berber dialects, French
RELIGIONS Islam 99%
CURRENCY Moroccan dirham = 100 centimes

GEOGRAPHY The Kingdom of Morocco lies in north-western Africa. Its name comes from the Arabic Maghreb-el-Aksa, meaning 'the farthest west'. Behind the western coastal plain the land rises to a broad plateau and ranges of the Atlas Mountains. The High (Haut) Atlas contains the highest peak, Djebel Toubkal, at 4,165 m [13,665 ft]. East of the mountains, the land descends to the arid Sahara.

The Atlantic coast of Morocco is cooled by the Canaries Current. Inland, summers are hot and dry, while winters are mild, with moderate rainfall between October and April. Snow often falls on the High Atlas Mountains.

POLITICS & ECONOMY The original people of Morocco were the Berbers. But in the 680s, Arab invaders introduced Islam and the Arabic language. By the early 20th century, France and Spain controlled Morocco, which became an independent kingdom in 1956. Although Morocco is a constitutional monarchy, King Hassan II ruled the country in a generally authoritarian way from the time of his accession to the throne in 1961 to his death in 1999. His son and successor, Mohamed VI, faced several problems, including the future of Western Sahara which Hassan II had vigorously claimed for Morocco. Relations with Spain became strained in 2002 over the disputed island of Leila (Perejil in Spanish) in the Strait of Gibraltar. But diplomatic relations were restored in 2003. Another problem faced by Morocco is activity by Islamic extremists. Its opposition to extremism led the United States to designate Morocco as a major non-NATO ally in 2004.

Morocco is classified as a 'lower-middle-income' developing country. It is the world's third largest producer of phosphate rock, which is used to make fertilizer. One of the reasons why Morocco wants to keep Western Sahara is that it, too, has large phosphate reserves. Farming employs 38% of Moroccans. Crops include barley, beans, citrus fruits, maize and wheat. Tourism is also important.

MOZAMBIQUE

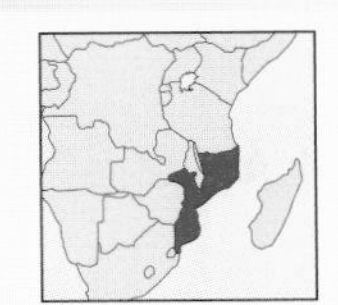

AREA 801,590 sq km [309,494 sq mi]
POPULATION 18,812,000
CAPITAL (POPULATION) Maputo (1,015,000)
GOVERNMENT Multiparty republic
ETHNIC GROUPS Indigenous tribal groups (Shangaan, Chokwe, Manyika, Sena, Makua, others) 99%
LANGUAGES Portuguese (official), many others
RELIGIONS Traditional beliefs 50%, Christianity 30%, Islam 20%
CURRENCY Metical = 100 centavos

GEOGRAPHY The Republic of Mozambique borders the Indian Ocean in south-eastern Africa. The coastal plains are narrow in the north but broaden in the south. Inland lie plateaux and hills, which make up another two-fifths of the land. Most of the country has a tropical climate.

POLITICS & ECONOMY In 1885, when the European powers divided Africa, Mozambique was recognized as a Portuguese colony. But black African opposition to European rule gradually increased. In 1961, the Front for the Liberation of Mozambique (FRELIMO) was founded to oppose Portuguese rule. A guerrilla war began in 1964 and continued for ten years. Mozambique became independent in 1975.

After independence, Mozambique became a one-party state. Its government aided African nationalists in Rhodesia (now Zimbabwe) and South Africa. But the white governments of these countries helped an opposition group, the Mozambique National Resistance Movement (RENAMO) to lead an armed struggle against Mozambique's government. Civil war, combined with droughts, caused much suffering in the 1980s. In 1989, FRELIMO declared that it had dropped its Communist policies and ended one-party rule. The war ended in 1992 and multiparty elections in 1994, 1999 and 2004 were all won by FRELIMO. In 1995, Mozambique became the 53rd member of the Commonwealth.

In the early 1990s, the UN rated Mozambique as one of the world's poorest countries. The second half of the 1990s saw a surge in economic growth, but huge floods in 2000 and 2001 proved to be a major setback. About 80% of the people are poor and agriculture is the main activity. Crops include cassava, cotton, maize, rice and tea.

NAMIBIA

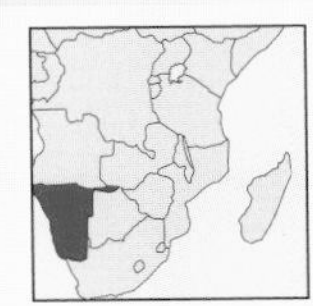

AREA 824,292 sq km [318,259 sq mi]
POPULATION 1,954,000
CAPITAL (POPULATION) Windhoek (147,000)
GOVERNMENT Multiparty republic
ETHNIC GROUPS Ovambo 50%, Kavango 9%, Herero 7%, Damara 7%, White 6%, Nama 5%
LANGUAGES English (official), Afrikaans, German, indigenous dialects
RELIGIONS Christianity 90% (Lutheran 51%)
CURRENCY Namibian dollar = 100 cents

GEOGRAPHY The Republic of Namibia was formerly ruled by South Africa, which called it South West Africa. The country became independent in 1990. The coastal region contains the arid Namib Desert, which is virtually uninhabited. Inland is a central plateau, bordered by a rugged spine of mountains stretching north–south. Eastern Namibia contains part of the Kalahari Desert. Namibia is a warm, arid country. Windhoek has an average annual rainfall of 370 mm [15 in]. Thunderstorms often occur in summer.

POLITICS & ECONOMY During World War I, South African troops defeated the Germans who ruled what is now Namibia. After World War II, many people challenged South Africa's right to govern the territory and a civil war began in the 1960s between African guerrillas and South African troops. A cease-fire was agreed in 1989 and Namibia became independent in 1990. In the 1990s, the government pursued a policy of 'national reconciliation'. An enclave on the coast, called Walvis Bay (Walvisbaai), remained part of South Africa until 1994, when it was transferred to Namibia. In 2004, Sam Nujoma, president since independence, retired. He was succeeded by Hifikepunye Pohama.

Namibia is rich in mineral reserves, including diamonds, uranium, zinc and copper. Minerals are major exports, but farming employs nearly 40% of the people. In 2003–4, the government revealed that it planned to speed up land reform by transferring commercial farmland from white to black Namibians. Sea fishing is important, but the country has few industries. Tourism is increasing.

NAURU

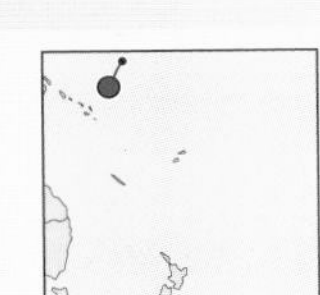

AREA 21 sq km [8 sq mi]
POPULATION 13,000
CAPITAL Yaren

A former UN Trust Territory ruled by Australia, Nauru became independent in 1968. Located in the western Pacific, close to the Equator, it is the world's smallest republic. Nauru's prosperity is based on phosphate mining, but the reserves are running out.

NEPAL

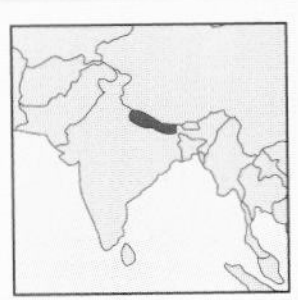

AREA 147,181 sq km [56,827 sq mi]
POPULATION 27,071,000
CAPITAL (POPULATION) Katmandu (695,000)
GOVERNMENT Constitutional monarchy
ETHNIC GROUPS Brahman, Chetri, Newar, Gurung, Magar, Tamang, Sherpa and others
LANGUAGES Nepali (official), local languages
RELIGIONS Hinduism 86%, Buddhism 8%, Islam 4%
CURRENCY Nepalese rupee = 100 paisa

GEOGRAPHY Over three-quarters of Nepal lies in the Himalayan region, culminating in the world's highest peak (Mount Everest, or Chomolongma in Nepali) at 8,850 m [29,035 ft]. As a result, climatic conditions vary widely according to the altitude.

POLITICS & ECONOMY Nepal was united in the late 18th century, although its complex topography has ensured that it remains a diverse patchwork of peoples. From the mid-19th century to 1951, power was held by the royal Rana family. Attempts to introduce a democratic system in the 1950s failed. The first democratic elections in 32 years were held in 1991, but, by the early 21st century, Nepal faced many problems, including the activities of Maoist guerrillas. In 2003, a brief cease-fire was agreed but fighting continued. In 2005, King Gyanendra seized power. He sacked the government, alleging that it had failed to defeat the Maoist rebels.

Agriculture remains the chief activity in this overwhelmingly rural country and the government is heavily dependent on aid. Tourism, centred around the high Himalaya, grows in importance each year, although Nepal was closed to foreigners until 1951. There are also plans to exploit the hydroelectric potential offered by the Himalayan rivers.

NETHERLANDS

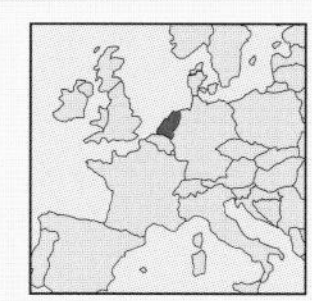

AREA 41,526 sq km [16,033 sq mi]
POPULATION 16,318,000
CAPITAL (POPULATION) Amsterdam (729,000); The Hague (seat of government, 440,000)
GOVERNMENT Constitutional monarchy
ETHNIC GROUPS Dutch 83%, Indonesian, Turkish, Moroccan and others
LANGUAGES Dutch (official), Frisian
RELIGIONS Roman Catholic 31%, Protestant 21%, Islam 4%, others
CURRENCY Euro = 100 cents

GEOGRAPHY The Netherlands lies at the western end of the North European Plain, which extends to the Ural Mountains in Russia. Except for the far south-eastern corner, the Netherlands is flat and about 40% lies below sea level at high tide. To prevent flooding, the Dutch have built dykes (sea walls) to hold back the waves. Large areas which were once under the sea, but which have been reclaimed, are called polders. Because of its position on the North Sea, the Netherlands has a temperate climate, with mild, rainy winters.

POLITICS & ECONOMY Before the 16th century, the area that is now the Netherlands was under a succession of foreign rulers, including the Romans, the Germanic Franks, the French and the Spanish. The Dutch declared their independence from Spain in 1581 and their status was finally recognized by Spain in 1648. In the 17th century, the Dutch built up a great overseas empire, especially in South-east Asia. But in the early 18th century, the Dutch lost control of the seas to England.

France controlled the Netherlands from 1795 to 1813. In 1815, the Netherlands, then containing Belgium and Luxembourg, became an independent kingdom. Belgium broke away in 1830 and Luxembourg followed in 1890.

The Netherlands was neutral in World War I (1914–18), but was occupied by Germany in World War II (1939–45). After the war, the Netherlands Indies became independent as Indonesia. The Netherlands became active in West European affairs. With Belgium and Luxembourg, it formed a customs union called Benelux in 1948. In 1949, it joined NATO (the North Atlantic Treaty Organization), and the European Coal and Steel Community (ECSC) in 1953. In 1957, it became a founder member of the European Economic Community (now the European Union) and, in 2002, it adopted the euro as its sole unit of currency. In 2002, an anti-immigration group made sweeping gains in national elections. It joined a coalition government, which collapsed later that year. The group's vote collapsed in new elections in 2003.

The Netherlands is a highly industrialized country and industry and commerce are the most valuable activities. Its resources include natural gas, some oil, salt and china clay. But the Netherlands imports many of the materials needed by its industries and it is, therefore, a major trading country. Industrial products are wide-ranging, including aircraft, chemicals, electronic equipment, machinery, textiles and vehicles. Agriculture employs only 5% of the people, but scientific methods are used and yields are high. Dairy farming is the leading farming activity. Major products include barley, flowers and bulbs, potatoes, sugar beet and wheat.

NETHERLANDS ANTILLES

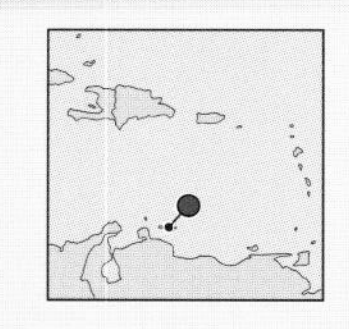

AREA 800 sq km [309 sq mi]
POPULATION 218,000
CAPITAL (POPULATION) Willemstad (130,000)

The Netherlands Antilles consists of two different island groups; one off the coast of Venezuela, and the other at the northern end of the Leeward Islands, some 800 km [500 mi] away. They remain a self-governing Dutch territory. The island of Aruba was once part of the territory, but it broke away in 1986 to become a separate Dutch territory. Oil refining and tourism are important activities.

NEW CALEDONIA

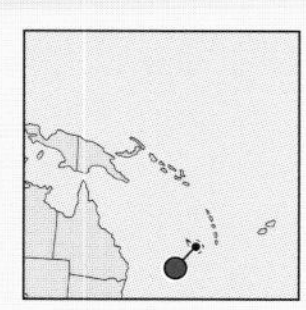

AREA 18,575 sq km [7,172 sq mi]
POPULATION 214,000
CAPITAL (POPULATION) Nouméa (76,000)

New Caledonia is the most southerly of the Melanesian countries in the Pacific. A French possession since 1853 and an Overseas Territory since 1958. In 1998, France announced an agreement with local Melanesians that a vote on independence would be postponed until 2014. The country is rich in mineral resources. Experts estimate that it has about a quarter of the world's nickel reserves.

NEW ZEALAND

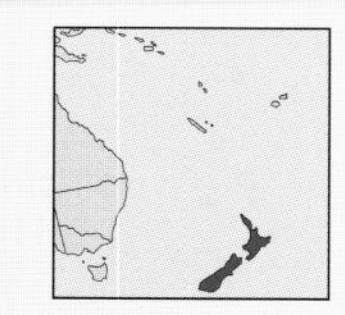

AREA 270,534 sq km [104,453 sq mi]
POPULATION 3,994,000
CAPITAL (POPULATION) Wellington (167,000)
GOVERNMENT Constitutional monarchy
ETHNIC GROUPS New Zealand European 74%, New Zealand Maori 10%, Polynesian 4%
LANGUAGES English and Maori (both official)
RELIGIONS Anglican 24%, Presbyterian 18%, Roman Catholic 15%, others
CURRENCY New Zealand dollar = 100 cents

GEOGRAPHY New Zealand lies about 1,600 km [994 mi] south-east of Australia. It consists of two main islands and several other small ones. Much of the North Island is volcanic. Active volcanoes include Ngauruhoe and Ruapehu. Hot springs and geysers are common, and steam from the ground is used to produce electricity. The Southern Alps, which contain the country's highest peak, Aoraki Mount Cook, at 3,753 m [12,313 ft], form the backbone of the South Island. The island also has some large, fertile plains.

Auckland in the north has a warm, humid climate throughout the year. Wellington has cooler summers, while in Dunedin, in the south-east, temperatures sometimes dip below freezing in winter. The rainfall is heaviest on the western highlands.

POLITICS & ECONOMY Evidence suggests that early Maori settlers arrived in New Zealand more than 1,000 years ago. The Dutch navigator Abel Tasman reached New Zealand in 1642, but his discovery was not followed up. In 1769, the British Captain James Cook rediscovered the islands. In the early 19th century, British settlers arrived and, in 1840, under the Treaty of Waitangi, Britain took possession of the islands. Clashes occurred with the Maoris in the 1860s but, from the 1870s, the Maoris were gradually integrated into society.

In 1907, New Zealand became a self-governing dominion in the British Commonwealth. The country's economy developed quickly and the people became increasingly prosperous. However, after Britain joined the European Economic Community in 1973, New Zealand's exports to Britain shrank and the country had to reassess its economic and defence strategies and seek new markets. The world recession led the government to cut back on welfare spending in the 1990s. The preservation of Maori culture and Maori rights are other political issues. Ties to Britain have been gradually reduced. In 2005, the country's prime minister, Helen Clark, stated that New Zealand would eventually abolish the monarchy and become a republic.

New Zealand's economy has traditionally depended on agriculture, but manufacturing now employs twice as many people as agriculture. Meat and dairy products are the most valuable items produced on farms. Sheep numbered less than 22 million in 2002. Their importance has greatly declined as the area under cattle, deer and vineyards has increased.

NICARAGUA

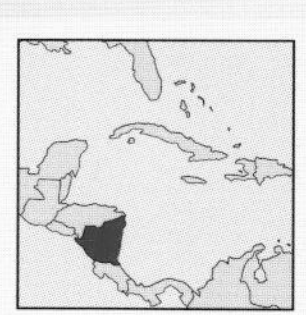

AREA 130,000 sq km [50,193 sq mi]
POPULATION 5,360,000
CAPITAL (POPULATION) Managua (1,009,000)
GOVERNMENT Multiparty republic
ETHNIC GROUPS Mestizo 69%, White 17%, Black 9%, Amerindian 5%
LANGUAGES Spanish (official)
RELIGIONS Roman Catholic 85%, Protestant
CURRENCY Córdoba oro (gold córdoba) = 100 centavos

GEOGRAPHY The Republic of Nicaragua is a large country in Central America. In the east is a broad plain bordering the Caribbean Sea. The plain is drained by rivers that flow from the Central Highlands. The fertile western Pacific region contains about 40 volcanoes, many of which are active, and earthquakes are common.

Nicaragua has a tropical climate. Managua is hot throughout the year and there is a marked rainy season from May to October. The Central Highlands and Caribbean region are cooler and wetter. The wettest region is the humid Caribbean plain.

POLITICS & ECONOMY In 1502, Christopher Columbus claimed the area for Spain, which ruled Nicaragua until 1821. By the early 20th century, the

United States had considerable influence in the country and, in 1912, US forces entered Nicaragua to protect US interests. From 1927 to 1933, rebels under General Augusto César Sandino, tried to drive US forces out of the country. In 1933, US marines set up a Nicaraguan army, the National Guard, to help to defeat the rebels. Its leader, Anastasio Somoza Garcia, had Sandino murdered in 1934 and, from 1937, Somoza ruled as a dictator.

In the mid-1970s, many people began to protest against Somoza's rule. Many joined a guerrilla force, called the Sandinista National Liberation Front, named after General Sandino. The rebels defeated the Somoza regime in 1979. In the 1980s, the US-supported forces, called the 'Contras', launched a campaign against the Sandinista government. The US government opposed the Sandinista regime, under Daniel José Ortega Saavedra, claiming that it was a Communist dictatorship. A coalition, the National Opposition Union, defeated the Sandinistas in elections in 1990. In 1996 and again in 2001, the Sandinista candidate Daniel Ortega was defeated in presidential elections.

In the early 1990s, Nicaragua faced many problems in rebuilding its shattered economy. Agriculture is the main activity, employing nearly 40% of the people. Coffee, cotton and sugar are exported, while beans, maize and rice are the main food crops. Managua has manufacturing industries that process farm products. Textiles and clothing are also important.

NIGER

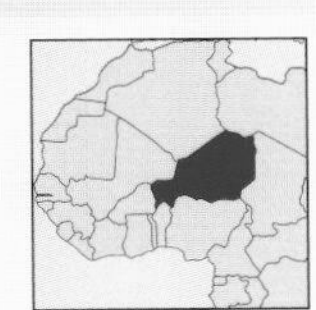

AREA 1,267,000 sq km [489,189 sq mi]
POPULATION 11,361,000
CAPITAL (POPULATION) Niamey (732,000)
GOVERNMENT Multiparty republic
ETHNIC GROUPS Hausa 56%, Djerma 22%, Tuareg 8%, Fula 8%, others
LANGUAGES French (official), Hausa, Djerma
RELIGIONS Islam 80%, indigenous beliefs, Christianity
CURRENCY CFA franc = 100 centimes

GEOGRAPHY The Republic of Niger is a landlocked nation in north-central Africa. The northern plateaux lie in the Sahara Desert, while Central Niger contains the rugged Aïr Mountains. The most fertile, densely populated region is the Niger valley in the south-west.

Niger has a tropical climate and the south has a rainy season between June and September. The north is practically rainless.

POLITICS & ECONOMY Since independence in 1960, Niger, a French territory from 1900, has suffered severe droughts. Food shortages and the collapse of the traditional nomadic way of life of some of Niger's people have caused political instability. After a period of military rule, a multiparty constitution was adopted in 1992, but the military again seized power in 1996. Later that year, the coup leader, Col. Ibrahim Barre Mainassara, was elected president. He was assassinated in 1999, but parliamentary rule was rapidly restored and Tandja Mamadou was elected president. Mamadou was re-elected president in December 2004.

Niger's chief resource is uranium and it is the world's fourth largest producer. Tin and tungsten are also mined, although other mineral resources are largely untouched. Despite its resources, Niger is one of the world's poorest countries. Farming employs about three-quarters of the population, but only 3% of the land can be farmed while 8% is used for grazing.

NIGERIA

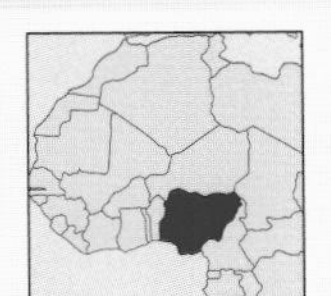

AREA 923,768 sq km [356,667 sq mi]
POPULATION 137,253,000
CAPITAL (POPULATION) Abuja (339,000)
GOVERNMENT Federal multiparty republic
ETHNIC GROUPS Hausa and Fulani 29%, Yoruba 21%, Ibo (or Igbo) 18%, Ijaw 10%, Kanuri 4%, many others
LANGUAGES English (official), Hausa, Yoruba, Ibo
RELIGIONS Islam 50%, Christianity 40%, traditional beliefs 10%
CURRENCY Naira = 100 kobo

GEOGRAPHY The Federal Republic of Nigeria is the most populous nation in Africa. The country's main rivers are the Niger and Benue, which meet in central Nigeria. North of the two river valleys are high plains and plateaux. The Lake Chad basin is in the north-east, with the Sokoto plains in the north-west. The south contains hilly areas and coastal plains. The south is hot and rainy throughout the year. The north is drier but often hotter than the south.

POLITICS & ECONOMY Nigeria has a long artistic tradition. Major cultures include the Nok (500 BC to AD 200), Ife, which developed about 1,000 years ago, and Benin, which flourished between the 15th and 17th centuries. Britain gradually extended its influence over the area in the second half of the 19th century.

Nigeria became independent in 1960 and a federal republic in 1963. A federal constitution dividing the country into regions was necessary because Nigeria contains more than 250 ethnic and linguistic groups, as well as several religious ones. Local rivalries have long been a threat to national unity, and six new states were created in 1996 in an attempt to overcome this. Civil war occurred between 1967 and 1970, when the people of the south-east attempted unsuccessfully to secede during the Biafran War. Between 1960 and 1998, Nigeria had only nine years of civilian government. In 1998–9, civilian rule was restored. A former general, Olusegun Obasanjo, was elected president and he was re-elected in 2003. His government faced many problems, including religious clashes in the north, where several states adopted *sharia* (Islamic law). In 2004, the government declared that it had put down an uprising in the north-east aimed at creating a Muslim state, while ethnic and religious conflict continued in other parts of the country.

Nigeria is a developing country with great potential. Its chief natural resource is oil, which accounts for most of its exports. Agriculture employs 43% of the people and the country is a major producer of cocoa, palm oil and palm kernels, groundnuts and rubber.

NORTHERN MARIANA ISLANDS

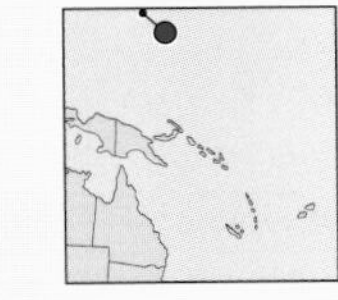

AREA 464 sq km [179 sq mi]
POPULATION 78,000
CAPITAL (POPULATION) Saipan (39,000)

The Commonwealth of the Northern Mariana Islands contains 16 mountainous islands north of Guam in the western Pacific Ocean. In a 1975 plebiscite, the islanders voted for Commonwealth status in union with the USA and, in 1986, they were granted US citizenship.

NORWAY

AREA 323,877 sq km [125,049 sq mi]
POPULATION 4,575,000
CAPITAL (POPULATION) Oslo (513,000)
GOVERNMENT Constitutional monarchy
ETHNIC GROUPS Norwegian 97%
LANGUAGES Norwegian (official)
RELIGIONS Evangelical Lutheran 86%
CURRENCY Norwegian krone = 100 ore

GEOGRAPHY The Kingdom of Norway forms the western part of the rugged Scandinavian peninsula. The deep inlets along the highly indented coastline were worn out by glaciers during the Ice Age.

The warm North Atlantic Drift off the coast of Norway moderates the climate, with mild winters and cool summers. Nearly all the ports are ice-free throughout the year. Inland, winters are colder and snow cover lasts for at least three months a year.

POLITICS & ECONOMY From about AD 800, for a period lasting about 300 years, Norwegian Vikings ravaged western Europe. Norway's first king, Harold I, united Norway in about 900. In 1380, Norway was united with Denmark. But under a treaty of 1814, Denmark handed Norway over to Sweden, though it kept Norway's colonies – Greenland, Iceland and the Færoe Islands. Norway briefly became independent, but Swedish forces defeated the Norwegians and Norway had to accept Sweden's king as its ruler.

The union between Norway and Sweden ended in 1903. During World War II (1939–45), Germany occupied Norway. Norway's economy developed quickly after the war and the country now enjoys one of the world's highest standards of living. In 1994, Norwegians voted against joining the EU. In the 1990s and 2000s, Norwegian diplomats sought to broker peace deals in Palestine and Sri Lanka.

Norway's chief resources and exports are oil and natural gas which come from wells under the North Sea. Farmland covers only 3% of the land. Dairy farming and meat production are important, but Norway has to import food. Norway has many industries powered by cheap hydroelectricity.

OMAN

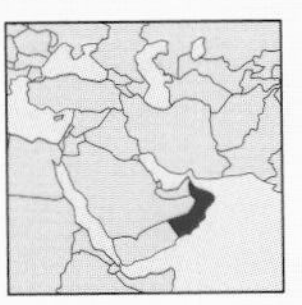

AREA 309,500 sq km [119,498 sq mi]
POPULATION 2,903,000
CAPITAL (POPULATION) Muscat (41,000)
GOVERNMENT Monarchy with consultative council
ETHNIC GROUPS Arab, Baluchi, Indian, Pakistani
LANGUAGES Arabic (official), Baluchi, English
RELIGIONS Islam (mainly Ibadhi), Hinduism
CURRENCY Omani rial = 100 baizas

GEOGRAPHY The Sultanate of Oman in the south-eastern Arabian peninsula also includes the tip of the Musandam peninsula. Oman has a hot tropical climate. In Muscat, temperatures may reach 47°C [117°F] in summer.

POLITICS & ECONOMY British influence in Oman dates back to the end of the 18th century, but the country became fully independent in 1971. Since then, using revenue from oil, which was discovered in 1964, the absolute ruler, Qaboos ibn Said, and his government have sought to modernize the country. In 2000, Oman held its first direct elections to its consultative parliament. In 2004, the Sultan appointed Oman's first woman minister with portfolio.

The World Bank classifies Oman as an 'upper-middle-income' country. Oil accounts for the bulk of the exports, but agriculture remains important. Major crops include alfalfa, bananas, coconuts, dates, limes, tobacco, vegetables and wheat. Some cattle are raised and fishing, especially for sardines, is important. But Oman still has to import food.

PAKISTAN

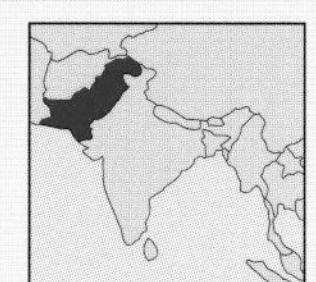

AREA 796,095 sq km [307,372 sq mi]
POPULATION 159,196,000
CAPITAL (POPULATION) Islamabad (529,000)
GOVERNMENT Military regime
ETHNIC GROUPS Punjabi, Sindhi, Pashtun (Pathan), Baluchi, Muhajir
LANGUAGES Urdu (official), many others
RELIGIONS Islam 97%, Christianity, Hinduism
CURRENCY Pakistani rupee = 100 paisa

GEOGRAPHY The Islamic Republic of Pakistan contains high mountains, fertile plains and rocky deserts. The Karakoram range, which contains K2, the world's second highest peak, lies in the northern part of Jammu and Kashmir, which is occupied by Pakistan but claimed by India. Other mountains rise in the west. Plains, drained by the River Indus and its tributaries, occupy much of the east. Most of Pakistan has hot summers and mild winters. The rainfall is sparse and deserts cover large areas.

POLITICS & ECONOMY Pakistan was the site of the Indus Valley civilization which developed about 4,500 years ago. But Pakistan's modern history dates from 1947, when British India was divided into India and Pakistan. Muslim Pakistan was divided into two parts: East and West Pakistan, but East Pakistan broke away in 1971 to become Bangladesh. In 1948–9, 1965 and 1971, Pakistan and India clashed over the disputed territory of Kashmir. In 1998, Pakistan responded in kind to a series of Indian nuclear weapon tests, provoking global controversy. However, in 2003–5, Pakistan launched a series of peace moves, raising hopes of a settlement in the disputed area, though militant activity continued on the ground.

Pakistan has been subject to several periods of military rule, but elections in 1988 led to Benazir Bhutto becoming prime minister. She was removed from office in 1990, but she returned as prime minister between 1993 and 1996. In 1997, Narwaz Sharif was elected prime minister, but a military coup in 1999 brought General Pervez Musharraf to power. In 2001, Pakistan supported the Western assault on Taliban forces in Afghanistan. In 2002, voters agreed to extend Musharraf's term in office by five years. He made constitutional changes to increase his own powers, but he received a setback in national elections when Islamic parties received substantial support. Pakistan's declaration that it supported the international coalition against terrorism also provoked a backlash by Islamic fundamentalists. In 2004, Musharraf announced, amid criticism, that he would remain army chief as well as head of state.

According to the World Bank, Pakistan is a 'low-income' developing country. The economy is based on farming or rearing goats and sheep. Agriculture employs nearly half the people. Major crops include cotton, fruits, rice, sugar cane and wheat.

PALAU

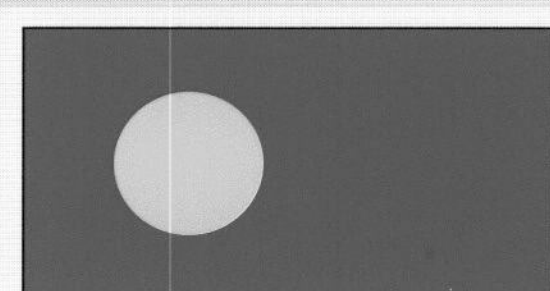

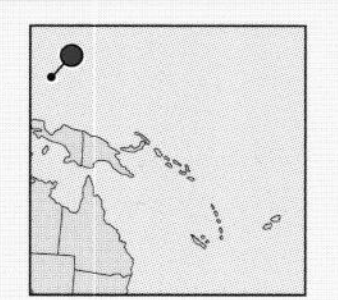

AREA 459 sq km [177 sq mi]
POPULATION 20,000
CAPITAL (POPULATION) Koror (11,000)

The Republic of Palau became fully independent in 1994, after the USA refused to accede to a 1979 referendum that declared this island nation a nuclear-free zone. The economy relies on US aid, tourism, fishing and subsistence agriculture. The main crops include cassava, coconuts and copra.

PANAMA

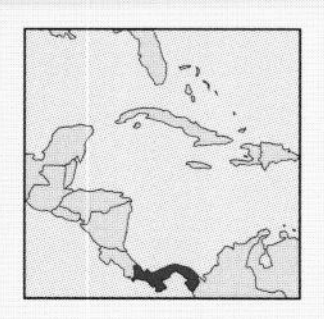

AREA 75,517 sq km [29,157 sq mi]
POPULATION 3,000,000
CAPITAL (POPULATION) Panamá (484,000)
GOVERNMENT Multiparty republic
ETHNIC GROUPS Mestizo 70%, Black and Mulatto 14%, White 10%, Amerindian 6%
LANGUAGES Spanish (official), English
RELIGIONS Roman Catholic 85%, Protestant 15%
CURRENCY US dollar; Balboa = 100 centésimos

GEOGRAPHY The Republic of Panama forms an isthmus linking Central America to South America. The Panama Canal, which is 81.6 km [50.7 mi] long, has made the country a major transport centre. Panama has a tropical climate and temperatures are high on the coastal plains. The main rainy season is between May and December.

POLITICS & ECONOMY Christopher Columbus landed in Panama in 1502 and Spain soon took control of the area. In 1821, Panama became independent from Spain and a province of Colombia.

In 1903, Colombia refused a request by the United States to build a canal. Panama then revolted against Colombia, and became independent. The United States then began to build the canal, which was opened in 1914. The United States administered the Panama Canal Zone, a strip of land along the canal. But many Panamanians resented US influence and, in 1979, the Canal Zone was returned to Panama. Control of the canal itself was handed over by the USA to Panama on 31 December 1999.

Panama's government has changed many times since independence, and there have been periods of military dictatorships. In 1983, General Manuel Antonio Noriega became Panama's leader. In 1988, two US grand juries in Florida indicted Noriega on charges of drug trafficking. In 1989, Noriega was apparently defeated in a presidential election, but the government declared the election invalid. After the killing of a US marine, US troops entered Panama and arrested Noriega, who was convicted by a Miami court of drug offences in 1992. In 1999, Mireya Moscoso became Panama's first woman president. She was succeeded in 2004 by Martin Torrijos, son of a former military dictator.

The World Bank classifies Panama as a 'lower-middle-income' developing country. The Panama Canal is an important source of revenue and it generates many jobs in commerce, trade, manufacturing and transport. Away from the Canal, the main activity is agriculture, which employs 16% of the people.

PAPUA NEW GUINEA

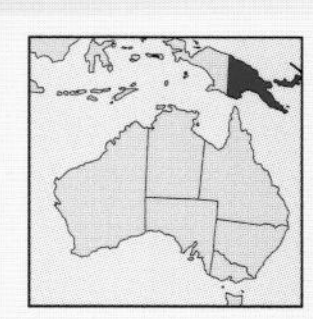

AREA 462,840 sq km [178,703 sq mi]
POPULATION 5,420,000
CAPITAL (POPULATION) Port Moresby (193,000)
GOVERNMENT Constitutional monarchy
ETHNIC GROUPS Papuan, Melanesian, Micronesian
LANGUAGES English (official), Melanesian Pidgin, more than 700 other indigenous languages
RELIGIONS Traditional beliefs 34%, Roman Catholic 22%, Lutheran 16%, others
CURRENCY Kina = 100 toea

GEOGRAPHY Papua New Guinea is an independent country in the Pacific Ocean, north of Australia. It is part of a Pacific island region called Melanesia. Papua New Guinea includes the eastern part of New Guinea, the Bismarck Archipelago, the northern Solomon Islands, the D'Entrecasteaux Islands and the Louisiade Archipelago. The land is largely mountainous. The climate is tropical. Most of the rain occurs during the monsoon season (December–April), when winds blow from the north-east. During the dry season, the winds blow from the south-west.

POLITICS & ECONOMY The Dutch took western New Guinea (now part of Indonesia) in 1828, but it was not until 1884 that Germany took north-eastern New Guinea and Britain took the south-east. In 1906, Britain handed the south-east over to Australia. It then became known as the Territory of Papua. When World War I broke out in 1914, Australia took German New Guinea and, in 1921, the League of Nations gave Australia a mandate to rule the area, which was named the Territory of New Guinea.

Japan invaded New Guinea in 1942, but the Allies reconquered the area in 1944. In 1949, Papua and New Guinea were combined. Papua New Guinea became independent in 1975. The new nation sought to develop its mineral reserves. One of the most valuable mines was on Bougainville, in the northern Solomon Islands, but a secessionist group declared the island independent. A peace treaty was agreed in 2001. In 2004, Australia sent police to the country to help fight crime after a report had stated that the country was heading for social and economic collapse.

The World Bank classifies Papua New Guinea as a 'lower-middle-income' developing country. Agriculture employs three out of every four people, many of whom produce little more than they need to feed their families. Minerals, notably copper and gold, are the most valuable exports.

PARAGUAY

AREA 406,752 sq km [157,047 sq mi]
POPULATION 6,191,000
CAPITAL (POPULATION) Asunción (547,000)
GOVERNMENT Multiparty republic
ETHNIC GROUPS Mestizo 95%
LANGUAGES Spanish and Guaraní (both official)
RELIGIONS Roman Catholic 90%, Protestant
CURRENCY Guaraní = 100 céntimos

GEOGRAPHY The Republic of Paraguay is a landlocked country and rivers, notably the Paraná, Pilcomayo (Brazo Sur) and Paraguay, form most of its borders. A flat region called the Gran Chaco lies in the north-west, while the south-east contains plains, hills and plateaux.

Northern Paraguay lies in the tropics, while the south is subtropical. Most of the country has a warm, humid climate.

POLITICS & ECONOMY In 1776, Paraguay became part of a large colony called the Vice-royalty of La Plata, with Buenos Aires as the capital. Paraguayans opposed this move and the country declared its independence in 1811.

For many years, Paraguay was torn by internal strife and conflict with its neighbours. A war against Brazil, Argentina and Uruguay (1865–70) led to the deaths of more than half of Paraguay's population, and a great loss of territory.

General Alfredo Stroessner took power in 1954 and ruled as a dictator. His government imprisoned many opponents. Stroessner was overthrown in 1989. Free multiparty elections were held in 1993, 1998 and 2003. However, the return to democracy often seemed precarious because of rivalries between politicians and army leaders, together with economic recession which arose partly from the problems experienced in neighbouring Argentina and Brazil.

The World Bank classifies Paraguay as a 'lower-middle-income' developing country. Farming and forestry are leading activities. Paraguay produces hydroelectricity and exports power to its neighbours.

PERU

AREA 1,285,216 sq km [496,222 sq mi]
POPULATION 27,544,000
CAPITAL (POPULATION) Lima (5,681,000)
GOVERNMENT Transitional republic
ETHNIC GROUPS Amerindian 45%, Mestizo 37%, White 15%
LANGUAGES Spanish and Quechua (both official), Aymara, other Amazonian languages
RELIGIONS Roman Catholic 90%
CURRENCY New sol = 100 centavos

GEOGRAPHY The Republic of Peru lies in the tropics in western South America. A narrow coastal plain borders the Pacific Ocean in the west. Inland are ranges of the Andes Mountains, which rise to 6,768 m [22,205 ft] at Mount Huascarán, an extinct volcano. East of the Andes lies the Amazon basin.

Lima, on the coastal plain, has an arid climate. The coastal region is chilled by the cold, offshore Humboldt Current. The rainfall increases inland and many mountains in the high Andes are snow-capped.

POLITICS & ECONOMY Spanish conquistadors conquered Peru in the 1530s. In 1820, an Argentinian, José de San Martín, led an army into Peru and declared it independent. But Spain still held large areas. In 1823, the Venezuelan Simon Bolívar led another army into Peru and, in 1824, one of his generals defeated the Spaniards at Ayacucho. The Spaniards surrendered in 1826. Peru suffered much instability throughout the 19th century.

Instability continued in the 20th century. In 1980, when civilian rule was restored, a left-wing group called the Sendero Luminoso, or the 'Shining Path', began guerrilla warfare against the government. In 1990, Alberto Fujimori, son of Japanese immigrants, became president. In 1992, he suspended the constitution and dismissed the legislature. The guerrilla leader, Abimael Guzmán, was arrested in 1992, but instability continued. Following his victory in disputed presidential elections in 2000, Fujimori resigned and sought sanctuary in Japan. In 2001, Alejandro Toledo became the first Peruvian of Amerindian descent to be elected president. Toledo faced many problems, including, in 2003–4, a resurgence in activity by the 'Shining Path' guerrillas.

The World Bank classifies Peru as a 'lower-middle-income' developing country. Major food crops include beans, maize, potatoes and rice. Fish products are exported, but the most valuable export is copper. Peru also produces lead, silver, zinc and iron ore.

PHILIPPINES

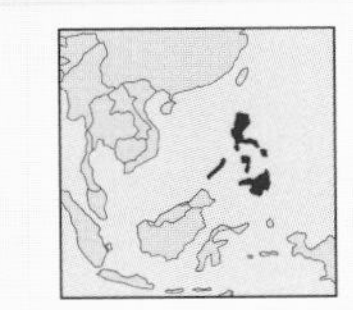

AREA 300,000 sq km [115,830 sq mi]
POPULATION 86,242,000
CAPITAL (POPULATION) Manila (1,581,000)
GOVERNMENT Multiparty republic
ETHNIC GROUPS Christian Malay 92%, Muslim Malay 4%, Chinese and others
LANGUAGES Filipino (Tagalog) and English (both official), Spanish, many others
RELIGIONS Roman Catholic 83%, Protestant 9%, Islam 5%
CURRENCY Philippine peso = 100 centavos

GEOGRAPHY The Republic of the Philippines is an island country in south-eastern Asia. It includes about 7,100 islands, of which 2,770 are named and about 1,000 are inhabited. Luzon and Mindanao, the two largest islands, make up more than two-thirds of the country. The land is mainly mountainous.

The country has a hot tropical climate. The dry season runs from December to April. The rest of the year is wet. Much of the rainfall comes from the typhoons which periodically strike the east coast.

POLITICS & ECONOMY The first European to reach the Philippines was the Portuguese navigator Ferdinand Magellan in 1521. Spanish explorers claimed the region in 1565 when they established a settlement on Cebu. The Spaniards ruled the country until 1898, when the United States took over at the end of the Spanish–American War. Japan invaded the Philippines in 1941, but US forces returned in 1944. The country became fully independent as the Republic of the Philippines in 1946.

Since independence, the country's problems have included armed uprisings by left-wing guerrillas demanding land reform, and Muslim separatist groups, crime, corruption and unemployment. The dominant figure in recent times was Ferdinand Marcos, who ruled in a dictatorial manner from 1965 to 1986. His successors were Corazon Aquino (1986–92), Fidel Ramos (1992–8), and Joseph Estrada, who resigned after massive public protests against his alleged corruption in 2001. He was succeeded by Vice-President Gloria Arroyo. She faced continuing problems in trying, with American help, to defeat the Muslim terrorist groups in the south. In 2003, the government put down a military rebellion. Gloria Arroyo was re-elected president in 2004 and a cease-fire was agreed in the south. However, the cease-fire was broken in 2005.

The Philippines is a developing country which has a 'lower-middle-income' economy. Agriculture employs 36% of the people. The main foods are rice and maize, while such crops as bananas, cocoa, coconuts, coffee, sugar cane and tobacco are all grown commercially. Manufacturing now plays an increasingly important role in the economy.

PITCAIRN

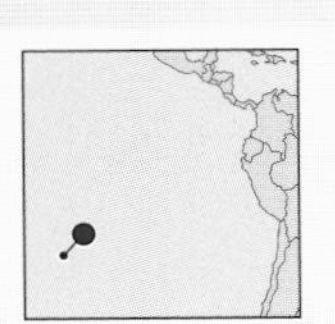

AREA 55 sq km [21 sq mi]
POPULATION 46
CAPITAL Adamstown

Pitcairn Island is a British overseas territory in the Pacific Ocean. Its inhabitants are descendants of the original settlers – nine mutineers from HMS *Bounty* and 18 Tahitians who arrived on this formerly uninhabited island in 1790.

POLAND

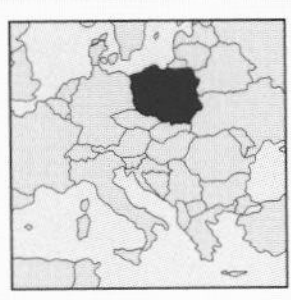

AREA 323,250 sq km [124,807 sq mi]
POPULATION 38,626,000
CAPITAL (POPULATION) Warsaw (1,615,000)
GOVERNMENT Multiparty republic
ETHNIC GROUPS Polish 97%, Belarusian, Ukrainian, German
LANGUAGES Polish (official)
RELIGIONS Roman Catholic 95%, Eastern Orthodox
CURRENCY Zloty = 100 groszy

GEOGRAPHY The Republic of Poland faces the Baltic Sea and, behind its lagoon-fringed coast, lies a broad plain. A plateau lies in the south-east, while the Sudeten Highlands straddle part of the border with the Czech Republic. Part of the Carpathian Range (the Tatra) lies in the south-east.

Poland's climate is influenced by its position in Europe. Warm, moist air masses come from the west, while cold air masses come from the north and east. Summers are warm, but winters are cold and snowy.

POLITICS & ECONOMY Poland's boundaries have changed several times in the last 200 years, partly as a result of its geographical location between the powers of Germany and Russia. It disappeared from the map in the late 18th century, when a Polish state called the Grand Duchy of Warsaw was set up. But in 1815, the country was partitioned, between Austria, Prussia and Russia. Poland became independent in 1918, but in 1939 it was divided between Germany and the Soviet Union. The country again became independent in 1945, when it lost land to Russia but gained some from Germany. Communists took power in 1948, but opposition mounted and eventually became focused through an organization called Solidarity.

Solidarity was led by a trade unionist, Lech Walesa. A coalition government was formed between Solidarity and the Communists in 1989. In 1990, the Communist party was dissolved and Walesa became president. But Walesa faced many problems in turning Poland towards a market economy. In presidential elections in 1995, Walesa was defeated by ex-Communist Aleksander Kwasniewski. However, Kwasniewski continued to follow westward-looking policies and he was re-elected president in 2000. Poland joined the North Atlantic Treaty Organization in 1999 and, on 1 May 2004, it became a member of the European Union.

Poland has large reserves of coal and deposits of various minerals which are used in its factories. Manufactures include chemicals, processed food, machinery, ships, steel and textiles.

PORTUGAL

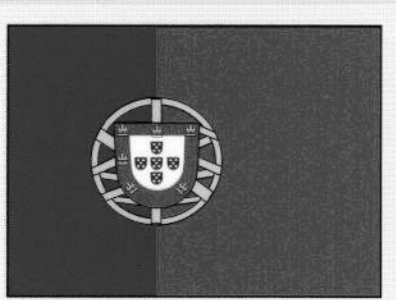
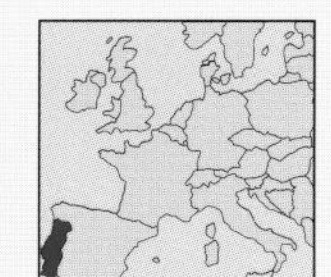

AREA 88,797 sq km [34,285 sq mi]
POPULATION 10,524,000
CAPITAL (POPULATION) Lisbon (663,000)
GOVERNMENT Multiparty republic
ETHNIC GROUPS Portuguese 99%
LANGUAGES Portuguese (official)
RELIGIONS Roman Catholic 94%, Protestant
CURRENCY Euro = 100 cents

GEOGRAPHY The Republic of Portugal is the most westerly of Europe's mainland countries. The land rises from the coastal plains on the Atlantic Ocean to the western edge of the huge plateau, or Meseta, which occupies most of the Iberian peninsula. Portugal also contains two autonomous regions, the Azores and Madeira island groups.

The climate is moderated by winds blowing from the Atlantic Ocean. Summers are cooler and winters are milder than in other Mediterranean lands.

POLITICS & ECONOMY Portugal became a separate country, independent of Spain, in 1143. In the 15th century, Portugal led the 'Age of European Exploration'. This led to the growth of a large Portuguese empire, with colonies in Africa, Asia and, most valuable of all, Brazil in South America. Portuguese power began to decline in the 16th century and, between 1580 and 1640, Portugal was ruled by Spain. Portugal lost Brazil in 1822 and, in 1910, Portugal became a republic. Instability hampered progress and army officers seized power in 1926. In 1928, they chose Antonio de Salazar to be minister of finance.

Salazar became prime minister in 1932 and ruled as a dictator from 1933 until 1968. In 1974, army officers mounted a coup. The new regime made most of Portugal's remaining colonies independent and free elections were held in 1978. Portugal joined the European Community (now the European Union) in 1986 and, on 1 January 2002, the euro replaced the escudo as the sole unit of currency. In 2005, the Socialists, led by a moderate, José Socrates, won a decisive victory in parliamentary elections.

Agriculture and fishing were the mainstays of the economy until the mid-20th century. Forest products, including timber and cork, are important and Portugal received a major setback in 2003 when forest fires caused damage estimated at US$1.1 billion. Manufacturing is now the most valuable sector.

PUERTO RICO

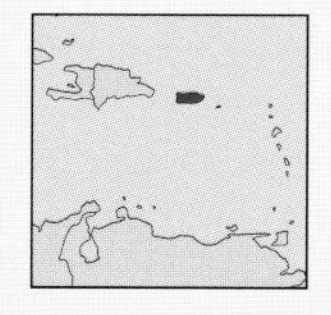

AREA 8,875 sq km [3,427 sq mi]
POPULATION 3,898,000
CAPITAL (POPULATION) San Juan (422,000)

The Commonwealth of Puerto Rico, a mainly mountainous island, is the easternmost of the Greater Antilles chain. The climate is hot and wet. Puerto Rico is a dependent territory of the USA and the people are US citizens. In 1998, 50.2% of the population voted in a referendum on possible statehood to maintain the status quo. Puerto Rico is the most industrialized country in the Caribbean. Tax exemptions attract US companies to the island and manufacturing is expanding.

QATAR

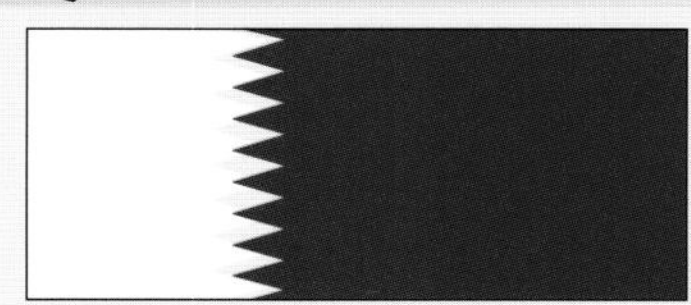
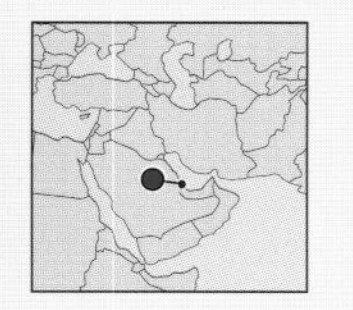

AREA 11,000 sq km [4,247 sq mi]
POPULATION 840,000
CAPITAL (POPULATION) Doha (217,000)

The State of Qatar occupies a low, barren peninsula that extends northwards from the Arabian peninsula into the Persian Gulf. The climate is hot and dry. Qatar became a British protectorate in 1916, but it became independent in 1971. Oil, first discovered in 1939, is the main resource of this prosperous nation. By the early 2000s, Qatar had formulated an independent foreign policy free from Saudi Arabian influence.

RÉUNION

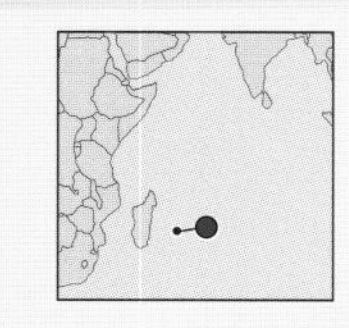

AREA 2,510 sq km [969 sq mi]
POPULATION 766,000
CAPITAL (POPULATION) St-Denis (122,000)

Réunion is a French overseas department in the Indian Ocean. The land is mainly mountainous, though the lowlands are intensely cultivated. Sugar and sugar products are the main exports, but French aid, given to the island in return for its use as a military base, is important to the economy.

ROMANIA

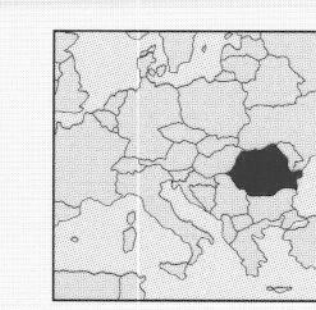

AREA 238,391 sq km [92,043 sq mi]
POPULATION 22,356,000
CAPITAL (POPULATION) Bucharest (2,001,000)
GOVERNMENT Multiparty republic
ETHNIC GROUPS Romanian 89%, Hungarian 7%, Roma 2%, Ukrainian
LANGUAGES Romanian (official), Hungarian, German
RELIGIONS Eastern Orthodox 87%, Protestant 7%, Roman Catholic 5%
CURRENCY Leu = 100 bani

GEOGRAPHY Romania is a country on the Black Sea in eastern Europe. Eastern and southern Romania form part of the Danube river basin. The delta region, near the mouths of the Danube, where the river flows into the Black Sea, is one of Europe's finest wetlands. The southern part of the coast contains several resorts. The heart of the country is called Transylvania. It is ringed in the east, south and west by scenic mountains which are part of the Carpathian mountain system.

Romania has hot summers and cold winters. The rainfall is heaviest in spring and early summer, when thundery showers are common.

POLITICS & ECONOMY From the late 18th century, the Turkish empire began to break up. The modern history of Romania began in 1861 when Walachia and Moldavia united. After World War I (1914–18), Romania, which had fought on the side of the victorious Allies, obtained large areas, including Transylvania, where most people were Romanians. This almost doubled the country's size and population. In 1939, Romania lost territory to Bulgaria, Hungary and the Soviet Union. Romania fought alongside Germany in World War II, and Soviet troops occupied the country in 1944. Hungary returned northern Transylvania to Romania in 1945, but Bulgaria and the Soviet Union kept former Romanian territory. In 1947, Romania officially became a Communist country.

In 1990, Romania held its first free elections since the end of World War II. The National Salvation Front, led by Ion Iliescu and containing many former Communist leaders, won a large majority. A new constitution, approved in 1991, made the country a democratic republic. Elections held under this constitution in 1992 again resulted in victory for Ion Iliescu, whose party was renamed the Party of Social Democracy in 1993. Iliescu was defeated in 1996, but he served again as president between 2000 and 2004, when he stood down. Romania became a member of NATO in 2004 and is expected to join the European Union in 2007.

According to the World Bank, Romania is a 'lower-middle-income' economy. Under Communist rule, industry, including mining and manufacturing, became more important than agriculture.

RUSSIA

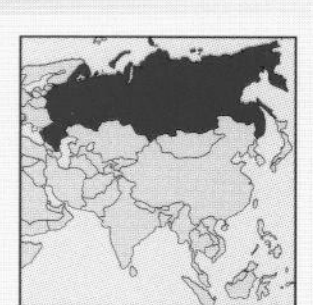

AREA 17,075,400 sq km [6,592,812 sq mi]
POPULATION 143,782,000
CAPITAL (POPULATION) Moscow (8,297,000)
GOVERNMENT Federal multiparty republic
ETHNIC GROUPS Russian 82%, Tatar 4%, Ukrainian 3%, Chuvash 1%, more than 100 others
LANGUAGES Russian (official), many others
RELIGIONS Mainly Russian Orthodox, Islam, Judaism
CURRENCY Russian ruble = 100 kopeks

GEOGRAPHY Russia is the world's largest country. About 25% lies west of the Ural Mountains in European Russia, where 80% of the population lives. It is mostly flat or undulating, but the land rises to the Caucasus Mountains in the south, where Russia's highest peak, Elbrus, at 5,633 m [18,481 ft], is found. Asian Russia, or Siberia, contains vast plains and plateaux, with mountains in the east and south. The Kamchatka peninsula in the far east has many active volcanoes. Russia contains many of the world's longest rivers, including the Yenisey-Angara and the Ob-Irtysh. It also includes part of the world's largest inland body of water, the Caspian Sea, and Lake Baikal, the world's deepest lake.

Moscow has a continental climate with cold and snowy winters and warm summers. Krasnoyarsk in south-central Siberia has a harsher, drier climate, but it is not as severe as parts of northern Siberia.

POLITICS & ECONOMY In the 9th century AD, a state called Kievan Rus was formed by a group of people called the East Slavs. Kiev, now capital of Ukraine, became a major trading centre, but, in 1237, Mongol armies conquered Russia and destroyed Kiev. Russia was part of the Mongol empire until the late 15th century. Under Mongol rule, Moscow became the leading Russian city.

In the 16th century, Moscow's grand prince was retitled 'tsar'. The first tsar, Ivan the Terrible, expanded Russian territory. In 1613, after a period of civil war, Michael Romanov became tsar, founding a dynasty which ruled until 1917. In the early 18th century, Tsar Peter the Great began to westernize Russia and, by 1812, when Napoleon failed to conquer the country,

Russia was a major European power. But during the 19th century, many Russians demanded reforms and discontent was widespread.

In World War I (1914–18), the Russian people suffered great hardships and, in 1917, Tsar Nicholas II was forced to abdicate. In November 1917, the Bolsheviks seized power under Vladimir Lenin. In 1922, the Bolsheviks set up a new nation, the Union of Soviet Socialist Republics (also called the USSR or the Soviet Union).

From 1924, Joseph Stalin introduced a socialist economic programme, suppressing all opposition. In 1939, the Soviet Union and Germany signed a non-aggression pact, but Germany invaded the Soviet Union in 1941. Soviet forces pushed the Germans back, occupying eastern Europe. They reached Berlin in May 1945. From the late 1940s, tension between the Soviet Union and its allies and Western nations developed into a 'Cold War'. This continued until 1991, when the Soviet Union was dissolved.

The Soviet Union collapsed because of the failure of its economic policies. From 1991, President Boris Yeltsin introduced democratic and economic reforms. Yeltsin retired in 1999 and, in 2000, was succeeded by Vladimir Putin. Putin, who was re-elected by a landslide in 2004, has sought to develop increasing contacts with the West. He supported the US-declared war on terrorism, though relations soured when Russia opposed the attack on Iraq in 2003. However, the secessionist conflict in Chechenia mounted in the 21st century and the occupation of a school by Muslim extremists in 2004, which led to more than 300 deaths, caused international outrage. The situation confirmed that Russia's sheer size and diversity makes national unity hard to achieve.

Russia's economy was thrown into disarray after the collapse of the Soviet Union, and in the early 1990s the World Bank described Russia as a 'lower-middle-income' economy. Russia was admitted to the Council of Europe in 1997, essentially to discourage instability in the Caucasus. In 1997, Russia attended the G7 summit, suggesting that Russia was now counted among the world's leading economies. Industry is the chief activity, though, under Communist rule, manufacturing was less efficient than in the West, with an emphasis on heavy industry. Today, light industries producing consumer goods are becoming important. Russia's resources include oil and natural gas, coal, timber, metal ores and hydroelectric power. Russia is a major producer of farm products, though it imports grains. Major crops include barley, flax, fruits, oats, rye, potatoes, sugar beet, sunflower seeds, vegetables and wheat.

RWANDA

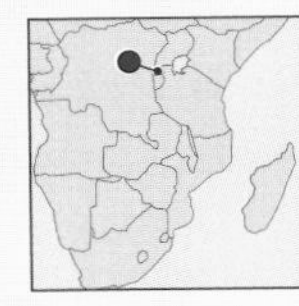

AREA 26,338 sq km [10,169 sq mi]
POPULATION 7,954,000
CAPITAL (POPULATION) Kigali (234,000)
GOVERNMENT Republic
ETHNIC GROUPS Hutu 84%, Tutsi 15%, Twa 1%
LANGUAGES French, English and Kinyarwanda (all official)
RELIGIONS Roman Catholic 57%, Protestant 26%, Adventist 11%, Islam 5%
CURRENCY Rwandan franc = 100 centimes

GEOGRAPHY The Republic of Rwanda is a small, landlocked country in east-central Africa. Lake Kivu and the River Ruzizi in the Great African Rift Valley form Rwanda's western border. Temperatures are moderated by the altitude. The rainfall is abundant.

POLITICS & ECONOMY Germany conquered the area, called Ruanda-Urundi, in the 1890s. However, Belgium occupied the region during World War I (1914–18) and ruled it until 1961, when the people of Ruanda voted for their country to become a republic, called Rwanda. This decision followed a rebellion by the majority Hutu people against the Tutsi monarchy. About 150,000 deaths resulted from this conflict. Many Tutsis fled to Uganda, where they formed a rebel army. Burundi became independent as a monarchy, though it became a republic in 1966.

Relations between Hutus and Tutsis deteriorated and, in 1994, between 500,000 and 800,000 people were massacred. After the Tutsis had restored order, many Hutu rebels fled into the Democratic Republic of the Congo (then Zaïre). Rwanda intervened in the Congo in 1996–2002. In the 2000s, Paul Kagame, the country's effective leader since 1994, worked to create unity and restore stability in Rwanda.

According to the World Bank, Rwanda is a 'low-income' developing country. Most people are poor farmers. Food crops include bananas, beans, cassava and sorghum. Some cattle are raised.

ST HELENA

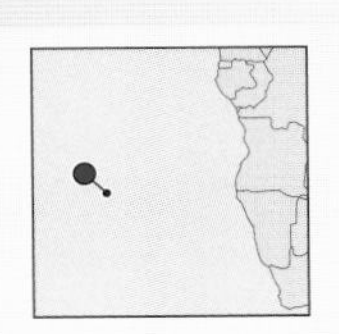

AREA 122 sq km [47 sq mi]
POPULATION 7,000
CAPITAL (POPULATION) Jamestown (1,000)

St Helena, which became a British colony in 1834, is an isolated volcanic island in the south Atlantic Ocean. Now a British overseas territory, it is also the administrative centre of Ascension to the north and Tristan da Cunha to the south.

ST KITTS AND NEVIS

AREA 261 sq km [101 sq mi]
POPULATION 39,000
CAPITAL (POPULATION) Basseterre (12,000)

The Federation of St Kitts and Nevis were settled by Britain in the 1620s, though British ownership was later disputed with France. The nation became independent in 1983. In 1998, a vote for the secession of Nevis did not meet the two-thirds required.

ST LUCIA

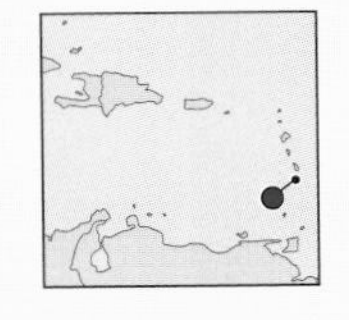

AREA 539 sq km [208 sq mi]
POPULATION 164,000
CAPITAL (POPULATION) Castries (13,000)

From the 16th century, St Lucia often changed hands between Britain and France, but it finally became British in 1814. It became independent in 1979. St Lucia is a mountainous, forested island of extinct volcanoes. It exports bananas and coconuts, and now attracts many tourists.

ST VINCENT AND THE GRENADINES

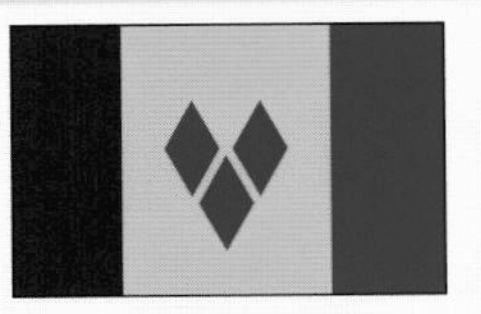

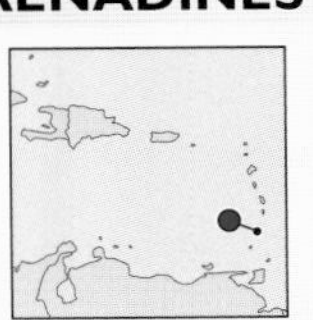

AREA 388 sq km [150 sq mi]
POPULATION 117,000
CAPITAL (POPULATION) Kingstown (15,000)

The island of St Vincent was settled in the 1620s by both British and French settlers. Its ownership was disputed, but it finally became a British territory. St Vincent and the Grenadines achieved independence in 1979. Tourism is growing, but this island country is less prosperous than its neighbours.

SAMOA

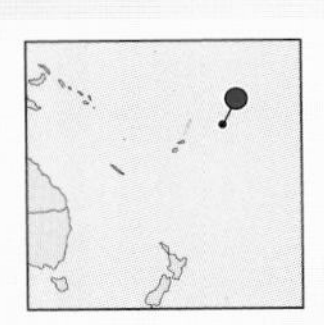

AREA 2,831 sq km [1,093 sq mi]
POPULATION 178,000
CAPITAL (POPULATION) Apia (32,000)

The Independent State of Samoa (formerly Western Samoa) comprises two islands in the South Pacific Ocean. The ownership of these Polynesian islands was disputed by European powers but Germany took control in 1900. Following Germany's defeat in World War I (1914–18), New Zealand governed Western Samoa from 1920 until 1961. The country became independent on 1 January 1962. The economy is based on agriculture, which employs more than 60% of the population, as well as fishing, copra, coconut oil and other coconut products.

SAN MARINO

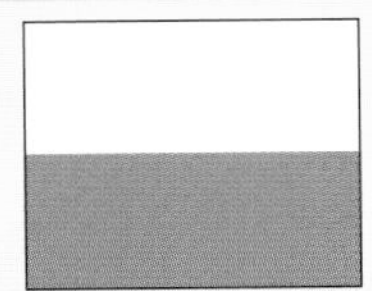

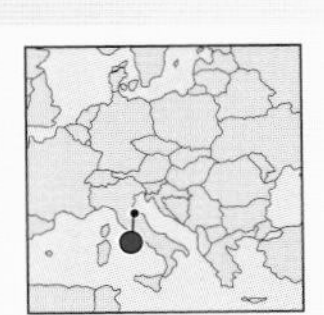

AREA 61 sq km [24 sq mi]
POPULATION 29,000
CAPITAL (POPULATION) San Marino (5,000)

San Marino in northern Italy has been independent since 885 and a republic since the 14th century. It is the world's oldest republic. Tourism is the mainstay of the economy, followed by farming. San Marino also obtains revenue from its postage stamps and annual payment from Italy for certain privileges.

SÃO TOMÉ AND PRÍNCIPE

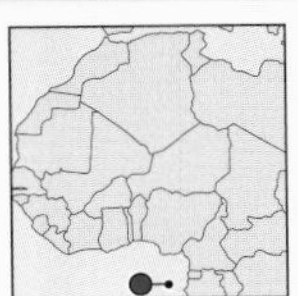

AREA 964 sq km [372 sq mi]
POPULATION 182,000
CAPITAL (POPULATION) São Tomé (43,000)

The Democratic Republic of São Tomé and Príncipe, a mountainous island territory west of Gabon, became Portuguese in 1522. After independence in 1975, the islands became a one-party Marxist state. Multiparty elections were held in 1991. The prospect of offshore oilfields holds out hope for the future.

SAUDI ARABIA

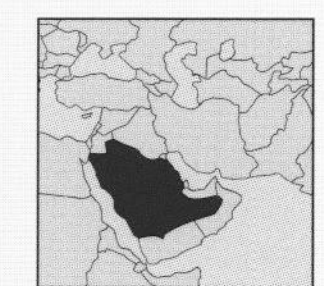

AREA 2,149,690 sq km [829,995 sq mi]
POPULATION 25,796,000
CAPITAL (POPULATION) Riyadh (3,000,000)
GOVERNMENT Absolute monarchy with consultative assembly
ETHNIC GROUPS Arab 90%, Afro-Asian 10%
LANGUAGES Arabic (official)
RELIGIONS Islam 100%
CURRENCY Saudi riyal = 100 halalas

GEOGRAPHY The Kingdom of Saudi Arabia occupies about three-quarters of the Arabian peninsula in south-west Asia. The land is mostly desert, with mountains in the west bordering the Red Sea plains. The climate is hot and dry. In the summer months, temperatures in Riyadh often exceed 40°C [104°F], though the nights are cool.

POLITICS & ECONOMY Saudi Arabia contains the two holiest places in Islam – Mecca (or Makka), the birthplace of the Prophet Muhammad in AD 570, and Medina (Al Madinah) where Muhammad went in 622. These places are visited by many pilgrims.

Saudi Arabia was poor until the oil industry began to operate on the eastern plains in 1933. Oil revenues have been used to develop the country. In the first Gulf War (1980–8), Saudi Arabia supported Iraq against Iran. But when Iraq invaded Kuwait in 1990, it joined the alliance against Iraq. Relations with the US became strained after the terrorist attacks on 11 September 2001, partly because many alleged terrorists were Saudi nationals. But Saudi Arabia denounced the attacks. In 2003 and 2004, Saudi Arabia was itself hit by Islamic attacks, but the government held nationwide municipal elections in 2005.

Saudi Arabia has about 25% of the world's known oil reserves, and oil and oil products make up nearly 90% of its exports. Irrigation and desalination schemes have increased food production.

SENEGAL

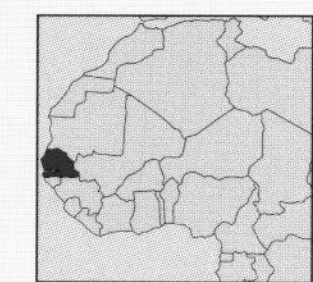

AREA 196,722 sq km [75,954 sq mi]
POPULATION 10,852,000
CAPITAL (POPULATION) Dakar (880,000)
GOVERNMENT Multiparty republic
ETHNIC GROUPS Wolof 44%, Pular 24%, Serer 15%
LANGUAGES French (official), tribal languages
RELIGIONS Islam 94%, Christianity (mainly Roman Catholic) 5%, traditional beliefs 1%
CURRENCY CFA franc = 100 centimes

GEOGRAPHY The Republic of Senegal is on the north-west coast of Africa. The volcanic Cape Verde (Cap Vert), on which Dakar stands, is the most westerly point in Africa. Plains cover most of Senegal, though the land rises gently in the south-east.

Dakar has a tropical climate, with a short rainy season between July and October.

POLITICS & ECONOMY In 1882, Senegal became a French colony, and from 1895 it was ruled as part of French West Africa, the capital of which, Dakar, developed as a major port and city.

In 1959, Senegal joined French Sudan (now Mali) to form the Federation of Mali. But Senegal withdrew in 1960 and became the separate Republic of Senegal. Its first president, Léopold Sédar Senghor, served until 1981, when he was succeeded by Abdou Diouf, who was later made 'president for life'. However, in 2000, Diouf was defeated in presidential elections by Abdoulaye Wade.

Senegal and The Gambia have always enjoyed close relations despite their differing French and British traditions. In 1981, Senegalese troops put down an attempted coup in The Gambia and, in 1982, the two countries set up a defence alliance, called the Confederation of Senegambia. But this confederation was dissolved in 1989.

According to the World Bank, Senegal is a 'lower-middle-income' developing country. It was badly hit in the 1960s and 1970s by droughts, which caused starvation. Agriculture still employs 65% of the population though many farmers produce little more than they need to feed their families. Food crops include groundnuts, millet and rice. Phosphates are the country's chief resource, but Senegal also refines oil which it imports from Gabon and Nigeria. Dakar is a busy port and has many industries.

SERBIA AND MONTENEGRO

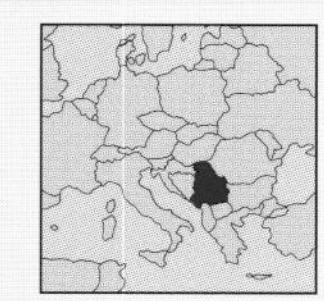

AREA 102,173 sq km [39,449 sq mi]
POPULATION 10,826,000
CAPITAL (POPULATION) Belgrade (1,594,000)
GOVERNMENT Federal republic
ETHNIC GROUPS Serb 62%, Albanian 17%, Montenegrin 5%, Hungarian 3%, others
LANGUAGES Serbian (official), Albanian
RELIGIONS Orthodox 65%, Islam 19%, Roman Catholic 4%, others
CURRENCY New dinar = 100 paras

GEOGRAPHY Serbia and Montenegro are two of the six republics which made up the country of Yugoslavia until it broke up in the early 1990s. From the early 1990s, Serbia and Montenegro were known as the Federal Republic of Yugoslavia. But, in 2003, the two republics became semi-independent and adopted the name of the Union of Serbia and Montenegro.

Behind the coastline on the Adriatic Sea lies an upland region, including the Dinaric Alps and part of the Balkan Mountains. The Pannonian plains, which are drained by the River Danube, are in the north. The coast has a Mediterranean climate. The interior highlands have bitterly cold winters and cool summers. The wettest season is the summer.

POLITICS & ECONOMY People who became known as the South Slavs began to move into the region around 1,500 years ago. Each group, including the Serbs and Croats, founded its own state. But, by the 15th century, foreign countries controlled the region. Serbia and Montenegro were under the Turkish Ottoman empire.

In the 19th century, many Slavs worked for independence and Slavic unity. In 1914, Austria–Hungary declared war on Serbia, blaming it for the assassination of Archduke Francis Ferdinand of Austria–Hungary. This led to World War I and the defeat of Austria–Hungary. In 1918, the South Slavs united in the Kingdom of the Serbs, Croats and Slovenes, which consisted of Bosnia-Herzegovina, Croatia, Dalmatia, Montenegro, Serbia and Slovenia. The country was renamed Yugoslavia in 1929.

Germany occupied Yugoslavia during World War II, but partisans, including a Communist force led by Josip Broz Tito, fought the invaders. From 1945, the Communists controlled the country, which was called the Federal People's Republic of Yugoslavia. But after Tito's death in 1980, the country faced many problems. In 1990, non-Communist parties were permitted and non-Communists won majorities in elections in all but Serbia and Montenegro, where Socialists (former Communists) won control. Yugoslavia split apart in 1991–2 with Bosnia-Herzegovina, Croatia, Macedonia and Slovenia proclaiming their independence. The two remaining republics of Serbia and Montenegro became the new Yugoslavia.

As rival groups struggled for power, fighting broke out in Croatia and Bosnia-Herzegovina. In 1992, the United Nations withdrew recognition of Yugoslavia because of its failure to halt atrocities committed by Serbs living in Croatia and Bosnia. In 1998, conflict flared up in Kosovo, a Yugoslav province where most people are ethnic Albanians. Serb ethnic cleansing in Kosovo led to a NATO offensive against Yugoslavia. Fighting broke out again in Kosovo in 2003 and the gulf between the two ethnic groups appeared to be wider than ever. In the early 21st century, many Montenegrins expressed the wish to secede from Yugoslavia. But, in 2003, Serbia and Montenegro set up a loose union and the name Yugoslavia passed into history.

Under Communist rule, manufacturing became increasingly important in Yugoslavia. But in the early 1990s, the World Bank described what is now Serbia and Montenegro as a 'lower-middle-income' economy. Resources include bauxite, coal, copper and other metals, oil and natural gas. Manufactures, which form the main exports, include aluminium, machinery, plastics, steel, textiles and vehicles. Farming remains important. Crops include fruits, maize, potatoes, tobacco and wheat. Cattle, pigs and sheep are raised.

SEYCHELLES

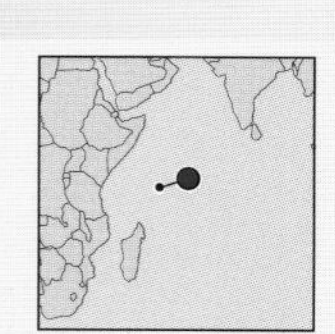

AREA 455 sq km [176 sq mi]
POPULATION 81,000
CAPITAL (POPULATION) Victoria (24,000)

The Republic of Seychelles in the western Indian Ocean achieved independence from Britain in 1976. Coconuts are the main cash crop and fishing and tourism are important.

SIERRA LEONE

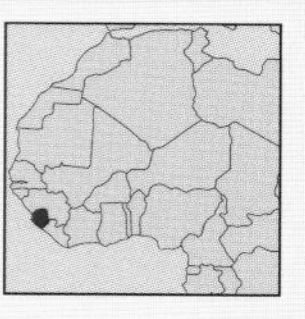

AREA 71,740 sq km [27,699 sq mi]
POPULATION 5,884,000
CAPITAL (POPULATION) Freetown (470,000)
GOVERNMENT Single-party republic
ETHNIC GROUPS Native African tribes 90%
LANGUAGES English (official), Mende, Temne, Krio
RELIGIONS Islam 60%, traditional beliefs 30%, Christianity 10%
CURRENCY Leone = 100 cents

GEOGRAPHY The Republic of Sierra Leone in West Africa is about the same size as the Republic of Ireland. The coast contains several deep estuaries in the north, with lagoons in the south. The most prominent feature is the mountainous Freetown (or Sierra Leone) peninsula. Sierra Leone has a tropical climate, with heavy rainfall between April and November.

POLITICS & ECONOMY A former British territory, Sierra Leone became independent in 1961 and a republic in 1971. It became a one-party state in 1978, but, in 1991, the people voted for the restoration of democracy. The military seized power in 1992 and a civil war caused much destruction in 1994–5. Elections in 1996 were followed by another military coup. In 1998, the West African Peace Force restored the deposed President Ahmed Tejan Kabbah. In 1999, a peace agreement followed further conflict. As part of this agreement, Foday Sankoh, one of the rebel leaders, became vice-president. However, he was arrested in 2000 and charged with war crimes. (He later died in custody in hospital in 2003, while another rebel leader, Johnny Paul Koroma, who was also wanted to stand trial for crimes against humanity, was killed in Liberia.) Conflict resumed, but another cease-fire was agreed. Disarmament continued through 2001. In 2002, the conflict appeared to be over – rebel raids from Liberia in 2003 failed to disturb the country's fragile peace. In 2004, President Kabbah declared a successful end to disarmament in Sierra Leone.

The World Bank classifies Sierra Leone among the 'low-income' economies. Agriculture provides a living for 70% of the people, though farming is mainly at subsistence level. The most valuable exports are minerals, including diamonds, bauxite and rutile (titanium ore). The country has few manufacturing industries.

SINGAPORE

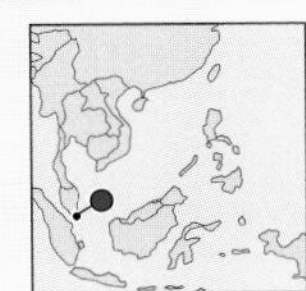

AREA 683 sq km [264 sq mi]
POPULATION 4,354,000
CAPITAL (POPULATION) Singapore City (3,894,000)
GOVERNMENT Multiparty republic
ETHNIC GROUPS Chinese 77%, Malay 14%, Indian 8%
LANGUAGES Chinese, Malay, Tamil and English (all official)
RELIGIONS Buddhism, Islam, Christianity, Hinduism
CURRENCY Singapore dollar = 100 cents

GEOGRAPHY The Republic of Singapore is an island country at the southern tip of the Malay peninsula. It consists of the large Singapore Island and 58 small islands, 20 of which are inhabited. The climate is hot and humid. Rainfall is heavy throughout the year.

POLITICS & ECONOMY In 1819, Sir Thomas Stamford Raffles (1781–1826), agent of the British East India Company, made a treaty with the Sultan of Johor allowing the British to build a settlement on Singapore Island. Singapore soon became the leading British trading centre in South-east Asia and it later became a naval base. Japanese forces seized the island in 1942, but British rule was restored in 1945. In 1963, Singapore became part of the Federation of Malaysia, which also included Malaya and the territories of Sabah and Sarawak on Borneo. In 1965, Singapore broke away and became independent.

The People's Action Party (PAP) has ruled Singapore since 1959. Its leader, Lee Kuan Yew, served as prime minister from 1959 until 1990, when he resigned and was succeeded by Goh Chok Tong. Under the PAP, the economy expanded rapidly, though some considered its rule rather dictatorial. In 2004, Lee Hsien Loong, eldest son of Lee Kuan Yew, succeeded Goh Chok Tong as prime minister and called for a more open society. He also called for more people to marry and have babies, a reflection of the country's falling birth rate.

The World Bank classifies Singapore as a 'high-income' economy. A skilled workforce has created a fast-growing economy, but the recession in 1997–8 was a setback. Trade and finance are leading activities. Manufactures include electronic products, machinery, scientific instruments, textiles and ships. Singapore has a large oil refinery. Petroleum products and manufactures are the main exports.

SLOVAK REPUBLIC

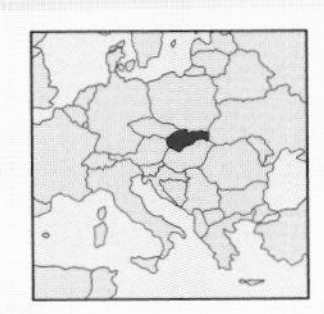

AREA 49,012 sq km [18,924 sq mi]
POPULATION 5,424,000
CAPITAL (POPULATION) Bratislava (449,000)
GOVERNMENT Multiparty republic
ETHNIC GROUPS Slovak 86%, Hungarian 11%
LANGUAGES Slovak (official), Hungarian
RELIGIONS Roman Catholic 60%, Protestant 8%, Orthodox 4%, others
CURRENCY Slovak koruna = 100 halierov

GEOGRAPHY The Slovak Republic is a predominantly mountainous country, consisting of part of the Carpathian range. The highest peak is Gerlachovka in the Tatra Mountains, which reaches 2,655 m [8,711 ft]. The south is a fertile lowland.

The Slovak Republic has cold winters and warm summers. Kosice, in the east, has average temperatures ranging from –3°C [27°F] in January to 20°C [68°F] in July. The highland areas are much colder. Snow or rain falls throughout the year. Kosice has an average annual rainfall of 600 mm [24 in], the wettest months being July and August.

POLITICS & ECONOMY Slavic peoples settled in the region in the 5th century AD. They were subsequently conquered by Hungary, beginning a millennium of Hungarian rule and suppression of Slovak culture.

In 1867, Hungary and Austria united to form Austria–Hungary, of which the present-day Slovak Republic was a part. Austria–Hungary collapsed at the end of World War I (1914–18). The Czech and Slovak people then united to form a new nation, Czechoslovakia. But Czech domination led to resentment by many Slovaks. In 1939, the Slovak Republic declared itself independent, but Germany occupied the country. At the end of World War II, the Slovak Republic again became part of Czechoslovakia.

The Communist party took control in 1948. In the 1960s, many people sought reform, but they were crushed by the Russians. In the late 1980s, demands for democracy mounted and a non-Communist government took office in 1990. Elections in 1992 led to victory for the Movement for a Democratic Slovakia headed by a former Communist and nationalist, Vladimir Meciar, and the independent Slovak Republic came into existence on 1 January 1993.

Independence raised national aspirations among Slovakia's Magyar-speaking community, but relations with Hungary deteriorated when the Magyars felt that administrative changes under-represented them politically. The government also made Slovak the only official language. The government's autocratic rule and human rights record provoked international criticism. In 1998, Meciar's party was defeated and Mikulas Dzurinda replaced Meciar as prime minister. Dzurinda narrowly held on to power in parliamentary elections in 2002 and his government continued its policy of strengthening its ties to the West. It achieved its aim in 2004, when it became a member of both the North Atlantic Treaty Organization and of the European Union.

Before 1948, the Slovak Republic's economy was based on farming, but Communist governments developed manufacturing industries, producing such things as chemicals, machinery, steel and weapons. Since the late 1980s, many state-run businesses have been handed over to private owners.

SLOVENIA

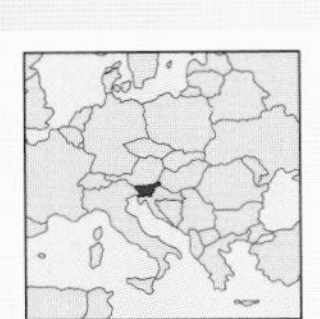

AREA 20,256 sq km [7,821 sq mi]
POPULATION 2,011,000
CAPITAL (POPULATION) Ljubljana (264,000)
GOVERNMENT Multiparty republic
ETHNIC GROUPS Slovene 92%, Croat 1%, Serb, Hungarian, Bosniak
LANGUAGES Slovenian (official), Serbo-Croatian
RELIGIONS Mainly Roman Catholic
CURRENCY Tolar = 100 stotin

GEOGRAPHY The Republic of Slovenia was one of the six republics which made up the former Yugoslavia. Much of the land is mountainous, rising to 2,863 m [9,393 ft] at Mount Triglav in the Julian Alps (Julijske Alpe) in the north-west. Central Slovenia contains the limestone Karst region. The Postojna caves near Ljubljana are among the largest in Europe. The coast has a mild Mediterranean climate, but inland the climate is more continental. The mountains are snow-capped in winter.

POLITICS & ECONOMY In the last 2,000 years, the Slovene people have been independent as a nation for less than 50 years. The Austrian Habsburgs ruled over the region from the 13th century until World War I. Slovenia became part of the Kingdom of the Serbs, Croats and Slovenes (later called Yugoslavia) in 1918. During World War II, Slovenia was invaded and partitioned between Italy, Germany and Hungary, but, after the war, Slovenia again became part of Yugoslavia.

From the late 1960s, some Slovenes demanded independence, but the central government opposed the break-up of the country. In 1990, when Communist governments had collapsed throughout Eastern Europe, elections were held and a non-Communist coalition government was set up. Slovenia then declared itself independent. This led to fighting between Slovenes and the federal army, but Slovenia did not become a battlefield like other parts of the former Yugoslavia. The European Community recognized Slovenia's independence in 1992. The electors returned a coalition led by the Liberal Democrats in 1992, 1996 and 2000. In 2004, Slovenia became a member of the North Atlantic Treaty Organization and the European Union. In October 2004, the centre-right Slovenian Democratic Party topped the polls in parliamentary elections. A centre-right coalition was formed, stating that it would continue Slovenia's westward-leaning stance.

The reform of the formerly state-run economy caused problems for Slovenia. However, it has enjoyed considerable economic progress, with one of Europe's fastest growing economies. In 1992, the World Bank classified Slovenia's economy as 'upper-middle-income'. Manufacturing is the leading activity and manufactures are the main exports. Manufactures include chemicals, machinery and transport equipment, metal goods and textiles. Agriculture and forestry employ 9% of the people. Fruits, maize, potatoes and wheat are the main crops.

SOLOMON ISLANDS

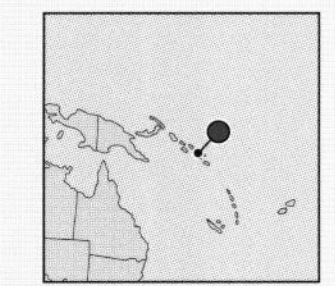

AREA 28,896 sq km [11,157 sq mi]
POPULATION 524,000
CAPITAL (POPULATION) Honiara (49,000)

The Solomon Islands, a chain of mainly volcanic islands in the Pacific Ocean, were a British territory between 1893 and 1978. The chain extends for some 2,250 km [1,400 mi]. They were the scene of fierce fighting in World War II. In 2003, an Australian peace-keeping force went to the Solomon Islands, which, the government believed, were threatened with anarchy. Fish, coconuts and cocoa are leading products, though economic development is hampered by the mountainous, forested terrain.

SOMALIA

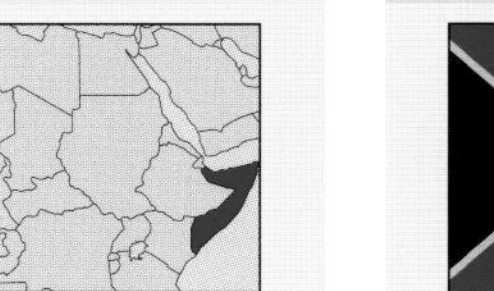

AREA 637,657 sq km [246,199 sq mi]
POPULATION 8,305,000
CAPITAL (POPULATION) Mogadishu (900,000)
GOVERNMENT Single-party republic, military dominated
ETHNIC GROUPS Somali 85%, Bantu, Arab and others
LANGUAGES Somali (official), Arabic, English, Italian
RELIGIONS Islam (Sunni Muslim)
CURRENCY Somali shilling = 100 cents

GEOGRAPHY The Somali Democratic Republic, or Somalia, is in a region known as the 'Horn of Africa'. It is more than twice the size of Italy, the country which once ruled the southern part of Somalia. The most mountainous part of the country is in the north, behind the narrow coastal plains that border the Gulf of Aden.

Rainfall is light throughout Somalia. The wettest regions are the south and the northern mountains, but droughts often occur. Temperatures are high on the low plateaux and plains.

POLITICS & ECONOMY European powers became interested in the Horn of Africa in the 19th century. In 1884, Britain made the northern part of what is now Somalia a protectorate, while Italy took the south in 1905. The new boundaries divided the Somalis into five areas: the two Somalilands, Djibouti (which was taken by France in the 1880s), Ethiopia and Kenya. Since then, many Somalis have longed for reunification in a Greater Somalia.

Italy entered World War II in 1940 and invaded British Somaliland. But British forces conquered the region in 1941 and ruled both Somalilands until 1950, when the United Nations asked Italy to take over the former Italian Somaliland for ten years. In 1960, both Somalilands became independent and united to become Somalia.

Somalia has faced many problems since independence. Economic problems led a military group to seize power in 1969. In the 1970s, Somalia supported an uprising of Somali-speaking people in the Ogaden region of Ethiopia. But Ethiopian forces prevailed and, in 1988, Somalia signed a peace treaty with Ethiopia. The cost of the fighting weakened Somalia's economy. In the 1990s, Somalia gradually broke apart. In 1991, the people in what was formerly British Somaliland set up the 'Somaliland Republic', although it never received international recognition. The north-east, which was called Puntland, also seceded from Somalia, while civil war, based on clan rivalry, raged in the south. US troops sent into the south by the UN in 1993 were forced to withdraw in 1994 and the clan warfare continued. A three-year transitional government set up in 2000 failed to bring peace. In 2004–5, a parliament, president and cabinet were formed in neighbouring Kenya, but the new regime feared violence if it returned to Somalia.

Somalia is a developing country, whose economy has been shattered by drought and war. Catastrophic flooding in late 1997 displaced tens of thousands of people, further damaging the country's infrastructure and destroying hopes of economic recovery.

Many Somalis are nomads who raise livestock. Live animals, meat and hides and skins are major exports, followed by bananas grown in the wetter south. Other crops include citrus fruits, cotton, maize and sugar cane. Mining and manufacturing remain relatively unimportant in the economy.

SOUTH AFRICA

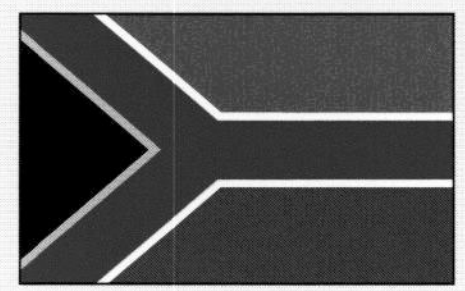

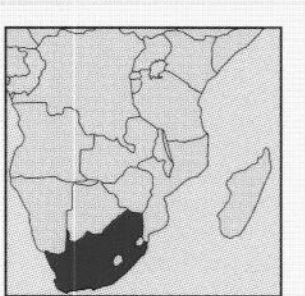

AREA 1,221,037 sq km [471,442 sq mi]
POPULATION 42,719,000
CAPITAL (POPULATION) Cape Town (legislative, 855,000); Tshwane/Pretoria (administrative, 692,000); Bloemfontein (judiciary, 350,000)
GOVERNMENT Multiparty republic
ETHNIC GROUPS Black 76%, White 13%, Coloured 9%, Asian 2%
LANGUAGES Afrikaans, English, Ndebele, Pedi, Sotho, Swazi, Tsonga, Tswana, Venda, Xhosa and Zulu (all official)
RELIGIONS Christianity 68%, Islam 2%, Hinduism 1%
CURRENCY Rand = 100 cents

GEOGRAPHY The Republic of South Africa is made up largely of the southern part of the huge plateau which makes up most of southern Africa. The highest peaks are in the Drakensberg range, which is formed by the uplifted rim of the plateau. The coastal plains include part of the Namib Desert in the north-west.

Most of South Africa has a mild, sunny climate. Much of the coastal strip, including the city of Cape Town, has warm, dry summers and mild, rainy winters. Inland, large areas are arid.

POLITICS & ECONOMY Early inhabitants in South Africa were the Khoisan. In the last 2,000 years, Bantu-speaking people moved into the area. Their descendants include the Zulu, Xhosa, Sotho and Tswana. The Dutch founded a settlement at the Cape in 1652, but Britain took over in the early 19th century, making the area a colony. The Dutch, called Boers or Afrikaners, resented British rule and moved inland. Rivalry between the groups led to Anglo-Boer Wars in 1880–1 and 1899–1902.

In 1910, the country was united as the Union of South Africa. In 1948, the National Party won power and introduced a policy known as apartheid, under which non-whites had no votes and their human rights were strictly limited. In 1990, Nelson Mandela, leader of the African National Congress (ANC), was released from prison. Multiracial elections were held in 1994 and Mandela became president. After Mandela's retirement in 1999, his successor, Thabo Mbeki, led the ANC to an emphatic victory in the elections in 1999 and again, by another landslide, in 2004. Its vote of almost 70% put it far ahead of its nearest rival, the Democratic Alliance, which took only 13%. The government still faced massive problems of poverty and under-development and maintaining national unity – the ANC failed to win outright control of Kwazulu-Natal province, where it was opposed by the nationalist Inkatha Freedom Party, and Western Cape province. South Africa also faces a major health crisis, with about 11% of the population infected with the HIV virus. It has the world's highest number of infected people. Until 2004, the government refused to provide anti-retroviral drugs to slow down the effects of the disease, citing cost and safety.

South Africa is Africa's most developed country. However, most of the black people are poor, with low standards of living. Natural resources include diamonds, gold and many other metals. Mining and manufacturing are the most valuable activities. Products include chemicals, iron and steel, metal goods, processed food, and vehicles. Major crops include fruits, maize, potatoes, sugar cane, tobacco and wheat. Livestock products are also important.

SPAIN

AREA 497,548 sq km [192,103 sq mi]
POPULATION 40,281,000
CAPITAL (POPULATION) Madrid (2,939,000)
GOVERNMENT Constitutional monarchy
ETHNIC GROUPS Composite of Mediterranean and Nordic types
LANGUAGES Castilian Spanish (official) 74%, Catalan 17%, Galician 7%, Basque 2%
RELIGIONS Roman Catholic 94%, others
CURRENCY Euro = 100 cents

GEOGRAPHY The Kingdom of Spain is the second largest country in Western Europe after France. It shares the Iberian peninsula with Portugal. A large plateau, called the Meseta, covers most of Spain. Much of the Meseta is flat, but it is crossed by several mountain ranges, called sierras.

The northern highlands include the Cantabrian Mountains (Cordillera Cantabrica) and the high Pyrenees, which form Spain's border with France. But Mulhacén, the highest peak on the Spanish mainland, is in the Sierra Nevada in the south-east. Spain also contains fertile coastal plains. Other major lowlands are the Ebro river basin in the north-east and the Guadalquivir river basin in the south-west. Spain also includes the Balearic Islands in the Mediterranean Sea and the Canary Islands off the north-west coast of Africa.

The Meseta has a continental climate, with hot summers and cold winters, when temperatures often fall below freezing point. Snow frequently covers the mountain ranges on the Meseta. The Mediterranean coasts have hot, dry summers and mild winters.

POLITICS & ECONOMY In the 16th century, Spain became a world power. At its peak, it controlled much of Central and South America, parts of Africa and the Philippines in Asia. Spain began to decline in the late 16th century. Its sea power was destroyed by a British fleet in the Battle of Trafalgar (1805). By the 20th century, it was a poor country.

Spain became a republic in 1931, but the republicans were defeated in the Spanish Civil War (1936–9). General Francisco Franco (1892–1975) became the country's dictator, though, technically, it was a monarchy. When Franco died, the monarchy was restored. Prince Juan Carlos became king.

Spain has several groups with their own languages

and cultures. Since the late 1970s, regional parliaments have been set up in the northern Basque Country (called Euskadi in the indigenous language and Pais Vasco in Spanish), in Catalonia in the north-east, and in Galicia in the north-west. Some Basque nationalists have committed terrorist acts in their quest for secession and, in 2003, Spain's Supreme Court voted to ban Batasuna, the Basque separatist party. In March 2004, bombings attributed to al Qaida terrorists killed about 200 people in Madrid. Following the bombings, the opposition socialists won the parliamentary elections. In 2005, the new government rejected proposals to make the Basque Country a 'free state' associated with Spain.

The revival of Spain's economy, which was shattered by the Civil War, began in the 1950s and 1960s, especially through the growth of tourism and manufacturing. Since the 1950s, Spain has changed from a poor country, dependent on agriculture, to a fairly prosperous industrial nation.

By the early 2000s, agriculture employed about 6% of the people, as compared with industry, 17%, and services, including tourism, 77%. Farmland, including pasture, makes up about two-thirds of the land, with forest making up most of the rest. Major crops include barley, citrus fruits, grapes for wine-making, olives, potatoes and wheat.

Spain has some high-grade iron ore in the north, though otherwise it lacks natural resources. But it has many manufacturing industries. Manufactures include cars, chemicals, clothing, electronics, processed food, metal goods, steel and textiles. The leading manufacturing centres are Barcelona, Bilbao and Madrid.

SRI LANKA

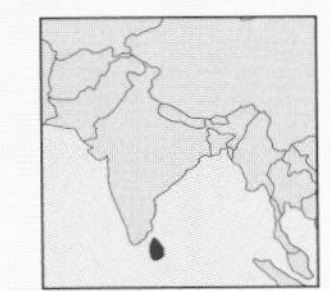

AREA 65,610 sq km [25,332 sq mi]
POPULATION 19,905,000
CAPITAL (POPULATION) Colombo (642,000)
GOVERNMENT Multiparty republic
ETHNIC GROUPS Sinhalese 74%, Tamil 18%, Moor 7%
LANGUAGES Sinhala and Tamil (both official)
RELIGIONS Buddhism 70%, Hinduism 15%, Christianity 8%, Islam 7%
CURRENCY Sri Lankan rupee = 100 cents

GEOGRAPHY The Democratic Socialist Republic of Sri Lanka is an island nation, separated from the south-east coast of India by the Palk Strait. The land is mostly low-lying, surrounding mountains in the south-centre. Western Sri Lanka has a wet equatorial climate. Temperatures are high and the rainfall is heavy. The east is drier than the west.

POLITICS & ECONOMY From the early 16th century, Ceylon (as Sri Lanka was then known) was ruled successively by the Portuguese, Dutch and British. Independence was achieved in 1948 and the country was renamed Sri Lanka in 1972.

After independence, rivalries between the two main ethnic groups, the Sinhalese and Tamils, marred progress. In the 1950s, the government made Sinhala the official language. Following protests, the prime minister made provisions for Tamil to be used in some areas. In 1959, the prime minister was assassinated by a Sinhalese extremist and he was succeeded by Sirimavo Bandanaraike, who became the world's first woman prime minister.

Conflict between Tamils and Sinhalese continued in the 1970s and 1980s. In 1987, India helped to engineer a cease-fire. Indian troops arrived to enforce the agreement, but withdrew in 1990 after failing to subdue the main guerrilla group, the Tamil Tigers, who wanted to set up an independent Tamil homeland in northern Sri Lanka. In 1993, the country's president was assassinated by a suspected Tamil separatist. Offensives against the Tamil Tigers continued until hopes of peace were raised in 2002, with the signing of a cease-fire. In late 2004, a tsunami, caused by a sudden movement of the plates underlying the eastern Indian Ocean, struck parts of the coast of Sri Lanka, killing more than 30,000 people. The tragedy failed to lead to a conciliation between the warring forces and, in 2005, the killing of some Tamil leaders threatened renewed conflict.

The World Bank classifies Sri Lanka as a 'low-income' developing country. Agriculture employs half of the workforce, and coconuts, rubber and tea are exported. Rice is the chief food crop. Textiles and clothing, petroleum products and jewellery are also exported.

SUDAN

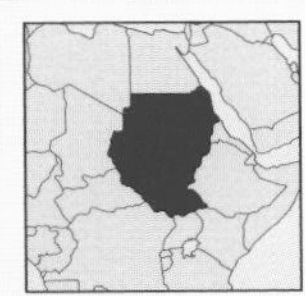

AREA 2,505,813 sq km [967,494 sq mi]
POPULATION 39,148,000
CAPITAL (POPULATION) Khartoum (947,000)
GOVERNMENT Military regime
ETHNIC GROUPS Black 52%, Arab 39%, Beja 6%, others
LANGUAGES Arabic (official), Nubian, Ta Bedawie
RELIGIONS Islam 70%, traditional beliefs 25%
CURRENCY Sudanese dinar = 10 Sudanese pounds

GEOGRAPHY The Republic of Sudan is the largest country in Africa. From north to south, it spans a vast area extending from the arid Sahara in the north to the wet equatorial region in the south. The land is mostly flat, with the highest mountains in the far south. The climate of Khartoum represents a transition between the virtually rainless northern deserts and the equatorial lands in the south.

POLITICS & ECONOMY In the 19th century, Egypt gradually took over Sudan. In 1881, a Muslim religious teacher, the Mahdi ('divinely appointed guide'), led an uprising. Britain and Egypt put the rebellion down in 1898. In 1899, they agreed to rule Sudan jointly as a condominium.

After independence in 1952, the black Africans in the south, who were either Christians or followers of traditional beliefs, feared domination by the Muslim northerners. For example, they objected to the government declaring that Arabic was the only official language. In 1964, civil war broke out and continued until 1972, when the south was given regional self-government, though executive power was still vested in the military government in Khartoum.

In 1983, the government established Islamic law throughout the country. This sparked off further conflict when the Sudan People's Liberation Army (SPLA) in the south launched attacks on government installations. In 2005, an agreement was signed, bringing peace to the south. But a major conflict, which had started in 2003, was raging in the western region of Darfur, where government-backed militias were attacking local people, driving more than 100,000 refugees into Chad.

The World Bank describes Sudan as a 'low-income' economy. Agriculture employs 60% of the people. The chief crop is cotton. Cotton, gum arabic and sesame seeds are exported, but the most valuable exports are oil and oil products. Manufacturing industries produce mainly items for home consumption.

SURINAME

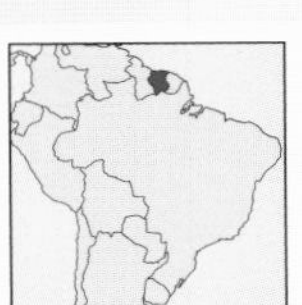

AREA 163,265 sq km [63,037 sq mi]
POPULATION 437,000
CAPITAL (POPULATION) Paramaribo (216,000)
GOVERNMENT Multiparty republic
ETHNIC GROUPS Hindustani/East Indian 37%, Creole (mixed White and Black) 31%, Javanese 15%, Black 10%, Amerindian 2%, Chinese 2%, others
LANGUAGES Dutch (official), Sranang Tonga
RELIGIONS Hinduism 27%, Protestant 25%, Roman Catholic 23%, Islam 20%
CURRENCY Surinamese dollar = 100 cents

GEOGRAPHY The Republic of Suriname is sandwiched between French Guiana and Guyana in north-eastern South America. The narrow coastal plain was once swampy, but it has been drained and now consists mainly of farmland. Inland lie hills and low mountains, which rise to 1,280 m [4,199 ft].

Suriname has a hot, wet and humid climate. Temperatures are high throughout the year.

POLITICS & ECONOMY In 1667, the British handed Suriname to the Dutch in return for New Amsterdam, an area that is now the state of New York. Slave revolts and Dutch neglect hampered development. In the early 19th century, Britain and the Netherlands disputed the ownership of the area. The British gave up their claims in 1813. Slavery was abolished in 1863 and, soon afterwards, Indian and Indonesian labourers were introduced to work on the plantations.

Suriname became fully independent in 1975, but the economy was weakened when thousands of skilled people emigrated from Suriname to the Netherlands. Following a coup in 1980, Suriname was ruled by a military dictator, Dési Bouterse. The adoption of a new constitution led to the restoration of democracy in 1988, though another military coup occurred in 1990. Elections were held in 1996 and 2000. In 1999, Bouterse was convicted *in absentia* in the Netherlands of having led a cocaine-trafficking ring during and after his tenure in office. In 2004, the government announced that he and others would face trial over the killings of 15 people in 1982.

The World Bank classifies Suriname as an 'upper-middle-income' developing country. Its economy is based on mining and metal processing. Suriname is a leading producer of bauxite, from which the metal aluminium is made.

SWAZILAND

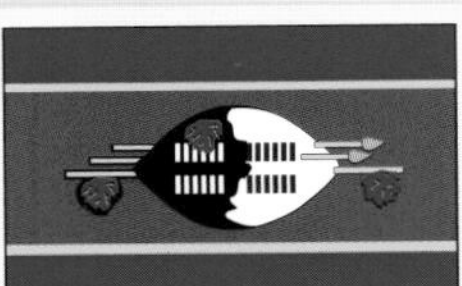

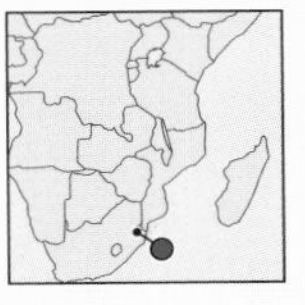

AREA 17,364 sq km [6,704 sq mi]
POPULATION 1,169,000
CAPITAL (POPULATION) Mbabane (38,000)
GOVERNMENT Monarchy
ETHNIC GROUPS African 97%, European 3%
LANGUAGES Siswati and English (both official)
RELIGIONS Zionist (a mix of Christianity and traditional beliefs) 40%, Roman Catholic 20%, Islam 10%
CURRENCY Lilangeni = 100 cents

GEOGRAPHY The Kingdom of Swaziland is a small, landlocked country in southern Africa. The country has four regions which run north–south. In the west, the Highveld, with an average height of

1,200 m [3,950 ft], makes up 30% of Swaziland. The Middleveld, between 350 m and 1,000 m [1,150 ft to 3,280 ft], covers 28% of the country. The Lowveld, with an average height of 270 m [886 ft], covers another 33%. Finally, the Lebombo Mountains reach 800 m [2,600 ft] in the east. The Lowveld is almost tropical, with an average annual temperature of 22°C [72°F] and low rainfall. The altitude moderates the climate in the west.

POLITICS & ECONOMY In 1894, Britain and the Boers of South Africa agreed to put Swaziland under the control of the South African Republic (the Transvaal). But at the end of the Anglo–Boer War (1899–1902), Britain took control of the country. In 1968, when Swaziland became fully independent as a constitutional monarchy, the head of state was King Sobhuza II. Sobhuza died in 1982 and was succeeded by one of his sons, Prince Makhosetive, who, in 1986, was installed as King Mswati III. Elections in 1993 and 1998, in which political parties were banned, failed to satisfy protesters who opposed the absolute monarchy. Mswati continued to rule by decree and, in 2004, he announced plans to build palaces for each of his 11 wives. At the same time, the government appealed for aid in the face of a national disaster caused by the spread of HIV/AIDS and a severe drought.

The World Bank classifies Swaziland as a 'lower-middle-income' developing country. Agriculture employs 50% of the people, and farm products and processed foods are the chief exports. Many farmers live at subsistence level. Swaziland's economy is heavily dependent on South Africa and the two countries are linked through a customs union.

SWEDEN

AREA 449,964 sq km [173,731 sq mi]
POPULATION 8,986,000
CAPITAL (POPULATION) Stockholm (744,000)
GOVERNMENT Constitutional monarchy
ETHNIC GROUPS Swedish 91%, Finnish, Sami
LANGUAGES Swedish (official), Finnish, Sami
RELIGIONS Lutheran 87%, Roman Catholic, Orthodox
CURRENCY Swedish krona = 100 öre

GEOGRAPHY The Kingdom of Sweden is the largest of the countries of Scandinavia in both area and population. It shares the Scandinavian peninsula with Norway. The western part of the country, along the border with Norway, is mountainous. The highest point is Kebnekaise, which reaches 2,117 m [6,946 ft] in the north-west. The climate of Sweden becomes more severe from south to north. Stockholm has cold winters and cool summers. The far south is much milder.

POLITICS & ECONOMY Swedish Vikings plundered areas to the south and east between the 9th and 11th centuries. Sweden, Denmark and Norway were united in 1397, but Sweden regained its independence in 1523. In 1809, Sweden lost Finland to Russia, but, in 1814, it gained Norway from Denmark. The union between Sweden and Norway was dissolved in 1905. Sweden was neutral in World Wars I and II. Since 1945, Sweden has become a prosperous country. In 1995, it joined the European Union. However, many people were sceptical about the advantages of EU membership and Sweden did not adopt the euro, the single EU currency, in 1999.

Sweden has wide-ranging welfare services. But many people are concerned about the high cost of these services and the high taxes they must pay. In 1991, the Social Democrats, who had built up the welfare state, were defeated. But the Social Democrats returned to power in 1994. In office, they sought to control public spending and expand the economy. In 2003, the government launched a referendum on replacing Sweden's unit of currency, the krona, with the euro, arguing that this change would help the economy. During the campaign, Sweden's foreign minister, Anna Lindh, was murdered. Shortly afterwards, the Swedish voters rejected the adoption of the euro by 56% to 42%.

Sweden is a highly developed industrial country. Major products include steel and steel goods. Steel is used in the engineering industry to manufacture aircraft, cars, machinery and ships. Sweden has some of the world's richest iron ore deposits. They are located near Kiruna in the far north. But most of this ore is exported, and Sweden imports most of the materials needed by its industries. In 1996, a decision was taken to decommission all of Sweden's nuclear power stations. This is said to be one of the boldest and most expensive environmental pledges ever made by a government.

SWITZERLAND

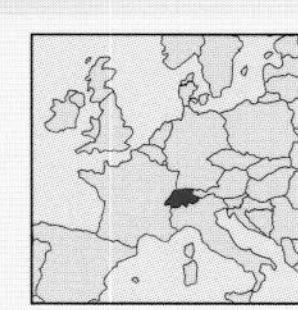

AREA 41,284 sq km [15,940 sq mi]
POPULATION 7,451,000
CAPITAL (POPULATION) Bern (124,000)
GOVERNMENT Federal republic
ETHNIC GROUPS German 65%, French 18%, Italian 10%, Romansch 1%, others
LANGUAGES French, German, Italian and Romansch (all official)
RELIGIONS Roman Catholic 46%, Protestant 40%
CURRENCY Swiss franc = 100 centimes

GEOGRAPHY The Swiss Confederation is a landlocked country in Western Europe. Much of the land is mountainous. The Jura Mountains lie along Switzerland's western border with France, while the Swiss Alps make up about 60% of the country in the south and east. Four-fifths of the people of Switzerland live on the fertile Swiss plateau, which contains most of Switzerland's large cities.

The climate varies according to the height of the land. The plateau region has warm summers and cold, snowy winters. Rain occurs throughout the year.

POLITICS & ECONOMY In 1291, three small cantons (states) united to defend their freedom against the Habsburg rulers of the Holy Roman Empire. They were Schwyz, Uri and Unterwalden, and they called the confederation they formed 'Switzerland'. Switzerland expanded and, in the 14th century, defeated Austria in three wars of independence. After a defeat by the French in 1515, the Swiss adopted a policy of neutrality, which they still follow. In 1815, the Congress of Vienna expanded Switzerland to 22 cantons and guaranteed its neutrality. Switzerland's 23rd canton, Jura, was created in 1979 from part of Bern. Neutrality combined with the vigour and independence of its people have made Switzerland prosperous. In 1993 and again in 2001, the Swiss people voted against starting negotiations to join the European Union. However, in 2002, the Swiss voted by a narrow majority to join the United Nations.

Although lacking in natural resources, Switzerland is a wealthy, industrialized country. Many workers are highly skilled. Major products include chemicals, electrical equipment, machinery and machine tools, precision instruments, processed food, watches and textiles. Farmers produce about three-fifths of the country's food – the rest is imported. Livestock raising, especially dairy farming, is the chief agricultural activity. Crops include fruits, potatoes and wheat. Tourism and banking are also important. Swiss banks attract investors from all over the world.

SYRIA

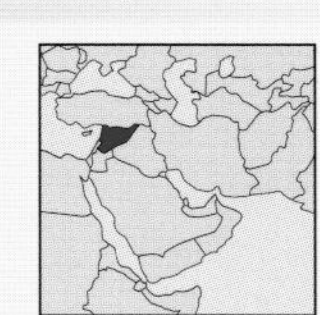

AREA 185,180 sq km [71,498 sq mi]
POPULATION 18,017,000
CAPITAL (POPULATION) Damascus (1,394,000)
GOVERNMENT Multiparty republic
ETHNIC GROUPS Arab 90%, Kurdish, Armenian, others
LANGUAGES Arabic (official), Kurdish, Armenian
RELIGIONS Sunni Muslim 74%, other Islam 16%
CURRENCY Syrian pound = 100 piastres

GEOGRAPHY The Syrian Arab Republic is a country in south-western Asia. The narrow coastal plain is overlooked by a low mountain range which runs north–south. Another range, the Jabal ash Sharqi, runs along the border with Lebanon. South of this range are the Golan Heights, which Israel has occupied since 1967. The coast has a Mediterranean climate, with dry, warm summers and wet, mild winters. The climate becomes drier towards the east.

POLITICS & ECONOMY After the collapse of the Turkish Ottoman empire in World War I, Syria was ruled by France. Since independence in 1946, Syria has been involved in the Arab–Israeli wars and, in 1967, it lost a strategic border area, the Golan Heights, to Israel. In 1970, Lieutenant-General Hafez al-Assad took power, establishing a stable but repressive regime. Following Assad's death in 2000, his son, Bashar Assad, succeeded him. The Israeli occupation of the Golan Heights continues to be one of Syria's main grievances. But Syria has been criticized for supporting Palestinian terrorist groups, keeping its troops in Lebanon and, possibly, having weapons of mass destruction. In 2005, following demonstrations against its continuing military presence in Lebanon, Syria announced a phased withdrawal of its troops.

The World Bank classifies Syria as a 'lower-middle-income' developing country. But it has great potential for development. Its main resources are oil, hydroelectricity from the dam at Lake Assad, and fertile land. Oil is the main export; farm products, textiles and phosphates are also important. Agriculture employs about 26% of the workforce.

TAIWAN

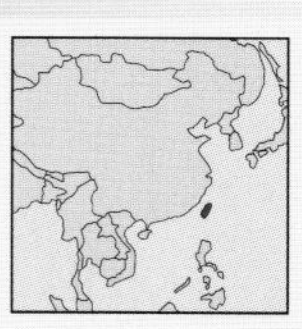

AREA 36,000 sq km [13,900 sq mi]
POPULATION 22,750,000
CAPITAL (POPULATION) Taipei (2,550,000)
GOVERNMENT Unitary multiparty republic
ETHNIC GROUPS Taiwanese 84%, mainland Chinese 14%
LANGUAGES Mandarin Chinese (official), Min, Hakka
RELIGIONS Buddhism, Taoism, Confucianism
CURRENCY New Taiwan dollar = 100 cents

GEOGRAPHY High mountain ranges run down the length of the island, with dense forest in many areas. The climate is warm, moist and suitable for agriculture.

POLITICS & ECONOMY Chinese settlers occupied

Taiwan from the 7th century. In 1895, Japan seized the territory from the Portuguese, who had named it Isla Formosa, or 'beautiful island'. China regained the island after World War II (1939–45). In 1949, China's Communists defeated the Nationalist forces under Chiang Kai-shek, who moved his government to Taiwan. Both regimes regarded themselves as China's legitimate rulers and that Taiwan was a province of China. In the early 1970s, the US favoured the admission of China to the United Nations. This led to the expulsion of the Nationalists from the UN. From the late 1980s, relations between Taiwan and mainland China began to improve. But in the early 21st century, some Taiwanese politicians wanted independence for Taiwan. China threatened to attack if Taiwan did not accept that it was part of China.

Since 1949, with US help, Taiwan has greatly expanded its economy. Despite its lack of natural resources, it produces a wide range of manufactured goods. Agriculture employs about 7% of the people, though only about a fourth of the land can be farmed.

TAJIKISTAN

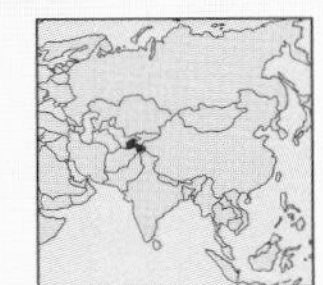

AREA 143,100 sq km [55,521 sq mi]
POPULATION 7,012,000
CAPITAL (POPULATION) Dushanbe (529,000)
GOVERNMENT Transitional democracy
ETHNIC GROUPS Tajik 65%, Uzbek 25%, Russian
LANGUAGES Tajik (official), Russian
RELIGIONS Islam (Sunni Muslim 85%)
CURRENCY Somoni = 100 dirams

GEOGRAPHY The Republic of Tajikistan is one of the five central Asian republics that formed part of the former Soviet Union. Only 7% of the land is below 1,000 m [3,280 ft], while almost all of eastern Tajikistan is above 3,000 m [9,840 ft]. Summers are hot and dry in the lower valleys, and winters are long and bitterly cold in the mountains.

POLITICS & ECONOMY Russia conquered parts of Tajikistan in the late 19th century and, by 1920, Russia took complete control. In 1924, Tajikistan became part of the Uzbek Soviet Socialist Republic, but, in 1929, it was expanded, taking in some areas populated by Uzbeks, becoming the Tajik Soviet Socialist Republic.

While the Soviet Union began to introduce reforms during the 1980s, many Tajiks demanded freedom. In 1989, the Tajik government made Tajik the official language instead of Russian and, in 1990, it stated that its local laws overruled Soviet laws. Tajikistan became fully independent in 1991, following the break-up of the Soviet Union. As the poorest of the ex-Soviet republics, Tajikistan faced many problems in trying to introduce a free-market system.

In 1992, civil war broke out between the government, which was run by former Communists, and an alliance of democrats and Islamic forces. A cease-fire was agreed in 1996, and in 1997 representatives of the opposition were brought into the government. In 2003, changes to the constitution enabled Emomali Rakhmanov, Tajikistan's president since 1994, to serve two more seven-year terms after elections in 2006. His party won parliamentary elections in 2005.

The World Bank classifies Tajikistan as a 'low-income' developing country. Agriculture, mainly on irrigated land, is the main activity and cotton is the chief product. Other crops include fruits, grains and vegetables. The country has large hydroelectric power resources and it produces aluminium.

TANZANIA

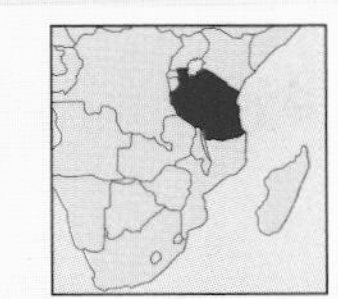

AREA 945,090 sq km [364,899 sq mi]
POPULATION 36,588,000
CAPITAL (POPULATION) Dodoma (204,000)
GOVERNMENT Multiparty republic
ETHNIC GROUPS Native African 99% (Bantu 95%)
LANGUAGES Swahili (Kiswahili) and English (both official)
RELIGIONS Islam 35% (99% in Zanzibar), traditional beliefs 35%, Christianity 30%
CURRENCY Tanzanian shilling = 100 cents

GEOGRAPHY The United Republic of Tanzania consists of the former mainland country of Tanganyika and the island nation of Zanzibar, which also includes the island of Pemba. Behind a narrow coastal plain, most of Tanzania is a plateau, which is broken by arms of the Great African Rift Valley. In the west, this valley contains lakes Nyasa and Tanganyika. The highest peak is Kilimanjaro, Africa's tallest mountain.

The coast has a hot and humid climate, with the greatest rainfall in April and May. The inland plateaux and mountains are cooler and less humid.

POLITICS & ECONOMY Mainland Tanganyika became a German territory in the 1880s, while Zanzibar and Pemba became a British protectorate in 1890. Following Germany's defeat in World War I, Britain took over Tanganyika, which remained a British territory until its independence in 1961. In 1964, Tanganyika and Zanzibar united to form the United Republic of Tanzania. The country's president, Julius Nyerere, pursued socialist policies of self-help (*ujamaa*) and egalitarianism. Many of its social reforms were successful, though the country failed to make economic progress. Nyerere resigned as president in 1985, although he retained much influence until his death in 1999. His successors, Ali Hassan Mwinyi and, from 1995, Benjamin Mkapa, introduced more liberal economic policies.

Tanzania is one of the world's poorest countries. Crops are grown on only 4.2% of the land, yet agriculture employs 80% of the people. Food crops include bananas, cassava, maize, millet and rice.

THAILAND

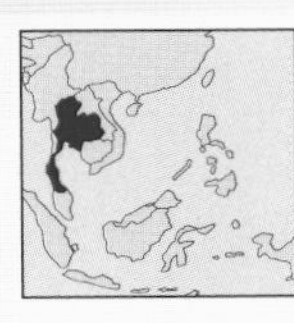

AREA 513,115 sq km [198,114 sq mi]
POPULATION 64,866,000
CAPITAL (POPULATION) Bangkok (6,320,000)
GOVERNMENT Constitutional monarchy
ETHNIC GROUPS Thai 75%, Chinese 14%, others 11%
LANGUAGES Thai (official), English, ethnic and regional dialects
RELIGIONS Buddhism 95%, Islam, Christianity
CURRENCY Baht = 100 satang

GEOGRAPHY The Kingdom of Thailand is one of the ten countries in South-east Asia. The highest land is in the north, where Doi Inthanon, the highest peak, reaches 2,595 m [8,514 ft]. The Khorat plateau, in the north-east, makes up about 30% of the country and is the most heavily populated part of Thailand. In the south, Thailand shares the finger-like Malay peninsula with Burma and Malaysia.

Thailand has a tropical climate. Monsoon winds from the south-west bring heavy rains between the months of May and October.

POLITICS & ECONOMY The first Thai state was set up in the 13th century. By 1350, it included most of what is now Thailand. European contact began in the early 16th century. But, in the late 17th century, the Thais, fearing interference in their affairs, forced all Europeans to leave. This policy continued for 150 years. In 1782, a Thai General, Chao Phraya Chakkri, became king, founding a dynasty which continues today. The country became known as Siam, and Bangkok became its capital. From the mid-19th century, contacts with the West were restored. In World War I, Siam supported the Allies. In 1941, the country was conquered by Japan and became its ally. However, after the end of World War II, it became an ally of the United States.

Since 1967, when Thailand became a member of ASEAN (the Association of South-east Asian Nations), its economy has grown, especially its manufacturing and service industries. However, from 1997, the country suffered economic recession which persisted into the 21st century. In 2004, the country was rocked by sectarian violence in the south where most people are Muslims, many of whom claim that they suffer discrimination by the central government.

Agriculture employs 40% of the people. Rice is the chief crop. Thailand also mines tin and other minerals. However, manufactures, including food products, machinery, timber products and textiles, are the main exports. Tourism is important, though the December 2004 tsunami, which killed more than 500 people, cast a shadow over its future growth.

TOGO

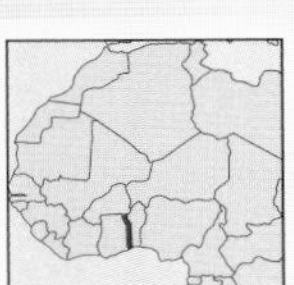

AREA 56,785 sq km [21,925 sq mi]
POPULATION 5,557,000
CAPITAL (POPULATION) Lomé (658,000)
GOVERNMENT Multiparty republic
ETHNIC GROUPS Native African 99% (largest tribes are Ewe, Mina and Kabre)
LANGUAGES French (official), African languages
RELIGIONS Traditional beliefs 51%, Christianity 29%, Islam 20%
CURRENCY CFA franc = 100 centimes

GEOGRAPHY The Republic of Togo is a long, narrow country in West Africa. From north to south, it extends about 500 km [311 mi]. Its coastline on the Gulf of Guinea is only 64 km [40 mi] long. Togo has a hot climate. The main wet season is March–July, with a minor wet season in October–November.

POLITICS & ECONOMY Togo became a German protectorate in 1884 but, in 1919, Britain took over the western third of the territory, while France took over the eastern two-thirds. In 1956, the people of British Togoland voted to join Ghana, while French Togoland became an independent republic in 1960.

A military regime took power in 1963. In 1967, General Gnassingbé Eyadéma became head of state and suspended the constitution. Under a new constitution, adopted in 1992, multiparty elections were held in 1994. In 1998, the count in presidential elections was stopped when it became clear that Eyadéma had been defeated. Leading opposition parties boycotted subsequent elections. Eyadéma died in 2005. His son, Faure, became president, but he soon stepped down after international pressure.

Togo is a poor, developing country dependent on agriculture. Phosphate rock is the leading export.

TONGA

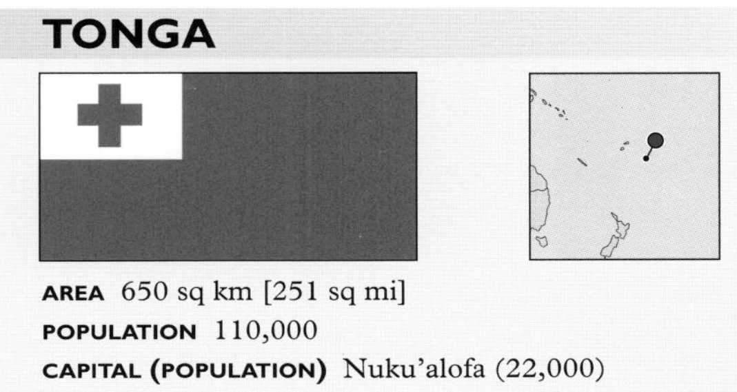

AREA 650 sq km [251 sq mi]
POPULATION 110,000
CAPITAL (POPULATION) Nuku'alofa (22,000)

Originally called the Friendly Islands, the Kingdom of Tonga became a British protectorate in 1900 and achieved independence in 1970. Situated in the South Pacific Ocean, it contains more than 170 islands, 36 of which are inhabited. Agriculture is the main activity – coconuts, copra, fruits and fish are leading products.

TRINIDAD AND TOBAGO

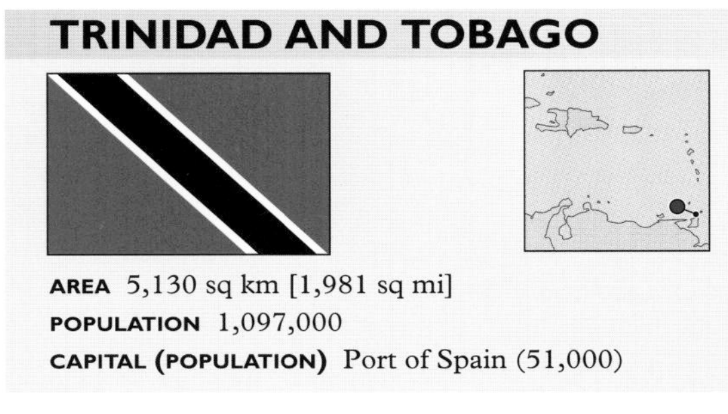

AREA 5,130 sq km [1,981 sq mi]
POPULATION 1,097,000
CAPITAL (POPULATION) Port of Spain (51,000)

Trinidad was captured from the French by the British in 1797, while Tobago was added in 1814. They became a single British colony in 1889. The Republic of Trinidad and Tobago became independent in 1962. These tropical islands, populated by people of African, Asian (mainly Indian) and European origin, are hilly and forested, though there are some fertile plains. Oil production is the main sector of the economy.

TUNISIA

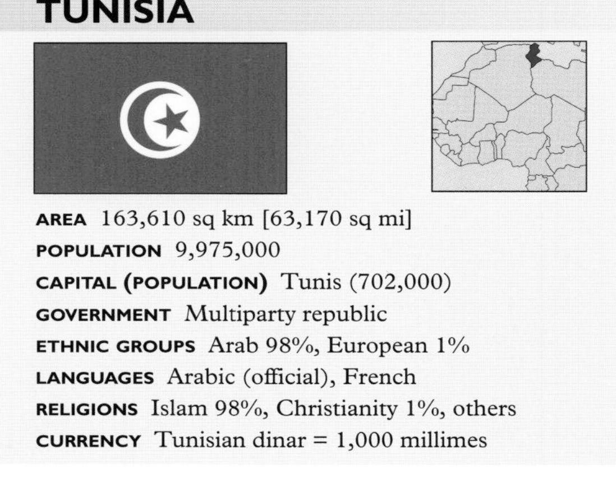

AREA 163,610 sq km [63,170 sq mi]
POPULATION 9,975,000
CAPITAL (POPULATION) Tunis (702,000)
GOVERNMENT Multiparty republic
ETHNIC GROUPS Arab 98%, European 1%
LANGUAGES Arabic (official), French
RELIGIONS Islam 98%, Christianity 1%, others
CURRENCY Tunisian dinar = 1,000 millimes

GEOGRAPHY The Republic of Tunisia is the smallest country in North Africa. The mountains in the north are an eastwards and comparatively low extension of the Atlas Mountains. To the north and east of the mountains lie fertile plains, especially between Sfax, Tunis and Bizerte. In the south, low-lying regions contain a vast salt pan, called the Chott Djerid, and part of the Sahara Desert.

Northern Tunisia has a Mediterranean climate, with dry, sunny summers, and mild winters with a moderate rainfall. The average yearly rainfall decreases towards the south.

POLITICS & ECONOMY In 1881, France established a protectorate over Tunisia and ruled the country until 1956. The new parliament abolished the monarchy and declared Tunisia to be a republic in 1957, with the nationalist leader, Habib Bourguiba, as president. His government introduced many reforms, including votes for women, but various problems arose, including unemployment among the middle class and fears that Western values introduced by tourists might undermine Muslim values. In 1987, the prime minister, Zine el Abidine Ben Ali, removed Bourguiba from office and succeeded him as president. He was elected in 1989 and re-elected in 1994, 1999 and 2004. His victories by landslide majorities provoked charges that the elections were not as democratic as they should have been.

The World Bank classifies Tunisia as a 'middle-income' developing country. The main resources and chief exports are phosphates and oil. Most industries are concerned with food processing. Agriculture employs 22% of the people; major crops being barley, dates, grapes, olives and wheat. Fishing is important, as is the tourist industry.

TURKEY

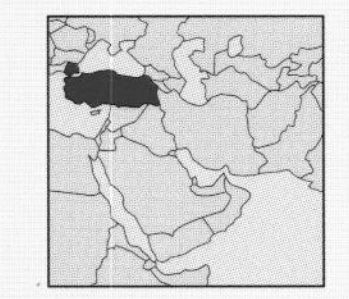

AREA 774,815 sq km [299,156 sq mi]
POPULATION 68,894,000
CAPITAL (POPULATION) Ankara (2,984,000)
GOVERNMENT Multiparty republic
ETHNIC GROUPS Turkish 80%, Kurdish 20%
LANGUAGES Turkish (official), Kurdish, Arabic
RELIGIONS Islam (mainly Sunni Muslim) 99%
CURRENCY New Turkish lira = 100 kurus

GEOGRAPHY The Republic of Turkey lies in two continents. European Turkey, also called Thrace, lies west of a waterway linking the Mediterranean and Black seas. Most of Asian Turkey consists of plateaux and mountains, which rise to 5,165 m [16,945 ft] at Mount Ararat (Agri Dagi) near the border with Armenia. Earthquakes are common.

Central Turkey has a dry climate, with hot, sunny summers and cold winters. The driest part of the central plateau lies south of the city of Ankara, around Lake Tuz. The west has a Mediterranean climate, but the Black Sea coast has cooler summers.

POLITICS & ECONOMY In AD 330, the Roman empire moved its capital to Byzantium, which it renamed Constantinople. Constantinople became capital of the East Roman (or Byzantine) empire in 395. Muslim Seljuk Turks from central Asia invaded Anatolia in the 11th century. In the 14th century, another group of Turks, the Ottomans, conquered the area. In 1453, the Ottoman Turks took Constantinople, which they called Istanbul.

The Ottoman Turks built up a large empire which finally collapsed during World War I (1914–18). In 1923, Turkey became a republic. Its leader Mustafa Kemal, or Atatürk ('father of the Turks'), launched policies to modernize and secularize the country.

Since the 1940s, Turkey has sought to strengthen its ties with Western powers. It joined NATO (North Atlantic Treaty Organization) in 1951 and it applied to join the European Economic Community in 1987. But Turkey's conflict with Greece, together with its invasion of northern Cyprus in 1974, have led many Europeans to treat Turkey's aspirations with caution. Political instability, military coups, conflict with Kurdish nationalists in eastern Turkey, and Turkey's human rights record are other problems.

Turkey has enjoyed democracy since 1983, though, in 1998, the government banned the Islamist Welfare Party, which it accused of violating secular principles. In 1999, the Muslim Virtue Party (successor to Islamist Welfare Party) lost ground. The largest numbers of parliamentary seats were won by the ruling Democratic Left Party and the far-right National Action Party. However, in the elections in 2002, the moderate Islamic Justice and Development Party (AKP) won 362 of the 500 seats in parliament, while none of the parties in the former ruling coalition won 10% of the vote. Turkey hopes to join the European Union. In 2003–4, to this end, it supported talks aimed at re-unifying the Turkish and Greek parts of Cyprus, prior to Cyprus's admission to the EU.

The World Bank classifies Turkey as a 'lower-middle-income' developing country. Agriculture employs 40% of the people, and barley, cotton, fruits, maize, tobacco and wheat are major crops. Livestock farming is important and wool is a leading product.

Turkey produces chromium, but manufacturing is the chief activity. Manufactures include processed farm products and textiles, cars, fertilizers, iron and steel, machinery, metal products and paper products.

TURKMENISTAN

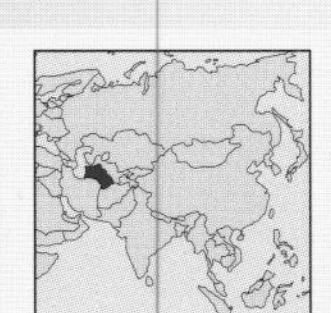

AREA 488,100 sq km [188,455 sq mi]
POPULATION 4,863,000
CAPITAL (POPULATION) Ashkhabad (521,000)
GOVERNMENT Single-party republic
ETHNIC GROUPS Turkmen 85%, Uzbek 5%, Russian 4%, others
LANGUAGES Turkmen (official), Russian, Uzbek, others
RELIGIONS Islam 89%, Eastern Orthodox 9%
CURRENCY Turkmen manat = 100 tenesi

GEOGRAPHY The Republic of Turkmenistan is one of the five central Asian republics which once formed part of the former Soviet Union. Most of the land is low-lying, with mountains lying on the southern and south-western borders. In the west lies the salty Caspian Sea. Most of Turkmenistan is arid and the Garagum, Asia's largest sand desert, covers about 80% of the country. Turkmenistan has a continental climate, with average annual rainfall varying from 80 mm [3 in] in the desert to 300 mm [12 in] in the mountains. Summer months are hot but winter temperatures drop well below freezing point.

POLITICS & ECONOMY Just over 1,000 years ago, Turkic people settled in the lands east of the Caspian Sea and the name 'Turkmen' comes from this time. Mongol armies conquered the area in the 13th century and Islam was introduced in the 14th century. Russia took over the area in the 1870s and 1880s. After the Russian Revolution of 1917, the area came under Communist rule and, in 1924, it became the Turkmen Soviet Socialist Republic. The Communists strictly controlled all aspects of life and discouraged religion. But they improved such services as education, health, housing and transport.

In the 1980s, when the Soviet Union began to introduce reforms, the Turkmen began to demand more freedom. In 1990, the Turkmen government stated that its laws overruled Soviet laws. In 1991, Turkmenistan became fully independent after the break-up of the Soviet Union. But the country kept ties with Russia through the Commonwealth of Independent States (CIS).

In 1992, Turkmenistan adopted a new constitution, allowing for the setting up of political parties, providing that they were not ethnic or religious in character. But, effectively, Turkmenistan remained a one-party state and, in 1992, Saparmurad Niyazov, the former Communist and now Democratic Party leader, was the only candidate. In 1994, a referendum prolonged Niyazov's term of office to 2002, while, in 1999, the parliament declared him president for life. In 2004, parliamentary elections were described as a 'sham', because all the candidates supported the president.

Faced with many economic problems, Turkmenistan began to look south rather than to the CIS for support. As part of this policy, it joined the Economic Co-operation Organization which had been set up in 1985 by Iran, Pakistan and Turkey. In 1996, the completion of a rail link from Turkmenistan to the Iranian coast was seen as an important step in the development of Central Asia. Oil and natural gas are Turkmenistan's chief resources, but agriculture is the main activity. Cotton is the main crop. Grain and vegetables are also important. Manufactures include cement, glass, petrochemicals and textiles.

TURKS AND CAICOS ISLANDS

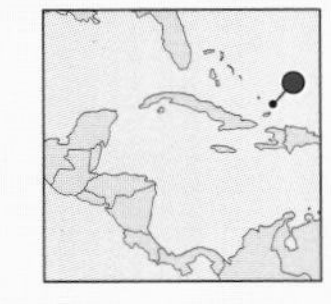

AREA 430 sq km [166 sq mi]
POPULATION 20,000
CAPITAL (POPULATION) Cockburn Town (4,000)

The Turks and Caicos Islands, a British territory in the Caribbean since 1776, are a group of about 30 islands. Fishing and tourism are major activities and lobsters are exported.

TUVALU

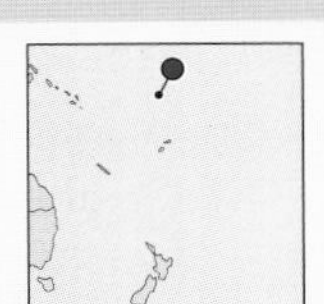

AREA 26 sq km [10 sq mi]
POPULATION 11,000
CAPITAL (POPULATION) Fongafale (3,000)

Tuvalu, formerly called the Ellice Islands, was a British territory from the 1890s until it became independent in 1978. It consists of nine low-lying coral atolls in the southern Pacific Ocean. Copra is the chief export. Rising sea levels caused by global warming are threatening the future of the country.

UGANDA

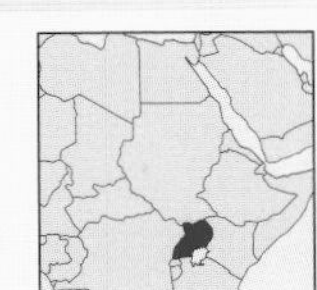

AREA 241,038 sq km [93,065 sq mi]
POPULATION 26,405,000
CAPITAL (POPULATION) Kampala (774,000)
GOVERNMENT Republic in transition
ETHNIC GROUPS Baganda 17%, Ankole 8%, Basogo 8%, Iteso 8%, Bakiga 7%, Langi 6%, Rwanda 6%, Bagisu 5%, Acholi 4%, Lugbara 4% and others
LANGUAGES English and Swahili (both official), Ganda
RELIGIONS Roman Catholic 33%, Protestant 33%, traditional beliefs 18%, Islam 16%
CURRENCY Ugandan shilling = 100 cents

GEOGRAPHY The Republic of Uganda is a landlocked country on the East African plateau. It contains part of Lake Victoria, Africa's largest lake and a source of the River Nile, which occupies a shallow depression in the plateau.

The equator runs through Uganda and the country is warm throughout the year, though the high altitude moderates the temperature. The wettest regions are the area to the north of Lake Victoria and the western mountains, especially the high Ruwenzori range.

POLITICS & ECONOMY Little is known of the early history of Uganda. When Europeans first reached the area in the 19th century, many of the people were organized in kingdoms, the most powerful of which was Buganda, the home of the Baganda people. Britain took over the country between 1894 and 1914, and ruled it until 1962.

In 1967, Uganda became a republic and Buganda's Kabaka (king), Sir Edward Mutesa II, was made president. But tensions between the Kabaka and the prime minister, Apollo Milton Obote, led to the dismissal of the Kabaka in 1966. Obote also abolished the traditional kingdoms, including Buganda. Obote was overthrown in 1971 by an army group led by General Idi Amin Dada. Amin ruled as a dictator. He forced most Ugandan Asians to leave the country and had many of his opponents killed.

In 1978, a border dispute between Uganda and Tanzania led Tanzanian troops to enter Uganda. With help from Ugandan opponents of Amin, they overthrew Amin's government. In 1980, Obote led his party to victory in national elections. But after charges of fraud, Obote's opponents began guerrilla warfare. A military group overthrew Obote in 1985, though strife continued until 1986, when Yoweri Museveni's National Resistance Movement seized power. In 1993, Museveni restored the traditional kingdoms. Elections were held in 1994, but political parties were forbidden. Museveni was elected in 1996 and 2001 and, in 2005, he announced a referendum on the restoration of multiparty democracy. Uganda has suffered in the 21st century from a conflict between government troops and the Lord's Resistance Army in the north, an anarchic organization whose objectives remain unclear.

Internal strife since the 1960s has greatly damaged the economy, but conditions improved during the relative stability of the 1990s and 2000s. Agriculture dominates the economy, employing 80% of the people. The chief export is coffee.

UKRAINE

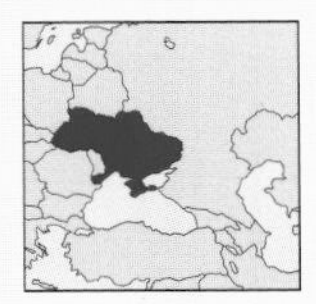

AREA 603,700 sq km [233,089 sq mi]
POPULATION 47,732,000
CAPITAL (POPULATION) Kiev (2,590,000)
GOVERNMENT Multiparty republic
ETHNIC GROUPS Ukrainian 78%, Russian 17%, Belarusian, Moldovan, Bulgarian, Hungarian, Polish
LANGUAGES Ukrainian (official), Russian
RELIGIONS Mostly Ukrainian Orthodox
CURRENCY Hryvnia = 100 kopiykas

GEOGRAPHY Ukraine is the second largest country in Europe after Russia. It was formerly part of the Soviet Union, which split apart in 1991. This mostly flat country faces the Black Sea in the south. The Crimean peninsula includes a highland region overlooking Yalta. Summers are warm, but winters are cold, becoming more severe from west to east. In summer, eastern Ukraine is often warmer than the west. The heaviest rainfall occurs in the summer.

POLITICS & ECONOMY Kiev was the original capital of the early Slavic civilization known as Kievan Rus. In the 17th and 18th centuries, parts of Ukraine came under Polish and Russian rule. But Russia gained most of Ukraine in the late 18th century. In 1918, Ukraine became independent, but in 1922 it became part of the Soviet Union. Millions of people died in the 1930s as a result of Soviet policies, while millions more died during the Nazi occupation (1941–4).

In the 1980s, Ukrainian people demanded more say over their affairs. The country became independent in 1991. Leonid Kuchma, who became president in 1994, came under fire in the early 2000s for maladministration and for his alleged involvement in the murder of a journalist. In 2004, the prime minister, a supporter of Kuchma, was declared the winner in presidential elections, but, after massive demonstrations, parliament declared the election invalid. In 2005, the opposition and pro-Western leader Victor Yuschenko was elected president.

The World Bank classifies Ukraine as a 'lower-middle-income' economy. Agriculture is important. Crops include wheat and sugar beet, which are the main exports. Livestock rearing and fishing are also important. But manufacturing is the chief economic activity. Manufactures include iron and steel, machinery and vehicles. Ukraine has large coalfields. The country imports oil and natural gas, but has hydro-electric and nuclear power stations. In 1986, an accident at the Chernobyl (Chornobyl) nuclear power plant caused widespread radiation. The plant was finally closed in 2000.

UNITED ARAB EMIRATES

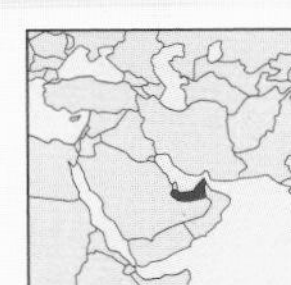

AREA 83,600 sq km [32,278 sq mi]
POPULATION 2,524,000
CAPITAL (POPULATION) Abu Dhabi (363,000)

The United Arab Emirates were formed in 1971 when the seven Trucial States of the Gulf (Abu Dhabi, Dubai, Sharjah, Ajman, Umm al Qawayn, Ra's al Khaymah and Al Fujayrah) opted to join together and form an independent country. The economy of this hot and dry country depends on oil production, and oil revenues give the United Arab Emirates one of the highest per capita GNPs in Asia.

UNITED KINGDOM

AREA 241,857 sq km [93,381 sq mi]
POPULATION 60,271,000
CAPITAL (POPULATION) London (8,089,000)
GOVERNMENT Constitutional monarchy
ETHNIC GROUPS English 82%, Scottish 10%, Irish 2%, Welsh 2%, Ulster 2%, West Indian, Indian, Pakistani and others
LANGUAGES English (official), Welsh, Gaelic
RELIGIONS Christianity, Islam, Sikhism, Hinduism, Judaism
CURRENCY Pound sterling = 100 pence

GEOGRAPHY The United Kingdom (or UK) is a union of four countries. Three of them – England, Scotland and Wales – make up Great Britain. The fourth country is Northern Ireland. The Isle of Man and the Channel Islands, including Jersey and Guernsey, are not part of the UK. They are self-governing British dependencies.

The land is highly varied. Much of Scotland and Wales is mountainous, and the highest peak is

Scotland's Ben Nevis at 1,342 m [4,404 ft]. England has some highland areas, including the Cumbrian Mountains (or Lake District) and the Pennine range in the north. But England also has large areas of fertile lowland. Northern Ireland is also a mixture of lowlands and uplands. It contains the UK's largest lake, Lough Neagh.

The UK has a mild climate, influenced by the warm Gulf Stream which flows across the Atlantic from the Gulf of Mexico, then past the British Isles. Moist winds from the south-west bring rain, but the rainfall decreases from west to east. Winds from the east and north bring cold weather in winter.

POLITICS & ECONOMY In ancient times, Britain was invaded by many peoples, including Iberians, Celts, Romans, Angles, Saxons, Jutes, Norsemen, Danes, and Normans, who arrived in 1066. The evolution of the United Kingdom spanned hundreds of years. The Normans finally overcame Welsh resistance in 1282, when King Edward I annexed Wales and united it with England. Union with Scotland was achieved by the Act of Union of 1707. This created a country known as the United Kingdom of Great Britain.

Ireland came under Norman rule in the 11th century, and much of its later history was concerned with a struggle against English domination. In 1801, Ireland became part of the United Kingdom of Great Britain and Ireland. But in 1921, southern Ireland broke away to become the Irish Free State. Most of the people in the Irish Free State were Roman Catholics. In Northern Ireland, where the majority of the people were Protestants, most people wanted to remain citizens of the United Kingdom. As a result, the country's official name changed to the United Kingdom of Great Britain and Northern Ireland.

The modern history of the UK began in the 18th century when the British empire began to develop, despite the loss in 1783 of its 13 North American colonies which became the core of the modern United States. The other major event occurred in the late 18th century, when the UK became the first country to industrialize its economy.

The British empire broke up after World War II (1939–45), though the UK still administers many small, mainly island, territories around the world. The empire was transformed into the Commonwealth of Nations, a free association of independent countries which numbered 54 in 2001.

The UK has retained an important world role. For example, in 2001, it played a prominent role in creating a broad alliance to counter international terrorism following the attacks on the United States. It was also a prominent member of the coalition force which invaded Iraq in 2003. However, the UK has recognized that its economic future lies within Europe. It became a member of the European Economic Community (now the European Union) in 1973. In the early 21st century, most people accepted the importance of the EU to the UK's economic future. But some feared a loss of British identity should the EU ever evolve into a political federation.

The UK is a major industrial and trading nation. It lacks natural resources apart from coal, iron ore, oil and natural gas, and has to import most of the materials it needs for its industries. The UK also has to import food, because it produces only about two-thirds of the food it needs. In the first half of the 20th century, Britain was a major exporter of cars, ships, steel and textiles. But many industries have suffered from competition from other countries, with lower labour costs. Today, industries have to use high-technology in order to compete on the world market.

The UK is one of the world's most urbanized countries, and agriculture employs only 1% of the people. Production is high because of the use of scientific methods and modern machinery. However, in the early 21st century, especially following the outbreak of foot-and-mouth disease in 2001, questions were raised about the future of rural industries. Major crops include barley, potatoes, sugar beet and wheat. Sheep are the leading livestock, but beef and dairy cattle, pigs and poultry are also important. Fishing is another major activity.

Service industries play a major part in the UK's economy. Financial and insurance services bring in much-needed foreign exchange, while tourism has become a major earner.

UNITED STATES OF AMERICA

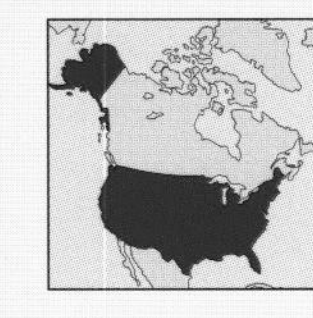

AREA 9,629,091 sq km [3,717,792 sq mi]
POPULATION 293,028,000
CAPITAL (POPULATION) Washington, DC (572,000)
GOVERNMENT Federal republic
ETHNIC GROUPS White 77%, African American 13%, Asian 4%, Amerindian 2%, others
LANGUAGES English (official), Spanish, more than 30 others
RELIGIONS Protestant 56%, Roman Catholic 28%, Islam 2%, Judaism 2%
CURRENCY US dollar = 100 cents

GEOGRAPHY The United States of America is the world's fourth largest country in area and the third largest in population. It contains 50 states, 48 of which lie between Canada and Mexico, plus Alaska in north-western North America, and Hawaii, a group of volcanic islands in the North Pacific Ocean. Densely populated coastal plains lie to the east and south of the Appalachian Mountains. The central lowlands drained by the Mississippi–Missouri rivers stretch from the Appalachians to the Rocky Mountains in the west. The Pacific region contains fertile valleys, separated by mountain ranges.

The climate varies greatly, ranging from the Arctic cold of Alaska to the intense heat of Death Valley, California. Of the 48 states between Canada and Mexico, winters are cold and snowy in the north, but mild in the south.

POLITICS & ECONOMY The first people in North America, the ancestors of the Native Americans (or American Indians) arrived perhaps 40,000 years ago from Asia. Although Vikings probably reached North America 1,000 years ago, European exploration proper did not begin until the late 15th century.

The first Europeans to settle in large numbers were the British, who founded settlements on the eastern coast in the early 17th century. British rule ended in the War of Independence (1775–83). The country expanded in 1803 when a vast territory in the south and west was acquired through the Louisiana Purchase, while the border with Mexico was fixed in the mid-19th century. The Civil War (1861–5) ended slavery and the serious threat that the nation might split into two parts. In the late 19th century, the West was opened up, while immigrants flooded in from Europe and elsewhere.

During the late 19th and early 20th centuries, industrialization led to the United States becoming the world's leading economic superpower and a pioneer in science and technology. It took on the mantle of the champion of Western democracy and, following the break-up of the former Soviet Union, it became the world's only superpower. But the attacks on the country on 11 September 2001 revealed its vulnerability to terrorists, especially those prepared to lose their lives in attacks, and also to the actions of rogue states. The response of the US government was vigorous. In 2001, it led a coalition force against the Taliban regime in Afghanistan, which was protecting al Qaida terrorists. Then, in 2003, it led another coalition force to overthrow the repressive regime of Saddam Hussein in Iraq. However, despite early military successes, the conflict continued. President George W. Bush was re-elected in 2004, and the 2005 elections in Iraq were hailed as a sign of the success of his policies.

The United States has the world's largest economy in terms of the total value of its production. Although agriculture employs only about 2% of the people, farming is highly mechanized and scientific, and the United States leads the world in farm production. Major products include beef and dairy cattle, together with such crops as cotton, fruits, groundnuts, maize, potatoes, soybeans, tobacco and wheat.

The country's natural resources include oil, natural gas and coal. There is also a wide range of metal ores that are used in manufacturing industries, together with timber, especially from the forests of the Pacific north-west. Manufacturing is the single most important activity, employing about 14% of the population. Major products include vehicles, food products, chemicals, machinery, printed goods, metal products and scientific instruments. California is now the leading manufacturing state. Many southern states, petroleum rich and climatically favoured, have also become highly prosperous in recent years.

URUGUAY

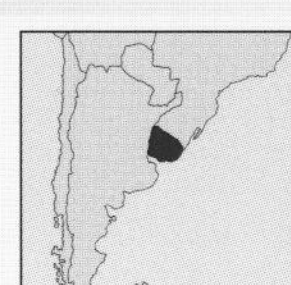

AREA 175,016 sq km [67,574 sq mi]
POPULATION 3,399,000
CAPITAL (POPULATION) Montevideo (1,303,000)
GOVERNMENT Multiparty republic
ETHNIC GROUPS White 88%, Mestizo 8%, Mulatto or Black 4%
LANGUAGES Spanish (official)
RELIGIONS Roman Catholic 66%, Protestant 2%, Judaism 1%
CURRENCY Uruguayan peso = 100 centésimos

GEOGRAPHY Uruguay is South America's second smallest independent country after Suriname. The land consists mainly of flat plains and hills. The River Uruguay, which forms the country's western border, flows into the Río de la Plata, a large estuary which leads into the South Atlantic Ocean.

Uruguay has a mild climate, with rain in every month, though droughts sometimes occur. Summers are pleasantly warm, especially near the coast. The weather remains relatively mild throughout the winter.

POLITICS & ECONOMY In 1726, Spanish settlers founded Montevideo in order to halt the Portuguese gaining influence in the area. By the late 18th century, Spaniards had settled in most of the country. Uruguay became part of a colony called the Viceroyalty of La Plata, which also included Argentina, Paraguay, and parts of Bolivia, Brazil and Chile. In 1820 Brazil annexed Uruguay, ending Spanish rule. In 1825, Uruguayans, supported by Argentina, began a struggle for independence. Finally, in 1828, Brazil and Argentina recognized Uruguay as an independent republic. Social and economic developments were slow in the 19th century, but, from 1903, Uruguay became stable and democratic.

From the 1950s, economic problems caused unrest. Terrorist groups, notably the Tupumaros, carried out murders and kidnappings. The army crushed the Tupumaros in 1972, but the army took over the government in 1973. Military rule continued until 1984 when elections were held. In the early 21st century, Uruguay faced many economic problems, many of which were the result of the economic crisis in neighbouring Argentina, and its imposition of banking controls. In 2004, Uruguay elected its first leftist president, Tabare Vasquez.

The World Bank classifies Uruguay as an 'upper-middle-income' developing country. Agriculture employs only 3% of the people, but farm products, notably hides and leather goods, beef and wool, are the leading exports, while the leading manufacturing industries process farm products. The main crops include maize, potatoes, wheat and sugar beet.

UZBEKISTAN

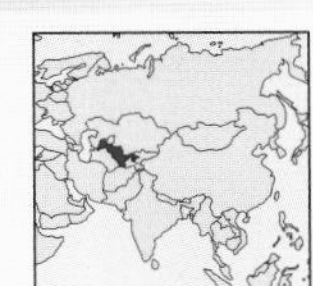

AREA 447,400 sq km [172,741 sq mi]
POPULATION 26,410,000
CAPITAL (POPULATION) Tashkent (2,143,000)
GOVERNMENT Socialist republic
ETHNIC GROUPS Uzbek 80%, Russian 5%, Tajik 5%, Kazakh 3%, Tatar 2%, Kara-Kalpak 2%
LANGUAGES Uzbek (official), Russian
RELIGIONS Islam 88%, Eastern Orthodox 9%
CURRENCY Uzbekistani sum = 100 tyiyn

GEOGRAPHY The Republic of Uzbekistan is one of the five republics in Central Asia which were once part of the Soviet Union. There are plains in the west and highlands in the east. The main rivers, the Amu (or Amu Darya) and Syr (or Syr Darya), drain into the Aral Sea. So much water has been taken from these rivers for irrigation that the Aral Sea is now only a quarter of its size in 1960. Much of the former sea is now desert. The climate is continental, with warm summers and cold winters. The west is arid, with an average annual rainfall of about 200 mm [8 in].

POLITICS & ECONOMY Russia took the area in the 19th century. After the Russian Revolution of 1917, the Communists took over and, in 1924, they set up the Uzbek Soviet Socialist Republic. Under Communism, all aspects of Uzbek life were controlled and religious worship was discouraged. But education, health, housing and transport were improved. In the late 1980s, the people demanded more freedom and, in 1990, the government stated that its laws overruled those of the Soviet Union. Uzbekistan became independent in 1991 when the Soviet Union broke up, but it retained links with Russia through the Commonwealth of Independent States. Islam Karimov, leader of the People's Democratic Party (formerly the Communist Party), was elected president in December 1991. In 1992–3, many opposition leaders were arrested because the government said that they threatened national stability. In 1994–5, the PDP was victorious in national elections and, in 1995, a referendum extended Karimov's term in office until 2000, when he was again re-elected. In 2001, Karimov declared his support for the United States in its campaign against terrorist bases in Afghanistan. But, in 2003, the New York-based Human Rights Watch criticized Karimov's record on human rights.

The World Bank classifies Uzbekistan as a 'lower-middle-income' developing country and the government still controls most economic activity. The country produces coal, copper, gold, oil and natural gas.

VANUATU

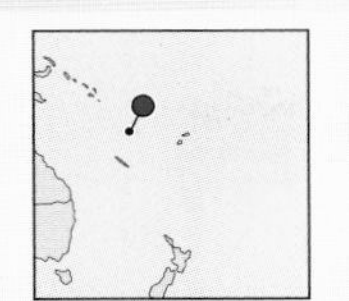

AREA 12,189 sq km [4,706 sq mi]
POPULATION 203,000
CAPITAL (POPULATION) Port-Vila (19,000)

The Republic of Vanuatu, formerly the Anglo-French Condominium of the New Hebrides, became independent in 1980. (Vanuatu is a word meaning 'Our Land Forever'.) The republic consists of a chain of 80 islands in the South Pacific Ocean. Its economy is based on agriculture and it exports copra, beef and veal, timber and cocoa.

VATICAN CITY

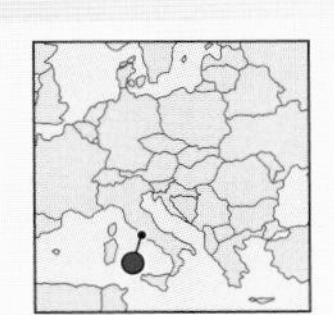

AREA 0.44 sq km [0.17 sq mi]
POPULATION 1,000

Vatican City State, the world's smallest independent nation, is an enclave on the west bank of the River Tiber in Rome. It forms an independent base for the Holy See, the governing body of the Roman Catholic Church. Vatican City contains St Peter's Basilica and museums with priceless works of art.

VENEZUELA

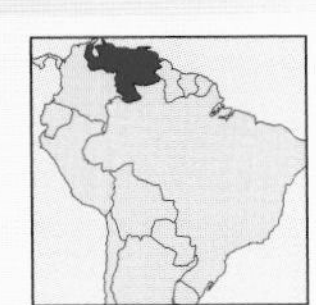

AREA 912,050 sq km [352,143 sq mi]
POPULATION 25,017,000
CAPITAL (POPULATION) Caracas (1,823,000)
GOVERNMENT Federal republic
ETHNIC GROUPS Spanish, Italian, Portuguese, Arab, German, African, indigenous people
LANGUAGES Spanish (official), indigenous dialects
RELIGIONS Roman Catholic 96%
CURRENCY Bolívar = 100 céntimos

GEOGRAPHY The Bolivarian Republic of Venezuela, in northern South America, contains the Maracaibo lowlands around the oil-rich Lake Maracaibo in the west. Andean ranges enclose the lowlands and extend across most of northern Venezuela. The Orinoco river basin, containing tropical grasslands called *llanos*, lies between the northern highlands and the Guiana Highlands in the south-east.

Venezuela has a tropical climate. Temperatures are high throughout the year on the lowlands, though the mountains are much cooler. Rainfall is heaviest in the mountains, but much of the country has a marked dry season between December and April.

POLITICS & ECONOMY In the early 19th century, Venezuelans, such as Simón Bolívar and Francisco de Miranda, began a struggle against Spanish rule. Venezuela declared its independence in 1811. But it only became truly independent in 1821, when the Spanish were defeated in a battle near Valencia.

The development of Venezuela in the 19th and the first half of the 20th centuries was marred by instability, violence and periods of harsh dictatorial rule. But Venezuela has had elected governments since 1958. The country has greatly benefited from its oil resources which were first exploited in 1917. In 1960, Venezuela helped to form OPEC (the Organization of Petroleum Exporting Countries) and, in 1976, the government of Venezuela took control of the entire oil industry. In 1999, Hugo Chavez, who had staged an unsuccessful coup in 1992, was elected president. Chavez survived an attempted coup in 2002 and, in 2004, he won a majority in a referendum that had been intended by the opposition to remove him from office.

The World Bank classifies Venezuela as an 'upper-middle-income' developing country. Oil accounts for 80% of the exports. Other exports include bauxite and aluminium, iron ore and farm products. Agriculture employs 9% of people and cattle ranching is important. The chief industry is petroleum refining. Other manufactures include cement, steel and textiles.

VIETNAM

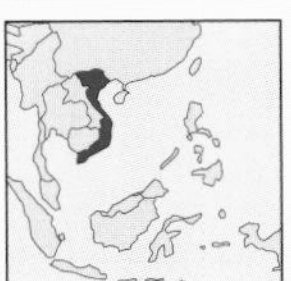

AREA 331,689 sq km [128,065 sq mi]
POPULATION 82,690,000
CAPITAL (POPULATION) Hanoi (1,074,000)
GOVERNMENT Socialist republic
ETHNIC GROUPS Vietnamese 87%, Chinese, Hmong, Thai, Khmer, Cham, mountain groups
LANGUAGES Vietnamese (official), English, Chinese
RELIGIONS Buddhism, Christianity, indigenous beliefs
CURRENCY Dong = 10 hao = 100 xu

GEOGRAPHY The Socialist Republic of Vietnam occupies an S-shaped strip of land facing the South China Sea in South-east Asia. The coastal plains include two densely populated, fertile delta regions: the Red (Hong) delta facing the Gulf of Tonkin in the north, and the Mekong delta in the south.

Vietnam has a tropical climate, though the driest months of January to March are a little cooler than the wet, hot summer months, when monsoon winds blow from the south-west. Typhoons (cyclones) sometimes hit the coast, causing much damage.

POLITICS & ECONOMY China dominated Vietnam for a thousand years before AD 939, when a Vietnamese state was founded. The French took over the area between the 1850s and 1880s. They ruled Vietnam as part of French Indo-China, which also included Cambodia and Laos.

Japan conquered Vietnam during World War II (1939–45). In 1946, war broke out between a nationalist group, called the Vietminh, and the French colonial government. France withdrew in 1954 and Vietnam was divided into a Communist North Vietnam, led by the Vietminh leader, Ho Chi Minh, and a non-Communist South.

A force called the Viet Cong rebelled against South Vietnam's government in 1957 and a war began, which gradually increased in intensity. The United States aided the South, but after it withdrew in 1975, South Vietnam surrendered. In 1976, the united Vietnam became a Socialist Republic. In 1978, Vietnam intervened in Cambodia to defeat the Khmer Rouge government, but it withdrew in 1989. In the 1990s, Vietnam launched reforms and its economy expanded rapidly in the 21st century. In 1995, the United States opened an embassy in Hanoi and, in 2002, it implemented a trade agreement, which normalized the trade status between the countries.

Agriculture employs 67% of the population. The main food crop is rice. Vietnam also produces chromium, oil (located off the south coast), tin and phosphates.

VIRGIN ISLANDS, BRITISH

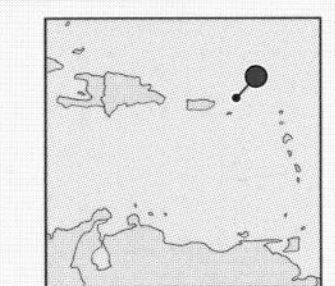

AREA 151 sq km [58 sq mi]
POPULATION 22,000
CAPITAL (POPULATION) Road Town (6,000)

The British Virgin Islands, the most northerly of the Lesser Antilles, comprise four low-lying islands and 36 islets and cays. The islands were 'discovered' by Christopher Columbus in 1493. Dutch from 1648 but British since 1666, they are now a British overseas territory, with a substantial measure of self-government. Tourism is the chief source of income.

VIRGIN ISLANDS, US

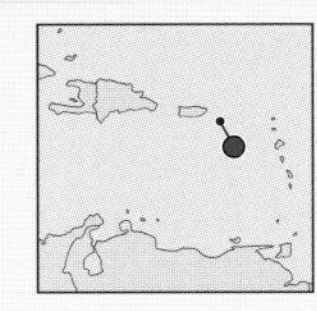

AREA 347 sq km [134 sq mi]
POPULATION 109,000
CAPITAL (POPULATION) Charlotte Amalie (12,000)

The Virgin Islands of the United States, a group of three islands and 65 small islets, are a self-governing US territory. Purchased from Denmark in 1917, its residents are US citizens and they elect a non-voting delegate to the House of Representatives. The tropical climate is pleasant throughout the year.

WALLIS AND FUTUNA ISLANDS

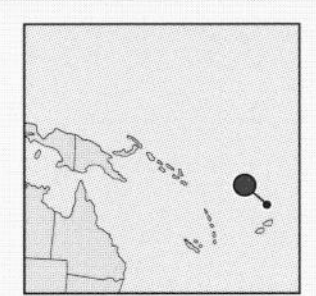

AREA 200 sq km [77 sq mi]
POPULATION 16,000
CAPITAL (POPULATION) Mata-Utu (1,000)

The Wallis and Futuna Islands, in the South Pacific Ocean, form the smallest and the poorest of France's overseas territories. A French dependency since 1842, the territory comprises two groups of islands: the Isles de Hoorn, north-east of the Fiji Islands, which includes Futuna; and the Wallis Archipelago.

YEMEN

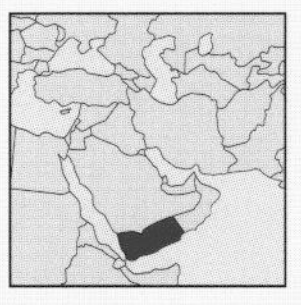

AREA 527,968 sq km [203,848 sq mi]
POPULATION 20,025,000
CAPITAL (POPULATION) Sana' (954,000)
GOVERNMENT Multiparty republic
ETHNIC GROUPS Predominantly Arab
LANGUAGES Arabic (official)
RELIGIONS Islam
CURRENCY Yemeni rial = 100 fils

GEOGRAPHY The Republic of Yemen faces the Red Sea and the Gulf of Aden in the south-western corner of the Arabian peninsula. Behind the narrow coastal plain along the Red Sea, the land rises to a mountain region called High Yemen.

The climate ranges from hot and often humid conditions on the coast to the cooler highlands. Most of the country is arid.

POLITICS & ECONOMY After World War I, northern Yemen, which had been ruled by Turkey, began to evolve into a separate state from the south, where Britain was in control. Britain withdrew in 1967 and a left-wing government took power in the south. North Yemen became a republic in 1962, when the monarchy was abolished.

Clashes occurred between the traditionalist Yemen Arab Republic in the north and the formerly British Marxist People's Democratic Republic of Yemen but, in 1990, the two Yemens merged to form a single country. Further conflict occurred in 1994, when southern secessionist forces were defeated. In 1998 and 1999, militants in the Aden-Abyan Islamic army sought to destabilize the country. In 2000, suicide bombers, thought to be part of the al Qaida network, steered a craft into a US destroyer in Aden harbour, killing 117 sailors, while other terrorist incidents occurred in 2002–4.

The World Bank classifies Yemen as a 'low-income' developing country. Agriculture employs about 48% of the people. Herders raise sheep and other animals, while farmers grow such crops as barley, fruits, wheat and vegetables in highland valleys and around oases. Cash crops include coffee and cotton.

Imported oil is refined at Aden and petroleum extraction began in the north-west in the 1980s. Handicrafts, leather goods and textiles are manufactured. Remittances from Yemenis abroad are a major source of revenue.

ZAMBIA

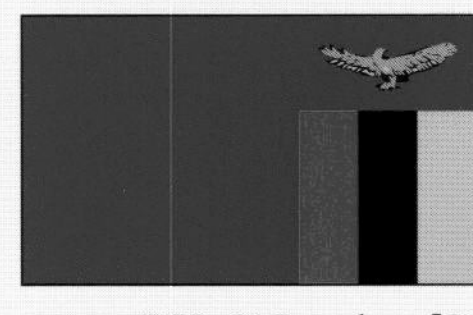
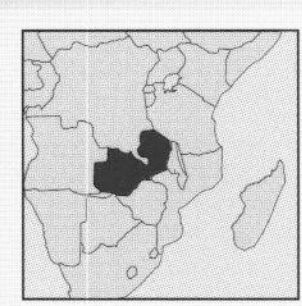

AREA 752,618 sq km [290,586 sq mi]
POPULATION 10,462,000
CAPITAL (POPULATION) Lusaka (1,270,000)
GOVERNMENT Multiparty republic
ETHNIC GROUPS Native African (Bemba, Tonga, Maravi/Nyanja)
LANGUAGES English (official), Bemba, Kaonda, Nyanja and about 70 others
RELIGIONS Christianity 70%, Islam, Hinduism
CURRENCY Zambian kwacha = 100 ngwee

GEOGRAPHY The Republic of Zambia is a landlocked country in southern Africa. Zambia lies on the plateau that makes up most of southern Africa. Much of the land is between 900 m and 1,500 m [2,950 ft to 4,920 ft] above sea level. The Muchinga Mountains in the north-east rise above this flat land. Lakes include Bangweulu, which is entirely within Zambia, together with parts of lakes Mweru and Tanganyika in the north.

Zambia lies in the tropics, but temperatures are moderated by the altitude. The rainy season runs from November to March.

POLITICS & ECONOMY European contact with Zambia began in the 19th century, when the explorer David Livingstone crossed the River Zambezi. In the 1890s, the British South Africa Company, set up by Cecil Rhodes (1853–1902), the British financier and statesman, made treaties with local chiefs and gradually took over the area. In 1911, the Company named the area Northern Rhodesia. In 1924, Britain took over the government of the country.

In 1953, Britain formed a federation of Northern Rhodesia, Southern Rhodesia (now Zimbabwe) and Nyasaland (now Malawi). Because of African opposition, the federation was dissolved in 1963 and Northern Rhodesia became independent as Zambia in 1964. Kenneth Kaunda became president and one-party rule was introduced in 1972. Under a new constitution, Frederick Chiluba was elected president in 1996. He stood down in 2001 and Levy Mwanawasa became president. In 2005, the Supreme Court rejected a challenge to his election, but stated that the 2001 ballot had been flawed.

Copper is the main resource, accounting for 49% of Zambia's exports in 1998. Zambia also produces cobalt, lead, zinc and gemstones. Agriculture employs 69% of workers, as compared with 4% in industry and mining. Maize is the chief crop.

ZIMBABWE

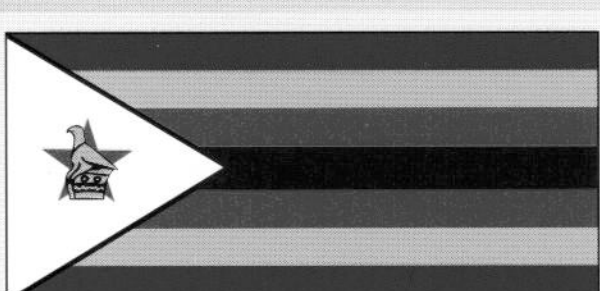
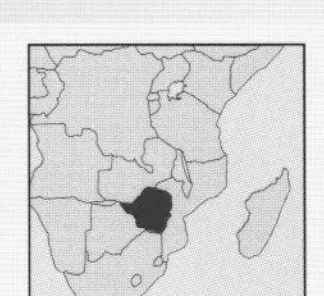

AREA 390,757 sq km [150,871 sq mi]
POPULATION 12,672,000
CAPITAL (POPULATION) Harare (1,189,000)
GOVERNMENT Multiparty republic
ETHNIC GROUPS Shona 82%, Ndebele 14%, other African groups 2%, mixed and Asian 1%
LANGUAGES English (official), Shona, Ndebele
RELIGIONS Christianity, traditional beliefs
CURRENCY Zimbabwean dollar = 100 cents

GEOGRAPHY The Republic of Zimbabwe is a landlocked country in southern Africa. Most of the country lies on a high plateau between the Zambezi and Limpopo rivers between 900 m to 1,500 m [2,950 ft to 4,920 ft] above sea level. From October to March, the weather is hot and wet. But daily temperatures may vary greatly in the winter.

POLITICS & ECONOMY The Shona people became dominant in the region about 1,000 years ago. The British South Africa Company, under the statesman Cecil Rhodes (1853–1902), occupied the area in the 1890s, after obtaining mineral rights from local chiefs. The area was named Rhodesia and later Southern Rhodesia. It became a self-governing British colony in 1923. Between 1953 and 1963, Southern and Northern Rhodesia (now Zambia) were joined to Nyasaland (Malawi) in the Central African Federation.

In 1965, the European government of Southern Rhodesia (then called Rhodesia) declared their country independent but Britain refused to accept this. Finally, after a civil war, the country became legally independent in 1980, though rivalries between the Shona and Ndebele people threatened stability. Order was restored when the Shona prime minister, Robert Mugabe, brought his Ndebele rivals into his government. In 1987, Mugabe became the country's executive president and, in 1991, the government renounced its Marxist ideology. Mugabe was re-elected president in 1990 and 1996. During the late 1990s, Mugabe threatened to seize white-owned farms without paying compensation to the owners. Despite international pressure, landless 'war veterans' began to occupy white farms. In 2002, Mugabe was re-elected amid accusations of electoral irregularities. The Commonwealth suspended Zimbabwe's membership and, in 2004, the European Union renewed sanctions against the country. In 2005, the United States named Zimbabwe as one of the world's six 'outposts of tyranny'. Zimbabwe rejected this accusation.

The World Bank classifies Zimbabwe as a 'low-income' developing country. The country has valuable mineral resources and mining accounts for a fifth of the country's exports. Agriculture employs 27% of working people. Maize is the chief food crop.

IMAGES OF EARTH

IJSSELMEER, NETHERLANDS
This unique feature was created in the 13th century when the sea breached a protective sand bar, flooding all the low-lying land. The remnants of the bar can still be seen as the chain of Frisian Islands at the top of the image. Large-scale reclamation started in 1932 with the completion of the causeway in the north. Since then, four 'polders' have been drained and reclaimed. The city of Amsterdam can be seen at bottom left. *[Map page 17]*

► **Iceland**
This winter image, captured in January, shows Iceland cloaked in snow, covering its four permanent ice-caps. The island sits astride the fault line between the North American and Eurasian tectonic plates. These plates are moving away from each other, resulting in a high level of volcanic activity, with much of the land covered in lava flows. Although situated just below the Arctic Circle, Iceland's climate in the south is modified by the relatively warm waters of the North Atlantic Drift Current. *[Map page 8]*

▼ **Rhône Delta, France**
The river Rhône reaches the Mediterranean to the west of Marseilles (seen at bottom centre) after flowing from its source, the Rhône Glacier, in Switzerland. To the west of its mouth, protected by sand bars, are the salt lagoons and marshes of the Camargue, a UNESCO World Heritage site. On the opposite bank, to the east, is a large lake, the Étang de Berre. The pink area between the lake and the river is the arid, boulder-strewn Plaine de Crau. *[Map page 21]*

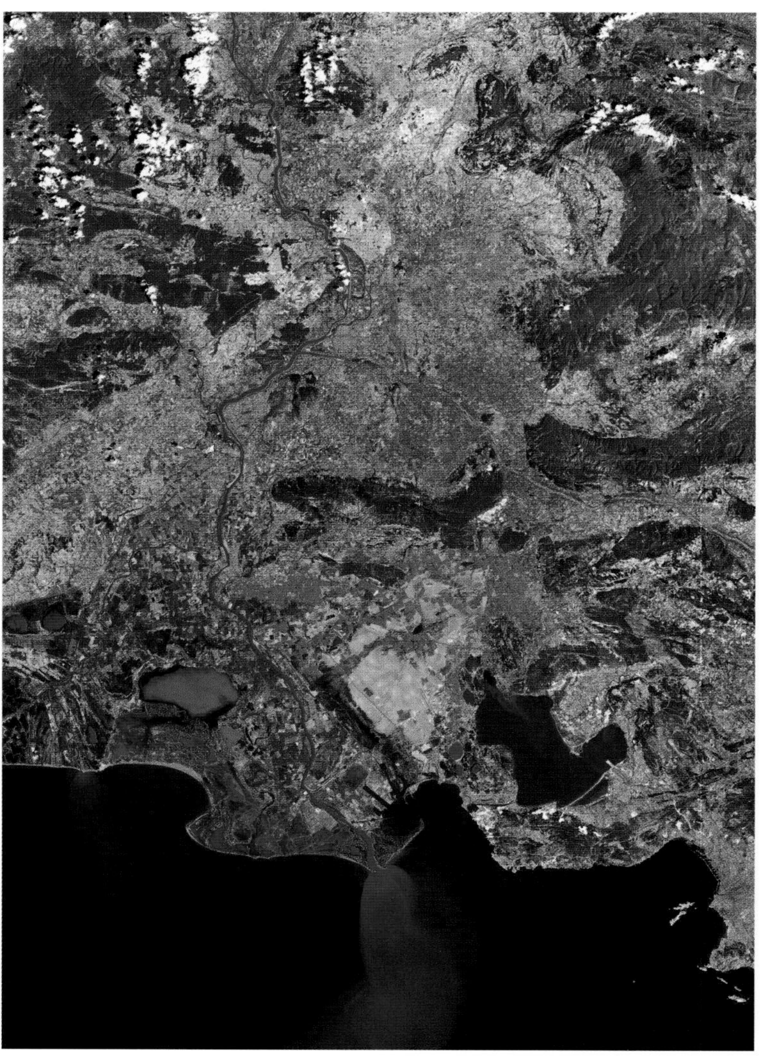

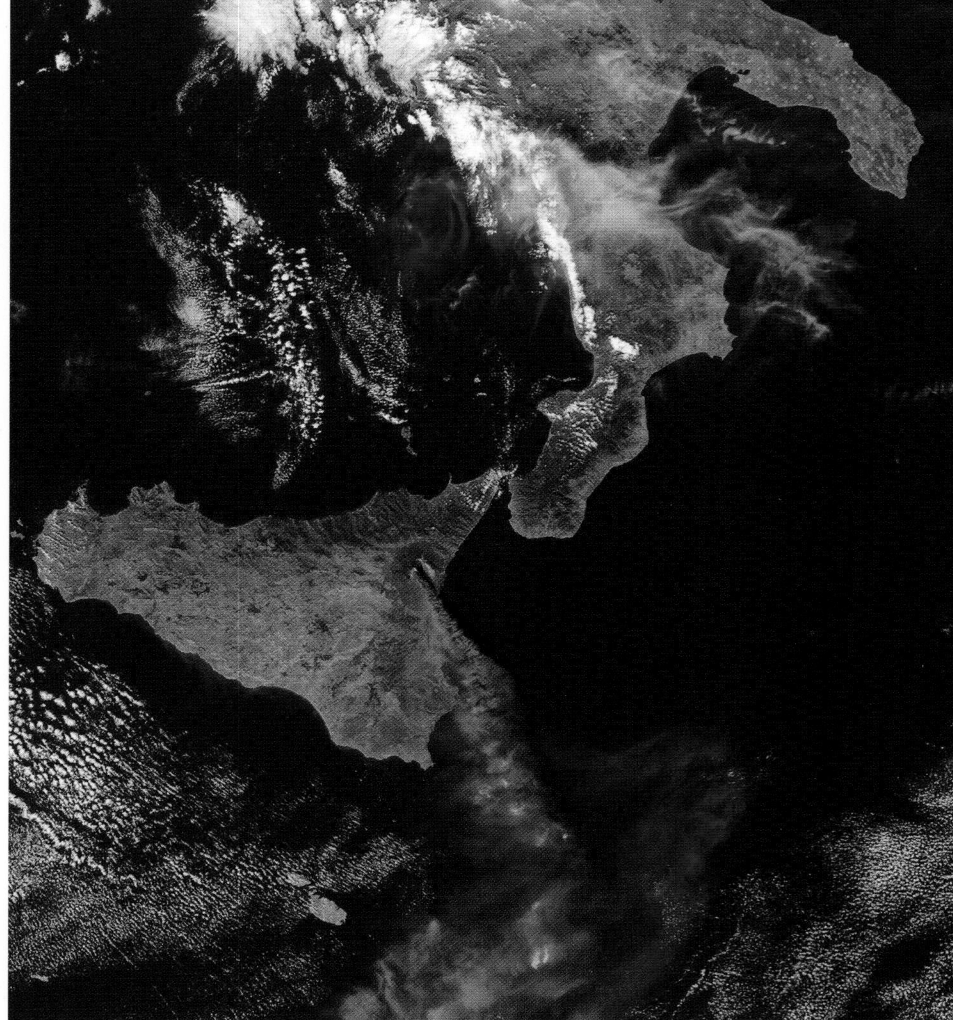

◄ **Kanin Peninsula, Russia**
The distinctive shape of this peninsula (Poluostrov Kanin in Russian) separates the White Sea (Beloye More) in the west from the Cheshskaya Guba in this false-colour image. Situated within the Arctic Circle, the area is flat, marshy tundra affected by permafrost, and serves as an important staging post for migrating birds. The local people are Nenets, with their own language and alphabet. Their traditional occupation is reindeer herding. *[Map page 52]*

◄ **Mount Etna, Sicily**
The most active volcano in Europe, Mount Etna, 3,323 m [10,906 ft] high, is shown here during the 2002–3 eruption, its plume of ash and smoke spreading southwards over the Mediterranean. Activity from Etna has been traced back by geologists to 1500 BC. As with many other volcanoes, the volcanic debris has weathered to produce highly fertile soils, resulting in productive vineyards, banana plantations and citrus groves around its base. *[Map pages 42–3]*

► **Western Crete, Greece**
Crete is largest of the Greek islands, stretching over 260 km [161 miles] long. The western end of the island is the most mountainous, with more than 50 peaks reaching over 2,000 m [6,564 ft]. Running north to south at right angles to the south coast, just to the west of the snow-capped mountains, can be seen one of Europe's longest gorges, 16 km [10 miles] long, now part of the Samaria National Park. On the bulbous peninsula to the north, the runways of Khanía airport are clearly visible. *[Map page 46]*

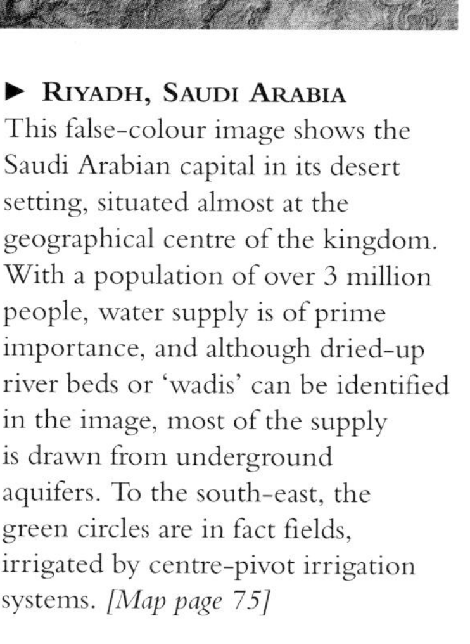

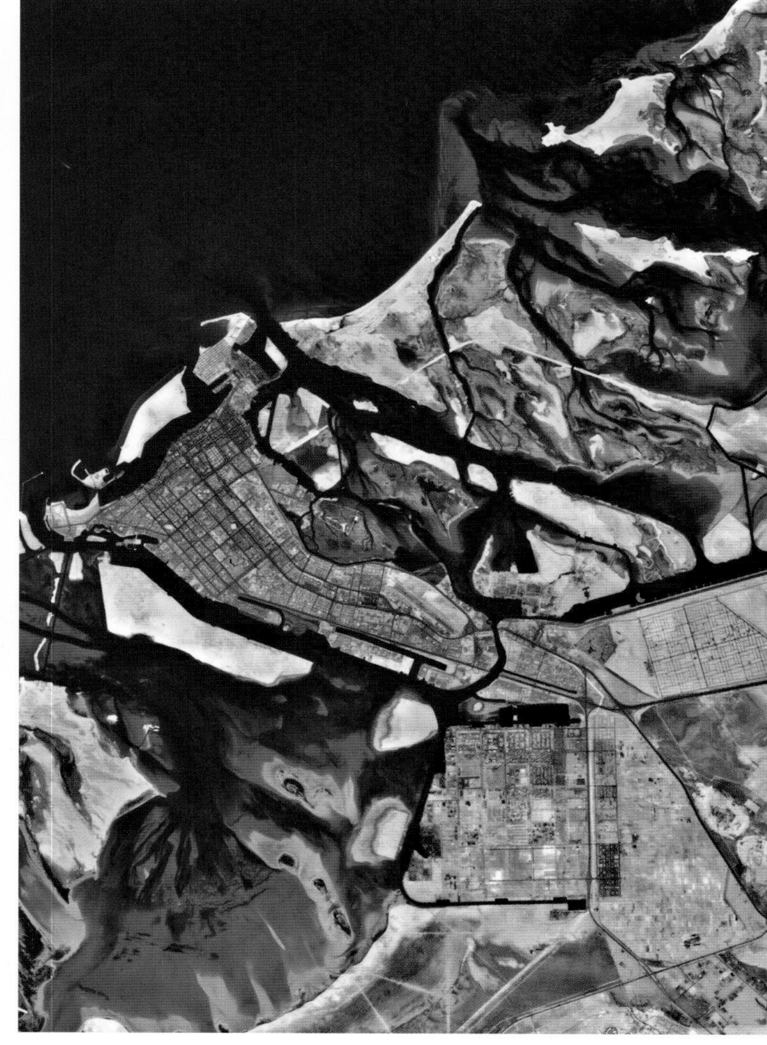

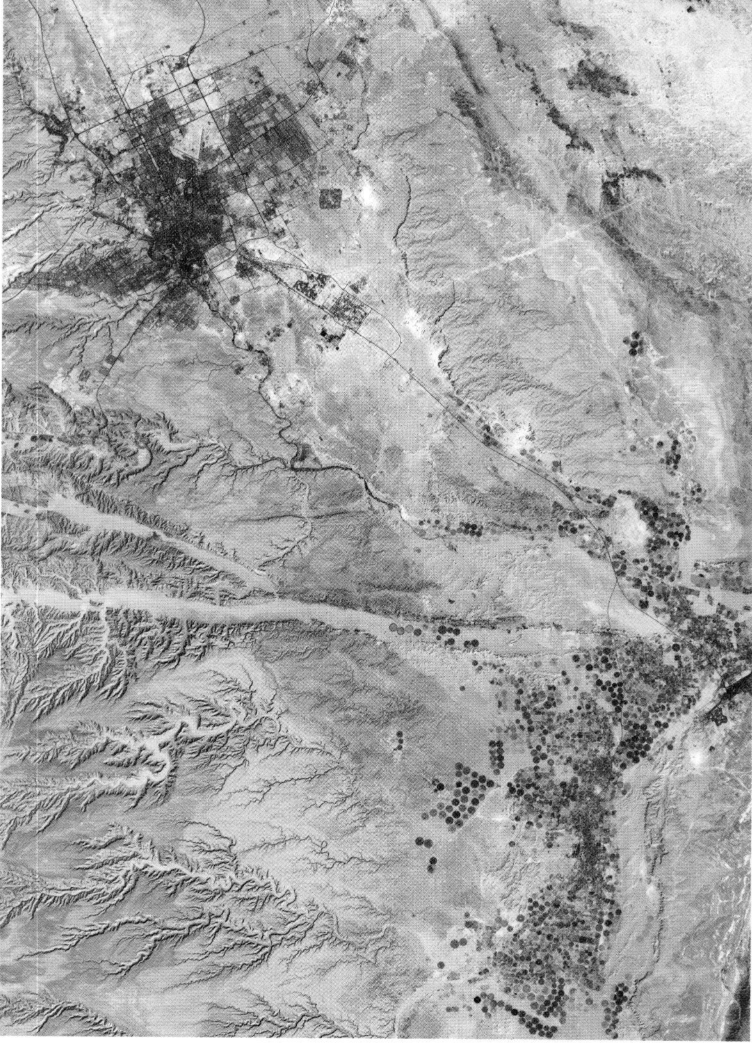

▲ **Dead Sea, Israel/Jordan**
At 411 m [1,349 ft] below sea level, the Dead Sea is the lowest body of water on the Earth's surface. As a result, there is no outlet for the water that flows into it. Despite this, its water level is dropping steadily due to water abstraction for irrigation on both the Israeli and Jordanian sides of the River Jordan, the main source. Due to the high surface evaporation, the water in the Dead Sea is five times as saline as ocean water and nothing can live in it, hence its name. *[Map page 74]*

► **Riyadh, Saudi Arabia**
This false-colour image shows the Saudi Arabian capital in its desert setting, situated almost at the geographical centre of the kingdom. With a population of over 3 million people, water supply is of prime importance, and although dried-up river beds or 'wadis' can be identified in the image, most of the supply is drawn from underground aquifers. To the south-east, the green circles are in fact fields, irrigated by centre-pivot irrigation systems. *[Map page 75]*

◄ Abu Dhabi, UAE
The green island at the centre of this image forms the core of the city of Abu Dhabi, the capital of the emirate of the same name. It is the richest of the United Arab Emirates and much effort has gone into the inclusion of many parks in the development of the capital. These are all irrigated with desalinated seawater. This part of the Persian Gulf coast is typified by its offshore islands and reefs. *[Map page 71]*

▼ Musandam Peninsula, Oman
Jutting northwards into the Strait of Hormuz towards Iran, this peninsula is an enclave of Oman, surrounded by the UAE. The strait is only 64 km [40 miles] wide at this point, but is important strategically as much of the region's oil production is exported through these waters. The distinctive coastline shape to the north and east is caused by the tilting of the land and the submergence of the coast. *[Map page 71]*

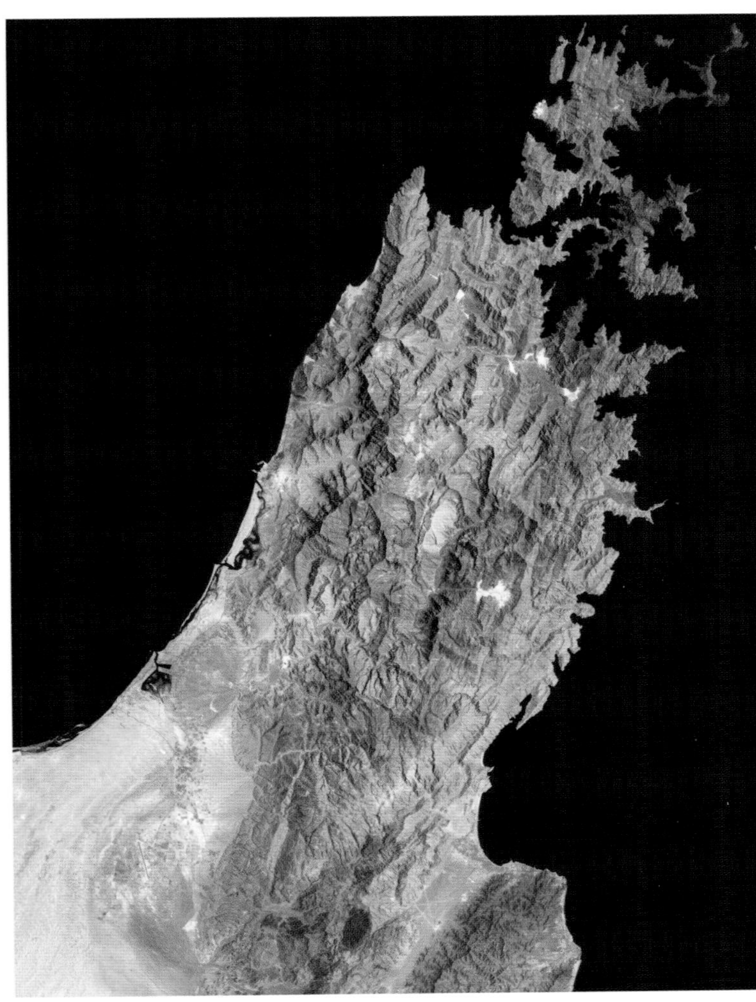

▲ Great Salt Desert, Iran
The area of this false-colour image is situated about 320 km [200 miles] south-east of Tehran. These amazing patterns are caused by the folding and subsequent wind erosion of layers of sediments. The blue salt lakes ('kavirs'), which dry out as salt flats in the hot season, can be seen in the south-west. An isolated road, crossing this otherwise uninhabited area from north to south, can also be identified. *[Map page 71]*

◄ Wadi Hadramawt, Yemen
Yemen is very arid, but images such as this show that its past was much wetter, enabling large river systems to evolve and carve out the deep, spectacular gorges and dried-up river beds seen here. These 'wadis' are still important for irrigation when it does rain in the interior mountains. This is one of the largest, stretching for over 550 km [340 miles] from the interior to the Gulf of Aden. *[Map page 75]*

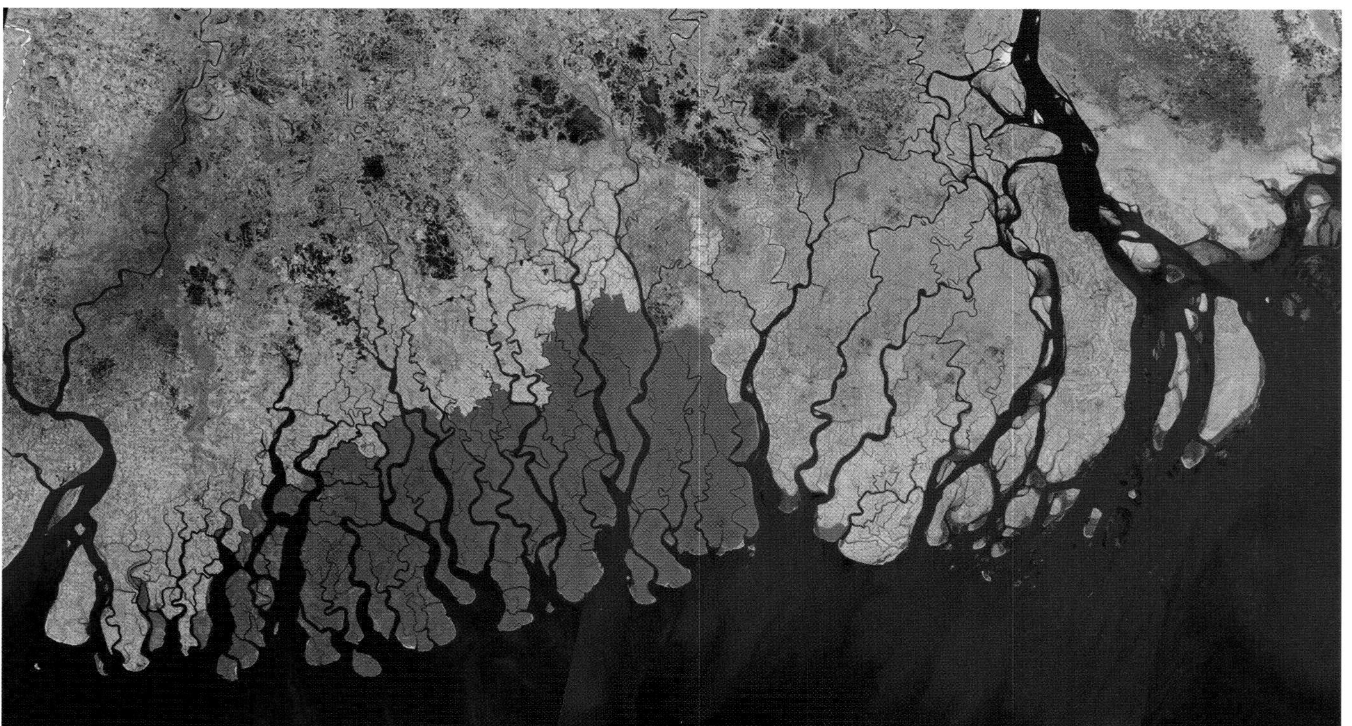

► **Turfan Depression, China**
The dark green folded areas in the north are the mountains of the Tian Shan range, which change abruptly into barren areas of overlapping alluvial fans, shown in mauve. Below these, steep rocky slopes fall to the depression floor, some 154 m [505 ft] below sea level. The yellow area is a sand desert. Despite these arid conditions, the dark green areas are fields irrigated by an ancient system of wells, growing grapes, melons and other crops.
[Map page 60]

▲ **Ganges Delta, India/Bangladesh**
Over 300 km [186 miles] wide, this is the world's largest delta, created by the River Ganges depositing sediment it has carried from the Himalayas. It is extremely vulnerable to frequent cyclones and tidal surges, but is densely populated because of the fertile land. On the western side of the image is the mouth of the Hugli, with the elongated city of Kolkata (Calcutta) showing as dark grey just to the north. The large red area indicates the presence of mangrove forests and swamps, and is divided between the countries of India and Bangladesh.
[Map page 69]

▼ **Singapore**
Three separate countries can be seen in this image. At the top, partially covered by cloud, is the southern end of Malaysia; the island in the centre is the state of Singapore; and the islands just visible at the bottom of the image are part of Indonesia. Singapore has developed a fast-growing economy based on the trans-shipment of goods between the Far East and the West. As a result, it is one of the world's major ports and much new development can be seen here, coloured grey.
[Map page 65]

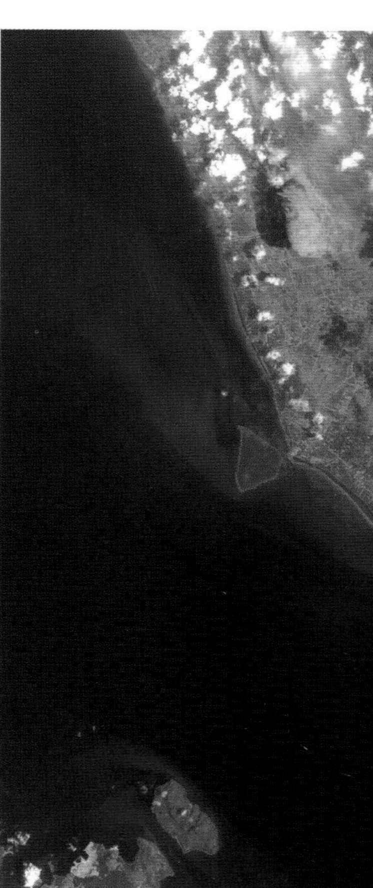

► **Chaiyaphum Province, Thailand**
Chaiyaphum is situated 332 km [206 miles] north of Bangkok, in a very fertile part of north-eastern Thailand. Vegetation is shown in red in this false-colour image, highlighting the steep slopes of the irregularly shaped plateau rising from the surrounding plain and covered with lush vegetation. On top of this more resistant rock, there is a dense patchwork of fields and lakes.
[Map page 64]

▲ **Mount Klyuchevskaya, Russia**

The snow-covered peaks are seen here protruding through low cloud. Klyuchevskaya's almost perfectly shaped cone casts the longest shadow. At 4,750 m [15,589 ft], it is the highest of the 29 volcanoes located in one of the most active regions in the world, the remote Kamchatka Peninsula in eastern Siberia. It forms part of the 'Ring of Fire' that surrounds the Pacific Ocean. *[Map page 53]*

► **Richat Structure, Mauritania**
When first seen from space by the Gemini spacecraft in 1965, this striking circular structure, about 50 km [30 miles] in diameter in north-eastern Mauritania, was thought to be a meteorite crater. Subsequent investigation, however, has confirmed that it is the heavily eroded remnant of a rock dome. It is about 200 m [656 ft] above the level of the desert, seen in the top left-hand corner of this image. *[Map page 78]*

▼ **Al Kufrah, Libya**
The Al Kufrah region contains the largest oases in the Libyan Desert. Beneath the desert are enormous freshwater reserves, which are held in porous rock layers called aquifers. This water collected when the climate in the Saharan region was much wetter. The false-colour image shows the characteristic round 'fields' that are irrigated by pumped water fed into centre-pivot irrigation systems, the crops showing up as red. The smoke on the right is gas burn-off from an oil well. *[Map page 79]*

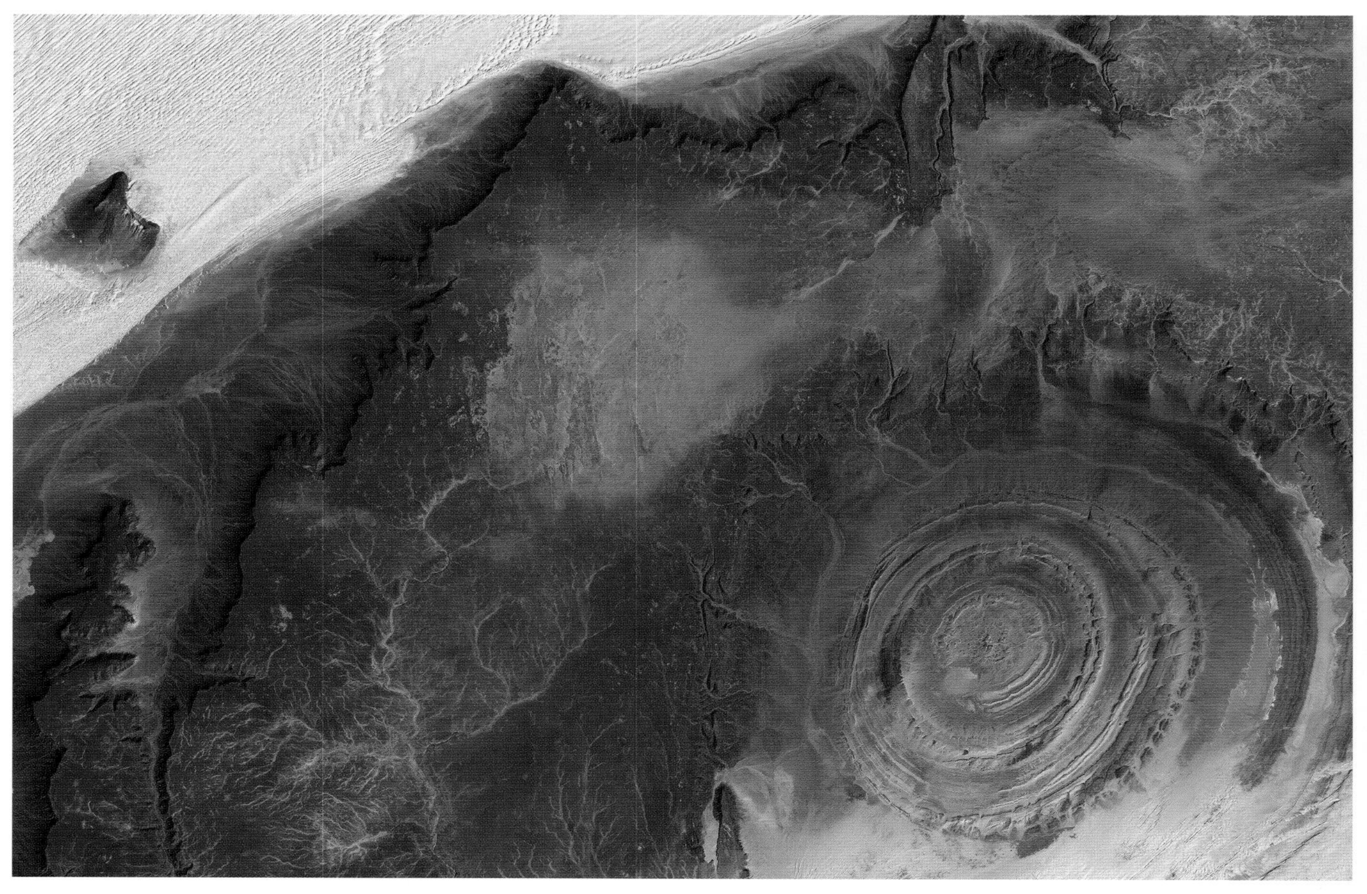

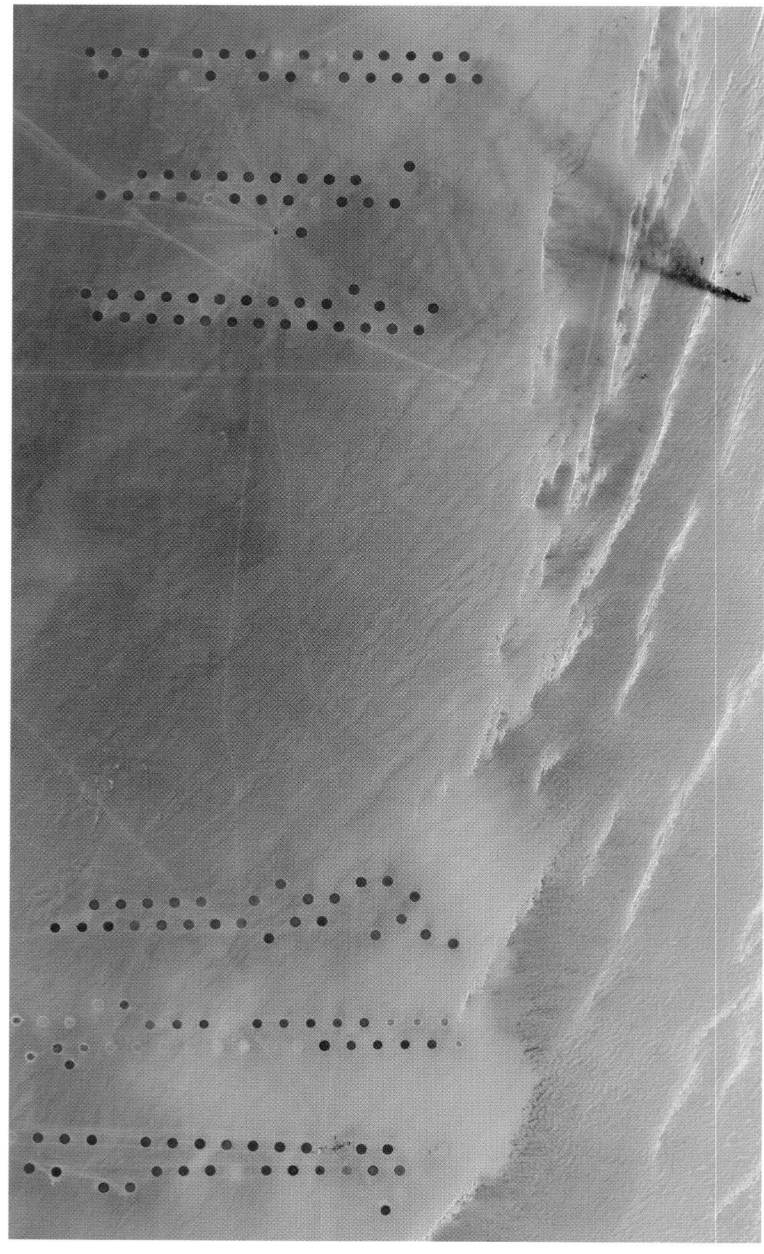

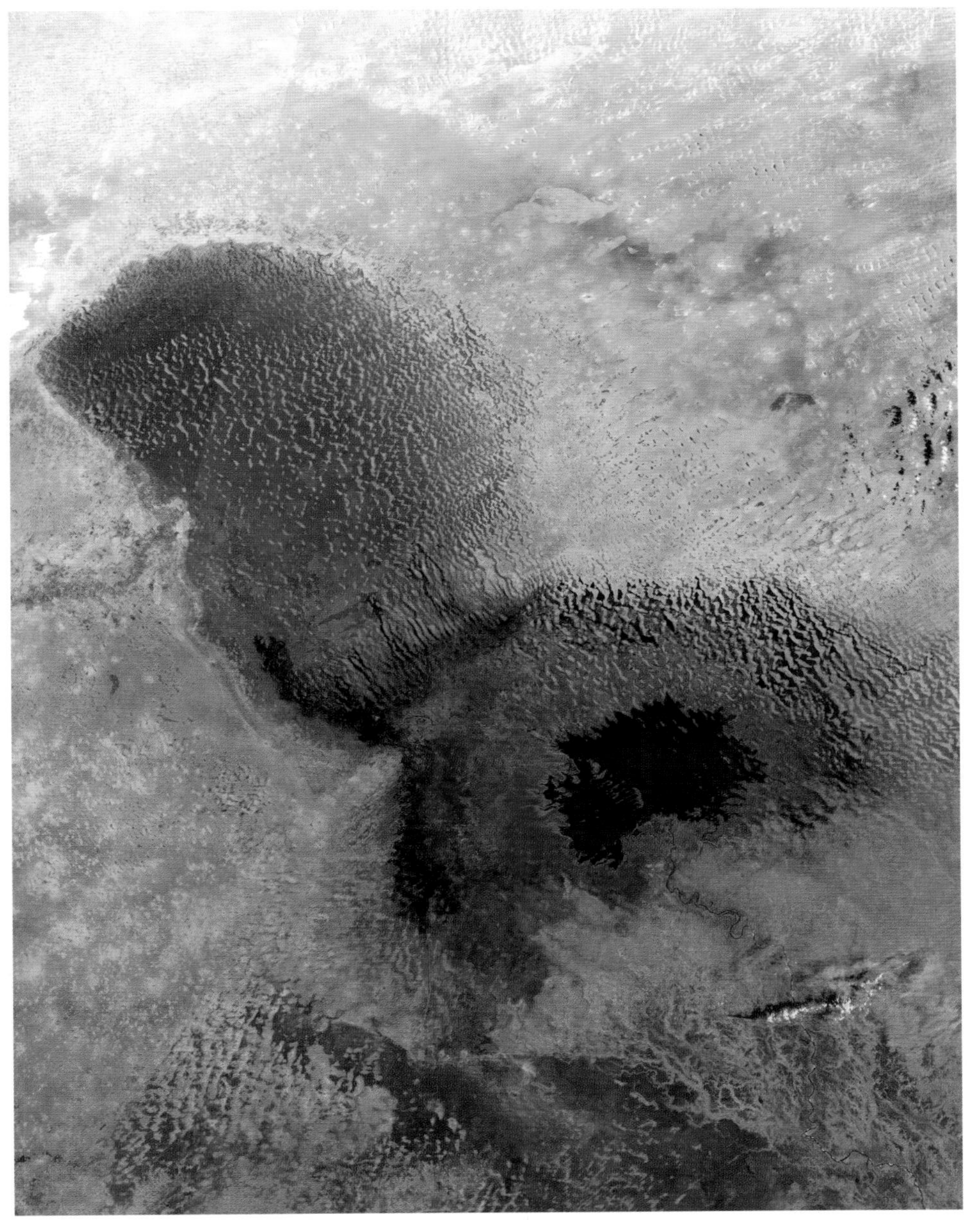

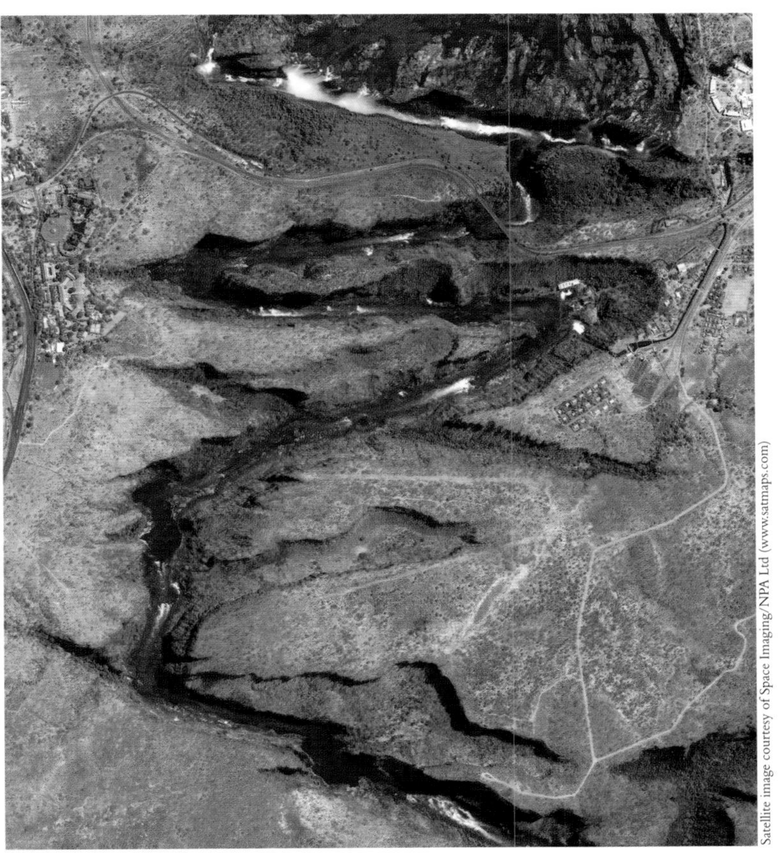

Satellite image courtesy of Space Imaging/NPA Ltd (www.satmaps.com)

▲ **Victoria Falls, Zambia/Zimbabwe**
At the top of the image, the Zambezi River plunges 105 m [345 ft] over a basalt cliff into a deep gorge. The falls are 1.6 km [1 mile] wide, but the chasm into which they fall is only 120 m [400 ft] wide, resulting in a fast turbulent torrent with many rapids. To the left of the river is Zimbabwe, with Zambia to its right. *[Map page 87]*

▼ **Cape Peninsula, South Africa**
The Cape Peninsula, seen running north to south on the far left of this image, is some 50 km [31 miles] long. Its southern extremity is the Cape of Good Hope, while the city of Cape Town sits at the northern end, beneath Table Mountain. Robben Island is clearly visible in Table Bay, to the north of the city. *[Map page 88]*

▲ **Lake Chad**
The lake, an inland drainage basin with no outlet to the sea, sits at the junction of four countries – Cameroon, Chad, Niger and Nigeria – and was once one of Africa's largest freshwater lakes, with an area of 25,000 sq km [9,650 sq miles] in 1963. However, sitting on the southern edge of the Sahara Desert, it has become susceptible to both the arid climate and increased abstraction of water for irrigation. By 2001, it had shrunk to only 1,350 sq km [839 sq miles] in area. *[Map page 83]*

◀ **Suez Canal, Egypt**
At the bottom of the image is the Gulf of Suez, at the northern end of the Red Sea. The port of Suez can be seen to the left of the line of the Suez Canal, which runs north to the Great Bitter Lakes, on its way to Port Said on the Mediterranean coast, 163 km [101 miles] away. Opened in 1869, the Suez Canal enables ships to travel between Europe and Asia without having to circumnavigate the whole of Africa. *[Map page 80]*

► Admiralty Gulf, Australia
Bordering the Timor Sea, the tropical coastline of this part of north-west Australia is one of the remotest on the continent. The rocks are very old and the cracks and fissures in them can clearly be seen in this image, enhanced by the vegetation growing along them. Western Australia, of which this is part, has an area of 2.5 million sq km [1 million sq miles], which makes it the largest state in the world. *[Map page 92]*

◄ Uluru (Ayers Rock), Australia
The remnant of a mountain range created some 500 million years ago and then eroded away, leaving only this huge outlier, Uluru rises 345 m [1,132 ft] above its surroundings and has a circumference of 9.4 km [5.8 miles]. The rock has been a centre of Aboriginal life for over 10,000 years. Its dramatic shape and coloration, caused by oxidized iron in the sandstone, now brings visitors from around the world to this remote site. The nearest town is Alice Springs, located 442 km [275 miles] to the east. *[Map page 93]*

Satellite image courtesy of Space Imaging/NPA Ltd (www.satmaps.com)

► New Zealand
This fine natural colour image shows the whole of New Zealand, or 'Aotearoa' ('Land of the Long White Cloud') as it is known to the indigenous Maori people. It is situated approximately 2,000 km [1,250 miles] south-east of Australia. Its rocks are ancient and the islands split away some 800 million years ago from the other continental land masses, allowing a unique variety of animal species, such as the flightless Kiwi, to develop. Polynesians are believed to have been the first settlers here, about 900 years ago. *[Map page 91]*

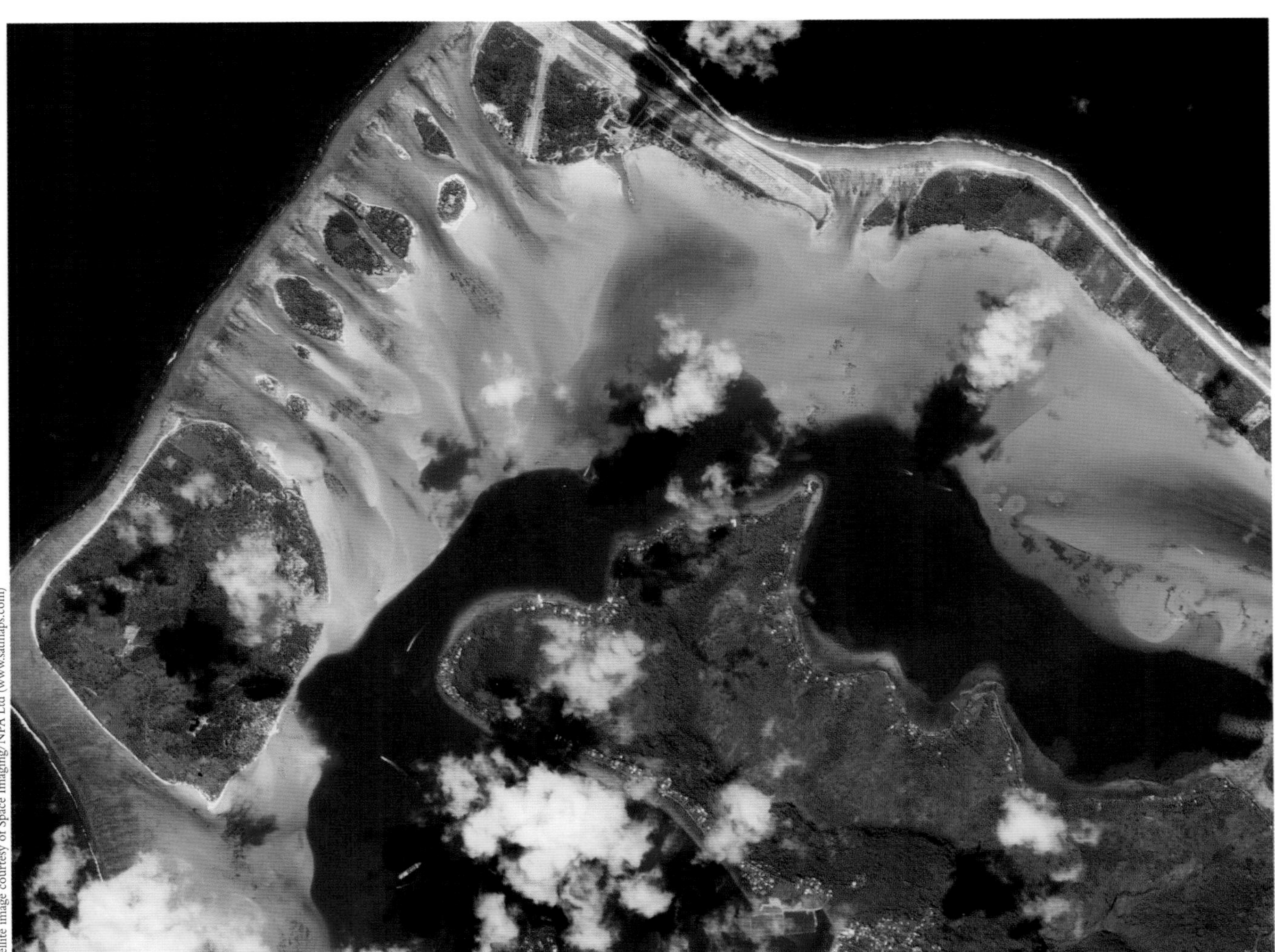

Satellite image courtesy of Space Imaging/NPA Ltd (www.satmaps.com)

◀ **Bora Bora, French Polynesia**
This image shows the northern tip of the island, its lagoon and fringing reef. The airport, visible at the top of the image, was built by US troops during World War II and can take international flights today. Situated 257 km [160 miles] north-west of Tahiti, Bora Bora is one of the Society Islands, part of French Polynesia. In the centre of the island, Mount Olemanu, the core of a long-extinct volcano, rises to a height of 725 m [2,380 ft]. *[Map page 97]*

▼ **Christchurch, New Zealand**
Situated on the east coast of the South Island, the city of Christchurch, with more than 300,000 inhabitants, lies between the braided Waimakariri River and the spectacular Banks Peninsula. The latter was formed by the erosion of two ancient volcanic cones by glaciers and their subsequent inundation by the sea to create the two large harbours of Lyttelton to the north and Akaroa in the south, as well as numerous flooded valleys. Inland, to the west, lie the fertile Canterbury Plains, New Zealand's prime sheep-rearing area. *[Map page 91]*

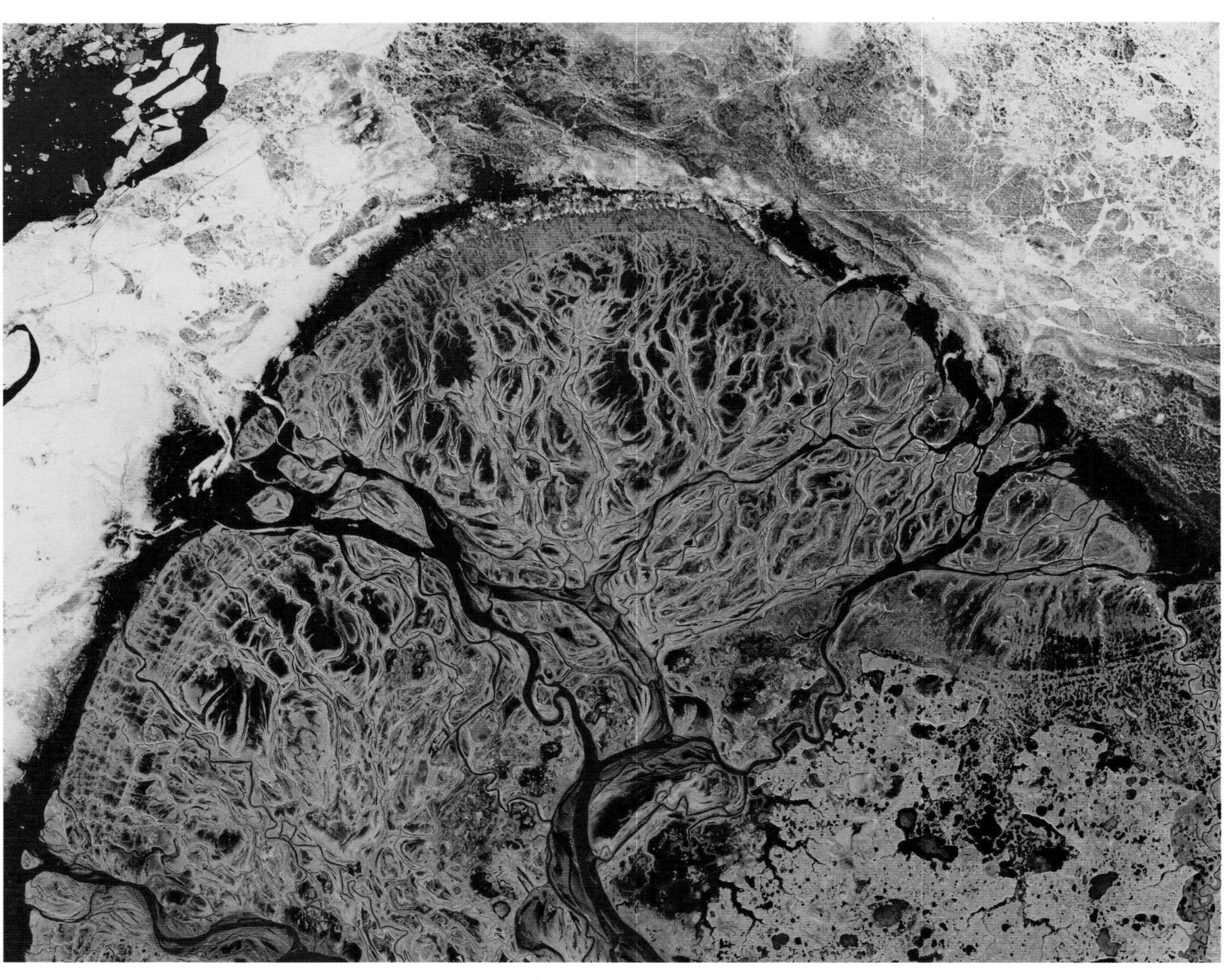

► **Lake Manicouagan, Canada**
This circular lake in Québec, some 70 km [43 miles] in diameter, is believed to be the result of a meteorite hitting the Earth some 214 million years ago. The central core is an area of uplifted rock that readjusted after the removal of thousands of tonnes of material above it by the impact. The crater shape has been further modified by glacial erosion during the last Ice Age. It is now used as a reservoir for a hydroelectric power station on the river to the south and for recreation. *[Map page 105]*

▼ **New Orleans, Louisiana**
Sometimes called 'the Crescent City', the settlement is situated between the south bank of Lake Pontchartrain (the largest in this view) and the Mississippi River. The brown sediment-laden water of the latter can be seen meandering sluggishly across the image, and each year it deposits over a million tonnes of material in its lower reaches and delta, which is to the south-east of the city. The river has the third-largest drainage basin in the world, after the Amazon and Congo. *[Map page 113]*

▲ **Yukon River Delta, Alaska**
At over 3,185 km [1,980 miles] long, the Yukon is one of North America's longest rivers, rising in Canada's McKenzie Mountains and flowing westwards across Alaska. It enters the Bering Sea via this complex delta, which is over 80 km [50 miles] wide. Lying just to the south of the Arctic Circle, sea ice can clearly be seen offshore, in light blue. *[Map page 100]*

► **San Francisco, California**
The whole of the 'Bay Area' is shown in this image: hilly San Francisco is at the top end of the southern peninsula, with the Golden Gate Bridge connecting it to Sausalito to the north. Alcatraz Island, former home of the infamous prison, can be seen as a small light area to the east of the bridge. On the opposite shore, connected by the double-decker Bay Bridge, are Oakland and Berkeley, while at the southern end of the bay is the city of San Jose. The bright green areas to the south of the bay are salt evaporation pans. *[Map page 110]*

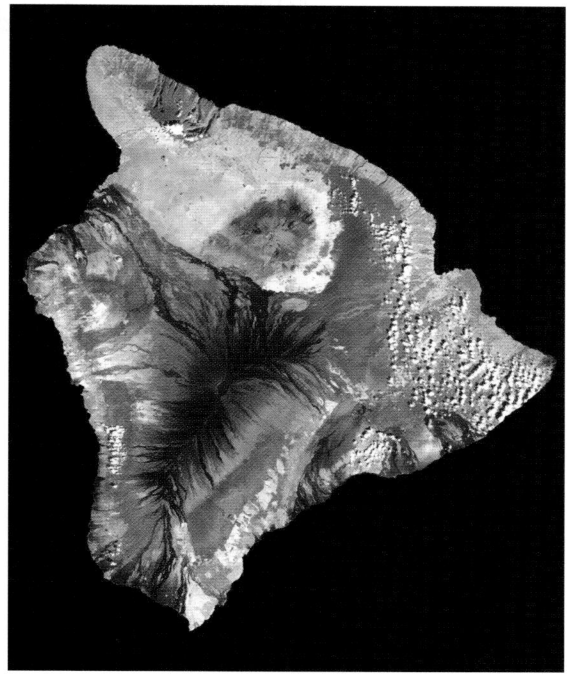

◄ **Hawai'i, USA**
Hawai'i is the largest of this group of mid-Pacific islands. Situated over a 'hot spot' on the Earth's crust, they are either active, dormant or extinct volcanoes. The blackened area to the south is lava from the largest active volcano, Mauna Loa, at 4,169 m [13,683 ft] high. *[Map page 106]*

▼ **Imperial Valley, USA/Mexico**
The Salton Sea is the dark area in the top left. It was inadvertently created in 1905 during an attempt to divert the flow of the Colorado River for irrigation. It lies 72 m [236 ft] below sea level and is very saline. To the south is a large area of productive land, showing bright red on this image. The abrupt colour change towards the bottom of this area marks the US–Mexico boundary. *[Map page 111]*

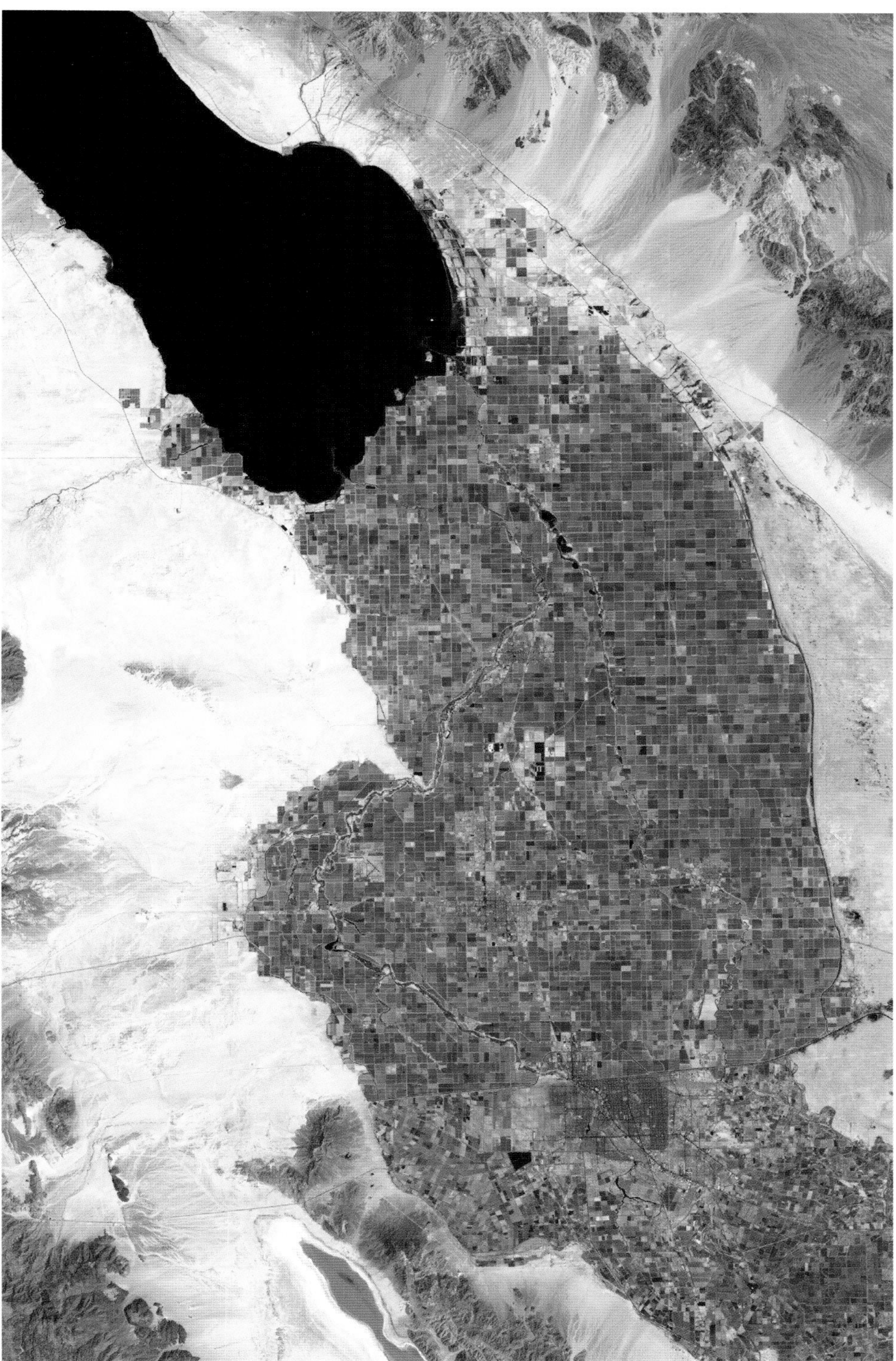

► BOLIVIA
Bolivia has over 250,000 sq km [100,000 sq miles] of dry tropical forest, home to animals such as jaguars and ocelots. It is, however, being cleared at a rate of over 2% per annum. This false-colour image shows an area that has been almost completely cleared. The darkest areas are remnants of the original forest, some retained as wind breaks between newly created arable fields. The radial patterns are fields with new villages at their centres, part of a government resettlement scheme. *[Map page 124]*

▼ SANTIAGO, CHILE
The Chilean capital city, Santiago, lies in a fertile valley at the foot of the Andes, some 60 km [37 miles] south-east of the main port of Valparaíso on the Pacific coast. To the east, the mountains rise to over 6,000 m [20,000 ft]. The city has expanded rapidly to its current population of over 5 million inhabitants and this resulted in air-pollution problems in the 1980s, though measures have since been taken to counter this. *[Map page 126]*

▼ WELLINGTON ISLAND, CHILE
This image shows part of Wellington Island, which is situated off the coast of southern Chile. This large island is approximately 5,556 sq km [2,145 sq miles] in extent, but is almost totally uninhabited. Experts believe its highly fractured surface is not simply the result of glaciation, since the fissures, valleys and fjords all run in varying directions. A more likely explanation is that it is the result of a collision between two tectonic plates. *[Map page 128]*

◄ **Manaus, Brazil**
The town, with a population of almost 1.5 million, shows up in light blue at the confluence of the Rio Negro or Black River (to the north) with the Amazon (to the south), some 1,600 km [1,000 miles] from its mouth. The main branch of the river to the south, sometimes also called the Solimões, is carrying a heavy load of sediment from the Andes, hence the marked colour difference. Ocean-going vessels can navigate this far upstream, and indeed continue a further 2,100 km [1,300 miles] up the Amazon to Iquitos, in northern Peru. *[Map page 124]*

▼ **Buenos Aires, Argentina**
Buenos Aires is situated where the continent's second-largest river system, the Paraná–Paraguay–Uruguay, flows into the flooded river valley that forms its estuary, the Río de la Plata (River Plate). The River Paraná flows in at the top left of the image. To the city's south and west is grazing land for livestock, while in the top right-hand corner, in Uruguay, wheat is the predominant crop grown locally. *[Map page 126]*

▲ **Patagonia, Chile**
This false-colour image shows many classic glacial features. As it flows slowly from the mountains towards the coast, the glacier is covered in fissures and crevasses. The bright-red semi-circular ridge, a little distance from its end, consists of loose rock debris and was pushed there by the ice. It is called a 'terminal moraine'. The blue-green areas around the tongues of the glacier are meltwater lakes, the colour coming from suspended silt, and they contain ice floes. Rivers drain these lakes, cutting through the moraine on their way to the sea. *[Map page 128]*

WORLD MAPS

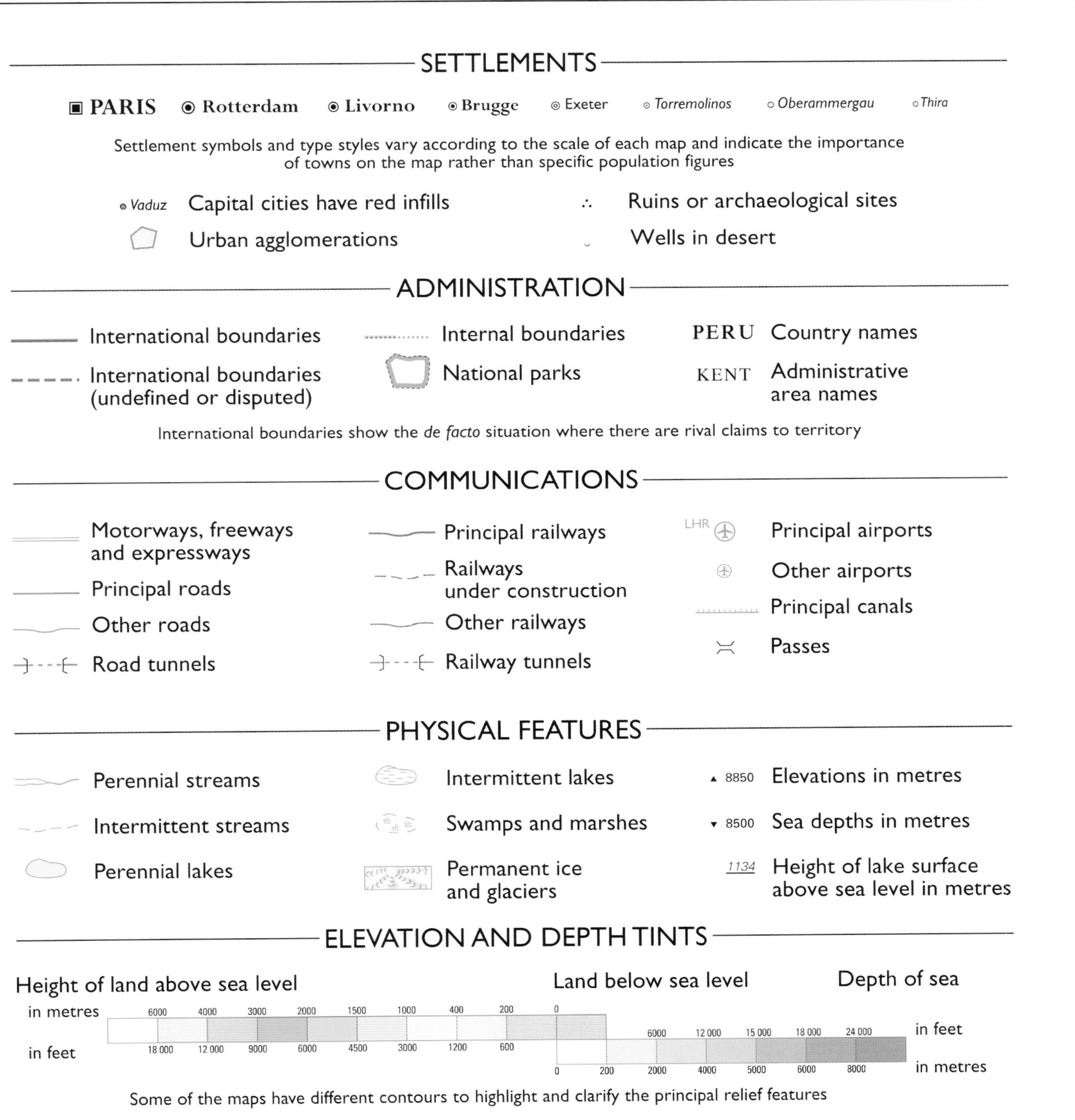
SETTLEMENTS
PARIS
Rotterdam
Livorno
Brugge
Exeter
Torremolinos
Oberammergau
Thira
Settlement symbols and type styles vary according to the scale of each map and indicate the importance of towns on the map rather than specific population figures
Vaduz
Capital cities have red infills
Ruins or archaeological sites
Urban agglomerations
Wells in desert
ADMINISTRATION
International boundaries
Internal boundaries
PERU
Country names
International boundaries (undefined or disputed)
National parks
KENT
Administrative area names
International boundaries show the de facto situation where there are rival claims to territory
COMMUNICATIONS
Motorways, freeways and expressways
Principal railways
LHR
Principal airports
Railways under construction
Other airports
Principal roads
Principal canals
Other roads
Other railways
Passes
Road tunnels
Railway tunnels
PHYSICAL FEATURES
Perennial streams
Intermittent lakes
8850
Elevations in metres
Intermittent streams
Swamps and marshes
8500
Sea depths in metres
Perennial lakes
Permanent ice and glaciers
1134
Height of lake surface above sea level in metres
ELEVATION AND DEPTH TINTS
Height of land above sea level
Land below sea level
Depth of sea
in metres
6000
4000
3000
2000
1500
1000
400
200
0
in feet
18 000
12 000
9000
6000
4500
3000
1200
600
6000
12 000
15 000
18 000
24 000
in feet
0
200
2000
4000
5000
6000
8000
in metres
Some of the maps have different contours to highlight and clarify the principal relief features

Equatorial Scale 1:84 000 000

Projection: *Hammer Equal Area*

Hanoi ● Capital Cities

4 ARCTIC OCEAN

100 0 200 400 600 800 1000 1200 1400 km

100 0 200 400 600 800 1000 miles

1:31 100 000

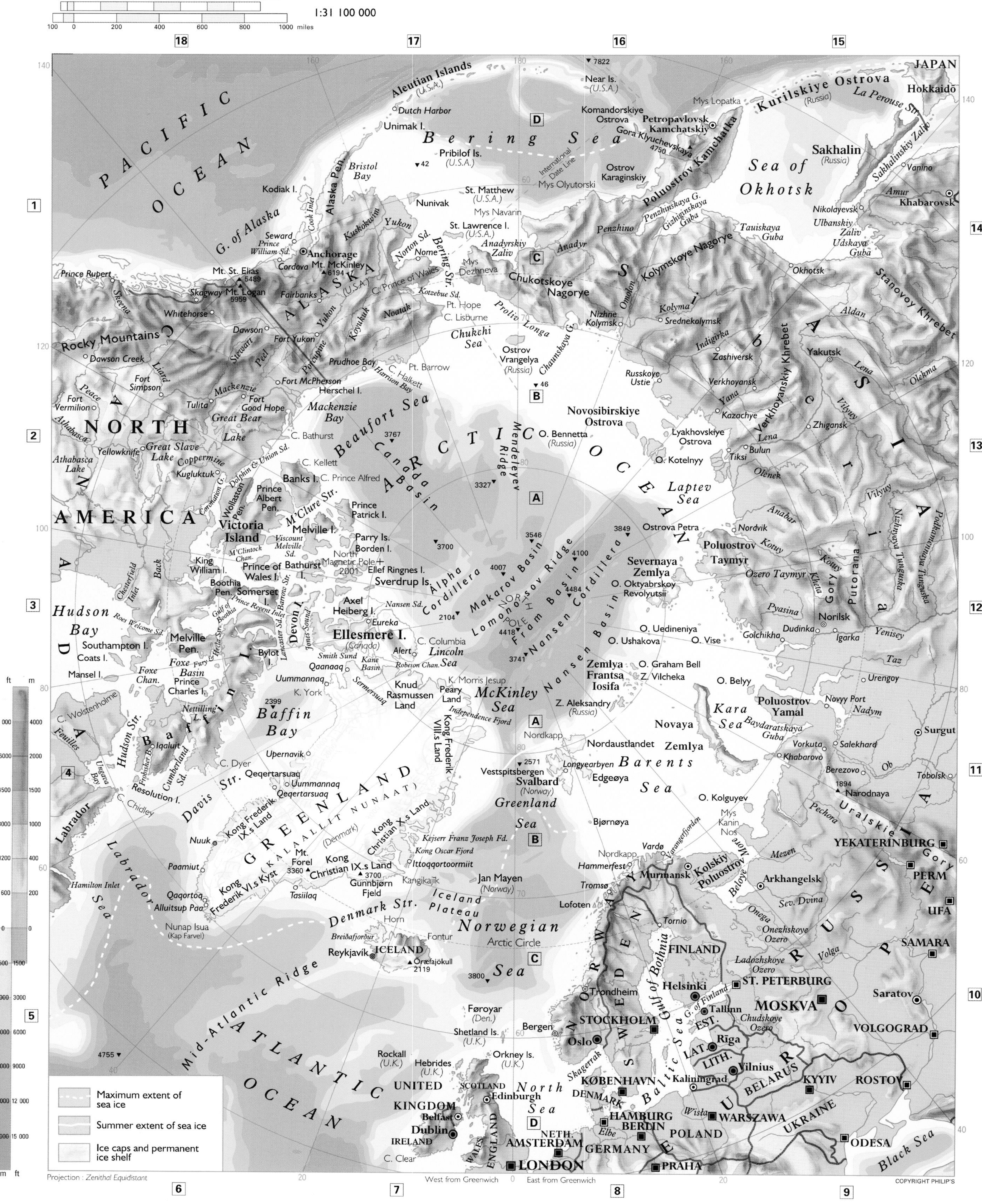

6 7 8 9

1:31 100 000

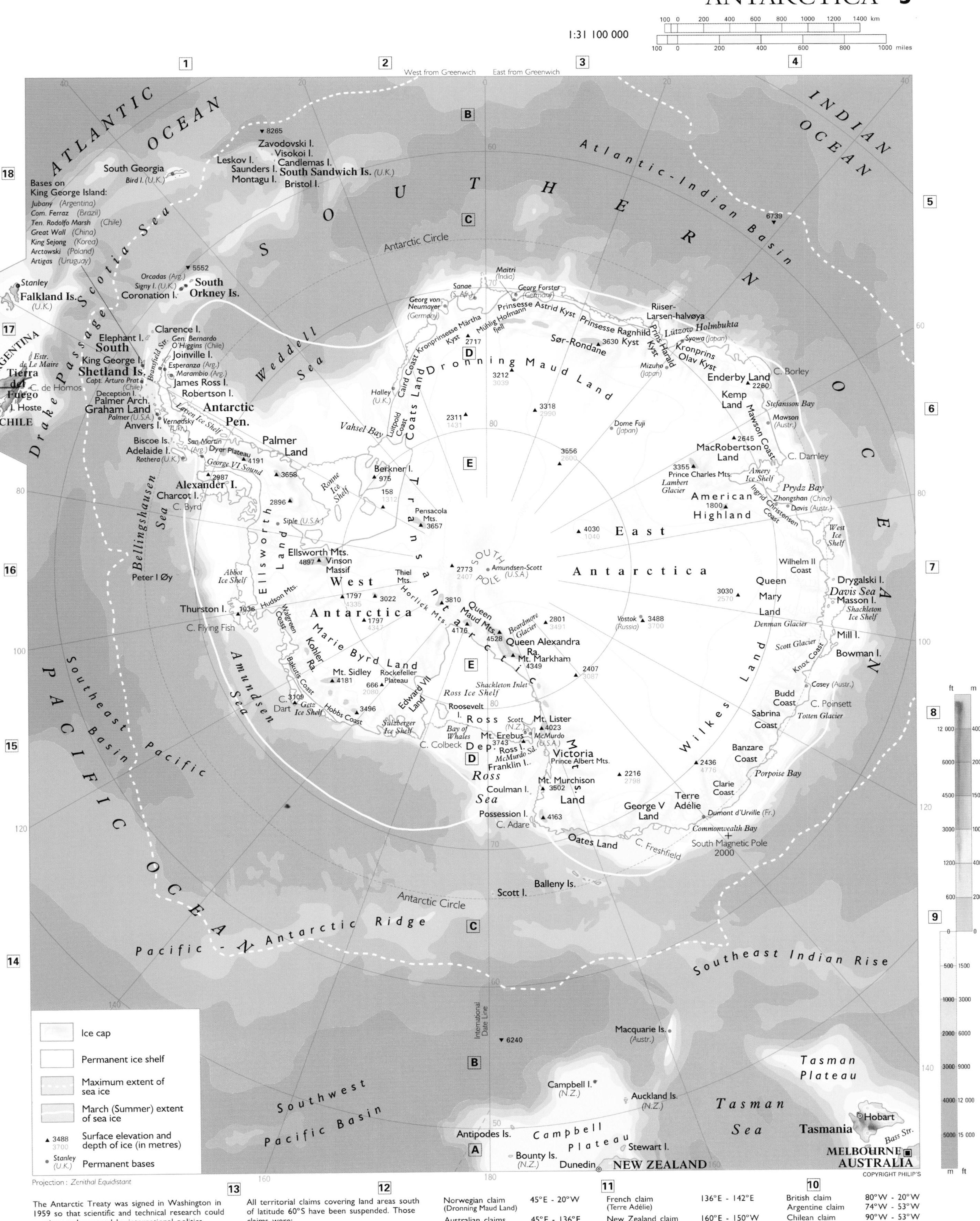

Projection: Zenithal Equidistant

The Antarctic Treaty was signed in Washington in 1959 so that scientific and technical research could continue unhampered by international politics.

All territorial claims covering land areas south of latitude 60°S have been suspended. Those claims were:

Norwegian claim (Dronning Maud Land)	45°E - 20°W
Australian claims	45°E - 136°E 142°E - 160°E
French claim (Terre Adélie)	136°E - 142°E
New Zealand claim (Ross Dependency)	160°E - 150°W
British claim	80°W - 20°W
Argentine claim	74°W - 53°W
Chilean claim	90°W - 53°W

EUROPE : Physical

100 0 100 200 300 400 500 600 700 800 km

100 0 100 200 300 400 500 miles

1:17 800 000

m	ft
5000	15 000
4000	12 000
2000	6000
1000	3000
400	1200
200	600
0	0
200	600
1000	3000
2000	6000
4000	12 000

Sea areas named in weather forecasts

Projection: Bonne

West from Greenwich | East from Greenwich

1:17 800 000

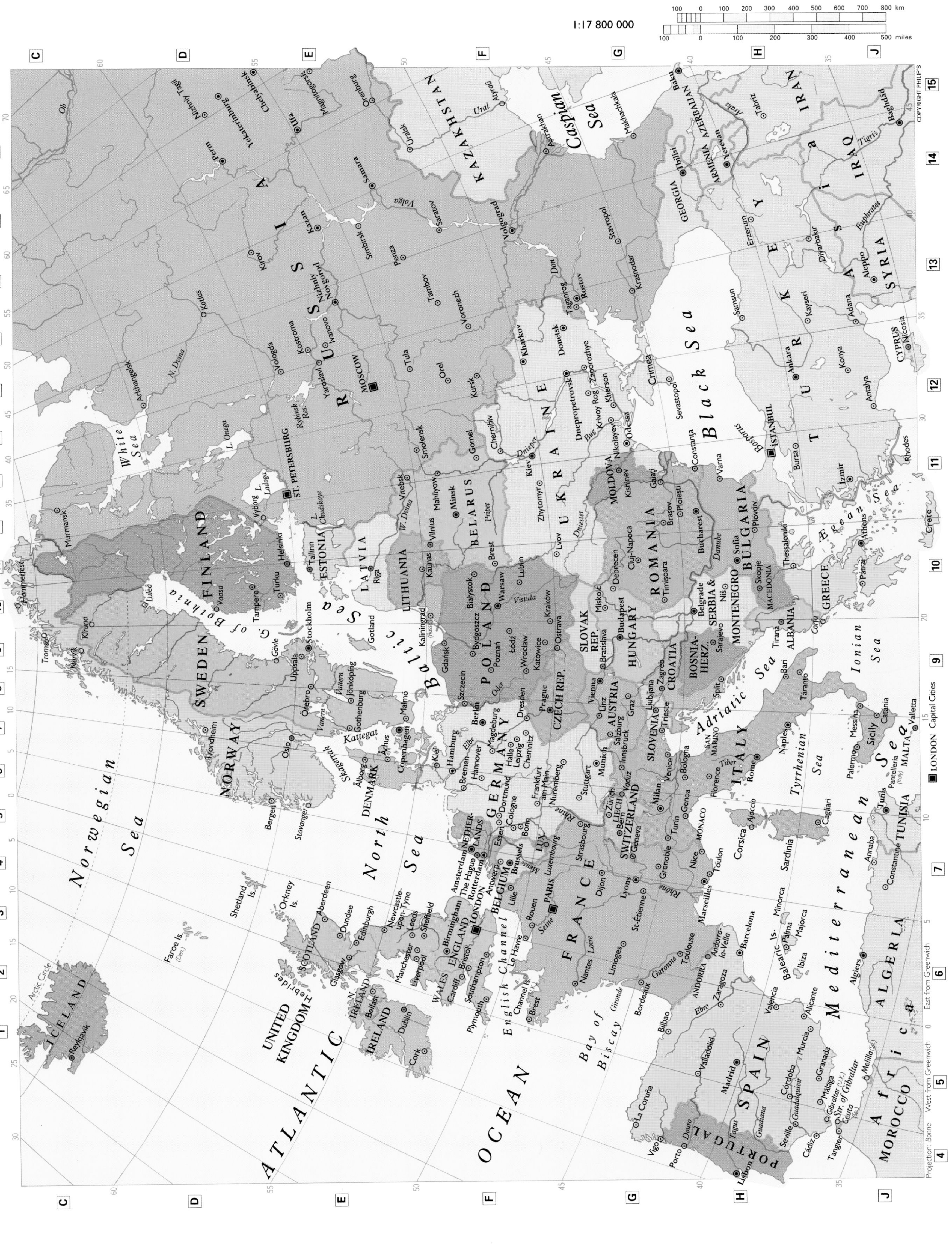

100 0 100 200 300 400 500 600 700 800 km

100 0 100 200 300 400 500 miles

■ LONDON Capital Cities

Projection: Bonne

West from Greenwich 0 East from Greenwich

ICELAND, Reykjavik, Arctic Circle, Faroe Is. (Den.), Shetland Is., Orkney Is., Hebrides, Norwegian Sea, North Sea, ATLANTIC OCEAN, Bay of Biscay, English Channel, Channel Is. (U.K.)

UNITED KINGDOM, SCOTLAND, ENGLAND, WALES, N. IRELAND, IRELAND, Aberdeen, Dundee, Edinburgh, Glasgow, Newcastle-upon-Tyne, Leeds, Sheffield, Manchester, Liverpool, Birmingham, Bristol, Cardiff, Southampton, Plymouth, LONDON, Belfast, Dublin, Cork

NORWAY, SWEDEN, FINLAND, DENMARK, Hammerfest, Tromsø, Narvik, Kiruna, Luleå, Trondheim, Bergen, Stavanger, Oslo, Gävle, Uppsala, Stockholm, Örebro, Vänern, Vättern, Jönköping, Gothenburg, Malmö, Kattegat, Skagerrak, Ålborg, Århus, Copenhagen, Vaasa, Tampere, Turku, Helsinki, G. of Bothnia, Baltic Sea, Gotland

ESTONIA, LATVIA, LITHUANIA, BELARUS, Tallinn, Riga, Kaunas, Vilnius, Minsk, Brest, Kaliningrad (Russia), Vitebsk, Mahilyow, Gomel, L. Chudskoye, W. Dvina, Pripet

RUSSIA, Murmansk, White Sea, L. Onega, L. Ladoga, Vyborg, ST. PETERSBURG, Arkhangelsk, N. Dvina, Kotlas, Vologda, Rybinsk Res., Yaroslavl, Kostroma, Ivanovo, MOSCOW, Smolensk, Tula, Orel, Kursk, Voronezh, Tambov, Penza, Nizhniy Novgorod, Kirov, Kazan, Simbirsk, Samara, Saratov, Volga, Volgograd, Perm, Ufa, Yekaterinburg, Nizhniy Tagil, Chelyabinsk, Magnitogorsk, Orenburg, Ob, Rostov, Taganrog, Don, Krasnodar, Stavropol, Makhachkala, Astrakhan

KAZAKHSTAN, Uralsk, Ural, Atyraū, Caspian Sea

UKRAINE, MOLDOVA, Kiev, Chernihiv, Kharkov, Donetsk, Zaporozhye, Dnepropetrovsk, Krivoy Rog, Kherson, Nikolayev, Odessa, Zhytomyr, Lvov, Dniester, Dnieper, Bug, Crimea, Sevastopol, Kishinev, Black Sea

GEORGIA, ARMENIA, AZERBAIJAN, Tbilisi, Yerevan, Baku, IRAN, Tabriz, Araks, IRAQ, Baghdād, Tigris, Euphrates, SYRIA, Aleppo, TURKEY, Erzurum, Diyarbakir, Samsun, Ankara, Kayseri, Konya, Adana, Antalya, Bursa, İzmir, ISTANBUL, Bosporus, CYPRUS, Nicosia, Rhodes, Crete

POLAND, Gdańsk, Szczecin, Bydgoszcz, Poznań, Białystok, Warsaw, Łódź, Lublin, Wrocław, Katowice, Kraków, Vistula, Oder, CZECH REP., Prague, Ostrava, SLOVAK REP., Bratislava, HUNGARY, Budapest, Miskolc, Debrecen, ROMANIA, Cluj-Napoca, Timişoara, Braşov, Ploieşti, Galaţi, Constanţa, Bucharest, Danube, BULGARIA, Sofia, Plovdiv, Varna, SERBIA & MONTENEGRO, Belgrade, Niš, MACEDONIA, Skopje, ALBANIA, Tirana, GREECE, Thessaloniki, Athens, Patrai, Corfu, Ægean Sea, Ionian Sea

GERMANY, Kiel, Hamburg, Bremen, Hannover, Berlin, Magdeburg, Halle, Leipzig, Dresden, Chemnitz, Essen, Dortmund, Cologne, Bonn, Frankfurt am Main, Nuremberg, Stuttgart, Munich, Elbe, Rhine, NETHERLANDS, Amsterdam, The Hague, Rotterdam, BELGIUM, Antwerp, Brussels, LUX., Luxembourg, Meuse

AUSTRIA, Vienna, Linz, Salzburg, Innsbruck, Graz, LIECH., Vaduz, SWITZERLAND, Zürich, Bern, Geneva, SLOVENIA, Ljubljana, CROATIA, Zagreb, Split, BOSNIA-HERZ., Sarajevo

FRANCE, Lille, Rouen, Le Havre, PARIS, Seine, Strasbourg, Brest, Nantes, Loire, Dijon, Lyons, St-Étienne, Grenoble, Limoges, Bordeaux, Gironde, Garonne, Toulouse, Rhône, Marseilles, Toulon, Nice, MONACO, Corsica, Ajaccio

ITALY, Milan, Turin, Genoa, Venice, Trieste, Bologna, Florence, SAN MARINO, Tiber, Rome, Naples, Bari, Taranto, Sardinia, Cagliari, Sicily, Palermo, Messina, Catania, Adriatic Sea, Tyrrhenian Sea, MALTA, Valletta, Pantelleria (Italy)

SPAIN, ANDORRA, Andorra-la-Vella, Barcelona, Zaragoza, Ebro, Bilbao, La Coruña, Vigo, Valladolid, Madrid, Valencia, Alicante, Murcia, Córdoba, Granada, Seville, Málaga, Cádiz, Guadalquivir, Guadiana, Tagus, Douro, Balearic Is., Minorca, Majorca, Palma, Ibiza, Gibraltar (U.K.), Str. of Gibraltar, Ceuta (Sp.), Melilla (Sp.)

PORTUGAL, Porto, Lisbon

Mediterranean Sea, Africa, MOROCCO, Tangier, ALGERIA, Algiers, Constantine, Annaba, TUNISIA, Tunis

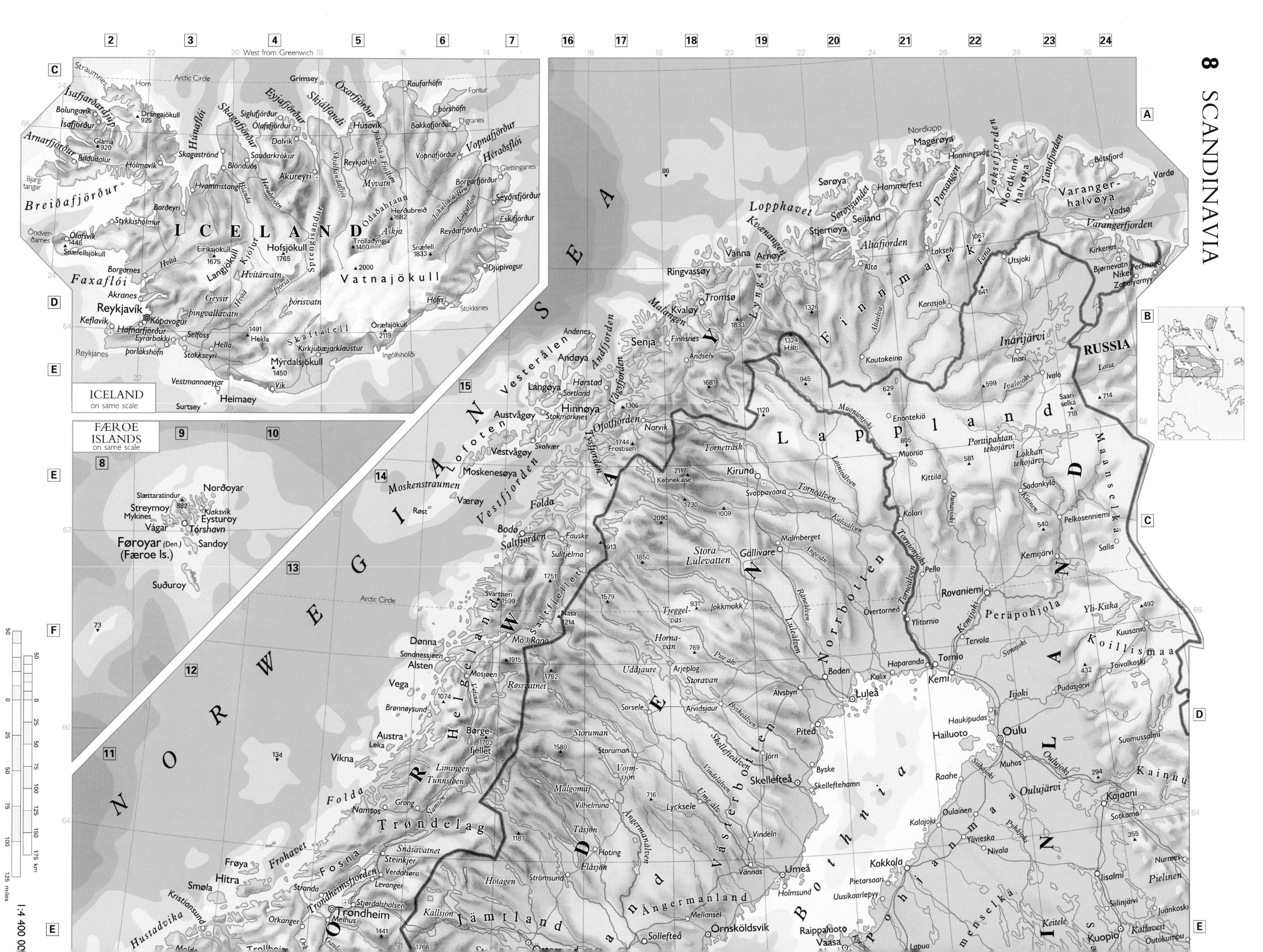

RUSSIA
Lappland
Finnmark
Norrbotten
Västerbotten
Ångermanland
Jämtland
Trøndelag
Helgeland
Lofoten
Vesterålen
NORWEGIAN SEA
Lopphavet
Vestfjorden
Maanselkä
Koillismaa
Peräpohjola
Kainuu
Pohjanmaa
Suomenselkä
Bothnia
ICELAND
Vatnajökull
Hofsjökull
Langjökull
Mýrdalsjökull
Faxaflói
Breiðafjörður
Húnaflói
Skagafjörður
Eyjafjörður
Skjálfandi
Öxarfjörður
Vopnafjörður
Héraðsflói
Reykjavík
Akureyri
Keflavík
Hafnarfjörður
Kópavogur
Selfoss
Húsavík
Höfn
Vík
Heimaey
Vestmannaeyjar
Surtsey
Hekla
Askja
Ísafjörður
West from Greenwich
ICELAND on same scale
FÆROE ISLANDS on same scale
Føroyar (Den.) (Færoe Is.)
Tórshavn
Streymoy
Eysturoy
Vágar
Sandoy
Suðuroy
Norðoyar
Vardø
Vadsø
Kirkenes
Varangerhalvøya
Varangerfjorden
Tanafjorden
Nordkinnhalvøya
Laksefjorden
Porsangen
Nordkapp
Magerøya
Hammerfest
Alta
Altafjorden
Sørøya
Stjernøya
Seiland
Kvænangen
Tromsø
Kvaløya
Ringvassøy
Vanna
Arnøy
Lyngen
Malangen
Finnsnes
Senja
Andselv
Narvik
Harstad
Hinnøya
Andøya
Andenes
Langøya
Sortland
Stokmarknes
Svolvær
Austvågøy
Vestvågøy
Moskenesøya
Moskenstraumen
Værøy
Røst
Ofotfjorden
Tysfjorden
Vågsfjorden
Andfjorden
Bodø
Fauske
Saltfjorden
Sulitjelma
Saltfjellet
Mo i Rana
Mosjøen
Vefsna
Svartisen
Dønna
Alsten
Vega
Brønnøysund
Austra
Leka
Vikna
Namsos
Grong
Steinkjer
Levanger
Trondheim
Trondheimsfjorden
Fosna
Frøya
Hitra
Smøla
Kristiansund
Børgefjellet
Limingen
Tunnsjøen
Kiruna
Gällivare
Malmberget
Jokkmokk
Kebnekaise
Torneträsk
Stora Lulevatten
Luleå
Boden
Kalix
Haparanda
Piteå
Skellefteå
Umeå
Örnsköldsvik
Sollefteå
Vännäs
Vindeln
Lycksele
Storuman
Sorsele
Arvidsjaur
Arjeplog
Vilhelmina
Hoting
Strömsund
Luleälven
Torneälven
Kalixälven
Skellefteälven
Ångermanälven
Oulu
Kemi
Tornio
Rovaniemi
Kemijärvi
Sodankylä
Ivalo
Inari
Inarijärvi
Kittilä
Muonio
Enontekiö
Pello
Ylitornio
Kuusamo
Kajaani
Oulujärvi
Kokkola
Raahe
Vaasa
Kuopio
Iisalmi
Kautokeino
Karasjok
Lakselv
Utsjoki
Nikel
Pechenga
Zapolyarnyy
Arctic Circle
1:4 400 00
km
miles

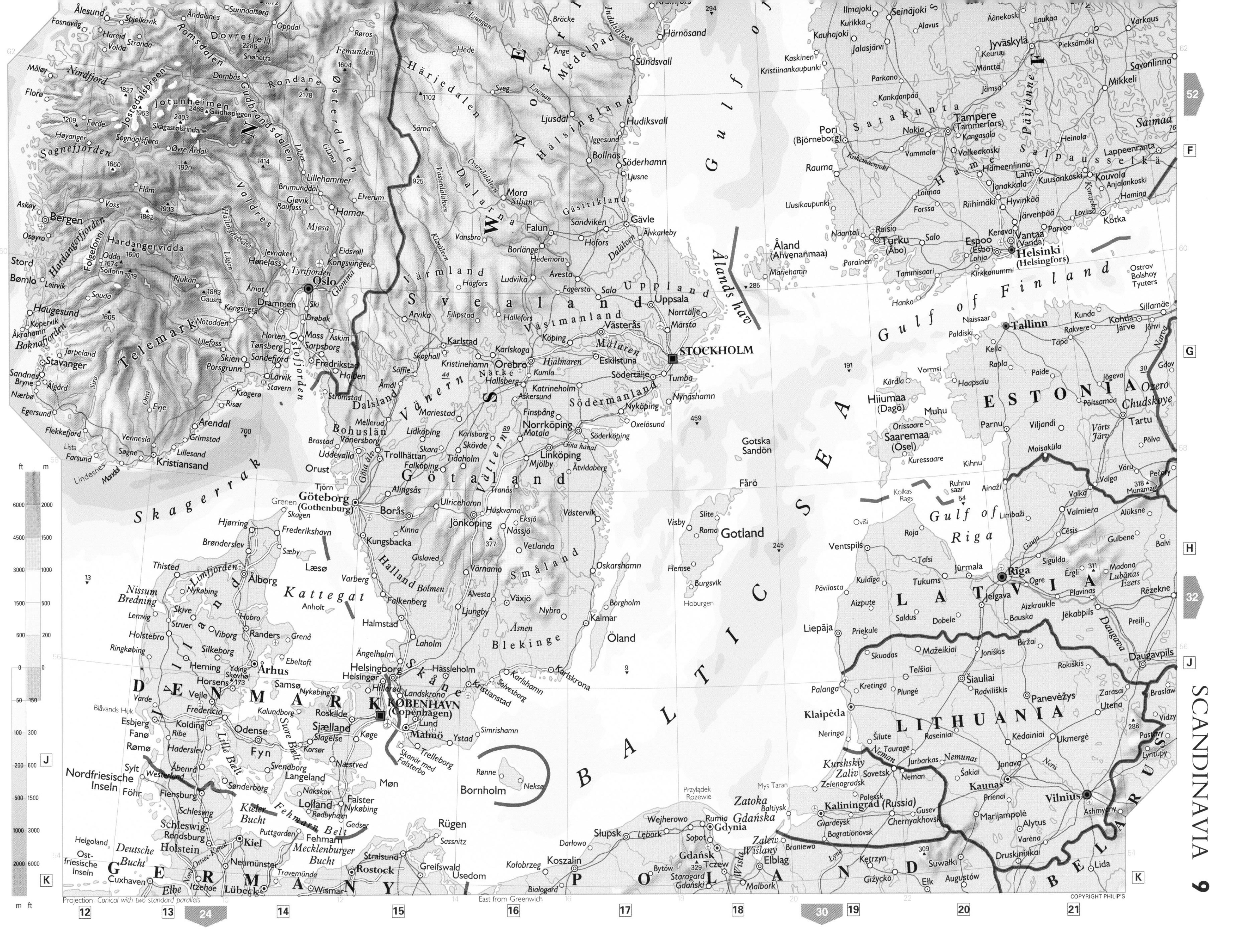
Gulf of Finland
Gulf of Riga
Ålands hav
Skagerrak
Kattegat
BALTIC SEA
ESTONIA
LATVIA
LITHUANIA
DENMARK
POLAND
GERMANY
BELARUS
Svealand
Götaland
STOCKHOLM
KØBENHAVN (Copenhagen)
Oslo
Helsinki (Helsingfors)
Tallinn
Riga
Vilnius
Göteborg (Gothenburg)
Gotland
Öland
Bornholm
Saaremaa (Ösel)
Hiiumaa (Dagö)
Åland (Ahvenanmaa)
Kaliningrad (Russia)
Gdańsk
Gdynia
Klaipėda
Kaunas
Tartu
Turku (Åbo)
Tampere (Tammerfors)
Bergen
Stavanger
Kristiansand
Uppsala
Malmö
Århus
Ålborg
Kiel
Lübeck
Rostock
Projection: Conical with two standard parallels
East from Greenwich
COPYRIGHT PHILIP'S
12
13
24
14
15
16
17
18
30
19
20
21
52
32
F
G
H
J
K

1:2 200 000
10 0 10 20 30 40 50 60 70 80 90 km
10 0 10 20 30 40 50 60 miles
Gulf of Bothnia
NORWAY
SWEDEN
STOCKHOLM
Oslo
Uppsala
Trondheim
Östersund
Sundsvall
Gävle
Falun
Borlänge
Karlstad
Örebro
Västerås
Eskilstuna
Drammen
Lillehammer
Hamar
Dovrefjell
Rondane
Jotunheimen
Härjedalen
Hälsingland
Medelpad
Gästrikland
Dalarna
Uppland
Närke
JÄMTLANDS LÄN
DALARNAS LÄN
GÄVLEBORGS LÄN
VÄSTERNORRLANDS LÄN
UPPSALA LÄN
STOCKHOLMS LÄN
VÄSTMANLANDS LÄN
VÄRMLANDS LÄN
ÖREBRO LÄN
SÖDERMANLANDS LÄN
SØR-TRØNDELAG
MØRE OG ROMSDAL
HEDMARK
OPPLAND
BUSKERUD
TELEMARK
AKERSHUS
ØSTFOLD
VESTFOLD
ft 6000 4500 3000 1500 600 0
m 2000 1500 1000 500 200 0

11
BALTIC SEA
Kattegat
Skagerrak
POLAND
GERMANY
DENMARK
SWEDEN
Öland (Sweden)
Gotland (Sweden)
GOTLANDS LÄN
Bornholm (Denmark)
BORNHOLMS AMT.
KØBENHAVN
Göteborg
Malmö
Helsingborg
Jönköping
Linköping
Norrköping
Kalmar
Karlskrona
Visby
Ålborg
Århus
Odense
Esbjerg
Flensburg
Sylt
Læsø (Denmark)
Anholt (Denmark)
Samsø
Sjælland
Fyn
Lolland
Falster
Møn
Fehmarn
Fehmarn Belt
Store Bælt
Lille Bælt
Øresund
Hanöbukten
Bornholmsgattet
ÖSTERGÖTLANDS LÄN
VÄSTRA GÖTALANDS LÄN
JÖNKÖPINGS LÄN
KRONOBERGS LÄN
KALMAR LÄN
BLEKINGE LÄN
SKÅNE LÄN
HALLANDS LÄN
Bohuslän
Dalsland
Småland
Götaland
AUST-AGDER
NORDJYLLANDS AMT.
VIBORG AMT.
ÅRHUS AMT.
RINGKØBING AMT.
VEJLE AMT.
RIBE AMT.
SØNDERJYLLANDS AMT.
FYNS AMT.
VESTSJÆLLANDS AMT.
STORSTRØMS AMT.
FREDERIKSBORG AMT.
ROSKILDE AMT.
Vättern
F G H J K
2 3 4 5 6 7 8 9 10 11
24
30
National Parks
East from Greenwich
Projection : Lambert's Conformal Conic
COPYRIGHT PHILIP'S

1:1 800 000

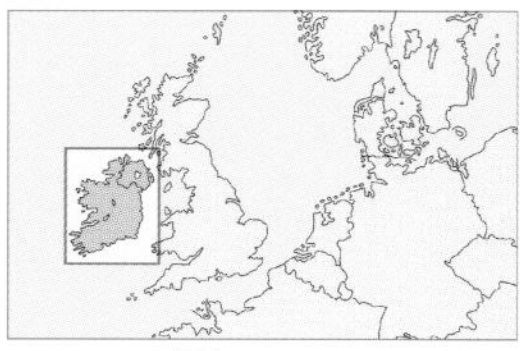

km: 10 0 10 20 30 40 50 60 70 80

miles: 10 0 10 20 30 40 50

ATLANTIC OCEAN

CELTIC SEA

IRISH SEA

North Channel

St. George's Channel

SCOTLAND

WALES

NORTHERN IRELAND

IRELAND

Ulster

Connacht

Leinster

Munster

DONEGAL, LONDONDERRY, ANTRIM, TYRONE, FERMANAGH, ARMAGH, DOWN, MONAGHAN, CAVAN, LEITRIM, SLIGO, MAYO, ROSCOMMON, LONGFORD, LOUTH, MEATH, WESTMEATH, GALWAY, OFFALY, KILDARE, DUBLIN, WICKLOW, LAOIS, CARLOW, CLARE, TIPPERARY, KILKENNY, WEXFORD, LIMERICK, KERRY, CORK, WATERFORD

Dublin, Belfast, Londonderry, Cork, Limerick, Galway, Waterford, Sligo, Dundalk, Drogheda, Wexford, Kilkenny, Tralee, Killarney, Athlone, Ennis

Projection : Lambert's Conformal Conic

West from Greenwich

National Parks

ft m: 1500 500, 600 200, 300 100, 0 0, 50 150, 100 300, 200 600, 500 1500, 1000 3000, 2000 6000

m ft

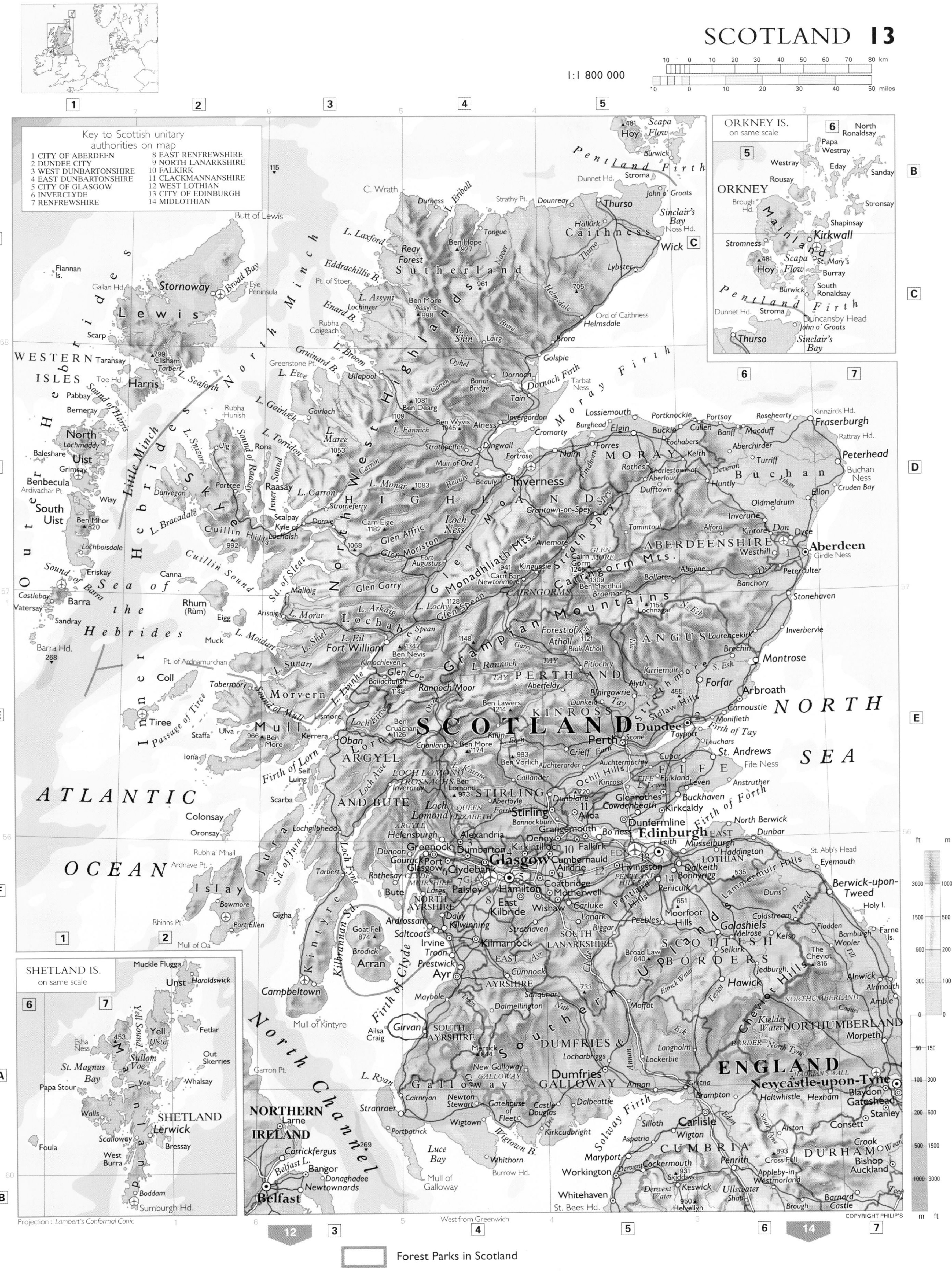

12
14

Forest Parks in Scotland

14 ENGLAND AND WALES

1:1 800 000

Key to English unitary authorities on map

25 HARTLEPOOL
26 DARLINGTON
27 STOCKTON-ON-TEES
28 MIDDLESBROUGH
29 REDCAR AND CLEVELAND
30 BLACKPOOL
31 BLACKBURN WITH DARWEN
32 HALTON
33 WARRINGTON
34 KINGSTON UPON HULL
35 NORTH EAST LINCOLNSHIRE
36 STOKE-ON-TRENT
37 TELFORD AND WREKIN
38 DERBY CITY
39 CITY OF NOTTINGHAM
40 LEICESTER CITY
41 RUTLAND
42 PETERBOROUGH
43 MILTON KEYNES
44 LUTON
45 NORTH SOMERSET
46 CITY OF BRISTOL
47 BATH AND NORTH EAST SOMERSET
48 SWINDON
49 READING
50 WOKINGHAM
51 WINDSOR AND MAIDENHEAD
52 SLOUGH
53 BRACKNELL FOREST
54 THURROCK
55 SOUTHEND-ON-SEA
56 MEDWAY
57 PLYMOUTH
58 TORBAY
59 POOLE
60 BOURNEMOUTH
61 SOUTHAMPTON
62 PORTSMOUTH
63 BRIGHTON AND HOVE

Key to Welsh unitary authorities on map

15 SWANSEA
16 NEATH PORT TALBOT
17 BRIDGEND
18 RHONDDA CYNON TAFF
19 MERTHYR TYDFIL
20 CAERPHILLY
21 BLAENAU GWENT
22 TORFAEN
23 CARDIFF
24 NEWPORT

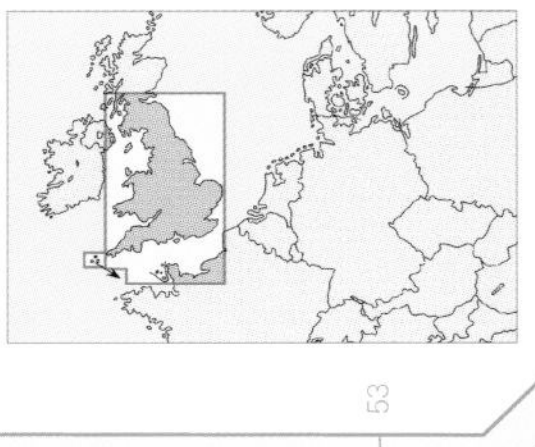

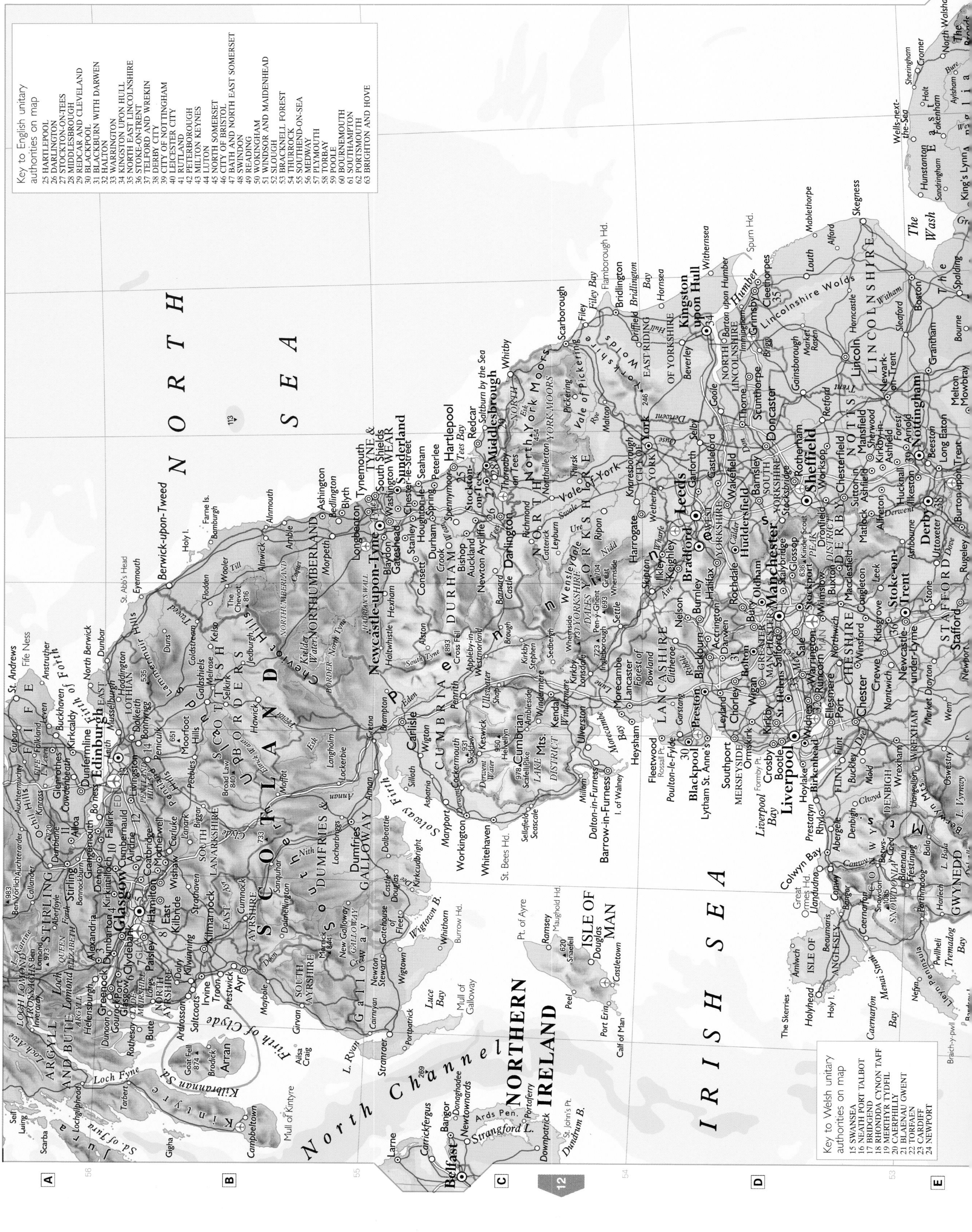

ENGLAND
WALES
FRANCE
ENGLISH CHANNEL
Bristol Channel
Cardigan Bay
Lyme Bay
Baie de la Seine
Baie de la Somme
Strait of Dover
Thames Estuary
Carmarthen Bay
Bridgwater Bay
CHANNEL ISLANDS
(U.K.)
ISLE OF WIGHT
LONDON
BIRMINGHAM
Bristol
Cardiff
Swansea
Plymouth
Exeter
Southampton
Portsmouth
Bournemouth
Brighton
Oxford
Cambridge
Northampton
Peterborough
Ipswich
Le Havre
Rouen
Caen
Cherbourg
Calais
Dieppe
Guernsey
Jersey
Alderney
Sark
Herm
HAUTE-NORMANDIE
CALVADOS
MANCHE
SEINE-MARITIME
CORNWALL
DEVON
DORSET
SOMERSET
WILTSHIRE
HANTS
SURREY
SUSSEX
KENT
ESSEX
SUFFOLK
NORFOLK
CAMBRIDGE
BEDFORD
NORTHAMPTON
OXFORD
BUCKS
HERTS
GLOUCS
HEREFORD
WORCESTER
WARWICK
SHROPSHIRE
POWYS
CEREDIGION
CARMARTHENSHIRE
PEMBROKESHIRE
ISLES OF SCILLY
on same scale
Isles of Scilly
Projection : Lambert's Conformal Conic
West from Greenwich
East from Greenwich
COPYRIGHT PHILIP'S
National Parks in England and Wales
Forest Parks in Scotland
ft
m
3000
1500
600
300
0
50
100
200
1000
500
200
100
0
150
300
600
m
ft
18
19

1:4 400 000
ATLANTIC OCEAN
NORTH SEA
CELTIC SEA
IRISH SEA
English Channel
UNITED KINGDOM
IRELAND
SCOTLAND
ENGLAND
WALES
NORTHERN IRELAND
FRANCE
BELGIUM
NETHERLANDS
Shetland Is.
Orkney Is.
Outer Hebrides
Inner Hebrides
Channel Is. (U.K.)
LONDON
Dublin
Edinburgh
Projection: Conical with two standard parallels
COPYRIGHT PHILIP'S

1:2 200 000

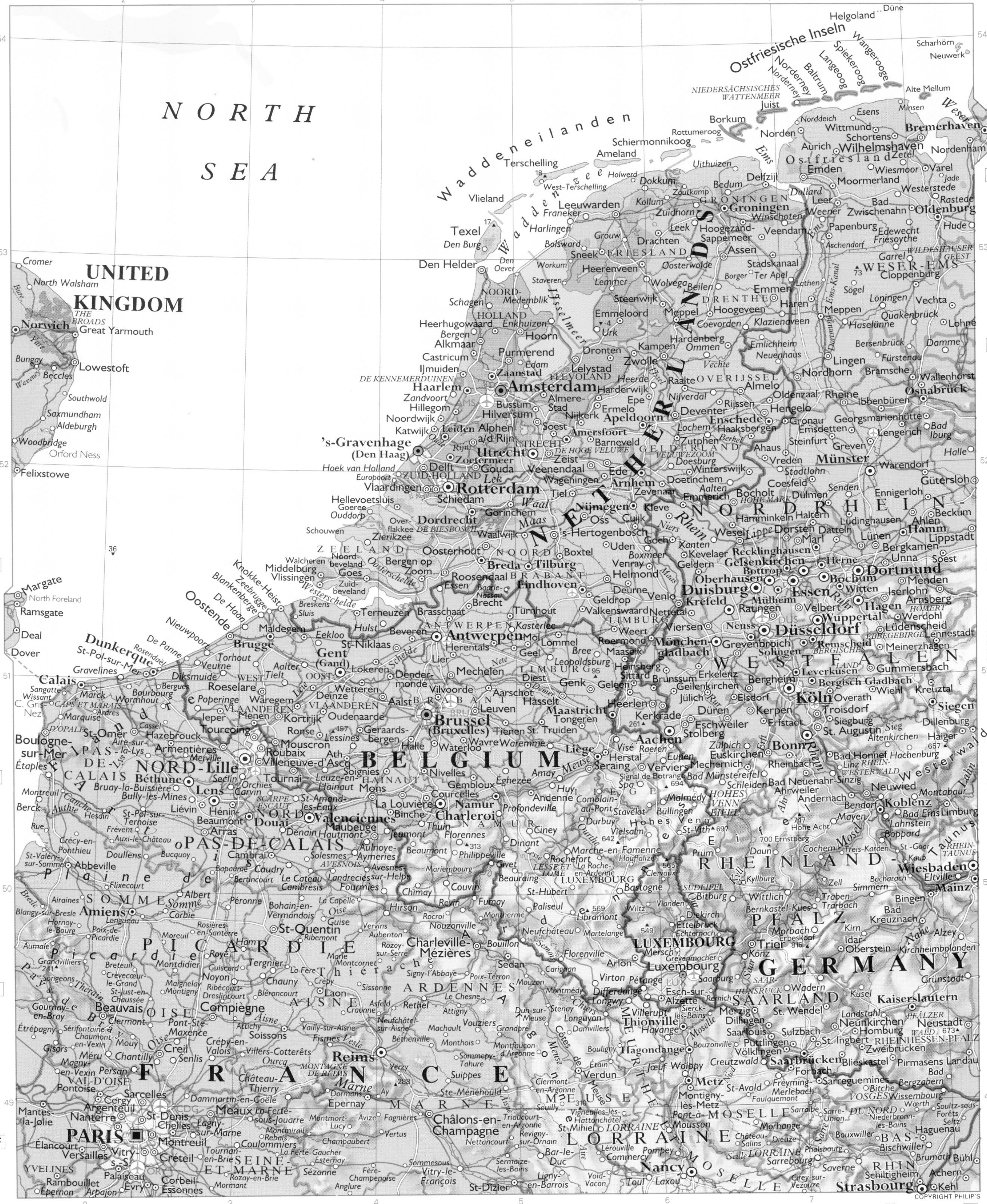

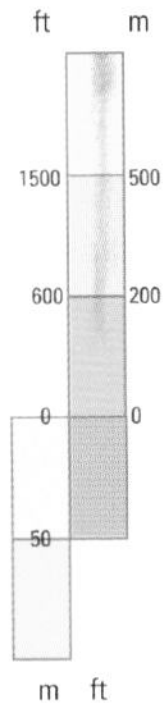

National Parks

Underlined towns give their name to the administrative area in which they stand.

NORTHERN FRANCE

1:2 200 000

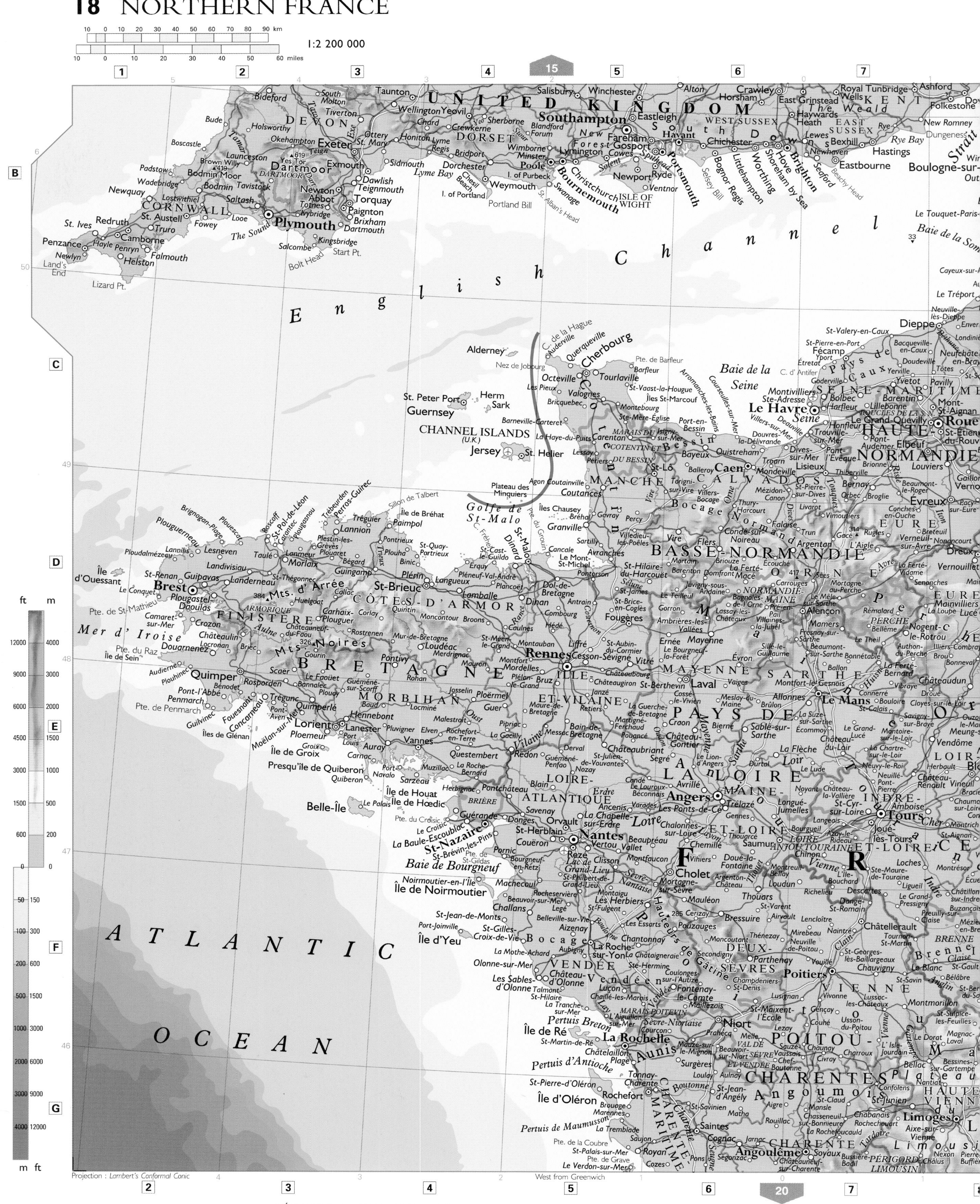

DÉPARTEMENTS IN THE PARIS AREA

1 Ville de Paris
2 Seine-St-Denis
3 Val-de-Marne
4 Hauts-de-Seine

17

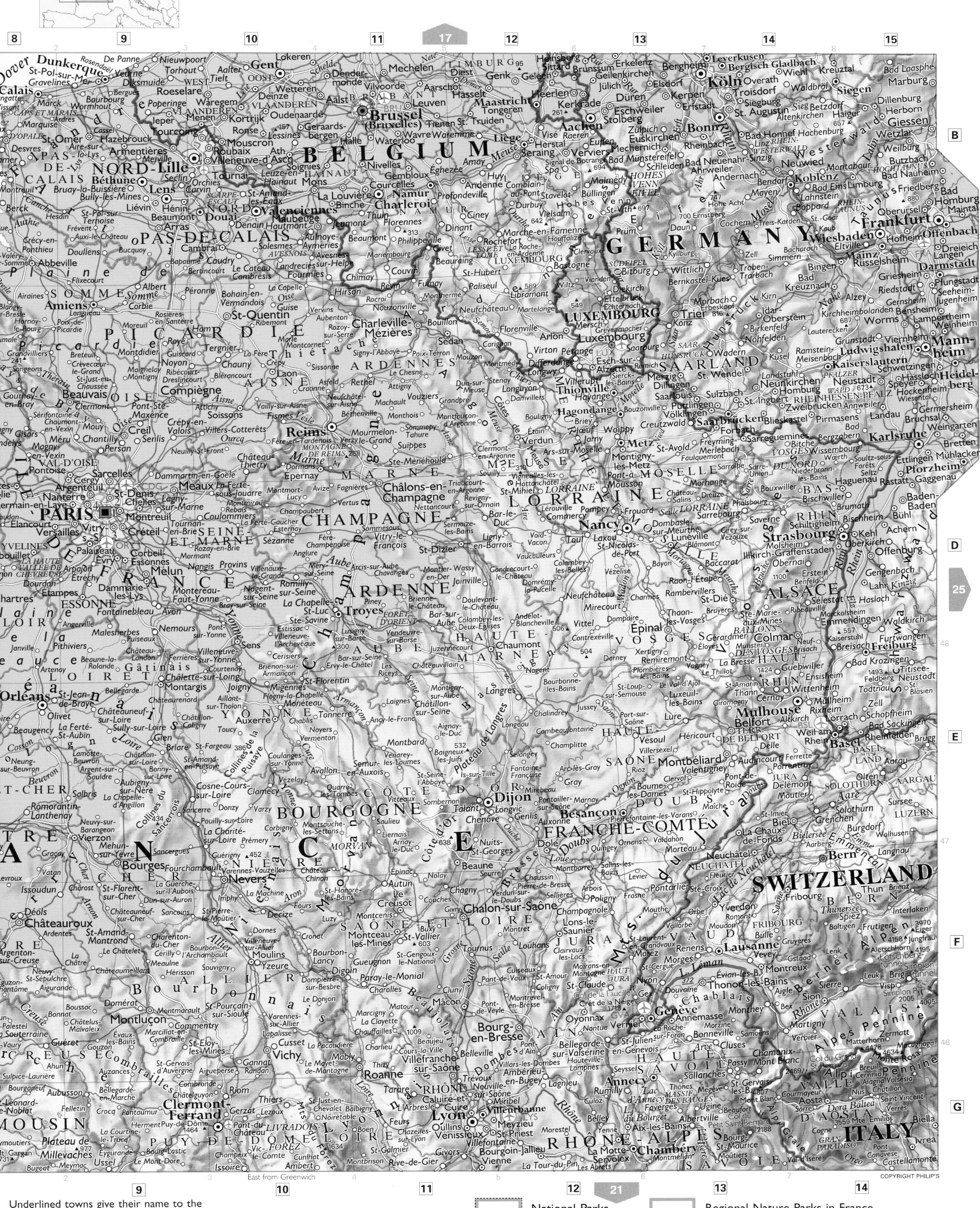

25

21

Underlined towns give their name to the administrative area in which they stand.

National Parks

Regional Nature Parks in France

1:2 200 000

ATLANTIC OCEAN
Golfe de Gascogne
FRANCE
SPAIN
ANDORRA
POITOU-CHARENTES
AQUITAINE
LIMOUSIN
AUVERGNE
MIDI-PYRÉNÉES
LANGUEDOC-ROUSSILLON
CATALUÑA
NAVARRA
ZARAGOZA
HUESCA
LLEIDA
GIRONA
BARCELONA
Nantes
Cholet
Poitiers
Niort
La Rochelle
Rochefort
Île de Ré
Île d'Oléron
Île d'Yeu
Angoulême
Limoges
Châteauroux
Bourges
Nevers
Montluçon
Vichy
Clermont-Ferrand
Périgueux
Brive-la-Gaillarde
Bordeaux
Arcachon
Agen
Montauban
Toulouse
Albi
Rodez
Millau
Aurillac
Cahors
Mont-de-Marsan
Bayonne
Biarritz
Pau
Tarbes
Lourdes
Carcassonne
Narbonne
Béziers
Perpignan
Pamplona
Donostia-San Sebastián
Zaragoza
Huesca
Lleida
Manresa
Girona
Figueres
Andorra la Vella
Massif Central
PYRÉNÉES
Costa Brava
Projection : Lambert's Conformal Conic
West from Greenwich
East from Greenwich

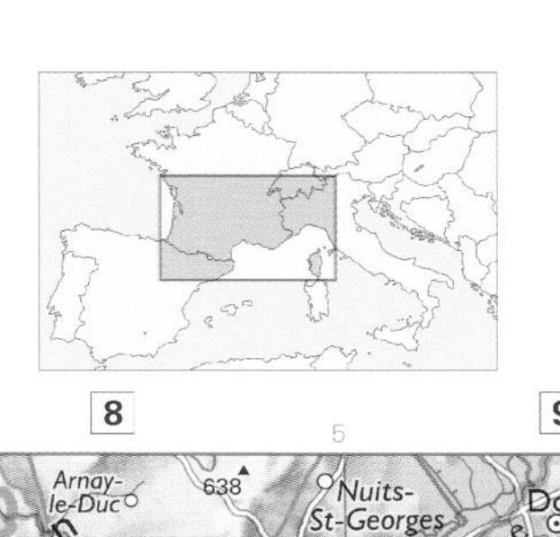

SWITZERLAND

FRANCE

ITALY

LIGURIAN SEA

MEDITERRANEAN SEA

CORSE

National Parks

Regional Nature Parks in France

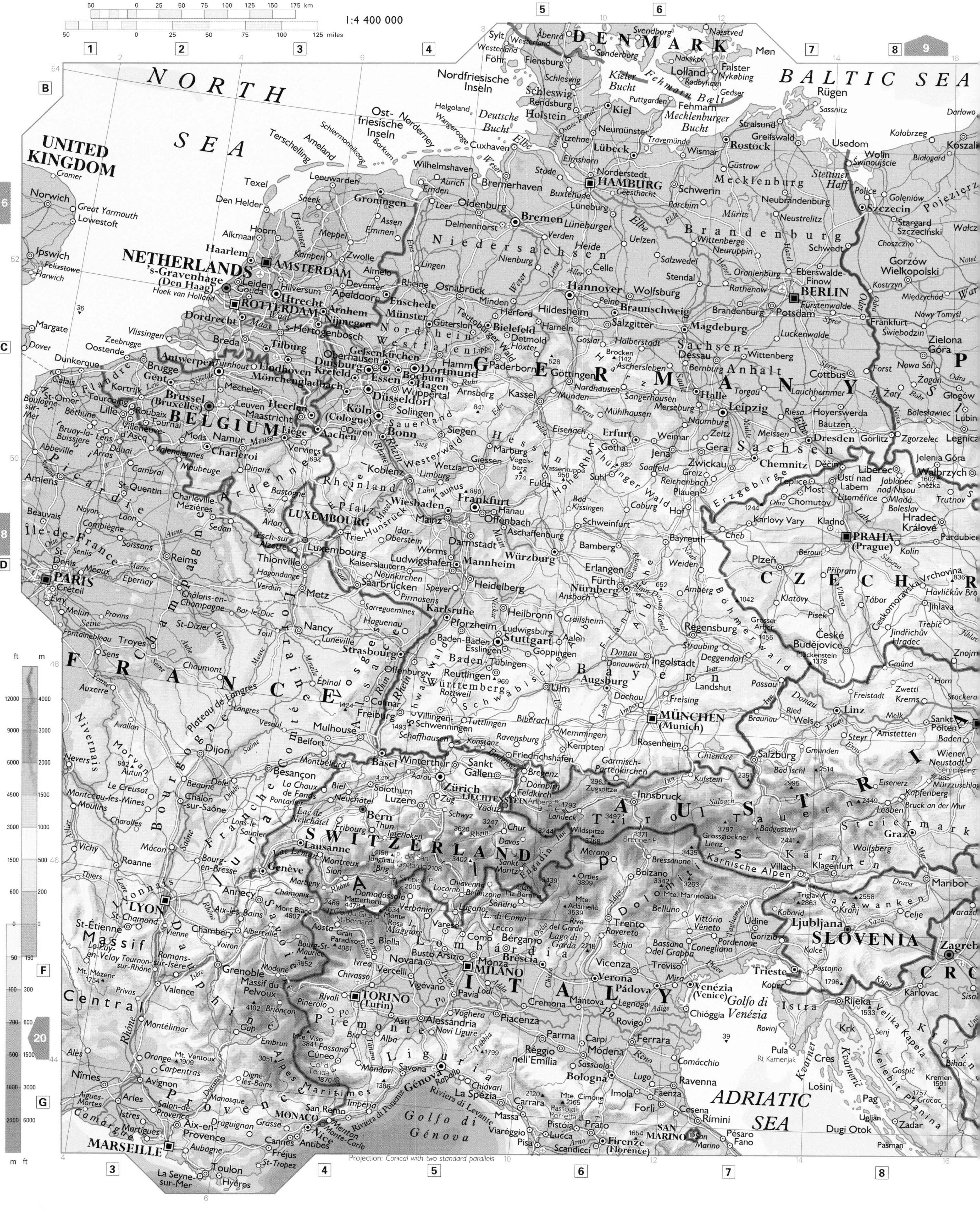

CENTRAL EUROPE

50 0 25 50 75 100 125 150 175 km

1:4 400 000

50 0 25 50 75 100 125 miles

1 2 3 4 5 6 7 8

B C D F G

ft m

12000 4000

9000 3000

6000 2000

4500 1500

3000 1000

1500 500

600 200

0 0

50 150

100 300

200 600

500 1500

1000 3000

2000 6000

m ft

Projection: *Conical with two standard parallels*

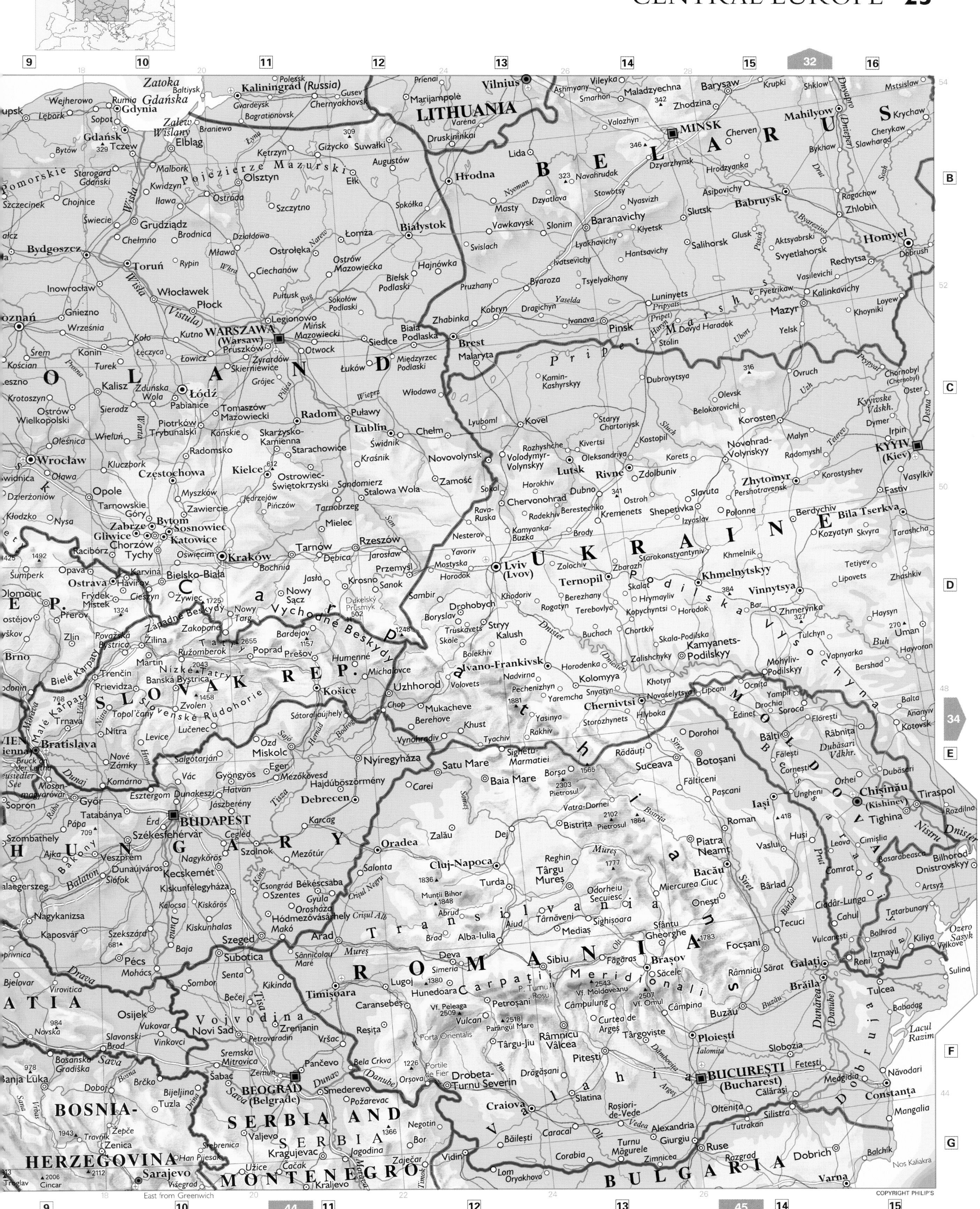
9
10
11
12
13
14
15
32
16
LITHUANIA
Vilnius
Kaliningrad (Russia)
Zatoka Gdańska
Gdynia
Gdańsk
Zalew Wiślany
Elbląg
Olsztyn
Pojezierze Mazurskie
Suwałki
Hrodna
Białystok
Bydgoszcz
Toruń
Włocławek
Płock
Poznań
WARSZAWA (Warsaw)
Łódź
Radom
Lublin
Kielce
Częstochowa
Wrocław
Opole
Katowice
Kraków
Tarnów
Rzeszów
Przemyśl
POLAND
BELARUS
MINSK
Maladzyechna
Barysaw
Mahilyow
Babruysk
Homyel
Baranavichy
Pinsk
Brest
Mazyr
Pripet Marshes
Lutsk
Rivne
Kovel
Lviv (Lvov)
Ternopil
Khmelnytskyy
Zhytomyr
Vinnytsya
KYYIV (Kiev)
Bila Tserkva
UKRAINE
Carpathians
Ivano-Frankivsk
Chernivtsi
Uzhhorod
Košice
Prešov
Poprad
Žilina
Tatry
Nízke Tatry
SLOVAK REP.
Bratislava
Ostrava
Brno
Vychodné Beskydy
Západné Beskydy
Miskolc
Debrecen
Nyíregyháza
BUDAPEST
Győr
Székesfehérvár
Balaton
Kecskemét
Szeged
Pécs
HUNGARY
Tisza
Dunaj
Subotica
Novi Sad
Vojvodina
BEOGRAD (Belgrade)
SERBIA AND MONTENEGRO
BOSNIA-HERZEGOVINA
Sarajevo
Osijek
Oradea
Cluj-Napoca
Satu Mare
Baia Mare
Suceava
Botoşani
Iaşi
Piatra Neamţ
Bacău
Târgu Mureş
Timişoara
Arad
Sibiu
Braşov
Transilvania
Carpaţii Meridionali
ROMANIA
Craiova
Piteşti
Ploieşti
BUCUREŞTI (Bucharest)
Walachia
Constanţa
Galaţi
Brăila
Dobrogea
Chişinău (Kishinev)
MOLDOVA
Tiraspol
Bălţi
Dnister
Prut
Siret
Danube
Ruse
Varna
Dobrich
BULGARIA
Vidin
34
E
B
C
D
F
G
COPYRIGHT PHILIP'S
East from Greenwich
44
45

10 0 10 20 30 40 50 60 70 80 90 km

1:2 200 000

10 0 10 20 30 40 50 60 miles

RHEINLAND-PFALZ
LUXEMBOURG
SAARLAND
LORRAINE
ALSACE
FRANCE
BADEN-WÜRTTEMBERG
BAYERN
CZECH REP.
PRAHA
SWITZERLAND
AUSTRIA
ITALY
SLOVENIA
TRENTINO-ALTO ADIGE
FRIULI-VENEZIA GIULIA
München
Stuttgart
Frankfurt
Nürnberg
Zürich
Bern
Basel
Genève
Strasbourg
Innsbruck
Salzburg
Linz
Projection : Lambert's Conformal Conic
East from Greenwich
COPYRIGHT PHILIP'S
Underlined towns give their name to the administrative area in which they stand.
National Parks
Nature Parks in Germany

1:2 200 000

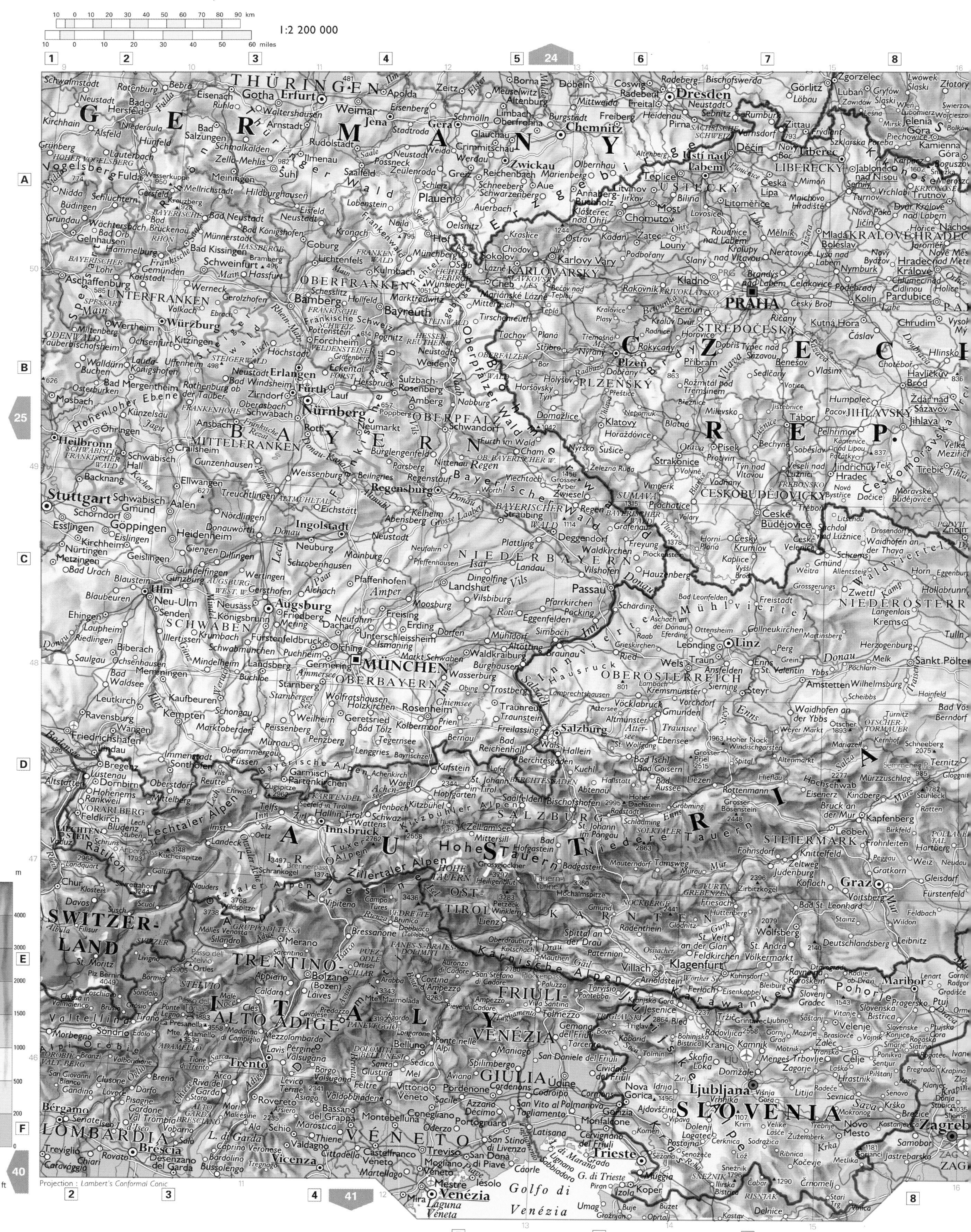

10 0 10 20 30 40 50 60 70 80 90 km
10 0 10 20 30 40 50 60 miles
GERMANY
THÜRINGEN
Erfurt
Weimar
Jena
Gera
Dresden
Chemnitz
Zwickau
Plauen
OBERFRANKEN
UNTERFRANKEN
MITTELFRANKEN
Würzburg
Bamberg
Bayreuth
Nürnberg
Erlangen
Fürth
Regensburg
Ingolstadt
Augsburg
MÜNCHEN
OBERBAYERN
NIEDERBAYERN
OBERPFALZ
SCHWABEN
BAYERN
Stuttgart
Heilbronn
Ulm
Passau
Landshut
CZECH REP.
PRAHA
STŘEDOČESKÝ
PLZEŇSKÝ
Plzeň
KARLOVARSKÝ
ÚSTECKÝ
Ústí nad Labem
LIBERECKÝ
Liberec
JIHLAVSKÝ
Jihlava
ČESKOBUDĚJOVICKÝ
České Budějovice
Pardubice
Hradec Králové
AUSTRIA
Linz
OBERÖSTERREICH
NIEDERÖSTERREICH
Salzburg
SALZBURG
Innsbruck
TIROL
VORARLBERG
STEIERMARK
Graz
KÄRNTEN
Klagenfurt
Villach
Hohe Tauern
Niedere Tauern
Zillertaler Alpen
Ötztaler Alpen
Lechtaler Alpen
Karnische Alpen
Karawanken
SWITZERLAND
ITALY
TRENTINO-ALTO ADIGE
Bolzano (Bozen)
Trento
FRIULI-VENEZIA GIULIA
Udine
Trieste
VENETO
Venézia
Vicenza
Treviso
LOMBARDIA
Brescia
Bergamo
Golfo di Venézia
SLOVENIA
Ljubljana
Maribor
Zagreb
Donau
Inn
Bodensee
Projection : Lambert's Conformal Conic

National Parks

Underlined towns give their name to the administrative area in which they stand.

1:2 200 000

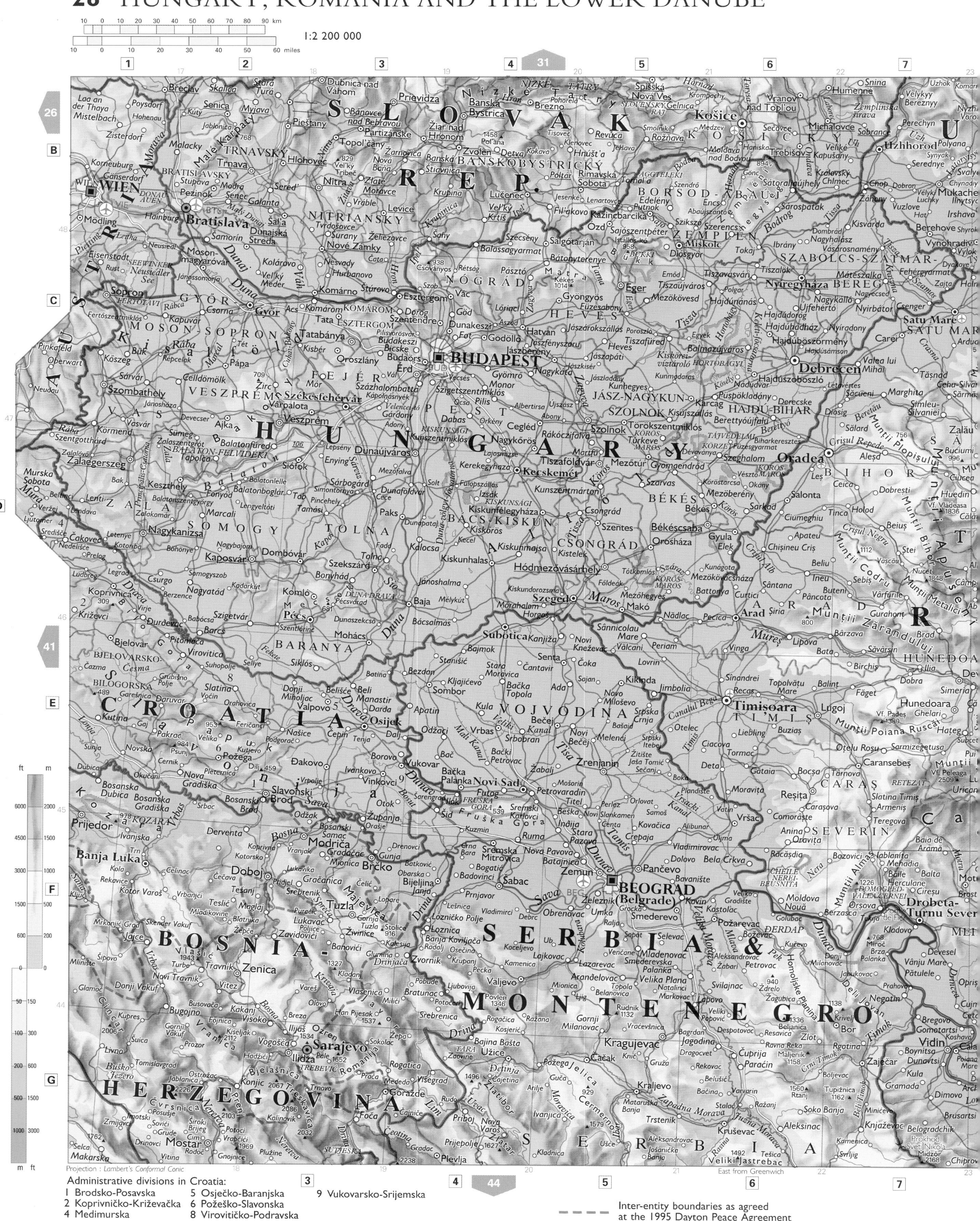

Projection : Lambert's Conformal Conic

Administrative divisions in Croatia:
1 Brodsko-Posavska
2 Koprivničko-Križevačka
4 Međimurska
5 Osječko-Baranjska
6 Požeško-Slavonska
8 Virovitičko-Podravska
9 Vukovarsko-Srijemska

Inter-entity boundaries as agreed at the 1995 Dayton Peace Agreement

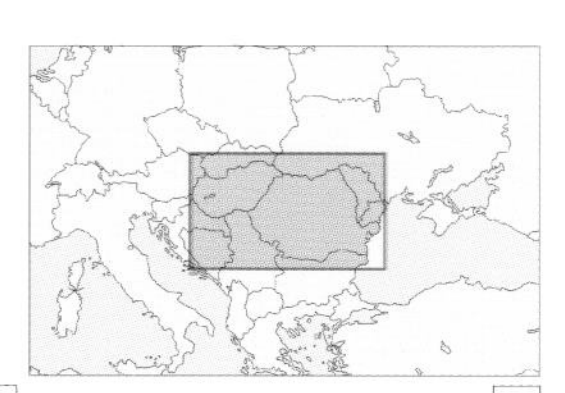

33

45

National Parks

Underlined towns give their name to the administrative area in which they stand.

10 0 10 20 30 40 50 60 70 80 90 km

10 0 10 20 30 40 50 60 miles

1:2 200 000

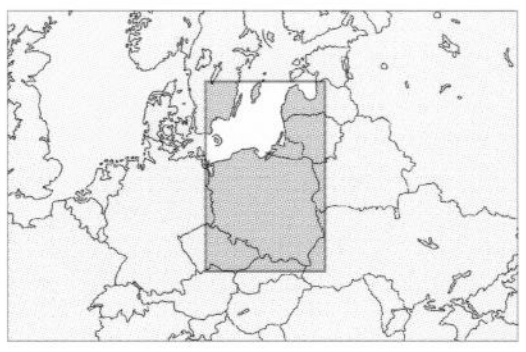

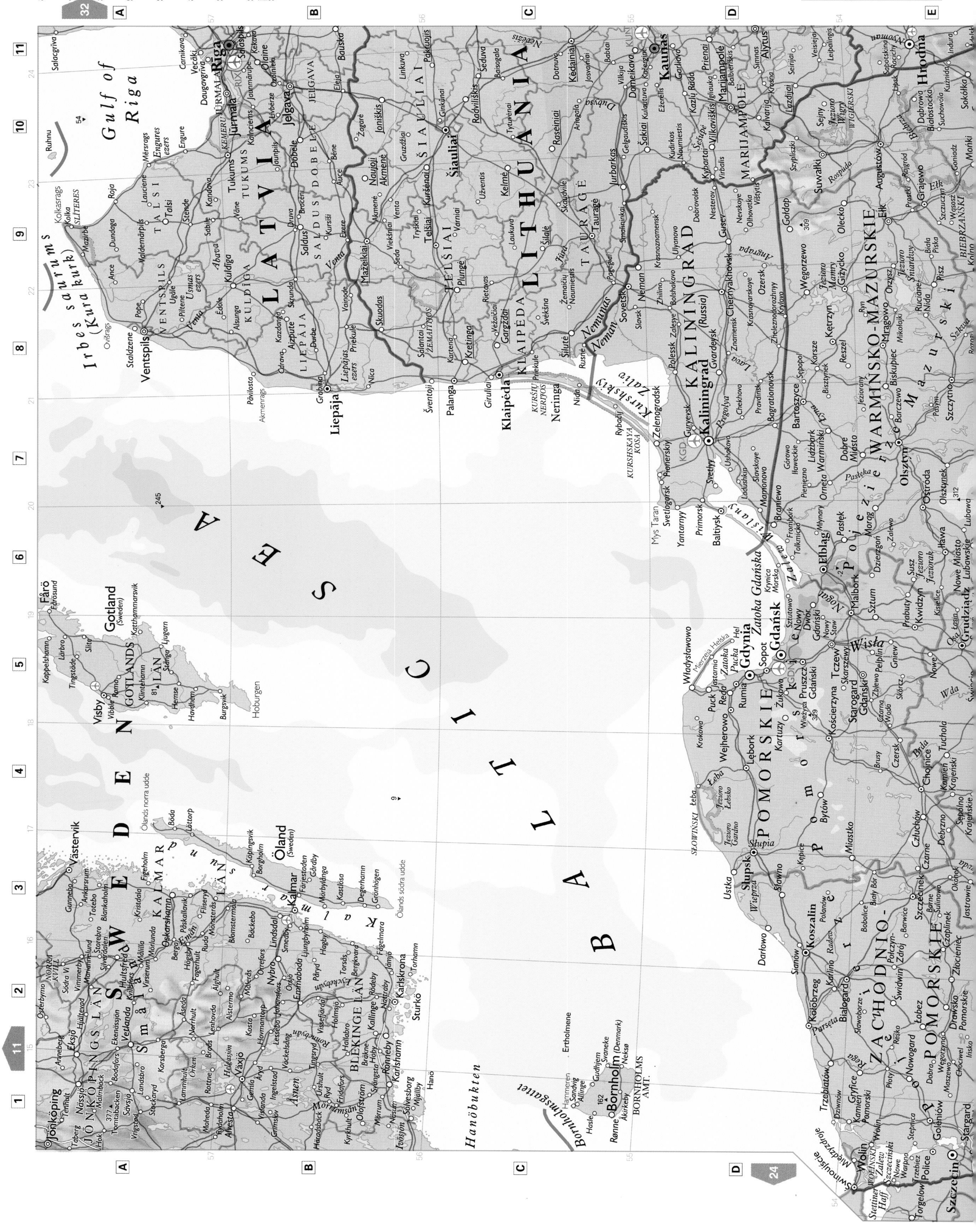

SWEDEN

LATVIA

LITHUANIA

KALININGRAD (Russia)

BALTIC SEA

Gulf of Riga

Irbes šaurums (Kura kurk)

Kurshskiy Zaliv

Zatoka Gdańska

Hanöbukten

Bornholmsgattet

Gotland (Sweden)

Öland (Sweden)

Bornholm (Denmark)

POMORSKIE

WARMIŃSKO-MAZURSKIE

ZACHODNIO-POMORSKIE

Riga

Jelgava

Liepāja

Ventspils

Šiauliai

Klaipėda

Kaunas

Kaliningrad

Gdańsk

Gdynia

Elbląg

Olsztyn

Koszalin

Słupsk

Szczecin

Kalmar

Karlskrona

Visby

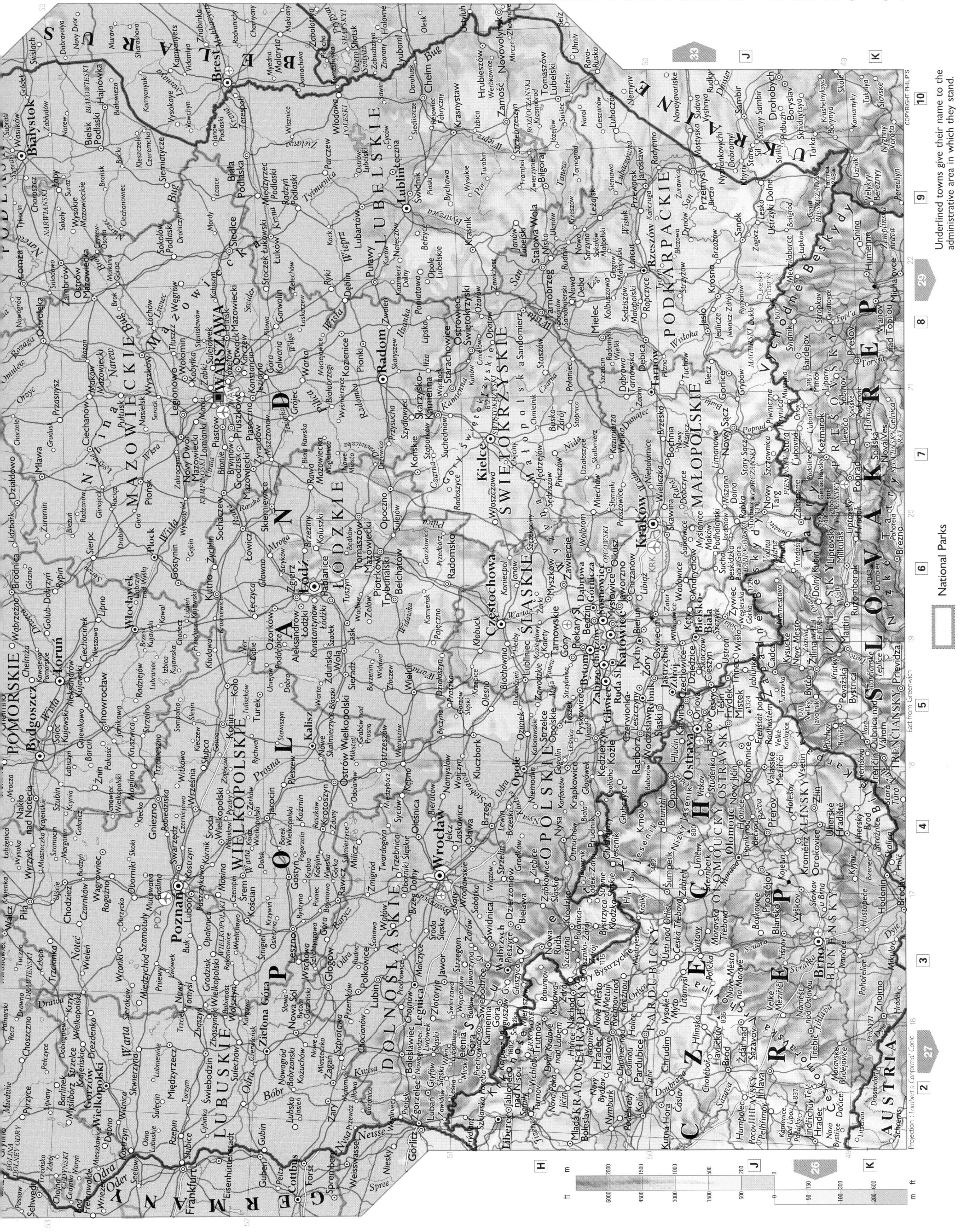

National Parks

Underlined towns give their name to the administrative area in which they stand.

Projection : Lambert's Conformal Conic

East from Greenwich

1:4 400 000

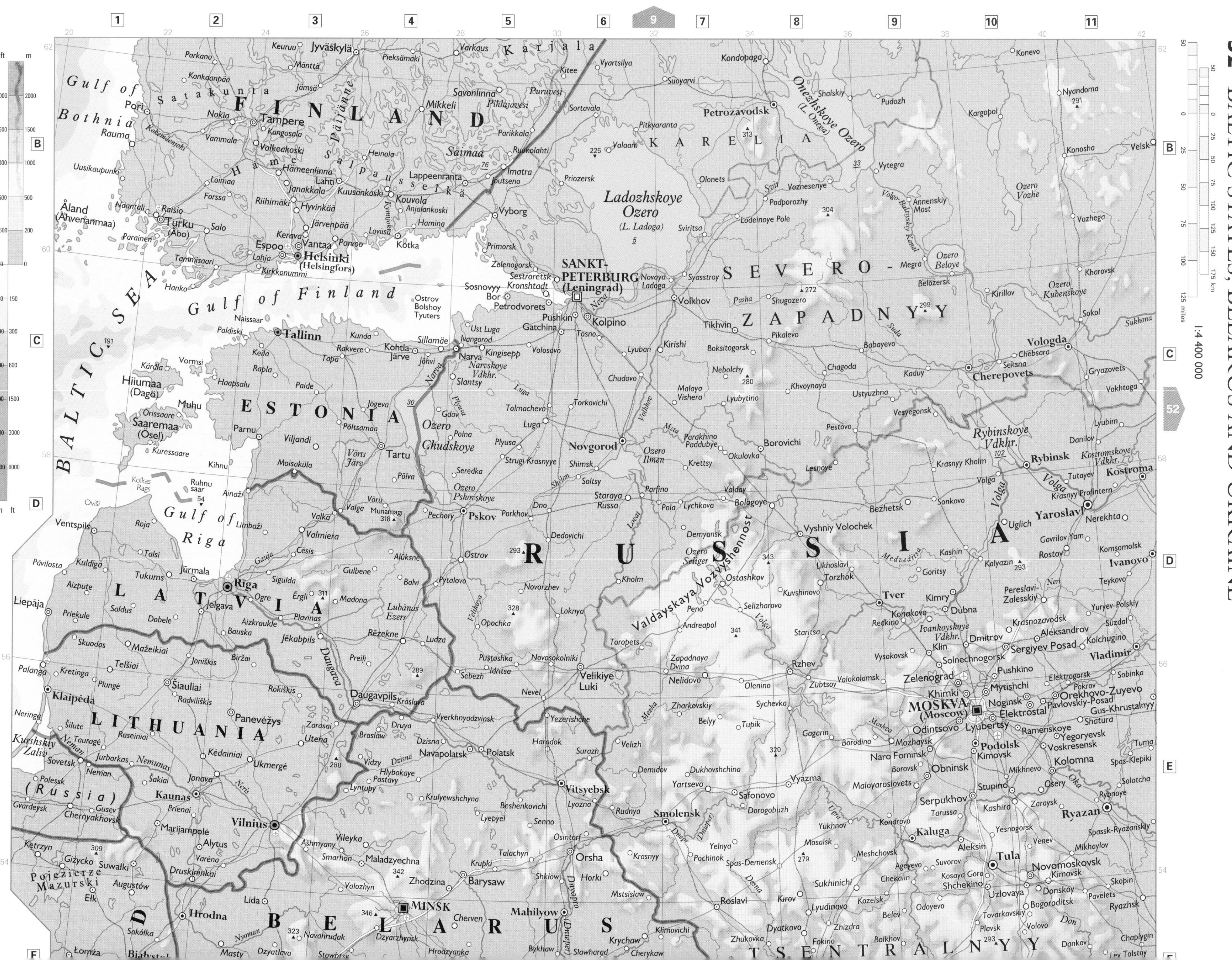
50 0 25 50 75 100 125 150 175 km
50 0 25 50 75 100 125 miles
52
9
FINLAND
ESTONIA
LATVIA
LITHUANIA
BELARUS
RUSSIA
KARELIA
SEVERO - ZAPADNYY
TSENTRALNYY
BALTIC SEA
Gulf of Finland
Gulf of Riga
Gulf of Bothnia
Ladozhskoye Ozero (L. Ladoga)
Onezhskoye Ozero (L. Onega)
Ozero Chudskoye
Ozero Pskovskoye
Ozero Ilmen
Ozero Beloye
Rybinskoye Vdkhr.
Valdayskaya Vozvyshennost
Daugava
Volga
Dnyapro (Dnieper)
Helsinki (Helsingfors)
Tallinn
Riga
Vilnius
MINSK
MOSKVA (Moscow)
SANKT-PETERBURG (Leningrad)
Novgorod
Pskov
Tartu
Narva
Vyborg
Petrozavodsk
Tver
Yaroslavl
Vologda
Cherepovets
Smolensk
Vitsyebsk
Mahilyow
Hrodna
Kaunas
Šiauliai
Klaipėda
Daugavpils
Liepāja
Ventspils
Parnu
Tampere
Turku (Åbo)
Lahti
Kaluga
Tula
Ryazan
Vladimir
Ivanovo
Kostroma
Rybinsk
Velikiye Luki
Orsha
Barysaw
Polatsk
Saaremaa (Osel)
Hiiumaa (Dagö)
Åland (Ahvenanmaa)
m ft
6000 2000
4500 1500
3000 1000
1500 500
600 200
0 0
50 150
100 300
200 600
500 1500
1000 3000
2000 6000

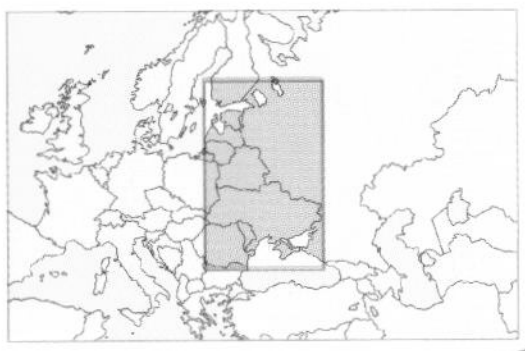

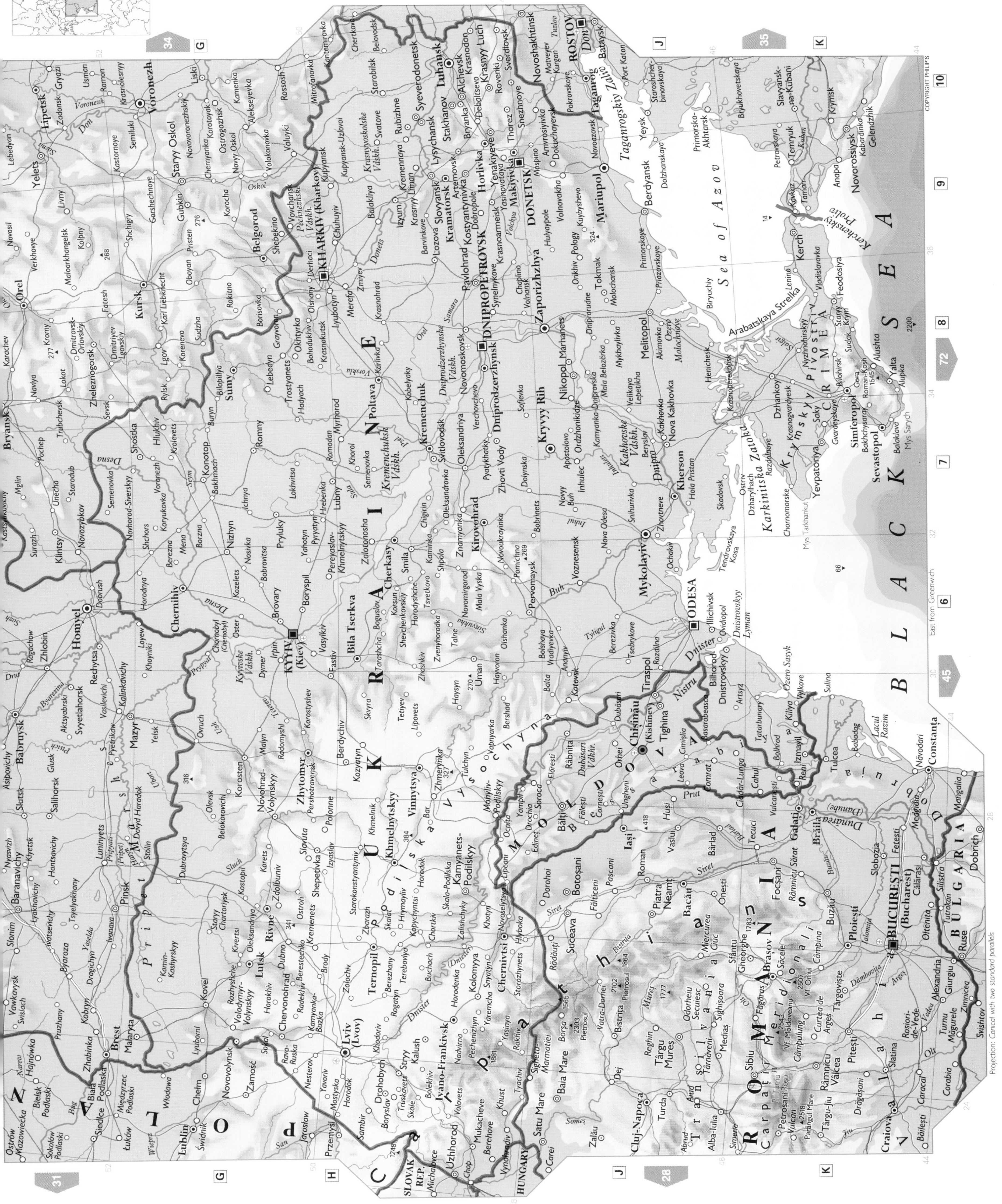

Projection: Conical with two standard parallels

East from Greenwich

34 THE VOLGA BASIN AND THE CAUCASUS

1:4 400 000

KAZAKHSTAN
Ryn Peski
Caspian Depression
YUZHNYY
KALMYKIA
Chernyye Zemli
CASPIAN SEA
BLACK SEA
Sea of Azov
Taganrogskiy Zaliv
Prikubanskaya Nizmennost
Caucasus Mountains
DAGESTAN
CHECHENIA
INGUSHETIA
NORTH OSSETIA
KABARDINO-BALKARIA
KARACHEY-CHERKESSIA
ADYGEA
ABKHAZIA
AJARIA
GEORGIA
ARMENIA
AZERBAIJAN
TURKEY
Kuzey Anadolu Dağları
VOLGOGRAD
Astrakhan
ROSTOV
Krasnodar
Stavropol
Elista
Makhachkala
Grozny
Vladikavkaz
Nalchik
TBILISI
YEREVAN
BAKI (Baku)
DONETSK
Luhansk
DNIPROPETROVSK
Zaporizhzhya
Mariupol
Sochi
Sokhumi
Batumi
Trabzon
Samsun
Projection: Conical with two standard parallels
East from Greenwich
COPYRIGHT PHILIP'S

10 0 10 20 30 40 50 60 70 80 90 km

1:2 200 000

10 0 10 20 30 40 50 60 miles

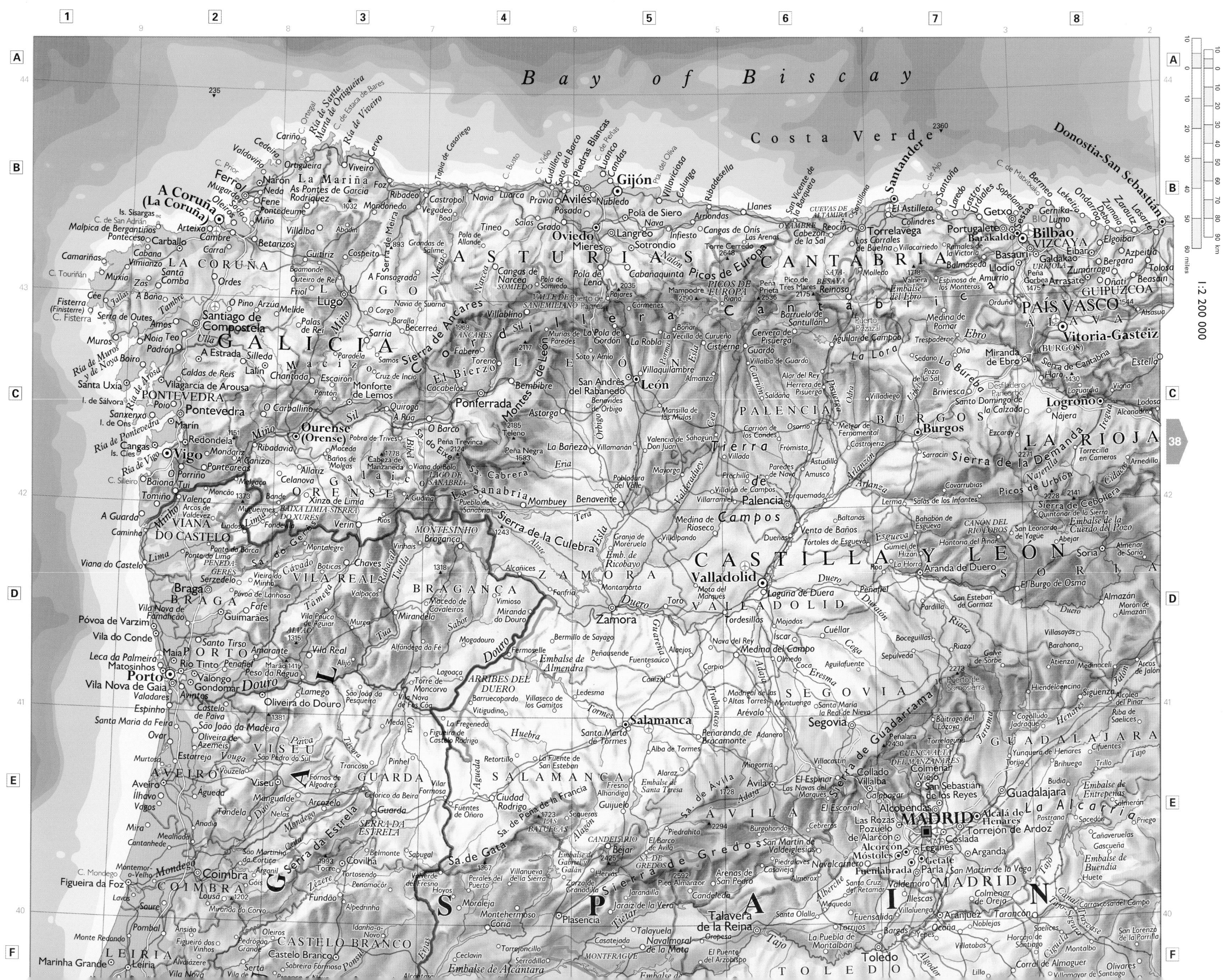

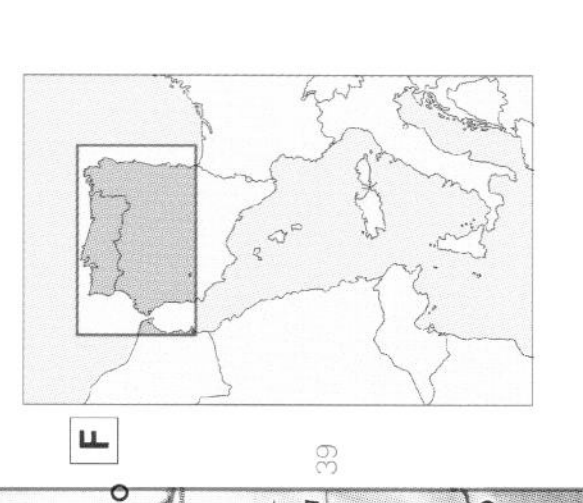

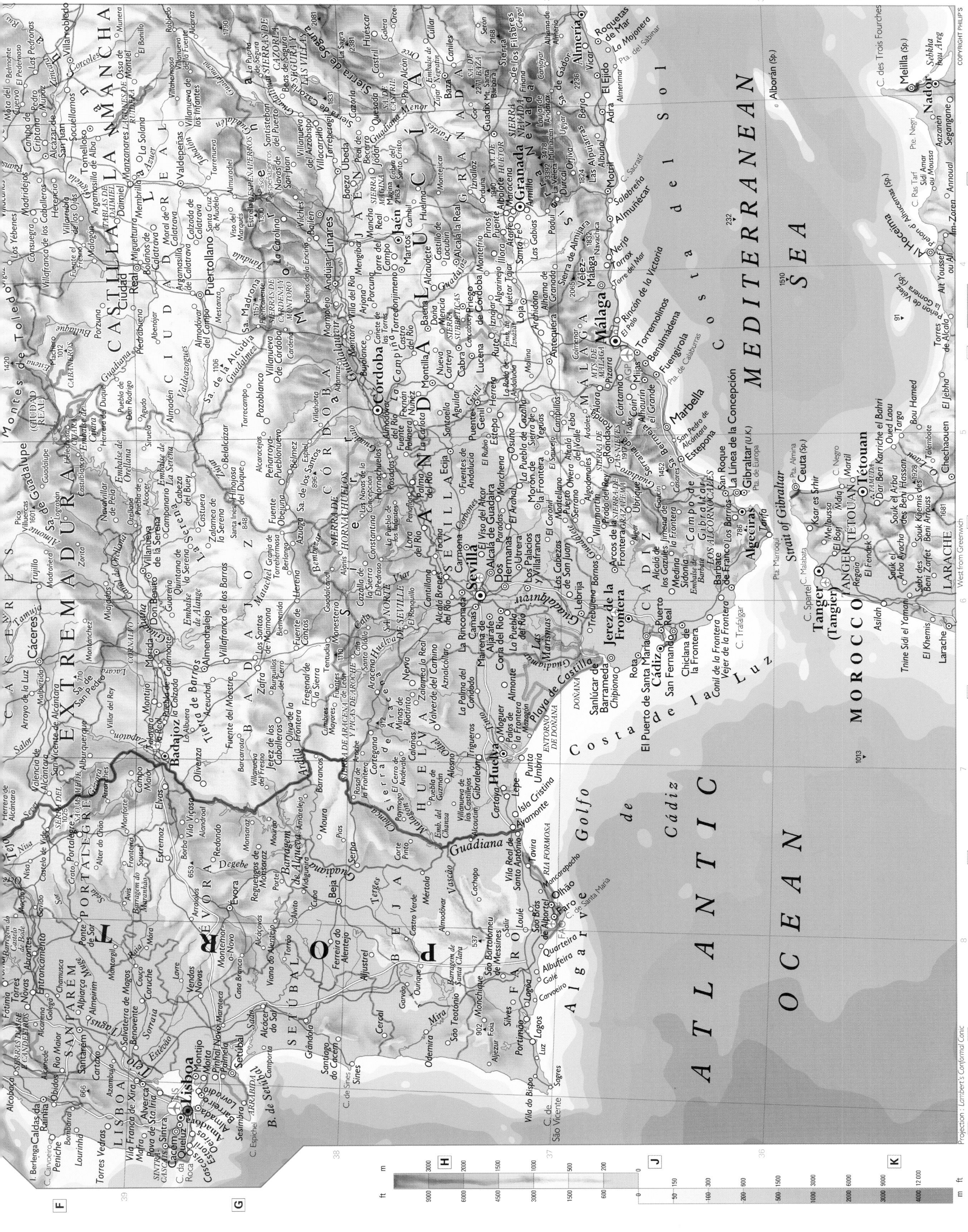

National Parks

Nature Parks in Spain and Portugal

Projection: Lambert's Conformal Conic

1:2 200 000

10 0 10 20 30 40 50 60 70 80 90 km

10 0 10 20 30 40 50 60 miles

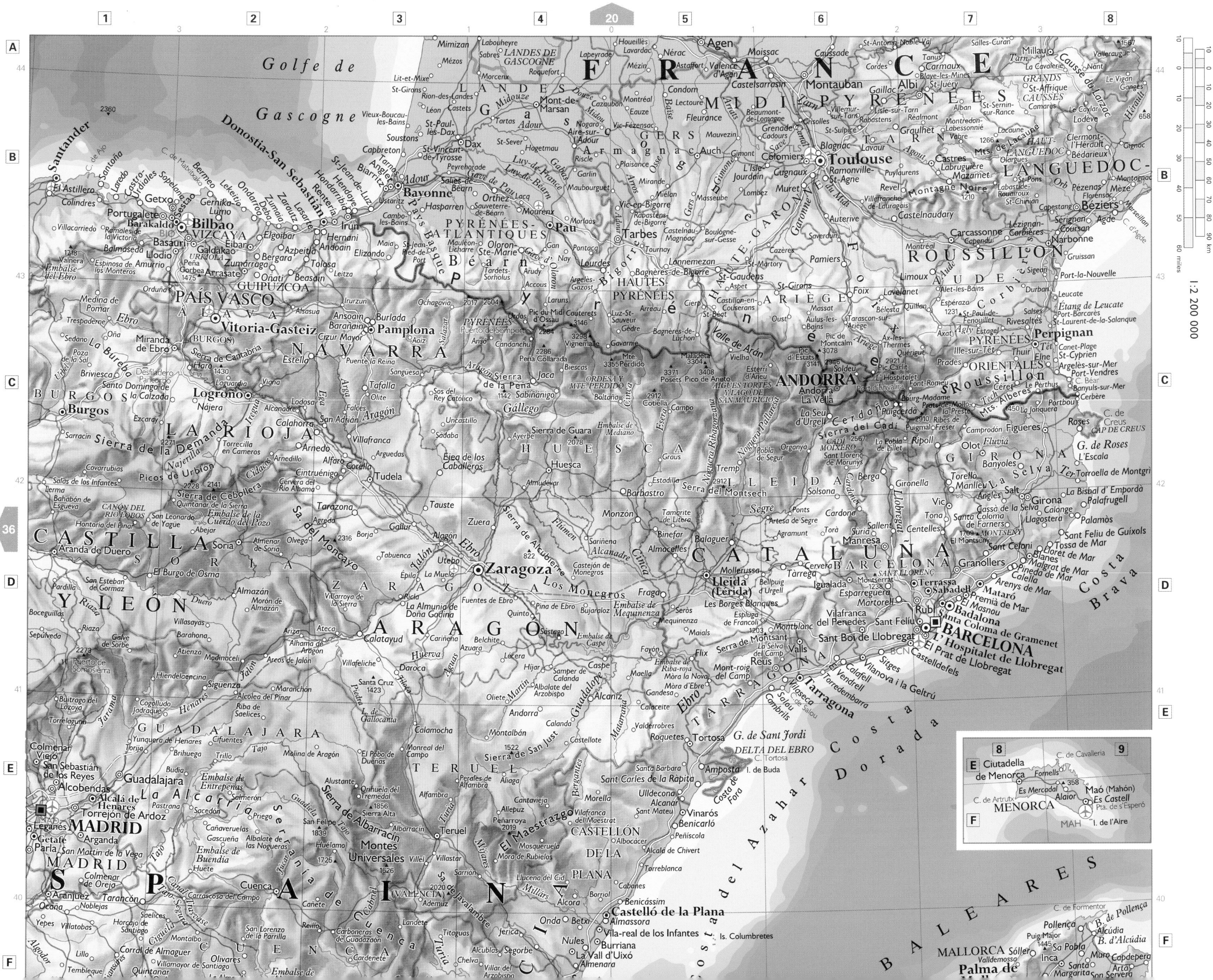

MEDITERRANEAN SEA
Golfo de Valencia
ISLAS
Costa Blanca
Costa del Sol
CASTILLA-LA MANCHA
CIUDAD REAL
ALBACETE
VALENCIA
ALICANTE
MURCIA
JAÉN
GRANADA
ALMERÍA
ALGERIA
ALGER (Algiers)
Valencia
Alicante
Elche
Murcia
Cartagena
Albacete
Granada
Almería
Lorca
Benidorm
Dénia
EIVISSA (IBIZA)
Eivissa (Ibiza)
Formentera
Cabrera
Palma
Mar Menor
G. de Mazarrón
G. de Almería
Sierra Nevada
Sierra de Segura
Sierra de Alcaraz
Sierra de los Filabres
Alborán (Sp.)
Melilla (Sp.)
Nador
Islas Chafarinas (Sp.)
Golfe d'Arzew
Oran (Ouahran)
Mostaganem
MOSTAGANEM
Relizane
RELIZANE
Ech Cheliff
ECH CHELIFF
AÏN DEFLA
AÏN TÉMOUCHENT
MASCARA
TISSEMSILT
TIPASA
MÉDÉA
TIARET
DJELFA
Blida
BLIDA
Médéa
Tiaret
Mascara
Sidi-bel-Abbès
National Parks
Nature Parks in Spain
Projection: Lambert's Conformal Conic
East from Greenwich
West from Greenwich
COPYRIGHT PHILIP'S
ft
m
37
78

1:2 200 000

Projection : Lambert's Conformal Conic

East from Greenwich

25
21
42

m 4000 3000 2000 1500 1000 500 200 0 50 100 200 500 1000 2000 m

ft 12 000 9000 6000 4500 3000 1500 600 0 150 300 600 1500 3000 6000 ft

National Parks

Underlined towns give their name to the administrative area in which they stand.

dministrative divisions in Croatia:

Brodsko-Posavska
Koprivničko-Križevačka
Krapinsko-Zagorska
4 Medimurska
6 Požeško-Slavonska
7 Varaždinska
8 Virovitičko-Podravska
10 Zagreba čka

Nature Parks in Italy

Inter-entity boundaries as agreed at the 1995 Dayton Peace Agreement

1:2 200 000

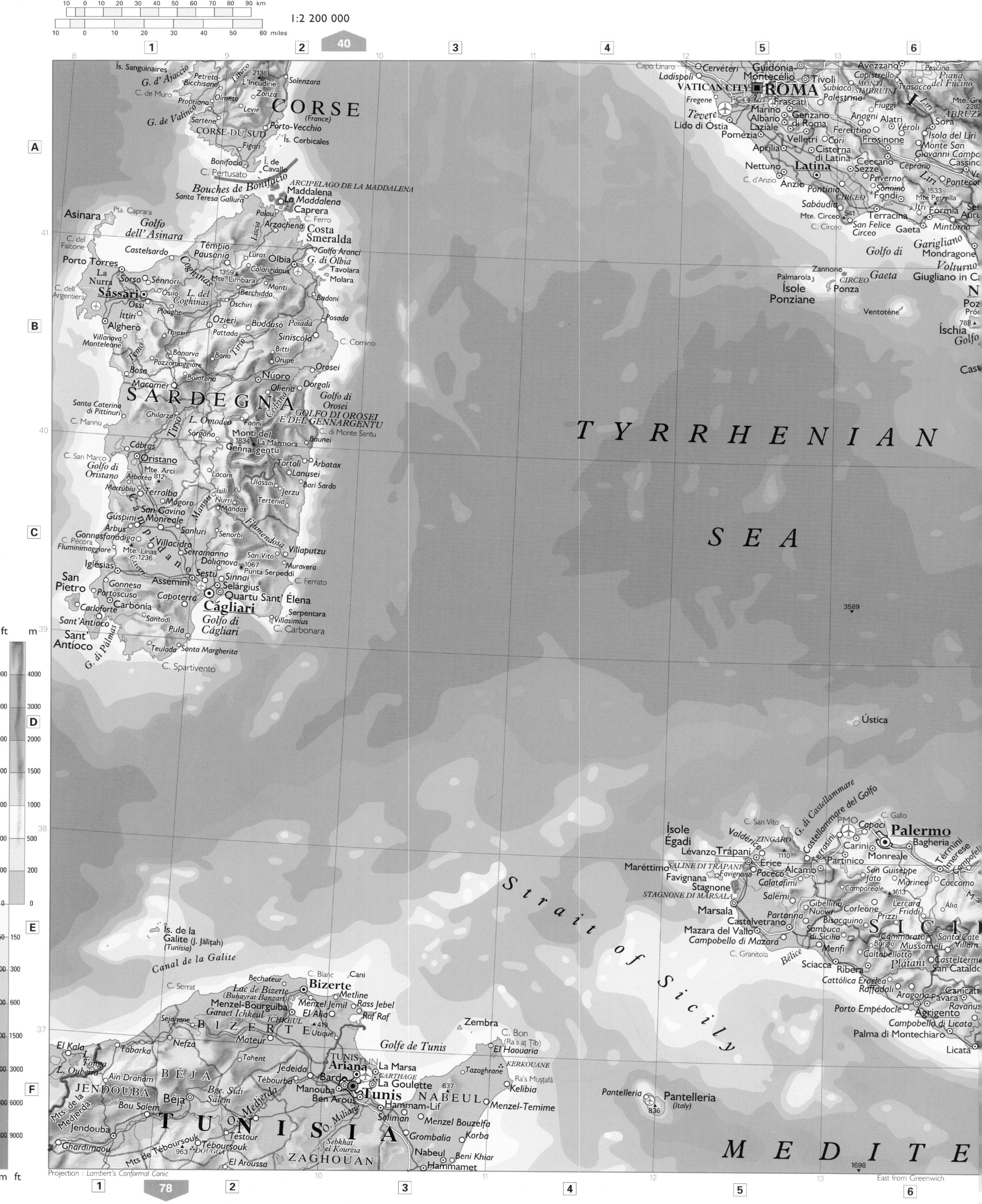
10 0 10 20 30 40 50 60 70 80 90 km
10 0 10 20 30 40 50 60 miles
40
78
Projection : Lambert's Conformal Conic
East from Greenwich
ft m
12000 4000
9000 3000
6000 2000
4500 1500
3000 1000
1500 500
600 200
0 0
50 150
100 300
200 600
500 1500
1000 3000
2000 6000
3000 9000
m ft
TYRRHENIAN
SEA
Strait of Sicily
MEDITE
CORSE
(France)
CORSE-DU-SUD
Îs. Sanguinaires
G. d' Ajaccio
Petreto-Bicchisano
C. de Muro
Propriano
Olmeto
Levie
Zonza
L'Incudine
2136
Solenzara
G. de Valinco
Sartène
Porto-Vecchio
Îs. Cerbicales
Figari
Bonifacio
Î. de Cavallo
C. Pertusato
Bouches de Bonifacio
ARCIPELAGO DE LA MADDALENA
Maddalena
La Maddalena
Caprera
Santa Teresa Gallura
Palau
C. Ferro
Arzachena
Costa Smeralda
Asinara
Pta. Caprara
Golfo dell' Asinara
C. del Falcone
Castelsardo
Tempio Pausania
Golfo Aranci
Olbia
G. di Olbia
Tavolara
Molara
Porto Torres
La Nurra
Sorso
Sennori
Sassari
Ossi
Ittiri
Alghero
C. dell' Argentiera
Mte. Limbara
1359
Berchidda
Oschiri
Ozieri
Pattada
Budduso
Posada
Siniscola
Budoni
C. Comino
Villanova Monteleone
Thiesi
Bonorva
Pozzomaggiore
Bono
Bitti
Orune
Bosa
Bolotana
Nuoro
Orosei
Macomer
Oliena
Dorgali
SARDEGNA
Golfo di Orosei
GOLFO DI OROSEI E DEL GENNARGENTU
Santa Caterina di Pittinuri
Ghilarza
L. Omodeo
Fonni
C. Mannu
Sorgono
Monti del Gennargentu
1834 La Marmora
C. di Monte Santu
Baunei
Cabras
Oristano
C. San Marco
Golfo di Oristano
Mte. Arci
Arborea 812
Tortolì
Arbatax
Lanusei
Laconi
Bari Sardo
Ulassai
Jerzu
Terralba
Isili
Nurri
Tertenia
Mogoro
Mandas
San Gavino Monreale
Guspini
Arbus
Sanluri
Senorbì
Gonnosfanadiga
C. Pecora
Fluminimaggiore
Mte. Linas 1236
Villacidro
Villaputzu
Serramanna
Dolianova
San Vito
Muravera
Iglesias
1067
Punta Serpeddi
San Pietro
Gonnesa
Assemini
Sestu
Sinnai
C. Ferrato
Portoscuso
Selargius
Capoterra
Quartu Sant' Elena
Carloforte
Carbonia
Cagliari
Serpentara
Golfo di Cagliari
Villasimius
C. Carbonara
Sant'Antioco
Santadi
Pula
Sant Antioco
G. di Palmas
Teulada
Santa Margherita
C. Spartivento
Capo Linaro
Ladispoli
Cerveteri
Guidonia-Montecelio
Tivoli
VATICAN CITY
ROMA
Subiaco
MONTI SIMBRUINI
Avezzano
Capistrello
Trasacco
Pescina
Piana del Fucino
Fregene
Frascati
Palestrina
Fiuggi
Tevere
Marino
Albano Laziale
Genzano di Roma
Anagni
Alatri
Veroli
Sora
Lido di Ostia
Pomezia
Ferentino
Velletri
Cori
Frosinone
Isola del Liri
Aprilia
Cisterna di Latina
Monte San Giovanni Campano
Cassino
Nettuno
Latina
Ceccano
Sezze
Anzio
C. d'Anzio
Pontinia
Priverno
Sonnino
Fondi
CIRCEO
1533
Mte Petrella
Sabaudia
Itri
Formia
Mte. Circeo 541
Terracina
C. Circeo
San Felice Circeo
Gaeta
Minturno
Garigliano
Golfo di Gaeta
Mondragone
Volturno
Palmarola
Zannone
CIRCEO
Isole Ponziane
Ponza
Giugliano in Ca
Ventotene
Ischia
788
Golfo
3589
Ustica
C. San Vito
C. Gallo
G. di Castellammare
Castellammare del Golfo
Isole Egadi
Valderice
ZINGARO
PMO
Capaci
Palermo
Bagheria
Levanzo
Trapani
1110
Carini
Monreale
Termini Imerese
Marettimo
SALINE DI TRAPANI
Erice
Partinico
Favignana
Paceco
Alcamo
San Giuseppe Jato
Marineo
Caccamo
Calatafimi
Camporeale
Stagnone
STAGNONE DI MARSALA
Salemi
1613
Marsala
Gibellina Nuova
Corleone
Lercara Friddi
Alia
Castelvetrano
Partanna
Bisacquino
Prizzi
Mazara del Vallo
Sambuca di Sicilia
Cammarata
Santa Cate
Campobello di Mazara
Burgio
Mussomeli
Villarro
C. Granitola
Belice
Menfi
Caltabellotta
Platani
Casteltermini
Sciacca
Ribera
San Cataldo
Cattolica Eraclea
Raffadali
Canicatti
Aragona
Favara
Porto Empedocle
Agrigento
Ravanusa
Campobello di Licata
Palma di Montechiaro
Licata
Îs. de la Galite (J. Jalitah)
(Tunisia)
Canal de la Galite
C. Blanc
Cani
Bechateur
Bizerte
C. Serrat
Lac de Bizerte (Buhayrat Banzart)
Metline
Menzel-Bourguiba
Menzel Jemil
Rass Jebel
Garaet Ichkeul
ICHKEUL
El Alia
Raf Raf
Sejenane
BIZERTE
419
Utique
Zembra
C. Bon (Ra's at Tib)
Nefza
Mateur
Golfe de Tunis
El Haouaria
El Kala
Tabarka
Tahent
KERKOUANE
Jedeida
TUNIS
Ariana
La Marsa
CARTHAGE
Tazoghrane
Ra's Mustafa
Ain Draham
BÉJA
Tebourba
Bardo
La Goulette
637
Kelibia
JENDOUBA
Bge. Sidi Salem
Manouba
Tunis
Ben Arous
Hammam-Lif
NABEUL
Menzel-Temime
Mts. de la Medjerda
Bou Salem
Béja
Medjerda
Soliman
Menzel Bouzelfa
Pantelleria
836
Pantelleria (Italy)
TUNISIA
Jendouba
O. Miliane
Testour
Grombalia
Korba
Ghardimaou
Mts de Teboursouk
963
Teboursouk
DOUGGA
Sebkhat el Kourzia
Nabeul
Beni Khiar
El Aroussa
ZAGHOUAN
Hammamet
1698
A
B
C
D
E
F
1
2
3
4
5
6
8
9
10
11
12
13
41
40
39
38
37

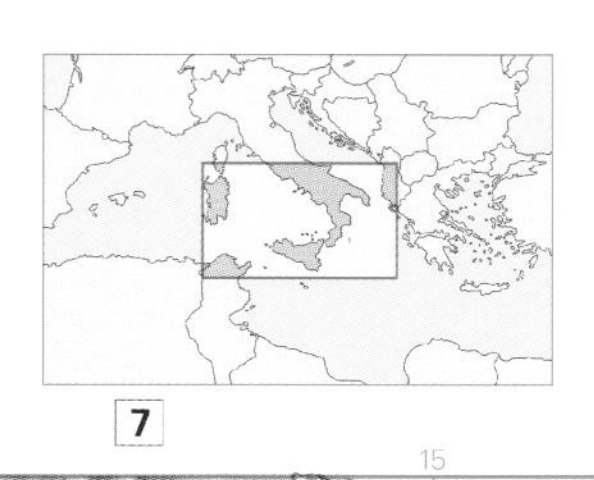

Nature Parks in Italy

National Parks

Underlined towns give their name to the administrative area in which they stand.

1:2 200 000
10 0 10 20 30 40 50 60 70 80 90 km
10 0 10 20 30 40 50 60 miles
28
41
43
46
CROATIA
BOSNIA-HERZEGOVINA
VOJVODINA
SERBIA & MONTENEGRO
MONTENEGRO
KOSOVO
ALBANIA
MACEDONIA
ITALY
ADRIATIC SEA
Strait of Otranto
BEOGRAD (Belgrade)
Sarajevo
Podgorica
Priština
Skopje
Tiranë
SOFIYA
Thessaloníki (Salonica)
Novi Sad
Niš
Kragujevac
Craiova
Durrës
Shkodër
Bitola
Kérkira (Corfu)
Brindisi
Lecce
KENTRIKÍ MAKEDHONÍA
DYTIKÍ MAKEDHONÍA
Thermaïkós Kólpos
Projection : Lambert's Conformal Conic
East from Greenwich
Inter-entity boundaries as agreed at the 1995 Dayton Peace Agreement

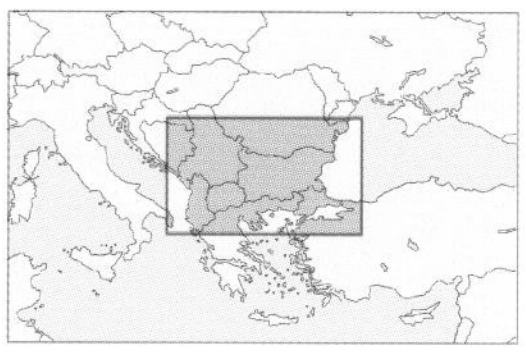

29

47

72

National Parks

Underlined towns give their name to the administrative area in which they stand.

1:2 200 000

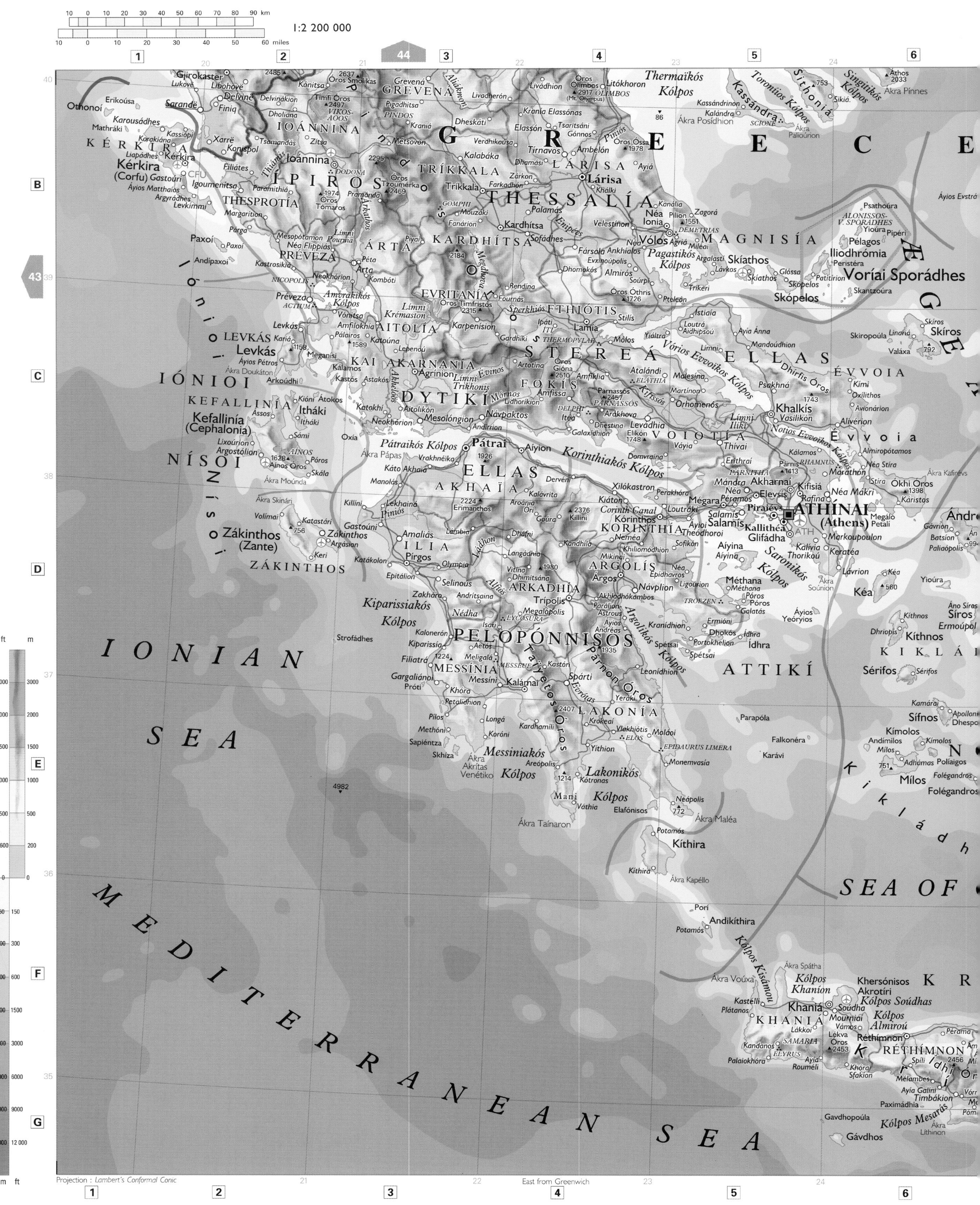
IONIAN SEA
MEDITERRANEAN SEA
SEA OF
GREECE
Ióniοi Nísoi
IÓNIOI NÍSOI
KÉRKIRA
Kérkira (Corfu)
Paxoí
Andípaxoi
LEVKÁS
Levkás
KEFALLINÍA
Kefallinía (Cephalonia)
Itháki
Zákinthos (Zante)
ZÁKINTHOS
Strofádhes
ÍPIROS
Ioánnina
IOÁNNINA
THESPROTÍA
PRÉVEZA
Préveza
ÁRTA
Árta
Amvrakikós Kólpos
AITOLÍA KAI AKARNANÍA
Agrínion
Mesolóngion
Pátrai
Pátraikós Kólpos
Korinthiakós Kólpos
DYTIKÍ ELLAS
AKHAÏA
ILIA
Pírgos
Kiparissiakós Kólpos
PELOPÓNNISOS
ARKADHÍA
Trípolis
ARGOLÍS
Árgos
Návplion
MESSÍNIA
Kalámai
Messiniakós Kólpos
LAKONÍA
Spárti
Lakonikós Kólpos
Kíthira
Andikíthira
KORINTHÍA
Kórinthos
Corinth Canal
ATTIKÍ
ATHÍNAI (Athens)
Piraiévs
Saronikós Kólpos
Aíyina
Salamís
Kéa
STERÉA ELLAS
FOKIS
VOIOTÍA
Thívai
Lamía
FTHIÓTIS
EVRITANÍA
THESSALÍA
Lárisa
LÁRISA
Tríkkala
TRÍKKALA
Kardhítsa
KARDHÍTSA
Vólos
MAGNISÍA
Pagastikós Kólpos
Skíathos
Skópelos
Vorίai Sporádhes
Alónnisos
Skíros
ÉVVOIA
Évvoia
Khalkís
Vórios Evvoïkós Kólpos
Thermaïkós Kólpos
Kassándra
Toronaíos Kólpos
Sithonía
Singitikós Kólpos
Athos
Óros Ólimbos (Mt. Olympus)
GREVENÁ
Pindhos
Kikládhes
KIKLÁDHES
Kíthnos
Sérifos
Sífnos
Mílos
Kímolos
Folégandros
Kólpos Khanión
Khaniá
KHANIÁ
Réthimnon
RÉTHIMNON
Kólpos Soúdhas
Kólpos Mesarás
Gávdhos
Gavdhopoúla
Sarandë
Gjirokastër
Projection : Lambert's Conformal Conic
East from Greenwich

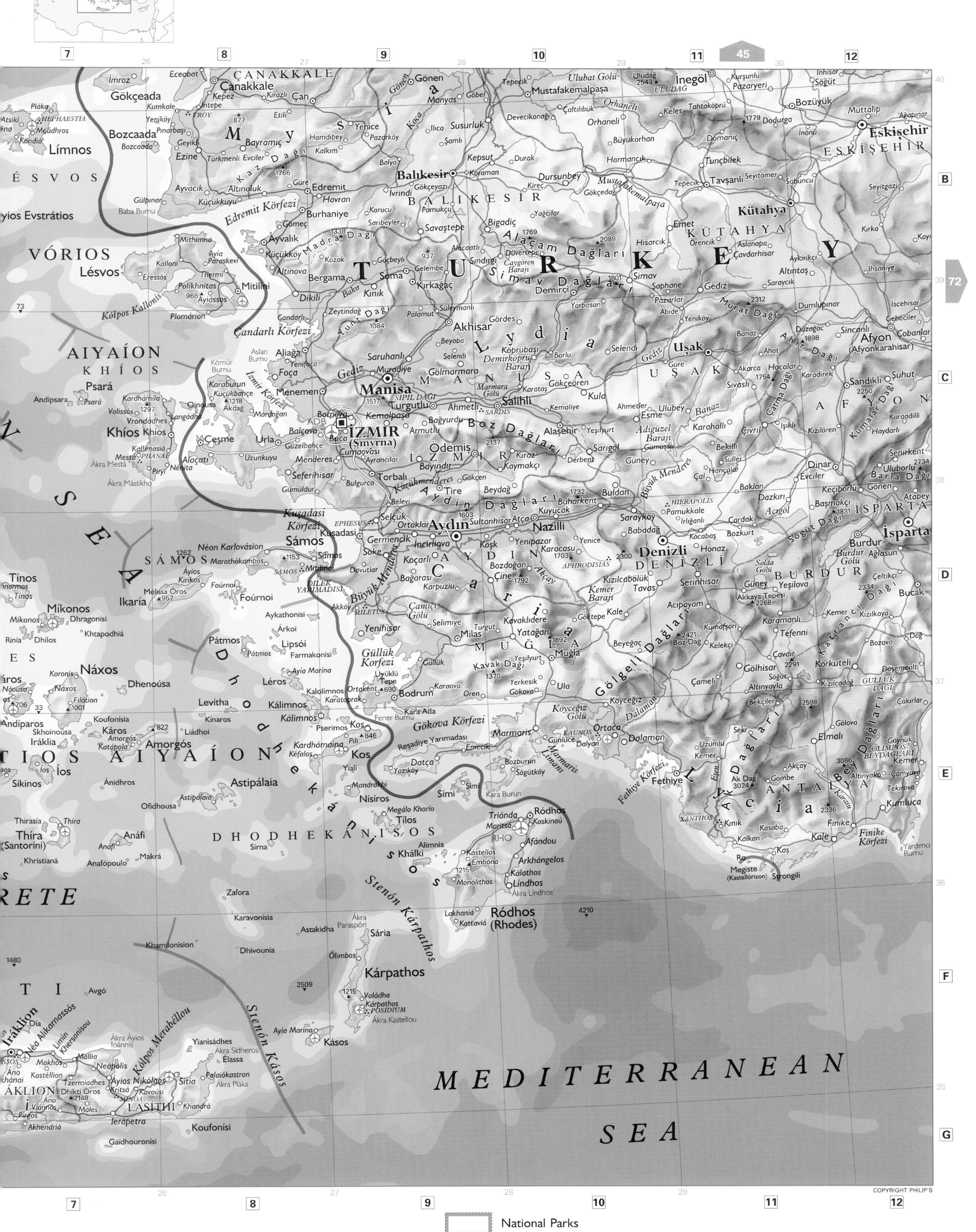

National Parks

Balearic Islands
Madeira
Canary Islands

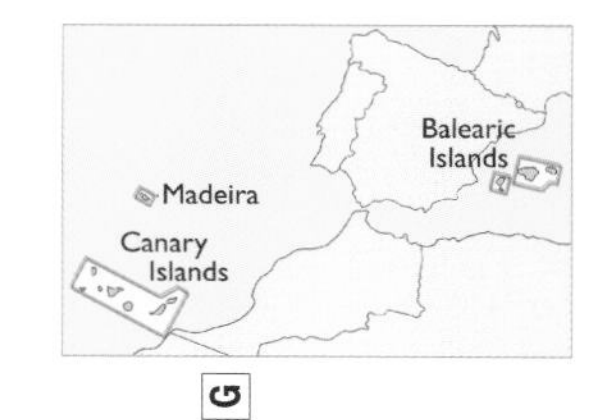

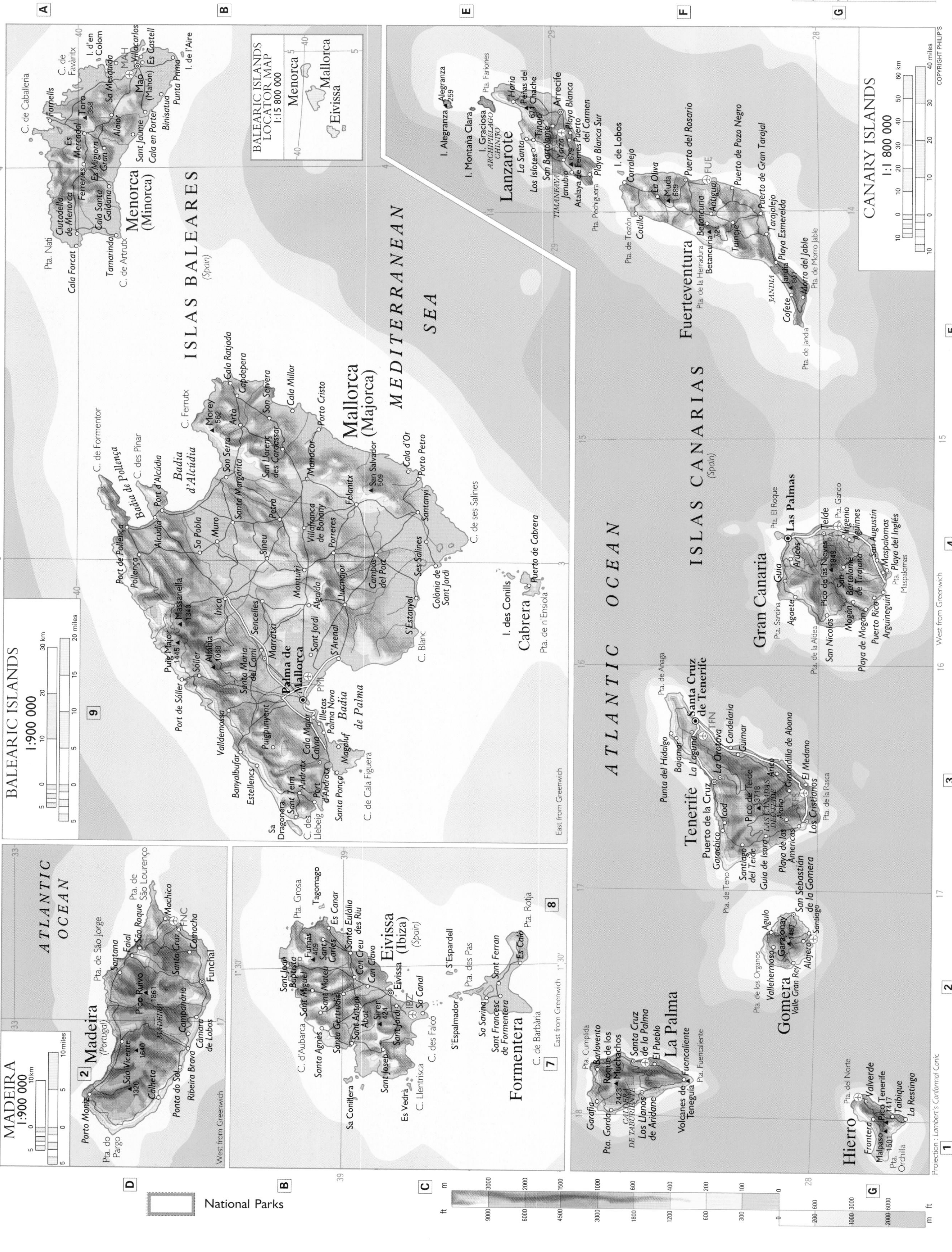

BALEARIC ISLANDS 1:900 000
BALEARIC ISLANDS LOCATOR MAP 1:15 800 000
CANARY ISLANDS 1:1 800 000
MADEIRA 1:900 000
ISLAS BALEARES (Spain)
MEDITERRANEAN SEA
ATLANTIC OCEAN
ISLAS CANARIAS (Spain)
Mallorca (Majorca)
Menorca (Minorca)
Eivissa (Ibiza)
Formentera
Cabrera
Palma de Mallorca
Maó (Mahón)
Ciutadella de Menorca
Lanzarote
Fuerteventura
Gran Canaria
Tenerife
Gomera
La Palma
Hierro
Santa Cruz de Tenerife
Las Palmas
Arrecife
Puerto del Rosario
Pico de Teide 3718
Madeira (Portugal)
Funchal
Pico Ruivo 1861
Projection : Lambert's Conformal Conic
COPYRIGHT PHILIP'S
National Parks

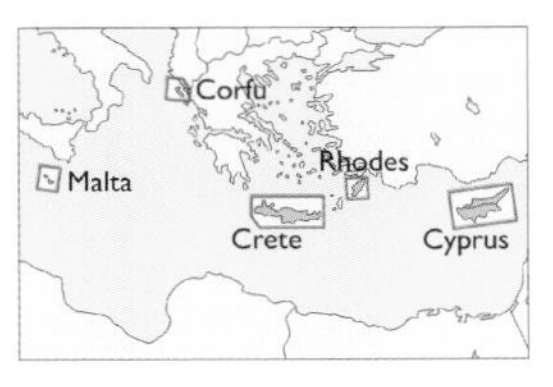

Corfu
Malta
Rhodes
Crete
Cyprus

CRETE
1:1 200 000
SEA OF CRETE
MEDITERRANEAN SEA
Kríti (Crete) (Greece)
KHANIÁ
RÉTHIMNON
IRÁKLION
LASÍTHI
Khaniá
Réthimnon
Iráklion
Áyios Nikólaos
Ierápetra
Sitía
Kólpos Khaníon
Kólpos Almiroú
Kólpos Mirabéllou
Kólpos Messarás
Gávdhos
Día
Koufonísi
Gaidhouronísi
Dhíkti Óros
2148
Psiloritis (Ídhi Óros) 2456
Levká Óri 2453
CYPRUS
1:1 200 000
MEDITERRANEAN SEA
CYPRUS
Nicosia (Levkosia)
Limassol
Larnaca
Famagusta (Ammochostos)
Paphos
Kyrenia
Morphou
Troodos
Olympus 1951
Kyrenia Range
Mesaoria
Famagusta Bay
Larnaca Bay
Morphou Bay
Khrysokhou Bay
Akrotiri Bay
Episkopi Bay
Karpas
Akrotiri Sovereign Base Area
Dhekelia Sovereign Base Area
(Under Turkish Administration)
C. Apostolos Andreas
C. Greco
C. Gata
C. Kormakiti
C. Arnauti
MALTA
1:900 000
Gozo
Comino
MALTA
Valletta
MEDITERRANEAN SEA
Filfla
Victoria (Rabat)
Mosta
Sliema
Birkirkara
Rabat
CORFU
1:900 000
Kérkira (Corfu) (Greece)
Kérkira
IONIAN SEA
ALBANIA
GREECE
Erikoúsa
Mathráki
Paleokastrítsa
Kassiópi
Lefkímmi
Sarandës (Santi-Quaranta)
RHODES
1:900 000
Ródhos (Rhodes) (Greece)
Ródhos
AEGEAN SEA
MEDITERRANEAN SEA
Líndhos
Alimnia
Ákra Prasonísi
Attáviros 1215
Projection : Lambert's Conformal Conic
East from Greenwich
COPYRIGHT PHILIP'S
m
ft
6000
4500
3000
1800
1200
600
300
0
2000
1500
1000
600
400
200
100
0

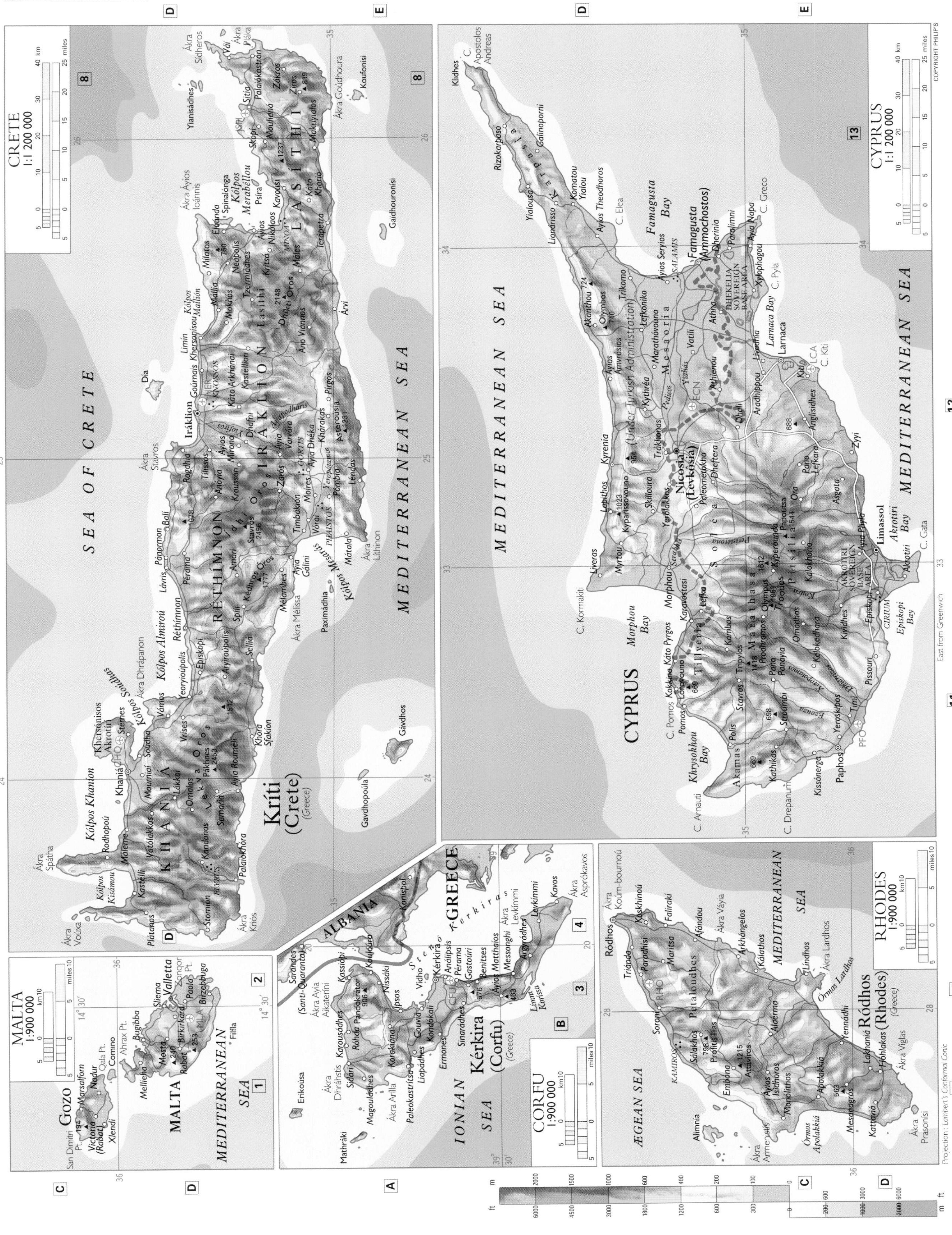

500 0 250 500 750 1000 1250 1500 1750 km

500 0 250 500 750 1000 1250 miles

1:44 400 000

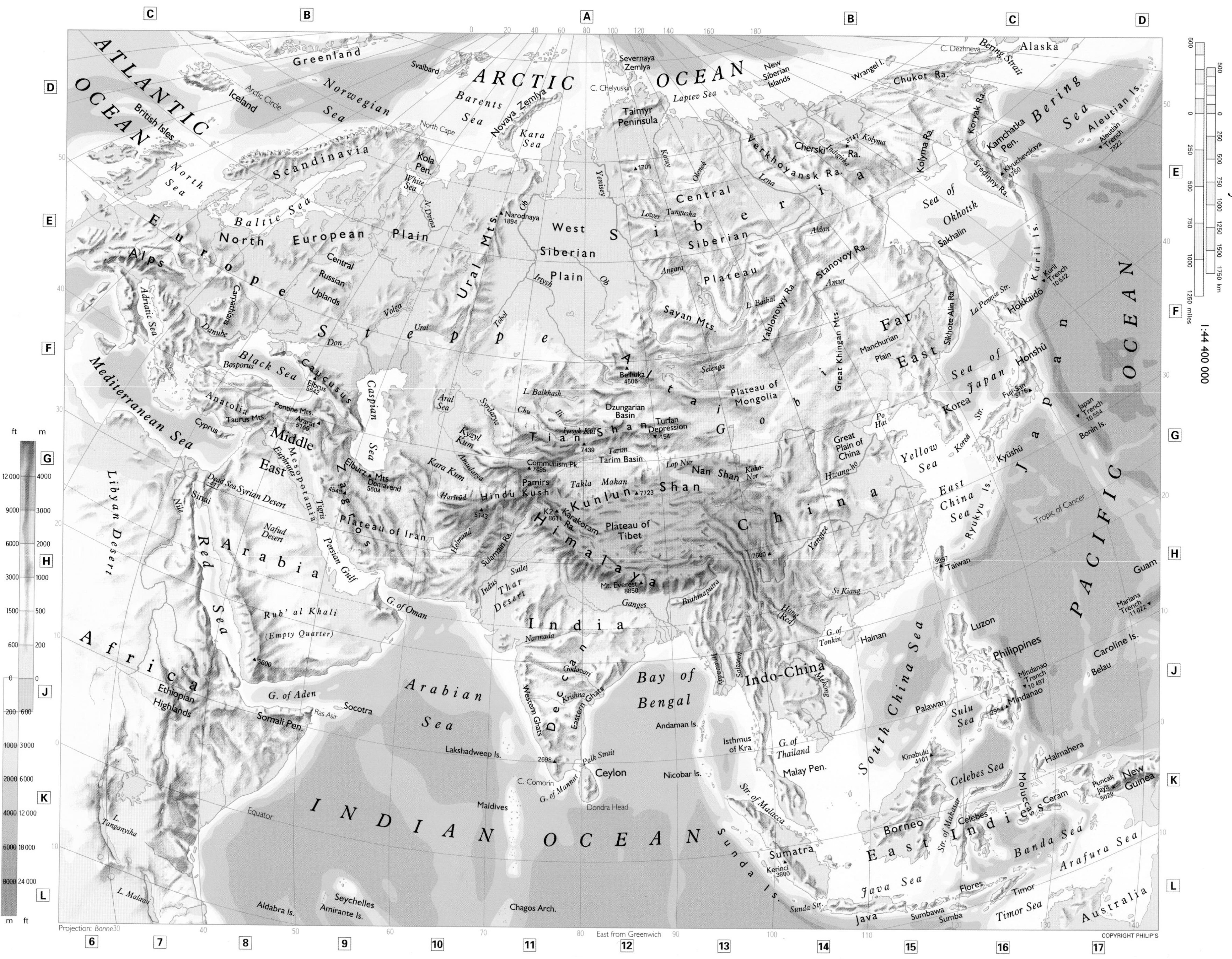

1:44 400 000

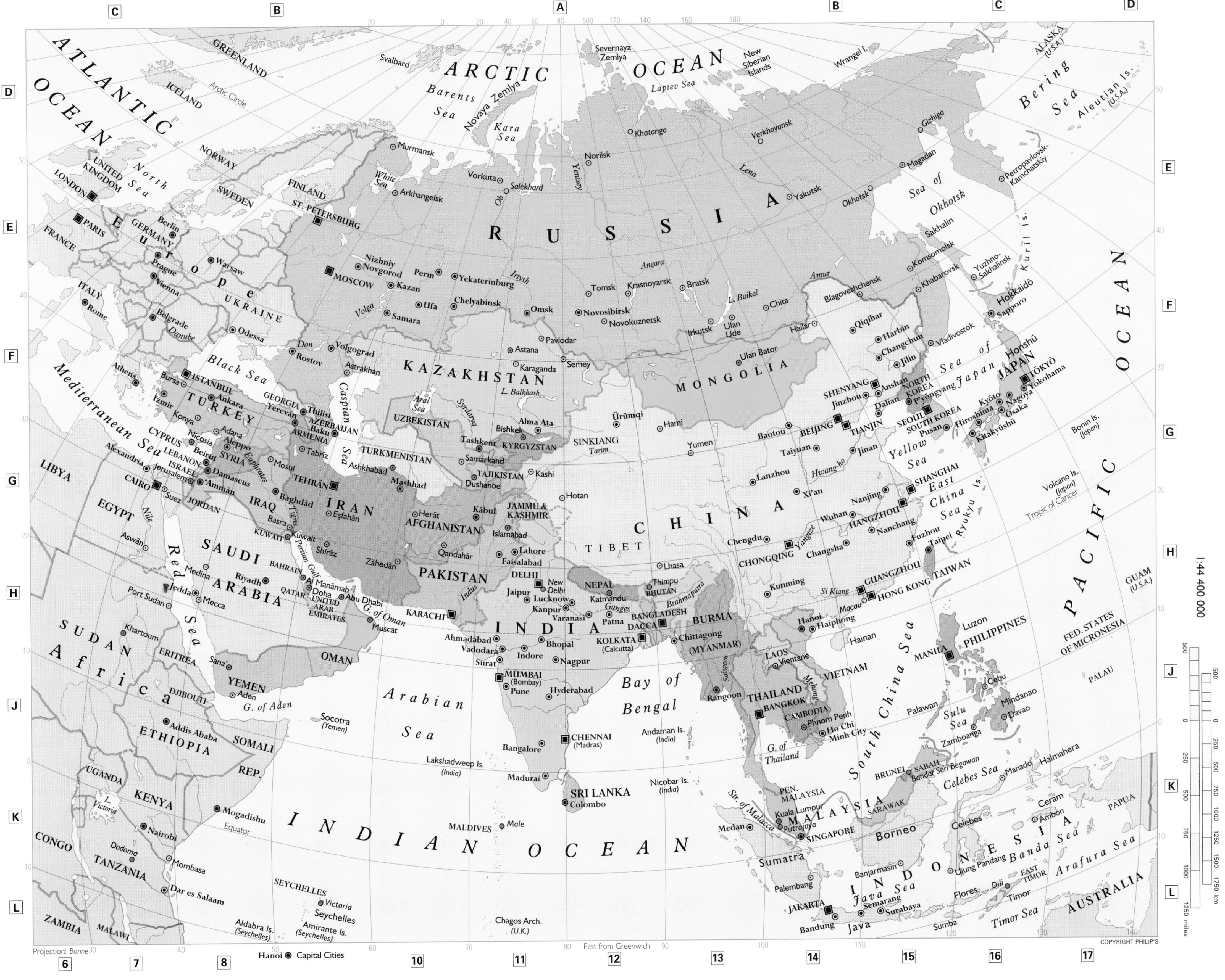

ATLANTIC OCEAN
ARCTIC OCEAN
PACIFIC OCEAN
INDIAN OCEAN
R U S S I A
C H I N A
I N D I A
I N D O N E S I A
KAZAKHSTAN
MONGOLIA
JAPAN
TOKYO
BEIJING
SHANGHAI
SEOUL
NORTH KOREA
SOUTH KOREA
MOSCOW
ST. PETERSBURG
IRAN
TEHRĀN
AFGHANISTAN
PAKISTAN
SAUDI ARABIA
TURKEY
IRAQ
SYRIA
JORDAN
ISRAEL
LEBANON
CYPRUS
OMAN
YEMEN
UZBEKISTAN
TURKMENISTAN
KYRGYZSTAN
TAJIKISTAN
JAMMU & KASHMIR
NEPAL
BHUTAN
BANGLADESH
BURMA (MYANMAR)
THAILAND
LAOS
VIETNAM
CAMBODIA
MALAYSIA
SINGAPORE
BRUNEI
PHILIPPINES
TAIWAN
SRI LANKA
MALDIVES
EAST TIMOR
AUSTRALIA
E u r o p e
A f r i c a
Bay of Bengal
Arabian Sea
South China Sea
Caspian Sea
Black Sea
Red Sea
Mediterranean Sea
Sea of Japan
Sea of Okhotsk
Bering Sea
Yellow Sea
East China Sea
Java Sea
Banda Sea
Arafura Sea
Timor Sea
Celebes Sea
Sulu Sea
TIBET
SINKIANG
Tropic of Cancer
Arctic Circle
Equator
Projection: Bonne
Hanoi ● Capital Cities
East from Greenwich
COPYRIGHT PHILIP'S

1:17 800 000
100 0 100 200 300 400 500 600 700 800 km
100 0 100 200 300 400 500 miles
RUSSIA
1 Adygea
2 Karachey-Cherkessia
3 Kabardino-Balkaria
4 North Ossetia
5 Ingushetia
6 Chechenia
7 Dagestan
8 Mordvinia
9 Chuvashia
10 Mari El
11 Tatarstan
12 Udmurtia
13 Khakassia
AZERBAIJAN
14 Naxçıvan
GEORGIA
15 Ajaria
16 Abkhazia
UKRAINE
17 Crimea
North Sea
Barents Sea
Kara Sea
Gulf of Bothnia
Baltic Sea
Beloye More
Black Sea
Sea of Azov
Caspian Sea
Aral Sea
NORWAY
SWEDEN
FINLAND
DENMARK
GERMANY
POLAND
LITHUANIA
LATVIA
ESTONIA
BELARUS
UKRAINE
MOLDOVA
ROMANIA
RUSSIA
GEORGIA
ARMENIA
AZERBAIJAN
TURKEY
IRAQ
IRAN
KAZAKHSTAN
UZBEKISTAN
TURKMENISTAN
KYRGYZSTAN
TAJIKISTAN
AFGHANISTAN
SEVERO-ZAPADNYY
TSENTRALNYY
PRIVOLZHSKIY
URALSKIY
YUZHNYY
MOSKVA
SANKT-PETERBURG
NIZHNIY NOVGOROD
VOLGOGRAD
YEKATERINBURG
CHELYABINSK
OMSK
NOVOSIBIRSK
ASTANA
ALMATY
TOSHKENT
BISHKEK
BAKI (Baku)
TEHRAN
KYIV
MINSK
STOCKHOLM
KØBENHAVN
BERLIN
WARSZAWA
Helsinki
Riga
Tallinn
Vilnius
Oslo
Projection: Conical Orthomorphic with two standard parallels
East from Greenwich

A
B
C
D
E
F
10
11
12
13
14
Mys Dezhneva (East C.)
Uelen
Chukchi Sea
Vankarem
Providenya
Anadyrskiy Zaliv
St. Lawrence I. (U.S.A.)
Ostrov Vrangelya
East Siberian Sea
Pevek
Chukotskoye Nagorye
Egvekinot
Anadyr
Beringovskiy
Ostrov Gennyetty
Ostrov Zhannetty
Ostrova Delonga
Ostrov Zhokhova
Ostrov Bennetta
Novosibirskiye Ostrova
Ostrov Faddeyevskiy
Ostrov Novaya Sibir
Ostrov Malyy Lyakhovskiy
Ostrov Bolshoy Lyakhovskiy
Ostrov Belkovskiy
Ostrov Kotelnyy
Ostrov Stolbovoy
Lyakhovskiye Ostrova
Proliv Dmitriya Lapteva
Laptev Sea
OCEAN
Ostrov Shmidta
Mys Arkticheskiy
Ostrov Komsomolets
Ostrov Pioner
Ostrov Oktyabrskoy Revolyutsii
Ostrov Bolshevik
Severnaya Zemlya
Proliv Vilkitskogo
Mys Chelyuskin
Gory Byrranga
Poluostrov Taymyr
Oz. Taymyr
Ostrov Bolshoy Begichev
Nordvik
Ust Olenek
Tiksi
Mys Buorkhaya
Ostrova Medvezhi
Ostrov Ayon
Ambarchik
Chersky
Bilibino
Ust Chaun
Bolshoy Anyuy
Yeropol
Markovo
Penzhino
Koryakskoye Nagorye
Khatyrka
Bering Sea
Nizhne Kolymsk
Chokurdakh
Indigirka
Kazachye
Ust Kuyga
Srednekolymsk
Khrebet Dalnevostochny
Kolymskoye Nagorye
Omolon
Kamenskoye
Tilichiki
Korf
Paren
Gizhiga
Penzhinskaya Guba
Sredinnyy Khrebet
Ossora
Ostrov Karaginskiy
Komandorskiye Ostrova
Ust-Kamchatsk
Nikolskoye
Klyuchevskaya Gora
Poluostrov Kamchatka
Petropavlovsk-Kamchatskiy
Tigil
Palana
Zaliv Shelikhova
Gizhiginskaya Guba
Evensk
Novorybnoye
Khatanga
Saskylakh
Olenek
Tit-Ary
Bulun
Kyusyur
Verkhoyanskiy Khrebet
Deputatskiy
Druzhina
Khonuu
Zyryanka
Kolyma
Pobeda
Ust-Nera
Taskan
Omsukchan
Orotukan
Seymchan
Volochanka
Kheta
Zhilinda
Verkhoyansk
Batagai
Gora Chen
Khrebet Cherskogo
Susuman
Yagodnoye
Atka
Palatka
Magadan
Ust Khayryuzovo
Norilsk
Gory Putorana
Yessey
Kystatyam
Oymyakon
Ust-Omchug
Zhigansk
Arctic Circle
Sangar
Batamay
Borogontsy
Khandyga
Okhotskiy Perevoz
Okhotsk
Arka
Kirovskiy
Ust-Bolsheretsk
Severo-Kurilsk
Ostrov Paramushir
Ostrov Onekotan
Sea of Okhotsk
Ulya
Ust Maya
Yakutsk
Vilyuysk
Verkhnevilyuysk
Namtsy
Pokrovsk
Nyurba
Suntar
Mirnyy
Chernyshevskiy
Noginsk
Tura
Yukta
Nizhnyaya Tunguska
Sinsk
Amga
Ust-Mil
Aim
Maya
Nelkan
Khrebet Dzhugdzur
Ayan
Ostrov Bolshoy Shantar
Sakhalinskiy Zaliv
Okha
Nikolayevsk-na-Amur
Sakhalin
Aleksandrovsk-Sakhalinskiy
Gora Lopatina
Poronaysk
Uglegorsk
Yuzhno-Sakhalinsk
Kholmsk
Korsakov
Kurilskiye Ostrova
Ostrov Simushir
Ostrov Urup
Ostrov Iturup
Kurilsk
Ostrov Kunashir
Yerbogachen
Olekminsk
Tommot
Chagda
Lensk
Aldan
Kuyumba
Mutoray
Vanavara
Podkamennaya Tunguska
Severo-Yeniseyskiy
Vitim
Yenyuka
Olekma
Neryungri
Chumikan
Tugur
Kezhma
Korshunovo
Mama
Bodaybo
Chara
Nagornyy
Stanovoy Khrebet
Yeniseysk
Boguchany
Ust-Ilimsk
Kirensk
Karalon
Ust-Nyukzha
Tynda
Zeya
Amgun
Amur
Khrebet Sikhote Alin
Kondratyevo
Zheleznogorsk-Ilimskiy
Makarovo
Ust-Kut
Magistralnyy
Kalakan
Skovorodino
Dzhalinda
Ushumun
Norsk
Komsomolsk
Amursk
Vanino
Kansk
Ilanskiy
Tayshet
Bratsk
Nizhneangarsk
Bagdarin
Mogocha
Yablonovyy Khrebet
Gulian
Shimanovsk
Svobodnyy
Belogorsk
Chegdomyn
Zavitinsk
Raychikhinsk
Obluchye
Birobidzhan
Smidovich
Khabarovsk
Krasnoyarsk
Achinsk
Nizhneudinsk
Tulun
Zima
Barguzin
Bukachacha
Shilka
Sretensk
Nerchinsk
Blagoveshchensk
Poyarkovo
Vyazemskiy
Bikin
Wakkanai
Abashiri
Kushiro
Rumoi
Obihiro
SAPPORO
Hokkaido
Otaru
Hakodate
Artemovsk
Vostochnyy Sayan
Chernogorsk
Minusinsk
Abakan
Cheremkhovo
Usolye Sibirskoye
Angarsk
Irkutsk
Ulan Ude
Chita
Aginskoye
Olovyannaya
Borzya
Zabaykalsk
Manzhouli
Hailar
Da Hinggan Ling
Nenjiang
QIQIHAR
Hegang
Jiamusi
Dalnerechensk
Lesozavodsk
Spassk
Dalniy
Ussuriysk
Artem
Vladivostok
Nakhodka
Terney
Dalnegorsk
Olga
Amgu
Munku-Sardyk
Turan
Toora-Khem
Kyzyl
Chadan
Slyudyanka
Gusinoozersk
Petrovsk-Zabaykalskiy
Kyakhta
Khilok
Khapcheranga
Hövsgöl Nuur
Hatgal
Zakamensk
Darhan
Hentiyn Nuruu
Onon
Choybalsan
Hulun Nur
Tamsagbulag
Uvs Nuur
Ulaangom
Erzin
Hyargas Nuur
Hangayn Nuruu
Döröö Nuur
Uliastay
Tsetserleg
Ulaanbaatar
Lun
Öndörhaan
MONGOLIA
Altay
Saynshand
Xilinhot
Linxi
Gobi
Erenhot
Dalandzadgad
Hami
Gaxun Nur
Ang'angxi
Nen Jiang
HARBIN
Songhua Jiang
Mudanjiang
Dongbei
Taonan
JILIN
Yanji
Kraskino
Chongjin
CHANGCHUN
Siping
FUSHUN
Tonghua
SHENYANG
ANSHAN
Chifeng
Dandong
NORTH KOREA
Wonsan
Kansong
Nampo
P'YONGYANG
SOUL (Seoul)
INCH'ON
SOUTH KOREA
TAEJON
TAEGU
PUSAN
DALIAN
Yingkou
Chengde
Zhangjiakou
BEIJING
Hohhot
Baotou
CHINA
Sea of Japan (East Sea)
Honshu
Aomori
Hachinohe
Akita
Niigata
Kanazawa
Fuji-San
JAPAN
OSAKA
ASIA
RUSSIA
YAKUTIA
BURYATIA
COPYRIGHT PHILIP'S

1:4 400 000
km
miles
SEA OF OKHOTSK
Sakhalin (Russia)
La Perouse Strait (Sōya-Kaikyō)
HOKKAIDŌ
Hokkaidō
SAPPORO
Hakodate
Tsugaru-Kaikyō
TŌHOKU
Honshū
Aomori
Hachinohe
Morioka
Akita
Sendai
Niigata
Sado
Kushiro
Obihiro
Asahikawa
Otaru
Muroran
Ostrov Kunashir
SEA OF JAPAN
(EAST SEA)
RUSSIA
CHINA
HEILONGJIANG
JILIN
NORTH KOREA
Lake Khanka
Vladivostok
Nakhodka
Ussuriysk
Zaliv Petra Velikogo
Jixi
Chŏngjin
Khrebet Sikhote Alin

53
57

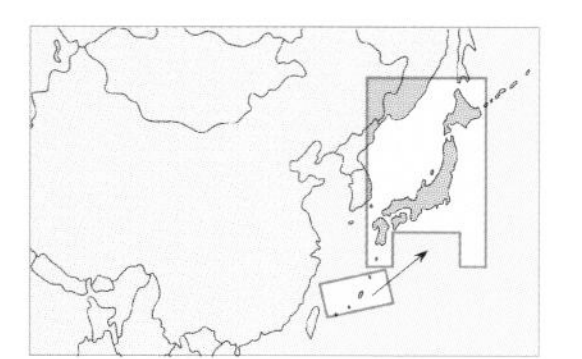

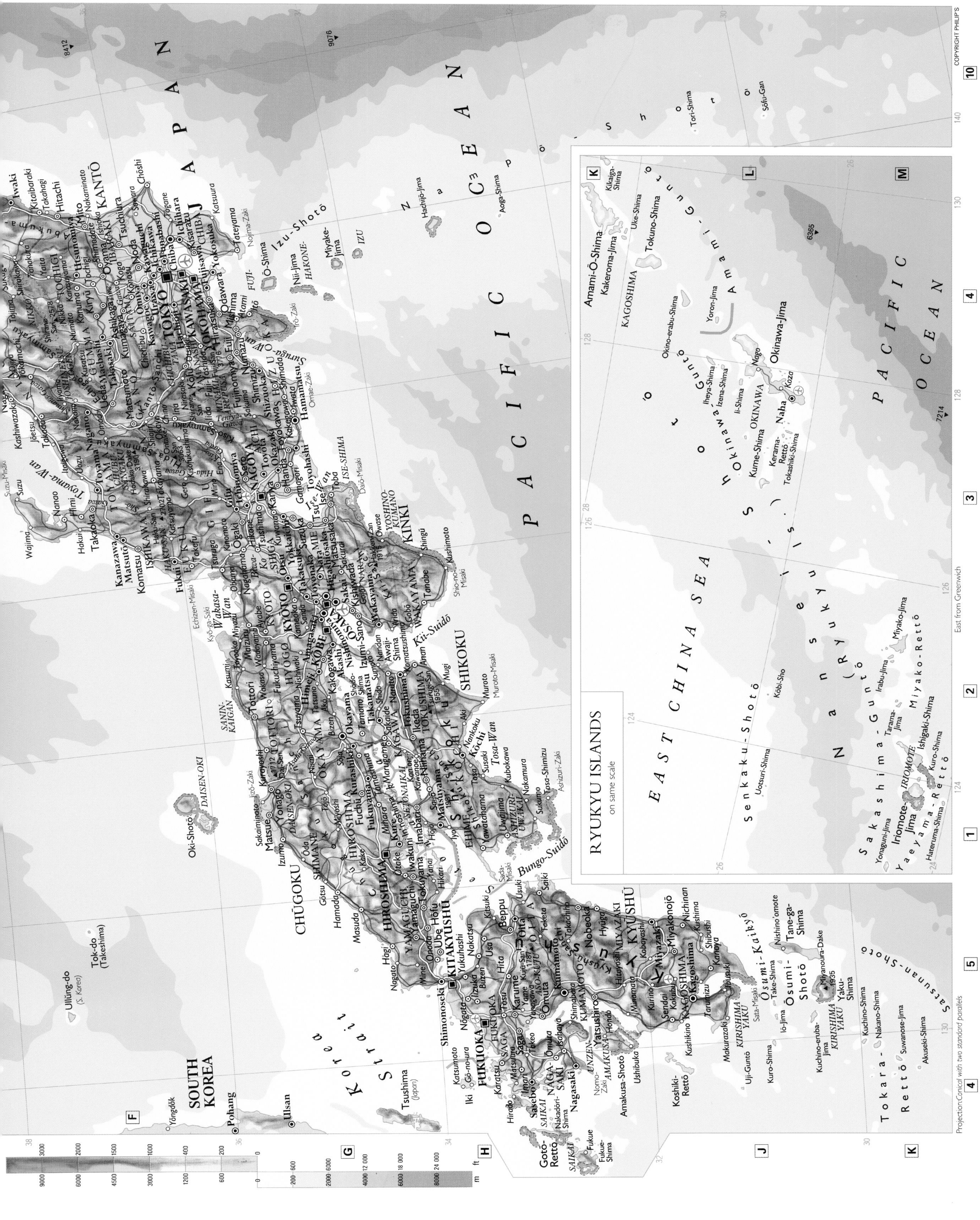

SEA OF JAPAN

PACIFIC OCEAN

EAST CHINA SEA

Korea Strait

SOUTH KOREA

HONSHU

SHIKOKU

KYUSHU

CHŪGOKU

KINKI

KANTŌ

TOKYO

YOKOHAMA

NAGOYA

KYOTO

ŌSAKA

KŌBE

HIROSHIMA

FUKUOKA

KITAKYŪSHŪ

KAGOSHIMA

Izu-Shotō

Nansei-Shotō (Ryukyu Is.)

RYUKYU ISLANDS

on same scale

Okinawa-Jima

Amami-Ō-Shima

Sakishima-Guntō

Senkaku-Shotō

Projection: Conical with two standard parallels

East from Greenwich

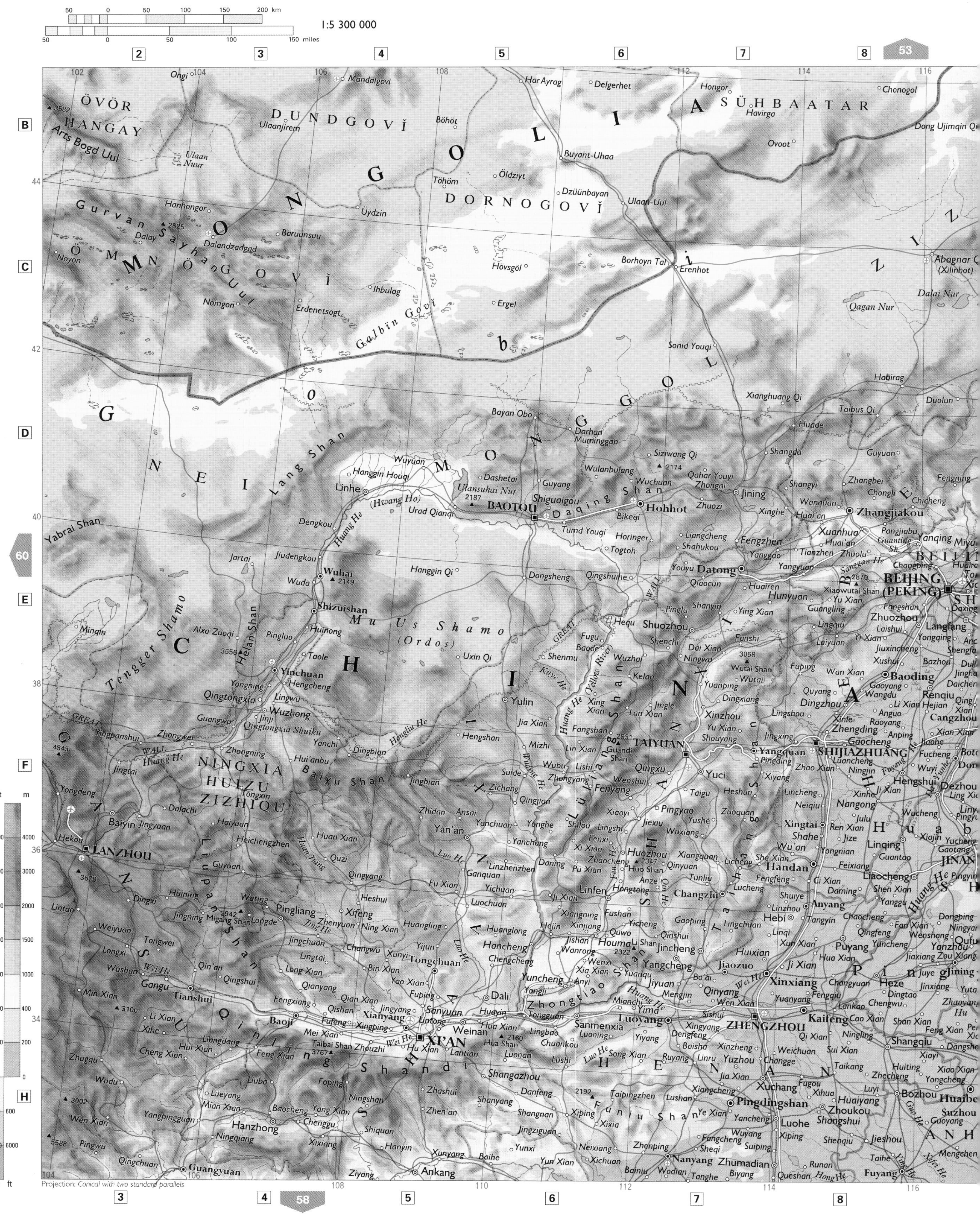

Projection: Conical with two standard parallels

9
10
11
12
13
14
15
16
B
C
D
E
F
G
H
55
59
HARBIN
Bin Xian
Acheng
Shuangcheng
Zhaoyuan
Maoxing
Da'an
Baicheng
Taonan
Tuquan
Horqin Youyi Qianqi
(Ulanhot)
Zhenlai
Nen Jiang
Hulingol
Hulin He
Anguang
Qagan Nur
Qian Gorlos
Qian an
Fuyu
Changchunling
Beitaolaizhao
Sanchahe
Yushu
Wuchang
Shanhetun
Lalin
Yimianpo
Shangzhi
Yanshou
Linkou
Jixi
Turiy Rog
Lake Khanka
RUSSIA
Muling
Mudanjiang
Hengdaohezi
Xiachengzi
Maqiaohe
Pogranichnyy
Suifenhe
Hailin
Ning'an
Suiyang
Dongning
Golenki
Ussuriysk
Dongjingcheng
Luozigou
Razdolnoye
Artem
Vladivostok
Zhangguangcai Ling
HEILONGJIANG
JILIN
Tongyu
Kaoshan
Shenjingzi
Nong'an
Dehui
Shulan
Zhanyu
Beizhenzhen
Jarud Qi
Changling
Fulongquan
Jiutai
Gangyao
Wulajie
Horqin Zuoyi Zhongqi
Maolin
Huaidezhen
CHANGCHUN
JILIN
Jiaohe
Xinzhan
Emu
Huangsongdian
Jingpo Hu
Chunyang
Daxinggou
Dunhua
Wangqing
Shixian
Tumen
Hunchun
Slavyanka
Xinkai He
Bairin Zuoqi
Kailu
Tongliao
Linxi
Bairin Youqi
Xiliao He
Xar Moron He
Shuangliao
Gongzhuling
Fanjiatun
Shuangyang
Yitong
Siping
Lishu
Dongliao He
Jargalang
Bamiancheng
Liaoyuan
Panshi
Huadian
Mingyuegue
Yanji
Longjing
Namyang
Helong
Kraskino
Posyet
Ongniud Qi
Laoha He
Wutonghaolai
Zhangwu
Xifeng
Kangping
Dongfeng
Huinan
Baishan
Antu
Hoeamdong
Unggi
Sŏsura
Najin
Hure Qi
Xiawa
Faku
Tiefa
Kaiyuan
Meihekou
Jingyu
Fusong
Baihe
Hoeryong
Musan
Puryong
Pugodong
Chifeng
Fuxin
Zhangwu
Xinlitun
Tieling
Qingyuan
Shanchengzhen
Liuhe
Changbai Shan
Paektu-san
Hunjiang
Linjiang
Chunggang-ŭp
Pochŏngdong
Nanam
Chŏngjin
Kyŏngsŏng
Chuuronjang
Hachon
Ondaejin
Heishui
Beipiao
Qinghemen
Xinmin
SHENYANG
FUSHUN
Xinbin
Tonghua
Weichang
Ningcheng
Heishan
Liaozhong
Qingshecheng
Changbai
Hyesan
Huch'ang
Kasan-dong
Irhyangdong
Hapsu
Simpungdong
Kapsan
Kilchu
Chaoyang
Beizhen
Yi Xian
Goubangzi
Liaoyang
Benxi
Huanren
Manp'o
Ji'an
Musudan
Chengde
Lingyuan
LIAONING
Jinzhou
Panjin
Anping
Tianshifu
ANSHAN
Lianshanguan
Kanggye
P'ungsan
Chail-bong
Kosŏngni
Kimch'aek
(Songjin)
Pingquan
Jianchang
Jinxi
Tianzhuangtai
Niuzhuang
Haicheng
Kuandian
Supung Shuiku
Usi
Ch'osan
Kuup-tong
Changjin-chosuji
Pujon-chosuji
Kwangdaeri
Tanch'ŏn
Luanping
Liugou
Shangbancheng
Kuancheng
Huludao
Yingkou
Dashiqiao
Pyŏktong
Koin-dong
Changjin
Chonghŭngni
Sinhung
Pukch'ŏng
Sinch'ang
Xinglong
Xingcheng
Liaodong Wan
Gaizhou
Fengcheng
Sakchu
Sinp'o
Sŏhori
Hongwon
Shuangshanzi
Suizhong
Xiongyuecheng
Wanfu
Xiuyan
Dandong
Sinŭiju
Uiju
Taegwan
NORTH KOREA
Pukchin
Hamhŭng
Hŭngnam
Oro
Zunhua
Jianchangying
Qinhuangdao
Buyun Shan
Gushan
Donggou
Yongamp'o
Kusŏng
Kujang
Tŏkch'ŏn
Tongchŏn-ni
SEA OF JAPAN
(EAST SEA)
Fengrun
Lulong
Funing
Luan Xian
Liaodong Bandao
Yalu Jiang
Sŏnch'ŏn
Chŏngju
Pakch'ŏn
Anju
Sunch'ŏn
Yŏnghŭng
Tongjosŏn Man
TANGSHAN
TIANJIN SHI
Changli
Leting
Wafangdian
Zhuanghe
Sukch'ŏn
Sinchang-ni
Songch'ŏn
Kowŏn
Munch'ŏn
Wŏnsan
Anbyŏn
Kojŏ
Hangu
Wuqing
TIANJIN
Tanggu
Dagu
Pulandian
Pikou
P'YŎNGYANG
Sunan
Kangdong
Tongyang
Singosan
Jin Xian
Lüshun
DALIAN
Korea Bay
Nampo
Chunghwa
Songnim
Suan
Koksan
Sepo-ri
Hoeyang
Changdo-ri
Kosŏng
Kansŏng
Sokch'o
Yangyang
Oikou
Bo Hai
Cho-do
Sariwŏn
Chaeryŏng
Sinmak
Chiha-ri
Pyŏnggang
Nam-ch'ŏn
Kŭmhwa
Ch'ŏrwŏn
Hwachon-chosuji
Chumunjin
Kangnŭng
Huanghua
Miaodao Qundao
Changyŏn
Sinch'ŏn
Kŭmch'ŏn
Haeju
Kaesŏng
Panmunjŏm
Ŭijŏngbu
Ch'unch'ŏn
Hongch'ŏn
Tonghae
Samch'ŏk
Ullŭng-do
(S. Korea)
Yanshan
Paengnyŏng-do
(S. Korea)
Ongjin
Yŏnan
Munsan
Kanghwa
SOUL
Songnam
Qingyun
Penglai
Wudi
Zhanhua
Huang He
Longkou
Daxindian
Yantai
Weihai
Puch'on
INCH'ŎN
Anyang
Hoengsŏng
Wŏnju
Chŏngsŏn
Laizhou Wan
Huang Xian
Fushan
Muping
Chengshan Jiao
Ansan
Suwŏn
Ich'on
Yoju
Osan
Yŏngwol
Ch'ungju
Chech'ŏn
Ulchin
Kenli
Huimin
Dongying
Zhaoyuan
Qixia
Wendeng
Rongcheng
Binzhou
Laizhou
Shandong Bandao
Rushan
P'yŏngt'aek
Ch'ŏnan
SOUTH KOREA
Yŏngju
Yechon
Shanghe
Gaoyuan
Guangrao
Shouguang
Nanhuang
Shidao
Sŏsan
Chŏngju
Andong
Yŏngdŏk
Huantai
Linzi
Changyi
Pingdu
Laiyang
Haiyang
Hongsŏng
Yesan
Kongju
Uisong
Zhoucun
ZIBO
Yidu
Weifang
Laixi
Anmyŏn-do
Taech'ŏn-ni
Nonsan
TAEJŎN
Sangju
Sŏnsan
Kimch'ŏn
Chŏngha
P'ohang
Changgi-Ap
Boshan
Fangzi
Anqiu
Gaomi
Jimo
Kanggyong
Yŏngdong
Yŏngch'ŏn
Kumi
Kyŏngju
Linqu
Lancun
Chengyang
Kunsan
Iri
Chŏnju
Waegwan
TAEGU
Laiwu
Zhucheng
Jiaozhou
QINGDAO
Kimje
Kochang
Koryong
Chŏngdo
Miryang
Ulsan
Xintai
Jiaozhou Wan
Puan
Hamyang
Mengyin
Yishui
Wulian
YELLOW SEA
(Huang Hai)
Chŏngŭp
Namwŏn
Chiri-san
Chinju
Masan
Kimhae
Tongnae
PUSAN
Ju Xian
Liangcheng
Rizhao
Tamyang
Sagŏ-ri
Songjŏng-ni
KWANGJU
Hadong
Ch'angwŏn
Samch'ŏnp'o
Ch'ungmu
Linyi
Tangtou
Shijiusuo
Andongwei
Naju
Sunch'ŏn
Mokp'o
Posŏng
Polgyo-ri
Yŏsu
Tsushima
Fei Xian
Tengzhou
Teng Xian
Zaozhuang
Ganyu
Haizhou Wan
Lianyungang
Changhŭng
Haenam
Chindo
Izuhara
Hŭksan-chedo
(S. Korea)
Korea Strait
Tancheng
Lianyungang
Chenjiagang
Iki
Haizhou
Guanyun
Xiangshui
Karatsu
Imari
Xuzhou
Yaowan
Guannan
Binhai
Cheju
Cheju-do (S. Korea)
Onpyŏng-ni
JAPAN
Sasebo
Kashima
Ōmura
Isahaya
Nagasaki
Kuchinotsu
Suqian
Shuyang
Shuanggou
Suining
Lianshui
Funing
Sheyang
Hallim
Taejŏng
Halla-san
Mosŭlpo
Sŏgwipo
Nakadōri-Shima
Fukue-Shima
JIANGSU
Lingbi
Huaiyin
Huai'an
Sixian
Hongze Hu
Guzhen
Wuhe
Baoying
Yancheng
Liuzhuang
Bengbu
Fengyang
Gaoyou Hu
Xinghua
Dongtai
118
120
122
124
126
128
130
132
East from Greenwich
44
42
40
38
36
34

1:5 300 000

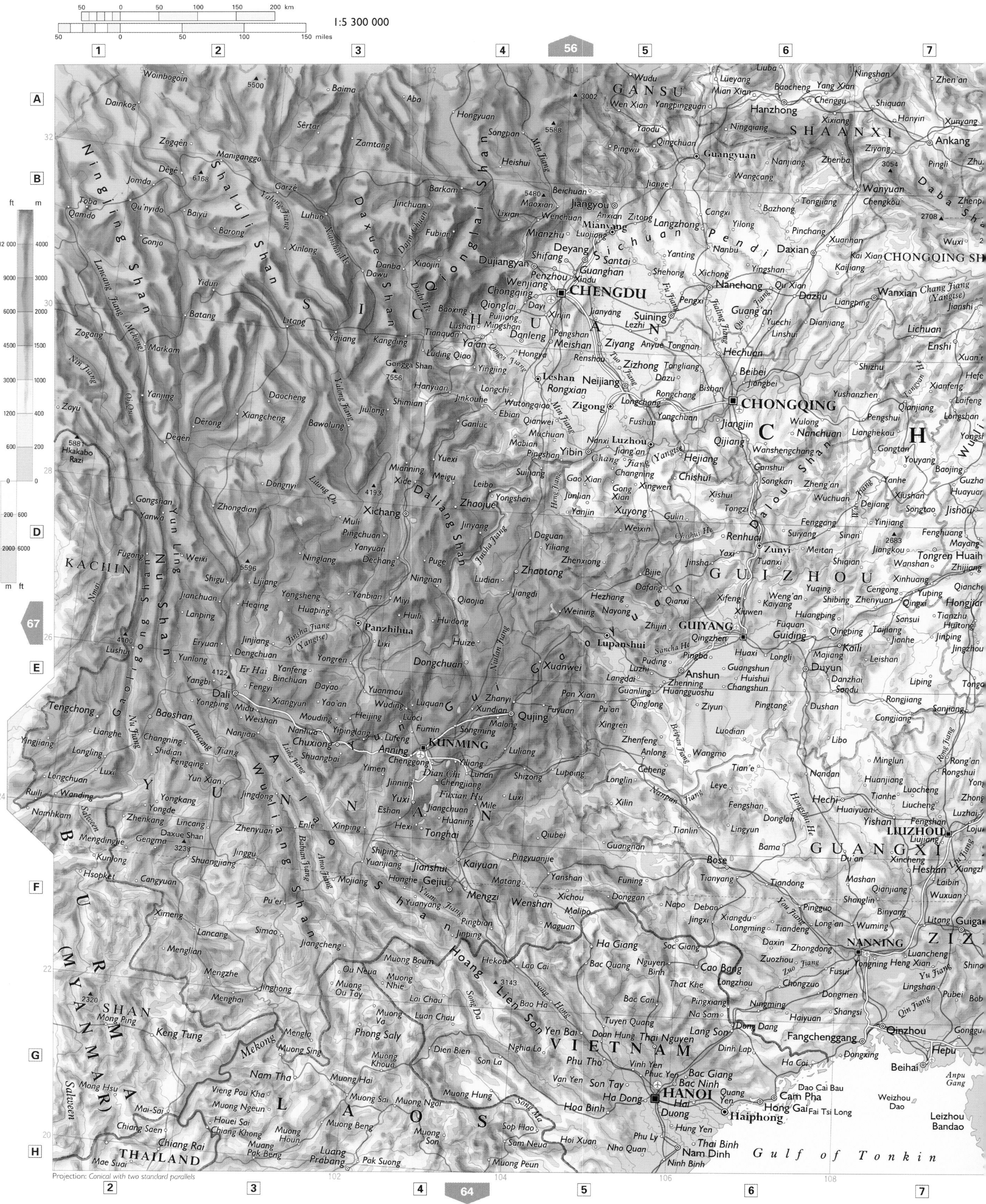

GANSU
SHAANXI
SICHUAN
Sichuan Pendi
CHENGDU
CHONGQING
GUIZHOU
GUIYANG
YUNNAN
KUNMING
GUANGXI
NANNING
LIUZHOU
KACHIN
SHAN
BURMA (MYANMAR)
LAOS
VIETNAM
HANOI
Haiphong
THAILAND
Gulf of Tonkin
Daxue Shan
Shaluli Shan
Ningjing Shan
Qionglai Shan
Daliang Shan
Nu Shan
Yun Ling
Gaoligong Shan
Wuliang Shan
Ailao Shan
Dalou Shan
Daba Shan
Hoang Lien Son
Gongga Shan
7556
Lancang Jiang (Mekong)
Jinsha Jiang (Yangtse)
Chang Jiang (Yangtse)
Yalong Jiang
Dadu He
Min Jiang
Nu Jiang
Salween
Song Hong
Song Da
Hongshui He
Nanpan Jiang
Projection: Conical with two standard parallels

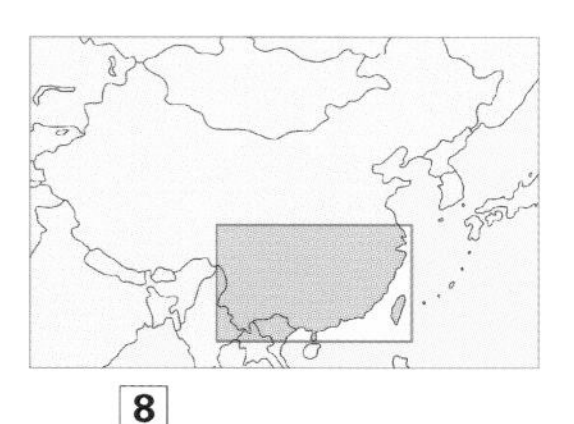

8 9 10 57 11 12 13 14

A B C D E F G H

HENAN
ANHUI
JIANGSU
HUBEI
HUNAN
JIANGXI
ZHEJIANG
FUJIAN
GUANGDONG
GUANGXI ZHUANGZU
TAIWAN

WUHAN
NANJING
SHANGHAI
SHANGHAI SHI
HANGZHOU
CHANGSHA
NANCHANG
GUANGZHOU
HONG KONG (XIANGGANG)
Kowloon
Macau
T'AIPEI
KAOHSIUNG

Dabie Shan
Dahong Shan
Jing Shan
Mufu Shan
Jiuling Shan
Wugong Shan
Luoxiao Shan
Wuyi Shan
Nan Ling
Yunkai Dashan
Chungyang Shanmo
Xuefeng Shan

Chang Jiang (Yangtse)
Han Shui
Huai He
Xi Jiang
Gan Jiang
Xiang Jiang
Min Jiang
Fuchun Jiang
Bei Jiang
Dong Jiang
Zhu Jiang

Dongting Hu
Poyang Hu
Tai Hu
Hongze Hu
Chao Hu

Three Gorges Dam

Hangzhou Wan
Xinghua Wan
Honghai Wan
Leizhou Wan

Taiwan Strait
Luzon Strait
SOUTH CHINA SEA
Tropic of Cancer

Matsu Tao (Taiwan)
Chinmen (Quemoy) Chinmen Tao (Taiwan)
P'enghu Ch'üntou (Pescadores) (Taiwan)
Dongsha Dao (Pratas I.) (China)
Chongming Dao
Zhoushan Dao
Daishan
Daqu Shan
Putuo
Taohua Dao
Liuheng Dao
Xiangshan
Niutou Shan
Taizhou Liedao
Yuhuan Dao
Dongtou
Nanji Shan
Haitan Dao
Nanri Dao
Fuying Dao
Dangan Liedao
Gaolan Dao
Shangchuan Dao
Xiachuan Dao
Hailing Dao
Donghai Dao
Naozhou Dao
Lü-Tao
Hungt'ou Hsü

112 114 116 118 120 122
32 30 28 26 24 22 20

East from Greenwich

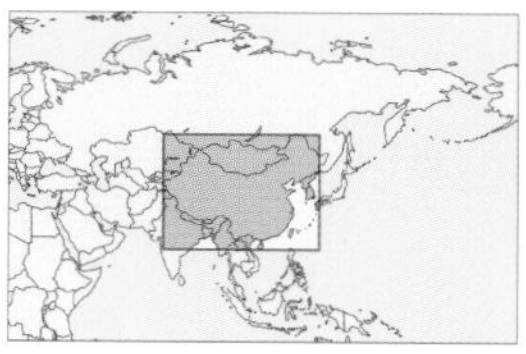

100 0 100 200 300 400 500 600 700 800 km

100 0 100 200 300 400 500 miles

1:17 800 000

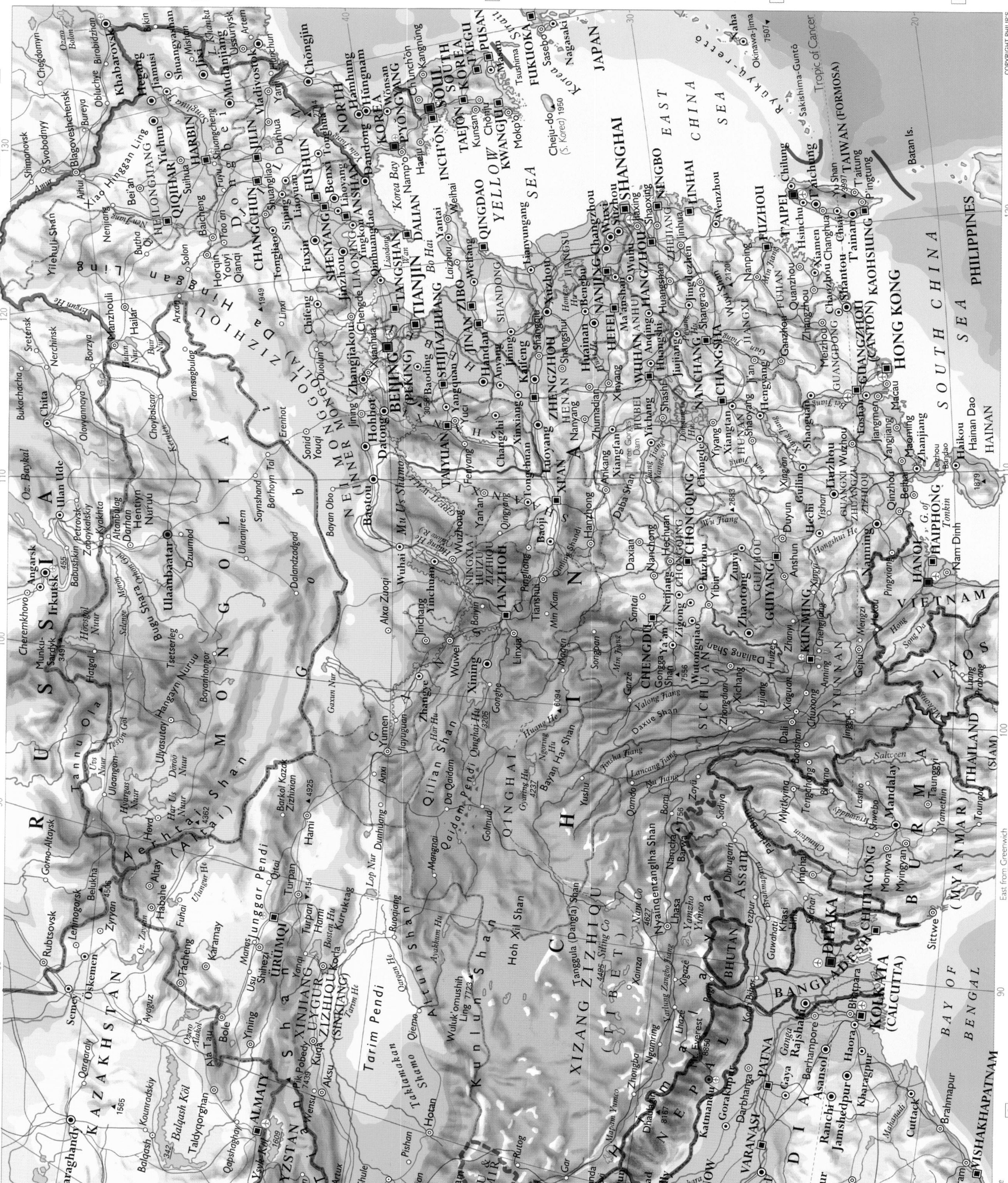

Projection: Bonne

East from Greenwich

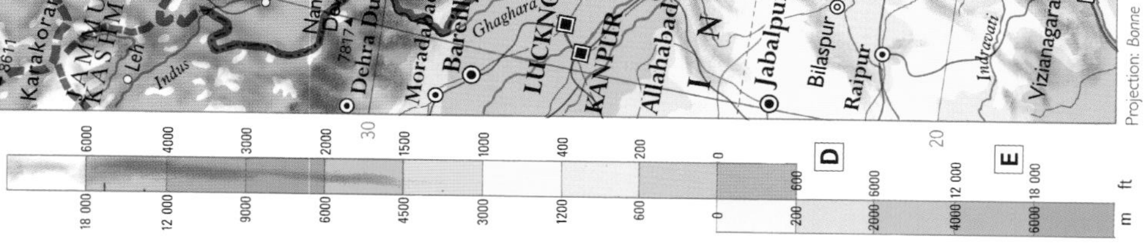

m 6000 4000 3000 2000 1500 1000 400 200 0 200 2000 4000 6000

ft 18 000 12 000 9000 6000 4500 3000 1200 600 0 600 6000 12 000 18 000

1:6 700 000

Projection: Lambert's Conformal Conic

East from Greenwich

COPYRIGHT PHILIP'S

1:11 100 000
100 0 100 200 300 400 500 km
100 0 50 100 150 200 250 300 350 miles
64
67
92
BURMA
(MYANMAR)
RANGOON
(YANGON)
Insein
Thaton
Moulmein
Mae Sot
Ma-ubin
Pyapon
G. of Martaban
Kyaikkami
Ye
Thoen
Uttaradit
Vientiane (Viangchan)
Nong Khai
Udon Thani
Loei
Sawankhalok
Phitsanulok
Tak
Phetchabun
Khon Kaen
THAILAND
Nakhon Sawan
Chaiyaphum
Roi Et
Nakhon Ratchasima
Buriram
Ubon Ratchathani
Nakhon Phanom
Sakon Nakhon
Savannakhet
Muang Khammouan
LAOS
Khemmarat
Saravan
Pakxe
Attapu
Sisaket
Khu Khan
Phnom Dangrek
Cheom Ksan
Ba Don
Dong Hoi
Quang Tri
Hue
Da Nang
Hoi An
VIETNAM
Chau O
Quang Ngai
Kon Tum
Bong Son
Binh Dinh
Plei Ku
Qui Nhon
Song Cau
A Yun Pa
Buon Ma Thuot
Nha Trang
Cam Ranh
Da Lat
Phan Rang
Mui Dinh
Phan Thiet
Bien Hoa
THANH PHO HO CHI MINH
Vung Tau
Natkyizin
Tavoy
Moscos Is.
Mali Kyun
Kadan Kyun
Mergui
Tenasserim
Letsôk-aw Kyun
Myeik
Lanbi Kyun
Kyunzu
(Mergui Arch.)
Zadetkyi Kyun
Nam Tok
Kanchanaburi
Phra Nakhon Si Ayutthaya
Saraburi
BANGKOK
Samut Songkhram
Samut Prakan
Chon Buri
Pattaya
Phet Buri
Sattahip
Rayong
Chanthaburi
Hua Hin
Prachuap Khiri Khan
Bang Saphan
Chumphon
Kho Khot Kra
(Isthmus of Kra)
Ranong
Aranyaprathet
Sisophon
Kulen
ANGKOR
Siemreab
Tonle Sap
Batdambang
CAMBODIA
Pouthisat
Kampong Chhnang
Kampong Thom
Krocheh
Senmonorom
Kampong Cham
Phnom Penh
(Phnum Penh)
Prey Veng
Svay Rieng
Takeo
Kampot
Long Xuyen
My Tho
Sa Dec
Can Tho
Soc Trang
Bac Lieu
Ca Mau
Mui Ca Mau
Con Son
Rach Gia
Hon Chong
Dao Phu Quoc
Ko Chang
Ko Kut
Phumi Koh Kong
Kaoh Kong
Sre Ambel
Chaak Kampong Saom
Kampong Saom
Gulf of Thailand
Ko Phangan
Ko Samui
Surat Thani
Nakhon Si Thammarat
Pak Phanang
Thung Song
Phatthalung
Thale Luang
Phangnga
Phuket
Trang
Ban Kantang
Songkhla
Hat Yai
Pattani
Satun
Yala
Narathiwat
Malay Pen.
ANDAMAN SEA
SOUTH CHINA SEA
Paracel Is.
Mui Nay
Nanshan I.
Loaita I.
Itu Aba I.
Sin Cowe I.
Spratly Is.
Spratly I.
Amboyna Cay
C. Buliluyan
Bugsuk
Balabac I.
Balabac Str.
Mt. Mantalingajan
Kudat
Kota Belud
Kota Kinabalu
Gunung Kinabalu
Labuan
Beaufort
Papar
Ranau
Beluran
SABAH
Melalap
Tenom
LABUAN
Bandar Seri Begawan
BRUNEI
Tutong
Lawas
Limbang
Kuala Belait
Seria
Miri
Marudi
Niah
Tawau
Bintulu
Mukah
SARAWAK
Oya
Sibu
Kanowit
Kapit
Bintangor
Sarikei
Saratok
Kuching
Lundu
Bau
Serian
Betung
Bandar Sri Aman
Tanjung Datu
Longnawan
Tanjungredeb
Tanjungselor
TIMUR
Sangkulirang
Straits of Malacca
Tarutao
Langkawi
Alor Setar
George Town
Butterworth
P. Pinang
Kota Bharu
Tumpat
Kep. Perhentian
P. Redang
Kuala Terengganu
Pasir Mas
Sungai Petani
PENINSULAR MALAYSIA
MALAYSIA
Kuala Kangsar
Taiping
Sepetang
Ipoh
Gunung Tahan
Dungun
Kemaman
Teluk Intan
Kampar
Kuala Lipis
Kuantan
Kota Kubu Bharu
Klang
KUALA LUMPUR
Putrajaya
Seremban
Port Dickson
Pulau Tioman
Segamat
Mersing
Melaka
Muar
Keluang
Kota Tinggi
Johor Bahru
SINGAPORE
Batu Pahat
Rupat
Dumai
Bengkalis
Laut
Kepulauan Natuna Besar
Telukbutun
Natuna Besar
Binjai
Matak
Siantan
Kepulauan Anambas
Midai
Subi
Kepulauan Natuna Selatan
Serasan
We
Sabang
Banda Aceh
Meureudu
Bireuen
Lhokseumawe
Sigli
Lhokkruet
Calang
Idi
Peureulak
Takengon
ACEH
Langsa
Meulaboh
Kualasimpang
G. Leuser
Pangkalanbrandan
Ujung Raja
Belawan
MEDAN
Tapaktuan
Kabanjahe
Tebingtinggi
Simeulue
Sinabang
Pematangsiantar
Prapat
Danau Toba
Tanjungbalai
Kepulauan Banyak
Tarutung
Sibolga
Rantauprapat
Musala
UTARA
Lahewa
Gunungsitoli
Nias
Padangsidempuan
Sumatera
Telukdalem
Siaksriindrapura
Pekanbaru
Bangkinang
Bintan
Tanjungpinang
Kepulauan Riau
Kepulauan Lingga
RIAU
Natal
Pini
Lubuksikaping
Tanahmasa
Kepulauan Batu
Tanahbala
Bukittinggi
Payakumbuh
Rengat
Lingga
Pasirkuning
Singkep
Selat Berhala
BARAT
Padangpanjang
Padang
Sawahlunto
Solok
Siberut
Sabulubbek
Muaratebo
JAMBI
Jambi
Muarabungo
Kerinci
Painan
Muaratembesi
Sungaipenuh
Sipura
Pulau Pagai Utara
Pulau Pagai Selatan
Kepulauan Mentawai
Bangko
Mukomuko
Sarolangun
PALEMBANG
Sungaigerong
SELATAN
Sekayu
Lubuklinggau
Curup
Tebingtinggi
Lahat
Muaraenim
Perabumulih
Bengkulu
BENGKULU
Dempo
Baturaja
Manna
Martapura
Kotabumi
Menggala
Bandar Lampung
LAMPUNG
Kotaagung
Kalianda
Enggano
Belinyu
Bangka
Sungailiat
Muntok
Pangkalpinang
BANGKA-BELITUNG
Tanjungpandan
Manggar
Dendang
Belitung
Toboali
Tg. Lumut
Selat Karimata
Kepulauan Karimata
INDONESIA
Sukadana
Ketapang
Nangatayap
Kendawangan
Tanjung Sambar
Kepulauan Tambelan
Sambas
Singkawang
Niut
Tebakang
Ngabang
Kepulauan Badas
Mempawah
Pontianak
BARAT
Sanggau
Putussibau
Semitau
Sintang
Nangapinoh
G. Saran
Muarajuloi
Kalimantan (Borneo)
TENGAH
Sukaraja
Pangkalanbuun
Sampit
Kumai
Kualajelai
Kualakapuas
Semuda
Kualapembuang
Teluk Sampit
Tanjung Puting
Palangkaraya
Banjarmasin
Martapura
Pelaihari
Jorong
Tg. Selatan
Pagatan
Satui
Kotabaru
Sebuku
Karambu
Pulau Laut
Muarakaman
Samarinda
Balikpapan
Tenggarong
Longiram
Purukcahu
Muaratewe
Kualakurun
Buntok
Tanahgrogot
Tanjung
Amuntai
Barabai
Kandangan
Besar
Kepulauan Balabalagan
Selat Makassar
Greater Sunda Islands
JAVA SEA
Kepulauan Laut Kecil
Kepulauan Masalima
Kepulauan Masalembo
Kepulauan Karimunjawa
Bawean
Sangkapura
Kepulauan Kangean
Kepulauan Tenga
Flores
Kepulauan Seribu
Merak
Serang
JAKARTA
Jatinegara
Purwakarta
Jatibarang
Tanjung Bugel
Selat Sunda
Pulau Rakata (Krakatau)
BANTEN
Panaitan
Bogor
Sukabumi
Teluk Pelabuhan Ratu
BANDUNG
JAWA BARAT
Cirebon
Brebes
Tegal
Pemalang
Pekalongan
Kendal
SEMARANG
Garut
Tasikmalaya
Cilacap
Slamet
JAWA TENGAH
Bojonegoro
Tuban
Gresik
Bangkalan
Madura
Sampang
SURABAYA
Pasuruan
Madiun
Kediri
Probolinggo
Lawu
Kebumen
Magelang
Yogyakarta
Surakarta
Tulungagung
Blitar
Malang
JAWA TIMUR
Semeru
Jember
Banyuwangi
Singaraja
BALI
Agung
Denpasar
Lombok
Rinjani
Mataram
Praya
Ampenan
Penida
Taliwang
Sumbawa Besar
Moyo
NUSA TENGGARA BARAT
Lesser Sunda Islands
Jawa (Java)
INDIAN OCEAN
Java Trench
Trung Son (Annam Range)
Dawna Ra.
Bilauktaung Range
Mekong
Chao Phraya
Pegunungan Muller
Pegunungan Schwaner
Kapuas
Barito
Mahakam
Kayan
Rajang
2080
2075
1813
1701
2598
1761
2405
4424
1835
2190
3381
3805
3159
6073
6650
3428
3265
2563
3670
3142
3726
1758
2278
2240
2988
2438
1892
4101
2086
100
105
110
115
15
10
5
0
1
2
3
4
5
A
B
C
D
E
F
ft m
12 000 4000
9000 3000
6000 2000
4500 1500
3000 1000
1200 400
600 200
0 0
200 600
2000 6000
4000 12 000
6000 18 000
8000 24 000
m ft
Projection: Mercator
East from Greenwich

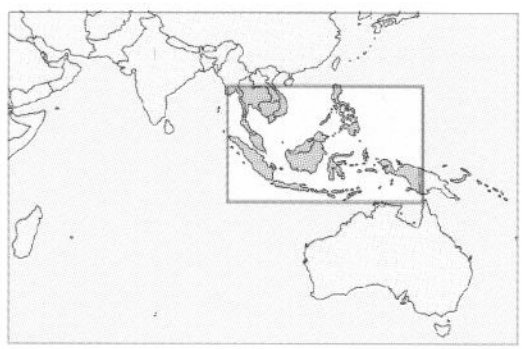

JAVA AND MADURA

1:6 700 000

BALI

1:1 800 000

94

50 0 50 100 150 200 km

1:5 300 000

50 0 50 100 150 miles

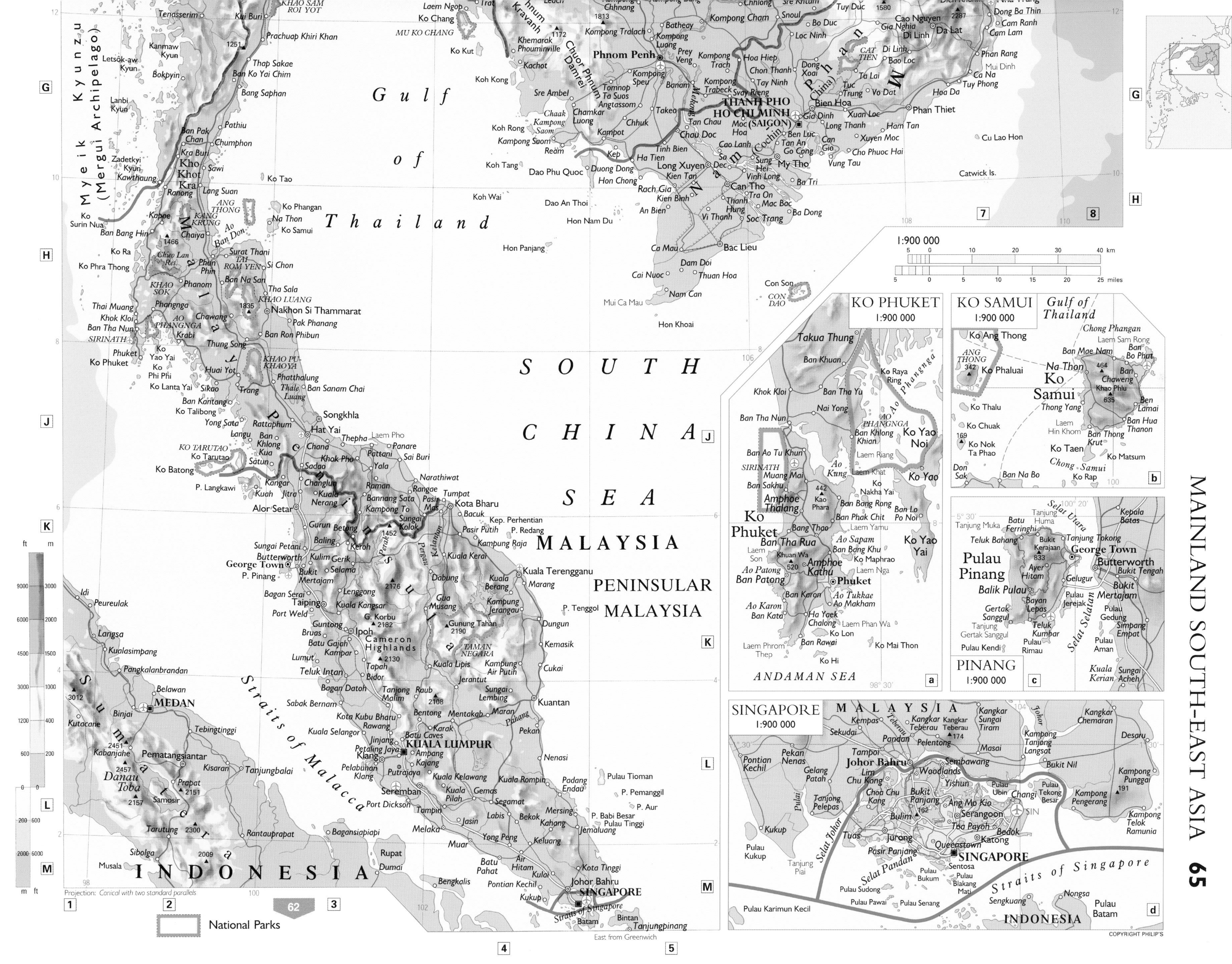
Gulf of Thailand
SOUTH CHINA SEA
MALAYSIA
PENINSULAR MALAYSIA
INDONESIA
Straits of Malacca
Myeik Kyunzu (Mergui Archipelago)
Phnom Penh
THANH PHO HO CHI MINH (SAIGON)
Phan Thiet
Da Lat
Bac Lieu
Nakhon Si Thammarat
Songkhla
Hat Yai
Kota Bharu
Kuala Terengganu
Kuantan
George Town
Butterworth
Ipoh
Cameron Highlands
KUALA LUMPUR
Seremban
Melaka
Johor Bahru
SINGAPORE
MEDAN
Danau Toba
Pulau Tioman
KO PHUKET
1:900 000
ANDAMAN SEA
KO SAMUI
1:900 000
Gulf of Thailand
PINANG
1:900 000
Pulau Pinang
SINGAPORE
1:900 000
Straits of Singapore
1:900 000
National Parks
Projection: Conical with two standard parallels
East from Greenwich
COPYRIGHT PHILIP'S

1:8 900 000

ARABIAN SEA
AFGHANISTAN
PAKISTAN
INDIA
SRI LANKA
KARACHI
DELHI
LAHORE
MUMBAI (BOMBAY)
CHENNAI (Madras)
BANGALORE
HYDERABAD
AHMADABAD
Kabul
Quetta
Islamabad
Rawalpindi
Peshawar
Hyderabad
Multan
Faisalabad
Colombo
Jaipur
Pune (Poona)
Srinagar
Herāt
Qandahār
Thar Desert
Rann of Kachchh
Gulf of Kachchh
Gulf of Khambhat
Gulf of Mannar
Palk Strait
Hindu Kush
Karakoram Range
Makran Coast Range
Central Makran Range
Siahan Range
Western Ghats
Malabar Coast
Coromandel Coast
Eastern Ghats
Continuation Southwards on same scale
Projection: Conical with two standard parallels

CHINA
XIZANG (TIBET)
QINGHAI
SICHUAN
YUNNAN
Huh Xil Shan
Bayan Har Shan
Tanggula (Dangla) Shan
Nyainqentanglha Shan
Kangri
Lhasa
Nagqu
Xigazê
Gyangzê
Qamdo
Yushu
Dainkog
Garzê
Baoshan
Lijiang
NEPAL
Katmandu
Mt. Everest 8850
Kanchenjunga 8598
Annapurna 8078
Dhaulagiri 8172
Siwalik Range
SIKKIM
Gangtok
BHUTAN
Thimphu
Punakha
ARUNACHAL PRADESH
ASSAM
Guwahati
Shillong
MEGHALAYA
NAGALAND
Kohima
MANIPUR
Imphal
MIZORAM
Aizawl
TRIPURA
Agartala
BANGLADESH
DHAKA
Chittagong
Cox's Bazar
Comilla
Khulna
Jessore
Rangpur
Dinajpur
Rajshahi
Mymensingh
Sylhet
Barisal
BIHAR
Patna
Gaya
Munger
Bhagalpur
Darbhanga
JHARKHAND
Ranchi
Jamshedpur
Dhanbad
Asansol
WEST BENGAL
KOLKATA (CALCUTTA)
Haora
Kharagpur
Durgapur
Barddhaman
Siliguri
Darjiling
Jalpaiguri
ORISSA
Cuttack
Bhubaneshwar
Puri
Brahmapur
Baleshwar
Raurkela
Sambalpur
CHHATTISGARH
Raipur
Durg
Lucknow
Faizabad
Varanasi
Allahabad
Jaunpur
Gorakhpur
Vishakhapatnam
Vizianagaram
Kakinada
Rajahmundry
Vijayawada
Machilipatnam
Tenali
Northern Circars
Mouths of the Ganges
The Sundarbans
Brahmaputra
Ganga
BAY OF BENGAL
INDIAN OCEAN
BURMA (MYANMAR)
KACHIN
SAGAING
CHIN
MAGWE
MANDALAY
SHAN
KAYAH
KAYIN
MON
IRRAWADDY
ARAKAN
PEGU
Mandalay
Monywa
Myitkyina
Bhamo
Lashio
Taunggyi
Meiktila
Magwe
Sittwe (Akyab)
Arakan Coast
Arakan Yoma
Chin Hills
Pegu Yoma
Irrawaddy
Salween
Henzada
Bassein
Pegu
RANGOON
Moulmein
Martaban
Amherst
G. of Martaban
Mouths of the Irrawaddy
Ramree I.
Cheduba I.
Preparis North Channel
Preparis South Channel
Paripari Kyun (Burma)
Koko Kyunzu (Burma)
Moscos Is.
Tavoy
THAILAND
Chiang Mai
Lamphun
Lampang
Tak
Tropic of Cancer
East from Greenwich
COPYRIGHT PHILIP'S

60
64
65

NORTHERN INDIA AND NEPAL

1:5 300 000

50 0 50 100 150 200 km

50 0 50 100 150 miles

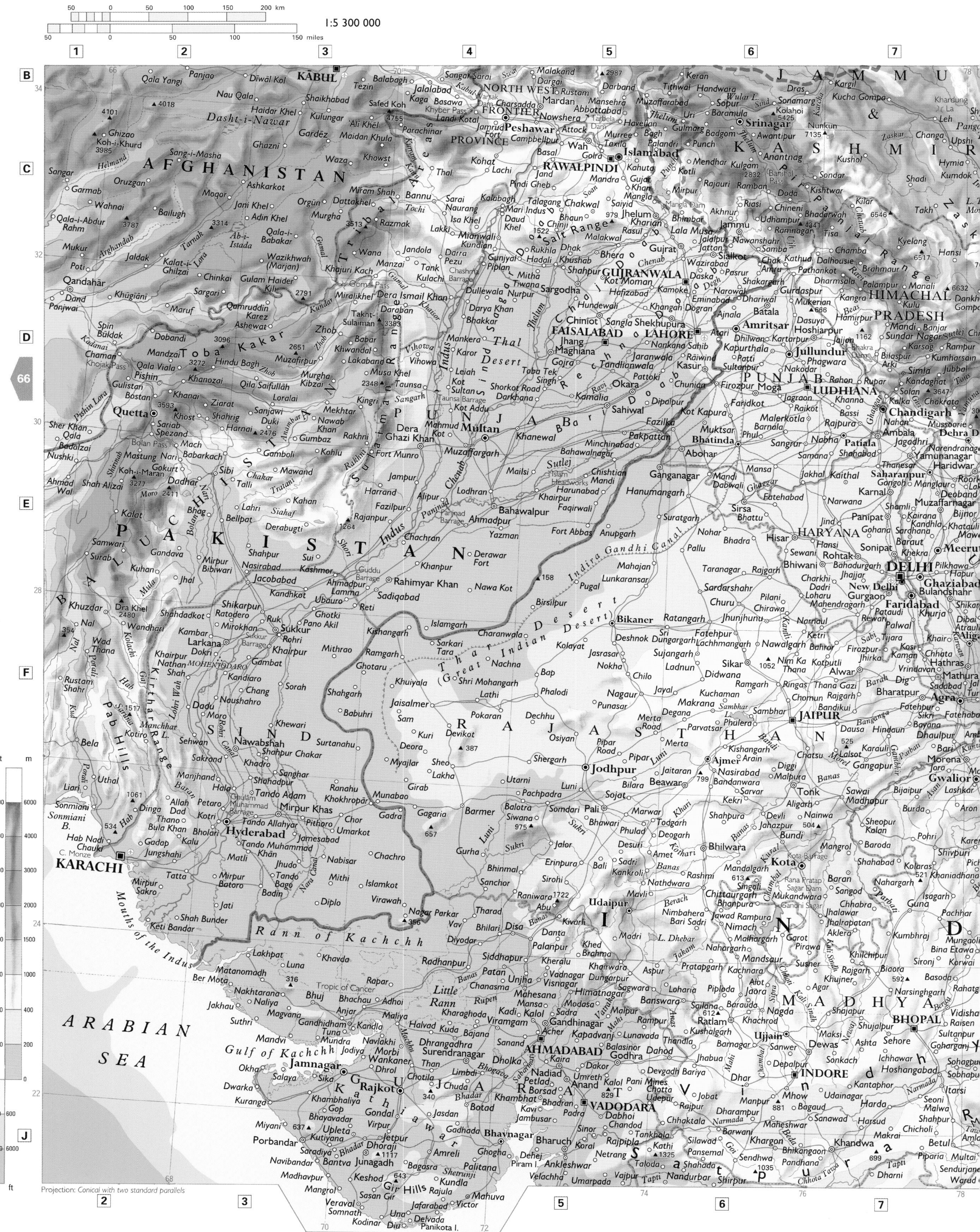

Projection: Conical with two standard parallels

JAMMU AND KASHMIR
on same scale
AFGHANISTAN
CHINA
NORTH WEST FRONTIER
Northern Areas
Azad Kashmir
PUNJAB
RAWALPINDI
Islamabad
Srinagar
Karakoram Range
JAMMU & KASHMIR
Zaskar Mountains
HIMACHAL PRADESH
Ladakh Range
Kunlun Shan
Aksai Chin
Siachen Glacier
Deosai Mts.
K2 8611
Gasherbrum 8068
Nanga Parbat 8126
Karakoram Pass
Leh
Jammu
Sialkot
Gujrat
Wazirabad
Gilgit
Skardu
Kargil
Nganglong Kangri
Gangdisê Shan
XIZANG ZIZHIQU (TIBET)
Yarlung Zangbo Jiang (Brahmaputra)
Maquan He (Brahmaputra)
Shiquan He (Indus)
Xiangquan He (Sutlej)
UTTARANCHAL
UTTAR PRADESH
NEPAL
Mahabharat Lekh
Siwalik Range
Katmandu
Mt. Everest (Chomolungma or Sagarmatha) 8850
Kanchenjunga 8598
Annapurna 8078
Dhaulagiri 8172
Makalu 8481
Nanda Devi 7817
Lhazê
Xigazê
SIKKIM
Gangtok
BHUTAN
Thimphu
ASSAM
Garo Hills
LUCKNOW
KANPUR
Allahabad
VARANASI
Gorakhpur
Bareilly
Moradabad
Shahjahanpur
Jhansi
Jabalpur
BIHAR
PATNA
Gaya
Bhagalpur
Muzaffarpur
Darbhanga
Purnia
JHARKHAND
Ranchi
Dhanbad
Jamshedpur
Rajmahal Hills
WEST BENGAL
KOLKATA
Haora
Kharagpur
Asansol
Durgapur
BANGLADESH
DHAKA
RAJSHAHI
Rajshahi
Khulna
KHULNA
Jessore
CHHATTISGARH
Bilaspur
Korba
Raigarh
Raurkela
Sambalpur
Kaimur Hills
Panna Hills
Maikala Ra.
Sundarbans
Mouths of the Ganges
The Sandheads
Ganga (Ganges)
Hugli (Hooghly)
East from Greenwich
COPYRIGHT PHILIP'S
A
B
C
E
F
G
H
J
8
9
10
5
6
60
7
11
12
13
66
67

1:6 200 000

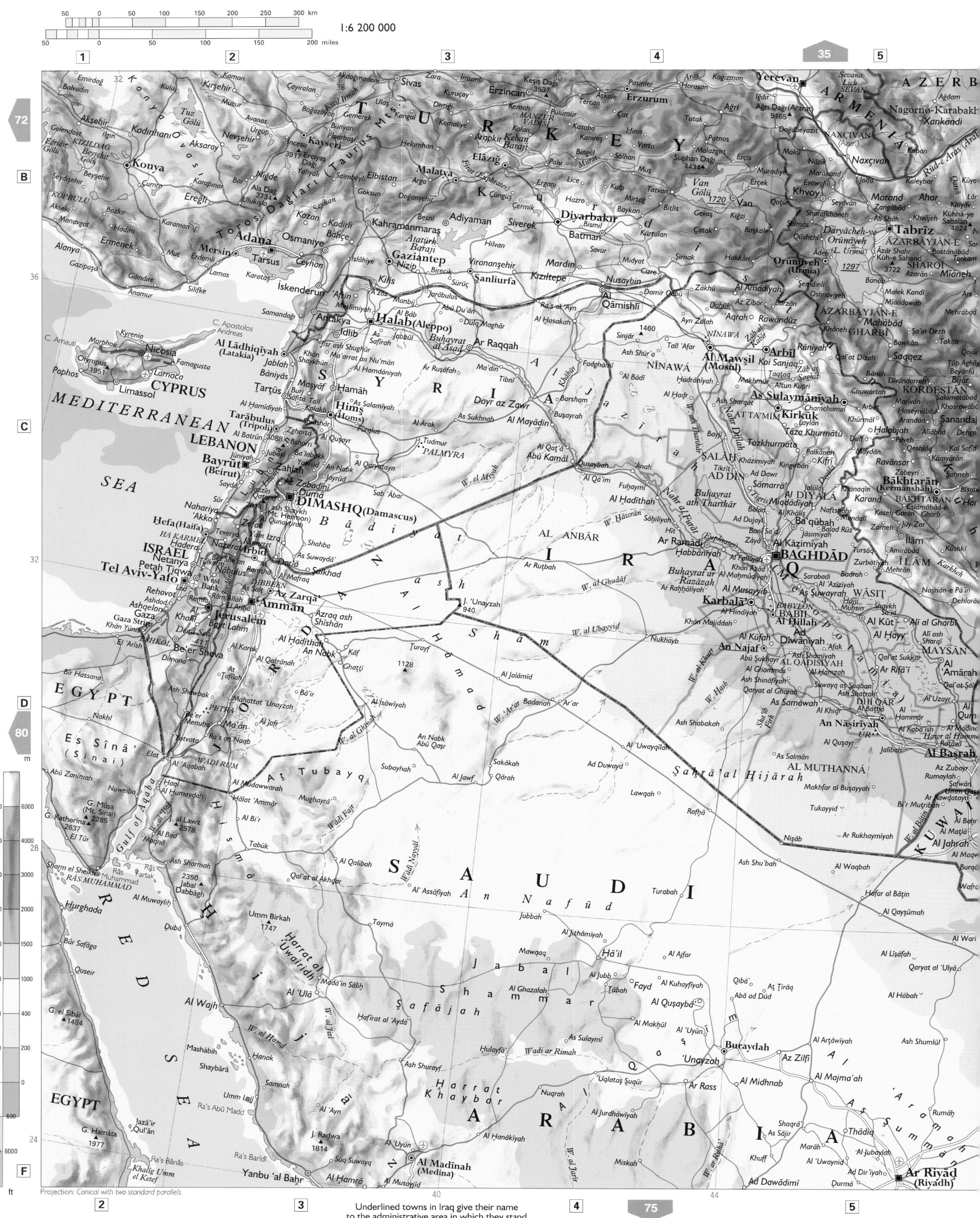

Projection: Conical with two standard parallels

Underlined towns in Iraq give their name to the administrative area in which they stand

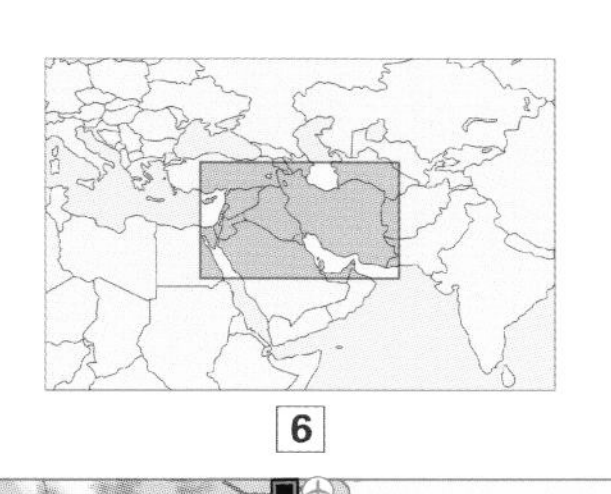

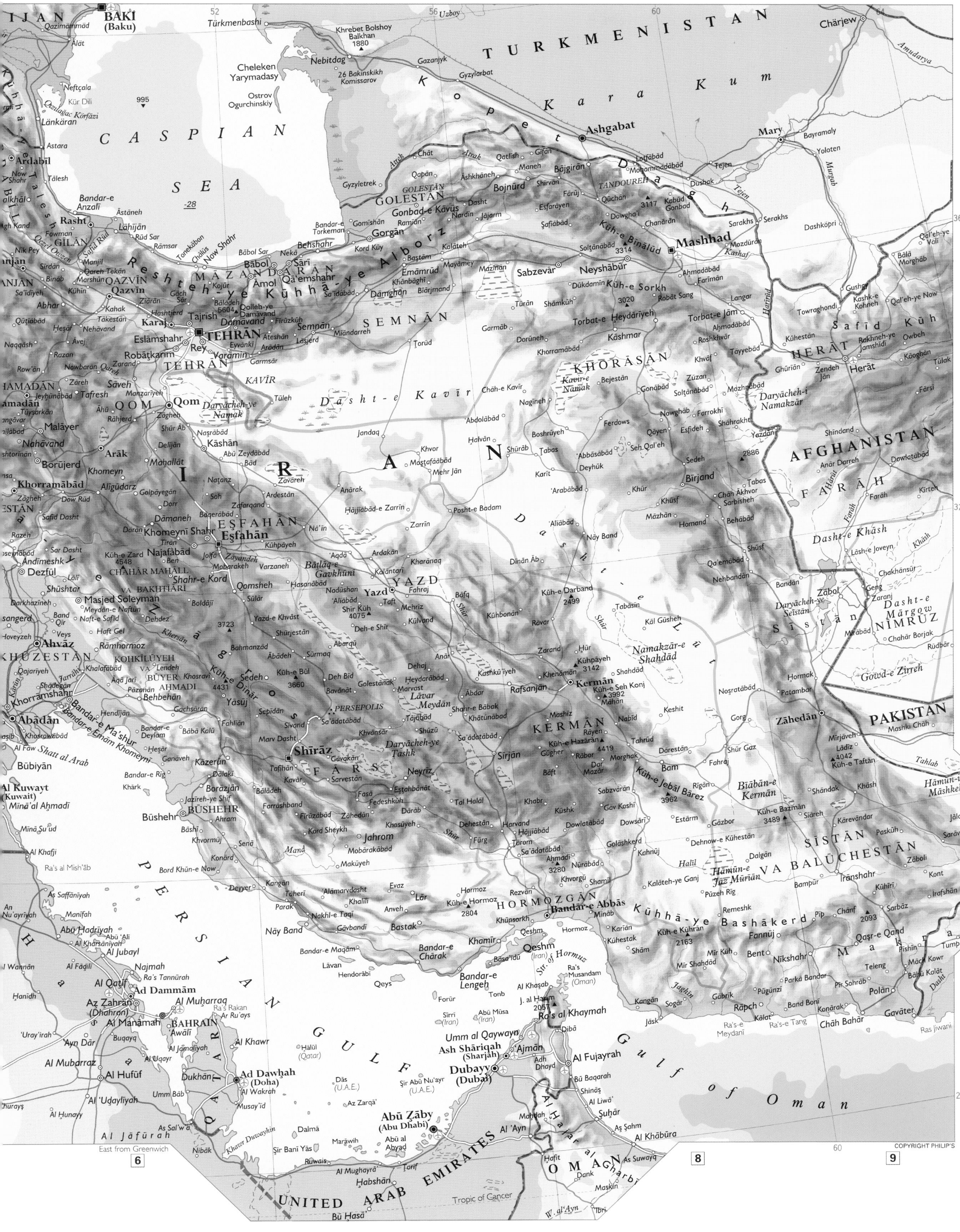

6
7
8
52
9
10

TURKMENISTAN
Kara Kum
Kopet Dagh
CASPIAN SEA
BAKI (Baku)
Türkmenbashi
Uzboy
Khrebet Bolshoy Balkhan 1880
Chärjew
Amudarya
Cheleken Yarymadasy
Nebitdag
26 Bakinskikh Komissarov
Gazanjyk
Gyzylarbat
Ostrov Ogurchinskiy
995
Neftçala
Kür Dili
Qızılağac Körfäzi
Länkäran
Astara
Ardabīl
Tālesh
Bandar-e Anzalī
Āstāneh
-28
Ashgabat
Mary
Bayramaly
Yoloten
Murgab
Tejen
Dushak
Serakhs
Sarakhs
Dashköpri
Lotfābād
Mohammadābād
TANDOUREH
Chāt
Atrak
Qotlīsh
Gifān
Maneh
Bājgīrān
Ashkhāneh
Qapān
Gyzyletrek
GOLESTĀN
Bojnūrd
Shīrvān
Fārūj
Qūchān
Kabūd Gonbad
3117
Gonbad-e Kāvūs
Nardīn
Dasht
Jājarm
Esfarāyen
Dowgha'ī
Chanārān
Bandar-e Torkeman
Gomīshān
Rāmiān
Gorgān
Şafīābād
Kūh-e Bīnālūd
3314
Mashhad
Mozdūrān
Kashaf
Rasht
Lāhījān
Fowman
Gīlān
Safīd Rūd
Rūd Sar
Rāmsar
Tonekābon
Chālūs
Now Shahr
Bābol Sar
Bābol
Neka
Behshahr
Kord Kūy
Kalāteh
Bastām
Māzandarān
Sārī
Qā'emshahr
Āmol
Reshteh-ye Kūhhā-ye Alborz
Khānbāghī
Emāmrūd
Mayāmey
Māzīnān
Sabzevār
Soltānābād
Neyshābūr
Ahmadābād
Farīmān
Dūkdamīn
Kūh-e Sorkh
3020
Robāt Sang
Langar
Harirūd
Qazvīn
Manjīl
Qareh Tekān
Marshūn
Zanjān
Sa'īdīyeh
Abhar
Kahak
Ziārān
Gach Sar
Bāladeh
5604
Dolleh-ye Damāvand
Damāvand
Fīrūzkūh
Semnān
Dāmghān
Biārjmand
Sa'īdābād
Hashtgerd
Tajrīsh
Karaj
TEHRĀN
Tehrān
Eslāmshahr
Rey
Varāmīn
Eyvānkī
Ārādān
Āteshān
Lasjerd
Mīāndarreh
SEMNĀN
Tūrān
Shāmkūh
Garmāb
Torbat-e Heydārīyeh
Torbat-e Jām
Aḥmadābād
Kāshmar
Dorūneh
Khorramābād
Roshkhvār
Tayyebād
KHORĀSĀN
Kavīr-e Namak
Bejestān
Gonābād
Kāvīr
Dasht-e Kavīr
Chāh-e Kavīr
Daryācheh-ye Namak
Qom
Tūleh
Ṭorūd
Saveh
Tafresh
Hamadān
Malāyer
Nahāvand
Borūjerd
Arāk
Khomeyn
Kāshān
Naşrābād
Delījān
Abū Zeydābād
Maḥallāt
Golpāyegān
Natanz
Ardestān
Khorramābād
Alīgūdarz
IRAN
Zavāreh
Anārak
Khvor
Mehr Jān
Jandaq
Tabas
Shūrāb
Halvān
'Abdolābād
Naginā
Boshrūyeh
Ferdows
Qāyen
Esfideh
Shāhrakht
Yazdān
Kīmī
Ahmad
Sedeh
Birjand
Khūsf
Mazhān
Homand
Chāh Akhvor
Sarbīsheh
Behābād
Tabas
Dowlatābād
Farāh
Herāt
Safīd Kūh
Ghūrīān
Zendeh Jān
Kūhestān
Towraghondī
Qal'eh-ye Now
Bālā Morghāb
Shindand
AFGHANISTAN
Anār Darreh
FARĀH
Farāh
Daryācheh-ye Namakzār
2886
Dasht-e Khāsh
Lāsh-e Joveyn
Chakhānsūr
Khāsh
Zābol
Daryācheh-ye Sīstān
Zaranj
Dasht-e Mārgow
NĪMRŪZ
Chahār Borjak
Rūdbār
Gowd-e Zirreh
Esfahān
ESFAHĀN
Najafābād
Khomeynī Shahr
Dāmaneh
Zāyandeh
Kūhpāyeh
Nā'īn
Posht-e Badam
Zarrīn
Ḥājjīābād-e Zarrīn
Ardakān
Yazd
YAZD
Fahraj
Mehrīz
Taft
Bāfq
Kūhbonān
Rāvar
Kūh-e Darband
2499
Tabasīn
Kāl Gūsheh
Dasht-e Lūt
Namakzār-e Shahdād
Shahdād
Kūhpāyeh
3142
Kermān
Kūh-e Seh Konj
3992
Māhān
Rafsanjān
KERMĀN
Kūh-e Hazārān
4419
Sīrjān
Bam
Zāhedān
PAKISTAN
Mashkī Chāh
Mīrjāveh
Lādīz
4042
Kūh-e Taftān
Hāmūn-i-Māshkel
Dezfūl
Shūshtar
Masjed Soleymān
Ahvāz
KHŪZESTĀN
Khorramshahr
Ābādān
Bandar-e Ma'shur
Bandar-e Emām Khomeynī
Shatt al Arab
Būbiyān
Al Kuwayt (Kuwait)
Mīnā' al Aḥmadī
Kūh-e Zard
4548
CHAHĀR MAHALL VA BAKHTĪĀRĪ
Shahr-e Kord
Qomsheh
Zāgros
KOHKĪLŪYEH VA BŪYER AḤMADĪ
Yāsūj
Kūh-e Dīnār
4431
3723
Ābādeh
Kūh-e Būl
3660
Eqlīd
Dehaj
Persepolis
Shīrāz
FĀRS
Daryācheh-ye Tashk
Neyrīz
Marv Dasht
Kāzerūn
Būshehr
BŪSHEHR
Borāzjān
Jahrom
Fasā
Lār
Bandar-e 'Abbās
HORMOZGĀN
Qeshm
Str. of Hormuz
Ra's Musandam (Oman)
Kūhhā-ye Bashākerd
Makran
SĪSTĀN VA BALŪCHESTĀN
Īrānshahr
Bampūr
Kūh-e Bazmān
3489
Bīābān-e Kermān
Hāmūn-e Jaz Mūrīān
Kūh-e Jebāl Bārez
3962
Nīkshahr
Chāh Bahār
Gavāter
Jāsk
Kūh-e Kūhrān
2163
2093
Ras Jiwani
PERSIAN GULF
Gulf of Oman
Al Khafjī
Ra's al Mish'āb
Al Jubayl
Ad Dammām
Az Zahrān (Dhahran)
Al Qaṭīf
Ra's Tannūrah
BAHRAIN
Al Manāmah
Al Muḥarraq
QATAR
Ad Dawḥah (Doha)
Al Hufūf
Al Mubarraz
Dukhān
Al Wakrah
Musay'īd
Al Jāfūrah
Bandar-e Lengeh
Ra's al Khaymah
Umm al Qaywayn
Ash Shāriqah (Sharjah)
'Ajmān
Dubayy (Dubai)
Al Fujayrah
Abū Ẓaby (Abu Dhabi)
Al 'Ayn
UNITED ARAB EMIRATES
OMAN
Ṣuḥār
Al Khābūra
Al Ḥajar al Gharbī
Tropic of Cancer
B
C
D
E
F
66
36
32
28
24
60
6
8
9
East from Greenwich
COPYRIGHT PHILIP'S

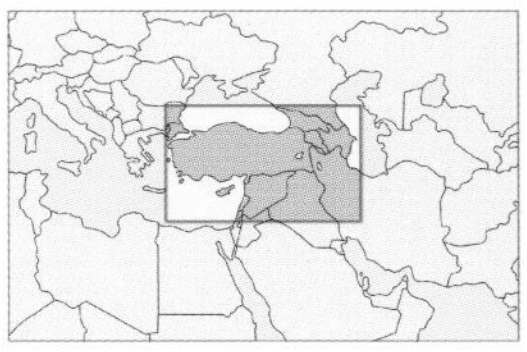

50 0 25 50 75 100 125 150 175 km

1: 4 400 000

50 0 25 50 75 100 125 miles

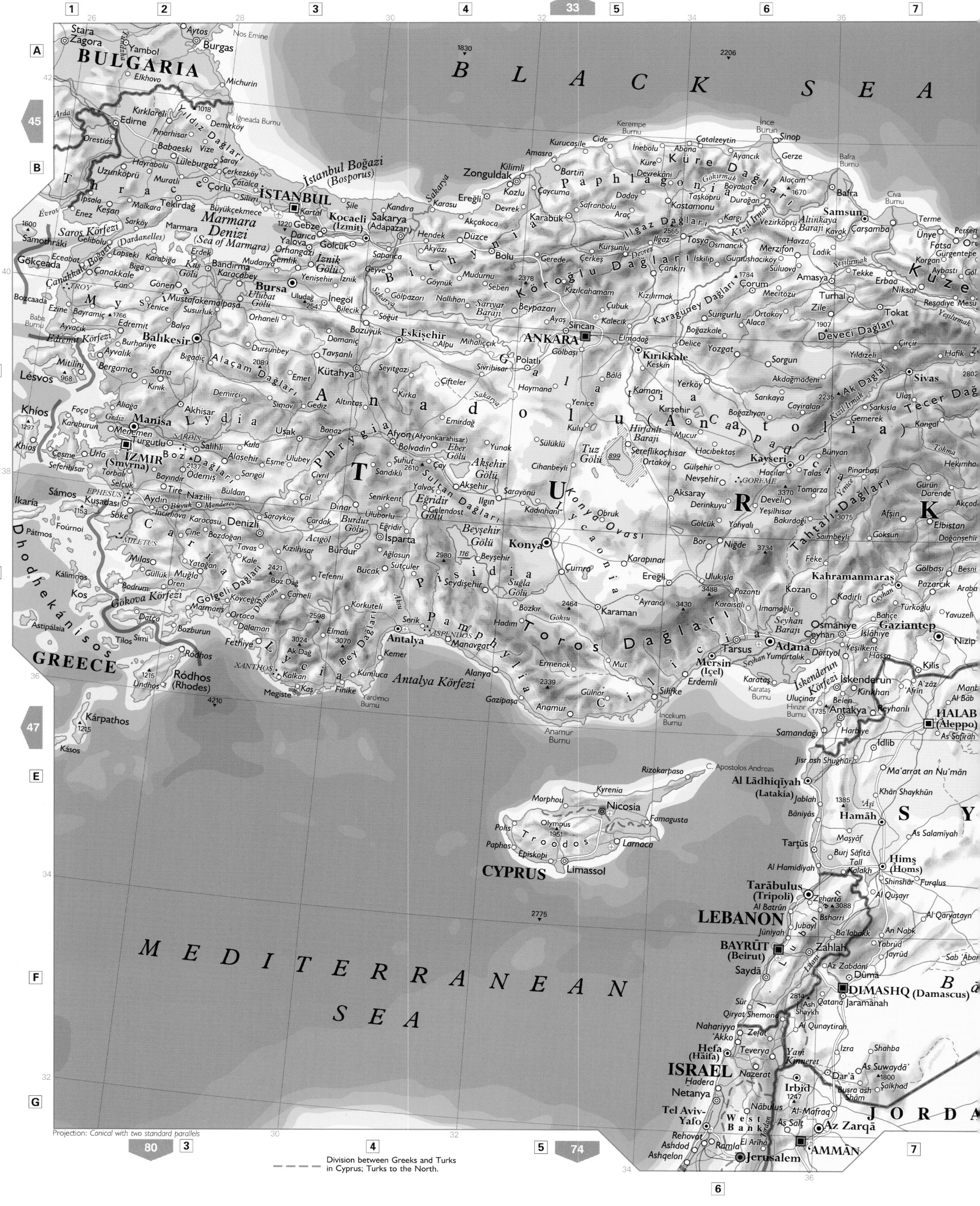

1 2 3 4 33 5 6 7

BULGARIA
BLACK SEA
İstanbul Boğazi (Bosporus)
ISTANBUL
Marmara Denizi (Sea of Marmara)
Çanakkale Boğazi (Dardanelles)
Thrace
Mysia
Lydia
Caria
Lycia
Pamphylia
Pisidia
Phrygia
Bithynia
Paphlagonia
Galatia
Lycaonia
Cilicia
Cappadocia
Anadolu (Anatolia)
TURKEY
ANKARA
Bursa
Eskişehir
Kütahya
Manisa
IZMIR (Smyrna)
Aydın
Denizli
Isparta
Antalya
Konya
Kayseri
Adana
Mersin (İçel)
Tarsus
Samsun
Sinop
Tokat
Sivas
Kahramanmaraş
Gaziantep
Kırıkkale
Zonguldak
Kastamonu
Çorum
Amasya
Yozgat
Niğde
Aksaray
Karaman
Iskenderun
Antakya
Tuz Gölü
Beyşehir Gölü
Eğridir Gölü
Burdur Gölü
Toros Dağları
Köroğlu Dağları
Küre Dağları
Antalya Körfezi
Iskenderun Körfezi
GREECE
Lésvos
Khíos
Sámos
Kos
Ródhos (Rhodes)
Kárpathos
Dhodhekánisos
CYPRUS
Nicosia
Limassol
Larnaca
Famagusta
Troodos
Kyrenia
MEDITERRANEAN SEA
SYRIA
HALAB (Aleppo)
Al Lādhiqīyah (Latakia)
Hamāh
Ḥimṣ (Homs)
DIMASHQ (Damascus)
LEBANON
BAYRŪT (Beirut)
Tarābulus (Tripoli)
Zahlah
Ṣaydā
ISRAEL
Hefa (Haifa)
Tel Aviv-Yafo
Jerusalem
West Bank
JORDAN
AMMĀN
Az Zarqā
Irbid

45
47

Projection: Conical with two standard parallels

80 3 4 5 74 6 7

Division between Greeks and Turks in Cyprus; Turks to the North.

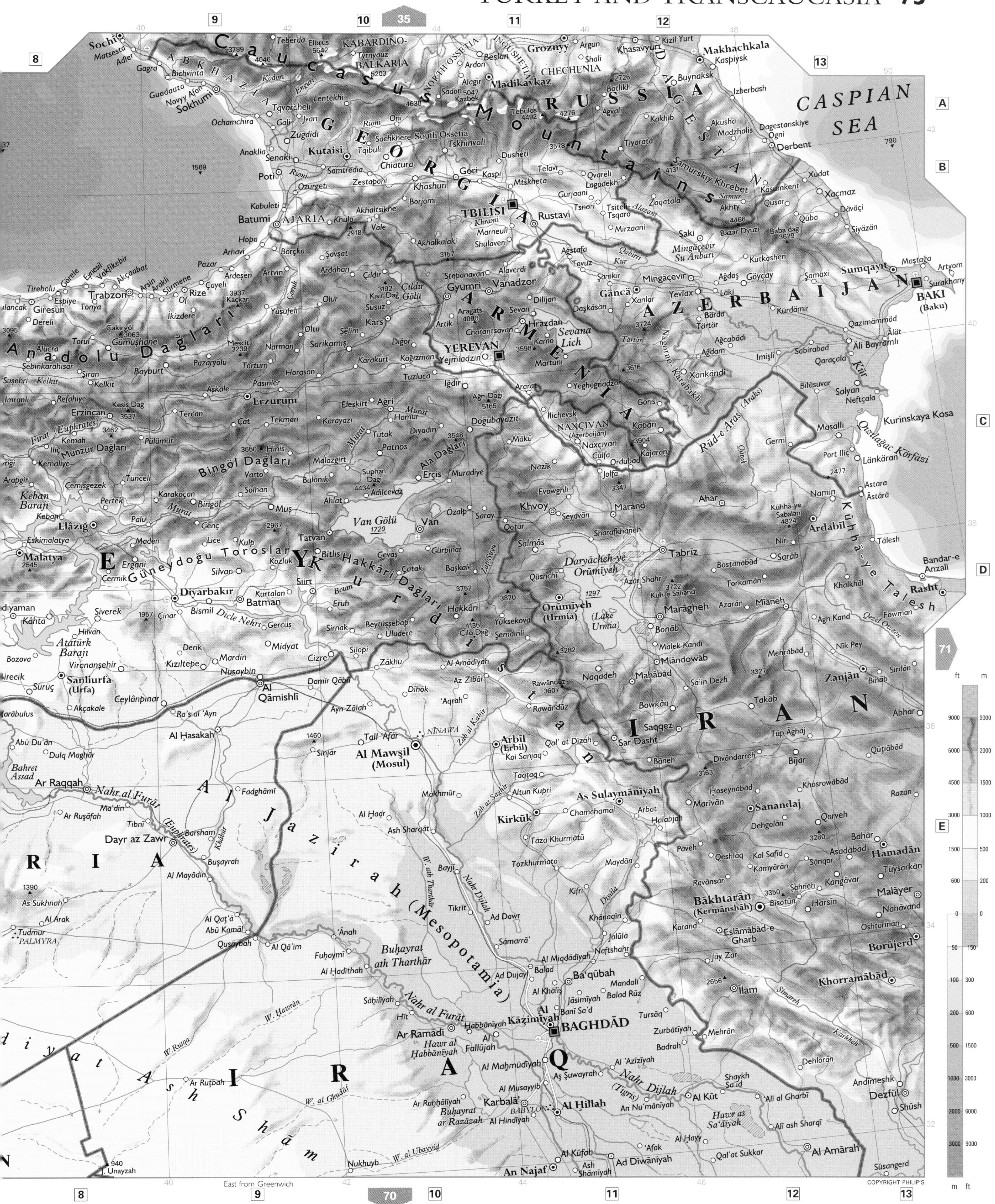

CASPIAN SEA
Caucasus Mountains
RUSSIA
GEORGIA
ARMENIA
AZERBAIJAN
TBILISI
YEREVAN
BAKI (Baku)
DAGESTAN
CHECHENIA
NORTH OSSETIA
INGUSHETIA
KABARDINO-BALKARIA
ABKHAZIA
AJARIA
South Ossetia
NAXÇIVAN (Azerbaijan)
Nagorno Karabakh
Sevana Lich
Anadolu Dağları
Güneydoğu Toroslar
Bingöl Dağları
Munzur Dağları
Hakkâri Dağları
Van Gölü
Erzurum
Trabzon
Diyarbakır
Malatya
Elâzığ
Sanlıurfa (Urfa)
Atatürk Barajı
Keban Barajı
Kurdistan
IRAN
Tabrīz
Orūmīyeh (Urmia)
Daryācheh-ye Orūmīyeh (Lake Urmia)
Ardabīl
Kūhhā-ye Tālesh
Rasht
Zanjān
Hamadān
Bākhtarān (Kermānshāh)
Sanandaj
Khorramābād
IRAQ
BAGHDĀD
Al Mawşil (Mosul)
Arbīl (Erbil)
Kirkūk
As Sulaymānīyah
Al Jazīrah (Mesopotamia)
Nahr al Furāt (Euphrates)
Nahr Dijlah (Tigris)
Buḩayrat ath Tharthār
Karbalā'
Al Ḩillah
An Najaf
Al Kūt
Al 'Amārah
Bādiyat Ash Shām
Dayr az Zawr
Ar Raqqah
Al Qāmishlī
Al Ḩasakah
Tudmur PALMYRA
East from Greenwich

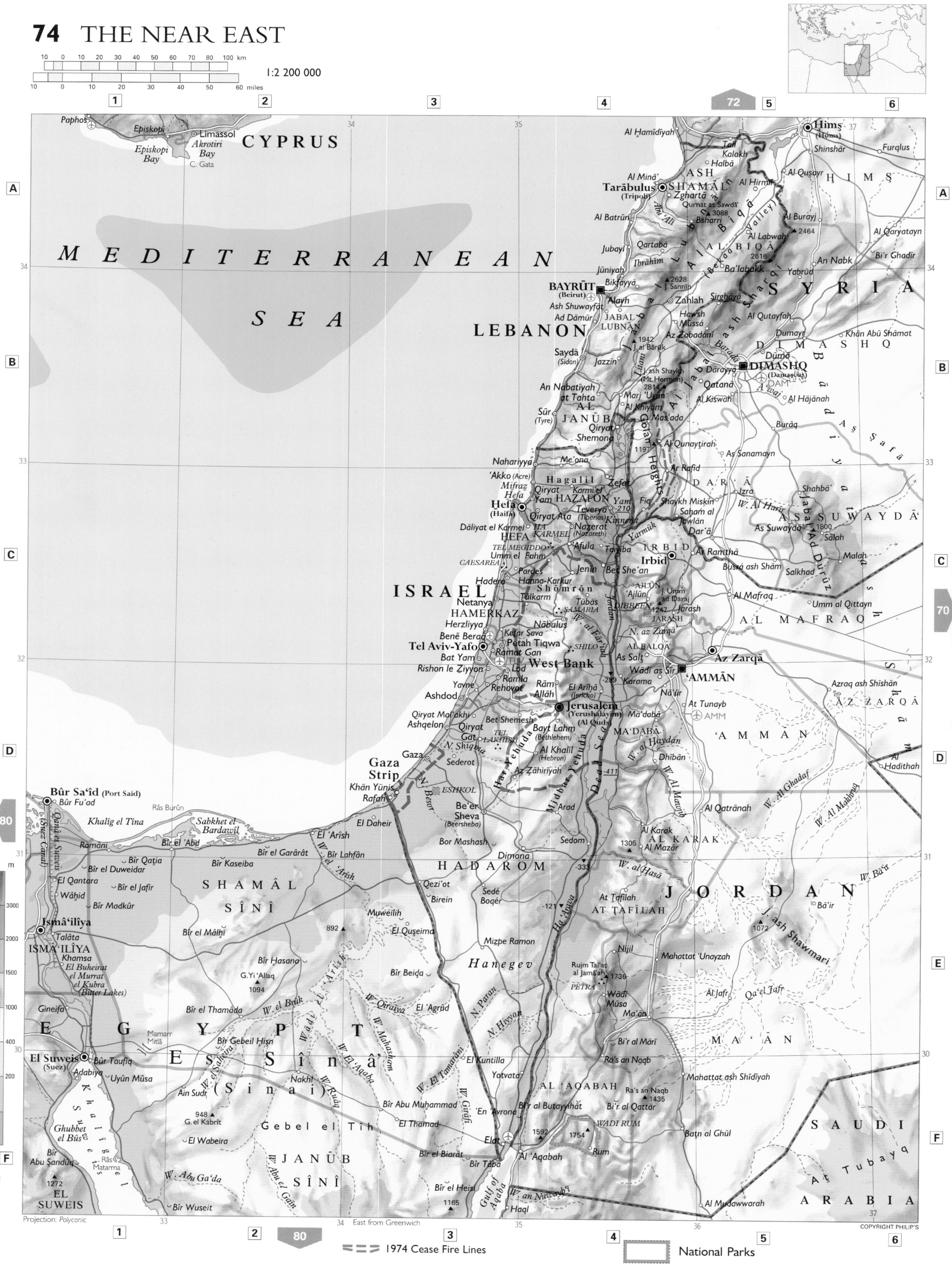
1:2 200 000
km
miles
CYPRUS
Paphos
Episkopi
Limassol
Episkopi Bay
Akrotiri Bay
C. Gata
MEDITERRANEAN
SEA
LEBANON
SYRIA
ISRAEL
JORDAN
EGYPT
SAUDI ARABIA
Al Ḩamīdīyah
Ḩimş (Homs)
Shinshār
Furqlus
Tall Kalakh
Ḩalbā
Al Minā'
Ţarābulus (Tripoli)
ASH SHAMĀL
Zghartā
Qurnat as Sawdā' 3088
Bsharri
Al Batrūn
Jubayl
Qartabā
Jūnīyah
Ibrāhīm
Bikfayyā
BAYRŪT (Beirut)
'Alayh
Ash Shuwayfāt
Ad Dāmūr
JABAL LUBNĀN
Zaḩlah
Ba'labakk
Al Hirmil
Al Qusayr
ḨIMŞ
Al Burayj
Al Qaryatayn
Al Labwah
Yabrūd
An Nabk
Bi'r Ghadīr
AL BIQĀ'
Jabal Lubnān
Al Jabal ash Sharqī
Ṣirghāyā
Ḩawsh Mūssá
Az Zabadānī
Al Quţayfah
Dumayr
Khān Abū Shāmat
DIMASHQ
Dūmā
DIMASHQ (Damascus)
Barada
Dārayyā
Qaţanā
Al Kiswah
Al Ḩājānah
Şaydā (Sidon)
Jazzīn
J. ash Shaykh (Mt. Hermon) 2814
An Nabaţīyah at Taḩtā
Marj 'Uyūn
Al Khiyām
Mas'ada
Şūr (Tyre)
AL JANŪB
Qiryat Shemona
Golan Heights
Al Qunayţirah
Buraq
Bādiyat ash Shām
Aş Şanamayn
Nahariyya
Me'ona
'Akko (Acre)
Hagalil
Zefat
Ar Rafīd
DAR'Ā
Izra
Shahbā'
Mifraz Hefa
Qiryat Yam
HAZAFON
Yam Kinneret -210
Fīq
Shaykh Miskīn
Saḩam al Jawlān
Dar'ā
Ḩefa (Haifa)
Qiryat Ata
Teverya (Tiberias)
Dāliyat el Karmel
HA KARMEL
HEFA
Nazerat (Nazareth)
Yarmūk
As Suwaydā'
AS SUWAYDĀ'
Jabal ad Durūz 1800
Şalkhad
TEL MEGIDDO
Afula
Ţaiyiba
IRBID
Irbid
Ar Ramthā
Busrá ash Shām
Umm el Fahm
CAESAREA
Malaḩ
Pardes Ḩanna-Karkur
Ḩadera
Jenin
Bet She'an
Shomron
Ţulkarm
'AJLŪN
'Ajlūn
J. Umm ad Daraj 1247
Al Mafraq
Umm al Qiţţayn
Netanya
HAMERKAZ
Ţūbās
SAMARIA
DIBBEEN
JARASH
Jarash
AL MAFRAQ
Herzliyya
Nābulus
N. az Zarqā
Benē Beraq
Kefar Sava
Petah Tiqwa
Tel Aviv-Yafo
SHILO
AL BALQĀ'
Az Zarqā
Ramat Gan
Bat Yam
West Bank
As Salţ
Wādī as Sīr
'AMMĀN
Rishon le Ziyyon
Lod
Ramla
Rām Allāh
Yavne
Reḩovot
El Arīḩā (Jericho)
-289
Karama
Nā'ūr
Azraq ash Shīshān
Ashdod
AZ ZARQĀ'
Jerusalem (Yerushalayim) (Al Quds)
At Tunayb
AMM
Qiryat Mal'akhi
Bet Shemesh
Mādabā
Ashqelon
Qiryat Gat
TEL LAKHISH
Bayt Laḩm (Bethlehem)
MA'DABĀ
'AMMAN
Al Khalīl (Hebron)
W. al Haydān
Gaza
N. Shiqma
Har Yehuda
Dhībān
Gaza Strip
Sederot
Aẓ Ẓāhirīyah
Midbar Yehuda
Dead Sea
-411
Al Ḩadīthah
Khān Yūnis
Rafah
N. Besor
ESHKOL
Be'er Sheva (Beersheba)
Arad
W. Al Mawjib
Al Qaţrānah
W. Al Ghadaf
Bûr Sa'îd (Port Said)
Bûr Fu'ad
Râs Burûn
Khalîg el Tîna
Sabkhet el Bardawîl
El 'Arîsh
El Daheir
Bor Mashash
Sedom
Al Karak
1305
Al Mazār
AL KARAK
W. Al Mukhraq
Qanât es Suweis (Suez Canal)
Români
Bîr el 'Abd
Bîr el Garârât
Bîr Lahfân
W. el 'Arîsh
Dimona
HADAROM
Bîr Qaṭia
Bîr el Duweidar
Bîr Kaseiba
-333
W. al Ḩasā
El Qantara
Bîr el Jafir
SHAMÂL SÎNÎ
Qezi'ot
Birein
Sedé Boqér
At Ţafīlah
AT ŢAFĪLAH
W. Bā'ir
Wâhid
Bîr Madkûr
-121
Bā'ir
Ismâ'ilîya
Talâta
ISMÂ'ILÎYA
Bîr el Mâlḥi
Muweilih
El Quseima
892
1072
J. ash Shawmarī
Khamsa
El Buheirat el Murrat el Kubra (Bitter Lakes)
Bîr Ḩasana
Miẕpe Ramon
Hanegev
Nijil
Mahattat 'Unayzah
G. Yi'Allaq 1094
Bîr Beiḍa
Rujm Tal'at al Jamā'ah 1736
PETRA
Wādī Mūsá
Ma'ān
Al Jafr
Qa'el Jafr
Gineifa
Bîr el Thamâda
W. el Brûk
W. Qurayya
El 'Agrûd
N. Paran
Wadi el 'Arîsh
Mamarr Mitlâ
Bîr Gebeil Ḩiṣn
W. Mahashsham
N. Ḩiyyon
MA'ĀN
Bi'r al Mārī
El Suweis (Suez)
Bûr Taufiq
W. el Sahtira
W. El 'Aqaba
El Kuntilla
Ra's an Naqb
Adabiya
'Uyûn Mûsa
Nakhl
W. Rûag
W. El Tamarâni
Yotvata
AL 'AQABAH
Mahattat ash Shīdīyah
Khalîg el Suweis
Ain Sudr
(Sinai)
Sînâ'
Bîr Abu Muḥammad
W. Girâfi
'En Avrona
Bi'r al Butayyihāt
Bi'r al Qattār
Ra's an Naqb 1435
948 G. el Kabrît
Gebel el Tîh
El Thamad
WADI RUM
Baţn al Ghūl
1592
1754
Ghubbet el Bûs
El Wabeira
Elat
Rum
Bîr Abu Sandûq
JANÛB SÎNÎ
Bîr el Biarât
Bîr Tâba
Al 'Aqabah
At Tubayq
Râs Matarma
W. Abu Ga'da
W. Abu el Gain
Bîr el Heisi
Gulf of Aqaba
W. an Nuwaybi'
1272
EL SUWEIS
Bîr Wuseit
1165
Ḩaql
Al Mudawwarah
Projection: Polyconic
East from Greenwich
COPYRIGHT PHILIP'S
1974 Cease Fire Lines
National Parks
72
70
80

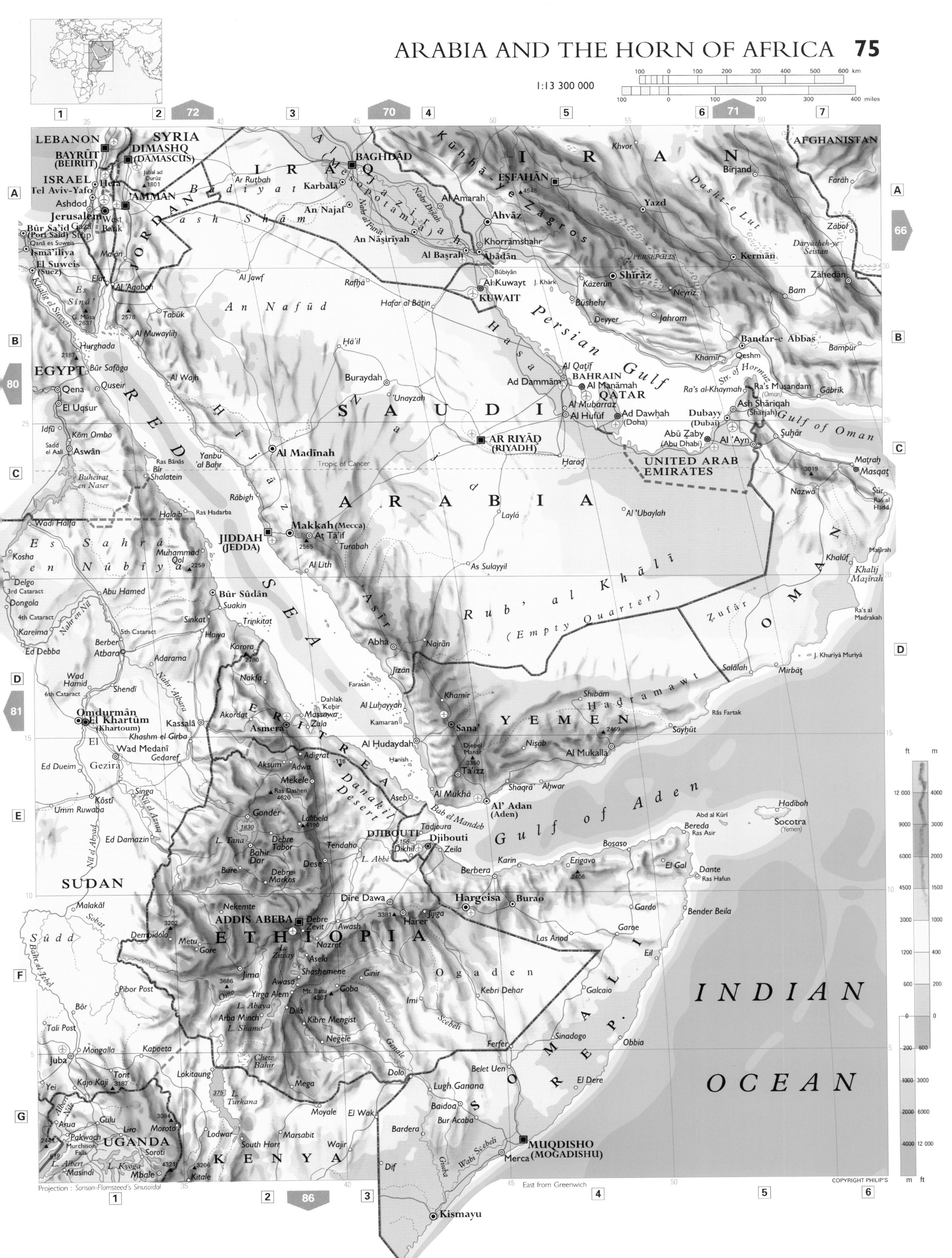
1:13 300 000
km
miles
LEBANON
SYRIA
DIMASHQ (DAMASCUS)
BAYRŪT (BEIRUT)
ISRAEL
Tel Aviv-Yafo
Ashdod
Jerusalem
West Bank
Gaza Strip
'AMMĀN
JORDAN
Bûr Sa'îd (Port Said)
Ismâ'iliya
El Suweis (Suez)
Elat
Al 'Aqabah
Ma'ān
IRAQ
BAGHDĀD
Karbalā'
An Najaf
Ar Rutbah
Bādiyat ash Shām
Al Jawf
An Nafūd
Al 'Amarah
An Nāşirīyah
Al Başrah
Ābādān
Khorramshahr
Ahvāz
IRAN
EŞFAHĀN
Yazd
Kermān
Shīrāz
Kāzerūn
Būshehr
Jahrom
Bandar-e Abbās
Zāhedān
Bīrjand
AFGHANISTAN
Farāh
Zābol
Dasht-e Lut
Kūhhā-ye Zāgros
Al Kuwayt
KUWAIT
Persian Gulf
Ḩafar al Bāţin
Ḩā'il
Buraydah
'Unayzah
Tabūk
Al Muwaylih
Al Wajh
SAUDI ARABIA
AR RIYĀD (RIYADH)
Al Madīnah
Yanbu 'al Baḩr
Tropic of Cancer
Rābigh
JIDDAH (JEDDA)
Makkah (Mecca)
Aţ Ţā'if
Al Līth
As Sulayyil
Laylá
Ad Dammām
BAHRAIN
Al Manāmah
QATAR
Ad Dawḩah (Doha)
Al Hufūf
Al Mubarraz
Dubayy (Dubai)
Abū Zaby (Abu Dhabi)
UNITED ARAB EMIRATES
Ash Shāriqah (Sharjah)
Ra's al-Khaymah
Str. of Hormuz
Gulf of Oman
Masqat
Maţraḩ
Şuḩār
OMAN
Nazwá
Rub' al Khālī (Empty Quarter)
Şalālah
Mirbāţ
Ẓufār
Abhā
Najrān
Jīzān
YEMEN
Şana'
Al Ḩudaydah
Ta'izz
Al Mukhā
Al' Adan (Aden)
Al Mukallā
Ḩaḑramawt
Gulf of Aden
Socotra
Hadiboh
EGYPT
Hurghada
Qena
Qusein
El Uqsur
Aswân
Buheirat en Naser
Wadi Halfa
Es Sahrâ en Nûbîya
RED SEA
Bûr Sûdân
Suakin
Atbara
Omdurmân
El Khartûm (Khartoum)
Kassalâ
Wad Medanî
Gedaref
Kôstî
SUDAN
Malakâl
Sûdd
Juba
ERITREA
Asmera
Massawa
Aseb
DJIBOUTI
Djibouti
Bab el Mandeb
ETHIOPIA
ADDIS ABEBA
Gonder
L. Tana
Bahir Dar
Dese
Dire Dawa
Harer
Jima
Awasa
Ogaden
Hargeisa
Berbera
Bosaso
SOMALI REP.
Galcaio
MUQDISHO (MOGADISHU)
Merca
Kismayu
Baidoa
KENYA
L. Turkana
UGANDA
Gulu
INDIAN OCEAN
Projection: Sanson-Flamsteed's Sinusoidal
East from Greenwich
COPYRIGHT PHILIP'S

1:37 300 000

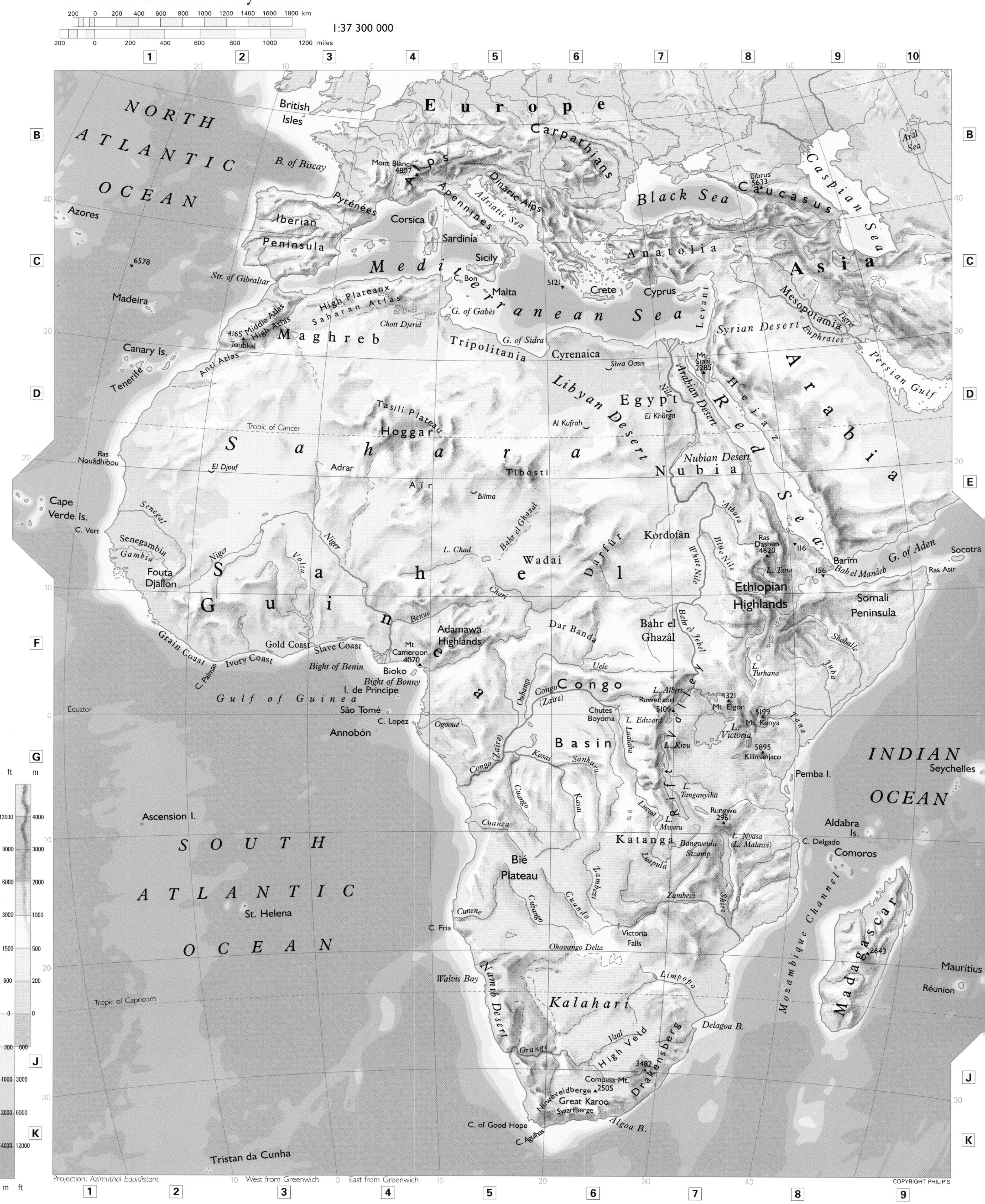

Projection: *Azimuthal Equidistant*

1:37 300 000
NORTH ATLANTIC OCEAN
SOUTH ATLANTIC OCEAN
INDIAN OCEAN
Mediterranean Sea
Black Sea
Caspian Sea
Red Sea
Sahara
ALGERIA
LIBYA
EGYPT
MOROCCO
WESTERN SAHARA
MAURITANIA
MALI
NIGER
CHAD
SUDAN
ETHIOPIA
SOMALI REP.
KENYA
UGANDA
TANZANIA
CONGO (DEM. REP. OF THE)
CONGO
GABON
CAMEROON
CENTRAL AFRICAN REP.
NIGERIA
BENIN
TOGO
GHANA
IVORY COAST
BURKINA FASO
GUINEA
SIERRA LEONE
LIBERIA
SENEGAL
GAMBIA
GUINEA-BISSAU
ANGOLA
ZAMBIA
ZIMBABWE
MOZAMBIQUE
MALAWI
NAMIBIA
BOTSWANA
SOUTH AFRICA
LESOTHO
SWAZ.
MADAGASCAR
ERITREA
DJIBOUTI
SAUDI ARABIA
YEMEN
Tropic of Cancer
Equator
Tropic of Capricorn
Projection: Azimuthal Equidistant
West from Greenwich
East from Greenwich
COPYRIGHT PHILIP'S
Dakar Capital Cities

1:13 300 000

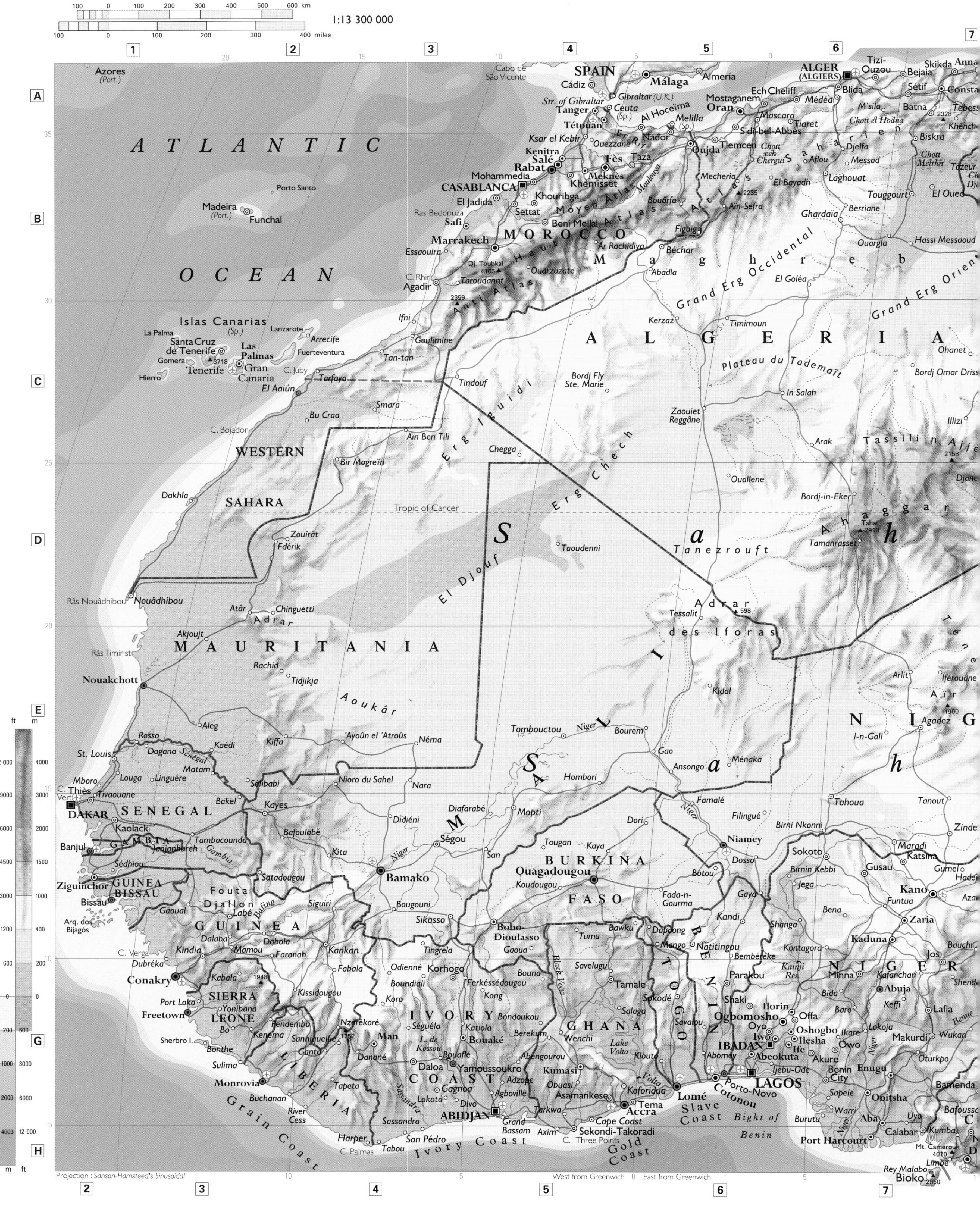
100 0 100 200 300 400 500 600 km
100 0 100 200 300 400 miles
ATLANTIC
OCEAN
Azores (Port.)
Madeira (Port.)
Porto Santo
Funchal
Islas Canarias (Sp.)
La Palma
Lanzarote
Arrecife
Fuerteventura
Santa Cruz de Tenerife
Las Palmas
Gran Canaria
Gomera
Tenerife
Hierro
3718
SPAIN
Cádiz
Málaga
Almería
Cabo de São Vicente
Str. of Gibraltar
Gibraltar (U.K.)
Tanger
Ceuta (Sp.)
Tétouan
Al Hoceïma
Melilla (Sp.)
Nador
Er Rif
Ksar el Kebir
Ouezzane
Kenitra
Salé
Rabat
Fès
Taza
Oujda
Meknès
Mohammedia
CASABLANCA
Khemisset
El Jadida
Khouribga
Settat
Ras Beddouza
Safi
Beni Mellal
Moyen Atlas
Moulouya
Haut Atlas
Marrakech
MOROCCO
Essaouira
Dj. Toubkal 4165
Ouarzazate
Ar Rachidiya
Taroudannt
C. Rhir
Agadir
Anti Atlas
2359
Ifni
Goulimine
Tan-tan
C. Juby
Tarfaya
El Aaiún
Smara
Bu Craa
C. Bojador
Ain Ben Tili
WESTERN
SAHARA
Bir Mogreïn
Dakhla
Tropic of Cancer
Zouîrât
Fdérik
Râs Nouâdhibou
Nouâdhibou
Atâr
Chinguetti
Adrar
Akjoujt
MAURITANIA
Râs Timirist
Rachid
Tidjikja
Nouakchott
Aoukâr
Aleg
Rosso
Kaédi
Kiffa
'Ayoûn el 'Atroûs
Néma
St. Louis
Dagana
Sénégal
Matam
Louga
Linguére
Mboro
C. Vert
Thiès
Tivaouane
DAKAR
SENEGAL
Bakel
Sélibabi
Nioro du Sahel
Nara
Kayes
Kaolack
Banjul
GAMBIA
Janjanbureh
Tambacounda
Gambia
Sédhiou
Bafoulabé
Kita
Ziguinchor
GUINEA-BISSAU
Bissau
Arq. dos Bijagós
Satadougou
Fouta Djallon
Labé
Bafing
Gaoual
Siguiri
GUINEA
Dalaba
Dabola
Mamou
Faranah
Kankan
Kindia
C. Verga
Dubréka
Conakry
Kabala
1948
SIERRA LEONE
Port Loko
Freetown
Yonibana
Bo
Kenema
Pendembu
Sherbro I.
Bonthe
Sulima
Monrovia
LIBERIA
Buchanan
River Cess
Harper
C. Palmas
Grain Coast
Bamako
Niger
Ségou
Didiéni
Diafarabé
Mopti
Bougouni
Sikasso
Tingrela
Kissidougou
Fabala
Odienné
Boundiali
Korhogo
Koro
Nzérékoré
1752
Man
Danané
Séguéla
Katiola
Bouaké
L. de Kossou
Daloa
Bouaflé
Yamoussoukro
IVORY COAST
Gagnoa
Divo
Lakota
Sassandra
Tapeta
Tabou
San Pédro
Ivory Coast
ABIDJAN
Grand Bassam
Agboville
Adzopé
Abengourou
Bondoukou
Ferkéssédougou
Kong
Bouna
Berekum
Kumasi
Obuasi
Asamankese
Tarkwa
Axim
C. Three Points
Sekondi-Takoradi
Cape Coast
Accra
Tema
Koforidua
Gold Coast
GHANA
Wenchi
Lake Volta
Volta
Kloutu
Salaga
Tamale
Savelugu
Black Volta
Tumu
Bawku
Bobo-Dioulasso
Gaoua
Koudougou
Ouagadougou
BURKINA FASO
Tougan
Kaya
San
Dori
Fada-n-Gourma
Dapaong
Mango
Natitingou
TOGO
Sokodé
Savalou
BENIN
Bembéréke
Parakou
Kandi
Lomé
Cotonou
Porto-Novo
Abomey
Slave Coast
Bight of Benin
Tombouctou
Bourem
Gao
Ansongo
Ménaka
Hombori
MALI
Taoudenni
El Djouf
Erg Iguidi
Erg Chech
Chegga
Tindouf
Tanezrouft
Adrar des Iforas
Tessalit
598
Kidal
SAHARA
Famalé
Filingué
Niamey
Dosso
Botou
Gaya
Birni Nkonni
Tahoua
Tanout
Zinder
Maradi
Katsina
Sokoto
Gusau
Birnin Kebbi
Jega
Kano
Funtua
Zaria
Bena
Kaduna
Shanga
Kontagora
Kainji Res.
Minna
Kafanchan
Abuja
Jos
Bauchi
Bida
Keffi
Lafia
Shaki
Ilorin
Ogbomosho
Oyo
Offa
Iwo
Oshogbo
Ilesha
Ife
Ikare
Lokoja
IBADAN
Abeokuta
Owo
Akure
Ijebu-Ode
LAGOS
Benin City
Enugu
Makurdi
Wukari
Otukpo
Sapele
Onitsha
Warri
Aba
Uyo
Burutu
Calabar
Port Harcourt
Bamenda
Bafoussa
Kumba
Mt. Cameroun 4070
Limbe
Rey Malabo
Bioko
2850
NIGERIA
NIGER
Agadez
Aïr
1900
Arlit
Iférouâne
I-n-Gall
ALGERIA
Ohanet
Bordj Omar Driss
In Salah
Plateau du Tademaït
Zaouiet Reggâne
Bordj Fly Ste. Marie
Kerzaz
Timimoun
Grand Erg Occidental
Grand Erg Oriental
Maghreb
Abadla
Béchar
Figuig
El Goléa
Ouargla
Hassi Messaoud
Ghardaïa
Berriane
Touggourt
El Oued
Laghouat
El Bayadh
Aflou
Messad
Djelfa
Chott ech Chergui
Saharien Atlas
Aïn-Sefra
2235
Mecheria
Tlemcen
Sidi-bel-Abbès
Tiaret
Mascara
Oran
Mostaganem
Ech Cheliff
Médéa
ALGER (ALGIERS)
Blida
Tizi-Ouzou
Bejaïa
Skikda
Annaba
Sétif
Constantine
M'sila
Batna
Tebessa
Chott el Hodna
2328
Khenchela
Biskra
Chott Melrhir
Tozeur
Illizi
Arak
Tassili n Ajjer
2158
Djanet
Ouallene
Bordj-in-Eker
Ahaggar
Tahat 2918
Tamanrasset
Ténéré
Projection : Sanson-Flamsteed's Sinusoidal
West from Greenwich 0 East from Greenwich
ft m
12 000 4000
9000 3000
6000 2000
4500 1500
3000 1000
1200 400
600 200
0 0
200 600
1000 3000
2000 6000
4000 12 000
m ft

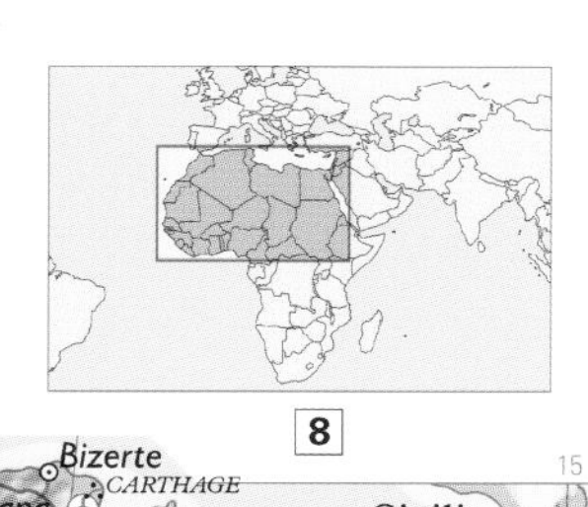

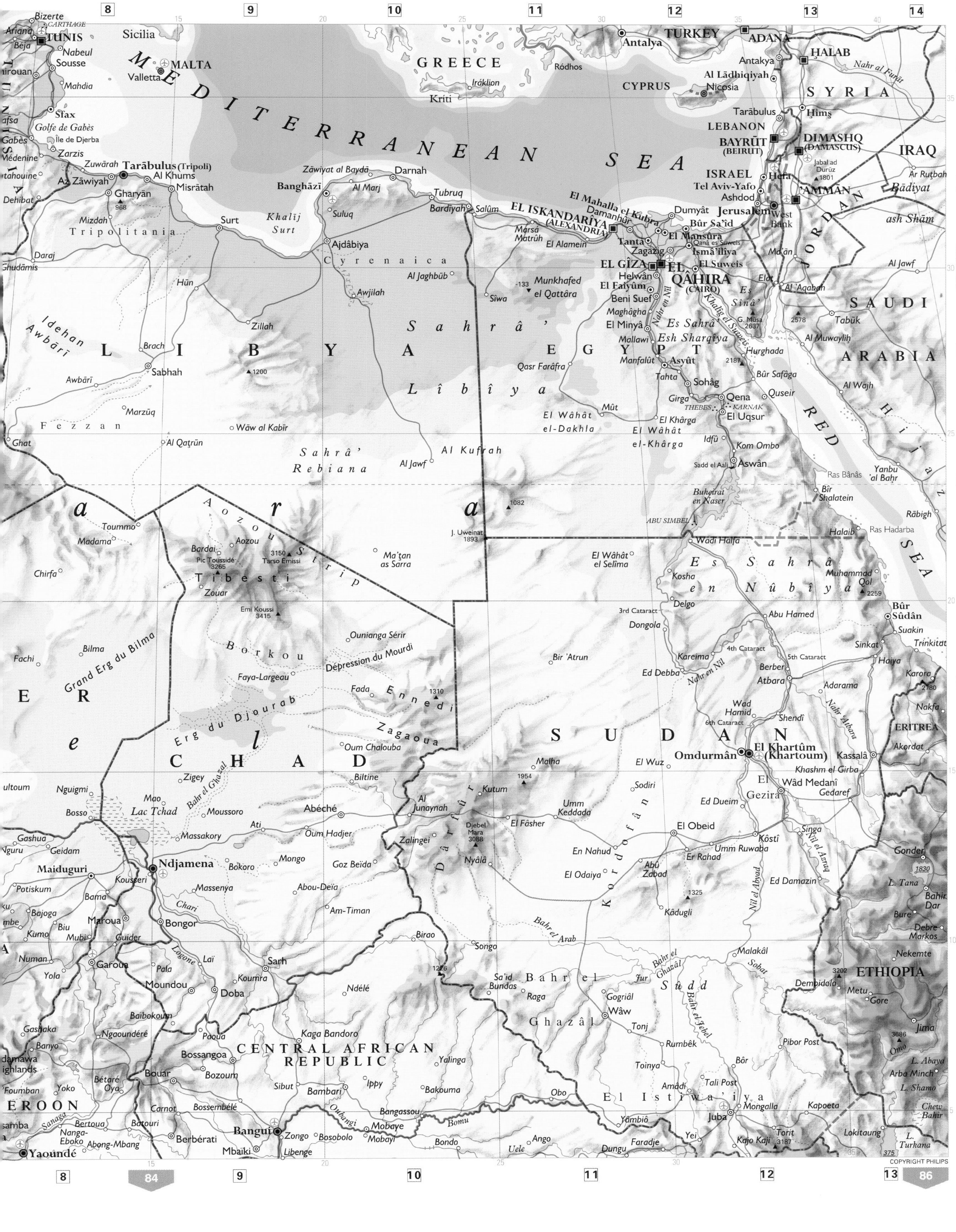

MEDITERRANEAN SEA
Sicilia
MALTA
Valletta
GREECE
Kríti
Iráklion
Ródhos
TURKEY
Antalya
ADANA
CYPRUS
Nicosia
Antakya
HALAB
Al Lādhiqiyah
SYRIA
Nahr al Furāt
Tarābulus
Hims
LEBANON
BAYRŪT (BEIRUT)
DIMASHQ (DAMASCUS)
IRAQ
Jabal ad Durūz
ISRAEL
Tel Aviv-Yafo
Haifa
Ashdod
Jerusalem
West Bank
'AMMĀN
JORDAN
Ar Rutbah
Bādiyat ash Shām
Bizerte
CARTHAGE
Ariana
TUNIS
Béja
Nabeul
Sousse
Kairouan
Mahdia
Sfax
Golfe de Gabès
Gabès
Île de Djerba
Médenine
Zarzis
Tataouine
Zuwārah
Az Zāwiyah
Tarābulus (Tripoli)
Al Khums
Misrātah
Gharyān
Dehibat
Mizdah
Tripolitania
Daraj
Ghudāmis
Surt
Khalīj Surt
Zāwiyat al Baydā
Darnah
Banghāzī
Al Marj
Tubruq
Bardiyah
Salûm
Suluq
Ajdābiya
Cyrenaica
Al Jaghbūb
Awjilah
Hūn
Zillah
Idehan Awbārī
Brach
LIBYA
Sabhah
Awbārī
Marzūq
Fezzan
Ghat
Wāw al Kabīr
Al Qaṭrūn
Sahrâ' Rebiana
Al Jawf
Al Kufrah
Sahrâ' Lîbîya
EL ISKANDARÎYA (ALEXANDRIA)
El Mahalla el Kubra
Damanhûr
Marsâ Matrûh
El Alamein
Dumyât
Bûr Sa'îd
El Mansûra
Tanta
Zagazig
Ismâ'ilîya
Qana es Suweis
EL GÎZA
EL QÂHIRA (CAIRO)
El Suweis
Siwa
Munkhafed el Qattâra
Helwân
El Faiyûm
Beni Suef
Maghâgha
El Minyâ
Mallawi
Nahr en Nil
Khalîg el Suweis
Es Sahrâ Esh Sharqîya
Es Sînâ'
G. Mûsa
Elat
Al 'Aqabah
EGYPT
Manfalût
Asyût
Qasr Farâfra
Tahta
Sohâg
Girga
Qena
Quseir
THEBES
KARNAK
El Uqsur
Hurghada
Bûr Safâga
Mût
El Wâhât el-Dakhla
El Khârga
El Wâhât el-Khârga
Idfû
Kom Ombo
Aswân
Sadd el Aali
Buheirat en Naser
ABU SIMBEL
SAUDI ARABIA
Tabūk
Al Muwaylih
Al Wajh
Hijaz
RED SEA
Ras Bânâs
Bîr Shalatein
Yanbu 'al Bahr
Rābigh
Halaib
Ras Hadarba
Wadi Halfa
J. Uweinat
Sahara
Tummo
Madama
Aozou Strip
Aozou
Bardai
Pic Toussidé
Tarso Emissi
Tibesti
Zouar
Emi Koussi
Chirfa
Ma'tan as Sarra
El Wâhât el Selîma
Es Sahrâ en Nûbîya
Kosha
Delgo
Muhammad Qol
3rd Cataract
Dongola
Abu Hamed
Bûr Sûdân
Suakin
Trinkitat
Sinkat
Haiya
Bir 'Atrun
Kareima
4th Cataract
5th Cataract
Berber
Atbara
Ed Debba
Karora
Adarama
Nakfa
Wad Hamid
Shendi
Nahr Atbara
6th Cataract
ERITREA
Akordat
SUDAN
Omdurmân
El Khartûm (Khartoum)
Kassalâ
Khashm el Girba
El Wuz
Sodiri
El Gezira
Wâd Medanî
Gedaref
Ed Dueim
Ounianga Sérir
Bilma
Grand Erg du Bilma
Fachi
Borkou
Dépression du Mourdi
Faya-Largeau
Fada
Ennedi
Erg du Djourab
Zagaoua
Oum Chalouba
NIGER
CHAD
Biltine
Zigey
Bahr el Ghazal
Malha
Ngulmi
Mao
Lac Tchad
Moussoro
Abéché
Al Junaynah
Kutum
Umm Keddada
Bosso
Ati
Oum Hadjer
Djebel Mara
El Fâsher
El Obeid
Kôstî
Singa
Gashua
Nguru
Geidam
Massakory
Zalingei
Dârfûr
En Nahud
Umm Ruwaba
Nil el Azraq
Gonder
Maiduguri
Ndjamena
Bokoro
Mongo
Goz Beïda
Nyâlâ
Er Rahad
Abû Zabad
Ed Damazin
L. Tana
Kordofân
El Odaiya
Nil el Abyad
Kousseri
Potiskum
Massenya
Abou-Deïa
Bahir Dar
Bama
Am-Timan
Kâdugli
Bure
Bajoga
Chari
Biu
Maroua
Bongor
Debre Markos
Kumo
Mubi
Guider
Bahr el Arab
Biroa
Songo
Numan
Garoua
Logone
Lai
Sarh
Malakâl
Nekemte
Yola
Pala
Koumra
Sa'id Bundas
Bahr el Ghazâl
Sobat
ETHIOPIA
Moundou
Doba
Ndélé
Raga
Jur
Sûdd
Dembidolo
Metu
Gore
Baïbokoum
Gogrial
Wâw
Bahr el Jebel
Ngaoundéré
Paoua
Kaga Bandoro
Tonj
Rumbek
Pibor Post
Jima
Gashaka
Banyo
Adamawa Highlands
Bossangoa
CENTRAL AFRICAN REPUBLIC
Yalinga
Bôr
Omo
L. Abaya
Arba Minch
Bouar
Bozoum
Toinya
Bétaré Oya
Foumban
Yoko
Sibut
Bambari
Ippy
Bakouma
Obo
Amâdi
Tali Post
L. Chamo
CAMEROON
Carnot
Bossembélé
El Istiwa'iya
Mongalla
Kapoeta
Chew Bahir
Bangassou
Bomu
Yambio
Juba
Sanaga
Bertoua
Batouri
Oubangui
Mobaye
Nanga-Eboko
Abong-Mbang
Berbérati
Bangui
Zongo
Bosobolo
Mobayi
Bondo
Ango
Faradje
Yei
Torit
Kajo Kaji
Lokitaung
L. Turkana
Yaoundé
Mbaïki
Libenge
Uele
Dungu

75
84
86

50 0 50 100 150 200 250 300 km

1:7 100 000

50 0 50 100 150 200 miles

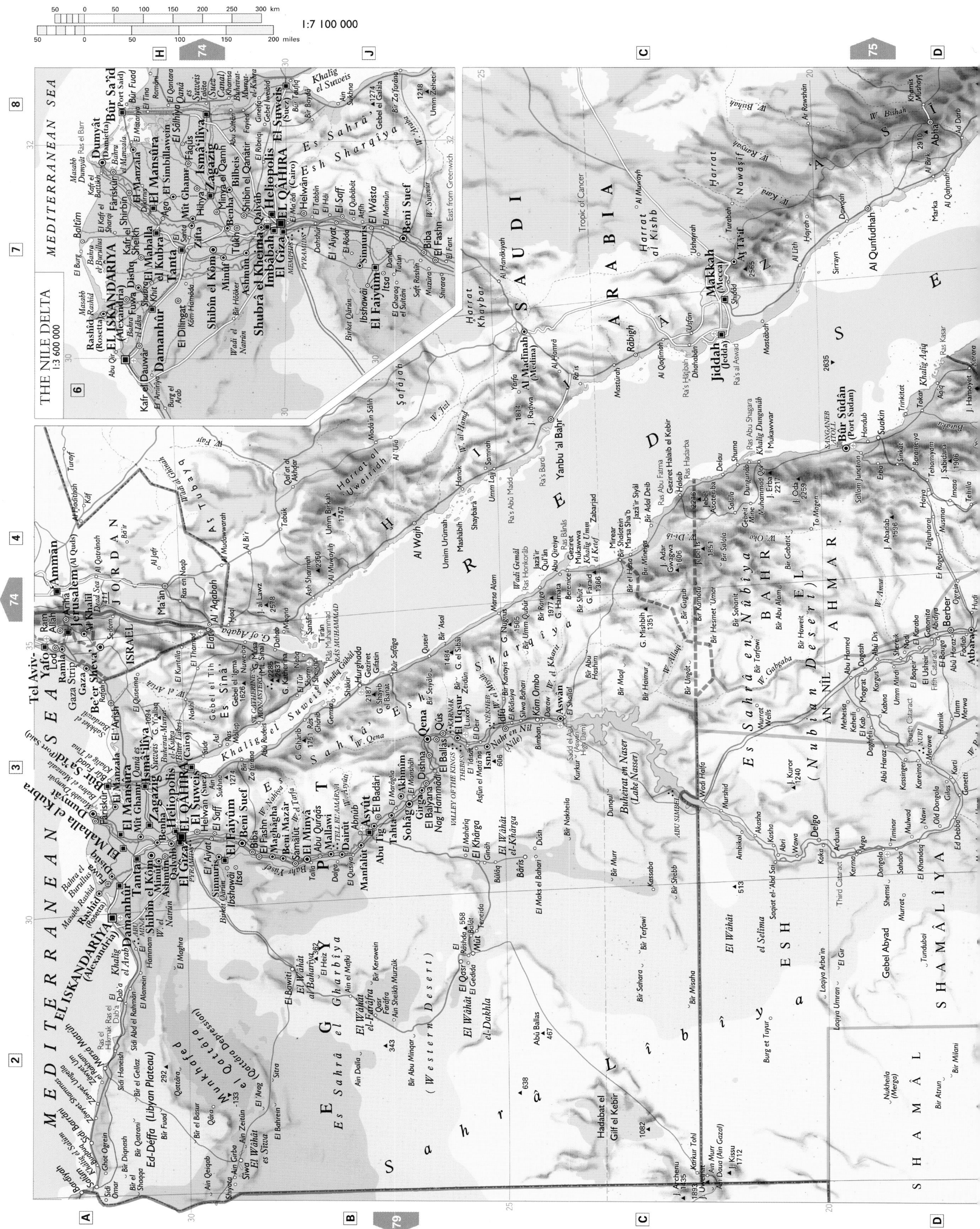

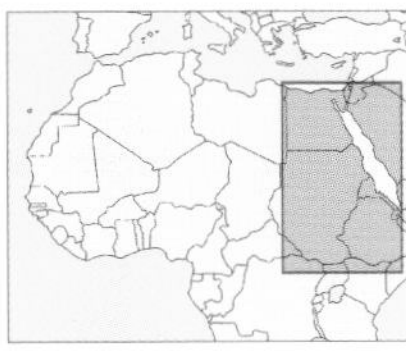

National Parks

Nature Reserves and Game Reserves

∴ UNESCO World Heritage Sites

m	ft
4000	12 000
3000	9000
2000	6000
1500	4500
1000	3000
400	1200
200	600
0	0
200	600

Projection: Lambert's Equivalent Azimuthal

1:7 100 000

MAURITANIA
SENEGAL
GAMBIA
GUINEA-BISSAU
GUINEA
SIERRA LEONE
LIBERIA
IVORY COAST
S A H A R A
ATLANTIC OCEAN
Grain Coast
Ivory Coast
Nouakchott
Dakar
Banjul
Bissau
Conakry
Freetown
Monrovia
Bamako
Abidjan
Yamoussoukro
Projection : Lambert's Equivalent Azimuthal
West from Greenwich

78

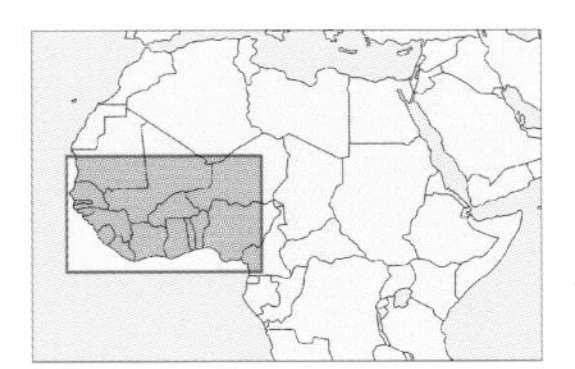

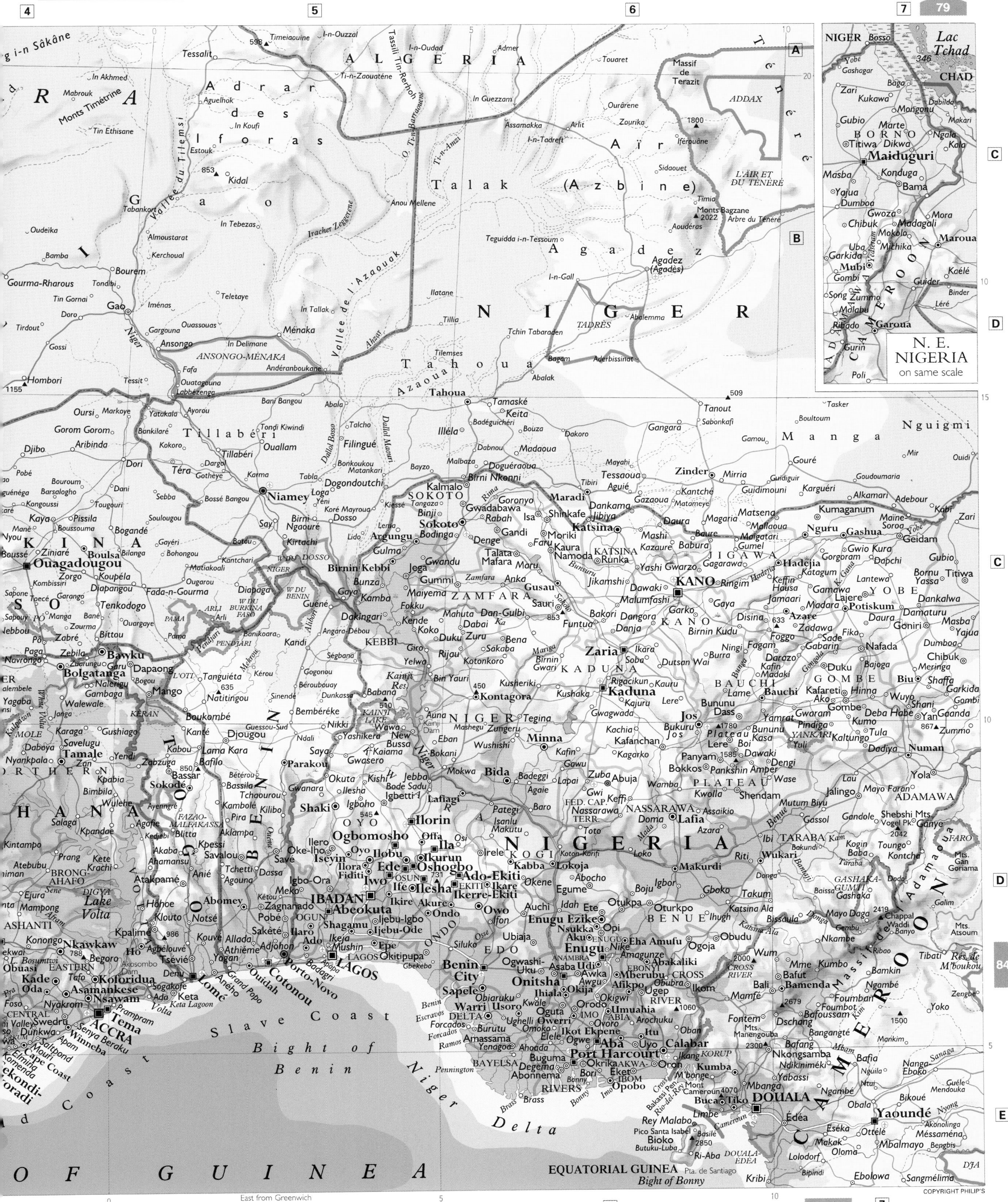

N. E. NIGERIA
on same scale

East from Greenwich

National Parks

Nature Reserves and Game Reserves

∴ UNESCO World Heritage Sites

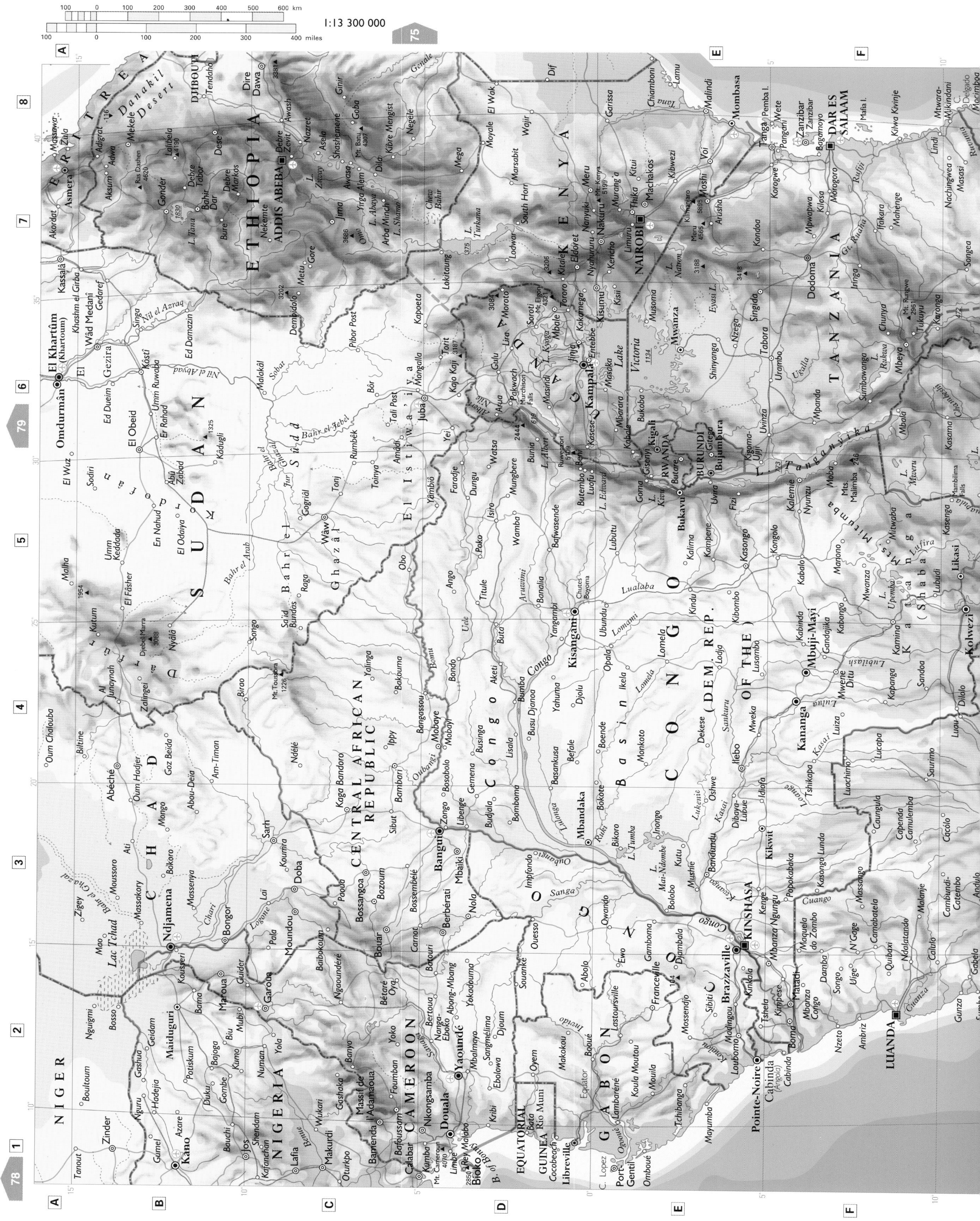
100 0 100 200 300 400 500 600 km
100 0 100 200 300 400 miles
1:13 300 000
75
79
78
ERITREA
DJIBOUTI
ETHIOPIA
ADDIS ABEBA
KENYA
NAIROBI
UGANDA
Kampala
Lake Victoria
TANZANIA
DAR ES SALAAM
SUDAN
El Khartûm (Khartoum)
Omdurmân
Juba
CHAD
Ndjamena
Lac Tchad
CENTRAL AFRICAN REPUBLIC
Bangui
NIGER
NIGERIA
Kano
CAMEROON
Yaoundé
Douala
EQUATORIAL GUINEA
Rio Muni
GABON
Libreville
CONGO
Brazzaville
CONGO (DEM. REP. OF THE)
KINSHASA
Kisangani
RWANDA
Kigali
BURUNDI
Bujumbura
L. Tanganyika
Cabinda (Angola)
LUANDA
Mombasa
Zanzibar
Congo Basin

ATLANTIC OCEAN
INDIAN OCEAN
Skeleton Coast
Namib Desert
Kalahari
NAMIBIA
BOTSWANA
SOUTH AFRICA
ZIMBABWE
ZAMBIA
MOZAMBIQUE
LESOTHO
SWAZI-LAND
MADAGASCAR
on same scale
Windhoek
Gaborone
PRETORIA (Tshwane)
JOHANNESBURG
Bloemfontein
Maseru
MAPUTO
HARARE
Lusaka
Bulawayo
DURBAN (eThekwini)
CAPE TOWN
Port Elizabeth
East London
Beira
Antananarivo
Toamasina
Walvis Bay
Swakopmund
Lüderitz
Livingstone
Victoria Falls
Caprivi Strip
Okavango Delta
Tropic of Capricorn
Cape of Good Hope
Cape Agulhas
Table Bay
Projection : Sanson-Flamsteed's Sinusoidal
East from Greenwich
COPYRIGHT PHILIPS

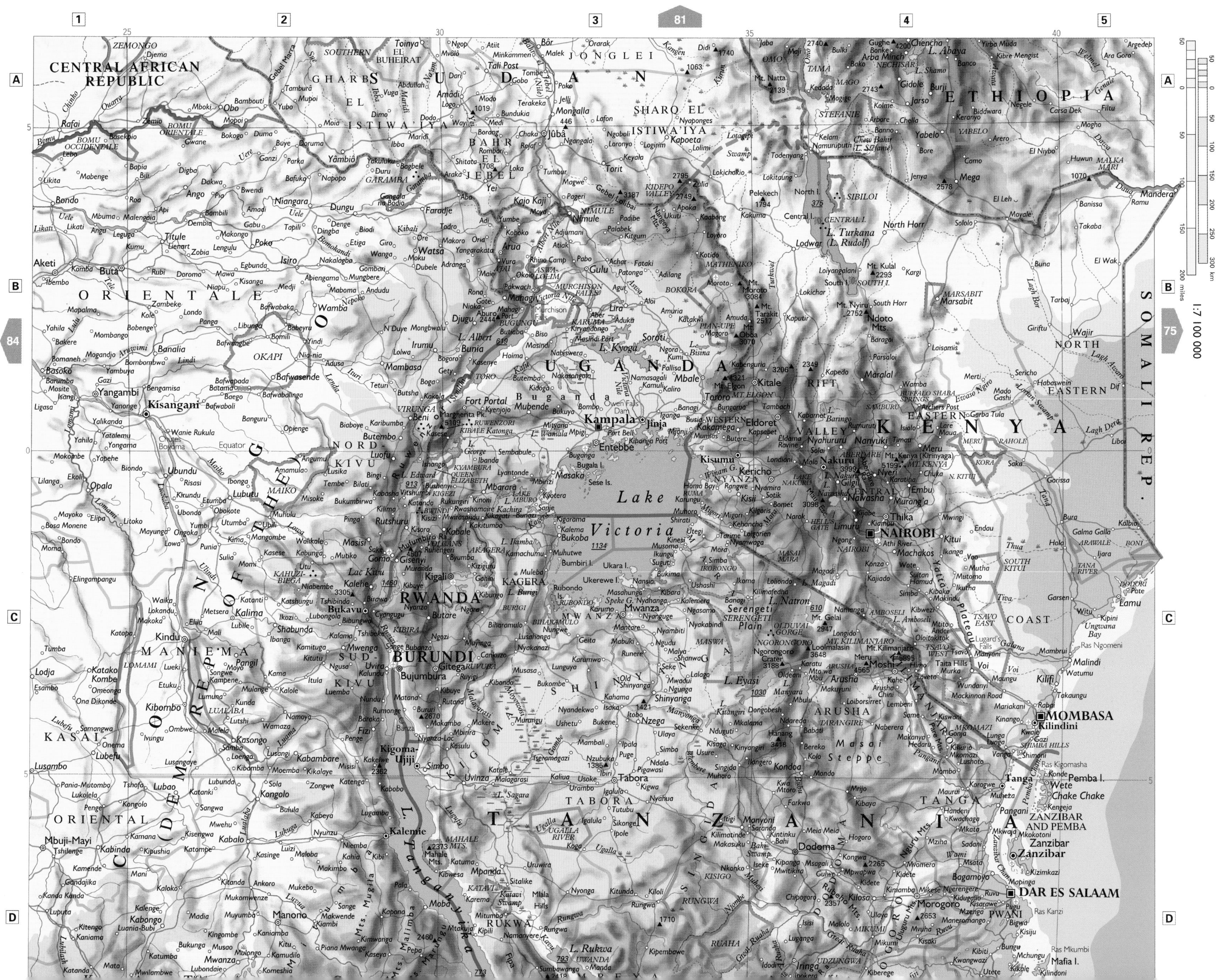

1:7 100 000
50 0 50 100 150 200 250 300 km
50 0 50 100 150 200 miles
1
2
3
4
5
A
B
C
D
81
84
75
CENTRAL AFRICAN REPUBLIC
SUDAN
ETHIOPIA
SOMALI REP.
UGANDA
KENYA
RWANDA
BURUNDI
TANZANIA
DEM. REP. OF THE CONGO
Lake Victoria
L. Turkana (L. Rudolf)
L. Albert
L. Edward
Lac Kivu
L. Kyoga
L. Tanganyika
L. Rukwa
L. Natron
L. Eyasi
NAIROBI
MOMBASA
DAR ES SALAAM
Zanzibar
Kampala
Kigali
Bujumbura
Dodoma
Kisangani
Tabora
Mwanza
Kigoma-Ujiji
Arusha
Moshi
Nakuru
Kisumu
Entebbe
Jinja
Jûbâ
Serengeti Plain
Masai Steppe
Equator

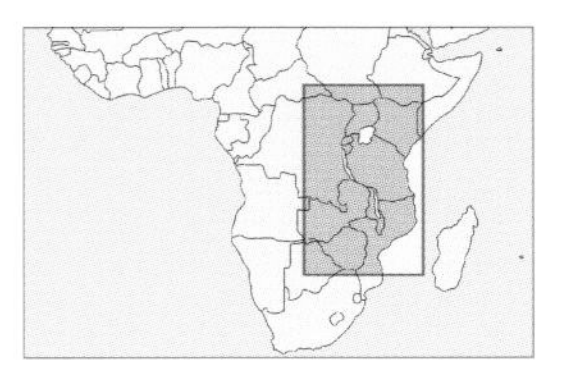

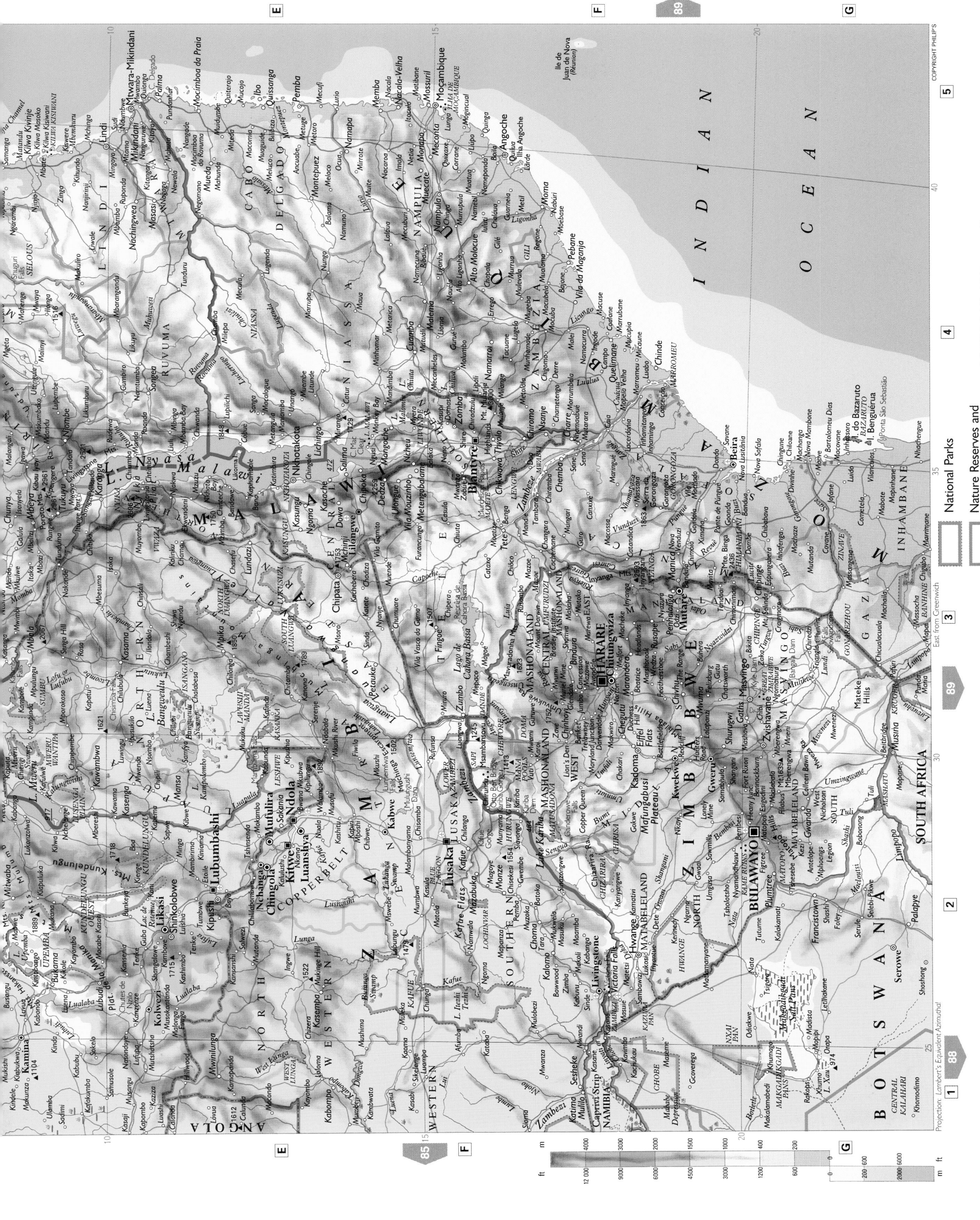

National Parks

Nature Reserves and Game Reserves

∴ UNESCO World Heritage Sites

m	ft
4000	12 000
3000	9000
2000	6000
1500	4500
1000	3000
400	1200
200	600
0	0
200	600
2000	6000

Projection: Lambert's Equivalent Azimuthal

East from Greenwich

1:7 100 000

50 0 50 100 150 200 250 300 km

50 0 50 100 150 200 miles

ft m
9000 3000
6000 2000
4500 1500
3000 1000
1200 400
600 200
0 0
200 600
2000 6000
4000 12 000
m ft

National Parks

Nature Reserves and Game Reserves

∴ UNESCO World Heritage Sites

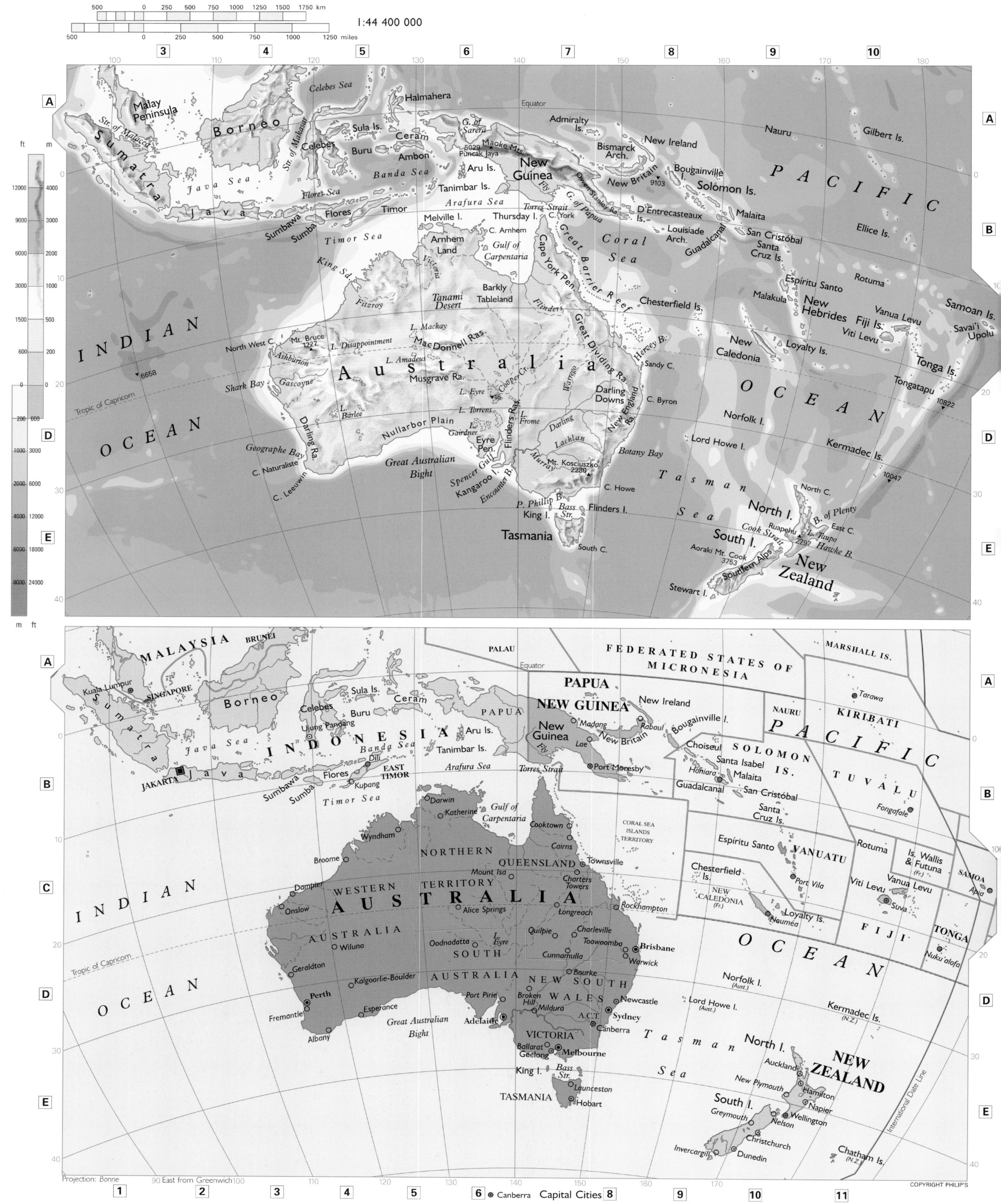
1:44 400 000
500 0 250 500 750 1000 1250 1500 1750 km
500 0 250 500 750 1000 1250 miles
Malay Peninsula
Str. of Malacca
Sumatra
Celebes Sea
Borneo
Str. of Makasar
Celebes
Halmahera
Sula Is.
Buru
Ceram
Ambon
Java Sea
Banda Sea
Java
Flores Sea
Sumbawa
Sumba
Flores
Timor
Timor Sea
Equator
G. of Sarera
5029 Puncak Jaya
Maoke Mts.
New Guinea
Aru Is.
Tanimbar Is.
Arafura Sea
Admiralty Is.
Bismarck Arch.
New Ireland
New Britain
Owen Stanley Ra.
G. of Papua
Bougainville I.
Solomon Is.
9103
Torres Strait
Thursday I.
C. York
Melville I.
C. Arnhem
Arnhem Land
Gulf of Carpentaria
Cape York Pen.
Great Barrier Reef
Coral Sea
D'Entrecasteaux Is.
Louisiade Arch.
Malaita
Guadalcanal
San Cristóbal
Santa Cruz Is.
Nauru
Gilbert Is.
PACIFIC
Ellice Is.
Rotuma
Espíritu Santo
Malakula
New Hebrides
Fiji Is.
Vanua Levu
Viti Levu
Samoan Is.
Savai'i
Upolu
King Sd.
Fitzroy
Victoria
Tanami Desert
Barkly Tableland
Flinders
Chesterfield Is.
New Caledonia
Loyalty Is.
Tonga Is.
Tongatapu
10822
INDIAN OCEAN
6658
North West C.
Mt. Bruce 1227
L. Disappointment
L. Mackay
MacDonnell Ras.
L. Amadeus
Ashburton
Australia
Musgrave Ra.
Cooper Cr.
Warrego
Great Dividing Ra.
Hervey B.
Sandy C.
Shark Bay
Gascoyne
Tropic of Capricorn
L. Eyre
-16
L. Torrens
L. Barlee
Darling Downs
C. Byron
New England Ra.
Norfolk I.
Darling Ra.
Nullarbor Plain
L. Gairdner
Flinders Ra.
L. Frome
Darling
Lachlan
Geographe Bay
C. Naturaliste
C. Leeuwin
Eyre Pen.
Great Australian Bight
Spencer Gulf
Kangaroo I.
Encounter B.
Murray
Mt. Kosciuszko 2230
Botany Bay
Lord Howe I.
Kermadec Is.
10047
C. Howe
Tasman Sea
P. Phillip B.
King I.
Bass Str.
Flinders I.
Tasmania
South C.
North C.
North I.
B. of Plenty
East C.
Ruapehu 2797
L. Taupo
Hawke B.
Cook Strait
South I.
Aoraki Mt. Cook 3753
Southern Alps
New Zealand
Stewart I.
ft m
12000 4000
9000 3000
6000 2000
3000 1000
1500 500
600 200
0 0
200 600
1000 3000
2000 6000
4000 12000
6000 18000
8000 24000
m ft
MALAYSIA
BRUNEI
PALAU
FEDERATED STATES OF MICRONESIA
MARSHALL IS.
Kuala Lumpur
SINGAPORE
Sumatra
Borneo
Celebes
Sula Is.
Ceram
Buru
Ujung Pandang
INDONESIA
Java Sea
Banda Sea
Aru Is.
Tanimbar Is.
JAKARTA
Java
Sumbawa
Sumba
Flores
Dili
Kupang
EAST TIMOR
Timor Sea
Arafura Sea
PAPUA
PAPUA NEW GUINEA
New Guinea
Madang
Lae
New Britain
Rabaul
New Ireland
Bougainville I.
Torres Strait
Port Moresby
Choiseul
SOLOMON IS.
Santa Isabel
Honiara
Malaita
Guadalcanal
San Cristóbal
Santa Cruz Is.
NAURU
Tarawa
KIRIBATI
PACIFIC
TUVALU
Fongafale
Darwin
Katherine
Gulf of Carpentaria
Cooktown
Cairns
CORAL SEA ISLANDS TERRITORY
Wyndham
NORTHERN TERRITORY
QUEENSLAND
Townsville
Mount Isa
Charters Towers
Espíritu Santo
VANUATU
Rotuma
Is. Wallis & Futuna (Fr.)
SAMOA
Apia
Broome
Chesterfield Is.
NEW CALEDONIA (Fr.)
Port Vila
Viti Levu
Vanua Levu
Suva
Dampier
WESTERN AUSTRALIA
AUSTRALIA
Alice Springs
Longreach
Rockhampton
Loyalty Is.
Nouméa
FIJI
TONGA
Nuku'alofa
INDIAN OCEAN
Onslow
Wiluna
Oodnadatta
L. Eyre
SOUTH AUSTRALIA
Quilpie
Charleville
Toowoomba
Cunnamulla
Brisbane
Warwick
Tropic of Capricorn
Geraldton
Kalgoorlie-Boulder
Bourke
NEW SOUTH WALES
Norfolk I. (Aust.)
Perth
Port Pirie
Broken Hill
Mildura
Newcastle
Lord Howe I. (Aust.)
Kermadec Is. (N.Z.)
Fremantle
Esperance
Great Australian Bight
Adelaide
A.C.T.
Sydney
Canberra
Albany
VICTORIA
Ballarat
Geelong
Melbourne
Tasman Sea
North I.
Auckland
NEW ZEALAND
King I.
Bass Str.
New Plymouth
Hamilton
Launceston
TASMANIA
Hobart
South I.
Greymouth
Napier
Nelson
Wellington
International Date Line
Christchurch
Invercargill
Dunedin
Chatham Is. (N.Z.)
Projection: Bonne
East from Greenwich
Canberra Capital Cities

1:5 300 000

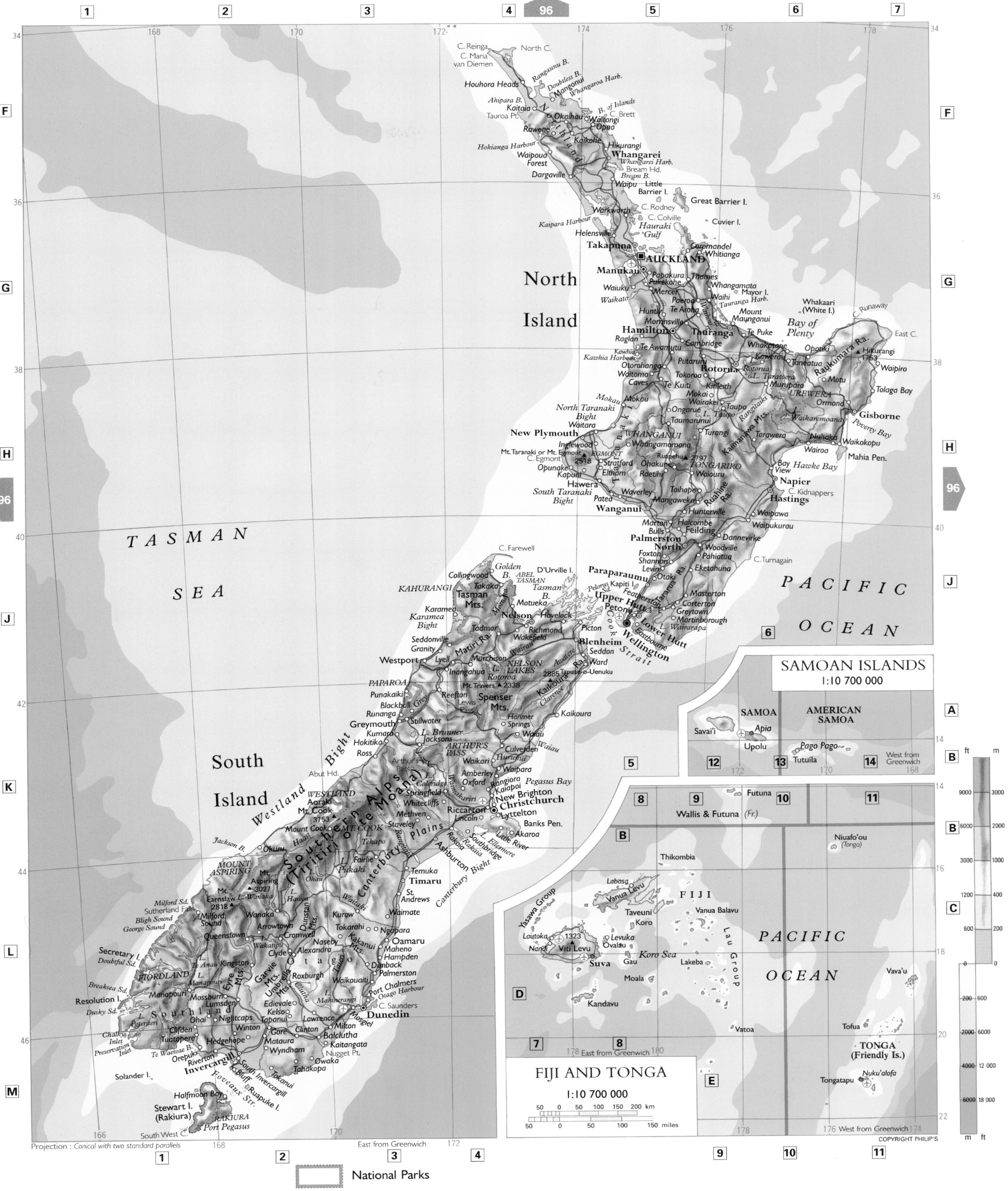

National Parks

1:7 100 000

50 0 50 100 150 200 250 300 km
50 0 50 100 150 200 miles
62
94
INDONESIA
TIMOR SEA
INDIAN OCEAN
NORTHERN TERRITORY
Bali
Lombok
Sumbawa
Waikabubak
Sumba
Waingapu
Melolo
Baing
Sawu
Raijua
Dana
Roti
Semau
Kupang
Timor
Hibernia Reef
Ashmore Reef
Ashmore and Cartier Is.
Cartier I.
Seringapatam Reef
Scott Reef
Browse I.
Lynher Reef
Adele I.
Rowley Shoals
Mermaid Reef
Clerke Reef
Imperieuse Reef
Bonaparte Archipelago
Joseph Bonaparte Gulf
Kimberley
King Leopold Ranges
Durack Range
Wyndham
Kununurra
Derby
Broome
Roebuck B.
Lagrange
Eighty Mile Beach
Sandfire Roadhouse
Port Hedland
Karratha
Dampier
Onslow
Exmouth
Exmouth Gulf
Newman
Hamersley Range
Great Sandy Desert
Little Sandy Desert
Gibson Desert
Tanami Desert
Tanami
Lake Mackay
Lake Disappointment
Tropic of Capricorn
Darwin
Palmerston
Katherine
Melville I.
Bathurst I.
Fitzroy Crossing
Halls Creek
Mt. Ord 937
Mt. Hann 776
Mt. Wells 970

WESTERN AUSTRALIA
SOUTH AUSTRALIA
INDIAN OCEAN
SOUTHERN OCEAN
Great Australian Bight
Great Victoria Desert
Nullarbor Plain
Hampton Tableland
PERTH
Fremantle
Rockingham
Mandurah
Kwinana
Midland
Wanneroo
Bunbury
Busselton
Albany
Geraldton
Carnarvon
Kalgoorlie-Boulder
Esperance
Norseman
Merredin
Northam
Collie
Narrogin
Katanning
Southern Cross
Coolgardie
Leonora
Laverton
Meekatharra
Wiluna
Cue
Mount Magnet
Kambalda
Menzies
Eucla
Ravensthorpe
Hopetoun
Dongara
Kalbarri
Denham
Nullarbor
Cook
Ooldea
Kata Tjuta (Mt. Olga) 1069
Uluru (Ayers Rock) 868
Petermann Ranges
Musgrave Ranges
Everard Ranges
Archipelago of the Recherche
Projection: Bonne
East from Greenwich
National Parks
COPYRIGHT PHILIP'S

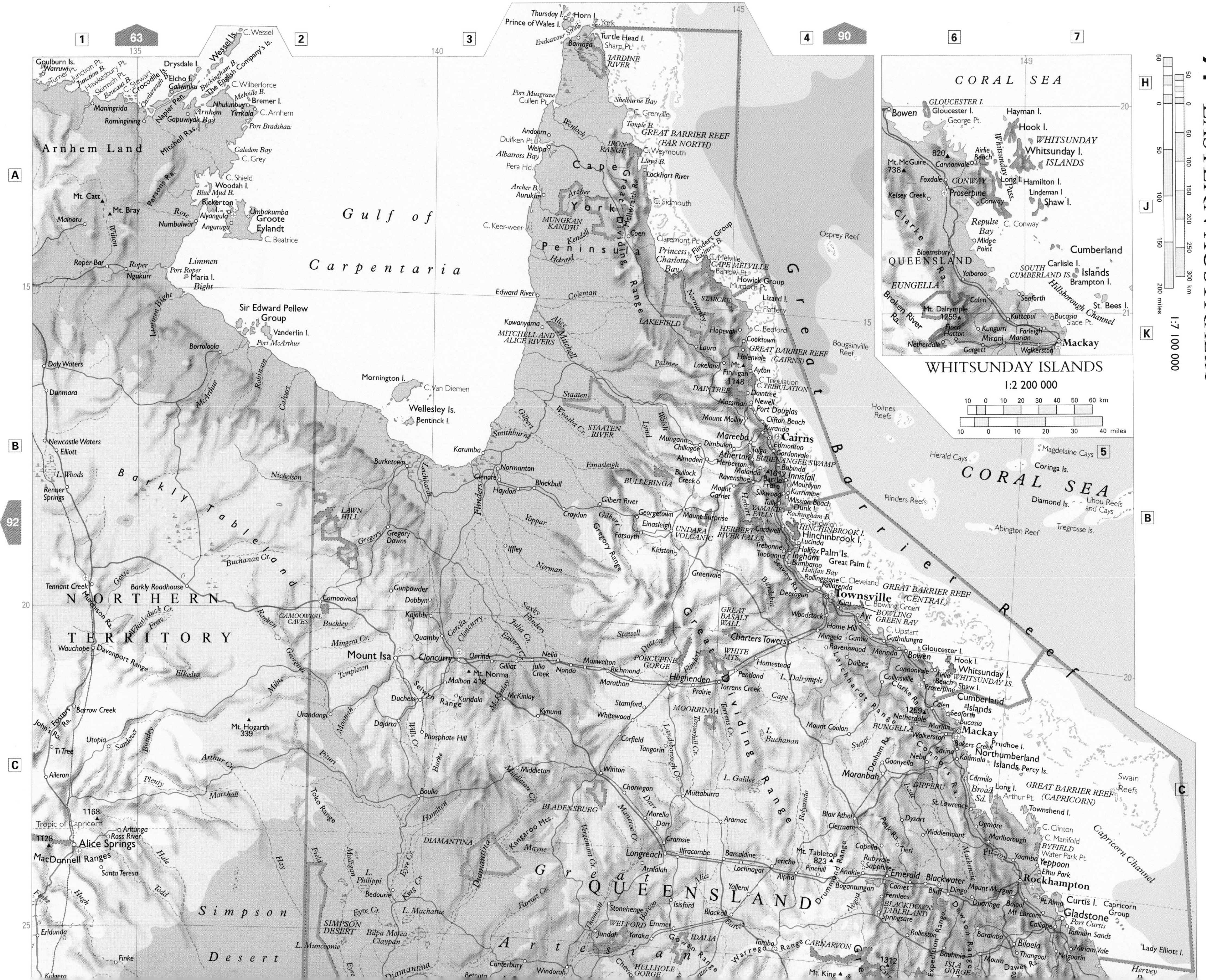

1:7 100 000
WHITSUNDAY ISLANDS
1:2 200 000
CORAL SEA
Gulf of Carpentaria
Great Barrier Reef
Great Dividing Range
Cape York Peninsula
QUEENSLAND
NORTHERN TERRITORY
Arnhem Land
Barkly Tableland
Simpson Desert
Great Artesian Basin
Cairns
Townsville
Mackay
Rockhampton
Gladstone
Mount Isa
Cloncurry
Longreach
Emerald
Charters Towers
Alice Springs
Tennant Creek
Bowen
Proserpine
Capricorn Channel
Wellesley Is.
Mornington I.
Groote Eylandt
Sir Edward Pellew Group
Tropic of Capricorn

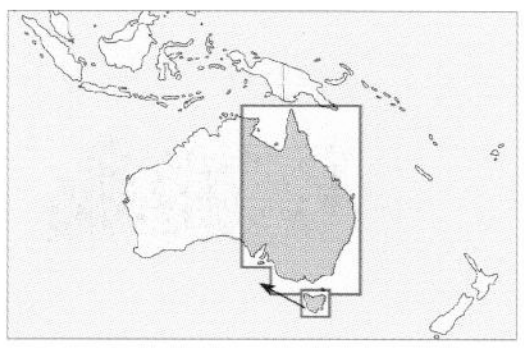

National Parks

m	ft
1500	4500
1000	3000
400	1200
200	600
0	0
200	600
2000	6000
4000	12 000

East from Greenwich

Projection: Bonne

93

Equatorial Scale 1:48 000 000

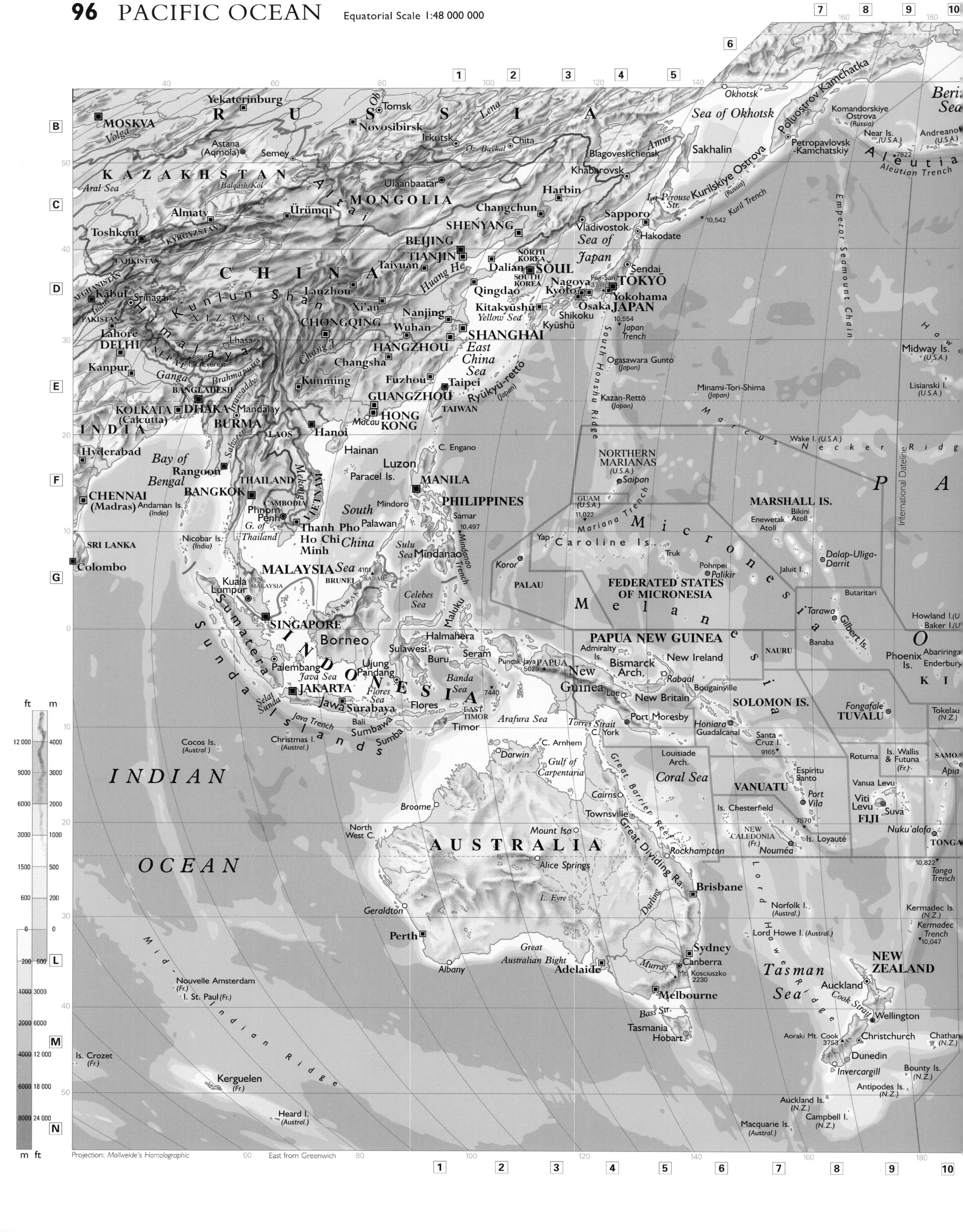

Arctic Circle
ALASKA (U.S.A.)
Anchorage
Bristol Bay
Gulf of Alaska
Juneau
Prince of Wales I. (U.S.A.)
Prince Rupert
Queen Charlotte Is. (Canada)
CANADA
ROCKY MTS.
Edmonton
Calgary
Regina
Winnipeg
L. Winnipeg
Vancouver
Vancouver I.
Victoria
Seattle
Portland
Boise
Salt Lake City
Denver
Kansas City
Minneapolis
Missouri
CHICAGO
L. Superior
L. Michigan
L. Huron
L. Erie
L. Ontario
Detroit
Toronto
Ottawa
Montréal
Québec
Buffalo
Boston
Pittsburgh
NEW YORK CITY
PHILADELPHIA
Baltimore
Washington D.C.
Cincinnati
St. Louis
Appalachian Mts.
St. Lawrence
Newfoundland
St. John's
NORTH ATLANTIC OCEAN
C. Mendocino
Sacramento
SAN FRANCISCO
UNITED STATES
Colorado
Snake
Oklahoma City
Memphis
Mississippi
Atlanta
C. Hatteras
Bermuda (U.K.)
LOS ANGELES
San Diego
Phoenix
Dallas
Ciudad Juárez
Houston
San Antonio
New Orleans
Jacksonville
Sargasso Sea
Guadalupe (Mex.)
Baja California
Golfo de California
MEXICO
Monterrey
Gulf of Mexico
Miami
Florida Str.
BAHAMAS
Tropic of Cancer
C. San Lucas
La Habana
Canal de Yucatán
CUBA
West Indies
Honolulu
Oahu
HAWAIIAN IS. (U.S.A.)
Hawaii
Guadalajara
MEXICO
Mérida
Puebla
Is. Revilla Gigedo (Mex.)
Acapulco
BELIZE
JAMAICA
Kingston
HAITI
DOMINICAN REP.
PUERTO RICO (U.S.A.)
Leeward Is.
Johnston I. (U.S.A.)
PACIFIC OCEAN
HONDURAS
Caribbean Sea
GUATEMALA
Guatemala
San Salvador
EL SALVADOR
NICARAGUA
Managua
BARBADOS
Windward Is.
I. Clipperton (Fr.)
Barranquilla
Maracaibo
Caracas
Orinoco
San José
Colón
Panamá
COSTA RICA
PANAMA
VENEZUELA
North West Christmas I. Ridge
Palmyra Is. (U.S.A.)
Teraina
Tabuaeran
Kiritimati
I. del Coco (Costa Rica)
Medellín
Bogotá
Cali
COLOMBIA
I. de Malpelo (Colombia)
Equator
Jarvis I. (U.S.A.)
Line Is.
KIRIBATI
Malden I.
Starbuck I.
Galápagos (Ecuador)
Quito
ECUADOR
Guayaquil
Iquitos
Amazonas
C. Paliñas
BRAZIL
East Pacific Ridge
Is. Marquises
Tongareva
Pukapuka
Manihiki
Vostok I.
Caroline I. (Millennium I.)
Flint I.
Trujillo
PERU
LIMA
Cuzco
L. Titicaca
Arequipa
Nevada Ancohuma
La Paz
BOLIVIA
AMER. SAMOA (U.S.A.)
Suwarrow Is.
Is. de la Société
Tahiti
Papeete
Is. Tuamotu
Tuamotu Ridge
Austral Seamount Chain
Cook Is. (N.Z.)
Niue (N.Z.)
FRENCH POLYNESIA
Peru-Chile Trench
Arica
Iquique
Rarotonga
Mururoa
Is. Tubuai
Tropic of Capricorn
Antofagasta
PARAGUAY
Asunción
Ducie I.
Pitcairn I. (U.K.)
Rapa
San Felix (Chile)
San Ambrosio (Chile)
San Miguel de Tucumán
Sala-y-Gómez (Chile)
I. de Pascua (Chile)
Porto Alegre
Córdoba
Aconcagua
Arch. de Juan Fernández (Chile)
Valparaíso
Rosario
SANTIAGO
BUENOS AIRES
URUGUAY
Montevideo
Río de la Plata
Concepción
ARGENTINA
ANDES
Chile Rise
SOUTH ATLANTIC OCEAN
Patagonia
Pacific-Antarctic Ridge
Falkland Is. (U.K.)
Punta Arenas
Est. de Magallanes
Tierra del Fuego
South Georgia (U.K.)
C. de Hornos
West from Greenwich

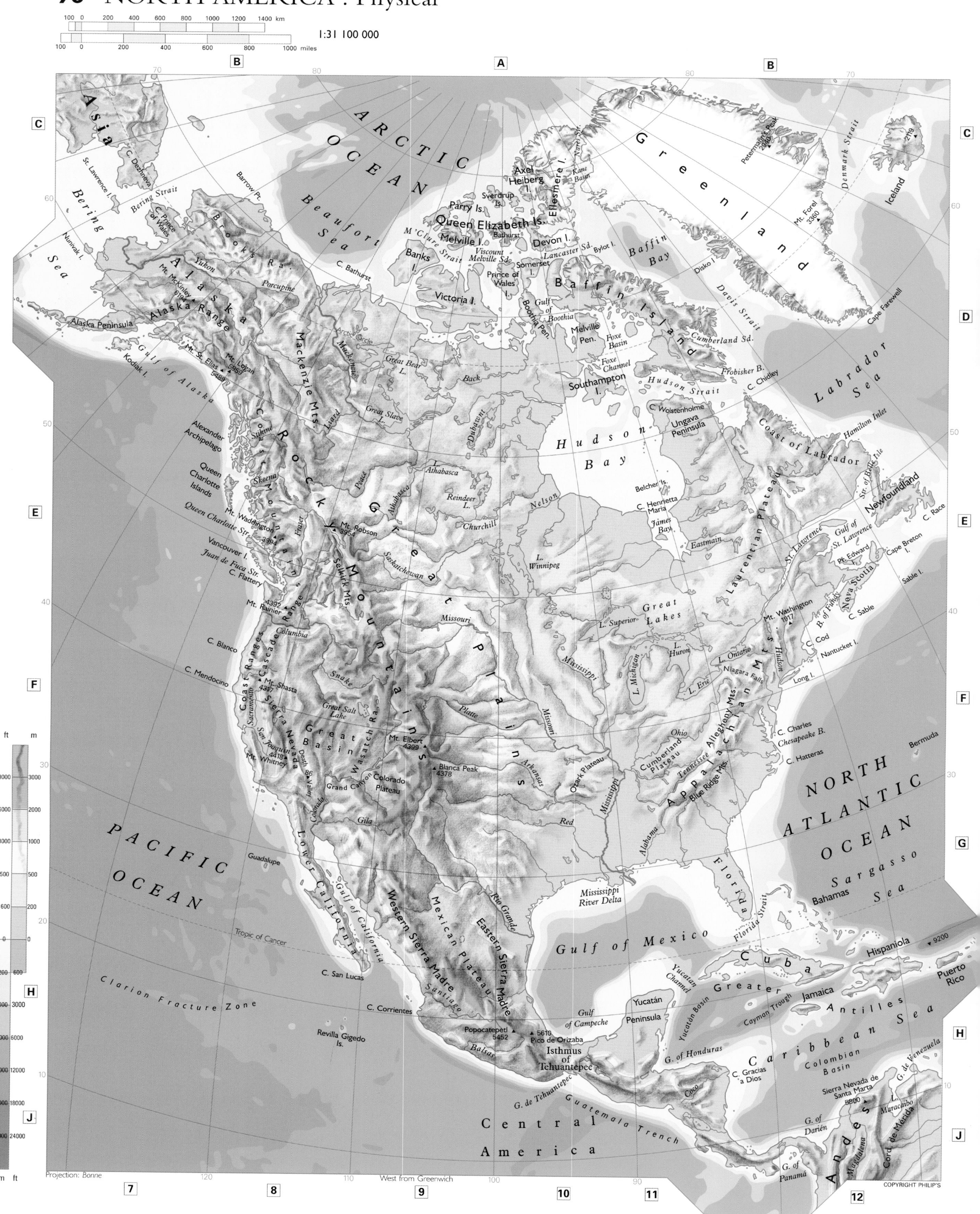

100 0 200 400 600 800 1000 1200 1400 km
100 0 200 400 600 800 1000 miles
1:31 100 000
ARCTIC OCEAN
Asia
C. Dezhneva
St. Lawrence I.
Bering Strait
Bering Sea
Nunivak I.
C. Prince of Wales
Barrow Pt.
Beaufort Sea
Brooks Ra.
Yukon
Porcupine
Alaska
Mt. McKinley 6194
Alaska Range
Alaska Peninsula
Kodiak I.
Gulf of Alaska
Mt. St. Elias 5489
Mt. Logan 5959
Mackenzie Mts.
Mackenzie
Arctic Circle
Great Bear L.
Great Slave L.
Back
Liard
Alexander Archipelago
Stikine
Coast Mountains
Rocky Mountains
Queen Charlotte Islands
Skeena
Queen Charlotte Str.
Mt. Waddington 3994
Fraser
Mt. Robson 3954
Vancouver I.
Juan de Fuca Str.
C. Flattery
Selkirk Mts
4392 Mt. Rainier
Cascade Range
Columbia
C. Blanco
C. Mendocino
Coast Ranges
Mt. Shasta 4317
Sierra Nevada
Sacramento
San Joaquin
Mt. Whitney 4418
Death Valley -86
Great Basin
Great Salt Lake
Snake
Wasatch Ra.
Grand Canyon
Colorado Plateau
Colorado
Gila
Mt. Elbert 4399
Blanca Peak 4378
Great Plains
Platte
Missouri
Arkansas
Red
PACIFIC OCEAN
Guadalupe
Lower California
Gulf of California
Tropic of Cancer
C. San Lucas
Clarion Fracture Zone
C. Corrientes
Revilla Gigedo Is.
Western Sierra Madre
Mexican Plateau
Eastern Sierra Madre
Santiago
Rio Grande
Balsas
Popocatepetl 5452
5610 Pico de Orizaba
Isthmus of Tehuantepec
G. de Tehuantepec
Guatemala Trench
Central America
Gulf of Campeche
Yucatán Peninsula
Yucatán Channel
Yucatán Basin
G. of Honduras
C. Gracias a Dios
Coco
Gulf of Mexico
Mississippi River Delta
Cuba
Greater Antilles
Cayman Trough
Jamaica
Hispaniola
9200
Puerto Rico
Caribbean Sea
Colombian Basin
G. de Venezuela
Sierra Nevada de Santa Marta 5800
L. Maracaibo
G. of Darién
G. of Panamá
Andes
Magdalena
Cord. de Mérida
Bahamas
Sargasso Sea
NORTH ATLANTIC OCEAN
Bermuda
Florida
Florida Strait
Alabama
Mississippi
Ozark Plateau
Tennessee
Cumberland Plateau
Ohio
Appalachian Mts.
Allegheny Mts.
Blue Ridge Mts.
C. Hatteras
Chesapeake B.
C. Charles
Long I.
Niagara Falls
L. Erie
L. Ontario
L. Huron
L. Michigan
L. Superior
Great Lakes
Hudson
Mt. Washington 1917
C. Cod
Nantucket I.
B. of Fundy
Nova Scotia
C. Sable
Sable I.
Cape Breton I.
Pt. Edward
Gulf of St. Lawrence
St. Lawrence
C. Race
Newfoundland
Str. of Belle Isle
Coast of Labrador
Hamilton Inlet
Laurentian Plateau
Eastmain
James Bay
C. Henrietta Maria
Belcher Is.
Hudson Bay
Nelson
L. Winnipeg
Saskatchewan
Churchill
Reindeer L.
L. Athabasca
Athabasca
Peace
Dubawnt
Ungava Peninsula
C. Wolstenholme
Hudson Strait
C. Chidley
Labrador Sea
Southampton I.
Foxe Channel
Foxe Basin
Melville Pen.
Gulf of Boothia
Boothia Pen.
Baffin Island
Cumberland Sd.
Frobisher B.
Baffin Bay
Bylot I.
Lancaster Sd.
Devon I.
Somerset I.
Prince of Wales I.
Viscount Melville Sd.
M'Clure Strait
Banks I.
C. Bathurst
Victoria I.
Melville I.
Bathurst I.
Queen Elizabeth Is.
Parry Is.
Sverdrup Is.
Axel Heiberg I.
Ellesmere I.
Kane Basin
Nares St.
Greenland
Petermanns Peak 2940
Mt. Forel 3360
Disko I.
Davis Strait
Cape Farewell
Denmark Strait
Iceland
2119
ft m
9000 3000
6000 2000
3000 1000
1500 500
600 200
0 0
200 600
1000 3000
2000 6000
4000 12000
6000 18000
8000 24000
m ft
Projection: Bonne
West from Greenwich
COPYRIGHT PHILIP'S

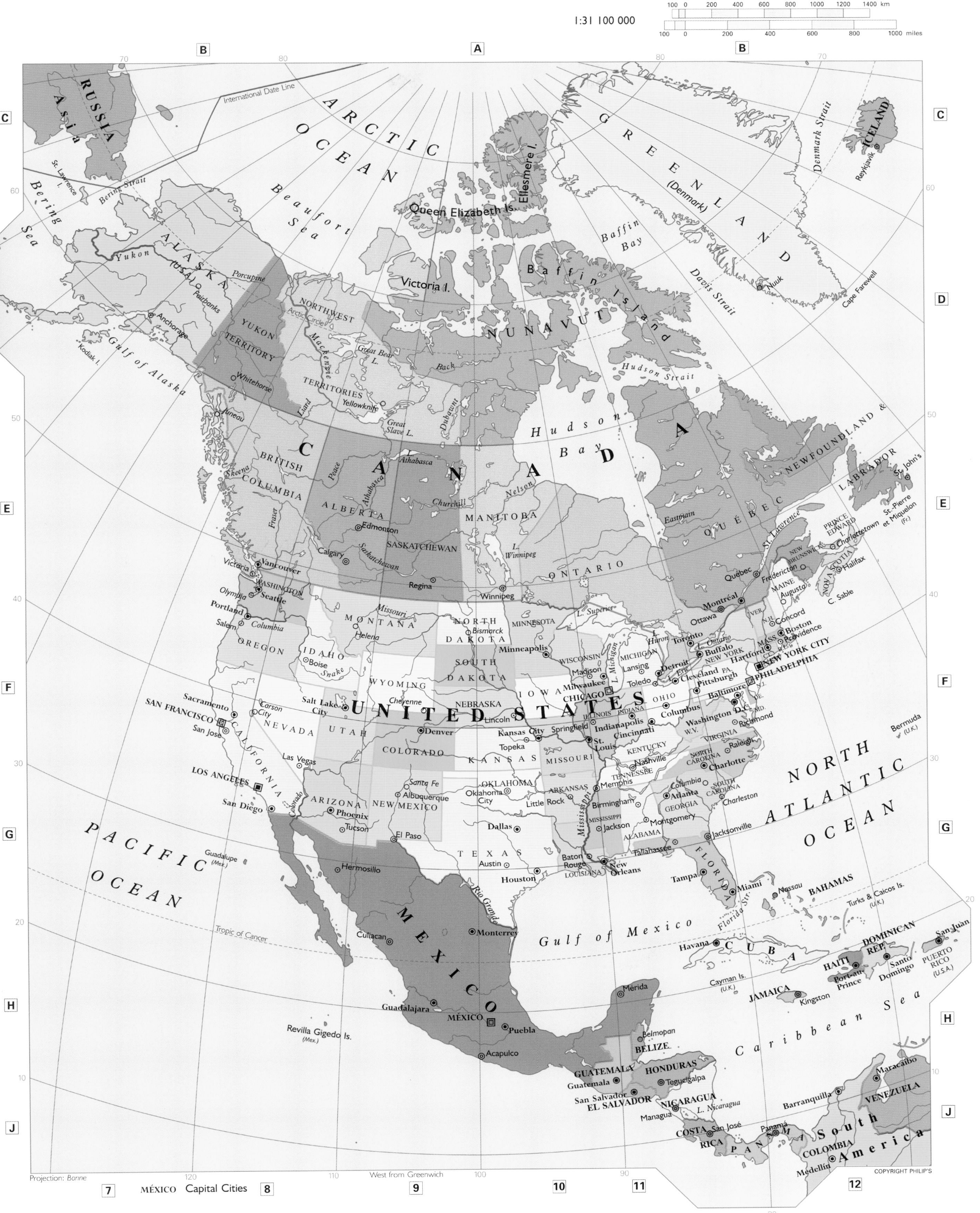
1:31 100 000
100 0 200 400 600 800 1000 1200 1400 km
100 0 200 400 600 800 1000 miles
A
B
C
D
E
F
G
H
J
7
8
9
10
11
12
RUSSIA
Asia
International Date Line
ARCTIC OCEAN
GREENLAND (Denmark)
ICELAND
Reykjavík
Denmark Strait
St. Lawrence I.
Bering Strait
Bering Sea
Beaufort Sea
Queen Elizabeth Is.
Ellesmere I.
Baffin Bay
Victoria I.
Baffin Island
Davis Strait
Nuuk
Cape Farewell
NUNAVUT
Yukon
ALASKA (U.S.A.)
Porcupine
Fairbanks
Anchorage
Kodiak I.
Gulf of Alaska
YUKON TERRITORY
Whitehorse
NORTHWEST TERRITORIES
Arctic Circle
Mackenzie
Great Bear L.
Back
Yellowknife
Great Slave L.
Liard
Dubawnt
Hudson Strait
Hudson Bay
Juneau
CANADA
BRITISH COLUMBIA
Skeena
Fraser
Peace
Athabasca
L. Athabasca
ALBERTA
Edmonton
Calgary
SASKATCHEWAN
Saskatchewan
Regina
Churchill
Nelson
MANITOBA
L. Winnipeg
Winnipeg
ONTARIO
Eastmain
QUÉBEC
St. Lawrence
NEWFOUNDLAND & LABRADOR
St. John's
PRINCE EDWARD I.
Charlottetown
St.-Pierre et Miquelon (Fr.)
NEW BRUNSWICK
Fredericton
NOVA SCOTIA
Halifax
C. Sable
Quebec
Montréal
Ottawa
Victoria
Vancouver
WASHINGTON
Olympia
Seattle
Portland
Salem
Columbia
OREGON
IDAHO
Boise
Snake
MONTANA
Helena
Missouri
NORTH DAKOTA
Bismarck
SOUTH DAKOTA
MINNESOTA
Minneapolis
L. Superior
WISCONSIN
Madison
Milwaukee
L. Michigan
MICHIGAN
Lansing
Detroit
L. Huron
Toronto
L. Ontario
Buffalo
NEW YORK
L. Erie
Toledo
Cleveland
PA.
Pittsburgh
MAINE
Augusta
VER.
N.H.
Concord
MASS.
Boston
Providence
Hartford
NEW YORK CITY
PHILADELPHIA
N.J.
DEL.
MD.
Baltimore
Washington D.C.
Richmond
WYOMING
Cheyenne
Salt Lake City
UNITED STATES
NEBRASKA
Lincoln
IOWA
CHICAGO
ILLINOIS
INDIANA
OHIO
Columbus
Indianapolis
Cincinnati
W.V.
VIRGINIA
Sacramento
SAN FRANCISCO
San Jose
Carson City
NEVADA
UTAH
Denver
COLORADO
Kansas City
Topeka
KANSAS
Springfield
St. Louis
MISSOURI
KENTUCKY
Nashville
TENNESSEE
NORTH CAROLINA
Raleigh
Charlotte
SOUTH CAROLINA
Columbia
Charleston
CALIFORNIA
Las Vegas
LOS ANGELES
San Diego
Colorado
ARIZONA
Phoenix
Tucson
NEW MEXICO
Santa Fe
Albuquerque
El Paso
OKLAHOMA
Oklahoma City
ARKANSAS
Little Rock
Memphis
Mississippi
MISSISSIPPI
Jackson
Birmingham
ALABAMA
Montgomery
GEORGIA
Atlanta
Jacksonville
Tallahassee
FLORIDA
Tampa
Miami
Dallas
TEXAS
Austin
Houston
Baton Rouge
LOUISIANA
New Orleans
Bermuda (U.K.)
NORTH ATLANTIC OCEAN
PACIFIC OCEAN
Guadalupe (Mex.)
Tropic of Cancer
Hermosillo
Rio Grande
MEXICO
Culiacan
Monterrey
Gulf of Mexico
Florida Str.
Nassau
BAHAMAS
Turks & Caicos Is. (U.K.)
Havana
CUBA
DOMINICAN REP.
Santo Domingo
HAITI
Port-au-Prince
San Juan
PUERTO RICO (U.S.A.)
Cayman Is. (U.K.)
JAMAICA
Kingston
Mérida
Guadalajara
MÉXICO
Puebla
Acapulco
Revilla Gigedo Is. (Mex.)
Belmopan
BELIZE
Caribbean Sea
GUATEMALA
Guatemala
HONDURAS
Tegucigalpa
San Salvador
EL SALVADOR
NICARAGUA
L. Nicaragua
Managua
COSTA RICA
San José
PANAMA
Panamá
Barranquilla
Maracaibo
VENEZUELA
COLOMBIA
Medellín
South America
Projection: Bonne
West from Greenwich
MÉXICO Capital Cities
COPYRIGHT PHILIP'S

1:13 300 000

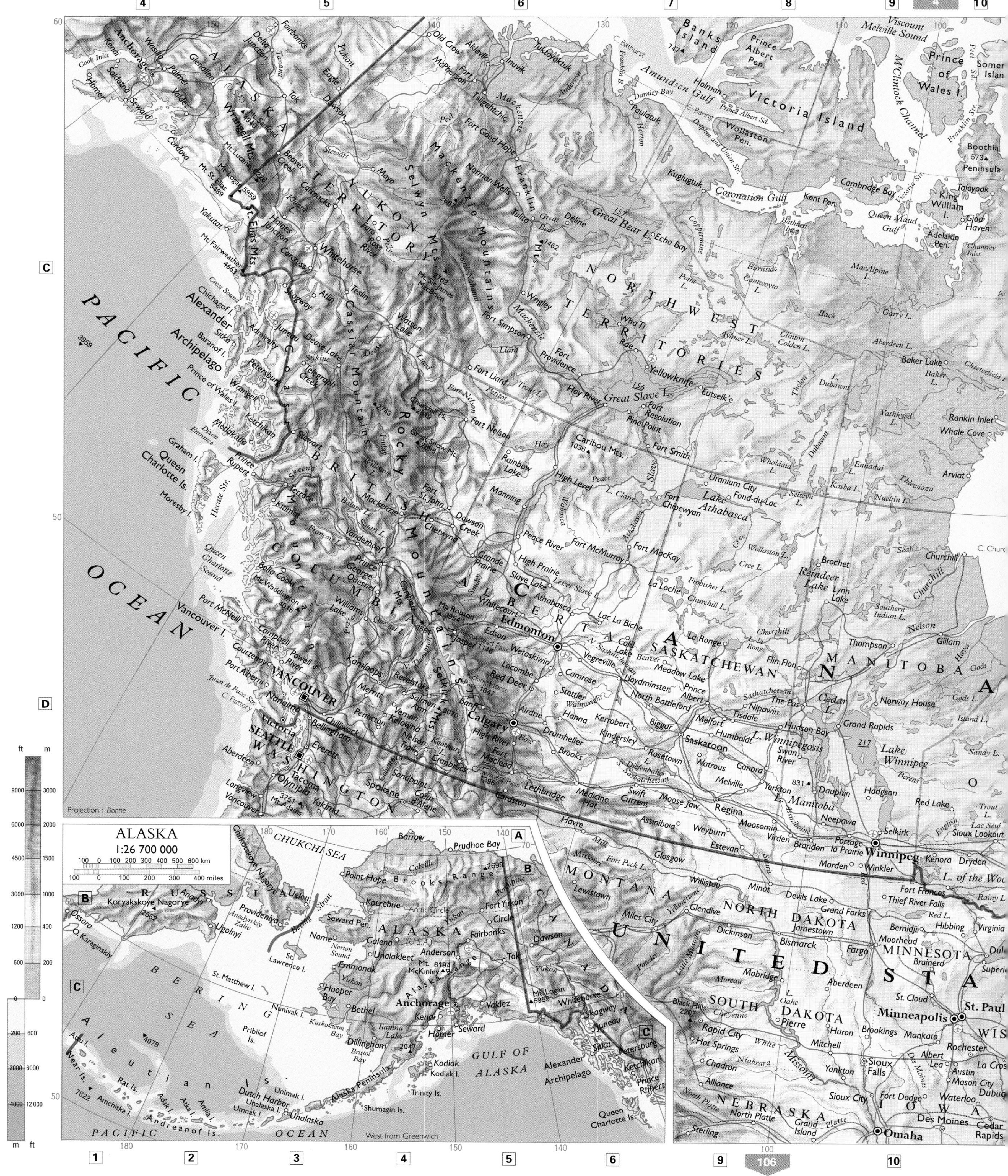

PACIFIC OCEAN
ALASKA
YUKON TERRITORY
NORTHWEST TERRITORIES
BRITISH COLUMBIA
ALBERTA
SASKATCHEWAN
MANITOBA
WASHINGTON
MONTANA
NORTH DAKOTA
SOUTH DAKOTA
NEBRASKA
MINNESOTA
IOWA
UNITED STATES
Victoria Island
Banks Island
Great Bear L.
Great Slave L.
Lake Athabasca
Lake Winnipeg
Mackenzie Mountains
Rocky Mountains
Coast Mountains
Cassiar Mountains
Selwyn Mts.
Queen Charlotte Is.
Vancouver I.
Alexander Archipelago
Anchorage
Fairbanks
Whitehorse
Yellowknife
Edmonton
Calgary
VANCOUVER
Victoria
SEATTLE
Regina
Saskatoon
Winnipeg
Minneapolis
St. Paul
Omaha
Projection : Bonne
ALASKA
1:26 700 000
RUSSIA
CHUKCHI SEA
BERING SEA
GULF OF ALASKA
Aleutian Is.
Brooks Range
CANADA
PACIFIC OCEAN
West from Greenwich

1:6 200 000

100

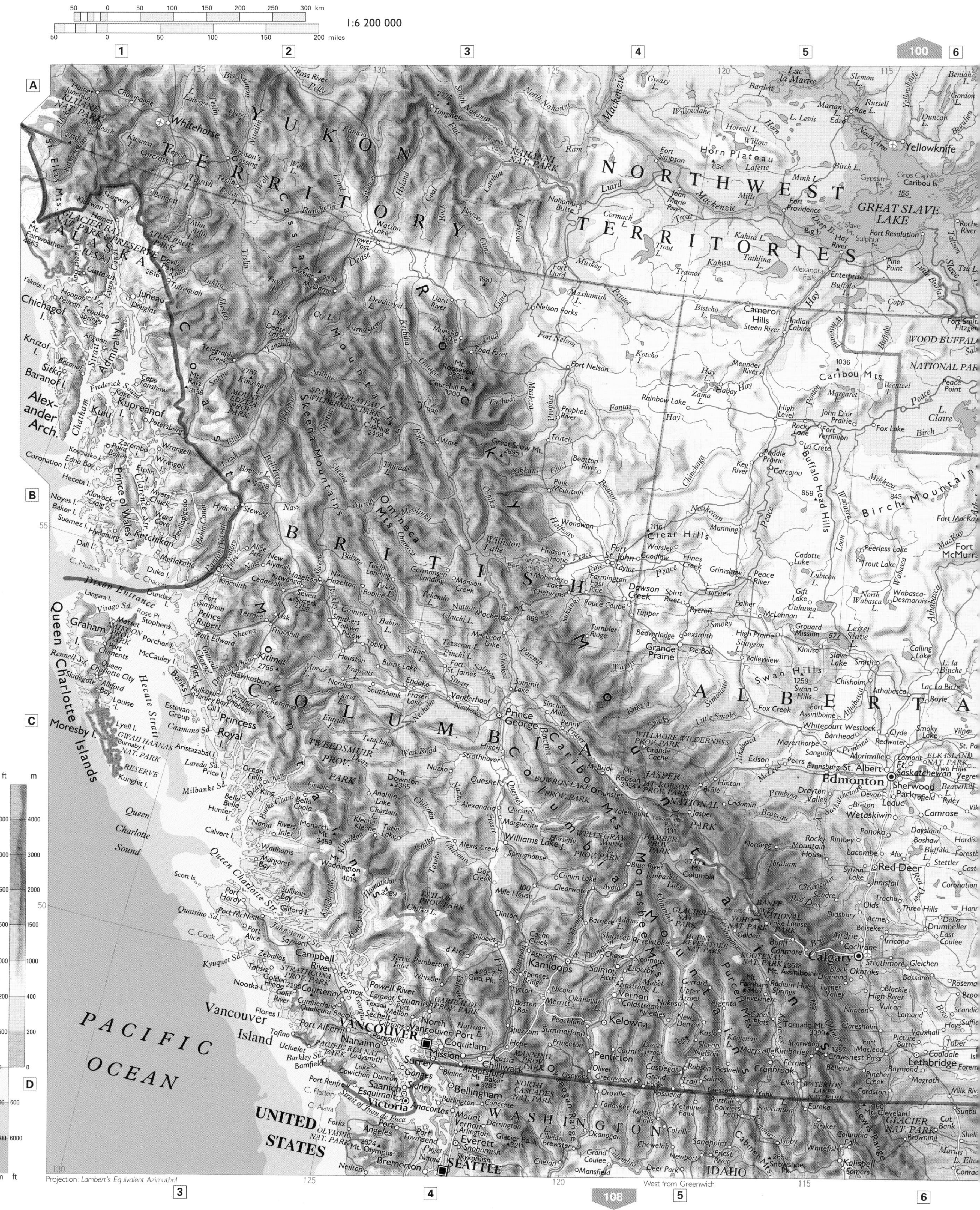

104

112

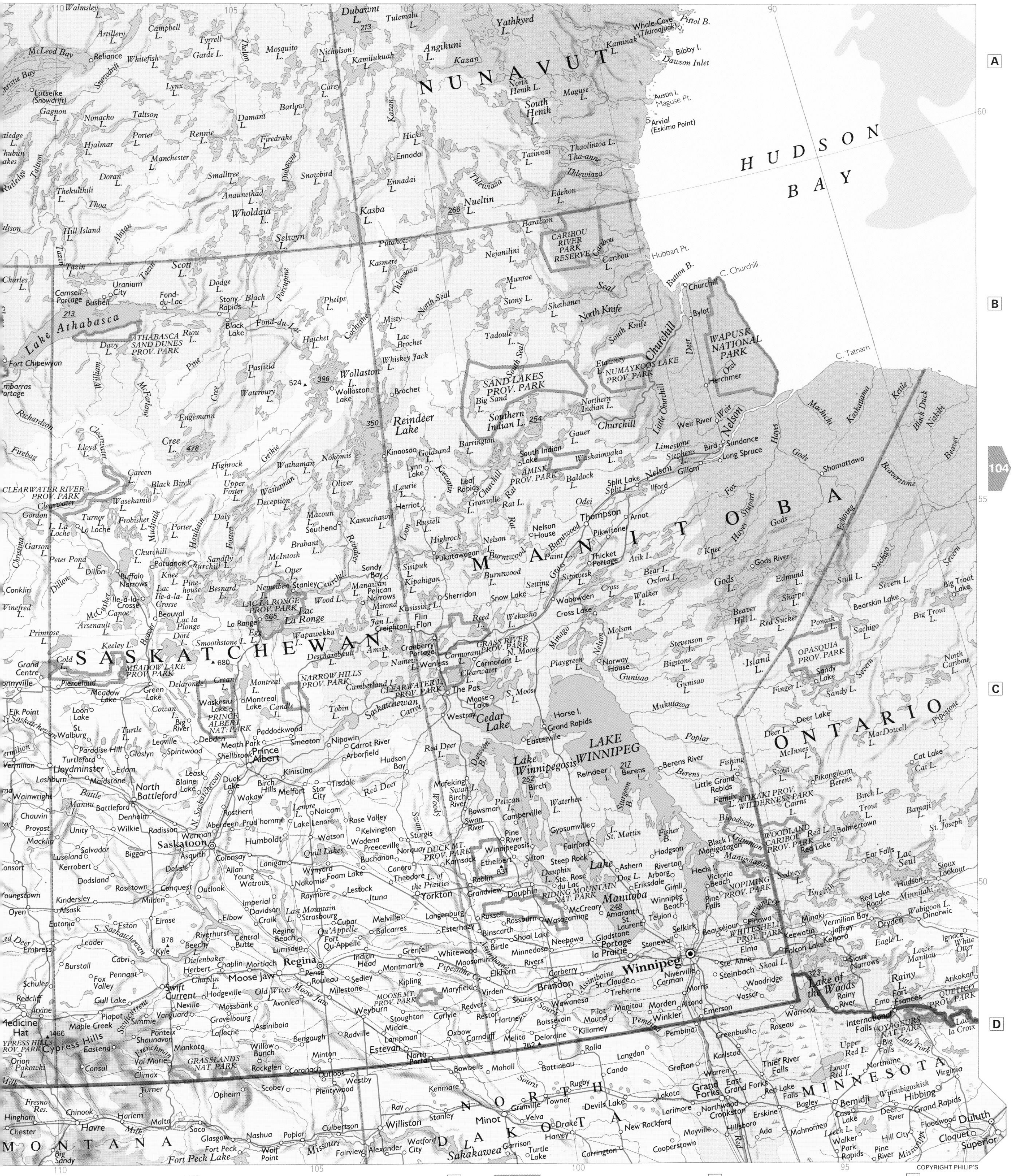

National Parks

1:6 200 000

National Parks

103
112
114

6 | 101 | 7 | 8 | 9

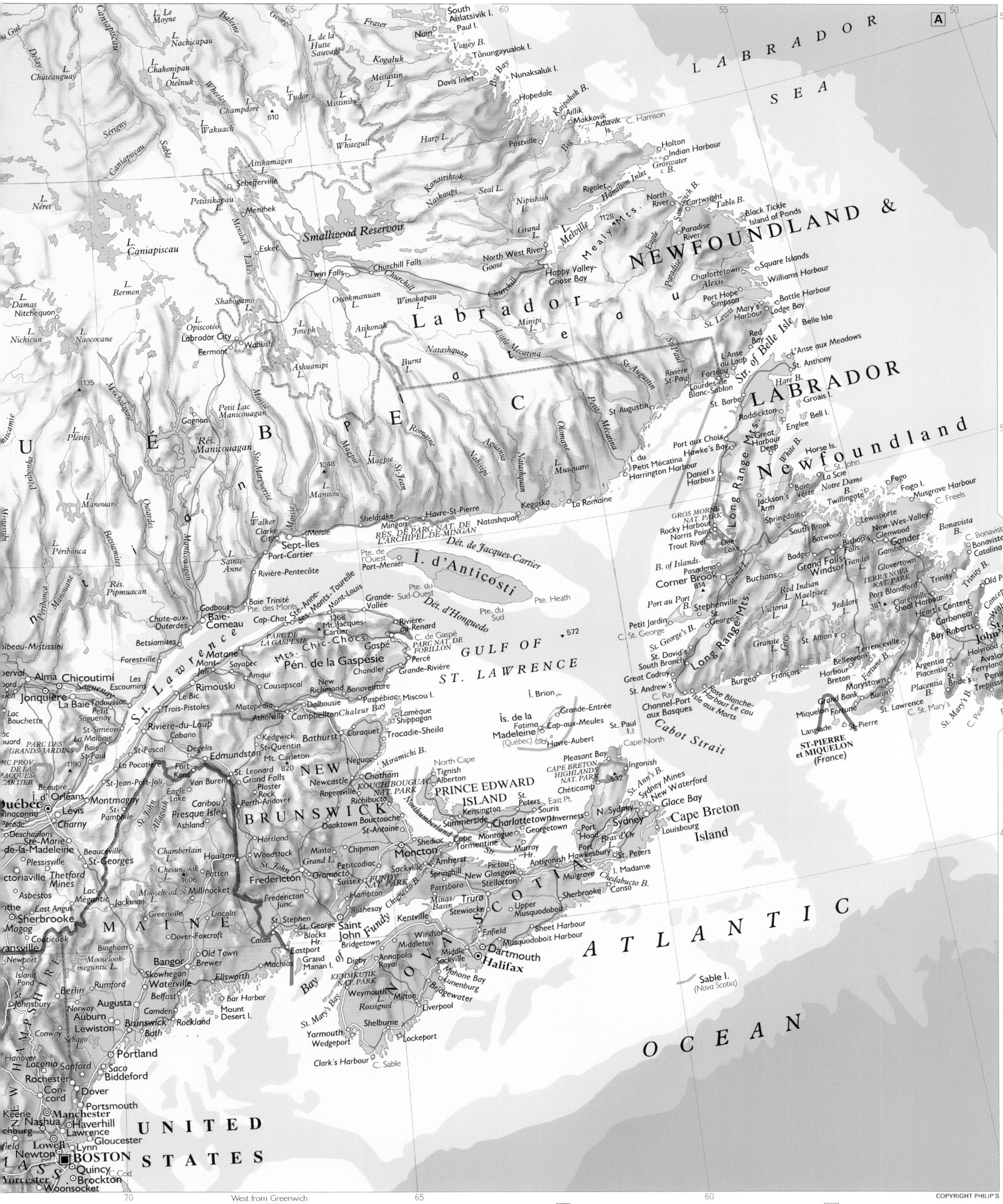

A | B | C | D

LABRADOR SEA

NEWFOUNDLAND & LABRADOR

Labrador

Newfoundland

QUÉBEC

NEW BRUNSWICK

PRINCE EDWARD ISLAND

NOVA SCOTIA

MAINE

NEW HAMPSHIRE

UNITED STATES

GULF OF ST. LAWRENCE

ATLANTIC OCEAN

Cabot Strait

Str. of Belle Isle

Bay of Fundy

Î. d'Anticosti

Cape Breton Island

ST-PIERRE et MIQUELON (France)

Smallwood Reservoir

Rés. Manicouagan

Pén. de la Gaspésie

Avalon Peninsula

Sable I. (Nova Scotia)

Long Range Mts.

Mealy Mts.

St. John's

Corner Brook

Gander

Grand Falls Windsor

Sydney

Halifax

Dartmouth

Charlottetown

Moncton

Fredericton

Saint John

Bangor

Augusta

Portland

BOSTON

Québec

Sherbrooke

Chicoutimi

Jonquière

Rimouski

Baie-Comeau

Sept-Îles

Labrador City

Happy Valley-Goose Bay

Churchill Falls

Schefferville

West from Greenwich

70 | 65 | 60 | 55 | 50 | 45

6 | 7 | 8

1:10 700 000

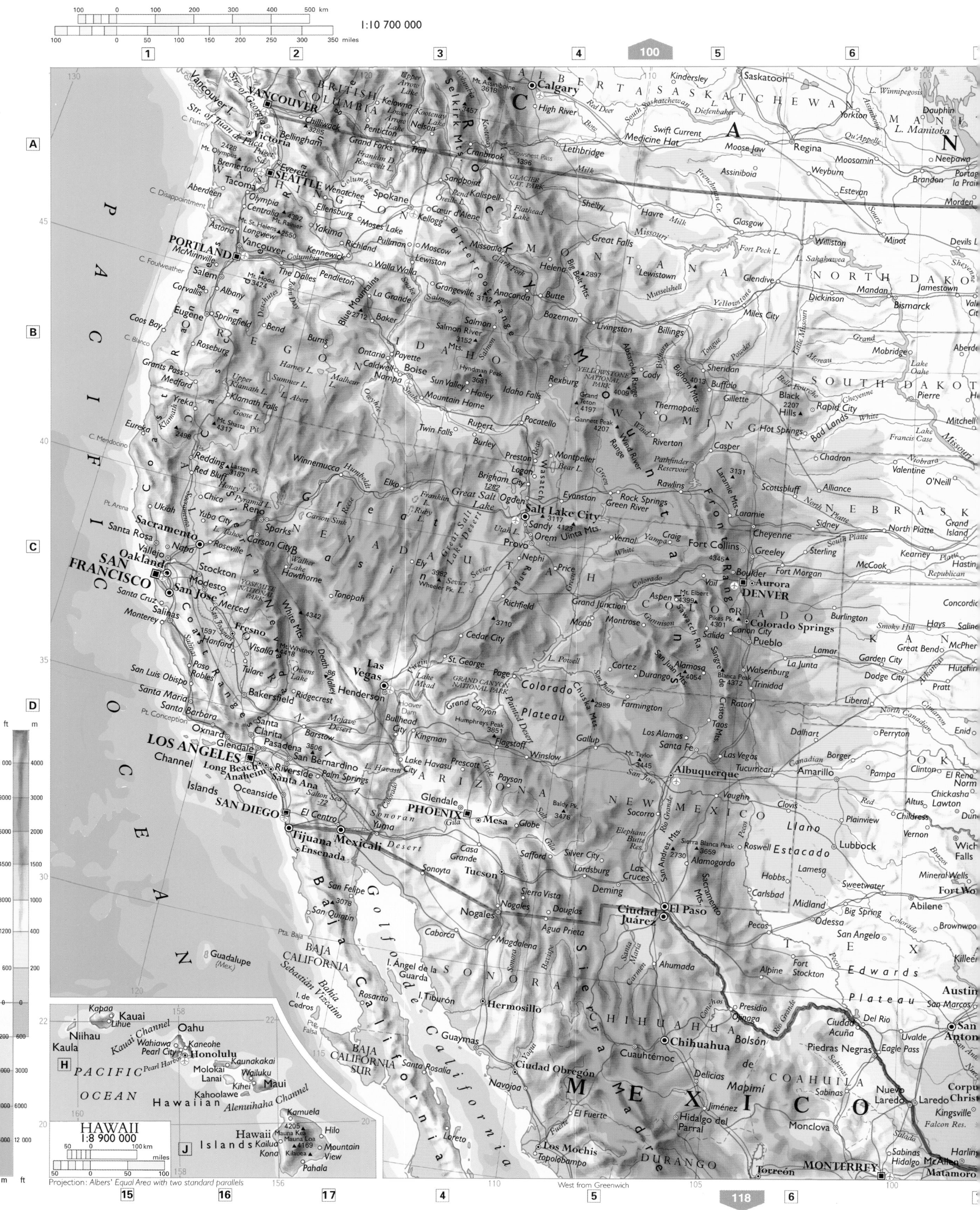

Projection: Albers' Equal Area with two standard parallels

West from Greenwich

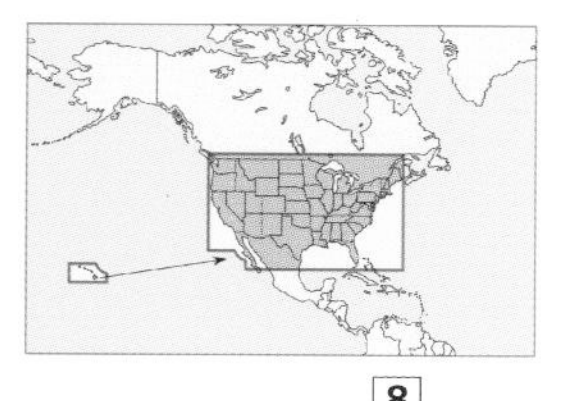

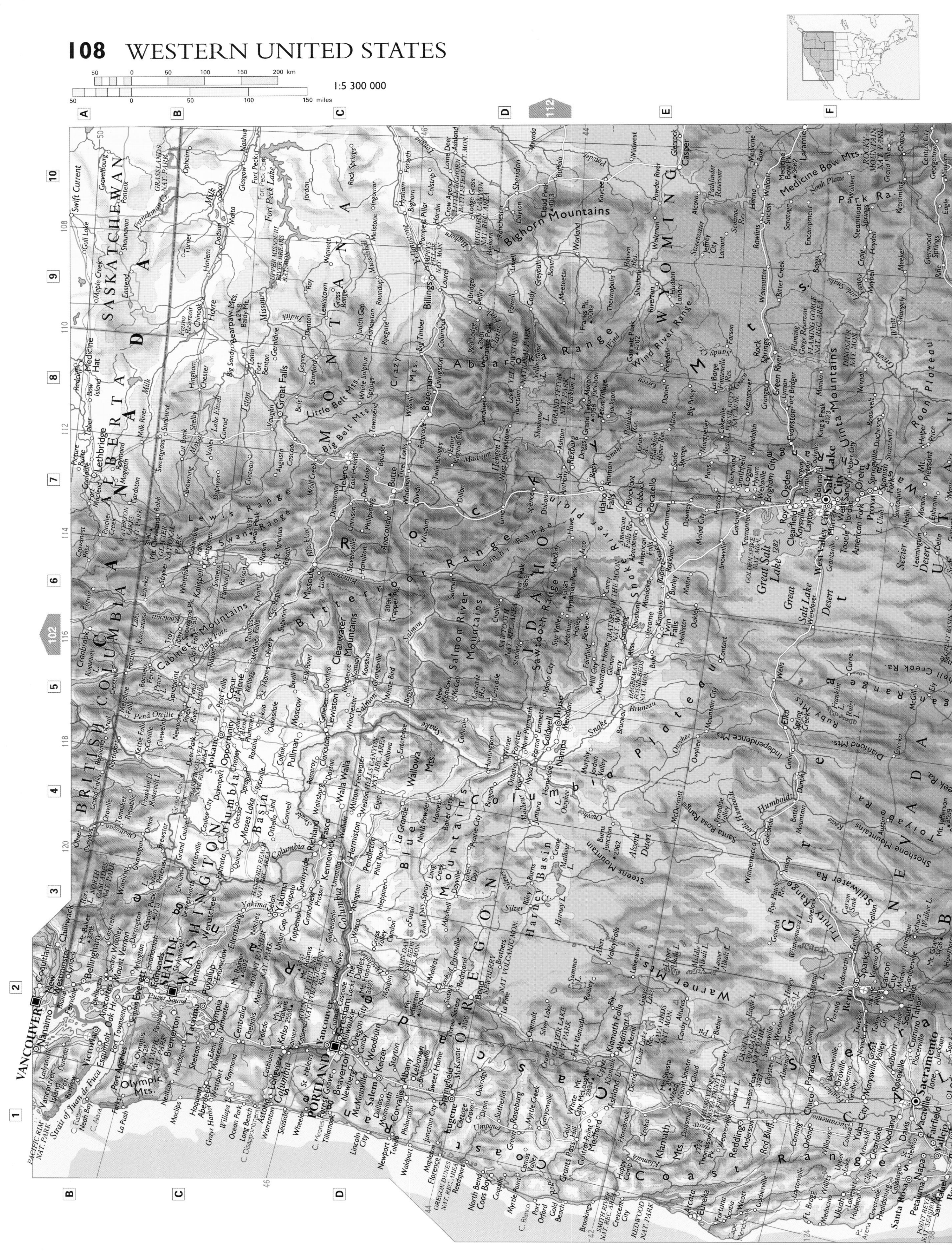

50 0 50 100 150 200 km
50 0 50 100 150 miles
1:5 300 000
A
B
C
D
E
F
112
102
1
2
3
4
5
6
7
8
9
10
BRITISH COLUMBIA
ALBERTA
SASKATCHEWAN
CANADA
WASHINGTON
OREGON
IDAHO
MONTANA
WYOMING
NEVADA
UTAH
CALIFORNIA
VANCOUVER
SEATTLE
PORTLAND
Sacramento
Salt Lake City
Boise
Spokane
Helena
Cheyenne
Casper
Billings
Great Falls
Reno
Great Salt Lake
Great Salt Lake Desert
Columbia Basin
Snake River Plain
Harney Basin
Bighorn Mountains
Wind River Range
Absaroka Range
Bitterroot Range
Salmon River Mountains
Sawtooth Range
Clearwater Mountains
Blue Mountains
Wallowa Mts.
Uinta Mountains
Medicine Bow Mts.
Rocky Mts.
Cascade Range
Klamath Mts.
Olympic Mts.
Steens Mountain
Ruby Mts.
Shoshone Mountains
Toiyabe Range
Stillwater Ra.
Trinity Range
Santa Rosa Range
Independence Mts.
Warner Mts.
Coast Ranges
Owyhee Plateau
Strait of Juan de Fuca
Puget Sound

PACIFIC
OCEAN
ARIZONA
NEW MEXICO
COLORADO
TEXAS
CHIHUAHUA
SONORA
MEXICO
BAJA CALIFORNIA
Golfo de California
Colorado Plateau
Painted Desert
Grand Canyon
Mojave Desert
Sonoran Desert
Desierto de Altar
Channel Is.
LOS ANGELES
SAN DIEGO
PHOENIX
Tucson
Albuquerque
Santa Fe
El Paso
Ciudad Juárez
Las Vegas
Tijuana
Mexicali
Hermosillo
Chihuahua
Isla Guadalupe (Mexico)
National Parks
West from Greenwich
Projection: Albers' Equal Area with two standard parallels
COPYRIGHT PHILIP'S

1:2 200 000

108
109

NEVADA
ARIZONA
CALIFORNIA
MEXICO
BAJA CALIFORNIA
PACIFIC OCEAN
Mojave Desert
Sonoran Desert
LAS VEGAS
Henderson
North Las Vegas
Lake Mead
Lake Mohave
LAKE MEAD NATIONAL RECREATION AREA
MOJAVE NATIONAL PRESERVE
JOSHUA TREE NATIONAL PARK
Death Valley
Amargosa Range
Avawatz Mts.
Providence Mts.
Chocolate Mts.
San Bernardino Mts.
San Gabriel Mts.
San Rafael Mts.
Tehachapi Mts.
Temblor Range
Channel Islands
CHANNEL ISLANDS NATIONAL PARK
SANTA MONICA MTS. NAT. REC. AREA
Santa Barbara Channel
San Pedro Channel
Salton Sea
Imperial Valley
Coachella Canal
Colorado River Aqueduct
Los Angeles Aqueduct
LOS ANGELES
SAN DIEGO
Tijuana
Mexicali
Bakersfield
Lancaster
Palmdale
Barstow
Victorville
Hesperia
San Bernardino
Riverside
Palm Springs
Indio
Santa Barbara
Ventura
Oxnard
Santa Maria
Lompoc
Long Beach
Anaheim
Santa Ana
Oceanside
Escondido
Chula Vista
Needles
Kingman
Lake Havasu City
Blythe
Yuma
El Centro
Calexico
Santa Catalina I.
San Clemente I.
San Nicolas I.
Santa Cruz I.
Santa Rosa I.
San Miguel I.
Santa Barbara I.
National Parks
West from Greenwich
Projection: Bonne
COPYRIGHT PHILIP'S
118
m
ft
12 000
9000
6000
4500
3000
1200
600
0
200
2000
6000
4000
3000
2000
1500
1000
400
200

50 0 50 100 150 200 km

1:5 300 000

50 0 50 100 150 miles

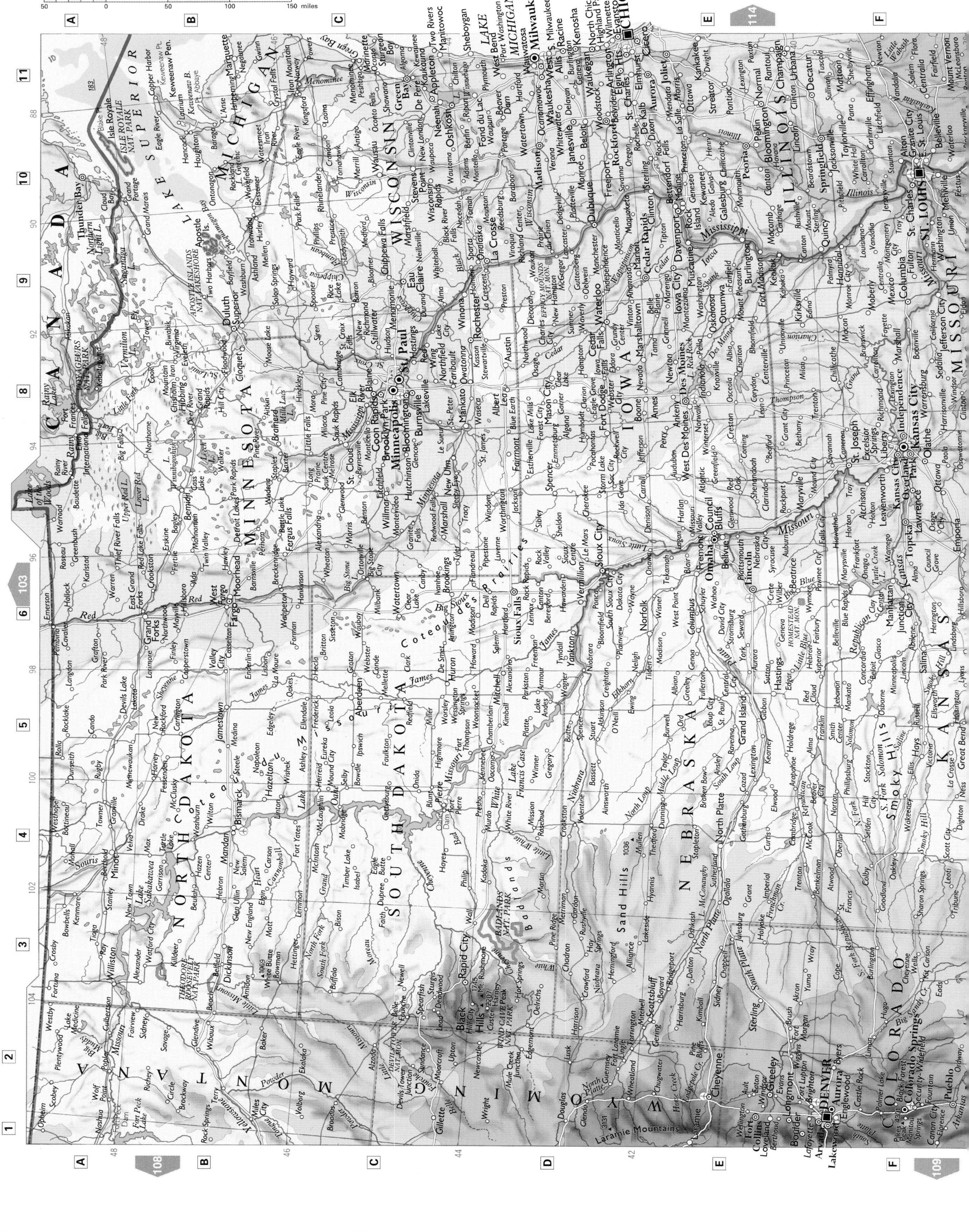

114

103

108

109

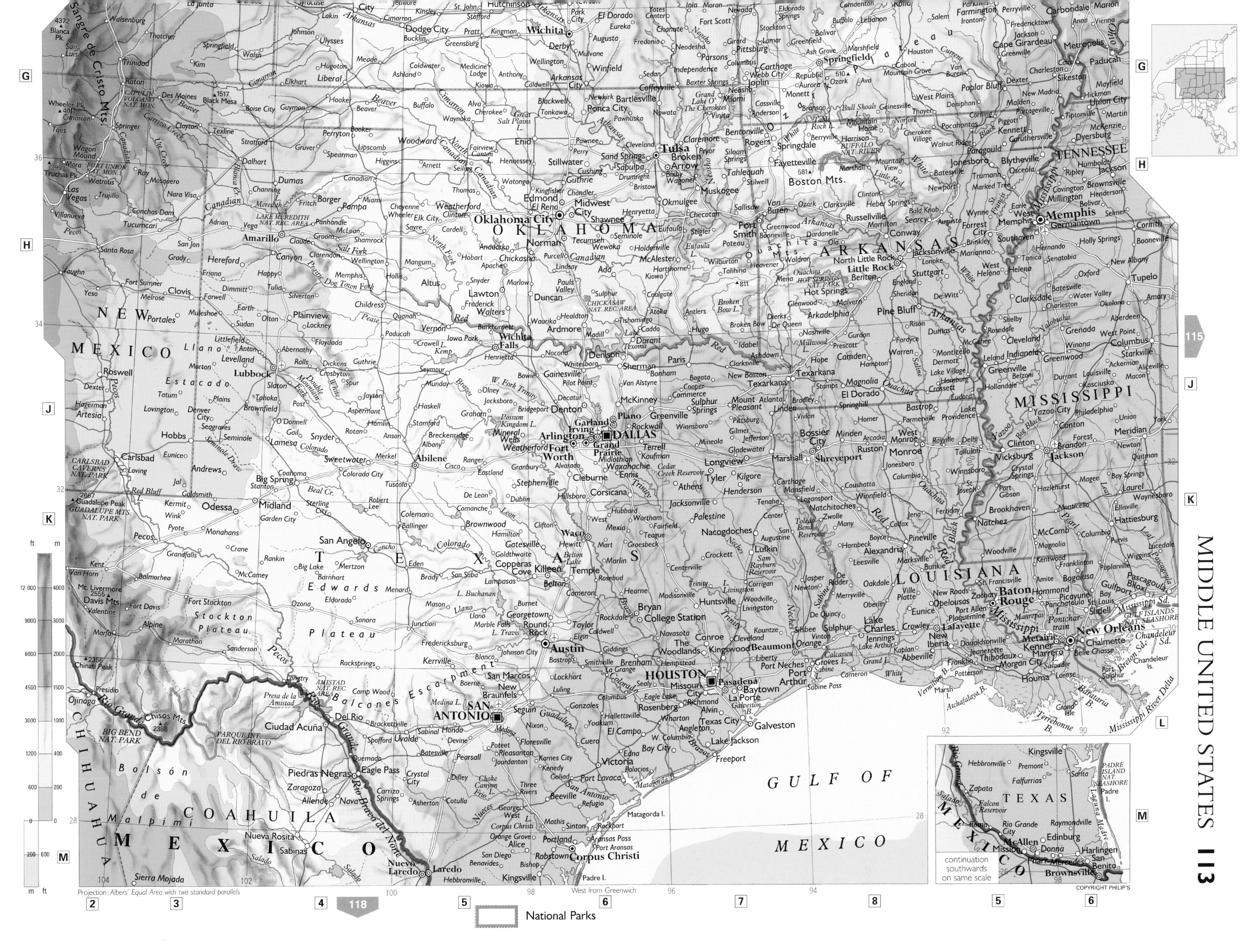
NEW MEXICO
OKLAHOMA
ARKANSAS
TENNESSEE
MISSISSIPPI
LOUISIANA
TEXAS
MEXICO
COAHUILA
CHIHUAHUA
GULF OF MEXICO
Wichita
Tulsa
Oklahoma City
Amarillo
Lubbock
Springfield
Memphis
Little Rock
Jackson
Shreveport
Dallas
Fort Worth
Arlington
Houston
San Antonio
Austin
Baton Rouge
New Orleans
Corpus Christi
Laredo
Brownsville
Sangre de Cristo Mts.
Boston Mts.
Ozark Plateau
Llano Estacado
Edwards Plateau
Stockton Plateau
Balcones Escarpment
Chisos Mts.
Bolsón de Mapimí
Rio Grande
Mississippi River Delta
115
118
National Parks
continuation southwards on same scale
West from Greenwich
Projection: Albers' Equal Area with two standard parallels
COPYRIGHT PHILIP'S

1:5 300 000
50 0 50 100 150 200 km
50 0 50 100 150 miles
LAKE SUPERIOR
LAKE HURON
LAKE MICHIGAN
LAKE ERIE
LAKE ONTARIO
Georgian Bay
ONTARIO
QUEBEC
MICHIGAN
WISCONSIN
ILLINOIS
INDIANA
OHIO
KENTUCKY
WEST VIRGINIA
VIRGINIA
PENNSYLVANIA
NEW YORK
VERMONT
NEW HAMPSHIRE
MASS.
R.I.
NEW JERSEY
MARYLAND
DELAWARE
CHICAGO
DETROIT
TORONTO
MONTREAL
Ottawa
Québec
BOSTON
NEW YORK
PHILADELPHIA
BALTIMORE
WASHINGTON D.C.
PITTSBURGH
CLEVELAND
Columbus
Cincinnati
Indianapolis
Louisville
Milwaukee
Grand Rapids
Buffalo
Rochester
Hamilton
Providence
Hartford
Norfolk
Virginia Beach
Chesapeake Bay
Delaware Bay
104
112

ATLANTIC OCEAN
GULF OF MEXICO
BAHAMAS
TENNESSEE
NORTH CAROLINA
SOUTH CAROLINA
GEORGIA
ALABAMA
FLORIDA
MISSISSIPPI
MAINE
NEW HAMPSHIRE
CANADA
Nashville
Knoxville
Chattanooga
Huntsville
Birmingham
Montgomery
Mobile
Pensacola
Tallahassee
Jacksonville
Savannah
Charleston
Columbia
Charlotte
Raleigh
Durham
Greensboro
Winston-Salem
Wilmington
ATLANTA
Augusta
Macon
Columbus
Orlando
TAMPA
St. Petersburg
Clearwater
Daytona Beach
West Palm Beach
Fort Lauderdale
MIAMI
Key Largo
Florida Keys
Portland
Bangor
Augusta
Grand Bahama
Freeport
Great Abaco I.
continuation eastwards on same scale
National Parks
West from Greenwich
Projection: Albers' Equal Area with two standard parallels
COPYRIGHT PHILIP'S
113
120

1:2 200 000
km
miles
Projection: Bonne
104
114
National Parks
LAKE HURON
LAKE ERIE
LAKE ONTARIO
Georgian Bay
ONTARIO
MICHIGAN
OHIO
PENNSYLVANIA
NEW YORK
BRUCE PENINSULA NAT. PARK
FATHOM FIVE NAT. MARINE PARK
GEORGIAN BAY ISLANDS NAT. PARK
ALGONQUIN PROVINCIAL PARK
POINT PELEE NAT. PARK
CUYAHOGA VALLEY NAT. PARK
Bruce Peninsula
Allegheny Plateau
Allegheny Mountains
Tuscarora Mts.
TORONTO
Mississauga
Hamilton
DETROIT
Windsor
CLEVELAND
PITTSBURGH
BUFFALO
ROCHESTER
London
Kitchener
Waterloo
Guelph
Brampton
Oakville
Burlington
St. Catharines
Niagara Falls
Erie
Akron
Canton
Youngstown
Sarnia
Port Huron
Barrie
Oshawa
Peterborough
Belleville
Altoona
State College
Mansfield
Wheeling
Steubenville

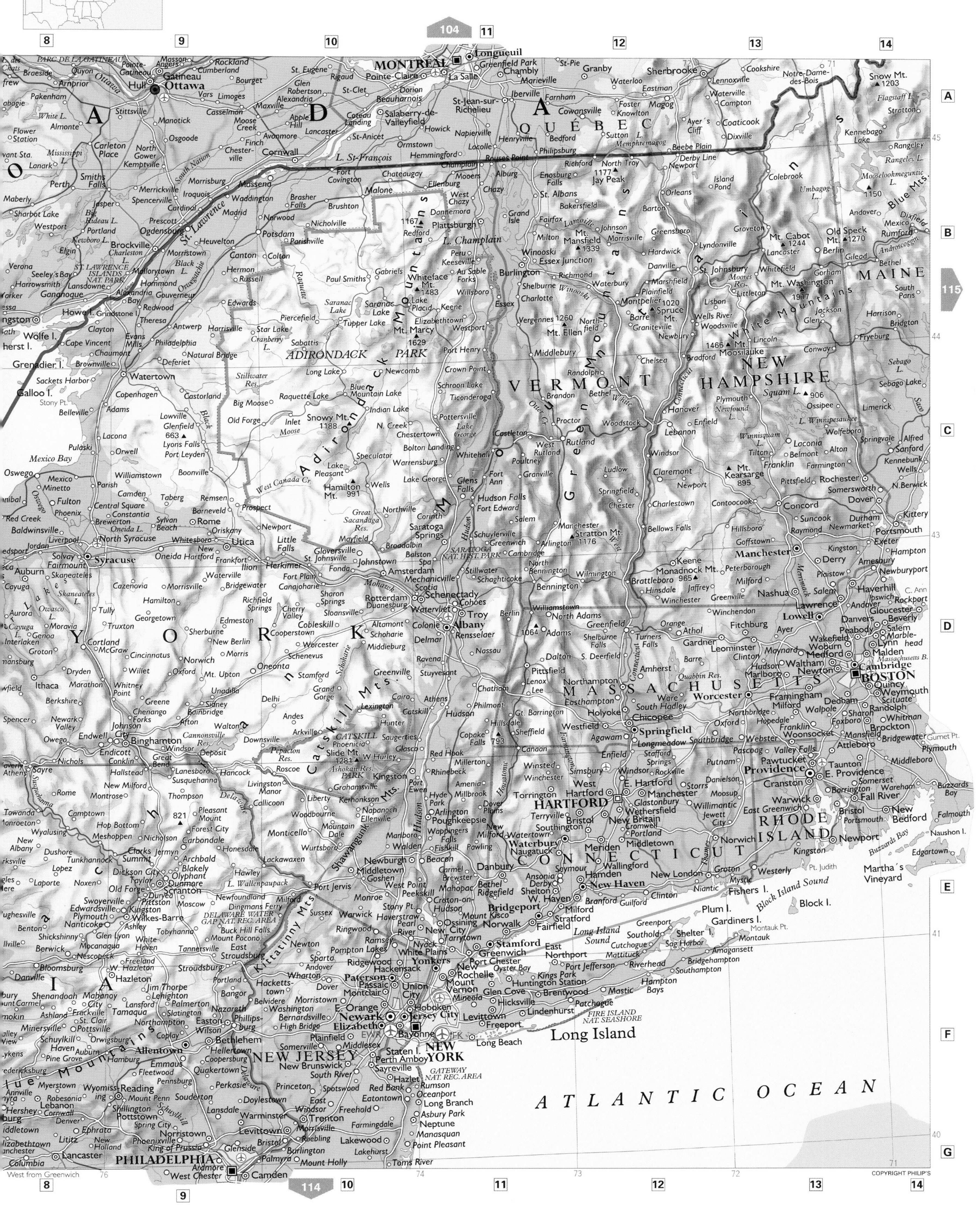
104
115
114
8 9 10 11 12 13 14
A B C D E F G
MONTREAL
Ottawa
Hull
Gatineau
Longueuil
La Salle
Pointe-Claire
Sherbrooke
Granby
Cornwall
Brockville
Kingston
QUÉBEC
ONTARIO
L. St-François
L. Champlain
St. Lawrence
ADIRONDACK PARK
Adirondack Mountains
Mt. Marcy 1629
Whiteface Mt. 1483
Lake Placid
Saranac Lake
Plattsburgh
Burlington
Montpelier
Barre
Mt. Mansfield 1339
Jay Peak 1177
VERMONT
Green Mountains
Rutland
Mt. Ellen 1260
Stratton Mt. 1176
NEW HAMPSHIRE
White Mountains
Mt. Washington 1917
Moosilauke 1466
Mt. Cabot 1244
Concord
Manchester
Nashua
Portsmouth
MAINE
Old Speck Mt. 1270
Snow Mt. 1203
Berlin
Watertown
Syracuse
Utica
Rome
Oswego
NORTH SYRACUSE
Mexico Bay
Schenectady
Albany
Troy
Saratoga Springs
SARATOGA NAT. HIST. PARK
Glens Falls
Catskill Mts.
CATSKILL PARK
Slide Mt. 1281
Binghamton
Ithaca
Cortland
Oneonta
Kingston
Poughkeepsie
Newburgh
Hudson
NEW YORK
Yonkers
Long Island
Long Island Sound
FIRE ISLAND NAT. SEASHORE
GATEWAY NAT. REC. AREA
Block Island Sound
Block I.
Fishers I.
Martha's Vineyard
MASSACHUSETTS
BOSTON
Cambridge
Worcester
Springfield
Lowell
Quincy
Brockton
Fall River
New Bedford
Pittsfield
Quabbin Res.
CONNECTICUT
HARTFORD
New Haven
Bridgeport
Stamford
Waterbury
Danbury
New London
RHODE ISLAND
Providence
Newport
Pawtucket
Cranston
NEW JERSEY
Newark
Jersey City
Elizabeth
Paterson
Trenton
Camden
PHILADELPHIA
Allentown
Bethlehem
Scranton
Wilkes-Barre
Kittatinny Mts.
Shawangunk Mts.
DELAWARE WATER GAP NAT. REC. AREA
Long Branch
Asbury Park
Toms River
ATLANTIC OCEAN
45
44
43
41
40
76
74
73
72
71
West from Greenwich

1:7 100 000

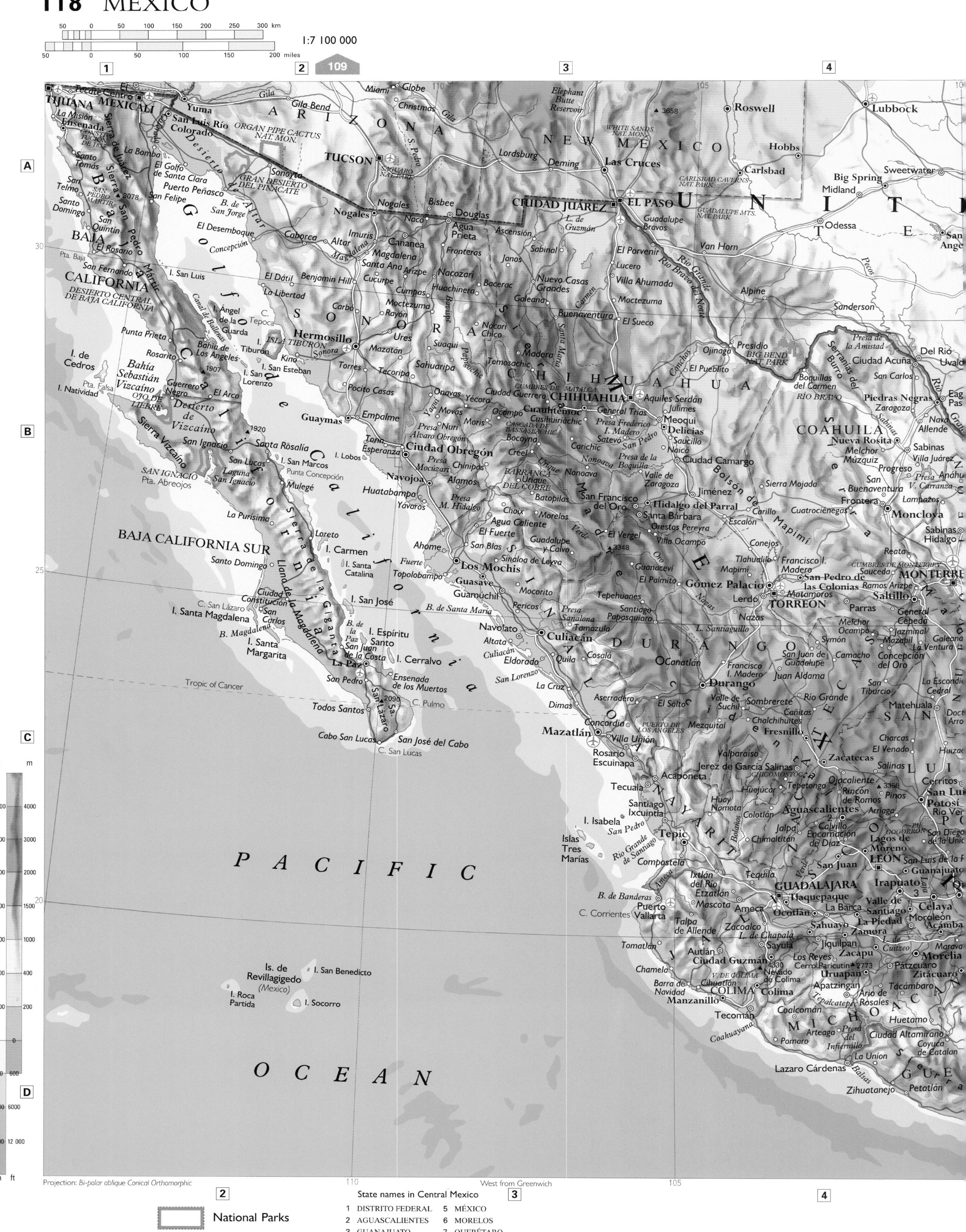

Projection: *Bi-polar oblique Conical Orthomorphic*

West from Greenwich

National Parks

State names in Central Mexico

1 DISTRITO FEDERAL
2 AGUASCALIENTES
3 GUANAJUATO
4 HIDALGO
5 MÉXICO
6 MORELOS
7 QUERÉTARO
8 TLAXCALA

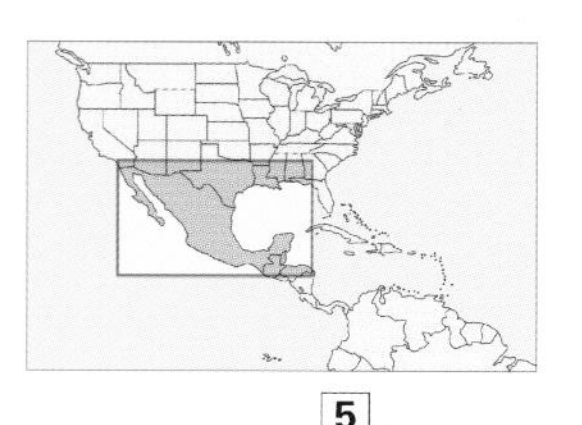

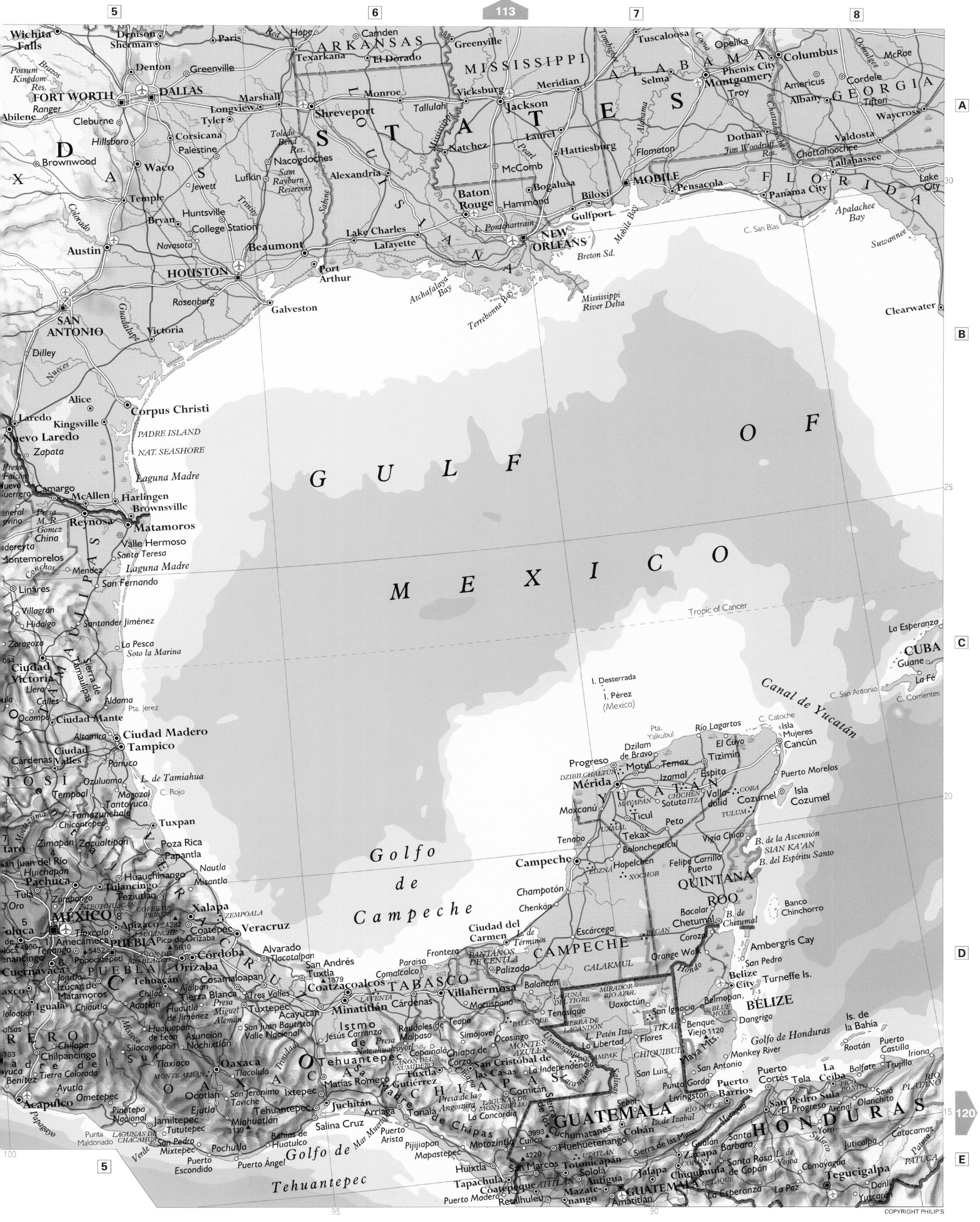

113

GULF OF MEXICO
Golfo de Campeche
Tropic of Cancer
Canal de Yucatán
Golfo de Honduras
Golfo de Tehuantepec
UNITED STATES
TEXAS
ARKANSAS
LOUISIANA
MISSISSIPPI
ALABAMA
GEORGIA
FLORIDA
TAMAULIPAS
VERACRUZ
PUEBLA
OAXACA
GUERRERO
TABASCO
CAMPECHE
YUCATÁN
QUINTANA ROO
CHIAPAS
BELIZE
GUATEMALA
HONDURAS
CUBA
MEXICO
DALLAS
FORT WORTH
HOUSTON
SAN ANTONIO
NEW ORLEANS
MOBILE
Corpus Christi
Galveston
Austin
Shreveport
Jackson
Montgomery
Tallahassee
Baton Rouge
Nuevo Laredo
Matamoros
Reynosa
Tampico
Ciudad Madero
Ciudad Victoria
Veracruz
Xalapa
Puebla
Oaxaca
Acapulco
Villahermosa
Campeche
Mérida
Cancún
Chetumal
Belize City
Belmopan
Tuxtla
Tapachula
GUATEMALA
Tegucigalpa
Mississippi River Delta
Breton Sd.
Atchafalaya Bay
Terrebonne Bay
Apalachee Bay
Mobile Bay
PADRE ISLAND NAT. SEASHORE
Laguna Madre
I. Desterrada
I. Pérez (Mexico)
Isla Mujeres
Isla Cozumel
Ambergris Cay
Turneffe Is.
Banco Chinchorro
Istmo de Tehuantepec
Sierra Madre de Chiapas
A
B
C
D
E
5
6
7
8
95
90
100
30
25
20
15

120

1:7 100 000
50 0 50 100 150 200 250 300 km
50 0 50 100 150 200 miles
JAMAICA
1:2 700 000
10 0 10 20 30 40 50 km
10 0 10 20 30 miles
a
CARIBBEAN SEA
Montego Bay
Lucea
Falmouth
Runaway Bay
St. Ann's Bay
Galina Point
Port Maria
Wakefield
Ocho Rios
Annotto Bay
South Negril Pt.
Negril
Cambridge
The Cockpit Country
Mount Denham 985
Dry Harbour Mountains
Moneague
Port Antonio
Savanna-la-Mar
Maggotty
Don Figuero Mts.
Linstead
The Blue Mountains
John Crow Mts.
Spanish Town
2256 Blue Mountain Peak
Black River
Mandeville
Portmore
KINGSTON
Morant Point
Santa Cruz Mts.
May Pen
Great Pedro Bluff
Alligator Pond
Portland Bight
Morant Bay
Port Morant
Portland Point
U. S. A.
L. Okeechobee
West Palm Beach
West End
Fort Myers
Boca Raton
Fort Lauderdale
Free-port
Grand Bahama
Hope Town
Little Abaco I.
Great Abaco I.
Naples
C. Romano
The Everglades
Hialeah
MIAMI
Northwest Providence Channel
Northeast Providence Channel
Bimini Is.
Berry Is.
EVERGLADES NAT. PARK
C. Sable
Florida Bay
Nicolls Town
Eleuthera I.
Nassau
New Providence
Adelaide
Dry Tortugas (U.S.A.)
Key West
Florida Keys
Straits of Florida
Great Bahama Bank
Andros Island
Andros Town
Exuma Sound
Great Guana Cay
Great Exuma I.
LA HABANA (Havana)
Marianao
Guanabacoa
Santa Cruz del Norte
Cay Sal Bank
Canal Nicholás
Santaren Channel
Matanzas
Cárdenas
Jovellanos
Colón
Sagua la Grande
Bahía Honda
La Esperanza
Guanajay
San Antonio de los Baños
Los Palacios
Güines
Batabanó
Jagüey Grande
Pinar del Río
Guane
San Luis
La Fé
C. Corrientes
C. San Antonio
Nueva Gerona
I. de la Juventud
Arch. de los Canarreos
Cienfuegos
Santa Clara
Placetas
Caibarién
Trinidad
Sancti Spíritus
Júcaro
Tunas de Zaza
Morón
Ciego de Ávila
Cayo Romano
Canal Viejo de Bahama
Duncan Town
Jumentos Cays
CUBA
Florida
Camagüey
Nuevitas
Puerto Manatí
Puerto Padre
Gibara
Arch. de Jardines de la Reina
Santa Cruz del Sur
Victoria de las Tunas
HOLGUÍN
Golfo de Guacanayabo
Bayamo
Manzanillo
Sierra Maestra
1994
SANTIAGO DE CUBA
C. Cruz
Greater
Cayman Islands (U.K.)
Cayman Brac
Little Cayman
George Town
Grand Cayman
7680
I. Desterrada
I. Pérez (Mexico)
GULF OF MEXICO
Canal de Yucatán
Punta Yalkubul
Río Lagartos
C. Catoche
Progreso
Dzilam de Bravo
El Cuyo
Tizimín
Cancún
Mérida
Motul
Temax
Izamal
Espita
El Diaz
YUCATÁN
Maxcanú
Sotuta
MAYAPÁN
CHICHEN ITZÁ
Valladolid
Puerto Morelos
Calkini
Ticul
Cozumel
Isla Cozumel
Tenabo
Tekax
Campeche
Peto
Bolonchenticul
Vigía Chico
Hopelchén
Champotón
San José Carpizo
Felipe Carrillo Puerto
B. de la Ascensión
SIAN KA'AN
B. del Espíritu Santo
Chenkán
Ciudad del Carmen
L. de Términos
MEXICO
QUINTANA ROO
Pedro Antonio Santos
Bacalar
Chetumal
B. de Chetumal
Corozal
Banco Chinchorro
Palizada
CAMPECHE
CALAKMUL
Balancán
Orange Walk
Ambergris Cay
MIRADOR-RÍO AZUL
Tenosique
LAGUNA DEL TIGRE
San Pedro
Uaxactún
Belmopan
Belize City
Turneffe Is.
BELIZE
San Ignacio
Ocosingo
SIERRA DEL LACANDÓN
L. Petén Itzá
TIKAL
Benque Viejo
Middlesex
Flores
1120
Dangriga
La Independencia
MONTES AZULES
La Libertad
CHIQUIBUL
Maya Mts.
Comitán
Golfo de Honduras
San Luis
Monkey River
San Antonio
Is. de la Bahía
Punta Gorda
Sebol
Livingston
Puerto Barrios
Puerto Cortés
Roatán
Puerto Castilla
Iriona
C. Camarón
GUATEMALA
3993
Cuilco
Cuchumatanes
Cobán
L. de Izabal
RÍO DULCE
Tela
La Ceiba
PICO BONITO
Balfate
Trujillo
RÍO PLÁTANO
Punta Patuca
Brus Laguna
Laguna Caratasca
San Marcos
Huehuetenango
Sierra de las Minas
San Pedro Sula
El Progreso
Savá
Olanchito
Arenal
Totonicapán
Sololá
Ayutla
Antigua
Jalapa
Zacapa
Santa Bárbara
El Jaral
Yoro
HONDURAS
Mosquitia
C. Falso
C. Gracias a Dios
Coatepeque
Retalhuleu
Mazatenango
GUATEMALA
Amatitlán
Escuintla
Chiquimula
Santa Rosa de Copán
L. de Yojoa
Juticalpa
Catacamas
Coco (Segovia)
Puerto Cabo Gracias á Dios
Kisalaya
San José
Santa Ana
La Esperanza
La Paz
Comayagua
Patuca
PATUCA
Cayos Miskitos (Nicaragua)
Ahuachapán
Sonsonate
Suchitoto
Cojutepeque
Tegucigalpa
Pta. Gorda
Puerto Cabezas
Acajutla
Nueva San Salvador
SAN SALVADOR
Zacatecoluca
Yuscarán
Danlí
Bonanza
Nacaome
Ocotal
Siuna
EL SALVADOR
Usulután
San Miguel
La Unión
Choluteca
Somoto
SASLAYA
Cord. Isabelia
Estelí
Jinotega
Tuma
Tungla
Prinzapolca
G. de Fonseca
Puerto Morazán
El Sauce
Matagalpa
Muy Muy
San Pedro del Norte
Río Grande
Chinandega
NICARAGUA
Corinto
León
Boaco
Siquia
La Paz Centro
L. de Managua
Santo Domingo
Punta de Perlas
MANAGUA
Masaya
Juigalpa
Rama
Is. del Maíz (Nicaragua)
Diriamba
Granada
Bluefields
Jinotepe
Lago de Nicaragua
I. de Ometepe
Cord. de Yolaina
El Bluff
Pta. Mico
Rivas
San Juan del Sur
B. de Salinas
GUANACASTE
La Cruz
C. Santa Elena
SANTA ROSA
G. de Papagayo
San Carlos
Los Chiles
San Juan
B. de San Juan del Norte
San Juan del Norte
C. Velas
Liberia
PALO VERDE
COSTA RICA
Cord. de Guanacaste
TORTUGUERO
Santa Cruz
Nicoya
Cord. Central
Guápiles
Siquirres
Carmona
Alajuela
San José
Limón
Puntarenas
Cartago
Pen. de Nicoya
Esparza
Pta. Mona
C. Blanco
G. de Nicoya
Pandora
Bribri
3837
Chirripó Grande
Cord. de Talamanca
AMISTAD
Bocas del Toro
L. de Chiriquí
Puerto Quepos
3374
Almirante
B. de Coronado
Buenos Aires
Chiriquí Grande
G. de los Mosquitos
Puerto Cortés
Volcán Barú
CORCOVADO
San Vito
Boquete
Pen. de Osa
Golfito
La Concepción
Serranía de Tabasará
G. Dulce
Puerto Armuelles
David
Remedios
Pta. Burica
Santiago
Soná
G. de Chiriquí
COIBA
I. de Coiba
I. Jicarón
Chitré
Pen. de Azuero
I. de Cebaco
Las Tablas
Pocri
Tonosí
Pta. Mala
CERRO HOYA
Punta Mariato
Bajo Nuevo (Colombia)
Is. Santanilla (Swan Islands) (Honduras)
Pedro Cays (Jamaica)
CARIB
Cayos Roncador (Colombia)
I. de Providencia (Colombia)
I. de San Andrés (Colombia)
Cayos de Albuquerque (Colombia)
Montego Bay
Falmouth
St. Ann's Bay
Port Maria
Annotto Bay
Lucea
Negril
South Negril Pt.
Cambridge
Port Antonio
Savanna-la-Mar
JAMAICA
Black River
Mandeville
May Pen
Spanish Town
KINGSTON
Port Morant
Pta. Manzanillo
Nombre de Dios
Portobelo
Archipiélago de San Blas
Panama Canal
CHAGRES
L. Gatún
Colón
Balboa
Chepo
Serranía del Darién
Golfo del Darién
PANAMÁ
La Chorrera
Chimán
PANAMA
Penonomé
Río Hato
Arch. de las Perlas
San Miguel
I. del Rey
Aguadulce
La Palma
Yaviza
Golfo de Panamá
Garachiné
El Real
DARIÉN
Jaqué
G. de Urabá
CARTAG
I. de San Bernardo
PACIFIC OCEAN
GUADELOUPE AND MARTINIQUE
1:1 800 000
10 0 10 20 30 40 50 60 km
10 0 10 20 30 40 miles
b
Pte. de la Grande Vigie
Port-Louis
Grande-Terre
Pointe Allègre
Petit-Canal
Moule
La Désirade
Ste-Rose
Pointe-à-Pitre
Pointe des Châteaux
Pointe-Noire
Ste-Anne
Gosier
Basse-Terre
Îles de la Petite Terre
Bouillante
GUADELOUPE (Fr.)
GUADELOUPE
Soufrière 1467
Capesterre-Belle-Eau
Marie-Galante
Basse-Terre
St-Louis
204
Trois-Rivières
Capesterre
Grand-Bourg
Îles des Saintes
Pte. des Basses
c
Cap St-Martin
Basse-Pointe
1463
Montagne Pelée
Ste-Marie
Le Prêcheur
Presqu'île de la Caravelle
St-Pierre
La Trinité
St-Joseph
Le Robert
Schœlcher
Le François
Fort-de-France
Le Lamentin
Rivière-Salée
Le St-Esprit
MARTINIQUE (Fr.)
Rivière-Pilote
Le Marin
Pte. d'Enfer
Projection: Conical with two standard parallels

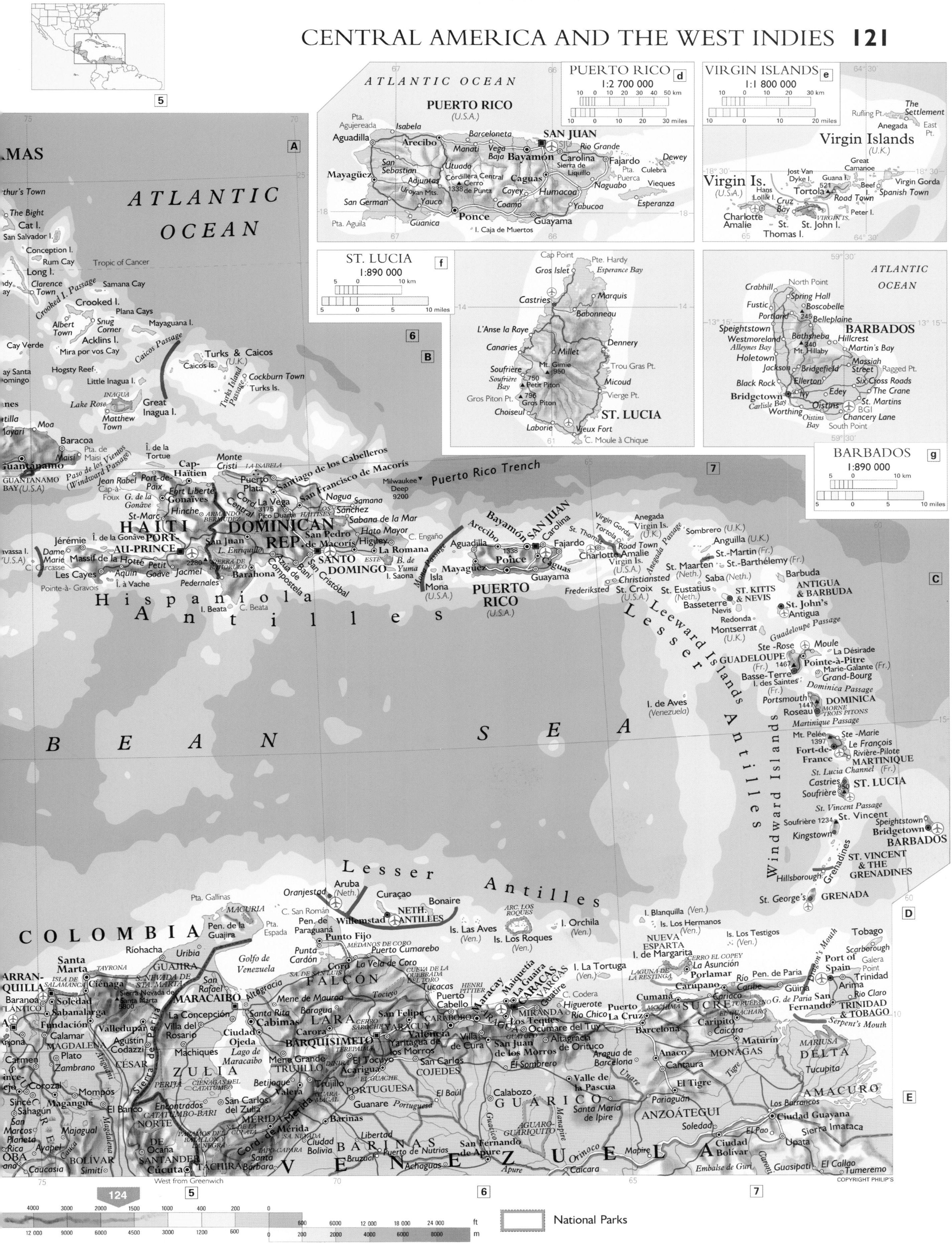

PUERTO RICO d
1:2 700 000

VIRGIN ISLANDS e
1:1 800 000

ST. LUCIA f
1:890 000

BARBADOS g
1:890 000

ATLANTIC OCEAN

CARIBBEAN SEA

Lesser Antilles

Leeward Islands

Windward Islands

West from Greenwich

National Parks

100 0 200 400 600 800 1000 1200 1400 km
100 0 200 400 600 800 1000 miles
1:31 100 000
Tropic of Cancer
Yucatan Channel
Cuba
Greater Antilles
Turks & Caicos Is.
Gulf of Campeche
Yucatán Peninsula
Hispaniola
9200
Puerto Rico
NORTH ATLANTIC OCEAN
Isthmus of Tehuantepec
G. de Honduras
Jamaica
Lesser Antilles
Guadeloupe
Dominica
Martinique
St. Lucia
St. Vincent
Barbados
C. Gracias a Dios
Caribbean Sea
Coco
Guatemala Trench
L. Nicaragua
C. de la Aguja
5800
Sierra Nevada de Santa Marta
L. Maracaibo
I. Margarita
Grenada
Tobago
Trinidad
Panama Canal
G. of Darién
Llanos
Orinoco
Card. de Mérida
Magdalena
Gulf of Panamá
Meta
Guiana Highlands
2810
Mt. Roraima
Sierra Pacaraima
Essequibo
Courantyne
Serra Tumucumaque
C. Orange
Cordillera Occidental
Cordillera Central
Cordillera Oriental
Guaviare
C. de San Francisco
Branco
Negro
Cotopaxi 5897
Chimborazo 6267
Caquetá
Equator
Japurá
Putumayo
Amazon
Marajó I.
Galapagos Is.
Napo
Amazon
G. of Guayaquil
Pta. Pariñas
Pta. Negra
Marañón
Tocantins
Tapajós
Xingu
Parnaíba
C. de São Roque
Juruá
Selvas
Purus
Madeira
Ucayali
Aripuanã
Roosevelt
Teles Pires
Huascarán 6768
Plat. of Borborema
São Francisco
Araguaia
Madre de Dios
Arinos
Guaporé
Plateau of Mato Grosso
Brazilian Highlands
Mamoré
Chincha Alta
L. Titicaca
Nevado Ancohuma 6550
Chile Peru Trench
Bolivian Plateau
L. de Poopó
PACIFIC OCEAN
Gran Chaco
Abrolhos Bank
Paraguay
Paraná
2890 Pico da Bandeira
Serra da Mantiqueira
Atacama Desert
8050
Pilcomayo
C. Frio
Tropic of Capricorn
Cerro Ojos del Salado 6863
San Félix
San Ambrosio
Iguaçu Falls
Uruguay
Serra do Mar
Salado
Paraná
Entre Ríos
Salinas Grandes
Andes
Sierra de Córdoba
L. Mar Chiquita
Mt. Aconcagua 6962
L. dos Patos
Arch. de Juan Fernández
Pampas
Río de la Plata
SOUTH ATLANTIC OCEAN
Colorado
Bahía Blanca
Negro
G. San Matías
Chile Rise
Chiloé I.
40
Valdés Peninsula
Chubut
Patagonia
Chonos Archipelago
Mte. San Valentín 4058
Argentine Basin
Taitao Peninsula
Gulf of San Jorge
Gulf of Penas
6212
Wellington I.
Madre de Dios I.
Falkland Is.
West Falkland
East Falkland
Magellan's Str.
Santa Inés I.
Tierra del Fuego
Staten I.
Canal Cockburn
Canal Beagle
C. Horn
South Georgia
ft m
12000 4000
9000 3000
6000 2000
3000 1000
1500 500
600 200
0 0
200 600
1000 3000
2000 6000
4000 12000
6000 18000
8000 24000
m ft
Projection: Lambert's Azimuthal Equal Area
West from Greenwich
COPYRIGHT PHILIP'S

1:31 100 000
NORTH ATLANTIC OCEAN
Caribbean Sea
PACIFIC OCEAN
SOUTH ATLANTIC OCEAN
BRAZIL
ARGENTINA
CHILE
PERU
BOLIVIA
COLOMBIA
VENEZUELA
ECUADOR
PARAGUAY
URUGUAY
GUYANA
SURINAME
FRENCH GUIANA
MEXICO
CUBA
Projection: Lambert's Azimuthal Equal Area
West from Greenwich
LIMA Capital Cities

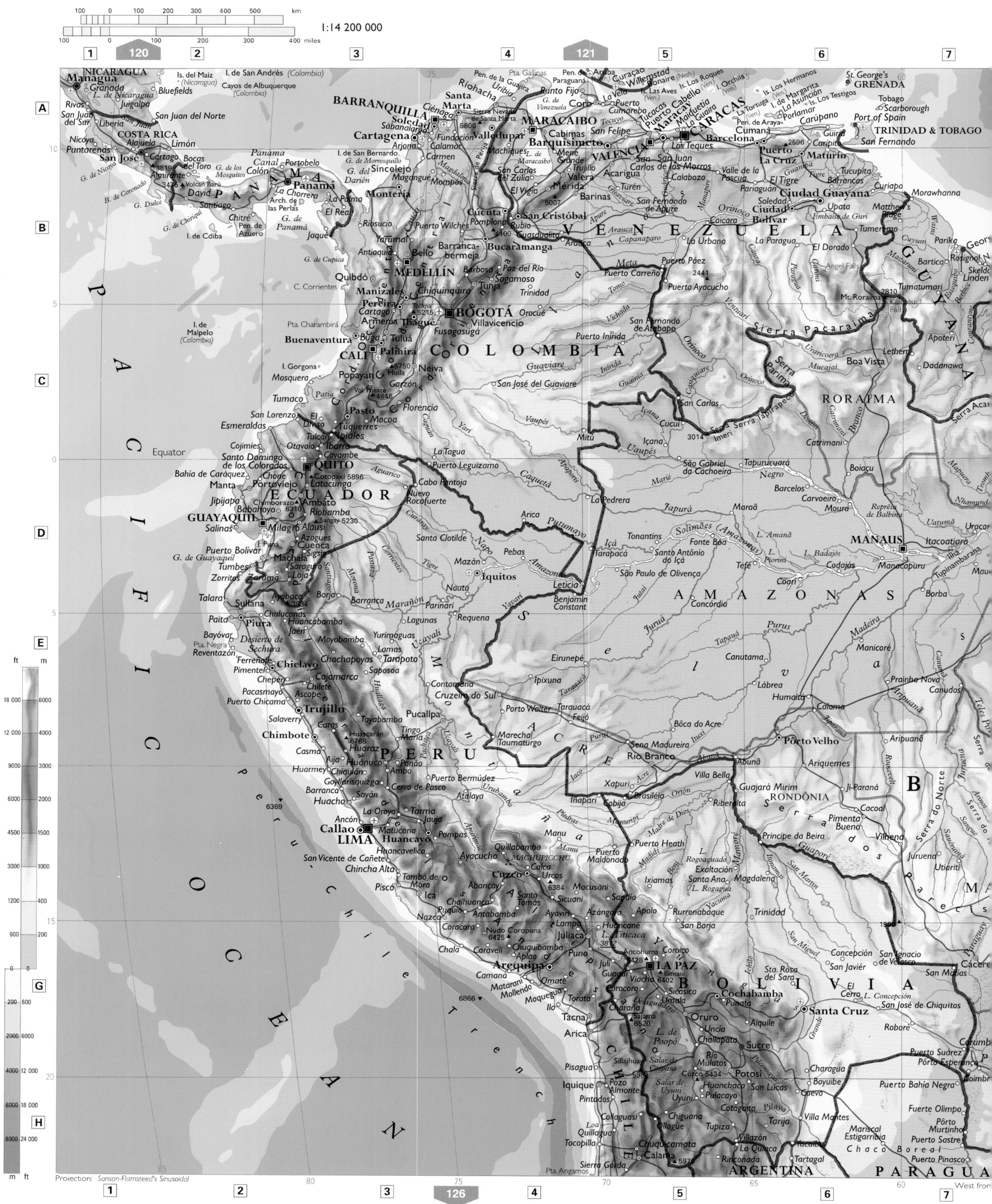
1:14 200 000
km
miles
120
121
126
NICARAGUA
Managua
Granada
L. de Nicaragua
Juigalpa
Bluefields
Is. del Maiz
I. de San Andrés (Colombia)
Cayos de Albuquerque (Colombia)
San Juan del Norte
COSTA RICA
Liberia
Alajuela
Limón
Puntarenas
San José
Cartago
Bocas del Toro
Colón
Panamá
PANAMA
David
Santiago
Chitré
I. de Coiba
G. de Panamá
Jaqué
Panama Canal
Portobelo
BARRANQUILLA
Cartagena
Santa Marta
Riohacha
Valledupar
Sincelejo
Montería
MARACAIBO
Barquisimeto
VALENCIA
CARACAS
Maracay
Barcelona
Cumaná
Maturín
Ciudad Guayana
Ciudad Bolívar
San Fernando de Apure
San Cristóbal
Mérida
Barinas
Cúcuta
Bucaramanga
MEDELLÍN
BOGOTÁ
Manizales
Pereira
Ibagué
Villavicencio
Quibdó
Buenaventura
CALI
Palmira
Popayán
Neiva
Pasto
Florencia
Tumaco
Puerto Ayacucho
Puerto Carreño
COLOMBIA
VENEZUELA
GUYANA
Port of Spain
TRINIDAD & TOBAGO
GRENADA
St. George's
Mt. Roraima
Sierra Pacaraima
RORAIMA
Boa Vista
Lethem
Esmeraldas
QUITO
Cotopaxi 5896
Chimborazo 6310
ECUADOR
GUAYAQUIL
Cuenca
Machala
Loja
Manta
Portoviejo
Ambato
Riobamba
Equator
Tumbes
Talara
Sullana
Piura
Chiclayo
Cajamarca
Trujillo
Chimbote
Huascarán 6768
Huaraz
Huánuco
Cerro de Pasco
Callao
LIMA
Huancayo
Ayacucho
Cuzco
MACHUPICCHU
Arequipa
Puno
Juliaca
L. Titicaca
Tacna
Arica
Iquique
PERU
Iquitos
Leticia
Pucallpa
Puerto Maldonado
Rio Branco
Porto Velho
MANAUS
Manacapuru
AMAZONAS
ACRE
RONDÔNIA
LA PAZ
Cochabamba
Oruro
Sucre
Potosí
Santa Cruz
Tarija
BOLIVIA
Trinidad
CHILE
Calama
ARGENTINA
PARAGUAY
PACIFIC OCEAN
Peru-Chile Trench
Projection: Sanson-Flamsteed's Sinusoidal

TRINIDAD AND TOBAGO
1:2 200 000
West from Greenwich
Tobago
Charlotteville
North Pt.
Little Tobago
Castara
Main Ridge
Roxborough
Plymouth
Scarborough
Buccoo Reef
Crown Pt.
Rockly Bay
Blanchisseuse
Sans Souci
Matelot
Toco
Galera Pt.
Redhead
Salibea
Northern Range
Mt. Aripo
Maracas Bay Village
La Vache Pt.
Chupara Pt.
Corozal Pt.
Monos I.
Dragon's Mouth
VENEZUELA
Pen. de Paria
Macuro
Güiria
Maraval
Port of Spain
San Juan
Tunapuna
Arima
Valencia
Matura Bay
Caroni
Guaico
Sangre Grande
Talparo
Upper Manzanilla
Chaguanas
Nariva Swamp
Cocos Bay
Couva
Golfo de Paria
Point Lisas
Otaheite Bay
Trinidad
San Fernando
Gasparillo
Rio Claro
Guatuaro Pt.
Brighton
Guapo Bay
La Brea
Pitch Lake
Princes Town
Pierreville
Mayaro Bay
Point Fortin
Penal
Basse Terre
Guayaguayare
Cedros Bay
Bonasse
Palo Seco
Siparia
Trinity Hills
Galeota Pt.
Icacos Pt.
Erin Pt.
La Lune
Moruga
Serpent's Mouth
Pta. Bombedor
ATLANTIC OCEAN
Paramaribo
Nieuw Amsterdam
Moengo
St-Laurent
Iracoubo
Sinnamary
Kourou
Cayenne
Kaw
C. Orange
St-Georges
Oiapoque
SURINAME
FRENCH GUIANA
Camopi
Amapá
I. de Maracá
AMAPÁ
Macapá
Equator
I. Caviana
I. Mexiana
C. Maguarinho
Salinópolis
Bragança
I. de Marajó
BELÉM
Abaetetuba
Cametá
Santarém
Altamira
PARÁ
Tucuruí
Itaituba
Marabá
São Luís
MARANHÃO
Imperatriz
Barra do Corda
Bacabal
Codó
Caxias
Parnaíba
Teresina
PIAUÍ
FORTALEZA
Sobral
CEARÁ
Mossoró
Natal
C. de São Roque
RIO GRANDE DO NORTE
João Pessoa
PARAÍBA
Campina Grande
RECIFE
Olinda
Jaboatão
PERNAMBUCO
Maceió
ALAGOAS
SERGIPE
Aracaju
Fernando de Noronha (Braz.)
Rocas
São Paulo (Braz.)
Petrolina
Juàzeiro
TOCANTINS
Palmas
BAHIA
Feira de Santana
SALVADOR
Vitória da Conquista
Ilhéus
Porto Seguro
BRASÍLIA
Anápolis
Goiânia
GOIÁS
MATO GROSSO
Cuiabá
Rondonópolis
MATO GROSSO DO SUL
Campo Grande
MINAS GERAIS
Montes Claros
Uberlândia
BELO HORIZONTE
Governador Valadares
ESPÍRITO SANTO
Vitória
Vila Velha
Cachoeiro de Itapemirim
Juiz de Fora
Campos
Ribeirão Prêto
SÃO PAULO
Campinas
Petrópolis
Nova Friburgo
RIO DE JANEIRO
Niterói
Cabo Frio
Trindade (Braz.)
Dourados
Ponta Porã
Presidente Prudente
Bauru
Piracicaba
Serra do Cachimbo
Planalto do Mato Grosso
Serra do Espinhaço
6059

1:7 100 000

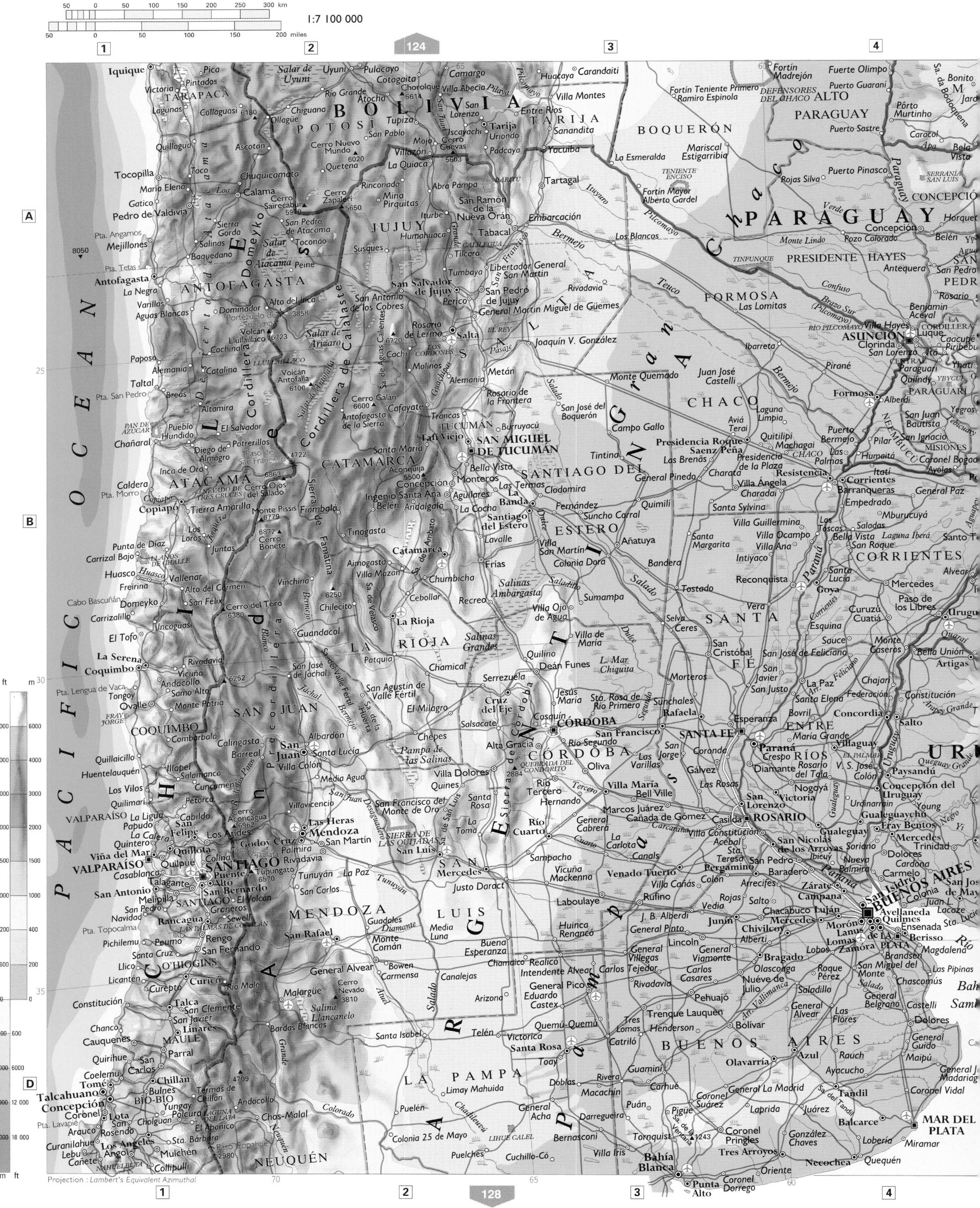
PACIFIC OCEAN
BOLIVIA
PARAGUAY
ARGENTINA
CHILE
Gran Chaco
Desierto de Atacama
Cordillera Domeyko
Cordillera de Calalaste
Precordillera
TARAPACÁ
ANTOFAGASTA
ATACAMA
COQUIMBO
VALPARAÍSO
SANTIAGO
O'HIGGINS
MAULE
BIO-BIO
POTOSÍ
TARIJA
BOQUERÓN
ALTO PARAGUAY
PRESIDENTE HAYES
JUJUY
SALTA
FORMOSA
CHACO
CATAMARCA
TUCUMÁN
SANTIAGO DEL ESTERO
CORRIENTES
LA RIOJA
SAN JUAN
CÓRDOBA
SANTA FE
ENTRE RÍOS
MENDOZA
SAN LUIS
LA PAMPA
BUENOS AIRES
NEUQUÉN
ASUNCIÓN
SAN MIGUEL DE TUCUMÁN
CÓRDOBA
SANTA FE
ROSARIO
BUENOS AIRES
SANTIAGO
VALPARAÍSO
Mendoza
Salta
San Salvador de Jujuy
Corrientes
Resistencia
Paraná
Antofagasta
Iquique
Calama
Copiapó
La Serena
Coquimbo
Concepción
Talcahuano
Mar del Plata
Bahía Blanca
Santa Rosa
San Luis
San Juan
La Rioja
Catamarca
Santiago del Estero
Formosa
Tarija
Concepción
Río Cuarto
Tandil
Chillán
Talca
Curicó
Rancagua
Los Ángeles
Projection : Lambert's Equivalent Azimuthal

125

5
6
7
A
B
C
D
BELO HORIZONTE
Nova Lima
Itabirito
Vitória
Vila Velha
Guarapari
Pico da Bandeira 2890
Cachoeiro de Itapemirim
Três Lagoas
Andradina
Araçatuba
Birigui
São José do Rio Prêto
Ribeirão Prêto
Passos
Oliveira
Conselheiro Lafaiete
Barbacena
Juiz de Fora
Cataguases
Ubá
Muriaé
Itaperuna
Leopoldina
CAMPOS
Cabo de São Tomé
Macaé
Cabo Frio
Nova Friburgo
Petrópolis
Duque de Caxias
NOVA IGUAÇU
Niterói
São Gonçalo
RIO DE JANEIRO
Tropic of Capricorn
Ilha Grande
Angra dos Reis
Baía da Ilha Grande
Volta Redonda
Barra Mansa
Taubaté
São José dos Campos
Jacareí
Moji das Cruzes
GUARULHOS
SÃO PAULO
SANTO ANDRÉ
São Bernardo do Campo
São Vicente
SANTOS
Guarujá
Ilha de São Sebastião
Sorocaba
Jundiaí
CAMPINAS
Piracicaba
Limeira
Americana
Rio Claro
Araraquara
São Carlos
Bauru
Jaú
Marília
Presidente Prudente
Assis
Ourinhos
Londrina
Maringá
Apucarana
Umuarama
Cascavel
Foz do Iguaçu
Ciudad del Este
Ponta Grossa
CURITIBA
Paranaguá
Joinville
São Francisco do Sul
Itajaí
Blumenau
Brusque
Florianópolis
Ilha de Santa Catarina
Lajes
Laguna
Tubarão
Criciúma
Cabo Santa Marta Grande
Torres
Caxias do Sul
Bento Gonçalves
Passo Fundo
Novo Hamburgo
São Leopoldo
Canoas
PORTO ALEGRE
Viamão
Santa Maria
Santa Cruz do Sul
Cachoeira do Sul
Lagoa dos Patos
Pelotas
Rio Grande
São José do Norte
Bagé
Jaguarão
Lagoa Mirim
Lagoa Mangueira
Santa Vitória do Palmar
Chuy
Castillos
Rocha
Maldonado
San Carlos
MONTEVIDEO
Plata
B R A Z I L
P A R A N Á
SANTA CATARINA
R I O   G R A N D E   D O   S U L
S Ã O   P A U L O
M A T O   G R O S S O   D O   S U L
MISIONES
UAY
Dourados
Ponta Porã
Pedro Juan Caballero
A T L A N T I C
O C E A N
5304
55
50
45
40
25
30
35
West from Greenwich
National Parks

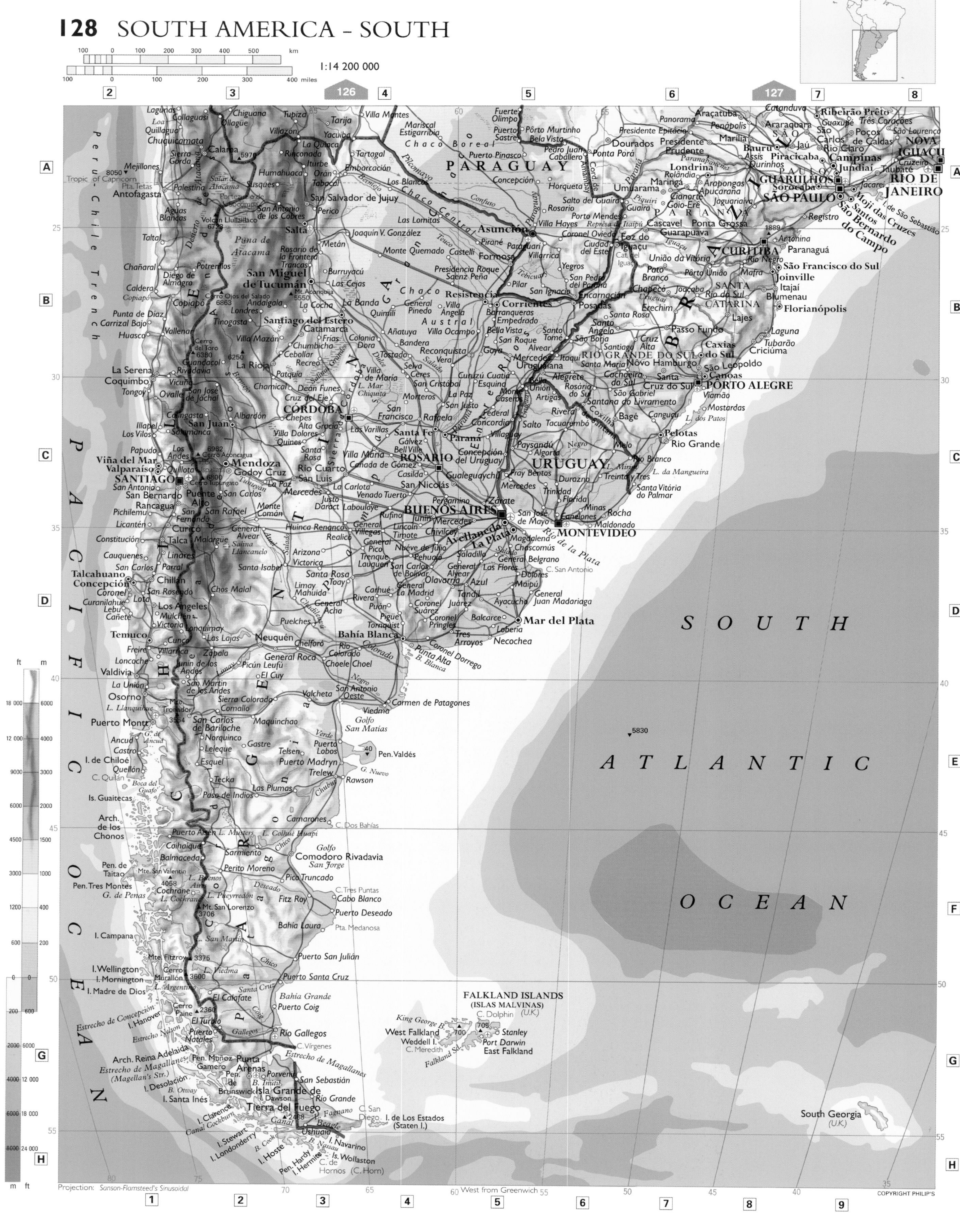
1:14 200 000
km
miles
126
127
PARAGUAY
URUGUAY
SOUTH
ATLANTIC
OCEAN
PACIFIC OCEAN
Peru-Chile Trench
Tropic of Capricorn
Chaco Boreal
Chaco Austral
Puna de Atacama
Desierto de Atacama
Antofagasta
Calama
Iquique
Chuquicamata
Taltal
Chañaral
Copiapó
Caldera
Vallenar
Huasco
La Serena
Coquimbo
Ovalle
Illapel
Los Vilos
Viña del Mar
Valparaíso
SANTIAGO
San Antonio
San Bernardo
Rancagua
Curicó
Talca
Linares
Cauquenes
Chillán
Talcahuano
Concepción
Coronel
Lota
Los Angeles
Temuco
Valdivia
Osorno
Puerto Montt
I. de Chiloé
Castro
Ancud
Quellón
Is. Guaitecas
Arch. de los Chonos
Puerto Aisén
Coihaique
Balmaceda
Pen. de Taitao
Pen.Tres Montes
G. de Penas
Cochrane
I. Campana
I. Wellington
I. Madre de Dios
I. Hanover
Estrecho de Concepción
Puerto Natales
Punta Arenas
Estrecho de Magallanes (Magellan's Str.)
I. Desolación
I. Santa Inés
Isla Grande de Tierra del Fuego
Porvenir
Ushuaia
Río Grande
I. Navarino
I. Hoste
I. Hermite
Is. Wollaston
C. de Hornos (C. Horn)
I. de Los Estados (Staten I.)
Río Gallegos
Cabo Vírgenes
El Calafate
Puerto Santa Cruz
Puerto San Julián
Puerto Deseado
Comodoro Rivadavia
Camarones
Rawson
Trelew
Puerto Madryn
Pen. Valdés
Golfo San Matías
Viedma
Carmen de Patagones
San Antonio Oeste
San Carlos de Bariloche
Esquel
Neuquén
General Roca
Bahía Blanca
Mar del Plata
Necochea
Tandil
Azul
Olavarría
La Plata
BUENOS AIRES
Mercedes
Zárate
Luján
Junín
Pergamino
San Nicolás
ROSARIO
Santa Fe
Paraná
CÓRDOBA
Río Cuarto
Villa María
San Luis
Mendoza
San Juan
San Rafael
La Rioja
Catamarca
Santiago del Estero
San Miguel de Tucumán
Salta
San Salvador de Jujuy
Tartagal
Resistencia
Corrientes
Formosa
Posadas
Asunción
Concepción
Encarnación
Ciudad del Este
Foz do Iguaçu
Río de la Plata
MONTEVIDEO
Maldonado
Paysandú
Salto
Rivera
Tacuarembó
Mercedes
Melo
L. Mirim
Pelotas
Rio Grande
PÔRTO ALEGRE
Canoas
Santa Maria
Passo Fundo
Caxias do Sul
Florianópolis
Blumenau
Joinville
CURITIBA
Paranaguá
Ponta Grossa
Londrina
Maringá
Cascavel
SÃO PAULO
GUARULHOS
Campinas
Santos
RIO DE JANEIRO
NOVA IGUAÇU
Sorocaba
Jundiaí
Piracicaba
Bauru
Ribeirão Prêto
Presidente Prudente
Dourados
Ponta Porã
Aconcagua 6962
Mt. Aconquija 5550
Cerro Ojos del Salado 6863
Cerro del Toro 6380
Mt. San Lorenzo 3706
Mte. Fitzroy 3375
5830
FALKLAND ISLANDS (ISLAS MALVINAS) (U.K.)
West Falkland
East Falkland
Stanley
Falkland Sd.
South Georgia (U.K.)
ft
m
Projection: Sanson-Flamsteed's Sinusoidal
West from Greenwich
COPYRIGHT PHILIP'S

INDEX TO WORLD MAPS

How to use the index

The index contains the names of all the principal places and features shown on the World Maps. Each name is followed by an additional entry in italics giving the country or region within which it is located. The alphabetical order of names composed of two or more words is governed primarily by the first word and then by the second. This is an example of the rule:

Mīr Kūh, *Iran* **71 E8**
Mīr Shahdād, *Iran* **71 E8**
Mira, *Italy* **41 C9**
Mira por vos Cay, *Bahamas* .. **121 B5**
Miraj, *India* **66 F2**

Physical features composed of a proper name (Erie) and a description (Lake) are positioned alphabetically by the proper name. The description is positioned after the proper name and is usually abbreviated:

Erie, L., *N. Amer.* **116 D4**

Where a description forms part of a settlement or administrative name however, it is always written in full and put in its true alphabetic position:

Mount Morris, *U.S.A.* **116 D7**

Names beginning with M' and Mc are indexed as if they were spelled Mac. Names beginning St. are alphabetised under Saint, but Sankt, Sint, Sant', Santa and San are all spelt in full and are alphabetised accordingly. If the same place name occurs two or more times in the index and all are in the same country, each is followed by the name of the administrative subdivision in which it is located. For example:

Jackson, Ky., *U.S.A.* **114 G4**
Jackson, Mich., *U.S.A.* **114 D3**
Jackson, Minn., *U.S.A.* **112 D7**

The number in bold type which follows each name in the index refers to the number of the map page where that feature or place will be found. This is usually the largest scale at which the place or feature appears.

The letter and figure which are in bold type immediately after the page number give the grid square on the map page, within which the feature is situated. The letter represents the latitude and the figure the longitude. A lower case letter immediately after the page number refers to an inset map on that page.

In some cases the feature itself may fall within the specified square, while the name is outside. This is usually the case only with features which are larger than a grid square.

Rivers are indexed to their mouths or confluences, and carry the symbol → after their names. The following symbols are also used in the index: ■ country, ☒ overseas territory or dependency, □ first order administrative area, △ national park, ⌓ other park (provincial park, nature reserve or game reserve), ✈ (LHR) principal airport (and location identifier).

How to pronounce place names

English-speaking people usually have no difficulty in reading and pronouncing correctly English place names. However, foreign place name pronunciations may present many problems. Such problems can be minimised by following some simple rules. However, these rules cannot be applied to all situations, and there will be many exceptions.

1. In general, stress each syllable equally, unless your experience suggests otherwise.
2. Pronounce the letter 'a' as a broad 'a' as in 'arm'.
3. Pronounce the letter 'e' as a short 'e' as in 'elm'.
4. Pronounce the letter 'i' as a cross between a short 'i' and long 'e', as the two 'i's in 'California'.
5. Pronounce the letter 'o' as an intermediate 'o' as in 'soft'.
6. Pronounce the letter 'u' as an intermediate 'u' as in 'sure'.
7. Pronounce consonants hard, except in the Romance-language areas where 'g's are likely to be pronounced softly like 'j' in 'jam'; 'j' itself may be pronounced as 'y'; and 'x's may be pronounced as 'h'.
8. For names in mainland China, pronounce 'q' like the 'ch' in 'chin', 'x' like the 'sh' in 'she', 'zh' like the 'j' in 'jam', and 'z' as if it were spelled 'dz'. In general pronounce 'a' as in 'father', 'e' as in 'but', 'i' as in 'keep', 'o' as in 'or', and 'u' as in 'rule'.

Moreover, English has no diacritical marks (accent and pronunciation signs), although some languages do. The following is a brief and general guide to the pronunciation of those most frequently used in the principal Western European languages.

		Pronunciation as in
French	é	day and shows that the e is to be pronounced; e.g. Orléans.
	è	mare
	î	used over any vowel and does not affect pronunciation; shows contraction of the name, usually omission of 's' following a vowel.
	ç	's' before 'a', 'o' and 'u'.
	ë, ï, ü	over 'e', 'i' and 'u' when they are used with another vowel and shows that each is to be pronounced.
German	ä	fate
	ö	fur
	ü	no English equivalent; like French 'tu'
Italian	à, é	over vowels and indicates stress.
Portuguese	ã, õ	vowels pronounced nasally.
	ç	boss
	á	shows stress
	ô	shows that a vowel has an 'i' or 'u' sound combined with it.
Spanish	ñ	canyon
	ü	pronounced as w and separately from adjoining vowels.
	á	usually indicates that this is a stressed vowel.

Abbreviations

A.C.T. – Australian Capital Territory
A.R. – Autonomous Region
Afghan. – Afghanistan
Afr. – Africa
Ala. – Alabama
Alta. – Alberta
Amer. – America(n)
Arch. – Archipelago
Ariz. – Arizona
Ark. – Arkansas
Atl. Oc. – Atlantic Ocean
B. – Baie, Bahía, Bay, Bucht, Bugt
B.C. – British Columbia
Bangla. – Bangladesh
Barr. – Barrage
Bos.-H. – Bosnia-Herzegovina
C. – Cabo, Cap, Cape, Coast
C.A.R. – Central African Republic
C. Prov. – Cape Province
Calif. – California
Cat. – Catarata
Cent. – Central
Chan. – Channel
Colo. – Colorado
Conn. – Connecticut
Cord. – Cordillera
Cr. – Creek
Czech. – Czech Republic
D.C. – District of Columbia
Del. – Delaware
Dem. – Democratic
Dep. – Dependency
Des. – Desert
Dét. – Détroit
Dist. – District
Dj. – Djebel
Domin. – Dominica
Dom. Rep. – Dominican Republic
E. – East
E. Salv. – El Salvador
Eq. Guin. – Equatorial Guinea
Est. – Estrecho
Falk. Is. – Falkland Is.
Fd. – Fjord
Fla. – Florida
Fr. – French
G. – Golfe, Golfo, Gulf, Guba, Gebel
Ga. – Georgia
Gt. – Great, Greater
Guinea-Biss. – Guinea-Bissau
H.K. – Hong Kong
H.P. – Himachal Pradesh
Hants. – Hampshire
Harb. – Harbor, Harbour
Hd. – Head
Hts. – Heights
I.(s). – Île, Ilha, Insel, Isla, Island, Isle
Ill. – Illinois
Ind. – Indiana
Ind. Oc. – Indian Ocean
Ivory C. – Ivory Coast
J. – Jabal, Jebel
Jaz. – Jazīrah
Junc. – Junction
K. – Kap, Kapp
Kans. – Kansas
Kep. – Kepulauan
Ky. – Kentucky
L. – Lac, Lacul, Lago, Lagoa, Lake, Limni, Loch, Lough
La. – Louisiana
Ld. – Land
Liech. – Liechtenstein
Lux. – Luxembourg
Mad. P. – Madhya Pradesh
Madag. – Madagascar
Man. – Manitoba
Mass. – Massachusetts
Md. – Maryland
Me. – Maine
Medit. S. – Mediterranean Sea
Mich. – Michigan
Minn. – Minnesota
Miss. – Mississippi
Mo. – Missouri
Mont. – Montana
Mozam. – Mozambique
Mt.(s) – Mont, Montaña, Mountain
Mte. – Monte
Mti. – Monti
N. – Nord, Norte, North, Northern, Nouveau
N.B. – New Brunswick
N.C. – North Carolina
N. Cal. – New Caledonia
N. Dak. – North Dakota
N.H. – New Hampshire
N.I. – North Island
N.J. – New Jersey
N. Mex. – New Mexico
N.S. – Nova Scotia
N.S.W. – New South Wales
N.W.T. – North West Territory
N.Y. – New York
N.Z. – New Zealand
Nac. – Nacional
Nat. – National
Nebr. – Nebraska
Neths. – Netherlands
Nev. – Nevada
Nfld. & L. – Newfoundland and Labrador
Nic. – Nicaragua
O. – Oued, Ouadi
Occ. – Occidentale
Okla. – Oklahoma
Ont. – Ontario
Or. – Orientale
Oreg. – Oregon
Os. – Ostrov
Oz. – Ozero
P. – Pass, Passo, Pasul, Pulau
P.E.I. – Prince Edward Island
Pa. – Pennsylvania
Pac. Oc. – Pacific Ocean
Papua N.G. – Papua New Guinea
Pass. – Passage
Peg. – Pegunungan
Pen. – Peninsula, Péninsule
Phil. – Philippines
Pk. – Peak
Plat. – Plateau
Prov. – Province, Provincial
Pt. – Point
Pta. – Ponta, Punta
Pte. – Pointe
Qué. – Québec
Queens. – Queensland
R. – Rio, River
R.I. – Rhode Island
Ra. – Range
Raj. – Rajasthan
Recr. – Recreational, Récréatif
Reg. – Region
Rep. – Republic
Res. – Reserve, Reservoir
Rhld-Pfz. – Rheinland-Pfalz
S. – South, Southern, Sur
Si. Arabia – Saudi Arabia
S.C. – South Carolina
S. Dak. – South Dakota
S.I. – South Island
S. Leone – Sierra Leone
Sa. – Serra, Sierra
Sask. – Saskatchewan
Scot. – Scotland
Sd. – Sound
Serbia & M.. – Serbia & Montenegro
Sev. – Severnaya
Sib. – Siberia
Sprs. – Springs
St. – Saint
Sta. – Santa
Ste. – Sainte
Sto. – Santo
Str. – Strait, Stretto
Switz. – Switzerland
Tas. – Tasmania
Tenn. – Tennessee
Terr. – Territory, Territoire
Tex. – Texas
Tg. – Tanjung
Trin. & Tob. – Trinidad & Tobago
U.A.E. – United Arab Emirates
U.K. – United Kingdom
U.S.A. – United States of America
Ut. P. – Uttar Pradesh
Va. – Virginia
Vdkhr. – Vodokhranilishche
Vdskh. – Vodoskhovyshche
Vf. – Vírful
Vic. – Victoria
Vol. – Volcano
Vt. – Vermont
W. – Wadi, West
W. Va. – West Virginia
Wall. & F. Is. – Wallis and Futuna Is.
Wash. – Washington
Wis. – Wisconsin
Wlkp. – Wielkopolski
Wyo. – Wyoming
Yorks. – Yorkshire

A

A 'Âli an Nîl □, *Sudan* 81 F3
A Baña, *Spain* 36 C2
A Cañiza, *Spain* 36 C2
A Coruña, *Spain* 36 B2
A Estrada, *Spain* 36 C2
A Fonsagrada, *Spain* 36 B3
A Guarda, *Spain* 36 D2
A Gudiña, *Spain* 36 C3
A Rúa, *Spain* 36 C3
Aachen, *Germany* 24 E2
Aalborg = Ålborg, *Denmark* 11 G3
Aalen, *Germany* 25 G6
Aalst, *Belgium* 17 D4
Aalten, *Neths.* 17 C6
Aalter, *Belgium* 17 C3
Äänekoski, *Finland* 9 E21
Aarau, *Switz.* 25 H4
Aarberg, *Switz.* 25 H3
Aare →, *Switz.* 25 H4
Aargau □, *Switz.* 25 H4
Aarhus = Århus, *Denmark* 11 H4
Aarschot, *Belgium* 17 D4
Aba, *China* 58 A3
Aba, *Dem. Rep. of the Congo* 86 B3
Aba, *Nigeria* 83 D6
Âbâ, Jazîrat, *Sudan* 81 E3
Abaco I., *Bahamas* 120 A4
Abadab, J., *Sudan* 80 D4
Ābādān, *Iran* 71 D6
Abade, *Ethiopia* 81 F4
Ābādeh, *Iran* 71 D7
Abadin, *Spain* 36 B3
Abadla, *Algeria* 78 B5
Abaetetuba, *Brazil* 125 D9
Abagnar Qi, *China* 56 C9
Abah, Tanjung, *Indonesia* 63 K18
Abai, *Paraguay* 127 B4
Abak, *Nigeria* 83 E6
Abakaliki, *Nigeria* 83 D6
Abakan, *Russia* 53 D10
Abala, *Niger* 83 C5
Abalak, *Niger* 83 B6
Abalemma, *Niger* 83 B6
Abana, *Turkey* 72 B6
Abancay, *Peru* 124 F4
Abano Terme, *Italy* 41 C8
Abarán, *Spain* 39 G3
Abariringa, *Kiribati* 96 H10
Abarqū, *Iran* 71 D7
Abashiri, *Japan* 54 B12
Abashiri-Wan, *Japan* 54 C12
Abaújszántó, *Hungary* 28 B6
Abava →, *Latvia* 30 A8
Ābay = Nîl el Azraq →, *Sudan* 81 D3
Abay, *Kazakhstan* 52 E8
Abaya, L., *Ethiopia* 81 F4
Abayita-Shala Lakes △, *Ethiopia* 81 F4
Abaza, *Russia* 52 D9
Abbadia di Fiastra ⌓, *Italy* 41 E10
Abbadia San Salvatore, *Italy* 41 F8
'Abbāsābād, *Iran* 71 C8
Abbay = Nîl el Azraq →, *Sudan* 81 D3
Abbaye, Pt., *U.S.A.* 114 B1
Abbé, L., *Ethiopia* 81 E5
Abbeville, *France* 19 B8
Abbeville, *Ala., U.S.A.* 115 K3
Abbeville, *La., U.S.A.* 113 L8
Abbeville, *S.C., U.S.A.* 115 H4
Abbiategrasso, *Italy* 40 C5
Abbot Ice Shelf, *Antarctica* 5 D16
Abbottabad, *Pakistan* 68 B5
Abd al Kūrī, *Yemen* 75 E5
Ābdar, *Iran* 71 D7
'Abdolābād, *Iran* 71 C8
Abdulpur, *Bangla.* 69 G13
Abéché, *Chad* 79 F10
Abejar, *Spain* 38 D2
Abekr, *Sudan* 81 E2
Abel Tasman △, *N.Z.* 91 J4
Abengourou, *Ivory C.* 82 D4
Abenójar, *Spain* 37 G6
Åbenrå, *Denmark* 11 J3
Abensberg, *Germany* 25 G7
Abeokuta, *Nigeria* 83 D5
Aber, *Uganda* 86 B3
Aberaeron, *U.K.* 15 E3
Aberayron = Aberaeron, *U.K.* 15 E3
Aberchirder, *U.K.* 13 D6
Abercorn, *Australia* 95 D5
Aberdare, *U.K.* 15 F4
Aberdare △, *Kenya* 86 C4
Aberdare Ra., *Kenya* 86 C4
Aberdeen, *Australia* 95 E5
Aberdeen, *Canada* 103 C7
Aberdeen, *S. Africa* 88 E3
Aberdeen, *U.K.* 13 D6
Aberdeen, *Ala., U.S.A.* 115 J1
Aberdeen, *Idaho, U.S.A.* 108 E7
Aberdeen, *Md., U.S.A.* 114 F7
Aberdeen, *S. Dak., U.S.A.* 112 C5
Aberdeen, *Wash., U.S.A.* 110 D3
Aberdeen, City of □, *U.K.* 13 D6
Aberdeenshire □, *U.K.* 13 D6
Aberdovey = Aberdyfi, *U.K.* 15 E3
Aberdyfi, *U.K.* 15 E3
Aberfeldy, *U.K.* 13 E5
Aberfoyle, *U.K.* 13 E4
Abergavenny, *U.K.* 15 F4
Abergele, *U.K.* 14 D4
Abernathy, *U.S.A.* 113 J4
Abert, L., *U.S.A.* 108 E3
Aberystwyth, *U.K.* 15 E3
Abhā, *Si. Arabia* 75 D3
Abhar, *Iran* 71 B6
Abhayapuri, *India* 69 F14
Abia □, *Nigeria* 83 D6
Abide, *Turkey* 47 C11
Abidiya, *Sudan* 80 D3
Abidjan, *Ivory C.* 82 D4
Abilene, *Kans., U.S.A.* 112 F6
Abilene, *Tex., U.S.A.* 113 J5
Abingdon, *U.K.* 15 F6
Abingdon, *U.S.A.* 115 G5
Abington Reef, *Australia* 94 B4
Abitau →, *Canada* 103 B7
Abitibi →, *Canada* 104 B3
Abitibi, L., *Canada* 104 C4
Abiy Adi, *Ethiopia* 81 E4
Abkhaz Republic = Abkhazia □, *Georgia* 35 J5
Abkhazia □, *Georgia* 35 J5
Abminga, *Australia* 95 D1
Abnûb, *Egypt* 80 B3
Åbo = Turku, *Finland* 9 F20
Abocho, *Nigeria* 83 D6
Abohar, *India* 68 D6
Aboisso, *Ivory C.* 82 D4
Abomey, *Benin* 83 D5
Abong-Mbang, *Cameroon* 84 D2
Abonnema, *Nigeria* 83 E6
Abony, *Hungary* 28 C5
Aboso, *Ghana* 82 D4
Abou-Deïa, *Chad* 79 F9
Aboyne, *U.K.* 13 D6
Abra Pampa, *Argentina* 126 A2
Abraham L., *Canada* 102 C5
Abrantes, *Portugal* 37 F2
Abreojos, Pta., *Mexico* 118 B2
Abri, *Esh Shamâliya, Sudan* 80 C3
Abri, *Janub Kordofân, Sudan* 81 E3
Abrolhos, Banka, *Brazil* 122 E7
Abrud, *Romania* 28 D8
Abruzzo □, *Italy* 41 F10
Absaroka Range, *U.S.A.* 108 D9
Abtenau, *Austria* 26 D6
Abu, *India* 68 G5
Abū al Abyad, *U.A.E.* 71 E7
Abū al Khaṣīb, *Iraq* 71 D6
Abū 'Alī, *Si. Arabia* 71 E6
Abū 'Alī →, *Lebanon* 74 A4
Abu Ballas, *Egypt* 80 C2
Abu Deleiq, *Sudan* 81 D3
Abu Dhabi = Abū Ẓāby, *U.A.E.* 71 E7
Abu Dis, *Sudan* 80 D3
Abu Dom, *Sudan* 81 D3
Abū Du'ān, *Syria* 70 B3
Abu el Gairi, W. →, *Egypt* 74 F2
Abu Fatma, Ras, *Sudan* 80 C4
Abu Gabra, *Sudan* 81 E2
Abu Ga'da, W. →, *Egypt* 74 F1
Abu Gelba, *Sudan* 81 E3
Abu Gubeiha, *Sudan* 81 E3
Abu Habl, Khawr →, *Sudan* 81 E3
Abū Ḥadrīyah, *Si. Arabia* 71 E6
Abu Hamed, *Sudan* 80 D3
Abu Haraz, *An Nîl el Azraq, Sudan* 80 D3
Abu Haraz, *El Gezira, Sudan* 81 E3
Abu Haraz, *Esh Shamâliya, Sudan* 80 D3
Abu Higar, *Sudan* 81 E3
Abū Kamāl, *Syria* 70 C4
Abu Kuleiwat, *Sudan* 81 E2
Abū Madd, Ra's, *Si. Arabia* 70 E3
Abu Matariq, *Sudan* 81 E2
Abu Mendi, *Ethiopia* 81 E4
Abū Mūsā, *U.A.E.* 71 E7
Abū Qaṣr, *Si. Arabia* 70 D3
Abu Qir, *Egypt* 80 H7
Abu Qireiya, *Egypt* 80 C4
Abu Qurqâs, *Egypt* 80 B3
Abu Shagara, Ras, *Sudan* 80 C4
Abu Shanab, *Sudan* 81 E2
Abu Simbel, *Egypt* 80 C3
Abū Şukhayr, *Iraq* 70 D5
Abu Sultân, *Egypt* 80 H8
Abu Tabari, *Sudan* 80 D2
Abu Tig, *Egypt* 80 B3
Abu Tiga, *Sudan* 81 E3
Abu Tineitin, *Sudan* 81 E3
Abu Uruq, *Sudan* 81 D3
Abu Zabad, *Sudan* 81 E2
Abū Ẓāby, *U.A.E.* 71 E7
Abū Zeydābād, *Iran* 71 C6
Abuja, *Nigeria* 83 D6
Abukuma-Gawa →, *Japan* 54 E10
Abukuma-Sammyaku, *Japan* 54 F10
Abunā, *Brazil* 124 E5
Abunā →, *Brazil* 124 E5
Abune Yosef, *Ethiopia* 81 E4
Aburo, *Dem. Rep. of the Congo* 86 B3
Abut Hd., *N.Z.* 91 K3
Abuye Meda, *Ethiopia* 81 E4
Abwong, *Sudan* 81 F3
Åby, *Sweden* 11 F10
Aby, Lagune, *Ivory C.* 82 D4
Abyad, *Sudan* 81 E2
Åbybro, *Denmark* 11 G3
Acadia △, *U.S.A.* 115 C11
Açailândia, *Brazil* 125 D9
Acajutla, *El Salv.* 120 D2
Acámbaro, *Mexico* 118 D4
Acanthus, *Greece* 44 F7
Acaponeta, *Mexico* 118 C3
Acapulco, *Mexico* 119 D5
Acarai, Serra, *Brazil* 124 C7
Acarigua, *Venezuela* 124 B5
Acatlán, *Mexico* 119 D5
Acayucan, *Mexico* 119 D6
Accéglio, *Italy* 40 D4
Accomac, *U.S.A.* 114 G8
Accous, *France* 20 E3
Accra, *Ghana* 83 D4
Accrington, *U.K.* 14 D5
Acebal, *Argentina* 126 C3
Aceh □, *Indonesia* 62 D1
Acerra, *Italy* 43 B7
Aceuchal, *Spain* 37 G4
Achalpur, *India* 66 J10
Acheng, *China* 57 B14
Achenkirch, *Austria* 26 D4
Achensee, *Austria* 26 D4
Acher, *India* 68 H5
Achern, *Germany* 25 G4
Achill Hd., *Ireland* 12 C1
Achill I., *Ireland* 12 C1
Achim, *Germany* 24 B5
Achinsk, *Russia* 53 D10
Acıgöl, *Turkey* 47 D11
Acıpayam, *Turkey* 47 D11
Acireale, *Italy* 43 E8
Ackerman, *U.S.A.* 113 J10
Acklins I., *Bahamas* 121 B5
Acme, *Canada* 102 C6
Acme, *U.S.A.* 116 F5
Aconcagua, Cerro, *Argentina* 126 C2
Aconquija, Mt., *Argentina* 126 B2
Açores, Is. dos, *Atl. Oc.* 78 A1
Acornhoek, *S. Africa* 89 C5
Acquapendente, *Italy* 41 F8
Acquasanta Terme, *Italy* 41 F10
Acquasparta, *Italy* 41 F9
Acquaviva delle Fonti, *Italy* 43 B9
Ácqui Terme, *Italy* 40 D5
Acraman, L., *Australia* 95 E2
Acre = 'Akko, *Israel* 74 C4
Acre □, *Brazil* 124 E4
Acre →, *Brazil* 124 E5
Acri, *Italy* 43 C9
Acs, *Hungary* 28 C3
Actium, *Greece* 46 C2
Acton, *Canada* 116 C4
Acuña, *Mexico* 118 B4
Ad Dammām, *Si. Arabia* 71 E6
Ad Dāmūr, *Lebanon* 74 B4
Ad Dawādimī, *Si. Arabia* 70 E5
Ad Dawḥah, *Qatar* 71 E6
Ad Dawr, *Iraq* 70 C4
Ad Dir'īyah, *Si. Arabia* 70 E5
Ad Dīwānīyah, *Iraq* 70 D5
Ad Dujayl, *Iraq* 70 C5
Ad Duwayd, *Si. Arabia* 70 D4
Ada, *Ghana* 83 D5
Ada, *Serbia & M.* 28 E5
Ada, *Minn., U.S.A.* 112 B6
Ada, *Okla., U.S.A.* 113 H6
Adabiya, *Egypt* 74 F1
Adair, C., *Canada* 101 A12
Adaja →, *Spain* 36 D6
Adak I., *U.S.A.* 100 C2
Adamaoua, Massif de l', *Cameroon* 83 D7
Adamawa □, *Nigeria* 83 D7
Adamawa Highlands = Adamaoua, Massif de l', *Cameroon* 83 D7
Adamello ⌓, *Italy* 40 B7
Adamello, Mte., *Italy* 40 B7
Adami Tulu, *Ethiopia* 81 F4
Adaminaby, *Australia* 95 F4
Adams, *Mass., U.S.A.* 117 D11
Adams, *N.Y., U.S.A.* 117 C8
Adams, *Wis., U.S.A.* 112 D10
Adams, Mt., *U.S.A.* 110 D5
Adam's Bridge, *Sri Lanka* 66 Q11
Adams L., *Canada* 102 C5
Adam's Peak, *Sri Lanka* 66 R12
Adamuz, *Spain* 37 G6
Adana, *Turkey* 70 B2
Adanero, *Spain* 36 E6
Adapazarı = Sakarya, *Turkey* 72 B4
Adar Gwagwa, J., *Sudan* 80 C4
Adarama, *Sudan* 81 D3
Adare, C., *Antarctica* 5 D11
Adarte, *Eritrea* 81 E5
Adaut, *Indonesia* 63 F8
Adavale, *Australia* 95 D3
Adda →, *Italy* 40 C6
Addis Ababa = Addis Abeba, *Ethiopia* 81 F4
Addis Abeba, *Ethiopia* 81 F4
Addis Alem, *Ethiopia* 81 F4
Addis Zemen, *Ethiopia* 81 E4
Addison, *U.S.A.* 116 D7
Addo, *S. Africa* 88 E4
Addo △, *S. Africa* 88 E4
Adebour, *Niger* 83 C7
Ādeh, *Iran* 70 B5
Adel, *U.S.A.* 115 K4
Adelaide, *Australia* 95 E2
Adelaide, *S. Africa* 88 E4
Adelaide I., *Antarctica* 5 C17
Adelaide Pen., *Canada* 100 B10
Adelaide River, *Australia* 92 B5
Adelaide Village, *Bahamas* 120 A4
Adelanto, *U.S.A.* 111 L9
Adele I., *Australia* 92 C3
Adélie, Terre, *Antarctica* 5 C10
Adélie Land = Adélie, Terre, *Antarctica* 5 C10
Adelsk, *Belarus* 30 E10
Ademuz, *Spain* 38 E3
Aden = Al 'Adan, *Yemen* 75 E4
Aden, G. of, *Asia* 75 E4
Adendorp, *S. Africa* 88 E3
Aderbissinat, *Niger* 83 B6
Adh Dhayd, *U.A.E.* 71 E7
Adhoi, *India* 68 H4
Adi, *Indonesia* 63 E8
Adi Arkai, *Ethiopia* 81 E4
Adi Daro, *Ethiopia* 81 E4
Adi Keyih, *Eritrea* 81 E4
Adi Kwala, *Eritrea* 81 E4
Adi Ugri, *Eritrea* 81 E4
Adieu, C., *Australia* 93 F5
Adieu Pt., *Australia* 92 C3
Adigala, *Ethiopia* 81 E5
Adige →, *Italy* 41 C9
Adigrat, *Ethiopia* 81 E4
Adıgüzel Barajı, *Turkey* 47 C11
Adilabad, *India* 66 K11
Adilcevaz, *Turkey* 73 C10
Adirondack ⌓, *U.S.A.* 117 C10
Adirondack Mts., *U.S.A.* 117 C10
Adis Abeba = Addis Abeba, *Ethiopia* 81 F4
Adıyaman, *Turkey* 73 D8
Adjohon, *Benin* 83 D5
Adjud, *Romania* 29 D12
Adjumani, *Uganda* 86 B3
Adjuntas, *Puerto Rico* 121 d
Adlavik Is., *Canada* 105 B8
Adler, *Russia* 35 J4
Admer, *Algeria* 83 A6
Admiralty G., *Australia* 92 B4
Admiralty I., *U.S.A.* 102 B2
Admiralty Is., *Papua N. G.* 96 H6
Adnan Menderes, İzmir ✕ (ADB), *Turkey* 47 C9
Ado, *Nigeria* 83 D5
Ado-Ekiti, *Nigeria* 83 D6
Adok, *Sudan* 81 F3
Adola, *Ethiopia* 81 E5
Adonara, *Indonesia* 63 F6
Adoni, *India* 66 M10
Adony, *Hungary* 28 C3
Adour →, *France* 20 E2
Adra, *India* 69 H12
Adra, *Spain* 37 J7
Adrano, *Italy* 43 E7
Adrar, *Mauritania* 78 D3
Adrar des Iforas, *Algeria* 78 C5
Ádria, *Italy* 41 C9
Adrian, *Mich., U.S.A.* 114 E3
Adrian, *Tex., U.S.A.* 113 H3
Adriatic Sea, *Medit. S.* 6 G9
Adua, *Indonesia* 63 E7
Adwa, *Ethiopia* 81 E4
Adygea □, *Russia* 35 H5
Adzhar Republic = Ajaria □, *Georgia* 35 K6
Adzopé, *Ivory C.* 82 D4
Ægean Sea, *Medit. S.* 47 C7
Aerhtai Shan, *Mongolia* 60 B4
Ærø, *Denmark* 11 K4
Ærøskøbing, *Denmark* 11 K4
Aëtós, *Greece* 46 D3
'Afak, *Iraq* 70 C5
Afándou, *Greece* 49 C10
Afar □, *Ethiopia* 81 E5
Afghanistan ■, *Asia* 66 C4
Afikpo, *Nigeria* 83 D6
Aflou, *Algeria* 78 B6
Afragóla, *Italy* 43 B7
Afram →, *Ghana* 83 D4
Afrera, *Ethiopia* 81 E5
Africa 76 E6
'Afrīn, *Syria* 70 B3
Afşin, *Turkey* 72 C7
Afton, *N.Y., U.S.A.* 117 D9
Afton, *Wyo., U.S.A.* 108 E8
Afuá, *Brazil* 125 D8
'Afula, *Israel* 74 C4
Afyon, *Turkey* 47 C12
Afyon □, *Turkey* 47 C12
Afyonkarahisar = Afyon, *Turkey* 47 C12
Aga, *Egypt* 80 H7
Agadès = Agadez, *Niger* 83 B6
Agadez, *Niger* 83 B6
Agadir, *Morocco* 78 B4
Agaete, *Canary Is.* 48 F4
Agaie, *Nigeria* 83 D6
Again, *Sudan* 81 F2
Agalega Is., *Mauritius* 3 E12
Ağapınar, *Turkey* 47 B12
Agar, *India* 68 H7
Agaro, *Ethiopia* 81 F4
Agartala, *India* 67 H17
Agăş, *Romania* 29 D11
Agassiz, *Canada* 102 D4
Agats, *Indonesia* 63 F9
Agawam, *U.S.A.* 117 D12
Agbélouvé, *Togo* 83 D5
Agboville, *Ivory C.* 82 D4
Ağcabädi, *Azerbaijan* 35 K8
Ağdam, *Azerbaijan* 35 L8
Ağdaş, *Azerbaijan* 35 K8
Agde, *France* 20 E7
Agde, C. d', *France* 20 E7
Agdzhabedi = Ağcabädi, *Azerbaijan* 35 K8
Agen, *France* 20 D4
Agerbæk, *Denmark* 11 J2
Agersø, *Denmark* 11 J5
Ageyevo, *Russia* 32 E9
Ággteleki △, *Hungary* 28 B5
Āgh Kand, *Iran* 71 B6
Aghireşu, *Romania* 29 D8
Aginskoye, *Russia* 53 D12
Ağlasun, *Turkey* 47 D12
Agly →, *France* 20 F7
Agnew, *Australia* 93 E3
Agnibilékrou, *Ivory C.* 82 D4
Agnita, *Romania* 29 E9
Agnone, *Italy* 41 G11
Agofie, *Ghana* 83 D5
Agogna →, *Italy* 40 C5
Agogo, *Sudan* 81 F2
Agön, *Sweden* 10 C11
Agon Coutainville, *France* 18 C5
Ágordo, *Italy* 41 B9
Agori, *India* 69 G10
Agouna, *Benin* 83 D5
Agout →, *France* 20 E5
Agra, *India* 68 F7
Agrakhanskiy Poluostrov, *Russia* 35 J8
Agramunt, *Spain* 38 D6
Agreda, *Spain* 38 D3
Ağri, *Turkey* 73 C10
Agri →, *Italy* 43 B9
Ağri Dağı, *Turkey* 70 B5
Ağri Karakose = Ağri, *Turkey* 73 C10
Agriá, *Greece* 46 B5
Agrigento, *Italy* 42 E6
Agrínion, *Greece* 46 C3
Agrópoli, *Italy* 43 B7
Ağstafa, *Azerbaijan* 35 K7
Agua Caliente, *Baja Calif., Mexico* 111 N10
Agua Caliente, *Sinaloa, Mexico* 118 B3
Agua Caliente Springs, *U.S.A.* 111 N10
Água Clara, *Brazil* 125 H8
Agua Fria ⌓, *U.S.A.* 109 J8
Agua Hechicero, *Mexico* 111 N10
Agua Prieta, *Mexico* 118 A3
Aguadilla, *Puerto Rico* 121 d
Aguadulce, *Panama* 120 E3
Aguanga, *U.S.A.* 111 M10
Aguanish, *Canada* 105 B7
Aguanus →, *Canada* 105 B7
Aguapey →, *Argentina* 126 B4
Aguaray Guazú →, *Paraguay* 126 A4
Aguarico →, *Ecuador* 124 D3
Aguaro-Guariquito △, *Venezuela* 121 E6
Aguas →, *Spain* 38 D4
Aguas Blancas, *Chile* 126 A2
Aguas Calientes, Sierra de, *Argentina* 126 B2
Aguascalientes, *Mexico* 118 C4
Aguascalientes □, *Mexico* 118 C4
Agudo, *Spain* 37 G6
Águeda, *Portugal* 36 E2
Agueda →, *Spain* 36 D4
Aguelhok, *Mali* 83 B5
Aguié, *Niger* 83 C6
Aguila, Punta, *Puerto Rico* 121 d
Aguilafuente, *Spain* 36 D6
Aguilar, *Spain* 37 H6
Aguilar de Campóo, *Spain* 36 C6
Aguilares, *Argentina* 126 B2
Aguilas, *Spain* 39 H3
Agüimes, *Canary Is.* 48 G4
Aguja, C. de la, *Colombia* 122 B3
Agujereada, Pta., *Puerto Rico* 121 d
Agulaa, *Ethiopia* 81 E4
Agulhas, C., *S. Africa* 88 E3
Agulo, *Canary Is.* 48 F2
Agung, Gunung, *Indonesia* 63 J18
Agur, *Uganda* 86 B3
Agusan →, *Phil.* 61 G6
Ağva, *Turkey* 45 E13
Agvali, *Russia* 35 J8
Aha Mts., *Botswana* 88 B3
Ahaggar, *Algeria* 78 D7
Ahamansu, *Ghana* 83 D5
Ahar, *Iran* 70 B5
Ahat, *Turkey* 47 C11
Ahaus, *Germany* 24 C2
Ahipara B., *N.Z.* 91 F4
Ahir Dağı, *Turkey* 47 C12
Ahiri, *India* 66 K12
Ahlat, *Turkey* 73 C10
Ahlen, *Germany* 24 D3
Ahmad Wal, *Pakistan* 68 E1
Ahmadabad, *India* 68 H5
Aḥmadābād, *Khorāsān, Iran* 71 C9
Aḥmadābād, *Khorāsān, Iran* 71 C8
Aḥmadī, *Iran* 71 E8
Ahmadnagar, *India* 66 K9
Ahmadpur, *Pakistan* 68 E4
Ahmadpur Lamma, *Pakistan* 68 E4
Ahmar, *Ethiopia* 81 F5
Ahmedabad = Ahmadabad, *India* 68 H5
Ahmednagar = Ahmadnagar, *India* 66 K9
Ahmetbey, *Turkey* 45 E11
Ahmetler, *Turkey* 47 C11
Ahmetli, *Turkey* 47 C9
Ahoada, *Nigeria* 83 D6
Ahome, *Mexico* 118 B3
Ahoskie, *U.S.A.* 115 G7
Ahr →, *Germany* 24 E3
Ahram, *Iran* 71 D6
Ahrax Pt., *Malta* 49 D1
Ahrensbök, *Germany* 24 A6
Ahrensburg, *Germany* 24 B6
Āhū, *Iran* 71 C6
Ahuachapán, *El Salv.* 120 D2
Ahun, *France* 19 F9
Åhus, *Sweden* 11 J8
Ahvāz, *Iran* 71 D6
Ahvenanmaa, *Finland* 9 F19
Aḥwar, *Yemen* 75 E4
Ahzar →, *Mali* 83 B5
Ai →, *India* 69 F14
Ai-Ais, *Namibia* 88 D2
Ai-Ais and Fish River Canyon △, *Namibia* 88 C2
Aichach, *Germany* 25 G7
Aichi □, *Japan* 55 G8
Aigle, *Switz.* 25 J2
Aignay-le-Duc, *France* 19 E11
Aigoual, Mt., *France* 20 D7
Aigre, *France* 20 C4
Aigua, *Uruguay* 127 C5
Aigueperse, *France* 19 F10
Aigues →, *France* 21 D8
Aigues-Mortes, *France* 21 E8
Aigues-Mortes, G. d', *France* 21 E8
Aigües Tortes y Lago San Mauricio △, *Spain* 38 C4
Aiguilles, *France* 21 D10
Aiguillon, *France* 20 D4
Aigurande, *France* 19 F8
Aihui, *China* 60 A7
Aija, *Peru* 124 E3
Aikawa, *Japan* 54 E9
Aiken, *U.S.A.* 115 J5
Ailao Shan, *China* 58 F3
Aileron, *Australia* 94 C1
Aillant-sur-Tholon, *France* 19 E10
Aillik, *Canada* 105 A8
Ailsa Craig, *U.K.* 13 F3
Aim, *Russia* 53 D14
Aimere, *Indonesia* 63 F6

Aimogasta, *Argentina* 126 B2
Ain □, *France* 19 F12
Ain →, *France* 21 C9
Aïn Ben Tili, *Mauritania* 78 C4
Ain Dalla, *Egypt* 80 B2
Ain el Mafki, *Egypt* 80 B2
Ain Girba, *Egypt* 80 B2
Ain Murr, *Sudan* 80 C2
Ain Qeiqab, *Egypt* 80 B1
Aïn Sefra, *Algeria* 78 B5
Ain Sheikh Murzûk, *Egypt* 80 B2
Ain Sudr, *Egypt* 74 F2
Ain Sukhna, *Egypt* 80 J8
Ain Zeitûn, *Egypt* 80 B2
Ainaži, *Latvia* 9 H21
Aínos Óros, *Greece* 46 C2
Ainsworth, *U.S.A.* 112 D5
Aiquile, *Bolivia* 124 G5
Aïr, *Niger* 83 B6
Air Force I., *Canada* 101 B12
Air Hitam, *Malaysia* 65 M4
Airaines, *France* 19 C8
Airdrie, *Canada* 102 C6
Airdrie, *U.K.* 13 F5
Aire →, *France* 19 C11
Aire →, *U.K.* 14 D7
Aire, I. de l', *Spain* 48 B11
Aire-sur-la-Lys, *France* 19 B9
Aire-sur-l'Adour, *France* 20 E3
Airlie Beach, *Australia* 94 J6
Airvault, *France* 18 F6
Aisch →, *Germany* 25 F6
Aisne □, *France* 19 C10
Aisne →, *France* 19 C9
Ait, *India* 69 G8
Aitana, Sierra de, *Spain* 39 G4
Aitkin, *U.S.A.* 112 B8
Aitolía kai Akarnanía □, *Greece* 46 C3
Aitolikón, *Greece* 46 C3
Aiud, *Romania* 29 D8
Aix-en-Provence, *France* 21 E9
Aix-la-Chapelle = Aachen, *Germany* 24 E2
Aix-les-Bains, *France* 21 C9
Aixe-sur-Vienne, *France* 20 C5
Aíyina, *Greece* 46 D5
Aiyínion, *Greece* 44 F6
Aíyion, *Greece* 46 C4
Aizawl, *India* 67 H18
Aizenay, *France* 18 F5
Aizkraukle, *Latvia* 9 H21
Aizpute, *Latvia* 9 H19
Aizuwakamatsu, *Japan* 54 F9
Ajaccio, *France* 21 G12
Ajaccio, G. d', *France* 21 G12
Ajai ⌓, *Uganda* 86 B3
Ajaigarh, *India* 69 G9
Ajalpan, *Mexico* 119 D5
Ajanta Ra., *India* 66 J9
Ajari Rep. = Ajaria □, *Georgia* 35 K6
Ajaria □, *Georgia* 35 K6
Ajax, *Canada* 116 C5
Ajdābiyā, *Libya* 79 B10
Ajdovščina, *Slovenia* 41 C10
Ajibar, *Ethiopia* 81 E4
Ajka, *Hungary* 28 C2
'Ajlūn, *Jordan* 74 C4
'Ajlūn □, *Jordan* 74 C4
'Ajmān, *U.A.E.* 71 E7
Ajmer, *India* 68 F6
Ajnala, *India* 68 D6
Ajo, *U.S.A.* 109 K7
Ajo, C. de, *Spain* 36 B7
Ajok, *Sudan* 81 F2
Ajuy, *Phil.* 61 F5
Ak Dağ, *Turkey* 47 E11
Ak Dağları, *Muğla, Turkey* 47 E11
Ak Dağları, *Sivas, Turkey* 72 C7
Akaba, *Togo* 83 D5
Akabira, *Japan* 54 C11
Akagera △, *Rwanda* 86 C3
Akaki Beseka, *Ethiopia* 81 F4
Akala, *Sudan* 81 D4
Akamas, *Cyprus* 49 D11
Akan △, *Japan* 54 C12
Akanthou, *Cyprus* 49 D12
Akarca, *Turkey* 47 C11
Akaroa, *N.Z.* 91 K4
Akasha, *Sudan* 80 C3
Akashi, *Japan* 55 G7
Akbarpur, *Bihar, India* 69 G10
Akbarpur, *Ut. P., India* 69 F10
Akçaabat, *Turkey* 73 B8
Akçadağ, *Turkey* 72 C7
Akçakale, *Turkey* 73 D8
Akçakoca, *Turkey* 72 B4
Akçaova, *Turkey* 45 E13
Akçay, *Turkey* 47 E11
Akçay →, *Turkey* 47 D10
Akdağ, *Turkey* 47 C8
Akdağmadeni, *Turkey* 72 C6
Akelamo, *Indonesia* 63 D7
Åkers styckebruk, *Sweden* 10 E11
Åkersberga, *Sweden* 10 E12
Aketi, *Dem. Rep. of the Congo* 84 D4
Akhaïa □, *Greece* 46 C3
Akhalkalaki, *Georgia* 35 K6
Akhaltsikhe, *Georgia* 35 K6
Akharnaí, *Greece* 46 C5
Akhelóös →, *Greece* 46 C3
Akhendriá, *Greece* 47 G7
Akhisar, *Turkey* 47 C9
Akhladhókambos, *Greece* 46 D4
Akhmîm, *Egypt* 80 B3
Akhnur, *India* 69 C6
Akhtopol, *Bulgaria* 45 D11
Akhtuba →, *Russia* 35 G8
Akhtubinsk, *Russia* 35 F8
Akhty, *Russia* 35 K8
Akhtyrka = Okhtyrka, *Ukraine* 33 G8
Aki, *Japan* 55 H6
Akimiski I., *Canada* 104 B3
Akimovka, *Ukraine* 33 J8
Åkirkeby, *Denmark* 11 J8
Akita, *Japan* 54 E10
Akita □, *Japan* 54 E10
Akjoujt, *Mauritania* 82 B2
Akka, *Mali* 82 B4
Akkaya Tepesi, *Turkey* 47 D11
Akkeshi, *Japan* 54 C12
'Akko, *Israel* 74 C4
Akköy, *Turkey* 47 D9
Aklampa, *Benin* 83 D5
Aklavik, *Canada* 100 B6
Aklera, *India* 68 G7
Akmenė, *Lithuania* 30 B9
Akmenrags, *Latvia* 30 B8
Akmonte = Almonte, *Spain* 37 H4
Akō, *Japan* 55 G7
Ako, *Nigeria* 83 C7
Akôbô, *Sudan* 81 F3
Akobo →, *Ethiopia* 81 F3
Akola, *India* 66 J10
Akonolinga, *Cameroon* 83 E7
Akor, *Mali* 82 C3
Akordat, *Eritrea* 81 D4
Akosombo Dam, *Ghana* 83 D5
Akot, *Sudan* 81 F3
Akoupé, *Ivory C.* 82 D4
Akpatok I., *Canada* 101 B13
Åkrahamn, *Norway* 9 G11
Akranes, *Iceland* 8 D2
Akreïjit, *Mauritania* 82 B3
Akrítas Venétiko, Ákra, *Greece* 46 E3
Akron, *Colo., U.S.A.* 112 E3
Akron, *Ohio, U.S.A.* 116 E3
Akrotiri, *Cyprus* 49 E11
Akrotíri, Ákra, *Greece* 45 F9
Akrotiri Bay, *Cyprus* 49 E12
Aksai Chin, *China* 69 B8
Aksaray, *Turkey* 70 B2
Aksay, *Kazakhstan* 52 D6
Akşehir, *Turkey* 70 B1
Akşehir Gölü, *Turkey* 72 C4
Akstafa = Ağstafa, *Azerbaijan* 35 K7
Aksu, *China* 60 B3
Aksu →, *Turkey* 72 D4
Aksum, *Ethiopia* 81 E4
Aktash, *Russia* 34 C11
Aktogay, *Kazakhstan* 52 E8
Aktsyabrski, *Belarus* 33 F5
Aktyubinsk = Aqtöbe, *Kazakhstan* 52 D6
Aku, *Nigeria* 83 D6
Akure, *Nigeria* 83 D6
Akureyri, *Iceland* 8 D4
Akuseki-Shima, *Japan* 55 K4
Akusha, *Russia* 35 J8
Akwa-Ibom □, *Nigeria* 83 E6
Akyab = Sittwe, *Burma* 67 J18
Akyazı, *Turkey* 72 B4
Al 'Adan, *Yemen* 75 E4
Al Aḩsā = Hasa □, *Si. Arabia* 71 E6
Al Ajfar, *Si. Arabia* 70 E4
Al Amādīyah, *Iraq* 70 B4
Al 'Amārah, *Iraq* 70 D5
Al 'Aqabah, *Jordan* 74 F4
Al 'Aqabah □, *Jordan* 74 F4
Al Arak, *Syria* 70 C3
Al 'Aramah, *Si. Arabia* 70 E5
Al 'Arţāwīyah, *Si. Arabia* 70 E5
Al 'Āşimah = 'Ammān □, *Jordan* 74 D5
Al 'Assāfīyah, *Si. Arabia* 70 D3
Al 'Ayn, *Si. Arabia* 70 E3
Al 'Ayn, *U.A.E.* 71 E7
Al 'Azīzīyah, *Iraq* 70 C5
Al Bāb, *Syria* 70 B3
Al Bad', *Si. Arabia* 70 D2
Al Bādī, *Iraq* 70 C4
Al Baḩrah, *Kuwait* 70 D5
Al Baḩral Mayyit = Dead Sea, *Asia* 74 D4
Al Balqā' □, *Jordan* 74 C4
Al Bārūk, J., *Lebanon* 74 B4
Al Başrah, *Iraq* 70 D5
Al Baţḩā, *Iraq* 70 D5
Al Batrūn, *Lebanon* 74 A4
Al Bayḑā, *Libya* 79 B10
Al Biqā, *Lebanon* 74 A5
Al Bi'r, *Si. Arabia* 70 D3
Al Burayj, *Syria* 74 A5
Al Faḑilī, *Si. Arabia* 71 E6
Al Fallūjah, *Iraq* 70 C4
Al Fāw, *Iraq* 71 D6
Al Fujayrah, *U.A.E.* 71 E8
Al Ghadaf, W. →, *Jordan* 74 D5
Al Ghammās, *Iraq* 70 D5
Al Ghazālah, *Si. Arabia* 70 E4
Al Ḩadīthah, *Iraq* 70 C4
Al Ḩadīthah, *Si. Arabia* 74 D6
Al Ḩaḑr, *Iraq* 70 C4
Al Ḩājānah, *Syria* 74 B5
Al Ḩajar al Gharbī, *Oman* 71 E8
Al Ḩāmad, *Si. Arabia* 70 D3
Al Hamdānīyah, *Syria* 70 C3
Al Ḩamīdīyah, *Syria* 74 A4
Al Ḩammār, *Iraq* 70 D5
Al Ḩamrā', *Si. Arabia* 70 E3
Al Ḩamzah, *Iraq* 70 D5
Al Ḩanākīyah, *Si. Arabia* 70 E4
Al Ḩarīr, W. →, *Syria* 74 C4
Al Ḩasā, W. →, *Jordan* 74 D4
Al Ḩasakah, *Syria* 70 B4
Al Ḩaydān, W. →, *Jordan* 74 D4
Al Ḩayy, *Iraq* 70 C5
Al Ḩijarah, *Asia* 70 D4
Al Ḩillah, *Iraq* 70 C5
Al Ḩillah, *Si. Arabia* 75 B4
Al Hindīyah, *Iraq* 70 C5
Al Hirmil, *Lebanon* 74 A5
Al Hoceïma, *Morocco* 78 A5
Al Ḩudaydah, *Yemen* 75 E3
Al Hufūf, *Si. Arabia* 71 E6
Al Ḩumayḑah, *Si. Arabia* 70 D2
Al Ḩunayy, *Si. Arabia* 71 E6
Al Īsāwīyah, *Si. Arabia* 70 D3
Al Jafr, *Jordan* 74 E5
Al Jāfūrah, *Si. Arabia* 71 E7
Al Jaghbūb, *Libya* 79 C10
Al Jahrah, *Kuwait* 70 D5
Al Jalāmīd, *Si. Arabia* 70 D3
Al Jamalīyah, *Qatar* 71 E6
Al Janūb □, *Lebanon* 74 B4
Al Jawf, *Libya* 79 D10
Al Jawf, *Si. Arabia* 70 D3
Al Jazirah, *Iraq* 70 C5
Al Jithāmīyah, *Si. Arabia* 70 E4
Al Jubayl, *Si. Arabia* 71 E6
Al Jubaylah, *Si. Arabia* 70 E5
Al Jubb, *Si. Arabia* 70 E4
Al Junaynah, *Sudan* 79 F10
Al Kabā'ish, *Iraq* 70 D5
Al Karak, *Jordan* 74 D4
Al Karak □, *Jordan* 74 E5
Al Kāẓimīyah, *Iraq* 70 C5
Al Khābūra, *Oman* 71 F8
Al Khafji, *Si. Arabia* 71 E6
Al Khalīl, *West Bank* 74 D4
Al Khāliş, *Iraq* 70 C5
Al Kharsānīyah, *Si. Arabia* 71 E6
Al Khaşab, *Oman* 71 E8
Al Khawr, *Qatar* 71 E6
Al Khiḑr, *Iraq* 70 D5
Al Khiyām, *Lebanon* 74 B4
Al Khums, *Libya* 79 B8
Al Kiswah, *Syria* 74 B5
Al Kūfah, *Iraq* 70 C5
Al Kufrah, *Libya* 79 D10
Al Kuhayfīyah, *Si. Arabia* 70 E4
Al Kūt, *Iraq* 70 C5
Al Kuwayt, *Kuwait* 70 D5
Al Labwah, *Lebanon* 74 A5
Al Lādhiqīyah, *Syria* 70 C2
Al Līth, *Si. Arabia* 75 C3
Al Liwā', *Oman* 71 E8
Al Luḩayyah, *Yemen* 75 D3
Al Madīnah, *Iraq* 70 D5
Al Madīnah, *Si. Arabia* 70 E3
Al Mafraq, *Jordan* 74 C5
Al Mafraq □, *Jordan* 74 C5
Al Maḩmūdīyah, *Iraq* 70 C5
Al Majma'ah, *Si. Arabia* 70 E5
Al Makhruq, W. →, *Jordan* 74 D6
Al Makhūl, *Si. Arabia* 70 E4
Al Manāmah, *Bahrain* 71 E6
Al Maqwa', *Kuwait* 70 D5
Al Marj, *Libya* 79 B10
Al Maţlā, *Kuwait* 70 D5
Al Mawjib, W. →, *Jordan* 74 D4
Al Mawşil, *Iraq* 70 B4
Al Mayādin, *Syria* 70 C4
Al Mazār, *Jordan* 74 D4
Al Midhnab, *Si. Arabia* 70 E5
Al Minā', *Lebanon* 74 A4
Al Miqdādīyah, *Iraq* 70 C5
Al Mubarraz, *Si. Arabia* 71 E6
Al Mudawwarah, *Jordan* 74 F5
Al Mughayrā', *U.A.E.* 71 E7
Al Muḩarraq, *Bahrain* 71 E6
Al Mukallā, *Yemen* 75 E4
Al Mukhā, *Yemen* 75 E3
Al Musayjīd, *Si. Arabia* 70 E3
Al Musayyib, *Iraq* 70 C5
Al Muthannā □, *Iraq* 70 D5
Al Muwayh, *Si. Arabia* 80 C5
Al Muwayliḩ, *Si. Arabia* 70 E2
Al Owuho = Otukpa, *Nigeria* 83 D6
Al Qādisīyah □, *Iraq* 70 D5
Al Qā'im, *Iraq* 70 C4
Al Qalībah, *Si. Arabia* 70 D3
Al Qāmishlī, *Syria* 70 B4
Al Qaryatayn, *Syria* 74 A6
Al Qaşīm, *Si. Arabia* 70 E4
Al Qaţ'ā, *Syria* 70 C4
Al Qaţīf, *Si. Arabia* 71 E6
Al Qatrānah, *Jordan* 74 D5
Al Qaţrūn, *Libya* 79 D9
Al Qayşūmah, *Si. Arabia* 70 D5
Al Quds = Jerusalem, *Israel* 74 D4
Al Qunayţirah, *Syria* 74 C4
Al Qunfudhah, *Si. Arabia* 80 D5
Al Qurnah, *Iraq* 70 D5
Al Quşayr, *Iraq* 70 D5
Al Quşayr, *Syria* 74 A5
Al Qutayfah, *Syria* 74 B5
Al 'Ubaylah, *Si. Arabia* 75 C5
Al 'Uḑaylīyah, *Si. Arabia* 71 E6
Al 'Ulā, *Si. Arabia* 70 E3
Al 'Uqayr, *Si. Arabia* 71 E6
Al 'Uwaynid, *Si. Arabia* 70 E5
Al 'Uwayqīlah, *Si. Arabia* 70 D4
Al 'Uyūn, *Ḩijāz, Si. Arabia* 70 E3
Al 'Uyūn, *Najd, Si. Arabia* 70 E4
Al 'Uzayr, *Iraq* 70 D5
Al Wajh, *Si. Arabia* 70 E3
Al Wakrah, *Qatar* 71 E6
Al Waqbah, *Si. Arabia* 70 D5
Al Wari'āh, *Si. Arabia* 70 E5
Ala, *Italy* 40 C8
Ala Dağ, *Turkey* 70 B2
Ala Dağları, *Turkey* 73 C10
Alabama □, *U.S.A.* 115 J2
Alabama →, *U.S.A.* 115 K2
Alabaster, *U.S.A.* 115 J2
Alaca, *Turkey* 72 B6
Alacaatlı, *Turkey* 47 B10
Alaçam, *Turkey* 72 B6
Alaçam Dağları, *Turkey* 47 B10
Alacant = Alicante, *Spain* 39 G4
Alaçatı, *Turkey* 47 C8
Alachua, *U.S.A.* 115 L4
Alaejos, *Spain* 36 D5
Alaérma, *Greece* 49 C9
Alagir, *Russia* 35 J7
Alagna Valsésia, *Italy* 40 C4
Alagoa Grande, *Brazil* 125 E11
Alagoas □, *Brazil* 125 E11
Alagoinhas, *Brazil* 125 F11
Alagón, *Spain* 38 D3
Alagón →, *Spain* 36 F4
Alaior, *Spain* 48 B11
Alajero, *Canary Is.* 48 F2
Alajuela, *Costa Rica* 120 D3
Alakamisy, *Madag.* 89 C8
Alaknanda →, *India* 69 D8
Alakol, Ozero, *Kazakhstan* 60 B3
Alamarvdasht, *Iran* 71 E7
Alamata, *Ethiopia* 81 E4
Alameda, *Calif., U.S.A.* 110 H4
Alameda, *N. Mex., U.S.A.* 109 J10
Alaminos, *Phil.* 61 C3
Alamo, *U.S.A.* 111 J11
Alamo Crossing, *U.S.A.* 111 L13
Alamogordo, *U.S.A.* 109 K11
Alamos, *Mexico* 118 B3
Alamosa, *U.S.A.* 109 H11
Åland = Ahvenanmaa, *Finland* 9 F19
Alandroal, *Portugal* 37 G3
Ålands hav, *Europe* 9 F18
Alange, Embalse d', *Spain* 37 G4
Alania = North Ossetia □, *Russia* 35 J7
Alanís, *Spain* 37 G5
Alanya, *Turkey* 70 B1
Alaotra, Farihin', *Madag.* 89 B8
Alapayevsk, *Russia* 52 D7
Alappuzha = Alleppey, *India* 66 Q10
Alar del Rey, *Spain* 36 C6
Alaraz, *Spain* 36 E5
Alarcón, Embalse de, *Spain* 38 F2
Alarobia-Vohiposa, *Madag.* 89 C8
Alaşehir, *Turkey* 47 C10
Alaska □, *U.S.A.* 100 B5
Alaska, G. of, *Pac. Oc.* 100 C5
Alaska Peninsula, *U.S.A.* 100 C4
Alaska Range, *U.S.A.* 100 B4
Alássio, *Italy* 40 E5
Älät, *Azerbaijan* 35 L9
Alatri, *Italy* 41 G10
Alatyr, *Russia* 34 C8
Alatyr →, *Russia* 34 C8
Alausi, *Ecuador* 124 D3
Álava □, *Spain* 38 C2
Alava, C., *U.S.A.* 108 B1
Alaverdi, *Armenia* 35 K7
Alavo = Alavus, *Finland* 9 E20
Alavus, *Finland* 9 E20
Alawoona, *Australia* 95 E3
'Alayh, *Lebanon* 74 B4
Alazani →, *Azerbaijan* 35 K8
Alba, *Italy* 40 D5
Alba □, *Romania* 29 D8
Alba Adriática, *Italy* 41 F10
Alba de Tormes, *Spain* 36 E5
Alba-Iulia, *Romania* 29 D8
Albac, *Romania* 28 D7
Albacete, *Spain* 39 F3
Albacete □, *Spain* 39 G3
Albacutya, L., *Australia* 95 F3
Ålbæk, *Denmark* 11 G4
Ålbæk Bugt, *Denmark* 11 G4
Albaida, *Spain* 39 G4
Albalate de las Nogueras, *Spain* 38 E2
Albalate del Arzobispo, *Spain* 38 D4
Alban, *France* 20 E6
Albanel, L., *Canada* 104 B5
Albania ■, *Europe* 44 E4
Albano Laziale, *Italy* 41 G9
Albany, *Australia* 93 G2
Albany, *Ga., U.S.A.* 115 K3
Albany, *N.Y., U.S.A.* 117 D11
Albany, *Oreg., U.S.A.* 108 D2
Albany, *Tex., U.S.A.* 113 J5
Albany →, *Canada* 104 B3
Albardón, *Argentina* 126 C2
Albarracín, *Spain* 38 E3
Albarracín, Sierra de, *Spain* 38 E3
Albatera, *Spain* 39 G4
Albatross B., *Australia* 94 A3
Albegna →, *Italy* 41 F8
Albemarle, *U.S.A.* 115 H5
Albemarle Sd., *U.S.A.* 115 H7
Albenga, *Italy* 40 D5
Alberche →, *Spain* 36 F6
Alberdi, *Paraguay* 126 B4
Albères, Mts., *France* 20 F6
Ålberga, *Sweden* 11 F10
Alberga, The →, *Australia* 95 D2
Albersdorf, *Germany* 24 A5
Albert, *France* 19 C9
Albert, L., *Africa* 86 B3
Albert, L., *Australia* 95 F2
Albert Edward Ra., *Australia* 92 C4
Albert Lea, *U.S.A.* 112 D8
Albert Nile →, *Uganda* 86 B3
Albert Town, *Bahamas* 121 B5
Alberta □, *Canada* 102 C6
Alberti, *Argentina* 126 D3
Albertinia, *S. Africa* 88 E3
Albertirsa, *Hungary* 28 C4
Alberton, *Canada* 105 C7
Albertville, *France* 21 C10
Albertville, *U.S.A.* 115 H2
Albi, *France* 20 E6
Albia, *U.S.A.* 112 E8
Albina, *Suriname* 125 B8
Albina, Ponta, *Angola* 88 B1
Albino, *Italy* 40 C6
Albion, *Mich., U.S.A.* 114 D3
Albion, *Nebr., U.S.A.* 112 E6
Albion, *Pa., U.S.A.* 116 E4
Albocácer, *Spain* 38 E5
Albolote, *Spain* 37 H7
Alborán, *Medit. S.* 37 K7
Alborea, *Spain* 39 F3
Ålborg, *Denmark* 11 G3
Ålborg Bugt, *Denmark* 11 H4
Alborz, Reshteh-ye Kūhhā-ye, *Iran* 71 C7
Albox, *Spain* 39 H2
Albufeira, *Portugal* 37 H2
Albula →, *Switz.* 25 J5
Albuñol, *Spain* 37 J7
Albuquerque, *U.S.A.* 109 J10
Albuquerque, Cayos de, *Caribbean* 120 D3
Alburg, *U.S.A.* 117 B11
Alburno, Mte., *Italy* 43 B8
Alburquerque, *Spain* 37 F4
Albury = Albury-Wodonga, *Australia* 95 F4
Albury-Wodonga, *Australia* 95 F4
Alcácer do Sal, *Portugal* 37 G2
Alcáçovas, *Portugal* 37 G2
Alcalá de Chivert, *Spain* 38 E5
Alcalá de Guadaira, *Spain* 37 H5
Alcalá de Henares, *Spain* 36 E7
Alcalá de los Gazules, *Spain* 37 J5
Alcalá del Júcar, *Spain* 39 F3
Alcalá del Río, *Spain* 37 H5
Alcalá del Valle, *Spain* 37 J5
Alcalá la Real, *Spain* 37 H7
Álcamo, *Italy* 42 E5
Alcanadre, *Spain* 38 C2
Alcanadre →, *Spain* 38 D4
Alcanar, *Spain* 38 E5
Alcanede, *Portugal* 37 F2
Alcanena, *Portugal* 37 F2
Alcañices, *Spain* 36 D4
Alcañiz, *Spain* 38 D4
Alcântara, *Brazil* 125 D10
Alcántara, *Spain* 36 F4
Alcántara, Embalse de, *Spain* 36 F4
Alcantarilla, *Spain* 39 H3
Alcaracejos, *Spain* 37 G6
Alcaraz, *Spain* 39 G2
Alcaraz, Sierra de, *Spain* 39 G2
Alcaudete, *Spain* 37 H6
Alcázar de San Juan, *Spain* 37 F7
Alchevsk, *Ukraine* 33 H10
Alcira = Alzira, *Spain* 39 F4
Alcobaça, *Portugal* 37 F2
Alcobendas, *Spain* 36 E7
Alcolea del Pinar, *Spain* 38 D2
Alcora, *Spain* 38 E4
Alcorcón, *Spain* 36 E7
Alcoutim, *Portugal* 37 H3
Alcova, *U.S.A.* 108 E10
Alcoy, *Spain* 39 G4
Alcubierre, Sierra de, *Spain* 38 D4
Alcublas, *Spain* 38 F4
Alcúdia, *Spain* 48 B10
Alcúdia, B. d', *Spain* 48 B10
Alcudia, Sierra de la, *Spain* 37 G6
Aldabra Is., *Seychelles* 77 G8
Aldama, *Mexico* 119 C5
Aldan, *Russia* 53 D13
Aldan →, *Russia* 53 C13
Aldea, Pta. de la, *Canary Is.* 48 G4
Aldeburgh, *U.K.* 15 E9
Alder Pk., *U.S.A.* 110 K5
Alderney, *U.K.* 15 H5
Aldershot, *U.K.* 15 F7
Åled, *Sweden* 11 H6
Aledo, *U.S.A.* 112 E9
Alefa, *Ethiopia* 81 E4
Aleg, *Mauritania* 82 B2
Alegranza, *Canary Is.* 48 E6
Alegranza, I., *Canary Is.* 48 E6
Alegre, *Brazil* 127 A7
Alegrete, *Brazil* 127 B4
Aleisk, *Russia* 52 D9
Aleksandriya = Oleksandriya, *Kirovohrad, Ukraine* 33 H7
Aleksandriya = Oleksandriya, *Rivne, Ukraine* 33 G4
Aleksandriyskaya, *Russia* 35 J8
Aleksandrov, *Russia* 32 D10
Aleksandrov Gay, *Russia* 34 E9
Aleksandrovac, *Serbia & M.* 44 C5
Aleksandrovac, *Serbia & M.* 44 B5
Aleksandrovka = Oleksandrovka, *Ukraine* 33 H7
Aleksandrovo, *Bulgaria* 45 C8
Aleksandrovsk-Sakhalinskiy, *Russia* 53 D15
Aleksandrów Kujawski, *Poland* 31 F5
Aleksandrów Łódźki, *Poland* 31 G6
Aleksandry, Z., *Russia* 4 A10
Alekseyevka, *Samara, Russia* 34 D10
Alekseyevka, *Voronezh, Russia* 33 G10
Aleksin, *Russia* 32 E9
Aleksinac, *Serbia & M.* 44 C5
Além Paraíba, *Brazil* 127 A7
Alemania, *Argentina* 126 B2
Alemania, *Chile* 126 B2
Alençon, *France* 18 D7
Alenquer, *Brazil* 125 D8
Alenuihaha Channel, *U.S.A.* 106 H17
Alépé, *Ivory C.* 82 D4
Aleppo = Ḩalab, *Syria* 70 B3
Aléria, *France* 21 F13
Alert, *Canada* 4 A4
Alès, *France* 21 D8
Aleşd, *Romania* 28 C7
Alessándria, *Italy* 40 D5
Ålestrup, *Denmark* 11 H3
Ålesund, *Norway* 9 E12
Alet-les-Bains, *France* 20 F6
Aletschhorn, *Switz.* 25 J4
Aleutian Is., *Pac. Oc.* 100 C2
Aleutian Trench, *Pac. Oc.* 96 C10
Alexander, *U.S.A.* 112 B3
Alexander, Mt., *Australia* 93 E3
Alexander Arch., *U.S.A.* 100 C6
Alexander Bay, *S. Africa* 88 D2
Alexander City, *U.S.A.* 115 J3
Alexander I., *Antarctica* 5 C17
Alexandra, *Australia* 95 F4
Alexandra, *N.Z.* 91 L2
Alexandra Falls, *Canada* 102 A5

Alexandria = El Iskandarîya, Egypt 80 H7
Alexandria, B.C., Canada 102 C4
Alexandria, Ont., Canada 117 A10
Alexandria, Romania 29 G10
Alexandria, S. Africa 88 E4
Alexandria, U.K. 13 F4
Alexandria, La., U.S.A. 113 K8
Alexandria, Minn., U.S.A. 112 C7
Alexandria, S. Dak., U.S.A. 112 D6
Alexandria, Va., U.S.A. 114 F7
Alexandria Bay, U.S.A. 117 B9
Alexandrina, L., Australia 95 F2
Alexandroúpolis, Greece 45 F9
Alexis →, Canada 105 B8
Alexis Creek, Canada 102 C4
Alfabia, Spain 48 B9
Alfambra, Spain 38 E3
Alfândega da Fé, Portugal 36 D4
Alfaro, Spain 38 C3
Alfatar, Bulgaria 45 C11
Alfaz del Pi, Spain 39 G4
Alfeld, Germany 24 D5
Alfenas, Brazil 127 A6
Alfiós →, Greece 46 D3
Alföld, Hungary 28 D5
Alfonsine, Italy 41 D9
Alford, Aberds., U.K. 13 D6
Alford, Lincs., U.K. 14 D8
Alfred, Maine, U.S.A. 117 C14
Alfred, N.Y., U.S.A. 116 D7
Alfreton, U.K. 14 D6
Alfta, Sweden 10 C10
Alga, Kazakhstan 52 E6
Algaida, Spain 48 B9
Algar, Spain 37 J5
Ålgård, Norway 9 G11
Algarinejo, Spain 37 H6
Algarve, Portugal 37 J2
Algeciras, Spain 37 J5
Algemesí, Spain 39 F4
Alger, Algeria 78 A6
Alger ✕ (ALG), Algeria 39 J8
Algeria ■, Africa 78 C6
Alghero, Italy 42 B1
Älghult, Sweden 11 G9
Algiers = Alger, Algeria 78 A6
Algoa B., S. Africa 88 E4
Algodonales, Spain 37 J5
Algodor →, Spain 36 F7
Algoma, U.S.A. 114 C2
Algona, U.S.A. 112 D7
Algonac, U.S.A. 116 D2
Algonquin ⌓, Canada 104 C4
Algorta, Uruguay 128 C5
Alhama de Almería, Spain 37 J8
Alhama de Aragón, Spain 38 D3
Alhama de Granada, Spain 37 H7
Alhama de Murcia, Spain 39 H3
Alhambra, U.S.A. 111 L8
Alhaurín el Grande, Spain 37 J6
Alhucemas = Al Hoceïma, Morocco 78 A5
'Alī al Gharbī, Iraq 70 C5
'Alī ash Sharqī, Iraq 70 C5
Äli Bayramlı, Azerbaijan 35 L9
'Alī Khēl, Afghan. 68 C3
Ali Sahîh, Djibouti 81 E5
Alī Shāh, Iran 70 B5
Ália, Italy 42 E6
'Alīābād, Khorāsān, Iran 71 C8
'Alīābād, Kordestān, Iran 70 C5
'Alīābād, Yazd, Iran 71 D7
Aliaga, Spain 38 E4
Aliağa, Turkey 47 C8
Aliákmon →, Greece 44 F6
Alibo, Ethiopia 81 F4
Alibori →, Benin 83 C5
Alibunar, Serbia & M. 28 E5
Alicante, Spain 39 G4
Alicante □, Spain 39 G4
Alicante ✕ (ALC), Spain 39 G4
Alice, S. Africa 88 E4
Alice, U.S.A. 113 M5
Alice →, Queens., Australia 94 C3
Alice →, Queens., Australia 94 B3
Alice, Punta, Italy 43 C10
Alice Arm, Canada 102 B3
Alice Springs, Australia 94 C1
Alicedale, S. Africa 88 E4
Aliceville, U.S.A. 115 J1
Alicudi, Italy 43 D7
Aliganj, India 69 F8
Aligarh, Raj., India 68 G7
Aligarh, Ut. P., India 68 F8
Alīgūdarz, Iran 71 C6
Alijó, Portugal 36 D3
Alimnía, Greece 49 C9
Alingsås, Sweden 11 G6
Alipur, Pakistan 68 E4
Alipur Duar, India 67 F16
Aliquippa, U.S.A. 116 F4
Alishan, Taiwan 59 F13
Aliste →, Spain 36 D5
Alitus = Alytus, Lithuania 9 J21
Alivérion, Greece 46 C6
Aliwal North, S. Africa 88 E4
Alix, Canada 102 C6
Aljezur, Portugal 37 H2
Aljustrel, Portugal 37 H2
Alkamari, Niger 83 C7
Alkmaar, Neths. 17 B4
All American Canal, U.S.A. 109 K6
Allada, Benin 83 D5
Allagash →, U.S.A. 115 B11
Allah Dad, Pakistan 68 G2
Allahabad, India 69 G9
Allan, Canada 103 C7
Allanche, France 20 C6
Allanridge, S. Africa 88 D4
Allaqi, Wadi →, Egypt 80 C3
Allariz, Spain 36 C3
Allassac, France 20 C5
Ålleberg, Sweden 11 F7
Allegany, U.S.A. 116 D6
Allegheny →, U.S.A. 116 F5
Allegheny Mts., U.S.A. 114 G6
Allegheny Reservoir, U.S.A. 116 E6
Allègre, France 20 C7
Allègre, Pte., Guadeloupe 120 b
Allen, Bog of, Ireland 12 C5
Allen, L., Ireland 12 B3
Allendale, U.S.A. 115 J5
Allende, Mexico 118 B4
Allentown, U.S.A. 117 F9
Allentsteig, Austria 26 C8
Alleppey, India 66 Q10
Allepuz, Spain 38 E4
Aller →, Germany 24 C5
Alleynes B., Barbados 121 g
Alliance, Nebr., U.S.A. 112 D3
Alliance, Ohio, U.S.A. 116 F3
Allier □, France 19 F9
Allier →, France 19 F10
Alliford Bay, Canada 102 C2
Alligator Pond, Jamaica 120 a
Allinge, Denmark 11 J8
Alliston = New Tecumseth, Canada 116 B5
Alloa, U.K. 13 E5
Allones, France 18 D8
Allora, Australia 95 D5
Allos, France 21 D10
Alluitsup Paa, Greenland 101 B15
Alma, Canada 105 C5
Alma, Ga., U.S.A. 115 K4
Alma, Kans., U.S.A. 112 F6
Alma, Mich., U.S.A. 114 D3
Alma, Nebr., U.S.A. 112 E5
Alma Ata = Almaty, Kazakhstan 52 E8
Almacelles, Spain 38 D5
Almada, Portugal 37 G1
Almaden, Australia 94 B3
Almadén, Spain 37 G6
Almanor, L., U.S.A. 108 F3
Almansa, Spain 39 G3
Almanza, Spain 36 C5
Almanzor, Pico, Spain 36 E5
Almanzora →, Spain 39 H3
Almaş, Munţii, Romania 28 F7
Almassora, Spain 38 F4
Almaty, Kazakhstan 52 E8
Almazán, Spain 38 D2
Almeirim, Brazil 125 D8
Almeirim, Portugal 37 F2
Almelo, Neths. 17 B6
Almenar de Soria, Spain 38 D2
Almenara, Spain 38 F4
Almenara, Sierra de la, Spain 39 H3
Almendra, Embalse de, Spain 36 D4
Almendralejo, Spain 37 G4
Almere-Stad, Neths. 17 B5
Almería, Spain 37 J8
Almería □, Spain 39 H2
Almería, G. de, Spain 39 J2
Almetyevsk, Russia 34 C11
Älmhult, Sweden 11 H8
Almirante, Panama 120 E3
Almiropótamos, Greece 46 C6
Almirós, Greece 46 B4
Almiroú, Kólpos, Greece 49 D6
Almodôvar, Portugal 37 H2
Almodóvar del Campo, Spain 37 G6
Almodóvar del Río, Spain 37 H5
Almond, U.S.A. 116 D7
Almont, U.S.A. 116 D1
Almonte, Canada 117 A8
Almonte, Spain 37 H4
Almora, India 69 E8
Almoradí, Spain 39 G4
Almorox, Spain 36 E6
Almoustarat, Mali 83 B5
Älmsta, Sweden 10 E12
Almudévar, Spain 38 C4
Almuñécar, Spain 37 J7
Almunge, Sweden 10 E12
Almuradiel, Spain 37 G7
Alness, U.K. 13 D4
Alnmouth, U.K. 14 B6
Alnwick, U.K. 14 B6
Aloi, Uganda 86 B3
Alon, Burma 67 H19
Alonissos-Voríai Sporades △, Greece 46 B6
Alor, Indonesia 63 F6
Alor Setar, Malaysia 65 J3
Álora, Spain 37 J6
Alosno, Spain 37 H3
Alot, India 68 H6
Aloysius, Mt., Australia 93 E4
Alpaugh, U.S.A. 110 K7
Alpe Apuane ⌓, Italy 40 D7
Alpedrinha, Portugal 36 E3
Alpena, U.S.A. 114 C4
Alpes-de-Haute-Provence □, France 21 D10
Alpes-Maritimes □, France 21 E11
Alpha, Australia 94 C4
Alpha Cordillera, Arctic 4 A2
Alphen aan den Rijn, Neths. 17 B4
Alpiarça, Portugal 37 F2
Alpine, Ariz., U.S.A. 109 K9
Alpine, Calif., U.S.A. 111 N10
Alpine, Tex., U.S.A. 113 K3
Alps, Europe 6 F7
Alpu, Turkey 72 C4
Alqueta, Barragem do, Portugal 37 G3
Alrø, Denmark 11 J4
Als, Denmark 11 K3
Alsace □, France 19 D14
Alsask, Canada 103 C7
Alsasua, Spain 38 C2
Alsek →, U.S.A. 102 B1
Alsfeld, Germany 24 E5
Alsten, Norway 8 D15
Alstermo, Sweden 11 H9
Alston, U.K. 14 C5
Alta, Norway 8 B20
Alta, Sierra, Spain 38 E3
Alta Gracia, Argentina 126 C3
Alta Sierra, U.S.A. 111 K8
Altaelva →, Norway 8 B20
Altafjorden, Norway 8 A20
Altai = Aerhtai Shan, Mongolia 60 B4
Altamaha →, U.S.A. 115 K5
Altamira, Brazil 125 D8
Altamira, Chile 126 B2
Altamira, Mexico 119 C5
Altamira, Cuevas de, Spain 36 B6
Altamont, U.S.A. 117 D10
Altamura, Italy 43 B9
Altanbulag, Mongolia 60 A5
Altar, Mexico 118 A2
Altar, Desierto de, Mexico 118 B2
Altata, Mexico 118 C3
Altavista, U.S.A. 114 G6
Altay, China 60 B3
Altdorf, Switz. 25 J4
Alte Mellum, Germany 24 B4
Altea, Spain 39 G4
Altenberg, Germany 24 E9
Altenbruch, Germany 24 B4
Altenburg, Germany 24 E8
Altenkirchen, Mecklenburg-Vorpommern, Germany 24 A9
Altenkirchen, Rhld-Pfz., Germany 24 E3
Altenmarkt, Austria 26 D7
Alter do Chão, Portugal 37 F3
Altınoluk, Turkey 47 B8
Altınova, Turkey 47 B8
Altıntaş, Turkey 47 B12
Altınyaka, Turkey 47 E12
Altınyayla, Turkey 47 D11
Altiplano, Bolivia 122 E4
Altkirch, France 19 E14
Altmark, Germany 24 C7
Altmühl →, Germany 25 G7
Altmühltal ⌓, Germany 25 G7
Altmunster, Austria 26 D6
Alto Adige = Trentino-Alto Adige □, Italy 41 B8
Alto Araguaia, Brazil 125 G8
Alto Cuchumatanes = Cuchumatanes, Sierra de los, Guatemala 120 C1
Alto del Carmen, Chile 126 B1
Alto del Inca, Chile 126 A2
Alto Garda Bresciano ⌓, Italy 40 C7
Alto Ligonha, Mozam. 87 F4
Alto Molocue, Mozam. 87 F4
Alto Paraguay □, Paraguay 126 A4
Alto Paraná □, Paraguay 127 B5
Alton, Canada 116 C4
Alton, U.K. 15 F7
Alton, Ill., U.S.A. 112 F9
Alton, N.H., U.S.A. 117 C13
Altona, Canada 103 D9
Altoona, U.S.A. 116 F6
Altötting, Germany 25 G8
Altstätten, Switz. 25 H5
Altun Kupri, Iraq 70 C5
Altun Shan, China 60 C3
Alturas, U.S.A. 108 F3
Altus, U.S.A. 113 H5
Alubijid, Phil. 61 G6
Alucra, Turkey 73 B8
Aluk, Sudan 81 F2
Alūksne, Latvia 9 H22
Alunda, Sweden 10 D12
Alunite, U.S.A. 111 K12
Aluoro →, Ethiopia 81 F3
Alupka, Ukraine 33 K8
Alushta, Ukraine 33 K8
Alusi, Indonesia 63 F8
Alustante, Spain 38 E3
Alva, U.S.A. 113 G5
Alvaiázere, Portugal 36 F2
Älvängen, Sweden 11 G6
Alvão ⌓, Portugal 36 D3
Alvarado, Mexico 119 D5
Alvarado, U.S.A. 113 J6
Alvaro Obregón, Presa, Mexico 118 B3
Älvdalen, Sweden 10 C8
Alvear, Argentina 126 B4
Alverca, Portugal 37 G1
Alvesta, Sweden 11 H8
Alvin, U.S.A. 113 L7
Alvinston, Canada 116 D3
Alvito, Portugal 37 G3
Älvkarleby, Sweden 10 D11
Alvord Desert, U.S.A. 108 E4
Älvros, Sweden 10 B8
Älvsbyn, Sweden 8 D19
Alwar, India 68 F7
Alxa Zuoqi, China 56 E3
Alyangula, Australia 94 A2
Alyata = Älät, Azerbaijan 35 L9
Alyth, U.K. 13 E5
Alytus, Lithuania 9 J21
Alzada, U.S.A. 112 C2
Alzey, Germany 25 F4
Alzira, Spain 39 F4
Am Timan, Chad 79 F10
Amadeus, L., Australia 93 D5
Amadi, Dem. Rep. of the Congo 86 B2
Amâdi, Sudan 81 F3
Amadjuak L., Canada 101 B12
Amadora, Portugal 37 G1
Amagansett, U.S.A. 117 F12
Amagasaki, Japan 55 G7
Amager, Denmark 11 J6
Amagunze, Nigeria 83 D6
Amahai, Indonesia 63 E7
Amakusa-Shotō, Japan 55 H5
Åmål, Sweden 10 E6
Amalfi, Italy 43 B7
Amaliás, Greece 46 D3
Amalner, India 66 J9
Amamapare, Indonesia 63 E9
Amambaí, Brazil 127 A4
Amambaí →, Brazil 127 A5
Amambay □, Paraguay 127 A4
Amambay, Cordillera de, S. Amer. 127 A4
Amami-Guntō, Japan 55 L4
Amami-Ō-Shima, Japan 55 L4
Aman, Pulau, Malaysia 65 c
Amanã, L., Brazil 124 D6
Amanat →, India 69 G11
Amanda Park, U.S.A. 110 C3
Amangeldy, Kazakhstan 52 D7
Amantea, Italy 43 C9
Amapá, Brazil 125 C8
Amapá □, Brazil 125 C8
Amara, Sudan 81 E3
Amara □, Ethiopia 81 E4
Amarante, Brazil 125 E10
Amarante, Portugal 36 D2
Amaranth, Canada 103 C9
Amareleja, Portugal 37 G3
Amargosa →, U.S.A. 111 J10
Amargosa Range, U.S.A. 111 J10
Amári, Greece 49 D6
Amarillo, U.S.A. 113 H4
Amarkantak, India 69 H9
Amârna, Tell el', Sudan 80 B3
Amaro, Mte., Italy 41 F11
Amarpur, India 69 G12
Amarti, Eritrea 81 E5
Amarwara, India 69 H8
Amasra, Turkey 72 B5
Amassama, Nigeria 83 D6
Amasya, Turkey 72 B6
Amata, Australia 93 E5
Amatikulu, S. Africa 89 D5
Amatitlán, Guatemala 120 D1
Amatrice, Italy 41 F10
Amay, Belgium 17 D5
Amazon = Amazonas →, S. Amer. 125 D9
Amazonas □, Brazil 124 E6
Amazonas →, S. Amer. 125 D9
Amba Ferit, Ethiopia 81 E4
Ambah, India 68 F8
Ambahakily, Madag. 89 C7
Ambahita, Madag. 89 C8
Ambala, India 68 D7
Ambalavao, Madag. 89 C8
Ambanja, Madag. 89 A8
Ambararata, Madag. 89 B8
Ambarchik, Russia 53 C17
Ambarijeby, Madag. 89 A8
Ambaro, Helodranon', Madag. 89 A8
Ambato, Ecuador 124 D3
Ambato, Madag. 89 A8
Ambato, Sierra de, Argentina 126 B2
Ambato Boeny, Madag. 89 B8
Ambatofinandrahana, Madag. 89 C8
Ambatolampy, Madag. 89 B8
Ambatomainty, Madag. 89 B8
Ambatomanoina, Madag. 89 B8
Ambatondrazaka, Madag. 89 B8
Ambatosoratra, Madag. 89 B8
Ambelón, Greece 46 B4
Ambenja, Madag. 89 B8
Amberg, Germany 25 F7
Ambergris Cay, Belize 119 D7
Ambérieu-en-Bugey, France 21 C9
Amberley, N.Z. 91 K4
Ambert, France 20 C7
Ambidédi, Mali 82 C2
Ambikapur, India 69 H10
Ambikol, Sudan 80 C3
Ambilobé, Madag. 89 A8
Ambinanindrano, Madag. 89 C8
Ambinanitelo, Madag. 89 B8
Ambinda, Madag. 89 B8
Amble, U.K. 14 B6
Ambleside, U.K. 14 C5
Ambo, Peru 124 F3
Amboahangy, Madag. 89 C8
Ambodifototra, Madag. 89 B8
Ambodilazana, Madag. 89 B8
Ambodiriana, Madag. 89 B8
Ambohidratrimo, Madag. 89 B8
Ambohidray, Madag. 89 B8
Ambohimahamasina, Madag. 89 C8
Ambohimahasoa, Madag. 89 C8
Ambohimanga, Madag. 89 C8
Ambohimitombo, Madag. 89 C8
Ambohitra, Madag. 89 A8
Amboise, France 18 E8
Ambon, Indonesia 63 E7
Ambondro, Madag. 89 D8
Amboseli △, Kenya 86 C4
Amboseli, L., Kenya 86 C4
Ambositra, Madag. 89 C8
Ambovombe, Madag. 89 D8
Amboy, U.S.A. 111 L11
Amboyna Cay, S. China Sea 62 C4
Ambridge, U.S.A. 116 F4
Ambriz, Angola 84 F2
Amchitka I., U.S.A. 100 C1
Amderma, Russia 52 C7
Amdhi, India 69 H9
Ameca, Mexico 118 C4
Ameca →, Mexico 118 C3
Amecameca, Mexico 119 D5
Ameland, Neths. 17 A5
Amélia, Italy 41 F9
Amendolara, Italy 43 C9
Amenia, U.S.A. 117 E11
American Falls, U.S.A. 108 E7
American Falls Reservoir, U.S.A. 108 E7
American Fork, U.S.A. 108 F8
American Highland, Antarctica 5 D6
American Samoa ⊠, Pac. Oc. 91 B13
Americana, Brazil 127 A6
Americus, U.S.A. 115 K3
Amerigo Vespucci, Firenze ✕ (FLR), Italy 40 E8
Amersfoort, Neths. 17 B5
Amersfoort, S. Africa 89 D4
Amery Ice Shelf, Antarctica 5 C6
Ames, Spain 36 C2
Ames, U.S.A. 112 E8
Amesbury, U.S.A. 117 D14
Amet, India 68 G5
Amfíklia, Greece 46 C4
Amfilokhía, Greece 46 C3
Amfípolis, Greece 44 F7
Ámfissa, Greece 46 C4
Amga, Russia 53 C14
Amga →, Russia 53 C14
Amgu, Russia 53 E14
Amgun →, Russia 53 D14
Amherst, Canada 105 C7
Amherst, Mass., U.S.A. 117 D12
Amherst, N.Y., U.S.A. 116 D6
Amherst, Ohio, U.S.A. 116 E2
Amherst I., Canada 117 B8
Amherstburg, Canada 104 D3
Amiata, Mte., Italy 41 F8
Amidon, U.S.A. 112 B3
Amiens, France 19 C9
Amindaion, Greece 44 F5
Åminne, Sweden 11 G7
Amino, Ethiopia 81 G5
Aminuis, Namibia 88 C2
Amīrābād, Iran 70 C5
Amirante Is., Seychelles 50 K9
Amisk ⌓, Canada 103 B9
Amisk L., Canada 103 C8
Amistad ⌓, U.S.A. 113 L4
Amistad, Presa de la, Mexico 118 B4
Amite, U.S.A. 113 K9
Amla, India 68 J8
Amlapura = Karangasem, Indonesia 63 J18
Amlia I., U.S.A. 100 C2
Amlwch, U.K. 14 D3
Amm Adam, Sudan 81 D4
'Ammān, Jordan 74 D4
'Ammān □, Jordan 74 D5
'Ammān ✕ (AMM), Jordan 74 D5
Ammanford, U.K. 15 F4
Ammassalik = Tasiilaq, Greenland 4 C6
Ammerån →, Sweden 10 A10
Ammersee, Germany 25 G7
Ammochostos = Famagusta, Cyprus 49 D12
Ammon, U.S.A. 108 E8
Amnat Charoen, Thailand 64 E5
Amnura, Bangla. 69 G13
Amo Jiang →, China 58 F3
Āmol, Iran 71 B7
Amorgós, Greece 47 E7
Amory, U.S.A. 115 J1
Amos, Canada 104 C4
Åmot, Norway 9 G13
Åmotfors, Sweden 10 E6
Amoy = Xiamen, China 59 E12
Ampanavoana, Madag. 89 B9
Ampang, Malaysia 65 L3
Ampangalana, Lakandranon', Madag. 89 C8
Ampanihy, Madag. 89 C7
Amparafaravola, Madag. 89 B8
Ampasinambo, Madag. 89 C8
Ampasindava, Helodranon', Madag. 89 A8
Ampasindava, Saikanosy, Madag. 89 A8
Ampenan, Indonesia 63 K18
Amper, Nigeria 83 D6
Amper →, Germany 25 G7
Ampezzo, Italy 41 B9
Amphoe Kathu, Thailand 65 a
Amphoe Thalang, Thailand 65 a
Ampitsikinana, Réunion 89 A8
Ampombiantambo, Madag. 89 A8
Amposta, Spain 38 E5
Ampotaka, Madag. 89 D7
Ampoza, Madag. 89 C7
Amqui, Canada 105 C6
Amravati, India 66 J10
Amreli, India 68 J4
Amritsar, India 68 D6
Amroha, India 69 E8
Amrum, Germany 24 A4
Amsterdam, Neths. 17 B4
Amsterdam, U.S.A. 117 D10
Amsterdam ✕ (AMS), Neths. 17 B4
Amsterdam, I. = Nouvelle-Amsterdam, Î., Ind. Oc. 3 F13
Amstetten, Austria 26 C7
Amudarya →, Uzbekistan 52 E6
Amundsen Gulf, Canada 100 A7
Amundsen-Scott, Antarctica 5 E
Amundsen Sea, Antarctica 5 D15
Amungen, Sweden 10 C9
Amuntai, Indonesia 62 E5
Amur →, Russia 53 D15
Amur, W. →, Sudan 80 D3
Amurang, Indonesia 63 D6
Amurrio, Spain 38 B1
Amursk, Russia 53 D14
Amusco, Spain 36 C6
Amvrakikós Kólpos, Greece 46 C2
Amvrosiyivka, Ukraine 33 J10
Amyderya = Amudarya →, Uzbekistan 52 E6
An Anbār □, Iraq 70 C4
An Bien, Vietnam 65 H5
An Hoa, Vietnam 64 E7
An Nabatīyah at Tahta, Lebanon 74 B4
An Nabk, Si. Arabia 70 D3
An Nabk, Syria 74 A5

An Nafūd, *Si. Arabia* 70 D4
An Najaf, *Iraq* 70 C5
An Nāṣirīyah, *Iraq* 70 D5
An Nhon, *Vietnam* 64 F7
An Nîl □, *Sudan* 80 D3
An Nîl el Abyad □, *Sudan* 81 E3
An Nîl el Azraq □, *Sudan* 81 E3
An Nu'ayrīyah, *Si. Arabia* 71 E6
An Nu'mānīyah, *Iraq* 73 F11
An Nuwayb'ī, W. →, *Si. Arabia* 74 F3
An Thoi, Dao, *Vietnam* 65 H4
An Uaimh, *Ireland* 12 C5
Anabar →, *Russia* 53 B12
'Anabtā, *West Bank* 74 C4
Anaconda, *U.S.A.* 108 C7
Anacortes, *U.S.A.* 110 B4
Anacuao, Mt., *Phil.* 61 C4
Anadarko, *U.S.A.* 113 H5
Anadia, *Portugal* 36 E2
Anadolu, *Turkey* 72 C5
Anadyr, *Russia* 53 C18
Anadyr →, *Russia* 53 C18
Anadyrskiy Zaliv, *Russia* 53 C19
Anáfi, *Greece* 47 E7
Anafópoulo, *Greece* 47 E7
Anaga, Pta. de, *Canary Is.* 48 F3
Anagni, *Italy* 41 G10
'Ānah, *Iraq* 70 C4
Anaheim, *U.S.A.* 111 M9
Anahim Lake, *Canada* 102 C3
Anáhuac, *Mexico* 118 B4
Anakapalle, *India* 67 L13
Anakie, *Australia* 94 C4
Anaklia, *Georgia* 35 J5
Analalava, *Madag.* 89 A8
Analavoka, *Madag.* 89 C8
Análipsis, *Greece* 49 A3
Anambar →, *Pakistan* 68 D3
Anambas, Kepulauan, *Indonesia* 62 D3
Anambas Is. = Anambas, Kepulauan, *Indonesia* 62 D3
Anambra □, *Nigeria* 83 D6
Anamosa, *U.S.A.* 112 D9
Anamur, *Turkey* 70 B2
Anamur Burnu, *Turkey* 72 D5
Anan, *Japan* 55 H7
Anand, *India* 68 H5
Anánes, *Greece* 46 E6
Anantapur, *India* 66 M10
Anantnag, *India* 69 C6
Ananyiv, *Ukraine* 29 C14
Anapa, *Russia* 33 K9
Anapodháris →, *Greece* 49 E7
Anápolis, *Brazil* 125 G9
Anapu →, *Brazil* 125 D8
Anār, *Iran* 71 D7
Anārak, *Iran* 71 C7
Anarisfjällen, *Sweden* 10 A7
Anas →, *India* 68 H5
Anatolia = Anadolu, *Turkey* 72 C5
Anatsogno, *Madag.* 89 C7
Añatuya, *Argentina* 126 B3
Anaunethad L., *Canada* 103 A8
Anbyŏn, *N. Korea* 57 E14
Ancares ⌂, *Spain* 36 C4
Ancares, Sierra de, *Spain* 36 C4
Ancaster, *Canada* 116 C5
Ancenis, *France* 18 E5
Anchor Bay, *U.S.A.* 110 G3
Anchorage, *U.S.A.* 100 B5
Anci, *China* 56 E9
Ancohuma, Nevado, *Bolivia* 124 G5
Ancón, *Peru* 124 F3
Ancona, *Italy* 41 E10
Ancud, *Chile* 128 E2
Ancud, G. de, *Chile* 128 E2
Ancy-le-Franc, *France* 19 E11
Andacollo, *Argentina* 126 D1
Andacollo, *Chile* 126 C1
Andaingo, *Madag.* 89 B8
Andalgalá, *Argentina* 126 B2
Åndalsnes, *Norway* 9 E12
Andalucía □, *Spain* 37 H6
Andalusia = Andalucía □, *Spain* 37 H6
Andalusia, *U.S.A.* 115 K2
Andaman Is., *Ind. Oc.* 50 H13
Andaman Sea, *Ind. Oc.* 62 B1
Andamooka Opal Fields, *Australia* 95 E2
Andapa, *Madag.* 89 A8
Andara, *Namibia* 88 B3
Andelot-Blancheville, *France* 19 D12
Andenes, *Norway* 8 B17
Andenne, *Belgium* 17 D5
Andéranboukane, *Mali* 83 B5
Andermatt, *Switz.* 25 J4
Andernach, *Germany* 24 E3
Andernos-les-Bains, *France* 20 D2
Anderslöv, *Sweden* 11 J7
Anderson, *Alaska, U.S.A.* 100 B5
Anderson, *Calif., U.S.A.* 108 F2
Anderson, *Ind., U.S.A.* 114 E3
Anderson, *Mo., U.S.A.* 113 G7
Anderson, *S.C., U.S.A.* 115 H4
Anderson →, *Canada* 100 B7
Anderstorp, *Sweden* 11 G7
Andes, *U.S.A.* 117 D10
Andes, Cord. de los, *S. Amer.* 124 H5
Andfjorden, *Norway* 8 B17
Andhra Pradesh □, *India* 66 L11
Andijon, *Uzbekistan* 52 E8
Andikíthira, *Greece* 46 F5
Andilamena, *Madag.* 89 B8
Andīmeshk, *Iran* 71 C6
Andímilos, *Greece* 46 E6
Andíparos, *Greece* 47 D7
Andípaxoi, *Greece* 46 B2
Andípsara, *Greece* 47 C7
Andírrion, *Greece* 46 C3
Andizhan = Andijon, *Uzbekistan* 52 E8
Andoain, *Spain* 38 B2
Andoany, *Madag.* 89 A8
Andohahela ⌂, *Madag.* 89 C8
Andong, *S. Korea* 57 F15
Andongwei, *China* 57 G10
Andoom, *Australia* 94 A3
Andorra, *Spain* 38 E4
Andorra ■, *Europe* 20 F5
Andorra La Vella, *Andorra* 20 F5
Andover, *U.K.* 15 F6
Andover, *Maine, U.S.A.* 117 B14
Andover, *Mass., U.S.A.* 117 D13
Andover, *N.J., U.S.A.* 117 F10
Andover, *N.Y., U.S.A.* 116 D7
Andover, *Ohio, U.S.A.* 116 E4
Andøya, *Norway* 8 B16
Andradina, *Brazil* 125 H8
Andrahary, Mt., *Madag.* 89 A8
Andramasina, *Madag.* 89 B8
Andranopasy, *Madag.* 89 C7
Andranovory, *Madag.* 89 C7
Andratx, *Spain* 48 B9
Andreanof Is., *U.S.A.* 100 C2
Andreapol, *Russia* 32 D7
Andrews, *S.C., U.S.A.* 115 J6
Andrews, *Tex., U.S.A.* 113 J3
Andreyevka, *Russia* 34 D10
Ándria, *Italy* 43 A9
Andriamena, *Madag.* 89 B8
Andriandampy, *Madag.* 89 C8
Andriba, *Madag.* 89 B8
Andrijevica, *Serbia & M.* 44 D3
Andringitra ⌂, *Madag.* 89 C8
Andrítsaina, *Greece* 46 D3
Androka, *Madag.* 89 C7
Ándros, *Greece* 46 D6
Andros I., *Bahamas* 120 B4
Andros Town, *Bahamas* 120 B4
Androscoggin →, *U.S.A.* 117 C14
Andrychów, *Poland* 31 J6
Andselv, *Norway* 8 B18
Andújar, *Spain* 37 G6
Andulo, *Angola* 84 G3
Aneby, *Sweden* 11 G8
Anegada, *Br. Virgin Is.* 121 e
Anegada Passage, *W. Indies* 121 C7
Anéhо, *Togo* 83 D5
Anenni-Noi, *Moldova* 29 D14
Aneto, Pico de, *Spain* 38 C5
Anfu, *China* 59 D10
Ang Mo Kio, *Singapore* 65 d
Ang Thong, *Thailand* 64 E3
Ang Thong △, *Thailand* 65 H2
Ang Thong, Ko, *Thailand* 65 b
Angamos, Punta, *Chile* 126 A1
Angara →, *Russia* 53 D10
Angara-Débou, *Benin* 83 C5
Angarab, *Ethiopia* 81 E4
Angarbaka, *Sudan* 81 F1
Angarsk, *Russia* 53 D11
Angas Hills, *Australia* 92 D4
Angaston, *Australia* 95 E2
Ånge, *Sweden* 10 B9
Ángel, Salto = Angel Falls, *Venezuela* 124 B6
Ángel de la Guarda, I., *Mexico* 118 B2
Angel Falls, *Venezuela* 124 B6
Angeles, *Phil.* 61 D4
Ängelholm, *Sweden* 11 H6
Angels Camp, *U.S.A.* 110 G6
Ängelsberg, *Sweden* 10 E10
Anger →, *Ethiopia* 81 F4
Angereb →, *Ethiopia* 81 E4
Ångermanälven →, *Sweden* 10 B11
Ångermanland, *Sweden* 8 E18
Angermünde, *Germany* 24 B9
Angers, *Canada* 117 A9
Angers, *France* 18 E6
Angerville, *France* 19 D9
Ängesån →, *Sweden* 8 C20
Angikuni L., *Canada* 103 A9
Angkor, *Cambodia* 64 F4
Anglès, *Spain* 38 D7
Anglesey, Isle of □, *U.K.* 14 D3
Anglet, *France* 20 E2
Angleton, *U.S.A.* 113 L7
Anglin →, *France* 20 B4
Anglisidhes, *Cyprus* 49 E12
Anglure, *France* 19 D10
Angmagssalik = Tasiilaq, *Greenland* 4 C6
Ango, *Dem. Rep. of the Congo* 86 B2
Angoche, *Mozam.* 87 F4
Angoche, I., *Mozam.* 87 F4
Angol, *Chile* 126 D1
Angola, *Ind., U.S.A.* 114 E3
Angola, *N.Y., U.S.A.* 116 D5
Angola ■, *Africa* 85 G3
Angoulême, *France* 20 C4
Angoumois, *France* 20 C4
Angra dos Reis, *Brazil* 127 A7
Angrapa →, *Russia* 30 D8
Angren, *Uzbekistan* 52 E8
Angtassom, *Cambodia* 65 G5
Angu, *Dem. Rep. of the Congo* 86 B1
Anguang, *China* 57 B12
Anguilla ☒, *W. Indies* 121 C7
Anguo, *China* 56 E8
Angurugu, *Australia* 94 A2
Angus □, *U.K.* 13 E6
Angwa →, *Zimbabwe* 89 B5
Anhanduí →, *Brazil* 127 A5
Anholt, *Denmark* 11 H5
Anhua, *China* 59 C8
Anhui □, *China* 59 B11
Anhwei = Anhui □, *China* 59 B11
Anichab, *Namibia* 88 C1
Ánidhros, *Greece* 47 E7
Anié, *Togo* 83 D5
Animas →, *U.S.A.* 109 H9
Anina, *Romania* 28 E6
Aninoasa, *Romania* 29 F9
Anivorano, *Madag.* 89 B8
Anjalankoski, *Finland* 9 F22
Anjar, *India* 68 H4
Anji, *China* 59 B12
Anjou, *France* 18 E6
Anjozorobe, *Madag.* 89 B8
Anju, *N. Korea* 57 E13
Anka, *Nigeria* 83 C6
Ankaboa, Tanjona, *Madag.* 89 C7
Ankang, *China* 56 H5
Ankara, *Turkey* 72 C5
Ankarafantsika ⌂, *Madag.* 89 B8
Ankaramena, *Madag.* 89 C8
Ankaratra, *Madag.* 85 H9
Ankarsrum, *Sweden* 11 G10
Ankasakasa, *Madag.* 89 B7
Ankavandra, *Madag.* 89 B8
Ankazoabo, *Madag.* 89 C7
Ankazobe, *Madag.* 89 B8
Ankeny, *U.S.A.* 112 E8
Ankilimalinika, *Madag.* 89 C7
Ankilizato, *Madag.* 89 C8
Ankisabe, *Madag.* 89 B8
Anklam, *Germany* 24 B9
Ankober, *Ethiopia* 81 F4
Ankoro, *Dem. Rep. of the Congo* 86 D2
Ankororoka, *Madag.* 89 D8
Anlong, *China* 58 E5
Anlu, *China* 59 B9
Anmyŏn-do, *S. Korea* 57 F14
Ånn, *Sweden* 10 A6
Ann, C., *U.S.A.* 117 D14
Ann Arbor, *U.S.A.* 114 D4
Anna, *Russia* 34 E5
Anna, *U.S.A.* 113 G10
Annaba, *Algeria* 78 A7
Annaberg-Buchholz, *Germany* 24 E9
Annalee →, *Ireland* 12 B4
Annam, *Vietnam* 64 E7
Annamitique, Chaîne, *Asia* 64 D6
Annan, *U.K.* 13 G5
Annan →, *U.K.* 13 G5
Annapolis, *U.S.A.* 114 F7
Annapolis Royal, *Canada* 105 D6
Annapurna, *Nepal* 69 E10
Annean, L., *Australia* 93 E2
Anneberg, *Sweden* 11 G8
Annecy, *France* 21 C10
Annecy, Lac d', *France* 21 C10
Annemasse, *France* 19 F13
Annenskiy Most, *Russia* 32 B9
Anning, *China* 58 E4
Anniston, *U.S.A.* 115 J3
Annobón, *Atl. Oc.* 77 G4
Annonay, *France* 21 C8
Annot, *France* 21 E10
Annotto B., *Jamaica* 120 a
Ånnsjön, *Sweden* 10 A6
Annville, *U.S.A.* 117 F8
Annweiler, *Germany* 25 F3
Áno Arkhánai, *Greece* 47 F7
Áno Porróia, *Greece* 44 E7
Áno Síros, *Greece* 46 D6
Áno Viánnos, *Greece* 49 D7
Anorotsangana, *Madag.* 89 A8
Anosibe, *Madag.* 89 B8
Anou Mellene, *Mali* 83 B5
Anoumaba, *Ivory C.* 82 D4
Anóyia, *Greece* 49 D6
Anping, *Hebei, China* 56 E8
Anping, *Liaoning, China* 57 D12
Anpu Gang, *China* 58 G7
Anqing, *China* 59 B11
Anqiu, *China* 57 F10
Anren, *China* 59 D9
Ansager, *Denmark* 11 J2
Ansai, *China* 56 F5
Ansbach, *Germany* 25 F6
Anse la Raye, *St. Lucia* 121 f
Anseba →, *Eritrea* 81 D4
Ansfelden, *Austria* 26 C7
Anshan, *China* 57 D12
Anshun, *China* 58 D5
Ansião, *Portugal* 36 F2
Ansley, *U.S.A.* 112 E5
Ansó, *Spain* 38 C4
Ansoain, *Spain* 38 C3
Anson, *U.S.A.* 113 J5
Anson B., *Australia* 92 B5
Ansongo, *Mali* 83 B5
Ansongo-Ménaka ⌂, *Mali* 83 B5
Ansonia, *U.S.A.* 117 E11
Anstruther, *U.K.* 13 E6
Ansudu, *Indonesia* 63 E9
Antabamba, *Peru* 124 F4
Antakya, *Turkey* 70 B3
Antalaha, *Madag.* 89 A9
Antalya, *Turkey* 72 D4
Antalya □, *Turkey* 47 E12
Antalya Körfezi, *Turkey* 72 D4
Antambohobe, *Madag.* 89 C8
Antanambao-Manampotsy, *Madag.* 89 B8
Antanambe, *Madag.* 89 B8
Antananarivo, *Madag.* 89 B8
Antananarivo □, *Madag.* 89 B8
Antanifotsy, *Madag.* 89 B8
Antanimbaribe, *Madag.* 89 C7
Antanimora, *Madag.* 89 C8
Antarctic Pen., *Antarctica* 5 C18
Antarctica 5 E3
Antelope, *Zimbabwe* 87 G2
Antequera, *Paraguay* 126 A4
Antequera, *Spain* 37 H6
Antero, Mt., *U.S.A.* 109 G10
Antevamena, *Madag.* 89 C7
Anthemoús, *Greece* 44 F7
Anthony, *Kans., U.S.A.* 113 G5
Anthony, *N. Mex., U.S.A.* 109 K10
Anti Atlas, *Morocco* 78 C4
Anti-Lebanon = Ash Sharqi, Al Jabal, *Lebanon* 74 B5
Antibes, *France* 21 E11
Antibes, C. d', *France* 21 E11
Anticosti, Î. d', *Canada* 105 C7
Antifer, C. d', *France* 18 C7
Antigo, *U.S.A.* 112 C10
Antigonish, *Canada* 105 C7
Antigua, *Canary Is.* 48 F5
Antigua, *Guatemala* 120 D1
Antigua, *W. Indies* 121 C7
Antigua & Barbuda ■, *W. Indies* 121 C7
Antilla, *Cuba* 120 B4
Antilles = West Indies, *Cent. Amer.* 121 D7
Antioch, *U.S.A.* 110 G5
Antioche, Pertuis d', *France* 20 B2
Antioquia, *Colombia* 124 B3
Antipodes Is., *Pac. Oc.* 96 M9
Antlers, *U.S.A.* 113 H7
Antoetra, *Madag.* 89 C8
Antofagasta, *Chile* 126 A1
Antofagasta □, *Chile* 126 A2
Antofagasta de la Sierra, *Argentina* 126 B2
Antofalla, *Argentina* 126 B2
Antofalla, Salar de, *Argentina* 126 B2
Anton, *U.S.A.* 113 J3
Antongila, Helodrano, *Madag.* 89 B8
Antonibé, *Madag.* 89 B8
Antonibé, Presqu'île d', *Madag.* 89 A8
Antonina, *Brazil* 127 B6
Antrain, *France* 18 D5
Antrim, *U.K.* 12 B5
Antrim, *U.S.A.* 116 F3
Antrim □, *U.K.* 12 B5
Antrim, Mts. of, *U.K.* 12 A5
Antrim Plateau, *Australia* 92 C4
Antrodoco, *Italy* 41 F10
Antropovo, *Russia* 34 A6
Antsakabary, *Madag.* 89 B8
Antsalova, *Madag.* 89 B7
Antsenavolo, *Madag.* 89 C8
Antsiafabositra, *Madag.* 89 B8
Antsirabe, *Antananarivo, Madag.* 89 B8
Antsirabe, *Antsiranana, Madag.* 89 A8
Antsirabe, *Mahajanga, Madag.* 89 B8
Antsiranana, *Madag.* 89 A8
Antsiranana □, *Madag.* 89 A8
Antsohihy, *Madag.* 89 A8
Antsohimbondrona Seranana, *Madag.* 89 A8
Antu, *China* 57 C15
Antwerp = Antwerpen, *Belgium* 17 C4
Antwerp, *U.S.A.* 117 B9
Antwerpen, *Belgium* 17 C4
Antwerpen □, *Belgium* 17 C4
Anupgarh, *India* 68 E5
Anuppur, *India* 69 H9
Anuradhapura, *Sri Lanka* 66 Q12
Anveh, *Iran* 71 E7
Anvers = Antwerpen, *Belgium* 17 C4
Anvers I., *Antarctica* 5 C17
Anwen, *China* 59 C13
Anxi, *Fujian, China* 59 E12
Anxi, *Gansu, China* 60 B4
Anxian, *China* 58 B5
Anxiang, *China* 59 C9
Anxious B., *Australia* 95 E1
Anyama, *Ivory C.* 82 D4
Anyang, *China* 56 F8
Anyer-Kidul, *Indonesia* 63 G11
Anyi, *Jiangxi, China* 59 C10
Anyi, *Shanxi, China* 56 G6
Anyuan, *China* 59 E10
Anyue, *China* 58 B5
Anza, *U.S.A.* 111 M10
Anze, *China* 56 F7
Anzhero-Sudzhensk, *Russia* 52 D9
Ánzio, *Italy* 42 A5
Ao Makham, *Thailand* 65 a
Ao Phangnga △, *Thailand* 65 a
Aoga-Shima, *Japan* 55 H9
Aoiz, *Spain* 38 C3
Aomen = Macau, *China* 59 F9
Aomori, *Japan* 54 D10
Aomori □, *Japan* 54 D10
Aonla, *India* 69 E8
Aoraki Mount Cook, *N.Z.* 91 K3
Aosta, *Italy* 40 C4
Aotearoa = New Zealand ■, *Oceania* 91 J6
Aoudéras, *Niger* 83 B6
Aoukâr, *Mauritania* 82 B3
Aozou, Couloir d', *Chad* 79 D9
Apa →, *S. Amer.* 126 A4
Apache, *U.S.A.* 113 H5
Apache Junction, *U.S.A.* 109 K8
Apalachee B., *U.S.A.* 115 L4
Apalachicola, *U.S.A.* 115 L3
Apalachicola →, *U.S.A.* 115 L3
Apam, *Ghana* 83 D4
Apapa, *Nigeria* 83 D5
Apaporis →, *Colombia* 124 D5
Aparados da Serra △, *Brazil* 127 B5
Aparri, *Phil.* 61 B4
Apateu, *Romania* 28 D6
Apatin, *Serbia & M.* 28 E4
Apatity, *Russia* 52 C4
Apatzingán, *Mexico* 118 D4
Apeldoorn, *Neths.* 17 B5
Apen, *Germany* 24 B3
Apennines = Appennini, *Italy* 40 D7
Aphrodisias, *Turkey* 47 D10
Apia, *Samoa* 91 A13
Apiacás, Serra dos, *Brazil* 124 E7
Apies →, *S. Africa* 89 D4
Apizaco, *Mexico* 119 D5
Aplao, *Peru* 124 G4
Apo, Mt., *Phil.* 63 C7
Apolakkiá, *Greece* 49 C9
Apolakkiá, Órmos, *Greece* 49 C9
Apolda, *Germany* 24 D7
Apollonia, *Greece* 46 E6
Apolo, *Bolivia* 124 F5
Aporé →, *Brazil* 125 G8
Apostle Is., *U.S.A.* 112 B9
Apostle Islands ⌂, *U.S.A.* 112 B9
Apóstoles, *Argentina* 127 B4
Apostolos Andreas, C., *Cyprus* 49 D13
Apostolovo, *Ukraine* 33 J7
Apoteri, *Guyana* 124 C7
Appalachian Mts., *U.S.A.* 114 G6
Äppelbo, *Sweden* 10 D8
Appennini, *Italy* 40 D7
Appennino Ligure, *Italy* 40 D6
Appenzell-Ausser Rhoden □, *Switz.* 25 H5
Appenzell-Inner Rhoden □, *Switz.* 25 H5
Appiano, *Italy* 41 B8
Apple Hill, *Canada* 117 A10
Apple Valley, *U.S.A.* 111 L9
Appleby-in-Westmorland, *U.K.* 14 C5
Appledore, *U.K.* 15 F3
Appleton, *U.S.A.* 114 C1
Approuague →, *Fr. Guiana* 125 C8
Apricena, *Italy* 41 G12
Aprília, *Italy* 42 A5
Apsheronsk, *Russia* 35 H4
Apsley, *Canada* 116 B6
Apt, *France* 21 E9
Apuane, Alpi, *Italy* 40 D7
Apucarana, *Brazil* 127 A5
Apulia = Púglia □, *Italy* 43 A9
Apure →, *Venezuela* 124 B5
Apurimac →, *Peru* 124 F4
Apuseni, Munţii, *Romania* 28 D7
Āqā Jarī, *Iran* 71 D6
Aqaba = Al 'Aqabah, *Jordan* 74 F4
Aqaba, G. of, *Red Sea* 70 D2
'Aqabah, Khalīj al = Aqaba, G. of, *Red Sea* 70 D2
'Aqdā, *Iran* 71 C7
Aqiq, *Sudan* 80 D4
Aqīq, Khalīg, *Sudan* 80 D4
'Aqrah, *Iraq* 70 B4
Aqtaū, *Kazakhstan* 52 E6
Aqtöbe, *Kazakhstan* 52 D6
Aquidauana, *Brazil* 125 H7
Aquiles Serdán, *Mexico* 118 B3
Aquin, *Haiti* 121 C5
Aquitaine □, *France* 20 D3
Ar Rachidiya = Er Rachidia, *Morocco* 78 B5
Ar Rafīd, *Syria* 74 C4
Ar Raḥḥālīyah, *Iraq* 70 C4
Ar Ramādī, *Iraq* 70 C4
Ar Ramthā, *Jordan* 74 C5
Ar Raqqah, *Syria* 70 C3
Ar Rass, *Si. Arabia* 70 E4
Ar Rawshān, *Si. Arabia* 80 C5
Ar Rifā'ī, *Iraq* 70 D5
Ar Riyāḍ, *Si. Arabia* 70 E5
Ar Ru'ays, *Qatar* 71 E6
Ar Rukhaymīyah, *Iraq* 70 D5
Ar Ruṣāfah, *Syria* 70 C3
Ar Ruṭbah, *Iraq* 70 C4
Ara, *India* 69 G11
Ara Goro, *Ethiopia* 81 F5
Ara Tera, *Ethiopia* 81 F5
Arab, *U.S.A.* 115 H2
'Arab, Bahr el →, *Sudan* 81 F2
Arab, Khalîg el, *Egypt* 80 A2
Arab, Shatt al →, *Asia* 71 D6
'Araba, W. →, *Egypt* 80 J8
'Arabābād, *Iran* 71 C8
Araban, *Turkey* 72 D7
Arabatskaya Strelka, *Ukraine* 33 K8
Arabba, *Italy* 41 B8
Arabia, *Asia* 50 G8
Arabian Desert = Es Sahrâ' Esh Sharqîya, *Egypt* 80 B3
Arabian Gulf = Persian Gulf, *Asia* 71 E6
Arabian Sea, *Ind. Oc.* 50 H10
Araç, *Turkey* 72 B5
Aracaju, *Brazil* 125 F11
Aracati, *Brazil* 125 D11
Araçatuba, *Brazil* 127 A5
Aracena, *Spain* 37 H4
Aracena, Sierra de, *Spain* 37 H4
Aračinovo, *Macedonia* 44 D5
Araçuaí, *Brazil* 125 G10
'Arad, *Israel* 74 D4
Arad, *Romania* 28 D6
Arad □, *Romania* 28 D6
Arādān, *Iran* 71 C7
Aradhippou, *Cyprus* 49 E12
Arafura Sea, *E. Indies* 96 H5
Aragats, *Armenia* 35 K7
Aragón □, *Spain* 38 D4
Aragón →, *Spain* 38 C3
Aragona, *Italy* 42 E6
Araguacema, *Brazil* 125 E9
Araguaia →, *Brazil* 125 E9
Araguaína, *Brazil* 125 E9
Araguari, *Brazil* 125 G9
Araguari →, *Brazil* 125 C9
Arain, *India* 68 F6
Arak, *Algeria* 78 C6
Arāk, *Iran* 71 C6
Araka, *Sudan* 81 G3
Arakan Coast, *Burma* 67 K19
Arakan Yoma, *Burma* 67 K19
Arákhova, *Greece* 46 C4
Arakli, *Turkey* 73 B8
Araks = Aras, Rūd-e →, *Asia* 35 K9
Aral, *Kazakhstan* 52 E7
Aral Sea, *Asia* 52 E7
Aral Tengizi = Aral Sea, *Asia* 52 E7
Aralsk = Aral, *Kazakhstan* 52 E7
Aralskoye More = Aral Sea, *Asia* 52 E7
Aralsor, Ozero, *Kazakhstan* 35 F9
Aramac, *Australia* 94 C4
Aran I., *Ireland* 12 A3
Aran Is., *Ireland* 12 C2
Aranda de Duero, *Spain* 36 D7
Arandān, *Iran* 70 C5

Aranđelovac, *Serbia & M.* 44 B4
Aranjuez, *Spain* 36 E7
Aranos, *Namibia* 88 C2
Aransas Pass, *U.S.A.* 113 M6
Aranyaprathet, *Thailand* 64 F4
Araouane, *Mali* 82 B4
Arapahoe, *U.S.A.* 112 E5
Arapey Grande →, *Uruguay* 126 C4
Arapgir, *Turkey* 70 B3
Arapiraca, *Brazil* 125 E11
Arapongas, *Brazil* 127 A5
Ar'ar, *Si. Arabia* 70 D4
Araranguá, *Brazil* 127 B6
Araraquara, *Brazil* 125 H9
Ararás, Serra das, *Brazil* 127 B5
Ararat, *Armenia* 73 C11
Ararat, *Australia* 95 F3
Ararat, Mt. = Ağrı Dağı, *Turkey* 70 B5
Araria, *India* 69 F12
Araripe, Chapada do, *Brazil* 125 E11
Araruama, L. de, *Brazil* 127 A7
Aras, Rūd-e →, *Asia* 35 K9
Aratāne, *Mauritania* 82 B3
Arauca, *Colombia* 124 B4
Arauca →, *Venezuela* 124 B5
Arauco, *Chile* 126 D1
Arawa, *Ethiopia* 81 F5
Arawale ⌂, *Kenya* 86 C5
Araxá, *Brazil* 125 G9
Araya, Pen. de, *Venezuela* 124 A6
Arba Gugu, *Ethiopia* 81 F5
Arba Minch, *Ethiopia* 81 F4
Arbat, *Iraq* 70 C5
Árbatax, *Italy* 42 C2
Arbi, *Ethiopia* 81 F4
Arbīl, *Iraq* 70 B5
Arboga, *Sweden* 10 E9
Arbois, *France* 19 F12
Arbore, *Ethiopia* 81 F4
Arboréa, *Italy* 42 C1
Arborfield, *Canada* 103 C8
Arborg, *Canada* 103 C9
Arbre du Ténéré, *Niger* 83 B7
Arbroath, *U.K.* 13 E6
Arbuckle, *U.S.A.* 110 F4
Arbus, *Italy* 42 C1
Arc →, *France* 21 C10
Arc-lès-Gray, *France* 19 E12
Arcachon, *France* 20 D2
Arcachon, Bassin d', *France* 20 D2
Arcade, *Calif., U.S.A.* 111 L8
Arcade, *N.Y., U.S.A.* 116 D6
Arcadia, *Fla., U.S.A.* 115 M5
Arcadia, *La., U.S.A.* 113 J8
Arcadia, *Pa., U.S.A.* 116 F6
Arcata, *U.S.A.* 108 F1
Arcévia, *Italy* 41 E9
Archangel = Arkhangelsk, *Russia* 52 C5
Archar, *Bulgaria* 44 C6
Archbald, *U.S.A.* 117 E9
Archena, *Spain* 39 G3
Archer →, *Australia* 94 A3
Archer B., *Australia* 94 A3
Archer Bend = Mungkan Kandju △, *Australia* 94 A3
Archers Post, *Kenya* 86 B4
Arches △, *U.S.A.* 109 G9
Archidona, *Spain* 37 H6
Archipel-de-Mingan △, *Canada* 105 B7
Archipiélago Chinijo △, *Canary Is.* 48 E6
Archipiélago Los Roques △, *Venezuela* 121 D6
Arci, Mte., *Italy* 42 C1
Arcidosso, *Italy* 41 F8
Arcipelago de la Maddalena △, *Italy* 42 A2
Arcipelago Toscano △, *Italy* 40 F7
Arcis-sur-Aube, *France* 19 D11
Arckaringa Cr. →, *Australia* 95 D2
Arco, *Italy* 40 C7
Arco, *U.S.A.* 108 E7
Arcos de Jalón, *Spain* 38 D2
Arcos de la Frontera, *Spain* 37 J5
Arcos de Valdevez, *Portugal* 36 D2
Arcot, *India* 66 N11
Arcozelo, *Portugal* 36 E3
Arctic Bay, *Canada* 101 A11
Arctic Ocean, *Arctic* 4 B18
Arctic Red River = Tsiigehtchic, *Canada* 100 B6
Arctowski, *Antarctica* 5 C18
Arda →, *Bulgaria* 45 E10
Arda →, *Italy* 40 C7
Ardabīl, *Iran* 71 B6
Ardabīl □, *Iran* 71 B6
Ardahan, *Turkey* 73 B10
Ardakān = Sepīdān, *Iran* 71 D7
Ardakān, *Iran* 71 C7
Ardala, *Sweden* 11 F7
Ardales, *Spain* 37 J6
Ardèche □, *France* 21 D8
Ardèche →, *France* 21 D8
Ardee, *Ireland* 12 C5
Arden, *Canada* 116 B8
Arden, *Denmark* 11 H3
Arden, *Calif., U.S.A.* 110 G5
Arden, *Nev., U.S.A.* 111 J11
Ardenne, *Belgium* 17 E5
Ardennes = Ardenne, *Belgium* 17 E5
Ardennes □, *France* 19 C11
Ardentes, *France* 19 F8
Arderin, *Ireland* 12 C4
Ardeşen, *Turkey* 73 B9
Ardestān, *Iran* 71 C7
Árdhas →, *Greece* 45 E10
Ardhéa, *Greece* 44 F6
Ardila →, *Portugal* 37 G3
Ardino, *Bulgaria* 45 E9
Ardivachar Pt., *U.K.* 13 D1
Ardlethan, *Australia* 95 E4
Ardmore, *Okla., U.S.A.* 113 H6
Ardmore, *Pa., U.S.A.* 117 G9
Ardnamurchan, Pt. of, *U.K.* 13 E2
Ardnave Pt., *U.K.* 13 F2
Ardon, *Russia* 35 J7
Ardore, *Italy* 43 D9
Ardres, *France* 19 B8
Ardrossan, *Australia* 95 E2
Ardrossan, *U.K.* 13 F4
Ards Pen., *U.K.* 12 B6
Arduan, *Sudan* 80 D3
Ardud, *Romania* 28 C7
Åre, *Sweden* 10 A7
Arecibo, *Puerto Rico* 121 d
Areia Branca, *Brazil* 125 E11
Arena, Pt., *U.S.A.* 110 G3
Arenal, *Honduras* 120 C2
Arenas = Las Arenas, *Spain* 36 B6
Arenas de San Pedro, *Spain* 36 E5
Arendal, *Norway* 9 G13
Arendsee, *Germany* 24 C7
Arenys de Mar, *Spain* 38 D7
Arenzano, *Italy* 40 D5
Areópolis, *Greece* 46 E4
Arequipa, *Peru* 124 G4
Arero, *Ethiopia* 81 G4
Arès, *France* 20 D2
Arévalo, *Spain* 36 D6
Arezzo, *Italy* 41 E8
Arga, *Turkey* 70 B3
Arga →, *Spain* 38 C3
Argalastí, *Greece* 46 B5
Argamasilla de Alba, *Spain* 37 F7
Argamasilla de Calatrava, *Spain* 37 G6
Arganda, *Spain* 36 E7
Arganil, *Portugal* 36 E2
Argedeb, *Ethiopia* 81 F5
Argelès-Gazost, *France* 20 E3
Argelès-sur-Mer, *France* 20 F7
Argens →, *France* 21 E10
Argent-sur-Sauldre, *France* 19 E9
Argenta, *Canada* 102 C5
Argenta, *Italy* 41 D8
Argentan, *France* 18 D6
Argentário, Mte., *Italy* 41 F8
Argentat, *France* 20 C5
Argentera, *Italy* 40 D4
Argenteuil, *France* 19 D9
Argentia, *Canada* 105 C9
Argentiera, C. dell', *Italy* 42 B1
Argentina ■, *S. Amer.* 128 D3
Argentine Basin, *S. Amer.* 122 H5
Argentino, L., *Argentina* 128 G2
Argenton-Château, *France* 18 F6
Argenton-sur-Creuse, *France* 19 F8
Argeş □, *Romania* 29 F9
Argeş →, *Romania* 29 F11
Arghandab →, *Afghan.* 68 D1
Argheile, *Ethiopia* 81 F5
Argo, *Sudan* 80 D3
Argolikós Kólpos, *Greece* 46 D4
Argolís □, *Greece* 46 D4
Argonne, *France* 19 C12
Árgos, *Greece* 46 D4
Árgos Orestikón, *Greece* 44 F5
Argostólion, *Greece* 46 C2
Arguedas, *Spain* 38 C3
Arguello, Pt., *U.S.A.* 111 L6
Arguineguín, *Canary Is.* 48 G4
Argun, *Russia* 35 J7
Argun →, *Russia* 53 D13
Argungu, *Nigeria* 83 C5
Argus Pk., *U.S.A.* 111 K9
Argyle, L., *Australia* 92 C4
Argyll ⌂, *U.K.* 13 E4
Argyll & Bute □, *U.K.* 13 E3
Arhavi, *Turkey* 73 B9
Århus, *Denmark* 11 H4
Århus Amtskommune □, *Denmark* 11 H4
Ariadnoye, *Russia* 54 B7
Ariamsvlei, *Namibia* 88 D2
Ariano Irpino, *Italy* 43 A8
Aribinda, *Burkina Faso* 83 C4
Arica, *Chile* 124 G4
Arica, *Colombia* 124 D4
Arico, *Canary Is.* 48 F3
Arid, C., *Australia* 93 F3
Arida, *Japan* 55 G7
Ariège □, *France* 20 F5
Ariège →, *France* 20 E5
Arieş →, *Romania* 29 D8
Arihā, *Israel* 80 A4
Arilje, *Serbia & M.* 44 C4
Arílla, Ákra, *Greece* 49 A3
Arima, *Trin. & Tob.* 121 D7
Arinos →, *Brazil* 124 F7
Ario de Rosales, *Mexico* 118 D4
Ariogala, *Lithuania* 30 C10
Aripo, Mt., *Trin. & Tob.* 125 K15
Aripuanã, *Brazil* 124 E6
Aripuanã →, *Brazil* 124 E6
Ariquemes, *Brazil* 124 E6
Arisaig, *U.K.* 13 E3
Arîsh, W. el →, *Egypt* 80 A3
Arissa, *Ethiopia* 81 E5
Aristazabal I., *Canada* 102 C3
Arivonimamo, *Madag.* 89 B8
Ariza, *Spain* 38 D2
Arizaro, Salar de, *Argentina* 126 A2
Arizona, *Argentina* 126 D2
Arizona □, *U.S.A.* 109 J8
Arizpe, *Mexico* 118 A2
Årjäng, *Sweden* 10 E6
Arjeplog, *Sweden* 8 D18
Arjepluovve = Arjeplog, *Sweden* 8 D18
Arjona, *Colombia* 124 A3
Arjona, *Spain* 37 H6
Arjuna, *Indonesia* 63 G15
Arka, *Russia* 53 C15
Arkadak, *Russia* 34 E6
Arkadelphia, *U.S.A.* 113 H8
Arkadhía □, *Greece* 46 D4
Arkaig, L., *U.K.* 13 E3
Arkalyk = Arqalyk, *Kazakhstan* 52 D7
Arkansas □, *U.S.A.* 113 H8
Arkansas →, *U.S.A.* 113 J9
Arkansas City, *U.S.A.* 113 G6
Arkaroola, *Australia* 95 E2
Árkathos →, *Greece* 46 B3
Arkhángelos, *Greece* 49 C10
Arkhangelsk, *Russia* 52 C5
Arkhangelskoye, *Russia* 34 E5
Arki, *India* 68 D7
Arkiko, *Eritrea* 81 D4
Arklow, *Ireland* 12 D5
Árkoi, *Greece* 47 D8
Arkona, Kap, *Germany* 24 A9
Arkösund, *Sweden* 11 F10
Arkoúdhi Nisís, *Greece* 46 C2
Arkport, *U.S.A.* 116 D7
Arkticheskiy, Mys, *Russia* 53 A10
Arkul, *Russia* 34 B10
Arkville, *U.S.A.* 117 D10
Årla, *Sweden* 10 E10
Arlanda, Stockholm ✕ (ARN), *Sweden* 10 E11
Arlanza →, *Spain* 36 C6
Arlanzón →, *Spain* 36 C6
Arlbergpass, *Austria* 26 D3
Arles, *France* 21 E8
Arli, *Burkina Faso* 83 C5
Arli △, *Burkina Faso* 83 C5
Arlington, *S. Africa* 89 D4
Arlington, *N.Y., U.S.A.* 117 E11
Arlington, *Oreg., U.S.A.* 108 D3
Arlington, *S. Dak., U.S.A.* 112 C6
Arlington, *Tex., U.S.A.* 113 J6
Arlington, *Va., U.S.A.* 114 F7
Arlington, *Vt., U.S.A.* 117 C11
Arlington, *Wash., U.S.A.* 110 B4
Arlington Heights, *U.S.A.* 114 D2
Arlit, *Niger* 78 E7
Arlon, *Belgium* 17 E5
Arltunga, *Australia* 94 C1
Armagh, *U.K.* 12 B5
Armagh □, *U.K.* 12 B5
Armagnac, *France* 20 E4
Armançon →, *France* 19 E10
Armando Bermudez △, *Dom. Rep.* 121 C5
Armavir, *Russia* 35 H5
Armenia, *Colombia* 124 C3
Armenia ■, *Asia* 35 K7
Armeniş, *Romania* 28 E7
Armenistís, Ákra, *Greece* 49 C9
Armentières, *France* 19 B9
Armidale, *Australia* 95 E5
Armilla, *Spain* 37 H7
Armorique ⌂, *France* 18 D3
Armour, *U.S.A.* 112 D5
Armstrong, *B.C., Canada* 102 C5
Armstrong, *Ont., Canada* 104 B2
Armutlu, *Bursa, Turkey* 45 F12
Armutlu, *İzmir, Turkey* 47 C9
Arnaía, *Greece* 44 F7
Arnarfjörður, *Iceland* 8 D2
Arnaud →, *Canada* 101 B12
Arnauti, C., *Cyprus* 49 D11
Arnay-le-Duc, *France* 19 E11
Arnedillo, *Spain* 38 C2
Arnedo, *Spain* 38 C2
Arnett, *U.S.A.* 113 G5
Arnhem, *Neths.* 17 C5
Arnhem, C., *Australia* 94 A2
Arnhem B., *Australia* 94 A2
Arnhem Land, *Australia* 94 A1
Árnissa, *Greece* 44 F5
Arno →, *Italy* 40 E7
Arno Bay, *Australia* 95 E2
Arnold, *U.K.* 14 D6
Arnold, *U.S.A.* 110 G6
Arnoldstein, *Austria* 26 E6
Arnon →, *France* 19 E9
Arnot, *Canada* 103 B9
Arnøy, *Norway* 8 A19
Arnprior, *Canada* 117 A8
Arnsberg, *Germany* 24 D4
Arnsberger Wald ⌂, *Germany* 24 D4
Arnstadt, *Germany* 24 E6
Aroab, *Namibia* 88 D2
Aroánia Óri, *Greece* 46 D4
Aroche, *Spain* 37 H4
Arochuku, *Nigeria* 83 D6
Arolsen, *Germany* 24 D5
Aron, *India* 68 G6
Aron →, *France* 19 F10
Arona, *Canary Is.* 48 F3
Arona, *Italy* 40 C5
Aroroy, *Phil.* 61 E5
Arosa, Ría de, *Spain* 36 C2
Arpajon, *France* 19 D9
Arpajon-sur-Cère, *France* 20 D6
Arpaşu de Jos, *Romania* 29 E9
Arqalyk, *Kazakhstan* 52 D7
Arrah = Ara, *India* 69 G11
Arrah, *Ivory C.* 82 D4
Arraiolos, *Portugal* 37 G3
Arran, *U.K.* 13 F3
Arras, *France* 19 B9
Arrasate, *Spain* 38 B2
Arrats →, *France* 20 D4
Arreau, *France* 20 F4
Arrecife, *Canary Is.* 48 F6
Arrecifes, *Argentina* 126 C3
Arrée, Mts. d', *France* 18 D3
Arresø, *Denmark* 11 J6
Arriaga, *Chiapas, Mexico* 119 D6
Arriaga, *San Luis Potosí, Mexico* 118 C4
Arribes del Duero ⌂, *Spain* 36 D4
Arrilalah, *Australia* 94 C3
Arrino, *Australia* 93 E2
Arriondas, *Spain* 36 B5
Arromanches-les-Bains, *France* 18 C6
Arronches, *Portugal* 37 F3
Arros →, *France* 20 E3
Arrow, L., *Ireland* 12 B3
Arrowhead, L., *U.S.A.* 111 L9
Arrowtown, *N.Z.* 91 L2
Arroyo de la Luz, *Spain* 37 F4
Arroyo Grande, *U.S.A.* 111 K6
Års, *Denmark* 11 H3
Ars, *Iran* 70 B5
Ars-sur-Moselle, *France* 19 C13
Arsenault L., *Canada* 103 B7
Arsenev, *Russia* 54 B6
Arsi, *Ethiopia* 81 F4
Arsiero, *Italy* 41 C8
Arsin, *Turkey* 73 B8
Arsk, *Russia* 34 B9
Årsunda, *Sweden* 10 D10
Árta, *Greece* 46 B3
Artà, *Spain* 48 B10
Árta □, *Greece* 46 B3
Arteaga, *Mexico* 118 D4
Arteche, *Phil.* 61 E6
Arteijo = Arteixo, *Spain* 36 B2
Arteixo, *Spain* 36 B2
Artem = Artyom, *Azerbaijan* 35 K10
Artem, *Russia* 54 C6
Artemovsk, *Russia* 53 D10
Artemovsk, *Ukraine* 33 H9
Artemovskiy, *Russia* 35 G5
Artenay, *France* 19 D8
Artern, *Germany* 24 D7
Artesa de Segre, *Spain* 38 D6
Artesia = Mosomane, *Botswana* 88 C4
Artesia, *U.S.A.* 113 J2
Arthington, *Liberia* 82 D2
Arthur, *Canada* 116 C4
Arthur →, *Australia* 95 G3
Arthur Cr. →, *Australia* 94 C2
Arthur Pt., *Australia* 94 C5
Arthur River, *Australia* 93 F2
Arthur's Pass, *N.Z.* 91 K3
Arthur's Pass △, *N.Z.* 91 K3
Arthur's Town, *Bahamas* 121 B4
Artigas, *Antarctica* 5 C18
Artigas, *Uruguay* 126 C4
Artik, *Armenia* 35 K6
Artillery L., *Canada* 103 A7
Artois, *France* 19 B9
Artotína, *Greece* 46 C4
Artrutx, C. de, *Spain* 48 B10
Artsyz, *Ukraine* 29 D14
Artvin, *Turkey* 73 B9
Artyom, *Azerbaijan* 35 K10
Aru, Kepulauan, *Indonesia* 63 F8
Aru Is. = Aru, Kepulauan, *Indonesia* 63 F8
Arua, *Uganda* 86 B3
Aruanã, *Brazil* 125 F8
Aruba ☒, *W. Indies* 121 D6
Arucas, *Canary Is.* 48 F4
Arudy, *France* 20 E3
Arun →, *Nepal* 69 F12
Arun →, *U.K.* 15 G7
Arunachal Pradesh □, *India* 67 F19
Arusha, *Tanzania* 86 C4
Arusha □, *Tanzania* 86 C4
Arusha △, *Tanzania* 86 C4
Arusha Chini, *Tanzania* 86 C4
Aruwimi →, *Dem. Rep. of the Congo* 86 B1
Arvada, *Colo., U.S.A.* 112 F2
Arvada, *Wyo., U.S.A.* 108 D10
Arve →, *France* 19 F13
Árvi, *Greece* 49 E7
Arviat, *Canada* 103 A10
Arvidsjaur, *Sweden* 8 D18
Arvika, *Sweden* 10 E6
Arvin, *U.S.A.* 111 K8
Arwal, *India* 69 G11
Arxan, *China* 60 B6
Åryd, *Sweden* 11 H8
Aryirádhes, *Greece* 49 B3
Aryiroúpolis, *Greece* 49 D6
Arys, *Kazakhstan* 52 E7
Arzachena, *Italy* 42 A2
Arzamas, *Russia* 34 C6
Arzgir, *Russia* 35 H7
Arzignano, *Italy* 41 C8
Arzúa, *Spain* 36 C2
Aš, *Czech Rep.* 26 A5
Ås, *Sweden* 10 A8
As Pontes de García Rodríguez, *Spain* 36 B3
Aş Şafā, *Syria* 74 B6
As Saffānīyah, *Si. Arabia* 71 E6
As Safīrah, *Syria* 70 B3
Aş Şahm, *Oman* 71 E8
As Sājir, *Si. Arabia* 70 E5
As Salamīyah, *Syria* 70 C3
As Salmān, *Iraq* 70 D5
As Salt, *Jordan* 74 C4
As Sal'w'a, *Qatar* 71 E6
As Samāwah, *Iraq* 70 D5
As Sanamayn, *Syria* 74 B5
As Sohar = Şuḩār, *Oman* 71 E8
As Sukhnah, *Syria* 70 C3
As Sulaymānīyah, *Iraq* 70 C5
As Sulaymī, *Si. Arabia* 70 E4
As Sulayyil, *Si. Arabia* 75 C4
As Summān, *Si. Arabia* 70 E5
As Suwaydā', *Syria* 74 C5
As Suwaydā' □, *Syria* 74 C5
As Suwayq, *Oman* 71 F8
Aş Şuwayrah, *Iraq* 70 C5
Åsa, *Sweden* 11 G6
Asab, *Namibia* 88 D2
Asaba, *Nigeria* 83 D6
Asad, Buḩayrat al, *Syria* 70 C3
Asadābād, *Iran* 73 E13
Asafo, *Ghana* 82 D4
Asahi-Gawa →, *Japan* 55 G6
Asahigawa, *Japan* 54 C11
Asale, L., *Ethiopia* 81 E5
Asamankese, *Ghana* 83 D4
Asan →, *India* 69 F8
Asansol, *India* 69 H12
Åsarna, *Sweden* 10 B8
Asayita, *Ethiopia* 81 E5
Asbe Teferi, *Ethiopia* 81 F5
Asbesberge, *S. Africa* 88 D3
Asbestos, *Canada* 105 C5
Asbury Park, *U.S.A.* 117 F10
Ascea, *Italy* 43 B8
Ascensión, *Mexico* 118 A3
Ascensión, B. de la, *Mexico* 119 D7
Ascension I., *Atl. Oc.* 77 G2
Aschach an der Donau, *Austria* 26 C7
Aschaffenburg, *Germany* 25 F5
Aschendorf, *Germany* 24 B3
Aschersleben, *Germany* 24 D7
Asciano, *Italy* 41 E8
Áscoli Piceno, *Italy* 41 F10
Áscoli Satriano, *Italy* 43 A8
Ascope, *Peru* 124 E3
Ascotán, *Chile* 126 A2
Aseb, *Eritrea* 81 E5
Åseda, *Sweden* 11 G9
Asela, *Ethiopia* 81 F4
Åsen, *Sweden* 10 C7
Asenovgrad, *Bulgaria* 45 D8
Aserradero, *Mexico* 118 C3
Asfeld, *France* 19 C11
Asfûn el Matâ'na, *Egypt* 80 B3
Asgata, *Cyprus* 49 E12
Ash Fork, *U.S.A.* 109 J7
Ash Grove, *U.S.A.* 113 G8
Ash Shabakah, *Iraq* 70 D4
Ash Shamāl □, *Lebanon* 74 A5
Ash Shāmīyah, *Iraq* 70 D5
Ash Shāriqah, *U.A.E.* 71 E7
Ash Sharmah, *Si. Arabia* 70 D2
Ash Sharqāt, *Iraq* 70 C4
Ash Sharqi, Al Jabal, *Lebanon* 74 B5
Ash Shaṭrah, *Iraq* 70 D5
Ash Shawbak, *Jordan* 70 D2
Ash Shawmari, J., *Jordan* 74 E5
Ash Shināfīyah, *Iraq* 70 D5
Ash Shu'bah, *Si. Arabia* 70 D5
Ash Shumlūl, *Si. Arabia* 70 E5
Ash Shūr'a, *Iraq* 70 C4
Ash Shurayf, *Si. Arabia* 70 E3
Ash Shuwayfāt, *Lebanon* 74 B4
Ashanti □, *Ghana* 83 D4
Ashau, *Vietnam* 64 D6
Ashbourne, *U.K.* 14 D6
Ashburn, *U.S.A.* 115 K4
Ashburton, *N.Z.* 91 K3
Ashburton →, *Australia* 92 D1
Ashcroft, *Canada* 102 C4
Ashdod, *Israel* 74 D3
Ashdown, *U.S.A.* 113 J7
Asheboro, *U.S.A.* 115 H6
Ashern, *Canada* 103 C9
Asherton, *U.S.A.* 113 L5
Asheville, *U.S.A.* 115 H4
Ashewat, *Pakistan* 68 D3
Asheweig →, *Canada* 104 B2
Ashford, *Australia* 95 D5
Ashford, *U.K.* 15 F8
Ashgabat, *Turkmenistan* 52 F6
Ashibetsu, *Japan* 54 C11
Ashikaga, *Japan* 55 F9
Ashington, *U.K.* 14 B6
Ashizuri-Uwakai △, *Japan* 55 H6
Ashizuri-Zaki, *Japan* 55 H6
Ashkarkot, *Afghan.* 68 C2
Ashkhabad = Ashgabat, *Turkmenistan* 52 F6
Āshkhāneh, *Iran* 71 B8
Ashland, *Kans., U.S.A.* 113 G5
Ashland, *Ky., U.S.A.* 114 F4
Ashland, *Mont., U.S.A.* 108 D10
Ashland, *Ohio, U.S.A.* 116 F2
Ashland, *Oreg., U.S.A.* 108 E2
Ashland, *Pa., U.S.A.* 117 F8
Ashland, *Va., U.S.A.* 114 G7
Ashland, *Wis., U.S.A.* 112 B9
Ashley, *N. Dak., U.S.A.* 112 B5
Ashley, *Pa., U.S.A.* 117 E9
Ashmore and Cartier Is., *Ind. Oc.* 92 B3
Ashmore Reef, *Australia* 92 B3
Ashmûn, *Egypt* 80 H7
Ashmyany, *Belarus* 9 J21
Ashokan Reservoir, *U.S.A.* 117 E10
Ashqelon, *Israel* 74 D3
Ashta, *India* 68 H7
Ashtabula, *U.S.A.* 116 E4
Ashton, *S. Africa* 88 E3
Ashton, *U.S.A.* 108 D8
Ashuanipi, L., *Canada* 105 B6
Ashuapmushuan →, *Canada* 104 C5
Ashville, *U.S.A.* 116 F6
'Āṣī →, *Asia* 72 D6
Asia 50 E11
Asia, Kepulauan, *Indonesia* 63 D8
Asiago, *Italy* 41 C8
Asifabad, *India* 66 K11
Asinara, *Italy* 42 A1
Asinara, G. dell', *Italy* 42 A1
Asino, *Russia* 52 D9
Asipovichy, *Belarus* 32 F5
'Asīr □, *Si. Arabia* 75 D3
Asir, Ras, *Somali Rep.* 75 E5
Aşkale, *Turkey* 73 C9
Askersund, *Sweden* 11 F8
Askham, *S. Africa* 88 D3
Askim, *Norway* 9 G14
Askja, *Iceland* 8 D5
Askøy, *Norway* 9 F11
Asl, *Egypt* 80 B3
Aslan Burnu, *Turkey* 47 C8
Aslanapa, *Turkey* 47 B11
Asmara = Asmera, *Eritrea* 81 D4
Asmera, *Eritrea* 81 D4
Asnæs, *Denmark* 11 J4

Åsnen, Sweden 11 H8
Aso Kuju △, Japan 55 H5
Ásola, Italy 40 C7
Asosa, Ethiopia 81 E3
Asoteriba, Jebel, Sudan 80 C4
Aspatria, U.K. 14 C4
Aspe, Spain 39 G4
Aspen, U.S.A. 109 G10
Aspendos, Turkey 72 D4
Aspermont, U.S.A. 113 J4
Aspet, France 20 E4
Aspiring, Mt., N.Z. 91 L2
Aspres-sur-Buëch, France 21 D9
Asprókavos, Ákra, Greece 49 B4
Aspromonte △, Italy 43 D8
Aspur, India 68 H6
Asquith, Canada 103 C7
Assab = Aseb, Eritrea 81 E5
Assâba, Massif de l', Mauritania 82 B2
Assagny △, Ivory C. 82 D4
Assaikio, Nigeria 83 D6
Assal, L., Djibouti 81 E5
Assam □, India 67 G18
Assamakka, Niger 83 B6
Assateague Island ⌓, U.S.A. 114 F8
Asse, Belgium 17 D4
Assémini, Italy 42 C1
Assen, Neths. 17 A6
Assens, Denmark 11 J3
Assini, Ivory C. 82 D4
Assiniboia, Canada 103 D7
Assiniboine →, Canada 103 D9
Assiniboine, Mt., Canada 102 C5
Assis, Brazil 127 A5
Assisi, Italy 41 E9
Ássos, Greece 46 C2
Assynt, L., U.K. 13 C3
Astaffort, France 20 D4
Astakidha, Greece 47 F8
Astakós, Greece 46 C3
Astana, Kazakhstan 52 D8
Āstāneh, Iran 71 B6
Astara, Azerbaijan 71 B6
Āstārā, Iran 73 C13
Asteroúsia, Greece 49 E7
Asti, Italy 40 D5
Astipálaia, Greece 47 E8
Astorga, Spain 36 C4
Astoria, U.S.A. 110 D3
Åstorp, Sweden 11 H6
Astrakhan, Russia 35 G9
Astudillo, Spain 36 C6
Asturias □, Spain 36 B5
Asturias ✕ (OVD), Spain 36 B4
Asunción, Paraguay 126 B4
Asunción Nochixtlán, Mexico 119 D5
Åsunden, Sweden 11 F9
Asutri, Sudan 81 D4
Aswa →, Uganda 86 B3
Aswa-Lolim ⌓, Uganda 86 B3
Aswad, Ra's al, Si. Arabia 80 C4
Aswân, Egypt 80 C3
Aswan Dam = Sadd el Aali, Egypt 80 C3
Asyût, Egypt 80 B3
Asyûti, Wadi →, Egypt 80 B3
Aszód, Hungary 28 C4
At Ṭafīlah, Jordan 74 E4
At Ṭafīlah □, Jordan 74 E4
Aṭ Ṭā'if, Si. Arabia 75 C3
At Ta'mīm □, Iraq 70 C5
Aṭ Ṭirāq, Si. Arabia 70 E5
Aṭ Ṭubayq, Si. Arabia 70 D3
Atabey, Turkey 47 D12
Atacama □, Chile 126 B2
Atacama, Desierto de, Chile 126 A2
Atacama, Salar de, Chile 126 A2
Atakpamé, Togo 83 D5
Atalándi, Greece 46 C4
Atalaya, Peru 124 F4
Atalaya de Femes, Canary Is. 48 F6
Atami, Japan 55 G9
Atapupu, E. Timor 63 F6
Atâr, Mauritania 78 D3
Atarfe, Spain 37 H7
Atari, Pakistan 68 D6
Atascadero, U.S.A. 110 K6
Atasu, Kazakhstan 52 E8
Ataturk, Istanbul ✕ (IST), Turkey 45 F12
Atatürk Barajı, Turkey 73 D8
Atauro, E. Timor 63 F7
'Atbara, Sudan 80 D3
'Atbara, Nahr →, Sudan 80 D3
Atbasar, Kazakhstan 52 D7
Atça, Turkey 47 D10
Atchafalaya B., U.S.A. 113 L9
Atchison, U.S.A. 112 F7
Atebubu, Ghana 83 D4
Ateca, Spain 38 D3
Aterno →, Italy 41 F10
Āteshān, Iran 71 C7
Atesine, Alpi, Italy 41 B8
Atessa, Italy 41 F11
Atfîh, Egypt 80 J7
Ath, Belgium 17 D3
Athabasca, Canada 102 C6
Athabasca →, Canada 103 B6
Athabasca, L., Canada 103 B7
Athabasca Sand Dunes ⌓, Canada 103 B7
Athboy, Ireland 12 C5
Athenry, Ireland 12 C3
Athens = Athínai, Greece 46 D5
Athens, Ala., U.S.A. 115 H2
Athens, Ga., U.S.A. 115 J4
Athens, N.Y., U.S.A. 117 D11
Athens, Ohio, U.S.A. 114 F4
Athens, Pa., U.S.A. 117 E8
Athens, Tenn., U.S.A. 115 H3
Athens, Tex., U.S.A. 113 J7
Atherley, Canada 116 B5
Atherton, Australia 94 B4
Athiéme, Benin 83 D5
Athienou, Cyprus 49 D12
Athínai, Greece 46 D5
Athínai ✕ (ATH), Greece 46 D5
Athlone, Ireland 12 C4
Athna, Cyprus 49 D12
Athol, U.S.A. 117 D12
Atholl, Forest of, U.K. 13 E5
Atholville, Canada 105 C6
Áthos, Greece 45 F8
Athy, Ireland 12 C5
Ati, Chad 79 F9
Ati, Sudan 81 E2
Atiak, Uganda 86 B3
Atienza, Spain 38 D2
Atiit, Sudan 81 F3
Atik L., Canada 103 B9
Atikaki ⌓, Canada 103 C9
Atikameg →, Canada 104 B3
Atikokan, Canada 104 C1
Atikonak L., Canada 105 B7
Atimonan, Phil. 61 E4
Atitlán △, Cent. Amer. 119 E6
Atka, Russia 53 C16
Atka I., U.S.A. 100 C2
Atkarsk, Russia 34 E7
Atkinson, U.S.A. 112 D5
Atlanta, Ga., U.S.A. 115 J3
Atlanta, Tex., U.S.A. 113 J7
Atlantic, U.S.A. 112 E7
Atlantic City, U.S.A. 114 F8
Atlantic-Indian Basin, Antarctica 5 B4
Atlantic-Indian Ridge, Atl. Oc. 5 B3
Atlantic Ocean 2 E9
Atlas Mts. = Haut Atlas, Morocco 78 B4
Atlin, Canada 102 B2
Atlin ⌓, Canada 102 B2
Atlin, L., Canada 102 B2
Atmore, U.S.A. 115 K2
Atoka, U.S.A. 113 H6
Átokos Nisís, Greece 46 C2
Atolia, U.S.A. 111 K9
Atrai →, Bangla. 69 G13
Atrak = Atrek →, Turkmenistan 71 B8
Ätran, Sweden 11 G6
Ätran →, Sweden 11 H6
Atrauli, India 68 E8
Atrek →, Turkmenistan 71 B8
Atri, Italy 41 F10
Atsikí, Greece 47 B7
Atsoum, Mts., Cameroon 83 D7
Atsuta, Japan 54 C10
Attalla, U.S.A. 115 H2
Attapu, Laos 64 E6
Attáviros, Greece 49 C9
Attawapiskat, Canada 104 B3
Attawapiskat →, Canada 104 B3
Attawapiskat L., Canada 104 B2
Attersee, Austria 26 D6
Attica, Ind., U.S.A. 114 E2
Attica, Ohio, U.S.A. 116 E2
Attichy, France 19 C10
Attigny, France 19 C11
Attika = Attikí □, Greece 46 D5
Attikamagen L., Canada 105 B6
Attikí □, Greece 46 D5
Attleboro, U.S.A. 117 E13
Attock, Pakistan 68 C5
Attopeu = Attapu, Laos 64 E6
Attu I., U.S.A. 100 C1
Attur, India 66 P11
Atuel →, Argentina 126 D2
Åtvidaberg, Sweden 11 F10
Atwater, U.S.A. 110 H6
Atwood, Canada 116 C3
Atwood, U.S.A. 112 F4
Atyraū, Kazakhstan 52 E6
Au Sable, U.S.A. 116 B1
Au Sable →, U.S.A. 114 C4
Au Sable Forks, U.S.A. 117 B11
Au Sable Pt., U.S.A. 116 B1
Aubagne, France 21 E9
Aubarca, C. d', Spain 48 B7
Aube □, France 19 D11
Aube →, France 19 D10
Aubenas, France 21 D8
Aubenton, France 19 C11
Auberry, U.S.A. 110 H7
Aubigny-sur-Nère, France 19 E9
Aubin, France 20 D6
Aubrac, Mts. d', France 20 D7
Auburn, Ala., U.S.A. 115 J3
Auburn, Calif., U.S.A. 110 G5
Auburn, Ind., U.S.A. 114 E3
Auburn, Maine, U.S.A. 115 C10
Auburn, N.Y., U.S.A. 117 D8
Auburn, Nebr., U.S.A. 112 E7
Auburn, Pa., U.S.A. 117 F8
Auburn, Wash., U.S.A. 110 C4
Auburn Ra., Australia 95 D5
Auburndale, U.S.A. 115 L5
Aubusson, France 20 C6
Auce, Latvia 30 B9
Auch, France 20 E4
Auchi, Nigeria 83 D6
Auchterarder, U.K. 13 E5
Auchtermuchty, U.K. 13 E5
Auckland, N.Z. 91 G5
Auckland Is., Pac. Oc. 96 N8
Aude □, France 20 E6
Aude →, France 20 E7
Auden, Canada 104 B2
Auderville, France 18 C5
Audierne, France 18 D2
Audincourt, France 19 E13
Audo Ra., Ethiopia 81 F5
Audubon, U.S.A. 112 E7
Aue, Germany 24 E8
Auerbach, Germany 24 E8
Augathella, Australia 95 D4
Aughnacloy, U.K. 12 B5
Augrabies Falls, S. Africa 88 D3
Augrabies Falls △, S. Africa 88 D3
Augsburg, Germany 25 G6
Augsburg-Westliche Wälder ⌓, Germany 25 G6
Augusta, Australia 93 F2
Augusta, Italy 43 E8
Augusta, Ark., U.S.A. 113 H9
Augusta, Ga., U.S.A. 115 J5
Augusta, Kans., U.S.A. 113 G6
Augusta, Maine, U.S.A. 101 D13
Augusta, Mont., U.S.A. 108 C7
Augustenborg, Denmark 11 K3
Augustów, Poland 30 E9
Augustus, Mt., Australia 93 D2
Augustus I., Australia 92 C3
Aukan, Eritrea 81 D5
Aukrug ⌓, Germany 24 A5
Aukum, U.S.A. 110 G6
Auld, L., Australia 92 D3
Aulla, Italy 40 D6
Aulnay, France 20 B3
Aulne →, France 18 D2
Aulnoye-Aymeries, France 19 B10
Ault, France 18 B8
Ault, U.S.A. 112 E2
Aulus-les-Bains, France 20 F5
Aumale, France 19 C8
Aumont-Aubrac, France 20 D7
Auna, Nigeria 83 C5
Auning, Denmark 11 H4
Aunis, France 20 B3
Auponhia, Indonesia 63 E7
Aups, France 21 E10
Aur, Pulau, Malaysia 65 L5
Auraiya, India 69 F8
Aurangabad, Bihar, India 69 G11
Aurangabad, Maharashtra, India 66 K9
Auray, France 18 E4
Aurich, Germany 24 B3
Aurillac, France 20 D6
Auronzo di Cadore, Italy 41 B9
Aurora, Canada 116 C5
Aurora, S. Africa 88 E2
Aurora, Colo., U.S.A. 112 F2
Aurora, Ill., U.S.A. 114 E1
Aurora, Mo., U.S.A. 113 G8
Aurora, N.Y., U.S.A. 117 D8
Aurora, Nebr., U.S.A. 112 E6
Aurora, Ohio, U.S.A. 116 E3
Aurukun, Australia 94 A3
Aus, Namibia 88 D2
Ausable →, Canada 116 C3
Auschwitz = Oświęcim, Poland 31 H6
Austerlitz = Slavkov u Brna, Czech Rep. 27 B9
Austin, Minn., U.S.A. 112 D8
Austin, Nev., U.S.A. 108 G5
Austin, Pa., U.S.A. 116 E6
Austin, Tex., U.S.A. 113 K6
Austin, L., Australia 93 E2
Austin I., Canada 103 A10
Austra, Norway 8 D14
Austral Is. = Tubuai Is., French Polynesia 97 K13
Austral Seamount Chain, Pac. Oc. 97 K13
Australia ■, Oceania 96 K5
Australian Capital Territory □, Australia 95 F4
Australind, Australia 93 F2
Austria ■, Europe 26 E7
Austvågøy, Norway 8 B16
Auterive, France 20 E5
Authie →, France 19 B8
Authon-du-Perche, France 18 D7
Autlán, Mexico 118 D4
Autun, France 19 F11
Auvergne □, France 20 C7
Auvergne, Mts. d', France 20 C6
Auvézère →, France 20 C4
Auxerre, France 19 E10
Auxi-le-Château, France 19 B9
Auxonne, France 19 E12
Auzances, France 19 F9
Ava, U.S.A. 113 G8
Avallon, France 19 E10
Avalon, U.S.A. 111 M8
Avalon Pen., Canada 105 C9
Avanos, Turkey 70 B2
Avaré, Brazil 127 A6
Ávas, Greece 45 F9
Avawatz Mts., U.S.A. 111 K10
Avdan Dağı, Turkey 45 F13
Aveiro, Brazil 125 D7
Aveiro, Portugal 36 E2
Aveiro □, Portugal 36 E2
Āvej, Iran 71 C6
Avellaneda, Argentina 126 C4
Avellino, Italy 43 B7
Avenal, U.S.A. 110 K6
Aversa, Italy 43 B7
Avery, U.S.A. 108 C6
Aves, I. de, W. Indies 121 C7
Aves, Is. las, Venezuela 121 D6
Avesnes-sur-Helpe, France 19 B10
Avesnois ⌓, France 19 B10
Avesta, Sweden 10 D10
Aveyron □, France 20 D6
Aveyron →, France 20 D5
Avezzano, Italy 41 F10
Avgó, Greece 47 F7
Aviá Terai, Argentina 126 B3
Aviano, Italy 41 B9
Aviemore, U.K. 13 D5
Avigliana, Italy 40 C4
Avigliano, Italy 43 B8
Avignon, France 21 E8
Ávila, Spain 36 E6
Ávila □, Spain 36 E6
Ávila, Sierra de, Spain 36 E5
Avila Beach, U.S.A. 111 K6
Avilés, Spain 36 B5
Avintes, Portugal 36 D2
Avionárion, Greece 46 C6
Avis, Portugal 37 F3
Avis, U.S.A. 116 E7
Avísio →, Italy 40 B8
Aviz = Avis, Portugal 37 F3
Avize, France 19 D11
Avlum, Denmark 11 H2
Avoca, U.S.A. 116 D7
Avoca →, Australia 95 F3
Avoca →, Ireland 12 D5
Avola, Canada 102 C5
Avola, Italy 43 F8
Avon, U.S.A. 116 D7
Avon →, Australia 93 F2
Avon →, Bristol, U.K. 15 F5
Avon →, Dorset, U.K. 15 G6
Avon →, Warks., U.K. 15 E5
Avon Park, U.S.A. 115 M5
Avondale, Zimbabwe 87 F3
Avonlea, Canada 103 D8
Avonmore, Canada 117 A10
Avonmouth, U.K. 15 F5
Avramov, Bulgaria 45 D10
Avranches, France 18 D5
Avre →, France 18 D8
Avrig, Romania 29 E9
Avrillé, France 18 E6
Avtovac, Bos.-H. 44 C2
Awag el Baqar, Sudan 81 E3
A'waj →, Syria 74 B5
Awaji-Shima, Japan 55 G7
'Awālī, Bahrain 71 E6
Awantipur, India 69 C6
Awasa, Ethiopia 81 F4
Awasa, L., Ethiopia 81 F4
Awash, Ethiopia 81 F5
Awash △, Ethiopia 81 F5
Awash →, Ethiopia 81 E5
Awaso, Ghana 82 D4
Awatere →, N.Z. 91 J5
Awbārī, Libya 79 C8
Awbārī, Idehan, Libya 79 C8
Awe, L., U.K. 13 E3
Aweil, Sudan 81 F2
Awgu, Nigeria 83 D6
Awjilah, Libya 79 C10
Awka, Nigeria 83 D6
Ax-les-Thermes, France 20 F5
Axat, France 20 F6
Axe →, U.K. 15 F5
Axel Heiberg I., Canada 98 A10
Axim, Ghana 82 E4
Axintele, Romania 29 F11
Axiós →, Greece 44 F6
Axminster, U.K. 15 G4
Axvall, Sweden 11 F7
Ay, France 19 C11
Ayabaca, Peru 124 D3
Ayabe, Japan 55 G7
Ayacucho, Argentina 126 D4
Ayacucho, Peru 124 F4
Ayaguz, Kazakhstan 52 E9
Ayamé, Ivory C. 82 D4
Ayamonte, Spain 37 H3
Ayan, Russia 53 D14
Ayancık, Turkey 72 B6
Ayas, Turkey 72 B5
Ayaviri, Peru 124 F4
Aybastı, Turkey 72 B7
Aydın, Turkey 72 D2
Aydin □, Turkey 47 D9
Aydin Dağları, Turkey 47 D10
Ayelu, Ethiopia 81 E5
Ayenngré, Togo 83 D5
Ayer, U.S.A. 117 D13
Ayer Hitam, Malaysia 65 c
Ayerbe, Spain 38 C4
Ayer's Cliff, Canada 117 A12
Ayers Rock, Australia 93 E5
Ayiá, Greece 46 B4
Ayia Aikateríni, Ákra, Greece 49 A3
Ayia Ánna, Greece 46 C5
Ayía Dhéka, Greece 49 D6
Ayia Gálini, Greece 49 D6
Ayía Marína, Kásos, Greece 47 F8
Ayía Marína, Léros, Greece 47 D8
Áyia Napa, Cyprus 49 E13
Ayía Paraskeví, Greece 47 B8
Áyia Phyla, Cyprus 49 E12
Ayía Rouméli, Greece 46 F5
Ayía Varvára, Greece 49 D7
Ayiássos, Greece 47 B8
Áyioi Theódhoroi, Greece 46 D5
Áyion Óros □, Greece 45 F8
Áyios Amvrósios, Cyprus 49 D12
Áyios Andréas, Greece 46 D4
Áyios Evstrátios, Greece 46 B6
Áyios Ioánnis, Ákra, Greece 49 D7
Áyios Isidhoros, Greece 49 C9
Áyios Kiríkos, Greece 47 D8
Áyios Matthaíos, Greece 49 B3
Áyios Mírono, Greece 47 F7
Áyios Nikólaos, Greece 49 D7
Áyios Pétros, Greece 46 C2
Áyios Seryios, Cyprus 49 D12
Áyios Theodhoros, Cyprus 49 D13
Áyios Yeóryios, Greece 46 D5
Aykathonisi, Greece 47 D8
Aykirikçi, Turkey 47 B12
Aylesbury, U.K. 15 F7
Aylmer, Canada 116 D4
Aylmer, L., Canada 100 B8
'Ayn, Wādī al, Oman 71 F7
Ayn Dār, Si. Arabia 71 E7
Ayn Zālah, Iraq 70 B4
Ayna, Spain 39 G2
Ayod, Sudan 81 F3
Ayolas, Paraguay 126 B4
Ayom, Sudan 81 F2
Ayon, Ostrov, Russia 53 C17
Ayora, Spain 39 F3
Ayorou, Niger 83 C5
'Ayoûn el 'Atroûs, Mauritania 82 B3
Ayr, Australia 94 B4
Ayr, Canada 116 C4
Ayr, U.K. 13 F4
Ayr →, U.K. 13 F4
Ayrancı, Turkey 72 D5
Ayrancılar, Turkey 47 C9
Ayre, Pt. of, I. of Man 14 C3
Aysha, Ethiopia 81 E5
Ayton, Australia 94 B4
Aytos, Bulgaria 45 D11
Aytoska Planina, Bulgaria 45 D11
Ayu, Kepulauan, Indonesia 63 D8
Ayutla, Guatemala 120 D1
Ayutla, Mexico 119 D5
Ayvacık, Turkey 72 C2
Ayvalık, Turkey 47 B8
Az Zabadānī, Syria 74 B5
Aẓ Ẓāhirīyah, West Bank 74 D3
Aẓ Ẓahrān, Si. Arabia 71 E6
Az Zarqā, Jordan 74 C5
Az Zarqā', U.A.E. 71 E7
Az Zarqā □, Jordan 74 C5
Az Zāwiyah, Libya 79 B8
Az Zībār, Iraq 70 B5
Az Zilfī, Si. Arabia 70 E5
Az Zubayr, Iraq 70 D5
Az Zuqur, Yemen 81 E5
Azad Kashmir □, Pakistan 69 C5
Azambuja, Portugal 37 F2
Azamgarh, India 69 F10
Azangaro, Peru 124 F4
Azaoua, Niger 83 B5
Azaouad, Mali 82 B4
Azaouak, Vallée de l', Mali 83 B5
Āzār Shahr, Iran 70 B5
Azara, Nigeria 83 D6
Azarān, Iran 70 B5
Azärbayjan = Azerbaijan ■, Asia 35 K9
Āzarbāyjān-e Gharbī □, Iran 70 B5
Āzarbāyjān-e Sharqī □, Iran 70 B5
Azare, Nigeria 83 C7
Azay-le-Rideau, France 18 E7
A'zāz, Syria 70 B3
Azbine = Aïr, Niger 83 B6
Azerbaijan ■, Asia 35 K9
Azerbaijchan = Azerbaijan ■, Asia 35 K9
Azezo, Ethiopia 81 E4
Azimganj, India 69 G13
Aznalcóllar, Spain 37 H4
Azogues, Ecuador 124 D3
Azores = Açores, Is. dos, Atl. Oc. 78 A1
Azov, Russia 35 G4
Azov, Sea of, Europe 33 J9
Azovskoye More = Azov, Sea of, Europe 33 J9
Azpeitia, Spain 38 B2
Azraq ash Shīshān, Jordan 74 D5
Aztec, U.S.A. 109 H10
Azúa de Compostela, Dom. Rep. 121 C5
Azuaga, Spain 37 G5
Azuara, Spain 38 D4
Azuer →, Spain 37 F7
Azuero, Pen. de, Panama 120 E3
Azuga, Romania 29 E10
Azul, Argentina 126 D4
Azusa, U.S.A. 111 L9
Azzano Décimo, Italy 41 C9

B

Ba Be △, Vietnam 64 A5
Ba Don, Vietnam 64 D6
Ba Dong, Vietnam 65 H6
Ba Ngoi = Cam Lam, Vietnam 65 G7
Ba Tri, Vietnam 65 G6
Ba Vi △, Vietnam 64 B5
Ba Xian = Bazhou, China 56 E9
Baa, Indonesia 63 F6
Baamonde, Spain 36 B3
Baardeere = Bardera, Somali Rep. 75 G3
Baarle-Nassau, Belgium 17 C4
Bab el Mandeb, Red Sea 75 E3
Baba, Bulgaria 44 D7
Bābā, Koh-i-, Afghan. 66 B5
Baba Burnu, Turkey 47 B8
Baba dag, Azerbaijan 35 K9
Bābā Kalū, Iran 71 D6
Babadag, Romania 29 F13
Babadağ, Turkey 47 D10
Babaeski, Turkey 45 E11
Babahoyo, Ecuador 124 D3
Babai = Sarju →, India 69 F9
Babana, Nigeria 83 C5
Babanusa, Sudan 81 E2
Babar, Indonesia 63 F7
Babar, Pakistan 68 D3
Babarkach, Pakistan 68 E3
Babayevo, Russia 32 C8
Babb, U.S.A. 108 B7
Babenhausen, Germany 25 F4
Băbeni, Romania 29 F9
Baberu, India 69 G9
Babi Besar, Pulau, Malaysia 65 L4
Babia Gora, Europe 31 J6
Babian Jiang →, China 58 F3
Babīl □, Iraq 70 C5
Babile, Ethiopia 81 F5
Babimost, Poland 31 F2
Babinda, Australia 94 B4
Babine, Canada 102 B3
Babine →, Canada 102 B3
Babine L., Canada 102 C3
Babiogórski △, Poland 31 J6
Babo, Indonesia 63 E8
Babócsa, Hungary 28 D2
Bābol, Iran 71 B7
Bābol Sar, Iran 71 B7

Baborów, *Poland* 31 H5
Babruysk, *Belarus* 33 F5
Babuhri, *India* 68 F3
Babuna, *Macedonia* 44 E5
Babura, *Nigeria* 83 C6
Babusar Pass, *Pakistan* 69 B5
Babushkin, *Russia* 60 A5
Babušnica, *Serbia & M.* 44 C6
Babuyan Chan., *Phil.* 61 B4
Babylon, *Iraq* 70 C5
Bač, *Serbia & M.* 28 E4
Bâc →, *Moldova* 29 D14
Bac Can, *Vietnam* 58 F5
Bac Giang, *Vietnam* 58 G6
Bac Lieu, *Vietnam* 65 H5
Bac Ninh, *Vietnam* 58 G6
Bac Phan, *Vietnam* 64 B5
Bac Quang, *Vietnam* 58 F5
Bacabal, *Brazil* 125 D10
Bacalar, *Mexico* 119 D7
Bacan, Kepulauan, *Indonesia* 63 E7
Bacarra, *Phil.* 61 B4
Bacău, *Romania* 29 D11
Bacău □, *Romania* 29 D11
Baccarat, *France* 19 D13
Bacerac, *Mexico* 118 A3
Băceşti, *Romania* 29 D12
Bach Long Vi, Dao, *Vietnam* 64 B6
Bach Ma △, *Vietnam* 64 D6
Bacharach, *Germany* 25 E3
Bachhwara, *India* 69 G11
Bachuma, *Ethiopia* 81 F4
Bačina, *Serbia & M.* 44 C5
Back →, *Canada* 100 B9
Bačka Palanka, *Serbia & M.* 28 E4
Bačka Topola, *Serbia & M.* 28 E4
Bäckebo, *Sweden* 11 H10
Bäckefors, *Sweden* 11 F6
Bäckhammar, *Sweden* 10 E8
Bački Petrovac, *Serbia & M.* 28 E4
Backnang, *Germany* 25 G5
Baco, Mt., *Phil.* 61 E4
Bacolod, *Phil.* 61 F5
Bacqueville-en-Caux, *France* 18 C8
Bács-Kiskun □, *Hungary* 28 D4
Bácsalmás, *Hungary* 28 D4
Bacuag = Placer, *Phil.* 61 G6
Bacuk, *Malaysia* 65 J4
Bād, *Iran* 71 C7
Bad →, *U.S.A.* 112 C4
Bad Aussee, *Austria* 26 D6
Bad Axe, *U.S.A.* 116 C2
Bad Bergzabern, *Germany* 25 F3
Bad Berleburg, *Germany* 24 D4
Bad Bevensen, *Germany* 24 B6
Bad Bramstedt, *Germany* 24 B5
Bad Brückenau, *Germany* 25 E5
Bad Doberan, *Germany* 24 A7
Bad Driburg, *Germany* 24 D5
Bad Ems, *Germany* 25 E3
Bad Frankenhausen, *Germany* 24 D7
Bad Freienwalde, *Germany* 24 C10
Bad Goisern, *Austria* 26 D6
Bad Harzburg, *Germany* 24 D6
Bad Hersfeld, *Germany* 24 E5
Bad Hofgastein, *Austria* 26 D6
Bad Homburg, *Germany* 25 E4
Bad Honnef, *Germany* 24 E3
Bad Iburg, *Germany* 24 C4
Bad Ischl, *Austria* 26 D6
Bad Kissingen, *Germany* 25 E6
Bad Königshofen, *Germany* 25 E6
Bad Kreuznach, *Germany* 25 F3
Bad Krozingen, *Germany* 25 H3
Bad Laasphe, *Germany* 24 E4
Bad Lands, *U.S.A.* 112 D3
Bad Langensalza, *Germany* 24 D6
Bad Lauterberg, *Germany* 24 D6
Bad Leonfelden, *Austria* 26 C7
Bad Liebenwerda, *Germany* 24 D9
Bad Mergentheim, *Germany* 25 F5
Bad Münstereifel, *Germany* 24 E2
Bad Nauheim, *Germany* 25 E4
Bad Neuenahr-Ahrweiler, *Germany* 24 E3
Bad Neustadt, *Germany* 25 E6
Bad Oeynhausen, *Germany* 24 C4
Bad Oldesloe, *Germany* 24 B6
Bad Orb, *Germany* 25 E5
Bad Pyrmont, *Germany* 24 D5
Bad Reichenhall, *Germany* 25 H8
Bad Säckingen, *Germany* 25 H3
Bad Salzuflen, *Germany* 24 C4
Bad Salzungen, *Germany* 24 E6
Bad Schwartau, *Germany* 24 B6
Bad Segeberg, *Germany* 24 B6
Bad St. Leonhard, *Austria* 26 E7
Bad Tölz, *Germany* 25 H7
Bad Urach, *Germany* 25 G5
Bad Vöslau, *Austria* 27 D9
Bad Waldsee, *Germany* 25 H5
Bad Wildungen, *Germany* 24 D5
Bad Wimpfen, *Germany* 25 F5
Bad Windsheim, *Germany* 25 F6
Bad Zwischenahn, *Germany* 24 B4
Bada Barabil, *India* 69 H11
Badagara, *India* 66 P9
Badagri, *Nigeria* 83 D5
Badajós, L., *Brazil* 124 D6
Badajoz, *Spain* 37 G4
Badajoz □, *Spain* 37 G4
Badakhshān □, *Afghan.* 66 A7
Badalona, *Spain* 38 D7
Badalzai, *Afghan.* 68 E1
Badampahar, *India* 67 H15
Badanah, *Si. Arabia* 70 D4
Badarinath, *India* 69 D8
Badas, Kepulauan, *Indonesia* 62 D3
Baddo →, *Pakistan* 66 F4
Bade, *Indonesia* 63 F9
Badeggi, *Nigeria* 83 D6
Badéguichéri, *Niger* 83 C6
Baden, *Austria* 27 C9
Baden, *Switz.* 25 H4
Baden, *U.S.A.* 116 F4
Baden-Baden, *Germany* 25 G4
Baden-Württemberg □, *Germany* 25 G4
Badgastein, *Austria* 26 D6
Badger, *Canada* 105 C8
Badger, *U.S.A.* 110 J7
Bādghīs □, *Afghan.* 66 B3
Badgingarra △, *Australia* 93 F2
Badgom, *India* 69 B6
Badia Polésine, *Italy* 41 C8
Badiar △, *Guinea* 82 C2
Badin, *Pakistan* 68 G3
Badinka ⌂, *Mali* 82 C3
Badlands △, *U.S.A.* 112 D3
Badogo, *Mali* 82 C3
Badoumbé, *Mali* 82 C2
Badrah, *Iraq* 70 C5
Badrinath, *India* 69 D8
Badulla, *Sri Lanka* 66 R12
Badung, Selat, *Indonesia* 63 K18
Baena, *Spain* 37 H6
Baeza, *Spain* 37 H7
Bafang, *Cameroon* 83 D7
Bafatá, *Guinea-Biss.* 82 C2
Baffin B., *Canada* 101 A13
Baffin I., *Canada* 101 B12
Bafia, *Cameroon* 83 E7
Bafilo, *Togo* 83 D5
Bafing △, *Mali* 82 C2
Bafing →, *Mali* 82 C2
Bafliyūn, *Syria* 70 B3
Bafoulabé, *Mali* 82 C2
Bafoussam, *Cameroon* 83 D7
Bāfq, *Iran* 71 D7
Bafra, *Turkey* 72 B6
Bafra Burnu, *Turkey* 72 B7
Bāft, *Iran* 71 D8
Bafut, *Cameroon* 83 D7
Bafwasende, *Dem. Rep. of the Congo* 86 B2
Bagam, *Niger* 83 B6
Bagamoyo, *Tanzania* 86 D4
Bagan Datoh, *Malaysia* 65 L3
Bagan Serai, *Malaysia* 65 K3
Baganga, *Phil.* 61 H7
Bagani, *Namibia* 88 B3
Bagansiapiapi, *Indonesia* 62 D2
Bagasra, *India* 68 J4
Bagaud, *India* 68 H6
Bagawi, *Sudan* 81 E3
Bagbag, *Sudan* 81 D3
Bagdad, *U.S.A.* 111 L11
Bagdarin, *Russia* 53 D12
Bagé, *Brazil* 127 C5
Bagenalstown = Muine Bheag, *Ireland* 12 D5
Baggs, *U.S.A.* 108 F10
Bagh, *Pakistan* 69 C5
Baghain →, *India* 69 G9
Baghdād, *Iraq* 70 C5
Bagheria, *Italy* 42 D6
Baghlān, *Afghan.* 66 A6
Baghlān □, *Afghan.* 66 B6
Bagley, *U.S.A.* 112 B7
Bagnara Cálabra, *Italy* 43 D8
Bagnasco, *Italy* 40 D5
Bagnères-de-Bigorre, *France* 20 E4
Bagnères-de-Luchon, *France* 20 F4
Bagni di Lucca, *Italy* 40 D7
Bagno di Romagna, *Italy* 41 E8
Bagnoles-de-l'Orne, *France* 18 D6
Bagnols-sur-Cèze, *France* 21 D8
Bagnorégio, *Italy* 41 F9
Bago = Pegu, *Burma* 67 L20
Bagodar, *India* 69 G11
Bagrationovsk, *Russia* 9 J19
Bagrdan, *Serbia & M.* 44 B5
Baguio, *Phil.* 61 C4
Bağyurdu, *Turkey* 47 C9
Bagzane, Monts, *Niger* 83 B6
Bah, *India* 69 F8
Bahabón de Esgueva, *Spain* 36 D7
Bahadurganj, *India* 69 F12
Bahadurgarh, *India* 68 E7
Bahama, Canal Viejo de, *W. Indies* 120 B4
Bahamas ■, *N. Amer.* 121 B5
Bahār, *Iran* 73 E13
Baharampur, *India* 69 G13
Baharîya, El Wâhât al, *Egypt* 80 B2
Baharu Pandan = Pandan, *Malaysia* 65 d
Bahawalnagar, *Pakistan* 68 E5
Bahawalpur, *Pakistan* 68 E4
Bahçe, *Turkey* 72 D7
Bahçecik, *Turkey* 45 F13
Baheri, *India* 69 E8
Bahgul →, *India* 69 F8
Bahi, *Tanzania* 86 D4
Bahi Swamp, *Tanzania* 86 D4
Bahía = Salvador, *Brazil* 125 F11
Bahía □, *Brazil* 125 F10
Bahía, Is. de la, *Honduras* 120 C2
Bahía Blanca, *Argentina* 126 D3
Bahía de Caráquez, *Ecuador* 124 D2
Bahía Honda, *Cuba* 120 B3
Bahía Laura, *Argentina* 128 F3
Bahía Negra, *Paraguay* 124 H7
Bahir Dar, *Ethiopia* 81 E4
Bahmanzād, *Iran* 71 D6
Bahr el Ahmar □, *Sudan* 80 D4
Bahr el Ghazâl □, *Sudan* 81 F2
Bahr el Jabal □, *Sudan* 81 G3
Bahraich, *India* 69 F9
Bahrain ■, *Asia* 71 E6
Bahror, *India* 68 F7
Bāhū Kalāt, *Iran* 71 E9
Bai, *Mali* 82 C4
Bai Bung, Mui = Ca Mau, Mui, *Vietnam* 65 H5
Bai Duc, *Vietnam* 64 C5
Bai Thuong, *Vietnam* 64 C5
Baia de Aramă, *Romania* 28 E7
Baia Mare, *Romania* 29 C8
Baia-Sprie, *Romania* 29 C8
Baião, *Brazil* 125 D9
Baïbokoum, *Chad* 79 G9
Baicheng, *China* 57 B12
Băicoi, *Romania* 29 E10
Baidoa, *Somali Rep.* 75 G3
Baie-Comeau, *Canada* 105 C6
Baie-St-Paul, *Canada* 105 C5
Baie-Trinité, *Canada* 105 C6
Baie Verte, *Canada* 105 C8
Baignes-Ste-Radegonde, *France* 20 C3
Baigneux-les-Juifs, *France* 19 E11
Baihar, *India* 69 H9
Baihe, *China* 56 H6
Baijnath, *India* 69 E8
Baikal, L. = Baykal, Oz., *Russia* 53 D11
Baikunthpur, *India* 69 H10
Baile Atha Cliath = Dublin, *Ireland* 12 C5
Băile Govora, *Romania* 29 E9
Băile Herculane, *Romania* 28 F7
Băile Olăneşti, *Romania* 29 E9
Băile Tuşnad, *Romania* 29 D10
Bailén, *Spain* 37 G7
Băileşti, *Romania* 29 F8
Baima, *China* 58 A3
Bain-de-Bretagne, *France* 18 E5
Bainbridge, *Ga., U.S.A.* 115 K3
Bainbridge, *N.Y., U.S.A.* 117 D9
Baing, *Indonesia* 63 F6
Bainiu, *China* 56 H7
Baiona, *Spain* 36 C2
Bā'ir, *Jordan* 74 E5
Bairiki = Tarawa, *Kiribati* 96 G9
Bairin Youqi, *China* 57 C10
Bairin Zuoqi, *China* 57 C10
Bairnsdale, *Australia* 95 F4
Bais, *Phil.* 61 G5
Baisha, *China* 56 G7
Baissa, *Nigeria* 83 D7
Baitadi, *Nepal* 69 E9
Baixa Limia-Sierra do Xurés ⌂, *Spain* 36 D2
Baiyin, *China* 56 F3
Baiyü, *China* 58 B2
Baiyu Shan, *China* 56 F4
Baiyuda, *Sudan* 80 D3
Baj Baj, *India* 69 H13
Baja, *Hungary* 28 D3
Baja, Pta., *Mexico* 118 B1
Baja California, *Mexico* 118 A1
Baja California □, *Mexico* 118 B2
Baja California Sur □, *Mexico* 118 B2
Bajag, *India* 69 H9
Bajamar, *Canary Is.* 48 F3
Bajana, *India* 68 H4
Bajatrejo, *Indonesia* 63 J17
Bajera, *Indonesia* 63 J18
Bājgīrān, *Iran* 71 B8
Bajimba, Mt., *Australia* 95 D5
Bajina Bašta, *Serbia & M.* 44 C3
Bajmok, *Serbia & M.* 28 E4
Bajo Nuevo, *Caribbean* 120 C4
Bajoga, *Nigeria* 83 C7
Bajool, *Australia* 94 C5
Bak, *Hungary* 28 D1
Bakar, *Croatia* 41 C11
Bakasi Pen., *Cameroon* 83 E6
Bakel, *Senegal* 82 C2
Baker, *Calif., U.S.A.* 111 K10
Baker, *Mont., U.S.A.* 112 B2
Baker, L., *Canada* 100 B10
Baker, Mt., *U.S.A.* 108 B3
Baker City, *U.S.A.* 108 D5
Baker I., *Pac. Oc.* 96 G10
Baker I., *U.S.A.* 102 B2
Baker L., *Australia* 93 E4
Baker Lake, *Canada* 100 B10
Bakers Creek, *Australia* 94 C4
Bakers Dozen Is., *Canada* 104 A4
Bakersfield, *Calif., U.S.A.* 111 K8
Bakersfield, *Vt., U.S.A.* 117 B12
Bakhchysaray, *Ukraine* 33 K7
Bakhmach, *Ukraine* 33 G7
Bākhtarān, *Iran* 70 C5
Bākhtarān □, *Iran* 70 C5
Bakı, *Azerbaijan* 35 K9
Bakır →, *Turkey* 47 C9
Bakırdaği, *Turkey* 72 C6
Bakkafjörður, *Iceland* 8 C6
Baklan, *Turkey* 47 C11
Bako, *Ethiopia* 81 F4
Bako, *Ivory C.* 82 D3
Bakony, *Hungary* 28 C2
Bakony Forest = Bakony, *Hungary* 28 C2
Bakori, *Nigeria* 83 C6
Bakouma, *C.A.R.* 84 C4
Baksan, *Russia* 35 J6
Bakswaho, *India* 69 G8
Baku = Bakı, *Azerbaijan* 35 K9
Bakundi, *Nigeria* 83 D7
Bakutis Coast, *Antarctica* 5 D15
Baky = Bakı, *Azerbaijan* 35 K9
Bala, *Canada* 116 A5
Bala, *Senegal* 82 C2
Bâlâ, *Turkey* 72 C5
Bala, *U.K.* 14 E4
Bala, L., *U.K.* 14 E4
Balabac I., *Phil.* 62 C5
Balabac Str., *E. Indies* 62 C5
Balabagh, *Afghan.* 68 B4
Ba'labakk, *Lebanon* 74 B5
Balabalangan, Kepulauan, *Indonesia* 62 E5
Bălăciţa, *Romania* 29 F8
Balad, *Iraq* 70 C5
Balad Rūz, *Iraq* 70 C5
Bālādeh, *Fārs, Iran* 71 D6
Bālādeh, *Māzandaran, Iran* 71 B6
Balaghat, *India* 66 J12
Balaghat Ra., *India* 66 K10
Balaguer, *Spain* 38 D5
Balakhna, *Russia* 34 B6
Balaklava, *Ukraine* 33 K7
Balakliya, *Ukraine* 33 H9
Balakovo, *Russia* 34 D8
Balamau, *India* 69 F9
Bălan, *Romania* 29 D10
Balancán, *Mexico* 119 D6
Balanivka, *Ukraine* 29 B14
Balashov, *Russia* 34 E6
Balasinor, *India* 68 H5
Balasore = Baleshwar, *India* 67 J15
Balassagyarmat, *Hungary* 28 B4
Balât, *Egypt* 80 B2
Balaton, *Hungary* 28 D2
Balaton-Felvidéki △, *Hungary* 28 D2
Balatonboglár, *Hungary* 28 D2
Balatonfüred, *Hungary* 28 D2
Balatonszentgyörgy, *Hungary* 28 D2
Balayan, *Phil.* 61 E4
Balazote, *Spain* 39 G2
Balbieriškis, *Lithuania* 30 D10
Balbigny, *France* 21 C8
Balbina, Reprêsa de, *Brazil* 124 D7
Balboa, *Panama* 120 E4
Balbriggan, *Ireland* 12 C5
Balcarce, *Argentina* 126 D4
Balcarres, *Canada* 103 C8
Bălceşti, *Romania* 29 F8
Balchik, *Bulgaria* 45 C12
Balclutha, *N.Z.* 91 M2
Balcones Escarpment, *U.S.A.* 113 L5
Balçova, *Turkey* 47 C9
Bald Hd., *Australia* 93 G2
Bald I., *Australia* 93 F2
Bald Knob, *U.S.A.* 113 H9
Baldock L., *Canada* 103 B9
Baldwin, *Mich., U.S.A.* 114 D3
Baldwin, *Pa., U.S.A.* 116 F5
Baldwinsville, *U.S.A.* 117 C8
Baldy Mt., *U.S.A.* 108 B9
Baldy Peak, *U.S.A.* 109 K9
Bale, *Croatia* 41 C10
Bale, *Ethiopia* 81 F5
Bale, *Ethiopia* 81 F5
Bale Mts. △, *Ethiopia* 81 F4
Baleares, Is., *Spain* 48 B10
Balearic Is. = Baleares, Is., *Spain* 48 B10
Baleine = Whale →, *Canada* 105 A6
Baleine, Petite R. de la →, *Canada* 104 A4
Băleni, *Romania* 29 E12
Baler, *Phil.* 61 D4
Baler Bay, *Phil.* 61 D4
Baleshare, *U.K.* 13 D1
Baleshwar, *India* 67 J15
Balezino, *Russia* 34 B11
Balfate, *Honduras* 120 C2
Bali, *Cameroon* 83 D7
Balí, *Greece* 49 D6
Bali, *India* 68 G5
Bali, *Indonesia* 63 J18
Bali □, *Indonesia* 63 J18
Bali, Selat, *Indonesia* 63 J17
Bali Sea, *Indonesia* 63 J17
Balia, *S. Leone* 82 D2
Baliapal, *India* 69 J12
Baligród, *Poland* 31 J9
Balik Pulau, *Malaysia* 65 c
Balıkeşir, *Turkey* 47 B9
Balıkeşir □, *Turkey* 47 B9
Balıklıçeşme, *Turkey* 45 F11
Balikpapan, *Indonesia* 62 E5
Balimbing, *Phil.* 63 C5
Baling, *Malaysia* 65 K3
Balingen, *Germany* 25 G4
Balinţ, *Romania* 28 E6
Balintang Channel, *Phil.* 61 B4
Balipara, *India* 67 F18
Balkan Mts. = Stara Planina, *Bulgaria* 44 C7
Balkhash = Balqash, *Kazakhstan* 52 E8
Balkhash, Ozero = Balqash Köl, *Kazakhstan* 52 E8
Balla, *Bangla.* 67 G17
Ballachulish, *U.K.* 13 E3
Balladonia, *Australia* 93 F3
Ballaghaderreen, *Ireland* 12 C3
Ballarat, *Australia* 95 F3
Ballard, L., *Australia* 93 E3
Ballater, *U.K.* 13 D5
Ballé, *Mali* 82 B3
Ballena Gris = Ojo de Liebre ⌂, *Mexico* 118 B2
Ballenas, Canal de, *Mexico* 118 B2
Balleny Is., *Antarctica* 5 C11
Balleroy, *France* 18 C6
Ballerup, *Denmark* 11 J6
Ballı, *Turkey* 45 F11
Ballia, *India* 69 G11
Ballina, *Australia* 95 D5
Ballina, *Ireland* 12 B2
Ballinasloe, *Ireland* 12 C3
Ballinger, *U.S.A.* 113 K5
Ballinrobe, *Ireland* 12 C2
Ballinskelligs B., *Ireland* 12 E1
Ballon, *France* 18 D7
Ballons des Vosges ⌂, *France* 19 E14
Ballsh, *Albania* 44 F3
Ballston Spa, *U.S.A.* 117 D11
Ballybunion, *Ireland* 12 D2
Ballycastle, *U.K.* 12 A5
Ballyclare, *U.K.* 12 B5
Ballyhaunis, *Ireland* 12 C3
Ballymena, *U.K.* 12 B5
Ballymoney, *U.K.* 12 A5
Ballymote, *Ireland* 12 B3
Ballynahinch, *U.K.* 12 B6
Ballyquintin Pt., *U.K.* 12 B6
Ballyshannon, *Ireland* 12 B3
Balmaceda, *Chile* 128 F2
Balmaseda, *Spain* 38 B1
Balmazújváros, *Hungary* 28 C6
Balmertown, *Canada* 103 C10
Balmoral, *Australia* 95 F3
Balmorhea, *U.S.A.* 113 K3
Balochistan = Baluchistan □, *Pakistan* 66 F4
Balonne →, *Australia* 95 D4
Balotra, *India* 68 G5
Balqash, *Kazakhstan* 52 E8
Balqash Köl, *Kazakhstan* 52 E8
Balrampur, *India* 69 F10
Balranald, *Australia* 95 E3
Balş, *Romania* 29 F9
Balsas, *Mexico* 119 D5
Balsas →, *Brazil* 125 E9
Balsas →, *Mexico* 118 D4
Bålsta, *Sweden* 10 E11
Balston Spa, *U.S.A.* 117 D11
Balta, *Romania* 28 F7
Balta, *Ukraine* 29 B14
Baltanás, *Spain* 36 D6
Bălţi, *Moldova* 29 C12
Baltic Sea, *Europe* 9 H18
Baltîm, *Egypt* 80 H7
Baltimore, *Ireland* 12 E2
Baltimore, *Md., U.S.A.* 114 F7
Baltimore, *Ohio, U.S.A.* 116 G2
Baltit, *Pakistan* 69 A6
Baltiysk, *Russia* 9 J18
Baltrum, *Germany* 24 B3
Baluchistan □, *Pakistan* 66 F4
Balurghat, *India* 69 G13
Balvi, *Latvia* 9 H22
Balya, *Turkey* 47 B9
Bam, *Iran* 71 D8
Bama, *China* 58 E6
Bama, *Nigeria* 83 C7
Bamaga, *Australia* 94 A3
Bamaji L., *Canada* 104 B1
Bamako, *Mali* 82 C3
Bamba, *Mali* 83 B4
Bambara Maoundé, *Mali* 82 B4
Bambari, *C.A.R.* 84 C4
Bambaroo, *Australia* 94 B4
Bambaya, *Guinea* 82 D2
Bamberg, *Germany* 25 F6
Bamberg, *U.S.A.* 115 J5
Bambesi, *Ethiopia* 81 F3
Bambey, *Senegal* 82 C1
Bambili, *Dem. Rep. of the Congo* 86 B2
Bamboi, *Ghana* 82 D4
Bamburgh, *U.K.* 14 B6
Bamenda, *Cameroon* 83 D7
Bamfield, *Canada* 102 D3
Bāmīān □, *Afghan.* 66 B5
Bamiancheng, *China* 57 C13
Bamkin, *Cameroon* 83 D7
Bampūr, *Iran* 71 E9
Ban, *Burkina Faso* 82 C4
Ban Ao Tu Khun, *Thailand* 65 a
Ban Ban, *Laos* 64 C4
Ban Bang Hin, *Thailand* 65 H2
Ban Bang Khu, *Thailand* 65 a
Ban Bang Rong, *Thailand* 65 a
Ban Bo Phut, *Thailand* 65 b
Ban Chaweng, *Thailand* 65 b
Ban Chiang Klang, *Thailand* 64 C3
Ban Chik, *Laos* 64 D4
Ban Choho, *Thailand* 64 E4
Ban Dan Lan Hoi, *Thailand* 64 D2
Ban Don = Surat Thani, *Thailand* 65 H2
Ban Don, *Vietnam* 64 F6
Ban Don, Ao →, *Thailand* 65 H2
Ban Dong, *Thailand* 64 C3
Ban Hong, *Thailand* 64 C2
Ban Hua Thanon, *Thailand* 65 b
Ban Kaeng, *Thailand* 64 D3
Ban Kantang, *Thailand* 65 J2
Ban Karon, *Thailand* 65 a
Ban Kata, *Thailand* 65 a
Ban Keun, *Laos* 64 C4
Ban Khai, *Thailand* 64 F3
Ban Kheun, *Laos* 64 B3
Ban Khlong Khian, *Thailand* 65 a
Ban Khlong Kua, *Thailand* 65 J3
Ban Khuan, *Thailand* 65 a
Ban Khuan Mao, *Thailand* 65 J2
Ban Ko Yai Chim, *Thailand* 65 G2
Ban Kok, *Thailand* 64 D4
Ban Laem, *Thailand* 64 F2
Ban Lamai, *Thailand* 65 b
Ban Lao Ngam, *Laos* 64 E6
Ban Le Kathe, *Thailand* 64 E2
Ban Lo Po Noi, *Thailand* 65 a
Ban Mae Chedi, *Thailand* 64 C2
Ban Mae Laeng, *Thailand* 64 B2
Ban Mae Nam, *Thailand* 65 b
Ban Mae Sariang, *Thailand* 64 C1
Ban Mê Thuôt = Buon Ma Thuot, *Vietnam* 64 F7
Ban Mi, *Thailand* 64 E3
Ban Muong Mo, *Laos* 64 C4
Ban Na Bo, *Thailand* 65 b
Ban Na Mo, *Laos* 64 D5
Ban Na San, *Thailand* 65 H2
Ban Na Tong, *Laos* 64 B3
Ban Nam Bac, *Laos* 64 B4
Ban Nam Ma, *Laos* 64 A3
Ban Ngang, *Laos* 64 E6
Ban Nong Bok, *Laos* 64 D5
Ban Nong Boua, *Laos* 64 E6
Ban Nong Pling, *Thailand* 64 E3
Ban Pak Chan, *Thailand* 65 G2
Ban Patong, *Thailand* 65 a
Ban Phai, *Thailand* 64 D4
Ban Phak Chit, *Thailand* 65 a
Ban Pong, *Thailand* 64 F2
Ban Rawai, *Thailand* 65 a

Ban Ron Phibun, *Thailand* 65 H2
Ban Sakhu, *Thailand* 65 a
Ban Sanam Chai, *Thailand* 65 J3
Ban Sangkha, *Thailand* 64 E4
Ban Tak, *Thailand* 64 D2
Ban Tako, *Thailand* 64 E4
Ban Tha Dua, *Thailand* 64 D2
Ban Tha Li, *Thailand* 64 D3
Ban Tha Nun, *Thailand* 65 a
Ban Tha Rua, *Thailand* 65 a
Ban Tha Yu, *Thailand* 65 a
Ban Thahine, *Laos* 64 E5
Ban Thong Krut, *Thailand* 65 b
Ban Xien Kok, *Laos* 64 B3
Ban Yen Nhan, *Vietnam* 64 B6
Banaba, *Kiribati* 96 H8
Banalia, *Dem. Rep. of the Congo* 86 B2
Banam, *Cambodia* 65 G5
Banamba, *Mali* 82 C3
Banana Is., *S. Leone* 82 D2
Bananal, I. do, *Brazil* 125 F8
Banaras = Varanasi, *India* 69 G10
Banas →, *Gujarat, India* 68 H4
Banas →, *Mad. P., India* 69 G9
Bânâs, Ras, *Egypt* 80 C4
Banaz, *Turkey* 47 C11
Banaz →, *Turkey* 47 C11
Banbridge, *U.K.* 12 B5
Banbury, *U.K.* 15 E6
Banchory, *U.K.* 13 D6
Banco, *Ethiopia* 81 F4
Bancroft, *Canada* 116 A7
Band, *Romania* 29 D9
Band Bonī, *Iran* 71 E8
Band Qīr, *Iran* 71 D6
Banda, *Mad. P., India* 69 G8
Banda, *Ut. P., India* 69 G9
Banda, Kepulauan, *Indonesia* 63 E7
Banda Aceh, *Indonesia* 62 C1
Banda Banda, Mt., *Australia* 95 E5
Banda Elat, *Indonesia* 63 F8
Banda Is. = Banda, Kepulauan, *Indonesia* 63 E7
Banda Sea, *Indonesia* 63 F7
Bandai-Asahi △, *Japan* 54 F10
Bandai-San, *Japan* 54 F10
Bandama →, *Ivory C.* 82 D3
Bandama Blanc →, *Ivory C.* 82 D3
Bandama Rouge →, *Ivory C.* 82 D4
Bandān, *Iran* 71 D9
Bandanaira, *Indonesia* 63 E7
Bandanwara, *India* 68 F6
Bandar = Machilipatnam, *India* 67 L12
Bandar-e Abbās, *Iran* 71 E8
Bandar-e Anzalī, *Iran* 71 B6
Bandar-e Bushehr = Būshehr, *Iran* 71 D6
Bandar-e Chārak, *Iran* 71 E7
Bandar-e Deylam, *Iran* 71 D6
Bandar-e Emām Khomeynı, *Iran* 71 D6
Bandar-e Lengeh, *Iran* 71 E7
Bandar-e Maqām, *Iran* 71 E7
Bandar-e Ma'shur, *Iran* 71 D6
Bandar-e Rīg, *Iran* 71 D6
Bandar-e Torkeman, *Iran* 71 B7
Bandar Lampung = Tanjungkarang Telukbetung, *Indonesia* 62 F3
Bandar Maharani = Muar, *Malaysia* 65 L4
Bandar Penggaram = Batu Pahat, *Malaysia* 65 M4
Bandar Seri Begawan, *Brunei* 62 C4
Bandar Sri Aman, *Malaysia* 62 D4
Bandawe, *Malawi* 87 E3
Bande, *Spain* 36 C3
Bandeira, Pico da, *Brazil* 127 A7
Bandera, *Argentina* 126 B3
Banderas, B. de, *Mexico* 118 C3
Bandhogarh, *India* 69 H9
Bandi →, *India* 68 F6
Bandiagara, *Mali* 82 C4
Bandikui, *India* 68 F7
Bandırma, *Turkey* 45 F11
Bandjarmasin = Banjarmasin, *Indonesia* 62 E4
Bandol, *France* 21 E9
Bandon, *Ireland* 12 E3
Bandon →, *Ireland* 12 E3
Bandula, *Mozam.* 87 F3
Bandundu, *Dem. Rep. of the Congo* 84 E3
Bandung, *Indonesia* 63 G12
Bané, *Burkina Faso* 83 C4
Băneasa, *Romania* 29 E12
Bāneh, *Iran* 70 C5
Bañeres, *Spain* 39 G4
Banes, *Cuba* 121 B4
Banff, *Canada* 102 C5
Banff, *U.K.* 13 D6
Banff △, *Canada* 102 C5
Banfora, *Burkina Faso* 82 C4
Bang Fai →, *Laos* 64 D5
Bang Hieng →, *Laos* 64 D5
Bang Krathum, *Thailand* 64 D3
Bang Lamung, *Thailand* 64 F3
Bang Mun Nak, *Thailand* 64 D3
Bang Pa In, *Thailand* 64 E3
Bang Rakam, *Thailand* 64 D3
Bang Saphan, *Thailand* 65 G2
Bang Thao, *Thailand* 65 a
Bangaduni I., *India* 69 J13
Bangala Dam, *Zimbabwe* 87 G3
Bangalore, *India* 66 N10
Banganga →, *India* 68 F6
Bangangté, *Cameroon* 83 D7
Bangaon, *India* 69 H13
Bangassou, *C.A.R.* 84 D4
Banggai, *Indonesia* 63 E6
Banggai, Kepulauan, *Indonesia* 63 E6
Banggai Arch. = Banggai, Kepulauan, *Indonesia* 63 E6
Banggi, *Malaysia* 62 C5
Banghāzī, *Libya* 79 B10
Bangjang, *Sudan* 81 E3
Bangka, *Sulawesi, Indonesia* 63 D7
Bangka, *Sumatera, Indonesia* 62 E3
Bangka, Selat, *Indonesia* 62 E3
Bangka-Belitung □, *Indonesia* 62 E3
Bangkalan, *Indonesia* 63 G15
Bangkinang, *Indonesia* 62 D2
Bangko, *Indonesia* 62 E2
Bangkok, *Thailand* 64 F3
Bangladesh ■, *Asia* 67 H17
Bangli, *Indonesia* 63 J18
Bangolo, *Ivory C.* 82 D3
Bangong Co, *India* 69 B8
Bangor, *Down, U.K.* 12 B6
Bangor, *Gwynedd, U.K.* 14 D3
Bangor, *Maine, U.S.A.* 101 D13
Bangor, *Pa., U.S.A.* 117 F9
Bangued, *Phil.* 61 C4
Bangui, *C.A.R.* 84 D3
Bangui, *Phil.* 61 B4
Banguru, *Dem. Rep. of the Congo* 86 B2
Bangweulu, L., *Zambia* 87 E3
Bangweulu Swamp, *Zambia* 87 E3
Banhine △, *Mozam.* 89 C5
Baní, *Dom. Rep.* 121 C5
Bani →, *Mali* 82 C4
Bani Bangou, *Niger* 83 B5
Banī Sa'd, *Iraq* 70 C5
Bania, *Ivory C.* 82 D4
Banihal Pass, *India* 69 C6
Banikoara, *Benin* 83 C5
Bāniyās, *Syria* 70 C3
Banja Luka, *Bos.-H.* 28 F2
Banjar, *India* 68 D7
Banjar →, *India* 69 H9
Banjarmasin, *Indonesia* 62 E4
Banjul, *Gambia* 82 C1
Banka, *India* 69 G12
Bankas, *Mali* 82 C4
Bankeryd, *Sweden* 11 G8
Banket, *Zimbabwe* 87 F3
Bankilaré, *Niger* 83 C5
Bankipore, *India* 67 G14
Banks I., *B.C., Canada* 102 C3
Banks I., *N.W.T., Canada* 100 A7
Banks Pen., *N.Z.* 91 K4
Banks Str., *Australia* 95 G4
Bankura, *India* 69 H12
Bankya, *Bulgaria* 44 D7
Banmankhi, *India* 69 G12
Bann →, *Arm., U.K.* 12 B5
Bann →, *L'derry., U.K.* 12 A5
Bannalec, *France* 18 E3
Bannang Sata, *Thailand* 65 J3
Banning, *U.S.A.* 111 M10
Banno, *Ethiopia* 81 G4
Bannockburn, *Canada* 116 B7
Bannockburn, *U.K.* 13 E5
Bannockburn, *Zimbabwe* 87 G2
Bannu, *Pakistan* 66 C7
Bano, *India* 69 H11
Bañolas = Banyoles, *Spain* 38 C7
Banon, *France* 21 D9
Baños de la Encina, *Spain* 37 G7
Baños de Molgas, *Spain* 36 C3
Bánovce nad Bebravou, *Slovak Rep.* 27 C11
Banovići, *Bos.-H.* 28 F3
Bansgaon, *India* 69 F10
Banská Bystrica, *Slovak Rep.* 27 C12
Banská Štiavnica, *Slovak Rep.* 27 C11
Bansko, *Bulgaria* 44 E7
Banskobystrický □, *Slovak Rep.* 27 C12
Banswara, *India* 68 H6
Banteang, *Indonesia* 63 F5
Bantaji, *Nigeria* 83 D7
Bantayan, *Phil.* 61 F5
Banten □, *Indonesia* 63 G11
Bantry, *Ireland* 12 E2
Bantry B., *Ireland* 12 E2
Bantul, *Indonesia* 63 G14
Bantva, *India* 68 J4
Banya, *Bulgaria* 45 D8
Banyak, Kepulauan, *Indonesia* 62 D1
Banyalbufar, *Spain* 48 B9
Banyo, *Cameroon* 83 D7
Banyoles, *Spain* 38 C7
Banyuls-sur-Mer, *France* 20 F7
Banyumas, *Indonesia* 63 G13
Banyuwangi, *Indonesia* 63 J17
Banzare Coast, *Antarctica* 5 C9
Bao Ha, *Vietnam* 58 F5
Bao Lac, *Vietnam* 64 A5
Bao Loc, *Vietnam* 65 G6
Bao'an = Shenzhen, *China* 59 F10
Baocheng, *China* 56 H4
Baode, *China* 56 E6
Baodi, *China* 57 E9
Baoding, *China* 56 E8
Baoji, *China* 56 G4
Baojing, *China* 58 C7
Baokang, *China* 59 B8
Baoshan, *Shanghai, China* 59 B13
Baoshan, *Yunnan, China* 58 E2
Baotou, *China* 56 D6
Baoxing, *China* 58 B4
Baoying, *China* 57 H10
Bap, *India* 68 F5
Bapatla, *India* 67 M12
Bapaume, *France* 19 B9
Bāqerābād, *Iran* 71 C6
Ba'qūbah, *Iraq* 70 C5
Baquedano, *Chile* 126 A2
Bar, *Serbia & M.* 44 D3
Bar, *Ukraine* 33 H4
Bar Bigha, *India* 69 G11
Bar Harbor, *U.S.A.* 115 C11
Bar-le-Duc, *France* 19 D12
Bar-sur-Aube, *France* 19 D11
Bar-sur-Seine, *France* 19 D11
Bara, *India* 69 G9
Bâra, *Romania* 29 C12
Bara Banki, *India* 69 F9
Barabai, *Indonesia* 62 E5
Baraboo, *U.S.A.* 112 D10
Baracoa, *Cuba* 121 B5
Baradā →, *Syria* 74 B5
Baradero, *Argentina* 126 C4
Baraga, *U.S.A.* 112 B10
Bărăganul, *Romania* 29 F12
Barah →, *India* 68 F6
Barahona, *Dom. Rep.* 121 C5
Barahona, *Spain* 38 D2
Barail Range, *India* 67 G18
Barajas, Madrid ✕ (MAD), *Spain* 36 E7
Baraka, *Sudan* 81 E2
Baraka →, *Sudan* 80 D4
Barakaldo, *Spain* 38 B2
Barakar →, *India* 69 G12
Barakhola, *India* 67 G18
Barakot, *India* 69 J11
Barakpur, *India* 69 H13
Baralaba, *Australia* 94 C4
Baralla, *Spain* 36 C3
Baralzon L., *Canada* 103 B9
Barameiya, *Sudan* 80 D4
Baramula, *India* 69 B6
Baran, *India* 68 G7
Baran →, *Pakistan* 68 G3
Barañain, *Spain* 38 C3
Baranavichy, *Belarus* 33 F4
Barani, *Burkina Faso* 82 C4
Baranof, *U.S.A.* 102 B2
Baranof I., *U.S.A.* 100 C6
Baranów Sandomierski, *Poland* 31 H8
Baranya □, *Hungary* 28 E3
Baraolt, *Romania* 29 D10
Barapasi, *Indonesia* 63 E9
Barasat, *India* 69 H13
Barat Daya, Kepulauan, *Indonesia* 63 F7
Barataria B., *U.S.A.* 113 L10
Barauda, *India* 68 H6
Baraut, *India* 68 E7
Barbacena, *Brazil* 127 A7
Barbados ■, *W. Indies* 121 g
Barban, *Croatia* 41 C11
Barbària, C. de, *Spain* 48 C7
Barbaros, *Turkey* 45 F11
Barbastro, *Spain* 38 C5
Barbate de Franco, *Spain* 37 J5
Barberino di Mugello, *Italy* 41 E8
Barberton, *S. Africa* 89 D5
Barberton, *U.S.A.* 116 E3
Barbezieux-St-Hilaire, *France* 20 C3
Barbosa, *Colombia* 124 B4
Barbourville, *U.S.A.* 115 G4
Barbuda, *W. Indies* 121 C7
Bârca, *Romania* 29 G8
Barcaldine, *Australia* 94 C4
Barcarrota, *Spain* 37 G4
Barcellona Pozzo di Gotto, *Italy* 43 D8
Barcelona, *Spain* 38 D7
Barcelona, *Venezuela* 124 A6
Barcelona □, *Spain* 38 D7
Barcelona ✕ (BCN), *Spain* 38 D7
Barceloneta, *Puerto Rico* 121 d
Barcelonette, *France* 21 D10
Barcelos, *Brazil* 124 D6
Barcin, *Poland* 31 F4
Barclayville, *Liberia* 82 E3
Barcoo →, *Australia* 94 D3
Barcs, *Hungary* 28 E2
Barczewo, *Poland* 30 E7
Bärdä, *Azerbaijan* 35 K8
Bardaï, *Chad* 79 D9
Bardas Blancas, *Argentina* 126 D2
Bardawîl, Sabkhet el, *Egypt* 74 D2
Barddhaman, *India* 69 H12
Bardejov, *Slovak Rep.* 27 B14
Bardera, *Somali Rep.* 75 G3
Bardi, *Italy* 40 D6
Bardīyah, *Libya* 79 B10
Bardolino, *Italy* 40 C7
Bardonécchia, *Italy* 40 C3
Bardsey I., *U.K.* 14 E3
Bardstown, *U.S.A.* 114 G3
Bareilly, *India* 69 E8
Barela, *India* 69 H9
Barentin, *France* 18 C7
Barenton, *France* 18 D6
Barents Sea, *Arctic* 50 B7
Barentu, *Eritrea* 81 D4
Barfleur, *France* 18 C5
Barfleur, Pte. de, *France* 18 C5
Barga, *Italy* 40 D7
Bargara, *Australia* 94 C5
Bargas, *Spain* 36 F6
Bârgăului Bistriţa, *Romania* 29 C9
Barge, *Italy* 40 D4
Bargnop, *Sudan* 81 F2
Bargteheide, *Germany* 24 B6
Barguzin, *Russia* 53 D11
Barh, *India* 69 G11
Barhaj, *India* 69 F10
Barharwa, *India* 69 G12
Barhi, *India* 69 G11
Bari, *India* 68 F7
Bari, *Italy* 43 A9
Bari Doab, *Pakistan* 68 D5
Bari Sadri, *India* 68 G6
Bari Sardo, *Italy* 42 C2
Barīdī, Ra's, *Si. Arabia* 70 E3
Barīm, *Yemen* 76 E8
Barinas, *Venezuela* 124 B4
Baring, C., *Canada* 100 B8
Baringo, L., *Kenya* 86 B4
Bârîs, *Egypt* 80 C3
Barisal, *Bangla.* 67 H17
Barisal □, *Bangla.* 67 H17
Barisan, Bukit, *Indonesia* 62 E2
Barito →, *Indonesia* 62 E4
Baritú △, *Argentina* 126 A3
Barjac, *France* 21 D8
Barjols, *France* 21 E10
Bark L., *Canada* 116 A7
Barka = Baraka →, *Sudan* 80 D4
Barkakana, *India* 69 H11
Barkam, *China* 58 B4
Barker, *U.S.A.* 116 C6
Barkley, L., *U.S.A.* 115 G2
Barkley Sound, *Canada* 102 D3
Barkly East, *S. Africa* 88 E4
Barkly Roadhouse, *Australia* 94 B2
Barkly Tableland, *Australia* 94 B2
Barkly West, *S. Africa* 88 D3
Barkol, Wadi →, *Sudan* 80 D3
Barla Dağı, *Turkey* 47 C12
Bârlad, *Romania* 29 D12
Bârlad →, *Romania* 29 E12
Barlee, L., *Australia* 93 E2
Barlee, Mt., *Australia* 93 D4
Barletta, *Italy* 43 A9
Barlinek, *Poland* 31 F2
Barlovento, *Canary Is.* 48 F2
Barlow L., *Canada* 103 A8
Barmedman, *Australia* 95 E4
Barmer, *India* 68 G4
Barmera, *Australia* 95 E3
Barmouth, *U.K.* 14 E3
Barmstedt, *Germany* 24 B5
Barna →, *India* 69 G10
Barnagar, *India* 68 H6
Barnala, *India* 68 D6
Barnard Castle, *U.K.* 14 C6
Barnaul, *Russia* 52 D9
Barnesville, *U.S.A.* 115 J3
Barnet □, *U.K.* 15 F7
Barneveld, *Neths.* 17 B5
Barneveld, *U.S.A.* 117 C9
Barneville-Cartevert, *France* 18 C5
Barnhart, *U.S.A.* 113 K4
Barnsley, *U.K.* 14 D6
Barnstaple, *U.K.* 15 F3
Barnstaple Bay = Bideford Bay, *U.K.* 15 F3
Barnsville, *U.S.A.* 112 B6
Barnwell, *U.S.A.* 115 J5
Baro, *Nigeria* 83 D6
Baro →, *Ethiopia* 81 F3
Baroda = Vadodara, *India* 68 H5
Baroda, *India* 68 G7
Baroe, *S. Africa* 88 E3
Baron Ra., *Australia* 92 D4
Barong, *China* 58 B2
Barotseland, *Zambia* 85 H4
Barouéli, *Mali* 82 C3
Barpeta, *India* 67 F17
Barques, Pt. Aux, *U.S.A.* 116 B2
Barquísimeto, *Venezuela* 124 A5
Barr, Ras el, *Egypt* 80 H7
Barr Smith Range, *Australia* 93 E3
Barra, *Brazil* 125 F10
Barra, *U.K.* 13 E1
Barra, Sd. of, *U.K.* 13 D1
Barra de Navidad, *Mexico* 118 D4
Barra do Corda, *Brazil* 125 E9
Barra do Piraí, *Brazil* 127 A7
Barra Falsa, Pta. da, *Mozam.* 89 C6
Barra Hd., *U.K.* 13 E1
Barra Mansa, *Brazil* 127 A7
Barraba, *Australia* 95 E5
Barrackpur = Barakpur, *India* 69 H13
Barradale Roadhouse, *Australia* 92 D1
Barrafranca, *Italy* 43 E7
Barraigh = Barra, *U.K.* 13 E1
Barranca, *Lima, Peru* 124 F3
Barranca, *Loreto, Peru* 124 D3
Barranca del Cobre ⌂, *Mexico* 118 B3
Barrancabermeja, *Colombia* 124 B4
Barrancas, *Venezuela* 124 B6
Barrancos, *Portugal* 37 G4
Barranqueras, *Argentina* 126 B4
Barranquilla, *Colombia* 124 A4
Barraute, *Canada* 104 C4
Barre, *Mass., U.S.A.* 117 D12
Barre, *Vt., U.S.A.* 117 B12
Barreal, *Argentina* 126 C2
Barreiras, *Brazil* 125 F10
Barreirinhas, *Brazil* 125 D10
Barreiro, *Portugal* 37 G1
Barrême, *France* 21 E10
Barren, Nosy, *Madag.* 89 B7
Barretos, *Brazil* 125 H9
Barrhead, *Canada* 102 C6
Barrie, *Canada* 116 B5
Barrier Ra., *Australia* 95 E3
Barrière, *Canada* 102 C4
Barrington, *U.S.A.* 117 E13
Barrington L., *Canada* 103 B8
Barrington Tops, *Australia* 95 E5
Barringun, *Australia* 95 D4
Barro do Garças, *Brazil* 125 G8
Barron, *U.S.A.* 112 C9
Barrow, *U.S.A.* 100 A4
Barrow →, *Ireland* 12 D5
Barrow Creek, *Australia* 94 C1
Barrow I., *Australia* 92 D2
Barrow-in-Furness, *U.K.* 14 C4
Barrow Pt., *Australia* 94 A3
Barrow Pt., *U.S.A.* 98 B4
Barrow Ra., *Australia* 93 E4
Barrow Str., *Canada* 4 B3
Barruecopardo, *Spain* 36 D4
Barruelo de Santullán, *Spain* 36 C6
Barry, *U.K.* 15 F4
Barry's Bay, *Canada* 116 A7
Barsalogho, *Burkina Faso* 83 C4
Barsat, *Pakistan* 69 A5
Barsham, *Syria* 70 C4
Barsi, *India* 66 K9
Barsinghausen, *Germany* 24 C5
Barsoi, *India* 67 G15
Barstow, *U.S.A.* 111 L9
Barth, *Germany* 24 A8
Barthélemy, Col, *Vietnam* 64 C5
Bartica, *Guyana* 124 B7
Bartin, *Turkey* 72 B5
Bartle Frere, *Australia* 94 B4
Bartlesville, *U.S.A.* 113 G7
Bartlett, *U.S.A.* 110 J8
Bartlett, L., *Canada* 102 A5
Bartolomeu Dias, *Mozam.* 87 G4
Barton, *U.S.A.* 117 B12
Barton upon Humber, *U.K.* 14 D7
Bartoszyce, *Poland* 30 D7
Bartow, *U.S.A.* 115 M5
Barú, Volcan, *Panama* 120 E3
Barumba, *Dem. Rep. of the Congo* 86 B1
Baruth, *Germany* 24 C9
Baruunsuu, *Mongolia* 56 C3
Barvinkove, *Ukraine* 33 H9
Barwani, *India* 68 H6
Barwice, *Poland* 30 E3
Barycz →, *Poland* 31 G3
Barysaw, *Belarus* 32 E5
Barysh, *Russia* 34 D8
Barzān, *Iraq* 70 B5
Bârzava, *Romania* 28 D6
Bas-Rhin □, *France* 19 D14
Bašaid, *Serbia & M.* 28 E5
Bāsa'idū, *Iran* 71 E7
Basal, *Pakistan* 68 C5
Basankusa, *Dem. Rep. of the Congo* 84 D3
Basarabeasca, *Moldova* 29 D13
Basarabi, *Romania* 29 F13
Basarabia = Bessarabiya, *Moldova* 33 J5
Basauri, *Spain* 38 B2
Basawa, *Afghan.* 68 B4
Bascuñán, C., *Chile* 126 B1
Basel, *Switz.* 25 H3
Basel, Euroairport ✕ (BSL), *Europe* 19 E14
Basel-Landschaft □, *Switz.* 25 H3
Basento →, *Italy* 43 B9
Bashākerd, Kūhhā-ye, *Iran* 71 E8
Bashaw, *Canada* 102 C6
Bāshī, *Iran* 71 D6
Bashkir Republic = Bashkortostan □, *Russia* 52 D6
Bashkortostan □, *Russia* 52 D6
Bashtanivka, *Ukraine* 29 E14
Basibasy, *Madag.* 89 C7
Basilan I., *Phil.* 61 H5
Basilan Str., *Phil.* 61 H5
Basildon, *U.K.* 15 F8
Basile, *Eq. Guin.* 83 E6
Basilicata □, *Italy* 43 B9
Basim = Washim, *India* 66 J10
Basin, *U.S.A.* 108 D9
Basingstoke, *U.K.* 15 F6
Baška, *Croatia* 41 D11
Başkale, *Turkey* 73 C10
Baskatong, Rés., *Canada* 104 C4
Basle = Basel, *Switz.* 25 H3
Başmakçı, *Turkey* 47 D12
Basoda, *India* 68 H7
Basoko, *Dem. Rep. of the Congo* 86 B1
Basque, Pays, *France* 20 E2
Basque Provinces = País Vasco □, *Spain* 38 C2
Basra = Al Başrah, *Iraq* 70 D5
Bass Str., *Australia* 95 F4
Bassano, *Canada* 102 C6
Bassano del Grappa, *Italy* 41 C8
Bassar, *Togo* 83 D5
Bassas da India, *Ind. Oc.* 85 J7
Basse-Normandie □, *France* 18 D6
Basse-Pointe, *Martinique* 120 c
Basse Santa-Su, *Gambia* 82 C2
Basse-Terre, *Guadeloupe* 120 b
Basse Terre, *Trin. & Tob.* 125 K15
Bassein, *Burma* 67 L19
Basses, Pte. des, *Guadeloupe* 120 b
Basseterre, *St. Kitts & Nevis* 121 C7
Bassett, *U.S.A.* 112 D5
Bassi, *India* 68 D7
Bassigny, *France* 19 E12
Bassikounou, *Mauritania* 82 B3
Bassila, *Benin* 83 D5
Bassum, *Germany* 24 C4
Båstad, *Sweden* 11 H6
Bastak, *Iran* 71 E7
Baştām, *Iran* 71 B7
Bastar, *India* 67 K12
Bastelica, *France* 21 F13
Basti, *India* 69 F10
Bastia, *France* 21 F13
Bastogne, *Belgium* 17 D5
Bastrop, *La., U.S.A.* 113 J9
Bastrop, *Tex., U.S.A.* 113 K6
Bat Yam, *Israel* 74 C3
Bata, *Eq. Guin.* 84 D1
Bata, *Romania* 28 D7
Bataan □, *Phil.* 61 D4
Batabanó, *Cuba* 120 B3
Batabanó, G. de, *Cuba* 120 B3
Batac, *Phil.* 61 B4
Batagai, *Russia* 53 C14
Batajnica, *Serbia & M.* 44 B4
Batak, *Bulgaria* 45 E8
Batala, *India* 68 D6
Batalha, *Portugal* 36 F2
Batama, *Dem. Rep. of the Congo* 86 B2
Batamay, *Russia* 53 C13
Batang, *China* 58 B2
Batang, *Indonesia* 63 G13
Batangas, *Phil.* 61 E4
Batanta, *Indonesia* 63 E8
Batatais, *Brazil* 127 A6
Batavia, *U.S.A.* 116 D6
Bataysk, *Russia* 33 J10
Batchelor, *Australia* 92 B5
Batdambang, *Cambodia* 64 F4

Batemans B., *Australia* 95 F5
Batemans Bay, *Australia* 95 F5
Bates Ra., *Australia* 93 E3
Batesburg-Leesville, *U.S.A.* 115 J5
Batesville, *Ark., U.S.A.* 113 H9
Batesville, *Miss., U.S.A.* 113 H10
Batesville, *Tex., U.S.A.* 113 L5
Bath, *Canada* 117 B8
Bath, *U.K.* 15 F5
Bath, *Maine, U.S.A.* 115 D11
Bath, *N.Y., U.S.A.* 116 D7
Bath & North East Somerset □, *U.K.* 15 F5
Batheay, *Cambodia* 65 G5
Bathsheba, *Barbados* 121 g
Bathurst, *Australia* 95 E4
Bathurst, *Canada* 105 C6
Bathurst, *S. Africa* 88 E4
Bathurst, C., *Canada* 100 A7
Bathurst B., *Australia* 94 A3
Bathurst Harb., *Australia* 95 G4
Bathurst I., *Australia* 92 B5
Bathurst I., *Canada* 98 B9
Bathurst Inlet, *Canada* 100 B9
Bati, *Ethiopia* 81 E5
Batie, *Burkina Faso* 82 D4
Batlow, *Australia* 95 F4
Batman, *Turkey* 70 B4
Baṭn al Ghūl, *Jordan* 74 F4
Batna, *Algeria* 78 A7
Batobato = San Isidro, *Phil.* 61 H7
Batočina, *Serbia & M.* 44 B5
Batoka, *Zambia* 87 F2
Baton Rouge, *U.S.A.* 113 K9
Batong, Ko, *Thailand* 65 J2
Bátonyterenye, *Hungary* 28 C4
Batopilas, *Mexico* 118 B3
Batouri, *Cameroon* 84 D2
Båtsfjord, *Norway* 8 A23
Battambang = Batdambang, *Cambodia* 64 F4
Batticaloa, *Sri Lanka* 66 R12
Battipáglia, *Italy* 43 B7
Battle, *U.K.* 15 G8
Battle →, *Canada* 103 C7
Battle Creek, *U.S.A.* 114 D3
Battle Ground, *U.S.A.* 110 E4
Battle Harbour, *Canada* 105 B8
Battle Lake, *U.S.A.* 112 B7
Battle Mountain, *U.S.A.* 108 F5
Battlefields, *Zimbabwe* 87 F2
Battleford, *Canada* 103 C7
Battonya, *Hungary* 28 D6
Batu, *Ethiopia* 81 F4
Batu, Kepulauan, *Indonesia* 62 E1
Batu Caves, *Malaysia* 65 L3
Batu Ferringhi, *Malaysia* 65 c
Batu Gajah, *Malaysia* 65 K3
Batu Is. = Batu, Kepulauan, *Indonesia* 62 E1
Batu Pahat, *Malaysia* 65 M4
Batuata, *Indonesia* 63 F6
Batugondang, Tanjung, *Indonesia* 63 J17
Batukau, Gunung, *Indonesia* 63 J18
Batumi, *Georgia* 35 K5
Batur, *Indonesia* 63 J18
Batur, Gunung, *Indonesia* 63 J18
Baturaja, *Indonesia* 62 E2
Baturité, *Brazil* 125 D11
Baturiti, *Indonesia* 63 J18
Bau, *Malaysia* 62 D4
Baubau, *Indonesia* 63 F6
Baucau, *E. Timor* 63 F7
Bauchi, *Nigeria* 83 C6
Bauchi □, *Nigeria* 83 C7
Baud, *France* 18 E3
Baudette, *U.S.A.* 112 A7
Bauer, C., *Australia* 95 E1
Bauhinia, *Australia* 94 C4
Baukau = Baucau, *E. Timor* 63 F7
Bauld, C., *Canada* 101 C14
Baume-les-Dames, *France* 19 E13
Baunatal, *Germany* 24 D5
Baunei, *Italy* 42 B2
Baure, *Nigeria* 83 C6
Bauru, *Brazil* 127 A6
Bausi, *India* 69 G12
Bauska, *Latvia* 9 H21
Bautino, *Kazakhstan* 35 H10
Bautzen, *Germany* 24 D10
Bauya, *S. Leone* 82 D2
Bavānāt, *Iran* 71 D7
Bavanište, *Serbia & M.* 28 F5
Bavaria = Bayern □, *Germany* 25 G7
Båven, *Sweden* 10 E10
Bavispe →, *Mexico* 118 B3
Bawdwin, *Burma* 67 H20
Bawean, *Indonesia* 62 F4
Bawku, *Ghana* 83 C4
Bawlake, *Burma* 67 K20
Bawolung, *China* 58 C3
Baxley, *U.S.A.* 115 K4
Baxoi, *China* 58 B1
Baxter, *U.S.A.* 112 B7
Baxter Springs, *U.S.A.* 113 G7
Baxter State ⌂, *U.S.A.* 115 B11
Bay, L. de, *Phil.* 61 D4
Bay City, *Mich., U.S.A.* 114 D4
Bay City, *Tex., U.S.A.* 113 L7
Bay Minette, *U.S.A.* 115 K2
Bay Roberts, *Canada* 105 C9
Bay St. Louis, *U.S.A.* 113 K10
Bay Springs, *U.S.A.* 113 K10
Bay View, *N.Z.* 91 H6
Baya, *Dem. Rep. of the Congo* 87 E2
Bayamo, *Cuba* 120 B4
Bayamón, *Puerto Rico* 121 d
Bayan Har Shan, *China* 60 C4
Bayan Hot = Alxa Zuoqi, *China* 56 E3
Bayan Lepas, *Malaysia* 65 c
Bayan Obo, *China* 56 D5
Bayan-Ovoo = Erdenetsogt, *Mongolia* 56 C4
Bayana, *India* 68 F7
Bayanaūyl, *Kazakhstan* 52 D8
Bayandalay, *Mongolia* 56 C2
Bayanhongor, *Mongolia* 60 B5
Bayard, *N. Mex., U.S.A.* 109 K9
Bayard, *Nebr., U.S.A.* 112 E3
Bayawan, *Phil.* 61 G5
Baybay, *Phil.* 61 F6
Bayburt, *Turkey* 73 B9
Baydhabo = Baidoa, *Somali Rep.* 75 G3
Bayelsa □, *Nigeria* 83 E6
Bayerische Alpen, *Germany* 25 H7
Bayerische Rhön ⌂, *Germany* 25 E6
Bayerischer Spessart ⌂, *Germany* 25 F6
Bayerischer Wald, *Germany* 25 G8
Bayern □, *Germany* 25 G7
Bayeux, *France* 18 C6
Bayfield, *Canada* 116 C3
Bayfield, *U.S.A.* 112 B9
Bayındır, *Turkey* 47 C9
Bayjī, *Iraq* 70 C4
Baykal, Oz., *Russia* 53 D11
Baykan, *Turkey* 70 B4
Baykonur = Bayqongyr, *Kazakhstan* 52 E7
Baynes Mts., *Namibia* 88 B1
Bayombong, *Phil.* 61 C4
Bayon, *France* 19 D13
Bayona = Baiona, *Spain* 36 C2
Bayonne, *France* 20 E2
Bayonne, *U.S.A.* 117 F10
Bayovar, *Peru* 124 E2
Bayqongyr, *Kazakhstan* 52 E7
Bayram-Ali = Bayramaly, *Turkmenistan* 52 F7
Bayramaly, *Turkmenistan* 52 F7
Bayramiç, *Turkey* 47 B8
Bayreuth, *Germany* 25 F7
Bayrischzell, *Germany* 25 H8
Bayrūt, *Lebanon* 74 B4
Bays, L. of, *Canada* 116 A5
Baysville, *Canada* 116 A5
Bayt Lahm, *West Bank* 74 D4
Baytown, *U.S.A.* 113 L7
Bayun, *Indonesia* 63 J18
Bayzo, *Niger* 83 C5
Baza, *Spain* 37 H8
Bazar Dyuzi, *Russia* 35 K8
Bazardüzü = Bazar Dyuzi, *Russia* 35 K8
Bazarny Karabulak, *Russia* 34 D8
Bazarnyy Syzgan, *Russia* 34 D8
Bazaruto △, *Mozam.* 89 C6
Bazaruto, I. do, *Mozam.* 89 C6
Bazas, *France* 20 D3
Bazhong, *China* 58 B6
Bazhou, *China* 56 E9
Bazmān, Kūh-e, *Iran* 71 D9
Beach, *U.S.A.* 112 B3
Beach City, *U.S.A.* 116 F3
Beachport, *Australia* 95 F3
Beachy Hd., *U.K.* 15 G8
Beacon, *Australia* 93 F2
Beacon, *U.S.A.* 117 E11
Beaconsfield, *Australia* 95 G4
Beagle, Canal, *S. Amer.* 128 H3
Beagle Bay, *Australia* 92 C3
Bealanana, *Madag.* 89 A8
Beals Cr. →, *U.S.A.* 113 J4
Beamsville, *Canada* 116 C5
Bear →, *Calif., U.S.A.* 110 G5
Bear →, *Utah, U.S.A.* 106 B4
Béar, C., *France* 20 F7
Bear I., *Ireland* 12 E2
Bear L., *Canada* 103 B9
Bear L., *U.S.A.* 108 F8
Beardmore, *Canada* 104 C2
Beardmore Glacier, *Antarctica* 5 E11
Beardstown, *U.S.A.* 112 F9
Bearma →, *India* 69 G8
Béarn, *France* 20 E3
Bearpaw Mts., *U.S.A.* 108 B9
Bearskin Lake, *Canada* 104 B1
Beas →, *India* 68 D6
Beas de Segura, *Spain* 37 G8
Beasain, *Spain* 38 B2
Beata, C., *Dom. Rep.* 121 C5
Beata, I., *Dom. Rep.* 121 C5
Beatrice, *U.S.A.* 112 E6
Beatrice, *Zimbabwe* 87 F3
Beatrice, C., *Australia* 94 A2
Beatton →, *Canada* 102 B4
Beatton River, *Canada* 102 B4
Beatty, *U.S.A.* 110 J10
Beaucaire, *France* 21 E8
Beauce, Plaine de la, *France* 19 D8
Beauceville, *Canada* 105 C5
Beaudesert, *Australia* 95 D5
Beaufort, *France* 21 C10
Beaufort, *Malaysia* 62 C5
Beaufort, *N.C., U.S.A.* 115 H7
Beaufort, *S.C., U.S.A.* 115 J5
Beaufort Sea, *Arctic* 98 B5
Beaufort West, *S. Africa* 88 E3
Beaugency, *France* 19 E8
Beauharnois, *Canada* 117 A11
Beaujeu, *France* 19 F11
Beaujolais, *France* 19 F11
Beaulieu →, *Canada* 102 A6
Beaulieu-sur-Dordogne, *France* 20 D5
Beaulieu-sur-Mer, *France* 21 E11
Beauly, *U.K.* 13 D4
Beauly →, *U.K.* 13 D4
Beaumaris, *U.K.* 14 D3
Beaumont, *Belgium* 17 D4
Beaumont, *France* 20 D4
Beaumont, *U.S.A.* 113 K7
Beaumont-de-Lomagne, *France* 20 E5
Beaumont-le-Roger, *France* 18 C7
Beaumont-sur-Sarthe, *France* 18 D7
Beaune, *France* 19 E11
Beaune-la-Rolande, *France* 19 D9
Beaupré, *Canada* 105 C5
Beaupréau, *France* 18 E6
Beauraing, *Belgium* 17 D4
Beaurepaire, *France* 21 C9
Beausejour, *Canada* 103 C9
Beauvais, *France* 19 C9
Beauval, *Canada* 103 B7
Beauvoir-sur-Mer, *France* 18 F4
Beauvoir-sur-Niort, *France* 20 B3
Beaver, *Okla., U.S.A.* 113 G4
Beaver, *Pa., U.S.A.* 116 F4
Beaver, *Utah, U.S.A.* 109 G7
Beaver →, *B.C., Canada* 102 B4
Beaver →, *Ont., Canada* 104 A2
Beaver →, *Sask., Canada* 103 B7
Beaver →, *U.S.A.* 113 G5
Beaver City, *U.S.A.* 112 E5
Beaver Creek, *Canada* 100 B5
Beaver Dam, *U.S.A.* 112 D10
Beaver Falls, *U.S.A.* 116 F4
Beaver Hill L., *Canada* 103 C10
Beaver I., *U.S.A.* 114 C3
Beaverhill L., *Canada* 102 C6
Beaverlodge, *Canada* 102 B5
Beaverstone →, *Canada* 104 B2
Beaverton, *Canada* 116 B5
Beaverton, *U.S.A.* 110 E4
Beawar, *India* 68 F6
Bebedouro, *Brazil* 127 A6
Bebera, Tanjung, *Indonesia* 63 K18
Beboa, *Madag.* 89 B7
Bebra, *Germany* 24 E5
Becan, *Mexico* 119 D7
Beccles, *U.K.* 15 E9
Bečej, *Serbia & M.* 28 E5
Beceni, *Romania* 29 E11
Becerreá, *Spain* 36 C3
Béchar, *Algeria* 78 B5
Bechyně, *Czech Rep.* 26 B7
Beckley, *U.S.A.* 114 G5
Beckum, *Germany* 24 D4
Beclean, *Romania* 29 C9
Bečov nad Teplou, *Czech Rep.* 26 A5
Bečva →, *Czech Rep.* 27 B10
Bédar, *Spain* 39 H3
Bédarieux, *France* 20 E7
Beddouza, Ras, *Morocco* 78 B4
Bedele, *Ethiopia* 81 F4
Bederkesa, *Germany* 24 B4
Bedeso, *Ethiopia* 81 F5
Bedford, *Canada* 117 A12
Bedford, *S. Africa* 88 E4
Bedford, *U.K.* 15 E7
Bedford, *Ind., U.S.A.* 114 F2
Bedford, *Iowa, U.S.A.* 112 E7
Bedford, *Ohio, U.S.A.* 116 E3
Bedford, *Pa., U.S.A.* 116 F6
Bedford, *Va., U.S.A.* 114 G6
Bedford, C., *Australia* 94 B4
Bedfordshire □, *U.K.* 15 E7
Będków, *Poland* 31 G6
Bednja →, *Croatia* 41 B13
Bednodemyanovsk, *Russia* 34 D6
Bedok, *Singapore* 65 d
Bedónia, *Italy* 40 D6
Bedourie, *Australia* 94 C2
Bedum, *Neths.* 17 A6
Będzin, *Poland* 31 H6
Beebe Plain, *Canada* 117 A12
Beech Creek, *U.S.A.* 116 E7
Beef I., *Br. Virgin Is.* 121 e
Beelitz, *Germany* 24 C8
Beenleigh, *Australia* 95 D5
Be'er Menuha, *Israel* 70 D2
Be'er Sheva, *Israel* 74 D3
Beersheba = Be'er Sheva, *Israel* 74 D3
Beeskow, *Germany* 24 C10
Beestekraal, *S. Africa* 89 D4
Beeston, *U.K.* 14 E6
Beetzendorf, *Germany* 24 C7
Beeville, *U.S.A.* 113 L6
Befale, *Dem. Rep. of the Congo* 84 D4
Befandriana, *Mahajanga, Madag.* 89 B8
Befandriana, *Toliara, Madag.* 89 C7
Befasy, *Madag.* 89 C7
Befotaka, *Antsiranana, Madag.* 89 A8
Befotaka, *Fianarantsoa, Madag.* 89 C8
Bega, *Australia* 95 F4
Bega, Canalul, *Romania* 28 E5
Bégard, *France* 18 D3
Beğendik, *Turkey* 45 F10
Begoro, *Ghana* 83 D4
Begusarai, *India* 69 G12
Behābād, *Iran* 71 C8
Behala, *India* 69 H13
Behara, *Madag.* 89 C8
Behbehān, *Iran* 71 D6
Behm Canal, *U.S.A.* 102 B2
Behshahr, *Iran* 71 B7
Bei Jiang →, *China* 59 F9
Bei'an, *China* 60 B7
Beibei, *China* 58 C6
Beichuan, *China* 58 B5
Beihai, *China* 58 G7
Beijing, *China* 56 E9
Beijing □, *China* 56 E9
Beilen, *Neths.* 17 B6
Beiliu, *China* 59 F8
Beilngries, *Germany* 25 F7
Beilpajah, *Australia* 95 E3
Beilul, *Eritrea* 81 E5
Beinn na Faoghla = Benbecula, *U.K.* 13 D1
Beipan Jiang, *China* 58 E5
Beipiao, *China* 57 D11
Beira, *Mozam.* 87 F3
Beirut = Bayrūt, *Lebanon* 74 B4
Beiseker, *Canada* 102 C6
Beitaolaizhao, *China* 57 B13
Beitbridge, *Zimbabwe* 87 G3
Beiuş, *Romania* 28 D7
Beizhen = Binzhou, *China* 57 F10
Beizhen, *China* 57 D11
Beizhengzhen, *China* 57 B12
Beja, *Portugal* 37 G3
Béja, *Tunisia* 79 A7
Beja □, *Portugal* 37 H3
Bejaïa, *Algeria* 78 A7
Béjar, *Spain* 36 E5
Bejestān, *Iran* 71 C8
Bekaa Valley = Al Biqā, *Lebanon* 74 A5
Bekçiler, *Turkey* 47 E11
Békés, *Hungary* 28 D6
Békés □, *Hungary* 28 D6
Békéscsaba, *Hungary* 28 D6
Bekilli, *Turkey* 47 C11
Bekily, *Madag.* 89 C8
Bekisopa, *Madag.* 89 C8
Bekitro, *Madag.* 89 C8
Bekodoka, *Madag.* 89 B8
Bekoji, *Ethiopia* 81 F4
Bekok, *Malaysia* 65 L4
Bekopaka, *Madag.* 89 B7
Bekuli, *Indonesia* 63 J17
Bekwai, *Ghana* 83 D4
Bela, *India* 69 G10
Bela, *Pakistan* 68 F2
Bela Bela, *S. Africa* 89 C4
Bela Crkva, *Serbia & M.* 28 F6
Bela Palanka, *Serbia & M.* 44 C6
Bela Vista, *Brazil* 126 A4
Bela Vista, *Mozam.* 89 D5
Bélâbre, *France* 20 B5
Belalcázar, *Spain* 37 G5
Belan →, *India* 69 G9
Belanovica, *Serbia & M.* 44 B4
Belarus ■, *Europe* 32 F4
Belau = Palau ■, *Pac. Oc.* 96 G5
Belavenona, *Madag.* 89 C8
Belawan, *Indonesia* 62 D1
Belaya, *Ethiopia* 81 E4
Belaya Glina, *Russia* 35 G5
Belaya Kalitva, *Russia* 35 F5
Belaya Tserkov = Bila Tserkva, *Ukraine* 33 H6
Belceşti, *Romania* 29 C12
Bełchatów, *Poland* 31 G6
Belcher Is., *Canada* 104 A3
Belchite, *Spain* 38 D4
Belden, *U.S.A.* 110 E5
Beled Weyne = Belet Uen, *Somali Rep.* 75 G4
Belém, *Brazil* 125 D9
Belén, *Argentina* 126 B2
Belén, *Paraguay* 126 A4
Belen, *U.S.A.* 109 J10
Belene, *Bulgaria* 45 C9
Beleni, *Turkey* 72 D7
Bélesta, *France* 20 F5
Belet Uen, *Somali Rep.* 75 G4
Belev, *Russia* 32 F9
Belevi, *Turkey* 47 C9
Belfair, *U.S.A.* 110 C4
Belfast, *S. Africa* 89 D5
Belfast, *U.K.* 12 B6
Belfast, *Maine, U.S.A.* 115 C11
Belfast, *N.Y., U.S.A.* 116 D6
Belfast L., *U.K.* 12 B6
Belfield, *U.S.A.* 112 B3
Belfort, *France* 19 E13
Belfort, Territoire de □, *France* 19 E13
Belfry, *U.S.A.* 108 D9
Belgaum, *India* 66 M9
Belgioioso, *Italy* 40 C6
Belgium ■, *Europe* 17 D4
Belgodère, *France* 21 F13
Belgorod, *Russia* 33 G9
Belgorod-Dnestrovskiy = Bilhorod-Dnistrovskyy, *Ukraine* 33 J6
Belgrade = Beograd, *Serbia & M.* 44 B4
Belgrade, *U.S.A.* 108 D8
Belhaven, *U.S.A.* 115 H7
Beli Drim →, *Europe* 44 D4
Beli Manastir, *Croatia* 28 E3
Beli Timok →, *Serbia & M.* 44 C6
Bélice →, *Italy* 42 E5
Belimbing, *Indonesia* 63 J18
Belinskiy, *Russia* 34 D6
Belinyu, *Indonesia* 62 E3
Beliton Is. = Belitung, *Indonesia* 62 E3
Belitung, *Indonesia* 62 E3
Beliu, *Romania* 28 D6
Belize ■, *Cent. Amer.* 119 D7
Belize City, *Belize* 119 D7
Beljakovci, *Macedonia* 44 D5
Beljanica, *Serbia & M.* 44 B5
Belkovskiy, Ostrov, *Russia* 53 B14
Bell →, *Canada* 104 C4
Bell I., *Canada* 105 B8
Bell-Irving →, *Canada* 102 B3
Bell Peninsula, *Canada* 101 B11
Bell Ville, *Argentina* 126 C3
Bella, *Italy* 43 B8
Bella Bella, *Canada* 102 C3
Bella Coola, *Canada* 102 C3
Bella Unión, *Uruguay* 126 C4
Bella Vista, *Corrientes, Argentina* 126 B4
Bella Vista, *Tucuman, Argentina* 126 B2
Bellac, *France* 20 B5
Bellágio, *Italy* 40 C6
Bellaire, *U.S.A.* 116 F4
Bellária, *Italy* 41 D9
Bellary, *India* 66 M10
Bellata, *Australia* 95 D4
Belle-Chasse, *U.S.A.* 113 L10
Belle Fourche, *U.S.A.* 112 C3
Belle Fourche →, *U.S.A.* 112 C3
Belle Glade, *U.S.A.* 115 M5
Belle-Île, *France* 18 E3
Belle Isle, *Canada* 105 B8
Belle Isle, Str. of, *Canada* 105 B8
Belle Plaine, *U.S.A.* 112 E8
Belle Yella, *Liberia* 82 D3
Belledonne, *France* 21 C10
Bellefontaine, *U.S.A.* 114 E4
Bellefonte, *U.S.A.* 116 F7
Bellegarde, *France* 19 E9
Bellegarde-en-Marche, *France* 20 C6
Bellegarde-sur-Valserine, *France* 19 F12
Bellême, *France* 18 D7
Belleoram, *Canada* 105 C8
Belleplaine, *Barbados* 121 g
Belleville, *Canada* 116 B7
Belleville, *France* 19 F11
Belleville, *Ill., U.S.A.* 112 F10
Belleville, *Kans., U.S.A.* 112 F6
Belleville, *N.Y., U.S.A.* 117 C8
Belleville-sur-Vie, *France* 18 F5
Bellevue, *Canada* 102 D6
Bellevue, *Idaho, U.S.A.* 108 E6
Bellevue, *Nebr., U.S.A.* 112 E7
Bellevue, *Ohio, U.S.A.* 116 E2
Bellevue, *Wash., U.S.A.* 110 C4
Belley, *France* 21 C9
Bellin = Kangirsuk, *Canada* 101 B13
Bellinge, *Denmark* 11 J4
Bellingen, *Australia* 95 E5
Bellingham, *U.S.A.* 100 D7
Bellingshausen Sea, *Antarctica* 5 C17
Bellinzona, *Switz.* 25 J5
Bello, *Colombia* 124 B3
Bellows Falls, *U.S.A.* 117 C12
Bellpat, *Pakistan* 68 E3
Bellpuig d'Urgell, *Spain* 38 D6
Belluno, *Italy* 41 B9
Bellwood, *U.S.A.* 116 F6
Bélmez, *Spain* 37 G5
Belmont, *Canada* 116 D3
Belmont, *S. Africa* 88 D3
Belmont, *U.S.A.* 116 D6
Belmonte, *Brazil* 125 G11
Belmonte, *Portugal* 36 E3
Belmonte, *Spain* 39 F2
Belmopan, *Belize* 119 D7
Belmullet, *Ireland* 12 B2
Belo Horizonte, *Brazil* 125 G10
Belo-sur-Mer, *Madag.* 89 C7
Belo-Tsiribihina, *Madag.* 89 B7
Belogorsk = Bilohirsk, *Ukraine* 33 K8
Belogorsk, *Russia* 53 D13
Belogradchik, *Bulgaria* 44 C6
Belogradets, *Bulgaria* 45 C11
Beloha, *Madag.* 89 D8
Beloit, *Kans., U.S.A.* 112 F5
Beloit, *Wis., U.S.A.* 112 D10
Belokorovichi, *Ukraine* 33 G5
Belomorsk, *Russia* 52 C4
Belonia, *India* 67 H17
Belopolye = Bilopillya, *Ukraine* 33 G8
Belorechensk, *Russia* 35 H4
Belorussia = Belarus ■, *Europe* 32 F4
Beloslav, *Bulgaria* 45 C11
Belovo, *Bulgaria* 45 D8
Belovo, *Russia* 52 D9
Belovodsk, *Ukraine* 33 H10
Beloye, Ozero, *Russia* 32 B9
Beloye More, *Russia* 52 C4
Belozem, *Bulgaria* 45 D9
Belozersk, *Russia* 32 B9
Belpasso, *Italy* 43 E7
Belpre, *U.S.A.* 114 F5
Belrain, *India* 69 E9
Belt, *U.S.A.* 108 C8
Beltana, *Australia* 95 E2
Belterra, *Brazil* 125 D8
Beltinci, *Slovenia* 41 B13
Belton, *U.S.A.* 113 K6
Belton L., *U.S.A.* 113 K6
Beltsy = Bălţi, *Moldova* 29 C12
Belturbet, *Ireland* 12 B4
Belukha, *Russia* 52 E9
Beluran, *Malaysia* 62 C5
Beluša, *Slovak Rep.* 27 B11
Belušić, *Serbia & M.* 44 C5
Belvedere Maríttimo, *Italy* 43 C8
Belvès, *France* 20 D5
Belvidere, *Ill., U.S.A.* 112 D10
Belvidere, *N.J., U.S.A.* 117 F9
Belvis de la Jara, *Spain* 36 F6
Belyando →, *Australia* 94 C4
Belyy, *Russia* 32 E7
Belyy, Ostrov, *Russia* 52 B8
Belyy Yar, *Russia* 52 D9
Belz, *Ukraine* 31 H11
Bełżec, *Poland* 31 H10
Belzig, *Germany* 24 C8
Belzoni, *U.S.A.* 113 J9
Bełżyce, *Poland* 31 G9
Bemaraha, Lembalemban' i, *Madag.* 89 B7
Bemarivo, *Madag.* 89 C7
Bemarivo →, *Antsiranana, Madag.* 89 A9
Bemarivo →, *Mahajanga, Madag.* 89 B8
Bemavo, *Madag.* 89 C8
Bembéréke, *Benin* 83 C5
Bembesi, *Zimbabwe* 87 G2
Bembesi →, *Zimbabwe* 87 F2
Bembézar →, *Spain* 37 H5
Bembibre, *Spain* 36 C4
Bemetara, *India* 69 J9
Bemidji, *U.S.A.* 112 B7
Bemolanga, *Madag.* 89 B8
Ben, *Iran* 71 C6
Ben Cruachan, *U.K.* 13 E3
Ben Dearg, *U.K.* 13 D4
Ben En △, *Vietnam* 64 C5
Ben Hope, *U.K.* 13 C4
Ben Lawers, *U.K.* 13 E4
Ben Lomond, *N.S.W., Australia* 95 E5
Ben Lomond, *Tas., Australia* 95 G4
Ben Lomond, *U.K.* 13 E4
Ben Lomond △, *Australia* 95 G4
Ben Luc, *Vietnam* 65 G6

Ben Macdhui, U.K. 13 D5
Ben Mhor, U.K. 13 D1
Ben More, Arg. & Bute, U.K. 13 E2
Ben More, Stirl., U.K. 13 E4
Ben More Assynt, U.K. 13 C4
Ben Nevis, U.K. 13 E3
Ben Quang, Vietnam 64 D6
Ben Vorlich, U.K. 13 E4
Ben Wyvis, U.K. 13 D4
Bena, Nigeria 83 C6
Benalla, Australia 95 F4
Benalmádena, Spain 37 J6
Benares = Varanasi, India 69 G10
Bénat, C., France 21 E10
Benavente, Portugal 37 G2
Benavente, Spain 36 C5
Benavides, U.S.A. 113 M5
Benavides de Órbigo, Spain 36 C5
Benbecula, U.K. 13 D1
Benbonyathe, Australia 95 E2
Bend, U.S.A. 108 D3
Bender Beila, Somali Rep. 75 F5
Bendery = Tighina, Moldova 29 D14
Bendigo, Australia 95 F3
Bendorf, Germany 24 E3
Benē Beraq, Israel 74 C3
Bénéna, Mali 82 C4
Benenitra, Madag. 89 C8
Benešov, Czech Rep. 26 B7
Benevento, Italy 43 A7
Benfeld, France 19 D14
Benga, Mozam. 87 F3
Bengal, Bay of, Ind. Oc. 67 M17
Bengalūru = Bangalore, India 66 N10
Bengbis, Cameroon 83 E7
Bengbu, China 57 H9
Benghazi = Banghāzī, Libya 79 B10
Bengkalis, Indonesia 62 D2
Bengkulu, Indonesia 62 E2
Bengkulu □, Indonesia 62 E2
Bengough, Canada 103 D7
Bengtsfors, Sweden 10 E6
Benguela, Angola 85 G2
Benguérua, I., Mozam. 89 C6
Benha, Egypt 80 H7
Beni, Dem. Rep. of the Congo 86 B2
Beni →, Bolivia 124 F5
Beni Mazâr, Egypt 80 B3
Beni Mellal, Morocco 78 B4
Beni Suef, Egypt 80 J7
Beniah L., Canada 102 A6
Benicarló, Spain 38 E5
Benicássim, Spain 38 E5
Benicia, U.S.A. 110 G4
Benidorm, Spain 39 G4
Benin ■, Africa 83 D5
Benin →, Nigeria 83 D6
Benin, Bight of, W. Afr. 83 E5
Benin City, Nigeria 83 D6
Benisa, Spain 39 G5
Benitses, Greece 49 A3
Benjamin Aceval, Paraguay 126 A4
Benjamin Constant, Brazil 124 D4
Benjamin Hill, Mexico 118 A2
Benkelman, U.S.A. 112 E4
Benkovac, Croatia 41 D12
Bennett, Canada 102 B2
Bennett, L., Australia 92 D5
Bennetta, Ostrov, Russia 53 B15
Bennettsville, U.S.A. 115 H6
Bennichchāb, Mauritania 82 B1
Bennington, N.H., U.S.A. 117 D11
Bennington, Vt., U.S.A. 117 D11
Bénodet, France 18 E2
Benoni, S. Africa 89 D4
Benque Viejo del Carmen, Belize 119 D7
Bensheim, Germany 25 F4
Benson, Ariz., U.S.A. 109 L8
Benson, Minn., U.S.A. 112 C7
Bent, Iran 71 E8
Benteng, Indonesia 63 F6
Bentinck I., Australia 94 B2
Bentiu, Sudan 81 F2
Bento Gonçalves, Brazil 127 B5
Benton, Ark., U.S.A. 113 H8
Benton, Calif., U.S.A. 110 H8
Benton, Ill., U.S.A. 112 G10
Benton, Pa., U.S.A. 117 E8
Benton Harbor, U.S.A. 114 D2
Bentong, Malaysia 65 L3
Bentonville, U.S.A. 113 G7
Bentu Liben, Ethiopia 81 F4
Benue □, Nigeria 83 D6
Benue →, Nigeria 83 D6
Benxi, China 57 D12
Beo, Indonesia 63 D7
Beograd, Serbia & M. 44 B4
Beograd ✕ (BEG), Serbia & M. 44 C4
Beoumi, Ivory C. 82 D3
Bepan Jiang →, China 58 E6
Beppu, Japan 55 H5
Beqaa Valley = Al Biqā, Lebanon 74 A5
Ber Mota, India 68 H3
Berach →, India 68 G6
Beraketa, Madag. 89 C7
Berane, Serbia & M. 44 D3
Berat, Albania 44 F3
Berau, Teluk, Indonesia 63 E8
Beravina, Madag. 89 B8
Berber, Sudan 80 D3
Berbera, Somali Rep. 75 E4
Berbérati, C.A.R. 84 D3
Berbice →, Guyana 124 B7
Berceto, Italy 40 D6
Berchidda, Italy 42 B2
Berchtesgaden, Germany 25 H8
Berchtesgaden △, Germany 25 H8
Berck, France 19 B8
Berdichev = Berdychiv, Ukraine 33 H5
Berdsk, Russia 52 D9
Berdyansk, Ukraine 33 J9
Berdychiv, Ukraine 33 H5
Berea, U.S.A. 114 G3
Berebere, Indonesia 63 D7
Bereda, Somali Rep. 75 E5
Berehomet, Ukraine 29 B10
Berehove, Ukraine 28 B7
Berekum, Ghana 82 D4
Berenice, Egypt 80 C4
Berens →, Canada 103 C9
Berens I., Canada 103 C9
Berens River, Canada 103 C9
Beresford, U.S.A. 112 D6
Berestechko, Ukraine 33 G3
Bereşti, Romania 29 D12
Beretău →, Romania 28 C6
Berettyó →, Hungary 28 D6
Berettyóújfalu, Hungary 28 C6
Berevo, Mahajanga, Madag. 89 B7
Berevo, Toliara, Madag. 89 B7
Bereza = Byaroza, Belarus 33 F3
Berezhany, Ukraine 33 H3
Berezina = Byarezina →, Belarus 33 F6
Berezivka, Ukraine 33 J6
Berezna, Ukraine 33 G6
Bereznik, Russia 52 C5
Berezniki, Russia 52 D6
Berezovo, Russia 52 C7
Berezyne, Ukraine 29 D14
Berga, Spain 38 C6
Berga, Sweden 11 G10
Bergama, Turkey 47 B9
Bérgamo, Italy 40 C6
Bergara, Spain 38 B2
Bergby, Sweden 10 D11
Bergedorf, Germany 24 B6
Bergeforsen, Sweden 10 B11
Bergen, Mecklenburg-Vorpommern, Germany 24 A9
Bergen, Niedersachsen, Germany 24 C5
Bergen, Neths. 17 B4
Bergen, Norway 9 F11
Bergen, U.S.A. 116 C7
Bergen op Zoom, Neths. 17 C4
Bergerac, France 20 D4
Bergheim, Germany 24 E2
Bergholz, U.S.A. 116 F4
Bergisch Gladbach, Germany 17 D7
Bergisches Land ⌂, Germany 24 E3
Bergkamen, Germany 24 D3
Bergkvara, Sweden 11 H10
Bergshamra, Sweden 10 E12
Bergsjö, Sweden 10 C11
Bergstrasse-Odenwald ⌂, Germany 25 F1
Bergues, France 19 B9
Bergviken, Sweden 10 C10
Bergville, S. Africa 89 D4
Berhala, Selat, Indonesia 62 E2
Berhampore = Baharampur, India 69 G13
Berhampur = Brahmapur, India 67 K14
Berheci →, Romania 29 E12
Bering Sea, Pac. Oc. 100 C1
Bering Strait, Pac. Oc. 100 B3
Beringovskiy, Russia 53 C18
Berisso, Argentina 126 C4
Berja, Spain 37 J8
Berkeley, U.S.A. 110 H4
Berkner I., Antarctica 5 D18
Berkovitsa, Bulgaria 44 C7
Berkshire, U.S.A. 117 D8
Berkshire Downs, U.K. 15 F6
Berlanga, Spain 37 G5
Berlenga, I., Portugal 37 F1
Berlin, Germany 24 C9
Berlin, Md., U.S.A. 114 F8
Berlin, N.H., U.S.A. 117 B13
Berlin, N.Y., U.S.A. 117 D11
Berlin, Wis., U.S.A. 114 D1
Berlin □, Germany 24 C9
Berlin L., U.S.A. 116 E4
Berlin Tegel ✕ (TXL), Germany 24 C9
Bermeja, Sierra, Spain 37 J5
Bermejo →, Formosa, Argentina 126 B4
Bermejo →, San Juan, Argentina 126 C2
Bermen, L., Canada 105 B6
Bermeo, Spain 38 B2
Bermillo de Sayago, Spain 36 D4
Bermuda ☒, Atl. Oc. 98 F13
Bern, Switz. 25 J3
Bern □, Switz. 25 J3
Bernalda, Italy 43 B9
Bernalillo, U.S.A. 109 J10
Bernardo de Irigoyen, Argentina 127 B5
Bernardo O'Higgins □, Chile 126 C1
Bernardsville, U.S.A. 117 F10
Bernasconi, Argentina 126 D3
Bernau, Bayern, Germany 25 H8
Bernau, Brandenburg, Germany 24 C9
Bernay, France 18 C7
Bernburg, Germany 24 D7
Berndorf, Austria 26 D9
Berne = Bern, Switz. 25 J3
Berne = Bern □, Switz. 25 J3
Berner Alpen, Switz. 25 J3
Berneray, U.K. 13 D1
Bernier I., Australia 93 D1
Bernina, Piz, Switz. 25 J5
Bernkastel-Kues, Germany 25 F3
Beroroha, Madag. 89 C8
Béroubouay, Benin 83 C5
Beroun, Czech Rep. 26 B7
Berounka →, Czech Rep. 26 B7
Berovo, Macedonia 44 E6
Berre, Étang de, France 21 E9
Berre-l'Étang, France 21 E9
Berri, Australia 95 E3
Berriane, Algeria 78 B6
Berry, Australia 95 E5
Berry, France 19 F8
Berry Is., Bahamas 120 A4
Berryessa L., U.S.A. 110 G4
Berryville, U.S.A. 113 G8
Berseba, Namibia 88 D2
Bersenbrück, Germany 24 C3
Bershad, Ukraine 29 B14
Berthold, U.S.A. 112 A4
Berthoud, U.S.A. 112 E2
Bertincourt, France 19 B9
Bertoua, Cameroon 84 D2
Bertraghboy B., Ireland 12 C2
Berwick, U.S.A. 117 E8
Berwick-upon-Tweed, U.K. 14 B6
Berwyn Mts., U.K. 14 E4
Beryslav, Ukraine 33 J7
Berzasca, Romania 28 F6
Berzence, Hungary 28 D2
Besal, Pakistan 69 B5
Besalampy, Madag. 89 B7
Besançon, France 19 E13
Besar, Indonesia 62 E5
Beshenkovichi, Belarus 32 E5
Beška, Serbia & M. 28 E5
Beslan, Russia 35 J7
Besna Kobila, Serbia & M. 44 D6
Besnard L., Canada 103 B7
Besni, Turkey 70 B3
Besor, N. →, Egypt 74 D3
Bessarabiya, Moldova 33 J5
Bessarabka = Basarabeasca, Moldova 29 D13
Bessèges, France 21 D8
Bessemer, Ala., U.S.A. 115 J2
Bessemer, Mich., U.S.A. 112 B9
Bessemer, Pa., U.S.A. 116 F4
Bessin, France 18 C6
Bessines-sur-Gartempe, France 20 B5
Beswick, Australia 92 B5
Bet She'an, Israel 74 C4
Bet Shemesh, Israel 74 D4
Betafo, Madag. 89 B8
Betancuria, Canary Is. 48 F5
Betanzos, Spain 36 B2
Bétaré Oya, Cameroon 84 C2
Betatao, Madag. 89 B8
Bétera, Spain 39 F4
Bétérou, Benin 83 D5
Bethal, S. Africa 89 D4
Bethanien, Namibia 88 D2
Bethany, Canada 116 B6
Bethany, U.S.A. 112 E7
Bethel, Alaska, U.S.A. 100 B3
Bethel, Conn., U.S.A. 117 E11
Bethel, Maine, U.S.A. 117 B14
Bethel, Vt., U.S.A. 117 C12
Bethel Park, U.S.A. 116 F4
Béthenville, France 19 C11
Bethlehem = Bayt Lahm, West Bank 74 D4
Bethlehem, S. Africa 89 D4
Bethlehem, U.S.A. 117 F9
Bethulie, S. Africa 88 E4
Béthune, France 19 B9
Béthune →, France 18 C8
Betioky, Madag. 89 C7
Betong, Thailand 65 K3
Betoota, Australia 94 D3
Betor, Ethiopia 81 E4
Betroka, Madag. 89 C8
Betsiamites, Canada 105 C6
Betsiamites →, Canada 105 C6
Betsiboka →, Madag. 89 B8
Bettendorf, U.S.A. 112 E9
Bettiah, India 69 F11
Bettna, Sweden 11 F10
Béttola, Italy 40 D6
Betul, India 66 J10
Betung, Malaysia 62 D4
Betws-y-Coed, U.K. 14 D4
Betxi, Spain 38 F4
Betzdorf, Germany 24 E3
Beuil, France 21 D10
Beulah, Mich., U.S.A. 114 C2
Beulah, N. Dak., U.S.A. 112 B4
Beuvron →, France 18 E8
Beveren, Belgium 17 C4
Beverley, Australia 93 F2
Beverley, U.K. 14 D7
Beverley Hills, U.S.A. 115 L4
Beverly, U.S.A. 117 D14
Beverly Hills, U.S.A. 111 L8
Beverungen, Germany 24 D5
Bevoalavo, Madag. 89 D7
Bewas →, India 69 H8
Bex, Switz. 25 J3
Bexhill, U.K. 15 G8
Bey Dağları, Turkey 47 E12
Beyānlū, Iran 70 C5
Beyazköy, Turkey 45 E11
Beyçayırı, Turkey 45 F10
Beydağ, Turkey 47 C10
Beyeğaç, Turkey 47 D10
Beyin, Ghana 82 D4
Beykoz, Turkey 45 E13
Beyla, Guinea 82 D3
Beynat, France 20 C5
Beyneu, Kazakhstan 52 E6
Beyoba, Turkey 47 C9
Beyoğlu, Turkey 45 E12
Beypazarı, Turkey 72 B4
Beyşehir, Turkey 72 D4
Beyşehir Gölü, Turkey 70 B1
Beytüşşebap, Turkey 73 D10
Bezdan, Serbia & M. 28 E3
Bezhetsk, Russia 32 D9
Béziers, France 20 E7
Bezwada = Vijayawada, India 67 L12
Bhabua, India 69 G10
Bhachau, India 66 H7
Bhadar →, Gujarat, India 68 H5
Bhadar →, Gujarat, India 68 J3
Bhadarwah, India 69 C6
Bhadgaon = Bhaktapur, Nepal 69 F11
Bhadohi, India 69 G10
Bhadra, India 68 E6
Bhadrakh, India 67 J15
Bhadran, India 68 H5
Bhadravati, India 66 N9
Bhag, Pakistan 68 E2
Bhagalpur, India 69 G12
Bhagirathi →, Uttaranchal, India 69 D8
Bhagirathi →, W. Bengal, India 69 H13
Bhakkar, Pakistan 68 D4
Bhakra Dam, India 68 D7
Bhaktapur, Nepal 69 F11
Bhamo, Burma 67 G20
Bhandara, India 66 J11
Bhanpura, India 68 G6
Bhanrer Ra., India 69 H8
Bhaptiahi, India 69 F12
Bharat = India ■, Asia 66 K11
Bharatpur, Chhattisgarh, India 69 H9
Bharatpur, Raj., India 68 F7
Bharno, India 69 H11
Bharuch, India 66 J8
Bhatinda, India 68 D6
Bhatpara, India 69 H13
Bhattu, India 68 E6
Bhaun, Pakistan 68 C5
Bhaunagar = Bhavnagar, India 66 J8
Bhavnagar, India 66 J8
Bhawari, India 68 G5
Bhayavadar, India 68 J4
Bhera, Pakistan 68 C5
Bhikangaon, India 68 J6
Bhilsa = Vidisha, India 68 H7
Bhilwara, India 68 G6
Bhima →, India 66 L10
Bhimbar, Pakistan 69 C6
Bhind, India 69 F8
Bhinga, India 69 F9
Bhinmal, India 68 G5
Bhiwandi, India 66 K8
Bhiwani, India 68 E7
Bhogava →, India 68 H5
Bhola, Bangla. 67 H17
Bholari, Pakistan 68 G3
Bhopal, India 68 H7
Bhubaneshwar, India 67 J14
Bhuj, India 68 H3
Bhumiphol Res., Thailand 64 D2
Bhusawal, India 66 J9
Bhutan ■, Asia 67 F17
Biafra, B. of = Bonny, Bight of, Africa 83 E6
Biak, Indonesia 63 E9
Biała, Poland 31 H4
Biała →, Poland 31 H7
Biała Piska, Poland 30 E9
Biała Podlaska, Poland 31 F10
Biała Rawska, Poland 31 G7
Białobrzegi, Poland 31 G7
Białogard, Poland 30 D2
Białowieski △, Poland 31 F10
Białowieża, Poland 31 F10
Biały Bór, Poland 30 E3
Białystok, Poland 31 E10
Biancavilla, Italy 43 E7
Bianco, Italy 43 D9
Biankouma, Ivory C. 82 D3
Biaora, India 68 H7
Bīārjmand, Iran 71 B7
Biaro, Indonesia 63 D7
Biarritz, France 20 E2
Bias, Indonesia 63 J18
Biasca, Switz. 25 J4
Biba, Egypt 80 J7
Bibai, Japan 54 C10
Bibbiena, Italy 41 E8
Bibby I., Canada 103 A10
Bibel →, Spain 36 C3
Biberach, Germany 25 G5
Bibiani, Ghana 82 D4
Bibungwa, Dem. Rep. of the Congo 86 C2
Bicaj, Albania 44 E4
Bicaz, Romania 29 D11
Bicazu Ardelean, Romania 29 D10
Bíccari, Italy 43 A8
Bicester, U.K. 15 F6
Bichena, Ethiopia 81 E4
Bicheno, Australia 95 G4
Bichia, India 69 H9
Bichvinta, Georgia 35 J5
Bickerton I., Australia 94 A2
Bicske, Hungary 28 C3
Bida, Nigeria 83 D6
Bidar, India 66 L10
Biddeford, U.S.A. 115 D10
Biddwara, Ethiopia 81 F4
Bideford, U.K. 15 F3
Bideford Bay, U.K. 15 F3
Bidhuna, India 69 F8
Bidor, Malaysia 65 K3
Bie, Sweden 10 E10
Bié, Planalto de, Angola 85 G3
Bieber, U.S.A. 108 F3
Biebrza →, Poland 31 E9
Biebrzański △, Poland 30 E9
Biecz, Poland 31 J8
Biel, Switz. 25 H3
Bielawa, Poland 31 H3
Bielefeld, Germany 24 C4
Bielersee, Switz. 25 H3
Biella, Italy 40 C5
Bielsk Podlaski, Poland 31 F10
Bielsko-Biała, Poland 31 J6
Bien Hoa, Vietnam 65 G6
Bienne = Biel, Switz. 25 H3
Bienvenida, Spain 37 G4
Bienville, L., Canada 104 A5
Bierné, France 18 E6
Bierun, Poland 31 H6
Bierutów, Poland 31 G4
Biescas, Spain 38 C4
Biese →, Germany 24 C7
Biesiesfontein, S. Africa 88 E2
Bieszczadzki △, Poland 31 J9
Bietigheim-Bissingen, Germany 25 G5
Bieżuń, Poland 31 F6
Biferno →, Italy 41 G12
Big →, Canada 105 B8
Big B., Canada 105 A7
Big Bear City, U.S.A. 111 L10
Big Bear Lake, U.S.A. 111 L10
Big Belt Mts., U.S.A. 108 C8
Big Bend, Swaziland 89 D5
Big Bend △, U.S.A. 113 L3
Big Black →, U.S.A. 113 K9
Big Blue →, U.S.A. 112 F6
Big Creek, U.S.A. 110 H7
Big Cypress ⌂, U.S.A. 115 M5
Big Cypress Swamp, U.S.A. 115 M5
Big Falls, U.S.A. 112 A8
Big Fork →, U.S.A. 112 A8
Big Horn Mts. = Bighorn Mts., U.S.A. 108 D10
Big I., Canada 102 A5
Big Lake, U.S.A. 113 K4
Big Moose, U.S.A. 117 C10
Big Muddy Cr. →, U.S.A. 112 A2
Big Pine, U.S.A. 110 H8
Big Piney, U.S.A. 108 E8
Big Rapids, U.S.A. 114 D3
Big Rideau L., Canada 117 B8
Big River, Canada 103 C7
Big Run, U.S.A. 116 F6
Big Sable Pt., U.S.A. 114 C2
Big Salmon →, Canada 102 A2
Big Sand L., Canada 103 B9
Big Sandy, U.S.A. 108 B8
Big Sandy →, U.S.A. 114 F4
Big Sandy Cr. →, U.S.A. 112 F3
Big Sioux →, U.S.A. 112 D6
Big South Fork △, U.S.A. 115 G3
Big Spring, U.S.A. 113 J4
Big Stone City, U.S.A. 112 C6
Big Stone Gap, U.S.A. 115 G4
Big Stone L., U.S.A. 112 C6
Big Sur, U.S.A. 110 J5
Big Timber, U.S.A. 108 D9
Big Trout L., Canada 104 B2
Big Trout Lake, Canada 104 B2
Biğa, Turkey 45 F11
Biga →, Turkey 45 F11
Bigadiç, Turkey 47 B10
Biganos, France 20 D3
Biggar, Canada 103 C7
Biggar, U.K. 13 F5
Bigge I., Australia 92 B4
Biggenden, Australia 95 D5
Biggleswade, U.K. 15 E7
Biggs, U.S.A. 110 F5
Bighorn, U.S.A. 108 C10
Bighorn →, U.S.A. 108 C10
Bighorn Canyon ⌂, U.S.A. 108 D9
Bighorn L., U.S.A. 108 D9
Bighorn Mts., U.S.A. 108 D10
Bignona, Senegal 82 C1
Bigorre, France 20 E4
Bigstone L., Canada 103 C9
Biguglia, Étang de, France 21 F13
Bigwa, Tanzania 86 D4
Bihać, Bos.-H. 41 D12
Bihar, India 69 G11
Bihar □, India 69 G12
Biharamulo, Tanzania 86 C3
Biharamulo ⌂, Tanzania 86 C3
Bihariganj, India 69 G12
Biharkeresztes, Hungary 28 C6
Bihor □, Romania 28 D7
Bihor, Munţii, Romania 28 D7
Bijagós, Arquipélago dos, Guinea-Biss. 82 C1
Bijaipur, India 68 F7
Bijapur, Chhattisgarh, India 67 K12
Bijapur, Karnataka, India 66 L9
Bījār, Iran 70 C5
Bijawar, India 69 G8
Bijeljina, Bos.-H. 28 F4
Bijelo Polje, Serbia & M. 44 C3
Bijie, China 58 D5
Bijnor, India 68 E8
Bikaner, India 68 E5
Bikapur, India 69 F10
Bikeqi, China 56 D6
Bikfayyā, Lebanon 74 B4
Bikin, Russia 53 E14
Bikin →, Russia 54 A7
Bikini Atoll, Marshall Is. 96 F8
Bikita, Zimbabwe 89 C5
Bikoué, Cameroon 83 E7
Bila Tserkva, Ukraine 33 H6
Bilanga, Burkina Faso 83 C4
Bilara, India 68 F5
Bilaspur, Chhattisgarh, India 69 H10
Bilaspur, Punjab, India 68 D7
Biläsuvar, Azerbaijan 73 C13
Bilauk Taungdan, Thailand 64 F2
Bilbao, Spain 38 B2
Bilbao ✕ (BIO), Spain 36 B8
Bilbeis, Egypt 80 H7
Bilbo = Bilbao, Spain 38 B2
Bilbor, Romania 29 C10
Bilche-Zolote, Ukraine 29 B10
Bilciureşti, Romania 29 F10
Bíldudalur, Iceland 8 D2
Bílé Karpaty, Europe 27 B11
Bileća, Bos.-H. 44 D2
Bilecik, Turkey 72 B4
Biłgoraj, Poland 31 H9
Bilgram, India 69 F9
Bilhaur, India 69 F9
Bilhorod-Dnistrovskyy, Ukraine 33 J6
Bilibino, Russia 53 C17
Bilibiza, Mozam. 87 E5
Bilisht, Albania 44 F5
Billabong Roadhouse, Australia 93 E2
Billdal, Sweden 11 G5

Billiluna, *Australia* 92 C4
Billings, *U.S.A.* 108 D9
Billiton Is. = Belitung, *Indonesia* 62 E3
Billsta, *Sweden* 10 A12
Billund, *Denmark* 11 J3
Bilma, *Niger* 79 E8
Bilo Gora, *Croatia* 28 E2
Biloela, *Australia* 94 C5
Bilohirsk, *Ukraine* 33 K8
Bilopillya, *Ukraine* 33 G8
Biloxi, *U.S.A.* 113 K10
Bilpa Morea Claypan, *Australia* 94 D3
Biltine, *Chad* 79 F10
Bilyarsk, *Russia* 34 C10
Bima, *Indonesia* 63 F5
Bimban, *Egypt* 80 C3
Bimbila, *Ghana* 83 D5
Bimini Is., *Bahamas* 120 A4
Bin Xian, *Heilongjiang, China* 57 B14
Bin Xian, *Shaanxi, China* 56 G5
Bin Yauri, *Nigeria* 83 C5
Bina-Etawah, *India* 68 G8
Bināb, *Iran* 71 B6
Binalbagan, *Phil.* 61 F5
Binalong, *Australia* 95 E4
Bīnālūd, Kūh-e, *Iran* 71 B8
Binatang = Bintangor, *Malaysia* 62 D4
Binche, *Belgium* 17 D4
Binchuan, *China* 58 E3
Binder, *Chad* 83 D7
Bindki, *India* 69 F9
Bindslev, *Denmark* 11 G4
Bindura, *Zimbabwe* 87 F3
Binefar, *Spain* 38 D5
Bingara, *Australia* 95 D5
Bingen, *Germany* 25 F3
Bingerville, *Ivory C.* 82 D4
Bingham, *U.S.A.* 115 C11
Binghamton, *U.S.A.* 117 D9
Bingöl, *Turkey* 70 B4
Bingöl Dağları, *Turkey* 73 C9
Bingsjö, *Sweden* 10 C9
Binh Dinh = An Nhon, *Vietnam* 64 F7
Binh Khe, *Vietnam* 64 F7
Binh Son, *Vietnam* 64 E7
Binhai, *China* 57 G10
Binic, *France* 18 D4
Binisatua, *Spain* 48 B11
Binjai, *Indonesia* 62 D3
Binji, *Nigeria* 83 C5
Binnaway, *Australia* 95 E4
Binongko, *Indonesia* 63 F6
Binscarth, *Canada* 103 C8
Binshangul Gumuz □, *Ethiopia* 81 E4
Bint Goda, *Sudan* 81 E3
Bintan, *Indonesia* 62 D2
Bintangor, *Malaysia* 62 D4
Bintulu, *Malaysia* 62 D4
Bintuni, *Indonesia* 63 E8
Binyang, *China* 58 F7
Binz, *Germany* 24 A9
Binzert = Bizerte, *Tunisia* 79 A7
Binzhou, *China* 57 F10
Bío Bío □, *Chile* 126 D1
Biograd na Moru, *Croatia* 41 E12
Biogradska Gora △, *Serbia & M.* 44 D3
Bioko, *Eq. Guin.* 83 E6
Biokovo, *Croatia* 41 E14
Bipindi, *Cameroon* 83 E7
Bir, *India* 66 K9
Bir, Ras, *Djibouti* 81 E5
Bîr Abu Hashim, *Egypt* 80 C3
Bîr Abu Minqar, *Egypt* 80 B2
Bîr Abu Muḥammad, *Egypt* 74 F3
Bi'r ad Dabbāghāt, *Jordan* 74 E4
Bîr Adal Deib, *Sudan* 80 C4
Bi'r al Butayyihāt, *Jordan* 74 F4
Bi'r al Mārī, *Jordan* 74 E4
Bi'r al Qattār, *Jordan* 74 F4
Bîr 'Asal, *Egypt* 80 B3
Bir Atrun, *Sudan* 80 D2
Bîr Beiḍa, *Egypt* 74 E3
Bîr Diqnash, *Egypt* 80 A2
Bîr el 'Abd, *Egypt* 74 D2
Bîr el Basur, *Egypt* 80 B2
Bîr el Biarât, *Egypt* 74 F3
Bîr el Duweidar, *Egypt* 74 E1
Bîr el Garârât, *Egypt* 74 D2
Bîr el Gellaz, *Egypt* 80 A2
Bîr el Heisi, *Egypt* 74 F3
Bîr el Jafir, *Egypt* 74 E1
Bîr el Mâlḥi, *Egypt* 74 E2
Bîr el Shaqqa, *Egypt* 80 A2
Bîr el Thamâda, *Egypt* 74 E2
Bîr Fuad, *Egypt* 80 A2
Bîr Gebeil Ḥiṣn, *Egypt* 74 E2
Bi'r Ghadīr, *Syria* 74 A6
Bîr Haimur, *Egypt* 80 C3
Bîr Ḥasana, *Egypt* 74 E2
Bîr Hööker, *Egypt* 80 H7
Bîr Kanayis, *Egypt* 80 C3
Bîr Kaseiba, *Egypt* 74 E2
Bîr Kerawein, *Egypt* 80 B2
Bîr Lahfân, *Egypt* 74 E2
Bîr Madkûr, *Egypt* 74 E1
Bîr Maql, *Egypt* 80 C3
Bîr Mîneiga, *Sudan* 80 C4
Bîr Misaha, *Egypt* 80 C2
Bîr Mogreïn, *Mauritania* 78 C3
Bîr Murr, *Egypt* 80 C3
Bi'r Muṭribah, *Kuwait* 70 D5
Bîr Nakheila, *Egypt* 80 C3
Bîr Qaṭia, *Egypt* 74 E1
Bîr Qatrani, *Egypt* 80 A2
Bîr Ranga, *Egypt* 80 C4
Bîr Sahara, *Egypt* 80 C2
Bîr Seiyâla, *Egypt* 80 B3
Bîr Shalatein, *Egypt* 80 C4
Bîr Shebb, *Egypt* 80 C2
Bîr Shût, *Egypt* 80 C4
Bîr Terfawi, *Egypt* 80 C2
Bîr Umm Qubûr, *Egypt* 80 C3
Bîr Ungât, *Egypt* 80 C3
Bîr Za'farâna, *Egypt* 80 J8
Bîr Zeidûn, *Egypt* 80 B3
Biramféro, *Guinea* 82 C3
Biratnagar, *Nepal* 69 F12
Birawa, *Dem. Rep. of the Congo* 86 C2
Birch →, *Canada* 102 B6
Birch Hills, *Canada* 103 C7
Birch I., *Canada* 103 C9
Birch L., *N.W.T., Canada* 102 A5
Birch L., *Ont., Canada* 104 B1
Birch Mts., *Canada* 102 B6
Birch River, *Canada* 103 C8
Birchip, *Australia* 95 F3
Birchiş, *Romania* 28 E7
Bird, *Canada* 103 B10
Bird I. = Aves, I. de, *W. Indies* 121 C7
Bird I., *Antarctica* 5 B1
Birdsville, *Australia* 94 D2
Birdum Cr. →, *Australia* 92 C5
Birecik, *Turkey* 70 B3
Birein, *Israel* 74 E3
Bireuen, *Indonesia* 62 C1
Biri →, *Sudan* 81 F2
Birifo, *Gambia* 82 C2
Birigui, *Brazil* 127 A5
Birjand, *Iran* 71 C8
Birkenfeld, *Germany* 25 F3
Birkenhead, *U.K.* 14 D4
Birkerød, *Denmark* 11 J6
Birket Qârûn, *Egypt* 80 J7
Birkfeld, *Austria* 26 D8
Bîrlad = Bârlad, *Romania* 29 D12
Birmingham, *U.K.* 15 E6
Birmingham, *U.S.A.* 115 J2
Birmingham International ✕ (BHX), *U.K.* 15 E6
Birmitrapur, *India* 67 H14
Birni Ngaouré, *Niger* 83 C5
Birni Nkonni, *Niger* 83 C6
Birnin Gwari, *Nigeria* 83 C6
Birnin Kebbi, *Nigeria* 83 C5
Birnin Kudu, *Nigeria* 83 C6
Birobidzhan, *Russia* 53 E14
Birr, *Ireland* 12 C4
Birrie →, *Australia* 95 D4
Birsilpur, *India* 68 E5
Birsk, *Russia* 52 D6
Birštonas, *Lithuania* 30 D11
Birtle, *Canada* 103 C8
Birur, *India* 66 N9
Biryuchiy, *Ukraine* 33 J8
Biržai, *Lithuania* 9 H21
Birzebbugga, *Malta* 49 D2
Bisa, *Indonesia* 63 E7
Bisáccia, *Italy* 43 A8
Bisacquino, *Italy* 42 E6
Bisalpur, *India* 69 E8
Bisbee, *U.S.A.* 109 L9
Biscarrosse, *France* 20 D2
Biscarrosse et de Parentis, Étang de, *France* 20 D2
Biscay, B. of, *Atl. Oc.* 6 F5
Biscayne B., *U.S.A.* 115 N5
Biscéglie, *Italy* 43 A9
Bischheim, *France* 19 D14
Bischofshofen, *Austria* 26 D6
Bischofswerda, *Germany* 24 D10
Bischwiller, *France* 19 D14
Biscoe Is., *Antarctica* 5 C17
Biscotasing, *Canada* 104 C3
Biševo, *Croatia* 41 F13
Bisha, *Eritrea* 81 D4
Bishah, W. →, *Si. Arabia* 80 C5
Bishan, *China* 58 C6
Bishkek, *Kyrgyzstan* 52 E8
Bishnupur, *India* 69 H12
Bisho, *S. Africa* 89 E4
Bishop, *Calif., U.S.A.* 110 H8
Bishop, *Tex., U.S.A.* 113 M6
Bishop Auckland, *U.K.* 14 C6
Bishop's Falls, *Canada* 105 C8
Bishop's Stortford, *U.K.* 15 F8
Bisignano, *Italy* 43 C9
Bisina, L., *Uganda* 86 B3
Biskra, *Algeria* 78 B7
Biskupiec, *Poland* 30 E7
Bismarck, *U.S.A.* 112 B4
Bismarck Arch., *Papua N. G.* 96 H7
Bismark, *Germany* 24 C7
Bismil, *Turkey* 73 D9
Biso, *Uganda* 86 B3
Bison, *U.S.A.* 112 C3
Bīsotūn, *Iran* 70 C5
Bispgården, *Sweden* 10 A10
Bissagos = Bijagós, Arquipélago dos, *Guinea-Biss.* 82 C1
Bissau, *Guinea-Biss.* 82 C1
Bissaula, *Nigeria* 83 D7
Bissikrima, *Guinea* 82 C2
Bissorã, *Guinea-Biss.* 82 C1
Bistcho L., *Canada* 102 B5
Bistreţ, *Romania* 29 G8
Bistrica = Ilirska-Bistrica, *Slovenia* 41 C11
Bistriţa, *Romania* 29 C9
Bistriţa →, *Romania* 29 D11
Bistriţa Năsăud □, *Romania* 29 C9
Bistriţei, Munţii, *Romania* 29 C10
Biswan, *India* 69 F9
Bisztynek, *Poland* 30 D7
Bitburg, *Germany* 25 F2
Bitche, *France* 19 C14
Bithynia, *Turkey* 72 B4
Bitlis, *Turkey* 70 B4
Bitola, *Macedonia* 44 E5
Bitolj = Bitola, *Macedonia* 44 E5
Bitonto, *Italy* 43 A9
Bitter Creek, *U.S.A.* 108 F9
Bitter L. = Buheirat-Murrat-el-Kubra, *Egypt* 80 H8
Bitterfeld, *Germany* 24 D8
Bitterfontein, *S. Africa* 88 E2
Bitterroot →, *U.S.A.* 108 C6
Bitterroot Range, *U.S.A.* 108 D6
Bitterwater, *U.S.A.* 110 J6
Bitti, *Italy* 42 B2
Bittou, *Burkina Faso* 83 C4
Biu, *Nigeria* 83 C7
Bivolari, *Romania* 29 C12
Bivolu, Vf., *Romania* 29 C10
Biwa-Ko, *Japan* 55 G8
Biwabik, *U.S.A.* 112 B8
Bixad, *Romania* 29 C8
Bixby, *U.S.A.* 113 H7
Biyang, *China* 56 H7
Biysk, *Russia* 52 D9
Bizana, *S. Africa* 89 E4
Bizen, *Japan* 55 G7
Bizerte, *Tunisia* 79 A7
Bjargtangar, *Iceland* 8 D1
Bjärnum, *Sweden* 11 H7
Bjästa, *Sweden* 10 A12
Bjelasica, *Serbia & M.* 44 D3
Bjelašnica, *Bos.-H.* 28 G3
Bjelovar, *Croatia* 41 C13
Bjerringbro, *Denmark* 11 H3
Björbo, *Sweden* 10 D8
Björklinge, *Sweden* 10 D11
Björneborg = Pori, *Finland* 9 F19
Björneborg, *Sweden* 10 E8
Bjørnevatn, *Norway* 8 B23
Bjørnøya, *Arctic* 4 B8
Bjursås, *Sweden* 10 D9
Bjuv, *Sweden* 11 H6
Bla, *Mali* 82 C3
Blace, *Serbia & M.* 44 C5
Blachownia, *Poland* 31 H5
Black = Da →, *Vietnam* 58 G5
Black →, *Canada* 116 B5
Black →, *Ariz., U.S.A.* 109 K8
Black →, *Ark., U.S.A.* 113 H9
Black →, *Mich., U.S.A.* 116 D2
Black →, *N.Y., U.S.A.* 117 C8
Black →, *Wis., U.S.A.* 112 D9
Black Bay Pen., *Canada* 104 C2
Black Birch L., *Canada* 103 B7
Black Canyon of the Gunnison ⌂, *U.S.A.* 109 G10
Black Diamond, *Canada* 102 C6
Black Duck →, *Canada* 104 A2
Black Forest = Schwarzwald, *Germany* 25 G4
Black Forest, *U.S.A.* 112 F2
Black Hd., *Ireland* 12 C2
Black Hills, *U.S.A.* 112 D3
Black I., *Canada* 103 C9
Black L., *Canada* 103 B7
Black L., *Mich., U.S.A.* 114 C3
Black L., *N.Y., U.S.A.* 117 B9
Black Lake, *Canada* 103 B7
Black Mesa, *U.S.A.* 113 G3
Black Mt. = Mynydd Du, *U.K.* 15 F4
Black Mts., *U.K.* 15 F4
Black Range, *U.S.A.* 109 K10
Black River, *Jamaica* 120 a
Black River Falls, *U.S.A.* 112 C9
Black Rock, *Barbados* 121 g
Black Sea, *Eurasia* 6 G12
Black Tickle, *Canada* 105 B8
Black Volta →, *Africa* 82 D4
Black Warrior →, *U.S.A.* 115 J2
Blackall, *Australia* 94 C4
Blackball, *N.Z.* 91 K3
Blackbull, *Australia* 94 B3
Blackburn, *U.K.* 14 D5
Blackburn with Darwen □, *U.K.* 14 D5
Blackdown Tableland △, *Australia* 94 C4
Blackfoot, *U.S.A.* 108 E7
Blackfoot →, *U.S.A.* 108 C7
Blackfoot River Reservoir, *U.S.A.* 108 E8
Blackpool, *U.K.* 14 D4
Blackpool □, *U.K.* 14 D4
Blackriver, *U.S.A.* 116 B1
Blacks Harbour, *Canada* 105 C6
Blacksburg, *U.S.A.* 114 G5
Blacksod B., *Ireland* 12 B1
Blackstone, *U.S.A.* 114 G7
Blackstone Ra., *Australia* 93 E4
Blackwater = West Road →, *Canada* 102 C4
Blackwater, *Australia* 94 C4
Blackwater →, *Meath, Ireland* 12 C4
Blackwater →, *Waterford, Ireland* 12 D4
Blackwater →, *U.K.* 12 B5
Blackwell, *U.S.A.* 113 G6
Blackwells Corner, *U.S.A.* 111 K7
Bladensburg △, *Australia* 94 C3
Blaenau Ffestiniog, *U.K.* 14 E4
Blaenau Gwent □, *U.K.* 15 F4
Blagaj, *Bos.-H.* 44 C1
Blagnac, *France* 20 E5
Blagnac, Toulouse ✕ (TLS), *France* 20 E5
Blagodarnoye = Blagodarnyy, *Russia* 35 H6
Blagodarnyy, *Russia* 35 H6
Blagoevgrad, *Bulgaria* 44 D7
Blagoveshchensk, *Russia* 53 D13
Blahkiuh, *Indonesia* 63 J18
Blain, *France* 18 E5
Blain, *U.S.A.* 116 F7
Blaine, *Minn., U.S.A.* 112 C8
Blaine, *Wash., U.S.A.* 110 B4
Blaine Lake, *Canada* 103 C7
Blair, *U.S.A.* 112 E6
Blair Athol, *Australia* 94 C4
Blair Atholl, *U.K.* 13 E5
Blairgowrie, *U.K.* 13 E5
Blairsden, *U.S.A.* 110 F6
Blairsville, *U.S.A.* 116 F5
Blaj, *Romania* 29 D8
Blakang Mati, Pulau, *Singapore* 65 d
Blake Pt., *U.S.A.* 112 A10
Blakely, *Ga., U.S.A.* 115 K3
Blakely, *Pa., U.S.A.* 117 E9
Blâmont, *France* 19 D13
Blanc, C., *Spain* 48 B9
Blanc, Mont, *Europe* 21 C10
Blanc-Sablon, *Canada* 105 B8
Blanca, B., *Argentina* 128 D4
Blanca Peak, *U.S.A.* 109 H11
Blanche, C., *Australia* 95 E1
Blanche, L., *S. Austral., Australia* 95 D2
Blanche, L., *W. Austral., Australia* 92 D3
Blanchisseuse, *Trin. & Tob.* 125 K15
Blanco, *S. Africa* 88 E3
Blanco, *U.S.A.* 113 K5
Blanco →, *Argentina* 126 C2
Blanco, C., *Costa Rica* 120 E2
Blanco, C., *U.S.A.* 108 E1
Blanda →, *Iceland* 8 D3
Blandford Forum, *U.K.* 15 G5
Blanding, *U.S.A.* 109 H9
Blanes, *Spain* 38 D7
Blangy-sur-Bresle, *France* 19 C8
Blanice →, *Czech Rep.* 26 B7
Blankaholm, *Sweden* 11 G10
Blankenberge, *Belgium* 17 C3
Blankenburg, *Germany* 24 D6
Blanquefort, *France* 20 D3
Blanquillo, *Uruguay* 127 C4
Blansko, *Czech Rep.* 27 B9
Blantyre, *Malawi* 87 F4
Blarney, *Ireland* 12 E3
Blasdell, *U.S.A.* 116 D6
Błaszki, *Poland* 31 G5
Blatná, *Czech Rep.* 26 B6
Blato, *Croatia* 41 F13
Blaubeuren, *Germany* 25 G5
Blaustein, *Germany* 25 G5
Blåvands Huk, *Denmark* 11 J2
Blaydon, *U.K.* 14 C6
Blaye, *France* 20 C3
Blaye-les-Mines, *France* 20 D6
Blayney, *Australia* 95 E4
Blaze, Pt., *Australia* 92 B5
Błażowa, *Poland* 31 J9
Bleckede, *Germany* 24 B6
Bled, *Slovenia* 41 B11
Bleiburg, *Austria* 26 E7
Blejeşti, *Romania* 29 F10
Blekinge, *Sweden* 9 H16
Blekinge län □, *Sweden* 11 H9
Blenheim, *Canada* 116 D3
Blenheim, *N.Z.* 91 J4
Bléone →, *France* 21 D10
Blérancourt, *France* 19 C10
Bletchley, *U.K.* 15 F7
Blida, *Algeria* 78 A6
Blidö, *Sweden* 10 E12
Blidsberg, *Sweden* 11 G7
Blieskastel, *Germany* 25 F3
Bligh Sound, *N.Z.* 91 L1
Blind River, *Canada* 104 C3
Blinisht, *Albania* 44 E3
Bliss, *Idaho, U.S.A.* 108 E6
Bliss, *N.Y., U.S.A.* 116 D6
Blissfield, *U.S.A.* 116 F3
Blitar, *Indonesia* 63 H15
Blitta, *Togo* 83 D5
Block I., *U.S.A.* 117 E13
Block Island Sd., *U.S.A.* 117 E13
Bloemfontein, *S. Africa* 88 D4
Bloemhof, *S. Africa* 88 D4
Blois, *France* 18 E8
Blomskog, *Sweden* 10 E6
Blomstermåla, *Sweden* 11 H10
Blönduós, *Iceland* 8 D3
Blongas, *Indonesia* 63 K19
Błonie, *Poland* 31 F7
Bloodvein →, *Canada* 103 C9
Bloody Foreland, *Ireland* 12 A3
Bloomer, *U.S.A.* 112 C9
Bloomfield, *Canada* 116 C7
Bloomfield, *Iowa, U.S.A.* 112 E8
Bloomfield, *N. Mex., U.S.A.* 109 H10
Bloomfield, *Nebr., U.S.A.* 112 D6
Bloomington, *Ill., U.S.A.* 112 E10
Bloomington, *Ind., U.S.A.* 114 F2
Bloomington, *Minn., U.S.A.* 112 C8
Bloomsburg, *U.S.A.* 117 F8
Bloomsbury, *Australia* 94 J6
Blora, *Indonesia* 63 G14
Blossburg, *U.S.A.* 116 E7
Blouberg, *S. Africa* 89 C4
Blountstown, *U.S.A.* 115 K3
Bludenz, *Austria* 26 D2
Blue Earth, *U.S.A.* 112 D8
Blue Hole △, *Belize* 120 C2
Blue Lagoon △, *Zambia* 87 F2
Blue Mesa Reservoir, *U.S.A.* 109 G10
Blue Mountain Lake, *U.S.A.* 117 C10
Blue Mountain Pk., *Jamaica* 120 a
Blue Mts., *Jamaica* 120 a
Blue Mts., *Maine, U.S.A.* 117 B14
Blue Mts., *Oreg., U.S.A.* 108 D4
Blue Mts., *Pa., U.S.A.* 117 F8
Blue Mud B., *Australia* 94 A2
Blue Nile = Nîl el Azraq →, *Sudan* 81 D3
Blue Rapids, *U.S.A.* 112 F6
Blue Ridge Mts., *U.S.A.* 115 G5
Blue River, *Canada* 102 C5
Bluefield, *U.S.A.* 114 G5
Bluefields, *Nic.* 120 D3
Bluff, *Australia* 94 C4
Bluff, *N.Z.* 91 M2
Bluff, *U.S.A.* 109 H9
Bluff Knoll, *Australia* 93 F2
Bluff Pt., *Australia* 93 E1
Bluffton, *U.S.A.* 114 E3
Blumenau, *Brazil* 127 B6
Blunt, *U.S.A.* 112 C5
Bly, *U.S.A.* 108 E3
Blyde River Canyon ⌂, *S. Africa* 89 C5
Blyth, *Canada* 116 C3
Blyth, *U.K.* 14 B6
Blythe, *U.S.A.* 111 M12
Blytheville, *U.S.A.* 113 H10
Bo, *S. Leone* 82 D2
Bo Duc, *Vietnam* 65 G6
Bo Hai, *China* 57 E10
Bo Xian = Bozhou, *China* 56 H8
Boa Vista, *Brazil* 124 C6
Boac, *Phil.* 61 E4
Boaco, *Nic.* 120 D2
Bo'ai, *China* 56 G7
Boal, *Spain* 36 B4
Boalsburg, *U.S.A.* 116 F7
Boane, *Mozam.* 89 D5
Boardman, *U.S.A.* 116 E4
Bobadah, *Australia* 95 E4
Bobai, *China* 58 F7
Bobbili, *India* 67 K13
Bóbbio, *Italy* 40 D6
Bobcaygeon, *Canada* 116 B6
Böblingen, *Germany* 25 G5
Bobo-Dioulasso, *Burkina Faso* 82 C4
Bobolice, *Poland* 30 E3
Boboshevo, *Bulgaria* 44 D7
Bobov Dol, *Bulgaria* 44 D6
Bóbr →, *Poland* 31 F2
Bobraomby, Tanjon' i, *Madag.* 89 A8
Bobrinets, *Ukraine* 33 H7
Bobrov, *Russia* 34 E5
Bobrovitsa, *Ukraine* 33 G6
Bobruysk = Babruysk, *Belarus* 33 F5
Boby, Pic, *Madag.* 85 J9
Boca de Drago, *Venezuela* 125 K15
Bôca do Acre, *Brazil* 124 E5
Boca Raton, *U.S.A.* 115 M5
Bocanda, *Ivory C.* 82 D4
Bocas del Toro, *Panama* 120 E3
Boceguillas, *Spain* 36 D7
Bochmanivka, *Ukraine* 29 C14
Bochnia, *Poland* 31 J7
Bocholt, *Germany* 24 D2
Bochum, *Germany* 24 D3
Bockenem, *Germany* 24 C6
Boćki, *Poland* 31 F10
Bocognano, *France* 21 F13
Bocoyna, *Mexico* 118 B3
Bocşa, *Romania* 28 E6
Boda, *Dalarna, Sweden* 10 C9
Böda, *Kalmar, Sweden* 11 G11
Boda, *Västernorrland, Sweden* 10 B10
Bodafors, *Sweden* 11 G8
Bodaybo, *Russia* 53 D12
Boddam, *U.K.* 13 B7
Boddington, *Australia* 93 F2
Bode Sadu, *Nigeria* 83 D5
Bodega Bay, *U.S.A.* 110 G3
Boden, *Sweden* 8 D19
Bodensee, *Europe* 25 H5
Bodenteich, *Germany* 24 C6
Bodhan, *India* 66 K10
Bodinga, *Nigeria* 83 C6
Bodmin, *U.K.* 15 G3
Bodmin Moor, *U.K.* 15 G3
Bodø, *Norway* 8 C16
Bodrog →, *Hungary* 28 B6
Bodrum, *Turkey* 47 D9
Bódva →, *Hungary* 28 B5
Boën, *France* 21 C8
Boende, *Dem. Rep. of the Congo* 84 E4
Boerne, *U.S.A.* 113 L5
Boesmans →, *S. Africa* 88 E4
Boffa, *Guinea* 82 C2
Bogalusa, *U.S.A.* 113 K10
Bogan →, *Australia* 95 D4
Bogan Gate, *Australia* 95 E4
Bogandé, *Burkina Faso* 83 C4
Bogantungan, *Australia* 94 C4
Bogata, *U.S.A.* 113 J7
Bogatić, *Serbia & M.* 44 B3
Boğazkale, *Turkey* 72 B6
Boğazlıyan, *Turkey* 72 C6
Bogen, *Sweden* 10 D6
Bogense, *Denmark* 11 J4
Bogetići, *Serbia & M.* 44 D2
Boggabilla, *Australia* 95 D5
Boggabri, *Australia* 95 E5
Boggeragh Mts., *Ireland* 12 D3
Boglan = Solhan, *Turkey* 70 B4
Bognor Regis, *U.K.* 15 G7
Bogo, *Phil.* 61 F6
Bogodukhov = Bohodukhiv, *Ukraine* 33 G8
Bogol Manya, *Ethiopia* 81 G5
Bogong, Mt., *Australia* 95 F4
Bogor, *Indonesia* 63 G12
Bogoroditsk, *Russia* 32 F10
Bogorodsk, *Russia* 34 B6
Bogoso, *Ghana* 82 D4
Bogotá, *Colombia* 124 C4
Bogotol, *Russia* 52 D9
Bogou, *Togo* 83 C5
Bogra, *Bangla.* 67 G16
Boguchany, *Russia* 53 D10
Boguchar, *Russia* 34 F5
Bogué, *Mauritania* 82 B2
Boguslav, *Ukraine* 33 H6
Boguszów-Gorce, *Poland* 31 H3
Bohain-en-Vermandois, *France* 19 C10
Bohdan, *Ukraine* 29 B9
Bohemian Forest = Böhmerwald, *Germany* 25 F9
Bohinjska Bistrica, *Slovenia* 41 B11
Böhmerwald, *Germany* 25 F9
Bohmte, *Germany* 24 C4
Bohodukhiv, *Ukraine* 33 G8
Bohol □, *Phil.* 61 G6
Bohol Sea, *Phil.* 63 C6
Bohongou, *Burkina Faso* 83 C5
Böhönye, *Hungary* 28 D2
Bohorodchany, *Ukraine* 29 B9

Bohuslän, Sweden 11 F5
Boi, Nigeria 83 D6
Boi, Pta. de, Brazil 127 A6
Boiaçu, Brazil 124 D6
Boileau, C., Australia 92 C3
Boing'o, Sudan 81 F3
Boiro, Spain 36 C2
Boise, U.S.A. 108 E5
Boise City, U.S.A. 113 G3
Boissevain, Canada 103 D8
Bóite →, Italy 41 B9
Boitzenburg, Germany 24 B9
Boizenburg, Germany 24 B6
Bojador, C., W. Sahara 78 C3
Bojana →, Albania 44 E3
Bojano, Italy 43 A7
Bojanowo, Poland 31 G3
Bøjden, Denmark 11 J4
Bojnūrd, Iran 71 B8
Bojonegoro, Indonesia 63 G14
Boju, Nigeria 83 D6
Boka, Serbia & M. 28 E5
Boka Kotorska, Serbia & M. 44 D2
Bokala, Ivory C. 82 D4
Bokani, Nigeria 83 D6
Bokaro, India 69 H11
Boké, Guinea 82 C2
Bokhara →, Australia 95 D4
Bokkos, Nigeria 83 D6
Boknafjorden, Norway 9 G11
Bokora ⌓, Uganda 86 B3
Bokoro, Chad 79 F9
Bokpyin, Burma 65 G2
Boksitogorsk, Russia 32 C7
Bol, Croatia 41 E13
Bolama, Guinea-Biss. 82 C1
Bolan →, Pakistan 68 E2
Bolan Pass, Pakistan 66 E5
Bolaños →, Mexico 118 C4
Bolaños de Calatrava, Spain 37 G7
Bolayır, Turkey 45 F10
Bolbec, France 18 C7
Boldājī, Iran 71 D6
Boldeşti-Scăeni, Romania 29 E11
Bole, China 60 B3
Bole, Ethiopia 81 F4
Bole, Ghana 82 D4
Bolekhiv, Ukraine 33 H2
Bolesławiec, Poland 31 G2
Bolgatanga, Ghana 83 C4
Bolgrad = Bolhrad, Ukraine 29 E13
Bolhrad, Ukraine 29 E13
Bolinao, Phil. 61 C3
Bolintin-Vale, Romania 29 F10
Bolívar, Argentina 126 D3
Bolivar, Mo., U.S.A. 113 G8
Bolivar, N.Y., U.S.A. 116 D6
Bolivar, Tenn., U.S.A. 113 H10
Bolivia ■, S. Amer. 124 G6
Bolivian Plateau = Altiplano, Bolivia 122 E4
Boljevac, Serbia & M. 44 C5
Bolkhov, Russia 32 F9
Bolków, Poland 31 H3
Bollebygd, Sweden 11 G6
Bollène, France 21 D8
Bollnäs, Sweden 10 C10
Bollon, Australia 95 D4
Bollstabruk, Sweden 10 B11
Bolmen, Sweden 11 H7
Bolobo, Dem. Rep. of the Congo 84 E3
Bologna, Italy 41 D8
Bologna ✕ (BLQ), Italy 41 D8
Bologoye, Russia 32 D8
Bolomba, Dem. Rep. of the Congo 84 D3
Bolon, Ozero, Russia 60 B8
Boloncheniticul, Mexico 119 D7
Bolótana, Italy 42 B1
Boloven, Cao Nguyen, Laos 64 E6
Bolpur, India 69 H12
Bolsena, Italy 41 F8
Bolsena, L. di, Italy 41 F8
Bolshakovo, Russia 30 D8
Bolshaya Chernigovka, Russia 34 D10
Bolshaya Glushitsa, Russia 34 D10
Bolshaya Martynovka, Russia 35 G5
Bolshaya Vradiyevka, Ukraine 33 J6
Bolshevik, Ostrov, Russia 53 B11
Bolshoy Anyuy →, Russia 53 C17
Bolshoy Begichev, Ostrov, Russia 53 B12
Bolshoy Kavkas = Caucasus Mountains, Eurasia 35 J7
Bolshoy Lyakhovskiy, Ostrov, Russia 53 B15
Bolshoy Tyuters, Ostrov, Russia 9 G22
Bolsward, Neths. 17 A5
Bolt Head, U.K. 15 G4
Boltaña, Spain 38 C5
Boltigen, Switz. 25 J3
Bolton, Canada 116 C5
Bolton, U.K. 14 D5
Bolton Landing, U.S.A. 117 C11
Bolu, Turkey 72 B4
Bolungavík, Iceland 8 C2
Boluo, China 59 F10
Bolvadin, Turkey 70 B1
Bolzano, Italy 41 B8
Bom Jesus da Lapa, Brazil 125 F10
Boma, Dem. Rep. of the Congo 84 F2
Bombala, Australia 95 F4
Bombarral, Portugal 37 F1
Bombay = Mumbai, India 66 K8
Bombedor, Pta., Venezuela 125 L15
Bomboma, Dem. Rep. of the Congo 84 D3
Bombombwa, Dem. Rep. of the Congo 86 B2
Bomi Hills, Liberia 82 D2
Bomili, Dem. Rep. of the Congo 86 B2
Bømlo, Norway 9 G11
Bomokandi →, Dem. Rep. of the Congo 86 B2
Bomu →, C.A.R. 84 D4
Bon, C., Tunisia 76 C5
Bon Sar Pa, Vietnam 64 F6
Bonāb, Iran 73 D12
Bonaigarh, India 69 J11
Bonaire, Neth. Ant. 121 D6
Bonampak, Mexico 119 D6
Bonang, Australia 95 F4
Bonanza, Nic. 120 D3
Bonaparte Arch., Australia 92 B3
Boñar, Spain 36 C5
Bonar Bridge, U.K. 13 D4
Bonasse, Trin. & Tob. 125 K15
Bonaventure, Canada 105 C6
Bonavista, Canada 105 C9
Bonavista, C., Canada 105 C9
Bonavista B., Canada 105 C9
Bondeno, Italy 41 D8
Bondo, Dem. Rep. of the Congo 86 B1
Bondoukou, Ivory C. 82 D4
Bondowoso, Indonesia 63 G15
Bone, Teluk, Indonesia 63 E6
Bonerate, Indonesia 63 F6
Bonerate, Kepulauan, Indonesia 63 F6
Bo'ness, U.K. 13 E5
Bonete, Cerro, Argentina 126 B2
Bong Son = Hoai Nhon, Vietnam 64 E7
Bonga, Ethiopia 81 F4
Bongabong, Phil. 61 E4
Bongor, Chad 79 F9
Bongouanou, Ivory C. 82 D4
Bonham, U.S.A. 113 J6
Boni, Mali 82 B4
Boni ⌓, Kenya 86 C5
Bonifacio, France 21 G13
Bonifacio, Bouches de, Medit. S. 42 A2
Bonin Is. = Ogasawara Gunto, Pac. Oc. 96 E6
Bonke, Ethiopia 81 F4
Bonkoukou, Niger 83 C5
Bonn, Germany 24 E3
Bonnat, France 19 F8
Bonne Terre, U.S.A. 113 G9
Bonners Ferry, U.S.A. 108 B5
Bonnétable, France 18 D7
Bonneval, France 21 C11
Bonneval-sur-Arc, France 18 D8
Bonneville, France 19 F13
Bonney, L., Australia 95 F3
Bonnie Rock, Australia 93 F2
Bonny, Nigeria 83 E6
Bonny →, Nigeria 83 E6
Bonny, Bight of, Africa 83 E6
Bonny-sur-Loire, France 19 E9
Bonnyrigg, U.K. 13 F5
Bonnyville, Canada 103 C6
Bono, Italy 42 B2
Bonoi, Indonesia 63 E9
Bonorva, Italy 42 B1
Bonsall, U.S.A. 111 M9
Bontang, Indonesia 62 D5
Bontebok △, S. Africa 88 E3
Bonthe, S. Leone 82 D2
Bontoc, Phil. 61 C4
Bonyeri, Ghana 82 D4
Bonyhád, Hungary 28 D3
Bonython Ra., Australia 92 D4
Bookabie, Australia 93 F5
Booker, U.S.A. 113 G4
Boola, Guinea 82 D3
Booligal, Australia 95 E3
Boonah, Australia 95 D5
Boone, Iowa, U.S.A. 112 D8
Boone, N.C., U.S.A. 115 G5
Booneville, Ark., U.S.A. 113 H8
Booneville, Miss., U.S.A. 115 H1
Boonville, Calif., U.S.A. 110 F3
Boonville, Ind., U.S.A. 114 F2
Boonville, Mo., U.S.A. 112 F8
Boonville, N.Y., U.S.A. 117 C9
Boorabbin △, Australia 93 F4
Boorindal, Australia 95 E4
Boorowa, Australia 95 E4
Boosaaso = Bosaso, Somali Rep. 75 E4
Boothia, Gulf of, Canada 101 A11
Boothia Pen., Canada 100 A10
Bootle, U.K. 14 D4
Booué, Gabon 84 E2
Boppard, Germany 25 E3
Boquete, Panama 120 E3
Boquilla, Presa de la, Mexico 118 B3
Boquillas del Carmen, Mexico 118 B4
Bor, Czech Rep. 26 B5
Bor, Russia 34 B7
Bor, Serbia & M. 44 B6
Bôr, Sudan 81 F3
Bor, Sweden 11 G8
Bor, Turkey 72 D6
Bor Mashash, Israel 74 D3
Borah Peak, U.S.A. 108 D7
Borang, Sudan 81 G3
Borås, Sweden 11 G6
Borāzjān, Iran 71 D6
Borba, Brazil 124 D7
Borba, Portugal 37 G3
Borborema, Planalto da, Brazil 122 D7
Borcea, Romania 29 F12
Borçka, Turkey 73 B9
Bord Khūn-e Now, Iran 71 D6
Borda, C., Australia 95 F2
Bordeaux, France 20 D3
Bordeaux ✕ (BOD), France 20 D3
Borden, Australia 93 F2
Borden-Carleton, Canada 105 C7
Borden I., Canada 4 B2
Borden Pen., Canada 101 A11
Border Ranges △, Australia 95 D5
Borders = Scottish Borders □, U.K. 13 F6
Bordertown, Australia 95 F3
Borðeyri, Iceland 8 D3
Bordighera, Italy 40 E4
Bordj Fly Ste. Marie, Algeria 78 C5
Bordj-in-Eker, Algeria 78 D7
Bordj Omar Driss, Algeria 78 C7
Bore, Ethiopia 81 G4
Borehamwood, U.K. 15 F7
Borek Wielkopolski, Poland 31 G4
Borensberg, Sweden 11 F9
Borgå = Porvoo, Finland 9 F21
Borgarfjörður, Iceland 8 D7
Borgarnes, Iceland 8 D3
Børgefjellet, Norway 8 D15
Borger, Neths. 17 B6
Borger, U.S.A. 113 H4
Borgholm, Sweden 11 H10
Bórgia, Italy 43 D9
Borgo San Dalmazzo, Italy 40 D4
Borgo San Lorenzo, Italy 41 E8
Borgo Val di Taro, Italy 40 D6
Borgo Valsugana, Italy 41 B8
Borgomanero, Italy 40 C5
Borgorose, Italy 41 F10
Borgosésia, Italy 40 C5
Borhoyn Tal, Mongolia 56 C6
Bori, Nigeria 83 E6
Borikhane, Laos 64 C4
Borisoglebsk, Russia 34 E6
Borisov = Barysaw, Belarus 32 E5
Borisovka, Russia 33 G9
Borja, Peru 124 D3
Borja, Spain 38 D3
Borjas Blancas = Les Borges Blanques, Spain 38 D5
Borjomi, Georgia 35 K6
Børkop, Denmark 11 J3
Borkou, Chad 79 E9
Borkum, Germany 24 B2
Borlänge, Sweden 10 D9
Borley, C., Antarctica 5 C5
Borlu, Turkey 47 C10
Bormida →, Italy 40 D5
Bórmio, Italy 40 B7
Borna, Germany 24 D8
Borne Sulinowo, Poland 30 E3
Borneo, E. Indies 62 D5
Bornholm, Denmark 11 J8
Bornholms Amtskommune □, Denmark 11 J8
Bornholmsgattet, Europe 11 J8
Borno □, Nigeria 83 C7
Bornos, Spain 37 J5
Bornova, Turkey 47 C9
Bornu Yassa, Nigeria 83 C7
Boro →, Sudan 81 F2
Borodino, Russia 32 E8
Borodino, Ukraine 29 D14
Borogontsy, Russia 53 C14
Boromo, Burkina Faso 82 C4
Boron, U.S.A. 111 L9
Borongan, Phil. 61 F6
Borotangba Mts., C.A.R. 81 F2
Borotou, Ivory C. 82 D3
Borovan, Bulgaria 44 C7
Borovichi, Russia 32 C7
Borovsk, Russia 32 E9
Borrby, Sweden 11 J8
Borrego Springs, U.S.A. 111 M10
Borriol, Spain 38 E4
Borroloola, Australia 94 B2
Borşa, Cluj, Romania 29 D8
Borşa, Maramureş, Romania 29 C9
Borsad, India 68 H5
Borsec, Romania 29 D10
Borshchiv, Ukraine 29 B11
Borsod-Abaúj-Zemplén □, Hungary 28 B6
Bort-les-Orgues, France 20 C6
Borth, U.K. 15 E3
Börtnan, Sweden 10 B7
Borūjerd, Iran 71 C6
Borynya, Ukraine 31 J10
Boryslav, Ukraine 31 J10
Boryspil, Ukraine 33 G6
Borzhomi = Borjomi, Georgia 35 K6
Borzna, Ukraine 33 G7
Borzya, Russia 53 D12
Bosa, Italy 42 B1
Bosanska Dubica, Bos.-H. 41 C13
Bosanska Gradiška, Bos.-H. 28 E2
Bosanska Kostajnica, Bos.-H. 41 C13
Bosanska Krupa, Bos.-H. 41 D13
Bosanski Brod, Bos.-H. 28 E2
Bosanski Novi, Bos.-H. 41 C13
Bosanski Petrovac, Bos.-H. 41 D13
Bosanski Šamac, Bos.-H. 28 E3
Bosansko Grahovo, Bos.-H. 41 D13
Bosaso, Somali Rep. 75 E4
Boscastle, U.K. 15 G3
Boscobelle, Barbados 121 g
Bose, China 58 F6
Boshan, China 57 F9
Boshof, S. Africa 88 D4
Boshrūyeh, Iran 71 C8
Bosilegrad, Serbia & M. 44 D6
Boskovice, Czech Rep. 27 B9
Bosna →, Bos.-H. 28 E3
Bosna i Hercegovina = Bosnia-Herzegovina ■, Europe 28 G2
Bosnia-Herzegovina ■, Europe 28 G2
Bosnik, Indonesia 63 E9
Bosobolo, Dem. Rep. of the Congo 84 D3
Bosporus = İstanbul Boğazı, Turkey 45 E13
Bosque Farms, U.S.A. 109 J10
Bossangoa, C.A.R. 84 C3
Bossé Bangou, Niger 83 C5
Bossier City, U.S.A. 113 J8
Bosso, Niger 83 C7
Bosso, Dallol →, Niger 83 C5
Bostan, Pakistan 68 D2
Bostānābād, Iran 70 B5
Bosten Hu, China 60 B3
Boston, U.K. 14 E7
Boston, U.S.A. 117 D13
Boston Bar, Canada 102 D4
Boston Mts., U.S.A. 113 H8
Bosumtwi, L., Ghana 83 D4
Bosut →, Croatia 28 E3
Boswell, Canada 102 D5
Boswell, U.S.A. 116 F5
Botad, India 68 H4
Botan →, Turkey 73 D10
Botene, Laos 64 D3
Botev, Bulgaria 45 D8
Botevgrad, Bulgaria 44 D7
Bothaville, S. Africa 88 D4
Bothnia, G. of, Europe 8 E19
Bothwell, Australia 95 G4
Bothwell, Canada 116 D3
Boticas, Portugal 36 D3
Botletle →, Botswana 88 C3
Botlikh, Russia 35 J8
Botna →, Moldova 29 D14
Botoroaga, Romania 29 F10
Botoşani, Romania 29 C11
Botoşani □, Romania 29 C11
Botou, Burkina Faso 83 C5
Botricello, Italy 43 D9
Botro, Ivory C. 82 D3
Botswana ■, Africa 88 C3
Bottineau, U.S.A. 112 A4
Bottnaryd, Sweden 11 G7
Bottrop, Germany 17 C6
Botucatu, Brazil 127 A6
Botwood, Canada 105 C8
Bou Djébéha, Mali 82 B4
Boû Rjeïmât, Mauritania 82 B1
Bouaflé, Ivory C. 82 D3
Bouaké, Ivory C. 82 D3
Bouar, C.A.R. 84 C3
Bouârfa, Morocco 78 B5
Boucaut B., Australia 94 A1
Bouches-du-Rhône □, France 21 E9
Boucle de Baoulé △, Mali 82 C3
Boucles de la Seine Normande ⌓, France 18 C7
Bouctouche, Canada 105 C7
Bougainville, C., Australia 92 B4
Bougainville I., Papua N. G. 96 H7
Bougainville Reef, Australia 94 B4
Bougie = Bejaïa, Algeria 78 A7
Bougouni, Mali 82 C3
Bouillon, Belgium 17 E5
Boukombé, Benin 83 C5
Boulal, Mali 82 B3
Boulazac, France 20 C4
Boulder, Colo., U.S.A. 112 E2
Boulder, Mont., U.S.A. 108 C7
Boulder City, U.S.A. 111 K12
Boulder Creek, U.S.A. 110 H4
Boulder Dam = Hoover Dam, U.S.A. 111 K12
Bouli, Mauritania 82 B2
Boulia, Australia 94 C2
Bouligny, France 19 C12
Boulogne →, France 18 E5
Boulogne-sur-Gesse, France 20 E4
Boulogne-sur-Mer, France 19 B8
Bouloire, France 18 E7
Boulouli, Mali 82 B3
Boulsa, Burkina Faso 83 C4
Boultoum, Niger 83 C7
Boûmdeïd, Mauritania 82 B2
Boun Neua, Laos 64 B3
Boun Tai, Laos 64 B3
Bouna, Ivory C. 82 D4
Boundary Peak, U.S.A. 110 H8
Boundiali, Ivory C. 82 D3
Bountiful, U.S.A. 108 F8
Bounty Is., Pac. Oc. 96 M9
Boura, Mali 82 C4
Bourbon-Lancy, France 19 F10
Bourbon-l'Archambault, France 19 F10
Bourbonnais, France 19 F10
Bourbonne-les-Bains, France 19 E12
Bourbourg, France 19 B9
Bourdel L., Canada 104 A5
Bourem, Mali 83 B4
Bourg, France 20 C3
Bourg-Argental, France 21 C8
Bourg-de-Péage, France 21 C9
Bourg-en-Bresse, France 19 F12
Bourg-Lastic, France 20 C6
Bourg-Madame, France 20 F5
Bourg-St-Andéol, France 21 D8
Bourg-St-Maurice, France 21 C10
Bourganeuf, France 20 C5
Bourges, France 19 E9
Bourget, Canada 117 A9
Bourget, Lac du, France 21 C9
Bourgneuf, B. de, France 18 E4
Bourgneuf-en-Retz, France 18 E5
Bourgogne □, France 19 F11
Bourgoin-Jallieu, France 21 C9
Bourgueil, France 18 E7
Bourke, Australia 95 E4
Bourne, U.K. 14 E7
Bournemouth, U.K. 15 G6
Bournemouth □, U.K. 15 G6
Bouroum, Burkina Faso 83 C4
Bouse, U.S.A. 111 M13
Boussac, France 19 F9
Boussé, Burkina Faso 83 C4
Boussouma, Burkina Faso 83 C4
Boutilimit, Mauritania 82 B2
Boutonne →, France 20 C3
Bouvet I. = Bouvetøya, Antarctica 3 G10
Bouvetøya, Antarctica 3 G10
Bouxwiller, France 19 D14
Bouza, Niger 83 C6
Bouzonville, France 19 C13
Bova Marina, Italy 43 E8
Bovalino Marina, Italy 43 D9
Bovec, Slovenia 41 B10
Bovill, U.S.A. 108 C5
Bovino, Italy 43 A8
Bovril, Argentina 126 C4
Bow →, Canada 102 C6
Bow Island, Canada 102 D6
Bowbells, U.S.A. 112 A3
Bowdle, U.S.A. 112 C5
Bowelling, Australia 93 F2
Bowen, Argentina 126 D2
Bowen, Australia 94 J6
Bowen Mts., Australia 95 F4
Bowie, Ariz., U.S.A. 109 K9
Bowie, Tex., U.S.A. 113 J6
Bowkān, Iran 70 B5
Bowland, Forest of, U.K. 14 D5
Bowling Green, Ky., U.S.A. 114 G2
Bowling Green, Ohio, U.S.A. 114 E4
Bowling Green, C., Australia 94 B4
Bowling Green Bay △, Australia 94 B4
Bowman, U.S.A. 112 B3
Bowman I., Antarctica 5 C8
Bowmanville = Clarington, Canada 116 C6
Bowmore, U.K. 13 F2
Bowral, Australia 95 E5
Bowraville, Australia 95 E5
Bowron →, Canada 102 C4
Bowron Lake ⌓, Canada 102 C4
Bowser L., Canada 102 B3
Bowsman, Canada 103 C8
Bowwood, Zambia 87 F2
Box Cr. →, Australia 95 E3
Boxholm, Sweden 11 F9
Boxmeer, Neths. 17 C5
Boxtel, Neths. 17 C5
Boyabat, Turkey 72 B6
Boyalıca, Turkey 45 F13
Boyang, China 59 C11
Boyany, Ukraine 29 B11
Boyce, U.S.A. 113 K8
Boyd L., Canada 104 B4
Boyle, Canada 102 C6
Boyle, Ireland 12 C3
Boyne →, Ireland 12 C5
Boyne City, U.S.A. 114 C3
Boynitsa, Bulgaria 44 C6
Boynton Beach, U.S.A. 115 M5
Boyolali, Indonesia 63 G14
Boyoma, Chutes, Dem. Rep. of the Congo 86 B2
Boysen Reservoir, U.S.A. 108 E9
Boyuibe, Bolivia 124 G6
Boyup Brook, Australia 93 F2
Boz Burun, Turkey 45 F12
Boz Dağ, Turkey 47 D11
Boz Dağları, Turkey 47 C10
Bozburun, Turkey 47 E10
Bozcaada, Turkey 72 C2
Bozdoğan, Turkey 47 D10
Bozeman, U.S.A. 108 D8
Bozen = Bolzano, Italy 41 B8
Boževac, Serbia & M. 44 B5
Bozhou, China 56 H8
Bozkır, Turkey 72 D5
Bozkurt, Turkey 47 D11
Bozouls, France 20 D6
Bozoum, C.A.R. 84 C3
Bozova, Antalya, Turkey 47 D12
Bozova, Sanliurfa, Turkey 73 D8
Bozovici, Romania 28 F7
Bozüyük, Turkey 47 B12
Bra, Italy 40 D4
Braås, Sweden 11 G9
Brabant □, Belgium 17 D4
Brabant L., Canada 103 B8
Brabrand, Denmark 11 H4
Brač, Croatia 41 E13
Bracadale, L., U.K. 13 D2
Bracciano, Italy 41 F9
Bracciano, L. di, Italy 41 F9
Bracebridge, Canada 116 A5
Brach, Libya 79 C8
Bracieux, France 18 E8
Bräcke, Sweden 10 B9
Brackettville, U.S.A. 113 L4
Bracki Kanal, Croatia 41 E13
Bracknell, U.K. 15 F7
Bracknell Forest □, U.K. 15 F7
Brad, Romania 28 D7
Brádano →, Italy 43 B9
Bradenton, U.S.A. 115 M4
Bradford, Canada 116 B5
Bradford, U.K. 14 D6
Bradford, Pa., U.S.A. 116 E6
Bradford, Vt., U.S.A. 117 C12
Bradley, Ark., U.S.A. 113 J8
Bradley, Calif., U.S.A. 110 K6
Bradley Institute, Zimbabwe 87 F3
Brady, U.S.A. 113 K5
Brædstrup, Denmark 11 J3
Braeside, Canada 117 A8
Braga, Portugal 36 D2
Braga □, Portugal 36 D2
Bragadiru, Romania 29 G10
Bragado, Argentina 126 D3
Bragança, Brazil 125 D9
Bragança, Portugal 36 D4
Bragança □, Portugal 36 D4
Bragança Paulista, Brazil 127 A6
Brahestad = Raahe, Finland 8 D21
Brahmanbaria, Bangla. 67 H17
Brahmani →, India 67 J15
Brahmapur, India 67 K14
Brahmaputra →, Asia 69 H13
Braich-y-pwll, U.K. 14 E3
Braidwood, Australia 95 F4
Brăila, Romania 29 E12
Brăila □, Romania 29 E12
Brainerd, U.S.A. 112 B7
Braintree, U.K. 15 F8
Braintree, U.S.A. 117 D14
Brak →, S. Africa 88 D3
Brake, Germany 24 B4

Brakel, *Germany* 24 D5
Bräkne-Hoby, *Sweden* 11 H9
Brakwater, *Namibia* 88 C2
Brålanda, *Sweden* 11 F6
Bramberg, *Germany* 25 E6
Bramdrupdam, *Denmark* 11 J3
Bramming, *Denmark* 11 J2
Brämön, *Sweden* 10 B11
Brampton, *Canada* 116 C5
Brampton, *U.K.* 14 C5
Bramsche, *Germany* 24 C3
Bramton I., *Australia* 94 J7
Branco →, *Brazil* 124 D6
Brandberg, *Namibia* 88 C1
Brandberg ⌓, *Namibia* 88 C1
Brande, *Denmark* 11 J3
Brandenburg = Neubrandenburg, *Germany* 24 B9
Brandenburg, *Germany* 24 C8
Brandenburg □, *Germany* 24 C9
Brandfort, *S. Africa* 88 D4
Brando, *France* 21 F13
Brandon, *Canada* 103 D9
Brandon, *U.S.A.* 117 C11
Brandon B., *Ireland* 12 D1
Brandon Mt., *Ireland* 12 D1
Brandsen, *Argentina* 126 D4
Brandvlei, *S. Africa* 88 E3
Brandýs nad Labem, *Czech Rep.* 26 A7
Brănești, *Romania* 29 F11
Branford, *U.S.A.* 117 E12
Braniewo, *Poland* 30 D6
Bransfield Str., *Antarctica* 5 C18
Brańsk, *Poland* 31 F9
Branson, *U.S.A.* 113 G8
Brantford, *Canada* 116 C4
Brantôme, *France* 20 C4
Branzi, *Italy* 40 B6
Bras d'Or L., *Canada* 105 C7
Brasher Falls, *U.S.A.* 117 B10
Brasil, Planalto, *Brazil* 122 E6
Brasiléia, *Brazil* 124 F5
Brasília, *Brazil* 125 G9
Brasília Legal, *Brazil* 125 D7
Braslaw, *Belarus* 9 J22
Braslovče, *Slovenia* 41 B12
Brașov, *Romania* 29 E10
Brașov □, *Romania* 29 E10
Brass, *Nigeria* 83 E6
Brass →, *Nigeria* 83 E6
Brassac-les-Mines, *France* 20 C7
Brasschaat, *Belgium* 17 C4
Brassey, Banjaran, *Malaysia* 62 D5
Brassey Ra., *Australia* 93 E3
Brasstown Bald, *U.S.A.* 115 H4
Brastad, *Sweden* 11 F5
Brastavățu, *Romania* 29 G9
Bratan = Morozov, *Bulgaria* 45 D9
Brateș, *Romania* 29 E11
Bratislava, *Slovak Rep.* 27 C10
Bratislava M.R. Stefanik ✕ (BTS), *Slovak Rep.* 27 C10
Bratislavský □, *Slovak Rep.* 27 C10
Bratsigovo, *Bulgaria* 45 D8
Bratsk, *Russia* 53 D11
Brattleboro, *U.S.A.* 117 D12
Bratunac, *Bos.-H.* 28 F4
Braunau, *Austria* 26 C6
Braunschweig, *Germany* 24 C6
Braunton, *U.K.* 15 F3
Bravicea, *Moldova* 29 C13
Bråviken, *Sweden* 11 F10
Bravo del Norte, Rio = Grande, Rio →, *U.S.A.* 113 N6
Brawley, *U.S.A.* 111 N11
Bray, *Ireland* 12 C5
Bray, Mt., *Australia* 94 A1
Bray-sur-Seine, *France* 19 D10
Brazeau →, *Canada* 102 C5
Brazil, *U.S.A.* 114 F2
Brazil ■, *S. Amer.* 125 F9
Brazilian Highlands = Brasil, Planalto, *Brazil* 122 E6
Brazo Sur →, *S. Amer.* 126 B4
Brazos →, *U.S.A.* 113 L7
Brazzaville, *Congo* 84 E3
Brčko, *Bos.-H.* 28 F3
Brda →, *Poland* 31 E5
Brdy, *Czech Rep.* 26 B6
Breaden, L., *Australia* 93 E4
Breaksea Sd., *N.Z.* 91 L1
Bream B., *N.Z.* 91 F5
Bream Hd., *N.Z.* 91 F5
Breas, *Chile* 126 B1
Breaza, *Romania* 29 E10
Brebes, *Indonesia* 63 G13
Brechin, *Canada* 116 B5
Brechin, *U.K.* 13 E6
Brecht, *Belgium* 17 C4
Breckenridge, *Colo., U.S.A.* 108 G10
Breckenridge, *Minn., U.S.A.* 112 B6
Breckenridge, *Tex., U.S.A.* 113 J5
Breckland, *U.K.* 15 E8
Břeclav, *Czech Rep.* 27 C9
Brecon, *U.K.* 15 F4
Brecon Beacons, *U.K.* 15 F4
Brecon Beacons △, *U.K.* 15 F4
Breda, *Neths.* 17 C4
Bredaryd, *Sweden* 11 G7
Bredasdorp, *S. Africa* 88 E3
Bredebro, *Denmark* 11 J2
Bredstedt, *Germany* 24 A4
Bree, *Belgium* 17 C5
Bregalnica →, *Macedonia* 44 E6
Bregenz, *Austria* 26 D2
Bregovo, *Bulgaria* 44 B6
Bréhal, *France* 18 D5
Bréhat, Î. de, *France* 18 D4
Breiðafjörður, *Iceland* 8 D2
Breil-sur-Roya, *France* 21 E11
Breisach, *Germany* 25 G3
Brejo, *Brazil* 125 D10
Bremen, *Germany* 24 B4
Bremen □, *Germany* 24 B4
Bremer Bay, *Australia* 93 F2
Bremer I., *Australia* 94 A2
Bremerhaven, *Germany* 24 B4
Bremerton, *U.S.A.* 110 C4
Bremervörde, *Germany* 24 B5
Brenes, *Spain* 37 H5
Brenham, *U.S.A.* 113 K6
Brenne, *France* 20 B5
Brenne ⌓, *France* 20 B5
Brennerpass, *Austria* 26 D4
Breno, *Italy* 40 C7
Brent, *U.S.A.* 115 J2
Brenta →, *Italy* 41 C9
Brentwood, *U.K.* 15 F8
Brentwood, *Calif., U.S.A.* 110 H5
Brentwood, *N.Y., U.S.A.* 117 F11
Bréscia, *Italy* 40 C7
Breskens, *Neths.* 17 C3
Breslau = Wrocław, *Poland* 31 G4
Bresle →, *France* 18 B8
Bressanone, *Italy* 41 B8
Bressay, *U.K.* 13 A7
Bresse, *France* 19 F12
Bressuire, *France* 18 F6
Brest, *Belarus* 33 F2
Brest, *France* 18 D2
Brest-Litovsk = Brest, *Belarus* 33 F2
Bretagne □, *France* 18 D3
Bretçu, *Romania* 29 D11
Bretenoux, *France* 20 D5
Breteuil, *Eure, France* 18 D7
Breteuil, *Oise, France* 19 C9
Breton, *Canada* 102 C6
Breton, Pertuis, *France* 20 B2
Breton Sd., *U.S.A.* 113 L10
Brett, C., *N.Z.* 91 F5
Bretten, *Germany* 25 F4
Breuil-Cervínia, *Italy* 40 C4
Brevard, *U.S.A.* 115 H4
Breves, *Brazil* 125 D8
Brewarrina, *Australia* 95 E4
Brewer, *U.S.A.* 115 C11
Brewer, Mt., *U.S.A.* 110 J8
Brewerville, *Liberia* 82 D2
Brewster, *N.Y., U.S.A.* 117 E11
Brewster, *Ohio, U.S.A.* 116 F3
Brewster, *Wash., U.S.A.* 108 B4
Brewster, Kap = Kangikajik, *Greenland* 4 B6
Brewton, *U.S.A.* 115 K2
Breyten, *S. Africa* 89 D5
Breza, *Bos.-H.* 28 F3
Brežice, *Slovenia* 41 C12
Březnice, *Czech Rep.* 26 B6
Breznik, *Bulgaria* 44 D6
Brezno, *Slovak Rep.* 27 C12
Brezoi, *Romania* 29 E9
Brezovica, *Serbia & M.* 44 D5
Brezovo, *Bulgaria* 45 D9
Briançon, *France* 21 D10
Briare, *France* 19 E9
Briático, *Italy* 43 D9
Bribie I., *Australia* 95 D5
Bribri, *Costa Rica* 120 E3
Briceni, *Moldova* 29 B12
Bricquebec, *France* 18 C5
Bridgefield, *Barbados* 121 g
Bridgehampton, *U.S.A.* 117 F12
Bridgend, *U.K.* 15 F4
Bridgend □, *U.K.* 15 F4
Bridgeport, *Calif., U.S.A.* 110 G7
Bridgeport, *Conn., U.S.A.* 117 E11
Bridgeport, *Nebr., U.S.A.* 112 E3
Bridgeport, *Tex., U.S.A.* 113 J6
Bridger, *U.S.A.* 108 D9
Bridgeton, *U.S.A.* 114 F8
Bridgetown, *Australia* 93 F2
Bridgetown, *Barbados* 121 g
Bridgetown, *Canada* 105 D6
Bridgewater, *Canada* 105 D7
Bridgewater, *Mass., U.S.A.* 117 E14
Bridgewater, *N.Y., U.S.A.* 117 D9
Bridgewater, C., *Australia* 95 F3
Bridgewater-Gagebrook, *Australia* 95 G4
Bridgnorth, *U.K.* 15 E5
Bridgton, *U.S.A.* 117 B14
Bridgwater, *U.K.* 15 F5
Bridgwater B., *U.K.* 15 F4
Bridlington, *U.K.* 14 C7
Bridlington B., *U.K.* 14 C7
Bridport, *Australia* 95 G4
Bridport, *U.K.* 15 G5
Briec, *France* 18 D2
Brienne-le-Château, *France* 19 D11
Brienon-sur-Armançon, *France* 19 E10
Brienz, *Switz.* 25 J4
Brienzersee, *Switz.* 25 J3
Brière ⌓, *France* 18 E4
Brig, *Switz.* 25 J3
Brigg, *U.K.* 14 D7
Brigham City, *U.S.A.* 108 F7
Bright, *Australia* 95 F4
Brighton, *Australia* 95 F2
Brighton, *Canada* 116 B7
Brighton, *Trin. & Tob.* 125 K15
Brighton, *U.K.* 15 G7
Brighton, *Colo., U.S.A.* 112 F2
Brighton, *N.Y., U.S.A.* 116 C7
Brignogan-Plage, *France* 18 D2
Brignoles, *France* 21 E10
Brihuega, *Spain* 38 E2
Brikama, *Gambia* 82 C1
Brilliant, *U.S.A.* 116 F4
Brilon, *Germany* 24 D4
Bríndisi, *Italy* 43 B10
Brinje, *Croatia* 41 D12
Brinkley, *U.S.A.* 113 H9
Brinnon, *U.S.A.* 110 C4
Brion, Î., *Canada* 105 C7
Brionne, *France* 18 C7
Brionski, *Croatia* 41 D10
Brioude, *France* 20 C7
Briouze, *France* 18 D6
Brisbane, *Australia* 95 D5
Brisbane →, *Australia* 95 D5
Brisighella, *Italy* 41 D8
Bristol, *U.K.* 15 F5
Bristol, *Conn., U.S.A.* 117 E12
Bristol, *Pa., U.S.A.* 117 F10
Bristol, *R.I., U.S.A.* 117 E13
Bristol, *Tenn., U.S.A.* 115 G4
Bristol, City of □, *U.K.* 15 F5
Bristol B., *U.S.A.* 100 C4
Bristol Channel, *U.K.* 15 F3
Bristol I., *Antarctica* 5 B1
Bristol L., *U.S.A.* 109 J5
Bristow, *U.S.A.* 113 H6
Britain = Great Britain, *Europe* 6 E5
British Columbia □, *Canada* 102 C3
British Indian Ocean Terr. = Chagos Arch. ☒, *Ind. Oc.* 50 K11
British Isles, *Europe* 6 D4
British Virgin Is. ☒, *W. Indies* 121 e
Brits, *S. Africa* 89 D4
Britstown, *S. Africa* 88 E3
Britt, *Canada* 104 C3
Brittany = Bretagne □, *France* 18 D3
Britton, *U.S.A.* 112 C6
Brive-la-Gaillarde, *France* 20 C5
Briviesca, *Spain* 36 C7
Brixen = Bressanone, *Italy* 41 B8
Brixham, *U.K.* 15 G4
Brnaze, *Croatia* 41 E13
Brnenský □, *Czech Rep.* 27 B9
Brno, *Czech Rep.* 27 B9
Broach = Bharuch, *India* 66 J8
Broad →, *U.S.A.* 115 J5
Broad Arrow, *Australia* 93 F3
Broad B., *U.K.* 13 C2
Broad Haven, *Ireland* 12 B2
Broad Law, *U.K.* 13 F5
Broad Sd., *Australia* 94 C4
Broadalbin, *U.S.A.* 117 C10
Broadback →, *Canada* 104 B4
Broadhurst Ra., *Australia* 92 D3
Broads △, *U.K.* 15 E9
Broads, The, *U.K.* 14 E9
Broadus, *U.S.A.* 112 C2
Broager, *Denmark* 11 K3
Broby, *Sweden* 11 H8
Brocēni, *Latvia* 30 B9
Brochet, *Canada* 103 B8
Brochet, L., *Canada* 103 B8
Brocken, *Germany* 24 D6
Brockport, *U.S.A.* 116 C7
Brockton, *U.S.A.* 117 D13
Brockville, *Canada* 117 B9
Brockway, *Mont., U.S.A.* 112 B2
Brockway, *Pa., U.S.A.* 116 E6
Brocton, *U.S.A.* 116 D5
Brod, *Macedonia* 44 E5
Brodarevo, *Serbia & M.* 44 C3
Brodeur Pen., *Canada* 101 A11
Brodhead, Mt., *U.S.A.* 116 E7
Brodick, *U.K.* 13 F3
Brodnica, *Poland* 31 E6
Brody, *Ukraine* 33 G3
Brogan, *U.S.A.* 108 D5
Broglie, *France* 18 C7
Brok, *Poland* 31 F8
Broken Arrow, *U.S.A.* 113 G7
Broken Bow, *Nebr., U.S.A.* 112 E5
Broken Bow, *Okla., U.S.A.* 113 H7
Broken Bow Lake, *U.S.A.* 113 H7
Broken Hill, *Australia* 95 E3
Broken River Ra., *Australia* 94 K6
Brokind, *Sweden* 11 F9
Bromley □, *U.K.* 15 F8
Bromo, *Indonesia* 63 G15
Bromölla, *Sweden* 11 H8
Bromsgrove, *U.K.* 15 E5
Brønderslev, *Denmark* 11 G3
Brong-Ahafo □, *Ghana* 82 D4
Broni, *Italy* 40 C6
Bronkhorstspruit, *S. Africa* 89 D4
Brønnøysund, *Norway* 8 D15
Bronte, *Italy* 43 E7
Brook Park, *U.S.A.* 116 E4
Brookhaven, *U.S.A.* 113 K9
Brookings, *Oreg., U.S.A.* 108 E1
Brookings, *S. Dak., U.S.A.* 112 C6
Brooklin, *Canada* 116 C6
Brooklyn Park, *U.S.A.* 112 C8
Brooks, *Canada* 102 C6
Brooks Range, *U.S.A.* 100 B5
Brooksville, *U.S.A.* 115 L4
Brookton, *Australia* 93 F2
Brookville, *U.S.A.* 116 E5
Broom, L., *U.K.* 13 D3
Broome, *Australia* 92 C3
Broons, *France* 18 D4
Brora, *U.K.* 13 C5
Brora →, *U.K.* 13 C5
Brørup, *Denmark* 11 J2
Brösarp, *Sweden* 11 J8
Brosna →, *Ireland* 12 C4
Broșteni, *Mehedinți, Romania* 28 F7
Broșteni, *Suceava, Romania* 29 C10
Brothers, *U.S.A.* 108 E3
Brou, *France* 18 D8
Brouage, *France* 20 C2
Brough, *U.K.* 14 C5
Brough Hd., *U.K.* 13 B5
Broughton Island = Qikiqtarjuaq, *Canada* 101 B13
Broumov, *Czech Rep.* 27 A9
Brovary, *Ukraine* 33 G6
Brovst, *Denmark* 11 G3
Brown, L., *Australia* 93 F2
Brown, Pt., *Australia* 95 E1
Brown City, *U.S.A.* 116 C2
Brown Willy, *U.K.* 15 G3
Brownfield, *U.S.A.* 113 J3
Browning, *U.S.A.* 108 B7
Brownsville, *Oreg., U.S.A.* 108 D2
Brownsville, *Pa., U.S.A.* 116 F5
Brownsville, *Tenn., U.S.A.* 113 H10
Brownsville, *Tex., U.S.A.* 113 N6
Brownville, *U.S.A.* 117 C9
Brownwood, *U.S.A.* 113 K5
Browse I., *Australia* 92 B3
Bruas, *Malaysia* 65 K3
Bruay-la-Buissière, *France* 19 B9
Bruce, Mt., *Australia* 92 D2
Bruce Pen., *Canada* 116 B3
Bruce Peninsula △, *Canada* 116 A3
Bruce Rock, *Australia* 93 F2
Bruche →, *France* 19 D14
Bruchsal, *Germany* 25 F4
Bruck an der Leitha, *Austria* 27 C9
Bruck an der Mur, *Austria* 26 D8
Brue →, *U.K.* 15 F5
Bruges = Brugge, *Belgium* 17 C3
Brugg, *Switz.* 25 H4
Brugge, *Belgium* 17 C3
Bruin, *U.S.A.* 116 E5
Brûlé, *Canada* 102 C5
Brûlon, *France* 18 E6
Brumado, *Brazil* 125 F10
Brumath, *France* 19 D14
Brumunddal, *Norway* 9 F14
Bruneau, *U.S.A.* 108 E6
Bruneau →, *U.S.A.* 108 E6
Bruneck = Brunico, *Italy* 41 B8
Brunei = Bandar Seri Begawan, *Brunei* 62 C4
Brunei ■, *Asia* 62 D4
Brunflo, *Sweden* 10 A8
Brunico, *Italy* 41 B8
Brunna, *Sweden* 10 E11
Brunnen, *Switz.* 25 J4
Brunner, L., *N.Z.* 91 K3
Brunsbüttel, *Germany* 24 B5
Brunssum, *Neths.* 17 D5
Brunswick = Braunschweig, *Germany* 24 C6
Brunswick, *Ga., U.S.A.* 115 K5
Brunswick, *Maine, U.S.A.* 115 D11
Brunswick, *Md., U.S.A.* 114 F7
Brunswick, *Mo., U.S.A.* 112 F8
Brunswick, *Ohio, U.S.A.* 116 E3
Brunswick, Pen. de, *Chile* 128 G2
Brunswick B., *Australia* 92 C3
Brunswick Junction, *Australia* 93 F2
Bruntál, *Czech Rep.* 27 B10
Bruny I., *Australia* 95 G4
Brus Laguna, *Honduras* 120 C3
Brusartsi, *Bulgaria* 44 C7
Brush, *U.S.A.* 112 E3
Brushton, *U.S.A.* 117 B10
Brusio, *Switz.* 25 J6
Brusque, *Brazil* 127 B6
Brussel, *Belgium* 17 D4
Brussel ✕ (BRU), *Belgium* 17 D5
Brussels = Brussel, *Belgium* 17 D4
Brussels, *Canada* 116 C3
Brusy, *Poland* 30 E4
Bruthen, *Australia* 95 F4
Bruxelles = Brussel, *Belgium* 17 D4
Bruyères, *France* 19 D13
Bruz, *France* 18 D5
Brwinów, *Poland* 31 F7
Bryagovo, *Bulgaria* 45 E9
Bryan, *Ohio, U.S.A.* 114 E3
Bryan, *Tex., U.S.A.* 113 K6
Bryan, Mt., *Australia* 95 E2
Bryanka, *Ukraine* 33 H10
Bryansk, *Bryansk, Russia* 33 F8
Bryansk, *Dagestan, Russia* 35 H8
Bryanskoye = Bryansk, *Russia* 35 H8
Bryce Canyon △, *U.S.A.* 109 H7
Bryne, *Norway* 9 G11
Bryson City, *U.S.A.* 115 H4
Bryukhovetskaya, *Russia* 33 K10
Brza Palanka, *Serbia & M.* 44 B6
Brzeg, *Poland* 31 H4
Brzeg Dolny, *Poland* 31 G3
Brześć Kujawski, *Poland* 31 F5
Brzesko, *Poland* 31 J7
Brzeziny, *Poland* 31 G6
Brzozów, *Poland* 31 J9
Bsharri, *Lebanon* 74 A5
Bū Baqarah, *U.A.E.* 71 E8
Bu Craa, *W. Sahara* 78 C3
Bū Ḩasā, *U.A.E.* 71 F7
Bua, *Sweden* 11 G6
Bua Yai, *Thailand* 64 E4
Buapinang, *Indonesia* 63 E6
Buba, *Guinea-Biss.* 82 C2
Bubanza, *Burundi* 86 C2
Bubaque, *Guinea-Biss.* 82 C1
Bube, *Ethiopia* 81 F4
Būbiyān, *Kuwait* 71 D6
Buca, *Turkey* 47 C9
Bucak, *Turkey* 47 D12
Bucaramanga, *Colombia* 124 B4
Bucas Grande I., *Phil.* 61 G6
Bucasia, *Australia* 94 K7
Buccaneer Arch., *Australia* 92 C3
Buccino, *Italy* 43 B8
Buccoo Reef, *Trin. & Tob.* 125 J16
Bucecea, *Romania* 29 C11
Bucegi △, *Romania* 29 E10
Buchach, *Ukraine* 33 H3
Buchan, *U.K.* 13 D6
Buchan Ness, *U.K.* 13 D7
Buchanan, *Canada* 103 C8
Buchanan, *Liberia* 82 D2
Buchanan, L., *Queens., Australia* 94 C4
Buchanan, L., *W. Austral., Australia* 93 E3
Buchanan, L., *U.S.A.* 113 K5
Buchanan Cr. →, *Australia* 94 B2
Buchans, *Canada* 105 C8
Bucharest = București, *Romania* 29 F11
Buchen, *Germany* 25 F5
Buchholz, *Germany* 24 B5
Buchloe, *Germany* 25 G6
Buchon, Pt., *U.S.A.* 110 K6
Buciumi, *Romania* 28 C8
Buck Hill Falls, *U.S.A.* 117 E9
Bückeburg, *Germany* 24 C5
Buckeye, *U.S.A.* 109 K7
Buckeye Lake, *U.S.A.* 116 G2
Buckhannon, *U.S.A.* 114 F5
Buckhaven, *U.K.* 13 E5
Buckhorn L., *Canada* 116 B6
Buckie, *U.K.* 13 D6
Buckingham, *Canada* 104 C4
Buckingham, *U.K.* 15 F7
Buckingham B., *Australia* 94 A2
Buckinghamshire □, *U.K.* 15 F7
Buckle Hd., *Australia* 92 B4
Buckleboo, *Australia* 95 E2
Buckley, *U.K.* 14 D4
Buckley →, *Australia* 94 C2
Bucklin, *U.S.A.* 113 G5
Bucks L., *U.S.A.* 110 F5
Bucquoy, *France* 19 B9
București, *Romania* 29 F11
București Otopeni ✕ (OTP), *Romania* 45 B10
Bucyrus, *U.S.A.* 114 E4
Budacu, Vf., *Romania* 29 C10
Budalin, *Burma* 67 H19
Budaörs, *Hungary* 28 C3
Budapest, *Hungary* 28 C4
Budapest □, *Hungary* 28 C4
Budapest ✕ (BUD), *Hungary* 28 C4
Budaun, *India* 69 E8
Budd Coast, *Antarctica* 5 C8
Buddusò, *Italy* 42 B2
Bude, *U.K.* 15 G3
Budennovsk, *Russia* 35 H7
Budești, *Romania* 29 F11
Budeyi, *Ukraine* 29 B14
Budge Budge = Baj Baj, *India* 69 H13
Budgewoi, *Australia* 95 E5
Budia, *Spain* 38 E2
Büdingen, *Germany* 25 E5
Budjala, *Dem. Rep. of the Congo* 84 D3
Budoni, *Italy* 42 B2
Búdrio, *Italy* 41 D8
Budva, *Serbia & M.* 44 D2
Budzyń, *Poland* 31 F3
Buea, *Cameroon* 83 E6
Buellton, *U.S.A.* 111 L6
Buena Esperanza, *Argentina* 126 C2
Buena Park, *U.S.A.* 111 M9
Buena Vista, *Colo., U.S.A.* 109 G10
Buena Vista, *Va., U.S.A.* 114 G6
Buena Vista Lake Bed, *U.S.A.* 111 K7
Buenaventura, *Colombia* 124 C3
Buenaventura, *Mexico* 118 B3
Buendía, Embalse de, *Spain* 38 E2
Buenos Aires, *Argentina* 126 C4
Buenos Aires, *Costa Rica* 120 E3
Buenos Aires □, *Argentina* 126 D4
Buenos Aires, L., *Chile* 128 F2
Buffalo, *Mo., U.S.A.* 113 G8
Buffalo, *N.Y., U.S.A.* 116 D6
Buffalo, *Okla., U.S.A.* 113 G5
Buffalo, *S. Dak., U.S.A.* 112 C3
Buffalo, *Wyo., U.S.A.* 108 D10
Buffalo △, *U.S.A.* 113 G8
Buffalo →, *Canada* 102 A5
Buffalo →, *S. Africa* 89 D5
Buffalo Head Hills, *Canada* 102 B5
Buffalo L., *Alta., Canada* 102 C6
Buffalo L., *N.W.T., Canada* 102 A5
Buffalo Narrows, *Canada* 103 B7
Buffalo Springs ⌓, *Kenya* 86 B4
Buffels →, *S. Africa* 88 D2
Buford, *U.S.A.* 115 H4
Bug = Buh →, *Ukraine* 33 J6
Bug →, *Poland* 31 F8
Buga, *Colombia* 124 C3
Bugala I., *Uganda* 86 C3
Buganda, *Uganda* 86 C3
Buganga, *Uganda* 86 C3
Bugasong, *Phil.* 61 F5
Bugeat, *France* 20 C5
Bugel, Tanjung, *Indonesia* 63 G14
Bugibba, *Malta* 49 D1
Bugojno, *Bos.-H.* 28 F2
Bugsuk, *Phil.* 62 C5
Buguma, *Nigeria* 83 E6
Bugun Shara, *Mongolia* 60 B5
Bugungu ⌓, *Uganda* 86 B3
Buguruslan, *Russia* 52 D6
Buh →, *Ukraine* 33 J6
Buharkent, *Turkey* 47 D10
Buheirat-Murrat-el-Kubra, *Egypt* 80 H8
Buhera, *Zimbabwe* 89 B5
Bühl, *Germany* 25 G4
Buhl, *U.S.A.* 108 E6
Buhuși, *Romania* 29 D11
Bui △, *Ghana* 82 D4
Builth Wells, *U.K.* 15 E4
Buinsk, *Russia* 34 C9
Buir Nur, *Mongolia* 60 B6
Buis-les-Baronnies, *France* 21 D9
Buitrago del Lozoya, *Spain* 36 E7
Bujalance, *Spain* 37 H6
Bujanovac, *Serbia & M.* 44 D5
Bujaraloz, *Spain* 38 D4
Buje, *Croatia* 41 C10
Bujumbura, *Burundi* 86 C2
Bük, *Hungary* 28 C1
Buk, *Poland* 31 F3
Bukachacha, *Russia* 53 D12
Bukama, *Dem. Rep. of the Congo* 87 D2
Bukavu, *Dem. Rep. of the Congo* 86 C2
Bukene, *Tanzania* 86 C3
Bukhara = Bukhoro, *Uzbekistan* 52 F7

Bukhoro, *Uzbekistan* 52 F7
Bukima, *Tanzania* 86 C3
Bukit Badung, *Indonesia* 63 K18
Bukit Kerajaan, *Malaysia* 65 c
Bukit Mertajam, *Malaysia* 65 c
Bukit Ni, *Malaysia* 65 d
Bukit Panjang, *Singapore* 65 d
Bukit Tengah, *Malaysia* 65 c
Bukittinggi, *Indonesia* 62 E2
Bükk, *Hungary* 28 B5
Bükki △, *Hungary* 28 B5
Bukoba, *Tanzania* 86 C3
Bukum, Pulau, *Singapore* 65 d
Bukuru, *Nigeria* 83 D6
Bukuya, *Uganda* 86 B3
Būl, Kuh-e, *Iran* 71 D7
Bula, *Guinea-Biss.* 82 C1
Bula, *Indonesia* 63 E8
Bülach, *Switz.* 25 H4
Bulahdelah, *Australia* 95 E5
Bulan, *Phil.* 61 E5
Bulancak, *Turkey* 73 B8
Bulandshahr, *India* 68 E7
Bulanık, *Turkey* 73 C10
Bûlâq, *Egypt* 80 B3
Bulawayo, *Zimbabwe* 87 G2
Buldan, *Turkey* 47 C10
Bulgar, *Russia* 34 C9
Bulgaria ■, *Europe* 45 D9
Bulgheria, Monte, *Italy* 43 B8
Bulgurca, *Turkey* 47 C9
Buli, Teluk, *Indonesia* 63 D7
Buliluyan, C., *Phil.* 61 G2
Bulim, *Singapore* 65 d
Bulki, *Ethiopia* 81 F4
Bulkley →, *Canada* 102 B3
Bull Shoals L., *U.S.A.* 113 G8
Bullaque →, *Spain* 37 G6
Bullas, *Spain* 39 G3
Bulle, *Switz.* 25 J3
Bulleringa △, *Australia* 94 B3
Bullhead City, *U.S.A.* 111 K12
Büllingen, *Belgium* 17 D6
Bullock Creek, *Australia* 94 B3
Bulloo →, *Australia* 95 D3
Bulloo L., *Australia* 95 D3
Bulls, *N.Z.* 91 J5
Bully-les-Mines, *France* 19 B9
Bulnes, *Chile* 126 D1
Bulqizë, *Albania* 44 E4
Bulsar = Valsad, *India* 66 J8
Bultfontein, *S. Africa* 88 D4
Bulukumba, *Indonesia* 63 F6
Bulun, *Russia* 53 B13
Bumba, *Dem. Rep. of the Congo* 84 D4
Bumbeşti-Jiu, *Romania* 29 E8
Bumbiri I., *Tanzania* 86 C3
Bumbuna, *S. Leone* 82 D2
Bumhpa Bum, *Burma* 67 F20
Bumi →, *Zimbabwe* 87 F2
Buna, *Kenya* 86 B4
Bunawan, *Phil.* 61 G6
Bunazi, *Tanzania* 86 C3
Bunbury, *Australia* 93 F2
Bunclody, *Ireland* 12 D5
Buncrana, *Ireland* 12 A4
Bundaberg, *Australia* 95 C5
Bünde, *Germany* 24 C4
Bundey →, *Australia* 94 C2
Bundi, *India* 68 G6
Bundjalung △, *Australia* 95 D5
Bundoran, *Ireland* 12 B3
Bundukia, *Sudan* 81 F3
Bung Kan, *Thailand* 64 C4
Bunga →, *Nigeria* 83 C6
Bungay, *U.K.* 15 E9
Bungil Cr. →, *Australia* 95 D4
Bungle Bungle = Purnululu △, *Australia* 92 C4
Bungo-Suidō, *Japan* 55 H6
Bungoma, *Kenya* 86 B3
Bungotakada, *Japan* 55 H5
Bungu, *Tanzania* 86 D4
Bunia, *Dem. Rep. of the Congo* 86 B3
Bunji, *Pakistan* 69 B6
Bunkie, *U.S.A.* 113 K8
Bunnell, *U.S.A.* 115 L5
Buñol, *Spain* 39 F4
Bunsuru, *Nigeria* 83 C5
Buntok, *Indonesia* 62 E4
Bununu Dass, *Nigeria* 83 C6
Bununu Kasa, *Nigeria* 83 D6
Bunya Mts. △, *Australia* 95 D5
Bünyan, *Turkey* 72 C6
Bunyu, *Indonesia* 62 D5
Bunza, *Nigeria* 83 C5
Buol, *Indonesia* 63 D6
Buon Brieng, *Vietnam* 64 F7
Buon Ma Thuot, *Vietnam* 64 F7
Buong Long, *Cambodia* 64 F6
Buorkhaya, Mys, *Russia* 53 B14
Buqayq, *Si. Arabia* 71 E6
Buqbuq, *Egypt* 80 A2
Bur Acaba, *Somali Rep.* 75 G3
Bûr Fuad, *Egypt* 80 H8
Bûr Safâga, *Egypt* 70 E2
Bûr Sa'îd, *Egypt* 80 H8
Bûr Sûdân, *Sudan* 80 D4
Bûr Taufiq, *Egypt* 80 J8
Bura, *Kenya* 86 C4
Burakin, *Australia* 93 F2
Buram, *Sudan* 81 E2
Burao, *Somali Rep.* 75 F4
Burāq, *Syria* 74 B5
Buraydah, *Si. Arabia* 70 E4
Burbank, *U.S.A.* 111 L8
Burda, *India* 68 G6
Burdekin →, *Australia* 94 B4
Burdur, *Turkey* 47 D12
Burdur □, *Turkey* 47 D12
Burdur Gölü, *Turkey* 47 D12
Burdwan = Barddhaman, *India* 69 H12
Bure, *Gojam, Ethiopia* 81 E4
Bure, *Ilubabor, Ethiopia* 81 F4
Bure →, *U.K.* 14 E9
Büren, *Germany* 24 D4
Bureya →, *Russia* 53 E13
Burford, *Canada* 116 C4
Burg, *Germany* 24 C7
Burg auf Fehmarn, *Germany* 24 A7
Burg el Arab, *Egypt* 80 H6
Burg et Tuyur, *Sudan* 80 C2
Burg Stargard, *Germany* 24 B9
Buşra ash Shām, *Syria* 74 C5
Burgas, *Bulgaria* 45 D11
Burgas □, *Bulgaria* 45 D10
Burgaski Zaliv, *Bulgaria* 45 D11
Burgdorf, *Germany* 24 C6
Burgdorf, *Switz.* 25 H3
Burgenland □, *Austria* 27 D9
Burgeo, *Canada* 105 C8
Burgersdorp, *S. Africa* 88 E4
Burges, Mt., *Australia* 93 F3
Burghausen, *Germany* 25 G8
Burghead, *U.K.* 13 D5
Búrgio, *Italy* 42 E6
Burglengenfeld, *Germany* 25 F8
Burgohondo, *Spain* 36 E6
Burgos, *Spain* 36 C7
Burgos □, *Spain* 36 C7
Burgstädt, *Germany* 24 E8
Burgsvik, *Sweden* 11 G12
Burguillos del Cerro, *Spain* 37 G4
Burgundy = Bourgogne □, *France* 19 F11
Burhaniye, *Turkey* 47 B8
Burhanpur, *India* 66 J10
Burhi Gandak →, *India* 69 G12
Burhner →, *India* 69 H9
Buri Pen., *Eritrea* 81 D4
Burias I., *Phil.* 61 E5
Burica, Pta., *Costa Rica* 120 E3
Burien, *U.S.A.* 110 C4
Burigi ⌂, *Tanzania* 86 C3
Burigi, L., *Tanzania* 86 C3
Burin, *Canada* 105 C8
Buriram, *Thailand* 64 E4
Burj Sāfitā, *Syria* 70 C3
Burji, *Ethiopia* 81 F4
Burkburnett, *U.S.A.* 113 H5
Burke →, *Australia* 94 C2
Burke Chan., *Canada* 102 C3
Burketown, *Australia* 94 B2
Burkina Faso ■, *Africa* 82 C4
Burk's Falls, *Canada* 104 C4
Burlada, *Spain* 38 C3
Burleigh Falls, *Canada* 116 B6
Burley, *U.S.A.* 108 E7
Burlingame, *U.S.A.* 110 H4
Burlington, *Canada* 116 C5
Burlington, *Colo., U.S.A.* 112 F3
Burlington, *Iowa, U.S.A.* 112 E9
Burlington, *Kans., U.S.A.* 112 F7
Burlington, *N.C., U.S.A.* 115 G6
Burlington, *N.J., U.S.A.* 117 F10
Burlington, *Vt., U.S.A.* 117 B11
Burlington, *Wash., U.S.A.* 110 B4
Burlington, *Wis., U.S.A.* 114 D1
Burlyu-Tyube, *Kazakhstan* 52 E8
Burma ■, *Asia* 67 J20
Burnaby I., *Canada* 102 C2
Burnet, *U.S.A.* 113 K5
Burney, *U.S.A.* 108 F3
Burnham, *U.S.A.* 116 F7
Burnham-on-Sea, *U.K.* 15 F5
Burnie, *Australia* 95 G4
Burnley, *U.K.* 14 D5
Burns, *U.S.A.* 108 E4
Burns Lake, *Canada* 102 C3
Burnside →, *Canada* 100 B9
Burnside, L., *Australia* 93 E3
Burnsville, *U.S.A.* 112 C8
Burnt, L., *Canada* 105 B7
Burnt River, *Canada* 116 B6
Burntwood →, *Canada* 103 B9
Burntwood L., *Canada* 103 B8
Burqān, *Kuwait* 70 D5
Burra, *Australia* 95 E2
Burra, *Nigeria* 83 C6
Burray, *U.K.* 13 C6
Burrel, *Albania* 44 E4
Burren △, *Ireland* 12 C3
Burren Junction, *Australia* 95 E4
Burriana, *Spain* 38 F4
Burrinjuck Res., *Australia* 95 F4
Burro, Serranías del, *Mexico* 118 B4
Burrow Hd., *U.K.* 13 G4
Burrum Coast △, *Australia* 95 D5
Burruyacú, *Argentina* 126 B3
Burry Port, *U.K.* 15 F3
Bursa, *Turkey* 45 F13
Burseryd, *Sweden* 11 G7
Burstall, *Canada* 103 C7
Burton, *Ohio, U.S.A.* 116 E3
Burton, *S.C., U.S.A.* 115 J5
Burton, L., *Canada* 104 B4
Burton upon Trent, *U.K.* 14 E6
Buru, *Indonesia* 63 E7
Burullus, Bahra el, *Egypt* 80 H7
Burûn, Râs, *Egypt* 74 D2
Burundi ■, *Africa* 86 C3
Bururi, *Burundi* 86 C2
Burutu, *Nigeria* 83 D6
Burwell, *U.S.A.* 112 E5
Burwick, *U.K.* 13 C5
Bury, *U.K.* 14 D5
Bury St. Edmunds, *U.K.* 15 E8
Buryatia □, *Russia* 53 D11
Buryn, *Ukraine* 33 G7
Burzenin, *Poland* 31 G5
Busalla, *Italy* 40 D5
Busan = Pusan, *S. Korea* 57 G15
Busango Swamp, *Zambia* 87 E2
Buşayrah, *Syria* 70 C4
Busca, *Italy* 40 D4
Bushat, *Albania* 44 E3
Būshehr, *Iran* 71 D6
Būshehr □, *Iran* 71 D6
Bushell, *Canada* 103 B7
Bushenyi, *Uganda* 86 C3
Bushire = Būshehr, *Iran* 71 D6
Bushtyna, *Ukraine* 29 B8
Busie, *Ghana* 82 C4
Businga, *Dem. Rep. of the Congo* 84 D4
Busko-Zdrój, *Poland* 31 H7
Busovača, *Bos.-H.* 28 F2
Busselton, *Australia* 93 F2
Busseri →, *Sudan* 81 F2
Busseto, *Italy* 40 D7
Bussière-Badil, *France* 20 C4
Bussolengo, *Italy* 40 C7
Bussum, *Neths.* 17 B5
Buşteni, *Romania* 29 E10
Busto, C., *Spain* 36 B4
Busto Arsízio, *Italy* 40 C5
Busu Djanoa, *Dem. Rep. of the Congo* 84 D4
Busuanga I., *Phil.* 61 E3
Büsum, *Germany* 24 A4
Busungbiu, *Indonesia* 63 J17
Buta, *Dem. Rep. of the Congo* 86 B1
Butare, *Rwanda* 86 C2
Butaritari, *Kiribati* 96 G9
Bute, *U.K.* 13 F3
Bute Inlet, *Canada* 102 C4
Butemba, *Uganda* 86 B3
Butembo, *Dem. Rep. of the Congo* 86 B2
Buteni, *Romania* 28 D7
Butera, *Italy* 43 E7
Butha Qi, *China* 60 B7
Butiaba, *Uganda* 86 B3
Butler, *Mo., U.S.A.* 112 F7
Butler, *Pa., U.S.A.* 116 F5
Buton, *Indonesia* 63 E6
Butte, *Mont., U.S.A.* 108 C7
Butte, *Nebr., U.S.A.* 112 D5
Butte Creek →, *U.S.A.* 110 F5
Butterworth = Gcuwa, *S. Africa* 89 E4
Butterworth, *Malaysia* 65 c
Buttevant, *Ireland* 12 D3
Buttfield, Mt., *Australia* 93 D4
Button B., *Canada* 103 B10
Buttonwillow, *U.S.A.* 111 K7
Butty Hd., *Australia* 93 F3
Butuan, *Phil.* 61 G6
Butuku-Luba, *Eq. Guin.* 83 E6
Butung = Buton, *Indonesia* 63 E6
Buturlinovka, *Russia* 34 E5
Butzbach, *Germany* 25 E4
Bützow, *Germany* 24 B7
Buur Hakaba = Bur Acaba, *Somali Rep.* 75 G3
Buxa Duar, *India* 69 F13
Buxar, *India* 69 G10
Buxtehude, *Germany* 24 B5
Buxton, *U.K.* 14 D6
Buxy, *France* 19 F11
Buy, *Russia* 34 A5
Buynaksk, *Russia* 35 J8
Buyo, *Ivory C.* 82 D3
Buyo, L. de, *Ivory C.* 82 D3
Büyük Menderes →, *Turkey* 47 D9
Büyükçekmece, *Turkey* 45 E12
Büyükkariştiran, *Turkey* 45 E11
Büyükkemikli Burnu, *Turkey* 45 F10
Büyükorhan, *Turkey* 47 B10
Büyükyoncalı, *Turkey* 45 E11
Buzançais, *France* 18 F8
Buzău, *Romania* 29 E11
Buzău □, *Romania* 29 E11
Buzău →, *Romania* 29 E12
Buzău, Pasul, *Romania* 29 E11
Buzen, *Japan* 55 H5
Buzet, *Croatia* 41 C10
Buzi →, *Mozam.* 87 F3
Buziaş, *Romania* 28 E6
Buzuluk, *Russia* 52 D6
Buzuluk →, *Russia* 34 E6
Buzzards B., *U.S.A.* 117 E14
Buzzards Bay, *U.S.A.* 117 E14
Bwana Mkubwe, *Dem. Rep. of the Congo* 87 E2
Bwindi △, *Uganda* 86 C2
Byala, *Ruse, Bulgaria* 45 C9
Byala, *Varna, Bulgaria* 45 D11
Byala Slatina, *Bulgaria* 44 C7
Byarezina →, *Belarus* 33 F6
Byaroza, *Belarus* 33 F3
Bychawa, *Poland* 31 G9
Byczyna, *Poland* 31 G5
Bydgoszcz, *Poland* 31 E5
Byelarus = Belarus ■, *Europe* 32 F4
Byelorussia = Belarus ■, *Europe* 32 F4
Byers, *U.S.A.* 112 F2
Byesville, *U.S.A.* 116 G3
Byfield △, *Australia* 94 C5
Byford, *Australia* 93 F2
Bykhaw, *Belarus* 32 F6
Bykhov = Bykhaw, *Belarus* 32 F6
Bykovo, *Russia* 34 F7
Bylas, *U.S.A.* 109 K8
Bylot, *Canada* 103 B10
Bylot I., *Canada* 101 A12
Byrd, C., *Antarctica* 5 C17
Byrock, *Australia* 95 E4
Byron, C., *Australia* 95 D5
Byron Bay, *Australia* 95 D5
Byrranga, Gory, *Russia* 53 B11
Byrranga Mts. = Byrranga, Gory, *Russia* 53 B11
Byrum, *Denmark* 11 G5
Byske, *Sweden* 8 D19
Byskeälven →, *Sweden* 8 D19
Bystrytsya, *Ukraine* 29 B9
Bystrzyca →, *Dolnośląskie, Poland* 31 G3
Bystrzyca →, *Lubelskie, Poland* 31 G9
Bystrzyca Kłodzka, *Poland* 31 H3
Bytča, *Slovak Rep.* 27 B11
Bytkiv, *Ukraine* 29 B9
Bytom, *Poland* 31 H5
Bytom Odrzański, *Poland* 31 G2
Bytów, *Poland* 30 D4
Byumba, *Rwanda* 86 C3
Bzenec, *Czech Rep.* 27 C10
Bzura →, *Poland* 31 F7

C

Ca →, *Vietnam* 64 C5
Ca Mau, *Vietnam* 65 H5
Ca Mau, Mui, *Vietnam* 65 H5
Ca Na, *Vietnam* 65 G7
Caacupé, *Paraguay* 126 B4
Caaguazú △, *Paraguay* 127 B4
Caála, *Angola* 85 G3
Caamaño Sd., *Canada* 102 C3
Caazapá, *Paraguay* 126 B4
Caazapá □, *Paraguay* 127 B4
Cabadbaran, *Phil.* 61 G6
Cabalian = San Juan, *Phil.* 61 F6
Caballeria, C. de, *Spain* 48 A11
Cabana, *Spain* 36 B2
Cabañaquinta, *Spain* 36 B5
Cabanatuan, *Phil.* 61 D4
Cabañeros ⌂, *Spain* 37 F6
Cabanes, *Spain* 38 E5
Cabano, *Canada* 105 C6
Čabar, *Croatia* 41 C11
Cabazon, *U.S.A.* 111 M10
Cabedelo, *Brazil* 125 E12
Cabeza del Buey, *Spain* 37 G5
Cabezón de la Sal, *Spain* 36 B6
Cabildo, *Chile* 126 C1
Cabimas, *Venezuela* 124 A4
Cabinda, *Angola* 84 F2
Cabinda □, *Angola* 84 F2
Cabinet Mts., *U.S.A.* 108 C6
Cabo Blanco, *Argentina* 128 F3
Cabo de Gata-Níjar ⌂, *Spain* 39 J2
Cabo Frio, *Brazil* 127 A7
Cabo Pantoja, *Peru* 124 D3
Cabonga, Réservoir, *Canada* 104 C4
Cabool, *U.S.A.* 113 G8
Caboolture, *Australia* 95 D5
Cabora Bassa Dam = Cahora Bassa, Reprêsa de, *Mozam.* 87 F3
Caborca, *Mexico* 118 A2
Cabot, Mt., *U.S.A.* 117 B13
Cabot Hd., *Canada* 116 A3
Cabot Str., *Canada* 105 C8
Cabra, *Spain* 37 H6
Cabra del Santo Cristo, *Spain* 37 H7
Cábras, *Italy* 42 C1
Cabrera, *Spain* 48 B9
Cabrera △, *Spain* 39 F7
Cabrera, Sierra, *Spain* 36 C4
Cabri, *Canada* 103 C7
Cabriel →, *Spain* 39 F3
Cabugao, *Phil.* 61 C4
Cacabelos, *Spain* 36 C4
Caçador, *Brazil* 127 B5
Čačak, *Serbia & M.* 44 C4
Caçapava do Sul, *Brazil* 127 C5
Cáccamo, *Italy* 42 E6
Cacém, *Portugal* 37 G1
Cáceres, *Brazil* 124 G7
Cáceres, *Spain* 37 F4
Cáceres □, *Spain* 36 F5
Cache Bay, *Canada* 104 C4
Cache Cr. →, *U.S.A.* 110 G5
Cache Creek, *Canada* 102 C4
Cacheu, *Guinea-Biss.* 82 C1
Cachi, *Argentina* 126 B2
Cachimbo, Serra do, *Brazil* 125 E7
Cachinal de la Sierra, *Chile* 126 A2
Cachoeira, *Brazil* 125 F11
Cachoeira do Sul, *Brazil* 127 C5
Cachoeiro de Itapemirim, *Brazil* 127 A7
Cachopo, *Portugal* 37 H3
Cacine, *Guinea-Biss.* 82 C1
Cacoal, *Brazil* 124 F6
Cacólo, *Angola* 84 G3
Caconda, *Angola* 85 G3
Čadca, *Slovak Rep.* 27 B11
Caddo, *U.S.A.* 113 H6
Cader Idris, *U.K.* 15 E4
Cadereyta, *Mexico* 118 B5
Cadí, Sierra del, *Spain* 38 C6
Cadí-Moixeró ⌂, *Spain* 38 C3
Cadibarrawirracanna, L., *Australia* 95 D2
Cadillac, *France* 20 D3
Cadillac, *U.S.A.* 114 C3
Cadiz, *Phil.* 61 F5
Cádiz, *Spain* 37 J4
Cadiz, *Calif., U.S.A.* 111 L11
Cadiz, *Ohio, U.S.A.* 116 F4
Cádiz □, *Spain* 37 J5
Cádiz, G. de, *Spain* 37 J3
Cadiz L., *U.S.A.* 109 J6
Cadney Park, *Australia* 95 D1
Cadomin, *Canada* 102 C5
Cadotte Lake, *Canada* 102 B5
Cadours, *France* 20 E5
Cadoux, *Australia* 93 F2
Caen, *France* 18 C6
Caernarfon, *U.K.* 14 D3
Caernarfon B., *U.K.* 14 D3
Caernarvon = Caernarfon, *U.K.* 14 D3
Caerphilly, *U.K.* 15 F4
Caerphilly □, *U.K.* 15 F4
Caesarea, *Israel* 74 C3
Caetité, *Brazil* 125 F10
Cafayate, *Argentina* 126 B2
Cafu, *Angola* 88 B2
Cagayan →, *Phil.* 61 B4
Cagayan de Oro, *Phil.* 61 G6
Cagayan Is., *Phil.* 61 G4
Cagayan Sulu I., *Phil.* 61 H3
Cagli, *Italy* 41 E9
Cágliari, *Italy* 42 C2
Cágliari, G. di, *Italy* 42 C2
Cagnano Varano, *Italy* 41 G12
Cagnes-sur-Mer, *France* 21 E11
Caguán →, *Colombia* 124 D4
Caguas, *Puerto Rico* 121 d
Caha Mts., *Ireland* 12 E2
Cahama, *Angola* 88 B1
Caher, *Ireland* 12 D4
Caherciveen, *Ireland* 12 E1
Cahora Bassa, L. de, *Mozam.* 87 F3
Cahora Bassa, Reprêsa de, *Mozam.* 87 F3
Cahore Pt., *Ireland* 12 D5
Cahors, *France* 20 D5
Cahul, *Moldova* 29 E13
Cai Bau, Dao, *Vietnam* 58 G6
Cai Nuoc, *Vietnam* 65 H5
Caia, *Mozam.* 87 F4
Caianda, *Angola* 87 E1
Caibarién, *Cuba* 120 B4
Caibiran, *Phil.* 61 F6
Caicara, *Venezuela* 124 B5
Caicó, *Brazil* 125 E11
Caicos Is., *Turks & Caicos* 121 B5
Caicos Passage, *W. Indies* 121 B5
Caidian, *China* 59 B10
Căinari, *Moldova* 29 D14
Caird Coast, *Antarctica* 5 D1
Cairn Gorm, *U.K.* 13 D5
Cairngorm Mts., *U.K.* 13 D5
Cairngorms △, *U.K.* 13 D5
Cairnryan, *U.K.* 13 G3
Cairns, *Australia* 94 B4
Cairns L., *Canada* 103 C10
Cairo = El Qâhira, *Egypt* 80 H7
Cairo, *Ga., U.S.A.* 115 K3
Cairo, *Ill., U.S.A.* 113 G10
Cairo, *N.Y., U.S.A.* 117 D11
Cairo Montenotte, *Italy* 40 D5
Caithness, *U.K.* 13 C5
Caithness, Ord of, *U.K.* 13 C5
Caja de Muertos, I., *Puerto Rico* 121 d
Cajamarca, *Peru* 124 E3
Cajarc, *France* 20 D5
Cajàzeiras, *Brazil* 125 E11
Ćajetina, *Serbia & M.* 44 C3
Çakirgol, *Turkey* 73 B8
Çakırlar, *Turkey* 47 E12
Čakovec, *Croatia* 41 B13
Çal, *Turkey* 47 C11
Cala, *Spain* 37 H4
Cala →, *Spain* 37 H4
Cala Cadolar, Punta de = Rotja, Pta., *Spain* 39 G6
Cala d'Or, *Spain* 48 B10
Cala en Porter, *Spain* 48 B11
Cala Figuera, C. de, *Spain* 48 B9
Cala Forcat, *Spain* 48 B10
Cala Major, *Spain* 48 B9
Cala Mezquida = Sa Mesquida, *Spain* 48 B11
Cala Millor, *Spain* 48 B10
Cala Ratjada, *Spain* 48 B10
Cala Santa Galdana, *Spain* 48 B10
Calabanga, *Phil.* 61 E5
Calabar, *Nigeria* 83 E6
Calabogie, *Canada* 117 A8
Calabozo, *Venezuela* 124 B5
Calábria □, *Italy* 43 C9
Calábria △, *Italy* 43 C9
Calaburras, Pta. de, *Spain* 37 J6
Calaceite, *Spain* 38 D5
Calacuccia, *France* 21 F13
Calafat, *Romania* 28 G7
Calafate, *Argentina* 128 G2
Calafell, *Spain* 38 D6
Calahorra, *Spain* 38 C3
Calais, *France* 19 B8
Calais, *U.S.A.* 115 C12
Calakmul ⌂, *Mexico* 119 D7
Calalaste, Cord. de, *Argentina* 126 B2
Calama, *Brazil* 124 E6
Calama, *Chile* 126 A2
Calamar, *Colombia* 124 A4
Calamian Group, *Phil.* 61 F3
Calamocha, *Spain* 38 E3
Calamonte, *Spain* 37 G4
Călan, *Romania* 28 E7
Calañas, *Spain* 37 H4
Calanda, *Spain* 38 E4
Calang, *Indonesia* 62 D1
Calangiánus, *Italy* 42 B2
Calapan, *Phil.* 61 E4
Călărasi, *Moldova* 29 C13
Călăraşi, *Romania* 29 F12
Călăraşi □, *Romania* 29 F12
Calasparra, *Spain* 39 G3
Calatafimi, *Italy* 42 E5
Calatayud, *Spain* 38 D3
Călăţele, *Romania* 28 D8
Calato = Kálathos, *Greece* 47 E10
Calauag, *Phil.* 61 E5
Calavà, C., *Italy* 43 D7
Calavite, C., *Phil.* 61 E4
Calayan, *Phil.* 61 B4
Calbayog, *Phil.* 61 E6
Calca, *Peru* 124 F4
Calcasieu L., *U.S.A.* 113 L8
Calcutta = Kolkata, *India* 69 H13
Calcutta, *U.S.A.* 116 F4
Caldaro, *Italy* 41 B8
Caldas da Rainha, *Portugal* 37 F1
Caldas de Reis, *Spain* 36 C2
Calder →, *U.K.* 14 D6
Caldera, *Chile* 126 B1

Caldera de Taburiente △, *Canary Is.* 48 F2
Caldwell, *Idaho, U.S.A.* 108 E5
Caldwell, *Kans., U.S.A.* 113 G6
Caldwell, *Tex., U.S.A.* 113 K6
Caledon, *S. Africa* 88 E2
Caledon →, *S. Africa* 88 E4
Caledon B., *Australia* 94 A2
Caledonia, *Canada* 116 C5
Caledonia, *U.S.A.* 116 D7
Calella, *Spain* 38 D7
Calemba, *Angola* 88 B2
Calen, *Australia* 94 J6
Calenzana, *France* 21 F12
Caletones, *Chile* 126 C1
Calexico, *U.S.A.* 111 N11
Calf of Man, *I. of Man* 14 C3
Calgary, *Canada* 102 C6
Calheta, *Madeira* 48 D2
Calhoun, *U.S.A.* 115 H3
Cali, *Colombia* 124 C3
Calicut, *India* 66 P9
Caliente, *U.S.A.* 109 H6
California, *Mo., U.S.A.* 112 F8
California, *Pa., U.S.A.* 116 F5
California □, *U.S.A.* 110 H7
California, Baja, *Mexico* 118 A1
California, Baja, T.N. = Baja California □, *Mexico* 118 B2
California, Baja, T.S. = Baja California Sur □, *Mexico* 118 B2
California, G. de, *Mexico* 118 B2
California City, *U.S.A.* 111 K9
California Hot Springs, *U.S.A.* 111 K8
Calilegua △, *Argentina* 126 B3
Călimăneşti, *Romania* 29 E9
Călimani, Munţii, *Romania* 29 C10
Calingasta, *Argentina* 126 C2
Calipatria, *U.S.A.* 111 M11
Calistoga, *U.S.A.* 110 G4
Calitri, *Italy* 43 B8
Calitzdorp, *S. Africa* 88 E3
Callabonna, L., *Australia* 95 D3
Callac, *France* 18 D3
Callan, *Ireland* 12 D4
Callander, *U.K.* 13 E4
Callao, *Peru* 124 F3
Calles, *Mexico* 119 C5
Callicoon, *U.S.A.* 117 E9
Calling Lake, *Canada* 102 B6
Calliope, *Australia* 94 C5
Callosa de Ensarriá, *Spain* 39 G4
Callosa de Segura, *Spain* 39 G4
Calne, *U.K.* 15 F6
Calola, *Angola* 88 B2
Calolbon = San Andres, *Phil.* 61 E6
Calonge, *Spain* 38 D8
Caloocan, *Phil.* 61 D4
Calore →, *Italy* 43 A7
Caloundra, *Australia* 95 D5
Calpe, *Spain* 39 G5
Calpella, *U.S.A.* 110 F3
Calpine, *U.S.A.* 110 F6
Calstock, *Canada* 104 C3
Caltabellotta, *Italy* 42 E6
Caltagirone, *Italy* 43 E7
Caltanissetta, *Italy* 43 E7
Çaltılıbük, *Turkey* 45 G12
Caluire-et-Cuire, *France* 19 G11
Calulo, *Angola* 84 G2
Caluso, *Italy* 40 C4
Calvados □, *France* 18 C6
Calvert →, *Australia* 94 B2
Calvert I., *Canada* 102 C3
Calvert Ra., *Australia* 92 D3
Calvi, *France* 21 F12
Calviá, *Spain* 39 F7
Calvillo, *Mexico* 118 C4
Calvinia, *S. Africa* 88 E2
Calvo, Mte., *Italy* 41 G12
Calwa, *U.S.A.* 110 J7
Calzada Almuradiel = Almuradiel, *Spain* 37 G7
Calzada de Calatrava, *Spain* 37 G7
Cam →, *U.K.* 15 E8
Cam Lam, *Vietnam* 65 G7
Cam Pha, *Vietnam* 58 G6
Cam Ranh, *Vietnam* 65 G7
Cam Xuyen, *Vietnam* 64 C6
Camabatela, *Angola* 84 F3
Camacha, *Madeira* 48 D3
Camacho, *Mexico* 118 C4
Camacupa, *Angola* 85 G3
Camagüey, *Cuba* 120 B4
Camaiore, *Italy* 40 E7
Camaná, *Peru* 124 G4
Camanche Reservoir, *U.S.A.* 110 G6
Camaquã, *Brazil* 127 C5
Camaquã →, *Brazil* 127 C5
Câmara de Lobos, *Madeira* 48 D3
Camarat, C., *France* 21 E10
Camarès, *France* 20 E6
Camaret-sur-Mer, *France* 18 D2
Camargo, *Mexico* 119 B5
Camargue, *France* 21 E8
Camargue ⌂, *France* 21 E8
Camarillo, *U.S.A.* 111 L7
Camariñas, *Spain* 36 B1
Camarón, C., *Honduras* 120 C2
Camarones, *Argentina* 128 E3
Camas, *Spain* 37 H4
Camas, *U.S.A.* 110 E4
Camas Valley, *U.S.A.* 108 E2
Camballin, *Australia* 92 C3
Cambará, *Brazil* 127 A5
Cambay = Khambhat, *India* 68 H5
Cambay, G. of = Khambhat, G. of, *India* 66 J8
Cambil, *Spain* 37 H7
Cambo-les-Bains, *France* 20 E2
Cambodia ■, *Asia* 64 F5
Camborne, *U.K.* 15 G2
Cambrai, *France* 19 B10
Cambre, *Spain* 36 B2
Cambria, *U.S.A.* 110 K5
Cambrian Mts., *U.K.* 15 E4
Cambridge, *Canada* 116 C4
Cambridge, *Jamaica* 120 a
Cambridge, *N.Z.* 91 G5
Cambridge, *U.K.* 15 E8
Cambridge, *Mass., U.S.A.* 117 D13
Cambridge, *Minn., U.S.A.* 112 C8
Cambridge, *N.Y., U.S.A.* 117 C11
Cambridge, *Nebr., U.S.A.* 112 E4
Cambridge, *Ohio, U.S.A.* 116 F3
Cambridge Bay = Ikaluktutiak, *Canada* 100 B9
Cambridge G., *Australia* 92 B4
Cambridge Springs, *U.S.A.* 116 E4
Cambridgeshire □, *U.K.* 15 E7
Cambrils, *Spain* 38 D6
Cambuci, *Brazil* 127 A7
Cambundi-Catembo, *Angola* 84 G3
Camden, *Ala., U.S.A.* 115 K2
Camden, *Ark., U.S.A.* 113 J8
Camden, *Maine, U.S.A.* 115 C11
Camden, *N.J., U.S.A.* 117 G9
Camden, *N.Y., U.S.A.* 117 C9
Camden, *S.C., U.S.A.* 115 H5
Camden Sd., *Australia* 92 C3
Camdenton, *U.S.A.* 113 F8
Camelford, *U.K.* 15 G3
Çameli, *Turkey* 47 D11
Camenca, *Moldova* 29 B13
Camerino, *Italy* 41 E10
Cameron, *Ariz., U.S.A.* 109 J8
Cameron, *La., U.S.A.* 113 L8
Cameron, *Mo., U.S.A.* 112 F7
Cameron, *Tex., U.S.A.* 113 K6
Cameron Highlands, *Malaysia* 65 K3
Cameron Hills, *Canada* 102 B5
Cameroon ■, *Africa* 79 G7
Camerota, *Italy* 43 B8
Cameroun →, *Cameroon* 83 E6
Cameroun, Mt., *Cameroon* 83 E6
Cametá, *Brazil* 125 D9
Çamiçi Gölü, *Turkey* 47 D9
Camiguin □, *Phil.* 61 G6
Camiguin I., *Phil.* 61 B4
Camiling, *Phil.* 61 D4
Camilla, *U.S.A.* 115 K3
Caminha, *Portugal* 36 D2
Camino, *U.S.A.* 110 G6
Camira Creek, *Australia* 95 D5
Cammal, *U.S.A.* 116 E7
Cammarata, *Italy* 42 E6
Camocim, *Brazil* 125 D10
Camooweal, *Australia* 94 B2
Camooweal Caves △, *Australia* 94 C2
Camopi, *Fr. Guiana* 125 C8
Camotes Is., *Phil.* 61 F6
Camotes Sea, *Phil.* 61 F6
Camp Borden, *Canada* 116 B5
Camp Hill, *U.S.A.* 116 F8
Camp Nelson, *U.S.A.* 111 J8
Camp Pendleton, *U.S.A.* 111 M9
Camp Verde, *U.S.A.* 109 J8
Camp Wood, *U.S.A.* 113 L5
Campagna, *Italy* 43 B8
Campana, *Argentina* 126 C4
Campana, I., *Chile* 128 F1
Campanário, *Madeira* 48 D2
Campanario, *Spain* 37 G5
Campània □, *Italy* 43 B7
Campbell, *S. Africa* 88 D3
Campbell, *Calif., U.S.A.* 110 H5
Campbell, *Ohio, U.S.A.* 116 E4
Campbell I., *Pac. Oc.* 96 N8
Campbell L., *Canada* 103 A7
Campbell River, *Canada* 102 C3
Campbell Town, *Australia* 95 G4
Campbellford, *Canada* 116 B7
Campbellpur, *Pakistan* 68 C5
Campbellsville, *U.S.A.* 114 G3
Campbellton, *Canada* 105 C6
Campbelltown, *Australia* 95 E5
Campbeltown, *U.K.* 13 F3
Campeche, *Mexico* 119 D6
Campeche □, *Mexico* 119 D6
Campeche, Golfo de, *Mexico* 119 D6
Campello, *Spain* 39 G4
Câmpeni, *Romania* 28 D8
Camperdown, *Australia* 95 F3
Camperville, *Canada* 103 C8
Campi Salentina, *Italy* 43 B11
Câmpia Turzii, *Romania* 29 D8
Campidano, *Italy* 42 C1
Campíglia Maríttima, *Italy* 40 E7
Campillo de Altobuey, *Spain* 39 F3
Campillos, *Spain* 37 H6
Câmpina, *Romania* 29 E10
Campina Grande, *Brazil* 125 E11
Campinas, *Brazil* 127 A6
Campli, *Italy* 41 F10
Campo, *Spain* 38 C5
Campo de Criptana, *Spain* 37 F7
Campo de Gibraltar, *Spain* 37 J5
Campo Grande, *Brazil* 125 H8
Campo Maior, *Brazil* 125 D10
Campo Maior, *Portugal* 37 F3
Campo Mourão, *Brazil* 127 A5
Campo Túres, *Italy* 41 B8
Campobasso, *Italy* 43 A7
Campobello di Licata, *Italy* 42 E6
Campobello di Mazara, *Italy* 42 E5
Campofelice di Roccella, *Italy* 42 E6
Campomarino, *Italy* 41 G12
Camporeale, *Italy* 42 E6
Camporrobles, *Spain* 38 F3
Campos, *Brazil* 127 A7
Campos Belos, *Brazil* 125 F9
Campos del Port, *Spain* 48 B10
Campos Novos, *Brazil* 127 B5
Camprodón, *Spain* 38 C7
Camptonville, *U.S.A.* 110 F5
Camptown, *U.S.A.* 117 E8
Câmpulung, *Argeş, Romania* 29 E10
Câmpulung, *Suceava, Romania* 29 C10
Câmpuri, *Romania* 29 D11
Camrose, *Canada* 102 C6
Camsell Portage, *Canada* 103 B7
Çamyuva, *Turkey* 47 E12
Çan, *Turkey* 45 F11
Can Clavo, *Spain* 48 C7
Can Creu, *Spain* 48 C7
Can Gio, *Vietnam* 65 G6
Can Tho, *Vietnam* 65 G5
Canaan, *U.S.A.* 117 D11
Canada ■, *N. Amer.* 100 C10
Canada Basin, *Arctic* 4 B18
Cañada de Gómez, *Argentina* 126 C3
Canadian, *U.S.A.* 113 H4
Canadian →, *U.S.A.* 113 H7
Canajoharie, *U.S.A.* 117 D10
Çanakkale, *Turkey* 45 F10
Çanakkale □, *Turkey* 45 F10
Çanakkale Boğazı, *Turkey* 45 F10
Canal Flats, *Canada* 102 C5
Canalejas, *Argentina* 126 D2
Canals, *Argentina* 126 C3
Canals, *Spain* 39 G4
Canandaigua, *U.S.A.* 116 D7
Canandaigua L., *U.S.A.* 116 D7
Cananea, *Mexico* 118 A2
Canarias, Is., *Atl. Oc.* 48 F4
Canaries, *St. Lucia* 121 f
Canarreos, Arch. de los, *Cuba* 120 B3
Canary Is. = Canarias, Is., *Atl. Oc.* 48 F4
Canaseraga, *U.S.A.* 116 D7
Canatlán, *Mexico* 118 C4
Canaveral ⌂, *U.S.A.* 115 L5
Canaveral, C., *U.S.A.* 115 L5
Cañaveruelas, *Spain* 38 E2
Canavieiras, *Brazil* 125 G11
Canberra, *Australia* 95 F4
Canby, *Calif., U.S.A.* 108 F3
Canby, *Minn., U.S.A.* 112 C6
Canby, *Oreg., U.S.A.* 110 E4
Cancale, *France* 18 D5
Canche →, *France* 19 B8
Cancún, *Mexico* 119 C7
Candanchu, *Spain* 38 C4
Çandarlı, *Turkey* 47 C8
Çandarlı Körfezi, *Turkey* 47 C8
Candas, *Spain* 36 B5
Candé, *France* 18 E5
Candela, *Italy* 43 A8
Candelaria, *Argentina* 127 B4
Candelaria, *Canary Is.* 48 F3
Candelario ⌂, *Spain* 36 E5
Candeleda, *Spain* 36 E5
Candelo, *Australia* 95 F4
Candi Dasa, *Indonesia* 63 J18
Candia = Iráklion, *Greece* 49 D7
Candia, Sea of = Crete, Sea of, *Greece* 47 E7
Candle L., *Canada* 103 C7
Candlemas I., *Antarctica* 5 B1
Cando, *U.S.A.* 112 A5
Candon, *Phil.* 61 C4
Canea = Khaniá, *Greece* 49 D6
Canelli, *Italy* 40 D5
Canelones, *Uruguay* 127 C4
Canet-Plage, *France* 20 F7
Cañete, *Chile* 126 D1
Cañete, *Peru* 124 F3
Cañete, *Spain* 38 E3
Cañete de las Torres, *Spain* 37 H6
Cangas, *Spain* 36 C2
Cangas de Narcea, *Spain* 36 B4
Cangas de Onís, *Spain* 36 B5
Cangnan, *China* 59 D13
Canguaretama, *Brazil* 125 E11
Canguçu, *Brazil* 127 C5
Canguçu, Serra do, *Brazil* 127 C5
Cangwu, *China* 59 F8
Cangxi, *China* 58 B5
Cangyuan, *China* 58 F2
Cangzhou, *China* 56 E9
Caniapiscau →, *Canada* 105 A6
Caniapiscau, L. de, *Canada* 105 B6
Canicattì, *Italy* 42 E6
Canicattini Bagni, *Italy* 43 E8
Caniles, *Spain* 37 H8
Canim Lake, *Canada* 102 C4
Canindeyu □, *Paraguay* 127 A5
Canino, *Italy* 41 F8
Canisteo, *U.S.A.* 116 D7
Canisteo →, *U.S.A.* 116 D7
Cañitas, *Mexico* 118 C4
Cañizal, *Spain* 36 D5
Canjáyar, *Spain* 37 H8
Çankırı, *Turkey* 72 B5
Cankuzo, *Burundi* 86 C3
Canmore, *Canada* 102 C5
Cann River, *Australia* 95 F4
Canna, *U.K.* 13 D2
Cannanore, *India* 66 P9
Cannes, *France* 21 E11
Canning Town = Port Canning, *India* 69 H13
Cannington, *Canada* 116 B5
Cannóbio, *Italy* 40 B5
Cannock, *U.K.* 15 E5
Cannon Ball →, *U.S.A.* 112 B4
Cannondale Mt., *Australia* 94 D4
Cannonsville Reservoir, *U.S.A.* 117 D9
Cannonvale, *Australia* 94 J6
Canoas, *Brazil* 127 B5
Canoe L., *Canada* 103 B7
Canon City, *U.S.A.* 112 F2
Cañón de Rio Blanco △, *Mexico* 119 D5
Cañón del Río Lobos ⌂, *Spain* 36 D7
Cañón del Sumidero △, *Mexico* 119 D5
Canora, *Canada* 103 C8
Canosa di Púglia, *Italy* 43 A9
Canowindra, *Australia* 95 E4
Canso, *Canada* 105 C7
Cantabria □, *Spain* 36 B7
Cantabria, Sierra de, *Spain* 38 C2
Cantabrian Mts. = Cantábrica, Cordillera, *Spain* 36 C5
Cantábrica, Cordillera, *Spain* 36 C5
Cantal □, *France* 20 C6
Cantal, Plomb du, *France* 20 C6
Cantanhede, *Portugal* 36 E2
Cantavieja, *Spain* 38 E4
Čantavir, *Serbia & M.* 28 E4
Cantemir, *Moldova* 29 D13
Canterbury, *Australia* 94 D3
Canterbury, *U.K.* 15 F9
Canterbury Bight, *N.Z.* 91 L3
Canterbury Plains, *N.Z.* 91 K3
Cantil, *U.S.A.* 111 K9
Cantillana, *Spain* 37 H5
Canton = Guangzhou, *China* 59 F9
Canton, *Ga., U.S.A.* 115 H3
Canton, *Ill., U.S.A.* 112 E9
Canton, *Miss., U.S.A.* 113 J9
Canton, *Mo., U.S.A.* 112 E9
Canton, *N.Y., U.S.A.* 117 B9
Canton, *Ohio, U.S.A.* 116 F3
Canton, *Pa., U.S.A.* 116 E8
Canton, *S. Dak., U.S.A.* 112 D6
Canton L., *U.S.A.* 113 G5
Cantù, *Italy* 40 C6
Canudos, *Brazil* 124 E7
Canumã →, *Brazil* 124 D7
Canutama, *Brazil* 124 E6
Canutillo, *U.S.A.* 109 L10
Canvey, *U.K.* 15 F8
Canyon, *U.S.A.* 113 H4
Canyon De Chelly ⌂, *U.S.A.* 109 H9
Canyon of the Ancients ⌂, *U.S.A.* 109 H9
Canyonlands △, *U.S.A.* 109 G9
Canyonville, *U.S.A.* 108 E2
Cao Bang, *Vietnam* 58 F6
Cao He →, *China* 57 D13
Cao Lanh, *Vietnam* 65 G5
Cao Xian, *China* 56 G8
Cáorle, *Italy* 41 C9
Cap-aux-Meules, *Canada* 105 C7
Cap-Chat, *Canada* 105 C6
Cap-de-la-Madeleine, *Canada* 104 C5
Cap-Haïtien, *Haiti* 121 C5
Cap Pt., *St. Lucia* 121 f
Capac, *U.S.A.* 116 C2
Capáccio, *Italy* 43 B8
Capaci, *Italy* 42 D6
Capanaparo →, *Venezuela* 124 B5
Capánnori, *Italy* 40 E7
Capbreton, *France* 20 E2
Capdenac, *France* 20 D6
Capdepera, *Spain* 38 F8
Cape →, *Australia* 94 C4
Cape Arid △, *Australia* 93 F3
Cape Barren I., *Australia* 95 G4
Cape Breton Highlands △, *Canada* 105 C7
Cape Breton I., *Canada* 105 C7
Cape Charles, *U.S.A.* 114 G8
Cape Coast, *Ghana* 83 D4
Cape Cod ⌂, *U.S.A.* 114 E10
Cape Coral, *U.S.A.* 115 M5
Cape Dorset, *Canada* 101 B12
Cape Fear →, *U.S.A.* 115 H6
Cape Girardeau, *U.S.A.* 113 G10
Cape Hatteras ⌂, *U.S.A.* 115 H8
Cape Lee △, *Australia* 93 F3
Cape Lookout ⌂, *U.S.A.* 115 H7
Cape May, *U.S.A.* 114 F8
Cape May Point, *U.S.A.* 114 F8
Cape Melville △, *Australia* 94 A3
Cape Mount △, *Liberia* 82 D2
Cape Peninsula △, *S. Africa* 88 E2
Cape Range △, *Australia* 92 D1
Cape Tormentine, *Canada* 105 C7
Cape Town, *S. Africa* 88 E2
Cape Tribulation △, *Australia* 94 B4
Cape Verde Is. ■, *Atl. Oc.* 77 E1
Cape Vincent, *U.S.A.* 117 B8
Cape York Peninsula, *Australia* 94 A3
Capela, *Brazil* 125 F11
Capella, *Australia* 94 C4
Capendu, *France* 20 E6
Capestang, *France* 20 E7
Capesterre-Belle-Eau, *Guadeloupe* 120 b
Capesterre-de-Marie-Galante, *Guadeloupe* 120 b
Capim →, *Brazil* 125 D9
Capistrello, *Italy* 41 G10
Capitan, *U.S.A.* 109 K11
Capitán Arturo Prat, *Antarctica* 5 C17
Capitol Reef △, *U.S.A.* 109 G8
Capitola, *U.S.A.* 110 J5
Capizzi, *Italy* 43 E7
Capoche →, *Mozam.* 87 F3
Capodichino, Nápoli ✕ (NAP), *Italy* 43 B7
Capoterra, *Italy* 42 C1
Cappadocia, *Turkey* 72 C6
Capraia, *Italy* 40 E6
Caprara, Pta., *Italy* 42 A1
Caprarola, *Italy* 41 F9
Capreol, *Canada* 104 C3
Caprera, *Italy* 42 A2
Capri, *Italy* 43 B7
Capricorn Group, *Australia* 94 C5
Capricorn Ra., *Australia* 92 D2
Caprino Veronese, *Italy* 40 C7
Caprivi Game ⌂, *Namibia* 88 B3
Caprivi Strip, *Namibia* 88 B3
Caps et Marais d'Opale ⌂, *France* 19 B9
Captain's Flat, *Australia* 95 F4
Captieux, *France* 20 D3
Capulin Volcano ⌂, *U.S.A.* 113 G3
Caquetá →, *Colombia* 124 D5
Caracal, *Romania* 29 F9
Caracas, *Venezuela* 124 A5
Caracol, *Mato Grosso do Sul, Brazil* 126 A4
Caracol, *Piauí, Brazil* 125 E10
Caráglio, *Italy* 40 D4
Carajas, *Brazil* 125 E8
Carajás, Serra dos, *Brazil* 125 E8
Carangola, *Brazil* 127 A7
Caransebeş, *Romania* 28 E7
Carantec, *France* 18 D3
Caraquet, *Canada* 105 C6
Caras, *Peru* 124 E3
Caraş Severin □, *Romania* 28 E7
Caraşova, *Romania* 28 E6
Caratasca, L., *Honduras* 120 C3
Caratinga, *Brazil* 125 G10
Caraúbas, *Brazil* 125 E11
Caravaca de la Cruz, *Spain* 39 G3
Caravággio, *Italy* 40 C6
Caravela, *Guinea-Biss.* 82 C1
Caravelas, *Brazil* 125 G11
Caraveli, *Peru* 124 G4
Caravelle, Presqu'île de la, *Martinique* 120 c
Caràzinho, *Brazil* 127 B5
Carballino = O Carballiño, *Spain* 36 C2
Carballo, *Spain* 36 B2
Carberry, *Canada* 103 D9
Carbó, *Mexico* 118 B2
Carbonara, C., *Italy* 42 C2
Carbondale, *Colo., U.S.A.* 108 G10
Carbondale, *Ill., U.S.A.* 113 G10
Carbondale, *Pa., U.S.A.* 117 E9
Carbonear, *Canada* 105 C9
Carboneras, *Spain* 39 J3
Carboneras de Guadazaón, *Spain* 38 F3
Carbónia, *Italy* 42 C1
Carcabuey, *Spain* 37 H6
Carcagente = Carcaixent, *Spain* 39 F4
Carcaixent, *Spain* 39 F4
Carcajou, *Canada* 102 B5
Carcar, *Phil.* 61 F5
Carcarana →, *Argentina* 126 C3
Carcasse, C., *Haiti* 121 C5
Carcassonne, *France* 20 E6
Carcross, *Canada* 102 A2
Çardak, *Çanakkale, Turkey* 45 F10
Çardak, *Denizli, Turkey* 47 D11
Cardamon Hills, *India* 66 Q10
Cardeña, *Spain* 37 G6
Cárdenas, *Cuba* 120 B3
Cárdenas, *San Luis Potosí, Mexico* 119 C5
Cárdenas, *Tabasco, Mexico* 119 D6
Cardenete, *Spain* 38 F3
Cardiff, *U.K.* 15 F4
Cardiff □, *U.K.* 15 F4
Cardiff-by-the-Sea, *U.S.A.* 111 M9
Cardigan, *U.K.* 15 E3
Cardigan B., *U.K.* 15 E3
Cardinal, *Canada* 117 B9
Cardona, *Spain* 38 D6
Cardona, *Uruguay* 126 C4
Cardoner →, *Spain* 38 D6
Cardoso, Ilha do, *Brazil* 127 B5
Cardston, *Canada* 102 D6
Cardwell, *Australia* 94 B4
Careen L., *Canada* 103 B7
Carei, *Romania* 28 C7
Careme = Ciremay, *Indonesia* 63 G13
Carentan, *France* 18 C5
Carey, *U.S.A.* 108 E7
Carey, L., *Australia* 93 E3
Carey L., *Canada* 103 A8
Careysburg, *Liberia* 82 D2
Cargèse, *France* 21 F12
Carhaix-Plouguer, *France* 18 D3
Carhué, *Argentina* 126 D3
Caria, *Turkey* 47 D10
Cariacica, *Brazil* 125 H10
Cariati, *Italy* 43 C9
Caribbean Sea, *W. Indies* 121 D5
Cariboo Mts., *Canada* 102 C4
Caribou, *U.S.A.* 115 B12
Caribou →, *Man., Canada* 103 B10
Caribou →, *N.W.T., Canada* 102 A3
Caribou I., *Canada* 104 C2
Caribou Is., *Canada* 102 A6
Caribou L., *Man., Canada* 103 B9
Caribou L., *Ont., Canada* 104 B2
Caribou Mts., *Canada* 102 B5
Caribou River ⌂, *Canada* 103 B9
Caribrod = Dimitrovgrad, *Serbia & M.* 44 C6
Carichic, *Mexico* 118 B3
Carigara, *Phil.* 61 F6
Carignan, *France* 19 C12
Carignano, *Italy* 40 D4
Carillo, *Mexico* 118 B4
Carinda, *Australia* 95 E4
Cariñena, *Spain* 38 D3
Carinhanha, *Brazil* 125 F10
Carinhanha →, *Brazil* 125 F10
Carini, *Italy* 42 D6
Cariño, *Spain* 36 B3
Carínola, *Italy* 42 A6
Carinthia = Kärnten □, *Austria* 26 E6
Caripito, *Venezuela* 124 A6
Carlet, *Spain* 39 F4
Carleton, Mt., *Canada* 105 C6
Carleton Place, *Canada* 117 A8
Carletonville, *S. Africa* 88 D4
Cârlibaba, *Romania* 29 C10
Carlin, *U.S.A.* 108 F5
Carlingford L., *U.K.* 12 B5
Carlinville, *U.S.A.* 112 F10
Carlisle, *U.K.* 14 C5
Carlisle, *U.S.A.* 116 F7
Carlisle B., *Barbados* 121 g
Carlisle I., *Australia* 94 J7
Carlit, Pic, *France* 20 F5

Carloforte, *Italy* 42 C1
Carlos Casares, *Argentina* 126 D3
Carlos Tejedor, *Argentina* 126 D3
Carlow, *Ireland* 12 D5
Carlow □, *Ireland* 12 D5
Carlsbad, *Calif., U.S.A.* 111 M9
Carlsbad, *N. Mex., U.S.A.* 113 J2
Carlsbad Caverns △, *U.S.A.* 113 J2
Carluke, *U.K.* 13 F5
Carlyle, *Canada* 103 D8
Carmacks, *Canada* 100 B6
Carmagnola, *Italy* 40 D4
Carman, *Canada* 103 D9
Carmarthen, *U.K.* 15 F3
Carmarthen B., *U.K.* 15 F3
Carmarthenshire □, *U.K.* 15 F3
Carmaux, *France* 20 D6
Carmel, *U.S.A.* 117 E11
Carmel-by-the-Sea, *U.S.A.* 110 J5
Carmel Valley, *U.S.A.* 110 J5
Carmelo, *Uruguay* 126 C4
Carmen, *Colombia* 124 B3
Carmen, *Paraguay* 127 B4
Carmen →, *Mexico* 118 A3
Carmen, I., *Mexico* 118 B2
Carmen de Patagones, *Argentina* 128 E4
Cármenes, *Spain* 36 C5
Carmensa, *Argentina* 126 D2
Carmi, *Canada* 102 D5
Carmi, *U.S.A.* 114 F1
Carmichael, *U.S.A.* 110 G5
Carmila, *Australia* 94 C4
Carmona, *Costa Rica* 120 E2
Carmona, *Spain* 37 H5
Carn Ban, *U.K.* 13 D4
Carn Eige, *U.K.* 13 D3
Carnamah, *Australia* 93 E2
Carnarvon, *Australia* 93 D1
Carnarvon, *S. Africa* 88 E3
Carnarvon △, *Australia* 94 C4
Carnarvon Ra., *Queens., Australia* 94 D4
Carnarvon Ra., *W. Austral., Australia* 93 E3
Carnation, *U.S.A.* 110 C5
Carndonagh, *Ireland* 12 A4
Carnduff, *Canada* 103 D8
Carnegie, *U.S.A.* 116 F4
Carnegie, L., *Australia* 93 E3
Carnic Alps = Karnische Alpen, *Europe* 26 E6
Carniche Alpi = Karnische Alpen, *Europe* 26 E6
Carnot, *C.A.R.* 84 D3
Carnot, C., *Australia* 95 E2
Carnot B., *Australia* 92 C3
Carnoustie, *U.K.* 13 E6
Carnsore Pt., *Ireland* 12 D5
Caro, *U.S.A.* 114 D4
Carol City, *U.S.A.* 115 N5
Carolina, *Brazil* 125 E9
Carolina, *Puerto Rico* 121 d
Carolina, *S. Africa* 89 D5
Caroline I., *Kiribati* 97 H12
Caroline Is., *Micronesia* 96 G7
Caroni, *Trin. & Tob.* 125 K15
Caroni →, *Venezuela* 124 B6
Caronie = Nébrodi, Monti, *Italy* 43 E7
Caroona, *Australia* 95 E5
Carpathians, *Europe* 6 F10
Carpaţii Meridionali, *Romania* 29 E9
Carpentaria, G. of, *Australia* 94 A2
Carpentras, *France* 21 D9
Carpi, *Italy* 40 D7
Cărpineni, *Moldova* 29 D13
Carpinteria, *U.S.A.* 111 L7
Carpio, *Spain* 36 D5
Carr Boyd Ra., *Australia* 92 C4
Carrabelle, *U.S.A.* 115 L3
Carral, *Spain* 36 B2
Carranza, Presa V., *Mexico* 118 B4
Carrara, *Italy* 40 D7
Carrascal, *Phil.* 61 G6
Carrascosa del Campo, *Spain* 38 E2
Carrauntoohill, *Ireland* 12 D2
Carrick-on-Shannon, *Ireland* 12 C3
Carrick-on-Suir, *Ireland* 12 D4
Carrickfergus, *U.K.* 12 B6
Carrickmacross, *Ireland* 12 C5
Carrieton, *Australia* 95 E2
Carrington, *U.S.A.* 112 B5
Carrión →, *Spain* 36 D6
Carrión de los Condes, *Spain* 36 C6
Carrizal Bajo, *Chile* 126 B1
Carrizalillo, *Chile* 126 B1
Carrizo Cr. →, *U.S.A.* 113 G3
Carrizo Plain ⌓, *U.S.A.* 110 K7
Carrizo Springs, *U.S.A.* 113 L5
Carrizozo, *U.S.A.* 109 K11
Carroll, *U.S.A.* 112 D7
Carrollton, *Ga., U.S.A.* 115 J3
Carrollton, *Ill., U.S.A.* 112 F9
Carrollton, *Ky., U.S.A.* 114 F3
Carrollton, *Mo., U.S.A.* 112 F8
Carrollton, *Ohio, U.S.A.* 116 F3
Carron →, *U.K.* 13 D4
Carron, L., *U.K.* 13 D3
Carrot →, *Canada* 103 C8
Carrot River, *Canada* 103 C8
Carrouges, *France* 18 D6
Carrù, *Italy* 40 D4
Carruthers, *Canada* 103 C7
Carsa Dek, *Ethiopia* 81 F4
Çarşamba, *Turkey* 72 B7
Carsóli, *Italy* 41 F10
Carson, *Calif., U.S.A.* 111 M8
Carson, *N. Dak., U.S.A.* 112 B4
Carson →, *U.S.A.* 110 F8
Carson City, *U.S.A.* 110 F7
Carson Sink, *U.S.A.* 108 G4
Cartagena, *Colombia* 124 A3
Cartagena, *Spain* 39 H4
Cartago, *Colombia* 124 C3
Cartago, *Costa Rica* 120 E3
Cártama, *Spain* 37 J6
Cartaxo, *Portugal* 37 F2
Cartaya, *Spain* 37 H3
Cartersville, *U.S.A.* 115 H3
Carterton, *N.Z.* 91 J5
Carthage, *Tunisia* 42 F3
Carthage, *Ill., U.S.A.* 112 E9
Carthage, *Mo., U.S.A.* 113 G7
Carthage, *N.Y., U.S.A.* 114 D8
Carthage, *Tex., U.S.A.* 113 J7
Cartier I., *Australia* 92 B3
Cartwright, *Canada* 105 B8
Caruaru, *Brazil* 125 E11
Carúpano, *Venezuela* 124 A6
Caruthersville, *U.S.A.* 113 G10
Carvin, *France* 19 B9
Carvoeiro, *Brazil* 124 D6
Carvoeiro, C., *Portugal* 37 F1
Cary, *U.S.A.* 115 H6
Casa, Pas de la = Envalira, Port d', *Europe* 38 C6
Casa Branca, *Portugal* 37 G2
Casa Grande, *U.S.A.* 109 K8
Casablanca, *Chile* 126 C1
Casablanca, *Morocco* 78 B4
Casacalenda, *Italy* 41 G11
Casalbordino, *Italy* 41 F11
Casale Monferrato, *Italy* 40 C5
Casalmaggiore, *Italy* 40 D7
Casalpusterlengo, *Italy* 40 C6
Casamance →, *Senegal* 82 C1
Casarano, *Italy* 43 B11
Casares, *Spain* 37 J5
Casas Ibáñez, *Spain* 39 F3
Casasimarro, *Spain* 39 F2
Casatejada, *Spain* 36 F5
Casavieja, *Spain* 36 E6
Cascada de Basaseachic △, *Mexico* 118 B3
Cascade, *Idaho, U.S.A.* 108 D5
Cascade, *Mont., U.S.A.* 108 C8
Cascade Locks, *U.S.A.* 110 E5
Cascade Ra., *U.S.A.* 110 D5
Cascade Reservoir, *U.S.A.* 108 D5
Cascais, *Portugal* 37 G1
Cascavel, *Brazil* 127 A5
Cáscina, *Italy* 40 E7
Casco B., *U.S.A.* 115 D10
Caselle Torinese, *Italy* 40 C4
Caserta, *Italy* 43 A7
Casey, *Antarctica* 5 C8
Caseyr, Raas = Asir, Ras, *Somali Rep.* 75 E5
Cashel, *Ireland* 12 D4
Casiguran, *Phil.* 61 C5
Casilda, *Argentina* 126 C3
Casimcea, *Romania* 29 F13
Casino, *Australia* 95 D5
Casiquiare →, *Venezuela* 124 C5
Čáslav, *Czech Rep.* 26 B8
Casma, *Peru* 124 E3
Casmalia, *U.S.A.* 111 L6
Cásola Valsénio, *Italy* 41 D8
Cásoli, *Italy* 41 F11
Caspe, *Spain* 38 D4
Casper, *U.S.A.* 108 E10
Caspian Depression, *Eurasia* 35 G9
Caspian Sea, *Eurasia* 52 E6
Cass Lake, *U.S.A.* 112 B7
Cassà de la Selva, *Spain* 38 D7
Cassadaga, *U.S.A.* 116 D5
Cassano allo Iónio, *Italy* 43 C9
Cassel, *France* 19 B9
Casselman, *Canada* 117 A9
Casselton, *U.S.A.* 112 B6
Cassiar, *Canada* 102 B3
Cassiar Mts., *Canada* 102 B2
Cassino, *Italy* 42 A6
Cassis, *France* 21 E9
Cassville, *U.S.A.* 113 G8
Castagneto Carducci, *Italy* 40 E7
Castaic, *U.S.A.* 111 L8
Castalia, *U.S.A.* 116 E2
Castanhal, *Brazil* 125 D9
Castara, *Trin. & Tob.* 125 J16
Castéggio, *Italy* 40 C6
Castejón de Monegros, *Spain* 38 D4
Castèl di Sangro, *Italy* 41 G11
Castèl San Giovanni, *Italy* 40 C6
Castèl San Pietro Terme, *Italy* 41 D8
Castelbuono, *Italy* 43 E7
Castelfidardo, *Italy* 41 E10
Castelfiorentino, *Italy* 40 E7
Castelfranco Emília, *Italy* 40 D8
Castelfranco Véneto, *Italy* 41 C8
Casteljaloux, *France* 20 D4
Castellabate, *Italy* 43 B7
Castellammare, G. di, *Italy* 42 D5
Castellammare del Golfo, *Italy* 42 D5
Castellammare di Stábia, *Italy* 43 B7
Castellamonte, *Italy* 40 C4
Castellane, *France* 21 E10
Castellaneta, *Italy* 43 B9
Castelli, *Argentina* 126 D4
Castelló de la Plana, *Spain* 38 F4
Castellón de la Plana □, *Spain* 38 E4
Castellote, *Spain* 38 E4
Castelmáuro, *Italy* 41 G11
Castelnau-de-Médoc, *France* 20 C3
Castelnau-Magnoac, *France* 20 E4
Castelnaudary, *France* 20 E5
Castelnovo ne' Monti, *Italy* 40 D7
Castelnuovo di Val di Cécina, *Italy* 40 E7
Castelo, *Brazil* 127 A7
Castelo Branco, *Portugal* 36 F3
Castelo Branco □, *Portugal* 36 F3
Castelo de Paiva, *Portugal* 36 D2
Castelo de Vide, *Portugal* 37 F3
Castelsardo, *Italy* 42 B1
Castelsarrasin, *France* 20 D5
Casteltérmini, *Italy* 42 E6
Castelvetrano, *Italy* 42 E5
Casterton, *Australia* 95 F3
Castets, *France* 20 E2
Castiglion Fiorentino, *Italy* 41 E8
Castiglione del Lago, *Italy* 41 E9
Castiglione della Pescáia, *Italy* 40 F7
Castiglione delle Stiviere, *Italy* 40 C7
Castilblanco, *Spain* 37 F5
Castile, *U.S.A.* 116 D6
Castilla, Playa de, *Spain* 37 J4
Castilla-La Mancha □, *Spain* 6 H5
Castilla y Leon □, *Spain* 36 D6
Castillo de Locubín, *Spain* 37 H7
Castillon-en-Couserans, *France* 20 F5
Castillonès, *France* 20 D4
Castillos, *Uruguay* 127 C5
Castle Dale, *U.S.A.* 108 G8
Castle Douglas, *U.K.* 13 G5
Castle Rock, *Colo., U.S.A.* 112 F2
Castle Rock, *Wash., U.S.A.* 110 D4
Castlebar, *Ireland* 12 C2
Castlebay, *U.K.* 13 E1
Castleblaney, *Ireland* 12 B5
Castlederg, *U.K.* 12 B4
Castleford, *U.K.* 14 D6
Castlegar, *Canada* 102 D5
Castlemaine, *Australia* 95 F3
Castlepollard, *Ireland* 12 C4
Castlerea, *Ireland* 12 C3
Castlereagh →, *Australia* 95 E4
Castlereagh B., *Australia* 94 A2
Castleton, *U.S.A.* 117 C11
Castletown, *I. of Man* 14 C3
Castletown Bearhaven, *Ireland* 12 E2
Castor, *Canada* 102 C6
Castor →, *Canada* 104 B4
Castorland, *U.S.A.* 117 C9
Castres, *France* 20 E6
Castricum, *Neths.* 17 B4
Castries, *St. Lucia* 121 f
Castril, *Spain* 37 H8
Castro, *Brazil* 127 A6
Castro, *Chile* 128 E2
Castro Alves, *Brazil* 125 F11
Castro del Río, *Spain* 37 H6
Castro-Urdiales, *Spain* 36 B7
Castro Verde, *Portugal* 37 H2
Castrojeriz, *Spain* 36 C6
Castropol, *Spain* 36 B4
Castroreale, *Italy* 43 D8
Castrovíllari, *Italy* 43 C9
Castroville, *U.S.A.* 110 J5
Castuera, *Spain* 37 G5
Çat, *Turkey* 73 C9
Cat Ba △, *Vietnam* 64 B6
Cat Ba, Dao, *Vietnam* 64 B6
Cat I., *Bahamas* 121 B4
Cat L., *Canada* 104 B1
Cat Lake, *Canada* 104 B1
Cat Tien △, *Vietnam* 65 G6
Čata, *Slovak Rep.* 27 D11
Catacamas, *Honduras* 120 D2
Cataguases, *Brazil* 127 A7
Çatak, *Turkey* 73 C10
Catalão, *Brazil* 125 G9
Çatalca, *Turkey* 45 E12
Catalina, *Canada* 105 C9
Catalina, *Chile* 126 B2
Catalina, *U.S.A.* 109 K8
Catalonia = Cataluña □, *Spain* 38 D6
Cataluña □, *Spain* 38 D6
Çatalzeytin, *Turkey* 72 B6
Catamarca, *Argentina* 126 B2
Catamarca □, *Argentina* 126 B2
Catanauan, *Phil.* 61 E5
Catanduanes □, *Phil.* 61 E6
Catanduva, *Brazil* 127 A6
Catánia, *Italy* 43 E8
Catánia, G. di, *Italy* 43 E8
Catanzaro, *Italy* 43 D9
Catarman, *Phil.* 61 E6
Catatumbo-Bari △, *Colombia* 121 E5
Catbalogan, *Phil.* 61 F6
Cateel, *Phil.* 61 H7
Catembe, *Mozam.* 89 D5
Caterham, *U.K.* 15 F7
Cathcart, *S. Africa* 88 E4
Cathlamet, *U.S.A.* 110 D3
Catio, *Guinea-Biss.* 82 C1
Catlettsburg, *U.S.A.* 114 F4
Çatma Dağı, *Turkey* 47 C11
Catoche, C., *Mexico* 119 C7
Cátria, Mte., *Italy* 41 E9
Catriló, *Argentina* 126 D3
Catrimani, *Brazil* 124 C6
Catrimani →, *Brazil* 124 C6
Catskill, *U.S.A.* 117 D11
Catskill ⌓, *U.S.A.* 117 D10
Catskill Mts., *U.S.A.* 117 D10
Catt, Mt., *Australia* 94 A1
Cattaraugus, *U.S.A.* 116 D6
Catterick, *U.K.* 14 C6
Cattólica, *Italy* 41 E9
Cattólica Eraclea, *Italy* 42 E6
Catuala, *Angola* 88 B2
Catuane, *Mozam.* 89 D5
Catur, *Mozam.* 87 E4
Catwick Is., *Vietnam* 65 G7
Cauca →, *Colombia* 124 B4
Caucaia, *Brazil* 125 D11
Caucasus Mountains, *Eurasia* 35 J7
Caudete, *Spain* 39 G3
Caudry, *France* 19 B10
Caulnes, *France* 18 D4
Caulónia, *Italy* 43 D9
Caungula, *Angola* 84 F3
Cauquenes, *Chile* 126 D1
Caura →, *Venezuela* 124 B6
Cauresi →, *Mozam.* 87 F3
Căuşani, *Moldova* 29 D14
Causapscal, *Canada* 105 C6
Caussade, *France* 20 D5
Causse-Méjean, *France* 20 D7
Causses du Quercy ⌓, *France* 20 D5
Cauterets, *France* 20 F3
Cauvery →, *India* 66 P11
Caux, Pays de, *France* 18 C7
Cava de' Tirreni, *Italy* 43 B7
Cávado →, *Portugal* 36 D2
Cavagrande del Cassibile ⌓, *Italy* 43 F8
Cavaillon, *France* 21 E9
Cavalaire-sur-Mer, *France* 21 E10
Cavalese, *Italy* 41 B8
Cavalier, *U.S.A.* 112 A6
Cavalla = Cavally →, *Africa* 82 E3
Cavallo, Î. de, *France* 21 G13
Cavally →, *Africa* 82 E3
Cavan, *Ireland* 12 B4
Cavan □, *Ireland* 12 C4
Cavárzere, *Italy* 41 C9
Çavdarhisar, *Turkey* 47 B11
Çavdır, *Turkey* 47 D11
Cave Creek, *U.S.A.* 109 K7
Cavenagh Ra., *Australia* 93 E4
Cavendish, *Australia* 95 F3
Caviana, I., *Brazil* 125 C8
Cavite, *Phil.* 61 D4
Cavnic, *Romania* 29 C8
Cavour, *Italy* 40 D4
Cavtat, *Croatia* 44 D2
Cawndilla L., *Australia* 95 E3
Cawnpore = Kanpur, *India* 69 F9
Caxias, *Brazil* 125 D10
Caxias do Sul, *Brazil* 127 B5
Çay, *Turkey* 72 C4
Cay Sal Bank, *Bahamas* 120 B4
Cayambe, *Ecuador* 124 C3
Çaycuma, *Turkey* 72 B5
Çayeli, *Turkey* 73 B9
Cayenne, *Fr. Guiana* 125 B8
Cayey, *Puerto Rico* 121 d
Caygören Barajı, *Turkey* 47 B10
Cayiralan, *Turkey* 72 C6
Caylus, *France* 20 D5
Cayman Brac, *Cayman Is.* 120 C4
Cayman Is. ⊠, *W. Indies* 120 C3
Cayman Trough, *Caribbean* 98 H11
Cayres, *France* 20 D7
Cayuga, *U.S.A.* 117 D8
Cayuga L., *U.S.A.* 117 D8
Cazalla de la Sierra, *Spain* 37 H5
Căzăneşti, *Romania* 29 F12
Cazaubon, *France* 20 E3
Cazaux et de Sanguinet, Étang de, *France* 20 D2
Cazenovia, *U.S.A.* 117 D9
Cazères, *France* 20 E5
Cazin, *Bos.-H.* 41 D12
Čazma, *Croatia* 41 C13
Cazombo, *Angola* 85 G4
Cazorla, *Spain* 37 H7
Cazorla, Sierra de, *Spain* 37 G8
Cea →, *Spain* 36 C5
Ceamurlia de Jos, *Romania* 29 F13
Ceanannus Mor, *Ireland* 12 C5
Ceará = Fortaleza, *Brazil* 125 D11
Ceará □, *Brazil* 125 E11
Ceará Mirim, *Brazil* 125 E11
Ceauru, L., *Romania* 29 F8
Cebaco, I. de, *Panama* 120 E3
Cebollar, *Argentina* 126 B2
Cebollera, Sierra de, *Spain* 38 D2
Cebreros, *Spain* 36 E6
Cebu, *Phil.* 61 F5
Čečava, *Bos.-H.* 28 F2
Ceccano, *Italy* 42 A6
Cece, *Hungary* 28 D3
Cechi, *Ivory C.* 82 D4
Cecil Plains, *Australia* 95 D5
Cécina, *Italy* 40 E7
Cécina →, *Italy* 40 E7
Ceclavín, *Spain* 36 F4
Cedar →, *U.S.A.* 112 E9
Cedar City, *U.S.A.* 109 H7
Cedar Creek Reservoir, *U.S.A.* 113 J6
Cedar Falls, *Iowa, U.S.A.* 112 D8
Cedar Falls, *Wash., U.S.A.* 110 C5
Cedar Key, *U.S.A.* 115 L4
Cedar L., *Canada* 103 C9
Cedar Rapids, *U.S.A.* 112 E9
Cedartown, *U.S.A.* 115 H3
Cedarvale, *Canada* 102 B3
Cedarville, *S. Africa* 89 E4
Cedeira, *Spain* 36 B2
Cedral, *Mexico* 118 C4
Cedrino →, *Italy* 42 B2
Cedro, *Brazil* 125 E11
Cedros, I. de, *Mexico* 118 B1
Cedros B., *Trin. & Tob.* 125 K15
Ceduna, *Australia* 95 E1
Cedynia, *Poland* 31 F1
Cée, *Spain* 36 C1
Ceerigaabo = Erigavo, *Somali Rep.* 75 E4
Cefalù, *Italy* 43 D7
Cega →, *Spain* 36 D6
Cegléd, *Hungary* 28 C4
Céglie Messápico, *Italy* 43 B10
Cehegín, *Spain* 39 G3
Ceheng, *China* 58 E5
Cehu-Silvaniei, *Romania* 29 C8
Ceica, *Romania* 28 D7
Ceira →, *Portugal* 36 E2
Cekik, *Indonesia* 63 J17
Čelákovice, *Czech Rep.* 26 A7
Celano, *Italy* 41 F10
Celanova, *Spain* 36 C3
Celaque △, *Honduras* 120 D2
Celaya, *Mexico* 118 C4
Celebes = Sulawesi, *Indonesia* 63 E6
Celebes Sea, *Indonesia* 63 D6
Čelić, *Bos.-H.* 28 F3
Celina, *U.S.A.* 114 E3
Celinac, *Bos.-H.* 28 F2
Celje, *Slovenia* 41 B12
Celldömölk, *Hungary* 28 C2
Celle, *Germany* 24 C6
Celorico da Beira, *Portugal* 36 E3
Celtic Sea, *Atl. Oc.* 6 E4
Çeltikçi, *Turkey* 47 D12
Çemişgezek, *Turkey* 73 C8
Cenderwasih, Teluk, *Indonesia* 63 E9
Cengong, *China* 58 D7
Ceno →, *Italy* 40 D7
Centallo, *Italy* 40 D4
Centelles, *Spain* 38 D7
Center, *N. Dak., U.S.A.* 112 B4
Center, *Tex., U.S.A.* 113 K7
Centerburg, *U.S.A.* 116 F2
Centerville, *Calif., U.S.A.* 110 J7
Centerville, *Iowa, U.S.A.* 112 E8
Centerville, *Pa., U.S.A.* 116 F5
Centerville, *Tenn., U.S.A.* 115 H2
Centerville, *Tex., U.S.A.* 113 K7
Cento, *Italy* 41 D8
Central = Tsentralnyy □, *Russia* 34 D4
Central □, *Ghana* 83 D4
Central □, *Kenya* 86 C4
Central □, *Malawi* 87 E3
Central □, *Zambia* 87 E2
Central, Cordillera, *Colombia* 124 C4
Central, Cordillera, *Costa Rica* 120 D3
Central, Cordillera, *Dom. Rep.* 121 C5
Central, Cordillera, *Phil.* 61 C4
Central, Cordillera, *Puerto Rico* 121 d
Central African Rep. ■, *Africa* 79 G9
Central America, *America* 98 H11
Central Butte, *Canada* 103 C7
Central City, *Colo., U.S.A.* 108 G11
Central City, *Ky., U.S.A.* 114 G2
Central City, *Nebr., U.S.A.* 112 E6
Central I., *Kenya* 86 B4
Central Island △, *Kenya* 86 B4
Central Kalahari ⌓, *Botswana* 88 C3
Central Makran Range, *Pakistan* 66 F4
Central Patricia, *Canada* 104 B1
Central Point, *U.S.A.* 108 E2
Central Russian Uplands, *Europe* 6 E13
Central Siberian Plateau, *Russia* 50 C14
Central Square, *U.S.A.* 117 C8
Centralia, *Ill., U.S.A.* 112 F10
Centralia, *Mo., U.S.A.* 112 F8
Centralia, *Wash., U.S.A.* 110 D4
Cenxi, *China* 59 F8
Čeotina →, *Bos.-H.* 44 C2
Cephalonia = Kefallinía, *Greece* 46 C2
Čepin, *Croatia* 28 E3
Ceprano, *Italy* 42 A6
Ceptura, *Romania* 29 E11
Cepu, *Indonesia* 63 G14
Ceram = Seram, *Indonesia* 63 E7
Ceram Sea = Seram Sea, *Indonesia* 63 E7
Cerbère, *France* 20 F7
Cerbicales, Îs., *France* 21 G13
Cercal, *Portugal* 37 H2
Cerdaña, *Spain* 38 C6
Cère →, *France* 20 D5
Cerea, *Italy* 41 C8
Ceredigion □, *U.K.* 15 E3
Ceres, *Argentina* 126 B3
Ceres, *S. Africa* 88 E2
Ceres, *U.S.A.* 110 H6
Céret, *France* 20 F6
Cergy, *France* 19 C9
Cerignola, *Italy* 43 A8
Cerigo = Kíthira, *Greece* 46 E5
Cérilly, *France* 19 F9
Cerisiers, *France* 19 D10
Cerizay, *France* 18 F6
Çerkeş, *Turkey* 72 B5
Çerkezköy, *Turkey* 45 E12
Cerknica, *Slovenia* 41 C11
Cerkovica, *Bulgaria* 45 C8
Cermerno, *Serbia & M.* 44 C4
Çermik, *Turkey* 73 C8
Cerna, *Romania* 29 E13
Cerna →, *Romania* 29 F8
Cernavodă, *Romania* 29 F13
Cernay, *France* 19 E14
Cernik, *Croatia* 28 E2
Cerralvo, I., *Mexico* 118 C3
Cërrik, *Albania* 44 E3
Cerritos, *Mexico* 118 C4
Cerro Chato, *Uruguay* 127 C4
Cerro Corá △, *Paraguay* 127 A4
Cerro el Copey △, *Venezuela* 121 D7
Cerro Hoya △, *Panama* 120 E3
Cerro Saroche △, *Venezuela* 121 D6
Certaldo, *Italy* 40 E8
Cervaro →, *Italy* 43 A8
Cervati, Monte, *Italy* 43 B8
Cerventes, *Australia* 93 F2
Cervera, *Spain* 38 D6
Cervera de Pisuerga, *Spain* 36 C6
Cervera del Río Alhama, *Spain* 38 C3
Cervéteri, *Italy* 41 F9
Cérvia, *Italy* 41 D9
Cervignano del Friuli, *Italy* 41 C10
Cervinara, *Italy* 43 A7
Cervione, *France* 21 F13
Cervo, *Spain* 36 B3
Cesarò, *Italy* 43 E7
Cesena, *Italy* 41 D9
Cesenático, *Italy* 41 D9
Cēsis, *Latvia* 9 H21
Česká Lípa, *Czech Rep.* 26 A7
Česká Třebová, *Czech Rep.* 27 B9
České Budějovice, *Czech Rep.* 26 C7
České Velenice, *Czech Rep.* 26 C7
Českobudějovický □, *Czech Rep.* 26 B7
Českomoravská Vrchovina, *Czech Rep.* 26 B8
Český Brod, *Czech Rep.* 26 A7
Český Krumlov, *Czech Rep.* 26 C7

Český Těšín, Czech Rep. 27 B11
Česma →, Croatia 41 C13
Çeşme, Turkey 47 C8
Cessnock, Australia 95 E5
Cesson-Sévigné, France 18 D5
Cestas, France 20 D3
Cestos →, Liberia 82 D3
Cestos Sehnkwehn △, Liberia 82 D3
Cetate, Romania 28 F8
Cetin Grad, Croatia 41 C12
Cetina →, Croatia 41 E13
Cetinje, Serbia & M. 44 D2
Cetraro, Italy 43 C8
Ceuta, N. Afr. 78 A4
Ceva, Italy 40 D5
Cévennes, France 20 D7
Cévennes △, France 20 D7
Ceyhan, Turkey 70 B2
Ceyhan →, Turkey 72 D6
Ceylânpınar, Turkey 73 D9
Ceylon = Sri Lanka ■, Asia 66 R12
Cèze →, France 21 D8
Cha-am, Thailand 64 F2
Cha Pa, Vietnam 64 A4
Chabanais, France 20 C4
Chabeuil, France 21 D9
Chablais, France 19 F13
Chablis, France 19 E10
Chacabuco, Argentina 126 C3
Chachapoyas, Peru 124 E3
Chachoengsao, Thailand 64 F3
Chachran, Pakistan 66 E7
Chachro, Pakistan 68 G4
Chaco △, Argentina 126 B4
Chaco □, Argentina 126 B3
Chaco □, Paraguay 126 B4
Chaco →, U.S.A. 109 H9
Chaco Austral, S. Amer. 128 B4
Chaco Boreal, S. Amer. 124 H6
Chaco Central, S. Amer. 128 A4
Chaco Culture △, U.S.A. 109 H10
Chacon, C., U.S.A. 102 C2
Chad ■, Africa 79 F8
Chad, L. = Tchad, L., Chad 79 F8
Chadan, Russia 53 D10
Chadileuvú →, Argentina 126 D2
Chadiza, Zambia 87 E3
Chadron, U.S.A. 112 D3
Chadyr-Lunga = Ciadâr-Lunga, Moldova 29 D13
Chae Hom, Thailand 64 C2
Chae Son △, Thailand 64 C2
Chaem →, Thailand 64 C2
Chaeryŏng, N. Korea 57 E13
Chagai Hills = Chāh Gay Hills, Afghan. 66 E3
Chagda, Russia 53 D14
Chaghcharān, Afghan. 66 B4
Chagny, France 19 F11
Chagoda, Russia 32 C8
Chagos Arch. ☒, Ind. Oc. 50 K11
Chagres △, Panama 120 E4
Chagrin Falls, U.S.A. 116 E3
Chaguanas, Trin. & Tob. 125 K15
Chāh Ākhvor, Iran 71 C8
Chāh Bahar, Iran 71 E9
Chāh-e Kavīr, Iran 71 C8
Chāh Gay Hills, Afghan. 66 E3
Chahar Burjak, Afghan. 66 D3
Chahār Mahāll va Bakhtīarī □, Iran 71 C6
Chaibasa, India 67 H14
Chaillé-les-Marais, France 20 B2
Chainat, Thailand 64 E3
Chaiya, Thailand 65 H2
Chaiyaphum, Thailand 64 E4
Chaj Doab, Pakistan 68 C5
Chajari, Argentina 126 C4
Chak Amru, Pakistan 68 C6
Chaka, Sudan 81 G3
Chakar →, Pakistan 68 E3
Chakari, Zimbabwe 89 B4
Chake Chake, Tanzania 86 D4
Chakhānsūr, Afghan. 66 D3
Chakonipau, L., Canada 105 A6
Chakradharpur, India 69 H11
Chakrata, India 68 D7
Chakwal, Pakistan 68 C5
Chala, Peru 124 G4
Chalais, France 20 C4
Chalchihuites, Mexico 118 C4
Chalcis = Khalkís, Greece 46 C5
Châlette-sur-Loing, France 19 D9
Chaleur B., Canada 105 C6
Chalfant, U.S.A. 110 H8
Chalhuanca, Peru 124 F4
Chalindrey, France 19 E12
Chaling, China 59 D9
Chalisgaon, India 66 J9
Chalk River, Canada 104 C4
Chalky Inlet, N.Z. 91 M1
Challans, France 18 F5
Challapata, Bolivia 124 G5
Challis, U.S.A. 108 D6
Chalmette, U.S.A. 113 L10
Chalon-sur-Saône, France 19 F11
Chalonnes-sur-Loire, France 18 E6
Châlons-en-Champagne, France 19 D11
Châlus, France 20 C4
Chālūs, Iran 71 B6
Cham, Germany 25 F8
Cham, Cu Lao, Vietnam 64 E7
Chama, U.S.A. 109 H10
Chamaicó, Argentina 126 D3
Chaman, Pakistan 66 D5
Chamba, India 68 C7
Chamba, Tanzania 87 E4
Chambal →, India 69 F8
Chamberlain, U.S.A. 112 D5
Chamberlain →, Australia 92 C4
Chamberlain L., U.S.A. 115 B11
Chambers, U.S.A. 109 J9
Chambersburg, U.S.A. 114 F7
Chambéry, France 21 C9
Chambeshi →, Zambia 84 G6
Chambly, Canada 117 A11
Chambord, Canada 105 C5
Chamboulive, France 20 C5
Chamchamal, Iraq 70 C5
Chamela, Mexico 118 D3
Chamical, Argentina 126 C2
Chamkar Luong, Cambodia 65 G4
Chamoli, India 69 D8
Chamonix-Mont Blanc, France 21 C10
Champa, India 69 H10
Champagne, Canada 102 A1
Champagne, France 19 D11
Champagnole, France 19 F12
Champaign, U.S.A. 114 E1
Champassak, Laos 64 E5
Champaubert, France 19 D10
Champawat, India 69 E9
Champdeniers-St-Denis, France 20 B3
Champdoré, L., Canada 105 A6
Champeix, France 20 C7
Champion, U.S.A. 116 E4
Champlain, U.S.A. 117 B11
Champlain, L., U.S.A. 117 B11
Champlitte, France 19 E12
Champotón, Mexico 119 D6
Champua, India 69 H11
Chamusca, Portugal 37 F2
Chana, Thailand 65 J3
Chañaral, Chile 126 B1
Chanārān, Iran 71 B8
Chanasma, India 68 H5
Chancery Lane, Barbados 121 g
Chanco, Chile 126 D1
Chand, India 69 J8
Chandan, India 69 G12
Chandan Chauki, India 69 E9
Chandannagar, India 69 H13
Chandausi, India 69 E8
Chandeleur Is., U.S.A. 113 L10
Chandeleur Sd., U.S.A. 113 L10
Chandigarh, India 68 D7
Chandil, India 69 H12
Chandler, Australia 95 D1
Chandler, Canada 105 C7
Chandler, Ariz., U.S.A. 109 K8
Chandler, Okla., U.S.A. 113 H6
Chandod, India 68 J5
Chandpur, Bangla. 67 H17
Chandrapur, India 66 K11
Chānf, Iran 71 E9
Chang, Pakistan 68 F3
Chang, Ko, Thailand 65 F4
Ch'ang Chiang = Chang Jiang →, China 59 B13
Chang Jiang →, China 59 B13
Changa, India 69 C7
Changanacheri, India 66 Q10
Changane →, Mozam. 89 C5
Changbai, China 57 D15
Changbai Shan, China 57 C15
Changchiak'ou = Zhangjiakou, China 56 D8
Ch'angchou = Changzhou, China 59 B12
Changchun, China 57 C13
Changchunling, China 57 B13
Changde, China 59 C8
Changdo-ri, N. Korea 57 E14
Changfeng, China 59 A11
Changhai = Shanghai, China 59 B13
Changhua, China 59 B12
Changhua, Taiwan 59 E13
Changhŭng, S. Korea 57 G14
Changhŭngni, N. Korea 57 D15
Changi, Singapore 65 d
Changi, Singapore ✕ (SIN), Singapore 65 M4
Changjiang, China 64 C7
Changjin, N. Korea 57 D14
Changjin-chŏsuji, N. Korea 57 D14
Changle, China 59 E12
Changli, China 57 E10
Changling, China 57 B12
Changlun, Malaysia 65 J3
Changning, Hunan, China 59 D9
Changning, Sichuan, China 58 C5
Changning, Yunnan, China 58 E2
Changping, China 56 D9
Changsha, China 59 C9
Changshan, China 59 C12
Changshu, China 59 B13
Changshun, China 58 D6
Changtai, China 59 E11
Changting, China 59 E11
Changwu, China 56 G4
Changxing, China 59 B12
Changyang, China 59 B8
Changyi, China 57 F10
Changyŏn, N. Korea 57 E13
Changyuan, China 56 G8
Changzhi, China 56 F7
Changzhou, China 59 B12
Chanhanga, Angola 88 B1
Chania = Khaniá, Greece 49 D6
Chanlar = Xanlar, Azerbaijan 35 K8
Channapatna, India 66 N10
Channel Is., U.K. 15 H5
Channel Is., U.S.A. 111 M7
Channel Islands △, U.S.A. 111 L7
Channel-Port aux Basques, Canada 105 C8
Channel Tunnel, Europe 15 F9
Channing, U.S.A. 113 H3
Chantada, Spain 36 C3
Chanthaburi, Thailand 64 F4
Chantilly, France 19 C9
Chantonnay, France 18 F5
Chantrey Inlet, Canada 100 B10
Chanute, U.S.A. 113 G7
Chanza →, Spain 37 H3
Chao Hu, China 59 B11
Chao Phraya →, Thailand 64 F3
Chao Phraya Lowlands, Thailand 64 E3
Chaocheng, China 56 F8
Chaohu, China 59 B11
Chaoyang, Guangdong, China 59 F11
Chaoyang, Liaoning, China 57 D11
Chaozhou, China 59 F11
Chapais, Canada 104 C5
Chapala, Mozam. 87 F4
Chapala, L. de, Mexico 118 C4
Chapayev, Kazakhstan 34 E10
Chapayevsk, Russia 34 D9
Chapecó, Brazil 127 B5
Chapel Hill, U.S.A. 115 H6
Chapleau, Canada 104 C3
Chaplin, Canada 103 C7
Chaplin L., Canada 103 C7
Chaplino, Ukraine 33 H9
Chaplygin, Russia 32 F11
Chappell, U.S.A. 112 E3
Chapra = Chhapra, India 69 G11
Chara, Russia 53 D12
Charadai, Argentina 126 B4
Charagua, Bolivia 124 G6
Charambirá, Punta, Colombia 124 C3
Charaña, Bolivia 124 G5
Charantsavan, Armenia 35 K7
Charanwala, India 68 F5
Charata, Argentina 126 B3
Charcas, Mexico 118 C4
Charcot I., Antarctica 5 C17
Chard, U.K. 15 G5
Chardon, U.S.A. 116 E3
Chardzhou = Chärjew, Turkmenistan 52 F7
Charente □, France 20 C4
Charente →, France 20 C2
Charente-Maritime □, France 20 C3
Charenton-du-Cher, France 19 F9
Chari →, Chad 79 F8
Chārīkār, Afghan. 66 B6
Chariton →, U.S.A. 112 F8
Chärjew, Turkmenistan 52 F7
Charkhari, India 69 G8
Charkhi Dadri, India 68 E7
Charleroi, Belgium 17 D4
Charleroi, U.S.A. 116 F5
Charles, C., U.S.A. 114 G8
Charles City, U.S.A. 112 D8
Charles de Gaulle, Paris ✕ (CDG), France 19 D9
Charles L., Canada 103 B6
Charles Town, U.S.A. 114 F7
Charleston, Ill., U.S.A. 114 F1
Charleston, Miss., U.S.A. 113 H9
Charleston, Mo., U.S.A. 113 G10
Charleston, S.C., U.S.A. 115 J6
Charleston, W. Va., U.S.A. 114 F5
Charleston L., Canada 117 B9
Charleston Peak, U.S.A. 111 J11
Charlestown, Ireland 12 C3
Charlestown, S. Africa 89 D4
Charlestown, Ind., U.S.A. 114 F3
Charlestown, N.H., U.S.A. 117 C12
Charlestown of Aberlour, U.K. 13 D5
Charleville = Rath Luirc, Ireland 12 D3
Charleville, Australia 95 D4
Charleville-Mézières, France 19 C11
Charlevoix, U.S.A. 114 C3
Charlieu, France 19 F11
Charlotte, Mich., U.S.A. 114 D3
Charlotte, N.C., U.S.A. 115 H5
Charlotte, Vt., U.S.A. 117 B11
Charlotte Amalie, U.S. Virgin Is. 121 e
Charlotte Harbor, U.S.A. 115 M4
Charlotte L., Canada 102 C3
Charlottenberg, Sweden 10 E6
Charlottesville, U.S.A. 114 F6
Charlottetown, Nfld. & L., Canada 105 B8
Charlottetown, P.E.I., Canada 105 C7
Charlotteville, Trin. & Tob. 125 J16
Charlton, Australia 95 F3
Charlton, U.S.A. 112 E8
Charlton I., Canada 104 B4
Charmes, France 19 D13
Charny, Canada 105 C5
Charnyany, Belarus 31 G11
Charolles, France 19 F11
Chârost, France 19 F9
Charre, Mozam. 87 F4
Charroux, France 20 B4
Charsadda, Pakistan 68 B4
Charters Towers, Australia 94 C4
Chartres, France 18 D8
Chartreuse ⌓, France 21 C9
Chascomús, Argentina 126 D4
Chasefu, Zambia 87 E3
Chashma Barrage, Pakistan 68 C4
Chasseneuil-sur-Bonnieure, France 20 C4
Chāt, Iran 71 B7
Chatal Balkan = Udvoy Balkan, Bulgaria 45 D10
Château-Arnoux-St-Auban, France 21 D10
Château-Chinon, France 19 E10
Château-d'Olonne, France 20 B2
Château-du-Loir, France 18 E7
Château-Gontier, France 18 E6
Château-la-Vallière, France 18 E7
Château-Landon, France 19 D9
Château-Renard, France 19 E9
Château-Renault, France 18 E7
Château-Salins, France 19 D13
Château-Thierry, France 19 C10
Châteaubourg, France 18 D5
Châteaubriant, France 18 E5
Châteaudun, France 18 D8
Chateaugay, U.S.A. 117 B10
Châteaugiron, France 18 D5
Châteauguay, L., Canada 105 A5
Châteaulin, France 18 D2
Châteaumeillant, France 19 F9
Châteauneuf-du-Faou, France 18 D3
Châteauneuf-sur-Charente, France 20 C3
Châteauneuf-sur-Cher, France 19 F9
Châteauneuf-sur-Loire, France 19 E9
Châteaurenard, France 21 E8
Châteauroux, France 19 F8
Châteauvillain, France 19 D11
Châteaux, Pte. des, Guadeloupe 120 b
Châtelaillon-Plage, France 20 B2
Châtelguyon, France 20 C7
Châtellerault, France 18 F7
Châtelus-Malvaleix, France 19 F9
Chatham = Chatham-Kent, Canada 116 D2
Chatham = Miramichi, Canada 105 C6
Chatham, U.K. 15 F8
Chatham, U.S.A. 117 D11
Chatham Is., Pac. Oc. 96 M10
Chatham-Kent, Canada 116 D2
Châtillon, Italy 40 C4
Châtillon-Coligny, France 19 E9
Châtillon-en-Diois, France 21 D9
Châtillon-sur-Indre, France 18 F8
Châtillon-sur-Loire, France 19 E9
Châtillon-sur-Seine, France 19 E11
Chatmohar, Bangla. 69 G13
Chatra, India 69 G11
Chatrapur, India 67 K14
Chats, L. des, Canada 117 A8
Chatsu, India 68 F6
Chatsworth, Canada 116 B4
Chatsworth, Zimbabwe 87 F3
Chāttagām = Chittagong, Bangla. 67 H17
Chattahoochee, U.S.A. 115 K3
Chattahoochee →, U.S.A. 115 K3
Chattanooga, U.S.A. 115 H3
Chatteris, U.K. 15 E8
Chaturat, Thailand 64 E3
Chau Doc, Vietnam 65 G5
Chaudes-Aigues, France 20 D7
Chauffailles, France 19 F11
Chaukan Pass, Burma 67 F20
Chaumont, France 19 D12
Chaumont, U.S.A. 117 B8
Chaumont-en-Vexin, France 19 C8
Chaumont-sur-Loire, France 18 E8
Chaunay, France 20 B4
Chaunskaya G., Russia 4 C16
Chauny, France 19 C10
Chausey, Îs., France 18 D5
Chaussin, France 19 F12
Chautauqua L., U.S.A. 116 D5
Chauvigny, France 18 F7
Chauvin, Canada 103 C6
Chavanges, France 19 D11
Chaves, Brazil 125 D9
Chaves, Portugal 36 D3
Chawang, Thailand 65 H2
Chazelles-sur-Lyon, France 21 C8
Chazy, U.S.A. 117 B11
Cheb, Czech Rep. 26 A5
Cheboksarskoye Vdkhr., Russia 34 B8
Cheboksary, Russia 34 B8
Cheboygan, U.S.A. 114 C3
Chebsara, Russia 32 C10
Chech, Erg, Africa 78 D5
Chechelnyk, Ukraine 29 B14
Chechen, Ostrov, Russia 35 H8
Chechenia □, Russia 35 J7
Checheno-Ingush Republic = Chechenia □, Russia 35 J7
Chechnya = Chechenia □, Russia 35 J7
Chech'ŏn, S. Korea 57 F15
Chęciny, Poland 31 H7
Checotah, U.S.A. 113 H7
Chedabucto B., Canada 105 C7
Cheduba I., Burma 67 K18
Cheepie, Australia 95 D4
Chef-Boutonne, France 20 B3
Chegdomyn, Russia 53 D14
Chegga, Mauritania 78 C4
Chegutu, Zimbabwe 87 F3
Chehalis, U.S.A. 110 D4
Chehalis →, U.S.A. 110 D3
Cheile Nerei-Beusnita △, Romania 28 F6
Cheiron, Mt., France 21 E10
Cheju do, S. Korea 57 H14
Chekalin, Russia 32 E9
Chekhovo, Russia 30 D7
Chekiang = Zhejiang □, China 59 C13
Chel = Kuru, Bahr el →, Sudan 81 F2
Chela, Sa. da, Angola 88 B1
Chelan, U.S.A. 108 C4
Chelan, L., U.S.A. 108 B3
Cheleken, Turkmenistan 52 F6
Cheleken Yarymadasy, Turkmenistan 71 B7
Chelforó, Argentina 128 D3
Chelkar = Shalqar, Kazakhstan 52 E6
Chelkar Tengiz, Solonchak, Kazakhstan 52 E7
Chella, Ethiopia 81 F4
Chelles, France 19 D9
Chełm, Poland 31 G10
Chełmno, Poland 31 E5
Chelmsford, U.K. 15 F8
Chełmża, Poland 31 E5
Chelsea, U.S.A. 117 C12
Cheltenham, U.K. 15 F5
Chelva, Spain 38 F4
Chelyabinsk, Russia 52 D7
Chelyuskin, C. = Chelyuskin, Mys, Russia 53 B11
Chelyuskin, Mys, Russia 53 B11
Chemainus, Canada 110 B3
Chemba, Mozam. 85 H6
Chembar = Belinskiy, Russia 34 D6
Chemillé, France 18 E6
Chemnitz, Germany 24 E8
Chemult, U.S.A. 108 E3
Chen, Gora, Russia 53 C15
Chenab →, Pakistan 68 D4
Chenango Forks, U.S.A. 117 D9
Chencha, Ethiopia 81 F4
Chenchiang = Zhenjiang, China 59 A12
Cheney, U.S.A. 108 C5
Cheng Xian, China 56 H3
Chengbu, China 59 D8
Chengcheng, China 56 G5
Chengchou = Zhengzhou, China 56 G7
Chengde, China 57 D9
Chengdong Hu, China 59 A11
Chengdu, China 58 B5
Chenggong, China 58 E4
Chenggu, China 56 H4
Chenghai, China 59 F11
Chengjiang, China 58 E4
Chengkou, China 58 B7
Ch'engmai, China 64 C7
Ch'engtu = Chengdu, China 58 B5
Chengwu, China 56 G8
Chengxi Hu, China 59 A11
Chengyang, China 57 F11
Chenjiagang, China 57 G10
Chenkán, Mexico 119 D6
Chennai, India 66 N12
Chenôve, France 19 E12
Chenxi, China 59 C8
Chenzhou, China 59 E9
Cheo Reo, Vietnam 62 B3
Cheom Ksan, Cambodia 64 E5
Chepelare, Bulgaria 45 E8
Chepén, Peru 124 E3
Chepes, Argentina 126 C2
Chepo, Panama 120 E4
Chepstow, U.K. 15 F5
Chequamegon B., U.S.A. 112 B9
Cher □, France 19 E9
Cher →, France 18 E7
Chéradi, Italy 43 B10
Cherasco, Italy 40 D4
Cheraw, U.S.A. 115 H6
Cherbourg, France 18 C5
Cherdakly, Russia 34 C9
Cherdyn, Russia 52 C6
Cheremkhovo, Russia 53 D11
Cherepanovo, Russia 52 D9
Cherepovets, Russia 32 C9
Chergui, Chott ech, Algeria 78 B6
Cherikov = Cherykaw, Belarus 32 F6
Cherkasy, Ukraine 33 H7
Cherkessk, Russia 35 H6
Cherlak, Russia 52 D8
Chernaya, Russia 53 B9
Chernelytsya, Ukraine 29 B10
Cherni, Bulgaria 44 D7
Chernigov = Chernihiv, Ukraine 33 G6
Chernihiv, Ukraine 33 G6
Chernivetska □, Ukraine 29 B10
Chernivtsi, Ukraine 29 B13
Chernivtsi, Ukraine 29 B10
Chernobyl = Chornobyl, Ukraine 33 G6
Chernogorsk, Russia 53 D10
Chernomorskoye = Chornomorske, Ukraine 33 K7
Chernovtsy = Chernivtsi, Ukraine 29 B10
Chernyakhovsk, Russia 9 J19
Chernyanka, Russia 33 G9
Chernysheyskiy, Russia 53 C12
Chernyye Zemli, Russia 35 H8
Cherokee, Iowa, U.S.A. 112 D7
Cherokee, Okla., U.S.A. 113 G5
Cherokee Village, U.S.A. 113 G9
Cherokees, Grand Lake O' The, U.S.A. 113 G7
Cherrapunji, India 67 G17
Cherry Valley, Calif., U.S.A. 111 M10
Cherry Valley, N.Y., U.S.A. 117 D10
Cherskiy, Russia 53 C17
Cherskogo Khrebet, Russia 53 C15
Chertkovo, Russia 33 H11
Cherven, Belarus 32 F5
Cherven-Bryag, Bulgaria 45 C8
Chervonoarmiyske, Ukraine 29 E13
Chervonohrad, Ukraine 33 G3
Cherwell →, U.K. 15 F6
Cherykaw, Belarus 32 F6
Chesapeake, U.S.A. 114 G7
Chesapeake B., U.S.A. 114 G7
Cheshire □, U.K. 14 D5
Cheshskaya Guba, Russia 52 C5
Cheshunt, U.K. 15 F7
Chesil Beach, U.K. 15 G5
Chesley, Canada 116 B3
Cheste, Spain 39 F4
Chester, U.K. 14 D5
Chester, Calif., U.S.A. 108 F3
Chester, Ill., U.S.A. 113 G10
Chester, Mont., U.S.A. 108 B8
Chester, Pa., U.S.A. 114 F8
Chester, S.C., U.S.A. 115 H5
Chester, Vt., U.S.A. 117 C12
Chester, W. Va., U.S.A. 116 F4
Chester-le-Street, U.K. 14 C6
Chesterfield, U.K. 14 D6
Chesterfield, Is., N. Cal. 96 J7
Chesterfield Inlet, Canada 100 B10
Chesterton Ra., Australia 95 D4
Chesterton Range △, Australia 95 D4
Chestertown, U.S.A. 117 C11
Chesterville, Canada 117 A9
Chestnut Ridge, U.S.A. 116 F5
Chesuncook L., U.S.A. 115 C11
Chéticamp, Canada 105 C7
Chetrosu, Moldova 29 B12
Chetumal, Mexico 119 D7
Chetumal, B. de, Mexico 119 D7
Chetwynd, Canada 102 B4
Chevanceaux, France 20 C3

Cheviot, The, U.K. 14 B5
Cheviot Hills, U.K. 14 B5
Cheviot Ra., Australia 94 D3
Chew Bahir, Ethiopia 81 G4
Chewelah, U.S.A. 108 B5
Chewore ⌓, Zimbabwe 87 F2
Cheyenne, Okla., U.S.A. 113 H5
Cheyenne, Wyo., U.S.A. 112 E2
Cheyenne →, U.S.A. 112 C4
Cheyenne Wells, U.S.A. 112 F3
Cheyne B., Australia 93 F2
Chhabra, India 68 G7
Chhaktala, India 68 H6
Chhapra, India 69 G11
Chhata, India 68 F7
Chhatarpur, Jharkhand, India 69 G11
Chhatarpur, Mad. P., India 69 G8
Chhattisgarh □, India 69 J10
Chhep, Cambodia 64 F5
Chhindwara, Mad. P., India 69 H8
Chhindwara, Mad. P., India 69 H8
Chhlong, Cambodia 65 F5
Chhota Tawa →, India 68 H7
Chhoti Kali Sindh →, India 68 G6
Chhuikhadan, India 69 J9
Chhuk, Cambodia 65 G5
Chi →, Thailand 64 E5
Chiai, Taiwan 59 F13
Chiali, Taiwan 59 F13
Chiamboni, Somali Rep. 84 E8
Chianciano Terme, Italy 41 E8
Chiang Dao, Thailand 64 C2
Chiang Kham, Thailand 64 C3
Chiang Khan, Thailand 64 D3
Chiang Khong, Thailand 58 G3
Chiang Mai, Thailand 64 C2
Chiang Rai, Thailand 58 H2
Chiang Saen, Thailand 58 G3
Chianti, Italy 41 E8
Chiapa →, Mexico 119 D6
Chiapa de Corzo, Mexico 119 D6
Chiapas □, Mexico 119 D6
Chiaramonte Gulfi, Italy 43 E7
Chiaravalle, Italy 41 E10
Chiaravalle Centrale, Italy 43 D9
Chiari, Italy 40 C6
Chiatura, Georgia 35 J6
Chiautla, Mexico 119 D5
Chiávari, Italy 40 D6
Chiavenna, Italy 40 B6
Chiba, Japan 55 G10
Chiba □, Japan 55 G10
Chibabava, Mozam. 89 C5
Chibemba, Cunene, Angola 85 H2
Chibemba, Huila, Angola 88 B2
Chibi, Zimbabwe 89 C5
Chibia, Angola 85 H2
Chibougamau, Canada 104 C5
Chibougamau, L., Canada 104 C5
Chibuk, Nigeria 83 C7
Chibuto, Mozam. 89 C5
Chic-Chocs, Mts., Canada 105 C6
Chicacole = Srikakulam, India 67 K13
Chicago, U.S.A. 114 E2
Chicago Heights, U.S.A. 114 E2
Chichagof I., U.S.A. 100 C6
Chichén-Itzá, Mexico 119 C7
Chicheng, China 56 D8
Chichester, U.K. 15 G7
Chichester Ra., Australia 92 D2
Chichibu, Japan 55 F9
Chichibu-Tama △, Japan 55 G9
Ch'ich'ihaerh = Qiqihar, China 53 E13
Chicholi, India 68 H8
Chickasaw ⌓, U.S.A. 113 H6
Chickasha, U.S.A. 113 H6
Chiclana de la Frontera, Spain 37 J4
Chiclayo, Peru 124 E3
Chico, U.S.A. 110 F5
Chico →, Chubut, Argentina 128 E3
Chico →, Santa Cruz, Argentina 128 G3
Chicomo, Mozam. 89 C5
Chicomostoc, Mexico 118 C4
Chicontepec, Mexico 119 C5
Chicopee, U.S.A. 117 D12
Chicoutimi, Canada 105 C5
Chicualacuala, Mozam. 89 C5
Chidambaram, India 66 P11
Chidenguele, Mozam. 89 C5
Chidley, C., Canada 101 B13
Chiducuane, Mozam. 89 C5
Chiede, Angola 88 B2
Chiefs Pt., Canada 116 B3
Chiem Hoa, Vietnam 64 A5
Chiemsee, Germany 25 H8
Chiengi, Zambia 87 D2
Chiengmai = Chiang Mai, Thailand 64 C2
Chienti →, Italy 41 E10
Chieri, Italy 40 C4
Chiers →, France 19 C11
Chiesa in Valmalenco, Italy 40 B6
Chiese →, Italy 40 C7
Chieti, Italy 41 F11
Chifeng, China 57 C10
Chigirin, Ukraine 33 H7
Chignecto B., Canada 105 C7
Chiguana, Bolivia 126 A2
Chigwell, U.K. 15 F8
Chiha-ri, N. Korea 57 E14
Chihli, G. of = Bo Hai, China 57 E10
Chihuahua, Mexico 118 B3
Chihuahua □, Mexico 118 B3
Chiili = Shīeli, Kazakhstan 52 E7
Chik Bollapur, India 66 N10
Chikmagalur, India 66 N9
Chikwawa, Malawi 87 F3
Chilac, Mexico 119 D5
Chilam Chavki, Pakistan 69 B6
Chilanga, Zambia 87 F2
Chilapa, Mexico 119 D5
Chilas, Pakistan 69 B6
Chilaw, Sri Lanka 66 R11
Chilcotin →, Canada 102 C4
Childers, Australia 95 D5
Childress, U.S.A. 113 H4
Chile ■, S. Amer. 128 D2
Chile Rise, Pac. Oc. 97 L18
Chilecito, Argentina 126 B2
Chilete, Peru 124 E3
Chilia, Braţul →, Romania 29 E14
Chililabombwe, Zambia 87 E2
Chilin = Jilin, China 57 C14
Chilka L., India 67 K14
Chilko →, Canada 102 C4
Chilko L., Canada 102 C4
Chillagoe, Australia 94 B3
Chillán, Chile 126 D1
Chillicothe, Ill., U.S.A. 112 E10
Chillicothe, Mo., U.S.A. 112 F8
Chillicothe, Ohio, U.S.A. 114 F4
Chilliwack, Canada 102 D4
Chilo, India 68 F5
Chiloane, I., Mozam. 89 C5
Chiloé, I. de, Chile 128 E2
Chilpancingo, Mexico 119 D5
Chiltern Hills, U.K. 15 F7
Chilton, U.S.A. 114 C1
Chilubi, Zambia 87 E2
Chilubula, Zambia 87 E3
Chilumba, Malawi 87 E3
Chilung, Taiwan 59 E13
Chilwa, L., Malawi 87 F4
Chimaltitán, Mexico 118 C4
Chimán, Panama 120 E4
Chimanimani, Zimbabwe 89 B5
Chimanimani △, Zimbabwe 87 F3
Chimay, Belgium 17 D4
Chimayo, U.S.A. 109 H11
Chimbay, Uzbekistan 52 E6
Chimborazo, Ecuador 124 D3
Chimbote, Peru 124 E3
Chimkent = Shymkent, Kazakhstan 52 E7
Chimoio, Mozam. 87 F3
Chimpembe, Zambia 87 D2
Chin □, Burma 67 J18
Chin Ling Shan = Qinling Shandi, China 56 H5
China, Mexico 119 B5
China ■, Asia 60 D6
China, Great Plain of, Asia 50 F15
China Lake, U.S.A. 111 K9
Chinan = Jinan, China 56 F9
Chinandega, Nic. 120 D2
Chinati Peak, U.S.A. 113 L2
Chincha Alta, Peru 124 F3
Chinchaga →, Canada 102 B5
Chinchilla, Australia 95 D5
Chinchilla de Monte Aragón, Spain 39 G3
Chinchorro, Banco, Mexico 119 D7
Chinchou = Jinzhou, China 57 D11
Chincoteague, U.S.A. 114 G8
Chinde, Mozam. 87 F4
Chindo, S. Korea 57 G14
Chindwin →, Burma 67 J19
Chineni, India 69 C6
Chinga, Mozam. 87 F4
Chingola, Zambia 87 E2
Chingole, Malawi 87 E3
Ch'ingtao = Qingdao, China 57 F11
Chinguetti, Mauritania 78 D3
Chingune, Mozam. 89 C5
Chinhae, S. Korea 57 G15
Chinhanguanine, Mozam. 89 D5
Chinhoyi, Zimbabwe 87 F3
Chini, India 68 D8
Chiniot, Pakistan 68 D5
Chínipas, Mexico 118 B3
Chinji, Pakistan 68 C5
Chinju, S. Korea 57 G15
Chinle, U.S.A. 109 H9
Chinmen, Taiwan 59 E13
Chinmen Tao, Taiwan 59 E12
Chinnampo = Namp'o, N. Korea 57 E13
Chino, Japan 55 G9
Chino, U.S.A. 111 L9
Chino Valley, U.S.A. 109 J7
Chinon, France 18 E7
Chinook, U.S.A. 108 B9
Chinsali, Zambia 87 E3
Chióggia, Italy 41 C9
Chíos = Khíos, Greece 47 C8
Chipata, Zambia 87 E3
Chiperceni, Moldova 29 C13
Chipinge, Zimbabwe 87 G3
Chipinge ⌓, Zimbabwe 87 G3
Chipiona, Spain 37 J4
Chipley, U.S.A. 115 K3
Chipman, Canada 105 C6
Chipoka, Malawi 87 E3
Chippenham, U.K. 15 F5
Chippewa →, U.S.A. 112 C8
Chippewa Falls, U.S.A. 112 C9
Chipping Norton, U.K. 15 F6
Chiprovtsi, Bulgaria 44 C6
Chiputneticook Lakes, U.S.A. 115 C11
Chiquián, Peru 124 F3
Chiquibul △, Belize 120 C2
Chiquimula, Guatemala 120 D2
Chiquinquira, Colombia 124 B4
Chir →, Russia 35 F6
Chirala, India 66 M12
Chiramba, Mozam. 87 F3
Chirawa, India 68 E6
Chirchiq, Uzbekistan 52 E7
Chiredzi, Zimbabwe 89 C5
Chiricahua ⌓, U.S.A. 109 K9
Chiricahua Peak, U.S.A. 109 L9
Chiriquí, G. de, Panama 120 E3
Chiriquí, L. de, Panama 120 E3
Chirisa ⌓, Zimbabwe 87 F2
Chirivira Falls, Zimbabwe 87 G3
Chirmiri, India 67 H13
Chirnogi, Romania 29 F11
Chirpan, Bulgaria 45 D9
Chirripó Grande, Cerro, Costa Rica 120 E3
Chirundu, Zimbabwe 89 B4
Chisamba, Zambia 87 E2
Chisapani Garhi, Nepal 67 F14
Chisasibi, Canada 104 B4
Ch'ishan, Taiwan 59 F13
Chisholm, Canada 102 C6
Chisholm, U.S.A. 112 B8
Chishtian Mandi, Pakistan 68 E5
Chishui, China 58 C5
Chishui He →, China 58 C5
Chisimaio, Somali Rep. 77 G8
Chisimba Falls, Zambia 87 E3
Chişinău, Moldova 29 C13
Chişinău ✖ (KIV), Moldova 29 C13
Chişineu Criş, Romania 28 D6
Chisone →, Italy 40 D4
Chisos Mts., U.S.A. 113 L3
Chistopol, Russia 34 C10
Chita, Russia 53 D12
Chitipa, Malawi 87 D3
Chitose, Japan 54 C10
Chitral, Pakistan 66 B7
Chitré, Panama 120 E3
Chittagong, Bangla. 67 H17
Chittagong □, Bangla. 67 G17
Chittaurgarh, India 68 G6
Chittoor, India 66 N11
Chitungwiza, Zimbabwe 87 F3
Chiusi, Italy 41 E8
Chiva, Spain 39 F4
Chivasso, Italy 40 C4
Chivhu, Zimbabwe 87 F3
Chivilcoy, Argentina 126 C4
Chiwanda, Tanzania 87 E3
Chixi, China 59 G9
Chizarira, Zimbabwe 87 F2
Chizarira △, Zimbabwe 87 F2
Chizera, Zambia 87 E2
Chkalov = Orenburg, Russia 52 D6
Chkolovsk, Russia 34 B6
Chloride, U.S.A. 111 K12
Chlumec nad Cidlinou, Czech Rep. 26 A8
Chmielnik, Poland 31 H7
Cho Bo, Vietnam 58 G5
Cho-do, N. Korea 57 E13
Cho Phuoc Hai, Vietnam 65 G6
Choa Chu Kang, Singapore 65 d
Choba, Kenya 86 B4
Chobe △, Botswana 88 B4
Choch'iwŏn, S. Korea 57 F14
Chocianów, Poland 31 G2
Chociwel, Poland 30 E2
Chocolate Mts., U.S.A. 111 M11
Choctawhatchee →, U.S.A. 115 K3
Chodecz, Poland 31 F6
Chodov, Czech Rep. 26 A5
Chodziez, Poland 31 F3
Choele Choel, Argentina 128 D3
Choiseul, St. Lucia 121 f
Choix, Mexico 118 B3
Chojna, Poland 31 F1
Chojnice, Poland 30 E4
Chojnów, Poland 31 G2
Chŏkai-San, Japan 54 E10
Choke Canyon L., U.S.A. 113 L5
Choke Mts., Ethiopia 81 E4
Chokurdakh, Russia 53 B15
Cholame, U.S.A. 110 K6
Cholet, France 18 E6
Cholguan, Chile 126 D1
Choluteca, Honduras 120 D2
Choluteca →, Honduras 120 D2
Chom Bung, Thailand 64 F2
Chom Thong, Thailand 64 C2
Choma, Zambia 87 F2
Chomolungma = Everest, Mt., Nepal 69 E12
Chomun, India 68 F6
Chomutov, Czech Rep. 26 A6
Chon Buri, Thailand 64 F3
Chon Thanh, Vietnam 65 G6
Ch'onan, S. Korea 57 F14
Chone, Ecuador 124 D3
Chong Kai, Cambodia 64 F4
Chong Mek, Thailand 64 E5
Chong Phangan, Thailand 65 b
Chong Samui, Thailand 65 b
Chongde, China 59 B13
Chŏngdo, S. Korea 57 G15
Chŏngha, S. Korea 57 F15
Chŏngjin, N. Korea 57 D15
Chŏngjiu, S. Korea 57 F14
Chŏngju, N. Korea 57 E13
Chongli, China 56 D8
Chongming, China 59 B13
Chongming Dao, China 59 B13
Chongqing, Chongqing, China 58 C6
Chongqing, Sichuan, China 58 B4
Chongqing Shi □, China 58 C6
Chongren, China 59 D11
Chonguene, Mozam. 89 C5
Chŏngŭp, S. Korea 57 G14
Chongyi, China 59 E10
Chongzuo, China 58 F6
Chŏnju, S. Korea 57 G14
Chonos, Arch. de los, Chile 128 F2
Chop, Ukraine 28 B7
Chopim →, Brazil 127 B5
Chor, Pakistan 68 G3
Chorbat La, India 69 B7
Chorley, U.K. 14 D5
Chorna, Ukraine 29 C14
Chornobyl, Ukraine 33 G6
Chornomorske, Ukraine 33 K7
Chorolque, Cerro, Bolivia 126 A2
Choroszcz, Poland 31 E9
Chorregon, Australia 94 C3
Chorro el Indio △, Venezuela 121 E5
Chortkiv, Ukraine 33 H3
Ch'ŏrwon, S. Korea 57 E14
Chorzele, Poland 31 E7
Chorzów, Poland 31 H5
Chos-Malal, Argentina 126 D1
Ch'osan, N. Korea 57 D13
Choszczno, Poland 31 E2
Choteau, U.S.A. 108 C7
Chotěboř, Czech Rep. 26 B8
Chotila, India 68 H4
Chotta Udepur, India 68 H6
Chowchilla, U.S.A. 110 H6
Choybalsan, Mongolia 60 B6
Christchurch, N.Z. 91 K4
Christchurch, U.K. 15 G6
Christian I., Canada 116 B4
Christiana, S. Africa 88 D4
Christiansfeld, Denmark 11 J3
Christiansted, U.S. Virgin Is. 121 C7
Christie B., Canada 103 A6
Christina →, Canada 103 B6
Christmas Cr. →, Australia 92 C4
Christmas I. = Kiritimati, Kiribati 97 G12
Christmas I., Ind. Oc. 96 J2
Christopher L., Australia 93 D4
Chrudim, Czech Rep. 26 B8
Chrzanów, Poland 31 H6
Chtimba, Malawi 87 E3
Chū = Shū, Kazakhstan 52 E8
Chū = Shū →, Kazakhstan 50 E10
Chu →, Vietnam 64 C5
Chu Lai, Vietnam 64 E7
Chuak, Ko, Thailand 65 b
Ch'uanchou = Quanzhou, China 59 E12
Chuankou, China 56 G6
Chubbuck, U.S.A. 108 E7
Chūbu □, Japan 55 F8
Chubu-Sangaku △, Japan 55 F8
Chubut →, Argentina 128 E3
Chuchi L., Canada 102 B4
Chuda, India 68 H4
Chudovo, Russia 32 C6
Chudskoye, Ozero, Russia 9 G22
Chūgoku □, Japan 55 G6
Chūgoku-Sanchi, Japan 55 G6
Chuguyev = Chuhuyiv, Ukraine 33 H9
Chugwater, U.S.A. 112 E2
Chuhuyiv, Ukraine 33 H9
Chukchi Sea, Russia 53 C19
Chukotskoye Nagorye, Russia 53 C18
Chula Vista, U.S.A. 111 N9
Chulucanas, Peru 124 E2
Chulym →, Russia 52 D9
Chum Phae, Thailand 64 D4
Chum Saeng, Thailand 64 E3
Chumar, India 69 C8
Chumbicha, Argentina 126 B2
Chumerna, Bulgaria 45 D9
Chumikan, Russia 53 D14
Chumphon, Thailand 65 G2
Chumuare, Mozam. 87 E3
Chumunjin, S. Korea 57 F15
Chuna →, Russia 53 D10
Chun'an, China 59 C12
Ch'unch'ŏn, S. Korea 57 F14
Chunchura, India 69 H13
Chunga, Zambia 87 F2
Chunggang-ŭp, N. Korea 57 D14
Chunghwa, N. Korea 57 E13
Ch'ungju, S. Korea 57 F14
Chungking = Chongqing, China 58 C6
Chungli, Taiwan 59 E13
Ch'ungmu, S. Korea 57 G15
Chungt'iaoshan = Zhongtiao Shan, China 56 G6
Chungyang Shanmo, Taiwan 59 F13
Chunian, Pakistan 68 D6
Chunya, Tanzania 87 D3
Chunyang, China 57 C15
Chupara Pt., Trin. & Tob. 125 K15
Chuquibamba, Peru 124 G4
Chuquicamata, Chile 126 A2
Chur, Switz. 25 J5
Churachandpur, India 67 G18
Church Stretton, U.K. 15 E5
Churchill, Canada 103 B10
Churchill →, Man., Canada 103 B10
Churchill →, Nfld. & L., Canada 105 B7
Churchill, C., Canada 103 B10
Churchill Falls, Canada 105 B7
Churchill L., Canada 103 B7
Churchill Pk., Canada 102 B3
Churki, India 69 H10
Churu, India 68 E6
Churún Merú = Angel Falls, Venezuela 124 B6
Chushal, India 69 C8
Chuska Mts., U.S.A. 109 H9
Chusovoy, Russia 52 D6
Chute-aux-Outardes, Canada 105 C6
Chuuronjang, N. Korea 57 D15
Chuvash Republic = Chuvashia □, Russia 34 C8
Chuvashia □, Russia 34 C8
Chuwārtah, Iraq 70 C5
Chuxiong, China 58 E3
Chuy, Uruguay 127 C5
Chuzhou, China 59 A12
Chynadiyeve, Ukraine 28 B7
Ci Xian, China 56 F8
Ciacova, Romania 28 E6
Ciadâr-Lunga, Moldova 29 D13
Ciamis, Indonesia 63 G13
Cianjur, Indonesia 63 G12
Cianorte, Brazil 127 A5
Cibola, U.S.A. 111 M12
Cicero, U.S.A. 114 E2
Cidacos →, Spain 38 C3
Cide, Turkey 72 B5
Ciégas del Cataumbo △, Venezuela 121 E5
Ciechanów, Poland 31 F7
Ciechanowiec, Poland 31 F9
Ciechocinek, Poland 31 F5
Ciego de Avila, Cuba 120 B4
Ciénaga, Colombia 124 A4
Cienfuegos, Cuba 120 B3
Cierp-Gaud, France 20 F4
Cíes, Is., Spain 36 C2
Cieszanów, Poland 31 H10
Cieszyn, Poland 31 J5
Cieza, Spain 39 G3
Çifteler, Turkey 72 C4
Cifuentes, Spain 38 E2
Cihanbeyli, Turkey 72 C5
Cihuatlán, Mexico 118 D4
Cijara ⌓, Spain 37 F6
Cijara, Embalse de, Spain 37 F6
Cijulang, Indonesia 63 G13
Cilacap, Indonesia 63 G13
Çıldır, Turkey 73 B10
Çıldır Gölü, Turkey 73 B10
Cilento e Vallo di Diano △, Italy 43 B8
Cili, China 59 C8
Cilibia, Romania 29 E12
Cilicia, Turkey 72 D5
Cill Chainnigh = Kilkenny, Ireland 12 D4
Cilo Dağı, Turkey 73 D10
Cima, U.S.A. 111 K11
Cimarron, Kans., U.S.A. 113 G4
Cimarron, N. Mex., U.S.A. 113 G2
Cimarron →, U.S.A. 113 G6
Cimişlia, Moldova 29 D13
Cimone, Mte., Italy 40 D7
Çinar, Turkey 73 D9
Çınarcık, Turkey 45 F13
Cinca →, Spain 38 D5
Cincar, Bos.-H. 28 G2
Cincinnati, U.S.A. 114 F3
Cincinnatus, U.S.A. 117 D9
Çine, Turkey 47 D10
Ciney, Belgium 17 D5
Cíngoli, Italy 41 E10
Cinigiano, Italy 41 F8
Cinto, Mte., France 21 F12
Cintruénigo, Spain 38 C3
Ciocile, Romania 29 F12
Ciolăneşti din Deal, Romania 29 F10
Ciorani, Romania 29 F11
Čiovo, Croatia 41 E13
Circeo, Mte., Italy 42 A6
Çirçir, Turkey 72 C7
Circle, Alaska, U.S.A. 100 B5
Circle, Mont., U.S.A. 112 B2
Circleville, U.S.A. 114 F4
Cirebon, Indonesia 63 G13
Ciremay, Indonesia 63 G13
Cirencester, U.K. 15 F6
Cireşu, Romania 28 F7
Cirey-sur-Vezouze, France 19 D13
Ciriè, Italy 40 C4
Cirium, Cyprus 49 E11
Cirò, Italy 43 C10
Cirò Marina, Italy 43 C10
Ciron →, France 20 D3
Cisco, U.S.A. 113 J5
Cislău, Romania 29 E11
Cisna, Poland 31 J9
Cisnădie, Romania 29 E9
Cisterna di Latina, Italy 42 A5
Cisternino, Italy 43 B10
Cistierna, Spain 36 C5
Citeli-Ckaro = Tsiteli-Tsqaro, Georgia 35 K8
Citlaltépetl = Orizaba, Pico de, Mexico 119 D5
Citrus Heights, U.S.A. 110 G5
Citrusdal, S. Africa 88 E2
Città della Pieve, Italy 41 F9
Città di Castello, Italy 41 E9
Città Sant' Angelo, Italy 41 F11
Cittadella, Italy 41 C8
Cittaducale, Italy 41 F9
Cittanova, Italy 43 D9
Ciuc, Munţii, Romania 29 D11
Ciucaş, Vf., Romania 29 E10
Ciucea, Romania 28 D7
Ciuciulea, Moldova 29 C12
Ciuciuleni, Moldova 29 C13
Ciudad Altamirano, Mexico 118 D4
Ciudad Bolívar, Venezuela 124 B6
Ciudad Camargo, Mexico 118 B3
Ciudad de Valles, Mexico 119 C5
Ciudad del Carmen, Mexico 119 D6
Ciudad del Este, Paraguay 127 B5
Ciudad Delicias = Delicias, Mexico 118 B3
Ciudad Guayana, Venezuela 124 B6
Ciudad Guerrero, Mexico 118 B3
Ciudad Guzmán, Mexico 118 D4
Ciudad Juárez, Mexico 118 A3
Ciudad Madero, Mexico 119 C5
Ciudad Mante, Mexico 119 C5
Ciudad Obregón, Mexico 118 B3
Ciudad Real, Spain 37 G7
Ciudad Real □, Spain 37 G7
Ciudad Rodrigo, Spain 36 E4
Ciudad Victoria, Mexico 119 C5
Ciudadela, Spain 48 B10
Ciulniţa, Romania 29 F12
Ciumeghiu, Romania 28 D6
Ciuperceni, Romania 28 F8
Civa Burnu, Turkey 72 B7
Cividale del Friuli, Italy 41 B10
Civita Castellana, Italy 41 F9
Civitanova Marche, Italy 41 E10
Civitavécchia, Italy 41 F8
Civray, France 20 B4
Çivril, Turkey 47 C11
Cixerri →, Italy 42 C1

Cixi, *China* 59 B13
Cizre, *Turkey* 70 B4
Cizur Mayor, *Spain* 38 C3
Clackmannanshire □, *U.K.* 13 E5
Clacton-on-Sea, *U.K.* 15 F9
Clain →, *France* 18 F7
Claire, L., *Canada* 102 B6
Clairton, *U.S.A.* 116 F5
Clairvaux-les-Lacs, *France* 19 F12
Claise →, *France* 20 B5
Clallam Bay, *U.S.A.* 110 B2
Clamecy, *France* 19 E10
Clanton, *U.S.A.* 115 J2
Clanwilliam, *S. Africa* 88 E2
Clara, *Ireland* 12 C4
Claraville, *U.S.A.* 111 K8
Clare, *Australia* 95 E2
Clare, *U.S.A.* 114 D3
Clare □, *Ireland* 12 D3
Clare →, *Ireland* 12 C2
Clare I., *Ireland* 12 C1
Claremont, *Calif., U.S.A.* 111 L9
Claremont, *N.H., U.S.A.* 117 C12
Claremont Pt., *Australia* 94 A3
Claremore, *U.S.A.* 113 G7
Claremorris, *Ireland* 12 C3
Clarence →, *Australia* 95 D5
Clarence →, *N.Z.* 91 K4
Clarence, I., *Chile* 128 G2
Clarence I., *Antarctica* 5 C18
Clarence Str., *Australia* 92 B5
Clarence Town, *Bahamas* 121 B5
Clarendon, *Pa., U.S.A.* 116 E5
Clarendon, *Tex., U.S.A.* 113 H4
Clarenville-Shoal Harbour, *Canada* 105 C9
Claresholm, *Canada* 102 D6
Clarie Coast, *Antarctica* 5 C9
Clarinda, *U.S.A.* 112 E7
Clarington, *Canada* 116 C6
Clarion, *Iowa, U.S.A.* 112 D8
Clarion, *Pa., U.S.A.* 116 E5
Clarion →, *U.S.A.* 116 E5
Clarion Fracture Zone, *Pac. Oc.* 98 H7
Clark, *U.S.A.* 112 C6
Clark, Pt., *Canada* 116 B3
Clark Fork, *U.S.A.* 108 B5
Clark Fork →, *U.S.A.* 108 B5
Clarkdale, *U.S.A.* 109 J7
Clarke City, *Canada* 105 B6
Clarke I., *Australia* 95 G4
Clarke Ra., *Australia* 94 J6
Clark's Fork →, *U.S.A.* 108 D9
Clark's Harbour, *Canada* 105 D6
Clarks Hill L., *U.S.A.* 115 J4
Clarks Summit, *U.S.A.* 117 E9
Clarksburg, *U.S.A.* 114 F5
Clarksdale, *U.S.A.* 113 H9
Clarksville, *Ark., U.S.A.* 113 H8
Clarksville, *Tenn., U.S.A.* 115 G2
Clarksville, *Tex., U.S.A.* 113 J7
Clatskanie, *U.S.A.* 110 D3
Claude, *U.S.A.* 113 H4
Claveria, *Phil.* 61 B4
Clay, *U.S.A.* 110 G5
Clay Center, *U.S.A.* 112 F6
Claypool, *U.S.A.* 109 K8
Claysburg, *U.S.A.* 116 F6
Claysville, *U.S.A.* 116 F4
Clayton, *N. Mex., U.S.A.* 113 G3
Clayton, *N.Y., U.S.A.* 117 B8
Clear, C., *Ireland* 12 E2
Clear, L., *Canada* 116 A7
Clear Hills, *Canada* 102 B5
Clear I., *Ireland* 12 E2
Clear L., *U.S.A.* 110 F4
Clear Lake, *Iowa, U.S.A.* 112 D8
Clear Lake, *S. Dak., U.S.A.* 112 C6
Clear Lake Reservoir, *U.S.A.* 108 F3
Clearfield, *Pa., U.S.A.* 116 E6
Clearfield, *Utah, U.S.A.* 108 F8
Clearlake, *U.S.A.* 108 G2
Clearlake Highlands, *U.S.A.* 110 G4
Clearwater, *Canada* 102 C4
Clearwater, *U.S.A.* 115 M4
Clearwater →, *Alta., Canada* 102 C6
Clearwater →, *Alta., Canada* 103 B6
Clearwater L., *Canada* 103 C9
Clearwater Lake ⌓, *Canada* 103 C8
Clearwater Mts., *U.S.A.* 108 C6
Clearwater River ⌓, *Canada* 103 B7
Cleburne, *U.S.A.* 113 J6
Clee Hills, *U.K.* 15 E5
Cleethorpes, *U.K.* 14 D7
Cleeve Cloud, *U.K.* 15 F6
Clelles, *France* 21 D9
Clemson, *U.S.A.* 115 H4
Clerke Reef, *Australia* 92 C2
Clermont, *Australia* 94 C4
Clermont, *France* 19 C9
Clermont, *U.S.A.* 115 L5
Clermont-en-Argonne, *France* 19 C12
Clermont-Ferrand, *France* 20 C7
Clermont-l'Hérault, *France* 20 E7
Clerval, *France* 19 E13
Clervaux, *Lux.* 17 D6
Cles, *Italy* 40 B8
Clevedon, *U.K.* 15 F5
Cleveland, *Miss., U.S.A.* 113 J9
Cleveland, *Ohio, U.S.A.* 116 E3
Cleveland, *Okla., U.S.A.* 113 G6
Cleveland, *Tenn., U.S.A.* 115 H3
Cleveland, *Tex., U.S.A.* 113 K7
Cleveland, C., *Australia* 94 B4
Cleveland, Mt., *U.S.A.* 108 B7
Cleveland Heights, *U.S.A.* 116 E3
Clevelândia, *Brazil* 127 B5
Clew B., *Ireland* 12 C2
Clewiston, *U.S.A.* 115 M5
Clifden, *Ireland* 12 C1
Clifden, *N.Z.* 91 M1
Cliffdell, *U.S.A.* 110 D5
Cliffy Hd., *Australia* 93 G2
Clifton, *Australia* 95 D5
Clifton, *Ariz., U.S.A.* 109 K9
Clifton, *Colo., U.S.A.* 109 G9
Clifton, *Tex., U.S.A.* 113 K6
Clifton Beach, *Australia* 94 B4
Climax, *Canada* 103 D7
Clinch →, *U.S.A.* 115 H3
Clingmans Dome, *U.S.A.* 115 H4
Clint, *U.S.A.* 109 L10
Clinton, *B.C., Canada* 102 C4
Clinton, *Ont., Canada* 116 C3
Clinton, *N.Z.* 91 M2
Clinton, *Ark., U.S.A.* 113 H8
Clinton, *Conn., U.S.A.* 117 E12
Clinton, *Ill., U.S.A.* 112 E10
Clinton, *Ind., U.S.A.* 114 F2
Clinton, *Iowa, U.S.A.* 112 E9
Clinton, *Mass., U.S.A.* 117 D13
Clinton, *Miss., U.S.A.* 113 J9
Clinton, *Mo., U.S.A.* 112 F8
Clinton, *N.C., U.S.A.* 115 H6
Clinton, *Okla., U.S.A.* 113 H5
Clinton, *S.C., U.S.A.* 115 H5
Clinton, *Tenn., U.S.A.* 115 G3
Clinton, *Wash., U.S.A.* 110 C4
Clinton C., *Australia* 94 C5
Clinton Colden L., *Canada* 100 B9
Clintonville, *U.S.A.* 112 C10
Clipperton, I., *Pac. Oc.* 97 F17
Clisham, *U.K.* 13 D2
Clisson, *France* 18 E5
Clitheroe, *U.K.* 14 D5
Clo-oose, *Canada* 110 B2
Cloates, Pt., *Australia* 92 D1
Clocolan, *S. Africa* 89 D4
Clodomira, *Argentina* 126 B3
Clogher Hd., *Ireland* 12 C5
Clonakilty, *Ireland* 12 E3
Clonakilty B., *Ireland* 12 E3
Cloncurry, *Australia* 94 C3
Cloncurry →, *Australia* 94 B3
Clondalkin, *Ireland* 12 C5
Clones, *Ireland* 12 B4
Clonmel, *Ireland* 12 D4
Cloppenburg, *Germany* 24 C4
Cloquet, *U.S.A.* 112 B8
Clorinda, *Argentina* 126 B4
Cloud Bay, *Canada* 104 C2
Cloud Peak, *U.S.A.* 108 D10
Cloudcroft, *U.S.A.* 109 K11
Cloverdale, *U.S.A.* 110 G4
Clovis, *Calif., U.S.A.* 110 J7
Clovis, *N. Mex., U.S.A.* 113 H3
Cloyes-sur-le-Loir, *France* 18 E8
Cloyne, *Canada* 116 B7
Cluj □, *Romania* 29 D8
Cluj-Napoca, *Romania* 29 D8
Clunes, *Australia* 95 F3
Cluny, *France* 19 F11
Cluses, *France* 19 F13
Clusone, *Italy* 40 C6
Clutha →, *N.Z.* 91 M2
Clwyd →, *U.K.* 14 D4
Clyde, *Canada* 102 C6
Clyde, *N.Z.* 91 L2
Clyde, *U.S.A.* 116 C8
Clyde →, *U.K.* 13 F4
Clyde, Firth of, *U.K.* 13 F3
Clyde Muirshiel ⌓, *U.K.* 13 F4
Clyde River, *Canada* 101 A13
Clydebank, *U.K.* 13 F4
Clymer, *N.Y., U.S.A.* 116 D5
Clymer, *Pa., U.S.A.* 116 D5
Ćmielów, *Poland* 31 H8
Côa →, *Portugal* 36 D3
Coachella, *U.S.A.* 111 M10
Coachella Canal, *U.S.A.* 111 N12
Coahoma, *U.S.A.* 113 J4
Coahuayana →, *Mexico* 118 D4
Coahuila □, *Mexico* 118 B4
Coal →, *Canada* 102 B3
Coalane, *Mozam.* 87 F4
Coalcomán, *Mexico* 118 D4
Coaldale, *Canada* 102 D6
Coalgate, *U.S.A.* 113 H6
Coalinga, *U.S.A.* 110 J6
Coalisland, *U.K.* 12 B5
Coalville, *U.K.* 14 E6
Coalville, *U.S.A.* 108 F8
Coamo, *Puerto Rico* 121 d
Coari, *Brazil* 124 D6
Coast □, *Kenya* 86 C4
Coast Mts., *Canada* 102 C3
Coast Ranges, *U.S.A.* 110 G4
Coatbridge, *U.K.* 13 F4
Coatepec, *Mexico* 119 D5
Coatepeque, *Guatemala* 120 D1
Coatesville, *U.S.A.* 114 F8
Coaticook, *Canada* 117 A13
Coats I., *Canada* 101 B11
Coats Land, *Antarctica* 5 D1
Coatzacoalcos, *Mexico* 119 D6
Coba, *Mexico* 119 C7
Cobadin, *Romania* 29 F13
Cobalt, *Canada* 104 C4
Cobán, *Guatemala* 120 C1
Çobanlar, *Turkey* 47 C12
Cobar, *Australia* 95 E4
Cóbh, *Ireland* 12 E3
Cobija, *Bolivia* 124 F5
Cobleskill, *U.S.A.* 117 D10
Coboconk, *Canada* 116 B6
Cobourg, *Canada* 116 C6
Cobourg ⌓, *Australia* 92 B5
Cobourg Pen., *Australia* 92 B5
Cobram, *Australia* 95 F4
Cóbué, *Mozam.* 87 E3
Coburg, *Germany* 25 E6
Coca, *Spain* 36 D6
Cocanada = Kakinada, *India* 67 L13
Cocentaina, *Spain* 39 G4
Cochabamba, *Bolivia* 124 G5
Cochem, *Germany* 25 E3
Cochemane, *Mozam.* 87 F3
Cochin, *India* 66 Q10
Cochin China = Nam-Phan, *Vietnam* 65 G6
Cochran, *U.S.A.* 115 J4
Cochrane, *Alta., Canada* 102 C6
Cochrane, *Ont., Canada* 104 C3
Cochrane, *Chile* 128 F2
Cochrane →, *Canada* 103 B8
Cochrane, L., *Chile* 128 F2
Cochranton, *U.S.A.* 116 E4
Cockburn, *Australia* 95 E3
Cockburn, Canal, *Chile* 128 G2
Cockburn I., *Canada* 104 C3
Cockburn Ra., *Australia* 92 C4
Cockermouth, *U.K.* 14 C4
Cocklebiddy, *Australia* 93 F4
Cockpit Country, The, *Jamaica* 120 a
Coco →, *Cent. Amer.* 120 D3
Coco, I. del, *Pac. Oc.* 97 G19
Cocoa, *U.S.A.* 115 L5
Cocobeach, *Gabon* 84 D1
Cocora, *Romania* 29 F12
Cocos B., *Trin. & Tob.* 125 K15
Cocos Is., *Ind. Oc.* 96 J1
Cod, C., *U.S.A.* 114 D10
Codajás, *Brazil* 124 D6
Codigoro, *Italy* 41 D9
Codlea, *Romania* 29 E10
Codó, *Brazil* 125 D10
Codogno, *Italy* 40 C6
Codróipo, *Italy* 41 C10
Codru, Munții, *Romania* 28 D7
Cody, *U.S.A.* 108 D9
Coe Hill, *Canada* 116 B7
Coelemu, *Chile* 126 D1
Coen, *Australia* 94 A3
Coesfeld, *Germany* 24 D3
Cœur d'Alene, *U.S.A.* 108 C5
Cœur d'Alene L., *U.S.A.* 108 C5
Coevorden, *Neths.* 17 B6
Cofete, *Canary Is.* 48 F5
Coffeyville, *U.S.A.* 113 G7
Coffin B., *Australia* 95 E2
Coffin Bay, *Australia* 95 E2
Coffin Bay △, *Australia* 95 E2
Coffin Bay Peninsula, *Australia* 95 E2
Coffs Harbour, *Australia* 95 E5
Cofre de Perote △, *Mexico* 119 D5
Cofrentes, *Spain* 39 F3
Cogalnic →, *Moldova* 29 E14
Cogealac, *Romania* 29 F13
Coghinas →, *Italy* 42 B1
Coghinas, L. del, *Italy* 42 B2
Cognac, *France* 20 C3
Cogne, *Italy* 40 C4
Cogolin, *France* 21 E10
Cogolludo, *Spain* 38 E1
Cohocton, *U.S.A.* 116 D7
Cohocton →, *U.S.A.* 116 D7
Cohoes, *U.S.A.* 117 D11
Cohuna, *Australia* 95 F3
Coiba, I., *Panama* 120 E3
Coig →, *Argentina* 128 G3
Coigeach, Rubha, *U.K.* 13 C3
Coihaique, *Chile* 128 F2
Coimbatore, *India* 66 P10
Coimbra, *Brazil* 124 G7
Coimbra, *Portugal* 36 E2
Coimbra □, *Portugal* 36 E2
Coín, *Spain* 37 J6
Coipasa, Salar de, *Bolivia* 124 G5
Cojimies, *Ecuador* 124 C3
Cojocna, *Romania* 29 D8
Cojutepequé, *El Salv.* 120 D2
Čoka, *Serbia & M.* 28 E5
Cokeville, *U.S.A.* 108 E8
Colac, *Australia* 95 F3
Colatina, *Brazil* 125 G10
Colbeck, C., *Antarctica* 5 D13
Colborne, *Canada* 116 C7
Colby, *U.S.A.* 112 F4
Colchester, *U.K.* 15 F8
Cold L., *Canada* 103 C7
Coldstream, *Canada* 102 C5
Coldstream, *U.K.* 13 F6
Coldwater, *Canada* 116 B5
Coldwater, *Kans., U.S.A.* 113 G5
Coldwater, *Mich., U.S.A.* 114 E3
Colebrook, *U.S.A.* 117 B13
Coleman, *U.S.A.* 113 K5
Coleman →, *Australia* 94 B3
Colenso, *S. Africa* 89 D4
Coleraine, *Australia* 95 F3
Coleraine, *U.K.* 12 A5
Coleridge, L., *N.Z.* 91 K3
Colesberg, *S. Africa* 88 E4
Coleville, *U.S.A.* 110 G7
Colfax, *Calif., U.S.A.* 110 F6
Colfax, *La., U.S.A.* 113 K8
Colfax, *Wash., U.S.A.* 108 C5
Colhué Huapi, L., *Argentina* 128 F3
Colibaşi, *Moldova* 29 E13
Colibaşi, *Romania* 29 F9
Cólico, *Italy* 40 B6
Coligny, *France* 19 F12
Coligny, *S. Africa* 89 D4
Colima, *Mexico* 118 D4
Colima □, *Mexico* 118 D4
Colima, Nevado de, *Mexico* 118 D4
Colina, *Chile* 126 C1
Colina do Norte, *Guinea-Biss.* 82 C2
Colinas, *Brazil* 125 E10
Colindres, *Spain* 36 B7
Coll, *U.K.* 13 E2
Collaguasi, *Chile* 126 A2
Collarada, Peña, *Spain* 38 C4
Collarenebri, *Australia* 95 D4
Colle di Val d'Elsa, *Italy* 40 E8
Collécchio, *Italy* 40 D7
Colleen Bawn, *Zimbabwe* 87 G2
College Park, *U.S.A.* 115 J3
College Station, *U.S.A.* 113 K6
Collesalvetti, *Italy* 40 E7
Colli Euganei ⌓, *Italy* 41 C8
Collie, *Australia* 93 F2
Collier B., *Australia* 92 C3
Collier Ra., *Australia* 93 D2
Collier Range △, *Australia* 93 D2
Collina, Passo di, *Italy* 40 D7
Collingwood, *Canada* 116 B4
Collingwood, *N.Z.* 91 J4
Collins, *Canada* 104 B2
Collinsville, *Australia* 94 C4
Collipulli, *Chile* 126 D1
Collooney, *Ireland* 12 B3
Colmar, *France* 19 D14
Colmars, *France* 21 D10
Colmenar, *Spain* 37 J6
Colmenar de Oreja, *Spain* 36 E7
Colmenar Viejo, *Spain* 36 E7
Colo →, *Australia* 95 E5
Cologne = Köln, *Germany* 24 E2
Colom, I. d'en, *Spain* 48 B11
Coloma, *U.S.A.* 110 G6
Colomb-Béchar = Béchar, *Algeria* 78 B5
Colombey-les-Belles, *France* 19 D12
Colombey-les-Deux-Églises, *France* 19 D11
Colombia ■, *S. Amer.* 124 C4
Colombian Basin, *S. Amer.* 98 H12
Colombo, *Sri Lanka* 66 R11
Colomiers, *France* 20 E5
Colón, *Buenos Aires, Argentina* 126 C3
Colón, *Entre Ríos, Argentina* 126 C4
Colón, *Cuba* 120 B3
Colón, *Panama* 120 E4
Colón, Arch. de, *Ecuador* 97 H18
Colònia de Sant Jordi, *Spain* 48 B9
Colonia del Sacramento, *Uruguay* 126 C4
Colonia Dora, *Argentina* 126 B3
Colonial Beach, *U.S.A.* 114 F7
Colonie, *U.S.A.* 117 D11
Colonna, C., *Italy* 43 C10
Colonsay, *Canada* 103 C7
Colonsay, *U.K.* 13 E2
Colorado □, *U.S.A.* 109 G10
Colorado →, *Argentina* 128 D4
Colorado →, *N. Amer.* 109 L6
Colorado →, *U.S.A.* 113 L7
Colorado City, *U.S.A.* 113 J4
Colorado Plateau, *U.S.A.* 109 H8
Colorado River Aqueduct, *U.S.A.* 111 L12
Colorado Springs, *U.S.A.* 112 F2
Colorno, *Italy* 40 D7
Colotlán, *Mexico* 118 C4
Colstrip, *U.S.A.* 108 D10
Colton, *U.S.A.* 117 B10
Columbia, *Ky., U.S.A.* 114 G3
Columbia, *La., U.S.A.* 113 J8
Columbia, *Miss., U.S.A.* 113 K10
Columbia, *Mo., U.S.A.* 112 F8
Columbia, *Pa., U.S.A.* 117 F8
Columbia, *S.C., U.S.A.* 115 J5
Columbia, *Tenn., U.S.A.* 115 H2
Columbia →, *N. Amer.* 110 D2
Columbia, C., *Canada* 4 A4
Columbia, District of □, *U.S.A.* 114 F7
Columbia, Mt., *Canada* 102 C5
Columbia Basin, *U.S.A.* 108 C4
Columbia Falls, *U.S.A.* 108 B6
Columbia Mts., *Canada* 102 C5
Columbia Plateau, *U.S.A.* 108 D5
Columbiana, *U.S.A.* 116 F4
Columbretes, Is., *Spain* 38 F5
Columbus, *Ga., U.S.A.* 115 J3
Columbus, *Ind., U.S.A.* 114 F3
Columbus, *Kans., U.S.A.* 113 G7
Columbus, *Miss., U.S.A.* 115 J1
Columbus, *Mont., U.S.A.* 108 D9
Columbus, *N. Mex., U.S.A.* 109 L10
Columbus, *Nebr., U.S.A.* 112 E6
Columbus, *Ohio, U.S.A.* 114 F4
Columbus, *Tex., U.S.A.* 113 L6
Colunga, *Spain* 36 B5
Colusa, *U.S.A.* 110 F4
Colville, *U.S.A.* 108 B5
Colville →, *U.S.A.* 100 A4
Colville, C., *N.Z.* 91 G5
Colwood, *Canada* 110 B3
Colwyn Bay, *U.K.* 14 D4
Coma, *Ethiopia* 81 F4
Comácchio, *Italy* 41 D9
Comalcalco, *Mexico* 119 D6
Comallo, *Argentina* 128 E2
Comana, *Romania* 29 F11
Comanche, *U.S.A.* 113 K5
Comandante Ferraz, *Antarctica* 5 C18
Comăneşti, *Romania* 29 D11
Comarnic, *Romania* 29 E10
Comayagua, *Honduras* 120 D2
Combahee →, *U.S.A.* 115 J5
Combarbalá, *Chile* 126 C1
Combe Martin, *U.K.* 15 F3
Combeaufontaine, *France* 19 E12
Comber, *Canada* 116 D2
Comber, *U.K.* 12 B6
Combermere, *Canada* 116 A7
Comblain-au-Pont, *Belgium* 17 D5
Combourg, *France* 18 D5
Combrailles, *France* 19 F9
Combronde, *France* 20 C7
Comeragh Mts., *Ireland* 12 D4
Comet, *Australia* 94 C4
Comilla, *Bangla.* 67 H17
Comino, *Malta* 49 C1
Comino, C., *Italy* 42 B2
Cómiso, *Italy* 43 F7
Comitán, *Mexico* 119 D6
Commentry, *France* 19 F9
Commerce, *Ga., U.S.A.* 115 H4
Commerce, *Tex., U.S.A.* 113 J7
Commercy, *France* 19 D12
Committee B., *Canada* 101 B11
Commonwealth B., *Antarctica* 5 C10
Commoron Cr. →, *Australia* 95 D5
Communism Pk. = Kommunizma, Pik, *Tajikistan* 52 F8
Como, *Italy* 40 C6
Como, Lago di, *Italy* 40 B6
Comodoro Rivadavia, *Argentina* 128 F3
Comoé △, *Ivory C.* 82 D4
Comorâşte, *Romania* 28 E6
Comorin, C., *India* 66 Q10
Comoro Is. = Comoros ■, *Ind. Oc.* 77 H8
Comoros ■, *Ind. Oc.* 77 H8
Comox, *Canada* 102 D4
Compiègne, *France* 19 C9
Comporta, *Portugal* 37 G2
Compostela, *Mexico* 118 C4
Comprida, I., *Brazil* 127 A6
Compton, *Canada* 117 A13
Compton, *U.S.A.* 111 M8
Comrat, *Moldova* 29 D13
Con Cuong, *Vietnam* 64 C5
Con Dao △, *Vietnam* 65 H6
Con Son, *Vietnam* 65 H6
Conakry, *Guinea* 82 D2
Conara, *Australia* 95 G4
Concarneau, *France* 18 E3
Conceição, *Mozam.* 87 F4
Conceição da Barra, *Brazil* 125 G11
Conceição do Araguaia, *Brazil* 125 E9
Concepción, *Argentina* 126 B2
Concepción, *Bolivia* 124 G6
Concepción, *Chile* 126 D1
Concepción, *Mexico* 119 D6
Concepción, *Paraguay* 126 A4
Concepción □, *Chile* 126 D1
Concepción →, *Mexico* 118 A2
Concepción, Est. de, *Chile* 128 G2
Concepción, L., *Bolivia* 124 G6
Concepción, Punta, *Mexico* 118 B2
Concepción del Oro, *Mexico* 118 C4
Concepción del Uruguay, *Argentina* 126 C4
Conception, Pt., *U.S.A.* 111 L6
Conception B., *Canada* 105 C9
Conception B., *Namibia* 88 C1
Conception I., *Bahamas* 121 B4
Concession, *Zimbabwe* 87 F3
Conchas Dam, *U.S.A.* 113 H2
Conches-en-Ouche, *France* 18 D7
Concho, *U.S.A.* 109 J9
Concho →, *U.S.A.* 113 K5
Conchos →, *Chihuahua, Mexico* 118 B4
Conchos →, *Tamaulipas, Mexico* 119 B5
Concord, *Calif., U.S.A.* 110 H4
Concord, *N.C., U.S.A.* 115 H5
Concord, *N.H., U.S.A.* 117 C13
Concordia, *Argentina* 126 C4
Concórdia, *Brazil* 124 D5
Concordia, *Mexico* 118 C3
Concordia, *U.S.A.* 112 F6
Concrete, *U.S.A.* 108 B3
Condamine, *Australia* 95 D5
Condat, *France* 20 C6
Conde, *U.S.A.* 112 C5
Condé-sur-Noireau, *France* 18 D6
Condeúba, *Brazil* 125 F10
Condobolin, *Australia* 95 E4
Condom, *France* 20 E4
Condon, *U.S.A.* 108 D3
Conegliano, *Italy* 41 C9
Conejera, I. = Conills, I. des, *Spain* 48 B9
Conejos, *Mexico* 118 B4
Conemaugh →, *U.S.A.* 116 F5
Conero ⌓, *Italy* 41 E10
Confolens, *France* 20 B4
Confuso →, *Paraguay* 126 B4
Congaz, *Moldova* 29 D13
Conghua, *China* 59 F9
Congjiang, *China* 58 E7
Congleton, *U.K.* 14 D5
Congo (Kinshasa) = Congo, Dem. Rep. of the ■, *Africa* 84 E4
Congo ■, *Africa* 84 E3
Congo →, *Africa* 84 F2
Congo, Dem. Rep. of the ■, *Africa* 84 E4
Congo Basin, *Africa* 84 E4
Congonhas, *Brazil* 127 A7
Congress, *U.S.A.* 109 J7
Conil de la Frontera, *Spain* 37 J4
Conills, I. des, *Spain* 48 B9
Coniston, *Canada* 104 C3
Conjeeveram = Kanchipuram, *India* 66 N11
Conklin, *Canada* 103 B6
Conklin, *U.S.A.* 117 D9
Conn, L., *Ireland* 12 B2
Connacht □, *Ireland* 12 C2
Conneaut, *U.S.A.* 116 E4
Connecticut □, *U.S.A.* 117 E12
Connecticut →, *U.S.A.* 117 E12
Connell, *U.S.A.* 108 C4
Connellsville, *U.S.A.* 116 F5
Connemara, *Ireland* 12 C2
Connemara △, *Ireland* 12 C2
Connerré, *France* 18 D7
Connersville, *U.S.A.* 114 F3
Connors Ra., *Australia* 94 C4
Conques, *France* 20 D6
Conquest, *Canada* 103 C7
Conrad, *U.S.A.* 108 B8
Conran, C., *Australia* 95 F4
Conroe, *U.S.A.* 113 K7
Consecon, *Canada* 116 C7
Conselheiro Lafaiete, *Brazil* 127 A7
Conselve, *Italy* 41 C8
Consett, *U.K.* 14 C6
Consort, *Canada* 103 C6

Constance = Konstanz, *Germany* 25 H5
Constance, L. = Bodensee, *Europe* 25 H5
Constanța, *Romania* 29 F13
Constanța □, *Romania* 29 F13
Constantia, *U.S.A.* 117 C8
Constantina, *Spain* 37 H5
Constantine, *Algeria* 78 A7
Constitución, *Chile* 126 D1
Constitución, *Uruguay* 126 C4
Constitucion de 1857 △, *Mexico* 118 A1
Consuegra, *Spain* 37 F7
Consul, *Canada* 103 D7
Contact, *U.S.A.* 108 F6
Contai, *India* 69 J12
Contamana, *Peru* 124 E4
Contarina, *Italy* 41 C9
Contas ➛, *Brazil* 125 F11
Contes, *France* 21 E11
Contoocook, *U.S.A.* 117 C13
Contra Costa, *Mozam.* 89 D5
Contres, *France* 18 E8
Contrexéville, *France* 19 D12
Contwoyto L., *Canada* 100 B8
Conversano, *Italy* 43 B10
Conway = Conwy, *U.K.* 14 D4
Conway = Conwy ➛, *U.K.* 14 D4
Conway, *Australia* 94 J6
Conway, *Ark., U.S.A.* 113 H8
Conway, *N.H., U.S.A.* 117 C13
Conway, *S.C., U.S.A.* 115 J6
Conway, C., *Australia* 94 J6
Conway, L., *Australia* 95 D2
Conwy, *U.K.* 14 D4
Conwy □, *U.K.* 14 D4
Conwy ➛, *U.K.* 14 D4
Coober Pedy, *Australia* 95 D1
Cooch Behar = Koch Bihar, *India* 67 F16
Cooinda, *Australia* 92 B5
Cook, *Australia* 93 F5
Cook, *U.S.A.* 112 B8
Cook, B., *Chile* 128 H3
Cook, C., *Canada* 102 C3
Cook, Mt. = Aoraki Mount Cook, *N.Z.* 91 K3
Cook Inlet, *U.S.A.* 100 C4
Cook Is., *Pac. Oc.* 97 J12
Cook Strait, *N.Z.* 91 J5
Cookeville, *U.S.A.* 115 G3
Cookhouse, *S. Africa* 88 E4
Cookshire, *Canada* 117 A13
Cookstown, *U.K.* 12 B5
Cooksville, *Canada* 116 C5
Cooktown, *Australia* 94 B4
Coolabah, *Australia* 95 E4
Cooladdi, *Australia* 95 D4
Coolah, *Australia* 95 E4
Coolamon, *Australia* 95 E4
Coolgardie, *Australia* 93 F3
Coolidge, *U.S.A.* 109 K8
Coolidge Dam, *U.S.A.* 109 K8
Cooloola △, *Australia* 95 D5
Cooma, *Australia* 95 F4
Coon Rapids, *U.S.A.* 112 C8
Coonabarabran, *Australia* 95 E4
Coonamble, *Australia* 95 E4
Coonana, *Australia* 93 F3
Coondapoor, *India* 66 N9
Cooninie, L., *Australia* 95 D2
Cooper, *U.S.A.* 113 J7
Cooper Cr. ➛, *Australia* 95 D2
Cooperstown, *N. Dak., U.S.A.* 112 B5
Cooperstown, *N.Y., U.S.A.* 117 D10
Coorabie, *Australia* 93 F5
Coorong, The, *Australia* 95 F2
Coorow, *Australia* 93 E2
Cooroy, *Australia* 95 D5
Coos Bay, *U.S.A.* 108 E1
Coosa ➛, *U.S.A.* 115 J2
Cootamundra, *Australia* 95 E4
Cootehill, *Ireland* 12 B4
Copahue Paso, *Argentina* 126 D1
Copainalá, *Mexico* 119 D6
Copake Falls, *U.S.A.* 117 D11
Copalnic Mănăştur, *Romania* 29 C8
Copán, *Honduras* 120 D2
Cope, *U.S.A.* 112 F3
Cope, C., *Spain* 39 H3
Copenhagen = København, *Denmark* 11 J6
Copenhagen, *U.S.A.* 117 C9
Copertino, *Italy* 43 B11
Copiapó, *Chile* 126 B1
Copiapó ➛, *Chile* 126 B1
Coplay, *U.S.A.* 117 F9
Copp L., *Canada* 102 A6
Copparo, *Italy* 41 D8
Coppename ➛, *Suriname* 125 B7
Copper Harbor, *U.S.A.* 114 B2
Copper Queen, *Zimbabwe* 87 F2
Copperas Cove, *U.S.A.* 113 K6
Copperbelt □, *Zambia* 87 E2
Coppermine = Kugluktuk, *Canada* 100 B8
Coppermine ➛, *Canada* 100 B8
Copperopolis, *U.S.A.* 110 H6
Copşa Mică, *Romania* 29 D9
Coquet ➛, *U.K.* 14 B6
Coquille, *U.S.A.* 108 E1
Coquimbo, *Chile* 126 C1
Coquimbo □, *Chile* 126 C1
Corabia, *Romania* 29 G9
Coracora, *Peru* 124 G4
Coraki, *Australia* 95 D5
Coral, *U.S.A.* 116 F5
Coral Gables, *U.S.A.* 115 N5
Coral Harbour, *Canada* 101 B11
Coral Sea, *Pac. Oc.* 96 J7
Coral Springs, *U.S.A.* 115 M5
Coraopolis, *U.S.A.* 116 F4
Corato, *Italy* 43 A9
Corbeil-Essonnes, *France* 19 D9
Corbie, *France* 19 C9
Corbières, *France* 20 F6
Corbigny, *France* 19 E10
Corbin, *U.S.A.* 114 G3
Corbones ➛, *Spain* 37 H5
Corbu, *Romania* 29 F13
Corby, *U.K.* 15 E7
Corcaigh = Cork, *Ireland* 12 E3
Corcoran, *U.S.A.* 110 J7
Corcovado △, *Costa Rica* 120 E3
Cordele, *U.S.A.* 115 K4
Cordell, *U.S.A.* 113 H5
Cordenòns, *Italy* 41 C9
Cordes-sur-Ciel, *France* 20 D5
Córdoba, *Argentina* 126 C3
Córdoba, *Mexico* 119 D5
Córdoba, *Spain* 37 H6
Córdoba □, *Argentina* 126 C3
Córdoba □, *Spain* 37 G6
Córdoba, Sierra de, *Argentina* 126 C3
Cordon, *Phil.* 61 C4
Cordova, *U.S.A.* 100 B5
Corella, *Spain* 38 C3
Corella ➛, *Australia* 94 B3
Corfield, *Australia* 94 C3
Corfu = Kérkira, *Greece* 49 A3
Corfu ✈ (CFU), *Greece* 46 B1
Corfu, Str. of, *Greece* 49 A4
Corgo = O Corgo, *Spain* 36 C3
Cori, *Italy* 42 A5
Coria, *Spain* 36 F4
Coria del Río, *Spain* 37 H4
Corigliano Cálabro, *Italy* 43 C9
Coringa Is., *Australia* 94 B4
Corinth = Kórinthos, *Greece* 46 D4
Corinth, *Miss., U.S.A.* 115 H1
Corinth, *N.Y., U.S.A.* 117 C11
Corinth, G. of = Korinthiakós Kólpos, *Greece* 46 C4
Corinth Canal, *Greece* 46 D4
Corinto, *Brazil* 125 G10
Corinto, *Nic.* 120 D2
Cork, *Ireland* 12 E3
Cork □, *Ireland* 12 E3
Cork Harbour, *Ireland* 12 E3
Corlay, *France* 18 D3
Corleone, *Italy* 42 E6
Corleto Perticara, *Italy* 43 B9
Çorlu, *Turkey* 45 E11
Cormack L., *Canada* 102 A4
Cormòns, *Italy* 41 C10
Cormorant, *Canada* 103 C8
Cormorant L., *Canada* 103 C8
Corn Is. = Maiz, Is. del, *Nic.* 120 D3
Cornalvo ⌓, *Spain* 37 F4
Cornélio Procópio, *Brazil* 127 A5
Corner Brook, *Canada* 105 C8
Corneşti, *Moldova* 29 C13
Corníglio, *Italy* 40 D7
Corning, *Ark., U.S.A.* 113 G9
Corning, *Calif., U.S.A.* 108 G2
Corning, *Iowa, U.S.A.* 112 E7
Corning, *N.Y., U.S.A.* 116 D7
Corno Grande, *Italy* 41 F10
Cornwall, *Canada* 117 A10
Cornwall, *U.S.A.* 117 F8
Cornwall □, *U.K.* 15 G3
Corny Pt., *Australia* 95 E2
Coro, *Venezuela* 124 A5
Coroatá, *Brazil* 125 D10
Corocoro, *Bolivia* 124 G5
Coroico, *Bolivia* 124 G5
Coromandel, *N.Z.* 91 G5
Coromandel Coast, *India* 66 N12
Corona, *Calif., U.S.A.* 111 M9
Corona, *N. Mex., U.S.A.* 109 J11
Coronach, *Canada* 103 D7
Coronado, *U.S.A.* 111 N9
Coronado, B. de, *Costa Rica* 120 E3
Coronados, Is. los, *U.S.A.* 111 N9
Coronation, *Canada* 102 C6
Coronation Gulf, *Canada* 100 B8
Coronation I., *Antarctica* 5 C18
Coronation Is., *Australia* 92 B3
Coronda, *Argentina* 126 C3
Coronel, *Chile* 126 D1
Coronel Bogado, *Paraguay* 126 B4
Coronel Dorrego, *Argentina* 126 D3
Coronel Oviedo, *Paraguay* 126 B4
Coronel Pringles, *Argentina* 126 D3
Coronel Suárez, *Argentina* 126 D3
Coronel Vidal, *Argentina* 126 D4
Coropuna, Nevado, *Peru* 124 G4
Çorovodë, *Albania* 44 F4
Corowa, *Australia* 95 F4
Corozal □, *Belize* 119 D7
Corozal Pt., *Trin. & Tob.* 125 K15
Corps, *France* 21 D9
Corpus, *Argentina* 127 B4
Corpus Christi, *U.S.A.* 113 M6
Corpus Christi, L., *U.S.A.* 113 L6
Corral de Almaguer, *Spain* 36 F7
Corralejo, *Canary Is.* 48 F6
Corraun Pen., *Ireland* 12 C2
Corréggio, *Italy* 40 D7
Correntes, C. das, *Mozam.* 89 C6
Corrèze □, *France* 20 C5
Corrèze ➛, *France* 20 C5
Corrib, L., *Ireland* 12 C2
Corridónia, *Italy* 41 E10
Corrientes, *Argentina* 126 B4
Corrientes □, *Argentina* 126 B4
Corrientes ➛, *Argentina* 126 C4
Corrientes ➛, *Peru* 124 D4
Corrientes, C., *Colombia* 124 B3
Corrientes, C., *Cuba* 120 B3
Corrientes, C., *Mexico* 118 C3
Corrigan, *U.S.A.* 113 K7
Corrigin, *Australia* 93 F2
Corry, *U.S.A.* 116 E5
Corse ⌓, *France* 21 F13
Corse □, *France* 21 G13
Corse, C., *France* 21 E13
Corse-du-Sud □, *France* 21 G13
Corsica = Corse □, *France* 21 G13
Corsicana, *U.S.A.* 113 J6
Corte, *France* 21 F13
Corte Pinto, *Portugal* 37 H3
Cortegana, *Spain* 37 H4
Cortés, Mar de = California, G. de, *Mexico* 118 B2
Cortez, *U.S.A.* 109 H9
Cortina d'Ampezzo, *Italy* 41 B9
Cortland, *N.Y., U.S.A.* 117 D8
Cortland, *Ohio, U.S.A.* 116 E4
Cortona, *Italy* 41 E8
Corubal ➛, *Guinea-Biss.* 82 C2
Coruche, *Portugal* 37 G2
Çoruh ➛, *Turkey* 35 K5
Çorum, *Turkey* 72 B6
Corumbá, *Brazil* 124 G7
Corund, *Romania* 29 D10
Corunna = A Coruña, *Spain* 36 B2
Corvallis, *U.S.A.* 108 D2
Corvette, L. de la, *Canada* 104 B5
Corydon, *U.S.A.* 112 E8
Cosalá, *Mexico* 118 C3
Cosamaloapan, *Mexico* 119 D5
Cosenza, *Italy* 43 C9
Coşereni, *Romania* 29 F11
Coshocton, *U.S.A.* 116 F3
Cosmo Newberry, *Australia* 93 E3
Cosne-Cours-sur-Loire, *France* 19 E9
Coso Junction, *U.S.A.* 111 J9
Coso Pk., *U.S.A.* 111 J9
Cospeito, *Spain* 36 B3
Cosquín, *Argentina* 126 C3
Cossato, *Italy* 40 C5
Cossé-le-Vivien, *France* 18 E6
Cosson ➛, *France* 18 E8
Costa Blanca, *Spain* 39 G4
Costa Brava, *Spain* 38 D8
Costa del Sol, *Spain* 37 J6
Costa Dorada, *Spain* 38 D6
Costa Mesa, *U.S.A.* 111 M9
Costa Rica ■, *Cent. Amer.* 120 E3
Costa Smeralda, *Italy* 42 A2
Costeşti, *Romania* 29 F9
Costigliole d'Asti, *Italy* 40 D5
Cosumnes ➛, *U.S.A.* 110 G5
Coswig, *Sachsen, Germany* 24 D9
Coswig, *Sachsen-Anhalt, Germany* 24 D8
Cotabato, *Phil.* 61 H6
Cotagaita, *Bolivia* 126 A2
Côte d'Azur, *France* 21 E11
Côte-d'Ivoire = Ivory Coast ■, *Africa* 82 D4
Côte d'Or, *France* 19 E11
Côte-d'Or □, *France* 19 E11
Coteau des Prairies, *U.S.A.* 112 C6
Coteau du Missouri, *U.S.A.* 112 B4
Cotentin, *France* 18 C5
Côtes-d'Armor □, *France* 18 D4
Côtes de Meuse, *France* 19 C12
Côtes-du-Nord = Côtes-d'Armor □, *France* 18 D4
Cotiella, *Spain* 38 C5
Cotillo, *Canary Is.* 48 F5
Cotiujeni, *Moldova* 29 C13
Cotonou, *Benin* 83 D5
Cotopaxi, *Ecuador* 124 D3
Cotronei, *Italy* 43 C9
Cotswold Hills, *U.K.* 15 F5
Cottage Grove, *U.S.A.* 108 E2
Cottbus, *Germany* 24 D10
Cottonwood, *U.S.A.* 109 J7
Cotulla, *U.S.A.* 113 L5
Coubre, Pte. de la, *France* 20 C2
Couches, *France* 19 F11
Couço, *Portugal* 37 G2
Coudersport, *U.S.A.* 116 E6
Couedic, C. du, *Australia* 95 F2
Couëron, *France* 18 E5
Couesnon ➛, *France* 18 D5
Couhé, *France* 20 B4
Coulanges-sur-Yonne, *France* 19 E10
Coulee City, *U.S.A.* 108 C4
Coulman I., *Antarctica* 5 D11
Coulommiers, *France* 19 D10
Coulon ➛, *France* 21 E9
Coulonge ➛, *Canada* 104 C4
Coulonges-sur-l'Autize, *France* 20 B3
Coulounieix-Chamiers, *France* 20 C4
Coulterville, *U.S.A.* 110 H6
Council, *U.S.A.* 108 D5
Council Bluffs, *U.S.A.* 112 E7
Council Grove, *U.S.A.* 112 F6
Coupeville, *U.S.A.* 110 B4
Courantyne ➛, *S. Amer.* 124 B7
Courcelles, *Belgium* 17 D4
Courchevel, *France* 21 C10
Courçon, *France* 20 B3
Courmayeur, *Italy* 40 C3
Couronne, C., *France* 21 E9
Cours-la-Ville, *France* 19 F11
Coursan, *France* 20 E7
Courseulles-sur-Mer, *France* 18 C6
Courtenay, *Canada* 102 D4
Courtenay, *France* 19 D10
Courtland, *U.S.A.* 110 G5
Courtrai = Kortrijk, *Belgium* 17 D3
Courtright, *Canada* 116 D2
Coushatta, *U.S.A.* 113 J8
Coutances, *France* 18 C5
Coutras, *France* 20 C3
Coutts Crossing, *Australia* 95 D5
Couva, *Trin. & Tob.* 125 K15
Couvin, *Belgium* 17 D4
Covarrubias, *Spain* 36 C7
Covasna, *Romania* 29 E11
Covasna □, *Romania* 29 E10
Cove I., *Canada* 116 A3
Coventry, *U.K.* 15 E6
Covilhã, *Portugal* 36 E3
Covington, *Ga., U.S.A.* 115 J4
Covington, *Ky., U.S.A.* 114 F3
Covington, *Okla., U.S.A.* 113 G6
Covington, *Tenn., U.S.A.* 113 H10
Covington, *Va., U.S.A.* 114 G5
Cowal, L., *Australia* 95 E4
Cowan, L., *Australia* 93 F3
Cowan L., *Canada* 103 C7
Cowangie, *Australia* 95 F3
Cowansville, *Canada* 117 A12
Coward Springs, *Australia* 95 D2
Cowcowing Lakes, *Australia* 93 F2
Cowdenbeath, *U.K.* 13 E5
Cowell, *Australia* 95 E2
Cowes, *U.K.* 15 G6
Cowichan L., *Canada* 110 B2
Cowlitz ➛, *U.S.A.* 110 D4
Cowra, *Australia* 95 E4
Cox, *Spain* 39 G4
Coxilha Grande, *Brazil* 127 B5
Coxim, *Brazil* 125 G8
Cox's Bazar, *Bangla.* 67 J17
Coyote Wells, *U.S.A.* 111 N11
Coyuca de Benítez, *Mexico* 119 D4
Coyuca de Catalan, *Mexico* 118 D4
Cozad, *U.S.A.* 112 E5
Cozes, *France* 20 C3
Cozumel, *Mexico* 119 C7
Cozumel, Isla, *Mexico* 119 C7
Crab Hill, *Barbados* 121 g
Cracow = Kraków, *Poland* 31 H6
Cracow, *Australia* 95 D5
Cradle Mt.-Lake St. Clair △, *Australia* 95 G4
Cradock, *Australia* 95 E2
Cradock, *S. Africa* 88 E4
Craig, *U.S.A.* 108 F10
Craigavon, *U.K.* 12 B5
Craigmore, *Zimbabwe* 87 G3
Craik, *Canada* 103 C7
Crailsheim, *Germany* 25 F6
Craiova, *Romania* 29 F8
Cramsie, *Australia* 94 C3
Cranberry L., *U.S.A.* 117 B10
Cranberry Portage, *Canada* 103 C8
Cranbrook, *Australia* 93 F2
Cranbrook, *Canada* 102 D5
Crandon, *U.S.A.* 112 C10
Crane, *Oreg., U.S.A.* 108 E4
Crane, *Tex., U.S.A.* 113 K3
Cranston, *U.S.A.* 117 E13
Craon, *France* 18 E6
Craonne, *France* 19 C10
Craponne-sur-Arzon, *France* 20 C7
Crasna, *Romania* 29 D12
Crasna ➛, *Romania* 28 C7
Crasnei, Munții, *Romania* 29 C8
Crater L., *U.S.A.* 108 E2
Crater Lake △, *U.S.A.* 108 E2
Craters of the Moon △, *U.S.A.* 108 E7
Crateús, *Brazil* 125 E10
Crati ➛, *Italy* 43 C9
Crato, *Brazil* 125 E11
Crato, *Portugal* 37 F3
Craven, L., *Canada* 104 B4
Crawford, *U.S.A.* 112 D3
Crawfordsville, *U.S.A.* 114 E2
Crawley, *U.K.* 15 F7
Crazy Mts., *U.S.A.* 108 C8
Crean L., *Canada* 103 C7
Crécy-en-Ponthieu, *France* 19 B8
Crediton, *Canada* 116 C3
Crediton, *U.K.* 15 G4
Cree ➛, *Canada* 103 B7
Cree ➛, *U.K.* 13 G4
Cree L., *Canada* 103 B7
Creede, *U.S.A.* 109 H10
Creekside, *U.S.A.* 116 F5
Creel, *Mexico* 118 B3
Creemore, *Canada* 116 B4
Creighton, *Canada* 103 C8
Creighton, *U.S.A.* 112 D6
Creil, *France* 19 C9
Crema, *Italy* 40 C6
Cremona, *Italy* 40 C7
Crepaja, *Serbia & M.* 28 E5
Crépy, *France* 19 C10
Crépy-en-Valois, *France* 19 C9
Cres, *Croatia* 41 D11
Crescent City, *U.S.A.* 108 F1
Crescentino, *Italy* 40 C5
Crespo, *Argentina* 126 C3
Cresson, *U.S.A.* 116 F6
Crest, *France* 21 D9
Cresta, Mt., *Phil.* 61 C5
Crestline, *Calif., U.S.A.* 111 L9
Crestline, *Ohio, U.S.A.* 116 F2
Creston, *Canada* 102 D5
Creston, *Calif., U.S.A.* 110 K6
Creston, *Iowa, U.S.A.* 112 E7
Crestview, *Calif., U.S.A.* 110 H8
Crestview, *Fla., U.S.A.* 115 K2
Crêt de la Neige, *France* 19 F12
Crete = Kríti, *Greece* 49 D7
Crete, *U.S.A.* 112 E6
Crete, Sea of, *Greece* 47 E7
Créteil, *France* 19 D9
Creus, C. de, *Spain* 38 C8
Creuse □, *France* 19 F9
Creuse ➛, *France* 20 B4
Creutzwald, *France* 19 C13
Creuzburg, *Germany* 24 D6
Crèvecœur-le-Grand, *France* 19 C9
Crevillente, *Spain* 39 G4
Crewe, *U.K.* 14 D5
Crewkerne, *U.K.* 15 G5
Crianlarich, *U.K.* 13 E4
Criciúma, *Brazil* 127 B6
Cricova, *Moldova* 29 C13
Crieff, *U.K.* 13 E5
Crikvenica, *Croatia* 41 C11
Crimea □, *Ukraine* 33 K8
Crimean Pen. = Krymskyy Pivostriv, *Ukraine* 33 K8
Crimmitschau, *Germany* 24 E8
Cristuru Secuiesc, *Romania* 29 D10
Crişul Alb ➛, *Romania* 28 D6
Crişul Negru ➛, *Romania* 28 D6
Crişul Repede ➛, *Romania* 28 D5
Criuleni, *Moldova* 29 C14
Crivitz, *Germany* 24 B7
Crna ➛, *Macedonia* 44 E5
Crna Gora = Montenegro □, *Serbia & M.* 44 D3
Crna Gora, *Macedonia* 44 D5
Crna Reka = Crna ➛, *Macedonia* 44 E5
Crna Trava, *Serbia & M.* 44 D6
Crni Drim ➛, *Macedonia* 44 E4
Crni Timok ➛, *Serbia & M.* 44 C6
Crnoljeva Planina, *Serbia & M.* 44 D5
Črnomelj, *Slovenia* 41 C12
Croagh Patrick, *Ireland* 12 C2
Croatia ■, *Europe* 41 C13
Crocker, Banjaran, *Malaysia* 62 C5
Crockett, *U.S.A.* 113 K7
Crocodile = Krokodil ➛, *Mozam.* 89 D5
Crocodile Is., *Australia* 94 A1
Crocq, *France* 20 C6
Crodo, *Italy* 40 B5
Crohy Hd., *Ireland* 12 B3
Croisette, C., *France* 21 E9
Croisic, Pte. du, *France* 18 E4
Croix, L. La, *Canada* 104 C1
Croker, C., *Australia* 92 B5
Croker, C., *Canada* 116 B4
Croker I., *Australia* 92 B5
Cromarty, *U.K.* 13 D4
Cromer, *U.K.* 14 E9
Cromwell, *N.Z.* 91 L2
Cromwell, *U.S.A.* 117 E12
Cronat, *France* 19 F10
Crook, *U.K.* 14 C6
Crooked ➛, *Canada* 102 C4
Crooked ➛, *U.S.A.* 108 D3
Crooked I., *Bahamas* 121 B5
Crooked Island Passage, *Bahamas* 121 B5
Crookston, *Minn., U.S.A.* 112 B6
Crookston, *Nebr., U.S.A.* 112 D4
Crookwell, *Australia* 95 E4
Cropane-Micone ⌓, *Italy* 43 D9
Crosby, *U.K.* 14 D4
Crosby, *N. Dak., U.S.A.* 112 A3
Crosby, *Pa., U.S.A.* 116 E6
Crosbyton, *U.S.A.* 113 J4
Crosía, *Italy* 43 C9
Cross ➛, *Nigeria* 83 E6
Cross City, *U.S.A.* 115 L4
Cross Fell, *U.K.* 14 C5
Cross L., *Canada* 103 C9
Cross Lake, *Canada* 103 C9
Cross River □, *Nigeria* 83 D6
Cross River △, *Nigeria* 83 D6
Cross Sound, *U.S.A.* 100 C6
Crossett, *U.S.A.* 113 J9
Crosshaven, *Ireland* 12 E3
Crossville, *U.S.A.* 115 G3
Croswell, *U.S.A.* 116 C2
Croton-on-Hudson, *U.S.A.* 117 E11
Crotone, *Italy* 43 C10
Crow ➛, *Canada* 102 B4
Crow Agency, *U.S.A.* 108 D10
Crow Hd., *Ireland* 12 E1
Crowell, *U.S.A.* 113 J5
Crowley, *U.S.A.* 113 K8
Crowley, L., *U.S.A.* 110 H8
Crown Point, *Ind., U.S.A.* 114 E2
Crown Point, *N.Y., U.S.A.* 117 C11
Crown Pt., *Trin. & Tob.* 125 J16
Crownpoint, *U.S.A.* 109 J9
Crows Landing, *U.S.A.* 110 H5
Crows Nest, *Australia* 95 D5
Crowsnest Pass, *Canada* 102 D6
Croydon, *Australia* 94 B3
Croydon □, *U.K.* 15 F7
Crozet, Is., *Ind. Oc.* 3 G12
Crozon, *France* 18 D2
Cruz, C., *Cuba* 120 C4
Cruz Alta, *Brazil* 127 B5
Cruz Bay, *U.S. Virgin Is.* 121 e
Cruz de Incio, *Spain* 36 C3
Cruz del Eje, *Argentina* 126 C3
Cruzeiro, *Brazil* 127 A7
Cruzeiro do Oeste, *Brazil* 127 A5
Cruzeiro do Sul, *Brazil* 124 E4
Cry L., *Canada* 102 B3
Crystal Bay, *U.S.A.* 110 F7
Crystal Brook, *Australia* 95 E2
Crystal City, *U.S.A.* 113 L5
Crystal Falls, *U.S.A.* 114 B1
Crystal River, *U.S.A.* 115 L4
Crystal Springs, *U.S.A.* 113 K9
Csenger, *Hungary* 28 C7
Csongrád, *Hungary* 28 D5
Csongrád □, *Hungary* 28 D5
Csorna, *Hungary* 28 C2
Csurgo, *Hungary* 28 D2
Cu Lao Hon, *Vietnam* 65 G7
Cua Rao, *Vietnam* 64 C5
Cuácua ➛, *Mozam.* 87 F4
Cuamato, *Angola* 88 B2
Cuamba, *Mozam.* 87 E4
Cuando ➛, *Angola* 85 H4
Cuando Cubango □, *Angola* 88 B3
Cuangar, *Angola* 88 B2
Cuango = Kwango ➛, *Dem. Rep. of the Congo* 84 E3
Cuanza ➛, *Angola* 84 F2
Cuarto ➛, *Argentina* 126 C3
Cuatrociénegas, *Mexico* 118 B4
Cuauhtémoc, *Mexico* 118 B3
Cuba, *Portugal* 37 G3
Cuba, *N. Mex., U.S.A.* 109 J10
Cuba, *N.Y., U.S.A.* 116 D6
Cuba ■, *W. Indies* 120 B4

Cubango →, *Africa* 88 B3
Çubuk, *Turkey* 72 B5
Cuc Phuong △, *Vietnam* 64 B5
Cuchumatanes, Sierra de los, *Guatemala* 120 C1
Cuckfield, *U.K.* 15 F7
Cucuí, *Brazil* 124 C5
Cucurpe, *Mexico* 118 A2
Cúcuta, *Colombia* 124 B4
Cudalbi, *Romania* 29 E12
Cuddalore, *India* 66 P11
Cuddapah, *India* 66 M11
Cuddapan, L., *Australia* 94 D3
Cudillero, *Spain* 36 B4
Cue, *Australia* 93 E2
Cuéllar, *Spain* 36 D6
Cuenca, *Ecuador* 124 D3
Cuenca, *Spain* 38 E2
Cuenca □, *Spain* 38 F3
Cuenca, Serranía de, *Spain* 38 F3
Cuenca Alta del Manzanares ⌓, *Spain* 36 E7
Cuerdo del Pozo, Embalse de la, *Spain* 38 D2
Cuernavaca, *Mexico* 119 D5
Cuero, *U.S.A.* 113 L6
Cuers, *France* 21 E10
Cueva de la Quebrada del Toro △, *Venezuela* 121 D6
Cuevas del Almanzora, *Spain* 39 H3
Cuevo, *Bolivia* 124 H6
Cugir, *Romania* 29 E8
Cugnaux, *France* 20 E5
Cuhai-Bakony →, *Hungary* 28 C2
Cuiabá, *Brazil* 125 G7
Cuiabá →, *Brazil* 125 G7
Cuijk, *Neths.* 17 C5
Cuilco, *Guatemala* 120 C1
Cuillin Hills, *U.K.* 13 D2
Cuillin Sd., *U.K.* 13 D2
Cuiseaux, *France* 19 F12
Cuito →, *Angola* 88 B3
Cuitzeo, L. de, *Mexico* 118 D4
Cujmir, *Romania* 28 F7
Cukai, *Malaysia* 65 K4
Culbertson, *U.S.A.* 112 A2
Culcairn, *Australia* 95 F4
Culebra, Isla de, *Puerto Rico* 121 d
Culebra, Sierra de la, *Spain* 36 D4
Culfa, *Azerbaijan* 73 C11
Culgoa →, *Australia* 95 D4
Culgoa Flood Plain △, *Australia* 95 D4
Culiacán, *Mexico* 118 C3
Culiacán →, *Mexico* 118 C3
Culik, *Indonesia* 63 J18
Culion, *Phil.* 61 F4
Cúllar, *Spain* 37 H8
Cullarin Ra., *Australia* 95 E4
Cullen, *U.K.* 13 D6
Cullen Pt., *Australia* 94 A3
Cullera, *Spain* 39 F4
Cullman, *U.S.A.* 115 H2
Cullompton, *U.K.* 15 G4
Culoz, *France* 21 C9
Culpeper, *U.S.A.* 114 F7
Culuene →, *Brazil* 125 F8
Culver, Pt., *Australia* 93 F3
Culverden, *N.Z.* 91 K4
Cumaná, *Venezuela* 124 A6
Cumaovası, *Turkey* 47 C9
Cumberland, *B.C., Canada* 102 D4
Cumberland, *Ont., Canada* 117 A9
Cumberland, *U.S.A.* 114 F6
Cumberland →, *U.S.A.* 115 G2
Cumberland, L., *U.S.A.* 115 G3
Cumberland Gap △, *U.S.A.* 115 G4
Cumberland I., *U.S.A.* 115 K5
Cumberland Is., *Australia* 94 J7
Cumberland Island ⌓, *U.S.A.* 115 K5
Cumberland L., *Canada* 103 C8
Cumberland Pen., *Canada* 101 B13
Cumberland Plateau, *U.S.A.* 115 H3
Cumberland Sd., *Canada* 101 B13
Cumbernauld, *U.K.* 13 F5
Cumborah, *Australia* 95 D4
Cumbres de Majalca △, *Mexico* 118 B3
Cumbres de Monterrey △, *Mexico* 118 B4
Cumbres Mayores, *Spain* 37 G4
Cumbria □, *U.K.* 14 C5
Cumbrian Mts., *U.K.* 14 C5
Cumbum, *India* 66 M11
Cuminá →, *Brazil* 125 D7
Cummings Mt., *U.S.A.* 111 K8
Cummins, *Australia* 95 E2
Cumnock, *Australia* 95 E4
Cumnock, *U.K.* 13 F4
Cumpas, *Mexico* 118 B3
Cumplida, Pta., *Canary Is.* 48 F2
Çumra, *Turkey* 72 D5
Cunco, *Chile* 128 D2
Cuncumén, *Chile* 126 C1
Cunderdin, *Australia* 93 F2
Cunene →, *Angola* 88 B1
Cúneo, *Italy* 40 D4
Çüngüş, *Turkey* 70 B3
Cunillera, I. = Sa Conillera, *Spain* 48 C7
Cunlhat, *France* 20 C7
Cunnamulla, *Australia* 95 D4
Cuorgnè, *Italy* 40 C4
Cupar, *Canada* 103 C8
Cupar, *U.K.* 13 E5
Cupcini, *Moldova* 29 B12
Cupica, G. de, *Colombia* 124 B3
Ćuprija, *Serbia & M.* 44 C5
Curaçao, *Neth. Ant.* 121 D6
Curanilahue, *Chile* 126 D1
Curaray →, *Peru* 124 D4
Cure →, *France* 19 E10
Curepto, *Chile* 126 D1
Curiapo, *Venezuela* 124 B6
Curicó, *Chile* 126 C1
Curinga, *Italy* 43 D9
Curitiba, *Brazil* 127 B6
Curitibanos, *Brazil* 127 B5
Currabubula, *Australia* 95 E5
Currais Novos, *Brazil* 125 E11
Curralinho, *Brazil* 125 D9
Currant, *U.S.A.* 108 G6
Currawinya △, *Australia* 95 D3
Current →, *U.S.A.* 113 G9
Currie, *Australia* 95 F3
Currie, *U.S.A.* 108 F6
Curtea de Argeş, *Romania* 29 E9
Curtici, *Romania* 28 D6
Curtis, *U.S.A.* 112 E4
Curtis Group, *Australia* 95 F4
Curtis I., *Australia* 94 C5
Curuápanema →, *Brazil* 125 D7
Curuçá, *Brazil* 125 D9
Curuguaty, *Paraguay* 127 A4
Curup, *Indonesia* 62 E2
Cururupu, *Brazil* 125 D10
Curuzú Cuatiá, *Argentina* 126 B4
Curvelo, *Brazil* 125 G10
Cushing, *U.S.A.* 113 H6
Cushing, Mt., *Canada* 102 B3
Cusihuiriáchic, *Mexico* 118 B3
Cusna, Mte., *Italy* 40 D7
Cusset, *France* 19 F10
Custer, *U.S.A.* 112 D3
Cut Bank, *U.S.A.* 108 B7
Cutchogue, *U.S.A.* 117 E12
Cuthbert, *U.S.A.* 115 K3
Cutler, *U.S.A.* 110 J7
Cutro, *Italy* 43 C9
Cuttaburra →, *Australia* 95 D3
Cuttack, *India* 67 J14
Cuvier, C., *Australia* 93 D1
Cuvier I., *N.Z.* 91 G5
Cuxhaven, *Germany* 24 B4
Cuyahoga Falls, *U.S.A.* 116 E3
Cuyahoga Valley △, *U.S.A.* 116 E3
Cuyapo, *Phil.* 61 D4
Cuyo, *Phil.* 61 F4
Cuyo East Pass, *Phil.* 61 F4
Cuyo West Pass, *Phil.* 61 F4
Cuyuni →, *Guyana* 124 B7
Cuzco, *Bolivia* 124 H5
Cuzco, *Peru* 124 F4
Čvrsnica, *Bos.-H.* 28 G2
Cwmbran, *U.K.* 15 F4
Cyangugu, *Rwanda* 86 C2
Cybinka, *Poland* 31 F1
Cyclades = Kikládhes, *Greece* 46 E6
Cygnet, *Australia* 95 G4
Cynthiana, *U.S.A.* 114 F3
Cypress Hills, *Canada* 103 D7
Cypress Hills ⌓, *Canada* 103 D7
Cyprus ■, *Asia* 49 E12
Cyrenaica, *Libya* 79 C10
Czaplinek, *Poland* 30 E3
Czar, *Canada* 103 C6
Czarna →, *Łódzkie, Poland* 31 G6
Czarna →, *Świętokrzyskie, Poland* 31 H8
Czarna Białostocka, *Poland* 31 E10
Czarna Woda, *Poland* 30 E5
Czarne, *Poland* 30 E3
Czarnków, *Poland* 31 F3
Czech Rep. ■, *Europe* 26 B8
Czechowice-Dziedzice, *Poland* 31 J5
Czempiń, *Poland* 31 F3
Czeremcha, *Poland* 31 F10
Czerniejewo, *Poland* 31 F4
Czersk, *Poland* 30 E4
Czerwieńsk, *Poland* 31 F2
Czerwionka-Leszczyny, *Poland* 31 H5
Częstochowa, *Poland* 31 H6
Człopa, *Poland* 31 E3
Człuchów, *Poland* 30 E4
Czyżew-Osada, *Poland* 31 F9

D

Da →, *Vietnam* 58 G5
Da Hinggan Ling, *China* 60 B7
Da Lat, *Vietnam* 65 G7
Da Nang, *Vietnam* 64 D7
Da Qaidam, *China* 60 C4
Da Yunhe →, *China* 57 G11
Da'an, *China* 57 B13
Daan Viljoen ⌓, *Namibia* 88 C2
Dab'a, Ras el, *Egypt* 80 H6
Daba Shan, *China* 58 B7
Dabai, *Nigeria* 83 C6
Dabakala, *Ivory C.* 82 D4
Dabas, *Hungary* 28 C4
Dabat, *Ethiopia* 81 E4
Dabbagh, Jabal, *Si. Arabia* 70 E2
Dabhoi, *India* 68 H5
Dąbie, *Poland* 31 F5
Dabie Shan, *China* 59 B10
Dabilda, *Cameroon* 83 C7
Dabnou, *Niger* 83 C6
Dabo = Pasirkuning, *Indonesia* 62 E2
Dabola, *Guinea* 82 C2
Dabou, *Ivory C.* 82 D4
Daboya, *Ghana* 83 D4
Dabravolya, *Belarus* 31 F10
Dąbrowa Białostocka, *Poland* 30 E10
Dąbrowa Górnicza, *Poland* 31 H6
Dąbrowa Tarnowska, *Poland* 31 H7
Dabu, *China* 59 E11
Dabung, *Malaysia* 65 K4
Dabus →, *Ethiopia* 81 E4
Dacato →, *Ethiopia* 81 F5
Dacca = Dhaka, *Bangla.* 69 H14
Dacca = Dhaka □, *Bangla.* 69 G14
Dachau, *Germany* 25 G7
Dachstein, Hoher, *Austria* 26 D6
Dačice, *Czech Rep.* 26 B8
Dadanawa, *Guyana* 124 C7
Daday, *Turkey* 72 B5
Dade City, *U.S.A.* 115 L4
Dadhar, *Pakistan* 68 E2
Dadiya, *Nigeria* 83 D7
Dadra & Nagar Haveli □, *India* 66 J8
Dadri = Charkhi Dadri, *India* 68 E7
Dadu, *Pakistan* 68 F2
Dadu He →, *China* 58 C4
Daet, *Phil.* 61 D5
Dafang, *China* 58 D5
Dağ, *Turkey* 47 D12
Dagana, *Senegal* 82 B1
Dagash, *Sudan* 80 D3
Dagestan □, *Russia* 35 J8
Dagestanskiye Ogni, *Russia* 35 J9
Daggett, *U.S.A.* 111 L10
Daghestan Republic = Dagestan □, *Russia* 35 J8
Daghfeli, *Sudan* 80 D3
Dağlıq Qarabağ = Nagorno-Karabakh □, *Azerbaijan* 70 B5
Dagö = Hiiumaa, *Estonia* 9 G20
Dagu, *China* 57 E9
Daguan, *China* 58 D4
Dagupan, *Phil.* 61 C4
Daguragu, *Australia* 92 C5
Dahab, *Egypt* 80 B3
Dahlak △, *Eritrea* 81 D5
Dahlak Kebir, *Eritrea* 81 D5
Dahlenburg, *Germany* 24 B6
Dahlonega, *U.S.A.* 115 H4
Dahme, *Germany* 24 D9
Dahod, *India* 68 H6
Dahong Shan, *China* 59 B9
Dahra, *Senegal* 82 B1
Dahshûr, *Egypt* 80 J7
Dahūk, *Iraq* 70 B3
Dai Hao, *Vietnam* 64 C6
Dai-Sen, *Japan* 55 G6
Dai Shan, *China* 59 B14
Dai Xian, *China* 56 E7
Daicheng, *China* 56 E9
Daimiel, *Spain* 37 F7
Daingean, *Ireland* 12 C4
Dainkog, *China* 58 A1
Daintree, *Australia* 94 B4
Daintree △, *Australia* 94 B4
Daiō-Misaki, *Japan* 55 G8
Dair, J. ed, *Sudan* 81 E3
Dairût, *Egypt* 80 B3
Daisen-Oki △, *Japan* 55 G6
Daisetsu-Zan, *Japan* 54 C11
Daisetsu-Zan △, *Japan* 54 C11
Dajarra, *Australia* 94 C2
Dajin Chuan →, *China* 58 B3
Dak Dam, *Cambodia* 64 F6
Dak Nhe, *Vietnam* 64 E6
Dak Pek, *Vietnam* 64 E6
Dak Song, *Vietnam* 65 F6
Dak Sui, *Vietnam* 64 E6
Dakar, *Senegal* 82 C1
Dakhla, *W. Sahara* 78 D2
Dakhla, El Wâhât el-, *Egypt* 80 B2
Dakingari, *Nigeria* 83 C5
Dakor, *India* 68 H5
Dakoro, *Niger* 83 C6
Dakota City, *U.S.A.* 112 D6
Đakovica, *Serbia & M.* 44 D4
Đakovo, *Croatia* 28 E3
Dalaba, *Guinea* 82 C2
Dalachi, *China* 56 F3
Dalai Nur, *China* 56 C9
Dālakī, *Iran* 71 D6
Dalälven →, *Sweden* 10 D10
Dalaman, *Turkey* 47 E10
Dalaman →, *Turkey* 47 E10
Dalandzadgad, *Mongolia* 56 C3
Dalap-Uliga-Darrit, *Marshall Is.* 96 G9
Dalarna, *Sweden* 10 D8
Dalarnas län □, *Sweden* 10 C8
Dālbandīn, *Pakistan* 66 E4
Dalbeattie, *U.K.* 13 G5
Dalbeg, *Australia* 94 C4
Dalbosjön, *Sweden* 11 F6
Dalby, *Australia* 95 D5
Dalby, *Sweden* 11 J7
Dalby Söderskog △, *Sweden* 11 J7
Dale City, *U.S.A.* 114 F7
Dale Hollow L., *U.S.A.* 115 G3
Dalga, *Egypt* 80 B3
Dalgān, *Iran* 71 E8
Dalhart, *U.S.A.* 113 G3
Dalhousie, *Canada* 105 C6
Dalhousie, *India* 68 C6
Dali, *Shaanxi, China* 56 G5
Dali, *Yunnan, China* 58 E3
Dalian, *China* 57 E11
Daliang Shan, *China* 58 D4
Daling He →, *China* 57 D11
Dāliyat el Karmel, *Israel* 74 C4
Dalj, *Croatia* 28 E3
Dalkeith, *U.K.* 13 F5
Dallas, *Oreg., U.S.A.* 108 D2
Dallas, *Tex., U.S.A.* 113 J6
Dallol, *Ethiopia* 81 E5
Dalmā, *U.A.E.* 71 E7
Dalmacija, *Croatia* 41 E13
Dalmas, L., *Canada* 105 B5
Dalmatia = Dalmacija, *Croatia* 41 E13
Dalmau, *India* 69 F9
Dalmellington, *U.K.* 13 F4
Dalnegorsk, *Russia* 53 E14
Dalnerechensk, *Russia* 53 E14
Dalnevostochnyy □, *Russia* 53 C14
Daloa, *Ivory C.* 82 D3
Dalou Shan, *China* 58 C6
Dalry, *U.K.* 13 F4
Dalrymple, L., *Australia* 94 C4
Dalrymple, Mt., *Australia* 94 K6
Dals Långed, *Sweden* 11 F6
Dalsjöfors, *Sweden* 11 G7
Dalsland, *Sweden* 11 F6
Daltenganj, *India* 69 H11
Dalton, *Ga., U.S.A.* 115 H3
Dalton, *Mass., U.S.A.* 117 D11
Dalton, *Nebr., U.S.A.* 112 E3
Dalton-in-Furness, *U.K.* 14 C4
Dalupiri I., *Phil.* 61 B4
Dalvík, *Iceland* 8 D4
Dálvvadis = Jokkmokk, *Sweden* 8 C18
Dalwallinu, *Australia* 93 F2
Daly →, *Australia* 92 B5
Daly City, *U.S.A.* 110 H4
Daly L., *Canada* 103 B7
Daly River, *Australia* 92 B5
Daly Waters, *Australia* 94 B1
Dalyan, *Turkey* 47 E10
Dam Doi, *Vietnam* 65 H5
Dam Ha, *Vietnam* 64 B6
Damachova, *Belarus* 31 G10
Daman, *India* 66 J8
Dāmaneh, *Iran* 71 C6
Damanhûr, *Egypt* 80 H7
Damant L., *Canada* 103 A7
Damanzhuang, *China* 56 E9
Damar, *Indonesia* 63 F7
Damaraland, *Namibia* 88 C2
Damascus = Dimashq, *Syria* 74 B5
Damaturu, *Nigeria* 83 C7
Damāvand, *Iran* 71 C7
Damāvand, Qolleh-ye, *Iran* 71 C7
Damba, *Angola* 84 F3
Dâmboviţa □, *Romania* 29 F10
Dâmboviţa →, *Romania* 29 F11
Dâmbovnic →, *Romania* 29 F10
Dame Marie, *Haiti* 121 C5
Dāmghān, *Iran* 71 B7
Dămienesti, *Romania* 29 D11
Damietta = Dumyât, *Egypt* 80 H7
Daming, *China* 56 F8
Damīr Qābū, *Syria* 70 B4
Dammam = Ad Dammām, *Si. Arabia* 71 E6
Dammarie-les-Lys, *France* 19 D9
Dammartin-en-Goële, *France* 19 C9
Damme, *Germany* 24 C4
Damodar →, *India* 69 H12
Damoh, *India* 69 H8
Dampier, *Australia* 92 D2
Dampier, Selat, *Indonesia* 63 E8
Dampier Arch., *Australia* 92 D2
Damrei, Chuor Phnum, *Cambodia* 65 G4
Damvillers, *France* 19 C12
Dan-Gulbi, *Nigeria* 83 C6
Dan Xian, *China* 64 C7
Dana, *Indonesia* 63 F6
Dana, L., *Canada* 104 B4
Dana, Mt., *U.S.A.* 110 H7
Danakil Desert, *Ethiopia* 81 E5
Danané, *Ivory C.* 82 D3
Danao, *Phil.* 61 F6
Danau Poso, *Indonesia* 63 E6
Danba, *China* 58 B3
Danbury, *U.S.A.* 117 E11
Danby L., *U.S.A.* 109 J6
Dand, *Afghan.* 68 D1
Dande ⌓, *Zimbabwe* 87 F3
Dandeldhura, *Nepal* 69 E9
Dandeli, *India* 66 M9
Dandenong, *Australia* 95 F4
Dandîl, *Egypt* 80 J7
Dandong, *China* 57 D13
Danfeng, *China* 56 H6
Dangan Liedao, *China* 59 F10
Dangé-St-Romain, *France* 20 B4
Dângeni, *Romania* 29 C11
Danger Is. = Pukapuka, *Cook Is.* 97 J11
Danger Pt., *S. Africa* 88 E2
Danginpuri, *Indonesia* 63 K18
Dangla, *Ethiopia* 81 E4
Dangla Shan = Tanggula Shan, *China* 60 C4
Dangora, *Nigeria* 83 C6
Dangouadougou, *Burkina Faso* 82 D4
Dangrek, Phnom, *Thailand* 64 E5
Dangriga, *Belize* 119 D7
Dangshan, *China* 56 G9
Dangtu, *China* 59 B12
Dangyang, *China* 59 B8
Dani, *Burkina Faso* 83 C4
Daniel, *U.S.A.* 108 E8
Daniel's Harbour, *Canada* 105 B8
Danielskuil, *S. Africa* 88 D3
Danielson, *U.S.A.* 117 E13
Danilov, *Russia* 32 C11
Danilovgrad, *Serbia & M.* 44 D3
Danilovka, *Russia* 34 E7
Daning, *China* 56 F6
Danja, *Nigeria* 83 C6
Danjiangkou, *China* 59 A8
Danjiangkou Shuiku, *China* 59 A8
Ḍank, *Oman* 71 F8
Dankalwa, *Nigeria* 83 C7
Dankama, *Nigeria* 83 C6
Dankhar Gompa, *India* 66 C11
Dankov, *Russia* 32 F10
Danleng, *China* 58 B4
Danlí, *Honduras* 120 D2
Dannemora, *U.S.A.* 117 B11
Dannenberg, *Germany* 24 B7
Dannevirke, *N.Z.* 91 J6
Dannhauser, *S. Africa* 89 D5
Dansville, *U.S.A.* 116 D7
Danta, *India* 68 G5
Dantan, *India* 69 J12
Danube = Dunărea →, *Europe* 29 E14
Danvers, *U.S.A.* 117 D14
Danville, *Ill., U.S.A.* 114 E2
Danville, *Ky., U.S.A.* 114 G3
Danville, *Pa., U.S.A.* 117 F8
Danville, *Va., U.S.A.* 115 G6
Danville, *Vt., U.S.A.* 117 B12
Danyang, *China* 59 B12
Danzhai, *China* 58 D6
Danzig = Gdańsk, *Poland* 30 D5
Dão →, *Portugal* 36 E2
Dao Xian, *China* 59 E8
Daocheng, *China* 58 C3
Daoukro, *Ivory C.* 82 D4
Dapaong, *Togo* 83 C5
Dapchi, *Nigeria* 83 C7
Dapitan, *Phil.* 61 G5
Daqing Shan, *China* 56 D6
Daqu Shan, *China* 59 B14
Dar Banda, *Africa* 76 F6
Dar el Beida = Casablanca, *Morocco* 78 B4
Dar es Salaam, *Tanzania* 86 D4
Dar Mazār, *Iran* 71 D8
Dar'ā, *Syria* 74 C5
Dar'ā □, *Syria* 74 C5
Dārāb, *Iran* 71 D7
Daraban, *Pakistan* 68 D4
Darabani, *Romania* 29 B11
Daraina, *Madag.* 89 A8
Daraj, *Libya* 79 B8
Dārān, *Iran* 71 C6
Daravica, *Serbia & M.* 44 D4
Daraw, *Egypt* 80 C3
Dārayyā, *Syria* 74 B5
Darazo, *Nigeria* 83 C7
Darband, *Pakistan* 68 B5
Darband, Kūh-e, *Iran* 71 D8
Darbhanga, *India* 69 F11
D'Arcy, *Canada* 102 C4
Darda, *Croatia* 28 E3
Dardanelle, *Ark., U.S.A.* 113 H8
Dardanelle, *Calif., U.S.A.* 110 G7
Dardanelles = Çanakkale Boğazı, *Turkey* 45 F10
Dare →, *Ethiopia* 81 F5
Darende, *Turkey* 72 C7
Dārestān, *Iran* 71 D8
Darfo, *Italy* 40 C7
Dârfûr, *Sudan* 79 F10
Dargai, *Pakistan* 68 B4
Dargan Ata, *Turkmenistan* 52 E7
Dargaville, *N.Z.* 91 F4
Dargol, *Niger* 83 C5
Darhan, *Mongolia* 60 B5
Darhan Muminggan Lianheqi, *China* 56 D6
Dari, *Sudan* 81 F3
Darıca, *Turkey* 72 B3
Darién △, *Panama* 120 E4
Darién, G. del, *Colombia* 124 B3
Dariganga = Ovoot, *Mongolia* 56 B7
Darinskoye, *Kazakhstan* 34 E10
Darjeeling = Darjiling, *India* 69 F13
Darjiling, *India* 69 F13
Darkan, *Australia* 93 F2
Darkhana, *Pakistan* 68 D5
Darkhazīneh, *Iran* 71 D6
Darkot Pass, *Pakistan* 69 A5
Darling →, *Australia* 95 E3
Darling Downs, *Australia* 95 D5
Darling Ra., *Australia* 93 F2
Darlington, *U.K.* 14 C6
Darlington, *U.S.A.* 115 H6
Darlington □, *U.K.* 14 C6
Darlington, L., *S. Africa* 88 E4
Darlot, L., *Australia* 93 E3
Darłowo, *Poland* 30 D3
Dărmăneşti, *Bacău, Romania* 29 D11
Dărmăneşti, *Suceava, Romania* 29 C11
Darmstadt, *Germany* 25 F4
Darnah, *Libya* 79 B10
Darnall, *S. Africa* 89 D5
Darney, *France* 19 D13
Darnley, C., *Antarctica* 5 C6
Darnley B., *Canada* 100 B7
Daroca, *Spain* 38 D3
Darou-Mousti, *Senegal* 82 B1
Darr →, *Australia* 94 C3
Darra Pezu, *Pakistan* 68 C4
Darrequeira, *Argentina* 126 D3
Darrington, *U.S.A.* 108 B3
Darsser Ort, *Germany* 24 A8
Dart →, *U.K.* 15 G4
Dart, C., *Antarctica* 5 D14
Dartford, *U.K.* 15 F8
Dartmoor, *U.K.* 15 G4
Dartmoor △, *U.K.* 15 G4
Dartmouth, *Canada* 105 D7
Dartmouth, *U.K.* 15 G4
Dartmouth Res., *Australia* 95 D4
Dartuch, C. = Artrutx, C. de, *Spain* 48 B10
Daruvar, *Croatia* 28 E2
Darvaza, *Turkmenistan* 52 E6
Darvel, Teluk = Lahad Datu, Teluk, *Malaysia* 63 D5
Darwen, *U.K.* 14 D5
Darwendale, *Zimbabwe* 89 B5
Darwha, *India* 66 J10
Darwin, *Australia* 92 B5
Darwin, *U.S.A.* 111 J9
Darya Khan, *Pakistan* 68 D4
Daryoi Amu = Amudarya →, *Uzbekistan* 52 E6
Dās, *U.A.E.* 71 E7
Dashen, Ras, *Ethiopia* 81 E4
Dashetai, *China* 56 D5
Dashhowuz, *Turkmenistan* 52 E6
Dashkesan = Daşkäsän, *Azerbaijan* 35 K7
Dashköpri, *Turkmenistan* 71 B9
Dasht, *Iran* 71 B8
Dasht →, *Pakistan* 66 G2
Daska, *Pakistan* 68 C6
Daşkäsän, *Azerbaijan* 35 K7
Dassa, *Benin* 83 D5
Dasuya, *India* 68 D6

Datça, *Turkey* 47 E9
Datia, *India* 69 G8
Datian, *China* 59 E11
Datong, *Anhui, China* 59 B11
Datong, *Shanxi, China* 56 D7
Dattakhel, *Pakistan* 68 C3
Datteln, *Germany* 24 D3
Datu, Tanjung, *Indonesia* 62 D3
Datu Piang, *Phil.* 61 H6
Datuk, Tanjong = Datu, Tanjung, *Indonesia* 62 D3
Daua = Dawa →, *Africa* 81 G5
Daud Khel, *Pakistan* 68 C4
Daudnagar, *India* 69 G11
Daugava →, *Latvia* 9 H21
Daugavpils, *Latvia* 9 J22
Daulpur, *India* 68 F7
Daun, *Germany* 25 E2
Dauphin, *Canada* 103 C8
Dauphin, *U.S.A.* 116 F8
Dauphin L., *Canada* 103 C9
Dauphiné, *France* 21 C9
Daura, *Borno, Nigeria* 83 C7
Daura, *Katsina, Nigeria* 83 C6
Dausa, *India* 68 F7
Däväçi, *Azerbaijan* 35 K9
Davangere, *India* 66 M9
Davao, *Phil.* 61 H6
Davao G., *Phil.* 61 H6
Dāvar Panāh = Sarāvān, *Iran* 71 E9
Davenport, *Calif., U.S.A.* 110 H4
Davenport, *Iowa, U.S.A.* 112 E9
Davenport, *Wash., U.S.A.* 108 C4
Davenport Ra., *Australia* 94 C1
Daventry, *U.K.* 15 E6
David, *Panama* 120 E3
David City, *U.S.A.* 112 E6
David Gorodok = Davyd Haradok, *Belarus* 33 F4
Davidson, *Canada* 103 C7
Davis, *Antarctica* 5 C6
Davis, *U.S.A.* 110 G5
Davis Dam, *U.S.A.* 111 K12
Davis Inlet, *Canada* 105 A7
Davis Mts., *U.S.A.* 113 K2
Davis Sea, *Antarctica* 5 C7
Davis Str., *N. Amer.* 101 B14
Davo →, *Ivory C.* 82 D3
Davos, *Switz.* 25 J5
Davutlar, *Turkey* 47 D9
Davy L., *Canada* 103 B7
Davyd Haradok, *Belarus* 33 F4
Dawa →, *Africa* 81 G5
Dawaki, *Bauchi, Nigeria* 83 D6
Dawaki, *Kano, Nigeria* 83 C6
Dawei = Tavoy, *Burma* 64 E2
Dawes Ra., *Australia* 94 C5
Dawlish, *U.K.* 15 G4
Dawna Ra., *Burma* 64 D2
Dawros Hd., *Ireland* 12 B3
Dawson, *Canada* 100 B6
Dawson, *U.S.A.* 115 K3
Dawson, I., *Chile* 128 G2
Dawson B., *Canada* 103 C8
Dawson Creek, *Canada* 102 B4
Dawson Inlet, *Canada* 103 A10
Dawson Ra., *Australia* 94 C4
Dawu, *Hubei, China* 59 B9
Dawu, *Sichuan, China* 58 B3
Dax, *France* 20 E2
Daxian, *China* 58 B6
Daxin, *China* 58 F6
Daxindian, *China* 57 F11
Daxinggou, *China* 57 C15
Daxue Shan, *Sichuan, China* 58 B3
Daxue Shan, *Yunnan, China* 58 F2
Dayao, *China* 58 E3
Daye, *China* 59 B10
Dayet en Naharat, *Mali* 82 B4
Dayi, *China* 58 B4
Daylesford, *Australia* 95 F3
Dayong, *China* 59 C8
Dayr az Zawr, *Syria* 70 C4
Daysland, *Canada* 102 C6
Dayton, *Nev., U.S.A.* 110 F7
Dayton, *Ohio, U.S.A.* 114 F3
Dayton, *Pa., U.S.A.* 116 F5
Dayton, *Tenn., U.S.A.* 115 H3
Dayton, *Wash., U.S.A.* 108 C4
Dayton, *Wyo., U.S.A.* 108 D10
Daytona Beach, *U.S.A.* 115 L5
Dayu, *China* 59 E10
Dayville, *U.S.A.* 108 D4
Dazhu, *China* 58 B6
Dazkırı, *Turkey* 47 D11
Dazu, *China* 58 C5
De Aar, *S. Africa* 88 E3
De Biesbosch △, *Neths.* 17 C4
De Funiak Springs, *U.S.A.* 115 K2
De Grey →, *Australia* 92 D2
De Haan, *Belgium* 17 C3
De Hoge Veluwe △, *Neths.* 17 B5
De Hoop ⌂, *S. Africa* 88 E3
De Kalb, *U.S.A.* 112 E10
De Kennemerduinen △, *Neths.* 17 B4
De Land, *U.S.A.* 115 L5
De Leon, *U.S.A.* 113 J5
De Panne, *Belgium* 17 C2
De Pere, *U.S.A.* 114 C1
De Queen, *U.S.A.* 113 H7
De Quincy, *U.S.A.* 113 K8
De Ridder, *U.S.A.* 113 K8
De Smet, *U.S.A.* 112 C6
De Soto, *U.S.A.* 112 F9
De Tour Village, *U.S.A.* 114 C4
De Witt, *U.S.A.* 113 H9
Dead Sea, *Asia* 74 D4
Deadwood, *U.S.A.* 112 C3
Deadwood L., *Canada* 102 B3
Deal, *U.K.* 15 F9
Deal I., *Australia* 95 F4
Dealesville, *S. Africa* 88 D4
De'an, *China* 59 C10
Dean →, *Canada* 102 C3
Dean, Forest of, *U.K.* 15 F5
Dean Chan., *Canada* 102 C3
Deán Funes, *Argentina* 126 C3
Dease →, *Canada* 102 B3
Dease L., *Canada* 102 B2
Dease Lake, *Canada* 102 B2
Death Valley, *U.S.A.* 111 J10
Death Valley △, *U.S.A.* 111 J10
Death Valley Junction, *U.S.A.* 111 J10
Deauville, *France* 18 C7
Deba, *Spain* 38 B2
Deba Habe, *Nigeria* 83 C7
Debaltsevo, *Ukraine* 33 H10
Debao, *China* 58 F6
Debar, *Macedonia* 44 E4
Debark, *Ethiopia* 81 E4
Debden, *Canada* 103 C7
Dębica, *Poland* 31 H8
Dęblin, *Poland* 31 G8
Dębno, *Poland* 31 F1
Débo, L., *Mali* 82 B4
DeBolt, *Canada* 102 B5
Deborah East, L., *Australia* 93 F2
Deborah West, L., *Australia* 93 F2
Debrc, *Serbia & M.* 44 B3
Debre Birhan, *Ethiopia* 81 F4
Debre Markos, *Ethiopia* 81 E4
Debre May, *Ethiopia* 81 E4
Debre Sina, *Ethiopia* 81 F4
Debre Tabor, *Ethiopia* 81 E4
Debre Zebit, *Ethiopia* 81 E4
Debre Zevit, *Ethiopia* 81 F4
Debrecen, *Hungary* 28 C6
Debrzno, *Poland* 30 E4
Dečani, *Serbia & M.* 44 D4
Decatur, *Ala., U.S.A.* 115 H2
Decatur, *Ga., U.S.A.* 115 J3
Decatur, *Ill., U.S.A.* 112 F10
Decatur, *Ind., U.S.A.* 114 E3
Decatur, *Tex., U.S.A.* 113 J6
Decazeville, *France* 20 D6
Deccan, *India* 66 L11
Deception Bay, *Australia* 95 D5
Deception I., *Antarctica* 5 C17
Deception L., *Canada* 103 B8
Dechang, *China* 58 D4
Dechhu, *India* 68 F5
Děčín, *Czech Rep.* 26 A7
Decize, *France* 19 F10
Deckerville, *U.S.A.* 116 C2
Decollatura, *Italy* 43 C9
Decorah, *U.S.A.* 112 D9
Deda, *Romania* 29 D9
Dedéagach = Alexandroúpolis, *Greece* 45 F9
Deder, *Ethiopia* 81 F5
Dedham, *U.S.A.* 117 D13
Dédougou, *Burkina Faso* 82 C4
Dedovichi, *Russia* 32 D5
Dedza, *Malawi* 87 E3
Dee →, *Aberds., U.K.* 13 D6
Dee →, *Dumf. & Gall., U.K.* 13 G4
Dee →, *Wales, U.K.* 14 D4
Deep B., *Canada* 102 A5
Deepwater, *Australia* 95 D5
Deer →, *Canada* 103 B10
Deer L., *Canada* 103 C10
Deer Lake, *Nfld. & L., Canada* 105 C8
Deer Lake, *Ont., Canada* 103 C10
Deer Lodge, *U.S.A.* 108 C7
Deer Park, *U.S.A.* 108 C5
Deer River, *U.S.A.* 112 B8
Deeragun, *Australia* 94 B4
Deerdepoort, *S. Africa* 88 C4
Deferiet, *U.S.A.* 117 B9
Defiance, *U.S.A.* 114 E3
Degana, *India* 68 F6
Dêgê, *China* 58 B2
Degebe →, *Portugal* 37 G3
Degeberga, *Sweden* 11 J8
Dégelis, *Canada* 105 C6
Degema, *Nigeria* 83 E6
Degerfors, *Sweden* 10 E8
Degerhamn, *Sweden* 11 H10
Deggendorf, *Germany* 25 G8
Degh →, *Pakistan* 68 D5
Değirmendere, *Turkey* 45 F13
Deh Bīd, *Iran* 71 D7
Deh-e Shīr, *Iran* 71 D7
Dehaj, *Iran* 71 D7
Dehak, *Iran* 71 E9
Dehdez, *Iran* 71 D6
Dehej, *India* 68 J5
Dehestān, *Iran* 71 D7
Dehgolān, *Iran* 70 C5
Dehibat, *Tunisia* 79 B8
Dehlorān, *Iran* 70 C5
Dehnow-e Kūhestān, *Iran* 71 E8
Dehra Dun, *India* 68 D8
Dehri, *India* 69 G11
Dehua, *China* 59 E12
Dehui, *China* 57 B13
Deim Zubeir, *Sudan* 81 F2
Deinze, *Belgium* 17 D3
Dej, *Romania* 29 C8
Deje, *Sweden* 10 E7
Dejiang, *China* 58 C7
Deka →, *Zimbabwe* 88 B4
Dekemhare, *Eritrea* 81 D4
Dekese, *Dem. Rep. of the Congo* 84 E4
Del Mar, *U.S.A.* 111 N9
Del Norte, *U.S.A.* 109 H10
Del Rio, *U.S.A.* 113 L4
Delai, *Sudan* 80 D4
Delambre I., *Australia* 92 D2
Delami, *Sudan* 81 E3
Delano, *U.S.A.* 111 K7
Delano Peak, *U.S.A.* 109 G7
Delareyville, *S. Africa* 88 D4
Delaronde L., *Canada* 103 C7
Delavan, *U.S.A.* 112 D10
Delaware, *U.S.A.* 114 E4
Delaware □, *U.S.A.* 114 F8
Delaware →, *U.S.A.* 117 G9
Delaware B., *U.S.A.* 114 F8
Delaware Water Gap ⌂, *U.S.A.* 117 E10
Delay →, *Canada* 105 A5
Delbrück, *Germany* 24 D4
Delčevo, *Macedonia* 44 E6
Delegate, *Australia* 95 F4
Delémont, *Switz.* 25 H3
Delevan, *U.S.A.* 116 D6
Delft, *Neths.* 17 B4
Delfzijl, *Neths.* 17 A6
Delgado, C., *Mozam.* 87 E5
Delgerhet, *Mongolia* 56 B6
Delgo, *Sudan* 80 C3
Delhi, *Canada* 116 D4
Delhi, *India* 68 E7
Delhi, *La., U.S.A.* 113 J9
Delhi, *N.Y., U.S.A.* 117 D10
Deli Jovan, *Serbia & M.* 44 B6
Delia, *Canada* 102 C6
Delice, *Turkey* 72 C6
Delicias, *Mexico* 118 B3
Delījān, *Iran* 71 C6
Déline, *Canada* 100 B7
Delisle, *Canada* 103 C7
Delitzsch, *Germany* 24 D8
Dell City, *U.S.A.* 109 L11
Dell Rapids, *U.S.A.* 112 D6
Delle, *France* 19 E14
Delmar, *U.S.A.* 117 D11
Delmenhorst, *Germany* 24 B4
Delnice, *Croatia* 41 C11
Delonga, Ostrova, *Russia* 53 B15
Deloraine, *Australia* 95 G4
Deloraine, *Canada* 103 D8
Delphi, *Greece* 46 C4
Delphi, *U.S.A.* 114 E2
Delphos, *U.S.A.* 114 E3
Delportshoop, *S. Africa* 88 D3
Delray Beach, *U.S.A.* 115 M5
Delsbo, *Sweden* 10 C10
Delta, *Colo., U.S.A.* 109 G9
Delta, *Utah, U.S.A.* 108 G7
Delta □, *Nigeria* 83 D6
Delta del Ebro ⌂, *Spain* 38 E5
Delta del Po ⌂, *Italy* 41 D9
Delta du Saloum △, *Senegal* 82 C1
Delta Dunărea ⌂, *Romania* 29 E14
Delta Junction, *U.S.A.* 100 B5
Deltona, *U.S.A.* 115 L5
Delungra, *Australia* 95 D5
Delvada, *India* 68 J4
Delvinákion, *Greece* 46 B2
Delvinë, *Albania* 44 G4
Delyatyn, *Ukraine* 29 B9
Demak, *Indonesia* 63 G14
Demanda, Sierra de la, *Spain* 38 C2
Demavend = Damāvand, Qolleh-ye, *Iran* 71 C7
Dembecha, *Ethiopia* 81 E4
Dembi, *Ethiopia* 81 F4
Dembia, *Dem. Rep. of the Congo* 86 B2
Dembidolo, *Ethiopia* 81 F3
Demchok, *India* 69 C8
Demer →, *Belgium* 17 D4
Demetrias, *Greece* 46 B5
Demidov, *Russia* 32 E6
Deming, *N. Mex., U.S.A.* 109 K10
Deming, *Wash., U.S.A.* 110 B4
Demini →, *Brazil* 124 D6
Demirci, *Turkey* 47 B10
Demirköprü Barajı, *Turkey* 47 C10
Demirköy, *Turkey* 45 E11
Demmin, *Germany* 24 B9
Demonte, *Italy* 40 D4
Demopolis, *U.S.A.* 115 J2
Dempo, *Indonesia* 62 E2
Demyansk, *Russia* 32 D7
Den Burg, *Neths.* 17 A4
Den Chai, *Thailand* 64 D3
Den Haag = 's-Gravenhage, *Neths.* 17 B4
Den Helder, *Neths.* 17 B4
Den Oever, *Neths.* 17 B5
Denain, *France* 19 B10
Denair, *U.S.A.* 110 H6
Denau, *Uzbekistan* 52 F7
Denbigh, *Canada* 116 A7
Denbigh, *U.K.* 14 D4
Denbighshire □, *U.K.* 14 D4
Dendang, *Indonesia* 62 E3
Dendermonde, *Belgium* 17 C4
Deneba, *Ethiopia* 81 F4
Dengchuan, *China* 58 E3
Denge, *Nigeria* 83 C6
Dengfeng, *China* 56 G7
Dengi, *Nigeria* 83 D6
Dengkou, *China* 56 D4
Dengzhou, *China* 59 A9
Denham, *Australia* 93 E1
Denham, Mt., *Jamaica* 120 a
Denham Ra., *Australia* 94 C4
Denham Sd., *Australia* 93 E1
Denholm, *Canada* 103 C7
Denia, *Spain* 39 G5
Denial B., *Australia* 95 E1
Deniliquin, *Australia* 95 F3
Denison, *Iowa, U.S.A.* 112 E7
Denison, *Tex., U.S.A.* 113 J6
Denison Plains, *Australia* 92 C4
Denizli, *Turkey* 47 D11
Denizli □, *Turkey* 47 D11
Denman Glacier, *Antarctica* 5 C7
Denmark, *Australia* 93 F2
Denmark ■, *Europe* 11 J3
Denmark Str., *Atl. Oc.* 4 C6
Dennery, *St. Lucia* 121 f
Dennison, *U.S.A.* 116 F3
Denny, *U.K.* 13 E5
Denpasar, *Indonesia* 63 K18
Denpasar ✕ (DPS), *Indonesia* 63 K18
Denton, *Mont., U.S.A.* 108 C9
Denton, *Tex., U.S.A.* 113 J6
D'Entrecasteaux △, *Australia* 93 F2
D'Entrecasteaux, Pt., *Australia* 93 F2
Denu, *Ghana* 83 D5
Denver, *Colo., U.S.A.* 112 F2
Denver, *Pa., U.S.A.* 117 F8
Denver City, *U.S.A.* 113 J3
Deoband, *India* 68 E7
Deogarh, *India* 68 G5
Deoghar, *India* 69 G12
Deolali, *India* 66 K8
Deoli = Devli, *India* 68 G6
Déols, *France* 19 F8
Deora, *India* 68 F4
Deori, *India* 69 H8
Deoria, *India* 69 F10
Deosai Mts., *Pakistan* 69 B6
Deosri, *India* 69 F14
Depalpur, *India* 68 H6
Deping, *China* 57 F9
Deposit, *U.S.A.* 117 D9
Depuch I., *Australia* 92 D2
Deputatskiy, *Russia* 53 C14
Dêqên, *China* 58 C2
Deqing, *China* 59 F8
Dera Ghazi Khan, *Pakistan* 68 D4
Dera Ismail Khan, *Pakistan* 68 D4
Derabugti, *Pakistan* 68 E3
Derawar Fort, *Pakistan* 68 E4
Derbent, *Russia* 35 J9
Derbent, *Turkey* 47 C10
Derby, *Australia* 92 C3
Derby, *U.K.* 14 E6
Derby, *Conn., U.S.A.* 117 E11
Derby, *Kans., U.S.A.* 113 G6
Derby, *N.Y., U.S.A.* 116 D6
Derby City □, *U.K.* 14 E6
Derby Line, *U.S.A.* 117 B12
Derbyshire □, *U.K.* 14 D6
Đerdap △, *Serbia & M.* 44 B6
Derdepoort, *S. Africa* 88 C4
Derecske, *Hungary* 28 C6
Dereham, *U.K.* 15 E8
Dereköy, *Turkey* 45 E11
Dereli, *Turkey* 73 B8
Derg →, *U.K.* 12 B4
Derg, L., *Ireland* 12 D3
Dergachi = Derhaci, *Ukraine* 33 G9
Dergaon, *India* 67 F19
Derhaci, *Ukraine* 33 G9
Derik, *Turkey* 73 D9
Derinkuyu, *Turkey* 72 C6
Dermantsi, *Bulgaria* 45 C8
Dermott, *U.S.A.* 113 J9
Dêrong, *China* 58 C2
Derry = Londonderry, *U.K.* 12 B4
Derry = Londonderry □, *U.K.* 12 B4
Derry, *N.H., U.S.A.* 117 D13
Derry, *Pa., U.S.A.* 116 F5
Derryveagh Mts., *Ireland* 12 B3
Derudub, *Sudan* 80 D4
Derval, *France* 18 E5
Dervéni, *Greece* 46 C4
Derventa, *Bos.-H.* 28 F2
Derwent →, *Cumb., U.K.* 14 C4
Derwent →, *Derby, U.K.* 14 E6
Derwent →, *N. Yorks., U.K.* 14 D7
Derwent Water, *U.K.* 14 C4
Des Moines, *Iowa, U.S.A.* 112 E8
Des Moines, *N. Mex., U.S.A.* 113 G3
Des Moines →, *U.S.A.* 112 E9
Desa, *Romania* 28 G8
Desaguadero →, *Argentina* 126 C2
Desaguadero →, *Bolivia* 124 G5
Desantne, *Ukraine* 29 E14
Desar, *Malaysia* 65 d
Descanso, Pta., *Mexico* 111 N9
Descartes, *France* 20 B4
Deschaillons-sur-St-Laurent, *Canada* 105 C5
Deschambault L., *Canada* 103 C8
Deschutes →, *U.S.A.* 108 D3
Dese, *Ethiopia* 81 E4
Deseado →, *Argentina* 128 F3
Desenzano del Garda, *Italy* 40 C7
Desert Center, *U.S.A.* 111 M11
Desert Hot Springs, *U.S.A.* 111 M10
Deshnok, *India* 68 F5
Desierto Central de Baja California ⌂, *Mexico* 118 B2
Desna →, *Ukraine* 33 G6
Desnătui →, *Romania* 29 G8
Desolación, I., *Chile* 128 G2
Despeñaperros ⌂, *Spain* 37 G7
Despeñaperros, Paso, *Spain* 37 G7
Despotovac, *Serbia & M.* 44 B5
Dessau, *Germany* 24 D8
Dessye = Dese, *Ethiopia* 81 E4
D'Estrees B., *Australia* 95 F2
Desuri, *India* 68 G5
Desvres, *France* 19 B8
Det Udom, *Thailand* 64 E5
Deta, *Romania* 28 E6
Dete, *Zimbabwe* 88 B4
Đetinja →, *Serbia & M.* 44 C4
Detmold, *Germany* 24 D4
Detour, Pt., *U.S.A.* 114 C2
Detroit, *U.S.A.* 116 D1
Detroit Lakes, *U.S.A.* 112 B7
Detva, *Slovak Rep.* 27 C12
Deurne, *Neths.* 17 C5
Deutsch-Luxemburgischer ⌂, *Germany* 25 F2
Deutsche Bucht, *Germany* 24 A4
Deutschlandsberg, *Austria* 26 E8
Deux-Sèvres □, *France* 18 F6
Deva, *Romania* 28 E7
Devakottai, *India* 66 Q11
Devaprayag, *India* 69 D8
Dévaványa, *Hungary* 28 C5
Deveci Dağları, *Turkey* 72 B7
Devecikonağı, *Turkey* 45 G12
Devecser, *Hungary* 28 C2
Develi, *Turkey* 72 C6
Deventer, *Neths.* 17 B6
Deveron →, *U.K.* 13 D6
Devesel, *Romania* 28 F7
Devgadh Bariya, *India* 68 H5
Devikot, *India* 68 F4
Devils Den, *U.S.A.* 110 K7
Devils Lake, *U.S.A.* 112 A5
Devils Paw, *Canada* 102 B2
Devils Postpile ⌂, *U.S.A.* 110 H7
Devils Tower ⌂, *U.S.A.* 112 C2
Devils Tower Junction, *U.S.A.* 112 C2
Devin, *Bulgaria* 45 E8
Devine, *U.S.A.* 113 L5
Devizes, *U.K.* 15 F6
Devli, *India* 68 G6
Devnya, *Bulgaria* 45 C11
Devoll →, *Albania* 44 F4
Devon, *Canada* 102 C6
Devon □, *U.K.* 15 G4
Devon I., *Canada* 98 B11
Devonport, *Australia* 95 G4
Devonport, *N.Z.* 91 G5
Devrek, *Turkey* 72 B4
Devrekâni, *Turkey* 72 B5
Devrez →, *Turkey* 72 B6
Dewas, *India* 68 H7
Dewetsdorp, *S. Africa* 88 D4
Dewey, *Puerto Rico* 121 d
Dexing, *China* 59 C11
Dexter, *Maine, U.S.A.* 115 C11
Dexter, *Mo., U.S.A.* 113 G10
Dexter, *N. Mex., U.S.A.* 113 J2
Dey-Dey, L., *Australia* 93 E5
Deyang, *China* 58 B5
Deyhūk, *Iran* 71 C8
Deyyer, *Iran* 71 E6
Dezadeash L., *Canada* 102 A1
Dezfūl, *Iran* 71 C6
Dezhneva, Mys, *Russia* 53 C19
Dezhou, *China* 56 F9
Dhadhar →, *India* 69 G11
Dháfni, *Kríti, Greece* 49 D7
Dháfni, *Pelóponnisos, Greece* 46 D4
Dhahabān, *Si. Arabia* 80 C4
Dhahiriya = Az̧ Z̧āhirīyah, *West Bank* 74 D3
Dhahran = Az̧ Z̧ahrān, *Si. Arabia* 71 E6
Dhak, *Pakistan* 68 C5
Dhaka, *Bangla.* 69 H14
Dhaka □, *Bangla.* 69 G14
Dhali, *Cyprus* 49 D12
Dhamási, *Greece* 46 B4
Dhampur, *India* 69 E8
Dhamtari, *India* 67 J12
Dhanbad, *India* 69 H12
Dhangarhi, *Nepal* 67 E12
Dhankuta, *Nepal* 69 F12
Dhar, *India* 68 H6
Dharampur, *India* 68 H6
Dharamsala = Dharmsala, *India* 68 C7
Dhariwal, *India* 68 D6
Dharla →, *Bangla.* 69 G13
Dharmapuri, *India* 66 N11
Dharmjaygarh, *India* 69 H10
Dharmsala, *India* 68 C7
Dharni, *India* 68 J7
Dharwad, *India* 66 M9
Dhasan →, *India* 69 G8
Dhaulagiri, *Nepal* 69 E10
Dhebar, L., *India* 68 G6
Dheftera, *Cyprus* 49 D12
Dhenkanal, *India* 67 J14
Dhenoúsa, *Greece* 47 D7
Dherinia, *Cyprus* 49 D12
Dheskáti, *Greece* 44 G5
Dhespotikó, *Greece* 46 E6
Dhestina, *Greece* 46 C4
Dhī Qār □, *Iraq* 70 D5
Dhiarrizos →, *Cyprus* 49 E11
Dhībān, *Jordan* 74 D4
Dhidhimótikhon, *Greece* 45 E10
Dhíkti Óros, *Greece* 49 D7
Dhilianáta, *Greece* 46 C2
Dhílos, *Greece* 47 D7
Dhilwan, *India* 68 D6
Dhimarkhera, *India* 69 H9
Dhimitsána, *Greece* 46 D4
Dhírfis Óros, *Greece* 46 C5
Dhodhekánisos, *Greece* 47 E8
Dhodhekánisos □, *Greece* 47 E8
Dhokós, *Greece* 46 D5
Dholiana, *Greece* 46 B2
Dholka, *India* 68 H5
Dhomokós, *Greece* 46 B4
Dhoraji, *India* 68 J4
Dhoxáton, *Greece* 45 E8
Dhragonísi, *Greece* 47 D7
Dhráhstis, Ákra, *Greece* 49 A3
Dhrangadhra, *India* 68 H4
Dhrápanon, Ákra, *Greece* 49 D6
Dhriopís, *Greece* 46 D6
Dhrol, *India* 68 H4
Dhuburi, *India* 67 F16
Dhule, *India* 66 J9
Di-ib, W. →, *Sudan* 80 C4
Di Linh, *Vietnam* 65 G7
Di Linh, Cao Nguyen, *Vietnam* 65 G7
Día, *Greece* 49 D7
Diabakania, *Guinea* 82 C2
Diablo, Mt., *U.S.A.* 110 H5
Diablo Range, *U.S.A.* 110 J5
Diafarabé, *Mali* 82 C4
Diala, *Mali* 82 C3
Dialakoro, *Mali* 82 C3
Dialakoto, *Senegal* 82 C2
Diallassagou, *Mali* 82 C4
Diamante, *Argentina* 126 C3

Diamante, *Italy* 43 **C8**
Diamante →, *Argentina* 126 **C2**
Diamantina, *Brazil* 125 **G10**
Diamantina △, *Australia* 94 **C3**
Diamantina →, *Australia* 95 **D2**
Diamantino, *Brazil* 125 **F7**
Diamond Bar, *U.S.A.* 111 **L9**
Diamond Harbour, *India* 69 **H13**
Diamond Is., *Australia* 94 **B5**
Diamond Mts., *U.S.A.* 108 **G6**
Diamond Springs, *U.S.A.* 110 **G6**
Dian Chi, *China* 58 **E4**
Dianalund, *Denmark* 11 **J5**
Dianbai, *China* 59 **G8**
Diancheng, *China* 59 **G8**
Dianjiang, *China* 58 **B6**
Diano Marina, *Italy* 40 **E5**
Dianra, *Ivory C.* 82 **D3**
Diapaga, *Burkina Faso* 83 **C5**
Diapangou, *Burkina Faso* 83 **C5**
Diariguila, *Guinea* 82 **C2**
Dībā, *U.A.E.* 71 **E8**
Dibai, *India* 68 **E8**
Dibaya-Lubue, *Dem. Rep. of the Congo* 84 **E3**
Dibbeen △, *Jordan* 74 **C4**
Dibete, *Botswana* 88 **C4**
Dibrugarh, *India* 67 **F19**
Dickens, *U.S.A.* 113 **J4**
Dickinson, *U.S.A.* 112 **B3**
Dickson, *U.S.A.* 115 **G2**
Dickson City, *U.S.A.* 117 **E9**
Dicle Nehri →, *Turkey* 73 **D9**
Dicomano, *Italy* 41 **E8**
Didesa, W. →, *Ethiopia* 81 **E4**
Didi, *Sudan* 81 **F3**
Didiéni, *Mali* 82 **C3**
Didsbury, *Canada* 102 **C6**
Didwana, *India* 68 **F6**
Die, *France* 21 **D9**
Diébougou, *Burkina Faso* 82 **C4**
Diecke, *Guinea* 82 **D3**
Diefenbaker, L., *Canada* 103 **C7**
Diego de Almagro, *Chile* 126 **B1**
Diego Garcia, *Ind. Oc.* 3 **E13**
Diekirch, *Lux.* 17 **E6**
Diéma, *Mali* 82 **C3**
Diembéring, *Senegal* 82 **C1**
Diemelsee ⌂, *Germany* 24 **D4**
Dien Ban, *Vietnam* 64 **E7**
Dien Bien, *Vietnam* 58 **G4**
Dien Khanh, *Vietnam* 65 **F7**
Diepholz, *Germany* 24 **C4**
Dieppe, *France* 18 **C8**
Dierks, *U.S.A.* 113 **H8**
Diest, *Belgium* 17 **D5**
Dietikon, *Switz.* 25 **H4**
Dieulefit, *France* 21 **D9**
Dieuze, *France* 19 **D13**
Dif, *Somali Rep.* 75 **G3**
Differdange, *Lux.* 17 **E5**
Dig, *India* 68 **F7**
Digba, *Dem. Rep. of the Congo* 86 **B2**
Digby, *Canada* 105 **D6**
Diggi, *India* 68 **F6**
Dighinala, *Bangla.* 67 **H18**
Dighton, *U.S.A.* 112 **F4**
Digna, *Mali* 82 **C3**
Digne-les-Bains, *France* 21 **D10**
Digoin, *France* 19 **F11**
Digor, *Turkey* 73 **B10**
Digos, *Phil.* 61 **H6**
Digranes, *Iceland* 8 **C6**
Digul →, *Indonesia* 63 **F9**
Digya △, *Ghana* 83 **D5**
Dihang = Brahmaputra →, *Asia* 69 **H13**
Dijlah, Nahr →, *Asia* 70 **D5**
Dijon, *France* 19 **E12**
Dikhil, *Djibouti* 81 **E5**
Dikili, *Turkey* 47 **B8**
Dikirnis, *Egypt* 80 **H7**
Dikkil = Dikhil, *Djibouti* 81 **E5**
Dikodougou, *Ivory C.* 82 **D3**
Diksmuide, *Belgium* 17 **C2**
Dikson, *Russia* 52 **B9**
Dikwa, *Nigeria* 83 **C7**
Dila, *Ethiopia* 81 **F4**
Dilek Yarimadisi △, *Turkey* 47 **D9**
Dili, *E. Timor* 63 **F7**
Dilijan, *Armenia* 35 **K7**
Dilizhan = Dilijan, *Armenia* 35 **K7**
Dilj, *Croatia* 28 **E3**
Dillenburg, *Germany* 24 **E4**
Dilley, *U.S.A.* 113 **L5**
Dilli = Delhi, *India* 68 **E7**
Dilling, *Sudan* 81 **E2**
Dillingen, *Bayern, Germany* 25 **G6**
Dillingen, *Saarland, Germany* 25 **F2**
Dillingham, *U.S.A.* 100 **C4**
Dillon, *Canada* 103 **B7**
Dillon, *Mont., U.S.A.* 108 **D7**
Dillon, *S.C., U.S.A.* 115 **H6**
Dillon →, *Canada* 103 **B7**
Dillsburg, *U.S.A.* 116 **F7**
Dilly, *Mali* 82 **C3**
Dilolo, *Dem. Rep. of the Congo* 84 **G4**
Dilove, *Ukraine* 29 **C9**
Dimas, *Mexico* 118 **C3**
Dimashq, *Syria* 74 **B5**
Dimashq ☐, *Syria* 74 **B5**
Dimbaza, *S. Africa* 89 **E4**
Dimbokro, *Ivory C.* 82 **D4**
Dimboola, *Australia* 95 **F3**
Dîmbovița = Dâmbovița →, *Romania* 29 **F11**
Dimbulah, *Australia* 94 **B4**
Dimitrovgrad, *Bulgaria* 45 **D9**
Dimitrovgrad, *Russia* 34 **C9**
Dimitrovgrad, *Serbia & M.* 44 **C6**
Dimitrovo = Pernik, *Bulgaria* 44 **D7**
Dimmitt, *U.S.A.* 113 **H3**
Dimo, *Sudan* 81 **F2**
Dimona, *Israel* 74 **D4**
Dimovo, *Bulgaria* 44 **C6**
Dinagat, *Phil.* 61 **F6**
Dinajpur, *Bangla.* 67 **G16**
Dinan, *France* 18 **D4**
Dīnān Āb, *Iran* 71 **C8**
Dinant, *Belgium* 17 **D4**
Dinapur, *India* 69 **G11**
Dinar, *Turkey* 47 **C12**
Dīnār, Kūh-e, *Iran* 71 **D6**
Dinara Planina, *Croatia* 41 **D13**
Dinard, *France* 18 **D4**
Dinaric Alps = Dinara Planina, *Croatia* 41 **D13**
Dindanko, *Mali* 82 **C3**
Dinder △, *Sudan* 81 **E4**
Dinder, Nahr ed →, *Sudan* 81 **E3**
Dindigul, *India* 66 **P11**
Dindori, *India* 69 **H9**
Ding Xian = Dingzhou, *China* 56 **E8**
Dinga, *Pakistan* 68 **G2**
Dingalan, *Phil.* 61 **D4**
Dingbian, *China* 56 **F4**
Dingelstädt, *Germany* 24 **D6**
Dingle, *Ireland* 12 **D1**
Dingle, *Sweden* 11 **F5**
Dingle B., *Ireland* 12 **D1**
Dingmans Ferry, *U.S.A.* 117 **E10**
Dingnan, *China* 59 **E10**
Dingo, *Australia* 94 **C4**
Dingolfing, *Germany* 25 **G8**
Dingtao, *China* 56 **G8**
Dinguira, *Mali* 82 **C2**
Dinguiraye, *Guinea* 82 **C2**
Dingwall, *U.K.* 13 **D4**
Dingxi, *China* 56 **G3**
Dingxiang, *China* 56 **E7**
Dingyuan, *China* 59 **A11**
Dingzhou, *China* 56 **E8**
Dinh, Mui, *Vietnam* 65 **G7**
Dinh Lap, *Vietnam* 58 **G6**
Dinira △, *Venezuela* 121 **E6**
Dinokwe, *Botswana* 88 **C4**
Dinorwic, *Canada* 103 **D10**
Dinosaur ⌂, *Canada* 102 **C6**
Dinosaur ⌂, *U.S.A.* 108 **F9**
Dinuba, *U.S.A.* 110 **J7**
Diö, *Sweden* 11 **H8**
Dioïla, *Mali* 82 **C3**
Dioka, *Mali* 82 **C2**
Diongoï, *Mali* 82 **C3**
Diósgyör, *Hungary* 28 **B5**
Diosig, *Romania* 28 **C7**
Diougani, *Mali* 82 **C4**
Diouloulou, *Senegal* 82 **C1**
Dioura, *Mali* 82 **C3**
Diourbel, *Senegal* 82 **C1**
Dipalpur, *Pakistan* 68 **D5**
Diplo, *Pakistan* 68 **G3**
Dipolog, *Phil.* 61 **G5**
Dipperu △, *Australia* 94 **C4**
Dir, *Pakistan* 66 **B7**
Diré, *Mali* 82 **B4**
Dire Dawa, *Ethiopia* 81 **F5**
Diriamba, *Nic.* 120 **D2**
Dirk Hartog I., *Australia* 93 **E1**
Dirranbandi, *Australia* 95 **D4**
Disa, *India* 68 **G5**
Disa, *Sudan* 81 **E3**
Disappointment, C., *U.S.A.* 108 **C2**
Disappointment, L., *Australia* 92 **D3**
Disaster B., *Australia* 95 **F4**
Discovery B., *Australia* 95 **F3**
Disentis Muster, *Switz.* 25 **J4**
Dishna, *Egypt* 80 **B3**
Disina, *Nigeria* 83 **C6**
Disko = Qeqertarsuaq, *Greenland* 101 **B5**
Disna = Dzisna →, *Belarus* 32 **E5**
Diss, *U.K.* 15 **E9**
Disteghil Sar, *Pakistan* 69 **A6**
Distrito Federal ☐, *Brazil* 125 **G9**
Distrito Federal ☐, *Mexico* 119 **D5**
Disûq, *Egypt* 80 **H7**
Diu, *India* 68 **J4**
Dīvāndarreh, *Iran* 70 **C5**
Dives →, *France* 18 **C6**
Dives-sur-Mer, *France* 18 **C6**
Divichi = Däväçi, *Azerbaijan* 35 **K9**
Divide, *U.S.A.* 108 **D7**
Dividing Ra., *Australia* 93 **E2**
Divinópolis, *Brazil* 125 **H10**
Divjake, *Albania* 44 **F3**
Divnoye, *Russia* 35 **H6**
Divo, *Ivory C.* 82 **D3**
Divriği, *Turkey* 73 **C8**
Dīwāl Kol, *Afghan.* 68 **B2**
Dixie Mt., *U.S.A.* 110 **F6**
Dixon, *Calif., U.S.A.* 110 **G5**
Dixon, *Ill., U.S.A.* 112 **E10**
Dixon Entrance, *U.S.A.* 100 **C6**
Dixville, *Canada* 117 **A13**
Diyadin, *Turkey* 73 **C10**
Diyālā ☐, *Iraq* 70 **C5**
Diyālā →, *Iraq* 70 **C5**
Diyarbakır, *Turkey* 70 **B4**
Diyodar, *India* 68 **G4**
Djakarta = Jakarta, *Indonesia* 63 **G12**
Djamba, *Angola* 88 **B1**
Djambala, *Congo* 84 **E2**
Djanet, *Algeria* 78 **D7**
Djawa = Jawa, *Indonesia* 62 **F3**
Djelfa, *Algeria* 78 **B6**
Djema, *C.A.R.* 86 **A2**
Djenné, *Mali* 82 **C4**
Djerba, I. de, *Tunisia* 79 **B8**
Djerid, Chott, *Tunisia* 78 **B7**
Djibo, *Burkina Faso* 83 **C4**
Djibouti, *Djibouti* 81 **E5**
Djibouti ■, *Africa* 81 **E5**
Djolu, *Dem. Rep. of the Congo* 84 **D4**
Djougou, *Benin* 83 **D5**
Djoum, *Cameroon* 84 **D2**
Djourab, Erg du, *Chad* 79 **E9**
Djugu, *Dem. Rep. of the Congo* 86 **B3**
Djúpivogur, *Iceland* 8 **D6**
Djurås, *Sweden* 10 **D9**
Djurö △, *Sweden* 11 **F7**
Djursland, *Denmark* 11 **H4**
Dmitriya Lapteva, Proliv, *Russia* 53 **B15**
Dmitriyev Lgovskiy, *Russia* 33 **F8**
Dmitrov, *Russia* 32 **D9**
Dmitrovsk-Orlovskiy, *Russia* 33 **F8**
Dnepr = Dnipro →, *Ukraine* 33 **J7**
Dneprodzerzhinsk = Dniprodzerzhynsk, *Ukraine* 33 **H8**
Dneprodzerzhinskoye Vdkhr. = Dniprodzerzhynske Vdskh., *Ukraine* 33 **H8**
Dnepropetrovsk = Dnipropetrovsk, *Ukraine* 33 **H8**
Dneprorudnoye = Dniprorudne, *Ukraine* 33 **J8**
Dnestr = Dnister →, *Europe* 33 **J6**
Dnieper = Dnipro →, *Ukraine* 33 **J7**
Dniester = Dnister →, *Europe* 33 **J6**
Dnipro →, *Ukraine* 33 **J7**
Dniprodzerzhynsk, *Ukraine* 33 **H8**
Dniprodzerzhynske Vdskh., *Ukraine* 33 **H8**
Dnipropetrovsk, *Ukraine* 33 **H8**
Dniprorudne, *Ukraine* 33 **J8**
Dnister →, *Europe* 33 **J6**
Dnistrovskyy Lyman, *Ukraine* 33 **J6**
Dno, *Russia* 32 **D5**
Dnyapro = Dnipro →, *Ukraine* 33 **J7**
Doaktown, *Canada* 105 **C6**
Doan Hung, *Vietnam* 58 **G5**
Doany, *Madag.* 89 **A8**
Doba, *Chad* 79 **G9**
Dobandi, *Pakistan* 68 **D2**
Dobbiaco, *Italy* 41 **B9**
Dobbyn, *Australia* 94 **B3**
Dobczyce, *Poland* 31 **J7**
Dobele, *Latvia* 9 **H20**
Dobele ☐, *Latvia* 30 **B10**
Döbeln, *Germany* 24 **D9**
Doberai, Jazirah, *Indonesia* 63 **E8**
Dobiegniew, *Poland* 31 **F2**
Doblas, *Argentina* 126 **D3**
Dobo, *Indonesia* 63 **F8**
Doboj, *Bos.-H.* 28 **F3**
Dobra, *Wielkopolskie, Poland* 31 **G5**
Dobra, *Zachodnio-Pomorskie, Poland* 30 **E2**
Dobra, *Dâmbovita, Romania* 29 **F10**
Dobra, *Hunedoara, Romania* 28 **E7**
Dobre Miasto, *Poland* 30 **E7**
Dobrești, *Romania* 28 **D7**
Dobrich, *Bulgaria* 45 **C11**
Dobrinishta, *Bulgaria* 44 **E7**
Dobříš, *Czech Rep.* 26 **B7**
Dobrodzień, *Poland* 31 **H5**
Dobromyl, *Ukraine* 31 **J9**
Dobron, *Ukraine* 28 **B7**
Dobropole, *Ukraine* 33 **H9**
Dobrovolsk, *Russia* 30 **D9**
Dobruja, *Europe* 29 **F13**
Dobrush, *Belarus* 33 **F6**
Dobrzany, *Poland* 30 **E2**
Dobrzyń nad Wisłą, *Poland* 31 **F6**
Doc, Mui, *Vietnam* 64 **D6**
Docker River, *Australia* 93 **D4**
Docksta, *Sweden* 10 **A12**
Doctor Arroyo, *Mexico* 118 **C4**
Doda, *India* 69 **C6**
Doda, L., *Canada* 104 **C4**
Dodecanese = Dhodhekánisos, *Greece* 47 **E8**
Dodge City, *U.S.A.* 113 **G5**
Dodge L., *Canada* 103 **B7**
Dodgeville, *U.S.A.* 112 **D9**
Dodo, *Cameroon* 83 **D7**
Dodo, *Sudan* 81 **F2**
Dodola, *Ethiopia* 81 **F4**
Dodoma, *Tanzania* 86 **D4**
Dodoma ☐, *Tanzania* 86 **D4**
Dodona, *Greece* 46 **B2**
Dodori ⌂, *Kenya* 86 **C5**
Dodsland, *Canada* 103 **C7**
Dodson, *U.S.A.* 108 **B9**
Dodurga, *Turkey* 47 **B11**
Doesburg, *Neths.* 17 **B6**
Doetinchem, *Neths.* 17 **C6**
Dog Creek, *Canada* 102 **C4**
Dog L., *Man., Canada* 103 **C9**
Dog L., *Ont., Canada* 104 **C2**
Doğanşehir, *Turkey* 72 **C7**
Dogliani, *Italy* 40 **D4**
Dogondoutchi, *Niger* 83 **C5**
Dogran, *Pakistan* 68 **D5**
Doğubayazıt, *Turkey* 70 **B5**
Doguéraoua, *Niger* 83 **C6**
Doha = Ad Dawḩah, *Qatar* 71 **E6**
Dohazari, *Bangla.* 67 **H18**
Dohrighat, *India* 69 **F10**
Doi, *Indonesia* 63 **D7**
Doi Inthanon △, *Thailand* 64 **C2**
Doi Khuntan △, *Thailand* 64 **C2**
Doi Luang, *Thailand* 64 **C3**
Doi Luang △, *Thailand* 64 **C2**
Doi Saket, *Thailand* 64 **C2**
Doi Suthep △, *Thailand* 64 **C2**
Dois Irmãos, Sa., *Brazil* 125 **E10**
Dojransko Jezero, *Macedonia* 44 **E6**
Dokkum, *Neths.* 17 **A5**
Dokri, *Pakistan* 68 **F3**
Dokuchayevsk, *Ukraine* 33 **J9**
Dol-de-Bretagne, *France* 18 **D5**
Dolac, *Serbia & M.* 44 **D4**
Dolak, Pulau, *Indonesia* 63 **F9**
Dolbeau-Mistassini, *Canada* 105 **C5**
Dole, *France* 19 **E12**
Doleib, Wadi →, *Sudan* 81 **E3**
Dolenji Logatec, *Slovenia* 41 **C11**
Dolgellau, *U.K.* 14 **E4**
Dolgelley = Dolgellau, *U.K.* 14 **E4**
Dolhasca, *Romania* 29 **C11**
Dolianova, *Italy* 42 **C2**
Dolinskaya = Dolynska, *Ukraine* 33 **H7**
Dolj ☐, *Romania* 29 **F8**
Dollard, *Neths.* 17 **A7**
Dolna Banya, *Bulgaria* 44 **D7**
Dolni Chiflik, *Bulgaria* 45 **D11**
Dolni Dŭbnik, *Bulgaria* 45 **C8**
Dolnośląskie ☐, *Poland* 31 **G3**
Dolný Kubín, *Slovak Rep.* 27 **B12**
Dolo, *Ethiopia* 81 **G5**
Dolo, *Italy* 41 **C9**
Dolomites = Dolomiti, *Italy* 41 **B8**
Dolomiti, *Italy* 41 **B8**
Dolomiti Bellunesi △, *Italy* 41 **B9**
Dolores, *Argentina* 126 **D4**
Dolores, *Uruguay* 126 **C4**
Dolores, *U.S.A.* 109 **H9**
Dolores →, *U.S.A.* 109 **G9**
Dolovo, *Serbia & M.* 28 **F5**
Dolphin, C., *Falk. Is.* 128 **G5**
Dolphin and Union Str., *Canada* 100 **B8**
Dolsk, *Poland* 31 **G4**
Dolyna, *Ukraine* 29 **B9**
Dolynska, *Ukraine* 33 **H7**
Dolynske, *Ukraine* 29 **C14**
Dolzhanskaya, *Russia* 33 **J9**
Dom Pedrito, *Brazil* 127 **C5**
Doma, *Nigeria* 83 **D6**
Doma ⌂, *Zimbabwe* 87 **F3**
Domaniç, *Turkey* 47 **B11**
Domariaganj →, *India* 69 **F10**
Domasi, *Malawi* 87 **F4**
Domažlice, *Czech Rep.* 26 **B5**
Dombarovskiy, *Russia* 52 **D6**
Dombås, *Norway* 9 **E13**
Dombasle-sur-Meurthe, *France* 19 **D13**
Dombes, *France* 21 **C9**
Dombóvár, *Hungary* 28 **D3**
Dombrád, *Hungary* 28 **B6**
Dome Fuji, *Antarctica* 5 **D5**
Domel I. = Letsôk-aw Kyun, *Burma* 65 **G2**
Domérat, *France* 19 **F9**
Domeyko, *Chile* 126 **B1**
Domeyko, Cordillera, *Chile* 126 **A2**
Domfront, *France* 18 **D6**
Dominador, *Chile* 126 **A2**
Dominica ■, *W. Indies* 121 **C7**
Dominica Passage, *W. Indies* 121 **C7**
Dominican Rep. ■, *W. Indies* 121 **C5**
Dömitz, *Germany* 24 **B7**
Domme, *France* 20 **D5**
Domnești, *Romania* 29 **E9**
Domodóssola, *Italy* 40 **B5**
Domogled-Valea Cernei △, *Romania* 28 **F7**
Dompaire, *France* 19 **D13**
Dompierre-sur-Besbre, *France* 19 **F10**
Dompim, *Ghana* 82 **D4**
Domrémy-la-Pucelle, *France* 19 **D12**
Domville, Mt., *Australia* 95 **D5**
Domvraína, *Greece* 46 **C4**
Domžale, *Slovenia* 41 **B11**
Don →, *Russia* 33 **J10**
Don →, *Aberds., U.K.* 13 **D6**
Don →, *S. Yorks., U.K.* 14 **D7**
Don, C., *Australia* 92 **B5**
Don Benito, *Spain* 37 **G5**
Don Figuerero Mts., *Jamaica* 120 **a**
Don Sak, *Thailand* 65 **b**
Dona Ana = Nhamaabué, *Mozam.* 87 **F4**
Doña Mencía, *Spain* 37 **H6**
Donaghadee, *U.K.* 12 **B6**
Donald, *Australia* 95 **F3**
Donaldsonville, *U.S.A.* 113 **K9**
Donalsonville, *U.S.A.* 115 **K3**
Doñana △, *Spain* 37 **J4**
Donau = Dunărea →, *Europe* 29 **E14**
Donau →, *Austria* 27 **C10**
Donau Auen △, *Austria* 27 **C9**
Donaueschingen, *Germany* 25 **H4**
Donauwörth, *Germany* 25 **G6**
Doncaster, *U.K.* 14 **D6**
Dondo, *Mozam.* 87 **F3**
Dondo, Teluk, *Indonesia* 63 **D6**
Dondra Head, *Sri Lanka* 66 **S12**
Dondușeni, *Moldova* 29 **B12**
Donegal, *Ireland* 12 **B3**
Donegal ☐, *Ireland* 12 **B4**
Donegal B., *Ireland* 12 **B3**
Donets →, *Russia* 35 **G5**
Donets Basin, *Ukraine* 6 **F13**
Donetsk, *Ukraine* 33 **J9**
Dong Ba Thin, *Vietnam* 65 **F7**
Dong Dang, *Vietnam* 58 **G6**
Dong Giam, *Vietnam* 64 **C5**
Dong Ha, *Vietnam* 64 **D6**
Dong Hene, *Laos* 64 **D5**
Dong Hoi, *Vietnam* 64 **D6**
Dong Jiang →, *China* 59 **F10**
Dong Khe, *Vietnam* 64 **A6**
Dong Ujimqin Qi, *China* 56 **B9**
Dong Van, *Vietnam* 64 **A5**
Dong Xoai, *Vietnam* 65 **G6**
Donga, *Nigeria* 83 **D7**
Donga →, *Nigeria* 83 **D7**
Dong'an, *China* 59 **D8**
Dongara, *Australia* 93 **E1**
Dongbei, *China* 53 **E13**
Dongchuan, *China* 58 **D4**
Donges, *France* 18 **E4**
Dongfang, *China* 64 **C7**
Dongfeng, *China* 57 **C13**
Donggala, *Indonesia* 63 **E5**
Donggan, *China* 58 **F5**
Donggou, *China* 57 **E13**
Dongguan, *China* 59 **F9**
Dongguang, *China* 56 **F9**
Donghai Dao, *China* 59 **G8**
Dongjingcheng, *China* 57 **B15**
Dongkou, *China* 59 **D8**
Donglan, *China* 58 **E6**
Dongliu, *China* 59 **B11**
Dongmen, *China* 58 **F6**
Dongning, *China* 57 **B16**
Dongnyi, *China* 58 **C3**
Dongola, *Sudan* 80 **D3**
Dongping, *China* 56 **G9**
Dongsha Dao, *China* 59 **G11**
Dongshan, *China* 59 **F11**
Dongsheng, *China* 56 **E6**
Dongtai, *China* 57 **H11**
Dongting Hu, *China* 59 **C9**
Dongtou, *China* 59 **D13**
Dongxiang, *China* 59 **C11**
Dongxing, *China* 58 **G7**
Dongyang, *China* 59 **C13**
Dongzhi, *China* 59 **B11**
Donington, C., *Australia* 95 **E2**
Doniphan, *U.S.A.* 113 **G9**
Donja Stubica, *Croatia* 41 **C12**
Donji Dušnik, *Serbia & M.* 44 **C6**
Donji Miholjac, *Croatia* 28 **E3**
Donji Milanovac, *Serbia & M.* 44 **B6**
Donji Vakuf, *Bos.-H.* 28 **F2**
Dønna, *Norway* 8 **C15**
Donna, *U.S.A.* 113 **M5**
Donnacona, *Canada* 105 **C5**
Donnelly's Crossing, *N.Z.* 91 **F4**
Donnybrook, *Australia* 93 **F2**
Donnybrook, *S. Africa* 89 **D4**
Donora, *U.S.A.* 116 **F5**
Donostia = Donostia-San Sebastián, *Spain* 38 **B3**
Donostia-San Sebastián, *Spain* 38 **B3**
Donskoy, *Russia* 32 **F10**
Donsol, *Phil.* 61 **E5**
Donzère, *France* 21 **D8**
Donzy, *France* 19 **E10**
Doon →, *U.K.* 13 **F4**
Dora, L., *Australia* 92 **D3**
Dora Báltea →, *Italy* 40 **C5**
Dora Ripária →, *Italy* 40 **C4**
Doran L., *Canada* 103 **A7**
Dorchester, *U.K.* 15 **G5**
Dorchester, C., *Canada* 101 **B12**
Dordabis, *Namibia* 88 **C2**
Dordogne ☐, *France* 20 **C4**
Dordogne →, *France* 20 **C3**
Dordrecht, *Neths.* 17 **C4**
Dordrecht, *S. Africa* 88 **E4**
Dore →, *France* 20 **C7**
Dore, Mts., *France* 20 **C6**
Doré L., *Canada* 103 **C7**
Doré Lake, *Canada* 103 **C7**
Dorfen, *Germany* 25 **G8**
Dorgali, *Italy* 42 **B2**
Dori, *Burkina Faso* 83 **C4**
Doring →, *S. Africa* 88 **E2**
Doringbos, *S. Africa* 88 **E2**
Dorking, *U.K.* 15 **F7**
Dormaa-Ahenkro, *Ghana* 82 **D4**
Dormans, *France* 19 **C10**
Dormo, Ras, *Eritrea* 81 **E5**
Dornbirn, *Austria* 26 **D2**
Dornes, *France* 19 **F10**
Dornești, *Romania* 29 **C11**
Dornie, *U.K.* 13 **D3**
Dornoch, *U.K.* 13 **D4**
Dornoch Firth, *U.K.* 13 **D4**
Dornogovĭ ☐, *Mongolia* 56 **C6**
Doro, *Mali* 83 **B4**
Dorog, *Hungary* 28 **C3**
Dorogobuzh, *Russia* 32 **E7**
Dorohoi, *Romania* 29 **C11**
Döröö Nuur, *Mongolia* 60 **B4**
Dorr, *Iran* 71 **C6**
Dorre I., *Australia* 93 **E1**
Dorrigo, *Australia* 95 **E5**
Dorris, *U.S.A.* 108 **F3**
Dorset, *Canada* 116 **A6**
Dorset, *U.S.A.* 116 **E4**
Dorset ☐, *U.K.* 15 **G5**
Dorsten, *Germany* 24 **D2**
Dortmund, *Germany* 24 **D3**
Dortmund-Ems-Kanal →, *Germany* 24 **D3**
Dörtyol, *Turkey* 72 **D7**
Dorum, *Germany* 24 **B4**
Doruma, *Dem. Rep. of the Congo* 86 **B2**
Dorūneh, *Iran* 71 **C8**
Dos Bahías, C., *Argentina* 128 **E3**
Dos Hermanas, *Spain* 37 **H5**
Dos Palos, *U.S.A.* 110 **J6**
Döşemealtı, *Turkey* 47 **D12**
Dosso, *Niger* 83 **C5**
Dosso ⌂, *Niger* 83 **C5**
Dothan, *U.S.A.* 115 **K3**
Doty, *U.S.A.* 110 **D3**
Douai, *France* 19 **B10**
Douako, *Guinea* 82 **D2**
Douala, *Cameroon* 83 **E6**
Douarnenez, *France* 18 **D2**
Doubabougou, *Mali* 82 **C3**
Double Island Pt., *Australia* 95 **D5**
Double Mountain Fork →, *U.S.A.* 113 **J4**
Doubrava →, *Czech Rep.* 26 **A8**
Doubs ☐, *France* 19 **E13**
Doubs →, *France* 19 **F12**
Doubtful Sd., *N.Z.* 91 **L1**
Doubtless B., *N.Z.* 91 **F4**
Doudeville, *France* 18 **C7**
Doué-la-Fontaine, *France* 18 **E6**
Douentza, *Mali* 82 **C4**
Douentza ⌂, *Mali* 82 **B4**
Douglas, *I. of Man* 14 **C3**
Douglas, *S. Africa* 88 **D3**
Douglas, *Ariz., U.S.A.* 109 **L9**
Douglas, *Ga., U.S.A.* 115 **K4**

Douglas, *Wyo., U.S.A.* 112 D2
Douglas Apsley △, *Australia* 95 G4
Douglas Chan., *Canada* 102 C3
Douglas Pt., *Canada* 116 B3
Douglasville, *U.S.A.* 115 J3
Doukáton, Ákra, *Greece* 46 C2
Doulevant-le-Château, *France* 19 D11
Doullens, *France* 19 B9
Doumen, *China* 59 F9
Douna, *Mali* 82 C3
Dounreay, *U.K.* 13 C5
Dourada, Serra, *Brazil* 125 F9
Dourados, *Brazil* 127 A5
Dourados →, *Brazil* 127 A5
Dourados, Serra dos, *Brazil* 127 A5
Dourdan, *France* 19 D9
Douro →, *Europe* 36 D2
Douvaine, *France* 19 F13
Douvres-la-Délivrande, *France* 18 C6
Douze →, *France* 20 E3
Dove →, *U.K.* 14 E6
Dove Creek, *U.S.A.* 109 H9
Dover, *Australia* 95 G4
Dover, *U.K.* 15 F9
Dover, *Del., U.S.A.* 114 F8
Dover, *N.H., U.S.A.* 117 C14
Dover, *N.J., U.S.A.* 117 F10
Dover, *Ohio, U.S.A.* 116 F3
Dover, Pt., *Australia* 93 F4
Dover, Str. of, *Europe* 15 G9
Dover-Foxcroft, *U.S.A.* 115 C11
Dover Plains, *U.S.A.* 117 E11
Dovey = Dyfi →, *U.K.* 15 E3
Dovhe, *Ukraine* 29 B8
Dovrefjell, *Norway* 9 E13
Dow Rūd, *Iran* 71 C6
Dowa, *Malawi* 87 E3
Dowagiac, *U.S.A.* 114 E2
Dowerin, *Australia* 93 F2
Dowgha'i, *Iran* 71 B8
Dowlatābād, *Iran* 71 D8
Down □, *U.K.* 12 B5
Downey, *Calif., U.S.A.* 111 M8
Downey, *Idaho, U.S.A.* 108 E7
Downham Market, *U.K.* 15 E8
Downieville, *U.S.A.* 110 F6
Downpatrick, *U.K.* 12 B6
Downpatrick Hd., *Ireland* 12 B2
Downsville, *U.S.A.* 117 D10
Downton, Mt., *Canada* 102 C4
Dowsārī, *Iran* 71 D8
Doyle, *U.S.A.* 110 E6
Doylestown, *U.S.A.* 117 F9
Dozois, Rés., *Canada* 104 C4
Dra Khel, *Pakistan* 68 F2
Drac →, *France* 21 C9
Dračevo, *Macedonia* 44 E5
Drachten, *Neths.* 17 A6
Drăgănești, *Moldova* 29 C13
Drăgănești-Olt, *Romania* 29 F9
Drăgănești-Vlașca, *Romania* 29 F10
Dragaš, *Serbia & M.* 44 D4
Drăgășani, *Romania* 29 F9
Dragichyn, *Belarus* 33 F3
Dragocvet, *Serbia & M.* 44 C5
Dragon's Mouth = Boca de Drago, *Venezuela* 125 K15
Dragovishtitsa, *Bulgaria* 44 D6
Draguignan, *France* 21 E10
Drahove, *Ukraine* 29 B8
Drain, *U.S.A.* 108 E2
Drake, *U.S.A.* 112 B4
Drake Passage, *S. Ocean* 5 B17
Drakensberg, *S. Africa* 89 D4
Dráma, *Greece* 45 E8
Dráma □, *Greece* 45 E8
Drammen, *Norway* 9 G14
Drangajökull, *Iceland* 8 C2
Dranov, Ostrov, *Romania* 29 F14
Dras, *India* 69 B6
Drau = Drava →, *Croatia* 28 E3
Drava →, *Croatia* 28 E3
Dravograd, *Slovenia* 41 B12
Drawa →, *Poland* 31 F2
Drawieński △, *Poland* 31 E2
Drawno, *Poland* 31 E2
Drawsko Pomorskie, *Poland* 30 E2
Drayton Valley, *Canada* 102 C6
Dreieich, *Germany* 25 E4
Dren, *Serbia & M.* 44 C4
Drenthe □, *Neths.* 17 B6
Drepanum, C., *Cyprus* 49 E11
Dresden, *Canada* 116 D2
Dresden, *Germany* 24 D9
Dreux, *France* 18 D8
Drezdenko, *Poland* 31 F2
Driffield, *U.K.* 14 C7
Driftwood, *U.S.A.* 116 E6
Driggs, *U.S.A.* 108 E8
Drin →, *Albania* 44 D3
Drin i Zi →, *Albania* 44 E4
Drina →, *Bos.-H.* 44 B3
Drincea →, *Romania* 28 F7
Drinjača →, *Bos.-H.* 28 F4
Drissa = Vyerkhnyadzvinsk, *Belarus* 32 E4
Drniš, *Croatia* 41 E13
Drøbak, *Norway* 9 G14
Drobeta-Turnu Severin, *Romania* 28 F7
Drobin, *Poland* 31 F6
Drochia, *Moldova* 29 B12
Drogheda, *Ireland* 12 C5
Drogichin = Dragichyn, *Belarus* 33 F3
Drogobych = Drohobych, *Ukraine* 31 J10
Drohiczyn, *Poland* 31 F9
Drohobych, *Ukraine* 31 J10
Droichead Atha = Drogheda, *Ireland* 12 C5
Droichead Nua, *Ireland* 12 C5
Droitwich, *U.K.* 15 E5
Drôme □, *France* 21 D9
Drôme →, *France* 21 D8
Dromedary, C., *Australia* 95 F5
Drömling ⌓, *Germany* 24 C7
Dromore, *U.K.* 12 B4
Dromore West, *Ireland* 12 B3
Dronero, *Italy* 40 D4
Dronfield, *U.K.* 14 D6
Dronne →, *France* 20 C3
Dronning Maud Land, *Antarctica* 5 D3
Dronninglund, *Denmark* 11 G4
Dronten, *Neths.* 17 B5
Dropt →, *France* 20 D3
Drosendorf, *Austria* 26 C8
Droué, *France* 18 D8
Drumbo, *Canada* 116 C4
Drumheller, *Canada* 102 C6
Drummond, *U.S.A.* 108 C7
Drummond I., *U.S.A.* 114 C4
Drummond Pt., *Australia* 95 E2
Drummond Ra., *Australia* 94 C4
Drummondville, *Canada* 104 C5
Drumright, *U.S.A.* 113 H6
Druskininkai, *Lithuania* 9 J20
Drut →, *Belarus* 33 F6
Druya, *Belarus* 32 E4
Druzhba, *Bulgaria* 45 C12
Druzhina, *Russia* 53 C15
Drvar, *Bos.-H.* 41 D13
Drvenik, *Croatia* 41 E13
Drwęca →, *Poland* 31 E5
Dry Harbour Mts., *Jamaica* 120 a
Dry Tortugas, *U.S.A.* 120 B3
Dryanovo, *Bulgaria* 45 D9
Dryden, *Canada* 103 D10
Dryden, *U.S.A.* 117 D8
Drygalski I., *Antarctica* 5 C7
Drysdale →, *Australia* 92 B4
Drysdale I., *Australia* 94 A2
Drysdale River △, *Australia* 92 B4
Drzewica, *Poland* 31 G7
Drzewiczka →, *Poland* 31 G7
Dschang, *Cameroon* 83 D7
Du Bois, *U.S.A.* 116 E6
Du Gué →, *Canada* 104 A5
Du He, *China* 59 A8
Du Quoin, *U.S.A.* 112 G10
Du'an, *China* 58 F7
Duanesburg, *U.S.A.* 117 D10
Duaringa, *Australia* 94 C4
Duarte, Pico, *Dom. Rep.* 121 D5
Ḍubā, *Si. Arabia* 70 E2
Dubai = Dubayy, *U.A.E.* 71 E7
Dubăsari, *Moldova* 29 C14
Dubăsari Vdkhr., *Moldova* 29 C13
Dubawnt →, *Canada* 103 A8
Dubawnt L., *Canada* 103 A8
Dubayy, *U.A.E.* 71 E7
Dubbo, *Australia* 95 E4
Dubele, *Dem. Rep. of the Congo* 86 B2
Dübendorf, *Switz.* 25 H4
Dubica, *Croatia* 41 C13
Dublin, *Ireland* 12 C5
Dublin, *Ga., U.S.A.* 115 J4
Dublin, *Tex., U.S.A.* 113 J5
Dublin □, *Ireland* 12 C5
Dublin ✕ (DUB), *Ireland* 12 C5
Dubna, *Russia* 32 D9
Dubnica nad Váhom, *Slovak Rep.* 27 C11
Dubno, *Ukraine* 33 G3
Dubois, *U.S.A.* 108 D7
Dubossary = Dubăsari, *Moldova* 29 C14
Dubossary Vdkhr. = Dubăsari Vdkhr., *Moldova* 29 C13
Dubove, *Ukraine* 29 B8
Dubovka, *Russia* 35 F7
Dubovskoye, *Russia* 35 G6
Dubrajpur, *India* 69 H12
Dubréka, *Guinea* 82 D2
Dubrovitsa = Dubrovytsya, *Ukraine* 33 G4
Dubrovnik, *Croatia* 44 D2
Dubrovytsya, *Ukraine* 33 G4
Dubuque, *U.S.A.* 112 D9
Dubysa →, *Lithuania* 30 C10
Duchang, *China* 59 C11
Duchesne, *U.S.A.* 108 F8
Duchess, *Australia* 94 C2
Ducie I., *Pac. Oc.* 97 K15
Duck →, *U.S.A.* 115 G2
Duck Cr. →, *Australia* 92 D2
Duck Lake, *Canada* 103 C7
Duck Mountain ⌓, *Canada* 103 C8
Duckwall, Mt., *U.S.A.* 110 H6
Duderstadt, *Germany* 24 D6
Dudhi, *India* 67 G13
Dudinka, *Russia* 53 C9
Dudley, *U.K.* 15 E5
Dudwa, *India* 69 E9
Duékoué, *Ivory C.* 82 D3
Dueñas, *Spain* 36 D6
Duero = Douro →, *Europe* 36 D2
Dufftown, *U.K.* 13 D5
Dufourspitz, *Switz.* 25 K3
Dūghī Kalā, *Afghan.* 66 C3
Dugi Otok, *Croatia* 41 D11
Dugo Selo, *Croatia* 41 C13
Duifken Pt., *Australia* 94 A3
Duisburg, *Germany* 24 D2
Duiwelskloof, *S. Africa* 89 C5
Dujiangyan, *China* 58 B4
Duk Fadiat, *Sudan* 81 F3
Duk Faiwil, *Sudan* 81 F3
Dukat, *Albania* 44 F3
Dūkdamīn, *Iran* 71 C8
Dukelský Průsmyk, *Slovak Rep.* 27 B14
Dukhān, *Qatar* 71 E6
Dukhovshchina, *Russia* 32 E7
Duki, *Pakistan* 66 D6
Dukla, *Poland* 31 J8
Duku, *Bauchi, Nigeria* 83 C7
Duku, *Sokoto, Nigeria* 83 C5
Dulag, *Phil.* 61 F6
Dulce, *U.S.A.* 109 H10
Dulce →, *Argentina* 126 C3
Dulce, G., *Costa Rica* 120 E3
Dulf, *Iraq* 70 C5
Dŭlgopol, *Bulgaria* 45 C11
Dulit, Banjaran, *Malaysia* 62 D4
Duliu, *China* 56 E9
Dullewala, *Pakistan* 68 D4
Dullstroom, *S. Africa* 89 D5
Dülmen, *Germany* 24 D3
Dulovo, *Bulgaria* 45 C11
Dulq Maghār, *Syria* 70 B3
Duluth, *U.S.A.* 112 B8
Dum Dum, *India* 69 H13
Dum Duma, *India* 67 F19
Dūmā, *Syria* 74 B5
Dumaguete, *Phil.* 61 G5
Dumai, *Indonesia* 62 D2
Dumaran, *Phil.* 61 F3
Dumas, *Ark., U.S.A.* 113 J9
Dumas, *Tex., U.S.A.* 113 H4
Ḍumayr, *Syria* 74 B5
Dumbarton, *U.K.* 13 F4
Ďumbier, *Slovak Rep.* 27 C12
Dumbleyung, *Australia* 93 F2
Dumboa, *Nigeria* 83 C7
Dumbrăveni, *Romania* 29 D9
Dumfries, *U.K.* 13 F5
Dumfries & Galloway □, *U.K.* 13 F5
Dumitrești, *Romania* 29 E11
Dumka, *India* 69 G12
Dumlupınar, *Turkey* 47 C12
Dümmer, *Germany* 24 C4
Dümmer ⌓, *Germany* 24 C4
Dumoine →, *Canada* 104 C4
Dumoine, L., *Canada* 104 C4
Dumont d'Urville, *Antarctica* 5 C10
Dumraon, *India* 69 G11
Dumyât, *Egypt* 80 H7
Dumyât, Masabb, *Egypt* 80 H7
Dún Dealgan = Dundalk, *Ireland* 12 B5
Dún Laoghaire, *Ireland* 12 C5
Dun-le-Palestel, *France* 19 F8
Dun-sur-Auron, *France* 19 F9
Dun-sur-Meuse, *France* 19 C12
Duna = Dunărea →, *Europe* 29 E14
Duna →, *Hungary* 28 E3
Duna-Drava △, *Hungary* 28 D3
Duna-völgyi-főcsatorna, *Hungary* 28 D4
Dunaföldvár, *Hungary* 28 D3
Dunagiri, *India* 69 D8
Dunaj = Dunărea →, *Europe* 29 E14
Dunaj →, *Slovak Rep.* 27 D11
Dunajec →, *Poland* 31 H7
Dunajská Streda, *Slovak Rep.* 27 C10
Dunakeszi, *Hungary* 28 C4
Dunapataj, *Hungary* 28 D4
Dunărea →, *Europe* 29 E14
Dunaszekcső, *Hungary* 28 D3
Dunaújváros, *Hungary* 28 D3
Dunav = Dunărea →, *Europe* 29 E14
Dunavațu de Jos, *Romania* 29 F14
Dunavtsi, *Bulgaria* 44 C6
Dunay, *Russia* 54 C6
Dunayivtsi, *Ukraine* 29 B11
Dunback, *N.Z.* 91 L3
Dunbar, *U.K.* 13 E6
Dunblane, *U.K.* 13 E5
Duncan, *Canada* 102 D4
Duncan, *Ariz., U.S.A.* 109 K9
Duncan, *Okla., U.S.A.* 113 H6
Duncan, L., *Canada* 104 B4
Duncan L., *Canada* 102 A6
Duncan Town, *Bahamas* 120 B4
Duncannon, *U.S.A.* 116 F7
Duncansby Head, *U.K.* 13 C5
Duncansville, *U.S.A.* 116 F6
Dundaga, *Latvia* 30 A9
Dundalk, *Canada* 116 B4
Dundalk, *Ireland* 12 B5
Dundalk, *U.S.A.* 114 F7
Dundalk Bay, *Ireland* 12 C5
Dundas = Uummannaq, *Greenland* 4 B4
Dundas = Uummannaq, *Greenland* 4 B5
Dundas, *Canada* 116 C5
Dundas, L., *Australia* 93 F3
Dundas I., *Canada* 102 C2
Dundas Str., *Australia* 92 B5
Dundee, *S. Africa* 89 D5
Dundee, *U.K.* 13 E6
Dundee, *U.S.A.* 116 D8
Dundee City □, *U.K.* 13 E6
Dundgovĭ □, *Mongolia* 56 B4
Dundrum, *U.K.* 12 B6
Dundrum B., *U.K.* 12 B6
Dunedin, *N.Z.* 91 L3
Dunedin, *U.S.A.* 115 L4
Dunfermline, *U.K.* 13 E5
Dungannon, *Canada* 116 C3
Dungannon, *U.K.* 12 B5
Dungarpur, *India* 68 H5
Dungarvan, *Ireland* 12 D4
Dungarvan Harbour, *Ireland* 12 D4
Dungeness, *U.K.* 15 G8
Dungo, L. do, *Angola* 88 B2
Dungog, *Australia* 95 E5
Dungu, *Dem. Rep. of the Congo* 86 B2
Dungun, *Malaysia* 65 K4
Dungunâb, *Sudan* 80 C4
Dungunâb, Khalîg, *Sudan* 80 C4
Dunhua, *China* 57 C15
Dunhuang, *China* 60 B4
Dunk I., *Australia* 94 B4
Dunkassa, *Benin* 83 C5
Dunkeld, *Australia* 95 E4
Dunkeld, *U.K.* 13 E5
Dunkerque, *France* 19 A9
Dunkery Beacon, *U.K.* 15 F4
Dunkirk = Dunkerque, *France* 19 A9
Dunkirk, *U.S.A.* 116 D5
Dunkuj, *Sudan* 81 E3
Dunkwa, *Central, Ghana* 82 D4
Dunkwa, *Central, Ghana* 83 D4
Dúnleary = Dún Laoghaire, *Ireland* 12 C5
Dunleer, *Ireland* 12 C5
Dunmanus B., *Ireland* 12 E2
Dunmanway, *Ireland* 12 E2
Dunmara, *Australia* 94 B1
Dunmore, *U.S.A.* 117 E9
Dunmore Hd., *Ireland* 12 D1
Dunmore Town, *Bahamas* 120 A4
Dunn, *U.S.A.* 115 H6
Dunnellon, *U.S.A.* 115 L4
Dunnet Hd., *U.K.* 13 C5
Dunning, *U.S.A.* 112 E4
Dunnville, *Canada* 116 D5
Dunolly, *Australia* 95 F3
Dunoon, *U.K.* 13 F4
Dunphy, *U.S.A.* 108 F5
Dunqul, *Egypt* 80 C3
Duns, *U.K.* 13 F6
Dunseith, *U.S.A.* 112 A4
Dunsmuir, *U.S.A.* 108 F2
Dunstable, *U.K.* 15 F7
Dunstan Mts., *N.Z.* 91 L2
Dunster, *Canada* 102 C5
Dunvegan, *U.K.* 13 D2
Dunvegan L., *Canada* 103 A7
Duolun, *China* 56 C9
Duong Dong, *Vietnam* 65 G4
Dupree, *U.S.A.* 112 C4
Dupuyer, *U.S.A.* 108 B7
Duque de Caxias, *Brazil* 127 A7
Durack →, *Australia* 92 C4
Durack Ra., *Australia* 92 C4
Durağan, *Turkey* 72 B6
Durak, *Turkey* 47 B10
Đurakovac, *Serbia & M.* 44 D4
Durance →, *France* 21 E8
Durand, *U.S.A.* 112 C9
Durango, *Mexico* 118 C4
Durango, *U.S.A.* 109 H10
Durango □, *Mexico* 118 C4
Durankulak, *Bulgaria* 45 C12
Durant, *Miss., U.S.A.* 113 J10
Durant, *Okla., U.S.A.* 113 J6
Duratón →, *Spain* 36 D6
Durazno, *Uruguay* 126 C4
Durazzo = Durrës, *Albania* 44 E3
Durban, *France* 20 F6
Durban, *S. Africa* 89 D5
Durbuy, *Belgium* 17 D5
Dúrcal, *Spain* 37 J7
Đurđevac, *Croatia* 28 D2
Düren, *Germany* 24 E2
Durg, *India* 67 J12
Durgapur, *India* 69 H12
Durham, *Canada* 116 B4
Durham, *U.K.* 14 C6
Durham, *Calif., U.S.A.* 110 F5
Durham, *N.C., U.S.A.* 115 H6
Durham, *N.H., U.S.A.* 117 C14
Durham □, *U.K.* 14 C6
Durlești, *Moldova* 29 C13
Ḍurmā, *Si. Arabia* 70 E5
Durmitor, *Serbia & M.* 44 C2
Durmitor △, *Serbia & M.* 44 C3
Durness, *U.K.* 13 C4
Durrës, *Albania* 44 E3
Durrow, *Ireland* 12 D4
Dursey I., *Ireland* 12 E1
Dursley, *U.K.* 15 F5
Dursunbey, *Turkey* 47 B10
Durtal, *France* 18 E6
Duru, *Dem. Rep. of the Congo* 86 B2
Duru Gölü, *Turkey* 45 E12
Durusu, *Turkey* 45 E12
Durūz, Jabal ad, *Jordan* 74 C5
D'Urville, Tanjung, *Indonesia* 63 E9
D'Urville I., *N.Z.* 91 J4
Duryea, *U.S.A.* 117 E9
Dûsh, *Egypt* 80 C3
Dushak, *Turkmenistan* 52 F7
Dushan, *China* 58 E6
Dushanbe, *Tajikistan* 52 F7
Dusheti, *Georgia* 35 J7
Dushore, *U.S.A.* 117 E8
Dusky Sd., *N.Z.* 91 L1
Dussejour, C., *Australia* 92 B4
Düsseldorf, *Germany* 24 D2
Düsseldorf Rhein-Ruhr ✕ (DUS), *Germany* 24 D2
Duszniki-Zdrój, *Poland* 31 H3
Dutch Harbor, *U.S.A.* 100 C3
Dutlwe, *Botswana* 88 C3
Dutsan Wai, *Nigeria* 83 C6
Dutton, *Canada* 116 D3
Dutton →, *Australia* 94 C3
Duved, *Sweden* 10 A6
Düvertepe, *Turkey* 47 B10
Duwayhin, Khawr, *U.A.E.* 71 E6
Duyun, *China* 58 D6
Düzağac, *Turkey* 47 C12
Düzce, *Turkey* 72 B4
Dve Mogili, *Bulgaria* 45 C9
Dvina, Severnaya →, *Russia* 52 C5
Dvinsk = Daugavpils, *Latvia* 9 J22
Dvor, *Croatia* 41 C13
Dvůr Králové nad Labem, *Czech Rep.* 26 A8
Dwarka, *India* 68 H3
Dwellingup, *Australia* 93 F2
Dwight, *Canada* 116 A5
Dwight, *U.S.A.* 114 E1
Dyakove, *Ukraine* 28 B7
Dyatkovo, *Russia* 32 F8
Dyatlovo = Dzyatlava, *Belarus* 32 F3
Dyce, *U.K.* 13 D6
Dyer, C., *Canada* 101 B13
Dyer Bay, *Canada* 116 A3
Dyer Plateau, *Antarctica* 5 D17
Dyersburg, *U.S.A.* 113 G10
Dyfi →, *U.K.* 15 E3
Dyje →, *Czech Rep.* 27 C9
Dymer, *Ukraine* 33 G6
Dynów, *Poland* 31 J9
Dysart, *Australia* 94 C4
Dyviziya 29 E14
Dzerzhinsk, *Russia* 34 B6
Dzhalinda, *Russia* 53 D13
Dzhambul = Taraz, *Kazakhstan* 52 E8
Dzhankoy, *Ukraine* 33 K8
Dzhanybek, *Kazakhstan* 34 F8
Dzharylhach, Ostriv, *Ukraine* 33 J7
Dzhezkazgan = Zhezqazghan, *Kazakhstan* 52 E7
Dzhizak = Jizzakh, *Uzbekistan* 52 E7
Dzhugdzur, Khrebet, *Russia* 53 D14
Dzhulynk, *Ukraine* 29 B14
Dzhuryn, *Ukraine* 29 B13
Dzhvari = Jvari, *Georgia* 35 J6
Działdowo, *Poland* 31 E7
Działoszyce, *Poland* 31 H7
Działoszyn, *Poland* 31 G5
Dzibilchaltún, *Mexico* 119 C7
Dzibilchaltun, *Yucatán, Mexico* 119 C7
Dzierzgoń, *Poland* 30 E6
Dzierżoniów, *Poland* 31 H3
Dzilam de Bravo, *Mexico* 119 C7
Dzisna, *Belarus* 32 E5
Dzisna →, *Belarus* 32 E5
Dziwnów, *Poland* 30 D1
Dzungaria = Junggar Pendi, *China* 60 B3
Dzungarian Basin = Junggar Pendi, *China* 60 B3
Dzuumod, *Mongolia* 60 B5
Dzyarzhynsk, *Belarus* 32 F4
Dzyatlava, *Belarus* 32 F3

E

E.C. Manning ⌓, *Canada* 102 D4
Eabamet L., *Canada* 104 B2
Eads, *U.S.A.* 112 F3
Eagar, *U.S.A.* 109 J9
Eagle, *Alaska, U.S.A.* 100 B5
Eagle, *Colo., U.S.A.* 108 G10
Eagle →, *Canada* 105 B8
Eagle Butte, *U.S.A.* 112 C4
Eagle Grove, *U.S.A.* 112 D8
Eagle L., *Canada* 103 D10
Eagle L., *Calif., U.S.A.* 108 F3
Eagle L., *Maine, U.S.A.* 115 B11
Eagle Lake, *Canada* 116 A6
Eagle Lake, *Maine, U.S.A.* 115 B11
Eagle Lake, *Tex., U.S.A.* 113 L6
Eagle Mountain, *U.S.A.* 111 M11
Eagle Nest, *U.S.A.* 109 H11
Eagle Pass, *U.S.A.* 113 L4
Eagle Pk., *U.S.A.* 110 G7
Eagle Pt., *Australia* 92 C3
Eagle River, *Mich., U.S.A.* 114 B1
Eagle River, *Wis., U.S.A.* 112 C10
Eaglehawk, *Australia* 95 F3
Eagles Mere, *U.S.A.* 117 E8
Ealing □, *U.K.* 15 F7
Ear Falls, *Canada* 103 C10
Earle, *U.S.A.* 113 H9
Earlimart, *U.S.A.* 111 K7
Earn →, *U.K.* 13 E5
Earn, L., *U.K.* 13 E4
Earnslaw, Mt., *N.Z.* 91 L2
Earth, *U.S.A.* 113 H3
Easley, *U.S.A.* 115 H4
East Anglia, *U.K.* 14 E9
East Angus, *Canada* 105 C5
East Antarctica, *Antarctica* 5 D7
East Aurora, *U.S.A.* 116 D6
East Ayrshire □, *U.K.* 13 F4
East Bengal, *Bangla.* 67 H17
East Beskids = Vychodné Beskydy, *Europe* 27 B15
East Brady, *U.S.A.* 116 F5
East C., *N.Z.* 91 G7
East Chicago, *U.S.A.* 114 E2
East China Sea, *Asia* 60 C7
East Coulee, *Canada* 102 C6
East Dereham = Dereham, *U.K.* 15 E8
East Dunbartonshire □, *U.K.* 13 F4
East Falkland, *Falk. Is.* 128 G5
East Grand Forks, *U.S.A.* 112 B6
East Greenwich, *U.S.A.* 117 E13
East Grinstead, *U.K.* 15 F8
East Hartford, *U.S.A.* 117 E12
East Helena, *U.S.A.* 108 C8
East Indies, *Asia* 50 K15
East Kilbride, *U.K.* 13 F4
East Lansing, *U.S.A.* 114 D3
East Liverpool, *U.S.A.* 116 F4
East London, *S. Africa* 89 E4
East Lothian □, *U.K.* 13 F6
East Main = Eastmain, *Canada* 104 B4
East Northport, *U.S.A.* 117 F11
East Orange, *U.S.A.* 117 F10
East Pacific Ridge, *Pac. Oc.* 97 J17
East Palestine, *U.S.A.* 116 F4
East Pine, *Canada* 102 B4
East Point, *U.S.A.* 115 J3
East Providence, *U.S.A.* 117 E13
East Pt., *Br. Virgin Is.* 121 e
East Pt., *Canada* 105 C7
East Renfrewshire □, *U.K.* 13 F4
East Retford = Retford, *U.K.* 14 D7
East Riding of Yorkshire □, *U.K.* 14 D7
East Rochester, *U.S.A.* 116 C7
East St. Louis, *U.S.A.* 112 F9
East Schelde = Oosterschelde →, *Neths.* 17 C4
East Sea = Japan, Sea of, *Asia* 54 E7
East Siberian Sea, *Russia* 53 B17

East Stroudsburg, *U.S.A.* 117 E9
East Sussex □, *U.K.* 15 G8
East Tawas, *U.S.A.* 114 C4
East Timor ■, *Asia* 63 F7
East Toorale, *Australia* 95 E4
East Walker →, *U.S.A.* 110 G7
East Windsor, *U.S.A.* 117 F10
Eastbourne, *N.Z.* 91 J5
Eastbourne, *U.K.* 15 G8
Eastend, *Canada* 103 D7
Easter I. = Pascua, I. de, *Chile* 97 K17
Eastern □, *Ghana* 83 D4
Eastern □, *Kenya* 86 C4
Eastern □, *S. Leone* 82 D2
Eastern Cape □, *S. Africa* 88 E4
Eastern Cr. →, *Australia* 94 C3
Eastern Ghats, *India* 66 N11
Eastern Group = Lau Group, *Fiji* 91 C9
Eastern Group, *Australia* 93 F3
Eastern Transvaal = Mpumalanga □, *S. Africa* 89 D5
Easterville, *Canada* 103 C9
Easthampton, *U.S.A.* 117 D12
Eastlake, *U.S.A.* 116 E3
Eastland, *U.S.A.* 113 J5
Eastleigh, *U.K.* 15 G6
Eastmain, *Canada* 104 B4
Eastmain →, *Canada* 104 B4
Eastman, *Canada* 117 A12
Eastman, *U.S.A.* 115 J4
Easton, *Md., U.S.A.* 114 F7
Easton, *Pa., U.S.A.* 117 F9
Easton, *Wash., U.S.A.* 110 C5
Eastpointe, *U.S.A.* 116 D2
Eastport, *U.S.A.* 115 C12
Eastsound, *U.S.A.* 110 B4
Eaton, *U.S.A.* 112 E2
Eatonia, *Canada* 103 C7
Eatonton, *U.S.A.* 115 J4
Eatontown, *U.S.A.* 117 F10
Eatonville, *U.S.A.* 110 D4
Eau Claire, *U.S.A.* 112 C9
Eau Claire, L. à l', *Canada* 104 A5
Eauze, *France* 20 E4
Eban, *Nigeria* 83 D5
Ebbegebirge ⌓, *Germany* 24 D3
Ebbw Vale, *U.K.* 15 F4
Ebeltoft, *Denmark* 11 H4
Ebeltoft Vig, *Denmark* 11 H4
Ebensburg, *U.S.A.* 116 F6
Ebensee, *Austria* 26 D6
Eber Gölü, *Turkey* 72 C4
Eberbach, *Germany* 25 F4
Eberswalde-Finow, *Germany* 24 C9
Ebetsu, *Japan* 54 C10
Ebey's Landing ⌓, *U.S.A.* 110 B4
Ebian, *China* 58 C4
Ebingen, *Germany* 25 G5
Éboli, *Italy* 43 B8
Ebolowa, *Cameroon* 83 E7
Ebonyi □, *Nigeria* 83 D6
Ebrach, *Germany* 25 F6
Ébrié, Lagune, *Ivory C.* 82 D4
Ebro →, *Spain* 38 E5
Ebro, Embalse del, *Spain* 36 C7
Ebstorf, *Germany* 24 B6
Eceabat, *Turkey* 45 F10
Ech Chéliff, *Algeria* 78 A6
Echigo-Sammyaku, *Japan* 55 F9
Échirolles, *France* 21 C9
Echizen-Misaki, *Japan* 55 G7
Echmiadzin = Yejmiadzin, *Armenia* 35 K7
Echo Bay, *N.W.T., Canada* 100 B8
Echo Bay, *Ont., Canada* 104 C3
Echoing →, *Canada* 104 B1
Echterdingen, Stuttgart ✕ (STR), *Germany* 25 G5
Echternach, *Lux.* 17 E6
Echuca, *Australia* 95 F3
Ecija, *Spain* 37 H5
Eckental, *Germany* 25 F7
Eckernförde, *Germany* 24 A5
Eclipse I., *Australia* 93 G2
Eclipse Is., *Australia* 92 B4
Eclipse Sd., *Canada* 101 A11
Écommoy, *France* 18 E7
Écouché, *France* 18 D6
Ecrins △, *France* 21 D10
Ecuador ■, *S. Amer.* 124 D3
Écueillé, *France* 18 E8
Ed, *Sweden* 11 F5
Ed Dabbura, *Sudan* 80 D3
Ed Da'ein, *Sudan* 81 E2
Ed Damazin, *Sudan* 79 F12
Ed Dâmer, *Sudan* 80 D3
Ed Dar el Beida = Casablanca, *Morocco* 78 B4
Ed Debba, *Sudan* 80 D3
Ed-Déffa, *Egypt* 80 A2
Ed Deim, *Sudan* 81 E2
Ed Dueim, *Sudan* 81 E3
Edam, *Canada* 103 C7
Edam, *Neths.* 17 B5
Edane, *Sweden* 10 E6
Eday, *U.K.* 13 B6
Edd, *Eritrea* 81 E5
Eddrachillis B., *U.K.* 13 C3
Eddystone, *U.K.* 15 G3
Eddystone Pt., *Australia* 95 G4
Ede, *Neths.* 17 B5
Ede, *Nigeria* 83 D5
Édéa, *Cameroon* 83 E7
Edebäck, *Sweden* 10 D7
Edehon L., *Canada* 103 A9
Edelény, *Hungary* 28 B5
Eden, *Australia* 95 F4
Eden, *N.C., U.S.A.* 115 G6
Eden, *N.Y., U.S.A.* 116 D6
Eden, *Tex., U.S.A.* 113 K5
Eden →, *U.K.* 14 C4
Edenburg, *S. Africa* 88 D4
Edendale, *S. Africa* 89 D5
Edenderry, *Ireland* 12 C4
Edenton, *U.S.A.* 115 G7
Edenville, *S. Africa* 89 D4
Eder →, *Germany* 24 D5
Eder-Stausee, *Germany* 24 D4
Edewecht, *Germany* 24 B3
Edgar, *U.S.A.* 112 E6
Edgartown, *U.S.A.* 117 E14
Edge Hill, *U.K.* 15 E6
Edgefield, *U.S.A.* 115 J5
Edgeley, *U.S.A.* 112 B5
Edgemont, *U.S.A.* 112 D3
Edgeøya, *Svalbard* 4 B9
Édhessa, *Greece* 44 F6
Edievale, *N.Z.* 91 L2
Edina, *Liberia* 82 D2
Edina, *U.S.A.* 112 E8
Edinboro, *U.S.A.* 116 E4
Edinburg, *U.S.A.* 113 M5
Edinburgh, *U.K.* 13 F5
Edinburgh ✕ (EDI), *U.K.* 13 F5
Edinburgh, City of □, *U.K.* 13 F5
Edineţ, *Moldova* 29 B12
Edirne, *Turkey* 45 E10
Edirne □, *Turkey* 45 E10
Edison, *U.S.A.* 110 B4
Edithburgh, *Australia* 95 F2
Edmeston, *U.S.A.* 117 D9
Edmond, *U.S.A.* 113 H6
Edmonds, *U.S.A.* 110 C4
Edmonton, *Australia* 94 B4
Edmonton, *Canada* 102 C6
Edmund L., *Canada* 104 B1
Edmundston, *Canada* 105 C6
Edna, *U.S.A.* 113 L6
Edo □, *Nigeria* 83 D6
Edolo, *Italy* 40 B7
Edremit, *Turkey* 47 B9
Edremit Körfezi, *Turkey* 47 B8
Edsbro, *Sweden* 10 E12
Edsbyn, *Sweden* 10 C9
Edson, *Canada* 102 C5
Eduardo Castex, *Argentina* 126 D3
Edward →, *Australia* 95 F3
Edward, L., *Africa* 86 C2
Edward River, *Australia* 94 A3
Edward VII Land, *Antarctica* 5 E13
Edwards, *Calif., U.S.A.* 111 L9
Edwards, *N.Y., U.S.A.* 117 B9
Edwards Air Force Base, *U.S.A.* 111 L9
Edwards Plateau, *U.S.A.* 113 K4
Edwardsville, *U.S.A.* 117 E9
Edzná, *Mexico* 119 D6
Edzo, *Canada* 102 A5
Eeklo, *Belgium* 17 C3
Eferding, *Austria* 26 C7
Effigy Mounds ⌓, *U.S.A.* 112 D9
Effingham, *U.S.A.* 114 F1
Eforie, *Romania* 29 F13
Ega →, *Spain* 38 C3
Égadi, Ísole, *Italy* 42 E5
Egan Range, *U.S.A.* 108 G6
Eganville, *Canada* 116 A7
Eger = Cheb, *Czech Rep.* 26 A5
Eger, *Hungary* 28 C5
Eger →, *Hungary* 28 C5
Egersund, *Norway* 9 G12
Egg L., *Canada* 103 B7
Eggegebirge Südlicher Teutoburger Wald ⌓, *Germany* 24 D4
Eggenburg, *Austria* 26 C8
Eggenfelden, *Germany* 25 G8
Éghezée, *Belgium* 17 D4
Égletons, *France* 20 C6
Egmont, *Canada* 102 D4
Egmont △, *N.Z.* 91 H5
Egmont, C., *N.Z.* 91 H4
Egmont, Mt. = Taranaki, Mt., *N.Z.* 91 H5
Egra, *India* 69 J12
Eğridir, *Turkey* 72 D4
Eğridir Gölü, *Turkey* 70 B1
Egtved, *Denmark* 11 J3
Egume, *Nigeria* 83 D6
Éguzon-Chantôme, *France* 19 F8
Egvekinot, *Russia* 53 C19
Egyek, *Hungary* 28 C5
Egypt ■, *Africa* 80 B3
Eha Amufu, *Nigeria* 83 D6
Ehime □, *Japan* 55 H6
Ehingen, *Germany* 25 G5
Ehrenberg, *U.S.A.* 111 M12
Ehrwald, *Austria* 26 D3
Eibar, *Spain* 38 B2
Eichstätt, *Germany* 25 G7
Eider →, *Germany* 24 A4
Eidsvold, *Australia* 95 D5
Eidsvoll, *Norway* 9 F14
Eifel, *Germany* 25 E2
Eiffel Flats, *Zimbabwe* 87 F3
Eiger, *Switz.* 40 B5
Eigg, *U.K.* 13 E2
Eighty Mile Beach, *Australia* 92 C3
Eil, *Somali Rep.* 75 F4
Eil, L., *U.K.* 13 E3
Eildon, L., *Australia* 95 F4
Eilenburg, *Germany* 24 D8
Ein el Luweiqa, *Sudan* 81 E3
Einasleigh, *Australia* 94 B3
Einasleigh →, *Australia* 94 B3
Einbeck, *Germany* 24 D5
Eindhoven, *Neths.* 17 C5
Einsiedeln, *Switz.* 25 H4
Eire = Ireland ■, *Europe* 12 C4
Eiríksjökull, *Iceland* 8 D3
Eirunepé, *Brazil* 124 E5
Eiseb →, *Namibia* 88 C2
Eisenach, *Germany* 24 E6
Eisenberg, *Germany* 24 E7
Eisenerz, *Austria* 26 D7
Eisenhüttenstadt, *Germany* 24 C10
Eisenkappel, *Austria* 26 E7
Eisenstadt, *Austria* 27 D9
Eisfeld, *Germany* 25 E6
Eisleben, *Germany* 24 D7
Eislingen, *Germany* 25 G5
Eivissa, *Spain* 48 C7
Eixe, Serra do, *Spain* 36 C4
Ejea de los Caballeros, *Spain* 38 C3
Ejeda, *Madag.* 89 C7
Ejura, *Ghana* 83 D4
Ejutla, *Mexico* 119 D5
Ekalaka, *U.S.A.* 112 C2
Ekenäs = Tammisaari, *Finland* 9 F20
Ekenässjön, *Sweden* 11 G9
Ekerö, *Sweden* 10 E11
Eket, *Nigeria* 83 E6
Eketahuna, *N.Z.* 91 J5
Ekhínos, *Greece* 45 E9
Ekibastuz, *Kazakhstan* 52 D8
Ekiti □, *Nigeria* 83 D6
Ekoli, *Dem. Rep. of the Congo* 86 C1
Ekoln, *Sweden* 10 E11
Ekshärad, *Sweden* 10 D7
Eksjö, *Sweden* 11 G8
Ekuma →, *Namibia* 88 B2
Ekwan →, *Canada* 104 B3
Ekwan Pt., *Canada* 104 B3
El Aaiún, *W. Sahara* 78 C3
El Abanico, *Chile* 126 D1
El Abbasiya, *Sudan* 81 E3
El 'Agrûd, *Egypt* 74 E3
El Ait, *Sudan* 81 E2
El 'Aiyat, *Egypt* 80 J7
El 'Alamein, *Egypt* 80 A2
El 'Aqaba, W. →, *Egypt* 74 E2
El 'Arag, *Egypt* 80 B2
El Arahal, *Spain* 37 H5
El Arīḥā, *West Bank* 74 D4
El 'Arîsh, *Egypt* 74 D2
El 'Arîsh, W. →, *Egypt* 74 D2
El Asnam = Ech Chéliff, *Algeria* 78 A6
El Astillero, *Spain* 36 B7
El Badâri, *Egypt* 80 B3
El Bahrein, *Egypt* 80 B2
El Ballâs, *Egypt* 80 B3
El Balyana, *Egypt* 80 B3
El Baqeir, *Sudan* 80 D3
El Barco de Ávila, *Spain* 36 E5
El Barco de Valdeorras = O Barco, *Spain* 36 C4
El Bauga, *Sudan* 80 D3
El Bawiti, *Egypt* 80 B2
El Bayadh, *Algeria* 78 B6
El Bierzo, *Spain* 36 C4
El Bluff, *Nic.* 120 D3
El Bonillo, *Spain* 39 G2
El Brûk, W. →, *Egypt* 74 E2
El Buheirat □, *Sudan* 81 F3
El Burgo de Osma, *Spain* 38 D1
El Cajon, *U.S.A.* 111 N10
El Campo, *U.S.A.* 113 L6
El Centro, *U.S.A.* 111 N11
El Cerro, *Bolivia* 124 G6
El Cerro de Andévalo, *Spain* 37 H4
El Compadre, *Mexico* 111 N10
El Coronil, *Spain* 37 H5
El Cuy, *Argentina* 128 D3
El Cuyo, *Mexico* 119 C7
El Dab'a, *Egypt* 80 H6
El Daheir, *Egypt* 74 D3
El Dátil, *Mexico* 118 B2
El Deir, *Egypt* 80 B3
El Dere, *Somali Rep.* 75 G4
El Descanso, *Mexico* 111 N10
El Desemboque, *Mexico* 118 A2
El Dilingat, *Egypt* 80 H7
El Diviso, *Colombia* 124 C3
El Djouf, *Mauritania* 78 D4
El Dorado, *Ark., U.S.A.* 113 J8
El Dorado, *Kans., U.S.A.* 113 G6
El Dorado, *Venezuela* 124 B6
El 'Ein, *Sudan* 81 D2
El Ejido, *Spain* 37 J8
El Escorial, *Spain* 36 E6
El Espinar, *Spain* 36 D6
El Faiyûm, *Egypt* 80 J7
El Fâsher, *Sudan* 81 E2
El Fashn, *Egypt* 80 J7
El Ferrol = Ferrol, *Spain* 36 B2
El Fifi, *Sudan* 81 E2
El Fuerte, *Mexico* 118 B3
El Ga'a, *Sudan* 81 E2
El Gal, *Somali Rep.* 75 E5
El Garef, *Sudan* 81 E3
El Gebir, *Sudan* 81 E2
El Gedida, *Egypt* 80 B2
El Geneina = Al Junaynah, *Sudan* 79 F10
El Geteina, *Sudan* 81 E3
El Gezira □, *Sudan* 81 E3
El Gir, *Sudan* 80 D2
El Gîza, *Egypt* 80 J7
El Gogorron △, *Mexico* 118 C4
El Goléa, *Algeria* 78 B6
El Grau, *Spain* 39 G4
El Guácharo △, *Venezuela* 121 D7
El Guache △, *Venezuela* 121 E6
El Hagiz, *Sudan* 81 D4
El Hâi, *Egypt* 80 J7
El Hammam, *Egypt* 80 A2
El Hawata, *Sudan* 81 E3
El Heiz, *Egypt* 80 B2
El Hideib, *Sudan* 81 E3
El Hilla, *Sudan* 81 E2
El 'Idisât, *Egypt* 80 B3
El Iskandarîya, *Egypt* 80 H7
El Istiwa'iya, *Sudan* 79 G11
El Jadida, *Morocco* 78 B4
El Jardal, *Honduras* 120 D2
El Jebelein, *Sudan* 81 E3
El Kab, *Sudan* 80 D3
El Kabrît, G., *Egypt* 74 F2
El Kafr el Sharqi, *Egypt* 80 H7
El Kamlin, *Sudan* 81 D3
El Karaba, *Sudan* 80 D3
El Kere, *Ethiopia* 81 F5
El Khandaq, *Sudan* 80 D3
El Khârga, *Egypt* 80 B3
El Khartûm, *Sudan* 81 D3
El Khartûm □, *Sudan* 81 D3
El Khartûm Bahrî, *Sudan* 81 D3
El Kuntilla, *Egypt* 74 E3
El Laqâwa, *Sudan* 81 E2
El Leh, *Ethiopia* 81 G4
El Leiya, *Sudan* 81 D4
El Maestrazgo, *Spain* 38 E4
El Mafâza, *Sudan* 81 E3
El Maghra, *Egypt* 80 A2
El Mahalla el Kubra, *Egypt* 80 H7
El Mahârîq, *Egypt* 80 B3
El Maîmûn, *Egypt* 80 J7
El Maks el Bahari, *Egypt* 80 C3
El Malpais ⌓, *U.S.A.* 109 J10
El Manshâh, *Egypt* 80 B3
El Mansûra, *Egypt* 80 H7
El Manzala, *Egypt* 80 H7
El Marâgha, *Egypt* 80 B3
El Masid, *Sudan* 81 D3
El Masnou, *Spain* 38 D7
El Matariya, *Egypt* 80 H8
El Meda, *Ethiopia* 81 F5
El Medano, *Canary Is.* 48 F3
El Metemma, *Sudan* 81 D3
El Milagro, *Argentina* 126 C2
El Minyâ, *Egypt* 80 B3
El Monte, *U.S.A.* 111 L8
El Montseny, *Spain* 38 D7
El Mreyye, *Mauritania* 82 B3
El Niybo, *Ethiopia* 81 G4
El Obeid, *Sudan* 81 E3
El Odaiya, *Sudan* 81 E2
El Oro, *Mexico* 119 D4
El Oued, *Algeria* 78 B7
El Palmar △, *Argentina* 126 C4
El Palmito, Presa, *Mexico* 118 B3
El Paso, *U.S.A.* 109 L10
El Paso Robles, *U.S.A.* 110 K6
El Pedernoso, *Spain* 39 F2
El Pedroso, *Spain* 37 H5
El Pinacate y Gran Desierto de Altar = Gran Desierto del Pinacate ⌓, *Mexico* 118 A2
El Pobo de Dueñas, *Spain* 38 E3
El Portal, *U.S.A.* 110 H7
El Porvenir, *Mexico* 118 A3
El Prat de Llobregat, *Spain* 38 D7
El Progreso, *Honduras* 120 C2
El Pueblito, *Mexico* 118 B3
El Pueblo, *Canary Is.* 48 F2
El Puente del Arzobispo, *Spain* 36 F5
El Puerto de Santa María, *Spain* 37 J4
El Qâhira, *Egypt* 80 H7
El Qantara, *Egypt* 74 E1
El Qasr, *Egypt* 80 B2
El Qubâbât, *Egypt* 80 J7
El Quseima, *Egypt* 74 E3
El Qusîya, *Egypt* 80 B3
El Râshda, *Egypt* 80 B2
El Real, *Panama* 124 B3
El Reno, *U.S.A.* 113 H6
El Rey △, *Argentina* 126 A3
El Rîdisiya, *Egypt* 80 C3
El Rio, *U.S.A.* 111 L7
El Ronquillo, *Spain* 37 H4
El Roque, Pta., *Canary Is.* 48 F4
El Rosarito, *Mexico* 118 B2
El Rubio, *Spain* 37 H5
El Saff, *Egypt* 80 J7
El Saheira, W. →, *Egypt* 74 E2
El Salto, *Mexico* 118 C3
El Salvador ■, *Cent. Amer.* 120 D2
El Sauce, *Nic.* 120 D2
El Saucejo, *Spain* 37 H5
El Shallal, *Egypt* 80 C3
El Simbillawein, *Egypt* 80 H7
El Sueco, *Mexico* 118 B3
El Suweis, *Egypt* 80 J8
El Tabbîn, *Egypt* 80 J7
El Tamarâni, W. →, *Egypt* 74 E3
El Thamad, *Egypt* 74 F3
El Tigre, *Venezuela* 124 B6
El Tîh, Gebal, *Egypt* 74 F2
El Tîna, *Egypt* 80 H8
El Tîna, Khalîg, *Egypt* 74 D1
El Tofo, *Chile* 126 B1
El Tránsito, *Chile* 126 B1
El Tûr, *Egypt* 70 D2
El Turbio, *Argentina* 128 G2
El Uqsur, *Egypt* 80 B3
El Valle ⌓, *Spain* 39 H3
El Venado, *Mexico* 118 C4
El Vendrell, *Spain* 38 D6
El Vergel, *Mexico* 118 B3
El Vigía, *Venezuela* 124 B4
El Viso del Alcor, *Spain* 37 H5
El Wabeira, *Egypt* 74 F2
El Wak, *Kenya* 86 B5
El Waqf, *Egypt* 80 B3
El Weguet, *Ethiopia* 81 F5
El Wuz, *Sudan* 81 D3
Elafónisos, *Greece* 46 E4
Élancourt, *France* 19 D8
Élassa, *Greece* 47 F8
Elassón, *Greece* 46 B4
Elat, *Israel* 74 F3
Eláthia, *Greece* 46 C4
Elâzığ, *Turkey* 70 B3
Elba, *Italy* 40 F7
Elba, *U.S.A.* 115 K2
Elbasan, *Albania* 44 E4
Elbe, *U.S.A.* 110 D4
Elbe →, *Europe* 24 B4
Elbe-Seitenkanal, *Germany* 24 C6
Elbert, Mt., *U.S.A.* 109 G10
Elberton, *U.S.A.* 115 H4
Elbeuf, *France* 18 C8
Elbidtan, *Turkey* 70 B3
Elbing = Elbląg, *Poland* 30 D6
Elbistan, *Turkey* 72 C7
Elbląg, *Poland* 30 D6
Elbow, *Canada* 103 C7
Elbrus, *Asia* 35 J6
Elbufer-Drawehn ⌓, *Germany* 24 B6
Elburz Mts. = Alborz, Reshteh-ye Kūhhā-ye, *Iran* 71 C7
Elche, *Spain* 39 G4
Elche de la Sierra, *Spain* 39 G2
Elcho I., *Australia* 94 A2
Elda, *Spain* 39 G4
Elde →, *Germany* 24 B7
Eldon, *Mo., U.S.A.* 112 F8
Eldon, *Wash., U.S.A.* 110 C3
Eldora, *U.S.A.* 112 D8
Eldorado, *Argentina* 127 B5
Eldorado, *Canada* 116 B7
Eldorado, *Mexico* 118 C3
Eldorado, *Ill., U.S.A.* 114 G1
Eldorado, *Tex., U.S.A.* 113 K4
Eldorado Springs, *U.S.A.* 113 G8
Eldoret, *Kenya* 86 B4
Eldred, *U.S.A.* 116 E6
Elea, C., *Cyprus* 49 D13
Eleanora, Pk., *Australia* 93 F3
Elefantes →, *Africa* 89 C5
Elektrogorsk, *Russia* 32 E10
Elektrostal, *Russia* 32 E10
Elele, *Nigeria* 83 D6
Elena, *Bulgaria* 45 D9
Elephant Butte Reservoir, *U.S.A.* 109 K10
Elephant I., *Antarctica* 5 C18
Eleshnitsa, *Bulgaria* 44 E7
Eleşkirt, *Turkey* 73 C10
Eleuthera, *Bahamas* 120 B4
Elevsís, *Greece* 46 C5
Elevtheroúpolis, *Greece* 45 F8
Elgin, *Canada* 117 B8
Elgin, *U.K.* 13 D5
Elgin, *Ill., U.S.A.* 114 D1
Elgin, *N. Dak., U.S.A.* 112 B4
Elgin, *Oreg., U.S.A.* 108 D5
Elgin, *Tex., U.S.A.* 113 K6
Elgoibar, *Spain* 38 B2
Elgon, Mt., *Africa* 86 B3
Eliase, *Indonesia* 63 F8
Elikón, *Greece* 46 C4
Elim, *Namibia* 88 B2
Elim, *S. Africa* 88 E2
Elin Pelin, *Bulgaria* 44 D7
Elista, *Russia* 35 G7
Elizabeth, *Australia* 95 E2
Elizabeth, *U.S.A.* 117 F10
Elizabeth City, *U.S.A.* 115 G7
Elizabethton, *U.S.A.* 115 G4
Elizabethtown, *Ky., U.S.A.* 114 G3
Elizabethtown, *N.Y., U.S.A.* 117 B11
Elizabethtown, *Pa., U.S.A.* 117 F8
Elizondo, *Spain* 38 B3
Ełk, *Poland* 30 E9
Elk →, *Canada* 102 C5
Ełk →, *Poland* 30 E9
Elk →, *U.S.A.* 115 H2
Elk City, *U.S.A.* 113 H5
Elk Creek, *U.S.A.* 110 F4
Elk Grove, *U.S.A.* 110 G5
Elk Island △, *Canada* 102 C6
Elk Lake, *Canada* 104 C3
Elk Point, *Canada* 103 C6
Elk River, *Idaho, U.S.A.* 108 C5
Elk River, *Minn., U.S.A.* 112 C8
Elkedra →, *Australia* 94 C2
Elkhart, *Ind., U.S.A.* 114 E3
Elkhart, *Kans., U.S.A.* 113 G4
Elkhorn, *Canada* 103 D8
Elkhorn →, *U.S.A.* 112 E6
Elkhovo, *Bulgaria* 45 D10
Elkin, *U.S.A.* 115 G5
Elkins, *U.S.A.* 114 F6
Elkland, *U.S.A.* 116 E7
Elko, *Canada* 102 D5
Elko, *U.S.A.* 108 F6
Elkton, *U.S.A.* 116 C1
Ell, L., *Australia* 93 E4
Ellef Ringnes I., *Canada* 4 B2
Ellen, Mt., *U.S.A.* 117 B12
Ellenburg, *U.S.A.* 117 B11
Ellendale, *U.S.A.* 112 B5
Ellensburg, *U.S.A.* 108 C3
Ellenville, *U.S.A.* 117 E10
Ellerton, *Barbados* 121 g
Ellery, Mt., *Australia* 95 F4
Ellesmere, L., *N.Z.* 91 M4
Ellesmere I., *Canada* 98 B11
Ellesmere Port, *U.K.* 14 D5
Ellice Is. = Tuvalu ■, *Pac. Oc.* 96 H9
Ellicottville, *U.S.A.* 116 D6
Elliot, *Australia* 94 B1
Elliot, *S. Africa* 89 E4
Elliot Lake, *Canada* 104 C3
Elliotdale = Xhora, *S. Africa* 89 E4
Ellis, *U.S.A.* 112 F5
Elliston, *Australia* 95 E1
Ellisville, *U.S.A.* 113 K10
Ellon, *U.K.* 13 D6
Ellore = Eluru, *India* 67 L12
Ellsworth, *Kans., U.S.A.* 112 F5
Ellsworth, *Maine, U.S.A.* 115 C11
Ellsworth Land, *Antarctica* 5 D16
Ellsworth Mts., *Antarctica* 5 D16
Ellwangen, *Germany* 25 G6
Ellwood City, *U.S.A.* 116 F4
Elm, *Switz.* 25 J5
Elm-Lappwald ⌓, *Germany* 24 C6
Elma, *Canada* 103 D9
Elma, *U.S.A.* 110 D3
Elmadağ, *Turkey* 72 C5
Elmalı, *Turkey* 47 E11

Elmhurst, *U.S.A.* 114 E2
Elmina, *Ghana* 83 D4
Elmira, *Canada* 116 C4
Elmira, *U.S.A.* 116 D8
Elmira Heights, *U.S.A.* 116 D8
Elmore, *Australia* 95 F3
Elmore, *U.S.A.* 111 M11
Elmshorn, *Germany* 24 B5
Elmvale, *Canada* 116 B5
Elne, *France* 20 F6
Elora, *Canada* 116 C4
Elos, *Greece* 46 E4
Eloúnda, *Greece* 49 D7
Eloy, *U.S.A.* 109 K8
Éloyes, *France* 19 D13
Elrose, *Canada* 103 C7
Elsdorf, *Germany* 24 E2
Elsie, *U.S.A.* 110 E3
Elsinore = Helsingør, *Denmark* 11 H6
Elster →, *Germany* 24 D7
Elsterwerda, *Germany* 24 D9
Eltham, *N.Z.* 91 H5
Elton, *Russia* 35 F8
Elton, Ozero, *Russia* 35 F8
Eltville, *Germany* 25 E4
Eluru, *India* 67 L12
Elvas, *Portugal* 37 G3
Elven, *France* 18 E4
Elverum, *Norway* 9 F14
Elvire →, *Australia* 92 C4
Elvire, Mt., *Australia* 93 E2
Elvo →, *Italy* 40 C5
Elwell, L., *U.S.A.* 108 B8
Elwood, *Ind., U.S.A.* 114 E3
Elwood, *Nebr., U.S.A.* 112 E5
Elx = Elche, *Spain* 39 G4
Ely, *U.K.* 15 E8
Ely, *Minn., U.S.A.* 112 B9
Ely, *Nev., U.S.A.* 108 G6
Elyria, *U.S.A.* 116 E2
Elyrus, *Greece* 46 F5
Elz →, *Germany* 25 G3
Emådalen, *Sweden* 10 C8
Emāmrūd, *Iran* 71 B7
Emån →, *Sweden* 11 G10
Emba, *Kazakhstan* 52 E6
Emba →, *Kazakhstan* 52 E6
Embarcación, *Argentina* 126 A3
Embarras Portage, *Canada* 103 B6
Embetsu, *Japan* 54 B10
Embi = Emba, *Kazakhstan* 52 E6
Embi = Emba →, *Kazakhstan* 52 E6
Embóna, *Greece* 49 C9
Embrun, *France* 21 D10
Embu, *Kenya* 86 C4
Emden, *Germany* 24 B3
Emecik, *Turkey* 47 E9
Emerald, *Australia* 94 C4
Emerson, *Canada* 103 D9
Emet, *Turkey* 47 B11
Emi Koussi, *Chad* 79 E9
Emília-Romagna □, *Italy* 40 D8
Emilius, Mte., *Italy* 40 C4
Eminabad, *Pakistan* 68 C6
Emine, Nos, *Bulgaria* 45 D11
Emirdağ, *Turkey* 72 C4
Emissi, Tarso, *Chad* 79 D9
Emlenton, *U.S.A.* 116 E5
Emlichheim, *Germany* 24 C2
Emmaboda, *Sweden* 11 H9
Emmaus, *S. Africa* 88 D4
Emmaus, *U.S.A.* 117 F9
Emme →, *Switz.* 25 H3
Emmeloord, *Neths.* 17 B5
Emmen, *Neths.* 17 B6
Emmen, *Switz.* 25 H4
Emmendingen, *Germany* 25 G3
Emmental, *Switz.* 25 J3
Emmerich, *Germany* 24 D2
Emmet, *Australia* 94 C3
Emmetsburg, *U.S.A.* 112 D7
Emmett, *Idaho, U.S.A.* 108 E5
Emmett, *Mich., U.S.A.* 116 D2
Emmonak, *U.S.A.* 100 B3
Emo, *Canada* 103 D10
Emőd, *Hungary* 28 C5
Emona, *Bulgaria* 45 D11
Empalme, *Mexico* 118 B2
Empangeni, *S. Africa* 89 D5
Empedrado, *Argentina* 126 B4
Emperor Seamount Chain, *Pac. Oc.* 96 D9
Empoli, *Italy* 40 E7
Emporia, *Kans., U.S.A.* 112 F6
Emporia, *Va., U.S.A.* 115 G7
Emporium, *U.S.A.* 116 E6
Empress, *Canada* 103 C7
Empty Quarter = Rub' al Khālī, *Si. Arabia* 75 D4
Ems →, *Germany* 24 B3
Emsdale, *Canada* 116 A5
Emsdetten, *Germany* 24 C3
Emu, *China* 57 C15
Emu Park, *Australia* 94 C5
'En 'Avrona, *Israel* 74 F4
En Nahud, *Sudan* 81 E2
En Nofalab, *Sudan* 81 D3
Ena, *Japan* 55 G8
Enana, *Namibia* 88 B2
Enånger, *Sweden* 10 C11
Enard B., *U.K.* 13 C3
Enare = Inarijärvi, *Finland* 8 B22
Enarotali, *Indonesia* 63 E9
Encampment, *U.S.A.* 108 F10
Encantadas, Serra, *Brazil* 127 C5
Encarnación, *Paraguay* 127 B4
Encarnación de Diaz, *Mexico* 118 C4
Enchi, *Ghana* 82 D4
Encinitas, *U.S.A.* 111 M9
Encino, *U.S.A.* 109 J11
Encounter B., *Australia* 95 F2
Encs, *Hungary* 28 B6
Endako, *Canada* 102 C3
Ende, *Indonesia* 63 F6
Endeavour Str., *Australia* 94 A3
Endelave, *Denmark* 11 J4
Enderbury I., *Kiribati* 96 H10
Enderby, *Canada* 102 C5
Enderby I., *Australia* 92 D2
Enderby Land, *Antarctica* 5 C5
Enderlin, *U.S.A.* 112 B6
Endicott, *U.S.A.* 117 D8
Endwell, *U.S.A.* 117 D8
Endyalgout I., *Australia* 92 B5
Eneabba, *Australia* 93 E2
Enewetak Atoll, *Marshall Is.* 96 F8
Enez, *Turkey* 45 F10
Enfer, Pte. d', *Martinique* 120 c
Enfield, *Canada* 105 D7
Enfield, *Conn., U.S.A.* 117 E12
Enfield, *N.H., U.S.A.* 117 C12
Engadin, *Switz.* 25 J6
Engaño, C., *Dom. Rep.* 121 C6
Engaño, C., *Phil.* 63 A6
Engaru, *Japan* 54 B11
Engcobo, *S. Africa* 89 E4
Engelberg, *Switz.* 25 J4
Engels, *Russia* 34 E8
Engemann L., *Canada* 103 B7
Engershatu, *Eritrea* 81 D4
Enggano, *Indonesia* 62 F2
England, *U.S.A.* 113 H9
England □, *U.K.* 15 E5
Englee, *Canada* 105 B8
Englehart, *Canada* 104 C4
Englewood, *U.S.A.* 112 F2
English →, *Canada* 103 C10
English Bazar = Ingraj Bazar, *India* 69 G13
English Channel, *Europe* 15 G6
English Company's Is., The, *Australia* 94 A2
English River, *Canada* 104 C1
Engures ezers, *Latvia* 30 A10
Enguri →, *Georgia* 35 J5
Enid, *U.S.A.* 113 G6
Enipévs →, *Greece* 46 B4
Enkhuizen, *Neths.* 17 B5
Enköping, *Sweden* 10 E11
Enle, *China* 58 F3
Enna, *Italy* 43 E7
Ennadai, *Canada* 103 A8
Ennadai L., *Canada* 103 A8
Ennedi, *Chad* 79 E10
Enngonia, *Australia* 95 D4
Ennigerloh, *Germany* 24 D4
Ennis, *Ireland* 12 D3
Ennis, *Mont., U.S.A.* 108 D8
Ennis, *Tex., U.S.A.* 113 J6
Enniscorthy, *Ireland* 12 D5
Enniskillen, *U.K.* 12 B4
Ennistimon, *Ireland* 12 D2
Enns, *Austria* 26 C7
Enns →, *Austria* 26 C7
Enontekiö, *Finland* 8 B20
Enosburg Falls, *U.S.A.* 117 B12
Enping, *China* 59 F9
Enriquillo, L., *Dom. Rep.* 121 C5
Enschede, *Neths.* 17 B6
Ensenada, *Argentina* 126 C4
Ensenada, *Mexico* 118 A1
Ensenada de los Muertos, *Mexico* 118 C2
Enshi, *China* 58 B7
Ensiola, Pta. de n', *Spain* 48 B9
Ensisheim, *France* 19 E14
Entebbe, *Uganda* 86 B3
Enterprise, *Canada* 102 A5
Enterprise, *Ala., U.S.A.* 115 K3
Enterprise, *Oreg., U.S.A.* 108 D5
Entorno de Doñana △, *Spain* 37 J4
Entraygues-sur-Truyère, *France* 20 D6
Entre Ríos, *Bolivia* 126 A3
Entre Ríos □, *Argentina* 126 C4
Entrepeñas, Embalse de, *Spain* 38 E2
Entroncamento, *Portugal* 37 F2
Enugu, *Nigeria* 83 D6
Enugu □, *Nigeria* 83 D6
Enugu Ezike, *Nigeria* 83 D6
Enumclaw, *U.S.A.* 110 C5
Envalira, Port d', *Europe* 38 C6
Envermeu, *France* 18 C8
Enviken, *Sweden* 10 D9
Enying, *Hungary* 28 D3
Enza →, *Italy* 40 D7
Eólie, Ís., *Italy* 43 D7
Epanomí, *Greece* 44 F6
Epe, *Neths.* 17 B5
Epe, *Nigeria* 83 D5
Épernay, *France* 19 C10
Épernon, *France* 19 D8
Ephesus, *Turkey* 47 D9
Ephraim, *U.S.A.* 108 G8
Ephrata, *Pa., U.S.A.* 117 F8
Ephrata, *Wash., U.S.A.* 108 C4
Epidaurus Limera, *Greece* 46 E5
Épila, *Spain* 38 D3
Épinac, *France* 19 F11
Épinal, *France* 19 D13
Episkopi, *Cyprus* 49 E11
Episkopí, *Greece* 49 D6
Episkopi Bay, *Cyprus* 49 E11
Epitálion, *Greece* 46 D3
Eppan = Appiano, *Italy* 41 B8
Eppingen, *Germany* 25 F4
Epsom, *U.K.* 15 F7
Epukiro, *Namibia* 88 C2
Equatoria = El Istiwa'iya, *Sudan* 79 G11
Equatorial Guinea ■, *Africa* 84 D1
Er Hai, *China* 58 E3
Er Rachidia, *Morocco* 78 B5
Er Rahad, *Sudan* 81 E3
Er Rif, *Morocco* 78 A5
Er Rogel, *Sudan* 80 D4
Er Roseires, *Sudan* 81 E3
Er Rua'at, *Sudan* 81 E3
Eraclea, *Italy* 41 C9
Erāwadī Myit = Irrawaddy →, *Burma* 67 M19
Erāwadī Myitwanya = Irrawaddy, Mouths of the, *Burma* 67 M19
Erba, *Italy* 40 C6
Erba, *Sudan* 80 D4
Erba, J., *Sudan* 80 C4
Erbaa, *Turkey* 72 B7
Erbeskopf, *Germany* 25 F3
Erbil = Arbīl, *Iraq* 70 B5
Erbu, *Ethiopia* 81 E3
Erçek, *Turkey* 70 B4
Erçiş, *Turkey* 73 C10
Erciyaş Dağı, *Turkey* 70 B2
Érd, *Hungary* 28 C3
Erdao Jiang →, *China* 57 C14
Erdek, *Turkey* 45 F11
Erdemli, *Turkey* 72 D6
Erdene = Ulaan-Uul, *Mongolia* 56 B6
Erdenetsogt, *Mongolia* 56 C4
Erding, *Germany* 25 G7
Erdre →, *France* 18 E5
Erebus, Mt., *Antarctica* 5 D11
Erechim, *Brazil* 127 B5
Ereğli, *Konya, Turkey* 70 B2
Ereğli, *Zonguldak, Turkey* 72 B4
Erei, Monti, *Italy* 43 E7
Erenhot, *China* 56 C7
Eresma →, *Spain* 36 D6
Eressós, *Greece* 47 B7
Erfenisdam, *S. Africa* 88 D4
Erfstadt, *Germany* 24 E2
Erft →, *Germany* 24 D2
Erfurt, *Germany* 24 E7
Ergani, *Turkey* 70 B3
Ergel, *Mongolia* 56 C5
Ergene →, *Turkey* 45 E10
Ergeni Vozvyshennost, *Russia* 35 G7
Ērgli, *Latvia* 9 H21
Erhlin, *Taiwan* 59 F13
Eria →, *Spain* 36 C5
Eriba, *Sudan* 81 D4
Eriboll, L., *U.K.* 13 C4
Érice, *Italy* 42 D5
Erie, *U.S.A.* 116 D4
Erie, L., *N. Amer.* 116 D4
Erie Canal, *U.S.A.* 116 C7
Erieau, *Canada* 116 D3
Erigavo, *Somali Rep.* 75 E4
Erikoúsa, *Greece* 49 A3
Eriksdale, *Canada* 103 C9
Erímanthos, *Greece* 46 D3
Erimo-misaki, *Japan* 54 D11
Erin Pt., *Trin. & Tob.* 125 K15
Erinpura, *India* 68 G5
Eriskay, *U.K.* 13 D1
Erithraí, *Greece* 46 C5
Eritrea ■, *Africa* 81 E4
Erjas →, *Portugal* 36 F3
Erkelenz, *Germany* 24 D2
Erkner, *Germany* 24 C9
Erlangen, *Germany* 25 F6
Erldunda, *Australia* 94 D1
Ermelo, *Neths.* 17 B5
Ermelo, *S. Africa* 89 D4
Ermenek, *Turkey* 70 B2
Ermil, *Sudan* 81 E2
Ermióni, *Greece* 46 D5
Ermones, *Greece* 49 A3
Ernakulam, *India* 66 Q10
Erne →, *Ireland* 12 B3
Erne, Lower L., *U.K.* 12 B4
Erne, Upper L., *U.K.* 12 B4
Ernée, *France* 18 D6
Ernest Giles Ra., *Australia* 93 E3
Ernstberg, *Germany* 25 E2
Erode, *India* 66 P10
Eromanga, *Australia* 95 D3
Erongo, *Namibia* 88 C2
Erquy, *France* 18 D4
Erramala Hills, *India* 66 M11
Errer →, *Ethiopia* 81 F5
Errigal, *Ireland* 12 A3
Erris Hd., *Ireland* 12 B1
Ersekë, *Albania* 44 F4
Erskine, *U.S.A.* 112 B7
Erstein, *France* 19 D14
Ertholmene, *Denmark* 11 J9
Ertil, *Russia* 34 E5
Ertis = Irtysh →, *Russia* 52 C7
Eruh, *Turkey* 73 D10
Eruwa, *Nigeria* 83 D5
Ervy-le-Châtel, *France* 19 D10
Erwin, *U.S.A.* 115 G4
Eryuan, *China* 58 D2
Erzgebirge, *Germany* 24 E8
Erzin, *Russia* 53 D10
Erzincan, *Turkey* 70 B3
Erzurum, *Turkey* 70 B4
Es Caló, *Spain* 48 C8
Es Canar, *Spain* 48 B8
Es Mercadal, *Spain* 48 B11
Es Migjorn Gran, *Spain* 48 B11
Es Safiya, *Sudan* 81 D3
Es Sahrâ' Esh Sharqîya, *Egypt* 80 B3
Es Sînâ', *Egypt* 74 F3
Es Sûkî, *Sudan* 81 E3
Es Vedrà, *Spain* 48 C7
Esambo, *Dem. Rep. of the Congo* 86 C1
Esan-Misaki, *Japan* 54 D10
Esashi, *Hokkaidō, Japan* 54 B11
Esashi, *Hokkaidō, Japan* 54 D10
Esbjerg, *Denmark* 11 J2
Esbo = Espoo, *Finland* 9 F21
Escalante, *U.S.A.* 109 H8
Escalante →, *U.S.A.* 109 H8
Escalón, *Mexico* 118 B4
Escambia →, *U.S.A.* 115 K2
Escanaba, *U.S.A.* 114 C2
Esch-sur-Alzette, *Lux.* 17 E6
Eschede, *Germany* 24 C6
Eschwege, *Germany* 24 D6
Eschweiler, *Germany* 24 E2
Escondido, *U.S.A.* 111 M9
Escravos →, *Nigeria* 83 D6
Escuinapa, *Mexico* 118 C3
Escuintla, *Guatemala* 120 D1
Eséka, *Cameroon* 83 E7
Eşen →, *Turkey* 47 E11
Esenguly, *Turkmenistan* 52 F6
Esens, *Germany* 24 B3
Esenyurt, *Turkey* 45 E12
Esera →, *Spain* 38 C5
Eşfahān, *Iran* 71 C6
Eşfahān □, *Iran* 71 C6
Esfarāyen, *Iran* 71 B8
Esfīdeh, *Iran* 71 C8
Esgueva →, *Spain* 36 D6
Esh Sham = Dimashq, *Syria* 74 B5
Esh Shamâlîya □, *Sudan* 80 D2
Esha Ness, *U.K.* 13 A7
Eshan, *China* 58 E4
Esher, *U.K.* 15 F7
Eshkol △, *Israel* 74 D3
Eshowe, *S. Africa* 89 D5
Esiama, *Ghana* 82 E4
Esigodini, *Zimbabwe* 89 C4
Esil = Ishim →, *Russia* 52 D8
Esino →, *Italy* 41 E10
Esira, *Madag.* 89 C8
Esk →, *Cumb., U.K.* 13 G5
Esk →, *N. Yorks., U.K.* 14 C7
Eskān, *Iran* 71 E9
Esker, *Canada* 105 B6
Eskifjörður, *Iceland* 8 D7
Eskilsäter, *Sweden* 11 F7
Eskilstuna, *Sweden* 10 E10
Eskimalatya, *Turkey* 73 C8
Eskimo Point = Arviat, *Canada* 103 A10
Eskişehir, *Turkey* 47 B12
Eskişehir □, *Turkey* 47 B12
Esla →, *Spain* 36 D4
Eslāmābād-e Gharb, *Iran* 70 C5
Eslāmshahr, *Iran* 71 C6
Eslöv, *Sweden* 11 J7
Eşme, *Turkey* 47 C10
Esmeraldas, *Ecuador* 124 C3
Esnagi L., *Canada* 104 C3
Espalion, *France* 20 D6
Espanola, *Canada* 104 C3
Espanola, *U.S.A.* 109 H10
Esparreguera, *Spain* 38 D6
Esparta, *Costa Rica* 120 E3
Espelkamp, *Germany* 24 C4
Esperance, *Australia* 93 F3
Esperance B., *Australia* 93 F3
Esperance Harbour, *St. Lucia* 121 f
Esperanza, *Antarctica* 5 C18
Esperanza, *Argentina* 126 C3
Esperanza, *Phil.* 61 G6
Esperanza, *Puerto Rico* 121 d
Espéraza, *France* 20 F6
Espichel, C., *Portugal* 37 G1
Espiel, *Spain* 37 G5
Espigão, Serra do, *Brazil* 127 B5
Espinazo, Sierra del = Espinhaço, Serra do, *Brazil* 125 G10
Espinhaço, Serra do, *Brazil* 125 G10
Espinho, *Portugal* 36 D2
Espinilho, Serra do, *Brazil* 127 B5
Espinosa de los Monteros, *Spain* 36 B7
Espírito Santo □, *Brazil* 125 H10
Espíritu Santo, *Vanuatu* 96 J8
Espíritu Santo, B. del, *Mexico* 119 D7
Espíritu Santo, I., *Mexico* 118 C2
Espita, *Mexico* 119 C7
Espiye, *Turkey* 73 B8
Espluga de Francolí, *Spain* 38 D6
Espoo, *Finland* 9 F21
Espuña, Sierra de, *Spain* 39 H3
Espungabera, *Mozam.* 89 C5
Esquel, *Argentina* 128 E2
Esquimalt, *Canada* 102 D4
Esquina, *Argentina* 126 C4
Essaouira, *Morocco* 78 B4
Essebie, *Dem. Rep. of the Congo* 86 B3
Essen, *Belgium* 17 C4
Essen, *Germany* 24 D3
Essendon, Mt., *Australia* 93 E3
Essequibo →, *Guyana* 124 B7
Essex, *Canada* 116 D2
Essex, *Calif., U.S.A.* 111 L11
Essex, *N.Y., U.S.A.* 117 B11
Essex □, *U.K.* 15 F8
Essex Junction, *U.S.A.* 117 B11
Esslingen, *Germany* 25 G5
Essonne □, *France* 19 D9
Estaca de Bares, C. de, *Spain* 36 B3
Estadilla, *Spain* 38 C5
Estados, I. de Los, *Argentina* 128 G4
Estagel, *France* 20 F6
Eştahbānāt, *Iran* 71 D7
Estância, *Brazil* 125 F11
Estancia, *U.S.A.* 109 J10
Estārm, *Iran* 71 D8
Estarreja, *Portugal* 36 E2
Estats, Pic d', *Spain* 38 C6
Estcourt, *S. Africa* 89 D4
Este, *Italy* 41 C8
Este △, *Dom. Rep.* 121 C6
Estelí, *Nic.* 120 D2
Estella, *Spain* 38 C2
Estellencs, *Spain* 48 B9
Estena →, *Spain* 37 F6
Estepa, *Spain* 37 H6
Estepona, *Spain* 37 J5
Esterhazy, *Canada* 103 C8
Esternay, *France* 19 D10
Esterri d'Aneu, *Spain* 38 C6
Estevan, *Canada* 103 D8
Estevan Group, *Canada* 102 C3
Estherville, *U.S.A.* 112 D7
Estissac, *France* 19 D10
Eston, *Canada* 103 C7
Estonia ■, *Europe* 9 G21
Estoril, *Portugal* 37 G1
Estouk, *Mali* 83 B5
Estreito, *Brazil* 125 E9
Estrela, Serra da, *Portugal* 36 E3
Estrella, *Spain* 37 G7
Estremoz, *Portugal* 37 G3
Estrondo, Serra do, *Brazil* 125 E9
Esztergom, *Hungary* 28 C3
Et Tîdra, *Mauritania* 82 B1
Etah, *India* 69 F8
Étain, *France* 19 C12
Étampes, *France* 19 D9
Etanga, *Namibia* 88 B1
Étaples, *France* 19 B8
Etawah, *India* 69 F8
Etawney L., *Canada* 103 B9
Ete, *Nigeria* 83 D6
eThekwini = Durban, *S. Africa* 89 D5
Ethel, *U.S.A.* 110 D4
Ethelbert, *Canada* 103 C8
Ethiopia ■, *Africa* 75 F3
Ethiopian Highlands, *Ethiopia* 50 J7
Etili, *Turkey* 45 G10
Etive, L., *U.K.* 13 E3
Etna, *Italy* 43 E7
Etoile, *Dem. Rep. of the Congo* 87 E2
Etosha △, *Namibia* 88 B2
Etosha Pan, *Namibia* 88 B2
Etowah, *U.S.A.* 115 H3
Étréchy, *France* 19 D9
Étrépagny, *France* 19 C8
Étretat, *France* 18 C7
Etropole, *Bulgaria* 45 D8
Ettelbruck, *Lux.* 17 E6
Ettlingen, *Germany* 25 G4
Ettrick Water →, *U.K.* 13 F6
Etuku, *Dem. Rep. of the Congo* 86 C2
Etulia, *Moldova* 29 E13
Etzatlán, *Mexico* 118 C4
Etzná, *Mexico* 119 D6
Etzná-Tixmucuy = Edzná, *Mexico* 119 D6
Eu, *France* 18 B8
Eubenangee Swamp △, *Australia* 94 B4
Euboea = Évvoia, *Greece* 46 C6
Eucla, *Australia* 93 F4
Euclid, *U.S.A.* 116 E3
Eucumbene, L., *Australia* 95 F4
Eudora, *U.S.A.* 113 J9
Eufaula, *Ala., U.S.A.* 115 K3
Eufaula, *Okla., U.S.A.* 113 H7
Eufaula L., *U.S.A.* 113 H7
Eugene, *U.S.A.* 108 E2
Eugowra, *Australia* 95 E4
Eulo, *Australia* 95 D4
Eungella △, *Australia* 94 C4
Eunice, *La., U.S.A.* 113 K8
Eunice, *N. Mex., U.S.A.* 113 J3
Eupen, *Belgium* 17 D6
Euphrates = Furāt, Nahr al →, *Asia* 70 D5
Eure □, *France* 18 C8
Eure →, *France* 18 C8
Eure-et-Loir □, *France* 18 D8
Eureka, *Canada* 4 B3
Eureka, *Calif., U.S.A.* 108 F1
Eureka, *Kans., U.S.A.* 113 G6
Eureka, *Mont., U.S.A.* 108 B6
Eureka, *Nev., U.S.A.* 108 G5
Eureka, *S. Dak., U.S.A.* 112 C5
Eureka, Mt., *Australia* 93 E3
Euroa, *Australia* 95 F4
Europa, Île, *Ind. Oc.* 85 J8
Europa, Picos de, *Spain* 36 B6
Europa, Pta. de, *Gib.* 37 J5
Europe 6 E10
Europoort, *Neths.* 17 C4
Euskirchen, *Germany* 24 E2
Eustis, *U.S.A.* 115 L5
Eutin, *Germany* 24 A6
Eutsuk L., *Canada* 102 C3
Evale, *Angola* 88 B2
Evans, *U.S.A.* 112 E2
Evans, L., *Canada* 104 B4
Evans City, *U.S.A.* 116 F4
Evans Head, *Australia* 95 D5
Evans Mills, *U.S.A.* 117 B9
Evansburg, *Canada* 102 C5
Evanston, *Ill., U.S.A.* 114 E2
Evanston, *Wyo., U.S.A.* 108 F8
Evansville, *U.S.A.* 114 G2
Évaux-les-Bains, *France* 19 F9
Evaz, *Iran* 71 E7
Evciler, *Afyon, Turkey* 47 C11
Evciler, *Çanakkale, Turkey* 47 B8
Eveleth, *U.S.A.* 112 B8
Evensk, *Russia* 53 C16
Everard, L., *Australia* 95 E2
Everard Ranges, *Australia* 93 E5
Everest, Mt., *Nepal* 69 E12
Everett, *Pa., U.S.A.* 116 F6
Everett, *Wash., U.S.A.* 110 C4
Everglades △, *U.S.A.* 115 N5
Everglades, The, *U.S.A.* 115 N5
Everglades City, *U.S.A.* 115 N5
Evergreen, *Ala., U.S.A.* 115 K2
Evergreen, *Mont., U.S.A.* 108 B6
Everöd, *Sweden* 11 J8
Evertsberg, *Sweden* 10 C7
Evesham, *U.K.* 15 E6
Évian-les-Bains, *France* 19 F13
Évinos →, *Greece* 46 C3
Évisa, *France* 21 F12
Evje, *Norway* 9 G12
Évora, *Portugal* 37 G3
Évora □, *Portugal* 37 G3
Evowghlī, *Iran* 70 B5
Évreux, *France* 18 C8
Evritanía □, *Greece* 46 B3
Évron, *France* 18 D6

Évros □, *Greece* 45 E10
Évros →, *Greece* 72 B2
Evrótas →, *Greece* 46 E4
Évry, *France* 19 D9
Évvoia, *Greece* 46 C6
Évvoia □, *Greece* 46 C5
Evxinoúpolis, *Greece* 46 B4
Ewe, L., *U.K.* 13 D3
Ewing, *U.S.A.* 112 D5
Ewo, *Congo* 84 E2
Exaltación, *Bolivia* 124 F5
Excelsior Springs, *U.S.A.* 112 F7
Excideuil, *France* 20 C5
Exe →, *U.K.* 15 G4
Exeter, *Canada* 116 C3
Exeter, *U.K.* 15 G4
Exeter, *Calif., U.S.A.* 110 J7
Exeter, *N.H., U.S.A.* 117 D14
Exmoor, *U.K.* 15 F4
Exmoor ∆, *U.K.* 15 F4
Exmouth, *Australia* 92 D1
Exmouth, *U.K.* 15 G4
Exmouth G., *Australia* 92 D1
Expedition ∆, *Australia* 95 D4
Expedition Ra., *Australia* 94 C4
Extremadura □, *Spain* 37 F4
Exuma Sound, *Bahamas* 120 B4
Eyasi, L., *Tanzania* 86 C4
Eye Pen., *U.K.* 13 C2
Eyemouth, *U.K.* 13 F6
Eygues = Aigues →, *France* 21 D8
Eygurande, *France* 19 G9
Eyjafjörður, *Iceland* 8 C4
Eymet, *France* 20 D4
Eymoutiers, *France* 20 C5
Eynesil, *Turkey* 73 B8
Eyre (North), L., *Australia* 95 D2
Eyre (South), L., *Australia* 95 D2
Eyre Mts., *N.Z.* 91 L2
Eyre Pen., *Australia* 95 E2
Eysturoy, *Færoe Is.* 8 E9
Eyvānkī, *Iran* 71 C6
Ez Zeidab, *Sudan* 80 D3
Ezcaray, *Spain* 38 C1
Ežerėlis, *Lithuania* 30 D10
Ezhou, *China* 59 B10
Ezine, *Turkey* 47 B8
Ezouza →, *Cyprus* 49 E11

F

F.Y.R.O.M. = Macedonia ■, *Europe* 44 E5
Fabala, *Guinea* 82 D3
Fabens, *U.S.A.* 109 L10
Fabero, *Spain* 36 C4
Fåborg, *Denmark* 11 J4
Fabriano, *Italy* 41 E9
Făcăeni, *Romania* 29 F12
Fachi, *Niger* 79 E8
Fada, *Chad* 79 E10
Fada-n-Gourma, *Burkina Faso* 83 C5
Fadd, *Hungary* 28 D3
Faddeyevskiy, Ostrov, *Russia* 53 B15
Faddor, *Sudan* 81 F3
Fadghāmī, *Syria* 70 C4
Fadlab, *Sudan* 80 D3
Faenza, *Italy* 41 D8
Færoe Is. = Føroyar, *Atl. Oc.* 8 F9
Fafa, *Mali* 83 B5
Fafe, *Portugal* 36 D2
Fagam, *Nigeria* 83 C7
Făgăras, *Romania* 29 E9
Făgăras, Munţii, *Romania* 29 E9
Fågelmara, *Sweden* 11 H9
Fagerhult, *Sweden* 11 G9
Fagersta, *Sweden* 10 D9
Făget, *Romania* 28 E7
Făget, Munţii, *Romania* 29 C8
Fagnano, L., *Argentina* 128 G3
Fagnières, *France* 19 D11
Faguibine, L., *Mali* 82 B4
Fahlīān, *Iran* 71 D6
Fahraj, *Kermān, Iran* 71 D8
Fahraj, *Yazd, Iran* 71 D7
Fai Tsi Long, *Vietnam* 58 G6
Faial, *Madeira* 48 D3
Fair Haven, *U.S.A.* 114 D9
Fair Hd., *U.K.* 12 A5
Fair Oaks, *U.S.A.* 110 G5
Fairbanks, *U.S.A.* 100 B5
Fairbury, *U.S.A.* 112 E6
Fairfax, *U.S.A.* 117 B11
Fairfield, *Ala., U.S.A.* 115 J2
Fairfield, *Calif., U.S.A.* 110 G4
Fairfield, *Conn., U.S.A.* 117 E11
Fairfield, *Idaho, U.S.A.* 108 E6
Fairfield, *Ill., U.S.A.* 114 F1
Fairfield, *Iowa, U.S.A.* 112 E9
Fairfield, *Tex., U.S.A.* 113 K7
Fairford, *Canada* 103 C9
Fairhope, *U.S.A.* 115 K2
Fairlie, *N.Z.* 91 L3
Fairmead, *U.S.A.* 110 H6
Fairmont, *Minn., U.S.A.* 112 D7
Fairmont, *W. Va., U.S.A.* 114 F5
Fairmount, *Calif., U.S.A.* 111 L8
Fairmount, *N.Y., U.S.A.* 117 C8
Fairplay, *U.S.A.* 109 G11
Fairport, *U.S.A.* 116 C7
Fairport Harbor, *U.S.A.* 116 E3
Fairview, *Canada* 102 B5
Fairview, *Mont., U.S.A.* 112 B2
Fairview, *Okla., U.S.A.* 113 G5
Fairweather, Mt., *U.S.A.* 102 B1
Faisalabad, *Pakistan* 68 D5
Faith, *U.S.A.* 112 C3
Faizabad, *India* 69 F10
Fajardo, *Puerto Rico* 121 d
Fajr, W. →, *Si. Arabia* 70 D3
Fakenham, *U.K.* 14 E8
Fåker, *Sweden* 10 A8
Fakfak, *Indonesia* 63 E8
Fakiya, *Bulgaria* 45 D11
Fakobli, *Ivory C.* 82 D3
Fakse, *Denmark* 11 J6
Fakse Bugt, *Denmark* 11 J6
Fakse Ladeplads, *Denmark* 11 J6
Faku, *China* 57 C12
Falaba, *S. Leone* 82 D2
Falaise, *France* 18 D6
Falaise, Mui, *Vietnam* 64 C5
Falakrón Óros, *Greece* 44 E7
Falam, *Burma* 67 H18
Falces, *Spain* 38 C3
Fălciu, *Romania* 29 D13
Falcó, C. des, *Spain* 48 C7
Falcón, Presa, *Mexico* 119 B5
Falcon Lake, *Canada* 103 D9
Falcon Reservoir, *U.S.A.* 113 M5
Falconara Maríttima, *Italy* 41 E10
Falcone, C. del, *Italy* 42 B1
Falconer, *U.S.A.* 116 D5
Faléa, *Mali* 82 C2
Falémé →, *Senegal* 82 C2
Falerum, *Sweden* 11 F10
Faleshty = Făleşti, *Moldova* 29 C12
Făleşti, *Moldova* 29 C12
Falfurrias, *U.S.A.* 113 M5
Falher, *Canada* 102 B5
Falirakí, *Greece* 49 C10
Falkenberg, *Germany* 24 D9
Falkenberg, *Sweden* 11 H6
Falkensee, *Germany* 24 C9
Falkirk, *U.K.* 13 F5
Falkirk □, *U.K.* 13 F5
Falkland, *U.K.* 13 E5
Falkland Is. ☒, *Atl. Oc.* 128 G5
Falkland Sd., *Falk. Is.* 128 G5
Falkonéra, *Greece* 46 E5
Falköping, *Sweden* 11 F7
Fall River, *U.S.A.* 117 E13
Fallbrook, *U.S.A.* 111 M9
Fallon, *U.S.A.* 108 G4
Falls City, *U.S.A.* 112 E7
Falls Creek, *U.S.A.* 116 E6
Falmouth, *Jamaica* 120 a
Falmouth, *U.K.* 15 G2
Falmouth, *U.S.A.* 117 E14
Falsa, Pta., *Mexico* 118 B1
False B., *S. Africa* 88 E2
Falso, C., *Honduras* 120 C3
Falster, *Denmark* 11 K5
Falsterbo, *Sweden* 9 J15
Fălticeni, *Romania* 29 C11
Falun, *Sweden* 10 D9
Famagusta, *Cyprus* 49 D12
Famagusta Bay, *Cyprus* 49 D13
Famalé, *Niger* 78 F6
Famatina, Sierra de, *Argentina* 126 B2
Family L., *Canada* 103 C9
Famoso, *U.S.A.* 111 K7
Fan Xian, *China* 56 G8
Fana, *Mali* 82 C3
Fanad Hd., *Ireland* 12 A4
Fanárion, *Greece* 46 B3
Fandriana, *Madag.* 89 C8
Fánes-Sénnes e Braies ⌓, *Italy* 41 B9
Fang, *Thailand* 58 H2
Fang Xian, *China* 59 A8
Fangaga, *Sudan* 80 D4
Fangak, *Sudan* 81 F3
Fangchang, *China* 59 B12
Fangcheng, *China* 56 H7
Fangchenggang, *China* 58 G7
Fangliao, *Taiwan* 59 F13
Fangshan, *China* 56 E6
Fangzi, *China* 57 F10
Fani i Madh →, *Albania* 44 E4
Fanjakana, *Madag.* 89 C8
Fanjiatun, *China* 57 C13
Fannich, L., *U.K.* 13 D4
Fannūj, *Iran* 71 E8
Fanø, *Denmark* 11 J2
Fano, *Italy* 41 E10
Fanshi, *China* 56 E7
Fao = Al Fāw, *Iraq* 71 D6
Faqirwali, *Pakistan* 68 E5
Fâqûs, *Egypt* 80 H7
Far East = Dalnevostochnyy □, *Russia* 53 C14
Far East, *Asia* 50 E16
Fara in Sabina, *Italy* 41 F9
Faradje, *Dem. Rep. of the Congo* 86 B2
Farafangana, *Madag.* 89 C8
Farâfra, El Wâhât el-, *Egypt* 80 B2
Farāh, *Afghan.* 66 C3
Farāh □, *Afghan.* 66 C3
Farahalana, *Madag.* 89 A9
Faraid, Gebel, *Egypt* 80 C4
Farako, *Ivory C.* 82 D4
Faramana, *Burkina Faso* 82 C4
Faranah, *Guinea* 82 C2
Farasān, Jazā'ir, *Si. Arabia* 75 D3
Farasan Is. = Farasān, Jazā'ir, *Si. Arabia* 75 D3
Faratsiho, *Madag.* 89 B8
Fardes →, *Spain* 37 H7
Fareham, *U.K.* 15 G6
Farewell, C., *N.Z.* 91 J4
Farewell C. = Nunap Isua, *Greenland* 101 C15
Färgelanda, *Sweden* 11 F5
Farghona, *Uzbekistan* 52 E8
Fargo, *U.S.A.* 112 B6
Fār'iah, W. al →, *West Bank* 74 C4
Faribault, *U.S.A.* 112 C8
Faridabad, *India* 68 E6
Faridkot, *India* 68 D6
Faridpur, *Bangla.* 69 H13
Faridpur, *India* 69 E8
Färila, *Sweden* 10 C9
Farim, *Guinea-Biss.* 82 C1
Farīmān, *Iran* 71 C8
Farina, *Australia* 95 E2
Fariones, Pta., *Canary Is.* 48 E6
Fâriskûr, *Egypt* 80 H7
Färjestaden, *Sweden* 11 H10
Farkadhón, *Greece* 46 B4
Farleigh, *Australia* 94 K7
Farmakonisi, *Greece* 47 D9
Farmerville, *U.S.A.* 113 J8
Farmingdale, *U.S.A.* 117 F10
Farmington, *Canada* 102 B4
Farmington, *Calif., U.S.A.* 110 H6
Farmington, *Maine, U.S.A.* 115 C10
Farmington, *Mo., U.S.A.* 113 G9
Farmington, *N.H., U.S.A.* 117 C13
Farmington, *N. Mex., U.S.A.* 109 H9
Farmington, *Utah, U.S.A.* 108 F8
Farmington →, *U.S.A.* 117 E12
Farmville, *U.S.A.* 114 G6
Färnäs, *Sweden* 10 D8
Farne Is., *U.K.* 14 B6
Färnebofjärden ∆, *Sweden* 10 D10
Farnham, *Canada* 117 A12
Farnham, Mt., *Canada* 102 C5
Faro, *Brazil* 125 D7
Faro, *Canada* 100 B6
Faro, *Portugal* 37 H3
Fårö, *Sweden* 9 H18
Faro □, *Portugal* 37 H2
Faro ✕ (FAO), *Portugal* 37 H3
Fårösund, *Sweden* 11 G13
Farquhar, C., *Australia* 93 D1
Farrars Cr. →, *Australia* 94 D3
Farrāshband, *Iran* 71 D7
Farrell, *U.S.A.* 116 E4
Farrokhī, *Iran* 71 C8
Farruch, C. = Ferrutx, C., *Spain* 48 B10
Fārs □, *Iran* 71 D7
Fársala, *Greece* 46 B4
Farsø, *Denmark* 11 H3
Farson, *U.S.A.* 108 E9
Farsund, *Norway* 9 G12
Fartak, Râs, *Si. Arabia* 70 D2
Fartak, Ra's, *Yemen* 75 D5
Fârţăneşti, *Romania* 29 E12
Fartura, Serra da, *Brazil* 127 B5
Faru, *Nigeria* 83 C6
Fārūj, *Iran* 71 B8
Fårup, *Denmark* 11 H3
Farvel, Kap = Nunap Isua, *Greenland* 101 C15
Farwell, *U.S.A.* 113 H3
Fāryāb □, *Afghan.* 66 B4
Fasā, *Iran* 71 D7
Fasano, *Italy* 43 B10
Fashoda, *Sudan* 81 F3
Fassa, *Mali* 82 C3
Fastiv, *Ukraine* 33 G5
Fastnet Rock, *Ireland* 12 E2
Fastov = Fastiv, *Ukraine* 33 G5
Fatagar, Tanjung, *Indonesia* 63 E8
Fatehabad, *Haryana, India* 68 E6
Fatehabad, *Ut. P., India* 68 F8
Fatehgarh, *India* 69 F8
Fatehpur, *Bihar, India* 69 G11
Fatehpur, *Raj., India* 68 F6
Fatehpur, *Ut. P., India* 69 G9
Fatehpur, *Ut. P., India* 69 F9
Fatehpur Sikri, *India* 68 F6
Fatesh, *Russia* 33 F8
Fathai, *Sudan* 81 F3
Fathom Five ⌓, *Canada* 116 A3
Fatick, *Senegal* 82 C1
Fatima, *Canada* 105 C7
Fátima, *Portugal* 37 F2
Fatoya, *Guinea* 82 C3
Fatsa, *Turkey* 72 B7
Faucille, Col de la, *France* 19 F13
Faulkton, *U.S.A.* 112 C5
Faulquemont, *France* 19 C13
Faure I., *Australia* 93 E1
Făurei, *Romania* 29 E12
Fauresmith, *S. Africa* 88 D4
Fauske, *Norway* 8 C16
Favara, *Italy* 42 E6
Faváritx, C. de, *Spain* 48 B11
Faverges, *France* 21 C10
Favignana, *Italy* 42 E5
Favignana, I., *Italy* 42 E5
Fawcett, Pt., *Australia* 92 B5
Fawn →, *Canada* 104 A2
Fawnskin, *U.S.A.* 111 L10
Faxaflói, *Iceland* 8 D2
Faxälven →, *Sweden* 10 A10
Faya-Largeau, *Chad* 79 E9
Fayd, *Si. Arabia* 70 E4
Fayence, *France* 21 E10
Fayette, *Ala., U.S.A.* 115 J2
Fayette, *Mo., U.S.A.* 112 F8
Fayetteville, *Ark., U.S.A.* 113 G7
Fayetteville, *N.C., U.S.A.* 115 H6
Fayetteville, *Tenn., U.S.A.* 115 H2
Fayied, *Egypt* 80 H8
Fayón, *Spain* 38 D5
Fazao-Malfakassa ∆, *Togo* 83 D5
Fazilka, *India* 68 D6
Fazilpur, *Pakistan* 68 E4
Fdérik, *Mauritania* 78 D3
Feale →, *Ireland* 12 D2
Fear, C., *U.S.A.* 115 J7
Feather →, *U.S.A.* 108 G3
Feather Falls, *U.S.A.* 110 F5
Featherston, *N.Z.* 91 J5
Featherstone, *Zimbabwe* 87 F3
Fécamp, *France* 18 C7
Fedala = Mohammedia, *Morocco* 78 B4
Federación, *Argentina* 126 C4
Féderal, *Argentina* 128 C5
Federal Capital Terr. □, *Nigeria* 83 D6
Federal Way, *U.S.A.* 110 C4
Fedeshkūh, *Iran* 71 D7
Fehérgyarmat, *Hungary* 28 C7
Fehmarn, *Germany* 24 A7
Fehmarn Bælt, *Europe* 11 K5
Fehmarn Belt = Fehmarn Bælt, *Europe* 11 K5
Fei Xian, *China* 57 G9
Feijó, *Brazil* 124 E4
Feilding, *N.Z.* 91 J5
Feira de Santana, *Brazil* 125 F11
Feixi, *China* 59 B11
Feixiang, *China* 56 F8
Fejér □, *Hungary* 28 C3
Fejø, *Denmark* 11 K5
Feke, *Turkey* 72 D6
Fekete →, *Hungary* 28 E3
Felanitx, *Spain* 48 B10
Feldbach, *Austria* 26 E8
Feldberg, *Baden-W., Germany* 25 H3
Feldberg, *Mecklenburg-Vorpommern, Germany* 24 B9
Feldkirch, *Austria* 26 D2
Feldkirchen, *Austria* 26 E7
Felipe Carrillo Puerto, *Mexico* 119 D7
Felixburg, *Zimbabwe* 89 B5
Felixstowe, *U.K.* 15 F9
Felletin, *France* 20 C6
Fellingsbro, *Sweden* 10 E9
Felton, *U.S.A.* 110 H4
Feltre, *Italy* 41 B8
Femer Bælt = Fehmarn Bælt, *Europe* 11 K5
Femø, *Denmark* 11 K5
Femunden, *Norway* 9 E14
Fen He →, *China* 56 G6
Fene, *Spain* 36 B2
Fenelon Falls, *Canada* 116 B6
Fener Burnu, *Turkey* 47 E9
Feneroa, *Ethiopia* 81 E4
Feng Xian, *Jiangsu, China* 56 G9
Feng Xian, *Shaanxi, China* 56 H4
Fengári, *Greece* 45 F9
Fengcheng, *Jiangxi, China* 59 C10
Fengcheng, *Liaoning, China* 57 D13
Fengfeng, *China* 56 F8
Fenggang, *China* 58 D6
Fenghua, *China* 59 C13
Fenghuang, *China* 58 D7
Fengkai, *China* 59 F8
Fengkang, *Taiwan* 59 F13
Fengle, *China* 59 B9
Fenglin, *Taiwan* 59 F13
Fengning, *China* 56 D9
Fengqing, *China* 58 E2
Fengqiu, *China* 56 G8
Fengrun, *China* 57 E10
Fengshan, *Guangxi Zhuangzu, China* 58 E7
Fengshan, *Guangxi Zhuangzu, China* 58 E6
Fengshan, *Taiwan* 59 F13
Fengshun, *China* 59 F11
Fengtai, *Anhui, China* 59 A11
Fengtai, *Beijing, China* 56 E9
Fengxian, *China* 59 B13
Fengxiang, *China* 56 G4
Fengxin, *China* 59 C10
Fengyang, *China* 57 H9
Fengyi, *China* 58 E3
Fengyüan, *Taiwan* 59 E13
Fengzhen, *China* 56 D7
Feno, C. de, *France* 21 G12
Fenoarivo, *Fianarantsoa, Madag.* 89 C8
Fenoarivo, *Fianarantsoa, Madag.* 89 C8
Fenoarivo Afovoany, *Madag.* 89 B8
Fenoarivo Atsinanana, *Madag.* 89 B8
Fens, The, *U.K.* 14 E7
Fensmark, *Denmark* 11 J5
Fenton, *U.S.A.* 114 D4
Fenxi, *China* 56 F6
Fenyang, *China* 56 F6
Fenyi, *China* 59 D10
Feodosiya, *Ukraine* 33 K8
Ferdows, *Iran* 71 C8
Fère-Champenoise, *France* 19 D10
Fère-en-Tardenois, *France* 19 C10
Ferentino, *Italy* 41 G10
Ferfer, *Somali Rep.* 75 F4
Fergana = Farghona, *Uzbekistan* 52 E8
Fergus, *Canada* 116 C4
Fergus Falls, *U.S.A.* 112 B6
Feričanci, *Croatia* 28 E2
Ferihegy, Budapest ✕ (BUD), *Hungary* 28 C4
Ferkéssédougou, *Ivory C.* 82 D3
Ferlach, *Austria* 26 E7
Ferland, *Canada* 104 B2
Ferlo, Vallée du, *Senegal* 82 B2
Ferlo-Nord ⌓, *Senegal* 82 B2
Ferlo-Sud ⌓, *Senegal* 82 B2
Fermanagh □, *U.K.* 12 B4
Fermo, *Italy* 41 E10
Fermont, *Canada* 105 B6
Fermoselle, *Spain* 36 D4
Fermoy, *Ireland* 12 D3
Fernán Nuñéz, *Spain* 37 H6
Fernández, *Argentina* 126 B3
Fernandina Beach, *U.S.A.* 115 K5
Fernando de Noronha, *Brazil* 125 D12
Fernando Póo = Bioko, *Eq. Guin.* 83 E6
Ferndale, *U.S.A.* 110 B4
Fernie, *Canada* 102 D5
Fernlees, *Australia* 94 C4
Fernley, *U.S.A.* 108 G4
Ferozepore = Firozpur, *India* 68 D6
Férrai, *Greece* 45 F10
Ferrandina, *Italy* 43 B9
Ferrara, *Italy* 41 D8
Ferrato, C., *Italy* 42 C2
Ferreira do Alentejo, *Portugal* 37 G2
Ferreñafe, *Peru* 124 E3
Ferrerías, *Spain* 48 B11
Ferret, C., *France* 20 D2
Ferrette, *France* 19 E14
Ferriday, *U.S.A.* 113 K9
Ferriere, *Italy* 40 D6
Ferrières, *France* 19 D9
Ferro, Capo, *Italy* 42 A2
Ferrol, *Spain* 36 B2
Ferron, *U.S.A.* 109 G8
Ferrutx, C., *Spain* 48 B10
Ferryland, *Canada* 105 C9
Fertile, *U.S.A.* 112 B6
Fertőszentmiklós, *Hungary* 28 C1
Fertotavi ∆, *Hungary* 28 C1
Fès, *Morocco* 78 B5
Fessenden, *U.S.A.* 112 B5
Festus, *U.S.A.* 112 F9
Feté Bowé, *Senegal* 82 C2
Feteşti, *Romania* 29 F12
Fethiye, *Turkey* 47 E11
Fethiye Körfezi, *Turkey* 47 E10
Fetlar, *U.K.* 13 A8
Feuilles →, *Canada* 101 C12
Feurs, *France* 21 C8
Fez = Fès, *Morocco* 78 B5
Fezzan, *Libya* 79 C8
Fiambalá, *Argentina* 126 B2
Fianarantsoa, *Madag.* 89 C8
Fianarantsoa □, *Madag.* 89 B8
Fiche, *Ethiopia* 81 F4
Fichtelgebirge, *Germany* 25 E7
Fichtelgebirge ⌓, *Germany* 25 E8
Ficksburg, *S. Africa* 89 D4
Fidenza, *Italy* 40 D7
Fiditi, *Nigeria* 83 D5
Field →, *Australia* 94 C2
Field I., *Australia* 92 B5
Fieni, *Romania* 29 E10
Fier, *Albania* 44 F3
Fierzë, *Albania* 44 D4
Fife ⌓, *U.K.* 13 E5
Fife □, *U.K.* 13 E5
Fife Ness, *U.K.* 13 E6
Fifth Cataract, *Sudan* 80 D3
Figari, *France* 21 G13
Figeac, *France* 20 D6
Figeholm, *Sweden* 11 G10
Figline Valdarno, *Italy* 41 E8
Figtree, *Zimbabwe* 87 G2
Figueira Castelo Rodrigo, *Portugal* 36 E4
Figueira da Foz, *Portugal* 36 E2
Figueiró dos Vinhos, *Portugal* 36 F2
Figueres, *Spain* 38 C7
Figuig, *Morocco* 78 B5
Fihaonana, *Madag.* 89 B8
Fiherenana, *Madag.* 89 B8
Fiherenana →, *Madag.* 89 C7
Fiji ■, *Pac. Oc.* 91 C8
Fik, *Ethiopia* 81 E5
Fika, *Nigeria* 83 C7
Filabres, Sierra de los, *Spain* 37 H8
Filabusi, *Zimbabwe* 89 C4
Filadélfia, *Italy* 43 D9
Fil'akovo, *Slovak Rep.* 27 C12
Filey, *U.K.* 14 C7
Filey B., *U.K.* 14 C7
Filfla, *Malta* 49 D1
Filiaşi, *Romania* 29 F8
Filiátes, *Greece* 46 B2
Filiatrá, *Greece* 46 D3
Filicudi, *Italy* 43 D7
Filingué, *Niger* 83 C5
Filiourí →, *Greece* 45 E9
Filipstad, *Sweden* 10 E8
Filisur, *Switz.* 25 J5
Fillmore, *Calif., U.S.A.* 111 L8
Fillmore, *Utah, U.S.A.* 109 G7
Filótion, *Greece* 47 D7
Filottrano, *Italy* 41 E10
Filtu, *Ethiopia* 81 F5
Fina ⌓, *Mali* 82 C3
Finale Emília, *Italy* 41 D8
Finale Lígure, *Italy* 40 D5
Fiñana, *Spain* 37 H8
Finch, *Canada* 117 A9
Finch Hatton, *Australia* 94 K6
Findhorn →, *U.K.* 13 D5
Findlay, *U.S.A.* 114 E4
Finger L., *Canada* 104 B1
Finger Lakes, *U.S.A.* 117 D8
Fíngoè, *Mozam.* 87 E3
Finike, *Turkey* 47 E12
Finike Körfezi, *Turkey* 47 E12
Finiq, *Albania* 44 G4
Finistère □, *France* 18 D3
Finisterre = Fisterra, *Spain* 36 C1
Finisterre, C. = Fisterra, C., *Spain* 36 C1
Finke, *Australia* 94 D1
Finke Gorge ∆, *Australia* 92 D5
Finland ■, *Europe* 8 E22
Finland, G. of, *Europe* 9 G21
Finlay →, *Canada* 102 B3
Finley, *Australia* 95 F4
Finley, *U.S.A.* 112 B6
Finn →, *Ireland* 12 B4
Finnerödja, *Sweden* 11 F8
Finnigan, Mt., *Australia* 94 B4
Finniss, C., *Australia* 95 E1
Finnmark, *Norway* 8 B20
Finnsnes, *Norway* 8 B18
Finspång, *Sweden* 11 F9
Finsteraarhorn, *Switz.* 25 J4
Finsterwalde, *Germany* 24 D9
Fiora →, *Italy* 41 F8
Fiordland ∆, *N.Z.* 91 L1
Fiorenzuola d'Arda, *Italy* 40 D6
Fīq, *Syria* 74 C4

Firat = Furāt, Nahr al →, *Asia* 70 D5
Fire Island ⌂, *U.S.A.* 117 F11
Firebag →, *Canada* 103 B6
Firebaugh, *U.S.A.* 110 J6
Firedrake L., *Canada* 103 A8
Firenze, *Italy* 41 E8
Firenze Amerigo Vespucci ✕ (FLR), *Italy* 40 E8
Firenze Pisa ✕ (PSA), *Italy* 40 E7
Firenzuola, *Italy* 41 D8
Firk, Sha'ib →, *Iraq* 70 D5
Firmi, *France* 20 D6
Firminy, *France* 21 C8
Firozabad, *India* 69 F8
Firozpur, *India* 68 D6
Firozpur-Jhirka, *India* 68 F7
Fīrūzābād, *Iran* 71 D7
Fīrūzkūh, *Iran* 71 C7
Firvale, *Canada* 102 C3
Fish →, *Namibia* 88 D2
Fish →, *S. Africa* 88 E3
Fish River Canyon, *Namibia* 88 D2
Fisher, *Australia* 93 F5
Fisher B., *Canada* 103 C9
Fishers I., *U.S.A.* 117 E13
Fishguard, *U.K.* 15 E3
Fishing L., *Canada* 103 C9
Fishkill, *U.S.A.* 117 E11
Fismes, *France* 19 C10
Fisterra, *Spain* 36 C1
Fisterra, C., *Spain* 36 C1
Fitchburg, *U.S.A.* 117 D13
Fitz Roy, *Argentina* 128 F3
Fitzgerald, *Canada* 102 B6
Fitzgerald, *U.S.A.* 115 K4
Fitzgerald River △, *Australia* 93 F3
Fitzmaurice →, *Australia* 92 B5
Fitzroy →, *Queens., Australia* 94 C5
Fitzroy →, *W. Austral., Australia* 92 C3
Fitzroy, Mte., *Argentina* 128 F2
Fitzroy Crossing, *Australia* 92 C4
Fitzwilliam I., *Canada* 116 A3
Fiuggi, *Italy* 41 G10
Fiume = Rijeka, *Croatia* 41 C11
Fiumicino, Roma ✕ (FCO), *Italy* 41 G9
Five Points, *U.S.A.* 110 J6
Fivizzano, *Italy* 40 D7
Fizi, *Dem. Rep. of the Congo* 86 C2
Fjällbacka, *Sweden* 11 F5
Fjärdhundra, *Sweden* 10 E10
Fjellerup, *Denmark* 11 H4
Fjerritslev, *Denmark* 11 G3
Fjugesta, *Sweden* 10 E8
Flagstaff, *U.S.A.* 109 J8
Flagstaff L., *U.S.A.* 115 C10
Flaherty I., *Canada* 104 A4
Flåm, *Norway* 9 F12
Flambeau →, *U.S.A.* 112 C9
Flamborough Hd., *U.K.* 14 C7
Fläming, *Germany* 24 C8
Flaming Gorge ⌂, *U.S.A.* 108 F9
Flaming Gorge Reservoir, *U.S.A.* 108 F9
Flamingo, Teluk, *Indonesia* 63 F9
Flanders = Flandre, *Europe* 19 B9
Flandre, *Europe* 19 B9
Flandre-Occidentale = West-Vlaanderen □, *Belgium* 17 D2
Flandre-Orientale = Oost-Vlaanderen □, *Belgium* 17 C3
Flandreau, *U.S.A.* 112 C6
Flanigan, *U.S.A.* 110 E7
Flannan Is., *U.K.* 13 C1
Flåsjön, *Sweden* 8 D16
Flat →, *Canada* 102 A3
Flathead L., *U.S.A.* 108 C7
Flattery, C., *Australia* 94 A4
Flattery, C., *U.S.A.* 110 B2
Flatwoods, *U.S.A.* 114 F4
Fleetwood, *U.K.* 14 D4
Fleetwood, *U.S.A.* 117 F9
Flekkefjord, *Norway* 9 G12
Flemington, *U.S.A.* 116 E7
Flen, *Sweden* 10 E10
Flensburg, *Germany* 24 A5
Flers, *France* 18 D6
Flesherton, *Canada* 116 B4
Flesko, Tanjung, *Indonesia* 63 D6
Fleurance, *France* 20 E4
Fleurier, *Switz.* 25 J2
Fleurieu Pen., *Australia* 95 F2
Flevoland □, *Neths.* 17 B5
Flin Flon, *Canada* 103 C8
Flinders →, *Australia* 94 B3
Flinders B., *Australia* 93 F2
Flinders Group, *Australia* 94 A3
Flinders I., *S. Austral., Australia* 95 E1
Flinders I., *Tas., Australia* 95 G4
Flinders Ranges, *Australia* 95 E2
Flinders Reefs, *Australia* 94 B4
Flint, *U.K.* 14 D4
Flint, *U.S.A.* 114 D4
Flint →, *U.S.A.* 115 K3
Flint I., *Kiribati* 97 J12
Flintshire □, *U.K.* 14 D4
Fliseryd, *Sweden* 11 G10
Flix, *Spain* 38 D5
Flixecourt, *France* 19 B9
Floby, *Sweden* 11 F7
Floda, *Sweden* 11 G6
Flodden, *U.K.* 14 B5
Flogny-la-Chapelle, *France* 19 E10
Floodwood, *U.S.A.* 112 B8
Flora, *U.S.A.* 114 F1
Florac, *France* 20 D7
Florala, *U.S.A.* 115 K2
Florence = Firenze, *Italy* 41 E8
Florence, *Ala., U.S.A.* 115 H2
Florence, *Ariz., U.S.A.* 109 K8
Florence, *Colo., U.S.A.* 112 F2
Florence, *Oreg., U.S.A.* 108 E1
Florence, *S.C., U.S.A.* 115 H6
Florence, L., *Australia* 95 D2
Florencia, *Colombia* 124 C3
Florennes, *Belgium* 17 D4
Florensac, *France* 20 E7
Florenville, *Belgium* 17 E5
Flores, *Guatemala* 120 C2
Flores, *Indonesia* 63 F6
Flores I., *Canada* 102 D3
Flores Sea, *Indonesia* 63 F6
Floreşti, *Moldova* 29 C13
Floresville, *U.S.A.* 113 L5
Floriano, *Brazil* 125 E10
Florianópolis, *Brazil* 127 B6
Florida, *Cuba* 120 B4
Florida, *Uruguay* 127 C4
Florida □, *U.S.A.* 115 L5
Florida, Straits of, *U.S.A.* 120 B4
Florida B., *U.S.A.* 120 B3
Florida Keys, *U.S.A.* 115 N5
Florídia, *Italy* 43 E8
Flórina, *Greece* 44 F5
Flórina □, *Greece* 44 F5
Florø, *Norway* 9 F11
Flower Station, *Canada* 117 A8
Flowerpot I., *Canada* 116 A3
Floydada, *U.S.A.* 113 J4
Fluk, *Indonesia* 63 E7
Flúmen →, *Spain* 38 D4
Flumendosa →, *Italy* 42 C2
Fluminimaggiore, *Italy* 42 C1
Flushing = Vlissingen, *Neths.* 17 C3
Fluviá →, *Spain* 38 C8
Flying Fish, C., *Antarctica* 5 D15
Foam Lake, *Canada* 103 C8
Foča, *Bos.-H.* 44 C2
Foça, *Turkey* 47 C8
Fochabers, *U.K.* 13 D5
Focşani, *Romania* 29 E12
Fodécontéa, *Guinea* 82 C2
Fogang, *China* 59 F9
Fóggia, *Italy* 43 A8
Foggo, *Nigeria* 83 C6
Foglia →, *Italy* 41 E9
Fogo, *Canada* 105 C9
Fogo I., *Canada* 105 C9
Fohnsdorf, *Austria* 26 D7
Föhr, *Germany* 24 A4
Foia, *Portugal* 37 H2
Foix, *France* 20 E5
Fojnica, *Bos.-H.* 28 G2
Fokino, *Russia* 32 F8
Fokís □, *Greece* 46 C4
Fokku, *Nigeria* 83 C5
Folda, *Nord-Trøndelag, Norway* 8 D14
Folda, *Nordland, Norway* 8 C16
Földeák, *Hungary* 28 D5
Folégandros, *Greece* 46 E6
Foley, *Botswana* 88 C4
Foley, *U.S.A.* 115 K2
Foleyet, *Canada* 104 C3
Folgefonni, *Norway* 9 F12
Foligno, *Italy* 41 F9
Folkestone, *U.K.* 15 F9
Folkston, *U.S.A.* 115 K5
Follansbee, *U.S.A.* 116 F4
Follónica, *Italy* 40 F7
Follónica, G. di, *Italy* 40 F7
Folsom L., *U.S.A.* 110 G5
Folteşti, *Romania* 29 E13
Fond-du-Lac, *Canada* 103 B7
Fond du Lac, *U.S.A.* 112 D10
Fond-du-Lac →, *Canada* 103 B7
Fonda, *U.S.A.* 117 D10
Fondi, *Italy* 42 A6
Fonfría, *Spain* 36 D4
Fongafale, *Tuvalu* 96 H9
Fonni, *Italy* 42 B2
Fonsagrada = A Fonsagrada, *Spain* 36 B3
Fonseca, G. de, *Cent. Amer.* 120 D2
Font-Romeu-Odeillo-Via, *France* 20 F5
Fontaine-Française, *France* 19 E12
Fontainebleau, *France* 19 D9
Fontana, *U.S.A.* 111 L9
Fontas →, *Canada* 102 B4
Fonte Boa, *Brazil* 124 D5
Fontem, *Cameroon* 83 D6
Fontenay-le-Comte, *France* 20 B3
Fontenelle Reservoir, *U.S.A.* 108 E8
Fontur, *Iceland* 8 C6
Fonyód, *Hungary* 28 D2
Foochow = Fuzhou, *China* 59 D12
Foping, *China* 56 H5
Forbach, *France* 19 C13
Forbes, *Australia* 95 E4
Forbesganj, *India* 69 F12
Forcados, *Nigeria* 83 D6
Forcados →, *Nigeria* 83 D6
Forcalquier, *France* 21 E9
Forchheim, *Germany* 25 F7
Ford City, *Calif., U.S.A.* 111 K7
Ford City, *Pa., U.S.A.* 116 F5
Førde, *Norway* 9 F11
Ford's Bridge, *Australia* 95 D4
Fordyce, *U.S.A.* 113 J8
Forécariah, *Guinea* 82 D2
Forel, Mt., *Greenland* 98 C16
Foremost, *Canada* 102 D6
Forest, *Canada* 116 C3
Forest, *U.S.A.* 113 J10
Forest City, *Iowa, U.S.A.* 112 D8
Forest City, *N.C., U.S.A.* 115 H5
Forest City, *Pa., U.S.A.* 117 E9
Forest Grove, *U.S.A.* 110 E3
Forestburg, *Canada* 102 C6
Foreste Casentinesi-Monte Falterona-Campigna △, *Italy* 41 E8
Foresthill, *U.S.A.* 110 F6
Forestier Pen., *Australia* 95 G4
Forestville, *Canada* 105 C6
Forestville, *Calif., U.S.A.* 110 G4
Forestville, *N.Y., U.S.A.* 116 D5
Forêt d'Orient ⌂, *France* 19 D11
Forez, Mts. du, *France* 20 C7
Forfar, *U.K.* 13 E6
Forillon △, *Canada* 105 C7
Forks, *U.S.A.* 110 C2
Forksville, *U.S.A.* 117 E8
Forlì, *Italy* 41 D9
Forman, *U.S.A.* 112 B6
Formazza, *Italy* 40 B5
Formby Pt., *U.K.* 14 D4
Formentera, *Spain* 48 C7
Formentor, C. de, *Spain* 48 B10
Former Yugoslav Republic of Macedonia = Macedonia ■, *Europe* 44 E5
Fórmia, *Italy* 42 A6
Formígine, *Italy* 40 D7
Formosa = Taiwan ■, *Asia* 59 F13
Formosa, *Argentina* 126 B4
Formosa, *Brazil* 125 G9
Formosa □, *Argentina* 126 B4
Formosa, Serra, *Brazil* 125 F8
Formosa B. = Ungwana B., *Kenya* 86 C5
Fornells, *Spain* 48 A11
Fornos de Algodres, *Portugal* 36 E3
Fornovo di Taro, *Italy* 40 D7
Føroyar, *Atl. Oc.* 8 F9
Forres, *U.K.* 13 D5
Forrest, *Australia* 93 F4
Forrest, Mt., *Australia* 93 D4
Forrest City, *U.S.A.* 113 H9
Fors, *Sweden* 10 D10
Forsayth, *Australia* 94 B3
Forshaga, *Sweden* 10 E7
Förslöv, *Sweden* 11 H6
Forsmo, *Sweden* 10 A11
Forssa, *Finland* 9 F20
Forst, *Germany* 24 D10
Forsvik, *Sweden* 11 F8
Forsyth, *U.S.A.* 108 C10
Fort Abbas, *Pakistan* 68 E5
Fort Albany, *Canada* 104 B3
Fort Ann, *U.S.A.* 117 C11
Fort Assiniboine, *Canada* 102 C6
Fort Augustus, *U.K.* 13 D4
Fort Beaufort, *S. Africa* 88 E4
Fort Benton, *U.S.A.* 108 C8
Fort Bragg, *U.S.A.* 108 G2
Fort Bridger, *U.S.A.* 108 F8
Fort Chipewyan, *Canada* 103 B6
Fort Clatsop ⌂, *U.S.A.* 110 D3
Fort Collins, *U.S.A.* 112 E2
Fort-Coulonge, *Canada* 104 C4
Fort Covington, *U.S.A.* 117 B10
Fort Davis, *U.S.A.* 113 K3
Fort-de-France, *Martinique* 120 c
Fort Defiance, *U.S.A.* 109 J9
Fort Dodge, *U.S.A.* 112 D7
Fort Edward, *U.S.A.* 117 C11
Fort Erie, *Canada* 116 D6
Fort Fairfield, *U.S.A.* 115 B12
Fort Frances, *Canada* 103 D10
Fort Franklin = Déline, *Canada* 100 B7
Fort Garland, *U.S.A.* 109 H11
Fort George = Chisasibi, *Canada* 104 B4
Fort Good Hope, *Canada* 100 B7
Fort Hancock, *U.S.A.* 109 L11
Fort Hope, *Canada* 104 B2
Fort Irwin, *U.S.A.* 111 K10
Fort Kent, *U.S.A.* 115 B11
Fort Klamath, *U.S.A.* 108 E3
Fort Laramie, *U.S.A.* 112 D2
Fort Lauderdale, *U.S.A.* 115 M5
Fort Liard, *Canada* 102 A4
Fort Liberté, *Haiti* 121 C5
Fort Lupton, *U.S.A.* 112 E2
Fort MacKay, *Canada* 102 B6
Fort Macleod, *Canada* 102 D6
Fort McMurray, *Canada* 102 B6
Fort McPherson, *Canada* 100 B6
Fort Madison, *U.S.A.* 112 E9
Fort Meade, *U.S.A.* 115 M5
Fort Morgan, *U.S.A.* 112 E3
Fort Myers, *U.S.A.* 115 M5
Fort Nelson, *Canada* 102 B4
Fort Nelson →, *Canada* 102 B4
Fort Norman = Tulita, *Canada* 100 B7
Fort Payne, *U.S.A.* 115 H3
Fort Peck, *U.S.A.* 108 B10
Fort Peck Dam, *U.S.A.* 108 C10
Fort Peck L., *U.S.A.* 108 C10
Fort Pierce, *U.S.A.* 115 M5
Fort Pierre, *U.S.A.* 112 C4
Fort Plain, *U.S.A.* 117 D10
Fort Portal, *Uganda* 86 B3
Fort Providence, *Canada* 102 A5
Fort Qu'Appelle, *Canada* 103 C8
Fort Resolution, *Canada* 102 A6
Fort Rixon, *Zimbabwe* 87 G2
Fort Ross, *U.S.A.* 110 G3
Fort Rupert = Waskaganish, *Canada* 104 B4
Fort St. James, *Canada* 102 C4
Fort St. John, *Canada* 102 B4
Fort Saskatchewan, *Canada* 102 C6
Fort Scott, *U.S.A.* 113 G7
Fort Severn, *Canada* 104 A2
Fort Shevchenko, *Kazakhstan* 35 H10
Fort Simpson, *Canada* 102 A4
Fort Smith, *Canada* 102 B6
Fort Smith, *U.S.A.* 113 H7
Fort Stockton, *U.S.A.* 113 K3
Fort Sumner, *U.S.A.* 113 H2
Fort Thompson, *U.S.A.* 112 C5
Fort Union ⌂, *U.S.A.* 113 H2
Fort Valley, *U.S.A.* 115 J4
Fort Vermilion, *Canada* 102 B5
Fort Walton Beach, *U.S.A.* 115 K2
Fort Wayne, *U.S.A.* 114 E3
Fort William, *U.K.* 13 E3
Fort Worth, *U.S.A.* 113 J6
Fort Yates, *U.S.A.* 112 B4
Fort Yukon, *U.S.A.* 100 B5
Fortaleza, *Brazil* 125 D11
Forteau, *Canada* 105 B8
Fortescue →, *Australia* 92 D2
Forth →, *U.K.* 13 E5
Forth, Firth of, *U.K.* 13 E6
Fortore →, *Italy* 41 G12
Fortrose, *U.K.* 13 D4
Fortuna, *Spain* 39 G3
Fortuna, *Calif., U.S.A.* 108 F1
Fortuna, *N. Dak., U.S.A.* 112 A3
Fortune, *Canada* 105 C8
Fortune B., *Canada* 105 C8
Forūr, *Iran* 71 E7
Fos-sur-Mer, *France* 21 E8
Foshan, *China* 59 F9
Fosna, *Norway* 8 E14
Fosnavåg, *Norway* 9 E11
Foso, *Ghana* 83 D4
Fossano, *Italy* 40 D4
Fossil, *U.S.A.* 108 D3
Fossil Butte ⌂, *U.S.A.* 108 F8
Fossombrone, *Italy* 41 E9
Foster, *Canada* 117 A12
Foster →, *Canada* 103 B7
Fosters Ra., *Australia* 94 C1
Fostoria, *U.S.A.* 114 E4
Fotadrevo, *Madag.* 89 C8
Fouesnant, *France* 18 E2
Fougères, *France* 18 D5
Foul Pt., *Sri Lanka* 66 Q12
Foula, *U.K.* 13 A6
Foulalaba, *Mali* 82 C3
Foulness I., *U.K.* 15 F8
Foulpointe, *Madag.* 89 B8
Foulweather, C., *U.S.A.* 106 B2
Foumban, *Cameroon* 83 D7
Foumbot, *Cameroon* 83 D7
Foundiougne, *Senegal* 82 C1
Fountain, *U.S.A.* 112 F2
Fountain Springs, *U.S.A.* 111 K8
Fourchambault, *France* 19 E10
Fouriesburg, *S. Africa* 88 D4
Fourmies, *France* 19 B11
Fournás, *Greece* 46 B3
Foúrnoi, *Greece* 47 D8
Fours, *France* 19 F10
Fourth Cataract, *Sudan* 80 D3
Fouta Djallon, *Guinea* 82 C2
Foux, Cap-à-, *Haiti* 121 C5
Foveaux Str., *N.Z.* 91 M2
Fowey, *U.K.* 15 G3
Fowler, *Calif., U.S.A.* 110 J7
Fowler, *Colo., U.S.A.* 112 F3
Fowlers B., *Australia* 93 F5
Fowman, *Iran* 71 B6
Fox →, *Canada* 103 B10
Fox Creek, *Canada* 102 C5
Fox Lake, *Canada* 102 B6
Fox Valley, *Canada* 103 C7
Foxboro, *U.S.A.* 117 D13
Foxdale, *Australia* 94 J6
Foxe Basin, *Canada* 101 B12
Foxe Chan., *Canada* 101 B11
Foxe Pen., *Canada* 101 B12
Foxen, *Sweden* 10 E5
Foxton, *N.Z.* 91 J5
Foyle, Lough, *U.K.* 12 A4
Foynes, *Ireland* 12 D2
Foz, *Spain* 36 B3
Foz do Cunene, *Angola* 88 B1
Foz do Iguaçu, *Brazil* 127 B5
Frackville, *U.S.A.* 117 F8
Fraga, *Spain* 38 D5
Fraile Muerto, *Uruguay* 127 C5
Fram Basin, *Arctic* 4 A
Framingham, *U.S.A.* 117 D13
Frampol, *Poland* 31 H9
Franca, *Brazil* 125 H9
Francavilla al Mare, *Italy* 41 F11
Francavilla Fontana, *Italy* 43 B10
France ■, *Europe* 7 F6
Frances, *Australia* 95 F3
Frances →, *Canada* 102 A3
Frances L., *Canada* 102 A3
Franceville, *Gabon* 84 E2
Franche-Comté □, *France* 19 F12
Francis Case, L., *U.S.A.* 112 D5
Francisco Beltrão, *Brazil* 127 B5
Francisco I. Madero, *Coahuila, Mexico* 118 B4
Francisco I. Madero, *Durango, Mexico* 118 C4
Francistown, *Botswana* 89 C4
Francofonte, *Italy* 43 E7
François, *Canada* 105 C8
François L., *Canada* 102 C3
Francois Peron △, *Australia* 93 E1
Franeker, *Neths.* 17 A5
Frank Hann △, *Australia* 93 F3
Frankado, *Djibouti* 81 E5
Frankenberg, *Germany* 24 D4
Frankenhöhe ⌂, *Germany* 25 F6
Frankenwald, *Germany* 25 E7
Frankenwald ⌂, *Germany* 25 E7
Frankford, *Canada* 116 B7
Frankfort, *S. Africa* 89 D4
Frankfort, *Ind., U.S.A.* 114 E2
Frankfort, *Kans., U.S.A.* 112 F6
Frankfort, *Ky., U.S.A.* 114 F3
Frankfort, *N.Y., U.S.A.* 117 C9
Frankfurt, *Brandenburg, Germany* 24 C10
Frankfurt, *Hessen, Germany* 25 E4
Frankfurt ✕ (FRA), *Germany* 25 E4
Fränkische Alb, *Germany* 25 F7
Fränkische Rezat →, *Germany* 25 F7
Fränkische Saale →, *Germany* 25 E5
Fränkische Schweiz, *Germany* 25 F7
Fränkische Schweiz-Veldensteiner Forst ⌂, *Germany* 25 F7
Frankland →, *Australia* 93 G2
Franklin, *Ky., U.S.A.* 115 G2
Franklin, *La., U.S.A.* 113 L9
Franklin, *Mass., U.S.A.* 117 D13
Franklin, *N.H., U.S.A.* 117 C13
Franklin, *Nebr., U.S.A.* 112 E5
Franklin, *Pa., U.S.A.* 116 E5
Franklin, *Va., U.S.A.* 115 G7
Franklin, *W. Va., U.S.A.* 114 F6
Franklin B., *Canada* 100 B7
Franklin D. Roosevelt L., *U.S.A.* 108 B4
Franklin-Gordon Wild Rivers △, *Australia* 95 G4
Franklin I., *Antarctica* 5 D11
Franklin L., *U.S.A.* 108 F6
Franklin Mts., *Canada* 100 B7
Franklin Str., *Canada* 100 A10
Franklinton, *U.S.A.* 113 K9
Franklinville, *U.S.A.* 116 D6
Franks Pk., *U.S.A.* 108 E9
Frankston, *Australia* 95 F4
Frånö, *Sweden* 10 B11
Fransfontein, *Namibia* 88 C2
Fränsta, *Sweden* 10 B10
Frantsa Iosifa, Zemlya, *Russia* 52 A6
Franz, *Canada* 104 C3
Franz Josef Land = Frantsa Iosifa, Zemlya, *Russia* 52 A6
Franz Josef Strauss, München ✕ (MUC), *Germany* 25 G7
Franzburg, *Germany* 24 A8
Frascati, *Italy* 41 G9
Fraser, *U.S.A.* 116 D2
Fraser →, *B.C., Canada* 102 D4
Fraser →, *Nfld. & L., Canada* 105 A7
Fraser, Mt., *Australia* 93 E2
Fraser I., *Australia* 95 D5
Fraser Lake, *Canada* 102 C4
Fraserburg, *S. Africa* 88 E3
Fraserburgh, *U.K.* 13 D6
Fraserdale, *Canada* 104 C3
Frashër, *Albania* 44 F4
Frasne, *France* 19 F13
Frăteşti, *Romania* 29 G10
Frauenfeld, *Switz.* 25 H4
Fray Bentos, *Uruguay* 126 C4
Fray Jorge △, *Chile* 126 C1
Frechilla, *Spain* 36 C6
Fredericia, *Denmark* 11 J3
Frederick, *Md., U.S.A.* 114 F7
Frederick, *Okla., U.S.A.* 113 H5
Frederick, *S. Dak., U.S.A.* 112 C5
Fredericksburg, *Pa., U.S.A.* 117 F8
Fredericksburg, *Tex., U.S.A.* 113 K5
Fredericksburg, *Va., U.S.A.* 114 F7
Fredericktown, *Mo., U.S.A.* 113 G9
Fredericktown, *Ohio, U.S.A.* 116 F2
Frederico I. Madero, Presa, *Mexico* 118 B3
Frederico Westphalen, *Brazil* 127 B5
Fredericton, *Canada* 105 C6
Fredericton Junction, *Canada* 105 C6
Frederiksborg Amtskommune □, *Denmark* 11 J6
Frederikshåb = Paamiut, *Greenland* 101 B15
Frederikshamn = Hamina, *Finland* 9 F22
Frederikshavn, *Denmark* 11 G4
Frederikssund, *Denmark* 11 J6
Frederiksted, *U.S. Virgin Is.* 121 C7
Frederiksværk, *Denmark* 11 J6
Fredonia, *Ariz., U.S.A.* 109 H7
Fredonia, *Kans., U.S.A.* 113 G7
Fredonia, *N.Y., U.S.A.* 116 D5
Fredriksberg, *Sweden* 10 D8
Fredrikstad, *Norway* 9 G14
Free State □, *S. Africa* 88 D4
Freehold, *U.S.A.* 117 F10
Freel Peak, *U.S.A.* 110 G7
Freeland, *U.S.A.* 117 E9
Freels, C., *Canada* 105 C9
Freeman, *Calif., U.S.A.* 111 K9
Freeman, *S. Dak., U.S.A.* 112 D6
Freeport, *Bahamas* 120 A4
Freeport, *Ill., U.S.A.* 112 D10
Freeport, *N.Y., U.S.A.* 117 F11
Freeport, *Ohio, U.S.A.* 116 F3
Freeport, *Pa., U.S.A.* 116 F5
Freeport, *Tex., U.S.A.* 113 L7
Freetown, *S. Leone* 82 D2
Frégate, L. de la, *Canada* 104 B5
Fregenal de la Sierra, *Spain* 37 G4
Fregene, *Italy* 41 G9
Fréhel, C., *France* 18 D4
Freiberg, *Germany* 24 E9
Freibourg = Fribourg, *Switz.* 25 J3
Freiburg, *Baden-W., Germany* 25 H3
Freiburg, *Niedersachsen, Germany* 24 B5
Freilassing, *Germany* 25 H8
Freire, *Chile* 128 D2
Freirina, *Chile* 126 B1
Freising, *Germany* 25 G7
Freistadt, *Austria* 26 C7
Freital, *Germany* 24 D9
Fréjus, *France* 21 E10
Fremantle, *Australia* 93 F2
Fremont, *Calif., U.S.A.* 110 H4
Fremont, *Mich., U.S.A.* 114 D3
Fremont, *Nebr., U.S.A.* 112 E6
Fremont, *Ohio, U.S.A.* 114 E4
Fremont →, *U.S.A.* 109 G8
French Camp, *U.S.A.* 110 H5
French Cays = Plana Cays, *Bahamas* 121 B5
French Creek →, *U.S.A.* 116 E5
French Guiana ▨, *S. Amer.* 125 C8

French Polynesia ☒, *Pac. Oc.* 97 K13
Frenchman Cr. →, *N. Amer.* 108 B10
Frenchman Cr. →, *U.S.A.* 112 E4
Frenštát pod Radhoštěm, *Czech Rep.* 27 B11
Fresco, *Ivory C.* 82 D3
Fresco →, *Brazil* 125 E8
Freshfield, C., *Antarctica* 5 C10
Fresnay-sur-Sarthe, *France* 18 D7
Fresnillo, *Mexico* 118 C4
Fresno, *U.S.A.* 110 J7
Fresno Alhandiga, *Spain* 36 E5
Fresno Reservoir, *U.S.A.* 108 B9
Freudenstadt, *Germany* 25 G4
Frévent, *France* 19 B9
Frew →, *Australia* 94 C2
Frewsburg, *U.S.A.* 116 D5
Freycinet △, *Australia* 95 G4
Freycinet Pen., *Australia* 95 G4
Freyming-Merlebach, *France* 19 C13
Freyung, *Germany* 25 G9
Fria, *Guinea* 82 C2
Fria, C., *Namibia* 88 B1
Friant, *U.S.A.* 110 J7
Frías, *Argentina* 126 B2
Fribourg, *Switz.* 25 J3
Fribourg ☐, *Switz.* 25 J3
Fridafors, *Sweden* 11 H8
Friday Harbor, *U.S.A.* 110 B3
Friedberg, *Bayern, Germany* 25 G6
Friedberg, *Hessen, Germany* 25 E4
Friedens, *U.S.A.* 116 F6
Friedland, *Germany* 24 B9
Friedrichshafen, *Germany* 25 H5
Friedrichskoog, *Germany* 24 A4
Friedrichstadt, *Germany* 24 A5
Friendship, *U.S.A.* 116 D6
Friesach, *Austria* 26 E7
Friesack, *Germany* 24 C8
Friesland ☐, *Neths.* 17 A5
Friesoythe, *Germany* 24 B3
Friggesund, *Sweden* 10 C10
Frillesås, *Sweden* 11 G6
Frinnaryd, *Sweden* 11 G8
Frio →, *U.S.A.* 113 L5
Frio, C., *Brazil* 122 F6
Friol, *Spain* 36 B3
Friona, *U.S.A.* 113 H3
Fristad, *Sweden* 11 G6
Fritch, *U.S.A.* 113 H4
Fritsla, *Sweden* 11 G6
Fritzlar, *Germany* 24 D5
Friuli-Venézia Giulia ☐, *Italy* 41 B9
Frobisher B., *Canada* 101 B13
Frobisher Bay = Iqaluit, *Canada* 101 B13
Frobisher L., *Canada* 103 B7
Frohavet, *Norway* 8 E13
Frohnleiten, *Austria* 26 D8
Frolovo, *Russia* 34 F6
Frombork, *Poland* 30 D6
Frome, *U.K.* 15 F5
Frome →, *U.K.* 15 G5
Frome, L., *Australia* 95 E2
Frome, The →, *Australia* 95 D2
Frómista, *Spain* 36 C6
Front Range, *U.S.A.* 106 C5
Front Royal, *U.S.A.* 114 F6
Fronteira, *Portugal* 37 F3
Frontera, *Canary Is.* 48 G2
Frontera, *Mexico* 119 D6
Fronteras, *Mexico* 118 A3
Frontignan, *France* 20 E7
Frosinone, *Italy* 42 A6
Frostburg, *U.S.A.* 114 F6
Frostisen, *Norway* 8 B17
Frouard, *France* 19 D13
Frövi, *Sweden* 10 E9
Frøya, *Norway* 8 E13
Frumoasa, *Romania* 29 D10
Frunze = Bishkek, *Kyrgyzstan* 52 E8
Frunzivka, *Ukraine* 29 C14
Fruška Gora, *Serbia & M.* 28 E4
Fruška Gora △, *Serbia & M.* 44 A3
Frutal, *Brazil* 125 H9
Frutigen, *Switz.* 25 J3
Frýdek-Místek, *Czech Rep.* 27 B11
Frýdlant, *Czech Rep.* 26 A8
Fryeburg, *U.S.A.* 117 B14
Fryvaldov = Jeseník, *Czech Rep.* 27 A10
Fthiótis ☐, *Greece* 46 C4
Fu Jiang →, *China* 58 C6
Fu Xian = Wafangdian, *China* 57 E11
Fu Xian, *China* 56 G5
Fu'an, *China* 59 D12
Fubian, *China* 58 B4
Fucécchio, *Italy* 40 E7
Fucheng, *China* 56 F9
Fuchou = Fuzhou, *China* 59 D12
Fuchū, *Japan* 55 G6
Fuchuan, *China* 59 E8
Fuchun Jiang →, *China* 59 B13
Fúcino, Piana del, *Italy* 41 F10
Fuding, *China* 59 D13
Fuencaliente, *Canary Is.* 48 F2
Fuencaliente, *Spain* 37 G6
Fuencaliente, Pta., *Canary Is.* 48 F2
Fuengirola, *Spain* 37 J6
Fuenlabrada, *Spain* 36 E7
Fuensalida, *Spain* 36 E6
Fuente-Álamo, *Spain* 39 G3
Fuente-Álamo de Murcia, *Spain* 39 H3
Fuente de Cantos, *Spain* 37 G4
Fuente del Maestre, *Spain* 37 G4
Fuente el Fresno, *Spain* 37 F7
Fuente Obejuna, *Spain* 37 G5
Fuente Palmera, *Spain* 37 H5
Fuentes de Andalucía, *Spain* 37 H5
Fuentes de Ebro, *Spain* 38 D4
Fuentes de León, *Spain* 37 G4
Fuentes de Oñoro, *Spain* 36 E4
Fuentesaúco, *Spain* 36 D5
Fuerte →, *Mexico* 118 B3
Fuerte Olimpo, *Paraguay* 126 A4
Fuerteventura, *Canary Is.* 48 F6
Fuerteventura ✕ (FUE), *Canary Is.* 48 F6
Fufeng, *China* 56 G5
Fuga I., *Phil.* 61 B4
Fugong, *China* 58 D2
Fugou, *China* 56 G8
Fugu, *China* 56 E6
Fuhai, *China* 60 B3
Fuḩaymī, *Iraq* 70 C4
Fuhlsbüttel, Hamburg ✕ (HAM), *Germany* 24 B5
Fuji, *Japan* 55 G9
Fuji-Hakone-Izu △, *Japan* 55 G9
Fuji-San, *Japan* 55 G9
Fuji-Yoshida, *Japan* 55 G9
Fujian ☐, *China* 59 E12
Fujinomiya, *Japan* 55 G9
Fujisawa, *Japan* 55 G9
Fujiyama, Mt. = Fuji-San, *Japan* 55 G9
Fukagawa, *Japan* 54 C11
Fukien = Fujian ☐, *China* 59 E12
Fukuchiyama, *Japan* 55 G7
Fukue-Shima, *Japan* 55 H4
Fukui, *Japan* 55 F8
Fukui ☐, *Japan* 55 G8
Fukuoka, *Japan* 55 H5
Fukuoka ☐, *Japan* 55 H5
Fukushima, *Japan* 54 F10
Fukushima ☐, *Japan* 54 F10
Fukuyama, *Japan* 55 G6
Fulacunda, *Guinea-Biss.* 82 C1
Fulda, *Germany* 24 E5
Fulda →, *Germany* 24 D5
Fulford Harbour, *Canada* 110 B3
Fuliang, *China* 59 C11
Fullerton, *Calif., U.S.A.* 111 M9
Fullerton, *Nebr., U.S.A.* 112 E6
Fulongquan, *China* 57 B13
Fülöpszállás, *Hungary* 28 D4
Fulton, *Mo., U.S.A.* 112 F9
Fulton, *N.Y., U.S.A.* 117 C8
Fuluälven →, *Sweden* 10 C7
Fulufjället, *Sweden* 10 C6
Fumay, *France* 19 C11
Fumel, *France* 20 D4
Fumin, *China* 58 E4
Funabashi, *Japan* 55 G10
Funafuti = Fongafale, *Tuvalu* 96 H9
Funäsdalen, *Sweden* 10 B6
Funchal, *Madeira* 48 D3
Funchal ✕ (FNC), *Madeira* 48 D3
Fundación, *Colombia* 124 A4
Fundão, *Portugal* 36 E3
Fundu Moldovei, *Romania* 29 C10
Fundulea, *Romania* 29 F11
Fundy △, *Canada* 105 C6
Fundy, B. of, *Canada* 105 D6
Funhalouro, *Mozam.* 89 C5
Funing, *Hebei, China* 57 E10
Funing, *Jiangsu, China* 57 H10
Funing, *Yunnan, China* 58 F5
Funiu Shan, *China* 56 H7
Funsi, *Ghana* 82 C4
Funtua, *Nigeria* 83 C6
Fuping, *Hebei, China* 56 E8
Fuping, *Shaanxi, China* 56 G5
Fuqing, *China* 59 E12
Fuquan, *China* 58 D6
Furano, *Japan* 54 C11
Furāt, Nahr al →, *Asia* 70 D5
Fūrg, *Iran* 71 D7
Furmanov, *Russia* 34 B5
Furmanovo, *Kazakhstan* 34 F9
Furnás, *Spain* 48 B8
Furnas, Represa de, *Brazil* 127 A6
Furneaux Group, *Australia* 95 G4
Furqlus, *Syria* 74 A6
Fürstenau, *Germany* 24 C3
Fürstenberg, *Germany* 24 B9
Fürstenfeld, *Austria* 26 D9
Fürstenfeldbruck, *Germany* 25 G7
Fürstenwalde, *Germany* 24 C10
Fürth, *Germany* 25 F6
Furth im Wald, *Germany* 25 F8
Furtwangen, *Germany* 25 G4
Furudal, *Sweden* 10 C9
Furukawa, *Japan* 54 E10
Furulund, *Sweden* 11 J7
Fury and Hecla Str., *Canada* 101 B11
Fusagasuga, *Colombia* 124 C4
Fuscaldo, *Italy* 43 C9
Fushan, *Shandong, China* 57 F11
Fushan, *Shanxi, China* 56 G6
Fushë Arrëz, *Albania* 44 D4
Fushë Krujë, *Albania* 44 E3
Fushun, *Liaoning, China* 57 D12
Fushun, *Sichuan, China* 58 C5
Fusong, *China* 57 C14
Füssen, *Germany* 25 H6
Fustic, *Barbados* 121 g
Fusui, *China* 58 F6
Futog, *Serbia & M.* 28 E4
Futuna, *Wall. & F. Is.* 91 B8
Fuwa, *Egypt* 80 H7
Fuxian Hu, *China* 58 E4
Fuxin, *China* 57 C11
Fuyang, *Anhui, China* 56 H8
Fuyang, *Zhejiang, China* 59 B12
Fuyang He →, *China* 56 E9
Fuying Dao, *China* 59 D13
Fuyu, *China* 57 B13
Fuyuan, *China* 58 E5
Füzesgyarmat, *Hungary* 28 C6
Fuzhou, *China* 59 D12
Fylde, *U.K.* 14 D5
Fyn, *Denmark* 11 J4
Fyne, L., *U.K.* 13 F3
Fyns Amtskommune ☐, *Denmark* 11 J4
Fynshav, *Denmark* 11 K3

G

Ga, *Ghana* 82 D4
Gaanda, *Nigeria* 83 C7
Gabarin, *Nigeria* 83 C7
Gabas →, *France* 20 E3
Gabela, *Angola* 84 G2
Gabès, *Tunisia* 79 B8
Gabès, G. de, *Tunisia* 79 B8
Gabgaba, W. →, *Egypt* 80 C3
Gąbin, *Poland* 31 F6
Gabon ■, *Africa* 84 E2
Gaborone, *Botswana* 88 C4
Gabriels, *U.S.A.* 117 B10
Gābrīk, *Iran* 71 E8
Gabrovo, *Bulgaria* 45 D9
Gacé, *France* 18 D7
Gāch Sār, *Iran* 71 B6
Gachsārān, *Iran* 71 D6
Gacko, *Bos.-H.* 44 C2
Gadag, *India* 66 M9
Gadamai, *Sudan* 81 D4
Gadap, *Pakistan* 68 G2
Gadarwara, *India* 69 H8
Gadebusch, *Germany* 24 B7
Gadein, *Sudan* 81 F2
Gadhada, *India* 68 J4
Gádor, Sierra de, *Spain* 37 J8
Gadra, *Pakistan* 68 G4
Gadsden, *U.S.A.* 115 H3
Gadwal, *India* 66 L10
Gadyach = Hadyach, *Ukraine* 33 G8
Găeşti, *Romania* 29 F10
Gaeta, *Italy* 42 A6
Gaeta, G. di, *Italy* 42 A6
Gaffney, *U.S.A.* 115 H5
Gafsa, *Tunisia* 78 B7
Gagarawa, *Nigeria* 83 C6
Gagaria, *India* 68 G4
Gagarin, *Russia* 32 E8
Găgăuzia ☐, *Moldova* 29 D13
Gaggenau, *Germany* 25 G4
Gaghamni, *Sudan* 81 E2
Gagino, *Russia* 34 C7
Gagliano del Capo, *Italy* 43 C11
Gagnef, *Sweden* 10 D9
Gagnoa, *Ivory C.* 82 D3
Gagnon, *Canada* 105 B6
Gagnon, L., *Canada* 103 A6
Gagra, *Georgia* 35 J5
Gahini, *Rwanda* 86 C3
Gahmar, *India* 69 G10
Gai Xian = Gaizhou, *China* 57 D12
Gaïdhouronísi, *Greece* 49 E7
Gail, *U.S.A.* 113 J4
Gail →, *Austria* 26 E6
Gaillac, *France* 20 E5
Gaillimh = Galway, *Ireland* 12 C2
Gaillon, *France* 18 C8
Gaines, *U.S.A.* 116 E7
Gainesville, *Fla., U.S.A.* 115 L4
Gainesville, *Ga., U.S.A.* 115 H4
Gainesville, *Mo., U.S.A.* 113 G8
Gainesville, *Tex., U.S.A.* 113 J6
Gainsborough, *U.K.* 14 D7
Gairdner, L., *Australia* 95 E2
Gairloch, *U.K.* 13 D3
Gairloch, L., *U.K.* 13 D3
Gaizhou, *China* 57 D12
Gaj, *Croatia* 28 E2
Gaj →, *Pakistan* 68 F2
Gakuch, *Pakistan* 69 A5
Galala, Gebel el, *Egypt* 80 J8
Galán, Cerro, *Argentina* 126 B2
Galana →, *Kenya* 86 C5
Galanta, *Slovak Rep.* 27 C10
Galapagar, *Spain* 36 E7
Galápagos = Colón, Arch. de, *Ecuador* 97 H18
Galashiels, *U.K.* 13 F6
Galatás, *Greece* 46 D5
Galaţi, *Romania* 29 E13
Galaţi ☐, *Romania* 29 E12
Galatia, *Turkey* 72 C5
Galatina, *Italy* 43 B11
Galátone, *Italy* 43 B11
Galax, *U.S.A.* 115 G5
Galaxídhion, *Greece* 46 C4
Galcaio, *Somali Rep.* 75 F4
Galdhøpiggen, *Norway* 9 F12
Galeana, *Chihuahua, Mexico* 118 A3
Galeana, *Nuevo León, Mexico* 118 A3
Galegu, *Sudan* 81 E4
Galela, *Indonesia* 63 D7
Galena, *U.S.A.* 100 B4
Galeota Pt., *Trin. & Tob.* 125 K16
Galera, *Spain* 39 H2
Galera Pt., *Trin. & Tob.* 121 D7
Galesburg, *U.S.A.* 112 E9
Galeton, *U.S.A.* 116 E7
Galga, *Ethiopia* 81 F4
Gali, *Georgia* 35 J5
Galicea Mare, *Romania* 29 F8
Galich, *Russia* 34 A6
Galiche, *Bulgaria* 44 C7
Galicia ☐, *Spain* 36 C3
Galičica △, *Macedonia* 44 E4
Galilee = Hagalil, *Israel* 74 C4
Galilee, L., *Australia* 94 C4
Galilee, Sea of = Yam Kinneret, *Israel* 74 C4
Galim, *Cameroon* 83 D7
Galina Pt., *Jamaica* 120 a
Galinoporni, *Cyprus* 49 D13
Galion, *U.S.A.* 116 F2
Galiuro Mts., *U.S.A.* 109 K8
Galiwinku, *Australia* 94 A2
Gallabat, *Sudan* 81 E4
Gallan Hd., *U.K.* 13 C1
Gallarate, *Italy* 40 C5
Gallatin, *U.S.A.* 115 G2
Galle, *Sri Lanka* 66 R12
Gállego →, *Spain* 38 D4
Gallegos →, *Argentina* 128 G3
Galletti →, *Ethiopia* 81 F5
Galley Hd., *Ireland* 12 E3
Galliate, *Italy* 40 C5
Gallinas, Pta., *Colombia* 124 A4
Gallipoli = Gelibolu, *Turkey* 45 F10
Gallípoli, *Italy* 43 B10
Gallipolis, *U.S.A.* 114 F4
Gällivare, *Sweden* 8 C19
Gallneukirchen, *Austria* 26 C7
Gällö, *Sweden* 10 B9
Gallo, C., *Italy* 42 D6
Gallocanta, L. de, *Spain* 38 E3
Galloo I., *U.S.A.* 117 C8
Galloway, *U.K.* 13 F4
Galloway ⌓, *U.K.* 13 F4
Galloway, Mull of, *U.K.* 13 G4
Gallup, *U.S.A.* 109 J9
Gallur, *Spain* 38 D3
Galoya, *Sri Lanka* 66 Q12
Galt, *U.S.A.* 110 G5
Galten, *Denmark* 11 H3
Galtür, *Austria* 26 E3
Galty Mts., *Ireland* 12 D3
Galtymore, *Ireland* 12 D3
Galva, *U.S.A.* 112 E9
Galve de Sorbe, *Spain* 38 D1
Galveston, *U.S.A.* 113 L7
Galveston B., *U.S.A.* 113 L7
Gálvez, *Argentina* 126 C3
Galway, *Ireland* 12 C2
Galway ☐, *Ireland* 12 C2
Galway B., *Ireland* 12 C2
Gam →, *Vietnam* 64 B5
Gamagōri, *Japan* 55 G8
Gamari, L., *Ethiopia* 81 E5
Gamawa, *Nigeria* 83 C7
Gamay, *Phil.* 61 E6
Gambaga, *Ghana* 83 C4
Gambat, *Pakistan* 68 F3
Gambela, *Ethiopia* 81 F3
Gambela △, *Ethiopia* 81 F3
Gambela-Hizboch ☐, *Ethiopia* 81 F3
Gambhir →, *India* 68 F6
Gambia ■, *W. Afr.* 82 C1
Gambia →, *W. Afr.* 82 C1
Gambier, *U.S.A.* 116 F2
Gambier, C., *Australia* 92 B5
Gambier Is., *Australia* 95 F2
Gambo, *Canada* 105 C9
Gamboli, *Pakistan* 68 E3
Gamboma, *Congo* 84 E3
Gamka →, *S. Africa* 88 E3
Gamkab →, *Namibia* 88 D2
Gamla Uppsala, *Sweden* 10 E11
Gamlakarleby = Kokkola, *Finland* 8 E20
Gamleby, *Sweden* 11 G10
Gammon →, *Canada* 103 C9
Gammon Ranges △, *Australia* 95 E2
Gamo-Gofa, *Ethiopia* 81 F4
Gamou, *Niger* 83 C6
Gamtoos →, *S. Africa* 88 E4
Gan, *France* 20 E3
Gan Goriama, Mts., *Cameroon* 83 D7
Gan Jiang →, *China* 59 C11
Ganado, *U.S.A.* 109 J9
Gananita, *Sudan* 80 D3
Gananoque, *Canada* 117 B8
Ganāveh, *Iran* 71 D6
Gäncä, *Azerbaijan* 35 K8
Gancheng, *China* 64 C7
Gand = Gent, *Belgium* 17 C3
Ganda, *Angola* 85 G2
Gandajika, *Dem. Rep. of the Congo* 84 F4
Gandak →, *India* 69 G11
Gandava, *Pakistan* 68 E2
Gander, *Canada* 105 C9
Gander L., *Canada* 105 C9
Ganderkesee, *Germany* 24 B4
Ganderowe Falls, *Zimbabwe* 87 F2
Gandesa, *Spain* 38 D5
Gandhi Sagar, *India* 68 G6
Gandhinagar, *India* 68 H5
Gandi, *Nigeria* 83 C6
Gandía, *Spain* 39 G4
Gandino, *Italy* 40 C6
Gando, Pta., *Canary Is.* 48 G4
Gandole, *Nigeria* 83 D7
Gâneb, *Mauritania* 82 B2
Ganedidalem = Gani, *Indonesia* 63 E7
Ganetti, *Sudan* 80 D3
Ganga →, *India* 69 H14
Ganga Sagar, *India* 69 J13
Gangafani, *Mali* 82 C4
Gangan →, *India* 69 E8
Ganganagar, *India* 68 E5
Gangapur, *India* 68 F7
Gangara, *Niger* 83 C6
Gangaw, *Burma* 67 H19
Gangdisê Shan, *China* 67 D12
Ganges = Ganga →, *India* 69 H14
Ganges, *Canada* 102 D4
Ganges, *France* 20 E7
Ganges, Mouths of the, *India* 69 J14
Gånghester, *Sweden* 11 G7
Gangi, *Italy* 43 E7
Gângiova, *Romania* 29 G8
Gangoh, *India* 68 E7
Gangotri, *India* 69 D8
Gangtok, *India* 67 F16
Gangu, *China* 56 G3
Gangyao, *China* 57 B14
Gani, *Indonesia* 63 E7
Ganj, *India* 69 F8
Ganluc, *China* 58 C4
Gannat, *France* 19 F10
Gannett Peak, *U.S.A.* 108 E9
Ganquan, *China* 56 F5
Gänserdorf, *Austria* 27 C9
Ganshui, *China* 58 C6
Gansu ☐, *China* 56 G3
Ganta, *Liberia* 82 D3
Gantheaume, C., *Australia* 95 F2
Gantheaume B., *Australia* 93 E1
Gantsevichi = Hantsavichy, *Belarus* 33 F4
Ganye, *Nigeria* 83 D7
Ganyem = Genyem, *Indonesia* 63 E10
Ganyu, *China* 57 G10
Ganyushkino, *Kazakhstan* 35 G9
Ganzhou, *China* 59 E10
Gao, *Mali* 83 B4
Gao Xian, *China* 58 C5
Gao'an, *China* 59 C10
Gaochun, *China* 59 B12
Gaohe, *China* 59 F9
Gaohebu, *China* 59 B11
Gaokeng, *China* 59 D9
Gaolan Dao, *China* 59 G9
Gaoligong Shan, *China* 58 E2
Gaomi, *China* 57 F10
Gaoming, *China* 59 F9
Gaoping, *China* 56 G7
Gaotang, *China* 56 F9
Gaoua, *Burkina Faso* 82 C4
Gaoual, *Guinea* 82 C2
Gaoxiong = Kaohsiung, *Taiwan* 59 F13
Gaoyang, *China* 56 E8
Gaoyao, *China* 59 F9
Gaoyou, *China* 59 A12
Gaoyou Hu, *China* 57 H10
Gaoyuan, *China* 57 F9
Gaozhou, *China* 59 G8
Gap, *France* 21 D10
Gapan, *Phil.* 61 D4
Gapat →, *India* 69 G10
Gapuwiyak, *Australia* 94 A2
Gar, *China* 60 C2
Garabogazköl Aylagy, *Turkmenistan* 52 E6
Garachico, *Canary Is.* 48 F3
Garachiné, *Panama* 120 E4
Garafia, *Canary Is.* 48 F2
Garah, *Australia* 95 D4
Garajonay, *Canary Is.* 48 F2
Garamba △, *Dem. Rep. of the Congo* 86 B2
Garango, *Burkina Faso* 83 C4
Garanhuns, *Brazil* 125 E11
Garautha, *India* 69 G8
Garawe, *Liberia* 82 E3
Garba Tula, *Kenya* 86 B4
Garberville, *U.S.A.* 108 F2
Garbiyang, *India* 69 D9
Garbsen, *Germany* 24 C5
Gard ☐, *France* 21 D8
Gard →, *France* 21 E8
Garda, L. di, *Italy* 40 C7
Gardanne, *France* 21 E9
Gårdby, *Sweden* 11 H10
Garde L., *Canada* 103 A7
Gardelegen, *Germany* 24 C7
Garden City, *Ga., U.S.A.* 115 J5
Garden City, *Kans., U.S.A.* 113 G4
Garden City, *Tex., U.S.A.* 113 K4
Garden Grove, *U.S.A.* 111 M9
Gardēz, *Afghan.* 68 C3
Gardhíki, *Greece* 46 C3
Gardiner, *Maine, U.S.A.* 115 C11
Gardiner, *Mont., U.S.A.* 108 D8
Gardiners I., *U.S.A.* 117 E12
Gardner, *U.S.A.* 117 D13
Gardner Canal, *Canada* 102 C3
Gardnerville, *U.S.A.* 110 G7
Gardno, Jezioro, *Poland* 30 D4
Gardo, *Somali Rep.* 75 F4
Gardone Val Trómpia, *Italy* 40 C7
Gárdony, *Hungary* 28 C3
Garešnica, *Croatia* 41 C13
Garéssio, *Italy* 40 D5
Garey, *U.S.A.* 111 L6
Garfield, *U.S.A.* 108 C5
Garforth, *U.K.* 14 D6
Gargaliánoi, *Greece* 46 D3
Gargan, Mt., *France* 20 C5
Gargano △, *Italy* 41 G12
Gargett, *Australia* 94 K6
Gargouna, *Mali* 83 B5
Gargždai, *Lithuania* 30 C8
Garibaldi ⌓, *Canada* 102 D4
Gariep, L., *S. Africa* 88 E4
Garies, *S. Africa* 88 E2
Garigliano →, *Italy* 42 A6
Garissa, *Kenya* 86 C4
Garkida, *Nigeria* 83 C7
Garko, *Nigeria* 83 C6
Garland, *Tex., U.S.A.* 113 J6
Garland, *Utah, U.S.A.* 108 F7
Garlasco, *Italy* 40 C5
Garliava, *Lithuania* 30 D10
Garlin, *France* 20 E3
Garm, *Tajikistan* 52 F8
Garmāb, *Iran* 71 C8
Garmisch-Partenkirchen, *Germany* 25 H7
Garmo, Qullai = Kommunizma, Pik, *Tajikistan* 52 F8
Garmsār, *Iran* 71 C7
Garner, *U.S.A.* 112 D8
Garnett, *U.S.A.* 112 F7
Garo Hills, *India* 69 G14
Garoe, *Somali Rep.* 75 F4
Garonne →, *France* 20 C3
Garonne, Canal Latéral à la, *France* 20 D4
Garoowe = Garoe, *Somali Rep.* 75 F4
Garot, *India* 68 G6
Garoua, *Cameroon* 83 D7
Garpenberg, *Sweden* 10 D10
Garphyttan, *Sweden* 10 E8

Garrauli, *India* 69 G8
Garrel, *Germany* 24 C4
Garrigues, *France* 20 E7
Garrison, *Mont., U.S.A.* 108 C7
Garrison, *N. Dak., U.S.A.* 112 B4
Garrison Res. = Sakakawea, L., *U.S.A.* 112 B4
Garron Pt., *U.K.* 12 A6
Garrovillas, *Spain* 37 F4
Garrucha, *Spain* 39 H3
Garry →, *U.K.* 13 E5
Garry, L., *Canada* 100 B9
Garsen, *Kenya* 86 C5
Gärsnäs, *Sweden* 11 J8
Garson L., *Canada* 103 B6
Garstang, *U.K.* 14 D5
Gartempe →, *France* 20 B4
Gartz, *Germany* 24 B10
Garu, *Ghana* 83 C4
Garu, *India* 69 H11
Garub, *Namibia* 88 D2
Garut, *Indonesia* 63 G12
Garvão, *Portugal* 37 H2
Garvie Mts., *N.Z.* 91 L2
Garwa = Garoua, *Cameroon* 83 D7
Garwa, *India* 69 G10
Garwolin, *Poland* 31 G8
Gary, *U.S.A.* 114 E2
Garz, *Germany* 24 A9
Garzê, *China* 58 B3
Garzón, *Colombia* 124 C3
Gas-San, *Japan* 54 E10
Gasan Kuli = Esenguly, *Turkmenistan* 52 F6
Gascogne, *France* 20 E4
Gascogne, G. de, *Europe* 20 E2
Gascony = Gascogne, *France* 20 E4
Gascoyne →, *Australia* 93 D1
Gascoyne Junction, *Australia* 93 E2
Gascueña, *Spain* 38 E2
Gash, Wadi →, *Ethiopia* 81 D4
Gash-Setit ⌂, *Eritrea* 81 D4
Gashagar, *Nigeria* 83 C7
Gashaka, *Nigeria* 83 D7
Gashaka-Gumti △, *Nigeria* 83 D7
Gasherbrum, *Pakistan* 69 B7
Gashua, *Nigeria* 83 C7
Gasparillo, *Trin. & Tob.* 125 K15
Gaspé, *Canada* 105 C7
Gaspé, C., *Canada* 105 C7
Gaspé Pen. = Gaspésie, Pén. de la, *Canada* 105 C6
Gaspésie ⌂, *Canada* 105 C6
Gaspésie, Pén. de la, *Canada* 105 C6
Gassan, *Burkina Faso* 82 C4
Gassol, *Nigeria* 83 D7
Gasteiz = Vitoria-Gasteiz, *Spain* 38 C2
Gastonia, *U.S.A.* 115 H5
Gastoúni, *Greece* 46 D3
Gastoúri, *Greece* 46 B1
Gastre, *Argentina* 128 E3
Gästrikland, *Sweden* 10 D10
Gata, C., *Cyprus* 49 E12
Gata, C. de, *Spain* 39 J2
Gata, Sierra de, *Spain* 36 E4
Gataga →, *Canada* 102 B3
Gătaia, *Romania* 28 E6
Gatchina, *Russia* 32 C6
Gatehouse of Fleet, *U.K.* 13 G4
Gates, *U.S.A.* 116 C7
Gateshead, *U.K.* 14 C6
Gatesville, *U.S.A.* 113 K6
Gateway ⌂, *U.S.A.* 117 F11
Gaths, *Zimbabwe* 87 G3
Gatico, *Chile* 126 A1
Gâtinais, *France* 19 D9
Gâtine, Hauteurs de, *France* 20 B3
Gatineau, *Canada* 117 A9
Gatineau △, *Canada* 104 C4
Gatineau →, *Canada* 104 C4
Gattaran, *Phil.* 61 B4
Gattinara, *Italy* 40 C5
Gatton, *Australia* 95 D5
Gatun, L., *Panama* 120 E4
Gatwick, London ✕ (LGW), *U.K.* 15 F7
Gatyana, *S. Africa* 89 E4
Gau, *Fiji* 91 D8
Gaucín, *Spain* 37 J5
Gauer L., *Canada* 103 B9
Gauhati = Guwahati, *India* 67 F17
Gauja →, *Latvia* 9 H21
Gaula →, *Norway* 8 E14
Gauri Phanta, *India* 69 E9
Gausta, *Norway* 9 G13
Gauteng □, *S. Africa* 89 D4
Gāv Koshī, *Iran* 71 D8
Gāvakān, *Iran* 71 D7
Gavallai △, *Liberia* 82 D3
Gavarnie, *France* 20 F3
Gavāter, *Iran* 71 E9
Gāvbandī, *Iran* 71 E7
Gavdhopoúla, *Greece* 49 E6
Gávdhos, *Greece* 49 E6
Gavi, *Italy* 40 D5
Gavião, *Portugal* 37 F3
Gaviota, *U.S.A.* 111 L6
Gāvkhūnī, Bāţlāq-e, *Iran* 71 C7
Gävle, *Sweden* 10 D11
Gävleborgs län □, *Sweden* 10 C10
Gävlebukten, *Sweden* 10 D11
Gavorrano, *Italy* 40 F7
Gavray, *France* 18 D5
Gavrilov Yam, *Russia* 32 D10
Gávrion, *Greece* 46 D6
Gawachab, *Namibia* 88 D2
Gawilgarh Hills, *India* 66 J10
Gawler, *Australia* 95 E2
Gawu, *Nigeria* 83 D6
Gaxun Nur, *China* 60 B5
Gaya, *India* 69 G11
Gaya, *Niger* 83 C5
Gaya, *Nigeria* 83 C6
Gayéri, *Burkina Faso* 83 C5
Gaylord, *U.S.A.* 114 C3
Gayndah, *Australia* 95 D5
Gaysin = Haysyn, *Ukraine* 29 B14
Gayvoron = Hayvoron, *Ukraine* 29 B14
Gaza, *Gaza Strip* 74 D3
Gaza □, *Mozam.* 89 C5
Gaza Strip ☒, *Asia* 74 D3
Gazanjyk, *Turkmenistan* 71 B7
Gazaoua, *Niger* 83 C6
Gāzbor, *Iran* 71 D8
Gazi, *Dem. Rep. of the Congo* 86 B1
Gaziantep, *Turkey* 70 B3
Gazimağosa = Famagusta, *Cyprus* 49 D12
Gazipaşa, *Turkey* 72 D5
Gbarnga, *Liberia* 82 D3
Gbekebo, *Nigeria* 83 D5
Gboko, *Nigeria* 83 D6
Gbongan, *Nigeria* 83 D5
Gcoverega, *Botswana* 88 B3
Gcuwa, *S. Africa* 89 E4
Gdańsk, *Poland* 30 D5
Gdansk ✕ (GDN), *Poland* 30 D5
Gdańska, Zatoka, *Poland* 30 D6
Gdov, *Russia* 9 G22
Gdynia, *Poland* 30 D5
Geba →, *Guinea-Biss.* 82 C1
Gebe, *Indonesia* 63 D7
Gebeciler, *Turkey* 47 C12
Gebeit Mine, *Sudan* 80 C4
Gebel Abyad, *Sudan* 80 D2
Gebel Iweibid, *Egypt* 80 H8
Gebze, *Turkey* 45 F13
Gecha, *Ethiopia* 81 F4
Gedaref, *Sudan* 81 E4
Gedaref □, *Sudan* 81 E4
Gediz, *Turkey* 47 B11
Gediz →, *Turkey* 47 C8
Gedo, *Ethiopia* 81 F4
Gèdre, *France* 20 F4
Gedser, *Denmark* 11 K5
Gedung, Pulau, *Malaysia* 65 c
Geegully Cr. →, *Australia* 92 C3
Geel, *Belgium* 17 C4
Geelong, *Australia* 95 F3
Geelvink B. = Cenderwasih, Teluk, *Indonesia* 63 E9
Geelvink Chan., *Australia* 93 E1
Geesthacht, *Germany* 24 B6
Geidam, *Nigeria* 83 C7
Geikie →, *Canada* 103 B8
Geikie Gorge △, *Australia* 92 C4
Geilenkirchen, *Germany* 24 E2
Geili, *Sudan* 81 D3
Geisingen, *Germany* 25 H4
Geislingen, *Germany* 25 G5
Geistown, *U.S.A.* 116 F6
Geita, *Tanzania* 86 C3
Gejiu, *China* 58 F4
Gel →, *Sudan* 81 F2
Gel, Meydān-e, *Iran* 71 D7
Gel River, *Sudan* 81 F2
Gela, *Italy* 43 E7
Gela, G. di, *Italy* 43 F7
Gelahun, *Liberia* 82 D2
Gelang Patah, *Malaysia* 65 d
Gelderland □, *Neths.* 17 B6
Geldern, *Germany* 24 D2
Geldrop, *Neths.* 17 C5
Geleen, *Neths.* 17 D5
Gelehun, *S. Leone* 82 D2
Gelembe, *Turkey* 47 B9
Gelemso, *Ethiopia* 81 F5
Gelendost, *Turkey* 72 C4
Gelendzhik, *Russia* 33 K10
Gelibolu, *Turkey* 45 F10
Gelibolu Yarımadası, *Turkey* 45 F10
Gelidonya Burnu, *Turkey* 72 D4
Gelnhausen, *Germany* 25 E5
Gelnica, *Slovak Rep.* 27 C13
Gelsenkirchen, *Germany* 24 D3
Gelting, *Germany* 24 A5
Gelugur, *Malaysia* 65 c
Gemas, *Malaysia* 65 L4
Gembloux, *Belgium* 17 D4
Gembu, *Nigeria* 83 D7
Gemena, *Dem. Rep. of the Congo* 84 D3
Gemerek, *Turkey* 70 B3
Gemla, *Sweden* 11 H8
Gemlik, *Turkey* 45 F13
Gemlik Körfezi, *Turkey* 45 F12
Gemona del Friuli, *Italy* 41 B10
Gemsa, *Egypt* 80 B3
Gemsbok △, *Botswana* 88 D3
Gemünden, *Germany* 25 E5
Genale →, *Ethiopia* 81 F4
Genç, *Turkey* 73 C9
Gençay, *France* 20 B4
Geneina, Gebel, *Egypt* 80 B3
General Acha, *Argentina* 126 D3
General Alvear, *Buenos Aires, Argentina* 126 D4
General Alvear, *Mendoza, Argentina* 126 D2
General Artigas, *Paraguay* 126 B4
General Belgrano, *Argentina* 126 D4
General Bernardo O'Higgins, *Antarctica* 5 C18
General Cabrera, *Argentina* 126 C3
General Cepeda, *Mexico* 118 B4
General Guido, *Argentina* 126 D4
General Juan Madariaga, *Argentina* 126 D4
General La Madrid, *Argentina* 126 D3
General MacArthur, *Phil.* 61 F6
General Martin Miguel de Güemes, *Argentina* 126 A3
General Paz, *Argentina* 126 B4
General Pico, *Argentina* 126 D3
General Pinedo, *Argentina* 126 B3
General Pinto, *Argentina* 126 C3
General Roca, *Argentina* 128 D3
General Santos, *Phil.* 61 H6
General Toshevo, *Bulgaria* 45 C12
General Trevino, *Mexico* 119 B5
General Trías, *Mexico* 118 B3
General Viamonte, *Argentina* 126 D3
General Villegas, *Argentina* 126 D3
Genesee, *Idaho, U.S.A.* 108 C5
Genesee, *Pa., U.S.A.* 116 E7
Genesee →, *U.S.A.* 116 C7
Geneseo, *Ill., U.S.A.* 112 E9
Geneseo, *N.Y., U.S.A.* 116 D7
Geneva = Genève, *Switz.* 25 J2
Geneva, *Ala., U.S.A.* 115 K3
Geneva, *N.Y., U.S.A.* 116 D8
Geneva, *Nebr., U.S.A.* 112 E6
Geneva, *Ohio, U.S.A.* 116 E4
Geneva, L. = Léman, L., *Europe* 19 F13
Geneva, L., *U.S.A.* 114 D1
Genève, *Switz.* 25 J2
Gengenbach, *Germany* 25 G4
Gengma, *China* 58 F2
Genichesk = Henichesk, *Ukraine* 33 J8
Genil →, *Spain* 37 H5
Genk, *Belgium* 17 D5
Genlis, *France* 19 E12
Gennargentu, Mti. del, *Italy* 42 B2
Gennes, *France* 18 E6
Genoa = Génova, *Italy* 40 D5
Genoa, *Australia* 95 F4
Genoa, *N.Y., U.S.A.* 117 D8
Genoa, *Nebr., U.S.A.* 112 E6
Genoa, *Nev., U.S.A.* 110 F7
Génova, *Italy* 40 D5
Genova ✕ (GOA), *Italy* 40 D5
Génova, G. di, *Italy* 40 E6
Genriyetty, Ostrov, *Russia* 53 B16
Gent, *Belgium* 17 C3
Genteng, *Bali, Indonesia* 63 J17
Genteng, *Jawa, Indonesia* 63 G12
Genthin, *Germany* 24 C8
Genyem, *Indonesia* 63 E10
Genzano di Lucánia, *Italy* 43 B9
Genzano di Roma, *Italy* 41 G9
Geoagiu, *Romania* 29 E8
Geographe B., *Australia* 93 F2
Geographe Chan., *Australia* 93 D1
Geokchay = Göyçay, *Azerbaijan* 35 K8
Georg Forster, *Antarctica* 5 D3
Georg von Neumayer, *Antarctica* 5 D17
Georga, Zemlya, *Russia* 52 A5
George, *S. Africa* 88 E3
George →, *Canada* 105 A6
George, L., *N.S.W., Australia* 95 F4
George, L., *S. Austral., Australia* 95 F3
George, L., *W. Austral., Australia* 92 D3
George, L., *Uganda* 86 B3
George, L., *Fla., U.S.A.* 115 L5
George, L., *N.Y., U.S.A.* 117 C11
George Gill Ra., *Australia* 92 D5
George Pt., *Australia* 94 J6
George River = Kangiqsualujjuaq, *Canada* 101 C13
George Sound, *N.Z.* 91 L1
George Town, *Australia* 95 G4
George Town, *Bahamas* 120 B4
George Town, *Cayman Is.* 120 C3
George Town, *Malaysia* 65 c
George V Land, *Antarctica* 5 C10
George VI Sound, *Antarctica* 5 D17
George West, *U.S.A.* 113 L5
Georgetown = Janjanbureh, *Gambia* 82 C2
Georgetown, *Australia* 94 B3
Georgetown, *Ont., Canada* 116 C5
Georgetown, *P.E.I., Canada* 105 C7
Georgetown, *Guyana* 124 B7
Georgetown, *Calif., U.S.A.* 110 G6
Georgetown, *Colo., U.S.A.* 108 G11
Georgetown, *Ky., U.S.A.* 114 F3
Georgetown, *N.Y., U.S.A.* 117 D9
Georgetown, *Ohio, U.S.A.* 114 F4
Georgetown, *S.C., U.S.A.* 115 J6
Georgetown, *Tex., U.S.A.* 113 K6
Georgia □, *U.S.A.* 115 K5
Georgia ■, *Asia* 35 J6
Georgia, Str. of, *Canada* 102 D4
Georgian B., *Canada* 116 A4
Georgian Bay Islands △, *Canada* 116 B5
Georgina →, *Australia* 94 C2
Georgina I., *Canada* 116 B5
Georgiyevsk, *Russia* 35 H6
Georgsmarienhütte, *Germany* 24 C4
Gera, *Germany* 24 E8
Geraardsbergen, *Belgium* 17 D3
Geral, Serra, *Brazil* 127 B6
Geral de Goiás, Serra, *Brazil* 125 F9
Geraldine, *U.S.A.* 108 C8
Geraldton, *Australia* 93 E1
Geraldton, *Canada* 104 C2
Gérardmer, *France* 19 D13
Gercüş, *Turkey* 73 D9
Gerede, *Turkey* 72 B5
Gerês, Sierra do, *Portugal* 36 D3
Gereshk, *Afghan.* 66 D4
Geretsried, *Germany* 25 H7
Gérgal, *Spain* 39 H2
Gerik, *Malaysia* 65 K3
Gering, *U.S.A.* 112 E3
Gerlach, *U.S.A.* 108 F4
Gerlachovský štit, *Slovak Rep.* 27 B13
German Planina, *Macedonia* 44 D6
Germansen Landing, *Canada* 102 B4
Germantown, *U.S.A.* 113 M10
Germany ■, *Europe* 24 E6
Germencik, *Turkey* 47 D9
Germering, *Germany* 25 G7
Germersheim, *Germany* 25 F4
Germī, *Iran* 71 B6
Germiston, *S. Africa* 89 D4
Gernika-Lumo, *Spain* 38 B2
Gernsheim, *Germany* 25 F4
Gero, *Japan* 55 G8
Gerokgak, *Indonesia* 63 J17
Gerolzhofen, *Germany* 25 F6
Gerona = Girona, *Spain* 38 D7
Gerrard, *Canada* 102 C5
Gers □, *France* 20 E4
Gers →, *France* 20 D4
Gersfeld, *Germany* 24 E5
Gersthofen, *Germany* 25 G6
Gertak Sanggul, *Malaysia* 65 c
Gertak Sanggul, Tanjung, *Malaysia* 65 c
Gerung, *Indonesia* 63 K19
Gerzat, *France* 20 C7
Gerze, *Turkey* 72 B6
Geseke, *Germany* 24 D4
Geser, *Indonesia* 63 E8
Gesso →, *Italy* 40 D4
Gestro, Wabi →, *Ethiopia* 81 G5
Getafe, *Spain* 36 E7
Getinge, *Sweden* 11 H6
Gettysburg, *Pa., U.S.A.* 114 F7
Gettysburg, *S. Dak., U.S.A.* 112 C5
Getxo, *Spain* 38 B2
Getz Ice Shelf, *Antarctica* 5 D14
Gevaş, *Turkey* 73 C10
Gévaudan, *France* 20 D7
Gevgelija, *Macedonia* 44 E6
Gévora →, *Spain* 37 G4
Gewani, *Ethiopia* 81 E5
Gex, *France* 19 F13
Geyikli, *Turkey* 47 B8
Geyser, *U.S.A.* 108 C8
Geyserville, *U.S.A.* 110 G4
Geyve, *Turkey* 72 B4
Ghâbat el Arab = Wang Kai, *Sudan* 81 F2
Ghabeish, *Sudan* 81 E2
Ghaggar →, *India* 68 E6
Ghaghara →, *India* 69 G11
Ghaghat →, *Bangla.* 69 G13
Ghagra, *India* 69 H11
Ghagra →, *India* 69 F9
Ghalla, Wadi el →, *Sudan* 81 E2
Ghana ■, *W. Afr.* 83 D4
Ghansor, *India* 69 H9
Ghanzi, *Botswana* 88 C3
Gharb el Istiwa'iya □, *Sudan* 81 G3
Gharb Kordofân □, *Sudan* 81 E2
Gharbîya, Es Sahrâ el, *Egypt* 80 B2
Ghardaïa, *Algeria* 78 B6
Ghârib, G., *Egypt* 80 B3
Gharig, *Sudan* 81 E2
Gharyān, *Libya* 79 B8
Ghat, *Libya* 79 D8
Ghatal, *India* 69 H12
Ghatampur, *India* 69 F9
Ghats, Eastern, *India* 66 N11
Ghats, Western, *India* 66 N9
Ghatsila, *India* 69 H12
Ghaţţī, *Si. Arabia* 70 D3
Ghawdex = Gozo, *Malta* 49 C1
Ghazal, Bahr el →, *Chad* 79 F9
Ghazâl, Bahr el →, *Sudan* 81 F3
Ghaziabad, *India* 68 E7
Ghazipur, *India* 69 G10
Ghaznī, *Afghan.* 68 C3
Ghaznī □, *Afghan.* 66 C6
Ghedi, *Italy* 40 C7
Ghelari, *Romania* 28 E7
Ghent = Gent, *Belgium* 17 C3
Gheorghe Gheorghiu-Dej = Oneşti, *Romania* 29 D11
Gheorgheni, *Romania* 29 D10
Gherla, *Romania* 29 C8
Ghidigeni, *Romania* 29 D12
Ghilarza, *Italy* 42 B1
Ghimeş-Făget, *Romania* 29 D11
Ghīnah, Wādī al →, *Si. Arabia* 70 D3
Ghisonaccia, *France* 21 F13
Ghisoni, *France* 21 F13
Ghizao, *Afghan.* 68 C1
Ghizar →, *Pakistan* 69 A5
Ghot Ogrein, *Egypt* 80 A2
Ghotaru, *India* 68 F4
Ghotki, *Pakistan* 68 E3
Ghowr □, *Afghan.* 66 C4
Ghudāf, W. al →, *Iraq* 70 C4
Ghudāmis, *Libya* 77 C4
Ghudāmis □, *Libya* 79 B8
Ghughri, *India* 69 H9
Ghugus, *India* 66 K11
Ghulam Mohammad Barrage, *Pakistan* 68 G3
Ghūrīān, *Afghan.* 66 B2
Gia Dinh, *Vietnam* 65 G6
Gia Lai = Plei Ku, *Vietnam* 64 F7
Gia Nghia, *Vietnam* 65 G6
Gia Ngoc, *Vietnam* 64 E7
Gia Vuc, *Vietnam* 64 E7
Giannutri, *Italy* 40 F8
Giant Forest, *U.S.A.* 110 J8
Giant Mts. = Krkonoše, *Czech Rep.* 26 A8
Giant Sequoia ⌂, *U.S.A.* 110 K8
Giants Causeway, *U.K.* 12 A5
Gianyar, *Indonesia* 63 K18
Giarabub = Al Jaghbūb, *Libya* 79 C10
Giarre, *Italy* 43 E8
Giaveno, *Italy* 40 C4
Gibara, *Cuba* 120 B4
Gibb River, *Australia* 92 C4
Gibbon, *U.S.A.* 112 E5
Gibe →, *Ethiopia* 81 F4
Gibellina Nuova, *Italy* 42 E5
Gibeon, *Namibia* 88 D2
Gibraleón, *Spain* 37 H4
Gibraltar ☒, *Europe* 37 J5
Gibraltar, Str. of, *Medit. S.* 37 K5
Gibraltar Range △, *Australia* 95 D5
Gibson Desert, *Australia* 92 D4
Gibsons, *Canada* 102 D4
Gibsonville, *U.S.A.* 110 F6
Giddings, *U.S.A.* 113 K6
Gidole, *Ethiopia* 81 F4
Giebnegáisi = Kebnekaise, *Sweden* 8 C18
Gien, *France* 19 E9
Giengen, *Germany* 25 G6
Giessen, *Germany* 24 E4
Gīfān, *Iran* 71 B8
Gifatin, Geziret, *Egypt* 80 B3
Gifhorn, *Germany* 24 C6
Gift Lake, *Canada* 102 B5
Gifu, *Japan* 55 G8
Gifu □, *Japan* 55 G8
Gigant, *Russia* 35 G5
Giganta, Sa. de la, *Mexico* 118 B2
Gigen, *Bulgaria* 45 C8
Gigha, *U.K.* 13 F3
Gíglio, *Italy* 40 F7
Gignac, *France* 20 E7
Gigüela →, *Spain* 37 F7
Gijón, *Spain* 36 B5
Gil I., *Canada* 102 C3
Gila →, *U.S.A.* 109 K6
Gila Bend, *U.S.A.* 109 K7
Gila Bend Mts., *U.S.A.* 109 K7
Gila Cliff Dwellings ⌂, *U.S.A.* 109 K9
Gīlān □, *Iran* 71 B6
Gilău, *Romania* 29 D8
Gilbert →, *Australia* 94 B3
Gilbert Is., *Kiribati* 96 G9
Gilbert River, *Australia* 94 B3
Gilead, *U.S.A.* 117 B14
Gilf el Kebîr, Hadabat el, *Egypt* 80 C2
Gilford I., *Canada* 102 C3
Gilgandra, *Australia* 95 E4
Gilgil, *Kenya* 86 C4
Gilgit, *India* 69 B6
Gilgit →, *Pakistan* 69 B6
Gili ⌂, *Mozam.* 87 F4
Gilimanuk, *Indonesia* 63 J17
Giljeva Planina, *Serbia & M.* 44 C3
Gillam, *Canada* 103 B10
Gilleleje, *Denmark* 11 H6
Gillen, L., *Australia* 93 E3
Gilles, L., *Australia* 95 E2
Gillette, *U.S.A.* 112 C2
Gilliat, *Australia* 94 C3
Gillingham, *U.K.* 15 F8
Gilmer, *U.S.A.* 113 J7
Gilmore, L., *Australia* 93 F3
Gilo →, *Ethiopia* 81 F3
Gilort →, *Romania* 29 F8
Gilroy, *U.S.A.* 110 H5
Gimbi, *Ethiopia* 81 F4
Gimie, Mt, *St. Lucia* 121 f
Gimli, *Canada* 103 C9
Gimo, *Sweden* 10 D12
Gimone →, *France* 20 E5
Gimont, *France* 20 E4
Gin Gin, *Australia* 95 D5
Ginâh, *Egypt* 80 B3
Gineifa, *Egypt* 80 H8
Gingin, *Australia* 93 F2
Gingindlovu, *S. Africa* 89 D5
Ginir, *Ethiopia* 81 F5
Ginosa, *Italy* 43 B9
Ginzo de Limia = Xinzo de Limia, *Spain* 36 C3
Gióia, G. di, *Italy* 43 D8
Gióia del Colle, *Italy* 43 B9
Gióia Táuro, *Italy* 43 D8
Gioiosa Iónica, *Italy* 43 D9
Gioiosa Marea, *Italy* 43 D7
Gióna, Óros, *Greece* 46 C4
Giovi, Passo dei, *Italy* 40 D5
Giovinazzo, *Italy* 43 A9
Gir Hills, *India* 68 J4
Girab, *India* 68 F4
Girâfi, W. →, *Egypt* 74 F3
Giraltovce, *Slovak Rep.* 27 B14
Girard, *Kans., U.S.A.* 113 G7
Girard, *Ohio, U.S.A.* 116 E4
Girard, *Pa., U.S.A.* 116 E4
Girdle Ness, *U.K.* 13 D6
Giresun, *Turkey* 73 B8
Girga, *Egypt* 80 B3
Giri →, *India* 68 D7
Giridih, *India* 69 G12
Girifalco, *Italy* 43 D9
Girne = Kyrenia, *Cyprus* 49 D12
Giro, *Nigeria* 83 C5
Giromagny, *France* 19 E13
Giron = Kiruna, *Sweden* 8 C19
Girona, *Spain* 38 D7
Girona □, *Spain* 38 C7
Gironde □, *France* 20 D3
Gironde →, *France* 20 C2
Gironella, *Spain* 38 C6
Girraween △, *Australia* 95 D5
Giru, *Australia* 94 B4
Girvan, *U.K.* 13 F4
Gisborne, *N.Z.* 91 H7
Gisenyi, *Rwanda* 86 C2
Gislaved, *Sweden* 11 G7
Gisors, *France* 19 C8
Gitega, *Burundi* 86 C2
Giuba →, *Somali Rep.* 75 G3
Giugliano in Campania, *Italy* 43 B7
Giulianova, *Italy* 41 F10
Giurgeni, *Romania* 29 F12
Giurgiu, *Romania* 29 G10
Giurgiu □, *Romania* 29 F10
Giurgiuleşti, *Moldova* 29 E13
Give, *Denmark* 11 J3
Givet, *France* 19 B11
Givors, *France* 21 C8
Givry, *France* 19 F11
Giyon, *Ethiopia* 81 F4
Giza = El Gîza, *Egypt* 80 J7
Gizhiga, *Russia* 53 C17
Gizhiginskaya Guba, *Russia* 53 C16
Giżycko, *Poland* 30 D8

Gizzeria, Italy 43 D9
Gjalicë e Lumës, Mal., Albania 44 D4
Gjegjan, Albania 44 E4
Gjirokastër, Albania 44 F4
Gjoa Haven, Canada 100 B10
Gjøvik, Norway 9 F14
Gjuhës, Kep i, Albania 44 F3
Glace Bay, Canada 105 C8
Glacier △, Canada 102 C5
Glacier △, U.S.A. 108 B7
Glacier Bay △, U.S.A. 102 B1
Glacier Peak, U.S.A. 108 B3
Gladewater, U.S.A. 113 J7
Gladstone, Queens., Australia 94 C5
Gladstone, S. Austral., Australia 95 E2
Gladstone, Canada 103 C9
Gladstone, U.S.A. 114 C2
Gladwin, U.S.A. 114 D3
Glafsfjorden, Sweden 10 E6
Glagah, Indonesia 63 J17
Głogów Małapolski, Poland 31 H8
Glåma = Glomma →, Norway 9 G14
Gláma, Iceland 8 D2
Glamis, U.S.A. 111 N11
Glamoč, Bos.-H. 41 D13
Glamorgan, Vale of □, U.K. 15 F4
Glamsbjerg, Denmark 11 J4
Glarus, Switz. 25 H5
Glarus □, Switz. 25 J5
Glasco, Kans., U.S.A. 112 F6
Glasco, N.Y., U.S.A. 117 D11
Glasgow, U.K. 13 F4
Glasgow, Ky., U.S.A. 114 G3
Glasgow, Mont., U.S.A. 108 B10
Glasgow, City of □, U.K. 13 F4
Glasgow International ✕ (GLA), U.K. 13 F4
Glaslyn, Canada 103 C7
Glastonbury, U.K. 15 F5
Glastonbury, U.S.A. 117 E12
Glauchau, Germany 24 E8
Glava, Sweden 10 E6
Glavice, Croatia 41 E13
Glazov, Russia 34 A11
Gleichen, Canada 102 C6
Gleisdorf, Austria 26 D8
Gleiwitz = Gliwice, Poland 31 H5
Glen, U.S.A. 117 B13
Glen Affric, U.K. 13 D3
Glen Canyon, U.S.A. 109 H8
Glen Canyon ⌓, U.S.A. 109 H8
Glen Canyon Dam, U.S.A. 109 H8
Glen Coe, U.K. 13 E3
Glen Cove, U.S.A. 117 F11
Glen Garry, U.K. 13 D3
Glen Innes, Australia 95 D5
Glen Lyon, U.S.A. 117 E8
Glen Mor, U.K. 13 D4
Glen More ⌓, U.K. 13 D5
Glen Moriston, U.K. 13 D4
Glen Robertson, Canada 117 A10
Glen Spean, U.K. 13 E4
Glen Ullin, U.S.A. 112 B4
Glénan, Îs. de, France 18 E3
Glenariff △, Ireland 12 A5
Glencoe, Canada 116 D3
Glencoe, S. Africa 89 D5
Glencoe, U.S.A. 112 C7
Glendale, Ariz., U.S.A. 109 K7
Glendale, Calif., U.S.A. 111 L8
Glendale, Zimbabwe 87 F3
Glendive, U.S.A. 112 B2
Glendo, U.S.A. 112 D2
Glenelg →, Australia 95 F3
Glenfield, U.S.A. 117 C9
Glengarriff, Ireland 12 E2
Glenmont, U.S.A. 116 F2
Glenmorgan, Australia 95 D4
Glenn, U.S.A. 110 F4
Glennallen, U.S.A. 100 B5
Glennamaddy, Ireland 12 C3
Glenns Ferry, U.S.A. 108 E6
Glenore, Australia 94 B3
Glenreagh, Australia 95 E5
Glenrock, U.S.A. 108 E11
Glenrothes, U.K. 13 E5
Glens Falls, U.S.A. 117 C11
Glenside, U.S.A. 117 F9
Glenties, Ireland 12 B3
Glenveagh △, Ireland 12 A3
Glenville, U.S.A. 114 F5
Glenwood, Canada 105 C9
Glenwood, Ark., U.S.A. 113 H8
Glenwood, Iowa, U.S.A. 112 E7
Glenwood, Minn., U.S.A. 112 C7
Glenwood, Wash., U.S.A. 110 D5
Glenwood Springs, U.S.A. 108 G10
Glettinganes, Iceland 8 D7
Glifádha, Greece 46 D5
Glimåkra, Sweden 11 H8
Glina, Croatia 41 C13
Glinojeck, Poland 31 F7
Gliwice, Poland 31 H5
Globe, U.S.A. 109 K8
Glodeanu Siliştea, Romania 29 F11
Glodeni, Moldova 29 C12
Glödnitz, Austria 26 E7
Gloggnitz, Austria 26 D8
Głogów, Poland 31 G3
Głogówek, Poland 31 H4
Glomma →, Norway 9 G14
Glorieuses, Is., Ind. Oc. 89 A8
Glóssa, Greece 46 B5
Glossop, U.K. 14 D6
Gloucester, Australia 95 E5
Gloucester, U.K. 15 F5
Gloucester, U.S.A. 117 D14
Gloucester I., Australia 94 J6
Gloucester Island △, Australia 94 J6
Gloucester Point, U.S.A. 114 G7
Gloucestershire □, U.K. 15 F5
Gloversville, U.S.A. 117 C10
Glovertown, Canada 105 C9
Głowno, Poland 31 G6
Głubczyce, Poland 31 H4
Glubokiy, Russia 35 F5
Glubokoye = Hlybokaye, Belarus 32 E4
Głuchołazy, Poland 31 H4
Glücksburg, Germany 24 A5
Glückstadt, Germany 24 B5
Glukhov = Hlukhiv, Ukraine 33 G7
Glusk, Belarus 33 F5
Głuszyca, Poland 31 H3
Glyngøre, Denmark 11 H2
Gmünd, Kärnten, Austria 26 E6
Gmünd, Niederösterreich, Austria 26 C8
Gmunden, Austria 26 D6
Gnarp, Sweden 10 B11
Gnesta, Sweden 10 E11
Gniew, Poland 30 E5
Gniewkowo, Poland 31 F5
Gniezno, Poland 31 F4
Gnjilane, Serbia & M. 44 D5
Gnoien, Germany 24 B8
Gnosjö, Sweden 11 G7
Gnowangerup, Australia 93 F2
Go Cong, Vietnam 65 G6
Gō-no-ura, Japan 55 H4
Goa, India 66 M8
Goa □, India 66 M8
Goalen Hd., Australia 95 F5
Goalpara, India 67 F17
Goaltor, India 69 H12
Goalundo Ghat, Bangla. 69 H13
Goaso, Ghana 82 D4
Goat Fell, U.K. 13 F3
Goba, Ethiopia 81 F4
Goba, Mozam. 89 D5
Gobabis, Namibia 88 C2
Göbel, Turkey 45 F12
Gobi, Asia 56 C6
Gobō, Japan 55 H7
Gobo, Sudan 81 F3
Göçbeyli, Turkey 47 B9
Goch, Germany 24 D2
Gochas, Namibia 88 C2
Godalming, U.K. 15 F7
Godavari →, India 67 L13
Godavari Pt., India 67 L13
Godbout, Canada 105 C6
Godda, India 69 G12
Godech, Bulgaria 44 C7
Goderich, Canada 116 C3
Goderville, France 18 C7
Godfrey Ra., Australia 93 D2
Godhavn = Qeqertarsuaq, Greenland 101 B14
Godhra, India 68 H5
Gödöllő, Hungary 28 C4
Godoy Cruz, Argentina 126 C2
Gods →, Canada 104 A1
Gods L., Canada 104 B1
Gods River, Canada 103 C10
Godthåb = Nuuk, Greenland 101 B14
Goeie Hoop, Kaap die = Good Hope, C. of, S. Africa 88 E2
Goéland, L. au, Canada 104 C4
Goélands, L. aux, Canada 105 A7
Goeree, Neths. 17 C3
Goes, Neths. 17 C3
Goffstown, U.S.A. 117 C13
Gogama, Canada 104 C3
Gogebic, L., U.S.A. 112 B10
Goggetti, Ethiopia 81 F4
Gogolin, Poland 31 H5
Gogonou, Benin 83 C5
Gogra = Ghaghara →, India 69 G11
Gogriâl, Sudan 81 F2
Gogti, Ethiopia 81 E5
Gohana, India 68 E7
Goharganj, India 68 H7
Goi →, India 68 H6
Goiânia, Brazil 125 G9
Goiás, Brazil 125 G8
Goiás □, Brazil 125 F9
Goio-Erê, Brazil 127 A5
Góis, Portugal 36 E2
Gojam, Ethiopia 81 E4
Gojeb, Wabi →, Ethiopia 81 F4
Gojō, Japan 55 G7
Gojra, Pakistan 68 D5
Gökçeada, Turkey 45 F9
Gökçedağ, Turkey 47 B10
Gökçen, Turkey 47 C9
Gökçeören, Turkey 47 C10
Gökçeyazı, Turkey 47 B9
Gökırmak →, Turkey 72 B6
Gökova, Turkey 47 D10
Gökova Körfezi, Turkey 47 E9
Göksu →, Turkey 72 D6
Göksun, Turkey 72 C7
Gokteik, Burma 67 H20
Göktepe, Turkey 47 D10
Gokurt, Pakistan 68 E2
Gokwe, Zimbabwe 89 B4
Gola, India 69 E9
Golakganj, India 69 F13
Golan Heights = Hagolan, Syria 74 C4
Gołańcz, Poland 31 F4
Golāshkerd, Iran 71 E8
Golaya Pristen = Hola Pristan, Ukraine 33 J7
Gölbaşı, Adiyaman, Turkey 72 D7
Gölbaşı, Ankara, Turkey 72 C5
Golchikha, Russia 4 B12
Golconda, U.S.A. 108 F5
Gölcük, Kocaeli, Turkey 45 F13
Gölcük, Niğde, Turkey 72 C6
Gold, U.S.A. 116 E7
Gold Beach, U.S.A. 108 E1
Gold Coast, W. Afr. 83 E4
Gold Hill, U.S.A. 108 E2
Gold River, Canada 102 D3
Gołdap, Poland 30 D9
Goldberg, Germany 24 B8
Golden, Canada 102 C5
Golden B., N.Z. 91 J4
Golden Gate, U.S.A. 108 H2
Golden Gate Highlands △, S. Africa 89 D4
Golden Hinde, Canada 102 D3
Golden Lake, Canada 116 A7
Golden Spike ⌓, U.S.A. 108 F7
Golden Vale, Ireland 12 D3
Goldendale, U.S.A. 108 D3
Goldfield, U.S.A. 109 H5
Goldsand L., Canada 103 B8
Goldsboro, U.S.A. 115 H7
Goldsmith, U.S.A. 113 K3
Goldsworthy, Australia 92 D2
Goldthwaite, U.S.A. 113 K5
Golegã, Portugal 37 F2
Goleniów, Poland 30 E1
Golestān □, Iran 71 B7
Golestānak, Iran 71 D7
Goleta, U.S.A. 111 L7
Golfito, Costa Rica 120 E3
Golfo Aranci, Italy 42 B2
Golfo di Orosei e del Gennargentu △, Italy 42 B2
Gölgeli Dağları, Turkey 47 D10
Gölhisar, Turkey 47 D11
Goliad, U.S.A. 113 L6
Golija, Serbia & M. 44 C2
Golija, Serbia & M. 44 C4
Golina, Poland 31 F5
Gölköy, Turkey 72 B7
Göllersdorf, Austria 26 C9
Gölmarmara, Turkey 47 C9
Golo →, France 21 F13
Gölova, Turkey 47 E12
Golpāyegān, Iran 71 C6
Gölpazarı, Turkey 72 B4
Golra, Pakistan 68 C5
Golspie, U.K. 13 D5
Golub-Dobrzyń, Poland 31 E6
Golubac, Serbia & M. 44 B5
Golyam Perelik, Bulgaria 45 E8
Golyama Kamchiya →, Bulgaria 45 C11
Goma, Dem. Rep. of the Congo 86 C2
Gomal Pass, Pakistan 68 D3
Gomati →, India 69 G10
Gombari, Dem. Rep. of the Congo 86 B2
Gombe, Nigeria 83 C7
Gömbe, Turkey 47 E11
Gombe □, Nigeria 83 C7
Gombe →, Tanzania 86 C3
Gombi, Nigeria 83 C7
Gomel = Homyel, Belarus 33 F6
Gomera, Canary Is. 48 F2
Gómez Palacio, Mexico 118 B4
Gomīshān, Iran 71 B7
Gommern, Germany 24 C7
Gomogomo, Indonesia 63 F8
Gomoh, India 67 H15
Gomotartsi, Bulgaria 44 B6
Gompa = Ganta, Liberia 82 D3
Gomphi, Greece 46 B3
Gonābād, Iran 71 C8
Gonaïves, Haiti 121 C5
Gonarezhou △, Zimbabwe 87 G3
Gonâve, G. de la, Haiti 121 C5
Gonâve, Île de la, Haiti 121 C5
Gonbad-e Kāvūs, Iran 71 B7
Gönc, Hungary 28 B6
Gonda, India 69 F9
Gondal, India 68 J4
Gonder, Ethiopia 81 E4
Gondia, India 66 J12
Gondola, Mozam. 87 F3
Gondomar, Portugal 36 D2
Gondrecourt-le-Château, France 19 D12
Gönen, Balıkesir, Turkey 45 F11
Gönen, Isparta, Turkey 47 D12
Gönen →, Turkey 45 F11
Gong Xian, China 58 C5
Gong'an, China 59 B9
Gongcheng, China 59 E8
Gongga Shan, China 58 C3
Gongguan, China 58 G7
Gonghe, China 60 C5
Gongola →, Nigeria 83 D7
Gongolgon, Australia 95 E4
Gongshan, China 58 D2
Gongtan, China 58 C7
Gongzhuling, China 57 C13
Goniadz, Poland 30 E9
Goniri, Nigeria 83 C7
Gonjo, China 58 B2
Gonnesa, Italy 42 C1
Gónnos, Greece 46 B4
Gonnosfanádiga, Italy 42 C1
Gonzaga, Phil. 61 B5
Gonzales, Calif., U.S.A. 110 J5
Gonzales, Tex., U.S.A. 113 L6
González Chaves, Argentina 126 D3
Good Hope, C. of, S. Africa 88 E2
Gooderham, Canada 116 B6
Goodhouse, S. Africa 88 D2
Gooding, U.S.A. 108 E6
Goodland, U.S.A. 112 F4
Goodlow, Canada 102 B4
Goodooga, Australia 95 D4
Goodsprings, U.S.A. 111 K11
Goole, U.K. 14 D7
Goolgowi, Australia 95 E4
Goomalling, Australia 93 F2
Goomeri, Australia 95 D5
Goonda, Mozam. 87 F3
Goondiwindi, Australia 95 D5
Goongarrie △, Australia 93 F3
Goongarrie, L., Australia 93 F3
Goonyella, Australia 94 C4
Goose →, Canada 105 B7
Goose Creek, U.S.A. 115 J5
Goose L., U.S.A. 108 F3
Gop, India 66 H6
Gopalganj, India 69 F11
Göppingen, Germany 25 G5
Gor, Spain 37 H8
Góra, Dolnośląskie, Poland 31 G3
Góra, Mazowieckie, Poland 31 F7
Góra Kalwaria, Poland 31 G8
Gorakhpur, India 69 F10
Goražde, Bos.-H. 28 G3
Gorbatov, Russia 34 B6
Gorbea, Peña, Spain 38 B2
Gorczański △, Poland 31 J7
Gorda, U.S.A. 110 K5
Gorda, Pta., Canary Is. 48 F2
Gorda, Pta., Nic. 120 D3
Gordan B., Australia 92 B5
Gördes, Turkey 47 C10
Gordon, U.S.A. 112 D3
Gordon →, Australia 95 G4
Gordon L., Alta., Canada 103 B6
Gordon L., N.W.T., Canada 102 A6
Gordonvale, Australia 94 B4
Gore, Ethiopia 81 F4
Gore, N.Z. 91 M2
Gore Bay, Canada 104 C3
Görele, Turkey 73 B8
Goreme, Turkey 72 C6
Gorey, Ireland 12 D5
Gorg, Iran 71 D8
Gorgān, Iran 71 B7
Gorgona, Italy 40 E6
Gorgona, I., Colombia 124 C3
Gorgora, Ethiopia 81 E4
Gorgoram, Nigeria 83 C7
Gorham, U.S.A. 117 B13
Gori, Georgia 35 J7
Goriganga →, India 69 E9
Gorinchem, Neths. 17 C4
Goris, Armenia 73 C12
Goritsy, Russia 32 D9
Gorízia, Italy 41 C10
Gorj □, Romania 29 E8
Gorki = Horki, Belarus 32 E6
Gorki = Nizhniy Novgorod, Russia 34 B7
Gorkiy = Nizhniy Novgorod, Russia 34 B7
Gorkovskoye Vdkhr., Russia 34 B6
Gorleston, U.K. 15 E9
Gorlice, Poland 31 J8
Görlitz, Germany 24 D10
Gorlovka = Horlivka, Ukraine 33 H10
Gorman, U.S.A. 111 L8
Gorna Dzhumayo = Blagoevgrad, Bulgaria 44 D7
Gorna Oryakhovitsa, Bulgaria 45 C9
Gornja Radgona, Slovenia 41 B13
Gornja Tuzla, Bos.-H. 28 F3
Gornji Grad, Slovenia 41 B11
Gornji Milanovac, Serbia & M. 44 B4
Gornji Vakuf, Bos.-H. 28 G2
Gorno Ablanovo, Bulgaria 45 C9
Gorno-Altay □, Russia 52 D9
Gorno-Altaysk, Russia 52 D9
Gornyatskiy, Russia 35 F5
Gornyy, Saratov, Russia 34 E9
Gornyy, Sib., Russia 54 B6
Gorodenka = Horodenka, Ukraine 29 B10
Gorodets, Russia 34 B6
Gorodishche = Horodyshche, Ukraine 33 H6
Gorodishche, Russia 34 D7
Gorodnya = Horodnya, Ukraine 33 G6
Gorodok = Haradok, Belarus 32 E6
Gorodok = Horodok, Ukraine 33 H2
Gorodovikovsk, Russia 35 G5
Gorokhov = Horokhiv, Ukraine 33 G3
Gorokhovets, Russia 34 B6
Gorom Gorom, Burkina Faso 83 C4
Goromonzi, Zimbabwe 87 F3
Gorong, Kepulauan, Indonesia 63 E8
Gorongosa △, Mozam. 89 B5
Gorongose →, Mozam. 89 C5
Gorongoza, Mozam. 87 F3
Gorongoza, Sa. da, Mozam. 87 F3
Gorontalo, Indonesia 63 D6
Gorontalo □, Indonesia 63 D6
Goronyo, Nigeria 83 C6
Górowo Iławeckie, Poland 30 D7
Gorron, France 18 D6
Gorshechnoye, Russia 33 G10
Gort, Ireland 12 C3
Gortis, Greece 49 D6
Góry Bystrzyckie, Poland 31 H3
Goryachiy Klyuch, Russia 35 H4
Gorzkowice, Poland 31 G6
Górzno, Poland 31 E6
Gorzów Śląski, Poland 31 G5
Gorzów Wielkopolski, Poland 31 F2
Gosford, Australia 95 E5
Goshen, Calif., U.S.A. 110 J7
Goshen, Ind., U.S.A. 114 E3
Goshen, N.Y., U.S.A. 117 E10
Goshogawara, Japan 54 D10
Goslar, Germany 24 D6
Gospič, Croatia 41 D12
Gosport, U.K. 15 G6
Gossas, Senegal 82 C1
Gosse →, Australia 94 B1
Gossi, Mali 83 B4
Gossinga, Sudan 81 F2
Gostivar, Macedonia 44 E4
Gostyń, Poland 31 G4
Gostynin, Poland 31 F6
Göta älv →, Sweden 11 G5
Göta kanal, Sweden 11 F9
Götaland, Sweden 11 G8
Göteborg, Sweden 11 G5
Götene, Sweden 11 F7
Goteşti, Moldova 29 D13
Gotha, Germany 24 E6
Gothenburg = Göteborg, Sweden 11 G5
Gothenburg, U.S.A. 112 E4
Gothèye, Niger 83 C5
Gotland, Sweden 11 G12
Gotlands län □, Sweden 11 G12
Gotō-Rettō, Japan 55 H4
Gotse Delchev, Bulgaria 44 E7
Gotska Sandön, Sweden 9 G18
Gōtsu, Japan 55 G6
Gott Pk., Canada 102 C4
Góttero, Monte, Italy 40 D6
Göttingen, Germany 24 D5
Gottwald = Zmiyev, Ukraine 33 H9
Gottwaldov = Zlín, Czech Rep. 27 B10
Goubangzi, China 57 D11
Gouda, Neths. 17 B4
Goúdhoura, Ákra, Greece 49 E8
Goudiry, Senegal 82 C2
Goudoumaria, Niger 83 C7
Gouéké, Guinea 82 D3
Gough I., Atl. Oc. 2 G9
Gouin, Rés., Canada 104 C5
Gouitafla, Ivory C. 82 D3
Goulburn, Australia 95 E4
Goulburn Is., Australia 94 A1
Goulia, Ivory C. 82 C3
Goulimine, Morocco 78 C3
Goumbou, Mali 82 B3
Gouménissa, Greece 44 F6
Goundam, Mali 82 B4
Goúra, Greece 46 D4
Gourbassi, Mali 82 C2
Gourdon, France 20 D5
Gouré, Niger 83 C7
Gourin, France 18 D3
Gourits →, S. Africa 88 E3
Gourma-Rharous, Mali 83 B4
Goúrnais, Greece 49 D7
Gournay-en-Bray, France 19 C8
Gourock, U.K. 13 F4
Goursi, Burkina Faso 82 C4
Gouverneur, U.S.A. 117 B9
Gouviá, Greece 49 A3
Gouzon, France 19 F9
Governador Valadares, Brazil 125 G10
Governor's Harbour, Bahamas 120 A4
Govindgarh, India 69 G9
Gowan Ra., Australia 94 D4
Gowanda, U.S.A. 116 D6
Gower, U.K. 15 F3
Gowna, L., Ireland 12 C4
Goya, Argentina 126 B4
Göyçay, Azerbaijan 35 K8
Goyder Lagoon, Australia 95 D2
Goyllarisquisga, Peru 124 F3
Göynük, Antalya, Turkey 47 E12
Göynük, Bolu, Turkey 72 B4
Goz Beïda, Chad 79 F10
Goz Regeb, Sudan 81 D4
Gozdnica, Poland 31 G2
Gozo, Malta 49 C1
Graaff-Reinet, S. Africa 88 E3
Grabo, Ivory C. 82 D3
Grabow, Germany 24 B7
Grabów nad Prosną, Poland 31 G5
Gračac, Croatia 41 D12
Gračanica, Bos.-H. 28 F3
Graçay, France 19 E8
Gracias a Dios, C., Honduras 120 D3
Graciosa, I., Canary Is. 48 E6
Grad Sofiya □, Bulgaria 44 D7
Gradac, Serbia & M. 44 C3
Gradačac, Bos.-H. 28 F3
Gradeška Planina, Macedonia 44 E6
Gradets, Bulgaria 45 D10
Gradišče, Slovenia 41 B12
Grădiştea de Munte, Romania 29 E8
Grado, Italy 41 C10
Grado, Spain 36 B4
Grady, U.S.A. 113 H3
Graeca, Lacul, Romania 29 F11
Grafenau, Germany 25 G9
Gräfenberg, Germany 25 F7
Grafham Water, U.K. 15 E7
Grafton, Australia 95 D5
Grafton, N. Dak., U.S.A. 112 A6
Grafton, W. Va., U.S.A. 114 F5
Graham, Canada 104 C1
Graham, U.S.A. 113 J5
Graham, Mt., U.S.A. 109 K9
Graham Bell, Ostrov = Greem-Bell, Ostrov, Russia 52 A7
Graham I., Canada 102 C2
Graham Land, Antarctica 5 C17
Grahamstown, S. Africa 88 E4
Grahamsville, U.S.A. 117 E10
Grahovo, Serbia & M. 44 D2
Graie, Alpi, Europe 21 C11
Grain Coast, W. Afr. 82 E3
Grajagan, Indonesia 63 K17
Grajagan, Teluk, Indonesia 63 K17
Grajaú, Brazil 125 E9
Grajaú →, Brazil 125 D10
Grajewo, Poland 30 E9
Gramada, Bulgaria 44 C6
Gramat, France 20 D5
Grammichele, Italy 43 E7
Grámmos, Óros, Greece 44 F4
Grampian, U.S.A. 116 F6
Grampian Highlands = Grampian Mts., U.K. 13 E5
Grampian Mts., U.K. 13 E5
Grampians, The, Australia 95 F3
Gramsh, Albania 44 F4
Gran Canaria, Canary Is. 48 G4
Gran Chaco, S. Amer. 126 B3
Gran Desierto del Pinacate ⌓, Mexico 118 A2
Gran Paradiso, Italy 40 C4
Gran Sasso d'Itália, Italy 41 F10
Gran Sasso e Monti Della Laga △, Italy 41 F10

Granada, *Nic.* 120 D2
Granada, *Spain* 37 H7
Granada, *U.S.A.* 113 F3
Granada □, *Spain* 37 H7
Granadilla de Abona, *Canary Is.* 48 F3
Granard, *Ireland* 12 C4
Granbury, *U.S.A.* 113 J6
Granby, *Canada* 117 A12
Granby, *U.S.A.* 108 F11
Grand →, *Canada* 116 D5
Grand →, *Mo., U.S.A.* 112 F8
Grand →, *S. Dak., U.S.A.* 112 C4
Grand Bahama I., *Bahamas* 120 A4
Grand Bank, *Canada* 105 C8
Grand Bassam, *Ivory C.* 82 D4
Grand Béréby, *Ivory C.* 82 E3
Grand-Bourg, *Guadeloupe* 120 b
Grand Canal = Yun Ho →, *China* 57 E9
Grand Canyon, *U.S.A.* 109 H7
Grand Canyon △, *U.S.A.* 109 H7
Grand Canyon-Parashant ⌓, *U.S.A.* 109 H7
Grand Cayman, *Cayman Is.* 120 C3
Grand Centre, *Canada* 103 C6
Grand Cess, *Liberia* 82 E3
Grand Coulee, *U.S.A.* 108 C4
Grand Coulee Dam, *U.S.A.* 108 C4
Grand Falls, *Canada* 105 C6
Grand Falls-Windsor, *Canada* 105 C8
Grand Forks, *Canada* 102 D5
Grand Forks, *U.S.A.* 112 B6
Grand Gorge, *U.S.A.* 117 D10
Grand Haven, *U.S.A.* 114 D2
Grand I., *Mich., U.S.A.* 114 B2
Grand I., *N.Y., U.S.A.* 116 D6
Grand Island, *U.S.A.* 112 E5
Grand Isle, *La., U.S.A.* 113 L9
Grand Isle, *Vt., U.S.A.* 117 B11
Grand Junction, *U.S.A.* 109 G9
Grand L., *N.B., Canada* 105 C6
Grand L., *Nfld. & L., Canada* 105 C8
Grand L., *Nfld. & L., Canada* 105 B7
Grand L., *U.S.A.* 113 L8
Grand Lahou, *Ivory C.* 82 D3
Grand Lake, *U.S.A.* 108 F11
Grand-Lieu, L. de, *France* 18 E5
Grand Manan I., *Canada* 105 D6
Grand Marais, *Canada* 112 B9
Grand Marais, *U.S.A.* 114 B3
Grand-Mère, *Canada* 104 C5
Grand Popo, *Benin* 83 D5
Grand Portage, *U.S.A.* 112 B10
Grand Prairie, *U.S.A.* 113 J6
Grand Rapids, *Canada* 103 C9
Grand Rapids, *Mich., U.S.A.* 114 D2
Grand Rapids, *Minn., U.S.A.* 112 B8
Grand St-Bernard, Col du, *Europe* 25 K3
Grand Staircase-Escalante ⌓, *U.S.A.* 109 H8
Grand Teton, *U.S.A.* 108 E8
Grand Teton △, *U.S.A.* 108 D8
Grand Union Canal, *U.K.* 15 E7
Grand-Vigie, Pte. de la, *Guadeloupe* 120 b
Grandas de Salime, *Spain* 36 B4
Grande →, *Jujuy, Argentina* 126 A2
Grande →, *Mendoza, Argentina* 126 D2
Grande →, *Bolivia* 124 G6
Grande →, *Bahia, Brazil* 125 F10
Grande →, *Minas Gerais, Brazil* 125 H8
Grande, B., *Argentina* 128 G3
Grande, Rio →, *U.S.A.* 113 N6
Grande Baleine, R. de la →, *Canada* 104 A4
Grande Cache, *Canada* 102 C5
Grande Casse, Pte. de la, *France* 21 C10
Grande-Entrée, *Canada* 105 C7
Grande Prairie, *Canada* 102 B5
Grande-Rivière, *Canada* 105 C7
Grande-Terre, *Guadeloupe* 120 b
Grande-Vallée, *Canada* 105 C6
Grandfalls, *U.S.A.* 113 K3
Grândola, *Portugal* 37 G2
Grandpré, *France* 19 C11
Grands Causses ⌓, *France* 20 D6
Grands-Jardins ⌓, *Canada* 105 C5
Grandview, *Canada* 103 C8
Grandview, *U.S.A.* 108 C4
Grandvilliers, *France* 19 C8
Graneros, *Chile* 126 C1
Grangemouth, *U.K.* 13 E5
Granger, *U.S.A.* 108 F9
Grängesberg, *Sweden* 10 D9
Grangeville, *U.S.A.* 108 D5
Granisle, *Canada* 102 C3
Granite City, *U.S.A.* 112 F9
Granite Falls, *U.S.A.* 112 C7
Granite L., *Canada* 105 C8
Granite Mt., *U.S.A.* 111 M10
Granite Pk., *U.S.A.* 108 D9
Graniteville, *U.S.A.* 117 B12
Granitola, C., *Italy* 42 E5
Granity, *N.Z.* 91 J3
Granja, *Brazil* 125 D10
Granja de Moreruela, *Spain* 36 D5
Granja de Torrehermosa, *Spain* 37 G5
Gränna, *Sweden* 11 F8
Granollers, *Spain* 38 D7
Gransee, *Germany* 24 B9
Grant, *U.S.A.* 112 E4
Grant, Mt., *U.S.A.* 108 G4
Grant City, *U.S.A.* 112 E7
Grant I., *Australia* 92 B5
Grant Range, *U.S.A.* 109 G6
Grantham, *U.K.* 14 E7
Grantown-on-Spey, *U.K.* 13 D5
Grants, *U.S.A.* 109 J10
Grants Pass, *U.S.A.* 108 E2
Grantsville, *U.S.A.* 108 F7
Granville, *France* 18 D5
Granville, *N. Dak., U.S.A.* 112 A4
Granville, *N.Y., U.S.A.* 117 C11
Granville, *Ohio, U.S.A.* 116 F2
Granville L., *Canada* 103 B8
Graskop, *S. Africa* 89 C5
Gräsö, *Sweden* 10 D12
Grass →, *Canada* 103 B9
Grass Range, *U.S.A.* 108 C9
Grass River ⌓, *Canada* 103 C8
Grass Valley, *Calif., U.S.A.* 110 F6
Grass Valley, *Oreg., U.S.A.* 108 D3
Grassano, *Italy* 43 B9
Grasse, *France* 21 E10
Grassflat, *U.S.A.* 116 F6
Grasslands △, *Canada* 103 D7
Grassy, *Australia* 95 G3
Gråsten, *Denmark* 11 K3
Grästorp, *Sweden* 11 F6
Gratkorn, *Austria* 26 D8
Graubünden □, *Switz.* 25 J5
Graulhet, *France* 20 E5
Graus, *Spain* 38 C5
Grave, Pte. de, *France* 20 C2
Gravelbourg, *Canada* 103 D7
Gravelines, *France* 19 A9
's-Gravenhage, *Neths.* 17 B4
Gravenhurst, *Canada* 116 B5
Gravesend, *Australia* 95 D5
Gravesend, *U.K.* 15 F8
Gravina in Púglia, *Italy* 43 B9
Gravois, Pointe-à-, *Haiti* 121 C5
Gravone →, *France* 21 G12
Gray, *France* 19 E12
Grayling, *U.S.A.* 114 C3
Grays, *U.K.* 15 F8
Grays Harbor, *U.S.A.* 108 C1
Grays L., *U.S.A.* 108 E8
Grays River, *U.S.A.* 110 D3
Grayvoron, *Russia* 33 G8
Graz, *Austria* 26 D8
Grdelica, *Serbia & M.* 44 D6
Greasy L., *Canada* 102 A4
Great Abaco I. = Abaco I., *Bahamas* 120 A4
Great Artesian Basin, *Australia* 94 C3
Great Australian Bight, *Australia* 93 F5
Great Bahama Bank, *Bahamas* 120 B4
Great Barrier I., *N.Z.* 91 G5
Great Barrier Reef, *Australia* 94 B4
Great Barrier Reef ⌓, *Australia* 94 B4
Great Barrington, *U.S.A.* 117 D11
Great Basalt Wall △, *Australia* 94 B4
Great Basin, *U.S.A.* 108 G5
Great Basin △, *U.S.A.* 108 G6
Great Bear →, *Canada* 100 B7
Great Bear L., *Canada* 100 B7
Great Belt = Store Bælt, *Denmark* 11 J4
Great Bend, *Kans., U.S.A.* 112 F5
Great Bend, *Pa., U.S.A.* 117 E9
Great Blasket I., *Ireland* 12 D1
Great Britain, *Europe* 6 E5
Great Camanoe, *Br. Virgin Is.* 121 e
Great Codroy, *Canada* 105 C8
Great Dividing Ra., *Australia* 94 C4
Great Driffield = Driffield, *U.K.* 14 C7
Great Exuma I., *Bahamas* 120 B4
Great Falls, *U.S.A.* 108 C8
Great Fish = Groot Vis →, *S. Africa* 88 E4
Great Guana Cay, *Bahamas* 120 B4
Great Inagua I., *Bahamas* 121 B5
Great Indian Desert = Thar Desert, *India* 68 F5
Great Karoo, *S. Africa* 88 E3
Great Khingan Mts. = Da Hinggan Ling, *China* 60 B7
Great Lake, *Australia* 95 G4
Great Lakes, *N. Amer.* 98 E11
Great Malvern, *U.K.* 15 E5
Great Miami →, *U.S.A.* 114 F3
Great Ormes Head, *U.K.* 14 D4
Great Ouse →, *U.K.* 14 E8
Great Palm I., *Australia* 94 B4
Great Pedro Bluff, *Jamaica* 120 a
Great Plains, *N. Amer.* 98 E9
Great Ruaha →, *Tanzania* 86 D4
Great Sacandaga L., *U.S.A.* 117 C10
Great Saint Bernard Pass = Grand St-Bernard, Col du, *Europe* 25 K3
Great Salt L., *U.S.A.* 108 F7
Great Salt Lake Desert, *U.S.A.* 108 F7
Great Salt Plains L., *U.S.A.* 113 G5
Great Sand Dunes ⌓, *U.S.A.* 109 H11
Great Sandy △, *Australia* 95 D5
Great Sandy Desert, *Australia* 92 D3
Great Sangi = Sangihe, Pulau, *Indonesia* 63 D7
Great Scarcies →, *S. Leone* 82 D2
Great Skellig, *Ireland* 12 E1
Great Slave L., *Canada* 102 A5
Great Smoky Mts. △, *U.S.A.* 115 H4
Great Snow Mt., *Canada* 102 B4
Great Stour = Stour →, *U.K.* 15 F9
Great Victoria Desert, *Australia* 93 E4
Great Wall, *Antarctica* 5 C18
Great Wall, *China* 56 E5
Great Whernside, *U.K.* 14 C6
Great Yarmouth, *U.K.* 15 E9
Great Zab = Zāb al Kabīr →, *Iraq* 70 C4
Great Zimbabwe, *Zimbabwe* 87 G3
Greater Antilles, *W. Indies* 121 C5
Greater London □, *U.K.* 15 F7
Greater Manchester □, *U.K.* 14 D5
Greater St. Lucia Wetlands ⌓, *S. Africa* 89 D5
Greater Sudbury = Sudbury, *Canada* 104 C3
Greater Sunda Is., *Indonesia* 62 F4
Grebbestad, *Sweden* 11 F5
Grebenka = Hrebenka, *Ukraine* 33 G7
Greco, C., *Cyprus* 49 E13
Greco, Mte., *Italy* 41 G10
Gredos, Sierra de, *Spain* 36 E6
Greece, *U.S.A.* 116 C7
Greece ■, *Europe* 46 B3
Greeley, *Colo., U.S.A.* 112 E2
Greeley, *Nebr., U.S.A.* 112 E5
Greem-Bell, Ostrov, *Russia* 52 A7
Green, *U.S.A.* 108 E2
Green →, *Ky., U.S.A.* 114 G2
Green →, *Utah, U.S.A.* 109 G9
Green B., *U.S.A.* 114 C2
Green Bay, *U.S.A.* 114 C2
Green C., *Australia* 95 F5
Green Cove Springs, *U.S.A.* 115 L5
Green Lake, *Canada* 103 C7
Green Mts., *U.S.A.* 117 C12
Green River, *Utah, U.S.A.* 109 G8
Green River, *Wyo., U.S.A.* 108 F9
Green Valley, *U.S.A.* 109 L8
Greenbank, *U.S.A.* 110 B4
Greenbush, *Mich., U.S.A.* 116 B1
Greenbush, *Minn., U.S.A.* 112 A6
Greencastle, *U.S.A.* 114 F2
Greene, *U.S.A.* 117 D9
Greenfield, *Calif., U.S.A.* 110 J5
Greenfield, *Calif., U.S.A.* 111 K8
Greenfield, *Ind., U.S.A.* 114 F3
Greenfield, *Iowa, U.S.A.* 112 E7
Greenfield, *Mass., U.S.A.* 117 D12
Greenfield, *Mo., U.S.A.* 113 G8
Greenfield Park, *Canada* 117 A11
Greenland ⊠, *N. Amer.* 4 C5
Greenland Sea, *Arctic* 4 B7
Greenock, *U.K.* 13 F4
Greenore, *Ireland* 12 B5
Greenore Pt., *Ireland* 12 D5
Greenough, *Australia* 93 E1
Greenough →, *Australia* 93 E1
Greenough Pt., *Canada* 116 B3
Greenport, *U.S.A.* 117 E12
Greensboro, *Ga., U.S.A.* 115 J4
Greensboro, *N.C., U.S.A.* 115 G6
Greensboro, *Vt., U.S.A.* 117 B12
Greensburg, *Ind., U.S.A.* 114 F3
Greensburg, *Kans., U.S.A.* 113 G5
Greensburg, *Pa., U.S.A.* 116 F5
Greenstone Pt., *U.K.* 13 D3
Greenvale, *Australia* 94 B4
Greenville, *Liberia* 82 D3
Greenville, *Ala., U.S.A.* 115 K2
Greenville, *Calif., U.S.A.* 110 E6
Greenville, *Maine, U.S.A.* 115 C11
Greenville, *Mich., U.S.A.* 114 D3
Greenville, *Miss., U.S.A.* 113 J9
Greenville, *Mo., U.S.A.* 113 G9
Greenville, *N.C., U.S.A.* 115 H7
Greenville, *N.H., U.S.A.* 117 D13
Greenville, *N.Y., U.S.A.* 117 D10
Greenville, *Ohio, U.S.A.* 114 E3
Greenville, *Pa., U.S.A.* 116 E4
Greenville, *S.C., U.S.A.* 115 H4
Greenville, *Tenn., U.S.A.* 115 G4
Greenville, *Tex., U.S.A.* 113 J6
Greenwater Lake ⌓, *Canada* 103 C8
Greenwich, *Conn., U.S.A.* 117 E11
Greenwich, *N.Y., U.S.A.* 117 C11
Greenwich, *Ohio, U.S.A.* 116 E2
Greenwich □, *U.K.* 15 F8
Greenwood, *Canada* 102 D5
Greenwood, *Ark., U.S.A.* 113 H7
Greenwood, *Ind., U.S.A.* 114 F2
Greenwood, *Miss., U.S.A.* 113 J9
Greenwood, *S.C., U.S.A.* 115 H4
Greenwood, Mt., *Australia* 92 B5
Gregbe, *Ivory C.* 82 D3
Gregory, *U.S.A.* 112 D5
Gregory △, *Australia* 92 C5
Gregory →, *Australia* 94 B2
Gregory, L., *S. Austral., Australia* 95 D2
Gregory, L., *W. Austral., Australia* 93 E2
Gregory Downs, *Australia* 94 B2
Gregory L., *Australia* 92 D4
Gregory Ra., *Queens., Australia* 94 B3
Gregory Ra., *W. Austral., Australia* 92 D3
Greiffenberg, *Germany* 24 B9
Greifswald, *Germany* 24 A9
Greifswalder Bodden, *Germany* 24 A9
Grein, *Austria* 26 C7
Greiz, *Germany* 24 E8
Gremikha, *Russia* 52 C4
Grenå, *Denmark* 11 H4
Grenada, *U.S.A.* 113 J10
Grenada ■, *W. Indies* 121 D7
Grenade, *France* 20 E5
Grenadier I., *U.S.A.* 117 B8
Grenadines, The, *St. Vincent* 121 D7
Grenchen, *Switz.* 25 H3
Grenen, *Denmark* 11 G4
Grenfell, *Australia* 95 E4
Grenfell, *Canada* 103 C8
Grenoble, *France* 21 C9
Grenville, C., *Australia* 94 A3
Grenville Chan., *Canada* 102 C3
Gréoux-les-Bains, *France* 21 E9
Gresham, *U.S.A.* 110 E4
Gresik, *Indonesia* 63 G15
Gretna, *U.K.* 13 F5
Greven, *Germany* 24 C3
Grevená, *Greece* 44 F5
Grevená □, *Greece* 44 F5
Grevenbroich, *Germany* 24 D2
Grevenmacher, *Lux.* 17 E6
Grevesmühlen, *Germany* 24 B7
Grevestrand, *Denmark* 11 J6
Grey →, *Canada* 105 C8
Grey →, *N.Z.* 91 K3
Grey, C., *Australia* 94 A2
Grey Ra., *Australia* 95 D3
Greybull, *U.S.A.* 108 D9
Greymouth, *N.Z.* 91 K3
Greystones, *Ireland* 12 C5
Greytown, *N.Z.* 91 J5
Greytown, *S. Africa* 89 D5
Gribanovskiy, *Russia* 34 E5
Gribbell I., *Canada* 102 C3
Gribës, Mal i, *Albania* 44 F3
Gridley, *U.S.A.* 110 F5
Griekwastad, *S. Africa* 88 D3
Griesheim, *Germany* 25 F4
Grieskirchen, *Austria* 26 C6
Griffin, *U.S.A.* 115 J3
Griffith, *Australia* 95 E4
Griffith, *Canada* 116 A7
Griffith I., *Canada* 116 B4
Grignols, *France* 20 D3
Grigoriopol, *Moldova* 29 C14
Grimaylov = Hrymayliv, *Ukraine* 33 H4
Grimes, *U.S.A.* 110 F5
Grimma, *Germany* 24 D8
Grimmen, *Germany* 24 A9
Grimsay, *U.K.* 13 D1
Grimsby, *Canada* 116 C5
Grimsby, *U.K.* 14 D7
Grímsey, *Iceland* 8 C5
Grimshaw, *Canada* 102 B5
Grimslöv, *Sweden* 11 H8
Grimstad, *Norway* 9 G13
Grindelwald, *Switz.* 25 J4
Grindsted, *Denmark* 11 J2
Grindstone I., *Canada* 117 B8
Grindu, *Romania* 29 F11
Grinnell, *U.S.A.* 112 E8
Grintavec, *Slovenia* 41 B11
Gris-Nez, C., *France* 19 B8
Grisolles, *France* 20 E5
Grisons = Graubünden □, *Switz.* 25 J5
Grisslehamn, *Sweden* 10 D12
Grmeč Planina, *Bos.-H.* 41 D13
Groais I., *Canada* 105 B8
Grobiņa, *Latvia* 30 B8
Groblersdal, *S. Africa* 89 D4
Grobming, *Austria* 26 D6
Grocka, *Serbia & M.* 44 B4
Gródek, *Poland* 31 E10
Grodków, *Poland* 31 H4
Grodno = Hrodna, *Belarus* 30 E10
Grodzisk Mazowiecki, *Poland* 31 F7
Grodzisk Wielkopolski, *Poland* 31 F3
Grodzyanka = Hrodzyanka, *Belarus* 32 F5
Groesbeck, *U.S.A.* 113 K6
Groix, *France* 18 E3
Groix, Î. de, *France* 18 E3
Grójec, *Poland* 31 G7
Gronau, *Niedersachsen, Germany* 24 C5
Gronau, *Nordrhein-Westfalen, Germany* 24 C3
Grong, *Norway* 8 D15
Grönhögen, *Sweden* 11 H10
Groningen, *Neths.* 17 A6
Groningen □, *Neths.* 17 A6
Groom, *U.S.A.* 113 H4
Groot →, *S. Africa* 88 E3
Groot Berg →, *S. Africa* 88 E2
Groot-Brakrivier, *S. Africa* 88 E3
Groot Karasberge, *Namibia* 88 D2
Groot-Kei →, *S. Africa* 89 E4
Groot Vis →, *S. Africa* 88 E4
Grootdrink, *S. Africa* 88 D3
Groote Eylandt, *Australia* 94 A2
Grootfontein, *Namibia* 88 B2
Grootlaagte →, *Africa* 88 C3
Grootvloer →, *S. Africa* 88 E3
Gros C., *Canada* 102 A6
Gros Islet, *St. Lucia* 121 f
Gros Morne △, *Canada* 105 C8
Gros Piton, *St. Lucia* 121 f
Gros Piton Pt., *St. Lucia* 121 f
Grósio, *Italy* 40 B7
Grosne →, *France* 19 F11
Grossa, Pta., *Spain* 48 B8
Grossenbrode, *Germany* 24 A7
Grossenhain, *Germany* 24 D9
Grosser Arber, *Germany* 25 F9
Grosser Plöner See, *Germany* 24 A6
Grosseto, *Italy* 41 F8
Grossgerungs, *Austria* 26 C7
Grossglockner, *Austria* 26 D5
Groswater B., *Canada* 105 B8
Groton, *Conn., U.S.A.* 117 E12
Groton, *N.Y., U.S.A.* 117 D8
Groton, *S. Dak., U.S.A.* 112 C5
Grottáglie, *Italy* 43 B10
Grottaminarda, *Italy* 43 A8
Grottammare, *Italy* 41 F10
Grouard Mission, *Canada* 102 B5
Grouin, Pte. du, *France* 18 D5
Groundhog →, *Canada* 104 C3
Grouw, *Neths.* 17 A5
Grove City, *U.S.A.* 116 E4
Grove Hill, *U.S.A.* 115 K2
Groveland, *U.S.A.* 110 H6
Grover City, *U.S.A.* 111 K6
Groves, *U.S.A.* 113 L8
Groveton, *U.S.A.* 117 B13
Grožnjan, *Croatia* 41 C10
Groznyy, *Russia* 35 J7
Grubišno Polje, *Croatia* 28 E2
Grudovo, *Bulgaria* 45 D11
Grudusk, *Poland* 31 E7
Grudziądz, *Poland* 30 E5
Gruinard B., *U.K.* 13 D3
Gruissan, *France* 20 E7
Grumo Áppula, *Italy* 43 A9
Grums, *Sweden* 10 E7
Grünberg, *Germany* 24 E4
Gründau, *Germany* 25 E5
Grundy Center, *U.S.A.* 112 D8
Grünstadt, *Germany* 25 F4
Gruppo di Tessa ⌓, *Italy* 40 B8
Gruvberget, *Sweden* 10 C10
Gruver, *U.S.A.* 113 G4
Gruyères, *Switz.* 25 J3
Gruža, *Serbia & M.* 44 C4
Gryazi, *Russia* 33 F10
Gryazovets, *Russia* 32 C11
Grybów, *Poland* 31 J7
Grycksbo, *Sweden* 10 D9
Gryfice, *Poland* 30 E2
Gryfino, *Poland* 31 E1
Gryfów Śląski, *Poland* 31 G2
Grythyttan, *Sweden* 10 E8
Gstaad, *Switz.* 25 J3
Gua, *India* 67 H14
Gua Musang, *Malaysia* 65 K3
Guacanayabo, G. de, *Cuba* 120 B4
Guachípas →, *Argentina* 126 B2
Guadajoz →, *Spain* 37 H6
Guadalajara, *Mexico* 118 C4
Guadalajara, *Spain* 38 E1
Guadalajara □, *Spain* 38 E2
Guadalcanal, *Solomon Is.* 96 H8
Guadalcanal, *Spain* 37 G5
Guadalén →, *Spain* 37 G7
Guadales, *Argentina* 126 C2
Guadalete →, *Spain* 37 J4
Guadalimar →, *Spain* 37 G7
Guadalmena →, *Spain* 37 G8
Guadalmez →, *Spain* 37 G5
Guadalope →, *Spain* 38 D4
Guadalquivir →, *Spain* 37 J4
Guadalupe = Guadeloupe ⊠, *W. Indies* 120 b
Guadalupe, *Mexico* 111 N10
Guadalupe, *Spain* 37 F5
Guadalupe, *U.S.A.* 111 L6
Guadalupe →, *Mexico* 111 N10
Guadalupe →, *U.S.A.* 113 L6
Guadalupe, Sierra de, *Spain* 37 F5
Guadalupe Bravos, *Mexico* 118 A3
Guadalupe I., *Pac. Oc.* 98 G8
Guadalupe Mts. △, *U.S.A.* 113 K2
Guadalupe Peak, *U.S.A.* 113 K2
Guadalupe y Calvo, *Mexico* 118 B3
Guadarrama, Sierra de, *Spain* 36 E7
Guadauta, *Georgia* 35 J5
Guadeloupe △, *Guadeloupe* 120 b
Guadeloupe ⊠, *W. Indies* 120 b
Guadeloupe Passage, *W. Indies* 121 C7
Guadiamar →, *Spain* 37 J4
Guadiana →, *Portugal* 37 H3
Guadiana Menor →, *Spain* 37 H7
Guadiaro →, *Spain* 37 J5
Guadiato →, *Spain* 37 H5
Guadiela →, *Spain* 38 E2
Guadix, *Spain* 37 H7
Guafo, Boca del, *Chile* 128 E2
Guaico, *Trin. & Tob.* 125 K15
Guainía →, *Colombia* 124 C5
Guaíra, *Brazil* 127 A5
Guaíra □, *Paraguay* 126 B4
Guaitecas, Is., *Chile* 128 E2
Guajará-Mirim, *Brazil* 124 F5
Guajira, Pen. de la, *Colombia* 124 A4
Gualán, *Guatemala* 120 C2
Gualdo Tadino, *Italy* 41 E9
Gualeguay, *Argentina* 126 C4
Gualeguaychú, *Argentina* 126 C4
Gualequay →, *Argentina* 126 C4
Guam ⊠, *Pac. Oc.* 96 F6
Guaminí, *Argentina* 126 D3
Guamúchil, *Mexico* 118 B3
Guana I., *Br. Virgin Is.* 121 e
Guanabacoa, *Cuba* 120 B3
Guanacaste △, *Costa Rica* 120 D2
Guanacaste, Cordillera del, *Costa Rica* 120 D2
Guanaceví, *Mexico* 118 B3
Guanahani = San Salvador I., *Bahamas* 121 B5
Guanajay, *Cuba* 120 B3
Guanajuato, *Mexico* 118 C4
Guanajuato □, *Mexico* 118 C4
Guandacol, *Argentina* 126 B2
Guane, *Cuba* 120 B3
Guang'an, *China* 58 B6
Guangchang, *China* 59 D11
Guangde, *China* 59 B12
Guangdong □, *China* 59 F9
Guangfeng, *China* 59 C12
Guanghan, *China* 58 B5
Guangling, *China* 56 E8
Guangnan, *China* 58 E5
Guangning, *China* 59 F9
Guangrao, *China* 57 F10
Guangshui, *China* 59 B9
Guangshun, *China* 58 D6
Guangwu, *China* 56 F3
Guangxi Zhuangzu Zizhiqu □, *China* 58 F7
Guangyuan, *China* 58 A5
Guangze, *China* 59 D11
Guangzhou, *China* 59 F9
Guánica, *Puerto Rico* 121 d
Guanipa →, *Venezuela* 124 B6
Guanling, *China* 58 E5
Guannan, *China* 57 G10
Guantánamo, *Cuba* 121 B4
Guantánamo B., *Cuba* 121 C4
Guantao, *China* 56 F8
Guanyang, *China* 59 E8
Guanyun, *China* 57 G10
Guápiles, *Costa Rica* 120 D3
Guapo B., *Trin. & Tob.* 125 K15
Guaporé, *Brazil* 127 B5
Guaporé →, *Brazil* 124 F5
Guaqui, *Bolivia* 124 G5
Guara, Sierra de, *Spain* 38 C4
Guaramacal △, *Venezuela* 121 E5
Guarapari, *Brazil* 127 A7
Guarapuava, *Brazil* 127 B5
Guaratinguetá, *Brazil* 127 A6
Guaratuba, *Brazil* 127 B6
Guarda, *Portugal* 36 E3
Guarda □, *Portugal* 36 E3

Guardafui, C. = Asir, Ras, *Somali Rep.* 75 E5
Guardamar del Segura, *Spain* 39 G4
Guardavalle, *Italy* 43 D9
Guárdia Sanframondi, *Italy* 43 A7
Guardiagrele, *Italy* 41 F11
Guardo, *Spain* 36 C6
Guareña, *Spain* 37 G4
Guareña →, *Spain* 36 D5
Guárico □, *Venezuela* 124 B5
Guarujá, *Brazil* 127 A6
Guarulhos, *Brazil* 127 A6
Guarus, *Brazil* 127 A7
Guasave, *Mexico* 118 B3
Guasdualito, *Venezuela* 124 B4
Guastalla, *Italy* 40 D7
Guatemala, *Guatemala* 120 D1
Guatemala ■, *Cent. Amer.* 120 C1
Guatemala Trench, *Pac. Oc.* 98 H10
Guatopo △, *Venezuela* 121 D6
Guatuaro Pt., *Trin. & Tob.* 125 K16
Guaviare →, *Colombia* 124 C5
Guaxupé, *Brazil* 127 A6
Guayaguayare, *Trin. & Tob.* 125 K15
Guayama, *Puerto Rico* 121 d
Guayaquil, *Ecuador* 124 D3
Guayaquil, G. de, *Ecuador* 124 D2
Guaymas, *Mexico* 118 B2
Guba, *Dem. Rep. of the Congo* 87 E2
Guba, *Ethiopia* 81 E4
Gûbâl, Madîq, *Egypt* 80 B3
Gubat, *Phil.* 61 E6
Gúbbio, *Italy* 41 E9
Guben, *Germany* 24 D10
Gubin, *Poland* 31 G1
Gubio, *Nigeria* 83 C7
Gubkin, *Russia* 33 G9
Guča, *Serbia & M.* 44 C4
Gucheng, *China* 59 A8
Gudata = Guadauta, *Georgia* 35 J5
Gudbrandsdalen, *Norway* 9 F14
Guddu Barrage, *Pakistan* 66 E6
Gudenå →, *Denmark* 11 H4
Gudermes, *Russia* 35 J8
Gudhjem, *Denmark* 11 J8
Gudur, *India* 66 M11
Guebwiller, *France* 19 E14
Guecho = Getxo, *Spain* 38 B2
Guékédou, *Guinea* 82 D2
Guéle Mendouka, *Cameroon* 83 E7
Guelmine = Goulimine, *Morocco* 78 C3
Guelph, *Canada* 116 C4
Guéméné-Penfao, *France* 18 E5
Guéméné-sur-Scorff, *France* 18 D3
Guéné, *Benin* 83 C5
Guer, *France* 18 E4
Guérande, *France* 18 E4
Guéret, *France* 19 F8
Guérigny, *France* 19 E10
Guerneville, *U.S.A.* 110 G4
Guernica = Gernika-Lumo, *Spain* 38 B2
Guernsey, *U.K.* 15 H5
Guernsey, *U.S.A.* 112 D2
Guerrero □, *Mexico* 119 D5
Gueussou-Sud, *Benin* 83 C5
Gueugnon, *France* 19 F11
Guéyo, *Ivory C.* 82 D3
Gughe, *Ethiopia* 81 F4
Gügher, *Iran* 71 D8
Guglionesi, *Italy* 41 G11
Guhakolak, Tanjung, *Indonesia* 63 G11
Gui Jiang →, *China* 59 F8
Guia, *Canary Is.* 48 F4
Guia de Isora, *Canary Is.* 48 F3
Guia Lopes da Laguna, *Brazil* 127 A4
Guiana Highlands, *S. Amer.* 122 C4
Guibéroua, *Ivory C.* 82 D3
Guichi, *China* 59 B11
Guider, *Cameroon* 83 D7
Guidiguir, *Niger* 83 C6
Guidimouni, *Niger* 83 C6
Guiding, *China* 58 D6
Guidong, *China* 59 D9
Guidónia-Montecélio, *Italy* 41 F9
Guiers, L. de, *Senegal* 82 B1
Guigang, *China* 58 F7
Guiglo, *Ivory C.* 82 D3
Guihulñgan, *Phil.* 61 F5
Guijá, *Mozam.* 89 C5
Guijuelo, *Spain* 36 E5
Guildford, *U.K.* 15 F7
Guilford, *U.S.A.* 117 E12
Guilin, *China* 59 E8
Guillaume-Delisle, L., *Canada* 104 A4
Guillaumes, *France* 21 D10
Guillestre, *France* 21 D10
Guilvinec, *France* 18 E2
Güimar, *Canary Is.* 48 F3
Guimarães, *Portugal* 36 D2
Guimaras □, *Phil.* 61 F5
Guinda, *U.S.A.* 110 G4
Guinea, *Africa* 76 F4
Guinea ■, *W. Afr.* 82 C2
Guinea, Gulf of, *Atl. Oc.* 83 E5
Guinea-Bissau ■, *Africa* 82 C2
Güines, *Cuba* 120 B3
Guingamp, *France* 18 D3
Guinguinéo, *Senegal* 82 C1
Guipavas, *France* 18 D2
Guiping, *China* 59 F8
Guipúzcoa □, *Spain* 38 B2
Guir, *Mali* 82 B4
Guirel, *Mauritania* 82 B3
Güiria, *Venezuela* 124 A6
Guiscard, *France* 19 C10
Guise, *France* 19 C10
Guitiriz, *Spain* 36 B3
Guitri, *Ivory C.* 82 D3
Guiuan, *Phil.* 61 F6
Guixi, *China* 59 C11
Guiyang, *Guizhou, China* 58 D6
Guiyang, *Hunan, China* 59 E9
Guizhou □, *China* 58 D6
Gujan-Mestras, *France* 20 D2
Gujar Khan, *Pakistan* 68 C5
Gujarat □, *India* 68 H4
Gujiang, *China* 59 D10
Gujranwala, *Pakistan* 68 C6
Gujrat, *Pakistan* 68 C6
Gukovo, *Russia* 35 F5
Gulbarga, *India* 66 L10
Gulbene, *Latvia* 9 H22
Gulf, The = Persian Gulf, *Asia* 71 E6
Gulf Islands ⌓, *U.S.A.* 115 E2
Gulfport, *U.S.A.* 113 K10
Gulgong, *Australia* 95 E4
Gulin, *China* 58 C5
Gulistan, *Pakistan* 68 D2
Gull Lake, *Canada* 103 C7
Gullbrandstorp, *Sweden* 11 H6
Gullspång, *Sweden* 11 F8
Güllük, *Turkey* 47 D9
Güllük Daği △, *Turkey* 47 E12
Güllük Korfezi, *Turkey* 47 D9
Gulma, *Nigeria* 83 C5
Gulmarg, *India* 69 B6
Gülnar, *Turkey* 72 D5
Gülpınar, *Turkey* 47 B8
Gülşehir, *Turkey* 72 C6
Gulshad, *Kazakhstan* 52 E8
Gulu, *Uganda* 86 B3
Gŭlŭbovo, *Bulgaria* 45 D9
Gulud, J., *Sudan* 81 E2
Gulwe, *Tanzania* 86 D4
Gulyaypole = Hulyaypole, *Ukraine* 33 J9
Gumal →, *Pakistan* 68 D4
Gumbaz, *Pakistan* 68 D3
Gumel, *Nigeria* 83 C6
Gumiel de Hizán, *Spain* 36 D7
Gumla, *India* 69 H11
Gumlu, *Australia* 94 B4
Gumma □, *Japan* 55 F9
Gummersbach, *Germany* 24 D3
Gummi, *Nigeria* 83 C6
Gümüldür, *Turkey* 47 C9
Gümüşçay, *Turkey* 45 F11
Gümüşhacıköy, *Turkey* 72 B6
Gümüşhane, *Turkey* 73 B8
Gümüşsu, *Turkey* 47 C11
Gumzai, *Indonesia* 63 F8
Guna, *Ethiopia* 81 F4
Guna, *India* 68 G7
Gundelfingen, *Germany* 25 G6
Güney, *Burdur, Turkey* 47 D11
Güney, *Denizli, Turkey* 47 C11
Güneydoğu Toroslar, *Turkey* 73 C9
Gunisao →, *Canada* 103 C9
Gunisao L., *Canada* 103 C9
Gunjyal, *Pakistan* 68 C4
Günlüce, *Turkey* 47 E10
Gunnarskog, *Sweden* 10 E6
Gunnbjørn Fjeld, *Greenland* 4 C6
Gunnebo, *Sweden* 11 G10
Gunnedah, *Australia* 95 E5
Gunnewin, *Australia* 95 D4
Gunningbar Cr. →, *Australia* 95 E4
Gunnison, *Colo., U.S.A.* 109 G10
Gunnison, *Utah, U.S.A.* 108 G8
Gunnison →, *U.S.A.* 109 G9
Gunpowder, *Australia* 94 B2
Guntakal, *India* 66 M10
Guntersville, *U.S.A.* 115 H2
Guntong, *Malaysia* 65 K3
Guntur, *India* 67 L12
Gunungapi, *Indonesia* 63 F7
Gunungsitoli, *Indonesia* 62 D1
Günz →, *Germany* 25 G6
Gunza, *Angola* 84 G2
Günzburg, *Germany* 25 G6
Gunzenhausen, *Germany* 25 F6
Guo He →, *China* 57 H9
Guoyang, *China* 56 H9
Gupis, *Pakistan* 69 A5
Gura Humorului, *Romania* 29 C10
Gura-Teghii, *Romania* 29 E11
Gurag, *Ethiopia* 81 F4
Gurahonţ, *Romania* 28 D7
Gurdaspur, *India* 68 C6
Gurdon, *U.S.A.* 113 J8
Güre, *Balıkesir, Turkey* 47 B8
Güre, *Uşak, Turkey* 47 C11
Gurgaon, *India* 68 E7
Gürgentepe, *Turkey* 72 B7
Gurghiu, Munţii, *Romania* 29 D10
Gurgueia →, *Brazil* 125 E10
Gurha, *India* 68 G4
Guri, Embalse de, *Venezuela* 124 B6
Gurig △, *Australia* 92 B5
Gurin, *Nigeria* 83 D7
Gurjaani, *Georgia* 35 K7
Gurk →, *Austria* 26 E7
Gurkha, *Nepal* 69 E11
Gurley, *Australia* 95 D4
Gurnet Point, *U.S.A.* 117 D14
Guro, *Mozam.* 87 F3
Gürpınar, *Ist., Turkey* 45 F12
Gürpınar, *Van, Turkey* 73 C10
Gürsu, *Turkey* 45 F13
Gurué, *Mozam.* 87 F4
Gurun, *Malaysia* 65 K3
Gürün, *Turkey* 72 C7
Gurupá, *Brazil* 125 D8
Gurupá, I. Grande de, *Brazil* 125 D8
Gurupi, *Brazil* 125 F9
Gurupi →, *Brazil* 125 D9
Guruwe, *Zimbabwe* 89 B5
Guryev = Atyraū, *Kazakhstan* 52 E6
Gurvevsk, *Russia* 30 D7
Gus-Khrustalnyy, *Russia* 34 C5
Gusau, *Nigeria* 83 C6
Gusev, *Russia* 9 J20
Gushan, *China* 57 E12
Gushgy, *Turkmenistan* 52 F7
Gushi, *China* 59 A10
Gushiago, *Ghana* 83 D4
Gusinje, *Serbia & M.* 44 D3
Gusinoozersk, *Russia* 53 D11
Gúspini, *Italy* 42 C1
Güssing, *Austria* 27 D9
Gustavsberg, *Sweden* 10 E12
Gustavus, *U.S.A.* 102 B1
Gustine, *U.S.A.* 110 H6
Güstrow, *Germany* 24 B8
Gusum, *Sweden* 11 F10
Guta = Kolárovo, *Slovak Rep.* 27 D10
Gütersloh, *Germany* 24 D4
Gutha, *Australia* 93 E2
Guthalungra, *Australia* 94 B4
Guthrie, *Okla., U.S.A.* 113 H6
Guthrie, *Tex., U.S.A.* 113 J4
Gutian, *China* 59 D12
Guttenberg, *U.S.A.* 112 D9
Gutu, *Zimbabwe* 89 B5
Guwahati, *India* 67 F17
Guy Fawkes River △, *Australia* 95 D5
Guyana ■, *S. Amer.* 124 C7
Guyane française = French Guiana ⊠, *S. Amer.* 125 C8
Guyang, *China* 56 D6
Guyenne, *France* 20 D4
Guymon, *U.S.A.* 113 G4
Guyra, *Australia* 95 E5
Guyuan, *Hebei, China* 56 D8
Guyuan, *Ningxia Huizu, China* 56 G4
Güzelbahçe, *Turkey* 47 C8
Güzelyurt = Morphou, *Cyprus* 49 D11
Guzhang, *China* 58 C7
Guzhen, *China* 57 H9
Guzmán, L. de, *Mexico* 118 A3
Gvardeysk, *Russia* 9 J19
Gvardeyskoye, *Ukraine* 33 K8
Gwa, *Burma* 67 L19
Gwaai, *Zimbabwe* 87 F2
Gwaai →, *Zimbabwe* 87 F2
Gwabegar, *Australia* 95 E4
Gwadabawa, *Nigeria* 83 C6
Gwādar, *Pakistan* 66 G3
Gwagwada, *Nigeria* 83 C6
Gwaii Haanas △, *Canada* 102 C2
Gwalior, *India* 68 F8
Gwanara, *Nigeria* 83 D5
Gwanda, *Zimbabwe* 87 G2
Gwandu, *Nigeria* 83 C5
Gwane, *Dem. Rep. of the Congo* 86 B2
Gwaram, *Nigeria* 83 C7
Gwarzo, *Nigeria* 83 C6
Gwasero, *Nigeria* 83 D5
Gwda →, *Poland* 31 E3
Gweebarra B., *Ireland* 12 B3
Gweedore, *Ireland* 12 A3
Gweru, *Zimbabwe* 87 F2
Gwi, *Nigeria* 83 D6
Gwinn, *U.S.A.* 114 B2
Gwio Kura, *Nigeria* 83 C7
Gwoza, *Nigeria* 83 C7
Gwydir →, *Australia* 95 D4
Gwynedd □, *U.K.* 14 E3
Gyandzha = Gäncä, *Azerbaijan* 35 K8
Gyaring Hu, *China* 60 C4
Gydanskiy Poluostrov, *Russia* 52 C8
Gympie, *Australia* 95 D5
Gyomaendrőd, *Hungary* 28 D5
Gyöngyös, *Hungary* 28 C4
Győr, *Hungary* 28 C2
Győr-Moson-Sopron □, *Hungary* 28 C2
Gypsum Pt., *Canada* 102 A6
Gypsumville, *Canada* 103 C9
Gyueshevo, *Bulgaria* 44 D6
Gyula, *Hungary* 28 D6
Gyumri, *Armenia* 35 K6
Gyzylarbat, *Turkmenistan* 52 F6
Gyzyletrek, *Turkmenistan* 71 B7
Gzhatsk = Gagarin, *Russia* 32 E8

H

Ha 'Arava →, *Israel* 74 E4
Ha Coi, *Vietnam* 58 G6
Ha Dong, *Vietnam* 58 G5
Ha Giang, *Vietnam* 58 F5
Ha Karmel △, *Israel* 74 C4
Ha Tien, *Vietnam* 65 G5
Ha Tinh, *Vietnam* 64 C5
Ha Trung, *Vietnam* 64 C5
Ha Yaek Chalong, *Thailand* 65 a
Haaksbergen, *Neths.* 17 B6
Haapsalu, *Estonia* 9 G20
Haarlem, *Neths.* 17 B4
Haast →, *N.Z.* 91 K2
Haast Bluff, *Australia* 92 D5
Hab →, *Pakistan* 68 G3
Hab Nadi Chauki, *Pakistan* 68 G2
Habahe, *China* 60 B3
Habaswein, *Kenya* 86 B4
Habay, *Canada* 102 B5
Ḩabbānīyah, *Iraq* 70 C4
Ḩabbānīyah, Hawr al, *Iraq* 73 F10
Habichtswald ⌓, *Germany* 24 D5
Habo, *Sweden* 11 G8
Haboro, *Japan* 54 B10
Ḩabshān, *U.A.E.* 71 F7
Hachenburg, *Germany* 24 E3
Hachijō-Jima, *Japan* 55 H9
Hachinohe, *Japan* 54 D10
Hachiōji, *Japan* 55 G9
Hachŏn, *N. Korea* 57 D15
Hacıbektaş, *Turkey* 72 C6
Hacılar, *Turkey* 72 C6
Hackås, *Sweden* 10 B8
Hackensack, *U.S.A.* 117 F10
Hackettstown, *U.S.A.* 117 F10
Hadali, *Pakistan* 68 C5
Hadarba, Ras, *Sudan* 80 C4
Hadarom □, *Israel* 74 E4
Ḩadd, Ra's al, *Oman* 75 C6
Haddington, *U.K.* 13 F6
Hadejia, *Nigeria* 83 C7
Hadejia →, *Nigeria* 83 C7
Ḩadera, *Israel* 74 C3
Ḩadera, N. →, *Israel* 74 C3
Haderslev, *Denmark* 11 J3
Hadhramaut = Ḩaḑramawt, *Yemen* 75 D4
Hadiboh, *Yemen* 75 E5
Hadım, *Turkey* 72 D5
Hadong, *S. Korea* 57 G14
Ḩaḑramawt, *Yemen* 75 D4
Ḩadrānīyah, *Iraq* 70 C4
Hadrian's Wall, *U.K.* 14 B5
Hadsten, *Denmark* 11 H4
Hadsund, *Denmark* 11 H4
Hadyach, *Ukraine* 33 G8
Haeju, *N. Korea* 57 E13
Haenam, *S. Korea* 57 G14
Haenertsburg, *S. Africa* 89 C4
Haerhpin = Harbin, *China* 57 B14
Hafar al Bāţin, *Si. Arabia* 70 D5
Hafik, *Turkey* 72 C7
Ḩafīrat al 'Aydā, *Si. Arabia* 70 E3
Ḩafit, *Oman* 71 F7
Hafizabad, *Pakistan* 68 C5
Haflong, *India* 67 G18
Hafnarfjörður, *Iceland* 8 D3
Haft Gel, *Iran* 71 D6
Hafun, Ras, *Somali Rep.* 75 E5
Hagalil, *Israel* 74 C4
Hagby, *Sweden* 11 H10
Hagen, *Germany* 24 D3
Hagenow, *Germany* 24 B7
Hagerman, *U.S.A.* 113 J2
Hagerman Fossil Beds ⌓, *U.S.A.* 108 E6
Hagerstown, *U.S.A.* 114 F7
Hagersville, *Canada* 116 D4
Hagetmau, *France* 20 E3
Hagfors, *Sweden* 10 D7
Hagi, *Japan* 55 G5
Hagolan, *Syria* 74 C4
Hagondange, *France* 19 C13
Hags Hd., *Ireland* 12 D2
Hague, C. de la, *France* 18 C5
Hague, The = 's-Gravenhage, *Neths.* 17 B4
Haguenau, *France* 19 D14
Hai Duong, *Vietnam* 58 G6
Hai'an, *Guangdong, China* 59 G8
Hai'an, *Jiangsu, China* 59 A13
Haicheng, *Fujian, China* 59 E11
Haicheng, *Liaoning, China* 57 D12
Haidar Khel, *Afghan.* 68 C3
Haidarâbâd = Hyderabad, *India* 66 L11
Haidargarh, *India* 69 F9
Haifa = Ḩefa, *Israel* 74 C4
Haifeng, *China* 59 F10
Haiger, *Germany* 24 E4
Haikou, *China* 60 D6
Ḩā'il, *Si. Arabia* 70 E4
Hailar, *China* 60 B6
Hailey, *U.S.A.* 108 E6
Haileybury, *Canada* 104 C4
Hailin, *China* 57 B15
Hailing Dao, *China* 59 G8
Hailong, *China* 57 C13
Hailuoto, *Finland* 8 D21
Haimen, *Guangdong, China* 59 F11
Haimen, *Jiangsu, China* 59 B13
Hainan □, *China* 60 E5
Hainaut □, *Belgium* 17 D4
Hainburg, *Austria* 27 C9
Haines, *Alaska, U.S.A.* 102 B1
Haines, *Oreg., U.S.A.* 108 D5
Haines City, *U.S.A.* 115 L5
Haines Junction, *Canada* 102 A1
Hainfeld, *Austria* 26 C8
Haining, *China* 59 B13
Haiphong, *Vietnam* 58 G6
Haitan Dao, *China* 59 E12
Haiti ■, *W. Indies* 121 C5
Haiya, *Sudan* 80 D4
Haiyan, *China* 59 B13
Haiyang, *China* 57 F11
Haiyuan, *Guangxi Zhuangzu, China* 58 F6
Haiyuan, *Ningxia Huizu, China* 56 F3
Haizhou, *China* 57 G10
Haizhou Wan, *China* 57 G10
Hajdú-Bihar □, *Hungary* 28 C6
Hajdúböszörmény, *Hungary* 28 C6
Hajdúdorog, *Hungary* 28 C6
Hajdúhadház, *Hungary* 28 C6
Hajdúnánás, *Hungary* 28 C6
Hajdúsámson, *Hungary* 28 C6
Hajdúszoboszló, *Hungary* 28 C6
Hajipur, *India* 69 G11
Ḩājjī Muḩsin, *Iraq* 70 C5
Ḩājjīābād, *Iran* 71 D7
Ḩājjīābād-e Zarrīn, *Iran* 71 C7
Hajnówka, *Poland* 31 F10
Hakansson, Mts., *Dem. Rep. of the Congo* 87 D2
Hakkâri, *Turkey* 70 B4
Hakkâri Dağları, *Turkey* 73 C10
Hakken-Zan, *Japan* 55 G7
Hakodate, *Japan* 54 D10
Hakos, *Namibia* 88 C2
Håksberg, *Sweden* 10 D9
Haku-San, *Japan* 55 F8
Haku-San △, *Japan* 55 F8
Hakui, *Japan* 55 F8
Hala, *Pakistan* 66 G6
Ḩalab, *Syria* 70 B3
Ḩalabjah, *Iraq* 70 C5
Halaib, *Sudan* 80 C4
Halasa, *Sudan* 81 E3
Ḩālat 'Ammār, *Si. Arabia* 70 D3
Halbā, *Lebanon* 74 A5
Halberstadt, *Germany* 24 D7
Halcombe, *N.Z.* 91 J5
Halcon, *Phil.* 63 B6
Halde Fjäll = Haltiatunturi, *Finland* 8 B19
Halden, *Norway* 9 G14
Haldensleben, *Germany* 24 C7
Haldia, *India* 67 H16
Haldimand, *Canada* 116 D5
Haldwani, *India* 69 E8
Hale →, *Australia* 94 C2
Halesowen, *U.K.* 15 E5
Halesworth, *U.K.* 15 E9
Haleyville, *U.S.A.* 115 H2
Half Assini, *Ghana* 82 D4
Halfmoon Bay, *N.Z.* 91 M2
Halfway →, *Canada* 102 B4
Halia, *India* 69 G10
Haliburton, *Canada* 116 A6
Halifax, *Australia* 94 B4
Halifax, *Canada* 105 D7
Halifax, *U.K.* 14 D6
Halifax, *U.S.A.* 116 F8
Halifax B., *Australia* 94 B4
Halifax I., *Namibia* 88 D2
Halīl →, *Iran* 71 E8
Halkirk, *U.K.* 13 C5
Hall Beach = Sanirajak, *Canada* 101 B11
Hall in Tirol, *Austria* 26 D4
Hall Pen., *Canada* 101 B13
Hall Pt., *Australia* 92 C3
Hallabro, *Sweden* 11 H9
Halland, *Sweden* 9 H15
Hallands län □, *Sweden* 11 H6
Hallands Väderö, *Sweden* 11 H6
Hallandsås, *Sweden* 11 H7
Hällbybrunn, *Sweden* 10 E10
Halle, *Belgium* 17 D4
Halle, *Nordrhein-Westfalen, Germany* 24 C4
Halle, *Sachsen-Anhalt, Germany* 24 D7
Hällefors, *Sweden* 10 E8
Hälleforsnäs, *Sweden* 10 E10
Hallein, *Austria* 26 D6
Hällekis, *Sweden* 11 F7
Hallen, *Sweden* 10 A8
Hallett, *Australia* 95 E2
Hallettsville, *U.S.A.* 113 L6
Hallim, *S. Korea* 57 H14
Hallingdalselvi →, *Norway* 9 F13
Hallock, *U.S.A.* 112 A6
Halls Creek, *Australia* 92 C4
Hallsberg, *Sweden* 10 E9
Hallstahammar, *Sweden* 10 E10
Hallstatt, *Austria* 26 D6
Hallstavik, *Sweden* 10 D12
Hallstead, *U.S.A.* 117 E9
Halmahera, *Indonesia* 63 D7
Halmeu, *Romania* 28 C8
Halmstad, *Sweden* 11 H6
Hals, *Denmark* 11 H4
Hälsingborg = Helsingborg, *Sweden* 11 H6
Hälsingland, *Sweden* 10 C10
Halstead, *U.K.* 15 F8
Haltern, *Germany* 24 D3
Haltiatunturi, *Finland* 8 B19
Halton □, *U.K.* 14 D5
Haltwhistle, *U.K.* 14 C5
Ḩālūl, *Qatar* 71 E7
Halvad, *India* 68 H4
Ḩalvān, *Iran* 71 C8
Ham, *France* 19 C10
Ham Tan, *Vietnam* 65 G6
Ham Yen, *Vietnam* 64 A5
Hamab, *Namibia* 88 D2
Hamad, *Sudan* 81 D3
Hamada, *Japan* 55 G6
Hamadān, *Iran* 71 C6
Hamadān □, *Iran* 71 C6
Hamāh, *Syria* 70 C3
Hamamatsu, *Japan* 55 G8
Hamar, *Norway* 9 F14
Hamâta, Gebel, *Egypt* 70 E2
Hambantota, *Sri Lanka* 66 R12
Hamber ⌓, *Canada* 102 C5
Hamburg, *Germany* 24 B5
Hamburg, *Ark., U.S.A.* 113 J9
Hamburg, *N.Y., U.S.A.* 116 D6
Hamburg, *Pa., U.S.A.* 117 F9
Hamburg □, *Germany* 24 B5
Hamburg Fuhlsbüttel ✕ (HAM), *Germany* 24 B5
Ḩamḑ, W. al →, *Si. Arabia* 70 E3
Hamden, *U.S.A.* 117 E12
Hamdibey, *Turkey* 47 B9
Häme, *Finland* 9 F20
Hämeenlinna, *Finland* 9 F21
Hamélé, *Ghana* 82 C4
Hamelin Pool, *Australia* 93 E1
Hameln, *Germany* 24 C5
Hamerkaz □, *Israel* 74 C3
Hamersley Ra., *Australia* 92 D2
Hamhung, *N. Korea* 57 E14
Hami, *China* 60 B4
Hamilton, *Australia* 95 F3
Hamilton, *Canada* 116 C5
Hamilton, *N.Z.* 91 G5
Hamilton, *U.K.* 13 F4
Hamilton, *Ala., U.S.A.* 115 H1
Hamilton, *Mont., U.S.A.* 108 C6
Hamilton, *N.Y., U.S.A.* 117 D9
Hamilton, *Ohio, U.S.A.* 114 F3
Hamilton, *Tex., U.S.A.* 113 K5
Hamilton →, *Australia* 94 C2
Hamilton, The →, *Australia* 95 D2
Hamilton City, *U.S.A.* 110 F4
Hamilton I., *Australia* 94 J6
Hamilton Inlet, *Canada* 105 B8
Hamilton Mt., *U.S.A.* 117 C10

Hamina, *Finland* 9 F22
Hamirpur, *H.P., India* 68 D7
Hamirpur, *Ut. P., India* 69 G9
Hamitabat, *Turkey* 45 E11
Hamlet, *U.S.A.* 115 H6
Hamley Bridge, *Australia* 95 E2
Hamlin = Hameln, *Germany* 24 C5
Hamlin, *N.Y., U.S.A.* 116 C7
Hamlin, *Tex., U.S.A.* 113 J4
Hamm, *Germany* 24 D3
Ḩammār, Hawr al, *Iraq* 70 D5
Hammarstrand, *Sweden* 10 A10
Hammelburg, *Germany* 25 E5
Hammeren, *Denmark* 11 J8
Hammerfest, *Norway* 8 A20
Hammerum, *Denmark* 11 H3
Hamminkeln, *Germany* 24 D2
Hammond, *Ind., U.S.A.* 114 E2
Hammond, *La., U.S.A.* 113 K9
Hammond, *N.Y., U.S.A.* 117 B9
Hammondsport, *U.S.A.* 116 D7
Hammonton, *U.S.A.* 114 F8
Hamneda, *Sweden* 11 H7
Hamoyet, Jebel, *Sudan* 80 D4
Hampden, *N.Z.* 91 L3
Hampshire □, *U.K.* 15 F6
Hampshire Downs, *U.K.* 15 F6
Hampton, *N.B., Canada* 105 C6
Hampton, *Ont., Canada* 116 C6
Hampton, *Ark., U.S.A.* 113 J8
Hampton, *Iowa, U.S.A.* 112 D8
Hampton, *N.H., U.S.A.* 117 D14
Hampton, *S.C., U.S.A.* 115 J5
Hampton, *Va., U.S.A.* 114 G7
Hampton Bays, *U.S.A.* 117 F12
Hampton Tableland, *Australia* 93 F4
Hamra, *Sweden* 10 C8
Hamrat esh Sheykh, *Sudan* 81 E2
Hamur, *Turkey* 73 C10
Hamyang, *S. Korea* 57 G14
Han Jiang →, *China* 59 F11
Han Shui, *China* 58 A7
Han Shui →, *China* 59 B10
Hanak, *Si. Arabia* 70 E3
Hanamaki, *Japan* 54 E10
Hanang, *Tanzania* 86 C4
Hanau, *Germany* 25 E4
Hanbogd = Ihbulag, *Mongolia* 56 C4
Hançalar, *Turkey* 47 C11
Hânceşti, *Moldova* 29 D13
Hancheng, *China* 56 G6
Hanchuan, *China* 59 B9
Hancock, *Mich., U.S.A.* 112 B10
Hancock, *N.Y., U.S.A.* 117 E9
Handa, *Japan* 55 G8
Handan, *China* 56 F8
Handeni, *Tanzania* 86 D4
Handlová, *Slovak Rep.* 27 C11
Handub, *Sudan* 80 D4
Handwara, *India* 69 B6
Hanegev, *Israel* 74 E4
Hanford, *U.S.A.* 110 J7
Hanford Reach ⌓, *U.S.A.* 108 C4
Hang Chat, *Thailand* 64 C2
Hang Dong, *Thailand* 64 C2
Hangang →, *S. Korea* 57 F14
Hangayn Nuruu, *Mongolia* 60 B4
Hangchou = Hangzhou, *China* 59 B13
Hanggin Houqi, *China* 56 D4
Hanggin Qi, *China* 56 E5
Hangu, *China* 57 E9
Hangzhou, *China* 59 B13
Hangzhou Wan, *China* 59 B13
Hanhongor, *Mongolia* 56 C3
Ḩanīdh, *Si. Arabia* 71 E6
Ḩanīsh, *Yemen* 75 E3
Haniska, *Slovak Rep.* 27 C14
Hanjiang, *China* 59 E12
Hankinson, *U.S.A.* 112 B6
Hankö, *Finland* 9 G20
Hankou, *China* 59 B10
Hanksville, *U.S.A.* 109 G8
Hanle, *India* 69 C8
Hanmer Springs, *N.Z.* 91 K4
Hann →, *Australia* 92 C4
Hann, Mt., *Australia* 92 C4
Hanna, *Canada* 102 C6
Hanna, *U.S.A.* 108 F10
Hannah B., *Canada* 104 B4
Hannibal, *Mo., U.S.A.* 112 F9
Hannibal, *N.Y., U.S.A.* 117 C8
Hannik, *Sudan* 80 D3
Hannover, *Germany* 24 C5
Hanö, *Sweden* 11 H8
Hanöbukten, *Sweden* 11 J8
Hanoi, *Vietnam* 58 G5
Hanover = Hannover, *Germany* 24 C5
Hanover, *Canada* 116 B3
Hanover, *S. Africa* 88 E3
Hanover, *N.H., U.S.A.* 117 C12
Hanover, *Ohio, U.S.A.* 116 F2
Hanover, *Pa., U.S.A.* 114 F7
Hanover, I., *Chile* 128 G2
Hans Lollik I., *U.S. Virgin Is.* 121 e
Hansdiha, *India* 69 G12
Hanshou, *China* 59 C8
Hansi, *India* 68 E6
Hanson, L., *Australia* 95 E2
Hanstholm, *Denmark* 11 G2
Hantsavichy, *Belarus* 33 F4
Hanumangarh, *India* 68 E6
Hanyin, *China* 58 A7
Hanyuan, *China* 58 C4
Hanzhong, *China* 56 H4
Hanzhuang, *China* 57 G9
Haora, *India* 69 H13
Haoxue, *China* 59 B9
Haparanda, *Sweden* 8 D21
Happy, *U.S.A.* 113 H4
Happy Camp, *U.S.A.* 108 F2
Happy Valley-Goose Bay, *Canada* 105 B7
Hapsu, *N. Korea* 57 D15
Hapur, *India* 68 E7
Ḩaql, *Si. Arabia* 74 F3
Har, *Indonesia* 63 F8
Har-Ayrag, *Mongolia* 56 B5
Har Hu, *China* 60 C4
Har Us Nuur, *Mongolia* 60 B4
Har Yehuda, *Israel* 74 D3
Ḩaraḑ, *Si. Arabia* 75 C4
Haradok, *Belarus* 32 E6
Häradsbäck, *Sweden* 11 H8
Haranomachi, *Japan* 54 F10
Harare, *Zimbabwe* 87 F3
Harat, *Eritrea* 81 D4
Harbin, *China* 57 B14
Harbiye, *Turkey* 72 D7
Harbo, *Sweden* 10 D11
Harbøør, *Denmark* 11 H2
Harbor Beach, *U.S.A.* 116 C2
Harbour Breton, *Canada* 105 C8
Harbour Deep, *Canada* 105 B8
Harburg, *Germany* 24 B5
Harburger Berge ⌓, *Germany* 24 B5
Hårby, *Denmark* 11 J4
Harda, *India* 68 H7
Hardangerfjorden, *Norway* 9 F12
Hardangervidda, *Norway* 9 F12
Hardap ⌓, *Namibia* 88 C2
Hardap Dam, *Namibia* 88 C2
Hardenberg, *Neths.* 17 B6
Harderwijk, *Neths.* 17 B5
Hardey →, *Australia* 92 D2
Hardin, *U.S.A.* 108 D10
Harding, *S. Africa* 89 E4
Harding Ra., *Australia* 92 C3
Hardisty, *Canada* 102 C6
Hardoi, *India* 69 F9
Hardwar = Haridwar, *India* 68 E8
Hardwick, *U.S.A.* 117 B12
Hardy, Pen., *Chile* 128 H3
Hardy, Pte., *St. Lucia* 121 f
Hare B., *Canada* 105 B8
Hareid, *Norway* 9 E12
Haren, *Germany* 24 C3
Harer, *Ethiopia* 81 F5
Harerge, *Ethiopia* 81 F5
Hareto, *Ethiopia* 81 F4
Harfleur, *France* 18 C7
Hargeisa, *Somali Rep.* 75 F3
Harghita □, *Romania* 29 D10
Harghita, Munţii, *Romania* 29 D10
Hargshamn, *Sweden* 10 D12
Hari →, *Indonesia* 62 E2
Haria, *Canary Is.* 48 E6
Haridwar, *India* 68 E8
Harim, Jabal al, *Oman* 71 E8
Haringhata →, *Bangla.* 67 J16
Harīrūd →, *Asia* 66 A2
Härjedalen, *Sweden* 10 B7
Harlan, *Iowa, U.S.A.* 112 E7
Harlan, *Ky., U.S.A.* 115 G4
Hârlău, *Romania* 29 C11
Harlech, *U.K.* 14 E3
Harlem, *U.S.A.* 108 B9
Hårlev, *Denmark* 11 J6
Harlingen, *Neths.* 17 A5
Harlingen, *U.S.A.* 113 M6
Harlow, *U.K.* 15 F8
Harlowton, *U.S.A.* 108 C9
Harmancık, *Turkey* 47 B11
Harmånger, *Sweden* 10 C11
Harmil, *Eritrea* 81 D5
Harnai, *Pakistan* 68 D2
Harney Basin, *U.S.A.* 108 E4
Harney L., *U.S.A.* 108 E4
Harney Peak, *U.S.A.* 112 D3
Härnön, *Sweden* 10 B12
Härnösand, *Sweden* 10 B11
Haro, *Spain* 38 C2
Haroldswick, *U.K.* 13 A8
Harp L., *Canada* 105 A7
Harper, *Liberia* 82 E3
Harplinge, *Sweden* 11 H6
Harr, *Mauritania* 82 B2
Harrai, *India* 69 H8
Harrand, *Pakistan* 68 E4
Ḩarrat Khaybar, *Si. Arabia* 80 B5
Ḩarrat Nawāşīf, *Si. Arabia* 80 C5
Harricana →, *Canada* 104 B4
Harriman, *U.S.A.* 115 H3
Harrington Harbour, *Canada* 105 B8
Harris, *U.K.* 13 D2
Harris, L., *Australia* 95 E2
Harris, Sd. of, *U.K.* 13 D1
Harris Pt., *Canada* 116 C2
Harrisburg, *Ill., U.S.A.* 113 G10
Harrisburg, *Nebr., U.S.A.* 112 E3
Harrisburg, *Pa., U.S.A.* 116 F8
Harrismith, *S. Africa* 89 D4
Harrison, *Ark., U.S.A.* 113 G8
Harrison, *Maine, U.S.A.* 117 B14
Harrison, *Nebr., U.S.A.* 112 D3
Harrison, C., *Canada* 105 B8
Harrison L., *Canada* 102 D4
Harrisonburg, *U.S.A.* 114 F6
Harrisonville, *U.S.A.* 112 F7
Harriston, *Canada* 116 C4
Harrisville, *Mich., U.S.A.* 116 B1
Harrisville, *N.Y., U.S.A.* 117 B9
Harrisville, *Pa., U.S.A.* 116 E5
Harrodsburg, *U.S.A.* 114 G3
Harrogate, *U.K.* 14 C6
Harrow □, *U.K.* 15 F7
Harrowsmith, *Canada* 117 B8
Harry S. Truman Reservoir, *U.S.A.* 112 F7
Harsefeld, *Germany* 24 B5
Harsewinkel, *Germany* 24 D4
Harsīn, *Iran* 70 C5
Hârşova, *Romania* 29 F12
Harstad, *Norway* 8 B17
Harsud, *India* 68 H7
Hart, *U.S.A.* 114 D2
Hart, L., *Australia* 95 E2
Hartbees →, *S. Africa* 88 D3
Hartberg, *Austria* 26 D8
Hartford, *Conn., U.S.A.* 117 E12
Hartford, *Ky., U.S.A.* 114 G2
Hartford, *S. Dak., U.S.A.* 112 D6
Hartford, *Wis., U.S.A.* 112 D10
Hartford City, *U.S.A.* 114 E3
Hartland, *Canada* 105 C6
Hartland Pt., *U.K.* 15 F3
Hartlepool, *U.K.* 14 C6
Hartlepool □, *U.K.* 14 C6
Hartley Bay, *Canada* 102 C3
Hartmannberge, *Namibia* 88 B1
Hartney, *Canada* 103 D8
Hârtop, *Moldova* 29 D13
Harts →, *S. Africa* 88 D3
Hartselle, *U.S.A.* 115 H2
Hartshorne, *U.S.A.* 113 H7
Hartstown, *U.S.A.* 116 E4
Hartsville, *U.S.A.* 115 H5
Hartswater, *S. Africa* 88 D3
Hartwell, *U.S.A.* 115 H4
Harunabad, *Pakistan* 68 E5
Harvand, *Iran* 71 D7
Harvey, *Australia* 93 F2
Harvey, *Ill., U.S.A.* 114 E2
Harvey, *N. Dak., U.S.A.* 112 B5
Harwich, *U.K.* 15 F9
Haryana □, *India* 68 E7
Haryn →, *Belarus* 33 F4
Harz, *Germany* 24 D6
Harz △, *Germany* 24 D6
Harzgerode, *Germany* 24 D7
Hasa □, *Si. Arabia* 71 E6
Hasaheisa, *Sudan* 81 E3
Ḩasanābād, *Iran* 71 C7
Ḩasb, W. →, *Iraq* 70 D5
Hasdo →, *India* 69 J10
Haselünne, *Germany* 24 C3
Hashimoto, *Japan* 55 G7
Hashtjerd, *Iran* 71 C6
Haskell, *U.S.A.* 113 J5
Hasköy, *Turkey* 45 E10
Haslach, *Germany* 25 G4
Hasle, *Denmark* 11 J8
Haslemere, *U.K.* 15 F7
Haslev, *Denmark* 11 J5
Hasparren, *France* 20 E2
Hassa, *Turkey* 72 D7
Hassberge ⌓, *Germany* 25 E6
Hassela, *Sweden* 10 B10
Hasselt, *Belgium* 17 D5
Hassfurt, *Germany* 25 E6
Hassi Messaoud, *Algeria* 78 B7
Hässleholm, *Sweden* 11 H7
Hassloch, *Germany* 25 F4
Hästholmen, *Sweden* 11 F8
Hastings, *N.Z.* 91 H6
Hastings, *U.K.* 15 G8
Hastings, *Mich., U.S.A.* 114 D3
Hastings, *Minn., U.S.A.* 112 C8
Hastings, *Nebr., U.S.A.* 112 E5
Hastings Ra., *Australia* 95 E5
Hästveda, *Sweden* 11 H7
Hat, *Ukraine* 28 B7
Hat Yai, *Thailand* 65 J3
Hatanbulag = Ergel, *Mongolia* 56 C5
Hatay = Antalya, *Turkey* 72 D4
Hatch, *U.S.A.* 109 K10
Hatchet L., *Canada* 103 B8
Haţeg, *Romania* 28 E7
Hateruma-Shima, *Japan* 55 M1
Hatfield P.O., *Australia* 95 E3
Hatgal, *Mongolia* 60 A5
Hathras, *India* 68 F8
Hatia, *Bangla.* 67 H17
Ḩāţibah, Ra's, *Si. Arabia* 80 C4
Hato Mayor, *Dom. Rep.* 121 C6
Hatta, *India* 69 G8
Hattah, *Australia* 95 E3
Hatteras, C., *U.S.A.* 115 H8
Hattiesburg, *U.S.A.* 113 K10
Hatvan, *Hungary* 28 C4
Hau Bon = Cheo Reo, *Vietnam* 62 B3
Hau Duc, *Vietnam* 64 E7
Haugesund, *Norway* 9 G11
Haukipudas, *Finland* 8 D21
Haultain →, *Canada* 103 B7
Hauraki G., *N.Z.* 91 G5
Hausruck, *Austria* 26 C6
Haut Atlas, *Morocco* 78 B4
Haut-Jura ⌓, *France* 19 F9
Haut-Languedoc ⌓, *France* 20 E6
Haut Niger △, *Guinea* 82 C2
Haut-Rhin □, *France* 19 E14
Haute-Corse □, *France* 21 F13
Haute-Garonne □, *France* 20 E5
Haute-Loire □, *France* 20 C7
Haute-Marne □, *France* 19 D12
Haute-Normandie □, *France* 18 C7
Haute-Saône □, *France* 19 E13
Haute-Savoie □, *France* 21 C10
Haute-Vienne □, *France* 20 C5
Hautes-Alpes □, *France* 21 D10
Hautes Fagnes = Hohe Venn, *Belgium* 17 D6
Hautes Fagnes = Hohes Venn-Eifel ⌓, *Europe* 24 E2
Hautes-Pyrénées □, *France* 20 F4
Hauteville-Lompnès, *France* 21 C9
Hautmont, *France* 19 B10
Hauts-de-Seine □, *France* 19 D9
Hauts Plateaux, *Algeria* 76 C4
Hauzenberg, *Germany* 25 G9
Havana = La Habana, *Cuba* 120 B3
Havana, *U.S.A.* 112 E9
Havant, *U.K.* 15 G7
Havârna, *Romania* 29 B11
Havasor = Kığzı, *Turkey* 70 B4
Havasu, L., *U.S.A.* 111 L12
Havdhem, *Sweden* 11 G12
Havel →, *Germany* 24 C8
Havelian, *Pakistan* 68 B5
Havelock, *Canada* 116 B7
Havelock, *N.Z.* 91 J4
Havelock, *U.S.A.* 115 H7
Haverfordwest, *U.K.* 15 F3
Haverhill, *U.K.* 15 E8
Haverhill, *U.S.A.* 117 D13
Haverstraw, *U.S.A.* 117 E11
Håverud, *Sweden* 11 F6
Havirga, *Mongolia* 56 B7
Havířov, *Czech Rep.* 27 B11
Havlíčkův Brod, *Czech Rep.* 26 B8
Havneby, *Denmark* 11 J2
Havran, *Turkey* 47 B9
Havre, *U.S.A.* 108 B9
Havre-Aubert, *Canada* 105 C7
Havre-St.-Pierre, *Canada* 105 B7
Havsa, *Turkey* 45 E10
Havza, *Turkey* 72 B6
Haw →, *U.S.A.* 115 H6
Hawaii □, *U.S.A.* 106 H16
Hawaii I., *Pac. Oc.* 106 J17
Hawaiian Is., *Pac. Oc.* 106 H17
Hawaiian Ridge, *Pac. Oc.* 97 E11
Hawarden, *U.S.A.* 112 D6
Hawea, L., *N.Z.* 91 L2
Hawera, *N.Z.* 91 H5
Hawick, *U.K.* 13 F6
Hawk Junction, *Canada* 104 C3
Hawke B., *N.Z.* 91 H6
Hawker, *Australia* 95 E2
Hawkesbury, *Canada* 104 C5
Hawkesbury I., *Canada* 102 C3
Hawkesbury Pt., *Australia* 94 A1
Hawkinsville, *U.S.A.* 115 J4
Hawley, *Minn., U.S.A.* 112 B6
Hawley, *Pa., U.S.A.* 117 E9
Ḩawrān, W. →, *Iraq* 70 C4
Hawsh Mūssá, *Lebanon* 74 B4
Hawthorne, *U.S.A.* 108 G4
Hay, *Australia* 95 E3
Hay →, *Australia* 94 C2
Hay →, *Canada* 102 A5
Hay, C., *Australia* 92 B4
Hay I., *Canada* 116 B4
Hay L., *Canada* 102 B5
Hay-on-Wye, *U.K.* 15 E4
Hay River, *Canada* 102 A5
Hay Springs, *U.S.A.* 112 D3
Haya = Tehoru, *Indonesia* 63 E7
Hayachine-San, *Japan* 54 E10
Hayange, *France* 19 C13
Haydarlı, *Turkey* 47 C12
Hayden, *U.S.A.* 108 F10
Haydon, *Australia* 94 B3
Hayes, *U.S.A.* 112 C4
Hayes →, *Canada* 104 A1
Hayes Creek, *Australia* 92 B5
Hayle, *U.K.* 15 G2
Hayling I., *U.K.* 15 G7
Haymana, *Turkey* 72 C5
Haymen I., *Australia* 94 J6
Hayrabolu, *Turkey* 45 E11
Hays, *Canada* 102 C6
Hays, *U.S.A.* 112 F5
Haysyn, *Ukraine* 29 B14
Hayvoron, *Ukraine* 29 B14
Hayward, *Calif., U.S.A.* 110 H4
Hayward, *Wis., U.S.A.* 112 B9
Haywards Heath, *U.K.* 15 G7
Haẓafon □, *Israel* 74 C4
Hazārān, Kūh-e, *Iran* 71 D8
Hazard, *U.S.A.* 114 G4
Hazaribag, *India* 69 H11
Hazaribag Road, *India* 69 G11
Hazebrouck, *France* 19 B9
Hazelton, *Canada* 102 B3
Hazelton, *U.S.A.* 112 B4
Hazen, *U.S.A.* 112 B4
Hazlehurst, *Ga., U.S.A.* 115 K4
Hazlehurst, *Miss., U.S.A.* 113 K9
Hazlet, *U.S.A.* 117 F10
Hazleton, *U.S.A.* 117 F9
Hazlett, L., *Australia* 92 D4
Hazro, *Turkey* 70 B4
He Xian, *Anhui, China* 59 B12
He Xian, *Guangxi Zhuangzu, China* 59 E8
Head of Bight, *Australia* 93 F5
Headlands, *Zimbabwe* 87 F3
Healdsburg, *U.S.A.* 110 G4
Healdton, *U.S.A.* 113 H6
Healesville, *Australia* 95 F4
Heany Junction, *Zimbabwe* 89 C4
Heard I., *Ind. Oc.* 3 G13
Hearne, *U.S.A.* 113 K6
Hearst, *Canada* 104 C3
Heart →, *U.S.A.* 112 B4
Heart's Content, *Canada* 105 C9
Heath, Pte., *Canada* 105 C7
Heathrow, London ✕ (LHR), *U.K.* 15 F7
Heavener, *U.S.A.* 113 H7
Hebbronville, *U.S.A.* 113 M5
Hebei □, *China* 56 E9
Hebel, *Australia* 95 D4
Heber, *U.S.A.* 111 N11
Heber City, *U.S.A.* 108 F8
Heber Springs, *U.S.A.* 113 H9
Hebert, *Canada* 103 C7
Hebgen L., *U.S.A.* 108 D8
Hebi, *China* 56 G8
Hebrides, *U.K.* 6 D4
Hebrides, Sea of the, *U.K.* 13 D2
Hebron = Al Khalīl, *West Bank* 74 D4
Hebron, *Canada* 101 C13
Hebron, *N. Dak., U.S.A.* 112 B3
Hebron, *Nebr., U.S.A.* 112 E6
Heby, *Sweden* 10 E10
Hecate Str., *Canada* 102 C2
Heceta I., *U.S.A.* 102 B2
Hechi, *China* 58 E7
Hechingen, *Germany* 25 G4
Hechuan, *China* 58 B6
Hecla, *U.S.A.* 112 C5
Hecla I., *Canada* 103 C9
Hédé, *France* 18 D5
Hede, *Sweden* 10 B7
Hedemora, *Sweden* 10 D9
Hedensted, *Denmark* 11 J3
Hedesunda, *Sweden* 10 D10
Heerde, *Neths.* 17 B6
Heerenveen, *Neths.* 17 B5
Heerhugowaard, *Neths.* 17 B4
Heerlen, *Neths.* 17 D5
Ḩefa, *Israel* 74 C4
Ḩefa □, *Israel* 74 C4
Hefei, *China* 59 B11
Hefeng, *China* 59 C8
Hegalig, *Sudan* 81 E3
Hegang, *China* 60 B8
Heiban, *Sudan* 81 E3
Heichengzhen, *China* 56 F4
Heide, *Germany* 24 A5
Heidelberg, *Germany* 25 F4
Heidelberg, *S. Africa* 88 E3
Heidenau, *Germany* 24 E9
Heidenheim, *Germany* 25 G6
Heijing, *China* 58 E3
Heilbad Heiligenstadt, *Germany* 24 D6
Heilbron, *S. Africa* 89 D4
Heilbronn, *Germany* 25 F5
Heiligenblut, *Austria* 26 D5
Heiligenhafen, *Germany* 24 A6
Heilongjiang □, *China* 60 B7
Heilunkiang = Heilongjiang □, *China* 60 B7
Heimaey, *Iceland* 8 E3
Heinola, *Finland* 9 F22
Heinsberg, *Germany* 24 D2
Heinze Kyun, *Burma* 64 E1
Heishan, *China* 57 D12
Heishui, *Liaoning, China* 57 C10
Heishui, *Sichuan, China* 58 A4
Hejaz = Ḩijāz □, *Si. Arabia* 70 E3
Hejian, *China* 56 E9
Hejiang, *China* 58 C5
Hejin, *China* 56 G6
Hekımhan, *Turkey* 70 B3
Hekla, *Iceland* 8 E4
Hekou, *Guangdong, China* 59 F9
Hekou, *Yunnan, China* 58 F4
Hel, *Poland* 30 D5
Helagsfjället, *Sweden* 10 B6
Helan Shan, *China* 56 E3
Helechosa, *Spain* 37 F6
Helen Atoll, *Pac. Oc.* 63 D8
Helena, *Ark., U.S.A.* 113 H9
Helena, *Mont., U.S.A.* 108 C7
Helendale, *U.S.A.* 111 L9
Helensburgh, *U.K.* 13 E4
Helensville, *N.Z.* 91 G5
Helenvale, *Australia* 94 B4
Helgasjön, *Sweden* 11 H8
Helgeland, *Norway* 8 C15
Helgoland, *Germany* 24 A3
Heligoland = Helgoland, *Germany* 24 A3
Heligoland B. = Deutsche Bucht, *Germany* 24 A4
Heliopolis, *Egypt* 80 H7
Hella, *Iceland* 8 E3
Hellertown, *U.S.A.* 117 F9
Hellespont = Çanakkale Boğazı, *Turkey* 45 F10
Hellevoetsluis, *Neths.* 17 C4
Hellhole Gorge △, *Australia* 94 D3
Hellín, *Spain* 39 G3
Hells Canyon ⌓, *U.S.A.* 108 D5
Hell's Gate △, *Kenya* 86 C4
Helmand □, *Afghan.* 66 D4
Helmand →, *Afghan.* 66 D2
Helme →, *Germany* 24 D7
Helmeringhausen, *Namibia* 88 D2
Helmond, *Neths.* 17 C5
Helmsdale, *U.K.* 13 C5
Helmsdale →, *U.K.* 13 C5
Helmstedt, *Germany* 24 C7
Helong, *China* 57 C15
Helper, *U.S.A.* 108 G8
Helsingborg, *Sweden* 11 H6
Helsinge, *Denmark* 11 H6
Helsingfors = Helsinki, *Finland* 9 F21
Helsingør, *Denmark* 11 H6
Helsinki, *Finland* 9 F21
Helska, Mierzeja, *Poland* 30 D5
Helston, *U.K.* 15 G2
Helvellyn, *U.K.* 14 C4
Helwân, *Egypt* 80 J7
Hemel Hempstead, *U.K.* 15 F7
Hemet, *U.S.A.* 111 M10
Hemingford, *U.S.A.* 112 D3
Hemmingford, *Canada* 117 A11
Hempstead, *U.S.A.* 113 K6
Hemse, *Sweden* 11 G12
Hemsön, *Sweden* 10 B12
Henån, *Sweden* 11 F5
Henan □, *China* 56 H8
Henares →, *Spain* 36 E7
Henashi-Misaki, *Japan* 54 D9
Hendaye, *France* 20 E2
Hendek, *Turkey* 72 B4
Henderson, *Argentina* 126 D3
Henderson, *Ky., U.S.A.* 114 G2
Henderson, *N.C., U.S.A.* 115 G6
Henderson, *Nev., U.S.A.* 111 J12
Henderson, *Tenn., U.S.A.* 115 H1
Henderson, *Tex., U.S.A.* 113 J7
Hendersonville, *N.C., U.S.A.* 115 H4
Hendersonville, *Tenn., U.S.A.* 115 G2
Hendījān, *Iran* 71 D6

Hendorābī, *Iran* 71 E7
Heng Jiang, *China* 58 C5
Heng Xian, *China* 58 F7
Hengcheng, *China* 56 E4
Hëngchun, *Taiwan* 59 F13
Hengdaohezi, *China* 57 B15
Hengelo, *Neths.* 17 B6
Hengfeng, *China* 59 C10
Hengshan, *Hunan, China* 59 D9
Hengshan, *Shaanxi, China* 56 F5
Hengshui, *China* 56 F8
Hengyang, *China* 59 D9
Henichesk, *Ukraine* 33 J8
Hénin-Beaumont, *France* 19 B9
Henley-on-Thames, *U.K.* 15 F7
Henlopen, C., *U.S.A.* 114 F8
Hennan, *Sweden* 10 B9
Hennebont, *France* 18 E3
Hennenman, *S. Africa* 88 D4
Hennessey, *U.S.A.* 113 G6
Hennigsdorf, *Germany* 24 C9
Henri Pittier △, *Venezuela* 121 D6
Henrietta, *U.S.A.* 113 J5
Henrietta, Ostrov = Genriyetty, Ostrov, *Russia* 53 B16
Henrietta Maria, C., *Canada* 104 A3
Henry, *U.S.A.* 112 E10
Henryetta, *U.S.A.* 113 H7
Henryville, *Canada* 117 A11
Hensall, *Canada* 116 C3
Henstedt-Ulzburg, *Germany* 24 B6
Hentiesbaai, *Namibia* 88 C1
Hentiyn Nuruu, *Mongolia* 60 B5
Henty, *Australia* 95 F4
Henzada, *Burma* 67 L19
Hephaestia, *Greece* 47 B7
Heping, *China* 59 E10
Heppner, *U.S.A.* 108 D4
Hepu, *China* 58 G7
Hepworth, *Canada* 116 B3
Heqing, *China* 58 D3
Hequ, *China* 56 E6
Héraðsflói, *Iceland* 8 D6
Héraðsvötn →, *Iceland* 8 D4
Heraklion = Iráklion, *Greece* 49 D7
Herald Cays, *Australia* 94 B4
Herāt, *Afghan.* 66 B3
Herāt □, *Afghan.* 66 B3
Hérault □, *France* 20 E7
Hérault →, *France* 20 E7
Herbault, *France* 18 E8
Herbert →, *Australia* 94 B4
Herbert River Falls △, *Australia* 94 B4
Herberton, *Australia* 94 B4
Herbertsdale, *S. Africa* 88 E3
Herbignac, *France* 18 E4
Herborn, *Germany* 24 E4
Herby, *Poland* 31 H5
Herceg-Novi, *Serbia & M.* 44 D2
Herchmer, *Canada* 103 B10
Herðubreið, *Iceland* 8 D5
Hereford, *U.K.* 15 E5
Hereford, *U.S.A.* 113 H3
Herefordshire □, *U.K.* 15 E5
Hereke, *Turkey* 45 F13
Herencia, *Spain* 37 F7
Herentals, *Belgium* 17 C4
Herford, *Germany* 24 C4
Héricourt, *France* 19 E13
Herington, *U.S.A.* 112 F6
Herisau, *Switz.* 25 H5
Hérisson, *France* 19 F9
Herkimer, *U.S.A.* 117 D10
Herlong, *U.S.A.* 110 E6
Herm, *U.K.* 15 H5
Hermakivka, *Ukraine* 29 B11
Hermann, *U.S.A.* 112 F9
Hermannsburg, *Australia* 92 D5
Hermannsburg, *Germany* 24 C6
Hermanus, *S. Africa* 88 E2
Herment, *France* 20 C6
Hermidale, *Australia* 95 E4
Hermiston, *U.S.A.* 108 D4
Hermite, I., *Chile* 128 H3
Hermon, *U.S.A.* 117 B9
Hermon, Mt. = Shaykh, J. ash, *Lebanon* 74 B4
Hermosillo, *Mexico* 118 B2
Hernád →, *Hungary* 28 C6
Hernandarias, *Paraguay* 127 B5
Hernandez, *U.S.A.* 110 J6
Hernando, *Argentina* 126 C3
Hernando, *U.S.A.* 113 H10
Hernani, *Spain* 38 B3
Herndon, *U.S.A.* 116 F8
Herne, *Germany* 17 C7
Herne Bay, *U.K.* 15 F9
Herning, *Denmark* 11 H2
Heroica = Caborca, *Mexico* 118 A2
Heroica Nogales = Nogales, *Mexico* 118 A2
Heron Bay, *Canada* 104 C2
Herradura, Pta. de la, *Canary Is.* 48 F5
Herreid, *U.S.A.* 112 C4
Herrenberg, *Germany* 25 G4
Herrera, *Spain* 37 H6
Herrera de Alcántara, *Spain* 37 F3
Herrera de Pisuerga, *Spain* 36 C6
Herrera del Duque, *Spain* 37 F5
Herrestad, *Sweden* 11 F5
Herrin, *U.S.A.* 113 G10
Herriot, *Canada* 103 B8
Herrljunga, *Sweden* 11 F7
Hersbruck, *Germany* 25 F7
Herschel I., *Canada* 4 C1
Hershey, *U.S.A.* 117 F8
Hersonissos, *Greece* 49 D7
Herstal, *Belgium* 17 D5
Hertford, *U.K.* 15 F7
Hertfordshire □, *U.K.* 15 F7
's-Hertogenbosch, *Neths.* 17 C5
Hertsa, *Ukraine* 29 B11
Hertzogville, *S. Africa* 88 D4
Hervás, *Spain* 36 E5
Hervey B., *Australia* 94 C5
Herzberg, *Brandenburg, Germany* 24 D9
Herzberg, *Niedersachsen, Germany* 24 D6
Herzliyya, *Israel* 74 C3
Herzogenburg, *Austria* 26 C8
Ḩeşār, *Fārs, Iran* 71 D6
Ḩeşār, *Markazī, Iran* 71 C6
Hesdin, *France* 19 B9
Heshan, *China* 58 F7
Heshui, *China* 56 G5
Heshun, *China* 56 F7
Hesperia, *U.S.A.* 111 L9
Hesse = Hessen □, *Germany* 24 E4
Hessen □, *Germany* 24 E4
Hessenreuther und Manteler Wald ⌓, *Germany* 25 F8
Hestra, *Sweden* 11 G7
Hetch Hetchy Aqueduct, *U.S.A.* 110 H5
Hettinger, *U.S.A.* 112 C3
Hettstedt, *Germany* 24 D7
Heuvelton, *U.S.A.* 117 B9
Heves, *Hungary* 28 C5
Heves □, *Hungary* 28 C5
Hewitt, *U.S.A.* 113 K6
Hexham, *U.K.* 14 C5
Hexi, *Yunnan, China* 58 E4
Hexi, *Zhejiang, China* 59 D12
Hexigten Qi, *China* 57 C9
Ḩeydarābād, *Iran* 71 D7
Heysham, *U.K.* 14 C5
Heyuan, *China* 59 F10
Heywood, *Australia* 95 F3
Heze, *China* 56 G8
Hezhang, *China* 58 D5
Hi, Ko, *Thailand* 65 a
Hi Vista, *U.S.A.* 111 L9
Hialeah, *U.S.A.* 115 N5
Hiawatha, *U.S.A.* 112 F7
Hibbing, *U.S.A.* 112 B8
Hibbs B., *Australia* 95 G4
Hibernia Reef, *Australia* 92 B3
Hickman, *U.S.A.* 113 G10
Hickory, *U.S.A.* 115 H5
Hicks, Pt., *Australia* 95 F4
Hicks L., *Canada* 103 A9
Hicksville, *U.S.A.* 117 F11
Hida, *Romania* 29 C8
Hida-Gawa →, *Japan* 55 G8
Hida-Sammyaku, *Japan* 55 F8
Hidaka-Sammyaku, *Japan* 54 C11
Hidalgo, *Mexico* 119 C5
Hidalgo □, *Mexico* 119 C5
Hidalgo, Presa M., *Mexico* 118 B3
Hidalgo del Parral, *Mexico* 118 B3
Hiddensee, *Germany* 24 A9
Hieflau, *Austria* 26 D7
Hiendelaencina, *Spain* 38 D2
Hierro, *Canary Is.* 48 G1
Higashiajima-San, *Japan* 54 F10
Higashiōsaka, *Japan* 55 G7
Higgins, *U.S.A.* 113 G4
Higgins Corner, *U.S.A.* 110 F5
High Bridge, *U.S.A.* 117 F10
High Level, *Canada* 102 B5
High Point, *U.S.A.* 115 H6
High Prairie, *Canada* 102 B5
High River, *Canada* 102 C6
High Tatra = Tatry, *Slovak Rep.* 27 B13
High Veld, *Africa* 76 J6
High Wycombe, *U.K.* 15 F7
Highland □, *U.K.* 13 D4
Highland Park, *U.S.A.* 114 D2
Highmore, *U.S.A.* 112 C5
Highrock L., *Man., Canada* 103 B8
Highrock L., *Sask., Canada* 103 B7
Higüey, *Dom. Rep.* 121 C6
Hihya, *Egypt* 80 H7
Hiiumaa, *Estonia* 9 G20
Híjar, *Spain* 38 D4
Ḩijāz □, *Si. Arabia* 70 E3
Hijo = Tagum, *Phil.* 61 H6
Hikari, *Japan* 55 H5
Hikmak, Ras el, *Egypt* 80 A2
Hiko, *U.S.A.* 110 H11
Hikone, *Japan* 55 G8
Hikurangi, *Gisborne, N.Z.* 91 H6
Hikurangi, *Northland, N.Z.* 91 F5
Hildburghausen, *Germany* 24 E6
Hildesheim, *Germany* 24 C5
Hill →, *Australia* 93 F2
Hill City, *Idaho, U.S.A.* 108 E6
Hill City, *Kans., U.S.A.* 112 F5
Hill City, *S. Dak., U.S.A.* 112 D3
Hill Island L., *Canada* 103 A7
Hillaby, Mt., *Barbados* 121 g
Hillared, *Sweden* 11 G7
Hillcrest, *Barbados* 121 g
Hillcrest Center, *U.S.A.* 111 K8
Hillegom, *Neths.* 17 B4
Hillerød, *Denmark* 11 J6
Hillerstorp, *Sweden* 11 G7
Hillsboro, *Kans., U.S.A.* 112 F6
Hillsboro, *N. Dak., U.S.A.* 112 B6
Hillsboro, *Ohio, U.S.A.* 114 F4
Hillsboro, *Oreg., U.S.A.* 110 E4
Hillsboro, *Tex., U.S.A.* 113 J6
Hillsborough, *Grenada* 121 D7
Hillsborough, *U.S.A.* 117 C13
Hillsborough Channel, *Australia* 94 J7
Hillsdale, *Mich., U.S.A.* 114 E3
Hillsdale, *N.Y., U.S.A.* 117 D11
Hillsport, *Canada* 104 C2
Hillston, *Australia* 95 E4
Hilo, *U.S.A.* 106 J17
Hilton, *U.S.A.* 116 C7
Hilton Head Island, *U.S.A.* 115 J5
Hilvan, *Turkey* 73 D8
Hilversum, *Neths.* 17 B5
Himachal Pradesh □, *India* 68 D7
Himalaya, *Asia* 69 E11
Himamaylan, *Phil.* 61 F5
Himarë, *Albania* 44 F3
Himatnagar, *India* 66 H8
Himeji, *Japan* 55 G7
Himi, *Japan* 55 F8
Himmerland, *Denmark* 11 H3
Ḩimş, *Syria* 74 A5
Ḩimş □, *Syria* 74 A6
Hinche, *Haiti* 121 C5
Hinchinbrook I., *Australia* 94 B4
Hinchinbrook Island △, *Australia* 94 B4
Hinckley, *U.K.* 15 E6
Hinckley, *U.S.A.* 112 B8
Hindaun, *India* 68 F7
Hindmarsh, L., *Australia* 95 F3
Hindsholm, *Denmark* 11 J4
Hindu Bagh, *Pakistan* 68 D2
Hindu Kush, *Asia* 66 B7
Hindupur, *India* 66 N10
Hines Creek, *Canada* 102 B5
Hinesville, *U.S.A.* 115 K5
Hinganghat, *India* 66 J11
Hingham, *U.S.A.* 108 B8
Hingir, *India* 69 J10
Hingoli, *India* 66 K10
Hinigaran, *Phil.* 61 F5
Hinis, *Turkey* 73 C9
Hinna = Imi, *Ethiopia* 81 F5
Hinna, *Nigeria* 83 C7
Hinnerup, *Denmark* 11 H4
Hinnøya, *Norway* 8 B16
Hinojosa del Duque, *Spain* 37 G5
Hinsdale, *U.S.A.* 117 D12
Hinterrhein →, *Switz.* 25 J5
Hinton, *Canada* 102 C5
Hinton, *U.S.A.* 114 G5
Hınzır Burnu, *Turkey* 72 D6
Hirado, *Japan* 55 H4
Hirakud Dam, *India* 67 J13
Hiran →, *India* 69 H8
Hirapur, *India* 69 G8
Hiratsuka, *Japan* 55 G9
Hirfanlı Barajı, *Turkey* 72 C5
Hiroo, *Japan* 54 C11
Hirosaki, *Japan* 54 D10
Hiroshima, *Japan* 55 G6
Hiroshima □, *Japan* 55 G6
Hirson, *France* 19 C11
Hirtshals, *Denmark* 11 G3
Hisar, *India* 68 E6
Hisarcık, *Turkey* 47 B11
Hisaria, *Bulgaria* 45 D8
Hisb, Sha'ib = Ḩasb, W. →, *Iraq* 70 D5
Ḩismá, *Si. Arabia* 70 D3
Hispaniola, *W. Indies* 121 C5
Hīt, *Iraq* 70 C4
Hita, *Japan* 55 H5
Hitachi, *Japan* 55 F10
Hitchin, *U.K.* 15 F7
Hitoyoshi, *Japan* 55 H5
Hitra, *Norway* 8 E13
Hitzacker, *Germany* 24 B7
Hixon, *Canada* 102 C4
Ḩiyyon, N. →, *Israel* 74 E4
Hjalmar L., *Canada* 103 A7
Hjälmaren, *Sweden* 10 E9
Hjältevad, *Sweden* 11 G9
Hjo, *Sweden* 11 F8
Hjørring, *Denmark* 11 G3
Hjortkvarn, *Sweden* 11 F9
Hkakabo Razi, *Burma* 67 E20
Hlinsko, *Czech Rep.* 26 B8
Hlobane, *S. Africa* 89 D5
Hlohovec, *Slovak Rep.* 27 C10
Hlučín, *Czech Rep.* 27 B11
Hluhluwe, *S. Africa* 89 D5
Hluhluwe ⌓, *S. Africa* 89 C5
Hlukhiv, *Ukraine* 33 G7
Hlyboka, *Ukraine* 29 B10
Hlybokaye, *Belarus* 32 E4
Hnúšt'a, *Slovak Rep.* 27 C12
Ho, *Ghana* 83 D5
Ho Chi Minh City = Thanh Pho Ho Chi Minh, *Vietnam* 65 G6
Ho Thuong, *Vietnam* 64 C5
Hoa Binh, *Vietnam* 58 G5
Hoa Da, *Vietnam* 65 G7
Hoa Hiep, *Vietnam* 65 G5
Hoai Nhon, *Vietnam* 64 E7
Hoang Lien Son, *Vietnam* 58 F4
Hoanib →, *Namibia* 88 B2
Hoare B., *Canada* 101 B13
Hoarusib →, *Namibia* 88 B2
Hobart, *Australia* 95 G4
Hobart, *U.S.A.* 113 H5
Hobbs, *U.S.A.* 113 J3
Hobbs Coast, *Antarctica* 5 D14
Hobe Sound, *U.S.A.* 115 M5
Hoboken, *U.S.A.* 117 F10
Hobro, *Denmark* 11 H3
Hoburgen, *Sweden* 11 H12
Hocalar, *Turkey* 47 C11
Hochfeld, *Namibia* 88 C2
Hochharz △, *Germany* 24 D6
Hochschwab, *Austria* 26 D8
Höchstadt, *Germany* 25 F6
Hochtaunus ⌓, *Germany* 25 E4
Hockenheim, *Germany* 25 F4
Hodaka-Dake, *Japan* 55 F8
Hodeida = Al Ḩudaydah, *Yemen* 75 E3
Hodgeville, *Canada* 103 C7
Hodgson, *Canada* 103 C9
Hódmezővásárhely, *Hungary* 28 D5
Hodna, Chott el, *Algeria* 78 A6
Hodonín, *Czech Rep.* 27 C10
Hoeamdong, *N. Korea* 57 C16
Hœdic, Î. de, *France* 18 E4
Hoek van Holland, *Neths.* 17 C4
Hoengsŏng, *S. Korea* 57 F14
Hoeryong, *N. Korea* 57 C15
Hoeyang, *N. Korea* 57 E14
Hof, *Germany* 25 E7
Hofgeismar, *Germany* 24 D5
Hofheim, *Germany* 25 E4
Hofmeyr, *S. Africa* 88 E4
Höfn, *Iceland* 8 D6
Hofors, *Sweden* 10 D10
Hofsjökull, *Iceland* 8 D4
Hōfu, *Japan* 55 G5
Hogan Group, *Australia* 95 F4
Höganäs, *Sweden* 11 H6
Hogarth, Mt., *Australia* 94 C2
Hoggar = Ahaggar, *Algeria* 78 D7
Högsäter, *Sweden* 11 F6
Högsby, *Sweden* 11 G10
Högsjö, *Sweden* 10 E9
Hogsty Reef, *Bahamas* 121 B5
Hoh →, *U.S.A.* 110 C2
Hohe Acht, *Germany* 25 E3
Hohe Tauern, *Austria* 26 D5
Hohe Tauern △, *Austria* 26 D5
Hohe Venn, *Belgium* 17 D6
Hohenau, *Austria* 27 C9
Hohenems, *Austria* 26 D2
Hohenloher Ebene, *Germany* 25 F5
Hohenwald, *U.S.A.* 115 H2
Hohenwestedt, *Germany* 24 A5
Hoher Rhön = Rhön, *Germany* 24 E5
Hoher Vogelsberg ⌓, *Germany* 24 D5
Hohes Venn-Eifel ⌓, *Europe* 24 E2
Hohhot, *China* 56 D6
Hóhlakas, *Greece* 49 D9
Hohoe, *Ghana* 83 D5
Hoi An, *Vietnam* 64 E7
Hoi Xuan, *Vietnam* 58 G5
Hoisington, *U.S.A.* 112 F5
Højer, *Denmark* 11 K2
Hōjō, *Japan* 55 H6
Hok, *Sweden* 11 G8
Hökensås, *Sweden* 11 G8
Hökerum, *Sweden* 11 G7
Hokianga Harbour, *N.Z.* 91 F4
Hokitika, *N.Z.* 91 K3
Hokkaidō □, *Japan* 54 C11
Hol-Hol, *Djibouti* 81 E5
Hola Pristan, *Ukraine* 33 J7
Holbæk, *Denmark* 11 J5
Holbrook, *Australia* 95 F4
Holbrook, *U.S.A.* 109 J8
Holden, *U.S.A.* 108 G7
Holdenville, *U.S.A.* 113 H6
Holdrege, *U.S.A.* 112 E5
Holešov, *Czech Rep.* 27 B10
Holetown, *Barbados* 121 g
Holguín, *Cuba* 120 B4
Holíč, *Slovak Rep.* 27 C10
Holice, *Czech Rep.* 26 A8
Höljes, *Sweden* 10 D6
Hollabrunn, *Austria* 26 C9
Hollams Bird I., *Namibia* 88 C1
Holland, *Mich., U.S.A.* 114 D2
Holland, *N.Y., U.S.A.* 116 D6
Hollandale, *U.S.A.* 113 J9
Holley, *U.S.A.* 116 C6
Hollfeld, *Germany* 25 F7
Hollidaysburg, *U.S.A.* 116 F6
Hollis, *U.S.A.* 113 H5
Hollister, *Calif., U.S.A.* 110 J5
Hollister, *Idaho, U.S.A.* 108 E6
Höllviken = Höllviksnäs, *Sweden* 11 J6
Höllviksnäs, *Sweden* 11 J6
Holly Hill, *U.S.A.* 115 L5
Holly Springs, *U.S.A.* 113 H10
Hollywood, *U.S.A.* 115 N5
Holman, *Canada* 100 A8
Hólmavík, *Iceland* 8 D3
Holmen, *U.S.A.* 112 D9
Holmes Reefs, *Australia* 94 B4
Holmsjö, *Sweden* 11 H9
Holmsjön, *Västernorrland, Sweden* 10 B10
Holmsjön, *Västernorrland, Sweden* 10 B9
Holmsland Klit, *Denmark* 11 J2
Holmsund, *Sweden* 8 E19
Holod, *Romania* 28 D7
Holovne, *Ukraine* 31 G11
Holozubyntsi, *Ukraine* 29 B11
Holroyd →, *Australia* 94 A3
Holstebro, *Denmark* 11 H2
Holsteinische Schweiz ⌓, *Germany* 24 A6
Holsworthy, *U.K.* 15 G3
Holton, *Canada* 105 B8
Holton, *U.S.A.* 112 F7
Holtville, *U.S.A.* 111 N11
Holwerd, *Neths.* 17 A5
Holy I., *Angl., U.K.* 14 D3
Holy I., *Northumberland, U.K.* 14 B6
Holyhead, *U.K.* 14 D3
Holyoke, *Colo., U.S.A.* 112 E3
Holyoke, *Mass., U.S.A.* 117 D12
Holyrood, *Canada* 105 C9
Holzkirchen, *Germany* 25 H7
Holzminden, *Germany* 24 D5
Homa Bay, *Kenya* 86 C3
Homalin, *Burma* 67 G19
Homand, *Iran* 71 C8
Homathko →, *Canada* 102 C4
Homberg, *Germany* 24 D5
Hombori, *Mali* 83 B4
Homburg, *Germany* 25 F3
Home B., *Canada* 101 B13
Home Hill, *Australia* 94 B4
Homedale, *U.S.A.* 108 E5
Homer, *Alaska, U.S.A.* 100 C4
Homer, *La., U.S.A.* 113 J8
Homer City, *U.S.A.* 116 F5
Homert ⌓, *Germany* 24 D4
Homestead, *Australia* 94 C4
Homestead, *U.S.A.* 115 N5
Homestead ⌓, *U.S.A.* 112 E6
Homewood, *U.S.A.* 110 F6
Homoine, *Mozam.* 89 C6
Homoljske Planina, *Serbia & M.* 44 B5
Homorod, *Romania* 29 D10
Homs = Ḩimş, *Syria* 74 A5
Homyel, *Belarus* 33 F6
Hon Chong, *Vietnam* 65 G5
Hon Me, *Vietnam* 64 C5
Honan = Henan □, *China* 56 H8
Honaz, *Turkey* 47 D11
Honbetsu, *Japan* 54 C11
Honcut, *U.S.A.* 110 F5
Honda Bay, *Phil.* 61 G3
Hondarribia, *Spain* 38 B3
Hondeklipbaai, *S. Africa* 88 E2
Hondo, *Japan* 55 H5
Hondo, *U.S.A.* 113 L5
Hondo, Rio →, *Belize* 119 D7
Honduras ■, *Cent. Amer.* 120 D2
Honduras, G. de, *Caribbean* 120 C2
Hønefoss, *Norway* 9 F14
Honesdale, *U.S.A.* 117 E9
Honey L., *U.S.A.* 110 E6
Honfleur, *France* 18 C7
Høng, *Denmark* 11 J5
Hong →, *Vietnam* 58 F5
Hong Gai, *Vietnam* 58 G6
Hong He →, *China* 56 H8
Hong Hu, *China* 59 C9
Hong Kong □, *China* 59 F10
Hong'an, *China* 59 B10
Hongch'ŏn, *S. Korea* 57 F14
Honghai Wan, *China* 59 F10
Honghe, *China* 58 F4
Honghu, *China* 59 C9
Hongjiang, *China* 58 D7
Hongliu He →, *China* 56 F5
Hongor, *Mongolia* 56 B7
Hongsa, *Laos* 64 C3
Hongshui He →, *China* 58 F7
Hongsŏng, *S. Korea* 57 F14
Hongtong, *China* 56 F6
Hongwedo, Détroit d', *Canada* 105 C7
Hongwon, *N. Korea* 57 E14
Hongya, *China* 58 C4
Hongyuan, *China* 58 A4
Hongze Hu, *China* 57 H10
Honiara, *Solomon Is.* 96 H7
Honiton, *U.K.* 15 G4
Honjō, *Japan* 54 E10
Honkorâb, Ras, *Egypt* 80 C4
Honningsvåg, *Norway* 8 A21
Hönö, *Sweden* 11 G5
Honolulu, *U.S.A.* 106 H16
Hontoria del Pinar, *Spain* 38 D1
Hood, Mt., *U.S.A.* 108 D3
Hood, Pt., *Australia* 93 F2
Hood River, *U.S.A.* 108 D3
Hoodsport, *U.S.A.* 110 C3
Hooge, *Germany* 24 A4
Hoogeveen, *Neths.* 17 B6
Hoogezand-Sappemeer, *Neths.* 17 A6
Hooghly = Hugli →, *India* 69 J13
Hooghly-Chinsura = Chunchura, *India* 69 H13
Hook Hd., *Ireland* 12 D5
Hook I., *Australia* 94 J6
Hook of Holland = Hoek van Holland, *Neths.* 17 C4
Hooker, *U.S.A.* 113 G4
Hooker Creek, *Australia* 92 C5
Hoonah, *U.S.A.* 102 B1
Hooper Bay, *U.S.A.* 100 B3
Hoopeston, *U.S.A.* 114 E2
Hoopstad, *S. Africa* 88 D4
Höör, *Sweden* 11 J7
Hoorn, *Neths.* 17 B5
Hoover, *U.S.A.* 115 J2
Hoover Dam, *U.S.A.* 111 K12
Hooversville, *U.S.A.* 116 F6
Hop Bottom, *U.S.A.* 117 E9
Hopa, *Turkey* 73 B9
Hope, *Canada* 102 D4
Hope, *Ariz., U.S.A.* 111 M13
Hope, *Ark., U.S.A.* 113 J8
Hope, L., *S. Austral., Australia* 95 D2
Hope, L., *W. Austral., Australia* 93 F3
Hope, Pt., *U.S.A.* 4 C17
Hope I., *Canada* 116 B4
Hope Town, *Bahamas* 120 A4
Hopedale, *Canada* 105 A7
Hopedale, *U.S.A.* 117 D13
Hopefield, *S. Africa* 88 E2
Hopei = Hebei □, *China* 56 E9
Hopelchén, *Mexico* 119 D7
Hopetoun, *Vic., Australia* 95 F3
Hopetoun, *W. Austral., Australia* 93 F3
Hopetown, *S. Africa* 88 D3
Hopevale, *Australia* 94 B4
Hopewell, *U.S.A.* 114 G7
Hopfgarten, *Austria* 26 D5
Hopkins, L., *Australia* 92 D4
Hopkinsville, *U.S.A.* 115 G2
Hopland, *U.S.A.* 110 G3
Hoquiam, *U.S.A.* 110 D3
Hora Hoverla, *Ukraine* 29 B9
Horasan, *Turkey* 73 B10
Horažďovice, *Czech Rep.* 26 B6
Horb, *Germany* 25 G4
Hörby, *Sweden* 11 J7
Horcajo de Santiago, *Spain* 38 F1
Horden Hills, *Australia* 92 D5
Horezu, *Romania* 29 E8
Horgen, *Switz.* 25 H4
Horgoš, *Serbia & M.* 28 D4
Hořice, *Czech Rep.* 26 A8
Horinchove, *Ukraine* 29 B8
Horinger, *China* 56 D6

Horki, *Belarus* 32 E6
Horlick Mts., *Antarctica* 5 E15
Horlivka, *Ukraine* 33 H10
Hormak, *Iran* 71 D9
Hormoz, *Iran* 71 E7
Hormoz, Jaz.-ye, *Iran* 71 E8
Hormozgān □, *Iran* 71 E8
Hormuz, Kūh-e, *Iran* 71 E7
Hormuz, Str. of, *The Gulf* 71 E8
Horn, *Austria* 26 C8
Horn, *Iceland* 8 C2
Horn, *Sweden* 11 G9
Horn →, *Canada* 102 A5
Horn, Cape = Hornos, C. de, *Chile* 128 H3
Horn Head, *Ireland* 12 A3
Horn I., *Australia* 94 A3
Horn Plateau, *Canada* 102 A5
Hornachuelos, *Spain* 37 H5
Hornavan, *Sweden* 8 C17
Hornbeck, *U.S.A.* 113 K8
Hornbrook, *U.S.A.* 108 F2
Hornburg, *Germany* 24 C6
Horncastle, *U.K.* 14 D7
Horndal, *Sweden* 10 D10
Hornell, *U.S.A.* 116 D7
Hornell L., *Canada* 102 A5
Hornepayne, *Canada* 104 C3
Horní Planá, *Czech Rep.* 26 C7
Hornings Mills, *Canada* 116 B4
Hornitos, *U.S.A.* 110 H6
Hornos, C. de, *Chile* 128 H3
Hornoy-le-Bourg, *France* 19 C8
Hornsea, *U.K.* 14 D7
Hornslandet, *Sweden* 10 C11
Hörnum, *Germany* 24 A4
Horobetsu = Noboribetsu, *Japan* 54 C10
Horodenka, *Ukraine* 29 B10
Horodnya, *Ukraine* 33 G6
Horodok, *Khmelnytskyy, Ukraine* 33 H4
Horodok, *Lviv, Ukraine* 33 H2
Horodyshche, *Ukraine* 33 H6
Horokhiv, *Ukraine* 33 G3
Horovice, *Czech Rep.* 26 B6
Horqin Youyi Qianqi, *China* 57 A12
Horqueta, *Paraguay* 126 A4
Horred, *Sweden* 11 G6
Horse Creek, *U.S.A.* 112 E3
Horse I., *Canada* 103 C9
Horse Is., *Canada* 105 B8
Horsefly L., *Canada* 102 C4
Horseheads, *U.S.A.* 116 D8
Horsens, *Denmark* 11 J3
Horsham, *Australia* 95 F3
Horsham, *U.K.* 15 F7
Horšovský Týn, *Czech Rep.* 26 B5
Horten, *Norway* 9 G14
Hortobágy →, *Hungary* 28 C6
Hortobágyi △, *Hungary* 28 C6
Horton, *U.S.A.* 112 F7
Horton →, *Canada* 100 B7
Horwood L., *Canada* 104 C3
Hosaina, *Ethiopia* 81 F4
Hose, Gunung-Gunung, *Malaysia* 62 D4
Ḩoseynābād, *Khuzestān, Iran* 71 C6
Ḩoseynābād, *Kordestān, Iran* 70 C5
Hoshangabad, *India* 68 H7
Hoshiarpur, *India* 68 D6
Hospet, *India* 66 M10
Hoste, I., *Chile* 128 H3
Hostens, *France* 20 D3
Hot, *Thailand* 64 C2
Hot Creek Range, *U.S.A.* 108 G6
Hot Springs, *Ark., U.S.A.* 113 H8
Hot Springs, *S. Dak., U.S.A.* 112 D3
Hot Springs △, *U.S.A.* 113 H8
Hotagen, *Sweden* 8 E16
Hotan, *China* 60 C2
Hotazel, *S. Africa* 88 D3
Hotchkiss, *U.S.A.* 109 G10
Hotham, C., *Australia* 92 B5
Hoting, *Sweden* 8 D17
Hotolisht, *Albania* 44 E4
Hotte, Massif de la, *Haiti* 121 C5
Hottentotsbaai, *Namibia* 88 D1
Houat, Î. de, *France* 18 E4
Houdan, *France* 19 D8
Houei Sai, *Laos* 58 G3
Houeillès, *France* 20 D4
Houffalize, *Belgium* 17 D5
Houghton, *Mich., U.S.A.* 112 B10
Houghton, *N.Y., U.S.A.* 116 D6
Houghton L., *U.S.A.* 114 C3
Houghton-le-Spring, *U.K.* 14 C6
Houhora Heads, *N.Z.* 91 F4
Houlton, *U.S.A.* 115 B12
Houma, *U.S.A.* 113 L9
Houndé, *Burkina Faso* 82 C4
Hourtin, *France* 20 C2
Hourtin-Carcans, Étang d', *France* 20 C2
Housatonic →, *U.S.A.* 117 E11
Houston, *Canada* 102 C3
Houston, *Mo., U.S.A.* 113 G9
Houston, *Tex., U.S.A.* 113 L7
Hout →, *S. Africa* 89 C4
Houtkraal, *S. Africa* 88 E3
Houtman Abrolhos, *Australia* 93 E1
Hovd, *Mongolia* 60 B4
Hove, *U.K.* 15 G7
Hovenweep ⌂, *U.S.A.* 109 H9
Hoveyzeh, *Iran* 71 D6
Hovmantorp, *Sweden* 11 H9
Hövsgöl, *Mongolia* 56 C5
Hövsgöl Nuur, *Mongolia* 60 A5
Hovsta, *Sweden* 10 E9
Howakil, *Eritrea* 81 D5
Howar, Wadi →, *Sudan* 81 D2
Howard, *Australia* 95 D5
Howard, *Pa., U.S.A.* 116 F7
Howard, *S. Dak., U.S.A.* 112 C6
Howe, *U.S.A.* 108 E7
Howe, C., *Australia* 95 F5
Howe I., *Canada* 117 B8
Howell, *U.S.A.* 114 D4
Howick, *Canada* 117 A11
Howick, *S. Africa* 89 D5
Howick Group, *Australia* 94 A4
Howitt, L., *Australia* 95 D2
Howland I., *Pac. Oc.* 96 G10
Howrah = Haora, *India* 69 H13
Howth Hd., *Ireland* 12 C5
Höxter, *Germany* 24 D5
Hoy, *U.K.* 13 C5
Hoya, *Germany* 24 C5
Høyanger, *Norway* 9 F12
Hoyerswerda, *Germany* 24 D10
Hoylake, *U.K.* 14 D4
Hoyos, *Spain* 36 E4
Hpa-an = Pa-an, *Burma* 67 L20
Hpungan Pass, *Burma* 67 F20
Hradec Králové, *Czech Rep.* 26 A8
Hrádek, *Czech Rep.* 27 C9
Hranice, *Czech Rep.* 27 B10
Hrazdan, *Armenia* 35 K7
Hrebenka, *Ukraine* 33 G7
Hrodna, *Belarus* 30 E10
Hrodzyanka, *Belarus* 32 F5
Hron →, *Slovak Rep.* 27 D11
Hrubieszów, *Poland* 31 H10
Hrubý Jeseník, *Czech Rep.* 27 A10
Hrvatska = Croatia ■, *Europe* 41 C13
Hrymayliv, *Ukraine* 33 H4
Hrynyava, *Ukraine* 29 C9
Hsenwi, *Burma* 67 H20
Hsiamen = Xiamen, *China* 59 E12
Hsian = Xi'an, *China* 56 G5
Hsinchu, *Taiwan* 59 E13
Hsinhailien = Lianyungang, *China* 57 G10
Hsinying, *Taiwan* 59 F13
Hsopket, *Burma* 58 F2
Hsüchou = Xuzhou, *China* 57 G9
Hu Xian, *China* 56 G5
Hua Hin, *Thailand* 64 F2
Hua Xian, *Henan, China* 56 G8
Hua Xian, *Shaanxi, China* 56 G5
Hua'an, *China* 59 E11
Huab →, *Namibia* 88 B2
Huacheng, *China* 59 E10
Huachinera, *Mexico* 118 A3
Huacho, *Peru* 124 F3
Huade, *China* 56 D7
Huadian, *China* 57 C14
Huadu, *China* 59 F9
Huai Had △, *Thailand* 64 D5
Huai He →, *China* 59 A12
Huai Nam Dang △, *Thailand* 64 C2
Huai Yot, *Thailand* 65 J2
Huai'an, *Hebei, China* 56 D8
Huai'an, *Jiangsu, China* 57 H10
Huaibei, *China* 56 G9
Huaibin, *China* 59 A10
Huaide = Gongzhuling, *China* 57 C13
Huaidezhen, *China* 57 C13
Huaihua, *China* 58 D7
Huaiji, *China* 59 F9
Huainan, *China* 59 A11
Huaining, *China* 59 B11
Huairen, *China* 56 E7
Huairou, *China* 56 D9
Huaiyang, *China* 56 H8
Huaiyin, *China* 57 H10
Huaiyuan, *Anhui, China* 57 H9
Huaiyuan, *Guangxi Zhuangzu, China* 58 E7
Huajianzi, *China* 57 D13
Huajuapan de Leon, *Mexico* 119 D5
Hualapai Peak, *U.S.A.* 109 J7
Hualien, *Taiwan* 59 E13
Huallaga →, *Peru* 124 E3
Huambo, *Angola* 85 G3
Huan Jiang →, *China* 56 G5
Huan Xian, *China* 56 F4
Huancabamba, *Peru* 124 E3
Huancane, *Peru* 124 G5
Huancavelica, *Peru* 124 F3
Huancayo, *Peru* 124 F3
Huanchaca, *Bolivia* 124 H5
Huang Hai = Yellow Sea, *China* 57 G12
Huang He →, *China* 57 F10
Huang Xian, *China* 57 F11
Huangchuan, *China* 59 A10
Huanggang, *China* 59 B10
Huangguoshu, *China* 58 E5
Huangling, *China* 56 G5
Huanglong, *China* 56 G5
Huanglongtan, *China* 59 A8
Huangmei, *China* 59 B10
Huangpi, *China* 59 B10
Huangping, *China* 58 D6
Huangshan, *China* 59 C12
Huangshi, *China* 59 B10
Huangsongdian, *China* 57 C14
Huangyan, *China* 59 C13
Huangyangsi, *China* 59 D8
Huaning, *China* 58 E4
Huanjiang, *China* 58 E7
Huantai, *China* 57 F9
Huánuco, *Peru* 124 E3
Huaping, *China* 58 D3
Huaraz, *Peru* 124 E3
Huarmey, *Peru* 124 F3
Huarong, *China* 59 C9
Huascarán, *Peru* 124 E3
Huasco, *Chile* 126 B1
Huasco →, *Chile* 126 B1
Huasna, *U.S.A.* 111 K6
Huatabampo, *Mexico* 118 B3
Huauchinango, *Mexico* 119 C5
Huautla de Jiménez, *Mexico* 119 D5
Huaxi, *China* 58 D6
Huay Namota, *Mexico* 118 C4
Huayin, *China* 56 G6
Huayuan, *China* 58 C7
Huayun, *China* 58 B6
Huazhou, *China* 59 G8
Hubbard, *Ohio, U.S.A.* 116 E4
Hubbard, *Tex., U.S.A.* 113 K6
Hubbart Pt., *Canada* 103 B10
Hubei □, *China* 59 B9
Hubli, *India* 66 M9
Huch'ang, *N. Korea* 57 D14
Hucknall, *U.K.* 14 D6
Huddersfield, *U.K.* 14 D6
Hude, *Germany* 24 B4
Hudi, *Sudan* 80 D3
Hudiksvall, *Sweden* 10 C11
Hudson, *Canada* 104 B1
Hudson, *Mass., U.S.A.* 117 D13
Hudson, *N.Y., U.S.A.* 117 D11
Hudson, *Wis., U.S.A.* 112 C8
Hudson, *Wyo., U.S.A.* 108 E9
Hudson →, *U.S.A.* 117 F10
Hudson Bay, *Nunavut, Canada* 101 C11
Hudson Bay, *Sask., Canada* 103 C8
Hudson Falls, *U.S.A.* 117 C11
Hudson Mts., *Antarctica* 5 D16
Hudson Str., *Canada* 101 B13
Hudson's Hope, *Canada* 102 B4
Hue, *Vietnam* 64 D6
Huebra →, *Spain* 36 D4
Huedin, *Romania* 28 D8
Huehuetenango, *Guatemala* 120 C1
Huejúcar, *Mexico* 118 C4
Huélamo, *Spain* 38 E3
Huelgoat, *France* 18 D3
Huelma, *Spain* 37 H7
Huelva, *Spain* 37 H4
Huelva □, *Spain* 37 H4
Huelva →, *Spain* 37 H5
Huentelauquén, *Chile* 126 C1
Huércal-Overa, *Spain* 39 H3
Huerta, Sa. de la, *Argentina* 126 C2
Huertas, C. de las, *Spain* 39 G4
Huerva →, *Spain* 38 D4
Huesca, *Spain* 38 C4
Huesca □, *Spain* 38 C5
Huéscar, *Spain* 39 H2
Huetamo, *Mexico* 118 D4
Huete, *Spain* 38 E2
Hugh →, *Australia* 94 D1
Hughenden, *Australia* 94 C3
Hughes, *Australia* 93 F4
Hughesville, *U.S.A.* 117 E8
Hugli →, *India* 69 J13
Hugo, *Colo., U.S.A.* 112 F3
Hugo, *Okla., U.S.A.* 113 H7
Hugoton, *U.S.A.* 113 G4
Hui Xian = Huixian, *China* 56 G7
Hui Xian, *China* 56 H4
Hui'an, *China* 59 E12
Hui'anbu, *China* 56 F4
Huichang, *China* 59 E10
Huichapán, *Mexico* 119 C5
Huidong, *Guangdong, China* 59 F10
Huidong, *Sichuan, China* 58 D4
Huifa He →, *China* 57 C14
Huila, Nevado del, *Colombia* 124 C3
Huilai, *China* 59 F11
Huili, *China* 58 D4
Huimin, *China* 57 F9
Huinan, *China* 57 C14
Huinca Renancó, *Argentina* 126 C3
Huining, *China* 56 G3
Huinong, *China* 56 E4
Huisache, *Mexico* 118 C4
Huishui, *China* 58 D6
Huisne →, *France* 18 E7
Huiting, *China* 56 G9
Huitong, *China* 58 D7
Huixian, *China* 56 G7
Huixtla, *Mexico* 119 D6
Huize, *China* 58 D4
Huizhou, *China* 59 F10
Hukawng Valley, *Burma* 67 F20
Hukou, *China* 59 C11
Hŭksan-chedo, *S. Korea* 57 G13
Hukuntsi, *Botswana* 88 C3
Ḩulayfā', *Si. Arabia* 70 E4
Hulin He →, *China* 57 B12
Hull = Kingston upon Hull, *U.K.* 14 D7
Hull, *Canada* 117 A9
Hull →, *U.K.* 14 D7
Hulst, *Neths.* 17 C4
Hultsfred, *Sweden* 11 G9
Hulun Nur, *China* 60 B6
Hulyaypole, *Ukraine* 33 J9
Huma, Tanjung, *Malaysia* 65 c
Humacao, *Puerto Rico* 121 d
Humahuaca, *Argentina* 126 A2
Humaitá, *Brazil* 124 E6
Humaitá, *Paraguay* 126 B4
Humansdorp, *S. Africa* 88 E3
Humara, J., *Sudan* 81 D3
Humbe, *Angola* 88 B1
Humber →, *U.K.* 14 D7
Humboldt, *Canada* 103 C7
Humboldt, *Iowa, U.S.A.* 112 D7
Humboldt, *Tenn., U.S.A.* 113 H10
Humboldt →, *U.S.A.* 108 F4
Humboldt Gletscher = Sermersuaq, *Greenland* 4 B4
Hume, *U.S.A.* 110 J8
Hume, L., *Australia* 95 F4
Humenné, *Slovak Rep.* 27 C14
Hummelsta, *Sweden* 10 E10
Humphreys, Mt., *U.S.A.* 110 H8
Humphreys Peak, *U.S.A.* 109 J8
Humpolec, *Czech Rep.* 26 B8
Humptulips, *U.S.A.* 110 C3
Hūn, *Libya* 79 C9
Hun Jiang →, *China* 57 D13
Húnaflói, *Iceland* 8 D3
Hunan □, *China* 59 D9
Hunchun, *China* 57 C16
Hundested, *Denmark* 11 J5
Hundewali, *Pakistan* 68 D5
Hundred Mile House, *Canada* 102 C4
Hunedoara, *Romania* 28 E7
Hunedoara □, *Romania* 28 E7
Hünfeld, *Germany* 24 E5
Hung Yen, *Vietnam* 58 G6
Hungary ■, *Europe* 27 D12
Hungary, Plain of, *Europe* 6 F10
Hungerford, *Australia* 95 D3
Hŭngnam, *N. Korea* 57 E14
Hungt'ou Hsü, *Taiwan* 59 G13
Huni Valley, *Ghana* 82 D4
Hunneberg, *Sweden* 11 F6
Hunnebostrand, *Sweden* 11 F5
Hunsberge, *Namibia* 88 D2
Hunsrück, *Germany* 25 F3
Hunstanton, *U.K.* 14 E8
Hunte →, *Germany* 24 B4
Hunter, *U.S.A.* 117 D10
Hunter I., *Australia* 95 G3
Hunter I., *Canada* 102 C3
Hunter Ra., *Australia* 95 E5
Hunters Road, *Zimbabwe* 87 F2
Hunterville, *N.Z.* 91 H5
Huntingburg, *U.S.A.* 114 F2
Huntingdon, *Canada* 104 C5
Huntingdon, *U.K.* 15 E7
Huntingdon, *U.S.A.* 116 F6
Huntington, *Ind., U.S.A.* 114 E3
Huntington, *N.Y., U.S.A.* 117 F11
Huntington, *Oreg., U.S.A.* 108 D5
Huntington, *Utah, U.S.A.* 108 G8
Huntington, *W. Va., U.S.A.* 114 F4
Huntington Beach, *U.S.A.* 111 M9
Huntly, *N.Z.* 91 G5
Huntly, *U.K.* 13 D6
Huntsville, *Canada* 116 A5
Huntsville, *Ala., U.S.A.* 115 H2
Huntsville, *Tex., U.S.A.* 113 K7
Hunyani →, *Zimbabwe* 87 F3
Hunyuan, *China* 56 E7
Hunza →, *India* 69 B6
Huo Xian = Huozhou, *China* 56 F6
Huong Khe, *Vietnam* 64 C5
Huonville, *Australia* 95 G4
Huoqiu, *China* 59 A11
Huoshan, *Anhui, China* 59 A12
Huoshan, *Anhui, China* 59 B11
Huoshao Dao = Lü-Tao, *Taiwan* 59 F13
Huozhou, *China* 56 F6
Hupeh = Hubei □, *China* 59 B9
Ḩūr, *Iran* 71 D8
Hurbanovo, *Slovak Rep.* 27 D11
Hurd, C., *Canada* 116 A3
Hure Qi, *China* 57 C11
Hurezani, *Romania* 29 F8
Hurghada, *Egypt* 80 B3
Hurley, *N. Mex., U.S.A.* 109 K9
Hurley, *Wis., U.S.A.* 112 B9
Huron, *Calif., U.S.A.* 110 J6
Huron, *Ohio, U.S.A.* 116 E2
Huron, *S. Dak., U.S.A.* 112 C5
Huron, L., *U.S.A.* 116 B2
Huron East, *Canada* 116 C3
Hurricane, *U.S.A.* 109 H7
Hurso, *Ethiopia* 81 F5
Hurungwe ⌂, *Zimbabwe* 87 F2
Hurunui →, *N.Z.* 91 K4
Hurup, *Denmark* 11 H2
Húsavík, *Iceland* 8 C5
Huşi, *Romania* 29 D13
Huskvarna, *Sweden* 11 G8
Hustadvika, *Norway* 8 E12
Hustontown, *U.S.A.* 116 F6
Hustopeče, *Czech Rep.* 27 C9
Husum, *Germany* 24 A5
Husum, *Sweden* 10 A13
Hutchinson, *Kans., U.S.A.* 113 F6
Hutchinson, *Minn., U.S.A.* 112 C7
Hutte Sauvage, L. de la, *Canada* 105 A7
Hüttenberg, *Austria* 26 E7
Hüttener Berge ⌂, *Germany* 24 A5
Hutton, Mt., *Australia* 95 D4
Huwun, *Ethiopia* 81 G5
Huy, *Belgium* 17 D5
Huzhou, *China* 59 B13
Hvalpsund, *Denmark* 11 H3
Hvammstangi, *Iceland* 8 D3
Hvar, *Croatia* 41 E13
Hvarski Kanal, *Croatia* 41 E13
Hvítá →, *Iceland* 8 D3
Hvizdets, *Ukraine* 29 B10
Hwachŏn-chŏsuji, *S. Korea* 57 E14
Hwang Ho = Huang He →, *China* 57 F10
Hwange, *Zimbabwe* 87 F2
Hwange △, *Zimbabwe* 88 B4
Hyannis, *Mass., U.S.A.* 114 E10
Hyannis, *Nebr., U.S.A.* 112 E4
Hyargas Nuur, *Mongolia* 60 B4
Hybo, *Sweden* 10 C10
Hydaburg, *U.S.A.* 102 B2
Hyde Park, *U.S.A.* 117 E11
Hyden, *Australia* 93 F2
Hyder, *U.S.A.* 102 B2
Hyderabad, *India* 66 L11
Hyderabad, *Pakistan* 68 G3
Hyères, *France* 21 E10
Hyères, Îs. d', *France* 21 F10
Hyesan, *N. Korea* 57 D15
Hyland →, *Canada* 102 B3
Hyltebruk, *Sweden* 11 H7
Hymia, *India* 69 C8
Hyndman Peak, *U.S.A.* 108 E6
Hyōgo □, *Japan* 55 G7
Hyrum, *U.S.A.* 108 F8
Hysham, *U.S.A.* 108 C10
Hythe, *U.K.* 15 F9
Hyūga, *Japan* 55 H5
Hyvinge = Hyvinkää, *Finland* 9 F21
Hyvinkää, *Finland* 9 F21

I

I-n-Gall, *Niger* 83 B6
I-n-Oudad, *Algeria* 83 A5
I-n-Ouzzal, *Algeria* 83 A5
I-n-Tadreft, *Niger* 83 B6
Iablaniţa, *Romania* 28 F7
Iaco →, *Brazil* 124 E5
Iacobeni, *Romania* 29 C10
Iakora, *Madag.* 89 C8
Ialomiţa □, *Romania* 29 F12
Ialomiţa →, *Romania* 29 F12
Ialoveni, *Moldova* 29 D13
Ialpug →, *Moldova* 29 E13
Ianca, *Romania* 29 E12
Iara, *Romania* 29 D8
Iarda, *Ethiopia* 81 E4
Iargara, *Moldova* 29 D13
Iaşi, *Romania* 29 C12
Iaşi □, *Romania* 29 C12
Íasmos, *Greece* 45 E9
Ib →, *India* 69 J10
Iba, *Phil.* 61 D3
Ibadan, *Nigeria* 83 D5
Ibagué, *Colombia* 124 C3
Iballë, *Albania* 44 D4
Ibăneşti, *Botoşani, Romania* 29 B11
Ibăneşti, *Mureş, Romania* 29 D9
Ibar →, *Serbia & M.* 44 C4
Ibaraki □, *Japan* 55 F10
Ibarra, *Ecuador* 124 C3
Ibba, *Sudan* 81 G2
Ibba, Bahr el →, *Sudan* 81 F2
Ibbenbüren, *Germany* 24 C3
Ibembo, *Dem. Rep. of the Congo* 86 B1
Ibera, L., *Argentina* 126 B4
Iberian Peninsula, *Europe* 6 H5
Iberville, *Canada* 117 A11
Iberville, Lac d', *Canada* 104 A5
Ibi, *Nigeria* 83 D6
Ibi, *Spain* 39 G4
Ibiá, *Brazil* 125 G9
Ibiapaba, Sa. da, *Brazil* 125 D10
Ibicuí →, *Brazil* 127 B4
Ibicuy, *Argentina* 126 C4
Ibiza = Eivissa, *Spain* 48 C7
Ibiza ✕ (IBZ), *Spain* 39 G6
Íblei, Monti, *Italy* 43 E7
Ibo, *Mozam.* 87 E5
Ibonma, *Indonesia* 63 E8
Ibotirama, *Brazil* 125 F10
Ibrāhīm →, *Lebanon* 74 A4
'Ibrī, *Oman* 71 F8
Ibriktepe, *Turkey* 45 E10
Ibshawâi, *Egypt* 80 J7
Ibu, *Indonesia* 63 D7
Ibusuki, *Japan* 55 J5
Ica, *Peru* 124 F3
Iça →, *Brazil* 124 D5
Icacos Pt., *Trin. & Tob.* 125 K15
Içana, *Brazil* 124 C5
Içana →, *Brazil* 124 C5
Içel = Mersin, *Turkey* 70 B2
Iceland ■, *Europe* 8 D4
Iceland Plateau, *Arctic* 4 C7
Ich'ang = Yichang, *China* 59 B8
Ichchapuram, *India* 67 K14
Ichhawar, *India* 68 H7
Ichihara, *Japan* 55 G10
Ichikawa, *Japan* 55 G9
Ichilo →, *Bolivia* 124 G6
Ichinohe, *Japan* 54 D10
Ichinomiya, *Japan* 55 G8
Ichinoseki, *Japan* 54 E10
Ichnya, *Ukraine* 33 G7
Icod, *Canary Is.* 48 F3
Ida Grove, *U.S.A.* 112 D7
Idabel, *U.S.A.* 113 J7
Idaga Hamus, *Ethiopia* 81 E4
Idah, *Nigeria* 83 D6
Idaho □, *U.S.A.* 108 D7
Idaho City, *U.S.A.* 108 E6
Idaho Falls, *U.S.A.* 108 E7
Idalia △, *Australia* 94 C3
Idanha-a-Nova, *Portugal* 36 F3
Idar-Oberstein, *Germany* 25 F3
Idensalmi = Iisalmi, *Finland* 8 E22
Idfû, *Egypt* 80 C3
Ídhi Óros, *Greece* 49 D6
Ídhra, *Greece* 46 D5
Idi, *Indonesia* 62 C1
Idiofa, *Dem. Rep. of the Congo* 84 E3
Idkerberget, *Sweden* 10 D9
Idku, Bahra el, *Egypt* 80 H7
Idlib, *Syria* 70 C3
Idre, *Sweden* 10 C6
Idria, *U.S.A.* 110 J6
Idrija, *Slovenia* 41 C11
Idritsa, *Russia* 32 D5
Idutywa, *S. Africa* 89 E4
Ieper, *Belgium* 17 D2
Ierápetra, *Greece* 49 E7
Ierissós, *Greece* 44 F7
Ierissóu Kólpos, *Greece* 44 F7
Iernut, *Romania* 29 D9
Iesi, *Italy* 41 E10
Iésolo, *Italy* 41 C9
Ifach, Peñón de, *Spain* 39 G5
Ifakara, *Tanzania* 84 F7
'Ifāl, W. al →, *Si. Arabia* 70 D2
Ifanadiana, *Madag.* 89 C8
Ife, *Nigeria* 83 D5
Iférouâne, *Niger* 83 B6
Iffley, *Australia* 94 B3
Ifon, *Nigeria* 83 D6
Iforas, Adrar des, *Africa* 83 B5
Ifould, L., *Australia* 93 F5
Iganga, *Uganda* 86 B3
Igarapava, *Brazil* 125 H9
Igarka, *Russia* 52 C9

Igatimi, *Paraguay* 127 A4
Igbetti, *Nigeria* 83 D5
Igbo-Ora, *Nigeria* 83 D5
Igboho, *Nigeria* 83 D5
Igbor, *Nigeria* 83 D6
Iğdır, *Turkey* 73 C11
Igelfors, *Sweden* 11 F9
Iggesund, *Sweden* 10 C11
Iglésias, *Italy* 42 C1
Igloolik, *Canada* 101 B11
Igluligaarjuk = Chesterfield Inlet, *Canada* 100 B10
Iglulik = Igloolik, *Canada* 101 B11
'Igma, Gebel el, *Egypt* 80 B3
Ignace, *Canada* 104 C1
İğneada, *Turkey* 45 E11
İğneada Burnu, *Turkey* 45 E12
Igoumenítsa, *Greece* 46 B2
Igra, *Russia* 34 B11
Iguaçu △, *Brazil* 127 B5
Iguaçu →, *Brazil* 127 B5
Iguaçu, Cat. del, *Brazil* 127 B5
Iguaçu Falls = Iguaçu, Cat. del, *Brazil* 127 B5
Iguala, *Mexico* 119 D5
Igualada, *Spain* 38 D6
Iguassu = Iguaçu →, *Brazil* 127 B5
Iguatu, *Brazil* 125 E11
Iguazú △, *Argentina* 127 B5
Iguidi, Erg, *Africa* 78 C4
Iharana, *Madag.* 89 A9
Ihbulag, *Mongolia* 56 C4
Iheya-Shima, *Japan* 55 L3
Ihiala, *Nigeria* 83 D6
Ihosy, *Madag.* 89 C8
Ihotry, Farihy, *Madag.* 89 C7
Ihugh, *Nigeria* 83 D6
Ii, *Finland* 8 D21
Ii-Shima, *Japan* 55 L3
Iida, *Japan* 55 G8
Iijoki →, *Finland* 8 D21
Iisalmi, *Finland* 8 E22
Iiyama, *Japan* 55 F9
Iizuka, *Japan* 55 H5
Ijebu-Igbo, *Nigeria* 83 D5
Ijebu-Ode, *Nigeria* 83 D5
IJmuiden, *Neths.* 17 B4
Ijo älv = Iijoki →, *Finland* 8 D21
IJssel →, *Neths.* 17 B5
IJsselmeer, *Neths.* 17 B5
Ijuí, *Brazil* 127 B5
Ijuí →, *Brazil* 127 B4
Ikalamavony, *Madag.* 89 C8
Ikale, *Nigeria* 83 D6
Ikaluktutiak, *Canada* 100 B9
Ikang, *Nigeria* 83 E6
Ikara, *Nigeria* 83 C6
Ikare, *Nigeria* 83 D6
Ikaría, *Greece* 47 D8
Ikast, *Denmark* 11 H3
Ikeda, *Japan* 55 G6
Ikeja, *Nigeria* 83 D5
Ikela, *Dem. Rep. of the Congo* 84 E4
Ikerre-Ekiti, *Nigeria* 83 D6
Ikhtiman, *Bulgaria* 44 D7
Iki, *Japan* 55 H4
Ikimba L., *Tanzania* 86 C3
Ikire, *Nigeria* 83 D5
İkizdere, *Turkey* 73 B9
Ikom, *Nigeria* 83 D6
Ikongo, *Madag.* 89 C8
Ikopa →, *Madag.* 89 B8
Ikorongo ⌂, *Tanzania* 86 C3
Ikot Ekpene, *Nigeria* 83 D6
Ikparjuk = Arctic Bay, *Canada* 101 A11
Ikungu, *Tanzania* 86 C3
Ikurun, *Nigeria* 83 D5
Ila, *Nigeria* 83 D5
Ilagan, *Phil.* 61 C4
Ilaka, *Madag.* 89 B8
Īlām, *Iran* 70 C5
Ilam, *Nepal* 69 F12
Īlām □, *Iran* 70 C5
Ilan, *Taiwan* 59 E13
Ilanskiy, *Russia* 53 D10
Ilaro, *Nigeria* 83 D5
Ilatane, *Niger* 83 B5
Iława, *Poland* 30 E6
Ile →, *Kazakhstan* 52 E8
Île-à-la-Crosse, *Canada* 103 B7
Île-à-la-Crosse, Lac, *Canada* 103 B7
Île-de-France □, *France* 19 D9
Ileanda, *Romania* 29 C8
Ilebo, *Dem. Rep. of the Congo* 84 E4
Ilek, *Russia* 52 D6
Ilero, *Nigeria* 83 D5
Ilesha, *Kwara, Nigeria* 83 D5
Ilesha, *Oyo, Nigeria* 83 D5
Ilford, *Canada* 103 B9
Ilfracombe, *Australia* 94 C3
Ilfracombe, *U.K.* 15 F3
Ilgaz, *Turkey* 72 B5
Ilgaz Dağları, *Turkey* 72 B5
Ilgın, *Turkey* 72 C4
Ilha de Moçambique, *Mozam.* 87 F5
Ílhavo, *Portugal* 36 E2
Ilhéus, *Brazil* 125 F11
Ili = Ile →, *Kazakhstan* 52 E8
Ilia, *Romania* 28 E7
Ilia □, *Greece* 46 D3
Iliamna L., *U.S.A.* 100 C4
Iliç, *Turkey* 73 C8
Ilıca, *Turkey* 47 B9
Ilichevsk, *Azerbaijan* 73 C11
Iligan, *Phil.* 61 G6
Iligan Bay, *Phil.* 61 G6
Ilíki, L., *Greece* 46 C5
Ilin I., *Phil.* 61 E4
Iliodhrómia, *Greece* 46 B5
Ilion, *U.S.A.* 117 D9
Ilirska-Bistrica, *Slovenia* 41 C11
Ilkeston, *U.K.* 14 E6
Ilkley, *U.K.* 14 D6
Illampu = Ancohuma, Nevado, *Bolivia* 124 G5
Illana B., *Phil.* 61 H5
Illapel, *Chile* 126 C1
Ille-et-Vilaine □, *France* 18 D5
Ille-sur-Têt, *France* 20 F6
Illéla, *Niger* 83 C6
Iller →, *Germany* 25 G5
Illertissen, *Germany* 25 G6
Illescas, *Spain* 36 E7
Illetas, *Spain* 48 B9
Illichivsk, *Ukraine* 33 J6
Illiers-Combray, *France* 18 D8
Illimani, Nevado, *Bolivia* 124 G5
Illinois □, *U.S.A.* 112 E10
Illinois →, *U.S.A.* 112 F9
Illizi, *Algeria* 78 C7
Illkirch-Graffenstaden, *France* 19 D14
Íllora, *Spain* 37 H7
Ilm →, *Germany* 24 D7
Ilmajoki, *Finland* 9 E20
Ilmen, Ozero, *Russia* 32 C6
Ilmenau, *Germany* 24 E6
Ilnytsya, *Ukraine* 28 B8
Ilo, *Peru* 124 G4
Ilobu, *Nigeria* 83 D5
Iloilo, *Phil.* 61 F5
Ilora, *Nigeria* 83 D5
Ilorin, *Nigeria* 83 D5
Ilovatka, *Russia* 34 E7
Ilovlya, *Russia* 35 F7
Ilovlya →, *Russia* 35 F7
Iłowa, *Poland* 31 G2
Ilubabor, *Ethiopia* 81 F4
Ilva Mică, *Romania* 29 C9
Ilwaco, *U.S.A.* 110 D2
Ilwaki, *Indonesia* 63 F7
Ilyichevsk = Illichivsk, *Ukraine* 33 J6
Iłża, *Poland* 31 G8
Iłżanka →, *Poland* 31 G8
Imabari, *Japan* 55 G6
Imaloto →, *Madag.* 89 C8
İmamoğlu, *Turkey* 72 D6
Imandra, Ozero, *Russia* 52 C4
Imanombo, *Madag.* 89 C8
Imari, *Japan* 55 H4
Imasa, *Sudan* 80 D4
Imathía □, *Greece* 44 F6
Imatra, *Finland* 32 B5
Iménas, *Mali* 83 B5
imeni 26 Bakinskikh Komissarov = Neftçala, *Azerbaijan* 71 B6
imeni 26 Bakinskikh Komissarov, *Turkmenistan* 71 B7
Imeri, Serra, *Brazil* 124 C5
Imerimandroso, *Madag.* 89 B8
Imi, *Ethiopia* 81 F5
Imishly = İmişli, *Azerbaijan* 35 L9
İmişli, *Azerbaijan* 35 L9
Imlay, *U.S.A.* 108 F4
Imlay City, *U.S.A.* 116 D1
Immaseri, *Sudan* 81 D2
Immenstadt, *Germany* 25 H6
Immingham, *U.K.* 14 D7
Immokalee, *U.S.A.* 115 M5
Imo □, *Nigeria* 83 D6
Imo →, *Nigeria* 83 E6
Ímola, *Italy* 41 D8
Imotski, *Croatia* 41 E14
Imperatriz, *Brazil* 125 E9
Impéria, *Italy* 40 E5
Imperial, *Canada* 103 C7
Imperial, *Calif., U.S.A.* 111 N11
Imperial, *Nebr., U.S.A.* 112 E4
Imperial Beach, *U.S.A.* 111 N9
Imperial Dam, *U.S.A.* 111 N12
Imperial Reservoir, *U.S.A.* 111 N12
Imperial Valley, *U.S.A.* 111 N11
Imperieuse Reef, *Australia* 92 C2
Impfondo, *Congo* 84 D3
Imphal, *India* 67 G18
Imphy, *France* 19 F10
İmranlı, *Turkey* 73 C8
İmroz = Gökçeada, *Turkey* 45 F9
İmroz, *Turkey* 45 F9
Imst, *Austria* 26 D3
Imuris, *Mexico* 118 A2
Imuruan B., *Phil.* 63 B5
In Akhmed, *Mali* 83 B4
In Aleï, *Mali* 82 B4
In Delimane, *Mali* 83 B5
In Guezzam, *Algeria* 83 B6
In Koufi, *Mali* 83 B5
In Salah, *Algeria* 78 C6
In Tallak, *Mali* 83 B5
In Tebezas, *Mali* 83 B5
Ina, *Japan* 55 G8
Inagua △, *Bahamas* 121 B5
Inangahua, *N.Z.* 91 J3
Inanwatan, *Indonesia* 63 E8
Iñapari, *Peru* 124 F5
Inari, *Finland* 8 B22
Inarijärvi, *Finland* 8 B22
Inawashiro-Ko, *Japan* 54 F10
Inca, *Spain* 48 B9
Inca de Oro, *Chile* 126 B2
Incaguasi, *Chile* 126 B1
İnce Burun, *Turkey* 72 A6
İncekum Burnu, *Turkey* 72 D5
Incesu, *Turkey* 70 B2
Inch'ŏn, *S. Korea* 57 F14
Incio = Cruz de Incio, *Spain* 36 C3
Incirliova, *Turkey* 47 D9
Incline Village, *U.S.A.* 108 G4
Incomáti →, *Mozam.* 89 D5
Incudine, Mte., *France* 21 G13
Inda Silase, *Ethiopia* 81 E4
Indal, *Sweden* 10 B11
Indalsälven →, *Sweden* 10 B11
Indaw, *Burma* 67 G20
Indbir, *Ethiopia* 81 F4
Independence, *Calif., U.S.A.* 110 J8
Independence, *Iowa, U.S.A.* 112 D9
Independence, *Kans., U.S.A.* 113 G7
Independence, *Ky., U.S.A.* 114 F3
Independence, *Mo., U.S.A.* 112 F7
Independence Fjord, *Greenland* 4 A6
Independence Mts., *U.S.A.* 108 F5
Independenţa, *Romania* 29 E12
Index, *U.S.A.* 110 C5
India ■, *Asia* 66 K11
Indian →, *U.S.A.* 115 M5
Indian Cabins, *Canada* 102 B5
Indian Harbour, *Canada* 105 B8
Indian Head, *Canada* 103 C8
Indian Lake, *U.S.A.* 117 C10
Indian Ocean 50 K11
Indian Springs, *U.S.A.* 111 J11
Indiana, *U.S.A.* 116 F5
Indiana □, *U.S.A.* 114 F3
Indianapolis, *U.S.A.* 114 F2
Indianola, *Iowa, U.S.A.* 112 E8
Indianola, *Miss., U.S.A.* 113 J9
Indigirka →, *Russia* 53 B15
Inđija, *Serbia & M.* 28 E5
Indio, *U.S.A.* 111 M10
Indira Gandhi Canal, *India* 68 F5
Indo-China, *Asia* 50 H14
Indonesia ■, *Asia* 62 F5
Indore, *India* 68 H6
Indramayu, *Indonesia* 63 G13
Indravati →, *India* 67 K12
Indre □, *France* 19 F8
Indre →, *France* 18 E7
Indre-et-Loire □, *France* 18 E7
Indulkana, *Australia* 95 D1
Indura, *Belarus* 30 E10
Indus →, *Pakistan* 68 G2
Indus, Mouths of the, *Pakistan* 68 H3
İnebolu, *Turkey* 72 B5
İnecik, *Turkey* 45 F11
İnegöl, *Turkey* 45 F13
Ineu, *Romania* 28 D6
Infantes = Villanueva de los Infantes, *Spain* 37 G7
Infiernillo, Presa del, *Mexico* 118 D4
Infiesto, *Spain* 36 B5
Ingelstad, *Sweden* 11 H8
Ingenio, *Canary Is.* 48 G4
Ingenio Santa Ana, *Argentina* 126 B2
Ingersoll, *Canada* 116 C4
Ingham, *Australia* 94 B4
Ingleborough, *U.K.* 14 C5
Inglewood, *Queens., Australia* 95 D5
Inglewood, *Vic., Australia* 95 F3
Inglewood, *N.Z.* 91 H5
Inglewood, *U.S.A.* 111 M8
Ingólfshöfði, *Iceland* 8 E5
Ingolstadt, *Germany* 25 G7
Ingomar, *U.S.A.* 108 C10
Ingonish, *Canada* 105 C7
Ingore, *Guinea-Biss.* 82 C1
Ingraj Bazar, *India* 69 G13
Ingrid Christensen Coast, *Antarctica* 5 C6
Ingul = Inhul →, *Ukraine* 33 J7
Ingulec = Inhulec, *Ukraine* 33 J7
Ingulets = Inhulets →, *Ukraine* 33 J7
Inguri = Enguri →, *Georgia* 35 J5
Ingushetia □, *Russia* 35 J7
Ingwavuma, *S. Africa* 89 D5
Inhaca, *Mozam.* 89 D5
Inhafenga, *Mozam.* 89 C5
Inhambane, *Mozam.* 89 C6
Inhambane □, *Mozam.* 89 C5
Inhaminga, *Mozam.* 87 F4
Inharrime, *Mozam.* 89 C6
Inharrime →, *Mozam.* 89 C6
Inhisar, *Turkey* 47 A12
Inhul →, *Ukraine* 33 J7
Inhulec, *Ukraine* 33 J7
Inhulets →, *Ukraine* 33 J7
Iniesta, *Spain* 39 F3
Ining = Yining, *China* 52 E9
Inírida →, *Colombia* 124 C5
Inishbofin, *Ireland* 12 C1
Inisheer, *Ireland* 12 C2
Inishfree B., *Ireland* 12 A3
Inishkea North, *Ireland* 12 B1
Inishkea South, *Ireland* 12 B1
Inishmaan, *Ireland* 12 C2
Inishmore, *Ireland* 12 C2
Inishowen Pen., *Ireland* 12 A4
Inishshark, *Ireland* 12 C1
Inishturk, *Ireland* 12 C1
Inishvickillane, *Ireland* 12 D1
Injibara, *Ethiopia* 81 E4
Injune, *Australia* 95 D4
Inklin →, *Canada* 102 B2
Inland Kaikoura Ra., *N.Z.* 91 J4
Inland Sea = Setonaikai, *Japan* 55 G6
Inle L., *Burma* 67 J20
Inlet, *U.S.A.* 117 C10
Inn →, *Austria* 26 C6
Innamincka, *Australia* 95 D3
Inner Hebrides, *U.K.* 13 E2
Inner Mongolia = Nei Monggol Zizhiqu □, *China* 56 D7
Inner Sound, *U.K.* 13 D3
Innerkip, *Canada* 116 C4
Innetalling I., *Canada* 104 A4
Innisfail, *Australia* 94 B4
Innisfail, *Canada* 102 C6
In'noshima, *Japan* 55 G6
Innsbruck, *Austria* 26 D4
Innviertel, *Austria* 26 C6
Inny →, *Ireland* 12 C4
Inongo, *Dem. Rep. of the Congo* 84 E3
İnönü, *Turkey* 47 B12
Inoucdjouac = Inukjuak, *Canada* 101 C12
Inowrocław, *Poland* 31 F5
Inpundong, *N. Korea* 57 D14
Inscription, C., *Australia* 93 E1
Insein, *Burma* 67 L20
Insjön, *Sweden* 10 D9
Ińsko, *Poland* 30 E2
Însurăţei, *Romania* 29 F12
Inta, *Russia* 52 C6
Intendente Alvear, *Argentina* 126 D3
Intepe, *Turkey* 47 A8
Interlaken, *Switz.* 25 J3
Interlaken, *U.S.A.* 117 D8
International Falls, *U.S.A.* 112 A8
Intiyaco, *Argentina* 126 B3
Întorsura Buzăului, *Romania* 29 E11
Inukjuak, *Canada* 101 C12
Inútil, B., *Chile* 128 G2
Inuvik, *Canada* 100 B6
Inveraray, *U.K.* 13 E3
Inverbervie, *U.K.* 13 E6
Invercargill, *N.Z.* 91 M2
Inverclyde □, *U.K.* 13 F4
Inverell, *Australia* 95 D5
Invergordon, *U.K.* 13 D4
Inverloch, *Australia* 95 F4
Invermere, *Canada* 102 C5
Inverness, *Canada* 105 C7
Inverness, *U.K.* 13 D4
Inverness, *U.S.A.* 115 L4
Inverurie, *U.K.* 13 D6
Investigator Group, *Australia* 95 E1
Investigator Str., *Australia* 95 F2
Inya, *Russia* 52 D9
Inyanga, *Zimbabwe* 87 F3
Inyangani, *Zimbabwe* 87 F3
Inyantue, *Zimbabwe* 88 B4
Inyo Mts., *U.S.A.* 110 J9
Inyokern, *U.S.A.* 111 K9
Inza, *Russia* 34 D8
Inzhavino, *Russia* 34 D6
Iō-Jima, *Japan* 55 J5
Ioánnina, *Greece* 46 B2
Ioánnina □, *Greece* 46 B2
Iola, *U.S.A.* 113 G7
Ion Corvin, *Romania* 29 F12
Iona, *U.K.* 13 E2
Ione, *U.S.A.* 110 G6
Ionia, *U.S.A.* 114 D3
Ionian Is. = Iónioi Nísoi, *Greece* 46 C2
Ionian Sea, *Medit. S.* 6 H9
Iónioi Nísoi, *Greece* 46 C2
Iónioi Nísoi □, *Greece* 46 C2
Íos, *Greece* 47 E7
Iowa □, *U.S.A.* 112 D8
Iowa →, *U.S.A.* 112 E9
Iowa City, *U.S.A.* 112 E9
Iowa Falls, *U.S.A.* 112 D8
Iowa Park, *U.S.A.* 113 J5
Ipala, *Tanzania* 86 C3
Ipameri, *Brazil* 125 G9
Ipáti, *Greece* 46 C4
Ipatinga, *Brazil* 125 G10
Ipatovo, *Russia* 35 H6
Ipel' →, *Europe* 27 D11
Ipiales, *Colombia* 124 C3
Ipin = Yibin, *China* 58 C5
Ípiros □, *Greece* 46 B2
Ipixuna, *Brazil* 124 E4
Ipoh, *Malaysia* 65 K3
Ippy, *C.A.R.* 84 C4
Ipsala, *Turkey* 45 F10
Ipsárion, Óros, *Greece* 45 F8
Ipswich, *Australia* 95 D5
Ipswich, *U.K.* 15 E9
Ipswich, *Mass., U.S.A.* 117 D14
Ipswich, *S. Dak., U.S.A.* 112 C5
Ipu, *Brazil* 125 D10
Iqaluit, *Canada* 101 B13
Iquique, *Chile* 124 H4
Iquitos, *Peru* 124 D4
Irabu-Jima, *Japan* 55 M2
Iracoubo, *Fr. Guiana* 125 B8
Īrafshān, *Iran* 71 E9
Irahuan, *Phil.* 61 G3
Iráklia, *Kikládhes, Greece* 47 E7
Iráklia, *Sérrai, Greece* 44 E7
Iráklion, *Greece* 49 D7
Iráklion □, *Greece* 49 D7
Irala, *Paraguay* 127 B5
Iran ■, *Asia* 71 C7
Iran, Gunung-Gunung, *Malaysia* 62 D4
Iran, Plateau of, *Asia* 50 F9
Iran Ra. = Iran, Gunung-Gunung, *Malaysia* 62 D4
Īrānshahr, *Iran* 71 E9
Irapuato, *Mexico* 118 C4
Iraq ■, *Asia* 70 C5
Irati, *Brazil* 127 B5
Irbes saurums, *Latvia* 30 A9
Irbid, *Jordan* 74 C4
Irbid □, *Jordan* 74 C5
Iregua →, *Spain* 38 C7
Ireland ■, *Europe* 12 C4
Irele, *Nigeria* 83 D6
Irgiz, Bolshaya →, *Russia* 34 D9
Irhyangdong, *N. Korea* 57 D15
Iri, *S. Korea* 57 G14
Irian Jaya = Papua □, *Indonesia* 63 E9
Irié, *Guinea* 82 D3
Iriga, *Phil.* 61 E5
Iringa, *Tanzania* 86 D4
Iringa □, *Tanzania* 86 D4
Iriomote △, *Japan* 55 M1
Iriomote-Jima, *Japan* 55 M1
Iriona, *Honduras* 120 C2
Iriri →, *Brazil* 125 D8
Irish Republic ■, *Europe* 12 C4
Irish Sea, *Europe* 14 D3
Irkutsk, *Russia* 53 D11
Irlıganlı, *Turkey* 47 D11
Irma, *Canada* 103 C6
Irō-Zaki, *Japan* 55 G9
Iroise, Mer d', *France* 18 D2
Iron Baron, *Australia* 95 E2
Iron Gate = Portile de Fier, *Europe* 28 F7
Iron Knob, *Australia* 95 E2
Iron Mountain, *U.S.A.* 114 C1
Iron Range △, *Australia* 94 A3
Iron River, *U.S.A.* 112 B10
Irondequoit, *U.S.A.* 116 C7
Ironton, *Mo., U.S.A.* 113 G9
Ironton, *Ohio, U.S.A.* 114 F4
Ironwood, *U.S.A.* 112 B9
Ironwood Forest ⌂, *U.S.A.* 109 K8
Iroquois, *Canada* 117 B9
Iroquois Falls, *Canada* 104 C3
Irosin, *Phil.* 61 E6
Irpin, *Ukraine* 33 G6
Irrara Cr. →, *Australia* 95 D4
Irrawaddy □, *Burma* 67 L19
Irrawaddy →, *Burma* 67 M19
Irrawaddy, Mouths of the, *Burma* 67 M19
Irricana, *Canada* 102 C6
Irshava, *Ukraine* 28 B8
Irsina, *Italy* 43 B9
Irtysh →, *Russia* 52 C7
Irumu, *Dem. Rep. of the Congo* 86 B2
Irún, *Spain* 38 B3
Irunea = Pamplona, *Spain* 38 C3
Irurzun, *Spain* 38 C3
Irvine, *U.K.* 13 F4
Irvine, *Calif., U.S.A.* 111 M9
Irvine, *Ky., U.S.A.* 114 G4
Irvinestown, *U.K.* 12 B4
Irving, *U.S.A.* 113 J6
Irvona, *U.S.A.* 116 F6
Irwin →, *Australia* 93 E1
Irymple, *Australia* 95 E3
Is, Jebel, *Sudan* 80 C4
Is-sur-Tille, *France* 19 E12
Isa, *Nigeria* 83 C6
Isa Khel, *Pakistan* 68 C4
Isaac →, *Australia* 94 C4
Isabel, *U.S.A.* 112 C4
Isabela, *Phil.* 61 H5
Isabela, *Puerto Rico* 121 d
Isabela, I., *Mexico* 118 C3
Isabelia, Cord., *Nic.* 120 D2
Isabella Ra., *Australia* 92 D3
Isaccea, *Romania* 29 E13
Ísafjarðardjúp, *Iceland* 8 C2
Ísafjörður, *Iceland* 8 C2
Isagarh, *India* 68 G7
Isahaya, *Japan* 55 H5
Isaka, *Tanzania* 86 C3
Işalniţa, *Romania* 29 F8
Isalo △, *Madag.* 89 C8
Isan →, *India* 69 F9
Isana = Içana →, *Brazil* 124 C5
Isangano △, *Zambia* 87 E3
Isanlu Makutu, *Nigeria* 83 D6
Isar →, *Germany* 25 G8
Isarco →, *Italy* 41 B8
Ísari, *Greece* 46 D3
Íscar, *Spain* 36 D6
İscehisar, *Turkey* 47 C12
Íschia, *Italy* 42 B6
Isdell →, *Australia* 92 C3
Ise, *Japan* 55 G8
Ise-Shima △, *Japan* 55 G8
Ise-Wan, *Japan* 55 G8
Isefjord, *Denmark* 11 J5
Isel →, *Austria* 26 E5
Iseo, *Italy* 40 C7
Iseo, L. d', *Italy* 40 C7
Iseramagazi, *Tanzania* 86 C3
Isère □, *France* 21 C9
Isère →, *France* 21 D8
Iserlohn, *Germany* 24 D3
Isérnia, *Italy* 43 A7
Iseyin, *Nigeria* 83 D5
Isfahan = Eşfahān, *Iran* 71 C6
Ishëm, *Albania* 44 E3
Ishigaki-Shima, *Japan* 55 M2
Ishikari-Gawa →, *Japan* 54 C10
Ishikari-Sammyaku, *Japan* 54 C11
Ishikari-Wan, *Japan* 54 C10
Ishikawa □, *Japan* 55 F8
Ishim, *Russia* 52 D7
Ishim →, *Russia* 52 D8
Ishinomaki, *Japan* 54 E10
Ishioka, *Japan* 55 F10
Ishkuman, *Pakistan* 69 A5
Ishpeming, *U.S.A.* 114 B2
Isigny-sur-Mer, *France* 18 C5
Işıklar Dağı, *Turkey* 45 F11
Işıklı, *Turkey* 47 C11
Isil Kul, *Russia* 52 D8
Ísili, *Italy* 42 C2
Isiolo, *Kenya* 86 B4
Isiro, *Dem. Rep. of the Congo* 86 B2
Isisford, *Australia* 94 C3
İskenderun, *Turkey* 70 B3
İskenderun Körfezi, *Turkey* 72 D6
İskilip, *Turkey* 72 B6
Iskŭr →, *Bulgaria* 45 C8
Iskŭr, Yazovir, *Bulgaria* 44 D7
Iskut →, *Canada* 102 B2
Isla →, *U.K.* 13 E5
Isla Coiba △, *Panama* 120 E3
Isla Cristina, *Spain* 37 H3
Isla de Salamanca △, *Colombia* 121 D5
Isla Gorge △, *Australia* 94 D4
Isla Tiburón y San Esteban ⌂, *Mexico* 118 B2
Isla Vista, *U.S.A.* 111 L7
Islâhiye, *Turkey* 72 D7
Islam Headworks, *Pakistan* 68 E5
Islamabad, *Pakistan* 68 C5
Islamgarh, *Pakistan* 68 F4
Islamkot, *Pakistan* 68 G4
Islampur, *India* 69 G11
Island L., *Canada* 103 C10
Island Lagoon, *Australia* 95 E2
Island Pond, *U.S.A.* 117 B13

Islands, B. of, Canada 105 C8
Islands, B. of, N.Z. 91 F5
Islay, U.K. 13 F2
Isle →, France 20 D3
Isle aux Morts, Canada 105 C8
Isle of Wight □, U.K. 15 G6
Isle Royale △, U.S.A. 114 B1
Isleton, U.S.A. 110 G5
Ismail = Izmayil, Ukraine 29 E13
Ismâ'ilîya, Egypt 80 H8
Ismaning, Germany 25 G7
Isna, Egypt 80 B3
Isoanala, Madag. 89 C8
Isogstalo, India 69 B8
Ísola del Liri, Italy 41 G10
Ísola della Scala, Italy 40 C7
Ísola di Capo Rizzuto, Italy 43 D10
Isparta, Turkey 47 D12
Isperikh, Bulgaria 45 C10
Íspica, Italy 43 F7
Israel ■, Asia 74 D3
Isratu, Eritrea 81 D4
Issakly, Russia 34 C10
Issia, Ivory C. 82 D3
Issoire, France 20 C7
Issoudun, France 19 F8
Issyk-Kul, Ozero = Ysyk-Köl, Kyrgyzstan 52 E8
Ist, Croatia 41 D11
Istállós-kő, Hungary 28 B5
İstanbul, Turkey 45 E12
İstanbul □, Turkey 45 E12
İstanbul ✕ (IST), Turkey 45 F12
İstanbul Boğazı, Turkey 45 E13
Istiaía, Greece 46 C5
Istok, Serbia & M. 44 D4
Istokpoga, L., U.S.A. 115 M5
Istra, Croatia 41 C10
Istres, France 21 E8
Istria = Istra, Croatia 41 C10
Itá, Paraguay 126 B4
Itaberaba, Brazil 125 F10
Itabira, Brazil 125 G10
Itabirito, Brazil 127 A7
Itabuna, Brazil 125 F11
Itacaunas →, Brazil 125 E9
Itacoatiara, Brazil 124 D7
Itaipú, Reprêsa de, Brazil 127 B5
Itaituba, Brazil 125 D7
Itajaí, Brazil 127 B6
Itajubá, Brazil 127 A6
Itaka, Tanzania 87 D3
Itala ⌂, S. Africa 89 D5
Italy ■, Europe 7 G8
Itamaraju, Brazil 125 G11
Itampolo, Madag. 89 C7
Itandrano, Madag. 89 C8
Itapecuru-Mirim, Brazil 125 D10
Itaperuna, Brazil 127 A7
Itapetininga, Brazil 127 A6
Itapeva, Brazil 127 A6
Itapicuru →, Bahia, Brazil 125 F11
Itapicuru →, Maranhão, Brazil 125 D10
Itapipoca, Brazil 125 D11
Itapuá □, Paraguay 127 B4
Itaquari, Brazil 127 A7
Itaquí, Brazil 126 B4
Itararé, Brazil 127 A6
Itarsi, India 68 H7
Itatí, Argentina 126 B4
Itatiaia △, Brazil 127 A7
Itbayat, Phil. 61 A4
Itchen →, U.K. 15 G6
Itéa, Greece 46 C4
Itezhi Tezhi, L., Zambia 87 F2
Ithaca = Itháki, Greece 46 C2
Ithaca, U.S.A. 117 D8
Itháki, Greece 46 C2
Íti △, Greece 46 C4
Itiquira →, Brazil 125 G7
Itō, Japan 55 G9
Itoigawa, Japan 55 F8
Iton →, France 18 C8
Itonamas →, Bolivia 124 F6
Itri, Italy 42 A6
Itsa, Egypt 80 J7
Ittiri, Italy 42 B1
Ittoqqortoormiit, Greenland 4 B6
Itu, Brazil 127 A6
Itu, Nigeria 83 D6
Itu Aba I., S. China Sea 62 B4
Ituiutaba, Brazil 125 G9
Itumbiara, Brazil 125 G9
Ituna, Canada 103 C8
Itunge Port, Tanzania 87 D3
Iturbe, Argentina 126 A2
Ituri →, Dem. Rep. of the Congo 86 B2
Iturup, Ostrov, Russia 53 E15
Ituxi →, Brazil 124 E6
Ituyuro →, Argentina 126 A3
Itzehoe, Germany 24 B5
Ivahona, Madag. 89 C8
Ivaí →, Brazil 127 A5
Ivalo, Finland 8 B22
Ivalojoki →, Finland 8 B22
Ivanava, Belarus 33 F3
Ivančice, Czech Rep. 27 B9
Ivane-Puste, Ukraine 29 B11
Ivănești, Romania 29 D12
Ivangorod, Russia 32 C5
Ivanhoe, Australia 95 E3
Ivanhoe, Calif., U.S.A. 110 J7
Ivanhoe, Minn., U.S.A. 112 C6
Ivanhorod, Ukraine 29 B14
Ivanić Grad, Croatia 41 C13
Ivanjica, Serbia & M. 44 C4
Ivanjska, Bos.-H. 28 F2
Ivankoyskoye Vdkhr., Russia 32 D9
Ivano-Frankivsk, Ukraine 29 B9
Ivano-Frankivska □, Ukraine 29 B9
Ivanovo = Ivanava, Belarus 33 F3
Ivanovo, Russia 32 D11
Ivanščica, Croatia 41 B13
Ivato, Madag. 89 C8
Ivatsevichy, Belarus 33 F3
Ivaylovgrad, Bulgaria 45 E10
Ivinheima →, Brazil 127 A5
Ivinhema, Brazil 127 A5
Ivohibe, Madag. 89 C8
Ivory Coast, W. Afr. 82 E4
Ivory Coast ■, Africa 82 D4
Ivösjön, Sweden 11 H8
Ivrea, Italy 40 C4
Ivrindi, Turkey 47 B9
Ivujivik, Canada 101 B12
Ivybridge, U.K. 15 G4
Iwaizumi, Japan 54 E10
Iwaki, Japan 55 F10
Iwakuni, Japan 55 G6
Iwamizawa, Japan 54 C10
Iwanai, Japan 54 C10
Iwata, Japan 55 G8
Iwate □, Japan 54 E10
Iwate-San, Japan 54 E10
Iwo, Nigeria 83 D5
Iwonicz-Zdrój, Poland 31 J8
Ixiamas, Bolivia 124 F5
Ixopo, S. Africa 89 E5
Ixtepec, Mexico 119 D5
Ixtlán del Río, Mexico 118 C4
Iyal Bakhit, Sudan 81 E2
Iyo, Japan 55 H6
Izabal, L. de, Guatemala 120 C2
Izamal, Mexico 119 C7
Izberbash, Russia 35 J8
Izbica, Poland 31 H10
Izbica Kujawska, Poland 31 F5
Izbiceni, Romania 29 G9
Izena-Shima, Japan 55 L3
Izgrev, Bulgaria 45 C10
Izhevsk, Russia 52 D6
Izmayil, Ukraine 29 E13
Izmir, Turkey 47 C9
Izmir □, Turkey 47 C9
Izmir Adnan Menderes ✕ (ADB), Turkey 47 C9
Izmir Körfezi, Turkey 47 C8
Izmit = Kocaeli, Turkey 45 F13
Iznájar, Spain 37 H6
Iznalloz, Spain 37 H7
Iznik, Turkey 72 B3
Iznik Gölü, Turkey 45 F13
Izobil'nyy, Russia 35 H5
Izola, Slovenia 41 C10
Izra, Syria 74 C5
Iztochni Rodopi, Bulgaria 45 E9
Izu-Shotō, Japan 55 G10
Izúcar de Matamoros, Mexico 119 D5
Izumi-Sano, Japan 55 G7
Izumo, Japan 55 G6
Izyaslav, Ukraine 33 G4
Izyum, Ukraine 33 H9

J

Jaba, Ethiopia 81 F4
Jabal at Tā'ir, Red Sea 81 D5
Jabalón →, Spain 37 G6
Jabalpur, India 69 H8
Jabbūl, Syria 70 B3
Jabiru, Australia 92 B5
Jablah, Syria 70 C3
Jablanac, Croatia 41 D11
Jablanica, Bos.-H. 28 G2
Jablonec nad Nisou, Czech Rep. 26 A8
Jablonica, Slovak Rep. 27 C10
Jabłonowo Pomorskie, Poland 30 E6
Jablunkov, Czech Rep. 27 B11
Jaboatão, Brazil 125 E11
Jaboticabal, Brazil 127 A6
Jabukovac, Serbia & M. 44 B6
Jaca, Spain 38 C4
Jacareí, Brazil 127 A6
Jacarèzinho, Brazil 127 A6
Jackman, U.S.A. 115 C10
Jacksboro, U.S.A. 113 J5
Jackson, Barbados 121 g
Jackson, Ala., U.S.A. 115 K2
Jackson, Calif., U.S.A. 110 G6
Jackson, Ky., U.S.A. 114 G4
Jackson, Mich., U.S.A. 114 D3
Jackson, Minn., U.S.A. 112 D7
Jackson, Miss., U.S.A. 113 J9
Jackson, Mo., U.S.A. 113 G10
Jackson, N.H., U.S.A. 117 B13
Jackson, Ohio, U.S.A. 114 F4
Jackson, Tenn., U.S.A. 115 H1
Jackson, Wyo., U.S.A. 108 E8
Jackson B., N.Z. 91 K2
Jackson L., U.S.A. 108 E8
Jacksons, N.Z. 91 K3
Jackson's Arm, Canada 105 C8
Jacksonville, Ala., U.S.A. 115 J3
Jacksonville, Ark., U.S.A. 113 H8
Jacksonville, Calif., U.S.A. 110 H6
Jacksonville, Fla., U.S.A. 115 K5
Jacksonville, Ill., U.S.A. 112 F9
Jacksonville, N.C., U.S.A. 115 H7
Jacksonville, Tex., U.S.A. 113 K7
Jacksonville Beach, U.S.A. 115 K5
Jacmel, Haiti 121 C5
Jacob Lake, U.S.A. 109 H7
Jacobabad, Pakistan 68 E3
Jacobina, Brazil 125 F10
Jacques-Cartier ⌂, Canada 105 C5
Jacques-Cartier, Dét. de, Canada 105 C7
Jacques-Cartier, Mt., Canada 105 C6
Jacqueville, Ivory C. 82 D4
Jacuí →, Brazil 127 C5
Jacumba, U.S.A. 111 N10
Jacundá →, Brazil 125 D8
Jade, Germany 24 B4
Jadebusen, Germany 24 B4
Jadovnik, Serbia & M. 44 C3
Jadraque, Spain 38 E2
Jaén, Peru 124 E3
Jaén, Spain 37 H7
Jaén □, Spain 37 H7
Jafarabad, India 68 J4
Jaffa = Tel Aviv-Yafo, Israel 74 C3
Jaffa, C., Australia 95 F2
Jaffna, Sri Lanka 66 Q12
Jaffray, Canada 103 D10
Jaffrey, U.S.A. 117 D12
Jagadhri, India 68 D7
Jagadishpur, India 69 G11
Jagdalpur, India 67 K13
Jagersfontein, S. Africa 88 D4
Jaghīn →, Iran 71 E8
Jagodina, Serbia & M. 44 B5
Jagraon, India 66 D9
Jagst →, Germany 25 F5
Jagtial, India 66 K11
Jaguariaíva, Brazil 127 A6
Jaguaribe →, Brazil 125 D11
Jagüey Grande, Cuba 120 B3
Jahanabad, India 69 G11
Jahazpur, India 68 G6
Jahrom, Iran 71 D7
Jaijon, India 68 D7
Jailolo, Indonesia 63 D7
Jailolo, Selat, Indonesia 63 D7
Jaipur, India 68 F6
Jais, India 69 F9
Jaisalmer, India 68 F4
Jaisinghnagar, India 69 H8
Jaitaran, India 68 F5
Jaithari, India 69 H8
Jājarm, Iran 71 B8
Jajce, Bos.-H. 28 F2
Jakam →, India 68 H6
Jakarta, Indonesia 63 G12
Jakhal, India 68 E6
Jakhau, India 68 H3
Jakobstad = Pietarsaari, Finland 8 E20
Jakupica, Macedonia 44 E5
Jal, U.S.A. 113 J3
Jalālābād, Afghan. 68 B4
Jalalabad, India 69 F8
Jalalpur Jattan, Pakistan 68 C6
Jalama, U.S.A. 111 L6
Jalapa, Guatemala 120 D2
Jalapa Enríquez = Xalapa, Mexico 119 D5
Jalasjärvi, Finland 9 E20
Jalaun, India 69 F8
Jaldhaka →, Bangla. 69 F13
Jalesar, India 68 F8
Jaleswar, Nepal 69 F11
Jalgaon, India 66 J9
Jalībah, Iraq 70 D5
Jalingo, Nigeria 83 D7
Jalisco □, Mexico 118 D4
Jalkot, Pakistan 69 B5
Jallas →, Spain 36 C1
Jalna, India 66 K9
Jalón →, Spain 38 D3
Jalor, India 68 G5
Jalpa, Mexico 118 C4
Jalpaiguri, India 67 F16
Jaluit I., Marshall Is. 96 G8
Jalūlā, Iraq 70 C5
Jamaari, Nigeria 83 C6
Jamaica ■, W. Indies 120 a
Jamalpur, Bangla. 67 G16
Jamalpur, India 69 G12
Jamalpurganj, India 69 H13
Jamanxim →, Brazil 125 D7
Jambewangi, Indonesia 63 J17
Jambi, Indonesia 62 E2
Jambi □, Indonesia 62 E2
Jambusar, India 68 H5
James →, S. Dak., U.S.A. 112 D6
James →, Va., U.S.A. 114 G7
James B., Canada 104 B3
James Ranges, Australia 92 D5
James Ross I., Antarctica 5 C18
Jamesabad, Pakistan 68 G3
Jamestown, Australia 95 E2
Jamestown, S. Africa 88 E4
Jamestown, N. Dak., U.S.A. 112 B5
Jamestown, N.Y., U.S.A. 116 D5
Jamestown, Pa., U.S.A. 116 E4
Jamīlābād, Iran 71 C6
Jamiltepec, Mexico 119 D5
Jamira →, India 69 J13
Jämjö, Sweden 11 H9
Jamkhandi, India 66 L9
Jammerbugt, Denmark 11 G3
Jammu, India 68 C6
Jammu & Kashmir □, India 69 B7
Jamnagar, India 68 H4
Jamni →, India 69 G8
Jampur, Pakistan 68 E4
Jamrud, Pakistan 68 C4
Jämsä, Finland 9 F21
Jamshedpur, India 69 H12
Jamtara, India 69 H12
Jämtland, Sweden 8 E15
Jämtlands län □, Sweden 10 B7
Jan L., Canada 103 C8
Jan Mayen, Arctic 4 B7
Janakkala, Finland 9 F21
Janaúba, Brazil 125 G10
Jand, Pakistan 68 C5
Jandaq, Iran 71 C7
Jandía, Canary Is. 48 F5
Jandía △, Canary Is. 48 F5
Jandía, Pta. de, Canary Is. 48 F5
Jandola, Pakistan 68 C4
Jandowae, Australia 95 D5
Jándula →, Spain 37 G6
Janesville, U.S.A. 112 D10
Janga, Ghana 83 C4
Jangamo, Mozam. 89 C6
Janghai, India 69 G10
Janikowo, Poland 31 F5
Janinà = Ioánnina □, Greece 46 B2
Janja, Bos.-H. 28 F4
Janjanbureh, Gambia 82 C2
Janjevo, Serbia & M. 44 D5
Janjgir, India 69 J10
Janjina, Croatia 41 F14
Janjina, Madag. 89 C8
Janos, Mexico 118 A3
Jánoshalma, Hungary 28 D4
Jánosháza, Hungary 28 C2
Jánossomorja, Hungary 28 C2
Janów, Poland 31 H6
Janów Lubelski, Poland 31 H9
Janów Podlaski, Poland 31 F10
Janowiec Wielkopolski, Poland 31 F4
Januária, Brazil 125 G10
Janub △, Sudan 81 F2
Janub Dârfûr □, Sudan 81 E2
Janub Kordofân □, Sudan 81 E3
Janûb Sînî □, Egypt 74 F2
Janubio, Canary Is. 48 F6
Janville, France 19 D8
Janzé, France 18 E5
Jaora, India 68 H6
Japan ■, Asia 55 G8
Japan, Sea of, Asia 54 E7
Japan Trench, Pac. Oc. 96 D6
Japen = Yapen, Indonesia 63 E9
Japla, India 69 G11
Japurá →, Brazil 124 D5
Jaquarão, Brazil 127 C5
Jaqué, Panama 120 E4
Jarābulus, Syria 70 B3
Jaraicejo, Spain 37 F5
Jaraíz de la Vera, Spain 36 E5
Jarama →, Spain 36 E7
Jaramānah, Syria 72 F7
Jarandilla, Spain 36 E5
Jaranwala, Pakistan 68 D5
Jarash, Jordan 74 C4
Jarash □, Jordan 74 C4
Järbo, Sweden 10 D10
Jardim, Brazil 126 A4
Jardín →, Spain 39 G2
Jardine River △, Australia 94 A3
Jardines de la Reina, Arch. de los, Cuba 120 B4
Jargalang, China 57 C12
Jari →, Brazil 125 D8
Jarīr, W. al →, Si. Arabia 70 E4
Järlåsa, Sweden 10 E11
Jarmen, Germany 24 B9
Järna, Dalarna, Sweden 10 D8
Järna, Stockholm, Sweden 10 E11
Jarnac, France 20 C3
Jarny, France 19 C12
Jarocin, Poland 31 G4
Jaroměř, Czech Rep. 26 A8
Jarosław, Poland 31 H9
Järpås, Sweden 11 F6
Järpen, Sweden 10 A7
Jarrahdale, Australia 93 F2
Jarrahi →, Iran 71 D6
Jarres, Plaine des, Laos 64 C4
Jarso, Ethiopia 81 F4
Jartai, China 56 E3
Jarud Qi, China 57 B11
Järvenpää, Finland 9 F21
Jarvis, Canada 116 D4
Jarvis I., Pac. Oc. 97 H12
Jarvorník, Czech Rep. 27 A10
Järvsö, Sweden 10 C10
Jarwa, India 69 F10
Jaša Tomić, Serbia & M. 28 E5
Jasdan, India 68 H4
Jashpurnagar, India 69 H11
Jasidih, India 69 G12
Jasień, Poland 31 G2
Jāsimīyah, Iraq 70 C5
Jasin, Malaysia 65 L4
Jāsk, Iran 71 E8
Jasło, Poland 31 J8
Jasmund, Germany 24 A9
Jasmund △, Germany 24 A9
Jaso, India 69 G9
Jasper, Alta., Canada 102 C5
Jasper, Ont., Canada 117 B9
Jasper, Ala., U.S.A. 115 J2
Jasper, Fla., U.S.A. 115 K4
Jasper, Ind., U.S.A. 114 F2
Jasper, Tex., U.S.A. 113 K8
Jasper △, Canada 102 C5
Jasrasar, India 68 F5
Jastarnia, Poland 30 D5
Jastrebarsko, Croatia 41 C12
Jastrowie, Poland 30 E3
Jastrzębie Zdrój, Poland 31 J5
Jász-Nagykun-Szolnok □, Hungary 28 C5
Jászapáti, Hungary 28 C5
Jászárokszállás, Hungary 28 C4
Jászberény, Hungary 28 C4
Jászkisér, Hungary 28 C5
Jászladány, Hungary 28 C5
Jataí, Brazil 125 G8
Jati, Pakistan 68 G3
Jatibarang, Indonesia 63 G13
Jatiluwih, Indonesia 63 J18
Jatinegara, Indonesia 63 G12
Játiva = Xátiva, Spain 39 G4
Jättendal, Sweden 10 C11
Jaú, Brazil 127 A6
Jauja, Peru 124 F3
Jaunpur, India 69 G10
Java = Jawa, Indonesia 62 F3
Java Sea, Indonesia 62 E3
Java Trench, Ind. Oc. 62 F3
Javalambre, Sa. de, Spain 38 E4
Jávea, Spain 39 G5
Jawa, Indonesia 62 F3
Jawa Barat □, Indonesia 63 G12
Jawa Tengah □, Indonesia 63 G14
Jawa Timur □, Indonesia 63 G15
Jawad, India 68 G6
Jawor, Poland 31 G3
Jaworzno, Poland 31 H6
Jaworzyna Śląska, Poland 31 H3
Jay Peak, U.S.A. 117 B12
Jaya, Puncak, Indonesia 63 E9
Jayanti, India 67 F16
Jayapura, Indonesia 63 E10
Jayawijaya, Pegunungan, Indonesia 63 E9
Jaynagar, India 67 F15
Jayrūd, Syria 70 C3
Jayton, U.S.A. 113 J4
Jāz Mūrīān, Hāmūn-e, Iran 71 E8
Jazīreh-ye Shīf, Iran 71 D6
Jazminal, Mexico 118 C4
Jazzīn, Lebanon 74 B4
Jean, U.S.A. 111 K11
Jean Marie River, Canada 102 A4
Jean-Rabel, Haiti 121 C5
Jeanerette, U.S.A. 113 L9
Jeanette, Ostrov = Zhannetty, Ostrov, Russia 53 B16
Jeannette, U.S.A. 116 F5
Jebāl Bārez, Kūh-e, Iran 71 D8
Jebba, Nigeria 83 D5
Jebel, Bahr el →, Sudan 81 F3
Jebel Dud, Sudan 81 E3
Jebel Qerri, Sudan 81 D3
Jedburgh, U.K. 13 F6
Jedda = Jiddah, Si. Arabia 75 C2
Jeddore L., Canada 105 C8
Jedlicze, Poland 31 J8
Jędrzejów, Poland 31 H7
Jedwabne, Poland 31 E9
Jeetzel →, Germany 24 B7
Jefferson, Iowa, U.S.A. 112 D7
Jefferson, Ohio, U.S.A. 116 E4
Jefferson, Tex., U.S.A. 113 J7
Jefferson, Mt., Nev., U.S.A. 108 G5
Jefferson, Mt., Oreg., U.S.A. 108 D3
Jefferson City, Mo., U.S.A. 112 F8
Jefferson City, Tenn., U.S.A. 115 G4
Jeffersontown, U.S.A. 114 F3
Jeffersonville, U.S.A. 114 F3
Jeffrey City, U.S.A. 108 E10
Jega, Nigeria 83 C5
Jeju = Cheju do, S. Korea 57 H14
Jēkabpils, Latvia 9 H21
Jekyll I., U.S.A. 115 K5
Jelcz-Laskowice, Poland 31 G4
Jelenia Góra, Poland 31 H2
Jelgava, Latvia 9 H20
Jelgava □, Latvia 30 B10
Jelica, Serbia & M. 44 C4
Jelli, Sudan 81 F3
Jelšava, Slovak Rep. 27 C13
Jemaja, Indonesia 65 L5
Jemaluang, Malaysia 65 L4
Jember, Indonesia 63 H15
Jembongan, Malaysia 62 C5
Jena, Germany 24 E7
Jena, U.S.A. 113 K8
Jenbach, Austria 26 D4
Jenīn, West Bank 74 C4
Jenkins, U.S.A. 114 G4
Jenner, U.S.A. 110 G3
Jennings, U.S.A. 113 K8
Jepara, Indonesia 63 G14
Jeparit, Australia 95 F3
Jequié, Brazil 125 F10
Jequitinhonha, Brazil 125 G10
Jequitinhonha →, Brazil 125 G11
Jerantut, Malaysia 65 L4
Jerejak, Pulau, Malaysia 65 c
Jérémie, Haiti 121 C5
Jerez, Punta, Mexico 119 C5
Jerez de García Salinas, Mexico 118 C4
Jerez de la Frontera, Spain 37 J4
Jerez de los Caballeros, Spain 37 G4
Jericho = El Arīḥā, West Bank 74 D4
Jericho, Australia 94 C4
Jerichow, Germany 24 C8
Jerid, Chott el = Djerid, Chott, Tunisia 78 B7
Jerilderie, Australia 95 F4
Jermyn, U.S.A. 117 E9
Jerome, U.S.A. 108 E6
Jerramungup, Australia 93 F2
Jersey, U.K. 15 H5
Jersey City, U.S.A. 117 F10
Jersey Shore, U.S.A. 116 E7
Jerseyville, U.S.A. 112 F9
Jerusalem, Israel 74 D4
Jervis B., Australia 95 F5
Jervis Inlet, Canada 102 C4
Jerzu, Italy 42 C2
Jesenice, Slovenia 41 B11
Jeseník, Czech Rep. 27 A10
Jesenké, Slovak Rep. 27 C13
Jesi = Iesi, Italy 41 E10
Jessnitz, Germany 24 D8
Jessore, Bangla. 67 H16
Jesup, U.S.A. 115 K5
Jesús Carranza, Mexico 119 D5
Jesús María, Argentina 126 C3
Jetmore, U.S.A. 113 F5
Jetpur, India 68 J4
Jeumont, France 19 B11
Jevnaker, Norway 9 F14
Jewett, U.S.A. 116 F3
Jewett City, U.S.A. 117 E13
Jeyḥūnābād, Iran 71 C6
Jeypore, India 67 K13
Jeziorak, Jezioro, Poland 30 E6
Jeziorany, Poland 30 E7
Jeziorka →, Poland 31 F8

Jha Jha, India 69 G12
Jhaarkand = Jharkhand □, India 69 H11
Jhabua, India 68 H6
Jhajjar, India 68 E7
Jhal, Pakistan 68 E2
Jhal Jhao, Pakistan 66 F4
Jhalawar, India 68 G7
Jhalida, India 69 H11
Jhalrapatan, India 68 G7
Jhang Maghiana, Pakistan 68 D5
Jhansi, India 69 G8
Jhargram, India 69 H12
Jharia, India 69 H12
Jharkhand □, India 69 H11
Jharsuguda, India 67 J14
Jhelum, Pakistan 68 C5
Jhelum →, Pakistan 68 D5
Jhilmilli, India 69 H10
Jhudo, Pakistan 68 G3
Jhunjhunu, India 68 E6
Ji-Paraná, Brazil 124 F6
Ji Xian, Hebei, China 56 F8
Ji Xian, Henan, China 56 G8
Ji Xian, Shanxi, China 56 F6
Jia Xian, Henan, China 56 H7
Jia Xian, Shaanxi, China 56 E6
Jiading, China 59 B13
Jiahe, China 59 E9
Jialing Jiang →, China 58 C6
Jiamusi, China 60 B8
Ji'an, Jiangxi, China 59 D10
Ji'an, Jilin, China 57 D14
Jianchang, China 57 D11
Jianchangying, China 57 D10
Jianchuan, China 58 D2
Jiande, China 59 C12
Jiang'an, China 58 C5
Jiangbei, China 58 C6
Jiangcheng, China 58 F3
Jiangchuan, China 58 E4
Jiangdi, China 58 D4
Jiangdu, China 59 A12
Jiange, China 58 A5
Jianghua, China 59 E8
Jiangjin, China 58 C6
Jiangkou, China 58 D7
Jiangle, China 59 D11
Jiangling, China 59 B9
Jiangmen, China 59 F9
Jiangning, China 59 B12
Jiangshan, China 59 C12
Jiangsu □, China 57 H11
Jiangxi □, China 59 D11
Jiangyan, China 59 A13
Jiangyin, China 59 B13
Jiangyong, China 59 E8
Jiangyou, China 58 B5
Jianhe, China 58 D7
Jianli, China 59 C9
Jianning, China 59 D11
Jian'ou, China 59 D12
Jianshi, China 58 B7
Jianshui, China 58 F4
Jianyang, Fujian, China 59 D12
Jianyang, Sichuan, China 58 B5
Jiao Xian = Jiaozhou, China 57 F11
Jiaohe, Hebei, China 56 E9
Jiaohe, Jilin, China 57 C14
Jiaojiang, China 59 C13
Jiaoling, China 59 E11
Jiaozhou, China 57 F11
Jiaozhou Wan, China 57 F11
Jiaozuo, China 56 G7
Jiashan, China 59 B13
Jiawang, China 57 G9
Jiaxiang, China 56 G9
Jiaxing, China 59 B13
Jiayi = Chiai, Taiwan 59 F13
Jiayu, China 59 C9
Jibiya, Nigeria 83 C6
Jibou, Romania 29 C8
Jibuti = Djibouti ■, Africa 81 E5
Jicarón, I., Panama 120 E3
Jičín, Czech Rep. 26 A8
Jiddah, Si. Arabia 75 C2
Jido, India 67 E19
Jieshou, China 56 H8
Jiexiu, China 56 F6
Jieyang, China 59 F11
Jigawa □, Nigeria 83 C6
Jiggalong, Australia 92 D3
Jigni, India 69 G8
Jihlava, Czech Rep. 26 B8
Jihlava →, Czech Rep. 27 C9
Jihlavský □, Czech Rep. 26 B8
Jihočeský □, Czech Rep. 26 B7
Jihomoravský □, Czech Rep. 27 B9
Jijiga, Ethiopia 75 F3
Jikamshi, Nigeria 83 C6
Jikau, Sudan 81 F3
Jilin, China 57 C14
Jilin □, China 57 C14
Jiloca →, Spain 38 D3
Jilong = Chilung, Taiwan 59 E13
Jim Thorpe, U.S.A. 117 F9
Jima, Ethiopia 81 F4
Jimbaran, Teluk, Indonesia 63 K18
Jimbolia, Romania 28 E5
Jimena de la Frontera, Spain 37 J5
Jiménez, Mexico 118 B4
Jimo, China 57 F11
Jin Jiang →, China 59 C10
Jin Xian = Jinzhou, China 56 E8
Jin Xian, China 57 E11
Jinan, China 56 F9
Jinchang, China 60 C5
Jincheng, China 56 G7
Jinchuan, China 58 B4
Jind, India 68 E7
Jindabyne, Australia 95 F4
Jindřichův Hradec, Czech Rep. 26 B8
Jing He →, China 56 G5
Jing Shan, China 59 B8
Jing Xian, China 59 B12
Jing'an, China 59 C10
Jingbian, China 56 F5
Jingchuan, China 56 G4
Jingde, China 59 B12
Jingdezhen, China 59 C11
Jingdong, China 58 E3
Jinggangshan, China 59 D10
Jinggu, China 58 F3
Jinghai, China 56 E9
Jinghong, China 58 G3
Jingjiang, China 59 A13
Jingle, China 56 E6
Jingmen, China 59 B9
Jingning, China 56 G3
Jingpo Hu, China 57 C15
Jingshan, China 59 B9
Jingtai, China 56 F3
Jingxi, China 58 F6
Jingxing, China 56 E8
Jingyang, China 56 G5
Jingyu, China 57 C14
Jingyuan, China 56 F3
Jingzhou, China 58 D7
Jingziguan, China 56 H6
Jinhua, China 59 C12
Jining, Nei Monggol Zizhiqu, China 56 D7
Jining, Shandong, China 56 G9
Jinja, Uganda 86 B3
Jinjang, Malaysia 65 L3
Jinji, China 56 F4
Jinjiang, Fujian, China 59 E12
Jinjiang, Yunnan, China 58 D3
Jinjini, Ghana 82 D4
Jinkou, China 59 B10
Jinkouhe, China 58 C4
Jinmen Dao, China 59 E12
Jinnah Barrage, Pakistan 66 C7
Jinning, China 58 E4
Jinotega, Nic. 120 D2
Jinotepe, Nic. 120 D2
Jinping, Guizhou, China 58 D7
Jinping, Yunnan, China 58 F4
Jinsha, China 58 D6
Jinsha Jiang →, China 58 C5
Jinshan, China 59 B13
Jinshi, China 59 C8
Jintan, China 59 B12
Jinxi, Jiangxi, China 59 D11
Jinxi, Liaoning, China 57 D11
Jinxian, China 59 C11
Jinxiang, China 56 G9
Jinyang, China 58 D4
Jinyun, China 59 C13
Jinzhai, China 59 B10
Jinzhou, Hebei, China 56 E8
Jinzhou, Liaoning, China 57 D11
Jiparaná →, Brazil 124 E6
Jipijapa, Ecuador 124 D2
Jiquilpan, Mexico 118 D4
Jishan, China 56 G6
Jishou, China 58 C7
Jishui, China 59 D10
Jisr ash Shughūr, Syria 70 C3
Jitarning, Australia 93 F2
Jitra, Malaysia 65 J3
Jiu →, Romania 29 G8
Jiudengkou, China 56 E4
Jiujiang, Guangdong, China 59 F9
Jiujiang, Jiangxi, China 59 C10
Jiuling Shan, China 59 C10
Jiulong = Kowloon, China 59 F10
Jiulong, China 58 C3
Jiutai, China 57 B13
Jiuxincheng, China 56 E8
Jiuyuhang, China 59 B12
Jixi, Anhui, China 59 B12
Jixi, Heilongjiang, China 57 B16
Jiyang, China 57 F9
Jiyuan, China 56 G7
Jīzān, Si. Arabia 75 D3
Jize, China 56 F8
Jizera →, Czech Rep. 26 A7
Jizl, Wādī al →, Si. Arabia 70 E3
Jizō-Zaki, Japan 55 G6
Jizzakh, Uzbekistan 52 E7
Joaçaba, Brazil 127 B5
Joal Fadiout, Senegal 82 C1
João Pessoa, Brazil 125 E12
Joaquín V. González, Argentina 126 B3
Jobat, India 68 H6
Jobourg, Nez de, France 18 C5
Jódar, Spain 37 H7
Jodhpur, India 68 F5
Jodiya, India 68 H4
Jōetsu, Japan 55 F9
Jœuf, France 19 C12
Jofane, Mozam. 89 C5
Jogbani, India 69 F12
Jõgeva, Estonia 9 G22
Jogjakarta = Yogyakarta, Indonesia 63 G14
Johannesburg, S. Africa 89 D4
Johannesburg, U.S.A. 111 K9
Johansfors, Sweden 11 H9
Johilla →, India 69 H9
John Crow Mts., Jamaica 120 a
John Day, U.S.A. 108 D4
John Day →, U.S.A. 108 D3
John Day Fossil Beds ⌂, U.S.A. 108 D4
John D'Or Prairie, Canada 102 B5
John F. Kennedy International, New York ✕ (JFK), U.S.A. 117 F11
John H. Kerr Reservoir, U.S.A. 115 G6
John o' Groats, U.K. 13 C5
Johnnie, U.S.A. 111 J10
John's Ra., Australia 94 C1
Johnson, Kans., U.S.A. 113 G4
Johnson, Vt., U.S.A. 117 B12
Johnson City, N.Y., U.S.A. 117 D9
Johnson City, Tenn., U.S.A. 115 G4
Johnson City, Tex., U.S.A. 113 K5
Johnsonburg, U.S.A. 116 E6
Johnsondale, U.S.A. 111 K8
Johnsons Crossing, Canada 102 A2
Johnston, L., Australia 93 F3
Johnston Falls = Mambilima Falls, Zambia 87 E2
Johnston I., Pac. Oc. 97 F11
Johnstone Str., Canada 102 C3
Johnstown, N.Y., U.S.A. 117 C10
Johnstown, Ohio, U.S.A. 116 F2
Johnstown, Pa., U.S.A. 116 F6
Johor, Selat, Asia 65 d
Johor Bahru, Malaysia 65 d
Jõhvi, Estonia 9 G22
Joigny, France 19 E10
Joinville, Brazil 127 B6
Joinville, France 19 D12
Joinville I., Antarctica 5 C18
Jojutla, Mexico 119 D5
Jokkmokk, Sweden 8 C18
Jökulsá á Bru →, Iceland 8 D6
Jökulsá á Fjöllum →, Iceland 8 C5
Jolfā, Āzarbājān-e Sharqī, Iran 70 B5
Jolfā, Eşfahan, Iran 71 C6
Joliet, U.S.A. 114 E1
Joliette, Canada 104 C5
Jolo, Phil. 61 J4
Jolon, U.S.A. 110 K5
Jomalig I., Phil. 61 D5
Jombang, Indonesia 63 G15
Jomda, China 58 B2
Jonava, Lithuania 9 J21
Jones Sound, Canada 4 B3
Jonesboro, Ark., U.S.A. 113 H9
Jonesboro, La., U.S.A. 113 J8
Jong →, S. Leone 82 D2
Jonglei, Sudan 81 F3
Jonglei □, Sudan 81 F3
Joniškis, Lithuania 9 H20
Jönköping, Sweden 11 G8
Jönköpings län □, Sweden 11 G8
Jonquière, Canada 105 C5
Jonsered, Sweden 11 G6
Jonzac, France 20 C3
Joplin, U.S.A. 113 G7
Jora, India 68 F6
Jordan, Mont., U.S.A. 108 C10
Jordan, N.Y., U.S.A. 117 C8
Jordan ■, Asia 74 E5
Jordan →, Asia 74 D4
Jordan Valley, U.S.A. 108 E5
Jordanów, Poland 31 J6
Jorhat, India 67 F19
Jörn, Sweden 8 D19
Jorong, Indonesia 62 E4
Jørpeland, Norway 9 G11
Jorquera →, Chile 126 B2
Jos, Nigeria 83 D6
Jos Plateau, Nigeria 83 D6
Jošanička Banja, Serbia & M. 44 C4
José Batlle y Ordóñez, Uruguay 127 C4
Joseni, Romania 29 D10
Joseph, L., Nfld. & L., Canada 105 B6
Joseph, L., Ont., Canada 116 A5
Joseph Bonaparte G., Australia 92 B4
Joshinath, India 69 D8
Joshinetsu-Kōgen △, Japan 55 F9
Joshua Tree, U.S.A. 111 L10
Joshua Tree △, U.S.A. 111 M10
Josselin, France 18 E4
Jost Van Dyke, Br. Virgin Is. 121 e
Jostedalsbreen, Norway 9 F12
Jotunheimen, Norway 9 F13
Joubertberge, Namibia 88 B1
Joué-lès-Tours, France 18 E7
Jourdanton, U.S.A. 113 L5
Joutseno, Finland 32 B5
Jovellanos, Cuba 120 B3
Joyeuse, France 21 D8
Józefów, Lubelskie, Poland 31 H10
Józefów, Mazowieckie, Poland 31 F8
Ju Xian, China 57 F10
Juan Aldama, Mexico 118 C4
Juan Bautista Alberdi, Argentina 126 C3
Juan de Fuca Str., Canada 110 B3
Juan de Nova, Ind. Oc. 89 B7
Juan Fernández, Arch. de, Pac. Oc. 97 L20
Juan José Castelli, Argentina 126 B3
Juan L. Lacaze, Uruguay 126 C4
Juankoski, Finland 8 E23
Juárez, Argentina 126 D4
Juárez, Mexico 111 N11
Juárez, Sierra de, Mexico 118 A1
Juàzeiro, Brazil 125 E10
Juàzeiro do Norte, Brazil 125 E11
Juba = Giuba →, Somali Rep. 75 G3
Juba, Sudan 81 G3
Jubany, Antarctica 5 C18
Jubayl, Lebanon 74 A4
Jubbah, Si. Arabia 70 D4
Jubbal, India 68 D7
Jubbulpore = Jabalpur, India 69 H8
Jübek, Germany 24 A5
Jubga, Russia 35 H4
Jubilee L., Australia 93 E4
Juby, C., Morocco 78 C3
Júcar = Xúquer →, Spain 39 F4
Júcaro, Cuba 120 B4
Juchitán, Mexico 119 D5
Judaea = Har Yehuda, Israel 74 D3
Judenburg, Austria 26 D7
Judith →, U.S.A. 108 C9
Judith, Pt., U.S.A. 117 E13
Judith Gap, U.S.A. 108 C9
Juelsminde, Denmark 11 J4
Jugoslavia = Serbia & Montenegro ■, Europe 44 C4
Juigalpa, Nic. 120 D2
Juillac, France 20 C5
Juist, Germany 24 B2
Juiz de Fora, Brazil 127 A7
Jujuy □, Argentina 126 A2
Julesburg, U.S.A. 112 E3
Juli, Peru 124 G5
Julia Cr. →, Australia 94 C3
Julia Creek, Australia 94 C3
Juliaca, Peru 124 G4
Julian, U.S.A. 111 M10
Julian, L., Canada 104 B4
Julian Alps = Julijske Alpe, Slovenia 41 B11
Julianatop, Suriname 125 C7
Julianehåb = Qaqortoq, Greenland 101 B6
Jülich, Germany 24 E2
Julijske Alpe, Slovenia 41 B11
Julimes, Mexico 118 B3
Jullundur, India 68 D6
Julu, China 56 F8
Jumbo, Zimbabwe 87 F3
Jumbo Pk., U.S.A. 111 J12
Jumentos Cays, Bahamas 120 B4
Jumilla, Spain 39 G3
Jumla, Nepal 69 E10
Jumna = Yamuna →, India 69 G9
Junagadh, India 68 J4
Junction, Tex., U.S.A. 113 K5
Junction, Utah, U.S.A. 109 G7
Junction B., Australia 94 A1
Junction City, Kans., U.S.A. 112 F6
Junction City, Oreg., U.S.A. 108 D2
Junction Pt., Australia 94 A1
Jundah, Australia 94 C3
Jundiaí, Brazil 127 A6
Juneau, U.S.A. 102 B2
Junee, Australia 95 E4
Jungfrau, Switz. 25 J3
Junggar Pendi, China 60 B3
Jungshahi, Pakistan 68 G2
Juniata →, U.S.A. 116 F7
Junín, Argentina 126 C3
Junín de los Andes, Argentina 128 D2
Jūniyah, Lebanon 74 B4
Junlian, China 58 C5
Juntas, Chile 126 B2
Juntura, U.S.A. 108 E4
Jur, Nahr el →, Sudan 81 F2
Jura = Jura, Mts. du, Europe 19 F13
Jura = Schwäbische Alb, Germany 25 G5
Jura, U.K. 13 F3
Jura □, France 19 F12
Jura □, Switz. 25 H3
Jūra →, Lithuania 30 C9
Jura, Mts. du, Europe 19 F13
Jura, Sd. of, U.K. 13 F3
Jurbarkas, Lithuania 9 J20
Jurien, Australia 93 F2
Jurilovca, Romania 29 F13
Jūrmala, Latvia 9 H20
Jurong, China 59 B12
Jurong, Singapore 65 d
Juruá →, Brazil 124 D5
Juruena, Brazil 124 F7
Juruena →, Brazil 124 E7
Juruti, Brazil 125 D7
Jussey, France 19 E12
Justo Daract, Argentina 126 C2
Jutaí →, Brazil 124 D5
Jüterbog, Germany 24 D9
Juticalpa, Honduras 120 D2
Jutland = Jylland, Denmark 11 H3
Juventud, I. de la, Cuba 120 B3
Juvigny-sous-Andaine, France 18 D6
Jūy Zar, Iran 70 C5
Juye, China 56 G9
Juzennecourt, France 19 D11
Jvari, Georgia 35 J6
Jwaneng, Botswana 85 J4
Jyderup, Denmark 11 J5
Jylland, Denmark 11 H3
Jyväskylä, Finland 9 E21

K

K2, Pakistan 69 B7
Ka →, Nigeria 83 C5
Kaap Plateau, S. Africa 88 D3
Kaapkruis, Namibia 88 C1
Kaapstad = Cape Town, S. Africa 88 E2
Kaba, Guinea 82 C2
Kabaena, Indonesia 63 F6
Kabala, S. Leone 82 D2
Kabale, Uganda 86 C3
Kabalo, Dem. Rep. of the Congo 86 D2
Kabambare, Dem. Rep. of the Congo 86 C2
Kabango, Dem. Rep. of the Congo 87 D2
Kabanjahe, Indonesia 62 D1
Kabankalan, Phil. 61 G5
Kabara, Mali 82 B4
Kabardinka, Russia 33 K10
Kabardino-Balkar Republic = Kabardino-Balkaria □, Russia 35 J6
Kabardino-Balkaria □, Russia 35 J6
Kabarega Falls = Murchison Falls, Uganda 86 B3
Kabasalan, Phil. 61 H5
Kabat, Indonesia 63 J17
Kabba, Nigeria 83 D6
Kabetogama, U.S.A. 112 A8
Kabi, Niger 83 C7
Kabin Buri, Thailand 64 F3
Kabinakagami L., Canada 104 C3
Kabinda, Dem. Rep. of the Congo 84 F4
Kabna, Sudan 80 D3
Kabompo, Zambia 87 E1
Kabompo →, Zambia 85 G4
Kabondo, Dem. Rep. of the Congo 87 D2
Kabongo, Dem. Rep. of the Congo 86 D2
Kabot, Guinea 82 C2
Kabou, Togo 83 D5
Kabr, Sudan 81 E2
Kabrousse, Senegal 82 C1
Kabūd Gonbad, Iran 71 B8
Kabugao, Phil. 61 B4
Kābul, Afghan. 68 B3
Kābul □, Afghan. 66 B6
Kābul →, Pakistan 68 C5
Kabunga, Dem. Rep. of the Congo 86 C2
Kaburuang, Indonesia 63 D7
Kabushiya, Sudan 81 D3
Kabwe, Zambia 87 E2
Kačanik, Serbia & M. 44 D5
Kačergine, Lithuania 30 D10
Kachchh, Gulf of, India 68 H3
Kachchh, Rann of, India 68 H4
Kachchhidhana, India 69 J8
Kachebera, Zambia 87 E3
Kachia, Nigeria 83 D6
Kachikau, Botswana 88 B3
Kachin □, Burma 58 D1
Kachira, L., Uganda 86 C3
Kachiry, Kazakhstan 52 D8
Kachisi, Ethiopia 81 F4
Kachnara, India 68 H6
Kachot, Cambodia 65 G4
Kaçkar, Turkey 73 B9
Kadan, Czech Rep. 26 A6
Kadan Kyun, Burma 64 F2
Kadanai →, Afghan. 68 D1
Kadarkút, Hungary 28 D2
Kadavu, Fiji 91 D8
Kade, Ghana 83 D4
Kadhimain = Al Kāzimīyah, Iraq 70 C5
Kadi, India 68 H5
Kadina, Australia 95 E2
Kadınhanı, Turkey 72 C5
Kadiolo, Mali 82 C3
Kadipur, India 69 F10
Kadirli, Turkey 70 B3
Kadiyevka = Stakhanov, Ukraine 33 H10
Kadodo, Sudan 81 E2
Kadoka, U.S.A. 112 D4
Kadom, Russia 34 C6
Kadoma, Zimbabwe 87 F2
Kâdugli, Sudan 81 E2
Kaduna, Nigeria 83 C6
Kaduna □, Nigeria 83 C6
Kaduy, Russia 32 C9
Kaédi, Mauritania 82 B2
Kaélé, Cameroon 83 C7
Kaeng Khoï, Thailand 64 E3
Kaeng Kra Chan △, Thailand 64 F2
Kaeng Tana △, Thailand 64 E5
Kaesŏng, N. Korea 57 F14
Kāf, Si. Arabia 70 D3
Kafan = Kapan, Armenia 70 B5
Kafanchan, Nigeria 83 D6
Kafareti, Nigeria 83 C7
Kaffrine, Senegal 82 C1
Kafin, Nigeria 83 D6
Kafin Madaki, Nigeria 83 C6
Kafinda, Zambia 87 E3
Kafirévs, Ákra, Greece 46 C6
Kafr el Battikh, Egypt 80 H7
Kafr el Dauwâr, Egypt 80 H7
Kafr el Sheikh, Egypt 80 H7
Kafue, Zambia 87 F2
Kafue △, Zambia 87 F2
Kafue →, Zambia 85 H5
Kafue Flats, Zambia 87 F2
Kafulwe, Zambia 87 D2
Kaga, Afghan. 68 B4
Kaga Bandoro, C.A.R. 84 C3
Kagan, Uzbekistan 52 F7
Kagarko, Nigeria 83 D6
Kagawa □, Japan 55 G7
Kagera □, Tanzania 86 C3
Kagera →, Uganda 86 C3
Kağızman, Turkey 70 B4
Kagmar, Sudan 81 E3
Kagoshima, Japan 55 J5
Kagoshima □, Japan 55 J5
Kagul = Cahul, Moldova 29 E13
Kahak, Iran 71 B6
Kahama, Tanzania 86 C3
Kahan, Pakistan 68 E3
Kahang, Malaysia 65 L4
Kahayan →, Indonesia 62 E4
Kahe, Tanzania 86 C4
Kahnūj, Iran 71 E8
Kahoka, U.S.A. 112 E9
Kahoolawe, U.S.A. 106 H16
Kahramanmaraş, Turkey 70 B3
Kâhta, Turkey 73 D8
Kahul, Ozero, Ukraine 29 E13
Kahurangi △, N.Z. 91 J4
Kahuta, Pakistan 68 C5
Kahuzi-Biega △, Dem. Rep. of the Congo 86 C2
Kai, Kepulauan, Indonesia 63 F8
Kai Besar, Indonesia 63 F8
Kai Is. = Kai, Kepulauan, Indonesia 63 F8
Kai Kecil, Indonesia 63 F8
Kai Xian, China 58 B7
Kaiama, Nigeria 83 D5
Kaiapoi, N.Z. 91 K4
Kaieteur Falls, Guyana 124 B7
Kaifeng, China 56 G8
Kaihua, China 59 C12
Kaijiang, China 58 B6
Kaikohe, N.Z. 91 F4
Kaikoura, N.Z. 91 K4
Kailahun, S. Leone 82 D2
Kailash = Kangrinboqe Feng, China 69 D9
Kaili, China 58 D6
Kailu, China 57 C11

Kailua Kona, *U.S.A.* 106 J17
Kaimana, *Indonesia* 63 E8
Kaimanawa Mts., *N.Z.* 91 H5
Kaimganj, *India* 69 F8
Kaimur Hills, *India* 69 G10
Kainab →, *Namibia* 88 D2
Kainji Dam, *Nigeria* 83 D5
Kainji Lake △, *Nigeria* 83 C5
Kainji Res., *Nigeria* 83 C5
Kainuu, *Finland* 8 D23
Kaipara Harbour, *N.Z.* 91 G5
Kaiping, *China* 59 F9
Kaipokok B., *Canada* 105 B8
Kaira, *India* 68 H5
Kairana, *India* 68 E7
Kaironi, *Indonesia* 63 E8
Kairouan, *Tunisia* 79 A8
Kaiserslautern, *Germany* 25 F3
Kaiserstuhl, *Germany* 25 G3
Kaitaia, *N.Z.* 91 F4
Kaitangata, *N.Z.* 91 M2
Kaithal, *India* 68 E7
Kaitu →, *Pakistan* 68 C4
Kaiyang, *China* 58 D6
Kaiyuan, *Liaoning, China* 57 C13
Kaiyuan, *Yunnan, China* 58 F4
Kajaani, *Finland* 8 D22
Kajabbi, *Australia* 94 C3
Kajana = Kajaani, *Finland* 8 D22
Kajang, *Malaysia* 65 L3
Kajaran, *Armenia* 73 C12
Kajiado, *Kenya* 86 C4
Kajo Kaji, *Sudan* 81 G3
Kajuru, *Nigeria* 83 C6
Kaka, *Sudan* 81 E3
Kakabeka Falls, *Canada* 104 C2
Kakadu △, *Australia* 92 B5
Kakamas, *S. Africa* 88 D3
Kakamega, *Kenya* 86 B3
Kakanj, *Bos.-H.* 28 F3
Kakanui Mts., *N.Z.* 91 L3
Kakata, *Liberia* 82 D2
Kakdwip, *India* 69 J13
Kake, *Japan* 55 G6
Kake, *U.S.A.* 102 B2
Kakegawa, *Japan* 55 G9
Kakeroma-Jima, *Japan* 55 K4
Kakhib, *Russia* 35 J8
Kakhovka, *Ukraine* 33 J7
Kakhovske Vdskh., *Ukraine* 33 J7
Kakinada, *India* 67 L13
Kakisa →, *Canada* 102 A5
Kakisa L., *Canada* 102 A5
Kakogawa, *Japan* 55 G7
Kakum △, *Ghana* 83 D4
Kakwa →, *Canada* 102 C5
Kāl Güsheh, *Iran* 71 D8
Kal Safīd, *Iran* 70 C5
Kala, *Nigeria* 83 C7
Kalaallit Nunaat = Greenland ⊠, *N. Amer.* 4 C5
Kalabagh, *Pakistan* 68 C4
Kalabahi, *Indonesia* 63 F6
Kalabáka, *Greece* 46 B3
Kalabana, *Mali* 82 C3
Kalach, *Russia* 34 E5
Kalach na Donu, *Russia* 35 F6
Kaladan →, *Burma* 67 J18
Kaladar, *Canada* 116 B7
Kalahari, *Africa* 88 C3
Kalahari Gemsbok △, *S. Africa* 88 D3
Kalajoki, *Finland* 8 D20
Kalakamati, *Botswana* 89 C4
Kalakan, *Russia* 53 D12
K'alak'unlun Shank'ou = Karakoram Pass, *Asia* 69 B7
Kalam, *Pakistan* 69 B5
Kalama, *Dem. Rep. of the Congo* 86 C2
Kalama, *U.S.A.* 110 E4
Kalámai, *Greece* 46 D4
Kalamariá, *Greece* 44 F6
Kalamazoo, *U.S.A.* 114 D3
Kalamazoo →, *U.S.A.* 114 D2
Kalambo Falls, *Tanzania* 87 D3
Kálamos, *Greece* 46 C5
Kálamos Nisís, *Greece* 46 C2
Kalan, *Turkey* 70 B3
Kalankalan, *Guinea* 82 C3
Kalannie, *Australia* 93 F2
Kalāntarī, *Iran* 71 C7
Kalao, *Indonesia* 63 F6
Kalaotoa, *Indonesia* 63 F6
Kälarne, *Sweden* 10 B10
Kalasin, *Thailand* 64 D4
Kālat, *Iran* 71 E8
Kalat, *Pakistan* 66 E5
Kalāteh, *Iran* 71 B7
Kalāteh-ye Ganj, *Iran* 71 E8
Kálathos, *Greece* 47 E10
Kalaus →, *Russia* 35 H7
Kalávrita, *Greece* 46 C4
Kalbarri, *Australia* 93 E1
Kalbarri △, *Australia* 93 E1
Kale, *Antalya, Turkey* 47 E12
Kale, *Denizli, Turkey* 47 D10
Kalecik, *Turkey* 72 B5
Kalegauk Kyun, *Burma* 67 M20
Kalehe, *Dem. Rep. of the Congo* 86 C2
Kalema, *Tanzania* 86 C3
Kalemie, *Dem. Rep. of the Congo* 86 D2
Kalety, *Poland* 31 H5
Kalewa, *Burma* 67 H19
Kaleybar, *Iran* 70 B5
Kalgoorlie-Boulder, *Australia* 93 F3
Kali →, *India* 69 F8
Kali Sindh →, *India* 68 G6
Kaliakra, Nos, *Bulgaria* 45 C12
Kalianda, *Indonesia* 62 F3
Kalibo, *Phil.* 61 F5
Kalima, *Dem. Rep. of the Congo* 86 C2
Kalimantan, *Indonesia* 62 E4
Kalimantan Barat □, *Indonesia* 62 E4
Kalimantan Selatan □, *Indonesia* 62 E5
Kalimantan Tengah □, *Indonesia* 62 E4
Kalimantan Timur □, *Indonesia* 62 D5
Kálimnos, *Greece* 47 D8
Kalimpong, *India* 69 F13
Kaliningrad, *Russia* 9 J19
Kaliningrad ✕ (KGD), *Russia* 30 D7
Kalininsk, *Russia* 34 E7
Kalinkavichy, *Belarus* 33 F5
Kalinkovichi = Kalinkavichy, *Belarus* 33 F5
Kalinovik, *Bos.-H.* 44 C2
Kalipetrovo, *Bulgaria* 45 B11
Kaliro, *Uganda* 86 B3
Kalirrákhi, *Greece* 45 F8
Kalispell, *U.S.A.* 108 B6
Kalisz, *Poland* 31 G5
Kalisz Pomorski, *Poland* 31 E2
Kaliua, *Tanzania* 86 D3
Kalívia Thorikoú, *Greece* 46 D5
Kalix = Kalixälven →, *Sweden* 8 D20
Kalix, *Sweden* 8 D20
Kalixälven →, *Sweden* 8 D20
Kalka, *India* 68 D7
Kalkan, *Turkey* 47 E11
Kalkarindji, *Australia* 92 C5
Kalkaska, *U.S.A.* 114 C3
Kalkfeld, *Namibia* 88 C2
Kalkfontein, *Botswana* 88 C3
Kalkım, *Turkey* 47 B9
Kalkrand, *Namibia* 88 C2
Kållandsö, *Sweden* 11 F7
Kallavesi, *Finland* 8 E22
Källby, *Sweden* 11 F7
Kållered, *Sweden* 11 G6
Kallimasiá, *Greece* 47 C8
Kallinge, *Sweden* 11 H9
Kallithéa, *Greece* 46 D5
Kallmet, *Albania* 44 E3
Kalloní, *Greece* 47 B8
Kallonís, Kólpos, *Greece* 47 B8
Kallsjön, *Sweden* 8 E15
Kalmalo, *Nigeria* 83 C6
Kalmar, *Sweden* 11 H10
Kalmar län □, *Sweden* 11 G10
Kalmar sund, *Sweden* 11 H10
Kalmyk Republic = Kalmykia □, *Russia* 35 G8
Kalmykia □, *Russia* 35 G8
Kalmykovo, *Kazakhstan* 52 E6
Kalna, *India* 69 H13
Kalnai, *India* 69 H10
Kalocsa, *Hungary* 28 D4
Kalofer, *Bulgaria* 45 D8
Kalokhorio, *Cyprus* 49 E12
Kaloko, *Dem. Rep. of the Congo* 86 D2
Kalol, *Gujarat, India* 68 H5
Kalol, *Gujarat, India* 68 H5
Kalolímnos, *Greece* 47 D9
Kalomo, *Zambia* 87 F2
Kalonerón, *Greece* 46 D3
Kalpi, *India* 69 F8
Kaltern = Caldaro, *Italy* 41 B8
Kaltungo, *Nigeria* 83 D7
Kalu, *Pakistan* 68 G2
Kaluga, *Russia* 32 E9
Kalulushi, *Zambia* 87 E2
Kalundborg, *Denmark* 11 J5
Kalush, *Ukraine* 33 H3
Kałuszyn, *Poland* 31 F8
Kalutara, *Sri Lanka* 66 R12
Kalvarija, *Lithuania* 30 D10
Kalyan, *India* 66 K8
Kalyazin, *Russia* 32 D9
Kam, *Albania* 44 D4
Kam →, *Nigeria* 83 D7
Kama, *Dem. Rep. of the Congo* 86 C2
Kama →, *Russia* 6 D16
Kamachumu, *Tanzania* 86 C3
Kamaishi, *Japan* 54 E10
Kamalia, *Pakistan* 68 D5
Kaman, *India* 68 F6
Kaman, *Turkey* 72 C5
Kamanjab, *Namibia* 88 B2
Kamapanda, *Zambia* 87 E1
Kamarān, *Yemen* 75 D3
Kamativi, *Zimbabwe* 88 B4
Kamba, *Nigeria* 83 C5
Kambalda, *Australia* 93 F3
Kambar, *Pakistan* 68 F3
Kambia, *S. Leone* 82 D2
Kambolé, *Togo* 83 D5
Kambolé, *Zambia* 87 D3
Kambos, *Cyprus* 49 D11
Kambove, *Dem. Rep. of the Congo* 87 E2
Kamchatka, Poluostrov, *Russia* 53 D16
Kamchatka Pen. = Kamchatka, Poluostrov, *Russia* 53 D16
Kamchiya →, *Bulgaria* 45 C11
Kame Ruins, *Zimbabwe* 87 G2
Kamen, *Russia* 52 D9
Kamen-Rybolov, *Russia* 54 B6
Kamenica, *Serbia & M.* 44 C6
Kamenica, *Serbia & M.* 44 B3
Kamenice nad Lipou, *Czech Rep.* 26 B8
Kamenjak, Rt, *Croatia* 41 D10
Kamenka = Kaminka, *Ukraine* 33 H7
Kamenka, *Kazakhstan* 34 E10
Kamenka, *Penza, Russia* 34 D6
Kamenka, *Voronezh, Russia* 33 G10
Kamenka Bugskaya = Kamyanka-Buzka, *Ukraine* 33 G3
Kamenka Dneprovskaya = Kamyanka-Dniprovska, *Ukraine* 33 J8
Kamennomostskiy, *Russia* 35 H5
Kameno, *Bulgaria* 45 D11
Kamenolomini, *Russia* 35 G5
Kamensk-Shakhtinskiy, *Russia* 35 F5
Kamensk Uralskiy, *Russia* 52 D7
Kamenskiy, *Russia* 34 E7
Kamenskoye, *Russia* 53 C17
Kamenyak, *Bulgaria* 45 C10
Kamenz, *Germany* 24 D10
Kameoka, *Japan* 55 G7
Kamiah, *U.S.A.* 108 C5
Kamień Krajeński, *Poland* 30 E4
Kamień Pomorski, *Poland* 30 E1
Kamienna →, *Poland* 31 G8
Kamienna Góra, *Poland* 31 H3
Kamieńsk, *Poland* 31 G6
Kamieskroon, *S. Africa* 88 E2
Kamilukuak L., *Canada* 103 A8
Kamin-Kashyrskyy, *Ukraine* 33 G3
Kamina, *Dem. Rep. of the Congo* 87 D2
Kaminak L., *Canada* 103 A10
Kaministiquia, *Canada* 104 C1
Kaminka, *Ukraine* 33 H7
Kaminoyama, *Japan* 54 E10
Kamiros, *Greece* 49 C9
Kamituga, *Dem. Rep. of the Congo* 86 C2
Kamla →, *India* 69 G12
Kamloops, *Canada* 102 C4
Kamnik, *Slovenia* 41 B11
Kamo, *Armenia* 35 K7
Kamo, *Japan* 54 F9
Kamoke, *Pakistan* 68 C6
Kamp →, *Austria* 26 C8
Kampala, *Uganda* 86 B3
Kampar, *Malaysia* 65 K3
Kampar →, *Indonesia* 62 D2
Kampen, *Neths.* 17 B5
Kampene, *Dem. Rep. of the Congo* 84 E5
Kamphaeng Phet, *Thailand* 64 D2
Kampinoski △, *Poland* 31 F7
Kampolombo, L., *Zambia* 87 E2
Kampong Chhnang, *Cambodia* 65 F5
Kampong Pengerang, *Malaysia* 65 d
Kampong Punggai, *Malaysia* 65 d
Kampong Saom, *Cambodia* 65 G4
Kampong Saom, Chaak, *Cambodia* 65 G4
Kampong Tanjong Langsat, *Malaysia* 65 d
Kampong Telok Ramunia, *Malaysia* 65 d
Kampong To, *Thailand* 65 J3
Kampot, *Cambodia* 65 G5
Kampti, *Burkina Faso* 82 C4
Kampuchea = Cambodia ■, *Asia* 64 F5
Kampung Air Putih, *Malaysia* 65 K4
Kampung Jerangau, *Malaysia* 65 K4
Kampung Raja, *Malaysia* 65 K4
Kampungbaru = Tolitoli, *Indonesia* 63 D6
Kamrau, Teluk, *Indonesia* 63 E8
Kamsack, *Canada* 103 C8
Kamsai, *Guinea* 82 C2
Kamskoye Ustye, *Russia* 34 C9
Kamuchawie L., *Canada* 103 B8
Kamui-Misaki, *Japan* 54 C10
Kamyanets-Podilskyy, *Ukraine* 29 B11
Kamyanka-Buzka, *Ukraine* 33 G3
Kamyanka-Dniprovska, *Ukraine* 33 J8
Kamyanyets, *Belarus* 31 F10
Kamyanyuki, *Belarus* 31 F10
Kāmyārān, *Iran* 70 C5
Kamyshin, *Russia* 34 E7
Kamyzyak, *Russia* 35 G9
Kan, *Sudan* 81 F3
Kanaaupscow, *Canada* 101 C12
Kanaaupscow →, *Canada* 104 B4
Kanab, *U.S.A.* 109 H7
Kanab →, *U.S.A.* 109 H7
Kanagi, *Japan* 54 D10
Kanairiktok →, *Canada* 105 A7
Kanália, *Greece* 46 B4
Kananga, *Dem. Rep. of the Congo* 84 F4
Kanash, *Russia* 34 C8
Kanaskat, *U.S.A.* 110 C5
Kanastraíon, Ákra = Paliouríon, Ákra, *Greece* 44 G7
Kanawha →, *U.S.A.* 114 F4
Kanazawa, *Japan* 55 F8
Kanchanaburi, *Thailand* 64 E2
Kanchenjunga, *Nepal* 69 F13
Kanchipuram, *India* 66 N11
Kańczuga, *Poland* 31 J9
Kandaghat, *India* 68 D7
Kandahar = Qandahār, *Afghan.* 66 D4
Kandalaksha, *Russia* 52 C4
Kandangan, *Indonesia* 62 E5
Kandanghaur, *Indonesia* 63 G13
Kandanos, *Greece* 49 D5
Kandava, *Latvia* 30 A9
Kandavu = Kadavu, *Fiji* 91 D8
Kandhíla, *Greece* 46 D4
Kandhkot, *Pakistan* 68 E3
Kandhla, *India* 68 E7
Kandi, *Benin* 83 C5
Kandi, *India* 69 H13
Kandiaro, *Pakistan* 68 F3
Kandıra, *Turkey* 72 B4
Kandla, *India* 68 H4
Kandos, *Australia* 95 E4
Kandreho, *Madag.* 89 B8
Kandy, *Sri Lanka* 66 R12
Kane, *U.S.A.* 116 E6
Kane Basin, *Greenland* 98 B12
Kanel, *Senegal* 82 B2
Kaneohe, *U.S.A.* 106 H16
Kanevskaya, *Russia* 35 G4
Kanfanar, *Croatia* 41 C10
Kang, *Botswana* 88 C3
Kang Krung △, *Thailand* 65 H2
Kangaba, *Mali* 82 C3
Kangal, *Turkey* 72 C7
Kangān, *Fārs, Iran* 71 E7
Kangān, *Hormozgān, Iran* 71 E8
Kangar, *Malaysia* 65 J3
Kangaré, *Mali* 82 C3
Kangaroo I., *Australia* 95 F2
Kangaroo Mts., *Australia* 94 C3
Kangasala, *Finland* 9 F21
Kangāvar, *Iran* 71 C6
Kangding, *China* 58 B3
Kangdong, *N. Korea* 57 E14
Kangean, Kepulauan, *Indonesia* 62 F5
Kangean Is. = Kangean, Kepulauan, *Indonesia* 62 F5
Kangen →, *Sudan* 81 F3
Kanggye, *N. Korea* 57 D14
Kanggyŏng, *S. Korea* 57 F14
Kanghwa, *S. Korea* 57 F14
Kangikajik, *Greenland* 4 B6
Kangiqliniq = Rankin Inlet, *Canada* 100 B10
Kangiqsualujjuaq, *Canada* 101 C13
Kangiqsujuaq, *Canada* 101 B12
Kangiqtugaapik = Clyde River, *Canada* 101 A13
Kangirsuk, *Canada* 101 B13
Kangkar Chemaran, *Malaysia* 65 d
Kangkar Sungai Tiram, *Malaysia* 65 d
Kangkar Teberau, *Malaysia* 65 d
Kangnŭng, *S. Korea* 57 F15
Kangping, *China* 57 C12
Kangra, *India* 68 C7
Kangrinboqe Feng, *China* 69 D9
Kangto, *India* 67 F18
Kanhar →, *India* 69 G10
Kani, *Ivory C.* 82 D3
Kaniama, *Dem. Rep. of the Congo* 86 D1
Kaniapiskau = Caniapiscau →, *Canada* 105 A6
Kaniapiskau, L. = Caniapiscau, L. de, *Canada* 105 B6
Kanin, Poluostrov, *Russia* 52 C5
Kanin Nos, Mys, *Russia* 52 C5
Kanin Pen. = Kanin, Poluostrov, *Russia* 52 C5
Kaninë, *Albania* 44 F3
Kaniva, *Australia* 95 F3
Kanjiža, *Serbia & M.* 28 D5
Kanjut Sar, *Pakistan* 69 A6
Kankaanpää, *Finland* 9 F20
Kankakee, *U.S.A.* 114 E2
Kankakee →, *U.S.A.* 114 E1
Kankan, *Guinea* 82 C3
Kankendy = Xankändi, *Azerbaijan* 70 B5
Kanker, *India* 67 J12
Kankossa, *Mauritania* 82 B2
Kankroli, *India* 68 G5
Kannapolis, *U.S.A.* 115 H5
Kannauj, *India* 69 F8
Kannod, *India* 66 H10
Kano, *Nigeria* 83 C6
Kano □, *Nigeria* 83 C6
Kan'onji, *Japan* 55 G6
Kanoroba, *Ivory C.* 82 D3
Kanowit, *Malaysia* 62 D4
Kanoya, *Japan* 55 J5
Kanpetlet, *Burma* 67 J18
Kanpur, *India* 69 F9
Kansas □, *U.S.A.* 112 F6
Kansas →, *U.S.A.* 112 F7
Kansas City, *Kans., U.S.A.* 112 F7
Kansas City, *Mo., U.S.A.* 112 F7
Kansenia, *Dem. Rep. of the Congo* 87 E2
Kansk, *Russia* 53 D10
Kansŏng, *S. Korea* 57 E15
Kansu = Gansu □, *China* 56 G3
Kantaphor, *India* 68 H7
Kantchari, *Burkina Faso* 83 C5
Kantché, *Niger* 83 C6
Kanté, *Togo* 83 D5
Kantemirovka, *Russia* 33 H10
Kantharalak, *Thailand* 64 E5
Kantli →, *India* 68 E6
Kantō □, *Japan* 55 F9
Kantō-Sanchi, *Japan* 55 G9
Kanturk, *Ireland* 12 D3
Kanuma, *Japan* 55 F9
Kanus, *Namibia* 88 D2
Kanye, *Botswana* 88 C4
Kanzenze, *Dem. Rep. of the Congo* 87 E2
Kanzi, Ras, *Tanzania* 86 D4
Kao Phara, *Thailand* 65 a
Kaohsiung, *Taiwan* 59 F13
Kaokoveld, *Namibia* 88 B1
Kaolack, *Senegal* 82 C1
Kaoshan, *China* 57 B13
Kapaa, *U.S.A.* 106 G15
Kapadvanj, *India* 68 H5
Kapaklı, *Turkey* 45 E11
Kapan, *Armenia* 70 B5
Kapanga, *Dem. Rep. of the Congo* 84 F4
Kapchagai = Qapshaghay, *Kazakhstan* 52 E8
Kapela = Velika Kapela, *Croatia* 41 C12
Kapéllo, Ákra, *Greece* 46 E5
Kapema, *Dem. Rep. of the Congo* 87 E2
Kapfenberg, *Austria* 26 D8
Kapı Dağı, *Turkey* 45 F11
Kapiri Mposhi, *Zambia* 87 E2
Kāpīsā □, *Afghan.* 66 B6
Kapiskau →, *Canada* 104 B3
Kapit, *Malaysia* 62 D4
Kapiti I., *N.Z.* 91 J5
Kaplan, *U.S.A.* 113 K8
Kaplice, *Czech Rep.* 26 C7
Kapoe, *Thailand* 65 H2
Kapoeta, *Sudan* 81 G3
Kápolnásnyék, *Hungary* 28 C3
Kapos →, *Hungary* 28 D3
Kaposvár, *Hungary* 28 D2
Kapowsin, *U.S.A.* 110 D4
Kappeln, *Germany* 24 A5
Kappelshamn, *Sweden* 11 G12
Kapps, *Namibia* 88 C2
Kaprije, *Croatia* 41 E12
Kapsan, *N. Korea* 57 D15
Kapsukas = Marijampolė, *Lithuania* 9 J20
Kaptai L., *Bangla.* 67 H18
Kapuas →, *Indonesia* 62 E3
Kapuas Hulu, Pegunungan, *Malaysia* 62 D4
Kapuas Hulu Ra. = Kapuas Hulu, Pegunungan, *Malaysia* 62 D4
Kapulo, *Dem. Rep. of the Congo* 87 D2
Kapunda, *Australia* 95 E2
Kapuni, *N.Z.* 91 H5
Kapurthala, *India* 68 D6
Kapuskasing, *Canada* 104 C3
Kapuskasing →, *Canada* 104 C3
Kapustin Yar, *Russia* 35 F7
Kaputar, *Australia* 95 E5
Kaputir, *Kenya* 86 B4
Kapuvár, *Hungary* 28 C2
Kara, *Russia* 52 C7
Karā, W. →, *Si. Arabia* 80 C5
Kara Ada, *Turkey* 47 E9
Kara Bogaz Gol, Zaliv = Garabogazköl Aylagy, *Turkmenistan* 52 E6
Kara Burun, *Turkey* 47 E9
Kara Kalpak Republic = Qoraqalpoghistan □, *Uzbekistan* 52 E6
Kara Kum, *Turkmenistan* 52 F6
Kara Sea, *Russia* 52 B7
Karaadilli, *Turkey* 47 C12
Karabiğa, *Turkey* 45 F11
Karabük, *Turkey* 72 B5
Karaburun, *Albania* 44 F3
Karaburun, *Turkey* 47 C8
Karabutak = Qarabutaq, *Kazakhstan* 52 E7
Karacabey, *Turkey* 45 F12
Karacakılavuz, *Turkey* 45 E11
Karacaköy, *Turkey* 45 E12
Karacasu, *Turkey* 47 D10
Karachala = Qaraçala, *Azerbaijan* 35 L9
Karachayevsk, *Russia* 35 J5
Karachev, *Russia* 33 F8
Karachey-Cherkessia □, *Russia* 35 J5
Karachi, *Pakistan* 68 G2
Karad, *India* 66 L9
Karadirek, *Turkey* 47 C12
Karaga, *Ghana* 83 D4
Karaganda = Qaraghandy, *Kazakhstan* 52 E8
Karagayly = Qaraghayly, *Kazakhstan* 52 E8
Karaginskiy, Ostrov, *Russia* 53 D17
Karagola Road, *India* 69 G12
Karagüney Dağları, *Turkey* 72 B6
Karahallı, *Turkey* 47 C11
Karaikal, *India* 66 P11
Karaikkudi, *India* 66 P11
Karaisali, *Turkey* 72 D6
Karaj, *Iran* 71 C6
Karak, *Malaysia* 65 L4
Karakalpakstan = Qoraqalpoghistan □, *Uzbekistan* 52 E6
Karakelong, *Indonesia* 63 D7
Karakitang, *Indonesia* 63 D7
Karakoçan, *Turkey* 73 C9
Karakol, *Kyrgyzstan* 52 E8
Karakoram Pass, *Asia* 69 B7
Karakoram Ra., *Pakistan* 69 B7
Karakurt, *Turkey* 73 B10
Karakuwisa, *Namibia* 88 B2
Karalon, *Russia* 53 D12
Karama, *Jordan* 74 D4
Karaman, *Balıkesir, Turkey* 47 B9
Karaman, *Konya, Turkey* 70 B2
Karamanlı, *Turkey* 47 D11
Karamay, *China* 60 B3
Karambu, *Indonesia* 62 E5
Karamea Bight, *N.Z.* 91 J3
Karamnasa →, *India* 69 G10
Karamürsel, *Turkey* 45 F13
Karand, *Iran* 70 C5
Karangana, *Mali* 82 C3
Karanganyar, *Indonesia* 63 G13
Karangasem, *Indonesia* 63 J18
Karanjia, *India* 69 J11
Karankasso, *Burkina Faso* 82 C4
Karaova, *Turkey* 47 D9
Karapınar, *Turkey* 72 D5
Karasburg, *Namibia* 88 D2
Karasino, *Russia* 52 C9
Karasjok, *Norway* 8 B21
Karasu, *Turkey* 72 B4
Karasu →, *Turkey* 47 E12
Karasuk, *Russia* 52 D8
Karasuyama, *Japan* 55 F10
Karataş, *Adana, Turkey* 72 D6
Karataş, *Manisa, Turkey* 47 C10
Karataş Burnu, *Turkey* 72 D6
Karatau, Khrebet = Qarataū, *Kazakhstan* 52 E7
Karatoprak, *Turkey* 47 D9
Karatsu, *Japan* 55 H5
Karaul, *Russia* 52 B9
Karauli, *India* 68 F7
Karavastasë, L. e, *Albania* 44 F3
Karávi, *Greece* 46 E5
Karavostasi, *Cyprus* 49 D11
Karawang, *Indonesia* 63 G12
Karawanken, *Europe* 26 E7
Karayazı, *Turkey* 73 C10
Karazhal, *Kazakhstan* 52 E8
Karbalā', *Iraq* 70 C5
Kårböle, *Sweden* 10 C9
Karcag, *Hungary* 28 C5
Karcha →, *Pakistan* 69 B7
Karchana, *India* 69 G9
Karczew, *Poland* 31 F8
Kardam, *Bulgaria* 45 C12

Kardeljovo = Ploče, Croatia 41 E14
Kardhámila, Greece 47 C8
Kardhamíli, Greece 46 E4
Kardhítsa, Greece 46 B3
Kardhítsa □, Greece 46 B3
Kärdla, Estonia 9 G20
Kareeberge, S. Africa 88 E3
Kareha →, India 69 G12
Kareima, Sudan 80 D3
Karelia □, Russia 52 C4
Karelian Republic = Karelia □, Russia 52 C4
Karera, India 68 G8
Kārevāndar, Iran 71 E9
Kargasok, Russia 52 D9
Kargat, Russia 52 D9
Kargı, Turkey 72 B6
Kargil, India 69 B7
Kargopol, Russia 32 B10
Kargowa, Poland 31 F2
Karguéri, Niger 83 C7
Karhal, India 69 F8
Kariá, Greece 46 C2
Kariaí, Greece 45 F8
Karīān, Iran 71 E8
Karianga, Madag. 89 C8
Kariba, Zimbabwe 87 F2
Kariba, L., Zimbabwe 87 F2
Kariba Dam, Zimbabwe 87 F2
Kariba Gorge, Zambia 87 F2
Karibib, Namibia 88 C2
Karijini △, Australia 92 D2
Karimata, Kepulauan, Indonesia 62 E3
Karimata, Selat, Indonesia 62 E3
Karimata Is. = Karimata, Kepulauan, Indonesia 62 E3
Karimnagar, India 66 K11
Karimun Kecil, Pulau, Indonesia 65 d
Karimunjawa, Kepulauan, Indonesia 62 F4
Karin, Somali Rep. 75 E4
Káristos, Greece 46 C6
Karīt, Iran 71 C8
Kariya, Japan 55 G8
Kariyangwe, Zimbabwe 89 B4
Karjala, Finland 32 A5
Karkaralinsk = Qarqaraly, Kazakhstan 52 E8
Karkheh →, Iran 70 D5
Karkinitska Zatoka, Ukraine 33 K7
Karkinitskiy Zaliv = Karkinitska Zatoka, Ukraine 33 K7
Karkuk = Kirkūk, Iraq 70 C5
Karkur Tohl, Egypt 80 C2
Karl Liebknecht, Russia 33 G8
Karleby = Kokkola, Finland 8 E20
Karlholmsbruk, Sweden 10 D11
Karlino, Poland 30 D2
Karlivka, Ukraine 33 H8
Karlobag, Croatia 41 D12
Karlovac, Croatia 41 C12
Karlovarský □, Czech Rep. 26 A5
Karlovka = Karlivka, Ukraine 33 H8
Karlovo, Bulgaria 45 D8
Karlovy Vary, Czech Rep. 26 A5
Karlsbad = Karlovy Vary, Czech Rep. 26 A5
Karlsborg, Sweden 11 F8
Karlshamn, Sweden 11 H8
Karlskoga, Sweden 10 E8
Karlskrona, Sweden 11 H9
Karlsruhe, Germany 25 F4
Karlstad, Sweden 10 E7
Karlstad, U.S.A. 112 A6
Karlstadt, Germany 25 F5
Karma, Niger 83 C5
Karmėlava, Lithuania 30 D11
Karmi'el, Israel 74 C4
Karnak, Egypt 80 B3
Karnal, India 68 E7
Karnali →, Nepal 69 E9
Karnaphuli Res. = Kaptai L., Bangla. 67 H18
Karnaprayag, India 69 D8
Karnataka □, India 66 N10
Karnes City, U.S.A. 113 L6
Karnische Alpen, Europe 26 E6
Karnobat, Bulgaria 45 D10
Kärnten □, Austria 26 E6
Karo, Mali 82 C4
Karoi, Zimbabwe 87 F2
Karon, Ao, Thailand 65 a
Karonga, Malawi 87 D3
Karoo △, S. Africa 88 E3
Karoonda, Australia 95 F2
Karor, Pakistan 68 D4
Karora, Sudan 80 D4
Káros, Greece 47 E7
Karounga, Mali 82 B3
Karousádhes, Greece 46 B1
Karpacz, Poland 31 H2
Karpasia, Cyprus 49 D13
Kárpathos, Greece 47 F9
Kárpathos, Stenón, Greece 47 F9
Karpatsky △, Ukraine 29 B9
Karpenísion, Greece 46 C3
Karpuz Burnu = Apostolos Andreas, C., Cyprus 49 D13
Karpuzlu, Turkey 47 D9
Karratha, Australia 92 D2
Kars, Turkey 73 B10
Karsakpay, Kazakhstan 52 E7
Karsha, Kazakhstan 34 F10
Karshi = Qarshi, Uzbekistan 52 F7
Karsiyang, India 69 F13
Karsog, India 68 D7
Karst = Kras, Croatia 41 C10
Kartal, Turkey 45 F13
Kartál Óros, Greece 45 E9
Kartaly, Russia 52 D7
Kartapur, India 68 D6
Karthaus, U.S.A. 116 E6
Kartuzy, Poland 30 D5
Karufa, Indonesia 63 E8
Karuma ⌓, Uganda 86 B3
Karumba, Australia 94 B3
Karumo, Tanzania 86 C3
Karumwa, Tanzania 86 C3
Kārūn →, Iran 71 D6
Karungu, Kenya 86 C3
Karup, Denmark 11 H3
Karviná, Czech Rep. 27 B11
Karwan →, India 68 F8
Karwar, India 66 M9
Karwendel ⌓, Austria 26 D4
Karwi, India 69 G9
Kaş, Turkey 47 E11
Kasaba, Turkey 47 E11
Kasache, Malawi 87 E3
Kasai →, Dem. Rep. of the Congo 84 E3
Kasai-Oriental □, Dem. Rep. of the Congo 86 D1
Kasaji, Dem. Rep. of the Congo 87 E1
Kasama, Zambia 87 E3
Kasan-dong, N. Korea 57 D14
Kasane, Namibia 88 B3
Kasanga, Tanzania 87 D3
Kasanka △, Zambia 87 E3
Kasar, Ras, Sudan 80 D4
Kasaragod, India 66 N9
Kasba L., Canada 103 A8
Kāseh Garān, Iran 70 C5
Kasempa, Zambia 87 E2
Kasenga, Dem. Rep. of the Congo 87 E2
Kasese, Uganda 86 B3
Kasewa, Zambia 87 E2
Kasganj, India 69 F8
Kashabowie, Canada 104 C1
Kashaf, Iran 71 C9
Kāshān, Iran 71 C6
Kashechewan, Canada 104 B3
Kashgar = Kashi, China 60 C2
Kashi, China 60 C2
Kashimbo, Dem. Rep. of the Congo 87 E2
Kashin, Russia 32 D9
Kashipur, India 69 E8
Kashira, Russia 32 E10
Kashiwazaki, Japan 55 F9
Kashk-e Kohneh, Afghan. 66 B3
Kashkū'īyeh, Iran 71 D7
Kāshmar, Iran 71 C8
Kashmir, Asia 69 C7
Kashmor, Pakistan 68 E3
Kashpirovka, Russia 34 D9
Kashun Noerh = Gaxun Nur, China 60 B5
Kasiari, India 69 H12
Kasimov, Russia 34 C5
Kasinge, Dem. Rep. of the Congo 86 D2
Kasiruta, Indonesia 63 E7
Kaskaskia →, U.S.A. 112 G10
Kaskattama →, Canada 103 B10
Kaskinen, Finland 9 E19
Kaskö = Kaskinen, Finland 9 E19
Kaslo, Canada 102 D5
Kasmere L., Canada 103 B8
Kasongo, Dem. Rep. of the Congo 86 C2
Kasongo Lunda, Dem. Rep. of the Congo 84 F3
Kásos, Greece 47 F8
Kásos, Stenón, Greece 47 F8
Kaspi, Georgia 35 K7
Kaspichan, Bulgaria 45 C11
Kaspiysk, Russia 35 J8
Kaspiyskiy, Russia 35 H8
Kassab ed Doleib, Sudan 81 E3
Kassaba, Egypt 80 C2
Kassalâ, Sudan 81 D4
Kassalâ □, Sudan 81 D4
Kassándra, Greece 44 F7
Kassándrinon, Greece 44 F7
Kassel, Germany 24 D5
Kassinger, Sudan 80 D3
Kassiópi, Greece 49 A3
Kasson, U.S.A. 112 C8
Kastamonu, Turkey 72 B5
Kastav, Croatia 41 C11
Kastélli, Greece 49 D5
Kastéllion, Greece 49 D7
Kastellórizon = Megiste, Greece 47 E11
Kástellos, Greece 47 E9
Kastellou, Ákra, Greece 47 F9
Kasterlee, Belgium 17 C4
Kastlösa, Sweden 11 H10
Kastóri, Greece 46 D4
Kastoría, Greece 44 F5
Kastoría □, Greece 44 F5
Kastorías, Límni, Greece 44 F5
Kastornoye, Russia 33 G10
Kastós Nisís, Greece 46 C2
Kastrosikiá, Greece 46 B2
Kastrup, København ✕ (CPH), Denmark 11 J6
Kastsyukovichy, Belarus 32 F7
Kasulu, Tanzania 86 C3
Kasumi, Japan 55 G7
Kasumkent, Russia 35 K9
Kasungu, Malawi 87 E3
Kasungu △, Malawi 87 E3
Kasur, Pakistan 68 D6
Kata Tjuta = Olga, Mt., Australia 93 E5
Kataba, Zambia 87 F2
Katagum, Nigeria 83 C7
Katahdin, Mt., U.S.A. 115 C11
Katako Kombe, Dem. Rep. of the Congo 86 C1
Katákolon, Greece 46 D3
Katale, Tanzania 86 C3
Katanda, Katanga, Dem. Rep. of the Congo 86 D1
Katanda, Nord-Kivu, Dem. Rep. of the Congo 86 C2
Katanga □, Dem. Rep. of the Congo 86 D2
Katangi, India 66 J11
Katanning, Australia 93 F2
Katastári, Greece 46 D2
Katavi △, Tanzania 86 D3
Katavi Swamp, Tanzania 86 D3
Kateríni, Greece 44 F6
Katghora, India 69 H10
Katha, Burma 67 G20
Katherîna, Gebel, Egypt 70 D2
Katherine, Australia 92 B5
Katherine Gorge, Australia 92 B5
Kathi, India 68 J6
Kathiawar, India 68 H4
Kathikas, Cyprus 49 E11
Kathmandu = Katmandu, Nepal 69 F11
Kathua, India 68 C6
Kati, Mali 82 C3
Katihar, India 69 G12
Katima Mulilo, Zambia 88 B3
Katimbira, Malawi 87 E3
Katingan = Mendawai →, Indonesia 62 E4
Katiola, Ivory C. 82 D3
Katlabukh, Ozero, Ukraine 29 E14
Katlanovo, Macedonia 44 E5
Katmandu, Nepal 69 F11
Katni, India 69 H9
Káto Akhaïa, Greece 46 C3
Káto Arkhánai, Greece 49 D7
Káto Khorió, Greece 49 D7
Káto Pyrgos, Cyprus 49 D11
Káto Stavros, Greece 44 F7
Katokhí, Greece 46 C3
Katompe, Dem. Rep. of the Congo 86 D2
Katong, Singapore 65 d
Katonga →, Uganda 86 B3
Katoomba, Australia 95 E5
Katoúna, Greece 46 C3
Katowice, Poland 31 H6
Katrancı Dağı, Turkey 47 D12
Katrine, L., U.K. 13 E4
Katrineholm, Sweden 10 E10
Katsepe, Madag. 89 B8
Katsina, Nigeria 83 C6
Katsina □, Nigeria 83 C6
Katsina Ala, Nigeria 83 D6
Katsina Ala →, Nigeria 83 D6
Katsumoto, Japan 55 H4
Katsuura, Japan 55 G10
Katsuyama, Japan 55 F8
Kattaviá, Greece 49 D9
Kattegat, Denmark 11 H5
Katthammarsvik, Sweden 11 G12
Katul, J., Sudan 81 E2
Katumba, Dem. Rep. of the Congo 86 D2
Katwa, India 69 H13
Katwijk, Neths. 17 B4
Kąty Wrocławskie, Poland 31 G3
Kauai, U.S.A. 106 H15
Kauai Channel, U.S.A. 106 H15
Kaub, Germany 25 E3
Kaudom ⌓, Namibia 88 B3
Kaufbeuren, Germany 25 H6
Kaufman, U.S.A. 113 J6
Kauhajoki, Finland 9 E20
Kaukauna, U.S.A. 114 C1
Kaukauveld, Namibia 88 C3
Kaunakakai, U.S.A. 106 H16
Kaunas, Lithuania 9 J20
Kaunas ✕ (KUN), Lithuania 30 D11
Kaunia, Bangla. 69 G13
Kaunos, Turkey 47 E10
Kaura Namoda, Nigeria 83 C6
Kauru, Nigeria 83 C6
Kautokeino, Norway 8 B20
Kauwapur, India 69 F10
Kavacha, Russia 53 C17
Kavadarci, Macedonia 44 E6
Kavajë, Albania 44 E3
Kavak, Turkey 72 B7
Kavak Dağı, Turkey 47 D10
Kavaklı, Turkey 45 E11
Kavaklıdere, Turkey 47 D10
Kavalerovo, Russia 54 B7
Kavali, India 66 M12
Kavála, Greece 45 F8
Kavála □, Greece 45 E8
Kavála Kólpos, Greece 45 F8
Kavār, Iran 71 D7
Kavarna, Bulgaria 45 C12
Kavi, India 68 H5
Kavimba, Botswana 88 B3
Kavīr, Dasht-e, Iran 71 C7
Kavkaz, Russia 33 K9
Kävlinge, Sweden 11 J7
Kavos, Greece 49 B4
Kavoúsi, Greece 47 F7
Kaw, Fr. Guiana 125 C8
Kawa, Sudan 81 E3
Kawagama L., Canada 116 A6
Kawagoe, Japan 55 G9
Kawaguchi, Japan 55 G9
Kawambwa, Zambia 87 D2
Kawanoe, Japan 55 G6
Kawardha, India 69 J9
Kawasaki, Japan 55 G9
Kawasi, Indonesia 63 E7
Kawerau, N.Z. 91 H6
Kawhia, N.Z. 91 H5
Kawhia Harbour, N.Z. 91 H5
Kawio, Kepulauan, Indonesia 63 D7
Kawnro, Burma 67 H21
Kawthaung, Burma 65 H2
Kawthoolei = Kayin □, Burma 67 L20
Kawthule = Kayin □, Burma 67 L20
Kaxholmen, Sweden 11 G8
Kaya, Burkina Faso 83 C4
Kayah □, Burma 67 K20
Kayalıköy Barajı, Turkey 45 E11
Kayan →, Indonesia 62 D5
Kaycee, U.S.A. 108 E10
Kayeli, Indonesia 63 E7
Kayenta, U.S.A. 109 H8
Kayes, Mali 82 C2
Kayı, Turkey 47 B12
Kayima, S. Leone 82 D2
Kayin □, Burma 67 L20
Kaymakçı, Turkey 47 C10
Kayoa, Indonesia 63 D7
Kayomba, Zambia 87 E1
Kaysatskoye, Russia 34 F8
Kayseri, Turkey 70 B2
Kaysville, U.S.A. 108 F8
Kaz Dağı, Turkey 47 B8
Kazachye, Russia 53 B14
Kazakhstan ■, Asia 52 E7
Kazan, Russia 34 C9
Kazan →, Canada 103 A9
Kazan-Rettō, Pac. Oc. 96 E6
Kazanlŭk, Bulgaria 45 D9
Kazanskaya, Russia 34 F5
Kazatin = Kozyatyn, Ukraine 33 H5
Kazaure, Nigeria 83 C6
Kazbek, Russia 35 J7
Kāzerūn, Iran 71 D6
Kazi Magomed = Qazimämmäd, Azerbaijan 35 K9
Kazimierz Dolny, Poland 31 G8
Kazimierza Wielka, Poland 31 H7
Kazincbarcika, Hungary 28 B5
Kazlų Rūda, Lithuania 30 D10
Kaztalovka, Kazakhstan 34 F9
Kazuma Pan △, Zimbabwe 87 F2
Kazuno, Japan 54 D10
Kazym →, Russia 52 C7
Kcynia, Poland 31 F4
Ké-Macina, Mali 82 C3
Kéa, Greece 46 D6
Keady, U.K. 12 B5
Kearney, U.S.A. 112 E5
Kearny, U.S.A. 109 K8
Kearsarge, Mt., U.S.A. 117 C13
Keban, Turkey 73 C8
Keban Barajı, Turkey 70 B3
Kebbi □, Nigeria 83 C5
Kébi, Ivory C. 82 D3
Kebnekaise, Sweden 8 C18
Kebri Dehar, Ethiopia 75 F3
Kebumen, Indonesia 63 G13
Kecel, Hungary 28 D4
Kechika →, Canada 102 B3
Keçiborlu, Turkey 47 D12
Kecskemét, Hungary 28 D4
Kedada, Ethiopia 81 F4
Kėdainiai, Lithuania 9 J21
Kedarnath, India 69 D8
Kedgwick, Canada 105 C6
Kédhros Óros, Greece 49 D6
Kediri, Indonesia 63 G15
Kedjebi, Ghana 83 D5
Kédougou, Senegal 82 C2
Kędzierzyn-Koźle, Poland 31 H5
Keeler, U.S.A. 110 J9
Keeley L., Canada 103 C7
Keeling Is. = Cocos Is., Ind. Oc. 96 J1
Keelung = Chilung, Taiwan 59 E13
Keene, Canada 116 B6
Keene, Calif., U.S.A. 111 K8
Keene, N.H., U.S.A. 117 D12
Keene, N.Y., U.S.A. 117 B11
Keep River △, Australia 92 C4
Keeper Hill, Ireland 12 D3
Keer-Weer, C., Australia 94 A3
Keeseville, U.S.A. 117 B11
Keetmanshoop, Namibia 88 D2
Keewatin, Canada 103 D10
Keewatin →, Canada 103 B8
Kefa, Ethiopia 81 F4
Kefallinía, Greece 46 C2
Kefallinía □, Greece 46 C2
Kéfalos, Greece 47 E8
Kefamenanu, Indonesia 63 F6
Kefar Sava, Israel 74 C3
Keffi, Nigeria 83 D6
Keffin Hausa, Nigeria 83 C6
Keflavík, Iceland 8 D2
Keftya, Ethiopia 81 E4
Keg River, Canada 102 B5
Kegaska, Canada 105 B7
Keheili, Sudan 80 D3
Kehl, Germany 25 G3
Keighley, U.K. 14 D6
Keila, Estonia 9 G21
Keimoes, S. Africa 88 D3
Keita, Niger 83 C6
Keitele, Finland 8 E22
Keith, Australia 95 F3
Keith, U.K. 13 D6
Keizer, U.S.A. 108 D2
Kejimkujik △, Canada 105 D6
Kejserr Franz Joseph Fd., Greenland 4 B6
Kekri, India 68 G6
Kelam, Ethiopia 81 G4
Kelamet, Eritrea 81 D4
Kelan, China 56 E6
Kelang = Klang, Malaysia 65 L3
Kelantan →, Malaysia 65 J4
Këlcyrë, Albania 44 F4
Kelekçi, Turkey 47 D11
Keles, Turkey 45 G13
Keleti-főcsatorna, Hungary 28 C6
Kelheim, Germany 25 G7
Kelkit, Turkey 73 B8
Kelkit →, Turkey 72 B7
Kellerberrin, Australia 93 F2
Kellett, C., Canada 4 B1
Kelleys I., U.S.A. 116 E2
Kellogg, U.S.A. 108 C5
Kells = Ceanannus Mor, Ireland 12 C5
Kelmė, Lithuania 30 C9
Kelmentsi, Ukraine 29 B11
Kelokedhara, Cyprus 49 E11
Kelowna, Canada 102 D5
Kelsey Creek, Australia 94 J6
Kelseyville, U.S.A. 110 G4
Kelso, N.Z. 91 L2
Kelso, U.K. 13 F6
Kelso, U.S.A. 110 D4
Keluang, Malaysia 65 L4
Kelvington, Canada 103 C8
Kem, Russia 52 C4
Kema, Indonesia 63 D7
Kemah, Turkey 70 B3
Kemaliye, Erzincan, Turkey 73 C8
Kemaliye, Manisa, Turkey 47 C10
Kemalpaşa, Turkey 47 C9
Kemaman, Malaysia 62 D2
Kemano, Canada 102 C3
Kemasik, Malaysia 65 K4
Kembolcha, Ethiopia 81 E4
Kemer, Antalya, Turkey 47 E12
Kemer, Burdur, Turkey 47 D12
Kemer, Muğla, Turkey 47 E11
Kemer Barajı, Turkey 47 D10
Kemerovo, Russia 52 D9
Ķemeru △, Latvia 30 B10
Kemi, Finland 8 D21
Kemi älv = Kemijoki →, Finland 8 D21
Kemi träsk = Kemijärvi, Finland 8 C22
Kemijärvi, Finland 8 C22
Kemijoki →, Finland 8 D21
Kemmerer, U.S.A. 108 F8
Kemmuna = Comino, Malta 49 C1
Kemp, L., U.S.A. 113 J5
Kemp Land, Antarctica 5 C5
Kempas, Malaysia 65 d
Kempsey, Australia 95 E5
Kempt, L., Canada 104 C5
Kempten, Germany 25 H6
Kempton, Australia 95 G4
Kemptville, Canada 117 B9
Ken →, India 69 G9
Kenai, U.S.A. 100 B4
Kendai, India 69 H10
Kendal, Indonesia 63 G14
Kendal, U.K. 14 C5
Kendall, Australia 95 E5
Kendall, U.S.A. 115 N5
Kendall →, Australia 94 A3
Kendallville, U.S.A. 114 E3
Kendari, Indonesia 63 E6
Kendawangan, Indonesia 62 E4
Kende, Nigeria 83 C5
Kendi, Pulau, Malaysia 65 c
Kendrapara, India 67 J15
Këndrevicës, Maja e, Albania 44 F3
Kendrew, S. Africa 88 E3
Kene Thao, Laos 64 D3
Kenedy, U.S.A. 113 L6
Kenema, S. Leone 82 D2
Keng Kok, Laos 64 D5
Keng Tawng, Burma 67 J21
Keng Tung, Burma 58 G2
Kengeja, Tanzania 86 D4
Kenhardt, S. Africa 88 D3
Kéniéba, Mali 82 C2
Kenitra, Morocco 78 B4
Kenli, China 57 F10
Kenmare, Ireland 12 E2
Kenmare, U.S.A. 112 A3
Kenmare River, Ireland 12 E2
Kennebago Lake, U.S.A. 117 A14
Kennebec, U.S.A. 112 D5
Kennebec →, U.S.A. 115 D11
Kennebunk, U.S.A. 117 C14
Kennedy, Zimbabwe 88 B4
Kennedy Ra., Australia 93 D2
Kennedy Range △, Australia 93 D2
Kenner, U.S.A. 113 L9
Kennet →, U.K. 15 F7
Kenneth Ra., Australia 93 D2
Kennett, U.S.A. 113 G9
Kennewick, U.S.A. 108 C4
Kenogami →, Canada 104 B3
Kenora, Canada 103 D10
Kenosha, U.S.A. 114 D2
Kensington, Canada 105 C7
Kent, Ohio, U.S.A. 116 E3
Kent, Tex., U.S.A. 113 K2
Kent, Wash., U.S.A. 110 C4
Kent □, U.K. 15 F8
Kent Group, Australia 95 F4
Kent Pen., Canada 100 B9
Kentaū, Kazakhstan 52 E7
Kentland, U.S.A. 114 E2
Kenton, U.S.A. 114 E4
Kentucky □, U.S.A. 114 G3
Kentucky →, U.S.A. 114 F3
Kentucky L., U.S.A. 115 G2
Kentville, Canada 105 C7
Kentwood, U.S.A. 113 K9
Kenya ■, Africa 86 B4
Kenya, Mt., Kenya 86 C4
Keo Neua, Deo, Vietnam 64 C5
Keokuk, U.S.A. 112 E9
Keonjhargarh, India 69 J11
Kep, Cambodia 65 G5
Kep, Vietnam 64 B6
Kepala Batas, Malaysia 65 c
Kepez, Turkey 45 F10
Kepi, Indonesia 63 F9
Kępice, Poland 30 D3
Kępno, Poland 31 G4
Kepsut, Turkey 47 B10
Kerala □, India 66 P10
Kerama-Rettō, Japan 55 L3
Keran, Pakistan 69 B5
Keran △, Togo 83 C5
Kerang, Australia 95 F3
Keranyo, Ethiopia 81 F4
Kerao →, Sudan 81 E3
Keratéa, Greece 46 D5
Keraudren, C., Australia 92 C2

Kerava, Finland 9 F21
Kerch, Ukraine 33 K9
Kerchenskiy Proliv, Black Sea 33 K9
Kerchoual, Mali 83 B5
Kerempe Burnu, Turkey 72 A5
Keren, Eritrea 81 D4
Kerewan, Gambia 82 C1
Kerguelen, Ind. Oc. 3 G13
Keri, Greece 46 D2
Keri Kera, Sudan 81 E3
Kericho, Kenya 86 C4
Kerinci, Indonesia 62 E2
Kerki, Turkmenistan 52 F7
Kerkinítis, Límni, Greece 44 E7
Kérkira, Greece 49 A3
Kérkira □, Greece 46 B1
Kérkira ✕ (CFU), Greece 46 B1
Kerkouane, Tunisia 42 F4
Kerkrade, Neths. 17 D6
Kerma, Sudan 80 D3
Kermadec Is., Pac. Oc. 96 L10
Kermadec Trench, Pac. Oc. 96 L10
Kermān, Iran 71 D8
Kerman, U.S.A. 110 J6
Kermān □, Iran 71 D8
Kermān, Bīābān-e, Iran 71 D8
Kermānshāh = Bākhtarān, Iran 70 C5
Kermen, Bulgaria 45 D10
Kermit, U.S.A. 113 K3
Kern →, U.S.A. 111 K7
Kernhof, Austria 26 D8
Kernow = Cornwall □, U.K. 15 G3
Kernville, U.S.A. 111 K8
Keroh, Malaysia 65 K3
Kérou, Benin 83 C5
Kérouane, Guinea 82 D3
Kerpen, Germany 24 E2
Kerrera, U.K. 13 E3
Kerrobert, Canada 103 C7
Kerrville, U.S.A. 113 K5
Kerry □, Ireland 12 D2
Kerry Hd., Ireland 12 D2
Kersa, Ethiopia 81 F5
Kerulen →, Asia 60 B6
Kervo = Kerava, Finland 9 F21
Kerzaz, Algeria 78 C5
Kesagami →, Canada 104 B4
Kesagami L., Canada 104 B3
Keşan, Turkey 45 F10
Kesennuma, Japan 54 E10
Keshit, Iran 71 D8
Keşiş Dağ, Turkey 73 C8
Keskin, Turkey 72 C5
Kestell, S. Africa 89 D4
Kestenga, Russia 52 C4
Keswick, U.K. 14 C4
Keszthely, Hungary 28 D2
Ket →, Russia 52 D9
Keta, Ghana 83 D5
Keta Lagoon, Ghana 83 D5
Ketapang, Bali, Indonesia 63 J17
Ketapang, Kalimantan, Indonesia 62 E4
Ketchenery, Russia 35 G7
Ketchikan, U.S.A. 102 B2
Ketchum, U.S.A. 108 E6
Kete Krachi, Ghana 83 D4
Ketef, Khalîg Umm el, Egypt 70 F2
Keti Bandar, Pakistan 68 G2
Kétou, Benin 83 D5
Ketri, India 68 E6
Kętrzyn, Poland 30 D8
Kettering, U.K. 15 E7
Kettering, U.S.A. 114 F3
Kettle →, Canada 103 B11
Kettle Falls, U.S.A. 108 B4
Kettle Pt., Canada 116 C2
Kettleman City, U.S.A. 110 J7
Kęty, Poland 31 J6
Keuka L., U.S.A. 116 D7
Keuruu, Finland 9 E21
Kevelaer, Germany 24 D2
Kewanee, U.S.A. 112 E10
Kewaunee, U.S.A. 114 C2
Keweenaw B., U.S.A. 114 B1
Keweenaw Pen., U.S.A. 114 B2
Keweenaw Pt., U.S.A. 114 B2
Key Largo, U.S.A. 115 N5
Key West, U.S.A. 107 F10
Keyala, Sudan 81 G3
Keynsham, U.K. 15 F5
Keyser, U.S.A. 114 F6
Kezhma, Russia 53 D11
Kezi, Zimbabwe 89 C4
Kežmarok, Slovak Rep. 27 B13
Kgalagadi Transfrontier ⌓, Africa 88 D3
Khabarovsk, Russia 53 E14
Khabr, Iran 71 D8
Khābūr →, Syria 70 C4
Khachmas = Xaçmaz, Azerbaijan 35 K9
Khachrod, India 68 H6
Khadari, W. el →, Sudan 81 E2
Khadro, Pakistan 68 F3
Khadyzhensk, Russia 35 H4
Khadzhilyangar, China 69 B8
Khaga, India 69 G9
Khagaria, India 69 G12
Khaipur, Pakistan 68 E5
Khair, India 68 F7
Khairabad, India 69 F9
Khairagarh, India 69 J9
Khairpur, Pakistan 68 F3
Khairpur Nathan Shah, Pakistan 68 F2
Khairwara, India 68 H5
Khaisor →, Pakistan 68 D3
Khajuri Kach, Pakistan 68 C3
Khakassia □, Russia 52 D9
Khakhea, Botswana 88 C3
Khalafābād, Iran 71 D6
Khalilabad, India 69 F10
Khalīlī, Iran 71 E7
Khalkhāl, Iran 71 B6
Khálki, Dhodhekánisos, Greece 47 E9
Khálki, Thessalía, Greece 46 B4
Khalkidhikí □, Greece 44 F7
Khalkís, Greece 46 C5
Khalmer Yu, Russia 52 C7
Khalūf, Oman 75 C6
Kham Keut, Laos 64 C5
Khamaria, India 69 H9
Khambhaliya, India 68 H3
Khambhat, India 68 H5
Khambhat, G. of, India 66 J8
Khamilonísion, Greece 47 F8
Khamīr, Iran 71 E7
Khamir, Yemen 75 D3
Khamsa, Egypt 74 E1
Khan →, Namibia 88 C2
Khān Abū Shāmat, Syria 74 B5
Khān Azād, Iraq 70 C5
Khān Mujiddah, Iraq 70 C4
Khān Shaykhūn, Syria 70 C3
Khān Yūnis, Gaza Strip 74 D3
Khanai, Pakistan 68 D2
Khānaqīn, Iraq 70 C5
Khānbāghī, Iran 71 B7
Khandrá, Greece 47 F8
Khandwa, India 66 J10
Khandyga, Russia 53 C14
Khāneh, Iran 70 B5
Khanewal, Pakistan 68 D4
Khangah Dogran, Pakistan 68 D5
Khanh Duong, Vietnam 64 F7
Khaniá, Greece 49 D6
Khaniá □, Greece 49 D6
Khaniadhana, India 68 G8
Khaníon, Kólpos, Greece 49 D5
Khanka, L., Asia 53 E14
Khankendy = Xankändi, Azerbaijan 70 B5
Khanna, India 68 D7
Khanozai, Pakistan 68 D2
Khanpur, Pakistan 68 E4
Khanty-Mansiysk, Russia 52 C7
Khao Laem △, Thailand 64 E2
Khao Laem Res., Thailand 64 E2
Khao Luang △, Thailand 65 H2
Khao Phlu, Thailand 65 b
Khao Pu-Khao Ya △, Thailand 65 J2
Khao Sam Roi Yot △, Thailand 65 F2
Khao Sok △, Thailand 65 H2
Khao Yai △, Thailand 64 E3
Khaoen Si Nakarin △, Thailand 64 E2
Khapalu, Pakistan 69 B7
Khapcheranga, Russia 53 E12
Kharabali, Russia 35 G8
Kharaghoda, India 68 H4
Kharagpur, India 69 H12
Khárakas, Greece 49 D7
Kharan Kalat, Pakistan 66 E4
Kharānaq, Iran 71 C7
Kharda, India 66 K9
Khardung La, India 69 B7
Kharg = Khārk, Jazīreh-ye, Iran 71 D6
Khârga, El Wâhât-el, Egypt 80 B3
Khargon, India 66 J9
Khari →, India 68 G6
Kharian, Pakistan 68 C5
Kharit, Wadi el →, Egypt 80 C3
Khārk, Jazīreh-ye, Iran 71 D6
Kharkiv, Ukraine 33 H9
Kharkov = Kharkiv, Ukraine 33 H9
Kharmanli, Bulgaria 45 E9
Kharovsk, Russia 32 C11
Kharsawangarh, India 69 H11
Kharta, Turkey 72 B3
Khartoum = El Khartûm, Sudan 81 D3
Khasan, Russia 54 C5
Khasavyurt, Russia 35 J8
Khāsh, Iran 66 E2
Khashm el Girba, Sudan 81 E4
Khashum, Sudan 81 E2
Khashuri, Georgia 35 J6
Khaskovo, Bulgaria 45 E9
Khaskovo □, Bulgaria 45 E9
Khatanga, Russia 53 B11
Khatanga →, Russia 53 B11
Khatauli, India 68 E7
Khatra, India 69 H12
Khātūnābād, Iran 71 D7
Khatyrka, Russia 53 C18
Khavda, India 68 H3
Khaybar, Ḥarrat, Si. Arabia 70 E4
Khayelitsha, S. Africa 85 L3
Khāzimiyah, Iraq 70 C4
Khazzān Jabal al Awliyā, Sudan 81 D3
Khe Bo, Vietnam 64 C5
Khe Long, Vietnam 64 B5
Khe Sanh, Vietnam 64 D6
Khed Brahma, India 66 G8
Khekra, India 68 E7
Khemarak Phouminville, Cambodia 65 G4
Khemisset, Morocco 78 B4
Khemmarat, Thailand 64 D5
Khenāmān, Iran 71 D8
Khenchela, Algeria 78 A7
Khersān →, Iran 71 D6
Khérson, Greece 44 E6
Kherson, Ukraine 33 J7
Khersónisos Akrotíri, Greece 49 D6
Kheta →, Russia 53 B11
Khewari, Pakistan 68 F3
Khilchipur, India 68 G7
Khiliomódhion, Greece 46 D4
Khilok, Russia 53 D12
Khimki, Russia 32 E9
Khíos, Greece 47 C8
Khíos □, Greece 47 C8
Khirsadoh, India 69 H8
Khiuma = Hiiumaa, Estonia 9 G20
Khiva, Uzbekistan 52 E7
Khīyāv, Iran 70 B5
Khlebarovo, Bulgaria 45 C10
Khlong Khlung, Thailand 64 D2
Khmelnik, Ukraine 33 H4
Khmelnitskiy = Khmelnytskyy, Ukraine 33 H4
Khmelnytskyy, Ukraine 33 H4
Khmer Rep. = Cambodia ■, Asia 64 F5
Khoai, Hon, Vietnam 65 H5
Khodoriv, Ukraine 33 H3
Khodzent = Khŭjand, Tajikistan 52 E7
Khojak Pass, Afghan. 68 D2
Khok Kloi, Thailand 65 a
Khok Pho, Thailand 65 J3
Kholm, Russia 32 D6
Kholmsk, Russia 53 E15
Khomas Hochland, Namibia 88 C2
Khombole, Senegal 82 C1
Khomeyn, Iran 71 C6
Khomeynī Shahr, Iran 71 C6
Khomodino, Botswana 88 C3
Khon Kaen, Thailand 64 D4
Khong →, Cambodia 64 F5
Khong Sedone, Laos 64 E5
Khonuu, Russia 53 C15
Khoper →, Russia 34 F6
Khor el 'Atash, Sudan 81 E3
Khóra, Greece 46 D3
Khóra Sfakíon, Greece 49 D6
Khorāsān □, Iran 71 C8
Khorat = Nakhon Ratchasima, Thailand 64 E4
Khorat, Cao Nguyen, Thailand 64 E4
Khorixas, Namibia 88 C1
Khorol, Ukraine 33 H7
Khorramābād, Khorāsān, Iran 71 C8
Khorramābād, Lorestān, Iran 71 C6
Khorrāmshahr, Iran 71 D6
Khorugh, Tajikistan 52 F8
Khosravī, Iran 71 D6
Khosrowābād, Khuzestān, Iran 71 D6
Khosrowābād, Kordestān, Iran 70 C5
Khost, Pakistan 68 D2
Khosūyeh, Iran 71 D7
Khotyn, Ukraine 29 B11
Khouribga, Morocco 78 B4
Khowst, Afghan. 68 C3
Khowst □, Afghan. 66 C6
Khoyniki, Belarus 33 G5
Khrami →, Georgia 35 K7
Khrenovoye, Russia 34 E5
Khrisoúpolis, Greece 45 F8
Khristianá, Greece 47 E7
Khrysokhou B., Cyprus 49 D11
Khtapodhiá, Greece 47 D7
Khu Khan, Thailand 64 E5
Khuan Wa, Thailand 65 a
Khudzhand = Khŭjand, Tajikistan 52 E7
Khuff, Si. Arabia 70 E5
Khūgīānī, Afghan. 68 D2
Khuis, Botswana 88 D3
Khuiyala, India 68 F4
Khŭjand, Tajikistan 52 E7
Khujner, India 68 H7
Khulna, Bangla. 67 H16
Khulna □, Bangla. 67 H16
Khulo, Georgia 35 K6
Khumago, Botswana 88 C3
Khūnsorkh, Iran 71 E8
Khunti, India 69 H11
Khūr, Iran 71 C8
Khurai, India 68 G8
Khurayş, Si. Arabia 71 E6
Khureit, Sudan 81 E2
Khurīyā Murīyā, Jazā'ir, Oman 75 D6
Khurja, India 68 E7
Khūrmāl, Iraq 70 C5
Khurr, Wādī al, Iraq 70 C4
Khūsf, Iran 71 C8
Khush, Afghan. 66 C3
Khushab, Pakistan 68 C5
Khust, Ukraine 29 B8
Khutse ⌓, Botswana 88 C3
Khuzdar, Pakistan 68 F2
Khūzestān □, Iran 71 D6
Khvāf, Iran 71 C9
Khvājeh, Iran 70 B5
Khvalynsk, Russia 34 D9
Khvānsār, Iran 71 D7
Khvatovka, Russia 34 D8
Khvor, Iran 71 C7
Khvorgū, Iran 71 E8
Khvormūj, Iran 71 D6
Khvoy, Iran 70 B5
Khvoynaya, Russia 32 C8
Khyber Pass, Afghan. 68 B4
Khyriv, Ukraine 28
Kiabukwa, Dem. Rep. of the Congo 87 D1
Kiama, Australia 95 E5
Kiamba, Phil. 61 H6
Kiambi, Dem. Rep. of the Congo 86 D2
Kiambu, Kenya 86 C4
King West △, Gambia 82 C1
Kiangara, Madag. 89 B8
Kiangsi = Jiangxi □, China 59 D11
Kiangsu = Jiangsu □, China 57 H11
Kiáton, Greece 46 C4
Kibæk, Denmark 11 H2
Kibale △, Uganda 86 B3
Kibanga Port, Uganda 86 B3
Kibara, Tanzania 86 C3
Kibare, Mts., Dem. Rep. of the Congo 86 D2
Kibira △, Burundi 86 C3
Kibombo, Dem. Rep. of the Congo 86 C2
Kibondo, Tanzania 86 C3
Kibre Mengist, Ethiopia 81 F4
Kibumbu, Burundi 86 C2
Kibungo, Rwanda 86 C3
Kibuye, Burundi 86 C2
Kibuye, Rwanda 86 C2
Kibwesa, Tanzania 86 D2
Kibwezi, Kenya 86 C4
Kicasalih, Turkey 45 E10
Kičevo, Macedonia 44 E4
Kichha, India 69 E8
Kichha →, India 69 E8
Kicking Horse Pass, Canada 102 C5
Kidal, Mali 83 B5
Kidderminster, U.K. 15 E5
Kidepo Valley △, Uganda 86 B3
Kidete, Tanzania 86 D4
Kidira, Senegal 82 C2
Kidnappers, C., N.Z. 91 H6
Kidsgrove, U.K. 14 D5
Kidston, Australia 94 B3
Kidugallo, Tanzania 86 D4
Kiel, Germany 24 A6
Kiel Canal = Nord-Ostsee-Kanal, Germany 24 A5
Kielce, Poland 31 H7
Kielder Water, U.K. 14 B5
Kieler Bucht, Germany 24 A6
Kiembara, Burkina Faso 82 C4
Kien Binh, Vietnam 65 H5
Kien Tan, Vietnam 65 G5
Kienge, Dem. Rep. of the Congo 87 E2
Kiessé, Niger 83 C5
Kiev = Kyyiv, Ukraine 33 G6
Kifaya, Guinea 82 C2
Kiffa, Mauritania 82 B2
Kifisiá, Greece 46 C5
Kifissós →, Greece 46 C5
Kifrī, Iraq 70 C5
Kigali, Rwanda 86 C3
Kigarama, Tanzania 86 C3
Kiggo, Sudan 81 F3
Kigezi ⌓, Uganda 86 C2
Kigoma □, Tanzania 86 D3
Kigoma-Ujiji, Tanzania 86 C2
Kigomasha, Ras, Tanzania 86 C4
Kığzı, Turkey 70 B4
Kihei, U.S.A. 106 H16
Kihnu, Estonia 9 G21
Kii-Sanchi, Japan 55 G8
Kii-Suidō, Japan 55 H7
Kikaiga-Shima, Japan 55 K4
Kikinda, Serbia & M. 28 E5
Kikládhes, Greece 46 E6
Kikládhes □, Greece 46 D6
Kikwit, Dem. Rep. of the Congo 84 E3
Kil, Sweden 10 E7
Kilafors, Sweden 10 C10
Kilar, India 68 C7
Kilauea Crater, U.S.A. 106 J17
Kilbrannan Sd., U.K. 13 F3
Kilchu, N. Korea 57 D15
Kilcoy, Australia 95 D5
Kildare, Ireland 12 C5
Kildare □, Ireland 12 C5
Kileikli, Sudan 81 E2
Kilfinnane, Ireland 12 D3
Kilgore, U.S.A. 113 J7
Kilibo, Benin 83 D5
Kilifi, Kenya 86 C4
Kilimanjaro, Tanzania 86 C4
Kilimanjaro □, Tanzania 86 C4
Kilimli, Turkey 72 B4
Kilindini, Kenya 86 C4
Kilis, Turkey 70 B3
Kiliya, Ukraine 29 E14
Kilkee, Ireland 12 D2
Kilkeel, U.K. 12 B5
Kilkenny, Ireland 12 D4
Kilkenny □, Ireland 12 D4
Kilkieran B., Ireland 12 C2
Kilkís, Greece 44 F6
Kilkís □, Greece 44 E6
Killala, Ireland 12 B2
Killala B., Ireland 12 B2
Killaloe, Canada 116 A7
Killaloe, Ireland 12 D3
Killarney, Australia 95 D5
Killarney, Canada 103 D9
Killarney, Ireland 12 D2
Killarney △, Ireland 12 D2
Killary Harbour, Ireland 12 C2
Killdeer, U.S.A. 112 B3
Killeberg, Sweden 11 H8
Killeen, U.S.A. 113 K6
Killin, U.K. 13 E4
Killíni, Ilía, Greece 46 D3
Killíni, Korinthía, Greece 46 D4
Killorglin, Ireland 12 D2
Killybegs, Ireland 12 B3
Kilmarnock, U.K. 13 F4
Kilmez, Russia 34 B10
Kilmez →, Russia 34 B10
Kilmore, Australia 95 F3
Kilondo, Tanzania 87 D3
Kilosa, Tanzania 86 D4
Kilrush, Ireland 12 D2
Kilwa Kisiwani, Tanzania 87 D4
Kilwa Kivinje, Tanzania 87 D4
Kilwa Masoko, Tanzania 87 D4
Kilwinning, U.K. 13 F4
Kim, U.S.A. 113 G3
Kim →, Cameroon 83 D7
Kimaam, Indonesia 63 F9
Kimamba, Tanzania 86 D4
Kimba, Australia 95 E2
Kimball, Nebr., U.S.A. 112 E3
Kimball, S. Dak., U.S.A. 112 D5
Kimberley, Australia 92 C4
Kimberley, Canada 102 D5
Kimberley, S. Africa 88 D3
Kimberly, U.S.A. 108 E6
Kimch'aek, N. Korea 57 D15
Kimch'ŏn, S. Korea 57 F15
Kími, Greece 46 C6
Kimje, S. Korea 57 G14
Kimmirut, Canada 101 B13
Kímolos, Greece 46 E6
Kimovsk, Moskva, Russia 32 E9
Kimovsk, Tula, Russia 32 E10
Kimparana, Mali 82 C4
Kimpese, Dem. Rep. of the Congo 84 F2
Kimry, Russia 32 D9
Kimstad, Sweden 11 F9
Kinabalu, Gunung, Malaysia 62 C5
Kínaros, Greece 47 E8
Kinaskan L., Canada 102 B2
Kinbasket L., Canada 102 C5
Kincardine, Canada 116 B3
Kincolith, Canada 102 C3
Kinda, Dem. Rep. of the Congo 87 D2
Kindberg, Austria 26 D8
Kinde, U.S.A. 116 C2
Kinder Scout, U.K. 14 D6
Kindersley, Canada 103 C7
Kindia, Guinea 82 D2
Kindu, Dem. Rep. of the Congo 86 C2
Kinel, Russia 34 D10
Kineshma, Russia 34 B6
Kinesi, Tanzania 86 C3
King, L., Australia 93 F2
King, Mt., Australia 94 D4
King City, U.S.A. 110 J5
King Cr. →, Australia 94 C2
King Edward →, Australia 92 B4
King Frederick VI Land = Kong Frederik VI Kyst, Greenland 101 B15
King George B., Falk. Is. 128 G4
King George I., Antarctica 5 C18
King George Is., Canada 101 C11
King I. = Kadan Kyun, Burma 64 F2
King I., Australia 95 F3
King I., Canada 102 C3
King Leopold Ranges, Australia 92 C4
King of Prussia, U.S.A. 117 F9
King Sd., Australia 92 C3
King Sejong, Antarctica 5 C18
King William I., Canada 100 B10
King William's Town, S. Africa 88 E4
Kingait = Cape Dorset, Canada 101 B12
Kingaok = Bathurst Inlet, Canada 100 B9
Kingaroy, Australia 95 D5
Kingfisher, U.S.A. 113 H6
Kingirbān, Iraq 70 C5
Kingisepp = Kuressaare, Estonia 9 G20
Kingisepp, Russia 32 C5
Kingman, Ariz., U.S.A. 111 K12
Kingman, Kans., U.S.A. 113 G5
Kingoonya, Australia 95 E2
Kingri, Pakistan 68 D3
Kings →, U.S.A. 110 J7
Kings Canyon △, U.S.A. 110 J8
King's Lynn, U.K. 14 E8
Kings Mountain, U.S.A. 115 H5
Kings Park, U.S.A. 117 F11
King's Peak, U.S.A. 108 F8
Kingsbridge, U.K. 15 G4
Kingsburg, U.S.A. 110 J7
Kingscote, Australia 95 F2
Kingscourt, Ireland 12 C5
Kingsford, U.S.A. 114 C1
Kingsland, U.S.A. 115 K5
Kingsley, U.S.A. 112 D7
Kingsport, U.S.A. 115 G4
Kingston, Canada 117 B8
Kingston, Jamaica 120 a
Kingston, N.Z. 91 L2
Kingston, N.H., U.S.A. 117 D13
Kingston, N.Y., U.S.A. 117 E11
Kingston, Pa., U.S.A. 117 E9
Kingston, R.I., U.S.A. 117 E13
Kingston Pk., U.S.A. 111 K11
Kingston South East, Australia 95 F2
Kingston upon Hull, U.K. 14 D7
Kingston upon Hull □, U.K. 14 D7
Kingston-upon-Thames □, U.K. 15 F7
Kingstown, St. Vincent 121 D7
Kingstree, U.S.A. 115 J6
Kingsville, Canada 116 D2
Kingsville, U.S.A. 113 M6
Kingussie, U.K. 13 D4
Kingwood, U.S.A. 113 K7
Kınık, Antalya, Turkey 47 E11
Kınık, İzmir, Turkey 47 B9
Kinistino, Canada 103 C7
Kinkala, Congo 84 E2
Kinki □, Japan 55 H8
Kinleith, N.Z. 91 H5
Kinlochleven, U.K. 13 E4
Kinmount, Canada 116 B6
Kinna, Sweden 11 G6
Kinnairds Hd., U.K. 13 D6
Kinnared, Sweden 11 G7
Kinnarp, Sweden 11 F7
Kinneviken, Sweden 11 F7
Kino, Mexico 118 B2
Kinoje →, Canada 104 B3
Kinomoto, Japan 55 G8
Kinoni, Uganda 86 C3
Kinoosao, Canada 103 B8
Kinross, U.K. 13 E5
Kinsale, Ireland 12 E3
Kinsale, Old Hd. of, Ireland 12 E3
Kinsha = Chang Jiang →, China 59 B13
Kinshasa, Dem. Rep. of the Congo 84 E3
Kinsley, U.S.A. 113 G5
Kinsman, U.S.A. 116 E4
Kinston, U.S.A. 115 H7
Kintamani, Indonesia 63 J18
Kintampo, Ghana 83 D4
Kintore, U.K. 13 D6
Kintore Ra., Australia 92 D4
Kintyre, U.K. 13 F3
Kintyre, Mull of, U.K. 13 F3
Kinushseo →, Canada 104 A3
Kinuso, Canada 102 B5
Kinyangiri, Tanzania 86 C3
Kinyeti, Sudan 81 G3
Kinzig →, Germany 25 G3
Kinzua, U.S.A. 116 E6
Kinzua Dam, U.S.A. 116 E6
Kióni, Greece 46 C2

Kiosk, *Canada* 104 C4
Kiowa, *Kans., U.S.A.* 113 G5
Kiowa, *Okla., U.S.A.* 113 H7
Kipahigan L., *Canada* 103 B8
Kipanga, *Tanzania* 86 D4
Kiparissía, *Greece* 46 D3
Kiparissiakós Kólpos, *Greece* 46 D3
Kipawa, L., *Canada* 104 C4
Kipembawe, *Tanzania* 86 D3
Kipengere Ra., *Tanzania* 87 D3
Kipili, *Tanzania* 86 D3
Kipini, *Kenya* 86 C5
Kipling, *Canada* 103 C8
Kippure, *Ireland* 12 C5
Kipushi, *Dem. Rep. of the Congo* 87 E2
Kirane, *Mali* 82 B2
Kiranomena, *Madag.* 89 B8
Kiraz, *Turkey* 47 C10
Kirazlı, *Turkey* 45 F10
Kirchhain, *Germany* 24 E4
Kirchheim, *Germany* 25 G5
Kirchheimbolanden, *Germany* 25 F3
Kirchschlag, *Austria* 27 D9
Kireç, *Turkey* 47 B10
Kirensk, *Russia* 53 D11
Kirghizia = Kyrgyzstan ■, *Asia* 52 E8
Kirghizstan = Kyrgyzstan ■, *Asia* 52 E8
Kiribati ■, *Pac. Oc.* 96 H10
Kırıkhan, *Turkey* 72 D7
Kırıkkale, *Turkey* 72 C5
Kirillov, *Russia* 32 C10
Kirin = Jilin, *China* 57 C14
Kirinyaga = Kenya, Mt., *Kenya* 86 C4
Kirishi, *Russia* 32 C7
Kirishima Yaku △, *Japan* 55 J5
Kiritimati, *Kiribati* 97 G12
Kırka, *Turkey* 47 B12
Kırkağaç, *Turkey* 47 B9
Kirkby, *U.K.* 14 D5
Kirkby-in-Ashfield, *U.K.* 14 D6
Kirkby Lonsdale, *U.K.* 14 C5
Kirkby Stephen, *U.K.* 14 C5
Kirkcaldy, *U.K.* 13 E5
Kirkcudbright, *U.K.* 13 G4
Kirkee, *India* 66 K8
Kirkenes, *Norway* 8 B23
Kirkfield, *Canada* 116 B6
Kirkintilloch, *U.K.* 13 F4
Kirkjubæjarklaustur, *Iceland* 8 E4
Kirkkonummi, *Finland* 9 F21
Kirkland Lake, *Canada* 104 C3
Kırklareli, *Turkey* 45 E11
Kırklareli □, *Turkey* 45 E11
Kirksville, *U.S.A.* 112 E8
Kirkūk, *Iraq* 70 C5
Kirkwall, *U.K.* 13 C6
Kirkwood, *S. Africa* 88 E4
Kirn, *Germany* 25 F3
Kirov, *Kaluga, Russia* 32 E8
Kirov, *Kirov, Russia* 52 D5
Kirovabad = Gäncä, *Azerbaijan* 35 K8
Kirovograd = Kirovohrad, *Ukraine* 33 H7
Kirovohrad, *Ukraine* 33 H7
Kirovskiy, *Astrakhan, Russia* 35 H9
Kirovskiy, *Kamchatka, Russia* 53 D16
Kirovskiy, *Primorsk, Russia* 54 B6
Kirriemuir, *U.K.* 13 E5
Kirsanov, *Russia* 34 D6
Kırşehir, *Turkey* 70 B2
Kirtachi, *Niger* 83 C5
Kirthar Range, *Pakistan* 68 F2
Kirtland, *U.S.A.* 109 H9
Kiruna, *Sweden* 8 C19
Kirundu, *Dem. Rep. of the Congo* 86 C2
Kirya, *Russia* 34 C8
Kiryū, *Japan* 55 F9
Kisa, *Sweden* 11 G9
Kisaga, *Tanzania* 86 C3
Kisalaya, *Nic.* 120 D3
Kisalföld, *Hungary* 28 C2
Kisámou, Kólpos, *Greece* 49 D5
Kisanga, *Dem. Rep. of the Congo* 86 B2
Kisangani, *Dem. Rep. of the Congo* 86 B2
Kisar, *Indonesia* 63 F7
Kisarawe, *Tanzania* 86 D4
Kisarazu, *Japan* 55 G9
Kisbér, *Hungary* 28 C3
Kishanganga →, *Pakistan* 69 B5
Kishanganj, *India* 69 F13
Kishangarh, *Raj., India* 68 F6
Kishangarh, *Raj., India* 68 F4
Kishi, *Nigeria* 83 D5
Kishinev = Chişinău, *Moldova* 29 C13
Kishiwada, *Japan* 55 G7
Kishtwar, *India* 69 C6
Kisielice, *Poland* 30 E6
Kisigo ⌂, *Tanzania* 86 D3
Kisii, *Kenya* 86 C3
Kisiju, *Tanzania* 86 D4
Kisir, *Turkey* 73 B10
Kisizi, *Uganda* 86 C2
Kiskomárom = Zalakomár, *Hungary* 28 D2
Kiskőrei-víztároló, *Hungary* 28 C5
Kiskőrös, *Hungary* 28 D4
Kiskundorozsma, *Hungary* 28 D5
Kiskunfélegyháza, *Hungary* 28 D4
Kiskunhalas, *Hungary* 28 D4
Kiskunmajsa, *Hungary* 28 D4
Kiskunsági △, *Hungary* 28 D4
Kislovodsk, *Russia* 35 J6
Kismayu = Chisimaio, *Somali Rep.* 77 G8
Kiso-Gawa →, *Japan* 55 G8
Kiso-Sammyaku, *Japan* 55 G8
Kisofukushima, *Japan* 55 G8
Kisoro, *Uganda* 86 C2
Kissidougou, *Guinea* 82 D2
Kissimmee, *U.S.A.* 115 L5
Kissimmee →, *U.S.A.* 115 M5
Kississing L., *Canada* 103 B8
Kissónerga, *Cyprus* 49 E11
Kissu, J., *Sudan* 80 C2
Kistanje, *Croatia* 41 E12
Kisújszállás, *Hungary* 28 C5
Kisumu, *Kenya* 86 C3
Kisvárda, *Hungary* 28 B7
Kiswani, *Tanzania* 86 C4
Kiswere, *Tanzania* 87 D4
Kit Carson, *U.S.A.* 112 F3
Kita, *Mali* 82 C3
Kitaibaraki, *Japan* 55 F10
Kitakami, *Japan* 54 E10
Kitakami-Gawa →, *Japan* 54 E10
Kitakami-Sammyaku, *Japan* 54 E10
Kitakata, *Japan* 54 F9
Kitakyūshū, *Japan* 55 H5
Kitale, *Kenya* 86 B4
Kitami, *Japan* 54 C11
Kitami-Sammyaku, *Japan* 54 B11
Kitangiri, L., *Tanzania* 86 C3
Kitaya, *Tanzania* 87 E5
Kitchener, *Canada* 116 C4
Kitee, *Finland* 32 A6
Kitega = Gitega, *Burundi* 86 C2
Kitengo, *Dem. Rep. of the Congo* 86 D1
Kitgum, *Uganda* 86 B3
Kíthira, *Greece* 46 E5
Kíthnos, *Greece* 46 D6
Kiti, *Cyprus* 49 E12
Kiti, C., *Cyprus* 49 E12
Kitimat, *Canada* 102 C3
Kitinen →, *Finland* 8 C22
Kitiyab, *Sudan* 81 D3
Kítros, *Greece* 44 F6
Kitsman, *Ukraine* 29 B10
Kitsuki, *Japan* 55 H5
Kittakittaooloo, L., *Australia* 95 D2
Kittanning, *U.S.A.* 116 F5
Kittatinny Mts., *U.S.A.* 117 F10
Kittery, *U.S.A.* 115 D10
Kittilä, *Finland* 8 C21
Kitui, *Kenya* 86 C4
Kitwanga, *Canada* 102 B3
Kitwe, *Zambia* 87 E2
Kitzbühel, *Austria* 26 D5
Kitzbühler Alpen, *Austria* 26 D5
Kitzingen, *Germany* 25 F6
Kivarli, *India* 68 G5
Kivertsi, *Ukraine* 33 G3
Kividhes, *Cyprus* 49 E11
Kivik, *Sweden* 11 J8
Kivotós, *Greece* 44 F5
Kivu, L., *Dem. Rep. of the Congo* 86 C2
Kiyev = Kyyiv, *Ukraine* 33 G6
Kiyevskoye Vdkhr. = Kyyivske Vdskh., *Ukraine* 33 G6
Kıyıköy, *Turkey* 45 E12
Kiziguru, *Rwanda* 86 C3
Kızıl Adalar, *Turkey* 45 F13
Kızıl Irmak →, *Turkey* 72 B6
Kizil Jilga, *China* 69 B8
Kizil Yurt, *Russia* 35 J8
Kızılcabölük, *Turkey* 47 D11
Kızılcadağ, *Turkey* 47 D11
Kızılcahamam, *Turkey* 72 B5
Kızılhisar, *Turkey* 72 D3
Kızılırmak, *Turkey* 72 B5
Kızılkaya, *Turkey* 47 D12
Kızılören, *Turkey* 47 C12
Kızıltepe, *Turkey* 70 B4
Kizimkazi, *Tanzania* 86 D4
Kizlyar, *Russia* 35 J8
Kizyl-Arvat = Gyzylarbat, *Turkmenistan* 52 F6
Kjellerup, *Denmark* 11 H3
Kjölur, *Iceland* 8 D4
Kladanj, *Bos.-H.* 28 F3
Kladnica, *Serbia & M.* 44 C4
Kladno, *Czech Rep.* 26 A7
Kladovo, *Serbia & M.* 44 B6
Klaeng, *Thailand* 64 F3
Klagenfurt, *Austria* 26 E7
Klaipėda, *Lithuania* 9 J19
Klaipėda □, *Lithuania* 30 C8
Klaksvík, *Færoe Is.* 8 E9
Klamath →, *U.S.A.* 108 F1
Klamath Falls, *U.S.A.* 108 E3
Klamath Mts., *U.S.A.* 108 F2
Klamono, *Indonesia* 63 E8
Klang, *Malaysia* 65 L3
Klanjec, *Croatia* 41 B12
Klappan →, *Canada* 102 B3
Klarälven →, *Sweden* 10 E7
Klässbol, *Sweden* 10 E6
Klatovy, *Czech Rep.* 26 B6
Klawer, *S. Africa* 88 E2
Klazienaveen, *Neths.* 17 B6
Klé, *Mali* 82 C3
Klecko, *Poland* 31 F4
Kleczew, *Poland* 31 F5
Kleena Kleene, *Canada* 102 C4
Klein-Karas, *Namibia* 88 D2
Klekovača, *Bos.-H.* 41 D13
Klembivka, *Ukraine* 29 B13
Klenoec, *Macedonia* 44 E4
Klenovec, *Slovak Rep.* 27 C12
Klerksdorp, *S. Africa* 88 D4
Kleszczele, *Poland* 31 F10
Kletnya, *Russia* 32 F7
Kletsk = Klyetsk, *Belarus* 33 F4
Kletskiy, *Russia* 35 F6
Kleve, *Germany* 24 D2
Klickitat, *U.S.A.* 108 D3
Klickitat →, *U.S.A.* 110 E5
Klidhes, *Cyprus* 49 D13
Klimovichi, *Belarus* 32 F6
Klin, *Russia* 32 D9
Klina, *Serbia & M.* 44 D4
Klinaklini →, *Canada* 102 C3
Klintehamn, *Sweden* 11 G12
Klintsy, *Russia* 33 F7
Klip →, *S. Africa* 89 D4
Klipdale, *S. Africa* 88 E2
Klippan, *Sweden* 11 H7
Klipplaat, *S. Africa* 88 E3
Klishkivtsi, *Ukraine* 29 B11
Klisura, *Bulgaria* 45 D8
Kljajićevo, *Serbia & M.* 28 E4
Ključ, *Bos.-H.* 41 D13
Kłobuck, *Poland* 31 H5
Klockestrand, *Sweden* 10 B11
Kłodawa, *Poland* 31 F5
Kłodzko, *Poland* 31 H3
Klong Wang Chao △, *Thailand* 64 D2
Klos, *Albania* 44 E4
Klosterneuburg, *Austria* 27 C9
Klosters, *Switz.* 25 J5
Klötze, *Germany* 24 C7
Klouto, *Togo* 83 D5
Kluane △, *Canada* 102 A1
Kluane L., *Canada* 100 B6
Kluczbork, *Poland* 31 H5
Klukwan, *U.S.A.* 102 B1
Klungkung, *Indonesia* 63 K18
Klyetsk, *Belarus* 33 F4
Klyuchevskaya, Gora, *Russia* 53 D17
Knäred, *Sweden* 11 H7
Knaresborough, *U.K.* 14 C6
Knee L., *Man., Canada* 104 A1
Knee L., *Sask., Canada* 103 B7
Knezha, *Bulgaria* 45 C8
Knight Inlet, *Canada* 102 C3
Knighton, *U.K.* 15 E4
Knights Ferry, *U.S.A.* 110 H6
Knights Landing, *U.S.A.* 110 G5
Knin, *Croatia* 41 D13
Knislinge, *Sweden* 11 H8
Knittelfeld, *Austria* 26 D7
Knivsta, *Sweden* 10 E11
Knjaževac, *Serbia & M.* 44 C6
Knob, C., *Australia* 93 F2
Knock, *Ireland* 12 C3
Knockmealdown Mts., *Ireland* 12 D4
Knokke-Heist, *Belgium* 17 C3
Knossós, *Greece* 49 D7
Knowlton, *Canada* 117 A12
Knox, *U.S.A.* 114 E2
Knox Coast, *Antarctica* 5 C8
Knoxville, *Iowa, U.S.A.* 112 E8
Knoxville, *Pa., U.S.A.* 116 E7
Knoxville, *Tenn., U.S.A.* 115 H4
Knud Rasmussen Land, *Greenland* 4 A5
Knysna, *S. Africa* 88 E3
Knyszyn, *Poland* 30 E9
Ko Kha, *Thailand* 64 C2
Ko Tarutao △, *Thailand* 65 J2
Ko Yao, *Thailand* 65 a
Koartac = Quaqtaq, *Canada* 101 B13
Koba, *Indonesia* 63 F8
Kobarid, *Slovenia* 41 B10
Kobayashi, *Japan* 55 J5
Kōbe, *Japan* 55 G7
Kobelyaky, *Ukraine* 33 H8
København, *Denmark* 11 J6
København ✕ (CPH), *Denmark* 11 J6
Københavns Amtskommune □, *Denmark* 11 J6
Kobenni, *Mauritania* 82 B3
Kōbi-Sho, *Japan* 55 M1
Koblenz, *Germany* 25 E3
Kobo, *Ethiopia* 81 E4
Kobryn, *Belarus* 33 F3
Kobuleti, *Georgia* 35 K5
Kobyletska Polyana, *Ukraine* 29 B9
Kobylin, *Poland* 31 G4
Kobyłka, *Poland* 31 F8
Kobylkino, *Russia* 34 C6
Koca →, *Turkey* 45 F11
Kocabaş, *Turkey* 47 D11
Kocaeli, *Turkey* 45 F13
Kocaeli □, *Turkey* 45 F13
Kočane, *Serbia & M.* 44 C5
Kočani, *Macedonia* 44 E6
Koçarlı, *Turkey* 47 D9
Koceljevo, *Serbia & M.* 44 B3
Kočevje, *Slovenia* 41 C11
Koch Bihar, *India* 67 F16
Kochang, *S. Korea* 57 G14
Kochas, *India* 69 G10
Kocher →, *Germany* 25 F5
Kochi = Cochin, *India* 66 Q10
Kōchi, *Japan* 55 H6
Kōchi □, *Japan* 55 H6
Kochiu = Gejiu, *China* 58 F4
Kock, *Poland* 31 G9
Kodarma, *India* 69 G11
Kode, *Sweden* 11 G5
Kodiak, *U.S.A.* 100 C4
Kodiak I., *U.S.A.* 100 C4
Kodinar, *India* 68 J4
Kodok, *Sudan* 81 F3
Kodori →, *Georgia* 35 J5
Kodyma, *Ukraine* 29 B14
Koedoesberge, *S. Africa* 88 E3
Koes, *Namibia* 88 D2
Kofçaz, *Turkey* 45 E11
Koffiefontein, *S. Africa* 88 D4
Kofiau, *Indonesia* 63 E7
Köflach, *Austria* 26 D8
Koforidua, *Ghana* 83 D4
Kōfu, *Japan* 55 G9
Koga, *Japan* 55 F9
Kogaluc →, *Canada* 105 A7
Køge, *Denmark* 11 J6
Køge Bugt, *Denmark* 11 J6
Kogi □, *Nigeria* 83 D6
Kogin Baba, *Nigeria* 83 D7
Koh-i-Khurd, *Afghan.* 68 C1
Koh-i-Maran, *Pakistan* 68 E2
Kohat, *Pakistan* 68 C4
Kohima, *India* 67 G19
Kohkīlūyeh va Būyer Aḥmadi □, *Iran* 71 D6
Kohler Ra., *Antarctica* 5 D15
Kohlu, *Pakistan* 68 E3
Kohtla-Järve, *Estonia* 9 G22
Kohylnyk →, *Ukraine* 29 E14
Koi Sanjaq, *Iraq* 70 B5
Koillismaa, *Finland* 8 D23
Koin-dong, *N. Korea* 57 D14
Koinare, *Bulgaria* 45 C8
Koindu, *S. Leone* 82 D2
Kojetín, *Czech Rep.* 27 B10
Kojō, *N. Korea* 57 E14
Kojonup, *Australia* 93 F2
Kojūr, *Iran* 71 B6
Koka, *Sudan* 80 C3
Kokand = Qūqon, *Uzbekistan* 52 E8
Kokas, *Indonesia* 63 E8
Kokava, *Slovak Rep.* 27 C12
Kokchetav = Kökshetaū, *Kazakhstan* 52 D7
Kokemäenjoki →, *Finland* 9 F19
Kokhma, *Russia* 34 B5
Koki, *Senegal* 82 B1
Kokkola, *Finland* 8 E20
Koko, *Nigeria* 83 C5
Koko Kyunzu, *Burma* 67 M18
Kokolopozo, *Ivory C.* 82 D3
Kokomo, *U.S.A.* 114 E2
Kokoro, *Niger* 83 C5
Koksan, *N. Korea* 57 E14
Kökshetaū, *Kazakhstan* 52 D7
Koksoak →, *Canada* 101 C13
Kokstad, *S. Africa* 89 E4
Kokubu, *Japan* 55 J5
Kola, *Indonesia* 63 F8
Kola Pen. = Kolskiy Poluostrov, *Russia* 52 C4
Kolachi →, *Pakistan* 68 F2
Kolahoi, *India* 69 B6
Kolahun, *Liberia* 82 D2
Kolaka, *Indonesia* 63 E6
Kolar, *India* 66 N11
Kolar Gold Fields, *India* 66 N11
Kolaras, *India* 68 G6
Kolari, *Finland* 8 C20
Kolárovo, *Slovak Rep.* 27 D10
Kolašin, *Serbia & M.* 44 D3
Kolayat, *India* 66 F8
Kolbäck, *Sweden* 10 E10
Kolbäcksån →, *Sweden* 10 E10
Kolbermoor, *Germany* 25 H8
Kolbuszowa, *Poland* 31 H8
Kolchugino, *Russia* 32 D10
Kolda, *Senegal* 82 C2
Koldegi, *Sudan* 81 E3
Kolding, *Denmark* 11 J3
Kolepom = Dolak, Pulau, *Indonesia* 63 F9
Kolguyev, Ostrov, *Russia* 52 C5
Kolhapur, *India* 66 L9
Kolia, *Ivory C.* 82 D3
Kolín, *Czech Rep.* 26 A8
Kolind, *Denmark* 11 H4
Kolkas rags, *Latvia* 9 H20
Kolkata, *India* 69 H13
Kollam = Quilon, *India* 66 Q10
Kölleda, *Germany* 24 D7
Kollum, *Neths.* 17 A6
Kolmanskop, *Namibia* 88 D2
Köln, *Germany* 24 E2
Kolno, *Poland* 30 E8
Koło, *Poland* 31 F5
Kołobrzeg, *Poland* 30 D2
Kolochava, *Ukraine* 29 B8
Kolokani, *Mali* 82 C3
Koloko, *Burkina Faso* 82 C3
Kololo, *Ethiopia* 81 F5
Kolomna, *Russia* 32 E10
Kolomyya, *Ukraine* 29 B10
Kolondiéba, *Mali* 82 C3
Kolonodale, *Indonesia* 63 E6
Kolonowskie, *Poland* 31 H5
Kolosib, *India* 67 G18
Kolpashevo, *Russia* 52 D9
Kolpino, *Russia* 32 C6
Kolpny, *Russia* 33 F9
Kolskiy Poluostrov, *Russia* 52 C4
Kolsva, *Sweden* 10 E9
Kolubara →, *Serbia & M.* 44 B4
Koluszki, *Poland* 31 G6
Kolwezi, *Dem. Rep. of the Congo* 87 E2
Kolyma →, *Russia* 53 C17
Kolymskoye Nagorye, *Russia* 53 C16
Kôm Hamâda, *Egypt* 80 H7
Kôm Ombo, *Egypt* 80 C3
Komadugu Gana →, *Nigeria* 83 C7
Komandorskiye Is. = Komandorskiye Ostrova, *Russia* 53 D17
Komandorskiye Ostrova, *Russia* 53 D17
Komárno, *Slovak Rep.* 27 D11
Komarnyky, *Ukraine* 28 B8
Komárom, *Hungary* 28 C3
Komárom-Esztergom □, *Hungary* 28 C3
Komatipoort, *S. Africa* 89 D5
Komatou Yialou, *Cyprus* 49 D13
Komatsu, *Japan* 55 F8
Komatsushima, *Japan* 55 H7
Kombissiri, *Burkina Faso* 83 C4
Kombori, *Burkina Faso* 82 C4
Kombóti, *Greece* 46 B3
Komen, *Slovenia* 41 C10
Komenda, *Ghana* 83 D4
Komi □, *Russia* 52 C6
Komiža, *Croatia* 41 E13
Komló, *Hungary* 28 D3
Kommunarsk = Alchevsk, *Ukraine* 33 H10
Kommunizma, Pik, *Tajikistan* 52 F8
Komodo, *Indonesia* 63 F5
Komoé →, *Ivory C.* 82 D4
Komoran, Pulau, *Indonesia* 63 F9
Komoro, *Japan* 55 F9
Komotini, *Greece* 45 E9
Komovi, *Serbia & M.* 44 D3
Kompasberg, *S. Africa* 88 E3
Kompong Bang, *Cambodia* 65 F5
Kompong Cham, *Cambodia* 65 F5
Kompong Chhnang = Kampong Chhnang, *Cambodia* 65 F5
Kompong Chikreng, *Cambodia* 64 F5
Kompong Kleang, *Cambodia* 64 F5
Kompong Luong, *Cambodia* 65 G5
Kompong Pranak, *Cambodia* 64 F5
Kompong Som = Kampong Saom, *Cambodia* 65 G4
Kompong Som, Chhung = Kampong Saom, Chaak, *Cambodia* 65 G4
Kompong Speu, *Cambodia* 65 G5
Kompong Sralau, *Cambodia* 64 E5
Kompong Thom, *Cambodia* 64 F5
Kompong Trabeck, *Cambodia* 64 F5
Kompong Trabeck, *Cambodia* 65 G5
Kompong Trach, *Cambodia* 65 G5
Kompong Tralach, *Cambodia* 65 G5
Komrat = Comrat, *Moldova* 29 D13
Komsberg, *S. Africa* 88 E3
Komsomolets, Ostrov, *Russia* 53 A10
Komsomolsk, *Amur, Russia* 53 D14
Komsomolsk, *Ivanovo, Russia* 32 D11
Komsomolskiy, *Russia* 34 C7
Kömür Burnu, *Turkey* 47 C8
Kon Tum, *Vietnam* 64 E7
Kon Tum, Plateau du, *Vietnam* 64 E7
Kona, *Mali* 82 C4
Konakovo, *Russia* 32 D9
Konarhā □, *Afghan.* 66 B7
Konārī, *Iran* 71 D6
Konch, *India* 69 G8
Konde, *Tanzania* 86 C4
Kondiá, *Greece* 47 B7
Kondinin, *Australia* 93 F2
Kondoa, *Tanzania* 86 C4
Kondókali, *Greece* 49 A3
Kondopaga, *Russia* 32 A8
Kondratyevo, *Russia* 53 D10
Kondrovo, *Russia* 32 E8
Konduga, *Nigeria* 83 C7
Köneürgench, *Turkmenistan* 52 E6
Konevo, *Russia* 32 A10
Kong = Khong →, *Cambodia* 64 F5
Kong, *Ivory C.* 82 D4
Kong, Koh, *Cambodia* 65 G4
Kong Christian IX Land, *Greenland* 4 C6
Kong Christian X Land, *Greenland* 4 B6
Kong Frederik IX Land, *Greenland* 4 C5
Kong Frederik VI Kyst, *Greenland* 101 B15
Kong Frederik VIII Land, *Greenland* 4 B6
Kong Oscar Fjord, *Greenland* 4 B6
Kongeå →, *Denmark* 11 J2
Kongerslev, *Denmark* 11 H4
Kongju, *S. Korea* 57 F14
Konglu, *Burma* 67 F20
Kongola, *Namibia* 88 B3
Kongolo, *Kasai-Or., Dem. Rep. of the Congo* 86 D1
Kongolo, *Katanga, Dem. Rep. of the Congo* 86 D2
Kongor, *Sudan* 81 F3
Kongoussi, *Burkina Faso* 83 C4
Kongsberg, *Norway* 9 G13
Kongsvinger, *Norway* 9 F15
Kongwa, *Tanzania* 86 D4
Koni, *Dem. Rep. of the Congo* 87 E2
Koni, Mts., *Dem. Rep. of the Congo* 87 E2
Koniakari, *Mali* 82 C2
Koniecpol, *Poland* 31 H6
Königs Wusterhausen, *Germany* 24 C9
Königsbrunn, *Germany* 25 G6
Königslutter, *Germany* 24 C6
Konin, *Poland* 31 F5
Konispol, *Albania* 44 G4
Kónitsa, *Greece* 46 A2
Konjic, *Bos.-H.* 28 G2
Konkiep, *Namibia* 88 D2
Konkouré →, *Guinea* 82 D2
Könnern, *Germany* 24 D7
Kono, *S. Leone* 82 D2
Konongo, *Ghana* 83 D4
Konosha, *Russia* 32 B11
Kōnosu, *Japan* 55 F9
Konotop, *Ukraine* 33 G7
Konsankoro, *Guinea* 82 D3
Końskie, *Poland* 31 G7
Konstancin-Jeziorna, *Poland* 31 F8
Konstantinovka = Kostyantynivka, *Ukraine* 33 H9
Konstantinovsk, *Russia* 35 G5
Konstantynów Łódźki, *Poland* 31 G6
Konstanz, *Germany* 25 H5
Kont, *Iran* 71 E9
Kontagora, *Nigeria* 83 C6
Kontcha, *Cameroon* 83 D7
Konya, *Turkey* 70 B2
Konya Ovası, *Turkey* 72 C5
Konz, *Germany* 25 F2
Konza, *Kenya* 86 C4
Koocanusa, L., *Canada* 108 B6
Kookynie, *Australia* 93 E3
Koolyanobbing, *Australia* 93 F2
Koonibba, *Australia* 95 E1
Koorawatha, *Australia* 95 E4
Koorda, *Australia* 93 F2
Kooskia, *U.S.A.* 108 C6
Kootenay △, *Canada* 102 C5
Kootenay →, *U.S.A.* 102 D5

Kootenay L., *Canada* 102 D5
Kootjieskolk, *S. Africa* 88 E3
Kopanovka, *Russia* 35 G8
Kopaonik, *Serbia & M.* 44 C4
Kopaonik △, *Serbia & M.* 44 C4
Kópavogur, *Iceland* 8 D3
Kopayhorod, *Ukraine* 29 B12
Koper, *Slovenia* 41 C10
Kopervik, *Norway* 9 G11
Kopet Dagh, *Asia* 71 B8
Kopi, *Australia* 95 E2
Köping, *Sweden* 10 E10
Köpingsvik, *Sweden* 11 H10
Kopište, *Croatia* 41 F13
Koplik, *Albania* 44 D3
Köpmanholmen, *Sweden* 10 A12
Kopparberg, *Sweden* 10 E9
Koppeh Dāgh = Kopet Dagh, *Asia* 71 B8
Koppies, *S. Africa* 89 D4
Koppom, *Sweden* 10 E6
Koprivlen, *Bulgaria* 44 E7
Koprivnica, *Croatia* 41 B13
Kopřivnice, *Czech Rep.* 27 B11
Koprivshtitsa, *Bulgaria* 45 D8
Köprübaşı, *Turkey* 47 C10
Kopychyntsi, *Ukraine* 33 H3
Kora △, *Kenya* 86 C4
Korab, *Macedonia* 44 E4
Korakiána, *Greece* 49 A3
Koral, *India* 68 J5
Korarou, L., *Mali* 82 B4
Korba, *India* 69 H10
Korbach, *Germany* 24 D4
Korbu, G., *Malaysia* 65 K3
Korçë, *Albania* 44 F4
Korčula, *Croatia* 41 F13
Korčulanski Kanal, *Croatia* 41 E13
Kord Kūy, *Iran* 71 B7
Kord Sheykh, *Iran* 71 D7
Kordestan = Kurdistan, *Asia* 73 D10
Kordestān □, *Iran* 70 C5
Kordofân, *Sudan* 79 F11
Koré Mayroua, *Niger* 83 C5
Korea, North ■, *Asia* 57 E14
Korea, South ■, *Asia* 57 G15
Korea Bay, *Korea* 57 E13
Korea Strait, *Asia* 57 H15
Korem, *Ethiopia* 81 E4
Korenevo, *Russia* 33 G8
Korenovsk, *Russia* 35 H4
Korets, *Ukraine* 33 G4
Korfantów, *Poland* 31 H4
Korgan, *Turkey* 72 B7
Korgus, *Sudan* 80 D3
Korhogo, *Ivory C.* 82 D3
Koribundu, *S. Leone* 82 D2
Korienzé, *Mali* 82 B4
Korinthía □, *Greece* 46 D4
Korinthiakós Kólpos, *Greece* 46 C4
Kórinthos, *Greece* 46 D4
Korioumé, *Mali* 82 B4
Koríssa, Límni, *Greece* 49 B3
Kōriyama, *Japan* 54 F10
Korkuteli, *Turkey* 47 D12
Kormakiti, C., *Cyprus* 49 D11
Körmend, *Hungary* 28 C1
Kornat, *Croatia* 41 E12
Kornat △, *Croatia* 41 E12
Korneshty = Corneşti, *Moldova* 29 C13
Korneuburg, *Austria* 27 C9
Kórnik, *Poland* 31 F4
Koro, *Fiji* 91 C8
Koro, *Ivory C.* 82 D3
Koro, *Mali* 82 C4
Koro Sea, *Fiji* 91 C9
Korocha, *Russia* 33 G9
Köroğlu Dağları, *Turkey* 72 B5
Korogwe, *Tanzania* 86 D4
Koroleve, *Ukraine* 29 B8
Koronadal, *Phil.* 61 H6
Koróni, *Greece* 46 E3
Korónia, Limni, *Greece* 44 F7
Koronís, *Greece* 47 D7
Koronowo, *Poland* 31 E4
Koropets, *Ukraine* 29 B10
Koror, *Palau* 96 G5
Körös →, *Hungary* 28 D5
Körös Maros △, *Hungary* 28 C5
Köröstarcsa, *Hungary* 28 D6
Korosten, *Ukraine* 33 G5
Korostyshev, *Ukraine* 33 G5
Korotoyak, *Russia* 33 G10
Korraraika, Helodranon' i, *Madag.* 89 B7
Korsakov, *Russia* 53 E15
Korsberga, *Sweden* 11 G9
Korshiv, *Ukraine* 29 B10
Korshunovo, *Russia* 53 D12
Korsør, *Denmark* 11 J5
Korsun Shevchenkovskiy, *Ukraine* 33 H6
Korsze, *Poland* 30 D8
Korti, *Sudan* 80 D3
Kortrijk, *Belgium* 17 D3
Korucu, *Turkey* 47 B9
Korwai, *India* 68 G8
Koryakskoye Nagorye, *Russia* 53 C18
Koryŏng, *S. Korea* 57 G15
Koryukovka, *Ukraine* 33 G7
Kos, *Greece* 47 E9
Kosa, *Ethiopia* 81 F4
Kosaya Gora, *Russia* 32 E9
Kościan, *Poland* 31 F3
Kościerzyna, *Poland* 30 D4
Kosciusko, *U.S.A.* 113 J10
Kosciuszko, Mt., *Australia* 95 F4
Kösély →, *Hungary* 28 C6
Kosha, *Sudan* 80 C3
Koshava, *Bulgaria* 44 B7
K'oshih = Kashi, *China* 60 C2
Koshiki-Rettō, *Japan* 55 J4
Kosi, *India* 68 F7
Kosi →, *India* 69 E8
Košice, *Slovak Rep.* 27 C14
Košický □, *Slovak Rep.* 27 C14
Kosiv, *Ukraine* 29 B10
Kosjerić, *Serbia & M.* 44 B3
Köşk, *Turkey* 47 D10
Koskinoú, *Greece* 49 C10
Koslan, *Russia* 52 C5
Kosmach, *Ukraine* 29 B9
Kosŏng, *N. Korea* 57 E15
Kosovo □, *Serbia & M.* 44 D4
Kosovo Polje, *Serbia & M.* 44 D5
Kosovska Kamenica, *Serbia & M.* 44 D5
Kosovska Mitrovica, *Serbia & M.* 44 D4
Kossou, L. de, *Ivory C.* 82 D3
Kosta, *Sweden* 11 H9
Kostajnica, *Croatia* 41 C13
Kostanjevica, *Slovenia* 41 C12
Kostenets, *Bulgaria* 44 D7
Koster, *S. Africa* 88 D4
Kôstî, *Sudan* 81 E3
Kostinbrod, *Bulgaria* 44 D7
Kostolac, *Serbia & M.* 44 B5
Kostopil, *Ukraine* 33 G4
Kostroma, *Russia* 32 D11
Kostromskoye Vdkhr., *Russia* 32 D11
Kostryzhivka, *Ukraine* 29 B10
Kostrzyn, *Lubuskie, Poland* 31 F1
Kostrzyn, *Wielkopolskie, Poland* 31 F4
Kostyantynivka, *Ukraine* 33 H9
Kostyukovichi = Kastsyukovichy, *Belarus* 32 F7
Koszalin, *Poland* 30 D3
Kőszeg, *Hungary* 28 C1
Kot Addu, *Pakistan* 68 D4
Kot Kapura, *India* 68 D6
Kot Moman, *Pakistan* 68 C5
Kot Sultan, *Pakistan* 68 D4
Kota, *India* 68 G6
Kota Barrage, *India* 68 G6
Kota Belud, *Malaysia* 62 C5
Kota Bharu, *Malaysia* 65 J4
Kota Kinabalu, *Malaysia* 62 C5
Kota Kubu Bharu, *Malaysia* 65 L3
Kota Tinggi, *Malaysia* 65 M4
Kotaagung, *Indonesia* 62 F2
Kotabaru, *Indonesia* 62 E5
Kotabumi, *Indonesia* 62 E2
Kotamobagu, *Indonesia* 63 D6
Kotcho L., *Canada* 102 B4
Kotdwara, *India* 69 E8
Kotel, *Bulgaria* 45 D10
Kotelnich, *Russia* 34 A9
Kotelnikovo, *Russia* 35 G6
Kotelnyy, Ostrov, *Russia* 53 B14
Kothari →, *India* 68 G6
Köthen, *Germany* 24 D7
Kothi, *Chhattisgarh, India* 69 H10
Kothi, *Mad. P., India* 69 G9
Kotiro, *Pakistan* 68 F2
Kotka, *Finland* 9 F22
Kotlas, *Russia* 52 C5
Kotlenska Planina, *Bulgaria* 45 D10
Kotli, *Pakistan* 68 C5
Kotma, *India* 69 H9
Kotmul, *Pakistan* 69 B6
Koton-Karifi, *Nigeria* 83 D6
Kotonkoro, *Nigeria* 83 C6
Kotor, *Serbia & M.* 44 D2
Kotor Varoš, *Bos.-H.* 28 F2
Kotoriba, *Croatia* 41 B13
Kotovo, *Russia* 34 E7
Kotovsk, *Russia* 34 D5
Kotovsk, *Ukraine* 33 J5
Kotputli, *India* 68 F7
Kotri, *Pakistan* 68 G3
Kótronas, *Greece* 46 E4
Kötschach-Mauthen, *Austria* 26 E6
Kotturu, *India* 66 M10
Kotuy →, *Russia* 53 B11
Kotyuzhany, *Ukraine* 29 B12
Kotzebue, *U.S.A.* 100 B3
Kouchibouguac △, *Canada* 105 C6
Koudougou, *Burkina Faso* 82 C4
Koufonísi, *Greece* 49 E8
Koufonísia, *Greece* 47 E7
Kougaberge, *S. Africa* 88 E3
Kouibli, *Ivory C.* 82 D3
Kouilou →, *Congo* 84 E2
Koula Moutou, *Gabon* 84 E2
Koulen = Kulen, *Cambodia* 64 F5
Koulikoro, *Mali* 82 C3
Kouloúra, *Greece* 49 A3
Koúm-bournoú, Ákra, *Greece* 49 C10
Koumala, *Australia* 94 C4
Koumankou, *Mali* 82 C3
Koumbia, *Burkina Faso* 82 C4
Koumbia, *Guinea* 82 C2
Koumboum, *Guinea* 82 C2
Koumpenntoum, *Senegal* 82 C2
Koumra, *Chad* 79 G9
Koun-Fao, *Ivory C.* 82 D4
Koundara, *Guinea* 82 C2
Koundian, *Guinea* 82 C3
Koungheul, *Senegal* 82 C2
Kounradskiy, *Kazakhstan* 52 E8
Kountze, *U.S.A.* 113 K7
Koupéla, *Burkina Faso* 83 C4
Kourémalé, *Mali* 82 C3
Kouris →, *Cyprus* 49 E11
Kourou, *Fr. Guiana* 125 B8
Kourouba, *Mali* 82 C2
Kouroukoto, *Mali* 82 C2
Kourouma, *Burkina Faso* 82 C4
Kourouninkoto, *Mali* 82 C3
Kouroussa, *Guinea* 82 C3
Koussanar, *Senegal* 82 C2
Koussané, *Mali* 82 C2
Koussane, *Senegal* 82 C2
Kousseri, *Cameroon* 79 F8
Koutiala, *Mali* 82 C3
Kouto, *Ivory C.* 82 D3
Kouvé, *Togo* 83 D5
Kouvola, *Finland* 9 F22
Kovačica, *Serbia & M.* 28 E5
Kovel, *Ukraine* 33 G3
Kovin, *Serbia & M.* 28 F5
Kovrov, *Russia* 34 B5
Kowal, *Poland* 31 F6
Kowalewo Pomorskie, *Poland* 31 E5
Kowanyama, *Australia* 94 B3
Kowloon, *China* 59 F10
Kowŏn, *N. Korea* 57 E14
Koyampattur = Coimbatore, *India* 66 P10
Köyceğiz, *Turkey* 47 E10
Köyceğiz Gölü, *Turkey* 47 E10
Koyulhisar, *Turkey* 72 B7
Koyunyeri, *Turkey* 45 F10
Koza, *Japan* 55 L3
Kozak, *Turkey* 47 B9
Kozan, *Turkey* 70 B2
Kozáni, *Greece* 44 F5
Kozáni □, *Greece* 44 F5
Kozara, *Bos.-H.* 41 D14
Kozara △, *Bos.-H.* 28 F2
Kozarac, *Bos.-H.* 41 D13
Kozelets, *Ukraine* 33 G6
Kozelsk, *Russia* 32 E8
Kozhikode = Calicut, *India* 66 P9
Koziegłowy, *Poland* 31 H6
Kozienice, *Poland* 31 G8
Kozje, *Slovenia* 41 B12
Kozloduy, *Bulgaria* 44 C7
Kozlovets, *Bulgaria* 45 C9
Kozlovka, *Russia* 34 C9
Kozlu, *Turkey* 72 B4
Kozluk, *Turkey* 73 C9
Koźmin, *Poland* 31 G4
Kozmodemyansk, *Russia* 34 B8
Kożuchów, *Poland* 31 G2
Kozyatyn, *Ukraine* 33 H5
Kpabia, *Ghana* 83 D4
Kpalimé, *Togo* 83 D5
Kpandae, *Ghana* 83 D4
Kpessi, *Togo* 83 D5
Kra, Isthmus of = Kra, Kho Khot, *Thailand* 65 G2
Kra, Kho Khot, *Thailand* 65 G2
Kra Buri, *Thailand* 65 G2
Kraai →, *S. Africa* 88 E4
Krabi, *Thailand* 65 H2
Kracheh, *Cambodia* 64 F6
Kragan, *Indonesia* 63 G14
Kragerø, *Norway* 9 G13
Kragujevac, *Serbia & M.* 44 B4
Krajenka, *Poland* 31 E3
Krakatau = Rakata, Pulau, *Indonesia* 62 F3
Krakatoa = Rakata, Pulau, *Indonesia* 62 F3
Krakor, *Cambodia* 64 F5
Kraków, *Poland* 31 H6
Kraków ✕ (KRK), *Poland* 31 H6
Kralanh, *Cambodia* 64 F4
Králíky, *Czech Rep.* 27 A9
Kraljevo, *Serbia & M.* 44 C4
Královéhradecký □, *Czech Rep.* 26 A8
Královský Chlmec, *Slovak Rep.* 27 C14
Kralupy nad Vltavou, *Czech Rep.* 26 A7
Kramatorsk, *Ukraine* 33 H9
Kramfors, *Sweden* 10 B11
Kraniá, *Greece* 44 G5
Kranía Elassónas, *Greece* 46 B4
Kranídhion, *Greece* 46 D5
Kranj, *Slovenia* 41 B11
Kranjska Gora, *Slovenia* 41 B10
Krankskop, *S. Africa* 89 D5
Krapina, *Croatia* 41 B12
Krapina →, *Croatia* 41 C12
Krapkowice, *Poland* 31 H4
Kras, *Croatia* 41 C10
Kraskino, *Russia* 53 E14
Krāslava, *Latvia* 32 E4
Kraslice, *Czech Rep.* 26 A5
Krasnaya Gorbatka, *Russia* 34 C5
Krasnaya Polyana, *Russia* 35 J5
Krasne, *Ukraine* 29 D14
Krasni Okny, *Ukraine* 29 C14
Kraśnik, *Poland* 31 H9
Krasnoarmeisk, *Ukraine* 33 H9
Krasnoarmeysk, *Russia* 34 E7
Krasnoarmeyskiy, *Russia* 35 G6
Krasnobrod, *Poland* 31 H10
Krasnodar, *Russia* 35 H4
Krasnodon, *Ukraine* 33 H10
Krasnogorskiy, *Russia* 34 B9
Krasnograd = Krasnohrad, *Ukraine* 33 H8
Krasnogvardeysk, *Ukraine* 33 K8
Krasnogvardeyskoye, *Russia* 35 H5
Krasnohrad, *Ukraine* 33 H8
Krasnokutsk, *Ukraine* 33 G8
Krasnolesnyy, *Russia* 33 G10
Krasnoperekopsk, *Ukraine* 33 J7
Krasnorechenskiy, *Russia* 54 B7
Krasnoselkup, *Russia* 52 C9
Krasnoslobodsk, *Mordvinia, Russia* 34 C6
Krasnoslobodsk, *Volgograd, Russia* 35 F7
Krasnoturinsk, *Russia* 52 D7
Krasnoyarsk, *Russia* 53 D10
Krasnoyarskoye, *Russia* 30 D8
Krasnoye = Krasnyy, *Russia* 32 E6
Krasnoyilsk 29 C10
Krasnozavodsk, *Russia* 32 D10
Krasnoznamensk, *Russia* 30 D9
Krasny Sulin, *Russia* 33 J11
Krasnystaw, *Poland* 31 H10
Krasnyy, *Russia* 32 E6
Krasnyy Kholm, *Russia* 32 C9
Krasnyy Kut, *Russia* 34 E8
Krasnyy Liman, *Ukraine* 33 H9
Krasnyy Luch, *Ukraine* 33 H10
Krasnyy Profintern, *Russia* 32 D11
Krasnyy Yar, *Astrakhan, Russia* 35 G9
Krasnyy Yar, *Samara, Russia* 34 D10
Krasnyy Yar, *Volgograd, Russia* 34 E7
Krasnyye Baki, *Russia* 34 B7
Krasnyyoskolske Vdskh., *Ukraine* 33 H9
Kraszna →, *Hungary* 28 B7
Kratie = Kracheh, *Cambodia* 64 F6
Kratovo, *Macedonia* 44 D6
Krau, *Indonesia* 63 E10
Kravanh, Chuor Phnum, *Cambodia* 65 G4
Krefeld, *Germany* 24 D2
Krémaston, Límni, *Greece* 46 C3
Kremen, *Croatia* 41 D12
Kremenchuk, *Ukraine* 33 H7
Kremenchuksk Vdskh., *Ukraine* 33 H7
Kremenets, *Ukraine* 33 G3
Kremennaya, *Ukraine* 33 H10
Kremges = Svitlovodsk, *Ukraine* 33 H7
Kremmen, *Germany* 24 C9
Kremmling, *U.S.A.* 108 F10
Kremnica, *Slovak Rep.* 27 C11
Krems, *Austria* 26 C8
Kremsmünster, *Austria* 26 C7
Kretinga, *Lithuania* 9 J19
Krettsy, *Russia* 32 C7
Kreuzberg, *Germany* 25 E5
Kreuztal, *Germany* 24 E4
Kría Vrísi, *Greece* 44 F6
Kribi, *Cameroon* 83 E6
Krichem, *Bulgaria* 45 D8
Krichev = Krychaw, *Belarus* 32 F6
Krim, *Slovenia* 41 C11
Kriós, Ákra, *Greece* 49 D5
Krishna →, *India* 67 M12
Krishnanagar, *India* 69 H13
Kristdala, *Sweden* 11 G10
Kristiansand, *Norway* 9 G13
Kristianstad, *Sweden* 11 H8
Kristiansund, *Norway* 8 E12
Kristiinankaupunki, *Finland* 9 E19
Kristinehamn, *Sweden* 10 E8
Kristinestad = Kristiinankaupunki, *Finland* 9 E19
Kríti, *Greece* 49 D7
Kritsá, *Greece* 49 D7
Kriva →, *Macedonia* 44 D5
Kriva Palanka, *Macedonia* 44 D6
Krivaja →, *Bos.-H.* 28 F3
Krivelj, *Serbia & M.* 44 B6
Křivoklátsko ⌓, *Czech Rep.* 26 A6
Krivoy Rog = Kryvyy Rih, *Ukraine* 33 J7
Križevci, *Croatia* 41 B13
Krk, *Croatia* 41 C11
Krka △, *Croatia* 41 E12
Krka →, *Slovenia* 41 C12
Krkonoše, *Czech Rep.* 26 A8
Krkonoše △, *Czech Rep.* 26 A8
Krnov, *Czech Rep.* 27 A10
Krobia, *Poland* 31 G3
Krokeaí, *Greece* 46 E4
Krokek, *Sweden* 11 F10
Krokodil →, *Mozam.* 89 D5
Krokom, *Sweden* 10 A8
Krokowa, *Poland* 30 D5
Krolevets, *Ukraine* 33 G7
Kroměříž, *Czech Rep.* 27 B10
Krompachy, *Slovak Rep.* 27 C13
Kromy, *Russia* 33 F8
Kronach, *Germany* 25 E7
Krong Kaoh Kong, *Cambodia* 62 B2
Kronobergs län □, *Sweden* 11 H8
Kronprins Olav Kyst, *Antarctica* 5 C5
Kronprinsesse Märtha Kyst, *Antarctica* 5 D2
Kronshtadt, *Russia* 32 C5
Kroonstad, *S. Africa* 88 D4
Kröpelin, *Germany* 24 A7
Kropotkin, *Russia* 35 H5
Kropp, *Germany* 24 A5
Krosna, *Lithuania* 30 D10
Krośniewice, *Poland* 31 F6
Krosno, *Poland* 31 J8
Krosno Odrzańskie, *Poland* 31 F2
Krotoszyn, *Poland* 31 G4
Krotovka, *Russia* 34 D10
Kroussón, *Greece* 49 D6
Krrabë, *Albania* 44 E3
Krško, *Slovenia* 41 C12
Krstača, *Serbia & M.* 44 D4
Kruger △, *S. Africa* 89 C5
Krugersdorp, *S. Africa* 89 D4
Kruisfontein, *S. Africa* 88 E3
Krujë, *Albania* 44 E3
Krulevshchina = Krulyewshchyna, *Belarus* 32 E4
Krulyewshchyna, *Belarus* 32 E4
Krumbach, *Germany* 25 G6
Krumë, *Albania* 44 D4
Krumovgrad, *Bulgaria* 45 E9
Krung Thep = Bangkok, *Thailand* 64 F3
Krupanj, *Serbia & M.* 44 B3
Krupina, *Slovak Rep.* 27 C12
Krupinica →, *Slovak Rep.* 27 C11
Krupki, *Belarus* 32 E5
Kruševac, *Serbia & M.* 44 C5
Kruševo, *Macedonia* 44 E5
Krushelnyksya, *Ukraine* 31 J10
Kruszwica, *Poland* 31 F5
Krychaw, *Belarus* 32 F6
Krymsk, *Russia* 33 K10
Krymskiy Poluostrov = Krymskyy Pivostriv, *Ukraine* 33 K8
Krymskyy Pivostriv, *Ukraine* 33 K8
Krynica, *Poland* 31 J7
Krynica Morska, *Poland* 30 D6
Krynki, *Poland* 31 E10
Krynychne, *Ukraine* 29 E13
Kryvyy Rih, *Ukraine* 33 J7
Kryzhopil, *Ukraine* 29 B13
Krzepice, *Poland* 31 H5
Krzeszów, *Poland* 31 H9
Krzna →, *Poland* 31 F10
Krzywiń, *Poland* 31 G3
Krzyż Wielkopolski, *Poland* 31 F2
Ksar el Kebir, *Morocco* 78 B4
Ksar es Souk = Er Rachidia, *Morocco* 78 B5
Książ Wielkopolski, *Poland* 31 F4
Kstovo, *Russia* 34 B7
Ku, W. el →, *Sudan* 81 E2
Kuah, *Malaysia* 65 J2
Kuala Belait, *Malaysia* 62 D4
Kuala Berang, *Malaysia* 65 K4
Kuala Dungun = Dungun, *Malaysia* 65 K4
Kuala Kangsar, *Malaysia* 65 K3
Kuala Kelawang, *Malaysia* 65 L4
Kuala Kerai, *Malaysia* 65 K4
Kuala Kerian, *Malaysia* 65 c
Kuala Lipis, *Malaysia* 65 K4
Kuala Lumpur, *Malaysia* 65 L3
Kuala Nerang, *Malaysia* 65 J3
Kuala Pilah, *Malaysia* 65 L4
Kuala Rompin, *Malaysia* 65 L4
Kuala Selangor, *Malaysia* 65 L3
Kuala Sepetang, *Malaysia* 65 K3
Kuala Terengganu, *Malaysia* 65 K4
Kualajelai, *Indonesia* 62 E4
Kualakapuas, *Indonesia* 62 E4
Kualakurun, *Indonesia* 62 E4
Kualapembuang, *Indonesia* 62 E4
Kualasimpang, *Indonesia* 62 D1
Kuancheng, *China* 57 D10
Kuandang, *Indonesia* 63 D6
Kuandian, *China* 57 D13
Kuangchou = Guangzhou, *China* 59 F9
Kuanshan, *Taiwan* 59 F13
Kuantan, *Malaysia* 65 L4
Kuba = Quba, *Azerbaijan* 35 K9
Kuban →, *Russia* 33 K9
Kuban Depression = Prikubanskaya Nizmennost, *Russia* 35 H4
Kubenskoye, Ozero, *Russia* 32 C10
Kubokawa, *Japan* 55 H6
Kubrat, *Bulgaria* 45 C10
Kubu, *Indonesia* 63 J18
Kubutambahan, *Indonesia* 63 J18
Kucar, Tanjung, *Indonesia* 63 K18
Kučevo, *Serbia & M.* 44 B5
Kucha Gompa, *India* 69 B7
Kuchaman, *India* 68 F6
Kuchenspitze, *Austria* 26 D3
Kuchinda, *India* 69 J11
Kuching, *Malaysia* 62 D4
Kuchino-eruba-Jima, *Japan* 55 J5
Kuchino-Shima, *Japan* 55 K4
Kuchinotsu, *Japan* 55 H5
Kuchl, *Austria* 26 D6
Kuchurhan →, *Ukraine* 29 D14
Kucing = Kuching, *Malaysia* 62 D4
Kuçovë, *Albania* 44 F3
Küçükbahçe, *Turkey* 47 C8
Küçükköy, *Turkey* 47 B8
Küçükkuyu, *Turkey* 47 B8
Küçükmenderes →, *Turkey* 47 D9
Kud →, *Pakistan* 68 F2
Kuda, *India* 66 H7
Kudat, *Malaysia* 62 C5
Kudirkos Naumiestis, *Lithuania* 30 D9
Kudowa-Zdrój, *Poland* 31 H3
Kudus, *Indonesia* 63 G14
Kudymkar, *Russia* 52 D6
Kueiyang = Guiyang, *China* 58 D6
Kufra Oasis = Al Kufrah, *Libya* 79 D10
Kufstein, *Austria* 26 D5
Kugaaruk = Pelly Bay, *Canada* 101 B11
Kugluktuk, *Canada* 100 B8
Kugong I., *Canada* 104 A4
Kūhak, *Iran* 66 F3
Kuhan, *Pakistan* 68 E2
Kūhbonān, *Iran* 71 D8
Kūhestak, *Iran* 71 E8
Kuhin, *Iran* 71 B6
Kūhīrī, *Iran* 71 E9
Kuhnsdorf, *Austria* 26 E7
Kūhpāyeh, *Eşfahan, Iran* 71 C7
Kūhpāyeh, *Kermān, Iran* 71 D8
Kūhrān, Kūh-e, *Iran* 71 E8
Kui Buri, *Thailand* 65 F2
Kuiseb →, *Namibia* 88 C1
Kuito, *Angola* 85 G3
Kuiu I., *U.S.A.* 102 B2
Kujang, *N. Korea* 57 E14
Kujawsko-Pomorskie □, *Poland* 30 E5
Kuji, *Japan* 54 D10
Kujū-San, *Japan* 55 H5
Kukava, *Ukraine* 29 B12
Kukavica, *Serbia & M.* 44 D5
Kukawa, *Nigeria* 83 C7
Kukës, *Albania* 44 D4
Kukmor, *Russia* 34 B10
Kukup, *Malaysia* 65 d
Kukup, Pulau, *Malaysia* 65 d
Kukvidze, *Russia* 34 E6
Kula, *Bulgaria* 44 C6
Kula, *Serbia & M.* 28 E4
Kula, *Turkey* 47 C10
Kulachi, *Pakistan* 68 D4
Kulai, *Malaysia* 65 M4
Kulaly, Ostrov, *Kazakhstan* 35 H10
Kulasekarappattinam, *India* 66 Q11
Kulautuva, *Lithuania* 30 D10
Kuldīga, *Latvia* 9 H19
Kuldīga □, *Latvia* 30 B8
Kuldu, *Sudan* 81 E2
Kulebaki, *Russia* 34 C6
Kulen, *Cambodia* 64 F5
Kulen Vakuf, *Bos.-H.* 41 D13
Kulgam, *India* 69 C6

Kulgera, *Australia* 94 D1
Kulim, *Malaysia* 65 K3
Kulin, *Australia* 93 F2
Kulkayu = Hartley Bay, *Canada* 102 C3
Kullen, *Sweden* 11 H6
Kulmbach, *Germany* 25 E7
Kŭlob, *Tajikistan* 52 F7
Kulp, *Turkey* 73 C9
Kulpawn →, *Ghana* 83 D4
Kulsary, *Kazakhstan* 52 E6
Kulti, *India* 69 H12
Kulu, *India* 68 D7
Kulu, *Turkey* 72 C5
Kulumbura, *Australia* 92 B4
Kulunda, *Russia* 52 D8
Kulungar, *Afghan.* 68 C3
Kūlvand, *Iran* 71 D7
Kulwin, *Australia* 95 F3
Kulyab = Kŭlob, *Tajikistan* 52 F7
Kuma →, *Russia* 35 H8
Kumafşarı, *Turkey* 47 D11
Kumaganum, *Nigeria* 83 C7
Kumagaya, *Japan* 55 F9
Kumai, *Indonesia* 62 E4
Kumalar Dağı, *Turkey* 47 C12
Kumamba, Kepulauan, *Indonesia* 63 E9
Kumamoto, *Japan* 55 H5
Kumamoto □, *Japan* 55 H5
Kumanovo, *Macedonia* 44 D5
Kumara, *N.Z.* 91 K3
Kumarina, *Australia* 93 D2
Kumasi, *Ghana* 82 D4
Kumba, *Cameroon* 83 E6
Kumbağ, *Turkey* 45 F11
Kumbakonam, *India* 66 P11
Kumbarilla, *Australia* 95 D5
Kumbhraj, *India* 68 G7
Kumbia, *Australia* 95 D5
Kumbo, *Cameroon* 83 D7
Kŭmch'ŏn, *N. Korea* 57 E14
Kumdok, *India* 69 C8
Kume-Shima, *Japan* 55 L3
Kumeny, *Russia* 34 A9
Kumharsain, *India* 68 D7
Kŭmhwa, *S. Korea* 57 E14
Kumi, *Uganda* 86 B3
Kumkale, *Turkey* 45 G10
Kumla, *Sweden* 10 E9
Kumluca, *Turkey* 47 E12
Kummerower See, *Germany* 24 B8
Kumo, *Nigeria* 83 C7
Kumo älv = Kokemäenjoki →, *Finland* 9 F19
Kumon Bum, *Burma* 67 F20
Kumylzhenskaya, *Russia* 34 F6
Kunágota, *Hungary* 28 D6
Kunashir, Ostrov, *Russia* 53 E15
Kunda, *Estonia* 9 G22
Kunda, *India* 69 G9
Kundar →, *Pakistan* 68 D3
Kundelungu △, *Dem. Rep. of the Congo* 87 E2
Kundelungu Ouest △, *Dem. Rep. of the Congo* 87 D2
Kundian, *Pakistan* 68 C4
Kundla, *India* 68 J4
Kung, Ao, *Thailand* 65 a
Kunga →, *Bangla.* 69 J13
Kungälv, *Sweden* 11 G5
Kunghit I., *Canada* 102 C2
Kungrad = Qŭnghirot, *Uzbekistan* 52 E6
Kungsängen, *Sweden* 10 E11
Kungsbacka, *Sweden* 11 G6
Kungsgården, *Sweden* 10 D10
Kungshamn, *Sweden* 11 F5
Kungsör, *Sweden* 10 E10
Kungur, *Russia* 52 D6
Kungurri, *Australia* 94 K6
Kunhar →, *Pakistan* 69 B5
Kunhegyes, *Hungary* 28 C5
Kuningan, *Indonesia* 63 G13
Kunlong, *Burma* 58 F2
Kunlun Shan, *Asia* 60 C3
Kunmadaras, *Hungary* 28 C5
Kunming, *China* 58 E4
Kunów, *Poland* 31 H8
Kunsan, *S. Korea* 57 G14
Kunshan, *China* 59 B13
Kunszentmárton, *Hungary* 28 D5
Kunszentmiklós, *Hungary* 28 C4
Kuntaur, *Senegal* 82 C2
Kununurra, *Australia* 92 C4
Kunwari →, *India* 69 F8
Kunya-Urgench = Köneürgench, *Turkmenistan* 52 E6
Künzelsau, *Germany* 25 F5
Kuopio, *Finland* 8 E22
Kupa →, *Croatia* 41 C13
Kupang, *Indonesia* 63 F6
Kupreanof I., *U.S.A.* 102 B2
Kupres, *Bos.-H.* 28 G2
Kupyansk, *Ukraine* 33 H9
Kupyansk-Uzlovoi, *Ukraine* 33 H9
Kuqa, *China* 60 B3
Kür →, *Azerbaijan* 73 C13
Kür Dili, *Azerbaijan* 71 B6
Kura = Kür →, *Azerbaijan* 73 C13
Kuranda, *Australia* 94 B4
Kuranga, *India* 68 H3
Kurashiki, *Japan* 55 G6
Kurayoshi, *Japan* 55 G6
Kürdämir, *Azerbaijan* 35 K9
Kurdistan, *Asia* 73 D10
Kŭrdzhali, *Bulgaria* 45 E9
Kure, *Japan* 55 G6
Küre, *Turkey* 72 B5
Küre Dağları, *Turkey* 72 B6
Kuressaare, *Estonia* 9 G20
Kurgan, *Russia* 52 D7
Kurganinsk, *Russia* 35 H5
Kurgannaya = Kurganinsk, *Russia* 35 H5
Kuri, *India* 68 F4
Kuria Maria Is. = Khurīyā Murīyā, Jazā'ir, *Oman* 75 D6
Kuridala, *Australia* 94 C3
Kurigram, *Bangla.* 67 G16
Kurikka, *Finland* 9 E20
Kuril Is. = Kurilskiye Ostrova, *Russia* 53 E15
Kuril Trench, *Pac. Oc.* 96 C7
Kurilsk, *Russia* 53 E15
Kurilskiye Ostrova, *Russia* 53 E15
Kurino, *Japan* 55 J5
Kurinskaya Kosa = Kür Dili, *Azerbaijan* 71 B6
Kurkur, *Egypt* 80 C3
Kurlovskiy, *Russia* 34 C5
Kurmuk, *Sudan* 81 E3
Kurnool, *India* 66 M11
Kuro-Shima, *Kagoshima, Japan* 55 J4
Kuro-Shima, *Okinawa, Japan* 55 M2
Kuror, J., *Sudan* 80 C3
Kurow, *N.Z.* 91 L3
Kurów, *Poland* 31 G9
Kurram →, *Pakistan* 68 C4
Kurri Kurri, *Australia* 95 E5
Kurrimine, *Australia* 94 B4
Kursavka, *Russia* 35 H6
Kurshskaya Kosa ⌂, *Russia* 30 C7
Kurshskiy Zaliv, *Russia* 9 J19
Kuršių Nerijos △, *Lithuania* 30 C8
Kursk, *Russia* 33 G9
Kuršumlija, *Serbia & M.* 44 C5
Kuršumlijska Banja, *Serbia & M.* 44 C5
Kurşunlu, *Bursa, Turkey* 45 F13
Kurşunlu, *Çankırı, Turkey* 72 B5
Kurtalan, *Turkey* 73 D9
Kurtbey, *Turkey* 45 E10
Kuru, *Sudan* 81 F2
Kuru, Bahr el →, *Sudan* 81 F2
Kurucaşile, *Turkey* 72 B5
Kuruçay, *Turkey* 70 B3
Kuruktag, *China* 60 B3
Kuruman, *S. Africa* 88 D3
Kuruman →, *S. Africa* 88 D3
Kurume, *Japan* 55 H5
Kurun →, *Sudan* 81 F3
Kurunegala, *Sri Lanka* 66 R12
Kurya, *Russia* 52 C6
Kus Gölü, *Turkey* 45 F11
Kuşadası, *Turkey* 72 D2
Kuşadası Körfezı, *Turkey* 47 D8
Kusamba, *Indonesia* 63 K18
Kusatsu, *Japan* 55 F9
Kusawa L., *Canada* 102 A1
Kusel, *Germany* 25 F3
Kushaka, *Nigeria* 83 C6
Kushalgarh, *India* 68 H6
Kushchevskaya, *Russia* 35 G4
Kusheriki, *Nigeria* 83 C6
Kushikino, *Japan* 55 J5
Kushima, *Japan* 55 J5
Kushimoto, *Japan* 55 H7
Kushiro, *Japan* 54 C12
Kushiro-Gawa →, *Japan* 54 C12
Kushiro Shitsugen △, *Japan* 54 C12
Kūshk, *Iran* 71 D8
Kushka = Gushgy, *Turkmenistan* 52 F7
Kūshkī, *Iran* 70 C5
Kushnytsya, *Ukraine* 29 B8
Kushol, *India* 69 C7
Kushtia, *Bangla.* 67 H16
Kushum →, *Kazakhstan* 34 F10
Kuskokwim B., *U.S.A.* 100 C3
Kusmi, *India* 69 H10
Kussharo-Ko, *Japan* 54 C12
Kustanay = Qostanay, *Kazakhstan* 52 D7
Kut, Ko, *Thailand* 65 G4
Kuta, *Indonesia* 63 K18
Kütahya, *Turkey* 47 B12
Kütahya □, *Turkey* 47 B11
Kutaisi, *Georgia* 35 J6
Kutaraja = Banda Aceh, *Indonesia* 62 C1
Kutch, Gulf of = Kachchh, Gulf of, *India* 68 H3
Kutch, Rann of = Kachchh, Rann of, *India* 68 H4
Kutina, *Croatia* 41 C13
Kutiyana, *India* 68 J4
Kutjevo, *Croatia* 28 E2
Kutkashen, *Azerbaijan* 35 K8
Kutná Hora, *Czech Rep.* 26 B8
Kutno, *Poland* 31 F6
Kutse, *Botswana* 88 C3
Kuttabul, *Australia* 94 K6
Kutu, *Dem. Rep. of the Congo* 84 E3
Kutum, *Sudan* 81 E1
Kúty, *Slovak Rep.* 27 C10
Kuty, *Ukraine* 29 B10
Kuujjuaq, *Canada* 101 C13
Kuujjuarapik, *Canada* 104 A4
Kuŭp-tong, *N. Korea* 57 D14
Kuusamo, *Finland* 8 D23
Kuusankoski, *Finland* 9 F22
Kuvshinovo, *Russia* 32 D8
Kuwait = Al Kuwayt, *Kuwait* 70 D5
Kuwait ■, *Asia* 70 D5
Kuwana, *Japan* 55 G8
Kuwana →, *India* 69 F10
Kuybyshev = Samara, *Russia* 34 D10
Kuybyshev, *Russia* 52 D8
Kuybyshevo, *Ukraine* 33 J9
Kuybyshevskoye Vdkhr., *Russia* 34 C9
Kuye He →, *China* 56 E6
Kūyeh, *Iran* 70 B5
Kuyucak, *Turkey* 47 D10
Kuyumba, *Russia* 53 C10
Kuzey Anadolu Dağları, *Turkey* 72 B7
Kuzmin, *Serbia & M.* 28 E4
Kuznetsk, *Russia* 34 D8
Kuzomen, *Russia* 52 C4
Kvænangen, *Norway* 8 A19
Kværndrup, *Denmark* 11 J4
Kvaløy, *Norway* 8 B18
Kvänum, *Sweden* 11 F7
Kvareli = Qvareli, *Georgia* 35 K7
Kvarner, *Croatia* 41 D11
Kvarnerič, *Croatia* 41 D11
Kvicksund, *Sweden* 10 E10
Kvillsfors, *Sweden* 11 G9
Kvismare kanal, *Sweden* 10 E9
Kvissleby, *Sweden* 10 B11
Kwa-Nobuhle, *S. Africa* 85 L5
Kwabhaca, *S. Africa* 89 E4
Kwakhanai, *Botswana* 88 C3
Kwakoegron, *Suriname* 125 B7
Kwale, *Kenya* 86 C4
Kwale, *Nigeria* 83 D6
KwaMashu, *S. Africa* 89 D5
Kwando →, *Africa* 88 B3
Kwangchow = Guangzhou, *China* 59 F9
Kwangdaeri, *N. Korea* 57 D14
Kwangju, *S. Korea* 57 G14
Kwango →, *Dem. Rep. of the Congo* 84 E3
Kwangsi-Chuang = Guangxi Zhuangzu Zizhiqu □, *China* 58 F7
Kwangtung = Guangdong □, *China* 59 F9
Kwara □, *Nigeria* 83 D6
Kwataboahegan →, *Canada* 104 B3
Kwatisore, *Indonesia* 63 E8
KwaZulu Natal □, *S. Africa* 89 D5
Kweichow = Guizhou □, *China* 58 D6
Kwekwe, *Zimbabwe* 87 F2
Kwidzyn, *Poland* 30 E5
Kwiha, *Ethiopia* 81 E4
Kwinana New Town, *Australia* 93 F2
Kwisa →, *Poland* 31 G2
Kwoka, *Indonesia* 63 E8
Kwolla, *Nigeria* 83 D6
Kyabra Cr. →, *Australia* 95 D3
Kyabram, *Australia* 95 F4
Kyaikto, *Burma* 64 D1
Kyakhta, *Russia* 53 D11
Kyambura ⌂, *Uganda* 86 C3
Kyancutta, *Australia* 95 E2
Kyaukpadaung, *Burma* 67 J19
Kyaukpyu, *Burma* 67 K18
Kyaukse, *Burma* 67 J20
Kybartai, *Lithuania* 30 D9
Kyburz, *U.S.A.* 110 G6
Kyelang, *India* 68 C7
Kyenjojo, *Uganda* 86 B3
Kyjov, *Czech Rep.* 27 B10
Kyle, *Canada* 103 C7
Kyle Dam, *Zimbabwe* 87 G3
Kyle of Lochalsh, *U.K.* 13 D3
Kyll →, *Germany* 25 F2
Kyllburg, *Germany* 25 E2
Kymijoki →, *Finland* 9 F22
Kymmene älv = Kymijoki →, *Finland* 9 F22
Kyneton, *Australia* 95 F3
Kynuna, *Australia* 94 C3
Kyō-ga-Saki, *Japan* 55 G7
Kyoga, L., *Uganda* 86 B3
Kyogle, *Australia* 95 D5
Kyom →, *Sudan* 81 F2
Kyongju, *S. Korea* 57 G15
Kyongpyaw, *Burma* 67 L19
Kyŏngsŏng, *N. Korea* 57 D15
Kyōto, *Japan* 55 G7
Kyōto □, *Japan* 55 G7
Kyparissovouno, *Cyprus* 49 D12
Kyperounda, *Cyprus* 49 E11
Kyrenia, *Cyprus* 49 D12
Kyrgyzstan ■, *Asia* 52 E8
Kyritz, *Germany* 24 C8
Kyrkhult, *Sweden* 11 H8
Kyrnasivka, *Ukraine* 29 B13
Kyrnychky, *Ukraine* 29 E14
Kyro älv = Kyrönjoki →, *Finland* 8 E19
Kyrönjoki →, *Finland* 8 E19
Kystatyam, *Russia* 53 C13
Kysucké Nové Mesto, *Slovak Rep.* 27 B11
Kytay, Ozero, *Ukraine* 29 E14
Kythréa, *Cyprus* 49 D12
Kyunhla, *Burma* 67 H19
Kyuquot Sound, *Canada* 102 D3
Kyurdamir = Kürdämir, *Azerbaijan* 35 K9
Kyūshū, *Japan* 55 H5
Kyūshū □, *Japan* 55 H5
Kyūshū-Sanchi, *Japan* 55 H5
Kyustendil, *Bulgaria* 44 D6
Kyusyur, *Russia* 53 B13
Kyyiv, *Ukraine* 33 G6
Kyyivske Vdskh., *Ukraine* 33 G6
Kyzyl, *Russia* 53 D10
Kyzyl Kum, *Uzbekistan* 52 E7
Kyzyl-Kyya, *Kyrgyzstan* 52 E8
Kyzyl-Orda = Qyzylorda, *Kazakhstan* 52 E7

L

La Albuera, *Spain* 37 G4
La Alcarria, *Spain* 38 E2
La Almarcha, *Spain* 38 F2
La Almunia de Doña Godina, *Spain* 38 D3
La Amistad △, *Cent. Amer.* 120 E3
La Asunción, *Venezuela* 124 A6
La Baie, *Canada* 105 C5
La Banda, *Argentina* 126 B3
La Bañeza, *Spain* 36 C5
La Barca, *Mexico* 118 C4
La Barge, *U.S.A.* 108 E8
La Bastide-Puylaurent, *France* 20 D7
La Baule, *France* 18 E4
La Belle, *U.S.A.* 115 M5
La Biche →, *Canada* 102 B4
La Biche, L., *Canada* 102 C6
La Bisbal d'Empordà, *Spain* 38 D8
La Blanquilla, *Venezuela* 121 D7
La Bomba, *Mexico* 118 A1
La Brea, *Trin. & Tob.* 125 K15
La Brède, *France* 20 D3
La Bresse, *France* 19 D13
La Bureba, *Spain* 36 C7
La Calera, *Chile* 126 C1
La Campana △, *Chile* 126 C1
La Campiña, *Spain* 37 H6
La Canal = Sa Canal, *Spain* 48 C7
La Cañiza = A Cañiza, *Spain* 36 C2
La Canourgue, *France* 20 D7
La Capelle, *France* 19 C10
La Carlota, *Argentina* 126 C3
La Carlota, *Phil.* 61 F5
La Carlota, *Spain* 37 H6
La Carolina, *Spain* 37 G7
La Cavalerie, *France* 20 D7
La Ceiba, *Honduras* 120 C2
La Chaise-Dieu, *France* 20 C7
La Chapelle d'Angillon, *France* 19 E9
La Chapelle-St-Luc, *France* 19 D11
La Chapelle-sur-Erdre, *France* 18 E5
La Charité-sur-Loire, *France* 19 E10
La Chartre-sur-le-Loir, *France* 18 E7
La Châtaigneraie, *France* 20 B3
La Châtre, *France* 19 F9
La Chaux-de-Fonds, *Switz.* 25 H2
La Chorrera, *Panama* 120 E4
La Ciotat, *France* 21 E9
La Clayette, *France* 19 F11
La Cocha, *Argentina* 126 B2
La Concepción, *Panama* 120 E3
La Concordia, *Mexico* 119 D6
La Coruña = A Coruña, *Spain* 36 B2
La Coruña □, *Spain* 36 B2
La Côte-St-André, *France* 21 C9
La Courtine, *France* 20 C6
La Crau, *Bouches-du-Rhône, France* 21 E8
La Crau, *Var, France* 21 E10
La Crescent, *U.S.A.* 112 D9
La Crete, *Canada* 102 B5
La Crosse, *Kans., U.S.A.* 112 F5
La Crosse, *Wis., U.S.A.* 112 D9
La Cruz, *Costa Rica* 120 D2
La Cruz, *Mexico* 118 C3
La Désirade, *Guadeloupe* 120 b
La Escondida, *Mexico* 118 C5
La Esmeralda, *Paraguay* 126 A3
La Esperanza, *Cuba* 120 B3
La Esperanza, *Honduras* 120 D2
La Estrada = A Estrada, *Spain* 36 C2
La Faouët, *France* 18 D3
La Fayette, *U.S.A.* 115 H3
La Fé, *Cuba* 120 B3
La Fère, *France* 19 C10
La Ferté-Bernard, *France* 18 D7
La Ferté-Gaucher, *France* 19 D10
La Ferté-Macé, *France* 18 D6
La Ferté-St-Aubin, *France* 19 E8
La Ferté-sous-Jouarre, *France* 19 D10
La Ferté-Vidame, *France* 18 D7
La Flèche, *France* 18 E6
La Follette, *U.S.A.* 115 G3
La Fregeneda, *Spain* 36 E4
La Fuente de San Esteban, *Spain* 36 E4
La Gacilly, *France* 18 E4
La Gineta, *Spain* 39 F2
La Grand'Combe, *France* 21 D8
La Grande, *U.S.A.* 108 D4
La Grande →, *Canada* 104 B5
La Grande Deux, Rés., *Canada* 104 B4
La Grande-Motte, *France* 21 E8
La Grande Quatre, Rés., *Canada* 104 B5
La Grande Trois, Rés., *Canada* 104 B4
La Grange, *Calif., U.S.A.* 110 H6
La Grange, *Ga., U.S.A.* 115 J3
La Grange, *Ky., U.S.A.* 114 F3
La Grange, *Tex., U.S.A.* 113 L6
La Grave, *France* 21 C10
La Guaira, *Venezuela* 124 A5
La Guardia = A Guarda, *Spain* 36 D2
La Gudiña = A Gudiña, *Spain* 36 C3
La Guerche-de-Bretagne, *France* 18 E5
La Guerche-sur-l'Aubois, *France* 19 F9
La Habana, *Cuba* 120 B3
La Haute Vallée de Chevreuse ⌂, *France* 19 D8
La Haye-du-Puits, *France* 18 C5
La Horra, *Spain* 36 D7
La Independencia, *Mexico* 119 D6
La Isabela, *Dom. Rep.* 121 C5
La Jonquera, *Spain* 38 C7
La Junta, *U.S.A.* 113 F3
La Laguna, *Canary Is.* 48 F3
La Libertad, *Guatemala* 120 C1
La Libertad, *Mexico* 118 B2
La Ligua, *Chile* 126 C1
La Línea de la Concepción, *Spain* 37 J5
La Loche, *Canada* 103 B7
La Londe-les-Maures, *France* 21 E10
La Lora, *Spain* 36 C7
La Loupe, *France* 18 D8
La Louvière, *Belgium* 17 D4
La Lune, *Trin. & Tob.* 125 K15
La Machine, *France* 19 F10
La Maddalena, *Italy* 42 A2
La Malbaie, *Canada* 105 C5
La Malinche △, *Mexico* 119 D5
La Mancha, *Spain* 39 F2
La Mariña, *Spain* 36 B3
La Martre, L., *Canada* 102 A5
La Mesa, *U.S.A.* 111 N9
La Misión, *Mexico* 118 A1
La Mothe-Achard, *France* 18 F5
La Motte-Chalançon, *France* 21 D9
La Motte-du-Caire, *France* 21 D10
La Motte-Servolex, *France* 21 C9
La Moure, *U.S.A.* 112 B5
La Muela, *Spain* 38 D3
La Mure, *France* 21 D9
La Negra, *Chile* 126 A1
La Oliva, *Canary Is.* 48 F6
La Orotava, *Canary Is.* 48 F3
La Oroya, *Peru* 124 F3
La Pacaudière, *France* 19 F10
La Palma, *Canary Is.* 48 F2
La Palma, *Panama* 120 E4
La Palma del Condado, *Spain* 37 H4
La Paloma, *Chile* 126 C1
La Pampa □, *Argentina* 126 D2
La Paragua, *Venezuela* 124 B6
La Paz, *Entre Ríos, Argentina* 126 C4
La Paz, *San Luis, Argentina* 126 C2
La Paz, *Bolivia* 124 G5
La Paz, *Honduras* 120 D2
La Paz, *Mexico* 118 C2
La Paz, *Phil.* 61 D4
La Paz Centro, *Nic.* 120 D2
La Pedrera, *Colombia* 124 D5
La Pérade, *Canada* 105 C5
La Perouse Str., *Asia* 54 B11
La Pesca, *Mexico* 119 C5
La Piedad, *Mexico* 118 C4
La Pine, *U.S.A.* 108 E3
La Plata, *Argentina* 126 D4
La Pobla de Lillet, *Spain* 38 C6
La Pocatière, *Canada* 105 C5
La Pola de Gordón, *Spain* 36 C5
La Porta, *France* 21 F13
La Porte, *Ind., U.S.A.* 114 E2
La Porte, *Tex., U.S.A.* 113 L7
La Presanella, *Italy* 40 B7
La Puebla = Sa Pobla, *Spain* 38 F8
La Puebla de Cazalla, *Spain* 37 H5
La Puebla de los Infantes, *Spain* 37 H5
La Puebla de Montalbán, *Spain* 36 F6
La Puebla del Río, *Spain* 37 H4
La Puerta de Segura, *Spain* 37 G8
La Purísima, *Mexico* 118 B2
La Push, *U.S.A.* 110 C2
La Quiaca, *Argentina* 126 A2
La Réole, *France* 20 D3
La Restinga, *Canary Is.* 48 G2
La Rioja, *Argentina* 126 B2
La Rioja □, *Argentina* 126 B2
La Rioja □, *Spain* 38 C2
La Robla, *Spain* 36 C5
La Roche-Bernard, *France* 18 E4
La Roche-Canillac, *France* 20 C5
La Roche-en-Ardenne, *Belgium* 17 D5
La Roche-sur-Foron, *France* 19 F13
La Roche-sur-Yon, *France* 18 F5
La Rochefoucauld, *France* 20 C4
La Rochelle, *France* 20 B2
La Roda, *Spain* 39 F2
La Roda de Andalucía, *Spain* 37 H6
La Romana, *Dom. Rep.* 121 C6
La Ronge, *Canada* 103 B7
La Rumorosa, *Mexico* 111 N10
La Sabina = Sa Savina, *Spain* 48 C7
La Sagra, *Spain* 39 H2
La Salle, *U.S.A.* 112 E10
La Sanabria, *Spain* 36 C4
La Santa, *Canary Is.* 48 E6
La Sarre, *Canada* 104 C4
La Scie, *Canada* 105 C8
La Selva, *Spain* 38 C7
La Selva Beach, *U.S.A.* 110 J5
La Selva del Camp, *Spain* 38 D6
La Serena, *Chile* 126 B1
La Serena, *Spain* 37 G5
La Seu d'Urgell, *Spain* 38 C6
La Seyne-sur-Mer, *France* 21 E9
La Sila, *Italy* 43 C9
La Solana, *Spain* 37 G7
La Soufrière, *St. Vincent* 121 D7
La Souterraine, *France* 19 F8
La Spézia, *Italy* 40 D6
La Suze-sur-Sarthe, *France* 18 E7
La Tagua, *Colombia* 124 C4
La Teste-de-Buch, *France* 20 D2
La Tortuga, *Venezuela* 121 D6
La Tour-du-Pin, *France* 21 C9
La Tranche-sur-Mer, *France* 18 F5
La Tremblade, *France* 20 C2
La Trinité, *Martinique* 120 c
La Tuque, *Canada* 104 C5
La Unión, *Chile* 128 E2
La Unión, *El Salv.* 120 D2
La Unión, *Mexico* 118 D4
La Unión, *Spain* 39 H4
La Urbana, *Venezuela* 124 B5
La Vache Pt., *Trin. & Tob.* 125 K15
La Vall d'Uixó, *Spain* 38 F4
La Vecilla de Curveño, *Spain* 36 C5
La Vega, *Dom. Rep.* 121 C5
La Vela de Coro, *Venezuela* 124 A5
La Veleta, *Spain* 37 H7
La Venta, *Mexico* 119 D6
La Ventura, *Mexico* 118 C4
La Voulte-sur-Rhône, *France* 21 D8
Laa an der Thaya, *Austria* 27 C9
Laaber, Grosse →, *Germany* 25 G8
Laage, *Germany* 24 B8
Laas Caanood = Las Anod, *Somali Rep.* 75 F4
Laatzen, *Germany* 24 C5
Laba →, *Russia* 35 H4
Labasa, *Fiji* 91 C8
Labason, *Phil.* 61 G5
Labastide-Murat, *France* 20 D5
Labastide-Rouairoux, *France* 20 E6
Labbézenga, *Mali* 83 B5
Labe = Elbe →, *Europe* 24 B4
Labé, *Guinea* 82 C2
Laberge, L., *Canada* 102 A1
Labin, *Croatia* 41 C11

Labinsk, *Russia* 35 H5
Labis, *Malaysia* 65 L4
Łabiszyn, *Poland* 31 F4
Labo, *Phil.* 61 D5
Laboe, *Germany* 24 A6
Laborec →, *Slovak Rep.* 27 C14
Laborie, *St. Lucia* 121 f
Labouheyre, *France* 20 D3
Laboulaye, *Argentina* 126 C3
Labrador, *Canada* 105 B7
Labrador City, *Canada* 105 B6
Labrador Sea, *Atl. Oc.* 101 C14
Lábrea, *Brazil* 124 E6
Labruguière, *France* 20 E6
Labuan, *Malaysia* 62 C5
Labuan, Pulau, *Malaysia* 62 C5
Labuha, *Indonesia* 63 E7
Labuhan, *Indonesia* 63 G11
Labuhanbajo, *Indonesia* 63 F6
Labuk, Telok, *Malaysia* 62 C5
Labyrinth, L., *Australia* 95 E2
Labytnangi, *Russia* 52 C7
Laç, *Albania* 44 E3
Lac-Bouchette, *Canada* 105 C5
Lac Édouard, *Canada* 104 C5
Lac La Biche, *Canada* 102 C6
Lac la Martre = Wha Ti, *Canada* 100 B8
Lac La Ronge ⌓, *Canada* 103 B7
Lac-Mégantic, *Canada* 105 C5
Lac Thien, *Vietnam* 64 F7
Lacanau, *France* 20 D2
Lacanau, Étang de, *France* 20 D2
Lacantúm →, *Mexico* 119 D6
Lacara →, *Spain* 37 G4
Lacaune, *France* 20 E6
Lacaune, Mts. de, *France* 20 E6
Laccadive Is. = Lakshadweep Is., *India* 50 H11
Lacepede B., *Australia* 95 F2
Lacepede Is., *Australia* 92 C3
Lacerdónia, *Mozam.* 87 F4
Lacey, *U.S.A.* 110 C4
Lachhmangarh, *India* 68 F6
Lachi, *Pakistan* 68 C4
Lachine, *Canada* 104 C5
Lachlan →, *Australia* 95 E3
Lachute, *Canada* 104 C5
Lackawanna, *U.S.A.* 116 D6
Lackawaxen, *U.S.A.* 117 E10
Lacolle, *Canada* 117 A11
Lacombe, *Canada* 102 C6
Lacona, *U.S.A.* 117 C8
Láconi, *Italy* 42 C2
Laconia, *U.S.A.* 117 C13
Lacq, *France* 20 E3
Ladakh Ra., *India* 69 C8
Lądek-Zdrój, *Poland* 31 H3
Ládhon →, *Greece* 46 D3
Ladik, *Turkey* 72 B6
Ladismith, *S. Africa* 88 E3
Ladíspoli, *Italy* 41 G9
Lādīz, *Iran* 71 D9
Ladnun, *India* 68 F6
Ladoga, L. = Ladozhskoye Ozero, *Russia* 32 B6
Ladozhskoye Ozero, *Russia* 32 B6
Ladushkin, *Russia* 30 D7
Lady Elliott I., *Australia* 94 C5
Lady Grey, *S. Africa* 88 E4
Ladybrand, *S. Africa* 88 D4
Ladysmith, *Canada* 102 D4
Ladysmith, *S. Africa* 89 D4
Ladysmith, *U.S.A.* 112 C9
Ladyznyn, *Ukraine* 29 B14
Lae, *Papua N. G.* 96 H6
Laem Hin Khom, *Thailand* 65 b
Laem Khat, *Thailand* 65 a
Laem Nga, *Thailand* 65 a
Laem Ngop, *Thailand* 65 F4
Laem Phan Wa, *Thailand* 65 a
Laem Pho, *Thailand* 65 J3
Laem Phrom Thep, *Thailand* 65 a
Laem Riang, *Thailand* 65 a
Laem Sam Rong, *Thailand* 65 b
Laem Son, *Thailand* 65 a
Laem Yamu, *Thailand* 65 a
Læsø, *Denmark* 11 G5
Læsø Rende, *Denmark* 11 G4
Lafayette, *Colo., U.S.A.* 112 F2
Lafayette, *Ind., U.S.A.* 114 E2
Lafayette, *La., U.S.A.* 113 K9
Lafayette, *Tenn., U.S.A.* 115 G2
Laferte →, *Canada* 102 A5
Lafia, *Nigeria* 83 D6
Lafiagi, *Nigeria* 83 D6
Lafleche, *Canada* 103 D7
Lafon, *Sudan* 81 F3
Lagan, *Sweden* 11 H7
Lagan →, *Sweden* 11 H6
Lagan →, *U.K.* 12 B6
Lagarfljót →, *Iceland* 8 D6
Lage, *Germany* 24 D4
Lågen →, *Oppland, Norway* 9 F14
Lågen →, *Vestfold, Norway* 9 G14
Lägerdorf, *Germany* 24 B5
Laghouat, *Algeria* 78 B6
Lagnieu, *France* 21 C9
Lagny-sur-Marne, *France* 19 D9
Lago, *Italy* 43 C9
Lago de Sanabria y Entorno ⌓, *Spain* 36 C4
Lagôa, *Portugal* 37 H2
Lagoa do Peixe △, *Brazil* 127 C5
Lagoa Vermelha, *Brazil* 127 B5
Lagoaça, *Portugal* 36 D4
Lagodekhi, *Georgia* 35 K8
Lagónegro, *Italy* 43 B8
Lagonoy G., *Phil.* 61 E5
Lagos, *Nigeria* 83 D5
Lagos, *Portugal* 37 H2
Lagos ☐, *Nigeria* 83 D5
Lagos de Moreno, *Mexico* 118 C4
Lagrange, *Australia* 92 C3
Lagrange B., *Australia* 92 C3
Laguardia, *Spain* 38 C2
Laguépie, *France* 20 D5
Laguna, *Brazil* 127 B6
Laguna, *U.S.A.* 109 J10
Laguna Beach, *U.S.A.* 111 M9
Laguna de Duera, *Spain* 36 D6
Laguna de la Restinga △, *Venezuela* 121 D6
Laguna del Laja △, *Chile* 126 D1
Laguna del Tigre △, *Guatemala* 120 C1
Laguna Limpia, *Argentina* 126 B4
Lagunas, *Chile* 126 A2
Lagunas, *Peru* 124 E3
Lagunas de Chacahua △, *Mexico* 119 D5
Lagunas de Montebello △, *Mexico* 119 D6
Lagunas de Ruidera ⌓, *Spain* 39 G2
Lahad Datu, *Malaysia* 63 C5
Lahad Datu, Teluk, *Malaysia* 63 D5
Lahan Sai, *Thailand* 64 E4
Lahanam, *Laos* 64 D5
Lahar, *India* 69 F8
Laharpur, *India* 69 F9
Lahat, *Indonesia* 62 E2
Lahewa, *Indonesia* 62 D1
Lāhījān, *Iran* 71 B6
Lahn →, *Germany* 25 E3
Lahnstein, *Germany* 25 E3
Laholm, *Sweden* 11 H7
Laholmsbukten, *Sweden* 11 H6
Lahore, *Pakistan* 68 D6
Lahr, *Germany* 25 G3
Lahri, *Pakistan* 68 E3
Lahti, *Finland* 9 F21
Lahtis = Lahti, *Finland* 9 F21
Laï, *Chad* 79 G9
Lai Chau, *Vietnam* 58 F4
Lai'an, *China* 59 A12
Laibin, *China* 58 F7
Laifeng, *China* 58 C7
L'Aigle, *France* 18 D7
Laignes, *France* 19 E11
L'Aiguillon-sur-Mer, *France* 20 B2
Laila = Layla, *Si. Arabia* 75 C4
Laingsburg, *S. Africa* 88 E3
Lainioälven →, *Sweden* 8 C20
Lairg, *U.K.* 13 C4
Laishui, *China* 56 E8
Laissac, *France* 20 D6
Láives, *Italy* 41 B8
Laiwu, *China* 57 F9
Laixi, *China* 57 F11
Laiyang, *China* 57 F11
Laiyuan, *China* 56 E8
Laizhou, *China* 57 F10
Laizhou Wan, *China* 57 F10
Laja →, *Mexico* 118 C4
Lajere, *Nigeria* 83 C7
Lajes, *Brazil* 127 B5
Lajkovac, *Serbia & M.* 44 B4
Lajosmizse, *Hungary* 28 C4
Lak Sao, *Laos* 64 C5
Lakaband, *Pakistan* 68 D3
Lakamané, *Mali* 82 C3
Lake Alpine, *U.S.A.* 110 G7
Lake Andes, *U.S.A.* 112 D5
Lake Arthur, *U.S.A.* 113 K8
Lake Bindegolly △, *Australia* 95 D3
Lake Cargelligo, *Australia* 95 E4
Lake Charles, *U.S.A.* 113 K8
Lake City, *Colo., U.S.A.* 109 G10
Lake City, *Fla., U.S.A.* 115 K4
Lake City, *Mich., U.S.A.* 114 C3
Lake City, *Minn., U.S.A.* 112 C8
Lake City, *Pa., U.S.A.* 116 D4
Lake City, *S.C., U.S.A.* 115 J6
Lake Cowichan, *Canada* 102 D4
Lake District △, *U.K.* 14 C4
Lake Elsinore, *U.S.A.* 111 M9
Lake Eyre △, *Australia* 95 D2
Lake Gairdner △, *Australia* 95 E2
Lake George, *U.S.A.* 117 C11
Lake Grace, *Australia* 93 F2
Lake Harbour = Kimmirut, *Canada* 101 B13
Lake Havasu City, *U.S.A.* 111 L12
Lake Hughes, *U.S.A.* 111 L8
Lake Isabella, *U.S.A.* 111 K8
Lake Jackson, *U.S.A.* 113 L7
Lake Junction, *U.S.A.* 108 D8
Lake King, *Australia* 93 F2
Lake Lenore, *Canada* 103 C8
Lake Louise, *Canada* 102 C5
Lake Malawi △, *Malawi* 87 E3
Lake Mburo △, *Uganda* 86 C3
Lake Mead ⌓, *U.S.A.* 111 K12
Lake Meredith ⌓, *U.S.A.* 113 H4
Lake Mills, *U.S.A.* 112 D8
Lake Nakura △, *Kenya* 86 C4
Lake Placid, *U.S.A.* 117 B11
Lake Pleasant, *U.S.A.* 117 C10
Lake Providence, *U.S.A.* 113 J9
Lake Roosevelt ⌓, *U.S.A.* 108 C4
Lake St. Peter, *Canada* 116 A6
Lake Superior ⌓, *Canada* 104 C3
Lake Torrens △, *Australia* 95 E2
Lake Village, *U.S.A.* 113 J9
Lake Wales, *U.S.A.* 115 M5
Lake Worth, *U.S.A.* 115 M5
Lakeba, *Fiji* 91 D9
Lakefield, *Canada* 116 B6
Lakefield △, *Australia* 94 B3
Lakehurst, *U.S.A.* 117 F10
Lakeland, *Australia* 94 B3
Lakeland, *U.S.A.* 115 M5
Lakemba = Lakeba, *Fiji* 91 D9
Lakeport, *Calif., U.S.A.* 110 F4
Lakeport, *Mich., U.S.A.* 116 C2
Lakes Entrance, *Australia* 95 F4
Lakeside, *Ariz., U.S.A.* 109 J9
Lakeside, *Calif., U.S.A.* 111 N10
Lakeside, *Nebr., U.S.A.* 112 D3
Lakeside, *Ohio, U.S.A.* 116 E2
Lakeview, *U.S.A.* 108 E3
Lakeville, *U.S.A.* 112 C8
Lakewood, *Colo., U.S.A.* 112 F2
Lakewood, *N.J., U.S.A.* 117 F10
Lakewood, *N.Y., U.S.A.* 116 D5
Lakewood, *Ohio, U.S.A.* 116 E3
Lakewood, *Wash., U.S.A.* 110 C4
Lakha, *India* 68 F4
Lakhaniá, *Greece* 49 D9
Lakhimpur, *India* 69 F9
Lakhnadon, *India* 69 H8
Lakhnau = Lucknow, *India* 69 F9
Lakhonpheng, *Laos* 64 E5
Lakhpat, *India* 68 H3
Läki, *Azerbaijan* 35 K8
Lakin, *U.S.A.* 113 G4
Lakitusaki →, *Canada* 104 B3
Lakki, *Pakistan* 68 C4
Lákkoi, *Greece* 49 D5
Lakonía ☐, *Greece* 46 E4
Lakonikós Kólpos, *Greece* 46 E4
Lakor, *Indonesia* 63 F7
Lakota, *Ivory C.* 82 D3
Lakota, *U.S.A.* 112 A5
Laksar, *India* 68 E8
Laksefjorden, *Norway* 8 A22
Lakselv, *Norway* 8 A21
Lakshadweep Is., *India* 50 H11
Lakshmanpur, *India* 69 H10
Lakshmikantapur, *India* 69 H13
Lala Musa, *Pakistan* 68 C5
Lalaghat, *India* 67 G18
Lalago, *Tanzania* 86 C3
Lalapanzi, *Zimbabwe* 87 F3
Lalapaşa, *Turkey* 45 E10
Lalbenque, *France* 20 D5
L'Albufera, *Spain* 39 F4
Lalganj, *India* 69 G11
Lalgola, *India* 69 G13
Lālī, *Iran* 71 C6
Lalibela, *Ethiopia* 81 E4
Lalin, *China* 57 B14
Lalín, *Spain* 36 C2
Lalin He →, *China* 57 B13
Lalinde, *France* 20 D4
Lalitapur, *Nepal* 69 F11
Lalitpur, *India* 69 G8
Lalkua, *India* 69 E8
Lalsot, *India* 68 F7
Lam, *Vietnam* 64 B6
Lam Pao Res., *Thailand* 64 D4
Lama Kara, *Togo* 83 D5
Lamaing, *Burma* 67 M20
Lamar, *Colo., U.S.A.* 112 F3
Lamar, *Mo., U.S.A.* 113 G7
Lamas, *Peru* 124 E3
Lamastre, *France* 21 D8
Lambach, *Austria* 26 C6
Lamballe, *France* 18 D4
Lambaréné, *Gabon* 84 E2
Lambasa = Labasa, *Fiji* 91 C8
Lambay I., *Ireland* 12 C5
Lambert Glacier, *Antarctica* 5 D6
Lambert's Bay, *S. Africa* 88 E2
Lambesc, *France* 21 E9
Lambeth, *Canada* 116 D3
Lámbia, *Greece* 46 D3
Lambomakondro, *Madag.* 89 C7
Lambro →, *Italy* 40 C6
Lambton Shores, *Canada* 116 C3
Lame, *Nigeria* 83 C6
Lame Deer, *U.S.A.* 108 D10
Lamego, *Portugal* 36 D3
Lamèque, *Canada* 105 C7
Lameroo, *Australia* 95 F3
Lamesa, *U.S.A.* 113 J4
Lamía, *Greece* 46 C4
Lamington △, *Australia* 95 D5
Lamitan, *Phil.* 61 H5
Lammermuir Hills, *U.K.* 13 F6
Lammhult, *Sweden* 11 G8
Lamoille →, *U.S.A.* 117 B11
Lamon B., *Phil.* 61 D5
Lamont, *Canada* 102 C6
Lamont, *Calif., U.S.A.* 111 K8
Lamont, *Wyo., U.S.A.* 108 E10
Lamotte-Beuvron, *France* 19 E9
Lampa, *Peru* 124 G4
Lampang, *Thailand* 64 C2
Lampasas, *U.S.A.* 113 K5
Lampazos de Naranjo, *Mexico* 118 B4
Lampertheim, *Germany* 25 F4
Lampeter, *U.K.* 15 E3
Lampman, *Canada* 103 D8
Lamprechtshausen, *Austria* 26 D5
Lampung ☐, *Indonesia* 62 F2
Lamta, *India* 69 H9
Lamu, *Kenya* 86 C5
Lamy, *U.S.A.* 109 J11
Lan Xian, *China* 56 E6
Lan Yu = Hungt'ou Hsü, *Taiwan* 59 G13
Lanak La, *China* 69 B8
Lanak'o Shank'ou = Lanak La, *China* 69 B8
Lanao, L., *Phil.* 61 H6
Lanark, *Canada* 117 A8
Lanark, *U.K.* 13 F5
Lanbi Kyun, *Burma* 65 G2
Lancang, *China* 58 F2
Lancang Jiang →, *China* 58 G3
Lancashire ☐, *U.K.* 14 D5
Lancaster, *Canada* 117 A10
Lancaster, *U.K.* 14 C5
Lancaster, *Calif., U.S.A.* 111 L8
Lancaster, *Ky., U.S.A.* 114 G3
Lancaster, *N.H., U.S.A.* 117 B13
Lancaster, *N.Y., U.S.A.* 116 D6
Lancaster, *Ohio, U.S.A.* 114 F4
Lancaster, *Pa., U.S.A.* 117 F8
Lancaster, *S.C., U.S.A.* 115 H5
Lancaster, *Wis., U.S.A.* 112 D9
Lancaster Sd., *Canada* 101 A11
Lancelin, *Australia* 93 F2
Lanchow = Lanzhou, *China* 56 F2
Lanchyn, *Ukraine* 29 B9
Lanciano, *Italy* 41 F11
Lancun, *China* 57 F11
Łańcut, *Poland* 31 H9
Land Between the Lakes ⌓, *U.S.A.* 115 G1
Landau, *Bayern, Germany* 25 G8
Landau, *Rhld-Pfz., Germany* 25 F4
Landeck, *Austria* 26 D3
Lander, *U.S.A.* 108 E9
Lander →, *Australia* 92 D5
Landerneau, *France* 18 D2
Landeryd, *Sweden* 11 G7
Landes, *France* 20 D2
Landes ☐, *France* 20 E3
Landes de Gascogne ⌓, *France* 20 D3
Landete, *Spain* 38 F3
Landi Kotal, *Pakistan* 68 B4
Landisburg, *U.S.A.* 116 F7
Landivisiau, *France* 18 D2
Landquart, *Switz.* 25 J5
Landrecies, *France* 19 B10
Land's End, *U.K.* 15 G2
Landsberg, *Germany* 25 G6
Landsborough Cr. →, *Australia* 94 C3
Landsbro, *Sweden* 11 G8
Landshut, *Germany* 25 G8
Landskrona, *Sweden* 11 J6
Landstuhl, *Germany* 25 F3
Landvetter, *Sweden* 11 G6
Lanesboro, *U.S.A.* 117 E9
Lanester, *France* 18 E3
Lanett, *U.S.A.* 115 J3
Lang Qua, *Vietnam* 64 A5
Lang Shan, *China* 56 D4
Lang Son, *Vietnam* 58 G6
Lang Suan, *Thailand* 65 H2
Langå, *Denmark* 11 H3
La'nga Co, *China* 67 D12
Lángadhás, *Greece* 44 F7
Langádhia, *Greece* 46 D4
Långan →, *Sweden* 10 A8
Langano, L., *Ethiopia* 81 F4
Langar, *Iran* 71 C9
Langara I., *Canada* 102 C2
Långås, *Sweden* 11 H6
Langdai, *China* 58 D5
Langdon, *U.S.A.* 112 A5
Långe Jan = Ölands södra udde, *Sweden* 11 H10
Langeac, *France* 20 C7
Langeais, *France* 18 E7
Langeb Baraka →, *Sudan* 80 D4
Langeberg, *S. Africa* 88 E3
Langeberge, *S. Africa* 88 D3
Langeland, *Denmark* 11 K4
Langelands Bælt, *Denmark* 11 K4
Langen, *Hessen, Germany* 25 F4
Langen, *Niedersachsen, Germany* 24 B4
Langenburg, *Canada* 103 C8
Langeneß, *Germany* 24 A4
Langenlois, *Austria* 26 C8
Langeoog, *Germany* 24 B3
Langeskov, *Denmark* 11 J4
Länghem, *Sweden* 11 G7
Langhirano, *Italy* 40 D7
Langholm, *U.K.* 13 F5
Langjökull, *Iceland* 8 D3
Langkawi, Pulau, *Malaysia* 65 J2
Langklip, *S. Africa* 88 D3
Langkon, *Malaysia* 62 C5
Langlade, *St-P. & M.* 105 C8
Langley, *Canada* 110 A4
Langnau, *Switz.* 25 J3
Langogne, *France* 20 D7
Langon, *France* 20 D3
Langøya, *Norway* 8 B16
Langreo, *Spain* 36 B5
Langres, *France* 19 E12
Langres, Plateau de, *France* 19 E12
Langsa, *Indonesia* 62 D1
Långsele, *Sweden* 10 A11
Långshyttan, *Sweden* 10 D10
Langtry, *U.S.A.* 113 L4
Langu, *Thailand* 65 J2
Langue de Barbarie △, *Senegal* 82 C1
Languedoc, *France* 20 E7
Languedoc-Roussillon ☐, *France* 20 E6
Langxi, *China* 59 B12
Langxiangzhen, *China* 56 E9
Langzhong, *China* 58 B5
Lanigan, *Canada* 103 C7
Lankao, *China* 56 G8
Länkäran, *Azerbaijan* 71 B6
Lanmeur, *France* 18 D3
Lannemezan, *France* 20 E4
Lannilis, *France* 18 D2
Lannion, *France* 18 D3
L'Annonciation, *Canada* 104 C5
Lanouaille, *France* 20 C5
Lanping, *China* 58 D2
Lansdale, *U.S.A.* 117 F9
Lansdowne, *Australia* 95 E5
Lansdowne, *Canada* 117 B8
Lansdowne, *India* 69 E8
Lansdowne House, *Canada* 104 B2
L'Anse, *U.S.A.* 114 B1
L'Anse au Loup, *Canada* 105 B8
L'Anse aux Meadows, *Canada* 105 B8
Lansford, *U.S.A.* 117 F9
Lanshan, *China* 59 E9
Lansing, *U.S.A.* 114 D3
Lanslebourg-Mont-Cenis, *France* 21 C10
Lanta Yai, Ko, *Thailand* 65 J2
Lantewa, *Nigeria* 83 C7
Lantian, *China* 56 G5
Lanus, *Argentina* 126 C4
Lanusei, *Italy* 42 C2
Lanuza, *Phil.* 61 G7
Lanxi, *China* 59 C12
Lanzarote, *Canary Is.* 48 F6
Lanzarote ✕ (ACE), *Canary Is.* 48 F6
Lanzhou, *China* 56 F2
Lanzo Torinese, *Italy* 40 C4
Lao →, *Italy* 43 C8
Lao Bao, *Laos* 64 D6
Lao Cai, *Vietnam* 58 F4
Laoag, *Phil.* 61 B4
Laoang, *Phil.* 61 E6
Laoha He →, *China* 57 C11
Laohekou, *China* 59 A8
Laois ☐, *Ireland* 12 D4
Laon, *France* 19 C10
Laona, *U.S.A.* 114 C1
Laos ■, *Asia* 64 D5
Lapa, *Brazil* 127 B6
Lapai, *Nigeria* 83 D6
Lapalisse, *France* 19 F10
Lapeer, *U.S.A.* 114 D4
Lapeyrade, *France* 20 D3
Lapithos, *Cyprus* 49 D12
Lapland = Lappland, *Europe* 8 B21
Laporte, *U.S.A.* 117 E8
Lapovo, *Serbia & M.* 44 B5
Lappeenranta, *Finland* 9 F23
Lappland, *Europe* 8 B21
Lappo = Lapua, *Finland* 8 E20
Laprida, *Argentina* 126 D3
Lapseki, *Turkey* 45 F10
Laptev Sea, *Russia* 53 B13
Lapua, *Finland* 8 E20
Lăpuş →, *Romania* 29 C8
Lapuş, Munţii, *Romania* 29 C8
Lăpuşna, *Moldova* 29 D13
Łapy, *Poland* 31 F9
Laqiya Arba'in, *Sudan* 80 C2
Laqiya Umran, *Sudan* 80 D2
L'Áquila, *Italy* 41 F10
Lār, *Āzarbājān-e Sharqī, Iran* 70 B5
Lār, *Fārs, Iran* 71 E7
Larabanga, *Ghana* 82 D4
Laragne-Montéglin, *France* 21 D9
Laramie, *U.S.A.* 112 E2
Laramie →, *U.S.A.* 108 F11
Laramie Mts., *U.S.A.* 112 E2
Laranjeiras do Sul, *Brazil* 127 B5
Larantuka, *Indonesia* 63 F6
Larat, *Indonesia* 63 F8
L'Arbresle, *France* 21 C8
Lärbro, *Sweden* 11 G12
Larde, *Mozam.* 87 F4
Larder Lake, *Canada* 104 C4
Lardhos, Ákra = Líndhos, Ákra, *Greece* 49 C10
Lardhos, Órmos, *Greece* 49 C10
Laredo, *Spain* 36 B7
Laredo, *U.S.A.* 113 M5
Laredo Sd., *Canada* 102 C3
Largentière, *France* 21 D8
L'Argentière-la-Bessée, *France* 21 D10
Largo, *U.S.A.* 115 M4
Largs, *U.K.* 13 F4
Lari, *Italy* 40 E7
Lariang, *Indonesia* 63 E5
Larimore, *U.S.A.* 112 B6
Larino, *Italy* 41 G11
Lárisa, *Greece* 46 B4
Lárisa ☐, *Greece* 46 B4
Larkana, *Pakistan* 68 F3
Larnaca, *Cyprus* 49 E12
Larnaca Bay, *Cyprus* 49 E12
Larne, *U.K.* 12 B6
Larned, *U.S.A.* 112 F5
Laroquebrou, *France* 20 D6
Larose, *U.S.A.* 113 L9
Larrimah, *Australia* 92 C5
Larsen Ice Shelf, *Antarctica* 5 C17
Laruns, *France* 20 F3
Larvik, *Norway* 9 G14
Larzac, Causse du, *France* 20 E7
Las Alpujarras, *Spain* 37 J1
Las Animas, *U.S.A.* 112 F3
Las Anod, *Somali Rep.* 75 F4
Las Arenas, *Spain* 36 B6
Las Batuecas ⌓, *Spain* 36 E4
Las Brenãs, *Argentina* 126 B3
Las Cabezas de San Juan, *Spain* 37 J5
Las Cañadas del Teide △, *Canary Is.* 48 F3
Las Cejas, *Argentina* 128 B4
Las Chimeneas, *Mexico* 111 N10
Las Cruces, *U.S.A.* 109 K10
Las Flores, *Argentina* 126 D4
Las Heras, *Argentina* 126 C2
Las Lajas, *Argentina* 128 D2
Las Lomitas, *Argentina* 126 A3
Las Marismas, *Spain* 37 H4
Las Minas, *Spain* 39 G3
Las Navas de la Concepción, *Spain* 37 H5
Las Navas del Marqués, *Spain* 36 E6
Las Palmas, *Argentina* 126 B4
Las Palmas, *Canary Is.* 48 F4
Las Palmas →, *Mexico* 111 N10
Las Palmas ✕ (LPA), *Canary Is.* 48 G4
Las Palmas de Cocalán △, *Chile* 126 C1
Las Pedroñas, *Spain* 39 F2
Las Piedras, *Uruguay* 127 C4
Las Pipinas, *Argentina* 126 D4
Las Plumas, *Argentina* 128 E3
Las Rosas, *Argentina* 126 C3
Las Rozas, *Spain* 36 E7
Las Tablas, *Panama* 120 E3
Las Termas, *Argentina* 126 B3
Las Toscas, *Argentina* 126 B4
Las Truchas, *Mexico* 118 D4
Las Varillas, *Argentina* 126 C3
Las Vegas, *N. Mex., U.S.A.* 109 J11
Las Vegas, *Nev., U.S.A.* 111 J11

Las Vegas McCarran International ✈ (LAS), *U.S.A.* 111 J11
Lasarte, *Spain* 38 B2
Lascano, *Uruguay* 127 C5
Lash-e Joveyn, *Afghan.* 66 D2
Lashburn, *Canada* 103 C7
Lashio, *Burma* 67 H20
Lashkar, *India* 68 F8
Łasin, *Poland* 30 E6
Lasíthi, *Greece* 49 D7
Lasíthi □, *Greece* 49 D7
Lāsjerd, *Iran* 71 C7
Lask, *Poland* 31 G6
Łaskarzew, *Poland* 31 G8
Laško, *Slovenia* 41 B12
Lassay-les-Châteaux, *France* 18 D6
Lassen Pk., *U.S.A.* 108 F3
Lassen Volcanic △, *U.S.A.* 108 F3
Last Mountain L., *Canada* 103 C7
Lastchance Cr. →, *U.S.A.* 110 E5
Lastoursville, *Gabon* 84 E2
Lastovo, *Croatia* 41 F13
Lastovski Kanal, *Croatia* 41 F14
Lat Yao, *Thailand* 64 E2
Latacunga, *Ecuador* 124 D3
Latakia = Al Lādhiqīyah, *Syria* 70 C2
Latchford, *Canada* 104 C4
Latehar, *India* 69 H11
Laterza, *Italy* 43 B9
Latham, *Australia* 93 E2
Lathen, *Germany* 24 C3
Lathi, *India* 68 F4
Lathrop Wells, *U.S.A.* 111 J10
Latiano, *Italy* 43 B10
Latina, *Italy* 42 A5
Latisana, *Italy* 41 C10
Latium = Lazio □, *Italy* 41 F9
Laton, *U.S.A.* 110 J7
Latorytsya →, *Slovak Rep.* 27 C14
Latouche Treville, C., *Australia* 92 C3
Latrobe, *Australia* 95 G4
Latrobe, *U.S.A.* 116 F5
Latrónico, *Italy* 43 B9
Latvia ■, *Europe* 9 H20
Lau, *Nigeria* 83 D7
Lau Group, *Fiji* 91 C9
Lauchhammer, *Germany* 24 D9
Lauda-Königshofen, *Germany* 25 F5
Lauenburg, *Germany* 24 B6
Lauenburgische Seen ⌓, *Germany* 24 B6
Lauf, *Germany* 25 F7
Laughlin, *U.S.A.* 109 J6
Laujar de Andarax, *Spain* 39 H2
Laukaa, *Finland* 9 E21
Launceston, *Australia* 95 G4
Launceston, *U.K.* 15 G3
Laune →, *Ireland* 12 D2
Launglon Bok, *Burma* 64 F1
Laupheim, *Germany* 25 G5
Laura, *Australia* 94 B3
Laureana di Borrello, *Italy* 43 D9
Laurel, *Miss., U.S.A.* 113 K10
Laurel, *Mont., U.S.A.* 108 D9
Laurencekirk, *U.K.* 13 E6
Laurens, *U.S.A.* 115 H4
Laurentian Plateau, *Canada* 105 B6
Lauria, *Italy* 43 B8
Laurie L., *Canada* 103 B8
Laurinburg, *U.S.A.* 115 H6
Laurium, *U.S.A.* 114 B1
Lausanne, *Switz.* 25 J2
Laut, *Indonesia* 62 D3
Laut, Pulau, *Indonesia* 62 E5
Laut Kecil, Kepulauan, *Indonesia* 62 E5
Lauterbach, *Germany* 24 E5
Lauterecken, *Germany* 25 F3
Lautoka, *Fiji* 91 C7
Lauzès, *France* 20 D5
Lava →, *Russia* 30 D8
Lava Beds ⌓, *U.S.A.* 108 F3
Lavagh More, *Ireland* 12 B3
Lavagna, *Italy* 40 D6
Laval, *France* 18 D6
Lavalle, *Argentina* 126 B2
Lavant Station, *Canada* 117 A8
Lāvar Meydān, *Iran* 71 D7
Lávara, *Greece* 45 E10
Lavardac, *France* 20 D4
Lavaur, *France* 20 E5
Lavelanet, *France* 20 F5
Lavello, *Italy* 43 A8
Laverton, *Australia* 93 E3
Lavìs, *Italy* 40 B8
Lávkos, *Greece* 46 B5
Lavos, *Portugal* 36 E2
Lavradio, *Portugal* 37 G1
Lavras, *Brazil* 127 A7
Lavre, *Portugal* 37 G2
Lávrion, *Greece* 46 D6
Lávris, *Greece* 49 D6
Lavumisa, *Swaziland* 89 D5
Lavushi Manda △, *Zambia* 87 E3
Lawas, *Malaysia* 62 D5
Lawele, *Indonesia* 63 F6
Lawn Hill △, *Australia* 94 B2
Lawng Pit, *Burma* 67 G20
Lawqah, *Si. Arabia* 70 D4
Lawra, *Ghana* 82 C4
Lawrence, *N.Z.* 91 L2
Lawrence, *Kans., U.S.A.* 112 F7
Lawrence, *Mass., U.S.A.* 117 D13
Lawrenceburg, *Ind., U.S.A.* 114 F3
Lawrenceburg, *Tenn., U.S.A.* 115 H2
Lawrenceville, *Ga., U.S.A.* 115 J4
Lawrenceville, *Pa., U.S.A.* 116 E7
Laws, *U.S.A.* 110 H8
Lawton, *U.S.A.* 113 H5
Lawu, *Indonesia* 63 G14
Lawz, J. al, *Si. Arabia* 80 B4
Laxå, *Sweden* 11 F8
Laxford, L., *U.K.* 13 C3
Laxou, *France* 19 D13
Lay →, *France* 20 B2
Layla, *Si. Arabia* 75 C4
Laylān, *Iraq* 70 C5
Layon →, *France* 18 E6
Layton, *U.S.A.* 108 F7
Laytonville, *U.S.A.* 108 G2
Lazarevac, *Serbia & M.* 44 B4
Lazarevskoye, *Russia* 35 J4
Lazarivo, *Madag.* 89 C8
Lazdijai, *Lithuania* 30 D10
Lazio □, *Italy* 41 F9
Lazo, *Moldova* 29 C13
Lazo, *Russia* 54 C6
Le Beausset, *France* 21 E9
Le Bic, *Canada* 105 C6
Le Blanc, *France* 20 B5
Le Bleymard, *France* 20 D7
Le Bourgneuf-la-Fôret, *France* 18 D6
Le Bugue, *France* 20 D4
Le Cateau Cambrésis, *France* 19 B10
Le Caylar, *France* 20 E7
Le Chambon-Feugerolles, *France* 21 C8
Le Châtelet, *France* 19 F9
Le Chesne, *France* 19 C11
Le Cheylard, *France* 21 D8
Le Conquet, *France* 18 D2
Le Creusot, *France* 19 F11
Le Croisic, *France* 18 E4
Le Donjon, *France* 19 F10
Le Dorat, *France* 20 B5
Le François, *Martinique* 120 c
Le Gosier, *Guadeloupe* 120 b
Le Grand-Lucé, *France* 18 E7
Le Grand-Pressigny, *France* 18 F7
Le Grand-Quevilly, *France* 18 C8
Le Havre, *France* 18 C7
Le Lamentin, *Martinique* 120 c
Le Lavandou, *France* 21 E10
Le Lion-d'Angers, *France* 18 E6
Le Louroux-Béconnais, *France* 18 E6
Le Luc, *France* 21 E10
Le Lude, *France* 18 E7
Le Mans, *France* 18 E7
Le Marin, *Martinique* 120 c
Le Mars, *U.S.A.* 112 D6
Le Mayet-de-Montagne, *France* 19 F10
Le Mêle-sur-Sarthe, *France* 18 D7
Le Monastier-sur-Gazeille, *France* 20 D7
Le Monêtier-les-Bains, *France* 21 D10
Le Mont-Dore, *France* 20 C6
Le Mont-St-Michel, *France* 18 D5
Le Moule, *Guadeloupe* 120 b
Le Muy, *France* 21 E10
Le Palais, *France* 18 E3
Le Perthus, *France* 20 F6
Le Prêcheur, *Martinique* 120 c
Le Puy-en-Velay, *France* 20 C7
Le Robert, *Martinique* 120 c
Le St-Esprit, *Martinique* 120 c
Le Sueur, *U.S.A.* 112 C8
Le Teil, *France* 21 D8
Le Teilleul, *France* 18 D6
Le Theil, *France* 18 D7
Le Thillot, *France* 19 E13
Le Thuy, *Vietnam* 64 D6
Le Touquet-Paris-Plage, *France* 19 B8
Le Tréport, *France* 18 B8
Le Val-d'Ajol, *France* 19 E13
Le Verdon-sur-Mer, *France* 20 C2
Le Vigan, *France* 20 E7
Lea →, *U.K.* 15 F8
Leach, *Cambodia* 65 F4
Lead, *U.S.A.* 112 C3
Leader, *Canada* 103 C7
Leadville, *U.S.A.* 109 G10
Leaf →, *U.S.A.* 113 K10
Leaf Rapids, *Canada* 103 B9
Leamington, *Canada* 116 D2
Leamington, *U.S.A.* 108 G7
Leamington Spa = Royal Leamington Spa, *U.K.* 15 E6
Le'an, *China* 59 D10
Leandro Norte Alem, *Argentina* 127 B4
Leane, L., *Ireland* 12 D2
Learmonth, *Australia* 92 D1
Leask, *Canada* 103 C7
Leatherhead, *U.K.* 15 F7
Leavenworth, *Kans., U.S.A.* 112 F7
Leavenworth, *Wash., U.S.A.* 108 C3
Łeba, *Poland* 30 D4
Łeba →, *Poland* 30 D4
Lebach, *Germany* 25 F2
Lebak, *Phil.* 61 H6
Lebam, *U.S.A.* 110 D3
Lebane, *Serbia & M.* 44 D5
Lebanon, *Ind., U.S.A.* 114 E2
Lebanon, *Kans., U.S.A.* 112 F5
Lebanon, *Ky., U.S.A.* 114 G3
Lebanon, *Mo., U.S.A.* 113 G8
Lebanon, *N.H., U.S.A.* 117 C12
Lebanon, *Oreg., U.S.A.* 108 D2
Lebanon, *Pa., U.S.A.* 117 F8
Lebanon, *Tenn., U.S.A.* 115 G2
Lebanon ■, *Asia* 74 B5
Lebec, *U.S.A.* 111 L8
Lebedyan, *Russia* 33 F10
Lebedyn, *Ukraine* 33 G8
Lebel-sur-Quévillon, *Canada* 104 C4
Lebomboberge, *S. Africa* 89 C5
Lębork, *Poland* 30 D4
Lebrija, *Spain* 37 J4
Łebsko, Jezioro, *Poland* 30 D4
Lebu, *Chile* 126 D1
Leca da Palmeira, *Portugal* 36 D2
Lecce, *Italy* 43 B11
Lecco, *Italy* 40 C6
Lecco, L. di, *Italy* 40 C6
Lécera, *Spain* 38 D4
Lech, *Austria* 26 D3
Lech →, *Germany* 25 G6
Lechang, *China* 59 E9
Lechtaler Alpen, *Austria* 26 D3
Lecontes Mills, *U.S.A.* 116 E6
Lectoure, *France* 20 E4
Łęczna, *Poland* 31 G9
Łęczyca, *Poland* 31 F6
Ledesma, *Spain* 36 D5
Ledong, *China* 64 C7
Leduc, *Canada* 102 C6
Lee, *U.S.A.* 117 D11
Lee →, *Ireland* 12 E3
Lee Vining, *U.S.A.* 110 H7
Leech L., *U.S.A.* 112 B7
Leechburg, *U.S.A.* 116 F5
Leeds, *U.K.* 14 D6
Leeds, *U.S.A.* 115 J2
Leek, *Neths.* 17 A6
Leek, *U.K.* 14 D5
Leeman, *Australia* 93 E1
Leeper, *U.S.A.* 116 E5
Leer, *Germany* 24 B3
Leesburg, *U.S.A.* 115 L5
Leesville, *U.S.A.* 113 K8
Leeton, *Australia* 95 E4
Leetonia, *U.S.A.* 116 F4
Leeu Gamka, *S. Africa* 88 E3
Leeuwarden, *Neths.* 17 A5
Leeuwin, C., *Australia* 93 F2
Leeuwin Naturaliste △, *Australia* 93 F2
Leeward Is., *Atl. Oc.* 121 C7
Lefka, *Cyprus* 49 D11
Lefkoniko, *Cyprus* 49 D12
Lefroy, *Canada* 116 B5
Lefroy, L., *Australia* 93 F3
Łeg →, *Poland* 31 H8
Leganés, *Spain* 36 E7
Legazpi, *Phil.* 61 E5
Lège-Cap-Ferret, *France* 20 D2
Lege Hida, *Ethiopia* 81 F5
Legendre I., *Australia* 92 D2
Leghorn = Livorno, *Italy* 40 E7
Legionowo, *Poland* 31 F7
Legnago, *Italy* 41 C8
Legnano, *Italy* 40 C5
Legnica, *Poland* 31 G3
Legrad, *Croatia* 41 B13
Leh, *India* 69 B7
Lehigh Acres, *U.S.A.* 115 M5
Lehighton, *U.S.A.* 117 F9
Lehliu, *Romania* 29 F11
Leho, *Sudan* 81 F3
Lehrte, *Germany* 24 C5
Lehututu, *Botswana* 88 C3
Lei Shui →, *China* 59 D9
Leiah, *Pakistan* 68 D4
Leibnitz, *Austria* 26 E8
Leibo, *China* 58 C4
Leicester, *U.K.* 15 E6
Leicester City □, *U.K.* 15 E6
Leicestershire □, *U.K.* 15 E6
Leichhardt →, *Australia* 94 B2
Leichhardt Ra., *Australia* 94 C4
Leiden, *Neths.* 17 B4
Leie →, *Belgium* 17 C3
Leifers = Láives, *Italy* 41 B8
Leimen, *Germany* 25 F4
Leine →, *Germany* 24 C5
Leinefelde, *Germany* 24 D6
Leinster, *Australia* 93 E3
Leinster □, *Ireland* 12 C4
Leinster, Mt., *Ireland* 12 D5
Leipalingis, *Lithuania* 30 D10
Leipzig, *Germany* 24 D8
Leiria, *Portugal* 36 F2
Leiria □, *Portugal* 36 F2
Leirvik, *Norway* 9 G11
Leishan, *China* 58 D7
Leisler, Mt., *Australia* 92 D4
Leith, *U.K.* 13 F5
Leith Hill, *U.K.* 15 F7
Leitha →, *Europe* 27 D10
Leitrim, *Ireland* 12 B3
Leitrim □, *Ireland* 12 B4
Leitza, *Spain* 38 B3
Leiyang, *China* 59 D9
Leizhou, *China* 59 G8
Leizhou Bandao, *China* 58 G7
Leizhou Wan, *China* 59 G8
Lek →, *Neths.* 17 C4
Leka, *Norway* 8 D14
Lekáni, *Greece* 45 E8
Lekbibaj, *Albania* 44 D3
Lekeitio, *Spain* 38 B2
Lekhainá, *Greece* 46 D3
Lekoui, *Burkina Faso* 82 C4
Leksand, *Sweden* 10 D9
Lékva Óros, *Greece* 49 D6
Leland, *Mich., U.S.A.* 114 C3
Leland, *Miss., U.S.A.* 113 J9
Lelång, *Sweden* 10 E6
Leleque, *Argentina* 128 E2
Lelystad, *Neths.* 17 B5
Lem, *Denmark* 11 H2
Lema, *Nigeria* 83 C5
Lema Shilindi, *Ethiopia* 81 G5
Léman, L., *Europe* 19 F13
Lembar, *Indonesia* 63 K19
Lembuak, *Indonesia* 63 K19
Lemera, *Dem. Rep. of the Congo* 86 C2
Lemery, *Phil.* 61 E4
Lemhi Ra., *U.S.A.* 108 D7
Lemmer, *Neths.* 17 B5
Lemmon, *U.S.A.* 112 C3
Lemon Grove, *U.S.A.* 111 N9
Lemoore, *U.S.A.* 110 J7
Lempdes, *France* 20 C7
Lemvig, *Denmark* 11 H2
Lena →, *Russia* 53 B13
Lenart, *Slovenia* 41 B12
Lenartovce, *Slovak Rep.* 27 C13
Lencloître, *France* 18 F7
Léndas, *Greece* 49 E6
Lendava, *Slovenia* 41 B13
Lendeh, *Iran* 71 D6
Lendinara, *Italy* 41 C8
Lengerich, *Germany* 24 C3
Lenggong, *Malaysia* 65 K3
Lenggries, *Germany* 25 H7
Lengshuijiang, *China* 59 D8
Lengshuitan, *China* 59 D8
Lengua de Vaca, Pta., *Chile* 126 C1
Lengwe △, *Malawi* 87 F3
Lengyeltóti, *Hungary* 28 D2
Lenhovda, *Sweden* 11 G9
Lenina, Kanal →, *Russia* 35 J7
Lenino, *Ukraine* 33 K8
Leninogorsk, *Kazakhstan* 52 D9
Leninsk, *Russia* 35 F7
Leninsk-Kuznetskiy, *Russia* 52 D9
Leninskoye, *Russia* 34 A8
Lenk, *Switz.* 25 J3
Lenkoran = Länkäran, *Azerbaijan* 71 B6
Lenmalu, *Indonesia* 63 E8
Lenne →, *Germany* 24 D3
Lennestadt, *Germany* 24 D4
Lennox, *U.S.A.* 112 D6
Lennoxville, *Canada* 117 A13
Leno, *Italy* 40 C7
Lenoir, *U.S.A.* 115 H5
Lenoir City, *U.S.A.* 115 H3
Lenore L., *Canada* 103 C8
Lenox, *U.S.A.* 117 D11
Lens, *France* 19 B9
Lensahn, *Germany* 24 A6
Lensk, *Russia* 53 C12
Lentekhi, *Georgia* 35 J6
Lenti, *Hungary* 28 D1
Lentini, *Italy* 43 E8
Lenwood, *U.S.A.* 111 L9
Lenya, *Burma* 62 B1
Lenzen, *Germany* 24 B7
Léo, *Burkina Faso* 82 C4
Leoben, *Austria* 26 D8
Leodhas = Lewis, *U.K.* 13 C2
Leola, *U.S.A.* 112 C5
Leominster, *U.K.* 15 E5
Leominster, *U.S.A.* 117 D13
Léon, *France* 20 E2
León, *Mexico* 118 C4
León, *Nic.* 120 D2
León, *Spain* 36 C5
Leon, *U.S.A.* 112 E8
León □, *Spain* 36 C5
Leon →, *U.S.A.* 113 K6
León, Montes de, *Spain* 36 C4
Leonardo da Vinci, Roma ✈ (FCO), *Italy* 41 G9
Leonardtown, *U.S.A.* 114 F7
Leonardville, *Namibia* 88 C2
Leonberg, *Germany* 25 G5
Leonding, *Austria* 26 C7
Leonessa, *Italy* 41 F9
Leonforte, *Italy* 43 E7
Leongatha, *Australia* 95 F4
Leonídhion, *Greece* 46 D4
Leonora, *Australia* 93 E3
Leopoldina, *Brazil* 127 A7
Leopoldsburg, *Belgium* 17 C5
Leoti, *U.S.A.* 112 F4
Leova, *Moldova* 29 D13
Leoville, *Canada* 103 C7
Lepe, *Spain* 37 H3
Lepel = Lyepyel, *Belarus* 32 E5
Lepenoú, *Greece* 46 C3
Leping, *China* 59 C11
Lépo, L. do, *Angola* 88 B2
Lepontine, Alpi, *Italy* 40 B5
Leppävirta, *Finland* 9 E22
Lepsény, *Hungary* 28 D3
Lequeitio = Lekeitio, *Spain* 38 B2
Lercara Friddi, *Italy* 42 E6
Lerdo, *Mexico* 118 B4
Léré, *Chad* 83 D7
Léré, *Mali* 82 B4
Lere, *Bauchi, Nigeria* 83 D6
Lere, *Kaduna, Nigeria* 83 C6
Leribe, *Lesotho* 89 D4
Lérici, *Italy* 40 D6
Lérida = Lleida, *Spain* 38 D5
Lérins, Îs. de, *France* 21 E11
Lerma, *Spain* 36 C7
Léros, *Greece* 47 D8
Lérouville, *France* 19 D12
Lerum, *Sweden* 11 G6
Lerwick, *U.K.* 13 A7
Leş, *Romania* 28 D6
Les Abrets, *France* 21 C9
Les Andelys, *France* 18 C8
Les Borges Blanques, *Spain* 38 D5
Les Cayes, *Haiti* 121 C5
Les Coteaux, *Canada* 117 A10
Les Essarts, *France* 18 F5
Les Herbiers, *France* 18 F5
Les Minquiers, Plateau des, *Chan. Is.* 18 D4
Les Pieux, *France* 18 C5
Les Ponts-de-Cé, *France* 18 E6
Les Riceys, *France* 19 E11
Les Sables-d'Olonne, *France* 20 B2
Les Vans, *France* 21 D8
Lesbos = Lésvos, *Greece* 47 B8
L'Escala, *Spain* 38 C8
Leshan, *China* 58 C4
Leshwe ⌓, *Dem. Rep. of the Congo* 87 E2
Lésina, *Italy* 41 G12
Lésina, L. di, *Italy* 41 G12
Lesjöfors, *Sweden* 10 E8
Lesko, *Poland* 31 J9
Leskov I., *Antarctica* 5 B1
Leskovac, *Serbia & M.* 44 C5
Leskovik, *Albania* 44 F4
Leśna, *Poland* 31 G2
Lesneven, *France* 18 D2
Leśnica, *Poland* 31 H5
Lešnica, *Serbia & M.* 44 B3
Lesnoye, *Russia* 32 C8
Lesopilnoye, *Russia* 54 A7
Lesotho ■, *Africa* 89 D4
Lesozavodsk, *Russia* 53 E14
Lesparre-Médoc, *France* 20 C3
Lessay, *France* 18 C5
Lesse →, *Belgium* 17 D4
Lesse et Lomme ⌓, *Belgium* 17 D5
Lessebo, *Sweden* 11 H9
Lesser Antilles, *W. Indies* 121 D7
Lesser Slave L., *Canada* 102 B5
Lesser Sunda Is., *Indonesia* 63 F6
Lessines, *Belgium* 17 D3
Lester, *U.S.A.* 110 C5
Lester B. Pearson International, Toronto ✈ (YYZ), *Canada* 116 C5
Lestock, *Canada* 103 C8
Lesuer I., *Australia* 92 B4
Lesueur △, *Australia* 93 F2
Lésvos, *Greece* 47 B8
Leszno, *Poland* 31 G3
Letaba, *S. Africa* 89 C5
Letälven, *Sweden* 10 E8
Létavértes, *Hungary* 28 C6
Letchworth, *U.K.* 15 F7
Letea, Ostrov, *Romania* 29 E14
Lethbridge, *Canada* 102 D6
Lethem, *Guyana* 124 C7
Leti, Kepulauan, *Indonesia* 63 F7
Leti Is. = Leti, Kepulauan, *Indonesia* 63 F7
Letiahau →, *Botswana* 88 C3
Leticia, *Colombia* 124 D5
Leting, *China* 57 E10
Letjiesbos, *S. Africa* 88 E3
Letlhakane, *Botswana* 88 C4
Letlhakeng, *Botswana* 88 C3
Letong, *Indonesia* 62 D3
Letpadan, *Burma* 67 L19
Letpan, *Burma* 67 K19
Letsôk-aw Kyun, *Burma* 65 G2
Letterkenny, *Ireland* 12 B4
Leu, *Romania* 29 F9
Leucadia, *U.S.A.* 111 M9
Leucate, *France* 20 F7
Leucate, Étang de, *France* 20 F7
Leuchars, *U.K.* 13 E6
Leuk, *Switz.* 25 J3
Leuşeni, *Moldova* 29 D13
Leuser, G., *Indonesia* 62 D1
Leutkirch, *Germany* 25 H6
Leuven, *Belgium* 17 D4
Leuze-en-Hainaut, *Belgium* 17 D3
Lev Tolstoy, *Russia* 32 F10
Levádhia, *Greece* 46 C4
Levan, *Albania* 44 F3
Levanger, *Norway* 8 E14
Levant, Î. du, *France* 21 E10
Lévanto, *Italy* 40 D6
Lévanzo, *Italy* 42 D5
Levelland, *U.S.A.* 113 J3
Leven, *U.K.* 13 E6
Leven, L., *U.K.* 13 E5
Leven, Toraka, *Madag.* 89 A8
Leveque C., *Australia* 92 C3
Leverano, *Italy* 43 B10
Leverkusen, *Germany* 24 D3
Levice, *Slovak Rep.* 27 C11
Lévico Terme, *Italy* 41 C8
Levie, *France* 21 G13
Levier, *France* 19 F13
Levin, *N.Z.* 91 J5
Lévis, *Canada* 105 C5
Levis, L., *Canada* 102 A5
Levítha, *Greece* 47 D8
Levittown, *N.Y., U.S.A.* 117 F11
Levittown, *Pa., U.S.A.* 117 F10
Levka, *Bulgaria* 45 E10
Levkás, *Greece* 46 C2
Levkás □, *Greece* 46 C2
Levkímmi, *Greece* 49 B4
Levkímmi, Ákra, *Greece* 49 B4
Levkôsia = Nicosia, *Cyprus* 49 D12
Levoča, *Slovak Rep.* 27 B13
Levroux, *France* 19 F8
Levski, *Bulgaria* 45 C9
Levskigrad = Karlovo, *Bulgaria* 45 D8
Lewes, *U.K.* 15 G8
Lewes, *U.S.A.* 114 F8
Lewin Brzeski, *Poland* 31 H4
Lewis, *U.K.* 13 C2
Lewis →, *U.S.A.* 110 E4
Lewis, Butt of, *U.K.* 13 C2
Lewis Ra., *Australia* 92 D4
Lewis Range, *U.S.A.* 108 C7
Lewis Run, *U.S.A.* 116 E6
Lewisburg, *Pa., U.S.A.* 116 F8
Lewisburg, *Tenn., U.S.A.* 115 H2
Lewisburg, *W. Va., U.S.A.* 114 G5
Lewisporte, *Canada* 105 C8
Lewiston, *Idaho, U.S.A.* 108 C5
Lewiston, *Maine, U.S.A.* 115 C11
Lewiston, *N.Y., U.S.A.* 116 C5
Lewistown, *Mont., U.S.A.* 108 C9
Lewistown, *Pa., U.S.A.* 116 F7
Lexington, *Ill., U.S.A.* 112 E10
Lexington, *Ky., U.S.A.* 114 F3
Lexington, *Mich., U.S.A.* 116 C2
Lexington, *Mo., U.S.A.* 112 F8
Lexington, *N.C., U.S.A.* 115 H5
Lexington, *N.Y., U.S.A.* 117 D10
Lexington, *Nebr., U.S.A.* 112 E5
Lexington, *Ohio, U.S.A.* 116 F2
Lexington, *Tenn., U.S.A.* 115 H1
Lexington, *Va., U.S.A.* 114 G6
Lexington Park, *U.S.A.* 114 F7
Leyburn, *U.K.* 14 C6
Leye, *China* 58 E6
Leyland, *U.K.* 14 D5
Leyre →, *France* 20 D2
Leyte □, *Phil.* 61 F6
Leyte Gulf, *Phil.* 61 F6

Leżajsk, Poland 31 H9
Lezay, France 20 B3
Lezhë, Albania 44 E3
Lezhi, China 58 B5
Lézignan-Corbières, France 20 E6
Lezoux, France 20 C7
Lgov, Russia 33 G8
Lhasa, China 60 D4
Lhazê, China 60 D3
Lhokkruet, Indonesia 62 D1
Lhokseumawe, Indonesia 62 C1
L'Hospitalet de Llobregat, Spain 38 D7
Li, Thailand 64 D2
Li Shui →, China 59 C9
Li Xian, Gansu, China 56 G3
Li Xian, Hebei, China 56 E8
Li Xian, Hunan, China 59 C8
Liádhoi, Greece 47 E8
Liancheng, China 59 E11
Liancourt Rocks = Tok-do, Asia 55 F5
Lianga, Phil. 61 G7
Liangcheng, Nei Monggol Zizhiqu, China 56 D7
Liangcheng, Shandong, China 57 G10
Liangdang, China 56 H4
Lianghe, China 58 E2
Lianghekou, China 58 C7
Liangping, China 58 B6
Liangpran, Indonesia 62 D4
Lianhua, China 59 D9
Lianjiang, Fujian, China 59 D12
Lianjiang, Guangdong, China 59 G8
Lianping, China 59 E10
Lianshan, China 59 E9
Lianshanguan, China 57 D12
Lianshui, China 57 H10
Lianyuan, China 59 D8
Lianyungang, China 57 G10
Lianzhou, China 59 E9
Liao He →, China 57 D11
Liaocheng, China 56 F8
Liaodong Bandao, China 57 E12
Liaodong Wan, China 57 D11
Liaoning □, China 57 D12
Liaotung, G. of = Liaodong Wan, China 57 D11
Liaoyang, China 57 D12
Liaoyuan, China 57 C13
Liaozhong, China 57 D12
Liapádhes, Greece 46 B1
Liard →, Canada 102 A4
Liard River, Canada 102 B3
Liari, Pakistan 68 G2
Libau = Liepāja, Latvia 9 H19
Libby, U.S.A. 108 B6
Libenge, Dem. Rep. of the Congo 84 D3
Liberal, U.S.A. 113 G4
Liberec, Czech Rep. 26 A8
Liberecký □, Czech Rep. 26 A8
Liberia, Costa Rica 120 D2
Liberia ■, W. Afr. 82 D3
Liberty, Mo., U.S.A. 112 F7
Liberty, N.Y., U.S.A. 117 E10
Liberty, Pa., U.S.A. 116 E7
Liberty, Tex., U.S.A. 113 K7
Libiąż, Poland 31 H6
Lîbîya, Sahrâ', Africa 79 C10
Libo, China 58 E6
Libobo, Tanjung, Indonesia 63 E7
Libode, S. Africa 89 E4
Libohovë, Albania 44 F4
Libourne, France 20 D3
Libramont, Belgium 17 E5
Librazhd, Albania 44 E4
Libreville, Gabon 84 D1
Libya ■, N. Afr. 79 C9
Libyan Desert = Lîbîya, Sahrâ', Africa 79 C10
Libyan Plateau = Ed-Déffa, Egypt 80 A2
Licantén, Chile 126 D1
Licata, Italy 42 E6
Lice, Turkey 73 C9
Licheng, China 56 F7
Lichfield, U.K. 15 E6
Lichinga, Mozam. 87 E4
Lichtenburg, S. Africa 88 D4
Lichtenfels, Germany 25 E7
Lichuan, Hubei, China 58 B7
Lichuan, Jiangxi, China 59 D11
Licking →, U.S.A. 114 F3
Licosa, Punta, Italy 43 B7
Licungo →, Mozam. 87 F4
Lida, Belarus 9 K21
Liden, Sweden 10 B10
Lidhoríkion, Greece 46 C4
Lidhult, Sweden 11 H7
Lidköping, Sweden 11 F7
Lido, Italy 41 C9
Lido, Niger 83 C5
Lido di Roma = Óstia, Lido di, Italy 41 G9
Lidzbark, Poland 31 E6
Lidzbark Warmiński, Poland 30 D7
Liebenwalde, Germany 24 C9
Lieberose, Germany 24 D10
Liebig, Mt., Australia 92 D5
Liebling, Romania 28 E6
Liechtenstein ■, Europe 25 H5
Liège, Belgium 17 D5
Liège □, Belgium 17 D5
Liegnitz = Legnica, Poland 31 G3
Lienart, Dem. Rep. of the Congo 86 B2
Lienyünchiangshih = Lianyungang, China 57 G10
Lienz, Austria 26 E5
Liepāja, Latvia 9 H19
Liepāja □, Latvia 30 B8
Liepājas ezers, Latvia 30 B8
Lier, Belgium 17 C4
Liernais, France 19 E11
Lieşti, Romania 29 E12
Liévin, France 19 B9
Lièvre →, Canada 104 C4
Liezen, Austria 26 D7
Liffey →, Ireland 12 C5
Lifford, Ireland 12 B4
Liffré, France 18 D5
Lifudzin, Russia 54 B7
Ligao, Phil. 61 E5
Lightning Ridge, Australia 95 D4
Lignano Sabbiadoro, Italy 41 C10
Ligny-en-Barrois, France 19 D12
Ligonha →, Mozam. 87 F4
Ligonier, U.S.A. 116 F5
Ligoúrion, Greece 46 D5
Ligueil, France 18 E7
Liguria □, Italy 40 D5
Ligurian Sea, Medit. S. 6 G7
Lihou Reefs and Cays, Australia 94 B5
Lihue, U.S.A. 106 H15
Lihué Calel △, Argentina 126 D2
Lijiang, China 58 D3
Likasi, Dem. Rep. of the Congo 87 E2
Likenäs, Sweden 10 D7
Likhoslavl, Russia 32 D8
Likhovskoy, Russia 33 H11
Likoma I., Malawi 87 E3
Likumburu, Tanzania 87 D4
L'Île-Bouchard, France 18 E7
L'Île-Rousse, France 21 F12
Liling, China 59 D9
Lilla Edet, Sweden 11 F6
Lille, France 19 B10
Lille Bælt, Denmark 11 J3
Lillebonne, France 18 C7
Lillehammer, Norway 9 F14
Lillesand, Norway 9 G13
Lillhärdal, Sweden 10 C8
Lillian Pt., Australia 93 E4
Lillo, Spain 36 F7
Lillooet, Canada 102 C4
Lillooet →, Canada 102 D4
Lilongwe, Malawi 87 E3
Liloy, Phil. 63 C6
Lim →, Bos.-H. 44 C3
Lim Chu Kang, Singapore 65 d
Lima, Indonesia 63 E7
Lima, Peru 124 F3
Lima, Mont., U.S.A. 108 D7
Lima, Ohio, U.S.A. 114 E3
Lima →, Portugal 36 D2
Liman, Indonesia 63 G14
Liman, Russia 35 H8
Limanowa, Poland 31 J7
Limassol, Cyprus 49 E12
Limavady, U.K. 12 A5
Limay →, Argentina 128 D3
Limay Mahuida, Argentina 126 D2
Limbach-Oberfrohna, Germany 24 E8
Limbang, Brunei 62 D5
Limbara, Mte., Italy 42 B2
Limbaži, Latvia 9 H21
Limbdi, India 68 H4
Limbe, Cameroon 83 E6
Limburg, Germany 25 E4
Limburg □, Belgium 17 C5
Limburg □, Neths. 17 C5
Limedsforsen, Sweden 10 D7
Limeira, Brazil 127 A6
Limenária, Greece 45 F8
Limerick, Ireland 12 D3
Limerick, U.S.A. 117 C14
Limerick □, Ireland 12 D3
Limestone, U.S.A. 116 D6
Limestone →, Canada 103 B10
Limfjorden, Denmark 11 H3
Limia = Lima →, Portugal 36 D2
Limín Khersonísou, Greece 47 F7
Limingen, Norway 8 D15
Limmared, Sweden 11 G7
Limmen Bight, Australia 94 A2
Limmen Bight →, Australia 94 B2
Límni, Greece 46 C5
Límnos, Greece 47 B7
Limoges, Canada 117 A9
Limoges, France 20 C5
Limón, Costa Rica 120 E3
Limon, U.S.A. 112 F3
Limone Piemonte, Italy 40 D4
Limousin □, France 20 C5
Limousin, Plateaux du, France 20 C5
Limoux, France 20 E6
Limpopo □, S. Africa 89 C4
Limpopo →, Africa 89 D5
Limuru, Kenya 86 C4
Lin Xian, China 56 F6
Lin'an, China 59 B12
Linapacan I., Phil. 61 F3
Linapacan Str., Phil. 61 F3
Linares, Chile 126 D1
Linares, Mexico 119 C5
Linares, Spain 37 G7
Linaro, Capo, Italy 41 F8
Línas Mte., Italy 42 C1
Linate, Milano ✕ (LIN), Italy 40 C6
Lincang, China 58 F3
Lincheng, China 56 F8
Linchuan, China 59 D11
Lincoln = Beamsville, Canada 116 C5
Lincoln, Argentina 126 C3
Lincoln, N.Z. 91 K4
Lincoln, U.K. 14 D7
Lincoln, Calif., U.S.A. 110 G5
Lincoln, Ill., U.S.A. 112 E10
Lincoln, Kans., U.S.A. 112 F5
Lincoln, Maine, U.S.A. 115 C11
Lincoln, N.H., U.S.A. 117 B13
Lincoln, N. Mex., U.S.A. 109 K11
Lincoln, Nebr., U.S.A. 112 E6
Lincoln City, U.S.A. 108 D1
Lincoln Hav = Lincoln Sea, Arctic 4 A5
Lincoln Sea, Arctic 4 A5
Lincolnshire □, U.K. 14 D7
Lincolnshire Wolds, U.K. 14 D7
Lincolnton, U.S.A. 115 H5
Lind, U.S.A. 108 C4
Linda, U.S.A. 110 F5
Lindau, Germany 25 H5
Lindeman I., Australia 94 J7
Linden, Guyana 124 B7
Linden, Ala., U.S.A. 115 J2
Linden, Calif., U.S.A. 110 G5
Linden, Tex., U.S.A. 113 J7
Lindenhurst, U.S.A. 117 F11
Lindesberg, Sweden 10 E9
Lindesnes, Norway 9 H12
Líndhos, Greece 49 C10
Líndhos, Ákra, Greece 49 C10
Lindi, Tanzania 87 D4
Lindi □, Tanzania 87 D4
Lindi →, Dem. Rep. of the Congo 86 B2
Lindö, Sweden 11 F10
Lindome, Sweden 11 G6
Lindoso, Portugal 36 D2
Lindow, Germany 24 C8
Lindsay, Canada 116 B6
Lindsay, Calif., U.S.A. 110 J7
Lindsay, Okla., U.S.A. 113 H6
Lindsborg, U.S.A. 112 F6
Lindsdal, Sweden 11 H10
Line Islands, Pac. Oc. 97 H12
Linesville, U.S.A. 116 E4
Linfen, China 56 F6
Ling Xian, Hunan, China 59 D9
Ling Xian, Shandong, China 56 F9
Lingao, China 64 C7
Lingayen, Phil. 63 A6
Lingayen G., Phil. 61 C4
Lingbi, China 57 H9
Lingbo, Sweden 10 C10
Lingchuan, Guangxi Zhuangzu, China 59 E8
Lingchuan, Shanxi, China 56 G7
Lingen, Germany 24 C3
Lingga, Indonesia 62 E2
Lingga, Kepulauan, Indonesia 62 E2
Lingga Arch. = Lingga, Kepulauan, Indonesia 62 E2
Linghem, Sweden 11 F9
Lingle, U.S.A. 112 D2
Lingqiu, China 56 E8
Lingshan, China 58 F7
Lingshi, China 56 F6
Lingshou, China 56 E8
Lingshui, China 64 C8
Lingtai, China 56 G4
Linguère, Senegal 82 B1
Lingui, China 59 E8
Lingwu, China 56 E4
Lingyuan, China 57 D10
Lingyun, China 58 E6
Linhai, China 59 C13
Linhares, Brazil 125 G10
Linhe, China 56 D4
Linjiang, China 57 D14
Linköping, Sweden 11 F9
Linkou, China 57 B16
Linli, China 59 C8
Linnhe, L., U.K. 13 E3
Linqi, China 56 G7
Linqing, China 56 F8
Linqu, China 57 F10
Linru, China 56 G7
Lins, Brazil 127 A6
Linshui, China 58 B6
Linstead, Jamaica 120 a
Linta →, Madag. 89 D7
Linth →, Switz. 25 H5
Linthal, Switz. 25 J5
Linton, Ind., U.S.A. 114 F2
Linton, N. Dak., U.S.A. 112 B4
Lintong, China 56 G5
Linwood, Canada 116 C4
Linwu, China 59 E9
Linxi, China 57 C10
Linxia, China 60 C5
Linxiang, China 59 C9
Linyanti →, Africa 88 B4
Linyi, China 57 G10
Linz, Austria 26 C7
Linz, Germany 24 E3
Linzhenzhen, China 56 F5
Linzi, China 57 F10
Lion, G. du, France 20 E7
Lionárisso, Cyprus 49 D13
Lioni, Italy 43 B8
Lions, G. of = Lion, G. du, France 20 E7
Lion's Den, Zimbabwe 87 F3
Lion's Head, Canada 116 B3
Liozno = Lyozna, Belarus 32 E6
Lipa, Phil. 61 E4
Lipali, Mozam. 87 F4
Lipany, Slovak Rep. 27 B13
Lipari, Italy 43 D7
Lipari, I., Italy 43 D7
Lipari, Is. = Eólie, Ís., Italy 43 D7
Lipcani, Moldova 29 B11
Lipetsk, Russia 33 F10
Lipiany, Poland 31 E1
Liping, China 58 D7
Lipkany = Lipcani, Moldova 29 B11
Lipljan, Serbia & M. 44 D5
Lipník nad Bečvou, Czech Rep. 27 B10
Lipno, Poland 31 F6
Lipova, Romania 28 D6
Lipovcy Manzovka, Russia 54 B5
Lipovets, Ukraine 33 H5
Lippe →, Germany 24 D2
Lippstadt, Germany 24 D4
Lipscomb, U.S.A. 113 G4
Lipsk, Poland 30 E10
Lipsko, Poland 31 G8
Lipsói, Greece 47 D8
Liptovský Hrádok, Slovak Rep. 27 B12
Liptovský Milkuláš, Slovak Rep. 27 B12
Liptrap, C., Australia 95 F4
Lipu, China 59 E8
Liquillo, Sierra de, Puerto Rico 121 d
Lira, Uganda 86 B3
Liri →, Italy 42 A6
Liria = Lliria, Spain 39 F4
Lisala, Dem. Rep. of the Congo 84 D4
Lisboa, Portugal 37 G1
Lisboa □, Portugal 37 F1
Lisboa ✕ (LIS), Portugal 37 G1
Lisbon = Lisboa, Portugal 37 G1
Lisbon, N. Dak., U.S.A. 112 B6
Lisbon, N.H., U.S.A. 117 B13
Lisbon, Ohio, U.S.A. 116 F4
Lisbon Falls, U.S.A. 115 D10
Lisburn, U.K. 12 B5
Lisburne, C., U.S.A. 4 C17
Liscannor B., Ireland 12 D2
Liscia →, Italy 42 A2
Lishe Jiang →, China 58 E3
Lishi, China 56 F6
Lishu, China 57 C13
Lishui, Jiangsu, China 59 B12
Lishui, Zhejiang, China 59 C12
Lisianski I., Pac. Oc. 96 E10
Lisichansk = Lysychansk, Ukraine 33 H10
Lisieux, France 18 C7
Liski, Russia 33 G10
L'Isle-Jourdain, Gers, France 20 E5
L'Isle-Jourdain, Vienne, France 20 B4
L'Isle-sur-la-Sorgue, France 21 E9
Lisle-sur-Tarn, France 20 E5
Lismore, Australia 95 D5
Lismore, Ireland 12 D4
Lista, Norway 9 G12
Lister, Mt., Antarctica 5 D11
Liston, Australia 95 D5
Listowel, Canada 116 C4
Listowel, Ireland 12 D2
Lit, Sweden 10 A8
Lit-et-Mixe, France 20 D2
Litang, Guangxi Zhuangzu, China 58 F7
Litang, Sichuan, China 58 B3
Litang Qu →, China 58 C3
Litani →, Lebanon 74 B4
Litchfield, Calif., U.S.A. 110 E6
Litchfield, Conn., U.S.A. 117 E11
Litchfield, Ill., U.S.A. 112 F10
Litchfield, Minn., U.S.A. 112 C7
Litchfield △, Australia 92 B5
Liteni, Romania 29 C11
Lithgow, Australia 95 E5
Líthinon, Ákra, Greece 49 E6
Lithuania ■, Europe 9 J20
Litija, Slovenia 41 B11
Lititz, U.S.A. 117 F8
Litókhoron, Greece 44 F6
Litoměřice, Czech Rep. 26 A7
Litomyšl, Czech Rep. 27 B9
Litschau, Austria 26 C8
Little Abaco, Bahamas 120 A4
Little Barrier I., N.Z. 91 G5
Little Belt Mts., U.S.A. 108 C8
Little Bighorn Battlefield ⌂, U.S.A. 108 D10
Little Blue →, U.S.A. 112 F6
Little Buffalo →, Canada 102 A6
Little Cayman, Cayman Is. 120 C3
Little Churchill →, Canada 103 B9
Little Colorado →, U.S.A. 109 H8
Little Current, Canada 104 C3
Little Current →, Canada 104 B3
Little Falls, Minn., U.S.A. 112 C7
Little Falls, N.Y., U.S.A. 117 C10
Little Fork →, U.S.A. 112 A8
Little Grand Rapids, Canada 103 C9
Little Humboldt →, U.S.A. 108 F5
Little Inagua I., Bahamas 121 B5
Little Karoo, S. Africa 88 E3
Little Khingan Mts. = Xiao Hinggan Ling, China 60 B7
Little Lake, U.S.A. 111 K9
Little Laut Is. = Laut Kecil, Kepulauan, Indonesia 62 E5
Little Mecatina = Petit-Mécatina →, Canada 105 B8
Little Minch, U.K. 13 D2
Little Missouri →, U.S.A. 112 B3
Little Ouse →, U.K. 15 E9
Little Rann, India 68 H4
Little Red →, U.S.A. 113 H9
Little River, N.Z. 91 K4
Little Rock, U.S.A. 113 H8
Little Ruaha →, Tanzania 86 D4
Little Sable Pt., U.S.A. 114 D2
Little Scarcies →, S. Leone 82 D2
Little Sioux →, U.S.A. 112 E6
Little Smoky →, Canada 102 C5
Little Snake →, U.S.A. 108 F9
Little Tobago, Trin. & Tob. 125 J16
Little Valley, U.S.A. 116 D6
Little Wabash →, U.S.A. 114 G1
Little White →, U.S.A. 112 D4
Little Zab = Zāb aş Şaghīr →, Iraq 70 C4
Littlefield, U.S.A. 113 J3
Littlehampton, U.K. 15 G7
Littleton, U.S.A. 117 B13
Litvinov, Czech Rep. 26 A6
Liu He →, China 57 D11
Liu Jiang →, China 58 F7
Liuba, China 56 H4
Liucheng, China 58 E7
Liugou, China 57 D10
Liuhe, China 57 C13
Liuheng Dao, China 59 C14
Liujiang, China 58 E7
Liukang Tenggaja = Sabalana, Kepulauan, Indonesia 63 F5
Liuli, Tanzania 87 E3
Liuwa Plain, Zambia 85 G4
Liuyang, China 59 C9
Liuzhou, China 58 E7
Liuzhuang, China 57 H11
Livada, Romania 28 C8
Livadherón, Greece 44 F5
Livadhia, Cyprus 49 E12
Livádhion, Greece 46 A4
Livarot, France 18 D7
Live Oak, Calif., U.S.A. 110 F5
Live Oak, Fla., U.S.A. 115 K4
Liveras, Cyprus 49 D11
Livermore, U.S.A. 110 H5
Livermore, Mt., U.S.A. 113 K2
Livermore Falls, U.S.A. 115 C11
Liverpool, Canada 105 D7
Liverpool, U.K. 14 D4
Liverpool, U.S.A. 117 C8
Liverpool Bay, U.K. 14 D4
Liverpool Ra., Australia 95 E5
Livigno, Italy 40 B7
Livingston, Guatemala 120 C2
Livingston, U.K. 13 F5
Livingston, Ala., U.S.A. 115 J1
Livingston, Calif., U.S.A. 110 H6
Livingston, Mont., U.S.A. 108 D8
Livingston, S.C., U.S.A. 115 J5
Livingston, Tenn., U.S.A. 115 G3
Livingston, Tex., U.S.A. 113 K7
Livingston, L., U.S.A. 113 K7
Livingston Manor, U.S.A. 117 E10
Livingstone, Zambia 87 F2
Livingstone Mts., Tanzania 87 D3
Livingstonia, Malawi 87 E3
Livno, Bos.-H. 28 G2
Livny, Russia 33 F9
Livonia, Mich., U.S.A. 114 D4
Livonia, N.Y., U.S.A. 116 D7
Livorno, Italy 40 E7
Livradois-Forez ⌂, France 20 E7
Livramento, Brazil 127 C4
Livron-sur-Drôme, France 21 D8
Livyntsi, Ukraine 29 B11
Liwale, Tanzania 87 D4
Liwiec →, Poland 31 F8
Liwonde △, Malawi 87 E4
Lixi, China 58 D3
Lixian, China 58 B4
Lixoúrion, Greece 46 C2
Liyang, China 59 B12
Lizard I., Australia 94 A4
Lizard Pt., U.K. 15 H2
Lizzano, Italy 43 B10
Ljig, Serbia & M. 44 B4
Ljubija, Bos.-H. 41 D13
Ljubinje, Bos.-H. 44 D2
Ljubljana, Slovenia 41 B11
Ljubljana ✕ (LJU), Slovenia 41 B11
Ljubno, Slovenia 41 B11
Ljubovija, Serbia & M. 44 B3
Ljugarn, Sweden 11 G12
Ljung, Sweden 11 G7
Ljungan →, Sweden 10 B11
Ljungaverk, Sweden 10 B10
Ljungby, Sweden 11 H7
Ljungbyholm, Sweden 11 H10
Ljungdalen, Sweden 10 B6
Ljungsbro, Sweden 11 F9
Ljungskile, Sweden 11 F5
Ljusdal, Sweden 10 C10
Ljusfallshammar, Sweden 11 F9
Ljusnan →, Sweden 10 C11
Ljusne, Sweden 10 C11
Ljutomer, Slovenia 41 B13
Llagostera, Spain 38 D7
Llancanelo, Salina, Argentina 126 D2
Llandeilo, U.K. 15 F4
Llandovery, U.K. 15 F4
Llandrindod Wells, U.K. 15 E4
Llandudno, U.K. 14 D4
Llanelli, U.K. 15 F3
Llanes, Spain 36 B6
Llangollen, U.K. 14 E4
Llanidloes, U.K. 15 E4
Llano, U.S.A. 113 K5
Llano →, U.S.A. 113 K5
Llano Estacado, U.S.A. 113 J3
Llanos, S. Amer. 124 C4
Llanos de Challe △, Chile 126 B1
Llanquihue, L., Chile 128 E1
Llanwrtyd Wells, U.K. 15 E4
Llebeig, C. des, Spain 48 B9
Lleida, Spain 38 D5
Lleida □, Spain 38 C6
Llentrisca, C., Spain 48 C7
Llera, Mexico 119 C5
Llerena, Spain 37 G5
Lleyn Peninsula, U.K. 14 E3
Llico, Chile 126 C1
Lliria, Spain 39 F4
Llobregat →, Spain 38 D7
Llodio, Spain 38 B2
Lloret de Mar, Spain 38 D7
Lloyd B., Australia 94 A3
Lloyd L., Canada 103 B7
Lloydminster, Canada 103 C7
Llucena del Cid, Spain 38 E4
Llucmajor, Spain 48 B9
Llullaillaco △, Chile 126 A2
Llullaillaco, Volcán, S. Amer. 126 A2
Lo →, Vietnam 64 B5
Loa, U.S.A. 109 G8
Loa →, Chile 126 A1
Loaita I., S. China Sea 62 B4
Loange →, Dem. Rep. of the Congo 84 E4
Loano, Italy 40 D5
Lobatse, Botswana 88 D4
Löbau, Germany 24 D10
Lobenstein, Germany 24 E7
Lobería, Argentina 126 D4
Löberöd, Sweden 11 J7
Łobez, Poland 30 E2
Lobito, Angola 85 G2
Lobo →, Ivory C. 82 D3

Lobos, *Argentina* 126 D4
Lobos, I., *Mexico* 118 B2
Lobos, I. de, *Canary Is.* 48 F6
Łobżenica, *Poland* 31 E4
Loc Binh, *Vietnam* 64 B6
Loc Ninh, *Vietnam* 65 G6
Locarno, *Switz.* 25 J4
Loch Baghasdail = Lochboisdale, *U.K.* 13 D1
Loch Garman = Wexford, *Ireland* 12 D5
Loch Lomond and the Trossachs △, *U.K.* 13 E4
Loch Nam Madadh = Lochmaddy, *U.K.* 13 D1
Lochaber, *U.K.* 13 E3
Locharbriggs, *U.K.* 13 F5
Lochboisdale, *U.K.* 13 D1
Loche, L. La, *Canada* 103 B7
Lochem, *Neths.* 17 B6
Loches, *France* 18 E7
Lochgilphead, *U.K.* 13 E3
Lochinvar △, *Zambia* 87 F2
Lochinver, *U.K.* 13 C3
Lochmaddy, *U.K.* 13 D1
Lochnagar, *Australia* 94 C4
Lochnagar, *U.K.* 13 E5
Łochów, *Poland* 31 F8
Lochy, L., *U.K.* 13 E4
Lock, *Australia* 95 E2
Lock Haven, *U.S.A.* 116 E7
Lockeford, *U.S.A.* 110 G5
Lockeport, *Canada* 105 D6
Lockerbie, *U.K.* 13 F5
Lockhart, *U.S.A.* 113 L6
Lockhart, L., *Australia* 93 F2
Lockhart River, *Australia* 94 A3
Lockney, *U.S.A.* 113 H4
Lockport, *U.S.A.* 116 C6
Locminé, *France* 18 E4
Locri, *Italy* 43 D9
Locronan, *France* 18 D2
Lod, *Israel* 74 D3
Lodeinoye Pole, *Russia* 32 B7
Lodève, *France* 20 E7
Lodge Bay, *Canada* 105 B8
Lodge Grass, *U.S.A.* 108 D10
Lodgepole Cr. →, *U.S.A.* 112 E2
Lodhran, *Pakistan* 68 E4
Lodi, *Italy* 40 C6
Lodi, *Calif., U.S.A.* 110 G5
Lodi, *Ohio, U.S.A.* 116 E3
Lodja, *Dem. Rep. of the Congo* 86 C1
Lodosa, *Spain* 38 C2
Lödöse, *Sweden* 11 F6
Lodwar, *Kenya* 86 B4
Łódź, *Poland* 31 G6
Łódzkie □, *Poland* 31 G6
Loei, *Thailand* 64 D3
Loengo, *Dem. Rep. of the Congo* 86 C2
Loeriesfontein, *S. Africa* 88 E2
Lofa →, *Liberia* 83 D2
Lofa Mano △, *Liberia* 82 D2
Lofer, *Austria* 26 D5
Lofoten, *Norway* 8 B15
Lofsdalen, *Sweden* 10 B7
Lofsen →, *Sweden* 10 B7
Loftahammar, *Sweden* 11 G10
Loga, *Niger* 83 C5
Logan, *Iowa, U.S.A.* 112 E7
Logan, *Ohio, U.S.A.* 114 F4
Logan, *Utah, U.S.A.* 108 F8
Logan, *W. Va., U.S.A.* 114 G5
Logan, Mt., *Canada* 100 B5
Logandale, *U.S.A.* 111 J12
Logansport, *Ind., U.S.A.* 114 E2
Logansport, *La., U.S.A.* 113 K8
Logirim, *Sudan* 81 G3
Logo, *Sudan* 81 F3
Logone →, *Chad* 79 F9
Logroño, *Spain* 38 C2
Logrosán, *Spain* 37 F5
Løgstør, *Denmark* 11 H3
Løgumkloster, *Denmark* 11 J2
Lohals, *Denmark* 11 J4
Lohardaga, *India* 69 H11
Loharia, *India* 68 H6
Loharu, *India* 68 E6
Lohja, *Finland* 9 F21
Löhne, *Germany* 24 C4
Lohr, *Germany* 25 F5
Lohri Wah →, *Pakistan* 68 F2
Loi-kaw, *Burma* 67 K20
Loimaa, *Finland* 9 F20
Loir →, *France* 18 E6
Loir-et-Cher □, *France* 18 E8
Loire □, *France* 21 C8
Loire →, *France* 18 E4
Loire Anjou Touraine ⌓, *France* 18 E6
Loire-Atlantique □, *France* 18 E5
Loiret □, *France* 19 E9
Loitz, *Germany* 24 B9
Loja, *Ecuador* 124 D3
Loja, *Spain* 37 H6
Loji = Kawasi, *Indonesia* 63 E7
Lojo = Lohja, *Finland* 9 F21
Løjt Kirkeby, *Denmark* 11 J3
Lojung, *China* 58 E7
Loka, *Sudan* 81 G3
Lokandu, *Dem. Rep. of the Congo* 86 C2
Lokeren, *Belgium* 17 C3
Lokgwabe, *Botswana* 88 C3
Lokhvitsa, *Ukraine* 33 G7
Lokichokio, *Kenya* 86 B3
Lokitaung, *Kenya* 86 B4
Lokkan tekojärvi, *Finland* 8 C22
Løkken, *Denmark* 11 G3
Loknya, *Russia* 32 D6
Loko, *Nigeria* 83 D6
Lokoja, *Nigeria* 83 D6
Lokot, *Russia* 33 F8
Lol →, *Sudan* 81 F2
Lola, *Guinea* 82 D3
Lola, Mt., *U.S.A.* 110 F6
Lolibai, Gebel, *Sudan* 81 G3
Lolimi, *Sudan* 81 G3
Loliondo, *Tanzania* 86 C4
Lolland, *Denmark* 11 K5
Lollar, *Germany* 24 E4
Lolo, *U.S.A.* 108 C6
Lolodorf, *Cameroon* 83 E7
Lom, *Bulgaria* 44 C7
Lom →, *Bulgaria* 44 C7
Lom Kao, *Thailand* 64 D3
Lom Sak, *Thailand* 64 D3
Loma, *U.S.A.* 108 C8
Loma Linda, *U.S.A.* 111 L9
Lomami →, *Dem. Rep. of the Congo* 86 B1
Lomas de Zamóra, *Argentina* 126 C4
Lombadina, *Australia* 92 C3
Lombárdia □, *Italy* 40 C6
Lombardy = Lombárdia □, *Italy* 40 C6
Lombez, *France* 20 E4
Lomblen, *Indonesia* 63 F6
Lombok, *Indonesia* 62 F5
Lombok, Selat, *Indonesia* 63 K18
Lomé, *Togo* 83 D5
Lomela, *Dem. Rep. of the Congo* 84 E4
Lomela →, *Dem. Rep. of the Congo* 84 E4
Lomianki, *Poland* 31 F7
Lomma, *Sweden* 11 J7
Lommel, *Belgium* 17 C5
Lomond, *Canada* 102 C6
Lomond, L., *U.K.* 13 E4
Lomonosov Ridge, *Arctic* 4 A
Lomphat, *Cambodia* 64 F6
Lompobatang, *Indonesia* 63 F5
Lompoc, *U.S.A.* 111 L6
Łomża, *Poland* 31 E9
Lon, Ko, *Thailand* 65 a
Loncoche, *Chile* 128 D2
Londa, *India* 66 M9
Londiani, *Kenya* 86 C4
Londinières, *France* 18 C8
London, *Canada* 116 D3
London, *U.K.* 15 F7
London, *Ky., U.S.A.* 114 G3
London, *Ohio, U.S.A.* 114 F4
London, Greater □, *U.K.* 15 F7
London Gatwick ✕ (LGW), *U.K.* 15 F7
London Heathrow ✕ (LHR), *U.K.* 15 F7
London Stansted ✕ (STN), *U.K.* 15 F8
Londonderry, *U.K.* 12 B4
Londonderry □, *U.K.* 12 B4
Londonderry, C., *Australia* 92 B4
Londonderry, I., *Chile* 128 H2
Londres, *Argentina* 128 B3
Londrina, *Brazil* 127 A5
Lone Pine, *U.S.A.* 110 J8
Lonely Mine, *Zimbabwe* 89 B4
Long B., *U.S.A.* 115 J6
Long Beach, *Calif., U.S.A.* 111 M8
Long Beach, *N.Y., U.S.A.* 117 F11
Long Beach, *Wash., U.S.A.* 110 D2
Long Branch, *U.S.A.* 117 F11
Long Creek, *U.S.A.* 108 D4
Long Eaton, *U.K.* 14 E6
Long I., *Australia* 94 J6
Long I., *Bahamas* 121 B4
Long I., *Canada* 104 B4
Long I., *Ireland* 12 E2
Long I., *U.S.A.* 117 F11
Long Island Sd., *U.S.A.* 117 E12
Long L., *Canada* 104 C2
Long Lake, *U.S.A.* 117 C10
Long Point B., *Canada* 116 D4
Long Prairie →, *U.S.A.* 112 C7
Long Pt., *Canada* 116 D4
Long Range Mts., *Canada* 105 C8
Long Reef, *Australia* 92 B4
Long Spruce, *Canada* 103 B10
Long Str. = Longa, Proliv, *Russia* 4 C16
Long Thanh, *Vietnam* 65 G6
Long Xian, *China* 56 G4
Long Xuyen, *Vietnam* 65 G5
Longá, *Greece* 46 E3
Longa, Proliv, *Russia* 4 C16
Long'an, *China* 58 F6
Longarone, *Italy* 41 B9
Longbenton, *U.K.* 14 B6
Longboat Key, *U.S.A.* 115 M4
Longchang, *China* 58 C5
Longchi, *China* 58 C4
Longchuan, *Guangdong, China* 59 E10
Longchuan, *Yunnan, China* 58 E1
Longde, *China* 56 G4
Longeau, *France* 19 E12
Longford, *Australia* 95 G4
Longford, *Ireland* 12 C4
Longford □, *Ireland* 12 C4
Longhai, *China* 59 E11
Longhua, *China* 57 D9
Longhui, *China* 59 D8
Longido, *Tanzania* 86 C4
Longiram, *Indonesia* 62 E5
Longkou, *Jiangxi, China* 59 D10
Longkou, *Shandong, China* 57 F11
Longlac, *Canada* 104 C2
Longli, *China* 58 D6
Longlin, *China* 58 E5
Longling, *China* 58 E2
Longmeadow, *U.S.A.* 117 D12
Longmen, *China* 59 F10
Longming, *China* 58 F6
Longmont, *U.S.A.* 112 E2
Longnan, *China* 59 E10
Longnawan, *Indonesia* 62 D4
Longobucco, *Italy* 43 C9
Longquan, *China* 59 C12
Longreach, *Australia* 94 C3
Longshan, *China* 58 C7
Longsheng, *China* 59 E8
Longué-Jumelles, *France* 18 E6
Longueau, *France* 19 C9
Longueuil, *Canada* 117 A11
Longuyon, *France* 19 C12
Longvic, *France* 19 E12
Longview, *Tex., U.S.A.* 113 J7
Longview, *Wash., U.S.A.* 110 D4
Longwy, *France* 19 C12
Longxi, *China* 56 G3
Longyan, *China* 59 E11
Longyearbyen, *Svalbard* 4 B8
Longyou, *China* 59 C12
Longzhou, *China* 58 F6
Lonigo, *Italy* 41 C8
Löningen, *Germany* 24 C3
Lonja →, *Croatia* 41 C13
Lonoke, *U.S.A.* 113 H9
Lonquimay, *Chile* 128 D2
Lons-le-Saunier, *France* 19 F12
Lönsboda, *Sweden* 11 H8
Looe, *U.K.* 15 G3
Lookout, C., *Canada* 104 A3
Lookout, C., *U.S.A.* 115 H7
Loolmalasin, *Tanzania* 86 C4
Loon →, *Alta., Canada* 102 B5
Loon →, *Man., Canada* 103 B8
Loon Lake, *Canada* 103 C7
Loongana, *Australia* 93 F4
Loop Hd., *Ireland* 12 D2
Lop Buri, *Thailand* 64 E3
Lop Nor = Lop Nur, *China* 60 B4
Lop Nur, *China* 60 B4
Lopare, *Bos.-H.* 28 F3
Lopatin, *Russia* 35 J8
Lopatina, Gora, *Russia* 53 D15
Lopaye, *Sudan* 81 F3
Lopez, *Phil.* 61 E5
Lopez, *U.S.A.* 117 E8
Lopez, C., *Gabon* 84 E1
Lopphavet, *Norway* 8 A19
Lora →, *Afghan.* 66 D4
Lora, Hāmūn-i-, *Pakistan* 66 E4
Lora Cr. →, *Australia* 95 D2
Lora del Río, *Spain* 37 H5
Lorain, *U.S.A.* 116 E2
Loralai, *Pakistan* 68 D3
Lorca, *Spain* 39 H3
Lord Howe I., *Pac. Oc.* 96 L7
Lord Howe Ridge, *Pac. Oc.* 96 L8
Lordsburg, *U.S.A.* 109 K9
Lorestan □, *Iran* 71 C6
Loreto, *Brazil* 125 E9
Loreto, *Italy* 41 E10
Loreto, *Mexico* 118 B2
Lorgues, *France* 21 E10
Lorhosso, *Burkina Faso* 82 C4
Lorient, *France* 18 E3
Lőrinci, *Hungary* 28 C4
Lormi, *India* 69 H9
Lorn, *U.K.* 13 E3
Lorn, Firth of, *U.K.* 13 E3
Lorne, *Australia* 95 F3
Loronyo, *Sudan* 81 G3
Lorovouno, *Cyprus* 49 D11
Lörrach, *Germany* 25 H3
Lorraine ⌓, *France* 19 D12
Lorraine □, *France* 19 D13
Los, *Sweden* 10 C9
Los, Îles de, *Guinea* 82 D2
Los Alamos, *Calif., U.S.A.* 111 L6
Los Alamos, *N. Mex., U.S.A.* 109 J10
Los Alcornocales ⌓, *Spain* 37 J5
Los Altos, *U.S.A.* 110 H4
Los Andes, *Chile* 126 C1
Los Angeles, *Chile* 126 D1
Los Angeles, *U.S.A.* 111 M8
Los Angeles, Bahia de, *Mexico* 118 B2
Los Angeles Aqueduct, *U.S.A.* 111 K9
Los Angeles International ✕ (LAX), *U.S.A.* 111 M8
Los Banos, *U.S.A.* 110 H6
Los Barrios, *Spain* 37 J5
Los Blancos, *Argentina* 126 A3
Los Cardones △, *Argentina* 126 B2
Los Chiles, *Costa Rica* 120 D3
Los Corrales de Buelna, *Spain* 36 B6
Los Cristianos, *Canary Is.* 48 F3
Los Gallardos, *Spain* 39 H3
Los Gatos, *U.S.A.* 110 H5
Los Haïtises △, *Dom. Rep.* 121 C6
Los Hermanos Is., *Venezuela* 121 D7
Los Islotes, *Canary Is.* 48 E6
Los Llanos de Aridane, *Canary Is.* 48 F2
Los Loros, *Chile* 126 B1
Los Lunas, *U.S.A.* 109 J10
Los Mochis, *Mexico* 118 B3
Los Monegros, *Spain* 38 D4
Los Nietos, *Spain* 39 H4
Los Olivos, *U.S.A.* 111 L6
Los Palacios, *Cuba* 120 B3
Los Palacios y Villafranca, *Spain* 37 H5
Los Reyes, *Mexico* 118 D4
Los Roques Is., *Venezuela* 121 D6
Los Santos de Maimona, *Spain* 37 G4
Los Teques, *Venezuela* 124 A5
Los Testigos, Is., *Venezuela* 124 A6
Los Vilos, *Chile* 126 C1
Los Yébenes, *Spain* 37 F7
Łosice, *Poland* 31 F9
Loskop Dam, *S. Africa* 89 D4
Løsning, *Denmark* 11 J3
Lossiemouth, *U.K.* 13 D5
Lossnen △, *Sweden* 10 B6
Lostwithiel, *U.K.* 15 G3
Lot □, *France* 20 D5
Lot →, *France* 20 D4
Lot-et-Garonne □, *France* 20 D4
Lota, *Chile* 126 D1
Lotagipi Swamp, *Sudan* 81 G3
Lotfābād, *Iran* 71 B8
Lothair, *S. Africa* 89 D5
Lotorp, *Sweden* 11 F9
Lötschbergtunnel, *Switz.* 25 J3
Löttorp, *Sweden* 11 G11
Lotung, *Taiwan* 59 E13
Loubomo, *Congo* 84 E2
Loudéac, *France* 18 D4
Loudi, *China* 59 D8
Loudonville, *U.S.A.* 116 F2
Loudun, *France* 18 E7
Loue →, *France* 19 E12
Louga, *Senegal* 82 B1
Loughborough, *U.K.* 14 E6
Loughrea, *Ireland* 12 C3
Loughros More B., *Ireland* 12 B3
Louhans, *France* 19 F12
Louis Trichardt, *S. Africa* 89 C4
Louis XIV, Pte., *Canada* 104 B4
Louisa, *U.S.A.* 114 F4
Louisbourg, *Canada* 105 C8
Louise I., *Canada* 102 C2
Louiseville, *Canada* 104 C5
Louisiade Arch., *Papua N. G.* 96 J7
Louisiana, *U.S.A.* 112 F9
Louisiana □, *U.S.A.* 113 K9
Louisville, *Ky., U.S.A.* 114 F3
Louisville, *Miss., U.S.A.* 113 J10
Louisville, *Ohio, U.S.A.* 116 F3
Loulay, *France* 20 B3
Loulé, *Portugal* 37 H3
Louny, *Czech Rep.* 26 A6
Loup City, *U.S.A.* 112 E5
Loups Marins, Lacs des, *Canada* 104 A5
Lourdes, *France* 20 E3
Lourinhã, *Portugal* 37 F1
Lousã, *Portugal* 36 E2
Louta, *Burkina Faso* 82 C4
Louth, *Australia* 95 E4
Louth, *Ireland* 12 C5
Louth, *U.K.* 14 D7
Louth □, *Ireland* 12 C5
Loutrá Aidhipsoú, *Greece* 46 C5
Loutráki, *Greece* 46 D4
Louvain = Leuven, *Belgium* 17 D4
Louviers, *France* 18 C8
Louwsburg, *S. Africa* 89 D5
Lovat →, *Russia* 32 C6
Lovćen, *Serbia & M.* 44 D2
Lovćen △, *Serbia & M.* 44 D2
Lovech, *Bulgaria* 45 C8
Lovech □, *Bulgaria* 45 C8
Loveland, *U.S.A.* 112 E2
Lovell, *U.S.A.* 108 D9
Lovelock, *U.S.A.* 108 F4
Lóvere, *Italy* 40 C7
Lövestad, *Sweden* 11 J7
Loviisa, *Finland* 9 F22
Loving, *U.S.A.* 113 J2
Lovington, *U.S.A.* 113 J3
Lovisa = Loviisa, *Finland* 9 F22
Lovosice, *Czech Rep.* 26 A7
Lovran, *Croatia* 41 C11
Lovrin, *Romania* 28 E5
Lövstabruk, *Sweden* 10 D11
Lövstabukten, *Sweden* 10 D11
Low, L., *Canada* 104 B4
Low Pt., *Australia* 93 F4
Low Tatra = Nízké Tatry, *Slovak Rep.* 27 C12
Lowa, *Dem. Rep. of the Congo* 86 C2
Lowa →, *Dem. Rep. of the Congo* 86 C2
Lowell, *U.S.A.* 117 D13
Lowellville, *U.S.A.* 116 E4
Löwen →, *Namibia* 88 D2
Lower Alkali L., *U.S.A.* 108 F3
Lower Arrow L., *Canada* 102 D5
Lower Austria = Niederösterreich □, *Austria* 26 C8
Lower California = Baja California, *Mexico* 118 A1
Lower Hutt, *N.Z.* 91 J5
Lower Lake, *U.S.A.* 110 G4
Lower Manitou L., *Canada* 103 D10
Lower Post, *Canada* 102 B3
Lower Red L., *U.S.A.* 112 B7
Lower Saxony = Niedersachsen □, *Germany* 24 C4
Lower Tunguska = Tunguska, Nizhnyaya →, *Russia* 53 C9
Lower Zambezi △, *Zambia* 87 F2
Lowestoft, *U.K.* 15 E9
Lowgar □, *Afghan.* 66 B6
Łowicz, *Poland* 31 F6
Lowville, *U.S.A.* 117 C9
Loxton, *Australia* 95 E3
Loxton, *S. Africa* 88 E3
Loyalton, *U.S.A.* 110 F6
Loyalty Is. = Loyauté, Îs., *N. Cal.* 96 K8
Loyang = Luoyang, *China* 56 G7
Loyauté, Îs., *N. Cal.* 96 K8
Loyev = Loyew, *Belarus* 33 G6
Loyew, *Belarus* 33 G6
Loyoro, *Uganda* 86 B3
Lož, *Slovenia* 41 C11
Lozère □, *France* 20 D7
Loznica, *Serbia & M.* 44 B3
Lozova, *Ukraine* 33 H9
Lü Shan, *China* 59 C11
Lü-Tao, *Taiwan* 59 F13
Luachimo, *Angola* 84 F4
Luajan →, *India* 69 G11
Lualaba →, *Dem. Rep. of the Congo* 86 B2
Luampa, *Zambia* 87 F1
Lu'an, *China* 59 B11
Luan Chau, *Vietnam* 58 G4
Luan He →, *China* 57 E10
Luan Xian, *China* 57 E10
Luancheng, *Guangxi Zhuangzu, China* 58 F7
Luancheng, *Hebei, China* 56 F8
Luanco, *Spain* 36 B5
Luanda, *Angola* 84 F2
Luang, Thale, *Thailand* 65 J3
Luang Prabang, *Laos* 58 H4
Luangwa, *Zambia* 87 F3
Luangwa →, *Zambia* 87 E3
Luangwa Valley, *Zambia* 87 E3
Luanne, *China* 57 D9
Luanping, *China* 57 D9
Luanshya, *Zambia* 87 E2
Luapula □, *Zambia* 87 E2
Luapula →, *Africa* 87 D2
Luarca, *Spain* 36 B4
Luashi, *Dem. Rep. of the Congo* 87 E1
Luau, *Angola* 84 G4
Lubaczów, *Poland* 31 H10
Lubań, *Poland* 31 G2
Lubana, Ozero = Lubānas Ezers, *Latvia* 9 H22
Lubānas Ezers, *Latvia* 9 H22
Lubang, *Phil.* 61 E4
Lubang Is., *Phil.* 63 B6
Lubango, *Angola* 85 G2
Lubao, *Dem. Rep. of the Congo* 86 D2
Lubartów, *Poland* 31 G9
Lubawa, *Poland* 30 E6
Lübbecke, *Germany* 24 C4
Lübben, *Germany* 24 D9
Lübbenau, *Germany* 24 D9
Lubbock, *U.S.A.* 113 J4
Lübeck, *Germany* 24 B6
Lübecker Bucht, *Germany* 24 A6
Lubefu, *Dem. Rep. of the Congo* 86 C1
Lubefu →, *Dem. Rep. of the Congo* 86 C1
Lubelskie □, *Poland* 31 G9
Lubero = Luofu, *Dem. Rep. of the Congo* 86 C2
Luberon ⌓, *France* 21 E9
Lubersac, *France* 20 C5
Lubicon L., *Canada* 102 B5
Lubień Kujawski, *Poland* 31 F6
Lubilash →, *Dem. Rep. of the Congo* 84 F4
Lubin, *Poland* 31 G3
Lublin, *Poland* 31 G9
Lubliniec, *Poland* 31 H5
Lubnān, Jabal, *Lebanon* 74 B4
Lubniewice, *Poland* 31 F2
Lubny, *Ukraine* 33 G7
Lubomierz, *Poland* 31 G2
Luboń, *Poland* 31 F3
Lubongola, *Dem. Rep. of the Congo* 86 C2
L'ubotín, *Slovak Rep.* 27 B13
Lubraniec, *Poland* 31 F5
Lubsko, *Poland* 31 G1
Lübtheen, *Germany* 24 B7
Lubuagan, *Phil.* 61 C4
Lubudi, *Dem. Rep. of the Congo* 84 F5
Lubudi →, *Dem. Rep. of the Congo* 87 D2
Lubuklinggau, *Indonesia* 62 E2
Lubuksikaping, *Indonesia* 62 D2
Lubumbashi, *Dem. Rep. of the Congo* 87 E2
Lubunda, *Dem. Rep. of the Congo* 86 D2
Lubungu, *Zambia* 87 E2
Lubuskie □, *Poland* 31 F2
Lubutu, *Dem. Rep. of the Congo* 86 C2
Luc An Chau, *Vietnam* 64 A5
Luc-en-Diois, *France* 21 D9
Lucan, *Canada* 116 C3
Lucania, Mt., *Canada* 100 B5
Lucas Channel, *Canada* 116 A3
Lucban, *Phil.* 61 D4
Lucca, *Italy* 40 E7
Lucé, *France* 18 D8
Luce Bay, *U.K.* 13 G4
Lucea, *Jamaica* 120 a
Lucedale, *U.S.A.* 115 K1
Lucena, *Phil.* 61 E4
Lucena, *Spain* 37 H6
Lučenec, *Slovak Rep.* 27 C12
Lucera, *Italy* 43 A8
Lucerne = Luzern, *Switz.* 25 H4
Lucerne, *U.S.A.* 110 F4
Lucerne Valley, *U.S.A.* 111 L10
Lucero, *Mexico* 118 A3
Luchena →, *Spain* 39 H3
Lucheng, *China* 56 F7
Lucheringo →, *Mozam.* 87 E4
Lüchow, *Germany* 24 C7
Luchuan, *China* 59 F8
Lucia, *U.S.A.* 110 J5
Lucinda, *Australia* 94 B4
Luckau, *Germany* 24 D9
Luckenwalde, *Germany* 24 C9
Luckhoff, *S. Africa* 88 D3
Lucknow, *Canada* 116 C3
Lucknow, *India* 69 F9
Luçon, *France* 20 B2
Lüda = Dalian, *China* 57 E11
Luda Kamchiya →, *Bulgaria* 45 C11
Ludbreg, *Croatia* 41 B13
Lüdenscheid, *Germany* 24 D3
Lüderitz, *Namibia* 88 D2
Lüderitzbaai, *Namibia* 88 D2
Ludhiana, *India* 68 D6
Ludian, *China* 58 D4
Luding Qiao, *China* 58 C4
Lüdinghausen, *Germany* 24 D3
Ludington, *U.S.A.* 114 D2
Ludlow, *U.K.* 15 E5
Ludlow, *Calif., U.S.A.* 111 L10
Ludlow, *Pa., U.S.A.* 116 E6
Ludlow, *Vt., U.S.A.* 117 C12
Ludus, *Romania* 29 D9
Ludvika, *Sweden* 10 D9
Ludwigsburg, *Germany* 25 G5
Ludwigsfelde, *Germany* 24 C9
Ludwigshafen, *Germany* 25 F4
Ludwigslust, *Germany* 24 B7
Ludza, *Latvia* 32 D4
Lueki, *Dem. Rep. of the Congo* 86 C2

Luena, *Dem. Rep. of the Congo* 87 D2
Luena, *Zambia* 87 E3
Luenha = Ruenya →, *Africa* 87 F3
Lüeyang, *China* 56 H4
Lufeng, *Guangdong, China* 59 F10
Lufeng, *Yunnan, China* 58 E4
Lufira →, *Dem. Rep. of the Congo* 87 D2
Lufkin, *U.S.A.* 113 K7
Lufupa, *Dem. Rep. of the Congo* 87 E1
Luga, *Russia* 32 C5
Luga →, *Russia* 32 C5
Lugano, *Switz.* 25 J4
Lugano, L. di, *Switz.* 40 C6
Lugansk = Luhansk, *Ukraine* 33 H10
Lugard's Falls, *Kenya* 86 C4
Lugela, *Mozam.* 87 F4
Lugenda →, *Mozam.* 87 E4
Lugh Ganana, *Somali Rep.* 75 G3
Lugnaquillia, *Ireland* 12 D5
Lugo, *Italy* 41 D8
Lugo, *Spain* 36 B3
Lugo □, *Spain* 36 C3
Lugoj, *Romania* 28 E6
Lugovoy = Qulan, *Kazakhstan* 52 E8
Luhansk, *Ukraine* 33 H10
Luhe, *China* 59 A12
Luhe →, *Germany* 24 B6
Luhuo, *China* 58 B3
Luiana, *Angola* 88 B3
Luichow Pen. = Leizhou Bandao, *China* 58 G7
Luimneach = Limerick, *Ireland* 12 D3
Luing, *U.K.* 13 E3
Luino, *Italy* 40 C5
Luís Correia, *Brazil* 125 D10
Luitpold Coast, *Antarctica* 5 D1
Luiza, *Dem. Rep. of the Congo* 84 F4
Luizi, *Dem. Rep. of the Congo* 86 D2
Luján, *Argentina* 126 C4
Lujiang, *China* 59 B11
Lukang, *Taiwan* 59 E13
Lukanga Swamp, *Zambia* 87 E2
Lukavac, *Bos.-H.* 28 F3
Lukenie →, *Dem. Rep. of the Congo* 84 E3
Lukhisaral, *India* 69 G12
Lŭki, *Bulgaria* 45 E8
Lukolela, *Dem. Rep. of the Congo* 86 D1
Lukosi, *Zimbabwe* 87 F2
Lukovë, *Albania* 44 G3
Lukovit, *Bulgaria* 45 C8
Łuków, *Poland* 31 G9
Lukoyanov, *Russia* 34 C7
Lukusuzi △, *Zambia* 87 E3
Luleå, *Sweden* 8 D20
Luleälven →, *Sweden* 8 D19
Lüleburgaz, *Turkey* 45 E11
Luliang, *China* 58 E4
Luling, *U.S.A.* 113 L6
Lulong, *China* 57 E10
Lulonga →, *Dem. Rep. of the Congo* 84 D3
Lulua →, *Dem. Rep. of the Congo* 84 E4
Lumajang, *Indonesia* 63 H15
Lumbala N'guimbo, *Angola* 85 G4
Lumberton, *U.S.A.* 115 H6
Lumsden, *Canada* 103 C8
Lumsden, *N.Z.* 91 L2
Lumut, *Malaysia* 65 K3
Lumut, Tanjung, *Indonesia* 62 E3
Luna, *India* 68 H3
Lunan, *China* 58 E4
Lunavada, *India* 68 H5
Lunca, *Romania* 29 C10
Lunca Corbului, *Romania* 29 F9
Lund, *Sweden* 11 J7
Lundazi, *Zambia* 87 E3
Lunderskov, *Denmark* 11 J3
Lundi →, *Zimbabwe* 87 G3
Lundu, *Malaysia* 62 D3
Lundy, *U.K.* 15 F3
Lune →, *U.K.* 14 C5
Lüneburg, *Germany* 24 B6
Lüneburg Heath = Lüneburger Heide, *Germany* 24 B6
Lüneburger Heide, *Germany* 24 B6
Lunel, *France* 21 E8
Lünen, *Germany* 24 D3
Lunenburg, *Canada* 105 D7
Lunéville, *France* 19 D13
Lunga →, *Zambia* 87 E2
Lungi Airport, *S. Leone* 82 D2
Lunglei, *India* 67 H18
Luni, *India* 68 G5
Luni →, *India* 68 G4
Luninets = Luninyets, *Belarus* 33 F4
Luning, *U.S.A.* 108 G4
Lunino, *Russia* 34 D7
Luninyets, *Belarus* 33 F4
Lunkaransar, *India* 68 E5
Lunsemfwa →, *Zambia* 87 E3
Lunsemfwa Falls, *Zambia* 87 E2
Luo He →, *China* 56 G6
Luocheng, *China* 58 E7
Luochuan, *China* 56 G5
Luoci, *China* 58 E4
Luodian, *China* 58 E6
Luoding, *China* 59 F8
Luofu, *Dem. Rep. of the Congo* 86 C2
Luohe, *China* 56 H8
Luojiang, *China* 58 B5
Luonan, *China* 56 G6
Luoning, *China* 56 G6
Luoshan, *China* 59 A10
Luotian, *China* 59 B10
Luoxiao Shan, *China* 59 D10
Luoyang, *China* 56 G7
Luoyuan, *China* 59 D12
Luozigou, *China* 57 C16
Lupanshui, *China* 58 D5
Lupeni, *Romania* 29 E8
Lupilichi, *Mozam.* 87 E4
Łupków, *Poland* 31 J9
Lupoing, *China* 58 E5
Luquan, *China* 58 E4
Luque, *Paraguay* 126 B4
Lúras, *Italy* 42 B2
Luray, *U.S.A.* 114 F6
Lure, *France* 19 E13
Lurgan, *U.K.* 12 B5
Lusaka, *Zambia* 87 F2
Lusaka □, *Zambia* 87 F2
Lusambo, *Dem. Rep. of the Congo* 86 C1
Lusangaye, *Dem. Rep. of the Congo* 86 C2
Luseland, *Canada* 103 C7
Lusenga Plain △, *Zambia* 87 D2
Lushan, *Henan, China* 56 H7
Lushan, *Sichuan, China* 58 B4
Lushi, *China* 56 G6
Lushnjë, *Albania* 44 F3
Lushoto, *Tanzania* 86 C4
Lushui, *China* 58 E2
Lüshun, *China* 57 E11
Lusignan, *France* 20 B4
Lusigny-sur-Barse, *France* 19 D11
Lusk, *U.S.A.* 112 D2
Lussac-les-Châteaux, *France* 20 B4
Lustenau, *Austria* 26 D2
Lūt, Dasht-e, *Iran* 71 D8
Luta = Dalian, *China* 57 E11
Lutherstadt Wittenberg, *Germany* 24 D8
Luton, *U.K.* 15 F7
Luton □, *U.K.* 15 F7
Łutselk'e, *Canada* 103 A6
Lutsk, *Ukraine* 33 G3
Lützow Holmbukta, *Antarctica* 5 C4
Lutzputs, *S. Africa* 88 D3
Luuq = Lugh Ganana, *Somali Rep.* 75 G3
Luverne, *Ala., U.S.A.* 115 K2
Luverne, *Minn., U.S.A.* 112 D6
Luvua, *Dem. Rep. of the Congo* 87 D2
Luvua →, *Dem. Rep. of the Congo* 86 D2
Luvuvhu →, *S. Africa* 89 C5
Luwegu →, *Tanzania* 87 D4
Luwuk, *Indonesia* 63 E6
Luxembourg, *Lux.* 17 E6
Luxembourg □, *Belgium* 17 E5
Luxembourg ■, *Europe* 7 F7
Luxembourg ✕ (LUX), *Lux.* 17 E6
Luxeuil-les-Bains, *France* 19 E13
Luxi, *Hunan, China* 59 C8
Luxi, *Yunnan, China* 58 E4
Luxi, *Yunnan, China* 58 E2
Luxor = El Uqsur, *Egypt* 80 B3
Luy-de-Béarn →, *France* 20 E3
Luy-de-France →, *France* 20 E3
Luyi, *China* 56 H8
Luz-St-Sauveur, *France* 20 F4
Luzern, *Switz.* 25 H4
Luzern □, *Switz.* 25 H3
Luzhai, *China* 58 E7
Luzhany, *Ukraine* 29 B10
Luzhi, *China* 58 D5
Luzhou, *China* 58 C5
Luziânia, *Brazil* 125 G9
Lužnice →, *Czech Rep.* 26 B7
Luzon, *Phil.* 61 D4
Luzon Strait, *Asia* 59 G13
Luzy, *France* 19 F10
Luzzi, *Italy* 43 C9
Lviv, *Ukraine* 33 H3
Lvov = Lviv, *Ukraine* 33 H3
Lwówek, *Poland* 31 F3
Lwówek Śląski, *Poland* 31 G2
Lyakhavichy, *Belarus* 33 F4
Lyakhovskiye, Ostrova, *Russia* 53 B15
Lyaki = Läki, *Azerbaijan* 35 K8
Lyal I., *Canada* 116 B3
Lyaskovets, *Bulgaria* 45 C9
Lyasnaya, *Belarus* 31 F10
Lybster, *U.K.* 13 C5
Lycaonia, *Turkey* 72 D5
Lychen, *Germany* 24 B9
Lychkova, *Russia* 32 D7
Lycia, *Turkey* 47 E11
Lyckebyån →, *Sweden* 11 H9
Lycksele, *Sweden* 8 D18
Lycosura, *Greece* 46 D4
Lydda = Lod, *Israel* 74 D3
Lydenburg, *S. Africa* 89 D5
Lydia, *Turkey* 47 C10
Łydynia →, *Poland* 31 F7
Lyell, *N.Z.* 91 J4
Lyell I., *Canada* 102 C2
Lyepyel, *Belarus* 32 E5
Lygnern, *Sweden* 11 G6
Lykens, *U.S.A.* 117 F8
Lyman, *Ukraine* 29 E14
Lyman, *U.S.A.* 108 F8
Lymanske, *Ukraine* 29 D14
Lyme B., *U.K.* 15 G4
Lyme Regis, *U.K.* 15 G5
Lymington, *U.K.* 15 G6
Łyna →, *Poland* 9 J19
Lynchburg, *U.S.A.* 114 G6
Lynd →, *Australia* 94 B3
Lynd Ra., *Australia* 95 D4
Lynden, *Canada* 116 C4
Lynden, *U.S.A.* 110 B4
Lyndhurst, *Australia* 95 E2
Lyndon →, *Australia* 93 D1
Lyndonville, *N.Y., U.S.A.* 116 C6
Lyndonville, *Vt., U.S.A.* 117 B12
Lyngen, *Norway* 8 B19
Lynher Reef, *Australia* 92 C3
Lynn, *U.S.A.* 117 D14
Lynn Lake, *Canada* 103 B8
Lynnwood, *U.S.A.* 110 C4
Lynton, *U.K.* 15 F4
Lyntupy, *Belarus* 9 J22
Lynx L., *Canada* 103 A7
Lyon, *France* 21 C8
Lyon St-Exupery ✕ (LYS), *France* 21 C9
Lyonnais, *France* 21 C8
Lyons = Lyon, *France* 21 C8
Lyons, *Ga., U.S.A.* 115 J4
Lyons, *Kans., U.S.A.* 112 F5
Lyons, *N.Y., U.S.A.* 116 C8
Lyons →, *Australia* 93 E2
Lyons Falls, *U.S.A.* 117 C9
Lyozna, *Belarus* 32 E6
Lys = Leie →, *Belgium* 17 C3
Lysá nad Labem, *Czech Rep.* 26 A7
Lysekil, *Sweden* 11 F5
Lyskovo, *Russia* 34 B7
Lystrup, *Denmark* 11 H4
Lysvik, *Sweden* 10 D7
Lysychansk, *Ukraine* 33 H10
Lytham St. Anne's, *U.K.* 14 D4
Lyttelton, *N.Z.* 91 K4
Lytton, *Canada* 102 C4
Lyuban, *Russia* 32 C6
Lyubertsy, *Russia* 32 E9
Lyubim, *Russia* 32 C11
Lyubimets, *Bulgaria* 45 E10
Lyuboml, *Ukraine* 31 G11
Lyubotyn, *Ukraine* 33 H8
Lyubytino, *Russia* 32 C7
Lyudinovo, *Russia* 32 F8

M

M.R. Gomez, Presa, *Mexico* 119 B5
M.R. Stefanik, Bratislava ✕ (BTS), *Slovak Rep.* 27 C10
Ma →, *Vietnam* 58 H5
Ma'adaba, *Jordan* 74 E4
Maamba, *Zambia* 88 B4
Ma'ān, *Jordan* 74 E4
Ma'ān □, *Jordan* 74 F5
Maanselkä, *Finland* 8 C23
Ma'anshan, *China* 59 B12
Maarianhamina, *Finland* 9 F18
Ma'arrat an Nu'mān, *Syria* 70 C3
Maas →, *Neths.* 17 C4
Maaseik, *Belgium* 17 C5
Maasin, *Phil.* 63 B6
Maastricht, *Neths.* 17 D5
Maave, *Mozam.* 89 C5
Mababe Depression, *Botswana* 88 B3
Mabalane, *Mozam.* 89 C5
Mabel L., *Canada* 102 C5
Mabenge, *Dem. Rep. of the Congo* 86 B1
Maberly, *Canada* 117 B8
Mabian, *China* 58 C4
Mabil, *Ethiopia* 81 E4
Mablethorpe, *U.K.* 14 D8
Mably, *France* 19 F11
Maboma, *Dem. Rep. of the Congo* 86 B2
Mabonto, *S. Leone* 82 D2
Mabrouk, *Mali* 83 B4
Mabuasehube ⌓, *Botswana* 88 D3
Mac Bac, *Vietnam* 65 H6
Macachín, *Argentina* 126 D3
Macaé, *Brazil* 127 A7
Macael, *Spain* 39 H2
McAlester, *U.S.A.* 113 H7
McAllen, *U.S.A.* 113 M5
MacAlpine L., *Canada* 100 B9
Macamic, *Canada* 104 C4
Macao = Macau, *China* 59 F9
Mação, *Portugal* 37 F3
Macapá, *Brazil* 125 C8
Macarao △, *Venezuela* 121 D6
McArthur →, *Australia* 94 B2
McArthur, Port, *Australia* 94 B2
Macau, *Brazil* 125 E11
Macau, *China* 59 F9
McBride, *Canada* 102 C4
McCall, *U.S.A.* 108 D5
McCamey, *U.S.A.* 113 K3
McCammon, *U.S.A.* 108 E7
McCauley I., *Canada* 102 C2
McCleary, *U.S.A.* 110 C3
Macclenny, *U.S.A.* 115 K4
Macclesfield, *U.K.* 14 D5
M'Clintock Chan., *Canada* 100 A9
McClintock Ra., *Australia* 92 C4
McCloud, *U.S.A.* 108 F2
McCluer I., *Australia* 92 B5
McClure, *U.S.A.* 116 F7
McClure, L., *U.S.A.* 110 H6
M'Clure Str., *Canada* 98 B8
McClusky, *U.S.A.* 112 B4
McComb, *U.S.A.* 113 K9
McConaughy, L., *U.S.A.* 112 E4
McCook, *U.S.A.* 112 E4
McCreary, *Canada* 103 C9
McCullough Mt., *U.S.A.* 111 K11
McCusker →, *Canada* 103 B7
McDame, *Canada* 102 B3
McDermitt, *U.S.A.* 108 F5
McDonald, *U.S.A.* 116 F4
Macdonald, L., *Australia* 92 D4
McDonald Is., *Ind. Oc.* 3 G13
MacDonnell Ranges, *Australia* 92 D5
MacDowell L., *Canada* 104 B1
Macduff, *U.K.* 13 D6
Maceda, *Spain* 36 C3
Macedonia, *U.S.A.* 116 E3
Macedonia ■, *Europe* 44 E5
Maceió, *Brazil* 125 E11
Maceira, *Portugal* 36 F2
Macenta, *Guinea* 82 D3
Macerata, *Italy* 41 E10
McFarland, *U.S.A.* 111 K7
McFarlane →, *Canada* 103 B7
Macfarlane, L., *Australia* 95 E2
McGehee, *U.S.A.* 113 J9
McGill, *U.S.A.* 108 G6
Macgillycuddy's Reeks, *Ireland* 12 E2
McGraw, *U.S.A.* 117 D8
McGregor, *U.S.A.* 112 D9
McGregor Ra., *Australia* 95 D3
McGuire, Mt, *Australia* 94 J6
Mach, *Pakistan* 66 E5
Māch Kowr, *Iran* 71 E9
Machado = Jiparaná →, *Brazil* 124 E6
Machagai, *Argentina* 126 B3
Machakos, *Kenya* 86 C4
Machala, *Ecuador* 124 D3
Machanga, *Mozam.* 89 C6
Machattie, L., *Australia* 94 C2
Machault, *France* 19 C11
Machava, *Mozam.* 89 D5
Machece, *Mozam.* 87 F4
Machecoul, *France* 18 F5
Macheke, *Zimbabwe* 89 B5
Macheng, *China* 59 B10
Machero, *Spain* 37 F6
Machhu →, *India* 68 H4
Machias, *Maine, U.S.A.* 115 C12
Machias, *N.Y., U.S.A.* 116 D6
Machichi →, *Canada* 103 B10
Machico, *Madeira* 48 D3
Machilipatnam, *India* 67 L12
Machiques, *Venezuela* 124 A4
Machupicchu, *Peru* 124 F4
Machynlleth, *U.K.* 15 E4
Macia, *Mozam.* 89 D5
Maciejowice, *Poland* 31 G8
McIlwraith Ra., *Australia* 94 A3
Măcin, *Romania* 29 E13
Macina, *Mali* 82 C4
McInnes L., *Canada* 103 C10
McIntosh, *U.S.A.* 112 C4
McIntosh L., *Canada* 103 B8
Macintosh Ra., *Australia* 93 E4
Macintyre →, *Australia* 95 D5
Macizo Galaico, *Spain* 36 C3
Mackay, *Australia* 94 K7
Mackay, *U.S.A.* 108 E7
MacKay →, *Canada* 102 B6
Mackay, L., *Australia* 92 D4
McKay Ra., *Australia* 92 D3
McKeesport, *U.S.A.* 116 F5
McKellar, *Canada* 116 A5
McKenna, *U.S.A.* 110 D4
Mackenzie, *Canada* 102 B4
McKenzie, *U.S.A.* 115 G1
Mackenzie →, *Australia* 94 C4
Mackenzie →, *Canada* 100 B6
McKenzie →, *U.S.A.* 108 D2
Mackenzie Bay, *Canada* 4 B1
Mackenzie City = Linden, *Guyana* 124 B7
Mackenzie Mts., *Canada* 100 B6
Mackinaw City, *U.S.A.* 114 C3
McKinlay, *Australia* 94 C3
McKinlay →, *Australia* 94 C3
McKinley, Mt., *U.S.A.* 100 B4
McKinley Sea, *Arctic* 4 A7
McKinney, *U.S.A.* 113 J6
Mackinnon Road, *Kenya* 86 C4
McKittrick, *U.S.A.* 111 K7
Macklin, *Canada* 103 C7
Macksville, *Australia* 95 E5
McLaughlin, *U.S.A.* 112 C4
Maclean, *Australia* 95 D5
McLean, *U.S.A.* 113 H4
McLeansboro, *U.S.A.* 112 F10
Maclear, *S. Africa* 89 E4
Maclear, C., *Malawi* 87 E3
Macleay →, *Australia* 95 E5
McLennan, *Canada* 102 B5
McLeod →, *Canada* 102 C5
MacLeod, B., *Canada* 103 A7
McLeod, L., *Australia* 93 D1
MacLeod Lake, *Canada* 102 C4
McLoughlin, Mt., *U.S.A.* 108 E2
McMechen, *U.S.A.* 116 G4
McMinnville, *Oreg., U.S.A.* 108 D2
McMinnville, *Tenn., U.S.A.* 115 H3
McMurdo Sd., *Antarctica* 5 D11
McMurray = Fort McMurray, *Canada* 102 B6
McMurray, *U.S.A.* 110 B4
Macodoene, *Mozam.* 89 C6
Macomb, *U.S.A.* 112 E9
Macomer, *Italy* 42 B1
Mâcon, *France* 19 F11
Macon, *Ga., U.S.A.* 115 J4
Macon, *Miss., U.S.A.* 115 J1
Macon, *Mo., U.S.A.* 112 F8
Macossa, *Mozam.* 87 F3
Macoun L., *Canada* 103 B8
Macovane, *Mozam.* 89 C6
McPherson, *U.S.A.* 112 F6
McPherson Pk., *U.S.A.* 111 L7
McPherson Ra., *Australia* 95 D5
Macquarie →, *Australia* 95 E4
Macquarie Harbour, *Australia* 95 G4
Macquarie Is., *Pac. Oc.* 96 N7
MacRobertson Land, *Antarctica* 5 D6
Macroom, *Ireland* 12 E3
MacTier, *Canada* 116 A5
Macubela, *Mozam.* 87 F4
Macugnaga, *Italy* 40 C4
Macuira △, *Colombia* 121 D5
Macuiza, *Mozam.* 87 F3
Macumba, The →, *Australia* 95 D2
Macuro, *Venezuela* 125 K15
Macusani, *Peru* 124 F4
Macuse, *Mozam.* 87 F4
Macuspana, *Mexico* 119 D6
Macusse, *Angola* 88 B3
Mada →, *Nigeria* 83 D6
Ma'dabā, *Jordan* 74 D4
Madadeni, *S. Africa* 89 D5
Madagali, *Nigeria* 83 C7
Madagascar ■, *Africa* 89 C8
Madā'in Sālih, *Si. Arabia* 70 E3
Madama, *Niger* 79 D8
Madame, I., *Canada* 105 C7
Madan, *Bulgaria* 45 E8
Madaoua, *Niger* 83 C6
Madara, *Nigeria* 83 C7
Madaripur, *Bangla.* 67 H17
Madauk, *Burma* 67 L20
Madawaska, *Canada* 116 A7
Madawaska →, *Canada* 116 A8
Madaya, *Burma* 67 H20
Madbar, *Sudan* 81 F3
Maddalena, *Italy* 42 A2
Maddaloni, *Italy* 43 A7
Madeira, *Atl. Oc.* 48 D3
Madeira →, *Brazil* 124 D7
Madeleine, Îs. de la, *Canada* 105 C7
Maden, *Turkey* 73 C8
Madera, *Mexico* 118 B3
Madera, *Calif., U.S.A.* 110 J6
Madera, *Pa., U.S.A.* 116 F6
Madha, *India* 66 L9
Madhavpur, *India* 68 J3
Madhepura, *India* 69 F12
Madhubani, *India* 69 F12
Madhupur, *India* 69 G12
Madhya Pradesh □, *India* 68 J8
Madidi →, *Bolivia* 124 F5
Madikeri, *India* 66 N9
Madikwe ⌓, *S. Africa* 89 D5
Madill, *U.S.A.* 113 H6
Madimba, *Dem. Rep. of the Congo* 84 E3
Ma'din, *Syria* 70 C3
Madina, *Mali* 82 C3
Madinani, *Ivory C.* 82 D3
Madingou, *Congo* 84 E2
Madirovalo, *Madag.* 89 B8
Madison, *Calif., U.S.A.* 110 G5
Madison, *Fla., U.S.A.* 115 K4
Madison, *Ind., U.S.A.* 114 F3
Madison, *Nebr., U.S.A.* 112 E6
Madison, *Ohio, U.S.A.* 116 E3
Madison, *S. Dak., U.S.A.* 112 D6
Madison, *Wis., U.S.A.* 112 D10
Madison →, *U.S.A.* 108 D8
Madison Heights, *U.S.A.* 114 G6
Madisonville, *Ky., U.S.A.* 114 G2
Madisonville, *Tex., U.S.A.* 113 K7
Madista, *Botswana* 88 C4
Madiun, *Indonesia* 63 G14
Madoc, *Canada* 116 B7
Madol, *Sudan* 81 F2
Madon →, *France* 19 D13
Madona, *Latvia* 9 H22
Madonie, *Italy* 42 E6
Madonna di Campíglio, *Italy* 40 B7
Madra Dağı, *Turkey* 47 B9
Madrakah, Ra's al, *Oman* 75 D6
Madras = Chennai, *India* 66 N12
Madras = Tamil Nadu □, *India* 66 P10
Madras, *U.S.A.* 108 D3
Madre, Laguna, *U.S.A.* 113 M6
Madre, Sierra, *Phil.* 61 C5
Madre de Dios →, *Bolivia* 124 F5
Madre de Dios, I., *Chile* 128 G1
Madre del Sur, Sierra, *Mexico* 119 D5
Madre Occidental, Sierra, *Mexico* 118 B3
Madre Oriental, Sierra, *Mexico* 118 C5
Madri, *India* 68 G5
Madrid, *Spain* 36 E7
Madrid, *U.S.A.* 117 B9
Madrid □, *Spain* 36 E7
Madrid Barajas ✕ (MAD), *Spain* 36 E7
Madridejos, *Spain* 37 F7
Madrigal de las Altas Torres, *Spain* 36 D6
Madrona, Sierra, *Spain* 37 G6
Madroñera, *Spain* 37 F5
Madu, *Sudan* 81 E2
Madura, *Australia* 93 F4
Madura, *Indonesia* 63 G15
Madura, Selat, *Indonesia* 63 G15
Madurai, *India* 66 Q11
Madurantakam, *India* 66 N11
Madzhalis, *Russia* 35 J8
Mae Chan, *Thailand* 64 B2
Mae Hong Son, *Thailand* 64 C2
Mae Khlong →, *Thailand* 64 F3
Mae Phrik, *Thailand* 64 D2
Mae Ping △, *Thailand* 64 D2
Mae Ramat, *Thailand* 64 D2
Mae Rim, *Thailand* 64 C2
Mae Sot, *Thailand* 64 D2
Mae Suai, *Thailand* 58 H2
Mae Tha, *Thailand* 64 C2
Mae Wong △, *Thailand* 64 E2
Mae Yom △, *Thailand* 64 C3
Maebashi, *Japan* 55 F9
Maella, *Spain* 38 D5
Maesteg, *U.K.* 15 F4
Maestra, Sierra, *Cuba* 120 B4
Maevatanana, *Madag.* 89 B8
Mafeking = Mafikeng, *S. Africa* 88 D4
Mafeking, *Canada* 103 C8
Maféré, *Ivory C.* 82 D4
Mafeteng, *Lesotho* 88 D4
Maffra, *Australia* 95 F4
Mafia I., *Tanzania* 86 D4
Mafikeng, *S. Africa* 88 D4
Mafra, *Brazil* 127 B6
Mafra, *Portugal* 37 G1
Mafungabusi Plateau, *Zimbabwe* 87 F2
Magadan, *Russia* 53 D16
Magadi, *Kenya* 86 C4
Magadi, L., *Kenya* 86 C4
Magaliesburg, *S. Africa* 89 D4
Magallanes, Estrecho de, *Chile* 128 G2
Magaluf, *Spain* 39 F7
Magangué, *Colombia* 124 B4
Magaria, *Niger* 83 C6

Magburaka, *S. Leone* 82 D2
Magdalen Is. = Madeleine, Îs. de la, *Canada* 105 C7
Magdalena, *Argentina* 126 D4
Magdalena, *Bolivia* 124 F6
Magdalena, *Mexico* 118 A2
Magdalena, *U.S.A.* 109 J10
Magdalena →, *Colombia* 124 A4
Magdalena →, *Mexico* 118 A2
Magdalena, B., *Mexico* 118 C2
Magdalena, Llano de la, *Mexico* 118 C2
Magdeburg, *Germany* 24 C7
Magdelaine Cays, *Australia* 94 B5
Magdub, *Sudan* 81 E2
Magee, *U.S.A.* 113 K10
Magelang, *Indonesia* 63 G14
Magellan's Str. = Magallanes, Estrecho de, *Chile* 128 G2
Magenta, *Italy* 40 C5
Magenta, L., *Australia* 93 F2
Magerøya, *Norway* 8 A21
Maggia →, *Switz.* 25 J4
Maggiorasca, Mte., *Italy* 40 D6
Maggiore, Lago, *Italy* 40 B5
Maggotty, *Jamaica* 120 a
Maghâgha, *Egypt* 80 B3
Maghama, *Mauritania* 82 B2
Magherafelt, *U.K.* 12 B5
Maghreb, *N. Afr.* 78 B5
Magione, *Italy* 41 E9
Magistralnyy, *Russia* 53 D11
Maglaj, *Bos.-H.* 28 F3
Magliano in Toscana, *Italy* 41 F8
Máglie, *Italy* 43 B11
Magnac-Laval, *France* 20 B5
Magnetic Pole (North), *Canada* 4 A2
Magnetic Pole (South), *Antarctica* 5 C9
Magnisía □, *Greece* 46 B5
Magnitogorsk, *Russia* 52 D6
Magnolia, *Ark., U.S.A.* 113 J8
Magnolia, *Miss., U.S.A.* 113 K9
Magny-en-Vexin, *France* 19 C8
Mago △, *Ethiopia* 81 F4
Magog, *Canada* 117 A12
Magoro, *Uganda* 86 B3
Magoša = Famagusta, *Cyprus* 49 D12
Magouládhes, *Greece* 49 A3
Magoye, *Zambia* 87 F2
Magozal, *Mexico* 119 C5
Magpie, L., *Canada* 105 B7
Magrath, *Canada* 102 D6
Magre →, *Spain* 39 F4
Magrur, *Sudan* 81 E3
Magrur, Wadi →, *Sudan* 81 D2
Magta Lahjar, *Mauritania* 82 B2
Maguan, *China* 58 F5
Maguarinho, C., *Brazil* 125 D9
Magude, *Mozam.* 89 D5
Magurski △, *Poland* 31 J8
Mağusa = Famagusta, *Cyprus* 49 D12
Maguse L., *Canada* 103 A9
Maguse Pt., *Canada* 103 A10
Magvana, *India* 68 H3
Magwe, *Burma* 67 J19
Magwe, *Sudan* 81 G3
Maha Sarakham, *Thailand* 64 D4
Mahābād, *Iran* 70 B5
Mahabharat Lekh, *Nepal* 69 E10
Mahabo, *Madag.* 89 C7
Mahadeo Hills, *India* 69 H8
Mahaffey, *U.S.A.* 116 F6
Mahagi, *Dem. Rep. of the Congo* 86 B3
Mahajamba →, *Madag.* 89 B8
Mahajamba, Helodranon' i, *Madag.* 89 B8
Mahajan, *India* 68 E5
Mahajanga, *Madag.* 89 B8
Mahajanga □, *Madag.* 89 B8
Mahajilo →, *Madag.* 89 B8
Mahakam →, *Indonesia* 62 E5
Mahalapye, *Botswana* 88 C4
Mahale Mts., *Tanzania* 86 D3
Mahale Mts. △, *Tanzania* 86 D2
Maḩallāt, *Iran* 71 C6
Māhān, *Iran* 71 D8
Mahan →, *India* 69 H10
Mahanadi →, *India* 67 J15
Mahananda →, *India* 69 G12
Mahanoro, *Madag.* 89 B8
Mahanoy City, *U.S.A.* 117 F8
Maharashtra □, *India* 66 J9
Mahasham, W. →, *Egypt* 74 E3
Mahasoa, *Madag.* 89 C8
Mahasolo, *Madag.* 89 B8
Mahattat ash Shīdīyah, *Jordan* 74 F4
Mahattat 'Unayzah, *Jordan* 74 E4
Mahavavy →, *Madag.* 89 B8
Mahaxay, *Laos* 64 D5
Mahbubnagar, *India* 66 L10
Maḩḑah, *Oman* 71 E7
Mahdia, *Tunisia* 79 A8
Mahe, *India* 69 C8
Mahendragarh, *India* 68 E7
Mahenge, *Tanzania* 87 D4
Maheno, *N.Z.* 91 L3
Mahesana, *India* 68 H5
Maheshwar, *India* 68 H6
Mahgawan, *India* 69 F8
Mahi →, *India* 68 H5
Mahia Pen., *N.Z.* 91 H6
Mahilyow, *Belarus* 32 F6
Mahinerangi, L., *N.Z.* 91 L2
Mahmiya, *Sudan* 81 D3
Mahmud Kot, *Pakistan* 68 D4
Mahmudia, *Romania* 29 E14
Mahmudiye, *Turkey* 47 B12
Mahmutbey, *Turkey* 45 E12
Mahnomen, *U.S.A.* 112 B7
Mahoba, *India* 69 G8
Mahón = Maó, *Spain* 48 B11
Mahon, Menorca ✕ (MAH), *Spain* 38 F9
Mahone Bay, *Canada* 105 D7
Mahopac, *U.S.A.* 117 E11
Mahuta, *Nigeria* 83 C5
Mahuva, *India* 68 J4
Mahya Daği, *Turkey* 45 E11
Mai-Ndombe, L., *Dem. Rep. of the Congo* 84 E3
Mai-Sai, *Thailand* 58 G2
Mai Thon, Ko, *Thailand* 65 a
Maia, *Portugal* 36 D2
Maia, *Spain* 38 B3
Maials, *Spain* 38 D5
Maîche, *France* 19 E13
Maicurú →, *Brazil* 125 D8
Máida, *Italy* 43 D9
Maidan Khula, *Afghan.* 68 C3
Maidenhead, *U.K.* 15 F7
Maidstone, *Canada* 103 C7
Maidstone, *U.K.* 15 F8
Maiduguri, *Nigeria* 83 C7
Maiella △, *Italy* 41 F11
Măieruş, *Romania* 29 E10
Maigatari, *Nigeria* 83 C6
Maignelay Montigny, *France* 19 C9
Maigo, *Phil.* 61 G5
Maigudo, *Ethiopia* 81 F4
Maihar, *India* 69 G9
Maijdi, *Bangla.* 67 H17
Maikala Ra., *India* 67 J12
Maiko △, *Dem. Rep. of the Congo* 86 C2
Mailani, *India* 69 E9
Maillezais, *France* 20 B3
Mailsi, *Pakistan* 68 E5
Main →, *Germany* 25 F4
Main →, *U.K.* 12 B5
Main Range △, *Australia* 95 D5
Main Ridge, *Trin. & Tob.* 125 J16
Mainburg, *Germany* 25 G7
Maine, *France* 18 D6
Maine □, *U.S.A.* 115 C11
Maine →, *Ireland* 12 D2
Maine-et-Loire □, *France* 18 E6
Maïne-Soroa, *Niger* 83 C7
Maingkwan, *Burma* 67 F20
Mainit, L., *Phil.* 61 G6
Mainland, *Orkney, U.K.* 13 C5
Mainland, *Shet., U.K.* 13 A7
Mainoru, *Australia* 94 A1
Mainpuri, *India* 69 F8
Maintal, *Germany* 25 E4
Maintenon, *France* 19 D8
Maintirano, *Madag.* 89 B7
Mainz, *Germany* 25 E4
Maipú, *Argentina* 126 D4
Maiquetía, *Venezuela* 124 A5
Máira →, *Italy* 40 D4
Mairabari, *India* 67 F18
Maisí, *Cuba* 121 B5
Maisí, Pta. de, *Cuba* 121 B5
Maitland, *N.S.W., Australia* 95 E5
Maitland, *S. Austral., Australia* 95 E2
Maitland →, *Canada* 116 C3
Maitri, *Antarctica* 5 D3
Maiyema, *Nigeria* 83 C5
Maiyuan, *China* 59 E11
Maiz, Is. del, *Nic.* 120 D3
Maizuru, *Japan* 55 G7
Majalengka, *Indonesia* 63 G13
Majene, *Indonesia* 63 E5
Majete ⌓, *Malawi* 87 F3
Majevica, *Bos.-H.* 28 F3
Maji, *Ethiopia* 81 F4
Majiang, *China* 58 D6
Majorca = Mallorca, *Spain* 48 B10
Maka, *Senegal* 82 C2
Makaha, *Zimbabwe* 89 B5
Makak, *Cameroon* 83 E7
Makalamabedi, *Botswana* 88 C3
Makale, *Indonesia* 63 E5
Makamba, *Burundi* 86 C2
Makari, *Cameroon* 83 C7
Makarikari = Makgadikgadi Salt Pans, *Botswana* 88 C4
Makarov Basin, *Arctic* 4 A
Makarovo, *Russia* 53 D11
Makarska, *Croatia* 41 E14
Makaryev, *Russia* 34 B6
Makasar = Ujung Pandang, *Indonesia* 63 F5
Makasar, Selat, *Indonesia* 63 E5
Makasar, Str. of = Makasar, Selat, *Indonesia* 63 E5
Makat, *Kazakhstan* 52 E6
Makedonija = Macedonia ■, *Europe* 44 E5
Makeni, *S. Leone* 82 D2
Makeyevka = Makiyivka, *Ukraine* 33 H9
Makgadikgadi △, *Botswana* 88 C3
Makgadikgadi Salt Pans, *Botswana* 88 C4
Makhachkala, *Russia* 35 J8
Makhado = Louis Trichardt, *S. Africa* 89 C4
Makharadze = Ozurgeti, *Georgia* 35 K5
Makhfar al Buşayyah, *Iraq* 70 D5
Makhmūr, *Iraq* 70 C4
Makian, *Indonesia* 63 D7
Makindu, *Kenya* 86 C4
Makinsk, *Kazakhstan* 52 D8
Makiv, *Ukraine* 29 B11
Makiyivka, *Ukraine* 33 H9
Makkah, *Si. Arabia* 75 C2
Makkovik, *Canada* 105 A8
Makó, *Hungary* 28 D5
Mako, *Senegal* 82 C2
Makokou, *Gabon* 84 D2
Makongo, *Dem. Rep. of the Congo* 86 B2
Makoro, *Dem. Rep. of the Congo* 86 B2
Maków Mazowiecki, *Poland* 31 F8
Maków Podhalański, *Poland* 31 J6
Makrá, *Greece* 47 E7
Makrai, *India* 66 H10
Makran Coast Range, *Pakistan* 66 G4
Makrana, *India* 68 F6
Makrany, *Belarus* 31 G11
Mákri, *Greece* 45 F9
Makriyialos, *Greece* 49 D7
Mākū, *Iran* 70 B5
Makunda, *Botswana* 88 C3
Makung, *Taiwan* 59 F12
Makurazaki, *Japan* 55 J5
Makurdi, *Nigeria* 83 D6
Makūyeh, *Iran* 71 D7
Makwassie, *S. Africa* 88 D4
Makwiro, *Zimbabwe* 89 B5
Mâl, *Mauritania* 82 B2
Mal B., *Ireland* 12 D2
Mala, Pta., *Panama* 120 E3
Mala Belozërka, *Ukraine* 33 J8
Malá Fatra △, *Slovak Rep.* 27 B12
Mala Kapela, *Croatia* 41 D12
Mała Panew →, *Poland* 31 H4
Mala Vyska, *Ukraine* 33 H6
Malabang, *Phil.* 61 H6
Malabar Coast, *India* 66 P9
Malabon, *Phil.* 61 D4
Malabu, *Nigeria* 83 D7
Malacca, Straits of, *Indonesia* 65 L3
Malacky, *Slovak Rep.* 27 C10
Malad City, *U.S.A.* 108 E7
Maladeta, *Spain* 38 C5
Maladzyechna, *Belarus* 32 E4
Málaga, *Spain* 37 J6
Málaga □, *Spain* 37 J6
Malagarasi, *Tanzania* 86 D3
Malagarasi →, *Tanzania* 86 D2
Malagasy Rep. = Madagascar ■, *Africa* 89 C8
Malagón, *Spain* 37 F7
Malagón →, *Spain* 37 H3
Malahide, *Ireland* 12 C5
Malaimbandy, *Madag.* 89 C8
Malakâl, *Sudan* 81 F3
Malakand, *Pakistan* 68 B4
Malakwal, *Pakistan* 68 C5
Malamala, *Indonesia* 63 E6
Malanda, *Australia* 94 B4
Malang, *Indonesia* 63 G15
Malangen, *Norway* 8 B18
Malanje, *Angola* 84 F3
Mälaren, *Sweden* 10 E11
Malargüe, *Argentina* 126 D2
Malartic, *Canada* 104 C4
Malaryta, *Belarus* 31 G11
Malatya, *Turkey* 70 B3
Malawi ■, *Africa* 87 E3
Malawi, L. = Nyasa, L., *Africa* 87 E3
Malay Pen., *Asia* 65 J3
Malaya Belozërka = Mala Belozërka, *Ukraine* 33 J8
Malaya Vishera, *Russia* 32 C7
Malaya Viska = Mala Vyska, *Ukraine* 33 H6
Malaybalay, *Phil.* 61 G6
Malāyer, *Iran* 71 C6
Malaysia ■, *Asia* 65 K4
Malazgirt, *Turkey* 70 B4
Malbaza, *Niger* 83 C6
Malbon, *Australia* 94 C3
Malbooma, *Australia* 95 E1
Malbork, *Poland* 30 D6
Malcésine, *Italy* 40 C7
Malchin, *Germany* 24 B8
Malchow, *Germany* 24 B8
Malcolm, *Australia* 93 E3
Malcolm, Pt., *Australia* 93 F3
Malczyce, *Poland* 31 G3
Maldah, *India* 69 G13
Maldegem, *Belgium* 17 C3
Malden, *Mass., U.S.A.* 117 D13
Malden, *Mo., U.S.A.* 113 G10
Malden I., *Kiribati* 97 H12
Maldives ■, *Ind. Oc.* 50 J11
Maldon, *U.K.* 15 F8
Maldonado, *Uruguay* 127 C5
Maldonado, Punta, *Mexico* 119 D5
Malè, *Italy* 40 B7
Male, *Maldives* 51 J11
Malé Karpaty, *Slovak Rep.* 27 C10
Maléa, Ákra, *Greece* 46 E5
Malegaon, *India* 66 J9
Malei, *Mozam.* 87 F4
Malek, *Sudan* 81 F3
Malek Kandī, *Iran* 70 B5
Malela, *Dem. Rep. of the Congo* 86 C2
Malema, *Mozam.* 87 E4
Máleme, *Greece* 49 D5
Mälerås, *Sweden* 11 H9
Malerkotla, *India* 68 D6
Máles, *Greece* 49 D7
Malesherbes, *France* 19 D9
Maleshevska Planina, *Europe* 44 E7
Malesína, *Greece* 46 C5
Malestroit, *France* 18 E4
Malfa, *Italy* 43 D7
Malgobek, *Russia* 35 J7
Malgomaj, *Sweden* 8 D17
Malgrat de Mar, *Spain* 38 D7
Malha, *Sudan* 81 D2
Malhargarh, *India* 68 G6
Malheur →, *U.S.A.* 108 D5
Malheur L., *U.S.A.* 108 E4
Mali, *Guinea* 82 C2
Mali ■, *Africa* 82 B4
Mali →, *Burma* 67 G20
Mali Kanal, *Serbia & M.* 28 E4
Mali Kyun, *Burma* 64 F2
Malibu, *U.S.A.* 111 L8
Maliku, *Indonesia* 63 E6
Malili, *Indonesia* 63 E6
Målilla, *Sweden* 11 G9
Malimba, Mts., *Dem. Rep. of the Congo* 86 D2
Malin Hd., *Ireland* 12 A4
Malin Pen., *Ireland* 12 A4
Malindi, *Kenya* 86 C5
Malines = Mechelen, *Belgium* 17 C4
Malino, *Indonesia* 63 D6
Malinyi, *Tanzania* 87 D4
Malipo, *China* 58 F5
Maliq, *Albania* 44 F4
Malita, *Phil.* 63 C7
Maliwun, *Burma* 62 B1
Maliya, *India* 68 H4
Maljenik, *Serbia & M.* 44 C5
Malka Mari △, *Kenya* 86 B5
Malkara, *Turkey* 45 F10
Małkinia Górna, *Poland* 31 F9
Malko Tŭrnovo, *Bulgaria* 45 E11
Mallacoota Inlet, *Australia* 95 F4
Mallaig, *U.K.* 13 D3
Mallaoua, *Niger* 83 C6
Mallawan, *India* 69 F9
Mallawi, *Egypt* 80 B3
Mallemort, *France* 21 E9
Málles Venosta, *Italy* 40 B7
Mállia, *Greece* 49 D7
Mallión, Kólpos, *Greece* 49 D7
Mallorca, *Spain* 48 B10
Mallorytown, *Canada* 117 B9
Mallow, *Ireland* 12 D3
Malmbäck, *Sweden* 11 G8
Malmberget, *Sweden* 8 C19
Malmédy, *Belgium* 17 D6
Malmesbury, *S. Africa* 88 E2
Malmivaara = Malmberget, *Sweden* 8 C19
Malmköping, *Sweden* 10 E10
Malmö, *Sweden* 11 J7
Malmslätt, *Sweden* 11 F9
Malmyzh, *Russia* 34 B10
Malnaş, *Romania* 29 D10
Malo Konare, *Bulgaria* 45 D8
Maloarkhangelsk, *Russia* 33 F9
Malolos, *Phil.* 63 B6
Malolotja ⌓, *Swaziland* 89 D5
Malombe L., *Malawi* 87 E4
Małomice, *Poland* 31 G2
Malomir, *Bulgaria* 45 D10
Malone, *U.S.A.* 117 B10
Malong, *China* 58 E4
Małopolskie □, *Poland* 31 J7
Malorad, *Bulgaria* 44 C7
Måløy, *Norway* 9 F11
Maloyaroslovets, *Russia* 32 E9
Malpartida, *Spain* 37 F4
Malpaso, *Canary Is.* 48 G1
Malpelo, I. de, *Colombia* 124 C2
Malpica de Bergantiños, *Spain* 36 B2
Malpur, *India* 68 H5
Malpura, *India* 68 F6
Mals = Málles Venosta, *Italy* 40 B7
Malta, *Idaho, U.S.A.* 108 E7
Malta, *Mont., U.S.A.* 108 B10
Malta ■, *Europe* 49 D2
Maltahöhe, *Namibia* 88 C2
Maltepe, *Turkey* 45 F13
Malton, *Canada* 116 C5
Malton, *U.K.* 14 C7
Maluku, *Indonesia* 63 E7
Maluku □, *Indonesia* 63 E7
Maluku Sea = Molucca Sea, *Indonesia* 63 E6
Maluku Utara □, *Indonesia* 63 D7
Malumfashi, *Nigeria* 83 C6
Malung, *Sweden* 10 D7
Malungsfors, *Sweden* 10 D7
Maluwe, *Ghana* 82 D4
Malvan, *India* 66 L8
Malvern, *U.S.A.* 113 H8
Malvern Hills, *U.K.* 15 E5
Malvinas, Is. = Falkland Is. ☑, *Atl. Oc.* 128 G5
Malý Dunaj →, *Slovak Rep.* 27 D11
Malya, *Tanzania* 86 C3
Malye Derbety, *Russia* 35 G7
Malyn, *Ukraine* 33 G5
Malyy Lyakhovskiy, Ostrov, *Russia* 53 B15
Mama, *Russia* 53 D12
Mamadysh, *Russia* 34 C10
Mamanguape, *Brazil* 125 E11
Mamarr Mitlā, *Egypt* 74 E1
Mamasa, *Indonesia* 63 E5
Mambasa, *Dem. Rep. of the Congo* 86 B2
Mamberamo →, *Indonesia* 63 E9
Mambilima Falls, *Zambia* 87 E2
Mambirima, *Dem. Rep. of the Congo* 87 E2
Mambo, *Tanzania* 86 C4
Mambrui, *Kenya* 86 C5
Mamburao, *Phil.* 61 E4
Mameigwess L., *Canada* 104 B2
Mamers, *France* 18 D7
Mamfé, *Cameroon* 83 D6
Mammoth, *U.S.A.* 109 K8
Mammoth Cave △, *U.S.A.* 114 G3
Mamonovo, *Russia* 30 D6
Mamoré →, *Bolivia* 124 F5
Mamou, *Guinea* 82 C2
Mamoudzou, *Mayotte* 77 H8
Mampatá, *Guinea-Biss.* 82 C2
Mampikony, *Madag.* 89 B8
Mampong, *Ghana* 83 D4
Mamry, Jezioro, *Poland* 30 D8
Mamuju, *Indonesia* 63 E5
Mamuno, *Botswana* 88 C3
Mamuras, *Albania* 44 E3
Man, *Ivory C.* 82 D3
Man, I. of, *U.K.* 14 C3
Man-Bazar, *India* 69 H12
Man Na, *Burma* 67 H20
Mana →, *Fr. Guiana* 125 B8
Mana Pools △, *Zimbabwe* 87 F2
Manaar, G. of = Mannar, G. of, *Asia* 66 Q11
Manacapuru, *Brazil* 124 D6
Manacor, *Spain* 48 B10
Manado, *Indonesia* 63 D6
Managua, *Nic.* 120 D2
Managua, L. de, *Nic.* 120 D2
Manakara, *Madag.* 89 C8
Manali, *India* 68 C7
Manama = Al Manāmah, *Bahrain* 71 E6
Manambao →, *Madag.* 89 B7
Manambato, *Madag.* 89 A8
Manambolo →, *Madag.* 89 B7
Manambolosy, *Madag.* 89 B8
Mananara, *Madag.* 89 B8
Mananara ⌓, *Madag.* 89 B8
Mananara →, *Madag.* 89 C8
Mananjary, *Madag.* 89 C8
Manankoro, *Mali* 82 C3
Manantenina, *Madag.* 89 C8
Manaos = Manaus, *Brazil* 124 D7
Manapire →, *Venezuela* 124 B5
Manapouri, *N.Z.* 91 L1
Manapouri, L., *N.Z.* 91 L1
Manaqil, *Sudan* 81 E3
Manār, Jabal, *Yemen* 75 E3
Manaravolo, *Madag.* 89 C8
Manas, *China* 60 B3
Manas →, *India* 67 F17
Manaslu, *Nepal* 69 E11
Manasquan, *U.S.A.* 117 F10
Manassa, *U.S.A.* 109 H11
Manatí, *Puerto Rico* 121 d
Manaung, *Burma* 67 K18
Manaus, *Brazil* 124 D7
Manavgat, *Turkey* 72 D4
Manawan L., *Canada* 103 B8
Manay, *Phil.* 61 H7
Manbij, *Syria* 70 B3
Mancha Real, *Spain* 37 H7
Manche □, *France* 18 C5
Manchegorsk, *Russia* 52 C4
Manchester, *U.K.* 14 D5
Manchester, *Calif., U.S.A.* 110 G3
Manchester, *Conn., U.S.A.* 117 E12
Manchester, *Ga., U.S.A.* 115 J3
Manchester, *Iowa, U.S.A.* 112 D9
Manchester, *Ky., U.S.A.* 114 G4
Manchester, *N.H., U.S.A.* 117 D13
Manchester, *N.Y., U.S.A.* 116 D7
Manchester, *Pa., U.S.A.* 117 F8
Manchester, *Tenn., U.S.A.* 115 H2
Manchester, *Vt., U.S.A.* 117 C11
Manchester International ✕ (MAN), *U.K.* 14 D5
Manchester L., *Canada* 103 A7
Manchhar L., *Pakistan* 68 F2
Manchuria = Dongbei, *China* 53 E13
Manchurian Plain, *China* 50 E16
Manciano, *Italy* 41 F8
Mancifa, *Ethiopia* 81 F5
Mand →, *India* 69 J10
Mand →, *Iran* 71 D7
Manda, *Ludewe, Tanzania* 87 E3
Manda, *Mbeya, Tanzania* 86 D3
Manda, *Mbeya, Tanzania* 87 D3
Mandabé, *Madag.* 89 C7
Mandaguari, *Brazil* 127 A5
Mandah = Töhöm, *Mongolia* 56 B5
Mandal, *Norway* 9 G12
Mandala, Puncak, *Indonesia* 63 E10
Mandalay, *Burma* 67 J20
Mandale = Mandalay, *Burma* 67 J20
Mandalgarh, *India* 68 G6
Mandalgovi, *Mongolia* 56 B4
Mandalī, *Iraq* 70 C5
Mandan, *U.S.A.* 112 B4
Mandaon, *Phil.* 61 E5
Mandar, Teluk, *Indonesia* 63 E5
Mándas, *Italy* 42 C2
Mandaue, *Phil.* 61 F5
Mandelieu-la-Napoule, *France* 21 E10
Mandera, *Kenya* 86 B5
Mandeville, *Jamaica* 120 a
Mandi, *India* 68 D7
Mandi Dabwali, *India* 68 E6
Mandiana, *Guinea* 82 C3
Mandimba, *Mozam.* 87 E4
Mandioli, *Indonesia* 63 E7
Mandla, *India* 69 H9
Mandø, *Denmark* 11 J2
Mandorah, *Australia* 92 B5
Mandoto, *Madag.* 89 B8
Mandoúdhion, *Greece* 46 C5
Mándra, *Greece* 46 C5
Mandra, *Pakistan* 68 C5
Mandrákhi, *Greece* 47 E9
Mandrare →, *Madag.* 89 D8
Mandritsara, *Madag.* 89 B8
Mandronarivo, *Madag.* 89 C8
Mandsaur, *India* 68 G6
Mandurah, *Australia* 93 F2
Mandúria, *Italy* 43 B10
Mandvi, *India* 68 H3
Mandya, *India* 66 N10
Mandzai, *Pakistan* 68 D2
Mané, *Burkina Faso* 83 C4
Maneh, *Iran* 71 B8
Manengouba, Mts., *Cameroon* 83 E6
Manera, *Madag.* 89 C7
Manérbio, *Italy* 40 C7
Maneroo Cr. →, *Australia* 94 C3
Manfalût, *Egypt* 80 B3
Manfredónia, *Italy* 41 G12
Manfredónia, G. di, *Italy* 41 G13
Manga, *Burkina Faso* 83 C4
Manga, *Niger* 83 C7
Mangabeiras, Chapada das, *Brazil* 125 F9
Mangalia, *Romania* 29 G13
Mangalore, *India* 66 N9
Mangan, *India* 69 F13
Mangaung, *S. Africa* 85 K5

Mangawan, *India* 69 G9
Mangaweka, *N.Z.* 91 H5
Manggar, *Indonesia* 62 E3
Manggawitu, *Indonesia* 63 E8
Manggis, *Indonesia* 63 J18
Mangindrano, *Madag.* 89 A8
Mangkalihat, Tanjung, *Indonesia* 63 D5
Mangla, *Pakistan* 68 C5
Mangla Dam, *Pakistan* 69 C5
Manglaur, *India* 68 E7
Mangnai, *China* 60 C4
Mango, *Togo* 83 C5
Mangoche, *Malawi* 87 E4
Mangoky →, *Madag.* 89 C7
Mangole, *Indonesia* 63 E6
Mangombe, *Dem. Rep. of the Congo* 86 C2
Mangonui, *N.Z.* 91 F4
Mangoro →, *Madag.* 89 B8
Mangrol, *Mad. P., India* 68 J4
Mangrol, *Raj., India* 68 G6
Mangualde, *Portugal* 36 E3
Mangueira, L. da, *Brazil* 127 C5
Mangum, *U.S.A.* 113 H5
Mangyshlak, Poluostrov, *Kazakhstan* 52 E6
Manhattan, *U.S.A.* 112 F6
Manhiça, *Mozam.* 89 D5
Mania →, *Madag.* 89 B8
Maniago, *Italy* 41 B9
Manica, *Mozam.* 89 B5
Manica □, *Mozam.* 89 B5
Manicaland □, *Zimbabwe* 87 F3
Manicoré, *Brazil* 124 E6
Manicouagan →, *Canada* 105 C6
Manicouagan, Rés., *Canada* 105 B6
Maniema □, *Dem. Rep. of the Congo* 86 C2
Manīfah, *Si. Arabia* 71 E6
Manifold, C., *Australia* 94 C5
Maniganggo, *China* 58 B2
Manigotagan, *Canada* 103 C9
Manigotagan →, *Canada* 103 C9
Manihari, *India* 69 G12
Manihiki, *Cook Is.* 97 J11
Manika, Plateau de la, *Dem. Rep. of the Congo* 87 E2
Manikpur, *India* 69 G9
Manila, *Phil.* 61 D4
Manila, *U.S.A.* 108 F9
Manila B., *Phil.* 61 D4
Manilla, *Australia* 95 E5
Manimpé, *Mali* 82 C3
Maningrida, *Australia* 94 A1
Maninian, *Ivory C.* 82 C3
Manipur □, *India* 67 G19
Manipur →, *Burma* 67 H19
Manisa, *Turkey* 47 C9
Manisa □, *Turkey* 47 C9
Manistee, *U.S.A.* 114 C2
Manistee →, *U.S.A.* 114 C2
Manistique, *U.S.A.* 114 C2
Manitoba □, *Canada* 103 B9
Manitoba, L., *Canada* 103 C9
Manitou, *Canada* 103 D9
Manitou, L., *Canada* 105 B6
Manitou Is., *U.S.A.* 114 C3
Manitou L., *Canada* 103 C7
Manitou Springs, *U.S.A.* 112 F2
Manitoulin I., *Canada* 104 C3
Manitouwadge, *Canada* 104 C2
Manitowoc, *U.S.A.* 114 C2
Manizales, *Colombia* 124 B3
Manja, *Madag.* 89 C7
Manjacaze, *Mozam.* 89 C5
Manjakandriana, *Madag.* 89 B8
Manjhand, *Pakistan* 68 G3
Manjil, *Iran* 71 B6
Manjimup, *Australia* 93 F2
Manjra →, *India* 66 K10
Mankato, *Kans., U.S.A.* 112 F5
Mankato, *Minn., U.S.A.* 112 C8
Mankayane, *Swaziland* 89 D5
Mankera, *Pakistan* 68 D4
Mankim, *Cameroon* 83 D7
Mankono, *Ivory C.* 82 D3
Mankota, *Canada* 103 D7
Manlay = Üydzin, *Mongolia* 56 B4
Manlleu, *Spain* 38 C7
Manmad, *India* 66 J9
Mann Ranges, *Australia* 93 E5
Manna, *Indonesia* 62 E2
Mannahill, *Australia* 95 E3
Mannar, *Sri Lanka* 66 Q11
Mannar, G. of, *Asia* 66 Q11
Mannar I., *Sri Lanka* 66 Q11
Mannheim, *Germany* 25 F4
Manning, *Canada* 102 B5
Manning, *Oreg., U.S.A.* 110 E3
Manning, *S.C., U.S.A.* 115 J5
Mannu →, *Italy* 42 C2
Mannu, C., *Italy* 42 B1
Mannum, *Australia* 95 E2
Mano, *S. Leone* 82 D2
Mano →, *Liberia* 82 D2
Mano River, *Liberia* 82 D2
Manoharpur, *India* 69 H11
Manokwari, *Indonesia* 63 E8
Manolás, *Greece* 46 C3
Manombo, *Madag.* 89 C7
Manono, *Dem. Rep. of the Congo* 86 D2
Manoppello, *Italy* 41 F11
Manosque, *France* 21 E9
Manotick, *Canada* 117 A9
Manouane →, *Canada* 105 C5
Manouane, L., *Canada* 105 B5
Manp'o, *N. Korea* 57 D14
Manpojin = Manp'o, *N. Korea* 57 D14
Manpur, *Chhattisgarh, India* 69 H10
Manpur, *Mad. P., India* 68 H6
Manresa, *Spain* 38 D6
Mansa, *Gujarat, India* 68 H5
Mansa, *Punjab, India* 68 E6
Mansa, *Zambia* 87 E2
Månsåsen, *Sweden* 10 A8
Mansehra, *Pakistan* 68 B5
Mansel I., *Canada* 101 B11
Mansfield, *Australia* 95 F4
Mansfield, *U.K.* 14 D6
Mansfield, *La., U.S.A.* 113 J8
Mansfield, *Mass., U.S.A.* 117 D13
Mansfield, *Ohio, U.S.A.* 116 F2
Mansfield, *Pa., U.S.A.* 116 E7
Mansfield, Mt., *U.S.A.* 117 B12
Mansilla de las Mulas, *Spain* 36 C5
Mansle, *France* 20 C4
Mansoa, *Guinea-Biss.* 82 C1
Manson Creek, *Canada* 102 B4
Manta, *Ecuador* 124 D2
Mantadia △, *Madag.* 89 B8
Mantalingajan, Mt., *Phil.* 61 G2
Mantare, *Tanzania* 86 C3
Manteca, *U.S.A.* 110 H5
Manteo, *U.S.A.* 115 H8
Mantes-la-Jolie, *France* 19 D8
Manthani, *India* 66 K11
Manti, *U.S.A.* 108 G8
Mantiqueira, Serra da, *Brazil* 127 A7
Manton, *U.S.A.* 114 C3
Mantorp, *Sweden* 11 F9
Mántova, *Italy* 40 C7
Mänttä, *Finland* 9 E21
Mantua = Mántova, *Italy* 40 C7
Manturovo, *Russia* 34 A7
Manu, *Peru* 124 F4
Manu →, *Peru* 124 F4
Manu'a Is., *Amer. Samoa* 91 B14
Manuel Alves →, *Brazil* 125 F9
Manui, *Indonesia* 63 E6
Manukau, *N.Z.* 91 G5
Manuripi →, *Bolivia* 124 F5
Many, *U.S.A.* 113 K8
Manyara, L., *Tanzania* 86 C4
Manyas, *Turkey* 45 F11
Manyava, *Ukraine* 29 B9
Manych →, *Russia* 35 G5
Manych-Gudilo, Ozero, *Russia* 35 G6
Manyonga →, *Tanzania* 86 C3
Manyoni, *Tanzania* 86 D3
Manzai, *Pakistan* 68 C4
Manzala, Bahra el, *Egypt* 80 H7
Manzanar ⌂, *U.S.A.* 110 J7
Manzanares, *Spain* 37 F7
Manzaneda, *Spain* 36 C3
Manzanillo, *Cuba* 120 B4
Manzanillo, *Mexico* 118 D4
Manzanillo, Pta., *Panama* 120 E4
Manzano Mts., *U.S.A.* 109 J10
Manzarīyeh, *Iran* 71 C6
Manzhouli, *China* 60 B6
Manzini, *Swaziland* 89 D5
Mao, *Chad* 79 F9
Maó, *Spain* 48 B11
Maoke, Pegunungan, *Indonesia* 63 E9
Maolin, *China* 57 C12
Maoming, *China* 59 G8
Maopi T'ou, *China* 59 G13
Maouri, Dallol →, *Niger* 83 C5
Maoxian, *China* 58 B4
Maoxing, *China* 57 B13
Mapam Yumco, *China* 60 C3
Mapastepec, *Mexico* 119 D6
Maphrao, Ko, *Thailand* 65 a
Mapia, Kepulauan, *Indonesia* 63 D8
Mapimí, *Mexico* 118 B4
Mapimí, Bolsón de, *Mexico* 118 B4
Maping, *China* 59 B9
Mapinga, *Tanzania* 86 D4
Mapinhane, *Mozam.* 89 C6
Maple Creek, *Canada* 103 D7
Maple Valley, *U.S.A.* 110 C4
Mapleton, *U.S.A.* 108 D2
Mapuera →, *Brazil* 124 D7
Mapulanguene, *Mozam.* 89 C5
Maputo, *Mozam.* 89 D5
Maputo ⌂, *Mozam.* 89 D5
Maputo □, *Mozam.* 89 D5
Maputo, B. de, *Mozam.* 89 D5
Maqiaohe, *China* 57 B16
Maqnā, *Si. Arabia* 70 D2
Maquan He = Brahmaputra →, *Asia* 69 H13
Maqueda, *Spain* 36 E6
Maquela do Zombo, *Angola* 84 F3
Maquinchao, *Argentina* 128 E3
Maquoketa, *U.S.A.* 112 D9
Mar, Serra do, *Brazil* 127 B6
Mar Chiquita, L., *Argentina* 126 C3
Mar del Plata, *Argentina* 126 D4
Mar Menor, *Spain* 39 H4
Mara, *Tanzania* 86 C3
Mara □, *Tanzania* 86 C3
Maraã, *Brazil* 124 D5
Marabá, *Brazil* 125 E9
Maracá, I. de, *Brazil* 125 C8
Maracaibo, *Venezuela* 124 A4
Maracaibo, L. de, *Venezuela* 124 B4
Maracaju, *Brazil* 127 A4
Maracas Bay Village, *Trin. & Tob.* 125 K15
Maracay, *Venezuela* 124 A5
Maracena, *Spain* 37 H7
Maradi, *Niger* 83 C6
Marāgheh, *Iran* 70 B5
Marāh, *Si. Arabia* 70 E5
Marahoue △, *Ivory C.* 82 D3
Marais du Cotentin et du Bessin ⌂, *France* 18 C5
Marais Poitevin, Val de Sèvre et Vendée ⌂, *France* 20 B3
Marajó, I. de, *Brazil* 125 D9
Marākand, *Iran* 70 B5
Marakele △, *S. Africa* 89 E4
Maralal, *Kenya* 86 B4
Maralinga, *Australia* 93 F5
Maramaraereğlisi, *Turkey* 45 F11
Marambio, *Antarctica* 5 C18
Marampa, *S. Leone* 82 D2
Maramureş □, *Romania* 29 C9
Maran, *Malaysia* 65 L4
Marana, *U.S.A.* 109 K8
Maranboy, *Australia* 92 B5
Maranchón, *Spain* 38 D2
Marand, *Iran* 70 B5
Marang, *Malaysia* 65 K4
Maranguape, *Brazil* 125 D11
Maranhão = São Luís, *Brazil* 125 D10
Maranhão □, *Brazil* 125 E9
Marano, L. di, *Italy* 41 C10
Maranoa →, *Australia* 95 D4
Marañón →, *Peru* 124 D4
Marão, *Mozam.* 89 C5
Maraş = Kahramanmaraş, *Turkey* 70 B3
Mărăşeşti, *Romania* 29 E12
Maratea, *Italy* 43 C8
Marateca, *Portugal* 37 G2
Marathasa, *Cyprus* 49 E11
Marathókambos, *Greece* 47 D8
Marathon, *Australia* 94 C3
Marathon, *Canada* 104 C2
Marathón, *Greece* 46 C5
Marathon, *N.Y., U.S.A.* 117 D8
Marathon, *Tex., U.S.A.* 113 K3
Marathóvouno, *Cyprus* 49 D12
Maratua, *Indonesia* 63 D5
Maraval, *Trin. & Tob.* 125 K15
Maravatío, *Mexico* 118 D4
Marawi City, *Phil.* 61 G6
Marāwih, *U.A.E.* 71 E7
Marazliyivka 29 D15
Marbella, *Spain* 37 J6
Marble Bar, *Australia* 92 D2
Marble Falls, *U.S.A.* 113 K5
Marblehead, *U.S.A.* 117 D14
Marburg, *Germany* 24 E4
Marcal →, *Hungary* 28 C2
Marcali, *Hungary* 28 D2
Marcaria, *Italy* 40 C7
Mărcăuţi, *Moldova* 29 B12
March, *U.K.* 15 E8
Marche, *France* 20 B5
Marche □, *Italy* 41 E10
Marche-en-Famenne, *Belgium* 17 D5
Marchena, *Spain* 37 H5
Marches = Marche □, *Italy* 41 E10
Marchesale ⌂, *Italy* 43 D9
Marciana Marina, *Italy* 40 F7
Marcianise, *Italy* 43 A7
Marcigny, *France* 19 F11
Marcillat-en-Combraille, *France* 19 F9
Marck, *France* 19 B8
Marckolsheim, *France* 19 D14
Marco, *U.S.A.* 115 N5
Marcos Juárez, *Argentina* 126 C3
Mărculeşti, *Moldova* 29 C13
Marcus I. = Minami-Tori-Shima, *Pac. Oc.* 96 E7
Marcus Necker Ridge, *Pac. Oc.* 96 F9
Marcy, Mt., *U.S.A.* 117 B11
Mardan, *Pakistan* 68 B5
Mardarivka, *Ukraine* 29 C14
Mardin, *Turkey* 70 B4
Mårdsjö, *Sweden* 10 A9
Marécchia →, *Italy* 41 D9
Maree, L., *U.K.* 13 D3
Mareeba, *Australia* 94 B4
Mareetsane, *S. Africa* 88 D4
Maremma, *Italy* 41 F8
Maremma ⌂, *Italy* 40 F8
Maréna, *Kayes, Mali* 82 C2
Maréna, *Koulikouro, Mali* 82 C3
Marengo, *U.S.A.* 112 E8
Marennes, *France* 20 C2
Marerano, *Madag.* 89 C7
Marettimo, *Italy* 42 E5
Mareuil, *France* 20 C4
Marfa, *U.S.A.* 113 K2
Marfa Pt., *Malta* 49 D1
Marganets = Marhanets, *Ukraine* 33 J8
Margaret →, *Australia* 92 C4
Margaret Bay, *Canada* 102 C3
Margaret L., *Canada* 102 B5
Margaret River, *Australia* 93 F2
Margarita, I. de, *Venezuela* 124 A6
Margaríticn, *Greece* 46 B2
Margaritovo, *Russia* 54 C7
Margate, *S. Africa* 89 E5
Margate, *U.K.* 15 F9
Margeride, Mts. de la, *France* 20 D7
Margherita di Savóia, *Italy* 43 A9
Margherita Pk., *Uganda* 86 B3
Marghita, *Romania* 28 C7
Margonin, *Poland* 31 F4
Margosatubig, *Phil.* 61 H5
Märgow, Dasht-e, *Afghan.* 66 D3
Marguerite, *Canada* 102 C4
Marhanets, *Ukraine* 33 J8
Mari El □, *Russia* 34 B8
Mari Indus, *Pakistan* 68 C4
Mari Republic = Mari El □, *Russia* 34 B8
María, Sa. de, *Spain* 39 H2
María Elena, *Chile* 126 A2
María Grande, *Argentina* 126 C4
Maria I., *N. Terr., Australia* 94 A2
Maria I., *Tas., Australia* 95 G4
Maria Island △, *Australia* 95 G4
Maria van Diemen, C., *N.Z.* 91 F4
Mariager, *Denmark* 11 H3
Mariager Fjord, *Denmark* 11 H4
Mariakani, *Kenya* 86 C4
Mariala △, *Australia* 95 D4
Marian, *Australia* 94 K6
Marian L., *Canada* 102 A5
Mariana Trench, *Pac. Oc.* 96 F6
Marianao, *Cuba* 120 B3
Marianna, *Ark., U.S.A.* 113 H9
Marianna, *Fla., U.S.A.* 115 K3
Mariannelund, *Sweden* 11 G9
Mariánské Lázně, *Czech Rep.* 26 B5
Marias →, *U.S.A.* 108 C8
Mariato, Punta, *Panama* 120 E3
Mariazell, *Austria* 26 D8
Maribo, *Denmark* 11 K5
Maribor, *Slovenia* 41 B12
Marico →, *Africa* 88 C4
Maricopa, *Ariz., U.S.A.* 109 K7
Maricopa, *Calif., U.S.A.* 111 K7
Marīdī, *Sudan* 81 G2
Marīdī, Wadi →, *Sudan* 81 F2
Marié →, *Brazil* 124 D5
Marie Byrd Land, *Antarctica* 5 D14
Marie-Galante, *Guadeloupe* 120 b
Mariecourt = Kangiqsujuaq, *Canada* 101 B12
Mariefred, *Sweden* 10 E11
Mariehamn = Maarianhamina, *Finland* 9 F18
Marieholm, *Sweden* 11 J7
Mariembourg, *Belgium* 17 D4
Marienbad = Mariánské Lázně, *Czech Rep.* 26 B5
Marienberg, *Germany* 24 E9
Mariental, *Namibia* 88 C2
Marienville, *U.S.A.* 116 E5
Mariestad, *Sweden* 11 F7
Marietta, *Ga., U.S.A.* 115 J3
Marietta, *Ohio, U.S.A.* 114 F5
Marieville, *Canada* 117 A11
Mariga →, *Nigeria* 83 C6
Marignane, *France* 21 E9
Marihatag, *Phil.* 61 G7
Mariinsk, *Russia* 52 D9
Mariinskiy Posad, *Russia* 34 B8
Marijampolė, *Lithuania* 9 J20
Marijampolės □, *Lithuania* 30 D10
Marília, *Brazil* 127 A6
Marín, *Spain* 36 C2
Marina, *U.S.A.* 110 J5
Marinduque, *Phil.* 63 B6
Marine City, *U.S.A.* 116 D2
Marineo, *Italy* 42 E6
Marinette, *U.S.A.* 114 C2
Maringá, *Brazil* 127 A5
Marinha Grande, *Portugal* 36 F2
Marino, *Italy* 41 G9
Marion, *Ala., U.S.A.* 115 J2
Marion, *Ill., U.S.A.* 113 G10
Marion, *Ind., U.S.A.* 114 E3
Marion, *Iowa, U.S.A.* 112 D9
Marion, *Kans., U.S.A.* 112 F6
Marion, *N.C., U.S.A.* 115 H5
Marion, *Ohio, U.S.A.* 114 E4
Marion, *S.C., U.S.A.* 115 H6
Marion, *Va., U.S.A.* 115 G5
Marion, L., *U.S.A.* 115 J5
Mariposa, *U.S.A.* 110 H7
Mariscal Estigarribia, *Paraguay* 126 A3
Maritime Alps = Maritimes, Alpes, *Europe* 21 D11
Maritimes, Alpes, *Europe* 21 D11
Maritsa = Évros →, *Greece* 72 B2
Maritsá, *Greece* 49 C10
Mariupol, *Ukraine* 33 J9
Mariusa △, *Venezuela* 121 E7
Marīvān, *Iran* 70 C5
Marj 'Uyūn, *Lebanon* 74 B4
Marka = Merca, *Somali Rep.* 75 G3
Marka, *Si. Arabia* 80 D5
Markam, *China* 58 C2
Markaryd, *Sweden* 11 H7
Markdale, *Canada* 116 B4
Marked Tree, *U.S.A.* 113 H9
Markelsdorfer Huk, *Germany* 24 A7
Market Drayton, *U.K.* 14 E5
Market Harborough, *U.K.* 15 E7
Market Rasen, *U.K.* 14 D7
Markham, *Canada* 116 C5
Markham, Mt., *Antarctica* 5 E11
Marki, *Poland* 31 F8
Märkische Schweiz ⌂, *Germany* 24 C10
Markkleeberg, *Germany* 24 D8
Markleeville, *U.S.A.* 110 G7
Markoupoulon, *Greece* 46 D5
Markovac, *Serbia & M.* 44 B5
Markovo, *Russia* 53 C17
Markoye, *Burkina Faso* 83 C5
Marks, *Russia* 34 E8
Marksville, *U.S.A.* 113 K8
Markt Schwaben, *Germany* 25 G7
Marktoberdorf, *Germany* 25 H6
Marktredwitz, *Germany* 25 E8
Marl, *Germany* 24 D3
Marla, *Australia* 95 D1
Marlbank, *Canada* 116 B7
Marlboro, *Mass., U.S.A.* 117 D13
Marlboro, *N.Y., U.S.A.* 117 E11
Marlborough, *Australia* 94 C4
Marlborough, *U.K.* 15 F6
Marlborough Downs, *U.K.* 15 F6
Marle, *France* 19 C10
Marlin, *U.S.A.* 113 K6
Marlow, *Germany* 24 A8
Marlow, *U.K.* 15 F7
Marlow, *U.S.A.* 113 H6
Marmagao, *India* 66 M8
Marmande, *France* 20 D4
Marmara, *Turkey* 45 F11
Marmara, Sea of = Marmara Denizi, *Turkey* 45 F12
Marmara Denizi, *Turkey* 45 F12
Marmara Gölü, *Turkey* 47 C10
Marmaris, *Turkey* 47 E10
Marmaris Limanı, *Turkey* 47 E10
Marmion, Mt., *Australia* 93 E2
Marmion L., *Canada* 104 C1
Marmolada, Mte., *Italy* 41 B8
Marmolejo, *Spain* 37 G6
Marmora, *Canada* 116 B7
Mármora, La, *Italy* 42 C2
Marnay, *France* 19 E12
Marne, *Germany* 24 B5
Marne □, *France* 19 D11
Marne →, *France* 19 D9
Marneuli, *Georgia* 35 K7
Maroala, *Madag.* 89 B8
Maroantsetra, *Madag.* 89 B8
Maroelaboom, *Namibia* 88 B2
Marofandilia, *Madag.* 89 C7
Marojejy ⌂, *Madag.* 89 A8
Marolambo, *Madag.* 89 C8
Maromandia, *Madag.* 89 A8
Maromokotro, *Madag.* 89 A8
Marondera, *Zimbabwe* 87 F3
Maroni →, *Fr. Guiana* 125 B8
Marónia, *Greece* 45 F9
Maronne →, *France* 20 C5
Maroochydore, *Australia* 95 D5
Maroona, *Australia* 95 F3
Maros →, *Hungary* 28 D5
Marosakoa, *Madag.* 89 B8
Maroseranana, *Madag.* 89 B8
Maróstica, *Italy* 41 C8
Marotandrano, *Madag.* 89 B8
Marotaolano, *Madag.* 89 A8
Maroua, *Cameroon* 83 C7
Marovato, *Madag.* 89 B8
Marovoay, *Madag.* 89 B8
Marquard, *S. Africa* 88 D4
Marquesas Is. = Marquises, Îs., *French Polynesia* 97 H14
Marquette, *U.S.A.* 114 B2
Marquis, *St. Lucia* 121 f
Marquise, *France* 19 B8
Marquises, Îs., *French Polynesia* 97 H14
Marra, Djebel, *Sudan* 79 F10
Marra, Gebel, *Sudan* 81 F2
Marracuene, *Mozam.* 89 D5
Marradi, *Italy* 41 D8
Marrakech, *Morocco* 78 B4
Marratxi, *Spain* 38 F7
Marrawah, *Australia* 95 G3
Marree, *Australia* 95 D2
Marrero, *U.S.A.* 113 L9
Marrimane, *Mozam.* 89 C5
Marromeu, *Mozam.* 89 B6
Marromeu ⌂, *Mozam.* 89 B6
Marroquí, Punta, *Spain* 37 K5
Marrowie Cr. →, *Australia* 95 E4
Marrubane, *Mozam.* 87 F4
Marrúbiu, *Italy* 42 C1
Marrupa, *Mozam.* 87 E4
Mars Hill, *U.S.A.* 115 B12
Marsá 'Alam, *Egypt* 80 B3
Marsá Matrûh, *Egypt* 80 A2
Marsá Sha'b, *Sudan* 80 C4
Marsabit, *Kenya* 86 B4
Marsabit △, *Kenya* 86 B4
Marsala, *Italy* 42 E5
Marsalforn, *Malta* 49 C1
Mârşani, *Romania* 29 F9
Marsberg, *Germany* 24 D4
Marsciano, *Italy* 41 F9
Marsden, *Australia* 95 E4
Marseillan, *France* 20 E7
Marseille, *France* 21 E9
Marseille ✕ (MRS), *France* 21 E9
Marseilles = Marseille, *France* 21 E9
Marsh I., *U.S.A.* 113 L9
Marshall, *Liberia* 82 D2
Marshall, *Ark., U.S.A.* 113 H8
Marshall, *Mich., U.S.A.* 114 D3
Marshall, *Minn., U.S.A.* 112 C7
Marshall, *Mo., U.S.A.* 112 F8
Marshall, *Tex., U.S.A.* 113 J7
Marshall →, *Australia* 94 C2
Marshall Is. ■, *Pac. Oc.* 96 G9
Marshalltown, *U.S.A.* 112 D8
Marshbrook, *Zimbabwe* 89 B5
Marshfield, *Mo., U.S.A.* 113 G8
Marshfield, *Vt., U.S.A.* 117 B12
Marshfield, *Wis., U.S.A.* 112 C9
Marshūn, *Iran* 71 B6
Mársico Nuovo, *Italy* 43 B8
Märsta, *Sweden* 10 E11
Marstal, *Denmark* 11 K4
Marstrand, *Sweden* 11 G5
Mart, *U.S.A.* 113 K6
Marta →, *Italy* 41 F8
Martaban, *Burma* 67 L20
Martaban, G. of, *Burma* 67 L20
Martano, *Italy* 43 B11
Martapura, *Kalimantan, Indonesia* 62 E4
Martapura, *Sumatera, Indonesia* 62 E2
Marte, *Nigeria* 83 C7
Martel, *France* 20 D5
Martelange, *Belgium* 17 E5
Martellago, *Italy* 41 C9
Martés, Sierra, *Spain* 39 F4
Martfű, *Hungary* 28 C5
Martha's Vineyard, *U.S.A.* 117 E14
Martigné-Ferchaud, *France* 18 E5
Martigny, *Switz.* 25 J3
Martigues, *France* 21 E9
Martin, *Slovak Rep.* 27 B11
Martin, *S. Dak., U.S.A.* 112 D4
Martin, *Tenn., U.S.A.* 113 G10
Martín →, *Spain* 38 D4
Martin, L., *U.S.A.* 115 J3
Martina Franca, *Italy* 43 B10
Martinborough, *N.Z.* 91 J5
Martinez, *Calif., U.S.A.* 110 G4
Martinez, *Ga., U.S.A.* 115 J4
Martinique ☒, *W. Indies* 120 c
Martinique Passage, *W. Indies* 121 C7
Martínon, *Greece* 46 C5
Martinópolis, *Brazil* 127 A5
Martin's Bay, *Barbados* 121 g
Martins Ferry, *U.S.A.* 116 F4
Martinsberg, *Austria* 26 C8

Martinsburg, *Pa., U.S.A.* 116 F6
Martinsburg, *W. Va., U.S.A.* 114 F7
Martinsicuro, *Italy* 41 F10
Martinsville, *Ind., U.S.A.* 114 F2
Martinsville, *Va., U.S.A.* 115 G6
Marton, *N.Z.* 91 J5
Martorell, *Spain* 38 D6
Martos, *Spain* 37 H7
Martuni, *Armenia* 35 K7
Maru, *Nigeria* 83 C6
Marudi, *Malaysia* 62 D4
Maruf, *Afghan.* 66 D5
Marugame, *Japan* 55 G6
Marunga, *Angola* 88 B3
Marungu, Mts., *Dem. Rep. of the Congo* 86 D3
Marv Dasht, *Iran* 71 D7
Marvast, *Iran* 71 D7
Marvejols, *France* 20 D7
Marvel Loch, *Australia* 93 F2
Marwar, *India* 68 G5
Mary, *Turkmenistan* 52 F7
Maryborough = Port Laoise, *Ireland* 12 C4
Maryborough, *Queens., Australia* 95 D5
Maryborough, *Vic., Australia* 95 F3
Maryfield, *Canada* 103 D8
Maryland □, *U.S.A.* 114 F7
Maryland Junction, *Zimbabwe* 87 F3
Maryport, *U.K.* 14 C4
Mary's Harbour, *Canada* 105 B8
Marystown, *Canada* 105 C8
Marysville, *Canada* 102 D5
Marysville, *Calif., U.S.A.* 110 F5
Marysville, *Kans., U.S.A.* 112 F6
Marysville, *Mich., U.S.A.* 116 D2
Marysville, *Ohio, U.S.A.* 114 E4
Marysville, *Wash., U.S.A.* 110 B4
Maryville, *Mo., U.S.A.* 112 E7
Maryville, *Tenn., U.S.A.* 115 H4
Marzūq, *Libya* 79 C8
Masahunga, *Tanzania* 86 C3
Masai, *Malaysia* 65 d
Masai Mara △, *Kenya* 86 C4
Masai Steppe, *Tanzania* 86 C4
Masaka, *Uganda* 86 C3
Masalembo, Kepulauan, *Indonesia* 62 F4
Masalima, Kepulauan, *Indonesia* 62 F5
Masallı, *Azerbaijan* 73 C13
Masamba, *Indonesia* 63 E6
Masan, *S. Korea* 57 G15
Masandam, Ra's, *Oman* 71 E8
Masasi, *Tanzania* 87 E4
Masaya, *Nic.* 120 D2
Masba, *Nigeria* 83 C7
Masbate, *Phil.* 61 E5
Máscali, *Italy* 43 E8
Mascara, *Algeria* 78 A6
Mascota, *Mexico* 118 C4
Masela, *Indonesia* 63 F7
Maseru, *Lesotho* 88 D4
Mashaba, *Zimbabwe* 87 G3
Mashābih, *Si. Arabia* 70 E3
Mashan, *China* 58 F7
Mashar, *Sudan* 81 F2
Mashatu ⌂, *Botswana* 89 C4
Mashegu, *Nigeria* 83 D6
Masherbrum, *Pakistan* 69 B7
Mashhad, *Iran* 71 B8
Mashi, *Nigeria* 83 C6
Mashīz, *Iran* 71 D8
Māshkel, Hāmūn-i-, *Pakistan* 66 E3
Mashki Chāh, *Pakistan* 66 E3
Mashonaland, *Zimbabwe* 85 H6
Mashonaland Central □, *Zimbabwe* 89 B5
Mashonaland East □, *Zimbabwe* 89 B5
Mashonaland West □, *Zimbabwe* 89 B4
Mashrakh, *India* 69 F11
Mashtaga = Maştağa, *Azerbaijan* 35 K10
Masindi, *Uganda* 86 B3
Masindi Port, *Uganda* 86 B3
Maşīrah, *Oman* 75 C6
Maşīrah, Khalīj, *Oman* 75 C6
Masisi, *Dem. Rep. of the Congo* 86 C2
Masjed Soleyman, *Iran* 71 D6
Mask, L., *Ireland* 12 C2
Maskin, *Oman* 71 F8
Maslen Nos, *Bulgaria* 45 D11
Maslinica, *Croatia* 41 E13
Masnou = El Masnou, *Spain* 38 D7
Masoala △, *Madag.* 89 B9
Masoala, Tanjon' i, *Madag.* 89 B9
Masoarivo, *Madag.* 89 B7
Masohi = Amahai, *Indonesia* 63 E7
Masomeloka, *Madag.* 89 C8
Mason, *Nev., U.S.A.* 110 G7
Mason, *Tex., U.S.A.* 113 K5
Mason City, *U.S.A.* 112 D8
Maspalomas, *Canary Is.* 48 G4
Maspalomas, Pta., *Canary Is.* 48 G4
Masqat, *Oman* 75 C6
Massa, *Italy* 40 D7
Massa Marítima, *Italy* 40 E7
Massachusetts □, *U.S.A.* 117 D13
Massachusetts B., *U.S.A.* 117 D14
Massafra, *Italy* 43 B10
Massakory, *Chad* 79 F9
Massanella, *Spain* 48 B9
Massangena, *Mozam.* 89 C5
Massango, *Angola* 84 F3
Massat, *France* 20 F5
Massawa = Mitsiwa, *Eritrea* 81 D4
Massena, *U.S.A.* 117 B10
Massénya, *Chad* 79 F9
Masset, *Canada* 102 C2
Masseube, *France* 20 E4
Massiac, *France* 20 C7
Massiah Street, *Barbados* 121 g
Massif Central, *France* 20 D7
Massif des Bauges ⌂, *France* 19 G13
Massigui, *Mali* 82 C3
Massillon, *U.S.A.* 116 F3
Massinga, *Mozam.* 89 C6
Massingir, *Mozam.* 89 C5
Masson-Angers, *Canada* 117 A9
Masson I., *Antarctica* 5 C7
Maştağa, *Azerbaijan* 35 K10
Mastanli = Momchilgrad, *Bulgaria* 45 E9
Masterton, *N.Z.* 91 J5
Mastic, *U.S.A.* 117 F12
Mástikho, Ákra, *Greece* 47 C8
Mastuj, *Pakistan* 69 A5
Mastung, *Pakistan* 66 E5
Mastūrah, *Si. Arabia* 80 C4
Masty, *Belarus* 32 F3
Masuda, *Japan* 55 G5
Masvingo, *Zimbabwe* 87 G3
Masvingo □, *Zimbabwe* 87 G3
Maswa ⌂, *Tanzania* 86 C3
Maşyāf, *Syria* 70 C3
Maszewo, *Poland* 30 E2
Mat →, *Albania* 44 E3
Matabeleland, *Zimbabwe* 85 H5
Matabeleland North □, *Zimbabwe* 87 F2
Matabeleland South □, *Zimbabwe* 87 G2
Matachel →, *Spain* 37 G4
Matachewan, *Canada* 104 C3
Matadi, *Dem. Rep. of the Congo* 84 F2
Matagalpa, *Nic.* 120 D2
Matagami, *Canada* 104 C4
Matagami, L., *Canada* 104 C4
Matagorda B., *U.S.A.* 113 L6
Matagorda I., *U.S.A.* 113 L6
Matak, *Indonesia* 62 D3
Mátala, *Greece* 49 E6
Matam, *Senegal* 82 B2
Matameye, *Niger* 83 C6
Matamoros, *Campeche, Mexico* 119 D6
Matamoros, *Coahuila, Mexico* 118 B4
Matamoros, *Tamaulipas, Mexico* 119 B5
Ma'ṭan as Sarra, *Libya* 79 D10
Matandu →, *Tanzania* 87 D3
Matane, *Canada* 105 C6
Matang, *China* 58 F5
Matankari, *Niger* 83 C5
Matanomadh, *India* 68 H3
Matanzas, *Cuba* 120 B3
Matapa, *Botswana* 88 C3
Matapan, C. = Taínaron, Ákra, *Greece* 46 E4
Matapédia, *Canada* 105 C6
Matapo △, *Zimbabwe* 87 G2
Matara, *Sri Lanka* 66 S12
Mataram, *Indonesia* 63 K19
Matarani, *Peru* 124 G4
Mataranka, *Australia* 92 B5
Matarma, Râs, *Egypt* 74 E1
Mataró, *Spain* 38 D7
Matarraña →, *Spain* 38 D5
Mataruška Banja, *Serbia & M.* 44 C4
Matatiele, *S. Africa* 89 E4
Mataura, *N.Z.* 91 M2
Matehuala, *Mexico* 118 C4
Mateke Hills, *Zimbabwe* 87 G3
Matelot, *Trin. & Tob.* 125 K15
Matera, *Italy* 43 B9
Matese ⌂, *Italy* 43 A7
Matese, Monti del, *Italy* 43 A7
Mátészalka, *Hungary* 28 C7
Matetsi, *Zimbabwe* 87 F2
Matfors, *Sweden* 10 B11
Matha, *France* 20 C3
Matheniko ⌂, *Uganda* 86 B3
Mathis, *U.S.A.* 113 L6
Mathráki, *Greece* 49 A3
Mathura, *India* 68 F7
Mati, *Phil.* 61 H7
Matiakoali, *Burkina Faso* 83 C5
Matiali, *India* 69 F13
Matías Romero, *Mexico* 119 D5
Matibane, *Mozam.* 87 E5
Matiri Ra., *N.Z.* 91 J4
Matjiesfontein, *S. Africa* 88 E3
Matla →, *India* 69 J13
Matlamanyane, *Botswana* 88 B4
Matli, *Pakistan* 68 G3
Matlock, *U.K.* 14 D6
Matna, *Sudan* 81 E4
Mato Grosso □, *Brazil* 125 F8
Mato Grosso, Planalto do, *Brazil* 125 G8
Mato Grosso do Sul □, *Brazil* 125 G8
Matobo = Matapo △, *Zimbabwe* 87 G2
Matochkin Shar, *Russia* 52 B6
Matopo Hills, *Zimbabwe* 87 G2
Matopos, *Zimbabwe* 87 G2
Matosinhos, *Portugal* 36 D2
Matour, *France* 19 F11
Matroosberg, *S. Africa* 88 E2
Maṭruḥ, *Oman* 75 C6
Matsena, *Nigeria* 83 C7
Matsesta, *Russia* 35 J4
Matsu Tao, *Taiwan* 59 E13
Matsue, *Japan* 55 G6
Matsum, Ko, *Thailand* 65 b
Matsumae, *Japan* 54 D10
Matsumoto, *Japan* 55 F9
Matsusaka, *Japan* 55 G8
Matsuura, *Japan* 55 H4
Matsuyama, *Japan* 55 H6
Mattagami →, *Canada* 104 B3
Mattancheri, *India* 66 Q10
Mattawa, *Canada* 104 C4
Matterhorn, *Switz.* 25 K3
Mattersburg, *Austria* 27 D9
Matthew Town, *Bahamas* 121 B5
Matthews Ridge, *Guyana* 124 B6
Mattice, *Canada* 104 C3
Mattituck, *U.S.A.* 117 F12
Mattō, *Japan* 55 F8
Mattoon, *U.S.A.* 114 F1
Matuba, *Mozam.* 89 C5
Matucana, *Peru* 124 F3
Matūn = Khowst, *Afghan.* 68 C3
Matura B., *Trin. & Tob.* 125 K15
Maturín, *Venezuela* 124 B6
Matusadona △, *Zimbabwe* 87 F2
Matveyev Kurgan, *Russia* 33 J10
Matxitxako, C., *Spain* 38 B2
Mau, *Mad. P., India* 69 F8
Mau, *Ut. P., India* 69 G10
Mau, *Ut. P., India* 69 G9
Mau Escarpment, *Kenya* 86 C4
Mau Ranipur, *India* 69 G8
Maubeuge, *France* 19 B10
Maubourguet, *France* 20 E4
Maud, Pt., *Australia* 92 D1
Maude, *Australia* 95 E3
Maudin Sun, *Burma* 67 M19
Maués, *Brazil* 124 D7
Mauganj, *India* 67 G12
Maughold Hd., *I. of Man* 14 C3
Mauguio, *France* 20 E7
Maui, *U.S.A.* 106 H16
Maulamyaing = Moulmein, *Burma* 67 L20
Maule □, *Chile* 126 D1
Mauléon-Licharre, *France* 20 E3
Maumee, *U.S.A.* 114 E4
Maumee →, *U.S.A.* 114 E4
Maumere, *Indonesia* 63 F6
Maumusson, Pertuis de, *France* 20 C2
Maun, *Botswana* 88 C3
Mauna Kea, *U.S.A.* 106 J17
Mauna Loa, *U.S.A.* 106 J17
Maungmagan Kyunzu, *Burma* 64 E1
Maupin, *U.S.A.* 108 D3
Maure-de-Bretagne, *France* 18 E5
Maurepas, L., *U.S.A.* 113 K9
Maures, *France* 21 E10
Mauriac, *France* 20 C6
Maurice, L., *Australia* 93 E5
Mauricie △, *Canada* 104 C5
Maurienne, *France* 21 C10
Mauritania ■, *Africa* 78 E3
Mauritius ■, *Ind. Oc.* 77 J9
Mauron, *France* 18 D4
Maurs, *France* 20 D6
Mauston, *U.S.A.* 112 D9
Mauterndorf, *Austria* 26 D6
Mauthen, *Austria* 26 E6
Mauvezin, *France* 20 E4
Mauzé-sur-le-Mignon, *France* 20 B3
Mavli, *India* 68 G5
Mavrovë, *Albania* 44 F3
Mavrovo △, *Macedonia* 44 E4
Mavuradonha Mts., *Zimbabwe* 87 F3
Mawa, *Dem. Rep. of the Congo* 86 B2
Mawai, *India* 69 H9
Mawana, *India* 68 E7
Mawand, *Pakistan* 68 E3
Mawk Mai, *Burma* 67 J20
Mawlaik, *Burma* 67 H19
Mawlamyine = Moulmein, *Burma* 67 L20
Mawqaq, *Si. Arabia* 70 E4
Mawson Base, *Antarctica* 5 C6
Mawson Coast, *Antarctica* 5 C6
Max, *U.S.A.* 112 B4
Maxcanú, *Mexico* 119 C6
Maxesibeni, *S. Africa* 89 E4
Maxhamish L., *Canada* 102 B4
Maxixe, *Mozam.* 89 C6
Maxville, *Canada* 117 A10
Maxwell, *U.S.A.* 110 F4
Maxwelton, *Australia* 94 C3
May, C., *U.S.A.* 114 F8
May Pen, *Jamaica* 120 a
Maya →, *Russia* 53 D14
Maya Mts., *Belize* 119 D7
Mayaguana, *Bahamas* 121 B5
Mayagüez, *Puerto Rico* 121 d
Mayahi, *Niger* 83 C6
Mayaky, *Ukraine* 29 C14
Mayals = Maials, *Spain* 38 D5
Mayāmey, *Iran* 71 B7
Mayang, *China* 58 D7
Mayanup, *Australia* 93 F2
Mayapán, *Mexico* 119 C7
Mayapan, *Yucatán, Mexico* 119 C7
Mayarí, *Cuba* 121 B4
Mayaro B., *Trin. & Tob.* 125 K16
Maybell, *U.S.A.* 108 F9
Maybole, *U.K.* 13 F4
Maychew, *Ethiopia* 81 E4
Maydān, *Iraq* 70 C5
Maydan, *Ukraine* 29 B8
Maydena, *Australia* 95 G4
Mayen, *Germany* 25 E3
Mayenne, *France* 18 D6
Mayenne □, *France* 18 D6
Mayenne →, *France* 18 E6
Mayer, *U.S.A.* 109 J7
Mayerthorpe, *Canada* 102 C5
Mayfield, *Ky., U.S.A.* 115 G1
Mayfield, *N.Y., U.S.A.* 117 C10
Mayhill, *U.S.A.* 109 K11
Maykop, *Russia* 35 H5
Maymyo, *Burma* 64 A1
Maynard, *Mass., U.S.A.* 117 D13
Maynard, *Wash., U.S.A.* 110 C4
Maynard Hills, *Australia* 93 E2
Mayne →, *Australia* 94 C3
Maynooth, *Ireland* 12 C5
Mayo, *Canada* 100 B6
Mayo □, *Ireland* 12 C2
Mayo Daga, *Nigeria* 83 D7
Mayo Faran, *Nigeria* 83 D7
Mayon Volcano, *Phil.* 61 E5
Mayor I., *N.Z.* 91 G6
Mayorga, *Spain* 36 C5
Mayotte ☑, *Ind. Oc.* 85 G9
Mayraira Pt., *Phil.* 61 B4
Maysān □, *Iraq* 70 D5
Mayskiy, *Russia* 35 J7
Maysville, *U.S.A.* 114 F4
Mayu, *Indonesia* 63 D7
Mayville, *N. Dak., U.S.A.* 112 B6
Mayville, *N.Y., U.S.A.* 116 D5
Mayya, *Russia* 53 C14
Mazabuka, *Zambia* 87 F2
Mazagán = El Jadida, *Morocco* 78 B4
Mazagão, *Brazil* 125 D8
Mazamet, *France* 20 E6
Mazán, *Peru* 124 D4
Māzandarān □, *Iran* 71 B7
Mazapil, *Mexico* 118 C4
Mazara del Vallo, *Italy* 42 E5
Mazarrón, *Spain* 39 H3
Mazarrón, G. de, *Spain* 39 H3
Mazaruni →, *Guyana* 124 B7
Mazatán, *Mexico* 118 B2
Mazatenango, *Guatemala* 120 D1
Mazatlán, *Mexico* 118 C3
Mažeikiai, *Lithuania* 9 H20
Māzhān, *Iran* 71 C8
Mazīnān, *Iran* 71 B8
Mazoe, *Mozam.* 87 F3
Mazoe →, *Mozam.* 87 F3
Mazowe, *Zimbabwe* 87 F3
Mazowieckie □, *Poland* 31 F8
Mazrûb, *Sudan* 81 E2
Mazu Dao, *China* 59 D12
Mazurian Lakes = Mazurski, Pojezierze, *Poland* 30 E7
Mazurski, Pojezierze, *Poland* 30 E7
Mazyr, *Belarus* 33 F5
Mbaba, *Senegal* 82 C1
Mbabane, *Swaziland* 89 D5
Mbagne, *Mauritania* 82 B2
M'bahiakro, *Ivory C.* 82 D4
Mbaïki, *C.A.R.* 84 D3
Mbala, *Zambia* 87 D3
Mbalabala, *Zimbabwe* 89 C4
Mbale, *Uganda* 86 B3
Mbalmayo, *Cameroon* 83 E7
Mbam →, *Cameroon* 83 E7
Mbamba Bay, *Tanzania* 87 E3
Mbandaka, *Dem. Rep. of the Congo* 84 D3
Mbanga, *Cameroon* 83 E6
Mbanza Congo, *Angola* 84 F2
Mbanza Ngungu, *Dem. Rep. of the Congo* 84 F2
Mbarangandu, *Tanzania* 87 D4
Mbarara, *Uganda* 86 C3
Mbashe →, *S. Africa* 89 E4
Mbatto, *Ivory C.* 82 D4
Mbenkuru →, *Tanzania* 87 D4
Mberengwa, *Zimbabwe* 87 G2
Mberengwa, Mt., *Zimbabwe* 87 G2
Mberubu, *Nigeria* 83 D6
Mbesuma, *Zambia* 87 E3
Mbeya, *Tanzania* 87 D3
Mbeya □, *Tanzania* 86 D3
M'bili, *Sudan* 81 F2
Mbinga, *Tanzania* 87 E4
Mbini = Río Muni □, *Eq. Guin.* 84 D2
Mboki, *C.A.R.* 81 F2
M'bonge, *Cameroon* 83 E6
Mboro, *Senegal* 82 B1
M'boukou, Rés. de, *Cameroon* 83 D7
Mboune, *Senegal* 82 C2
Mbour, *Senegal* 82 C1
Mbout, *Mauritania* 82 B2
Mbuji-Mayi, *Dem. Rep. of the Congo* 86 D1
Mbulu, *Tanzania* 86 C4
Mburucuyá, *Argentina* 126 B4
McCarran International, Las Vegas ✕ (LAS), *U.S.A.* 111 J11
Mchinja, *Tanzania* 87 D4
Mchinji, *Malawi* 87 E3
McMurdo, *Antarctica* 5 D11
Mdantsane, *S. Africa* 85 L5
Mead, L., *U.S.A.* 111 J12
Meade, *U.S.A.* 113 G4
Meadow Lake, *Canada* 103 C7
Meadow Lake ⌂, *Canada* 103 C7
Meadow Valley Wash →, *U.S.A.* 111 J12
Meadville, *U.S.A.* 116 E4
Meaford, *Canada* 116 B4
Mealhada, *Portugal* 36 E2
Mealy Mts., *Canada* 105 B8
Meander River, *Canada* 102 B5
Meares, C., *U.S.A.* 108 D2
Mearim →, *Brazil* 125 D10
Meath □, *Ireland* 12 C5
Meath Park, *Canada* 103 C7
Meaulne, *France* 19 F9
Meaux, *France* 19 D9
Mebechi-Gawa →, *Japan* 54 D10
Mebulu, Tanjung, *Indonesia* 63 K18
Mecanhelas, *Mozam.* 87 F4
Mecca = Makkah, *Si. Arabia* 75 C2
Mecca, *U.S.A.* 111 M10
Mechanicsburg, *U.S.A.* 116 F8
Mechanicville, *U.S.A.* 117 D11
Mechara, *Ethiopia* 81 F5
Mechelen, *Belgium* 17 C4
Mecheria, *Algeria* 78 B5
Mechernich, *Germany* 24 E2
Mechetinskaya, *Russia* 35 G5
Mecidiye, *Turkey* 45 F10
Mecitözü, *Turkey* 72 B6
Mecklenburg-Vorpommern □, *Germany* 24 B8
Mecklenburger Bucht, *Germany* 24 A7
Meconta, *Mozam.* 87 E4
Mecsek, *Hungary* 28 D3
Meda, *Portugal* 36 E3
Medan, *Indonesia* 62 D1
Médanos de Coro △, *Venezuela* 121 D6
Medanosa, Pta., *Argentina* 128 F3
Mede, *Italy* 40 C5
Médéa, *Algeria* 78 A6
Mededa, *Bos.-H.* 28 G4
Medellín, *Colombia* 124 B3
Medelpad, *Sweden* 10 B10
Medemblik, *Neths.* 17 B5
Mederdra, *Mauritania* 82 B1
Medford, *Mass., U.S.A.* 117 D13
Medford, *Oreg., U.S.A.* 108 E2
Medford, *Wis., U.S.A.* 112 C9
Medgidia, *Romania* 29 F13
Medi, *Sudan* 81 F3
Media Agua, *Argentina* 126 C2
Media Luna, *Argentina* 126 C2
Medianeira, *Brazil* 127 B5
Mediaş, *Romania* 29 D9
Medicina, *Italy* 41 D8
Medicine Bow, *U.S.A.* 108 F10
Medicine Bow Pk., *U.S.A.* 108 F10
Medicine Bow Ra., *U.S.A.* 108 F10
Medicine Hat, *Canada* 103 D6
Medicine Lake, *U.S.A.* 112 A2
Medicine Lodge, *U.S.A.* 113 G5
Medina = Al Madīnah, *Si. Arabia* 70 E3
Medina, *N. Dak., U.S.A.* 112 B5
Medina, *N.Y., U.S.A.* 116 C6
Medina, *Ohio, U.S.A.* 116 E3
Medina →, *U.S.A.* 113 L5
Medina de Pomar, *Spain* 36 C7
Medina de Ríoseco, *Spain* 36 D5
Medina del Campo, *Spain* 36 D6
Medina L., *U.S.A.* 113 L5
Medina Sidonia, *Spain* 37 J5
Medinaceli, *Spain* 38 D2
Medinipur, *India* 69 H12
Mediterranean Sea, *Europe* 6 H7
Médoc, *France* 20 C3
Medulin, *Croatia* 41 D10
Medveđa, *Serbia & M.* 44 D5
Medvedevo, *Russia* 34 B8
Medveditsa →, *Tver, Russia* 32 D9
Medveditsa →, *Volgograd, Russia* 34 F6
Medvedok, *Russia* 34 B10
Medvezhi, Ostrava, *Russia* 53 B17
Medvezhyegorsk, *Russia* 52 C4
Medway □, *U.K.* 15 F8
Medway →, *U.K.* 15 F8
Medzev, *Slovak Rep.* 27 C13
Medzilaborce, *Slovak Rep.* 27 B14
Medžitlija, *Macedonia* 44 F5
Meekatharra, *Australia* 93 E2
Meeker, *U.S.A.* 108 F10
Meelpaeg Res., *Canada* 105 C8
Meersburg, *Germany* 25 H5
Meerut, *India* 68 E7
Meeteetse, *U.S.A.* 108 D9
Mega, *Ethiopia* 81 G4
Megálo Khorío, *Greece* 47 E9
Megálo Petalí, *Greece* 46 D6
Megalópolis, *Greece* 46 D4
Meganísi Nisís, *Greece* 46 C2
Mégara, *Greece* 46 D5
Megasini, *India* 69 J12
Megdhova →, *Greece* 46 B3
Megève, *France* 21 C10
Meghalaya □, *India* 67 G17
Meghezez, *Ethiopia* 81 F4
Meghna →, *Bangla.* 67 H17
Mégiscane, L., *Canada* 104 C4
Megiste, *Greece* 47 E11
Megra, *Russia* 32 B9
Mehadia, *Romania* 28 F7
Meharry, Mt., *Australia* 92 D2
Mehedeby, *Sweden* 10 D11
Mehedinţi □, *Romania* 28 F7
Meheisa, *Sudan* 80 D3
Mehlville, *U.S.A.* 112 F9
Mehndawal, *India* 69 F10
Mehr Jān, *Iran* 71 C7
Mehrābād, *Iran* 70 B5
Mehrān, *Iran* 70 C5
Mehrīz, *Iran* 71 D7
Mehun-sur-Yèvre, *France* 19 E9
Mei Jiang →, *China* 59 E11
Mei Xian, *China* 56 G4
Meicheng, *China* 59 C12
Meichengzhen, *China* 59 C8
Meichuan, *China* 59 B10
Meigu, *China* 58 C4
Meiktila, *Burma* 67 J19
Meinerzhagen, *Germany* 24 D3
Meiningen, *Germany* 24 E6
Meira, Serra de, *Spain* 36 B3
Meiringen, *Switz.* 25 J4
Meishan, *China* 58 B4
Meissen, *Germany* 24 D9
Meissner, *Germany* 24 D5
Meissner-Kaufunger Wald ⌂, *Germany* 24 D5
Meitan, *China* 58 D6
Meizhou, *China* 59 E11
Meja, *India* 69 G10
Mejillones, *Chile* 126 A1
Mekdela, *Ethiopia* 81 E4
Mekele, *Ethiopia* 81 E4
Mekhtar, *Pakistan* 66 D6
Meknès, *Morocco* 78 B4
Meko, *Nigeria* 83 D5
Mekong →, *Asia* 65 H6
Mekongga, *Indonesia* 63 E6
Mekrou →, *Benin* 83 C5
Mekvari = Kür →, *Azerbaijan* 73 C13
Mel, *Italy* 41 B9
Melagiri Hills, *India* 66 N10
Melaka, *Malaysia* 65 L4
Melalap, *Malaysia* 62 C5
Mélambes, *Greece* 49 D6
Melanesia, *Pac. Oc.* 96 H7
Melaya, *Indonesia* 63 J17
Melbourne, *Australia* 95 F4
Melbourne, *U.S.A.* 115 L5
Melchor Múzquiz, *Mexico* 118 B4
Melchor Ocampo, *Mexico* 118 C4
Méldola, *Italy* 41 D9

Meldorf, Germany 24 A5
Melegnano, Italy 40 C6
Melenci, Serbia & M. 28 E5
Melenki, Russia 34 C5
Mélèzes →, Canada 104 A5
Melfi, Italy 43 B8
Melfort, Canada 103 C8
Melfort, Zimbabwe 87 F3
Melgaço, Portugal 36 C2
Melgar de Fernamental, Spain 36 C6
Melhus, Norway 8 E14
Melide, Spain 36 C2
Meligalá, Greece 46 D3
Melilla, N. Afr. 78 A5
Melilli, Italy 43 E8
Melipilla, Chile 126 C1
Mélissa, Ákra, Greece 49 D6
Mélissa Óros, Greece 47 D8
Melita, Canada 103 D8
Mélito di Porto Salvo, Italy 43 E8
Melitopol, Ukraine 33 J8
Melk, Austria 26 C8
Mellan Fryken, Sweden 10 E7
Mellansel, Sweden 8 E18
Mellbystrand, Sweden 11 H6
Melle, France 20 B3
Melle, Germany 24 C4
Mellen, U.S.A. 112 B9
Mellerud, Sweden 11 F6
Mellette, U.S.A. 112 C5
Mellid = Melide, Spain 36 C2
Mellieħa, Malta 49 D1
Mellit, Sudan 81 E2
Mellrichstadt, Germany 24 E6
Melnik, Bulgaria 44 E7
Mělník, Czech Rep. 26 A7
Melnytsya Podilska, Ukraine 29 B11
Melo, Uruguay 127 C5
Melolo, Indonesia 63 F6
Melouprey, Cambodia 64 F5
Melrose, Australia 95 E4
Melrose, U.K. 13 F6
Melrose, Minn., U.S.A. 112 C7
Melrose, N. Mex., U.S.A. 113 H3
Melstone, U.S.A. 108 C10
Melsungen, Germany 24 D5
Melton Mowbray, U.K. 14 E7
Melun, France 19 D9
Melut, Sudan 81 E3
Melville, Canada 103 C8
Melville, C., Australia 94 A3
Melville, L., Canada 105 B8
Melville B., Australia 94 A2
Melville I., Australia 92 B5
Melville I., Canada 98 B8
Melville Pen., Canada 101 B11
Mélykút, Hungary 28 D4
Memaliaj, Albania 44 F3
Memba, Mozam. 87 E5
Memboro, Indonesia 63 F5
Membrilla, Spain 37 G7
Memel = Klaipėda, Lithuania 9 J19
Memel, S. Africa 89 D4
Memmingen, Germany 25 H6
Mempawah, Indonesia 62 D3
Memphis, Egypt 80 J7
Memphis, Mich., U.S.A. 116 D2
Memphis, Tenn., U.S.A. 113 H10
Memphis, Tex., U.S.A. 113 H4
Memphremagog, L., U.S.A. 117 B12
Mena, Ukraine 33 G7
Mena, U.S.A. 113 H7
Mena →, Ethiopia 81 F5
Menai Strait, U.K. 14 D3
Ménaka, Mali 83 B5
Menan = Chao Phraya →, Thailand 64 F3
Menarandra →, Madag. 89 D7
Menard, U.S.A. 113 K5
Menawashei, Sudan 81 E1
Mendawai →, Indonesia 62 E4
Mende, France 20 D7
Mendebo Mts., Ethiopia 81 F4
Mendeleyev Ridge, Arctic 4 B17
Menden, Germany 24 D3
Menderes, Turkey 47 C9
Mendez, Mexico 119 B5
Mendhar, India 69 C6
Mendi, Ethiopia 81 F4
Mendip Hills, U.K. 15 F5
Mendocino, U.S.A. 108 G2
Mendocino, C., U.S.A. 108 F1
Mendota, Calif., U.S.A. 110 J6
Mendota, Ill., U.S.A. 112 E10
Mendoyo, Indonesia 63 J17
Mendoza, Argentina 126 C2
Mendoza □, Argentina 126 C2
Mene Grande, Venezuela 124 B4
Menemen, Turkey 47 C9
Menen, Belgium 17 D3
Menfi, Italy 42 E5
Mengdingjie, China 58 F2
Mengeš, Slovenia 41 B11
Menggala, Indonesia 62 E3
Menghai, China 58 G3
Mengíbar, Spain 37 H7
Mengjin, China 56 G7
Mengla, China 58 G3
Menglian, China 58 F2
Mengshan, China 59 E8
Mengyin, China 57 G9
Mengzhe, China 58 F3
Mengzi, China 58 F4
Menihek, Canada 105 B6
Menihek L., Canada 105 B6
Menin = Menen, Belgium 17 D3
Menindee, Australia 95 E3
Menindee L., Australia 95 E3
Meningie, Australia 95 F2
Menjangan, Pulau, Indonesia 63 J17
Menlo Park, U.S.A. 110 H4
Menominee, U.S.A. 114 C2
Menominee →, U.S.A. 114 C2
Menomonie, U.S.A. 112 C9
Menongue, Angola 85 G3
Menorca, Spain 48 B11
Menorca ✕ (MAH), Spain 38 F9
Mentakab, Malaysia 65 L4
Mentawai, Kepulauan, Indonesia 62 E1
Menton, France 21 E11
Mentor, U.S.A. 116 E3
Menzies, Australia 93 E3
Meob B., Namibia 88 C1
Me'ona, Israel 74 B4
Meoqui, Mexico 118 B3
Mepaco, Mozam. 87 F3
Meppel, Neths. 17 B6
Meppen, Germany 24 C3
Mequinenza, Spain 38 D5
Mequinenza, Embalse de, Spain 38 D5
Mer, France 18 E8
Merabéllou, Kólpos, Greece 49 D7
Merak, Indonesia 63 F12
Meramangye, L., Australia 93 E5
Meran = Merano, Italy 41 B8
Merano, Italy 41 B8
Merate, Italy 40 C6
Merauke, Indonesia 63 F10
Merbein, Australia 95 E3
Merbuk, Gunung, Indonesia 63 J17
Merca, Somali Rep. 75 G3
Mercantour △, France 21 D10
Mercato Saraceno, Italy 41 E9
Merced, U.S.A. 110 H6
Merced →, U.S.A. 110 H6
Merced Pk., U.S.A. 110 H7
Mercedes, Buenos Aires, Argentina 126 C4
Mercedes, Corrientes, Argentina 126 B4
Mercedes, San Luis, Argentina 126 C2
Mercedes, Uruguay 126 C4
Mercedes, U.S.A. 113 M6
Merceditas, Chile 126 B1
Mercer, N.Z. 91 G5
Mercer, U.S.A. 116 E4
Mercer Island, U.S.A. 110 C4
Mercury, U.S.A. 111 J11
Mercy, C., Canada 101 B13
Merdrignac, France 18 D4
Mere, U.K. 15 F5
Meredith, C., Falk. Is. 128 G4
Meredith, L., U.S.A. 113 H4
Merefa, Ukraine 33 H9
Merei, Romania 29 E11
Merga = Nukheila, Sudan 80 D2
Mergui, Burma 64 F2
Mergui Arch. = Myeik Kyunzu, Burma 65 G1
Méribel-les-Allues, France 21 C10
Meriç, Turkey 45 E10
Meriç →, Turkey 45 F10
Mérida, Mexico 119 C7
Mérida, Spain 37 G4
Mérida, Venezuela 124 B4
Mérida, Cord. de, Venezuela 124 B4
Meriden, U.K. 15 E6
Meriden, U.S.A. 117 E12
Meridian, Calif., U.S.A. 110 F5
Meridian, Idaho, U.S.A. 108 E5
Meridian, Miss., U.S.A. 115 J1
Mérignac, France 20 D3
Mérinaghène, Senegal 82 B1
Merinda, Australia 94 C4
Mering, Germany 25 G6
Meringa, Nigeria 83 C7
Merir, Pac. Oc. 63 D8
Merirumã, Brazil 125 C8
Merkel, U.S.A. 113 J5
Mermaid Reef, Australia 92 C2
Merowe, Sudan 80 D3
Merredin, Australia 93 F2
Merrick, U.K. 13 F4
Merrickville, Canada 117 B9
Merrill, Oreg., U.S.A. 108 E3
Merrill, Wis., U.S.A. 112 C10
Merrimack →, U.S.A. 117 D14
Merriman, U.S.A. 112 D4
Merritt, Canada 102 C4
Merritt Island, U.S.A. 115 L5
Merriwa, Australia 95 E5
Merry I., Canada 104 A4
Merryville, U.S.A. 113 K8
Mersa Fatma, Eritrea 81 E5
Mersch, Lux. 17 E6
Merse →, Italy 41 E8
Mersea I., U.K. 15 F8
Merseburg, Germany 24 D7
Mersey →, U.K. 14 D4
Merseyside □, U.K. 14 D4
Mersin, Turkey 70 B2
Mersing, Malaysia 65 L4
Merta, India 68 F6
Merta Road, India 68 F5
Merthyr Tydfil, U.K. 15 F4
Merthyr Tydfil □, U.K. 15 F4
Mértola, Portugal 37 H3
Mertzon, U.S.A. 113 K4
Méru, France 19 C9
Meru, Kenya 86 B4
Meru, Tanzania 86 C4
Meru △, Kenya 86 B4
Merville, France 19 B9
Méry-sur-Seine, France 19 D10
Merzifon, Turkey 72 B6
Merzig, Germany 25 F2
Mesa, U.S.A. 109 K8
Mesa Verde △, U.S.A. 109 H9
Mesagne, Italy 43 B10
Mesanagrós, Greece 49 C9
Mesaoría, Cyprus 49 D12
Mesarás, Kólpos, Greece 49 D6
Meschede, Germany 24 D4
Mescit, Turkey 73 B9
Mesfinto, Ethiopia 81 E4
Mesgouez, L., Canada 104 B5
Meshchovsk, Russia 32 E8
Meshed = Mashhad, Iran 71 B8
Meshoppen, U.S.A. 117 E8
Meshra er Req, Sudan 81 F2
Mesilinka →, Canada 102 B4
Mesilla, U.S.A. 109 K10
Meslay-du-Maine, France 18 E6
Mesocco, Switz. 25 J5
Mesolóngion, Greece 46 C3
Mesopotamia = Al Jazirah, Iraq 70 C5
Mesopotamia, U.S.A. 116 E4
Mesopótamon, Greece 46 B2
Mesoraca, Italy 43 C9
Mésou Volímais = Volímai, Greece 46 D2
Mesquite, U.S.A. 109 H6
Messaad, Algeria 78 B6
Messac, France 18 E5
Messalo →, Mozam. 87 E4
Méssaména, Cameroon 83 E7
Messeue, Greece 46 D3
Messina = Musina, S. Africa 89 C5
Messina, Italy 43 D8
Messina, Str. di, Italy 43 D8
Messíni, Greece 46 D4
Messínia □, Greece 46 D3
Messiniakós Kólpos, Greece 46 E4
Messkirch, Germany 25 H5
Messlingen, Sweden 10 B6
Messonghi, Greece 49 B3
Mesta →, Bulgaria 44 E7
Mestá, Ákra, Greece 47 C7
Mestanza, Spain 37 G6
Mestre, Italy 41 C9
Mesudiye, Turkey 72 B7
Meta →, S. Amer. 124 B5
Meta Incognita Pen., Canada 101 B13
Metabetchouan, Canada 105 C5
Metairie, U.S.A. 113 L9
Metalici, Munţii, Romania 28 D7
Metaline Falls, U.S.A. 108 B5
Metallifere, Colline, Italy 40 E8
Metán, Argentina 126 B3
Metangula, Mozam. 87 E3
Metauro →, Italy 41 E10
Metema, Ethiopia 81 E4
Metengobalame, Mozam. 87 E3
Méthana, Greece 46 D5
Methóni, Greece 46 E3
Methven, N.Z. 91 K3
Metil, Mozam. 87 F4
Metkovets, Bulgaria 44 C7
Metković, Croatia 41 E14
Metlakatla, U.S.A. 100 C6
Metlika, Slovenia 41 C12
Metropolis, U.S.A. 113 G10
Métsovon, Greece 46 B3
Metu, Ethiopia 81 F4
Metz, France 19 C13
Metzingen, Germany 25 G5
Meulaboh, Indonesia 62 D1
Meung-sur-Loire, France 19 E8
Meureudu, Indonesia 62 C1
Meurthe →, France 19 D13
Meurthe-et-Moselle □, France 19 D13
Meuse □, France 19 C12
Meuse →, Europe 17 D5
Meuselwitz, Germany 24 D8
Mexia, U.S.A. 113 K6
Mexiana, I., Brazil 125 D9
Mexicali, Mexico 111 N11
Mexican Plateau, Mexico 98 G9
Mexican Water, U.S.A. 109 H9
México, Mexico 119 D5
Mexico, Maine, U.S.A. 117 B14
Mexico, Mo., U.S.A. 112 F9
Mexico, N.Y., U.S.A. 117 C8
México □, Mexico 119 D5
Mexico ■, Cent. Amer. 118 C4
Mexico, G. of, Cent. Amer. 119 C7
Mexico B., U.S.A. 117 C8
Meydān-e Naftūn, Iran 71 D6
Meydani, Ra's-e, Iran 71 E8
Meyenburg, Germany 24 B8
Meymac, France 20 C6
Meymaneh, Afghan. 66 B4
Meyrueis, France 20 D7
Meyssac, France 20 C5
Meyzieu, France 21 C8
Mezdra, Bulgaria 44 C7
Mèze, France 20 E7
Mezen, Russia 52 C5
Mezen →, Russia 52 C5
Mézenc, Mt., France 21 D8
Mezeş, Munţii, Romania 28 C8
Mezha →, Russia 32 E6
Mezhdurechenskiy, Russia 52 D7
Mézidon-Canon, France 18 C6
Mézières-en-Brenne, France 20 B5
Mézilhac, France 21 D8
Mézin, France 20 D4
Mezőberény, Hungary 28 D6
Mezőfalva, Hungary 28 D3
Mezőhegyes, Hungary 28 D5
Mezőkövácsháza, Hungary 28 D5
Mezőkövesd, Hungary 28 C5
Mézos, France 20 D2
Mezőtúr, Hungary 28 C5
Mezquital, Mexico 118 C4
Mezzolombardo, Italy 40 B8
Mfolozi →, S. Africa 89 D5
Mgeta, Tanzania 87 D4
Mglin, Russia 33 F7
Mhlaba Hills, Zimbabwe 87 F3
Mhow, India 68 H6
Miahuatlán, Mexico 119 D5
Miajadas, Spain 37 F5
Miami, Fla., U.S.A. 115 N5
Miami, Okla., U.S.A. 113 G7
Miami, Tex., U.S.A. 113 H4
Miami Beach, U.S.A. 115 N5
Mian Xian, China 56 H4
Mianchi, China 56 G6
Mīāndarreh, Iran 71 C7
Mīāndowāb, Iran 70 B5
Miandrivazo, Madag. 89 B8
Mīāneh, Iran 70 B5
Mianning, China 58 C4
Mianwali, Pakistan 68 C4
Mianyang, China 58 B5
Mianzhu, China 58 B5
Miaoli, Taiwan 59 E13
Miarinarivo, Antananarivo, Madag. 89 B8
Miarinarivo, Toamasina, Madag. 89 B8
Miariravaratra, Madag. 89 C8
Miass, Russia 52 D7
Miasteczko Krajeńskie, Poland 31 E4
Miastko, Poland 30 E3
Mica, S. Africa 89 C5
Micăsasa, Romania 29 D9
Michalovce, Slovak Rep. 27 C14
Michigan □, U.S.A. 114 C3
Michigan, L., U.S.A. 114 D2
Michigan City, U.S.A. 114 E2
Michika, Nigeria 83 C7
Michipicoten I., Canada 104 C2
Michoacan □, Mexico 118 D4
Michurin, Bulgaria 45 D11
Michurinsk, Russia 34 D5
Mico, Pta., Nic. 120 D3
Micoud, St. Lucia 121 f
Micronesia, Pac. Oc. 96 G7
Micronesia, Federated States of ■, Pac. Oc. 96 G7
Mid-Oceanic Ridge, Ind. Oc. 96 M1
Midai, Indonesia 62 D3
Midale, Canada 103 D8
Middelburg, Neths. 17 C3
Middelburg, Eastern Cape, S. Africa 88 E4
Middelburg, Mpumalanga, S. Africa 89 D4
Middelfart, Denmark 11 J3
Middelpos, S. Africa 88 E3
Middelwit, S. Africa 88 C4
Middle Alkali L., U.S.A. 108 F3
Middle Bass I., U.S.A. 116 E2
Middle East, Asia 50 F7
Middle Fork Feather →, U.S.A. 110 F5
Middle I., Australia 93 F3
Middle Loup →, U.S.A. 112 E5
Middle Sackville, Canada 105 D7
Middleboro, U.S.A. 117 E14
Middleburg, Fla., U.S.A. 115 K5
Middleburg, Pa., U.S.A. 116 F7
Middleburgh, U.S.A. 117 D10
Middlebury, U.S.A. 117 B11
Middlemount, Australia 94 C4
Middleport, N.Y., U.S.A. 116 C6
Middleport, Ohio, U.S.A. 114 F4
Middlesboro, U.S.A. 115 G4
Middlesbrough, U.K. 14 C6
Middlesbrough □, U.K. 14 C6
Middlesex, Belize 120 C2
Middlesex, N.J., U.S.A. 117 F10
Middlesex, N.Y., U.S.A. 116 D7
Middleton, Australia 94 C3
Middleton, Canada 105 D6
Middleton Cr. →, Australia 94 C3
Middletown, U.K. 12 B5
Middletown, Calif., U.S.A. 110 G4
Middletown, Conn., U.S.A. 117 E12
Middletown, N.Y., U.S.A. 117 E10
Middletown, Ohio, U.S.A. 114 F3
Middletown, Pa., U.S.A. 117 F8
Midge Point, Australia 94 J6
Midhurst, U.K. 15 G7
Midī, Yemen 81 D5
Midi, Canal du →, France 20 E5
Midi d'Ossau, Pic du, France 20 F3
Midi-Pyrénées □, France 20 E5
Midland, Australia 93 F2
Midland, Canada 116 B5
Midland, Calif., U.S.A. 111 M12
Midland, Mich., U.S.A. 114 D3
Midland, Pa., U.S.A. 116 F4
Midland, Tex., U.S.A. 113 K3
Midlands □, Zimbabwe 87 F2
Midleton, Ireland 12 E3
Midlothian, U.S.A. 113 J6
Midlothian □, U.K. 13 F5
Midongy, Tangorombohitr' i, Madag. 89 C8
Midongy Atsimo, Madag. 89 C8
Midou →, France 20 E3
Midouze →, France 20 E3
Midsayap, Phil. 61 H6
Midu, China 58 E3
Midway Is., Pac. Oc. 96 E10
Midway Wells, U.S.A. 111 N11
Midwest, U.S.A. 107 B9
Midwest, Wyo., U.S.A. 108 E10
Midwest City, U.S.A. 113 H6
Midyat, Turkey 70 B4
Midzŏr, Bulgaria 44 C6
Mie □, Japan 55 G8
Miechów, Poland 31 H7
Miedwie, Jezioro, Poland 31 E1
Międzybórz, Poland 31 G4
Międzychód, Poland 31 F2
Międzylesie, Poland 31 H3
Międzyrzec Podlaski, Poland 31 G9
Międzyrzecz, Poland 31 F2
Międzyzdroje, Poland 30 E1
Miejska Górka, Poland 31 G3
Miélan, France 20 E4
Mielec, Poland 31 H8
Mienga, Angola 88 B2
Miercurea-Ciuc, Romania 29 D10
Miercurea Sibiului, Romania 29 E8
Mieres, Spain 36 B5
Mieroszów, Poland 31 H3
Mieso, Ethiopia 81 F5
Mieszkowice, Poland 31 F1
Mifflintown, U.S.A. 116 F7
Mifraz Hefa, Israel 74 C4
Migennes, France 19 E10
Migliarino, Italy 41 D8
Migliarino-San Rossore-Massaciuccoli ⌓, Italy 40 E7
Miguel Alemán, Presa, Mexico 119 D5
Miguelturra, Spain 37 G7
Mihăileni, Romania 29 C11
Mihăileşti, Romania 29 F10
Mihailovca, Moldova 29 D13
Mihalgazi, Turkey 47 A12
Mihaliççık, Turkey 72 C4
Mihara, Japan 55 G6
Miheşu de Cîmpie, Romania 29 D9
Mijas, Spain 37 J6
Mikese, Tanzania 86 D4
Mikha-Tskhakaya = Senaki, Georgia 35 J6
Mikhailovka = Mykhaylivka, Ukraine 33 J8
Mikhaylov, Russia 32 E10
Mikhaylovgrad = Montana, Bulgaria 44 C7
Mikhaylovka, Russia 34 E6
Mikhnevo, Russia 32 E9
Mikínai, Greece 46 D4
Mikkeli, Finland 9 F22
Mikkwa →, Canada 102 B6
Mikniya, Sudan 81 D3
Mikołajki, Poland 30 E8
Míkonos, Greece 47 D7
Mikrí Préspa, Límni, Greece 44 F5
Mikrón Dhérion, Greece 45 E10
Mikstat, Poland 31 G4
Mikulov, Czech Rep. 27 C9
Mikumi, Tanzania 86 D4
Mikumi △, Tanzania 86 D4
Milaca, U.S.A. 112 C8
Milagro, Ecuador 124 D3
Milagros, Phil. 61 E5
Milan = Milano, Italy 40 C6
Milan, Mo., U.S.A. 112 E8
Milan, Tenn., U.S.A. 115 H1
Milange, Mozam. 87 F4
Milano, Italy 40 C6
Milano Linate ✕ (LIN), Italy 40 C6
Milanoa, Madag. 89 A8
Milâs, Turkey 47 D9
Milatos, Greece 49 D7
Milazzo, Italy 43 D8
Milbank, U.S.A. 112 C6
Milbanke Sd., Canada 102 C3
Milden, Canada 103 C7
Mildenhall, U.K. 15 E8
Mildmay, Canada 116 B3
Mildura, Australia 95 E3
Mile, China 58 E4
Miléai, Greece 46 B5
Miles, Australia 95 D5
Miles City, U.S.A. 112 B2
Mileşti, Moldova 29 C13
Milestone, Canada 103 D8
Mileto, Italy 43 D9
Miletto, Mte., Italy 43 A7
Miletus, Turkey 47 D9
Milevsko, Czech Rep. 26 B7
Milford, Calif., U.S.A. 110 E6
Milford, Conn., U.S.A. 117 E11
Milford, Del., U.S.A. 114 F8
Milford, Mass., U.S.A. 117 D13
Milford, N.H., U.S.A. 117 D13
Milford, Pa., U.S.A. 117 E10
Milford, Utah, U.S.A. 109 G7
Milford Haven, U.K. 15 F2
Milford Sd., N.Z. 91 L1
Milford Sound, N.Z. 91 L1
Milḥ, Baḥr al = Razāzah, Buḥayrat ar, Iraq 70 C4
Milicz, Poland 31 G4
Milikapiti, Australia 92 B5
Miling, Australia 93 F2
Militello in Val di Catània, Italy 43 E7
Milk →, U.S.A. 108 B10
Milk, Wadi el →, Sudan 80 D3
Milk River, Canada 102 D6
Mill I., Antarctica 5 C8
Mill Valley, U.S.A. 110 H4
Millárs →, Spain 38 F4
Millau, France 20 D7
Millbridge, Canada 116 B7
Millbrook, Canada 116 B6
Millbrook, U.S.A. 117 E11
Mille Lacs, L. des, Canada 104 C1
Mille Lacs L., U.S.A. 112 B8
Milledgeville, U.S.A. 115 J4
Millen, U.S.A. 115 J5
Millennium I. = Caroline I., Kiribati 97 H12
Miller, U.S.A. 112 C5
Millerovo, Russia 35 F5
Millersburg, Ohio, U.S.A. 116 F3
Millersburg, Pa., U.S.A. 116 F8
Millerton, U.S.A. 117 E11
Millerton L., U.S.A. 110 J7
Millet, St. Lucia 121 f
Millevaches, Plateau de, France 20 C6
Millheim, U.S.A. 116 F7
Millicent, Australia 95 F3
Millington, U.S.A. 113 H10
Millinocket, U.S.A. 115 C11
Millmerran, Australia 95 D5
Millom, U.K. 14 C4
Mills L., Canada 102 A5
Millsboro, U.S.A. 116 G5
Millstream-Chichester △, Australia 92 D2
Milltown Malbay, Ireland 12 D2
Millville, N.J., U.S.A. 114 F8
Millville, Pa., U.S.A. 117 E8

Millwood L., *U.S.A.* 113 J8
Milna, *Croatia* 41 E13
Milne →, *Australia* 94 C2
Milo, *U.S.A.* 115 C11
Mílos, *Greece* 46 E6
Miłosław, *Poland* 31 F4
Milot, *Albania* 44 E3
Milparinka, *Australia* 95 D3
Miltenberg, *Germany* 25 F5
Milton, *N.S., Canada* 105 D7
Milton, *Ont., Canada* 116 C5
Milton, *N.Z.* 91 M2
Milton, *Calif., U.S.A.* 110 G6
Milton, *Fla., U.S.A.* 115 K2
Milton, *Pa., U.S.A.* 116 F8
Milton, *Vt., U.S.A.* 117 B11
Milton-Freewater, *U.S.A.* 108 D4
Milton Keynes, *U.K.* 15 E7
Milton Keynes □, *U.K.* 15 E7
Miluo, *China* 59 C9
Milverton, *Canada* 116 C4
Milwaukee, *U.S.A.* 114 D2
Milwaukee Deep, *Atl. Oc.* 121 C6
Milwaukie, *U.S.A.* 110 E4
Mim, *Ghana* 82 D4
Mimizan, *France* 20 D2
Mimoň, *Czech Rep.* 26 A7
Min Jiang →, *Fujian, China* 59 E12
Min Jiang →, *Sichuan, China* 58 C5
Min Xian, *China* 56 G3
Mina Pirquitas, *Argentina* 126 A2
Mīnā Su'ud, *Si. Arabia* 71 D6
Mīnā'al Aḩmadī, *Kuwait* 71 D6
Minago →, *Canada* 103 C9
Minaki, *Canada* 103 D10
Minamata, *Japan* 55 H5
Minami-Arapusa △, *Japan* 55 G9
Minami-Tori-Shima, *Pac. Oc.* 96 E7
Minas, *Uruguay* 127 C4
Minas, Sierra de las, *Guatemala* 120 C2
Minas Basin, *Canada* 105 C7
Minas de Riotinto, *Spain* 37 H4
Minas Gerais □, *Brazil* 125 G9
Minatitlán, *Mexico* 119 D6
Minbu, *Burma* 67 J19
Minchinabad, *Pakistan* 68 D5
Mincio →, *Italy* 40 C7
Minčol, *Slovak Rep.* 27 B13
Mindanao, *Phil.* 61 H6
Mindanao Sea = Bohol Sea, *Phil.* 63 C6
Mindanao Trench, *Pac. Oc.* 61 F7
Mindel →, *Germany* 25 G6
Mindelheim, *Germany* 25 G6
Minden, *Canada* 116 B6
Minden, *Germany* 24 C4
Minden, *La., U.S.A.* 113 J8
Minden, *Nev., U.S.A.* 110 G7
Mindiptana, *Indonesia* 63 F10
Mindoro, *Phil.* 61 E4
Mindoro Str., *Phil.* 61 E4
Mine, *Japan* 55 G5
Minehead, *U.K.* 15 F4
Mineola, *N.Y., U.S.A.* 117 F11
Mineola, *Tex., U.S.A.* 113 J7
Mineral King, *U.S.A.* 110 J8
Mineral Wells, *U.S.A.* 113 J5
Mineralnyye Vody, *Russia* 35 H6
Minersville, *U.S.A.* 117 F8
Minerva, *U.S.A.* 116 F3
Minervino Murge, *Italy* 43 A9
Minetto, *U.S.A.* 117 C8
Mingäçevir, *Azerbaijan* 35 K8
Mingäçevir Su Anbarı, *Azerbaijan* 35 K8
Mingan, *Canada* 105 B7
Mingechaur = Mingäçevir, *Azerbaijan* 35 K8
Mingechaurskoye Vdkhr. = Mingäçevir Su Anbarı, *Azerbaijan* 35 K8
Mingela, *Australia* 94 B4
Mingenew, *Australia* 93 E2
Mingera Cr. →, *Australia* 94 C2
Minggang, *China* 59 A10
Mingguang, *China* 59 A11
Mingin, *Burma* 67 H19
Mingir, *Moldova* 29 D13
Minglanilla, *Spain* 39 F3
Minglun, *China* 58 E7
Mingo Junction, *U.S.A.* 116 F4
Mingorria, *Spain* 36 E6
Mingshan, *China* 58 B4
Mingteke Daban = Mintaka Pass, *Pakistan* 69 A6
Mingxi, *China* 59 D11
Mingyuegue, *China* 57 C15
Minho = Miño →, *Spain* 36 D2
Minhou, *China* 59 E12
Minićevo, *Serbia & M.* 28 G7
Minidoka, *U.S.A.* 108 E7
Minigwal, L., *Australia* 93 E3
Minilya →, *Australia* 93 D1
Minilya Roadhouse, *Australia* 93 D1
Minipi L., *Canada* 105 B7
Mink L., *Canada* 102 A5
Minkammen, *Sudan* 81 F3
Minna, *Nigeria* 83 D6
Minneapolis, *Kans., U.S.A.* 112 F6
Minneapolis, *Minn., U.S.A.* 112 C8
Minnedosa, *Canada* 103 C9
Minnesota □, *U.S.A.* 112 B8
Minnesota →, *U.S.A.* 112 C8
Minnewaukan, *U.S.A.* 112 A5
Minnipa, *Australia* 95 E2
Minnitaki L., *Canada* 104 C1
Mino, *Japan* 55 G8
Miño, *Spain* 36 B2
Miño →, *Spain* 36 D2
Minoa, *Greece* 47 F7
Minorca = Menorca, *Spain* 48 B11
Minot, *U.S.A.* 112 A4
Minqin, *China* 56 E2
Minqing, *China* 59 D12
Minsen, *Germany* 24 B3
Minsk, *Belarus* 32 F4
Mińsk Mazowiecki, *Poland* 31 F8
Mintabie, *Australia* 95 D1
Mintaka Pass, *Pakistan* 69 A6
Minto, *Canada* 105 C6
Minto, L., *Canada* 104 A5
Minton, *Canada* 103 D8
Minturn, *U.S.A.* 108 G10
Minturno, *Italy* 42 A6
Minûf, *Egypt* 80 H7
Minusinsk, *Russia* 53 D10
Minutang, *India* 67 E20
Minya el Qamh, *Egypt* 80 H7
Minya Konka = Gongga Shan, *China* 58 C3
Mionica, *Bos.-H.* 28 F3
Mionica, *Serbia & M.* 44 B4
Miquelon, *Canada* 104 C4
Miquelon, *St-P. & M.* 105 C8
Mir, *Niger* 83 C7
Mīr Kūh, *Iran* 71 E8
Mīr Shahdād, *Iran* 71 E8
Mira, *Italy* 41 C9
Mira, *Portugal* 36 E2
Mira →, *Portugal* 37 H2
Mira por vos Cay, *Bahamas* 121 B5
Mirabella Eclano, *Italy* 43 A7
Mirador-Río Azul △, *Guatemala* 120 C2
Miraj, *India* 66 L9
Miram Shah, *Pakistan* 68 C4
Miramar, *Argentina* 126 D4
Miramar, *Mozam.* 89 C6
Miramas, *France* 21 E8
Mirambeau, *France* 20 C3
Miramichi, *Canada* 105 C6
Miramichi B., *Canada* 105 C7
Miramont-de-Guyenne, *France* 20 D4
Miranda, *Brazil* 125 H7
Miranda →, *Brazil* 124 G7
Miranda de Ebro, *Spain* 38 C2
Miranda do Corvo, *Portugal* 36 E2
Miranda do Douro, *Portugal* 36 D4
Mirande, *France* 20 E4
Mirandela, *Portugal* 36 D3
Mirándola, *Italy* 40 D8
Mirandópolis, *Brazil* 127 A5
Mirango, *Malawi* 87 E3
Mirani, *Australia* 94 K6
Mirano, *Italy* 41 C9
Miras, *Albania* 44 F4
Mirassol, *Brazil* 127 A6
Mirbāţ, *Oman* 75 D5
Mirear, *Egypt* 80 C4
Mirebeau, *France* 18 F7
Mirebeau-sur-Bèze, *France* 19 E12
Mirecourt, *France* 19 D13
Mirgorod = Myrhorod, *Ukraine* 33 H7
Miri, *Malaysia* 62 D4
Miriam Vale, *Australia* 94 C5
Miribel, *France* 19 G11
Mirim, L., *S. Amer.* 127 C5
Mirnyy, *Russia* 53 C12
Miroč, *Serbia & M.* 44 B6
Mirokhan, *Pakistan* 68 F3
Mirond L., *Canada* 103 B8
Mirosławiec, *Poland* 30 E3
Mirpur, *Pakistan* 69 C5
Mirpur Batoro, *Pakistan* 68 G3
Mirpur Bibiwari, *Pakistan* 68 E2
Mirpur Khas, *Pakistan* 68 G3
Mirpur Sakro, *Pakistan* 68 G2
Mirria, *Niger* 83 C6
Mirsk, *Poland* 31 H2
Mirtağ, *Turkey* 70 B4
Miryang, *S. Korea* 57 G15
Mirzaani, *Georgia* 35 K8
Mirzapur, *India* 69 G10
Mirzapur-cum-Vindhyachal = Mirzapur, *India* 69 G10
Misantla, *Mexico* 119 D5
Misawa, *Japan* 54 D10
Miscou I., *Canada* 105 C7
Mish'āb, Ra's al, *Si. Arabia* 71 D6
Mishan, *China* 60 B8
Mishawaka, *U.S.A.* 114 E2
Mishbih, Gebel, *Egypt* 80 C3
Mishima, *Japan* 55 G9
Misión, *Mexico* 111 N10
Misiones □, *Argentina* 127 B5
Misiones □, *Paraguay* 126 B4
Miskah, *Si. Arabia* 70 E4
Miskitos, Cayos, *Nic.* 120 D3
Miskolc, *Hungary* 28 B5
Misoke, *Dem. Rep. of the Congo* 86 C2
Misool, *Indonesia* 63 E8
Mişrātah, *Libya* 79 B9
Missanabie, *Canada* 104 C3
Missinaibi →, *Canada* 104 B3
Missinaibi L., *Canada* 104 C3
Mission, *Canada* 102 D4
Mission, *S. Dak., U.S.A.* 112 D4
Mission, *Tex., U.S.A.* 113 M5
Mission Beach, *Australia* 94 B4
Mission Viejo, *U.S.A.* 111 M9
Missirah, *Senegal* 82 C1
Missisa L., *Canada* 104 B2
Missisicabi →, *Canada* 104 B4
Mississagi →, *Canada* 104 C3
Mississauga, *Canada* 116 C5
Mississippi □, *U.S.A.* 113 J10
Mississippi →, *U.S.A.* 113 L10
Mississippi L., *Canada* 117 A8
Mississippi River Delta, *U.S.A.* 113 L9
Mississippi Sd., *U.S.A.* 113 K10
Missoula, *U.S.A.* 108 C7
Missouri □, *U.S.A.* 112 F8
Missouri →, *U.S.A.* 112 F9
Missouri City, *U.S.A.* 113 L7
Missouri Valley, *U.S.A.* 112 E7
Mist, *U.S.A.* 110 E3
Mistassibi →, *Canada* 105 B5
Mistassini →, *Canada* 105 C5
Mistassini, L., *Canada* 104 B5
Mistastin L., *Canada* 105 A7
Mistelbach, *Austria* 27 C9
Misterbianco, *Italy* 43 E8
Mistinibi, L., *Canada* 105 A7
Mistissini, *Canada* 105 C5
Mistretta, *Italy* 43 E7
Misty L., *Canada* 103 B8
Misurata = Mişrātah, *Libya* 79 B9
Mît Ghamr, *Egypt* 80 H7
Mitatib, *Sudan* 81 D4
Mitchell, *Australia* 95 D4
Mitchell, *Canada* 116 C3
Mitchell, *Nebr., U.S.A.* 112 E3
Mitchell, *Oreg., U.S.A.* 108 D3
Mitchell, *S. Dak., U.S.A.* 112 D6
Mitchell →, *Australia* 94 B3
Mitchell, Mt., *U.S.A.* 115 H4
Mitchell and Alice Rivers △, *Australia* 94 B3
Mitchell Ranges, *Australia* 94 A2
Mitchelstown, *Ireland* 12 D3
Mitha Tiwana, *Pakistan* 68 C5
Mithi, *Pakistan* 68 G3
Míthimna, *Greece* 47 B8
Mithrao, *Pakistan* 68 F3
Mitilíni, *Greece* 47 B8
Mitilinoí, *Greece* 47 D8
Mito, *Japan* 55 F10
Mitrofanovka, *Russia* 33 H10
Mitrovica = Kosovska Mitrovica, *Serbia & M.* 44 D4
Mitsinjo, *Madag.* 89 B8
Mitsiwa, *Eritrea* 81 D4
Mitsiwa Channel, *Eritrea* 81 D5
Mitsukaidō, *Japan* 55 F9
Mittagong, *Australia* 95 E5
Mittelberg, *Austria* 26 D3
Mittelfranken □, *Germany* 25 F6
Mittellandkanal →, *Germany* 24 C4
Mittenwalde, *Germany* 24 C9
Mittersill, *Austria* 26 D5
Mitterteich, *Germany* 25 F8
Mittimatalik = Pond Inlet, *Canada* 101 A12
Mittweida, *Germany* 24 E8
Mitú, *Colombia* 124 C4
Mitumba, *Tanzania* 86 D3
Mitumba, Mts., *Dem. Rep. of the Congo* 86 D2
Mitwaba, *Dem. Rep. of the Congo* 87 D2
Mityana, *Uganda* 86 B3
Mixteco →, *Mexico* 119 D5
Miyagi □, *Japan* 54 E10
Miyāh, W. el →, *Egypt* 80 C3
Miyāh, W. el →, *Syria* 70 C3
Miyake-Jima, *Japan* 55 G9
Miyako, *Japan* 54 E10
Miyako-Jima, *Japan* 55 M2
Miyako-Rettō, *Japan* 55 M2
Miyakonojō, *Japan* 55 J5
Miyani, *India* 68 J3
Miyanoura-Dake, *Japan* 55 J5
Miyazaki, *Japan* 55 J5
Miyazaki □, *Japan* 55 H5
Miyazu, *Japan* 55 G7
Miyet, Bahr el = Dead Sea, *Asia* 74 D4
Miyi, *China* 58 D4
Miyoshi, *Japan* 55 G6
Miyun, *China* 56 D9
Miyun Shuiku, *China* 57 D9
Mizan Teferi, *Ethiopia* 81 F4
Mizdah, *Libya* 79 B8
Mizen Hd., *Cork, Ireland* 12 E2
Mizen Hd., *Wicklow, Ireland* 12 D5
Mizhhirya, *Ukraine* 29 B8
Mizhi, *China* 56 F6
Mizil, *Romania* 29 F11
Mizoram □, *India* 67 H18
Mizpe Ramon, *Israel* 74 E3
Mizuho, *Antarctica* 5 D5
Mizusawa, *Japan* 54 E10
Mjällby, *Sweden* 11 H8
Mjöbäck, *Sweden* 11 G6
Mjölby, *Sweden* 11 F9
Mjörn, *Sweden* 11 G6
Mjøsa, *Norway* 9 F14
Mkata, *Tanzania* 86 D4
Mkhaya ⌂, *Swaziland* 89 D5
Mkokotoni, *Tanzania* 86 D4
Mkomazi, *Tanzania* 86 C4
Mkomazi ⌂, *Tanzania* 86 C3
Mkomazi →, *S. Africa* 89 E5
Mkulwe, *Tanzania* 87 D3
Mkumbi, Ras, *Tanzania* 86 D4
Mkushi, *Zambia* 87 E2
Mkushi River, *Zambia* 87 E2
Mkuze, *S. Africa* 89 D5
Mkuze ⌂, *S. Africa* 89 D4
Mladá Boleslav, *Czech Rep.* 26 A7
Mladenovac, *Serbia & M.* 44 B4
Mlala Hills, *Tanzania* 86 D3
Mlange = Mulanje, *Malawi* 87 F4
Mlanje, Pic, *Malawi* 85 H7
Mlava →, *Serbia & M.* 44 B5
Mława, *Poland* 31 E7
Mlawula ⌂, *Swaziland* 89 D5
Mliniště, *Bos.-H.* 41 D13
Mljet, *Croatia* 41 F14
Mljet △, *Croatia* 41 F14
Mljetski Kanal, *Croatia* 41 F14
Młynary, *Poland* 30 D6
Mmabatho, *S. Africa* 88 D4
Mme, *Cameroon* 83 D7
Mnichovo Hradiště, *Czech Rep.* 26 A7
Mo i Rana, *Norway* 8 C16
Moa, *Cuba* 121 B4
Moa, *Indonesia* 63 F7
Moa →, *S. Leone* 82 D2
Moab, *U.S.A.* 109 G9
Moala, *Fiji* 91 D8
Moama, *Australia* 95 F3
Moamba, *Mozam.* 89 D5
Moapa, *U.S.A.* 111 J12
Moate, *Ireland* 12 C4
Moba, *Dem. Rep. of the Congo* 86 D2
Mobārakābād, *Iran* 71 D7
Mobaye, *C.A.R.* 84 D4
Mobayi, *Dem. Rep. of the Congo* 84 D4
Moberley Lake, *Canada* 102 B4
Moberly, *U.S.A.* 112 F8
Mobile, *U.S.A.* 115 K1
Mobile B., *U.S.A.* 115 K2
Mobridge, *U.S.A.* 112 C4
Moc Chau, *Vietnam* 64 B5
Moc Hoa, *Vietnam* 65 G5
Mocabe Kasari, *Dem. Rep. of the Congo* 87 D2
Moçambique, *Mozam.* 87 F5
Mocanaqua, *U.S.A.* 117 E8
Mochima △, *Venezuela* 121 D7
Mochudi, *Botswana* 88 C4
Mocimboa da Praia, *Mozam.* 87 E5
Mociu, *Romania* 29 D9
Möckeln, *Sweden* 11 H8
Mockfjärd, *Sweden* 10 D8
Moclips, *U.S.A.* 110 C2
Mocoa, *Colombia* 124 C3
Mococa, *Brazil* 127 A6
Mocorito, *Mexico* 118 B3
Moctezuma, *Mexico* 118 B3
Moctezuma →, *Mexico* 119 C5
Mocuba, *Mozam.* 87 F4
Mocúzari, Presa, *Mexico* 118 B3
Modane, *France* 21 C10
Modasa, *India* 68 H5
Modder →, *S. Africa* 88 D3
Modderrivier, *S. Africa* 88 D3
Módena, *Italy* 40 D7
Modena, *U.S.A.* 109 H7
Modesto, *U.S.A.* 110 H6
Módica, *Italy* 43 F7
Modimolle, *S. Africa* 89 C4
Mödling, *Austria* 27 C9
Modo, *Sudan* 81 F3
Modra, *Slovak Rep.* 27 C10
Modriča, *Bos.-H.* 28 F3
Moe, *Australia* 95 F4
Moebase, *Mozam.* 87 F4
Moëlan-sur-Mer, *France* 18 E3
Moengo, *Suriname* 125 B8
Moffat, *U.K.* 13 F5
Moga, *India* 68 D6
Mogadishu = Muqdisho, *Somali Rep.* 75 G4
Mogador = Essaouira, *Morocco* 78 B4
Mogadouro, *Portugal* 36 D4
Mogalakwena →, *S. Africa* 89 C4
Mogami-Gawa →, *Japan* 54 E10
Mogán, *Canary Is.* 48 G4
Mogaung, *Burma* 67 G20
Mogente = Moixent, *Spain* 39 G4
Mogho, *Ethiopia* 81 G5
Mogi das Cruzes, *Brazil* 127 A6
Mogi-Guaçu →, *Brazil* 127 A6
Mogi-Mirim, *Brazil* 127 A6
Mogielnica, *Poland* 31 G7
Mogige, *Ethiopia* 81 F4
Mogilev = Mahilyow, *Belarus* 32 F6
Mogilev-Podolskiy = Mohyliv-Podilskyy, *Ukraine* 29 B12
Mogilno, *Poland* 31 F4
Mogincual, *Mozam.* 87 F5
Mogliano Véneto, *Italy* 41 C9
Mogocha, *Russia* 53 D12
Mogok, *Burma* 67 H20
Mogollon Rim, *U.S.A.* 109 J8
Mógoro, *Italy* 42 C1
Mograt, *Sudan* 80 D3
Moguer, *Spain* 37 H4
Mogumber, *Australia* 93 F2
Mohács, *Hungary* 28 E3
Mohales Hoek, *Lesotho* 88 E4
Mohall, *U.S.A.* 112 A4
Moḩammadābād, *Iran* 71 B8
Mohammedia, *Morocco* 78 B4
Mohana →, *India* 69 G11
Mohanlalganj, *India* 69 F9
Mohave, L., *U.S.A.* 111 K12
Mohawk →, *U.S.A.* 117 D11
Moheda, *Sweden* 11 G8
Mohenjodaro, *Pakistan* 68 F3
Moher, Cliffs of, *Ireland* 12 D2
Mohicanville Reservoir, *U.S.A.* 116 F3
Möhne →, *Germany* 24 D3
Mohoro, *Tanzania* 86 D4
Mohyliv-Podilskyy, *Ukraine* 29 B12
Moia, *Sudan* 81 F2
Moidart, L., *U.K.* 13 E3
Moineşti, *Romania* 29 D11
Moira →, *Canada* 116 B7
Moirans, *France* 21 C9
Moirans-en-Montagne, *France* 19 F12
Moíres, *Greece* 49 D6
Moisaküla, *Estonia* 9 G21
Moisie, *Canada* 105 B6
Moisie →, *Canada* 105 B6
Moissac, *France* 20 D5
Moita, *Portugal* 37 G2
Moixent, *Spain* 39 G4
Mōja, *Sweden* 10 E12
Mojácar, *Spain* 39 H3
Mojados, *Spain* 36 D6
Mojave, *U.S.A.* 111 K8
Mojave ⌂, *U.S.A.* 111 K11
Mojave Desert, *U.S.A.* 111 L10
Mojiang, *China* 58 F3
Mojjo →, *Ethiopia* 81 F5
Mojkovac, *Serbia & M.* 44 D3
Mojo, *Bolivia* 126 A2
Mojo, *Ethiopia* 81 F4
Mojokerto, *Indonesia* 63 G15
Mokai, *N.Z.* 91 H5
Mokambo, *Dem. Rep. of the Congo* 87 E2
Mokameh, *India* 69 G11
Mokau, *N.Z.* 91 H5
Mokelumne →, *U.S.A.* 110 G5
Mokelumne Hill, *U.S.A.* 110 G6
Mokhós, *Greece* 49 D7
Mokhotlong, *Lesotho* 89 D4
Möklinta, *Sweden* 10 D10
Mokokchung, *India* 67 F19
Mokolo, *Cameroon* 83 C7
Mokolo →, *S. Africa* 89 C4
Mokopane, *S. Africa* 89 C4
Mokp'o, *S. Korea* 57 G14
Mokra Gora, *Serbia & M.* 44 D4
Mokronog, *Slovenia* 41 C12
Moksha →, *Russia* 34 C6
Mokshan, *Russia* 34 D7
Mokwa, *Nigeria* 83 D6
Mol, *Belgium* 17 C5
Mola di Bari, *Italy* 43 A10
Molale, *Ethiopia* 81 E4
Moláoi, *Greece* 46 E4
Molara, *Italy* 42 B2
Molat, *Croatia* 41 D11
Molchanovo, *Russia* 52 D9
Mold, *U.K.* 14 D4
Moldava nad Bodvou, *Slovak Rep.* 27 C14
Moldavia = Moldova ■, *Europe* 29 C13
Moldavia, *Romania* 29 D12
Molde, *Norway* 8 E12
Moldova ■, *Europe* 29 C13
Moldova Nouă, *Romania* 28 F6
Moldoveanu, Vf., *Romania* 29 E9
Moldoviţa, *Romania* 29 C10
Mole △, *Ghana* 83 D4
Mole →, *U.K.* 15 F7
Mole Creek, *Australia* 95 G4
Molepolole, *Botswana* 88 C4
Molfetta, *Italy* 43 A9
Molina de Aragón, *Spain* 38 E3
Molina de Segura, *Spain* 39 G3
Moline, *U.S.A.* 112 E9
Molinella, *Italy* 41 D8
Molinos, *Argentina* 126 B2
Moliro, *Dem. Rep. of the Congo* 86 D3
Moliterno, *Italy* 43 B8
Molkom, *Sweden* 10 E7
Mölle, *Sweden* 11 H6
Molledo, *Spain* 36 B6
Mollendo, *Peru* 124 G4
Mollerin, L., *Australia* 93 F2
Mollerussa, *Spain* 38 D5
Mollina, *Spain* 37 H6
Mölln, *Germany* 24 B6
Mölltorp, *Sweden* 11 F8
Mölnlycke, *Sweden* 11 G6
Molochansk, *Ukraine* 33 J8
Molochnoye, Ozero, *Ukraine* 33 J8
Molodechno = Maladzyechna, *Belarus* 32 E4
Molodove, *Ukraine* 29 D14
Molokai, *U.S.A.* 106 H16
Molong, *Australia* 95 E4
Molopo →, *Africa* 88 D3
Mólos, *Greece* 46 C4
Molsheim, *France* 19 D14
Molson L., *Canada* 103 C9
Molteno, *S. Africa* 88 E4
Molu, *Indonesia* 63 F8
Molucca Sea, *Indonesia* 63 E6
Moluccas = Maluku, *Indonesia* 63 E7
Moma, *Dem. Rep. of the Congo* 86 C1
Moma, *Mozam.* 87 F4
Mombasa, *Kenya* 86 C4
Mombetsu, *Japan* 54 B11
Mombuey, *Spain* 36 C4
Momchilgrad, *Bulgaria* 45 E9
Momi, *Dem. Rep. of the Congo* 86 C2
Mompós, *Colombia* 124 B4
Møn, *Denmark* 11 K6
Mon □, *Burma* 67 L20
Mona, Canal de la = Mona Passage, *W. Indies* 121 C6
Mona, Isla, *Puerto Rico* 121 C6
Mona, Pta., *Costa Rica* 120 E3
Mona Passage, *W. Indies* 121 C6
Monaca, *U.S.A.* 116 F4
Monaco ■, *Europe* 21 E11
Monadhliath Mts., *U.K.* 13 D4
Monadnock, Mt., *U.S.A.* 117 D12
Monaghan, *Ireland* 12 B5
Monaghan □, *Ireland* 12 B5
Monahans, *U.S.A.* 113 K3
Monapo, *Mozam.* 87 E5
Monar, L., *U.K.* 13 D3
Monarch Mt., *Canada* 102 C3
Monashee Mts., *Canada* 102 C5
Monasterevin, *Ireland* 12 C4
Monastir = Bitola, *Macedonia* 44 E5
Moncada, *Phil.* 61 D4
Moncalieri, *Italy* 40 D4
Moncalvo, *Italy* 40 C5
Monção, *Portugal* 36 C2
Moncarapacho, *Portugal* 37 H3
Moncayo, Sierra del, *Spain* 38 D3
Mönchengladbach, *Germany* 24 D2
Monchique, *Portugal* 37 H2
Moncks Corner, *U.S.A.* 115 J5
Monclova, *Mexico* 118 B4
Moncontour, *France* 18 D4
Moncton, *Canada* 105 C7
Mondariz, *Spain* 36 C2
Mondego →, *Portugal* 36 E2
Mondego, C., *Portugal* 36 E2
Mondeodo, *Indonesia* 63 E6
Mondeville, *France* 18 C6
Mondolfo, *Italy* 41 E10
Mondoñedo, *Spain* 36 B3
Mondovì, *Italy* 40 D4
Mondragon, *Phil.* 61 E6

Mondragone, *Italy* 42 A6
Mondrain I., *Australia* 93 F3
Moneague, *Jamaica* 120 a
Monemvasía, *Greece* 46 E5
Monessen, *U.S.A.* 116 F5
Monesterio, *Spain* 37 G4
Monestier-de-Clermont, *France* 21 D9
Monett, *U.S.A.* 113 G8
Moneymore, *U.K.* 12 B5
Monfalcone, *Italy* 41 C10
Monflanquin, *France* 20 D4
Monforte, *Portugal* 37 F3
Monforte de Lemos, *Spain* 36 C3
Mong Cai, *Vietnam* 64 B6
Mong Hsu, *Burma* 58 G2
Mong Kung, *Burma* 67 J20
Mong Nai, *Burma* 67 J20
Mong Pawk, *Burma* 67 H21
Mong Ping, *Burma* 58 G2
Mong Ton, *Burma* 67 J21
Mong Wa, *Burma* 67 J22
Mong Yai, *Burma* 67 H21
Mongalla, *Sudan* 81 F3
Mongers, L., *Australia* 93 E2
Monghyr = Munger, *India* 69 G12
Mongibello = Etna, *Italy* 43 E7
Mongo, *Chad* 79 F9
Mongo →, *S. Leone* 82 D2
Mongolia ■, *Asia* 53 E10
Mongolia, Plateau of, *Asia* 50 E14
Mongonu, *Nigeria* 83 C7
Mongu, *Zambia* 85 H4
Môngua, *Angola* 88 B2
Monifieth, *U.K.* 13 E6
Monistrol-sur-Loire, *France* 21 C8
Monkey Bay, *Malawi* 87 E4
Monkey Mia, *Australia* 93 E1
Monkey River Town, *Belize* 119 D7
Mońki, *Poland* 30 E9
Monkoto, *Dem. Rep. of the Congo* 84 E4
Monkton, *Canada* 116 C3
Monmouth, *U.K.* 15 F5
Monmouth, *Ill., U.S.A.* 112 E9
Monmouth, *Oreg., U.S.A.* 108 D2
Monmouthshire □, *U.K.* 15 F5
Mono L., *U.S.A.* 110 H7
Monolith, *U.S.A.* 111 K8
Monólithos, *Greece* 49 C9
Monongahela, *U.S.A.* 116 F5
Monópoli, *Italy* 43 B10
Monor, *Hungary* 28 C4
Monos I., *Trin. & Tob.* 125 K15
Monóvar, *Spain* 39 G4
Monreal del Campo, *Spain* 38 E3
Monreale, *Italy* 42 D6
Monroe, *Ga., U.S.A.* 115 J4
Monroe, *La., U.S.A.* 113 J8
Monroe, *Mich., U.S.A.* 114 E4
Monroe, *N.C., U.S.A.* 115 H5
Monroe, *N.Y., U.S.A.* 117 E10
Monroe, *Utah, U.S.A.* 109 G7
Monroe, *Wash., U.S.A.* 110 C5
Monroe, *Wis., U.S.A.* 112 D10
Monroe City, *U.S.A.* 112 F9
Monroeton, *U.S.A.* 117 E8
Monroeville, *Ala., U.S.A.* 115 K2
Monroeville, *Pa., U.S.A.* 116 F5
Monrovia, *Liberia* 82 D2
Mons, *Belgium* 17 D3
Møns Klint, *Denmark* 11 K6
Monsaraz, *Portugal* 37 G3
Monse, *Indonesia* 63 E6
Monségur, *France* 20 D4
Monsélice, *Italy* 41 C8
Mönsterås, *Sweden* 11 G10
Mont Cenis, Col du, *France* 21 C10
Mont-de-Marsan, *France* 20 E3
Mont-Joli, *Canada* 105 C6
Mont-Laurier, *Canada* 104 C4
Mont-Louis, *Canada* 105 C6
Mont Peko △, *Ivory C.* 82 D3
Mont-roig del Camp, *Spain* 38 D5
Mont-St-Michel, Le, *France* 18 D5
Mont Sangbe △, *Ivory C.* 82 D3
Mont-Tremblant ⌓, *Canada* 104 C5
Montabaur, *Germany* 24 E3
Montagnac, *France* 20 E7
Montagnana, *Italy* 41 C8
Montagne d'Ambre △, *Madag.* 89 A8
Montagne de Reims ⌓, *France* 19 C11
Montagu, *S. Africa* 88 E3
Montagu I., *Antarctica* 5 B1
Montague, *Canada* 105 C7
Montague, I., *Mexico* 118 A2
Montague Ra., *Australia* 93 E2
Montague Sd., *Australia* 92 B4
Montaigu, *France* 18 F5
Montalbán, *Spain* 38 E4
Montalbano Iónico, *Italy* 43 B9
Montalbo, *Spain* 38 F2
Montalcino, *Italy* 41 E8
Montalegre, *Portugal* 36 D3
Montalto, *Italy* 43 D8
Montalto di Castro, *Italy* 41 F8
Montalto Uffugo, *Italy* 43 C9
Montalvo, *U.S.A.* 111 L7
Montamarta, *Spain* 36 D5
Montana, *Bulgaria* 44 C7
Montaña, *Peru* 124 E4
Montana □, *Bulgaria* 44 C7
Montana □, *U.S.A.* 108 C9
Montaña Clara, I., *Canary Is.* 48 E6
Montañas de Malaga ⌓, *Spain* 37 J6
Montánchez, *Spain* 37 F4
Montargil, *Portugal* 37 F2
Montargis, *France* 19 E9
Montauban, *France* 20 D5
Montauk, *U.S.A.* 117 E13
Montauk Pt., *U.S.A.* 117 E13
Montbard, *France* 19 E11
Montbarrey, *France* 19 E12
Montbéliard, *France* 19 E13
Montblanc, *Spain* 38 D6
Montbrison, *France* 21 C8
Montcalm, Pic de, *France* 20 F5
Montceau-les-Mines, *France* 19 F11
Montcenis, *France* 21 B8
Montclair, *U.S.A.* 117 F10
Montcornet, *France* 19 C11
Montcuq, *France* 20 D5
Montdidier, *France* 19 C9
Monte Albán, *Mexico* 119 D5
Monte Alegre, *Brazil* 125 D8
Monte Azul, *Brazil* 125 G10
Monte-Carlo, *Monaco* 21 E11
Monte Caseros, *Argentina* 126 C4
Monte Comán, *Argentina* 126 C2
Monte Cristi, *Dom. Rep.* 121 C5
Monte Cucco ⌓, *Italy* 41 E9
Monte Lindo →, *Paraguay* 126 A4
Monte Patria, *Chile* 126 C1
Monte Quemado, *Argentina* 126 B3
Monte Redondo, *Portugal* 36 F2
Monte Rio, *U.S.A.* 110 G4
Monte San Giovanni Campano, *Italy* 42 A6
Monte San Savino, *Italy* 41 E8
Monte Sant' Ángelo, *Italy* 41 G12
Monte Santu, C. di, *Italy* 42 B2
Monte Sibillini △, *Italy* 41 F10
Monte Subasio ⌓, *Italy* 41 E9
Monte Vista, *U.S.A.* 109 H10
Monteagudo, *Argentina* 127 B5
Montealegre del Castillo, *Spain* 39 G3
Montebello, *Canada* 104 C5
Montebello Iónico, *Italy* 43 E8
Montebello Is., *Australia* 92 D2
Montebelluna, *Italy* 41 C9
Montebourg, *France* 18 C5
Montecastrilli, *Italy* 41 F9
Montecatini Terme, *Italy* 40 E7
Montecito, *U.S.A.* 111 L7
Montecristo, *Italy* 40 F7
Montefalco, *Italy* 41 F9
Montefiascone, *Italy* 41 F9
Montefrío, *Spain* 37 H7
Montegiórgio, *Italy* 41 E10
Montego Bay, *Jamaica* 120 a
Montehermoso, *Spain* 36 E4
Montejicar, *Spain* 37 H7
Montélimar, *France* 21 D8
Montella, *Italy* 43 B8
Montellano, *Spain* 37 J5
Montello, *U.S.A.* 112 D10
Montemor-o-Novo, *Portugal* 37 G2
Montemor-o-Velho, *Portugal* 36 E2
Montemorelos, *Mexico* 119 B5
Montendre, *France* 20 C3
Montenegro, *Brazil* 127 B5
Montenegro □, *Serbia & M.* 44 D3
Montenero di Bisáccia, *Italy* 41 G11
Montepuez, *Mozam.* 87 E4
Montepuez →, *Mozam.* 87 E5
Montepulciano, *Italy* 41 E8
Montereale, *Italy* 41 F10
Montereau-Faut-Yonne, *France* 19 D9
Monterey, *U.S.A.* 110 J5
Monterey B., *U.S.A.* 110 J5
Montería, *Colombia* 124 B3
Monteros, *Argentina* 126 B2
Monterotondo, *Italy* 41 F9
Monterrey, *Mexico* 118 B4
Montes Azules ⌓, *Mexico* 119 D6
Montes Claros, *Brazil* 125 G10
Montesano, *U.S.A.* 110 D3
Montesano sulla Marcellana, *Italy* 43 B8
Montesárchio, *Italy* 43 A7
Montescaglioso, *Italy* 43 B9
Montesilvano, *Italy* 41 F11
Montesinho ⌓, *Portugal* 36 D4
Montevarchi, *Italy* 41 E8
Montevideo, *Uruguay* 127 C4
Montevideo, *U.S.A.* 112 C7
Montezuma, *U.S.A.* 112 E8
Montezuma Castle ⌓, *U.S.A.* 109 J8
Montfaucon, *France* 18 E5
Montfaucon-d'Argonne, *France* 19 C12
Montfaucon-en-Velay, *France* 21 C8
Montfort-le-Gesnois, *France* 18 D7
Montfort-sur-Meu, *France* 18 D5
Montfragüe ⌓, *Spain* 36 F5
Montgenèvre, *France* 21 D10
Montgomery, *U.K.* 15 E4
Montgomery, *Ala., U.S.A.* 115 J2
Montgomery, *Pa., U.S.A.* 116 E8
Montgomery, *W. Va., U.S.A.* 114 F5
Montgomery City, *U.S.A.* 112 F9
Montguyon, *France* 20 C3
Monthermé, *France* 19 C11
Monthey, *Switz.* 25 J2
Monthois, *France* 19 C11
Monti, *Italy* 42 B2
Monti Lucrétili ⌓, *Italy* 41 F9
Monti Picentini ⌓, *Italy* 43 B8
Monti Simbruini ⌓, *Italy* 41 G10
Monticelli d'Ongina, *Italy* 40 C6
Monticello, *Ark., U.S.A.* 113 J9
Monticello, *Fla., U.S.A.* 115 K4
Monticello, *Ind., U.S.A.* 114 E2
Monticello, *Iowa, U.S.A.* 112 D9
Monticello, *Ky., U.S.A.* 115 G3
Monticello, *Minn., U.S.A.* 112 C8
Monticello, *Miss., U.S.A.* 113 K9
Monticello, *N.Y., U.S.A.* 117 E10
Monticello, *Utah, U.S.A.* 109 H9
Montichiari, *Italy* 40 C7
Montier-en-Der, *France* 19 D11
Montignac, *France* 20 C5
Montigny-les-Metz, *France* 19 C13
Montigny-sur-Aube, *France* 19 E11
Montijo, *Portugal* 37 G2
Montijo, *Spain* 37 G4
Montilla, *Spain* 37 H6
Montivilliers, *France* 18 C7
Montluçon, *France* 19 F9
Montmagny, *Canada* 105 C5
Montmarault, *France* 19 F9
Montmartre, *Canada* 103 C8
Montmédy, *France* 19 C12
Montmélian, *France* 21 C10
Montmirail, *France* 19 D10
Montmoreau-St-Cybard, *France* 20 C4
Montmorillon, *France* 20 B4
Montmort-Lucy, *France* 19 D10
Monto, *Australia* 94 C5
Montoire-sur-le-Loir, *France* 18 E7
Montongbuwoh, *Indonesia* 63 K19
Montório al Vomano, *Italy* 41 F10
Montoro, *Spain* 37 G6
Montour Falls, *U.S.A.* 116 D8
Montoursville, *U.S.A.* 116 E8
Montpelier, *Idaho, U.S.A.* 108 E8
Montpelier, *Vt., U.S.A.* 117 B12
Montpellier, *France* 20 E7
Montpezat-de-Quercy, *France* 20 D5
Montpon-Ménestérol, *France* 20 D4
Montréal, *Canada* 117 A11
Montréal, *Aude, France* 20 E6
Montréal, *Gers, France* 20 E4
Montreal →, *Canada* 104 C3
Montreal L., *Canada* 103 C7
Montreal Lake, *Canada* 103 C7
Montredon-Labessonnié, *France* 20 E6
Montrésor, *France* 18 E8
Montret, *France* 19 F12
Montreuil, *Pas-de-Calais, France* 19 B8
Montreuil, *Seine-St-Denis, France* 19 D9
Montreuil-Bellay, *France* 18 E6
Montreux, *Switz.* 25 J2
Montrevel-en-Bresse, *France* 19 F12
Montrichard, *France* 18 E8
Montrose, *U.K.* 13 E6
Montrose, *Colo., U.S.A.* 109 G10
Montrose, *Pa., U.S.A.* 117 E9
Monts, Pte. des, *Canada* 105 C6
Montsalvy, *France* 20 D6
Montsant, Serra de, *Spain* 38 D6
Montsauche-les-Settons, *France* 19 E11
Montsec, Serra del, *Spain* 38 C5
Montseny ⌓, *Spain* 38 D2
Montserrat, *Spain* 38 D6
Montserrat ☒, *W. Indies* 121 C7
Montuenga, *Spain* 36 D6
Montuiri, *Spain* 48 B9
Monywa, *Burma* 67 H19
Monza, *Italy* 40 C6
Monze, *Zambia* 87 F2
Monze, C., *Pakistan* 68 G2
Monzón, *Spain* 38 D5
Mooers, *U.S.A.* 117 B11
Mooi →, *S. Africa* 89 D5
Mooi River, *S. Africa* 89 D4
Moonah →, *Australia* 94 C2
Moonda, L., *Australia* 94 D3
Moonie, *Australia* 95 D5
Moonie →, *Australia* 95 D4
Moonta, *Australia* 95 E2
Moora, *Australia* 93 F2
Moorcroft, *U.S.A.* 112 C2
Moore →, *Australia* 93 F2
Moore, L., *Australia* 93 E2
Moore Park, *Australia* 94 C5
Moore River △, *Australia* 93 F2
Moorefield, *U.S.A.* 114 F6
Moores Res., *U.S.A.* 117 B13
Moorfoot Hills, *U.K.* 13 F5
Moorhead, *U.S.A.* 112 B6
Moormerland, *Germany* 24 B3
Moorpark, *U.S.A.* 111 L8
Moorreesburg, *S. Africa* 88 E2
Moorrinya △, *Australia* 94 C3
Moosburg, *Germany* 25 G7
Moose →, *Canada* 104 B3
Moose →, *U.S.A.* 117 C9
Moose Creek, *Canada* 117 A10
Moose Factory, *Canada* 104 B3
Moose Jaw, *Canada* 103 C7
Moose Jaw →, *Canada* 103 C7
Moose Lake, *U.S.A.* 112 B8
Moose Mountain ⌓, *Canada* 103 D8
Moosehead L., *U.S.A.* 115 C11
Mooselookmeguntic L., *U.S.A.* 115 C10
Moosilauke, Mt., *U.S.A.* 117 B13
Moosomin, *Canada* 103 C8
Moosonee, *Canada* 104 B3
Moosup, *U.S.A.* 117 E13
Mopane, *S. Africa* 89 C4
Mopeia Velha, *Mozam.* 87 F4
Mopipi, *Botswana* 88 C3
Mopoi, *C.A.R.* 86 A2
Mopti, *Mali* 82 C4
Moqatta, *Sudan* 81 E4
Moqor, *Afghan.* 68 C2
Moquegua, *Peru* 124 G4
Mór, *Hungary* 28 C3
Mora, *Cameroon* 83 C7
Móra, *Portugal* 37 G2
Mora, *Spain* 37 F7
Mora, *Sweden* 10 C8
Mora, *Minn., U.S.A.* 112 C8
Mora, *N. Mex., U.S.A.* 109 J11
Mora →, *U.S.A.* 113 H2
Mora de Rubielos, *Spain* 38 E4
Móra d'Ebre, *Spain* 38 D5
Móra la Nova, *Spain* 38 D5
Morača →, *Serbia & M.* 44 D3
Moradabad, *India* 69 E8
Morafenobe, *Madag.* 89 B7
Morąg, *Poland* 30 E6
Moral de Calatrava, *Spain* 37 G7
Moraleja, *Spain* 36 E4
Moramanga, *Madag.* 89 B8
Moran, *Kans., U.S.A.* 113 G7
Moran, *Wyo., U.S.A.* 108 E8
Moranbah, *Australia* 94 C4
Morano Cálabro, *Italy* 43 C9
Morant Bay, *Jamaica* 120 a
Morant Cays, *Jamaica* 120 C4
Morant Pt., *Jamaica* 120 a
Morar, *India* 68 F8
Morar, L., *U.K.* 13 E3
Moratalla, *Spain* 39 G3
Moratuwa, *Sri Lanka* 66 R11
Morava →, *Slovak Rep.* 27 C9
Moravia, *U.S.A.* 117 D8
Moravian Hts. = Českomoravská Vrchovina, *Czech Rep.* 26 B8
Moravica →, *Serbia & M.* 44 C4
Moravița, *Romania* 28 E6
Moravská Třebová, *Czech Rep.* 27 B9
Moravské Budějovice, *Czech Rep.* 26 B8
Morawa, *Australia* 93 E2
Morawhanna, *Guyana* 124 B7
Moray □, *U.K.* 13 D5
Moray Firth, *U.K.* 13 D5
Morbach, *Germany* 25 F3
Morbegno, *Italy* 40 B6
Morbi, *India* 68 H4
Morbihan □, *France* 18 E4
Mörbylånga, *Sweden* 11 H10
Morcenx, *France* 20 D3
Morcone, *Italy* 43 A7
Mordelles, *France* 18 D5
Morden, *Canada* 103 D9
Mordoğan, *Turkey* 47 C8
Mordovian Republic = Mordvinia □, *Russia* 34 C7
Mordovo, *Russia* 34 D5
Mordvinia □, *Russia* 34 C7
Mordy, *Poland* 31 F9
Morea, *Greece* 6 H10
Moreau →, *U.S.A.* 112 C4
Morecambe, *U.K.* 14 C5
Morecambe B., *U.K.* 14 C5
Moree, *Australia* 95 D4
Morehead, *U.S.A.* 114 F4
Morehead City, *U.S.A.* 115 H7
Morel →, *India* 68 F7
Morelia, *Mexico* 118 D4
Morella, *Australia* 94 C3
Morella, *Spain* 38 E4
Morelos, *Mexico* 118 B3
Morelos □, *Mexico* 119 D5
Moremi ⌓, *Botswana* 88 B3
Morena, *India* 68 F8
Morena, Sierra, *Spain* 37 G7
Moreni, *Romania* 29 F10
Moreno Valley, *U.S.A.* 111 M10
Moresby I., *Canada* 102 C2
Morestel, *France* 21 C9
Moreton I., *Australia* 95 D5
Moreton Island △, *Australia* 95 D5
Moreuil, *France* 19 C9
Morey, *Spain* 48 B10
Morez, *France* 19 F13
Morgan, *U.S.A.* 108 F8
Morgan City, *U.S.A.* 113 L9
Morgan Hill, *U.S.A.* 110 H5
Morganfield, *U.S.A.* 114 G2
Morganton, *U.S.A.* 115 H5
Morgantown, *U.S.A.* 114 F6
Morgenzon, *S. Africa* 89 D4
Morges, *Switz.* 25 J2
Morghak, *Iran* 71 D8
Morgongåva, *Sweden* 10 E10
Morhange, *France* 19 D13
Morhar →, *India* 69 G11
Mori, *Italy* 40 C7
Mori, *Japan* 54 C10
Moriarty, *U.S.A.* 109 J10
Moribaya, *Guinea* 82 D3
Morice L., *Canada* 102 C3
Moriki, *Nigeria* 83 C6
Morinville, *Canada* 102 C6
Morioka, *Japan* 54 E10
Moris, *Mexico* 118 B3
Morlaàs, *France* 20 E3
Morlaix, *France* 18 D3
Mörlunda, *Sweden* 11 G9
Mormanno, *Italy* 43 C8
Mormant, *France* 19 D9
Mornington, *Australia* 95 F4
Mornington, I., *Chile* 128 F1
Mornington I., *Australia* 94 B2
Mórnos →, *Greece* 46 C3
Moro, *Pakistan* 68 F2
Moro, *Sudan* 81 E3
Moro →, *Pakistan* 68 E2
Moro G., *Phil.* 61 H5
Morocco ■, *N. Afr.* 78 B4
Morogoro, *Tanzania* 86 D4
Morogoro □, *Tanzania* 86 D4
Moroleón, *Mexico* 118 C4
Morombe, *Madag.* 89 C7
Moron, *Argentina* 126 C4
Morón, *Cuba* 120 B4
Morón de Almazán, *Spain* 38 D2
Morón de la Frontera, *Spain* 37 H5
Morona →, *Peru* 124 D3
Morondava, *Madag.* 89 C7
Morondo, *Ivory C.* 82 D3
Morongo Valley, *U.S.A.* 111 L10
Moroni, *Comoros Is.* 77 H8
Moroni, *U.S.A.* 108 G8
Moronou, *Ivory C.* 82 D4
Morotai, *Indonesia* 63 D7
Moroto, *Uganda* 86 B3
Moroto, Mt., *Uganda* 86 B3
Morozov, *Bulgaria* 45 D9
Morozovsk, *Russia* 35 F5
Morpeth, *U.K.* 14 B6
Morphou, *Cyprus* 49 D11
Morphou Bay, *Cyprus* 49 D11
Morrilton, *U.S.A.* 113 H8
Morrinhos, *Brazil* 125 G9
Morrinsville, *N.Z.* 91 G5
Morris, *Canada* 103 D9
Morris, *Ill., U.S.A.* 112 E10
Morris, *Minn., U.S.A.* 112 C7
Morris, *N.Y., U.S.A.* 117 D9
Morris, *Pa., U.S.A.* 116 E7
Morris, Mt., *Australia* 93 E5
Morris Jesup, Kap, *Greenland* 4 A5
Morrisburg, *Canada* 117 B9
Morristown, *Ariz., U.S.A.* 109 K7
Morristown, *N.J., U.S.A.* 117 F10
Morristown, *N.Y., U.S.A.* 117 B9
Morristown, *Tenn., U.S.A.* 115 G4
Morrisville, *N.Y., U.S.A.* 117 D9
Morrisville, *Pa., U.S.A.* 117 F10
Morrisville, *Vt., U.S.A.* 117 B12
Morro, Pta., *Chile* 126 B1
Morro Bay, *U.S.A.* 110 K6
Morro del Jable, *Canary Is.* 48 F5
Morro Jable, Pta. de, *Canary Is.* 48 F5
Morrocoy △, *Venezuela* 121 D6
Morrosquillo, G. de, *Colombia* 120 E4
Mörrum, *Sweden* 11 H8
Morrumbene, *Mozam.* 89 C6
Mörrumsån →, *Sweden* 11 H8
Mors, *Denmark* 11 H2
Morshansk, *Russia* 34 D5
Mörsil, *Sweden* 10 A7
Mortagne →, *France* 19 D13
Mortagne-au-Perche, *France* 18 D7
Mortagne-sur-Gironde, *France* 20 C3
Mortagne-sur-Sèvre, *France* 18 F6
Mortain, *France* 18 D6
Mortara, *Italy* 40 C5
Morteau, *France* 19 E13
Morteros, *Argentina* 126 C3
Mortlach, *Canada* 103 C7
Mortlake, *Australia* 95 F3
Morton, *Tex., U.S.A.* 113 J3
Morton, *Wash., U.S.A.* 110 D4
Moruga, *Trin. & Tob.* 125 K15
Morundah, *Australia* 95 E4
Moruya, *Australia* 95 F5
Morvan, *France* 19 E11
Morvan ⌓, *France* 19 E11
Morven, *Australia* 95 D4
Morvern, *U.K.* 13 E3
Morwell, *Australia* 95 F4
Moryń, *Poland* 31 F1
Morzine, *France* 19 F13
Mosalsk, *Russia* 32 E8
Mosbach, *Germany* 25 F5
Mošćenice, *Croatia* 41 C11
Mosciano Sant' Ángelo, *Italy* 41 F10
Moscos Is., *Burma* 64 E1
Moscow = Moskva, *Russia* 32 E9
Moscow, *Idaho, U.S.A.* 108 C5
Moscow, *Pa., U.S.A.* 117 E9
Mosel →, *Europe* 19 B14
Moselle = Mosel →, *Europe* 19 B14
Moselle □, *France* 19 D13
Moses Lake, *U.S.A.* 108 C4
Mosgiel, *N.Z.* 91 L3
Moshaweng →, *S. Africa* 88 D3
Moshi, *Tanzania* 86 C4
Moshupa, *Botswana* 88 C4
Mosina, *Poland* 31 F3
Mosjøen, *Norway* 8 D15
Moskenesøya, *Norway* 8 C15
Moskenstraumen, *Norway* 8 C15
Moskva, *Russia* 32 E9
Moskva →, *Russia* 32 E10
Moslavačka Gora, *Croatia* 41 C13
Mosomane, *Botswana* 88 C4
Mosonmagyaróvár, *Hungary* 28 C2
Mošorin, *Serbia & M.* 28 E5
Mospino, *Ukraine* 33 J9
Mosquera, *Colombia* 124 C3
Mosquero, *U.S.A.* 113 H3
Mosqueruela, *Spain* 38 E4
Mosquitia, *Honduras* 120 C3
Mosquito Coast = Mosquitia, *Honduras* 120 C3
Mosquito Creek L., *U.S.A.* 116 E4
Mosquito L., *Canada* 103 A8
Mosquitos, G. de los, *Panama* 120 E3
Moss, *Norway* 9 G14
Moss Vale, *Australia* 95 E5
Mossbank, *Canada* 103 D7
Mossburn, *N.Z.* 91 L2
Mosselbaai, *S. Africa* 88 E3
Mossendjo, *Congo* 84 E2
Mossgiel, *Australia* 95 E3
Mossingen, *Germany* 25 G5
Mossman, *Australia* 94 B4
Mossoró, *Brazil* 125 E11
Mossuril, *Mozam.* 87 E5
Most, *Czech Rep.* 26 A6
Mosta, *Malta* 49 D1
Mostaganem, *Algeria* 78 A6
Mostar, *Bos.-H.* 28 G2
Mostardas, *Brazil* 127 C5
Mostiska = Mostyska, *Ukraine* 31 J10
Móstoles, *Spain* 36 E7
Mosty = Masty, *Belarus* 32 F3
Mostyska, *Ukraine* 31 J10
Mosul = Al Mawşil, *Iraq* 70 B4
Mosŭlpo, *S. Korea* 57 H14
Mota, *Ethiopia* 81 E4
Mota del Cuervo, *Spain* 39 F2
Mota del Marqués, *Spain* 36 D5
Motagua →, *Guatemala* 120 C2
Motala, *Sweden* 11 F9
Motaze, *Mozam.* 89 C5
Moțca, *Romania* 29 C11
Moth, *India* 69 G8
Motherwell, *U.K.* 13 F5
Motihari, *India* 69 F11
Motilla del Palancar, *Spain* 39 F3
Motnik, *Slovenia* 41 B11
Motovun, *Croatia* 41 C10
Motozintla de Mendoza, *Mexico* 119 D6
Motril, *Spain* 37 J7
Motru, *Romania* 28 F7
Motru →, *Romania* 29 F8

Mott, U.S.A. 112 B3
Móttola, Italy 43 B10
Motueka, N.Z. 91 J4
Motueka →, N.Z. 91 J4
Motul, Mexico 119 C7
Mouchalagane →, Canada 105 B6
Moúdhros, Greece 47 B7
Mouding, China 58 E3
Moudjeria, Mauritania 82 B2
Moudon, Switz. 25 J2
Mouila, Gabon 84 E2
Moulamein, Australia 95 F3
Moule à Chique, C., St. Lucia 121 f
Moulianá, Greece 49 D7
Moulins, France 19 F10
Moulmein, Burma 67 L20
Moulouya, O. →, Morocco 78 B5
Moultrie, U.S.A. 115 K4
Moultrie, L., U.S.A. 115 J5
Mound City, Mo., U.S.A. 112 E7
Mound City, S. Dak., U.S.A. 112 C4
Moúnda, Ákra, Greece 46 C2
Moundou, Chad 79 G9
Moundsville, U.S.A. 116 G4
Moung, Cambodia 64 F4
Mount Airy, U.S.A. 115 G5
Mount Albert, Canada 116 B5
Mount Aspiring △, N.Z. 91 L2
Mount Barker, S. Austral., Australia 95 F2
Mount Barker, W. Austral., Australia 93 F2
Mount Brydges, Canada 116 D3
Mount Burr, Australia 95 F3
Mount Carmel = Ha Karmel △, Israel 74 C4
Mount Carmel, Ill., U.S.A. 114 F2
Mount Carmel, Pa., U.S.A. 117 F8
Mount Charleston, U.S.A. 111 J11
Mount Clemens, U.S.A. 116 D2
Mount Coolon, Australia 94 C4
Mount Darwin, Zimbabwe 87 F3
Mount Desert I., U.S.A. 115 C11
Mount Dora, U.S.A. 115 L5
Mount Edziza ⌂, Canada 102 B2
Mount Elgon △, E. Afr. 86 B3
Mount Field △, Australia 95 G4
Mount Fletcher, S. Africa 89 E4
Mount Forest, Canada 116 C4
Mount Gambier, Australia 95 F3
Mount Garnet, Australia 94 B4
Mount Holly, U.S.A. 117 G10
Mount Holly Springs, U.S.A. 116 F7
Mount Hope, N.S.W., Australia 95 E4
Mount Hope, S. Austral., Australia 95 E2
Mount Isa, Australia 94 C2
Mount Jewett, U.S.A. 116 E6
Mount Kaputar △, Australia 95 E5
Mount Kenya △, Kenya 86 C4
Mount Kilimanjaro △, Tanzania 86 C4
Mount Kisco, U.S.A. 117 E11
Mount Laguna, U.S.A. 111 N10
Mount Larcom, Australia 94 C5
Mount Lofty Ra., Australia 95 E2
Mount Magnet, Australia 93 E2
Mount Maunganui, N.Z. 91 G6
Mount Molloy, Australia 94 B4
Mount Morgan, Australia 94 C5
Mount Morris, U.S.A. 116 D7
Mount Pearl, Canada 105 C9
Mount Penn, U.S.A. 117 F9
Mount Perry, Australia 95 D5
Mount Pleasant, Iowa, U.S.A. 112 E9
Mount Pleasant, Mich., U.S.A. 114 D3
Mount Pleasant, Pa., U.S.A. 116 F5
Mount Pleasant, S.C., U.S.A. 115 J6
Mount Pleasant, Tenn., U.S.A. 115 H2
Mount Pleasant, Tex., U.S.A. 113 J7
Mount Pleasant, Utah, U.S.A. 108 G8
Mount Pocono, U.S.A. 117 E9
Mount Rainier △, U.S.A. 110 D5
Mount Revelstoke △, Canada 102 C5
Mount Robson ⌂, Canada 102 C5
Mount St. Helens ⌂, U.S.A. 110 D4
Mount Selinda, Zimbabwe 89 C5
Mount Shasta, U.S.A. 108 F2
Mount Signal, U.S.A. 111 N11
Mount Sterling, Ill., U.S.A. 112 F9
Mount Sterling, Ky., U.S.A. 114 F4
Mount Surprise, Australia 94 B3
Mount Union, U.S.A. 116 F7
Mount Upton, U.S.A. 117 D9
Mount Vernon, Ill., U.S.A. 114 F1
Mount Vernon, Ind., U.S.A. 112 F10
Mount Vernon, N.Y., U.S.A. 117 F11
Mount Vernon, Ohio, U.S.A. 116 F2
Mount Vernon, Wash., U.S.A. 110 B4
Mount William △, Australia 95 G4
Mountain Ash, U.K. 15 F4
Mountain Center, U.S.A. 111 M10
Mountain City, Nev., U.S.A. 108 F6
Mountain City, Tenn., U.S.A. 115 G5
Mountain Dale, U.S.A. 117 E10
Mountain Grove, U.S.A. 113 G8
Mountain Home, Ark., U.S.A. 113 G8
Mountain Home, Idaho, U.S.A. 108 E6
Mountain Iron, U.S.A. 112 B8
Mountain Pass, U.S.A. 111 K11
Mountain View, Ark., U.S.A. 113 H8
Mountain View, Calif., U.S.A. 110 H4
Mountain View, Hawaii, U.S.A. 106 J17
Mountain Zebra △, S. Africa 88 E4
Mountainair, U.S.A. 109 J10
Mountlake Terrace, U.S.A. 110 C4
Mountmellick, Ireland 12 C4
Mountrath, Ireland 12 D4
Moura, Australia 94 C4
Moura, Brazil 124 D6
Moura, Portugal 37 G3
Mourão, Portugal 37 G3
Mourdi, Dépression du, Chad 79 E10
Mourdiah, Mali 82 C3
Mourenx, France 20 E3
Mouri, Ghana 83 D4
Mourilyan, Australia 94 B4
Mourmelon-le-Grand, France 19 C11
Mourne →, U.K. 12 B4
Mourne Mts., U.K. 12 B5
Mourniaí, Greece 49 D6
Mournies = Mourniaí, Greece 49 D6
Mouscron, Belgium 17 D3
Moussoro, Chad 79 F9
Mouthe, France 19 F13
Moutier, Switz. 25 H3
Moûtiers, France 21 C10
Moutong, Indonesia 63 D6
Mouy, France 19 C9
Mouzáki, Greece 46 B3
Mouzon, France 19 C12
Movas, Mexico 118 B3
Moville, Ireland 12 A4
Mowandjum, Australia 92 C3
Moy →, Ireland 12 B2
Moyale, Kenya 81 G4
Moyamba, S. Leone 82 D2
Moyen Atlas, Morocco 78 B4
Moyne, L. le, Canada 105 A6
Moyo, Indonesia 62 F5
Moyobamba, Peru 124 E3
Moyyero →, Russia 53 C11
Moyynty, Kazakhstan 52 E8
Mozambique = Moçambique, Mozam. 87 F5
Mozambique ■, Africa 87 F4
Mozambique Chan., Africa 89 B7
Mozdok, Russia 35 J7
Mozdūrān, Iran 71 B9
Mozhaysk, Russia 32 E9
Mozhga, Russia 34 B11
Mozhnābād, Iran 71 C9
Mozirje, Slovenia 41 B11
Mozyr = Mazyr, Belarus 33 F5
Mpanda, Tanzania 86 D3
Mpésoba, Mali 82 C3
Mphoengs, Zimbabwe 89 C4
Mpika, Zambia 87 E3
Mpulungu, Zambia 87 D3
Mpumalanga, S. Africa 89 D5
Mpumalanga □, S. Africa 89 B5
Mpwapwa, Tanzania 86 D4
Mqanduli, S. Africa 89 E4
Mqinvartsveri = Kazbek, Russia 35 J7
Mrągowo, Poland 30 E8
Mramor, Serbia & M. 44 C5
Mrkonjić Grad, Bos.-H. 28 F2
Mrkopalj, Croatia 41 C11
Mrocza, Poland 31 E4
Msambansovu, Zimbabwe 87 F3
M'sila →, Algeria 78 A6
Msoro, Zambia 87 E3
Msta →, Russia 32 C6
Mstislavl = Mstsislaw, Belarus 32 E6
Mstsislaw, Belarus 32 E6
Mszana Dolna, Poland 31 J7
Mszczonów, Poland 31 G7
Mtama, Tanzania 87 E4
Mtamvuna →, S. Africa 89 E5
Mtilikwe →, Zimbabwe 87 G3
Mtsensk, Russia 32 F9
Mtskheta, Georgia 35 K7
Mtubatuba, S. Africa 89 D5
Mtwalume, S. Africa 89 E5
Mtwara-Mikindani, Tanzania 87 E5
Mu Gia, Deo, Vietnam 64 D5
Mu Ko Chang △, Thailand 65 G4
Mu Us Shamo, China 56 E5
Muang Chiang Rai = Chiang Rai, Thailand 58 H2
Muang Khong, Laos 64 E5
Muang Lamphun, Thailand 64 C2
Muang Mai, Thailand 65 a
Muang Pak Beng, Laos 58 H3
Muar, Malaysia 65 L4
Muarabungo, Indonesia 62 E2
Muaraenim, Indonesia 62 E2
Muarajuloi, Indonesia 62 E4
Muarakaman, Indonesia 62 E5
Muaratebo, Indonesia 62 E2
Muaratembesi, Indonesia 62 E2
Muaratewe, Indonesia 62 E4
Mubarakpur, India 69 F10
Mubarraz = Al Mubarraz, Si. Arabia 71 E6
Mubende, Uganda 86 B3
Mubi, Nigeria 83 C7
Mucajaí →, Brazil 124 C6
Muchachos, Roque de los, Canary Is. 48 F2
Mücheln, Germany 24 D7
Muchinga Mts., Zambia 87 E3
Muchkapskiy, Russia 34 E6
Muchuan, China 58 C5
Muck, U.K. 13 E2
Muckadilla, Australia 95 D4
Muckle Flugga, U.K. 13 A8
Mucur, Turkey 72 C6
Mucuri, Brazil 125 G11
Mucusso, Angola 88 B3
Muda, Canary Is. 48 F6
Mudanjiang, China 57 B15
Mudanya, Turkey 45 F12
Muddy Cr. →, U.S.A. 109 H8
Mudgee, Australia 95 E4
Mudjatik →, Canada 103 B7
Mudurnu, Turkey 72 B4
Muecate, Mozam. 87 E4
Mueda, Mozam. 87 E4
Mueller Ra., Australia 92 C4
Muende, Mozam. 87 E3
Muerto, Mar, Mexico 119 D6
Mufu Shan, China 59 C10
Mufulira, Zambia 87 E2
Mufumbiro Range, Africa 86 C2
Mugardos, Spain 36 B2
Muge →, Portugal 37 F2
Múggia, Italy 41 C10
Mughal Sarai, India 69 G10
Mughayrā', Si. Arabia 70 D3
Mugi, Japan 55 H7
Mugia = Muxía, Spain 36 B1
Mugila, Mts., Dem. Rep. of the Congo 86 D2
Muğla, Turkey 47 D10
Muğla □, Turkey 47 D10
Muglad, Sudan 81 E2
Müglizh, Bulgaria 45 D9
Mugu, Nepal 69 E10
Muhammad, Râs, Egypt 70 E2
Muhammad Qol, Sudan 80 C4
Muhammadabad, India 69 F10
Muhesi →, Tanzania 86 D4
Mühlacker, Germany 25 G4
Mühldorf, Germany 25 G8
Mühlhausen, Germany 24 D6
Mühlig Hofmann fjell, Antarctica 5 D3
Mühlviertel, Austria 26 C7
Muhos, Finland 8 D22
Muhu, Estonia 9 G20
Muhutwe, Tanzania 86 C3
Muine Bheag, Ireland 12 D5
Muir, L., Australia 93 F2
Muir of Ord, U.K. 13 D4
Mujnak = Muynak, Uzbekistan 52 E6
Muka, Tanjung, Malaysia 65 c
Mukacheve, Ukraine 28 B7
Mukachevo = Mukacheve, Ukraine 28 B7
Mukah, Malaysia 62 D4
Mukandwara, India 68 G6
Mukawwa, Geziret, Egypt 80 C4
Mukawwar, Sudan 80 C4
Mukdahan, Thailand 64 D5
Mukden = Shenyang, China 57 D12
Mukerian, India 68 D6
Mukhavyets, Belarus 31 F10
Mukhtolovo, Russia 34 C6
Mukinbudin, Australia 93 F2
Mukishi, Dem. Rep. of the Congo 87 D1
Mukomuko, Indonesia 62 E2
Mukomwenze, Dem. Rep. of the Congo 86 D2
Muktsar, India 68 D6
Mukur = Moqor, Afghan. 68 C2
Mukutawa →, Canada 103 C9
Mukwela, Zambia 87 F2
Mula, Spain 39 G3
Mula →, Pakistan 68 F2
Mulange, Dem. Rep. of the Congo 86 C2
Mulanje, Malawi 87 F4
Mulanje, Mt., Malawi 87 F4
Mulchén, Chile 126 D1
Mulde →, Germany 24 D8
Mule Creek Junction, U.S.A. 112 D2
Muleba, Tanzania 86 C3
Mulejé, Mexico 118 B2
Muleshoe, U.S.A. 113 H3
Muletta, Gara, Ethiopia 81 F5
Mulgrave, Canada 105 C7
Mulhacén, Spain 37 H7
Mülheim, Germany 24 D2
Mulhouse, France 19 E14
Muli, China 58 D3
Muling, China 57 B16
Mull, U.K. 13 E3
Mull, Sound of, U.K. 13 E3
Mullaittivu, Sri Lanka 66 Q12
Mullen, U.S.A. 112 D4
Mullens, U.S.A. 114 G5
Muller, Pegunungan, Indonesia 62 D4
Mullet Pen., Ireland 12 B1
Mullewa, Australia 93 E2
Müllheim, Germany 25 H3
Mulligan →, Australia 94 D2
Mullingar, Ireland 12 C4
Mullins, U.S.A. 115 H6
Mullsjö, Sweden 11 G7
Mullumbimby, Australia 95 D5
Mulobezi, Zambia 87 F2
Mulroy B., Ireland 12 A4
Multan, Pakistan 68 D4
Mulumbe, Mts., Dem. Rep. of the Congo 87 D2
Mulungushi Dam, Zambia 87 E2
Mulvane, U.S.A. 113 G6
Mulwad, Sudan 80 D3
Mumbai, India 66 K8
Mumbwa, Zambia 87 F2
Mumra, Russia 35 H8
Mun →, Thailand 64 E5
Muna, Indonesia 63 F6
Munabao, India 68 G4
Munamagi, Estonia 9 H22
Muncan, Indonesia 63 K18
Muncar, Indonesia 63 J17
Münchberg, Germany 25 E7
Müncheberg, Germany 24 C10
München, Germany 25 G7
Munchen-Gladbach = Mönchengladbach, Germany 24 D2
München International ✖ (MUC), Germany 25 G7
Muncho Lake, Canada 102 B3
Munch'ŏn, N. Korea 57 E14
Muncie, U.S.A. 114 E3
Muncoonie, L., Australia 94 D2
Mundabbera, Australia 95 D5
Munday, U.S.A. 113 J5
Münden, Germany 24 D5
Münden ⌂, Germany 24 D5
Mundiwindi, Australia 92 D3
Mundo →, Spain 39 G2
Mundo Novo, Brazil 125 F10
Mundra, India 68 H3
Mundrabilla, Australia 93 F4
Munera, Spain 39 F2
Mungallala, Australia 95 D4
Mungallala Cr. →, Australia 95 D4
Mungana, Australia 94 B3
Mungaoli, India 68 G8
Mungari, Mozam. 87 F3
Mungbere, Dem. Rep. of the Congo 86 B2
Mungeli, India 69 H9
Munger, India 69 G12
Mungkan Kandju △, Australia 94 A3
Munich = München, Germany 25 G7
Munising, U.S.A. 114 B2
Munka-Ljungby, Sweden 11 H6
Munkebo, Denmark 11 J4
Munkedal, Sweden 11 F5
Munkfors, Sweden 10 E7
Munku-Sardyk, Russia 53 D11
Münnerstadt, Germany 25 E6
Muñoz Gamero, Pen., Chile 128 G2
Munroe L., Canada 103 B9
Munsan, S. Korea 57 F14
Munster, France 19 D14
Münster, Niedersachsen, Germany 24 C6
Münster, Nordrhein-Westfalen, Germany 24 D3
Munster □, Ireland 12 D3
Muntadgin, Australia 93 F2
Muntele Mare, Vf., Romania 29 D8
Muntok, Indonesia 62 E3
Munyama, Zambia 87 F2
Munzur Dağları, Turkey 73 C8
Muong Beng, Laos 58 G3
Muong Boum, Vietnam 58 F4
Muong Et, Laos 64 B5
Muong Hai, Laos 58 G3
Muong Hiem, Laos 64 B4
Muong Houn, Laos 58 G3
Muong Hung, Vietnam 58 G4
Muong Kau, Laos 64 E5
Muong Khao, Laos 64 C4
Muong Khoua, Laos 58 G4
Muong Liep, Laos 64 C3
Muong May, Laos 64 E6
Muong Ngeun, Laos 58 G3
Muong Ngoi, Laos 58 G4
Muong Nhie, Vietnam 58 F4
Muong Nong, Laos 64 D6
Muong Ou Tay, Laos 58 F3
Muong Oua, Laos 64 C3
Muong Peun, Laos 58 G4
Muong Phalane, Laos 64 D5
Muong Phieng, Laos 64 C3
Muong Phine, Laos 64 D6
Muong Sai, Laos 58 G3
Muong Saiapoun, Laos 64 C3
Muong Sen, Vietnam 64 C5
Muong Sing, Laos 58 G3
Muong Son, Laos 58 G4
Muong Soui, Laos 64 C4
Muong Va, Laos 58 G4
Muong Xia, Vietnam 64 B5
Muonio, Finland 8 C20
Muonio älv = Muonionjoki →, Finland 8 C20
Muonioälven = Muonionjoki →, Finland 8 C20
Muonionjoki →, Finland 8 C20
Muping, China 57 F11
Mupoi, Sudan 81 F2
Muqaddam, Wadi →, Sudan 80 D3
Muqdisho, Somali Rep. 75 G4
Mur →, Austria 27 E9
Mûr-de-Bretagne, France 18 D4
Muradiye, Manisa, Turkey 47 C9
Muradiye, Van, Turkey 73 C10
Murakami, Japan 54 E9
Murallón, Cerro, Chile 128 F2
Muranda, Rwanda 86 C2
Murang'a, Kenya 86 C4
Murashi, Russia 52 D5
Murat, France 20 C6
Murat →, Turkey 73 C9
Murat Dağı, Turkey 47 C11
Muratlı, Turkey 45 E11
Murato, France 21 F13
Murau, Austria 26 D7
Murava, Belarus 31 F11
Muravera, Italy 42 C2
Murayama, Japan 54 E10
Murça, Portugal 36 D3
Murchison →, Australia 93 E1
Murchison, Mt., Antarctica 5 D11
Murchison Falls, Uganda 86 B3
Murchison Falls △, Uganda 86 B3
Murchison Ra., Australia 94 C1
Murchison Rapids, Malawi 87 F3
Murcia, Spain 39 G3
Murcia □, Spain 39 H3
Murdo, U.S.A. 112 D4
Murdoch Pt., Australia 94 A3
Mürefte, Turkey 45 F11
Mureş □, Romania 29 D9
Mureş →, Romania 28 D5
Mureşul = Mureş →, Romania 28 D5
Muret, France 20 E5
Murewa, Zimbabwe 89 B5
Murfreesboro, N.C., U.S.A. 115 G7
Murfreesboro, Tenn., U.S.A. 115 H2
Murgab = Murghob, Tajikistan 52 F8
Murgab →, Turkmenistan 71 B9
Murgenella, Australia 92 B5
Murgeni, Romania 29 D13
Murgha Kibzai, Pakistan 68 D3
Murghob, Tajikistan 52 F8
Murgon, Australia 95 D5
Muri, India 69 H11
Muria, Indonesia 63 G14
Muriaé, Brazil 127 A7
Murias de Paredes, Spain 36 C4
Muriel Mine, Zimbabwe 87 F3
Müritz, Germany 24 B8
Müritz △, Germany 24 B8
Murliganj, India 69 G12
Murmansk, Russia 52 C4
Murnau, Germany 25 H7
Muro, France 21 F12
Muro, Spain 48 B10
Muro, C. de, France 21 G12
Muro de Alcoy, Spain 39 G4
Muro Lucano, Italy 43 B8
Murom, Russia 34 C6
Muroran, Japan 54 C10
Muros, Spain 36 C1
Muros y de Noya, Ría de, Spain 36 C1
Muroto, Japan 55 H7
Muroto-Misaki, Japan 55 H7
Murovani Kurylivtsi, Ukraine 29 B12
Murowana Goślina, Poland 31 F3
Murphy, U.S.A. 108 E5
Murphys, U.S.A. 110 G6
Murrat, Sudan 80 D2
Murrat Wells, Sudan 80 C3
Murray, Ky., U.S.A. 115 G1
Murray, Utah, U.S.A. 108 F8
Murray →, Australia 95 F2
Murray, L., U.S.A. 115 H5
Murray Bridge, Australia 95 F2
Murray Harbour, Canada 105 C7
Murray River △, Australia 95 E3
Murraysburg, S. Africa 88 E3
Murree, Pakistan 68 C5
Murrieta, U.S.A. 111 M9
Murro di Porco, Capo, Italy 43 F8
Murrumbidgee →, Australia 95 E3
Murrumburrah, Australia 95 E4
Murrurundi, Australia 95 E5
Murshid, Sudan 80 C3
Murshidabad, India 69 G13
Murska Sobota, Slovenia 41 B13
Murtle L., Canada 102 C5
Murtoa, Australia 95 F3
Murtosa, Portugal 36 E2
Murungu, Tanzania 86 C3
Mururoa, French Polynesia 97 K14
Murwara, India 69 H9
Murwillumbah, Australia 95 D5
Mürz →, Austria 26 D8
Mürzzuschlag, Austria 26 D8
Muş, Turkey 70 B4
Mûsa, Gebel, Egypt 70 D2
Musa Khel, Pakistan 68 D3
Mūsa Qal'eh, Afghan. 66 C4
Musafirkhana, India 69 F9
Musala, Bulgaria 44 D7
Musala, Indonesia 62 D1
Musan, N. Korea 57 C15
Musangu, Dem. Rep. of the Congo 87 E1
Musasa, Tanzania 86 C3
Musay'īd, Qatar 71 E6
Muscat = Masqat, Oman 75 C6
Muscatine, U.S.A. 112 E9
Musengezi = Unsengedsi →, Zimbabwe 87 F3
Musgrave Harbour, Canada 105 C9
Musgrave Ranges, Australia 93 E5
Mushie, Dem. Rep. of the Congo 84 E3
Mushin, Nigeria 83 D5
Musi →, Indonesia 62 E2
Musina, S. Africa 89 C5
Muskeg →, Canada 102 A4
Muskegon, U.S.A. 114 D2
Muskegon →, U.S.A. 114 D2
Muskegon Heights, U.S.A. 114 D2
Muskogee, U.S.A. 113 H7
Muskoka, L., Canada 116 B5
Muskwa →, Canada 102 B4
Muslīmiyah, Syria 70 B3
Musmar, Sudan 80 D4
Musofu, Zambia 87 E2
Musoma, Tanzania 86 C3
Musquaro, L., Canada 105 B7
Musquodoboit Harbour, Canada 105 D7
Musselburgh, U.K. 13 F5
Musselshell →, U.S.A. 108 C10
Mussidan, France 20 C4
Mussomeli, Italy 42 E6
Mussoorie, India 68 D8
Mussuco, Angola 88 B2
Mustafakemalpaşa, Turkey 45 F12
Mustang, Nepal 69 E10
Musters, L., Argentina 128 F3
Musudan, N. Korea 57 D15
Muswellbrook, Australia 95 E5
Muszyna, Poland 31 J7
Mût, Egypt 80 B2
Mut, Turkey 70 B2
Mutanda, Mozam. 89 C5
Mutanda, Zambia 87 E2
Mutare, Zimbabwe 87 F3
Muting, Indonesia 63 F10
Mutki = Mirtağ, Turkey 70 B4
Mutoko, Zimbabwe 89 B5
Mutoray, Russia 53 C11
Mutshatsha, Dem. Rep. of the Congo 87 E1
Mutsu, Japan 54 D10
Mutsu-Wan, Japan 54 D10
Muttaburra, Australia 94 C3
Muttalip, Turkey 47 B12
Mutton I., Ireland 12 D2
Mutuáli, Mozam. 87 E4
Mutum Biyu, Nigeria 83 D7
Muweilih, Egypt 74 E3
Muxía, Spain 36 B1
Muy Muy, Nic. 120 D2
Muyinga, Burundi 86 C3
Muynak, Uzbekistan 52 E6
Muzaffarabad, Pakistan 69 B5
Muzaffargarh, Pakistan 68 D4
Muzaffarnagar, India 68 E7
Muzaffarpur, India 69 F11
Muzafirpur, Pakistan 68 D3
Muzhi, Russia 52 C7
Muzillac, France 18 E4

Muzūra, *Egypt* 80 J7
Mvôlô, *Sudan* 81 F2
Mvuma, *Zimbabwe* 87 F3
Mvurwi, *Zimbabwe* 87 F3
Mwabvi ⌂, *Malawi* 87 F3
Mwadui, *Tanzania* 86 C3
Mwambo, *Tanzania* 87 E5
Mwandi, *Zambia* 87 F1
Mwanza, *Dem. Rep. of the Congo* 86 D2
Mwanza, *Tanzania* 86 C3
Mwanza, *Zambia* 87 F1
Mwanza □, *Tanzania* 86 C3
Mwaya, *Tanzania* 87 D3
Mweelrea, *Ireland* 12 C2
Mweka, *Dem. Rep. of the Congo* 84 E4
Mwenezi, *Zimbabwe* 87 G3
Mwenezi →, *Mozam.* 87 G3
Mwenga, *Dem. Rep. of the Congo* 86 C2
Mweru, L., *Zambia* 87 D2
Mweru Wantipa △, *Zambia* 87 D2
Mweza Range, *Zimbabwe* 87 G3
Mwilambwe, *Dem. Rep. of the Congo* 86 D2
Mwimbi, *Tanzania* 87 D3
Mwinilunga, *Zambia* 87 E1
My Tho, *Vietnam* 65 G6
Myajlar, *India* 68 F4
Myanaung, *Burma* 67 K19
Myanmar = Burma ■, *Asia* 67 J20
Myaungmya, *Burma* 67 L19
Myedna, *Belarus* 31 G10
Myeik Kyunzu, *Burma* 65 G1
Myers Chuck, *U.S.A.* 102 B2
Myerstown, *U.S.A.* 117 F8
Myingyan, *Burma* 67 J19
Myitkyina, *Burma* 67 G20
Myjava, *Slovak Rep.* 27 C10
Mykhaylivka, *Ukraine* 33 J8
Mykines, *Færoe Is.* 8 E9
Mykolayiv, *Ukraine* 33 J7
Mymensingh, *Bangla.* 67 G17
Mynydd Du, *U.K.* 15 F4
Mýrdalsjökull, *Iceland* 8 E4
Myrhorod, *Ukraine* 33 H7
Myrtle Beach, *U.S.A.* 115 J6
Myrtle Creek, *U.S.A.* 108 E2
Myrtle Point, *U.S.A.* 108 E1
Myrtou, *Cyprus* 49 D12
Mysia, *Turkey* 45 G11
Myślenice, *Poland* 31 J6
Myślibórz, *Poland* 31 F1
Mysłowice, *Poland* 31 H6
Mysore = Karnataka □, *India* 66 N10
Mysore, *India* 66 N10
Mystic, *U.S.A.* 117 E13
Myszków, *Poland* 31 H6
Myszyniec, *Poland* 30 E8
Mytishchi, *Russia* 32 E9
Mývatn, *Iceland* 8 D5
Mže →, *Czech Rep.* 26 B6
Mzimba, *Malawi* 87 E3
Mzimkulu →, *S. Africa* 89 E5
Mzimvubu →, *S. Africa* 89 E4
Mzuzu, *Malawi* 87 E3

N

Na Hearadh = Harris, *U.K.* 13 D2
Na Noi, *Thailand* 64 C3
Na Phao, *Laos* 64 D5
Na Sam, *Vietnam* 58 F6
Na San, *Vietnam* 64 B5
Na Thon, *Thailand* 65 b
Naab →, *Germany* 25 F8
Na'am, *Sudan* 81 F2
Na'am →, *Sudan* 81 F2
Naantali, *Finland* 9 F19
Naas, *Ireland* 12 C5
Nababeep, *S. Africa* 88 D2
Nabadwip = Navadwip, *India* 69 H13
Nabawa, *Australia* 93 E1
Nabberu, L., *Australia* 93 E3
Nabburg, *Germany* 25 F8
Naberezhnyye Chelny, *Russia* 34 C11
Nabeul, *Tunisia* 79 A8
Nabha, *India* 68 D7
Nabīd, *Iran* 71 D8
Nabire, *Indonesia* 63 E9
Nabisar, *Pakistan* 68 G3
Nabisipi →, *Canada* 105 B7
Nabiswera, *Uganda* 86 B3
Nāblus = Nābulus, *West Bank* 74 C4
Naboomspruit, *S. Africa* 89 C4
Nabou, *Burkina Faso* 82 C4
Nabua, *Phil.* 61 E5
Nābulus, *West Bank* 74 C4
Nacala, *Mozam.* 87 E5
Nacala-Velha, *Mozam.* 87 E5
Nacaome, *Honduras* 120 D2
Nacaroa, *Mozam.* 87 E4
Naches, *U.S.A.* 108 C3
Naches →, *U.S.A.* 110 D6
Nachicapau, L., *Canada* 105 A6
Nachingwea, *Tanzania* 87 E4
Nachna, *India* 68 F4
Náchod, *Czech Rep.* 26 A9
Nacimiento L., *U.S.A.* 110 K6
Naco, *Mexico* 118 A3
Nacogdoches, *U.S.A.* 113 K7
Nácori Chico, *Mexico* 118 B3
Nacozari, *Mexico* 118 A3
Nådendal = Naantali, *Finland* 9 F19
Nadi, *Fiji* 91 C7
Nadi, *Sudan* 80 D3
Nadiad, *India* 68 H5
Nădlac, *Romania* 28 D5
Nador, *Morocco* 78 B5
Nadur, *Malta* 49 C1
Nadūshan, *Iran* 71 C7
Nadvirna, *Ukraine* 29 B9
Nadvornaya = Nadvirna, *Ukraine* 29 B9
Nadym, *Russia* 52 C8
Nadym →, *Russia* 52 C8
Nærbø, *Norway* 9 G11
Næstved, *Denmark* 11 J5
Nafada, *Nigeria* 83 C7
Naft-e Safīd, *Iran* 71 D6
Naftshahr, *Iran* 70 C5
Nafud Desert = An Nafūd, *Si. Arabia* 70 D4
Nag Hammâdi, *Egypt* 80 B3
Naga, *Phil.* 61 E5
Nagahama, *Japan* 55 G8
Nagai, *Japan* 54 E10
Nagaland □, *India* 67 G19
Nagano, *Japan* 55 F9
Nagano □, *Japan* 55 F9
Nagaoka, *Japan* 55 F9
Nagappattinam, *India* 66 P11
Nagar →, *Bangla.* 69 G13
Nagar Parkar, *Pakistan* 68 G4
Nagasaki, *Japan* 55 H4
Nagasaki □, *Japan* 55 H4
Nagato, *Japan* 55 G5
Nagaur, *India* 68 F5
Nagda, *India* 68 H6
Nagercoil, *India* 66 Q10
Nagina, *India* 69 E8
Nagīneh, *Iran* 71 C8
Nagir, *Pakistan* 69 A6
Naglarby, *Sweden* 10 D9
Nagod, *India* 69 G9
Nagold, *Germany* 25 G4
Nagold →, *Germany* 25 G4
Nagoorin, *Australia* 94 C5
Nagorno-Karabakh □, *Azerbaijan* 70 B5
Nagornyy, *Russia* 53 D13
Nagoya, *Japan* 55 G8
Nagpur, *India* 66 J11
Nagua, *Dom. Rep.* 121 C6
Naguabo, *Puerto Rico* 121 d
Nagyatád, *Hungary* 28 D2
Nagyecsed, *Hungary* 28 C7
Nagykálló, *Hungary* 28 C6
Nagykanizsa, *Hungary* 28 D2
Nagykáta, *Hungary* 28 C4
Nagykőrös, *Hungary* 28 C4
Naha, *Japan* 55 L3
Nahan, *India* 68 D7
Nahanni △, *Canada* 102 A4
Nahanni Butte, *Canada* 102 A4
Nahargarh, *Mad. P., India* 68 G6
Nahargarh, *Raj., India* 68 G7
Nahariyya, *Israel* 70 C2
Nahāvand, *Iran* 71 C6
Nahe →, *Germany* 25 F3
Nahirne, *Ukraine* 29 E13
Nahīya, W. →, *Egypt* 80 B3
Nahuelbuta △, *Chile* 126 D1
Nai Yong, *Thailand* 65 a
Naicá, *Mexico* 118 B3
Naicam, *Canada* 103 C8
Naikoon ⌂, *Canada* 102 C2
Naila, *Germany* 25 E7
Naimisharanya, *India* 69 F9
Nain, *Canada* 105 A7
Nā'īn, *Iran* 71 C7
Naini Tal, *India* 69 E8
Nainpur, *India* 66 H12
Naintré, *France* 18 F7
Nainwa, *India* 68 G6
Naipu, *Romania* 29 F10
Nairn, *U.K.* 13 D5
Nairobi, *Kenya* 86 C4
Nairobi △, *Kenya* 86 C4
Naissaar, *Estonia* 9 G21
Naita, Mt., *Ethiopia* 81 F4
Naivasha, *Kenya* 86 C4
Naivasha, L., *Kenya* 86 C4
Najac, *France* 20 D5
Najaf = An Najaf, *Iraq* 70 C5
Najafābād, *Iran* 71 C6
Najd, *Si. Arabia* 75 B3
Nájera, *Spain* 38 C2
Najerilla →, *Spain* 38 C2
Najibabad, *India* 68 E8
Najin, *N. Korea* 57 C16
Najmah, *Si. Arabia* 71 E6
Najrān, *Si. Arabia* 75 D3
Naju, *S. Korea* 57 G14
Nakadōri-Shima, *Japan* 55 H4
Nakalagba, *Dem. Rep. of the Congo* 86 B2
Nakaminato, *Japan* 55 F10
Nakamura, *Japan* 55 H6
Nakano, *Japan* 55 F9
Nakano-Shima, *Japan* 55 K4
Nakashibetsu, *Japan* 54 C12
Nakfa, *Eritrea* 81 D4
Nakfa ⌂, *Eritrea* 81 D4
Nakha Yai, Ko, *Thailand* 65 a
Nakhichevan = Naxçıvan, *Azerbaijan* 70 B5
Nakhichevan Rep. = Naxçıvan □, *Azerbaijan* 52 F5
Nakhl, *Egypt* 74 F2
Nakhl-e Taqī, *Iran* 71 E7
Nakhodka, *Russia* 53 E14
Nakhon Nayok, *Thailand* 64 E3
Nakhon Pathom, *Thailand* 64 F3
Nakhon Phanom, *Thailand* 64 D5
Nakhon Ratchasima, *Thailand* 64 E4
Nakhon Sawan, *Thailand* 64 E3
Nakhon Si Thammarat, *Thailand* 65 H3
Nakhon Thai, *Thailand* 64 D3
Nakhtarana, *India* 68 H3
Nakina, *Canada* 104 B2
Nakło nad Notecią, *Poland* 31 E4
Nako, *Burkina Faso* 82 C4
Nakodar, *India* 68 D6
Nakskov, *Denmark* 11 K5
Naktong →, *S. Korea* 57 G15
Nakuru, *Kenya* 86 C4
Nakuru, L., *Kenya* 86 C4
Nakusp, *Canada* 102 C5
Nal, *Pakistan* 68 F2
Nal →, *Pakistan* 68 G1
Nalázi, *Mozam.* 89 C5
Nalchik, *Russia* 35 J6
Nałęczów, *Poland* 31 G9
Nalerigu, *Ghana* 83 C4
Nalgonda, *India* 66 L11
Nalhati, *India* 69 G12
Naliya, *India* 68 H3
Nallamalai Hills, *India* 66 M11
Nallıhan, *Turkey* 72 B4
Nalón →, *Spain* 36 B4
Nam Can, *Vietnam* 65 H5
Nam-ch'on, *N. Korea* 57 E14
Nam Co, *China* 60 C4
Nam Dinh, *Vietnam* 58 G6
Nam Du, Hon, *Vietnam* 65 H5
Nam Nao △, *Thailand* 64 D3
Nam Ngum Dam, *Laos* 64 C4
Nam-Phan, *Vietnam* 65 G6
Nam Phong, *Thailand* 64 D4
Nam Tha, *Laos* 58 G3
Nam Tok, *Thailand* 64 E2
Namacunde, *Angola* 88 B2
Namacurra, *Mozam.* 89 B6
Namak, Daryācheh-ye, *Iran* 71 C7
Namak, Kavir-e, *Iran* 71 C8
Namakzār, Daryācheh-ye, *Iran* 71 C9
Namaland, *Namibia* 88 C2
Namangan, *Uzbekistan* 52 E8
Namapa, *Mozam.* 87 E4
Namaqualand, *S. Africa* 88 E2
Namasagali, *Uganda* 86 B3
Namber, *Indonesia* 63 E8
Nambour, *Australia* 95 D5
Nambucca Heads, *Australia* 95 E5
Nambung △, *Australia* 93 F2
Namche Bazar, *Nepal* 69 F12
Namchonjŏm = Nam-ch'on, *N. Korea* 57 E14
Namecunda, *Mozam.* 87 E4
Nameponda, *Mozam.* 87 F4
Náměšť nad Oslavou, *Czech Rep.* 27 B9
Námestovo, *Slovak Rep.* 27 B12
Nametil, *Mozam.* 87 F4
Namew L., *Canada* 103 C8
Namgia, *India* 69 D8
Namhkam, *Burma* 58 E1
Namib Desert, *Namibia* 88 C2
Namib-Naukluft ⌂, *Namibia* 88 C2
Namibe, *Angola* 85 H2
Namibe □, *Angola* 88 B1
Namibia ■, *Africa* 88 C2
Namibwoestyn = Namib Desert, *Namibia* 88 C2
Namīn, *Iran* 73 C13
Namlea, *Indonesia* 63 E7
Namoi →, *Australia* 95 E4
Nampa, *U.S.A.* 108 E5
Nampala, *Mali* 82 B3
Namp'o, *N. Korea* 57 E13
Nampō-Shotō, *Japan* 55 J10
Nampula, *Mozam.* 87 F4
Namrole, *Indonesia* 63 E7
Namse Shankou, *China* 67 E13
Namsen →, *Norway* 8 D14
Namsos, *Norway* 8 D14
Namtok Chat Trakan △, *Thailand* 64 D3
Namtok Mae Surin △, *Thailand* 64 C2
Namtsy, *Russia* 53 C13
Namtu, *Burma* 67 H20
Namtumbo, *Tanzania* 87 E4
Namu, *Canada* 102 C3
Namur, *Belgium* 17 D4
Namur □, *Belgium* 17 D4
Namutoni, *Namibia* 88 B2
Namwala, *Zambia* 87 F2
Namwŏn, *S. Korea* 57 G14
Namysłów, *Poland* 31 G4
Nan, *Thailand* 64 C3
Nan →, *Thailand* 64 E3
Nan-ch'ang = Nanchang, *China* 59 C10
Nan Ling, *China* 59 E8
Nan Xian, *China* 59 C9
Nana, *Romania* 29 F11
Nana Kru, *Liberia* 82 E3
Nanaimo, *Canada* 102 D4
Nanam, *N. Korea* 57 D15
Nanan, *China* 59 E12
Nanango, *Australia* 95 D5
Nan'ao, *China* 59 F11
Nanao, *Japan* 55 F8
Nanbu, *China* 58 B6
Nanchang, *Jiangxi, China* 59 C10
Nanchang, *Kiangsi, China* 59 C10
Nancheng, *China* 59 D11
Nanching = Nanjing, *China* 59 A12
Nanchong, *China* 58 B6
Nanchuan, *China* 58 C6
Nancy, *France* 19 D13
Nanda Devi, *India* 69 D8
Nanda Kot, *India* 69 D9
Nandan, *China* 58 E6
Nandan, *Japan* 55 G7
Nanded, *India* 66 K10
Nandewar Ra., *Australia* 95 E5
Nandi = Nadi, *Fiji* 91 C7
Nandigram, *India* 69 H12
Nandurbar, *India* 66 J9
Nandyal, *India* 66 M11
Nanfeng, *Guangdong, China* 59 F8
Nanfeng, *Jiangxi, China* 59 D11
Nanga-Eboko, *Cameroon* 83 E7
Nanga Parbat, *Pakistan* 69 B6
Nangade, *Mozam.* 87 E4
Nangapinoh, *Indonesia* 62 E4
Nangarhār □, *Afghan.* 66 B7
Nangatayap, *Indonesia* 62 E4
Nangeya Mts., *Uganda* 86 B3
Nangis, *France* 19 D10
Nangong, *China* 56 F8
Nanhua, *China* 58 E3
Nanhuang, *China* 57 F11
Nanhui, *China* 59 B13
Nanjeko, *Zambia* 87 F1
Nanji Shan, *China* 59 D13
Nanjian, *China* 58 E3
Nanjiang, *China* 58 A6
Nanjing, *Fujian, China* 59 E11
Nanjing, *Jiangsu, China* 59 A12
Nanjirinji, *Tanzania* 87 D4
Nankana Sahib, *Pakistan* 68 D5
Nankang, *China* 59 E10
Nanking = Nanjing, *China* 59 A12
Nankoku, *Japan* 55 H6
Nanling, *China* 59 B12
Nanning, *China* 58 F7
Nannup, *Australia* 93 F2
Nanpan Jiang →, *China* 58 E6
Nanpara, *India* 69 F9
Nanpi, *China* 56 E9
Nanping, *Fujian, China* 59 D12
Nanping, *Henan, China* 59 C9
Nanri Dao, *China* 59 E12
Nanripe, *Mozam.* 87 E4
Nansei-Shotō = Ryūkyū-rettō, *Japan* 55 M3
Nansen Basin, *Arctic* 4 A10
Nansen Cordillera, *Arctic* 4 A
Nansen Sd., *Canada* 4 A3
Nanshan I., *S. China Sea* 62 B5
Nansio, *Tanzania* 86 C3
Nant, *France* 20 D7
Nanterre, *France* 19 D9
Nantes, *France* 18 E5
Nantiat, *France* 20 B5
Nanticoke, *U.S.A.* 117 E8
Nanton, *Canada* 102 C6
Nantong, *China* 59 A13
Nantou, *Taiwan* 59 F13
Nantua, *France* 19 F12
Nantucket I., *U.S.A.* 114 E10
Nantwich, *U.K.* 14 D5
Nanty Glo, *U.S.A.* 116 F6
Nanuque, *Brazil* 125 G10
Nanusa, Kepulauan, *Indonesia* 63 D7
Nanutarra Roadhouse, *Australia* 92 D2
Nanxi, *China* 58 C5
Nanxiong, *China* 59 E10
Nanyang, *China* 56 H7
Nanyi Hu, *China* 59 B12
Nanyuki, *Kenya* 86 B4
Nanzhang, *China* 59 B8
Nao, C. de la, *Spain* 39 G5
Naococane, L., *Canada* 105 B5
Náousa, *Imathía, Greece* 44 F6
Náousa, *Kikládhes, Greece* 47 D7
Naozhou Dao, *China* 59 G8
Napa, *U.S.A.* 110 G4
Napa →, *U.S.A.* 110 G4
Napanee, *Canada* 116 B8
Napanoch, *U.S.A.* 117 E10
Nape, *Laos* 64 C5
Nape Pass = Keo Neua, Deo, *Vietnam* 64 C5
Napier, *N.Z.* 91 H6
Napier Broome B., *Australia* 92 B4
Napier Pen., *Australia* 94 A2
Napierville, *Canada* 117 A11
Naples = Nápoli, *Italy* 43 B7
Naples, *U.S.A.* 115 M5
Napo, *China* 58 F5
Napo →, *Peru* 124 D4
Napoleon, *N. Dak., U.S.A.* 112 B5
Napoleon, *Ohio, U.S.A.* 114 E3
Nápoli, *Italy* 43 B7
Nápoli, G. di, *Italy* 43 B7
Nápoli Capodichino ✕ (NAP), *Italy* 43 B7
Napopo, *Dem. Rep. of the Congo* 86 B2
Naqâda, *Egypt* 80 B3
Naqadeh, *Iran* 73 D11
Naqb, Ra's an, *Jordan* 74 F4
Naqqāsh, *Iran* 71 C6
Nara, *Japan* 55 G7
Nara, *Mali* 82 B3
Nara □, *Japan* 55 G8
Nara Canal, *Pakistan* 68 G3
Nara Visa, *U.S.A.* 113 H3
Naracoorte, *Australia* 95 F3
Naradhan, *Australia* 95 E4
Naraini, *India* 69 G9
Narasapur, *India* 67 L12
Narathiwat, *Thailand* 65 J3
Narayanganj, *Bangla.* 67 H17
Narayanpet, *India* 66 L10
Narberth, *U.K.* 15 F3
Narbonne, *France* 20 E7
Narcea →, *Spain* 36 B4
Nardīn, *Iran* 71 B7
Nardò, *Italy* 43 B11
Narembeen, *Australia* 93 F2
Narendranagar, *India* 68 D8
Nares Str., *Arctic* 98 A13
Naretha, *Australia* 93 F3
Narew →, *Poland* 31 F7
Nari →, *Pakistan* 68 F2
Narin, *Afghan.* 66 A6
Narindra, Helodranon' i, *Madag.* 89 A8
Narita, *Japan* 55 G10
Nariva Swamp, *Trin. & Tob.* 125 K15
Närke, *Sweden* 10 E8
Narmada →, *India* 68 J5
Narman, *Turkey* 73 B9
Narmland, *Sweden* 9 F15
Narnaul, *India* 68 E7
Narni, *Italy* 41 F9
Naro, *Ghana* 82 C4
Naro Fominsk, *Russia* 32 E9
Narodnaya, *Russia* 6 B17
Narok, *Kenya* 86 C4
Narón, *Spain* 36 B2
Narooma, *Australia* 95 F5
Narowal, *Pakistan* 68 C6
Narrabri, *Australia* 95 E4
Narran →, *Australia* 95 D4
Narrandera, *Australia* 95 E4
Narrogin, *Australia* 93 F2
Narromine, *Australia* 95 E4
Narrow Hills ⌂, *Canada* 103 C8
Narsimhapur, *India* 69 H8
Narsinghgarh, *India* 68 H7
Nartes, L. e, *Albania* 44 F3
Nartkala, *Russia* 35 J6
Naruto, *Japan* 55 G7
Narva, *Estonia* 32 C5
Narva →, *Russia* 9 G22
Narva Bay = Narva Laht, *Estonia* 9 G19
Narva Laht, *Estonia* 9 G19
Narvik, *Norway* 8 B17
Narvskoye Vdkhr., *Russia* 32 C5
Narwana, *India* 68 E7
Narwiański △, *Poland* 31 F9
Naryan-Mar, *Russia* 52 C6
Narym, *Russia* 52 D9
Naryn, *Kyrgyzstan* 52 E8
Nasa, *Norway* 8 C16
Năsăud, *Romania* 29 C9
Naseby, *N.Z.* 91 L3
Naselle, *U.S.A.* 110 D3
Naser, Buheirat en, *Egypt* 80 C3
Nashua, *Mont., U.S.A.* 108 B10
Nashua, *N.H., U.S.A.* 117 D13
Nashville, *Ark., U.S.A.* 113 J8
Nashville, *Ga., U.S.A.* 115 K4
Nashville, *Tenn., U.S.A.* 115 G2
Našice, *Croatia* 28 E3
Nasielsk, *Poland* 31 F7
Nasik, *India* 66 K8
Nasipit, *Phil.* 61 G6
Nasir, *Sudan* 81 F3
Nasirabad, *India* 68 F6
Nasirabad, *Pakistan* 68 E3
Nasiriyah = An Nāṣirīyah, *Iraq* 70 D5
Naskaupi →, *Canada* 105 B7
Naso, *Italy* 43 D7
Naṣrābād, *Iran* 71 C6
Naṣriān-e Pā'īn, *Iran* 70 C5
Nass →, *Canada* 102 C3
Nassarawa, *Nigeria* 83 D6
Nassarawa □, *Nigeria* 83 D6
Nassau, *Bahamas* 120 A4
Nassau, *U.S.A.* 117 D11
Nassau, B., *Chile* 128 H3
Nasser, L. = Naser, Buheirat en, *Egypt* 80 C3
Nassian, *Ivory C.* 82 D4
Nässjö, *Sweden* 11 G8
Nastapoka →, *Canada* 104 A4
Nastapoka, Is., *Canada* 104 A4
Nasugbu, *Phil.* 61 D4
Näsum, *Sweden* 11 H8
Näsviken, *Sweden* 10 C10
Nata, *Botswana* 88 C4
Nata →, *Botswana* 88 C4
Natal, *Brazil* 125 E11
Natal, *Indonesia* 62 D1
Natal, *S. Africa* 85 K6
Natal Drakensberg ⌂, *S. Africa* 89 D4
Natalinci, *Serbia & M.* 28 F5
Naṭanz, *Iran* 71 C6
Natashquan, *Canada* 105 B7
Natashquan →, *Canada* 105 B7
Natchez, *U.S.A.* 113 K9
Natchitoches, *U.S.A.* 113 K8
Nathalia, *Australia* 95 F4
Nathdwara, *India* 68 G5
Nati, Pta., *Spain* 48 A10
Natimuk, *Australia* 95 F3
Nation →, *Canada* 102 B4
National City, *U.S.A.* 111 N9
Natitingou, *Benin* 83 C5
Natividad, I., *Mexico* 118 B1
Natkyizin, *Burma* 64 E1
Natron, L., *Tanzania* 86 C4
Natrona Heights, *U.S.A.* 116 F5
Natrûn, W. el →, *Egypt* 80 H7
Nättraby, *Sweden* 11 H9
Natukanaoka Pan, *Namibia* 88 B2
Natuna Besar, Kepulauan, *Indonesia* 62 D3
Natuna Is. = Natuna Besar, Kepulauan, *Indonesia* 62 D3
Natuna Selatan, Kepulauan, *Indonesia* 62 D3
Natural Bridge, *U.S.A.* 117 B9
Natural Bridges ⌂, *U.S.A.* 109 H8
Naturaliste, C., *Australia* 95 G4
Nau Qala, *Afghan.* 68 B3
Naucelle, *France* 20 D6
Nauders, *Austria* 26 E3
Nauen, *Germany* 24 C8
Naugatuck, *U.S.A.* 117 E11
Naujaat = Repulse Bay, *Canada* 101 B11
Naujoji Akmenė, *Lithuania* 30 B9
Naumburg, *Germany* 24 D7
Nā'ūr at Tunayb, *Jordan* 74 D4
Nauru ■, *Pac. Oc.* 96 H8
Naushahra = Nowshera, *Pakistan* 66 C8
Naushahro, *Pakistan* 68 F3
Naushon I., *U.S.A.* 117 E14
Nauta, *Peru* 124 D4
Nautanwa, *India* 67 F13
Naute ⌂, *Namibia* 88 D2
Nautla, *Mexico* 119 C5
Nava, *Mexico* 118 B4
Nava, *Spain* 36 B5
Nava del Rey, *Spain* 36 D5
Navadwip, *India* 69 H13
Navahermosa, *Spain* 37 F6
Navahrudak, *Belarus* 32 F3

Navajo Reservoir, U.S.A. 109 H10
Navalcarnero, Spain 36 E6
Navalmoral de la Mata, Spain 36 F5
Navalvillar de Pela, Spain 37 F5
Navan = An Uaimh, Ireland 12 C5
Navapolatsk, Belarus 32 E5
Navarin, Mys, Russia 4 C16
Navarino, I., Chile 128 H3
Navarra □, Spain 38 C3
Navarre, U.S.A. 116 F3
Navarro →, U.S.A. 110 F3
Navas de San Juan, Spain 37 G7
Navasota, U.S.A. 113 K6
Navassa I., W. Indies 121 C5
Nävekvarn, Sweden 11 F10
Naver →, U.K. 13 C4
Navia, Spain 36 B4
Navia →, Spain 36 B4
Navia de Suarna, Spain 36 C3
Navibandar, India 68 J3
Navidad, Chile 126 C1
Naviraí, Brazil 127 A5
Navlakhi, India 68 H4
Navlya, Russia 33 F8
Năvodari, Romania 29 F13
Navoi = Nawoiy, Uzbekistan 52 E7
Navojoa, Mexico 118 B3
Navolato, Mexico 118 C3
Návpaktos, Greece 46 C3
Návplion, Greece 46 D4
Navrongo, Ghana 83 C4
Navsari, India 66 J8
Nawa Kot, Pakistan 68 E4
Nawab Khan, Pakistan 68 D3
Nawabganj, Ut. P., India 69 F9
Nawabganj, Ut. P., India 69 E8
Nawabshah, Pakistan 68 F3
Nawada, India 69 G11
Nawakot, Nepal 69 F11
Nawalgarh, India 68 F6
Nawanshahr, India 69 C6
Nawar, Dasht-i-, Afghan. 68 C3
Nawi, Sudan 80 D3
Nawoiy, Uzbekistan 52 E7
Naxçıvan, Azerbaijan 70 B5
Naxçıvan □, Azerbaijan 52 F5
Náxos, Greece 47 D7
Nay, France 20 E3
Nay, Mui, Vietnam 62 B3
Nāy Band, Būshehr, Iran 71 E7
Nāy Band, Khorāsān, Iran 71 C8
Nayakhan, Russia 53 C16
Nayarit □, Mexico 118 C4
Nayé, Senegal 82 C2
Nayong, China 58 D5
Nayoro, Japan 54 B11
Nayyāl, W. →, Si. Arabia 70 D3
Nazaré, Brazil 125 F11
Nazaré, Portugal 37 F1
Nazareth = Nazerat, Israel 74 C4
Nazareth, U.S.A. 117 F9
Nazas, Mexico 118 B4
Nazas →, Mexico 118 B4
Nazca, Peru 124 F4
Naze, The, U.K. 15 F9
Nazerat, Israel 74 C4
Nāzīk, Iran 70 B5
Nazilli, Turkey 47 D10
Nazko, Canada 102 C4
Nazko →, Canada 102 C4
Nazret, Ethiopia 81 F4
Nazwa, Oman 75 C6
Nchanga, Zambia 87 E2
Ncheu, Malawi 87 E3
Ndala, Tanzania 86 C3
Ndalatando, Angola 84 F2
Ndali, Benin 83 D5
Ndareda, Tanzania 86 C4
Ndélé, C.A.R. 84 C4
Ndiael ⌓, Senegal 82 B1
Ndikinimeki, Cameroon 83 E7
N'Dioum, Senegal 82 B2
Ndjamena, Chad 79 F8
Ndola, Zambia 87 E2
Ndoto Mts., Kenya 86 B4
Nduguti, Tanzania 86 C3
Ndumu ⌓, S. Africa 89 D5
Néa Alikarnassós, Greece 47 F7
Néa Ankhíalos, Greece 46 B4
Néa Epídhavros, Greece 46 D5
Néa Flippiás, Greece 46 B2
Néa Ionia, Greece 46 B4
Néa Kallikrátia, Greece 44 F7
Néa Mákri, Greece 46 C5
Néa Moudhaniá, Greece 44 F7
Néa Péramos, Attikí, Greece 46 C5
Néa Péramos, Kavála, Greece 45 F8
Néa Víssi, Greece 45 E10
Néa Zíkhna, Greece 44 E7
Neagh, Lough, U.K. 12 B5
Neah Bay, U.S.A. 110 B2
Neale, L., Australia 92 D5
Neales, The →, Australia 95 D2
Neamţ □, Romania 29 C11
Neápolis, Kozáni, Greece 44 F5
Neápolis, Kríti, Greece 49 D7
Neápolis, Lakonía, Greece 46 E5
Near Is., U.S.A. 100 C1
Neath, U.K. 15 F4
Neath Port Talbot □, U.K. 15 F4
Nebbou, Burkina Faso 83 C4
Nebelat el Hagana, Sudan 81 E2
Nebine Cr. →, Australia 95 D4
Nebitdag, Turkmenistan 52 F6
Nebo, Australia 94 C4
Nebolchy, Russia 32 C7
Nebraska □, U.S.A. 112 E5
Nebraska City, U.S.A. 112 E7
Nébrodi, Monti, Italy 43 E7
Necedah, U.S.A. 112 C9
Nechako →, Canada 102 C4
Neches →, U.S.A. 113 L8
Nechisar △, Ethiopia 81 F4
Neckar →, Germany 25 F4
Neckartal-Odenwald ⌓, Germany 25 F5
Necochea, Argentina 126 D4
Neda, Spain 36 B2
Nedelino, Bulgaria 45 E9
Nedelišće, Croatia 41 B13
Nédha →, Greece 46 D3
Nedoboyivtsi, Ukraine 29 B11
Needles, Canada 102 D5
Needles, U.S.A. 111 L12
Needles, The, U.K. 15 G6
Ñeembucú □, Paraguay 126 B4
Neemuch = Nimach, India 68 G6
Neenah, U.S.A. 114 C1
Neepawa, Canada 103 C9
Neftçala, Azerbaijan 71 B6
Neftegorsk, Russia 35 H4
Neftekumsk, Russia 35 H7
Nefyn, U.K. 14 E3
Négala, Mali 82 C3
Negapatam = Nagappattinam, India 66 P11
Negara, Indonesia 63 J17
Negaunee, U.S.A. 114 B2
Negele, Ethiopia 81 F4
Negev Desert = Hanegev, Israel 74 E4
Negoiul, Vf., Romania 29 E9
Negombo, Sri Lanka 66 R11
Negotin, Serbia & M. 44 B6
Negotino, Macedonia 44 E6
Negra, Peña, Spain 36 C4
Negra, Pta., Peru 124 E2
Negrais, C. = Maudin Sun, Burma 67 M19
Negreşti, Romania 29 D12
Negreşti-Oaş, Romania 29 C8
Negril, Jamaica 120 a
Negro →, Argentina 128 E4
Negro →, Brazil 124 D7
Negro →, Uruguay 127 C4
Negros, Phil. 61 G5
Negru Vodă, Romania 29 G13
Neguac, Canada 105 C6
Nehalem →, U.S.A. 110 E3
Nehāvand, Iran 71 C6
Nehbandān, Iran 71 D9
Nehoiu, Romania 29 E11
Nei Monggol Zizhiqu □, China 56 D7
Neijiang, China 58 C5
Neillsville, U.S.A. 112 C9
Neilton, U.S.A. 108 C2
Neiqiu, China 56 F8
Neiva, Colombia 124 C3
Neixiang, China 56 H6
Nejanilini L., Canada 103 B9
Nejd = Najd, Si. Arabia 75 B3
Nejo, Ethiopia 81 F4
Nekā, Iran 71 B7
Nekemte, Ethiopia 81 F4
Někheb, Egypt 80 B3
Neksø, Denmark 11 J9
Nelas, Portugal 36 E3
Nelia, Australia 94 C3
Nelidovo, Russia 32 D7
Neligh, U.S.A. 112 D5
Nelkan, Russia 53 D14
Nellore, India 66 M11
Nelson, Canada 102 D5
Nelson, N.Z. 91 J4
Nelson, U.K. 14 D5
Nelson, Ariz., U.S.A. 109 J7
Nelson, Nev., U.S.A. 111 K12
Nelson →, Canada 103 C9
Nelson, C., Australia 95 F3
Nelson, Estrecho, Chile 128 G2
Nelson Forks, Canada 102 B4
Nelson House, Canada 103 B9
Nelson L., Canada 103 B8
Nelson Lakes △, N.Z. 91 J4
Nelspoort, S. Africa 88 E3
Nelspruit, S. Africa 89 D5
Néma, Mauritania 82 B3
Neman = Nemunas →, Lithuania 9 J19
Neman, Russia 9 J20
Neméa, Greece 46 D4
Nemeiben L., Canada 103 B7
Nemërçkë, Mal, Albania 44 F4
Nemira, Vf., Romania 29 D11
Nemiscau, Canada 104 B4
Nemiscau, L., Canada 104 B4
Nemours, France 19 D9
Nemšová, Slovak Rep. 27 C11
Nemunas →, Lithuania 9 J19
Nemuro, Japan 54 C12
Nemuro-Kaikyō, Japan 54 C12
Nemyriv, Ukraine 31 H10
Nen Jiang →, China 57 B13
Nenagh, Ireland 12 D3
Nenasi, Malaysia 65 L4
Nene →, U.K. 15 E8
Nénita, Greece 47 C8
Nenjiang, China 60 B7
Neno, Malawi 87 F3
Neodesha, U.S.A. 113 G7
Neokhórion, Aitolía kai Akarnanía, Greece 46 C3
Neokhórion, Árta, Greece 46 B2
Néon Karlovásion, Greece 47 D8
Néon Petrítsi, Greece 44 E7
Neosho, U.S.A. 113 G7
Neosho →, U.S.A. 113 H7
Nepal ■, Asia 69 F11
Nepalganj, Nepal 69 E9
Nepalganj Road, India 69 E9
Nephi, U.S.A. 108 G8
Nephin, Ireland 12 B2
Nepi, Italy 41 F9
Nepomuk, Czech Rep. 26 B6
Neptune, U.S.A. 117 F10
Nera →, Italy 41 F9
Nera →, Romania 28 F6
Nérac, France 20 D4
Nerang, Australia 95 D5
Neratovice, Czech Rep. 26 A7
Nerchinsk, Russia 53 D12
Nereju, Romania 29 E11
Nerekhta, Russia 32 D11
Neresnytsya, Ukraine 29 B8
Néret, L., Canada 105 B5
Neretvanski Kanal, Croatia 41 E14
Neringa, Lithuania 9 J19
Neris →, Lithuania 9 J21
Nerja, Spain 37 J7
Nerl →, Russia 32 D11
Nerpio, Spain 39 G2
Nerva, Spain 37 H4
Nervi, Italy 40 D6
Neryungri, Russia 53 D13
Nescopeck, U.S.A. 117 E8
Nesebŭr, Bulgaria 45 D11
Ness, L., U.K. 13 D4
Ness City, U.S.A. 112 F5
Nesterov, Russia 30 D9
Nesterov, Ukraine 33 G2
Nestórion, Greece 44 F5
Néstos →, Greece 45 E8
Nesvady, Slovak Rep. 27 D11
Nesvizh = Nyasvizh, Belarus 33 F4
Netanya, Israel 74 C3
Netarhat, India 69 H11
Nete →, Belgium 17 C4
Netherdale, Australia 94 K6
Netherlands ■, Europe 17 C5
Netherlands Antilles ⊠, W. Indies 124 A5
Neto →, Italy 43 C10
Netrang, India 68 J5
Nettancourt, France 19 D11
Nettetal, Germany 24 D2
Nettilling L., Canada 101 B12
Nettuno, Italy 42 A5
Netzahualcoyotl, Presa, Mexico 119 D6
Neu-Isenburg, Germany 25 E4
Neu-Ulm, Germany 25 G6
Neubrandenburg, Germany 24 B9
Neubukow, Germany 24 A7
Neuburg, Germany 25 G7
Neuchâtel, Switz. 25 J2
Neuchâtel □, Switz. 25 J2
Neuchâtel, Lac de, Switz. 25 J2
Neudau, Austria 26 D9
Neuenhagen, Germany 24 C9
Neuenhaus, Germany 24 C2
Neuf-Brisach, France 19 D14
Neufahrn, Bayern, Germany 25 G8
Neufahrn, Bayern, Germany 25 G7
Neufchâteau, Belgium 17 E5
Neufchâteau, France 19 D12
Neufchâtel-en-Bray, France 18 C8
Neufchâtel-sur-Aisne, France 19 C11
Neuhaus, Germany 24 B6
Neuillé-Pont-Pierre, France 18 E7
Neuilly-St-Front, France 19 C10
Neukalen, Germany 24 B8
Neumarkt, Germany 25 F7
Neumünster, Germany 24 A5
Neung-sur-Beuvron, France 19 E8
Neunkirchen, Austria 26 D9
Neunkirchen, Germany 25 F3
Neuquén, Argentina 128 D3
Neuquén □, Argentina 126 D2
Neuruppin, Germany 24 C8
Neusäss, Germany 25 G6
Neuse →, U.S.A. 115 H7
Neusiedl, Austria 27 D9
Neusiedler See, Austria 27 D9
Neusiedler See-Seewinkel △, Austria 27 D9
Neuss, Germany 24 D2
Neussargues-Moissac, France 20 C7
Neustadt, Bayern, Germany 25 F8
Neustadt, Bayern, Germany 25 G7
Neustadt, Bayern, Germany 25 F6
Neustadt, Bayern, Germany 25 E7
Neustadt, Brandenburg, Germany 24 C8
Neustadt, Hessen, Germany 24 E5
Neustadt, Niedersachsen, Germany 24 C5
Neustadt, Rhld-Pfz., Germany 25 F4
Neustadt, Sachsen, Germany 24 D10
Neustadt, Schleswig-Holstein, Germany 24 A6
Neustadt, Thüringen, Germany 24 E7
Neustrelitz, Germany 24 B9
Neuvic, France 20 C6
Neuville-sur-Saône, France 21 C8
Neuvy-le-Roi, France 18 E7
Neuvy-St-Sépulchre, France 19 F8
Neuvy-sur-Barangeon, France 19 E9
Neuwerk, Germany 24 B4
Neuwied, Germany 24 E3
Neva →, Russia 32 C6
Nevada, Iowa, U.S.A. 112 D8
Nevada, Mo., U.S.A. 113 G7
Nevada □, U.S.A. 108 G5
Nevada City, U.S.A. 110 F6
Nevado, Cerro, Argentina 126 D2
Nevado de Colima = Volcán de Colima △, Mexico 118 D4
Nevado de Tres Cruces △, Chile 126 B2
Nevel, Russia 32 D5
Nevers, France 19 F10
Nevertire, Australia 95 E4
Nevesinje, Bos.-H. 44 C2
Neville, Canada 103 D7
Nevinnomyssk, Russia 35 H6
Nevis, St. Kitts & Nevis 121 C7
Nevrokop = Gotse Delchev, Bulgaria 44 E7
Nevşehir, Turkey 70 B2
Nevskoye, Russia 30 D9
New →, U.S.A. 114 F5
New Aiyansh, Canada 102 B3
New Albany, Ind., U.S.A. 114 F3
New Albany, Miss., U.S.A. 113 H10
New Albany, Pa., U.S.A. 117 E8
New Amsterdam, Guyana 124 B7
New Angledool, Australia 95 D4
New Baltimore, U.S.A. 116 D2
New Bedford, U.S.A. 117 E14
New Berlin, N.Y., U.S.A. 117 D9
New Berlin, Pa., U.S.A. 116 F8
New Bern, U.S.A. 115 H7
New Bethlehem, U.S.A. 116 F5
New Bloomfield, U.S.A. 116 F7
New Boston, U.S.A. 113 J7
New Braunfels, U.S.A. 113 L5
New Brighton, N.Z. 91 K4
New Brighton, U.S.A. 116 F4
New Britain, Papua N. G. 96 H7
New Britain, U.S.A. 117 E12
New Brunswick, U.S.A. 117 F10
New Brunswick □, Canada 105 C6
New Bussa, Nigeria 83 D5
New Caledonia ⊠, Pac. Oc. 96 K8
New Castile = Castilla-La Mancha □, Spain 6 H5
New Castle, Ind., U.S.A. 114 F3
New Castle, Pa., U.S.A. 116 F4
New City, U.S.A. 117 E11
New Concord, U.S.A. 116 G3
New Cumberland, U.S.A. 116 F4
New Cuyama, U.S.A. 111 L7
New Delhi, India 68 E7
New Denver, Canada 102 D5
New Don Pedro Reservoir, U.S.A. 110 H6
New England, U.S.A. 107 B12
New England, N. Dak., U.S.A. 112 B3
New England Ra., Australia 95 E5
New Forest, U.K. 15 G6
New Galloway, U.K. 13 F4
New Glasgow, Canada 105 C7
New Guinea, Oceania 96 H5
New Hamburg, Canada 116 C4
New Hampshire □, U.S.A. 117 C13
New Hampton, U.S.A. 112 D8
New Hanover, S. Africa 89 D5
New Hartford, U.S.A. 117 C9
New Haven, Conn., U.S.A. 117 E12
New Haven, Mich., U.S.A. 116 D2
New Hazelton, Canada 102 B3
New Hebrides = Vanuatu ■, Pac. Oc. 96 J8
New Holland, U.S.A. 117 F8
New Iberia, U.S.A. 113 K9
New Ireland, Papua N. G. 96 H7
New Jersey □, U.S.A. 114 E8
New Kensington, U.S.A. 116 F5
New Lexington, U.S.A. 114 F4
New Liskeard, Canada 104 C4
New London, Conn., U.S.A. 117 E12
New London, Ohio, U.S.A. 116 E2
New London, Wis., U.S.A. 112 C10
New Madrid, U.S.A. 113 G10
New Martinsville, U.S.A. 114 F5
New Meadows, U.S.A. 108 D5
New Melones L., U.S.A. 110 H6
New Mexico □, U.S.A. 109 J10
New Milford, Conn., U.S.A. 117 E11
New Milford, Pa., U.S.A. 117 E9
New Norcia, Australia 93 F2
New Norfolk, Australia 95 G4
New Orleans, U.S.A. 113 L9
New Philadelphia, U.S.A. 116 F3
New Plymouth, N.Z. 91 H5
New Plymouth, U.S.A. 108 E5
New Port Richey, U.S.A. 115 L4
New Providence, Bahamas 120 A4
New Quay, U.K. 15 E3
New Radnor, U.K. 15 E4
New Richmond, Canada 105 C6
New Richmond, U.S.A. 112 C8
New River Gorge △, U.S.A. 114 G5
New Roads, U.S.A. 113 K9
New Rochelle, U.S.A. 117 F11
New Rockford, U.S.A. 112 B5
New Romney, U.K. 15 G8
New Ross, Ireland 12 D5
New Salem, U.S.A. 112 B4
New Scone = Scone, U.K. 13 E5
New Siberian I. = Novaya Sibir, Ostrov, Russia 53 B16
New Siberian Is. = Novosibirskiye Ostrova, Russia 53 B15
New Smyrna Beach, U.S.A. 115 L5
New South Wales □, Australia 95 E4
New Tecumseth, Canada 116 B5
New Town, U.S.A. 112 B3
New Tredegar, U.K. 15 F4
New Ulm, U.S.A. 112 C7
New Waterford, Canada 105 C7
New-Wes-Valley, Canada 105 C9
New Westminster, Canada 110 A4
New York, U.S.A. 117 F11
New York □, U.S.A. 117 D9
New York J.F. Kennedy International ✕ (JFK), U.S.A. 117 F11
New York Mts., U.S.A. 109 J6
New Zealand ■, Oceania 91 J6
Newaj →, India 68 G7
Newala, Tanzania 87 E4
Newark, Del., U.S.A. 114 F8
Newark, N.J., U.S.A. 117 F10
Newark, N.Y., U.S.A. 116 C7
Newark, Ohio, U.S.A. 116 F2
Newark International ✕ (EWR), U.S.A. 117 F10
Newark-on-Trent, U.K. 14 D7
Newark Valley, U.S.A. 117 D8
Newberg, U.S.A. 108 D2
Newberry, Mich., U.S.A. 114 B3
Newberry, S.C., U.S.A. 115 H5
Newberry ⌓, U.S.A. 108 E2
Newberry Springs, U.S.A. 111 L10
Newboro L., Canada 117 B8
Newbridge = Droichead Nua, Ireland 12 C5
Newburgh, Canada 116 B8
Newburgh, U.S.A. 117 E10
Newbury, U.K. 15 F6
Newbury, N.H., U.S.A. 117 B12
Newbury, Vt., U.S.A. 117 B12
Newburyport, U.S.A. 115 D10
Newcastle, Australia 95 E5
Newcastle, N.B., Canada 105 C6
Newcastle, Ont., Canada 104 D4
Newcastle, S. Africa 89 D4
Newcastle, U.K. 12 B6
Newcastle, Calif., U.S.A. 110 G5
Newcastle, Wyo., U.S.A. 112 D2
Newcastle Emlyn, U.K. 15 E3
Newcastle Ra., Australia 92 C5
Newcastle-under-Lyme, U.K. 14 D5
Newcastle-upon-Tyne, U.K. 14 C6
Newcastle Waters, Australia 94 B1
Newcastle West, Ireland 12 D2
Newcomb, U.S.A. 117 C10
Newcomerstown, U.S.A. 116 F3
Newdegate, Australia 93 F2
Newell, Australia 94 B4
Newell, U.S.A. 112 C3
Newfane, U.S.A. 116 C6
Newfield, U.S.A. 117 D8
Newfound L., U.S.A. 117 C13
Newfoundland, Canada 105 C8
Newfoundland, U.S.A. 117 E9
Newfoundland & Labrador □, Canada 105 B8
Newhall, U.S.A. 111 L8
Newhaven, U.K. 15 G8
Newkirk, U.S.A. 113 G6
Newlyn, U.K. 15 G2
Newman, Australia 92 D2
Newman, U.S.A. 110 H5
Newmarket, Canada 116 B5
Newmarket, Ireland 12 D2
Newmarket, U.K. 15 E8
Newmarket, U.S.A. 117 C14
Newnan, U.S.A. 115 J3
Newport, Ireland 12 C2
Newport, I. of W., U.K. 15 G6
Newport, Newp., U.K. 15 F5
Newport, Ark., U.S.A. 113 H9
Newport, Ky., U.S.A. 114 F3
Newport, N.H., U.S.A. 117 C12
Newport, N.Y., U.S.A. 117 C9
Newport, Oreg., U.S.A. 108 D1
Newport, Pa., U.S.A. 116 F7
Newport, R.I., U.S.A. 117 E13
Newport, Tenn., U.S.A. 115 H4
Newport, Vt., U.S.A. 117 B12
Newport, Wash., U.S.A. 108 B5
Newport □, U.K. 15 F4
Newport Beach, U.S.A. 111 M9
Newport News, U.S.A. 114 G7
Newport Pagnell, U.K. 15 E7
Newquay, U.K. 15 G2
Newry, U.K. 12 B5
Newton, Ill., U.S.A. 112 F10
Newton, Iowa, U.S.A. 112 E8
Newton, Kans., U.S.A. 113 F6
Newton, Mass., U.S.A. 117 D13
Newton, Miss., U.S.A. 113 J10
Newton, N.C., U.S.A. 115 H5
Newton, N.J., U.S.A. 117 E10
Newton, Tex., U.S.A. 113 K8
Newton Abbot, U.K. 15 G4
Newton Aycliffe, U.K. 14 C6
Newton Falls, U.S.A. 116 E4
Newton Stewart, U.K. 13 G4
Newtonmore, U.K. 13 D4
Newtown, U.K. 15 E4
Newtownabbey, U.K. 12 B6
Newtownards, U.K. 12 B6
Newtownbarry = Bunclody, Ireland 12 D5
Newtownstewart, U.K. 12 B4
Newville, U.S.A. 116 F7
Nexon, France 20 C5
Neya, Russia 34 A6
Neyrīz, Iran 71 D7
Neyshābūr, Iran 71 B8
Nezhin = Nizhyn, Ukraine 33 G6
Nezperce, U.S.A. 108 C5
Nezvysko, Ukraine 29 B10
Ngabang, Indonesia 62 D3
Ngabordamlu, Tanjung, Indonesia 63 F8
N'Gage, Angola 84 F3
Ngala, Nigeria 83 C7
Ngambé, Centre, Cameroon 83 D7
Ngambé, Littoral, Cameroon 83 E7
Ngami Depression, Botswana 88 C3
Ngamo, Zimbabwe 87 F2
Ngangala, Sudan 81 G3
Nganglong Kangri, China 67 C12
Ngao, Thailand 64 C2
Ngaoundéré, Cameroon 84 C2
Ngapara, N.Z. 91 L3
Ngara, Tanzania 86 C3
Ngawi, Indonesia 63 G14
Nghia Lo, Vietnam 58 G5
Ngoboli, Sudan 81 G3
Ngoma, Malawi 87 E3
Ngomahura, Zimbabwe 87 G3
Ngomba, Tanzania 87 D3
Ngop, Sudan 81 F3
Ngoring Hu, China 60 C4
Ngorkou, Mali 82 B4
Ngorongoro, Tanzania 86 C4
Ngorongoro ⌓, Tanzania 86 C4
Ngozi, Burundi 86 C2
Ngudu, Tanzania 86 C3
Nguigmi, Niger 79 F8
Nguila, Cameroon 83 E7
Nguiu, Australia 92 B5
Ngukurr, Australia 94 A1
Ngunga, Tanzania 86 C3
Nguru, Nigeria 83 C7
Nguru Mts., Tanzania 86 D4

Ngusi, *Malawi* 87 E3
Nguyen Binh, *Vietnam* 58 F5
Nha Trang, *Vietnam* 65 F7
Nhacoongo, *Mozam.* 89 C6
Nhamaabué, *Mozam.* 87 F4
Nhamundá →, *Brazil* 125 D7
Nhangulaze, L., *Mozam.* 89 C5
Nhill, *Australia* 95 F3
Nho Quan, *Vietnam* 58 G5
Nhulunbuy, *Australia* 94 A2
Nia-nia, *Dem. Rep. of the Congo* 86 B2
Niafounké, *Mali* 82 B4
Niagara Falls, *Canada* 116 C5
Niagara Falls, *U.S.A.* 116 C6
Niagara-on-the-Lake, *Canada* 116 C5
Niah, *Malaysia* 62 D4
Niamey, *Niger* 83 C5
Niandan-Koro, *Guinea* 82 C3
Nianforando, *Guinea* 82 D2
Niangara, *Dem. Rep. of the Congo* 86 B2
Niangbo, *Ivory C.* 82 D3
Niangoloko, *Burkina Faso* 82 C4
Niantic, *U.S.A.* 117 E12
Niaro, *Sudan* 81 E3
Nias, *Indonesia* 62 D1
Niassa ⌓, *Mozam.* 87 E4
Niassa □, *Mozam.* 87 E4
Nibāk, *Si. Arabia* 71 E7
Nibe, *Denmark* 11 H3
Nicaragua ■, *Cent. Amer.* 120 D2
Nicaragua, L. de, *Nic.* 120 D2
Nicastro, *Italy* 43 D9
Nice, *France* 21 E11
Nice ✕ (NCE), *France* 21 E11
Niceville, *U.S.A.* 115 K2
Nichicun, L., *Canada* 105 B5
Nichinan, *Japan* 55 J5
Nicholas Channel, *W. Indies* 120 B3
Nicholasville, *U.S.A.* 114 G3
Nichols, *U.S.A.* 117 D8
Nicholson, *Australia* 92 C4
Nicholson, *U.S.A.* 117 E9
Nicholson →, *Australia* 94 B2
Nicholson L., *Canada* 103 A8
Nicholson Ra., *Australia* 93 E2
Nicholville, *U.S.A.* 117 B10
Nicobar Is., *Ind. Oc.* 50 J13
Nicola, *Canada* 102 C4
Nicolls Town, *Bahamas* 120 A4
Nicopolis, *Greece* 46 B2
Nicosia, *Cyprus* 49 D12
Nicosia, *Italy* 43 E7
Nicótera, *Italy* 43 D8
Nicoya, *Costa Rica* 120 D2
Nicoya, G. de, *Costa Rica* 120 E3
Nicoya, Pen. de, *Costa Rica* 120 E2
Nida, *Lithuania* 30 C8
Nidd →, *U.K.* 14 D6
Nidda, *Germany* 25 E5
Nidda →, *Germany* 25 E4
Nidwalden □, *Switz.* 25 J4
Nidzica, *Poland* 31 E7
Niebüll, *Germany* 24 A4
Nied →, *Germany* 19 C13
Niederaula, *Germany* 24 E5
Niederbayern □, *Germany* 25 G8
Niederbronn-les-Bains, *France* 19 D14
Niedere Tauern, *Austria* 26 D7
Niederlausitz, *Germany* 24 D9
Niederösterreich □, *Austria* 26 C8
Niedersachsen □, *Germany* 24 C4
Niedersächsisches Wattenmeer △, *Germany* 24 B3
Niekerkshoop, *S. Africa* 88 D3
Niellé, *Ivory C.* 82 C3
Niemba, *Dem. Rep. of the Congo* 86 D2
Niemen = Nemunas →, *Lithuania* 9 J19
Niemodlin, *Poland* 31 H4
Nienburg, *Germany* 24 C5
Niepołomice, *Poland* 31 H7
Niers →, *Germany* 24 D1
Niesky, *Germany* 24 D10
Nieszawa, *Poland* 31 F5
Nieu Bethesda, *S. Africa* 88 E3
Nieuw Amsterdam, *Suriname* 125 B7
Nieuw Nickerie, *Suriname* 125 B7
Nieuwoudtville, *S. Africa* 88 E2
Nieuwpoort, *Belgium* 17 C2
Nieves, Pico de las, *Canary Is.* 48 G4
Nièvre □, *France* 19 E10
Niga, *Mali* 82 C3
Niğde, *Turkey* 70 B2
Nigel, *S. Africa* 89 D4
Niger □, *Nigeria* 83 D6
Niger ■, *W. Afr.* 83 B7
Niger →, *W. Afr.* 83 D6
Niger Delta, *Africa* 83 E6
Nigeria ■, *W. Afr.* 83 D6
Nighasin, *India* 69 E9
Nightcaps, *N.Z.* 91 L2
Nigríta, *Greece* 44 F7
Nii-Jima, *Japan* 55 G9
Niigata, *Japan* 54 F9
Niigata □, *Japan* 55 F9
Niihama, *Japan* 55 H6
Niihau, *U.S.A.* 106 H14
Niimi, *Japan* 55 G6
Niitsu, *Japan* 54 F9
Níjar, *Spain* 39 J2
Nijil, *Jordan* 74 E4
Nijkerk, *Neths.* 17 B5
Nijmegen, *Neths.* 17 C5
Nijverdal, *Neths.* 17 B6
Nīk Pey, *Iran* 71 B6
Nike, *Nigeria* 83 D6
Nikiniki, *Indonesia* 63 F6
Nikísiani, *Greece* 45 F8
Nikítas, *Greece* 44 F7
Nikki, *Benin* 83 D5
Nikkō, *Japan* 55 F9
Nikkō △, *Japan* 55 F9
Nikolayev = Mykolayiv, *Ukraine* 33 J7
Nikolayevsk, *Russia* 34 E7
Nikolayevsk-na-Amur, *Russia* 53 D15
Nikolsk, *Russia* 34 D8
Nikolskoye, *Russia* 53 D17
Nikopol, *Bulgaria* 45 C8
Nikopol, *Ukraine* 33 J8
Niksar, *Turkey* 72 B7
Nīkshahr, *Iran* 71 E9
Nikšić, *Serbia & M.* 44 D2
Nîl, Nahr en →, *Africa* 80 H7
Nîl el Abyad →, *Sudan* 81 D3
Nîl el Azraq →, *Sudan* 81 D3
Nila, *Indonesia* 63 F7
Niland, *U.S.A.* 111 M11
Nile = Nîl, Nahr en →, *Africa* 80 H7
Nile Delta, *Egypt* 80 H7
Niles, *Mich., U.S.A.* 114 E2
Niles, *Ohio, U.S.A.* 116 E4
Nilüfer →, *Turkey* 45 F12
Nim Ka Thana, *India* 68 F6
Nimach, *India* 68 G6
Nimbahera, *India* 68 G6
Nîmes, *France* 21 E8
Nimfaíon, Ákra = Pínnes, Ákra, *Greece* 45 F8
Nimmitabel, *Australia* 95 F4
Nimule, *Sudan* 81 G3
Nimule △, *Sudan* 81 G3
Nin, *Croatia* 41 D12
Nīnawá, *Iraq* 70 B4
Nīnawá □, *Iraq* 70 B4
Nindigully, *Australia* 95 D4
Nineveh = Nīnawá, *Iraq* 70 B4
Ning Xian, *China* 56 G4
Ningaloo ⌓, *Australia* 92 D1
Ning'an, *China* 57 B15
Ningbo, *China* 59 C13
Ningcheng, *China* 57 D10
Ningde, *China* 59 D12
Ningdu, *China* 59 D10
Ninggang, *China* 59 D9
Ningguo, *China* 59 B12
Ninghai, *China* 59 C13
Ninghua, *China* 59 D11
Ningi, *Nigeria* 83 C6
Ningjin, *China* 56 F8
Ningjing Shan, *China* 58 C2
Ninglang, *China* 58 D3
Ningling, *China* 56 G8
Ningming, *China* 58 F6
Ningnan, *China* 58 D4
Ningpo = Ningbo, *China* 59 C13
Ningqiang, *China* 56 H4
Ningshan, *China* 56 H5
Ningsia Hui A.R. = Ningxia Huizu Zizhiqu □, *China* 56 F4
Ningwu, *China* 56 E7
Ningxia Huizu Zizhiqu □, *China* 56 F4
Ningxiang, *China* 59 C9
Ningyang, *China* 56 G9
Ningyuan, *China* 59 E8
Ninh Binh, *Vietnam* 58 G5
Ninh Giang, *Vietnam* 64 B6
Ninh Hoa, *Vietnam* 64 F7
Ninh Ma, *Vietnam* 64 F7
Nini-Suhien △, *Ghana* 82 D4
Ninove, *Belgium* 17 D4
Nioaque, *Brazil* 127 A4
Niobrara, *U.S.A.* 112 D6
Niobrara →, *U.S.A.* 112 D6
Niokolo-Koba △, *Senegal* 82 C2
Niono, *Mali* 82 C3
Nionsamoridougou, *Guinea* 82 D3
Nioro du Rip, *Senegal* 82 C1
Nioro du Sahel, *Mali* 82 B3
Niort, *France* 20 B3
Nipawin, *Canada* 103 C8
Nipfjället, *Sweden* 10 C6
Nipigon, *Canada* 104 C2
Nipigon, L., *Canada* 104 C2
Nipishish L., *Canada* 105 B7
Nipissing, L., *Canada* 104 C4
Nipomo, *U.S.A.* 111 K6
Nipton, *U.S.A.* 111 K11
Niquelândia, *Brazil* 125 F9
Nīr, *Iran* 70 B5
Nirasaki, *Japan* 55 G9
Nirmal, *India* 66 K11
Nirmali, *India* 69 F12
Niš, *Serbia & M.* 44 C5
Nisa, *Portugal* 37 F3
Nisāb, *Si. Arabia* 70 D5
Nisāb, *Yemen* 75 E4
Nišava →, *Serbia & M.* 44 C5
Niscemi, *Italy* 43 E7
Nishinomiya, *Japan* 55 G7
Nishino'omote, *Japan* 55 J5
Nishiwaki, *Japan* 55 G7
Nísíros, *Greece* 47 E9
Niška Banja, *Serbia & M.* 44 C6
Niskibi →, *Canada* 104 A2
Nisko, *Poland* 31 H9
Nisporeni, *Moldova* 29 C13
Nisqually →, *U.S.A.* 110 C4
Nissáki, *Greece* 49 A3
Nissan →, *Sweden* 11 H6
Nissum Bredning, *Denmark* 11 H2
Nissum Fjord, *Denmark* 11 H2
Nistru = Dnister →, *Europe* 33 J6
Nisutlin →, *Canada* 102 A2
Nitchequon, *Canada* 105 B5
Niterói, *Brazil* 127 A7
Nith →, *Canada* 116 C4
Nith →, *U.K.* 13 F5
Nitmiluk △, *Australia* 92 B5
Nitra, *Slovak Rep.* 27 C11
Nitra →, *Slovak Rep.* 27 D11
Nitriansky □, *Slovak Rep.* 27 C11
Nittenau, *Germany* 25 F8
Niuafo'ou, *Tonga* 91 B11
Niue, *Cook Is.* 97 J11
Niulan Jiang →, *China* 58 D4
Niut, *Indonesia* 62 D4
Niutou Shan, *China* 59 C13
Niuzhuang, *China* 57 D12
Nivala, *Finland* 8 E21
Nivelles, *Belgium* 17 D4
Nivernais, *France* 19 E10
Niwas, *India* 69 H9
Nixon, *U.S.A.* 113 L6
Nizamabad, *India* 66 K11
Nizamghat, *India* 67 E19
Nizhne Kolymsk, *Russia* 53 C17
Nizhneangarsk, *Russia* 53 D11
Nizhnegorskiy = Nyzhnohirskyy, *Ukraine* 33 K8
Nizhnekamsk, *Russia* 34 C10
Nizhneudinsk, *Russia* 53 D10
Nizhnevartovsk, *Russia* 52 C8
Nizhniy Chir, *Russia* 35 F6
Nizhniy Lomov, *Russia* 34 D6
Nizhniy Novgorod, *Russia* 34 B7
Nizhniy Tagil, *Russia* 52 D6
Nizhyn, *Ukraine* 33 G6
Nizina Mazowiecka, *Poland* 31 F8
Nizip, *Turkey* 70 B3
Nízké Tatry, *Slovak Rep.* 27 C12
Nízké Tatry △, *Slovak Rep.* 27 C12
Nízký Jeseník, *Czech Rep.* 27 B10
Nizza Monferrato, *Italy* 40 D5
Njakwa, *Malawi* 87 E3
Njanji, *Zambia* 87 E3
Njegoš, *Serbia & M.* 44 D2
Njinjo, *Tanzania* 87 D4
Njombe, *Tanzania* 87 D3
Njombe →, *Tanzania* 86 D4
Njurundabommen, *Sweden* 10 B11
Nkambe, *Cameroon* 83 D7
Nkana, *Zambia* 87 E2
Nkandla, *S. Africa* 89 D5
Nkawkaw, *Ghana* 83 D4
Nkayi, *Zimbabwe* 87 F2
Nkhotakota, *Malawi* 87 E3
Nkhotakota ⌓, *Malawi* 87 E3
Nkongsamba, *Cameroon* 83 E6
Nkurenkuru, *Namibia* 88 B2
Nkwanta, *Ghana* 82 D4
Nmai →, *Burma* 58 F2
Noakhali = Maijdi, *Bangla.* 67 H17
Nobel, *Canada* 116 A4
Nobeoka, *Japan* 55 H5
Noblejas, *Spain* 36 F7
Noblesville, *U.S.A.* 114 E3
Noboribetsu, *Japan* 54 C10
Noce →, *Italy* 40 B8
Nocera Inferiore, *Italy* 43 B7
Nocera Umbra, *Italy* 41 E9
Noci, *Italy* 43 B10
Nocona, *U.S.A.* 113 J6
Nocrich, *Romania* 29 E9
Noda, *Japan* 55 G9
Nogales, *Mexico* 118 A2
Nogales, *U.S.A.* 109 L8
Nogaro, *France* 20 E3
Nogat →, *Poland* 30 D6
Nōgata, *Japan* 55 H5
Nogent, *France* 19 D12
Nogent-le-Rotrou, *France* 18 D7
Nogent-sur-Seine, *France* 19 D10
Noggerup, *Australia* 93 F2
Noginsk, *Moskva, Russia* 32 E10
Noginsk, *Tunguska, Russia* 53 C10
Nogoa →, *Australia* 94 C4
Nogoyá, *Argentina* 126 C4
Nógrád □, *Hungary* 28 C4
Noguera Pallaresa →, *Spain* 38 D5
Noguera Ribagorzana →, *Spain* 38 D5
Nohar, *India* 68 E6
Nohfelden, *Germany* 25 F3
Nohta, *India* 69 H8
Noia, *Spain* 36 C2
Noire, Montagne, *France* 20 E6
Noires, Mts., *France* 18 D3
Noirétable, *France* 20 C7
Noirmoutier, Î. de, *France* 18 F4
Noirmoutier-en-l'Île, *France* 18 F4
Nojane, *Botswana* 88 C3
Nojima-Zaki, *Japan* 55 G9
Nok Kundi, *Pakistan* 66 E3
Nok Ta Phao, Ko, *Thailand* 65 b
Nokaneng, *Botswana* 88 B3
Nokia, *Finland* 9 F20
Nokomis, *Canada* 103 C8
Nokomis L., *Canada* 103 B8
Nola, *C.A.R.* 84 D3
Nola, *Italy* 43 B7
Nolay, *France* 19 F11
Noli, C. di, *Italy* 40 D5
Nolinsk, *Russia* 34 B9
Noma Omuramba →, *Namibia* 88 B3
Nombre de Dios, *Panama* 120 E4
Nome, *U.S.A.* 100 B3
Nomo-Zaki, *Japan* 55 H4
Nonacho L., *Canada* 103 A7
Nonancourt, *France* 18 D8
Nonda, *Australia* 94 C3
None, *Italy* 40 D4
Nong Chang, *Thailand* 64 E2
Nong Het, *Laos* 64 C4
Nong Khai, *Thailand* 64 D4
Nong'an, *China* 57 B13
Nongoma, *S. Africa* 89 D5
Nongsa, *Indonesia* 65 d
Nonoava, *Mexico* 118 B3
Nonoava →, *Mexico* 118 B3
Nonthaburi, *Thailand* 64 F3
Nontron, *France* 20 C4
Nonza, *France* 21 F13
Noonamah, *Australia* 92 B5
Noondie, L., *Australia* 93 E2
Noord Brabant □, *Neths.* 17 C5
Noord Holland □, *Neths.* 17 B4
Noordbeveland, *Neths.* 17 C3
Noordoostpolder, *Neths.* 17 B5
Noordwijk, *Neths.* 17 B4
Noosa Heads, *Australia* 95 D5
Nootka I., *Canada* 102 D3
Nopiming ⌓, *Canada* 103 C9
Nora, *Eritrea* 81 D5
Nora, *Sweden* 10 E9
Noralee, *Canada* 102 C3
Noranda = Rouyn-Noranda, *Canada* 104 C4
Norberg, *Sweden* 10 D9
Nórcia, *Italy* 41 F10
Norco, *U.S.A.* 111 M9
Nord □, *France* 19 B10
Nord-Kivu □, *Dem. Rep. of the Congo* 86 C2
Nord-Ostsee-Kanal, *Germany* 24 A5
Nord-Pas-de-Calais □, *France* 19 B9
Nordaustlandet, *Svalbard* 4 B9
Nordborg, *Denmark* 11 J3
Nordby, *Denmark* 11 J2
Norddeich, *Germany* 24 B3
Nordegg, *Canada* 102 C5
Norden, *Germany* 24 B3
Nordenham, *Germany* 24 B4
Norderney, *Germany* 24 B3
Norderstedt, *Germany* 24 B6
Nordfjord, *Norway* 9 F11
Nordfriesische Inseln, *Germany* 24 A4
Nordhausen, *Germany* 24 D6
Nordhorn, *Germany* 24 C3
Norðoyar, *Færoe Is.* 8 E9
Nördinge-Nol, *Sweden* 11 G6
Nordingrå, *Sweden* 10 B12
Nordjyllands Amtskommune □, *Denmark* 11 G4
Nordkapp, *Norway* 8 A21
Nordkapp, *Svalbard* 4 A9
Nordkinnhalvøya, *Norway* 8 A22
Nördlicher Teutoburger Wald-Wiehengebirge ⌓, *Germany* 24 C4
Nördlingen, *Germany* 25 G6
Nordrhein-Westfalen □, *Germany* 24 D3
Nordstrand, *Germany* 24 A4
Nordvik, *Russia* 53 B12
Nore →, *Ireland* 12 D4
Norfolk, *Canada* 116 D4
Norfolk, *Nebr., U.S.A.* 112 D6
Norfolk, *Va., U.S.A.* 114 G7
Norfolk □, *U.K.* 15 E8
Norfolk I., *Pac. Oc.* 96 K8
Norfork L., *U.S.A.* 113 G8
Norilsk, *Russia* 53 C9
Norma, Mt., *Australia* 94 C3
Normal, *U.S.A.* 112 E10
Norman, *U.S.A.* 113 H6
Norman →, *Australia* 94 B3
Norman Wells, *Canada* 100 B7
Normanby →, *Australia* 94 A3
Normandie-Maine ⌓, *France* 18 D6
Normandin, *Canada* 104 C5
Normanhurst, Mt., *Australia* 93 E3
Normanton, *Australia* 94 B3
Normétal, *Canada* 104 C4
Norquay, *Canada* 103 C8
Norquinco, *Argentina* 128 E2
Norra Dellen, *Sweden* 10 C10
Norra Kvill △, *Sweden* 11 G9
Norra Ulvön, *Sweden* 10 A12
Norrahammar, *Sweden* 11 G8
Norrbottens län □, *Sweden* 8 C19
Nørre Åby, *Denmark* 11 J3
Nørre Alslev, *Denmark* 11 K5
Nørresundby, *Denmark* 11 G3
Norrhult-Klavreström, *Sweden* 11 G9
Norris Point, *Canada* 105 C8
Norristown, *U.S.A.* 117 F9
Norrköping, *Sweden* 11 F10
Norrland, *Sweden* 9 E16
Norrsundet, *Sweden* 10 D11
Norrtälje, *Sweden* 10 E12
Norseman, *Australia* 93 F3
Norsk, *Russia* 53 D14
Norte, Pta. del, *Canary Is.* 48 G2
Norte, Serra do, *Brazil* 124 F7
North, C., *Canada* 105 C7
North Adams, *U.S.A.* 117 D11
North America 98 F10
North Arm, *Canada* 102 A5
North Atlantic Ocean, *Atl. Oc.* 2 C7
North Augusta, *U.S.A.* 115 J5
North Ayrshire □, *U.K.* 13 F4
North Bass I., *U.S.A.* 116 E2
North Battleford, *Canada* 103 C7
North Bay, *Canada* 104 C4
North Belcher Is., *Canada* 104 A4
North Bend, *Oreg., U.S.A.* 108 E1
North Bend, *Pa., U.S.A.* 116 E7
North Bend, *Wash., U.S.A.* 110 C5
North Bennington, *U.S.A.* 117 D11
North Berwick, *U.K.* 13 E6
North Berwick, *U.S.A.* 117 C14
North C., *Canada* 105 C7
North C., *N.Z.* 91 F4
North Canadian →, *U.S.A.* 113 H7
North Canton, *U.S.A.* 116 F3
North Cape = Nordkapp, *Norway* 8 A21
North Cape = Nordkapp, *Svalbard* 4 A9
North Caribou L., *Canada* 104 B1
North Carolina □, *U.S.A.* 115 H6
North Cascades △, *U.S.A.* 108 B3
North Channel, *Canada* 104 C3
North Channel, *U.K.* 13 F3
North Charleston, *U.S.A.* 115 J6
North Chicago, *U.S.A.* 114 D2
North Creek, *U.S.A.* 117 C11
North Dakota □, *U.S.A.* 112 B5
North Downs, *U.K.* 15 F8
North East, *U.S.A.* 116 D5
North East Frontier Agency = Arunachal Pradesh □, *India* 67 F19
North East Lincolnshire □, *U.K.* 14 D7
North Eastern □, *Kenya* 86 B5
North Esk →, *U.K.* 13 E6
North European Plain, *Europe* 6 E10
North Foreland, *U.K.* 15 F9
North Fork, *U.S.A.* 110 H7
North Fork American →, *U.S.A.* 110 G5
North Fork Feather →, *U.S.A.* 110 F5
North Fork Grand →, *U.S.A.* 112 C3
North Fork Red →, *U.S.A.* 113 H5
North Frisian Is. = Nordfriesische Inseln, *Germany* 24 A4
North Gower, *Canada* 117 A9
North Hd., *Australia* 93 F1
North Henik L., *Canada* 103 A9
North Highlands, *U.S.A.* 110 G5
North Horr, *Kenya* 86 B4
North I., *Kenya* 86 B4
North I., *N.Z.* 91 H5
North Kingsville, *U.S.A.* 116 E4
North Kitui ⌓, *Kenya* 86 C4
North Knife →, *Canada* 103 B10
North Koel →, *India* 69 G10
North Korea ■, *Asia* 57 E14
North Lakhimpur, *India* 67 F19
North Lanarkshire □, *U.K.* 13 F5
North Las Vegas, *U.S.A.* 111 J11
North Lincolnshire □, *U.K.* 14 D7
North Little Rock, *U.S.A.* 113 H8
North Loup →, *U.S.A.* 112 E5
North Luangwa △, *Zambia* 87 E3
North Magnetic Pole, *Canada* 4 A2
North Minch, *U.K.* 13 C3
North Moose L., *Canada* 103 C8
North Moose L., *Man., Canada* 103 C8
North Myrtle Beach, *U.S.A.* 115 J6
North Nahanni →, *Canada* 102 A4
North Olmsted, *U.S.A.* 116 E3
North Ossetia □, *Russia* 35 J7
North Pagai, I. = Pagai Utara, Pulau, *Indonesia* 62 E2
North Palisade, *U.S.A.* 110 H8
North Platte, *U.S.A.* 112 E4
North Platte →, *U.S.A.* 112 E4
North Pole, *Arctic* 4 A
North Portal, *Canada* 103 D8
North Powder, *U.S.A.* 108 D5
North Pt., *Barbados* 121 g
North Pt., *Trin. & Tob.* 125 J16
North Pt., *U.S.A.* 116 A1
North Rhine Westphalia = Nordrhein-Westfalen □, *Germany* 24 D3
North River, *Canada* 105 B8
North Ronaldsay, *U.K.* 13 B6
North Saskatchewan →, *Canada* 103 C7
North Sea, *Europe* 16
North Seal →, *Canada* 103 B9
North Somerset □, *U.K.* 15 F5
North Sporades = Vóriai Sporádhes, *Greece* 46 B5
North Sydney, *Canada* 105 C7
North Syracuse, *U.S.A.* 117 C8
North Taranaki Bight, *N.Z.* 91 H5
North Thompson →, *Canada* 102 C4
North Tonawanda, *U.S.A.* 116 C6
North Troy, *U.S.A.* 117 B12
North Truchas Pk., *U.S.A.* 109 J11
North Twin I., *Canada* 104 B4
North Tyne →, *U.K.* 14 B5
North Uist, *U.K.* 13 D1
North Vancouver, *Canada* 102 D4
North Vernon, *U.S.A.* 114 F3
North Wabasca L., *Canada* 102 B6
North Walsham, *U.K.* 14 E9
North West = Severo-Zapadnyy □, *Russia* 52 C4
North-West □, *S. Africa* 88 D4
North West C., *Australia* 92 D1
North West Christmas I. Ridge, *Pac. Oc.* 97 G11
North West Frontier □, *Pakistan* 68 C4
North West Highlands, *U.K.* 13 D4
North West River, *Canada* 105 B7
North Western □, *Zambia* 87 E2
North Wildwood, *U.S.A.* 114 F8
North York Moors, *U.K.* 14 C7
North York Moors △, *U.K.* 14 C7
North Yorkshire □, *U.K.* 14 C6
Northallerton, *U.K.* 14 C6
Northam, *Australia* 93 F2
Northam, *S. Africa* 88 C4
Northampton, *Australia* 93 E1
Northampton, *U.K.* 15 E7
Northampton, *Mass., U.S.A.* 117 D12
Northampton, *Pa., U.S.A.* 117 F9
Northamptonshire □, *U.K.* 15 E7
Northbridge, *U.S.A.* 117 D13
Northcliffe, *Australia* 93 F2
Northeast Providence Chan., *W. Indies* 120 A4
Northeim, *Germany* 24 D6
Northern = Limpopo □, *S. Africa* 89 C4
Northern □, *Ghana* 83 D4
Northern □, *Malawi* 87 E3
Northern □, *S. Leone* 82 D2
Northern □, *Zambia* 87 E3
Northern Areas □, *Pakistan* 69 A5
Northern Cape □, *S. Africa* 88 D3
Northern Circars, *India* 67 L13
Northern Indian L., *Canada* 103 B9
Northern Ireland □, *U.K.* 12 B5
Northern Light L., *Canada* 104 C1
Northern Marianas ⊠, *Pac. Oc.* 96 F6
Northern Mid-Atlantic Ridge, *Atl. Oc.* 4 D6
Northern Province □, *S. Africa* 89 C4
Northern Range, *Trin. & Tob.* 125 K15
Northern Territory □, *Australia* 92 D5
Northfield, *Minn., U.S.A.* 112 C8
Northfield, *Vt., U.S.A.* 117 B12
Northland □, *N.Z.* 91 F4
Northome, *U.S.A.* 112 B7

Northport, *Ala., U.S.A.* 115 J2
Northport, *Wash., U.S.A.* 108 B5
Northumberland □, *U.K.* 14 B6
Northumberland, C., *Australia* 95 F3
Northumberland Is., *Australia* 94 C4
Northumberland Str., *Canada* 105 C7
Northville, *U.S.A.* 117 C10
Northwest Providence Channel, *W. Indies* 120 A4
Northwest Territories □, *Canada* 100 B9
Northwich, *U.K.* 14 D5
Northwood, *Iowa, U.S.A.* 112 D8
Northwood, *N. Dak., U.S.A.* 112 B6
Norton, *U.S.A.* 112 F5
Norton, *Zimbabwe* 87 F3
Norton Sd., *U.S.A.* 100 B3
Nortorf, *Germany* 24 A5
Norwalk, *Calif., U.S.A.* 111 M8
Norwalk, *Conn., U.S.A.* 117 E11
Norwalk, *Iowa, U.S.A.* 112 E8
Norwalk, *Ohio, U.S.A.* 116 E2
Norway, *Maine, U.S.A.* 115 C10
Norway, *Mich., U.S.A.* 114 C2
Norway ■, *Europe* 8 E14
Norway House, *Canada* 103 C9
Norwegian Sea, *Atl. Oc.* 7 B6
Norwich, *Canada* 116 D4
Norwich, *U.K.* 15 E9
Norwich, *Conn., U.S.A.* 117 E12
Norwich, *N.Y., U.S.A.* 117 D9
Norwood, *Canada* 116 B7
Norwood, *U.S.A.* 117 B10
Noshiro, *Japan* 54 D10
Nosivka, *Ukraine* 33 G6
Nosovka = Nosivka, *Ukraine* 33 G6
Noşratābād, *Iran* 71 D8
Noss Hd., *U.K.* 13 C5
Nossebro, *Sweden* 11 F6
Nossob →, *S. Africa* 88 D3
Nossombougou, *Mali* 82 C3
Nosy Barren, *Madag.* 85 H8
Nosy Be, *Madag.* 85 G9
Nosy Boraha, *Madag.* 89 B8
Nosy Lava, *Madag.* 89 A8
Nosy Varika, *Madag.* 89 C8
Noteć →, *Poland* 31 F2
Notikewin →, *Canada* 102 B5
Notio Aigaio = Notios Aiyaíon □ 47 E7
Notios Aiyaíon □ 47 E7
Notios Evvoïkos Kólpos, *Greece* 46 C5
Noto, *Italy* 43 F8
Noto, G. di, *Italy* 43 F8
Notodden, *Norway* 9 G13
Notre Dame B., *Canada* 105 C8
Notre-Dame-de-Koartac = Quaqtaq, *Canada* 101 B13
Notre-Dame-des-Bois, *Canada* 117 A13
Notre-Dame-d'Ivugivic = Ivujivik, *Canada* 101 B12
Notre-Dame-du-Nord, *Canada* 104 C4
Notsé, *Togo* 83 D5
Nottawasaga B., *Canada* 116 B4
Nottaway →, *Canada* 104 B4
Nottingham, *U.K.* 14 E6
Nottingham, City of □, *U.K.* 14 E6
Nottingham I., *Canada* 101 B12
Nottinghamshire □, *U.K.* 14 D6
Nottoway →, *U.S.A.* 114 G7
Notwane →, *Botswana* 88 C4
Nouâdhibou, *Mauritania* 78 D2
Nouâdhibou, Ras, *Mauritania* 78 D2
Nouakchott, *Mauritania* 82 B1
Nouâmghâr, *Mauritania* 82 B1
Nouméa, *N. Cal.* 96 K8
Nouna, *Burkina Faso* 82 C4
Noupoort, *S. Africa* 88 E3
Nouveau Comptoir = Wemindji, *Canada* 104 B4
Nouvelle-Amsterdam, Î., *Ind. Oc.* 3 F13
Nouvelle-Calédonie = New Caledonia ☒, *Pac. Oc.* 96 K8
Nouzonville, *France* 19 C11
Nová Baňa, *Slovak Rep.* 27 C11
Nová Bystřice, *Czech Rep.* 26 B8
Nova Casa Nova, *Brazil* 125 E10
Nova Esperança, *Brazil* 127 A5
Nova Friburgo, *Brazil* 127 A7
Nova Gorica, *Slovenia* 41 C10
Nova Gradiška, *Croatia* 28 E2
Nova Iguaçu, *Brazil* 127 A7
Nova Iorque, *Brazil* 125 E10
Nova Kakhovka, *Ukraine* 33 J7
Nova Lamego, *Guinea-Biss.* 82 C2
Nova Lima, *Brazil* 127 A7
Nova Lusitânia, *Mozam.* 87 F3
Nova Mambone, *Mozam.* 89 C6
Nova Odesa, *Ukraine* 33 J6
Nová Paka, *Czech Rep.* 26 A8
Nova Pavova, *Serbia & M.* 28 F5
Nova Scotia □, *Canada* 105 C7
Nova Siri, *Italy* 43 B9
Nova Sofala, *Mozam.* 89 C5
Nova Ushytsya, *Ukraine* 29 B12
Nova Varoš, *Serbia & M.* 44 C3
Nova Venécia, *Brazil* 125 G10
Nova Zagora, *Bulgaria* 45 D10
Novaci, *Macedonia* 44 E5
Novaci, *Romania* 29 E8
Novaféltria, *Italy* 41 E9
Novannenskiy = Novoannenskiy, *Russia* 34 E6
Novar, *Canada* 116 A5
Novara, *Italy* 40 C5
Novato, *U.S.A.* 110 G4
Novaya Kakhovka = Nova Kakhovka, *Ukraine* 33 J7
Novaya Kazanka, *Kazakhstan* 35 F9
Novaya Ladoga, *Russia* 32 B7
Novaya Lyalya, *Russia* 52 D7
Novaya Sibir, Ostrov, *Russia* 53 B16
Novaya Zemlya, *Russia* 52 B6
Nové Město, *Slovak Rep.* 27 C10
Nové Město na Moravě, *Czech Rep.* 26 B9
Nové Město nad Metují, *Czech Rep.* 27 A9
Nové Zámky, *Slovak Rep.* 27 C11
Novelda, *Spain* 39 G4
Novellara, *Italy* 40 D7
Noventa Vicentina, *Italy* 41 C8
Novgorod, *Russia* 32 C6
Novgorod-Severskiy = Novhorod-Siverskyy, *Ukraine* 33 G7
Novhorod-Siverskyy, *Ukraine* 33 G7
Novi Bečej, *Serbia & M.* 28 E5
Novi Iskar, *Bulgaria* 44 D7
Novi Kneževac, *Serbia & M.* 28 D5
Novi Lígure, *Italy* 40 D5
Novi Pazar, *Bulgaria* 45 C11
Novi Pazar, *Serbia & M.* 44 C4
Novi Sad, *Serbia & M.* 28 E4
Novi Slankamen, *Serbia & M.* 28 E5
Novi Travnik, *Bos.-H.* 28 F2
Novi Vinodolski, *Croatia* 41 C11
Novigrad, *Istra, Croatia* 41 C10
Novigrad, *Zadar, Croatia* 41 D12
Novigradsko More, *Croatia* 41 D12
Novo Hamburgo, *Brazil* 127 B5
Novo Ivanivka, *Ukraine* 29 E14
Novo Mesto, *Slovenia* 41 C12
Novo Miloševo, *Serbia & M.* 28 E5
Novo Remanso, *Brazil* 125 E10
Novoaleksandrovsk, *Russia* 35 H5
Novoaleksandrovskaya = Novoaleksandrovsk, *Russia* 35 H5
Novoaltaysk, *Russia* 52 D9
Novoannenskiy, *Russia* 34 E6
Novoazovsk, *Ukraine* 33 J10
Novocheboksarsk, *Russia* 34 B8
Novocherkassk, *Russia* 35 G5
Novodevichye, *Russia* 34 D9
Novogrudok = Navahrudak, *Belarus* 32 F3
Novohrad-Volynskyy, *Ukraine* 33 G4
Novokachalinsk, *Russia* 54 B6
Novokhopersk, *Russia* 34 E5
Novokuybyshevsk, *Russia* 34 D9
Novokuznetsk, *Russia* 52 D9
Novomirgorod, *Ukraine* 33 H6
Novomoskovsk, *Russia* 32 E10
Novomoskovsk, *Ukraine* 33 H8
Novopolotsk = Navapolatsk, *Belarus* 32 E5
Novorossiysk, *Russia* 33 K9
Novorybnoye, *Russia* 53 B11
Novorzhev, *Russia* 32 D5
Novosej, *Albania* 44 E4
Novoselytsya, *Ukraine* 29 B11
Novoshakhtinsk, *Russia* 33 J10
Novosibirsk, *Russia* 52 D9
Novosibirskiye Ostrova, *Russia* 53 B15
Novosil, *Russia* 33 F9
Novosokolniki, *Russia* 32 D6
Novotitarovskaya, *Russia* 35 H4
Novotroitsk, *Russia* 52 D6
Novoukrayinka, *Ukraine* 33 H6
Novouljanovsk, *Russia* 34 C9
Novouzensk, *Russia* 34 E9
Novovolynsk, *Ukraine* 31 H11
Novovoronezhskiy, *Russia* 33 G10
Novoyavoriske, *Ukraine* 31 J10
Novozybkov, *Russia* 33 F6
Novska, *Croatia* 41 C14
Novvy Urengoy, *Russia* 52 C8
Nový Bor, *Czech Rep.* 26 A7
Novy Bug = Novyy Buh, *Ukraine* 33 J7
Nový Bydžov, *Czech Rep.* 26 A8
Novy Dvor, *Belarus* 31 F11
Novy Dwór Mazowiecki, *Poland* 31 F7
Nový Jičín, *Czech Rep.* 27 B11
Novyy Afon, *Georgia* 35 J5
Novyy Buh, *Ukraine* 33 J7
Novyy Oskol, *Russia* 33 G9
Novyy Port, *Russia* 52 C8
Now Shahr, *Iran* 71 B6
Nowa Deba, *Poland* 31 H8
Nowa Ruda, *Poland* 31 H3
Nowa Sarzyna, *Poland* 31 H9
Nowa Sól, *Poland* 31 G2
Nowata, *U.S.A.* 113 G7
Nowbarān, *Iran* 71 C6
Nowe, *Poland* 30 E5
Nowe Miasteczko, *Poland* 31 G2
Nowe Miasto, *Poland* 31 G7
Nowe Miasto Lubawskie, *Poland* 30 E6
Nowe Skalmierzyce, *Poland* 31 G4
Nowe Warpno, *Poland* 30 E1
Nowghāb, *Iran* 71 C8
Nowgong, *Assam, India* 67 F18
Nowgong, *Mad. P., India* 69 G8
Nowogard, *Poland* 30 E2
Nowogród, *Poland* 31 E8
Nowogród Bobrzanski, *Poland* 31 G2
Nowogrodziec, *Poland* 31 G2
Nowra, *Australia* 95 E5
Nowshera, *Pakistan* 66 C8
Nowy Dwór Gdański, *Poland* 30 D6
Nowy Sącz, *Poland* 31 J7
Nowy Staw, *Poland* 30 D6
Nowy Targ, *Poland* 31 J7
Nowy Tomyśl, *Poland* 31 F3
Nowy Wiśnicz, *Poland* 31 J7
Noxen, *U.S.A.* 117 E8
Noxon, *U.S.A.* 108 C6
Noyabr'sk, *Russia* 52 C8
Noyant, *France* 18 E7
Noyers, *France* 19 E10
Noyon, *France* 19 C9
Noyon, *Mongolia* 56 C2
Nozay, *France* 18 E5
Nqutu, *S. Africa* 89 D5
Nsanje, *Malawi* 87 F4
Nsawam, *Ghana* 83 D4
Nsomba, *Zambia* 87 E2
Nsukka, *Nigeria* 83 D6
Ntui, *Cameroon* 83 E7
Nu Jiang →, *China* 58 E2
Nu Shan, *China* 58 E2
Nuba Mts. = Nubah, Jibalan, *Sudan* 81 E3
Nubah, Jibalan, *Sudan* 81 E3
Nubia, *Africa* 76 D7
Nubian Desert = Nûbîya, Es Sahrâ en, *Sudan* 80 C3
Nûbîya, Es Sahrâ en, *Sudan* 80 C3
Nubledo, *Spain* 36 B5
Nuboai, *Indonesia* 63 E9
Nubra →, *India* 69 B7
Nucet, *Romania* 28 D7
Nueces →, *U.S.A.* 113 M6
Nueltin L., *Canada* 103 A9
Nueva Carteya, *Spain* 37 H6
Nueva Gerona, *Cuba* 120 B3
Nueva Palmira, *Uruguay* 126 C4
Nueva Rosita, *Mexico* 118 B4
Nueva San Salvador, *El Salv.* 120 D2
Nueva Tabarca, *Spain* 39 G4
Nuéve de Julio, *Argentina* 126 D3
Nuevitas, *Cuba* 120 B4
Nuevo, G., *Argentina* 128 E4
Nuevo Casas Grandes, *Mexico* 118 A3
Nuevo Guerrero, *Mexico* 119 B5
Nuevo Laredo, *Mexico* 119 B5
Nuevo León □, *Mexico* 118 C5
Nuevo Rocafuerte, *Ecuador* 124 D3
Nugget Pt., *N.Z.* 91 M2
Nugrus, Gebel, *Egypt* 80 C3
Nuhaka, *N.Z.* 91 H6
Nuits-St-Georges, *France* 19 E11
Nukey Bluff, *Australia* 95 E2
Nukhayb, *Iraq* 70 C4
Nukheila, *Sudan* 80 D2
Nuku'alofa, *Tonga* 91 E12
Nukus, *Uzbekistan* 52 E6
Nules, *Spain* 38 F4
Nullagine, *Australia* 92 D3
Nullagine →, *Australia* 92 D3
Nullarbor, *Australia* 93 F5
Nullarbor △, *Australia* 93 F2
Nullarbor Plain, *Australia* 93 F4
Numalla, L., *Australia* 95 D3
Numan, *Nigeria* 83 D7
Numata, *Japan* 55 F9
Numatinna →, *Sudan* 81 F2
Numaykoos Lake ⌓, *Canada* 103 B9
Numazu, *Japan* 55 G9
Numbulwar, *Australia* 94 A2
Numfoor, *Indonesia* 63 E8
Numurkah, *Australia* 95 F4
Nunaksaluk I., *Canada* 105 A7
Nunap Isua, *Greenland* 101 C15
Nunavut □, *Canada* 101 D8
Nunda, *U.S.A.* 116 D7
Nuneaton, *U.K.* 15 E6
Nungarin, *Australia* 93 F2
Nungo, *Mozam.* 87 E4
Nungwe, *Tanzania* 86 C3
Nunivak I., *U.S.A.* 100 B3
Nunkun, *India* 69 C7
Núoro, *Italy* 42 B2
Nūrābād, *Iran* 71 E8
Nure →, *Italy* 40 C6
Nuremberg = Nürnberg, *Germany* 25 F7
Nuri, *Mexico* 118 B3
Nuri, *Sudan* 80 D3
Nuriootpa, *Australia* 95 E2
Nuristān □, *Afghan.* 66 B7
Nurlat, *Russia* 34 C10
Nurmes, *Finland* 8 E23
Nürnberg, *Germany* 25 F7
Nurpur, *Pakistan* 68 D4
Nurra, La, *Italy* 42 B1
Nurran, L. = Terewah, L., *Australia* 95 D4
Nurrari Lakes, *Australia* 93 E5
Nurri, *Italy* 42 C2
Nürtingen, *Germany* 25 G5
Nurzec →, *Poland* 31 F9
Nus, *Italy* 40 C4
Nusa Barung, *Indonesia* 63 H15
Nusa Dua, *Indonesia* 63 K18
Nusa Kambangan, *Indonesia* 63 G13
Nusa Tenggara Barat □, *Indonesia* 62 F5
Nusa Tenggara Timur □, *Indonesia* 63 F6
Nusaybin, *Turkey* 73 D9
Nushki, *Pakistan* 68 E2
Nuuk, *Greenland* 101 B14
Nuwakot, *Nepal* 69 E10
Nuweiba', *Egypt* 70 D2
Nuwerus, *S. Africa* 88 E2
Nuweveldberge, *S. Africa* 88 E3
Nuyts, C., *Australia* 93 F5
Nuyts, Pt., *Australia* 93 G2
Nuyts Arch., *Australia* 95 E1
Nxai Pan △, *Botswana* 88 B3
Nxau-Nxau, *Botswana* 88 B3
Nyaake, *Liberia* 82 E3
Nyabing, *Australia* 93 F2
Nyack, *U.S.A.* 117 E11
Nyagan, *Russia* 52 C7
Nyahanga, *Tanzania* 86 C3
Nyahua, *Tanzania* 86 D3
Nyahururu, *Kenya* 86 B4
Nyainqentanglha Shan, *China* 60 C4
Nyakanazi, *Tanzania* 86 C3
Nyakrom, *Ghana* 83 D4
Nyâlâ, *Sudan* 81 E1
Nyamandhlovu, *Zimbabwe* 87 F2
Nyambiti, *Tanzania* 86 C3
Nyamlell, *Sudan* 81 F2
Nyamwaga, *Tanzania* 86 C3
Nyandekwa, *Tanzania* 86 C3
Nyanding →, *Sudan* 81 F3
Nyandoma, *Russia* 32 B11
Nyanga △, *Zimbabwe* 87 F3
Nyangana, *Namibia* 88 B3
Nyanguge, *Tanzania* 86 C3
Nyankpala, *Ghana* 83 D4
Nyanza, *Rwanda* 86 C2
Nyanza □, *Kenya* 86 C3
Nyanza-Lac, *Burundi* 86 C2
Nyaponges, *Sudan* 81 F3
Nyasa, L., *Africa* 87 E3
Nyasvizh, *Belarus* 33 F4
Nyazura, *Zimbabwe* 87 F3
Nyazwidzi →, *Zimbabwe* 87 G3
Nyborg, *Denmark* 11 J4
Nybro, *Sweden* 11 H9
Nyda, *Russia* 52 C8
Nyeri, *Kenya* 86 C4
Nyerol, *Sudan* 81 F3
Nyhammar, *Sweden* 10 D8
Nyika △, *Malawi* 87 E3
Nyinahin, *Ghana* 82 D4
Nyíradony, *Hungary* 28 C6
Nyírbátor, *Hungary* 28 C7
Nyíregyháza, *Hungary* 28 C6
Nykarleby = Uusikaarlepyy, *Finland* 8 E20
Nykøbing, *Storstrøm, Denmark* 11 K5
Nykøbing, *Vestsjælland, Denmark* 11 J5
Nykøbing, *Viborg, Denmark* 11 H2
Nyköping, *Sweden* 11 F11
Nykroppa, *Sweden* 10 E8
Nykvarn, *Sweden* 10 E11
Nyland, *Sweden* 10 A11
Nylstroom = Modimolle, *S. Africa* 89 C4
Nymagee, *Australia* 95 E4
Nymboida △, *Australia* 95 D5
Nymburk, *Czech Rep.* 26 A8
Nynäshamn, *Sweden* 11 F11
Nyngan, *Australia* 95 E4
Nyoma Rap, *India* 69 C8
Nyoman = Nemunas →, *Lithuania* 9 J19
Nyon, *Switz.* 25 J2
Nyong →, *Cameroon* 83 E6
Nyons, *France* 21 D9
Nyou, *Burkina Faso* 83 C4
Nýrsko, *Czech Rep.* 26 B6
Nysa, *Poland* 31 H4
Nysa →, *Europe* 24 C10
Nysa Kłodzka →, *Poland* 31 H4
Nysäter, *Sweden* 10 E6
Nyslott = Savonlinna, *Finland* 32 B5
Nyssa, *U.S.A.* 108 E5
Nystad = Uusikaupunki, *Finland* 9 F19
Nysted, *Denmark* 11 K5
Nyunzu, *Dem. Rep. of the Congo* 86 D2
Nyurba, *Russia* 53 C12
Nyzhankovychi, *Ukraine* 31 J9
Nyzhnohirskyy, *Ukraine* 33 K8
Nyzhny Vorota, *Ukraine* 29 B8
Nzébéla, *Guinea* 82 D3
Nzega, *Tanzania* 86 C3
Nzérékoré, *Guinea* 82 D3
Nzeto, *Angola* 84 F2
Nzilo, Chutes de, *Dem. Rep. of the Congo* 87 E2
N'zo ⌓, *Ivory C.* 82 D3
N'zo →, *Ivory C.* 82 D3
Nzubuka, *Tanzania* 86 C3

O

O Barco, *Spain* 36 C4
O Carballiño, *Spain* 36 C2
O Corgo, *Spain* 36 C3
O Pino, *Spain* 36 C2
O Porriño, *Spain* 36 C2
Ō-Shima, *Japan* 55 G9
Oa, Mull of, *U.K.* 13 F2
Oacoma, *U.S.A.* 112 D5
Oahe, L., *U.S.A.* 112 C4
Oahe Dam, *U.S.A.* 112 C4
Oahu, *U.S.A.* 106 H16
Oak Harbor, *U.S.A.* 110 B4
Oak Hill, *U.S.A.* 114 G5
Oak Ridge, *U.S.A.* 115 G3
Oak View, *U.S.A.* 111 L7
Oakan-Dake, *Japan* 54 C12
Oakdale, *Calif., U.S.A.* 110 H6
Oakdale, *La., U.S.A.* 113 K8
Oakes, *U.S.A.* 112 B5
Oakesdale, *U.S.A.* 108 C5
Oakey, *Australia* 95 D5
Oakfield, *U.S.A.* 116 C6
Oakham, *U.K.* 15 E7
Oakhurst, *U.S.A.* 110 H7
Oakland, *U.S.A.* 110 H4
Oakley, *Idaho, U.S.A.* 108 E7
Oakley, *Kans., U.S.A.* 112 F4
Oakover →, *Australia* 92 D3
Oakridge, *U.S.A.* 108 E2
Oakville, *Canada* 116 C5
Oakville, *U.S.A.* 110 D3
Oamaru, *N.Z.* 91 L3
Oancea, *Romania* 29 E12
Oasi Faunistica di Vendicari ⌓, *Italy* 43 F8
Oasis, *Calif., U.S.A.* 111 M10
Oasis, *Nev., U.S.A.* 110 H9
Oates Land, *Antarctica* 5 C11
Oatlands, *Australia* 95 G4
Oatman, *U.S.A.* 111 K12
Oaxaca, *Mexico* 119 D5
Oaxaca □, *Mexico* 119 D5
Ob →, *Russia* 52 C7
Oba, *Canada* 104 C3
Obala, *Cameroon* 83 E7
Obama, *Japan* 55 G7
Oban, *Nigeria* 83 D6
Oban, *U.K.* 13 E3
Obbia, *Somali Rep.* 75 F4
Obera, *Argentina* 127 B4
Oberammergau, *Germany* 25 H7
Oberasbach, *Germany* 25 F6
Oberbayern □, *Germany* 25 G7
Oberdrauburg, *Austria* 26 E5
Obere Donau ⌓, *Germany* 25 G5
Oberer Bayerischer Wald ⌓, *Germany* 25 F8
Oberfranken □, *Germany* 25 E7
Oberhausen, *Germany* 24 D2
Oberkirch, *Germany* 25 G4
Oberlausitz, *Germany* 24 D10
Oberlin, *Kans., U.S.A.* 112 F4
Oberlin, *La., U.S.A.* 113 K8
Oberlin, *Ohio, U.S.A.* 116 E2
Obernai, *France* 19 D14
Oberndorf, *Germany* 25 G4
Oberon, *Australia* 95 E4
Oberösterreich □, *Austria* 26 C7
Oberpfalz □, *Germany* 25 F8
Oberpfälzer Wald, *Germany* 25 F8
Oberpfälzer Wald ⌓, *Germany* 25 F8
Oberstdorf, *Germany* 25 H6
Obertyn, *Ukraine* 29 B10
Oberursel, *Germany* 25 E4
Oberwart, *Austria* 27 D9
Obi, *Indonesia* 63 E7
Obiaruku, *Nigeria* 83 D6
Óbidos, *Brazil* 125 D7
Óbidos, *Portugal* 37 F1
Obihiro, *Japan* 54 C11
Obilatu, *Indonesia* 63 E7
Obilnoye, *Russia* 35 G7
Obing, *Germany* 25 G8
Objat, *France* 20 C5
Obluchye, *Russia* 53 E14
Obninsk, *Russia* 32 E9
Obo, *C.A.R.* 86 A2
Oboa, Mt., *Uganda* 86 B3
Obock, *Djibouti* 81 E5
Obodivka, *Ukraine* 29 B14
Oborniki, *Poland* 31 F3
Oborniki Śląskie, *Poland* 31 G3
Oboyan, *Russia* 33 G9
Obozerskaya = Obozerskiy, *Russia* 52 C5
Obozerskiy, *Russia* 52 C5
Obrenovac, *Serbia & M.* 44 B4
Obrovac, *Croatia* 41 D12
Obruk, *Turkey* 72 C5
Obrzycko, *Poland* 31 F3
Observatory Inlet, *Canada* 102 B3
Obshchi Syrt, *Russia* 6 E16
Obskaya Guba, *Russia* 52 C8
Obuasi, *Ghana* 83 D4
Obubra, *Nigeria* 83 D6
Obudu, *Nigeria* 83 D6
Obwalden □, *Switz.* 25 J4
Obzor, *Bulgaria* 45 D11
Ocala, *U.S.A.* 115 L4
Ocampo, *Chihuahua, Mexico* 118 B3
Ocampo, *Tamaulipas, Mexico* 119 C5
Ocaña, *Spain* 36 F7
Ocanomowoc, *U.S.A.* 112 D10
Occidental, Cordillera, *Colombia* 124 C3
Occidental, Grand Erg, *Algeria* 78 B6
Ocean City, *Md., U.S.A.* 114 F8
Ocean City, *N.J., U.S.A.* 114 F8
Ocean City, *Wash., U.S.A.* 110 C2
Ocean Falls, *Canada* 102 C3
Ocean I. = Banaba, *Kiribati* 96 H8
Ocean Park, *U.S.A.* 110 D2
Oceano, *U.S.A.* 111 K6
Oceanport, *U.S.A.* 117 F10
Oceanside, *U.S.A.* 111 M9
Ochagavía, *Spain* 38 C3
Ochakiv, *Ukraine* 33 J6
Ochamchira, *Georgia* 35 J5
Ochil Hills, *U.K.* 13 E5
Ocho Rios, *Jamaica* 120 a
Ochsenfurt, *Germany* 25 F6
Ochsenhausen, *Germany* 25 G5
Ocilla, *U.S.A.* 115 K4
Ockelbo, *Sweden* 10 D10
Ocmulgee →, *U.S.A.* 115 K4
Ocna Mureş, *Romania* 29 D8
Ocna Sibiului, *Romania* 29 E9
Ocnele Mari, *Romania* 29 E9
Ocniţa, *Moldova* 29 B12
Oconee →, *U.S.A.* 115 K4
Oconto, *U.S.A.* 114 C2
Oconto Falls, *U.S.A.* 114 C1
Ocosingo, *Mexico* 119 D6
Ocotal, *Nic.* 120 D2
Ocotlán, *Mexico* 118 C4
Ocotlán de Morelos, *Mexico* 119 D5
Ocreza →, *Portugal* 37 F3
Öcsa, *Hungary* 28 C4
Octeville, *France* 18 C5
Oda, *Ghana* 83 D4
Oda, *Japan* 55 G6
Oda, J., *Sudan* 80 C4
Ódáðahraun, *Iceland* 8 D5
Ödåkra, *Sweden* 11 H6
Odate, *Japan* 54 D10
Odawara, *Japan* 55 G9
Odda, *Norway* 9 F12
Odder, *Denmark* 11 J4
Odei →, *Canada* 103 B9
Odemira, *Portugal* 37 H2
Ödemiş, *Turkey* 47 C9
Odendaalsrus, *S. Africa* 88 D4
Odensbacken, *Sweden* 10 E9
Odense, *Denmark* 11 J4
Odenwald = Neckartal-Odenwald ⌓, *Germany* 25 F5
Odenwald, *Germany* 25 F5
Oder →, *Europe* 24 B10
Oder-Havel Kanal, *Germany* 24 C10
Oderzo, *Italy* 41 C9

Odesa, *Ukraine* 33 J6
Ödeshög, *Sweden* 11 F8
Odessa = Odesa, *Ukraine* 33 J6
Odessa, *Canada* 117 B8
Odessa, *Tex., U.S.A.* 113 K3
Odessa, *Wash., U.S.A.* 108 C4
Odiakwe, *Botswana* 88 C4
Odiel →, *Spain* 37 H4
Odienné, *Ivory C.* 82 D3
Odintsovo, *Russia* 32 E9
Odiongan, *Phil.* 61 E4
Odobeşti, *Romania* 29 E12
Odolanów, *Poland* 31 G4
O'Donnell, *U.S.A.* 113 J4
Odorheiu Secuiesc, *Romania* 29 D10
Odoyevo, *Russia* 32 F9
Odra = Oder →, *Europe* 24 B10
Odra →, *Spain* 36 C6
Odžaci, *Serbia & M.* 28 E4
Odžak, *Bos.-H.* 28 E3
Odzi, *Zimbabwe* 89 B5
Odzi →, *Zimbabwe* 89 B5
Oebisfelde, *Germany* 24 C6
Oeiras, *Brazil* 125 E10
Oeiras, *Portugal* 37 G1
Oelrichs, *U.S.A.* 112 D3
Oelsnitz, *Germany* 25 E8
Oelwein, *U.S.A.* 112 D9
Oenpelli, *Australia* 92 B5
Oetz, *Austria* 26 D3
Of, *Turkey* 73 B9
Ofanto →, *Italy* 43 A9
Offa, *Nigeria* 83 D5
Offaly □, *Ireland* 12 C4
Offenbach, *Germany* 25 E4
Offenburg, *Germany* 25 G3
Officer, The →, *Australia* 93 E5
Offida, *Italy* 41 F10
Ofidhousa, *Greece* 47 E8
Ofotfjorden, *Norway* 8 B17
Ōfunato, *Japan* 54 E10
Oga, *Japan* 54 E9
Oga-Hantō, *Japan* 54 E9
Ogaden, *Ethiopia* 75 F3
Ōgaki, *Japan* 55 G8
Ogallala, *U.S.A.* 112 E4
Ogasawara Gunto, *Pac. Oc.* 96 E6
Ogbomosho, *Nigeria* 83 D5
Ogden, *U.S.A.* 108 F7
Ogdensburg, *U.S.A.* 117 B9
Ogeechee →, *U.S.A.* 115 K5
Ogilby, *U.S.A.* 111 N12
Oglio →, *Italy* 40 C7
Óglio Nord ⌓, *Italy* 40 C6
Óglio Sud ⌓, *Italy* 40 C7
Ogmore, *Australia* 94 C4
Ognon →, *France* 19 E12
Ogoja, *Nigeria* 83 D6
Ogoki, *Canada* 104 B2
Ogoki →, *Canada* 104 B2
Ogoki L., *Canada* 104 B2
Ogoki Res., *Canada* 104 B2
Ogooué →, *Gabon* 84 E1
Ogosta →, *Bulgaria* 44 C7
Ogowe = Ogooué →, *Gabon* 84 E1
Ogr = Sharafa, *Sudan* 81 E2
Ogražden, *Macedonia* 44 E6
Ogre, *Latvia* 9 H21
Ogrein, *Sudan* 80 D3
Ogulin, *Croatia* 41 C12
Ogun □, *Nigeria* 83 D5
Ogurchinskiy, Ostrov, *Turkmenistan* 71 B7
Oguta, *Nigeria* 83 D6
Ogwashi-Uku, *Nigeria* 83 D6
Ogwe, *Nigeria* 83 E6
Ohai, *N.Z.* 91 L2
Ohakune, *N.Z.* 91 H5
Ohata, *Japan* 54 D10
Ohau, L., *N.Z.* 91 L2
Ohio □, *U.S.A.* 116 F2
Ohio →, *U.S.A.* 114 G1
Ohře →, *Czech Rep.* 26 A7
Ohre →, *Germany* 24 C7
Ohrid, *Macedonia* 44 E4
Ohridsko Jezero, *Macedonia* 44 E4
Ohrigstad, *S. Africa* 89 C5
Öhringen, *Germany* 25 F5
Oi Qu, *China* 58 C2
Oiapoque, *Brazil* 125
Oikou, *China* 57 E9
Oil City, *U.S.A.* 116 E5
Oil Springs, *Canada* 116 D2
Oildale, *U.S.A.* 111 K7
Oinousa, *Greece* 47 C8
Oise □, *France* 19 C9
Oise →, *France* 19 C9
Oiseaux du Djoudj △, *Senegal* 82 B1
Oistins, *Barbados* 121 g
Oistins B., *Barbados* 121 g
Ōita, *Japan* 55 H5
Ōita □, *Japan* 55 H5
Oiticica, *Brazil* 125 E10
Ojacaliente, *Mexico* 118 C4
Ojai, *U.S.A.* 111 L7
Ojcowski △, *Poland* 31 H6
Ojinaga, *Mexico* 118 B4
Ojiya, *Japan* 55 F9
Ojo de Liebre ⌓, *Mexico* 118 B2
Ojos del Salado, Cerro, *Argentina* 126 B2
Oka →, *Russia* 34 B7
Okaba, *Indonesia* 63 F9
Okahandja, *Namibia* 88 C2
Okanagan L., *Canada* 102 D5
Okanogan, *U.S.A.* 108 B4
Okanogan →, *U.S.A.* 108 B4
Okány, *Hungary* 28 D6
Okapi △, *Dem. Rep. of the Congo* 86 B2
Okaputa, *Namibia* 88 C2
Okara, *Pakistan* 68 D5
Okaukuejo, *Namibia* 88 B2
Okavango Delta, *Botswana* 88 B3
Okavango Swamp = Okavango Delta, *Botswana* 88 B3
Okaya, *Japan* 55 F9
Okayama, *Japan* 55 G6
Okayama □, *Japan* 55 G6
Okazaki, *Japan* 55 G8
Oke-Iho, *Nigeria* 83 D5
Okęcie, Warszawa ✕ (WAW), *Poland* 31 F7
Okeechobee, *U.S.A.* 115 M5
Okeechobee, L., *U.S.A.* 115 M5
Okefenokee ⌓, *U.S.A.* 115 K4
Okefenokee Swamp, *U.S.A.* 115 K4
Okehampton, *U.K.* 15 G4
Okene, *Nigeria* 83 D6
Oker →, *Germany* 24 C6
Okha, *India* 68 H3
Okha, *Russia* 53 D15
Ókhi Óros, *Greece* 46 C6
Okhotsk, *Russia* 53 D15
Okhotsk, Sea of, *Asia* 53 D15
Okhotskiy Perevoz, *Russia* 53 C14
Okhtyrka, *Ukraine* 33 G8
Oki-Shotō, *Japan* 55 F6
Okiep, *S. Africa* 88 D2
Okigwi, *Nigeria* 83 D6
Okija, *Nigeria* 83 D6
Okinawa □, *Japan* 55 L4
Okinawa-Guntō, *Japan* 55 L4
Okinawa-Jima, *Japan* 55 L4
Okino-erabu-Shima, *Japan* 55 L4
Okitipupa, *Nigeria* 83 D5
Oklahoma □, *U.S.A.* 113 H6
Oklahoma City, *U.S.A.* 113 H6
Okmulgee, *U.S.A.* 113 H7
Oknitsa = Ocniţa, *Moldova* 29 B12
Oko, W. →, *Sudan* 80 C4
Okolo, *Uganda* 86 B3
Okolona, *U.S.A.* 113 J10
Okombahe, *Namibia* 88 C2
Okonek, *Poland* 30 E3
Okotoks, *Canada* 102 C6
Okrika, *Nigeria* 83 E6
Oksibil, *Indonesia* 63 E10
Oktabrsk = Oktyabrsk, *Kazakhstan* 52 E6
Oktyabrsk, *Kazakhstan* 52 E6
Oktyabrsk, *Russia* 34 D9
Oktyabrskiy = Aktsyabrski, *Belarus* 33 F5
Oktyabrskiy, *Russia* 35 G5
Oktyabrskoy Revolyutsii, Ostrov, *Russia* 53 B10
Oktyabrskoye = Zhovtneve, *Ukraine* 33 J7
Okulovka, *Russia* 32 C7
Okuru, *N.Z.* 91 K2
Okushiri-Tō, *Japan* 54 C9
Okuta, *Nigeria* 83 D5
Okwa →, *Botswana* 88 C3
Ola, *U.S.A.* 113 H8
Ólafsfjörður, *Iceland* 8 C4
Ólafsvík, *Iceland* 8 D2
Olaine, *Latvia* 30 B10
Olancha, *U.S.A.* 111 J8
Olancha Pk., *U.S.A.* 111 J8
Olanchito, *Honduras* 120 C2
Öland, *Sweden* 11 H10
Ölands norra udde, *Sweden* 11 G11
Ölands södra udde, *Sweden* 11 H10
Olargues, *France* 20 E6
Olary, *Australia* 95 E3
Olascoaga, *Argentina* 126 D3
Olathe, *U.S.A.* 112 F7
Olavarría, *Argentina* 126 D3
Oława, *Poland* 31 H4
Olbernhau, *Germany* 24 E9
Ólbia, *Italy* 42 B2
Ólbia, G. di, *Italy* 42 B2
Olching, *Germany* 25 G7
Olcott, *U.S.A.* 116 C6
Old Bahama Chan. = Bahama, Canal Viejo de, *W. Indies* 120 B4
Old Baldy Pk. = San Antonio, Mt., *U.S.A.* 111 L9
Old Castile = Castilla y Leon □, *Spain* 36 D6
Old Crow, *Canada* 100 B6
Old Dale, *U.S.A.* 111 L11
Old Forge, *N.Y., U.S.A.* 117 C10
Old Forge, *Pa., U.S.A.* 117 E9
Old Perlican, *Canada* 105 C9
Old Shinyanga, *Tanzania* 86 C3
Old Speck Mt., *U.S.A.* 117 B14
Old Town, *U.S.A.* 115 C11
Old Washington, *U.S.A.* 116 F3
Old Wives L., *Canada* 103 C7
Oldbury, *U.K.* 15 F5
Oldcastle, *Ireland* 12 C4
Oldeani, *Tanzania* 86 C4
Oldenburg, *Niedersachsen, Germany* 24 B4
Oldenburg, *Schleswig-Holstein, Germany* 24 A6
Oldenzaal, *Neths.* 17 B6
Oldham, *U.K.* 14 D5
Oldman →, *Canada* 102 D6
Oldmeldrum, *U.K.* 13 D6
Olds, *Canada* 102 C6
Olduvai Gorge, *Tanzania* 86 C4
Oldziyt, *Mongolia* 56 B5
Olean, *U.S.A.* 116 D6
Olecko, *Poland* 30 D9
Olèggio, *Italy* 40 C5
Oleiros, *Portugal* 36 F3
Oleiros, *Spain* 36 B2
Olekma →, *Russia* 53 C13
Olekminsk, *Russia* 53 C13
Oleksandriya, *Kirovohrad, Ukraine* 33 H7
Oleksandriya, *Rivne, Ukraine* 33 G4
Oleksandrovka, *Ukraine* 33 H7
Olema, *U.S.A.* 110 G4
Olenek, *Russia* 53 C12
Olenek →, *Russia* 53 B13
Olenino, *Russia* 32 D7
Oléron, Î. d', *France* 20 C2
Olesk, *Ukraine* 31 G11
Oleśnica, *Poland* 31 G4
Olesno, *Poland* 31 H5
Olevsk, *Ukraine* 33 G4
Olga, *Russia* 53 E14
Olga, L., *Canada* 104 C4
Olga, Mt., *Australia* 93 E5
Ølgod, *Denmark* 11 J2
Olhão, *Portugal* 37 H3
Olhopil, *Ukraine* 29 B14
Olhovatka, *Russia* 30 D9
Olib, *Croatia* 41 D11
Oliena, *Italy* 42 B2
Oliete, *Spain* 38 D4
Olifants = Elefantes →, *Africa* 89 C5
Olifants →, *Namibia* 88 C2
Olifantshoek, *S. Africa* 88 D3
Ólimbos, *Greece* 47 F9
Ólimbos, Óros, *Greece* 44 F6
Olímpia, *Brazil* 127 A6
Olimpos-Beydaglari △, *Turkey* 47 E12
Olinda, *Brazil* 125 E12
Olite, *Spain* 38 C3
Oliva, *Argentina* 126 C3
Oliva, *Spain* 39 G4
Oliva, Punta del, *Spain* 36 B5
Oliva de la Frontera, *Spain* 37 G4
Olivares, *Spain* 38 F2
Olivehurst, *U.S.A.* 110 F5
Oliveira de Azeméis, *Portugal* 36 E2
Oliveira do Douro, *Portugal* 36 D2
Olivenza, *Spain* 37 G3
Oliver, *Canada* 102 D5
Oliver L., *Canada* 103 B8
Olivet, *France* 19 E8
Olkhovka, *Russia* 34 F7
Olkusz, *Poland* 31 H6
Ollagüe, *Chile* 126 A2
Olmedo, *Spain* 36 D6
Olmeto, *France* 21 G12
Olney, *Ill., U.S.A.* 114 F1
Olney, *Tex., U.S.A.* 113 J5
Olofström, *Sweden* 11 H8
Oloma, *Cameroon* 83 E7
Olomane →, *Canada* 105 B7
Olomouc, *Czech Rep.* 27 B10
Olomoucký □, *Czech Rep.* 27 B10
Olonets, *Russia* 32 B7
Olongapo, *Phil.* 61 D4
Olonne-sur-Mer, *France* 20 B2
Oloron, Gave d' →, *France* 20 E2
Oloron-Ste-Marie, *France* 20 E3
Olot, *Spain* 38 C7
Olovo, *Bos.-H.* 28 F3
Olovyannaya, *Russia* 53 D12
Oloy →, *Russia* 53 C16
Olsberg, *Germany* 24 D4
Olshammar, *Sweden* 11 F8
Olshanka, *Ukraine* 33 H6
Olshany, *Ukraine* 33 G8
Olsztyn, *Poland* 30 E7
Olsztynek, *Poland* 30 E7
Olt □, *Romania* 29 F9
Olt →, *Romania* 29 G9
Olten, *Switz.* 25 H3
Olteniţa, *Romania* 29 F11
Olton, *U.S.A.* 113 H3
Oltu, *Turkey* 73 B9
Oluanpi, *Taiwan* 59 G13
Olula del Rio, *Spain* 39 H2
Olur, *Turkey* 73 B10
Olutanga, *Phil.* 61 H5
Olvega, *Spain* 38 D2
Olvera, *Spain* 37 J5
Olymbos, *Cyprus* 49 D12
Olympia, *Greece* 46 D3
Olympia, *U.S.A.* 110 D4
Olympic △, *U.S.A.* 110 C3
Olympic Dam, *Australia* 95 E2
Olympic Mts., *U.S.A.* 110 C3
Olympus, *Cyprus* 49 E11
Olympus, Mt. = Ólimbos, Óros, *Greece* 44 F6
Olympus, Mt. = Uludağ, *Turkey* 45 F13
Olympus, Mt., *U.S.A.* 110 C3
Olyphant, *U.S.A.* 117 E9
Om →, *Russia* 52 D8
Om Hajer, *Eritrea* 81 E4
Om Koi, *Thailand* 64 D2
Ōma, *Japan* 54 D10
Ōmachi, *Japan* 55 F8
Omae-Zaki, *Japan* 55 G9
Ōmagari, *Japan* 54 E10
Omagh, *U.K.* 12 B4
Omagh □, *U.K.* 12 B4
Omaha, *U.S.A.* 112 E7
Omak, *U.S.A.* 108 B4
Omalos, *Greece* 49 D5
Oman ■, *Asia* 75 C6
Oman, G. of, *Asia* 71 E8
Omaruru, *Namibia* 88 C2
Omaruru →, *Namibia* 88 C1
Omate, *Peru* 124 G4
Ombai, Selat, *Indonesia* 63 F6
Omboué, *Gabon* 84 E1
Ombrone →, *Italy* 40 F8
Omdurmân, *Sudan* 81 D3
Omegna, *Italy* 40 C5
Omemee, *Canada* 116 B6
Omeonga, *Dem. Rep. of the Congo* 86 C1
Ometepe, I. de, *Nic.* 120 D2
Ometepec, *Mexico* 119 D5
Ominato, *Japan* 54 D10
Omineca →, *Canada* 102 B4
Omiš, *Croatia* 41 E13
Omišalj, *Croatia* 41 C11
Omitara, *Namibia* 88 C2
Ōmiya, *Japan* 55 G9
Omme Å →, *Denmark* 11 J2
Ommen, *Neths.* 17 B6
Ömnögovĭ □, *Mongolia* 56 C3
Omo △, *Ethiopia* 81 F4
Omo →, *Ethiopia* 81 F4
Omo Valley, *Ethiopia* 81 F4
Omodeo, L., *Italy* 42 B1
Omodhos, *Cyprus* 49 E11
Omoko, *Nigeria* 83 D6
Omolon →, *Russia* 53 C16
Omono-Gawa →, *Japan* 54 E10
Omsk, *Russia* 52 D8
Omsukchan, *Russia* 53 C16
Ōmu, *Japan* 54 B11
Omul, Vf., *Romania* 29 E10
Omulew →, *Poland* 31 E8
Ōmura, *Japan* 55 H4
Omuramba Omatako →, *Namibia* 88 B2
Omuramba Ovambo →, *Namibia* 88 B2
Omurtag, *Bulgaria* 45 C10
Ōmuta, *Japan* 55 H5
Oña, *Spain* 36 C7
Onaga, *U.S.A.* 112 F6
Onalaska, *U.S.A.* 112 D9
Onancock, *U.S.A.* 114 G8
Onang, *Indonesia* 63 E5
Onaping L., *Canada* 104 C3
Oñati, *Spain* 38 B2
Onavas, *Mexico* 118 B3
Onawa, *U.S.A.* 112 D6
Oncócua, *Angola* 88 B1
Onda, *Spain* 38 F4
Ondaejin, *N. Korea* 57 D15
Ondangwa, *Namibia* 88 B2
Ondarroa, *Spain* 38 B2
Ondava →, *Slovak Rep.* 27 C14
Ondjiva, *Angola* 88 B2
Ondo, *Nigeria* 83 D5
Ondo □, *Nigeria* 83 D6
Öndörshil, *Mongolia* 56 B5
Öndverðarnes, *Iceland* 8 D1
One Tree, *Australia* 95 E3
Onega, *Russia* 52 C4
Onega →, *Russia* 6 C13
Onega, L. = Onezhskoye Ozero, *Russia* 32 B8
Oneida, *U.S.A.* 117 C9
Oneida L., *U.S.A.* 117 C9
O'Neill, *U.S.A.* 112 D5
Onekotan, Ostrov, *Russia* 53 E16
Onema, *Dem. Rep. of the Congo* 86 C1
Oneonta, *U.S.A.* 117 D9
Oneşti, *Romania* 29 D11
Onezhskoye Ozero, *Russia* 32 B8
Ongarue, *N.Z.* 91 H5
Ongers →, *S. Africa* 88 E3
Ongerup, *Australia* 93 F2
Ongjin, *N. Korea* 57 F13
Ongkharak, *Thailand* 64 E3
Ongniud Qi, *China* 57 C10
Ongoka, *Dem. Rep. of the Congo* 86 C2
Ongole, *India* 66 M12
Ongon = Havirga, *Mongolia* 56 B7
Oni, *Georgia* 35 J6
Onida, *U.S.A.* 112 C4
Onilahy →, *Madag.* 89 C7
Onitsha, *Nigeria* 83 D6
Onoda, *Japan* 55 G5
Onpyŏng-ni, *S. Korea* 57 H14
Ons, I. de, *Spain* 36 C2
Onsala, *Sweden* 11 G6
Onslow, *Australia* 92 D2
Onslow B., *U.S.A.* 115 H7
Ontake-San, *Japan* 55 G8
Ontario, *Calif., U.S.A.* 111 L9
Ontario, *Oreg., U.S.A.* 108 D5
Ontario □, *Canada* 104 B2
Ontario, L., *N. Amer.* 116 C7
Ontinyent, *Spain* 39 G4
Ontonagon, *U.S.A.* 112 B10
Ontur, *Spain* 39 G3
Onyx, *U.S.A.* 111 K8
Oodnadatta, *Australia* 95 D2
Ooldea, *Australia* 93 F5
Oombulgurri, *Australia* 92 C4
Oorindi, *Australia* 94 C3
Oost-Vlaanderen □, *Belgium* 17 C3
Oostende, *Belgium* 17 C2
Oosterhout, *Neths.* 17 C4
Oosterschelde →, *Neths.* 17 C4
Oosterwolde, *Neths.* 17 B6
Ootacamund = Udagamandalam, *India* 66 P10
Ootsa L., *Canada* 102 C3
Op Luang △, *Thailand* 64 C2
Opaka, *Bulgaria* 45 C10
Opala, *Dem. Rep. of the Congo* 86 C1
Opalenica, *Poland* 31 F3
Opan, *Bulgaria* 45 D9
Opanake, *Sri Lanka* 66 R12
Opasatika, *Canada* 104 C3
Opasquia ⌓, *Canada* 104 B1
Opatija, *Croatia* 41 C11
Opatów, *Poland* 31 H8
Opava, *Czech Rep.* 27 B10
Opelika, *U.S.A.* 115 J3
Opelousas, *U.S.A.* 113 K8
Opémisca, L., *Canada* 104 C5
Opheim, *U.S.A.* 108 B10
Ophthalmia Ra., *Australia* 92 D2
Opi, *Nigeria* 83 D6
Opinaca →, *Canada* 104 B4
Opinaca, Rés., *Canada* 104 B4
Opinnagau →, *Canada* 104 B3
Opiscotéo, L., *Canada* 105 B6
Opobo, *Nigeria* 83 E6
Opochka, *Russia* 32 D5
Opoczno, *Poland* 31 G7
Opol, *Phil.* 61 G6
Opole, *Poland* 31 H4
Opole Lubelskie, *Poland* 31 G8
Opolskie □, *Poland* 31 H5
Oponono L., *Namibia* 88 B2
Oporto = Porto, *Portugal* 36 D2
Opotiki, *N.Z.* 91 H6
Opp, *U.S.A.* 115 K2
Oppdal, *Norway* 9 E13
Óppido Mamertina, *Italy* 43 D8
Opportunity, *U.S.A.* 108 C5
Oprişor, *Romania* 28 F8
Oprtalj, *Croatia* 41 C10
Opua, *N.Z.* 91 F5
Opunake, *N.Z.* 91 H4
Opuwo, *Namibia* 88 B1
Opuzen, *Croatia* 41 E14
Ora, *Cyprus* 49 E12
Oracle, *U.S.A.* 109 K8
Oradea, *Romania* 28 C6
Öræfajökull, *Iceland* 8 D5
Orahovac, *Serbia & M.* 44 D4
Orahovica, *Croatia* 28 E2
Orai, *India* 69 G8
Oraison, *France* 21 E9
Oral = Zhayyq →, *Kazakhstan* 52 E6
Oral, *Kazakhstan* 34 E10
Oran, *Algeria* 78 A5
Orange, *Australia* 95 E4
Orange, *France* 21 D8
Orange, *Calif., U.S.A.* 111 M9
Orange, *Mass., U.S.A.* 117 D12
Orange, *Tex., U.S.A.* 113 K8
Orange, *Va., U.S.A.* 114 F6
Orange →, *S. Africa* 88 D2
Orange, C., *Brazil* 125 C8
Orange Cove, *U.S.A.* 110 J7
Orange Free State = Free State □, *S. Africa* 88 D4
Orange Grove, *U.S.A.* 113 M6
Orange Walk, *Belize* 119 D7
Orangeburg, *U.S.A.* 115 J5
Orangeville, *Canada* 116 C4
Orango, *Guinea-Biss.* 82 C1
Orani, *Phil.* 61 D4
Oranienburg, *Germany* 24 C9
Oranje = Orange →, *S. Africa* 88 D2
Oranjemund, *Namibia* 88 D2
Oranjerivier, *S. Africa* 88 D3
Oranjestad, *Aruba* 121 D5
Orapa, *Botswana* 85 J5
Orarak, *Sudan* 81 F3
Oras, *Phil.* 61 E6
Orašje, *Bos.-H.* 28 E3
Orăştie, *Romania* 29 E8
Orava →, *Slovak Rep.* 27 B12
Orava, Vodna nádrž, *Slovak Rep.* 27 B12
Oraviţa, *Romania* 28 E6
Orb →, *France* 20 E7
Orba →, *Italy* 40 D5
Ørbæk, *Denmark* 11 J4
Orbe, *Switz.* 25 J2
Orbec, *France* 18 C7
Orbetello, *Italy* 41 F8
Órbigo →, *Spain* 36 C5
Orbisonia, *U.S.A.* 116 F7
Orbost, *Australia* 95 F4
Örbyhus, *Sweden* 10 D11
Orcadas, *Antarctica* 5 C18
Orcas I., *U.S.A.* 110 B4
Orce, *Spain* 39 H2
Orce →, *Spain* 39 H2
Orchard City, *U.S.A.* 109 G10
Orchies, *France* 19 B10
Orchila, I., *Venezuela* 121 D6
Orchilla, Pta., *Canary Is.* 48 G1
Órcia →, *Italy* 41 F8
Orco →, *Italy* 40 C4
Orcutt, *U.S.A.* 111 L6
Ord, *U.S.A.* 112 E5
Ord →, *Australia* 92 C4
Ord, Mt., *Australia* 92 C4
Ordenes = Ordes, *Spain* 36 B2
Orderville, *U.S.A.* 109 H7
Ordes, *Spain* 36 B2
Ordesa y Monte Perido △, *Spain* 38 C4
Ording = St-Peter-Ording, *Germany* 24 A4
Ordos = Mu Us Shamo, *China* 56 E5
Ordu, *Turkey* 72 B7
Ordubad, *Azerbaijan* 73 C12
Orduña, *Álava, Spain* 38 C2
Orduña, *Granada, Spain* 37 H7
Ordway, *U.S.A.* 112 F3
Ordzhonikidze, *Ukraine* 33 J8
Ore, *Dem. Rep. of the Congo* 86 B2
Ore Mts. = Erzgebirge, *Germany* 24 E8
Orebić, *Croatia* 41 F14
Örebro, *Sweden* 10 E9
Örebro län □, *Sweden* 10 E8
Orecchiella ⌓, *Italy* 40 D7
Oregon, *U.S.A.* 112 D10
Oregon □, *U.S.A.* 108 E3
Oregon City, *U.S.A.* 110 E4
Oregon Dunes ⌓, *U.S.A.* 108 E1
Öregrund, *Sweden* 10 D12
Öregrundsgrepen, *Sweden* 10 D12
Orekhov = Orikhiv, *Ukraine* 33 J8
Orekhovo-Zuyevo, *Russia* 32 E10
Orel, *Russia* 33 F9
Orel →, *Ukraine* 33 H8
Orellana, *Spain* 37 F5
Orellana, Canal de, *Spain* 37 F5
Orellana, Embalse de, *Spain* 37 F5
Orem, *U.S.A.* 108 F8
Ören, *Turkey* 47 D9
Orenburg, *Russia* 52 D6
Örencik, *Turkey* 47 B11
Orense = Ourense, *Spain* 36 C3
Orense □, *Spain* 36 C3
Orepuki, *N.Z.* 91 M1
Orestiás, *Greece* 45 E10
Orestos Pereyra, *Mexico* 118 B3

Øresund, *Europe* 11 J6
Orford Ness, *U.K.* 15 E9
Organ Pipe Cactus ⌓, *U.S.A.* 109 K7
Organos, Pta. de los, *Canary Is.* 48 F2
Organyà, *Spain* 38 C6
Orgaz, *Spain* 37 F7
Orgeyev = Orhei, *Moldova* 29 C13
Orhaneli, *Turkey* 45 G12
Orhaneli →, *Turkey* 45 G12
Orhangazi, *Turkey* 45 F13
Orhei, *Moldova* 29 C13
Orhon Gol →, *Mongolia* 60 A5
Oria, *Italy* 43 B10
Oriental, Cordillera, *Colombia* 124 B4
Oriental, Grand Erg, *Algeria* 78 B7
Orientale □, *Dem. Rep. of the Congo* 86 B2
Oriente, *Argentina* 126 D3
Orihuela, *Spain* 39 G4
Orihuela del Tremedal, *Spain* 38 E3
Orikhiv, *Ukraine* 33 J8
Orikum, *Albania* 44 F3
Orillia, *Canada* 116 B5
Orinoco →, *Venezuela* 124 B6
Orion, *Canada* 103 D6
Oriskany, *U.S.A.* 117 C9
Orissa □, *India* 67 K14
Orissaare, *Estonia* 9 G20
Oristano, *Italy* 42 C1
Oristano, G. di, *Italy* 42 C1
Orizaba, *Mexico* 119 D5
Orizaba, Pico de, *Mexico* 119 D5
Orizare, *Bulgaria* 45 D11
Orjen, *Bos.-H.* 44 D2
Orjiva, *Spain* 37 J7
Orkanger, *Norway* 8 E13
Örkelljunga, *Sweden* 11 H7
Örken, *Sweden* 11 G9
Örkény, *Hungary* 28 C4
Orkla →, *Norway* 8 E13
Orkney, *S. Africa* 88 D4
Orkney □, *U.K.* 13 B5
Orkney Is., *U.K.* 13 B6
Orland, *U.S.A.* 110 F4
Orlando, *U.S.A.* 115 L5
Orlando, C. d', *Italy* 43 D7
Orléanais, *France* 19 E9
Orléans, *France* 19 E8
Orleans, *U.S.A.* 117 B12
Orléans, Î. d', *Canada* 105 C5
Orlice →, *Czech Rep.* 26 A8
Orlivka, *Ukraine* 29 E13
Orlov, *Slovak Rep.* 27 B13
Orlov Gay, *Russia* 34 E9
Orlová, *Czech Rep.* 27 B11
Orlovat, *Serbia & M.* 28 E5
Orly, Paris ✕ (ORY), *France* 19 D9
Ormara, *Pakistan* 66 G4
Ormea, *Italy* 40 D4
Ormília, *Greece* 44 F7
Ormoc, *Phil.* 61 F6
Ormond, *N.Z.* 91 H6
Ormond Beach, *U.S.A.* 115 L5
Ormož, *Slovenia* 41 B13
Ormskirk, *U.K.* 14 D5
Ormstown, *Canada* 117 A11
Ornans, *France* 19 E13
Orne □, *France* 18 D7
Orne →, *France* 18 C6
Orneta, *Poland* 30 D7
Ornö, *Sweden* 10 E12
Örnsköldsvik, *Sweden* 10 A12
Oro, *N. Korea* 57 D14
Oro →, *Mexico* 118 B3
Oro Grande, *U.S.A.* 111 L9
Oro Valley, *U.S.A.* 109 K8
Orobie, Alpi, *Italy* 40 B6
Orobie Bergamasche ⌓, *Italy* 40 C6
Orobie Valtellinesi ⌓, *Italy* 40 B6
Orocué, *Colombia* 124 C4
Orodara, *Burkina Faso* 82 C4
Orodo, *Nigeria* 83 D6
Orofino, *U.S.A.* 108 C5
Orol Dengizi = Aral Sea, *Asia* 52 E7
Oromiya □, *Ethiopia* 81 F5
Oromocto, *Canada* 105 C6
Oron, *Nigeria* 83 E6
Orono, *Canada* 116 C6
Orono, *U.S.A.* 115 C11
Oronsay, *U.K.* 13 E2
Oropesa, *Spain* 36 F5
Oroquieta, *Phil.* 61 G5
Orosei, *Italy* 42 B2
Orosei, G. di, *Italy* 42 B2
Orosháza, *Hungary* 28 D5
Oroszlány, *Hungary* 28 C3
Orotukan, *Russia* 53 C16
Oroville, *Calif., U.S.A.* 110 F5
Oroville, *Wash., U.S.A.* 108 B4
Oroville, L., *U.S.A.* 110 F5
Orrefors, *Sweden* 11 H9
Orroroo, *Australia* 95 E2
Orrviken, *Sweden* 10 A8
Orrville, *U.S.A.* 116 F3
Orsa, *Sweden* 10 C8
Orsara di Púglia, *Italy* 43 A8
Orsasjön, *Sweden* 10 C8
Orsha, *Belarus* 32 E6
Örsjö, *Sweden* 11 H9
Orsk, *Russia* 52 D6
Orşova, *Romania* 28 F7
Ørsted, *Denmark* 11 H4
Örsundsbro, *Sweden* 10 E11
Orta, L. d', *Italy* 40 C5
Orta Nova, *Italy* 43 A8
Ortaca, *Turkey* 47 E10
Ortakent, *Turkey* 47 D9
Ortaklar, *Turkey* 47 D9
Ortaköy, *Çorum, Turkey* 72 B6
Ortaköy, *Niğde, Turkey* 72 C6
Orte, *Italy* 41 F9
Ortegal, C., *Spain* 36 B3
Orthez, *France* 20 E3
Ortigueira, *Spain* 36 B3
Orting, *U.S.A.* 110 C4
Ortisei, *Italy* 41 B8
Ortles, *Italy* 40 B7
Ortón →, *Bolivia* 124 F5
Ortona, *Italy* 41 F11
Ortonville, *U.S.A.* 112 C6
Orūmīyeh, *Iran* 70 B5
Orūmīyeh, Daryācheh-ye, *Iran* 70 B5
Orune, *Italy* 42 B2
Oruro, *Bolivia* 124 G5
Orust, *Sweden* 11 F5
Oruzgān □, *Afghan.* 66 C5
Orvault, *France* 18 E5
Orvieto, *Italy* 41 F9
Orwell, *N.Y., U.S.A.* 117 C9
Orwell, *Ohio, U.S.A.* 116 E4
Orwell →, *U.K.* 15 F9
Orwigsburg, *U.S.A.* 117 F8
Oryakhovo, *Bulgaria* 44 C7
Orynyn, *Ukraine* 29 B11
Orzinuovi, *Italy* 40 C6
Orzyc →, *Poland* 31 F8
Orzysz, *Poland* 30 E8
Osa →, *Poland* 30 E5
Osa, Pen. de, *Costa Rica* 120 E3
Osage, *U.S.A.* 112 D8
Osage →, *U.S.A.* 112 F9
Osage City, *U.S.A.* 112 F7
Ōsaka, *Japan* 55 G7
Osan, *S. Korea* 57 F14
Osawatomie, *U.S.A.* 112 F7
Osborne, *U.S.A.* 112 F5
Osby, *Sweden* 11 H7
Osceola, *Ark., U.S.A.* 113 H10
Osceola, *Iowa, U.S.A.* 112 E8
Oschatz, *Germany* 24 D9
Oschersleben, *Germany* 24 C7
Óschiri, *Italy* 42 B2
Oscoda, *U.S.A.* 116 B1
Osečina, *Serbia & M.* 44 B3
Ösel = Saaremaa, *Estonia* 9 G20
Osery, *Russia* 32 E10
Osgoode, *Canada* 117 A9
Osh, *Kyrgyzstan* 52 E8
Oshakati, *Namibia* 85 H3
Oshawa, *Canada* 116 C6
Oshigambo, *Namibia* 88 B2
Oshkosh, *Nebr., U.S.A.* 112 E3
Oshkosh, *Wis., U.S.A.* 112 C10
Oshmyany = Ashmyany, *Belarus* 9 J21
Oshnovīyeh, *Iran* 70 B5
Oshogbo, *Nigeria* 83 D5
Oshtorīnān, *Iran* 71 C6
Oshwe, *Dem. Rep. of the Congo* 84 E3
Osi, *Nigeria* 83 D6
Osieczna, *Poland* 31 G3
Osijek, *Croatia* 28 E3
Ósilo, *Italy* 42 B1
Ósimo, *Italy* 41 E10
Osintorf, *Belarus* 32 E6
Osipovichi = Asipovichy, *Belarus* 32 F5
Osiyan, *India* 68 F5
Osizweni, *S. Africa* 89 D5
Oskaloosa, *U.S.A.* 112 E8
Oskarshamn, *Sweden* 11 G10
Oskarström, *Sweden* 11 H6
Oskélanéo, *Canada* 104 C4
Öskemen, *Kazakhstan* 52 E9
Oskol →, *Ukraine* 33 H9
Oslo, *Norway* 9 G14
Oslob, *Phil.* 61 G5
Oslofjorden, *Norway* 9 G14
Osmanabad, *India* 66 K10
Osmancık, *Turkey* 72 B6
Osmaniye, *Turkey* 70 B3
Osmanlı, *Turkey* 45 E10
Ösmo, *Sweden* 10 F11
Osnabrück, *Germany* 24 C4
Ośno Lubuskie, *Poland* 31 F1
Osoblaha, *Czech Rep.* 27 A10
Osogovska Planina, *Macedonia* 44 D6
Osor, *Italy* 41 D11
Osorio, *Brazil* 127 B5
Osorno, *Chile* 128 E2
Osorno, *Spain* 36 C6
Osoyoos, *Canada* 102 D5
Osøyro, *Norway* 9 F11
Ospika →, *Canada* 102 B4
Osprey Reef, *Australia* 94 A4
Oss, *Neths.* 17 C5
Ossa, Mt., *Australia* 95 G4
Óssa, Óros, *Greece* 46 B4
Ossa de Montiel, *Spain* 39 G2
Ossabaw I., *U.S.A.* 115 K5
Osse →, *France* 20 D4
Osse →, *Nigeria* 83 D6
Ossi, *Italy* 42 B1
Ossining, *U.S.A.* 117 E11
Ossipee, *U.S.A.* 117 C13
Ossokmanuan L., *Canada* 105 B7
Ossora, *Russia* 53 D17
Ostashkov, *Russia* 32 D7
Östavall, *Sweden* 10 B9
Oste →, *Germany* 24 B5
Ostend = Oostende, *Belgium* 17 C2
Oster, *Ukraine* 33 G6
Österbotten = Pohjanmaa, *Finland* 8 E20
Osterburg, *Germany* 24 C7
Osterburg, *U.S.A.* 116 F6
Osterburken, *Germany* 25 F5
Österbybruk, *Sweden* 10 D11
Österbymo, *Sweden* 11 G9
Österdalälven, *Sweden* 10 C7
Østerdalen, *Norway* 9 F14
Österfärnebo, *Sweden* 10 D10
Österforse, *Sweden* 10 A11
Östergötlands län □, *Sweden* 11 F9
Osterholz-Scharmbeck, *Germany* 24 B4
Østerild, *Denmark* 11 G2
Östermyra = Seinäjoki, *Finland* 9 E20
Osterode, *Germany* 24 D6
Östersund, *Sweden* 10 A8
Östervåla, *Sweden* 10 D11
Ostfriesische Inseln, *Germany* 24 B3
Ostfriesland, *Germany* 24 B3
Östhammar, *Sweden* 10 D12
Óstia, Lido di, *Italy* 41 G9
Ostíglia, *Italy* 41 C8
Östmark, *Sweden* 10 D6
Östra Husby, *Sweden* 11 F10
Ostrava, *Czech Rep.* 27 B11
Ostravský □, *Czech Rep.* 27 B10
Ostróda, *Poland* 30 E6
Ostrogozhsk, *Russia* 33 G10
Ostroh, *Ukraine* 33 G4
Ostrołęka, *Poland* 31 E8
Ostrov, *Bulgaria* 45 C8
Ostrov, *Czech Rep.* 26 A5
Ostrov, *Romania* 29 F12
Ostrov, *Russia* 32 D5
Ostrów Lubelski, *Poland* 31 G9
Ostrów Mazowiecka, *Poland* 31 F8
Ostrów Wielkopolski, *Poland* 31 G4
Ostrowiec-Świętokrzyski, *Poland* 31 H8
Ostrožac, *Bos.-H.* 28 G2
Ostrzeszów, *Poland* 31 G4
Ostseebad Kühlungsborn, *Germany* 24 A7
Osttirol □, *Austria* 26 E5
Ostuni, *Italy* 43 B10
Osum →, *Albania* 44 F4
Osŭm →, *Bulgaria* 45 C8
Ōsumi-Kaikyō, *Japan* 55 J5
Ōsumi-Shotō, *Japan* 55 J5
Osun □, *Nigeria* 83 D5
Osuna, *Spain* 37 H5
Oswegatchie →, *U.S.A.* 117 B9
Oswego, *U.S.A.* 117 C8
Oswego →, *U.S.A.* 117 C8
Oswestry, *U.K.* 14 E4
Oświęcim, *Poland* 31 H6
Otaci, *Moldova* 29 B12
Otago □, *N.Z.* 91 L2
Otago Harbour, *N.Z.* 91 L3
Otaheite B., *Trin. & Tob.* 125 K15
Ōtake, *Japan* 55 G6
Otaki, *N.Z.* 91 J5
Otaru, *Japan* 54 C10
Otaru-Wan = Ishikari-Wan, *Japan* 54 C10
Otava →, *Czech Rep.* 26 B7
Otavalo, *Ecuador* 124 C3
Otavi, *Namibia* 88 B2
Otchinjau, *Angola* 88 B1
Otelec, *Romania* 28 E5
Otelnuk, L., *Canada* 105 A6
Oţelu Roşu, *Romania* 28 E7
Otero de Rey = Outeiro de Rei, *Spain* 36 B3
Othello, *U.S.A.* 108 C4
Othonoí, *Greece* 46 B1
Óthris, Óros, *Greece* 46 B4
Oti ⌓, *Togo* 83 C5
Otjiwarongo, *Namibia* 88 C2
Otmuchów, *Poland* 31 H4
Otočac, *Croatia* 41 D12
Otoineppu, *Japan* 54 B11
Otok, *Croatia* 41 E13
Otopeni, Bucureşti ✕ (OTP), *Romania* 45 B10
Otorohanga, *N.Z.* 91 H5
Otoskwin →, *Canada* 104 B2
Otra →, *Norway* 9 G13
Otradnyy, *Russia* 34 D10
Otranto, *Italy* 43 B11
Otranto, C. d', *Italy* 43 B11
Otranto, Str. of, *Italy* 43 B11
Otrokovice, *Czech Rep.* 27 B10
Otse, *S. Africa* 88 D4
Ōtsu, *Japan* 55 G7
Ōtsuki, *Japan* 55 G9
Ottawa = Outaouais →, *Canada* 104 C5
Ottawa, *Canada* 117 A9
Ottawa, *Ill., U.S.A.* 112 E10
Ottawa, *Kans., U.S.A.* 112 F7
Ottawa Is., *Canada* 101 C11
Ottélé, *Cameroon* 83 E7
Ottensheim, *Austria* 26 C7
Otter Cr. →, *U.S.A.* 117 B11
Otter L., *Canada* 103 B8
Otterndorf, *Germany* 24 B4
Otterup, *Denmark* 11 J4
Otterville, *Canada* 116 D4
Ottery St. Mary, *U.K.* 15 G4
Otto Beit Bridge, *Zimbabwe* 87 F2
Ottosdal, *S. Africa* 88 D4
Ottumwa, *U.S.A.* 112 E8
Otu, *Nigeria* 83 D5
Otukpa, *Nigeria* 83 D6
Oturkpo, *Nigeria* 83 D6
Otway, B., *Chile* 128 G2
Otway, C., *Australia* 95 F3
Otwock, *Poland* 31 F8
Otyniya, *Ukraine* 29 B9
Ötztaler Ache →, *Austria* 26 D3
Ötztaler Alpen, *Austria* 26 E3
Ou →, *Laos* 64 B4
Ou Neua, *Laos* 58 F3
Ou-Sammyaku, *Japan* 54 E10
Ouachita →, *U.S.A.* 113 K9
Ouachita, L., *U.S.A.* 113 H8
Ouachita Mts., *U.S.A.* 113 H7
Ouagadougou, *Burkina Faso* 83 C4
Ouahigouya, *Burkina Faso* 82 C4
Ouahran = Oran, *Algeria* 78 A5
Oualâta, *Mauritania* 82 B3
Ouallam, *Niger* 83 C5
Ouallene, *Algeria* 78 D6
Ouargaye, *Burkina Faso* 83 C5
Ouargla, *Algeria* 78 B7
Ouarkoye, *Burkina Faso* 82 C4
Ouarzazate, *Morocco* 78 B4
Ouassouas, *Mali* 83 B5
Ouatagouna, *Mali* 83 B5
Oubangi →, *Dem. Rep. of the Congo* 84 E3
Ouche →, *France* 19 E12
Ouddorp, *Neths.* 17 C3
Oude Rijn →, *Neths.* 17 B4
Oudeïka, *Mali* 83 B4
Oudenaarde, *Belgium* 17 D3
Oudon →, *France* 18 E6
Oudtshoorn, *S. Africa* 88 E3
Ouellé, *Ivory C.* 82 D4
Ouémé →, *Benin* 83 D5
Ouessa, *Burkina Faso* 82 C4
Ouessant, Î. d', *France* 18 D1
Ouesso, *Congo* 84 D3
Ouest, Pte. de l', *Canada* 105 C7
Ouezzane, *Morocco* 78 B4
Ougarou, *Burkina Faso* 83 C5
Oughterard, *Ireland* 12 C2
Ouidah, *Benin* 83 D5
Ouidi, *Niger* 83 C7
Ouistreham, *France* 18 C6
Oujda, *Morocco* 78 B5
Oujeft, *Mauritania* 82 A2
Oulainen, *Finland* 8 D21
Ould Yenjé, *Mauritania* 82 B2
Oullins, *France* 21 C8
Oulu, *Finland* 8 D21
Oulujärvi, *Finland* 8 D22
Oulujoki →, *Finland* 8 D21
Oulx, *Italy* 40 C3
Oum Chalouba, *Chad* 79 E10
Oum Hadjer, *Chad* 79 F9
Oumé, *Ivory C.* 82 D3
Ounasjoki →, *Finland* 8 C21
Ounguati, *Namibia* 88 C2
Ounianga Sérir, *Chad* 79 E10
Our →, *Lux.* 17 E6
Ouranópolis, *Greece* 44 F7
Ourârene, *Niger* 83 B6
Ouray, *U.S.A.* 109 G10
Ourcq →, *France* 19 C10
Ourense, *Spain* 36 C3
Ouricuri, *Brazil* 125 E10
Ourinhos, *Brazil* 127 A6
Ourique, *Portugal* 37 H2
Ouro Fino, *Brazil* 127 A6
Ouro-Ndia, *Mali* 82 B4
Ouro Prêto, *Brazil* 127 A7
Ouro Sogui, *Senegal* 82 B2
Oursi, *Burkina Faso* 83 C4
Ourthe →, *Belgium* 17 D5
Ouse →, *E. Susx., U.K.* 15 G8
Ouse →, *N. Yorks., U.K.* 14 D7
Oust, *France* 20 F5
Oust →, *France* 18 E4
Outamba-Kilimi △, *S. Leone* 82 D2
Outaouais →, *Canada* 104 C5
Outardes →, *Canada* 105 C6
Outeiro de Rei, *Spain* 36 B3
Outer Hebrides, *U.K.* 13 D1
Outes = Serra de Outes, *Spain* 36 C2
Outjo, *Namibia* 88 C2
Outlook, *Canada* 103 C7
Outokumpu, *Finland* 8 E23
Outreau, *France* 19 B8
Ouvèze →, *France* 21 E8
Ouyen, *Australia* 95 F3
Ouzouer-le-Marché, *France* 19 E8
Ovada, *Italy* 40 D5
Ovalau, *Fiji* 91 C8
Ovalle, *Chile* 126 C1
Ovamboland, *Namibia* 88 B2
Ovar, *Portugal* 36 E2
Overath, *Germany* 24 E3
Overflakkee, *Neths.* 17 C4
Overijssel □, *Neths.* 17 B6
Overland Park, *U.S.A.* 112 F7
Overton, *U.S.A.* 111 J12
Övertorneå, *Sweden* 8 C20
Överum, *Sweden* 11 F10
Ovid, *U.S.A.* 117 D8
Ovidiopol, *Ukraine* 33 J6
Ovidiu, *Romania* 29 F13
Oviedo, *Spain* 36 B5
Oviksfjällen, *Sweden* 10 A7
Oviši, *Latvia* 9 H19
Ovoot, *Mongolia* 56 B7
Övör Hangay □, *Mongolia* 56 B2
Ovoro, *Nigeria* 83 D6
Øvre Årdal, *Norway* 9 F12
Övre Fryken, *Sweden* 10 E7
Ovruch, *Ukraine* 33 G5
Owaka, *N.Z.* 91 M2
Owambo = Ovamboland, *Namibia* 88 B2
Owasco L., *U.S.A.* 117 D8
Owase, *Japan* 55 G8
Owatonna, *U.S.A.* 112 C8
Owbeh, *Afghan.* 66 B3
Owego, *U.S.A.* 117 D8
Owen Falls Dam, *Uganda* 86 B3
Owen Sound, *Canada* 116 B4
Owens →, *U.S.A.* 110 J9
Owens L., *U.S.A.* 111 J9
Owensboro, *U.S.A.* 114 G2
Owerri, *Nigeria* 83 D6
Owl →, *Canada* 103 B10
Owo, *Nigeria* 83 D6
Owosso, *U.S.A.* 114 D3
Owyhee, *U.S.A.* 108 F5
Owyhee →, *U.S.A.* 108 E5
Owyhee, L., *U.S.A.* 108 E5
Ox Mts. = Slieve Gamph, *Ireland* 12 B3
Öxarfjörður, *Iceland* 8 C5
Oxbow, *Canada* 103 D8
Oxelösund, *Sweden* 11 F11
Oxford, *N.Z.* 91 K4
Oxford, *U.K.* 15 F6
Oxford, *Mass., U.S.A.* 117 D13
Oxford, *Miss., U.S.A.* 113 H10
Oxford, *N.C., U.S.A.* 115 G6
Oxford, *N.Y., U.S.A.* 117 D9
Oxford, *Ohio, U.S.A.* 114 F3
Oxford L., *Canada* 103 C9
Oxfordshire □, *U.K.* 15 F6
Oxía Nisís, *Greece* 46 C3
Oxie, *Sweden* 11 J7
Oxílithos, *Greece* 46 C6
Oxnard, *U.S.A.* 111 L7
Oxsjövålen, *Sweden* 10 B7
Oxus = Amudarya →, *Uzbekistan* 52 E6
Oya, *Malaysia* 62 D4
Oyama, *Japan* 55 F9
Oyambre ⌓, *Spain* 36 B6
Oyem, *Gabon* 84 D2
Oyen, *Canada* 103 C6
Oykel →, *U.K.* 13 D4
Oymyakon, *Russia* 53 C15
Oyo, *Nigeria* 83 D5
Oyo □, *Nigeria* 83 D5
Oyonnax, *France* 19 F12
Oyster Bay, *U.S.A.* 117 F11
Ōyübari, *Japan* 54 C11
Özalp, *Turkey* 73 C10
Ozamiz, *Phil.* 61 G5
Ozark, *Ala., U.S.A.* 115 K3
Ozark, *Ark., U.S.A.* 113 H8
Ozark, *Mo., U.S.A.* 113 G8
Ozark Plateau, *U.S.A.* 113 G9
Ozarks, L. of the, *U.S.A.* 112 F8
Ożarów, *Poland* 31 H8
Ózd, *Hungary* 28 B5
Ozernoye, *Russia* 34 E10
Ozero Svityaz, *Ukraine* 31 G10
Ozersk, *Russia* 30 D8
Ozette L., *U.S.A.* 110 B2
Ozieri, *Italy* 42 B2
Ozimek, *Poland* 31 H5
Ozinki, *Russia* 34 E9
Ozona, *U.S.A.* 113 K4
Ozorków, *Poland* 31 G6
Ozren, *Bos.-H.* 28 G3
Ozuluama, *Mexico* 119 C5
Ozun, *Romania* 29 E10
Ozurgeti, *Georgia* 35 K5

P

Pa, *Burkina Faso* 82 C4
Pa-an, *Burma* 67 L20
Pa Mong Dam, *Thailand* 64 D4
Pa Sak →, *Thailand* 62 B2
Paamiut, *Greenland* 101 B15
Paar →, *Germany* 25 G7
Paarl, *S. Africa* 88 E2
Pab Hills, *Pakistan* 68 F2
Pabbay, *U.K.* 13 D1
Pabianice, *Poland* 31 G6
Pabna, *Bangla.* 67 G16
Pabo, *Uganda* 86 B3
Pacaja →, *Brazil* 125 D8
Pacaraima, Sa., *S. Amer.* 124 C6
Pacasmayo, *Peru* 124 E3
Paceco, *Italy* 42 E5
Pachhar, *India* 68 G7
Pachino, *Italy* 43 F8
Pachitea →, *Peru* 124 E4
Pachmarhi, *India* 69 H8
Pachpadra, *India* 66 G8
Pachuca, *Mexico* 119 C5
Pacific, *Canada* 102 C3
Pacific-Antarctic Ridge, *Pac. Oc.* 97 M16
Pacific Grove, *U.S.A.* 110 J5
Pacific Ocean 97 G14
Pacific Rim △, *Canada* 102 D4
Pacifica, *U.S.A.* 110 H4
Pacitan, *Indonesia* 63 H14
Packwood, *U.S.A.* 110 D5
Pacov, *Czech Rep.* 26 B8
Pacy-sur-Eure, *France* 18 C8
Padaido, Kepulauan, *Indonesia* 63 E9
Padang, *Indonesia* 62 E2
Padang Endau, *Malaysia* 65 L4
Padangpanjang, *Indonesia* 62 E2
Padangsidempuan, *Indonesia* 62 D1
Padborg, *Denmark* 11 K3
Paddle Prairie, *Canada* 102 B5
Paddockwood, *Canada* 103 C7
Paderborn, *Germany* 24 D4
Padeş, Vf., *Romania* 28 E7
Padina, *Romania* 29 F12
Padma, *India* 69 G11
Pádova, *Italy* 41 C8
Padra, *India* 68 H5
Padrauna, *India* 69 F10
Padre I., *U.S.A.* 113 M6
Padre Island ⌓, *U.S.A.* 113 M6
Padrón, *Spain* 36 C2
Padstow, *U.K.* 15 G3
Padua = Pádova, *Italy* 41 C8
Paducah, *Ky., U.S.A.* 114 G1
Paducah, *Tex., U.S.A.* 113 H4
Padul, *Spain* 37 H7
Paengnyŏng-do, *S. Korea* 57 F13
Paeroa, *N.Z.* 91 G5
Paesana, *Italy* 40 D4
Pafúri, *Mozam.* 89 C5
Pag, *Croatia* 41 D12
Paga, *Ghana* 83 C4
Pagadian, *Phil.* 61 H5
Pagai Selatan, Pulau, *Indonesia* 62 E2
Pagai Utara, Pulau, *Indonesia* 62 E2
Pagalu = Annobón, *Atl. Oc.* 77 G4
Pagara, *India* 69 G9
Pagastikós Kólpos, *Greece* 46 B5
Pagatan, *Indonesia* 62 E5
Page, *U.S.A.* 109 H8
Pagėgiai, *Lithuania* 30 C8

Pago Pago, *Amer. Samoa* 91 B13
Pagosa Springs, *U.S.A.* 109 H10
Pagwa River, *Canada* 104 B2
Pahala, *U.S.A.* 106 J17
Pahang →, *Malaysia* 65 L4
Pahiatua, *N.Z.* 91 J5
Pahokee, *U.S.A.* 115 M5
Pahrump, *U.S.A.* 111 J11
Pahute Mesa, *U.S.A.* 110 H10
Pai, *Thailand* 64 C2
Paicines, *U.S.A.* 110 J5
Paide, *Estonia* 9 G21
Paignton, *U.K.* 15 G4
Paiho, *Taiwan* 59 F13
Päijänne, *Finland* 9 F21
Pailani, *India* 69 G9
Pailin, *Cambodia* 64 F4
Paimpol, *France* 18 D3
Painan, *Indonesia* 62 E2
Painesville, *U.S.A.* 116 E3
Paint Hills = Wemindji, *Canada* 104 B4
Paint L., *Canada* 103 B9
Painted Desert, *U.S.A.* 109 J8
Paintsville, *U.S.A.* 114 G4
País Vasco □, *Spain* 38 C2
Paisley, *Canada* 116 B3
Paisley, *U.K.* 13 F4
Paisley, *U.S.A.* 108 E3
Paita, *Peru* 124 E2
Paiva →, *Portugal* 36 D2
Paizhou, *China* 59 B9
Pajares, *Spain* 36 B5
Pajares, Puerto de, *Spain* 36 C5
Pajęczno, *Poland* 31 G5
Pak Lay, *Laos* 64 C3
Pak Phanang, *Thailand* 65 H3
Pak Sane, *Laos* 64 C4
Pak Song, *Laos* 64 E6
Pak Suong, *Laos* 58 H4
Pakaur, *India* 69 G12
Pakenham, *Canada* 117 A8
Pákhnes, *Greece* 49 D6
Pakhuis, *S. Africa* 88 E2
Pakistan ■, *Asia* 68 E4
Pakkading, *Laos* 64 C4
Paklenica △, *Croatia* 41 D12
Pakokku, *Burma* 67 J19
Pakość, *Poland* 31 F5
Pakowki L., *Canada* 103 D6
Pakpattan, *Pakistan* 68 D5
Pakrac, *Croatia* 28 E2
Pakruojis, *Lithuania* 30 C10
Paks, *Hungary* 28 D3
Paktīā □, *Afghan.* 66 C6
Paktīkā □, *Afghan.* 66 C6
Pakwach, *Uganda* 86 B3
Pakxe, *Laos* 64 E5
Pal Lahara, *India* 69 J11
Pala, *Chad* 79 G9
Pala, *Dem. Rep. of the Congo* 86 D2
Pala, *U.S.A.* 111 M9
Palabek, *Uganda* 86 B3
Palacios, *U.S.A.* 113 L6
Palafrugell, *Spain* 38 D8
Palagiano, *Italy* 43 B10
Palagonía, *Italy* 43 E7
Palagruža, *Croatia* 41 F13
Palaiókastron, *Greece* 49 D8
Palaiokhóra, *Greece* 49 D5
Pálairos, *Greece* 46 C2
Palaiseau, *France* 19 D9
Palam, *India* 66 K10
Palamás, *Greece* 46 B4
Palamòs, *Spain* 38 D8
Palampur, *India* 68 C7
Palamut, *Turkey* 47 C9
Palana, *Australia* 95 F4
Palana, *Russia* 53 D16
Palanan, *Phil.* 61 C5
Palanan Pt., *Phil.* 61 C5
Palandri, *Pakistan* 69 C5
Palanga, *Lithuania* 9 J19
Palangkaraya, *Indonesia* 62 E4
Palani Hills, *India* 66 P10
Palanpur, *India* 68 G5
Palapye, *Botswana* 88 C4
Palas, *Pakistan* 69 B5
Palas de Rei, *Spain* 36 C3
Palashi, *India* 69 H13
Palasponga, *India* 69 J11
Palatka, *Russia* 53 C16
Palatka, *U.S.A.* 115 L5
Palau, *Italy* 42 A2
Palau ■, *Pac. Oc.* 96 G5
Palauk, *Burma* 64 F2
Palawan, *Phil.* 61 G3
Palayankottai, *India* 66 Q10
Palazzo, Pte., *France* 21 F12
Palazzo San Gervásio, *Italy* 43 B8
Palazzolo Acréide, *Italy* 43 E7
Paldiski, *Estonia* 9 G21
Pale, *Bos.-H.* 28 G3
Paleleh, *Indonesia* 63 D6
Palembang, *Indonesia* 62 E2
Palencia, *Spain* 36 C6
Palencia □, *Spain* 36 C6
Palenque, *Mexico* 119 D6
Paleokastrítsa, *Greece* 49 A3
Paleometokho, *Cyprus* 49 D12
Palermo, *Italy* 42 D6
Palermo, *U.S.A.* 108 G3
Palermo ✕ (PMO), *Italy* 42 D6
Palestina, *Chile* 128 A3
Palestine, *Asia* 74 D4
Palestine, *U.S.A.* 113 K7
Palestrina, *Italy* 41 G9
Paletwa, *Burma* 67 J18
Palghat, *India* 66 P10
Palgrave, Mt., *Australia* 92 D2
Pali, *India* 68 G5
Palikir, *Micronesia* 96 G7
Palinuro, *Italy* 43 B8
Palinuro, C., *Italy* 43 B8
Palioúrion, Ákra, *Greece* 44 G7
Palisades Reservoir, *U.S.A.* 108 E8
Paliseul, *Belgium* 17 E5
Palitana, *India* 68 J4
Palizada, *Mexico* 119 D6
Palk Bay, *Asia* 66 Q11
Palk Strait, *Asia* 66 Q11
Palkānah, *Iraq* 70 C5
Palkot, *India* 69 H11
Pallanza = Verbánia, *Italy* 40 C5
Pallarenda, *Australia* 94 B4
Pallasovka, *Russia* 34 E8
Pallës, Bishti i, *Albania* 44 E3
Pallinup →, *Australia* 93 F2
Pallisa, *Uganda* 86 B3
Pallu, *India* 68 E6
Palm Bay, *U.S.A.* 115 L5
Palm Beach, *U.S.A.* 115 M6
Palm Coast, *U.S.A.* 115 L5
Palm Desert, *U.S.A.* 111 M10
Palm Is., *Australia* 94 B4
Palm Springs, *U.S.A.* 111 M10
Palma, *Mozam.* 87 E5
Palma, B. de, *Spain* 48 B9
Palma de Mallorca, *Spain* 48 B9
Palma de Mallorca ✕ (PMI), *Spain* 39 F7
Palma del Río, *Spain* 37 H5
Palma di Montechiaro, *Italy* 42 E6
Palma Soriano, *Cuba* 120 B4
Palmares, *Brazil* 125 E11
Palmarola, *Italy* 42 B5
Palmas, *Brazil* 127 B5
Palmas, C., *Liberia* 82 E3
Pálmas, G. di, *Italy* 42 D1
Palmdale, *U.S.A.* 111 L8
Palmeira das Missões, *Brazil* 127 B5
Palmeira dos Índios, *Brazil* 125 E11
Palmela, *Portugal* 37 G2
Palmer, *Antarctica* 5 C17
Palmer, *U.S.A.* 100 B5
Palmer →, *Australia* 94 B3
Palmer Arch., *Antarctica* 5 C17
Palmer Lake, *U.S.A.* 112 F2
Palmer Land, *Antarctica* 5 D18
Palmerston, *Australia* 92 B5
Palmerston, *Canada* 116 C4
Palmerston, *N.Z.* 91 L3
Palmerston North, *N.Z.* 91 J5
Palmerton, *U.S.A.* 117 F9
Palmetto, *U.S.A.* 115 M4
Palmi, *Italy* 43 D8
Palmira, *Argentina* 126 C2
Palmira, *Colombia* 124 C3
Palmyra = Tudmur, *Syria* 70 C3
Palmyra, *Mo., U.S.A.* 112 F9
Palmyra, *N.J., U.S.A.* 117 F9
Palmyra, *N.Y., U.S.A.* 116 C7
Palmyra, *Pa., U.S.A.* 117 F8
Palmyra Is., *Pac. Oc.* 97 G11
Palo Alto, *U.S.A.* 110 H4
Palo Seco, *Trin. & Tob.* 125 K15
Palo Verde, *U.S.A.* 111 M12
Palo Verde △, *Costa Rica* 120 D2
Paloich, *Sudan* 81 E3
Palomar Mt., *U.S.A.* 111 M10
Palompon, *Phil.* 61 F6
Palopo, *Indonesia* 63 E6
Palos, C. de, *Spain* 39 H4
Palos de la Frontera, *Spain* 37 H4
Palos Verdes, *U.S.A.* 111 M8
Palos Verdes, Pt., *U.S.A.* 111 M8
Pålsboda, *Sweden* 10 E9
Palu, *Indonesia* 63 E5
Palu, *Turkey* 70 B3
Paluke, *Liberia* 82 D3
Paluzza, *Italy* 41 B10
Palwal, *India* 68 E7
Pama, *Burkina Faso* 83 C5
Pama ⌓, *Burkina Faso* 83 C5
Pamanukan, *Indonesia* 63 G12
Pamekasan, *Indonesia* 63 G15
Pamenang, *Indonesia* 63 J19
Pamiers, *France* 20 E5
Pamir, *Tajikistan* 52 F8
Pamlico →, *U.S.A.* 115 H7
Pamlico Sd., *U.S.A.* 115 H8
Pampa, *U.S.A.* 113 H4
Pampa de las Salinas, *Argentina* 126 C2
Pampanua, *Indonesia* 63 E6
Pampas, *Argentina* 126 D3
Pampas, *Peru* 124 F4
Pamphylia, *Turkey* 72 D4
Pamplona, *Colombia* 124 B4
Pamplona, *Spain* 38 C3
Pampoenpoort, *S. Africa* 88 E3
Pamukçu, *Turkey* 47 B9
Pamukkale, *Turkey* 47 D11
Pan de Azúcar △, *Chile* 126 B1
Pan Xian, *China* 58 E5
Pana, *U.S.A.* 112 F10
Panabo, *Phil.* 61 H6
Panaca, *U.S.A.* 109 H6
Panagyurishte, *Bulgaria* 45 D8
Panaitan, *Indonesia* 63 G11
Panaji, *India* 66 M8
Panamá, *Panama* 120 E4
Panama ■, *Cent. Amer.* 120 E4
Panamá, G. de, *Panama* 120 E4
Panama Canal, *Panama* 120 E4
Panama City, *U.S.A.* 115 K3
Panamint Range, *U.S.A.* 111 J9
Panamint Springs, *U.S.A.* 111 J9
Panão, *Peru* 124 E3
Panaon I., *Phil.* 61 F6
Panare, *Thailand* 65 J3
Panarea, *Italy* 43 D8
Panaro →, *Italy* 41 D8
Panay, *Phil.* 61 F5
Panay, G., *Phil.* 63 B6
Pančevo, *Serbia & M.* 28 F5
Panch'iao, *Taiwan* 59 E13
Panciu, *Romania* 29 E12
Pancorbo, Desfiladero, *Spain* 36 C7
Pâncota, *Romania* 28 D6
Panda, *Mozam.* 89 C5
Pandan, *Malaysia* 65 d
Pandan, *Antique, Phil.* 61 F5
Pandan, *Catanduanes, Phil.* 61 D6
Pandan, Selat, *Singapore* 65 d
Pandan Tampoi = Tampoi, *Malaysia* 65 d
Pandegelang, *Indonesia* 63 G12
Pandhana, *India* 68 J7
Pandharpur, *India* 66 L9
Pando, *Uruguay* 127 C4
Pando, L. = Hope, L., *Australia* 95 D2
Pandokrátor, *Greece* 49 A3
Pandora, *Costa Rica* 120 E3
Pandrup, *Denmark* 11 G3
Panevéggio-Pale di San Martino ⌓, *Italy* 41 B8
Panevėžys, *Lithuania* 9 J21
Panfilov, *Kazakhstan* 52 E8
Panfilovo, *Russia* 34 E6
Pang-Long, *Burma* 67 H21
Pang Sida △, *Thailand* 64 E4
Pang-Yang, *Burma* 67 H21
Panga, *Dem. Rep. of the Congo* 86 B2
Pangaíon Óros, *Greece* 45 F8
Pangalanes, Canal des = Ampangalana, Lakandranon', *Madag.* 89 C8
Pangani, *Tanzania* 86 D4
Pangani →, *Tanzania* 86 D4
Pangfou = Bengbu, *China* 57 H9
Pangil, *Dem. Rep. of the Congo* 86 C2
Pangkah, Tanjung, *Indonesia* 63 G15
Pangkajene, *Indonesia* 63 E5
Pangkalanbrandan, *Indonesia* 62 D1
Pangkalanbuun, *Indonesia* 62 E4
Pangkalpinang, *Indonesia* 62 E3
Pangnirtung, *Canada* 101 B13
Pangong Tso, *India* 68 B8
Panguitch, *U.S.A.* 109 H7
Pangutaran Group, *Phil.* 61 H4
Panhandle, *U.S.A.* 113 H4
Pani Mines, *India* 68 H5
Pania-Mutombo, *Dem. Rep. of the Congo* 86 D1
Panikota I., *India* 68 J4
Panipat, *India* 68 E7
Panjal Range = Pir Panjal Range, *India* 68 C7
Panjang, Hon, *Vietnam* 65 H4
Panjgur, *Pakistan* 66 F4
Panjim = Panaji, *India* 66 M8
Panjin, *China* 57 D12
Panjinad Barrage, *Pakistan* 66 E7
Panjnad →, *Pakistan* 68 E4
Panjwai, *Afghan.* 68 D1
Pankshin, *Nigeria* 83 D6
Panmunjŏm, *N. Korea* 57 F14
Panna, *India* 69 G9
Panna Hills, *India* 69 G9
Pannawonica, *Australia* 92 D2
Pannga, Tanjung, *Indonesia* 63 K19
Pannirtuuq = Pangnirtung, *Canada* 101 B13
Pano Akil, *Pakistan* 68 F3
Pano Lefkara, *Cyprus* 49 E12
Pano Panayia, *Cyprus* 49 E11
Panorama, *Brazil* 127 A5
Pánormon, *Greece* 49 D6
Pansemal, *India* 68 J6
Panshan = Panjin, *China* 57 D12
Panshi, *China* 57 C14
Pantanal, *Brazil* 124 H7
Pantanos de Centla ⌓, *Mexico* 119 D6
Pantar, *Indonesia* 63 F6
Pante Macassar, *E. Timor* 63 F6
Pante Makasar = Pante Macassar, *E. Timor* 63 F6
Pantelleria, *Italy* 42 F4
Pantón, *Spain* 36 C3
Pánuco, *Mexico* 119 C5
Panyam, *Nigeria* 83 D6
Panyu, *China* 59 F9
Panzhihua, *China* 58 D3
Páola, *Italy* 43 C9
Paola, *Malta* 49 D2
Paola, *U.S.A.* 112 F7
Paonia, *U.S.A.* 109 G10
Paoting = Baoding, *China* 56 E8
Paot'ou = Baotou, *China* 56 D6
Paoua, *C.A.R.* 84 C3
Pápa, *Hungary* 28 C2
Papa Stour, *U.K.* 13 A7
Papa Westray, *U.K.* 13 B6
Papagayo →, *Mexico* 119 D5
Papagayo, G. de, *Costa Rica* 120 D2
Papakura, *N.Z.* 91 G5
Papantla, *Mexico* 119 C5
Papar, *Malaysia* 62 C5
Paparoa △, *N.Z.* 91 K3
Pápas, Ákra, *Greece* 46 C3
Papeete, *Tahiti* 97 J13
Papenburg, *Germany* 24 B3
Paphlagonia, *Turkey* 72 B5
Paphos, *Cyprus* 49 E11
Papigochic →, *Mexico* 118 B3
Paposo, *Chile* 126 B1
Papoutsa, *Cyprus* 49 E12
Papua □, *Indonesia* 63 E9
Papua New Guinea ■, *Oceania* 96 H6
Papudo, *Chile* 126 C1
Papuk, *Croatia* 28 E2
Papun, *Burma* 67 K20
Papunya, *Australia* 92 D5
Pará = Belém, *Brazil* 125 D9
Pará □, *Brazil* 125 D8
Paraburdoo, *Australia* 92 D2
Paracale, *Phil.* 61 D5
Paracatu, *Brazil* 125 G9
Paracel Is., *S. China Sea* 62 A4
Parachilna, *Australia* 95 E2
Parachinar, *Pakistan* 68 C4
Paraćin, *Serbia & M.* 44 C5
Paradas, *Spain* 37 H5
Paradela, *Spain* 36 C3
Paradhísi, *Greece* 49 C10
Paradip, *India* 67 J15
Paradise, *Calif., U.S.A.* 110 F5
Paradise, *Nev., U.S.A.* 111 J11
Paradise →, *Canada* 105 B8
Paradise Hill, *Canada* 103 C7
Paradise River, *Canada* 105 B8
Paradise Valley, *U.S.A.* 108 F5
Parado, *Indonesia* 63 F5
Paragould, *U.S.A.* 113 G9
Paragua →, *Venezuela* 124 B6
Paraguaçu →, *Brazil* 125 F11
Paraguaçu Paulista, *Brazil* 127 A5
Paraguaná, Pen. de, *Venezuela* 124 A5
Paraguarí, *Paraguay* 126 B4
Paraguarí □, *Paraguay* 126 B4
Paraguay ■, *S. Amer.* 126 A4
Paraguay →, *Paraguay* 126 B4
Paraíba = João Pessoa, *Brazil* 125 E12
Paraíba □, *Brazil* 125 E11
Paraíba do Sul →, *Brazil* 127 A7
Parainen, *Finland* 9 F20
Paraiso, *Mexico* 119 D6
Parak, *Iran* 71 E7
Parakhino Paddubye, *Russia* 32 C7
Parakou, *Benin* 83 D5
Paralimni, *Cyprus* 49 D12
Parálion-Astrous, *Greece* 46 D4
Paramaribo, *Suriname* 125 B7
Paramithiá, *Greece* 46 B2
Páramos del Batallón y La Negra △, *Venezuela* 121 E5
Paramushir, Ostrov, *Russia* 53 D16
Paran →, *Israel* 74 E4
Paraná, *Argentina* 126 C3
Paraná, *Brazil* 125 F9
Paraná □, *Brazil* 127 A5
Paraná →, *Argentina* 126 C4
Paranaguá, *Brazil* 127 B6
Paranaíba, *Brazil* 125 G8
Paranaíba →, *Brazil* 125 H8
Paranapanema →, *Brazil* 127 A5
Paranapiacaba, Serra do, *Brazil* 127 A6
Paranas, *Phil.* 61 F6
Paranavaí, *Brazil* 127 A5
Parang, *Maguindanao, Phil.* 63 C6
Parang, *Sulu, Phil.* 61 J4
Parângul Mare, Vf., *Romania* 29 E8
Paraparaumu, *N.Z.* 91 J5
Parapóla, *Greece* 46 E5
Paraspóri, Ákra, *Greece* 47 F9
Paray-le-Monial, *France* 19 F11
Parbati →, *Mad. P., India* 68 G7
Parbati →, *Raj., India* 68 F7
Parbhani, *India* 66 K10
Parchim, *Germany* 24 B7
Parczew, *Poland* 31 G9
Pardes Hanna-Karkur, *Israel* 74 C3
Pardilla, *Spain* 36 D7
Pardo →, *Bahia, Brazil* 125 G11
Pardo →, *Mato Grosso, Brazil* 127 A5
Pardubice, *Czech Rep.* 26 A8
Pardubický □, *Czech Rep.* 26 B8
Pare, *Indonesia* 63 G15
Pare Mts., *Tanzania* 86 C4
Parecis, Serra dos, *Brazil* 124 F7
Paredes de Nava, *Spain* 36 C6
Paren, *Russia* 53 C17
Parent, *Canada* 104 C5
Parent, L., *Canada* 104 C4
Parentis-en-Born, *France* 20 D2
Parepare, *Indonesia* 63 E5
Parfino, *Russia* 32 D6
Párga, *Greece* 46 B2
Pargas = Parainen, *Finland* 9 F20
Pargo, Pta. do, *Madeira* 48 D2
Paria, G. de, *Venezuela* 125 K14
Pariaguán, *Venezuela* 124 B6
Paricutín, Cerro, *Mexico* 118 D4
Parigi, *Indonesia* 63 E6
Parika, *Guyana* 124 B7
Parikkala, *Finland* 32 B5
Parima, Serra, *Brazil* 124 C6
Parinari, *Peru* 124 D4
Pariñas, Pta., *S. Amer.* 122 D2
Parincea, *Romania* 29 D12
Parintins, *Brazil* 125 D7
Pariparit Kyun, *Burma* 67 M18
Paris, *Canada* 116 C4
Paris, *France* 19 D9
Paris, *Idaho, U.S.A.* 108 E8
Paris, *Ky., U.S.A.* 114 F3
Paris, *Tenn., U.S.A.* 115 G1
Paris, *Tex., U.S.A.* 113 J7
Paris, Ville de □, *France* 19 D9
Paris Charles de Gaulle ✕ (CDG), *France* 19 D9
Paris Orly ✕ (ORY), *France* 19 D9
Parish, *U.S.A.* 117 C8
Parishville, *U.S.A.* 117 B10
Park, *U.S.A.* 110 B4
Park City, *U.S.A.* 113 G6
Park Falls, *U.S.A.* 112 C9
Park Head, *Canada* 116 B3
Park Hills, *U.S.A.* 113 G9
Park Range, *U.S.A.* 108 G10
Park Rapids, *U.S.A.* 112 B7
Park River, *U.S.A.* 112 A6
Park Rynie, *S. Africa* 89 E5
Parkā Bandar, *Iran* 71 E8
Parkano, *Finland* 9 E20
Parker, *Ariz., U.S.A.* 111 L12
Parker, *Pa., U.S.A.* 116 E5
Parker Dam, *U.S.A.* 111 L12
Parkersburg, *U.S.A.* 114 F5
Parkes, *Australia* 95 E4
Parkfield, *U.S.A.* 110 K6
Parkhill, *Canada* 116 C3
Parkland, *U.S.A.* 110 C4
Parkston, *U.S.A.* 112 D6
Parksville, *Canada* 102 D4
Parla, *Spain* 36 E7
Pârliţa, *Moldova* 29 C12
Parma, *Italy* 40 D7
Parma, *Idaho, U.S.A.* 108 E5
Parma, *Ohio, U.S.A.* 116 E3
Parma →, *Italy* 40 D7
Parnaguá, *Brazil* 125 F10
Parnaíba, *Brazil* 125 D10
Parnaíba →, *Brazil* 125 D10
Parnassós, *Greece* 46 C4
Párnis, *Greece* 46 C5
Párnitha △, *Greece* 46 C5
Párnon Óros, *Greece* 46 D4
Pärnu, *Estonia* 9 G21
Paroo →, *Australia* 95 E3
Páros, *Greece* 47 D7
Parowan, *U.S.A.* 109 H7
Parpaillon, *France* 21 D10
Parral, *Chile* 126 D1
Parras, *Mexico* 118 B4
Parrett →, *U.K.* 15 F4
Parris I., *U.S.A.* 115 J5
Parrsboro, *Canada* 105 C7
Parry I., *Canada* 116 A4
Parry Is., *Canada* 98 B8
Parry Sound, *Canada* 116 A5
Parsberg, *Germany* 25 F7
Parsęta →, *Poland* 30 D2
Parsnip →, *Canada* 102 B4
Parsons, *U.S.A.* 113 G7
Parsons Ra., *Australia* 94 A2
Partanna, *Italy* 42 E5
Partenio ⌓, *Italy* 43 B7
Parthenay, *France* 18 F6
Partinico, *Italy* 42 D6
Partizánske, *Slovak Rep.* 27 C11
Partridge I., *Canada* 104 A2
Paru →, *Brazil* 125 D8
Parvān □, *Afghan.* 66 B6
Parvatipuram, *India* 67 K13
Parvatsar, *India* 68 F6
Påryd, *Sweden* 11 H9
Parys, *S. Africa* 88 D4
Pas, Pta. des, *Spain* 48 C7
Pas-de-Calais □, *France* 19 B9
Pasada, *Spain* 36 B5
Pasadena, *Canada* 105 C8
Pasadena, *Calif., U.S.A.* 111 L8
Pasadena, *Tex., U.S.A.* 113 L7
Pasaje →, *Argentina* 126 B3
Paşalimanı, *Turkey* 45 F11
Pasar, *Indonesia* 63 J17
Pasay, *Phil.* 61 D4
Pascagoula, *U.S.A.* 113 K10
Pascagoula →, *U.S.A.* 113 K10
Paşcani, *Romania* 29 C11
Pasco, *U.S.A.* 108 C4
Pasco, Cerro de, *Peru* 124 F3
Pasco I., *Australia* 92 D2
Pascoag, *U.S.A.* 117 E13
Pascua, I. de, *Chile* 97 K17
Pasewalk, *Germany* 24 B9
Pasfield L., *Canada* 103 B7
Pasha →, *Russia* 32 B7
Pasinler, *Turkey* 73 C9
Pasir Mas, *Malaysia* 65 J4
Pasir Panjang, *Singapore* 65 d
Pasir Putih, *Malaysia* 65 K4
Pasirian, *Indonesia* 63 H15
Pasirkuning, *Indonesia* 62 E2
Påskallavik, *Sweden* 11 G10
Paskūh, *Iran* 71 E9
Pasłęk, *Poland* 30 D6
Pasłęka →, *Poland* 30 D6
Pasley, C., *Australia* 93 F3
Pašman, *Croatia* 41 E12
Pasni, *Pakistan* 66 G3
Paso Cantinela, *Mexico* 111 N11
Paso de Indios, *Argentina* 128 E3
Paso de los Libres, *Argentina* 126 B4
Paso de los Toros, *Uruguay* 126 C4
Paso Robles, *U.S.A.* 109 J3
Paspébiac, *Canada* 105 C6
Pasrur, *Pakistan* 68 C6
Passage West, *Ireland* 12 E3
Passaic, *U.S.A.* 117 F10
Passau, *Germany* 25 G9
Passero, C., *Italy* 43 F8
Passo Fundo, *Brazil* 127 B5
Passos, *Brazil* 125 H9
Passow, *Germany* 24 B10
Passy, *France* 21 C10
Pastavy, *Belarus* 9 J22
Pastaza →, *Peru* 124 D3
Pasto, *Colombia* 124 C3
Pastrana, *Spain* 38 E2
Pasuruan, *Indonesia* 63 G15
Pasym, *Poland* 30 E7
Pásztó, *Hungary* 28 C4
Patagonia, *Argentina* 128 F3
Patagonia, *U.S.A.* 109 L8
Patambar, *Iran* 71 D9
Patan = Lalitapur, *Nepal* 69 F11
Patan, *Gujarat, India* 66 H8
Patan, *Maharashtra, India* 68 H5
Patani, *Indonesia* 63 D7
Pătârlagele, *Romania* 29 E11
Pataudi, *India* 68 E7
Patchewollock, *Australia* 95 F3
Patchogue, *U.S.A.* 117 F11
Pate, *Kenya* 86 C5
Patea, *N.Z.* 91 H5
Pategi, *Nigeria* 83 D6
Patensie, *S. Africa* 88 E3
Paterna, *Spain* 39 F4
Paternion, *Austria* 26 E6

Paternò, *Italy* 43 E7
Pateros, *U.S.A.* 108 B4
Paterson, *U.S.A.* 117 F10
Paterson Ra., *Australia* 92 D3
Pathankot, *India* 68 C6
Pathein = Bassein, *Burma* 67 L19
Pathfinder Reservoir, *U.S.A.* 108 E10
Pathiu, *Thailand* 65 G2
Pathum Thani, *Thailand* 64 E3
Pati, *Indonesia* 63 G14
Patía →, *Colombia* 124 C3
Patiala, *Punjab, India* 68 D7
Patiala, *Ut. P., India* 69 F8
Patine Kouka, *Senegal* 82 C2
Patitíríon, *Greece* 46 B5
Patkai Bum, *India* 67 F19
Pátmos, *Greece* 47 D8
Patna, *India* 69 G11
Patnos, *Turkey* 73 C10
Pato Branco, *Brazil* 127 B5
Patong, Ao, *Thailand* 65 a
Patonga, *Uganda* 86 B3
Patos, *Albania* 44 F3
Patos, *Brazil* 125 E11
Patos, L. dos, *Brazil* 127 C5
Patos, Río de los →, *Argentina* 126 C2
Patos de Minas, *Brazil* 125 G9
Patquía, *Argentina* 126 C2
Pátrai, *Greece* 46 C3
Pátraikós Kólpos, *Greece* 46 C3
Patras = Pátrai, *Greece* 46 C3
Patrocínio, *Brazil* 125 G9
Pattada, *Italy* 42 B2
Pattani, *Thailand* 65 J3
Pattaya, *Thailand* 62 B2
Patten, *U.S.A.* 115 C11
Patterson, *Calif., U.S.A.* 110 H5
Patterson, *La., U.S.A.* 113 L9
Patterson, Mt., *U.S.A.* 110 G7
Patti, *Punjab, India* 68 D6
Patti, *Ut. P., India* 69 G10
Patti, *Italy* 43 D7
Pattoki, *Pakistan* 68 D5
Patton, *U.S.A.* 116 F6
Patuakhali, *Bangla.* 67 H17
Patuanak, *Canada* 103 B7
Patuca △, *Honduras* 120 D2
Patuca →, *Honduras* 120 C3
Patuca, Punta, *Honduras* 120 C3
Pătulele, *Romania* 28 F7
Pátzcuaro, *Mexico* 118 D4
Pau, *France* 20 E3
Pau, Gave de →, *France* 20 E2
Pauillac, *France* 20 C3
Pauk, *Burma* 67 J19
Paul I., *Canada* 105 A7
Paul Smiths, *U.S.A.* 117 B10
Paulatuk, *Canada* 100 B7
Paulhan, *France* 20 E7
Paulistana, *Brazil* 125 E10
Paulo Afonso, *Brazil* 125 E11
Paulpietersburg, *S. Africa* 89 D5
Pauls Valley, *U.S.A.* 113 H6
Pauma Valley, *U.S.A.* 111 M10
Pauri, *India* 69 D8
Pāveh, *Iran* 70 C5
Pavelets, *Russia* 32 F10
Pavia, *Italy* 40 C6
Pavilion, *U.S.A.* 116 D6
Pavilly, *France* 18 C7
Pāvilosta, *Latvia* 9 H19
Pavlikeni, *Bulgaria* 45 C9
Pavlodar, *Kazakhstan* 52 D8
Pavlograd = Pavlohrad, *Ukraine* 33 H8
Pavlohrad, *Ukraine* 33 H8
Pavlovo, *Russia* 34 C6
Pavlovsk, *Russia* 34 E5
Pavlovskaya, *Russia* 35 G4
Pavlovskiy-Posad, *Russia* 32 E10
Pavullo nel Frignano, *Italy* 40 D7
Pawai, Pulau, *Singapore* 65 d
Pawayan, *India* 69 E9
Pawhuska, *U.S.A.* 113 G6
Pawling, *U.S.A.* 117 E11
Pawnee, *U.S.A.* 113 G6
Pawnee City, *U.S.A.* 112 E6
Pawtucket, *U.S.A.* 117 E13
Paximádhia, *Greece* 49 E6
Paxoí, *Greece* 46 B2
Paxton, *Ill., U.S.A.* 114 E1
Paxton, *Nebr., U.S.A.* 112 E4
Payakumbuh, *Indonesia* 62 E2
Payerne, *Switz.* 25 J2
Payette, *U.S.A.* 108 D5
Paymogo, *Spain* 37 H3
Payne Bay = Kangirsuk, *Canada* 101 B13
Payne L., *Canada* 101 C12
Paynes Find, *Australia* 93 E2
Paynesville, *Liberia* 82 D2
Paynesville, *U.S.A.* 112 C7
Pays de la Loire □, *France* 18 E6
Paysandú, *Uruguay* 126 C4
Payson, *U.S.A.* 109 J8
Paz →, *Guatemala* 120 D1
Paz, B. de la, *Mexico* 118 C2
Pāzanān, *Iran* 71 D6
Pazar, *Turkey* 73 B9
Pazarcık, *Turkey* 72 D7
Pazardzhik, *Bulgaria* 45 D8
Pazarköy, *Turkey* 47 B9
Pazarlar, *Turkey* 47 C11
Pazaryeri, *Turkey* 47 B11
Pazaryolu, *Turkey* 73 B9
Pazin, *Croatia* 41 C10
Pčinja →, *Macedonia* 44 E5
Pe Ell, *U.S.A.* 110 D3
Peabody, *U.S.A.* 117 D14
Peace →, *Canada* 102 B6
Peace Point, *Canada* 102 B6
Peace River, *Canada* 102 B5
Peach Springs, *U.S.A.* 109 J7
Peachland, *Canada* 102 D5
Peachtree City, *U.S.A.* 115 J3
Peak, The = Kinder Scout, *U.K.* 14 D6
Peak Charles △, *Australia* 93 F3
Peak District △, *U.K.* 14 D6
Peak Hill, *N.S.W., Australia* 95 E4
Peak Hill, *W. Austral., Australia* 93 E2
Peak Ra., *Australia* 94 C4
Peake Cr. →, *Australia* 95 D2
Peal de Becerro, *Spain* 37 H7
Peale, Mt., *U.S.A.* 109 G9
Pearblossom, *U.S.A.* 111 L9
Pearl →, *U.S.A.* 113 K10
Pearl City, *U.S.A.* 106 H16
Pearl Harbor, *U.S.A.* 106 H16
Pearl River = Zhu Jiang →, *China* 59 F9
Pearl River, *U.S.A.* 117 E10
Pearsall, *U.S.A.* 113 L5
Peary Land, *Greenland* 4 A6
Pease →, *U.S.A.* 113 H5
Peawanuck, *Canada* 101 C11
Pebane, *Mozam.* 87 F4
Pebas, *Peru* 124 D4
Pebble Beach, *U.S.A.* 110 J5
Peć, *Serbia & M.* 44 D4
Péccioli, *Italy* 40 E7
Pechea, *Romania* 29 E12
Pechenga, *Russia* 52 C4
Pechenizhyn, *Ukraine* 29 B9
Pechiguera, Pta., *Canary Is.* 48 F6
Pechnezhskoye Vdkhr., *Ukraine* 33 G9
Pechora, *Russia* 52 C6
Pechora →, *Russia* 52 C6
Pechorskaya Guba, *Russia* 52 C6
Pechory, *Russia* 9 H22
Pecica, *Romania* 28 D6
Pecka, *Serbia & M.* 44 B3
Pécora, C., *Italy* 42 C1
Pecos, *U.S.A.* 113 K3
Pecos →, *U.S.A.* 113 L3
Pécs, *Hungary* 28 D3
Pedder, L., *Australia* 95 G4
Peddie, *S. Africa* 89 E4
Pedernales, *Dom. Rep.* 121 C5
Pedieos →, *Cyprus* 49 D12
Pedirka, *Australia* 95 D2
Pedra Azul, *Brazil* 125 G10
Pedreguer, *Spain* 39 G5
Pedreiras, *Brazil* 125 D10
Pedro Afonso, *Brazil* 125 E9
Pedro Cays, *Jamaica* 120 C4
Pedro de Valdivia, *Chile* 126 A2
Pedro Juan Caballero, *Paraguay* 127 A4
Pedro Muñoz, *Spain* 37 F8
Pedrógão Grande, *Portugal* 36 F2
Pee Dee →, *U.S.A.* 115 J6
Peebinga, *Australia* 95 E3
Peebles, *U.K.* 13 F5
Peekskill, *U.S.A.* 117 E11
Peel, *I. of Man* 14 C3
Peel →, *Australia* 95 E5
Peel →, *Canada* 100 B6
Peel Sd., *Canada* 100 A10
Peene →, *Germany* 24 A9
Peera Peera Poolanna L., *Australia* 95 D2
Peerless Lake, *Canada* 102 B6
Peers, *Canada* 102 C5
Pegasus Bay, *N.Z.* 91 K4
Peggau, *Austria* 26 D8
Pegnitz, *Germany* 25 F7
Pegnitz →, *Germany* 25 F6
Pego, *Spain* 39 G4
Pegu, *Burma* 67 L20
Pegu Yoma, *Burma* 67 K20
Pehčevo, *Macedonia* 44 E6
Pehlıvanköy, *Turkey* 45 E10
Pehuajó, *Argentina* 126 D3
Pei Xian = Pizhou, *China* 56 G9
Peine, *Chile* 126 A2
Peine, *Germany* 24 C6
Peip'ing = Beijing, *China* 56 E9
Peipus, L. = Chudskoye, Ozero, *Russia* 9 G22
Peissenberg, *Germany* 25 H7
Peitz, *Germany* 24 D10
Peixe, *Brazil* 125 F9
Peixe →, *Brazil* 125 H8
Pek →, *Serbia & M.* 44 B5
Pekalongan, *Indonesia* 63 G13
Pekan, *Malaysia* 65 L4
Pekan Nenas, *Malaysia* 65 d
Pekanbaru, *Indonesia* 62 D2
Pekang, *Taiwan* 59 F13
Pekin, *U.S.A.* 112 E10
Peking = Beijing, *China* 56 E9
Pekutatan, *Indonesia* 63 J17
Péla, *Guinea* 82 D3
Pelabuhan Klang, *Malaysia* 65 L3
Pelabuhan Ratu, Teluk, *Indonesia* 63 G12
Pelabuhanratu, *Indonesia* 63 G12
Pélagos, *Greece* 46 B6
Pelaihari, *Indonesia* 62 E4
Pelat, Mt., *France* 21 D10
Pełczyce, *Poland* 31 E2
Peleaga, Vf., *Romania* 28 E7
Pelée, Mt., *Martinique* 120 c
Pelee, Pt., *Canada* 104 D3
Pelee I., *Canada* 116 E2
Pelekech, *Kenya* 86 B4
Peleng, *Indonesia* 63 E6
Pelentong, *Malaysia* 65 d
Pélézi, *Ivory C.* 82 D3
Pelhřimov, *Czech Rep.* 26 B8
Pelican, *U.S.A.* 102 B1
Pelican L., *Canada* 103 C8
Pelican Narrows, *Canada* 103 B8
Pelister △, *Macedonia* 44 F5
Pelješac, *Croatia* 41 F14
Pelkosenniemi, *Finland* 8 C22
Pella, *Greece* 44 F6
Pella, *S. Africa* 88 D2
Pella, *U.S.A.* 112 E8
Pélla □, *Greece* 44 F6
Pello, *Finland* 8 C21
Pellworm, *Germany* 24 A4
Pelly →, *Canada* 100 B6
Pelly Bay, *Canada* 101 B11
Peloponnese = Pelopónnisos □, *Greece* 46 D4
Pelopónnisos □, *Greece* 46 D4
Peloritani, Monti, *Italy* 43 D8
Pelorus Sd., *N.Z.* 91 J4
Pelotas, *Brazil* 127 C5
Pelotas →, *Brazil* 127 B5
Pelovo, *Bulgaria* 45 C8
Pelplin, *Poland* 30 E5
Pelvoux, Massif du, *France* 21 D10
Pemalang, *Indonesia* 63 G13
Pemanggil, Pulau, *Malaysia* 65 L5
Pematangsiantar, *Indonesia* 62 D1
Pemba, *Mozam.* 87 E5
Pemba, *Zambia* 87 F2
Pemba Channel, *Tanzania* 86 D4
Pemba I., *Tanzania* 86 D4
Pemberton, *Australia* 93 F2
Pemberton, *Canada* 102 C4
Pembina, *U.S.A.* 112 A6
Pembroke, *Canada* 104 C4
Pembroke, *U.K.* 15 F3
Pembrokeshire □, *U.K.* 15 F3
Pembrokeshire Coast △, *U.K.* 15 F2
Pen-y-Ghent, *U.K.* 14 C5
Peña, Sierra de la, *Spain* 38 C4
Peña de Francia, Sierra de la, *Spain* 36 E4
Penafiel, *Portugal* 36 D2
Peñafiel, *Spain* 36 D6
Peñaflor, *Spain* 37 H5
Penal, *Trin. & Tob.* 125 K15
Peñalara, *Spain* 36 E7
Penamacôr, *Portugal* 36 E3
Penang = Pinang, *Malaysia* 65 c
Penápolis, *Brazil* 127 A6
Peñaranda de Bracamonte, *Spain* 36 E5
Peñarroya, *Spain* 38 E4
Peñarroya-Pueblonuevo, *Spain* 37 G5
Penarth, *U.K.* 15 F4
Peñas, C. de, *Spain* 36 B5
Penas, G. de, *Chile* 128 F2
Peñas de San Pedro, *Spain* 39 G3
Peñas del Chache, *Canary Is.* 48 E6
Peñausende, *Spain* 36 D5
Pench'i = Benxi, *China* 57 D12
Pend Oreille →, *U.S.A.* 108 B5
Pend Oreille, L., *U.S.A.* 108 C5
Pendálofon, *Greece* 44 F5
Pendembu, *Eastern, S. Leone* 82 D2
Pendembu, *Northern, S. Leone* 82 D2
Pender B., *Australia* 92 C3
Pendik, *Turkey* 45 F13
Pendjari △, *Benin* 83 C5
Pendjari →, *Benin* 83 C5
Pendleton, *U.S.A.* 108 D4
Pendra, *India* 69 H9
Peneda-Gerês △, *Portugal* 36 D2
Penedo, *Brazil* 125 F11
Penelokan, *Indonesia* 63 J18
Penetanguishene, *Canada* 116 B5
Penfield, *U.S.A.* 116 E6
Pengalengan, *Indonesia* 63 G12
Penge, *Kasai-Or., Dem. Rep. of the Congo* 86 D1
Penge, *Sud-Kivu, Dem. Rep. of the Congo* 86 C2
P'enghu Ch'üntou, *Taiwan* 59 F12
Penglai, *China* 57 F11
Pengshan, *China* 58 B4
Pengshui, *China* 58 C7
Penguin, *Australia* 95 G4
Pengxi, *China* 58 B5
Pengze, *China* 59 C11
Penhalonga, *Zimbabwe* 87 F3
Peniche, *Portugal* 37 F1
Penicuik, *U.K.* 13 F5
Penida, Nusa, *Indonesia* 63 K18
Peninnes, Alpes = Pennine, Alpi, *Alps* 25 J3
Peninsular Malaysia □, *Malaysia* 65 L4
Peñíscola, *Spain* 38 E5
Penitente, Serra do, *Brazil* 125 E9
Penkridge, *U.K.* 14 E5
Penmarch, *France* 18 E2
Penmarch, Pte. de, *France* 18 E2
Penn Hills, *U.S.A.* 116 F5
Penn Yan, *U.S.A.* 116 D7
Penna, Punta della, *Italy* 41 F11
Pennant, *Canada* 103 C7
Penne, *Italy* 41 F10
Penner →, *India* 66 M12
Pennine, Alpi, *Alps* 25 J3
Pennines, *U.K.* 14 C5
Pennington, *U.S.A.* 110 F5
Pennington →, *Nigeria* 83 E6
Pennino, Mte., *Italy* 41 E9
Pennsburg, *U.S.A.* 117 F9
Pennsylvania □, *U.S.A.* 114 E7
Penny, *Canada* 102 C4
Peno, *Russia* 32 D7
Penobscot →, *U.S.A.* 115 C11
Penobscot B., *U.S.A.* 115 C11
Penola, *Australia* 95 F3
Penong, *Australia* 93 F5
Penonomé, *Panama* 120 E3
Penrith, *Australia* 95 E5
Penrith, *U.K.* 14 C5
Penryn, *U.K.* 15 G2
Pensacola, *U.S.A.* 115 K2
Pensacola Mts., *Antarctica* 5 E1
Pense, *Canada* 103 C8
Penshurst, *Australia* 95 F3
Penticton, *Canada* 102 D5
Pentland, *Australia* 94 C4
Pentland Firth, *U.K.* 13 C5
Pentland Hills, *U.K.* 13 F5
Pentland Hills ⌓, *U.K.* 13 F5
Penza, *Russia* 34 D7
Penzance, *U.K.* 15 G2
Penzberg, *Germany* 25 H7
Penzhino, *Russia* 53 C17
Penzhinskaya Guba, *Russia* 53 C17
Penzhou, *China* 58 B4
Penzlin, *Germany* 24 B9
Peoria, *Ariz., U.S.A.* 109 K7
Peoria, *Ill., U.S.A.* 112 E10
Pepacton Reservoir, *U.S.A.* 117 D10
Pepani →, *S. Africa* 88 D3
Pepel, *S. Leone* 82 D2
Peqin, *Albania* 44 E3
Pera Hd., *Australia* 94 A3
Perabumulih, *Indonesia* 62 E2
Perak →, *Malaysia* 65 K3
Perakhóra, *Greece* 46 C4
Perales de Alfambra, *Spain* 38 E4
Perales del Puerto, *Spain* 36 E4
Pérama, *Kérkira, Greece* 49 A3
Pérama, *Kríti, Greece* 49 D6
Perancak, *Indonesia* 63 J17
Peräpohjola, *Finland* 8 C22
Perast, *Serbia & M.* 44 D2
Percé, *Canada* 105 C7
Perche, *France* 18 D8
Perche ⌓, *France* 18 D7
Perchtoldsdorf, *Austria* 27 C9
Percival Lakes, *Australia* 92 D4
Percy, *France* 18 D5
Percy Is., *Australia* 94 C5
Perdido, Mte., *Spain* 38 C5
Perdu, Mt. = Perdido, Mte., *Spain* 38 C5
Perechyn, *Ukraine* 28 B7
Perehinske, *Ukraine* 29 B9
Pereira, *Colombia* 124 C3
Perelazovskiy, *Russia* 35 F6
Perenjori, *Australia* 93 E2
Peresecina, *Moldova* 29 C13
Pereslavl-Zalesskiy, *Russia* 32 D10
Peretu, *Romania* 29 F10
Pereyaslav-Khmelnytskyy, *Ukraine* 33 G6
Pereyma, *Ukraine* 29 B14
Pérez, I., *Mexico* 119 C7
Perg, *Austria* 26 C7
Pergamino, *Argentina* 126 C3
Pergau →, *Malaysia* 65 K3
Pérgine Valsugana, *Italy* 41 B8
Pérgola, *Italy* 41 E9
Perham, *U.S.A.* 112 B7
Perhentian, Kepulauan, *Malaysia* 65 K4
Periam, *Romania* 28 D5
Péribonka →, *Canada* 105 C5
Péribonka, L., *Canada* 105 B5
Perico, *Argentina* 126 A2
Pericos, *Mexico* 118 B3
Périers, *France* 18 C5
Périgord, *France* 20 D4
Périgord-Limousin ⌓, *France* 20 C4
Périgueux, *France* 20 C4
Perijá △, *Venezuela* 121 E5
Perijá, Sierra de, *Colombia* 124 B4
Peristéra, *Greece* 46 B5
Peristerona →, *Cyprus* 49 D12
Perito Moreno, *Argentina* 128 F2
Perivol = Dragovishtitsa, *Bulgaria* 44 D6
Perkasie, *U.S.A.* 117 F9
Perković, *Croatia* 41 E13
Perlas, Arch. de las, *Panama* 120 E4
Perlas, Punta de, *Nic.* 120 D3
Perleberg, *Germany* 24 B7
Perlez, *Serbia & M.* 28 E5
Perm, *Russia* 52 D6
Përmet, *Albania* 44 F4
Pernambuco = Recife, *Brazil* 125 E12
Pernambuco □, *Brazil* 125 E11
Pernatty Lagoon, *Australia* 95 E2
Pernik, *Bulgaria* 44 D7
Peron Is., *Australia* 92 B5
Peron Pen., *Australia* 93 E1
Péronne, *France* 19 C9
Perosa Argentina, *Italy* 40 D4
Perow, *Canada* 102 C3
Perpignan, *France* 20 F6
Perris, *U.S.A.* 111 M9
Perros-Guirec, *France* 18 D3
Perry, *Fla., U.S.A.* 115 K4
Perry, *Ga., U.S.A.* 115 J4
Perry, *Iowa, U.S.A.* 112 E7
Perry, *Okla., U.S.A.* 113 G6
Perryton, *U.S.A.* 113 G4
Perryville, *U.S.A.* 113 G10
Persan, *France* 19 C9
Persberg, *Sweden* 10 E8
Perşembe, *Turkey* 72 B7
Persepolis, *Iran* 71 D7
Pershotravensk, *Ukraine* 33 G4
Persia = Iran ■, *Asia* 71 C7
Persian Gulf, *Asia* 71 E6
Perstorp, *Sweden* 11 H7
Pertek, *Turkey* 73 C8
Perth, *Australia* 93 F2
Perth, *Canada* 117 B8
Perth, *U.K.* 13 E5
Perth & Kinross □, *U.K.* 13 E5
Perth Amboy, *U.S.A.* 117 F10
Perth-Andover, *Canada* 105 C6
Pertuis, *France* 21 E9
Pertusato, C., *France* 21 G13
Peru, *Ind., U.S.A.* 114 E2
Peru, *N.Y., U.S.A.* 117 B11
Peru ■, *S. Amer.* 124 D4
Peru Basin, *Pac. Oc.* 97 J18
Peru-Chile Trench, *Pac. Oc.* 124 G3
Perúgia, *Italy* 41 E9
Perušić, *Croatia* 41 D12
Pervomaysk, *Russia* 34 C6
Pervomaysk, *Ukraine* 33 H6
Pervouralsk, *Russia* 52 D6
Pésaro, *Italy* 41 E9
Pescadores = P'enghu Ch'üntou, *Taiwan* 59 F12
Pescara, *Italy* 41 F11
Pescara →, *Italy* 41 F11
Peschanokopskoye, *Russia* 35 G5
Péscia, *Italy* 40 E7
Pescina, *Italy* 41 F10
Peshawar, *Pakistan* 68 B4
Peshkopi, *Albania* 44 E4
Peshtera, *Bulgaria* 45 D8
Peshtigo, *U.S.A.* 114 C2
Peski, *Russia* 34 E6
Pêso da Régua, *Portugal* 36 D3
Pesqueira, *Brazil* 125 E11
Pessac, *France* 20 D3
Pest □, *Hungary* 28 C4
Pestovo, *Russia* 32 C8
Pestravka, *Russia* 34 D9
Péta, *Greece* 46 B3
Petah Tiqwa, *Israel* 74 C3
Petalídhion, *Greece* 46 E3
Petaling Jaya, *Malaysia* 65 L3
Petaloudhes, *Greece* 49 C10
Petaluma, *U.S.A.* 110 G4
Pétange, *Lux.* 17 E5
Petaro, *Pakistan* 68 G3
Petatlán, *Mexico* 118 D4
Petauke, *Zambia* 87 E3
Petawawa, *Canada* 104 C4
Petén Itzá, L., *Guatemala* 120 C2
Peter I., *Br. Virgin Is.* 121 e
Peter I.s Øy, *Antarctica* 5 C16
Peter Pond L., *Canada* 103 B7
Peterbell, *Canada* 104 C3
Peterborough, *Australia* 95 E2
Peterborough, *Canada* 116 B6
Peterborough, *U.K.* 15 E7
Peterborough, *U.S.A.* 117 D13
Peterborough □, *U.K.* 15 E7
Peterculter, *U.K.* 13 D6
Peterhead, *U.K.* 13 D7
Peterlee, *U.K.* 14 C6
Petermann Ranges, *Australia* 92 E5
Petersburg, *Alaska, U.S.A.* 100 C6
Petersburg, *Pa., U.S.A.* 116 F6
Petersburg, *Va., U.S.A.* 114 G7
Petersburg, *W. Va., U.S.A.* 114 F6
Petersfield, *U.K.* 15 F7
Petershagen, *Germany* 24 C4
Petília Policastro, *Italy* 43 C9
Petit-Canal, *Guadeloupe* 120 b
Petit Goâve, *Haiti* 121 C5
Petit Jardin, *Canada* 105 C8
Petit Lac Manicouagan, *Canada* 105 B6
Petit-Mécatina →, *Canada* 105 B8
Petit-Mécatina, Î. du, *Canada* 105 B8
Petit Piton, *St. Lucia* 121 f
Petit-Saguenay, *Canada* 105 C5
Petit Saint Bernard, Col du, *Italy* 21 C10
Petitcodiac, *Canada* 105 C6
Petite Terre, Îles de la, *Guadeloupe* 120 b
Petitot →, *Canada* 102 A4
Petitsikapau L., *Canada* 105 B6
Petlad, *India* 68 H5
Peto, *Mexico* 119 C7
Petone, *N.Z.* 91 J5
Petorca, *Chile* 126 C1
Petoskey, *U.S.A.* 114 C3
Petra, *Jordan* 74 E4
Petra, *Spain* 48 B10
Petra, Ostrova, *Russia* 4 B13
Petra Velikogo, Zaliv, *Russia* 54 C6
Petrel = Petrer, *Spain* 39 G4
Petrella, Monte, *Italy* 42 A6
Petrer, *Spain* 39 G4
Petreto-Bicchisano, *France* 21 G12
Petrich, *Bulgaria* 44 E7
Petrified Forest △, *U.S.A.* 109 J9
Petrijanec, *Croatia* 41 B13
Petrikov = Pyetrikaw, *Belarus* 33 F5
Petrila, *Romania* 29 E8
Petrinja, *Croatia* 41 C13
Petrodvorets, *Russia* 32 C5
Petrolândia, *Brazil* 125 E11
Petrolia, *Canada* 116 D2
Petrolina, *Brazil* 125 E10
Petropavl, *Kazakhstan* 52 D7
Petropavlovsk = Petropavl, *Kazakhstan* 52 D7
Petropavlovsk-Kamchatskiy, *Russia* 53 D16
Petropavlovskiy = Akhtubinsk, *Russia* 35 F8
Petrópolis, *Brazil* 127 A7
Petroşani, *Romania* 29 E8
Petrova Gora, *Croatia* 41 C12
Petrovac, *Serbia & M.* 44 D2
Petrovac, *Serbia & M.* 44 B5
Petrovaradin, *Serbia & M.* 28 E4
Petrovsk, *Russia* 34 D7
Petrovsk-Zabaykalskiy, *Russia* 53 D11
Petrovskaya, *Russia* 33 K9
Petrozavodsk, *Russia* 32 B8
Petrus Steyn, *S. Africa* 89 D4
Petrusburg, *S. Africa* 88 D4
Petzeck, *Austria* 26 E5
Peumo, *Chile* 126 C1
Peureulak, *Indonesia* 62 D1
Pevek, *Russia* 53 C18
Peveragno, *Italy* 40 D4
Peyrehorade, *France* 20 E2
Peyruis, *France* 21 D9
Pézenas, *France* 20 E7
Pezinok, *Slovak Rep.* 27 C10
Pfaffenhofen, *Germany* 25 G7

Pfälzerwald ⌓, *Germany* 25 F5
Pfarrkirchen, *Germany* 25 G8
Pfeffenhausen, *Germany* 25 G7
Pforzheim, *Germany* 25 G4
Pfullendorf, *Germany* 25 H5
Pfungstadt, *Germany* 25 F4
Pha Taem △, *Thailand* 64 E5
Phagwara, *India* 66 D9
Phaistós, *Greece* 49 D6
Phala, *Botswana* 88 C4
Phalera = Phulera, *India* 68 F6
Phalodi, *India* 68 F5
Phalsbourg, *France* 19 D14
Phaluai, Ko, *Thailand* 65 b
Phan, *Thailand* 64 C2
Phan Rang, *Vietnam* 65 G7
Phan Ri = Hoa Da, *Vietnam* 65 G7
Phan Thiet, *Vietnam* 65 G7
Phanae, *Greece* 47 C7
Phanat Nikhom, *Thailand* 64 F3
Phangan, Ko, *Thailand* 65 H3
Phangnga, *Thailand* 65 H2
Phangnga, Ao, *Thailand* 65 a
Phanom Sarakham, *Thailand* 64 F3
Phaphund, *India* 69 F8
Pharenda, *India* 69 F10
Pharr, *U.S.A.* 113 M5
Phatthalung, *Thailand* 65 J3
Phayao, *Thailand* 64 C2
Phelps, *U.S.A.* 116 D7
Phelps L., *Canada* 103 B8
Phenix City, *U.S.A.* 115 J3
Phet Buri, *Thailand* 64 F2
Phetchabun, *Thailand* 64 D3
Phetchabun, Thiu Khao, *Thailand* 64 E3
Phetchaburi = Phet Buri, *Thailand* 64 F2
Phi Phi, Ko, *Thailand* 65 J2
Phiafay, *Laos* 64 E6
Phibun Mangsahan, *Thailand* 64 E5
Phichai, *Thailand* 64 D3
Phichit, *Thailand* 64 D3
Philadelphia, *Miss., U.S.A.* 113 J10
Philadelphia, *N.Y., U.S.A.* 117 B9
Philadelphia, *Pa., U.S.A.* 117 G9
Philip, *U.S.A.* 112 C4
Philippeville, *Belgium* 17 D4
Philippi, *Greece* 45 E8
Philippi, *U.S.A.* 114 F5
Philippi L., *Australia* 94 C2
Philippine Sea, *Pac. Oc.* 50 H16
Philippines ■, *Asia* 61 F5
Philippolis, *S. Africa* 88 E4
Philippopolis = Plovdiv, *Bulgaria* 45 D8
Philipsburg, *Canada* 117 A11
Philipsburg, *Mont., U.S.A.* 108 C7
Philipsburg, *Pa., U.S.A.* 116 F6
Philipstown = Daingean, *Ireland* 12 C4
Philipstown, *S. Africa* 88 E3
Phillip I., *Australia* 95 F4
Phillips, *U.S.A.* 112 C9
Phillipsburg, *Kans., U.S.A.* 112 F5
Phillipsburg, *N.J., U.S.A.* 117 F9
Philmont, *U.S.A.* 117 D11
Philomath, *U.S.A.* 108 D2
Phimai, *Thailand* 64 E4
Phitsanulok, *Thailand* 64 D3
Phnom Dangrek, *Thailand* 62 B2
Phnom Penh, *Cambodia* 65 G5
Phnum Penh = Phnom Penh, *Cambodia* 65 G5
Phoenicia, *U.S.A.* 117 D10
Phoenix, *Ariz., U.S.A.* 109 K7
Phoenix, *N.Y., U.S.A.* 117 C8
Phoenix Is., *Kiribati* 96 H10
Phoenixville, *U.S.A.* 117 F9
Phon, *Thailand* 64 E4
Phon Tiou, *Laos* 64 D5
Phong →, *Thailand* 64 D4
Phong Saly, *Laos* 58 G4
Phong Tho, *Vietnam* 64 A4
Phonhong, *Laos* 64 C4
Phonum, *Thailand* 65 H2
Phosphate Hill, *Australia* 94 C2
Photharam, *Thailand* 64 F2
Phra Nakhon Si Ayutthaya, *Thailand* 64 E3
Phra Thong, Ko, *Thailand* 65 H2
Phrae, *Thailand* 64 C3
Phrom Phiram, *Thailand* 64 D3
Phrygia, *Turkey* 72 C4
Phu Chong-Na Yoi △, *Thailand* 64 E5
Phu Dien, *Vietnam* 64 C5
Phu Hin Rang Kla △, *Thailand* 64 D3
Phu Kradung △, *Thailand* 64 D3
Phu Loi, *Laos* 64 B4
Phu Luang △, *Thailand* 64 D3
Phu Ly, *Vietnam* 58 G5
Phu Phan △, *Thailand* 64 D4
Phu Quoc, Dao, *Vietnam* 65 G4
Phu Tho, *Vietnam* 58 G5
Phuc Yen, *Vietnam* 58 G5
Phuket, *Thailand* 65 a
Phuket, Ko, *Thailand* 65 a
Phul, *India* 68 D6
Phulad, *India* 68 G5
Phulchari, *Bangla.* 69 G13
Phulera, *India* 68 F6
Phulpur, *India* 69 G10
Phun Phin, *Thailand* 65 H2
Piacenza, *Italy* 40 C6
Piai, Tanjung, *Malaysia* 65 d
Pian Cr. →, *Australia* 95 E4
Pian-Upe ⌓, *Uganda* 86 B3
Piana, *France* 21 F12
Pianella, *Italy* 41 F11
Pianosa, *Puglia, Italy* 41 F12
Pianosa, *Toscana, Italy* 40 F7
Piapot, *Canada* 103 D7
Pias, *Portugal* 37 G3
Piaseczno, *Poland* 31 F8
Piaski, *Poland* 31 G9
Piastów, *Poland* 31 F7
Piatra, *Romania* 29 G10
Piatra Craiului △, *Romania* 29 E10
Piatra Neamţ, *Romania* 29 D11
Piatra Olt, *Romania* 29 F9
Piauí □, *Brazil* 125 E10
Piauí →, *Brazil* 125 E10
Piave →, *Italy* 41 C9
Piazza Ármerina, *Italy* 43 E7
Pibor →, *Sudan* 81 F3
Pibor Post, *Sudan* 81 F3
Picardie □, *France* 19 C10
Picardie, Plaine de, *France* 19 C9
Picardy = Picardie □, *France* 19 C10
Picayune, *U.S.A.* 113 K10
Picerno, *Italy* 43 B8
Pichhor, *India* 69 G8
Pichilemu, *Chile* 126 C1
Pichor, *India* 68 G8
Pickerel L., *Canada* 104 C1
Pickering, *U.K.* 14 C7
Pickering, Vale of, *U.K.* 14 C7
Pickle Lake, *Canada* 104 B1
Pickwick L., *U.S.A.* 115 H1
Pico Bonito △, *Honduras* 120 C2
Pico Truncado, *Argentina* 128 F3
Picos, *Brazil* 125 E10
Picos de Europa △, *Spain* 36 B6
Picton, *Australia* 95 E5
Picton, *Canada* 116 B7
Picton, *N.Z.* 91 J5
Pictou, *Canada* 105 C7
Picture Butte, *Canada* 102 D6
Pictured Rocks ⌓, *U.S.A.* 114 B2
Picún Leufú, *Argentina* 128 D3
Pidbuzh, *Ukraine* 31 J10
Pidurutalagala, *Sri Lanka* 66 R12
Piechowice, *Poland* 31 H2
Piedimonte Matese, *Italy* 43 A7
Piedmont = Piemonte □, *Italy* 40 D5
Piedmont, *Ala., U.S.A.* 115 J3
Piedmont, *S.C., U.S.A.* 107 D10
Piedra →, *Spain* 38 D3
Piedrabuena, *Spain* 37 G6
Piedrahita, *Spain* 36 E5
Piedralaves, *Spain* 36 E6
Piedras Blancas, *Spain* 36 B5
Piedras Negras, *Mexico* 118 B4
Piekary Śląskie, *Poland* 31 H5
Pieksämäki, *Finland* 9 E22
Piemonte □, *Italy* 40 D5
Pienaarsrivier, *S. Africa* 89 D4
Pieniężno, *Poland* 30 D7
Pieninský △, *Europe* 27 B13
Pieńsk, *Poland* 31 G2
Piercefield, *U.S.A.* 117 B10
Pierceland, *Canada* 103 C7
Piería □, *Greece* 44 F6
Pierpont, *U.S.A.* 116 E4
Pierre, *U.S.A.* 112 C4
Pierre-Buffière, *France* 20 C5
Pierre-de-Bresse, *France* 19 F12
Pierrefontaine-les-Varans, *France* 19 E13
Pierrefort, *France* 20 D6
Pierrelatte, *France* 21 D8
Pierreville, *Trin. & Tob.* 125 K16
Pieštany, *Slovak Rep.* 27 C10
Piesting →, *Austria* 27 C9
Pieszyce, *Poland* 31 H3
Piet Retief, *S. Africa* 89 D5
Pietarsaari, *Finland* 8 E20
Pietermaritzburg, *S. Africa* 89 D5
Pietersburg = Polokwane, *S. Africa* 89 C4
Pietragalla, *Italy* 43 B8
Pietrasanta, *Italy* 40 E7
Pietroşiţa, *Romania* 29 E10
Pietrosul, Vf., *Maramureş, Romania* 29 C9
Pietrosul, Vf., *Suceava, Romania* 29 C10
Pieve di Cadore, *Italy* 41 B9
Pieve di Teco, *Italy* 40 D4
Pievepélago, *Italy* 40 D7
Pigadhítsa, *Greece* 44 G5
Pigeon L., *Canada* 116 B6
Piggott, *U.S.A.* 113 G9
Pigna, *Italy* 40 E4
Pigüe, *Argentina* 126 D3
Pihani, *India* 69 F9
Pihlajavesi, *Finland* 9 F23
Pijijiapan, *Mexico* 119 D6
Pikalevo, *Russia* 32 C8
Pikangikum Berens, *Canada* 103 C10
Pikes Peak, *U.S.A.* 112 F2
Piketberg, *S. Africa* 88 E2
Pikeville, *U.S.A.* 114 G4
Pikou, *China* 57 E12
Pikwitonei, *Canada* 103 B9
Piła, *Poland* 31 E3
Pila, *Spain* 39 G3
Pilaía, *Greece* 44 F6
Pilanesberg △, *S. Africa* 88 D4
Pilani, *India* 68 E6
Pilar, *Paraguay* 126 B4
Pilar de la Horadada, *Spain* 39 H4
Pilat ⌓, *France* 21 C8
Pilawa, *Poland* 31 G8
Pilaya →, *Bolivia* 124 H6
Pilbara, *Australia* 92 D2
Pilcomayo →, *Paraguay* 126 B4
Pilgrim's Rest, *S. Africa* 89 C5
Pilgrimstad, *Sweden* 10 B9
Píli, *Greece* 47 E9
Pilibhit, *India* 69 E8
Pilica →, *Poland* 31 G8
Pilion, *Greece* 46 B5
Pilis, *Hungary* 28 C4
Pilisvörösvár, *Hungary* 28 C3
Pilkhawa, *India* 68 E7
Pilliga, *Australia* 95 E4
Pílos, *Greece* 46 E3
Pilot Mound, *Canada* 103 D9
Pilot Point, *U.S.A.* 113 J6
Pilot Rock, *U.S.A.* 108 D4
Pilštanj, *Slovenia* 41 B12
Piltene, *Latvia* 30 A8
Pilzno, *Poland* 31 J8
Pima, *U.S.A.* 109 K9
Pimba, *Australia* 95 E2
Pimenta Bueno, *Brazil* 124 F6
Pimentel, *Peru* 124 E3
Pina de Ebro, *Spain* 38 D4
Pinamalayan, *Phil.* 61 E4
Pinang, *Malaysia* 65 c
Pinar, C. des, *Spain* 48 B10
Pinar del Río, *Cuba* 120 B3
Pınarbaşı, *Çanakkale, Turkey* 47 B8
Pınarbaşı, *Kayseri, Turkey* 72 C7
Pınarhisar, *Turkey* 45 E11
Pinatubo, Mt., *Phil.* 61 D3
Pincehely, *Hungary* 28 D3
Pinchang, *China* 58 B6
Pincher Creek, *Canada* 102 D6
Pinchi L., *Canada* 102 C4
Pinckneyville, *U.S.A.* 112 F10
Pińczów, *Poland* 31 H7
Pindar, *Australia* 93 E2
Pindi Gheb, *Pakistan* 68 C5
Pindiga, *Nigeria* 83 D7
Pindos △, *Greece* 46 B3
Pindos Óros, *Greece* 46 B3
Pindus Mts. = Pindos Óros, *Greece* 46 B3
Pine →, *B.C., Canada* 102 B4
Pine →, *Sask., Canada* 103 B7
Pine, C., *Canada* 105 C9
Pine Bluff, *U.S.A.* 113 H9
Pine Bluffs, *U.S.A.* 112 E2
Pine City, *U.S.A.* 112 C8
Pine Cr. →, *U.S.A.* 116 E7
Pine Creek, *Australia* 92 B5
Pine Falls, *Canada* 103 C9
Pine Flat Res., *U.S.A.* 110 J7
Pine Grove, *U.S.A.* 117 F8
Pine Pass, *Canada* 102 B4
Pine Point, *Canada* 102 A6
Pine Ridge, *U.S.A.* 112 D3
Pine River, *Canada* 103 C8
Pine River, *U.S.A.* 112 B7
Pine Valley, *U.S.A.* 111 N10
Pinecrest, *U.S.A.* 110 G6
Pineda de Mar, *Spain* 38 D7
Pinedale, *Calif., U.S.A.* 110 J7
Pinedale, *Wyo., U.S.A.* 108 E9
Pinega →, *Russia* 52 C5
Pinehill, *Australia* 94 C4
Pinehouse L., *Canada* 103 B7
Pineimuta →, *Canada* 104 B1
Pinerolo, *Italy* 40 D4
Pineto, *Italy* 41 F11
Pinetop, *U.S.A.* 109 J9
Pinetown, *S. Africa* 89 D5
Pineville, *U.S.A.* 113 K8
Piney, *France* 19 D11
Ping →, *Thailand* 64 E3
Pingaring, *Australia* 93 F2
Pingba, *China* 58 D6
Pingbian, *China* 58 F4
Pingchuan, *China* 58 D3
Pingding, *China* 56 F7
Pingdingshan, *China* 56 H7
Pingdong, *Taiwan* 59 F13
Pingdu, *China* 57 F10
Pingelly, *Australia* 93 F2
Pingguo, *China* 58 F6
Pinghe, *China* 59 E11
Pinghu, *China* 59 B13
Pingjiang, *China* 59 C9
Pingle, *China* 59 E8
Pingli, *China* 58 A7
Pingliang, *China* 56 G4
Pinglu, *China* 56 E7
Pingluo, *China* 56 E4
Pingnan, *Fujian, China* 59 D12
Pingnan, *Guangxi Zhuangzu, China* 59 F8
Pingquan, *China* 57 D10
Pingrup, *Australia* 93 F2
Pingshan, *China* 58 C5
Pingtan, *China* 59 E12
Pingtang, *China* 58 E6
P'ingtung, *Taiwan* 59 F13
Pingwu, *China* 56 H3
Pingxiang, *Guangxi Zhuangzu, China* 58 F6
Pingxiang, *Jiangxi, China* 59 D9
Pingyao, *China* 56 F7
Pingyi, *China* 57 G9
Pingyin, *China* 56 F9
Pingyuan, *Guangdong, China* 59 E10
Pingyuan, *Shandong, China* 56 F9
Pingyuanjie, *China* 58 F4
Pinhal, *Brazil* 127 A6
Pinhal Novo, *Portugal* 37 G2
Pinheiro, *Brazil* 125 D9
Pinheiro Machado, *Brazil* 127 C5
Pinhel, *Portugal* 36 E3
Pini, *Indonesia* 62 D1
Piniós →, *Ilía, Greece* 46 D3
Piniós →, *Trikkala, Greece* 46 B4
Pinjarra, *Australia* 93 F2
Pink Mountain, *Canada* 102 B4
Pinkafeld, *Austria* 27 D9
Pinnacles, *U.S.A.* 110 J5
Pinnacles ⌓, *U.S.A.* 110 J5
Pinnaroo, *Australia* 95 F3
Pinneberg, *Germany* 24 B5
Pínnes, Ákra, *Greece* 45 F8
Pinon Hills, *U.S.A.* 111 L9
Pinos, *Mexico* 118 C4
Pinos, Mt., *U.S.A.* 111 L7
Pinos Pt., *U.S.A.* 109 H3
Pinos Puente, *Spain* 37 H7
Pinotepa Nacional, *Mexico* 119 D5
Pinrang, *Indonesia* 63 E5
Pins, Pte. aux, *Canada* 116 D3
Pinsk, *Belarus* 33 F4
Pintados, *Chile* 124 H5
Pinyang, *China* 59 D13
Pinyug, *Russia* 52 C5
Pioche, *U.S.A.* 109 H6
Piombino, *Italy* 40 F7
Piombino, Canale di, *Italy* 40 F7
Pioner, Ostrov, *Russia* 53 B10
Pionerskiy, *Russia* 30 D7
Pionki, *Poland* 31 G8
Piorini, L., *Brazil* 124 D6
Piotrków Trybunalski, *Poland* 31 G6
Piove di Sacco, *Italy* 41 C9
Pīp, *Iran* 71 E9
Pipar, *India* 68 F5
Pipar Road, *India* 68 F5
Piparia, *Mad. P., India* 68 H8
Piparia, *Mad. P., India* 68 J7
Pipéri, *Greece* 46 B6
Pipestone, *U.S.A.* 112 D6
Pipestone →, *Canada* 104 B2
Pipestone Cr. →, *Canada* 103 D8
Piplan, *Pakistan* 68 C4
Piploda, *India* 68 H6
Pipmuacan, Rés., *Canada* 105 C5
Pippingarra, *Australia* 92 D2
Pipriac, *France* 18 E5
Piqua, *U.S.A.* 114 E3
Piquiri →, *Brazil* 127 A5
Pir Panjal Range, *India* 68 C7
Pīr Sohrāb, *Iran* 71 E9
Pira, *Benin* 83 D5
Piracicaba, *Brazil* 127 A6
Piracuruca, *Brazil* 125 D10
Piræus = Piraiévs, *Greece* 46 D5
Piraiévs, *Greece* 46 D5
Pirajuí, *Brazil* 127 A6
Piram I., *India* 68 J5
Piran, *Slovenia* 41 C10
Piranê, *Argentina* 126 B4
Pirano = Piran, *Slovenia* 41 C10
Pirapora, *Brazil* 125 G10
Pirawa, *India* 68 G7
Pirdop, *Bulgaria* 45 D8
Pírgos, *Ilía, Greece* 46 D3
Pírgos, *Kríti, Greece* 47 F7
Pirgovo, *Bulgaria* 45 C9
Piribebuy, *Paraguay* 126 B4
Pirimapun, *Indonesia* 63 F9
Pirin △, *Bulgaria* 44 E7
Pirin Planina, *Bulgaria* 44 E7
Píríneos = Pyrénées, *Europe* 20 F4
Piripiri, *Brazil* 125 D10
Pirmasens, *Germany* 25 F3
Pirna, *Germany* 24 E9
Pirot, *Serbia & M.* 44 C6
Piru, *Indonesia* 63 E7
Piru, *U.S.A.* 111 L8
Piryatin = Pyryatyn, *Ukraine* 33 G7
Piryí, *Greece* 47 C7
Pisa, *Italy* 40 E7
Pisa →, *Poland* 31 E8
Pisa, Firenze ✕ (PSA), *Italy* 40 E7
Pisagne, *Italy* 40 C7
Pisagua, *Chile* 124 G4
Pisarovina, *Croatia* 41 C12
Pisco, *Peru* 124 F3
Piscu, *Romania* 29 E12
Písek, *Czech Rep.* 26 B7
Pishan, *China* 60 C2
Pishcha, *Ukraine* 31 G10
Pishchanka, *Ukraine* 29 B13
Pīshīn, *Iran* 71 E9
Pishin, *Pakistan* 68 D2
Pishin Lora →, *Pakistan* 68 E1
Pisidia, *Turkey* 72 D4
Pising, *Indonesia* 63 F6
Pismo Beach, *U.S.A.* 111 K6
Piso, L., *Liberia* 82 D2
Pissila, *Burkina Faso* 83 C4
Pissis, Cerro, *Argentina* 126 B2
Pissos, *France* 20 D3
Pissouri, *Cyprus* 49 E11
Pisticci, *Italy* 43 B9
Pistóia, *Italy* 40 E7
Pistol B., *Canada* 103 A10
Pisuerga →, *Spain* 36 D6
Pisz, *Poland* 30 E8
Pit →, *U.S.A.* 108 F2
Pita, *Guinea* 82 C2
Pitarpunga, L., *Australia* 95 E3
Pitcairn I., *Pac. Oc.* 97 K14
Pitch L., *Trin. & Tob.* 125 K15
Piteå, *Sweden* 8 D19
Piteälven →, *Sweden* 8 D19
Piterka, *Russia* 34 E8
Piteşti, *Romania* 29 F9
Pithapuram, *India* 67 L13
Pithara, *Australia* 93 F2
Píthion, *Greece* 45 E10
Pithiviers, *France* 19 D9
Pithoragarh, *India* 69 E9
Pithoro, *Pakistan* 68 G3
Pitigliano, *Italy* 41 F8
Pitkyaranta, *Russia* 32 B6
Pitlochry, *U.K.* 13 E5
Pitsilia, *Cyprus* 49 E12
Pitt I., *Canada* 102 C3
Pittsburg, *Calif., U.S.A.* 110 G5
Pittsburg, *Kans., U.S.A.* 113 G7
Pittsburg, *Tex., U.S.A.* 113 J7
Pittsburgh, *U.S.A.* 116 F5
Pittsfield, *Ill., U.S.A.* 112 F9
Pittsfield, *Maine, U.S.A.* 115 C11
Pittsfield, *Mass., U.S.A.* 117 D11
Pittsfield, *N.H., U.S.A.* 117 C13
Pittston, *U.S.A.* 117 E9
Pittsworth, *Australia* 95 D5
Pituri →, *Australia* 94 C2
Piura, *Peru* 124 E2
Piva →, *Serbia & M.* 44 C2
Piwniczna, *Poland* 31 J7
Pixley, *U.S.A.* 110 K7
Piyai, *Greece* 46 B3
Pizarra, *Spain* 37 J6
Pizhou, *China* 56 G9
Pizzo, *Italy* 43 D9
Placentia, *Canada* 105 C9
Placentia B., *Canada* 105 C9
Placer, *Masbate, Phil.* 61 F5
Placer, *Surigao N., Phil.* 61 G6
Placerville, *U.S.A.* 110 G6
Placetas, *Cuba* 120 B4
Plačkovica, *Macedonia* 44 E6
Plainfield, *N.J., U.S.A.* 117 F10
Plainfield, *Ohio, U.S.A.* 116 F3
Plainfield, *Vt., U.S.A.* 117 B12
Plains, *Mont., U.S.A.* 108 C6
Plains, *Tex., U.S.A.* 113 J3
Plainview, *Nebr., U.S.A.* 112 D6
Plainview, *Tex., U.S.A.* 113 H4
Plainwell, *U.S.A.* 114 D3
Plaisance, *France* 20 E4
Plaistow, *U.S.A.* 117 D13
Pláka, *Greece* 47 B7
Pláka, Ákra, *Greece* 49 D8
Plakenska Planina, *Macedonia* 44 E5
Planá, *Czech Rep.* 26 B5
Plana Cays, *Bahamas* 121 B5
Planada, *U.S.A.* 110 H6
Plancoët, *France* 18 D4
Plandište, *Serbia & M.* 28 E6
Plano, *U.S.A.* 113 J6
Plant City, *U.S.A.* 115 M4
Plaquemine, *U.S.A.* 113 K9
Plasencia, *Spain* 36 E4
Plaški, *Croatia* 41 C12
Plaster City, *U.S.A.* 111 N11
Plaster Rock, *Canada* 105 C6
Plastun, *Russia* 54 B8
Plasy, *Czech Rep.* 26 B6
Plata, Río de la, *S. Amer.* 126 C4
Plátani →, *Italy* 42 E6
Plátanos, *Greece* 49 D5
Plateau □, *Nigeria* 83 D6
Platí, Ákra, *Greece* 45 F8
Platte, *U.S.A.* 112 D5
Platte →, *Mo., U.S.A.* 112 F7
Platte →, *Nebr., U.S.A.* 112 E7
Platteville, *U.S.A.* 112 D9
Plattling, *Germany* 25 G8
Plattsburgh, *U.S.A.* 117 B11
Plattsmouth, *U.S.A.* 112 E7
Plau, *Germany* 24 B8
Plauen, *Germany* 24 E8
Plauer See, *Germany* 24 B8
Plav, *Serbia & M.* 44 D3
Plavinas, *Latvia* 9 H21
Plavnica, *Serbia & M.* 44 D3
Plavno, *Croatia* 41 D13
Plavsk, *Russia* 32 F9
Playa Blanca, *Canary Is.* 48 F6
Playa Blanca Sur, *Canary Is.* 48 F6
Playa de las Americas, *Canary Is.* 48 F3
Playa de Mogán, *Canary Is.* 48 G4
Playa del Inglés, *Canary Is.* 48 G4
Playa Esmerelda, *Canary Is.* 48 F5
Playgreen L., *Canada* 103 C9
Pleasant Bay, *Canada* 105 C7
Pleasant Hill, *U.S.A.* 110 H4
Pleasant Mount, *U.S.A.* 117 E9
Pleasanton, *Calif., U.S.A.* 110 H5
Pleasanton, *Tex., U.S.A.* 113 L5
Pleasantville, *N.J., U.S.A.* 114 F8
Pleasantville, *Pa., U.S.A.* 116 E5
Pléaux, *France* 20 C6
Plei Ku, *Vietnam* 64 F7
Plélan-le-Grand, *France* 18 D4
Pléneuf-Val-André, *France* 18 D4
Pleniţa, *Romania* 29 F8
Plenty →, *Australia* 94 C2
Plenty, B. of, *N.Z.* 91 G6
Plentywood, *U.S.A.* 112 A2
Plérin, *France* 18 D4
Plessisville, *Canada* 105 C5
Plestin-les-Grèves, *France* 18 D3
Pleszew, *Poland* 31 G4
Pleternica, *Croatia* 28 E2
Plétipi, L., *Canada* 105 B5
Pleven, *Bulgaria* 45 C8
Plevlja, *Serbia & M.* 44 C3
Plevna, *Canada* 116 B8
Plitvička Jezera △, *Croatia* 41 D12
Plješevica, *Croatia* 41 D12
Ploaghe, *Italy* 42 B1
Ploče, *Croatia* 41 E14
Płock, *Poland* 31 F6
Plöckenpass, *Italy* 41 B9
Plöckenstein, *Germany* 25 G9
Ploemeur, *France* 18 E3
Ploërmel, *France* 18 E4
Ploieşti, *Romania* 29 F11
Plomárion, *Greece* 47 C8
Plombières-les-Bains, *France* 19 E13
Plomin, *Croatia* 41 C11
Plön, *Germany* 24 A6
Plonge, Lac la, *Canada* 103 B7
Płońsk, *Poland* 31 F7
Plopeni, *Romania* 29 E10
Plopişului, Munţii, *Romania* 28 C7
Płoty, *Poland* 30 E2
Plouaret, *France* 18 D3
Plouay, *France* 18 E3
Ploučnice →, *Czech Rep.* 26 A7
Ploudalmézeau, *France* 18 D2
Plouescat, *France* 18 D2
Plougasnou, *France* 18 D3
Plougastel-Daoulas, *France* 18 D2

Plouguerneau, *France* 18 D2
Plouha, *France* 18 D4
Plouhinec, *France* 18 E2
Plovdiv, *Bulgaria* 45 D8
Plovdiv □, *Bulgaria* 45 D8
Plum, *U.S.A.* 116 F5
Plum I., *U.S.A.* 117 E12
Plumas, *U.S.A.* 110 F7
Plummer, *U.S.A.* 108 C5
Plumtree, *Zimbabwe* 87 G2
Plungė, *Lithuania* 9 J19
Pluvigner, *France* 18 E3
Plymouth, *Trin. & Tob.* 125 J16
Plymouth, *U.K.* 15 G3
Plymouth, *Calif., U.S.A.* 110 G6
Plymouth, *Ind., U.S.A.* 114 E2
Plymouth, *Mass., U.S.A.* 117 E14
Plymouth, *N.C., U.S.A.* 115 H7
Plymouth, *N.H., U.S.A.* 117 C13
Plymouth, *Pa., U.S.A.* 117 E9
Plymouth, *Wis., U.S.A.* 114 D2
Plympton-Wyoming, *Canada* 116 D2
Plynlimon = Pumlumon Fawr, *U.K.* 15 E4
Plyusa, *Russia* 32 C5
Plyusa →, *Russia* 32 C5
Plzeň, *Czech Rep.* 26 B6
Plzeňský □, *Czech Rep.* 26 B6
Pniewy, *Poland* 31 F3
Pô, *Burkina Faso* 83 C4
Pô △, *Burkina Faso* 83 C4
Po →, *Italy* 41 D9
Po, Foci del, *Italy* 41 D9
Po Hai = Bo Hai, *China* 57 E10
Pobé, *Benin* 83 D5
Pobé, *Burkina Faso* 83 C4
Pobeda, *Russia* 53 C15
Pobedy, Pik, *Kyrgyzstan* 52 E8
Pobiedziska, *Poland* 31 F4
Pobla de Segur, *Spain* 38 C5
Pobladura del Valle, *Spain* 36 C5
Pobra de Trives, *Spain* 36 C3
Pocahontas, *Ark., U.S.A.* 113 G9
Pocahontas, *Iowa, U.S.A.* 112 D7
Pocatello, *U.S.A.* 108 E7
Počátky, *Czech Rep.* 26 B8
Pochep, *Russia* 33 F7
Pochinki, *Russia* 34 C7
Pochinok, *Russia* 32 E7
Pöchlarn, *Austria* 26 C8
Pochutla, *Mexico* 119 D5
Pocito Casas, *Mexico* 118 B2
Pocking, *Germany* 25 G9
Pocomoke City, *U.S.A.* 114 F8
Poços de Caldas, *Brazil* 127 A6
Podbořany, *Czech Rep.* 26 A6
Poddębice, *Poland* 31 G5
Poděbrady, *Czech Rep.* 26 A8
Podensac, *France* 20 D3
Podenzano, *Italy* 40 D6
Podgorač, *Croatia* 28 E3
Podgorica, *Serbia & M.* 44 D3
Podgorie, *Albania* 44 F4
Podilska Vysochyna, *Ukraine* 29 B13
Podkarpackie □, *Poland* 31 H9
Podkova, *Bulgaria* 45 E9
Podlapača, *Croatia* 41 D12
Podlaskie □, *Poland* 31 E10
Podoleni, *Romania* 29 D11
Podolínec, *Slovak Rep.* 27 B13
Podolsk, *Russia* 32 E9
Podor, *Senegal* 82 B1
Podporozhye, *Russia* 32 B8
Podu Iloaiei, *Romania* 29 C12
Podu Turcului, *Romania* 29 D12
Podujevo, *Serbia & M.* 44 D5
Podyji △, *Czech Rep.* 26 C8
Poel, *Germany* 24 B6
Pofadder, *S. Africa* 88 D2
Poggiardo, *Italy* 43 B11
Poggibonsi, *Italy* 40 E8
Póggio Mirteto, *Italy* 41 F9
Pogoanele, *Romania* 29 F12
Pogorzela, *Poland* 31 G4
Pogradec, *Albania* 44 F4
Pogranichnyy, *Russia* 54 B5
Poh, *Indonesia* 63 E6
P'ohang, *S. Korea* 57 F15
Pohjanmaa, *Finland* 8 E20
Pohnpei, *Micronesia* 96 G7
Pohorelá, *Slovak Rep.* 27 C13
Pohořelice, *Czech Rep.* 27 C9
Pohorje, *Slovenia* 41 B12
Pohri, *India* 68 G6
Poiana Mare, *Romania* 28 G8
Poiana Ruscăi, Munţii, *Romania* 28 E7
Poiana Stampei, *Romania* 29 C10
Poinsett, C., *Antarctica* 5 C8
Point Arena, *U.S.A.* 110 G3
Point Baker, *U.S.A.* 102 B2
Point Edward, *Canada* 104 D3
Point Fortin, *Trin. & Tob.* 125 K15
Point Hope, *U.S.A.* 100 B3
Point L., *Canada* 100 B8
Point Lisas, *Trin. & Tob.* 125 K15
Point Pedro, *Sri Lanka* 66 Q12
Point Pelee △, *Canada* 116 E2
Point Pleasant, *N.J., U.S.A.* 117 F10
Point Pleasant, *W. Va., U.S.A.* 114 F4
Point Reyes ⌒, *U.S.A.* 110 G2
Pointe-à-Pitre, *Guadeloupe* 120 b
Pointe-au-Pic = La Malbaie, *Canada* 105 C5
Pointe-Claire, *Canada* 117 A11
Pointe-Gatineau, *Canada* 117 A9
Pointe-Noire, *Congo* 84 E2
Pointe Noire, *Guadeloupe* 120 b
Poio, *Spain* 36 C2
Poirino, *Italy* 40 D4
Poisonbush Ra., *Australia* 92 D3
Poissonnier Pt., *Australia* 92 C2
Poitiers, *France* 18 F7
Poitou, *France* 20 B3
Poitou-Charentes □, *France* 20 B4
Poix-de-Picardie, *France* 19 C8
Poix-Terron, *France* 19 C11
Pojoaque, *U.S.A.* 109 J11
Pokaran, *India* 66 F7
Pokataroo, *Australia* 95 D4
Pokhara, *Nepal* 69 E10
Pokhvistnevo, *Russia* 34 D11
Poko, *Dem. Rep. of the Congo* 86 B2
Poko, *Sudan* 81 F3
Pokrov, *Russia* 32 E10
Pokrovsk, *Russia* 53 C13
Pokrovskoye, *Russia* 33 J10
Pola = Pula, *Croatia* 41 D10
Pola, *Russia* 32 D7
Pola de Allande, *Spain* 36 B4
Pola de Lena, *Spain* 36 B5
Pola de Siero, *Spain* 36 B5
Pola de Somiedo, *Spain* 36 B4
Polacca, *U.S.A.* 109 J8
Polan, *Iran* 71 E9
Pol'ana, *Slovak Rep.* 27 C12
Poland ■, *Europe* 31 G3
Polanica-Zdrój, *Poland* 31 H3
Połaniec, *Poland* 31 H8
Polanów, *Poland* 30 D3
Polar Bear ⌒, *Canada* 104 A2
Polatlı, *Turkey* 72 C5
Polatsk, *Belarus* 32 E5
Polcura, *Chile* 126 D1
Połczyn-Zdrój, *Poland* 30 E3
Poleski △, *Poland* 31 G10
Polessk, *Russia* 9 J19
Polesye = Pripet Marshes, *Europe* 33 F5
Polgar, *Hungary* 28 C6
Pŏlgyo-ri, *S. Korea* 57 G14
Poli, *Cameroon* 83 C7
Políaigos, *Greece* 46 E6
Policastro, G. di, *Italy* 43 C8
Police, *Poland* 30 E1
Polička, *Czech Rep.* 27 B9
Policoro, *Italy* 43 B9
Polignano a Mare, *Italy* 43 A9
Poligny, *France* 19 F12
Políkhnitas, *Greece* 47 B8
Polillo Is., *Phil.* 61 D4
Polillo Strait, *Phil.* 61 D4
Polis, *Cyprus* 49 D11
Polístena, *Italy* 43 D9
Políyiros, *Greece* 44 F7
Polk, *U.S.A.* 116 E5
Polkowice, *Poland* 31 G3
Polla, *Italy* 43 B8
Pollachi, *India* 66 P10
Pollença, *Spain* 48 B10
Pollença, B. de, *Spain* 48 B10
Póllica, *Italy* 43 B8
Pollino △, *Italy* 43 C9
Pollino, Mte., *Italy* 43 C9
Polna, *Russia* 32 C5
Polnovat, *Russia* 52 C7
Pology, *Ukraine* 33 J9
Polokwane, *S. Africa* 89 C4
Polonne, *Ukraine* 33 G4
Polonnoye = Polonne, *Ukraine* 33 G4
Polski Trŭmbesh, *Bulgaria* 45 C9
Polsko Kosovo, *Bulgaria* 45 C9
Polson, *U.S.A.* 108 C6
Poltár, *Slovak Rep.* 27 C12
Poltava, *Ukraine* 33 H8
Põltsamaa, *Estonia* 9 G21
Polunochnoye, *Russia* 52 C7
Põlva, *Estonia* 9 G22
Polyana, *Ukraine* 28 B7
Polynesia, *Pac. Oc.* 97 F11
Polynésie française = French Polynesia ☑, *Pac. Oc.* 97 K13
Pomarance, *Italy* 40 E7
Pomaro, *Mexico* 118 D4
Pombal, *Portugal* 36 F2
Pómbia, *Greece* 49 E6
Pomene, *Mozam.* 89 C6
Pomeroy, *Ohio, U.S.A.* 114 F4
Pomeroy, *Wash., U.S.A.* 108 C5
Pomézia, *Italy* 41 G9
Pomichna, *Ukraine* 33 H6
Pomona, *Australia* 95 D5
Pomona, *U.S.A.* 111 L9
Pomorie, *Bulgaria* 45 D11
Pomorskie □, *Poland* 30 D5
Pomorskie, Pojezierze, *Poland* 30 E3
Pomos, *Cyprus* 49 D11
Pomos, C., *Cyprus* 49 D11
Pompano Beach, *U.S.A.* 115 M5
Pompei, *Italy* 43 B7
Pompey, *France* 19 D13
Pompeys Pillar, *U.S.A.* 108 D10
Pompeys Pillar ⌒, *U.S.A.* 108 D10
Pompton Lakes, *U.S.A.* 117 F10
Ponape = Pohnpei, *Micronesia* 96 G7
Ponask L., *Canada* 104 B1
Ponca, *U.S.A.* 112 D6
Ponca City, *U.S.A.* 113 G6
Ponce, *Puerto Rico* 121 d
Ponchatoula, *U.S.A.* 113 K9
Poncheville, L., *Canada* 104 B4
Pond, *U.S.A.* 111 K7
Pond Inlet, *Canada* 101 A12
Pondicherry, *India* 66 P11
Ponds, I. of, *Canada* 105 B8
Ponferrada, *Spain* 36 C4
Pongo, Wadi →, *Sudan* 81 F2
Poniatowa, *Poland* 31 G9
Poniec, *Poland* 31 G3
Ponikva, *Slovenia* 41 B12
Ponnani, *India* 66 P9
Ponoka, *Canada* 102 C6
Ponorogo, *Indonesia* 63 G14
Pons = Ponts, *Spain* 38 D6
Pons, *France* 20 C3
Ponsul →, *Portugal* 36 F3
Pont-à-Mousson, *France* 19 D13
Pont-Audemer, *France* 18 C7
Pont-Aven, *France* 18 E3
Pont Canavese, *Italy* 40 C4
Pont-d'Ain, *France* 19 F12
Pont-de-Roide, *France* 19 E13
Pont-de-Salars, *France* 20 D6
Pont-de-Vaux, *France* 19 F11
Pont-de-Veyle, *France* 19 F11
Pont-du-Château, *France* 19 G10
Pont-l'Abbé, *France* 18 E2
Pont-l'Évêque, *France* 18 C7
Pont-St-Esprit, *France* 21 D8
Pont-St-Martin, *Italy* 40 C4
Pont-Ste-Maxence, *France* 19 C9
Pont-sur-Yonne, *France* 19 D10
Ponta do Sol, *Madeira* 48 D2
Ponta Grossa, *Brazil* 127 B5
Ponta Pora, *Brazil* 127 A4
Pontacq, *France* 20 E3
Pontailler-sur-Saône, *France* 19 E12
Pontarlier, *France* 19 F13
Pontassieve, *Italy* 41 E8
Pontaumur, *France* 20 C6
Pontcharra, *France* 21 C10
Pontchartrain L., *U.S.A.* 113 K10
Pontchâteau, *France* 18 E4
Ponte da Barca, *Portugal* 36 D2
Ponte de Sor, *Portugal* 37 F2
Ponte dell'Ólio, *Italy* 40 D6
Ponte di Legno, *Italy* 40 B7
Ponte do Lima, *Portugal* 36 D2
Ponte do Pungué, *Mozam.* 87 F3
Ponte-Leccia, *France* 21 F13
Ponte nelle Alpi, *Italy* 41 B9
Ponte Nova, *Brazil* 127 A7
Ponteareas, *Spain* 36 C2
Pontebba, *Italy* 41 B10
Ponteceso, *Spain* 36 B2
Pontecorvo, *Italy* 42 A6
Pontedeume, *Spain* 36 B2
Ponteix, *Canada* 103 D7
Pontevedra, *Spain* 36 C2
Pontevedra □, *Spain* 36 C2
Pontevedra, R. de →, *Spain* 36 C2
Pontevico, *Italy* 40 C7
Pontiac, *Ill., U.S.A.* 112 E10
Pontiac, *Mich., U.S.A.* 114 D4
Pontian Kechil, *Malaysia* 65 d
Pontianak, *Indonesia* 62 E3
Pontine Is. = Ponziane, Ísole, *Italy* 42 B5
Pontine Mts. = Kuzey Anadolu Dağları, *Turkey* 72 B7
Pontínia, *Italy* 42 A6
Pontivy, *France* 18 D4
Pontoise, *France* 19 C9
Ponton →, *Canada* 102 B5
Pontorson, *France* 18 D5
Pontrémoli, *Italy* 40 D6
Pontrieux, *France* 18 D3
Ponts, *Spain* 38 D6
Pontypool, *Canada* 116 B6
Pontypool, *U.K.* 15 F4
Ponza, *Italy* 42 B5
Ponziane, Ísole, *Italy* 42 B5
Poochera, *Australia* 95 E1
Poole, *U.K.* 15 G6
Poole □, *U.K.* 15 G6
Poona = Pune, *India* 66 K8
Pooncarie, *Australia* 95 E3
Poopelloe L., *Australia* 95 E3
Poopó, L. de, *Bolivia* 124 G5
Popayán, *Colombia* 124 C3
Poperinge, *Belgium* 17 D2
Popilta L., *Australia* 95 E3
Popina, *Bulgaria* 45 B10
Popio L., *Australia* 95 E3
Poplar, *U.S.A.* 112 A2
Poplar →, *Canada* 103 C9
Poplar Bluff, *U.S.A.* 113 G9
Poplarville, *U.S.A.* 113 K10
Popocatépetl, Volcán, *Mexico* 119 D5
Popokabaka, *Dem. Rep. of the Congo* 84 F3
Pópoli, *Italy* 41 F10
Popovača, *Croatia* 41 C13
Popovo, *Bulgaria* 45 C10
Poppberg, *Germany* 25 F7
Poppi, *Italy* 41 E8
Poprad, *Slovak Rep.* 27 B13
Poprad →, *Slovak Rep.* 27 B13
Porali →, *Pakistan* 68 G2
Porbandar, *India* 68 J3
Porcher I., *Canada* 102 C2
Porcuna, *Spain* 37 H6
Porcupine →, *Canada* 103 B8
Porcupine →, *U.S.A.* 100 B5
Porcupine Gorge △, *Australia* 94 C3
Pordenone, *Italy* 41 C9
Pordim, *Bulgaria* 45 C8
Poreč, *Croatia* 41 C10
Poretskoye, *Russia* 34 C8
Pori, *Finland* 9 F19
Porí, *Greece* 46 F5
Porkhov, *Russia* 32 D5
Porlamar, *Venezuela* 124 A6
Porlezza, *Italy* 40 B6
Porma →, *Spain* 36 C5
Pornic, *France* 18 E4
Poronaysk, *Russia* 53 E15
Póros, *Greece* 46 D5
Poroshiri-Dake, *Japan* 54 C11
Poroszló, *Hungary* 28 C5
Poroto Mts., *Tanzania* 87 D3
Porpoise B., *Antarctica* 5 C9
Porquerolles, Î. de, *France* 21 F10
Porrentruy, *Switz.* 25 H3
Porreres, *Spain* 48 B10
Porsangen, *Norway* 8 A21
Porsgrunn, *Norway* 9 G13
Port Alberni, *Canada* 102 D4
Port Alfred, *S. Africa* 88 E4
Port Alice, *Canada* 102 C3
Port Allegany, *U.S.A.* 116 E6
Port Allen, *U.S.A.* 113 K9
Port Alma, *Australia* 94 C5
Port Angeles, *U.S.A.* 110 B3
Port Antonio, *Jamaica* 120 a
Port Aransas, *U.S.A.* 113 M6
Port Arthur, *Australia* 95 G4
Port Arthur, *U.S.A.* 113 L8
Port au Choix, *Canada* 105 B8
Port au Port B., *Canada* 105 C8
Port-au-Prince, *Haiti* 121 C5
Port Augusta, *Australia* 95 E2
Port Austin, *U.S.A.* 116 B2
Port Bell, *Uganda* 86 B3
Port Bergé Vaovao, *Madag.* 89 B8
Port Blandford, *Canada* 105 C9
Port-Bouët, *Ivory C.* 82 D4
Port Bradshaw, *Australia* 94 A2
Port Broughton, *Australia* 95 E2
Port Burwell, *Canada* 116 D4
Port Canning, *India* 69 H13
Port-Cartier, *Canada* 105 B6
Port Chalmers, *N.Z.* 91 L3
Port Charlotte, *U.S.A.* 115 M4
Port Chester, *U.S.A.* 117 F11
Port Clements, *Canada* 102 C2
Port Clinton, *U.S.A.* 114 E4
Port Colborne, *Canada* 116 D5
Port Coquitlam, *Canada* 102 D4
Port Credit, *Canada* 116 C5
Port-Cros △, *France* 21 F10
Port Curtis, *Australia* 94 C5
Port d'Alcúdia, *Spain* 48 B10
Port Dalhousie, *Canada* 116 C5
Port d'Andratx, *Spain* 48 B9
Port Darwin, *Australia* 92 B5
Port Darwin, *Falk. Is.* 128 G5
Port Davey, *Australia* 95 G4
Port-de-Bouc, *France* 21 E8
Port-de-Paix, *Haiti* 121 C5
Port de Pollença, *Spain* 48 B10
Port de Sóller, *Spain* 48 B9
Port Dickson, *Malaysia* 65 L3
Port Douglas, *Australia* 94 B4
Port Dover, *Canada* 116 D4
Port Edward, *Canada* 102 C2
Port Elgin, *Canada* 116 B3
Port Elizabeth, *S. Africa* 88 E4
Port Ellen, *U.K.* 13 F2
Port-en-Bessin-Huppain, *France* 18 C6
Port Erin, *I. of Man* 14 C3
Port Essington, *Australia* 92 B5
Port Ewen, *U.S.A.* 117 E11
Port Fairy, *Australia* 95 F3
Port Fouâd = Bûr Fuad, *Egypt* 80 H8
Port Gamble, *U.S.A.* 110 C4
Port-Gentil, *Gabon* 84 E1
Port Germein, *Australia* 95 E2
Port Gibson, *U.S.A.* 113 K9
Port Glasgow, *U.K.* 13 F4
Port Harcourt, *Nigeria* 83 E6
Port Hardy, *Canada* 102 C3
Port Harrison = Inukjuak, *Canada* 101 C12
Port Hawkesbury, *Canada* 105 C7
Port Hedland, *Australia* 92 D2
Port Henry, *U.S.A.* 117 B11
Port Hood, *Canada* 105 C7
Port Hope, *Canada* 116 C6
Port Hope, *U.S.A.* 116 C2
Port Hope Simpson, *Canada* 105 B8
Port Hueneme, *U.S.A.* 111 L7
Port Huron, *U.S.A.* 116 D2
Port Iliç, *Azerbaijan* 73 C13
Port Jefferson, *U.S.A.* 117 F11
Port Jervis, *U.S.A.* 117 E10
Port-Joinville, *France* 18 F4
Port Katon, *Russia* 33 J10
Port Kelang = Pelabuhan Klang, *Malaysia* 65 L3
Port Kenny, *Australia* 95 E1
Port-la-Nouvelle, *France* 20 E7
Port Lairge = Waterford, *Ireland* 12 D4
Port Laoise, *Ireland* 12 C4
Port Lavaca, *U.S.A.* 113 L6
Port Leyden, *U.S.A.* 117 C9
Port Lincoln, *Australia* 95 E2
Port Loko, *S. Leone* 82 D2
Port Louis, *France* 18 E3
Port-Louis, *Guadeloupe* 120 b
Port Louis, *Mauritius* 77 H9
Port MacDonnell, *Australia* 95 F3
Port McNeill, *Canada* 102 C3
Port Macquarie, *Australia* 95 E5
Port Maria, *Jamaica* 120 a
Port Matilda, *U.S.A.* 116 F6
Port Mellon, *Canada* 102 D4
Port-Menier, *Canada* 105 C7
Port Moody, *Canada* 110 A4
Port Morant, *Jamaica* 120 a
Port Moresby, *Papua N. G.* 96 H6
Port Musgrave, *Australia* 94 A3
Port-Navalo, *France* 18 E4
Port Neches, *U.S.A.* 113 L8
Port Nolloth, *S. Africa* 88 D2
Port Nouveau-Québec = Kangiqsualujjuaq, *Canada* 101 C13
Port of Spain, *Trin. & Tob.* 121 D7
Port Orange, *U.S.A.* 115 L5
Port Orchard, *U.S.A.* 110 C4
Port Orford, *U.S.A.* 108 E1
Port Pegasus, *N.Z.* 91 M1
Port Perry, *Canada* 116 B6
Port Phillip B., *Australia* 95 F3
Port Pirie, *Australia* 95 E2
Port Renfrew, *Canada* 102 D4
Port Roper, *Australia* 94 A2
Port Rowan, *Canada* 116 D4
Port Safaga = Bûr Safâga, *Egypt* 70 E2
Port Said = Bûr Sa'îd, *Egypt* 80 H8
Port St. Joe, *U.S.A.* 115 L3
Port St. Johns = Umzimvubu, *S. Africa* 89 E4
Port-St-Louis-du-Rhône, *France* 21 E8
Port St. Lucie, *U.S.A.* 115 M5
Port-Ste-Marie, *France* 20 D4
Port Sanilac, *U.S.A.* 116 C2
Port Severn, *Canada* 116 B5
Port Shepstone, *S. Africa* 89 E5
Port Simpson, *Canada* 102 C2
Port Stanley = Stanley, *Falk. Is.* 128 G5
Port Stanley, *Canada* 116 D3
Port Sudan = Bûr Sûdân, *Sudan* 80 D4
Port Sulphur, *U.S.A.* 113 L10
Port-sur-Saône, *France* 19 E13
Port Talbot, *U.K.* 15 F4
Port Taufîq = Bûr Taufiq, *Egypt* 80 J8
Port Townsend, *U.S.A.* 110 B4
Port-Vendres, *France* 20 F7
Port Vila, *Vanuatu* 96 J8
Port Wakefield, *Australia* 95 E2
Port Washington, *U.S.A.* 114 D2
Portadown, *U.K.* 12 B5
Portaferry, *U.K.* 12 B6
Portage, *Pa., U.S.A.* 116 F6
Portage, *Wis., U.S.A.* 112 D10
Portage la Prairie, *Canada* 103 D9
Portageville, *U.S.A.* 113 G10
Portalegre, *Portugal* 37 F3
Portalegre □, *Portugal* 37 F3
Portales, *U.S.A.* 113 H3
Portarlington, *Ireland* 12 C4
Portbou, *Spain* 38 C8
Portel, *Portugal* 37 G3
Portela, Lisboa ✈ (LIS), *Portugal* 37 G1
Porter L., *N.W.T., Canada* 103 A7
Porter L., *Sask., Canada* 103 B7
Porterville, *S. Africa* 88 E2
Porterville, *U.S.A.* 110 J8
Portes-lès-Valence, *France* 21 D8
Porthcawl, *U.K.* 15 F4
Porthill, *U.S.A.* 108 B5
Porthmadog, *U.K.* 14 E3
Portile de Fier, *Europe* 28 F7
Portimão, *Portugal* 37 H2
Portishead, *U.K.* 15 F5
Portiţei, Gura, *Romania* 29 F14
Portknockie, *U.K.* 13 D6
Portland, *N.S.W., Australia* 95 E5
Portland, *Vic., Australia* 95 F3
Portland, *Canada* 117 B8
Portland, *Conn., U.S.A.* 117 E12
Portland, *Maine, U.S.A.* 101 D12
Portland, *Mich., U.S.A.* 114 D3
Portland, *Oreg., U.S.A.* 110 E4
Portland, *Pa., U.S.A.* 117 F9
Portland, *Tex., U.S.A.* 113 M6
Portland ✈ (PDX), *U.S.A.* 110 E4
Portland, I. of, *U.K.* 15 G5
Portland B., *Australia* 95 F3
Portland Bight, *Jamaica* 120 a
Portland Bill, *U.K.* 15 G5
Portland Canal, *U.S.A.* 102 B2
Portland Pt., *Jamaica* 120 a
Portmadoc = Porthmadog, *U.K.* 14 E3
Portmore, *Jamaica* 120 a
Porto, *France* 21 F12
Porto, *Portugal* 36 D2
Porto □, *Portugal* 36 D2
Porto, G. de, *France* 21 F12
Pôrto Alegre, *Brazil* 127 C5
Porto Azzurro, *Italy* 40 F7
Porto Cristo, *Spain* 48 B10
Pôrto de Móz, *Brazil* 125 D8
Porto Empédocle, *Italy* 42 E6
Pôrto Esperança, *Brazil* 124 G7
Pôrto Franco, *Brazil* 125 E9
Pôrto Lágos, *Greece* 45 E9
Pôrto Mendes, *Brazil* 127 A5
Porto Moniz, *Madeira* 48 D2
Pôrto Murtinho, *Brazil* 124 H7
Pôrto Nacional, *Brazil* 125 F9
Porto-Novo, *Benin* 83 D5
Porto Petro, *Spain* 48 B10
Porto San Giórgio, *Italy* 41 E10
Porto Sant' Elpídio, *Italy* 41 E10
Porto Santo, I. de, *Madeira* 78 B2
Porto Santo Stéfano, *Italy* 40 F8
Pôrto São José, *Brazil* 127 A5
Pôrto Seguro, *Brazil* 125 G11
Porto Tolle, *Italy* 41 D9
Porto Tórres, *Italy* 42 B1
Pôrto União, *Brazil* 127 B5
Pôrto Válter, *Brazil* 124 E4
Porto-Vecchio, *France* 21 G13
Pôrto Velho, *Brazil* 124 E6
Portobelo, *Panama* 120 E4
Portoferráio, *Italy* 40 F7
Portogruaro, *Italy* 41 C9
Portola, *U.S.A.* 110 F6
Portomaggiore, *Italy* 41 D8
Portoscuso, *Italy* 42 C1
Portovénere, *Italy* 40 D6
Portoviejo, *Ecuador* 124 D2
Portpatrick, *U.K.* 13 G3
Portree, *U.K.* 13 D2
Portrush, *U.K.* 12 A5
Portsmouth, *Dominica* 121 C7
Portsmouth, *U.K.* 15 G6
Portsmouth, *N.H., U.S.A.* 115 D10
Portsmouth, *Ohio, U.S.A.* 114 F4
Portsmouth, *R.I., U.S.A.* 117 E13
Portsmouth, *Va., U.S.A.* 114 G7
Portsmouth □, *U.K.* 15 G6
Portsoy, *U.K.* 13 D6
Portstewart, *U.K.* 12 A5
Porttipahdan tekojärvi, *Finland* 8 B22
Portugal ■, *Europe* 36 F3
Portugalete, *Spain* 38 B1

Portumna, *Ireland* 12 C3
Portville, *U.S.A.* 116 D6
Porvenir, *Chile* 128 G2
Porvoo, *Finland* 9 F21
Porzuna, *Spain* 37 F6
Posada, *Italy* 42 B2
Posada →, *Italy* 42 B2
Posadas, *Argentina* 127 B4
Posadas, *Spain* 37 H5
Poschiavo, *Switz.* 25 J6
Posets, *Spain* 38 C5
Posht-e Badam, *Iran* 71 C7
Posídhion, Ákra, *Greece* 44 G7
Posidium, *Greece* 47 F9
Poso, *Indonesia* 63 E6
Posong, *S. Korea* 57 G14
Posse, *Brazil* 125 F9
Possession I., *Antarctica* 5 D11
Pössneck, *Germany* 24 E7
Possum Kingdom L., *U.S.A.* 113 J5
Post, *U.S.A.* 113 J4
Post Falls, *U.S.A.* 108 C5
Postavy = Pastavy, *Belarus* 9 J22
Poste-de-la-Baleine = Kuujjuarapik, *Canada* 104 A4
Postmasburg, *S. Africa* 88 D3
Postojna, *Slovenia* 41 C11
Poston, *U.S.A.* 111 M12
Postville, *Canada* 105 B8
Potamós, *Andikíthira, Greece* 46 F5
Potamós, *Kíthira, Greece* 46 E4
Potchefstroom, *S. Africa* 88 D4
Potcoava, *Romania* 29 F9
Poteau, *U.S.A.* 113 H7
Poteet, *U.S.A.* 113 L5
Potenza, *Italy* 43 B8
Potenza →, *Italy* 41 E10
Potenza Picena, *Italy* 41 E10
Poteriteri, L., *N.Z.* 91 M1
Potgietersrus = Mokopane, *S. Africa* 89 C4
Poti, *Georgia* 35 J5
Potiskum, *Nigeria* 83 C7
Potlogi, *Romania* 29 F10
Potomac →, *U.S.A.* 114 G7
Potosí, *Bolivia* 124 G5
Potosi Mt., *U.S.A.* 111 K11
Pototan, *Phil.* 61 F5
Potrerillos, *Chile* 126 B2
Potsdam, *Germany* 24 C9
Potsdam, *U.S.A.* 117 B10
Pottenstein, *Germany* 25 F7
Pottersville, *U.S.A.* 117 C11
Pottstown, *U.S.A.* 117 F9
Pottsville, *U.S.A.* 117 F8
Pottuvil, *Sri Lanka* 66 R12
P'otzu, *Taiwan* 59 F13
Pouancé, *France* 18 E5
Pouce Coupé, *Canada* 102 B4
Poughkeepsie, *U.S.A.* 117 E11
Pouilly-sur-Loire, *France* 19 E9
Poulaphouca Res., *Ireland* 12 C5
Poulsbo, *U.S.A.* 110 C4
Poultney, *U.S.A.* 117 C11
Poulton-le-Fylde, *U.K.* 14 D5
Pouso Alegre, *Brazil* 127 A6
Pout, *Senegal* 82 C1
Pouthisat, *Cambodia* 64 F4
Pouzauges, *France* 18 F6
Pova de Santa Iria, *Portugal* 37 G1
Považská Bystrica, *Slovak Rep.* 27 B11
Poverty B., *N.Z.* 91 H7
Povlen, *Serbia & M.* 44 B3
Póvoa de Lanhosa, *Portugal* 36 D2
Póvoa de Varzim, *Portugal* 36 D2
Povorino, *Russia* 34 E6
Povungnituk = Puvirnituq, *Canada* 101 B12
Powassan, *Canada* 104 C4
Poway, *U.S.A.* 111 N9
Powder →, *U.S.A.* 112 B2
Powder River, *U.S.A.* 108 E10
Powell, *U.S.A.* 108 D9
Powell, L., *U.S.A.* 109 H8
Powell River, *Canada* 102 D4
Powers, *U.S.A.* 114 C2
Powys □, *U.K.* 15 E4
Poyang Hu, *China* 59 C11
Poyarkovo, *Russia* 53 E13
Poysdorf, *Austria* 27 C9
Poza de la Sal, *Spain* 36 C7
Poza Rica, *Mexico* 119 C5
Pozanti, *Turkey* 72 D6
Požarevac, *Serbia & M.* 44 B5
Pozazal, Puerto, *Spain* 36 C6
Požega, *Croatia* 28 E2
Požega, *Serbia & M.* 44 C4
Poznań, *Poland* 31 F3
Poznań ✈ (POZ), *Poland* 31 F3
Pozo, *U.S.A.* 111 K6
Pozo Alcón, *Spain* 37 H8
Pozo Almonte, *Chile* 124 H5
Pozo Colorado, *Paraguay* 126 A4
Pozoblanco, *Spain* 37 G6
Pozzallo, *Italy* 43 F7
Pozzomaggiore, *Italy* 42 B1
Pozzuoli, *Italy* 43 B7
Pra →, *Ghana* 83 D4
Prabuty, *Poland* 30 E6
Prača, *Bos.-H.* 28 G3
Prachatice, *Czech Rep.* 26 B6
Prachin Buri, *Thailand* 64 E3
Prachuap Khiri Khan, *Thailand* 65 G2
Pradelles, *France* 20 D7
Prades, *France* 20 F6
Prado, *Brazil* 125 G11
Prado del Rey, *Spain* 37 J5
Præstø, *Denmark* 11 J6
Pragersko, *Slovenia* 41 B12
Prague = Praha, *Czech Rep.* 26 A7
Praha, *Czech Rep.* 26 A7
Praha ✈ (PRG), *Czech Rep.* 26 A7
Prahecq, *France* 20 B3
Prahova □, *Romania* 29 E10
Prahova →, *Romania* 29 F10
Prahovo, *Serbia & M.* 44 B6
Praia, *C. Verde Is.* 77 E1
Práia a Mare, *Italy* 43 C8
Praid, *Romania* 29 D10
Prainha, *Amazonas, Brazil* 124 E6
Prainha, *Pará, Brazil* 125 D8
Prairie, *Australia* 94 C3
Prairie City, *U.S.A.* 108 D4
Prairie Dog Town Fork →, *U.S.A.* 113 H5
Prairie du Chien, *U.S.A.* 112 D9
Prairies, L. of the, *Canada* 103 C8
Pramánda, *Greece* 46 B3
Prampram, *Ghana* 83 D5
Pran Buri, *Thailand* 64 F2
Prang, *Ghana* 83 D4
Prapat, *Indonesia* 62 D1
Prasonísi, Ákra, *Greece* 49 D9
Prästmon, *Sweden* 10 A11
Praszka, *Poland* 31 G5
Prata, *Brazil* 125 G9
Pratabpur, *India* 69 H10
Pratapgarh, *Raj., India* 68 G6
Pratapgarh, *Ut. P., India* 69 G9
Pratas Is. = Dongsha Dao, *China* 59 G11
Prato, *Italy* 40 E8
Prátola Peligna, *Italy* 41 F10
Prats-de-Mollo-la-Preste, *France* 20 F6
Pratt, *U.S.A.* 113 G5
Prattville, *U.S.A.* 115 J2
Pravdinsk, *Russia* 30 D8
Pravdinsk, *Russia* 34 B6
Pravets, *Bulgaria* 44 D7
Pravia, *Spain* 36 B4
Praya, *Indonesia* 62 F5
Pré-en-Pail, *France* 18 D6
Precipice △, *Australia* 95 D5
Precordillera, *Argentina* 126 C2
Predáppio, *Italy* 41 D8
Predazzo, *Italy* 41 B8
Predeal, *Romania* 29 E10
Predejane, *Serbia & M.* 44 D6
Preeceville, *Canada* 103 C8
Preetz, *Germany* 24 A6
Pregolya →, *Russia* 30 D7
Pregrada, *Croatia* 41 B12
Preiļi, *Latvia* 9 H22
Preko, *Croatia* 41 D12
Prelog, *Croatia* 41 B13
Prémery, *France* 19 E10
Premià de Mar, *Spain* 38 D7
Premont, *U.S.A.* 113 M5
Premuda, *Croatia* 41 D11
Prentice, *U.S.A.* 112 C9
Prenzlau, *Germany* 24 B9
Preobrazheniye, *Russia* 54 C6
Preparis North Channel, *Ind. Oc.* 67 M18
Preparis South Channel, *Ind. Oc.* 67 M18
Přerov, *Czech Rep.* 27 B10
Prescott, *Canada* 117 B9
Prescott, *Ariz., U.S.A.* 109 J7
Prescott, *Ark., U.S.A.* 113 J8
Prescott Valley, *U.S.A.* 109 J7
Preservation Inlet, *N.Z.* 91 M1
Preševo, *Serbia & M.* 44 D5
Presho, *U.S.A.* 112 D4
Presicce, *Italy* 43 C11
Presidencia de la Plaza, *Argentina* 126 B4
Presidencia Roque Saenz Peña, *Argentina* 126 B3
Presidente Epitácio, *Brazil* 125 H8
Presidente Hayes □, *Paraguay* 126 A4
Presidente Prudente, *Brazil* 127 A5
Presidio, *Mexico* 118 B4
Presidio, *U.S.A.* 113 L2
Preslav, *Bulgaria* 45 C10
Preslavska Planina, *Bulgaria* 45 C10
Prešov, *Slovak Rep.* 27 B14
Prešovský □, *Slovak Rep.* 27 B13
Prespa, *Bulgaria* 45 E8
Préspa △, *Greece* 44 F5
Prespa, L. = Prespansko Jezero, *Macedonia* 44 F5
Prespansko Jezero, *Macedonia* 44 F5
Presque I., *U.S.A.* 116 D4
Presque Isle, *U.S.A.* 115 B12
Prestatyn, *U.K.* 14 D4
Prestea, *Ghana* 82 D4
Presteigne, *U.K.* 15 E5
Přeštice, *Czech Rep.* 26 B6
Preston, *Canada* 116 C4
Preston, *U.K.* 14 D5
Preston, *Idaho, U.S.A.* 108 E8
Preston, *Minn., U.S.A.* 112 D8
Preston, C., *Australia* 92 D2
Prestonburg, *U.S.A.* 114 G4
Prestwick, *U.K.* 13 F4
Pretoria, *S. Africa* 89 D4
Preuilly-sur-Claise, *France* 18 F7
Préveza, *Greece* 46 C2
Préveza □, *Greece* 46 B2
Prey Veng, *Cambodia* 65 G5
Priazovskoye, *Ukraine* 33 J8
Pribilof Is., *U.S.A.* 100 C2
Priboj, *Serbia & M.* 44 C3
Příbram, *Czech Rep.* 26 B7
Price, *U.S.A.* 108 G8
Price I., *Canada* 102 C3
Prichard, *U.S.A.* 115 K1
Priego, *Spain* 38 E2
Priego de Córdoba, *Spain* 37 H6
Priekule, *Latvia* 9 H19
Priekule, *Lithuania* 30 C8
Prien, *Germany* 25 H8
Prienai, *Lithuania* 9 J20
Prieska, *S. Africa* 88 D3
Priest L., *U.S.A.* 108 B5
Priest River, *U.S.A.* 108 B5
Priest Valley, *U.S.A.* 110 J6
Prievidza, *Slovak Rep.* 27 C11
Prignitz, *Germany* 24 B7
Prijedor, *Bos.-H.* 41 D13
Prijepolje, *Serbia & M.* 44 C3
Prikaspiyskaya Nizmennost = Caspian Depression, *Eurasia* 35 G9
Prikro, *Ivory C.* 82 D4
Prikubanskaya Nizmennost, *Russia* 35 H4
Prilep, *Macedonia* 44 E5
Priluki = Pryluky, *Ukraine* 33 G7
Prime Seal I., *Australia* 95 G4
Primorsk, *Russia* 30 D6
Primorsk, *Russia* 32 B5
Primorsko, *Bulgaria* 45 D11
Primorsko-Akhtarsk, *Russia* 33 J10
Primorskoye, *Ukraine* 33 J9
Primrose L., *Canada* 103 C7
Prince Albert, *Canada* 103 C7
Prince Albert, *S. Africa* 88 E3
Prince Albert △, *Canada* 103 C7
Prince Albert Mts., *Antarctica* 5 D11
Prince Albert Pen., *Canada* 100 A8
Prince Albert Sd., *Canada* 100 A8
Prince Alfred, C., *Canada* 4 B1
Prince Charles I., *Canada* 101 B12
Prince Charles Mts., *Antarctica* 5 D6
Prince Edward I. □, *Canada* 105 C7
Prince Edward Is., *Ind. Oc.* 3 G11
Prince Edward Pt., *Canada* 116 C8
Prince George, *Canada* 102 C4
Prince of Wales, C., *U.S.A.* 98 C3
Prince of Wales I., *Australia* 94 A3
Prince of Wales I., *Canada* 100 A10
Prince of Wales I., *U.S.A.* 100 C6
Prince Patrick I., *Canada* 4 B2
Prince Regent Inlet, *Canada* 4 B3
Prince Rupert, *Canada* 102 C2
Princes Town, *Trin. & Tob.* 125 K15
Princess Charlotte B., *Australia* 94 A3
Princess May Ranges, *Australia* 92 C4
Princess Royal I., *Canada* 102 C3
Princeton, *Canada* 102 D4
Princeton, *Calif., U.S.A.* 110 F4
Princeton, *Ill., U.S.A.* 112 E10
Princeton, *Ind., U.S.A.* 114 F2
Princeton, *Ky., U.S.A.* 114 G2
Princeton, *Mo., U.S.A.* 112 E8
Princeton, *N.J., U.S.A.* 117 F10
Princeton, *W. Va., U.S.A.* 114 G5
Principe, I. de, *Atl. Oc.* 76 F4
Principe da Beira, *Brazil* 124 F6
Prineville, *U.S.A.* 108 D3
Prins Harald Kyst, *Antarctica* 5 D4
Prinsesse Astrid Kyst, *Antarctica* 5 D3
Prinsesse Ragnhild Kyst, *Antarctica* 5 D4
Prinzapolca, *Nic.* 120 D3
Prior, C., *Spain* 36 B2
Priozersk, *Russia* 32 B6
Pripet = Prypyat →, *Europe* 33 G6
Pripet Marshes, *Europe* 33 F5
Pripyat Marshes = Pripet Marshes, *Europe* 33 F5
Pripyats = Prypyat →, *Europe* 33 G6
Prislop, Pasul, *Romania* 29 C9
Pristen, *Russia* 33 G9
Priština, *Serbia & M.* 44 D5
Pritzwalk, *Germany* 24 B8
Privas, *France* 21 D8
Priverno, *Italy* 42 A6
Privolzhsk, *Russia* 34 B5
Privolzhskaya Vozvyshennost, *Russia* 34 E7
Privolzhskiy, *Russia* 34 E8
Privolzhskiy □, *Russia* 34 B10
Privolzhye, *Russia* 34 D9
Priyutnoye, *Russia* 35 G6
Prizren, *Serbia & M.* 44 D4
Prizzi, *Italy* 42 E6
Prnjavor, *Bos.-H.* 28 F2
Probolinggo, *Indonesia* 63 G15
Prochowice, *Poland* 31 G3
Proctor, *U.S.A.* 117 C11
Proddatur, *India* 66 M11
Prodhromos, *Cyprus* 49 E11
Proença-a-Nova, *Portugal* 36 F3
Profítis Ilías, *Greece* 49 C9
Profondeville, *Belgium* 17 D4
Progreso, *Coahuila, Mexico* 118 B4
Progreso, *Yucatán, Mexico* 119 C7
Prokhladnyy, *Russia* 35 J7
Prokletije, *Albania* 44 D3
Prokopyevsk, *Russia* 52 D9
Prokuplje, *Serbia & M.* 44 C5
Proletarsk, *Russia* 35 G5
Proletarskaya = Proletarsk, *Russia* 35 G5
Prome, *Burma* 67 K19
Prophet →, *Canada* 102 B4
Prophet River, *Canada* 102 B4
Propriá, *Brazil* 125 F11
Propriano, *France* 21 G12
Proserpine, *Australia* 94 J6
Prosna →, *Poland* 31 F4
Prospect, *U.S.A.* 117 C9
Prosser, *U.S.A.* 108 C4
Prostějov, *Czech Rep.* 27 B10
Prostki, *Poland* 30 E9
Proston, *Australia* 95 D5
Proszowice, *Poland* 31 H7
Próti, *Greece* 46 D3
Provadiya, *Bulgaria* 45 C11
Provence, *France* 21 E9
Provence-Alpes-Côte d'Azur □, *France* 21 D10
Providence, *Ky., U.S.A.* 114 G2
Providence, *R.I., U.S.A.* 117 E13
Providence Bay, *Canada* 104 C3
Providence Mts., *U.S.A.* 111 K11
Providencia, I. de, *Colombia* 120 D3
Provideniya, *Russia* 53 C19
Provins, *France* 19 D10
Provo, *U.S.A.* 108 F8
Provost, *Canada* 103 C6
Prozor, *Bos.-H.* 28 G2
Prrenjas, *Albania* 44 E4
Prudhoe Bay, *U.S.A.* 100 A5
Prudhoe I., *Australia* 94 C4
Prud'homme, *Canada* 103 C7
Prudnik, *Poland* 31 H4
Prüm, *Germany* 25 E2
Prundu, *Romania* 29 F11
Pruszcz Gdański, *Poland* 30 D5
Pruszków, *Poland* 31 F7
Prut →, *Romania* 29 E13
Pruzhany, *Belarus* 33 F3
Prvič, *Croatia* 41 D11
Prydz B., *Antarctica* 5 C6
Pryluky, *Ukraine* 33 G7
Pryor, *U.S.A.* 113 G7
Prypyat →, *Europe* 33 G6
Przasnysz, *Poland* 31 E7
Przedbórz, *Poland* 31 G6
Przedecz, *Poland* 31 F5
Przemków, *Poland* 31 G2
Przemyśl, *Poland* 31 J9
Przeworsk, *Poland* 31 H9
Przewóz, *Poland* 31 G1
Przhevalsk = Karakol, *Kyrgyzstan* 52 E8
Przysucha, *Poland* 31 G7
Psakhná, *Greece* 46 C5
Psará, *Greece* 47 C7
Psathoúra, *Greece* 46 B6
Psel →, *Ukraine* 33 H7
Pserimos, *Greece* 47 E9
Psíra, *Greece* 49 D7
Pskov, *Russia* 32 D5
Pskovskoye, Ozero, *Russia* 32 D5
Psunj, *Croatia* 28 E2
Pteleón, *Greece* 46 B4
Ptich = Ptsich →, *Belarus* 33 F5
Ptolemaís, *Greece* 44 F5
Ptsich →, *Belarus* 33 F5
Ptuj, *Slovenia* 41 B12
Ptujska Gora, *Slovenia* 41 B12
Pu Xian, *China* 56 F6
Pua, *Thailand* 64 C3
Puán, *Argentina* 126 D3
Pu'an, *China* 58 E5
Puan, *S. Korea* 57 G14
Pubei, *China* 58 F7
Pucallpa, *Peru* 124 E4
Pucheng, *China* 59 D12
Pucheni, *Romania* 29 E10
Puchheim, *Germany* 25 G7
Púchov, *Slovak Rep.* 27 B11
Pucioasa, *Romania* 29 E10
Pučišća, *Croatia* 41 E13
Puck, *Poland* 30 D5
Pucka, Zatoka, *Poland* 30 D5
Puçol, *Spain* 39 F4
Pudasjärvi, *Finland* 8 D22
Puding, *China* 58 D5
Pudozh, *Russia* 32 B9
Puduchcheri = Pondicherry, *India* 66 P11
Pudukkottai, *India* 66 P11
Puebla, *Mexico* 119 D5
Puebla □, *Mexico* 119 D5
Puebla de Alcocer, *Spain* 37 G5
Puebla de Don Fadrique, *Spain* 39 H2
Puebla de Don Rodrigo, *Spain* 37 F6
Puebla de Guzmán, *Spain* 37 H3
Puebla de la Calzada, *Spain* 37 G4
Puebla de Sanabria, *Spain* 36 C4
Puebla de Trives = Pobra de Trives, *Spain* 36 C3
Pueblo, *U.S.A.* 112 F2
Pueblo Hundido, *Chile* 126 B1
Puelches, *Argentina* 126 D2
Puelén, *Argentina* 126 D2
Puente Alto, *Chile* 126 C1
Puente-Genil, *Spain* 37 H6
Puente la Reina, *Spain* 38 C3
Puenteareas = Ponteareas, *Spain* 36 C2
Puentedeume = Pontedeume, *Spain* 36 B2
Puentes de Garcia Rodriguez = As Pontes de García Rodríguez, *Spain* 36 B3
Pu'er, *China* 58 F3
Puerca, Pta., *Puerto Rico* 121 d
Puerco →, *U.S.A.* 109 J10
Puerto Aisén, *Chile* 128 F2
Puerto Ángel, *Mexico* 119 D5
Puerto Arista, *Mexico* 119 D6
Puerto Armuelles, *Panama* 120 E3
Puerto Ayacucho, *Venezuela* 124 B5
Puerto Barrios, *Guatemala* 120 C2
Puerto Bermejo, *Argentina* 126 B4
Puerto Bermúdez, *Peru* 124 F4
Puerto Bolívar, *Ecuador* 124 D3
Puerto Cabello, *Venezuela* 124 A5
Puerto Cabezas, *Nic.* 120 D3
Puerto Cabo Gracias á Dios, *Nic.* 120 D3
Puerto Carreño, *Colombia* 124 B5
Puerto Castilla, *Honduras* 120 C2
Puerto Chicama, *Peru* 124 E3
Puerto Coig, *Argentina* 128 G3
Puerto Cortés, *Costa Rica* 120 E3
Puerto Cortés, *Honduras* 120 C2
Puerto Cumarebo, *Venezuela* 124 A5
Puerto de Alcudia = Port d'Alcúdia, *Spain* 48 B10
Puerto de Cabrera, *Spain* 48 B9
Puerto de Gran Tarajal, *Canary Is.* 48 F5
Puerto de la Cruz, *Canary Is.* 48 F3
Puerto de los Angeles ⌂, *Mexico* 118 C3
Puerto de Mazarrón, *Spain* 39 H3
Puerto de Pozo Negro, *Canary Is.* 48 F6
Puerto de Sóller = Port de Sóller, *Spain* 48 B9
Puerto de Somosierra, *Spain* 36 D7
Puerto del Carmen, *Canary Is.* 48 F6
Puerto del Rosario, *Canary Is.* 48 F6
Puerto Deseado, *Argentina* 128 F3
Puerto Escondido, *Mexico* 119 D5
Puerto Heath, *Bolivia* 124 F5
Puerto Inírida, *Colombia* 124 C5
Puerto Juárez, *Mexico* 119 C7
Puerto La Cruz, *Venezuela* 124 A6
Puerto Leguízamo, *Colombia* 124 D4
Puerto Limón, *Colombia* 124 C4
Puerto Lobos, *Argentina* 128 E3
Puerto Lumbreras, *Spain* 39 H3
Puerto Madryn, *Argentina* 128 E3
Puerto Maldonado, *Peru* 124 F5
Puerto Manatí, *Cuba* 120 B4
Puerto Montt, *Chile* 128 E2
Puerto Morazán, *Nic.* 120 D2
Puerto Morelos, *Mexico* 119 C7
Puerto Natales, *Chile* 128 G2
Puerto Padre, *Cuba* 120 B4
Puerto Páez, *Venezuela* 124 B5
Puerto Peñasco, *Mexico* 118 A2
Puerto Pinasco, *Paraguay* 126 A4
Puerto Plata, *Dom. Rep.* 121 C5
Puerto Pollensa = Port de Pollença, *Spain* 48 B10
Puerto Princesa, *Phil.* 61 G3
Puerto Quepos, *Costa Rica* 120 E3
Puerto Real, *Spain* 37 J4
Puerto Rico, *Canary Is.* 48 G4
Puerto Rico ☒, *W. Indies* 121 d
Puerto Rico Trench, *Atl. Oc.* 121 C6
Puerto San Julián, *Argentina* 128 F3
Puerto Sastre, *Paraguay* 126 A4
Puerto Serrano, *Spain* 37 J5
Puerto Suárez, *Bolivia* 124 G7
Puerto Vallarta, *Mexico* 118 C3
Puerto Wilches, *Colombia* 124 B4
Puertollano, *Spain* 37 G6
Pueyrredón, L., *Argentina* 128 F2
Púez Odle ⌂, *Italy* 41 B8
Puffin I., *Ireland* 12 E1
Pugachev, *Russia* 34 D9
Pugal, *India* 68 E5
Puge, *China* 58 D4
Puge, *Tanzania* 86 C3
Puget Sound, *U.S.A.* 108 C2
Puget-Théniers, *France* 21 E10
Púglia □, *Italy* 43 A9
Pugŏdong, *N. Korea* 57 C16
Pugu, *Tanzania* 86 D4
Pūgūnzī, *Iran* 71 E8
Pui, *Romania* 28 E8
Puiești, *Romania* 29 D12
Puig Major, *Spain* 48 B9
Puigcerdà, *Spain* 38 C6
Puigmal, *Spain* 38 C7
Puigpunyent, *Spain* 48 B9
Puijiang, *China* 58 B4
Puisaye, Collines de la, *France* 19 E10
Puiseaux, *France* 19 D9
Pujehun, *S. Leone* 82 D2
Pujiang, *China* 59 C12
Pujols, *France* 20 D3
Pujon-chŏsuji, *N. Korea* 57 D14
Pukaki, L., *N.Z.* 91 L3
Pukapuka, *Cook Is.* 97 J11
Pukaskwa △, *Canada* 104 C2
Pukatawagan, *Canada* 103 B8
Pukchin, *N. Korea* 57 D13
Pukch'ŏng, *N. Korea* 57 D15
Pukë, *Albania* 44 D3
Pukekohe, *N.Z.* 91 G5
Pukhrayan, *India* 69 F8
Pukou, *China* 59 A12
Pula, *Croatia* 41 D10
Pula, *Italy* 42 C1
Pulacayo, *Bolivia* 124 H5
Pulai, *Malaysia* 65 d
Pulandian, *China* 57 E11
Pularumpi, *Australia* 92 B5
Pulaski, *N.Y., U.S.A.* 117 C8
Pulaski, *Tenn., U.S.A.* 115 H2
Pulaski, *Va., U.S.A.* 114 G5
Pulau →, *Indonesia* 63 F9
Puławy, *Poland* 31 G8
Pulga, *U.S.A.* 110 F5
Pulicat L., *India* 66 N12
Pullman, *U.S.A.* 108 C5
Pulog, Mt., *Phil.* 61 C4
Pułtusk, *Poland* 31 F8
Pülümür, *Turkey* 73 C8
Pumlumon Fawr, *U.K.* 15 E4
Puná, I., *Ecuador* 124 D2
Punakaiki, *N.Z.* 91 K3
Punakha, *Bhutan* 67 F16
Punasar, *India* 68 F5
Punata, *Bolivia* 124 G5
Punch, *India* 69 C6
Punch →, *Pakistan* 68 C5
Punda Maria, *S. Africa* 89 C5
Pune, *India* 66 K8
P'ungsan, *N. Korea* 57 D15
Pungue, Ponte de, *Mozam.* 87 F3
Puning, *China* 59 F11
Punjab □, *India* 68 D7
Punjab □, *Pakistan* 68 E6
Puno, *Peru* 124 G4
Punpun →, *India* 69 G11
Punta, Cerro de, *Puerto Rico* 121 d
Punta Alta, *Argentina* 128 D4
Punta Arenas, *Chile* 128 G2
Punta de Díaz, *Chile* 126 B1
Punta del Hidalgo, *Canary Is.* 48 F3
Punta Gorda, *Belize* 119 D7
Punta Gorda, *U.S.A.* 115 M5
Punta Prieta, *Mexico* 118 B2
Punta Prima, *Spain* 48 B11

Punta Umbria, *Spain* 37 H4
Puntarenas, *Costa Rica* 120 E3
Punto Fijo, *Venezuela* 124 A4
Punxsatawney, *U.S.A.* 116 F6
Pupuan, *Indonesia* 63 J18
Puqi, *China* 59 C9
Puquio, *Peru* 124 F4
Pur →, *Russia* 52 C8
Puracé, Vol., *Colombia* 124 C3
Puračić, *Bos.-H.* 28 F3
Puralia = Puruliya, *India* 69 H12
Puranpur, *India* 69 E9
Purbeck, Isle of, *U.K.* 15 G5
Purcell, *U.S.A.* 113 H6
Purcell Mts., *Canada* 102 D5
Puri, *India* 67 K14
Purmerend, *Neths.* 17 B4
Purnia, *India* 69 G12
Purnululu △, *Australia* 92 C4
Pursat = Pouthisat, *Cambodia* 64 F4
Purukcahu, *Indonesia* 62 E4
Puruliya, *India* 69 H12
Purus →, *Brazil* 124 D6
Puruvesi, *Finland* 32 B5
Purvis, *U.S.A.* 113 K10
Pŭrvomay, *Bulgaria* 45 D9
Purwa, *India* 69 F9
Purwakarta, *Indonesia* 63 G12
Purwo, Tanjung, *Indonesia* 63 K18
Purwodadi, *Indonesia* 63 G14
Purwokerto, *Indonesia* 63 G13
Puryŏng, *N. Korea* 57 C15
Pusa, *India* 69 G11
Pusan, *S. Korea* 57 G15
Pushkin, *Russia* 32 C6
Pushkino, *Moskva, Russia* 32 D9
Pushkino, *Saratov, Russia* 34 E8
Püspökladány, *Hungary* 28 C6
Pustoshka, *Russia* 32 D5
Puszczykowo, *Poland* 31 F3
Putahow L., *Canada* 103 B8
Putao, *Burma* 67 F20
Putaruru, *N.Z.* 91 H5
Putbus, *Germany* 24 A9
Putian, *China* 59 E12
Putignano, *Italy* 43 B10
Puting, Tanjung, *Indonesia* 62 E4
Putlitz, *Germany* 24 B8
Putna, *Romania* 29 C10
Putna →, *Romania* 29 E12
Putnam, *U.S.A.* 117 E13
Putnok, *Hungary* 28 B5
Putorana, Gory, *Russia* 53 C10
Putrajaya, *Malaysia* 65 L3
Puttalam, *Sri Lanka* 66 Q11
Puttgarden, *Germany* 24 A7
Püttlingen, *Germany* 25 F2
Putumayo →, *S. Amer.* 124 D5
Putuo, *China* 59 C14
Putussibau, *Indonesia* 62 D4
Putyla, *Ukraine* 29 B10
Puvirnituq, *Canada* 101 B12
Puy-de-Dôme, *France* 20 C6
Puy-de-Dôme □, *France* 20 C7
Puy-l'Évêque, *France* 20 D5
Puyallup, *U.S.A.* 110 C4
Puyang, *China* 56 G8
Puylaurens, *France* 20 E6
Pūzeh Rīg, *Iran* 71 E8
Puzhaykove, *Ukraine* 29 B14
Pwani □, *Tanzania* 86 D4
Pweto, *Dem. Rep. of the Congo* 87 D2
Pwllheli, *U.K.* 14 E3
Pyana →, *Russia* 34 C8
Pyapon, *Burma* 67 L19
Pyasina →, *Russia* 53 B9
Pyatigorsk, *Russia* 35 H6
Pyatykhatky, *Ukraine* 33 H7
Pydna, *Greece* 44 F6
Pyè = Prome, *Burma* 67 K19
Pyetrikaw, *Belarus* 33 F5
Pyhäjoki, *Finland* 8 D21
Pyinmana, *Burma* 67 K20
Pyla, C., *Cyprus* 49 E12
Pymatuning Reservoir, *U.S.A.* 116 E4
Pyŏktong, *N. Korea* 57 D13
Pyŏnggang, *N. Korea* 57 E14
P'yŏngt'aek, *S. Korea* 57 F14
P'yŏngyang, *N. Korea* 57 E13
Pyote, *U.S.A.* 113 K3
Pyramid L., *U.S.A.* 108 G4
Pyramid Pk., *U.S.A.* 111 J10
Pyramids, *Egypt* 80 J7
Pyrénées, *Europe* 20 F4
Pyrénées △, *France* 20 F3
Pyrénées-Atlantiques □, *France* 20 E3
Pyrénées-Orientales □, *France* 20 F6
Pyryatyn, *Ukraine* 33 G7
Pyrzyce, *Poland* 31 E1
Pyskowice, *Poland* 31 H5
Pytalovo, *Russia* 32 D4
Pyu, *Burma* 67 K20
Pyzdry, *Poland* 31 F4

Q

Qaanaaq, *Greenland* 4 B4
Qabirri →, *Azerbaijan* 35 K8
Qachasnek, *S. Africa* 89 E4
Qa'el Jafr, *Jordan* 74 E5
Qa'emābād, *Iran* 71 D9
Qā'emshahr, *Iran* 71 B7
Qagan Nur, *China* 56 C8
Qahar Youyi Zhongqi, *China* 56 D7
Qahremānshahr = Bākhtarān, *Iran* 70 C5
Qaidam Pendi, *China* 60 C4
Qajarīyeh, *Iran* 71 D6
Qala, Ras il, *Malta* 49 C1
Qala-i-Jadid = Spīn Būldak, *Afghan.* 68 D2
Qala Point = Qala, Ras il, *Malta* 49 C1
Qala Viala, *Pakistan* 68 D2
Qala Yangi, *Afghan.* 68 B2
Qal'at al Akhḑar, *Si. Arabia* 70 E3
Qal'at Dīzah, *Iraq* 70 B5
Qal'at Şāliḩ, *Iraq* 70 D5
Qal'at Sukkar, *Iraq* 70 D5
Qalyûb, *Egypt* 80 H7
Qamani'tuaq = Baker Lake, *Canada* 100 B10
Qamdo, *China* 58 B1
Qamruddin Karez, *Pakistan* 68 D3
Qandahār, *Afghan.* 66 D4
Qandahār □, *Afghan.* 66 D4
Qapān, *Iran* 71 B7
Qapshaghay, *Kazakhstan* 52 E8
Qaqortoq, *Greenland* 101 B6
Qâra, *Egypt* 80 B2
Qara Qash →, *China* 69 B8
Qarabutaq, *Kazakhstan* 52 E7
Qaraçala, *Azerbaijan* 35 L9
Qaraghandy, *Kazakhstan* 52 E8
Qaraghayly, *Kazakhstan* 52 E8
Qārah, *Si. Arabia* 70 D4
Qarataū, *Kazakhstan* 52 E8
Qarataū, *Kazakhstan* 52 E7
Qardho = Gardo, *Somali Rep.* 75 F4
Qardud, *Sudan* 81 E2
Qareh →, *Iran* 70 B5
Qareh Tekān, *Iran* 71 B6
Qarqan He →, *China* 60 C3
Qarqaraly, *Kazakhstan* 52 E8
Qarrasa, *Sudan* 81 E3
Qarshi, *Uzbekistan* 52 F7
Qartabā, *Lebanon* 74 A4
Qaryat al Gharab, *Iraq* 70 D5
Qaryat al 'Ulyā, *Si. Arabia* 70 E5
Qasr 'Amra, *Jordan* 70 D3
Qaşr-e Qand, *Iran* 71 E9
Qasr Farâfra, *Egypt* 80 B2
Qatanā, *Syria* 74 B5
Qatar ■, *Asia* 71 E6
Qatlīsh, *Iran* 71 B8
Qattâra, *Egypt* 80 A2
Qattâra, Munkhafed el, *Egypt* 80 B2
Qattâra Depression = Qattâra, Munkhafed el, *Egypt* 80 B2
Qawām al Ḩamzah = Al Ḩamzah, *Iraq* 70 D5
Qāyen, *Iran* 71 C8
Qazaqstan = Kazakhstan ■, *Asia* 52 E7
Qazimämmäd, *Azerbaijan* 35 K9
Qazvin, *Iran* 71 B6
Qazvin □, *Iran* 71 B6
Qeissan, *Sudan* 81 E3
Qena, *Egypt* 80 B3
Qena, W. →, *Egypt* 80 B3
Qeqertarsuaq, *Greenland* 101 B5
Qeqertarsuaq, *Greenland* 101 B14
Qeshlāq, *Iran* 70 C5
Qeshm, *Iran* 71 E8
Qeys, *Iran* 71 E7
Qezel Owzen →, *Iran* 71 B6
Qezi'ot, *Israel* 74 E3
Qi Xian, *China* 56 G8
Qian Gorlos, *China* 57 B13
Qian Xian, *China* 56 G5
Qiancheng, *China* 58 D7
Qianjiang, *Guangxi Zhuangzu, China* 58 F7
Qianjiang, *Hubei, China* 59 B9
Qianjiang, *Sichuan, China* 58 C7
Qianshan, *China* 59 B11
Qianwei, *China* 58 C4
Qianxi, *China* 58 D6
Qianyang, *Hunan, China* 59 D8
Qianyang, *Shaanxi, China* 56 G4
Qianyang, *Zhejiang, China* 59 B12
Qiaojia, *China* 58 D4
Qichun, *China* 59 B10
Qidong, *Hunan, China* 59 D9
Qidong, *Jiangsu, China* 59 B13
Qijiang, *China* 58 C6
Qikiqtarjuaq, *Canada* 101 B13
Qila Safed, *Pakistan* 66 E2
Qila Saifullāh, *Pakistan* 68 D3
Qilian Shan, *China* 60 C4
Qimen, *China* 59 C11
Qin He →, *China* 56 G7
Qin Jiang →, *Guangxi Zhuangzu, China* 58 F7
Qin Jiang →, *Jiangxi, China* 59 D10
Qin Ling = Qinling Shandi, *China* 56 H5
Qin'an, *China* 56 G3
Qing Xian, *China* 56 E9
Qingcheng, *China* 57 F9
Qingdao, *China* 57 F11
Qingfeng, *China* 56 G8
Qinghai □, *China* 60 C4
Qinghai Hu, *China* 60 C5
Qinghecheng, *China* 57 D13
Qinghemen, *China* 57 D11
Qingjian, *China* 56 F6
Qingjiang = Huaiyin, *China* 57 H10
Qingliu, *China* 59 D11
Qinglong, *China* 58 E5
Qingping, *China* 58 D6
Qingpu, *China* 59 B13
Qingshui, *China* 56 G4
Qingshuihe, *China* 56 E6
Qingtian, *China* 59 C13
Qingtongxia Shuiku, *China* 56 F3
Qingxi, *China* 58 D7
Qingxu, *China* 56 F7
Qingyang, *Anhui, China* 59 B11
Qingyang, *Gansu, China* 56 F4
Qingyi Jiang →, *China* 58 C4
Qingyuan, *Guangdong, China* 59 F9
Qingyuan, *Liaoning, China* 57 C13
Qingyuan, *Zhejiang, China* 59 D12
Qingyun, *China* 57 F9
Qingzhen, *China* 58 D6
Qinhuangdao, *China* 57 E10
Qinling Shandi, *China* 56 H5
Qinshui, *China* 56 G7
Qinyang = Jiyuan, *China* 56 G7
Qinyuan, *China* 56 F7
Qinzhou, *China* 58 G7
Qionghai, *China* 64 C8
Qionglai, *China* 58 B4
Qionglai Shan, *China* 58 B4
Qiongzhou Haixia, *China* 64 B8
Qiqihar, *China* 53 E13
Qiraîya, W. →, *Egypt* 74 E3
Qiryat Ata, *Israel* 74 C4
Qiryat Gat, *Israel* 74 D3
Qiryat Mal'akhi, *Israel* 74 D3
Qiryat Shemona, *Israel* 74 B4
Qiryat Yam, *Israel* 74 C4
Qishan, *China* 56 G4
Qitai, *China* 60 B3
Qiubei, *China* 58 E5
Qixia, *China* 57 F11
Qiyang, *China* 59 D8
Qızılağac Körfäzi, *Azerbaijan* 71 B6
Qojūr, *Iran* 70 B5
Qom, *Iran* 71 C6
Qom □, *Iran* 71 C6
Qomolangma Feng = Everest, Mt., *Nepal* 69 E12
Qomsheh, *Iran* 71 D6
Qoraqalpoghistan □, *Uzbekistan* 52 E6
Qorveh, *Iran* 73 E12
Qostanay, *Kazakhstan* 52 D7
Qoṭūr, *Iran* 73 C11
Qu Jiang →, *China* 58 B6
Qu Xian, *China* 58 B6
Quabbin Reservoir, *U.S.A.* 117 D12
Quairading, *Australia* 93 F2
Quakenbrück, *Germany* 24 C3
Quakertown, *U.S.A.* 117 F9
Qualicum Beach, *Canada* 102 D4
Quambatook, *Australia* 95 F3
Quambone, *Australia* 95 E4
Quamby, *Australia* 94 C3
Quan Long = Ca Mau, *Vietnam* 65 H5
Quanah, *U.S.A.* 113 H5
Quang Ngai, *Vietnam* 64 E7
Quang Tri, *Vietnam* 64 D6
Quang Yen, *Vietnam* 58 G6
Quannan, *China* 59 E10
Quantock Hills, *U.K.* 15 F4
Quanzhou, *Fujian, China* 59 E12
Quanzhou, *Guangxi Zhuangzu, China* 59 E8
Qu'Appelle, *Canada* 103 C8
Quaqtaq, *Canada* 101 B13
Quaraí, *Brazil* 126 C4
Quarré-les-Tombes, *France* 19 E11
Quarteira, *Portugal* 37 H2
Quartu Sant'Élena, *Italy* 42 C2
Quartzsite, *U.S.A.* 111 M12
Quatsino Sd., *Canada* 102 C3
Quba, *Azerbaijan* 35 K9
Qūchān, *Iran* 71 B8
Queanbeyan, *Australia* 95 F4
Québec, *Canada* 105 C5
Québec □, *Canada* 105 C6
Quebrada del Condorito △, *Argentina* 126 C3
Quedlinburg, *Germany* 24 D7
Queen Alexandra Ra., *Antarctica* 5 E11
Queen Charlotte City, *Canada* 102 C2
Queen Charlotte Is., *Canada* 102 C2
Queen Charlotte Sd., *Canada* 102 C3
Queen Charlotte Strait, *Canada* 102 C3
Queen Elizabeth ⌂, *U.K.* 13 E4
Queen Elizabeth △, *Uganda* 86 C3
Queen Elizabeth Is., *Canada* 98 B10
Queen Mary Land, *Antarctica* 5 D7
Queen Maud G., *Canada* 100 B9
Queen Maud Land = Dronning Maud Land, *Antarctica* 5 D3
Queen Maud Mts., *Antarctica* 5 E13
Queens Chan., *Australia* 92 C4
Queenscliff, *Australia* 95 F3
Queensland □, *Australia* 94 C3
Queenstown, *Australia* 95 G4
Queenstown, *N.Z.* 91 L2
Queenstown, *Singapore* 65 d
Queenstown, *S. Africa* 88 E4
Queets, *U.S.A.* 110 C2
Queguay Grande →, *Uruguay* 126 C4
Queimadas, *Brazil* 125 F11
Quelimane, *Mozam.* 87 F4
Quellón, *Chile* 128 E2
Quelpart = Cheju do, *S. Korea* 57 H14
Queluz, *Portugal* 37 G1
Quemado, *N. Mex., U.S.A.* 109 J9
Quemado, *Tex., U.S.A.* 113 L4
Quemoy = Chinmen, *Taiwan* 59 E13
Quemú-Quemú, *Argentina* 126 D3
Quequén, *Argentina* 126 D4
Querétaro, *Mexico* 118 C4
Querétaro □, *Mexico* 118 C5
Querfurt, *Germany* 24 D7
Quérigut, *France* 20 F6
Querqueville, *France* 18 C5
Quesada, *Spain* 37 H7
Queshan, *China* 56 H8
Quesnel, *Canada* 102 C4
Quesnel →, *Canada* 102 C4
Quesnel L., *Canada* 102 C4
Questa, *U.S.A.* 109 H11
Questembert, *France* 18 E4
Quetico ⌂, *Canada* 104 C1
Quetta, *Pakistan* 68 D2
Queyras ⌂, *France* 21 D10
Quezaltenango, *Guatemala* 120 D1
Quezon City, *Phil.* 61 D4
Qufār, *Si. Arabia* 70 E4
Qui Nhon, *Vietnam* 64 F7
Quibaxe, *Angola* 84 F2
Quibdo, *Colombia* 124 B3
Quiberon, *France* 18 E3
Quiberon, Presqu'île de, *France* 18 E3
Quickborn, *Germany* 24 B5
Quiet L., *Canada* 102 A2
Quiindy, *Paraguay* 126 B4
Quila, *Mexico* 118 C3
Quilán, C., *Chile* 128 E2
Quilcene, *U.S.A.* 110 C4
Quilimarí, *Chile* 126 C1
Quilino, *Argentina* 126 C3
Quill Lakes, *Canada* 103 C8
Quillabamba, *Peru* 124 F4
Quillagua, *Chile* 126 A2
Quillaicillo, *Chile* 126 C1
Quillan, *France* 20 F6
Quillota, *Chile* 126 C1
Quilmes, *Argentina* 126 C4
Quilon, *India* 66 Q10
Quilpie, *Australia* 95 D3
Quilpué, *Chile* 126 C1
Quilua, *Mozam.* 87 F4
Quimilí, *Argentina* 126 B3
Quimper, *France* 18 E2
Quimperlé, *France* 18 E3
Quinault →, *U.S.A.* 110 C2
Quincy, *Calif., U.S.A.* 110 F6
Quincy, *Fla., U.S.A.* 115 K3
Quincy, *Ill., U.S.A.* 112 F9
Quincy, *Mass., U.S.A.* 117 D14
Quincy, *Wash., U.S.A.* 108 C4
Quines, *Argentina* 126 C2
Quinga, *Mozam.* 87 F5
Quingey, *France* 19 E12
Quintana de la Serena, *Spain* 37 G5
Quintana Roo □, *Mexico* 119 D7
Quintanar de la Orden, *Spain* 37 F7
Quintanar de la Sierra, *Spain* 38 D2
Quintanar del Rey, *Spain* 39 F3
Quinte West, *Canada* 116 B7
Quintero, *Chile* 126 C1
Quintin, *France* 18 D4
Quinto, *Spain* 38 D4
Quípar →, *Spain* 39 G3
Quirihue, *Chile* 126 D1
Quirindi, *Australia* 95 E5
Quirinópolis, *Brazil* 125 G8
Quiroga, *Spain* 36 C3
Quissac, *France* 21 E8
Quissanga, *Mozam.* 87 E5
Quissico, *Mozam.* 89 C5
Quitilipi, *Argentina* 126 B3
Quitman, *U.S.A.* 115 K4
Quito, *Ecuador* 124 D3
Quixadá, *Brazil* 125 D11
Quixaxe, *Mozam.* 87 F5
Qujing, *China* 58 E4
Qulan, *Kazakhstan* 52 E8
Qul'ân, Jazâ'ir, *Egypt* 70 E2
Qumbu, *S. Africa* 89 E4
Quneitra, *Syria* 74 B4
Qŭnghirot, *Uzbekistan* 52 E6
Qu'nyido, *China* 58 B2
Quoin I., *Australia* 92 B4
Quoin Pt., *S. Africa* 88 E2
Quorn, *Australia* 95 E2
Qŭqon, *Uzbekistan* 52 E8
Qurein, *Sudan* 81 E3
Qurnat as Sawdā', *Lebanon* 74 A5
Qûs, *Egypt* 80 B3
Qusar, *Azerbaijan* 35 K9
Quşaybā', *Si. Arabia* 70 E4
Qusaybah, *Iraq* 70 C4
Quseir, *Egypt* 70 E2
Qūshchī, *Iran* 70 B5
Quthing, *Lesotho* 89 E4
Qūṭīābād, *Iran* 71 C6
Quwo, *China* 56 G6
Quyang, *China* 56 E8
Quynh Nhai, *Vietnam* 64 B4
Quyon, *Canada* 117 A8
Quzhou, *China* 59 C12
Quzi, *China* 56 F4
Qvareli, *Georgia* 35 K7
Qyzylorda, *Kazakhstan* 52 E7

R

Ra, Ko, *Thailand* 65 H2
Raab, *Austria* 26 C6
Raahe, *Finland* 8 D21
Raalte, *Neths.* 17 B6
Raasay, *U.K.* 13 D2
Raasay, Sd. of, *U.K.* 13 D2
Rab, *Croatia* 41 D11
Raba, *Indonesia* 63 F5
Rába →, *Hungary* 28 C2
Raba →, *Poland* 31 H7
Rabaçal →, *Portugal* 36 D3
Rabah, *Nigeria* 83 C6
Rabai, *Kenya* 86 C4
Rabak, *Sudan* 81 E3
Rabastens, *France* 20 E5
Rabastens-de-Bigorre, *France* 20 E4
Rabat = Victoria, *Malta* 49 C1
Rabat, *Malta* 49 D1
Rabat, *Morocco* 78 B4
Rabaul, *Papua N. G.* 96 H7
Rābigh, *Si. Arabia* 75 C2
Rabka, *Poland* 31 J6
Râbniţa, *Moldova* 29 C14
Rābor, *Iran* 71 D8
Rača, *Serbia & M.* 44 B4
Răcăciuni, *Romania* 29 D11
Răcăşdia, *Romania* 28 F6
Racconigi, *Italy* 40 D4
Race, C., *Canada* 105 C9
Rach Gia, *Vietnam* 65 G5
Rachid, *Mauritania* 82 B2
Raciąż, *Poland* 31 F7
Racibórz, *Poland* 31 H5
Racichy, *Belarus* 30 E10
Racine, *U.S.A.* 114 D2
Rackerby, *U.S.A.* 110 F5
Radama, Nosy, *Madag.* 89 A8
Radama, Saikanosy, *Madag.* 89 A8
Radan, *Serbia & M.* 44 D5
Rădăuţi, *Romania* 29 C10
Rădăuţi-Prut, *Romania* 29 B11
Radbuza →, *Czech Rep.* 26 B6
Radcliff, *U.S.A.* 114 G3
Radeberg, *Germany* 24 D9
Radebeul, *Germany* 24 D9
Radeče, *Slovenia* 41 B12
Radekhiv, *Ukraine* 33 G3
Radekhov = Radekhiv, *Ukraine* 33 G3
Radenthein, *Austria* 26 E6
Radew →, *Poland* 30 D2
Radford, *U.S.A.* 114 G5
Radhanpur, *India* 68 H4
Radhwa, Jabal, *Si. Arabia* 70 E3
Radika →, *Macedonia* 44 E4
Radisson, *Qué., Canada* 104 B4
Radisson, *Sask., Canada* 103 C7
Radium Hot Springs, *Canada* 102 C5
Radlje ob Dravi, *Slovenia* 41 B12
Radnevo, *Bulgaria* 45 D9
Radnice, *Czech Rep.* 26 B6
Radnor Forest, *U.K.* 15 E4
Radolfzell, *Germany* 25 H4
Radom, *Poland* 31 G8
Radomir, *Bulgaria* 44 D6
Radomka →, *Poland* 31 G8
Radomsko, *Poland* 31 G6
Radomyshl, *Ukraine* 33 G5
Radomyśl Wielki, *Poland* 31 H8
Radoszyce, *Poland* 31 G7
Radoviš, *Macedonia* 44 E6
Radovljica, *Slovenia* 41 B11
Radstadt, *Austria* 26 D6
Radstock, C., *Australia* 95 E1
Răducăneni, *Romania* 29 D12
Raduša, *Macedonia* 44 D5
Radvanichy, *Belarus* 31 F11
Radviliškis, *Lithuania* 9 J20
Radville, *Canada* 103 D8
Raḑwá, J., *Si. Arabia* 80 C4
Radymno, *Poland* 31 J9
Radzanów, *Poland* 31 F7
Radziejów, *Poland* 31 F5
Radzyń Chełmiński, *Poland* 30 E5
Radzyń Podlaski, *Poland* 31 G9
Rae, *Canada* 102 A5
Rae Bareli, *India* 69 F9
Rae Isthmus, *Canada* 101 B11
Raeren, *Belgium* 17 D6
Raeside, L., *Australia* 93 E3
Raetihi, *N.Z.* 91 H5
Rafaela, *Argentina* 126 C3
Rafah, *Gaza Strip* 74 D3
Rafai, *C.A.R.* 86 B1
Raffadali, *Italy* 42 E6
Raffili, *Sudan* 81 F2
Rafḩā, *Si. Arabia* 70 D4
Rafsanjān, *Iran* 71 D8
Raft Pt., *Australia* 92 C3
Râgâ, *Sudan* 81 F2
Raga →, *Sudan* 81 F2
Ragachow, *Belarus* 33 F6
Ragag, *Sudan* 81 E1
Ragama, *Sri Lanka* 66 R11
Ragged, Mt., *Australia* 93 F3
Ragged Pt., *Barbados* 121 g
Raghunathpalli, *India* 69 H11
Raghunathpur, *India* 69 H12
Raglan, *N.Z.* 91 G5
Ragusa, *Italy* 43 F7
Raha, *Indonesia* 63 E6
Rahad, Nahr ed →, *Sudan* 81 E3
Rahaeng = Tak, *Thailand* 64 D2
Rahatgarh, *India* 69 H8
Rahden, *Germany* 24 C4
Raheita, *Eritrea* 81 E5
Rahimyar Khan, *Pakistan* 68 E4
Rāhjerd, *Iran* 71 C6
Rahole ⌂, *Kenya* 86 B4
Rahon, *India* 68 D7
Raichur, *India* 66 L10
Raiganj, *India* 69 G13
Raigarh, *India* 67 J13
Raijua, *Indonesia* 63 F6
Raikot, *India* 68 D6
Railton, *Australia* 95 G4
Rainbow Bridge ⌂, *U.S.A.* 109 H8
Rainbow Lake, *Canada* 102 B5
Rainier, *U.S.A.* 110 D4
Rainier, Mt., *U.S.A.* 110 D5
Rainy L., *Canada* 103 D10
Rainy River, *Canada* 103 D10
Raippaluoto, *Finland* 8 E19
Raipur, *India* 67 J12
Ra'is, *Si. Arabia* 80 C4
Raisen, *India* 68 H8
Raisio, *Finland* 9 F20
Raj Nandgaon, *India* 67 J12
Raj Nilgiri, *India* 69 J12
Raja, Ujung, *Indonesia* 62 D1
Raja Ampat, Kepulauan, *Indonesia* 63 E7
Rajahmundry, *India* 67 L12
Rajang →, *Malaysia* 62 D4
Rajanpur, *Pakistan* 68 E4
Rajapalaiyam, *India* 66 Q10
Rajasthan □, *India* 68 F5
Rajasthan Canal = Indira Gandhi Canal, *India* 68 F5

Rajauri, *India* 69 C6
Rajgarh, *Mad. P., India* 68 G7
Rajgarh, *Raj., India* 68 F7
Rajgarh, *Raj., India* 68 E6
Rajgir, *India* 69 G11
Rajgród, *Poland* 30 E9
Rajkot, *India* 68 H4
Rajmahal Hills, *India* 69 G12
Rajpipla, *India* 66 J8
Rajpur, *India* 68 H6
Rajpura, *India* 68 D7
Rajshahi, *Bangla.* 67 G16
Rajshahi □, *Bangla.* 69 G13
Rajula, *India* 68 J4
Rakaia, *N.Z.* 91 K4
Rakaia →, *N.Z.* 91 K4
Rakan, Ra's, *Qatar* 71 E6
Rakaposhi, *Pakistan* 69 A6
Rakata, Pulau, *Indonesia* 62 F3
Rakhiv, *Ukraine* 29 B9
Rakhni, *Pakistan* 68 D3
Rakhni →, *Pakistan* 68 E3
Rakhny-Lisovi, *Ukraine* 29 B13
Rakitnoye, *Russia* 54 B7
Rakitovo, *Bulgaria* 45 E8
Rakiura △, *N.Z.* 91 M1
Rakoniewice, *Poland* 31 F3
Rakops, *Botswana* 88 C3
Rakovica, *Croatia* 41 D12
Rakovník, *Czech Rep.* 26 A6
Rakovski, *Bulgaria* 45 D8
Rakvere, *Estonia* 9 G22
Raleigh, *U.S.A.* 115 H6
Ralja, *Serbia & M.* 44 B4
Ralls, *U.S.A.* 113 J4
Ralston, *U.S.A.* 116 E8
Ram →, *Canada* 102 A4
Rām Allāh, *West Bank* 74 D4
Rama, *Nic.* 120 D3
Ramacca, *Italy* 43 E7
Ramakona, *India* 69 J8
Ramales de la Victoria, *Spain* 36 B7
Rāmallāh = Rām Allāh, *West Bank* 74 D4
Raman, *Thailand* 65 J3
Ramanathapuram, *India* 66 Q11
Ramanetaka, B. de, *Madag.* 89 A8
Ramanujganj, *India* 69 H10
Ramat Gan, *Israel* 74 C3
Ramatlhabama, *S. Africa* 88 D4
Ramban, *India* 69 C6
Rambervillers, *France* 19 D13
Rambipuji, *Indonesia* 63 H15
Rambouillet, *France* 19 D8
Rame Hd., *Australia* 95 F4
Ramechhap, *Nepal* 69 F12
Ramenskoye, *Russia* 32 E10
Ramganga →, *India* 69 F8
Ramgarh, *Jharkhand, India* 69 H11
Ramgarh, *Raj., India* 68 F6
Ramgarh, *Raj., India* 68 F4
Rāmhormoz, *Iran* 71 D6
Ramīān, *Iran* 71 B7
Ramingining, *Australia* 94 A2
Ramla, *Israel* 74 D3
Ramlu, *Eritrea* 81 E5
Ramm = Rum, *Jordan* 74 F4
Ramm, Jabal, *Jordan* 74 F4
Râmna →, *Romania* 29 E12
Ramnad = Ramanathapuram, *India* 66 Q11
Ramnagar, *Jammu & Kashmir, India* 69 C6
Ramnagar, *Uttaranchal, India* 69 E8
Ramnäs, *Sweden* 10 E10
Râmnicu Sărat, *Romania* 29 E12
Râmnicu Vâlcea, *Romania* 29 E9
Ramon, *Russia* 33 G10
Ramona, *U.S.A.* 111 M10
Ramonville-St-Agne, *France* 20 E5
Ramore, *Canada* 104 C3
Ramos →, *Nigeria* 83 D6
Ramotswa, *Botswana* 88 C4
Rampur, *H.P., India* 68 D7
Rampur, *Mad. P., India* 68 H5
Rampur, *Ut. P., India* 69 E8
Rampur Hat, *India* 69 G12
Rampura, *India* 68 G6
Ramrama Tola, *India* 69 J8
Ramree I., *Burma* 67 K19
Rāmsar, *Iran* 71 B6
Ramsey, *I. of Man* 14 C3
Ramsey, *U.S.A.* 117 E10
Ramsey L., *Canada* 104 C3
Ramsgate, *U.K.* 15 F9
Ramsjö, *Sweden* 10 B9
Ramstein, *Germany* 25 F3
Ramtek, *India* 66 J11
Ramvik, *Sweden* 10 B11
Rana Pratap Sagar Dam, *India* 68 G6
Ranaghat, *India* 69 H13
Ranahu, *Pakistan* 68 G3
Ranau, *Malaysia* 62 C5
Rancagua, *Chile* 126 C1
Rance →, *France* 18 D5
Rancheria →, *Canada* 102 A3
Ranchester, *U.S.A.* 108 D10
Ranchi, *India* 69 H11
Rancho Cucamonga, *U.S.A.* 111 L9
Randalstown, *U.K.* 12 B5
Randan, *France* 19 F10
Randazzo, *Italy* 43 E7
Randers, *Denmark* 11 H4
Randers Fjord, *Denmark* 11 H4
Randfontein, *S. Africa* 89 D4
Randle, *U.S.A.* 110 D5
Randolph, *Mass., U.S.A.* 117 D13
Randolph, *N.Y., U.S.A.* 116 D6
Randolph, *Utah, U.S.A.* 108 F8
Randolph, *Vt., U.S.A.* 117 C12
Randsburg, *U.S.A.* 111 K9
Râneälven →, *Sweden* 8 D20
Rangae, *Thailand* 65 J3
Rangaunu B., *N.Z.* 91 F4
Rangeley, *U.S.A.* 117 B14
Rangeley L., *U.S.A.* 117 B14
Rangely, *U.S.A.* 108 F9
Ranger, *U.S.A.* 113 J5
Rangia, *India* 67 F17
Rangiora, *N.Z.* 91 K4
Rangitaiki →, *N.Z.* 91 G6
Rangitata →, *N.Z.* 91 K3
Rangitoto ke te tonga = D'Urville I., *N.Z.* 91 J4
Rangkasbitung, *Indonesia* 63 G12
Rangon →, *Burma* 67 L20
Rangoon, *Burma* 67 L20
Rangpur, *Bangla.* 67 G16
Rangsit, *Thailand* 64 F3
Ranibennur, *India* 66 M9
Raniganj, *Ut. P., India* 69 F9
Raniganj, *W. Bengal, India* 67 H15
Ranikhet, *India* 69 E8
Raniwara, *India* 66 G8
Rāniyah, *Iraq* 70 B5
Ranka, *India* 69 H10
Ranken →, *Australia* 94 C2
Rankin, *U.S.A.* 113 K4
Rankin Inlet, *Canada* 100 B10
Rankins Springs, *Australia* 95 E4
Rankweil, *Austria* 26 D2
Rannoch, L., *U.K.* 13 E4
Rannoch Moor, *U.K.* 13 E4
Ranobe, Helodranon' i, *Madag.* 89 C7
Ranohira, *Madag.* 89 C8
Ranomafana, *Toamasina, Madag.* 89 B8
Ranomafana, *Toliara, Madag.* 89 C8
Ranomafana △, *Madag.* 89 C8
Ranomena, *Madag.* 89 C8
Ranong, *Thailand* 65 H2
Ranotsara Nord, *Madag.* 89 C8
Rānsa, *Iran* 71 C6
Ransiki, *Indonesia* 63 E8
Rantabe, *Madag.* 89 B8
Rantauprapat, *Indonesia* 62 D1
Rantemario, *Indonesia* 63 E5
Rantoul, *U.S.A.* 114 E1
Ranum, *Denmark* 11 H3
Ranyah, W. →, *Si. Arabia* 80 C5
Raon l'Étape, *France* 19 D13
Raoping, *China* 59 F11
Raoyang, *China* 56 E8
Rap, Ko, *Thailand* 65 b
Rapa, *French Polynesia* 97 K13
Rapa Nui = Pascua, I. de, *Chile* 97 K17
Rapallo, *Italy* 40 D6
Rapar, *India* 68 H4
Rāpch, *Iran* 71 E8
Raper, C., *Canada* 101 B13
Rapid City, *U.S.A.* 112 D3
Rapid River, *U.S.A.* 114 C2
Rapla, *Estonia* 9 G21
Rapti →, *India* 69 F10
Rapu Rapu I., *Phil.* 61 E6
Raqaba ez Zarqa →, *Sudan* 81 F2
Raquette →, *U.S.A.* 117 B10
Raquette Lake, *U.S.A.* 117 C10
Rarotonga, *Cook Is.* 97 K12
Ra's al 'Ayn, *Syria* 70 B4
Ra's al Khaymah, *U.A.E.* 71 E7
Râs el Mâ, *Mali* 82 B4
Râs Ghârib, *Egypt* 80 B3
Râs Mallap, *Egypt* 80 B3
Râs Muhammad △, *Egypt* 80 B3
Rasca, Pta. de la, *Canary Is.* 48 G3
Răşcani, *Moldova* 29 C12
Raseiniai, *Lithuania* 9 J20
Rashad, *Sudan* 81 E3
Rashîd, *Egypt* 80 H7
Rashîd, Masabb, *Egypt* 80 H7
Rashmi, *India* 68 G6
Rasht, *Iran* 71 B6
Rasi Salai, *Thailand* 64 E5
Raška, *Serbia & M.* 44 C4
Râsnov, *Romania* 29 E10
Rason L., *Australia* 93 E3
Raşova, *Romania* 29 F12
Rasovo, *Bulgaria* 44 C7
Rasra, *India* 69 G10
Rasskazovo, *Russia* 34 D5
Rast, *Romania* 29 G8
Rastatt, *Germany* 25 G4
Rastede, *Germany* 24 B4
Răstoliţa, *Romania* 29 D9
Rasul, *Pakistan* 68 C5
Raszków, *Poland* 31 G4
Rat Buri, *Thailand* 64 F2
Rat Islands, *U.S.A.* 100 C1
Rat L., *Canada* 103 B9
Rätan, *Sweden* 10 B8
Ratangarh, *India* 68 E6
Raţāwī, *Iraq* 70 D5
Rath, *India* 69 G8
Rath Luirc, *Ireland* 12 D3
Rathdrum, *Ireland* 12 D5
Rathenow, *Germany* 24 C8
Rathkeale, *Ireland* 12 D3
Rathlin I., *U.K.* 12 A5
Rathmelton, *Ireland* 12 A4
Ratibor = Racibórz, *Poland* 31 H5
Rätikon, *Austria* 26 D2
Ratingen, *Germany* 24 D2
Ratlam, *India* 68 H6
Ratnagiri, *India* 66 L8
Ratodero, *Pakistan* 68 F3
Raton, *U.S.A.* 113 G2
Rattaphum, *Thailand* 65 J3
Ratten, *Austria* 26 D8
Rattray Hd., *U.K.* 13 D7
Rättvik, *Sweden* 10 D9
Ratz, Mt., *Canada* 102 B2
Ratzeburg, *Germany* 24 B6
Raub, *Malaysia* 65 L3
Rauch, *Argentina* 126 D4
Raudales de Malpaso, *Mexico* 119 D6
Raufarhöfn, *Iceland* 8 C6
Raufoss, *Norway* 9 F14
Raukumara Ra., *N.Z.* 91 H6
Rauma, *Finland* 9 F19
Raumo = Rauma, *Finland* 9 F19
Raung, Gunung, *Indonesia* 63 J17
Raurkela, *India* 69 H11
Rausu-Dake, *Japan* 54 B12
Răut →, *Moldova* 29 C14
Rava-Ruska, *Ukraine* 31 H10
Rava Russkaya = Rava-Ruska, *Ukraine* 31 H10
Ravalli, *U.S.A.* 108 C6
Ravānsar, *Iran* 70 C5
Ravanusa, *Italy* 42 E6
Rāvar, *Iran* 71 D8
Ravena, *U.S.A.* 117 D11
Ravenna, *Italy* 41 D9
Ravenna, *Nebr., U.S.A.* 112 E5
Ravenna, *Ohio, U.S.A.* 116 E3
Ravensburg, *Germany* 25 H5
Ravenshoe, *Australia* 94 B4
Ravensthorpe, *Australia* 93 F3
Ravenswood, *Australia* 94 C4
Ravenswood, *U.S.A.* 114 F5
Ravi →, *Pakistan* 68 D4
Ravna Gora, *Croatia* 41 C11
Ravna Reka, *Serbia & M.* 44 B5
Ravne na Koroškem, *Slovenia* 41 B11
Rawa Mazowiecka, *Poland* 31 G7
Rawalpindi, *Pakistan* 68 C5
Rawāndūz, *Iraq* 70 B5
Rawang, *Malaysia* 65 L3
Rawene, *N.Z.* 91 F4
Rawicz, *Poland* 31 G3
Rawka →, *Poland* 31 F7
Rawlinna, *Australia* 93 F4
Rawlins, *U.S.A.* 108 F10
Rawlinson Ra., *Australia* 93 D4
Rawson, *Argentina* 128 E3
Raxaul, *India* 69 F11
Ray, *U.S.A.* 112 A3
Ray, C., *Canada* 105 C8
Raya Ring, Ko, *Thailand* 65 a
Rayadurg, *India* 66 M10
Rayagada, *India* 67 K13
Raychikhinsk, *Russia* 53 E13
Rāyen, *Iran* 71 D8
Rayleigh, *U.K.* 15 F8
Raymond, *Canada* 102 D6
Raymond, *Calif., U.S.A.* 110 H7
Raymond, *N.H., U.S.A.* 117 C13
Raymond, *Wash., U.S.A.* 110 D3
Raymondville, *U.S.A.* 113 M6
Raymore, *Canada* 103 C8
Rayón, *Mexico* 118 B2
Rayong, *Thailand* 64 F3
Rayville, *U.S.A.* 113 J9
Raz, Pte. du, *France* 18 D2
Razan, *Iran* 71 C6
Ražana, *Serbia & M.* 44 B3
Ražanj, *Serbia & M.* 44 C5
Razāzah, Buḩayrat ar, *Iraq* 70 C4
Razazah, L. = Razāzah, Buḩayrat ar, *Iraq* 70 C4
Razdelna, *Bulgaria* 45 C11
Razdel'naya = Rozdilna, *Ukraine* 29 D15
Razdolnoye, *Russia* 54 C5
Razdolnoye, *Ukraine* 33 K7
Razeh, *Iran* 71 C6
Razgrad, *Bulgaria* 45 C10
Razim, Lacul, *Romania* 29 F14
Razlog, *Bulgaria* 44 E7
Razmak, *Pakistan* 68 C3
Ré, Î. de, *France* 20 B2
Reading, *U.K.* 15 F7
Reading, *U.S.A.* 117 F9
Reading □, *U.K.* 15 F7
Realicó, *Argentina* 126 D3
Réalmont, *France* 20 E6
Ream, *Cambodia* 65 G4
Reata, *Mexico* 118 B4
Reay Forest, *U.K.* 13 C4
Rebais, *France* 19 D10
Rebi, *Indonesia* 63 F8
Rebiana, *Libya* 79 D10
Rebiana, Sahrâ', *Libya* 79 D10
Rebun-Tō, *Japan* 54 B10
Recanati, *Italy* 41 E10
Recaş, *Romania* 28 E6
Recco, *Italy* 40 D6
Recherche, Arch. of the, *Australia* 93 F3
Rechna Doab, *Pakistan* 68 D5
Rechytsa, *Belarus* 33 F6
Recife, *Brazil* 125 E12
Recklinghausen, *Germany* 17 C7
Reconquista, *Argentina* 126 B4
Recreo, *Argentina* 126 B2
Recz, *Poland* 31 E2
Red →, *La., U.S.A.* 113 K9
Red →, *N. Dak., U.S.A.* 100 C10
Red Bank, *U.S.A.* 117 F10
Red Bay, *Canada* 105 B8
Red Bluff, *U.S.A.* 108 F2
Red Bluff L., *U.S.A.* 113 K3
Red Cliffs, *Australia* 95 E3
Red Cloud, *U.S.A.* 112 E5
Red Creek, *U.S.A.* 117 C8
Red Deer, *Canada* 102 C6
Red Deer →, *Alta., Canada* 103 C7
Red Deer →, *Man., Canada* 103 C8
Red Deer L., *Canada* 103 C8
Red Hook, *U.S.A.* 117 E11
Red Indian L., *Canada* 105 C8
Red L., *Canada* 103 C10
Red Lake, *Canada* 103 C10
Red Lake Falls, *U.S.A.* 112 B6
Red Lake Road, *Canada* 103 C10
Red Lodge, *U.S.A.* 108 D9
Red Mountain, *U.S.A.* 111 K9
Red Oak, *U.S.A.* 112 E7
Red Rock, *Canada* 104 C2
Red Rock, L., *U.S.A.* 112 E8
Red Rocks Pt., *Australia* 93 F4
Red Sea, *Asia* 75 C2
Red Slate Mt., *U.S.A.* 110 H8
Red Sucker L., *Canada* 104 B1
Red Tower Pass = Turnu Roşu, P., *Romania* 29 E9
Red Wing, *U.S.A.* 112 C8
Reda, *Poland* 30 D5
Redang, *Malaysia* 65 K4
Redange, *Lux.* 17 E5
Redcar, *U.K.* 14 C6
Redcar & Cleveland □, *U.K.* 14 C7
Redcliff, *Canada* 103 C6
Redcliffe, *Australia* 95 D5
Redcliffe, Mt., *Australia* 93 E3
Reddersburg, *S. Africa* 88 D4
Redding, *U.S.A.* 108 F2
Redditch, *U.K.* 15 E6
Redfield, *U.S.A.* 112 C5
Redford, *U.S.A.* 117 B11
Redhead, *Trin. & Tob.* 125 K16
Redkino, *Russia* 32 D9
Redlands, *U.S.A.* 111 M9
Redmond, *Oreg., U.S.A.* 108 D3
Redmond, *Wash., U.S.A.* 110 C4
Redon, *France* 18 E4
Redonda, *Antigua & B.* 121 C7
Redondela, *Spain* 36 C2
Redondo, *Portugal* 37 G3
Redondo Beach, *U.S.A.* 111 M8
Redruth, *U.K.* 15 G2
Redvers, *Canada* 103 D8
Redwater, *Canada* 102 C6
Redwood, *U.S.A.* 117 B9
Redwood △, *U.S.A.* 108 F1
Redwood City, *U.S.A.* 110 H4
Redwood Falls, *U.S.A.* 112 C7
Ree, L., *Ireland* 12 C3
Reed, L., *Canada* 103 C8
Reed City, *U.S.A.* 114 D3
Reedley, *U.S.A.* 110 J7
Reedsburg, *U.S.A.* 112 D9
Reedsport, *U.S.A.* 108 E1
Reedsville, *U.S.A.* 116 F7
Reefton, *N.Z.* 91 K3
Rees, *Germany* 24 D2
Reese →, *U.S.A.* 108 F5
Refahiye, *Turkey* 73 C8
Reftele, *Sweden* 11 G7
Refugio, *U.S.A.* 113 L6
Rega →, *Poland* 30 D2
Regalbuto, *Italy* 43 E7
Regen, *Germany* 25 G9
Regen →, *Germany* 25 F8
Regensburg, *Germany* 25 F8
Regenstauf, *Germany* 25 F8
Reggâne = Zaouiet Reggâne, *Algeria* 78 C6
Reggello, *Italy* 41 E8
Réggio di Calábria, *Italy* 43 D8
Réggio nell'Emília, *Italy* 40 D7
Reghin, *Romania* 29 D9
Regina, *Canada* 103 C8
Regina Beach, *Canada* 103 C8
Registro, *Brazil* 127 A6
Reguengos de Monsaraz, *Portugal* 37 G3
Rehar →, *India* 69 H10
Rehli, *India* 69 H8
Rehoboth, *Namibia* 88 C2
Rehovot, *Israel* 74 D3
Reichenbach, *Germany* 24 E8
Reid, *Australia* 93 F4
Reidsville, *U.S.A.* 115 G6
Reigate, *U.K.* 15 F7
Reillo, *Spain* 38 F3
Reims, *France* 19 C11
Reina Adelaida, Arch., *Chile* 128 G2
Reina Sofia, Tenerife ✕ (TFS), *Canary Is.* 48 F3
Reinbek, *Germany* 24 B6
Reindeer →, *Canada* 103 B8
Reindeer I., *Canada* 103 C9
Reindeer L., *Canada* 103 B8
Reinga, C., *N.Z.* 91 F4
Reinosa, *Spain* 36 B6
Reitz, *S. Africa* 89 D4
Reivilo, *S. Africa* 88 D3
Rejaf, *Sudan* 81 G3
Rejmyre, *Sweden* 11 F9
Rejowiec Fabryczny, *Poland* 31 G10
Reka →, *Slovenia* 41 C11
Rekovac, *Serbia & M.* 44 C5
Reliance, *Canada* 103 A7
Rémalard, *France* 18 D7
Remarkable, Mt., *Australia* 95 E2
Rembang, *Indonesia* 63 G14
Remedios, *Panama* 120 E3
Remeshk, *Iran* 71 E8
Remetea, *Romania* 29 D10
Remich, *Lux.* 17 E6
Remiremont, *France* 19 D13
Remo, *Ethiopia* 81 F5
Remontnoye, *Russia* 35 G6
Remoulins, *France* 21 E8
Remscheid, *Germany* 17 C7
Ren Xian, *China* 56 F8
Rendang, *Indonesia* 63 J18
Rende, *Italy* 43 C9
Rendína, *Greece* 46 B3
Rendsburg, *Germany* 24 A5
Renfrew, *Canada* 117 A8
Renfrewshire □, *U.K.* 13 F4
Rengat, *Indonesia* 62 E2
Rengo, *Chile* 126 C1
Renhua, *China* 59 E9
Renhuai, *China* 58 D6
Reni, *Ukraine* 29 E13
Renk, *Sudan* 81 E3
Renmark, *Australia* 95 E3
Rennell Sd., *Canada* 102 C2
Renner Springs, *Australia* 94 B1
Rennes, *France* 18 D5
Rennie L., *Canada* 103 A7
Reno, *U.S.A.* 110 F7
Reno →, *Italy* 41 D9
Renovo, *U.S.A.* 116 E7
Renqiu, *China* 56 E9
Rens, *Denmark* 11 K3
Renshou, *China* 58 C5
Rensselaer, *Ind., U.S.A.* 114 E2
Rensselaer, *N.Y., U.S.A.* 117 D11
Rentería, *Spain* 38 B3
Renton, *U.S.A.* 110 C4
Réo, *Burkina Faso* 82 C4
Reocín, *Spain* 36 B6
Reotipur, *India* 69 G10
Répcelak, *Hungary* 28 C2
Republic, *Mo., U.S.A.* 113 G8
Republic, *Wash., U.S.A.* 108 B4
Republican →, *U.S.A.* 112 F6
Repulse B., *Australia* 94 J6
Repulse Bay, *Canada* 101 B11
Requena, *Peru* 124 E4
Requena, *Spain* 39 F3
Réquista, *France* 20 D6
Reşadiye = Datça, *Turkey* 47 E9
Reşadiye, *Turkey* 72 B7
Reşadiye Yarımadası, *Turkey* 47 E9
Resavica, *Serbia & M.* 44 B5
Resen, *Macedonia* 44 E5
Reserve, *U.S.A.* 109 K9
Resht = Rasht, *Iran* 71 B6
Resistencia, *Argentina* 126 B4
Reşiţa, *Romania* 28 E6
Resko, *Poland* 30 E2
Reso = Raisio, *Finland* 9 F20
Resolution I., *Canada* 101 B13
Resolution I., *N.Z.* 91 L1
Ressano Garcia, *Mozam.* 89 D5
Reston, *Canada* 103 D8
Reszel, *Poland* 30 D8
Retalhuleu, *Guatemala* 120 D1
Retenue, L. de, *Dem. Rep. of the Congo* 87 E2
Retezat △, *Romania* 28 E7
Retezat, Munţii, *Romania* 28 E8
Retford, *U.K.* 14 D7
Rethel, *France* 19 C11
Rethem, *Germany* 24 C5
Réthímnon, *Greece* 49 D6
Réthímnon □, *Greece* 49 D6
Reti, *Pakistan* 68 E3
Retiche, Alpi, *Switz.* 25 J6
Retiers, *France* 18 E5
Retortillo, *Spain* 36 E4
Retournac, *France* 21 C8
Rétság, *Hungary* 28 C4
Réunion ☒, *Ind. Oc.* 77 J9
Reus, *Spain* 38 D6
Reuterstadt Stavenhagen, *Germany* 24 B8
Reutlingen, *Germany* 25 G5
Reutte, *Austria* 26 D3
Reval = Tallinn, *Estonia* 9 G21
Revel, *France* 20 E6
Revelganj, *India* 69 G11
Revelstoke, *Canada* 102 C5
Reventazón, *Peru* 124 E2
Revigny-sur-Ornain, *France* 19 D11
Revillagigedo, Is. de, *Pac. Oc.* 118 D2
Revin, *France* 19 C11
Revúca, *Slovak Rep.* 27 C13
Revuè →, *Mozam.* 87 F3
Rewa, *India* 69 G9
Rewari, *India* 68 E7
Rexburg, *U.S.A.* 108 E8
Rey, *Iran* 71 C6
Rey, I. del, *Panama* 120 E4
Rey Malabo, *Eq. Guin.* 83 E6
Reyðarfjörður, *Iceland* 8 D6
Reyes, Pt., *U.S.A.* 110 H3
Reyhanlı, *Turkey* 72 D7
Reykjahlið, *Iceland* 8 D5
Reykjanes, *Iceland* 8 E2
Reykjavík, *Iceland* 8 D3
Reynolds Ra., *Australia* 92 D5
Reynoldsville, *U.S.A.* 116 E6
Reynosa, *Mexico* 119 B5
Rēzekne, *Latvia* 9 H22
Rezina, *Moldova* 29 C13
Rezovo, *Bulgaria* 45 D12
Rezvān, *Iran* 71 E8
Rgotina, *Serbia & M.* 44 B6
Rhamnus, *Greece* 46 C6
Rhayader, *U.K.* 15 E4
Rheda-Wiedenbrück, *Germany* 24 D4
Rhede, *Germany* 24 D2
Rhein →, *Europe* 17 C6
Rhein-Main-Donau-Kanal, *Germany* 25 F7
Rhein-Ruhr, Düsseldorf ✕ (DUS), *Germany* 24 D2
Rhein-Taunus ⌓, *Germany* 25 E4
Rhein-Westerwald ⌓, *Germany* 24 E3
Rheinbach, *Germany* 24 E2
Rheine, *Germany* 24 C3
Rheinfelden, *Germany* 25 H3
Rheinhessen-Pfalz □, *Germany* 25 F3
Rheinland-Pfalz □, *Germany* 25 E2
Rheinsberg, *Germany* 24 B8
Rhin = Rhein →, *Europe* 17 C6
Rhine = Rhein →, *Europe* 17 C6
Rhinebeck, *U.S.A.* 117 E11
Rhineland-Palatinate = Rheinland-Pfalz □, *Germany* 25 E2
Rhinelander, *U.S.A.* 112 C10
Rhinns Pt., *U.K.* 13 F2

Rhino Camp, Uganda 86 B3
Rhir, Cap, Morocco 78 B4
Rho, Italy 40 C6
Rhode Island □, U.S.A. 117 E13
Rhodes = Ródhos, Greece 49 C10
Rhodope Mts. = Rhodopi Planina, Bulgaria 45 E8
Rhodopi Planina, Bulgaria 45 E8
Rhön, Germany 24 E5
Rhondda, U.K. 15 F4
Rhondda Cynon Taff □, U.K. 15 F4
Rhône □, France 21 C8
Rhône →, France 21 E8
Rhône-Alpes □, France 21 C9
Rhum, U.K. 13 E2
Rhyl, U.K. 14 D4
Ri-Aba, Eq. Guin. 83 E6
Ria Formosa ⌓, Portugal 37 H3
Riachão, Brazil 125 E9
Riangnom, Sudan 81 F3
Riaño, Spain 36 C6
Rians, France 21 E9
Riansáres →, Spain 37 F7
Riasi, India 69 C6
Riau □, Indonesia 62 D2
Riau, Kepulauan, Indonesia 62 D2
Riau Arch. = Riau, Kepulauan, Indonesia 62 D2
Riaza, Spain 36 D7
Riaza →, Spain 36 D7
Riba de Saelices, Spain 38 E2
Riba-Roja de Turia, Spain 39 F4
Ribadavia, Spain 36 C2
Ribadeo, Spain 36 B3
Ribadesella, Spain 36 B5
Ribado, Nigeria 83 D7
Ribao, Cameroon 83 D7
Ribas = Ribes de Freser, Spain 38 C7
Ribas do Rio Pardo, Brazil 125 H8
Ribauè, Mozam. 87 E4
Ribble →, U.K. 14 D5
Ribe, Denmark 11 J2
Ribe Amtskommune □, Denmark 11 J2
Ribeauvillé, France 19 D14
Ribécourt-Dreslincourt, France 19 C9
Ribeira = Santa Uxía, Spain 36 C2
Ribeira Brava, Madeira 48 D2
Ribeirão Prêto, Brazil 127 A6
Ribemont, France 19 C10
Ribera, Italy 42 E6
Ribérac, France 20 C4
Riberalta, Bolivia 124 F5
Ribes de Freser, Spain 38 C7
Ribnica, Slovenia 41 C11
Ribnitz-Damgarten, Germany 24 A8
Říčany, Czech Rep. 26 B7
Riccarton, N.Z. 91 K4
Ríccia, Italy 43 A7
Riccione, Italy 41 E9
Rice, U.S.A. 111 L12
Rice L., Canada 116 B6
Rice Lake, U.S.A. 112 C9
Rich, C., Canada 116 B4
Richard Toll, Senegal 82 B1
Richards Bay, S. Africa 89 D5
Richardson →, Canada 103 B6
Richardson Lakes, U.S.A. 114 C10
Richardson Springs, U.S.A. 110 F5
Riche, C., Australia 93 F2
Richelieu, France 18 E7
Richey, U.S.A. 112 B2
Richfield, U.S.A. 109 G8
Richfield Springs, U.S.A. 117 D10
Richford, U.S.A. 117 B12
Richibucto, Canada 105 C7
Richland, Ga., U.S.A. 115 J3
Richland, Wash., U.S.A. 108 C4
Richland Center, U.S.A. 112 D9
Richlands, U.S.A. 114 G5
Richmond, Australia 94 C3
Richmond, N.Z. 91 J4
Richmond, U.K. 14 C6
Richmond, Calif., U.S.A. 110 H4
Richmond, Ind., U.S.A. 114 F3
Richmond, Ky., U.S.A. 114 G3
Richmond, Mich., U.S.A. 116 D2
Richmond, Mo., U.S.A. 112 F8
Richmond, Tex., U.S.A. 113 L7
Richmond, Utah, U.S.A. 108 F8
Richmond, Va., U.S.A. 114 G7
Richmond, Vt., U.S.A. 117 B12
Richmond Hill, Canada 116 C5
Richmond Ra., Australia 95 D5
Richtersveld △, S. Africa 88 D2
Richwood, U.S.A. 114 F5
Ricla, Spain 38 D3
Ridder = Leninogorsk, Kazakhstan 52 D9
Riddlesburg, U.S.A. 116 F6
Ridgecrest, U.S.A. 111 K9
Ridgefield, Conn., U.S.A. 117 E11
Ridgefield, Wash., U.S.A. 110 E4
Ridgeland, U.S.A. 115 J5
Ridgetown, Canada 116 D3
Ridgewood, U.S.A. 117 F10
Ridgway, U.S.A. 116 E6
Riding Mountain △, Canada 103 C9
Ridley, Mt., Australia 93 F3
Riebeek-Oos, S. Africa 88 E4
Ried, Austria 26 C6
Riedlingen, Germany 25 G5
Riedstadt, Germany 25 F4
Rienza →, Italy 41 B8
Riesa, Germany 24 D9
Riesi, Italy 43 E7
Riet →, S. Africa 88 D3
Rietavas, Lithuania 30 C8
Rietbron, S. Africa 88 E3
Rietfontein, Namibia 88 C3
Rieti, Italy 41 F9
Rieupeyroux, France 20 D6
Riez, France 21 E10
Rif = Er Rif, Morocco 78 A5
Riffe L., U.S.A. 110 D4
Rifle, U.S.A. 108 G10
Rift Valley, Africa 76 G7
Rift Valley □, Kenya 86 B4
Rīga, Latvia 9 H21
Riga ✕ (RIX), Latvia 30 B10
Riga, G. of, Latvia 9 H20
Rigacikun, Nigeria 83 C6
Rīgān, Iran 71 D8
Rīgas Jūras Līcis = Riga, G. of, Latvia 9 H20
Rigaud, Canada 117 A10
Rigby, U.S.A. 108 E8
Rīgestān, Afghan. 66 D4
Riggins, U.S.A. 108 D5
Rignac, France 20 D6
Rigolet, Canada 105 B8
Rihand Dam, India 69 G10
Riihimäki, Finland 9 F21
Riiser-Larsen-halvøya, Antarctica 5 C4
Rijau, Nigeria 83 C6
Rijeka, Croatia 41 C11
Rijeka Crnojevića, Serbia & M. 44 D3
Rijssen, Neths. 17 B6
Rika →, Ukraine 29 B8
Rike, Ethiopia 81 E4
Rikuchū-Kaigan △, Japan 54 E11
Rikuzentakada, Japan 54 E10
Rila, Bulgaria 44 D7
Rila Planina, Bulgaria 44 D7
Riley, U.S.A. 108 E4
Rima →, Nigeria 83 C6
Rimah, Wadi ar →, Si. Arabia 70 E4
Rimau, Pulau, Malaysia 65 c
Rimavská Sobota, Slovak Rep. 27 C13
Rimbey, Canada 102 C6
Rimbo, Sweden 10 E12
Rimersburg, U.S.A. 116 E5
Rimforsa, Sweden 11 F9
Rimi, Nigeria 83 C6
Rímini, Italy 41 D9
Rimouski, Canada 105 C6
Rimrock, U.S.A. 110 D5
Rinca, Indonesia 63 F5
Rincón de la Victoria, Spain 37 J6
Rincón de Romos, Mexico 118 C4
Rinconada, Argentina 126 A2
Rind →, India 69 G9
Ringarum, Sweden 11 F10
Ringas, India 68 F6
Ringe, Denmark 11 J4
Ringim, Nigeria 83 C6
Ringkøbing, Denmark 11 H2
Ringkøbing Amtskommune □, Denmark 11 H2
Ringkøbing Fjord, Denmark 11 H2
Ringsjön, Sweden 11 J7
Ringsted, Denmark 11 J5
Ringvassøy, Norway 8 B18
Ringwood, U.S.A. 117 E10
Rinía, Greece 47 D7
Rinjani, Indonesia 62 F5
Rinteln, Germany 24 C5
Río, Punta del, Spain 39 J2
Rio Branco, Brazil 124 E5
Río Branco, Uruguay 127 C5
Río Bravo ⌓, N. Amer. 118 B4
Río Bravo del Norte →, Mexico 119 B5
Rio Brilhante, Brazil 127 A5
Rio Claro, Brazil 127 A6
Rio Claro, Trin. & Tob. 121 D7
Río Colorado, Argentina 128 D4
Río Cuarto, Argentina 126 C3
Rio das Pedras, Mozam. 89 C6
Rio de Janeiro, Brazil 127 A7
Rio de Janeiro □, Brazil 127 A7
Rio do Sul, Brazil 127 B6
Río Dulce △, Guatemala 120 C2
Río Gallegos, Argentina 128 G3
Río Grande, Argentina 128 G3
Rio Grande, Brazil 127 C5
Río Grande, Mexico 118 C4
Río Grande, Nic. 120 D3
Río Grande, Puerto Rico 121 d
Rio Grande, U.S.A. 113 N6
Rio Grande City, U.S.A. 113 M5
Río Grande de Santiago →, Mexico 118 C3
Rio Grande do Norte □, Brazil 125 E11
Rio Grande do Sul □, Brazil 127 C5
Río Hato, Panama 120 E3
Río Lagartos, Mexico 119 C7
Rio Largo, Brazil 125 E11
Rio Maior, Portugal 37 F2
Rio Marina, Italy 40 F7
Río Mulatos, Bolivia 124 G5
Río Muni □, Eq. Guin. 84 D2
Rio Negro, Brazil 127 B6
Rio Pardo, Brazil 127 C5
Río Pilcomayo △, Argentina 126 B4
Río Platano ⌓, Honduras 120 C3
Rio Rancho, U.S.A. 109 J10
Río Segundo, Argentina 126 C3
Río Tercero, Argentina 126 C3
Rio Tinto, Portugal 36 D2
Rio Verde, Brazil 125 G8
Río Verde, Mexico 119 C5
Rio Vista, U.S.A. 110 G5
Ríobamba, Ecuador 124 D3
Ríohacha, Colombia 124 A4
Riom, France 20 C7
Riom-ès-Montagnes, France 20 C6
Rion-des-Landes, France 20 E3
Rionero in Vúlture, Italy 43 B8
Rioni →, Georgia 35 J5
Riós, Spain 36 D3
Ríosucio, Colombia 124 B3
Riou L., Canada 103 B7
Rioz, France 19 E13
Ripatransone, Italy 41 F10
Ripley, Canada 116 B3
Ripley, Calif., U.S.A. 111 M12
Ripley, N.Y., U.S.A. 116 D5
Ripley, Tenn., U.S.A. 113 H10
Ripley, W. Va., U.S.A. 114 F5
Ripoll, Spain 38 C7
Ripon, U.K. 14 C6
Ripon, Calif., U.S.A. 110 H5
Ripon, Wis., U.S.A. 114 D1
Riposto, Italy 43 E8
Risan, Serbia & M. 44 D2
Riscle, France 20 E3
Rishā', W. ar →, Si. Arabia 70 E5
Rishiri-Rebun-Sarobetsu △, Japan 54 B10
Rishiri-Tō, Japan 54 B10
Rishon le Ẕiyyon, Israel 74 D3
Risle →, France 18 C7
Risnjak △, Croatia 41 C11
Rison, U.S.A. 113 J8
Risør, Norway 9 G13
Rita Blanca Cr. →, U.S.A. 113 H3
Riti, Nigeria 83 D6
Ritter, Mt., U.S.A. 110 H7
Rittman, U.S.A. 116 F3
Ritzville, U.S.A. 108 C4
Riva del Garda, Italy 40 C7
Riva Lígure, Italy 40 E4
Rivadavia, Buenos Aires, Argentina 126 D3
Rivadavia, Mendoza, Argentina 126 C2
Rivadavia, Salta, Argentina 126 A3
Rivadavia, Chile 126 B1
Rivarolo Canavese, Italy 40 C4
Rivas, Nic. 120 D2
Rive-de-Gier, France 21 C8
River Cess, Liberia 82 D3
River Jordan, Canada 110 B2
Rivera, Argentina 126 D3
Rivera, Uruguay 127 C4
Riverbank, U.S.A. 110 H6
Riverdale, U.S.A. 110 J7
Riverhead, U.S.A. 117 F12
Riverhurst, Canada 103 C7
Rivers, Canada 103 C8
Rivers □, Nigeria 83 E6
Rivers Inlet, Canada 102 C3
Riversdale, S. Africa 88 E3
Riverside, U.S.A. 111 M9
Riverton, Australia 95 E2
Riverton, Canada 103 C9
Riverton, N.Z. 91 M2
Riverton, U.S.A. 108 E9
Riverton Heights, U.S.A. 110 C4
Rives, France 21 C9
Rivesaltes, France 20 F6
Riviera, U.S.A. 111 K12
Riviera di Levante, Italy 40 D6
Riviera di Ponente, Italy 40 D5
Rivière-au-Renard, Canada 105 C7
Rivière-du-Loup, Canada 105 C6
Rivière-Pentecôte, Canada 105 C6
Rivière-Pilote, Martinique 120 c
Rivière St-Paul, Canada 105 B8
Rivière-Salée, Martinique 120 c
Rivne, Ukraine 29 D14
Rivne, Ukraine 33 G4
Rívoli, Italy 40 C4
Rivoli B., Australia 95 F3
Rixheim, France 19 E14
Riyadh = Ar Riyāḍ, Si. Arabia 70 E5
Rize, Turkey 73 B9
Rizhao, China 57 G10
Rizokarpaso, Cyprus 49 D13
Rizzuto, C., Italy 43 D10
Rjukan, Norway 9 G13
Ro, Greece 47 E11
Roa, Spain 36 D7
Road Town, Br. Virgin Is. 121 e
Roan Plateau, U.S.A. 108 G9
Roanne, France 19 F11
Roanoke, Ala., U.S.A. 115 J3
Roanoke, Va., U.S.A. 114 G6
Roanoke →, U.S.A. 115 H7
Roanoke I., U.S.A. 115 H8
Roanoke Rapids, U.S.A. 115 G7
Roatán, Honduras 120 C2
Robāt Sang, Iran 71 C8
Robāṭkarīm, Iran 71 C6
Robāṭkarīm □, Iran 71 B6
Robbins I., Australia 95 G4
Róbbio, Italy 40 C5
Robe →, Australia 92 D2
Röbel, Germany 24 B8
Robert Lee, U.S.A. 113 K4
Robertsdale, U.S.A. 116 F6
Robertsganj, India 69 G10
Robertson, S. Africa 88 E2
Robertson I., Antarctica 5 C18
Robertson Ra., Australia 92 D3
Robertsport, Liberia 82 D2
Robertstown, Australia 95 E2
Roberval, Canada 105 C5
Robeson Chan., N. Amer. 4 A4
Robesonia, U.S.A. 117 F8
Robi, Ethiopia 81 F4
Robinson, U.S.A. 114 F2
Robinson →, Australia 94 B2
Robinson Ra., Australia 93 E2
Robinvale, Australia 95 E3
Robledo, Spain 39 G2
Roblin, Canada 103 C8
Roboré, Bolivia 124 G7
Robson, Canada 102 D5
Robson, Mt., Canada 102 C5
Robstown, U.S.A. 113 M6
Roca, C. da, Portugal 37 G1
Roca Partida, I., Mexico 118 D2
Rocamadour, France 20 D5
Rocas, I., Brazil 125 D12
Rocca San Casciano, Italy 41 D8
Roccadáspide, Italy 43 B8
Roccastrada, Italy 41 F8
Roccella Iónica, Italy 43 D9
Rocha, Uruguay 127 C5
Rochdale, U.K. 14 D5
Rochechouart, France 20 C4
Rochefort, Belgium 17 D5
Rochefort, France 20 C3
Rochefort-en-Terre, France 18 E4
Rochelle, U.S.A. 112 E10
Rocher River, Canada 102 A6
Rocheservière, France 18 F5
Rochester, U.K. 15 F8
Rochester, Ind., U.S.A. 114 E2
Rochester, Minn., U.S.A. 112 C8
Rochester, N.H., U.S.A. 117 C14
Rochester, N.Y., U.S.A. 116 C7
Rociu, Romania 29 F10
Rock →, Canada 102 A3
Rock Creek, U.S.A. 116 E4
Rock Falls, U.S.A. 112 E10
Rock Hill, U.S.A. 115 H5
Rock Island, U.S.A. 112 E9
Rock Rapids, U.S.A. 112 D6
Rock Sound, Bahamas 120 B4
Rock Springs, Mont., U.S.A. 108 C10
Rock Springs, Wyo., U.S.A. 108 F9
Rock Valley, U.S.A. 112 D6
Rockall, Atl. Oc. 6 D3
Rockdale, Tex., U.S.A. 113 K6
Rockdale, Wash., U.S.A. 110 C5
Rockeby = Mungkan Kandju △, Australia 94 A3
Rockefeller Plateau, Antarctica 5 E14
Rockford, U.S.A. 112 D10
Rockglen, Canada 103 D7
Rockhampton, Australia 94 C5
Rockingham, Australia 93 F2
Rockingham, U.S.A. 115 H6
Rockingham B., Australia 94 B4
Rocklake, U.S.A. 112 A5
Rockland, Canada 117 A9
Rockland, Idaho, U.S.A. 108 E7
Rockland, Maine, U.S.A. 115 C11
Rockland, Mich., U.S.A. 112 B10
Rocklin, U.S.A. 110 G5
Rockly B., Trin. & Tob. 125 J16
Rockmart, U.S.A. 115 H3
Rockport, Mass., U.S.A. 117 D14
Rockport, Mo., U.S.A. 112 E7
Rockport, Tex., U.S.A. 113 L6
Rocksprings, U.S.A. 113 K4
Rockville, Conn., U.S.A. 117 E12
Rockville, Md., U.S.A. 114 F7
Rockwall, U.S.A. 113 J6
Rockwell City, U.S.A. 112 D7
Rockwood, Canada 116 C4
Rockwood, Maine, U.S.A. 115 C11
Rockwood, Tenn., U.S.A. 115 H3
Rocky Ford, U.S.A. 112 F3
Rocky Gully, Australia 93 F2
Rocky Harbour, Canada 105 C8
Rocky Island L., Canada 104 C3
Rocky Lane, Canada 102 B5
Rocky Mount, U.S.A. 115 H7
Rocky Mountain △, U.S.A. 108 F11
Rocky Mountain House, Canada 102 C6
Rocky Mts., N. Amer. 108 G10
Rocky Point, Namibia 88 B2
Rocroi, France 19 C11
Rod, Pakistan 66 E3
Rødby, Denmark 11 K5
Rødbyhavn, Denmark 11 K5
Roddickton, Canada 105 B8
Rødding, Denmark 11 J3
Rödeby, Sweden 11 H9
Rødekro, Denmark 11 J3
Rodenkirchen, Germany 24 B4
Rodez, France 20 D6
Rodholívas, Greece 44 F7
Rodhópi □, Greece 45 E9
Rodhopoú, Greece 49 D5
Ródhos, Greece 49 C10
Ródhos ✕ (RHO), Greece 47 E10
Rodi Gargánico, Italy 41 G12
Rodna, Romania 29 C9
Rodnei, Munţii, Romania 29 C9
Rodney, Canada 116 D3
Rodney, C., N.Z. 91 G5
Rodniki, Russia 34 B5
Rodonit, Kepi i, Albania 44 E3
Rodriguez, Ind. Oc. 3 E13
Roe →, U.K. 12 A5
Roebling, U.S.A. 117 F10
Roebourne, Australia 92 D2
Roebuck B., Australia 92 C3
Roermond, Neths. 17 C6
Roes Welcome Sd., Canada 101 B11
Roeselare, Belgium 17 D3
Rogachev = Ragachow, Belarus 33 F6
Rogačica, Serbia & M. 44 B3
Rogagua, L., Bolivia 124 F5
Rogaška Slatina, Slovenia 41 B12
Rogatec, Slovenia 41 B12
Rogatica, Bos.-H. 28 G4
Rogatyn, Ukraine 33 H3
Rogdhia, Greece 49 D7
Rogers, U.S.A. 113 G7
Rogers City, U.S.A. 114 C4
Rogersville, Canada 105 C6
Roggan →, Canada 104 B4
Roggan L., Canada 104 B4
Roggeveldberge, S. Africa 88 E3
Roggiano Gravina, Italy 43 C9
Rogliano, France 21 F13
Rogliano, Italy 43 C9
Rogoaguado, L., Bolivia 124 F5
Rogojampi, Indonesia 63 J17
Rogoźno, Poland 31 F3
Rogue →, U.S.A. 108 E1
Rohan, France 18 D4
Róhda, Greece 49 A3
Rohnert Park, U.S.A. 110 G4
Rohri, Pakistan 68 F3
Rohri Canal, Pakistan 68 F3
Rohtak, India 68 E7
Roi Et, Thailand 64 D4
Roja, Latvia 9 H20
Rojas, Argentina 126 C3
Rojişte, Romania 29 F8
Rojo, C., Mexico 119 C5
Rokan →, Indonesia 62 D2
Rokel →, S. Leone 82 D2
Rokiškis, Lithuania 9 J21
Rokitno, Russia 33 G8
Rokycany, Czech Rep. 26 B6
Rolândia, Brazil 127 A5
Rolla, U.S.A. 113 G9
Rolleston, Australia 94 C4
Rollingstone, Australia 94 B4
Rom, Sudan 81 F3
Roma, Australia 95 D4
Roma, Italy 41 G9
Roma, Sweden 11 G12
Roma, U.S.A. 113 M5
Roma Fiumicino ✕ (FCO), Italy 41 G9
Romain C., U.S.A. 115 J6
Romaine, Canada 105 B7
Romaine →, Canada 105 B7
Roman, Bulgaria 44 C7
Roman, Romania 29 D11
Roman-Kosh, Gora, Ukraine 33 K8
Romanche →, France 21 C9
Romang, Indonesia 63 F7
Români, Egypt 74 E1
Romania ■, Europe 29 D10
Romanija, Bos.-H. 28 G3
Romano, Cayo, Cuba 120 B4
Romans-sur-Isère, France 21 C9
Romanshorn, Switz. 25 H5
Rombari, Sudan 81 G3
Romblon, Phil. 61 E5
Rome = Roma, Italy 41 G9
Rome, Ga., U.S.A. 115 H3
Rome, N.Y., U.S.A. 117 C9
Rome, Pa., U.S.A. 117 E8
Rometta, Italy 43 D8
Romilly-sur-Seine, France 19 D10
Romney, U.S.A. 114 F6
Romney Marsh, U.K. 15 F8
Romny, Ukraine 33 G7
Rømø, Denmark 11 J2
Romodan, Ukraine 33 G7
Romodanovo, Russia 34 C7
Romont, Switz. 25 J2
Romorantin-Lanthenay, France 19 E8
Romsdalen, Norway 9 E12
Romsey, U.K. 15 G6
Ron, Vietnam 64 D6
Rona, U.K. 13 D3
Ronan, U.S.A. 108 C6
Roncador, Cayos, Colombia 120 D3
Roncador, Serra do, Brazil 125 F8
Ronciglione, Italy 41 F9
Ronco →, Italy 41 D9
Ronda, Spain 37 J5
Ronda, Serranía de, Spain 37 J5
Rondane, Norway 9 F13
Rondônia □, Brazil 124 F6
Rondonópolis, Brazil 125 G8
Rong, Koh, Cambodia 65 G4
Rong Jiang →, China 58 E7
Rong Xian, Guangxi Zhuangzu, China 59 F8
Rong Xian, Sichuan, China 58 C5
Rong'an, China 58 E7
Rongchang, China 58 C5
Ronge, L. la, Canada 103 B7
Rongjiang, China 58 E7
Rongshui, China 58 E7
Rønne, Denmark 11 J8
Ronne Ice Shelf, Antarctica 5 D18
Ronneby, Sweden 11 H9
Ronnebyån →, Sweden 11 H9
Rönneshytta, Sweden 11 F9
Ronsard, C., Australia 93 D1
Ronse, Belgium 17 D3
Roodepoort, S. Africa 89 D4
Roof Butte, U.S.A. 109 H9
Rooiboklaagte →, Namibia 88 C3
Roorkee, India 68 E7
Roosendaal, Neths. 17 C4
Roosevelt, U.S.A. 108 F8
Roosevelt →, Brazil 124 E6
Roosevelt, Mt., Canada 102 B3
Roosevelt I., Antarctica 5 D12
Ropczyce, Poland 31 H8
Roper →, Australia 94 A2
Roper Bar, Australia 94 A1
Roque Pérez, Argentina 126 D4
Roquefort, France 20 D3
Roquemaure, France 21 D8
Roquetas de Mar, Spain 39 J2
Roquetes, Spain 38 E5
Roquevaire, France 21 E9
Roraima □, Brazil 124 C6
Roraima, Mt., Venezuela 124 B6
Røros, Norway 9 E14
Rorschach, Switz. 25 H5
Rosa, Zambia 87 D3
Rosa, L., Bahamas 121 B5
Rosa, Monte, Europe 40 C4
Rosal de la Frontera, Spain 37 H3
Rosalia, U.S.A. 108 C5
Rosamond, U.S.A. 111 L8
Rosans, France 21 D9
Rosario, Argentina 126 C3
Rosário, Brazil 125 D10
Rosario, Baja Calif., Mexico 118 B1
Rosario, Sinaloa, Mexico 118 C3
Rosario, Paraguay 126 A4

Rosario de la Frontera, *Argentina* 126 B3
Rosario de Lerma, *Argentina* 126 A2
Rosario del Tala, *Argentina* 126 C4
Rosário do Sul, *Brazil* 127 C5
Rosarito, *Mexico* 111 N9
Rosarno, *Italy* 43 D8
Rosas = Roses, *Spain* 38 C8
Roscoe, *U.S.A.* 117 E10
Roscoff, *France* 18 D3
Roscommon, *Ireland* 12 C3
Roscommon □, *Ireland* 12 C3
Roscrea, *Ireland* 12 D4
Rose →, *Australia* 94 A2
Rose Blanche-Harbour Le Cou, *Canada* 105 C8
Rose Pt., *Canada* 102 C2
Rose Valley, *Canada* 103 C8
Roseau, *Dominica* 121 C7
Roseau, *U.S.A.* 112 A7
Rosebery, *Australia* 95 G4
Rosebud, *S. Dak., U.S.A.* 112 D4
Rosebud, *Tex., U.S.A.* 113 K6
Roseburg, *U.S.A.* 108 E2
Rosedale, *U.S.A.* 113 J9
Rosehearty, *U.K.* 13 D6
Roseland, *U.S.A.* 110 G4
Rosemary, *Canada* 102 C6
Rosenberg, *U.S.A.* 113 L7
Rosendaël, *France* 19 A9
Rosenheim, *Germany* 25 H8
Roses, *Spain* 38 C8
Roses, G. de, *Spain* 38 C8
Roseto degli Abruzzi, *Italy* 41 F11
Rosetown, *Canada* 103 C7
Rosetta = Rashîd, *Egypt* 80 H7
Roseville, *Calif., U.S.A.* 110 G5
Roseville, *Mich., U.S.A.* 116 D2
Rosewood, *Australia* 95 D5
Roshkhvār, *Iran* 71 C8
Rosières-en-Santerre, *France* 19 C9
Rosignano Maríttimo, *Italy* 40 E7
Rosignol, *Guyana* 124 B7
Roşiori de Vede, *Romania* 29 F10
Rositsa, *Bulgaria* 45 C11
Rositsa →, *Bulgaria* 45 C9
Roskilde, *Denmark* 11 J6
Roskilde Amtskommune □, *Denmark* 11 J6
Roskovec, *Albania* 44 F3
Roslavl, *Russia* 32 F7
Rosmaninhal, *Portugal* 36 F3
Rosmead, *S. Africa* 88 E4
Røsnæs, *Denmark* 11 J4
Rosolini, *Italy* 43 F7
Rosporden, *France* 18 E3
Ross, *Australia* 95 G4
Ross, *N.Z.* 91 K3
Ross Béthio, *Mauritania* 82 B1
Ross Dependency, *Antarctica* 5 D12
Ross I., *Antarctica* 5 D11
Ross Ice Shelf, *Antarctica* 5 E12
Ross L., *U.S.A.* 108 B3
Ross-on-Wye, *U.K.* 15 F5
Ross River, *Australia* 94 C1
Ross River, *Canada* 102 A2
Ross Sea, *Antarctica* 5 D11
Rossall Pt., *U.K.* 14 D4
Rossan Pt., *Ireland* 12 B3
Rossano, *Italy* 43 C9
Rossburn, *Canada* 103 C8
Rosseau, *Canada* 116 A5
Rosseau, L., *Canada* 116 A5
Rosses, The, *Ireland* 12 A3
Rossignol, L., *Canada* 104 B5
Rossignol L., *Canada* 105 D6
Rossland, *Canada* 102 D5
Rosslare, *Ireland* 12 D5
Rosslare Harbour, *Ireland* 12 D5
Rosslau, *Germany* 24 D8
Rosso, *Mauritania* 82 B1
Rosso, C., *France* 21 F12
Rossosh, *Russia* 33 G10
Røssvatnet, *Norway* 8 D16
Røst, *Norway* 8 C15
Rosthern, *Canada* 103 C7
Rostock, *Germany* 24 A8
Rostov, *Don, Russia* 33 J10
Rostov, *Yaroslavl, Russia* 32 D10
Rostrenen, *France* 18 D3
Roswell, *Ga., U.S.A.* 115 H3
Roswell, *N. Mex., U.S.A.* 113 J2
Rota, *Spain* 37 J4
Rotan, *U.S.A.* 113 J4
Rotenburg, *Hessen, Germany* 24 E5
Rotenburg, *Niedersachsen, Germany* 24 B5
Roth, *Germany* 25 F7
Rothaargebirge, *Germany* 24 D4
Rothaargebirge ⌓, *Germany* 24 E4
Rothenburg ob der Tauber, *Germany* 25 F6
Rother →, *U.K.* 15 G8
Rothera, *Antarctica* 5 C17
Rotherham, *U.K.* 14 D6
Rothes, *U.K.* 13 D5
Rothesay, *Canada* 105 C6
Rothesay, *U.K.* 13 F3
Roti, *Indonesia* 63 F6
Rotja, Pta., *Spain* 39 G6
Roto, *Australia* 95 E4
Rotondo, Mte., *France* 21 F13
Rotoroa, L., *N.Z.* 91 J4
Rotorua, *N.Z.* 91 H6
Rotorua, L., *N.Z.* 91 H6
Rott →, *Germany* 25 G9
Rottenburg, *Germany* 25 G4
Rottenmann, *Austria* 26 D7
Rotterdam, *Neths.* 17 C4
Rotterdam, *U.S.A.* 117 D10
Rottne, *Sweden* 11 G8
Rottnest I., *Australia* 93 F2
Rottumeroog, *Neths.* 17 A6
Rottweil, *Germany* 25 G4
Rotuma, *Fiji* 96 J9
Roubaix, *France* 19 B10
Roudnice nad Labem, *Czech Rep.* 26 A7
Rouen, *France* 18 C8
Rouergue, *France* 20 D5
Rouillac, *France* 20 C3
Rouleau, *Canada* 103 C8
Round Mountain, *U.S.A.* 108 G5
Round Mt., *Australia* 95 E5
Round Rock, *U.S.A.* 113 K6
Roundup, *U.S.A.* 108 C9
Rousay, *U.K.* 13 B5
Rouses Point, *U.S.A.* 117 B11
Rouseville, *U.S.A.* 116 E5
Roussillon, *Isère, France* 21 C8
Roussillon, *Pyrénées-Or., France* 20 F6
Rouxville, *S. Africa* 88 E4
Rouyn-Noranda, *Canada* 104 C4
Rovaniemi, *Finland* 8 C21
Rovato, *Italy* 40 C7
Rovenki, *Ukraine* 33 H10
Rovereto, *Italy* 40 C8
Rovigo, *Italy* 41 C8
Rovinj, *Croatia* 41 C10
Rovno = Rivne, *Ukraine* 33 G4
Rovnoye, *Russia* 34 E8
Rovuma = Ruvuma →, *Tanzania* 87 E5
Row'ān, *Iran* 71 C6
Rowena, *Australia* 95 D4
Rowley Shoals, *Australia* 92 C2
Roxa, *Guinea-Biss.* 82 C1
Roxas, *Capiz, Phil.* 61 F5
Roxas, *Isabela, Phil.* 61 C4
Roxas, *Mind. Or., Phil.* 61 E4
Roxboro, *U.S.A.* 115 G6
Roxborough, *Trin. & Tob.* 125 J16
Roxburgh, *N.Z.* 91 L2
Roxbury, *U.S.A.* 116 F7
Roxen, *Sweden* 11 F9
Roy, *Mont., U.S.A.* 108 C9
Roy, *N. Mex., U.S.A.* 113 H2
Roy, *Utah, U.S.A.* 108 F7
Royal Canal, *Ireland* 12 C4
Royal Leamington Spa, *U.K.* 15 E6
Royal Natal △, *S. Africa* 89 D4
Royal Tunbridge Wells, *U.K.* 15 F8
Royale, Isle, *U.S.A.* 112 B10
Royan, *France* 20 C2
Roye, *France* 19 C9
Royston, *U.K.* 15 E7
Rožaj, *Serbia & M.* 44 D4
Różan, *Poland* 31 F8
Rozay-en-Brie, *France* 19 D9
Rozdilna, *Ukraine* 29 D15
Rozhnyativ, *Ukraine* 29 B9
Rozhyshche, *Ukraine* 33 G3
Rožmitál pod Třemšínem, *Czech Rep.* 26 B6
Rožňava, *Slovak Rep.* 27 C13
Rozogi, *Poland* 30 E8
Rozoy-sur-Serre, *France* 19 C11
Roztoczański △, *Poland* 31 H10
Rozzano, *Italy* 40 C6
Rrëshen, *Albania* 44 E3
Rrogozhine, *Albania* 44 E3
Rtanj, *Serbia & M.* 44 C5
Rtishchevo, *Russia* 34 D6
Rúa = A Rúa, *Spain* 36 C3
Ruacaná, *Namibia* 88 B1
Ruaha △, *Tanzania* 86 D3
Ruahine Ra., *N.Z.* 91 H6
Ruapehu, *N.Z.* 91 H5
Ruapuke I., *N.Z.* 91 M2
Ruâq, W. →, *Egypt* 74 F2
Rub' al Khālī, *Si. Arabia* 75 D4
Rubeho Mts., *Tanzania* 86 D4
Rubezhnoye = Rubizhne, *Ukraine* 33 H10
Rubh a' Mhail, *U.K.* 13 F2
Rubha Hunish, *U.K.* 13 D2
Rubha Robhanais = Lewis, Butt of, *U.K.* 13 C2
Rubi, *Spain* 38 D7
Rubicon →, *U.S.A.* 110 G5
Rubicone →, *Italy* 41 D9
Rubik, *Albania* 44 E3
Rubino, *Ivory C.* 82 D4
Rubio, *Venezuela* 124 B4
Rubizhne, *Ukraine* 33 H10
Rubondo △, *Tanzania* 86 C3
Rubtsovsk, *Russia* 52 D9
Ruby L., *U.S.A.* 108 F6
Ruby Mts., *U.S.A.* 108 F6
Rubyvale, *Australia* 94 C4
Rucheng, *China* 59 E9
Ruciane-Nida, *Poland* 30 E8
Rūd Sar, *Iran* 71 B6
Ruda, *Sweden* 11 G10
Ruda Śląska, *Poland* 31 H5
Rudall, *Australia* 95 E2
Rudall →, *Australia* 92 D3
Rudall River △, *Australia* 92 D3
Rüdersdorf, *Germany* 24 C9
Rudewa, *Tanzania* 87 E3
Rudkøbing, *Denmark* 11 K4
Rudky, *Ukraine* 31 J10
Rudna, *Poland* 31 G3
Rudnik, *Bulgaria* 45 D11
Rudnik, *Poland* 31 H9
Rudnik, *Serbia & M.* 44 B4
Rudnya, *Russia* 32 E6
Rudnytsa, *Ukraine* 29 B13
Rudnyy, *Kazakhstan* 52 D7
Rudo, *Bos.-H.* 28 G4
Rudolfa, Ostrov, *Russia* 52 A6
Rudolstadt, *Germany* 24 E7
Rudong, *China* 59 A13
Rudozem, *Bulgaria* 45 E8
Rudyard, *U.S.A.* 114 B3
Rue, *France* 19 B8
Ruenya →, *Africa* 87 F3
Rufa'a, *Sudan* 81 E3
Rufiji →, *Tanzania* 86 D4
Rufino, *Argentina* 126 C3
Rufisque, *Senegal* 82 C1
Rufling Pt., *Br. Virgin Is.* 121 e
Rufunsa, *Zambia* 87 F2
Rugao, *China* 59 A13
Rugby, *U.K.* 15 E6
Rugby, *U.S.A.* 112 A5
Rügen, *Germany* 24 A9
Rügen ⌓, *Germany* 24 A9
Rugles, *France* 18 D7
Ruhengeri, *Rwanda* 86 C2
Ruhla, *Germany* 24 E6
Ruhland, *Germany* 24 D9
Ruhnu, *Estonia* 9 H20
Ruhr →, *Germany* 24 D2
Ruhuhu →, *Tanzania* 87 E3
Rui'an, *China* 59 D13
Ruichang, *China* 59 C10
Ruidoso, *U.S.A.* 109 K11
Ruijin, *China* 59 E10
Ruili, *China* 58 E1
Ruivo, Pico, *Madeira* 48 D3
Ruj, *Bulgaria* 44 D6
Rujen, *Macedonia* 44 D6
Rujm Tal'at al Jamā'ah, *Jordan* 74 E4
Ruk, *Pakistan* 68 F3
Rukhla, *Pakistan* 68 C4
Ruki →, *Dem. Rep. of the Congo* 84 E3
Rukwa □, *Tanzania* 86 D3
Rukwa, L., *Tanzania* 86 D3
Rulhieres, C., *Australia* 92 B4
Rum = Rhum, *U.K.* 13 E2
Rum, *Jordan* 74 F4
Rum Cay, *Bahamas* 121 B5
Rum Jungle, *Australia* 92 B5
Ruma, *Serbia & M.* 28 E4
Ruma △, *Kenya* 86 C3
Rumāḥ, *Si. Arabia* 70 E5
Rumania = Romania ■, *Europe* 29 D10
Rumaylah, *Iraq* 70 D5
Rumbêk, *Sudan* 81 F2
Rumburk, *Czech Rep.* 26 A7
Rumford, *U.S.A.* 115 C10
Rumia, *Poland* 30 D5
Rumilly, *France* 21 C9
Rumoi, *Japan* 54 C10
Rumonge, *Burundi* 86 C2
Rumson, *U.S.A.* 117 F11
Rumuruti, *Kenya* 86 B4
Runan, *China* 56 H8
Runanga, *N.Z.* 91 K3
Runaway, C., *N.Z.* 91 G6
Runaway Bay, *Jamaica* 120 a
Runcorn, *U.K.* 14 D5
Rundu, *Namibia* 88 B2
Rungwa, *Tanzania* 86 D3
Rungwa ⌓, *Tanzania* 86 D3
Rungwa →, *Tanzania* 86 D3
Rungwe, *Tanzania* 87 D3
Rungwe, Mt., *Tanzania* 84 F6
Runka, *Nigeria* 83 C6
Runn, *Sweden* 10 D9
Runton Ra., *Australia* 92 D3
Ruokolahti, *Finland* 32 B5
Ruoqiang, *China* 60 C3
Rupa, *India* 67 F18
Rupar, *India* 68 D7
Rupat, *Indonesia* 62 D2
Rupea, *Romania* 29 D10
Rupen →, *India* 68 H4
Rupert, *U.S.A.* 108 E7
Rupert →, *Canada* 104 B4
Rupert B., *Canada* 104 B4
Rupert House = Waskaganish, *Canada* 104 B4
Rupsa, *India* 69 J12
Rur →, *Germany* 24 D1
Rurrenabaque, *Bolivia* 124 F5
Rus →, *Spain* 39 F2
Rusambo, *Zimbabwe* 87 F3
Rusape, *Zimbabwe* 87 F3
Ruschuk = Ruse, *Bulgaria* 45 C9
Ruse, *Bulgaria* 45 C9
Ruse □, *Bulgaria* 45 C10
Rusenski Lom △, *Bulgaria* 44 C7
Ruşeţu, *Romania* 29 F12
Rush, *Ireland* 12 C5
Rushan, *China* 57 F11
Rushden, *U.K.* 15 E7
Rushmore, Mt., *U.S.A.* 112 D3
Rushville, *Ill., U.S.A.* 112 E9
Rushville, *Ind., U.S.A.* 114 F3
Rushville, *Nebr., U.S.A.* 112 D3
Russas, *Brazil* 125 D11
Russell, *Canada* 103 C8
Russell, *Kans., U.S.A.* 112 F5
Russell, *N.Y., U.S.A.* 117 B9
Russell, *Pa., U.S.A.* 116 E5
Russell Cave ⌓, *U.S.A.* 115 H3
Russell L., *Man., Canada* 103 B8
Russell L., *N.W.T., Canada* 102 A5
Russellkonda, *India* 67 K14
Russellville, *Ala., U.S.A.* 115 H2
Russellville, *Ark., U.S.A.* 113 H8
Russellville, *Ky., U.S.A.* 115 G2
Rüsselsheim, *Germany* 25 F4
Russi, *Italy* 41 D9
Russia ■, *Eurasia* 53 C11
Russian →, *U.S.A.* 110 G3
Russkoye Ustie, *Russia* 4 B15
Rust, *Austria* 27 D9
Rustam, *Pakistan* 68 B5
Rustam Shahr, *Pakistan* 68 F2
Rustavi, *Georgia* 35 K7
Rustenburg, *S. Africa* 88 D4
Ruston, *U.S.A.* 113 J8
Rutana, *Burundi* 86 C3
Rute, *Spain* 37 H6
Ruteng, *Indonesia* 63 F6
Ruth, *U.S.A.* 116 C2
Rutherford, *U.S.A.* 110 G4
Rutland, *U.S.A.* 117 C12
Rutland □, *U.K.* 15 E7
Rutland Water, *U.K.* 15 E7
Rutledge →, *Canada* 103 A6
Rutledge L., *Canada* 103 A6
Rutqa, W. →, *Syria* 73 E9
Rutshuru, *Dem. Rep. of the Congo* 86 C2
Ruvo di Púglia, *Italy* 43 A9
Ruvu, *Tanzania* 86 D4
Ruvu →, *Tanzania* 86 D4
Ruvuba △, *Burundi* 86 C2
Ruvuma □, *Tanzania* 87 E4
Ruvuma →, *Tanzania* 87 E5
Ruwais, *U.A.E.* 71 E7
Ruwenzori, *Africa* 86 B2
Ruwenzori △, *Uganda* 86 B2
Ruya →, *Zimbabwe* 89 B5
Ruyigi, *Burundi* 86 C3
Ruyuan, *China* 59 E9
Ruzayevka, *Russia* 34 C7
Růzhevo Konare, *Bulgaria* 45 D8
Ružomberok, *Slovak Rep.* 27 B12
Ruzyne, Praha ✈ (PRG), *Czech Rep.* 26 A7
Rwanda ■, *Africa* 86 C3
Ryakhovo, *Bulgaria* 45 C10
Ryan, L., *U.K.* 13 G3
Ryazan, *Russia* 32 E10
Ryazhsk, *Russia* 32 F11
Rybache = Rybachye, *Kazakhstan* 52 E9
Rybachiy, *Russia* 30 C7
Rybachye, *Kazakhstan* 52 E9
Rybinsk, *Russia* 32 C10
Rybinskoye Vdkhr., *Russia* 32 C10
Rybnik, *Poland* 31 H5
Rybnitsa = Râbniţa, *Moldova* 29 C14
Rybnoye, *Russia* 32 E10
Rychnov nad Kněžnou, *Czech Rep.* 27 A9
Rychwał, *Poland* 31 F5
Rycroft, *Canada* 102 B5
Ryd, *Sweden* 11 H8
Rydaholm, *Sweden* 11 H8
Ryde, *U.K.* 15 G6
Ryderwood, *U.S.A.* 110 D3
Rydzyna, *Poland* 31 G3
Rye, *U.K.* 15 G8
Rye →, *U.K.* 14 C7
Rye Bay, *U.K.* 15 G8
Rye Patch Reservoir, *U.S.A.* 108 F4
Ryegate, *U.S.A.* 108 C9
Ryki, *Poland* 31 G8
Ryley, *Canada* 102 C6
Rylsk, *Russia* 33 G8
Rylstone, *Australia* 95 E4
Rymanów, *Poland* 31 J8
Ryn, *Poland* 30 E8
Ryn Peski, *Kazakhstan* 35 G9
Ryōtsu, *Japan* 54 E9
Rypin, *Poland* 31 E6
Ryssby, *Sweden* 11 H8
Rysy, *Europe* 27 B13
Ryūgasaki, *Japan* 55 G10
Ryūkyū Is. = Ryūkyū-rettō, *Japan* 55 M3
Ryūkyū-rettō, *Japan* 55 M3
Rzepin, *Poland* 31 F1
Rzeszów, *Poland* 31 H8
Rzhev, *Russia* 32 D8

S

Sa, *Thailand* 64 C3
Sa Canal, *Spain* 48 C7
Sa Conillera, *Spain* 48 C7
Sa Dec, *Vietnam* 65 G5
Sa Dragonera, *Spain* 48 B9
Sa Mesquida, *Spain* 48 B11
Sa Pobla, *Spain* 38 F8
Sa Savina, *Spain* 48 C7
Sa'ādatābād, *Fārs, Iran* 71 D7
Sa'ādatābād, *Hormozgān, Iran* 71 D7
Sa'ādatābād, *Kermān, Iran* 71 D7
Saale →, *Germany* 24 D7
Saaler Bodden, *Germany* 24 A8
Saalfeld, *Germany* 24 E7
Saalfelden, *Austria* 26 D5
Saane →, *Switz.* 25 H3
Saanich, *Canada* 110 B3
Saar →, *Europe* 17 E6
Saar-Hunsrück ⌓, *Germany* 25 F2
Saarbrücken, *Germany* 25 F2
Saarburg, *Germany* 25 F2
Saaremaa, *Estonia* 9 G20
Saarijärvi, *Finland* 9 E21
Saariselkä, *Finland* 8 B23
Saarland □, *Germany* 25 F2
Saarlouis, *Germany* 25 F2
Sab 'Ābar, *Syria* 70 C3
Saba, *W. Indies* 121 C7
Šabac, *Serbia & M.* 44 B3
Sabadell, *Spain* 38 D7
Sabah □, *Malaysia* 62 C5
Sabak Bernam, *Malaysia* 65 L3
Sabalān, Kūhhā-ye, *Iran* 70 B5
Sabalana, Kepulauan, *Indonesia* 63 F5
Sábana de la Mar, *Dom. Rep.* 121 C6
Sábanalarga, *Colombia* 124 A4
Sabang, *Indonesia* 62 C1
Săbăoani, *Romania* 29 C11
Sabará, *Brazil* 125 G10
Sabarmati →, *India* 68 H5
Sabattis, *U.S.A.* 117 B10
Sabáudia, *Italy* 42 A6
Saberania, *Indonesia* 63 E9
Sabhah, *Libya* 79 C8
Sabi →, *India* 68 E7
Sabidana, J., *Sudan* 80 D4
Sabie, *S. Africa* 89 D5
Sabinal, *Mexico* 118 A3
Sabinal, *U.S.A.* 113 L5
Sabiñánigo, *Spain* 38 C4
Sabinar, Punta del, *Spain* 39 J2
Sabinas, *Mexico* 118 B4
Sabinas →, *Mexico* 118 B4
Sabinas Hidalgo, *Mexico* 118 B4
Sabine →, *U.S.A.* 113 L8
Sabine L., *U.S.A.* 113 L8
Sabine Pass, *U.S.A.* 113 L8
Sabinov, *Slovak Rep.* 27 B14
Sabinsville, *U.S.A.* 116 E7
Sabirabad, *Azerbaijan* 35 K9
Sablayan, *Phil.* 61 E4
Sable, *Canada* 105 A6
Sable, C., *Canada* 105 D6
Sable, C., *U.S.A.* 107 E10
Sable I., *Canada* 105 D8
Sablé-sur-Sarthe, *France* 18 E6
Sabonkafi, *Niger* 83 C6
Sabor →, *Portugal* 36 D3
Sabou, *Burkina Faso* 82 C4
Sabres, *France* 20 D3
Sabrina Coast, *Antarctica* 5 C9
Sabugal, *Portugal* 36 E3
Sabulubbek, *Indonesia* 62 E1
Sabuncu, *Turkey* 47 B12
Sabzevār, *Iran* 71 B8
Sabzvārān, *Iran* 71 D8
Sac City, *U.S.A.* 112 D7
Sacedón, *Spain* 38 E2
Săcele, *Romania* 29 E10
Sachigo →, *Canada* 104 A2
Sachigo, L., *Canada* 104 B1
Sachkhere, *Georgia* 35 J6
Sachsen □, *Germany* 24 E9
Sachsen-Anhalt □, *Germany* 24 D7
Sächsische Schweiz △, *Germany* 24 E10
Sacile, *Italy* 41 C9
Sackets Harbor, *U.S.A.* 117 C8
Sackville, *Canada* 105 C7
Saco, *Maine, U.S.A.* 115 D10
Saco, *Mont., U.S.A.* 108 B10
Sacramento, *U.S.A.* 110 G5
Sacramento →, *U.S.A.* 110 G5
Sacramento Mts., *U.S.A.* 109 K11
Sacramento Valley, *U.S.A.* 110 G5
Sacratif, C., *Spain* 37 J7
Săcueni, *Romania* 28 C7
Sada, *Spain* 36 B2
Sada-Misaki, *Japan* 55 H6
Sádaba, *Spain* 38 C3
Sadabad, *India* 68 F8
Sadani, *Tanzania* 86 D4
Sadao, *Thailand* 65 J3
Sadd el Aali, *Egypt* 80 C3
Saddle Mt., *U.S.A.* 110 E3
Sade, *Nigeria* 83 C7
Sadimi, *Dem. Rep. of the Congo* 87 D1
Sadiola, *Mali* 82 C2
Sa'dīyah, Hawr as, *Iraq* 73 F12
Sado, *Japan* 54 F9
Sado →, *Portugal* 37 G2
Sadon, *Burma* 67 G20
Sadon, *Russia* 35 J6
Sadovoye, *Russia* 35 G7
Sadra, *India* 68 H5
Sadri, *India* 68 G5
Sæby, *Denmark* 11 G4
Saegertown, *U.S.A.* 116 E4
Saelices, *Spain* 38 F2
Safaalan, *Turkey* 45 E12
Safaga, *Egypt* 80 B3
Şafājah, *Si. Arabia* 70 E3
Šafárikovo = Tornal'a, *Slovak Rep.* 27 C13
Säffle, *Sweden* 10 E6
Safford, *U.S.A.* 109 K9
Saffron Walden, *U.K.* 15 E8
Safi, *Morocco* 78 B4
Şafīābād, *Iran* 71 B8
Safīd Dasht, *Iran* 71 C6
Safīd Kūh, *Afghan.* 66 B3
Safīd Rūd →, *Iran* 71 B6
Safipur, *India* 69 F9
Safonovo, *Russia* 32 E7
Safranbolu, *Turkey* 72 B5
Saft Rashîn, *Egypt* 80 J7
Şafwān, *Iraq* 70 D5
Sag Harbor, *U.S.A.* 117 F12
Saga, *Japan* 55 H5
Saga □, *Japan* 55 H5
Sagae, *Japan* 54 E10
Sagala, *Mali* 82 C3
Sagamartha = Everest, Mt., *Nepal* 69 E12
Sagamore, *U.S.A.* 116 F5
Sagar, *Karnataka, India* 66 M9
Sagar, *Mad. P., India* 69 H8
Sagara, L., *Tanzania* 86 D3
Sagay, *Phil.* 61 F5
Saginaw, *U.S.A.* 114 D4
Saginaw →, *U.S.A.* 114 D4
Saginaw B., *U.S.A.* 114 D4
Sagleipie, *Liberia* 82 D3
Saglouc = Salluit, *Canada* 101 B12
Sagŏ-ri, *S. Korea* 57 G14
Sagone, *France* 21 F12
Sagone, G. de, *France* 21 F12
Sagres, *Portugal* 37 J2
Sagua la Grande, *Cuba* 120 B3
Saguache, *U.S.A.* 109 G10
Saguaro △, *U.S.A.* 109 K8
Saguenay →, *Canada* 105 C5
Sagunt, *Spain* 38 F4
Sagunto = Sagunt, *Spain* 38 F4
Sagwara, *India* 68 H6
Sahaba, *Sudan* 80 D3

Sahagún, *Spain* 36 C5
Saḩam al Jawlān, *Syria* 74 C4
Sahamandrevo, *Madag.* 89 C8
Sahand, Kūh-e, *Iran* 70 B5
Sahara, *Africa* 78 D6
Saharan Atlas = Saharien, Atlas, *Algeria* 78 B6
Saharanpur, *India* 68 E7
Saharien, Atlas, *Algeria* 78 B6
Saharsa, *India* 69 G12
Sahasinaka, *Madag.* 89 C8
Sahaswan, *India* 69 E8
Sahel, *Africa* 78 E5
Sahel, Canal du, *Mali* 82 C3
Sahibganj, *India* 69 G12
Sāḩilīyah, *Iraq* 70 C4
Sahiwal, *Pakistan* 68 D5
Şahneh, *Iran* 70 C5
Sahrawi = Western Sahara ■, *Africa* 78 D3
Sahuaripa, *Mexico* 118 B3
Sahuarita, *U.S.A.* 109 L8
Sahuayo, *Mexico* 118 C4
Šahy, *Slovak Rep.* 27 C11
Sai →, *India* 69 G10
Sai Buri, *Thailand* 65 J3
Sa'id Bundas, *Sudan* 79 G10
Sa'īdābād = Sīrjān, *Iran* 71 D7
Sa'īdābād, *Iran* 71 B7
Sa'īdīyeh, *Iran* 71 B6
Saidpur, *Bangla.* 67 G16
Saidpur, *India* 69 G10
Saidu, *Pakistan* 69 B5
Saignes, *France* 20 C6
Saigon = Thanh Pho Ho Chi Minh, *Vietnam* 65 G6
Saijō, *Japan* 55 H6
Saikai △, *Japan* 55 H4
Saikanosy Masoala, *Madag.* 89 B9
Saikhoa Ghat, *India* 67 F19
Saiki, *Japan* 55 H5
Sailana, *India* 68 H6
Saillans, *France* 21 D9
Sailolof, *Indonesia* 63 E8
Saimaa, *Finland* 9 F23
Saimbeyli, *Turkey* 72 D7
Saimen = Saimaa, *Finland* 9 F23
Şa'in Dezh, *Iran* 70 B5
St. Abb's Head, *U.K.* 13 F6
St-Affrique, *France* 20 E6
St-Agrève, *France* 21 C8
St-Aignan, *France* 18 E8
St. Alban's, *Canada* 105 C8
St. Albans, *U.K.* 15 F7
St. Albans, *Vt., U.S.A.* 117 B11
St. Albans, *W. Va., U.S.A.* 114 F5
St. Alban's Head, *U.K.* 15 G5
St. Albert, *Canada* 102 C6
St-Amand-en-Puisaye, *France* 19 E10
St-Amand-les-Eaux, *France* 19 B10
St-Amand-Montrond, *France* 19 F9
St-Amarin, *France* 19 E14
St-Amour, *France* 19 F12
St-André-de-Cubzac, *France* 20 D3
St-André-les-Alpes, *France* 21 E10
St. Andrew's, *Canada* 105 C8
St. Andrews, *U.K.* 13 E6
St-Anicet, *Canada* 117 A10
St. Anns B., *Canada* 105 C7
St. Ann's Bay, *Jamaica* 120 a
St. Anthony, *Canada* 105 B8
St. Anthony, *U.S.A.* 108 E8
St-Antoine, *Canada* 105 C7
St-Antonin-Noble-Val, *France* 20 D5
St. Arnaud, *Australia* 95 F3
St-Astier, *France* 20 C4
St-Aubin-du-Cormier, *France* 18 D5
St-Augustin, *Canada* 105 B8
St-Augustin →, *Canada* 105 B8
St. Augustine, *U.S.A.* 115 L5
St-Aulaye, *France* 20 C4
St. Austell, *U.K.* 15 G3
St-Avold, *France* 19 C13
St. Barbe, *Canada* 105 B8
St-Barthélemy, *W. Indies* 121 C7
St-Béat, *France* 20 F4
St. Bees Hd., *U.K.* 14 C4
St. Bees I., *Australia* 94 J7
St-Benoît-du-Sault, *France* 20 B5
St-Bonnet-en-Champsaur, *France* 21 D10
St-Brevin-les-Pins, *France* 18 E4
St-Brice-en-Coglès, *France* 18 D5
St. Bride's, *Canada* 105 C9
St. Brides B., *U.K.* 15 F2
St-Brieuc, *France* 18 D4
St-Calais, *France* 18 E7
St-Cast-le-Guildo, *France* 18 D4
St. Catharines, *Canada* 116 C5
St. Catherines I., *U.S.A.* 115 K5
St. Catherine's Pt., *U.K.* 15 G6
St-Céré, *France* 20 D5
St-Cergue, *Switz.* 25 J2
St-Cernin, *France* 20 C6
St-Chamond, *France* 21 C8
St. Charles, *Ill., U.S.A.* 114 E1
St. Charles, *Mo., U.S.A.* 112 F9
St. Charles, *Va., U.S.A.* 114 F7
St-Chély-d'Apcher, *France* 20 D7
St-Chinian, *France* 20 E6
St. Christopher-Nevis = St. Kitts & Nevis ■, *W. Indies* 121 C7
St-Ciers-sur-Gironde, *France* 20 C3
St. Clair, *Mich., U.S.A.* 116 D2
St. Clair, *Pa., U.S.A.* 117 F8
St. Clair →, *U.S.A.* 116 D2
St. Clair, L., *Canada* 104 D3
St. Clair, L., *U.S.A.* 116 D2
St. Clairsville, *U.S.A.* 116 F4
St-Claud, *France* 20 C4
St. Claude, *Canada* 103 D9
St-Claude, *France* 19 F12
St. Clears, *U.K.* 15 F3
St-Clet, *Canada* 117 A10
St. Cloud, *Fla., U.S.A.* 115 L5
St. Cloud, *Minn., U.S.A.* 112 C7
St. Cricq, C., *Australia* 93 E1
St. Croix, *U.S. Virgin Is.* 121 C7
St. Croix →, *U.S.A.* 112 C8
St. Croix Falls, *U.S.A.* 112 C8
St-Cyprien, *France* 20 F7
St-Cyr-sur-Mer, *France* 21 E9
St. David's, *Canada* 105 C8
St. David's, *U.K.* 15 F2
St. David's Head, *U.K.* 15 F2
St-Denis, *France* 19 D9
St-Dié, *France* 19 D13
St-Dizier, *France* 19 D11
St-Égrève, *France* 21 C9
St. Elias, Mt., *U.S.A.* 100 B5
St. Elias Mts., *N. Amer.* 102 A1
St-Eloy-les-Mines, *France* 19 F9
St-Émilion, *France* 20 D3
St-Étienne, *France* 21 C8
St-Étienne-de-Tinée, *France* 21 D10
St-Étienne-du-Rouvray, *France* 18 C8
St. Eugène, *Canada* 117 A10
St. Eustatius, *W. Indies* 121 C7
St-Exupery, Lyon ✈ (LYS), *France* 21 C9
St-Fargeau, *France* 19 E10
St-Félicien, *Canada* 104 C5
St-Florent, *France* 21 F13
St-Florent, G. de, *France* 21 F13
St-Florent-sur-Cher, *France* 19 F9
St-Florentin, *France* 19 E10
St-Flour, *France* 20 C7
St. Francis, *U.S.A.* 112 F4
St. Francis →, *U.S.A.* 113 H9
St. Francis, C., *S. Africa* 88 E3
St. Francisville, *U.S.A.* 113 K9
St-François, L., *Canada* 117 A10
St-Fulgent, *France* 18 F5
St-Gabriel, *Canada* 104 C5
St. Gallen = Sankt Gallen, *Switz.* 25 H5
St-Galmier, *France* 19 G11
St-Gaudens, *France* 20 E4
St-Gaultier, *France* 18 F8
St-Gengoux-le-National, *France* 19 F11
St-Geniez-d'Olt, *France* 20 D6
St. George, *Australia* 95 D4
St. George, *Canada* 105 C6
St. George, *S.C., U.S.A.* 115 J5
St. George, *Utah, U.S.A.* 109 H7
St. George, C., *Canada* 105 C8
St. George, C., *U.S.A.* 115 L3
St. George Ra., *Australia* 92 C4
St. George's, *Canada* 105 C8
St-Georges, *Canada* 105 C5
St. George's, *Grenada* 121 D7
St. George's B., *Canada* 105 C8
St. Georges Basin, *N.S.W., Australia* 95 F5
St. Georges Basin, *W. Austral., Australia* 92 C4
St. George's Channel, *Europe* 12 E6
St. Georges Hd., *Australia* 95 F5
St-Georges-lès-Baillargeaux, *France* 20 B4
St-Germain-de-Calberte, *France* 20 D7
St-Germain-en-Laye, *France* 19 D9
St-Germain-Lembron, *France* 20 C7
St-Gervais-d'Auvergne, *France* 19 F9
St-Gervais-les-Bains, *France* 21 C10
St-Gildas, Pte. de, *France* 18 E4
St-Gilles, *France* 21 E8
St-Girons, *Ariège, France* 20 F5
St-Girons, *Landes, France* 20 E2
St. Gotthard P. = San Gottardo, P. del, *Switz.* 25 J4
St. Helena, *Atl. Oc.* 76 H3
St. Helena, *U.S.A.* 108 G2
St. Helena, Mt., *U.S.A.* 110 G4
St. Helena B., *S. Africa* 88 E2
St. Helens, *Australia* 95 G4
St. Helens, *U.K.* 14 D5
St. Helens, *U.S.A.* 110 E4
St. Helens, Mt., *U.S.A.* 110 D4
St. Helier, *U.K.* 15 H5
St-Herblain, *France* 18 E5
St-Hilaire-du-Harcouët, *France* 18 D5
St-Hippolyte, *France* 19 E13
St-Hippolyte-du-Fort, *France* 20 E7
St-Honoré-les-Bains, *France* 19 F10
St-Hubert, *Belgium* 17 D5
St-Hyacinthe, *Canada* 104 C5
St. Ignace, *U.S.A.* 114 C3
St. Ignace I., *Canada* 104 C2
St. Ignatius, *U.S.A.* 108 C6
St-Imier, *Switz.* 25 H2
St. Ives, *Cambs., U.K.* 15 E7
St. Ives, *Corn., U.K.* 15 G2
St-James, *France* 18 D5
St. James, *U.S.A.* 112 D7
St-Jean →, *Canada* 105 B7
St-Jean, L., *Canada* 105 C5
St-Jean-d'Angély, *France* 20 C3
St-Jean-de-Braye, *France* 19 E8
St-Jean-de-Luz, *France* 20 E2
St-Jean-de-Maurienne, *France* 21 C10
St-Jean-de-Monts, *France* 18 F4
St-Jean-du-Gard, *France* 20 D7
St-Jean-en-Royans, *France* 21 C9
St-Jean-Pied-de-Port, *France* 20 E2
St-Jean-Port-Joli, *Canada* 105 C5
St-Jean-sur-Richelieu, *Canada* 117 A11
St-Jérôme, *Canada* 104 C5
St. John, *Canada* 105 C6
St. John, *U.S.A.* 113 G5
St. John →, *Liberia* 82 D2
St. John →, *U.S.A.* 115 C12
St. John, C., *Canada* 105 C8
St. John I., *U.S. Virgin Is.* 121 e
St. John's, *Antigua & B.* 121 C7
St. John's, *Canada* 105 C9
St. Johns, *Ariz., U.S.A.* 109 J9
St. Johns, *Mich., U.S.A.* 114 D3
St. Johns →, *U.S.A.* 115 K5
St. John's Pt., *Ireland* 12 B3
St. Johnsbury, *U.S.A.* 117 B12
St. Johnsville, *U.S.A.* 117 D10
St-Joseph, *Martinique* 120 c
St. Joseph, *La., U.S.A.* 113 K9
St. Joseph, *Mo., U.S.A.* 112 F7
St. Joseph →, *U.S.A.* 114 D2
St. Joseph, I., *Canada* 104 C3
St. Joseph, L., *Canada* 104 B1
St-Jovite, *Canada* 104 C5
St-Juéry, *France* 20 E6
St-Julien-Chapteuil, *France* 21 C8
St-Julien-de-Vouvantes, *France* 18 E5
St-Julien-en-Genevois, *France* 19 F13
St-Junien, *France* 20 C4
St-Just-en-Chaussée, *France* 19 C9
St-Just-en-Chevalet, *France* 20 C7
St. Kitts & Nevis ■, *W. Indies* 121 C7
St. Laurent, *Canada* 103 C9
St-Laurent-de-la-Salanque, *France* 20 F6
St-Laurent-du-Pont, *France* 21 C9
St-Laurent-en-Grandvaux, *France* 19 F12
St-Laurent-Médoc, *France* 20 C3
St. Lawrence, *Australia* 94 C4
St. Lawrence, *Canada* 105 C8
St. Lawrence →, *Canada* 105 C6
St. Lawrence, Gulf of, *Canada* 105 C7
St. Lawrence I., *U.S.A.* 100 B3
St. Lawrence Islands △, *Canada* 117 B9
St. Leonard, *Canada* 105 C6
St-Léonard-de-Noblat, *France* 20 C5
St. Lewis →, *Canada* 105 B8
St-Lô, *France* 18 C5
St-Louis, *France* 19 E14
St-Louis, *Guadeloupe* 120 b
St. Louis, *Senegal* 82 B1
St. Louis, *U.S.A.* 112 F9
St. Louis →, *U.S.A.* 112 B8
St-Loup-sur-Semouse, *France* 19 E13
St. Lucia ■, *W. Indies* 121 f
St. Lucia, L., *S. Africa* 89 D5
St. Lucia Channel, *W. Indies* 121 D7
St. Maarten ⊠, *W. Indies* 121 C7
St. Magnus B., *U.K.* 13 A7
St-Maixent-l'École, *France* 20 B3
St-Malo, *France* 18 D4
St-Malo, G. de, *France* 18 D4
St-Mandrier-sur-Mer, *France* 21 E9
St-Marc, *Haiti* 121 C5
St-Marcellin, *France* 21 C9
St-Marcouf, Îs., *France* 18 C5
St. Maries, *U.S.A.* 108 C5
St-Martin ⊠, *W. Indies* 121 C7
St-Martin, C., *Martinique* 120 c
St. Martin, L., *Canada* 103 C9
St-Martin-de-Crau, *France* 21 E8
St-Martin-de-Ré, *France* 20 B2
St-Martin-d'Hères, *France* 21 C9
St-Martin-Vésubie, *France* 21 D11
St. Martins, *Barbados* 121 g
St-Martory, *France* 20 E4
St. Mary Pk., *Australia* 95 E2
St. Marys, *Australia* 95 G4
St. Marys, *Canada* 116 C3
St. Mary's, *Corn., U.K.* 15 H1
St. Mary's, *Orkney, U.K.* 13 C6
St. Marys, *Ga., U.S.A.* 115 K5
St. Marys, *Pa., U.S.A.* 116 E6
St. Mary's, C., *Canada* 105 C9
St. Mary's B., *Canada* 105 C9
St. Marys Bay, *Canada* 105 D6
St-Mathieu, Pte., *France* 18 D2
St. Matthew I., *U.S.A.* 100 B2
St-Maurice →, *Canada* 104 C5
St. Mawes, *U.K.* 15 G2
St-Maximin-la-Ste-Baume, *France* 21 E9
St-Médard-en-Jalles, *France* 20 D3
St-Méen-le-Grand, *France* 18 D4
St-Mihiel, *France* 19 D12
St. Moritz, *Switz.* 25 J5
St-Nazaire, *France* 18 E4
St. Neots, *U.K.* 15 E7
St-Nicolas-de-Port, *France* 19 D13
St-Niklaas, *Belgium* 17 C4
St-Omer, *France* 19 B9
St-Palais-sur-Mer, *France* 20 C2
St-Pamphile, *Canada* 105 C6
St-Pardoux-la-Rivière, *France* 20 C4
St-Pascal, *Canada* 105 C6
St. Paul, *Canada* 102 C6
St-Paul, *France* 21 D10
St. Paul, *Minn., U.S.A.* 112 C8
St. Paul, *Nebr., U.S.A.* 112 E5
St-Paul →, *Canada* 105 B8
St. Paul →, *Liberia* 82 D2
St. Paul, I., *Ind. Oc.* 3 F13
St-Paul-de-Fenouillet, *France* 20 F6
St. Paul I., *Canada* 105 C7
St-Paul-lès-Dax, *France* 20 E2
St-Péray, *France* 21 D8
St. Peter, *U.S.A.* 112 C8
St-Peter-Ording, *Germany* 24 A4
St. Peter Port, *U.K.* 15 H5
St. Peters, *N.S., Canada* 105 C7
St. Peters, *P.E.I., Canada* 105 C7
St. Petersburg = Sankt-Peterburg, *Russia* 32 C6
St. Petersburg, *U.S.A.* 115 M4
St-Philbert-de-Grand-Lieu, *France* 18 E5
St-Pie, *Canada* 117 A12
St-Pierre, *Martinique* 120 c
St-Pierre, *St-P. & M.* 105 C8
St-Pierre, L., *Canada* 104 C5
St-Pierre-d'Oléron, *France* 20 C2
St-Pierre-en-Port, *France* 18 C7
St-Pierre-et-Miquelon ⊠, *N. Amer.* 105 C8
St-Pierre-le-Moûtier, *France* 19 F10
St-Pierre-sur-Dives, *France* 18 C6
St-Pol-de-Léon, *France* 18 D3
St-Pol-sur-Mer, *France* 19 A9
St-Pol-sur-Ternoise, *France* 19 B9
St-Pons, *France* 20 E6
St-Pourçain-sur-Sioule, *France* 19 F10
St-Priest, *France* 21 C8
St-Quay-Portrieux, *France* 18 D4
St-Quentin, *Canada* 105 C6
St-Quentin, *France* 19 C10
St-Rambert-d'Albon, *France* 21 C8
St-Raphaël, *France* 21 E10
St. Regis, *U.S.A.* 108 C6
St-Renan, *France* 18 D2
St-Saëns, *France* 18 C8
St-Savin, *France* 20 B4
St-Savinien, *France* 20 C3
St. Sebastien, Tanjon' i, *Madag.* 89 A8
St-Seine-l'Abbaye, *France* 19 E11
St-Sernin-sur-Rance, *France* 20 E6
St-Sever, *France* 20 E3
St-Siméon, *Canada* 105 C6
St. Simons I., *U.S.A.* 115 K5
St. Simons Island, *U.S.A.* 115 K5
St. Stephen, *Canada* 105 C6
St-Sulpice, *France* 20 E5
St-Sulpice-Laurière, *France* 20 B5
St-Sulpice-les-Feuilles, *France* 20 B5
St-Syprien = St-Cyprien, *France* 20 F7
St-Thégonnec, *France* 18 D3
St. Thomas, *Canada* 116 D3
St. Thomas I., *U.S. Virgin Is.* 121 e
St-Tite, *Canada* 104 C5
St-Tropez, *France* 21 E10
St-Troud = St. Truiden, *Belgium* 17 D5
St. Truiden, *Belgium* 17 D5
St-Vaast-la-Hougue, *France* 18 C5
St-Valery-en-Caux, *France* 18 C7
St-Valéry-sur-Somme, *France* 19 B8
St-Vallier, *France* 19 F11
St-Vallier-de-Thiey, *France* 21 E10
St-Varent, *France* 18 F6
St-Vaury, *France* 20 B5
St. Vincent, *Italy* 40 C4
St. Vincent, G., *Australia* 95 F2
St. Vincent & the Grenadines ■, *W. Indies* 121 D7
St-Vincent-de-Tyrosse, *France* 20 E2
St. Vincent Passage, *W. Indies* 121 D7
St-Vith, *Belgium* 17 D6
St-Vivien-de-Médoc, *France* 20 C2
St. Walburg, *Canada* 103 C7
St-Yrieix-la-Perche, *France* 20 C5
Ste-Adresse, *France* 18 C7
Ste-Agathe-des-Monts, *Canada* 104 C5
Ste-Anne, *Guadeloupe* 120 b
Ste-Anne, L., *Canada* 105 B6
Ste-Anne-des-Monts-Tourelle, *Canada* 105 C6
Ste-Croix, *Switz.* 25 J2
Ste-Enimie, *France* 20 D7
Ste-Foy-la-Grande, *France* 20 D4
Ste. Genevieve, *U.S.A.* 112 G9
Ste-Hermine, *France* 20 B2
Ste-Livrade-sur-Lot, *France* 20 D4
Ste-Marguerite →, *Canada* 105 B6
Ste-Marie, *Canada* 105 C5
Ste-Marie, *Martinique* 120 c
Ste-Marie-aux-Mines, *France* 19 D14
Ste-Maure-de-Touraine, *France* 18 E7
Ste-Maxime, *France* 21 E10
Ste-Menehould, *France* 19 C11
Ste-Mère-Église, *France* 18 C5
Ste-Rose, *Guadeloupe* 120 b
Ste. Rose du Lac, *Canada* 103 C9
Ste-Savine, *France* 19 D11
Ste-Sigolène, *France* 21 C8
Saintes, *France* 20 C3
Saintes, Îs. des, *Guadeloupe* 120 b
Stes-Maries-de-la-Mer, *France* 21 E8
Saintfield, *U.K.* 12 B6
Saintonge, *France* 20 C3
Saipan, *Pac. Oc.* 96 F6
Sairang, *India* 67 H18
Sairecábur, Cerro, *Bolivia* 126 A2
Saitama □, *Japan* 55 F9
Saiteli = Kadınhanı, *Turkey* 72 C5
Saiţi, *Moldova* 29 D14
Saiyid, *Pakistan* 68 C5
Saja-Besaya △, *Spain* 36 B6
Sajama, *Bolivia* 124 G5
Sajan, *Serbia & M.* 28 E5
Sajó →, *Hungary* 28 C6
Sajószentpéter, *Hungary* 28 B5
Sajum, *India* 69 C8
Sak →, *S. Africa* 88 E3
Sakaba, *Nigeria* 83 C6
Sakai, *Japan* 55 G7
Sakaide, *Japan* 55 G6
Sakaiminato, *Japan* 55 G6
Sakākah, *Si. Arabia* 70 D4
Sakakawea, L., *U.S.A.* 112 B4
Sakami →, *Canada* 104 B4
Sakami, L., *Canada* 104 B4
Sâkâne, 'Erg i-n, *Mali* 83 A4
Sakania, *Dem. Rep. of the Congo* 87 E2
Sakaraha, *Madag.* 89 C7
Sakarya, *Turkey* 72 B4
Sakarya →, *Turkey* 72 B4
Sakashima-Guntō, *Japan* 55 M2
Sakassou, *Ivory C.* 82 D3
Sakata, *Japan* 54 E9
Sakchu, *N. Korea* 57 D13
Sakeny →, *Madag.* 89 C8
Sakété, *Benin* 83 D5
Sakha □, *Russia* 53 C13
Sakhalin, *Russia* 53 D15
Sakhalinskiy Zaliv, *Russia* 53 D15
Şaki, *Azerbaijan* 35 K8
Šakiai, *Lithuania* 9 J20
Sakon Nakhon, *Thailand* 64 D5
Sakrand, *Pakistan* 68 F3
Sakri, *India* 69 F12
Sakrivier, *S. Africa* 88 E3
Sakskøbing, *Denmark* 11 K5
Sakti, *India* 69 H10
Sakuma, *Japan* 55 G8
Sakurai, *Japan* 55 G7
Saky, *Ukraine* 33 K7
Sal →, *Russia* 35 G5
Sala, *Eritrea* 81 D4
Šal'a, *Slovak Rep.* 27 C10
Sala, *Sweden* 10 E10
Sala →, *Eritrea* 81 D4
Sala Consilina, *Italy* 43 B8
Sala-y-Gómez, *Pac. Oc.* 97 K17
Salaberry-de-Valleyfield, *Canada* 117 A10
Salacgrīva, *Latvia* 30 A11
Salada, L., *Mexico* 109 K6
Saladas, *Argentina* 126 B4
Saladillo, *Argentina* 126 D4
Salado →, *Buenos Aires, Argentina* 126 D4
Salado →, *La Pampa, Argentina* 128 D3
Salado →, *Santa Fe, Argentina* 126 C3
Salado →, *Mexico* 113 M5
Salaga, *Ghana* 83 D4
Şalāh, *Syria* 74 C5
Şalāḩ ad Dīn □, *Iraq* 70 C4
Sălaj □, *Romania* 28 C8
Sálakhos, *Greece* 49 C9
Salala, *Liberia* 82 D2
Salala, *Sudan* 80 C4
Salālah, *Oman* 75 D5
Salamanca, *Chile* 126 C1
Salamanca, *Spain* 36 E5
Salamanca, *U.S.A.* 116 D6
Salamanca □, *Spain* 36 E5
Salāmatābād, *Iran* 70 C5
Salamis, *Cyprus* 49 D12
Salamís, *Greece* 46 D5
Salar de Atacama, *Chile* 126 A2
Salar de Uyuni, *Bolivia* 124 H5
Sălard, *Romania* 28 C7
Salas, *Spain* 36 B4
Salas de los Infantes, *Spain* 36 C7
Salatiga, *Indonesia* 63 G14
Salaverry, *Peru* 124 E3
Salawati, *Indonesia* 63 E8
Salaya, *India* 68 H3
Salayar, *Indonesia* 63 F6
Salazar →, *Spain* 38 C3
Salbris, *France* 19 E9
Salcia, *Romania* 29 G9
Sălciua, *Romania* 29 D8
Salcombe, *U.K.* 15 G4
Saldaña, *Spain* 36 C6
Saldanha, *S. Africa* 88 E2
Saldanha B., *S. Africa* 88 E2
Saldus, *Latvia* 9 H20
Saldus □, *Latvia* 30 B9
Sale, *Australia* 95 F4
Sale, *Italy* 40 D5
Salé, *Morocco* 78 B4
Sale, *U.K.* 14 D5
Salekhard, *Russia* 52 C7
Salem, *India* 66 P11
Salem, *Ill., U.S.A.* 114 F1
Salem, *Ind., U.S.A.* 114 F2
Salem, *Mass., U.S.A.* 117 D14
Salem, *Mo., U.S.A.* 113 G9
Salem, *N.H., U.S.A.* 117 D13
Salem, *N.J., U.S.A.* 114 F8
Salem, *N.Y., U.S.A.* 117 C11
Salem, *Ohio, U.S.A.* 116 F4
Salem, *Oreg., U.S.A.* 108 D2
Salem, *S. Dak., U.S.A.* 112 D6
Salem, *Va., U.S.A.* 114 G5
Salemi, *Italy* 42 E5
Sälen, *Sweden* 10 C7
Salernes, *France* 21 E10
Salerno, *Italy* 43 B7
Salerno, G. di, *Italy* 43 B7
Salford, *U.K.* 14 D5
Salgir →, *Ukraine* 33 K8
Salgótarján, *Hungary* 28 B4
Salgueiro, *Brazil* 125 E11
Salibabu, *Indonesia* 63 D7
Salibea = Salybia, *Trin. & Tob.* 125 K15
Salida, *U.S.A.* 106 C5
Salies-de-Béarn, *France* 20 E3
Salihli, *Turkey* 72 C3
Salihorsk, *Belarus* 33 F4
Salima, *Malawi* 85 G6
Salina, *Italy* 43 D7
Salina, *Kans., U.S.A.* 112 F6
Salina, *Utah, U.S.A.* 109 G8
Salina Cruz, *Mexico* 119 D5
Salina di Margherita di Savoia ⌓, *Italy* 43 A9
Salinas, *Brazil* 125 G10
Salinas, *Chile* 126 A2
Salinas, *Ecuador* 124 D2
Salinas, *U.S.A.* 110 J5
Salinas →, *Guatemala* 119 D6
Salinas →, *U.S.A.* 110 J5
Salinas, B. de, *Nic.* 120 D2
Salinas, Pampa de las, *Argentina* 126 C2
Salinas Ambargasta, *Argentina* 126 B3
Salinas de Hidalgo, *Mexico* 118 C4
Salinas Grandes, *Argentina* 126 C3
Salinas Pueblo Missions ⌓, *U.S.A.* 109 J10
Saline →, *Ark., U.S.A.* 113 J8
Saline →, *Kans., U.S.A.* 112 F6
Saline di Trapani e Paceco ⌓, *Italy* 42 E5
Salines, C. de ses, *Spain* 48 B10
Salinópolis, *Brazil* 125 D9

Salins-les-Bains, *France* 19 F12
Salir, *Portugal* 37 H2
Salisbury, *U.K.* 15 F6
Salisbury, *Md., U.S.A.* 114 F8
Salisbury, *N.C., U.S.A.* 115 H5
Salisbury I., *Canada* 101 B12
Salisbury Plain, *U.K.* 15 F6
Săliște, *Romania* 29 E8
Salka, *Nigeria* 83 C5
Şalkhad, *Syria* 74 C5
Salkove, *Ukraine* 29 B14
Salla, *Finland* 8 C23
Sallanches, *France* 21 C10
Sallent, *Spain* 38 D6
Salles, *France* 20 D3
Salles-Curan, *France* 20 D6
Salling, *Denmark* 11 H2
Salliq = Coral Harbour, *Canada* 101 B11
Sallisaw, *U.S.A.* 113 H7
Sallom Junction, *Sudan* 80 D4
Salluit, *Canada* 101 B12
Salmās, *Iran* 70 B5
Salmerón, *Spain* 38 E2
Salmo, *Canada* 102 D5
Salmon, *U.S.A.* 108 D7
Salmon →, *Canada* 102 C4
Salmon →, *U.S.A.* 108 D5
Salmon Arm, *Canada* 102 C5
Salmon Gums, *Australia* 93 F3
Salmon River Mts., *U.S.A.* 108 D6
Salo, *Finland* 9 F20
Salò, *Italy* 40 C7
Salobreña, *Spain* 37 J7
Salome, *U.S.A.* 111 M13
Salon, *India* 69 F9
Salon-de-Provence, *France* 21 E9
Salonica = Thessaloníki, *Greece* 44 F6
Salonta, *Romania* 28 D6
Salor →, *Spain* 37 F3
Salou, *Spain* 38 D6
Salou, C. de, *Spain* 38 D6
Saloum →, *Senegal* 82 C1
Salpausselkä, *Finland* 9 F22
Salsacate, *Argentina* 126 C2
Salses, *France* 20 F6
Salsk, *Russia* 35 G5
Salso →, *Italy* 42 E6
Salsomaggiore Terme, *Italy* 40 D6
Salt, *Spain* 38 D7
Salt →, *Canada* 102 B6
Salt →, *U.S.A.* 109 K7
Salt L., The, *Australia* 95 E3
Salt Lake City, *U.S.A.* 108 F8
Salt Range, *Pakistan* 68 C5
Salta, *Argentina* 126 A2
Salta □, *Argentina* 126 A2
Saltara, *Italy* 41 E9
Saltash, *U.K.* 15 G3
Saltburn by the Sea, *U.K.* 14 C7
Saltcoats, *U.K.* 13 F4
Saltee Is., *Ireland* 12 D5
Saltfjellet, *Norway* 8 C16
Saltfjorden, *Norway* 8 C16
Saltholm, *Denmark* 11 J6
Saltillo, *Mexico* 118 B4
Salto, *Argentina* 126 C3
Salto, *Uruguay* 126 C4
Salto del Guaíra, *Paraguay* 127 A5
Salton City, *U.S.A.* 111 M11
Salton Sea, *U.S.A.* 111 M11
Saltpond, *Ghana* 83 D4
Saltsburg, *U.S.A.* 116 F5
Saltsjöbaden, *Sweden* 10 E12
Saluda →, *U.S.A.* 115 J5
Salûm, *Egypt* 80 A2
Salûm, Khâlig el, *Egypt* 80 A2
Salur, *India* 67 K13
Saluzzo, *Italy* 40 D4
Salvador, *Brazil* 125 F11
Salvador, *Canada* 103 C7
Salvador, El ■, *Cent. Amer.* 120 D2
Salvador, L., *U.S.A.* 113 L9
Salvaterra de Magos, *Portugal* 37 F2
Sálvora, I. de, *Spain* 36 C2
Salween →, *Burma* 67 L20
Salyan, *Azerbaijan* 52 F5
Salybia, *Trin. & Tob.* 125 K15
Salza →, *Austria* 26 D7
Salzach →, *Austria* 26 C5
Salzburg, *Austria* 26 D6
Salzburg □, *Austria* 26 D6
Salzgitter, *Germany* 24 C6
Salzkotten, *Germany* 24 D4
Salzwedel, *Germany* 24 C7
Sam, *India* 68 F4
Sam Neua, *Laos* 58 G5
Sam Ngao, *Thailand* 64 D2
Sam Rayburn Reservoir, *U.S.A.* 113 K7
Sam Son, *Vietnam* 64 C5
Sam Teu, *Laos* 64 C5
Sama de Langreo = Langreo, *Spain* 36 B5
Samagaltay, *Russia* 53 D10
Samales Group, *Phil.* 61 J4
Samâlût, *Egypt* 80 B3
Samana, *India* 68 D7
Samana Cay, *Bahamas* 121 B5
Samandağı, *Turkey* 72 D6
Samandıra, *Turkey* 45 F13
Samanga, *Tanzania* 87 D4
Samangān □, *Afghan.* 66 B5
Samangwa, *Dem. Rep. of the Congo* 86 C1
Samani, *Japan* 54 C11
Samanli Dağları, *Turkey* 45 F13
Samar, *Phil.* 61 F6
Samara, *Russia* 34 D10
Samara →, *Russia* 34 D10
Samara →, *Ukraine* 33 H8
Samaria = Shōmrōn, *West Bank* 74 C4
Samariá, *Greece* 49 D5
Samaria ∆, *Greece* 46 F5
Samarinda, *Indonesia* 62 E5
Samarkand = Samarqand, *Uzbekistan* 52 F7
Samarqand, *Uzbekistan* 52 F7
Sāmarrā', *Iraq* 70 C4
Samastipur, *India* 69 G11
Şamaxi, *Azerbaijan* 35 K9
Samba, *Dem. Rep. of the Congo* 86 C2
Samba, *India* 69 C6
Sambalpur, *India* 67 J14
Sambar, Tanjung, *Indonesia* 62 E4
Sambas, *Indonesia* 62 D3
Sambava, *Madag.* 89 A9
Sambawizi, *Zimbabwe* 87 F2
Sambhal, *India* 69 E8
Sambhar, *India* 68 F6
Sambhar L., *India* 68 F6
Sambiase, *Italy* 43 D9
Sambir, *Ukraine* 31 J10
Sambor, *Cambodia* 64 F6
Samborombón, B., *Argentina* 126 D4
Sambuca di Sicilia, *Italy* 42 E6
Samburu ⌓, *Kenya* 86 B4
Samch'ŏk, *S. Korea* 57 F15
Samch'onp'o, *S. Korea* 57 G15
Same, *Tanzania* 86 C4
Samer, *France* 19 B8
Samfya, *Zambia* 87 E2
Sámi, *Greece* 46 C2
Şämkir, *Azerbaijan* 35 K8
Şamlı, *Turkey* 47 B9
Samnah, *Si. Arabia* 70 E3
Samo Alto, *Chile* 126 C1
Samoa ■, *Pac. Oc.* 91 B13
Samoan Is., *Pac. Oc.* 91 A13
Samobor, *Croatia* 41 C12
Samoëns, *France* 19 F13
Samokov, *Bulgaria* 44 D7
Šamorín, *Slovak Rep.* 27 C10
Samorogouan, *Burkina Faso* 82 C4
Sámos, *Greece* 47 D8
Samoš, *Serbia & M.* 28 E5
Samos, *Spain* 36 C3
Sámos □, *Greece* 47 D8
Samothráki = Mathráki, *Greece* 49 A3
Samothráki, *Greece* 45 F9
Samoylovka, *Russia* 34 E6
Sampa, *Ghana* 82 D4
Sampacho, *Argentina* 126 C3
Sampalan, *Indonesia* 63 K18
Sampang, *Indonesia* 63 G15
Samper de Calanda, *Spain* 38 D4
Sampéyre, *Italy* 40 D4
Sampit, *Indonesia* 62 E4
Sampit, Teluk, *Indonesia* 62 E4
Samrong, *Cambodia* 64 E4
Samrong, *Thailand* 64 E3
Samsø, *Denmark* 11 J4
Samsø Bælt, *Denmark* 11 J4
Samsun, *Turkey* 72 B7
Samtredia, *Georgia* 35 J6
Samui, Ko, *Thailand* 65 b
Samur →, *Russia* 35 K9
Samurskiy Khrebet, *Russia* 35 K8
Samusole, *Dem. Rep. of the Congo* 87 E1
Samut Prakan, *Thailand* 64 F3
Samut Songkhram →, *Thailand* 62 B1
Samwari, *Pakistan* 68 E2
San, *Mali* 82 C4
San →, *Cambodia* 64 F5
San →, *Poland* 31 H8
San Adrián, *Spain* 38 C3
San Adrián, C. de, *Spain* 36 B2
San Agustin, C., *Phil.* 61 H7
San Agustín de Valle Fértil, *Argentina* 126 C2
San Ambrosio, *Pac. Oc.* 97 K20
San Andreas, *U.S.A.* 110 G6
San Andres, *Phil.* 61 E6
San Andrés, I. de, *Caribbean* 120 D3
San Andrês del Rabanedo, *Spain* 36 C5
San Andres Mts., *U.S.A.* 109 K10
San Andrés Tuxtla, *Mexico* 119 D5
San Angelo, *U.S.A.* 113 K4
San Anselmo, *U.S.A.* 110 H4
San Antonio, *Belize* 119 D7
San Antonio, *Chile* 126 C1
San Antonio, *Phil.* 61 D4
San Antonio, *N. Mex., U.S.A.* 109 K10
San Antonio, *Tex., U.S.A.* 113 L5
San Antonio →, *U.S.A.* 113 L6
San Antonio, C., *Argentina* 126 D4
San Antonio, C. de, *Cuba* 120 B3
San Antonio, C. de, *Spain* 39 G5
San Antonio, Mt., *U.S.A.* 111 L9
San Antonio de los Baños, *Cuba* 120 B3
San Antonio de los Cobres, *Argentina* 126 A2
San Antonio Oeste, *Argentina* 128 E4
San Arcángelo, *Italy* 43 B9
San Ardo, *U.S.A.* 110 J6
San Augustín, *Canary Is.* 48 G4
San Augustine, *U.S.A.* 113 K7
San Bartolomé, *Canary Is.* 48 F6
San Bartolomé de Tirajana, *Canary Is.* 48 G4
San Bartolomeo in Galdo, *Italy* 43 A8
San Benedetto del Tronto, *Italy* 41 F10
San Benedetto Po, *Italy* 40 C7
San Benedicto, I., *Mexico* 118 D2
San Benito, *U.S.A.* 113 M6
San Benito →, *U.S.A.* 110 J5
San Benito Mt., *U.S.A.* 110 J6
San Bernardino, *U.S.A.* 111 L9
San Bernardino Mts., *U.S.A.* 111 L10
San Bernardino Str., *Phil.* 61 E6
San Bernardo, *Chile* 126 C1
San Bernardo, I. de, *Colombia* 124 B3
San Blas, *Mexico* 118 B3
San Blas, Arch. de, *Panama* 120 E4
San Blas, C., *U.S.A.* 115 L3
San Bonifacio, *Italy* 41 C8
San Borja, *Bolivia* 124 F5
San Buenaventura = Ventura, *U.S.A.* 111 L7
San Buenaventura, *Mexico* 118 B4
San Carlos = Sant Carles, *Spain* 48 B8
San Carlos, *Argentina* 126 C2
San Carlos, *Chile* 126 D1
San Carlos, *Baja Calif. S., Mexico* 118 C2
San Carlos, *Coahuila, Mexico* 118 B4
San Carlos, *Nic.* 120 D3
San Carlos, *Neg. Occ., Phil.* 61 F5
San Carlos, *Pangasinan, Phil.* 61 D4
San Carlos, *Uruguay* 127 C5
San Carlos, *U.S.A.* 109 K8
San Carlos, *Venezuela* 124 B5
San Carlos de Bariloche, *Argentina* 128 E2
San Carlos de Bolívar, *Argentina* 128 D4
San Carlos de la Rápita = Sant Carles de la Ràpita, *Spain* 38 E5
San Carlos del Zulia, *Venezuela* 124 B4
San Carlos L., *U.S.A.* 109 K8
San Cataldo, *Italy* 42 E6
San Celoni = Sant Celoni, *Spain* 38 D7
San Clemente, *Chile* 126 D1
San Clemente, *Spain* 39 F2
San Clemente, *U.S.A.* 111 M9
San Clemente I., *U.S.A.* 111 N8
San Cristóbal = Es Migjorn Gran, *Spain* 48 B11
San Cristóbal, *Argentina* 126 C3
San Cristóbal, *Dom. Rep.* 121 C5
San Cristóbal, *Venezuela* 124 B4
San Cristóbal de la Casas, *Mexico* 119 D6
San Damiano d'Asti, *Italy* 40 D5
San Daniele del Friuli, *Italy* 41 B10
San Diego, *Calif., U.S.A.* 111 N9
San Diego, *Tex., U.S.A.* 113 M5
San Diego, C., *Argentina* 128 G3
San Diego de la Unión, *Mexico* 118 C4
San Diego International ✕ (SAN), *U.S.A.* 111 N9
San Dimitri, Ras, *Malta* 49 C1
San Dimitri Point = San Dimitri, Ras, *Malta* 49 C1
San Donà di Piave, *Italy* 41 C9
San Estanislao, *Paraguay* 126 A4
San Esteban de Gormaz, *Spain* 38 D1
San Felice Circeo, *Italy* 42 A6
San Felice sul Panaro, *Italy* 41 D8
San Felipe, *Chile* 126 C1
San Felipe, *Mexico* 118 A2
San Felipe, *Venezuela* 124 A5
San Felipe →, *U.S.A.* 111 M11
San Félix, *Chile* 126 B1
San Félix, *Pac. Oc.* 97 K20
San Fernando = Sant Ferran, *Spain* 48 C7
San Fernando, *Chile* 126 C1
San Fernando, *Baja Calif., Mexico* 118 B1
San Fernando, *Tamaulipas, Mexico* 119 C5
San Fernando, *La Union, Phil.* 61 C4
San Fernando, *Pampanga, Phil.* 61 D4
San Fernando, *Spain* 37 J4
San Fernando, *Trin. & Tob.* 121 D7
San Fernando, *U.S.A.* 111 L8
San Fernando de Apure, *Venezuela* 124 B5
San Fernando de Atabapo, *Venezuela* 124 C5
San Fernando di Púglia, *Italy* 43 A9
San Francisco, *Argentina* 126 C3
San Francisco, *U.S.A.* 110 H4
San Francisco →, *U.S.A.* 109 K9
San Francisco, C. de, *Colombia* 122 C3
San Francisco, Paso de, *S. Amer.* 126 B2
San Francisco de Macorís, *Dom. Rep.* 121 C5
San Francisco del Monte de Oro, *Argentina* 126 C2
San Francisco del Oro, *Mexico* 118 B3
San Francisco International ✕ (SFO), *U.S.A.* 110 H4
San Francisco Javier = Sant Francesc de Formentera, *Spain* 48 C7
San Fratello, *Italy* 43 D7
San Gabriel, *Chile* 126 C1
San Gabriel Mts., *U.S.A.* 111 L9
San Gavino Monreale, *Italy* 42 C1
San German, *Puerto Rico* 121 d
San Gimignano, *Italy* 40 E8
San Giórgio di Nogaro, *Italy* 41 C10
San Giórgio Iónico, *Italy* 43 B10
San Giovanni Bianco, *Italy* 40 C6
San Giovanni in Fiore, *Italy* 43 C9
San Giovanni in Persiceto, *Italy* 41 D8
San Giovanni Rotondo, *Italy* 41 G12
San Giovanni Valdarno, *Italy* 41 E8
San Giuliano Terme, *Italy* 40 E7
San Gorgonio Mt., *U.S.A.* 111 L10
San Gottardo, P. del, *Switz.* 25 J4
San Gregorio, *Uruguay* 127 C4
San Gregorio, *U.S.A.* 110 H4
San Guiseppe Jato, *Italy* 42 E6
San Ignacio, *Belize* 119 D7
San Ignacio, *Bolivia* 124 G6
San Ignacio, *Mexico* 118 B2
San Ignacio, *Paraguay* 120 C2
San Ignacio ⌓, *Mexico* 118 B2
San Ignacio, L., *Mexico* 118 B2
San Ildefonso, C., *Phil.* 61 C5
San Isidro, *Argentina* 126 C4
San Isidro, *Phil.* 61 H7
San Jacinto, *U.S.A.* 111 M10
San Jaime = Sant Jaume, *Spain* 48 B11
San Javier, *Misiones, Argentina* 127 B4
San Javier, *Santa Fe, Argentina* 126 C4
San Javier, *Bolivia* 124 G6
San Javier, *Chile* 126 D1
San Javier, *Spain* 39 H4
San Jeronimo Taviche, *Mexico* 119 D5
San Joaquin, *U.S.A.* 110 J6
San Joaquin →, *U.S.A.* 110 G5
San Joaquin Valley, *U.S.A.* 110 J6
San Jon, *U.S.A.* 113 H3
San Jordi = Sant Jordi, *Spain* 48 B9
San Jorge, *Argentina* 126 C3
San Jorge, B. de, *Mexico* 118 A2
San Jorge, G., *Argentina* 128 F3
San José = San Josep, *Spain* 48 C7
San José, *Costa Rica* 120 E3
San José, *Guatemala* 120 D1
San José, *Mexico* 118 C2
San Jose, *Mind. Occ., Phil.* 61 E4
San Jose, *Nueva Ecija, Phil.* 61 D4
San Jose, *U.S.A.* 110 H5
San Jose →, *U.S.A.* 109 J10
San Jose de Buenavista, *Phil.* 63 B6
San José de Chiquitos, *Bolivia* 124 G6
San José de Feliciano, *Argentina* 126 C4
San José de Jáchal, *Argentina* 126 C2
San José de Mayo, *Uruguay* 126 C4
San José del Cabo, *Mexico* 118 C3
San José del Guaviare, *Colombia* 124 C4
San Josep, *Spain* 48 C7
San Juan, *Argentina* 126 C2
San Juan, *Mexico* 118 C4
San Juan, *Phil.* 61 F6
San Juan, *Puerto Rico* 121 d
San Juan, *Trin. & Tob.* 125 K15
San Juan □, *Argentina* 126 C2
San Juan →, *Argentina* 126 C2
San Juan →, *Nic.* 120 D3
San Juan →, *U.S.A.* 109 H8
San Juan Bautista = Sant Joan Baptista, *Spain* 48 B8
San Juan Bautista, *Paraguay* 126 B4
San Juan Bautista, *U.S.A.* 110 J5
San Juan Bautista Valle Nacional, *Mexico* 119 D5
San Juan Capistrano, *U.S.A.* 111 M9
San Juan Cr. →, *U.S.A.* 110 J5
San Juan de Alicante, *Spain* 39 G4
San Juan de Guadalupe, *Mexico* 118 C4
San Juan de la Costa, *Mexico* 118 C2
San Juan de los Morros, *Venezuela* 124 B5
San Juan del Norte, *Nic.* 120 D3
San Juan del Norte, B. de, *Nic.* 120 D3
San Juan del Río, *Mexico* 119 C5
San Juan del Sur, *Nic.* 120 D2
San Juan I., *U.S.A.* 110 B3
San Juan Island ∆, *U.S.A.* 110 B4
San Juan Mts., *U.S.A.* 109 H10
San Just, Sierra de, *Spain* 38 E4
San Justo, *Argentina* 126 C3
San Kamphaeng, *Thailand* 64 C2
San Lázaro, C., *Mexico* 118 C2
San Lázaro, Sa., *Mexico* 118 C3
San Leandro, *U.S.A.* 110 H4
San Leonardo de Yagüe, *Spain* 38 D1
San Lorenzo = Sant Llorenç des Cardassar, *Spain* 48 B10
San Lorenzo, *Argentina* 126 C3
San Lorenzo, *Ecuador* 124 C3
San Lorenzo, *Paraguay* 126 B4
San Lorenzo →, *Mexico* 118 C3
San Lorenzo, I., *Mexico* 118 B2
San Lorenzo, Mte., *Argentina* 128 F2
San Lorenzo de la Parrilla, *Spain* 38 F2
San Lorenzo de Morunys = Sant Llorenç de Morunys, *Spain* 38 C6
San Lucas, *Bolivia* 124 H5
San Lucas, *Baja Calif. S., Mexico* 118 C3
San Lucas, *Baja Calif. S., Mexico* 118 B2
San Lucas, *U.S.A.* 110 J5
San Lucas, C., *Mexico* 118 C3
San Lúcido, *Italy* 43 C9
San Luis, *Argentina* 126 C2
San Luis, *Cuba* 120 B3
San Luis, *Guatemala* 120 C2
San Luis, *Ariz., U.S.A.* 109 K6
San Luis, *Colo., U.S.A.* 109 H11
San Luis □, *Argentina* 126 C2
San Luis, I., *Mexico* 118 B2
San Luis, Sierra de, *Argentina* 126 C2
San Luis de la Paz, *Mexico* 118 C4
San Luis Obispo, *U.S.A.* 111 K6
San Luis Potosí, *Mexico* 118 C4
San Luis Potosí □, *Mexico* 118 C4
San Luis Reservoir, *U.S.A.* 110 H5
San Luis Río Colorado, *Mexico* 118 A2
San Manuel, *U.S.A.* 109 K8
San Marco, C., *Italy* 42 C1
San Marco Argentano, *Italy* 43 C9
San Marco in Lámis, *Italy* 41 G12
San Marcos, *Guatemala* 120 D1
San Marcos, *Mexico* 118 B2
San Marcos, *Calif., U.S.A.* 111 M9
San Marcos, *Tex., U.S.A.* 113 L6
San Marino, *San Marino* 41 E9
San Marino ■, *Europe* 41 E9
San Martin, *Antarctica* 5 C17
San Martín, *Argentina* 126 C2
San Martín →, *Bolivia* 124 F6
San Martín, L., *Argentina* 128 F2
San Martín de la Vega, *Spain* 36 E7
San Martín de los Andes, *Argentina* 128 E2
San Martín de Valdeiglesias, *Spain* 36 E6
San Mateo = Sant Mateu, *Baleares, Spain* 48 B7
San Mateo = Sant Mateu, *Valencia, Spain* 38 E5
San Mateo, *Phil.* 61 C4
San Mateo, *U.S.A.* 110 H4
San Matías, *Bolivia* 124 G7
San Matías, G., *Argentina* 128 E4
San Miguel = Sant Miguel, *Spain* 48 B7
San Miguel, *El Salv.* 120 D2
San Miguel, *Panama* 120 E4
San Miguel, *U.S.A.* 110 K6
San Miguel →, *Bolivia* 124 F6
San Miguel de Tucumán, *Argentina* 126 B2
San Miguel del Monte, *Argentina* 126 D4
San Miguel I., *U.S.A.* 111 L6
San Miniato, *Italy* 40 E7
San Nicolás, *Canary Is.* 48 G4
San Nicolas, *Phil.* 61 B4
San Nicolás de los Arroyas, *Argentina* 126 C3
San Nicolas I., *U.S.A.* 111 M7
San Onofre, *U.S.A.* 111 M9
San Pablo, *Bolivia* 126 A2
San Pablo, *Phil.* 61 D4
San Pablo, *U.S.A.* 110 H4
San Páolo di Civitate, *Italy* 41 G12
San Pedro, *Buenos Aires, Argentina* 126 C4
San Pedro, *Misiones, Argentina* 127 B5
San Pedro, *Chile* 126 C1
San Pédro, *Ivory C.* 82 E3
San Pedro, *Mexico* 118 C2
San Pedro □, *Paraguay* 126 A4
San Pedro →, *Chihuahua, Mexico* 118 B3
San Pedro →, *Nayarit, Mexico* 118 C3
San Pedro →, *U.S.A.* 109 K8
San Pedro, Pta., *Chile* 126 B1
San Pedro, Sierra de, *Spain* 37 F4
San Pedro Channel, *U.S.A.* 111 M8
San Pedro de Atacama, *Chile* 126 A2
San Pedro de Jujuy, *Argentina* 126 A3
San Pedro de las Colonias, *Mexico* 118 B4
San Pedro de Macorís, *Dom. Rep.* 121 C6
San Pedro del Norte, *Nic.* 120 D3
San Pedro del Paraná, *Paraguay* 126 B4
San Pedro del Pinatar, *Spain* 39 H4
San Pedro Mártir ∆, *Mexico* 118 A1
San Pedro Mártir, Sierra, *Mexico* 118 A1
San Pedro Mixtepec, *Mexico* 119 D5
San Pedro Ocampo = Melchor Ocampo, *Mexico* 118 C4
San Pedro Sula, *Honduras* 120 C2
San Pietro, *Italy* 42 C1
San Pietro Vernótico, *Italy* 43 B11
San Quintín, *Mexico* 118 A1
San Rafael, *Argentina* 126 C2
San Rafael, *Calif., U.S.A.* 110 H4
San Rafael, *N. Mex., U.S.A.* 109 J10
San Rafael Mt., *U.S.A.* 111 L7
San Rafael Mts., *U.S.A.* 111 L7
San Ramón de la Nueva Orán, *Argentina* 126 A3
San Remo, *Italy* 40 E4
San Roque, *Argentina* 126 B4
San Roque, *Spain* 37 J5
San Rosendo, *Chile* 126 D1
San Saba, *U.S.A.* 113 K5
San Salvador, *El Salv.* 120 D2
San Salvador, *Spain* 48 B10
San Salvador de Jujuy, *Argentina* 126 A3
San Salvador I., *Bahamas* 121 B5
San Salvo, *Italy* 41 F11
San Sebastián = Donostia-San Sebastián, *Spain* 38 B3
San Sebastián, *Argentina* 128 G3
San Sebastián, *Puerto Rico* 121 d
San Sebastián de la Gomera, *Canary Is.* 48 F2
San Serra = Son Serra, *Spain* 48 B10
San Serverino Marche, *Italy* 41 E10
San Severo, *Italy* 41 G12
San Simeon, *U.S.A.* 110 K5
San Simon, *U.S.A.* 109 K9
San Stéfano di Cadore, *Italy* 41 B9
San Stino di Livenza, *Italy* 41 C9
San Telmo = Sant Telm, *Spain* 48 B9
San Telmo, *Mexico* 118 A1
San Tiburcio, *Mexico* 118 C4
San Valentin, Mte., *Chile* 128 F2
San Vicente de Alcántara, *Spain* 37 F3
San Vicente de la Barquera, *Spain* 36 B6
San Vincente del Raspeig, *Spain* 39 G4
San Vincenzo, *Italy* 40 E7
San Vito, *Costa Rica* 120 E3
San Vito, *Italy* 42 C2
San Vito, C., *Italy* 42 D5
San Vito al Tagliamento, *Italy* 41 C9
San Vito Chietino, *Italy* 41 F11
San Vito dei Normanni, *Italy* 43 B10
Sana', *Yemen* 75 D3
Sana →, *Bos.-H.* 41 C13
Sanaba, *Burkina Faso* 82 C4
Şanāfīr, *Si. Arabia* 80 B3
Sanaga →, *Cameroon* 83 E6
Sanaloa, Presa, *Mexico* 118 C3
Sanana, *Indonesia* 63 E7
Sanand, *India* 68 H5
Sanandaj, *Iran* 70 C5
Sanandita, *Bolivia* 126 A3
Sanary-sur-Mer, *France* 21 E9
Sanawad, *India* 68 H7
Sancellas = Sencelles, *Spain* 48 B9
Sancergues, *France* 19 E9
Sancerre, *France* 19 E9
Sancerrois, Collines du, *France* 19 E9
Sancha He →, *China* 58 D6
Sanchahe, *China* 57 B14
Sánchez, *Dom. Rep.* 121 C6
Sanchor, *India* 68 G4
Sancoins, *France* 19 F9
Sancti Spíritus, *Cuba* 120 B4
Sancy, Puy de, *France* 20 C6
Sand →, *S. Africa* 89 C5
Sand Hills, *U.S.A.* 112 D4
Sand Lakes ⌓, *Canada* 103 B9
Sand Springs, *U.S.A.* 113 G6

Sanda, *Japan* 55 G7
Sandakan, *Malaysia* 62 C5
Sandan = Sambor, *Cambodia* 64 F6
Sandanski, *Bulgaria* 44 E7
Sandaré, *Mali* 82 C2
Sandared, *Sweden* 11 G6
Sandarne, *Sweden* 10 C11
Sanday, *U.K.* 13 B6
Sandefjord, *Norway* 9 G14
Sanders, *U.S.A.* 109 J9
Sanderson, *U.S.A.* 113 K3
Sandersville, *U.S.A.* 115 J4
Sandfire Roadhouse, *Australia* 92 C3
Sandfly L., *Canada* 103 B7
Sandfontein, *Namibia* 88 C2
Sandhammaren, C., *Sweden* 11 J8
Sandheads, The, *India* 69 J13
Sandía, *Peru* 124 F5
Sandıklı, *Turkey* 47 C12
Sandila, *India* 69 F9
Sandnes, *Norway* 9 G11
Sandnessjøen, *Norway* 8 C15
Sandoa, *Dem. Rep. of the Congo* 84 F4
Sandomierz, *Poland* 31 H8
Sândominic, *Romania* 29 D10
Sandover →, *Australia* 94 C2
Sandoway, *Burma* 67 K19
Sandoy, *Færoe Is.* 8 F9
Sandpoint, *U.S.A.* 108 B5
Sandray, *U.K.* 13 E1
Sandringham, *U.K.* 14 E8
Sandstone, *Australia* 93 E2
Sandu, *China* 58 E6
Sandusky, *Mich., U.S.A.* 116 C2
Sandusky, *Ohio, U.S.A.* 116 E2
Sandvig, *Sweden* 11 J8
Sandviken, *Sweden* 10 D10
Sandwich, C., *Australia* 94 B4
Sandwich B., *Canada* 105 B8
Sandwich B., *Namibia* 88 C1
Sandy, *Oreg., U.S.A.* 110 E4
Sandy, *Pa., U.S.A.* 116 E6
Sandy, *Utah, U.S.A.* 108 F8
Sandy Bay, *Canada* 103 B8
Sandy Bight, *Australia* 93 F3
Sandy C., *Queens., Australia* 94 C5
Sandy C., *Tas., Australia* 95 G3
Sandy Cay, *Bahamas* 121 B4
Sandy Cr. →, *U.S.A.* 108 F9
Sandy L., *Canada* 104 B1
Sandy Lake, *Canada* 104 B1
Sandy Valley, *U.S.A.* 111 K11
Sånfjällets △, *Sweden* 10 B7
Sanford, *Fla., U.S.A.* 115 L5
Sanford, *Maine, U.S.A.* 115 D10
Sanford, *N.C., U.S.A.* 115 H6
Sanford →, *Australia* 93 E2
Sanford, Mt., *U.S.A.* 100 B5
Sang-i-Masha, *Afghan.* 68 C2
Sanga, *Mozam.* 87 E4
Sanga →, *Congo* 84 E3
Sangamner, *India* 66 K9
Sanganeb Atoll △, *Sudan* 80 D4
Sangar, *Afghan.* 68 C1
Sangar, *Russia* 53 C13
Sangar Sarai, *Afghan.* 68 B4
Sangaredi, *Guinea* 82 C2
Sangarh →, *Pakistan* 68 D4
Sangasso, *Mali* 82 C3
Sangatte, *France* 19 B8
Sangay, *Ecuador* 124 D3
Sange, *Dem. Rep. of the Congo* 86 D2
Sangeang, *Indonesia* 63 F5
Sângeorz-Băi, *Romania* 29 C9
Sanger, *U.S.A.* 110 J7
Sângera, *Moldova* 29 D13
Sangerhausen, *Germany* 24 D7
Sanggan He →, *China* 56 E9
Sanggau, *Indonesia* 62 D4
Sanghar, *Pakistan* 68 F3
Sangihe, Kepulauan, *Indonesia* 63 D7
Sangihe, Pulau, *Indonesia* 63 D7
Sangju, *S. Korea* 57 F15
Sangkapura, *Indonesia* 62 F4
Sangkhla, *Thailand* 64 E2
Sangkulirang, *Indonesia* 62 D5
Sangla, *Pakistan* 68 D5
Sangli, *India* 66 L9
Sangmélima, *Cameroon* 83 E7
Sangod, *India* 68 G7
Sangre de Cristo Mts., *U.S.A.* 113 G2
Sangre Grande, *Trin. & Tob.* 125 K15
Sangro →, *Italy* 41 F11
Sangrur, *India* 68 D6
Sangudo, *Canada* 102 C6
Sangue →, *Brazil* 124 F7
Sangüesa, *Spain* 38 C3
Sanguinaires, Îs., *France* 21 G12
Sangzhi, *China* 59 C8
Sanhala, *Ivory C.* 82 C3
Sanibel, *U.S.A.* 115 M4
Sanikiluaq, *Canada* 101 C12
Sanin-Kaigan △, *Japan* 55 G7
Sanirajak, *Canada* 101 B11
Sanjawi, *Pakistan* 68 D3
Sanje, *Uganda* 86 C3
Sanjiang, *China* 58 E7
Sanjo, *Japan* 54 F9
Sankh →, *India* 69 H11
Sankt Andrä, *Austria* 26 E7
Sankt Augustin, *Germany* 24 E3
Sankt Blasien, *Germany* 25 H4
Sankt Gallen, *Switz.* 25 H5
Sankt Gallen □, *Switz.* 25 H5
Sankt Goar, *Germany* 25 E3
Sankt Ingbert, *Germany* 25 F3
Sankt Johann im Pongau, *Austria* 26 D6
Sankt Johann in Tirol, *Austria* 26 D5
Sankt Michel = Mikkeli, *Finland* 9 F22
Sankt-Peterburg, *Russia* 32 C6
Sankt Pölten, *Austria* 26 C8
Sankt Ulrich = Ortisei, *Italy* 41 B8
Sankt Valentin, *Austria* 26 C7
Sankt Veit an der Glan, *Austria* 26 E7
Sankt Wendel, *Germany* 25 F3
Sankt Wolfgang, *Austria* 26 D6
Sankuru →, *Dem. Rep. of the Congo* 84 E4
Sanliurfa, *Turkey* 70 B3
Sanlúcar de Barrameda, *Spain* 37 J4
Sanluri, *Italy* 42 C1
Sânmartin, *Romania* 29 D10
Sanmen, *China* 59 C13
Sanmenxia, *China* 56 G6
Sanming, *China* 59 D11
Sannaspos, *S. Africa* 88 D4
Sannicandro Gargánico, *Italy* 41 G12
Sânnicolau Mare, *Romania* 28 D5
Sannieshof, *S. Africa* 88 D4
Sannīn, J., *Lebanon* 74 B4
Sanniquellie, *Liberia* 82 D3
Sannûr, W. →, *Egypt* 80 B3
Sanoe, *Antarctica* 5 D2
Sanok, *Poland* 31 J9
Sanquhar, *U.K.* 13 F5
Sans Souci, *Trin. & Tob.* 125 K16
Sansanding, *Mali* 82 C3
Sansepolcro, *Italy* 41 E9
Sansha, *China* 59 D13
Sanshui, *China* 59 F9
Sanski Most, *Bos.-H.* 41 D13
Sansui, *China* 58 D7
Sant Antoni Abat, *Spain* 48 C7
Sant Boi de Llobregat, *Spain* 38 D7
Sant Carles, *Spain* 48 B8
Sant Carles de la Ràpita, *Spain* 38 E5
Sant Celoni, *Spain* 38 D7
Sant Feliu de Guíxols, *Spain* 38 D8
Sant Feliu de Llobregat, *Spain* 38 D7
Sant Ferran, *Spain* 48 C7
Sant Francesc de Formentera, *Spain* 48 C7
Sant Jaume, *Spain* 48 B11
Sant Joan Baptista, *Spain* 48 B8
Sant Jordi, *Ibiza, Spain* 48 C7
Sant Jordi, *Mallorca, Spain* 48 B9
Sant Jordi, G. de, *Spain* 38 E6
Sant Llorenç de Morunys, *Spain* 38 C6
Sant Llorenç del Munt y l'Obac ⌂, *Spain* 38 D3
Sant Llorenç des Cardassar, *Spain* 48 B10
Sant Mateu, *Baleares, Spain* 48 B7
Sant Mateu, *Valencia, Spain* 38 E5
Sant Miguel, *Spain* 48 B7
Sant Telm, *Spain* 48 B9
Sant' Ágata Militello, *Italy* 43 D7
Santa Agnés, *Spain* 48 B7
Santa Ana, *Bolivia* 124 F5
Santa Ana, *El Salv.* 120 D2
Santa Ana, *Mexico* 118 A2
Santa Ana, *U.S.A.* 111 M9
Sant' Ángelo Lodigiano, *Italy* 40 C6
Sant' Antíoco, *Italy* 42 C1
Santa Bárbara, *Chile* 126 D1
Santa Bárbara, *Honduras* 120 D2
Santa Bárbara, *Mexico* 118 B3
Santa Bárbara, *Spain* 38 E5
Santa Barbara, *U.S.A.* 111 L7
Santa Bárbara, Mt., *Spain* 39 H2
Santa Barbara Channel, *U.S.A.* 111 L7
Santa Barbara I., *U.S.A.* 111 M7
Santa Catalina, Gulf of, *U.S.A.* 111 N9
Santa Catalina, I., *Mexico* 118 B2
Santa Catalina I., *U.S.A.* 111 M8
Santa Catarina □, *Brazil* 127 B6
Santa Catarina, I. de, *Brazil* 127 B6
Santa Caterina di Pittinuri, *Italy* 42 B1
Santa Caterina Villarmosa, *Italy* 43 E7
Santa Cecília, *Brazil* 127 B5
Santa Clara, *Cuba* 120 B4
Santa Clara, *Calif., U.S.A.* 110 H5
Santa Clara, *Utah, U.S.A.* 109 H7
Santa Clara, El Golfo de, *Mexico* 118 A2
Santa Clara de Olimar, *Uruguay* 127 C5
Santa Clarita, *U.S.A.* 111 L8
Santa Clotilde, *Peru* 124 D4
Santa Coloma de Farners, *Spain* 38 D7
Santa Coloma de Gramenet, *Spain* 38 D7
Santa Comba, *Spain* 36 B2
Santa Croce Camerina, *Italy* 43 F7
Santa Croce di Magliano, *Italy* 41 G11
Santa Cruz, *Argentina* 128 G3
Santa Cruz, *Bolivia* 124 G6
Santa Cruz, *Chile* 126 C1
Santa Cruz, *Costa Rica* 120 D2
Santa Cruz, *Madeira* 48 D3
Santa Cruz, *Phil.* 61 D4
Santa Cruz, *U.S.A.* 110 J4
Santa Cruz →, *Argentina* 128 G3
Santa Cruz de la Palma, *Canary Is.* 48 F2
Santa Cruz de la Palma ✕ (SPC), *Canary Is.* 48 F2
Santa Cruz de Mudela, *Spain* 37 G7
Santa Cruz de Tenerife, *Canary Is.* 48 F3
Santa Cruz del Norte, *Cuba* 120 B3
Santa Cruz del Retamar, *Spain* 36 E6
Santa Cruz del Sur, *Cuba* 120 B4
Santa Cruz do Rio Pardo, *Brazil* 127 A6
Santa Cruz do Sul, *Brazil* 127 B5
Santa Cruz I., *U.S.A.* 111 M7
Santa Cruz Is., *Solomon Is.* 96 J8
Santa Cruz Mts., *Jamaica* 120 a
Santa Domingo, Cay, *Bahamas* 120 B4
Sant' Egídio alla Vibrata, *Italy* 41 F10
Santa Elena, *Argentina* 126 C4
Santa Elena, C., *Costa Rica* 120 D2
Sant' Eufémia, G. di, *Italy* 43 D9
Santa Eulàlia des Riu, *Spain* 48 C8
Santa Fe, *Argentina* 126 C3
Santa Fe, *Spain* 37 H7
Santa Fe, *U.S.A.* 109 J11
Santa Fé □, *Argentina* 126 C3
Santa Fé do Sul, *Brazil* 125 H8
Santa Filomena, *Brazil* 125 E9
Santa Fiora, *Italy* 41 F8
Santa Gertrudis, *Spain* 48 C7
Santa Giustina, *Italy* 41 B9
Santa Inês, *Brazil* 125 F11
Santa Inés, *Spain* 37 G5
Santa Inés, I., *Chile* 128 G2
Santa Isabel, *Argentina* 126 D2
Santa Isabel, Pico, *Eq. Guin.* 83 E6
Santa Isabel do Morro, *Brazil* 125 F8
Santa Lucía, *Corrientes, Argentina* 126 B4
Santa Lucía, *San Juan, Argentina* 126 C2
Santa Lucía, *Spain* 39 H4
Santa Lucia, *Uruguay* 126 C4
Santa Lucia Range, *U.S.A.* 110 K5
Santa Magdalena, I., *Mexico* 118 C2
Santa Margarita, *Argentina* 126 D3
Santa Margarita, *Spain* 48 B10
Santa Margarita, *U.S.A.* 110 K6
Santa Margarita →, *U.S.A.* 111 M9
Santa Margarita, I., *Mexico* 118 C2
Santa Margherita, *Italy* 42 D1
Santa Margherita Ligure, *Italy* 40 D6
Santa María, *Argentina* 126 B2
Santa Maria, *Brazil* 127 B5
Santa Maria, *Phil.* 61 C4
Santa Maria, *U.S.A.* 111 L6
Santa María →, *Mexico* 118 A3
Santa María, B. de, *Mexico* 118 B3
Santa Maria, C. de, *Portugal* 37 J3
Santa Maria Cápua Vétere, *Italy* 43 A7
Santa Maria da Feira, *Portugal* 36 E2
Santa Maria da Vitória, *Brazil* 125 F10
Santa Maria del Camí, *Spain* 48 B9
Santa Maria di Léuca, C., *Italy* 43 C11
Santa María la Real de Nieva, *Spain* 36 D6
Santa Marinella, *Italy* 41 F8
Santa Marta, *Colombia* 124 A4
Santa Marta, Sierra Nevada de, *Colombia* 124 A4
Santa Marta de Tormes, *Spain* 36 E5
Santa Marta Grande, C., *Brazil* 127 B6
Santa Marta Ortigueira, Ría de, *Spain* 36 B3
Santa Maura = Levkás, *Greece* 46 C2
Santa Monica, *U.S.A.* 111 M8
Santa Monica Mts. ⌂, *U.S.A.* 111 L8
Santa Olalla, *Huelva, Spain* 37 H4
Santa Olalla, *Toledo, Spain* 36 E6
Santa Paula, *U.S.A.* 111 L7
Santa Pola, *Spain* 39 G4
Santa Ponça, *Spain* 48 B9
Santa Rita, *U.S.A.* 109 K10
Santa Rosa, *La Pampa, Argentina* 126 D3
Santa Rosa, *San Luis, Argentina* 126 C2
Santa Rosa, *Brazil* 127 B5
Santa Rosa, *Calif., U.S.A.* 110 G4
Santa Rosa, *N. Mex., U.S.A.* 113 H2
Santa Rosa and San Jacinto Mts. ⌂, *U.S.A.* 111 M10
Santa Rosa de Copán, *Honduras* 120 D2
Santa Rosa de Río Primero, *Argentina* 126 C3
Santa Rosa del Sara, *Bolivia* 124 G6
Santa Rosa I., *Calif., U.S.A.* 111 M6
Santa Rosa I., *Fla., U.S.A.* 115 K2
Santa Rosa Range, *U.S.A.* 108 F5
Santa Rosalía, *Mexico* 118 B2
Santa Sylvina, *Argentina* 126 B3
Santa Tecla = Nueva San Salvador, *El Salv.* 120 D2
Santa Teresa, *Argentina* 126 C3
Santa Teresa, *Australia* 94 C1
Santa Teresa, *Mexico* 119 B5
Santa Teresa △, *Uruguay* 127 C5
Santa Teresa di Riva, *Italy* 43 E8
Santa Teresa Gallura, *Italy* 42 A2
Santa Uxía, *Spain* 36 C2
Santa Vitória do Palmar, *Brazil* 127 C5
Santa Ynez →, *U.S.A.* 111 L6
Santa Ynez Mts., *U.S.A.* 111 L6
Santa Ysabel, *U.S.A.* 111 M10
Santadi, *Italy* 42 C1
Santaella, *Spain* 37 H6
Santai, *China* 58 B5
Santana, *Madeira* 48 D3
Sântana, *Romania* 28 D6
Santana, Coxilha de, *Brazil* 127 C4
Santana do Livramento, *Brazil* 127 C4
Santander, *Spain* 36 B7
Santander Jiménez, *Mexico* 119 C5
Santanilla, Is., *Honduras* 120 C3
Santanyí, *Spain* 48 B10
Santaquin, *U.S.A.* 108 G8
Santarcángelo di Romagna, *Italy* 41 D9
Santarém, *Brazil* 125 D8
Santarém, *Portugal* 37 F2
Santarém □, *Portugal* 37 F2
Santaren Channel, *W. Indies* 120 B4
Santee, *U.S.A.* 111 N10
Santee →, *U.S.A.* 115 J6
Santéramo in Colle, *Italy* 43 B9
Santerno →, *Italy* 41 D8
Santhià, *Italy* 40 C5
Santi-Quaranta = Sarandë, *Albania* 44 G3
Santiago, *Brazil* 127 B5
Santiago, *Canary Is.* 48 F2
Santiago, *Chile* 126 C1
Santiago, *Panama* 120 E3
Santiago, *Phil.* 61 C4
Santiago □, *Chile* 126 C1
Santiago →, *Mexico* 98 G9
Santiago →, *Peru* 124 D3
Santiago, Punta de, *Eq. Guin.* 83 E6
Santiago de Compostela, *Spain* 36 C2
Santiago de Cuba, *Cuba* 120 C4
Santiago de los Cabelleros, *Dom. Rep.* 121 C5
Santiago del Estero, *Argentina* 126 B3
Santiago del Estero □, *Argentina* 126 B3
Santiago del Teide, *Canary Is.* 48 F3
Santiago do Cacém, *Portugal* 37 G2
Santiago Ixcuintla, *Mexico* 118 C3
Santiago Papasquiaro, *Mexico* 118 C3
Santiaguillo, L. de, *Mexico* 118 C4
Santiguila, *Mali* 82 C3
Santillana, *Spain* 36 B6
Santisteban del Puerto, *Spain* 37 G7
Santo Amaro, *Brazil* 125 F11
Santo Anastácio, *Brazil* 127 A5
Santo André, *Brazil* 127 A6
Santo Ângelo, *Brazil* 127 B5
Santo Antônio do Içá, *Brazil* 124 D5
Santo Antônio do Leverger, *Brazil* 125 G7
Santo Domingo, *Dom. Rep.* 121 C6
Santo Domingo, *Baja Calif., Mexico* 118 A1
Santo Domingo, *Baja Calif. S., Mexico* 118 B2
Santo Domingo, *Nic.* 120 D3
Santo Domingo de la Calzada, *Spain* 38 C2
Santo Domingo de los Colorados, *Ecuador* 124 D3
Santo Domingo Pueblo, *U.S.A.* 109 J10
Santo Stéfano di Camastro, *Italy* 43 D7
Santo Tirso, *Portugal* 36 D2
Santo Tomás, *Mexico* 118 A1
Santo Tomás, *Peru* 124 F4
Santo Tomé, *Argentina* 127 B4
Santo Tomé de Guayana = Ciudad Guayana, *Venezuela* 124 B6
Santomera, *Spain* 39 G3
Santoña, *Spain* 36 B7
Santoríni = Thíra, *Greece* 47 E7
Santos, *Brazil* 127 A6
Santos, Sierra de los, *Spain* 37 G5
Santos Dumont, *Brazil* 127 A7
Sanur, *Indonesia* 63 K18
Sanwer, *India* 68 H6
Sanxenxo, *Spain* 36 C2
Sanyuan, *China* 56 G5
São Bartolomeu de Messines, *Portugal* 37 H2
São Bernardo do Campo, *Brazil* 127 A6
São Borja, *Brazil* 127 B4
São Brás de Alportel, *Portugal* 37 H3
São Carlos, *Brazil* 127 A6
São Cristóvão, *Brazil* 125 F11
São Domingos, *Brazil* 125 F9
São Domingos, *Guinea-Biss.* 82 C1
São Francisco, *Brazil* 125 G10
São Francisco →, *Brazil* 125 F11
São Francisco do Sul, *Brazil* 127 B6
São Gabriel, *Brazil* 127 C5
São Gonçalo, *Brazil* 127 A7
Sao Hill, *Tanzania* 87 D4
São João, *Guinea-Biss.* 82 C1
São João da Boa Vista, *Brazil* 127 A6
São João da Madeira, *Portugal* 36 E2
São João da Pesqueira, *Portugal* 36 D3
São João del Rei, *Brazil* 127 A7
São João do Araguaia, *Brazil* 125 E9
São João do Piauí, *Brazil* 125 E10
São Joaquim, *Brazil* 127 B6
São Joaquim △, *Brazil* 127 B6
São Jorge, Pta. de, *Madeira* 48 D3
São José, *Brazil* 127 B5
São José do Norte, *Brazil* 127 C5
São José do Rio Prêto, *Brazil* 127 A6
São José dos Campos, *Brazil* 127 A6
São Leopoldo, *Brazil* 127 B5
São Lourenço, *Brazil* 127 A6
São Lourenço →, *Brazil* 125 G7
São Lourenço, Pta. de, *Madeira* 48 D3
São Lourenço do Sul, *Brazil* 127 C5
São Luís, *Brazil* 125 D10
São Luís Gonzaga, *Brazil* 127 B5
São Marcos →, *Brazil* 125 G9
São Marcos, B. de, *Brazil* 125 D10
São Martinho da Cortiça, *Portugal* 36 E2
São Mateus, *Brazil* 125 G11
São Mateus do Sul, *Brazil* 127 B5
São Miguel do Oeste, *Brazil* 127 B5
São Paulo, *Brazil* 127 A6
São Paulo □, *Brazil* 127 A6
São Paulo, I., *Atl. Oc.* 2 D8
São Paulo de Olivença, *Brazil* 124 D5
São Pedro do Sul, *Portugal* 36 E2
São Roque, *Madeira* 48 D3
São Roque, C. de, *Brazil* 125 E11
São Sebastião, I. de, *Brazil* 127 A6
São Sebastião do Paraíso, *Brazil* 127 A6
São Teotónio, *Portugal* 37 H2
São Tomé, *São Tomé & Príncipe* 76 F4
São Tomé, C. de, *Brazil* 127 A7
São Tomé & Príncipe ■, *Africa* 77 F4
São Vicente, *Brazil* 127 A6
São Vicente, *Madeira* 48 D2
São Vicente, C. de, *Portugal* 37 H1
Saona, I., *Dom. Rep.* 121 C6
Saône →, *France* 19 G11
Saône-et-Loire □, *France* 19 F11
Saonek, *Indonesia* 63 E8
Sápai, *Greece* 45 E9
Sapam, Ao, *Thailand* 65 a
Sapanca, *Turkey* 72 B4
Saparua, *Indonesia* 63 E7
Sapele, *Nigeria* 83 D6
Sapelo I., *U.S.A.* 115 K5
Şaphane, *Turkey* 47 B11
Sapi ⌂, *Zimbabwe* 87 F2
Sapiéntza, *Greece* 46 E3
Sapo △, *Liberia* 82 D3
Sapone, *Burkina Faso* 83 C4
Saposoa, *Peru* 124 E3
Sapotskina, *Belarus* 30 E10
Sapouy, *Burkina Faso* 83 C4
Sapozhok, *Russia* 34 D5
Sapphire, *Australia* 94 C4
Sappho, *U.S.A.* 110 B2
Sapporo, *Japan* 54 C10
Sapri, *Italy* 43 B8
Sapulpa, *U.S.A.* 113 H6
Saqqez, *Iran* 70 B5
Sar Dasht, *Āzarbāyjān-e Gharbī, Iran* 73 D11
Sar Dasht, *Khuzestān, Iran* 71 C6
Sar-e Pol □, *Afghan.* 66 B4
Sar Gachīneh = Yāsūj, *Iran* 71 D6
Sar Planina, *Macedonia* 44 E4
Sara, *Burkina Faso* 82 C4
Sara, *Phil.* 61 F5
Šara △, *Serbia & M.* 44 D5
Sara Buri = Saraburi, *Thailand* 64 E3
Sarāb, *Iran* 70 B5
Sarabadi, *Iraq* 70 C5
Saraburi, *Thailand* 64 E3
Saradiya, *India* 68 J4
Saraféré, *Mali* 82 B4
Saragossa = Zaragoza, *Spain* 38 D4
Saraguro, *Ecuador* 124 D3
Sarai Naurang, *Pakistan* 68 C4
Saraikela, *India* 69 H11
Saraiu, *Romania* 29 F13
Sarajevo, *Bos.-H.* 28 G3
Sarakhs, *Turkmenistan* 71 B9
Saran, Gunung, *Indonesia* 62 E4
Saranac L., *U.S.A.* 117 B10
Saranac Lake, *U.S.A.* 117 B10
Saranda, *Tanzania* 86 D3
Sarandë, *Albania* 44 G3
Sarandí del Yi, *Uruguay* 127 C4
Sarandí Grande, *Uruguay* 126 C4
Sarangani B., *Phil.* 61 J6
Sarangani Is., *Phil.* 61 J6
Sarangarh, *India* 67 J13
Saransk, *Russia* 34 C7
Sarapul, *Russia* 52 D6
Sarasota, *U.S.A.* 115 M4
Sarata, *Ukraine* 29 D14
Sarata →, *Ukraine* 29 E14
Saratoga, *Calif., U.S.A.* 110 H4
Saratoga, *Wyo., U.S.A.* 108 F10
Saratoga △, *U.S.A.* 117 D11
Saratoga Springs, *U.S.A.* 117 C11
Saratok, *Malaysia* 62 D4
Saratov, *Russia* 34 E7
Sarāvān, *Iran* 71 E9
Saravane, *Laos* 64 E6
Sarawak □, *Malaysia* 62 D4
Saray, *Tekirdağ, Turkey* 45 E11
Saray, *Van, Turkey* 73 C11
Saraya, *Guinea* 82 C2
Saraya, *Senegal* 82 C2
Saraycık, *Turkey* 47 B11
Sarayköy, *Turkey* 47 D10
Saraylar, *Turkey* 45 F11
Sarayönü, *Turkey* 72 C5
Sarbāz, *Iran* 71 E9
Sarbīsheh, *Iran* 71 C8
Sárbogárd, *Hungary* 28 D3
Sarca →, *Italy* 40 C7
Sarcelles, *France* 19 D9
Sarda →, *India* 67 F12
Sardarshahr, *India* 68 E6
Sardegna □, *Italy* 42 B1
Sardhana, *India* 68 E7
Sardina, Pta., *Canary Is.* 48 F4
Sardinia = Sardegna □, *Italy* 42 B1
Sardis, *Turkey* 47 C10
Sārdūīyeh = Dar Mazār, *Iran* 71 D8
Saren, *Indonesia* 63 J18
S'Arenal, *Spain* 48 B9
Sarentino, *Italy* 41 B8
Saréyamou, *Mali* 82 B4
Sargasso Sea, *Atl. Oc.* 97 D20
Sargodha, *Pakistan* 68 C5
Sarh, *Chad* 79 G9
Sarhala, *Ivory C.* 82 D3
Sārī, *Iran* 71 B7
Sari d'Orcino, *France* 21 F12
Sária, *Greece* 47 F9
Saria, *India* 69 J10
Sariab, *Pakistan* 68 D2
Sarıbeyler, *Turkey* 47 B9
Sarıgöl, *Turkey* 72 C3
Sarikamiş, *Turkey* 73 B10
Sarıkaya, *Turkey* 72 C6
Sarikei, *Malaysia* 62 D4
Sarıköy, *Turkey* 45 F11
Sarila, *India* 69 G8
Sarina, *Australia* 94 C4
Sariñena, *Spain* 38 D4
Sarita, *U.S.A.* 113 M6
Sariwŏn, *N. Korea* 57 E13
Sariyar Barajı, *Turkey* 72 B4
Sarıyer, *Turkey* 45 E13
Sarju →, *India* 69 F9
Sark, *U.K.* 15 H5
Sarkad, *Hungary* 28 D6
Sarkari Tala, *India* 68 F4
Şarkışla, *Turkey* 72 C7
Şarköy, *Turkey* 45 F11
Sarlat-la-Canéda, *France* 20 D5
Sărmăşag, *Romania* 28 C7
Sărmaşu, *Romania* 29 D9
Sarmi, *Indonesia* 63 E9
Sarmiento, *Argentina* 128 F3
Sarmizegetusa, *Romania* 28 E7
Särna, *Sweden* 10 C7
Sarnano, *Italy* 41 E10
Sarnen, *Switz.* 25 J4
Sarnia, *Canada* 116 D2
Sarno, *Italy* 43 B7

Sarnthein = Sarentino, *Italy* **41 B8**
Särö, *Sweden* **11 G5**
Sarolangun, *Indonesia* **62 E2**
Saronikós Kólpos, *Greece* **46 D5**
Saronno, *Italy* **40 C6**
Saros Körfezi, *Turkey* **45 F10**
Sárospatak, *Hungary* **28 B6**
Sarpsborg, *Norway* **9 G14**
Sarracín, *Spain* **36 C7**
Sarralbe, *France* **19 D14**
Sarre = Saar →, *Europe* **17 E6**
Sarre, *Italy* **40 C4**
Sarre-Union, *France* **19 D14**
Sarrebourg, *France* **19 D14**
Sarreguemines, *France* **19 C14**
Sarria, *Spain* **36 C3**
Sarrión, *Spain* **38 E4**
Sarro, *Mali* **82 C3**
Sarstedt, *Germany* **24 C5**
Sartène, *France* **21 G12**
Sarthe □, *France* **18 D7**
Sarthe →, *France* **18 E6**
Sartilly, *France* **18 D5**
Saruhanlı, *Turkey* **47 C9**
Săruleşti, *Romania* **29 F11**
Saruna →, *Pakistan* **68 F2**
Sárvár, *Hungary* **28 C1**
Sarvar, *India* **68 F6**
Sarvestān, *Iran* **71 D7**
Särvfjället, *Sweden* **10 B7**
Sárviz →, *Hungary* **28 D3**
Sary-Tash, *Kyrgyzstan* **52 F8**
Sarych, Mys, *Ukraine* **33 K7**
Saryshagan, *Kazakhstan* **52 E8**
Sarzana, *Italy* **40 D6**
Sarzeau, *France* **18 E4**
Sasan Gir, *India* **68 J4**
Sasaram, *India* **69 G11**
Sasebo, *Japan* **55 H4**
Saser, *India* **69 B7**
Saskatchewan □, *Canada* **103 C7**
Saskatchewan →, *Canada* **103 C8**
Saskatoon, *Canada* **103 C7**
Saskylakh, *Russia* **53 B12**
Saslaya △, *Nic.* **120 D2**
Sasolburg, *S. Africa* **89 D4**
Sasovo, *Russia* **34 C5**
Sassandra, *Ivory C.* **82 E3**
Sassandra →, *Ivory C.* **82 E3**
Sássari, *Italy* **42 B1**
Sassnitz, *Germany* **24 A9**
Sasso Marconi, *Italy* **41 D8**
Sassocorvaro, *Italy* **41 E9**
Sassoferrato, *Italy* **41 E9**
Sasstown, *Liberia* **82 E3**
Sassuolo, *Italy* **40 D7**
Sástago, *Spain* **38 D4**
Sasyk, Ozero, *Ukraine* **29 E14**
Sata-Misaki, *Japan* **55 J5**
Satadougou, *Mali* **82 C2**
Satakunda = Satakunta, *Finland* . **9 F20**
Satakunta, *Finland* **9 F20**
Satama-Soukoura, *Ivory C.* **82 D4**
Satara, *India* **66 L8**
Satara, *S. Africa* **89 C5**
Satbarwa, *India* **69 H11**
Såtenäs, *Sweden* **11 F6**
Säter, *Sweden* **10 D9**
Satevó, *Mexico* **118 B3**
Satilla →, *U.S.A.* **115 K5**
Satmala Hills, *India* **66 J9**
Satna, *India* **69 G9**
Šator, *Bos.-H.* **41 D13**
Sátoraljaújhely, *Hungary* **28 B6**
Satpura Ra., *India* **66 J10**
Satrup, *Germany* **24 A5**
Satsuna-Shotō, *Japan* **55 K5**
Sattahip, *Thailand* **64 F3**
Satu Mare, *Romania* **28 C7**
Satu Mare □, *Romania* **28 C8**
Satui, *Indonesia* **62 E5**
Satun, *Thailand* **65 J3**
Saturnina →, *Brazil* **124 F7**
Sauce, *Argentina* **126 C4**
Sauceda, *Mexico* **118 B4**
Saucillo, *Mexico* **118 B3**
Sauda, *Norway* **9 G12**
Sauðarkrókur, *Iceland* **8 D4**
Saudi Arabia ■, *Asia* **70 B3**
Saugeen →, *Canada* **116 B3**
Saugerties, *U.S.A.* **117 D11**
Saugues, *France* **20 D7**
Saugus, *U.S.A.* **111 L8**
Saujon, *France* **20 C3**
Sauk Centre, *U.S.A.* **112 C7**
Sauk Rapids, *U.S.A.* **112 C7**
Saulgau, *Germany* **25 G5**
Saulieu, *France* **19 E11**
Sault, *France* **21 D9**
Sault Ste. Marie, *Canada* **104 C3**
Sault Ste. Marie, *U.S.A.* **101 D11**
Saumlaki, *Indonesia* **63 F8**
Saumur, *France* **18 E6**
Saunders, C., *N.Z.* **91 L3**
Saunders I., *Antarctica* **5 B1**
Saunders Point, *Australia* **93 E4**
Sauri, *Nigeria* **83 C6**
Saurimo, *Angola* **84 F4**
Sausalito, *U.S.A.* **110 H4**
Sauveterre-de-Béarn, *France* **20 E3**
Sauzé-Vaussais, *France* **20 B4**
Savá, *Honduras* **120 C2**
Sava, *Italy* **43 B10**
Sava →, *Serbia & M.* **28 F5**
Savage, *U.S.A.* **112 B2**
Savage I. = Niue, *Cook Is.* **97 J11**
Savage River, *Australia* **95 G4**
Savai'i, *Samoa* **91 A12**
Savalou, *Benin* **83 D5**
Savane, *Mozam.* **87 F4**
Savanna, *U.S.A.* **112 D9**
Savanna-la-Mar, *Jamaica* .... **120 a**
Savannah, *Ga., U.S.A.* **115 J5**
Savannah, *Mo., U.S.A.* **112 F7**
Savannah, *Tenn., U.S.A.* **115 H1**
Savannah →, *U.S.A.* **115 J5**
Savannakhet, *Laos* **64 D5**
Savant L., *Canada* **104 B1**
Savant Lake, *Canada* **104 B1**
Săvârşin, *Romania* **28 D7**
Savaştepe, *Turkey* **47 B9**
Savé, *Benin* **83 D5**
Save →, *France* **20 E5**
Save →, *Mozam.* **89 C5**
Sāveh, *Iran* **71 C6**
Savelugu, *Ghana* **83 D4**
Savenay, *France* **18 E5**
Săveni, *Romania* **29 C11**
Saverdun, *France* **20 E5**
Saverne, *France* **19 D14**
Savigliano, *Italy* **40 D4**
Savigny-sur-Braye, *France* **18 E7**
Sàvio →, *Italy* **41 D9**
Šavnik, *Serbia & M.* **44 D3**
Savo, *Finland* **8 E22**
Savoie □, *France* **21 C10**
Savolax = Savo, *Finland* **8 E22**
Savona, *Italy* **40 D5**
Savona, *U.S.A.* **116 D7**
Savonlinna, *Finland* **32 B5**
Savoy = Savoie □, *France* **21 C10**
Şavşat, *Turkey* **73 B10**
Sävsjö, *Sweden* **11 G8**
Savur, *Turkey* **70 B4**
Sawahlunto, *Indonesia* **62 E2**
Sawai, *Indonesia* **63 E7**
Sawai Madhopur, *India* **68 G7**
Sawang Daen Din, *Thailand* **64 D4**
Sawankhalok, *Thailand* **64 D2**
Sawara, *Japan* **55 G10**
Sawatch Range, *U.S.A.* **109 G10**
Sawel Mt., *U.K.* **12 B4**
Sawi, *Thailand* **65 G2**
Sawla, *Ghana* **82 D4**
Sawmills, *Zimbabwe* **87 F2**
Sawtooth ⌂, *U.S.A.* **108 D6**
Sawtooth Range, *U.S.A.* **108 E6**
Sawu, *Indonesia* **63 F6**
Sawu Sea, *Indonesia* **63 F6**
Saxby →, *Australia* **94 B3**
Saxmundham, *U.K.* **15 E9**
Saxony = Sachsen □, *Germany* .. **24 E9**
Saxony, Lower = Niedersachsen □, *Germany* **24 C4**
Saxton, *U.S.A.* **116 F6**
Say, *Mali* **82 C4**
Say, *Niger* **83 C5**
Saya, *Nigeria* **83 D5**
Sayabec, *Canada* **105 C6**
Sayaboury, *Laos* **64 C3**
Sayán, *Peru* **124 F3**
Sayan, Vostochnyy, *Russia* **53 D10**
Sayan, Zapadnyy, *Russia* **53 D10**
Saydā, *Lebanon* **74 B4**
Sayhandulaan = Oldziyt, *Mongolia* **56 B5**
Sayḩūt, *Yemen* **75 D5**
Saykhin, *Kazakhstan* **35 F8**
Saylac = Zeila, *Somali Rep.* **75 E3**
Saynshand, *Mongolia* **60 B6**
Sayre, *Okla., U.S.A.* **113 H5**
Sayre, *Pa., U.S.A.* **117 E8**
Sayreville, *U.S.A.* **117 F10**
Sayula, *Mexico* **118 D4**
Sayward, *Canada* **102 C3**
Sazanit, *Albania* **44 F3**
Sázava →, *Czech Rep.* **26 B7**
Sazin, *Pakistan* **69 B5**
Sazlika →, *Bulgaria* **45 E9**
Scaër, *France* **18 D3**
Scafell Pike, *U.K.* **14 C4**
Scalea, *Italy* **43 C8**
Scalloway, *U.K.* **13 A7**
Scalpay, *U.K.* **13 D3**
Scandia, *Canada* **102 C6**
Scandiano, *Italy* **40 D7**
Scandicci, *Italy* **41 E8**
Scandinavia, *Europe* **8 E16**
Scansano, *Italy* **41 F8**
Scapa Flow, *U.K.* **13 C5**
Scappoose, *U.S.A.* **110 E4**
Scarámia, Capo, *Italy* **43 F7**
Scarba, *U.K.* **13 E3**
Scarborough, *Trin. & Tob.* **121 D7**
Scarborough, *U.K.* **14 C7**
Scariff I., *Ireland* **12 E1**
Scarp, *U.K.* **13 C1**
Scarpe-Escaut ⌂, *France* **19 B10**
Scebeli, Wabi →, *Somali Rep.* .. **75 G3**
Šćedro, *Croatia* **41 E13**
Schaal See, *Germany* **24 B6**
Schaalsee ⌂, *Germany* **24 B6**
Schaffhausen, *Switz.* **25 H4**
Schagen, *Neths.* **17 B4**
Schaghticoke, *U.S.A.* **117 D11**
Schärding, *Austria* **26 C6**
Scharhörn, *Germany* **24 B4**
Scheessel, *Germany* **24 B5**
Schefferville, *Canada* **105 B6**
Scheibbs, *Austria* **26 C8**
Schelde →, *Belgium* **17 C4**
Schell Creek Ra., *U.S.A.* **108 G6**
Schellsburg, *U.S.A.* **116 F6**
Schenectady, *U.S.A.* **117 D11**
Schenevus, *U.S.A.* **117 D10**
Scherfede, *Germany* **24 D5**
Schesslitz, *Germany* **25 F7**
Schiedam, *Neths.* **17 C4**
Schiermonnikoog, *Neths.* **17 A6**
Schiltigheim, *France* **19 D14**
Schio, *Italy* **41 C8**
Schiphol, Amsterdam ✕ (AMS), *Neths.* **17 B4**
Schladming, *Austria* **26 D6**
Schlanders = Silandro, *Italy* **40 B7**
Schlei →, *Germany* **24 A5**
Schleiden, *Germany* **24 E2**
Schleiz, *Germany* **24 E7**
Schleswig, *Germany* **24 A5**
Schleswig-Holstein □, *Germany* . **24 A5**
Schlüchtern, *Germany* **25 E5**
Schmalkalden, *Germany* **24 E6**
Schmölln, *Germany* **24 E8**
Schneeberg, *Austria* **26 D8**
Schneeberg, *Germany* **24 E8**
Schneverdingen, *Germany* **24 B5**
Schœlcher, *Martinique* .... **120 c**
Schoharie, *U.S.A.* **117 D10**
Schoharie Cr. →, *U.S.A.* **117 D10**
Scholls, *U.S.A.* **110 E4**
Schönberg, *Mecklenburg-Vorpommern, Germany* **24 B6**
Schönberg, *Schleswig-Holstein, Germany* **24 A6**
Schönbuch ⌂, *Germany* **25 G5**
Schönebeck, *Germany* **24 C7**
Schongau, *Germany* **25 H6**
Schöningen, *Germany* **24 C6**
Schopfheim, *Germany* **25 H3**
Schorndorf, *Germany* **25 G5**
Schortens, *Germany* **24 B3**
Schouten I., *Australia* **95 G4**
Schouten Is. = Supiori, *Indonesia* **63 E9**
Schouwen, *Neths.* **17 C3**
Schramberg, *Germany* **25 G4**
Schrankogel, *Austria* **26 D4**
Schreiber, *Canada* **104 C2**
Schrems, *Austria* **26 C8**
Schrobenhausen, *Germany* **25 G7**
Schroffenstein, *Namibia* **88 D2**
Schroon Lake, *U.S.A.* **117 C11**
Schruns, *Austria* **26 D2**
Schuler, *Canada* **103 C6**
Schumacher, *Canada* **104 C3**
Schurz, *U.S.A.* **108 G4**
Schuyler, *U.S.A.* **112 E6**
Schuylerville, *U.S.A.* **117 C11**
Schuylkill →, *U.S.A.* **117 G9**
Schuylkill Haven, *U.S.A.* **117 F8**
Schwabach, *Germany* **25 F7**
Schwaben □, *Germany* **25 G6**
Schwäbisch-Fränkischer Wald ⌂, *Germany* **25 G5**
Schwäbisch Gmünd, *Germany* .. **25 G5**
Schwäbisch Hall, *Germany* **25 F5**
Schwäbische Alb, *Germany* **25 G5**
Schwabmünchen, *Germany* **25 G6**
Schwalmstadt, *Germany* **24 E5**
Schwandorf, *Germany* **25 F8**
Schwaner, Pegunungan, *Indonesia* **62 E4**
Schwanewede, *Germany* **24 B4**
Schwarmstedt, *Germany* **24 C5**
Schwarze Elster →, *Germany* **24 D8**
Schwarzenberg, *Germany* **24 E8**
Schwarzrand, *Namibia* **88 D2**
Schwarzwald, *Germany* **25 G4**
Schwaz, *Austria* **26 D4**
Schwechat, *Austria* **27 C9**
Schwechat, Wien ✕ (VIA), *Austria* **27 C9**
Schwedt, *Germany* **24 B10**
Schweinfurt, *Germany* **25 E6**
Schweizer-Reneke, *S. Africa* **88 D4**
Schwenningen = Villingen-Schwenningen, *Germany* **25 G4**
Schwerin, *Germany* **24 B7**
Schweriner See, *Germany* **24 B7**
Schwetzingen, *Germany* **25 F4**
Schwyz, *Switz.* **25 H4**
Schwyz □, *Switz.* **25 H4**
Sciacca, *Italy* **42 E6**
Scicli, *Italy* **43 F7**
Sciliar ⌂, *Italy* **41 B8**
Scilla, *Italy* **43 D8**
Scilly, Isles of, *U.K.* **15 H1**
Ścinawa, *Poland* **31 G3**
Scione, *Greece* **44 G7**
Scioto →, *U.S.A.* **114 F4**
Scituate, *U.S.A.* **117 D14**
Scobey, *U.S.A.* **112 A2**
Scone, *Australia* **95 E5**
Scone, *U.K.* **13 E5**
Scordia, *Italy* **43 E7**
Scoresbysund = Ittoqqortoormiit, *Greenland* **4 B6**
Scorniceşti, *Romania* **29 F9**
Scotia, *Calif., U.S.A.* **108 F1**
Scotia, *N.Y., U.S.A.* **117 D11**
Scotia Sea, *Antarctica* **5 B18**
Scotland, *Canada* **116 C4**
Scotland □, *U.K.* **13 E5**
Scott, *Antarctica* **5 D11**
Scott, C., *Australia* **92 B4**
Scott City, *U.S.A.* **112 F4**
Scott Glacier, *Antarctica* **5 C8**
Scott I., *Antarctica* **5 C11**
Scott Is., *Canada* **102 C3**
Scott L., *Canada* **103 B7**
Scott Reef, *Australia* **92 B3**
Scottburgh, *S. Africa* **89 E5**
Scottdale, *U.S.A.* **116 F5**
Scottish Borders □, *U.K.* **13 F6**
Scottsbluff, *U.S.A.* **112 E3**
Scottsboro, *U.S.A.* **115 H3**
Scottsburg, *U.S.A.* **114 F3**
Scottsdale, *Australia* **95 G4**
Scottsdale, *U.S.A.* **109 K7**
Scottsville, *Ky., U.S.A.* **115 G2**
Scottsville, *N.Y., U.S.A.* **116 C7**
Scottville, *U.S.A.* **114 D2**
Scranton, *U.S.A.* **117 E9**
Scugog, L., *Canada* **116 B6**
Sculeni, *Moldova* **29 C12**
Scunthorpe, *U.K.* **14 D7**
Scuol Schuls, *Switz.* **25 J6**
Scutari = Shkodër, *Albania* **44 D3**
Scutari = Üsküdar, *Turkey* **45 F13**
Seabrook, L., *Australia* **93 F2**
Seaford, *U.K.* **15 G8**
Seaford, *U.S.A.* **114 F8**
Seaforth, *Australia* **94 J6**
Seaforth, *Canada* **116 C3**
Seaforth, L., *U.K.* **13 D2**
Seagraves, *U.S.A.* **113 J3**
Seaham, *U.K.* **14 C6**
Seal →, *Canada* **103 B10**
Seal L., *Canada* **105 B7**
Sealy, *U.S.A.* **113 L6**
Searchlight, *U.S.A.* **111 K12**
Searcy, *U.S.A.* **113 H9**
Searles L., *U.S.A.* **111 K9**
Seascale, *U.K.* **14 C4**
Seaside, *Calif., U.S.A.* **110 J5**
Seaside, *Oreg., U.S.A.* **110 E3**
Seaspray, *Australia* **95 F4**
Seattle, *U.S.A.* **110 C4**
Seattle-Tacoma International ✕ (SEA), *U.S.A.* **110 C4**
Seaview Ra., *Australia* **94 B4**
Sebago L., *U.S.A.* **117 C14**
Sebago Lake, *U.S.A.* **117 C14**
Sebastián Vizcaíno, B., *Mexico* .. **118 B2**
Sebastopol = Sevastopol, *Ukraine* **33 K7**
Sebastopol, *U.S.A.* **110 G4**
Sebba, *Burkina Faso* **83 C5**
Sebderat, *Eritrea* **81 D4**
Sébékoro, *Mali* **82 C3**
Seben, *Turkey* **72 B4**
Sebeş, *Romania* **29 E8**
Sebeşului, Munţii, *Romania* **29 E8**
Sebewaing, *U.S.A.* **114 D4**
Sebezh, *Russia* **32 D5**
Sebha = Sabhah, *Libya* **79 C8**
Sébi, *Mali* **82 B4**
Şebinkarahisar, *Turkey* **73 B8**
Sebiş, *Romania* **28 D7**
Sebnitz, *Germany* **24 E10**
Sebring, *Fla., U.S.A.* **115 M5**
Sebring, *Ohio, U.S.A.* **116 F3**
Sebringville, *Canada* **116 C3**
Sebta = Ceuta, *N. Afr.* **78 A4**
Sebuku, *Indonesia* **62 E5**
Sebuku, Teluk, *Malaysia* **62 D5**
Sečanj, *Serbia & M.* **28 E5**
Secchia →, *Italy* **40 C8**
Sechelt, *Canada* **102 D4**
Sechura, Desierto de, *Peru* **124 E2**
Seclin, *France* **19 B10**
Secondigny, *France* **18 F6**
Sečovce, *Slovak Rep.* **27 C14**
Secretary I., *N.Z.* **91 L1**
Secunderabad, *India* **66 L11**
Security-Widefield, *U.S.A.* **112 F2**
Sedalia, *U.S.A.* **112 F8**
Sedan, *France* **19 C11**
Sedan, *U.S.A.* **113 G6**
Sedano, *Spain* **36 C7**
Sedbergh, *U.K.* **14 C5**
Seddon, *N.Z.* **91 J5**
Seddonville, *N.Z.* **91 J4**
Sedé Boqér, *Israel* **74 E3**
Sedeh, *Fārs, Iran* **71 D7**
Sedeh, *Khorāsān, Iran* **71 C8**
Séderon, *France* **21 D9**
Sederot, *Israel* **74 D3**
Sédhiou, *Senegal* **82 C1**
Sedico, *Italy* **41 B9**
Sedlčany, *Czech Rep.* **26 B7**
Sedley, *Canada* **103 C8**
Sedona, *U.S.A.* **109 J8**
Sedova, Pik, *Russia* **52 B6**
Sedro Woolley, *U.S.A.* **110 B4**
Šeduva, *Lithuania* **30 C10**
Sędziszów, *Poland* **31 H7**
Sędziszów Małapolski, *Poland* **31 H8**
Seebad Ahlbeck, *Germany* **24 B10**
Seefeld in Tirol, *Austria* **26 D4**
Seehausen, *Germany* **24 C7**
Seeheim, *Namibia* **88 D2**
Seeheim-Jugenheim, *Germany* **25 F4**
Seeis, *Namibia* **88 C2**
Seekoei →, *S. Africa* **88 E4**
Seeley's Bay, *Canada* **117 B8**
Seelow, *Germany* **24 C10**
Sées, *France* **18 D7**
Seesen, *Germany* **24 D6**
Seevetal, *Germany* **24 B6**
Seewinkel = Neusiedler See-Seewinkel △, *Austria* **27 D9**
Sefadu, *S. Leone* **82 D2**
Seferihisar, *Turkey* **47 C8**
Séfeto, *Mali* **82 C3**
Sefwi Bekwai, *Ghana* **82 D4**
Segamat, *Malaysia* **65 L4**
Şegarcea, *Romania* **29 F8**
Ségbana, *Benin* **83 C5**
Segbwema, *S. Leone* **82 D2**
Seget, *Indonesia* **63 E8**
Segonzac, *France* **20 C3**
Segorbe, *Spain* **38 F4**
Ségou, *Mali* **82 C3**
Segovia = Coco →, *Cent. Amer.* . **120 D3**
Segovia, *Spain* **36 E6**
Segovia □, *Spain* **36 E6**
Segré, *France* **18 E6**
Segre →, *Spain* **38 D5**
Séguéla, *Ivory C.* **82 D3**
Séguénéga, *Burkina Faso* **83 C4**
Seguin, *U.S.A.* **113 L6**
Segundo →, *Argentina* **126 C3**
Segura →, *Spain* **39 G4**
Segura, Sierra de, *Spain* **39 G2**
Seh Konj, Kūh-e, *Iran* **71 D8**
Seh Qal'eh, *Iran* **71 C8**
Sehitwa, *Botswana* **88 C3**
Sehlabathebe △, *Lesotho* **89 D4**
Sehore, *India* **68 H7**
Sehwan, *Pakistan* **68 F2**
Şeica Mare, *Romania* **29 D9**
Seil, *U.K.* **13 E3**
Seiland, *Norway* **8 A20**
Seilhac, *France* **20 C5**
Seiling, *U.S.A.* **113 G5**
Seille →, *Moselle, France* **19 C13**
Seille →, *Saône-et-Loire, France* **19 F11**
Sein, Î. de, *France* **18 D2**
Seinäjoki, *Finland* **9 E20**
Seine →, *France* **18 C7**
Seine, B. de la, *France* **18 C6**
Seine-et-Marne □, *France* **19 D10**
Seine-Maritime □, *France* **18 C7**
Seine-St-Denis □, *France* **19 D9**
Seini, *Romania* **29 C8**
Seirijai, *Lithuania* **30 D10**
Seistan = Sīstān, *Asia* **71 D9**
Seistan, Daryācheh-ye = Sīstān, Daryācheh-ye, *Iran* **71 D9**
Sejerø, *Denmark* **11 J5**
Sejerø Bugt, *Denmark* **11 J5**
Sejny, *Poland* **30 D10**
Seka, *Ethiopia* **81 F4**
Sekayu, *Indonesia* **62 E2**
Seke, *Tanzania* **86 C3**
Sekenke, *Tanzania* **86 C3**
Seki, *Turkey* **47 E11**
Sekondi-Takoradi, *Ghana* **82 E4**
Sekota, *Ethiopia* **81 E4**
Seksna, *Russia* **32 C10**
Sekudai, *Malaysia* .... **65 d**
Sekuma, *Botswana* **88 C3**
Selah, *U.S.A.* **108 C3**
Selama, *Malaysia* **65 K3**
Selárgius, *Italy* **42 C2**
Selaru, *Indonesia* **63 F8**
Selatan, Selat, *Malaysia* .... **65 c**
Selb, *Germany* **25 E8**
Selby, *U.K.* **14 D6**
Selby, *U.S.A.* **112 C4**
Selca, *Croatia* **41 E13**
Selçuk, *Turkey* **47 D9**
Selden, *U.S.A.* **112 F4**
Sele →, *Italy* **43 B7**
Selebi-Pikwe, *Botswana* **89 C4**
Selemdzha →, *Russia* **53 D13**
Selendi, *Manisa, Turkey* **47 C10**
Selendi, *Manisa, Turkey* **47 C9**
Selenga = Selenge Mörön →, *Asia* **60 A5**
Selenge Mörön →, *Asia* **60 A5**
Selenicë, *Albania* **44 F3**
Selenter See, *Germany* **24 A6**
Sélestat, *France* **19 D14**
Seletan, Tanjung, *Indonesia* **62 E4**
Selevac, *Serbia & M.* **44 B4**
Sélibabi, *Mauritania* **82 B2**
Seliger, Ozero, *Russia* **32 D7**
Seligman, *U.S.A.* **109 J7**
Şelim, *Turkey* **73 B10**
Selîma, El Wâhât el, *Sudan* **80 C2**
Selimiye, *Turkey* **47 D9**
Selinda Spillway →, *Botswana* .. **88 B3**
Selinoús, *Greece* **46 D3**
Selinsgrove, *U.S.A.* **116 F8**
Selizharovo, *Russia* **32 D7**
Selkirk, *Canada* **103 C9**
Selkirk, *U.K.* **13 F6**
Selkirk I. = Horse I., *Canada* **103 C9**
Selkirk Mts., *Canada* **100 C8**
Sellafield, *U.K.* **14 C4**
Sellama, *Sudan* **81 E2**
Selliá, *Greece* **49 D6**
Sellières, *France* **19 F12**
Sells, *U.S.A.* **109 L8**
Sellye, *Hungary* **28 E2**
Selma, *Ala., U.S.A.* **115 J2**
Selma, *Calif., U.S.A.* **110 J7**
Selma, *N.C., U.S.A.* **115 H6**
Selmer, *U.S.A.* **115 H1**
Selongey, *France* **19 E12**
Selous ⌂, *Tanzania* **87 D4**
Selowandoma Falls, *Zimbabwe* . **87 G3**
Selpele, *Indonesia* **63 E8**
Selsey Bill, *U.K.* **15 G7**
Seltso, *Russia* **32 F8**
Seltz, *France* **19 D15**
Selu, *Indonesia* **63 F8**
Sélune →, *France* **18 D5**
Selva = La Selva del Camp, *Spain* **38 D6**
Selva, *Argentina* **126 B3**
Selva Lancandona = Montes Azules ⌂, *Mexico* **119 D6**
Selvas, *Brazil* **124 E5**
Selwyn L., *Canada* **103 B8**
Selwyn Mts., *Canada* **100 B6**
Selwyn Ra., *Australia* **94 C3**
Selyatyn, *Ukraine* **29 C10**
Seman →, *Albania* **44 F3**
Semarang, *Indonesia* **63 G14**
Sembabule, *Uganda* **86 C3**
Sembawang, *Singapore* .... **65 d**
Sembung, *Indonesia* **63 J18**
Şemdinli, *Turkey* **73 D11**
Sémé, *Senegal* **82 B2**
Semeih, *Sudan* **81 E3**
Semenanjung Blambangan, *Indonesia* **63 K17**
Semenov, *Russia* **34 B7**
Semenovka, *Chernihiv, Ukraine* . **33 F7**
Semenovka, *Kremenchuk, Ukraine* **33 H7**
Semeru, *Indonesia* **63 H15**
Semey, *Kazakhstan* **52 D9**
Semikarakorskiy, *Russia* **35 G5**
Semiluki, *Russia* **33 G10**
Seminoe Reservoir, *U.S.A.* **108 F10**

Seminole, *Okla., U.S.A.* 113 H6
Seminole, *Tex., U.S.A.* 113 J3
Seminole Draw →, *U.S.A.* 113 J3
Semipalatinsk = Semey, *Kazakhstan* 52 D9
Semirara Is., *Phil.* 61 F4
Semitau, *Indonesia* 62 D4
Semiyarka, *Kazakhstan* 52 D8
Semiyarskoye = Semiyarka, *Kazakhstan* 52 D8
Semmering P., *Austria* 26 D8
Semnān, *Iran* 71 C7
Semnān □, *Iran* 71 C7
Semporna, *Malaysia* 63 D5
Semuda, *Indonesia* 62 E4
Semur-en-Auxois, *France* 19 E11
Sen →, *Cambodia* 62 B3
Senā, *Iran* 71 D6
Sena, *Mozam.* 87 F4
Sena Madureira, *Brazil* 124 E5
Senador Pompeu, *Brazil* 125 E11
Senaki, *Georgia* 35 J6
Senang, Pulau, *Singapore* 65 d
Senanga, *Zambia* 85 H4
Senatobia, *U.S.A.* 113 H10
Sencelles, *Spain* 48 B9
Sendafa, *Ethiopia* 81 F4
Sendai, *Kagoshima, Japan* 55 J5
Sendai, *Miyagi, Japan* 54 E10
Sendai-Wan, *Japan* 54 E10
Senden, *Bayern, Germany* 25 G6
Senden, *Nordrhein-Westfalen, Germany* 24 D3
Sendhwa, *India* 68 J6
Sene →, *Ghana* 83 D4
Senec, *Slovak Rep.* 27 C10
Seneca, *U.S.A.* 115 H4
Seneca Falls, *U.S.A.* 117 D8
Seneca L., *U.S.A.* 116 D8
Senecaville L., *U.S.A.* 116 G3
Senegal ■, *W. Afr.* 82 C2
Sénégal →, *W. Afr.* 82 B1
Senegambia, *Africa* 76 E2
Senekal, *S. Africa* 89 D4
Senftenberg, *Germany* 24 D10
Senga Hill, *Zambia* 87 D3
Senge Khambab = Indus →, *Pakistan* 68 G2
Sengiley, *Russia* 34 D9
Sengua →, *Zimbabwe* 87 F2
Senhor-do-Bonfim, *Brazil* 125 F10
Senica, *Slovak Rep.* 27 C10
Senigállia, *Italy* 41 E10
Senio →, *Italy* 41 D9
Senirkent, *Turkey* 47 C12
Senise, *Italy* 43 B9
Senj, *Croatia* 41 D11
Senja, *Norway* 8 B17
Senkaku-Shotō, *Japan* 55 L1
Senkuang, *Indonesia* 65 d
Senlis, *France* 19 C9
Senmonorom, *Cambodia* 64 F6
Sennâr, *Sudan* 81 E3
Sennar □, *Sudan* 81 E3
Senneterre, *Canada* 104 C4
Senno, *Belarus* 32 E5
Sènnori, *Italy* 42 B1
Seno, *Laos* 64 D5
Senonches, *France* 18 D8
Senorbì, *Italy* 42 C2
Senožeče, *Slovenia* 41 C11
Sens, *France* 19 D10
Senta, *Serbia & M.* 28 E5
Sentani, *Indonesia* 63 E10
Sentery = Lubao, *Dem. Rep. of the Congo* 86 D2
Sentinel, *U.S.A.* 109 K7
Šentjur, *Slovenia* 41 B12
Sentosa, *Singapore* 65 d
Senya Beraku, *Ghana* 83 D4
Seo de Urgel = La Seu d'Urgell, *Spain* 38 C6
Seohara, *India* 69 E8
Seonath →, *India* 69 J10
Seondha, *India* 69 F8
Seoni, *India* 69 H8
Seoni Malwa, *India* 68 H8
Seoul = Sŏul, *S. Korea* 57 F14
Sepīdān, *Iran* 71 D7
Sepo-ri, *N. Korea* 57 E14
Sępólno Krajeńskie, *Poland* 30 E4
Sepone, *Laos* 64 D6
Sępopol, *Poland* 30 D8
Sept-Îles, *Canada* 105 B6
Septemvri, *Bulgaria* 45 D8
Sepúlveda, *Spain* 36 D7
Sequeros, *Spain* 36 E4
Sequim, *U.S.A.* 110 B3
Sequoia △, *U.S.A.* 110 J8
Serafimovich, *Russia* 34 F6
Seraing, *Belgium* 17 D5
Serakhis →, *Cyprus* 49 D11
Seram, *Indonesia* 63 E7
Seram Sea, *Indonesia* 63 E7
Seranantsara, *Madag.* 89 B8
Serang, *Indonesia* 63 G12
Serangoon, *Singapore* 65 d
Serasan, *Indonesia* 62 D3
Seravezza, *Italy* 40 E7
Şerbettar, *Turkey* 45 E10
Serbia □, *Serbia & M.* 44 C5
Serbia & Montenegro ■, *Europe* 44 C4
Şercaia, *Romania* 29 E10
Serdo, *Ethiopia* 81 E5
Serdobsk, *Russia* 34 D7
Sered', *Slovak Rep.* 27 C10
Seredka, *Russia* 32 C5
Serednye, *Ukraine* 29
Şereflikoçhisar, *Turkey* 72 C5
Seregno, *Italy* 40 C6
Seremban, *Malaysia* 65 L3
Serengeti △, *Tanzania* 86 C3
Serengeti Plain, *Tanzania* 86 C4
Serenje, *Zambia* 87 E3
Seret →, *Ukraine* 29 B10
Sereth = Siret →, *Romania* 29 E12
Sergach, *Russia* 34 C7
Sergen, *Turkey* 45 E11
Sergino, *Russia* 52 C7
Sergipe □, *Brazil* 125 F11
Sergiyev Posad, *Russia* 32 D10
Seria, *Brunei* 62 D4
Serian, *Malaysia* 62 D4
Seriate, *Italy* 40 C6
Seribu, Kepulauan, *Indonesia* 62 F3
Sérifontaine, *France* 19 C8
Sérifos, *Greece* 46 D6
Sérignan, *France* 20 E7
Sérigny →, *Canada* 105 A6
Serik, *Turkey* 72 D4
Seringapatam Reef, *Australia* 92 B3
Serinhisar, *Turkey* 47 D11
Seririt, *Indonesia* 63 J17
Sermaize-les-Bains, *France* 19 D11
Sermata, *Indonesia* 63 F7
Sermersuaq, *Greenland* 4 B4
Sérmide, *Italy* 41 D8
Sernovodsk, *Russia* 34 D10
Sernur, *Russia* 34 B9
Serock, *Poland* 31 F8
Serón, *Spain* 39 H2
Seròs, *Spain* 38 D5
Serov, *Russia* 52 D7
Serowe, *Botswana* 88 C4
Serpa, *Portugal* 37 H3
Serpeddí, Punta, *Italy* 42 C2
Serpentara, *Italy* 42 C2
Serpentine Lakes, *Australia* 93 E4
Serpent's Mouth = Sierpe, Bocas de la, *Venezuela* 125 L15
Serpis →, *Spain* 39 G4
Serpneve, *Ukraine* 29 D14
Serpukhov, *Russia* 32 E9
Serra da Estrela ⌓, *Portugal* 36 E3
Serra de Outes, *Spain* 36 C2
Serra do Navio, *Brazil* 125 C8
Serra San Bruno, *Italy* 43 D9
Serradilla, *Spain* 36 F4
Sérrai, *Greece* 44 E7
Sérrai □, *Greece* 44 E7
Serramanna, *Italy* 42 C1
Serranía San Luís △, *Paraguay* 126 A4
Serras d'Aire e Candeeiros ⌓, *Portugal* 37 F2
Serravalle Scrívia, *Italy* 40 D5
Serre-Ponçon, L. de, *France* 21 D10
Serres, *France* 21 D9
Serrezuela, *Argentina* 126 C2
Serrinha, *Brazil* 125 F11
Sersale, *Italy* 43 C9
Sertã, *Portugal* 36 F2
Sertanópolis, *Brazil* 127 A5
Sêrtar, *China* 58 A3
Serua, *Indonesia* 63 F8
Serui, *Indonesia* 63 E9
Serule, *Botswana* 88 C4
Sérvia, *Greece* 44 F6
Serzedelo, *Portugal* 36 D2
Ses Salines, *Spain* 48 B10
Sese Is., *Uganda* 86 C3
Sesepe, *Indonesia* 63 E7
Sesfontein, *Namibia* 88 B1
Sesheke, *Zambia* 88 B3
Sésia →, *Italy* 40 C5
Sesimbra, *Portugal* 37 G1
S'Espalmador, *Spain* 48 C7
S'Espardell, *Spain* 48 C7
Sessa Aurunca, *Italy* 42 A6
S'Estanyol, *Spain* 48 B9
Sestao, *Spain* 38 B2
Sesto Calende, *Italy* 40 C5
Sesto San Giovanni, *Italy* 40 C6
Sestri Levante, *Italy* 40 D6
Sestriere, *Italy* 40 D3
Sestroretsk, *Russia* 32 B6
Sestrunj, *Croatia* 41 D11
Sestu, *Italy* 42 C2
Setana, *Japan* 54 C9
Sète, *France* 20 E7
Sete Lagôas, *Brazil* 125 G10
Sétif, *Algeria* 78 A7
Seto, *Japan* 55 G8
Setonaikai, *Japan* 55 G6
Setonaikai △, *Japan* 55 G6
Settat, *Morocco* 78 B4
Séttimo Torinese, *Italy* 40 C4
Setting L., *Canada* 103 C9
Settle, *U.K.* 14 C5
Settlement Pt., *Bahamas* 115 M6
Settlers, *S. Africa* 89 C4
Setúbal, *Portugal* 37 G2
Setúbal □, *Portugal* 37 G2
Setúbal, B. de, *Portugal* 37 G2
Seugne →, *France* 20 C3
Seul, Lac, *Canada* 104 B1
Seurre, *France* 19 F12
Sevan, *Armenia* 35 K7
Sevan, Ozero = Sevana Lich, *Armenia* 35 K7
Sevana Lich, *Armenia* 35 K7
Sevastopol, *Ukraine* 33 K7
Seven Sisters, *Canada* 102 C3
Sever →, *Spain* 37 F3
Sévérac-le-Château, *France* 20 D7
Severn →, *Canada* 104 A2
Severn →, *U.K.* 15 F5
Severn L., *Canada* 104 B1
Severnaya Zemlya, *Russia* 53 B10
Severo-Kurilsk, *Russia* 53 D16
Severo-Yeniseyskiy, *Russia* 53 C10
Severo-Zapadnyy □, *Russia* 52 C4
Severočeský □, *Czech Rep.* 26 A7
Severodonetsk = Syeverodonetsk, *Ukraine* 33 H10
Severodvinsk, *Russia* 52 C4
Severomoravský □, *Czech Rep.* 27 B10
Sevier, *U.S.A.* 109 G7
Sevier →, *U.S.A.* 109 G7
Sevier Desert, *U.S.A.* 108 G7
Sevier L., *U.S.A.* 108 G7
Sevilla, *Spain* 37 H5
Sevilla □, *Spain* 37 H5
Seville = Sevilla, *Spain* 37 H5
Sevlievo, *Bulgaria* 45 C9
Sevnica, *Slovenia* 41 B12
Sèvre-Nantaise →, *France* 18 E5
Sèvre-Niortaise →, *France* 20 B3
Sevsk, *Russia* 33 F8
Sewa →, *S. Leone* 82 D2
Sewani, *India* 68 E6
Seward, *Alaska, U.S.A.* 100 B5
Seward, *Nebr., U.S.A.* 112 E6
Seward, *Pa., U.S.A.* 116 F5
Seward Peninsula, *U.S.A.* 100 B3
Sewell, *Chile* 126 C1
Sewer, *Indonesia* 63 F8
Sewickley, *U.S.A.* 116 F4
Sexsmith, *Canada* 102 B5
Seychelles ■, *Ind. Oc.* 50 K9
Seyðisfjörður, *Iceland* 8 D6
Seydişehir, *Turkey* 72 D4
Seydvān, *Iran* 70 B5
Seyhan →, *Turkey* 70 B2
Seyhan Barajı, *Turkey* 72 D6
Seyitgazi, *Turkey* 47 B12
Seyitömer, *Turkey* 47 B11
Seym →, *Ukraine* 33 G7
Seymen, *Turkey* 45 E11
Seymour, *Australia* 95 F4
Seymour, *S. Africa* 89 E4
Seymour, *Conn., U.S.A.* 117 E11
Seymour, *Ind., U.S.A.* 114 F3
Seymour, *Tex., U.S.A.* 113 J5
Seyne, *France* 21 D10
Seyssel, *France* 21 C9
Sežana, *Slovenia* 41 C10
Sézanne, *France* 19 D10
Sezze, *Italy* 42 A6
Sfântu Gheorghe, *Covasna, Romania* 29 E10
Sfântu Gheorghe, *Tulcea, Romania* 29 F14
Sfântu Gheorghe, Braţul →, *Romania* 29 F14
Sfax, *Tunisia* 79 B8
Sha Xi →, *China* 59 D12
Sha Xian, *China* 59 D11
Shaanxi □, *China* 56 G5
Shaba = Katanga □, *Dem. Rep. of the Congo* 86 D2
Shaba ⌓, *Kenya* 86 B4
Shaballe = Scebeli, Wabi →, *Somali Rep.* 75 G3
Shabla, *Bulgaria* 45 C12
Shabogamo L., *Canada* 105 B6
Shabunda, *Dem. Rep. of the Congo* 86 C2
Shache, *China* 60 C2
Shackleton Ice Shelf, *Antarctica* 5 C8
Shackleton Inlet, *Antarctica* 5 E11
Shādegān, *Iran* 71 D6
Shadi, *China* 59 D10
Shadi, *India* 69 C7
Shadrinsk, *Russia* 52 D7
Shadyside, *U.S.A.* 116 G4
Shaffa, *Nigeria* 83 C7
Shafter, *U.S.A.* 111 K7
Shaftesbury, *U.K.* 15 F5
Shagamu, *Nigeria* 83 D5
Shagram, *Pakistan* 69 A5
Shah Alizai, *Pakistan* 68 E2
Shah Bunder, *Pakistan* 68 G2
Shahabad, *Punjab, India* 68 D7
Shahabad, *Raj., India* 68 G7
Shahabad, *Ut. P., India* 69 F8
Shahadpur, *Pakistan* 68 G3
Shahba, *Syria* 74 C5
Shahdād, *Iran* 71 D8
Shahdād, Namakzār-e, *Iran* 71 D8
Shahdadkot, *Pakistan* 68 F2
Shahdol, *India* 69 H9
Shahe, *China* 56 F8
Shahganj, *India* 69 F10
Shahgarh, *India* 66 F6
Shahjahanpur, *India* 69 F8
Shahpur, *India* 68 H7
Shahpur, *Baluchistan, Pakistan* 68 E3
Shahpur, *Punjab, Pakistan* 68 C5
Shahpur Chakar, *Pakistan* 68 F3
Shahpura, *Mad. P., India* 69 H9
Shahpura, *Raj., India* 68 G6
Shahr-e Bābak, *Iran* 71 D7
Shahr-e Kord, *Iran* 71 C6
Shāhrakht, *Iran* 71 C9
Shahrig, *Pakistan* 68 D2
Shahukou, *China* 56 D7
Shaikhabad, *Afghan.* 68 B3
Shajapur, *India* 68 H7
Shakargarh, *Pakistan* 68 C6
Shakawe, *Botswana* 88 B3
Shaker Heights, *U.S.A.* 116 E3
Shakhty, *Russia* 35 G5
Shakhunya, *Russia* 34 B8
Shaki, *Nigeria* 83 D5
Shākir, *Egypt* 80 B3
Shaksam Valley, *Asia* 69 A7
Shala, L., *Ethiopia* 81 F4
Shali, *Russia* 35 J7
Shallow Lake, *Canada* 116 B3
Shalqar, *Kazakhstan* 52 E6
Shalskiy, *Russia* 32 B8
Shaluli Shan, *China* 58 B2
Shām, *Iran* 71 E8
Shām, Bādiyat ash, *Asia* 70 C3
Shamâl Bahr el Ghazal □, *Sudan* 81 F2
Shamâl Dârfûr □, *Sudan* 81 E2
Shamâl Kordofân □, *Sudan* 81 E3
Shamâl Sînî □, *Egypt* 74 E2
Shamattawa, *Canada* 104 A1
Shamattawa →, *Canada* 104 A2
Shambe, *Sudan* 81 F3
Shambe △, *Sudan* 81 F3
Shambu, *Ethiopia* 81 F4
Shamīl, *Iran* 71 E8
Shamkhor = Şämkir, *Azerbaijan* 35 K8
Shāmkūh, *Iran* 71 C8
Shamli, *India* 68 E7
Shammar, Jabal, *Si. Arabia* 70 E4
Shamo = Gobi, *Asia* 56 C6
Shamo, L., *Ethiopia* 81 F4
Shamokin, *U.S.A.* 117 F8
Shamrock, *U.S.A.* 113 H4
Shamva, *Zimbabwe* 87 F3
Shan □, *Burma* 67 J21
Shan Xian, *China* 56 G9
Shanan →, *Ethiopia* 81 F5
Shanchengzhen, *China* 57 C13
Shāndak, *Iran* 71 D9
Shandon, *U.S.A.* 110 K6
Shandong □, *China* 57 G10
Shandong Bandao, *China* 57 F11
Shang Xian = Shangzhou, *China* 56 H5
Shanga, *Nigeria* 78 F6
Shangalowe, *Dem. Rep. of the Congo* 87 E2
Shangani, *Zimbabwe* 89 B4
Shangani →, *Zimbabwe* 87 F2
Shangbancheng, *China* 57 D10
Shangcheng, *China* 59 B10
Shangchuan Dao, *China* 59 G9
Shangdu, *China* 56 D7
Shanggao, *China* 59 C10
Shanghai, *China* 59 B13
Shanghai Shi □, *China* 59 B13
Shanghang, *China* 59 E11
Shanghe, *China* 57 F9
Shanglin, *China* 58 F7
Shangnan, *China* 56 H6
Shangqiu, *China* 56 G8
Shangrao, *China* 59 C11
Shangshui, *China* 60 C6
Shangsi, *China* 58 F6
Shangyou, *China* 59 E10
Shangyu, *China* 59 B13
Shangzhi, *China* 57 B14
Shangzhou, *China* 56 H5
Shanhetun, *China* 57 B14
Shani, *Nigeria* 83 C7
Shanklin, *U.K.* 15 G6
Shannon, *N.Z.* 91 J5
Shannon △, *Australia* 93 F2
Shannon →, *Ireland* 12 D2
Shannon, Mouth of the, *Ireland* 12 D2
Shannon Airport, *Ireland* 12 D3
Shansi = Shanxi □, *China* 56 F7
Shantar, Ostrov Bolshoy, *Russia* 53 D14
Shantipur, *India* 69 H13
Shantou, *China* 59 F11
Shantung = Shandong □, *China* 57 G10
Shanwei, *China* 59 F10
Shanxi □, *China* 56 F7
Shanyang, *China* 56 H5
Shanyin, *China* 56 E7
Shaodong, *China* 59 D8
Shaoguan, *China* 59 E9
Shaoshan, *China* 59 D9
Shaowu, *China* 59 D11
Shaoxing, *China* 59 C13
Shaoyang, *Hunan, China* 59 D8
Shaoyang, *Hunan, China* 59 D8
Shap, *U.K.* 14 C5
Shapinsay, *U.K.* 13 B6
Shaqq el Gi'eifer →, *Sudan* 81 D2
Shaqra', *Si. Arabia* 70 E5
Shaqrā', *Yemen* 75 E4
Sharafa, *Sudan* 81 E2
Sharafkhāneh, *Iran* 70 B5
Sharashova, *Belarus* 31 F11
Sharbot Lake, *Canada* 117 B8
Sharhorod, *Ukraine* 29 B13
Shari, *Japan* 54 C12
Sharjah = Ash Shāriqah, *U.A.E.* 71 E7
Shark B., *Australia* 93 E1
Shark Bay ⌓, *Australia* 93 F2
Sharm el Sheikh, *Egypt* 80 B3
Sharon, *Mass., U.S.A.* 117 D13
Sharon, *Pa., U.S.A.* 116 E4
Sharon Springs, *Kans., U.S.A.* 112 F4
Sharon Springs, *N.Y., U.S.A.* 117 D10
Sharp Pt., *Australia* 94 A3
Sharpe L., *Canada* 104 B1
Sharpsville, *U.S.A.* 116 E4
Sharq el Istiwa'iya □, *Sudan* 81 G3
Sharya, *Russia* 34 A7
Shasha, *Ethiopia* 81 F4
Shashemene, *Ethiopia* 81 F4
Shashi, *Botswana* 89 C4
Shashi, *China* 59 B9
Shashi →, *Africa* 87 G2
Shasta, Mt., *U.S.A.* 108 F2
Shasta L., *U.S.A.* 108 F2
Shatawi, *Sudan* 81 E3
Shatsk, *Russia* 34 C5
Shatsk, *Ukraine* 31 G10
Shatskyi ⌓, *Ukraine* 31 G10
Shatt al Arab, *Asia* 71 D6
Shatura, *Russia* 32 E10
Shaumyani = Shulaveri, *Georgia* 35 K7
Shaunavon, *Canada* 103 D7
Shaver L., *U.S.A.* 110 H7
Shaw →, *Australia* 92 D2
Shaw I., *Australia* 94 J7
Shawanaga, *Canada* 116 A4
Shawangunk Mts., *U.S.A.* 117 E10
Shawano, *U.S.A.* 114 C1
Shawinigan, *Canada* 104 C5
Shawnee, *U.S.A.* 113 H6
Shay Gap, *Australia* 92 D3
Shayang, *China* 59 B9
Shaybārā, *Si. Arabia* 70 E3
Shayib el Banat, Gebel, *Egypt* 80 B3
Shaykh, J. ash, *Lebanon* 74 B4
Shaykh Miskīn, *Syria* 74 C5
Shaykh Sa'īd, *Iraq* 70 C5
Shchekino, *Russia* 32 E9
Shchigry, *Russia* 33 G9
Shchors, *Ukraine* 33 G6
Shchuchinsk, *Kazakhstan* 52 D8
She Xian, *Anhui, China* 59 C12
She Xian, *Hebei, China* 56 F7
Shebekino, *Russia* 33 G9
Shebele = Scebeli, Wabi →, *Somali Rep.* 75 G3
Sheboygan, *U.S.A.* 114 D2
Shebshi Mts., *Nigeria* 83 D7
Shediac, *Canada* 105 C7
Sheelin, L., *Ireland* 12 C4
Sheep Haven, *Ireland* 12 A4
Sheerness, *U.K.* 15 F8
Sheet Harbour, *Canada* 105 D7
Sheffield, *U.K.* 14 D6
Sheffield, *Ala., U.S.A.* 115 H2
Sheffield, *Mass., U.S.A.* 117 D11
Sheffield, *Pa., U.S.A.* 116 E5
Shehojele, *Ethiopia* 81 E4
Shehong, *China* 58 B5
Sheikh Idris, *Sudan* 81 E3
Sheikhpura, *India* 69 G11
Shek Hasan, *Ethiopia* 81 E4
Shekhupura, *Pakistan* 68 D5
Sheki = Şaki, *Azerbaijan* 35 K8
Shelburne, *N.S., Canada* 105 D6
Shelburne, *Ont., Canada* 116 B4
Shelburne, *U.S.A.* 117 B11
Shelburne B., *Australia* 94 A3
Shelburne Falls, *U.S.A.* 117 D12
Shelby, *Mich., U.S.A.* 114 D2
Shelby, *Miss., U.S.A.* 113 J9
Shelby, *Mont., U.S.A.* 108 B8
Shelby, *N.C., U.S.A.* 115 H5
Shelby, *Ohio, U.S.A.* 116 F2
Shelbyville, *Ill., U.S.A.* 112 F10
Shelbyville, *Ind., U.S.A.* 114 F3
Shelbyville, *Ky., U.S.A.* 114 F3
Shelbyville, *Tenn., U.S.A.* 115 H2
Sheldon, *U.S.A.* 112 D7
Sheldrake, *Canada* 105 B7
Shelengo, Khawr →, *Sudan* 81 E2
Shelikhova, Zaliv, *Russia* 53 D16
Shell Lakes, *Australia* 93 E4
Shellbrook, *Canada* 103 C7
Shellharbour, *Australia* 95 E5
Shelon →, *Russia* 32 C6
Shelter I, *U.S.A.* 117 E12
Shelton, *Conn., U.S.A.* 117 E11
Shelton, *Wash., U.S.A.* 110 C3
Shemakha = Şamaxi, *Azerbaijan* 35 K9
Shëmri, *Albania* 44 D4
Shemsi, *Sudan* 80 D2
Shen Xian, *China* 56 F8
Shenandoah, *Iowa, U.S.A.* 112 E7
Shenandoah, *Pa., U.S.A.* 117 F8
Shenandoah, *Va., U.S.A.* 114 F6
Shenandoah △, *U.S.A.* 114 F6
Shenandoah →, *U.S.A.* 114 F7
Shenchi, *China* 56 E7
Shendam, *Nigeria* 83 D6
Shendî, *Sudan* 81 D3
Shenge, *S. Leone* 82 D2
Shengfang, *China* 56 E9
Shëngjergj, *Albania* 44 E4
Shëngjin, *Albania* 44 E3
Shengzhou, *China* 59 C13
Shenjingzi, *China* 57 B13
Shenmu, *China* 56 E6
Shennongjia, *China* 59 B8
Shenqiu, *China* 56 H8
Shensi = Shaanxi □, *China* 56 G5
Shenyang, *China* 57 D12
Shenzhen, *China* 59 F10
Sheo, *India* 68 F4
Sheopur Kalan, *India* 66 G10
Shepetivka, *Ukraine* 33 G4
Shepetovka = Shepetivka, *Ukraine* 33 G4
Shepparton, *Australia* 95 F4
Sheppey, I. of, *U.K.* 15 F8
Shepton Mallet, *U.K.* 15 F5
Sheqi, *China* 56 H7
Sher Qila, *Pakistan* 69 A6
Sherab, *Sudan* 81 E1
Sherborne, *U.K.* 15 G5
Sherbro →, *S. Leone* 82 D2
Sherbro I., *S. Leone* 82 D2
Sherbrooke, *N.S., Canada* 105 C7
Sherbrooke, *Qué., Canada* 117 A13
Sherburne, *U.S.A.* 117 D9
Shereik, *Sudan* 80 D3
Shergarh, *India* 68 F5
Sherghati, *India* 69 G11
Sheridan, *Ark., U.S.A.* 113 H8
Sheridan, *Wyo., U.S.A.* 108 D10
Sheringham, *U.K.* 14 E9
Sherkin I., *Ireland* 12 E2
Sherkot, *India* 69 E8
Sherman, *U.S.A.* 113 J6
Sherpur, *India* 69 G10
Sherridon, *Canada* 103 B8
Sherwood Forest, *U.K.* 14 D6
Sherwood Park, *Canada* 102 C6
Sheslay →, *Canada* 102 B2
Shethanei L., *Canada* 103 B9
Shetland □, *U.K.* 13 A7
Shetland Is., *U.K.* 13 A7
Shetrunji →, *India* 68 J5

Shevchenkovo, *Ukraine* 29 E14
Shewa, *Ethiopia* 81 F4
Shewa Gimira, *Ethiopia* 81 F4
Sheyenne →, *U.S.A.* 112 B6
Shibām, *Yemen* 75 D4
Shibata, *Japan* 54 F9
Shibecha, *Japan* 54 C12
Shibetsu, *Japan* 54 B11
Shibîn el Kôm, *Egypt* 80 H7
Shibîn el Qanâtir, *Egypt* 80 H7
Shibing, *China* 58 D7
Shibogama L., *Canada* 104 B2
Shibushi, *Japan* 55 J5
Shicheng, *China* 59 D11
Shickshinny, *U.S.A.* 117 E8
Shickshock Mts. = Chic-Chocs, Mts., *Canada* 105 C6
Shidao, *China* 57 F12
Shidian, *China* 58 E2
Shido, *Japan* 55 G7
Shiel, L., *U.K.* 13 E3
Shield, C., *Australia* 94 A2
Shīeli, *Kazakhstan* 52 E7
Shifang, *China* 58 B5
Shiga □, *Japan* 55 G8
Shigu, *China* 58 D2
Shiguaigou, *China* 56 D6
Shihchiachuangi = Shijiazhuang, *China* 56 E8
Shihezi, *China* 60 B3
Shijak, *Albania* 44 E3
Shijiazhuang, *China* 56 E8
Shijiu Hu, *China* 59 B12
Shikarpur, *India* 68 E8
Shikarpur, *Pakistan* 68 F3
Shikohabad, *India* 69 F8
Shikoku □, *Japan* 55 H6
Shikoku-Sanchi, *Japan* 55 H6
Shikotsu-Ko, *Japan* 54 C10
Shikotsu-Tōya △, *Japan* 54 C10
Shiliguri, *India* 67 F16
Shilka, *Russia* 53 D12
Shilka →, *Russia* 53 D13
Shillelagh, *Ireland* 12 D5
Shillington, *U.S.A.* 117 F9
Shillong, *India* 67 G17
Shilo, *West Bank* 74 C4
Shilong, *China* 59 F9
Shilou, *China* 56 F6
Shilovo, *Russia* 34 C5
Shimabara, *Japan* 55 H5
Shimada, *Japan* 55 G9
Shimane □, *Japan* 55 G6
Shimanovsk, *Russia* 53 D13
Shimba Hills ⌓, *Kenya* 86 C4
Shimen, *China* 59 C8
Shimenjie, *China* 59 C11
Shimian, *China* 58 C4
Shimizu, *Japan* 55 G9
Shimodate, *Japan* 55 F9
Shimoga, *India* 66 N9
Shimoni, *Kenya* 86 C4
Shimonoseki, *Japan* 55 H5
Shimpuru Rapids, *Namibia* 88 B2
Shimsk, *Russia* 32 C6
Shin, L., *U.K.* 13 C4
Shinan, *China* 58 F7
Shinano-Gawa →, *Japan* 55 F9
Shināş, *Oman* 71 E8
Shīndand, *Afghan.* 66 C3
Shinglehouse, *U.S.A.* 116 E6
Shingū, *Japan* 55 H7
Shingwidzi, *S. Africa* 89 C5
Shinjō, *Japan* 54 E10
Shinkafe, *Nigeria* 83 C6
Shinshār, *Syria* 74 A5
Shinyanga, *Tanzania* 86 C3
Shinyanga □, *Tanzania* 86 C3
Shio-no-Misaki, *Japan* 55 H7
Shiogama, *Japan* 54 E10
Shiojiri, *Japan* 55 F8
Shipchenski Prokhod, *Bulgaria* 45 D9
Shiping, *China* 58 F4
Shippagan, *Canada* 105 C7
Shippensburg, *U.S.A.* 116 F7
Shippenville, *U.S.A.* 116 E5
Shiprock, *U.S.A.* 109 H9
Shiqian, *China* 58 D7
Shiqma, N. →, *Israel* 74 D3
Shiquan, *China* 56 H5
Shiquan He = Indus →, *Pakistan* 68 G2
Shīr Kūh, *Iran* 71 D7
Shiragami-Misaki, *Japan* 54 D10
Shirakawa, *Fukushima, Japan* 55 F10
Shirakawa, *Gifu, Japan* 55 F8
Shirane-San, *Gumma, Japan* 55 F9
Shirane-San, *Yamanashi, Japan* 55 G9
Shiraoi, *Japan* 54 C10
Shīrāz, *Iran* 71 D7
Shirbîn, *Egypt* 80 H7
Shire →, *Africa* 87 F4
Shiretoko-Misaki, *Japan* 54 B12
Shirinab →, *Pakistan* 68 D2
Shiriya-Zaki, *Japan* 54 D10
Shiroishi, *Japan* 54 F10
Shīrvān, *Iran* 71 B8
Shirwa, L. = Chilwa, L., *Malawi* 87 F4
Shishi, *China* 59 E12
Shishou, *China* 59 C9
Shitai, *China* 59 B11
Shivpuri, *India* 68 G7
Shixian, *China* 57 C15
Shixing, *China* 59 E10
Shiyan, *China* 59 A8
Shiyata, *Egypt* 80 B2
Shizhu, *China* 58 C7
Shizong, *China* 58 E5
Shizuishan, *China* 56 E4
Shizuoka, *Japan* 55 G9
Shizuoka □, *Japan* 55 G9
Shklov = Shklow, *Belarus* 32 E6
Shklow, *Belarus* 32 E6
Shkodër, *Albania* 44 D3
Shkumbini →, *Albania* 44 E3
Shmidta, Ostrov, *Russia* 53 A10
Shō-Gawa →, *Japan* 55 F8
Shoal L., *Canada* 103 D9
Shoal Lake, *Canada* 103 C8
Shōdo-Shima, *Japan* 55 G7
Sholapur = Solapur, *India* 66 L9
Shōmrōn, *West Bank* 74 C4
Shoreham by Sea, *U.K.* 15 G7
Shori →, *Pakistan* 68 E3
Shorkot Road, *Pakistan* 68 D5
Shoshone, *Calif., U.S.A.* 111 K10
Shoshone, *Idaho, U.S.A.* 108 E6
Shoshone L., *U.S.A.* 108 D8
Shoshone Mts., *U.S.A.* 108 G5
Shoshong, *Botswana* 88 C4
Shoshoni, *U.S.A.* 108 E9
Shostka, *Ukraine* 33 G7
Shou Xian, *China* 59 A11
Shouchang, *China* 59 C12
Shouguang, *China* 57 F10
Shouning, *China* 59 D12
Shouyang, *China* 56 F7
Show Low, *U.S.A.* 109 J9
Shpola, *Ukraine* 33 H6
Shpykiv, *Ukraine* 29 B13
Shreveport, *U.S.A.* 113 J8
Shrewsbury, *U.K.* 15 E5
Shri Mohangarh, *India* 68 F4
Shrirampur, *India* 69 H13
Shropshire □, *U.K.* 15 E5
Shū, *Kazakhstan* 52 E8
Shū →, *Kazakhstan* 50 E10
Shuangbai, *China* 58 E3
Shuangcheng, *China* 57 B14
Shuangfeng, *China* 59 D9
Shuanggou, *China* 57 G9
Shuangjiang, *China* 58 F2
Shuangliao, *China* 57 C12
Shuangshanzi, *China* 57 D10
Shuangyang, *China* 57 C13
Shuangyashan, *China* 60 B8
Shubra el Kheima, *Egypt* 80 H7
Shubra Khit, *Egypt* 80 H7
Shucheng, *China* 59 B11
Shugozero, *Russia* 32 C8
Shuguri Falls, *Tanzania* 87 D4
Shuiji, *China* 59 D12
Shuiye, *China* 56 F8
Shujalpur, *India* 68 H7
Shukpa Kunzang, *India* 69 B8
Shulan, *China* 57 B14
Shulaveri, *Georgia* 35 K7
Shule, *China* 60 C2
Shumagin Is., *U.S.A.* 100 C4
Shumen, *Bulgaria* 45 C10
Shumerlya, *Russia* 34 C8
Shumikha, *Russia* 52 D7
Shunchang, *China* 59 D11
Shunde, *China* 59 F9
Shungay, *Kazakhstan* 35 F8
Shuo Xian = Shuozhou, *China* 56 E7
Shuozhou, *China* 56 E7
Shūr →, *Fārs, Iran* 71 D7
Shūr →, *Kermān, Iran* 71 D8
Shūr →, *Yazd, Iran* 71 D7
Shūr Āb, *Iran* 71 C6
Shūr Gaz, *Iran* 71 D8
Shūrāb, *Iran* 71 C8
Shūrjestān, *Iran* 71 D7
Shurugwi, *Zimbabwe* 87 F3
Shūsf, *Iran* 71 D9
Shūsh, *Iran* 73 F13
Shūshtar, *Iran* 71 D6
Shuswap L., *Canada* 102 C5
Shuya, *Russia* 34 B5
Shuyang, *China* 57 G10
Shūzū, *Iran* 71 D7
Shwebo, *Burma* 67 H19
Shwegu, *Burma* 67 G20
Shweli →, *Burma* 67 H20
Shymkent, *Kazakhstan* 52 E7
Shyok, *India* 69 B8
Shyok →, *Pakistan* 69 B6
Shyroke, *Ukraine* 28 B8
Shyroke, *Ukraine* 29 E15
Si Chon, *Thailand* 65 H2
Si Kiang = Xi Jiang →, *China* 59 F9
Si Lanna △, *Thailand* 64 C2
Si-ngan = Xi'an, *China* 56 G5
Si Prachan, *Thailand* 64 E3
Si Racha, *Thailand* 64 F3
Si Xian, *China* 57 H9
Siachen Glacier, *Asia* 69 B7
Siahaf →, *Pakistan* 68 E3
Siahan Range, *Pakistan* 66 F4
Siaksriindrapura, *Indonesia* 62 D2
Sialkot, *Pakistan* 68 C6
Siam = Thailand ■, *Asia* 64 E4
Sian = Xi'an, *China* 56 G5
Sian Ka'an ⌓, *Mexico* 119 D7
Sianów, *Poland* 30 D3
Siantan, *Indonesia* 62 D3
Sīāreh, *Iran* 71 D9
Siargao I., *Phil.* 61 G7
Siari, *Pakistan* 69 B7
Siasi, *Phil.* 63 C6
Siasi I., *Phil.* 61 J4
Siátista, *Greece* 44 F5
Siau, *Indonesia* 63 D7
Šiauliai, *Lithuania* 9 J20
Šiauliai □, *Lithuania* 30 C10
Siazan = Siyäzän, *Azerbaijan* 35 K9
Sibâi, Gebel el, *Egypt* 70 E2
Sibang, *Indonesia* 63 K18
Sibayi, L., *S. Africa* 89 D5
Sibdu, *Sudan* 81 E2
Šibenik, *Croatia* 41 E12
Siberia = Sibirskiy □, *Russia* 53 D10
Siberia, *Russia* 50 C13
Siberut, *Indonesia* 62 E1
Sibi, *Pakistan* 68 E2
Sibil = Oksibil, *Indonesia* 63 E10
Sibiloi △, *Kenya* 86 B4
Sibirskiy □, *Russia* 53 D10
Sibiti, *Congo* 84 E2
Sibiu, *Romania* 29 E9
Sibiu □, *Romania* 29 E9
Sibley, *U.S.A.* 112 D7
Sibolga, *Indonesia* 62 D1
Sibsagar, *India* 67 F19
Sibu, *Malaysia* 62 D4
Sibuco, *Phil.* 61 H5
Sibuguey B., *Phil.* 61 H5
Sibut, *C.A.R.* 84 C3
Sibutu, *Phil.* 63 D5
Sibutu Group, *Phil.* 61 J3
Sibutu Passage, *E. Indies* 63 D5
Sibuyan I., *Phil.* 61 E5
Sibuyan Sea, *Phil.* 61 E5
Sic, *Romania* 29 D8
Sicamous, *Canada* 102 C5
Siccus →, *Australia* 95 E2
Sichuan □, *China* 58 B5
Sichuan Pendi, *China* 58 B5
Sicilia, *Italy* 43 E7
Sicily = Sicilia, *Italy* 43 E7
Sicily, Str. of 42 E4
Sicuani, *Peru* 124 F4
Šid, *Serbia & M.* 28 E4
Sidamo, *Ethiopia* 81 G4
Sidaouet, *Niger* 83 B6
Sidári, *Greece* 49 A3
Siddhapur, *India* 68 H5
Siddipet, *India* 66 K11
Sidensjö, *Sweden* 10 A12
Sidéradougou, *Burkina Faso* 82 C4
Siderno, *Italy* 43 D9
Sidhauli, *India* 69 F9
Sídheros, Ákra, *Greece* 49 D8
Sidhi, *India* 69 G9
Sidhirókastron, *Greece* 44 E7
Sîdi Abd el Rahmân, *Egypt* 80 A2
Sîdi Barrâni, *Egypt* 80 A2
Sidi-bel-Abbès, *Algeria* 78 A5
Sidi Haneish, *Egypt* 80 A2
Sidi Ifni, *Morocco* 78 C3
Sîdi Omar, *Egypt* 80 A1
Sidlaw Hills, *U.K.* 13 E5
Sidley, Mt., *Antarctica* 5 D14
Sidmouth, *U.K.* 15 G4
Sidmouth, C., *Australia* 94 A3
Sidney, *Canada* 102 D4
Sidney, *Mont., U.S.A.* 112 B2
Sidney, *N.Y., U.S.A.* 117 D9
Sidney, *Nebr., U.S.A.* 112 E3
Sidney, *Ohio, U.S.A.* 114 E3
Sidney Lanier, L., *U.S.A.* 115 H4
Sido, *Mali* 82 C3
Sidoarjo, *Indonesia* 63 G15
Sidon = Saydā, *Lebanon* 74 B4
Sidra, G. of = Surt, Khalīj, *Libya* 79 B9
Siedlce, *Poland* 31 F9
Sieg →, *Germany* 24 E3
Siegburg, *Germany* 24 E3
Siegen, *Germany* 24 E4
Siem Pang, *Cambodia* 64 E6
Siem Reap = Siemreab, *Cambodia* 64 F4
Siemiatycze, *Poland* 31 F9
Siemreab, *Cambodia* 64 F4
Siena, *Italy* 41 E8
Sieniawa, *Poland* 31 H9
Sieradz, *Poland* 31 G5
Sieraków, *Poland* 31 F3
Sierck-les-Bains, *France* 19 C13
Sierning, *Austria* 26 C7
Sierpc, *Poland* 31 F6
Sierpe, Bocas de la, *Venezuela* 125 L15
Sierra Blanca, *U.S.A.* 109 L11
Sierra Blanca Peak, *U.S.A.* 109 K11
Sierra City, *U.S.A.* 110 F6
Sierra Colorada, *Argentina* 128 E3
Sierra de Aracena y Picas de Aroche ⌓, *Spain* 37 H4
Sierra de Bahoruco △, *Dom. Rep.* 121 C5
Sierra de Baza ⌓, *Spain* 39 H2
Sierra de Castril ⌓, *Spain* 39 H2
Sierra de Espuña ⌓, *Spain* 39 H3
Sierra de Grazalema ⌓, *Spain* 37 J5
Sierra de Gredos ⌓, *Spain* 36 E5
Sierra de Hornachuelos ⌓, *Spain* 37 H5
Sierra de Huétor ⌓, *Spain* 37 H7
Sierra de La Culata △, *Venezuela* 121 E5
Sierra de Lancandón △, *Guatemala* 120 C1
Sierra de las Nieves ⌓, *Spain* 37 J6
Sierra de las Quijadas △, *Argentina* 126 C2
Sierra de María-Los Vélez ⌓, *Spain* 39 H2
Sierra de San Luis △, *Venezuela* 121 D6
Sierra de Yeguas, *Spain* 37 H6
Sierra del São Mamede ⌓, *Portugal* 37 F3
Sierra Gorda, *Chile* 126 A2
Sierra Leone ■, *W. Afr.* 82 D2
Sierra Madre, *Mexico* 119 D6
Sierra Mágina ⌓, *Spain* 37 H7
Sierra Mojada, *Mexico* 118 B4
Sierra Nevada, *Spain* 37 H7
Sierra Nevada, *U.S.A.* 110 H8
Sierra Nevada ⌓, *Spain* 37 H7
Sierra Nevada △, *Venezuela* 121 E5
Sierra Nevada de Santa Marta △, *Colombia* 121 D5
Sierra Norte de Seville ⌓, *Spain* 37 H5
Sierra Subbéticas ⌓, *Spain* 37 H6
Sierra Vista, *U.S.A.* 109 L8
Sierras de Cardeña y Montoro ⌓, *Spain* 37 G6
Sierras de Cazorla, Segura y las Villas ⌓, *Spain* 39 J2
Sierraville, *U.S.A.* 110 F6
Sierre, *Switz.* 25 J3
Sifani, *Ethiopia* 81 E5
Sifié, *Ivory C.* 82 D3
Sífnos, *Greece* 46 E6
Sifton, *Canada* 103 C8
Sifton Pass, *Canada* 102 B3
Sigean, *France* 20 E6
Sighetu-Marmaţiei, *Romania* 29 C8
Sighişoara, *Romania* 29 D9
Sigli, *Indonesia* 62 C1
Siglufjörður, *Iceland* 8 C4
Sigmaringen, *Germany* 25 G5
Signa, *Italy* 40 E8
Signakhi = Tsnori, *Georgia* 35 K7
Signal, *U.S.A.* 111 L13
Signal de Botrang, *Belgium* 17 D6
Signal Pk., *U.S.A.* 111 M12
Signy I., *Antarctica* 5 C18
Signy-l'Abbaye, *France* 19 C11
Sigsig, *Ecuador* 124 D3
Sigüenza, *Spain* 38 D2
Siguiri, *Guinea* 82 C3
Sigulda, *Latvia* 9 H21
Sihora, *India* 69 H9
Sihui, *China* 59 F9
Siikajoki →, *Finland* 8 D21
Siilinjärvi, *Finland* 8 E22
Siirt, *Turkey* 73 D9
Sijarira Ra. = Chizarira, *Zimbabwe* 87 F2
Sika, *India* 68 H3
Sikani Chief →, *Canada* 102 B4
Sikao, *Thailand* 65 J2
Sikar, *India* 68 F6
Sikasso, *Mali* 82 C3
Sikeston, *U.S.A.* 113 G10
Sikhote Alin, Khrebet, *Russia* 53 E14
Sikhote Alin Ra. = Sikhote Alin, Khrebet, *Russia* 53 E14
Sikiá, *Greece* 44 F7
Síkinos, *Greece* 47 E7
Sikkim □, *India* 67 F16
Siklós, *Hungary* 28 E3
Sil →, *Spain* 36 C3
Silacayoapan, *Mexico* 119 D5
Šilalė, *Lithuania* 30 C9
Silandro, *Italy* 40 B7
Silawad, *India* 68 J6
Silay, *Phil.* 61 F5
Silba, *Croatia* 41 D11
Silchar, *India* 67 G18
Şile, *Turkey* 45 E13
Siler City, *U.S.A.* 115 H6
Silgarhi Doti, *Nepal* 69 E9
Silghat, *India* 67 F18
Sili, *Burkina Faso* 82 C4
Silifke, *Turkey* 70 B2
Siliguri = Shiliguri, *India* 67 F16
Siling Co, *China* 60 C3
Silistea Nouă, *Romania* 29 F10
Silistra, *Bulgaria* 45 B11
Silivri, *Turkey* 45 E12
Siljan, *Sweden* 10 D8
Siljansnäs, *Sweden* 10 D8
Silkeborg, *Denmark* 11 H3
Silkwood, *Australia* 94 B4
Silla, *Spain* 39 F4
Sillajhuay, Cordillera, *Chile* 124 G5
Sillamäe, *Estonia* 9 G22
Sillé-le-Guillaume, *France* 18 D6
Silleda, *Spain* 36 C2
Silloth, *U.K.* 14 C4
Sílo, *Greece* 45 E9
Siloam Springs, *U.S.A.* 113 G7
Silopi, *Turkey* 73 D10
Silsbee, *U.S.A.* 113 K7
Siluko, *Nigeria* 83 D6
Šilutė, *Lithuania* 9 J19
Silvan, *Turkey* 73 C9
Silvani, *India* 69 H8
Silver City, *U.S.A.* 109 K9
Silver Cr. →, *U.S.A.* 108 E4
Silver Creek, *U.S.A.* 116 D5
Silver L., *U.S.A.* 110 G6
Silver Lake, *Calif., U.S.A.* 111 K10
Silver Lake, *Oreg., U.S.A.* 108 E3
Silverdalen, *Sweden* 11 G9
Silverton, *Colo., U.S.A.* 109 H10
Silverton, *Tex., U.S.A.* 113 H4
Silves, *Portugal* 37 H2
Silvi Marina, *Italy* 41 F11
Silvies →, *U.S.A.* 108 E4
Silvrettahorn, *Switz.* 40 B7
Silwa Bahari, *Egypt* 80 C3
Silz, *Austria* 26 D3
Simaltala, *India* 69 G12
Simanggang = Bandar Sri Aman, *Malaysia* 62 D4
Simao, *China* 58 F3
Simard, L., *Canada* 104 C4
Şīmareh →, *Iran* 73 F12
Simav, *Turkey* 47 B10
Simav →, *Turkey* 45 F12
Simav Dağları, *Turkey* 47 B10
Simba, *Tanzania* 86 C4
Simbach, *Germany* 25 G9
Simbirsk, *Russia* 34 C9
Simbo, *Tanzania* 86 C2
Simcoe, *Canada* 116 D4
Simcoe, L., *Canada* 116 B5
Simdega, *India* 69 H11
Simeonovgrad, *Bulgaria* 45 D9
Simeria, *Romania* 28 E8
Simeto →, *Italy* 43 E8
Simeulue, *Indonesia* 62 D1
Simferopol, *Ukraine* 33 K8
Sími, *Greece* 47 E9
Simi Valley, *U.S.A.* 111 L8
Simien Mts. △, *Ethiopia* 81 E4
Simikot, *Nepal* 69 E9
Simitli, *Bulgaria* 44 E7
Simla, *India* 68 D7
Simlångsdalen, *Sweden* 11 H7
Şimleu-Silvaniei, *Romania* 28 C7
Simmern, *Germany* 25 F3
Simmie, *Canada* 103 D7
Simmler, *U.S.A.* 111 K7
Simnas, *Lithuania* 30 D10
Simo älv = Simojoki →, *Finland* 8 D21
Simojoki →, *Finland* 8 D21
Simojovel, *Mexico* 119 D6
Simonette →, *Canada* 102 B5
Simonstown, *S. Africa* 88 E2
Simontornya, *Hungary* 28 D3
Simpang Empat, *Malaysia* 65 c
Simplonpass, *Switz.* 25 J4
Simplontunnel, *Switz.* 25 J4
Simpson Desert, *Australia* 94 D2
Simpson Desert △, *Australia* 94 C2
Simpson Pen., *Canada* 101 B11
Simpungdong, *N. Korea* 57 D15
Simrishamn, *Sweden* 11 J8
Simsbury, *U.S.A.* 117 E12
Simushir, Ostrov, *Russia* 53 E16
Sin Cowe I., *S. China Sea* 62 C4
Sinabang, *Indonesia* 62 D1
Sinadogo, *Somali Rep.* 75 F4
Sinai = Es Sînâ', *Egypt* 74 F3
Sinai, Mt. = Mûsa, Gebel, *Egypt* 70 D2
Sinai Peninsula, *Egypt* 50 G7
Sinaia, *Romania* 29 E10
Sinaloa □, *Mexico* 118 C3
Sinaloa de Leyva, *Mexico* 118 B3
Sinalunga, *Italy* 41 E8
Sinan, *China* 58 D7
Sînandrei, *Romania* 28 E6
Sinarádhes, *Greece* 49 A3
Sincan, *Turkey* 72 B5
Sincanlı, *Turkey* 47 C12
Sincelejo, *Colombia* 124 B3
Sinch'ang, *N. Korea* 57 D15
Sinchang-ni, *N. Korea* 57 E14
Sinclair, *U.S.A.* 108 F10
Sinclair Mills, *Canada* 102 C4
Sinclair's B., *U.K.* 13 C5
Sinclairville, *U.S.A.* 116 D5
Sincorá, Serra do, *Brazil* 125 F10
Sind, *Pakistan* 68 G3
Sind □, *Pakistan* 68 G3
Sind →, *Jammu & Kashmir, India* 69 B6
Sind →, *Mad. P., India* 69 F8
Sind Sagar Doab, *Pakistan* 68 D4
Sindal, *Denmark* 11 G4
Sindangan, *Phil.* 61 G5
Sindangbarang, *Indonesia* 63 G12
Sinde, *Zambia* 87 F2
Sindelfingen, *Germany* 25 G4
Sindh = Sind □, *Pakistan* 68 G3
Sındırgı, *Turkey* 47 B10
Sindou, *Burkina Faso* 82 C3
Sindri, *India* 69 H12
Sine →, *Senegal* 82 C1
Sinegorskiy, *Russia* 35 G5
Sinekli, *Turkey* 45 E12
Sinelnikovo = Synelnykove, *Ukraine* 33 H8
Sinendé, *Benin* 83 C5
Sines, *Portugal* 37 H2
Sines, C. de, *Portugal* 37 H2
Sineu, *Spain* 48 B10
Sinfra, *Ivory C.* 82 D3
Sing Buri, *Thailand* 64 E3
Singa, *Sudan* 81 E3
Singapore ■, *Asia* 65 d
Singapore, Straits of, *Asia* 65 d
Singapore Changi ✕ (SIN), *Singapore* 65 M4
Singaraja, *Indonesia* 63 J18
Singen, *Germany* 25 H4
Singida, *Tanzania* 86 C3
Singida □, *Tanzania* 86 D3
Singitikós Kólpos, *Greece* 44 F7
Singkaling Hkamti, *Burma* 67 G19
Singkang, *Indonesia* 63 E6
Singkawang, *Indonesia* 62 D3
Singkep, *Indonesia* 62 E2
Singleton, *Australia* 95 E5
Singleton, Mt., *N. Terr., Australia* 92 D5
Singleton, Mt., *W. Austral., Australia* 93 E2
Singö, *Sweden* 10 D12
Singoli, *India* 68 G6
Singora = Songkhla, *Thailand* 65 J3
Singosan, *N. Korea* 57 E14
Sinhung, *N. Korea* 57 D14
Siniátsikon, Óros, *Greece* 44 F5
Siniscóla, *Italy* 42 B2
Sinj, *Croatia* 41 E13
Sinjai, *Indonesia* 63 F6
Sinjajevina, *Serbia & M.* 44 D3
Sinjār, *Iraq* 70 B4
Sinkat, *Sudan* 80 D4
Sinkiang Uighur = Xinjiang Uygur Zizhiqu □, *China* 60 B3
Sinmak, *N. Korea* 57 E14
Sínnai, *Italy* 42 C2
Sinnamary, *Fr. Guiana* 125 B8
Sinni →, *Italy* 43 B9
Sinnuris, *Egypt* 80 J7
Sinoie, Lacul, *Romania* 29 F13
Sinop, *Turkey* 72 A6
Sinor, *India* 68 J5
Sinp'o, *N. Korea* 57 E15
Sinsheim, *Germany* 25 F4
Sinsk, *Russia* 53 C13
Sintang, *Indonesia* 62 D4
Sinton, *U.S.A.* 113 L6
Sintra, *Portugal* 37 G1
Sintra-Cascais ⌓, *Portugal* 37 G1

Sinŭiju, *N. Korea* 57 D13
Sinyukha →, *Ukraine* 33 H6
Sinzig, *Germany* 24 E3
Sio →, *Hungary* 28 D3
Siocon, *Phil.* 61 H5
Siófok, *Hungary* 28 D3
Sion, *Switz.* 25 J3
Sion Mills, *U.K.* 12 B4
Sioux City, *U.S.A.* 112 D6
Sioux Falls, *U.S.A.* 112 D6
Sioux Lookout, *Canada* 104 B1
Sioux Narrows, *Canada* 103 D10
Sipalay, *Phil.* 61 G5
Šipan, *Croatia* 44 D1
Siparia, *Trin. & Tob.* 125 K15
Sipil Daği △, *Turkey* 47 C9
Siping, *China* 57 C13
Sipiwesk L., *Canada* 103 B9
Siple, *Antarctica* 5 D7
Šipovo, *Bos.-H.* 28 F2
Sipra →, *India* 68 H6
Sipura, *Indonesia* 62 E1
Siquia →, *Nic.* 120 D3
Siquijor, *Phil.* 61 G5
Siquirres, *Costa Rica* 120 D3
Şīr Abu Nu'ayr, *U.A.E.* 71 E7
Şīr Banī Yās, *U.A.E.* 71 E7
Sir Edward Pellew Group, *Australia* 94 B2
Sir Graham Moore Is., *Australia* 92 B4
Sir James MacBrien, Mt., *Canada* 100 B7
Sira →, *Norway* 9 G12
Siracusa, *Italy* 43 E8
Sirajganj, *Bangla.* 69 G13
Sirakoro, *Mali* 82 C3
Şiran, *Turkey* 73 B8
Sirasso, *Ivory C.* 82 D3
Sirathu, *India* 69 G9
Sīrdān, *Iran* 71 B6
Sirdaryo = Syrdarya →, *Kazakhstan* 52 E7
Sire, *Ethiopia* 81 F4
Siren, *U.S.A.* 112 C8
Sirente-Velino ⌓, *Italy* 41 F10
Sirer, *Spain* 48 C7
Siret, *Romania* 29 C11
Siret →, *Romania* 29 E12
Sirghāyā, *Syria* 74 B5
Şiria, *Romania* 28 D6
Sirinath △, *Thailand* 65 a
Sirino, Mte., *Italy* 43 B8
Sīrjān, *Iran* 71 D7
Sirmaur, *India* 69 G9
Sírna, *Greece* 47 E8
Şirnak, *Turkey* 73 D10
Sirohi, *India* 68 G5
Sironj, *India* 68 G7
Síros, *Greece* 46 D6
Sirretta Pk., *U.S.A.* 111 K8
Sīrrī, *Iran* 71 E7
Sirsa, *India* 68 E6
Sirsa →, *India* 69 F8
Siruela, *Spain* 37 G5
Sisak, *Croatia* 41 C13
Sisaket, *Thailand* 64 E5
Sisante, *Spain* 39 F2
Sisargas, Is., *Spain* 36 B2
Sishen, *S. Africa* 88 D3
Sishui, *Henan, China* 56 G7
Sishui, *Shandong, China* 57 G9
Sisipuk L., *Canada* 103 B8
Sisophon, *Cambodia* 64 F4
Sisseton, *U.S.A.* 112 C6
Sissonne, *France* 19 C10
Sīstān, *Asia* 71 D9
Sīstān, Daryācheh-ye, *Iran* 71 D9
Sīstān va Balūchestān □, *Iran* 71 E9
Sisteron, *France* 21 D9
Sisters, *U.S.A.* 108 D3
Siswa Bazar, *India* 69 F10
Sitakili, *Mali* 82 C2
Sitamarhi, *India* 69 F11
Sitampiky, *Madag.* 89 B8
Sitapur, *India* 69 F9
Siteki, *Swaziland* 89 D5
Sitges, *Spain* 38 D6
Sithoniá, *Greece* 44 F7
Sitía, *Greece* 49 D8
Sitka, *U.S.A.* 102 B1
Sitoti, *Botswana* 88 C3
Sitra, *Egypt* 80 B2
Sittang Myit →, *Burma* 67 L20
Sittard, *Neths.* 17 C5
Sittensen, *Germany* 24 B5
Sittingbourne, *U.K.* 15 F8
Sittona, *Eritrea* 81 E4
Sittoung = Sittang Myit →, *Burma* 67 L20
Sittwe, *Burma* 67 J18
Situbondo, *Indonesia* 63 G16
Siuna, *Nic.* 120 D3
Siuri, *India* 69 H12
Siutghiol, Lacul, *Romania* 29 F13
Sīvand, *Iran* 71 D7
Sivas, *Turkey* 70 B3
Sivaslı, *Turkey* 47 C11
Siverek, *Turkey* 70 B3
Sivrihisar, *Turkey* 72 C4
Sîwa, *Egypt* 80 B2
Sîwa, El Wâhât es, *Egypt* 80 B2
Siwa Oasis = Sîwa, El Wâhât es, *Egypt* 80 B2
Siwalik Range, *Nepal* 69 F10
Siwan, *India* 69 F11
Siwana, *India* 68 G5
Six Cross Roads, *Barbados* 121 g
Sixmilebridge, *Ireland* 12 D3
Sixth Cataract, *Sudan* 81 D3
Siyâl, Jazâ'ir, *Egypt* 80 C4
Siyäzän, *Azerbaijan* 35 K9
Siziwang Qi, *China* 56 D6
Sjælland, *Denmark* 11 J5
Sjællands Odde, *Denmark* 11 J5
Sjenica, *Serbia & M.* 44 C3
Sjöbo, *Sweden* 11 J7
Sjötofta, *Sweden* 11 G7
Sjötorp, *Sweden* 11 F8
Sjumen = Shumen, *Bulgaria* 45 C10
Sjuntorp, *Sweden* 11 F6
Skadarsko Jezero, *Serbia & M.* 44 D3
Skadovsk, *Ukraine* 33 J7
Skælskør, *Denmark* 11 J5
Skærbæk, *Denmark* 11 J2
Skaftafell, *Iceland* 8 D5
Skagafjörður, *Iceland* 8 D4
Skagastølstindane, *Norway* 9 F12
Skagaströnd, *Iceland* 8 D3
Skagen, *Denmark* 11 G4
Skagern, *Sweden* 10 E8
Skagerrak, *Denmark* 11 G2
Skagit →, *U.S.A.* 110 B4
Skagway, *U.S.A.* 100 C6
Skala-Podilska, *Ukraine* 29 B11
Skala Podolskaya = Skala-Podilska, *Ukraine* 29 B11
Skalat, *Ukraine* 33 H3
Skalbmierz, *Poland* 31 H7
Skälderviken, *Sweden* 11 H6
Skalica, *Slovak Rep.* 27 C10
Skallingen, *Denmark* 11 J2
Skalni Dol = Kamenyak, *Bulgaria* 45 C10
Skanderborg, *Denmark* 11 H3
Skåne, *Sweden* 11 J7
Skåne län □, *Sweden* 11 H7
Skaneateles, *U.S.A.* 117 D8
Skaneateles L., *U.S.A.* 117 D8
Skänninge, *Sweden* 11 F9
Skanör med Falsterbo, *Sweden* 11 J6
Skantzoúra, *Greece* 46 B6
Skara, *Sweden* 11 F7
Skärblacka, *Sweden* 11 F9
Skardu, *Pakistan* 69 B6
Skåre, *Sweden* 10 E7
Skärhamn, *Sweden* 11 G5
Skarszewy, *Poland* 30 D5
Skaryszew, *Poland* 31 G8
Skarżysko-Kamienna, *Poland* 31 G7
Skattkärr, *Sweden* 10 E7
Skattungbyn, *Sweden* 10 C8
Skawina, *Poland* 31 J6
Skebobruk, *Sweden* 10 E12
Skeena →, *Canada* 102 C2
Skeena Mts., *Canada* 102 B3
Skegness, *U.K.* 14 D8
Skeldon, *Guyana* 124 B7
Skeleton Coast, *Namibia* 85 H2
Skeleton Coast ⌓, *Namibia* 88 C1
Skellefteå, *Sweden* 8 D19
Skellefteälven →, *Sweden* 8 D19
Skelleftehamn, *Sweden* 8 D19
Skender Vakuf, *Bos.-H.* 28 F2
Skerries, The, *U.K.* 14 D3
Skhidnytsya, *Ukraine* 31 J10
Skhíza, *Greece* 46 E3
Skhoinoúsa, *Greece* 47 E7
Ski, *Norway* 9 G14
Skíathos, *Greece* 46 B5
Skibbereen, *Ireland* 12 E2
Skiddaw, *U.K.* 14 C4
Skidegate, *Canada* 102 C2
Skídhra, *Greece* 44 F6
Skien, *Norway* 9 G13
Skierniewice, *Poland* 31 G7
Skikda, *Algeria* 78 A7
Skillingaryd, *Sweden* 11 G8
Skillinge, *Sweden* 11 J8
Skilloura, *Cyprus* 49 D12
Skinári, Ákra, *Greece* 46 D2
Skinnskatteberg, *Sweden* 10 E9
Skipton, *U.K.* 14 D5
Skiring, C., *Senegal* 82 C1
Skirmish Pt., *Australia* 94 A1
Skiropoúla, *Greece* 46 C6
Skíros, *Greece* 46 C6
Skivarp, *Sweden* 11 J7
Skive, *Denmark* 11 H3
Skjálfandafljót →, *Iceland* 8 D5
Skjálfandi, *Iceland* 8 C5
Skjern, *Denmark* 11 J2
Skoczów, *Poland* 31 J5
Škofja Loka, *Slovenia* 41 B11
Skoghall, *Sweden* 10 E7
Skogstorp, *Sweden* 10 E10
Skoki, *Poland* 31 F4
Skole, *Ukraine* 33 H2
Skópelos, *Greece* 46 B5
Skopí, *Greece* 49 D8
Skopin, *Russia* 32 F10
Skopje, *Macedonia* 44 D5
Skopje ✕ (SKP), *Macedonia* 44 E5
Skórcz, *Poland* 30 E5
Skørping, *Denmark* 11 H3
Skövde, *Sweden* 11 F7
Skovorodino, *Russia* 53 D13
Skowhegan, *U.S.A.* 115 C11
Skradin, *Croatia* 41 E12
Skrea, *Sweden* 11 H6
Skrunda, *Latvia* 30 B9
Skrwa →, *Poland* 31 F6
Skuleskogen △, *Sweden* 10 A12
Skull, *Ireland* 12 E2
Skultorp, *Sweden* 11 F7
Skultuna, *Sweden* 10 E10
Skunk →, *U.S.A.* 112 E9
Skuodas, *Lithuania* 9 H19
Skurup, *Sweden* 11 J7
Skutskär, *Sweden* 10 D11
Skvyra, *Ukraine* 33 H5
Skwierzyna, *Poland* 31 F2
Skye, *U.K.* 13 D2
Skykomish, *U.S.A.* 108 C3
Skyros = Skíros, *Greece* 46 C6
Skyttorp, *Sweden* 10 D11
Slade Pt., *Australia* 94 K7
Slættaratindur, *Færoe Is.* 8 E9
Slagelse, *Denmark* 11 J5
Slamet, *Indonesia* 63 G13
Slaney →, *Ireland* 12 D5
Slangberge, *S. Africa* 88 E3
Slănic, *Romania* 29 E10
Slano, *Croatia* 44 D1
Slantsy, *Russia* 32 C5
Slaný, *Czech Rep.* 26 A7
Śląskie □, *Poland* 31 H6
Slätbaken, *Sweden* 11 F10
Slate Is., *Canada* 104 C2
Slatina, *Croatia* 28 E2
Slatina, *Romania* 29 F9
Slatina Timiş, *Romania* 28 E7
Slatington, *U.S.A.* 117 F9
Slaton, *U.S.A.* 113 J4
Slave →, *Canada* 102 A6
Slave Coast, *W. Afr.* 83 D5
Slave Lake, *Canada* 102 B6
Slave Pt., *Canada* 102 A5
Slavgorod, *Russia* 52 D8
Slavinja, *Serbia & M.* 44 C6
Slavkov u Brna, *Czech Rep.* 27 B9
Slavkovský Les ⌓, *Czech Rep.* 26 A5
Slavonija, *Europe* 28 E2
Slavonski Brod, *Croatia* 28 E3
Slavsk, *Russia* 30 C8
Slavska, *Ukraine* 29 B8
Slavskoye, *Russia* 30 D7
Slavuta, *Ukraine* 33 G4
Slavyanka, *Russia* 54 C5
Slavyanovo, *Bulgaria* 45 C8
Slavyansk = Slovyansk, *Ukraine* 33 H9
Slavyansk-na-Kubani, *Russia* 33 K10
Sława, *Poland* 31 G3
Slawharad, *Belarus* 32 F6
Sławno, *Poland* 30 D3
Sławoborze, *Poland* 30 E2
Sleaford, *U.K.* 14 D7
Sleaford B., *Australia* 95 E2
Sleat, Sd. of, *U.K.* 13 D3
Sleeper Is., *Canada* 101 C11
Sleeping Bear Dunes ⌓, *U.S.A.* 114 C2
Sleepy Eye, *U.S.A.* 112 C7
Slemon L., *Canada* 102 A5
Ślesin, *Poland* 31 F5
Slide Mt., *U.S.A.* 117 E10
Slidell, *U.S.A.* 113 K10
Sliema, *Malta* 49 D2
Slieve Aughty, *Ireland* 12 C3
Slieve Bloom, *Ireland* 12 C4
Slieve Donard, *U.K.* 12 B6
Slieve Gamph, *Ireland* 12 B3
Slieve Gullion, *U.K.* 12 B5
Slieve League, *Ireland* 12 B3
Slieve Mish, *Ireland* 12 D2
Slievenamon, *Ireland* 12 D4
Sligeach = Sligo, *Ireland* 12 B3
Sligo, *Ireland* 12 B3
Sligo, *U.S.A.* 116 E5
Sligo □, *Ireland* 12 B3
Sligo B., *Ireland* 12 B3
Slippery Rock, *U.S.A.* 116 E4
Slite, *Sweden* 11 G12
Slīteres ⌓, *Latvia* 30 A9
Sliven, *Bulgaria* 45 D10
Slivnitsa, *Bulgaria* 44 D7
Sljeme, *Croatia* 41 C12
Sloan, *U.S.A.* 111 K11
Sloansville, *U.S.A.* 117 D10
Slobidka, *Ukraine* 29 C14
Slobozia, *Moldova* 29 D14
Slobozia, *Argeş, Romania* 29 F10
Slobozia, *Ialomiţa, Romania* 29 F12
Slocan, *Canada* 102 D5
Słomniki, *Poland* 31 H7
Slonim, *Belarus* 33 F3
Slough, *U.K.* 15 F7
Slough □, *U.K.* 15 F7
Sloughhouse, *U.S.A.* 110 G5
Slovak Rep. ■, *Europe* 27 C13
Slovakia = Slovak Rep. ■, *Europe* 27 C13
Slovakian Ore Mts. = Slovenské Rudohorie, *Slovak Rep.* 27 C12
Slovenia ■, *Europe* 41 C11
Slovenija = Slovenia ■, *Europe* 41 C11
Slovenj Gradec, *Slovenia* 41 B12
Slovenska Bistrica, *Slovenia* 41 B12
Slovenské Konjice, *Slovenia* 41 B12
Slovenské Rudohorie, *Slovak Rep.* 27 C12
Slovenský Raj △, *Slovak Rep.* 27 C13
Slovyansk, *Ukraine* 33 H9
Słowiński △, *Poland* 30 D4
Słubice, *Poland* 31 F1
Sluch →, *Ukraine* 33 G4
Sluis, *Neths.* 17 C3
Slŭnchev Bryag, *Bulgaria* 45 D11
Slunj, *Croatia* 41 C12
Słupca, *Poland* 31 F4
Słupia →, *Poland* 30 D3
Słupsk, *Poland* 30 D4
Slurry, *S. Africa* 88 D4
Slutsk, *Belarus* 33 F4
Slyne Hd., *Ireland* 12 C1
Slyudyanka, *Russia* 53 D11
Småland, *Sweden* 11 G9
Smålandsfarvandet, *Denmark* 11 J5
Smålandsstenar, *Sweden* 11 G7
Smalltree L., *Canada* 103 A8
Smallwood Res., *Canada* 105 B7
Smarhon, *Belarus* 32 E4
Smarje, *Slovenia* 41 B12
Smartt Syndicate Dam, *S. Africa* 88 E3
Smartville, *U.S.A.* 110 F5
Smeaton, *Canada* 103 C8
Smedby, *Sweden* 11 H10
Smederevo, *Serbia & M.* 44 B4
Smederevska Palanka, *Serbia & M.* 44 B4
Smedjebacken, *Sweden* 10 D9
Smela = Smila, *Ukraine* 33 H6
Smerwick Harbour, *Ireland* 12 D1
Smethport, *U.S.A.* 116 E6
Smidovich, *Russia* 53 E14
Śmigiel, *Poland* 31 F3
Smila, *Ukraine* 33 H6
Smilyan, *Bulgaria* 45 E8
Smith, *Canada* 102 B6
Smith Center, *U.S.A.* 112 F5
Smith River ⌓, *U.S.A.* 108 F2
Smith Sd., *N. Amer.* 4 B4
Smithburne →, *Australia* 94 B3
Smithers, *Canada* 102 C3
Smithfield, *S. Africa* 89 E4
Smithfield, *N.C., U.S.A.* 115 H6
Smithfield, *Utah, U.S.A.* 108 F8
Smiths Falls, *Canada* 117 B9
Smithton, *Australia* 95 G4
Smithville, *Canada* 116 C5
Smithville, *U.S.A.* 113 K6
Smoky →, *Canada* 102 B5
Smoky Bay, *Australia* 95 E1
Smoky Hill →, *U.S.A.* 112 F6
Smoky Hills, *U.S.A.* 112 F5
Smoky Lake, *Canada* 102 C6
Smøla, *Norway* 8 E13
Smolensk, *Russia* 32 E7
Smolikas, Óros, *Greece* 44 F4
Smolník, *Slovak Rep.* 27 C13
Smolyan, *Bulgaria* 45 E8
Smooth Rock Falls, *Canada* 104 C3
Smoothstone L., *Canada* 103 C7
Smorgon = Smarhon, *Belarus* 32 E4
Smotrych, *Ukraine* 29 B11
Smotrych → 29 B11
Smulţi, *Romania* 29 E12
Smyadovo, *Bulgaria* 45 C11
Smygehamn, *Sweden* 11 J7
Smyrna = İzmir, *Turkey* 47 C9
Smyrna, *U.S.A.* 114 F8
Snæfell, *Iceland* 8 D6
Snaefell, *I. of Man* 14 C3
Snæfellsjökull, *Iceland* 8 D2
Snake →, *U.S.A.* 108 C4
Snake I., *Australia* 95 F4
Snake Range, *U.S.A.* 108 G6
Snake River Plain, *U.S.A.* 108 E7
Snasahögarna, *Sweden* 10 A6
Snåsavatnet, *Norway* 8 D14
Snedsted, *Denmark* 11 H2
Sneek, *Neths.* 17 A5
Sneeuberge, *S. Africa* 88 E3
Snejbjerg, *Denmark* 11 H2
Snelling, *U.S.A.* 110 H6
Snezhnoye, *Ukraine* 33 J10
Snežnik, *Slovenia* 41 C11
Śniadowo, *Poland* 31 E8
Śniardwy, Jezioro, *Poland* 30 E8
Śnieżka, *Europe* 26 A8
Snigirevka = Snihurivka, *Ukraine* 33 J7
Snihurivka, *Ukraine* 33 J7
Snina, *Slovak Rep.* 27 C15
Snizort, L., *U.K.* 13 D2
Snøhetta, *Norway* 9 E13
Snohomish, *U.S.A.* 110 C4
Snoul, *Cambodia* 65 F6
Snow Hill, *U.S.A.* 114 F8
Snow Lake, *Canada* 103 C8
Snow Mt., *Calif., U.S.A.* 110 F4
Snow Mt., *Maine, U.S.A.* 117 A14
Snow Shoe, *U.S.A.* 116 E7
Snowbird L., *Canada* 103 A8
Snowdon, *U.K.* 14 D3
Snowdonia △, *U.K.* 14 D4
Snowdrift = Łutselk'e, *Canada* 103 A6
Snowdrift →, *Canada* 103 A6
Snowflake, *U.S.A.* 109 J8
Snowshoe Pk., *U.S.A.* 108 B6
Snowtown, *Australia* 95 E2
Snowville, *U.S.A.* 108 F7
Snowy →, *Australia* 95 F4
Snowy Mt., *U.S.A.* 117 C10
Snowy Mts., *Australia* 95 F4
Snug Corner, *Bahamas* 121 B5
Snyatyn, *Ukraine* 29 B10
Snyder, *Okla., U.S.A.* 113 H5
Snyder, *Tex., U.S.A.* 113 J4
Soahanina, *Madag.* 89 B7
Soalala, *Madag.* 89 B8
Soaloka, *Madag.* 89 B8
Soamanonga, *Madag.* 89 C7
Soan →, *Pakistan* 68 C4
Soanierana-Ivongo, *Madag.* 89 B8
Soanindraniny, *Madag.* 89 B8
Şoarş, *Romania* 29 E9
Soavina, *Madag.* 89 C8
Soavinandriana, *Madag.* 89 B8
Sob →, *Ukraine* 29 B14
Soba, *Nigeria* 83 C6
Sobat, Nahr →, *Sudan* 81 F3
Soběslav, *Czech Rep.* 26 B7
Sobhapur, *India* 68 H8
Sobinka, *Russia* 32 E11
Sobótka, *Poland* 31 H3
Sobra, *Croatia* 41 F14
Sobradinho, Reprêsa de, *Brazil* 125 E10
Sobral, *Brazil* 125 D10
Sobrance, *Slovak Rep.* 27 C15
Sobreira Formosa, *Portugal* 36 F3
Soc Giang, *Vietnam* 58 F6
Soc Trang, *Vietnam* 65 H5
Soča →, *Europe* 26 E6
Socastee, *U.S.A.* 115 J6
Sochaczew, *Poland* 31 F7
Soch'e = Shache, *China* 60 C2
Sochi, *Russia* 35 J4
Société, Is. de la, *French Polynesia* 97 J12
Society Is. = Société, Is. de la, *French Polynesia* 97 J12
Socompa, Portezuelo de, *Chile* 126 A2
Socorro, *N. Mex., U.S.A.* 109 J10
Socorro, *Tex., U.S.A.* 109 L10
Socorro, I., *Mexico* 118 D2
Socotra, *Yemen* 75 E5
Socovos, *Spain* 39 G3
Socuéllamos, *Spain* 39 F2
Soda L., *U.S.A.* 109 J5
Soda Plains, *India* 69 B8
Soda Springs, *U.S.A.* 108 E8
Sodankylä, *Finland* 8 C22
Soddy-Daisy, *U.S.A.* 115 H3
Söderala, *Sweden* 10 C10
Söderåsen △, *Sweden* 11 H7
Söderbärke, *Sweden* 10 D9
Söderfors, *Sweden* 10 D11
Söderhamn, *Sweden* 10 C11
Söderköping, *Sweden* 11 F10
Södermanland, *Sweden* 9 G17
Södermanlands län □, *Sweden* 10 E10
Södertälje, *Sweden* 10 E11
Sodiri, *Sudan* 81 E2
Sodo, *Ethiopia* 81 F4
Södra Dellen, *Sweden* 10 C10
Södra Finnskoga, *Sweden* 10 D6
Södra Sandby, *Sweden* 11 J7
Södra Ulvön, *Sweden* 10 B12
Södra Vi, *Sweden* 11 G9
Sodražica, *Slovenia* 41 C11
Sodus, *U.S.A.* 116 C7
Sodwana Bay △, *S. Africa* 89 D5
Soekmekaar, *S. Africa* 89 C4
Soest, *Germany* 24 D4
Soest, *Neths.* 17 B5
Sofádhes, *Greece* 46 B4
Sofala □, *Mozam.* 89 B5
Sofara, *Mali* 82 C4
Sofia = Sofiya, *Bulgaria* 44 D7
Sofia →, *Madag.* 89 B8
Sofievka, *Ukraine* 33 H7
Sofikón, *Greece* 46 D5
Sofiya, *Bulgaria* 44 D7
Sofiya □, *Bulgaria* 44 D7
Sofiya ✕ (SOF), *Bulgaria* 44 D7
Sōfu-Gan, *Japan* 55 K10
Sogakofe, *Ghana* 83 D5
Sogamoso, *Colombia* 124 B4
Sogār, *Iran* 71 E8
Sögel, *Germany* 24 C3
Sogndalsfjøra, *Norway* 9 F12
Søgne, *Norway* 9 G12
Sognefjorden, *Norway* 9 F11
Söğüt, *Bilecik, Turkey* 47 A12
Söğüt, *Burdur, Turkey* 47 D11
Söğüt Dağı, *Turkey* 47 D11
Söğütköy, *Turkey* 47 E10
Sŏgwipo, *S. Korea* 57 H14
Soh, *Iran* 71 C6
Sohâg, *Egypt* 80 B3
Sohagpur, *India* 68 H8
Sŏhori, *N. Korea* 57 D15
Soignies, *Belgium* 17 D4
Soin, *Burkina Faso* 82 C4
Soira, *Eritrea* 81 E4
Soissons, *France* 19 C10
Sōja, *Japan* 55 G6
Sojat, *India* 68 G5
Sok →, *Russia* 34 D10
Sokal, *Ukraine* 33 G3
Söke, *Turkey* 47 D9
Sokelo, *Dem. Rep. of the Congo* 87 D1
Sokhós, *Greece* 44 F7
Sokhumi, *Georgia* 35 J5
Soko Banja, *Serbia & M.* 44 C5
Sokodé, *Togo* 83 D5
Sokol, *Russia* 32 C11
Sokolac, *Bos.-H.* 28 G3
Sokółka, *Poland* 30 E10
Sokolo, *Ségou, Mali* 82 C3
Sokolo, *Sikasso, Mali* 82 C3
Sokolov, *Czech Rep.* 26 A5
Sokołów Małpolski, *Poland* 31 H9
Sokołów Podlaski, *Poland* 31 F9
Sokoły, *Poland* 31 F9
Sokoto, *Nigeria* 83 C6
Sokoto □, *Nigeria* 83 C6
Sokoto →, *Nigeria* 83 C5
Sokyrnytsya, *Ukraine* 29 B8
Sokyryany, *Ukraine* 29 B12
Sol Iletsk, *Russia* 52 D6
Sola →, *Poland* 31 H6
Solai, *Kenya* 86 B4
Solan, *India* 68 D7
Solander I., *N.Z.* 91 M1
Solano, *Phil.* 61 C4
Solapur, *India* 66 L9
Solca, *Romania* 29 C10
Solda Gölü, *Turkey* 47 D11
Soldăneşti, *Moldova* 29 C13
Soldeu, *Andorra* 38 C6
Soldotna, *U.S.A.* 100 B4
Soléa, *Cyprus* 49 D12
Solec Kujawski, *Poland* 31 E5
Soledad, *Colombia* 124 A4
Soledad, *U.S.A.* 110 J5
Soledad, *Venezuela* 124 B6
Solent, The, *U.K.* 15 G6
Solenzara, *France* 21 G13
Solesmes, *France* 19 B10
Solfonn, *Norway* 9 F12
Solhan, *Turkey* 70 B4
Soligorsk = Salihorsk, *Belarus* 33 F4
Solihull, *U.K.* 15 E6
Solikamsk, *Russia* 52 D6
Solila, *Madag.* 89 C8
Solimões = Amazonas →, *S. Amer.* 125 D9
Solin, *Croatia* 41 E13
Solingen, *Germany* 24 D3
Sollebrunn, *Sweden* 11 F6
Sollefteå, *Sweden* 10 A11

Sollentuna, *Sweden* 10 **E11**
Söller, *Spain* 48 **B9**
Sollerön, *Sweden* 10 **D8**
Solling, *Germany* 24 **D5**
Solling-Vogler ⌓, *Germany* 24 **D5**
Solnechnogorsk, *Russia* 32 **D9**
Solo →, *Indonesia* 63 **G15**
Solofra, *Italy* 43 **B7**
Sologne, *France* 19 **E8**
Solok, *Indonesia* 62 **E2**
Sololá, *Guatemala* 120 **D1**
Solomon, N. Fork →, *U.S.A.* 112 **F5**
Solomon, S. Fork →, *U.S.A.* 112 **F5**
Solomon Is. ■, *Pac. Oc.* 96 **H7**
Solon, *China* 60 **B7**
Solon Springs, *U.S.A.* 112 **B9**
Solor, *Indonesia* 63 **F6**
Solotcha, *Russia* 32 **E10**
Solothurn, *Switz.* 25 **H3**
Solothurn □, *Switz.* 25 **H3**
Solotvyn, *Ukraine* 29 **B9**
Solsona, *Spain* 38 **C6**
Solt, *Hungary* 28 **D4**
Šolta, *Croatia* 41 **E13**
Solṭānābād, *Khorāsān, Iran* 71 **C8**
Solṭānābād, *Khorāsān, Iran* 71 **B8**
Soltau, *Germany* 24 **C5**
Soltsy, *Russia* 32 **C6**
Solunska Glava, *Macedonia* 44 **E5**
Solvang, *U.S.A.* 111 **L6**
Solvay, *U.S.A.* 117 **C8**
Sölvesborg, *Sweden* 11 **H8**
Solway Firth, *U.K.* 14 **C4**
Solwezi, *Zambia* 87 **E2**
Sōma, *Japan* 54 **F10**
Soma, *Turkey* 47 **B9**
Somabhula, *Zimbabwe* 89 **B4**
Somali Pen., *Africa* 76 **F8**
Somali Rep. ■, *Africa* 75 **F4**
Somalia = Somali Rep. ■, *Africa* 75 **F4**
Sombernon, *France* 19 **E11**
Sombor, *Serbia & M.* 28 **E4**
Sombra, *Canada* 116 **D2**
Sombrerete, *Mexico* 118 **C4**
Sombrero, *Anguilla* 121 **C7**
Şomcuta Mare, *Romania* 29 **C8**
Somdari, *India* 68 **G5**
Someido ⌓, *Spain* 36 **B4**
Somers, *U.S.A.* 108 **B6**
Somerset, *Ky., U.S.A.* 114 **G3**
Somerset, *Mass., U.S.A.* 117 **E13**
Somerset, *Pa., U.S.A.* 116 **F5**
Somerset □, *U.K.* 15 **F5**
Somerset East, *S. Africa* 88 **E4**
Somerset I., *Canada* 100 **A10**
Somerset West, *S. Africa* 88 **E2**
Somersworth, *U.S.A.* 117 **C14**
Somerton, *U.S.A.* 109 **K6**
Somerville, *U.S.A.* 117 **F10**
Someş →, *Romania* 28 **C7**
Someşul Mare →, *Romania* 29 **C8**
Somme □, *France* 19 **C9**
Somme →, *France* 19 **B8**
Somme, B. de la, *France* 18 **B8**
Sommen, *Jönköping, Sweden* 11 **F8**
Sommen, *Östergötland, Sweden* 11 **F9**
Sommepy-Tahure, *France* 19 **C11**
Sömmerda, *Germany* 24 **D7**
Sommesous, *France* 19 **D11**
Sommières, *France* 21 **E8**
Somnath, *India* 68 **J4**
Somogy □, *Hungary* 28 **D2**
Somogyszob, *Hungary* 28 **D2**
Somoto, *Nic.* 120 **D2**
Sompolno, *Poland* 31 **F5**
Somport, Puerto de, *Spain* 38 **C4**
Son →, *India* 69 **G11**
Son Ha, *Vietnam* 64 **E7**
Son Hoa, *Vietnam* 64 **F7**
Son La, *Vietnam* 58 **G4**
Son Serra, *Spain* 48 **B10**
Son Servera, *Spain* 38 **F8**
Son Tay, *Vietnam* 58 **G5**
Soná, *Panama* 120 **E3**
Sonamarg, *India* 69 **B6**
Sonamukhi, *India* 69 **H12**
Sonar →, *India* 69 **G8**
Sŏnch'ŏn, *N. Korea* 57 **E13**
Sondags →, *S. Africa* 88 **E4**
Sóndalo, *Italy* 40 **B7**
Sondar, *India* 69 **C6**
Sønder Felding, *Denmark* 11 **J2**
Sønder Omme, *Denmark* 11 **J2**
Sønderborg, *Denmark* 11 **K3**
Sønderjyllands Amtskommune □, *Denmark* 11 **J3**
Sondershausen, *Germany* 24 **D6**
Sóndrio, *Italy* 40 **B6**
Sone, *Mozam.* 87 **F3**
Sonepur, *India* 67 **J13**
Song, *Nigeria* 83 **D7**
Song, *Thailand* 64 **C3**
Song Cau, *Vietnam* 64 **F7**
Song Xian, *China* 56 **G7**
Songan, *Indonesia* 63 **J18**
Songch'ŏn, *N. Korea* 57 **E14**
Songea, *Tanzania* 87 **E4**
Songeons, *France* 19 **C8**
Songhua Hu, *China* 57 **C14**
Songhua Jiang →, *China* 60 **B8**
Songimvelo ⌓, *S. Africa* 89 **D5**
Songjiang, *China* 59 **B13**
Songjin, *N. Korea* 57 **D15**
Songjŏng-ni, *S. Korea* 57 **G14**
Songkan, *China* 58 **C6**
Songkhla, *Thailand* 65 **J3**
Songming, *China* 58 **E4**
Songnim, *N. Korea* 57 **E13**
Songo, *Mozam.* 85 **H6**
Songo, *Sudan* 79 **G10**
Songpan, *China* 58 **A4**
Songtao, *China* 58 **C7**
Songwe, *Dem. Rep. of the Congo* 86 **C2**
Songwe →, *Africa* 87 **D3**
Songxi, *China* 59 **D12**
Songzi, *China* 59 **B8**
Sonhat, *India* 69 **H10**
Sonid Youqi, *China* 56 **C7**
Sonipat, *India* 68 **E7**
Sonkach, *India* 68 **H7**
Sonkovo, *Russia* 32 **D9**
Sonmiani, *Pakistan* 68 **G2**
Sonmiani B., *Pakistan* 68 **G2**
Sonnino, *Italy* 42 **A6**
Sono →, *Brazil* 125 **E9**
Sonoma, *U.S.A.* 110 **G4**
Sonora, *Calif., U.S.A.* 110 **H6**
Sonora, *Tex., U.S.A.* 113 **K4**
Sonora □, *Mexico* 118 **B2**
Sonora →, *Mexico* 118 **B2**
Sonoran Desert, *U.S.A.* 111 **L12**
Sonoyta, *Mexico* 118 **A2**
Sonqor, *Iran* 73 **E12**
Sŏnsan, *S. Korea* 57 **F15**
Sonseca, *Spain* 37 **F7**
Sonsonate, *El Salv.* 120 **D2**
Sonstorp, *Sweden* 11 **F9**
Sonthofen, *Germany* 25 **H6**
Soochow = Suzhou, *China* 59 **B13**
Sooke, *Canada* 110 **B3**
Sop Hao, *Laos* 58 **G5**
Sop Prap, *Thailand* 64 **D2**
Sopelana, *Spain* 38 **B2**
Sopi, *Indonesia* 63 **D7**
Sopo, Nahr →, *Sudan* 81 **F2**
Sopot, *Bulgaria* 45 **D8**
Sopot, *Poland* 30 **D5**
Sopot, *Serbia & M.* 44 **B4**
Sopotnica, *Macedonia* 44 **E5**
Sopron, *Hungary* 28 **C1**
Sopur, *India* 69 **B6**
Sør-Rondane, *Antarctica* 5 **D4**
Sora, *Italy* 41 **G10**
Sorah, *Pakistan* 68 **F3**
Söråker, *Sweden* 10 **B11**
Sorano, *Italy* 41 **F8**
Soraon, *India* 69 **G9**
Sorbas, *Spain* 39 **H2**
Sörbygden, *Sweden* 10 **B10**
Sore, *France* 20 **D3**
Sorel-Tracy, *Canada* 104 **C5**
Soresina, *Italy* 40 **C6**
Sörforsa, *Sweden* 10 **C10**
Sórgono, *Italy* 42 **B2**
Sorgues, *France* 21 **D8**
Sorgun, *Turkey* 72 **C6**
Soria, *Spain* 38 **D2**
Soria □, *Spain* 38 **D2**
Soriano, *Uruguay* 126 **C4**
Soriano nel Cimino, *Italy* 41 **F9**
Sorkh, Kuh-e, *Iran* 71 **C8**
Sorø, *Denmark* 11 **J5**
Soro, *Guinea* 82 **C3**
Soroca, *Moldova* 29 **B13**
Sorocaba, *Brazil* 127 **A6**
Soroki = Soroca, *Moldova* 29 **B13**
Sorong, *Indonesia* 63 **E8**
Soroní, *Greece* 49 **C10**
Soroti, *Uganda* 86 **B3**
Sørøya, *Norway* 8 **A20**
Sørøysundet, *Norway* 8 **A20**
Sorraia →, *Portugal* 37 **G2**
Sorrell, *Australia* 95 **G4**
Sorrento, *Italy* 43 **B7**
Sorsele, *Sweden* 8 **D17**
Sörsjön, *Sweden* 10 **C7**
Sorso, *Italy* 42 **B1**
Sorsogon, *Phil.* 61 **E6**
Sortavala, *Russia* 32 **B6**
Sortino, *Italy* 43 **E8**
Sortland, *Norway* 8 **B16**
Sorvizhi, *Russia* 34 **B9**
Sos del Rey Católico, *Spain* 38 **C3**
Sŏsan, *S. Korea* 57 **F14**
Soscumica, L., *Canada* 104 **B4**
Sösdala, *Sweden* 11 **H7**
Sosna →, *Russia* 33 **F10**
Sosnovka, *Kirov, Russia* 34 **B10**
Sosnovka, *Tambov, Russia* 34 **D5**
Sosnovyy Bor, *Russia* 32 **C5**
Sosnowiec, *Poland* 31 **H6**
Sospel, *France* 21 **E11**
Sossus Vlei, *Namibia* 88 **C2**
Šoštanj, *Slovenia* 41 **B12**
Sŏsura, *N. Korea* 57 **C16**
Sot →, *India* 69 **F8**
Sotkamo, *Finland* 8 **D23**
Soto del Barco, *Spain* 36 **B4**
Soto la Marina →, *Mexico* 119 **C5**
Soto y Amío, *Spain* 36 **C5**
Sotrondio, *Spain* 36 **B5**
Sotuta, *Mexico* 119 **C7**
Souanké, *Congo* 84 **D2**
Soubré, *Ivory C.* 82 **D3**
Souderton, *U.S.A.* 117 **F9**
Soúdha, *Greece* 49 **D6**
Soúdhas, Kólpos, *Greece* 49 **D6**
Souflíon, *Greece* 45 **E10**
Soufrière, *Guadeloupe* 120 **b**
Soufrière, *St. Lucia* 121 **f**
Soufrière Bay, *Dominica* 121 **f**
Souillac, *France* 20 **D5**
Souilly, *France* 19 **C12**
Soukhouma, *Laos* 64 **E5**
Sŏul, *S. Korea* 57 **F14**
Soulac-sur-Mer, *France* 20 **C2**
Soulougou, *Burkina Faso* 83 **C5**
Soultz-sous-Forêts, *France* 19 **D14**
Sound, The = Øresund, *Europe* 11 **J6**
Sound, The, *U.K.* 15 **G3**
Soúnion, Ákra, *Greece* 46 **D6**
Sources, Mt. aux, *Lesotho* 89 **D4**
Soure, *Brazil* 125 **D9**
Soure, *Portugal* 36 **E2**
Souris, *Man., Canada* 103 **D8**
Souris, *P.E.I., Canada* 105 **C7**
Souris →, *Canada* 112 **A5**
Sourou →, *Africa* 82 **C4**
Soúrpi, *Greece* 46 **B4**
Sousa, *Brazil* 125 **E11**
Sousel, *Portugal* 37 **G3**
Sousse, *Tunisia* 79 **A8**
Soustons, *France* 20 **E2**
Sout →, *S. Africa* 88 **E2**
South Africa ■, *Africa* 88 **E3**
South America 122 **E5**
South Atlantic Ocean 2 **F8**
South Aulatsivik I., *Canada* 105 **A7**
South Australia □, *Australia* 95 **E2**
South Ayrshire □, *U.K.* 13 **F4**
South Baldy, *U.S.A.* 109 **J10**
South Bass I., *U.S.A.* 116 **E2**
South Bend, *Ind., U.S.A.* 114 **E2**
South Bend, *Wash., U.S.A.* 110 **D3**
South Boston, *U.S.A.* 115 **G6**
South Branch, *Canada* 105 **C8**
South Brook, *Canada* 105 **C8**
South Carolina □, *U.S.A.* 115 **J5**
South Charleston, *U.S.A.* 114 **F5**
South China Sea, *Asia* 62 **C4**
South Cumberland Is. △, *Australia* 94 **J7**
South Dakota □, *U.S.A.* 112 **C5**
South Deerfield, *U.S.A.* 117 **D12**
South Downs, *U.K.* 15 **G7**
South East C., *Australia* 95 **G4**
South-East Indian Rise, *Ind. Oc.* 5 **B10**
South East Is., *Australia* 93 **F3**
South Esk →, *U.K.* 13 **E6**
South Foreland, *U.K.* 15 **F9**
South Fork American →, *U.S.A.* 110 **G5**
South Fork Feather →, *U.S.A.* 110 **F5**
South Fork Grand →, *U.S.A.* 112 **C3**
South Fork Republican →, *U.S.A.* 112 **E4**
South Georgia, *Antarctica* 128 **G9**
South Gloucestershire □, *U.K.* 15 **F5**
South Hadley, *U.S.A.* 117 **D12**
South Haven, *U.S.A.* 114 **D2**
South Henik L., *Canada* 103 **A9**
South Honshu Ridge, *Pac. Oc.* 96 **E6**
South Horr, *Kenya* 86 **B4**
South I., *Kenya* 86 **B4**
South I., *N.Z.* 91 **L3**
South Indian Lake, *Canada* 103 **B9**
South Invercargill, *N.Z.* 91 **M2**
South Island △, *Kenya* 86 **B4**
South Kitui ⌓, *Kenya* 86 **C4**
South Knife →, *Canada* 103 **B10**
South Koel →, *India* 69 **H11**
South Korea ■, *Asia* 57 **G15**
South Lake Tahoe, *U.S.A.* 110 **G6**
South Lanarkshire □, *U.K.* 13 **F5**
South Loup →, *U.S.A.* 112 **E5**
South Luangwa △, *Zambia* 87 **E3**
South Magnetic Pole, *Antarctica* 5 **C9**
South Milwaukee, *U.S.A.* 114 **D2**
South Molton, *U.K.* 15 **F4**
South Moose L., *Canada* 103 **C8**
South Nahanni →, *Canada* 102 **A4**
South Nation →, *Canada* 117 **A9**
South Natuna Is. = Natuna Selatan, Kepulauan, *Indonesia* 62 **D3**
South Negril Pt., *Jamaica* 120 **a**
South Orkney Is., *Antarctica* 5 **C18**
South Ossetia □, *Georgia* 35 **J7**
South Pagai, I. = Pagai Selatan, Pulau, *Indonesia* 62 **E2**
South Paris, *U.S.A.* 117 **B14**
South Pittsburg, *U.S.A.* 115 **H3**
South Platte →, *U.S.A.* 112 **E4**
South Pole, *Antarctica* 5 **E**
South Porcupine, *Canada* 104 **C3**
South Portland, *U.S.A.* 115 **D10**
South Pt., *Barbados* 121 **g**
South Pt., *U.S.A.* 116 **B1**
South River, *Canada* 104 **C4**
South River, *U.S.A.* 117 **F10**
South Ronaldsay, *U.K.* 13 **C6**
South Sandwich Is., *Antarctica* 5 **B1**
South Saskatchewan →, *Canada* 103 **C7**
South Seal →, *Canada* 103 **B9**
South Shetland Is., *Antarctica* 5 **C18**
South Shields, *U.K.* 14 **C6**
South Sioux City, *U.S.A.* 112 **D6**
South Taranaki Bight, *N.Z.* 91 **H5**
South Thompson →, *Canada* 102 **C4**
South Twin I., *Canada* 104 **B4**
South Tyne →, *U.K.* 14 **C5**
South Uist, *U.K.* 13 **D1**
South West C., *Australia* 95 **G4**
South West C., *N.Z.* 91 **M1**
South Williamsport, *U.S.A.* 116 **E8**
South Yorkshire □, *U.K.* 14 **D6**
Southampton, *Canada* 116 **B3**
Southampton, *U.K.* 15 **G6**
Southampton, *U.S.A.* 117 **F12**
Southampton □, *U.K.* 15 **G6**
Southampton I., *Canada* 101 **B11**
Southaven, *U.S.A.* 113 **H9**
Southbank, *Canada* 102 **C3**
Southbridge, *N.Z.* 91 **K4**
Southbridge, *U.S.A.* 117 **D12**
Southeast Pacific Basin, *Pac. Oc.* 5 **C15**
Southend, *Canada* 103 **B8**
Southend-on-Sea, *U.K.* 15 **F8**
Southend-on-Sea □, *U.K.* 15 **F8**
Southern = Janub △, *Sudan* 81 **F2**
Southern = Yedebub Biheroch Bihereseboch na Hizboch □, *Ethiopia* 81 **F4**
Southern = Yuzhnyy □, *Russia* 35 **H5**
Southern □, *Malawi* 87 **F4**
Southern □, *S. Leone* 82 **D2**
Southern □, *Zambia* 87 **F2**
Southern Alps, *N.Z.* 91 **K3**
Southern Cross, *Australia* 93 **F2**
Southern Indian L., *Canada* 103 **B9**
Southern Ocean, *Antarctica* 5 **C6**
Southern Pines, *U.S.A.* 115 **H6**
Southern Uplands, *U.K.* 13 **F5**
Southington, *U.S.A.* 117 **E12**
Southland □, *N.Z.* 91 **L1**
Southold, *U.S.A.* 117 **E12**
Southport, *Australia* 95 **D5**
Southport, *U.K.* 14 **D4**
Southport, *Fla., U.S.A.* 115 **K3**
Southport, *N.Y., U.S.A.* 116 **D8**
Southwest △, *Australia* 95 **G4**
Southwestern Pacific Basin, *Pac. Oc.* 5 **A12**
Southwold, *U.K.* 15 **E9**
Southwood △, *Australia* 95 **D5**
Soutpansberg, *S. Africa* 89 **C4**
Souvigny, *France* 19 **F10**
Sovata, *Romania* 29 **D10**
Soverato, *Italy* 43 **D9**
Sovetsk, *Kaliningrad, Russia* 9 **J19**
Sovetsk, *Kirov, Russia* 34 **B9**
Sovetskaya Gavan = Vanino, *Russia* 53 **E15**
Sovicille, *Italy* 41 **E8**
Soweto, *S. Africa* 89 **D4**
Sōya-Kaikyō = La Perouse Str., *Asia* 54 **B11**
Sōya-Misaki, *Japan* 54 **B10**
Soyaux, *France* 20 **C4**
Sozh →, *Belarus* 33 **F6**
Sozopol, *Bulgaria* 45 **D11**
Spa, *Belgium* 17 **D5**
Spain ■, *Europe* 7 **H5**
Spalding, *Australia* 95 **E2**
Spalding, *U.K.* 14 **E7**
Spangler, *U.S.A.* 116 **F6**
Spanish, *Canada* 104 **C3**
Spanish Fork, *U.S.A.* 108 **F8**
Spanish Town, *Br. Virgin Is.* 121 **e**
Spanish Town, *Jamaica* 120 **a**
Sparks, *U.S.A.* 110 **F7**
Sparreholm, *Sweden* 10 **E10**
Sparta = Spárti, *Greece* 46 **D4**
Sparta, *Mich., U.S.A.* 114 **D3**
Sparta, *N.J., U.S.A.* 117 **E10**
Sparta, *Wis., U.S.A.* 112 **D9**
Spartanburg, *U.S.A.* 115 **H5**
Spartansburg, *U.S.A.* 116 **E5**
Spárti, *Greece* 46 **D4**
Spartivento, C., *Calabria, Italy* 43 **E9**
Spartivento, C., *Sard., Italy* 42 **D1**
Sparwood, *Canada* 102 **D6**
Spas-Demensk, *Russia* 32 **E7**
Spas-Klepiki, *Russia* 32 **E11**
Spassk Dalniy, *Russia* 53 **E14**
Spassk-Ryazanskiy, *Russia* 32 **E11**
Spátha, Ákra, *Greece* 49 **D5**
Spatsizi →, *Canada* 102 **B3**
Spatsizi Plateau Wilderness ⌓, *Canada* 102 **B3**
Spean →, *U.K.* 13 **E4**
Spearfish, *U.S.A.* 112 **C3**
Spearman, *U.S.A.* 113 **G4**
Speculator, *U.S.A.* 117 **C10**
Speia, *Moldova* 29 **D14**
Speightstown, *Barbados* 121 **g**
Speke Gulf, *Tanzania* 86 **C3**
Spello, *Italy* 41 **F9**
Spence Bay = Taloyoak, *Canada* 100 **B10**
Spencer, *Idaho, U.S.A.* 108 **D7**
Spencer, *Iowa, U.S.A.* 112 **D7**
Spencer, *N.Y., U.S.A.* 117 **D8**
Spencer, *Nebr., U.S.A.* 112 **D5**
Spencer, C., *Australia* 95 **F2**
Spencer B., *Namibia* 88 **D1**
Spencer G., *Australia* 95 **E2**
Spencerville, *Canada* 117 **B9**
Spences Bridge, *Canada* 102 **C4**
Spennymoor, *U.K.* 14 **C6**
Spenser Mts., *N.Z.* 91 **K4**
Spentrup, *Denmark* 11 **H4**
Sperkhiós →, *Greece* 46 **C4**
Sperrin Mts., *U.K.* 12 **B5**
Spessart, *Germany* 25 **F5**
Spétsai, *Greece* 46 **D5**
Spey →, *U.K.* 13 **D5**
Speyer, *Germany* 25 **F4**
Spezand, *Pakistan* 68 **E2**
Spezzano Albanese, *Italy* 43 **C9**
Spiekeroog, *Germany* 24 **B3**
Spiez, *Switz.* 25 **J3**
Spíli, *Greece* 49 **D6**
Spilimbergo, *Italy* 41 **B9**
Spīn Būldak, *Afghan.* 68 **D2**
Spinalónga, *Greece* 49 **D7**
Spinazzola, *Italy* 43 **B9**
Spineni, *Romania* 29 **F9**
Spirit Lake, *U.S.A.* 110 **D4**
Spirit River, *Canada* 102 **B5**
Spiritwood, *Canada* 103 **C7**
Spišská Nová Ves, *Slovak Rep.* 27 **C13**
Spišské Podhradie, *Slovak Rep.* 27 **B13**
Spital, *Austria* 26 **D7**
Spithead, *U.K.* 15 **G6**
Spittal an der Drau, *Austria* 26 **E6**
Spitzbergen = Svalbard, *Arctic* 51 **B5**
Spjelkavik, *Norway* 9 **E12**
Split, *Croatia* 41 **E13**
Split ✈ (SPU), *Croatia* 41 **E13**
Split L., *Canada* 103 **B9**
Split Lake, *Canada* 103 **B9**
Splitski Kanal, *Croatia* 41 **E13**
Splügenpass, *Switz.* 25 **J5**
Spofford, *U.S.A.* 113 **L4**
Spokane, *U.S.A.* 108 **C5**
Spoleto, *Italy* 41 **F9**
Spooner, *U.S.A.* 112 **C9**
Sporyy Navolok, Mys, *Russia* 52 **B7**
Sprague, *U.S.A.* 108 **C5**
Spratly I., *S. China Sea* 62 **C4**
Spratly Is., *S. China Sea* 62 **C4**
Spray, *U.S.A.* 108 **D4**
Spreča →, *Bos.-H.* 28 **F3**
Spree →, *Germany* 24 **C9**
Spreewald, *Germany* 24 **D9**
Spremberg, *Germany* 24 **D10**
Sprengisandur, *Iceland* 8 **D5**
Spring City, *U.S.A.* 117 **F9**
Spring Creek, *U.S.A.* 108 **F6**
Spring Garden, *U.S.A.* 110 **F6**
Spring Hall, *Barbados* 121 **g**
Spring Hill, *U.S.A.* 115 **L4**
Spring Mts., *U.S.A.* 109 **H6**
Spring Valley, *U.S.A.* 111 **N10**
Springbok, *S. Africa* 88 **D2**
Springboro, *U.S.A.* 116 **E4**
Springdale, *Canada* 105 **C8**
Springdale, *U.S.A.* 113 **G7**
Springe, *Germany* 24 **C5**
Springer, *U.S.A.* 113 **G2**
Springerville, *U.S.A.* 109 **J9**
Springfield, *Canada* 116 **D4**
Springfield, *N.Z.* 91 **K3**
Springfield, *Colo., U.S.A.* 113 **G3**
Springfield, *Ill., U.S.A.* 112 **F10**
Springfield, *Mass., U.S.A.* 117 **D12**
Springfield, *Mo., U.S.A.* 113 **G8**
Springfield, *Ohio, U.S.A.* 114 **F4**
Springfield, *Oreg., U.S.A.* 108 **D2**
Springfield, *Tenn., U.S.A.* 115 **G2**
Springfield, *Vt., U.S.A.* 117 **C12**
Springfontein, *S. Africa* 88 **E4**
Springhill, *Canada* 105 **C7**
Springhill, *U.S.A.* 113 **J8**
Springhouse, *Canada* 102 **C4**
Springs, *S. Africa* 89 **D4**
Springsure, *Australia* 94 **C4**
Springvale, *U.S.A.* 117 **C14**
Springville, *Calif., U.S.A.* 110 **J8**
Springville, *N.Y., U.S.A.* 116 **D6**
Springville, *Utah, U.S.A.* 108 **F8**
Springwater, *U.S.A.* 116 **D7**
Spruce-Creek, *U.S.A.* 116 **F6**
Spruce Knob-Seneca Rocks ⌓, *U.S.A.* 114 **F6**
Spruce Mt., *U.S.A.* 117 **B12**
Spur, *U.S.A.* 113 **J4**
Spurn Hd., *U.K.* 14 **D8**
Spuž, *Serbia & M.* 44 **D3**
Spuzzum, *Canada* 102 **D4**
Squam L., *U.S.A.* 117 **C13**
Squamish, *Canada* 102 **D4**
Square Islands, *Canada* 105 **B8**
Squillace, G. di, *Italy* 43 **D9**
Squinzano, *Italy* 43 **B11**
Squires, Mt., *Australia* 93 **E4**
Srbac, *Bos.-H.* 28 **E2**
Srbica, *Serbia & M.* 44 **D4**
Srbija = Serbia □, *Serbia & M.* 44 **C5**
Srbobran, *Serbia & M.* 28 **E4**
Sre Ambel, *Cambodia* 65 **G4**
Sre Khtum, *Cambodia* 65 **F6**
Sre Umbell = Sre Ambel, *Cambodia* 65 **G4**
Srebrenica, *Bos.-H.* 28 **F4**
Sredinny Ra. = Sredinnyy Khrebet, *Russia* 53 **D16**
Sredinnyy Khrebet, *Russia* 53 **D16**
Središče, *Slovenia* 41 **B13**
Sredna Gora, *Bulgaria* 45 **D8**
Srednekolymsk, *Russia* 53 **C16**
Sredni Rodopi, *Bulgaria* 45 **E8**
Srednogorie, *Bulgaria* 45 **D8**
Śrem, *Poland* 31 **F4**
Sremska Mitrovica, *Serbia & M.* 28 **F4**
Sremski Karlovci, *Serbia & M.* 28 **E4**
Srepok →, *Cambodia* 64 **F6**
Sretensk, *Russia* 53 **D12**
Sri Lanka ■, *Asia* 66 **R12**
Srikakulam, *India* 67 **K13**
Srinagar, *India* 69 **B6**
Srinagarind Res., *Thailand* 64 **E2**
Środa Śląska, *Poland* 31 **G3**
Środa Wielkopolski, *Poland* 31 **F4**
Srono, *Indonesia* 63 **J17**
Srpska Crnja, *Serbia & M.* 28 **E5**
Srpski Itebej, *Serbia & M.* 28 **E5**
Staaten →, *Australia* 94 **B3**
Staaten River △, *Australia* 94 **B3**
Staberhuk, *Germany* 24 **A7**
Stade, *Germany* 24 **B5**
Stadskanaal, *Neths.* 17 **A6**
Stadtallendorf, *Germany* 24 **E5**
Stadthagen, *Germany* 24 **C5**
Stadtlohn, *Germany* 24 **D2**
Stadtroda, *Germany* 24 **E7**
Staffa, *U.K.* 13 **E2**
Staffanstorp, *Sweden* 11 **J7**
Stafford, *U.K.* 14 **E5**
Stafford, *U.S.A.* 113 **G5**
Stafford Springs, *U.S.A.* 117 **E12**
Staffordshire □, *U.K.* 14 **E5**
Stagnone, *Italy* 42 **E5**
Stagnone di Marsala ⌓, *Italy* 42 **E5**
Staines, *U.K.* 15 **F7**
Stainz, *Austria* 26 **E8**
Stakhanov, *Ukraine* 33 **H10**
Stalać, *Serbia & M.* 44 **C5**
Stalis, *Greece* 49 **D7**
Stallarholmen, *Sweden* 10 **E11**
Ställdalen, *Sweden* 10 **E8**
Stalowa Wola, *Poland* 31 **H9**
Stalybridge, *U.K.* 14 **D5**
Stamford, *Australia* 94 **C3**
Stamford, *U.K.* 15 **E7**
Stamford, *Conn., U.S.A.* 117 **E11**
Stamford, *N.Y., U.S.A.* 117 **D10**

Stamford, *Tex., U.S.A.* 113 J5
Stampriet, *Namibia* 88 C2
Stamps, *U.S.A.* 113 J8
Stančevo = Kalipetrovo, *Bulgaria* 45 B11
Standerton, *S. Africa* 89 D4
Standish, *U.S.A.* 114 D4
Stanford, *S. Africa* 88 E2
Stanford, *U.S.A.* 108 C8
Stånga, *Sweden* 11 G12
Stanger, *S. Africa* 89 D5
Stängselåsen = Salpausselkä, *Finland* 9 F22
Stanišić, *Serbia & M.* 28 E4
Stanislaus →, *U.S.A.* 110 H5
Stanisławów, *Poland* 31 F8
Stanley, *Australia* 95 G4
Stanley, *Falk. Is.* 128 G5
Stanley, *U.K.* 14 C6
Stanley, *Idaho, U.S.A.* 108 D6
Stanley, *N. Dak., U.S.A.* 112 A3
Stanley, *N.Y., U.S.A.* 116 D7
Stanley Mission, *Canada* 103 B8
Stanovoy Khrebet, *Russia* 53 D13
Stanovoy Ra. = Stanovoy Khrebet, *Russia* 53 D13
Stansmore Ra., *Australia* 92 D4
Stansted, London ✕ (STN), *U.K.* 15 F8
Stanthorpe, *Australia* 95 D5
Stanton, *U.S.A.* 113 J4
Stanwood, *U.S.A.* 110 B4
Staples, *U.S.A.* 112 B7
Stąporków, *Poland* 31 G7
Star City, *Canada* 103 C8
Star Lake, *U.S.A.* 117 B9
Stará L'ubovňa, *Slovak Rep.* 27 B13
Stara Moravica, *Serbia & M.* 28 E4
Stara Pazova, *Serbia & M.* 28 F5
Stara Planina, *Bulgaria* 44 C7
Stara Sil, *Ukraine* 31 J9
Stará Turá, *Slovak Rep.* 27 C10
Stara Ushytsya, *Ukraine* 29 B12
Stara Zagora, *Bulgaria* 45 D9
Starachowice, *Poland* 31 G8
Staraya Russa, *Russia* 32 D6
Starbuck I., *Kiribati* 97 H12
Starchiojd, *Romania* 29 E11
Starcke △, *Australia* 94 A4
Stargard Szczeciński, *Poland* 30 E2
Stari Bar, *Serbia & M.* 44 D3
Stari Trg, *Slovenia* 41 C12
Staritsa, *Russia* 32 D8
Starke, *U.S.A.* 115 L4
Starnberg, *Germany* 25 H7
Starnberger See, *Germany* 25 H7
Starobilsk, *Ukraine* 33 H10
Starodub, *Russia* 33 F7
Starogard Gdański, *Poland* 30 E5
Starokonstantinov = Starokonstyantyniv, *Ukraine* 33 H4
Starokonstyantyniv, *Ukraine* 33 H4
Starokozache, *Ukraine* 29 D14
Starominskaya, *Russia* 33 J10
Staroshcherbinovskaya, *Russia* 33 J10
Start Pt., *U.K.* 15 G4
Stary Sącz, *Poland* 31 J7
Staryy Biryuzyak, *Russia* 35 H8
Staryy Chartoriysk, *Ukraine* 33 G3
Staryy Krym, *Ukraine* 33 K8
Staryy Oskol, *Russia* 33 G9
Staryy Sambir, *Ukraine* 31 J9
Stassfurt, *Germany* 24 D7
Staszów, *Poland* 31 H8
State College, *U.S.A.* 116 F7
Stateline, *U.S.A.* 110 G7
Staten, I. = Estados, I. de Los, *Argentina* 128 G4
Staten I., *U.S.A.* 117 F10
Statesboro, *U.S.A.* 115 J5
Statesville, *U.S.A.* 115 H5
Statia = St. Eustatius, *W. Indies* 121 C7
Stauffer, *U.S.A.* 111 L7
Staunton, *Ill., U.S.A.* 112 F10
Staunton, *Va., U.S.A.* 114 F6
Stavanger, *Norway* 9 G11
Staveley, *N.Z.* 91 K3
Stavelot, *Belgium* 17 D5
Stavern, *Norway* 9 G14
Stavoren, *Neths.* 17 B5
Stavropol, *Russia* 35 H6
Stavros, *Cyprus* 49 D11
Stavrós, *Greece* 49 D6
Stavrós, Ákra, *Greece* 49 D6
Stavroúpolis, *Greece* 45 E8
Stawell, *Australia* 95 F3
Stawell →, *Australia* 94 C3
Stawiski, *Poland* 30 E9
Stawiszyn, *Poland* 31 G5
Stayner, *Canada* 116 B4
Stayton, *U.S.A.* 108 D2
Steamboat Springs, *U.S.A.* 108 F10
Steblevë, *Albania* 44 E4
Steele, *U.S.A.* 112 B5
Steelton, *U.S.A.* 116 F8
Steen River, *Canada* 102 B5
Steens Mt., *U.S.A.* 108 E4
Steenwijk, *Neths.* 17 B6
Steep Pt., *Australia* 93 E1
Steep Rock, *Canada* 103 C9
Ştefan Vodă, *Moldova* 29 D14
Ştefănesti, *Romania* 29 C12
Stefanie △, *Ethiopia* 81 G4
Stefanie L. = Chew Bahir, *Ethiopia* 81 G4
Stefansson Bay, *Antarctica* 5 C5
Stege, *Denmark* 11 K6
Ştei, *Romania* 28 D7
Steiermark □, *Austria* 26 D8
Steigerwald, *Germany* 25 F6
Steigerwald ⌓, *Germany* 25 F6
Steilacoom, *U.S.A.* 110 C4
Steilrandberge, *Namibia* 88 B1
Steinbach, *Canada* 103 D9
Steinfurt, *Germany* 24 C3
Steinhausen, *Namibia* 88 C2
Steinheim, *Germany* 24 D5
Steinhuder Meer, *Germany* 24 C5
Steinhuder Meer ⌓, *Germany* 24 C5
Steinkjer, *Norway* 8 D14
Steinkopf, *S. Africa* 88 D2
Steinwald ⌓, *Germany* 25 F8
Stellarton, *Canada* 105 C7
Stellenbosch, *S. Africa* 88 E2
Stelvio, Paso dello, *Italy* 40 B7
Stenay, *France* 19 C12
Stendal, *Germany* 24 C7
Stende, *Latvia* 30 A9
Stenhamra, *Sweden* 10 E11
Stenshuvud △, *Sweden* 11 J8
Stenstorp, *Sweden* 11 F7
Stenungsund, *Sweden* 11 F5
Steornabhaigh = Stornoway, *U.K.* 13 C2
Stepanakert = Xankändi, *Azerbaijan* 70 B5
Stepanavan, *Armenia* 35 K7
Stephens Creek, *Australia* 95 E3
Stephens I., *Canada* 102 C2
Stephens L., *Canada* 103 B9
Stephenville, *Canada* 105 C8
Stephenville, *U.S.A.* 113 J5
Stepnica, *Poland* 30 E1
Steppe, *Asia* 50 D9
Stereá Ellas □, *Greece* 46 C4
Sterkstroom, *S. Africa* 88 E4
Sterling, *Colo., U.S.A.* 112 E3
Sterling, *Ill., U.S.A.* 112 E10
Sterling, *Kans., U.S.A.* 112 F5
Sterling City, *U.S.A.* 113 K4
Sterling Heights, *U.S.A.* 114 D4
Sterling Run, *U.S.A.* 116 E6
Sterlitamak, *Russia* 52 D6
Sternberg, *Germany* 24 B7
Šternberk, *Czech Rep.* 27 B10
Stérnes, *Greece* 49 D6
Sterzing = Vipiteno, *Italy* 41 B8
Stettin = Szczecin, *Poland* 30 E1
Stettiner Haff, *Germany* 24 B10
Stettler, *Canada* 102 C6
Steubenville, *U.S.A.* 116 F4
Stevenage, *U.K.* 15 F7
Stevens Point, *U.S.A.* 112 C10
Stevenson, *U.S.A.* 110 E5
Stevenson, The →, *Australia* 95 D2
Stevenson L., *Canada* 103 C9
Stevensville, *U.S.A.* 108 C6
Stevns Klint, *Denmark* 11 J6
Stewart, *Canada* 102 B3
Stewart, *U.S.A.* 110 F7
Stewart →, *Canada* 100 B6
Stewart, C., *Australia* 94 A1
Stewart, I., *Chile* 128 G2
Stewart I., *N.Z.* 91 M1
Stewarts Point, *U.S.A.* 110 G3
Stewartville, *U.S.A.* 112 D8
Stewiacke, *Canada* 105 C7
Steynsburg, *S. Africa* 88 E4
Steyr, *Austria* 26 C7
Steyr →, *Austria* 26 C7
Steytlerville, *S. Africa* 88 E3
Stia, *Italy* 41 E8
Stigler, *U.S.A.* 113 H7
Stigliano, *Italy* 43 B9
Stigtomta, *Sweden* 11 F10
Stikine →, *Canada* 102 B2
Stilfontein, *S. Africa* 88 D4
Stílis, *Greece* 46 C4
Stillwater, *N.Z.* 91 K3
Stillwater, *Minn., U.S.A.* 112 C8
Stillwater, *N.Y., U.S.A.* 117 D11
Stillwater, *Okla., U.S.A.* 113 G6
Stillwater Range, *U.S.A.* 108 G4
Stillwater Reservoir, *U.S.A.* 117 C9
Stilo, Pta., *Italy* 43 D9
Stilwell, *U.S.A.* 113 H7
Stînga Nistrului □, *Moldova* 29 C14
Štip, *Macedonia* 44 E6
Stíra, *Greece* 46 C6
Stirling, *Canada* 116 B7
Stirling, *U.K.* 13 E5
Stirling □, *U.K.* 13 E4
Stirling Ra., *Australia* 93 F2
Stirling Range △, *Australia* 93 F2
Stittsville, *Canada* 117 A9
Stjernøya, *Norway* 8 A20
Stjørdalshalsen, *Norway* 8 E14
Stockach, *Germany* 25 H5
Stockaryd, *Sweden* 11 G8
Stockerau, *Austria* 27 C9
Stockholm, *Sweden* 10 E12
Stockholm Arlanda ✕ (ARN), *Sweden* 10 E11
Stockholms län □, *Sweden* 10 E12
Stockport, *U.K.* 14 D5
Stocksbridge, *U.K.* 14 D6
Stockton, *Calif., U.S.A.* 110 H5
Stockton, *Kans., U.S.A.* 112 F5
Stockton, *Mo., U.S.A.* 113 G8
Stockton-on-Tees, *U.K.* 14 C6
Stockton-on-Tees □, *U.K.* 14 C6
Stockton Plateau, *U.S.A.* 113 K3
Stoczek Łukowski, *Poland* 31 G8
Stöde, *Sweden* 10 B10
Stoeng Treng, *Cambodia* 64 F5
Stoer, Pt. of, *U.K.* 13 C3
Stogovo, *Macedonia* 44 E4
Stoholm, *Denmark* 11 H3
Stoke-on-Trent, *U.K.* 14 D5
Stoke-on-Trent □, *U.K.* 14 D5
Stokes △, *Australia* 93 E2
Stokes Pt., *Australia* 95 G3
Stokes Ra., *Australia* 92 C5
Stokksnes, *Iceland* 8 D6
Stokmarknes, *Norway* 8 B16
Stolac, *Bos.-H.* 44 C1
Stolberg, *Germany* 24 E2
Stolbovoy, Ostrov, *Russia* 53 B14
Stolbtsy = Stowbtsy, *Belarus* 32 F4
Stolin, *Belarus* 33 G4
Stöllet, *Sweden* 10 D7
Stolnici, *Romania* 29 F9
Stomíon, *Greece* 49 D5
Ston, *Croatia* 41 F14
Stone, *U.K.* 14 E5
Stoneboro, *U.S.A.* 116 E4
Stonehaven, *U.K.* 13 E6
Stonehenge, *Australia* 94 C3
Stonehenge, *U.K.* 15 F6
Stonewall, *Canada* 103 C9
Stony L., *Man., Canada* 103 B9
Stony L., *Ont., Canada* 116 B6
Stony Point, *U.S.A.* 117 E11
Stony Pt., *U.S.A.* 117 C8
Stony Rapids, *Canada* 103 B7
Stony Tunguska = Tunguska, Podkamennaya →, *Russia* 53 C10
Stonyford, *U.S.A.* 110 F4
Stopnica, *Poland* 31 H7
Storå, *Sweden* 10 E9
Storå →, *Denmark* 11 H2
Stora Gla, *Sweden* 10 E6
Stora Le, *Sweden* 10 E5
Stora Lulevatten, *Sweden* 8 C18
Storavan, *Sweden* 8 D18
Stord, *Norway* 9 G11
Store Bælt, *Denmark* 11 J4
Store Heddinge, *Denmark* 11 J6
Store Mosse △, *Sweden* 11 G7
Storebro, *Sweden* 11 G9
Storfors, *Sweden* 10 E8
Storlien, *Sweden* 10 A6
Storm B., *Australia* 95 G4
Storm Lake, *U.S.A.* 112 D7
Stormberge, *S. Africa* 88 E4
Stormsrivier, *S. Africa* 88 E3
Stornoway, *U.K.* 13 C2
Storo, *Italy* 40 C7
Storozhinets = Storozhynets, *Ukraine* 29 B10
Storozhynets, *Ukraine* 29 B10
Storrs, *U.S.A.* 117 E12
Storsjön, *Gävleborg, Sweden* 10 D10
Storsjön, *Jämtland, Sweden* 10 B7
Storsjön, *Jämtland, Sweden* 10 A8
Storstrøms Amtskommune □, *Denmark* 11 J5
Storuman, *Sweden* 8 D17
Storuman, *Sweden* 8 D17
Storvätteshågna, *Sweden* 10 B6
Storvik, *Sweden* 10 D10
Storvreta, *Sweden* 10 E11
Stouffville, *Canada* 116 C5
Stoughton, *Canada* 103 D8
Stour →, *Dorset, U.K.* 15 G6
Stour →, *Kent, U.K.* 15 F9
Stour →, *Suffolk, U.K.* 15 F9
Stourbridge, *U.K.* 15 E5
Stout L., *Canada* 103 C10
Stove Pipe Wells Village, *U.S.A.* 111 J9
Støvring, *Denmark* 11 H3
Stow, *U.S.A.* 116 E3
Stowbtsy, *Belarus* 32 F4
Stowmarket, *U.K.* 15 E9
Strabane, *U.K.* 12 B4
Stracin, *Macedonia* 44 D6
Stradella, *Italy* 40 C6
Strahan, *Australia* 95 G4
Strajitsa, *Bulgaria* 45 C9
Strakonice, *Czech Rep.* 26 B6
Straldzha, *Bulgaria* 45 D10
Stralsund, *Germany* 24 A9
Strand, *S. Africa* 88 E2
Stranda, *Møre og Romsdal, Norway* 9 E12
Stranda, *Nord-Trøndelag, Norway* 8 E14
Strandby, *Denmark* 11 G4
Strangford L., *U.K.* 12 B6
Strängnäs, *Sweden* 10 E11
Stranraer, *U.K.* 13 G3
Strasbourg, *Canada* 103 C8
Strasbourg, *France* 19 D14
Strasburg, *Germany* 24 B9
Străşeni, *Moldova* 29 C13
Stråssa, *Sweden* 10 E9
Stratford, *Canada* 116 C4
Stratford, *N.Z.* 91 H5
Stratford, *Calif., U.S.A.* 110 J7
Stratford, *Conn., U.S.A.* 117 E11
Stratford, *Tex., U.S.A.* 113 G3
Stratford-upon-Avon, *U.K.* 15 E6
Strath Spey, *U.K.* 13 D5
Strathalbyn, *Australia* 95 F2
Strathaven, *U.K.* 13 F4
Strathcona ⌓, *Canada* 102 D3
Strathmore, *Canada* 102 C6
Strathmore, *U.K.* 13 E5
Strathmore, *U.S.A.* 110 J7
Strathnaver, *Canada* 102 C4
Strathpeffer, *U.K.* 13 D4
Strathroy, *Canada* 116 D3
Strathy Pt., *U.K.* 13 C4
Strattanville, *U.S.A.* 116 E5
Stratton, *U.S.A.* 117 A14
Stratton Mt., *U.S.A.* 117 C12
Straubing, *Germany* 25 G8
Straumnes, *Iceland* 8 C2
Strausberg, *Germany* 24 C9
Strawberry →, *U.S.A.* 108 F8
Strážnice, *Czech Rep.* 27 C10
Streaky B., *Australia* 95 E1
Streaky Bay, *Australia* 95 E1
Streator, *U.S.A.* 112 E10
Středočeský □, *Czech Rep.* 26 B7
Streetsboro, *U.S.A.* 116 E3
Streetsville, *Canada* 116 C5
Strehaia, *Romania* 29 F8
Strelcha, *Bulgaria* 45 D8
Strelka, *Russia* 53 D10
Streng →, *Cambodia* 64 F4
Stresa, *Italy* 40 C5
Streymoy, *Færoe Is.* 8 E9
Strezhevoy, *Russia* 52 C8
Stříbro, *Czech Rep.* 26 A6
Strilky, *Ukraine* 31 J9
Strimón →, *Greece* 44 F7
Strimonikós Kólpos, *Greece* 44 F7
Strofádhes, *Greece* 46 D3
Stroma, *U.K.* 13 C5
Stromberg-Heuchelberg ⌓, *Germany* 25 F4
Strómboli, *Italy* 43 D8
Stromeferry, *U.K.* 13 D3
Stromness, *U.K.* 13 C5
Strömsbruk, *Sweden* 10 C11
Stromsburg, *U.S.A.* 112 E6
Strömsnäsbruk, *Sweden* 11 H7
Strömstad, *Sweden* 11 F5
Strömsund, *Sweden* 8 E16
Strongilí, *Greece* 47 E11
Strongoli, *Italy* 43 C10
Strongsville, *U.S.A.* 116 E3
Stronie Śląskie, *Poland* 31 H3
Stronsay, *U.K.* 13 B6
Stropkov, *Slovak Rep.* 27 B14
Stroud, *U.K.* 15 F5
Stroud Road, *Australia* 95 E5
Stroudsburg, *U.S.A.* 117 F9
Stroumbi, *Cyprus* 49 E11
Struer, *Denmark* 11 H2
Struga, *Macedonia* 44 E4
Strugi Krasnyye, *Russia* 32 C5
Strumica, *Macedonia* 44 E6
Strumica →, *Europe* 44 E7
Strumok, *Ukraine* 29 E14
Struthers, *Canada* 104 C2
Struthers, *U.S.A.* 116 E4
Stryama, *Bulgaria* 45 D8
Stryker, *U.S.A.* 108 B6
Stryków, *Poland* 31 G6
Stryy, *Ukraine* 33 H2
Strzegom, *Poland* 31 H3
Strzelce Krajeńskie, *Poland* 31 F2
Strzelce Opolskie, *Poland* 31 H5
Strzelecki Cr. →, *Australia* 95 D2
Strzelin, *Poland* 31 H4
Strzelno, *Poland* 31 F5
Strzybnica, *Poland* 31 H5
Strzyżów, *Poland* 31 J8
Stuart, *Fla., U.S.A.* 115 M5
Stuart, *Nebr., U.S.A.* 112 D5
Stuart →, *Canada* 102 C4
Stuart Bluff Ra., *Australia* 92 D5
Stuart L., *Canada* 102 C4
Stuart Ra., *Australia* 95 D1
Stubbekøbing, *Denmark* 11 K6
Stuben, *Austria* 26 D3
Studen Kladenets, Yazovir, *Bulgaria* 45 E9
Studenka, *Czech Rep.* 27 B11
Stugun, *Sweden* 10 A9
Stuhr, *Germany* 24 B4
Stull L., *Canada* 104 B1
Stung Treng = Stoeng Treng, *Cambodia* 64 F5
Stupart →, *Canada* 104 A1
Stupava, *Slovak Rep.* 27 C10
Stupino, *Russia* 32 E10
Sturgeon B., *Canada* 103 C9
Sturgeon Bay, *U.S.A.* 114 C2
Sturgeon Falls, *Canada* 104 C4
Sturgeon L., *Alta., Canada* 102 B5
Sturgeon L., *Ont., Canada* 104 C1
Sturgeon L., *Ont., Canada* 116 B6
Sturgis, *Canada* 103 C8
Sturgis, *Mich., U.S.A.* 114 E3
Sturgis, *S. Dak., U.S.A.* 112 C3
Sturkö, *Sweden* 11 H9
Štúrovo, *Slovak Rep.* 27 D11
Sturt △, *Australia* 95 D3
Sturt Cr. →, *Australia* 92 C4
Sturt Stony Desert, *Australia* 95 D3
Stutterheim, *S. Africa* 88 E4
Stuttgart, *Germany* 25 G5
Stuttgart, *U.S.A.* 113 H9
Stuttgart Echterdingen ✕ (STR), *Germany* 25 G5
Stuyvesant, *U.S.A.* 117 D11
Stykkishólmur, *Iceland* 8 D2
Styria = Steiermark □, *Austria* 26 D8
Styrsö, *Sweden* 11 G5
Su Xian = Suzhou, *China* 56 H9
Suakin, *Sudan* 80 D4
Suan, *N. Korea* 57 E14
Suaqui, *Mexico* 118 B3
Suar, *India* 69 E8
Subang, *Indonesia* 63 G12
Subansiri →, *India* 67 F18
Subarnarekha →, *India* 69 H12
Subayhah, *Si. Arabia* 70 D3
Subcetate, *Romania* 28 E8
Subi, *Indonesia* 62 D3
Subiaco, *Italy* 41 G10
Subotica, *Serbia & M.* 28 D4
Suca, *Ethiopia* 81 F4
Suceava, *Romania* 29 C11
Suceava □, *Romania* 29 C10
Suceava →, *Romania* 29 C11
Sucha-Beskidzka, *Poland* 31 J6
Suchań, *Poland* 31 E2
Suchan, *Russia* 54 C6
Suchedniów, *Poland* 31 G7
Suchitoto, *El Salv.* 120 D2
Suchou = Suzhou, *China* 59 B13
Süchow = Xuzhou, *China* 57 G9
Suchowola, *Poland* 30 E10
Suck →, *Ireland* 12 C3
Sucre, *Bolivia* 124 G5
Sućuraj, *Croatia* 41 E14
Sucuriú →, *Brazil* 125 H8
Sud, Pte. du, *Canada* 105 C7
Sud-Kivu □, *Dem. Rep. of the Congo* 86 C2
Sud-Ouest, Pte., *Canada* 105 C7
Suda →, *Russia* 32 C9
Sudak, *Ukraine* 33 K8
Sudan, *U.S.A.* 113 H3
Sudan ■, *Africa* 81 E3
Sudbury, *Canada* 104 C3
Sudbury, *U.K.* 15 E8
Sûdd, *Sudan* 81 F3
Sudeifel = Deutsch-Luxemburgischer ⌓, *Germany* 25 F2
Süderbrarup, *Germany* 24 A5
Süderlügum, *Germany* 24 A4
Süderoogsand, *Germany* 24 A4
Sudeten Mts. = Sudety, *Europe* 27 A9
Sudety, *Europe* 27 A9
Südheide ⌓, *Germany* 24 C6
Suðuroy, *Færoe Is.* 8 F9
Sudi, *Tanzania* 87 E4
Sudirman, Pegunungan, *Indonesia* 63 E9
Sudiţi, *Romania* 29 F12
Sudogda, *Russia* 34 C5
Sudong, Pulau, *Singapore* 65 d
Sudova Vyshnya, *Ukraine* 31 J10
Sudr, *Egypt* 80 B3
Sudzha, *Russia* 33 G8
Sue →, *Sudan* 81 F2
Sueca, *Spain* 39 F4
Sŭedinenie, *Bulgaria* 45 D8
Suemez I., *U.S.A.* 102 B2
Suez = El Suweis, *Egypt* 80 J8
Suez, G. of = Suweis, Khalîg el, *Egypt* 80 J8
Suez Canal = Suweis, Qanâ es, *Egypt* 80 H8
Suffield, *Canada* 102 C6
Suffolk, *U.S.A.* 114 G7
Suffolk □, *U.K.* 15 E9
Şugag, *Romania* 29 E8
Sugargrove, *U.S.A.* 116 E5
Sugarive →, *India* 69 F12
Suğla Gölü, *Turkey* 72 D5
Sugluk = Salluit, *Canada* 101 B12
Suhaia, Lacul, *Romania* 29 G10
Şuḩār, *Oman* 71 E8
Sühbaatar □, *Mongolia* 56 B8
Suhl, *Germany* 24 E6
Şuhut, *Turkey* 47 C12
Sui, *Pakistan* 68 E3
Sui Xian, *China* 56 G8
Šuica, *Bos.-H.* 28 G2
Suichang, *China* 59 C12
Suichuan, *China* 59 D10
Suide, *China* 56 F6
Suifenhe, *China* 57 B16
Suihua, *China* 60 B7
Suijiang, *China* 58 C4
Suining, *Hunan, China* 59 D8
Suining, *Jiangsu, China* 57 H9
Suining, *Sichuan, China* 58 B5
Suiping, *China* 56 H7
Suippes, *France* 19 C11
Suir →, *Ireland* 12 D4
Suisun City, *U.S.A.* 110 G4
Suixi, *China* 59 G8
Suiyang, *Guizhou, China* 58 D6
Suiyang, *Heilongjiang, China* 57 B16
Suizhong, *China* 57 D11
Suizhou, *China* 59 B9
Sujangarh, *India* 68 F6
Sukabumi, *Indonesia* 63 G12
Sukadana, *Indonesia* 62 E3
Sukagawa, *Japan* 55 F10
Sukaraja, *Indonesia* 62 E4
Sukawati, *Indonesia* 63 K18
Sukch'ŏn, *N. Korea* 57 E13
Sukhindol, *Bulgaria* 45 C9
Sukhinichi, *Russia* 32 E8
Sukhona →, *Russia* 52 D4
Sukhothai, *Thailand* 64 D2
Sukhumi = Sokhumi, *Georgia* 35 J5
Sukkur, *Pakistan* 68 F3
Sukkur Barrage, *Pakistan* 68 F3
Sukovo, *Serbia & M.* 44 C6
Sukri →, *India* 68 G4
Sukumo, *Japan* 55 H6
Sukunka →, *Canada* 102 B4
Sula →, *Ukraine* 33 H7
Sula, Kepulauan, *Indonesia* 63 E7
Sulaco →, *Honduras* 120 C2
Sulaiman Range, *Pakistan* 68 D3
Sulak →, *Russia* 35 J8
Sūlār, *Iran* 71 D6
Sulawesi, *Indonesia* 63 E6
Sulawesi Sea = Celebes Sea, *Indonesia* 63 D6
Sulawesi Selatan □, *Indonesia* 63 E6
Sulawesi Tengah □, *Indonesia* 63 E6
Sulawesi Tenggara □, *Indonesia* 63 E6
Sulawesi Utara □, *Indonesia* 63 D6
Sulechów, *Poland* 31 F2
Sulęcin, *Poland* 31 F2
Sulejów, *Poland* 31 G6
Sulejówek, *Poland* 31 F8
Süleymanlı, *Turkey* 47 C9
Sulima, *S. Leone* 82 D2
Sulina, *Romania* 29 E14
Sulina, Braţul →, *Romania* 29 E14
Sulingen, *Germany* 24 C4
Suliţa, *Romania* 29 C11
Sulitjelma, *Norway* 8 C17
Sułkowice, *Poland* 31 J6
Sullana, *Peru* 124 D2
Süller, *Turkey* 47 C11
Sullivan, *Ill., U.S.A.* 112 F10

Sullivan, *Ind., U.S.A.* 114 F2
Sullivan, *Mo., U.S.A.* 112 F9
Sullivan Bay, *Canada* 102 C3
Sullivan I. = Lanbi Kyun, *Burma* 65 G2
Sullom Voe, *U.K.* 13 A7
Sully-sur-Loire, *France* 19 E9
Sulmierzyce, *Poland* 31 G4
Sulmona, *Italy* 41 F10
Süloğlu, *Turkey* 45 E10
Sulphur, *La., U.S.A.* 113 K8
Sulphur, *Okla., U.S.A.* 113 H6
Sulphur Pt., *Canada* 102 A6
Sulphur Springs, *U.S.A.* 113 J7
Sultan, *Canada* 104 C3
Sultan, *U.S.A.* 110 C5
Sultan Dağları, *Turkey* 72 C4
Sultanhisar, *Turkey* 47 D10
Sultanіça, *Turkey* 45 F10
Sultaniye, *Turkey* 45 F12
Sultanpur, *Mad. P., India* 68 H8
Sultanpur, *Punjab, India* 68 D6
Sultanpur, *Ut. P., India* 69 F10
Sulu Arch., *Phil.* 61 J4
Sulu Sea, *E. Indies* 61 G4
Sülüklü, *Turkey* 72 C5
Sululta, *Ethiopia* 81 F4
Suluova, *Turkey* 72 B6
Suluq, *Libya* 79 B10
Sulzbach, *Germany* 25 F3
Sulzbach-Rosenberg, *Germany* 25 F7
Sulzberger Ice Shelf, *Antarctica* 5 E13
Sumalata, *Indonesia* 63 D6
Sumampa, *Argentina* 126 B3
Sumatera, *Indonesia* 62 D2
Sumatera Barat □, *Indonesia* 62 E2
Sumatera Utara □, *Indonesia* 62 D1
Sumatra = Sumatera, *Indonesia* 62 D2
Šumava △, *Czech Rep.* 26 C6
Sumba, *Indonesia* 63 F5
Sumba, Selat, *Indonesia* 63 F5
Sumbawa, *Indonesia* 62 F5
Sumbawa Besar, *Indonesia* 62 F5
Sumbawanga □, *Tanzania* 84 F6
Sumbe, *Angola* 84 G2
Sumbu △, *Zambia* 87 D3
Sumburgh Hd., *U.K.* 13 B7
Sumdeo, *India* 69 D8
Sumdo, *China* 69 B8
Sumedang, *Indonesia* 63 G12
Sümeg, *Hungary* 28 D2
Sumeih, *Sudan* 81 F2
Šumen = Shumen, *Bulgaria* 45 C10
Sumenep, *Indonesia* 63 G15
Sumgait = Sumqayıt, *Azerbaijan* 35 K9
Summer L., *U.S.A.* 108 E3
Summerland, *Canada* 102 D5
Summerside, *Canada* 105 C7
Summersville, *U.S.A.* 114 F5
Summerville, *Ga., U.S.A.* 115 H3
Summerville, *S.C., U.S.A.* 115 J5
Summit Lake, *Canada* 102 C4
Summit Peak, *U.S.A.* 109 H10
Sumner, *Iowa, U.S.A.* 112 D8
Sumner, *Wash., U.S.A.* 110 C4
Sumoto, *Japan* 55 G7
Šumperk, *Czech Rep.* 27 B9
Sumqayıt, *Azerbaijan* 35 K9
Sumter, *U.S.A.* 115 J5
Sumy, *Ukraine* 33 G8
Sun City, *S. Africa* 88 D4
Sun City, *Ariz., U.S.A.* 109 K7
Sun City, *Calif., U.S.A.* 111 M9
Sun City Center, *U.S.A.* 115 M4
Sun Lakes, *U.S.A.* 109 K8
Sun Valley, *U.S.A.* 108 E6
Sunagawa, *Japan* 54 C10
Sunan, *N. Korea* 57 E13
Sunart, L., *U.K.* 13 E3
Sunburst, *U.S.A.* 108 B8
Sunbury, *Australia* 95 F3
Sunbury, *U.S.A.* 117 F8
Sunchales, *Argentina* 126 C3
Suncho Corral, *Argentina* 126 B3
Sunch'ŏn, *S. Korea* 57 G14
Suncook, *U.S.A.* 117 C13
Sunda, Selat, *Indonesia* 62 F3
Sunda Is., *Indonesia* 96 H2
Sunda Str. = Sunda, Selat, *Indonesia* 62 F3
Sundance, *Canada* 103 B10
Sundance, *U.S.A.* 112 C2
Sundar Nagar, *India* 68 D7
Sundarbans, *Asia* 67 J16
Sundargarh, *India* 67 H14
Sundays = Sondags →, *S. Africa* 88 E4
Sunderland, *Canada* 116 B5
Sunderland, *U.K.* 14 C6
Sundown △, *Australia* 95 D5
Sundre, *Canada* 102 C6
Sunds, *Denmark* 11 H3
Sundsvall, *Sweden* 10 B11
Sundsvallsbukten, *Sweden* 10 B11
Sung Hei, *Vietnam* 65 G6
Sungai Acheh, *Malaysia* 65 c
Sungai Kolok, *Thailand* 65 J3
Sungai Lembing, *Malaysia* 65 L4
Sungai Petani, *Malaysia* 65 K3
Sungaigerong, *Indonesia* 62 E2
Sungailiat, *Indonesia* 62 E3
Sungaipenuh, *Indonesia* 62 E2
Sungari = Songhua Jiang →, *China* 60 B8
Sunghua Chiang = Songhua Jiang →, *China* 60 B8
Sungikai, *Sudan* 81 E2
Sungurlu, *Turkey* 72 B6
Sunja, *Croatia* 41 C13
Sunland Park, *U.S.A.* 109 L10
Sunnansjö, *Sweden* 10 D8
Sunndalsøra, *Norway* 9 E13
Sunne, *Sweden* 10 E7
Sunnemo, *Sweden* 10 E7
Sunnyside, *U.S.A.* 108 C3
Sunnyvale, *U.S.A.* 110 H4
Suntar, *Russia* 53 C12
Sunyani, *Ghana* 82 D4
Suomenselkä, *Finland* 8 E21
Suomussalmi, *Finland* 8 D23
Suoyarvi, *Russia* 32 A7
Supai, *U.S.A.* 109 H7
Supaul, *India* 69 F12
Superior, *Ariz., U.S.A.* 109 K8
Superior, *Mont., U.S.A.* 108 C6
Superior, *Nebr., U.S.A.* 112 E5
Superior, *Wis., U.S.A.* 112 B8
Superior, L., *N. Amer.* 104 C2
Supetar, *Croatia* 41 E13
Suphan Buri, *Thailand* 64 E3
Suphan Dağı, *Turkey* 70 B4
Supiori, *Indonesia* 63 E9
Supraśl, *Poland* 31 E10
Supraśl →, *Poland* 31 E9
Supung Shuiku, *China* 57 D13
Sūq Suwayq, *Si. Arabia* 70 E3
Suqian, *China* 57 H10
Suquṭra = Socotra, *Yemen* 75 E5
Sūr, *Lebanon* 74 B4
Ṣūr, *Oman* 75 C6
Sur, Pt., *U.S.A.* 110 J5
Sura →, *Russia* 34 C8
Surab, *Pakistan* 68 E2
Surabaja = Surabaya, *Indonesia* 63 G15
Surabaya, *Indonesia* 63 G15
Surahammar, *Sweden* 10 E10
Suraia, *Romania* 29 E12
Surakarta, *Indonesia* 63 G14
Surakhany, *Azerbaijan* 35 K10
Šurany, *Slovak Rep.* 27 C11
Surat, *Australia* 95 D4
Surat, *India* 66 J8
Surat Thani, *Thailand* 65 H2
Suratgarh, *India* 68 E5
Suraż, *Poland* 31 F9
Surazh, *Belarus* 32 E6
Surazh, *Russia* 33 F7
Surduc, *Romania* 29 C8
Surduc Pasul, *Romania* 29 E8
Surdulica, *Serbia & M.* 44 D6
Surendranagar, *India* 68 H4
Surf, *U.S.A.* 111 L6
Surfers Paradise, *Australia* 95 D5
Surgères, *France* 20 B3
Surgut, *Russia* 52 C8
Sùria, *Spain* 38 D6
Suriapet, *India* 66 L11
Surigao, *Phil.* 61 G6
Surigao Strait, *Phil.* 61 F6
Surin, *Thailand* 64 E4
Surin Nua, Ko, *Thailand* 65 H1
Surinam = Suriname ■, *S. Amer.* 125 C7
Suriname ■, *S. Amer.* 125 C7
Suriname →, *Suriname* 125 B7
Sürmaq, *Iran* 71 D7
Sürmene, *Turkey* 73 B9
Surovikino, *Russia* 35 F6
Surrey, *Canada* 110 A4
Surrey □, *U.K.* 15 F7
Sursand, *India* 69 F11
Sursar →, *India* 69 F12
Sursee, *Switz.* 25 H4
Sursk, *Russia* 34 D7
Surskoye, *Russia* 34 C8
Surt, *Libya* 79 B9
Surt, Khalīj, *Libya* 79 B9
Surtanahu, *Pakistan* 68 F4
Surte, *Sweden* 11 G6
Surtsey, *Iceland* 8 E3
Sürüç, *Turkey* 73 D8
Suruga-Wan, *Japan* 55 G9
Susa, *Italy* 40 C4
Suså →, *Denmark* 11 J5
Sušac, *Croatia* 41 F13
Susak, *Croatia* 41 D11
Susaki, *Japan* 55 H6
Sūsangerd, *Iran* 71 D6
Susanville, *U.S.A.* 108 F3
Susch, *Switz.* 25 J6
Suşehri, *Turkey* 73 B8
Sušice, *Czech Rep.* 26 B6
Susleni, *Moldova* 29 C13
Susner, *India* 68 H7
Susong, *China* 59 B11
Susquehanna, *U.S.A.* 117 E9
Susquehanna →, *U.S.A.* 117 G8
Susques, *Argentina* 126 A2
Sussex, *Canada* 105 C6
Sussex, *U.S.A.* 117 E10
Sussex, E. □, *U.K.* 15 G8
Sussex, W. □, *U.K.* 15 G7
Sustut →, *Canada* 102 B3
Susuman, *Russia* 53 C15
Susunu, *Indonesia* 63 E8
Susurluk, *Turkey* 47 B10
Susuz, *Turkey* 73 B10
Susz, *Poland* 30 E6
Sütçüler, *Turkey* 72 D4
Şuţeşti, *Romania* 29 E12
Sutherland, *S. Africa* 88 E3
Sutherland, *U.K.* 13 C4
Sutherland, *U.S.A.* 112 E4
Sutherland Falls, *N.Z.* 91 L1
Sutherlin, *U.S.A.* 108 E2
Suthri, *India* 68 H3
Sutjeska △, *Bos.-H.* 28 G3
Sutlej →, *Pakistan* 68 E4
Sutter, *U.S.A.* 110 F5
Sutter Creek, *U.S.A.* 110 G6
Sutton, *Canada* 117 A12
Sutton, *Nebr., U.S.A.* 112 E6
Sutton, *W. Va., U.S.A.* 114 F5
Sutton →, *Canada* 104 A3
Sutton Coldfield, *U.K.* 15 E6
Sutton in Ashfield, *U.K.* 14 D6
Sutton L., *Canada* 104 B3
Suttor →, *Australia* 94 C4
Suttsu, *Japan* 54 C10
Suva, *Fiji* 91 D8
Suva Gora, *Macedonia* 44 E5
Suva Planina, *Serbia & M.* 44 C6
Suva Reka, *Serbia & M.* 44 D4
Suvorov, *Russia* 32 E9
Suvorov Is. = Suwarrow Is., *Cook Is.* 97 J11
Suvorove, *Ukraine* 29 E13
Suvorovo, *Bulgaria* 45 C11
Suwałki, *Poland* 30 D9
Suwana, *Indonesia* 63 K18
Suwannaphum, *Thailand* 64 E4
Suwannee →, *U.S.A.* 115 L4
Suwanose-Jima, *Japan* 55 K4
Suwarrow Is., *Cook Is.* 97 J11
Suwayq aş Şuqban, *Iraq* 70 D5
Suweis, Khalîg el, *Egypt* 80 J8
Suweis, Qanâ es, *Egypt* 80 H8
Suwŏn, *S. Korea* 57 F14
Suzdal, *Russia* 32 D11
Suzhou, *Anhui, China* 56 H9
Suzhou, *Jiangsu, China* 59 B13
Suzu, *Japan* 55 F8
Suzu-Misaki, *Japan* 55 F8
Suzuka, *Japan* 55 G8
Suzzara, *Italy* 40 D7
Svalbard, *Arctic* 51 B5
Svalbard Radio = Longyearbyen, *Svalbard* 4 B8
Svalöv, *Sweden* 11 J7
Svalyava, *Ukraine* 28 B7
Svaneke, *Denmark* 11 J9
Svängsta, *Sweden* 11 H8
Svanskog, *Sweden* 10 E6
Svappavaara, *Sweden* 8 C19
Svärdsjö, *Sweden* 10 D9
Svartå, *Sweden* 10 E8
Svartisen, *Norway* 8 C15
Svartvik, *Sweden* 10 B11
Svatove, *Ukraine* 33 H10
Svatovo = Svatove, *Ukraine* 33 H10
Svay Chek, *Cambodia* 64 F4
Svay Rieng, *Cambodia* 65 G5
Svealand □, *Sweden* 10 D9
Svedala, *Sweden* 11 J7
Sveg, *Sweden* 10 B8
Svendborg, *Denmark* 11 J4
Svenljunga, *Sweden* 11 G7
Svenstavik, *Sweden* 10 B8
Svenstrup, *Denmark* 11 H3
Sverdlovsk, *Ukraine* 33 H10
Sverdrup Is., *Canada* 98 B10
Svetac, *Croatia* 41 E12
Sveti Nikola, Prokhad, *Europe* 44 C6
Sveti Nikole, *Macedonia* 44 E5
Sveti Rok, *Croatia* 41 D12
Svetlaya, *Russia* 54 A9
Svetlogorsk = Svyetlahorsk, *Belarus* 33 F5
Svetlogorsk, *Russia* 30 D7
Svetlograd, *Russia* 35 H6
Svetlovodsk = Svitlovodsk, *Ukraine* 33 H7
Svetlyy, *Russia* 30 D7
Svidník, *Slovak Rep.* 27 B14
Svilaja Planina, *Croatia* 41 E13
Svilajnac, *Serbia & M.* 44 B5
Svilengrad, *Bulgaria* 45 E10
Svir →, *Russia* 32 B7
Sviritsa, *Russia* 32 B7
Svishtov, *Bulgaria* 45 C9
Svislach, *Belarus* 31 E11
Svitava →, *Czech Rep.* 27 B9
Svitavy, *Czech Rep.* 27 B9
Svitlovodsk, *Ukraine* 33 H7
Svobodnyy, *Russia* 53 D13
Svoge, *Bulgaria* 44 D7
Svolvær, *Norway* 8 B16
Svratka →, *Czech Rep.* 27 B9
Svrljig, *Serbia & M.* 44 C6
Svyetlahorsk, *Belarus* 33 F5
Swabian Alps = Schwäbische Alb, *Germany* 25 G5
Swaffham, *U.K.* 15 E8
Swainsboro, *U.S.A.* 115 J4
Swakop →, *Namibia* 88 C2
Swakopmund, *Namibia* 88 C1
Swale →, *U.K.* 14 C6
Swan →, *Australia* 93 F2
Swan →, *Canada* 103 C8
Swan Hill, *Australia* 95 F3
Swan Hills, *Canada* 102 C5
Swan Is. = Santanilla, Is., *Honduras* 120 C3
Swan L., *Canada* 103 C8
Swan Peak, *U.S.A.* 108 C7
Swan Ra., *U.S.A.* 108 C7
Swan River, *Canada* 103 C8
Swanage, *U.K.* 15 G6
Swansea, *Australia* 95 G4
Swansea, *Canada* 116 C5
Swansea, *U.K.* 15 F4
Swansea □, *U.K.* 15 F3
Swar →, *Pakistan* 69 B5
Swartberge, *S. Africa* 88 E3
Swartmodder, *S. Africa* 88 D3
Swartnossob →, *Namibia* 88 C2
Swartruggens, *S. Africa* 88 D4
Swarzędz, *Poland* 31 F4
Swastika, *Canada* 104 C3
Swatow = Shantou, *China* 59 F11
Swaziland ■, *Africa* 89 D5
Sweden ■, *Europe* 9 G16
Swedru, *Ghana* 83 D4
Sweet Home, *U.S.A.* 108 D2
Sweetgrass, *U.S.A.* 108 B8
Sweetwater, *Nev., U.S.A.* 110 G7
Sweetwater, *Tenn., U.S.A.* 115 H3
Sweetwater, *Tex., U.S.A.* 113 J4
Sweetwater →, *U.S.A.* 108 E10
Swellendam, *S. Africa* 88 E3
Swider →, *Poland* 31 F8
Świdnica, *Poland* 31 H3
Świdnik, *Poland* 31 G9
Świdwin, *Poland* 30 E2
Świebodzice, *Poland* 31 H3
Świebodzin, *Poland* 31 F2
Świecie, *Poland* 30 E5
Świerzawa, *Poland* 31 G2
Świętokrzyski △, *Poland* 31 H7
Świętokrzyskie □, *Poland* 31 H7
Świętokrzyskie, Góry, *Poland* 31 H7
Swift Current, *Canada* 103 C7
Swift Current →, *Canada* 103 C7
Swilly, L., *Ireland* 12 A4
Swindon, *U.K.* 15 F6
Swindon □, *U.K.* 15 F6
Swinemünde = Świnoujście, *Poland* 30 E1
Swinford, *Ireland* 12 C3
Świnoujście, *Poland* 30 E1
Switzerland ■, *Europe* 25 J4
Swords, *Ireland* 12 C5
Swoyerville, *U.S.A.* 117 E9
Syasstroy, *Russia* 32 B7
Sychevka, *Russia* 32 E8
Syców, *Poland* 31 G4
Sydenham →, *Canada* 116 D2
Sydney, *Australia* 95 E5
Sydney, *Canada* 105 C7
Sydney L., *Canada* 103 C10
Sydney Mines, *Canada* 105 C7
Sydprøven = Alluitsup Paa, *Greenland* 101 B15
Sydra, G. of = Surt, Khalīj, *Libya* 79 B9
Syeverodonetsk, *Ukraine* 33 H10
Syke, *Germany* 24 C4
Sykesville, *U.S.A.* 116 E6
Syktyvkar, *Russia* 52 C6
Sylacauga, *U.S.A.* 115 J2
Sylarna, *Sweden* 8 E15
Sylhet, *Bangla.* 67 G17
Sylhet □, *Bangla.* 67 G17
Sylt, *Germany* 24 A4
Sylvan Beach, *U.S.A.* 117 C9
Sylvan Lake, *Canada* 102 C6
Sylvania, *U.S.A.* 115 J5
Sylvester, *U.S.A.* 115 K4
Sym, *Russia* 52 C9
Symón, *Mexico* 118 C4
Synelnykove, *Ukraine* 33 H8
Synevyr △, *Ukraine* 29 B8
Synevyrska Polyana, *Ukraine* 29 B8
Synnott Ra., *Australia* 92 C4
Synyak, *Ukraine* 28 B7
Syowa, *Antarctica* 5 C5
Syracuse, *Kans., U.S.A.* 113 G4
Syracuse, *N.Y., U.S.A.* 117 C8
Syracuse, *Nebr., U.S.A.* 112 E6
Syrdarya →, *Kazakhstan* 52 E7
Syria ■, *Asia* 70 C3
Syrian Desert = Shām, Bādiyat ash, *Asia* 70 C3
Sysslebäck, *Sweden* 10 D6
Syzran, *Russia* 34 D9
Szabolcs-Szatmár-Bereg □, *Hungary* 28 B6
Szadek, *Poland* 31 G5
Szamocin, *Poland* 31 E4
Szamos →, *Hungary* 28 B7
Szamotuły, *Poland* 31 F3
Száraz →, *Hungary* 28 D6
Szarvas, *Hungary* 28 D5
Százhalombatta, *Hungary* 28 C3
Szczawnica, *Poland* 31 J7
Szczebrzeszyn, *Poland* 31 H9
Szczecin, *Poland* 30 E1
Szczecinek, *Poland* 30 E3
Szczeciński, Zalew = Stettiner Haff, *Germany* 24 B10
Szczekociny, *Poland* 31 H6
Szczucin, *Poland* 31 H8
Szczuczyn, *Poland* 30 E9
Szczyrk, *Poland* 31 J6
Szczytna, *Poland* 31 H3
Szczytno, *Poland* 30 E7
Szechuan Basin = Sichuan Pendi, *China* 58 B5
Szechwan = Sichuan □, *China* 58 B5
Szécsény, *Hungary* 28 B4
Szeged, *Hungary* 28 D5
Szeghalom, *Hungary* 28 C6
Székesfehérvár, *Hungary* 28 C3
Szekszárd, *Hungary* 28 D3
Szendrő, *Hungary* 28 B5
Szentendre, *Hungary* 28 C4
Szentes, *Hungary* 28 D5
Szentgotthárd, *Hungary* 28 D1
Szentlőrinc, *Hungary* 28 D3
Szerencs, *Hungary* 28 B6
Szigetszentmiklós, *Hungary* 28 C4
Szigetvár, *Hungary* 28 D2
Szikszó, *Hungary* 28 B5
Szklarska Poreba, *Poland* 31 H2
Szkwa →, *Poland* 31 E8
Szlichtyngowa, *Poland* 31 G3
Szob, *Hungary* 28 C3
Szolnok, *Hungary* 28 C5
Szombathely, *Hungary* 28 C1
Szprotawa, *Poland* 31 G2
Sztum, *Poland* 30 E6
Sztutowo, *Poland* 30 D6
Szubin, *Poland* 31 E4
Szydłowiec, *Poland* 31 G7
Szypliszki, *Poland* 30 D10

T

Ta Khli Khok, *Thailand* 64 E3
Ta Lai, *Vietnam* 65 G6
Tab, *Hungary* 28 D3
Tabacal, *Argentina* 126 A3
Tabaco, *Phil.* 61 E5
Tabagné, *Ivory C.* 82 D4
Ţābah, *Si. Arabia* 70 E4
Tabanan, *Indonesia* 63 K18
Tabankort, *Niger* 83 B5
Ţabas, *Khorāsān, Iran* 71 C9
Ţabas, *Khorāsān, Iran* 71 C8
Tabasará, Serranía de, *Panama* 120 E3
Tabasco □, *Mexico* 119 D6
Tabāsīn, *Iran* 71 D8
Tabatinga, Serra da, *Brazil* 125 F10
Taber, *Canada* 102 D6
Taberg, *Sweden* 11 G8
Taberg, *U.S.A.* 117 C9
Tabla, *Niger* 83 C5
Tablas de Daimiel △, *Spain* 37 F7
Tablas I., *Phil.* 61 E5
Tablas Strait, *Phil.* 61 E4
Table B., *Canada* 105 B8
Table B., *S. Africa* 88 E2
Table Mt., *S. Africa* 88 E2
Table Rock L., *U.S.A.* 113 G8
Tabletop, Mt., *Australia* 94 C4
Tábor, *Czech Rep.* 26 B7
Tabora, *Tanzania* 86 D3
Tabora □, *Tanzania* 86 D3
Tabou, *Ivory C.* 82 E3
Tabrīz, *Iran* 70 B5
Tabuaeran, *Kiribati* 97 G12
Tabuenca, *Spain* 38 D3
Tabūk, *Si. Arabia* 70 D3
Taburno-Camposauro ⌓, *Italy* 43 A7
Täby, *Sweden* 10 E12
Tacámbaro de Codallos, *Mexico* 118 D4
Tacheng, *China* 60 B3
Tach'i, *Taiwan* 59 E13
Tachia, *Taiwan* 59 E13
Tach'ing Shan = Daqing Shan, *China* 56 D6
Tachov, *Czech Rep.* 26 B5
Tácina →, *Italy* 43 D9
Tacloban, *Phil.* 61 F6
Tacna, *Peru* 124 G4
Tacoma, *U.S.A.* 110 C4
Tacuarembó, *Uruguay* 127 C4
Tademaït, Plateau du, *Algeria* 78 C6
Tadio, L., *Ivory C.* 82 D3
Tadjoura, *Djibouti* 81 E5
Tadjoura, Golfe de, *Djibouti* 81 E5
Tadmor, *N.Z.* 91 J4
Tadoule L., *Canada* 103 B9
Tadoussac, *Canada* 105 C6
Tadrés ⌓, *Niger* 83 B6
Tadzhikistan = Tajikistan ■, *Asia* 52 F8
Taechŏn-ni, *S. Korea* 57 F14
Taegu, *S. Korea* 57 G15
Taegwan, *N. Korea* 57 D13
Taejŏn, *S. Korea* 57 F14
Taen, Ko, *Thailand* 65 b
Tafalla, *Spain* 38 C3
Tafar, *Sudan* 81 F2
Tafelbaai = Table B., *S. Africa* 88 E2
Tafermaar, *Indonesia* 63 F8
Tafí Viejo, *Argentina* 126 B2
Tafīhān, *Iran* 71 D7
Tafiré, *Ivory C.* 82 D3
Tafo, *Ghana* 83 D4
Tafresh, *Iran* 71 C6
Taft, *Iran* 71 D7
Taft, *Phil.* 61 F6
Taft, *U.S.A.* 111 K7
Taftān, Kūh-e, *Iran* 71 D9
Taga Dzong, *Bhutan* 67 F16
Taganrog, *Russia* 33 J10
Taganrogskiy Zaliv, *Russia* 33 J10
Tagânt, *Mauritania* 82 B2
Tagatay, *Phil.* 61 D4
Tagbilaran, *Phil.* 61 G5
Tággia, *Italy* 40 E4
Tagish, *Canada* 102 A2
Tagish L., *Canada* 102 A2
Tagliacozzo, *Italy* 41 F10
Tagliamento →, *Italy* 41 C10
Táglio di Po, *Italy* 41 D9
Tago, *Phil.* 61 G7
Tagomago, *Spain* 48 B8
Tagourãret, *Mauritania* 82 B3
Taguatinga, *Brazil* 125 F10
Tagudin, *Phil.* 61 C4
Tagum, *Phil.* 61 H6
Tagus = Tejo →, *Europe* 37 F2
Tahakopa, *N.Z.* 91 M2
Tahan, Gunung, *Malaysia* 65 K4
Tahat, *Algeria* 78 D7
Tāherī, *Iran* 71 E7
Tahiti, *French Polynesia* 97 J13
Tahlequah, *U.S.A.* 113 H7
Tahoe, L., *U.S.A.* 110 G6
Tahoe City, *U.S.A.* 110 F6
Tahoka, *U.S.A.* 113 J4
Taholah, *U.S.A.* 110 C2
Tahoua, *Niger* 83 C6
Tahrūd, *Iran* 71 D8
Tahsis, *Canada* 102 D3
Tahta, *Egypt* 80 B3
Tahtaköprü, *Turkey* 45 G13
Tahtalı Dağları, *Turkey* 72 C7
Tahulandang, *Indonesia* 63 D7
Tahuna, *Indonesia* 63 D7
Taï, *Ivory C.* 82 D3
Taï △, *Ivory C.* 82 D3
Tai Hu, *China* 59 B12
Tai Rom Yen △, *Thailand* 65 H2

Tai Shan, *China* 57 F9
Tai'an, *China* 57 F9
Taibei = T'aipei, *Taiwan* 59 E13
Taibique, *Canary Is.* 48 G2
Taibus Qi, *China* 56 D8
Taicang, *China* 59 B13
T'aichung, *Taiwan* 59 E13
Taieri →, *N.Z.* 91 M3
Taigu, *China* 56 F7
Taihang Shan, *China* 56 G7
Taihape, *N.Z.* 91 H5
Taihe, *Anhui, China* 56 H8
Taihe, *Jiangxi, China* 59 D10
Taihu, *China* 59 B11
Taijiang, *China* 58 D7
Taikang, *China* 56 G8
Tailem Bend, *Australia* 95 F2
Tailfingen, *Germany* 25 G5
Tailuko, *Taiwan* 59 E13
Taimyr Peninsula = Taymyr, Poluostrov, *Russia* 53 B11
Tain, *U.K.* 13 D4
T'ainan, *Taiwan* 59 F13
Taínaron, Ákra, *Greece* 46 E4
Taining, *China* 59 D11
T'aipei, *Taiwan* 59 E13
Taiping, *China* 59 B12
Taiping, *Malaysia* 65 K3
Taipingzhen, *China* 56 H6
Tairbeart = Tarbert, *U.K.* 13 D2
Taishan, *China* 59 F9
Taishun, *China* 59 D12
Taita Hills, *Kenya* 86 C4
Taitao, Pen. de, *Chile* 128 F2
T'aitung, *Taiwan* 59 F13
Taivalkoski, *Finland* 8 D23
Taiwan ■, *Asia* 59 F13
Taiwan Strait, *Asia* 59 E12
Taixing, *China* 59 A13
Taiyara, *Sudan* 81 E3
Taïyetos Óros, *Greece* 46 D4
Taiyiba, *Israel* 74 C4
Taiyuan, *China* 56 F7
Taizhong = T'aichung, *Taiwan* 59 E13
Taizhou, *China* 59 A12
Taizhou Liedao, *China* 59 C13
Ta'izz, *Yemen* 75 E3
Tājābād, *Iran* 71 D7
Tajikistan ■, *Asia* 52 F8
Tajima, *Japan* 55 F9
Tajo = Tejo →, *Europe* 37 F2
Tajrīsh, *Iran* 71 C6
Tak, *Thailand* 64 D2
Takāb, *Iran* 70 B5
Takachiho, *Japan* 55 H5
Takachu, *Botswana* 88 C3
Takada, *Japan* 55 F9
Takahagi, *Japan* 55 F10
Takaka, *N.Z.* 91 J4
Takamatsu, *Japan* 55 G7
Takaoka, *Japan* 55 F8
Takapuna, *N.Z.* 91 G5
Takasaki, *Japan* 55 F9
Takatsuki, *Japan* 55 G7
Takaungu, *Kenya* 86 C4
Takayama, *Japan* 55 F8
Take-Shima, *Japan* 55 J5
Takefu, *Japan* 55 G8
Takengon, *Indonesia* 62 D1
Takeo, *Japan* 55 H5
Tåkern, *Sweden* 11 F8
Takeshima = Tok-do, *Asia* 55 F5
Tākestān, *Iran* 71 C6
Taketa, *Japan* 55 H5
Takev, *Cambodia* 65 G5
Takh, *India* 69 C7
Takht-Sulaiman, *Pakistan* 68 D3
Takikawa, *Japan* 54 C10
Takla L., *Canada* 102 B3
Takla Landing, *Canada* 102 B3
Takla Makan = Taklamakan Shamo, *China* 60 C3
Taklamakan Shamo, *China* 60 C3
Taku →, *Canada* 102 B2
Takua Thung, *Thailand* 65 a
Takum, *Nigeria* 83 D6
Tal Halāl, *Iran* 71 D7
Tala, *Uruguay* 127 C4
Talachyn, *Belarus* 32 E5
Talacogan, *Phil.* 61 G6
Talagang, *Pakistan* 68 C5
Talagante, *Chile* 126 C1
Talak, *Niger* 83 B6
Talamanca, Cordillera de, *Cent. Amer.* 120 E3
Talant, *France* 19 E11
Talara, *Peru* 124 D2
Talas, *Kyrgyzstan* 52 E8
Talas, *Turkey* 72 C6
Talâta, *Egypt* 74 E1
Talata Mafara, *Nigeria* 83 C6
Talaud, Kepulauan, *Indonesia* 63 D7
Talaud Is. = Talaud, Kepulauan, *Indonesia* 63 D7
Talavera de la Reina, *Spain* 36 F6
Talavera la Real, *Spain* 37 G4
Talayan, *Phil.* 61 H6
Talayuela, *Spain* 36 F5
Talbandh, *India* 69 H12
Talbert, Sillon de, *France* 18 D3
Talbot, C., *Australia* 92 B4
Talbragar →, *Australia* 95 E4
Talca, *Chile* 126 D1
Talcahuano, *Chile* 126 D1
Talcher, *India* 67 J14
Talcho, *Niger* 83 C5
Taldy Kurgan = Taldyqorghan, *Kazakhstan* 52 E8
Taldyqorghan, *Kazakhstan* 52 E8
Tālesh, *Iran* 71 B6
Tālesh, Kūhhā-ye, *Iran* 71 B6
Talguharai, *Sudan* 80 D4
Tali Post, *Sudan* 81 F3
Taliabu, *Indonesia* 63 E6
Talibon, *Phil.* 63 B6
Talibong, Ko, *Thailand* 65 J2
Talihina, *U.S.A.* 113 H7
Talisayan, *Phil.* 61 G6
Taliwang, *Indonesia* 62 F5
Tall 'Afar, *Iraq* 70 B4
Tall Kalakh, *Syria* 74 A5
Talla, *Egypt* 80 B3
Talladega, *U.S.A.* 115 J2
Tallahassee, *U.S.A.* 115 K3
Tallangatta, *Australia* 95 F4
Tallard, *France* 21 D10
Tällberg, *Sweden* 10 D9
Tallering Pk., *Australia* 93 E2
Talli, *Pakistan* 68 E3
Tallinn, *Estonia* 9 G21
Tallmadge, *U.S.A.* 116 E3
Tallulah, *U.S.A.* 113 J9
Tălmaciu, *Romania* 29 E9
Talmont-St-Hilaire, *France* 20 B2
Talne, *Ukraine* 33 H6
Talnoye = Talne, *Ukraine* 33 H6
Talodi, *Sudan* 81 E3
Talovaya, *Russia* 34 E5
Taloyoak, *Canada* 100 B10
Talpa de Allende, *Mexico* 118 C4
Talparo, *Trin. & Tob.* 125 K15
Talsi, *Latvia* 9 H20
Talsi □, *Latvia* 30 A9
Taltal, *Chile* 126 B1
Taltson →, *Canada* 102 A6
Talwood, *Australia* 95 D4
Talyawalka Cr. →, *Australia* 95 E3
Tam Ky, *Vietnam* 64 E7
Tam Quan, *Vietnam* 64 E7
Tama, *U.S.A.* 112 E8
Tama ⌓, *Ethiopia* 81 F4
Tamale, *Ghana* 83 D4
Taman, *Russia* 33 K9
Taman Negara △, *Malaysia* 65 K4
Tamani, *Mali* 82 C3
Tamano, *Japan* 55 G6
Tamanrasset, *Algeria* 78 D7
Tamaqua, *U.S.A.* 117 F9
Tamar →, *U.K.* 15 G3
Tamarinda, *Spain* 48 B10
Tamarite de Litera, *Spain* 38 D5
Tamashima, *Japan* 55 G6
Tamási, *Hungary* 28 D3
Tamaské, *Niger* 83 C6
Tamaulipas □, *Mexico* 119 C5
Tamaulipas, Sierra de, *Mexico* 119 C5
Tamazula, *Mexico* 118 C3
Tamazunchale, *Mexico* 119 C5
Tamba-Dabatou, *Guinea* 82 C2
Tambacounda, *Senegal* 82 C2
Tambelan, Kepulauan, *Indonesia* 62 D3
Tambellup, *Australia* 93 F2
Tambo, *Australia* 94 C4
Tambo de Mora, *Peru* 124 F3
Tambohorano, *Madag.* 89 B7
Tambora, *Indonesia* 62 F5
Tambov, *Russia* 34 D5
Tambre →, *Spain* 36 C2
Tambuku, *Indonesia* 63 G15
Tamburâ, *Sudan* 81 F2
Tâmchekket, *Mauritania* 82 B2
Tâmega →, *Portugal* 36 D2
Tamenglong, *India* 67 G18
Tamgué, Massif du, *Guinea* 82 C2
Tamiahua, L. de, *Mexico* 119 C5
Tamil Nadu □, *India* 66 P10
Tamis →, *Serbia & M.* 28 F5
Tamluk, *India* 69 H12
Tammerfors = Tampere, *Finland* 9 F20
Tammisaari, *Finland* 9 F20
Tämnaren, *Sweden* 10 D11
Tamo Abu, Pegunungan, *Malaysia* 62 D5
Tampa, *U.S.A.* 115 M4
Tampa, Tanjung, *Indonesia* 63 K19
Tampa B., *U.S.A.* 115 M4
Tampere, *Finland* 9 F20
Tampico, *Mexico* 119 C5
Tampin, *Malaysia* 65 L4
Tampoi, *Malaysia* 65 d
Tamsweg, *Austria* 26 D6
Tamu, *Burma* 67 G19
Tamuja →, *Spain* 37 F4
Tamworth, *Australia* 95 E5
Tamworth, *Canada* 116 B8
Tamworth, *U.K.* 15 E6
Tamyang, *S. Korea* 57 G14
Tan An, *Vietnam* 65 G6
Tan Chau, *Vietnam* 65 G5
Tan-Tan, *Morocco* 78 C3
Tana →, *Kenya* 86 C5
Tana →, *Norway* 8 A23
Tana, L., *Ethiopia* 81 E4
Tana River Primate ⌓, *Kenya* 86 C5
Tanabe, *Japan* 55 H7
Tanafjorden, *Norway* 8 A23
Tanahbala, *Indonesia* 62 E1
Tanahgrogot, *Indonesia* 62 E5
Tanahjampea, *Indonesia* 63 F6
Tanahmasa, *Indonesia* 62 E1
Tanahmerah, *Indonesia* 63 F10
Tanakpur, *India* 69 E9
Tanakura, *Japan* 55 F10
Tanami, *Australia* 92 C4
Tanami Desert, *Australia* 92 C5
Tanana →, *U.S.A.* 100 B4
Tananarive = Antananarivo, *Madag.* 89 B8
Tánaro →, *Italy* 40 D5
Tancheng, *China* 57 G10
Tanch'ŏn, *N. Korea* 57 D15
Tanda, *Ut. P., India* 69 F10
Tanda, *Ut. P., India* 69 E8
Tanda, *Ivory C.* 82 D4
Tandag, *Phil.* 61 G7
Tandaia, *Tanzania* 87 D3
Tăndărei, *Romania* 29 F12
Tandaué, *Angola* 88 B2
Tandil, *Argentina* 126 D4
Tandil, Sa. del, *Argentina* 126 D4
Tandlianwala, *Pakistan* 68 D5
Tando Adam, *Pakistan* 68 G3
Tando Allahyar, *Pakistan* 68 G3
Tando Bago, *Pakistan* 68 G3
Tando Mohommed Khan, *Pakistan* 68 G3
Tandou L., *Australia* 95 E3
Tandragee, *U.K.* 12 B5
Tandsjöborg, *Sweden* 10 C8
Tane-ga-Shima, *Japan* 55 J5
Taneatua, *N.Z.* 91 H6
Tanen Tong Dan = Dawna Ra., *Burma* 64 D2
Tanew →, *Poland* 31 H9
Tanezrouft, *Algeria* 78 D6
Tang, Koh, *Cambodia* 65 G4
Tang, Ra's-e, *Iran* 71 E8
Tang Krasang, *Cambodia* 64 F5
Tanga, *Tanzania* 86 D4
Tanga □, *Tanzania* 86 D4
Tanganyika, L., *Africa* 86 D3
Tangaza, *Nigeria* 83 C5
Tanger, *Morocco* 78 A4
Tangerang, *Indonesia* 63 G12
Tangerhütte, *Germany* 24 C7
Tangermünde, *Germany* 24 C7
Tanggu, *China* 57 E9
Tanggula Shan, *China* 60 C4
Tanghe, *China* 56 H7
Tanghla Range = Tanggula Shan, *China* 60 C4
Tangier = Tanger, *Morocco* 78 A4
Tangorin, *Australia* 94 C3
Tangorombohitr'i Makay, *Madag.* 89 C8
Tangshan, *China* 57 E10
Tangtou, *China* 57 G10
Tanguiéta, *Benin* 83 C5
Tangxi, *China* 59 C12
Tangyan He →, *China* 58 C7
Tanimbar, Kepulauan, *Indonesia* 63 F8
Tanimbar Is. = Tanimbar, Kepulauan, *Indonesia* 63 F8
Taninthari = Tenasserim, *Burma* 65 F2
Tanjay, *Phil.* 61 G5
Tanjong Malim, *Malaysia* 65 L3
Tanjong Pelepas, *Malaysia* 65 d
Tanjore = Thanjavur, *India* 66 P11
Tanjung, *Indonesia* 63 J19
Tanjung, *Phil.* 62 E5
Tanjung Tokong, *Malaysia* 65 c
Tanjungbalai, *Indonesia* 62 D1
Tanjungbatu, *Indonesia* 62 D5
Tanjungkarang Telukbetung, *Indonesia* 62 F3
Tanjungpandan, *Indonesia* 62 E3
Tanjungpinang, *Indonesia* 62 D2
Tanjungredeb, *Indonesia* 62 D5
Tanjungselor, *Indonesia* 62 D5
Tank, *Pakistan* 68 C4
Tankhala, *India* 68 J5
Tankwa-Karoo △, *S. Africa* 88 E2
Tännäs, *Sweden* 10 B6
Tannersville, *U.S.A.* 117 E9
Tannis Bugt, *Denmark* 11 G4
Tannu-Ola, *Russia* 53 D10
Tannum Sands, *Australia* 94 C5
Tano →, *Ghana* 82 D4
Tanon Str., *Phil.* 61 F5
Tanout, *Niger* 83 C6
Tanshui, *Taiwan* 59 E13
Tansilla, *Burkina Faso* 82 C4
Tanta, *Egypt* 80 H7
Tantoyuca, *Mexico* 119 C5
Tantung = Dandong, *China* 57 D13
Tanumshede, *Sweden* 11 F5
Tanunda, *Australia* 95 E2
Tanus, *France* 20 D6
Tanzania ■, *Africa* 86 D3
Tanzilla →, *Canada* 102 B2
Tao, Ko, *Thailand* 65 G2
Tao'an = Taonan, *China* 57 B12
Tao'er He →, *China* 57 B13
Taohua Dao, *China* 59 C14
Taolanaro, *Madag.* 89 D8
Taole, *China* 56 E4
Taonan, *China* 57 B12
Taormina, *Italy* 43 E8
Taos, *U.S.A.* 109 H11
Taoudenni, *Mali* 78 D5
Taoyuan, *China* 59 C8
T'aoyüan, *Taiwan* 59 E13
Tapa, *Estonia* 9 G21
Tapa Shan = Daba Shan, *China* 58 B7
Tapachula, *Mexico* 119 E6
Tapah, *Malaysia* 65 K3
Tapajós →, *Brazil* 125 D8
Tapaktuan, *Indonesia* 62 D1
Tapanahoni →, *Suriname* 125 C8
Tapanui, *N.Z.* 91 L2
Tapauá →, *Brazil* 124 E6
Tapes, *Brazil* 127 C5
Tapeta, *Liberia* 82 D3
Taphan Hin, *Thailand* 64 D3
Tapi →, *India* 66 J8
Tapia de Casariego, *Spain* 36 B4
Tapirapecó, Serra, *Venezuela* 124 C6
Tapo-Capara △, *Venezuela* 121 E5
Tapolca, *Hungary* 28 D2
Tapuae-o-Uenuku, *N.Z.* 91 K4
Tapul Group, *Phil.* 61 J4
Tapurucuará, *Brazil* 124 D5
Ţaqţaq, *Iraq* 70 C5
Taquara, *Brazil* 127 B5
Taquari →, *Brazil* 124 G7
Tara, *Australia* 95 D5
Tara, *Canada* 116 B3
Tara, *Russia* 52 D8
Tara, *Zambia* 87 F2
Tara △, *Serbia & M.* 44 C3
Tara →, *Serbia & M.* 44 C2
Taraba □, *Nigeria* 83 D7
Taraba →, *Nigeria* 83 D7
Tarābulus, *Lebanon* 74 A4
Tarābulus, *Libya* 79 B8
Taraclia, *Taraclia, Moldova* 29 E13
Taraclia, *Tighina, Moldova* 29 D14
Taradehi, *India* 69 H8
Tarajalejo, *Canary Is.* 48 F5
Tarakan, *Indonesia* 62 D5
Tarakit, Mt., *Kenya* 86 B4
Tarama-Jima, *Japan* 55 M2
Taran, Mys, *Russia* 9 J18
Taranagar, *India* 68 E6
Taranaki □, *N.Z.* 91 H5
Taranaki, Mt., *N.Z.* 91 H5
Tarancón, *Spain* 38 E1
Tarangire △, *Tanzania* 86 C4
Taransay, *U.K.* 13 D1
Táranto, *Italy* 43 B10
Táranto, G. di, *Italy* 43 B10
Tarapacá, *Colombia* 124 D5
Tarapacá □, *Chile* 126 A2
Tarapoto, *Peru* 124 E3
Tarare, *France* 21 C8
Tararua Ra., *N.Z.* 91 J5
Tarascon, *France* 21 E8
Tarascon-sur-Ariège, *France* 20 F5
Tarashcha, *Ukraine* 33 H6
Tarauacá, *Brazil* 124 E4
Tarauacá →, *Brazil* 124 E5
Taravo →, *France* 21 G12
Tarawa, *Kiribati* 96 G9
Tarawera, *N.Z.* 91 H6
Tarawera, L., *N.Z.* 91 H6
Taraz, *Kazakhstan* 52 E8
Tarazona, *Spain* 38 D3
Tarazona de la Mancha, *Spain* 39 F3
Tarbagatay, Khrebet, *Kazakhstan* 52 E9
Tarbat Ness, *U.K.* 13 D5
Tarbela Dam, *Pakistan* 68 B5
Tarbert, *Arg. & Bute, U.K.* 13 F3
Tarbert, *W. Isles, U.K.* 13 D2
Tarbes, *France* 20 E4
Tarboro, *U.S.A.* 115 H7
Tărcău, Munţii, *Romania* 29 D11
Tarcento, *Italy* 41 B10
Tarcoola, *Australia* 95 E1
Tarcoon, *Australia* 95 E4
Tardets-Sorholus, *France* 20 E3
Tardoire →, *France* 20 C4
Taree, *Australia* 95 E5
Tarfa, W. el →, *Egypt* 80 B3
Tarfaya, *Morocco* 78 C3
Târgovişte, *Romania* 29 F10
Târgu Bujor, *Romania* 29 E12
Târgu Cărbuneşti, *Romania* 29 F8
Târgu Frumos, *Romania* 29 C12
Târgu-Jiu, *Romania* 29 E8
Târgu Lăpuş, *Romania* 29 C8
Târgu Mureş, *Romania* 29 D9
Târgu Neamţ, *Romania* 29 C11
Târgu Ocna, *Romania* 29 D11
Târgu Secuiesc, *Romania* 29 E11
Târguşor, *Romania* 29 F13
Tărhăus, Vf., *Romania* 29 D11
Ţarif, *U.A.E.* 71 E7
Tarifa, *Spain* 37 J5
Tarija, *Bolivia* 126 A3
Tarija □, *Bolivia* 126 A3
Tariku →, *Indonesia* 63 E9
Tarim Basin = Tarim Pendi, *China* 60 C3
Tarim He →, *China* 60 C3
Tarim Pendi, *China* 60 C3
Taritatu →, *Indonesia* 63 E9
Tarka →, *S. Africa* 88 E4
Tarkastad, *S. Africa* 88 E4
Tarkhankut, Mys, *Ukraine* 33 K7
Tarko Sale, *Russia* 52 C8
Tarkwa, *Ghana* 82 D4
Tarlac, *Phil.* 61 D4
Tarm, *Denmark* 11 J2
Tarma, *Peru* 124 F3
Tarn □, *France* 20 E6
Tarn →, *France* 20 D5
Tarn-et-Garonne □, *France* 20 D5
Tarna →, *Hungary* 28 C4
Târnava Mare →, *Romania* 29 D8
Târnava Mică →, *Romania* 29 D8
Târnăveni, *Romania* 29 D9
Tarnica, *Poland* 31 J9
Tarnobrzeg, *Poland* 31 H8
Tarnogród, *Poland* 31 H9
Tarnos, *France* 20 E2
Târnova, *Moldova* 29 B12
Târnova, *Romania* 28 E6
Tarnów, *Poland* 31 H8
Tarnowskie Góry, *Poland* 31 H5
Tärnsjö, *Sweden* 10 D10
Táro →, *Italy* 40 C7
Ţārom, *Iran* 71 D7
Taroom, *Australia* 95 D4
Taroudannt, *Morocco* 78 B4
Tarp, *Germany* 24 A5
Tarpon Springs, *U.S.A.* 115 L4
Tarquínia, *Italy* 41 F8
Tarragona, *Spain* 38 D6
Tarragona □, *Spain* 38 D6
Tarraleah, *Australia* 95 G4
Tarrasa = Terrassa, *Spain* 38 D7
Tàrrega, *Spain* 38 D6
Tarrytown, *U.S.A.* 117 E11
Tårs, *Denmark* 11 G4
Tarshiha = Me'ona, *Israel* 74 B4
Tarsus, *Turkey* 70 B2
Tartagal, *Argentina* 126 A3
Tärtär, *Azerbaijan* 35 K8
Tärtär →, *Azerbaijan* 35 K8
Tartas, *France* 20 E3
Tartu, *Estonia* 9 G22
Ţarţūs, *Syria* 70 C2
Tarumizu, *Japan* 55 J5
Tarussa, *Russia* 32 E9
Tarutao = Ko Tarutao △, *Thailand* 65 J2
Tarutao, Ko, *Thailand* 65 J2
Tarutung, *Indonesia* 62 D1
Tarutyne, *Ukraine* 29 D14
Tarvísio, *Italy* 41 B10
Taseko →, *Canada* 102 C4
Tash-Kömür, *Kyrgyzstan* 52 E8
Tash-Kumyr = Tash-Kömür, *Kyrgyzstan* 52 E8
Tashauz = Dashhowuz, *Turkmenistan* 52 E6
Tashi Chho Dzong = Thimphu, *Bhutan* 67 F16
Ţashk, Daryācheh-ye, *Iran* 71 D7
Tashkent = Toshkent, *Uzbekistan* 52 E7
Tashtagol, *Russia* 52 D9
Tasiilaq, *Greenland* 4 C6
Tasikmalaya, *Indonesia* 63 G13
Tåsinge, *Denmark* 11 J4
Tåsjön, *Sweden* 8 D16
Taskan, *Russia* 53 C16
Tasker, *Niger* 83 C7
Taşköprü, *Turkey* 72 B6
Taşlâc, *Moldova* 29 C14
Tasman B., *N.Z.* 91 J4
Tasman Mts., *N.Z.* 91 J4
Tasman Pen., *Australia* 95 G4
Tasman Plateau, *S. Ocean* 5 A10
Tasman Sea, *Pac. Oc.* 96 L8
Tasmania □, *Australia* 95 G4
Tăşnad, *Romania* 28 C7
Tassili n'Ajjer, *Algeria* 78 C7
Tassili Tin-Rerhoh, *Algeria* 83 A5
Tata, *Hungary* 28 C3
Tatabánya, *Hungary* 28 C3
Tatahouine, *Tunisia* 79 B8
Tataouine, *Tunisia* 79 B8
Tatar Republic = Tatarstan □, *Russia* 34 C10
Tatarbunary, *Ukraine* 29 E14
Tatarsk, *Russia* 52 D8
Tatarstan □, *Russia* 34 C10
Tateyama, *Japan* 55 G9
Tathlina L., *Canada* 102 A5
Tathra, *Australia* 95 F4
Tatinnai L., *Canada* 103 A9
Tatla L., *Canada* 102 C4
Tatlısu, *Turkey* 45 F11
Tatnam, C., *Canada* 103 B10
Tatra = Tatry, *Slovak Rep.* 27 B13
Tatranský △, *Slovak Rep.* 27 B13
Tatry, *Slovak Rep.* 27 B13
Tatshenshini →, *Canada* 102 B1
Tatsuno, *Japan* 55 G7
Tatta, *Pakistan* 68 G2
Tatuí, *Brazil* 127 A6
Tatum, *U.S.A.* 113 J3
Tat'ung = Datong, *China* 56 D7
Tatvan, *Turkey* 70 B4
Taubaté, *Brazil* 127 A6
Tauberbischofsheim, *Germany* 25 F5
Taucha, *Germany* 24 D8
Tauern-tunnel, *Austria* 26 D6
Taufikia, *Sudan* 81 F3
Taulé, *France* 18 D3
Taumarunui, *N.Z.* 91 H5
Taumaturgo, *Brazil* 124 E4
Taung, *S. Africa* 88 D3
Taungdwingyi, *Burma* 67 J19
Taunggyi, *Burma* 67 J20
Taungup, *Burma* 67 K19
Taungup Taunggya, *Burma* 67 K18
Taunsa, *Pakistan* 68 D4
Taunsa Barrage, *Pakistan* 68 D4
Taunton, *U.K.* 15 F4
Taunton, *U.S.A.* 117 E13
Taunus, *Germany* 25 E4
Taupo, *N.Z.* 91 H6
Taupo, L., *N.Z.* 91 H5
Tauragė, *Lithuania* 9 J20
Tauragė □, *Lithuania* 30 C9
Tauranga, *N.Z.* 91 G6
Tauranga Harb., *N.Z.* 91 G6
Taureau, Rés., *Canada* 104 C5
Taurianova, *Italy* 43 D9
Taurus Mts. = Toros Dağları, *Turkey* 70 B2
Tauste, *Spain* 38 D3
Tauz = Tovuz, *Azerbaijan* 35 K7
Tavas, *Turkey* 47 D11
Tavastehus = Hämeenlinna, *Finland* 9 F21
Tavda, *Russia* 52 D7
Tavda →, *Russia* 52 D7
Tavernes de la Valldigna, *Spain* 39 F4
Taveta, *Tanzania* 86 C4
Taveuni, *Fiji* 91 C9
Taviano, *Italy* 43 C11
Tavignano →, *France* 21 F13
Tavira, *Portugal* 37 H3
Tavistock, *Canada* 116 C4
Tavistock, *U.K.* 15 G3
Tavolara, *Italy* 42 B2
Távora →, *Portugal* 36 D3
Tavoy, *Burma* 64 E2
Tavşanlı, *Turkey* 47 B11
Taw →, *U.K.* 15 F3
Tawa →, *India* 68 H8
Tawas City, *U.S.A.* 114 C4
Tawau, *Malaysia* 62 D5
Taweisha, *Sudan* 81 E2

Tawitawi, *Phil.* 63 B6
Tawu, *Taiwan* 59 F13
Taxco de Alarcón, *Mexico* 119 D5
Taxila, *Pakistan* 68 C5
Tay ⌓, *U.K.* 13 E5
Tay →, *U.K.* 13 E5
Tay, Firth of, *U.K.* 13 E5
Tay, L., *Australia* 93 F3
Tay, L., *U.K.* 13 E4
Tay Ninh, *Vietnam* 65 G6
Tayabamba, *Peru* 124 E3
Tayabas Bay, *Phil.* 61 E4
Taylakova, *Russia* 52 D8
Taylakovy = Taylakova, *Russia* 52 D8
Taylor, *Canada* 102 B4
Taylor, *Nebr., U.S.A.* 112 E5
Taylor, *Pa., U.S.A.* 117 E9
Taylor, *Tex., U.S.A.* 113 K6
Taylor, Mt., *U.S.A.* 109 J10
Taylorville, *U.S.A.* 112 F10
Taymā, *Si. Arabia* 70 E3
Taymyr, Oz., *Russia* 53 B11
Taymyr, Poluostrov, *Russia* 53 B11
Tayport, *U.K.* 13 E6
Tayrona △, *Colombia* 121 D5
Tayshet, *Russia* 53 D10
Taytay, *Phil.* 61 F3
Tāyyebād, *Iran* 71 C9
Tayyebād □, *Iran* 71 C9
Taz →, *Russia* 52 C8
Taza, *Morocco* 78 B5
Tāza Khurmātū, *Iraq* 70 C5
Tazawa-Ko, *Japan* 54 E10
Tazin, *Canada* 103 B7
Tazin L., *Canada* 103 B7
Tazovskiy, *Russia* 52 C8
Tbilisi, *Georgia* 35 K7
Tchad = Chad ■, *Africa* 79 F8
Tchad, L., *Chad* 79 F8
Tchaourou, *Benin* 83 D5
Tch'eng-tou = Chengdu, *China* 58 B5
Tchentlo L., *Canada* 102 B4
Tchetti, *Benin* 83 D5
Tchibanga, *Gabon* 84 E2
Tchien, *Liberia* 82 D3
Tchin Tabaraden, *Niger* 83 B6
Tch'ong-k'ing = Chongqing, *China* 58 C6
Tczew, *Poland* 30 D5
Te Anau, L., *N.Z.* 91 L1
Te Aroha, *N.Z.* 91 G5
Te Awamutu, *N.Z.* 91 H5
Te Ika a Maui = North I., *N.Z.* 91 H5
Te Kuiti, *N.Z.* 91 H5
Te-n-Dghâmcha, Sebkhet, *Mauritania* 82 B1
Te Puke, *N.Z.* 91 G6
Te Waewae B., *N.Z.* 91 M1
Te Wai Pounamu = South I., *N.Z.* 91 L3
Teaca, *Romania* 29 D9
Teague, *U.S.A.* 113 K6
Teano, *Italy* 43 A7
Teapa, *Mexico* 119 D6
Teba, *Spain* 37 J6
Tebakang, *Malaysia* 62 D4
Teberda, *Russia* 35 J5
Teberu, *Malaysia* 65 d
Tébessa, *Algeria* 78 A7
Tebicuary →, *Paraguay* 126 B4
Tebingtinggi, *Riau, Indonesia* 62 E2
Tebingtinggi, *Sumatera Utara, Indonesia* 62 D1
Tebulos, *Georgia* 35 J7
Tecate, *Mexico* 111 N10
Tecer Dağları, *Turkey* 72 C7
Tech →, *France* 20 F7
Techiman, *Ghana* 82 D4
Techirghiol, *Romania* 29 F13
Tecka, *Argentina* 128 E2
Tecomán, *Mexico* 118 D4
Tecopa, *U.S.A.* 111 K10
Tecoripa, *Mexico* 118 B3
Tecuala, *Mexico* 118 C3
Tecuci, *Romania* 29 E12
Tecumseh, *Canada* 116 D2
Tecumseh, *Mich., U.S.A.* 114 D4
Tecumseh, *Okla., U.S.A.* 113 H6
Tedzhen = Tejen, *Turkmenistan* 52 F7
Tees →, *U.K.* 14 C6
Tees B., *U.K.* 14 C6
Teeswater, *Canada* 116 C3
Tefé, *Brazil* 124 D6
Tefenni, *Turkey* 47 D11
Tegal, *Indonesia* 63 G13
Tegallalang, *Indonesia* 63 J18
Tegalsari, *Indonesia* 63 J17
Tegel, Berlin ✕ (TXL), *Germany* 24 C9
Tegernsee, *Germany* 25 H7
Teggiano, *Italy* 43 B8
Tegid, L. = Bala, L., *U.K.* 14 E4
Tegina, *Nigeria* 83 C6
Tegucigalpa, *Honduras* 120 D2
Teguidda i-n-Tessoum, *Niger* 83 B6
Tehachapi, *U.S.A.* 111 K8
Tehachapi Mts., *U.S.A.* 111 L8
Tehamiyam, *Sudan* 80 D4
Teheran = Tehrān, *Iran* 71 C6
Tehilla, *Sudan* 80 D4
Téhini, *Ivory C.* 82 D4
Tehoru, *Indonesia* 63 E7
Tehrān, *Iran* 71 C6
Tehran □, *Iran* 71 C6
Tehri, *India* 69 D8
Tehuacán, *Mexico* 119 D5
Tehuantepec, *Mexico* 119 D5
Tehuantepec, G. de, *Mexico* 119 D5
Tehuantepec, Istmo de, *Mexico* 119 D6
Teide, Pico de, *Canary Is.* 48 F3
Teifi →, *U.K.* 15 E3
Teign →, *U.K.* 15 G4
Teignmouth, *U.K.* 15 G4
Teiuş, *Romania* 29 D8
Teixeira Pinto, *Guinea-Biss.* 82 C1
Tejakula, *Indonesia* 63 J18
Tejam, *India* 69 E9
Tejen, *Turkmenistan* 52 F7
Tejen →, *Turkmenistan* 71 B9
Tejo →, *Europe* 37 F2
Tejon Pass, *U.S.A.* 111 L8
Tekamah, *U.S.A.* 112 E6
Tekapo, L., *N.Z.* 91 K3
Tekax, *Mexico* 119 C7
Teke, *Turkey* 45 E13
Tekeli, *Kazakhstan* 52 E8
Tekeze →, *Ethiopia* 81 E4
Tekija, *Serbia & M.* 44 B6
Tekirdağ, *Turkey* 45 F11
Tekirdağ □, *Turkey* 45 E11
Tekirova, *Turkey* 47 E12
Tekkali, *India* 67 K14
Tekke, *Turkey* 72 B7
Tekman, *Turkey* 73 C9
Tekoa, *U.S.A.* 108 C5
Tekong Besar, Pulau, *Singapore* 65 d
Tel Aviv ✕ (TLV), *Israel* 74 C3
Tel Aviv-Yafo, *Israel* 74 C3
Tel Lakhish, *Israel* 74 D3
Tel Megiddo, *Israel* 74 C4
Tela, *Honduras* 120 C2
Telanaipura = Jambi, *Indonesia* 62 E2
Telašćica ⌓, *Croatia* 41 E12
Telavi, *Georgia* 35 J7
Telč, *Czech Rep.* 26 B8
Telciu, *Romania* 29 C9
Telde, *Canary Is.* 48 G4
Telegraph Creek, *Canada* 102 B2
Telekhany = Tsyelyakhany, *Belarus* 33 F3
Telemark, *Norway* 9 G12
Telén, *Argentina* 126 D2
Teleneşti, *Moldova* 29 C13
Teleng, *Iran* 71 E9
Teleño, *Spain* 36 C4
Teleorman □, *Romania* 29 G10
Teleorman →, *Romania* 29 G10
Teles Pires →, *Brazil* 124 E7
Telescope Pk., *U.S.A.* 111 J9
Teletaye, *Mali* 83 B5
Telfer Mine, *Australia* 92 C3
Telford, *U.K.* 15 E5
Telford and Wrekin □, *U.K.* 14 E5
Telfs, *Austria* 26 D4
Télimélé, *Guinea* 82 C2
Teljo, J., *Sudan* 81 E2
Telkwa, *Canada* 102 C3
Tell City, *U.S.A.* 114 G2
Tellicherry, *India* 66 P9
Telluride, *U.S.A.* 109 H10
Teloloapán, *Mexico* 119 D5
Telpos Iz, *Russia* 6 C17
Telsen, *Argentina* 128 E3
Telšiai, *Lithuania* 9 H20
Telšiai □, *Lithuania* 30 C9
Teltow, *Germany* 24 C9
Teluk Anson = Teluk Intan, *Malaysia* 65 K3
Teluk Bahang, *Malaysia* 65 c
Teluk Betung = Tanjungkarang Telukbetung, *Indonesia* 62 F3
Teluk Intan, *Malaysia* 65 K3
Teluk Kumbar, *Malaysia* 65 c
Telukbutun, *Indonesia* 62 D3
Telukdalem, *Indonesia* 62 D1
Tema, *Ghana* 83 D5
Temax, *Mexico* 119 C7
Temba, *S. Africa* 89 D4
Tembagapura, *Indonesia* 63 E9
Tembe, *Dem. Rep. of the Congo* 86 C2
Tembe ⌓, *S. Africa* 89 D5
Tembleque, *Spain* 36 F7
Temblor Range, *U.S.A.* 111 K7
Teme →, *U.K.* 15 E5
Temecula, *U.S.A.* 111 M9
Temerloh, *Malaysia* 62 D2
Teminabuan, *Indonesia* 63 E8
Temir, *Kazakhstan* 52 E6
Temirtau, *Kazakhstan* 52 D8
Temirtau, *Russia* 52 D9
Témiscamie →, *Canada* 105 B5
Témiscaming, *Canada* 104 C4
Témiscamingue, L., *Canada* 104 C4
Temnikov, *Russia* 34 C6
Temo →, *Italy* 42 B1
Temosachic, *Mexico* 118 B3
Tempe, *U.S.A.* 109 K8
Témpio Pausánia, *Italy* 42 B2
Tempiute, *U.S.A.* 110 H11
Temple, *U.S.A.* 113 K6
Temple B., *Australia* 94 A3
Templemore, *Ireland* 12 D4
Templeton, *U.S.A.* 110 K6
Templeton →, *Australia* 94 C2
Templin, *Germany* 24 B9
Tempoal, *Mexico* 119 C5
Temryuk, *Russia* 33 K9
Temska →, *Serbia & M.* 44 C6
Temuco, *Chile* 128 D2
Temuka, *N.Z.* 91 L3
Tenabo, *Mexico* 119 C6
Tenaha, *U.S.A.* 113 K7
Tenakee Springs, *U.S.A.* 102 B1
Tenali, *India* 67 L12
Tenancingo, *Mexico* 119 D5
Tenango, *Mexico* 119 D5
Tenasserim, *Burma* 65 F2
Tenasserim □, *Burma* 64 F2
Tenby, *U.K.* 15 F3
Tenda, Colle di, *France* 21 D11
Tendaho, *Ethiopia* 81 E5
Tende, *France* 21 D11
Tendelti, *Sudan* 81 E3
Tendrovskaya Kosa, *Ukraine* 33 J6
Tendukhera, *India* 69 H8
Teneguía, Volcanes de, *Canary Is.* 48 F2
Teneida, *Egypt* 80 B2
Tenenkou, *Mali* 82 C4
Ténéré, *Niger* 83 B7
Tenerife, *Canary Is.* 48 F3
Tenerife, Pico, *Canary Is.* 48 G1
Tenerife Norte ✕ (TFN), *Canary Is.* 48 F3
Tenerife Sur ✕ (TFS), *Canary Is.* 48 F3
Teng Xian, *Guangxi Zhuangzu, China* 59 F8
Teng Xian, *Shandong, China* 57 G9
Tengah, Kepulauan, *Indonesia* 62 F5
Tengchong, *China* 58 E2
Tengchowfu = Penglai, *China* 57 F11
Tenggarong, *Indonesia* 62 E5
Tenggol, Pulau, *Malaysia* 65 K4
Tengiz, Ozero, *Kazakhstan* 52 D7
Tenhult, *Sweden* 11 G8
Teniente Enciso △, *Paraguay* 126 A3
Teniente Rodolfo Marsh, *Antarctica* 5 C18
Tenino, *U.S.A.* 110 D4
Tenkasi, *India* 66 Q10
Tenke, *Katanga, Dem. Rep. of the Congo* 87 E2
Tenke, *Katanga, Dem. Rep. of the Congo* 87 E2
Tenkodogo, *Burkina Faso* 83 C4
Tenna →, *Italy* 41 E10
Tennant Creek, *Australia* 94 B1
Tennessee □, *U.S.A.* 115 H2
Tennessee →, *U.S.A.* 114 G1
Teno, Pta. de, *Canary Is.* 48 F3
Tenom, *Malaysia* 62 C5
Tenosique, *Mexico* 119 D6
Tenryū-Gawa →, *Japan* 55 G8
Tenterden, *U.K.* 15 F8
Tenterfield, *Australia* 95 D5
Teo, *Spain* 36 C2
Teófilo Otoni, *Brazil* 125 G10
Tepa, *Indonesia* 63 F7
Tepalcatepec →, *Mexico* 118 D4
Tepecik, *Bursa, Turkey* 45 F12
Tepecik, *Kütahya, Turkey* 47 B11
Tepehuanes, *Mexico* 118 B3
Tepelenë, *Albania* 44 F4
Tepetongo, *Mexico* 118 C4
Tepic, *Mexico* 118 C4
Teplá, *Czech Rep.* 26 B5
Teplice, *Czech Rep.* 26 A6
Teplyk, *Ukraine* 29 B14
Tepoca, C., *Mexico* 118 A2
Tequila, *Mexico* 118 C4
Ter →, *Spain* 38 C8
Ter Apel, *Neths.* 17 B7
Téra, *Niger* 83 C5
Tera →, *Spain* 36 D5
Teraina, *Kiribati* 97 G11
Terakeka, *Sudan* 81 F3
Téramo, *Italy* 41 F10
Terang, *Australia* 95 F3
Terang, Teluk, *Indonesia* 63 K19
Terazit, Massif de, *Niger* 83 A6
Tercan, *Turkey* 73 C9
Tercero →, *Argentina* 126 C3
Terebovlya, *Ukraine* 33 H3
Teregova, *Romania* 28 E7
Tereida, *Sudan* 81 E3
Terek →, *Russia* 35 J8
Terepaima △, *Venezuela* 121 E6
Tereshka →, *Russia* 34 E8
Teresina, *Brazil* 125 E10
Terespol, *Poland* 31 F10
Teresva, *Ukraine* 29 B8
Terewah, L., *Australia* 95 D4
Terges →, *Portugal* 37 H3
Tergnier, *France* 19 C10
Teridgerie Cr. →, *Australia* 95 E4
Terlizzi, *Italy* 43 A9
Terme, *Turkey* 72 B7
Termez = Termiz, *Uzbekistan* 52 F7
Términi Imerese, *Italy* 42 E6
Términos, L. de, *Mexico* 119 D6
Termiz, *Uzbekistan* 52 F7
Térmoli, *Italy* 41 F12
Ternate, *Indonesia* 63 D7
Terneuzen, *Neths.* 17 C3
Terney, *Russia* 53 E14
Terni, *Italy* 41 F9
Ternitz, *Austria* 26 D9
Ternivka, *Ukraine* 29 B14
Ternopil, *Ukraine* 33 H3
Ternopol = Ternopil, *Ukraine* 33 H3
Terowie, *Australia* 95 E2
Terpní, *Greece* 44 F7
Terra Bella, *U.S.A.* 111 K7
Terra Nova △, *Canada* 105 C9
Terrace, *Canada* 102 C3
Terrace Bay, *Canada* 104 C2
Terracina, *Italy* 42 A6
Terralba, *Italy* 42 C1
Terrasini, *Italy* 42 D6
Terrassa, *Spain* 38 D7
Terrasson-la-Villedieu, *France* 20 C5
Terre Haute, *U.S.A.* 114 F2
Terrebonne B., *U.S.A.* 113 L9
Terrell, *U.S.A.* 113 J6
Terrenceville, *Canada* 105 C9
Terry, *U.S.A.* 112 B2
Terryville, *U.S.A.* 117 E11
Terschelling, *Neths.* 17 A5
Tersko-Kumskiy Kanal, *Russia* 35 H7
Tertenía, *Italy* 42 C2
Terter = Tārtār →, *Azerbaijan* 35 K8
Teruel, *Spain* 38 E3
Teruel □, *Spain* 38 E4
Tervel, *Bulgaria* 45 C11
Tervola, *Finland* 8 C21
Teryaweyna L., *Australia* 95 E3
Tešanj, *Bos.-H.* 28 F3
Teseney, *Eritrea* 81 D4
Tesha →, *Russia* 34 C6
Teshio, *Japan* 54 B10
Teshio-Gawa →, *Japan* 54 B10
Tešica, *Serbia & M.* 44 C5
Tesiyn Gol →, *Mongolia* 60 A4
Teslić, *Bos.-H.* 28 F2
Teslin, *Canada* 102 A2
Teslin →, *Canada* 102 A2
Teslin L., *Canada* 102 A2
Tessalit, *Mali* 83 A5
Tessaoua, *Niger* 83 C6
Tessin, *Germany* 24 A8
Tessit, *Mali* 83 B5
Test →, *U.K.* 15 G6
Testa del Gargano, *Italy* 41 G13
Testigos, Is. Las, *Venezuela* 121 D7
Tét, *Hungary* 28 C2
Têt →, *France* 20 F7
Tetachuck L., *Canada* 102 C3
Tetas, Pta., *Chile* 126 A1
Tete, *Mozam.* 87 F3
Tete □, *Mozam.* 87 F3
Teterev →, *Ukraine* 33 G6
Teterow, *Germany* 24 B8
Teteven, *Bulgaria* 45 D8
Tethul →, *Canada* 102 A6
Tetiyev, *Ukraine* 33 H5
Teton →, *U.S.A.* 108 C8
Tétouan, *Morocco* 78 A4
Tetovo, *Macedonia* 44 D4
Tetyushi, *Russia* 34 C9
Teuco →, *Argentina* 126 B3
Teulada, *Italy* 42 D1
Teulon, *Canada* 103 C9
Teun, *Indonesia* 63 F7
Teutoburger Wald, *Germany* 24 C4
Tevere ⌓, *Italy* 41 F9
Tevere →, *Italy* 41 G9
Teverya, *Israel* 74 C4
Teviot →, *U.K.* 13 F6
Tewantin, *Australia* 95 D5
Tewkesbury, *U.K.* 15 F5
Texada I., *Canada* 102 D4
Texarkana, *Ark., U.S.A.* 113 J8
Texarkana, *Tex., U.S.A.* 113 J7
Texas, *Australia* 95 D5
Texas □, *U.S.A.* 113 K5
Texas City, *U.S.A.* 113 L7
Texel, *Neths.* 17 A4
Texline, *U.S.A.* 113 G3
Texoma, L., *U.S.A.* 113 J6
Teykovo, *Russia* 32 D11
Teza →, *Russia* 34 B5
Tezin, *Afghan.* 68 B3
Teziutlán, *Mexico* 119 D5
Tezpur, *India* 67 F18
Tezzeron L., *Canada* 102 C4
Tha-anne →, *Canada* 103 A10
Tha Deua, *Laos* 64 D4
Tha Deua, *Laos* 64 C3
Tha Pla, *Thailand* 64 D3
Tha Rua, *Thailand* 64 E3
Tha Sala, *Thailand* 65 H2
Tha Song Yang, *Thailand* 64 D1
Thaba Putsoa, *Lesotho* 89 D4
Thabana Ntlenyana, *Lesotho* 89 D4
Thabazimbi, *S. Africa* 89 C4
Thādiq, *Si. Arabia* 70 E5
Thai Binh, *Vietnam* 58 G6
Thai Muang, *Thailand* 65 H2
Thai Nguyen, *Vietnam* 58 G5
Thailand ■, *Asia* 64 E4
Thailand, G. of, *Asia* 65 G3
Thakhek, *Laos* 64 D5
Thal, *Pakistan* 68 C4
Thal Desert, *Pakistan* 68 D4
Thala La = Hkakabo Razi, *Burma* 67 E20
Thalabarivat, *Cambodia* 64 F5
Thallon, *Australia* 95 D4
Thalu, Ko, *Thailand* 65 b
Thalwil, *Switz.* 25 H4
Thames, *N.Z.* 91 G5
Thames →, *Canada* 116 D2
Thames →, *U.K.* 15 F8
Thames →, *U.S.A.* 117 E12
Thames Estuary, *U.K.* 15 F8
Thamesford, *Canada* 116 C4
Thamesville, *Canada* 116 D3
Than, *India* 68 H4
Than Uyen, *Vietnam* 64 B4
Thana Gazi, *India* 68 F7
Thandla, *India* 68 H6
Thane, *India* 66 K8
Thanesar, *India* 68 D7
Thanet, I. of, *U.K.* 15 F9
Thangool, *Australia* 94 C5
Thanh Hoa, *Vietnam* 64 C5
Thanh Hung, *Vietnam* 65 H5
Thanh Pho Ho Chi Minh, *Vietnam* 65 G6
Thanh Thuy, *Vietnam* 64 A5
Thanjavur, *India* 66 P11
Thann, *France* 19 E14
Thano Bula Khan, *Pakistan* 68 G2
Thaolinta L., *Canada* 103 A9
Thaon-les-Vosges, *France* 19 D13
Thap Lan △, *Thailand* 64 E4
Thap Sakae, *Thailand* 65 G2
Thap Than, *Thailand* 64 E2
Thar Desert, *India* 68 F5
Tharad, *India* 68 G4
Thargomindah, *Australia* 95 D3
Tharrawaddy, *Burma* 67 L19
Tharthār, Buḩayrat ath, *Iraq* 70 C4
Tharthār, L. = Tharthār, Buḩayrat ath, *Iraq* 70 C4
Tharthār, W. ath →, *Iraq* 70 C4
Thasopoúla, *Greece* 45 F8
Thásos, *Greece* 45 F8
That Khe, *Vietnam* 58 F6
Thatcher, *Ariz., U.S.A.* 109 K9
Thatcher, *Colo., U.S.A.* 113 G2
Thaton, *Burma* 67 L20
Thau, Bassin de, *France* 20 E7
Thaungdut, *Burma* 67 G19
Thayer, *U.S.A.* 113 G9
Thayetmyo, *Burma* 67 K19
Thazi, *Burma* 67 J20
The Bight, *Bahamas* 121 B4
The Crane, *Barbados* 121 g
The Dalles, *U.S.A.* 108 D3
The Great Divide = Great Dividing Ra., *Australia* 94 C4
The Hague = 's-Gravenhage, *Neths.* 17 B4
The Pas, *Canada* 103 C8
The Range, *Zimbabwe* 87 F3
The Rock, *Australia* 95 F4
The Settlement, *Br. Virgin Is.* 121 e
The Woodlands, *U.S.A.* 113 K7
Thebes = Thívai, *Greece* 46 C5
Thebes, *Egypt* 80 B3
Thedford, *U.S.A.* 112 E4
Theebine, *Australia* 95 D5
Thekulthili L., *Canada* 103 A7
Thelon →, *Canada* 103 A8
Thénezay, *France* 18 F6
Thenon, *France* 20 C5
Theodore, *Australia* 94 C5
Theodore, *Canada* 103 C8
Theodore, *U.S.A.* 115 K1
Theodore Roosevelt △, *U.S.A.* 112 B3
Theodore Roosevelt L., *U.S.A.* 109 K8
Thepha, *Thailand* 65 J3
Thérain →, *France* 19 C9
Theresa, *U.S.A.* 117 B9
Thermaïkós Kólpos, *Greece* 44 F6
Thermí, *Greece* 47 B8
Thermopolis, *U.S.A.* 108 E9
Thermopylae P., *Greece* 46 C4
Thesprotía □, *Greece* 46 B2
Thessalía □, *Greece* 46 B4
Thessalon, *Canada* 104 C3
Thessaloníki, *Greece* 44 F6
Thessaloníki □, *Greece* 44 F7
Thessaloníki ✕ (SKG), *Greece* 44 F7
Thessaloníki, Gulf of = Thermaïkós Kólpos, *Greece* 44 F6
Thessaly = Thessalía □, *Greece* 46 B4
Thetford, *U.K.* 15 E8
Thetford Mines, *Canada* 105 C5
Theun →, *Laos* 64 C5
Theunissen, *S. Africa* 88 D4
Thevenard, *Australia* 95 E1
Thiámis →, *Greece* 46 B2
Thiberville, *France* 18 C7
Thibodaux, *U.S.A.* 113 L9
Thicket Portage, *Canada* 103 B9
Thief River Falls, *U.S.A.* 112 A6
Thiel Mts., *Antarctica* 5 E16
Thiene, *Italy* 41 C8
Thiérache, *France* 19 C10
Thiers, *France* 20 C7
Thiès, *Senegal* 82 C1
Thiesi, *Italy* 42 B1
Thiet, *Sudan* 81 F2
Thika, *Kenya* 86 C4
Thikombia, *Fiji* 91 B9
Thille-Boubacar, *Senegal* 82 B1
Thimphu, *Bhutan* 67 F16
Þingvallavatn, *Iceland* 8 D3
Thionville, *France* 19 C13
Thíra, *Greece* 47 E7
Thirasía, *Greece* 47 E7
Third Cataract, *Sudan* 80 D3
Thirsk, *U.K.* 14 C6
Thiruvananthapuram = Trivandrum, *India* 66 Q10
Thisted, *Denmark* 11 H2
Thistle I., *Australia* 95 F2
Thívai, *Greece* 46 C5
Thiviers, *France* 20 C4
Thizy, *France* 19 F11
Þjórsá →, *Iceland* 8 E3
Thlewiaza →, *Canada* 103 A10
Thmar Puok, *Cambodia* 64 F4
Tho Vinh, *Vietnam* 64 C5
Thoa →, *Canada* 103 A7
Thoen, *Thailand* 64 D2
Thoeng, *Thailand* 64 C3
Thohoyandou, *S. Africa* 85 J6
Tholdi, *Pakistan* 69 B7
Thomas, *U.S.A.* 113 H5
Thomas, L., *Australia* 95 D2
Thomaston, *U.S.A.* 115 J3
Thomasville, *Ala., U.S.A.* 115 K2
Thomasville, *Ga., U.S.A.* 115 K4
Thomasville, *N.C., U.S.A.* 115 H5
Thompson, *Canada* 103 B9
Thompson, *U.S.A.* 117 E9
Thompson →, *Canada* 102 C4
Thompson →, *U.S.A.* 112 F8
Thompson Falls, *U.S.A.* 108 C6
Thompson Pk., *U.S.A.* 108 F2
Thompson Springs, *U.S.A.* 109 G9
Thompsontown, *U.S.A.* 116 F7
Thomson, *U.S.A.* 115 J4
Thomson →, *Australia* 94 C3
Thônes, *France* 21 C10
Thong Yang, *Thailand* 65 b
Thonon-les-Bains, *France* 19 F13
Thorez, *Ukraine* 33 H10
Þórisvatn, *Iceland* 8 D4
Thornaby on Tees, *U.K.* 14 C6
Thornbury, *Canada* 116 B4
Thorne, *U.K.* 14 D7
Thornhill, *Canada* 102 C3
Thorold, *Canada* 116 C5
Þórshöfn, *Iceland* 8 C6
Thouarcé, *France* 18 E6
Thouars, *France* 18 F6

Thouet →, *France* 18 E6
Thouin, C., *Australia* 92 D2
Thousand Oaks, *U.S.A.* 111 L8
Thrace, *Turkey* 45 F10
Thrakikón Pélagos, *Greece* 45 F8
Three Forks, *U.S.A.* 108 D8
Three Gorges Dam, *China* 59 B8
Three Hills, *Canada* 102 C6
Three Hummock I., *Australia* 95 G3
Three Pagodas Pass, *Asia* 64 E2
Three Points, C., *Ghana* 82 E4
Three Rivers, *Calif., U.S.A.* 110 J8
Three Rivers, *Tex., U.S.A.* 113 L5
Three Sisters, *U.S.A.* 108 D3
Three Springs, *Australia* 93 E2
Throssell, L., *Australia* 93 E3
Throssell Ra., *Australia* 92 D3
Thrushton △, *Australia* 95 D4
Thuan Hoa, *Vietnam* 65 H5
Thubun Lakes, *Canada* 103 A6
Thueyts, *France* 21 D8
Thuin, *Belgium* 17 D4
Thuir, *France* 20 F6
Thule = Qaanaaq, *Greenland* 4 B4
Thule Air Base = Uummannaq, *Greenland* 4 B5
Thun, *Switz.* 25 J3
Thunder B., *U.S.A.* 116 B1
Thunder Bay, *Canada* 104 C2
Thunersee, *Switz.* 25 J3
Thung Salaeng Luang △, *Thailand* 64 D3
Thung Song, *Thailand* 65 H2
Thunkar, *Bhutan* 67 F17
Thuong Tra, *Vietnam* 64 D6
Thur →, *Switz.* 25 H5
Thurgau □, *Switz.* 25 H5
Thüringen □, *Germany* 24 D6
Thüringer Wald, *Germany* 24 E6
Thurles, *Ireland* 12 D4
Thurn P., *Austria* 26 D5
Thurrock □, *U.K.* 15 F8
Thursday I., *Australia* 94 A3
Thurso, *Canada* 104 C4
Thurso, *U.K.* 13 C5
Thurso →, *U.K.* 13 C5
Thurston I., *Antarctica* 5 D16
Thury-Harcourt, *France* 18 D6
Thutade L., *Canada* 102 B3
Thy, *Denmark* 11 H2
Thyborøn, *Denmark* 11 H2
Thyolo, *Malawi* 87 F4
Ti-n-Amzi →, *Niger* 83 B5
Ti-n-Barraouene, O. →, *Africa* 83 B5
Ti-n-Zaouatene, *Algeria* 83 B5
Ti Tree, *Australia* 94 C1
Tiadiaye, *Senegal* 82 C1
Tian Shan, *Asia* 60 B3
Tianchang, *China* 59 A12
Tiandeng, *China* 58 F6
Tiandong, *China* 58 F6
Tian'e, *China* 58 E6
Tianhe, *China* 58 E7
Tianjin, *China* 57 E9
Tiankoura, *Burkina Faso* 82 C4
Tianlin, *China* 58 E6
Tianmen, *China* 59 B9
Tianquan, *China* 58 B4
Tianshui, *China* 56 G3
Tiantai, *China* 59 C13
Tianyang, *China* 58 F6
Tianyar, *Indonesia* 63 J18
Tianzhen, *China* 56 D8
Tianzhu, *China* 58 D7
Tianzhuangtai, *China* 57 D12
Tiaret, *Algeria* 78 A6
Tiassalé, *Ivory C.* 82 D4
Tibagi, *Brazil* 127 A5
Tibagi →, *Brazil* 127 A5
Tibati, *Cameroon* 83 D7
Tibe, *Ethiopia* 81 F4
Tiber = Tevere →, *Italy* 41 G9
Tiberias = Teverya, *Israel* 74 C4
Tiberias, L. = Yam Kinneret, *Israel* 74 C4
Tibesti, *Chad* 79 D9
Tibet = Xizang Zizhiqu □, *China* 60 C3
Tibet, Plateau of, *Asia* 50 F12
Tibiao, *Phil.* 61 F5
Tibiri, *Niger* 83 C6
Ţibleş, Vf., *Romania* 29 C9
Ţibleşului, Munţii, *Romania* 29 C9
Tibnī, *Syria* 70 C3
Tibooburra, *Australia* 95 D3
Tibro, *Sweden* 11 F8
Tiburón, I., *Mexico* 118 B2
Ticao I., *Phil.* 61 E5
Tîchît, *Mauritania* 82 B3
Ticho, *Ethiopia* 81 F4
Ticino □, *Switz.* 25 J4
Ticino →, *Italy* 25 K5
Ticleni, *Romania* 29 F8
Ticonderoga, *U.S.A.* 117 C11
Ticul, *Mexico* 119 C7
Tidaholm, *Sweden* 11 F7
Tidan, *Sweden* 11 F8
Tiddim, *Burma* 67 H18
Tidioute, *U.S.A.* 116 E5
Tidjikja, *Mauritania* 82 B2
Tidore, *Indonesia* 63 D7
Tiébissou, *Ivory C.* 82 D3
Tiel, *Neths.* 17 C5
Tiel, *Senegal* 82 C1
Tieling, *China* 57 C12
Tielt, *Belgium* 17 C3
Tien Shan = Tian Shan, *Asia* 60 B3
Tien-tsin = Tianjin, *China* 57 E9
Tien Yen, *Vietnam* 64 B6
T'ienching = Tianjin, *China* 57 E9
Tienen, *Belgium* 17 D4
Tiénigbé, *Ivory C.* 82 D3
Tientsin = Tianjin, *China* 57 E9
Tieri, *Australia* 94 C4
Tierp, *Sweden* 10 D11
Tierra Amarilla, *Chile* 126 B1
Tierra Amarilla, *U.S.A.* 109 H10
Tierra Colorada, *Mexico* 119 D5
Tierra de Barros, *Spain* 37 G4
Tierra de Campos, *Spain* 36 C6
Tierra del Fuego, I. Gr. de, *Argentina* 128 G3
Tiétar →, *Spain* 36 F4
Tieté →, *Brazil* 127 A5
Tiffin, *U.S.A.* 114 E4
Tifton, *U.S.A.* 115 K4
Tifu, *Indonesia* 63 E7
Tighina, *Moldova* 29 D14
Tigil, *Russia* 53 D16
Tignish, *Canada* 105 C7
Tigray □, *Ethiopia* 81 E4
Tigre →, *Peru* 124 D4
Tigre →, *Venezuela* 124 B6
Tigris = Dijlah, Nahr →, *Asia* 70 D5
Tigveni, *Romania* 29 E9
Tigyaing, *Burma* 67 H20
Tîh, Gebel el, *Egypt* 80 B3
Tijara, *India* 68 F7
Tijuana, *Mexico* 111 N9
Tikal, *Guatemala* 120 C2
Tikal △, *Guatemala* 120 C2
Tikamgarh, *India* 69 G8
Tikaré, *Burkina Faso* 83 C4
Tikhoretsk, *Russia* 35 H5
Tikhvin, *Russia* 32 C7
Tikiraqjuaq = Whale Cove, *Canada* 103 A10
Tiko, *Cameroon* 83 E6
Tikrīt, *Iraq* 70 C4
Tiksi, *Russia* 53 B13
Tilamuta, *Indonesia* 63 D6
Tilburg, *Neths.* 17 C5
Tilbury, *Canada* 116 D2
Tilbury, *U.K.* 15 F8
Tilcara, *Argentina* 126 A2
Tilden, *U.S.A.* 112 D6
Tilemses, *Niger* 83 B5
Tilemsi, Vallée du, *Mali* 83 B5
Tilhar, *India* 69 F8
Tilichiki, *Russia* 53 C17
Tílissos, *Greece* 49 D7
Till →, *U.K.* 14 B5
Tillabéri, *Niger* 83 C5
Tillamook, *U.S.A.* 108 D2
Tillberga, *Sweden* 10 E10
Tillia, *Niger* 83 B5
Tillsonburg, *Canada* 116 D4
Tillyeria, *Cyprus* 49 D11
Tilogne, *Senegal* 82 B2
Tílos, *Greece* 47 E9
Tilpa, *Australia* 95 E3
Tilt →, *U.K.* 13 E5
Tilton, *U.S.A.* 117 C13
Tiltonsville, *U.S.A.* 116 F4
Tim, *Denmark* 11 H2
Timagami, L., *Canada* 104 C3
Timanfaya △, *Canary Is.* 48 F6
Timaru, *N.Z.* 91 L3
Timashevo, *Russia* 34 D10
Timashevsk, *Russia* 35 H4
Timau, *Kenya* 86 B4
Timbákion, *Greece* 49 D6
Timbedgha, *Mauritania* 82 B3
Timber Creek, *Australia* 92 C5
Timber Lake, *U.S.A.* 112 C4
Timber Mt., *U.S.A.* 110 H10
Timbo, *Guinea* 82 C2
Timbo, *Liberia* 82 D3
Timbuktu = Tombouctou, *Mali* 82 B4
Timeiaouine, *Algeria* 83 A5
Timétrine, Mts., *Mali* 83 B4
Timfi Óros, *Greece* 46 B2
Timfristós, Óros, *Greece* 46 C3
Timi, *Cyprus* 49 E11
Tîmia, *Niger* 83 B6
Timimoun, *Algeria* 78 C6
Timirist, Râs, *Mauritania* 82 B1
Timiş = Tamis →, *Serbia & M.* 28 F5
Timiş □, *Romania* 28 E6
Timiskaming, L. = Témiscamingue, L., *Canada* 104 C4
Timişoara, *Romania* 28 E6
Timmersdala, *Sweden* 11 F7
Timmins, *Canada* 104 C3
Timok →, *Serbia & M.* 44 B6
Timor, *Asia* 63 F7
Timor Leste = East Timor ■, *Asia* 63 F7
Timor Sea, *Ind. Oc.* 92 B4
Timrå, *Sweden* 10 B11
Tin Can Bay, *Australia* 95 D5
Tin Ethisane, *Mali* 83 B4
Tin Gornai, *Mali* 83 B4
Tin Mt., *U.S.A.* 110 J9
Tina →, *S. Africa* 89 E4
Tîna, Khalîg el, *Egypt* 80 A3
Tinaca Pt., *Phil.* 61 J6
Tinajo, *Canary Is.* 48 E6
Tinca, *Romania* 28 D6
Tindal, *Australia* 92 B5
Tindouf, *Algeria* 78 C4
Tinée →, *France* 21 E11
Tineo, *Spain* 36 B4
Tinfunque △, *Paraguay* 126 A3
Ting Jiang →, *China* 59 E11
Tinggi, Pulau, *Malaysia* 65 L5
Tinglev, *Denmark* 11 K3
Tingo Maria, *Peru* 124 E3
Tingrela, *Ivory C.* 82 C3
Tingsryd, *Sweden* 11 H9
Tingstäde, *Sweden* 11 G12
Tinh Bien, *Vietnam* 65 G5
Tinnevelly = Tirunelveli, *India* 66 Q10
Tinogasta, *Argentina* 126 B2
Tínos, *Greece* 47 D7
Tiñoso, C., *Spain* 39 H3
Tinpahar, *India* 69 G12
Tintina, *Argentina* 126 B3
Tintinara, *Australia* 95 F3
Tintioulé, *Guinea* 82 C3
Tinto →, *Spain* 37 H4
Tioga, *N. Dak., U.S.A.* 112 A3
Tioga, *Pa., U.S.A.* 116 E7
Tioman, Pulau, *Malaysia* 65 L5
Tione di Trento, *Italy* 40 B7
Tionesta, *U.S.A.* 116 E5
Tior, *Sudan* 81 F3
Tipongpani, *India* 67 F19
Tipperary, *Ireland* 12 D3
Tipperary □, *Ireland* 12 D4
Tipton, *Calif., U.S.A.* 110 J7
Tipton, *Iowa, U.S.A.* 112 E9
Tipton Mt., *U.S.A.* 111 K12
Tiptonville, *U.S.A.* 113 G10
Tīrān, *Iran* 71 C6
Tīrān, *Si. Arabia* 80 B3
Tiranë, *Albania* 44 E3
Tiranë ✕ (TIA), *Albania* 43 A12
Tirano, *Italy* 40 B7
Tiraspol, *Moldova* 29 D14
Tirdout, *Mali* 83 B4
Tire, *Turkey* 47 C9
Tirebolu, *Turkey* 73 B8
Tiree, *U.K.* 13 E2
Tiree, Passage of, *U.K.* 13 E2
Tîrgovişte = Târgovişte, *Romania* 29 F10
Tîrgu-Jiu = Târgu-Jiu, *Romania* 29 E8
Tîrgu Mureş = Târgu Mureş, *Romania* 29 D9
Tirich Mir, *Pakistan* 66 A7
Tiriolo, *Italy* 43 D9
Tiriro, *Guinea* 82 C3
Tiritiri o te Moana = Southern Alps, *N.Z.* 91 K3
Tírnavos, *Greece* 46 B4
Tirodi, *India* 66 J11
Tirol □, *Austria* 26 D3
Tirschenreuth, *Germany* 25 F8
Tirso →, *Italy* 42 C1
Tirstrup, *Denmark* 11 H4
Tiruchchirappalli, *India* 66 P11
Tirunelveli, *India* 66 Q10
Tirupati, *India* 66 N11
Tiruppur, *India* 66 P10
Tiruvannamalai, *India* 66 N11
Tisa, *India* 68 C7
Tisa →, *Serbia & M.* 28 E5
Tisdale, *Canada* 103 C8
Tishomingo, *U.S.A.* 113 H6
Tisjön, *Sweden* 10 D7
Tisnaren, *Sweden* 11 F9
Tišnov, *Czech Rep.* 27 B9
Tisovec, *Slovak Rep.* 27 C12
Tisza = Tisa →, *Serbia & M.* 28 E5
Tiszaföldvár, *Hungary* 28 D5
Tiszafüred, *Hungary* 28 C5
Tiszalök, *Hungary* 28 B6
Tiszavasvári, *Hungary* 28 C6
Tit-Ary, *Russia* 53 B13
Titaguas, *Spain* 38 F3
Titao, *Burkina Faso* 83 C4
Titel, *Serbia & M.* 28 E5
Tithwal, *Pakistan* 69 B5
Titicaca, L., *S. Amer.* 124 G5
Titisee, *Germany* 25 H4
Titiwa, *Nigeria* 83 C7
Tito, *Italy* 43 B8
Titova Korenica, *Croatia* 41 D12
Titu, *Romania* 29 F10
Titule, *Dem. Rep. of the Congo* 86 B2
Titusville, *Fla., U.S.A.* 115 L5
Titusville, *Pa., U.S.A.* 116 E5
Tivaouane, *Senegal* 82 C1
Tivat, *Serbia & M.* 44 D2
Tivedens △, *Sweden* 11 F8
Tiverton, *U.K.* 15 G4
Tívoli, *Italy* 41 G9
Tiyo, *Eritrea* 81 E5
Tizi-Ouzou, *Algeria* 78 A6
Tizimín, *Mexico* 119 C7
Tjæreborg, *Denmark* 11 J2
Tjällmo, *Sweden* 11 F9
Tjeggelvas, *Sweden* 8 C17
Tjieggelvas = Tjeggelvas, *Sweden* 8 C17
Tjirebon = Cirebon, *Indonesia* 63 G13
Tjluring, *Indonesia* 63 J17
Tjörn, *Sweden* 11 F5
Tkibuli = Tqibuli, *Georgia* 35 J6
Tkvarcheli = Tqvarcheli, *Georgia* 35 J5
Tlacotalpan, *Mexico* 119 D5
Tlahualilo, *Mexico* 118 B4
Tlaquepaque, *Mexico* 118 C4
Tlaxcala, *Mexico* 119 D5
Tlaxcala □, *Mexico* 119 D5
Tlaxiaco, *Mexico* 119 D5
Tlemcen, *Algeria* 78 B5
Tlumach, *Ukraine* 29 B10
Tłuszcz, *Poland* 31 F8
Tlyarata, *Russia* 35 J8
To Bong, *Vietnam* 64 F7
Toa Payoh, *Singapore* 65 d
Toad →, *Canada* 102 B4
Toad River, *Canada* 102 B3
Toamasina, *Madag.* 89 B8
Toamasina □, *Madag.* 89 B8
Toay, *Argentina* 126 D3
Toba, *China* 58 B1
Toba, *Japan* 55 G8
Toba, Danau, *Indonesia* 62 D1
Toba Kakar, *Pakistan* 68 D3
Toba Tek Singh, *Pakistan* 68 D5
Tobago, *Trin. & Tob.* 121 D7
Tobarra, *Spain* 39 G3
Tobelo, *Indonesia* 63 D7
Tobermory, *Canada* 116 A3
Tobermory, *U.K.* 13 E2
Tobi, *Pac. Oc.* 63 D8
Tobin, *U.S.A.* 110 F5
Tobin, L., *Australia* 92 D4
Tobin L., *Canada* 103 C8
Toblach = Dobbiaco, *Italy* 41 B9
Toboali, *Indonesia* 62 E3
Tobol →, *Russia* 52 D7
Toboli, *Indonesia* 63 E6
Tobolsk, *Russia* 52 D7
Tobor, *Senegal* 82 C1
Tobruk = Tubruq, *Libya* 79 B10
Tobyhanna, *U.S.A.* 117 E9
Tobyl = Tobol →, *Russia* 52 D7
Tocantinópolis, *Brazil* 125 E9
Tocantins □, *Brazil* 125 F9
Tocantins →, *Brazil* 125 D9
Toccoa, *U.S.A.* 115 H4
Toce →, *Italy* 40 C5
Tochi →, *Pakistan* 68 C4
Tochigi, *Japan* 55 F9
Tochigi □, *Japan* 55 F9
Tocina, *Spain* 37 H5
Töcksfors, *Sweden* 10 E5
Toco, *Trin. & Tob.* 125 K16
Toconao, *Chile* 126 A2
Tocopilla, *Chile* 126 A1
Tocumwal, *Australia* 95 F4
Tocuyo →, *Venezuela* 124 A5
Todd →, *Australia* 94 C2
Todeli, *Indonesia* 63 E6
Todenyang, *Kenya* 86 B4
Todgarh, *India* 68 G5
Todi, *Italy* 41 F9
Todos os Santos, B. de, *Brazil* 125 F11
Todos Santos, *Mexico* 118 C2
Todtnau, *Germany* 25 H3
Toe Hd., *U.K.* 13 D1
Toecé, *Burkina Faso* 83 C4
Tofield, *Canada* 102 C6
Tofino, *Canada* 102 D3
Töfsingdalens △, *Sweden* 10 B6
Tofua, *Tonga* 91 D11
Tōgane, *Japan* 55 G10
Togba, *Mauritania* 82 B2
Togian, Kepulauan, *Indonesia* 63 E6
Togliatti, *Russia* 34 D9
Togo ■, *W. Afr.* 83 D5
Togtoh, *China* 56 D6
Tohma →, *Turkey* 72 C7
Tōhoku □, *Japan* 54 E10
Töhöm, *Mongolia* 56 B5
Toinya, *Sudan* 81 F2
Toiyabe Range, *U.S.A.* 108 G5
Tojikiston = Tajikistan ■, *Asia* 52 F8
Tojo, *Indonesia* 63 E6
Tōjō, *Japan* 55 G6
Tok, *U.S.A.* 100 B5
Tok-do, *Asia* 55 F5
Tokachi-Dake, *Japan* 54 C11
Tokachi-Gawa →, *Japan* 54 C11
Tokaj, *Hungary* 28 B6
Tokala, *Indonesia* 63 E6
Tōkamachi, *Japan* 55 F9
Tokanui, *N.Z.* 91 M2
Tokar, *Sudan* 80 D4
Tokara-Rettō, *Japan* 55 K4
Tokarahi, *N.Z.* 91 L3
Tokashiki-Shima, *Japan* 55 L3
Tokat, *Turkey* 72 B7
Tŏkch'ŏn, *N. Korea* 57 E14
Tokeland, *U.S.A.* 110 D3
Tokelau Is., *Pac. Oc.* 96 H10
Tokmak, *Kyrgyzstan* 52 E8
Tokmak, *Ukraine* 33 J8
Toko Ra., *Australia* 94 C2
Tokoro-Gawa →, *Japan* 54 B12
Tokuno-Shima, *Japan* 55 L4
Tokushima, *Japan* 55 G7
Tokushima □, *Japan* 55 H7
Tokuyama, *Japan* 55 G5
Tōkyō, *Japan* 55 G9
Tolaga Bay, *N.Z.* 91 H7
Tolbukhin = Dobrich, *Bulgaria* 45 C11
Toledo, *Brazil* 127 A5
Toledo, *Spain* 36 F6
Toledo, *Ohio, U.S.A.* 114 E4
Toledo, *Oreg., U.S.A.* 108 D2
Toledo, *Wash., U.S.A.* 108 C2
Toledo, Montes de, *Spain* 37 F6
Toledo Bend Reservoir, *U.S.A.* 113 K8
Tolentino, *Italy* 41 E10
Tolfa, *Italy* 41 F8
Tolga, *Australia* 94 B4
Toliara, *Madag.* 89 C7
Toliara □, *Madag.* 89 C8
Tolima, *Colombia* 124 C3
Tolitoli, *Indonesia* 63 D6
Tolkmicko, *Poland* 30 D6
Tollarp, *Sweden* 11 J7
Tollensesee, *Germany* 24 B9
Tollhouse, *U.S.A.* 110 H7
Tolmachevo, *Russia* 32 C5
Tolmezzo, *Italy* 41 B10
Tolmin, *Slovenia* 41 B10
Tolna, *Hungary* 28 D3
Tolna □, *Hungary* 28 D3
Tolo, Teluk, *Indonesia* 63 E6
Tolochin = Talachyn, *Belarus* 32 E5
Tolosa, *Spain* 38 B2
Tolox, *Spain* 37 J6
Toluca, *Mexico* 119 D5
Tom Burke, *S. Africa* 89 C4
Tom Price, *Australia* 92 D2
Toma, *Burkina Faso* 82 C4
Tomah, *U.S.A.* 112 D9
Tomahawk, *U.S.A.* 112 C10
Tomai, *Moldova* 29 D13
Tomakomai, *Japan* 54 C10
Tomales, *U.S.A.* 110 G4
Tomales B., *U.S.A.* 110 G3
Tomar, *Portugal* 37 F2
Tómaros, Óros, *Greece* 46 B2
Tomarza, *Turkey* 72 C6
Tomashevka, *Belarus* 31 G10
Tomashpil, *Ukraine* 29 B13
Tomaszów Lubelski, *Poland* 31 H10
Tomaszów Mazowiecki, *Poland* 31 G7
Tomatlán, *Mexico* 118 D3
Tombadonkéa, *Guinea* 82 C2
Tombador, Serra do, *Brazil* 124 F7
Tombe, *Sudan* 81 F3
Tombigbee →, *U.S.A.* 115 K2
Tombouctou, *Mali* 82 B4
Tombstone, *U.S.A.* 109 L8
Tombua, *Angola* 88 B1
Tomé, *Chile* 126 D1
Tomelilla, *Sweden* 11 J7
Tomelloso, *Spain* 37 F7
Tomini, *Indonesia* 63 D6
Tomini, Teluk, *Indonesia* 63 E6
Tominian, *Mali* 82 C4
Tomiño, *Spain* 36 D2
Tomintoul, *U.K.* 13 D5
Tomislavgrad, *Bos.-H.* 28 G2
Tomkinson Ranges, *Australia* 93 E4
Tommot, *Russia* 53 D13
Tomnop Ta Suos, *Cambodia* 65 G5
Tomo →, *Colombia* 124 B5
Toms Place, *U.S.A.* 110 H8
Toms River, *U.S.A.* 117 G10
Tomsk, *Russia* 52 D9
Tomtabacken, *Sweden* 11 G8
Tona, *Spain* 38 D7
Tonalá, *Mexico* 119 D6
Tonale, Passo del, *Italy* 40 B7
Tonantins, *Brazil* 124 D5
Tonasket, *U.S.A.* 108 B4
Tonawanda, *U.S.A.* 116 D6
Tonb, *Iran* 71 E7
Tonbridge, *U.K.* 15 F8
Tondano, *Indonesia* 63 D6
Tondela, *Portugal* 36 E2
Tønder, *Denmark* 11 K2
Tondi Kiwindi, *Niger* 83 C5
Tondibi, *Mali* 83 B4
Tondoro, *Namibia* 88 B2
Tone →, *Australia* 93 F2
Tone-Gawa →, *Japan* 55 F9
Tonekābon, *Iran* 71 B6
Tong Xian, *China* 56 E9
Tongā, *Sudan* 81 F3
Tonga ■, *Pac. Oc.* 91 D11
Tonga Trench, *Pac. Oc.* 96 J10
Tongaat, *S. Africa* 89 D5
Tong'an, *China* 59 E12
Tongareva, *Cook Is.* 97 H12
Tongariro △, *N.Z.* 91 H5
Tongatapu Group, *Tonga* 91 E12
Tongbai, *China* 59 A9
Tongcheng, *Anhui, China* 59 B11
Tongcheng, *Hubei, China* 59 C9
Tongchŏn-ni, *N. Korea* 57 E14
Tongchuan, *China* 56 G5
Tongdao, *China* 58 D7
Tongeren, *Belgium* 17 D5
Tonggu, *China* 59 C10
Tongguan, *China* 56 G6
Tonghae, *S. Korea* 57 F15
Tonghai, *China* 58 E4
Tonghua, *China* 57 D13
Tongjiang, *China* 58 B6
Tongjosŏn Man, *N. Korea* 57 E15
Tongking, G. of = Tonkin, G. of, *Asia* 60 E5
Tongliang, *China* 58 C6
Tongliao, *China* 57 C12
Tongling, *China* 59 B11
Tonglu, *China* 59 C12
Tongnae, *S. Korea* 57 G15
Tongnan = Anyue, *China* 58 B5
Tongobory, *Madag.* 89 C7
Tongoy, *Chile* 126 C1
Tongren, *China* 58 D7
Tongres = Tongeren, *Belgium* 17 D5
Tongsa Dzong, *Bhutan* 67 F17
Tongue, *U.K.* 13 C4
Tongue →, *U.S.A.* 112 B2
Tongwei, *China* 56 G3
Tongxiang, *China* 59 B13
Tongxin, *China* 56 F3
Tongyang, *N. Korea* 57 E14
Tongyu, *China* 57 B12
Tongzi, *China* 58 C6
Tonj, *Sudan* 81 F2
Tonj →, *Sudan* 81 F2
Tonk, *India* 68 F6
Tonkawa, *U.S.A.* 113 G6
Tonkin = Bac Phan, *Vietnam* 64 B5
Tonkin, G. of, *Asia* 60 E5
Tonle Sap, *Cambodia* 64 F4
Tonnay-Charente, *France* 20 C3
Tonneins, *France* 20 D4
Tonnerre, *France* 19 E10
Tönning, *Germany* 24 A4
Tono, *Japan* 54 E10
Tonopah, *U.S.A.* 109 G5
Tonosí, *Panama* 120 E3
Tons →, *Haryana, India* 68 D7
Tons →, *Ut. P., India* 69 F10
Tønsberg, *Norway* 9 G14
Tonto ⌂, *U.S.A.* 109 K8
Tonya, *Turkey* 73 B8
Toobanna, *Australia* 94 B4
Toodyay, *Australia* 93 F2
Tooele, *U.S.A.* 108 F7
Toompine, *Australia* 95 D3
Toora, *Australia* 95 F4
Toora-Khem, *Russia* 53 D10
Toowoomba, *Australia* 95 D5
Top Springs, *Australia* 92 C5
Topalu, *Romania* 29 F13

Topaz, *U.S.A.* 110 G7
Topeka, *U.S.A.* 112 F7
Topl'a →, *Slovak Rep.* 27 C14
Topley, *Canada* 102 C3
Toplica →, *Serbia & M.* 44 C5
Toplița, *Romania* 29 D10
Topocalma, Pta., *Chile* 126 C1
Topock, *U.S.A.* 111 L12
Topola, *Serbia & M.* 44 B4
Topolčani, *Macedonia* 44 E5
Topol'čany, *Slovak Rep.* 27 C11
Topolnitsa →, *Bulgaria* 45 D8
Topolobampo, *Mexico* 118 B3
Topoloveni, *Romania* 29 F10
Topolovgrad, *Bulgaria* 45 D10
Topolvățu Mare, *Romania* 28 E6
Toppenish, *U.S.A.* 108 C3
Topraisar, *Romania* 29 F13
Topusko, *Croatia* 41 C12
Torà, *Spain* 38 D6
Tora Kit, *Sudan* 81 E3
Toraka Vestale, *Madag.* 89 B7
Torata, *Peru* 124 G4
Torbalı, *Turkey* 47 C9
Torbat-e Heydārīyeh, *Iran* 71 C8
Torbat-e Jām, *Iran* 71 C9
Torbay, *Canada* 105 C9
Torbay □, *U.K.* 15 G4
Torbjörntorp, *Sweden* 11 F7
Tordesillas, *Spain* 36 D6
Töreboda, *Sweden* 11 F8
Torekov, *Sweden* 11 H6
Torellò, *Spain* 38 C7
Toreno, *Spain* 36 C4
Torfaen □, *U.K.* 15 F4
Torgau, *Germany* 24 D8
Torgelow, *Germany* 24 B10
Torhamn, *Sweden* 11 H9
Torhout, *Belgium* 17 C3
Torhovytsya, *Ukraine* 29 B10
Tori, *Ethiopia* 81 F3
Tori-Shima, *Japan* 55 J10
Torigni-sur-Vire, *France* 18 C6
Torija, *Spain* 38 E1
Torin, *Mexico* 118 B2
Torino, *Italy* 40 C4
Torit, *Sudan* 81 G3
Torkamān, *Iran* 70 B5
Torkovichi, *Russia* 32 C6
Tormac, *Romania* 28 E6
Tormes →, *Spain* 36 D4
Tornado Mt., *Canada* 102 D6
Tornal'a, *Slovak Rep.* 27 C13
Torneå = Tornio, *Finland* 8 D21
Torneälven →, *Europe* 8 D21
Torneträsk, *Sweden* 8 B18
Tornio, *Finland* 8 D21
Tornionjoki = Torneälven →, *Europe* 8 D21
Tornquist, *Argentina* 126 D3
Toro, *Baleares, Spain* 48 B11
Toro, *Zamora, Spain* 36 D5
Torö, *Sweden* 11 F11
Toro ⌂, *Uganda* 86 C3
Toro, Cerro del, *Chile* 126 B2
Toro Pk., *U.S.A.* 111 M10
Törökszentmiklós, *Hungary* 28 C5
Toronîos Kólpos, *Greece* 44 F7
Toronto, *Canada* 116 C5
Toronto, *U.S.A.* 116 F4
Toronto Lester B. Pearson International ✕ (YYZ), *Canada* 116 C5
Toropets, *Russia* 32 D6
Tororo, *Uganda* 86 B3
Toros Dağları, *Turkey* 70 B2
Torpa, *India* 69 H11
Torquay, *U.K.* 15 G4
Torquemada, *Spain* 36 C6
Torrance, *U.S.A.* 111 M8
Torrão, *Portugal* 37 G2
Torre Annunziata, *Italy* 43 B7
Torre de Moncorvo, *Portugal* 36 D3
Torre del Campo, *Spain* 37 H7
Torre del Greco, *Italy* 43 B7
Torre del Mar, *Spain* 37 J6
Torre-Pacheco, *Spain* 39 H4
Torre Péllice, *Italy* 40 D4
Torreblanca, *Spain* 38 E5
Torrecampo, *Spain* 37 G6
Torrecilla en Cameros, *Spain* 38 C2
Torredembarra, *Spain* 38 D6
Torredonjimeno, *Spain* 37 H7
Torrejón de Ardoz, *Spain* 36 E7
Torrejoncillo, *Spain* 36 F4
Torrelaguna, *Spain* 36 E7
Torrelavega, *Spain* 36 B6
Torremaggiore, *Italy* 41 G12
Torremolinos, *Spain* 37 J6
Torrens, L., *Australia* 95 E2
Torrens Cr. →, *Australia* 94 C4
Torrens Creek, *Australia* 94 C4
Torrent, *Spain* 39 F4
Torrenueva, *Spain* 37 G7
Torreón, *Mexico* 118 B4
Torreperogil, *Spain* 37 G7
Torres, *Brazil* 127 B5
Torres, *Mexico* 118 B2
Torres Novas, *Portugal* 37 F2
Torres Strait, *Australia* 96 H6
Torres Vedras, *Portugal* 37 F1
Torrevieja, *Spain* 39 H4
Torrey, *U.S.A.* 109 G8
Torridge →, *U.K.* 15 G3
Torridon, L., *U.K.* 13 D3
Torrijos, *Spain* 36 F6
Tørring, *Denmark* 11 J3
Torrington, *Conn., U.S.A.* 117 E11
Torrington, *Wyo., U.S.A.* 112 D2
Torroella de Montgrì, *Spain* 38 C8
Torrox, *Spain* 37 J7
Torsås, *Sweden* 11 H9
Torsby, *Sweden* 10 D6
Torshälla, *Sweden* 10 E10
Tórshavn, *Færoe Is.* 8 E9
Torslanda, *Sweden* 11 G5
Torsö, *Sweden* 11 F7
Tortola, *Br. Virgin Is.* 121 e
Tórtoles de Esgueva, *Spain* 36 D6
Tortolì, *Italy* 42 C2
Tortona, *Italy* 40 D5
Tortorici, *Italy* 43 D7
Tortosa, *Spain* 38 E5
Tortosa, C., *Spain* 38 E5
Tortosendo, *Portugal* 36 E3
Tortue, I. de la, *Haiti* 121 B5
Tortuguero △, *Costa Rica* 120 D3
Tortum, *Turkey* 73 B9
Ţorūd, *Iran* 71 C7
Torul, *Turkey* 73 B8
Toruń, *Poland* 31 E5
Torun, *Ukraine* 29 B8
Tory I., *Ireland* 12 A3
Torysa →, *Slovak Rep.* 27 C14
Torzhok, *Russia* 32 D8
Torzym, *Poland* 31 F2
Tosa, *Japan* 55 H6
Tosa-Shimizu, *Japan* 55 H6
Tosa-Wan, *Japan* 55 H6
Toscana □, *Italy* 40 E8
Toscano, Arcipelago, *Italy* 40 F7
Toshkent, *Uzbekistan* 52 E7
Tosno, *Russia* 32 C6
Tossa de Mar, *Spain* 38 D7
Tösse, *Sweden* 11 F6
Tostado, *Argentina* 126 B3
Tostedt, *Germany* 24 B5
Tostón, Pta. de, *Canary Is.* 48 F5
Tosu, *Japan* 55 H5
Tosya, *Turkey* 72 B6
Toszek, *Poland* 31 H5
Totana, *Spain* 39 H3
Totebo, *Sweden* 11 G10
Toteng, *Botswana* 88 C3
Tôtes, *France* 18 C8
Tótkomlós, *Hungary* 28 D5
Totma, *Russia* 52 C5
Totnes, *U.K.* 15 G4
Totness, *Suriname* 125 B7
Toto, *Nigeria* 83 D6
Totonicapán, *Guatemala* 120 D1
Totten Glacier, *Antarctica* 5 C8
Tottenham, *Australia* 95 E4
Tottenham, *Canada* 116 B5
Tottori, *Japan* 55 G7
Tottori □, *Japan* 55 G7
Touaret, *Niger* 83 A6
Touba, *Ivory C.* 82 D3
Touba, *Senegal* 82 C1
Toubkal, Djebel, *Morocco* 78 B4
Toucy, *France* 19 E10
Tougan, *Burkina Faso* 82 C4
Touggourt, *Algeria* 78 B7
Tougouri, *Burkina Faso* 83 C4
Tougué, *Guinea* 82 C2
Toukoto, *Mali* 82 C3
Toul, *France* 19 D12
Toulepleu, *Ivory C.* 82 D3
Toulon, *France* 21 E9
Toulouse, *France* 20 E5
Toulouse Blagnac ✕ (TLS), *France* 20 E5
Toummo, *Niger* 79 D8
Toumodi, *Ivory C.* 82 D3
Tounan, *Taiwan* 59 F13
Toungo, *Nigeria* 83 D7
Toungoo, *Burma* 67 K20
Touques →, *France* 18 C7
Touraine, *France* 18 E7
Tourcoing, *France* 19 B10
Touriñán, C., *Spain* 36 B1
Tournai, *Belgium* 17 D3
Tournan-en-Brie, *France* 19 D9
Tournay, *France* 20 E4
Tournon-St-Martin, *France* 18 F7
Tournon-sur-Rhône, *France* 21 C8
Tournus, *France* 19 F11
Tours, *France* 18 E7
Toussora, Mt., *C.A.R.* 84 C4
Touws →, *S. Africa* 88 E3
Touwsrivier, *S. Africa* 88 E3
Tovarkovskiy, *Russia* 32 F10
Tovste, *Ukraine* 29 B10
Tovuz, *Azerbaijan* 35 K7
Towada, *Japan* 54 D10
Towada-Hachimantai △, *Japan* 54 D10
Towada-Ko, *Japan* 54 D10
Towanda, *U.S.A.* 117 E8
Towang, *India* 67 F17
Tower, *U.S.A.* 112 B8
Towerhill Cr. →, *Australia* 94 C3
Towner, *U.S.A.* 112 A4
Townsend, *U.S.A.* 108 C8
Townshend I., *Australia* 94 C5
Townsville, *Australia* 94 B4
Towraghondi, *Afghan.* 66 B3
Towson, *U.S.A.* 114 F7
Towuti, Danau, *Indonesia* 63 E6
Toya-Ko, *Japan* 54 C10
Toyama, *Japan* 55 F8
Toyama □, *Japan* 55 F8
Toyama-Wan, *Japan* 55 F8
Toyapakeh, *Indonesia* 63 K18
Toyohashi, *Japan* 55 G8
Toyokawa, *Japan* 55 G8
Toyonaka, *Japan* 55 G7
Toyooka, *Japan* 55 G7
Toyota, *Japan* 55 G8
Tozeur, *Tunisia* 78 B7
Tozkhurmato, *Iraq* 70 C5
Tqibuli, *Georgia* 35 J6
Tqvarcheli, *Georgia* 35 J5
Trá Li = Tralee, *Ireland* 12 D2
Tra On, *Vietnam* 65 H5
Trabancos →, *Spain* 36 D5
Traben-Trarbach, *Germany* 25 F3
Trabzon, *Turkey* 73 B8
Tracadie-Sheila, *Canada* 105 C7
Tracy, *Calif., U.S.A.* 110 H5
Tracy, *Minn., U.S.A.* 112 C7
Tradate, *Italy* 40 C5
Trade Town, *Liberia* 82 D3
Trafalgar, C., *Spain* 37 J4
Traian, *Brăila, Romania* 29 E12
Traian, *Tulcea, Romania* 29 E13
Trail, *Canada* 102 D5
Trainor L., *Canada* 102 A4
Trákhonas, *Cyprus* 49 D12
Tralee, *Ireland* 12 D2
Tralee B., *Ireland* 12 D2
Tramore, *Ireland* 12 D4
Tramore B., *Ireland* 12 D4
Tran Ninh, Cao Nguyen, *Laos* 64 C4
Tranås, *Sweden* 11 F8
Tranbjerg, *Denmark* 11 H4
Trancas, *Argentina* 126 B2
Trancoso, *Portugal* 36 E3
Tranebjerg, *Denmark* 11 J4
Tranemo, *Sweden* 11 G7
Trang, *Thailand* 65 J2
Trangahy, *Madag.* 89 B7
Trangan, *Indonesia* 63 F8
Trangie, *Australia* 95 E4
Trångsviken, *Sweden* 10 A7
Trani, *Italy* 43 A9
Tranoroa, *Madag.* 89 C8
Tranqueras, *Uruguay* 127 C4
Transantarctic Mts., *Antarctica* 5 E12
Transilvania, *Romania* 29 D9
Transilvanian Alps = Carpații Meridionali, *Romania* 29 E9
Transnistria = Stînga Nistrului □, *Moldova* 29 C14
Transtrand, *Sweden* 10 C7
Transtrandsfjällen, *Sweden* 10 C6
Transylvania = Transilvania, *Romania* 29 D9
Trápani, *Italy* 42 D5
Trapper Pk., *U.S.A.* 108 D6
Traralgon, *Australia* 95 F4
Trarza, *Mauritania* 82 B2
Trasacco, *Italy* 41 G10
Trăscău, Munții, *Romania* 29 D8
Trasimeno, L., *Italy* 41 E9
Träslövsläge, *Sweden* 11 G6
Trasvase Tajo-Segura, Canal de, *Spain* 38 E2
Trat, *Thailand* 65 F4
Tratani →, *Pakistan* 68 E3
Traun, *Austria* 26 C7
Traunreut, *Germany* 25 H8
Traunsee, *Austria* 26 D6
Traunstein, *Germany* 25 H8
Traveller's L., *Australia* 95 E3
Travemünde, *Germany* 24 B6
Travers, Mt., *N.Z.* 91 K4
Traverse City, *U.S.A.* 114 C3
Travis, L., *U.S.A.* 113 K5
Travnik, *Bos.-H.* 28 F2
Trbovlje, *Slovenia* 41 B12
Trébbia →, *Italy* 40 C6
Trebel →, *Germany* 24 B9
Trébeurden, *France* 18 D3
Trebević △, *Bos.-H.* 28 G3
Třebíč, *Czech Rep.* 26 B8
Trebinje, *Bos.-H.* 44 D2
Trebisacce, *Italy* 43 C9
Trebišnjica →, *Bos.-H.* 44 D2
Trebišov, *Slovak Rep.* 27 C14
Trebižat →, *Bos.-H.* 41 E14
Trebnje, *Slovenia* 41 C12
Třeboň, *Czech Rep.* 26 B7
Trebonne, *Australia* 94 B4
Třeboňsko ⌂, *Czech Rep.* 26 B7
Trebujena, *Spain* 37 J4
Trecate, *Italy* 40 C5
Tregaron, *U.K.* 15 E4
Tregnago, *Italy* 41 C8
Tregrosse Is., *Australia* 94 B5
Tréguier, *France* 18 D3
Trégunc, *France* 18 E3
Treherne, *Canada* 103 D9
Tréia, *Italy* 41 E10
Treignac, *France* 20 C5
Treinta y Tres, *Uruguay* 127 C5
Treis-karden, *Germany* 25 E3
Treklyano, *Bulgaria* 44 D6
Trelawney, *Zimbabwe* 89 B5
Trélazé, *France* 18 E6
Trelew, *Argentina* 128 E3
Trélissac, *France* 20 C4
Trelleborg, *Sweden* 11 J7
Tremadog Bay, *U.K.* 14 E3
Trémiti, *Italy* 41 F12
Tremonton, *U.S.A.* 108 F7
Tremp, *Spain* 38 C5
Trenche →, *Canada* 104 C5
Trenčiansky □, *Slovak Rep.* 27 C11
Trenčín, *Slovak Rep.* 27 C11
Trenggalek, *Indonesia* 63 H14
Trenque Lauquen, *Argentina* 126 D3
Trent →, *Canada* 116 B7
Trent →, *U.K.* 14 D7
Trentino-Alto Adige □, *Italy* 41 B8
Trento, *Italy* 40 B8
Trenton = Quinte West, *Canada* 116 B7
Trenton, *Mo., U.S.A.* 112 E8
Trenton, *N.J., U.S.A.* 117 F10
Trenton, *Nebr., U.S.A.* 112 E4
Trepassey, *Canada* 105 C9
Trepuzzi, *Italy* 43 B11
Tres Arroyos, *Argentina* 126 D3
Três Corações, *Brazil* 127 A6
Três Lagoas, *Brazil* 125 H8
Tres Lomas, *Argentina* 126 D3
Tres Marías, Islas, *Mexico* 118 C3
Tres Montes, C., *Chile* 128 F1
Tres Pinos, *U.S.A.* 110 J5
Três Pontas, *Brazil* 127 A6
Tres Puentes, *Chile* 126 B1
Tres Puntas, C., *Argentina* 128 F3
Três Rios, *Brazil* 127 A7
Tres Valles, *Mexico* 119 D5
Tresco, *U.K.* 15 H1
Treska →, *Macedonia* 44 E5
Treskavica, *Bos.-H.* 28 G3
Trespaderne, *Spain* 36 C7
Tresticklan △, *Sweden* 11 F5
Trets, *France* 21 E9
Treuchtlingen, *Germany* 25 G6
Treuenbrietzen, *Germany* 24 C8
Trevi, *Italy* 41 F9
Trevíglio, *Italy* 40 C6
Trevínca, Peña, *Spain* 36 C4
Treviso, *Italy* 41 C9
Trévoux, *France* 21 C8
Trgovište, *Serbia & M.* 44 D6
Triabunna, *Australia* 95 G4
Triánda, *Greece* 49 C10
Triangle, *Zimbabwe* 89 C5
Triaucourt-en-Argonne, *France* 19 D12
Tribal Areas □, *Pakistan* 68 C4
Tribsees, *Germany* 24 A8
Tribulation, C., *Australia* 94 B4
Tribune, *U.S.A.* 112 F4
Tricárico, *Italy* 43 B9
Tricase, *Italy* 43 C11
Trichinopoly = Tiruchchirappalli, *India* 66 P11
Trichur, *India* 66 P10
Trida, *Australia* 95 E4
Trier, *Germany* 25 F2
Trieste, *Italy* 41 C10
Trieste, G. di, *Italy* 41 C10
Trieux →, *France* 18 D3
Triggiano, *Italy* 43 A9
Triglav, *Slovenia* 41 B10
Triglavski △, *Slovenia* 41 B10
Trigno →, *Italy* 41 F11
Trigueros, *Spain* 37 H4
Tríkeri, *Greece* 46 B5
Trikhonis, Límni, *Greece* 46 C3
Tríkkala, *Greece* 46 B3
Tríkkala □, *Greece* 46 B3
Trikomo, *Cyprus* 49 D12
Trikora, Puncak, *Indonesia* 63 E9
Trilj, *Croatia* 41 E13
Trillo, *Spain* 38 E2
Trim, *Ireland* 12 C5
Trincomalee, *Sri Lanka* 66 Q12
Trindade, *Brazil* 125 G9
Trindade, I., *Atl. Oc.* 2 F8
Třinec, *Czech Rep.* 27 B11
Trinidad, *Bolivia* 124 F6
Trinidad, *Cuba* 120 B4
Trinidad, *Trin. & Tob.* 121 D7
Trinidad, *Uruguay* 126 C4
Trinidad, *U.S.A.* 113 G2
Trinidad →, *Mexico* 119 D5
Trinidad & Tobago ■, *W. Indies* 121 D7
Trinitápoli, *Italy* 43 A9
Trinity, *Canada* 105 C9
Trinity, *U.S.A.* 113 K7
Trinity →, *Calif., U.S.A.* 108 F2
Trinity →, *Tex., U.S.A.* 113 L7
Trinity B., *Canada* 105 C9
Trinity Hills, *Trin. & Tob.* 125 K15
Trinity Is., *U.S.A.* 100 C4
Trinity Range, *U.S.A.* 108 F4
Trinkitat, *Sudan* 80 D4
Trino, *Italy* 40 C5
Trinway, *U.S.A.* 116 F2
Trionto, C., *Italy* 43 C9
Triora, *Italy* 40 D4
Tripoli = Tarābulus, *Lebanon* 74 A4
Tripoli = Tarābulus, *Libya* 79 B8
Trípolis, *Greece* 46 D4
Tripolitania, *N. Afr.* 79 B8
Tripura □, *India* 67 H18
Tripylos, *Cyprus* 49 E11
Trischen, *Germany* 24 A4
Tristan da Cunha, *Atl. Oc.* 77 K2
Trisul, *India* 69 D8
Trivandrum, *India* 66 Q10
Trivento, *Italy* 41 G11
Trnava, *Slovak Rep.* 27 C10
Trnavský □, *Slovak Rep.* 27 C10
Troarn, *France* 18 C6
Trochu, *Canada* 102 C6
Trodely I., *Canada* 104 B4
Troezen, *Greece* 46 D5
Trogir, *Croatia* 41 E13
Troglav, *Croatia* 41 E13
Tróia, *Italy* 43 A8
Troilus, L., *Canada* 104 B5
Troina, *Italy* 43 E7
Trois-Pistoles, *Canada* 105 C6
Trois-Rivières, *Canada* 104 C5
Trois-Rivières, *Guadeloupe* 120 b
Troisdorf, *Germany* 24 E3
Troitsk, *Russia* 52 D7
Troitsko Pechorsk, *Russia* 52 C6
Troitskoye, *Russia* 35 G7
Trölladyngja, *Iceland* 8 D5
Trollhättan, *Sweden* 11 F6
Trollheimen, *Norway* 8 E13
Trombetas →, *Brazil* 125 D7
Tromsø, *Norway* 8 B18
Trona, *U.S.A.* 111 K9
Tronador, Mte., *Argentina* 128 E2
Trøndelag, *Norway* 8 D14
Trondheim, *Norway* 8 E14
Trondheimsfjorden, *Norway* 8 E14
Trönninge, *Sweden* 11 H6
Tronto →, *Italy* 41 F10
Troodos, *Cyprus* 49 E11
Troon, *U.K.* 13 F4
Tropea, *Italy* 43 D8
Tropic, *U.S.A.* 109 H7
Tropojë, *Albania* 44 D4
Trosa, *Sweden* 11 F11
Trostan, *U.K.* 12 A5
Trostberg, *Germany* 25 G8
Trostyanets, *Ukraine* 29 B14
Trostyanets, *Ukraine* 33 G8
Trou Gras Pt., *St. Lucia* 121 f
Trout →, *Canada* 102 A5
Trout L., *N.W.T., Canada* 102 A4
Trout L., *Ont., Canada* 103 C10
Trout Lake, *Canada* 102 B6
Trout Lake, *U.S.A.* 110 E5
Trout River, *Canada* 105 C8
Trout Run, *U.S.A.* 116 E7
Trouville-sur-Mer, *France* 18 C7
Trowbridge, *U.K.* 15 F5
Troy, *Turkey* 47 B8
Troy, *Ala., U.S.A.* 115 K3
Troy, *Kans., U.S.A.* 112 F7
Troy, *Mo., U.S.A.* 112 F9
Troy, *Mont., U.S.A.* 108 B6
Troy, *N.Y., U.S.A.* 117 D11
Troy, *Ohio, U.S.A.* 114 E3
Troy, *Pa., U.S.A.* 117 E8
Troyan, *Bulgaria* 45 D8
Troyes, *France* 19 D11
Trpanj, *Croatia* 41 E14
Trstenik, *Serbia & M.* 44 C5
Trubchevsk, *Russia* 33 F7
Truchas Peak, *U.S.A.* 113 H2
Trucial States = United Arab Emirates ■, *Asia* 71 F7
Truckee, *U.S.A.* 110 F6
Trudfront, *Russia* 35 H8
Trudovoye, *Russia* 54 C6
Trujillo, *Honduras* 120 C2
Trujillo, *Peru* 124 E3
Trujillo, *Spain* 37 F5
Trujillo, *U.S.A.* 113 H2
Trujillo, *Venezuela* 124 B4
Truk, *Micronesia* 96 G7
Trumann, *U.S.A.* 113 H9
Trumansburg, *U.S.A.* 117 D8
Trumbull, Mt., *U.S.A.* 109 H7
Trŭn, *Bulgaria* 44 D6
Trun, *France* 18 D7
Trundle, *Australia* 95 E4
Trung-Phan = Annam, *Vietnam* 64 E7
Truro, *Canada* 105 C7
Truro, *U.K.* 15 G2
Truskavets, *Ukraine* 33 H2
Trŭstenik, *Bulgaria* 45 C8
Trustrup, *Denmark* 11 H4
Trutch, *Canada* 102 B4
Truth or Consequences, *U.S.A.* 109 K10
Trutnov, *Czech Rep.* 26 A8
Truxton, *U.S.A.* 117 D8
Truyère →, *France* 20 D6
Tryavna, *Bulgaria* 45 D9
Tryonville, *U.S.A.* 116 E5
Trzcianka, *Poland* 31 E3
Trzciel, *Poland* 31 F2
Trzcińsko Zdrój, *Poland* 31 F1
Trzebiatów, *Poland* 30 D2
Trzebiez, *Poland* 30 E1
Trzebnica, *Poland* 31 G4
Trzemeszno, *Poland* 31 F4
Tržič, *Slovenia* 41 B11
Tsagan Aman, *Russia* 35 G8
Tsamandás, *Greece* 46 B2
Tsandi, *Namibia* 88 B1
Tsaratanana, *Madag.* 89 B8
Tsaratanana ⌂, *Madag.* 89 A8
Tsaratanana, Mt. de = Maromokotro, *Madag.* 89 A8
Tsarevo, *Bulgaria* 45 D9
Tsaritsáni, *Greece* 46 B4
Tsau, *Botswana* 88 C3
Tsavo East △, *Kenya* 86 C4
Tsavo West △, *Kenya* 86 C4
Tsebrykove, *Ukraine* 33 J6
Tsentralnyy □, *Russia* 34 D4
Tses, *Namibia* 88 D2
Tsetserleg, *Mongolia* 60 B5
Tsévié, *Togo* 83 D5
Tshabong, *Botswana* 88 D3
Tshane, *Botswana* 88 C3
Tshela, *Dem. Rep. of the Congo* 84 E2
Tshesebe, *Botswana* 89 C4
Tshibeke, *Dem. Rep. of the Congo* 86 C2
Tshibinda, *Dem. Rep. of the Congo* 86 C2
Tshikapa, *Dem. Rep. of the Congo* 84 F4
Tshilenge, *Dem. Rep. of the Congo* 86 D1
Tshinsenda, *Dem. Rep. of the Congo* 87 E2
Tshofa, *Dem. Rep. of the Congo* 86 D2
Tshwane = Pretoria, *S. Africa* 89 D4
Tshwane, *Botswana* 88 C3
Tsigara, *Botswana* 88 C4
Tsihombe, *Madag.* 89 D8
Tsiigehtchic, *Canada* 100 B6
Tsimlyansk, *Russia* 35 G6
Tsimlyansk Res. = Tsimlyanskoye Vdkhr., *Russia* 35 F6
Tsimlyanskoye Vdkhr., *Russia* 35 F6
Tsinan = Jinan, *China* 56 F9
Tsineng, *S. Africa* 88 D3
Tsínga, *Greece* 45 E8
Tsinghai = Qinghai □, *China* 60 C4
Tsingtao = Qingdao, *China* 57 F11
Tsingy de Bemaraha ⌂, *Madag.* 89 B8
Tsingy de Namoroka ⌂, *Madag.* 89 B8
Tsinjoarivo, *Madag.* 89 B8
Tsinjomitondraka, *Madag.* 89 B8
Tsiroanomandidy, *Madag.* 89 B8
Tsiteli-Tsqaro, *Georgia* 35 K8

Tsitondroina, *Madag.* 89 C8
Tsitsikamma △, *S. Africa* 88 E3
Tsivilsk, *Russia* 34 C8
Tsivory, *Madag.* 89 C8
Tskhinvali, *Georgia* 35 J7
Tsna →, *Russia* 34 C6
Tsnori, *Georgia* 35 K7
Tso Moriri, L., *India* 69 C8
Tsobis, *Namibia* 88 B2
Tsodilo Hill, *Botswana* 88 B3
Tsogttsetsiy = Baruunsuu, *Mongolia* 56 C3
Tsolo, *S. Africa* 89 E4
Tsomo, *S. Africa* 89 E4
Tsu, *Japan* 55 G8
Tsu L., *Canada* 102 A6
Tsuchiura, *Japan* 55 F10
Tsuen Wan, *China* 59 F10
Tsugaru-Kaikyō, *Japan* 54 D10
Tsumeb, *Namibia* 88 B2
Tsumis, *Namibia* 88 C2
Tsuruga, *Japan* 55 G8
Tsurugi-San, *Japan* 55 H7
Tsuruoka, *Japan* 54 E9
Tsushima, *Gifu, Japan* 55 G8
Tsushima, *Nagasaki, Japan* 55 G4
Tsuyama, *Japan* 55 G7
Tsvetkovo, *Ukraine* 33 H6
Tsyelyakhany, *Belarus* 33 F3
Tua →, *Portugal* 36 D3
Tual, *Indonesia* 63 F8
Tuam, *Ireland* 12 C3
Tuamotu Arch. = Tuamotu Is., *French Polynesia* 97 J13
Tuamotu Is., *French Polynesia* 97 J13
Tuamotu Ridge, *Pac. Oc.* 97 K14
Tuanfeng, *China* 59 B10
Tuanxi, *China* 58 D6
Tuao, *Phil.* 61 C4
Tuapse, *Russia* 35 H4
Tuas, *Singapore* 65 d
Tuatapere, *N.Z.* 91 M1
Tuba City, *U.S.A.* 109 H8
Tuban, *Indonesia* 63 G15
Tubani, *Botswana* 88 C3
Tubarão, *Brazil* 127 B6
Tūbās, *West Bank* 74 C4
Tubas →, *Namibia* 88 C2
Tübingen, *Germany* 25 G5
Tubruq, *Libya* 79 B10
Tubuai Is., *French Polynesia* 97 K13
Tuc Trung, *Vietnam* 65 G6
Tucacas, *Venezuela* 124 A5
T'uch'ang, *Taiwan* 59 E13
Tuchodi →, *Canada* 102 B4
Tuchola, *Poland* 30 E4
Tuchów, *Poland* 31 J8
Tuckanarra, *Australia* 93 E2
Tucson, *U.S.A.* 109 K8
Tucumán □, *Argentina* 126 B2
Tucumcari, *U.S.A.* 113 H3
Tucupita, *Venezuela* 124 B6
Tucuruí, *Brazil* 125 D9
Tucuruí, Reprêsa de, *Brazil* 125 D9
Tuczno, *Poland* 31 E3
Tudela, *Spain* 38 C3
Tudmur, *Syria* 70 C3
Tudor, L., *Canada* 105 A6
Tudora, *Romania* 29 C11
Tuella →, *Portugal* 36 D3
Tugela →, *S. Africa* 89 D5
Tuguegarao, *Phil.* 61 C4
Tugur, *Russia* 53 D14
Tui, *Spain* 36 C2
Tuineje, *Canary Is.* 48 F5
Tukangbesi, Kepulauan, *Indonesia* 63 F6
Tukarak I., *Canada* 104 A4
Tukayyid, *Iraq* 70 D5
Tûkh, *Egypt* 80 H7
Tukhlya, *Ukraine* 29 B8
Tukkae, Ao, *Thailand* 65 a
Tukobo, *Ghana* 82 D4
Tuktoyaktuk, *Canada* 100 B6
Tukums, *Latvia* 9 H20
Tukums □, *Latvia* 30 B10
Tukuyu, *Tanzania* 87 D3
Tula, *Hidalgo, Mexico* 119 C5
Tula, *Tamaulipas, Mexico* 119 C5
Tula, *Nigeria* 83 D7
Tula, *Russia* 32 E9
Tulancingo, *Mexico* 119 C5
Tulare, *Serbia & M.* 44 D5
Tulare, *U.S.A.* 110 J7
Tulare Lake Bed, *U.S.A.* 110 K7
Tularosa, *U.S.A.* 109 K10
Tulbagh, *S. Africa* 88 E2
Tulcán, *Ecuador* 124 C3
Tulcea, *Romania* 29 E13
Tulcea □, *Romania* 29 E13
Tulchyn, *Ukraine* 29 B13
Tūleh, *Iran* 71 C7
Tulemalu L., *Canada* 103 A9
Tulgheş, *Romania* 29 D10
Tuli, *Zimbabwe* 87 G2
Tulia, *U.S.A.* 113 H4
Tuliszków, *Poland* 31 F5
Tulita, *Canada* 100 B7
Ţūlkarm, *West Bank* 74 C4
Tulla, *Ireland* 12 D3
Tullahoma, *U.S.A.* 115 H2
Tullamore, *Australia* 95 E4
Tullamore, *Ireland* 12 C4
Tulle, *France* 20 C5
Tulln, *Austria* 26 C9
Tullow, *Ireland* 12 D5
Tullus, *Sudan* 81 E1
Tully, *Australia* 94 B4
Tully, *U.S.A.* 117 D8
Tulnici, *Romania* 29 E11
Tulovo, *Bulgaria* 45 D9
Tulsa, *U.S.A.* 113 G7
Tulsequah, *Canada* 102 B2
Tulu Milki, *Ethiopia* 81 F4
Tulu Welel, *Ethiopia* 81 F3
Tulua, *Colombia* 124 C3
Tuluceşti, *Romania* 29 E13
Tulun, *Russia* 53 D11
Tulungagung, *Indonesia* 63 H14
Tuma, *Russia* 32 E11
Tuma →, *Nic.* 120 D3
Tumacacori ⌂, *U.S.A.* 109 L8
Tumaco, *Colombia* 124 C3
Tumatumari, *Guyana* 124 B7
Tumba, *Sweden* 10 E11
Tumba, L., *Dem. Rep. of the Congo* 84 E3
Tumbarumba, *Australia* 95 F4
Tumbaya, *Argentina* 126 A2
Tumbes, *Peru* 124 D2
Tumbur, *Sudan* 81 G3
Tumbwe, *Dem. Rep. of the Congo* 87 E2
Tumby Bay, *Australia* 95 E2
Tumd Youqi, *China* 56 D6
Tumen, *China* 57 C15
Tumen Jiang →, *China* 57 C16
Tumeremo, *Venezuela* 124 B6
Tumkur, *India* 66 N10
Tump, *Pakistan* 66 F3
Tumpat, *Malaysia* 65 J4
Tumu, *Ghana* 82 C4
Tumucumaque, Serra, *Brazil* 125 C8
Tumut, *Australia* 95 F4
Tumwater, *U.S.A.* 110 C4
Tuna, *India* 68 H4
Tunadal, *Sweden* 10 B11
Tunapuna, *Trin. & Tob.* 125 K15
Tunas de Zaza, *Cuba* 120 B4
Tunbridge Wells = Royal Tunbridge Wells, *U.K.* 15 F8
Tunçbilek, *Turkey* 47 B11
Tunceli, *Turkey* 73 C8
Tuncurry, *Australia* 95 E5
Tundla, *India* 68 F8
Tundubai, *Sudan* 80 D2
Tunduru, *Tanzania* 87 E4
Tundzha →, *Bulgaria* 45 E10
Tungabhadra →, *India* 66 M11
Tungaru, *Sudan* 81 E3
Tungla, *Nic.* 120 D3
Tungsha Tao = Dongsha Dao, *China* 59 G11
Tungshih, *Taiwan* 59 E13
Tungsten, *Canada* 102 A3
Tunguska, Nizhnyaya →, *Russia* 53 C9
Tunguska, Podkamennaya →, *Russia* 53 C10
Tunica, *U.S.A.* 113 H9
Tunis, *Tunisia* 78 A7
Tunis ✈ (TUN), *Tunisia* 42 F3
Tunisia ■, *Africa* 78 B6
Tunja, *Colombia* 124 B4
Tunkhannock, *U.S.A.* 117 E9
Tunliu, *China* 56 F7
Tunnel Creek △, *Australia* 92 C4
Tunnsjøen, *Norway* 8 D15
Tunø, *Denmark* 11 J4
Tunungayualok I., *Canada* 105 A7
Tunuyán, *Argentina* 126 C2
Tunuyán →, *Argentina* 126 C2
Tuo Jiang →, *China* 58 C5
Tuolumne, *U.S.A.* 110 H6
Tuolumne →, *U.S.A.* 110 H5
Tūp Āghāj, *Iran* 70 B5
Tupã, *Brazil* 127 A5
Tupelo, *U.S.A.* 115 H1
Tupik, *Russia* 32 E7
Tupinambaranas, *Brazil* 124 D7
Tupiza, *Bolivia* 126 A2
Tupižnica, *Serbia & M.* 44 C6
Tupman, *U.S.A.* 111 K7
Tupper, *Canada* 102 B4
Tupper Lake, *U.S.A.* 117 B10
Tupungato, Cerro, *S. Amer.* 126 C2
Tuquan, *China* 57 B11
Túquerres, *Colombia* 124 C3
Tura, *Russia* 53 C11
Turabah, *Ḩā'il, Si. Arabia* 70 D4
Turabah, *Makkah, Si. Arabia* 80 C5
Tūrān, *Iran* 71 C8
Turan, *Russia* 53 D10
Ţurayf, *Si. Arabia* 70 D3
Turbacz, *Poland* 31 J7
Turbe, *Bos.-H.* 28 F2
Turčianske Teplice, *Slovak Rep.* 27 C11
Turcoaia, *Romania* 29 E13
Turda, *Romania* 29 D8
Turek, *Poland* 31 F5
Turen, *Venezuela* 124 B5
Turfan = Turpan, *China* 60 B3
Turfan Basin = Turpan Hami, *China* 50 E12
Turfan Depression = Turpan Hami, *China* 50 E12
Turgeon →, *Canada* 104 C4
Tŭrgovishte, *Bulgaria* 45 C10
Turgut, *Turkey* 47 D10
Turgutlu, *Turkey* 47 C9
Turgwe →, *Zimbabwe* 89 C5
Turhal, *Turkey* 72 B7
Turia →, *Spain* 39 F4
Turiaçu, *Brazil* 125 D9
Turiaçu →, *Brazil* 125 D9
Turiec →, *Slovak Rep.* 27 B11
Turin = Torino, *Italy* 40 C4
Turka, *Ukraine* 31 J10
Turkana, L., *Africa* 86 B4
Türkeli, *Turkey* 45 F11
Turkestan = Türkistan, *Kazakhstan* 52 E7
Túrkeve, *Hungary* 28 C5
Turkey ■, *Eurasia* 72 C7
Turkey Creek, *Australia* 92 C4
Turki, *Russia* 34 D6
Türkistan, *Kazakhstan* 52 E7
Türkmenbashi, *Turkmenistan* 52 E6
Turkmenistan ■, *Asia* 52 F6
Türkmenli, *Turkey* 47 B8
Türkoğlu, *Turkey* 72 D7
Turks & Caicos Is. ⊠, *W. Indies* 121 B5
Turks Island Passage, *W. Indies* 121 B5
Turku, *Finland* 9 F20
Turkwel →, *Kenya* 86 B4
Turlock, *U.S.A.* 110 H6
Turnagain →, *Canada* 102 B3
Turnagain, C., *N.Z.* 91 J6
Turneffe Is., *Belize* 119 D7
Turner, *U.S.A.* 108 B9
Turner Pt., *Australia* 94 A1
Turner Valley, *Canada* 102 C6
Turners Falls, *U.S.A.* 117 D12
Turnhout, *Belgium* 17 C4
Türnitz, *Austria* 26 D8
Turnor L., *Canada* 103 B7
Turnov, *Czech Rep.* 26 A8
Tŭrnovo = Veliko Tŭrnovo, *Bulgaria* 45 C9
Turnu Măgurele, *Romania* 29 G9
Turnu Roşu, P., *Romania* 29 E9
Turobin, *Poland* 31 H9
Turpan, *China* 60 B3
Turpan Hami, *China* 50 E12
Turrës, Kala e, *Albania* 44 E3
Turriff, *U.K.* 13 D6
Tursāq, *Iraq* 70 C5
Tursi, *Italy* 43 B9
Turtle Head I., *Australia* 94 A3
Turtle Is., *S. Leone* 82 D2
Turtle L., *Canada* 103 C7
Turtle Lake, *U.S.A.* 112 B4
Turtleford, *Canada* 103 C7
Turuépano △, *Venezuela* 121 D7
Turukhansk, *Russia* 53 C9
Turzovka, *Slovak Rep.* 27 B11
Tuscaloosa, *U.S.A.* 115 J2
Tuscánia, *Italy* 41 F8
Tuscany = Toscana □, *Italy* 40 E8
Tuscarawas →, *U.S.A.* 116 F3
Tuscarora Mt., *U.S.A.* 116 F7
Tuscola, *Ill., U.S.A.* 114 F1
Tuscola, *Tex., U.S.A.* 113 J5
Tuscumbia, *U.S.A.* 115 H2
Tuskegee, *U.S.A.* 115 J3
Tustin, *U.S.A.* 111 M9
Tuszyn, *Poland* 31 G6
Tutak, *Turkey* 73 C10
Tutayev, *Russia* 32 D10
Tuticorin, *India* 66 Q11
Tutin, *Serbia & M.* 44 D4
Tutóia, *Brazil* 125 D10
Tutong, *Brunei* 62 D4
Tutova →, *Romania* 29 D12
Tutrakan, *Bulgaria* 45 B10
Tuttle Creek L., *U.S.A.* 112 F6
Tuttlingen, *Germany* 25 H4
Tutuala, *E. Timor* 63 F7
Tutuila, *Amer. Samoa* 91 B13
Tutume, *Botswana* 85 J5
Tutun, *Egypt* 80 J7
Tututepec, *Mexico* 119 D5
Tuva □, *Russia* 53 D10
Tuvalu ■, *Pac. Oc.* 96 H9
Tuxer Alpen, *Austria* 26 D4
Tuxpan, *Mexico* 119 C5
Tuxtla Gutiérrez, *Mexico* 119 D6
Tuy = Tui, *Spain* 36 C2
Tuy An, *Vietnam* 64 F7
Tuy Duc, *Vietnam* 65 F6
Tuy Hoa, *Vietnam* 64 F7
Tuy Phong, *Vietnam* 65 G7
Tuya L., *Canada* 102 B2
Tuyen Hoa, *Vietnam* 64 D6
Tuyen Quang, *Vietnam* 58 G5
Tūysarkān, *Iran* 71 C6
Tuz Gölü, *Turkey* 72 C5
Ţūz Khurmātū = Tozkhurmato, *Iraq* 70 C5
Tuzi, *Serbia & M.* 44 D3
Tuzigoot ⌂, *U.S.A.* 109 J7
Tuzla, *Bos.-H.* 28 F3
Tuzlov →, *Russia* 33 J10
Tuzluca, *Turkey* 73 B10
Tuzly 29 E15
Tvååker, *Sweden* 11 G6
Tvardiţa, *Moldova* 29 D13
Tver, *Russia* 32 D8
Tvrdošin, *Slovak Rep.* 27 B12
Tvrdošovce, *Slovak Rep.* 27 C11
Tvŭrditsa, *Bulgaria* 45 D9
Twain, *U.S.A.* 110 E5
Twain Harte, *U.S.A.* 110 G6
Twardogóra, *Poland* 31 G4
Tweed, *Canada* 116 B7
Tweed →, *U.K.* 13 F6
Tweed Heads, *Australia* 95 D5
Tweedsmuir ⌂, *Canada* 102 C3
Twentynine Palms, *U.S.A.* 111 L10
Twillingate, *Canada* 105 C9
Twin Bridges, *U.S.A.* 108 D7
Twin Falls, *Canada* 105 B7
Twin Falls, *U.S.A.* 108 E6
Twin Valley, *U.S.A.* 112 B6
Twinsburg, *U.S.A.* 116 E3
Twistringen, *Germany* 24 C4
Twitchell Reservoir, *U.S.A.* 111 L6
Two Harbors, *U.S.A.* 112 B9
Two Hills, *Canada* 102 C6
Two Rivers, *U.S.A.* 114 C2
Two Rocks, *Australia* 93 F2
Twofold B., *Australia* 95 F4
Tyachiv, *Ukraine* 33 H2
Tychy, *Poland* 31 H5
Tyczyn, *Poland* 31 J9
Tykocin, *Poland* 31 E9
Tyler, *Minn., U.S.A.* 112 C6
Tyler, *Tex., U.S.A.* 113 J7
Tyligul →, *Ukraine* 33 J6
Tymanivka, *Ukraine* 29 B13
Týn nad Vltavou, *Czech Rep.* 26 B7
Tynda, *Russia* 53 D13
Tyndall, *U.S.A.* 112 D6
Tyne →, *U.K.* 14 C6
Tyne & Wear □, *U.K.* 14 B6
Týnec nad Sázavou, *Czech Rep.* 26 B7
Tynemouth, *U.K.* 14 B6
Tyre = Sūr, *Lebanon* 74 B4
Tyresta △, *Sweden* 10 E12
Tyrifjorden, *Norway* 9 F14
Tyringe, *Sweden* 11 H7
Tyrnyauz, *Russia* 35 J6
Tyrol = Tirol □, *Austria* 26 D3
Tyrone, *U.S.A.* 116 F6
Tyrone □, *U.K.* 12 B4
Tyrrell →, *Australia* 95 F3
Tyrrell, L., *Australia* 95 F3
Tyrrell L., *Canada* 103 A7
Tyrrhenian Sea, *Medit. S.* 6 G8
Tysfjorden, *Norway* 8 B17
Tysmenytsya, *Ukraine* 29 B9
Tystberga, *Sweden* 11 F11
Tytuvėnai, *Lithuania* 30 C10
Tyub Karagan, Mys, *Kazakhstan* 35 H10
Tyuleni, Ostrova, *Kazakhstan* 35 H10
Tyuleniy, *Russia* 35 H8
Tyuleniy, Mys, *Azerbaijan* 35 K10
Tyumen, *Russia* 52 D7
Tywi →, *U.K.* 15 F3
Tywyn, *U.K.* 15 E3
Tzaneen, *S. Africa* 89 C5
Tzermiádhes, *Greece* 49 D7
Tzoumérka, Óros, *Greece* 46 B3
Tzukong = Zigong, *China* 58 C5

U

U Taphao, *Thailand* 64 F3
U.S.A. = United States of America ■, *N. Amer.* 106 C7
U.S. Virgin Is. ⊠, *W. Indies* 121 e
Uatumã →, *Brazil* 124 D7
Uaupés, *Brazil* 124 D5
Uaupés →, *Brazil* 124 C5
Uaxactún, *Guatemala* 120 C2
Ub, *Serbia & M.* 44 B4
Ubá, *Brazil* 127 A7
Uba, *Nigeria* 83 C7
Ubaitaba, *Brazil* 125 F11
Ubangi = Oubangi →, *Dem. Rep. of the Congo* 84 E3
Ubauro, *Pakistan* 68 E3
Ubaye →, *France* 21 D10
Ubayyiḑ, W. al →, *Iraq* 70 C4
Ube, *Japan* 55 H5
Úbeda, *Spain* 37 G7
Uberaba, *Brazil* 125 G9
Uberlândia, *Brazil* 125 G9
Überlingen, *Germany* 25 H5
Ubiaja, *Nigeria* 83 D6
Ubin, Pulau, *Singapore* 65 d
Ubolratna Res., *Thailand* 64 D4
Ubombo, *S. Africa* 89 D5
Ubon Ratchathani, *Thailand* 64 E5
Ubondo, *Dem. Rep. of the Congo* 86 C2
Ubort →, *Belarus* 33 F5
Ubrique, *Spain* 37 J5
Ubud, *Indonesia* 63 J18
Ubundu, *Dem. Rep. of the Congo* 86 C2
Ucayali →, *Peru* 124 D4
Uchab, *Namibia* 88 B2
Uchiura-Wan, *Japan* 54 C10
Uchquduq, *Uzbekistan* 52 E7
Uchte, *Germany* 24 C4
Uchur →, *Russia* 53 D14
Uckermark, *Germany* 24 B9
Ucluelet, *Canada* 102 D3
Uda →, *Russia* 53 D14
Udagamandalam, *India* 66 P10
Udainagar, *India* 68 H7
Udaipur, *India* 68 G5
Udaipur Garhi, *Nepal* 69 F12
Udala, *India* 69 J12
Udbina, *Croatia* 41 D12
Uddeholm, *Sweden* 10 D7
Uddevalla, *Sweden* 11 F5
Uddjaure, *Sweden* 8 D17
Uden, *Neths.* 17 C5
Udgir, *India* 66 K10
Udhampur, *India* 69 C6
Udi, *Nigeria* 83 D6
Údine, *Italy* 41 B10
Udmurtia □, *Russia* 52 D6
Udon Thani, *Thailand* 64 D4
Udupi, *India* 66 N9
Udvoy Balkan, *Bulgaria* 45 D10
Udzungwa △, *Tanzania* 86 D4
Udzungwa Range, *Tanzania* 87 D4
Ueckermünde, *Germany* 24 B10
Ueda, *Japan* 55 F9
Uedineniya, Os., *Russia* 4 B12
Uele →, *Dem. Rep. of the Congo* 84 D4
Uelen, *Russia* 53 C19
Uelzen, *Germany* 24 C6
Uetersen, *Germany* 24 B5
Uetze, *Germany* 24 C6
Ufa, *Russia* 52 D6
Uffenheim, *Germany* 25 F6
Ugab →, *Namibia* 88 C1
Ugalla →, *Tanzania* 86 D3
Ugalla River ⌂, *Tanzania* 86 D3
Uganda ■, *Africa* 86 B3
Ugento, *Italy* 43 C11
Ugep, *Nigeria* 83 D6
Ughelli, *Nigeria* 83 D6
Ugie, *S. Africa* 89 E4
Ugíjar, *Spain* 37 J7
Ugine, *France* 21 C10
Uglegorsk, *Russia* 53 E15
Uglich, *Russia* 32 D10
Ugljan, *Croatia* 41 D12
Ugljane, *Croatia* 41 E13
Ugra →, *Russia* 32 E9
Ugŭrchin, *Bulgaria* 45 C8
Uh →, *Slovak Rep.* 27 C15
Uherské Hradiště, *Czech Rep.* 27 B10
Uherský Brod, *Czech Rep.* 27 B10
Úhlava →, *Czech Rep.* 26 B6
Uhlenhorst, *Namibia* 88 C2
Uhniv, *Ukraine* 31 H10
Uhrichsville, *U.S.A.* 116 F3
Uibhist a Deas = South Uist, *U.K.* 13 D1
Uibhist a Tuath = North Uist, *U.K.* 13 D1
Uig, *U.K.* 13 D2
Uíge, *Angola* 84 F2
Uijŏngbu, *S. Korea* 57 F14
Ŭiju, *N. Korea* 57 D13
Uinta Mts., *U.S.A.* 108 F8
Uis, *Namibia* 88 C1
Uitenhage, *S. Africa* 88 E4
Uithuizen, *Neths.* 17 A6
Ujazd, *Poland* 31 H5
Újfehértó, *Hungary* 28 C6
Ujh →, *India* 68 C6
Ujhani, *India* 69 F8
Uji-guntō, *Japan* 55 J4
Ujjain, *India* 68 H6
Ujście, *Poland* 31 E3
Újszász, *Hungary* 28 C5
Ujung Pandang, *Indonesia* 63 F5
Uka, *Russia* 53 D17
Ukara I., *Tanzania* 86 C3
Uke-Shima, *Japan* 55 K4
Ukerewe I., *Tanzania* 86 C3
Ukholovo, *Russia* 34 D5
Ukhrul, *India* 67 G19
Ukhta, *Russia* 52 C6
Ukiah, *U.S.A.* 110 F3
Ukmergė, *Lithuania* 9 J21
Ukraine ■, *Europe* 33 H7
Ukwi, *Botswana* 88 C3
Ulaan-Uul, *Mongolia* 56 B6
Ulaanbaatar, *Mongolia* 53 E11
Ulaangom, *Mongolia* 60 A4
Ulaanjirem, *Mongolia* 56 B3
Ulamba, *Dem. Rep. of the Congo* 87 D1
Ulan Bator = Ulaanbaatar, *Mongolia* 53 E11
Ulan Erge, *Russia* 35 G7
Ulan Khol, *Russia* 35 H8
Ulan Ude, *Russia* 53 D11
Ulanów, *Poland* 31 H9
Ulaş, *Sivas, Turkey* 72 C7
Ulaş, *Tekirdağ, Turkey* 45 E11
Ulaya, *Morogoro, Tanzania* 86 D4
Ulaya, *Tabora, Tanzania* 86 C3
Ulcinj, *Serbia & M.* 44 E3
Ulco, *S. Africa* 88 D3
Ule älv = Oulujoki →, *Finland* 8 D21
Ule träsk = Oulujärvi, *Finland* 8 D22
Uleåborg = Oulu, *Finland* 8 D21
Ulefoss, *Norway* 9 G13
Ulëz, *Albania* 44 E3
Ulfborg, *Denmark* 11 H2
Ulhasnagar, *India* 66 K8
Uliastay, *Mongolia* 60 B4
Uljma, *Serbia & M.* 28 E6
Ulla →, *Spain* 36 C2
Ulladulla, *Australia* 95 F5
Ullapool, *U.K.* 13 D3
Ullared, *Sweden* 11 G6
Ulldecona, *Spain* 38 E5
Ullswater, *U.K.* 14 C5
Ullŭng-do, *S. Korea* 55 F5
Ulm, *Germany* 25 G5
Ulmarra, *Australia* 95 D5
Ulmeni, *Buzău, Romania* 29 E11
Ulmeni, *Maramureş, Romania* 29 C8
Ulonguè, *Mozam.* 87 E3
Ulricehamn, *Sweden* 11 G7
Ulrika, *Sweden* 11 F9
Ulsan, *S. Korea* 57 G15
Ulsta, *U.K.* 13 A7
Ulster □, *U.K.* 12 B5
Ulstrem, *Bulgaria* 45 D10
Ulubat Gölü, *Turkey* 45 F12
Ulubey, *Turkey* 47 C11
Uluborlu, *Turkey* 47 C12
Uluçinar, *Turkey* 72 D6
Uludağ, *Turkey* 45 F13
Uludağ △, *Turkey* 45 F13
Uludere, *Turkey* 73 D10
Uluguru Mts., *Tanzania* 86 D4
Ulukışla, *Turkey* 72 D6
Ulungur He →, *China* 60 B3
Uluru = Ayers Rock, *Australia* 93 E5
Uluru-Kata Tjuta △, *Australia* 93 E5
Ulutau, *Kazakhstan* 52 E7
Uluwatu, *Indonesia* 63 K18
Ulva, *U.K.* 13 E2
Ulverston, *U.K.* 14 C4
Ulverstone, *Australia* 95 G4
Ulya, *Russia* 53 D15
Ulyanovo, *Russia* 30 D9
Ulyanovsk = Simbirsk, *Russia* 34 C9
Ulyasutay = Uliastay, *Mongolia* 60 B4
Ulysses, *U.S.A.* 113 G4
Umag, *Croatia* 41 C10
Umala, *Bolivia* 124 G5
Uman, *Ukraine* 33 H6
Umaria, *India* 67 H12
Umarkot, *Pakistan* 66 G6
Umarpada, *India* 68 J5

Umatilla, *U.S.A.* 108 **D4**
Umbagog L., *U.S.A.* 117 **B13**
Umbakumba, *Australia* 94 **A2**
Umbértide, *Italy* 41 **E9**
Umbrella Mts., *N.Z.* 91 **L2**
Umbria □, *Italy* 41 **F9**
Umeå, *Sweden* 8 **E19**
Umeälven →, *Sweden* 8 **E19**
Umera, *Indonesia* 63 **E7**
Umfolozi ⌓, *S. Africa* 89 **D5**
Umfuli →, *Zimbabwe* 87 **F2**
Umfurudzi ⌓, *Zimbabwe* 87 **F3**
Umgusa, *Zimbabwe* 87 **F2**
Umim Urūmah, *Si. Arabia* 80 **B4**
Umka, *Serbia & M.* 44 **B4**
Umkomaas, *S. Africa* 89 **E5**
Umlazi, *S. Africa* 85 **L6**
Umm ad Daraj, J., *Jordan* 74 **C4**
Umm al Qaywayn, *U.A.E.* 71 **E7**
Umm al Qittayn, *Jordan* 74 **C5**
Umm Arda, *Sudan* 81 **D3**
Umm Bāb, *Qatar* 71 **E6**
Umm Badr, *Sudan* 81 **E2**
Umm Baiyud, *Sudan* 81 **E3**
Umm Bel, *Sudan* 81 **E2**
Umm Birkah, *Si. Arabia* 80 **B4**
Umm Boim, *Sudan* 81 **E2**
Umm Dam, *Sudan* 81 **E3**
Umm Debi, *Sudan* 81 **E3**
Umm Dubban, *Sudan* 81 **D3**
Umm Durman = Omdurmân, *Sudan* 81 **D3**
Umm el Fahm, *Israel* 74 **C4**
Umm Gafala, *Sudan* 81 **E2**
Umm Gimala, *Sudan* 81 **E2**
Umm Inderaba, *Sudan* 80 **D3**
Umm Keddada, *Sudan* 81 **E2**
Umm Koweika, *Sudan* 81 **E3**
Umm Lajj, *Si. Arabia* 70 **E3**
Umm Merwa, *Sudan* 80 **D3**
Umm Qantur, *Sudan* 81 **E3**
Umm Qurein, *Sudan* 81 **F2**
Umm Ruwaba, *Sudan* 81 **E3**
Umm Saiyala, *Sudan* 81 **E3**
Umm Shanqa, *Sudan* 81 **E2**
Umm Shutur, *Sudan* 81 **F3**
Umm Sidr, *Sudan* 81 **E2**
Umm Zehetir, *Egypt* 80 **J8**
Umnak I., *U.S.A.* 100 **C3**
Umniati →, *Zimbabwe* 87 **F2**
Umpqua →, *U.S.A.* 108 **E1**
Umreth, *India* 68 **H5**
Umtata, *S. Africa* 89 **E4**
Umuahia, *Nigeria* 83 **D6**
Umuarama, *Brazil* 127 **A5**
Umurbey, *Turkey* 45 **F10**
Umvukwe Ra., *Zimbabwe* 87 **F3**
Umzimvubu, *S. Africa* 89 **E4**
Umzingwane →, *Zimbabwe* 87 **G2**
Umzinto, *S. Africa* 89 **E5**
Una, *India* 68 **J4**
Una →, *Bos.-H.* 41 **D13**
Unac →, *Bos.-H.* 41 **D13**
Unadilla, *U.S.A.* 117 **D9**
Unalakleet, *U.S.A.* 100 **B3**
Unalaska, *U.S.A.* 100 **C3**
Unalaska I., *U.S.A.* 100 **C3**
'Unayzah, *Si. Arabia* 70 **E4**
'Unayzah, J., *Asia* 70 **C3**
Uncastillo, *Spain* 38 **C3**
Uncía, *Bolivia* 124 **G5**
Uncompahgre Peak, *U.S.A.* 109 **G10**
Uncompahgre Plateau, *U.S.A.* 109 **G9**
Undara Volcanic △, *Australia* 94 **B3**
Unden, *Sweden* 11 **F8**
Underbool, *Australia* 95 **F3**
Undersaker, *Sweden* 10 **A7**
Unecha, *Russia* 33 **F7**
Ungarie, *Australia* 95 **E4**
Ungarra, *Australia* 95 **E2**
Ungava, Pén. d', *Canada* 101 **C12**
Ungava B., *Canada* 101 **C13**
Ungeny = Ungheni, *Moldova* 29 **C12**
Unggi, *N. Korea* 57 **C16**
Ungheni, *Moldova* 29 **C12**
Unguala →, *Ethiopia* 81 **F5**
Ungwana B., *Kenya* 86 **C5**
Ungwatiri, *Sudan* 81 **D4**
Uni, *Russia* 34 **B10**
União da Vitória, *Brazil* 127 **B5**
Uničov, *Czech Rep.* 27 **B10**
Uniejów, *Poland* 31 **G5**
Unije, *Croatia* 41 **D11**
Unimak I., *U.S.A.* 100 **C3**
Union, *Miss., U.S.A.* 113 **J10**
Union, *Mo., U.S.A.* 112 **F9**
Union, *S.C., U.S.A.* 115 **H5**
Union City, *Calif., U.S.A.* 110 **H4**
Union City, *N.J., U.S.A.* 117 **F10**
Union City, *Pa., U.S.A.* 116 **E5**
Union City, *Tenn., U.S.A.* 113 **G10**
Union Gap, *U.S.A.* 108 **C3**
Union Springs, *U.S.A.* 115 **J3**
Uniondale, *S. Africa* 88 **E3**
Uniontown, *U.S.A.* 114 **F6**
Unionville, *U.S.A.* 112 **E8**
Unirea, *Romania* 29 **F12**
United Arab Emirates ■, *Asia* 71 **F7**
United Kingdom ■, *Europe* 7 **E5**
United States of America ■, *N. Amer.* 106 **C7**
Unity, *Canada* 103 **C7**
Universales, Mtes., *Spain* 38 **E3**
University Park, *U.S.A.* 109 **K10**
Unjha, *India* 68 **H5**
Unna, *Germany* 24 **D3**
Unnao, *India* 69 **F9**
Uno, Ilha, *Guinea-Biss.* 82 **C1**
Unsengedsi →, *Zimbabwe* 87 **F3**
Unst, *U.K.* 13 **A8**
Unstrut →, *Germany* 24 **D7**
Unterfranken □, *Germany* 25 **F5**
Unterschleissheim, *Germany* 25 **G7**
Unuk →, *Canada* 102 **B2**
Ünye, *Turkey* 72 **B7**
Unzen-Amakusa △, *Japan* 55 **H5**
Unzha, *Russia* 34 **A7**
Unzha →, *Russia* 34 **B6**
Uozu, *Japan* 55 **F8**
Upata, *Venezuela* 124 **B6**
Upemba △, *Dem. Rep. of the Congo* 87 **D2**
Upemba, L., *Dem. Rep. of the Congo* 87 **D2**
Upernavik, *Greenland* 4 **B5**
Upington, *S. Africa* 88 **D3**
Upleta, *India* 68 **J4**
'Upolu, *Samoa* 91 **A13**
Upper □, *Ghana* 83 **C4**
Upper Alkali L., *U.S.A.* 108 **F3**
Upper Arrow L., *Canada* 102 **C5**
Upper Foster L., *Canada* 103 **B7**
Upper Hutt, *N.Z.* 91 **J5**
Upper Klamath L., *U.S.A.* 108 **E3**
Upper Lake, *U.S.A.* 110 **F4**
Upper Manzanilla, *Trin. & Tob.* 125 **K15**
Upper Missouri River Breaks ⌓, *U.S.A.* 108 **C9**
Upper Musquodoboit, *Canada* 105 **C7**
Upper Red L., *U.S.A.* 112 **A7**
Upper Sandusky, *U.S.A.* 114 **E4**
Upper Volta = Burkina Faso ■, *Africa* 82 **C4**
Upphärad, *Sweden* 11 **F6**
Uppland, *Sweden* 10 **D12**
Upplands-Väsby, *Sweden* 10 **E11**
Uppsala, *Sweden* 10 **E11**
Uppsala län □, *Sweden* 10 **D11**
Upshi, *India* 69 **C7**
Upstart, C., *Australia* 94 **B4**
Upton, *U.S.A.* 112 **C2**
Uqsuqtuuq = Gjoa Haven, *Canada* 100 **B10**
Ur, *Iraq* 70 **D5**
Urad Qianqi, *China* 56 **D5**
Urakawa, *Japan* 54 **C11**
Ural = Uralskiy □, *Russia* 52 **C7**
Ural = Zhayyq →, *Kazakhstan* 52 **E6**
Ural, *Australia* 95 **E4**
Ural Mts. = Uralskie Gory, *Eurasia* 52 **D6**
Uralla, *Australia* 95 **E5**
Uralsk = Oral, *Kazakhstan* 34 **E10**
Uralskie Gory, *Eurasia* 52 **D6**
Uralskiy □, *Russia* 52 **C7**
Urambo, *Tanzania* 86 **D3**
Urandangi, *Australia* 94 **C2**
Uranium City, *Canada* 103 **B7**
Uraricoera →, *Brazil* 124 **C6**
Urawa, *Japan* 55 **G9**
Uray, *Russia* 52 **C7**
'Uray'irah, *Si. Arabia* 71 **E6**
Urbana, *Ill., U.S.A.* 114 **E1**
Urbana, *Ohio, U.S.A.* 114 **E4**
Urbánia, *Italy* 41 **E9**
Urbel →, *Spain* 36 **C7**
Urbino, *Italy* 41 **E9**
Urbión, Picos de, *Spain* 38 **C2**
Urcos, *Peru* 124 **F4**
Urdinarrain, *Argentina* 126 **C4**
Urdos, *France* 20 **F3**
Urdzhar, *Kazakhstan* 52 **E9**
Ure →, *U.K.* 14 **C6**
Uren, *Russia* 34 **B7**
Ures, *Mexico* 118 **B2**
Urewera △, *N.Z.* 91 **H6**
Urfa = Sanliurfa, *Turkey* 70 **B3**
Urganch, *Uzbekistan* 52 **E7**
Urgench = Urganch, *Uzbekistan* 52 **E7**
Ürgüp, *Turkey* 70 **B2**
Uri, *India* 69 **B6**
Uri □, *Switz.* 25 **J4**
Uribia, *Colombia* 124 **A4**
Uricani, *Romania* 28 **E8**
Uriondo, *Bolivia* 126 **A3**
Urique, *Mexico* 118 **B3**
Urique →, *Mexico* 118 **B3**
Urk, *Neths.* 17 **B5**
Urkiola ⌓, *Spain* 38 **B3**
Urla, *Turkey* 47 **C8**
Urlaţi, *Romania* 29 **F11**
Urmia = Orūmīyeh, *Iran* 70 **B5**
Uroševac, *Serbia & M.* 44 **D5**
Uroyan, Montanas de, *Puerto Rico* 121 **d**
Urshult, *Sweden* 11 **H8**
Uruaçu, *Brazil* 125 **F9**
Uruapan, *Mexico* 118 **D4**
Urubamba →, *Peru* 124 **F4**
Uruçara, *Brazil* 124 **D7**
Uruçuí, *Brazil* 125 **E10**
Uruguai →, *Brazil* 127 **B5**
Uruguaiana, *Brazil* 126 **B4**
Uruguay ■, *S. Amer.* 126 **C4**
Uruguay →, *S. Amer.* 126 **C4**
Urumchi = Ürümqi, *China* 52 **E9**
Ürümqi, *China* 52 **E9**
Urup →, *Russia* 35 **H5**
Urup, Ostrov, *Russia* 53 **E16**
Uryupinsk, *Russia* 34 **E5**
Urzhum, *Russia* 34 **B9**
Urziceni, *Romania* 29 **F11**
Usa →, *Russia* 52 **C6**
Uşak, *Turkey* 47 **C11**
Uşak □, *Turkey* 47 **C11**
Usakos, *Namibia* 88 **C2**
Ušće, *Serbia & M.* 44 **C4**
Usedom, *Germany* 24 **B10**
Usedom ⌓, *Germany* 24 **B10**
Useless Loop, *Australia* 93 **E1**
'Usfān, *Si. Arabia* 80 **C4**
Ush-Tobe, *Kazakhstan* 52 **E8**
Ushakova, Ostrov, *Russia* 4 **A12**
Ushakovo, *Russia* 30 **D7**
Ushant = Ouessant, Î. d', *France* 18 **D1**
Ushashi, *Tanzania* 86 **C3**
Ushat, *Sudan* 81 **F2**
'Ushayrah, *Si. Arabia* 80 **C5**
Ushibuka, *Japan* 55 **H5**
Ushuaia, *Argentina* 128 **G3**
Ushumun, *Russia* 53 **D13**
Ushytsya →, *Ukraine* 29 **B12**
Usk, *Canada* 102 **C3**
Usk →, *U.K.* 15 **F5**
Uska, *India* 69 **F10**
Üsküdar, *Turkey* 45 **F13**
Uslar, *Germany* 24 **D5**
Usman, *Russia* 33 **F10**
Usoke, *Tanzania* 86 **D3**
Usolye Sibirskoye, *Russia* 53 **D11**
Usoro, *Nigeria* 83 **D6**
Uspallata, P. de, *Argentina* 126 **C2**
Uspenskiy, *Kazakhstan* 52 **E8**
Ussel, *France* 20 **C6**
Usson-du-Poitou, *France* 20 **B4**
Ussuri →, *Asia* 54 **A7**
Ussuriysk, *Russia* 53 **E14**
Ussurka, *Russia* 54 **B6**
Ust-Bolsheretsk, *Russia* 53 **D16**
Ust-Buzulukskaya, *Russia* 34 **E6**
Ust-Chaun, *Russia* 53 **C18**
Ust-Chorna, *Ukraine* 29 **B8**
Ust-Donetskiy, *Russia* 35 **G5**
Ust-Ilimsk, *Russia* 53 **D11**
Ust-Ishim, *Russia* 52 **D8**
Ust-Kamchatsk, *Russia* 53 **D17**
Ust-Kamenogorsk = Öskemen, *Kazakhstan* 52 **E9**
Ust-Khayryuzovo, *Russia* 53 **D16**
Ust-Kut, *Russia* 53 **D11**
Ust-Kuyga, *Russia* 53 **B14**
Ust-Labinsk, *Russia* 35 **H4**
Ust-Luga, *Russia* 32 **C5**
Ust-Maya, *Russia* 53 **C14**
Ust-Mil, *Russia* 53 **D14**
Ust-Nera, *Russia* 53 **C15**
Ust-Nyukzha, *Russia* 53 **D13**
Ust-Olenek, *Russia* 53 **B12**
Ust-Omchug, *Russia* 53 **C15**
Ust-Port, *Russia* 52 **C9**
Ust-Tsilma, *Russia* 52 **C6**
Ust Urt = Ustyurt Plateau, *Asia* 52 **E6**
Ustaritz, *France* 20 **E2**
Ustecký □, *Czech Rep.* 26 **A7**
Uster, *Switz.* 25 **H4**
Ústí nad Labem, *Czech Rep.* 26 **A7**
Ústí nad Orlicí, *Czech Rep.* 27 **B9**
Ústica, *Italy* 42 **D6**
Ustinov = Izhevsk, *Russia* 52 **D6**
Ustka, *Poland* 30 **D3**
Ustroń, *Poland* 31 **J5**
Ustrzyki Dolne, *Poland* 31 **J9**
Ustyluh, *Ukraine* 31 **H11**
Ustyurt Plateau, *Asia* 52 **E6**
Ustyuzhna, *Russia* 32 **C9**
Usu, *China* 60 **B3**
Usuki, *Japan* 55 **H5**
Usulután, *El Salv.* 120 **D2**
Usumacinta →, *Mexico* 119 **D6**
Usumbura = Bujumbura, *Burundi* 86 **C2**
Usure, *Tanzania* 86 **C3**
Usutuo →, *Mozam.* 89 **D5**
Uta, *Indonesia* 63 **E9**
Utah □, *U.S.A.* 108 **G8**
Utah L., *U.S.A.* 108 **F8**
Utansjö, *Sweden* 10 **B11**
Utara, Selat, *Malaysia* 65 **c**
Utarni, *India* 68 **F4**
Utatlan, *Guatemala* 120 **C1**
Ute Creek →, *U.S.A.* 113 **H3**
Utebo, *Spain* 38 **D3**
Utena, *Lithuania* 9 **J21**
Utete, *Tanzania* 86 **D4**
Uthai Thani, *Thailand* 64 **E3**
Uthal, *Pakistan* 68 **G2**
Utiariti, *Brazil* 124 **F7**
Utica, *N.Y., U.S.A.* 117 **C9**
Utica, *Ohio, U.S.A.* 116 **F2**
Utiel, *Spain* 39 **F3**
Utikuma L., *Canada* 102 **B5**
Utö, *Sweden* 10 **F12**
Utopia, *Australia* 94 **C1**
Utraula, *India* 69 **F10**
Utrecht, *Neths.* 17 **B5**
Utrecht, *S. Africa* 89 **D5**
Utrecht □, *Neths.* 17 **B5**
Utrera, *Spain* 37 **H5**
Utsjoki →, *Finland* 8 **B22**
Utsunomiya, *Japan* 55 **F9**
Uttar Pradesh □, *India* 69 **F9**
Uttaradit, *Thailand* 64 **D3**
Uttaranchal □, *India* 69 **D8**
Uttoxeter, *U.K.* 14 **E6**
Utuado, *Puerto Rico* 121 **d**
Uummannaq, *Greenland* 4 **B4**
Uummannaq, *Greenland* 4 **B5**
Uummannarsuaq = Nunap Isua, *Greenland* 101 **C15**
Uusikaarlepyy, *Finland* 8 **E20**
Uusikaupunki, *Finland* 9 **F19**
Uva, *Russia* 34 **B11**
Uvac →, *Serbia & M.* 44 **C3**
Uvalde, *U.S.A.* 113 **L5**
Uvarovo, *Russia* 34 **E6**
Uvat, *Russia* 52 **D7**
Uvinza, *Tanzania* 86 **D3**
Uvira, *Dem. Rep. of the Congo* 86 **C2**
Uvs Nuur, *Mongolia* 60 **A4**
'Uwairidh, Ḥarrat al, *Si. Arabia* 70 **E3**
Uwajima, *Japan* 55 **H6**
Uwanda ⌓, *Tanzania* 86 **D3**
Uweinat, Jebel, *Sudan* 80 **C1**
Uxbridge, *Canada* 116 **B5**
Uxin Qi, *China* 56 **E5**
Uxmal, *Mexico* 119 **C7**
Üydzin, *Mongolia* 56 **B4**
Uyo, *Nigeria* 83 **D6**
Üyüklü Tepe, *Turkey* 47 **D9**
Uyûn Mûsa, *Egypt* 74 **F1**
Uyuni, *Bolivia* 124 **H5**
Uzbekistan ■, *Asia* 52 **E7**
Uzen, Bolshoi →, *Kazakhstan* 35 **F9**
Uzen, Mal →, *Kazakhstan* 35 **F9**
Uzerche, *France* 20 **C5**
Uzès, *France* 21 **D8**
Uzh →, *Ukraine* 33 **G6**
Uzhgorod = Uzhhorod, *Ukraine* 28 **B7**
Uzhhorod, *Ukraine* 28 **B7**
Uzhok, *Ukraine* 28 **B7**
Užice, *Serbia & M.* 44 **C3**
Uzlovaya, *Russia* 32 **F10**
Üzümlü, *Turkey* 47 **E11**
Uzunköprü, *Turkey* 45 **E10**
Uzunkuyu, *Turkey* 47 **C8**

V

Vaal →, *S. Africa* 88 **D3**
Vaal Dam, *S. Africa* 89 **D4**
Vaalbos △, *S. Africa* 88 **D3**
Vaalwater, *S. Africa* 89 **C4**
Vaasa, *Finland* 8 **E19**
Vabre, *France* 20 **E6**
Vác, *Hungary* 28 **C4**
Vacaria, *Brazil* 127 **B5**
Vacaville, *U.S.A.* 110 **G5**
Vaccarès, Étang de, *France* 21 **E8**
Vach = Vakh →, *Russia* 52 **C8**
Vache, Î. à, *Haiti* 121 **C5**
Väckelsång, *Sweden* 11 **H8**
Väddö, *Sweden* 10 **D12**
Väderstad, *Sweden* 11 **F8**
Vadnagar, *India* 68 **H5**
Vado Lígure, *Italy* 40 **D5**
Vadodara, *India* 68 **H5**
Vadsø, *Norway* 8 **A23**
Vadstena, *Sweden* 11 **F8**
Vaduz, *Liech.* 25 **H5**
Værøy, *Norway* 8 **C15**
Vágar, *Færoe Is.* 8 **E9**
Vaggeryd, *Sweden* 11 **G8**
Vagney, *France* 19 **D13**
Vagnhärad, *Sweden* 11 **F11**
Vagos, *Portugal* 36 **E2**
Vågsfjorden, *Norway* 8 **B17**
Váh →, *Slovak Rep.* 27 **D11**
Vahsel B., *Antarctica* 5 **D1**
Váhtjer = Gällivare, *Sweden* 8 **C19**
Vái, *Greece* 49 **D8**
Vaigach, *Russia* 52 **B6**
Vaiges, *France* 18 **D6**
Vaihingen, *Germany* 25 **G4**
Vail, *U.S.A.* 106 **C5**
Vailly-sur-Aisne, *France* 19 **C10**
Vaisali →, *India* 69 **F8**
Vaison-la-Romaine, *France* 21 **D9**
Vakarel, *Bulgaria* 44 **D7**
Vakfıkebir, *Turkey* 73 **B8**
Vakh →, *Russia* 52 **C8**
Vakhtan, *Russia* 34 **B8**
Vál, *Hungary* 28 **C3**
Val-de-Marne □, *France* 19 **D9**
Val-d'Isère, *France* 21 **C10**
Val-d'Oise □, *France* 19 **C9**
Val-d'Or, *Canada* 104 **C4**
Val Grande △, *Italy* 40 **B5**
Val Marie, *Canada* 103 **D7**
Val Thorens, *France* 21 **C10**
Valaam, *Russia* 32 **B6**
Valadares, *Portugal* 36 **D2**
Valahia, *Romania* 29 **F9**
Valais □, *Switz.* 25 **J3**
Valais, Alpes du, *Switz.* 25 **J3**
Valandovo, *Macedonia* 44 **E6**
Valašské Meziříčí, *Czech Rep.* 27 **B10**
Valáxa, *Greece* 46 **C6**
Vålberg, *Sweden* 10 **E7**
Valbo, *Sweden* 10 **D10**
Valbondione, *Italy* 40 **B7**
Vâlcani, *Romania* 28 **D5**
Vâlcea □, *Romania* 29 **F9**
Valcheta, *Argentina* 128 **E3**
Valdagno, *Italy* 41 **C8**
Valdahon, *France* 19 **E13**
Valdai Hills = Valdayskaya Vozvyshennost, *Russia* 32 **D7**
Valday, *Russia* 32 **D7**
Valdayskaya Vozvyshennost, *Russia* 32 **D7**
Valdeazogues →, *Spain* 37 **G6**
Valdecañas, Embalse de, *Spain* 36 **F5**
Valdemarsvik, *Sweden* 11 **F10**
Valdemoro, *Spain* 36 **E7**
Valdepeñas, *Spain* 37 **G7**
Valderaduey →, *Spain* 36 **D5**
Valdérice, *Italy* 42 **D5**
Valderrobres, *Spain* 38 **E5**
Valdés, Pen., *Argentina* 128 **E4**
Valdez, *U.S.A.* 100 **B5**
Valdivia, *Chile* 128 **D2**
Valdobbiádene, *Italy* 41 **C8**
Valdosta, *U.S.A.* 115 **K4**
Valdoviño, *Spain* 36 **B2**
Valdres, *Norway* 9 **F13**
Vale, *Georgia* 35 **K6**
Vale, *U.S.A.* 108 **E5**
Vale of Glamorgan □, *U.K.* 15 **F4**
Valea lui Mihai, *Romania* 28 **C7**
Valea Mărului, *Romania* 29 **E12**
Valemount, *Canada* 102 **C5**
Valença, *Brazil* 125 **F11**
Valença, *Portugal* 36 **C2**
Valença do Piauí, *Brazil* 125 **E10**
Valençay, *France* 19 **E8**
Valence, *France* 21 **D8**
Valence d'Agen, *France* 20 **D4**
Valencia, *Spain* 39 **F4**
Valencia, *Trin. & Tob.* 125 **K15**
Valencia, *U.S.A.* 109 **J10**
Valencia, *Venezuela* 124 **A5**
Valencia □, *Spain* 39 **F4**
Valencia ✕ (VLC), *Spain* 39 **F4**
Valencia, G. de, *Spain* 39 **F5**
Valencia de Alcántara, *Spain* 37 **F3**
Valencia de Don Juan, *Spain* 36 **C5**
Valencia I., *Ireland* 12 **E1**
Valenciennes, *France* 19 **B10**
Văleni, *Romania* 29 **F9**
Vălenii de Munte, *Romania* 29 **E11**
Valensole, *France* 21 **E9**
Valentigney, *France* 19 **E13**
Valentim, Sa. do, *Brazil* 125 **E10**
Valentin, *Russia* 54 **C7**
Valentine, *U.S.A.* 113 **K2**
Valenza, *Italy* 40 **C5**
Valera, *Venezuela* 124 **B4**
Valga, *Estonia* 9 **H22**
Valguarnera Caropepe, *Italy* 43 **E7**
Valier, *U.S.A.* 108 **B7**
Valinco, G. de, *France* 21 **G12**
Valjevo, *Serbia & M.* 44 **B3**
Valka, *Latvia* 9 **H21**
Valkeakoski, *Finland* 9 **F20**
Valkenswaard, *Neths.* 17 **C5**
Vall de Uxó = La Vall d'Uixó, *Spain* 38 **F4**
Valla, *Sweden* 10 **E10**
Valladolid, *Mexico* 119 **C7**
Valladolid, *Spain* 36 **D6**
Valladolid □, *Spain* 36 **D6**
Vallata, *Italy* 43 **A8**
Valldemossa, *Spain* 48 **B9**
Valle d'Aosta □, *Italy* 40 **C4**
Valle de Arán, *Spain* 38 **C5**
Valle de la Pascua, *Venezuela* 124 **B5**
Valle de las Palmas, *Mexico* 111 **N10**
Valle de Santiago, *Mexico* 118 **C4**
Valle de Suchil, *Mexico* 118 **C4**
Valle de Zaragoza, *Mexico* 118 **B3**
Valle del Ticino ⌓, *Italy* 40 **C6**
Valle Fértil, Sierra del, *Argentina* 126 **C2**
Valle Gran Rey, *Canary Is.* 48 **F2**
Valle Hermoso, *Mexico* 119 **B5**
Valledupar, *Colombia* 124 **A4**
Vallehermoso, *Canary Is.* 48 **F2**
Vallejo, *U.S.A.* 110 **G4**
Vallenar, *Chile* 126 **B1**
Vallentuna, *Sweden* 10 **E12**
Valleraugue, *France* 20 **D7**
Vallet, *France* 18 **E5**
Valletta, *Malta* 49 **D2**
Valley Center, *U.S.A.* 111 **M9**
Valley City, *U.S.A.* 112 **B6**
Valley Falls, *Oreg., U.S.A.* 108 **E3**
Valley Falls, *R.I., U.S.A.* 117 **E13**
Valley of the Kings, *Egypt* 80 **B3**
Valley Springs, *U.S.A.* 110 **G6**
Valley View, *U.S.A.* 117 **F8**
Valley Wells, *U.S.A.* 111 **K11**
Valleyview, *Canada* 102 **B5**
Valli di Comácchio, *Italy* 41 **D9**
Vallimanca, Arroyo, *Argentina* 126 **D4**
Vallo della Lucánia, *Italy* 43 **B8**
Vallon-Pont-d'Arc, *France* 21 **D8**
Vallorbe, *Switz.* 25 **J2**
Valls, *Spain* 38 **D6**
Valmaseda = Balmaseda, *Spain* 38 **B1**
Valmiera, *Latvia* 9 **H21**
Valnera, *Spain* 36 **B7**
Valognes, *France* 18 **C5**
Valona = Vlorë, *Albania* 44 **F3**
Valongo, *Portugal* 36 **D2**
Valozhyn, *Belarus* 32 **E4**
Valpaços, *Portugal* 36 **D3**
Valparaíso, *Chile* 126 **C1**
Valparaíso, *Mexico* 118 **C4**
Valparaiso, *U.S.A.* 114 **E2**
Valparaíso □, *Chile* 126 **C1**
Valpovo, *Croatia* 28 **E3**
Valréas, *France* 21 **D9**
Vals, *Switz.* 25 **J5**
Vals →, *S. Africa* 88 **D4**
Vals, Tanjung, *Indonesia* 63 **F9**
Vals-les-Bains, *France* 21 **D8**
Valsad, *India* 66 **J8**
Valtellina, *Italy* 40 **B6**
Valuyki, *Russia* 33 **G10**
Valverde, *Canary Is.* 48 **G2**
Valverde del Camino, *Spain* 37 **H4**
Valverde del Fresno, *Spain* 36 **E4**
Vama, *Romania* 29 **C10**
Vamdrup, *Denmark* 11 **J3**
Vämhus, *Sweden* 10 **C8**
Vammala, *Finland* 9 **F20**
Vámos, *Greece* 49 **D6**
Van, *Turkey* 70 **B4**
Van, L. = Van Gölü, *Turkey* 70 **B4**
Van Alstyne, *U.S.A.* 113 **J6**
Van Blommestein Meer, *Suriname* 125 **C7**
Van Buren, *Canada* 105 **C6**
Van Buren, *Ark., U.S.A.* 113 **H7**
Van Buren, *Maine, U.S.A.* 115 **B11**
Van Buren, *Mo., U.S.A.* 113 **G9**
Van Canh, *Vietnam* 64 **F7**
Van Diemen, C., *N. Terr., Australia* 92 **B5**
Van Diemen, C., *Queens., Australia* 94 **B2**
Van Diemen G., *Australia* 92 **B5**
Van Gölü, *Turkey* 70 **B4**
Van Horn, *U.S.A.* 113 **K2**

Van Ninh, *Vietnam* 64 F7
Van Rees, Pegunungan, *Indonesia* 63 E9
Van Wert, *U.S.A.* 114 E3
Van Yen, *Vietnam* 58 G5
Vanadzor, *Armenia* 35 K7
Vanavara, *Russia* 53 C11
Vancouver, *Canada* 102 D4
Vancouver, *U.S.A.* 110 E4
Vancouver, C., *Australia* 93 G2
Vancouver I., *Canada* 102 D3
Vancouver International ✕
(YVR), *U.S.A.* 110 A3
Vanda = Vantaa, *Finland* 9 F21
Vandalia, *Ill., U.S.A.* 112 F10
Vandalia, *Mo., U.S.A.* 112 F9
Vandenburg, *U.S.A.* 111 L6
Vanderbijlpark, *S. Africa* 89 D4
Vandergrift, *U.S.A.* 116 F5
Vanderhoof, *Canada* 102 C4
Vanderkloof Dam, *S. Africa* 88 E3
Vanderlin I., *Australia* 94 B2
Vänern, *Sweden* 11 F7
Vänersborg, *Sweden* 11 F6
Vang Vieng, *Laos* 64 C4
Vanga, *Kenya* 86 C4
Vangaindrano, *Madag.* 89 C8
Vanguard, *Canada* 103 D7
Vanino, *Russia* 53 E15
Vânju Mare, *Romania* 28 F7
Vanna, *Norway* 8 A18
Vännäs, *Sweden* 8 E18
Vannes, *France* 18 E4
Vanoise, Massif de la, *France* 21 C10
Vanrhynsdorp, *S. Africa* 88 E2
Vansbro, *Sweden* 10 D8
Vansittart B., *Australia* 92 B4
Vantaa, *Finland* 9 F21
Vanua Balavu, *Fiji* 91 C9
Vanua Levu, *Fiji* 91 C8
Vanuatu ■, *Pac. Oc.* 96 J8
Vanwyksvlei, *S. Africa* 88 E3
Vanzylsrus, *S. Africa* 88 D3
Vapnyarka, *Ukraine* 29 B13
Var □, *France* 21 E10
Var →, *France* 21 E11
Vara, *Sweden* 11 F6
Varades, *France* 18 E5
Varáita →, *Italy* 40 D4
Varallo, *Italy* 40 C5
Varāmīn, *Iran* 71 C6
Varāmīn □, *Iran* 71 B6
Varanasi, *India* 69 G10
Varangerfjorden, *Norway* 8 A23
Varangerhalvøya, *Norway* 8 A23
Varano, Lago di, *Italy* 41 G12
Varaždin, *Croatia* 41 B13
Varazze, *Italy* 40 D5
Varberg, *Sweden* 11 G6
Vardak □, *Afghan.* 66 B6
Vardar = Axiós →, *Greece* 44 F6
Varde, *Denmark* 11 J2
Varde Å →, *Denmark* 11 J2
Vardø, *Norway* 8 A24
Varel, *Germany* 24 B4
Varella, Mui, *Vietnam* 64 F7
Varėna, *Lithuania* 9 J21
Varennes-sur-Allier, *France* 19 F10
Varennes-Vauzelles, *France* 19 E10
Vareš, *Bos.-H.* 28 F3
Varese, *Italy* 40 C5
Vârfurile, *Romania* 28 D7
Vårgårda, *Sweden* 11 F6
Varginha, *Brazil* 127 A6
Vargön, *Sweden* 11 F6
Varillas, *Chile* 126 A1
Varkaus, *Finland* 9 E22
Värmdölandet, *Sweden* 10 E12
Värmeln, *Sweden* 10 E6
Värmlands län □, *Sweden* 10 E6
Värmlandsbro, *Sweden* 10 E7
Varna, *Bulgaria* 45 C11
Varna □, *Bulgaria* 45 C11
Värnamo, *Sweden* 11 G8
Varnsdorf, *Czech Rep.* 26 A7
Várpalota, *Hungary* 28 C3
Vars, *Canada* 117 A9
Vars, *France* 21 D10
Varto, *Turkey* 73 C9
Varvarin, *Serbia & M.* 44 C5
Varysburg, *U.S.A.* 116 D6
Varzaneh, *Iran* 71 C7
Varzi, *Italy* 40 D6
Varzo, *Italy* 40 B5
Varzy, *France* 19 E10
Vas □, *Hungary* 28 C1
Vasa = Vaasa, *Finland* 8 E19
Vasa Barris →, *Brazil* 125 F11
Vásárosnamény, *Hungary* 28 B7
Vascão →, *Portugal* 37 H3
Vaşcău, *Romania* 28 D7
Vascongadas = País Vasco □,
Spain 38 C2
Vashkivtsi, *Ukraine* 29 B10
Vasht = Khāsh, *Iran* 66 E2
Vasilevichi, *Belarus* 33 F5
Vasilikón, *Greece* 46 C5
Vasilkov = Vasylkiv, *Ukraine* 33 G6
Vaslui, *Romania* 29 D12
Vaslui □, *Romania* 29 D12
Väsman, *Sweden* 10 D9
Vassar, *Canada* 103 D9
Vassar, *U.S.A.* 114 D4
Västerås, *Sweden* 10 E10
Västerbotten, *Sweden* 8 D18
Västerdalälven →, *Sweden* 10 D8
Västergötland, *Sweden* 11 F7
Västerhaninge, *Sweden* 10 E12
Västervik, *Sweden* 11 G10
Västmanland, *Sweden* 9 G16
Västmanlands län □, *Sweden* 10 E10
Vasto, *Italy* 41 F11
Västra Götalands Län □, *Sweden* 11 F6
Vasvár, *Hungary* 28 C1
Vasylivka, *Ukraine* 29 E13
Vasylkiv, *Ukraine* 33 G6
Vatan, *France* 19 E8
Vatersay, *U.K.* 13 E1
Váthia, *Greece* 46 E4
Vatican City ■, *Europe* 41 G9
Vaticano, C., *Italy* 43 D8
Vatili, *Cyprus* 49 D12
Vatin, *Serbia & M.* 28 E6
Vatnajökull, *Iceland* 8 D5
Vatoa, *Fiji* 91 D9
Vatólakkos, *Greece* 49 D5
Vatoloha, *Madag.* 89 B8
Vatomandry, *Madag.* 89 B8
Vatra-Dornei, *Romania* 29 C10
Vatrak →, *India* 68 H5
Vättern, *Sweden* 11 F8
Vaucluse □, *France* 21 E9
Vaucouleurs, *France* 19 D12
Vaud □, *Switz.* 25 J2
Vaudreuil-Dorion, *Canada* 117 A10
Vaughn, *Mont., U.S.A.* 108 C8
Vaughn, *N. Mex., U.S.A.* 109 J11
Vaujours L., *Canada* 104 A5
Vaupés = Uaupés →, *Brazil* 124 C5
Vaupes □, *Colombia* 124 C4
Vauvert, *France* 21 E8
Vauxhall, *Canada* 102 C6
Vav, *India* 68 G4
Vavatenina, *Madag.* 89 B8
Vava'u, *Tonga* 91 D12
Vavoua, *Ivory C.* 82 D3
Vawkavysk, *Belarus* 33 F3
Vaxholm, *Sweden* 10 E12
Växjö, *Sweden* 11 H8
Våxtorp, *Sweden* 11 H7
Vaygach, Ostrov, *Russia* 52 C6
Váyia, *Greece* 46 C5
Váyia, Ákra, *Greece* 49 C10
Veaikevárri = Svappavaara,
Sweden 8 C19
Vechelde, *Germany* 24 C6
Vechta, *Germany* 24 C4
Vechte →, *Neths.* 17 B6
Vecsés, *Hungary* 28 C4
Veddige, *Sweden* 11 G6
Vedea →, *Romania* 29 G10
Vedia, *Argentina* 126 C3
Vedrette di Ries-Aurina ⌓, *Italy* 41 B9
Vedum, *Sweden* 11 F7
Veendam, *Neths.* 17 A6
Veenendaal, *Neths.* 17 B5
Vefsna →, *Norway* 8 D15
Vega, *Norway* 8 D14
Vega, *U.S.A.* 113 H3
Vega Baja, *Puerto Rico* 121 d
Vegadeo, *Spain* 36 B3
Vegorrítis, Límni, *Greece* 44 F5
Vegreville, *Canada* 102 C6
Veinge, *Sweden* 11 H7
Veisiejai, *Lithuania* 30 D10
Vejbystrand, *Sweden* 11 H6
Vejen, *Denmark* 11 J3
Vejer de la Frontera, *Spain* 37 J5
Vejle, *Denmark* 11 J3
Vejle Amtskommune □,
Denmark 11 J3
Vejle Fjord, *Denmark* 11 J3
Vela Luka, *Croatia* 41 F13
Velas, C., *Costa Rica* 120 D2
Velasco, Sierra de, *Argentina* 126 B2
Velay, Mts. du, *France* 20 D7
Velbert, *Germany* 24 D3
Velddrif, *S. Africa* 88 E2
Velebit ⌓, *Croatia* 41 D12
Velebit Planina, *Croatia* 41 D12
Velebitski Kanal, *Croatia* 41 D11
Veleka →, *Bulgaria* 45 D11
Velencei-tó, *Hungary* 28 C3
Velenje, *Slovenia* 41 B12
Veles, *Macedonia* 44 E5
Velestínon, *Greece* 46 B4
Vélez-Málaga, *Spain* 37 J6
Vélez Rubio, *Spain* 39 H2
Velhas →, *Brazil* 125 G10
Velika, *Croatia* 28 E2
Velika Gorica, *Croatia* 41 C13
Velika Kapela, *Croatia* 41 C12
Velika Kladuša, *Bos.-H.* 41 C12
Velika Kruša, *Serbia & M.* 44 D4
Velika Morava →, *Serbia & M.* 44 B5
Velika Plana, *Serbia & M.* 44 B5
Velikaya →, *Russia* 32 D5
Velikaya Kema, *Russia* 54 B8
Velikaya Lepetikha, *Ukraine* 33 J7
Veliké Kapušany, *Slovak Rep.* 27 C15
Velike Lašče, *Slovenia* 41 C11
Veliki Jastrebac, *Serbia & M.* 44 C5
Veliki Kanal, *Serbia & M.* 28 E4
Veliki Popović, *Serbia & M.* 44 B5
Velikiye Luki, *Russia* 32 D6
Veliko Gradište, *Serbia & M.* 44 B5
Veliko Tŭrnovo, *Bulgaria* 45 C9
Velikonda Range, *India* 66 M11
Vélingara, *Kolda, Senegal* 82 C2
Vélingara, *Louga, Senegal* 82 B2
Velingrad, *Bulgaria* 44 D7
Velino, Mte., *Italy* 41 F10
Velizh, *Russia* 32 E6
Velké Karlovice, *Czech Rep.* 27 B11
Velké Meziříčí, *Czech Rep.* 26 B9
Vel'ký Javorník, *Slovak Rep.* 27 B11
Vel'ký Krtíš, *Slovak Rep.* 27 C12
Vel'ký Meder, *Slovak Rep.* 27 D10
Vel'ký Tribeč, *Slovak Rep.* 27 C11
Velletri, *Italy* 42 A5
Vellinge, *Sweden* 11 J6
Vellmar, *Germany* 24 D5
Vellore, *India* 66 N11
Velsk, *Russia* 32 B11
Velten, *Germany* 24 C9
Veluwezoom △, *Neths.* 17 B6
Velva, *U.S.A.* 112 A4
Velvendós, *Greece* 44 F6
Velyka Mykhaylivka, *Ukraine* 29 C14
Velyki Luchky, *Ukraine* 28 B7
Velykyy Bereznyy, *Ukraine* 28 B7
Velykyy Bychkiv, *Ukraine* 29 C9
Vemb, *Denmark* 11 H2
Vemdalen, *Sweden* 10 B7
Ven, *Sweden* 11 J6
Venaco, *France* 21 F13
Venado Tuerto, *Argentina* 126 C3
Venafro, *Italy* 43 A7
Venarey-les-Laumes, *France* 19 E11
Venaría, *Italy* 40 C4
Venčane, *Serbia & M.* 44 B4
Vence, *France* 21 E11
Vendas Novas, *Portugal* 37 G2
Vendée □, *France* 18 F5
Vendée →, *France* 18 F5
Vendéen, Bocage, *France* 20 B2
Vendeuvre-sur-Barse, *France* 19 D11
Vendôme, *France* 18 E8
Vendrell = El Vendrell, *Spain* 38 D6
Vendsyssel, *Denmark* 11 G4
Vendychany, *Ukraine* 29 B12
Venelles, *France* 21 E9
Véneta, L., *Italy* 41 C9
Véneto □, *Italy* 41 C9
Venev, *Russia* 32 E10
Venézia, *Italy* 41 C9
Venézia, G. di, *Italy* 41 C10
Venezuela ■, *S. Amer.* 124 B5
Venezuela, G. de, *Venezuela* 124 A4
Vengurla, *India* 66 M8
Venice = Venézia, *Italy* 41 C9
Venice, *U.S.A.* 115 M4
Vénissieux, *France* 21 C8
Venjansjön, *Sweden* 10 D8
Venkatapuram, *India* 67 K12
Venlo, *Neths.* 17 C6
Vennesla, *Norway* 9 G12
Venosa, *Italy* 43 B8
Venray, *Neths.* 17 C6
Venta, *Lithuania* 30 B9
Venta →, *Latvia* 30 A8
Venta de Baños, *Spain* 36 D6
Venta de Cardeña = Cardeña,
Spain 37 G6
Ventana, Punta de la, *Mexico* 118 C3
Ventana, Sa. de la, *Argentina* 126 D3
Ventersburg, *S. Africa* 88 D4
Venterstad, *S. Africa* 88 E4
Ventimíglia, *Italy* 40 E4
Ventnor, *U.K.* 15 G6
Ventotène, *Italy* 42 B6
Ventoux, Mt., *France* 21 D9
Ventspils, *Latvia* 9 H19
Ventspils □, *Latvia* 30 A8
Ventuarí →, *Venezuela* 124 C5
Ventucopa, *U.S.A.* 111 L7
Ventura, *U.S.A.* 111 L7
Venus B., *Australia* 95 F4
Vera, *Argentina* 126 B3
Vera, *Spain* 39 H3
Veracruz, *Mexico* 119 D5
Veracruz □, *Mexico* 119 D5
Veraval, *India* 68 J4
Verbánia, *Italy* 40 C5
Verbicaro, *Italy* 43 C8
Verbier, *Switz.* 25 J3
Vercelli, *Italy* 40 C5
Verchovchevo, *Ukraine* 33 H8
Vercors ⌓, *France* 21 D9
Verdalsøra, *Norway* 8 E14
Verde →, *Argentina* 128 E3
Verde →, *Goiás, Brazil* 125 G8
Verde →, *Mato Grosso do Sul,*
Brazil 125 H8
Verde →, *Chihuahua, Mexico* 118 B3
Verde →, *Oaxaca, Mexico* 119 D5
Verde →, *Veracruz, Mexico* 118 C4
Verde →, *Paraguay* 126 A4
Verde →, *U.S.A.* 106 D4
Verde, Cay, *Bahamas* 120 B4
Verde Island Pass, *Phil.* 61 E4
Verden, *Germany* 24 C5
Verdhikoúsa, *Greece* 46 B3
Verdi, *U.S.A.* 110 F7
Verdon ⌓, *France* 21 E10
Verdon →, *France* 21 E9
Verdun, *France* 19 C12
Verdun-sur-le-Doubs, *France* 19 F12
Vereeniging, *S. Africa* 89 D4
Verga, C., *Guinea* 82 C2
Vergara, *Uruguay* 127 C5
Vergato, *Italy* 40 D8
Vergemont Cr. →, *Australia* 94 C3
Vergennes, *U.S.A.* 117 B11
Vergt, *France* 20 C4
Verín, *Spain* 36 D3
Verkhnedvinsk =
Vyerkhnyadzvinsk, *Belarus* 32 E4
Verkhnevilyuysk, *Russia* 53 C13
Verkhniy Baskunchak, *Russia* 35 F8
Verkhovye, *Russia* 33 F9
Verkhovyna, *Ukraine* 29 B9
Verkhoyansk, *Russia* 53 C14
Verkhoyansk Ra. =
Verkhoyanskiy Khrebet, *Russia* 53 C13
Verkhoyanskiy Khrebet, *Russia* 53 C13
Vermenton, *France* 19 E10
Vermilion, *Canada* 103 C6
Vermilion, *U.S.A.* 116 E2
Vermilion →, *Canada* 103 C6
Vermilion, B., *U.S.A.* 113 L9
Vermilion Bay, *Canada* 103 D10
Vermilion L., *U.S.A.* 112 B8
Vermillion, *U.S.A.* 112 D6
Vermillion →, *Canada* 104 C5
Vermont □, *U.S.A.* 117 C12
Vermosh, *Albania* 44 D3
Vernadsky, *Antarctica* 5 C17
Vernal, *U.S.A.* 108 F9
Vernalis, *U.S.A.* 110 H5
Vernazza, *Italy* 40 D6
Verner, *Canada* 104 C3
Verneuil-sur-Avre, *France* 18 D7
Verneukpan, *S. Africa* 88 E3
Vernier, *Switz.* 25 J2
Vérnio, *Italy* 40 D8
Vernon, *Canada* 102 C5
Vernon, *France* 18 C8
Vernon, *U.S.A.* 113 H5
Vernonia, *U.S.A.* 110 E3
Vernouillet, *France* 18 D8
Vero Beach, *U.S.A.* 115 M5
Véroia, *Greece* 44 F6
Véroli, *Italy* 41 G10
Verona, *Canada* 117 B8
Verona, *Italy* 40 C7
Verona, *U.S.A.* 112 D10
Verrès, *Italy* 40 C4
Versailles, *France* 19 D9
Versmold, *Germany* 24 C4
Vert, C., *Senegal* 82 C1
Vertou, *France* 18 E5
Vertus, *France* 19 D11
Verulam, *S. Africa* 89 D5
Verviers, *Belgium* 17 D5
Vervins, *France* 19 C10
Veržej, *Slovenia* 41 B13
Verzy, *France* 19 C11
Vescovato, *France* 21 F13
Veselí nad Lužnicí, *Czech Rep.* 26 B7
Veselie, *Bulgaria* 45 D11
Veselovskoye Vdkhr., *Russia* 35 G5
Veshenskaya, *Russia* 34 F5
Vesle →, *France* 19 C10
Vesoul, *France* 19 E13
Vessigebro, *Sweden* 11 H6
Vesterålen, *Norway* 8 B16
Vestfjorden, *Norway* 8 C15
Vestmannaeyjar, *Iceland* 8 E3
Vestsjællands Amtskommune □,
Denmark 11 J5
Vestspitsbergen, *Svalbard* 4 B8
Vestvågøy, *Norway* 8 B15
Vesuvio, *Italy* 43 B7
Vesuvius, Mt. = Vesuvio, *Italy* 43 B7
Vesyegonsk, *Russia* 32 C9
Veszprém, *Hungary* 28 C2
Veszprém □, *Hungary* 28 C2
Vésztő, *Hungary* 28 D6
Vetlanda, *Sweden* 11 G9
Vetluga, *Russia* 34 B7
Vetlugu →, *Russia* 34 B8
Vetluzhskiy, *Kostroma, Russia* 34 A7
Vetluzhskiy, *Nizhniy Novgorod,*
Russia 34 B7
Vetovo, *Bulgaria* 45 C10
Vetralla, *Italy* 41 F9
Vetren, *Bulgaria* 45 D8
Vettore, Mte., *Italy* 41 F10
Veurne, *Belgium* 17 C2
Veveno →, *Sudan* 81 F3
Vevey, *Switz.* 25 J2
Vévi, *Greece* 44 F5
Veynes, *France* 21 D9
Veys, *Iran* 71 D6
Vézelay, *France* 19 E10
Vézelise, *France* 19 D13
Vézère →, *France* 20 D4
Vezhen, *Bulgaria* 45 D8
Vezirköprü, *Turkey* 72 B6
Vezzani, *France* 21 F13
Vi Thanh, *Vietnam* 65 H5
Viacha, *Bolivia* 124 G5
Viadana, *Italy* 40 D7
Viamão, *Brazil* 127 C5
Viana, *Brazil* 125 D10
Viana, *Spain* 38 C2
Viana do Alentejo, *Portugal* 37 G3
Viana do Bolo, *Spain* 36 C3
Viana do Castelo, *Portugal* 36 D2
Viana do Castelo □, *Portugal* 36 D2
Vianden, *Lux.* 17 E6
Viangchan = Vientiane, *Laos* 64 D4
Vianópolis, *Brazil* 125 G9
Viar →, *Spain* 37 H5
Viaréggio, *Italy* 40 E7
Viaur →, *France* 20 D5
Vibble, *Sweden* 11 G12
Vibo Valéntia, *Italy* 43 D9
Viborg, *Denmark* 11 H3
Viborg Amtskommune □,
Denmark 11 H3
Vibraye, *France* 18 D7
Vic, *Spain* 38 D7
Vic, Étang de, *France* 20 E7
Vic-en-Bigorre, *France* 20 E4
Vic-Fezensac, *France* 20 E4
Vic-le-Comte, *France* 19 G10
Vic-sur-Cère, *France* 20 D6
Vícar, *Spain* 39 J2
Vicenza, *Italy* 41 C8
Vich = Vic, *Spain* 38 D7
Vichada →, *Colombia* 124 C5
Vichuga, *Russia* 34 B5
Vichy, *France* 19 F10
Vicksburg, *Ariz., U.S.A.* 111 M13
Vicksburg, *Miss., U.S.A.* 113 J9
Vico, *France* 21 F12
Vico, L. di, *Italy* 41 F9
Vico del Gargano, *Italy* 41 G12
Vicovu de Sus, *Romania* 29 C10
Victor, *India* 68 J4
Victor, *U.S.A.* 116 D7
Victor Harbor, *Australia* 95 F2
Victoria, *Argentina* 126 C3
Victoria, *Canada* 102 D4
Victoria, *Chile* 128 D2
Victoria, *Guinea* 82 C2
Victoria, *Malta* 49 C1
Victoria, *Phil.* 61 D4
Victoria, *Romania* 29 E9
Victoria, *Kans., U.S.A.* 112 F5
Victoria, *Tex., U.S.A.* 113 L6
Victoria □, *Australia* 95 F3
Victoria →, *Australia* 92 C4
Victoria, Grand L., *Canada* 104 C4
Victoria, L., *Africa* 86 C3
Victoria, L., *Australia* 95 E3
Victoria, Mt., *Burma* 67 J18
Victoria Beach, *Canada* 103 C9
Victoria de Durango = Durango,
Mexico 118 C4
Victoria de las Tunas, *Cuba* 120 B4
Victoria Falls, *Zimbabwe* 87 F2
Victoria Harbour, *Canada* 116 B5
Victoria I., *Canada* 100 A8
Victoria L., *Canada* 105 C8
Victoria Ld., *Antarctica* 5 D11
Victoria Nile →, *Uganda* 86 B3
Victoria River, *Australia* 92 C5
Victoria Str., *Canada* 100 B9
Victoria West, *S. Africa* 88 E3
Victorias, *Phil.* 61 F5
Victoriaville, *Canada* 105 C5
Victorica, *Argentina* 126 D2
Victorville, *U.S.A.* 111 L9
Vicuña, *Chile* 126 C1
Vicuña Mackenna, *Argentina* 126 C3
Vidal, *U.S.A.* 111 L12
Vidal Junction, *U.S.A.* 111 L12
Vidalia, *U.S.A.* 115 J4
Vidamlya, *Belarus* 31 F10
Vidauban, *France* 21 E10
Videbæk, *Denmark* 11 H2
Videle, *Romania* 29 F10
Vídho, *Greece* 49 A3
Vidigueira, *Portugal* 37 G3
Vidin, *Bulgaria* 44 C6
Vidio, C., *Spain* 36 B4
Vidisha, *India* 68 H7
Vidra, *Romania* 29 E11
Viduša, *Bos.-H.* 44 D2
Vidzy, *Belarus* 9 J22
Viechtach, *Germany* 25 F8
Viedma, *Argentina* 128 E4
Viedma, L., *Argentina* 128 F2
Vieira do Minho, *Portugal* 36 D2
Vielha, *Spain* 38 C5
Viella = Vielha, *Spain* 38 C5
Vielsalm, *Belgium* 17 D5
Vienenburg, *Germany* 24 D6
Vieng Pou Kha, *Laos* 58 G3
Vienna = Wien, *Austria* 27 C9
Vienna, *Ill., U.S.A.* 113 G10
Vienna, *Mo., U.S.A.* 112 F9
Vienne, *France* 21 C8
Vienne □, *France* 20 B4
Vienne →, *France* 18 E7
Vientiane, *Laos* 64 D4
Vientos, Paso de los, *Caribbean* 121 C5
Vieques, Isla de, *Puerto Rico* 121 d
Vierge Pt., *St. Lucia* 121 f
Viernheim, *Germany* 25 F4
Viersen, *Germany* 24 D2
Vierwaldstättersee, *Switz.* 25 J4
Vierzon, *France* 19 E9
Vieste, *Italy* 41 G13
Vietnam ■, *Asia* 64 C6
Vieux-Boucau-les-Bains, *France* 20 E2
Vieux Fort, *St. Lucia* 121 f
Vif, *France* 21 C9
Vigan, *Phil.* 61 C4
Vigévano, *Italy* 40 C5
Vigia, *Brazil* 125 D9
Vigía Chico, *Mexico* 119 D7
Víglas, Ákra, *Greece* 49 D9
Vignemalle, *France* 20 F3
Vigneulles-lès-Hattonchâtel,
France 19 D12
Vignola, *Italy* 40 D8
Vigo, *Spain* 36 C2
Vigo, Ría de, *Spain* 36 C2
Vigsø Bugt, *Denmark* 11 G2
Vihiers, *France* 18 E6
Vihowa, *Pakistan* 68 D4
Vihowa →, *Pakistan* 68 D4
Vijayawada, *India* 67 L12
Vijosë →, *Albania* 44 F3
Vík, *Iceland* 8 E4
Vika, *Sweden* 10 D8
Vikarbyn, *Sweden* 10 D9
Vikeke = Viqueque, *E. Timor* 63 F7
Viken, *Skåne, Sweden* 11 H6
Viken, *Västra Götaland, Sweden* 11 F8
Viking, *Canada* 102 C6
Vikmanshyttan, *Sweden* 10 D9
Vikna, *Norway* 8 D14
Vikos-Aoos △, *Greece* 46 B2
Vila da Maganja, *Mozam.* 87 F4
Vila de Rei, *Portugal* 36 F2
Vila do Bispo, *Portugal* 37 H2
Vila do Conde, *Portugal* 36 D2
Vila Franca de Xira, *Portugal* 37 G2
Vila Gamito, *Mozam.* 87 E3
Vila Gomes da Costa, *Mozam.* 89 C5
Vila Machado, *Mozam.* 87 F3
Vila Mouzinho, *Mozam.* 87 E3
Vila Nova de Famalicão, *Portugal* 36 D2
Vila Nova de Fos Côa, *Portugal* 36 D3
Vila Nova de Gaia, *Portugal* 36 D2
Vila Nova de Ourém, *Portugal* 36 F2
Vila Pouca de Aguiar, *Portugal* 36 D3
Vila Real, *Portugal* 36 D3
Vila Real □, *Portugal* 36 D3
Vila-real de los Infantes, *Spain* 38 F4
Vila Real de Santo António,
Portugal 37 H3
Vila Vasco da Gama, *Mozam.* 87 E3
Vila Velha, *Brazil* 127 A7

Vila Viçosa, *Portugal* 37 G3
Vilafranca del Maestrat, *Spain* 38 E4
Vilafranca del Penedès, *Spain* 38 D6
Vilagarcía de Arousa, *Spain* 36 C2
Vilaine →, *France* 18 E4
Vilanandro, Tanjona, *Madag.* 89 B7
Vilanculos, *Mozam.* 89 C6
Vilanova de Castelló, *Spain* 39 F4
Vilanova i la Geltrú, *Spain* 38 D6
Vilar Formosa, *Portugal* 36 E4
Vilaseca, *Spain* 38 D6
Vilaseca-Salou = Vilaseca, *Spain* 38 D6
Vilbjerg, *Denmark* 11 H2
Vilcheka, Zemlya, *Russia* 4 A11
Vilches, *Spain* 37 G7
Vileyka, *Belarus* 32 E4
Vilhelmina, *Sweden* 8 D17
Vilhena, *Brazil* 124 F6
Viliya = Neris →, *Lithuania* 9 J21
Viljandi, *Estonia* 9 G21
Vilkaviškis, *Lithuania* 30 D10
Vilkija, *Lithuania* 30 C10
Vilkitskogo, Proliv, *Russia* 53 B11
Vilkovo = Vylkove, *Ukraine* 29 E14
Villa Abecia, *Bolivia* 126 A2
Villa Ahumada, *Mexico* 118 A3
Villa Ana, *Argentina* 126 B4
Villa Ángela, *Argentina* 126 B3
Villa Bella, *Bolivia* 124 F5
Villa Cañás, *Argentina* 126 C3
Villa Colón, *Argentina* 126 C2
Villa Constitución, *Argentina* 126 C3
Villa de María, *Argentina* 126 B3
Villa del Rio, *Spain* 37 H6
Villa Dolores, *Argentina* 126 C2
Villa Frontera, *Mexico* 118 B4
Villa Guillermina, *Argentina* 126 B4
Villa Hayes, *Paraguay* 126 B4
Villa Iris, *Argentina* 126 D3
Villa Juárez, *Mexico* 118 B4
Villa María, *Argentina* 126 C3
Villa Mazán, *Argentina* 126 B2
Villa Minozzo, *Italy* 40 D7
Villa Montes, *Bolivia* 126 A3
Villa Ocampo, *Argentina* 126 B4
Villa Ocampo, *Mexico* 118 B3
Villa Ojo de Agua, *Argentina* 126 B3
Villa San Giovanni, *Italy* 43 D8
Villa San José, *Argentina* 126 C4
Villa San Martín, *Argentina* 126 B3
Villa Santina, *Italy* 41 B9
Villa Unión, *Mexico* 118 C3
Villablino, *Spain* 36 C4
Villacarlos, *Spain* 48 B11
Villacarriedo, *Spain* 36 B7
Villacarrillo, *Spain* 37 G7
Villacastín, *Spain* 36 E6
Villach, *Austria* 26 E6
Villacidro, *Italy* 42 C1
Villada, *Spain* 36 C6
Villadiego, *Spain* 36 C6
Villadóssola, *Italy* 40 B5
Villafeliche, *Spain* 38 D3
Villafranca, *Spain* 38 C3
Villafranca de los Barros, *Spain* 37 G4
Villafranca de los Caballeros, *Baleares, Spain* 48 B10
Villafranca de los Caballeros, *Toledo, Spain* 37 F7
Villafranca del Cid = Vilafranca del Maestrat, *Spain* 38 E4
Villafranca del Panadés = Vilafranca del Penedès, *Spain* 38 D6
Villafranca di Verona, *Italy* 40 C7
Villafranca Tirrena, *Italy* 43 D8
Villagrán, *Mexico* 119 C5
Villaguay, *Argentina* 126 C4
Villaharta, *Spain* 37 G6
Villahermosa, *Mexico* 119 D6
Villahermosa, *Spain* 39 G2
Villaines-la-Juhel, *France* 18 D6
Villajoyosa, *Spain* 39 G4
Villalba, *Spain* 36 B3
Villalba de Guardo, *Spain* 36 C6
Villalón de Campos, *Spain* 36 C5
Villalpando, *Spain* 36 D5
Villaluenga, *Spain* 36 E7
Villamanán, *Spain* 36 C5
Villamartín, *Spain* 37 J5
Villamayor de Santiago, *Spain* 38 F2
Villamblard, *France* 20 C4
Villanova Monteleone, *Italy* 42 B1
Villanueva, *U.S.A.* 113 H2
Villanueva de Castellón = Vilanova de Castelló, *Spain* 39 F4
Villanueva de Córdoba, *Spain* 37 G6
Villanueva de la Fuente, *Spain* 39 G2
Villanueva de la Serena, *Spain* 37 G5
Villanueva de la Sierra, *Spain* 36 E4
Villanueva de los Castillejos, *Spain* 37 H3
Villanueva de los Infantes, *Spain* 37 G7
Villanueva del Arzobispo, *Spain* 39 G2
Villanueva del Fresno, *Spain* 37 G3
Villanueva y Geltrú = Vilanova i la Geltrú, *Spain* 38 D6
Villaputzu, *Italy* 42 C2
Villaquilambre, *Spain* 36 C5
Villar del Arzobispo, *Spain* 38 F4
Villar del Rey, *Spain* 37 F4
Villard-de-Lans, *France* 21 C9
Villarramiel, *Spain* 36 C6
Villarreal = Vila-real de los Infantes, *Spain* 38 F4
Villarrica, *Chile* 128 D2
Villarrica, *Paraguay* 126 B4
Villarrobledo, *Spain* 39 F2
Villarroya de la Sierra, *Spain* 38 D3
Villarrubia de los Ojos, *Spain* 37 F7
Villars-les-Dombes, *France* 19 F12
Villasayas, *Spain* 38 D2
Villaseca de los Gamitos = Villaseco de los Gamitos, *Spain* 36 D4
Villaseco de los Gamitos, *Spain* 36 D4
Villasimíus, *Italy* 42 C2
Villastar, *Spain* 38 E3
Villatobas, *Spain* 36 F7
Villavicencio, *Argentina* 126 C2
Villavicencio, *Colombia* 124 C4
Villaviciosa, *Spain* 36 B5
Villazón, *Bolivia* 126 A2
Ville-Marie, *Canada* 104 C4
Ville Platte, *U.S.A.* 113 K8
Villedieu-les-Poêles, *France* 18 D5
Villefort, *France* 20 D7
Villefranche-de-Lauragais, *France* 20 E5
Villefranche-de-Rouergue, *France* 20 D6
Villefranche-du-Périgord, *France* 20 D5
Villefranche-sur-Saône, *France* 21 C8
Villel, *Spain* 38 E3
Villemur-sur-Tarn, *France* 20 E5
Villena, *Spain* 39 G4
Villenauxe-la-Grande, *France* 19 D10
Villenave-d'Ornon, *France* 20 D3
Villeneuve-d'Ascq, *France* 19 B10
Villeneuve-l'Archevêque, *France* 19 D10
Villeneuve-lès-Avignon, *France* 21 E8
Villeneuve-sur-Allier, *France* 19 F10
Villeneuve-sur-Lot, *France* 20 D4
Villeneuve-sur-Yonne, *France* 19 D10
Villeréal, *France* 20 D4
Villers-Bocage, *France* 18 C6
Villers-Cotterêts, *France* 19 C10
Villers-sur-Mer, *France* 18 C6
Villersexel, *France* 19 E13
Villerupt, *France* 19 C12
Villeurbanne, *France* 21 C8
Villiers, *S. Africa* 89 D4
Villingen-Schwenningen, *Germany* 25 G4
Villmanstrand = Lappeenranta, *Finland* 9 F23
Vilna, *Canada* 102 C6
Vilnius, *Lithuania* 9 J21
Vils, *Austria* 26 D3
Vils →, *Bayern, Germany* 25 G9
Vils →, *Bayern, Germany* 25 F7
Vilsbiburg, *Germany* 25 G8
Vilshofen, *Germany* 25 G9
Vilusi, *Serbia & M.* 44 D2
Vilvoorde, *Belgium* 17 D4
Vilyuy →, *Russia* 53 C13
Vilyuysk, *Russia* 53 C13
Vimianzo, *Spain* 36 B1
Vimioso, *Portugal* 36 D4
Vimmerby, *Sweden* 11 G9
Vimoutiers, *France* 18 D7
Vimperk, *Czech Rep.* 26 B6
Viña del Mar, *Chile* 126 C1
Vinarós, *Spain* 38 E5
Vincennes, *U.S.A.* 114 F2
Vincent, *U.S.A.* 111 L8
Vinchina, *Argentina* 126 B2
Vindelälven →, *Sweden* 8 E18
Vindeln, *Sweden* 8 D18
Vinderup, *Denmark* 11 H2
Vindhya Ra., *India* 68 H7
Vineland, *U.S.A.* 114 F8
Vineuil, *France* 18
Vinga, *Romania* 28 D6
Vingåker, *Sweden* 10 E9
Vinh, *Vietnam* 64 C5
Vinh Linh, *Vietnam* 64 D6
Vinh Long, *Vietnam* 65 G5
Vinh Yen, *Vietnam* 58 G5
Vinhais, *Portugal* 36 D3
Vinica, *Croatia* 41 B13
Vinica, *Macedonia* 44 E6
Vinica, *Slovenia* 41 C12
Vinita, *U.S.A.* 113 G7
Vinkovci, *Croatia* 28 E3
Vinnitsa = Vinnytsya, *Ukraine* 33 H5
Vinnytsya, *Ukraine* 33 H5
Vinslöv, *Sweden* 11 H7
Vinson Massif, *Antarctica* 5 D16
Vintjärn, *Sweden* 10 D10
Vinton, *Calif., U.S.A.* 110 F6
Vinton, *Iowa, U.S.A.* 112 D8
Vinton, *La., U.S.A.* 113 K8
Vințu de Jos, *Romania* 29 D8
Viöl, *Germany* 24 A5
Vipava, *Slovenia* 41 C10
Vipiteno, *Italy* 41 B8
Viqueque, *E. Timor* 63 F7
Vir, *Croatia* 41 D12
Virac, *Phil.* 61 E6
Virachey, *Cambodia* 64 F6
Virachey △, *Cambodia* 64 E6
Virago Sd., *Canada* 102 C2
Viramgam, *India* 68 H5
Viranşehir, *Turkey* 70 B3
Virawah, *Pakistan* 68 G4
Virbalis, *Lithuania* 30 D9
Virden, *Canada* 103 D8
Vire, *France* 18 D6
Vire →, *France* 18 C5
Vírgenes, C., *Argentina* 128 G3
Virgin →, *U.S.A.* 109 H6
Virgin Gorda, *Br. Virgin Is.* 121 e
Virgin Is. (British) ☒, *W. Indies* 121 e
Virgin Is. (U.S.) ☒, *W. Indies* 121 e
Virgin Islands △, *U.S. Virgin Is.* 121 C7
Virginia, *S. Africa* 88 D4
Virginia, *U.S.A.* 112 B8
Virginia □, *U.S.A.* 114 G7
Virginia Beach, *U.S.A.* 114 G8
Virginia City, *Mont., U.S.A.* 108 D8
Virginia City, *Nev., U.S.A.* 110 F7
Virginia Falls, *Canada* 102 A3
Virginiatown, *Canada* 104 C4
Virje, *Croatia* 41 B13
Viroqua, *U.S.A.* 112 D9
Virovitica, *Croatia* 28 E2
Virpazar, *Serbia & M.* 44 D3
Virpur, *India* 68 J4
Virserum, *Sweden* 11 G9
Virton, *Belgium* 17 E5
Virudunagar, *India* 66 Q10
Virunga △, *Dem. Rep. of the Congo* 86 B2
Vis, *Croatia* 41 E13
Visalia, *U.S.A.* 110 J7
Visayan Sea, *Phil.* 61 F5
Visby, *Sweden* 11 G12
Viscount Melville Sd., *Canada* 98 B9
Visé, *Belgium* 17 D5
Višegrad, *Bos.-H.* 28 G4
Viseu, *Brazil* 125 D9
Viseu, *Portugal* 36 E3
Viseu □, *Portugal* 36 E3
Vişeu de Sus, *Romania* 29 C9
Vishakhapatnam, *India* 67 L13
Vişina, *Romania* 29 G9
Vişineşti, *Moldova* 29 D13
Visingsö, *Sweden* 11 F8
Viskafors, *Sweden* 11 G6
Viskan →, *Sweden* 11 G6
Viški Kanal, *Croatia* 41 E13
Vislanda, *Sweden* 11 H8
Visnagar, *India* 68 H5
Višnja Gora, *Slovenia* 41 C11
Viso, Mte., *Italy* 40 D4
Viso del Marqués, *Spain* 37 G7
Visoko, *Bos.-H.* 28 G3
Visokoi I., *Antarctica* 5 B1
Visp, *Switz.* 25 J3
Vissefjärda, *Sweden* 11 H9
Visselhövede, *Germany* 24 C5
Vissenbjerg, *Denmark* 11 J4
Vista, *U.S.A.* 111 M9
Vistonikos, Ormos = Vistonís, Límni, *Greece* 45 E9
Vistonís, Límni, *Greece* 45 E9
Vistula = Wisła →, *Poland* 30 D5
Vit →, *Bulgaria* 45 C8
Vitanje, *Slovenia* 41 B12
Vitebsk = Vitsyebsk, *Belarus* 32 E6
Viterbo, *Italy* 41 F9
Vitez, *Bos.-H.* 28 F2
Viti Levu, *Fiji* 91 C7
Vitigudino, *Spain* 36 D4
Vitim, *Russia* 53 D12
Vitim →, *Russia* 53 D12
Vitina, *Bos.-H.* 41 E14
Vitína, *Greece* 46 D4
Vítkov, *Czech Rep.* 27 B10
Vitória, *Brazil* 125 H10
Vitória da Conquista, *Brazil* 125 F10
Vitória de São Antão, *Brazil* 125 E11
Vitoria-Gasteiz, *Spain* 38 C2
Vitosha △, *Bulgaria* 44 D7
Vitré, *France* 18 D5
Vitry-le-François, *France* 19 D11
Vitry-sur-Seine, *France* 19 D9
Vitsand, *Sweden* 10 D7
Vitsi, Óros, *Greece* 44 F5
Vitsyebsk, *Belarus* 32 E6
Vittaryd, *Sweden* 11 H7
Vitteaux, *France* 19 E11
Vittel, *France* 19 D12
Vittória, *Italy* 43 F7
Vittório Véneto, *Italy* 41 C9
Vittsjö, *Sweden* 11 H7
Viveiro, *Spain* 36 B3
Vivian, *U.S.A.* 113 J8
Viviers, *France* 21 D8
Vivonne, *France* 20 B4
Vizcaíno, Desierto de, *Mexico* 118 B2
Vizcaíno, Sierra, *Mexico* 118 B2
Vizcaya □, *Spain* 38 B2
Vize, *Turkey* 45 E11
Vizianagaram, *India* 67 K13
Vizille, *France* 21 C9
Viziñada, *Croatia* 41 C10
Viziru, *Romania* 29 E12
Vizzini, *Italy* 43 E7
Vlaardingen, *Neths.* 17 C4
Vlădeasa, Vf., *Romania* 28 D7
Vladičin Han, *Serbia & M.* 44 D6
Vladikavkaz, *Russia* 35 J7
Vladimir, *Russia* 32 D11
Vladimir Volynskiy = Volodymyr-Volynskyy, *Ukraine* 33 G3
Vladimirci, *Serbia & M.* 44 B3
Vladimirovac, *Serbia & M.* 28 E5
Vladimirovka, *Russia* 35 F8
Vladimirovo, *Bulgaria* 44 C7
Vladimorvka, *Kazakhstan* 34 E10
Vladislavovka, *Ukraine* 33 K8
Vladivostok, *Russia* 53 E14
Vlăhiţa, *Romania* 29 D10
Vlakhiótis, *Greece* 46 E4
Vlasenica, *Bos.-H.* 28 F3
Vlašić, *Bos.-H.* 28 F2
Vlašim, *Czech Rep.* 26 B7
Vlasinsko Jezero, *Serbia & M.* 44 D6
Vlasotince, *Serbia & M.* 44 D6
Vlieland, *Neths.* 17 A4
Vlissingen, *Neths.* 17 C3
Vlorë, *Albania* 44 F3
Vlorës, Gjiri i, *Albania* 44 F3
Vltava →, *Czech Rep.* 26 A7
Vo Dat, *Vietnam* 65 G6
Vobarno, *Italy* 40 C7
Vočin, *Croatia* 28 E2
Vöcklabruck, *Austria* 26 C6
Vodice, *Croatia* 41 E12
Vodňany, *Czech Rep.* 26 B7
Vodnjan, *Croatia* 41 D10
Voe, *U.K.* 13 A7
Vogel Pk., *Nigeria* 83 D7
Vogelkop = Doberai, Jazirah, *Indonesia* 63 E8
Vogelsberg, *Germany* 24 E5
Voghera, *Italy* 40 D6
Vohibinany, *Madag.* 89 B8
Vohilava, *Madag.* 89 C8
Vohimarina = Iharana, *Madag.* 89 A9
Vohimena, Tanjon' i, *Madag.* 89 D8
Vohipeno, *Madag.* 89 C8
Voi, *Kenya* 86 C4
Void-Vacon, *France* 19 D12
Voineşti, *Iaşi, Romania* 29 C12
Voineşti, *Prahova, Romania* 29 E10
Voiotía □, *Greece* 46 C5
Voiron, *France* 21 C9
Voisey B., *Canada* 105 A7
Voitsberg, *Austria* 26 D8
Vojens, *Denmark* 11 J3
Vojmsjön, *Sweden* 8 D17
Vojnić, *Croatia* 41 C12
Vojnik, *Italy* 41 B12
Vojvodina □, *Serbia & M.* 28 E5
Vokhtoga, *Russia* 32 C11
Volary, *Czech Rep.* 26 C6
Volborg, *U.S.A.* 112 C2
Volcán de Colima △, *Mexico* 118 D4
Volcano Is. = Kazan-Rettō, *Pac. Oc.* 96 E6
Volcans △, *Rwanda* 86 C2
Volcans d'Auvergne ⌓, *France* 20 C6
Volchansk = Vovchansk, *Ukraine* 33 G9
Volchya →, *Ukraine* 33 H8
Volda, *Norway* 9 E12
Volga = Privolzhskiy □, *Russia* 34 B10
Volga, *Russia* 32 C10
Volga →, *Russia* 35 G9
Volga Hts. = Privolzhskaya Vozvyshennost, *Russia* 34 E7
Volgo-Baltiyskiy Kanal, *Russia* 32 B9
Volgo-Donskoy Kanal, *Russia* 35 F7
Volgodonsk, *Russia* 35 G6
Volgograd, *Russia* 35 F7
Volgogradskoye Vdkhr., *Russia* 34 E8
Volgorechensk, *Russia* 34 B5
Volímai, *Greece* 46 D2
Volintiri, *Moldova* 29 D14
Volissós, *Greece* 47 C7
Volkach, *Germany* 25 F6
Völkermarkt, *Austria* 26 E7
Volkhov, *Russia* 32 C7
Volkhov →, *Russia* 32 B7
Völklingen, *Germany* 25 F2
Volkovysk = Vawkavysk, *Belarus* 33 F3
Volksrust, *S. Africa* 89 D4
Volnansk, *Ukraine* 33 H8
Volnovakha, *Ukraine* 33 J9
Volochanka, *Russia* 53 B10
Volodarsk, *Russia* 34 B6
Volodymyr-Volynskyy, *Ukraine* 33 G3
Vologda, *Russia* 32 C10
Volokolamsk, *Russia* 32 D8
Volokonovka, *Russia* 33 G9
Vólos, *Greece* 46 B4
Volosovo, *Russia* 32 C5
Volovets, *Ukraine* 29 B8
Volovo, *Russia* 32 F10
Volozhin = Valozhyn, *Belarus* 32 E4
Volsk, *Russia* 34 D8
Volta □, *Ghana* 83 D5
Volta →, *Ghana* 83 D5
Volta, L., *Ghana* 83 D5
Volta Blanche = White Volta →, *Ghana* 83 D4
Volta Redonda, *Brazil* 127 A7
Voltaire, C., *Australia* 92 B4
Volterra, *Italy* 40 E7
Voltri, *Italy* 40 D5
Volturno →, *Italy* 42 A6
Vólvi, L., *Greece* 44 F7
Volyně, *Czech Rep.* 26 B6
Volzhsk, *Russia* 34 C9
Volzhskiy, *Russia* 35 F7
Vondrozo, *Madag.* 89 C8
Vónitsa, *Greece* 46 C2
Vopnafjörður, *Iceland* 8 D6
Vorarlberg □, *Austria* 26 D2
Vóras Óros, *Greece* 44 F5
Vorbasse, *Denmark* 11 J3
Vorchdorf, *Austria* 26 C6
Vorderrhein →, *Switz.* 25 J5
Vordingborg, *Denmark* 11 J5
Vorë, *Albania* 44 E3
Voreio Aigaio = Vórios Aiyaíon □, *Greece* 47 C7
Voreppe, *France* 21 C9
Vóriai Sporádhes, *Greece* 46 B5
Vórios Aiyaíon □, *Greece* 47 C7
Vórios Evvoïkos Kólpos, *Greece* 46 C5
Vorkuta, *Russia* 52 C7
Vormsi, *Estonia* 9 G20
Vóroi, *Greece* 46 F6
Vorona →, *Russia* 34 E6
Voronezh, *Russia* 33 G10
Voronezh, *Ukraine* 33 G7
Voronezh →, *Russia* 33 G10
Vorontsovo-Aleksandrovskoye = Zelenokumsk, *Russia* 35 H6
Vorpommersche Boddenlandschaft △, *Germany* 24 A8
Vorskla →, *Ukraine* 33 H8
Võrts Järv, *Estonia* 9 G22
Võru, *Estonia* 9 H22
Vosges, *France* 19 D14
Vosges □, *France* 19 D13
Vosges du Nord ⌓, *France* 19 D14
Voskopojë, *Albania* 44 F4
Voskresensk, *Russia* 32 E10
Voskresenskoye, *Russia* 34 B7
Voss, *Norway* 9 F12
Vostok, *Antarctica* 5 D8
Vostok I., *Kiribati* 97 J12
Votice, *Czech Rep.* 26 B7
Votsuri-Shima, *Japan* 55 M1
Vouga →, *Portugal* 36 E2
Vouillé, *France* 18 F7
Voúxa, Ákra, *Greece* 49 D5
Vouzela, *Portugal* 36 E2
Vouziers, *France* 19 C11
Vovchansk, *Ukraine* 33 G9
Vowchyn, *Belarus* 31 F10
Voyageurs △, *U.S.A.* 112 A8
Vozhe, Ozero, *Russia* 32 B10
Vozhega, *Russia* 32 B11
Voznesensk, *Ukraine* 33 J6
Voznesenye, *Russia* 32 B8
Vrå, *Denmark* 11 G3
Vráble, *Slovak Rep.* 27 C11
Vraćevšnica, *Serbia & M.* 44 B4
Vrakhnéïka, *Greece* 46 C3
Vrancea □, *Romania* 29 E11
Vrancei, Munţii, *Romania* 29 E11
Vrangelya, Ostrov, *Russia* 53 B19
Vranica, *Bos.-H.* 28 G2
Vranje, *Serbia & M.* 44 D5
Vranjska Banja, *Serbia & M.* 44 D6
Vranov nad Topl'ou, *Slovak Rep.* 27 C14
Vransko, *Slovenia* 41 B11
Vransko Jezero, *Croatia* 41 E12
Vrapčište, *Macedonia* 44 E4
Vratsa, *Bulgaria* 44 C7
Vrbas, *Serbia & M.* 28 E4
Vrbas →, *Bos.-H.* 28 E2
Vrbnik, *Croatia* 41 C11
Vrbovec, *Croatia* 41 C13
Vrbovsko, *Croatia* 41 C12
Vrchlabí, *Czech Rep.* 26 A8
Vrede, *S. Africa* 89 D4
Vredefort, *S. Africa* 88 D4
Vreden, *Germany* 24 C2
Vredenburg, *S. Africa* 88 E2
Vredendal, *S. Africa* 88 E2
Vretstorp, *Sweden* 10 E8
Vrgorac, *Croatia* 41 E14
Vrhnika, *Slovenia* 41 C11
Vrïdi, *Ivory C.* 82 D4
Vrigstad, *Sweden* 11 G8
Vrindavan, *India* 68 F7
Vríses, *Greece* 49 D6
Vrnograč, *Bos.-H.* 41 C12
Vrondádhes, *Greece* 47 C8
Vrpolje, *Croatia* 28 E3
Vršac, *Serbia & M.* 28 E6
Vrsacki Kanal, *Serbia & M.* 28 E5
Vrútky, *Slovak Rep.* 27 B11
Vryburg, *S. Africa* 88 D3
Vryheid, *S. Africa* 89 D5
Vsetín, *Czech Rep.* 27 B11
Vu Liet, *Vietnam* 64 C5
Vŭcha →, *Bulgaria* 45 D8
Vučitrn, *Serbia & M.* 44 D4
Vukovar, *Croatia* 28 E3
Vulcan, *Canada* 102 C6
Vulcan, *Romania* 29 E8
Vulcaneşti, *Moldova* 29 E13
Vulcano, *Italy* 43 D7
Vŭlchedruma, *Bulgaria* 44 C7
Vulkaneshty = Vulcaneşti, *Moldova* 29 E13
Vunduzi →, *Mozam.* 87 F3
Vung Tau, *Vietnam* 65 G6
Vŭrbitsa, *Bulgaria* 45 D10
Vurshets, *Bulgaria* 44 C7
Vutcani, *Romania* 29 D12
Vuya, *Sudan* 81 F2
Vuzlove, *Ukraine* 28 B7
Vwaza ⌓, *Malawi* 87 E3
Vyartsilya, *Russia* 32 A6
Vyatka = Kirov, *Russia* 52 D5
Vyatka →, *Russia* 34 C10
Vyatskiye Polyany, *Russia* 34 B10
Vyazemskiy, *Russia* 53 E14
Vyazma, *Russia* 32 E8
Vyazniki, *Russia* 34 B6
Vyborg, *Russia* 32 B5
Vychegda →, *Russia* 52 C5
Vychodné Beskydy, *Europe* 27 B15
Vyerkhnyadzvinsk, *Belarus* 32 E4
Vyhoda, *Ukraine* 29 B8
Vyksa, *Russia* 34 C6
Vylkove, *Ukraine* 29 E14
Vylok, *Ukraine* 28 B7
Vynohradiv, *Ukraine* 28 B8
Vyrnwy, L., *U.K.* 14 E4
Vyshkiv, *Ukraine* 29 B8
Vyshkove, *Ukraine* 29 B8
Vyshniy Volochek, *Russia* 32 D8
Vyshzha = imeni 26 Bakinskikh Komissarov, *Turkmenistan* 71 B7
Vyškov, *Czech Rep.* 27 B9
Vysokaye, *Belarus* 31 F10
Vysoké Mýto, *Czech Rep.* 27 B9
Vysokovsk, *Russia* 32 D9
Vyšší Brod, *Czech Rep.* 26 C7
Vytegra, *Russia* 32 B9
Vyzhnytsya, *Ukraine* 29 B10
Vyzhnytsya ⌓, *Ukraine* 29 B10

W

W du Benin △, *Benin* 83 C5
W du Burkina Faso △, *Burkina Faso* 83 C4
W du Niger △, *Niger* 83 C5
W.A.C. Bennett Dam, *Canada* 102 B4
Wa, *Ghana* 82 C4
Waal →, *Neths.* 17 C5
Waalwijk, *Neths.* 17 C5
Waat, *Sudan* 81 F3
Wabakimi △, *Canada* 104 B2
Wabana, *Canada* 105 C9
Wabasca →, *Canada* 102 B5
Wabasca-Desmarais, *Canada* 102 B6
Wabash, *U.S.A.* 114 E3
Wabash →, *U.S.A.* 114 G1

Wabi →, Ethiopia 81 F5
Wabigoon L., Canada 103 D10
Wabowden, Canada 103 C9
Wąbrzeźno, Poland 31 E5
Wabu Hu, China 59 A11
Wabuk Pt., Canada 104 A2
Wabush, Canada 105 B6
Wąchock, Poland 31 G8
Wächtersbach, Germany 25 E5
Waco, U.S.A. 113 K6
Waconichi, L., Canada 104 B5
Wad Ban Naqa, Sudan 81 D3
Wad Banda, Sudan 81 E2
Wad el Haddad, Sudan 81 E3
Wad en Nau, Sudan 81 E3
Wad Hamid, Sudan 81 D3
Wad Medanî, Sudan 81 E3
Wad Thana, Pakistan 68 F2
Wadai, Africa 76 E5
Wadayama, Japan 55 G7
Waddeneilanden, Neths. 17 A5
Waddenzee, Neths. 17 A5
Waddi, Chappal, Nigeria 83 D7
Waddington, U.S.A. 117 B9
Waddington, Mt., Canada 102 C3
Waddy Pt., Australia 95 C5
Wadebridge, U.K. 15 G3
Wadena, Canada 103 C8
Wadena, U.S.A. 112 B7
Wädenswil, Switz. 25 H4
Wadern, Germany 25 F2
Wadeye, Australia 92 B4
Wadhams, Canada 102 C3
Wādī as Sīr, Jordan 74 D4
Wadi Gemâl, Egypt 80 C4
Wadi Halfa, Sudan 80 C3
Wadi Rum △, Jordan 74 F4
Wadian, China 59 A9
Wadlew, Poland 31 G6
Wadowice, Poland 31 J6
Wadsworth, Nev., U.S.A. 108 G4
Wadsworth, Ohio, U.S.A. 116 E3
Waegwan, S. Korea 57 G15
Wafangdian, China 57 E11
Wafrah, Si. Arabia 70 D5
Wageningen, Neths. 17 C5
Wager B., Canada 101 B11
Wagga Wagga, Australia 95 F4
Waghete, Indonesia 63 E9
Wagin, Australia 93 F2
Wagner, U.S.A. 112 D5
Wagon Mound, U.S.A. 113 G2
Wagoner, U.S.A. 113 H7
Wągrowiec, Poland 31 F4
Wah, Pakistan 68 C5
Wahai, Indonesia 63 E7
Wahiawa, U.S.A. 106 H15
Wâḥid, Egypt 74 E1
Wahnai, Afghan. 68 C1
Wahni, Ethiopia 81 E4
Wahoo, U.S.A. 112 E6
Wahpeton, U.S.A. 112 B6
Waiau →, N.Z. 91 K4
Waibeem, Indonesia 63 E8
Waiblingen, Germany 25 G5
Waidhofen an der Thaya, Austria 26 C8
Waidhofen an der Ybbs, Austria 26 D7
Waigeo, Indonesia 63 E8
Waihi, N.Z. 91 G5
Waihou →, N.Z. 91 G5
Waika, Dem. Rep. of the Congo 86 C2
Waikabubak, Indonesia 63 F5
Waikaremoana, L., N.Z. 91 H6
Waikari, N.Z. 91 K4
Waikato →, N.Z. 91 G5
Waikerie, Australia 95 E3
Waikokopu, N.Z. 91 H6
Waikouaiti, N.Z. 91 L3
Wailuku, U.S.A. 106 H16
Waimakariri →, N.Z. 91 K4
Waimate, N.Z. 91 L3
Wainganga →, India 66 K11
Waingapu, Indonesia 63 F6
Waini →, Guyana 124 B7
Wainwright, Canada 103 C6
Waiouru, N.Z. 91 H5
Waipara, N.Z. 91 K4
Waipawa, N.Z. 91 H6
Waipiro, N.Z. 91 H7
Waipoua Forest, N.Z. 91 F4
Waipu, N.Z. 91 F5
Waipukurau, N.Z. 91 J6
Wairakei, N.Z. 91 H6
Wairarapa, L., N.Z. 91 J5
Wairoa, N.Z. 91 H6
Waitaki →, N.Z. 91 L3
Waitangi, N.Z. 91 F5
Waitara, N.Z. 91 H5
Waitomo Caves, N.Z. 91 H5
Waitsburg, U.S.A. 108 C5
Waiuku, N.Z. 91 G5
Wajima, Japan 55 F8
Wajir, Kenya 86 B5
Waka, Ethiopia 81 F4
Wakasa, Japan 55 G7
Wakasa-Wan, Japan 55 G7
Wakatipu, L., N.Z. 91 L2
Wakaw, Canada 103 C7
Wakayama, Japan 55 G7
Wakayama □, Japan 55 H7
Wake Forest, U.S.A. 115 H6
Wake I., Pac. Oc. 96 F8
WaKeeney, U.S.A. 112 F5
Wakefield, Jamaica 120 a
Wakefield, N.Z. 91 J4
Wakefield, U.K. 14 D6
Wakefield, Mass., U.S.A. 117 D13
Wakefield, Mich., U.S.A. 112 B10
Wakkanai, Japan 54 B10
Wakkerstroom, S. Africa 89 D5
Wakool, Australia 95 F3
Wakool →, Australia 95 F3
Wakre, Indonesia 63 E8
Wakuach, L., Canada 105 A6
Walamba, Zambia 87 E2
Wałbrzych, Poland 31 H3
Walbury Hill, U.K. 15 F6
Walcha, Australia 95 E5
Walcheren, Neths. 17 C3
Walcott, U.S.A. 108 F10
Wałcz, Poland 31 E3
Waldbröl, Germany 24 E3
Waldburg Ra., Australia 93 D2
Waldeck, Germany 24 D5
Walden, Colo., U.S.A. 108 F10
Walden, N.Y., U.S.A. 117 E10
Waldkirch, Germany 25 G3
Waldkirchen, Germany 25 G9
Waldkraiburg, Germany 25 G8
Waldport, U.S.A. 108 D1
Waldron, U.S.A. 113 H7
Waldviertel, Austria 26 C8
Walebing, Australia 93 F2
Walembele, Ghana 82 C4
Walensee, Switz. 25 H5
Wales □, U.K. 15 E3
Walewale, Ghana 83 C4
Walgett, Australia 95 E4
Walgreen Coast, Antarctica 5 D15
Walker, U.S.A. 112 B7
Walker, L., Canada 105 B6
Walker L., Canada 103 C9
Walker L., U.S.A. 108 G4
Walkerston, Australia 94 K7
Walkerton, Canada 116 B3
Wall, U.S.A. 112 D3
Walla Walla, U.S.A. 108 C4
Wallace, Idaho, U.S.A. 108 C6
Wallace, N.C., U.S.A. 115 H7
Wallaceburg, Canada 116 D2
Wallachia = Valahia, Romania 29 F9
Wallal, Australia 95 D4
Wallam Cr. →, Australia 95 D4
Wallambin, L., Australia 93 F2
Wallangarra, Australia 95 D5
Wallaroo, Australia 95 E2
Walldürn, Germany 25 F5
Wallenhorst, Germany 24 C4
Wallenpaupack, L., U.S.A. 117 E9
Wallingford, U.S.A. 117 E12
Wallis & Futuna, Is., Pac. Oc. 96 J10
Wallowa, U.S.A. 108 D5
Wallowa Mts., U.S.A. 108 D5
Walls, U.K. 13 A7
Walls of Jerusalem △, Australia 95 G4
Wallula, U.S.A. 108 C4
Wallumbilla, Australia 95 D4
Walmsley, L., Canada 103 A7
Walney, I. of, U.K. 14 C4
Walnut Canyon ⌓, U.S.A. 109 J8
Walnut Creek, U.S.A. 110 H4
Walnut Ridge, U.S.A. 113 G9
Walpole, Australia 93 F2
Walpole, U.S.A. 117 D13
Wals, Austria 26 D5
Walsall, U.K. 15 E6
Walsenburg, U.S.A. 113 G2
Walsh, U.S.A. 113 G3
Walsh →, Australia 94 B3
Walsrode, Germany 24 C5
Walterboro, U.S.A. 115 J5
Walters, U.S.A. 113 H5
Waltershausen, Germany 24 E6
Waltham, U.S.A. 117 D13
Waltman, U.S.A. 108 E10
Walton, U.S.A. 117 D9
Walton-on-the-Naze, U.K. 15 F9
Walvis Bay, Namibia 88 C1
Walvisbaai = Walvis Bay, Namibia 88 C1
Wamba, Dem. Rep. of the Congo 86 B2
Wamba, Kenya 86 B4
Wamba, Nigeria 83 D6
Wamego, U.S.A. 112 F6
Wamena, Indonesia 63 E9
Wamsutter, U.S.A. 108 F9
Wamulan, Indonesia 63 E7
Wan Xian, China 56 E8
Wana, Pakistan 68 C3
Wanaaring, Australia 95 D3
Wanaka, N.Z. 91 L2
Wanaka, L., N.Z. 91 L2
Wan'an, China 59 D10
Wanapitei L., Canada 104 C3
Wandel Sea = McKinley Sea, Arctic 4 A7
Wandérama, Ivory C. 82 D4
Wanderer, Zimbabwe 87 F3
Wandhari, Pakistan 68 F2
Wanding, China 58 E2
Wandoan, Australia 95 D4
Wanfu, China 57 D12
Wang →, Thailand 64 D2
Wang Kai, Sudan 81 F2
Wang Noi, Thailand 64 E3
Wang Saphung, Thailand 64 D3
Wang Thong, Thailand 64 D3
Wanga, Dem. Rep. of the Congo 86 B2
Wangal, Indonesia 63 F8
Wanganella, Australia 95 F3
Wanganui, N.Z. 91 H5
Wangaratta, Australia 95 F4
Wangary, Australia 95 E2
Wangcang, China 58 A6
Wangcheng, China 59 C9
Wangdu, China 56 E8
Wangen, Germany 25 H5
Wangerooge, Germany 24 B3
Wangiwangi, Indonesia 63 F6
Wangjiang, China 59 B11
Wangmo, China 58 E6
Wangolodougou, Ivory C. 82 D3
Wangqing, China 57 C15
Wankaner, India 68 H4
Wanless, Canada 103 C8
Wanneroo, Australia 93 F2
Wannian, China 59 C11
Wanning, China 64 C8
Wanon Niwat, Thailand 64 D4
Wanquan, China 56 D8
Wanrong, China 56 G6
Wanshan, China 58 D7
Wanshengchang, China 58 C6
Wantage, U.K. 15 F6
Wanxian, China 58 B7
Wanyuan, China 58 A7
Wanzai, China 59 C10
Wapakoneta, U.S.A. 114 E3
Wapato, U.S.A. 108 C3
Wapawekka L., Canada 103 C8
Wapikopa L., Canada 104 B2
Wapiti →, Canada 102 B5
Wappingers Falls, U.S.A. 117 E11
Wapsipinicon →, U.S.A. 112 E9
Wapusk △, Canada 103 B10
Warab □, Sudan 81 F2
Warangal, India 66 L11
Waraseoni, India 69 J9
Waratah, Australia 95 G4
Waratah B., Australia 95 F4
Warburg, Germany 24 D5
Warburton, Vic., Australia 95 F4
Warburton, W. Austral., Australia 93 E4
Warburton, The →, Australia 95 D2
Warburton Ra., Australia 93 E4
Ward, N.Z. 91 J5
Ward →, Australia 95 D4
Ward Mt., U.S.A. 110 H8
Warden, S. Africa 89 D4
Wardha, India 66 J11
Wardha →, India 66 K11
Ware, Canada 102 B3
Ware, U.K. 15 F8
Ware, U.S.A. 117 D12
Waregem, Belgium 17 D3
Wareham, U.S.A. 117 E14
Waremme, Belgium 17 D5
Waren, Germany 24 B8
Warendorf, Germany 24 D4
Warialda, Australia 95 D5
Wariap, Indonesia 63 E8
Warin Chamrap, Thailand 64 E5
Warka, Poland 31 G8
Warkopi, Indonesia 63 E8
Warm Springs, U.S.A. 109 G5
Warman, Canada 103 C7
Warmbad = Bela Bela, S. Africa 89 C4
Warmbad, Namibia 88 D2
Warmińsko-Mazurskie □, Poland 30 D8
Warminster, U.K. 15 F5
Warminster, U.S.A. 117 F9
Warnemünde, Germany 24 A8
Warner Mts., U.S.A. 108 F3
Warner Robins, U.S.A. 115 J4
Warnow →, Germany 24 A8
Waroona, Australia 93 F2
Warracknabeal, Australia 95 F3
Warragul, Australia 95 F4
Warrego →, Australia 95 E4
Warrego Ra., Australia 94 C4
Warren, Australia 95 E4
Warren, Ark., U.S.A. 113 J8
Warren, Mich., U.S.A. 114 D4
Warren, Minn., U.S.A. 112 A6
Warren, Ohio, U.S.A. 116 E4
Warren, Pa., U.S.A. 116 E5
Warrenpoint, U.K. 12 B5
Warrensburg, Mo., U.S.A. 112 F8
Warrensburg, N.Y., U.S.A. 117 C11
Warrenton, S. Africa 88 D3
Warrenton, U.S.A. 110 D3
Warri, Nigeria 83 D6
Warrina, Australia 95 D2
Warrington, U.K. 14 D5
Warrington, U.S.A. 115 K2
Warrington □, U.K. 14 D5
Warrnambool, Australia 95 F3
Warroad, U.S.A. 112 A7
Warruwi, Australia 94 A1
Warsa, Indonesia 63 E9
Warsak Dam, Pakistan 68 B4
Warsaw = Warszawa, Poland 31 F8
Warsaw, Ind., U.S.A. 114 E3
Warsaw, N.Y., U.S.A. 116 D6
Warsaw, Ohio, U.S.A. 116 F3
Warstein, Germany 24 D4
Warszawa, Poland 31 F8
Warszawa ✕ (WAW), Poland 31 F7
Warta, Poland 31 G5
Warta →, Poland 31 F1
Warthe = Warta →, Poland 31 F1
Waru, Indonesia 63 E8
Warwick, Australia 95 D5
Warwick, U.K. 15 E6
Warwick, N.Y., U.S.A. 117 E10
Warwick, R.I., U.S.A. 117 E13
Warwickshire □, U.K. 15 E6
Wasaga Beach, Canada 116 B4
Wasagaming, Canada 103 C9
Wasatch Ra., U.S.A. 108 F8
Wasbank, S. Africa 89 D5
Wasco, Calif., U.S.A. 111 K7
Wasco, Oreg., U.S.A. 108 D3
Wase, Nigeria 83 D6
Waseca, U.S.A. 112 C8
Wasekamio L., Canada 103 B7
Wash, The, U.K. 14 E8
Washago, Canada 116 B5
Washburn, N. Dak., U.S.A. 112 B4
Washburn, Wis., U.S.A. 112 B9
Washim, India 66 J10
Washington, U.K. 14 C6
Washington, D.C., U.S.A. 114 F7
Washington, Ga., U.S.A. 115 J4
Washington, Ind., U.S.A. 114 F2
Washington, Iowa, U.S.A. 112 E9
Washington, Mo., U.S.A. 112 F9
Washington, N.C., U.S.A. 115 H7
Washington, N.J., U.S.A. 117 F10
Washington, Pa., U.S.A. 116 F4
Washington, Utah, U.S.A. 109 H7
Washington □, U.S.A. 108 C3
Washington, Mt., U.S.A. 117 B13
Washington Court House, U.S.A. 114 F4
Washington I., U.S.A. 114 C2
Washougal, U.S.A. 110 E4
Washpool △, Australia 95 D5
Wasian, Indonesia 63 E8
Wasilków, Poland 31 E10
Wasilla, U.S.A. 100 B5
Wasior, Indonesia 63 E8
Wāsiţ □, Iraq 70 C5
Waskaganish, Canada 104 B4
Waskaiowaka, L., Canada 103 B9
Waskesiu Lake, Canada 103 C7
Wasserburg, Germany 25 G8
Wasserkuppe, Germany 24 E5
Wassy, France 19 D11
Waswanipi, Canada 104 C4
Waswanipi, L., Canada 104 C4
Watampone, Indonesia 63 E6
Watamu, Kenya 86 C5
Watarrka △, Australia 92 D5
Water Park Pt., Australia 94 C5
Water Valley, U.S.A. 113 H10
Waterberg Plateau ⌓, Namibia 88 C2
Waterberge, S. Africa 89 C4
Waterbury, Conn., U.S.A. 117 E11
Waterbury, Vt., U.S.A. 117 B12
Waterbury L., Canada 103 B8
Waterdown, Canada 116 C5
Waterford, Canada 116 D4
Waterford, Ireland 12 D4
Waterford, Calif., U.S.A. 110 H6
Waterford, Pa., U.S.A. 116 E5
Waterford □, Ireland 12 D4
Waterford Harbour, Ireland 12 D5
Waterhen L., Canada 103 C9
Waterloo, Belgium 17 D4
Waterloo, Ont., Canada 116 C4
Waterloo, Qué., Canada 117 A12
Waterloo, S. Leone 82 D2
Waterloo, Ill., U.S.A. 112 F9
Waterloo, Iowa, U.S.A. 112 D8
Waterloo, N.Y., U.S.A. 116 D8
Watersmeet, U.S.A. 112 B10
Waterton Lakes △, Canada 102 D6
Watertown, Conn., U.S.A. 117 E11
Watertown, N.Y., U.S.A. 117 C9
Watertown, S. Dak., U.S.A. 112 C6
Watertown, Wis., U.S.A. 112 D10
Waterval-Boven, S. Africa 89 D5
Waterville, Canada 117 A13
Waterville, Maine, U.S.A. 115 C11
Waterville, N.Y., U.S.A. 117 D9
Waterville, Pa., U.S.A. 116 E7
Waterville, Wash., U.S.A. 108 C3
Watervliet, U.S.A. 117 D11
Wates, Indonesia 63 G14
Watford, Canada 116 D3
Watford, U.K. 15 F7
Watford City, U.S.A. 112 B3
Wathaman →, Canada 103 B8
Wathaman L., Canada 103 B8
Watheroo, Australia 93 F2
Watheroo △, Australia 93 F2
Wating, China 56 G4
Watkins Glen, U.S.A. 116 D8
Watling I. = San Salvador I., Bahamas 121 B5
Watonga, U.S.A. 113 H5
Watrous, Canada 103 C7
Watrous, U.S.A. 113 H2
Watsa, Dem. Rep. of the Congo 86 B2
Watseka, U.S.A. 114 E2
Watson, Australia 93 F5
Watson, Canada 103 C8
Watson Lake, Canada 102 A3
Watsontown, U.S.A. 116 E8
Watsonville, U.S.A. 110 J5
Wattiwarriganna Cr. →, Australia 95 D2
Wattwil, Switz. 25 H5
Watuata = Batuata, Indonesia 63 F6
Watubela, Kepulauan, Indonesia 63 E8
Watubela Is. = Watubela, Kepulauan, Indonesia 63 E8
Wau = Wâw, Sudan 81 F2
Waubamik, Canada 116 A4
Waubay, U.S.A. 112 C6
Wauchope, N.S.W., Australia 95 E5
Wauchope, N. Terr., Australia 94 C1
Wauchula, U.S.A. 115 M5
Waukarlycarly, L., Australia 92 D3
Waukegan, U.S.A. 114 D2
Waukesha, U.S.A. 114 D1
Waukon, U.S.A. 112 D9
Waupaca, U.S.A. 112 C10
Waupun, U.S.A. 112 D10
Waurika, U.S.A. 113 H6
Wausau, U.S.A. 112 C10
Wautoma, U.S.A. 112 C10
Wauwatosa, U.S.A. 114 D2
Waveney →, U.K. 15 E9
Waverley, N.Z. 91 H5
Waverly, Iowa, U.S.A. 112 D8
Waverly, N.Y., U.S.A. 117 E8
Wavre, Belgium 17 D4
Wâw, Sudan 81 F2
Wāw al Kabīr, Libya 79 C9
Wawa, Canada 104 C3
Wawa, Nigeria 83 D5
Wawa, Sudan 80 C3
Wawanesa, Canada 103 D9
Wawona, U.S.A. 110 H7
Waxahachie, U.S.A. 113 J6
Way, L., Australia 93 E3
Waycross, U.S.A. 115 K4
Wayi, Sudan 81 F3
Wayland, U.S.A. 116 D7
Wayne, Nebr., U.S.A. 112 D6
Wayne, W. Va., U.S.A. 114 F4
Waynesboro, Ga., U.S.A. 115 J4
Waynesboro, Miss., U.S.A. 115 K1
Waynesboro, Pa., U.S.A. 114 F7
Waynesboro, Va., U.S.A. 114 F6
Waynesburg, U.S.A. 114 F5
Waynesville, U.S.A. 115 H4
Waynoka, U.S.A. 113 G5
Wazirabad, Pakistan 68 C6
Wda →, Poland 30 E5
We, Indonesia 62 C1
Weald, The, U.K. 15 F8
Wear →, U.K. 14 C6
Weatherford, Okla., U.S.A. 113 H5
Weatherford, Tex., U.S.A. 113 J6
Weaverville, U.S.A. 108 F2
Webb City, U.S.A. 113 G7
Webequie, Canada 104 B2
Webo = Nyaake, Liberia 82 E3
Webster, Mass., U.S.A. 117 D13
Webster, N.Y., U.S.A. 116 C7
Webster, S. Dak., U.S.A. 112 C6
Webster City, U.S.A. 112 D8
Webster Springs, U.S.A. 114 F5
Weda, Indonesia 63 D7
Weda, Teluk, Indonesia 63 D7
Weddell I., Falk. Is. 128 G4
Weddell Sea, Antarctica 5 D1
Wedderburn, Australia 95 F3
Wedel, Germany 24 B5
Wedemark, Germany 24 C5
Wedgeport, Canada 105 D6
Wedza, Zimbabwe 87 F3
Wee Waa, Australia 95 E4
Weed, U.S.A. 108 F2
Weed Heights, U.S.A. 110 G7
Weedsport, U.S.A. 117 C8
Weedville, U.S.A. 116 E6
Weenen, S. Africa 89 D5
Weener, Germany 24 B3
Weert, Neths. 17 C5
Węgierska-Górka, Poland 31 J6
Węgliniec, Poland 31 G2
Węgorzewo, Poland 30 D8
Węgorzyno, Poland 30 E2
Węgrów, Poland 31 F9
Wehda □, Sudan 81 F3
Wei He →, Hebei, China 56 F8
Wei He →, Shaanxi, China 56 G6
Weichang, China 57 D9
Weichuan, China 56 G7
Weida, Germany 24 E8
Weiden, Germany 25 F8
Weifang, China 57 F10
Weihai, China 57 F12
Weil, Germany 25 H3
Weilburg, Germany 24 E4
Weilheim, Germany 25 H7
Weimar, Germany 24 E7
Weinan, China 56 G5
Weingarten, Germany 25 F4
Weinheim, Germany 25 F4
Weining, China 58 D5
Weipa, Australia 94 A3
Weir →, Australia 95 D4
Weir →, Canada 103 B10
Weir River, Canada 103 B10
Weirton, U.S.A. 116 F4
Weiser, U.S.A. 108 D5
Weishan, Shandong, China 57 G9
Weishan, Yunnan, China 58 E3
Weissenburg, Germany 25 F6
Weissenfels, Germany 24 D7
Weisswasser, Germany 24 D10
Wéitra, Austria 26 C7
Weixi, China 58 D2
Weixin, China 58 D5
Weiyuan, China 56 G3
Weiz, Austria 26 D8
Weizhou Dao, China 58 G7
Wejherowo, Poland 30 D5
Wekusko L., Canada 103 C9
Welch, U.S.A. 114 G5
Weldya, Ethiopia 81 E4
Welega, Ethiopia 81 F3
Welford △, Australia 94 D3
Welkite, Ethiopia 81 F4
Welkom, S. Africa 88 D4
Welland, Canada 116 D5
Welland →, U.K. 15 E7
Wellesley Is., Australia 94 B2
Wellingborough, U.K. 15 E7
Wellington, Australia 95 E4
Wellington, Canada 116 C7
Wellington, N.Z. 91 J5
Wellington, S. Africa 88 E2
Wellington, Somst., U.K. 15 G4
Wellington, Telford & Wrekin, U.K. 15 E5
Wellington, Colo., U.S.A. 112 E2
Wellington, Kans., U.S.A. 113 G6
Wellington, Nev., U.S.A. 110 G7
Wellington, Ohio, U.S.A. 116 E2
Wellington, Tex., U.S.A. 113 H4
Wellington, I., Chile 128 F2
Wellington, L., Australia 95 F4
Wells, U.K. 15 F5
Wells, Maine, U.S.A. 117 C14
Wells, N.Y., U.S.A. 117 C10
Wells, Nev., U.S.A. 108 F6
Wells, L., Australia 93 E3
Wells, Mt., Australia 92 C4
Wells Gray ⌓, Canada 102 C4
Wells-next-the-Sea, U.K. 14 E8
Wells River, U.S.A. 117 B12
Wellsboro, U.S.A. 116 E7
Wellsburg, U.S.A. 116 F4
Wellsville, N.Y., U.S.A. 116 D7
Wellsville, Ohio, U.S.A. 116 F4
Wellsville, Utah, U.S.A. 108 F8

Wellton, *U.S.A.* 109 K6
Welmel, Wabi →, *Ethiopia* 81 F5
Welo, *Ethiopia* 81 E4
Wels, *Austria* 26 C7
Welshpool, *U.K.* 15 E4
Welwyn Garden City, *U.K.* 15 F7
Wem, *U.K.* 14 E5
Wembere →, *Tanzania* 86 C3
Wemindji, *Canada* 104 B4
Wen Xian, *China* 56 G7
Wenatchee, *U.S.A.* 108 C3
Wenchang, *China* 64 C8
Wencheng, *China* 59 D13
Wenchi, *Ghana* 82 D4
Wenchow = Wenzhou, *China* 59 D13
Wenchuan, *China* 58 B4
Wenden, *U.S.A.* 111 M13
Wendeng, *China* 57 F12
Wendesi, *Indonesia* 63 E8
Wendo, *Ethiopia* 81 F4
Wendover, *U.S.A.* 108 F6
Weng'an, *China* 58 D6
Wengcheng, *China* 59 E9
Wengyuan, *China* 59 E10
Wenjiang, *China* 58 B4
Wenling, *China* 59 C13
Wenlock →, *Australia* 94 A3
Wenshan, *China* 58 F5
Wenshang, *China* 56 G9
Wenshui, *China* 56 F7
Wensleydale, *U.K.* 14 C6
Wensu, *China* 60 B3
Wensum →, *U.K.* 14 E8
Wentworth, *Australia* 95 E3
Wentzel L., *Canada* 102 B6
Wenut, *Indonesia* 63 E8
Wenxi, *China* 56 G6
Wenxian, *China* 56 H3
Wenzhou, *China* 59 D13
Weott, *U.S.A.* 108 F2
Wepener, *S. Africa* 88 D4
Werda, *Botswana* 88 D3
Werdau, *Germany* 24 E8
Werder, *Germany* 24 C8
Werdohl, *Germany* 24 D3
Wereilu, *Ethiopia* 81 E4
Weri, *Indonesia* 63 E8
Werneck, *Germany* 25 F6
Wernigerode, *Germany* 24 D6
Werra →, *Germany* 24 D5
Werrimull, *Australia* 95 E3
Werris Creek, *Australia* 95 E5
Wertach →, *Germany* 25 G6
Wertheim, *Germany* 25 F5
Wertingen, *Germany* 25 G6
Wesel, *Germany* 24 D2
Weser →, *Germany* 24 B4
Weser-Ems □, *Germany* 24 C3
Weserbergland, *Germany* 24 C5
Weserbergland Schaumburg Hameln ⌓, *Germany* 24 C5
Wesiri, *Indonesia* 63 F7
Weslemkoon L., *Canada* 116 A7
Wesleyville, *U.S.A.* 116 D4
Wessel, C., *Australia* 94 A2
Wessel Is., *Australia* 94 A2
Wesselburen, *Germany* 24 A4
Wessington Springs, *U.S.A.* 112 C5
West, *U.S.A.* 113 K6
West →, *U.S.A.* 117 D12
West Antarctica, *Antarctica* 5 D15
West Baines →, *Australia* 92 C4
West Bank ▨, *Asia* 74 C4
West Bend, *U.S.A.* 114 D1
West Bengal □, *India* 69 H13
West Berkshire □, *U.K.* 15 F6
West Beskids = Západné Beskydy, *Europe* 27 B12
West Branch, *U.S.A.* 114 C3
West Branch Susquehanna →, *U.S.A.* 117 F8
West Bromwich, *U.K.* 15 E6
West Burra, *U.K.* 13 A7
West Canada Cr. →, *U.S.A.* 117 C10
West Cape Howe, *Australia* 93 G2
West Chazy, *U.S.A.* 117 B11
West Chester, *U.S.A.* 117 G9
West Coast ⌓, *Namibia* 88 C1
West Coast △, *S. Africa* 88 E2
West Columbia, *U.S.A.* 113 L7
West Covina, *U.S.A.* 111 L9
West Des Moines, *U.S.A.* 112 E8
West Dunbartonshire □, *U.K.* 13 F4
West End, *Bahamas* 120 A4
West Falkland, *Falk. Is.* 128 G5
West Fargo, *U.S.A.* 112 B6
West Farmington, *U.S.A.* 116 E4
West Fjord = Vestfjorden, *Norway* 8 C15
West Fork Trinity →, *U.S.A.* 113 J6
West Frankfort, *U.S.A.* 112 G10
West Hartford, *U.S.A.* 117 E12
West Haven, *U.S.A.* 117 E12
West Hazleton, *U.S.A.* 117 F9
West Helena, *U.S.A.* 113 H9
West Hurley, *U.S.A.* 117 E10
West Ice Shelf, *Antarctica* 5 C7
West Indies, *Cent. Amer.* 121 D7
West Jordan, *U.S.A.* 108 F8
West Lorne, *Canada* 116 D3
West Lothian □, *U.K.* 13 F5
West Lunga →, *Zambia* 87 E1
West MacDonnell △, *Australia* 92 D5
West Memphis, *U.S.A.* 113 H9
West Midlands □, *U.K.* 15 E6
West Mifflin, *U.S.A.* 116 F5
West Milton, *U.S.A.* 116 E8
West Monroe, *U.S.A.* 113 J8
West Newton, *U.S.A.* 116 F5
West Nicholson, *Zimbabwe* 87 G2
West Palm Beach, *U.S.A.* 115 M5
West Plains, *U.S.A.* 113 G9
West Point, *N.Y., U.S.A.* 117 E11
West Point, *Nebr., U.S.A.* 112 E6
West Point, *Va., U.S.A.* 114 G7
West Pt. = Ouest, Pte. de l', *Canada* 105 C7
West Pt., *Australia* 95 F2
West Road →, *Canada* 102 C4
West Rutland, *U.S.A.* 117 C11
West Schelde = Westerschelde →, *Neths.* 17 C3
West Seneca, *U.S.A.* 116 D6
West Siberian Plain, *Russia* 50 C11
West Sussex □, *U.K.* 15 G7
West-Terschelling, *Neths.* 17 A5
West Valley City, *U.S.A.* 108 F8
West Virginia □, *U.S.A.* 114 F5
West-Vlaanderen □, *Belgium* 17 D2
West Walker →, *U.S.A.* 110 G7
West Wyalong, *Australia* 95 E4
West Yellowstone, *U.S.A.* 108 D8
West Yorkshire □, *U.K.* 14 D6
Westall, Pt., *Australia* 95 E1
Westbrook, *U.S.A.* 115 D10
Westbury, *Australia* 95 G4
Westby, *U.S.A.* 112 A2
Westend, *U.S.A.* 111 K9
Westerland, *Germany* 9 J13
Westerly, *U.S.A.* 117 E13
Western □, *Ghana* 82 D4
Western □, *Kenya* 86 B3
Western □, *S. Leone* 82 D2
Western □, *Zambia* 87 F1
Western Australia □, *Australia* 93 E2
Western Cape □, *S. Africa* 88 E3
Western Dvina = Daugava →, *Latvia* 9 H21
Western Ghats, *India* 66 N9
Western Isles □, *U.K.* 13 D1
Western Sahara ■, *Africa* 78 D3
Western Samoa = Samoa ■, *Pac. Oc.* 91 B13
Westernport, *U.S.A.* 114 F6
Westerschelde →, *Neths.* 17 C3
Westerstede, *Germany* 24 B3
Westerwald, *Germany* 24 E3
Westfield, *Mass., U.S.A.* 117 D12
Westfield, *N.Y., U.S.A.* 116 D5
Westfield, *Pa., U.S.A.* 116 E7
Westhill, *U.K.* 13 D6
Westhope, *U.S.A.* 112 A4
Westland △, *N.Z.* 91 K2
Westland Bight, *N.Z.* 91 K3
Westlock, *Canada* 102 C6
Westmar, *Australia* 95 D4
Westmeath □, *Ireland* 12 C4
Westminster, *U.S.A.* 114 F7
Westmont, *U.S.A.* 116 F6
Westmoreland, *Barbados* 121 g
Westmorland, *U.S.A.* 111 M11
Weston, *Oreg., U.S.A.* 108 D4
Weston, *W. Va., U.S.A.* 114 F5
Weston I., *Canada* 104 B4
Weston-super-Mare, *U.K.* 15 F5
Westover, *U.S.A.* 116 F6
Westport, *Canada* 117 B8
Westport, *Ireland* 12 C2
Westport, *N.Z.* 91 J3
Westport, *N.Y., U.S.A.* 117 B11
Westport, *Oreg., U.S.A.* 110 D3
Westport, *Wash., U.S.A.* 110 D2
Westray, *Canada* 103 C8
Westray, *U.K.* 13 B5
Westree, *Canada* 104 C3
Westville, *U.S.A.* 110 F6
Westwood, *U.S.A.* 108 F3
Wetar, *Indonesia* 63 F7
Wetaskiwin, *Canada* 102 C6
Wete, *Tanzania* 84 F7
Wetherby, *U.K.* 14 D6
Wethersfield, *U.S.A.* 117 E12
Wetteren, *Belgium* 17 D3
Wetzlar, *Germany* 24 E4
Wewoka, *U.S.A.* 113 H6
Wexford, *Ireland* 12 D5
Wexford □, *Ireland* 12 D5
Wexford Harbour, *Ireland* 12 D5
Weyburn, *Canada* 103 D8
Weyer Markt, *Austria* 26 D7
Weyhe, *Germany* 24 C4
Weyib →, *Ethiopia* 81 F5
Weymouth, *Canada* 105 D6
Weymouth, *U.K.* 15 G5
Weymouth, *U.S.A.* 117 D14
Weymouth, C., *Australia* 94 A3
Wha Ti, *Canada* 100 B8
Whakaari = White I., *N.Z.* 91 G6
Whakatane, *N.Z.* 91 G6
Whale →, *Canada* 105 A6
Whale Cove, *Canada* 103 A10
Whales, B. of, *Antarctica* 5 D12
Whalsay, *U.K.* 13 A8
Whangamata, *N.Z.* 91 G5
Whangamomona, *N.Z.* 91 H5
Whanganui △, *N.Z.* 91 H5
Whangarei, *N.Z.* 91 F5
Whangarei Harb., *N.Z.* 91 F5
Wharfe →, *U.K.* 14 D6
Wharfedale, *U.K.* 14 C5
Wharton, *N.J., U.S.A.* 117 F10
Wharton, *Pa., U.S.A.* 116 E6
Wharton, *Tex., U.S.A.* 113 L6
Wheatland, *Calif., U.S.A.* 110 F5
Wheatland, *Wyo., U.S.A.* 112 D2
Wheatley, *Canada* 116 D2
Wheaton, *Md., U.S.A.* 114 F7
Wheaton, *Minn., U.S.A.* 112 C6
Wheelbarrow Pk., *U.S.A.* 110 H10
Wheeler, *Oreg., U.S.A.* 108 D2
Wheeler, *Tex., U.S.A.* 113 H4
Wheeler →, *Canada* 105 A6
Wheeler L., *U.S.A.* 115 H2
Wheeler Pk., *N. Mex., U.S.A.* 109 H11
Wheeler Pk., *Nev., U.S.A.* 109 G6
Wheeler Ridge, *U.S.A.* 111 L8
Wheeling, *U.S.A.* 116 F4
Whernside, *U.K.* 14 C5
Whiskey Jack L., *Canada* 103 B8
Whiskeytown-Shasta-Trinity ⌓, *U.S.A.* 108 F2
Whistleduck Cr. →, *Australia* 94 C2
Whistler, *Canada* 102 C4
Whitby, *Canada* 116 C6
Whitby, *U.K.* 14 C7
White →, *Ark., U.S.A.* 113 J9
White →, *Ind., U.S.A.* 114 F2
White →, *S. Dak., U.S.A.* 112 D5
White →, *Tex., U.S.A.* 113 J4
White →, *Utah, U.S.A.* 108 F9
White →, *Vt., U.S.A.* 117 C12
White →, *Wash., U.S.A.* 110 C4
White, L., *Australia* 92 D4
White B., *Canada* 105 C8
White Bird, *U.S.A.* 108 D5
White Butte, *U.S.A.* 112 B3
White City, *U.S.A.* 108 E2
White Cliffs, *Australia* 95 E3
White Hall, *U.S.A.* 112 F9
White Haven, *U.S.A.* 117 E9
White Horse, Vale of, *U.K.* 15 F6
White I., *N.Z.* 91 G6
White L., *Canada* 117 A8
White L., *U.S.A.* 113 L8
White Mountain Peak, *U.S.A.* 109 G4
White Mts., *Calif., U.S.A.* 110 H8
White Mts., *N.H., U.S.A.* 117 B13
White Mts. △, *Australia* 94 C4
White Nile = Nîl el Abyad →, *Sudan* 81 D3
White Nile Dam = Khazzān Jabal al Awliyā, *Sudan* 81 D3
White Otter L., *Canada* 104 C1
White Pass, *U.S.A.* 110 D5
White Plains, *U.S.A.* 117 E11
White River, *Canada* 104 C2
White River, *S. Africa* 89 D5
White River, *U.S.A.* 112 D4
White Rock, *Canada* 110 A4
White Russia = Belarus ■, *Europe* 32 F4
White Sands ⌓, *U.S.A.* 109 K10
White Sea = Beloye More, *Russia* 52 C4
White Sulphur Springs, *Mont., U.S.A.* 108 C8
White Sulphur Springs, *W. Va., U.S.A.* 114 G5
White Swan, *U.S.A.* 110 D6
White Volta →, *Ghana* 83 D4
Whitecliffs, *N.Z.* 91 K3
Whitecourt, *Canada* 102 C5
Whiteface Mt., *U.S.A.* 117 B11
Whitefield, *U.S.A.* 117 B13
Whitefish, *U.S.A.* 108 B6
Whitefish L., *Canada* 103 A7
Whitefish Point, *U.S.A.* 114 B3
Whitegull, L. = Goélands, L. aux, *Canada* 105 A7
Whitehall, *Mich., U.S.A.* 114 D2
Whitehall, *Mont., U.S.A.* 108 D7
Whitehall, *N.Y., U.S.A.* 117 C11
Whitehall, *Wis., U.S.A.* 112 C9
Whitehaven, *U.K.* 14 C4
Whitehorse, *Canada* 102 A1
Whitemark, *Australia* 95 G4
Whiteplains, *Liberia* 82 D2
Whiteriver, *U.S.A.* 109 K9
Whitesand →, *Canada* 102 A5
Whitesands, *S. Africa* 88 E3
Whitesboro, *N.Y., U.S.A.* 117 C9
Whitesboro, *Tex., U.S.A.* 113 J6
Whiteshell ⌓, *Canada* 103 D9
Whitesville, *U.S.A.* 116 D7
Whiteville, *U.S.A.* 115 H6
Whitewater, *U.S.A.* 114 D1
Whitewater Baldy, *U.S.A.* 109 K9
Whitewater L., *Canada* 104 B2
Whitewood, *Australia* 94 C3
Whitewood, *Canada* 103 C8
Whithorn, *U.K.* 13 G4
Whitianga, *N.Z.* 91 G5
Whitman, *U.S.A.* 117 D14
Whitney, *Canada* 116 A6
Whitney, Mt., *U.S.A.* 110 J8
Whitney Point, *U.S.A.* 117 D9
Whitstable, *U.K.* 15 F9
Whitsunday I., *Australia* 94 J7
Whitsunday Islands △, *Australia* 94 J7
Whitsunday Passage, *Australia* 94 J6
Whittier, *U.S.A.* 111 M8
Whittlesea, *Australia* 95 F4
Wholdaia L., *Canada* 103 A8
Whyalla, *Australia* 95 E2
Wiang Kosai △, *Thailand* 64 D2
Wiarton, *Canada* 116 B3
Wiawso, *Ghana* 82 D4
Wiay, *U.K.* 13 D1
Wiązów, *Poland* 31 H4
Wibaux, *U.S.A.* 112 B2
Wichian Buri, *Thailand* 64 E3
Wichita, *U.S.A.* 113 G6
Wichita Falls, *U.S.A.* 113 J5
Wick, *U.K.* 13 C5
Wicked Pt., *Canada* 116 C7
Wickenburg, *U.S.A.* 109 K7
Wickepin, *Australia* 93 F2
Wickham, *Australia* 92 D2
Wickham, C., *Australia* 95 F3
Wickliffe, *U.S.A.* 116 E3
Wicklow, *Ireland* 12 D5
Wicklow □, *Ireland* 12 D5
Wicklow Hd., *Ireland* 12 D6
Wicklow Mts., *Ireland* 12 C5
Wicklow Mts. △, *Ireland* 12 C5
Widawa, *Poland* 31 G5
Widawka →, *Poland* 31 G5
Widgeegoara Cr. →, *Australia* 95 D4
Widgiemooltha, *Australia* 93 F3
Widnes, *U.K.* 14 D5
Więcbork, *Poland* 31 E4
Wiehengebirge = Nördlicher Teutoburger Wald-Wiehengebirge ⌓, *Germany* 24 C4
Wiehl, *Germany* 24 E3
Wiek, *Germany* 24 A9
Wielbark, *Poland* 30 E7
Wieleń, *Poland* 31 F3
Wielichowo, *Poland* 31 F3
Wieliczka, *Poland* 31 J7
Wielkopolski △, *Poland* 31 F3
Wielkopolskie □, *Poland* 31 F4
Wieluń, *Poland* 31 G5
Wien, *Austria* 27 C9
Wien ✕ (VIA), *Austria* 27 C9
Wiener Neustadt, *Austria* 27 D9
Wieprz →, *Poland* 31 G8
Wieprza →, *Poland* 30 D3
Wieruszów, *Poland* 31 G5
Wiesbaden, *Germany* 25 E4
Wiesental, *Germany* 25 F4
Wiesloch, *Germany* 25 F4
Wiesmoor, *Germany* 24 B3
Wieżyca, *Poland* 30 D5
Wigan, *U.K.* 14 D5
Wiggins, *Colo., U.S.A.* 112 E2
Wiggins, *Miss., U.S.A.* 113 K10
Wight, I. of □, *U.K.* 15 G6
Wigierski △, *Poland* 30 D10
Wigry, Jezioro, *Poland* 30 D10
Wigston, *U.K.* 15 E6
Wigton, *U.K.* 14 C4
Wigtown, *U.K.* 13 G4
Wigtown B., *U.K.* 13 G4
Wil, *Switz.* 25 H5
Wilamowice, *Poland* 31 J6
Wilber, *U.S.A.* 112 E6
Wilberforce, *Canada* 116 A6
Wilberforce, C., *Australia* 94 A2
Wilburton, *U.S.A.* 113 H7
Wilcannia, *Australia* 95 E3
Wilcox, *U.S.A.* 116 E6
Wildbad, *Germany* 25 G4
Wildeshausen, *Germany* 24 C4
Wildeshauser Geest ⌓, *Germany* 24 C4
Wildon, *Austria* 26 E8
Wildrose, *U.S.A.* 111 J9
Wildspitze, *Austria* 26 E3
Wilga →, *Poland* 31 G8
Wilge →, *S. Africa* 89 D4
Wilhelm II Coast, *Antarctica* 5 C7
Wilhelmsburg, *Austria* 26 C8
Wilhelmshaven, *Germany* 24 B4
Wilhelmstal, *Namibia* 88 C2
Wilkes-Barre, *U.S.A.* 117 E9
Wilkes Land, *Antarctica* 5 D9
Wilkie, *Canada* 103 C7
Wilkinsburg, *U.S.A.* 116 F5
Wilkinson Lakes, *Australia* 93 E5
Willandra Creek →, *Australia* 95 E4
Willapa B., *U.S.A.* 108 C2
Willapa Hills, *U.S.A.* 110 D3
Willard, *N.Y., U.S.A.* 116 D8
Willard, *Ohio, U.S.A.* 116 E2
Willcox, *U.S.A.* 109 K9
Willemstad, *Neth. Ant.* 121 D6
Willet, *U.S.A.* 117 D9
William →, *Canada* 103 B7
William 'Bill' Dannely Res., *U.S.A.* 115 J2
William Creek, *Australia* 95 D2
Williams, *Australia* 93 F2
Williams, *Ariz., U.S.A.* 109 J7
Williams, *Calif., U.S.A.* 110 F4
Williams Harbour, *Canada* 105 B8
Williams Lake, *Canada* 102 C4
Williamsburg, *Ky., U.S.A.* 115 G3
Williamsburg, *Pa., U.S.A.* 116 F6
Williamsburg, *Va., U.S.A.* 114 G7
Williamson, *N.Y., U.S.A.* 116 C7
Williamson, *W. Va., U.S.A.* 114 G4
Williamsport, *U.S.A.* 116 E7
Williamston, *U.S.A.* 115 H7
Williamstown, *Australia* 95 F3
Williamstown, *Ky., U.S.A.* 114 F3
Williamstown, *Mass., U.S.A.* 117 D11
Williamstown, *N.Y., U.S.A.* 117 C9
Willimantic, *U.S.A.* 117 E12
Willingboro, *U.S.A.* 114 E8
Williston, *S. Africa* 88 E3
Williston, *Fla., U.S.A.* 115 L4
Williston, *N. Dak., U.S.A.* 112 A3
Williston L., *Canada* 102 B4
Willits, *U.S.A.* 108 G2
Willmar, *U.S.A.* 112 C7
Willmore Wilderness ⌓, *Canada* 102 C5
Willoughby, *U.S.A.* 116 E3
Willow Bunch, *Canada* 103 D7
Willow L., *Canada* 102 A5
Willow Wall, The, *China* 57 C12
Willowick, *U.S.A.* 116 E3
Willowlake →, *Canada* 102 A4
Willowmore, *S. Africa* 88 E3
Willows, *U.S.A.* 110 F4
Willowvale = Gatyana, *S. Africa* 89 E4
Wills, L., *Australia* 92 D4
Wills Cr. →, *Australia* 94 C3
Willsboro, *U.S.A.* 117 B11
Willunga, *Australia* 95 F2
Wilmette, *U.S.A.* 114 D2
Wilmington, *Australia* 95 E2
Wilmington, *Del., U.S.A.* 114 F8
Wilmington, *N.C., U.S.A.* 115 H7
Wilmington, *Ohio, U.S.A.* 114 F4
Wilmington, *Vt., U.S.A.* 117 D12
Wilmslow, *U.K.* 14 D5
Wilpena Cr. →, *Australia* 95 E2
Wilsall, *U.S.A.* 108 D8
Wilson, *N.C., U.S.A.* 115 H7
Wilson, *N.Y., U.S.A.* 116 C6
Wilson, *Pa., U.S.A.* 117 F9
Wilson →, *Australia* 92 C4
Wilson Bluff, *Australia* 93 F4
Wilson Inlet, *Australia* 93 G2
Wilsons Promontory, *Australia* 95 F4
Wilster, *Germany* 24 B5
Wilton, *U.S.A.* 112 B4
Wilton →, *Australia* 94 A1
Wiltshire □, *U.K.* 15 F6
Wiltz, *Lux.* 17 E5
Wiluna, *Australia* 93 E3
Wimborne Minster, *U.K.* 15 G6
Wimereux, *France* 19 B8
Wimmera →, *Australia* 95 F3
Winam G., *Kenya* 86 C3
Winburg, *S. Africa* 88 D4
Winchendon, *U.S.A.* 117 D12
Winchester, *U.K.* 15 F6
Winchester, *Conn., U.S.A.* 117 E11
Winchester, *Idaho, U.S.A.* 108 C5
Winchester, *Ind., U.S.A.* 114 E3
Winchester, *Ky., U.S.A.* 114 G3
Winchester, *N.H., U.S.A.* 117 D12
Winchester, *Nev., U.S.A.* 111 J11
Winchester, *Tenn., U.S.A.* 115 H2
Winchester, *Va., U.S.A.* 114 F6
Wind →, *U.S.A.* 108 E9
Wind Cave △, *U.S.A.* 112 D3
Wind River Range, *U.S.A.* 108 E9
Windau = Ventspils, *Latvia* 9 H19
Windber, *U.S.A.* 116 F6
Winder, *U.S.A.* 115 J4
Windermere, *U.K.* 14 C5
Windhoek, *Namibia* 88 C2
Windischgarsten, *Austria* 26 D7
Windom, *U.S.A.* 112 D7
Windorah, *Australia* 94 D3
Window Rock, *U.S.A.* 109 J9
Windrush →, *U.K.* 15 F6
Windsor, *Australia* 95 E5
Windsor, *N.S., Canada* 105 D7
Windsor, *Ont., Canada* 116 D2
Windsor, *U.K.* 15 F7
Windsor, *Colo., U.S.A.* 112 E2
Windsor, *Conn., U.S.A.* 117 E12
Windsor, *Mo., U.S.A.* 112 F8
Windsor, *N.Y., U.S.A.* 117 D9
Windsor, *Vt., U.S.A.* 117 C12
Windsor & Maidenhead □, *U.K.* 15 F7
Windsorton, *S. Africa* 88 D3
Windward Is., *W. Indies* 121 D7
Windward Passage = Vientos, Paso de los, *Caribbean* 121 C5
Winefred L., *Canada* 103 B6
Winejok, *Sudan* 81 F2
Winfield, *U.S.A.* 113 G6
Wingate Mts., *Australia* 92 B5
Wingham, *Australia* 95 E5
Wingham, *Canada* 116 C3
Winisk, *Canada* 104 A2
Winisk →, *Canada* 104 A2
Winisk L., *Canada* 104 B2
Wink, *U.S.A.* 113 K3
Winkler, *Canada* 103 D9
Winklern, *Austria* 26 E5
Winlock, *U.S.A.* 110 D4
Winneba, *Ghana* 83 D4
Winnebago, L., *U.S.A.* 114 D1
Winnecke Cr. →, *Australia* 92 C5
Winnemucca, *U.S.A.* 108 F5
Winnemucca L., *U.S.A.* 108 F4
Winnett, *U.S.A.* 108 C9
Winnfield, *U.S.A.* 113 K8
Winnibigoshish, L., *U.S.A.* 112 B7
Winnipeg, *Canada* 103 D9
Winnipeg →, *Canada* 103 C9
Winnipeg, L., *Canada* 103 C9
Winnipeg Beach, *Canada* 103 C9
Winnipegosis, *Canada* 103 C9
Winnipegosis L., *Canada* 103 C9
Winnipesaukee, L., *U.S.A.* 117 C13
Winnisquam L., *U.S.A.* 117 C13
Winnsboro, *La., U.S.A.* 113 J9
Winnsboro, *S.C., U.S.A.* 115 H5
Winnsboro, *Tex., U.S.A.* 113 J7
Winokapau, L., *Canada* 105 B7
Winona, *Minn., U.S.A.* 112 C9
Winona, *Miss., U.S.A.* 113 J10
Winooski, *U.S.A.* 117 B11
Winooski →, *U.S.A.* 117 B11
Winschoten, *Neths.* 17 A7
Winsen, *Germany* 24 B6
Winsford, *U.K.* 14 D5
Winslow, *Ariz., U.S.A.* 109 J8
Winslow, *Wash., U.S.A.* 110 C4
Winsted, *U.S.A.* 117 E11
Winston-Salem, *U.S.A.* 115 G5
Winter Garden, *U.S.A.* 115 L5
Winter Haven, *U.S.A.* 115 M5
Winter Park, *U.S.A.* 115 L5
Winterberg, *Germany* 24 D4
Winterhaven, *U.S.A.* 111 N12
Winters, *U.S.A.* 110 G5
Wintersville, *U.S.A.* 116 F4
Winterswijk, *Neths.* 17 C6
Winterthur, *Switz.* 25 H4
Winthrop, *U.S.A.* 108 B3
Winton, *Australia* 94 C3
Winton, *N.Z.* 91 M2
Wipper →, *Germany* 24 D7
Wirrulla, *Australia* 95 E1
Wisbech, *U.K.* 15 E8
Wisconsin □, *U.S.A.* 112 C10
Wisconsin →, *U.S.A.* 112 D9
Wisconsin Rapids, *U.S.A.* 112 C10
Wisdom, *U.S.A.* 108 D7
Wishaw, *U.K.* 13 F5
Wishek, *U.S.A.* 112 B5
Wisła, *Poland* 31 J5
Wisła →, *Poland* 30 D5
Wisłok →, *Poland* 31 H9

Wisłoka →, *Poland* 31 H8
Wismar, *Germany* 24 B7
Wisner, *U.S.A.* 112 E6
Wissant, *France* 19 B8
Wissembourg, *France* 19 C14
Wisznice, *Poland* 31 G10
Witbank, *S. Africa* 89 D4
Witdraai, *S. Africa* 88 D3
Witham, *U.K.* 15 F8
Witham →, *U.K.* 14 E7
Withernsea, *U.K.* 14 D8
Witjira △, *Australia* 95 D2
Witkowo, *Poland* 31 F4
Witney, *U.K.* 15 F6
Witnica, *Poland* 31 F1
Witnossob →, *Namibia* 88 D3
Wittdün, *Germany* 24 A4
Witten, *Germany* 24 D3
Wittenberge, *Germany* 24 B7
Wittenburg, *Germany* 24 B7
Wittenheim, *France* 19 E14
Wittenoom, *Australia* 92 D2
Wittingen, *Germany* 24 C6
Wittlich, *Germany* 25 F2
Wittmund, *Germany* 24 B3
Wittow, *Germany* 24 A9
Wittstock, *Germany* 24 B8
Witvlei, *Namibia* 88 C2
Witzenhausen, *Germany* 24 D5
Wkra →, *Poland* 31 F7
Władysławowo, *Poland* 30 D5
Wleń, *Poland* 31 G2
Wlingi, *Indonesia* 63 H15
Włocławek, *Poland* 31 F6
Włodawa, *Poland* 31 G10
Włoszczowa, *Poland* 31 H6
Woburn, *U.S.A.* 117 D13
Wodian, *China* 56 H7
Wodonga = Albury-Wodonga, *Australia* 95 F4
Wodzisław Śląski, *Poland* 31 H5
Wœrth, *France* 19 D14
Woinbogoin, *China* 58 A2
Woippy, *France* 19 C13
Wojcieszow, *Poland* 31 H2
Wokam, *Indonesia* 63 F8
Woking, *U.K.* 15 F7
Wokingham, *U.K.* 15 F7
Wokingham □, *U.K.* 15 F7
Wolbrom, *Poland* 31 H6
Wołczyn, *Poland* 31 G5
Woldegk, *Germany* 24 B9
Wolf →, *Canada* 102 A2
Wolf Creek, *U.S.A.* 108 C7
Wolf L., *Canada* 102 A2
Wolf Point, *U.S.A.* 112 A2
Wolfe I., *Canada* 117 B8
Wolfeboro, *U.S.A.* 117 C13
Wolfen, *Germany* 24 D8
Wolfenbüttel, *Germany* 24 C6
Wolfratshausen, *Germany* 25 H7
Wolfsberg, *Austria* 26 E7
Wolfsburg, *Germany* 24 C6
Wolgast, *Germany* 24 A9
Wolhusen, *Switz.* 25 H4
Wolin, *Poland* 30 E1
Woliński △, *Poland* 30 E1
Wollaston, Is., *Chile* 128 H3
Wollaston L., *Canada* 103 B8
Wollaston Lake, *Canada* 103 B8
Wollaston Pen., *Canada* 100 B8
Wollongong, *Australia* 95 E5
Wolmaransstad, *S. Africa* 88 D4
Wolmirstedt, *Germany* 24 C7
Wołomin, *Poland* 31 F8
Wołów, *Poland* 31 G3
Wolseley, *S. Africa* 88 E2
Wolsey, *U.S.A.* 112 C5
Wolstenholme, C., *Canada* 98 C12
Wolsztyn, *Poland* 31 F3
Wolvega, *Neths.* 17 B6
Wolverhampton, *U.K.* 15 E5
Wondai, *Australia* 95 D5
Wongalarroo L., *Australia* 95 E3
Wongan Hills, *Australia* 93 F2
Wŏnju, *S. Korea* 57 F14
Wonosari, *Indonesia* 63 G14
Wonosobo, *Indonesia* 63 G13
Wonowon, *Canada* 102 B4
Wŏnsan, *N. Korea* 57 E14
Wonthaggi, *Australia* 95 F4
Wood Buffalo △, *Canada* 102 B6
Wood Is., *Australia* 92 C3
Wood L., *Canada* 103 B8
Woodah I., *Australia* 94 A2
Woodbourne, *U.S.A.* 117 E10
Woodbridge, *Canada* 116 C5
Woodbridge, *U.K.* 15 E9
Woodburn, *U.S.A.* 108 D2
Woodenbong, *Australia* 95 D5
Woodend, *Australia* 95 F3
Woodford, *Australia* 95 D5
Woodfords, *U.S.A.* 110 G7
Woodlake, *U.S.A.* 110 J7
Woodland, *Calif., U.S.A.* 110 G5
Woodland, *Maine, U.S.A.* 115 C12
Woodland, *Pa., U.S.A.* 116 F6
Woodland, *Wash., U.S.A.* 110 E4
Woodland Caribou ⌓, *Canada* 103 C10
Woodlands, *Singapore* 65 d
Woodridge, *Canada* 103 D9
Woodroffe, Mt., *Australia* 93 E5
Woods, L., *Australia* 94 B1
Woods, L. of the, *Canada* 103 D10
Woodstock, *Australia* 94 B4
Woodstock, *N.B., Canada* 105 C6
Woodstock, *Ont., Canada* 116 C4
Woodstock, *U.K.* 15 F6
Woodstock, *Ill., U.S.A.* 112 D10
Woodstock, *Vt., U.S.A.* 117 C12
Woodsville, *U.S.A.* 117 B13
Woodville, *N.Z.* 91 J5
Woodville, *Miss., U.S.A.* 113 K9
Woodville, *Tex., U.S.A.* 113 K7
Woodward, *U.S.A.* 113 G5
Woody, *U.S.A.* 111 K8
Woody →, *Canada* 103 C8
Woolacombe, *U.K.* 15 F3
Woolamai, C., *Australia* 95 F4
Wooler, *U.K.* 14 B5
Woolgoolga, *Australia* 95 E5
Woomera, *Australia* 95 E2
Woonsocket, *R.I., U.S.A.* 117 E13
Woonsocket, *S. Dak., U.S.A.* 112 C5
Wooramel →, *Australia* 93 E1
Wooramel Roadhouse, *Australia* 93 E1
Wooster, *U.S.A.* 116 F3
Worcester, *S. Africa* 88 E2
Worcester, *U.K.* 15 E5
Worcester, *Mass., U.S.A.* 117 D13
Worcester, *N.Y., U.S.A.* 117 D10
Worcestershire □, *U.K.* 15 E5
Wörgl, *Austria* 26 D5
Workington, *U.K.* 14 C4
Worksop, *U.K.* 14 D6
Workum, *Neths.* 17 B5
Worland, *U.S.A.* 108 D10
Wormhout, *France* 19 B9
Worms, *Germany* 25 F4
Worsley, *Canada* 102 B5
Wörth, *Germany* 25 F8
Wortham, *U.S.A.* 113 K6
Wörther See, *Austria* 26 E7
Worthing, *Barbados* 121 g
Worthing, *U.K.* 15 G7
Worthington, *Minn., U.S.A.* 112 D7
Worthington, *Pa., U.S.A.* 116 F5
Wosi, *Indonesia* 63 E7
Wou-han = Wuhan, *China* 59 B10
Wousi = Wuxi, *China* 59 B13
Wowoni, *Indonesia* 63 E6
Wrangel I. = Vrangelya, Ostrov, *Russia* 53 B19
Wrangell, *U.S.A.* 102 B2
Wrangell Mts., *U.S.A.* 100 B5
Wrath, C., *U.K.* 13 C3
Wray, *U.S.A.* 112 E3
Wrekin, The, *U.K.* 15 E5
Wrens, *U.S.A.* 115 J4
Wrexham, *U.K.* 14 D4
Wrexham □, *U.K.* 14 D5
Wriezen, *Germany* 24 C10
Wright = Paranas, *Phil.* 61 F6
Wright, *U.S.A.* 112 D2
Wright Pt., *Canada* 116 C3
Wrightson, Mt., *U.S.A.* 109 L8
Wrightwood, *U.S.A.* 111 L9
Wrigley, *Canada* 100 B7
Wrocław, *Poland* 31 G4
Wronki, *Poland* 31 F3
Września, *Poland* 31 F4
Wschowa, *Poland* 31 G3
Wu Jiang →, *China* 58 C6
Wu'an, *China* 56 F8
Wubin, *Australia* 93 F2
Wubu, *China* 56 F6
Wuchang, *China* 57 B14
Wucheng, *China* 56 F9
Wuchuan, *Guangdong, China* 59 G8
Wuchuan, *Guizhou, China* 58 C7
Wuchuan, *Nei Monggol Zizhiqu, China* 56 D6
Wudi, *China* 57 F9
Wuding, *China* 58 E4
Wuding He →, *China* 56 F6
Wudinna, *Australia* 95 E2
Wudu, *China* 56 H3
Wufeng, *China* 59 B8
Wugang, *China* 59 D8
Wugong Shan, *China* 59 D9
Wuhan, *China* 59 B10
Wuhe, *China* 57 H9
Wuhsi = Wuxi, *China* 59 B13
Wuhu, *China* 59 B12
Wujiang, *China* 59 B13
Wukari, *Nigeria* 83 D6
Wulajie, *China* 57 B14
Wulanbulang, *China* 56 D6
Wular L., *India* 69 B6
Wulehe, *Ghana* 83 D5
Wulian, *China* 57 G10
Wuliang Shan, *China* 58 E3
Wuliaru, *Indonesia* 63 F8
Wuling Shan, *China* 58 C7
Wulong, *China* 58 C6
Wulumuchi = Ürümqi, *China* 52 E9
Wum, *Cameroon* 83 D7
Wuming, *China* 58 F7
Wun Rog, *Sudan* 81 F2
Wuning, *China* 59 C10
Wunnummin L., *Canada* 104 B2
Wunsiedel, *Germany* 25 E8
Wunstorf, *Germany* 24 C5
Wuntho, *Burma* 67 H19
Wupatki ⌓, *U.S.A.* 109 J8
Wuping, *China* 59 E11
Wuppertal, *Germany* 24 D3
Wuppertal, *S. Africa* 88 E2
Wuqing, *China* 57 E9
Wurtsboro, *U.S.A.* 117 E10
Würzburg, *Germany* 25 F5
Wurzen, *Germany* 24 D8
Wushan, *China* 56 G3
Wushishi, *Nigeria* 83 D6
Wusuli Jiang = Ussuri →, *Asia* 54 A7
Wutach →, *Germany* 25 H4
Wutai, *China* 56 E7
Wuting = Huimin, *China* 57 F9
Wutong, *China* 59 E8
Wutonghaolai, *China* 57 C11
Wutongqiao, *China* 58 C4
Wuwei, *Anhui, China* 59 B11
Wuwei, *Gansu, China* 60 C5
Wuxi, *Jiangsu, China* 59 B13
Wuxi, *Sichuan, China* 58 B7
Wuxiang, *China* 56 F7
Wuxuan, *China* 58 F7
Wuxue, *China* 59 C10
Wuyang, *China* 56 H7
Wuyi, *Hebei, China* 56 F8
Wuyi, *Zhejiang, China* 59 C12
Wuyi Shan, *China* 59 D11
Wuyishan, *China* 59 D12
Wuyo, *Nigeria* 83 C7
Wuyuan, *Jiangxi, China* 59 C11
Wuyuan, *Nei Monggol Zizhiqu, China* 56 D5
Wuzhai, *China* 56 E6
Wuzhi Shan, *China* 64 C7
Wuzhong, *China* 56 E4
Wuzhou, *China* 59 F8
Wyaaba Cr. →, *Australia* 94 B3
Wyalkatchem, *Australia* 93 F2
Wyalusing, *U.S.A.* 117 E8
Wyandotte, *U.S.A.* 114 D4
Wyandra, *Australia* 95 D4
Wyangala, L., *Australia* 95 E4
Wyara, L., *Australia* 95 D3
Wycheproof, *Australia* 95 F3
Wye →, *U.K.* 15 F5
Wyemandoo, *Australia* 93 E2
Wyk, *Germany* 24 A4
Wymondham, *U.K.* 15 E9
Wymore, *U.S.A.* 112 E6
Wyndham, *Australia* 92 C4
Wyndham, *N.Z.* 91 M2
Wynne, *U.S.A.* 113 H9
Wynyard, *Australia* 95 G4
Wynyard, *Canada* 103 C8
Wyola L., *Australia* 93 E5
Wyoming = Plympton-Wyoming, *Canada* 116 D2
Wyoming □, *U.S.A.* 108 E10
Wyomissing, *U.S.A.* 117 F9
Wyong, *Australia* 95 E5
Wyrzysk, *Poland* 31 E4
Wyśmierzyce, *Poland* 31 G7
Wysoka, *Poland* 31 E4
Wysokie, *Poland* 31 H9
Wysokie Mazowieckie, *Poland* 31 F9
Wyszków, *Poland* 31 F8
Wyszogród, *Poland* 31 F7
Wytheville, *U.S.A.* 114 G5
Wyżyna Małopolska, *Poland* 31 H7

X

Xaafuun, *Somali Rep.* 75 E5
Xaçmaz, *Azerbaijan* 35 K9
Xai-Xai, *Mozam.* 89 D5
Xainza, *China* 60 C3
Xalapa, *Mexico* 119 D5
Xangongo, *Angola* 88 B2
Xankändi, *Azerbaijan* 70 B5
Xanlar, *Azerbaijan* 35 K8
Xanten, *Germany* 24 D2
Xánthi, *Greece* 45 E8
Xánthi □, *Greece* 45 E8
Xanthos, *Turkey* 47 E11
Xanxerê, *Brazil* 127 B5
Xapuri, *Brazil* 124 F5
Xar Moron He →, *China* 57 C11
Xarrë, *Albania* 44 G4
Xátiva, *Spain* 39 G4
Xau, L., *Botswana* 88 C3
Xavantina, *Brazil* 127 A5
Xenia, *U.S.A.* 114 F4
Xeropotamos →, *Cyprus* 49 E11
Xertigny, *France* 19 D13
Xhora, *S. Africa* 89 E4
Xhumo, *Botswana* 88 C3
Xi Jiang →, *China* 59 F9
Xi Xian, *Henan, China* 59 A10
Xi Xian, *Shanxi, China* 56 F6
Xia Xian, *China* 56 G6
Xiachengzi, *China* 57 B16
Xiachuan Dao, *China* 59 G9
Xiaguan, *China* 60 D5
Xiajiang, *China* 59 D10
Xiajin, *China* 56 F9
Xiamen, *China* 59 E12
Xi'an, *China* 56 G5
Xian Xian, *China* 56 E9
Xianfeng, *China* 58 C7
Xiang Jiang →, *China* 59 C9
Xiangcheng, *Henan, China* 56 H8
Xiangcheng, *Henan, China* 56 H7
Xiangcheng, *Sichuan, China* 58 C2
Xiangdu, *China* 58 F6
Xiangfan, *China* 59 A9
Xianggang = Hong Kong □, *China* 59 F10
Xianghuang Qi, *China* 56 C7
Xiangning, *China* 56 G6
Xiangquan, *China* 56 F7
Xiangquan He = Sutlej →, *Pakistan* 68 E4
Xiangshan, *China* 59 C13
Xiangshui, *China* 57 G10
Xiangtan, *China* 59 D9
Xiangxiang, *China* 59 D9
Xiangyin, *China* 59 C9
Xiangyun, *China* 58 E3
Xiangzhou, *China* 58 F7
Xianju, *China* 59 C13
Xianning, *China* 59 C10
Xianshui He →, *China* 58 B3
Xiantao, *China* 59 B9
Xianyang, *China* 56 G5
Xianyou, *China* 59 E12
Xiao Hinggan Ling, *China* 60 B7
Xiao Xian, *China* 56 G9
Xiaofeng, *China* 59 B12
Xiaogan, *China* 59 B9
Xiaojin, *China* 58 B4
Xiaolan, *China* 59 F9
Xiaoshan, *China* 59 B13
Xiaoyi, *China* 56 F6
Xiapu, *China* 59 D12
Xiawa, *China* 57 C11
Xiayi, *China* 56 G9
Xichang, *China* 58 D4
Xichong, *China* 58 B5
Xichou, *China* 58 E5
Xichuan, *China* 56 H6
Xide, *China* 58 C4
Xiemahe, *China* 59 B8
Xieng Khouang, *Laos* 64 C4
Xifei He →, *China* 56 H9
Xifeng, *Gansu, China* 56 G4
Xifeng, *Guizhou, China* 58 D6
Xifeng, *Liaoning, China* 57 C13
Xifengzhen = Xifeng, *China* 56 G4
Xigazê, *China* 60 D3
Xihe, *China* 56 G3
Xihua, *China* 56 H8
Xilaganí, *Greece* 45 F9
Xiliao He →, *China* 57 C12
Xilin, *China* 58 E5
Xilókastron, *Greece* 46 C4
Ximana, *Mozam.* 87 F3
Xime, *Guinea-Biss.* 82 C2
Ximeng, *China* 58 F2
Xin Jiang →, *China* 59 C11
Xin Xian = Xinzhou, *China* 56 E7
Xinavane, *Mozam.* 89 D5
Xinbin, *China* 57 D13
Xincai, *China* 59 A10
Xinchang, *China* 59 C13
Xincheng, *Guangxi Zhuangzu, China* 58 E7
Xincheng, *Jiangxi, China* 59 D10
Xindu, *China* 58 B5
Xinfeng, *Guangdong, China* 59 E10
Xinfeng, *Jiangxi, China* 59 D11
Xinfeng, *Jiangxi, China* 59 E10
Xinfengjiang Skuiku, *China* 59 F10
Xing Xian, *China* 56 E6
Xing'an, *Guangxi Zhuangzu, China* 59 E8
Xingan, *Jiangxi, China* 59 D10
Xingcheng, *China* 57 D11
Xingguo, *China* 59 D10
Xinghe, *China* 56 D7
Xinghua, *China* 57 H10
Xinghua Wan, *China* 59 E12
Xinglong, *China* 57 D9
Xingning, *China* 59 E10
Xingping, *China* 56 G5
Xingren, *China* 58 E5
Xingshan, *China* 59 B8
Xingtai, *China* 56 F8
Xingu →, *Brazil* 125 D8
Xingwen, *China* 58 C5
Xingyang, *China* 56 G7
Xinhe, *China* 56 F8
Xinhua, *China* 59 D8
Xinhuang, *China* 58 D7
Xinhui, *China* 59 F9
Xining, *China* 60 C5
Xinjian, *China* 59 C10
Xinjiang, *China* 56 G6
Xinjiang Uygur Zizhiqu □, *China* 60 B3
Xinjie, *China* 58 D3
Xinjin = Pulandian, *China* 57 E11
Xinjin, *China* 58 B4
Xinkai He →, *China* 57 C12
Xinle, *China* 56 E8
Xinlitun, *China* 57 D12
Xinlong, *China* 58 B3
Xinmin, *China* 57 D12
Xinning, *China* 59 D8
Xinping, *China* 58 E3
Xinshao, *China* 59 D8
Xintai, *China* 57 G9
Xintian, *China* 59 E9
Xinxian, *China* 59 B10
Xinxiang, *China* 56 G7
Xinxing, *China* 59 F9
Xinyang, *China* 59 A10
Xinye, *China* 59 A9
Xinyi, *China* 59 F8
Xinyu, *China* 59 D10
Xinzhan, *China* 57 C14
Xinzheng, *China* 56 G7
Xinzhou, *Hubei, China* 59 B10
Xinzhou, *Shanxi, China* 56 E7
Xinzo de Limia, *Spain* 36 C3
Xiongyuecheng, *China* 57 D12
Xiping, *Henan, China* 56 H8
Xiping, *Henan, China* 56 H6
Xiping, *Zhejiang, China* 59 C12
Xique-Xique, *Brazil* 125 F10
Xisha Qundao = Paracel Is., *S. China Sea* 62 A4
Xishui, *Guizhou, China* 58 C6
Xishui, *Hubei, China* 59 B10
Xitole, *Guinea-Biss.* 82 C2
Xiu Shui →, *China* 59 C10
Xiuning, *China* 59 C12
Xiuren, *China* 59 E8
Xiushan, *China* 58 C7
Xiushui, *China* 59 C10
Xiuwen, *China* 58 D6
Xiuyan, *China* 57 D12
Xixabangma Feng, *China* 67 E14
Xixia, *China* 56 H6
Xixiang, *China* 56 H4
Xiyang, *China* 56 F7
Xizang Zizhiqu □, *China* 60 C3
Xlendi, *Malta* 49 C1
Xochob, *Mexico* 119 D7
Xu Jiang →, *China* 59 D11
Xuan Loc, *Vietnam* 65 G6
Xuan'en, *China* 58 C7
Xuanhan, *China* 58 B6
Xuanhua, *China* 56 D8
Xuanwei, *China* 58 C5
Xuanzhou, *China* 59 B12
Xuchang, *China* 56 G7
Xudat, *Azerbaijan* 35 K9
Xuefeng Shan, *China* 59 D8
Xuejiaping, *China* 59 B8
Xun Jiang →, *China* 59 F8
Xun Xian, *China* 56 G8
Xundian, *China* 58 E4
Xunwu, *China* 59 E10
Xunyang, *China* 56 H5
Xunyi, *China* 56 G5
Xupu, *China* 59 D8
Xúquer →, *Spain* 39 F4
Xushui, *China* 56 E8
Xuwen, *China* 59 G8
Xuyen Moc, *Vietnam* 65 G6
Xuyong, *China* 58 C5
Xuzhou, *China* 57 G9
Xylophagou, *Cyprus* 49 E12

Y

Ya Xian, *China* 64 C7
Yaamba, *Australia* 94 C5
Ya'an, *China* 58 C4
Yaapeet, *Australia* 95 F3
Yabassi, *Cameroon* 83 E6
Yabelo, *Ethiopia* 81 G4
Yabelo ⌓, *Ethiopia* 81 F4
Yablanitsa, *Bulgaria* 45 C8
Yablonovy Ra. = Yablonovyy Khrebet, *Russia* 53 D12
Yablonovyy Khrebet, *Russia* 53 D12
Yabluniv, *Ukraine* 29 B9
Yablunytsya, *Ukraine* 29 B9
Yabrai Shan, *China* 56 E2
Yabrūd, *Syria* 74 B5
Yabucoa, *Puerto Rico* 121 d
Yacambú △, *Venezuela* 121 E6
Yacheng, *China* 64 C7
Yacuiba, *Bolivia* 126 A3
Yacuma →, *Bolivia* 124 F5
Yadgir, *India* 66 L10
Yadkin →, *U.S.A.* 115 H5
Yadrin, *Russia* 34 C8
Yaeyama-Rettō, *Japan* 55 M1
Yagaba, *Ghana* 83 C4
Yağcılar, *Turkey* 47 B10
Yagodnoye, *Russia* 53 C15
Yahila, *Dem. Rep. of the Congo* 86 B1
Yahk, *Canada* 102 D5
Yahotyn, *Ukraine* 33 G6
Yahuma, *Dem. Rep. of the Congo* 84 D4
Yahyalı, *Turkey* 72 C6
Yaita, *Japan* 55 F9
Yaiza, *Canary Is.* 48 F6
Yajiang, *China* 58 B3
Yajua, *Nigeria* 83 C7
Yakima, *U.S.A.* 108 C3
Yakima →, *U.S.A.* 108 C3
Yako, *Burkina Faso* 82 C4
Yakobi I., *U.S.A.* 102 B1
Yakoruda, *Bulgaria* 44 D7
Yakovlevka, *Russia* 54 B6
Yaku-Shima, *Japan* 55 J5
Yakumo, *Japan* 54 C10
Yakutat, *U.S.A.* 100 C6
Yakutia = Sakha □, *Russia* 53 C13
Yakutsk, *Russia* 53 C13
Yala, *Thailand* 65 J3
Yalboroo, *Australia* 94 J6
Yale, *U.S.A.* 116 C2
Yalgoo, *Australia* 93 E2
Yalgorup △, *Australia* 93 D2
Yalinga, *C.A.R.* 84 C4
Yalkubul, Punta, *Mexico* 119 C7
Yalleroi, *Australia* 94 C4
Yalobusha →, *U.S.A.* 113 J9
Yalong Jiang →, *China* 58 D3
Yalova, *Turkey* 45 F13
Yalpuh, Ozero, *Ukraine* 29 E13
Yalta, *Ukraine* 33 K8
Yalu Jiang →, *China* 57 E13
Yalvaç, *Turkey* 72 C4
Yam Ha Melah = Dead Sea, *Asia* 74 D4
Yam Kinneret, *Israel* 74 C4
Yamada, *Japan* 55 H5
Yamagata, *Japan* 54 E10
Yamagata □, *Japan* 54 E10
Yamaguchi, *Japan* 55 G5
Yamaguchi □, *Japan* 55 G5
Yamal, Poluostrov, *Russia* 52 B8
Yamal Pen. = Yamal, Poluostrov, *Russia* 52 B8
Yamanashi □, *Japan* 55 G9
Yamanie Falls △, *Australia* 94 B4
Yamba, *Australia* 95 D5
Yambarran Ra., *Australia* 92 C5
Yambéring, *Guinea* 82 C2
Yâmbiô, *Sudan* 81 G2
Yambol, *Bulgaria* 45 D10
Yamdena, *Indonesia* 63 F8
Yame, *Japan* 55 H5
Yamethin, *Burma* 67 J20
Yamma-Yamma, L., *Australia* 95 D3
Yamoussoukro, *Ivory C.* 82 D3
Yampa →, *U.S.A.* 108 F9
Yampi Sd., *Australia* 92 C3
Yampil, *Moldova* 33 H5
Yampol = Yampil, *Moldova* 33 H5
Yamrat, *Nigeria* 83 C6
Yamrukchal = Botev, *Bulgaria* 45 D8
Yamuna →, *India* 69 G9
Yamunanagar, *India* 68 D7

Yamzho Yumco, *China* 60 D4
Yan, *Nigeria* 83 C7
Yana →, *Russia* 53 B14
Yanagawa, *Japan* 55 H5
Yanai, *Japan* 55 H6
Yan'an, *China* 56 F5
Yanbian, *China* 58 D3
Yanbu 'al Baḩr, *Si. Arabia* 70 F3
Yanchang, *China* 56 F6
Yancheng, *Henan, China* 56 H8
Yancheng, *Jiangsu, China* 57 H11
Yanchep Beach, *Australia* 93 F2
Yanchi, *China* 56 F4
Yanchuan, *China* 56 F6
Yanco Cr. →, *Australia* 95 F4
Yandicoogina, *Australia* 92 D2
Yandoon, *Burma* 67 L19
Yanfeng, *China* 58 E3
Yanfolila, *Mali* 82 C3
Yang Xian, *China* 56 H4
Yang-Yang, *Senegal* 82 B1
Yangambi, *Dem. Rep. of the Congo* 86 B1
Yangbi, *China* 58 E2
Yangcheng, *China* 56 G7
Yangch'ü = Taiyuan, *China* 56 F7
Yangchun, *China* 59 F8
Yanggao, *China* 56 D7
Yanggu, *China* 56 F8
Yangjiang, *China* 59 G8
Yangliuqing, *China* 57 E9
Yangon = Rangoon, *Burma* 67 L20
Yangping, *China* 59 B8
Yangpingguan, *China* 56 H4
Yangquan, *China* 56 F7
Yangshan, *China* 59 E9
Yangshuo, *China* 59 E8
Yangtse = Chang Jiang →, *China* 59 B13
Yangtze Kiang = Chang Jiang →, *China* 59 B13
Yangudi Rassa △, *Ethiopia* 81 E5
Yangxin, *China* 59 C10
Yangyang, *S. Korea* 57 E15
Yangyuan, *China* 56 D8
Yangzhong, *China* 59 A12
Yangzhou, *China* 59 A12
Yanhe, *China* 58 C7
Yanji, *China* 57 C15
Yanjin, *China* 58 C5
Yanjing, *China* 58 C2
Yankari △, *Nigeria* 83 D7
Yankton, *U.S.A.* 112 D6
Yanonge, *Dem. Rep. of the Congo* 86 B1
Yanqi, *China* 60 B3
Yanqing, *China* 56 D8
Yanshan, *Hebei, China* 57 E9
Yanshan, *Jiangxi, China* 59 C11
Yanshan, *Yunnan, China* 58 F5
Yanshou, *China* 57 B15
Yantabulla, *Australia* 95 D4
Yantai, *China* 57 F11
Yantarnyy, *Russia* 30 D6
Yanting, *China* 58 B5
Yantra →, *Bulgaria* 45 C9
Yanwa, *China* 58 D2
Yanyuan, *China* 58 D3
Yanzhou, *China* 56 G9
Yao Noi, Ko, *Thailand* 65 a
Yao Xian, *China* 56 G5
Yao Yai, Ko, *Thailand* 65 a
Yao'an, *China* 58 E3
Yaodu, *China* 58 A5
Yaoundé, *Cameroon* 83 E7
Yaowan, *China* 57 G10
Yap, *Pac. Oc.* 96 G5
Yapen, *Indonesia* 63 E9
Yapen, Selat, *Indonesia* 63 E9
Yapero, *Indonesia* 63 E9
Yappar →, *Australia* 94 B3
Yaqui →, *Mexico* 118 B2
Yar-Sale, *Russia* 52 C8
Yaraka, *Australia* 94 C3
Yaransk, *Russia* 34 B8
Yarbasan, *Turkey* 47 C10
Yardımcı Burnu, *Turkey* 47 E12
Yare →, *U.K.* 15 E9
Yaremcha, *Ukraine* 29 B9
Yarensk, *Russia* 52 C5
Yarfa, *Si. Arabia* 80 C4
Yarí →, *Colombia* 124 D4
Yarkand = Shache, *China* 60 C2
Yarker, *Canada* 117 B8
Yarkhun →, *Pakistan* 69 A5
Yarlung Ziangbo Jiang = Brahmaputra →, *Asia* 69 H13
Yarmouth, *Canada* 105 D6
Yarmūk →, *Syria* 74 C4
Yaroslavl, *Russia* 32 D10
Yarqa, W. →, *Egypt* 74 F2
Yarra Yarra Lakes, *Australia* 93 E2
Yarram, *Australia* 95 F4
Yarraman, *Australia* 95 D5
Yarras, *Australia* 95 E5
Yartsevo, *Sib., Russia* 53 C10
Yartsevo, *Smolensk, Russia* 32 E7
Yarumal, *Colombia* 124 B3
Yasawa Group, *Fiji* 91 C7
Yaselda, *Belarus* 33 F4
Yasen, *Ukraine* 29 B9
Yashi, *Nigeria* 83 C6
Yashikera, *Nigeria* 83 D5
Yashkul, *Russia* 35 G7
Yasin, *Pakistan* 69 A5
Yasinovataya, *Ukraine* 33 H9
Yasinski, L., *Canada* 104 B4
Yasinya, *Ukraine* 29 B9
Yasothon, *Thailand* 64 E5
Yass, *Australia* 95 E4
Yāsūj, *Iran* 71 D6
Yatağan, *Turkey* 47 D10
Yatakala, *Niger* 83 C5
Yates Center, *U.S.A.* 113 G7
Yathkyed L., *Canada* 103 A9
Yatsushiro, *Japan* 55 H5
Yatta Plateau, *Kenya* 86 C4
Yauco, *Puerto Rico* 121 d
Yavari →, *Peru* 124 D4
Yávaros, *Mexico* 118 B3
Yavatmal, *India* 66 J11
Yavne, *Israel* 74 D3
Yavoriv, *Ukraine* 31 J10
Yavorov = Yavoriv, *Ukraine* 31 J10
Yavuzeli, *Turkey* 72 D7
Yawatahama, *Japan* 55 H6
Yawri B., *S. Leone* 82 D2
Yaxi, *China* 58 D6
Yazd, *Iran* 71 D7
Yazd □, *Iran* 71 D7
Yazd-e Khvāst, *Iran* 71 D7
Yazıköy, *Turkey* 47 E9
Yazman, *Pakistan* 68 E4
Yazoo →, *U.S.A.* 113 J9
Yazoo City, *U.S.A.* 113 J9
Ybbs, *Austria* 26 C8
Ybycuí △, *Paraguay* 126 B4
Ybytyruzú △, *Paraguay* 127 B4
Yding Skovhøj, *Denmark* 11 J3
Ye, *Burma* 64 E1
Ye Xian, *China* 56 H7
Yebyu, *Burma* 64 E2
Yechŏn, *S. Korea* 57 F15
Yecla, *Spain* 39 G3
Yécora, *Mexico* 118 B3
Yedebub Biheroch Bihereseboch na Hizboch □, *Ethiopia* 81 F4
Yedintsy = Edineţ, *Moldova* 29 B12
Yedseram →, *Nigeria* 83 C7
Yefremov, *Russia* 32 F10
Yeghegnadzor, *Armenia* 73 C11
Yegorlyk →, *Russia* 35 G5
Yegorlykskaya, *Russia* 35 G5
Yegoryevsk, *Russia* 32 E10
Yegros, *Paraguay* 126 B4
Yehbuah, *Indonesia* 63 J17
Yehuda, Midbar, *Israel* 74 D4
Yei, *Sudan* 81 G3
Yei, Nahr →, *Sudan* 81 F3
Yejmiadzin, *Armenia* 35 K7
Yekaterinburg, *Russia* 52 D7
Yelabuga, *Russia* 34 C11
Yelan, *Russia* 34 E6
Yelarbon, *Australia* 95 D5
Yelatma, *Russia* 34 C5
Yelets, *Russia* 33 F10
Yélimané, *Mali* 82 B2
Yelizavetgrad = Kirovohrad, *Ukraine* 33 H7
Yell, *U.K.* 13 A7
Yell Sd., *U.K.* 13 A7
Yellow Sea, *China* 57 G12
Yellowhead Pass, *Canada* 102 C5
Yellowknife, *Canada* 102 A6
Yellowknife →, *Canada* 102 A6
Yellowstone △, *U.S.A.* 108 D9
Yellowstone →, *U.S.A.* 112 B3
Yellowstone L., *U.S.A.* 108 D8
Yelnya, *Russia* 32 E7
Yelsk, *Belarus* 33 G5
Yelwa, *Nigeria* 83 C5
Yemen ■, *Asia* 75 E3
Yen Bai, *Vietnam* 58 G5
Yenagoa, *Nigeria* 83 E6
Yenakiyeve, *Ukraine* 33 H10
Yenakiyevo = Yenakiyeve, *Ukraine* 33 H10
Yenangyaung, *Burma* 67 J19
Yenbo = Yanbu 'al Baḩr, *Si. Arabia* 70 F3
Yenda, *Australia* 95 E4
Yende Millimou, *Guinea* 82 D2
Yendéré, *Burkina Faso* 82 C4
Yendi, *Ghana* 83 D4
Yéni, *Niger* 83 C5
Yenice, *Ankara, Turkey* 72 C5
Yenice, *Aydın, Turkey* 47 D10
Yenice, *Çanakkale, Turkey* 47 B9
Yenice, *Edirne, Turkey* 45 F10
Yenice →, *Turkey* 72 D6
Yenifoça, *Turkey* 47 C8
Yenihisar, *Turkey* 47 D9
Yeniköy, *Bursa, Turkey* 45 F13
Yeniköy, *Çanakkale, Turkey* 47 B8
Yeniköy, *Kütahya, Turkey* 47 C11
Yenipazar, *Turkey* 47 D10
Yenisaía, *Greece* 45 E8
Yenişehir, *Turkey* 45 F13
Yenisey →, *Russia* 52 B9
Yeniseysk, *Russia* 53 D10
Yeniseyskiy Zaliv, *Russia* 52 B9
Yennádhi, *Greece* 49 C9
Yenne, *France* 21 C9
Yenotayevka, *Russia* 35 G8
Yenyuka, *Russia* 53 D13
Yeo →, *U.K.* 15 G5
Yeo, L., *Australia* 93 E3
Yeo I., *Canada* 116 A3
Yeola, *India* 66 J9
Yeoryioúpolis, *Greece* 49 D6
Yeovil, *U.K.* 15 G5
Yepes, *Spain* 36 F7
Yeppoon, *Australia* 94 C5
Yeráki, *Greece* 46 D4
Yerbent, *Turkmenistan* 52 F6
Yerbogachen, *Russia* 53 C11
Yerevan, *Armenia* 35 K7
Yerington, *U.S.A.* 108 G4
Yerkesik, *Turkey* 47 D10
Yerköy, *Turkey* 72 C6
Yermak, *Kazakhstan* 52 D8
Yermo, *U.S.A.* 111 L10
Yerólakkos, *Cyprus* 49 D12
Yeropol, *Russia* 53 C17
Yeropótamos →, *Greece* 49 D6
Yeroskipos, *Cyprus* 49 E11
Yershov, *Russia* 34 E9
Yerushalayim = Jerusalem, *Israel* 74 D4
Yerville, *France* 18 C7
Yes Tor, *U.K.* 15 G4
Yesan, *S. Korea* 57 F14
Yeşilhisar, *Turkey* 72 C6
Yeşilırmak →, *Turkey* 72 B7
Yeşilkent, *Turkey* 72 D7
Yeşilköy, *Turkey* 45 F12
Yeşilova, *Turkey* 47 D11
Yeşilyurt, *Manisa, Turkey* 47 C10
Yeşilyurt, *Muğla, Turkey* 47 D10
Yesnogorsk, *Russia* 32 E9
Yeso, *U.S.A.* 113 H2
Yessentuki, *Russia* 35 H6
Yessey, *Russia* 53 C11
Yeste, *Spain* 39 G2
Yetman, *Australia* 95 D5
Yeu, Î. d', *France* 18 F4
Yevlakh = Yevlax, *Azerbaijan* 35 K8
Yevlax, *Azerbaijan* 35 K8
Yevpatoriya, *Ukraine* 33 K7
Yeya →, *Russia* 33 J10
Yeysk, *Russia* 33 J10
Yezd = Yazd, *Iran* 71 D7
Yezerishche, *Belarus* 32 E5
Yhati, *Paraguay* 126 B4
Yhú, *Paraguay* 127 B4
Yi →, *Uruguay* 126 C4
Yi 'Allaq, G., *Egypt* 74 E2
Yi He →, *China* 57 G10
Yi Xian, *Anhui, China* 59 C11
Yi Xian, *Hebei, China* 56 E8
Yi Xian, *Liaoning, China* 57 D11
Yialí, *Greece* 47 E9
Yialiás →, *Cyprus* 49 D12
Yi'allaq, G., *Egypt* 80 A3
Yialousa, *Cyprus* 49 D13
Yiáltra, *Greece* 46 C4
Yianisádhes, *Greece* 49 D8
Yiannitsa, *Greece* 44 F6
Yibin, *China* 58 C5
Yichang, *China* 59 B8
Yicheng, *Henan, China* 59 B9
Yicheng, *Shanxi, China* 56 G6
Yichuan, *China* 56 F6
Yichun, *Heilongjiang, China* 60 B7
Yichun, *Jiangxi, China* 59 D10
Yidu, *China* 57 F10
Yidun, *China* 58 B2
Yifag, *Ethiopia* 81 E4
Yifeng, *China* 59 C10
Yihuang, *China* 59 D11
Yijun, *China* 56 G5
Yıldız Dağları, *Turkey* 45 E11
Yıldızeli, *Turkey* 72 C7
Yiliang, *Yunnan, China* 58 D5
Yiliang, *Yunnan, China* 58 E4
Yilong, *China* 58 B6
Yimen, *China* 58 E4
Yimianpo, *China* 57 B15
Yinchuan, *China* 56 E4
Yindarlgooda, L., *Australia* 93 F3
Ying He →, *China* 56 H9
Ying Xian, *China* 56 E7
Yingcheng, *China* 59 B9
Yingde, *China* 59 E9
Yingjiang, *China* 58 E1
Yingjing, *China* 58 C4
Yingkou, *China* 57 D12
Yingshan, *Henan, China* 59 B9
Yingshan, *Hubei, China* 59 B10
Yingshan, *Sichuan, China* 58 B6
Yingshang, *China* 59 A11
Yingtan, *China* 59 C11
Yining, *China* 52 E9
Yinjiang, *China* 58 C7
Yinmabin, *Burma* 67 H19
Yiofiros →, *Greece* 49 D7
Yioúra, *Nótios Aiyaíon, Greece* 46 D6
Yioúra, *Thessalía, Greece* 46 B6
Yipinglang, *China* 58 E3
Yirba Muda, *Ethiopia* 81 F4
Yirga Alem, *Ethiopia* 81 F4
Yirol, *Sudan* 81 F3
Yirrkala, *Australia* 94 A2
Yishan, *China* 58 E7
Yishui, *China* 57 G10
Yishun, *Singapore* 65 d
Yíthion, *Greece* 46 E4
Yitong, *China* 57 C13
Yiwu, *China* 59 C13
Yixing, *China* 59 B12
Yiyang, *Henan, China* 56 G7
Yiyang, *Hunan, China* 59 C9
Yiyang, *Jiangxi, China* 59 C11
Yizhang, *China* 59 E9
Yizheng, *China* 59 A12
Yli-Kitka, *Finland* 8 C23
Ylitornio, *Finland* 8 C20
Ylivieska, *Finland* 8 D21
Yngaren, *Sweden* 11 F10
Yoakum, *U.S.A.* 113 L6
Yob ⌓, *Eritrea* 81 D4
Yobe □, *Nigeria* 83 C7
Yog Pt., *Phil.* 63 B6
Yogan, *Togo* 83 D5
Yoğuntaş, *Turkey* 45 E11
Yogyakarta, *Indonesia* 63 G14
Yogyakarta □, *Indonesia* 63 G14
Yoho △, *Canada* 102 C5
Yojoa, L. de, *Honduras* 120 D2
Yŏju, *S. Korea* 57 F14
Yok Don △, *Vietnam* 64 F6
Yokadouma, *Cameroon* 84 D2
Yokkaichi, *Japan* 55 G8
Yoko, *Cameroon* 83 D7
Yokohama, *Japan* 55 G9
Yokosuka, *Japan* 55 G9
Yokote, *Japan* 54 E10
Yola, *Nigeria* 83 D7
Yolaina, Cordillera de, *Nic.* 120 D3
Yoloten, *Turkmenistan* 71 B9
Yom →, *Thailand* 62 A2
Yonago, *Japan* 55 G6
Yonaguni-Jima, *Japan* 55 M1
Yŏnan, *N. Korea* 57 F14
Yonezawa, *Japan* 54 F10
Yong Peng, *Malaysia* 65 L4
Yong Sata, *Thailand* 65 J2
Yongamp'o, *N. Korea* 57 E13
Yong'an, *China* 59 E11
Yongcheng, *China* 56 H9
Yŏngch'ŏn, *S. Korea* 57 G15
Yongchuan, *China* 58 C5
Yongchun, *China* 59 E12
Yongde, *China* 58 E2
Yongdeng, *China* 56 F2
Yongding, *China* 59 E11
Yŏngdŏk, *S. Korea* 57 F15
Yŏngdŭngpo, *S. Korea* 57 F14
Yongfeng, *China* 59 D10
Yongfu, *China* 58 E7
Yonghe, *China* 56 F6
Yŏnghŭng, *N. Korea* 57 E14
Yongji, *China* 56 G6
Yongjia, *China* 59 C13
Yŏngju, *S. Korea* 57 F15
Yongkang, *Yunnan, China* 58 E2
Yongkang, *Zhejiang, China* 59 C13
Yongnian, *China* 56 F8
Yongning, *Guangxi Zhuangzu, China* 58 F7
Yongning, *Ningxia Huizu, China* 56 E4
Yongping, *China* 58 E2
Yongqing, *China* 56 E9
Yongren, *China* 58 D3
Yongshan, *China* 58 C4
Yongsheng, *China* 58 D3
Yongshun, *China* 58 C7
Yongtai, *China* 59 E12
Yŏngwŏl, *S. Korea* 57 F15
Yongxin = Jinggangshan, *China* 59 D10
Yongxing, *China* 59 D9
Yongxiu, *China* 59 C10
Yongzhou, *China* 59 D8
Yonibana, *S. Leone* 82 D2
Yonkers, *U.S.A.* 117 F11
Yonne □, *France* 19 E10
Yonne →, *France* 19 D9
York, *Australia* 93 F2
York, *U.K.* 14 D6
York, *Ala., U.S.A.* 113 J10
York, *Nebr., U.S.A.* 112 E6
York, *Pa., U.S.A.* 114 F7
York, C., *Australia* 94 A3
York, City of □, *U.K.* 14 D6
York, Kap, *Greenland* 4 B4
York, Vale of, *U.K.* 14 C6
York Haven, *U.S.A.* 116 F8
York Sd., *Australia* 92 C4
Yorke Pen., *Australia* 95 E2
Yorkshire Dales △, *U.K.* 14 C5
Yorkshire Wolds, *U.K.* 14 C7
Yorkton, *Canada* 103 C8
Yorkville, *U.S.A.* 110 G3
Yoro, *Honduras* 120 C2
Yoron-Jima, *Japan* 55 L4
Yorosso, *Mali* 82 C4
Yos Sudarso, Pulau = Dolak, Pulau, *Indonesia* 63 F9
Yosemite △, *U.S.A.* 110 H7
Yosemite Village, *U.S.A.* 110 H7
Yoshino-Kumano △, *Japan* 55 H8
Yoshkar Ola, *Russia* 34 B8
Yŏsu, *S. Korea* 57 G14
Yotvata, *Israel* 74 F4
You Jiang →, *China* 58 F6
You Xian, *China* 59 D9
Youbou, *Canada* 110 B2
Youghal, *Ireland* 12 E4
Youghal B., *Ireland* 12 E4
Youkounkoun, *Guinea* 82 C2
Young, *Australia* 95 E4
Young, *Canada* 103 C7
Young, *Uruguay* 126 C4
Younghusband, L., *Australia* 95 E2
Younghusband Pen., *Australia* 95 F2
Youngstown, *Canada* 103 C6
Youngstown, *N.Y., U.S.A.* 116 C5
Youngstown, *Ohio, U.S.A.* 116 E4
Youngsville, *U.S.A.* 116 E5
Youngwood, *U.S.A.* 116 F5
Youxi, *China* 59 D12
Youyang, *China* 58 C7
Youyu, *China* 56 D7
Yozgat, *Turkey* 72 C6
Ypacaraí △, *Paraguay* 126 B4
Ypané →, *Paraguay* 126 A4
Yport, *France* 18 C7
Ypres = Ieper, *Belgium* 17 D2
Yreka, *U.S.A.* 108 F2
Yssingeaux, *France* 21 C8
Ystad, *Sweden* 11 J7
Ysyk-Köl, *Kyrgyzstan* 52 E8
Ythan →, *U.K.* 13 D7
Ytterhogdal, *Sweden* 10 B8
Ytyk-Kyuyel, *Russia* 53 C14
Yu Jiang →, *China* 58 F7
Yu Shan, *Taiwan* 59 F13
Yu Xian = Yuzhou, *China* 56 G7
Yu Xian, *Hebei, China* 56 E8
Yu Xian, *Shanxi, China* 56 E7
Yuan Jiang →, *Hunan, China* 59 C8
Yuan Jiang →, *Yunnan, China* 58 F4
Yuan'an, *China* 59 B8
Yuanjiang, *Hunan, China* 59 C9
Yuanjiang, *Yunnan, China* 58 F4
Yüanli, *Taiwan* 59 E13
Yüanlin, *Taiwan* 59 F13
Yuanling, *China* 59 C8
Yuanmou, *China* 58 E3
Yuanqu, *China* 56 G6
Yuanyang, *Henan, China* 56 G7
Yuanyang, *Yunnan, China* 58 F4
Yuba →, *U.S.A.* 110 F5
Yuba City, *U.S.A.* 110 F5
Yūbari, *Japan* 54 C10
Yubdo, *Ethiopia* 81 F4
Yūbetsu, *Japan* 54 B11
Yubo, *Sudan* 81 F2
Yucatán □, *Mexico* 119 C7
Yucatán, Canal de, *Caribbean* 120 B2
Yucatán, Península de, *Mexico* 98 H11
Yucatan Basin, *Cent. Amer.* 98 H11
Yucatan Channel = Yucatán, Canal de, *Caribbean* 120 B2
Yucca, *U.S.A.* 111 L12
Yucca Valley, *U.S.A.* 111 L10
Yucheng, *China* 56 F9
Yuci, *China* 56 F7
Yudu, *China* 59 E10
Yuechi, *China* 58 B6
Yuendumu, *Australia* 92 D5
Yueqing, *China* 59 C13
Yueqing Wan, *China* 59 D13
Yuexi, *Anhui, China* 59 B11
Yuexi, *Sichuan, China* 58 C4
Yueyang, *China* 59 C9
Yugan, *China* 59 C11
Yugoslavia = Serbia & Montenegro ■, *Europe* 44 C4
Yuhuan, *China* 59 C13
Yuhuan Dao, *China* 59 C13
Yujiang, *China* 59 C11
Yukhnov, *Russia* 32 E8
Yukon →, *U.S.A.* 100 B3
Yukon Territory □, *Canada* 100 B6
Yüksekova, *Turkey* 73 D11
Yukta, *Russia* 53 C11
Yukuhashi, *Japan* 55 H5
Yulara, *Australia* 93 E5
Yule →, *Australia* 92 D2
Yuleba, *Australia* 95 D4
Yuli, *Nigeria* 83 D7
Yuli, *Taiwan* 59 F13
Yulin, *Guangxi Zhuangzu, China* 59 F8
Yülin, *Hainan, China* 65 C7
Yulin, *Shaanxi, China* 56 E5
Yuma, *Ariz., U.S.A.* 111 N12
Yuma, *Colo., U.S.A.* 112 E3
Yuma, B. de, *Dom. Rep.* 121 C6
Yumbe, *Uganda* 86 B3
Yumbi, *Dem. Rep. of the Congo* 86 C2
Yumen, *China* 60 C4
Yumurtalık, *Turkey* 72 D6
Yun Gui Gaoyuan, *China* 58 E3
Yun Ho →, *China* 57 E9
Yun Ling, *China* 58 D2
Yun Xian, *Hubei, China* 59 A8
Yun Xian, *Yunnan, China* 58 E3
Yuna, *Australia* 93 E2
Yunak, *Turkey* 72 C4
Yunan, *China* 59 F8
Yuncheng, *Henan, China* 56 G8
Yuncheng, *Shanxi, China* 56 G6
Yunfu, *China* 59 F9
Yungas, *Bolivia* 124 G5
Yungay, *Chile* 126 D1
Yunhe, *China* 59 C12
Yunkai Dashan, *China* 59 F8
Yunlin, *Taiwan* 59 F13
Yunlong, *China* 58 E2
Yunmeng, *China* 59 B9
Yunnan □, *China* 58 E4
Yunquera de Henares, *Spain* 38 E1
Yunt Dağı, *Turkey* 47 C9
Yunta, *Australia* 95 E2
Yunxi, *China* 56 H6
Yunxiao, *China* 59 F11
Yuping, *China* 58 D7
Yupyongdong, *N. Korea* 57 D15
Yuqing, *China* 58 D6
Yuraygir △, *Australia* 95 D5
Yurga, *Russia* 52 D9
Yurimaguas, *Peru* 124 E3
Yurkiyka, *Ukraine* 29 B13
Yurubí △, *Venezuela* 121 D6
Yuryev-Polskiy, *Russia* 32 D10
Yuryevets, *Russia* 34 B6
Yuscarán, *Honduras* 120 D2
Yūsef, Bahr →, *Egypt* 80 B3
Yushan, *China* 59 C12
Yushanzhen, *China* 58 C7
Yushe, *China* 56 F7
Yushu, *Jilin, China* 57 B14
Yushu, *Qinghai, China* 60 C4
Yusufeli, *Turkey* 73 B9
Yutai, *China* 56 G9
Yutian, *China* 57 E9
Yuxarı Qarabağ = Nagorno-Karabakh □, *Azerbaijan* 70 B5
Yuxi, *China* 58 E4
Yuyao, *China* 59 B13
Yuzawa, *Japan* 54 E10
Yuzha, *Russia* 34 B6
Yuzhno-Sakhalinsk, *Russia* 53 E15
Yuzhnyy □, *Russia* 35 H5
Yuzhou, *China* 56 G7
Yvelines □, *France* 19 D8
Yverdon-les-Bains, *Switz.* 25 J2
Yvetot, *France* 18 C7
Yzeure, *France* 19 F10

Z

Zaanstad, *Neths.* 17 B4
Zāb al Kabīr →, *Iraq* 70 C4
Zāb aş Şaghīr →, *Iraq* 70 C4
Žabalj, *Serbia & M.* 28 E5
Žabari, *Serbia & M.* 44 B5
Zabarjad, *Egypt* 80 C4

Zabaykalsk, *Russia* 53 E12
Zabki, *Poland* 31 F8
Ząbkowice Śląskie, *Poland* 31 H3
Žabljak, *Serbia & M.* 44 C3
Zabłudów, *Poland* 31 F9
Żabno, *Poland* 31 H7
Zābol, *Iran* 71 D9
Zābol □, *Afghan.* 66 D5
Zābolī, *Iran* 71 E9
Zabolotiv, *Ukraine* 29 B10
Zabolottya, *Ukraine* 31 G11
Zabré, *Burkina Faso* 83 C4
Zábřeh, *Czech Rep.* 27 B9
Zabrze, *Poland* 31 H5
Zabuzhzhya, *Ukraine* 31 G10
Zabzuga, *Ghana* 83 D5
Zacapa, *Guatemala* 120 D2
Zacapu, *Mexico* 118 D4
Zacatecas, *Mexico* 118 C4
Zacatecas □, *Mexico* 118 C4
Zacatecoluca, *El Salv.* 120 D2
Zachary, *U.S.A.* 113 K9
Zachodnio-Pomorskie □, *Poland* 30 E2
Zacoalco, *Mexico* 118 C4
Zacualtipán, *Mexico* 119 C5
Zadar, *Croatia* 41 D12
Zadawa, *Nigeria* 83 C7
Zadetkyi Kyun, *Burma* 65 G2
Zadonsk, *Russia* 33 F10
Zafarqand, *Iran* 71 C7
Zafora, *Greece* 47 E8
Zafra, *Spain* 37 G4
Żagań, *Poland* 31 G2
Zagaoua, *Chad* 79 E10
Žagarė, *Lithuania* 30 B10
Zagazig, *Egypt* 80 H7
Zāgheh, *Iran* 71 C6
Zaglivérion, *Greece* 44 F7
Zagnanado, *Benin* 83 D5
Zagorá, *Greece* 46 B5
Zagorje, *Slovenia* 41 B11
Zagórów, *Poland* 31 F4
Zagórz, *Poland* 31 J9
Zagreb, *Croatia* 41 C12
Zagreb ✕ (ZAG), *Croatia* 41 C13
Zāgros, Kūhhā-ye, *Iran* 71 C6
Zagros Mts. = Zāgros, Kūhhā-ye, *Iran* 71 C6
Žagubica, *Serbia & M.* 44 B5
Zaguinaso, *Ivory C.* 82 C3
Zagyva →, *Hungary* 28 C5
Zahamena ⌂, *Madag.* 89 B8
Zāhedān, *Fārs, Iran* 71 D7
Zāhedān, *Sīstān va Balūchestān, Iran* 71 D9
Zahlah, *Lebanon* 74 B4
Zahna, *Germany* 24 D8
Záhony, *Hungary* 28 B7
Zainsk, *Russia* 34 C11
Zaïre = Congo →, *Africa* 84 F2
Zaječar, *Serbia & M.* 44 C6
Zaka, *Zimbabwe* 89 C5
Zakamensk, *Russia* 53 D11
Zakarpatska □, *Ukraine* 29 B8
Zakataly = Zaqatala, *Azerbaijan* 35 K8
Zakháro, *Greece* 46 D3
Zakhodnaya Dzvina = Daugava →, *Latvia* 9 H21
Zākhū, *Iraq* 70 B4
Zákinthos, *Greece* 46 D2
Zákinthos □, *Greece* 46 D2
Zakopane, *Poland* 31 J6
Zakroczym, *Poland* 31 F7
Zákros, *Greece* 49 D8
Zala, *Ethiopia* 81 F4
Zala □, *Hungary* 28 D1
Zala →, *Hungary* 28 D2
Zalaegerszeg, *Hungary* 28 D1
Zalakomár, *Hungary* 28 D2
Zalalövő, *Hungary* 28 D1
Zalamea de la Serena, *Spain* 37 G5
Zalamea la Real, *Spain* 37 H4
Zalău, *Romania* 28 C8
Žalec, *Slovenia* 41 B12
Zaleshchiki = Zalishchyky, *Ukraine* 29 B10
Zalesye, *Russia* 30 D8
Zalew Wiślany, *Poland* 30 D6
Zalewo, *Poland* 30 E6
Zalingei, *Sudan* 79 F10
Zalishchyky, *Ukraine* 29 B10
Zama L., *Canada* 102 B5
Zambeke, *Dem. Rep. of the Congo* 86 B2
Zambeze →, *Africa* 87 F4
Zambezi = Zambeze →, *Africa* 87 F4
Zambezi, *Zambia* 85 G4
Zambezi △, *Zimbabwe* 87 F2
Zambezia □, *Mozam.* 87 F4
Zambia ■, *Africa* 87 F2
Zamboanga, *Phil.* 61 H5
Zambrów, *Poland* 31 F9
Zametchino, *Russia* 34 D6
Zamfara □, *Nigeria* 83 C6
Zamfara →, *Nigeria* 83 C5
Zamora, *Mexico* 118 D4
Zamora, *Spain* 36 D5
Zamora □, *Spain* 36 D5
Zamość, *Poland* 31 H10
Zamtang, *China* 58 A3
Zan, *Ghana* 83 D4
Záncara →, *Spain* 39 F1
Zandvoort, *Neths.* 17 B4
Zanesville, *U.S.A.* 116 G2
Zangābād, *Iran* 70 B5
Zangue →, *Mozam.* 87 F4
Zanjān, *Iran* 71 B6
Zanjān □, *Iran* 71 B6
Zanjān →, *Iran* 71 B6
Zannone, *Italy* 42 B6
Zante = Zákinthos, *Greece* 46 D2
Zanthus, *Australia* 93 F3
Zanzibar, *Tanzania* 86 D4
Zaouiet El-Kala = Bordj Omar Driss, *Algeria* 78 C7
Zaouiet Reggâne, *Algeria* 78 C6
Zaoyang, *China* 59 A9
Zaozhuang, *China* 57 G9
Zap Suyu = Zāb al Kabīr →, *Iraq* 70 C4
Zapadna Morava →, *Serbia & M.* 44 C5
Zapadnaya Dvina = Daugava →, *Latvia* 9 H21
Zapadnaya Dvina, *Russia* 32 D7
Západné Beskydy, *Europe* 27 B12
Zapadni Rodopi, *Bulgaria* 44 E7
Západočeský □, *Czech Rep.* 26 B6
Zapala, *Argentina* 128 D2
Zapaleri, Cerro, *Bolivia* 126 A2
Zapata, *U.S.A.* 113 M5
Zapatón →, *Spain* 37 F4
Zaporizhzhya, *Ukraine* 33 J8
Zaporozhye = Zaporizhzhya, *Ukraine* 33 J8
Zaqatala, *Azerbaijan* 35 K8
Zara, *Turkey* 70 B3
Zaragoza, *Coahuila, Mexico* 118 B4
Zaragoza, *Nuevo León, Mexico* 119 C5
Zaragoza, *Spain* 38 D4
Zaragoza □, *Spain* 38 D4
Zarand, *Kermān, Iran* 71 D8
Zarand, *Markazī, Iran* 71 C6
Zărandului, Munţii, *Romania* 28 D7
Zaranj, *Afghan.* 66 D2
Zarasai, *Lithuania* 9 J22
Zárate, *Argentina* 126 C4
Zarautz, *Spain* 38 B2
Zaraysk, *Russia* 32 E10
Zard, Kūh-e, *Iran* 71 C6
Zāreh, *Iran* 71 C6
Zari, *Nigeria* 83 C7
Zaria, *Nigeria* 83 C6
Żarki, *Poland* 31 H6
Zárkon, *Greece* 46 B4
Zarneh, *Iran* 70 C5
Zărneşti, *Romania* 29 E10
Zarós, *Greece* 49 D6
Żarów, *Poland* 31 H3
Zarqā', Nahr az →, *Jordan* 74 C4
Zarrīn, *Iran* 71 C7
Zaruma, *Ecuador* 124 D3
Żary, *Poland* 31 G2
Zarza de Granadilla, *Spain* 36 E4
Zarzis, *Tunisia* 79 B8
Zas, *Spain* 36 B2
Zaskar →, *India* 69 B7
Zaskar Mts., *India* 69 C7
Zastavna, *Ukraine* 29 B10
Zastron, *S. Africa* 88 E4
Žatec, *Czech Rep.* 26 A6
Zaterechnyy, *Russia* 35 H7
Zator, *Poland* 31 J6
Zatyshshya, *Ukraine* 29 C14
Zavala, *Bos.-H.* 44 D1
Zavāreh, *Iran* 71 C7
Zave, *Zimbabwe* 89 B5
Zavetnoye, *Russia* 35 G6
Zavidovići, *Bos.-H.* 28 F3
Zavitinsk, *Russia* 53 D13
Zavodovski, I., *Antarctica* 5 B1
Zavolzhsk, *Russia* 34 B6
Zavolzhye, *Russia* 34 B6
Zawadzkie, *Poland* 31 H5
Zawichost, *Poland* 31 H8
Zawidów, *Poland* 31 G2
Zawiercie, *Poland* 31 H6
Zāwiyat al Baydā = Al Baydā, *Libya* 79 B10
Zâwyet Shammas, *Egypt* 80 A2
Zâwyet Um el Rakham, *Egypt* 80 A2
Zâwyet Ungeîla, *Egypt* 80 A2
Zāyā, *Iraq* 70 C5
Zāyandeh →, *Iran* 71 C7
Zaysan, *Kazakhstan* 52 E9
Zaysan, Oz., *Kazakhstan* 52 E9
Zayü, *China* 58 C1
Zazafotsy, *Madag.* 89 C8
Zázrivá, *Slovak Rep.* 27 B12
Zbarazh, *Ukraine* 33 H3
Zbąszyń, *Poland* 31 F2
Zbąszynek, *Poland* 31 F2
Zblewo, *Poland* 30 E5
Zbruch → 29 B11
Žďár nad Sázavou, *Czech Rep.* 26 B8
Zdolbuniv, *Ukraine* 33 G4
Ždrelo, *Serbia & M.* 44 B5
Zduńska Wola, *Poland* 31 G5
Zduny, *Poland* 31 G4
Zeballos, *Canada* 102 D3
Zebediela, *S. Africa* 89 C4
Zebila, *Ghana* 83 C4
Zeebrugge, *Belgium* 17 C3
Zeehan, *Australia* 95 G4
Zeeland □, *Neths.* 17 C3
Zeerust, *S. Africa* 88 D4
Zefat, *Israel* 74 C4
Zege, *Ethiopia* 81 E4
Zeggerene, Iracher, *Mali* 83 B5
Zégoua, *Mali* 82 C3
Zehdenick, *Germany* 24 C9
Zeil, Mt., *Australia* 92 D5
Zeila, *Somali Rep.* 75 E3
Zeist, *Neths.* 17 B5
Zeitz, *Germany* 24 D8
Żelechów, *Poland* 31 G8
Zelena, *Ukraine* 29 B9
Zelengora, *Bos.-H.* 44 C2
Zelenodolsk, *Russia* 34 C9
Zelenogorsk, *Russia* 32 B5
Zelenograd, *Russia* 32 D9
Zelenogradsk, *Russia* 9 J19
Zelenokumsk, *Russia* 35 H6
Železná Ruda, *Czech Rep.* 26 B6
Železnik, *Serbia & M.* 44 B4
Zelienople, *U.S.A.* 116 F4
Želiezovce, *Slovak Rep.* 27 C11
Zelina, *Croatia* 41 C13
Zell, *Baden-W., Germany* 25 H3
Zell, *Rhld-Pfz., Germany* 25 E3
Zell am See, *Austria* 26 D5
Zella-Mehlis, *Germany* 24 E6
Zelów, *Poland* 31 G6
Zeltweg, *Austria* 26 D7
Žemaitijos △, *Lithuania* 30 B8
Zémio, *C.A.R.* 86 A2
Zempléni-hegység, *Hungary* 28 B6
Zemplínska šírava, *Slovak Rep.* 27 C15
Zempoala, *Mexico* 119 D5
Zemun, *Serbia & M.* 44 B4
Zengbé, *Cameroon* 83 D7
Zengcheng, *China* 59 F9
Zenica, *Bos.-H.* 28 F2
Žepče, *Bos.-H.* 28 F3
Zeraf, Bahr ez →, *Sudan* 81 F3
Zerbst, *Germany* 24 D8
Żerków, *Poland* 31 F4
Zermatt, *Switz.* 25 J3
Zernez, *Switz.* 25 J6
Zernograd, *Russia* 35 G5
Zerqan, *Albania* 44 E4
Zestaponi, *Georgia* 35 J6
Zetel, *Germany* 24 B3
Zeulenroda, *Germany* 24 E7
Zeven, *Germany* 24 B5
Zevenaar, *Neths.* 17 C6
Zévio, *Italy* 40 C8
Zeya, *Russia* 53 D13
Zeya →, *Russia* 53 D13
Zeytinbaği, *Turkey* 45 F12
Zeytindağ, *Turkey* 47 C9
Zghartā, *Lebanon* 74 A4
Zgierz, *Poland* 31 G6
Zgorzelec, *Poland* 31 G2
Zguriţa, *Moldova* 29 B13
Zhabinka, *Belarus* 31 F11
Zhabokrych, *Ukraine* 29 B13
Zhailma, *Kazakhstan* 52 D7
Zhambyl = Taraz, *Kazakhstan* 52 E8
Zhangaly, *Kazakhstan* 35 G10
Zhangaqazaly, *Kazakhstan* 52 E7
Zhangbei, *China* 56 D8
Zhangguangcai Ling, *China* 57 B15
Zhangjiakou, *China* 56 D8
Zhangping, *China* 59 E11
Zhangpu, *China* 59 E11
Zhangshu, *China* 59 C10
Zhangwu, *China* 57 C12
Zhangye, *China* 60 C5
Zhangzhou, *China* 59 E11
Zhanhua, *China* 57 F10
Zhanjiang, *China* 59 G8
Zhannetty, Ostrov, *Russia* 53 B16
Zhanyi, *China* 58 E4
Zhanyu, *China* 57 B12
Zhao Xian, *China* 56 F8
Zhao'an, *China* 59 F11
Zhaocheng, *China* 56 F6
Zhaojue, *China* 58 C4
Zhaoping, *China* 59 E8
Zhaoqing, *China* 59 F9
Zhaotong, *China* 58 D4
Zhaoyuan, *Heilongjiang, China* 57 B13
Zhaoyuan, *Shandong, China* 57 F11
Zharkovskiy, *Russia* 32 E7
Zhashkiv, *Ukraine* 33 H6
Zhashui, *China* 56 H5
Zhayyq →, *Kazakhstan* 52 E6
Zhdanov = Mariupol, *Ukraine* 33 J9
Zhecheng, *China* 56 G8
Zhegao, *China* 59 B11
Zhejiang □, *China* 59 C13
Zheleznodorozhnyy, *Russia* 30 D8
Zheleznogorsk, *Russia* 33 F8
Zheleznogorsk-Ilimskiy, *Russia* 53 D11
Zheltyye Vody = Zhovti Vody, *Ukraine* 33 H7
Zhen'an, *China* 56 H5
Zhenba, *China* 58 A6
Zhenfeng, *China* 58 E5
Zheng'an, *China* 58 C6
Zhengding, *China* 56 E8
Zhenghe, *China* 59 D12
Zhengyang, *China* 59 A10
Zhengyangguan, *China* 59 A11
Zhengzhou, *China* 56 G7
Zhenhai, *China* 59 C13
Zhenjiang, *China* 59 A12
Zhenkang, *China* 58 F2
Zhenlai, *China* 57 B12
Zhenning, *China* 58 D5
Zhenping, *Henan, China* 56 H7
Zhenping, *Shaanxi, China* 58 B7
Zhenxiong, *China* 58 D5
Zhenyuan, *Gansu, China* 56 G4
Zhenyuan, *Guizhou, China* 58 D7
Zherdevka, *Russia* 34 E5
Zherebkove, *Ukraine* 29 C14
Zherong, *China* 59 D12
Zhetiqara, *Kazakhstan* 52 D7
Zhezqazghan, *Kazakhstan* 52 E7
Zhicheng, *China* 59 B8
Zhidan, *China* 56 F5
Zhigansk, *Russia* 53 C13
Zhigulevsk, *Russia* 34 D9
Zhijiang, *Hubei, China* 59 B8
Zhijiang, *Hunan, China* 58 D7
Zhijin, *China* 58 D5
Zhilinda, *Russia* 53 C12
Zhilino, *Russia* 30 D8
Zhirnovsk, *Russia* 34 E7
Zhitomir = Zhytomyr, *Ukraine* 33 G5
Zhizdra, *Russia* 32 F8
Zhlobin, *Belarus* 33 F6
Zhmerinka = Zhmerynka, *Ukraine* 33 H5
Zhmerynka, *Ukraine* 33 H5
Zhob, *Pakistan* 68 D3
Zhob →, *Pakistan* 68 C3
Zhodino = Zhodzina, *Belarus* 32 E5
Zhodzina, *Belarus* 32 E5
Zhokhova, Ostrov, *Russia* 53 B16
Zhongdian, *China* 58 D2
Zhongdong, *China* 58 F6
Zhongdu, *China* 58 E7
Zhongning, *China* 56 F3
Zhongshan, *Antarctica* 5 C6
Zhongshan, *Guangdong, China* 59 F9
Zhongshan, *Guangxi Zhuangzu, China* 59 E8
Zhongtiao Shan, *China* 56 G6
Zhongwei, *China* 56 F3
Zhongxiang, *China* 59 B9
Zhongyang, *China* 56 F6
Zhorany, *Ukraine* 31 G10
Zhoucun, *China* 57 F9
Zhouning, *China* 59 D12
Zhoushan, *China* 59 B14
Zhoushan Dao, *China* 59 C14
Zhouzhi, *China* 56 G5
Zhovti Vody, *Ukraine* 33 H7
Zhovtneve, *Ukraine* 31 H11
Zhovtneve, *Ukraine* 33 J7
Zhovtnevoye = Zhovtneve, *Ukraine* 33 J7
Zhu Jiang →, *China* 59 F9
Zhuanghe, *China* 57 E12
Zhucheng, *China* 57 G10
Zhugqu, *China* 56 H3
Zhuhai, *China* 59 F9
Zhuji, *China* 59 C13
Zhukovka, *Russia* 32 F7
Zhumadian, *China* 56 H8
Zhuo Xian = Zhuozhou, *China* 56 E8
Zhuolu, *China* 56 D8
Zhuozhou, *China* 56 E8
Zhuozi, *China* 56 D7
Zhushan, *China* 59 A8
Zhuxi, *China* 58 A7
Zhuzhou, *China* 59 D9
Zhvanets, *Ukraine* 29 B11
Zhytomyr, *Ukraine* 33 G5
Zi Shui →, *China* 59 C9
Žiar nad Hronom, *Slovak Rep.* 27 C11
Zīārān, *Iran* 71 B6
Ziarat, *Pakistan* 68 D2
Zibo, *China* 57 F10
Zichang, *China* 56 F5
Zidarovo, *Bulgaria* 45 D11
Zidi = Wandhari, *Pakistan* 68 F2
Ziębice, *Poland* 31 H4
Zielona Góra, *Poland* 31 G2
Zierikzee, *Neths.* 17 C3
Ziesar, *Germany* 24 C8
Zifta, *Egypt* 80 H7
Zigey, *Chad* 79 F9
Zigong, *China* 58 C5
Ziguinchor, *Senegal* 82 C1
Zihuatanejo, *Mexico* 118 D4
Zijin, *China* 59 F10
Zile, *Turkey* 72 B6
Žilina, *Slovak Rep.* 27 B11
Žilinský □, *Slovak Rep.* 27 B12
Zillah, *Libya* 79 C9
Zillertaler Alpen, *Austria* 26 D4
Zima, *Russia* 53 D11
Zimapán, *Mexico* 119 C5
Zimba, *Zambia* 87 F2
Zimbabwe, *Zimbabwe* 87 G3
Zimbabwe ■, *Africa* 87 F3
Zimi, *S. Leone* 82 D2
Zimnicea, *Romania* 29 G10
Zimovniki, *Russia* 35 G6
Zinave △, *Mozam.* 89 C5
Zinder, *Niger* 83 C6
Zinga, *Tanzania* 87 D4
Zingaro ⌂, *Italy* 42 D5
Zingst, *Germany* 24 A8
Ziniaré, *Burkina Faso* 83 C4
Zinnowitz, *Germany* 24 A9
Zion △, *U.S.A.* 109 H7
Zirbitzkogel, *Austria* 26 D7
Zirc, *Hungary* 28 C2
Žiri, *Slovenia* 41 B11
Žirje, *Croatia* 41 E12
Zirl, *Austria* 26 D4
Zirndorf, *Germany* 25 F6
Ziros, *Greece* 49 D8
Zirreh, Gowd-e, *Afghan.* 66 E3
Zisterdorf, *Austria* 27 C9
Zitácuaro, *Mexico* 118 D4
Žitava →, *Slovak Rep.* 27 C11
Žitište, *Serbia & M.* 28 E5
Zitong, *China* 58 B5
Zítsa, *Greece* 46 B2
Zittau, *Germany* 24 E10
Zitundo, *Mozam.* 89 D5
Živinice, *Bos.-H.* 28 F3
Ziwa Maghariba = Kagera □, *Tanzania* 86 C3
Ziway, L., *Ethiopia* 81 F4
Zixi, *China* 59 D11
Zixing, *China* 59 E9
Ziyang, *Shaanxi, China* 56 H5
Ziyang, *Sichuan, China* 58 B5
Ziyuan, *China* 59 D8
Ziyun, *China* 58 E6
Zizhong, *China* 58 C5
Zlarin, *Croatia* 41 E12
Zlatar, *Croatia* 41 B13
Zlatar, *Serbia & M.* 44 C3
Zlataritsa, *Bulgaria* 45 C9
Zlaté Moravce, *Slovak Rep.* 27 C11
Zlatibor, *Serbia & M.* 44 C3
Zlatitsa, *Bulgaria* 45 D8
Zlatna, *Romania* 29 D8
Zlatna Panega, *Bulgaria* 45 C8
Zlatni Pyasŭtsi, *Bulgaria* 45 C12
Zlatograd, *Bulgaria* 45 E9
Zlatoust, *Russia* 52 D6
Zletovo, *Macedonia* 44 E6
Zlín, *Czech Rep.* 27 B10
Zlínský □, *Czech Rep.* 27 B10
Złocieniec, *Poland* 30 E3
Złoczew, *Poland* 31 G5
Zlot, *Serbia & M.* 44 B5
Złotoryja, *Poland* 31 G2
Złotów, *Poland* 30 E4
Zmeinogorsk, *Kazakhstan* 52 D9
Żmigród, *Poland* 31 G3
Zmiyev, *Ukraine* 33 H9
Znamenka = Znamyanka, *Ukraine* 33 H7
Znamensk, *Russia* 30 D8
Znamyanka, *Ukraine* 33 H7
Żnin, *Poland* 31 F4
Znojmo, *Czech Rep.* 26 C9
Zobeyrī, *Iran* 70 C5
Zobia, *Dem. Rep. of the Congo* 86 B2
Zoetermeer, *Neths.* 17 B4
Zogang, *China* 58 C1
Zogno, *Italy* 40 C6
Zogqên, *China* 58 A2
Zolochev = Zolochiv, *Ukraine* 33 H3
Zolochiv, *Ukraine* 33 H3
Zolotonosha, *Ukraine* 33 H7
Zolotyy Potik, *Ukraine* 29 B10
Zomba, *Malawi* 87 F4
Zongo, *Dem. Rep. of the Congo* 84 D3
Zonguldak, *Turkey* 72 B4
Zongyang, *China* 59 B11
Zonqor Pt., *Malta* 49 D2
Zonza, *France* 21 G13
Zorgo, *Burkina Faso* 83 C4
Zorita, *Spain* 37 F5
Zorleni, *Romania* 29 D12
Zornitsa, *Bulgaria* 45 D10
Zorritos, *Peru* 124 D2
Żory, *Poland* 31 H5
Zorzor, *Liberia* 82 D3
Zossen, *Germany* 24 C9
Zou Xiang, *China* 56 G9
Zouan-Hounien, *Ivory C.* 82 D3
Zouar, *Chad* 79 D9
Zouérate = Zouîrât, *Mauritania* 78 D3
Zouîrât, *Mauritania* 78 D3
Zourika, *Niger* 83 B6
Zourma, *Burkina Faso* 83 C4
Zoutkamp, *Neths.* 17 A6
Zrenjanin, *Serbia & M.* 28 E5
Zuarungu, *Ghana* 83 C4
Zuba, *Nigeria* 83 D6
Zubayr, *Yemen* 81 D5
Zubtsov, *Russia* 32 D8
Zuénoula, *Ivory C.* 82 D3
Zuera, *Spain* 38 D4
Zufār, *Oman* 75 D5
Zug □, *Switz.* 25 H4
Zugdidi, *Georgia* 35 J5
Zugersee, *Switz.* 25 H4
Zugspitze, *Germany* 25 H6
Zuid-Holland □, *Neths.* 17 C4
Zuidbeveland, *Neths.* 17 C3
Zuidhorn, *Neths.* 17 A6
Zújar, *Spain* 37 H8
Zújar →, *Spain* 37 G5
Żukowo, *Poland* 30 D5
Zula, *Eritrea* 81 D4
Zülpich, *Germany* 24 E2
Zumaia, *Spain* 38 B2
Zumárraga, *Spain* 38 B2
Zumbo, *Mozam.* 87 F3
Zummo, *Nigeria* 83 D7
Zumpango, *Mexico* 119 D5
Zungeru, *Nigeria* 83 D6
Zunhua, *China* 57 D9
Zuni, *U.S.A.* 109 J9
Zunyi, *China* 58 D6
Zuo Jiang →, *China* 58 F6
Zuozhou, *China* 58 F6
Županja, *Croatia* 28 E3
Žur, *Serbia & M.* 44 D4
Zurbātīyah, *Iraq* 70 C5
Zürich, *Switz.* 25 H4
Zürich □, *Switz.* 25 H4
Zürichsee, *Switz.* 25 H4
Żuromin, *Poland* 31 E6
Žut, *Croatia* 41 E12
Zutphen, *Neths.* 17 B6
Zuurberg △, *S. Africa* 88 E4
Zuwārah, *Libya* 79 B8
Zūzan, *Iran* 71 C8
Žužemberk, *Slovenia* 41 C11
Zvenigorodka = Zvenyhorodka, *Ukraine* 33 H6
Zvenyhorodka, *Ukraine* 33 H6
Zverinogolovskoye, *Russia* 52 D7
Zvezdets, *Bulgaria* 45 D11
Zvishavane, *Zimbabwe* 87 G3
Zvolen, *Slovak Rep.* 27 C12
Zvonce, *Serbia & M.* 44 D6
Zvornik, *Bos.-H.* 28 F4
Zwedru = Tchien, *Liberia* 82 D3
Zweibrücken, *Germany* 25 F3
Zwelitsha, *S. Africa* 85 L5
Zwenkau, *Germany* 24 D8
Zwettl, *Austria* 26 C8
Zwickau, *Germany* 24 E8
Zwierzyniec, *Poland* 31 H9
Zwiesel, *Germany* 25 F9
Zwoleń, *Poland* 31 G8
Zwolle, *Neths.* 17 B6
Zwolle, *U.S.A.* 113 K8
Żychlin, *Poland* 31 F6
Żyrardów, *Poland* 31 F7
Zyryan, *Kazakhstan* 52 E9
Zyryanka, *Russia* 53 C16
Zyryanovsk = Zyryan, *Kazakhstan* 52 E9
Żywiec, *Poland* 31 J6
Zyyi, *Cyprus* 49 E12

KEY TO EUROPEAN MAP PAGES

Large scale maps
(>1:2 500 000)

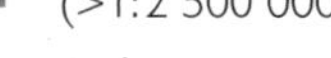
Medium scale maps
(1:2 800 000 – 1:9 900 000)

Small scale maps
(<1:10 000 000)

Arctic Circle

WORLD COUNTRY INDEX

Afghanistan 66
Albania 44
Algeria 78
Angola 84–85
Argentina 126, 128
Armenia 73
Australia 92–95
Austria 26–27
Azerbaijan 73

Bahamas 120–121
Bahrain 71
Bangladesh 67
Barbados 121
Belarus 32–33
Belgium 17
Belize 120
Benin 83
Bhutan 67
Bolivia 124
Bosnia-Herzegovina 41, 44
Botswana 88
Brazil 124–125, 127
Brunei 62
Bulgaria 44–45
Burkina Faso 82–83
Burma (Myanmar) 67
Burundi 86

Cambodia 64–65
Canary Is. 48
Cameroon 83, 84
Canada 100–105
Central African Republic 84
Chad 79
Chile 126–127, 128
China 56–60
Colombia 124
Congo 84
Congo, Dem. Rep. of the 84–85, 86–87
Costa Rica 120
Croatia 41
Cuba 120–121
Cyprus 49
Czech Republic 26–27

Denmark 11
Djibouti 81
Dominican Republic 121

East Timor 63
Ecuador 124
Egypt 80
El Salvador 120
England 14–15
Equatorial Guinea 84
Eritrea 80–81
Estonia 32
Ethiopia 75, 81

Fiji 91
Finland 8–9
France 18–21
French Guiana 125

Gabon 84
Gambia 82
Georgia 35
Germany 24–25
Ghana 82–83
Greece 44–47
Greenland 4
Guadeloupe 120
Guatemala 120
Guinea 82
Guinea-Bissau 82
Guyana 124

Haiti 121
Honduras 120
Hungary 28

Iceland 8
India 66–69
Indonesia 62–63
Iran 70–71, 73
Iraq 70–71, 73
Irish Republic 12
Israel 74
Italy 40–43
Ivory Coast 82

Jamaica 120
Japan 54–55
Jordan 74

Kazakhstan 52
Kenya 86
Korea, North 57
Korea, South 57
Kuwait 70–71
Kyrgyzstan 52

Laos 64
Latvia 32
Lebanon 74
Lesotho 89
Liberia 82
Libya 79
Lithuania 32
Luxembourg 17

Macedonia 44
Madagascar 89
Malawi 87
Malaysia 62–63, 65
Mali 78, 82–83
Malta 49
Martinique 120
Mauritania 78, 82
Mexico 118–119
Moldova 29
Mongolia 60
Morocco 78
Mozambique 87, 89

Namibia 88
Nepal 69
Netherlands 17
New Zealand 91
Nicaragua 120
Niger 78–79, 83
Nigeria 83
Northern Ireland 12
Norway 8–9

Oman 75

Pakistan 66, 68
Panama 120
Papua New Guinea 96
Paraguay 126–127
Peru 124
Philippines 61
Poland 30–31
Portugal 36–37
Puerto Rico 121

Qatar 71

Romania 28–29
Russia 32–35, 52–53
Rwanda 86

St. Lucia 121
Samoa 91
Saudi Arabia 70–71, 75
Scotland 13
Senegal 82
Serbia and Montenegro 28, 44
Sierra Leone 82
Singapore 65
Slovak Republic 27
Slovenia 41
Solomon Is. 96
Somali Republic 75
South Africa 88–89
Spain 36–39
Sri Lanka 66
Sudan 80–81
Suriname 124–125
Swaziland 89
Sweden 8–9
Switzerland 25
Syria 70, 72–73

Taiwan 59
Tajikistan 52
Tanzania 86–87
Thailand 64–65
Togo 83
Tonga 91
Trinidad and Tobago 125
Tunisia 78–79
Turkey 72–73
Turkmenistan 52

Uganda 86
Ukraine 33
United Arab Emirates 75
United Kingdom 12–16
USA 106–117
Uruguay 126–127
Uzbekistan 52

Vanuatu 96
Venezuela 124
Vietnam 64–65

Wales 14–15

Yemen 75

Zambia 85, 87
Zimbabwe 87